The
Gramophone
Good **CD** *Guide*
1 9 9 5

Published by

General Gramophone Publications Limited

177-179 Kenton Road, Harrow,

Middlesex HA3 0HA. Great Britain

Gramophone magazine, founded by the novelist and writer Compton Mackenzie and the broadcaster Christopher Stone, has been published monthly since 1923. As one of the first magazines devoted to the discussion of recorded music, Gramophone has maintained its position as the most informed and influential publication of its kind. Calling on the wealth of talent of a panel of the world's leading writers on music, Gramophone is, for many, the record collector's bible. Each month the magazine carries over 200 reviews of music across a wide spectrum and talks to the leading performers of the day.

Editorial Director	Christopher Pollard
Editor	Máire Taylor
Reviews Editor	Jonathan Swain
Editorial Consultant	Michael Stewart
Editorial Assistants	Ann Marks, Helen White
Production Editors	Dermot Jones, Ivor Humphreys, Christine Narain
Contributors	Andrew Achenbach, Nicholas Anderson, Mary Berry, Alan Blyth, Joan Chissell, Robert Cowan, Peter Dickinson, John Duarte, Jessica Duchen, Adrian Edwards, Richard T. Fairman, David Fallows, David J. Fanning, Iain Fenlon, Hilary Finch, Fabrice Fitch, Jonathan Freeman-Attwood, Robin Golding, Edward Greenfield, David Gutman, Douglas Hammond, Christopher Headington, Michael Jameson, Stephen Johnson, James Jolly, Lindsay Kemp, Robert Kenchington, Michael Kennedy, Tess Knighton, Andrew Lamb, Robert Layton, Ivan March, Peter Marchbank, James Methuen-Campbell, John Milsom, Ivan Moody, Bryce Morrison, Patrick O'Connor, Michael Oliver, Richard Osborne, David Patmore, Stephen Plaistow, Nicholas Rast, Guy Rickards, Marc Rochester, Julie-Anne Sadie, Stanley Sadie, Lionel Salter, Alan Sanders, Edward Seckerson, Robert Seeley, Keith Shadwick, Harriet Smith, John Steane, Michael Stewart, Jonathan Swain, John Warrack, Arnold Whittall, Mark Wiggins, Richard Wigmore and Ronald Woodley

General Gramophone Publications Limited 1994
UK ISBN 0-902470-50-7
USA ISBN 0-902470-49-3

Recording companies reserve the right to withdraw any Compact Disc without giving previous notice, and although every effort is made to obtain the latest information for inclusion in this book, no guarantee can be given that all the discs listed are immediately available. Any difficulties should be referred to the issuing company concerned. When ordering, purchasers are advised to quote all the relevant information in addition to the disc numbers. The publishers cannot accept responsibility for the consequences of any error.

Printed in Great Britain by William Clowes Ltd, Beccles, Suffolk, NR34 9QE.

Emanuel Ax and Yo-Yo Ma

Montserrat Caballé

James Levine

Introduction

Welcome to the 1995 edition of *The Gramophone Good CD Guide*, the most comprehensive and informative to date. Comprehensive it certainly needs to be, for the Compact Disc medium, now in its twelfth, hugely successful year, has swelled *The Gramophone Classical Catalogue* to almost unbelievable proportions with over 800, three-column pages of composer listings alone — a vast difference from the days of LP and cassette. The law of averages therefore dictates that when confronted with 95 available versions of Beethoven's Fifth Symphony (yes, 95, no less!), 58 accounts of the Brahms Violin Concerto or 52 versions of Mozart's *Requiem* there are going to be more than just a few exceptionally fine and recommendable recordings to choose from.

To that end we have expanded the "Additional recommendation" listings (introduced last year) as much as possible so as to give the reader the widest possible range of good recordings available — that is the best historical, modern and 'authentic' version of a particular work in the catalogue. Likewise, beyond the standard repertoire we have also expanded the "Further" and "Suggested" listing features in order to keep pace with the current focus of interest in recordings of music by non-mainstream, less familiar composers. Indeed, such is the interest in the more unfamiliar highways and byways of music at the moment (by larger companies as well as by the traditionally more adventurous smaller companies) that readers will find an increasing number of new reviews in the current *Guide* falling into this category — not a deliberate strategy on our part, but merely a reflection of the kind of exemplary commitment by musicians, engineers and record companies in presenting these less frequently heard composers in the best possible light.

Notable highlights from this year's releases include string quartets by Hans Krása and Pavel Haas, *page 326*, Berthold Goldschmidt's opera *Der gewaltige Hahnrei, page 309* — both of these from Decca's highly successful Entartete Musik series; RCA's issue of Charles Koechlin's masterly *Le Livre de la jungle* with David Zinman and the Berlin Radio Symphony Orchestra, *page 408*; two discs of concert works (as opposed to the more frequently recorded film scores) by the Hungarian composer Miklós Rózsa from Koch International, *page 646* and a splendid new recording of the Korngold Symphony from Chandos, *page 410*.

The resurgence of interest in the music of Busoni and Medtner which began a few years ago continues, the former being represented by a fine disc of orchestral and *concertante* works, *page 189*, featuring the Berlin Radio Symphony Orchestra this time under the direction of Gerd Albrecht (the first issue in a promised Complete Busoni Edition) and a two CD double-bill of the operas *Arlecchino* and *Turandot* from the winning team of Kent Nagano and Virgin Classics, *page 190*. The Medtner catalogue expands with a liberal sprinkling of new releases in just about every category from chamber to orchestral, a special highlight being the composer's own 1947 recordings of the Second and Third Piano Concertos which have been remastered and issued by Testament, *page 473*.

Contemporary music continues to attract interest and gain good coverage from most labels, as well. Among the most prominent ventures of the last year include NMC's recording of Robin Holloway's *Second Concerto for Orchestra*, *page 376*, John Tavener's two extraordinarily intense and moving works for string quartet, *The Last Sleep of the Virgin* and *The Hidden Treasure*, *page 776*, and the equally extraordinary and very different *Jesus' Blood never failed me yet* by Gavin Bryars which quickly established itself as a cult best-seller, *page 188*. The music of Alan Hovhaness has always had its followers, but it is only in the last year or so that it has managed to make inroads into the world of CD. It certainly seems to be making up for lost time, however, with no less than three new reviews appearing in this *Guide*, among them the internationally acclaimed recording of his *Mount St Helens* Symphony (his fiftieth no less!), which recalls the day the mountain literally blew its top (creating earth tremors of 5·1 on the Richter scale) in 1980, *page 382*.

Less familiar names pop up in the area of early music too, with discs devoted to music by composers such as Guillaume Bouzignac — whose Motets on the Harmonia Mundi label so enthralled and excited its *Gramophone* reviewer last year, *page 148* — and Cipriano de Rore whose *Missa Praeter rerum seriem* is performed by The Tallis Scholars on Gimell, *page 634*. Even when we think we're on more familiar territory we often have to think again, and such was the case with the appearance of the world première recording of Berlioz's recently rediscovered *Messe Solennelle* under the persuasive direction of John Eliot Gardiner on the Philips label, *page 122*.

There is a continued commitment from record companies to expand the recorded repertoire of American music too. Apart from new recordings of music by established composers such as Bernstein's *On the Town*, *page 127*, there are innumerable discs of lesser known composers awaiting general discovery: William Grant Still's Symphony *Afro American*, David Diamond's Symphony No. 1 and Violin Concerto No. 2, *page 241* and orchestral music by Irving Fine, *page 283*.

But what of more familiar fare? Well, there's still plenty to satisfy most tastes. Baroque enthusiasts, for instance, will not want to miss Pierre Hantaï's spirited account of Bach's *Goldberg Variations*, *page 51* or Tafelmusik's virtuosic reading of Handel's *Concerti grossi*, Op. 3, *page 329* whilst classical and romantic enthusiasts would be strongly advised to investigate Richard Goode's extraordinarily fine survey of the Beethoven piano sonatas on Elektra Nonesuch, *page 103*, Oestman's magical and spontaneous *Die Zauberflöte* on L'Oiseau-Lyre, *page 541*, a glowing account of Rachmaninov's Second Symphony from Mikhail Pletnev, *page 606* or Evgeni Kissin's remarkable Chopin recital on RCA, *page 207*.

So, we may not be falling over mountains of Mozart or bundles of Brahms this year but in terms of sheer variety and choice the 1994-95 period which this edition covers could well prove to be one of the richest and most exciting to date for the CD collector.

Michael Stewart

How to use the guide

In order to enhance the usefulness of this book and to cover as many 'good' CDs as possible from the huge range now available, this edition incorporates the following additional information: **Additional recommendations:** Under a full review, which is generally the top recommendation for a particular work, single or multiple additional alternative recommendations will follow where appropriate. **Further listening:** Contains details of further musical works worthy of consideration from the same composer. **Suggested listening:** Contains details of musical works by composers for whom no full reviews exist or where few recordings are available.

Details are given of composer(s), work(s), instrument(s), voice range(s), record company or label (see the listing of Labels/manufacturers and distributors), disc number (and previous number when the newcomer is a reissue) and review date(s) in *Gramophone*. Addresses of distributing companies are provided at the rear of this book.

On the musical staves following a heading, information is provided by a system of symbols as follows:

The symbols

Price	Quantity/availability	Timing	Mode	Review date
	② ②	lh 23m	DDD	6/88

Price

Full price: £10·00 and over

Medium price: £7·00–£9·99

Budget price: £5·00–£6·99

Super-budget price: below £4·99

Quantity/availability

If there is more than one disc, the number involved is shown here. The first type of circle indicates sets in which the individual discs are not available separately. The second type indicates that the discs are *only* available separately.

Timing

Calculated to the nearest minute.

Mode

This three-letter code is now used by almost all manufacturers to indicate the type of processing employed during manufacture. The letters A or D are used to denote Analogue or Digital and the letter sequence represents chronological steps in the chain: the recording session itself; the editing and/or mixing routines; and finally the mastering or transcription used in preparation of the master tape which is sent to the factory.

Review date

The month and year in which the recording was reviewed in *Gramophone*.

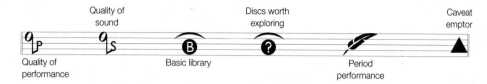

Quality of performance
Recordings which really brook no argument — 'musts' for the keen collector. Often the older recordings among these might well have won a *Gramophone* Award had the Awards existed when they first appeared.

Quality of sound
Those recordings which truly merit the epithet 'demonstration quality'.

Basic library
Recordings with which to begin building your CD collection.

Discs worth exploring
For the adventurous! Recordings which might easily be overlooked since they are not among the best-known works or by the better-known composers. But they could well provide some interesting surprises.

Period performance
Recordings in which some attempt is made at historical authenticity. Typically these involve the use of period instruments and/or original manuscript sources.

Caveat emptor
Performances which have stood the test of time but where the recording quality may not be up to the highest standards. This generally applies to pre-1960 recordings.

Two further symbols are used in the reviews:

Gramophone Award winners
The classical music world's most coveted accolades for recordings, these are awarded each year by *Gramophone* in categories ranging from Orchestral to Operatic, Baroque to Contemporary. One recording is also chosen from the overall list to be given the Award of Record of the Year.

Editor's choice
Gramophone's Editor, James Jolly, selects ten discs each month that have received particular praise from the critics in the magazine.

Comment utiliser ce guide?

Afin de rendre ce livre encore plus utile et de faire justice à autant de "bons" disques compacts que possible parmi la vaste gamme maintenant disponible, cette édition fournit les informations supplémentaires suivantes: **Recommandations supplémentaires:** Sous une critique complète, qui représente en général la plus haute recommandation pour une oeuvre donnée, une ou plusieurs autres oeuvres sont éventuellement conseillées. **A écouter également:** Des informations concernant d'autres oeuvres musicales du même compositeur, et qui méritent qu'on les écoute. **Conseils:** Des informations concernant des oeuvres musicales de compositeurs n'ayant pas fait l'objet de critiques complètes ou dont il existe peu d'enregistrements.

Compositeur(s), oeuvre(s), instrument(s), registre(s) de voix, maison de disques ou label (reportez-vous á la liste des labels/fabricants et sociétés de distribution), numéro de disque (et le numéro précédent lorsque le disque est ressorti) et date(s) de critique(s) dans *Gramophone* sont indiqués.

Les portées à la suite des titres vous fournissent des informations grâce au système de symboles suivant.

Les symboles

| Prix | Quantité/
disponibilité | Durée | Mode | Date de la
critique |

Prix

Prix normal   Prix moyen

Prix modique   Prix très modique

Quantité/disponiblité
S'il y a plus d'un disque, le nombre est indiqué ici. Le premier type de cercle indique des séries dont les disques ne sont pas vendus séparément. Le second type indique que les disques ne sont disponibles *que* séparément.

Durée
Calculée à la minute près.

Mode
Ce code de trois lettres est maintenant utilisé par presque tous les fabricants pour indiquer le procédé utilisé lors de la fabrication. Les lettres A ou D signifient 'analogique' ou 'numérique' et l'ordre des lettres correspond aux étapes, par ordre chronologique, dans la chaîne: la séance d'enregistrement à proprement parler, le mixage et/ou le montage, et enfin la gravure pour la préparation de la bande maîtresse envoyée à l'usine.

Date de la critique
Le mois et l'année de publication de la critique de l'enregistrement dans *Gramophone*.

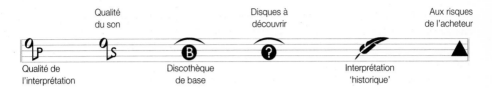

Qualité du son	Disques à découvrir	Aux risques de l'acheteur

Qualité de l'interprétation	Discothèque de base	Interprétation 'historique'

Qualité de l'interprétation
Des enregistrements dont la qualité est indiscutable – des 'musts' pour le collectionneur passionné. Les plus anciens parmi ceux-ci auraient souvent remporté le prix du disque *Gramophone* s'il avait existé à leur sortie.

Qualité du son
Des enregistrements dont on peut vraiment dire qu'ils sont de 'qualité démonstration'.

Discothèque de base
Des enregistrements qui constitueront les fondements de votre collection de disques compacts.

Disques à découvrir
Pour les touche-à-tout de la musique! Des enregistrements à côté desquels on aurait tendance à passer parce qu'on ne les doit pas aux compositeurs les plus célèbres, mais qui peuvent réserver de bien agréables surprises.

Interprétation 'historique'
Des enregistrements empreints de tentatives d'authenticité historique, généralement grâce à l'utilisation d'instruments d'époque et/ou de manuscrits d'origine.

Aux risques de l'acheteur
Des interprétations qui ont "bien vieilli", mais dont l'enregistrement n'est peut-être pas de la plus haute qualité. C'est généralement le cas des enregistrements datant d'avant 1960.

Deux autres symboles sont utilisés dans les critiques:

Lauréats du prix *Gramophone*
La distinction la plus convoitée dans le monde de la musique classique, décernée chaque année par le magazine dont nous sommes issus, par catégories allant d'Orchestral à Opéra en passant par Baroque et Contemporain. Un enregistrement est également sélectionné sur toute la liste pour le prix du disque de l'année.

La selection du Rédacteur en chef du *Gramophone*

Benutzungshinweise

Um die Nützlichkeit dieses Buches zu erhöhen und möglichst viele "gute" CDs aus dem riesigen nun erhältlichen Angebot zu erfassen, enthält diese Ausgabe folgende zusätzliche Informationen: **Weitere empfehlungen:** Bei einer vollständigen Besprechung, die im allgemeinen die höchste Empfehlung für ein bestimmtes Werk ist, werden gegebenenfalls zusätzlich alternative Einzel- oder Mehrfachempfehlungen folgen. **Weitere werke:** Einzelheiten über weitere beachtenswerte musikalische Werke desselben Komponisten. **Vorgeschlagene werke:** Einzelheiten über musikalische Werke von Komponisten, für die keine vollständigen Besprechungen vorliegen oder wo wenige Aufnahmen verfügbar sind.

Die angegebenen Einzelheiten betreffen Komponist(en), Werk(e), Instrument(e), Stimmumfang, Plattenfirma oder Label (siehe die Auflistung der Labels/Hersteller und Händler), CD-Nummer (plus alter Nummer, falls es sich um eine Wiederveröffentlichung handelt) und Besprechungsdatum in *Gramophone*.
Auf den Notenlinien unter einer überschrift werden folgende Informationen durch Symbole wiedergegeben:

Symbole

| Preis | Anzahl/verfügbarkeit | Dauer | Modus | Besprechungs-datum |

Preis

Normalpreis   Mittlere Preislage

Sparpreis   Super-Sparpreis

Anzahl/verfügbarkeit
Falls es sich um mehr als eine CD handelt, wird die entsprechende Zahl hier angegeben. Der erste Kreistyp zeigt Sets an, bei denen individuelle CDs nicht separat verfügbar sind. Der zweite Kreistyp zeigt an, daß die CDs *nur* separat verfügbar sind.

Dauer
Auf volle Minuten ab-oder aufgerundet.

Modus
Dieser Code aus drei Buchstaben wird heute von fast allen Herstellern verwendet, um Verfahren bei Aufnahme, Schnitt und Abmischung zu kennzeichnen. Die Buchstaben A und D stehen für Analog bzw Digital, und die Buchstabenfolge bezeichnet die chronologischen Schritte der Produktionskette: die Aufnahme selbst; das Schnitt- und/oder Abmischverfahren; und schließlich die Art der überspielung oder Transkription, die zur Vorbereitung des Originalbandes verwendet wird, welches dann die Vorlage für die Pressung bildet.

Besprechungsdatum
Monat und Jahr, in dem die Aufnahme in *Gramophone* besprochen wurde.

Beste
klangqualität

Lohnende
aufnahmen

Achtung!

Beste
interpretationen

Grundstock
authentizität

Historische

Beste interpretationen
Aufnahmen, die über jede Kritik erhaben sind – ein 'Muß' für jeden Sammler. Viele der älteren Aufnahmen hätten *Gramophone*-Preise gewonnen, hätte es diese Auszeichnung bei ihrem ersten Erscheinen bereits gegeben.

Beste klangqualität
Aufnahmen, die wirklich die Bezeichnung "Vorspielqualität" verdienen.

Grundstock
Aufnahmen, die die Basis für Ihre CD-Sammlung bilden sollten.

Lohnende aufnahmen
Nur für musikalisch Vielseitige! Diese Aufnahmen könnten leicht übersehen werden, da sie von weniger bekannten Komponisten stammen, sind jedoch oft für eine angenehme überraschung gut.

Historische authentizität
Aufnahmen, bei denen der Versuch historischer Authentizität unternommen wurde, etwa durch Verwendung von zeitgenössischen Instrumenten und/oder Originalmanuskripten.

Achtung!
Interpretationen, die die Zeiten überdauert haben, deren Aufnahmequalität jedoch eventuell nicht dem höchsten Standard entspricht. Dies betrifft im allgemeinen Aufnahmen von vor 1960.

Zwei weitere symbole werden in besprechungen verwendet:

Gramophone-Preisträger
Die begehrtesten Auszeichnungen für Aufnahmen im Bereich der klassischen Musik. Sie werden jedes Jahr von unserer Mutterzeitschrift in verschiedenen Kategorien verliehen, die von Orchestermusik bis Oper, von Barock- bis zu zeitgenössischer Musik reichen. Aus dieser Liste wird ebenfalls eine Aufnahme ausgewählt, die den Titel Platte des Jahres erhält.

Die Wahl des Redakteurs von *Gramophone*

Cómo valerse de esta guía

A fin de aumentar la utilidad de este libro y de cubrir tantos CD "buenos" como sea posible de la amplia gama actualmente disponible, esta edición incorpora la siguiente información adicional: **Recomendaciones adicionales:** Dentro de una revisión completa, que generalmente constituye la recomendación principal de una obra en especial, cuando sea adecuado habrá una o múltiples recomendaciones alternativas adicionales. **Audiciones adicionales:** Contiene detalles de otras obras musicales del mismo compositor que sean merecedoras de consideración. **Audiciones sugeridas:** Contiene detalles de obras musicales de aquellos compositores para los cuales no existen revisiones completas o de los que hay disponibles pocas grabaciones.

Se ofrecen detalles de los compositores, obras, instrumentos, escala vocal, compañía o etiqueta productora de los discos (véase de Etiquetas/Fabricantes y Distribuidores), número de disco (y número anterior cuando el nuevo es una reedición), así como la fecha o fechas de la revisión en *Gramophone*.
En los pentagramas musicales que siguen el título se facilita un índice informativo con el sistema de símbolos siguiente:

Los símbolos

Precio	Cantidad/ disponibilidad	Duración	Proceso	Fecha revisión
	② ②	lh 23m	DDD	6/88

Precio

Precio completo   Precio intermedio

Precio asequible   Precio módico

Cantidad/disponibilidad
Si hubiese más de un disco, el número de que se trate se mostrará aquí. El primer tipo de círculo indica los álbumes en que no están disponibles los discos por separado. El segundo tipo indica que los discos *solamente* están disponibles por separado.

Duración
Cálculo redondeado hasta el minuto más próximo.

Proceso
Este es un código formado por tres letras, que usan en la actualidad casi todos los fabricantes para indicar el tipo de proceso empleado en la manufactura. Las letras A ó D se emplean como denotadoras de Análogo o Digital, y la secuencia de las letras representa los pasos cronológicos en la cadena: la misma sesión de grabación, los procesos de edición y/o mezcla y, por último, la preparación del disco maestro de la transcripción, según el método de preparación de la cinta maestra que se envía a la fábrica.

Fecha de revisión
El mes y el año en qué se revisó la grabación en *Gramophone*.

Calidad de sonido | Disco que merece la pena explorar | Advertencia al comprador

Calidad de ejecución | Biblioteca básica | Ejecución con instrumentos de la época

Calidad de la ejecución

Grabaciones indiscutibles – 'obligatorias' para el buen coleccionista. A veces, las ediciones más antiguas hubieran merecido un Premio al Disco de *Gramophone* si dicho Premio hubiese existido cuando aparecieron.

Calidad de sonido

Estas grabaciones merecen verdaderamente el epíteto de 'parangones de buena calidad'.

Colección fundamental

Grabaciones con que comenzar a coleccionar discos compactos.

Discos que merece la pena explorar

Para el musicalmente promiscuo! Grabaciones que podrían pasarse por alto con facilidad puesto que no pertenecen a los compositores más conocidos. Pero quizá encierran agradables sorpresas.

Ejecución con instrumentos de la época

Grabaciones en que se ha intentado una autenticidad histórica. Habitualmente se han ejecutado con instrumentos de la época y/o empleando los manuscritos originales.

Advertencia al comprador

Interpretaciones que han resistido al paso del tiempo, pero en las que la calidad de la grabación puede no ser del más alto nivel. Esto generalmente se aplica a las grabaciones anteriores a 1960.

Dos símbolos más que se emplean en estas revisiones:

Ganadores de Premios *Gramophone*

Los más ambicionados en el mundo de la música clásica; se conceden todos los años por nuestra revista matriz en categorías desde Orquestal hasta Opera, Barroco y Contemporánea. Una grabación se escoge también en la lista general para recibir el Premio al Disco del Año.

Escogimiento del Redactor del *Gramophone*

Abbreviations

alto	counter-tenor	*ob*	oboe
anon	anonymous	*Op*	opus
arr	arranged	*orig*	original
attrib	attributed	*org*	organ
bar	baritone	*perc*	percussion
bass-bar	bass-baritone	*pf*	piano
bn	bassoon	*picc*	piccolo
c.	circa (about)	*pub*	publisher/published
cl	clarinet	*rec*	recorder
clav	clavichord	*rev*	revised
cont	continuo	*sax*	saxophone
contr	contralto	*sngr*	singer
cor ang	cor anglais	*sop*	soprano
cpte(d)	complete(d)	*spkr*	speaker
db	double bass	*stg*	string
dig pf	digital piano	*synth*	synthesizer
dir	director	*tbn*	trombone
ed	edited (by)/edition	*ten*	tenor
exc	excerpt	*timp*	timpani
fl	flute	*tpt*	trumpet
fp	fortepiano	*trad*	traditional
gtr	guitar	*trans*	transcribed
harm	harmonium	*treb*	treble
hn	horn	*va*	viola
hp	harp	*va da gamba*	viola da gamba
hpd	harpsichord	*vars*	variations
keybd	keyboard	*vc*	cello
lte	lute	*vib*	vibraphone
mez	mezzo-soprano	*vn*	violin
mndl	mandolin	*voc*	vocal/vocalist
narr	narrator	*wds*	words

Chamber music forms

string trio	violin, viola, cello
piano trio	violin, cello, piano
horn trio	horn, piano, violin
clarinet trio	clarinet, piano, cello
wind trio	oboe, clarinet, basssoon
baryton trio	baryton, viola, bass instrument
string quartet	2 violins, viola, cello
piano quartet	piano, string trio
wind quartet	flute, clarinet, horn, bassoon
string quintet	2 violins, 2 violas, cello
piano quintet	piano, string quartet
clarinet quintet	clarinet, string quartet
flute quartet	flute, string quartet
wind quintet	flute, oboe, clarinet, bassoon, horn
string sextet	2 violins, 2 violas, cello, double bass

Herbert von Karajan

Reviews

Bernard Haitink

Daniel Barenboim

Jascha Heifetz

About the Guide

The reviews

These indicate the best recordings available, in some instances the only recording, as in the case of John Adams's opera, *Nixon in China*, *page 20*. Reviews new to this edition of the *Guide* are clearly indicated.

Additional recommendations

These will include the same information as that provided on the staves following the main review headings: price category, number of discs, timing, original *Gramophone* review date and so on (see below). Full details are provided on *page 8* onwards and a brief explanation is provided at intervals throughout the book. An example of such recommendations are those following the new review of Adolphe Adam's ballet, *Giselle*, *opposite*.

Key to symbols

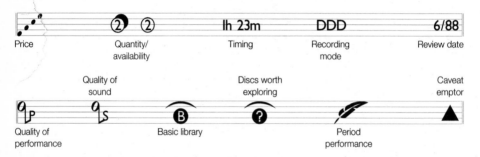

| Price | Quantity/availability | Timing | Recording mode | Review date |

② ②   lh 23m   DDD   6/88

Quality of sound   Discs worth exploring   Caveat emptor

Quality of performance   Basic library   Period performance

Suggested listening

Full title details are given of recordings of works by more obscure composers who merit attention but not, perhaps, a full review. An example of this is the first entry, *opposite*, for Carl Friedrich Abel. The date in brackets refers to the original *Gramophone* review date. A further example is the entry for Richard Addinsell, *page 21*, where the reader is referred to the Index to Reviews, *page 989*. Generally, where more than three composers are represented on a single disc, if it receives a full review this appears in the Collections section which starts on *page 871*.

Further listening

As this heading implies, these are works (again with full title information) by the same composer, listed at the end of a composer entry, which should be considered as worthwhile additions to a classical CD collection. An example of this is Adam's ballet, *Le corsaire*, *opposite*.

Carl Friedrich Abel

Suggested listening ...

Symphonies, Op. 7 — No. 1 in G major; No. 2 in B flat major; No. 3 in D major; No. 4 in F major; No. 5 in C major; No. 6 in E flat major. **Cantilena/Adrian Shepherd.** Chandos CHAN8648 (6/89).

Adolphe Adam

New review

Adam. Giselle. **Royal Opera House Orchestra, Covent Garden/Mark Ermler.** Royal Opera House Records ROH007. Recorded in 1993.

lh 14m DDD 4/94

Mark Ermler brings a Bolshoi Ballet director's experience to bear on the score, and with the Royal Opera House Orchestra likewise playing music it has in its blood the results are consistently impressive. The brass are especially good in the important hunting music in Act 1 and the galop towards the end of the same Act goes off in lively fashion. The score of *Giselle* is not a long one, which means that it can be accommodated virtually complete on one disc. Note, though, that the version of the score used here is that of Henri Busser, which means that there are some deviations of content and orchestration from other more recent recordings which go back to Adam's own score. Among these is Michael Tilson Thomas's version, which offers a no less alert and winning performance than Ermler. Tilson Thomas remains a strong competitor but no ballet enthusiast should have any reason to be disappointed with this well-filled, opulently recorded and well-documented disc.

Additional recommendations ...

Vienna Philharmonic Orchestra/Herbert von Karajan. Decca Ovation 417 738-2DM — lh ADD

London Symphony Orchestra/Michael Tilson Thomas. Sony Classical SK42450 — lh 17m DDD 3/92

Further listening ...

Le corsaire. **English Chamber Orchestra/Richard Bonynge.** Decca 430 286-2DH2 (10/92).

John Adams

New review

J. Adams. Harmonielehre. The Chairman Dances. Two Fanfares —Tromba lontana; Short Ride in a Fast Machine. **City of Birmingham Symphony Orchestra/Simon Rattle.** EMI CDC5 55051-2. Recorded in 1993.

lh 2m DDD 6/94

Harmonielehre was inspired by a dream vision of a massive tanker that suddenly took flight, displaying a "beautiful brownish-orange oxide on the bottom part of its hull"; the 'setting' was just off San Francisco Bay Bridge. "Those pounding E minor chords are like a grinding of gears," says John Adams of its violent, gunshot opening. Scored for a huge orchestra and structured in three contrasted sections, *Harmonielehre* is probably the nearest thing on offer to a minimalist symphony, and for that reason alone it could well appeal beyond the élite coterie of minimalist-fanciers. Rattle's recording has great heft and dynamic range, an informative balance and a vivid sense of aural perspective. The brass components of those opening chords (horns, trumpets, trombones and tubas) have enormous weight and presence, and the ringing marimbas thereafter, a bright complexion. Adams's frequent requests for subtle tempo transitions ("Tempo gradually picks up", "Slightly faster ... but still very flexible and fluid" and so on) are subtly honoured by the conductor. Rattle gives us three fill-ups: the Copland-inspired *Short Ride in a Fast Machine* and *Two Fanfares*, and *The Chairman Dances*, a 'foxtrot for orchestra' that utilizes material from Adams's opera, *Nixon in China*. Searching for a metaphor, one might suggest that Rattle's Mao does his foxtrot in tweeds and a pair of brogues. Rattle's view of Adams is recommended particularly to mainstream collectors who aren't yet sold on minimalism.

New review

Adams. Hoodoo Zephyr. Coast. Disappointment Lake. Tourist Song. Tundra. Bump. Cerulean. **John Adams** (bar/synth). Elektra Nonesuch 7559-79311-2. Texts included. Recorded 1992-93.

> **54m DDD 4/94**

This is music which depicts phases of travel. Each title indicates a place or area of the American West Coast which is then musically depicted. The music is wholly instrumental, is synthesizer-generated and within what can be loosely described as the minimalist tradition. What Adams achieves here is more human, more intimate and certainly more approachable than much of his recent work. There is less striving to borrow from past composers, and the apparent influences, whether ethnic or conservatory, are not bleeding chunks but part of a personal compositional tapestry which has its own character and cohesiveness. And Adams has solved the problem of moving a harmonically static composition through time and space by 'colouring' the rhythm with pitch and tone, like a great deal of pop, jazz and ethnic musics have done and continue to do. A small-scale but satisfying success, and one which is surprisingly pleasant on the ear for all but the most obdurate of anti-minimalists.

Adams. NIXON IN CHINA. **Sanford Sylvan** (bar) Chou en-Lai; **James Maddalena** (bar) Richard Nixon; **Thomas Hammons** (bar) Henry Kissinger; **Mari Opatz** (mez) Nancy T'ang (First Secretary to Mao); **Stephanie Friedman** (mez) Second Secretary to Mao; **Marion Dry** (mez) Third Secretary to Mao; **John Duykers** (ten) Mao Tse-Tung; **Carolann Page** (sop) Pat Nixon; **Trudy Ellen Craney** (sop) Chiang Ch'ing; **St Luke's Chorus and Orchestra/Edo de Waart.** Elektra Nonesuch 7559-79177-2. Notes and text included.

> **③ 2h 24m DDD 10/88** ?

If few operas deal with current affairs and even fewer address political issues, then *Nixon in China* takes the unusual risk of bordering on the documentary. But it is also a study in the psychology of its principal characters, and by peering into the personalities it goes well beyond fact alone, revealing instead a truly human drama. Alice Goodman's libretto is structured around the American presidential visit to Beijing in February 1972. At first all is a whirl of formalities, functions and fervent debate, but as the energy begins to flag so human vulnerabilities show through, and the opera ends in a state of lassitude, a strange super-imposition of bedroom scenes in which the protagonists share with one another their various reminiscences and dreams. Adams's score is particularly strong when the action is fast-moving: he is a master of energetic, sonorous music, and his minimalist leanings serve him well in those parts of the story that require movement or depend upon quick-fire exchanges. Less dynamic moments — and Goodman's libretto is rich in poetical soliloquies and dialogues — he perhaps handles less elegantly, though in the long final act the mood of intimacy and soul-searching is cleverly caught. Best of all, however, is the music that captures the mood of the public scenes. Adams revels in evoking tawdry glamour, and a hint of fox-trot often hangs deliciously in the air. The cast is a strong one; James Maddalena in particular faces us with a life-like Richard Nixon, and Trudy Ellen Craney is memorable in Adams's most exaggerated character, the coloratura Madame Mao. So familiar are the faces behind the names that *Nixon in China* cannot be an easy work to watch on stage. On disc, with a few photographs provided in the insert booklet to jog the memory, it's perhaps easier to reconcile historical truth with the fantasy-world of this curious opera.

Further listening ...

THE DEATH OF KLINGHOFFER. **Soloists; London Opera Chorus; Lyon Opera Orchestra/Kent Nagano.** Elektra Nonesuch 7559-79281-2 (3/93).

Richard Addinsell

Suggested listening ...

Warsaw Concerto. *Coupled with* **Gottschalk.** Grande fantaisie triomphale sur l'hymne national brésilien, RO108. **Litolff.** Concerto Symphonique No. 4 in D minor, Op. 102 — Scherzo. **Rachmaninov.** Piano Concerto No. 2 in C minor, Op. 18. **Cristina Ortiz** (pf). **Royal Philharmonic Orchestra/Moshe Atzmon.** Decca 414 348-2DH (9/86). *See review in the Collections section; refer to the Index to Reviews.*

Theodore Adorno

Suggested listening ...

Six Kurze Orchesterstücke, Op. 4[a]. Kinderjahr: sechs stücke aus Op. 68 von Robert Schumann (1941)[a]. Two Stücke — String Quartet, Op. 22[b]. Three Gedichte[c]. Der Schatz des Indianer-Joe — Singspiel[d]. [d]**Soloists;** [b]**Buchberger Quartet;** [c]**Frankfurt Chamber Choir/Hans Michael Beuerle;** [a]**Frankfurt Opera Orchestra/Gary Bertini.** Wergo WER173-2 (6/91).

Vladimir Agopov

Suggested listening ...

Cello Concerto, Op. 10, "Tres Viae"[a]. *Coupled with* **Dutilleux.** Cello Concerto, "Tout un monde lointain"[b]. **Arto Noras** (vc); **Finnish Radio Symphony Orchestra/Jukka-Pekka Saraste.** Finlandia FACD401 (10/92).

Alexander Agricola

Suggested listening ...

Vocal Works — Virgo sub ethereis. Je n'ay dueil. Revenez tous regretz. En actendant. Jam fulsit sol de sidere. Gardez voz bien. A la mignonne de fortune. In mijnen sin. *Instrumental Works* — De tous bien playne (two versions). Tandernaken al op den rijn. Pater meus agricola est. Dictes moi toutes. Cecus non judicat de coloribus. Helas madame. Fortuna desperata. **Ferrara Ensemble; Ensemble Este of the Schola Cantorum Basiliensis/Crawford Young.** Deutsche Harmonia Mundi RD77038 (7/90).

Kalevi Aho

Suggested listening ...

Symphonies — No. 5 (1975-76). No. 7, "Insect" (1988). **Leipzig Radio Symphony Orchestra/Max Pommer.** Ondine ODE765-2.

Jehan Alain

Suggested listening ...

Intermezzo. Litanies, Op. 79. *Coupled with* **Dupré.** Preludes and Fugues, Op. 7. **Franck.**
Prélude, fugue et variation in B minor, Op. 18. Fantaisie in A major. **Tournemire.** Petite
rapsodie improvisée. Cantilène improvisée. Improvisation sur le Te Deum. **Jane Watts** (org).
Priory PRCD286 (9/90).

Litanies, Op. 79. *Coupled with* **Sibelius** (arr. H. Fricker). Finlandia, Op. 26. **Sløgedal.**
Variations on a Norwegian Folk Tune. **Mulet.** Carillon-sortie in D major. **Lindberg.** Organ
Sonata in G minor, Op. 23 — Alla Sarabanda; Allegro con brio. **Mozart.** Orgelstück (Fantasia)
für eine Uhr, K608. **Lefébure-Wély.** Marche. **Nielsen.** Commotio, FS155. **Elgar.** Pomp
and Circumstance March in G major, Op. 39 No. 4. **Christopher Herrick** (org). Hyperion
CDA66676. *See review in the Collections section; refer to the Index to Reviews.*

Deuxième fantaisie. Le jardin suspendu. *Coupled with* **Franck.** Fantaisie in A major.
Mendelssohn. Organ Sonata in C major/minor. **Schumann.** Fugue on B-A-C-H, Op. 60
No. 3. **Andriessen.** Sonata da chiesa. **Saint-Saëns.** Fantaisie in C major, Op. 157.
Messiaen. Les corps glorieux — Joie et clarté des corps glorieux. **Piet Kee** (org). Chandos
CHAN9188 (10/93). *See review in the Collections section; refer to the Index to Reviews.*

Isaac Albéniz

Albéniz (orch. Halffter). Rapsodia española, Op. 70.
Falla. Noches en los jardins de España.
Turina. Rapsodia sinfónica, Op. 66. **Alicia de Larrocha** (pf); **London Philharmonic
Orchestra/Rafael Frühbeck de Burgos.** Decca 410 289-2DH. From 410 289-1DH (6/84).

⠶ 52m DDD 10/84 ⁹ₚ

The three magically beautiful nocturnes which make up Falla's *Nights in the gardens of Spain*
express the feelings and emotions evoked by contrasted surroundings, whilst Albéniz's enjoyably
colourful *Rapsodia española* is a loosely assembled sequence of Spanish dances such as the *jota* and
the *malagueña*. Like Falla's *Nights* the work was conceived as a piano solo, but this disc contains
a version with orchestra arranged by Cristobal Halffter. The disc is completed by Turina's short,
two-part work for piano and strings. All three pieces are excellently performed, but it is the
Falla work which brings out the quality of Larrocha's artistry; her ability to evoke the colour of
the Spanish atmosphere is remarkable. Frühbeck de Burgos supports her magnificently and
persuades the LPO to some very Latin-sounding playing. The recording is suitably atmospheric.

Albéniz. Iberiaᵃ (arr. Gray) — El Albaicín; Triana; Rondeña.
Granados. Seven Valses poéticos (trans. Williams).
Rodrigo. Invocación y Danza. En los trigales.
Anonymous (arr. Llobet): Ten Catalan Folk-songs — Cançó del lladre; El testament d'Amelia;
La filadora; El mestre; La nit de Nadal; L'hereu Riera; Lo fill del Ré; La Pastoreta; El Noi de la
Mare. **John Williams** (gtr); ᵃ**London Symphony Orchestra/Paul Daniels.** Sony Classical
SK48480.

⠶ 1h 11m DDD 7/92 ⁹ₚ ❓

The amalgam of technical guitaristic perfection in the face of daunting demands, fluid musicality
and exemplary tone-production, caught in this exceptionally lifelike recording, represents a
landmark in the instrument's march towards true parity with other instruments. Granados's
Valses are unabridged, Rodrigo's moody *Invocación y Danza* comes in its original and more
effective form, and two of the charming settings of Catalan folk-songs arranged by Llobet have
no other recording. Nothing in Albéniz's virtuosic *Iberia* is accessible to the solo guitar, but with
the aid of the London Symphony Orchestra and Gray's enchantingly evocative arrangements,

Williams shows three of its movements in a new and colourful light. To anyone with the slightest interest in the guitar or Spanish romantic music this disc is a required purchase.

Additional recommendations ...
Iberia. Navarra (compl. de Séverac). Suite española, Op. 47. **Alicia de Larrocha** (pf). Decca 417 887-2DH2 — ⁘ ② 2h 6m DDD 6/88 ⑨ₛ Ⓑ
Iberia. Cantos de España, Op. 232. **Rafael Orozco** (pf). Auvidis Valois V4663 — ⁘ ② 1h 2m DDD 11/92 Ⓑ

New review
Albéniz (arr. Byzantine). Suite española, Op. 47. Recuerdos de viaje, Op. 71. **Julian Byzantine** (gtr). Classics for Pleasure CD-CFP4631. Recorded in 1990.

⁙ 1h 18m DDD 4/94

Transferring these works to the guitar transmutes them into a semi-precious metal of another kind, one of which Albéniz himself warmly approved. Rather slower tempos in "Asturias" and "Aragón" suit the guitar, whilst in "Castilla" and "Cádiz" the two move happily at much the same rate, and Byzantine takes some pieces at both faster and slower than 'pianistic' tempos. He is a lyrical and utterly musical player whose clean fingers produce lovely sounds and he gives a cultured and thoughtful view of the music. With *Recuerdos de viaje* Byzantine has the field to himself — there is not even a piano version available. His arrangements and performances of them will do very nicely. At budget price this is strongly tempting.

Additional recommendation ...
Suite española. **Granados.** *Goyescas — excerpts.* **Falla.** *El amor brujo.* **New Philharmonia Orchestra/Rafael Frühbeck de Burgos.** Decca 417 786-2DM — ⁘ 1h 9m ADD 10/89

New review
Albéniz (trans. Bream). GUITAR WORKS.
Granados (trans. Bream). GUITAR WORKS. **Julian Bream** (gtr). RCA Julian Bream Edition 09026 61608-2. Recorded in 1982.
Albéniz: Mallorca, Op. 202. Suite española, Op. 47. Cantos de España, Op. 232 — Córdoba.
Granados: Cuentos de la juventud — Dedicatoria. 15 Tonadillas — El majo Olvidado. 12 Danzas españolas, Op. 37 — Villanesca; Andaluza (Playera). Seven Valses poéticos.

⁘ 1h 3m DDD 6/94   ⑨ₚ ⑨ₛ

In the early summer of 1982 Julian Bream recorded a solo recital of music by Albéniz and Granados in his favourite recording venue, Wardour Chapel in Wiltshire. The result turned out to be the finest of all his discs, a view endorsed by the artist himself. The recording is just about perfect — if one sets the correct level he appears to be sitting out there behind the speakers — and the playing itself has extraordinary electricity and magnetism. The two items to sample first are the hauntingly evocative "Córdoba" from the *Cantos de España* of Albéniz and the famous *Danza española* No. 5 ("Andaluza") of Granados, where in the middle section (against a silent background) Bream echoes himself gently in the most magical *pianissimo* — breathtaking. The other works included are all played with comparable spontaneity.

Sebastiàn de Albero
Spanish 1722-1756

New review
Albero. 14 Keyboard Sonatas. Three Keyboard Sonatas (misattributed to D. Scarlatti) — F sharp minor, Kk142; C major, Kk143; G major, Kk144. **Joseph Payne** (hpd). BIS CD629. Recorded in 1993.

⁘ 1h 9m DDD 4/94   ⑨ₚ ⑨ₛ ✒

This is a significant and attractive disc that will be wanted by all those interested in this little-known area of Spanish harpsichord music. Many characteristics of the present sonatas are similar to those of Domenico Scarlatti — an exuberant vitality, employment of Spanish dance rhythms, bold leaps up and down the keyboard, handcrossings, freedom of modulation (in the fashion of Scarlatti's "jesting with art", as in the second half of No. 4), repeated cadential formulas, 'scrunch' chords (in Nos. 8 and 10) and quasi-trumpet fanfares (in the buoyant No. 14). The spirited performances by the British-born, American-based Joseph Payne, divided equally between copies of a single-manual Italian instrument of 1693 and a two-manual Blanchet of 1730, are admirable throughout, and the recording is of the excellence we have come to expect from BIS.

Eugen d'Albert
British/German 1864-1932

Suggested listening ...

TIEFLAND. **Soloists; Berlin RIAS Chorus; Berlin Symphony Orchestra/Hans Zanotelli.** Eurodisc 353 240 (2/89).

Tomaso Albinoni
Italian 1671-1751

Albinoni. Concerti a cinque, Op. 7. Sinfonie e concerti a cinque, Op. 2 — No. 5 in D major; No. 6 in G minor. **Heinz Holliger, Maurice Bourgue** (obs); **I Musici.** Philips 432 115-2PH2. Recorded 1990-91.
No. 1 in D major. No. 2 in C major. No. 3 in B flat major. No. 4 in G major. No. 5 in C major. No. 6 in D major. No. 7 in A major. No. 8 in D major. No. 9 in F major. No. 10 in B flat major. No. 11 in C major. No. 12 in C major

② lh 34m DDD 1/93

Albinoni's 12 Concertos, Op. 7 fall into three distinct types: four of them are for strings alone, four for strings with a single oboe and four for strings with two oboes. More than in Vivaldi's oboe concertos, Albinoni's earlier examples of the form contain a greater interaction between the oboes and the violins. This repertory has been a stock-in-trade for I Musici for well over 30 years so, as we might expect, the performances are lively, well polished and, within certain boundaries, stylish. But it is above all the oboists on whom the success or failure of this set ultimately depends. In the partnership of Heinz Holliger and Maurice Bourgue we could hardly find stronger advocates. They phrase eloquently, shade effectively, ornament tastefully and unfailingly play in tune. Holliger also plays the four concertos for one oboe, bringing a wonder-ful sense of poetry to the music, wistful in slow movements, athletic in faster ones. I Musici are perhaps on occasion a little weighty in their accompaniments but clean ensemble and clear articulation are positive virtues. Two additional pieces in this release come from Albinoni's Op. 2. Both of them are attractive sonatas in five parts for strings only. In short an enjoyable issue, affectionately realized.

Additional recommendations ...
Op. 7 — Nos. 2, 3, 5, 6, 8, 9, 11 and 12. **Heinz Holliger, Hans Elhorst** (obs); **Berne Camerata.** Archiv Produktion Galleria 427 111-2AGA — 57m ADD 4/89
Op. 7 — Nos. 3, 6, 9 and 12. Op. 9 — No. 2 in D minor; No. 5 in C major; No. 8 in G minor; No. 11 in B flat major. **London Harpsichord Ensemble/Sarah Francis** (ob). Unicorn-Kanchana DKPCD9088 — lh 14m DDD 3/90

New review
Albinoni. Concerti a cinque, Op. 9. **Anthony Camden, ªJulia Girdwood** (obs); **London Virtuosi/John Georgiadis.** Naxos 8 550739. Recorded in 1992.
No. 2 in D minor. No. 3 in F major[a]. No. 5 in C major. No. 8 in G minor. No. 9 in C major[a]. No. 11 in B flat major.

lh 4m DDD 3/94

Both Vivaldi and Albinoni were generous to the oboe, but whilst the former wrote violinistically for it, the latter treated it like a human voice, as befitted the composer of more than 50 known operas — an association that is reflected in the presentation of the thematic material of the concertos. The oboe participates in, rather than dominates, these works in a chamber-music-like fashion. Each of the four groups of three into which the concertos of Op. 9 fall consists of one for the violin, one for solo oboe and one for two oboes, in that order. Albinoni was not in the business of springing harmonic surprises, but was a fluent writer of engaging tunes, particularly those in the *Adagios* — each of these works has one — and of elegant discourses between the soloist(s) and the upper strings. Anthony Camden and Julia Girdwood produce liquid sounds from their modern instruments and are as meltingly expressive in the slow movements as they are light on their feet in the flanking ones. The London Virtuosi, also using modern strings, have a nice, clean air about them and give the music neither more nor less than its due. The recording is bright and well balanced.

Additional recommendation …
No. 2; No. 6 in G major; No. 9. Concerto in C major. **Vivaldi.** Concertos — C major, RV560; F major, RV457; C major, RV559. **Paul Goodwin** (ob); **King's Consort/Robert King.**
Hyperion CDA66383 — .•´ Ih 10m DDD 6/91 ✍

Hugo Alfvén

Alfvén. Symphony No. 4, Op. 39, "From the Outermost Skerries"[a]. A legend of the Skerries, Op. 20. [a]**Christina Högman** (sop); [a]**Claes-Hakon Ahnsjö** (ten); [a]**Per-Olof Gillblad** (cor ang); [a]**Karl-Ove Mannberg** (vn); [a]**Elemér Lavotha** (vc); [a]**Lucia Negro** (pf); **Stockholm Philharmonic Orchestra/Neeme Järvi.** BIS CD505. Recorded in 1990.

.•´ Ih 4m DDD 8/92

The Fourth Symphony occupied Alfvén for the best part of a decade; the first ideas come from 1908 and he returned to the score in 1913. He put it into its final shape during 1918-19 after spending a great deal of time in the outer archipelago of Stockholm, that stretches out far into the Baltic. Anyone who has spent any time there will know just how magical it is. This is a highly romantic programme. Its opulence of colour and sumptuousness of texture has won it many admirers: there is a lot of Strauss in it, and a touch of Reger and even Debussy. There is a wordless vocalise, inspired no doubt by Nielsen's *Sinfonia Espansiva* (1912). The soloists in this performance are excellent and the orchestral playing under Neeme Järvi is very responsive. The recording is beautifully balanced with detail perfectly placed and plenty of air round the sound. *A legend of the Skerries* is an earlier piece, which comes from the same period as his *Midsummer Vigil* but does not have its independence of outlook. There is a lot of Wagner in this piece. Eminently recommendable to those who like to wallow in lush romantic sonorities.

New review
Alfvén. Symphony No. 5 in A minor, Op. 54. The Mountain King — Suite. Gustav II Adolf, Op. 49 — Elegy. **Royal Stockholm Philharmonic Orchestra/Neeme Järvi.** BIS CD585. Recorded in 1992.

.•´ Ih 8m DDD 1/94   ⁹s

The first movement of the Fifth Symphony (1942-52) is a long movement lasting over 17 minutes, with echoes of Wagner and Sibelius — and in the second group a reminder of Bax. Given the fervent advocacy it receives here from Neeme Järvi and the Royal Stockholm Philharmonic, it makes a strong impression. So, too, do the dreamy musings of the slow movement. Järvi is also at his most persuasive and gets marvellously responsive and committed playing from the Stockholm orchestra especially in the first two movements and *The Mountain King* — and the touching "Elegy" from *Gustav II Adolf*, perhaps Alfvén's most affecting and deeply felt piece. The BIS team have come up with a state-of-the-art recording, natural and lifelike. The perspective could hardly be improved upon and each orchestral strand has presence and is effortlessly truthful in timbre.

Further listening …

Symphony No. 2 in D major, R28. Midsummer Vigil — Swedish Rhapsody No. 1, R45.
Stockholm Philharmonic Orchestra/Neeme Järvi. BIS CD385 (7/88).

Charles-Valentin Alkan

French 1813-1888

Alkan. Grand duo concertante in F sharp minor, Op. 21[a]. Sonate de concert in E major, Op. 47[b]. Trio in G minor, Op. 30[c]. **ᶜTrio Alkan** ([a]Kolja Lessing, vn; [b]Bernhard Schwarz, vc; [ab]Rainer Klaas, pf). Marco Polo 8 223383.

1h 15m DDD 8/93

The first movement of Alkan's violin sonata, the *Grand duo concertante* suggests, at times, the harmonic world of Berlioz, but perhaps more strikingly looks forward, both here and in the final movement, to the melodic, Gallic charm, of the Fauré sonatas. The *Sonate de concert* for cello and piano is perhaps Alkan's finest and most important contribution to chamber music. It is some 32 minutes in length and has been described as "the missing link between the cello sonatas of Beethoven and Brahms". Despite dating from 1856 and containing an unusual degree of virtuosic display, the work is clearly rooted in the classical tradition. And yet the sonata shouts Alkan from every page: the second movement, in *siciliano* style, is a fine example of Alkan whimsy — a real teaser of a movement, and in the slow movement Alkan draws musical inspiration from his Jewish faith to create a serene oasis of calm before launching into the helter-skelter activity of the *saltarello* finale in which an almost continuous stream of triplets fly hither and thither in tarantella style. The earlier Piano Trio (1841) is even more classical in design. The performances, by members of the aptly named Trio Alkan, are quite superb and the recording is full-bodied and close, though not uncomfortably so.

Alkan. 25 Préludes dans les tons majeurs et mineur, Op. 31.
Shostakovich. 24 Preludes, Op. 34. **Olli Mustonen** (pf). Decca 433 055-2DH. Recorded in 1990.

1h 16m DDD 10/91

It was brave of Decca to launch the career of their then newly-signed pianist with a disc of miniatures few people actually know since the *oeuvre* of Charles-Valentin Alkan is usually confined to specialist labels and second-rate executants. The 25 Préludes are a reasonably benign introduction to Alkan's idiosyncratic world — elusive and quirky to be sure but less ruthlessly barnstorming than much of his output. They are by no means easy pieces to bring off, but you wouldn't know it from Mustonen's exceptionally assured, brilliantly poised readings. Where rival versions are content to offer the 25 Préludes without coupling, Mustonen adds deft and sparkling performances of Shostakovich's not exactly insubstantial Op. 34 Preludes. Exceptional pianism, excellent, bright recording and helpful notes.

Alkan. 12 Etudes dans les tons mineurs, Op. 39 Nos. 8-10. Concerto pour Piano Seul. **Marc-André Hamelin** (pf). Music and Arts CD724.

50m DDD 8/93

Alkan. 12 Etudes dans les tons mineurs, Op. 39 Nos. 3 and 12. 12 Etudes dans les tons majeurs, Op. 35. **Bernard Ringeissen** (pf). Marco Polo 8 223351.

1h 18m DDD 11/93

The extreme technical difficulties imposed upon any pianist rash enough to undertake a performance of the *Concerto* cannot be overstated. The effect is cumulative. Only after five to six minutes into the 30-minute first movement do we become aware of the almost superhuman feat unfolding before our ears. And then there's the key signature — G sharp minor — no easy key, ask any pianist. This is the *ne plus ultra* of piano *études* — it leaves all reeling in its wake: no wonder that Liszt was said to have feared the idea of playing before Alkan. Yet this is no mere showpiece, but a fully integrated and richly melodic example of sonata form. The second movement is a profoundly moving and expressive *Adagio* that builds to a powerful funereal central section presaging the sound-world of Mahler. Such pianism as one finds here really needs only the shortest of descriptions: Hamelin's is a stunningly monumental performance, an exhilarating experience not to be missed. Bernard Ringeissen's disc brings with it the first complete recording of the neglected *12 Etudes dans les tons majeurs*, Op. 35 of 1847. Of course, Alkan and the word *étude* spell technical difficulties of the most fearsome variety, but Ringeissen's formidable technique seems to know no bounds, and challenge after challenge appear to be swallowed up with yet still more in hand — for particularly dazzling examples try Studies Nos. 4, 5 (the famous *Allegro barbaro*), 6 and 12 and one wonders why we hear so little of this pianist. Fine performances of "Le festin d'Esope" and the "Scherzo diabolico" (both from the Op. 39 set of *études*) fill the remainder of this generous disc. The recorded sound is good on both discs.

Further listening ...

Concerti da Camera, Op. 10 — No. 1 in A minor; No. 2 in C sharp minor. *Coupled with* **Henselt.** Piano Concert in F minor, Op. 16. Variations de Concert, Op. 11, on "Quand je quittai la Normandie" from Meyerbeer's "Robert le Diable". **Marc-André Hamelin** (pf); **BBC Scottish Symphony Orchestra/Martyn Brabbins.** Hyperion CDA66717 (8/94). *See review under Henselt; refer to the Index to Reviews.*

Key to symbols

Quality of sound	Discs worth exploring	Caveat emptor
Quality of performance	Basic library	Period performance

Gregorio Allegri

Italian c.1582-1652

Allegri. Miserere mei.
Palestrina. MOTETS. **Roy Goodman** (treb); **King's College Choir, Cambridge/Sir David Willcocks.** Decca Ovation 421 147-2DM.
Palestrina: Stabat mater a 8. Hodie beata virgo. Senex puerum portabat. Magnificat a 8. Litaniae de Beata Vergine Mariae I a 8.

56m ADD 5/89

More than 30 years have passed since this recording of Allegri's *Miserere* was made yet it still has the power to enchant: it was one of the glories of Sir David Willcocks's influential tenure at King's, the days of a uniform sound of voices which blended seamlessly with each other, making here the perfect aural backdrop for the voice of a boy treble. Here it is Roy Goodman (who went on to become a successful violinist and director) whose clear tones soar effortlessly into the vaults of the College Chapel, creating arches of sound that mirror the architecture of the Chapel. It is recordings like this that draw visitors to the Chapel in Cambridge and listeners to the radio to hear the choir sing in the Service of Nine Lessons and Carols each Christmas and yet it is still regrettably the only piece generally known by this pupil of Palestrina (and from Palestrina we have some superbly sung and well-chosen motets). In short, for an endearing selection of Palestrina's art and Allegri's gem, both allied to the timeless quality of King's, this mid-price disc cannot be beaten.

Additional recommendations ...
Miserere (with Nicholas Thompson, treb; Wilfred Swansborough, alto; Timothy Jones, bass). **B. Rose.** Feast Song for St Cecilia (with Simon Hill, alto; Alan Green, ten). **Brahms.** Ein deutsches Requiem — Ich hab nun Traurigkeit. **Britten.** Festival Te Deum, Op. 32. **Harvey.** Come, Holy Ghost (with Andrew Burden, ten; Nigel Beaven, bass). **Mendelssohn.** Hear my prayer. **Stanford.** Evening Canticles in G major (with Timothy Jones). **Tavener.** I will lift up mine eyes.

Wise. *The way of Zion do mourn* (with Charles Gibbs, bass). **Jeremy Budd** (treb); **St Paul's Cathedral Choir/John Scott** with **Andrew Lucas** (org). Hyperion CDA66439 — ⋯ 1h 16m DDD 10/91 Ⓑ

Miserere. **Lotti.** *Crucifixus.* **Palestrina.** *Missa Papae Marcelli. Stabat mater a 8.* **The Sixteen/ Harry Christophers.** Collins Classics 5009-2 — ⋯ 56m DDD 10/90 Ⓑ

Francisco António de Almeida

Portuguese c.1702-1755

Almeida. La Giuditta. **Lena Lootens, Francesca Congiu** (sops); **Axel Köhler** (alto); **Martyn Hill** (ten); **Cologne Concerto/René Jacobs.** Harmonia Mundi HMC90 1411/2. Text and translation included. Recorded in 1992.

⋯ ② 2h 1m DDD 11/92 ♀P ❓ ✒

Francisco António de Almeida is a name that will be unfamiliar to all but the most ardent *aficionados* of baroque music. Born in Portugal, he spent some time in Rome which led to the composition of several comic operas and a large amount of sacred music, most of which has been lost. *La Giuditta*, based on the biblical story of Judith's victory over Holofernes, is his only surviving oratorio. Stylistically he is closest to Handel, with those characteristic Handelian harmonies in "Quella fiamma" on track 3, though *Giuditta* was written before any of Handel's oratorios except *La Resurrezione*. But Almeida establishes a style very much his own from the very first chord, here brilliantly brought to life by René Jacobs and his Cologne Concerto. Martyn Hill as Holofernes is appropriately war-like, though he is occasionally choppy, notably in "Invitti miei guerrieri". Axel Köhler as Ozia, beseiged by Holofernes's armies, is, however, superb, with a fine dramatic range: the gentleness of his "Tortorella, se rimira" is particularly moving. Lena Lootens in the title-role is wonderfully stylish, pure of voice throughout "Sento che dice al cor", with great strength and clean *fioriture* in her plea to God to defeat her enemies, "Dalla destra onnipotente". It is perhaps a pity that the part of Achiorre should have been written for a soprano: Francesca Congiu has a hard time convincing listeners that she is indeed Commander of the Ammonites, though this illusion would probably be easier to sustain on stage. René Jacobs guides the work with an unerring sense of pace and drama. From the attention-grabbing Overture through to the final notes, this is a totally committed, totally compelling performance of a newly discovered masterpiece.

William Alwyn

British 1905-1985

New review
Alwyn. Concerto for Flute and Eight Wind Instruments[a]. Suite for Oboe and Harp[b]. Music for Three Players[d]. Trio for Flute, Cello and Piano[e]. [ace]**Kate Hill** (fl); [d]**Joy Farrall** (cl); [d]**Leland Chen** (vn); [e]**Caroline Dearnley** (vc); [c]**Ieuan Jones** (hp); [bde]**Julius Drake** (pf); [a]**London Haffner Wind Ensemble/Nicholas Daniel** ([b]ob). Chandos CHAN9152. Recorded in 1992.

⋯ 1h 6m DDD 10/93 ♀S

Anyone familiar with the scale and spectacle of Alwyn's symphonies might wonder if his chamber music would prove to be inflated. Not so. Its scale is admirable and the part-writing and control of texture endlessly pleases the ear. The Concerto for Flute and Eight Wind Instruments is structurally as appealing as it is tuneful, while the Suite for Oboe and Harp is utterly charming. This leads us naturally into the peaceful opening "Prelude" of the *Music for Three Players* — violin, clarinet and piano. This is a suite of eight contrasted vignettes and the "Romance", which comes second, led by the violin, really tickles the ear. The final work, a two-movement Trio, has some soaring writing for the cello which brings lovely playing from Caroline Dearnley and there is an engaging interplay with the flute. The Haffner Wind Ensemble is very impressive indeed, both individually as personalities and as a team matching timbres expertly. Their playing is full of spontaneity and enjoyment and the recording is well balanced and very realistic, as we expect from Chandos. The acoustic seems just about perfect.

Alwyn (arr. Palmer). Odd Man Out — Suite. The History of Mr Polly — Suite. The Fallen Idol — Suite. The Rake's Progress — Calypso. **London Symphony Orchestra/Richard Hickox.** Chandos CHAN9243.

1h 12m DDD 3/94

William Alwyn, like Malcolm Arnold, made his name as a composer of film music in the great days of British cinema. In the immediate post-war years he wrote the scores on the present disc. British films in those days had 'symphonic' scores and were awash with orchestral sound. *Odd Man Out* inspired the most powerful and lyrically poignant music here, while *The History of Mr Polly* (a much-liked movie, with John Mills memorable in the title-role) is charmingly light-weight, especially in the "Punting scene", and is really rather touching in the "Utopian sunset" of the finale. *The Fallen Idol* (an outstanding movie, written by Graham Greene) is about a small boy who witnesses a death and is in danger of implicating his friend, the Butler (Ralph Richard-son). The music subtly underlines the action and feelings of the characters. The original scores were unwittingly destroyed at Pinewood Studios but Christopher Palmer has lovingly restored each one for this record. Hickox conducts all this music with total commitment and it is beautifully played and recorded.

Alwyn. Invocations[a]. A Leave-taking[b]. [a]**Jill Gomez** (sop); [b]**Anthony Rolfe Johnson** (ten); [a]**John Constable**, [b]**Graham Johnson** (pfs). Chandos CHAN9220. Texts included. From ABRD1117 (3/85).

46m DDD 6/94

Jill Gomez and Anthony Rolfe Johnson had both taken leading roles in Alwyn's opera *Miss Julie*, and the songs were offered as an expression of gratitude. Going with this is an appreciation of their voices and musicianship, Gomez so clear in tone and secure on high, and Rolfe Johnson so expert in coloration, with impressive resources of power to be drawn on at climaxes. The piano writing is also immensely skilful and both pianists make much of their opportunities and are as 'authentic' in their work as the singers themselves. Alwyn has a fine sense of the song-maker's art in establishing a unity and allowing a difference. Particularly attractive are the "Invocation to the Queen of Moonlight", where there is an uncloying, delicate sweetness, and "The Ocean Wood" where the piano part enacts the sea-fantasy and the voice, catching the marine mystery, grows to a resounding climax. The playing time is rather short but it is easy to think of discs that last longer and have less on them.

Alwyn. MISS JULIE. **Jill Gomez** (sop) Miss Julie; **Benjamin Luxon** (bar) Jean; **Della Jones** (mez) Kristin; **John Mitchinson** (ten) Ulrik; **Philharmonia Orchestra/Vilem Tausky.** Lyrita SRCD2218. Notes and text included. From SRCS121/2 (12/83). Recorded in 1979.

② 1h 58m ADD 3/93

A magnificent recorded presentation of Alwyn's strong and characterful adaptation of August Strindberg's drama which was three years in the making and first performed in 1977 for a BBC Radio 3 broadcast. The composer himself wrote the fluent (if somewhat over-sanitized) libretto, creating in the process an extra character in the personage of Ulrik, the gamekeeper; in the opera, Ulrik (off-stage) shoots the lap-dog Miss Julie wants to take with her when she elopes with her manservant Jean, whereas in Strindberg's original it is Jean who (on on-stage) horrific-ally kills Miss Julie's pet finch — both dramatically and symbolically a far more pungent gesture. As ever, Alwyn's idiom is approachable (there are strong echoes of Puccini and Walton) and impeccably crafted; certainly the Philharmonia seem to revel in the confident orchestral writing, and Vilem Tausky directs proceedings with real passion and conviction. The cast, too, is uniformly excellent: Benjamin Luxon is on commanding form as Jean, whilst Jill Gomez in the title-role produces the most ravishing sounds throughout (try sampling her gorgeous delivery of the Midsummer Night aria at the end of Act 1 Scene 1). The Kingsway Hall sessions took place over a four-day period in January 1979. The expertly-annotated booklet may say "ADD", but this is, technically speaking, as realistic a recording as you will ever hear, with soloists set in perfect relief against an impeccably balanced orchestral backdrop. From every conceivable point of view, then, this welcome CD reissue represents an unqualified success.

Further listening ...

String Quartets — No. 1 in D minor; No. 2, "Spring Waters". **London Quartet.** Chandos CHAN9219 (5/94).

Symphonies — No. 1 in D major; No. 4. **London Philharmonic Orchestra/ William Alwyn.** Lyrita SRCD227 (7/92).

Symphonies — No. 2[a]; No. 3[b]; No. 5, "Hydriotaphia"[c]. **London Philharmonic Orchestra/ William Alwyn.** Lyrita SRCD228 (10/92).

Violin Concerto[a]. Symphony No. 3. [a]**Lydia Mordkovitch** (vn). **London Symphony Orchestra/Richard Hickox.** Chandos CHAN9187 (1/94).

Lyra Angelica[a]. Autumn Legend[b]. Pastoral fantasia[c]. Tragic Interlude. [a]**Rachel Masters** (hp); [b]**Nicholas Daniel** (cor ang); [c]**Stephen Tees** (va); **City of London Sinfonia/ Richard Hickox.** Chandos CHAN9065 (10/92).

George Antheil
American 1900-1959

New review
Antheil. Ballet mécanique[a]. A Jazz Symphony[b]. Sonata No. 2 for Violin, Piano and Drum[c]. String Quartet No. 1[d]. [c]**Charles Castleman** (vn); [b]**Ivan Davis**, [c]**Randall Hodgkinson** (pfs); [a]**Rex Lawson** (pianola); [d]**Mendelssohn Quartet** (Ida Levin, Nicolas Mann, vns; Katherine Murdock, va; Marcy Rosen, vc); **New Palais Royale** [a]**Percussion Ensemble and** [ab]**Orchestra /Maurice Peress.** Music Masters 67094-2. Recorded in 1989.

Ih Im DDD 4/94

Ballet mécanique was Antheil's youthful response to the gloriously liberated atmosphere of Paris in the mid-1920s, when 'anything went', including compositions for pianola with multiple pianos, xylophones and percussion (hideously wailing sirens prominent). But it is the other, earlier works on the disc which reveal why Antheil's music is worth taking seriously. The First String Quartet may be inconsequential in form, but it has an appealing lyric quality, and its livelier episodes confirm that Antheil could digest, and not simply copy, the formidable influence of Stravinsky. The *Jazz Symphony* and the Second Violin Sonata enjoy themselves with collages of quotations and allusions. The symphony has more to do with dance music than with jazz 'proper' (no wonder Gershwin was puzzled by it) and also has clear links with mainstream French music — Ibert, even Ravel. The sonata is less anxious to please, and comparisons with Ives are therefore more appropriate: the imaginative reticence of the ending is particularly attractive. All is expertly performed and the engineers did well to contain *Ballet mécanique* within ear-stretching rather than ear-bursting bounds.

Further listening ...

String Quartets Nos. 1-3. **Mondriaan Quartet.** Etcetera KTC1093 (6/91).

Hans Erich Apostel
Austrian 1901-1972

Suggested listening ...

String Quartet No. 1, Op. 7[a]. *Coupled with* **Zemlinsky.** String Quartets — No. 1 in A major, Op. 4; No. 2, Op. 15; No. 3, Op. 19; No. 4, Op. 25. **LaSalle Quartet.** DG 427 421-2GC2 (8/89).

Anton Arensky
Russian 1861-1906

Suggested listening ...

String Quartet No. 2 in A minor, Op. 35. *Coupled with* **Tchaikovsky.** Souvenir de Florence, Op. 70ª. **Raphael Ensemble.** Hyperion CDA66648 (2/94).

Symphonies — No. 1 in B minor, Op. 4; No. 2 in A major, Op. 22. **USSR Academy Symphony Orchestra/Evgeni Svetlanov.** Olympia OCD167 (7/89).

Thomas Arne
British 1710-1778

Arne. INSTRUMENTAL WORKS. **Le Nouveau Quatuor** (Utako Ikeda, fl; Catherine Weiss, vn; Mark Caudle, vc; ªPaul Nicholson, hpd). Amon Ra CDSAR-42. Recorded in 1989. Favourite Concertos — No. 1 in C major (solo hpd version)ª. Keyboard Sonatas — No. 1 in F majorª. Trio Sonatas — No. 2 in G major; No. 5; No. 6 in B minor; No. 7 in E minor.

· 58m DDD 5/90

If the music history books offer little more than a passing reference to the slim repertoire of enchanting chamber music by Thomas Arne, the ordinary man in the street, who can at least whistle *Rule Britannia*, is unlikely even to have heard that any exists. This disc comes therefore as something of a revelation. The members of the Nouveau Quatuor perform on instruments dating from the composer's lifetime, tuned down a semitone. The trio sonatas, originally published for two violins and continuo, are played here by a mixed quartet: flute, violin, cello and harpsichord, which is believed to have been what the composer really intended. The introduction of the flute adds colour, brightness and definition to these charming pieces and gives the listener a chance to savour the admirable tone and phrasing of the flautist, Utako Ikeda. Paul Nicholson's harpsichord solos are distinguished as much by their elegance as by their extraordinary power and brilliance. A word, finally, in praise of Peter Holman's excellent sleeve-notes: they are both scholarly and extremely readable.

New review

Arne. VOCAL WORKS.
Lampe. Britannia — Welcome Marsª. Dione — Pretty warblersª.
Handel. VOCAL WORKS. ªEmma Kirkby (sop); **Academy of Ancient Music/ Christopher Hogwood.** L'Oiseau-Lyre 436 132-2OH. Texts and translations included.
Arne: Comus — By the rushy-fringed bank; Brightest Lady; Thrice upon thy Finger's Tipª. Rosamond — Rise, Glory, riseª. The Tempest — Ariel's songª. *Handel:* Ariodante — Neghittosi or voi che fate?ª. Alcina — Credete al mio dolore; Tornami a vagheggiarª. Alexander's Feast — War, he sung, is toil and troubleª. L'Allegro, il penseroso ed il moderato — Sweet birdª. Saul — Capricious manª. Overture, Allessandro Severo, HWVAnh13. Hornpipe in D major, HWV356. March in D major, HWV345.

· 1h 12m DDD 7/93

Emma Kirkby's voice has no longer the *ingénue* air, the charmingly demure quality through which a hint of passion enticingly peeps, with which she delighted so many of us in her earlier recordings. It is now fuller, and used with less inhibition (or pretence of it); and that means that a wider repertory, not to say a wider interpretative range, is open to her. The virtues of taste and technique and impeccable tuning however remain, still supported by a prodigious musical intelligence and a natural feeling for early eighteenth-century style (among others). This disc casts her in music composed, for the most part, for one of the most celebrated English singers of that era, Cecilia Young, one of several talented singing sisters and for a time the wife of Thomas Arne — famed in her day for the "sweetness and simplicity" (Dibdin's words) of her singing and her character. The impersonation seems a convincing one, to judge by the result here, which is uniformly delightful. Christopher Hogwood conducts in direct and unaffected fashion. A true desert island disc.

Further listening ...

Concertos — No. 1 in C major[a]; No. 2 in G major[b]; No. 3 in A major[c]; No. 4 in B flat major[b]; No. 5 in G minor[a]; No. 6 in B flat major[c]. **The Parley of Instruments/Paul Nicholson** ([a]hpd, [b]org, [c]fp). Hyperion CDA66509 (9/92).

Symphonies — No. 1 in C major; No. 2 in F major; No. 3 in E flat major; No. 4 in C minor. **Cantilena/Adrian Shepherd.** Chandos CHAN8403 (6/87).

Sir Malcolm Arnold

British 1921-

New review

Arnold. Clarinet Concertos — No. 1, Op. 20; No. 2, Op. 115. You know what sailors are — Scherzetto (arr. Palmer).
Britten (orch. Matthews). Movement for Clarinet and Orchestra.
Maconchy. Concertinos Nos. 1 and 2. **Thea King** (cl); **English Chamber Orchestra/ Barry Wordsworth.** Hyperion CDA66634. Recorded in 1992.

lh 5m DDD 12/93

Designed in part as a tribute to Frederick Thurston, who died just 40 years ago, this collection of short *concertante* works for clarinet makes an exceptionally attractive disc, beautifully recorded and superbly performed, with Thurston's widow and star-pupil, Thea King, as soloist. With her ever-seductive tone, at once sensuously beautiful yet clear, never letting you forget that this is a reed instrument, King perpetuates the qualities he sought to instil, not least in the works on the disc written for him. These include the first of Arnold's concertos and the first of Maconchy's concertinos, while the *Scherzetto,* a delightfully jaunty piece adapted by Christopher Palmer from Arnold's music for the film, *You know what sailors are,* also seems to have been inspired directly by Thurston's playing. The other direct influence here is Benny Goodman. He turned in 1942 to the young Benjamin Britten, then in the United States, to write a concerto for him. It is a highly attractive short piece, alternately energetic and poetic, with material adroitly interchanged, and with percussion used most imaginatively. The second of the Arnold concertos was written for Goodman too and it shows Arnold at his most endearing, with sharp ideas leading to broad, memorable melodies that echo popular music, without ever cheapening the result. Both King and the ECO under Barry Wordsworth bring out the warmth as well as the rhythmic drive of all this music.

Additional recommendation ...

No. 1[b]. *Concerto for Two Violins and Orchestra, Op. 77[d]. Concerto No. 1 for Flute and Strings, Op. 45[a]. Concerto No. 2 for Horn and Strings, Op. 58[c].*[a]**Karen Jones** (fl); [b]**Michael Collins** (cl); [c]**Richard Watkins** (hn); [d]**Kenneth Sillito,** [d]**Lyn Fletcher** (vns); **London Musici/Mark Stephenson.** Conifer CDCF172 — 56m DDD 8/89

New review

Arnold. Concertos — Flute and Chamber Orchestra No. 2, Op. 111[a]; Clarinet and Orchestra No. 2, Op. 115[b]; Horn and Orchestra No. 1, Op. 11[c]; Piano Duet and Strings, Op. 32[d]. [a]**Karen Jones** (fl); [b]**Michael Collins** (cl); [c]**Richard Watkins** (hn); [d]**David Nettle, [d]Richard Markham** (pfs); **London Musici/Mark Stephenson.** Conifer CDCF228. Recorded in 1993.

lh 12m DDD 12/93

Of the brief concertos which Arnold wrote for a whole range of instruments, the Horn Concerto No. 1 is the earliest work here. Written in 1946 for Charles Gregory, then Arnold's colleague in the London Philharmonic, it is also the longest of the works here, with an extended central *Andante* with dark overtones and a hunting-rhythm finale. Richard Watkins, Principal Horn of the Philharmonia, plays it with great panache and glorious tone. Karen Jones, Principal Flute of the Bournemouth orchestra and Shell/LSO prize-winner in 1985, is equally sympathetic in the Flute Concerto No. 2, the most original work on the disc, with a central scherzo flanked by an equivocal *Allegro moderato* and a final lyrical *Allegretto*. The Concerto for Piano Duet is full of characteristic Arnold touches. After an emphatic first movement a central Passacaglia brings craggy contrasts, leading to a jazzy finale with relaxed episodes. Nettle and Markham play as one at their single keyboard, and under Mark Stephenson the young musicians of London Musici perform throughout with understanding and precision.

New review

Arnold. Guitar Concerto, Op. 67.
Rodrigo. Concierto de Aranjuez.
Takemitsu. To the Edge of Dream. **Julian Bream** (gtr); **City of Birmingham Symphony Orchestra/Simon Rattle.** EMI CDC7 54661-2. Recorded in 1991.

58m DDD 7/93

There are nearly 40 extant versions of the Rodrigo and this is Bream's fourth recording of it. It is also his second version of the Arnold Concerto, and the energy, sparkle and clean delivery are undiminished. What differentiates these performances from others, including Bream's earlier ones, is the extraordinary accounts of their slow movements. Bream's views of the *sardana* and the smoky night club (respectively) come from within, to an extent that makes even the most expressive of others seem 'external', and they are conveyed with such wonderful fluidity of tone and phrasing that one might almost believe that one is hearing them for the first time. These are the desert-island versions of these two concertos, adding maturity to virtuosity. Takemitsu's *To the Edge of Dream* is scored for an unusually large orchestra but, as it most often alternates with, rather than opposes the guitar or is held to a breathless *pianissimo*, the guitar is always audible. It is a work of haunting beauty and if the composer is not delighted by Bream's playing (and EMI's recording) of it he is indeed a difficult man to please.

Arnold. ORCHESTRAL WORKS. [a]**Phyllis Sellick**, [a]**Cyril Smith** (pfs); [b]**Bournemouth Symphony Orchestra**, [c]**City of Birmingham Symphony Orchestra**, [d]**Philharmonia Orchestra/Malcolm Arnold.** EMI British Composers [abc]stereo/[d]mono CDM7 64044-2. Items marked [abc] recorded 1970-1979, [d] 1955.
Concerto for Two Pianos (three hands), Op. 104[ac] (from HMV ASD2612, 10/70). Symphony No. 1, Op. 22[b]. Solitaire[b] — Sarabande; Polka (all from ASD3823, 6/80). Tam O'Shanter — Overture, Op. 51[d]. English Dances[d] — No. 3, Op. 27 No. 3; No. 5, Op. 33 No. 1 (Columbia SED5529, 2/56).

1h 16m ADD 10/91

When Sir Malcolm celebrated his seventieth birthday in 1991, many people realized how badly he had been neglected by the stiff British establishment as too tuneful, uninhibited and (worst of all!) communicative to be 'serious'. These recordings under his own baton were ripe for this mid-price reissue, for although the sound is not new — the *Tam O'Shanter* Overture and *English Dances* are in mono and date from 1955 — it is surprisingly good. Newcomers to Arnold's music (or who think they are, for they've probably heard it in several famous British films) could well start with *Tam O'Shanter*, which was inspired by a Robert Burns poem about a Scotsman's wild night ride with the devil in pursuit. The boisterous and brilliant scoring here is a delight, as is the marvellous sense of atmosphere. The Double Piano Concerto was commis-sioned for the 1969 Proms and the duo of Phyllis Sellick and Cyril Smith, the "three hands" being because Smith had lost the use of his left hand after a stroke a decade before. Such is Arnold's skill that one is not conscious of a limitation, although his keyboard writing is more as if laid out for one three-handed pianist than for two players of whom one is at a disadvantage. As usual with him, there are contrasts of noisy high spirits and gentle lyricism, and no shortage of tunes, as in the cool, slow movement in slow waltz time. This concerto makes us realize that Arnold is the nearest British equivalent to Poulenc. But like Poulenc, he also had a darker and tougher side, and it comes across in the First Symphony which, for all its vigour, contains real bitterness too. One sometimes thinks of Sibelius and Nielsen as it unfolds, but the voice is still Arnold's and this is fine music if not by any means cosy listening (the end of the finale reaches unmistakable tragedy). The other, lighter pieces make up a valuable issue, with unfailingly strong, authentic-sounding performances.

Arnold. ARNOLD ON BRASS. **Grimethorpe Colliery Band/Elgar Howarth;** [a]**Sir Malcolm Arnold** Conifer CDCF222. Recorded in 1993.
Four Scottish Dances, Op. 59 (arr. Farr). Four English Dances, Op. 27 (arr. Farr). Four English Dances, Op. 33 (arr. Farr). Four Cornish Dances, Op. 91. Little Suites — No. 1, Op. 80; No. 2, Op. 93. Fantasy, Op. 114. The Padstow Lifeboat, Op. 94[a].

lh 6m DDD 12/93

The composer was present throughout these recordings and he conducted the final item, the *Padstow Lifeboat* march with its insistent off-key foghorn. The sheer ebullience of the playing is immediately breathtaking in the first of the *Scottish Dances*, and in the second the 'drunken' solo bass trombone is in the best tradition of the British brass experience. The eight *English Dances* are played with equal sophistication and brilliance. The *Mesto* (Op. 27 No. 3) is quite haunting and the players get round the colour problem in the first dance in Op. 33 by whistling the air themselves! The more melancholy atmosphere of the *Cornish Dances* is touchingly caught. The two *Little Suites* demonstrate how well the composer — once a trumpeter himself in the LPO — understands the medium. The finest of the original band works is the *Fantasy*, a highly imaginative series of joined vignettes. The recording is natural, and beautifully balanced, making the most of the hall's ambience without any loss of detail.

Additional recommendations ...
Cornish Dances. English Dances — Op. 27; Op. 33. Irish Dances, Op. 126. Scottish Dances. Solitaire — Sarabande; Polka. **London Philharmonic Orchestra/Malcolm Arnold.** Lyrita SRCD201 —
lh lm ADD/DDD 12/90
As Lyrita. **Philharmonia Orchestra/Bryden Thomson.** Chandos CHAN8867 —
48m DDD 10/90

Arnold. OVERTURES. **London Philharmonic Orchestra/Malcolm Arnold.** Reference Recordings RRCD48. Recorded in 1991.
A Sussex Overture, Op. 31. Beckus the Dandipratt, Op. 5. The Smoke, Op. 21. The Fair Field, Op. 110. Commonwealth Christmas Overture, Op. 64.

lh 3m DDD 6/92

Four of the overtures here are early pieces composed before 1960, while *The Fair Field* (written for the Fairfield Halls in Croydon, Surrey) dates from 1972. The earliest piece is *Beckus the Dandipratt* (a dandipratt was an Elizabethan coin, but the word was also used for a cheeky small boy) and was inspired by a youngster that the composer and his wife befriended on a wartime Cornish holiday. *The Smoke* (a Cockney term for London) has raucous jazz elements, while the *Commonwealth Christmas Overture* places cosy English chimes alongside the more urgent Christmas music of a Caribbean pop group. Though much of this music is cheerfully extrovert, by no means all of it is, and for all its tunefulness it is not easy-listening music in the usual sense. Under the composer, the London Philharmonic play it brilliantly and lovingly, and the recording is rich and detailed. The booklet note by the producer, Christopher Palmer, is a model of information, enthusiasm and style and complements a splendid issue.

Arnold. Symphony No. 6, Op. 95. Fantasy on a theme of John Field, Op. 116[a]. Sweeney Todd, Op. 68a. Tam O'Shanter, Op. 51. [a]**John Lill** (pf); **Royal Philharmonic Orchestra/ Vernon Handley.** Conifer CDCF224.

lh 18m DDD 2/94

Arnold's *Tam O'Shanter*, with its drunken carousing and a witches' sabbath complete with bagpipes, never fails to make an impact. The essentially good-natured, high-spirited music for the ballet, *Sweeney Todd*, is a far cry from the malignancy of Stephen Sondheim's musical. Arnold's score has a genuine music-hall flavour, with lots of gusto, a winning waltz theme, an Offenbachian can-can and even twittering bird effects in the tuneful pot-pourri towards the end of the suite. The powerful Sixth Symphony — even though it has an upbeat ending to its jovial rondo-like finale — is a work which broods a great deal. The composer has suggested that his writing carries an affinity with the jazz phrases of Charlie Parker, yet its character is essentially symphonic. The composer was present at the recording sessions and must have been impressed by the power, spontaneity and grip of all these performances, and certainly by John Lill's melting Irish delicacy in his *sotto voce* presentations of the John Field *Fantasy*. The recording, made in London's Henry Wood Hall, is in every way first class.

Further listening ...

Sinfoniettas — No. 1, Op. 48; No. 2, Op. 65; No. 3, Op. 81. Flute Concerto No. 1, Op. 45[a]. Oboe Concerto, Op. 39[b]. [a]**Edward Beckett** (fl); [b]**Malcolm Messiter** (ob); **London Festival Orchestra/Ross Pople.** Hyperion CDA66332 (3/90).

Symphonies — No. 7, Op. 113; No. 8, Op. 124. **Royal Philharmonic Orchestra/Vernon Handley.** Conifer CDCF177 (3/91).

Film Suites (arr. Palmer) — The Bridge on the River Kwai; The Inn of the Sixth Happiness; Hobson's Choice; Whistle down the Wind. The Sound Barrier, Op. 38.**London Symphony Orchestra/Richard Hickox.** Chandos CHAN9100 (2/93).

String Quartets — No. 1, Op. 23; No. 2, Op. 118. **McCapra Quartet**. Chandos CHAN9112 (10/92).

Juan Crisóstomo Arriaga   *Spanish 1806-1826*

Suggested listening ...

String Quartets — No. 1 in D minor; No. 2 in A major; No. 3 in E flat major. **Chilingirian Quartet.** CRD CRDC4012/3 (8/89).

Kurt Atterberg   *Swedish 1887-1974*

Suggested listening ...

Piano Quintet, Op. 31[a]. Suite No. 1, "Orientale"[b]. Sonata for Horn and Piano in B minor, Op. 27[c]. [c]**Imre Magyari** (hn); [b]**György Kertész** (vc); [ab]**Ilona Prunyi** (pf); [a]**New Budapest Quartet.** Marco Polo 8 223405 (9/93).

Daniel-François-Esprit Auber   *French 1782-1871*

Suggested listening ...

FRA DIAVOLO. **Soloists; Jean Laforge Chorale Ensemble; Monte Carlo Philharmonic Orchestra/Marc Soustrot.** EMI CDS7 54810-2 (1/94).

GUSTAV III. **Soloists; Intermezzo Vocal Ensemble; French Lyrique Orchestra/Michel Swierczewski.** Arion ARN368220 (9/93).

Edmond Audran   *French 1840-1901*

New review

Audran. MISS HELYETT[a]. **Lina Dachary** (sop) Miss Helyett; **Claudine Collart** (sop) Manuela Fernandez; **Gabrielle Ristori** (mez) Senora Fernandez; **Lise Arseguet** (sngr)

Norette; **Aimé Doniat** (bar) Paul; **Dominique Tirmont** (bar) Pasteur Smithson; **Michel Hamel** (ten) Puycardas; **René Lenoty** (ten) James Richter; **Gaston Rey** (bar) Bacarel; **French Radio Lyric Chorale and Orchestra/Marcel Cariven.**
LA POUPEE[b] — excerpts. **Huguette Hennetier, Gabrielle Ristori** (mezs); **Joseph Peyron, Duvaleix, René Lenoty** (tens); **Robert Massard, Jacques Pruvost** (bars); **Génio, Pierre Roi** (sngrs); **French Radio Lyric Chorus and Orchestra/Marcel Cariven.** Musidisc Gaieté-Lyrique 20240-2. Items recorded live in [a] 1963, [b] 1958.

2h 29m AAD 11/93

The plot of *Miss Helyett* concerns an American lady whose undergarments and more are glimpsed by a fellow-mountaineer during a climbing accident. Her father decrees that such is the intimate contact implied by this indiscreet glimpse, duet "Ah! le superbe point de vue", that the man must marry her. She, of course, was upside down and therefore cannot identify him. This naughty-nineties nonsense prompts from Audran a bubbling, totally delicious *opérette*. The English and American accents are hilarious as interpreted by the French singers and tune after tune tumbles out. The fill-up, extracts from Audran's 1899 *La Poupée*, is also charming. That elegant baritone, Robert Massard sings the role of Father Maximin who sends the blushing novice Lancelot out into the world to recover the fortunes of the monastery. Suffice it to say that by the end of the story he is no longer a novice in any sense of the word. It is such a special pleasure to hear the French language delivered in an operatic context by such seasoned performers, which makes one regret all the more the apparent lack in the intervening years of younger French singers able to master the opéra *comique-opérette* style, or perhaps the recording industry's failure to nurture those artists who could.

Charles Avison
British 1709-1770

New review

Avison. 12 Concerti grossi after D. Scarlatti. **Iona Brown, Malcolm Latchem** (vns); **Denis Vigay** (vc); **Nicholas Kraemer** (hpd); **Academy of St Martin in the Fields/Sir Neville Marriner.** Philips Duo 438 806-2PM2. From 6769 018 (9/79).

② 2h 23m ADD

Charles Avison issued his string arrangements of harpsichord sonatas by Domenico Scarlatti in 1744. The sonatas included only two slow movements and Avison, planning 12 concertos in the slow-fast-slow-fast scheme favoured by his teacher, Geminiani, required 24. So, at "extraordinary expence", Avison got hold of some manuscript copies of further sonatas by Scarlatti which provided him with additional slow pieces. In the end, however, he inserted a few of his own, albeit in some cases little more than cadential chords. Avison's arrangements are delightful and even as early as 1768 the novelist, Laurence Sterne had immortalized them in the Third Book of *Tristram Shandy* where he finds an ingenious analogy between Tristram's father's apoplectic rage and the *Con furia* movement of the Sixth Concerto. In a coda of some asperity Sterne then ticks off Avison for his use of such terms for, as he says, "What has 'con furia' — 'con strepito' [which Avison never used] — or any other hurly-burly whatever to do with harmony?". These performances are lively in spirit, bringing out much of the charm and vitality of some inventive musical ideas. Marriner adopts sensible tempos throughout and has a good feeling for dance measures. The concertino players are excellent and the performances are almost consistently reliable in matters of tuning and ensemble. All in all, this is an engaging issue of music that stands up to more than cursory investigation. Lovers of *Tristram Shandy* will require no further recommendations, but the set should have a wider appeal. The recorded sound is clear.

Grázyna Bacewicz
Spanish 1909-1969

Suggested listening ...

Violin Sonata No. 4[a]. Piano Sonata No. 2[b]. Concerto for String Orchestra[c]. Violin Concerto
No. 7[d]. [a]**Edward Statkiewicz**, [d]**Piotr Janowski** (vns); [a]**Aleksandra Utrecht**, [b]**Krystian**

Zimerman (pfs); ^c**Polish Chamber Orchestra/Jerzy Maksymiuk;** ^d**Warsaw Philharmonic Orchestra/Andrzej Markowski.** Olympia OCD392 (12/93).

String Quartets^a — No. 3; No. 5. Piano Quintet No. 2^b. ^a**Wilanow Quartet;** ^b**Warsaw Piano Quintet.** Olympia OCD387 (8/93).

Carl Philipp Emanuel Bach

German 1714-1788

C.P.E. Bach. Cello Concertos — A minor, Wq170; B flat major, Wq171; A major, Wq172. **Anner Bylsma** (vc); **Orchestra of the Age of Enlightenment/Gustav Leonhardt.** Virgin Classics Veritas VC7 59541-2.

Ih 10m   DDD   2/90

During his many years at the court of Frederick the Great, C.P.E. Bach composed these three cello concertos. The fact that they also exist in his transcriptions for harpsichord and flute hardly suggests very idiomatic writing for the cello and in a way the implied comment is true; nevertheless, they go very well on the tenor instrument and Anner Bylsma brings out their quirky charm (a quality never in short supply with this composer) while coping adequately with some tricky figuration in the quicker movements; he's also eloquent in the highly expressive slower ones that are especially characteristic of this Bach. This is perhaps not a CD for a basic collection, even of cello music, but it should give the pleasure which is itself audible in the music-making by players completely at home in the idiom. The recording was made in the well-tried location of All Saints' Church in Petersham in the UK; it places the cello rather far back, but convincingly, and has an agreeably warm sound. The period pitch is about a quarter of a tone lower than a modern one and the booklet gives the date and maker's name of the orchestra's 23 instruments, though, oddly, not those of the soloist's baroque cello.

Additional recommendation ...
Balázs Máté (vc); **Concerto Armonico/Péter Szüts, Miklós Spányi.** Hungaroton HCD31337 — .•´ Ih 9m DDD II/92

New review
C.P.E. Bach. Flute Concertos — D minor, H484 No. 1; A major, H438; G major, H445. **Jennifer Stinton** (fl); **Orchestra of St John's Smith Square/John Lubbock.** Collins Classics 1373-2. Recorded in 1992.

Ih 7m   DDD   10/93

The three concertos on this disc all exist in versions for solo instruments other than the flute. Which versions reflect Bach's original intentions is not clear but, bearing in mind his employer, Frederick the Great's passion for the flute, and the composer's equally fervent commitment to the keyboard, we may perhaps adjudge an element of expediency in the flute concerto versions. The flautist Jennifer Stinton finds plenty of interest in the music and interprets it with spirit and virtuosity. Her phrases are well thought out and her articulation clear and effective. It is in the outer movements that these performances are at their best with crisp, responsive orchestral playing, well-chosen tempos and clean, incisive ensemble, and the brooding intensity of the middle movements is at times startling. These are modern-instrument performances, but none the worse for that. The recording balance is pleasing, too, achieving an even dialogue between soloist and ripieno, without artificially highlighting the flute and the sound is clear and effective.

C.P.E. Bach. SONATAS. **London Baroque** (^aCharles Medlam, William Hunt, va da gambas; ^bRichard Egarr, hpd). Harmonia Mundi HMC90 1410. Recorded in 1991.
Viola da gamba Sonatas — C major, Wq136; D major, Wq137; G minor, Wq88^{ab}. Keyboard Sonatas — E major, H26^b; A minor, H30^b.

Ih 8m   DDD   1/93

C.P.E. Bach's three sonatas for viola da gamba must be among the very last solo pieces outside France for an instrument which had gradually been supplanted by the cello. Two of the sontatas

(Wq136/137) are of the continuo accompaniment type and date from the mid-1740s. The third (Wq88) written in 1759 is, by contrast more up-to-date in style with a fully written out harpsichord part on an equal footing with the gamba. From the gambist's viewpoint all three works are virtuoso pieces which explore pretty widely the expressive and technical range of the instrument. The partnership of Charles Medlam and Richard Egarr, with William Hunt in the two continuo sonatas, is an effective one. Medlam's tone is well-focused, he articulates clearly and has a lively rapport with the north German *Empfindsamer Stil*, present to a greater or lesser extent in almost all C.P.E. Bach's music after 1740 or so. Medlam responds to the music with a happy blend of head and heart, realizing at the same time one of Bach's own tenets for a good performance, "the ability through singing or playing to make the ear conscious of the true content and affect of a composition". Two keyboard sonatas complete this entertaining programme, one from the *Prussian* set, the other from the *Württemberg*. Richard Egarr plays them stylishly with a lively response to ornaments. Some listeners may find the interpretations understate Bach's characteristically temperamental gestures but the virtuosity of the playing is admirable.

Additional recommendation ...
Sonatas — Wq88; Wq136; Wq137. Fantasia in C major, Wq59 No. 6. **Siegfried Pank** (va da gamba); **Christiane Jaccottet** (clav, fp). Capriccio 10 102 — ⠶⠶ 56m DDD 10/88 ✎

Key to symbols

Price	Quantity/availability	Timing	Recording mode	Review date
⠶⠶	② ②	1h 23m	DDD	6/88

New review
C.P.E. Bach. FLUTE SONATAS. **Barthold Kuijken** (fl); **Bob van Asperen** (hpd). Sony Classical Vivarte S2K53964. Recorded in 1993.
C major, H504. D major, H505. E major, H506. G major, H508. G major, H509. C major, H515. G minor, H542 No. 5 (BWV1020). B flat major, H543. E flat major, H545 (BWV1031). B flat major, H578.

⠶⠶ ② 2h 20m DDD 5/94 ⧫P ✎

The title on this disc is misleading. This album contains nothing like the "Complete Flute Sonatas" of C.P.E. Bach but only the five for flute with obbligato harpsichord. That said, the playing is lively in spirit. Kuijken's tone is warmly coloured, softly spoken and pleasingly rounded and he clearly has much affection for Bach's expressive idiom. The balance between flute and harpsichord is effective, too, with Bob van Asperen proving himself an ideal partner both on account of his playing, which is particular in and attentive to detail, and his sympathy with the music. A first-rate recital, stylishly played with outstanding virtuosity and sympathetically recorded.

New review
C.P.E. Bach. Keyboard Sonatas — "Prussian", H24-29[a]; "Württemberg", H30-35[b].
Harpsichord Concerto in C major, H190[c]. **Bob van Asperen** (hpd). Teldec Das Alte Werk 9031-77623-2. Items marked [ac] recorded in 1978 and 1979, new to UK, [b] EK6 35378 (6/79).

⠶⠶ ③ 2h 55m ADD 7/93

New review
C.P.E. Bach. Keyboard Sonatas — B minor, H35; E major, H39; F minor, H40; C major, H41; B flat major, H51. **Colin Booth** (hpd). Soundboard Records SBCD921.

⠶⠶ 1h 18m DDD 8/93

C.P.E. Bach's sets of *Prussian* and *Württemberg* Sonatas played by Bob van Asperen typify why back catalogues are as important as ever; not only have these veracious performances of the earlier *Prussian* Sonatas never reached these shores before, but neither of these sets are currently available complete. In the *Württemburg* Sonatas van Asperen's playing is of the utmost brilliance and he rarely misses a trick in communicating Bach's variegated style with exuberance and refinement. Such qualities abound too in the dazzling *Concerto per il Cembalo solo*. The recorded sound is suitably clear and fresh throughout. One interesting feature of these keyboard sonatas is the stylistic variety that is contained within individual movements. Recitative-like passages jostle with orchestrally conceived ideas, lyricism with more robust, challenging gestures, counterpoint with homophonic texture and baroque disciplines with *galant* phraseology. Rhythmic and harmonic uncertainties abound and all this is placed at the service of expression. Colin Booth plays with technical fluency and a ready awareness of all the little quirks and pitfalls in Bach's style which can be the undoing of players with a more prosaic outlook. This is a worthy single disc alternative and a recital well worth becoming acquainted with, above all for the music but also for the sympathetic playing and the distinctive sound of the Mietke harpsichord.

C.P.E. Bach. ORGAN WORKS. **Jacques van Oortmerssen** (org). BIS CD569. Played on the Bätz organ of the Onze Lieve Vrouwe Kerk, Harderwijk, The Netherlands. Recorded 1992. Fantasia and Fugue a 4 in C minor, H103. Prelude in D major, H107. Sonatas — F major, H84; A minor, H85; D major, H86; G minor, H87.

1h 10m   DDD   5/93

It may have been a deliberate decision, a subconscious reaction or just simple coincidence, but the most famous of Bach's sons established his reputation as a composer without ever really trespassing on his father's territory. Thus while the complete organ works of J.S. Bach cover anything up to 20 CDs, C.P.E. Bach's can be accommodated on just one. Moreover with the exception of the grand *Fantasia and Fugue* in C minor there's little hint of Bach-the-elder's influence in these undeniably fine and distinctive pieces. C.P.E.'s keyboard *métier* was the sonata; for the organ he wrote four with a question mark hanging over several others. These are well-crafted, tuneful three-movement works for manuals only which thrive in the hands of an alert player and on a bright, colourful instrument. This disc provides first-rate interpretations of the Sonatas and the *Fantasia and Fugue* and would make a worthwhile addition to any CD collection. Jacques van Oortmerssen plays with great authority and seriousness of purpose. The recording is exemplary and the instrument makes a wonderful sound.

Further listening ...

Flute Concertos — D minor (original version of Harpsichord Concerto, Wq22); A major, Wq168; B flat major, Wq167; G major, Wq169; A minor, Wq166. **Konrad Hünteler** (fl); **Amsterdam Baroque Orchestra/Ton Koopman.** Erato 2292-45353-2 (7/89).

Concerto in E flat major for Harpsichord and Fortepiano, Wq47. Organ Concerto in G major, Wq34. Sonatina in D major for Two Harpsichords, Wq109. **Richard Fuller** (fp); **Ingomar Rainer** (hpd); **Vienna Akademie/Martin Haselböck** (hpd, org). Novalis 150 025-2 (2/89).

Oboe Concerto in E flat major, H468. *Coupled with* **Lebrun.** Oboe Concerto No. 1 in D minor. **Mozart.** Oboe Concerto in C major, K314/285d. **Paul Goodwin** (ob); **The English Concert/Trevor Pinnock.** Archiv Produktion 431 821-2AH (7/91).

Symphonies, Wq 182 — No. 1 in G major; No. 2 in B flat major; No. 3 in C major; No. 4 in A major; No. 5 in B minor; No. 6 in E major. **The English Concert/Trevor Pinnock.** Archiv Produktion 415 300-2AH (5/86).

Symphonies, Wq183 — No. 1 in D major; No. 2 in E flat major; No. 3 in F major; No. 4 in G major. **Carl Philipp Emanuel Bach Chamber Orchestra/Hartmut Haenchen.** Capriccio 10 175 (10/88).

Three Quartets, H537-9[a]. Fantasia in C major, H291. [a]**Nicholas McGegan** (fl); [a]**Catherine Mackintosh** (va); [a]**Anthony Pleeth** (vc); **Christopher Hogwood** (fp). L'Oiseau-Lyre 433 189-2OH (9/92).

Die Auferstehung und Himmelfahrt Jesu, H777. **Hillevi Martinpelto** (sop); **Christoph Prégardien** (ten); **Peter Harvey** (bass); **Ghent Collegium Vocale Choir; Orchestra of the Age of Enlightenment/Philippe Herreweghe.** Virgin Classics Veritas VC7 59069-2 (9/92).

Johann Christian Bach

New review
J.C. Bach. Adriano in Siria — Overture. Grand Overtures, Op. 18 — No. 1 in E flat major;
No. 4 in D major. Symphony in G minor, Op. 6 No. 6. Sinfonia concertante in C major, T289
No. 4 (ed. Maunder). **Academy of Ancient Music/Simon Standage.** Chandos Chaconne
CHAN0540. Recorded in 1993.

·· lh 5m DDD 12/93

There was no finer symphonist than J.C. Bach working anywhere in Europe at the end of the
1760s and the beginning of the 1770s. The G minor Symphony is a magnificently fiery piece,
similar in manner to Haydn's No. 39 and Mozart's No. 25; it is done here with plenty of *Sturm
und Drang*, notably in the very forceful finale, and the fine, noble ideas of the slow movement
are well caught too. The opening item is a three-movement D major Symphony, in effect, with
a well-worked first movement and an *Andante* with rich wind writing. No other composer,
besides of course Mozart, seems to have had as keen a feeling as J.C. Bach for the sensuous
beauty of wind textures. The *Sinfonia concertante* isn't quite as successful a piece, being rather
repetitive, but it is never less than charming and enjoyable music, again with some beautiful
windy textures in the *Larghetto* and a delightful "Two lovely black eyes" theme in the rondo. The
solo playing is admirable. Recommended to anyone sympathetic to J.C. Bach's music.

J.C. Bach. CHAMBER WORKS. **The English Concert** (Lisa Beznosiuk, fl; David
Reichenberg, ob; Anthony Halstead, David Cox, hns; Simon Standage, vn; Trevor Jones, va;
Anthony Pleeth, vc; Trevor Pinnock, hpd, fp, square pf). Archiv Produktion 423 385-2AH.
Recorded in 1987.
Quintet in D major for Flute, Oboe, Violin, Cello and Keyboard, Op. 22 No. 1. Sextet in
C major for Oboe, Two Horns, Violin, Cello and Keyboard. Quintets for Flute, Oboe, Violin,
Viola and Continuo, Op. 11 — No. 1 in C major; No. 6 in D major.

·· lh 9m DDD 5/88

Johann Christian Bach was the youngest of J.S. Bach's sons and the most widely travelled of them.
After studying with his father and with his half-brother C.P.E. Bach, Johann Christian worked in Italy
and in England where he settled in 1762. For the remaining 20 years of his life J.C. Bach played a
central role in London musical circles composing, playing and teaching. As well as operas, sacred
music, symphonies and concertos the "London Bach" as he became affectionately known, composed
various types of chamber music. Among the most engaging of these are the six Quintets, Op. 11,
those of Op. 22 and the Sextet in C major once thought to be the work of his elder brother J.C.F.
Bach. Trevor Pinnock and members of The English Concert give sparkling performances of music
conspicuous for its abundance of captivating melodies, transparent textures and fine craftsmanship.
Slow movements are especially beguiling and the subtly shaded dynamics, delicately contrived
instrumental sonorities and informed sense of style with which these artists bring the music to life
give the performances a rare delicacy and refinement. Pinnock himself plays a variety of keyboard
instruments whose contrasting sound adds another pleasing dimension to the interpretations. Each of
the artists makes a strong contribution but special praise, perhaps, should be given to the artistry of
the late David Reichenberg, an oboist with outstanding lyrical gifts. Good recorded sound.

New review
J.C. Bach. AMADIS DES GAULES (sung in German). **James Wagner** (ten) Amadis; **Ulrike
Sonntag** (sop) Oriane; **Elfrieda Hobarth** (sop) Coryphée; **Ibolya Verebics** (sop)
Arcabonne; **Wolfgang Schöne** (bass) Arcalaus; **Etsuko Matsushita** (sop) Temptress I; **Ruth
Altrock** (mez) Discord, Temptress II, Urgande; **Reinhard Hagen** (bass) Hatred; Voice from
the grave; **Stuttgart Gächinger Kantorei; Stuttgart Bach Collegium/Helmuth Rilling**.
Hänssler Classic 98 963. Text and translation included.

·· ② 2h 4m DDD 9/93

A French opera, often Italian in idiom, written by a German who spent most of his working life
in England: a real European Community piece, this! Gluck is the reference in terms of style: his
two *Iphigénies*, *Armide* and the French versions of *Alceste* and *Orfeo* had been heard in Paris not

long before, though Bach reverts at times to his more Italian manner and lacks the broad dramatic command and concentration that distinguish Gluck's greatest works. *Amadis* is a *tragédie-lyrique*, on a magical medieval theme with a number of Italian-style arias, some intensely eloquent airs, several duets and some fine choruses. Being a French opera, *Amadis* has no *secco* but rather orchestral recitative throughout, music in the manner of the recitative in *Idomeneo* though not, of course, dramatically as dense or as closely worked. But much of it is strong, taut, effective music, often very richly orchestrated, and there is plenty of imaginative and resourceful writing for the woodwind (which includes clarinets). Rilling directs a stylish reading, with a real sense of drama and he clearly relishes the variety of orchestral colour in the score. There is a lot of very fine, highly original and deeply serious music in this score; it's well worth trying.

Further listening ...

Symphonies — Op. 6 No. 3; Op. 9 No. 2; Op. 18 Nos. 2 and 4. **Bournemouth Sinfonietta/ Kenneth Montgomery.** Classics for Pleasure CD-CFP4550 (3/89).

Sinfonias concertante — G major for Two Violins and Cello, T284/1; E flat major for Two Clarinets and Bassoon, T290/9; A major for Violin and Cello, T284/4; E flat major for Two Violins, T288/4. **Soloists; London Festival Orchestra/Ross Pople.** ASV CDDCA651 (10/89).

Keyboard Sonatas — Op. 5 Nos. 5 and 6; Op. 17 Nos. 2, 3 and 5. **Virginia Black** (hpd). CRD CRD3453 (2/90).

Johann Sebastian Bach

German 1685-1750

Bach. Violin Concertos — No. 1 in A minor, BWV1041; No. 2 in E major, BWV1042. Double Violin Concerto in D minor, BWV1043[a]. Violin and Oboe Concerto in C minor, BWV1060[b]. [a]**John Tunnell** (vn); [b]**Robin Miller** (ob); **Scottish Chamber Orchestra/ Oscar Shumsky** (vn). Nimbus NI5325.

Ih 3m DDD 9/92

The three basic concertos BWV1041-43 are models of what a good baroque violin concert should be — and raised to the 'peerage' by Bach's genius, with eloquent slow movements framed by sturdy faster ones that are full of energy and unflagging invention. The two notes that begin the A minor Concerto are an unmistakable gesture of confidence and purpose, and who could invest a descending scale with more sublimity than does Bach in the *Largo, ma non tanto* of the Double Concerto? These are essential works in any collection that does not turn its back on baroque music. Together they take less than 45 minutes to play, and the Violin and Oboe Concerto BWV1060, another gem, is perhaps their best helpmate in completing a well-filled CD. Shumsky and his well-matched partners in the double concertos, John Tunnell and Robin Miller, are most successful in satisfying those who are comfortable with neither the sound of period instruments nor the excesses (no matter how slight) of romanticized performances, and period-instrument lovers who can happily accept outstandingly sensitive and stylish versions on modern instruments. Shumsky's is the view of one who has enjoyed a long love-affair with these works and, in the matters of ornamentation and use of vibrato (another form of ornamentation), has given thought to the status of every note. If this seems to suggest a studied, even dry, approach, you may rest assured that such is not the case; these performances are illuminated by serene love, expressed with singing tone. The Scottish Chamber Orchestra and those responsible for the recording itself have done their part in making this the memorable issue that it is.

Additional recommendations ...
As Nimbus. **Jaap Schröder, Christopher Hirons** (vns); **Academy of Ancient Music/ Christopher Hogwood.** L'Oiseau-Lyre 400 080-2OH — 45m DDD 3/83
As Nimbus. **Anne-Sophie Mutter** (vn); **English Chamber Orchestra/Salvatore Accardo** (vn). EMI CDC7 47005-2 — 53m DDD 2/84
As Nimbus. **José-Luis Garcia** (vn); **Neil Black** (ob); **English Chamber Orchestra/Dimitri Sitkovetsky** (vn). Novalis 150 017-2 — Ih 5m DDD 5/88

Violin Concertos. Double Violin Concerto. **Simon Standage, Elizabeth Wilcock** (vns); **The English Concert/Trevor Pinnock** (hpd). Archiv Produktion 410 646-2AH — .·˙ 46m DDD 8/84 Ⓑ ✍

No. 2. Double Violin Concerto. Harpsichord Concerto in F minor, BWV1056. **C.P.E. Bach.** *Cello Concerto in A major, Wq172.* **Jane Murdoch** (vn); **Caroline Dale** (vc); **Scottish Ensemble/Jonathan Rees.** Virgin Classics Virgo VJ7 59641-2 — . 1h 6m DDD 12/91 Ⓑ

Bach. Brandenburg Concertos, BWV1046-51[a]. Four Orchestral Suites, BWV1066-9[b]. **The English Concert/Trevor Pinnock.** Archiv Produktion 423 492-2AX3. Items marked [a] from 2742 003 (2/83), [b] 2533 410/1 (5/79).
Brandenburg Concertos — No. 1 in F major; No. 2 in F major; No. 3 in G major; No. 4 in G major; No. 5 in D major; No. 6 in B flat major. *Orchestral Suites* — No. 1 in C major; No. 2 in B minor; No. 3 in D major; No. 4 in D major.

.·˙ ③ 2h 53m DDD/ADD 10/88 ♩ₚ ♩ₛ Ⓑ ✍

These concertos, written in 1721, were Bach's response to a request from the Margrave of Brandenburg, whose name they now bear, but despite the dedication we do not know whether the Margrave acknowledged their receipt or ever heard them. Two, Concertos Nos. 3 and 6, are written for strings only, the latter without violins, but the others call for different combina-tions of other instrumental soloists. The music itself displays an amazing variety of form and use of instrumental colour, and since The English Concert use period instruments their performances must closely approach those which Bach may have heard, in both colour and balance — but he is unlikely to have heard them to greater advantage than we can through these excellent recordings.

Additional recommendations ...
Brandenburg Concertos. **English Chamber Orchestra/Raymond Leppard** (hpd). Philips Silver Line. *Nos. 1-3:* 420 345-2PM. *Nos. 4-6:* 420 346-2PM — .·˙ ② 54m 46m ADD 6/87 ♩ₚ Ⓑ
Brandenburg Concertos. **Orchestra of the Age of Enlightenment.** Virgin Classics Veritas VCD7 59260-2 — .·˙ ② 1h 33m DDD 7/89 Ⓑ ✍
Brandenburg Concertos. Overture in B flat major (from BWV194). Viola de gamba Sonata in C minor, BWV1029. **Taverner Players/Andrew Parrott.** EMI Reflexe CDS7 49806-2 — .·˙ ② 1h 50m DDD 1/90 Ⓑ ✍
Brandenburg Concertos. **Chamber Orchestra of Europe.** DG 431 660-2GH2 — .·˙ ② 1h 35m DDD 5/91 Ⓑ
Brandenburg Concertos. Orchestral Suites. **Adolf Busch Chamber Players/A. Busch.** EMI Références mono CHS7 64047-2 — .·˙ ③ 3h 15m ADD 12/91 Ⓑ ▲
Brandenburg Concertos. **Hanover Band/Anthony Halstead** (hpd). EMI Eminence. *Nos. 1, 3 and 4:* CD-EMX2200. *Nos. 2, 5 and 6:* CD-EMX2201 — .·˙ ② 44m 49m DDD 2/92 ♩ₚ Ⓑ
Brandenburg Concertos Nos. 1, 2 and 4. Orchestral Suite No. 2. **Vienna Concentus Musicus/ Nikolaus Harnoncourt.** Teldec Digital Experience 9031-75858-2 — .·˙ 1h 13m DDD 9/92 ♩ₛ Ⓑ ✍
Brandenburg Concertos Nos. 3, 5 and 6. Orchestral Suite No. 3. **Vienna Concentus Musicus/ Nikolaus Harnoncourt.** Teldec Digital Experience 9031-75859-2 — .·˙ 1h 15m DDD 9/92 ♩ₛ Ⓑ ✍
Brandenburg Concertos. **Vienna Concentus Musicus/Harnoncourt.** Teldec Das Alte Werk 9031-77611-2 — .·˙ ② 1h 45m ADD 7/93 Ⓑ ✍

Bach. Keyboard Concertos, BWV1052-58. **Chamber Orchestra of Europe/András Schiff** (pf). Decca 425 676-2DH2. Recorded in 1989.

.·˙ ② 1h 48m DDD 11/90 ♩ₚ

Although Bach's duties in Leipzig centred on the church he also wrote secular music for a series of coffee-house concerts, at which his keyboard concertos were probably first performed. The *Brandenburgs* were *concerti grossi*, in which the keyboard shares the limelight with other instruments; BWV1052-58 were the first-ever true keyboard concertos, a genre of which Bach was the 'father'. Practically all the music of the concertos was adapted from existing works of various kinds — cantatas and concertos (mostly for the violin) and the Fourth *Brandenburg* Concerto, a time-saving expedient for a hard-pressed composer. The instrument for which they were written was of course the harpsichord, but only the most rabid purist would now object to their presentation on the piano — providing that it embodies no stylistic anachronism. Schiff, with the attentive support of both the COE and the recording engineers, comes the closest yet to achieving that elusive goal.

Additional recommendations ...
BWV1052, 1057 and 1059. **Amsterdam Baroque Orchestra/Ton Koopman** (hpd). Erato 2292-45545-2 — ⠶ 5lm DDD 9ₚ ✒
BWV1052-54. **Melante Amsterdam/Bob van Asperen** (hpd). EMI Reflexe CDC7 54478-2 — ⠶ lh DDD 6/93 9ₚ 9ₛ ✒

Bach. DOUBLE CONCERTOS. [a]**Jaap Schröder,** [a]**Christopher Hirons,** [b]**Catherine Mackintosh** (vns); [b]**Stephen Hammer** (ob); [c]**Christophe Rousset** (hpd); **Academy of Ancient Music/Christopher Hogwood** ([c]hpd). L'Oiseau-Lyre Florilegium 421 500-2OH. Item marked [a] from DSDL702 (8/82), [b] and [c] new to UK.
D minor for Two Violins, BWV1043[a]; C minor for Violin and Oboe, BWV1060[b]; C minor for Two Harpsichords, BWV1060[c]; C minor for Two Harpsichords, BWV1062[c].

⠶ **58m DDD 9/89** ✒

The concept of a concerto with two or more soloists grew naturally out of the *concerto grosso*, and Bach was among those baroque composers who explored its possibilities. The Concerto in D minor, BWV1043 for two violins is perhaps the best known of his works in the *genre*, which Bach himself reworked as a Concerto for Two Harpsichords, BWV1062, in the key of C minor. No alternative version has survived in the case of the two-harpsichord Concerto BWV1060, also in C minor, but musicological evidence suggests that it was originally intended for two single-line instruments — two violins or one violin and an oboe. The work has thus been notionally reconstructed in the latter form. Baroque music never sounds better than when it is played on period instruments, in proper style, and by performers of the quality of those in this recording, not least the well matched soloists. The famous slow movement of BWV1043 is taken a little faster than usual, convincingly stripped of the specious sentimentality with which it is often invested. The recording is of suitably high quality.

Bach. OBOE CONCERTOS — F major, BWV1053; A major, BWV1055; D minor, BWV1059. **Chamber Orchestra of Europe/Douglas Boyd** (ob, ob d'amore). DG 429 225-2GH. Recorded in 1989.

⠶ **46m DDD 4/90**

Although Bach is not known to have written any concerto for the oboe he did entrust it with some beautiful *obbligato* parts, so he clearly did not underrate its expressive capacities. He did however rearrange many of his works for different instrumental media and there is musicological evidence that original oboe concertos were the (lost) sources from which other works were derived. The Harpsichord Concerto in A major, BWV1055, is believed originally to have been written for the oboe d'amore, whilst the other two Oboe Concertos have been reassembled from movements found in various cantatas. Whatever the validity of the academic reasoning, the results sound very convincing. Douglas Boyd is a superb oboist, with a clear sound that is free from stridency, and a fluency that belies the instrument's technical difficulty. He plays the faster, outer movements with winsome lightness of tongue and spirit, and with alertness to dynamic nuance; the slow ones, the hearts of these works, are given with sensitivity but without sentimentality — which can easily invade that of BWV1059, taken from Cantata No. 156, *Ich steh mit einem Fuss im Grabe*. The Chamber Orchestra of Europe partners him to perfection in this crisp recording.

New review
Bach. ORCHESTRAL SUITES Nos. 1-4, BWV1066-9. [a]**Wilbert Hazelzet** (fl); **Amsterdam Baroque Orchestra/Ton Koopman.** Deutsche Harmonia Mundi RD77864. Recorded 1988. No. 1 in C major; No. 2 in B minor[a]; No. 3 in D major; No. 4 in D major.

⠶ ② **lh 19m DDD 1/90** 9ₚ 9ₛ Ⓑ ✒

Bach's Orchestral Suites are deservedly well represented in the catalogue, with versions in plenty by orchestras of period and modern instruments alike. Koopman captures the contrasting colours and textures of these works with a sure feeling for orchestral sonority, but over and above that he is most persuasive in his gestures, graceful at times, ceremoniously pompous at others. Thus the Sarabande of the B minor Suite is one of the high-water marks of the entire set, exquisitely poised and lovingly articulated by the flautist, Wilbert Hazelzet, an artist of rare sensibility. Other dances in this suite fare equally well, with a Menuet redolent of courtly gesture and a Polonaise with ·an easy, carefree gait. As a general rule, Koopman favours rather slower tempos than many of his competing colleagues and he is to be applauded for doing so. The Rondeau of the B minor Suite is, comparatively speaking, slow yet avoiding monotony; the Forlane of the C major Suite is delightfully airy, as are the two Bourrées and the pleasingly leisurely Passepieds. Loveliest of all, perhaps, in this performance of the C major Suite, are the relaxed and affecting-ly articulated Courantes and the refined Menuets, whose kinetic energy is subtly realized under Koopman's direction. Koopman draws the strongest contrast between lighter textured dances and galanteries such as these, and the grandiose music contained in the two D major Suites. The Overtures in both instances are magnificent with commendably vibrant timpani and snarling trumpets which sets the blood coursing through the veins. This is robust Bach playing but without a hint of vulgarity and in no sense lacking in appropriate restraint. This is a considerable achievement and if some listeners are mildly irked by Koopman's own brilliant but perhaps over-busy keyboard continuo realizations, they are unlikely to be able to resist the subtle inflexions and ravishing inner-part understanding of Suite No. 2; and, it should be added, the sheer exuberant spirit of occasion which shines through the performances of the other three suites. The recorded sound is splendid.

Additional recommendations ...
Suites. **Cologne Musica Antiqua/Reinhard Goebel.** Archiv Produktion 415 671-2AH2 — ·· ② 1h 51m DDD 10/86 Ⓑ ✎
Suites. **Academy of St Martin in the Fields/Sir Neville Marriner.** Decca Serenata 430 378-2DM — ·· 1h 18m ADD 7/91 Ⓑ
Suites. Double Concertos, BWV1043 and BWV1060. **Heinz Holliger** (ob); **Gidon Kremer, Henryk Szeryng, Maurice Hasson** (vns); **Academy of St Martin in the Fields/Sir Neville Marriner.** Philips Baroque Classics 426 462-2PBQ2 — ·· ② 1h 54m ADD/DDD 11/91 Ⓑ
No. 2. Flute Concerto in A major, BWV1032 (orch. Mohr)[a]. Triple Concerto in A minor, BWV1044[b]. [ab]**James Galway** (fl); [b]**Rainer Wolters** (vn); [b]**Ursula Deutschler** (hpd); **Württemberg Chamber Orchestra/Jörg Faerber.** RCA Victor Red Seal 09026 60900-2 — ·· 56m DDD 6/93 Ⓑ

New review
Bach. Orchestral Suite No. 4 in D major, BWV1069. Concerto for Three Violins and Strings in D major, BWV1064. Cantata No. 42, Am Abend aber desselbigen Sabbats — Sinfonia. **Vivaldi.** Concertos — Strings in A major, RV158; Four Violins and Strings in B minor, Op. 3 No. 10. L'Olimpiade — Overture. **Freiburg Baroque Orchestra/Thomas Hengelbrock.** Deutsche Harmonia Mundi 05472 77289-2. Recorded 1991-92.

·· 1h 4m DDD 4/94 ✐

The Freiburg Baroque Orchestra score ten out of ten for vitality in their pleasingly varied programme. Bach's Orchestral Suite No. 4 is heard in what is probably a pre-Leipzig version, which excludes trumpets and drums. That may not sound too promising for readers who like their 'fix' of brass and timpani, yet the immensely rewarding sonorities created by strings, three oboes and bassoon together with invigorating rhythmic patterns, provides wonderful mental and aural refreshment. However, the two Menuets in the Leipzig version are also missing. Of the two Vivaldi concertos, the A major piece for ripieno strings foreshadows the style of the early Mannheim symphonists, with its tremolos, breaks and short runs punctuated by trills in the outer movements and the B minor, the tenth of the 12 which Vivaldi published under the title *L'estro armonico*, is among the most inventive of the set. This enjoyable release is well recorded and helpfully documented.

New review
Bach. ORCHESTRAL WORKS (arr. Stokowski). **BBC Philharmonic Orchestra/Matthias Bamert.** Chandos CHAN9259.
Toccata and Fugue in D minor, BWV565. Four Orchestral Suites, BWV1066-9 — No. 3 in D major: Air. Fugue in G minor, BWV578. Cantata No. 208, Was mir behagt, ist nur die

muntre Jagd, "Hunt Cantata", BWV208 — Schafe können sicher weiden. Das Wohltemperirte
Klavier, BWV846-93 — B minor, BWV869. Passacaglia and Fugue in C minor, BWV582.
Musicalisches Gesang-Buch G.C. Schemelli, BWV439-88 — Komm, süsser Tod, BWV478; Mein
Jesu! was für Seelenweh, BWV487. Cantata No. 4, Christ lag in Todesbanden, BWV4 — Wir
essen und leben wohl. Toccata, Adagio and Fugue in C major, BWV564 — Adagio. Clavier-
Ubung III, BWV669-89 — Wir glauben all'an einen Gott, BWV680. Six Violin Sonatas,
BWV1014-19 — No. 4 in C minor: Siciliano.

1h 10m DDD 3/94

Generations of new music-lovers must have experienced a thrill of discovery near the opening of the
Disney film, *Fantasia*, when Leopold Stokowski conducted his monumental orchestral transcription
of the Toccata and Fugue in D minor. It is sad that once the maestro himself stopped recording,
that and so many of his other Bach arrangements have been almost totally neglected on disc. This
ripely satisfying issue, opulently recorded by Chandos, superbly played by the BBC Philharmonic and
conducted by an erstwhile assistant to Stokowski, Matthias Bamert, fills an important gap. It is not
so much the unauthentic massiveness of these arrangements or the romantic manners (authentic for
Stokowski if not Bach) that strike one first, but the sheer beauty of the sound. Stokowski knew how
to make Bach glow. Plainly the members of the BBC Philharmonic relished throughout this
abandonment of modern authentic manners in Bach, playing with heartfelt expressiveness,
responding to Bamert's persuasive way with phrasing and rubato. If you have been feeling guilty
over not enjoying Bach as much as you did in pre-authentic days, this is just the disc for you.

Bach. The Art of Fugue, BWV1080[a]. A Musical Offering, BWV1079[b]. Canons, BWV1072-8;
1086-7[a]. **Cologne Musica Antiqua/Reinhard Goebel.** Archiv Produktion 413 642-2AH3.
Booklet included. Items marked [a] from 413 728-1AH2 (4/85); [b] 2533 422 (11/79).

③ 2h 20m ADD 4/85

The great compilation of fugues, canons and a trio sonata which Bach dedicated to King
Frederick the Great is one of the monuments of baroque instrumental music. Every contrapuntal
device of canon at various intervals, augmentation, inversion, retrograde motion and so on is
displayed here, and the performances are splendidly alive and authentic-sounding. It goes without
saying that period instruments or modern replicas are used. The intellectually staggering *Art of
Fugue* is a kind of testament to Bach's art and for this recording the instrumentation, unspecified
by the composer, has been well chosen. The 14 miniature Canons which close this issue are for
the most part a recent discovery and were written on a page of Bach's own copy of the *Goldberg
Variations*; of curiosity value certainly but not much more than that. Excellent recording for
these performances which have great authority.

Additional recommendations ...
The Art of Fugue. **Hespèrion XX/Jordi Savall.** Astrée Auvidis E2001 — ② 1h 32m ADD
11/88
The Art of Fugue. **Amsterdam Bach Soloists.** Ottavo OTRC48503 — 1h 12m DDD 8/89
The Art of Fugue. **Juilliard Quartet.** Sony Classical SK45937 — ② 1h 30m DDD 6/92
See further on in this section for The Art of Fugue (harpsichord and organ versions).

New review
Bach. FLUTE SONATAS, BWV1030-35. **William Bennett** (fl); **George Malcolm** (hpd);
[a]**Michael Evans** (vc). ASV Quicksilva CDQS6108. Recorded in 1978.
No. 1 in B minor. No. 2 in E flat major. No. 3 in A major. No. 4 in C major[a]. No. 5 in
E major[a]. No. 6 in E major[a].

1h 17m ADD 3/94

There is something special about the Bach flute sonatas and the more so when they are as well played
as they are here. They were obviously written during a happy period in Bach's life for they are
amiably inventive pieces, which is not to imply that they are slight, just very appealing. What matter
if the E flat, BWV1031 (possibly by C.P.E. Bach) and the C major, BWV1033 are probably spurious
— they still offer thoroughly worthwhile music. The first three sonatas (BWV1030-2) are played as a
simple duet for flute and harpsichord; in the last three (BWV1033-5), written for flute and bass
continuo, Michael Evans joins the ensemble and the balance — especially since his is not a baroque

instrument — is quite perfect. As for that superb flautist William Bennett, he too uses a modern instrument, yet is the soul of finesse as well as playing creatively and with consistently beautiful tone. The sound is forward but very convincing. At super-bargain price this disc should not be missed.

Additional recommendations ...
BWV1030-35. *Partita in A minor, BWV1013.* **Stephen Preston** (fl); [a]**Trevor Pinnock** (hpd); [b]**Jordi Savall** (va da gamba). CRD CRD3314/5 — .·' ② 1h 38m ADD 1/90 ✐
BWV1030-35. *G minor, BWV1020.* **Janet See** (fl); **Davitt Moroney** (hpd); **Mary Springfels** (va da gamba). Harmonia Mundi HMU90 7024/5 — .·' ② 1h 54m DDD 11/91 ✐
BWV1030-35. **Michala Petri** (rec); **Keith Jarrett** (hpd). RCA Victor Red Seal 09026 61274-2 · — .·' 1h 11m DDD 2/93

New review
Bach. VIOLIN SONATAS. **Elizabeth Blumenstock** (vn); **John Butt** (hpd) with [a]**Elisabeth Le Guin** (vc); [b]**Steven Lehning** (va da gamba). Harmonia Mundi HMU90 7084/5. Recorded 1991-92.
Violin Sonatas, BWV1014-19 — No. 1 in B minor; No. 1c — Andante; No. 2 in A major; No. 2c — Andante; No. 2d — Presto; No. 3 in E major; No. 4 in C minor; No. 4a — Siciliano: Largo; No. 5 in F minor; No. 6 in G major. Sonata in G major, BWV1019a. Sonatas for Violin and Continuo — G major, BWV1021[a]; E minor, BWV1023[b].

.·' ② 2h DDD 10/93 ⁹ₚ ✐

Bach's first biographer, Forkel, noted that the violin writing in these sonatas required a master to play it. Bach, he said, knew all the possibilities of the instrument, sparing it as little as he spared the harpsichord. Elizabeth Blumenstock has a bright tone, a clean, well-focused sound and an eloquent feeling for phrasing. These virtues can be heard to full advantage in the expressive *Adagio* of the Sonata in C minor. This is invigorating, perceptive and often very sensitive playing, controlled yet far from unrelaxed. Her expressive performances reach the heart of the music and her partner, John Butt is also impressive. A fine achievement.

Additional recommendations ...
BWV1014-19. **Susanne Lautenbacher** (vn); **Leonore Klinckerfuss** (hpd). Bayer BR100086/7 — .·' ② 1h 38m DDD 10/90 ✐
BWV1014-19. **Sigiswald Kuijken** (vn); **Gustav Leonhardt** (hpd). Deutsche Harmonia Mundi Editio Classica GD77170 — .·' ② 1h 34m ADD 10/90 ✐
BWV1017. **Beethoven.** *Violin Sonata No. 10 in major G, Op. 96.* **Schoenberg.** *Phantasy, Op. 47.* **Sir Yehudi Menuhin** (vn); **Glenn Gould** (pf). Sony Classical Glenn Gould Edition mono SMK52688 — .·' 48m ADD 10/93 ⁹ₚ ▲

New review
Bach. Keyboard Partitas, BWV825-30. **Christophe Rousset** (hpd). L'Oiseau-Lyre 440 217-2OH2.

.·' ② 2h 34m DDD 9/93

Christophe Rousset is impeccable in his finger work and lucid in his phrasing. He has abundant vitality, while eschewing extremes of tempo. He can be firmly rhythmic without becoming stiff, but he can also be flexible — there is freedom in the B flat Sarabande, the D major's elaborate Allemande and, particularly, its Sarabande. Altogether these are extremely impressive and deeply musicianly performances. The admirably warm but clean and natural sound of Rousset's very fine Hemsch harpsichord of 1751 is commendable.

Bach. The Art of Fugue, BWV1080. **Davitt Moroney** (hpd). Harmonia Mundi HMC90 1169/70.

.·' ② 1h 39m DDD 5/86 ⁹ₚ ✐

New review
Bach. The Art of Fugue, BWV1080. **Wolfgang Rübsam** (org). Naxos 8 550703/4. Played on the Flentrop organ of Duke University Chapel, Durham, USA. Recorded in 1992.

8 550703 — Contrapunctus 1-12, 14, 15. *8 550704* — Contrapunctus 13 and 17-19. Passacaglia and Fugue in C minor, BWV582. Sei gegrüsset, Jesu gütig, BWV768.

② 1h 12m 1h 18m DDD 1/94 q_P q_S

Bach died before the process of engraving his last great work had been completed, thus leaving a number of issues concerning performance in some doubt. However, Davitt Moroney is a performer-scholar who has a mature understanding of the complexity of Bach's work; in a lucid essay in the booklet, he discusses the problems of presenting *The Art of Fugue* whilst at the same time explaining his approach to performing it. Certain aspects of this version will be of particular importance to prospective buyers: Moroney, himself, has completed Contrapunctus 14 but he also plays the same Contrapunctus in its unfinished state as a fugue on three subjects. He omits Bach's own reworkings for two harpsichords of Contrapunctus 13 on the grounds that they do not play a part in the composer's logically-constructed fugue cycle; and he omits the Chorale Prelude in G major (BWV668*a*) which certainly had nothing to do with Bach's scheme but was added in the edition of 1751 so that the work should not end in an incomplete state. Moroney's performing technique is of a high order, placing emphasis on the beauty of the music which he reveals with passionate conviction. Exemplary presentation and an appropriate recorded sound enhance this fine achievement.

If a case has to be made to justify performing *The Art of Fugue* on the organ one need look no further than the Fugue subject itself. It fits naturally under the hands and the feet and cries out for the organ's unique sustaining qualities. Not that Wolfgang Rübsam relies overmuch on those sustaining qualities. Full-blown legato touch has no place in the scheme of things here; Rübsam's clearly defined, unpretentious phrasing is quite sufficient to trace the interweaving contrapuntal voices. He leads us unfalteringly through the most labyrinthine of Bach's contrapuntal mazes, yet his self-assured geniality makes it all seem, if not simple, at least accessible. Clearly the sumptuous organ sound helps, but in resisting any temptation to fall into a routine loud/soft/ loud pattern or to explore the more unusual stops Rübsam allows the music to flow uncluttered by external stimuli. It is incredible that the two magnificently recorded Naxos discs are available at super-budget price. Most collectors would happily pay well over the odds for this valuable addition to the catalogue.

Additional recommendations ...
The Art of Fugue (earlier version). **Kenneth Gilbert** (hpd). Archiv Produktion 427 673-2AH —
59m DDD 4/90

The Art of Fugue. Overture in the French style in B minor, BWV831. Italian Concerto in F major, BWV971. Prelude, Fugue and Allegro in E flat major, BWV998. **Gustav Leonhardt, Bob van Asperen** *(Art of Fugue)* (hpds). Deutsche Harmonia Mundi Editio Classica GD77013 — ②
2h 12m ADD 12/90

The Art of Fugue. **Gustav Leonhardt** (hpd). Vanguard Classics Bach Guild mono 08.2012.72 —
② 1h 27m ADD q_P ▲

Bach. SONATAS AND PARTITAS FOR SOLO VIOLIN, BWV1001-06. **Arthur Grumiaux** (vn). Philips Duo 438 736-2PM2. From A02205/7L (3/62). Recorded 1960-61.
Sonatas — No. 1 in G minor, BWV1001; No. 2 in A minor, BWV1003; No. 3 in C major, BWV1005. *Partitas* — No. 1 in B minor, BWV1002; No. 2 in D minor, BWV1004; No. 3 in E major, BWV1006.

② 1h 53m ADD 2/94 q_P

Bach. Partitas — No. 1 in B minor, BWV1002; No. 2 in D minor, BWV1004; No. 3 in E major, BWV1006. **Viktoria Mullova** (vn). Philips 434 075-2PH.

1h 17m DDD 6/94 q_P

The totally innocent ear, deprived of any comparison, could be forgiven for judging Grumiaux's to be definitive performances of Bach's Partitas and Sonatas. There is little of the sweetness of a Heifetz, the passing whimsy of a Shumsky here. And yet they define, indeed, as few other performances do, the structural frame and rhythmic working-out of each movement with extraordinary determination and authority. The purity of intonation is absolute; the energy locked into the sheer sound of the instrument startling. *And* two discs, as they say, for the price of one! Those who know and love the performances of the Belgian violinist Arthur Grumiaux will be thrilled to rediscover these Berlin recordings of the early 1960s, sharply remastered and sounding out in a roomy acoustic. The platinum gleam glancing off every moment of double-stopping, and the flinty brightness struck where contrapuntal voices meet ring out as never before. The arpeggios of the *Presto* of the G minor Sonata flash like light from the many facets of a prism; and the same mesmeric steadiness of *moto perpetuo* makes for a heady finish to the C major Sonata. What dominates, though, is the rhythmic rigour of Grumiaux's playing. His perfectionism, fused with a real sense of struggle, brings sheer might to the fugues of the Sonatas: it is rather like watching a climber scaling a vast rock face, securing himself with a pick and leaping across the next crevasse.

In a completely different way, Viktoria Mullova also comes as a breath of fresh air: her playing is as close to technical perfection as makes no difference, her lean tone favours transparent textures, her dance movements are light on their feet and her nuancing of tone and volume is full of subtlety — warmly expressive but with no trace of romanticism. She is not afraid to embellish the texts with discretion: and adorns the 'open spaces' of the Sarabande of the B minor Partita in delightful fashion but refrains from overloading the already ornate one in the D minor, the Chaconne of which here receives the finest performance available, majestic in its realization of the work's architecture and variety. In sum, Mullova's heart is rarely if ever on her sleeve, but, in tandem with her understanding is always in her violin. This disc could safely be added to a 'desert island' collection and the recording is worthy of the performances.

Additional recommendations ...
Oscar Shumsky. ASV CDDCD454 — ･ ② 2h 27m ADD 9/87 ♀ₚ
Jascha Heifetz. RCA Victor Gold Seal GD87708 — ･ ② 2h 5m ADD 9/88 ♀ₚ ▲
Henryk Szeryng. CBS Masterworks Portrait mono CD46721 — ･ ② 2h 8m ADD 12/91 ♀ₚ ▲
Sigiswald Kuijken. Deutsche Harmonia Mundi Editio Classica GD77043 — ･ ② 2h 8m ADD ♀ₚ ✎
Nathan Milstein. EMI mono ZDMB 64793-2 — ･ ② 1h 54m ADD 5/94 ♀ₚ ▲

Bach. SOLO CELLO SUITES, BWV1007-12. **Anner Bylsma** (vc). Sony Classical Vivarte SK48047. Recorded in 1992.
No. 1 in G major. No. 2 in D minor. No. 3 in C major. No. 4 in E flat major. No. 5 in C minor. No. 6 in D major.

･ ② 1h 55m DDD 1/93 ✎

This is the second complete version of Bach's six Cello Suites recorded by the Dutch virtuoso Anner Bylsma (the first is listed below). In a period of some 13 years between the first and second recordings, Bylsma's concept of these works has not undergone any fundamental changes. The difference between them is rather one of degree for, as Byslma himself says in a lively note accompanying the discs, "one keeps finding new relationships between the notes and every motif can be played in so many different ways — and always with meaning, too". In the new version Bylsma intensifies the musical gestures which characterized the earlier one. He is, if anything, more spontaneous in his playing here and he takes greater risks. What we have, in fact, are 'performances' as opposed to studio-correct readings; and so listeners concerned with niceties of intonation, for instance, may sometimes be mildly disconcerted by what they hear. But from a purely interpretative standpoint the new set is bolder, more relaxed and more broadly expressive. Indeed, were it not for his impeccable 'early music' credentials Bylsma might be targeted by critics for excessive romanticism. The late Pierre Fournier was thus condemned for his Bach playing, yet his performances of the *Preludes* of these Suites, made three decades ago (listed below), were in many respects far stricter than those of Bylsma. All this and much else make it clear that convenient generalizations and tidy compartments are less acceptable than ever before. Bylsma is an artist who is not afraid to express himself individually, intensely and even, at times audaciously. Open-minded readers will find much to admire and much that is satisfying in these passionate, warmly expressive performances. But neither the noble Fournier nor Bylsma's earlier recording is lightly to be cast aside, not to mention all the other recommend-able recordings in the catalogue.

Additional recommendations ...
Nos. 1-6. **Pierre Fournier.** DG 419 359-2GCM2 — ･ ② 2h 19m ADD 3/89 ♀ₚ
Nos. 1-6. **Pablo Casals.** EMI Références mono CHS7 61027-2 — ･ ② 2h 10m ADD 3/89 ♀ₚ ▲
Nos. 1-6. **Anner Bylsma.** RCA RD70950 — ･ ② 2h 6m DDD ♀ₚ

Nos. 1-6. **Robert Cohen.** Collins Classics 1081-2 — .•' ② 2h 26m DDD 5/90 ◖ₚ
Nos. 1-6. **Paul Tortelier.** EMI CMS7 69431-2 — .• ② 2h 5m ADD 3/92 ◖ₚ ▲
*(All arr. Söllscher): Nos. 1 and 2; No. 6 in D major — Sarabande; Gigue. Sonata for Solo Violin No. 3
in C major, BWV1005.* **Göran Söllscher** *(gtr).* DG 435 471-2GH — .•' 1h DDD 8/92 ◖ₛ

Bach. HARPSICHORD WORKS. **Davitt Moroney.** Virgin Classics Veritas VC7 59272-2.
Recorded in 1990.
Four Duets, BWV802-05. Overture in the French style in B minor, BWV831. Italian Concerto
in F major, BWV971. Prelude, Fugue and Allegro in E flat major, BWV998.

.•' 1h 11m DDD 9/92 ◖ₚ ✒

Davitt Moroney has established a reputation both for his stylish Bach playing and his lively interest
in background scholarship. In this recital his performance sits comfortably alongside those of his
rivals Kenneth Gilbert and Christophe Rousset. The *Italian Concerto* and the Overture (Partita) in
B minor come from the Second Part of Bach's *Clavier-Ubung* in which he provided the performer
with contrasting examples of his skill in transferring orchestral forms — concerto and suite — to
the keyboard. Moroney's interpretations are vivacious without being frenetic and he allows the
music to breathe naturally. He is also conscious of the inherent poetry of Bach's keyboard genius,
though the close recording balance favouring the lower register of the instrument sometimes
threatens both the evenness of sound and the eloquence of Moroney's approach. But this in itself
hardly deflects attention from disciplined, often passionate, and personally involved playing which
is sensitive to the nobility of Bach's writing. This is apparent, above all, in the great French
Overture itself which prefaces the B minor Suite. A musically satisfying disc.

Additional recommendations ...
Italian Concerto. French Overture. Four Duets. **Kenneth Gilbert.** Harmonia Mundi Musique
d'Abord HMA190 1278 — .•' 56m DDD 2/90 ◖ₚ ✒
Italian Concerto. French Overture. Four Duets. Chromatic Fantasia. **Christophe Rousset.** L'Oiseau-
Lyre 433 054-2OH — .•' 1h 8m DDD 5/92 ◖ₚ ◖ₛ ✒

Bach. HARPSICHORD WORKS. **Wanda Landowska** *(hpd).* RCA Victor Gold Seal mono
GD60919. Recorded 1945-57.
Goldberg Variations, BWV988 (from HMV ALP1139, 5/54). Concerto in D major, BWV972
(HMV DB6819, 12/48). Fantasias — C minor, BWV906 (RB16068, 9/58); C minor,
BWV919. Prelude, Fugue and Allegro in E flat major, BWV998 (both from ALP1246, 6/55).
Two-Part Inventions, BWV772-86. Three-Part Inventions, BWV787-801 — No. 1 in C major;
No. 2 in C minor; No. 5 in E flat major; No. 11 in G minor; No. 13 in A minor; No. 14 in B
flat major; No. 15 in B minor (all from RB16193, 7/60). Capriccio sopra la lontananza del suo
fratello dilettissimo in B flat major, BWV992. Partita No. 2 in C minor, BWV826 (RB16068).

.•' ② 2h 30m ADD 3/93 ◖ₚ ▲

The lady who played for Tolstoy, who rediscovered the harpsichord for a modern listening audience
and who enchanted generations of music-lovers with her engaging personality, was also one of the
century's great Bach interpreters. But her grand, flamboyant and highly demonstrative style is largely
out of step with modern theories on Bach performance, so these two discs — which are beautifully
transferred from late 78s and early tape originals — are likely to annoy as well as inspire. However,
the *Goldberg Variations* (the second of Landowska's two recordings of the work) are deeply poetic and
chock-full of imagination, while few keyboard players have injected quite so much pathos and
personality into Bach's autobiographical *Capriccio sopra la lontananza del suo fratello dilettissimo* ("Capriccio
on the Departure of His Beloved Brother") — his "departure" being *a* journey, as opposed to *the*
journey! — or the Concerto in D major "After Vivaldi". Landowska's 'harpsichord Pleyel' makes a big,
exciting sound, very unlike the softer, less dynamic sonority of a genuine period instrument. Few
apologies need be made for the later recordings on the album, which come across with considerable
presence, albeit in mono. One woman's Bach, perhaps ... but very much worth listening to.

Additional recommendations ...
*Prelude and Fugue in A minor, BWV894. Toccatas — F sharp minor, BWV910; C minor, BWV911;
G minor, BWV915. Aria variata in A minor, BWV989. Capriccio sopra ....* **Kenneth Gilbert** *(hpd).*
Archiv Produktion 437 555-2AH — .•' 1h 10m DDD 6/93 ✒

Two Part-Inventions. Three-Part Inventions. **Glenn Gould** (pf). Sony Classical Glenn Gould Edition. CD52596 — .·˙ 50m ADD 6/93 ⁹ₚ

Bach. The Well-tempered Clavier, Books 1 and 2, BWV846-93. **Davitt Moroney** (hpd). Harmonia Mundi HMC90 1285/8.

.·˙ ④ 4h 32m DDD 4/89   Ⓑ 🖋

For those wanting both books of the *48*, the choice is wide. With numerous versions currently available on CD the listener is confronted by a daunting process of selection. Davitt Moroney is a gifted and serious-minded artist whose performances are technically secure, stylistically informed and thoughtful. Empty rhetoric, uncalled-for flamboyance or superfluous gesture are not for him; indeed, on occasion listeners might feel that a degree of spontaneity is lacking. Yet where this playing is constantly impressive is in the successful marriage of virtuosity with the poetic content of the music. In short Moroney makes the music sing with carefully shaped phrases, admirable rhythmic suppleness and well-defined articulation. No listener will find all he wants from any one performance of these masterpieces since different registrations, tempos and indeed instruments bring out different colours and induce in us different responses. Moroney highlights many of the almost infinite contrasts which exist in the music with sensibility and affection. The instrument is effectively balanced, if a shade too closely, allowing listeners to discern subtle details in Bach's writing.

Additional recommendations ...
Books 1 and 2. **Kenneth Gilbert** (hpd). Archiv Produktion 413 439-2AH4 — .·˙ ④ 4h 16m 2/87 Ⓑ 🖋
Books 1 and 2. **Edwin Fischer** (pf). EMI Références mono CHS7 63188-2 — .·˙ ③ 3h 57m ADD 3/90 Ⓑ ▲
Book 1. **András Schiff** (pf). Decca 414 388-2DH2 — .·˙ ② 1h 50m DDD 9/86 Ⓑ
Book 2. **András Schiff** (pf). Decca 417 236-2DH2 — .·˙ ② 2h 24m DDD 3/87 Ⓑ
Books 1 and 2. **Colin Tilney** (clav/hpd). Hyperion CDA66351/4 — .·˙ ④ 5h 4m DDD 10/90 Ⓑ

Key to symbols

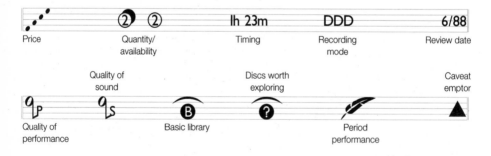

.·˙	② ②	1h 23m	DDD	6/88
Price	Quantity/ availability	Timing	Recording mode	Review date

| | Quality of
sound | | Discs worth
exploring | | Caveat
emptor |

⁹ₚ	⁹ₛ	Ⓑ	❓	🖋	▲
Quality of performance		Basic library		Period performance	

Bach. French Suites, BWV812-17. Suite in A minor, BWV818a. Suite in E flat major, BWV819a. **Davitt Moroney** (hpd). Virgin Classics Veritas VCD7 59011-2.

.·˙ ② 2h 24m DDD 4/91   ⁹ₛ 🖋

Bach compiled his *French Suites*, so-called — the composer himself did not give them this title — towards the end of his Cöthen period and at the beginning of his final appointment at Leipzig. As well as performing the customary six suites, five of which have survived in Bach's own hand, Davitt Moroney includes two further suites prepared by Bach's pupil, Heinrich Nikolaus Gerber, in 1725. These and extra movements to the well-known six suites belong to various surviving sources and though we can be sure that Bach himself had good reason to discard them from his final thoughts, so-to-speak, their presence in this album is nonetheless welcome. Moroney has given careful thought and preparation to the project and the results are often illuminating. His interpretations are relaxed, articulate and show a lively awareness of the music's poetic content. There is a clarity in these performances which stems from lucid punctuation highlighting the significance of every phrase. Shorter dance movements have poise and are allowed to breathe while longer ones, notably *allemandes,* have a taut rhythmic elasticity which enable the listener to savour their eloquent often pensive inflexions. Perhaps *sarabandes* are sometimes a little too weighty, but this is to some extent a matter of taste and few will be disappointed by Moroney's stylistically informed and technically fluent playing. The recording is excellent.

Additional recommendations ...
French Suites. **Gustav Leonhardt** (hpd). RCA Victor Seon GD71963 — .∙• ② lh 18m ADD 5/90
French Suites. Concerto in the Italian style, BWV971. Overture in the French style in B minor, BWV831.
András Schiff (pf). Decca 433 313-2DH2 — .∙• ② 2h 7m DDD 10/93 ℗

New review
Bach. Goldberg Variations, BWV988. **Pierre Hantaï** (hpd). Opus 111 OPS30-84.

.∙• lh 17m DDD 4/94 ℗ Ⓑ

Pierre Hantaï's approach to the *Goldberg Variations* is tremendously spirited and energetic but also disciplined. What is most appealing about this playing, though, is that Hantaï clearly finds the music great fun to perform; some players have been too inclined to make heavy weather over this music. He makes each and every one of the canons a piece of entertainment while in no sense glossing over Bach's consummate formal mastery. Other movements, such as Var. 7 (gigue) and Var. 11, effervesce with energy and good humour and he is careful to avoid anything in the nature of superficiality. Not for a moment is the listener given the impression that his view of the music is merely skin deep. Indeed, there is a marked concentration of thought in canons such as that at the fourth interval (Var. 12). Elsewhere his feeling for the fantasy and poetry of Bach's music is effective and well placed (such as in Var. 13). The character of Bruce Kennedy's copy of an early eighteenth-century instrument by the Berlin craftsman, Michael Mietke is admirably captured by the effectively resonant recorded sound.

Additional recommendations ...
Goldberg Variations. **Trevor Pinnock** (hpd). Archiv Produktion 415 130-2AH — .∙• lh lm ADD 8/85 ℗ Ⓑ
Goldberg Variations. **András Schiff** (pf). Decca 417 116-2DH — .∙• lh 13m DDD 12/86 ℗ Ⓑ
Goldberg Variations. **Kenneth Gilbert** (hpd). Harmonia Mundi HMC90 1240 — .∙• lh 7m DDD 6/87 ℗ Ⓑ
Goldberg Variations. Prelude in G major, BWV902/1. Fantasia in C minor, BWV906/1. Adagio in G major, BWV968. Chromatic Fantasia and Fugue in D minor, BWV903. **Virginia Black** (hpd). Collins Classics 7003-2 — .∙• ② lh 50m DDD 2/92 ℗ Ⓑ
Goldberg Variations. **Maggie Cole** (hpd). Virgin Classics Veritas VC7 59045-2 — .∙• lh 19m DDD 2/92 Ⓑ
Goldberg Variations. **Glenn Gould** (pf). Sony Classical Glenn Gould Edition mono SMK52594 — .∙• 46m ADD 4/93 ℗ Ⓑ ▲
Goldberg Variations. **Glenn Gould** (pf). Sony Classical Glenn Gould Edition SMK52619 — .∙• 5lm DDD 8/93 ℗ Ⓑ ▲

New review
Bach. PIANO WORKS. **János Sebestyén.** Naxos 8 550679.
Two-Part Inventions, BWV772-86. Three-Part Inventions, BWV787-801. Anna Magdalena Notenbüch — Minuets: G major, BWVAnh114, F major, BWVAnh115, G major, BWVAnh116, F major, BWVAnh132; Polonaises: G minor, BWVAnh119, G minor, BWVAnh125; March in D major, BWVAnh122; Musette in D major, BWVAnh126.

58m DDD 6/94

There is a place for a satisfactory piano version of the *Two-* and *Three-Part Inventions.* These are simple pieces, without a profound message, intended to assist Bach's son Wilhelm Friedemann to play clearly in two and three parts, and to develop his legato touch; Sebestyén wisely reads them in that spirit instead of looking for what is not there. His are clean performances in every sense, with well-balanced lines, no extravagant gradation of volume, with just enough (and that means very little) rubato to shape his phrases — and with no romantic dwelling to make a note more important than is its due. Had Sebestyén taken a more 'sophisticated' approach to these *Inventions* the simple pieces from Anna Magdalena's *Notenbüchlein* could have come either as an anticlimax or as a relief, according to one's point of view, but proper proportion is preserved so that they sound as though they belong there. So many of the items in this recording are used as piano-teaching material that it is well to have such excellent examples of their performance available — and so well recorded at that.

See the end of this section for details of availability of Complete Organ Works.

New review
Bach. FANTASIAS, PRELUDES AND FUGUES. **Christopher Herrick** (org). Hyperion CDA66791/2. Played on the organ of the Jesuitenkirche, Lucerne, Switzerland. Recorded 1993. Fantasias and Fugues — C minor, BWV537; G minor, BWV542; C minor, BWV562; G major, BWV572. Preludes and Fugues — D major, BWV532; F minor, BWV534; A major, BWV536; G major, BWV541; A minor, BWV543; B minor, BWV544; C major, BWV545; C minor, BWV546; C major, BWV547; E minor, BWV548, "Wedge"; E flat major, BWV552, "St Anne".

These 15 works constitute some of the finest and most important music ever written for the organ. They are such mainstays of the repertory that no serious lover of organ music could consider a world without them. Herrick's performances are authoritative, scholarly and perceptive, but if that were all it would merely be putting Bach on a pedestal, making him accessible only to those who already possess the key to the door. Herrick's genius is in bringing the music vividly to life, injecting it with a sense of fun and a directness of appeal without for a moment compromising artistic integrity. Few could fail to be captivated by the wonderfully vibrant and smiling countenance of the great E flat Prelude while those of us who have laboured long and hard just to get our feet round that most ankle-twisting of all fugue subjects must surely surrender in the face of Herrick's effortless fluency in BWV542. The glorious Swiss instrument has been brilliantly recorded, portraying not just the instrument itself but its sumptuous aural setting.

Bach. Orgelbüchlein, BWV599-644. **Simon Preston** (org). DG 431 816-2GH. Played on the Lorentz organ of Sorø Abbey, Denmark. Recorded in 1989.

Bach's *Orgelbüchlein* ("Little Organ Book") contains 46 short preludes based on the chorale melodies used in the Lutheran church. It is arranged to follow the course of the church's year, beginning in Advent, passing through Christmas, Lent, Easter, Ascension, Pentecost and Trinity and ending with those miscellaneous areas classified in most hymn-books as "General". But Bach was not merely providing the church organist with something useful (although its enduring usefulness is still evident today — walk into almost any church and at some point you are likely to find the organist delving into a copy of Bach's *Orgelbüchlein*), he also intended these as teaching pieces. The title page describes them as offering "instruction in the various ways of working out a chorale, and also practice in the use of the pedals". What wonderful teaching pieces these are for any organ student — training exercises of this calibre would surely be enough to tempt anyone into learning how to play the organ! Here with that accomplished organist, Simon Preston, playing a ravishing Danish instrument sumptuously recorded by DG, the full genius of Bach is revealed. At just over an hour and a quarter, this CD represents astonishing value not just in playing time, but also in the quality of the playing, the magnificent recorded sound and, above all, the wealth of truly great music.

Bach. ORGAN PARTITAS. **Simon Preston.** DG 429 775-2GH. Played on the Lorentz organ of Sorø Abbey, Denmark. Recorded in 1989.
Christ, der du bist der helle Tag, BWV766. O Gott, du frommer Gott, BWV767. Sei gegrüsset, Jesu gütig, BWV768. Ach, was soll ich Sünder machen?, BWV770.

At the last count the number of chorale preludes for organ believed to be by Bach was 239. In addition there are six Chorale Preludes — more extended sets of variations on the Lutheran chorales. These continue a tradition some of the greatest masters of which were Bach's immediate predecessors Böhm, Buxtehude and Pachelbel. While Bach's magnificent set on *Vom Himmel hoch, da komm ich her* (not included on this disc) is generally regarded as the pinnacle of the genre, the other partitas are all early works and with the exception of that based on *Sei gegrüsset* do not call for pedals. It seems that these pieces could just as easily have been intended for domestic consumption by harpsichordists as for church use by organists. As such, they have perhaps been somewhat overlooked by present-day organists, yet as this captivating disc shows most convincingly, the music contains an abundant wealth of variety, interest and charm. Simon Preston is on excellent form, showing his customary formidable technical mastery. His performances bring this music vividly to life and he unearths an astonishing variety of tone colours from a famous and historic organ. All of this is recorded with outstanding clarity and the overall sound is simply delicious.

Bach. ORGAN WORKS, Volume 1. **Kevin Bowyer.** Nimbus NI5280. Played on the Marcussen organ of St Hans Kirke, Odense, Denmark. Recorded in 1991.
Fantasia and Fugue in G minor, BWV542. Trio Sonata No. 1 in E flat major, BWV525. Toccata and Fugue in D minor, BWV565. Pastorale in F major, BWV590. Organ Concerto No. 1 in G major, BWV592. Chorale Prelude — Erbarm' dich mein, O Herre Gott, BWV721. Organ Chorale — Aus tiefer Not schrei ich zu dir, BWV1099.

lh 7m DDD 10/92 Ⓑ

Organist Kevin Bowyer and record company Nimbus have set out to record every note Bach wrote for the organ, is believed to have written or is now known not to but in the past was thought to have written. It is a mammoth project planned to take several years. The first disc, perhaps inevitably, includes the best-known of all Bach's organ pieces — although some would dispute that it is an organ piece or even that Bach wrote it; Bowyer's account of the *Toccata and Fugue* in D minor is invigorating, exciting and very fast. It sets the scene for a CD of virtuoso performances and sound musicianship. The whole is a well-chosen, self-contained programme which also includes an indisputably 'great' organ work, a Trio Sonata, a transcription Bach made of an effervescent concerto by Ernst, a youthful chorale prelude as well as one from a collection only discovered in 1985 and one real oddity. Much thought has gone into the choice of organ and this instrument serves its purpose admirably; roaring magnificently in the *Fantasia* and emulating the tranquil sounds so characteristic of the *Pastorale*. If the remaining discs are going to be this good then it's a series well worth collecting.

Additional recommendations ...
Toccatas and Fugues — BWV565; F major, BWV540; D minor, BWV538, "Dorian". Toccata, Adagio and Fugue in C major, BWV564. Passacaglia and Fugue in C minor, BWV582. **Christopher Herrick.** Hyperion CDA66434 — lh 4m DDD 4/91 ⁹ₚ ⁹ₛ Ⓑ
Organ works, Volume 3. Preludes and Fugues — F minor, BWV534; A minor, BWV543. Trio Sonata No. 2 in C minor, BWV526. Organ Concerto No. 5 in D minor, BWV596. Sei gegrüsset, Jesu gütig, BWV768. **Kevin Bowyer.** Nimbus NI5290 — lh 4m DDD 6/93 ⁹ₚ

New review
Bach. ORGAN WORKS, Volume 4. **Kevin Bowyer**. Nimbus NI5377. Played on the Marcussen organ of Sct. Hans Kirke, Odense, Denmark. Recorded in 1992.
Toccatas — G minor, BWV915; G major, BWV916. Fugues on themes of Albinoni — A major, BWV950; B minor, BWV951. Fugue in C minor, BWV575. Preludes and Fugues — C major, BWV553; D minor, BWV554; E minor, BWV555; F major, BWV556; G major, BWV557; G minor, BWV558; A minor, BWV559; B flat major, BWV560. Fantasia con imitazione in B minor, BWV563.

lh 14m DDD 2/94 ⁹ₚ

While critical opinion and academic argument may deter others, Bowyer is content to let the music speak for itself, whether it is "by J.S. Bach, J.L. Krebs or A.N. Other". On this disc the music speaks with absolute conviction. One thinks of the gloriously dramatic rhetoric Bowyer brings to the two Toccatas (BWV915 and 916). Harpsichordists may claim these as their own but who could deny this lovely Odense organ the opportunity to glitter with such flamboyant music? The eight 'short' Preludes and Fugues have a muscular, clean-shaven feel to them underlined by plain and simple registrations. While other recordings of such indefinable pieces seem like scraps from the cutting-room floor, Bowyer sets them firmly in the mainstream of high baroque organ music.

Bach. ORGAN WORKS, Volume 1. **Peter Hurford** (org). EMI Eminence CD-EMX2218. Played on the organ of Martinikerk, Groningen, Holland.
Toccata and Fugue in D minor, BWV565. Herzlich tut mich verlangen, BWV727. Fugue in G major, BWV577. Erbarm' dich mein, O Herre Gott, BWV721. Fugue on a theme by Corelli in B minor, BWV579. Prelude and Fugue in G major, BWV541. Pastorale in F major, BWV590. Clavier-Übung III, BWV669-89 — Wir glauben all'an einen Gott, BWV680. Orgel-Büchlein, BWV599-644 — O Mensch, bewein' dein Sünde gross, BWV622. Passacaglia and Fugue in C minor, BWV582.

1h 3m DDD 3/94

"Peter Hurford playing organs of Bach's Time". For his earlier recordings on Argo, Hurford played mainly modern, neo-baroque instruments and while Bach on 'authentic' instruments is no novelty, we certainly don't hear enough of the wondrous Ahrend organ which begins this new series in such style. Ahrend? Builders of Bach's time? Well we're obviously going to have to take the title with a hefty pinch of salt. Although it dates back over 500 years, in its present form the organ dates back only as far as 1984. Bach never played it, and even if he had he certainly wouldn't recognize it now, but it sounds wonderful; Henry Mitton and Mark Nations have recorded it magnificently, closely focusing the sound within an aura of spaciousness. Splendid playing by Hurford too, of course. He begins (as everyone does) with the ubiquitous Toccata and Fugue in D minor. But what a performance! Everything else is given warmly communicative, unpretentious and immensely appealing performances. Hurford knows and loves his Bach, something which shines out of every note he plays.

Bach. ORGAN WORKS, Volume 3. **Peter Hurford.** Decca Ovation 421 617-2DM3. From Argo D150D3 (7/79). Recorded 1974-1979.
Chorale Variations and Partitas, BWV766-71. The Schübler Chorale Preludes, BWV645-50. Chorale Preludes — Herr Jesu Christ, dich zu uns wend', BWV726; Herzlich tut mich verlangen, BWV727; Jesus, meine Zuversicht, BWV728; In dulci jubilo, BWV729; Liebster Jesu, wir sind hier, BWV730; Liebster Jesu, wir sind hier, BWV731; Lobt Gott, ihr Christen, allzugleich, BWV732; Meine Seele erhebt den Herrn, BWV733; Nun freut euch, lieben Christen g'mein, BWV734; Valet will ich dir geben, BWV735; Valet will ich dir geben, BWV736; Vater unser im Himmelreich, BWV737; Vom Himmel hoch, da komm'ich her, BWV738; Wie schön leuchtet der Morgenstern, BWV739; Wir glauben all' an einen Gott, BWV740. Concertos — No. 1 in G major, BWV592; No. 2 in A minor, BWV593; No. 3 in C major, BWV594; No. 4 in C major, BWV595; No. 5 in D minor, BWV596; No. 6 in E flat major, BWV597.

③ 3h 31m ADD 6/90

Most record collectors will be familiar with Bach's great organ works; not least the ubiquitous *Toccata and Fugue* in D minor. While these are undeniably essential ingredients in any CD collection they represent only a tiny fraction of Bach's enormous output for the instrument. Generally these are what are known as chorale preludes; miniature pieces reflecting both the chorale's melody and the character of its words. Here are some of Bach's most ingenious and personal creations. In more extended form are the six Chorale Partitas which provide variations for each of the verses of the original chorale. Unique among his organ works are the secular concertos, transcriptions of string concertos by Vivaldi and Ernst. While Bach made few changes to the original, his unique genius has turned typically Italianate violin writing (in the third even the violin cadenzas have been retained) into something utterly at ease on the organ. Here is some of the most charming and effervescent music in the entire repertoire. Peter Hurford's playing, Decca's superlative recordings and a selection of top-rate organs from around the world provide the best realization imaginable of these works. If a three-disc set of lesser-known Bach organ works (even at mid-price) seems a tall order, rest assured you are buying some of the finest organ music, organ playing and organ recordings available. Here is a recording to be dipped into time and time again; it never loses its freshness or ability to captivate.

Additional recommendations ...
Volume 4: Chorales from the Neumeister Collection Nos. 1-35. Chorale Preludes, BWV651-668, The "Eighteen". Chorale Preludes — O Lamm Gottes unschuldig, NBA; Ach Gott und Herr, BWV714; Allein Gott in der Höh' sei Ehr', BWV715; Allein Gott in der Höh' sei Ehr', BWV716; Allein Gott in der Höh', BWV717; Christ lag in Todesbanden, BWV718; Der Tag, der ist so freudenrich, BWV719; Ein' feste Burg ist unser Gott, BWV720; Erbarm' dich mein, o Herre Gott, BWV721; Gelobet seist du, Jesu Christ, BWV722; Gelobet seist du, Jesu Christ, BWV723; Gottes Sohn ist kommen, BWV724; Herr Gott, dich loben wir, BWV725. **Peter Hurford.** Decca Ovation 421 621-2DM3 — ⨟ ③ 3h 50m ADD/DDD 6/90 ⁹ₚ ⁹ₛ*

BWV565. BWV709/726. BWV727. Preludes and Fugues — E minor, BWV533; D minor, BWV539; C major, BWV531; C minor, BWV549; G major, BWV550. Wo soll ich fliehen hin, BWV694. Nun komm, der Heiden Heiland, BWV699. Gottes Sohn ist kommen, BWV703. Herr Christ, der einig Gottes Sohn, BWV698. Lob sei dem allmächtigen Gott, BWV704. Gelobet seist du Jesu Christ, BWV697; Vom Himmel hoch, da komm ich her, BWV701. Christum wir sollen loben schon, BWV696. In dulci jubilo, BWV751. **Lorenzo Ghielmi.** Deutsche Harmonia Mundi 05472 77278-2 — ⨟ 58m DDD 7/93*

Bach. ORGAN WORKS, Volume 3. **Ton Koopman.** Novalis 150036-2. Played on the organ of the Great Church, Leeuwarden, Holland. Recorded in 1988.
Toccata and Fugue in D minor, BWV538, "Dorian". Partita on "Sei gegrüsset, Jesu gutig", BWV768. Fantasia in G major, BWV572. Trio Sonata No. 6 in G major, BWV530. Chorale Preludes — "Vater Unser im Himmelreich", BWV682; "Jesu Christus unser Heiland", BWV688. Prelude and Fugue in A minor, BWV543.

⨟ 1h 10m DDD 8/89 — ⁹ₚ ✐

Bach. ORGAN WORKS. **Michael Murray.** Telarc CD80179. Played on the organ of the College of St Thomas, St Paul, Minnesota, USA.
Prelude and Fugues — C major, BWV531; G minor, BWV535; D minor, BWV539. Concerto No. 1 in G major, BWV592. Fantasia in G major, BWV572. Prelude in C major, BWV567. "Little" Fugue in G minor, BWV578. Canzona in D minor, BWV588. Chorale Prelude "In dulci jubilo", BWV751.

⨟ 58m DDD 8/89 — ⁹ₚ ⁹ₛ ✐

These two constitute 'Good CDs' from any standpoint. The playing is unwavering in its excellence, the instruments are well chosen, the combined programmes present a good cross-section of some of Bach's finest (if not exactly his best-known) organ compositions and the recordings are superlative (indeed Telarc's sound is nothing short of stunning). The one work common to both (the *Fantasia* in G) receives such utterly different interpretations that it is well worth having in both versions. Ton Koopman (playing on an instrument built when Bach was 42) is an acknowledged Bach expert and whilst his performances undoubtedly show scholarship and a keen appreciation of style, they are also exceedingly enjoyable in their own right. In fact, Koopman's playing is so compelling and vivacious that he manages to make accessible works which in lesser hands come across as dull and academic. Michael Murray uses a much more modern instrument. It has a bright, forthright tone which is ideally suited to this joyous and energetic music. Murray, too, plays with an infectious enthusiasm and allows the music to speak for itself, never allowing fussiness of detail or extravagant use of the organ to obscure the sheer ebullience of the writing.

Bach. ORGAN WORKS. **Nicholas Danby.** CBS Digital Masters CD45807. Played on the organ of Lübeck Cathedral, Germany. Recorded in 1989.
Chorale Preludes — Wachet auf, ruft uns die stimme, BWV645; Nun komm' der Heiden Heiland, BWV659; Dies sind die Heil'gen zehn gebot', BWV678; Liebster Jesu, wir sind hier, BWV706; Herr Jesu Christ, dich zu uns wend', BWV709; Erbarm' dich mein, O Herre Gott, BWV721; Herzlich tut mich verlangen, BWV727; Vater unser im Himmelreich, BWV737; Aus der tiefe rufe ich, BWV745. Fantasia in G major, BWV572. Prelude and Fugues — A minor, BWV543; C minor, BWV546. Toccata and Fugue in D minor, BWV565.

⨟ 1h 10m DDD 6/90 — ⁹ₚ ⁹ₛ Ⓑ

This is an excellent CD on every count. The music is wonderful, Bach at his most varied and interesting. The playing is sympathetic, tasteful, elegant and persuasive, with the organ making a really sumptuous sound. And the recording is exemplary, perfectly realizing the cathedral's warm atmosphere and the organ's splendid array of charms, but without any disturbing background thuds or clatters. Add to all this a generous playing time (forget about the useless accompanying booklet) and here is a disc for everyone's collection. Nicholas Danby has planned his programme with commendable good sense. It begins and ends with quiet reflective Chorale Preludes and passes through the powerful, quasi-orchestral C minor Prelude and Fugue, the exciting A minor Prelude and Fugue, the colourful Fantasia (one of the best performances of all, this) and numerous Chorale Preludes of widely differing moods before launching into everybody's favourite, the Toccata and Fugue in D minor. It makes compelling listening. This is not a disc from which to pick out your favourites; sit down, press 'play' and enjoy an hour and ten minutes' worth of unfettered pleasure.

Bach. TRIO SONATAS, BWV525-30. **Christopher Herrick** (org). Hyperion CDA66390. Played on the Metzler organ of the Parish Church of St Nikolaus, Bremgarten, Switzerland. Recorded in 1989.
No. 1 in E flat major. No. 2 in C minor. No. 3 in D minor. No. 4 in E minor. No. 5 in C major. No. 6 in G major.

Ih 12m   DDD   11/90   ♀ₚ ♀ₛ

The common assumption is that Bach wrote his six Trio Sonatas as training studies for his son Wilhelm Friedmann, and certainly to this day young organists regard the ability to play these pieces as a prerequisite in establishing proper organ technique. But if ever the notion that this is music "first to practise and secondly to admire" was shown to be false, this stunning disc presents an unanswerable argument. Christopher Herrick's performances are immense fun, brimming over with real affection for the music. He allows himself occasional displays of enthusiasm (adding a few exuberant glissandos in the last movement of the E flat major Sonata, for example) and he chooses his stops both to enhance the vitality of the quick movements and to underline the sheer beauty of the slower ones. Never has this music sounded less like a training study! The Hyperion recording of the sumptuous Swiss instrument makes this disc a worthwhile buy if only for its glorious sound; the organ speaks into a rich, opulent acoustic which treats each note as a priceless jewel, to be enhanced by its setting but not in any way to be obscured. A disc of rare beauty and a real gem in any collection.

Bach. Cantatas — No. 8, Liebster Gott, wann werd ich sterben?[a]; No. 156, Ich steh mit einem Fuss im Grabe[b]; No. 198, Lass, Fürstin, lass noch einen Strahl, "Trauer-Ode". [a]**Julianne Baird**, [c]**Judith Nelson** (sops); [c]**Judith Malafronte** (mez); [ab]**Steven Rickards** (alto); [c]**William Sharp** (bar); [ab]**James Weaver** (bass); **American Bach Soloists/Jeffrey Thomas** (ten). Koch International Classics 37163-2. Texts and translations included. Recorded in 1992.

Ih 8m   DDD   4/93   ♀ₚ 🖋

Jeffrey Thomas and his American Bach Soloists perform three of Bach's outstandingly beautiful sacred cantatas on this second disc in their series. These are all Leipzig works dating from the 1720s which, taken together, can only make us wonder at the sheer expressive range and far-flung terms of reference which Bach had at his disposal. Cantata No. 156 opens with a ravishing sinfonia for oboe and strings, better known in its version for harpsichord and strings in the Concerto in F minor (BWV1056); and the remainder of the work is of comparable expressive intensity. Cantata No. 8 begins with one of Bach's most miraculous poetic fantasies in which the composer's free-ranging imagination is cause for wonder. Cantata No. 198, the *Trauer-Ode* is no less impressive for its profoundly expressive qualities. Bach performed it in 1727 at the memorial service for the much loved and staunchly Protestant Christiane Eberhardine, Queen of Poland, Electoral Princess of Saxony and wife of Augustus the Strong. Each cantata is stylishly performed by these gifted artists and though there are a few weak moments the many instances of sensitive singing and playing far outweigh them. Thomas himself is an eloquent tenor and the sopranos Julianne Baird and Judith Nelson are both on strong form. The counter-tenor Steven Rickards sounds slightly less secure but the bass, James Weaver, gives a fine account of his robust aria in Cantata No. 8. Not only is this disc a marvellous introduction to Bach's cantatas but one which all Bach lovers will find very stimulating.

Additional recommendations ...
No. 5, Wo soll ich fliehen hin; No. 6, Bleib bei uns, denn ens will Abend werden; No. 7, Christ unser Herr zum Jordan kam; No. 8, Liebster Gott, wann werd' ich sterben. **Paul Esswood** (alto); **Kurt**

Equiluz (ten); **Max van Egmond** (bass); **Vienna Boys' Choir; Chorus Viennensis; Vienna Concentus Musicus/Nikolaus Harnoncourt; Regensburger Domspatzen; King's College Choir, Cambridge; Leonhardt Consort/Gustav Leonhardt.** Teldec 2292-42498-2 — ․•‘ ② lh 27m ADD 9/85 ℗

No. 8. No. 78, Jesu, der du meine Seele; No. 99, Was Gott tut, das ist wohlgetan. **Julianne Baird** (sop); **Allan Fast** (alto); **Frank Kelley** (ten); **Jan Opalach** (bass); **Bach Ensemble/Joshua Rifkin.** L'Oiseau-Lyre 421 728-2OH — ․•‘ 58m DDD 10/89 ℗

New review

Bach. Cantatas — No. 11, Lobet Gott in seinen Reichen; No. 43, Gott fähret auf mit Jauchzen; No. 44, Sie werden euch in den Bann tun. **Barbara Schlick** (sop); **Catherine Patriasz** (contr); **Christoph Prégardien** (ten); **Peter Kooy** (bass); **Collegium Vocale/ Philippe Herreweghe.** Harmonia Mundi HMC90 1479. Texts and translations included.

․•‘ **lh 7m DDD 3/94** ℗

Gott fähret auf mit Jauchzen is resonant in its joyful celebration of Christ's Ascension to Heaven and the right hand of God the Father. The orchestra includes three trumpets, drums and two oboes, as well as the basic string band, and these all play a part in the majestic opening chorus. By comparison, *Sie werden euch in den Bann tun* is a modestly conceived piece. The Ascension 'Oratorio' (No. 11), though listed among Bach's cantatas, is an oratorio in more than just name, making use of a narrator who relates the events surrounding Christ's Ascension. Like Bach's two other oratorios, this one makes extensive use of music which had previously been written for other contexts. It also contains the music which eventually was to become the *Agnus Dei* of the B minor Mass. Herreweghe paces all three works with assurance and fluency and is supported by the excellence of his singers and instrumentalists. Fine recorded sound and an informative booklet set the seal on an accomplished issue.

New review

Bach. CANTATAS, Volume 1. [a]**Edith Mathis,** [b]**Sheila Armstrong,** [c]**Lotte Schädle** (sops); [d]**Anna Reynolds,** [e]**Hertha Töpper** (mezzos); [f]**Peter Schreier,** [g]**Ernst Haefliger** (tens); [h]**Dietrich Fischer-Dieskau** (bar); [i]**Theo Adam** (bass-bar); **Munich Bach** [j]**Choir and Orchestra/Karl Richter.** Archiv Produktion 439 369-2AX4. All from 2722 005 (11/72) except No. 82, 198477 (4/70).

No. 13, Meine Seufzer, meine Tränen[adfhj]; No. 28, Gottlob! nun geht das Jahr zu Ende[aefhj]; No. 58, Ach Gott, wie manches Herzeleid[bh]; No. 61, Nun komm, der Heiden Heiland[afhj]; No. 63, Christen, ätzet diesen Tag[adfhj]; No. 64, Sehet, welch eine Liebe[adhj]; No. 65, Sie werden aus Saba alle kommen[gij]; No. 81, Jesus schläft, was soll ich hoffen?[dfhj]; No. 82, Ich habe genug[h]; No. 111, Was mein Gott will, das g'scheh allzeit[adfij]; No. 121, Christum wir sollen loben schon[adfhj]; No. 124, Meinen Jesum lass ich nicht[cegij]; No. 132, Bereitet die Wege, bereitet die Bahn[adfij]; No. 171, Gott, wie dein Name, so ist auch dein Ruhm[aefhj].

․•‘ ④ **4h 38m ADD 3/94** ℗

Richter's involvement in Bach's Passions, oratorios and cantatas spanned a period of almost 30 years, from the early 1950s until his untimely death in 1981. Altogether Richter recorded 76 cantatas for Archiv of which, happily, 75 have been transferred to CD. It is DG's intention to issue each volume to coincide with the major seasons of the Church year into which the package has been thoughtfully subdivided. Volume 1, containing cantatas for Advent, Christmas and Epiphany was recorded during the late 1960s and early 1970s and the level of executancy remains consistently high. Among the works that come off especially well are the Christmas cantata, *Christen, ätzet diesen Tag* (No. 63), the colourful Epiphany cantatas, *Sie werden aus Saba alle kommen* (No. 65) — still perhaps the most convincing version on disc — and *Was mein Gott will, das g'scheh allzeit* (No. 111). The tenor Ernst Haefliger is admirable in No. 65, Anna Reynolds and Peter Schreier superb in their surging, fervent G major duets, which steal the show in Nos. 63 and 111. The soprano, Edith Mathis, is never less than dependable throughout the series and is often very much more than that, while Dietrich Fischer-Dieskau, sometimes sensitive (Nos. 61 and 82), sometimes boisterous almost to the point of caricature (No. 121), is never dull. Richter's Munich Bach Choir and Orchestra usually make a satisfying conjunction though the vocal forces are arguably too large. The players are generally first rate and this is a feature of the recordings which remains absolutely constant. Readers who are satisfied that

Nikolaus Harnoncourt and Gustav Leonhardt on Teldec provide all the answers to the interpretation of these profoundly satisfying, infinitely varied pieces, perhaps need not bother themselves with discovering or rediscovering an approach which could hardly be further removed from theirs. Others of an enquiring disposition, and with a healthy scepticism of dogma or fashion, may well find much to admire in the concept of a Kantor and Kapellmeister whose firm grounding in Lutheran theology and intuitive feeling for the declamation and design of the many great choral movements result in a distinctive expressive intensity.

Bach. Cantatas — No. 36, Schwingt freudig euch empor[a]; No. 61, Nun komm, der Heiden Heiland; No. 62, Nun komm, der Heiden Heiland[a]. **Nancy Argenta** (sop); [a]**Petra Lang** (mez); **Anthony Rolfe Johnson** (ten); **Olaf Bär** (bar); **Monteverdi Choir; English Baroque Soloists/John Eliot Gardiner.** Archiv Produktion 437 327-2AH. Texts and translations included. Recorded in 1992.

⠠⠶ **Ih Im DDD 2/93**

This disc, the third in John Eliot Gardiner's series for DG, contains three of Bach's *Advent* Cantatas. Two of them, *Nun komm, der Heiden Heiland* (BWV61 and 62) are linked to Luther's metrical version of the fourth-century *Veni redemptor gentium*, while the third, *Schwingt freudig euch empor* (BWV36) is an adaptation of birthday music which Bach performed on several occasions during the mid- to late-1720s. The earliest and best known of them is Cantata No. 61, a masterpiece of Bach's Weimar years. None of its drama is lost on Gardiner who performs the work with affection and a lively sense of theatre. Were it not for the masterly nature of No. 61, its namesake of ten years later (Leipzig, 1724) would undoubtedly enjoy a higher profile. Gardiner brings to life the beautifully constructed, joyful opening chorus with crisply articulated phrasing and a feeling for the music's restless vivacity. The reverse side of this expressive coin is represented by an accompanied recitative for soprano and alto of affecting tenderness and intimacy. Cantata No. 36 is the most extended of the three and, perhaps, the least consistent in performance. Among the strongest features is the partnership of Nancy Argenta and the violinist Alison Bury in the aria "Auch mit gedämpften, schwachen Stimmen", though Gardiner sets a tempo which is dangerously slow. This is a captivating disc with many strong contributions from soloists and obbligato players. The recorded sound is warm and spacious.

New review

Bach. Cantatas — No. 39, Brich dem Hungrigen dein Brot; No. 93, Wer nur den lieben Gott lässt walten; No. 107, Was willst du dich betrüben. **Agnès Mellon** (sop); **Charles Brett** (alto); **Howard Crook** (ten); **Peter Kooy** (bass); **Collegium Vocale Chorus and Orchestra/Philippe Herreweghe.** Virgin Classics Veritas VC7 59320-2. Texts and translations included.

⠠⠶ **Ih Im DDD 3/94**

The three pieces included here are mature examples of Bach's cantata writing; two of them, Nos. 93 and 107, were written in 1724 for the Fifth and Seventh Sundays after Trinity respectively, and thus belong to Bach's great second cycle in which he concentrated on a chorale-based scheme. The remaining cantata, No. 39, is a masterly work, above all in the concerto-like construction of the opening chorus, scored for voices with treble recorders, oboes and strings. Agnès Mellon is beguiling both in her three arias — one per cantata — and in her duo with Charles Brett. Both Crook and Kooy are on characteristically fine form. Enjoyable, too, are the contributions from the chorus and orchestra, and, as usual, the oboe playing of Marcel Ponseele is a constant pleasure, above all for his poetic phrasing and communicative articulation. An excellent recorded sound sets the seal on a fine issue.

New review

Bach. Cantatas — No. 49, Ich gehe und suche mit Verlangen; No. 58, Ach Gott, wie manches Herzelied; No. 82, Ich habe genug. **Nancy Argenta** (sop); **Klaus Mertens** (bass); **La Petite Bande/Sigiswald Kuijken** (vn). Accent ACC9395D. Texts and translations included.

⠠⠶ **Ih 3m DDD 3/94**

Few readers will be disappointed either by the music or the performances on this disc. It
features one of Bach's very finest cantatas, *Ich habe genug* for solo baritone, and two 'Dialogue'

cantatas for soprano and bass, *Ich gehe und suche mit Verlangen* and *Ach Gott, wie manches Herzelied*. Sigiswald Kuijken is among the most thoughtful of present-day practitioners of baroque music, tempos are beautifully judged, the string sound is warmer than usual and the overall approach to the music is expressive and eloquently shaped. The soloist in *Ich habe genug* is Klaus Mertens who gives a fine performance, clearly articulated and resonantly declaimed. Kuijken has opted for the first of several versions of this cantata which Bach made subsequently for various voice pitches and with small instrumental adjustments. In the two 'Dialogue' cantatas Mertens is joined by Nancy Argenta, an effective piece of casting. Both voices are tonally well focused and project the music in a manner admirably free from needless affectation or contrivance. An outstanding achievement.

New review

Bach. Magnificat in D major, BWV243[a]. Cantatas — No. 50, Nun ist das Heil und die Kraft[b] No. 70, Wachet! betet! [a]**Mimi Coertse,** [c]**Anny Felbermayer** (sops); [a]**Margareta Sjöstedt,** [a]**Hilde Rössl-Majdan,** [e]**Erika Wien** (mezs); [a]**Anton Dermota,** [c]**Hugo Meyer-Welfing** (tens); [a]**Frederick Guthrie,** [c]**Norman Foster** (basses); **Vienna State Opera Chorus/Felix Prohaska.** Vanguard Classics Bach Guild mono/stereo 08.2010.71. Texts and translation included. Items marked [ab] from Top Rank XRK507 (8/59), [c] new to UK.

· **1h 3m ADD 9/93** ▲

Recorded in Vienna during the 1950s the disc suffers from some digital remastering problems, but in the Cantata *Wachet! betet!* the opening chorus is beautifully sung and sensitively handled by Felix Prohaska, who has a marvellous feeling for phrasing and punctuation, though the performance is compromised elsewhere by weak contributions from the tenor and the bass. Nevertheless, the disc is valuable for Prohaska's overview of the work, for the appealing voice of the soprano Anny Felbermayer, and for the tenor Anton Dermota's fine declamation of the "Deposuit potentes" of the *Magnificat*. An illuminating reissue which, apart from anything else, provides us with fascinating staging-posts by which we can chart changing attitudes and tastes in performance.

Bach. Cantatas — No. 51, Jauchzet Gott in allen Landen![a]; No. 54, Widerstehe doch der Sünde[b]. No. 55, Ich armer Mensch, ich Sündenknecht[c]; No. 82, Ich habe genug[d]. [a]**Julianne Baird** (sop); [b]**Drew Minter** (alto); [d]**William Sharp** (bar); [c]**Kathleen Kraft** (fl); [cd]**John Abberger** (ob); [a]**Barry Baugess** (tpt); **American Bach Soloists/Jeffrey Thomas** ([c]ten). Koch International Classics 37138-2. Texts and translations included. Recorded in 1990.

· **1h 2m DDD 12/92** 🖋

Jeffrey Thomas, the director of the American Bach Soloists is himself the excellent tenor in Bach's only solo cantata for tenor voice (BWV55). The remaining cantatas on the disc are for solo soprano (BWV51), solo alto (BWV54) and solo bass (BWV82). Readers may be startled initially by the brisk tempo set for the poignant opening aria of *Widerstehe doch der Sünde*; but musically it makes sense though at such a pace some may feel that Bach's searing and insistent dissonant sevenths above a tonic organ point do not make their full impact in their illustration of the text. The counter-tenor Drew Minter shapes the vocal line sensitively and with tonal precision. The soprano Julianne Baird and the baritone William Sharp are both appealing in their respective cantatas, *Jauchzet Gott in allen Landen!* and *Ich habe genug*, though there are occasional vocal insecurities. Throughout the programme the singers are sympathetically accompanied by the period instrumentalists of the American Bach Soloists; and there is some fine oboe obbligato playing from John Abberger.

Additional recommendation ...

No. 51. No. 140, Wachet auf, ruft uns die Stimme. **Julianne Baird** (sop); **Drew Minter** (alto); **Jeffrey Thomas** (ten); **Jan Opalach** (bass); **Fred Holmgren** (tpt); **Bach Ensemble/ Joshua Rifkin.** L'Oiseau-Lyre 417 616-2OH — **·** 43m DDD 11/87 🖋

Bach. Cantatas — Nos. 51, 80, 147 and 208. **Ingrid Kertesi,** [c]**Julia Pászthy** (sops); [ab]**Judit Németh** (mez); [abc]**Jozsef Mukk** (ten); [abc]**István Gáti** (bar); [abc]**Hungarian Radio Chorus; Failoni Chamber Orchestra, Budapest/Mátyás Antál.** Naxos 8 550642/3. Recorded in 1992.

8 550642 — No. 80, Ein feste Burg ist unser Gott[a]; No. 147, Herz und Mund und Tat und Leben[b]. *8 550643* — No. 51, Jauchzet Gott in allen Landen!; No. 208, Was mir behagt, ist nur die muntre Jagd[c].

(2) **54m 50m DDD 12/92**

On two separately available discs Naxos have included Bach's most celebrated and accessible cantatas. The performances are far removed in character and resources from the complete Teldec edition with Nikolaus Harnoncourt and Gustav Leonhardt: women rather than boys or male altos sing the soprano and alto solos, the Hungarian Radio Chorus is a mixed male and female ensemble and the Failoni Chamber Orchestra of Budapest plays modern instruments at today's concert pitch rather than period instruments at a lower baroque pitch. This is spirited music-making which, in its choice of tempos, its understanding of recitative and its feeling for lyricism in Bach's writing compares favourably with some rival versions. The general standard of executancy is seldom less than adequate and some of the solo vocal contributions are first-rate, but there are disappointments in store for enthusiasts who like to hear the instruments for which Bach wrote and who feel particular about performing texts. The celebrated aria from BWV208, "Sheep may safely graze", for instance is accompanied here by flutes rather than the recorders which Bach specified; and in the case of BWV80 the inflated version with brass and timpani of the first and fifth movements is preferred to Bach's own modest but no less effective scoring for woodwind and strings. This was, in fact, the work of his eldest son, Wilhelm Friedemann who undertook the revision shortly after his father's death. Much else comes across extremely well, however, and there is an outstandingly successful performance by the soprano, Ingrid Kertesi, of the brilliantly coloured *Jauchzet Gott in allen Landen* (BWV51). To sum up, here are two mainly very enjoyable discs which can be confidently recommended, though the absence of texts is regrettable.

New review
Bach. Cantatas — No. 56, Ich will den Kreuzstab gerne tragen; No. 82, Ich habe genug; No. 158, Der Friede sei mit dir. **Olaf Bär** (bar); **Scottish Chamber Orchestra/Peter Schreier.** EMI CDC7 54453-2. Texts and translations included.

48m DDD 6/93   P Ⓑ

Peter Schreier takes the opening aria of the *Kreuzstab* Cantata at a brisker pace than one can ever remember having heard before. What a good idea! Most performances focus on the cross-bearing but ignore the gladness of the text, the journey to the promised land and the laying of sorrow in the grave. Less convincing, perhaps, is the way in which Schreier articulates the music inducing a slightly breathless effect and a jauntiness which, however optimistic the text, does strike one as a little misplaced.The vivid word painting of the following accompanied recitative, which likens the mortal's journey through life to a sea voyage, is imaginatively done both by Olaf Bär and by Kevin McCrae, whose cello playing sympathetically complements the voice. And the partnership between Bär and the oboist Douglas Boyd in the following virtuoso aria is just as effective with plenty of light and shade in the dynamics and thoughtful shaping of phrases. Schreier uses a bassoon with organ as continuo here, instead of the more usual cello. Elsewhere in the pro-gramme he switches between organ and harpsichord, the latter being used mainly for recitative, accompanied and *semplice*. Second in the programme is *Der Friede sei mit dir*, both shorter and earlier in its composition than the two other solo bass cantatas sung here. The focal point of this piece is its single aria with a lyrical violin obbligato. This is provided by James Clark whose expressive and beautifully controlled playing is all that one could wish for. The concluding chorale is pleasingly sung, both in this and the previous cantata by the Scottish Chamber Orchestra Chorus or, at least, a section of it. Lastly comes *Ich habe genug*. Bär's declamation is beautifully controlled and eloquently punctuated and he is warmly supported by the strings of the Scottish Chamber Orchestra. There are many strong features in Schreier's approach and the singing of Olaf Bär is of such a calibre that one wants to return to it time and again. Recorded sound is spacious and effective and there is an informative note by Robin Stowell to guide you on an awe-inspiring musical journey. Not period instruments, but so what. Recommended.

Additional recommendations ...
Nos. 56 and 82. **Max van Egmond** (bar); **St Bavo's Cathedral Boys' Choir; Baroque Instrumental Ensemble/Franz Brüggen.** RCA Seon GD71956 — .·‘ 40m ADD 10/89 Ⓑ
Nos. 56 and 82. **Harry van der Kemp** (bass); **Bremen Vocal Ensemble; Fiori Musicali/ Thomas Albert.** Dabringhaus und Grimm L3297 — .·‘ 42m DDD 10/89 Ⓑ

Nos. 56, 82 and 158[a]. [a]**Laurie Monahan** (sop); [a]**Douglas Stevens** (alto); [a]**William Hite** (ten); **Jan Opalach** (bass); **The Bach Ensemble/Joshua Rifkin** (org). L'Oiseau-Lyre 425 822-2OH — .·˙ 5lm DDD 9/91 Ⓑ ✒

Nos. 56, 82 and 158. **Peter Kooy** (bass); **La Chapelle Royale Choir and Orchestra/ Philippe Herreweghe**. Harmonia Mundi HMC90 1365 — .·˙ 52m DDD 10/92 Ⓑ ✒

Bach. Cantatas — No. 67, Halt im Gedächtnis Jesum Christ[a]; No. 108, Es ist euch gut, dass ich hingehe[a]; No. 127, Herr Jesu Christ, wahr' Mensch und Gott[b]. [b]**Antonia Fahberg** (sop); [a]**Lilian Benningsen** (contr); **Sir Peter Pears** (ten); **Keith Engen** (bass); **Munich Bach Choir; Munich State Opera Orchestra/Karl Richter.** Teldec Das Alte Werk 9031-77614-2. Texts and translations included. Recorded in 1958. New to UK.

.·˙ 1h 1m ADD 5/93 ▲

Collectors of Bach's choral music have strong views on Richter's performances, especially the church cantatas which represented the majority of his recorded output for Archiv. Most would agree that Richter's special affinity with Bach's music found its mark most persuasively in the 1960s before his mysterious adoption of the cloudy neo-romantic sound which did little to project his profound understanding of Bach's inner strength. Here we have a rarity from the late 1950s (a 'one-off' from Teldec not available in this country before) which forces us to revise our opinions about Richter's rigidity. These three cantatas were caught before the Munich Bach Orchestra had been formed though you would not know that they were not Bachians to the core; this is a state opera orchestra inspired by invigorating musical expression, blessed with an ignorance of self-conscious fashion. Certainly there are a few distracting mannerisms and a voice, notably Lilian Benningsen, which in hindsight seem somewhat out of place but they never detract from the prevailing conviction of the performances. In Cantata No. 67 the spirit of the text is directly and lucidly communicated by a spruce and well-balanced choral group, supported by the inimitable Peter Pears (a treasure or two here for his fans). The bass Keith Engen is also a Bach singer out of the top drawer; the opening aria of Cantata No. 108 is lovingly sung and the legendary Edgar Shann delivers an obbligato oboe line which is worth the cost of the disc alone, even without the other priceless revelations here.

Bach. CANTATAS. **Thomas Hampson** (bar); [a]**Allan Bergius**, [b]**Christoph Wegmann**, [a]**Helmut Wittek**, [d]**Stefan Gienger** (trebs); [e]**Kurt Equiluz** (ten); **Vienna Concentus Musicus/Nikolaus Harnoncourt.** Teldec 9031-74798-2. Recorded 1983-87.
No. 140, Wachet auf! ruft uns die Stimme — Wann kommst du, mein Heil?[a]; Mein Freund ist mein![a]. No. 146, Wir müssen durch viel Trübsal in das Reich Gottes eingehen — Wie will ich mich freuen[e] (all from 6 35653, 1/85). No. 147, Herz und Mund und Tat und Leben — Ich will von Jesu Wundern singen (6 35654, 7/85). No. 152, Tritt auf die Glaubensahn — Tritt auf die Glaubensbahn; Wie soll ich dich, Liebster der Seelen[b]. No. 153, Schau, lieber Gott, wie meine Feind — Fürchte dich nicht, ich bin bei dir. No. 154, Mein liebster Jesus ist verloren — Wisset ihr nicht (6 35656, 4/86). No. 185, Barmherziges Herze der ewigen Liebes — Das ist der Christen Kunst (2292-44179-2, 9/89). No. 192, Nun danket alle Gott — Der ewig reiche Gott[c]. No. 194, Höchsterwünschtes Freudenfest — Was des Höchsten Glanz erfüllt; O wie wohl ist uns geschehn[d] (2292-44193-2, 5/90). No. 196, Der Herr denket an uns — Der Herr segne euch[e] (2292-44194-2, 5/90).

.·˙ 55m DDD 4/92 q|p Ⓑ ✒

This disc is both an alluring shop window for Teldec's complete series of Bach cantatas — though in no sense a substitute — and an attractive programme in its own right. Bach's sacred cantatas are richly endowed with vocal duets and the present issue offers only a selection from them. The common factor is the baritone, Thomas Hampson, who is partnered by some of the talented boy trebles who made such a distinctive contribution to the complete edition, and by the tenor, Kurt Equiluz. Hampson joined the team when the series was already two-thirds of the way through, so the earliest cantata to feature here is No. 140, *Wachet auf! ruft uns die Stimme*. That work, however, provides an auspicious starting-point since it contains two especially fine duets which are also among the most popular with audiences. Much else, though, will be comparatively unfamiliar to all but well-seasoned Bach cantata enthusiasts. In short, a very attractive compilation which, if it draws unsuspecting listeners into Bach's sacred dramatic wonderland will have more than fulfilled its purpose. Texts are not included, alas, but an accompanying note provides useful signposts to travellers in a strange land.

Additional recommendations ...

No. 80, *Ein feste Burg ist unser Gott*. No. 140. **Gabriele Fontana** (sop); **Júlia Hamari** (contr); **Gösta Winbergh** (ten); **Tom Krause** (bar); **Stuttgart Hymnus Boys' Choir; Stuttgart Chamber Orchestra/Karl Münchinger.** Decca Ovation 436 226-2DM— ꞏ•* 58m DDD II/85 ⓑ

Nos. 80 and 147. **Jane Bryden** (sop); **Drew Minter** (alto); **Jeffrey Thomas** (ten); **Jap Opalach** (bass); **Bach Ensemble/Joshua Rifkin.** L'Oiseau-Lyre 417 250-2OH — ꞏ•* DDD 2/87 ⓑ

No. 51, *Jauchzet Gott in allen landen*. No. 140. **Julianne Baird** (sop); **Drew Minter** (alto); **Jeffrey Thomas** (ten); **Jan Opalach** (bass); **Fred Holmgren** (tpt); **Bach Ensemble/Joshua Rifkin.** L'Oiseau-Lyre 417 616-2OH — ꞏ•* 43m DDD II/87 ⓑ

Nos. 140 and 147. **Ruth Holton** (sop); **Michael Chance** (alto); **Anthony Rolfe Johnson** (ten); **Stephen Varcoe** (bar); **Monteverdi Choir; English Baroque Soloists/John Eliot Gardiner.** Archiv Produktion 431 809-2AH — ꞏ•* 53m DDD 6/92 ⓑ ✒

Bach. Cantatas — No. 211, *Schweigt stille, plaudert nicht*, "Coffee"; No. 212, *Mer hahn en neue Oberkeet*, "Peasant". **Emma Kirkby** (sop); **Rogers Covey-Crump** (ten); **David Thomas** (bass); **Academy of Ancient Music/Christopher Hogwood.** L'Oiseau-Lyre 417 621-2OH. Texts and translation included.

ꞏ•* **52m DDD 10/89** ✒

These two most delightful of Bach's secular cantatas here receive sparkling performances fully alive to the humour and invention of the music. The *Coffee* Cantata illustrates a family altercation over a current enthusiasm, the drinking of coffee. A narrator tells the story whilst the soprano and bass soloists confront each other in a series of delightful arias. Thomas brings out the crabby dyspeptic side of Schlendrian's character imaginatively and Kirkby makes a charming minx-like Lieschen. Covey-Crump's sweet light tenor acts as a good foil. The *Peasant* Cantata also takes the form of a dialogue, here between a somewhat dull and simple young man and his sweetheart Mieke, a girl who intends to better herself. Through the 24 short movements Bach conjures up a wonderfully rustic picture with some vivid dance numbers and rumbustious ritornellos. The soloists' nicely rounded characterizations emerge with great humour and Hogwood directs with vitality and sprightly rhythmic control. The recording is excellent.

Additional recommendation ...

No. 202, *Weichet nur, betrübte Schatten*, "Wedding Cantata"[a]. No. 209, *Non sa che sia dolore*[a]. Nos. 211 and 212[abc]. [a]**Elly Ameling** (sop); [b]**Gerald English** (ten); [c]**Siegmund Nimsgern** (bass); **Collegium Aureum.** Deutsche Harmonia Mundi Editio Classica GD77151 — ꞏ•* ② lh 46m ADD 10/90 ✒

Bach. MOTETS, BWV225-30. **Greta de Reyghere, Katelijne van Laetham** (sops); **Martin van der Zeijst, Sytse Buwalda** (altos); **Hans Hermann Jansen** (ten); **Johannes-Christoph Happel** (bar); **La Petite Bande Choir; La Petite Bande/Sigiswald Kuijken.** Accent ACC9287D. Texts and translations included. Recorded in 1992.
Singet dem Herren, BWV225; Der Geist hilft unsrer Schwachheit auf, BWV226; Jesu meine Freude, BWV227; Fürchte dich nicht, BWV228; Komm, Jesu, komm, BWV229; Lobet den Herren, BWV230.

ꞏ•* **lh 5m DDD 5/93** ✒

Bach. MOTETS, BWV225-30. **Netherlands Chamber Choir/Ton Koopman.** Philips 434 165-2PH. Texts and translations included. Recorded 1986-87.
Singet dem Herren, BWV225; Der Geist hilft unsrer Schwachheit auf, BWV226; Jesu meine Freude, BWV227; Fürchte dich nicht, BWV228; Komm, Jesu, komm, BWV229; Lobet den Herren, BWV230.

ꞏ•* **lh 3m DDD 5/93** ✒

These two approaches to Bach's Motets differ strongly from one another. Sigiswald Kuijken directs performances with *colla parte* instrumental support, that is to say with instruments doubling each of the vocal strands. Ton Koopman, on the other hand, prefers the vocal strands *a cappella* with instruments providing only the basso continuo. The choir in each version is made up of women sopranos and countertenors with the men's voices. Choosing between the versions is difficult and, to a large extent must be a matter of which approach you prefer. Kuijken's performances are more relaxed than those of Koopman. He avoids anything in the nature of over-direction and, while neither singing nor playing is always quite as tidy as it might be, there is a lively spontaneity, especially rewarding in the radiant performance of *Singet dem Herren*. Koopman draws more sharply articulated singing than Kuijken from the Netherlands Chamber Choir though sometimes at the expense of natural declamation and spontaneity. But there is greater linear clarity here than in the other and it pays off handsomely in *Komm, Jesu, komm*. It is a pity that Koopman does not avail himself of the surviving instrumental parts for *Der Geist hilft* but, in other respects, the strengths and weaknesses of the two performances are fairly evenly distributed and both are highly recommended.

Additional recommendations …
As above. O Jesu Christ, meins Lebens Licht, BWV118. **Agnès Mellon, Greta de Reyghere** (sops); **Vincent Darras** (alto); **Howard Crook** (ten); **Peter Kooy** (bass); **Collegium Vocale; La Chapelle Royale Chorus and Orchestra/Philippe Herreweghe.** Harmonia Mundi HMC90 1231 — .⁺ lh 7m DDD 12/86 ✒
As above. **Trinity College Choir, Cambridge/Richard Marlow** with **Graham Jackson** and **Richard Pearce** (orgs). Conifer CDCF158 — .⁺ lh 6m DDD 12/88

Bach. Magnificat in D major, BWV243ᵃ.
Vivaldi. Ostro picta, RV642ᵇ. Gloria in D major, RV589ᶜ. ᵃᵇᶜ**Emma Kirkby,** ᵃᶜ**Tessa Banner** (sops); ᵃᶜ**Michael Chance** (alto); ᵃ**John Mark Ainsley** (ten); ᵃ**Stephen Varcoe** (bar); **Collegium Musicum 90 Chorus and Orchestra/Richard Hickox.** Chandos Chaconne CHAN0518. Texts and translations included. Recorded in 1990.

.⁺ lh 4m DDD 7/91 — Ⓑ ✒

This issue was the first CD release featuring the then newly founded Collegium Musicum 90 under its directors Richard Hickox and Simon Standage. The Collegium embraces both choir and orchestra who are joined in this programme of Bach and Vivaldi by a comparably fine team of soloists. Hickox sets effective tempos in Bach's *Magnificat* and points up the many striking contrasts in colour and texture with which the piece abounds. From among the many successful features of the recording Stephen Varcoe's "Quia fecit mihi magna" and the "Et misericordia" sung by Michael Chance and John Mark Ainsley stand out. Vivaldi's *Gloria*, RV589 is the better known of two settings by the composer in D major. In this programme it is prefaced by an introductory motet *Ostro picta*, which may well in fact belong to the *Gloria* and here sung with warmth and radiance by Emma Kirkby. Hickox's performance of this evergreen vocal master-piece comes over with conviction. It is gracefully phrased, sensitively sung and affectingly paced with an admirable rapport between vocalists and instrumentalists. The recorded sound is first-rate.

Additional recommendations …
Magnificat. Cantata No. 51, Jauchzet Gott in allen Landen!. **Soloists; English Baroque Soloists/John Eliot Gardiner.** Philips 411 458-2PH — .⁺ 4lm DDD 9/85 Ⓑ ✒
Magnificat. Cantata No. 21, Ich hatte viel Bekümmernis". **Soloists; Netherland Chamber Choir; La Petite Bande/Sigiswald Kuijken.** Virgin Classics Veritas VC7 59528-2 — .⁺ lh l3m DDD 2/90 Ⓑ ✒
*Magnificat. **Vivaldi.** Gloria.* **Soloists; Academy of St Martin in the Fields Chorus and Orchestra/Sir Neville Marriner.** EMI CDC7 54283-2 — .⁺ 56m DDD 3/92 Ⓑ
Magnificatᵃ. Cantatasᵇ — No. 67, Halt im Gedächtnis Jssum Christ; No. 130, Herr Gott, dich loben alle wir. **Soloists;** ᵃ**Vienna Academy Choir;** ᵃ**Stuttgart Chamber Orchestra/Karl Münchinger;** ᵇ**Lausanne Pro Arte Choir;** ᵇ**Suisse Romande Orchestra/Ernest Ansermet.** Decca Serenata 433 175-2DM — .⁺ lh 5m ADD 5/92 Ⓑ

Bach. Mass in B minor, BWV232. **Nancy Argenta** (sop); **Catherine Denley** (mez); **Mark Tucker** (ten); **Stephen Varcoe** (bar); **Collegium Musicum 90 Chorus and Orchestra/ Richard Hickox.** Chandos Chaconne CHAN0533/4. Texts and translation included. Recorded in 1992.

.⁺ ② lh 48m DDD 1/93 — Ⓑ

Chandos's early music label Chaconne is still, comparatively speaking, in its infancy but with recordings such as this in its catalogue its reputation for excellence is quickly being established.

Richard Hickox, his soloists and the Collegium Musicum 90 Chorus and Orchestra deliver a performance which is satisfying on many levels. Hickox has a proven track-record with choirs and here he comes across as an effective disciplinarian in his firm control both of voices and instruments. Yet he avoids imposing that autocratic will on his forces which sometimes lessens the spontaneity of rival performances. Perhaps Hickox's strength lies more in the handling of the extrovert and most joyful sections of the Mass than in the deeply contemplative ones. Thus the *Et in terra pax*, for instance comes over especially well with articulate and transparently textured choral singing supported by robust but none the less sympathetic orchestral playing. The solo vocalists make a strong, even team and the use of a mezzo-soprano offers a welcome alternative in the *Agnus Dei* which, in most period instrument performances has unjustly become the sole preserve of counter-tenors. It may be that some other versions intermittently achieve greater heights of intensity but, taken as a whole this lively, spontaneous and consistently accomplished version is a fine achievement.

Additional recommendations ...

Soloists; Taverner Consort; Taverner Players/Andrew Parrott. EMI Reflexe CDS7 47293-8 — ⌵ ② 1h 43m DDD 8/86 Ⓑ ✦

Monteverdi Choir; English Baroque Soloists/John Eliot Gardiner. Archiv Produktion 415 514-2AH2 — ⌵ ② DDD 2/86 Ⓑ ✦

Soloists; Netherlands Bach Society Collegium Musicum; La Petite Bande/Gustav Leonhardt. Deutsche Harmonia Mundi Editio Classica GD77040 — ⌵ ② 1h 51m ADD 6/90 Ⓑ ✦

Soloists; American Bach Soloists/Jeffrey Thomas. Koch International Classics 37194-2 — ⌵ ② 1h 48m DDD 4/93 Ⓑ ✦

Key to symbols

**The Gramophone
Awards winners**

**Gramophone
Editor's choice**

New review
Bach. Masses — G minor, BWV235; A major, BWV234. Sanctus in D major, BWV238. **Agnès Mellon** (sop); **Gérard Lesne** (alto); **Christoph Prégardien** (ten); **Peter Kooy** (bass); **Ghent Collegium Vocale Chorus and Orchestra/Philippe Herreweghe**. Virgin Classics Veritas VC7 91118-2. Texts and translations included.

⌵ 1h 4m DDD 1/91 ✦

That Bach's four short Masses have excited so little interest is doubtless a result of the bad press they have attracted over the years: "more barbaric parodies cannot be imagined" was Albert Schweitzer's opinion, and his evaluation — if rather blunt — is typical of the disdain felt for these works by Bach scholars who could not forgive the composer for re-cycling a few of his cantatas and thereby treading on their romantic notions of the original creative artist. But unless the B minor Mass itself — just as much a patchwork of secondhand material — is also to be classed as 'barbaric', few listeners today will be able to find much to object to in these charming pieces, in which Bach's personality shines through just as strongly as in any of his more reputable creations. And how many people *know* Cantata No. 187? Philippe Herreweghe's recordings of the Masses in G minor and A major — along with the sprightly (and original) D major Sanctus, BWV238 — should not, then, be of interest only to Bach enthusiasts. Both Masses share the same formal outline, the main contrast between them arising instead from their instrumental colouring, as Bach supplements the strings with oboes in BWV235, and flutes in BWV234. Herreweghe maximizes this gentle distinction by fixing his efforts on achieving a smooth blend and a rich, reverberant sound, in which he is undoubtedly helped by the echoing church acoustic of the Abbaye aux Dames in Saintes. If the sheer nobility and tenderness of Bach's church music appeals to you then you will have no problems with this disc.

Additional recommendation ...
BWV235[a]*; G major, BWV236*[b]. **Soloists; Stuttgart Gächinger Kantorei;** [a]**Stuttgart Bach Collegium;** [b]**Stuttgart Chamber Orchestra/Helmuth Rilling.** Hänssler Classic 98 962 — .·'· 52m DDD 10/93

Bach. St John Passion. **Nico van der Meel** (ten) Evangelist; **Kristin Sigmundsson** (bass) Jesus; **Annegeer Stumphius** (sop); **James Bowman** (alto); **Christoph Prégardien** (ten); **Peter Kooy** (bass); **Netherlands Chamber Choir; Orchestra of the Eighteenth Century/Frans Brüggen.** Philips 434 905-2PH2. Text and translation included. Recorded in 1992.

.·'· ② 1h 48m DDD 5/93 Ⓑ 🖋

At once striking in this thought-provoking performance of Bach's *St John Passion* is the softly spoken, lightly articulated continuo playing whose sensibility permeates all the remaining strands of the texture, instrumental and choral. The result is enlivening, especially in large choral movements where the director, Frans Brüggen, shapes the music expressively, introducing quite a wide dynamic range. A wonderfully affecting instance of this is demonstrated by the singing and playing of the opening chorus with its clear-textured, eloquent phrasing and its freedom from ponderous continuo gestures, symptomatic of excessive sentiment and laboured declamation. The solo vocal cast is strong with Nico van der Meel as an articulate and engaging Evangelist. No less impressive are contributions from James Bowman, Christoph Prégardien and Peter Kooy. The Netherlands Chamber Choir makes a more favourable impression here than on some previously issued recordings and the Orchestra of the Eighteenth Century is warmly and sensitively supportive of the voices. Choosing a *St John Passion* is a difficult proposition but Brüggen's version is a front-runner in the full-price bracket. At mid-price, versions by Harnoncourt and Kuijken are outstanding value.

Additional recommendations ...
Soloists; Monteverdi Choir; English Baroque Soloists/John Eliot Gardiner. Archiv Produktion 419 324-2AH2 — .·'· ② 1h 47m DDD 2/87 Ⓑ 🖋
Soloists; Vienna Boys' Choir; Chorus Viennensis; Vienna Concentus Musicus/ Nikolaus Harnoncourt. Teldec 2292-42492-2 — .·'· ② 1h 57m DDD 9/87 Ⓑ 🖋
Soloists; Ghent Collegium Vocale; La Chapelle Royale Orchestra/Philippe Herreweghe. Harmonia Mundi HMC90 1264/5 — .·'· ② 1h 55m DDD 5/88 Ⓑ 🖋
Soloists; La Petite Bande Choir and Orchestra/Sigiswald Kuijken. Deutsche Harmonia Mundi Editio Classica GD77041 — .·'· ② 2h 2m ADD 6/90 Ⓑ 🖋

Bach. St Matthew Passion, BWV244. **Anthony Rolfe Johnson** (ten) Evangelist; **Andreas Schmidt** (bar) Jesus; **Barbara Bonney, Anne Monoyios** (sops); **Anne Sofie von Otter** (mez); **Michael Chance** (alto); **Howard Crook** (ten); **Olaf Bär** (bar); **Cornelius Hauptmann** (bass); **London Oratory Junior Choir; Monteverdi Choir; English Baroque Soloists/John Eliot Gardiner.** Archiv Produktion 427 648-2AH3. Text and translation included.

.·'· ③ 2h 47m DDD 10/89 🄿 Ⓑ 🖋

What makes John Eliot Gardiner's *St Matthew Passion* stand out in the face of stiff competition is perhaps more than anything his vivid sense of theatre. Bach's score is, after all, a sacred drama and Gardiner interprets this aspect of the work with lively and colourful conviction. That in itself, of course, is not sufficient to ensure a fine performance but here we have a first-rate group of solo voices, immediately responsive choral groups in the Monteverdi Choir and the London Oratory Junior Choir — a distinctive element this — and refined obbligato and orchestral playing from the English Baroque Soloists. Anthony Rolfe Johnson declaims the Evangelist's role with clarity, authority and the subtle inflexion of an accomplished story-teller. Ann Monoyios, Howard Crook and Olaf Bär also make strong contributions but it is Michael Chance's "Erbarme dich", tenderly accompanied by the violin obbligato which sets the seal of distinction on the performance.

Singing and playing of this calibre deserve to win many friends and Gardiner's deeply-felt account of Bach's great Passion does the music considerable justice. Clear recorded sound.

Additional recommendations ...
Soloists; Ghent Collegium Vocale; Chapelle Royale Chorus and Orchestra/Philippe Herreweghe. Harmonia Mundi HMC90 1155/7 — ⠌ ③ 2h 51m DDD 11/85 Ⓑ ✐
Soloists; Berlin State and Cathedral Choirs; Vienna Singverein; Deutsche Oper Chorus; Berlin Philharmonic Orchestra/Herbert von Karajan. DG 419 789-2GH3 —
⠌ ③ 3h 24m ADD 3/88 Ⓑ
Soloists; Tölz Boys' Choir; La Petite Bande Men's Chorus and Orchestra/Gustav Leonhardt. Deutsche Harmonia Mundi RD77848 — ⠌ ③ 2h 52m DDD 5/90 Ⓑ ✐
Soloists; Breda Sacraments Choir; Netherlands Bach Society Choir; Amsterdam Baroque Orchestra/Ton Koopman. Erato 2292-45814-2 — ⠌ ③ DDD 5/93 Ⓑ ✐
Soloists; Munich Boys' Choir; Munich Bach Choir and Orchestra/Karl Richter. Archiv Produktion 439 338-2AX3 — ⠌ ③ 3h 17m ADD 6/94 ⁹ₚ Ⓑ
(In English; rev. Elgar and Atkins). **Soloists; Boy's voices of St Paul's Cathedral Choir; Bach Choir; Thames Chamber Orchestra/Sir David Willcocks.** ASV Quicksilva CDQSS324 —
. ③ 3h 8m ADD 7/94

Bach. Christmas Oratorio, BWV248. **Theo Altmeyer** (ten) Evangelist and arias; **Hans Buchhierl** (treb); **Andreas Stein** (boy alto); **Barry McDaniel** (bar); **Tölz Boys' Choir; Collegium Aureum/Gerhard Schmidt-Gaden.** Deutsche Harmonia Mundi Editio Classica GD77046. Notes, text and translation included. From EMI CDS7 49119-8 (4/88). Recorded in 1973.

⠌ ③ 2h 43m 4/88 ⁹ₚ Ⓑ ✐

This performance of Bach's *Christmas Oratorio* possesses a radiance and a spontaneity perhaps unrivalled by more modern and carefully contrived versions. It is not without its weaknesses, which lie mainly in passages of insecure instrumental playing; but these are outweighed by its merits chief among which, perhaps, are the contributions, both solo and choral, of the Tölz Boys' Choir. All the soprano and alto solos are sung by boys and in the choruses it is boys rather than countertenors who sing the alto line. Gerhard Schmidt-Gaden, the chorusmaster and conductor, effectively relaxed tempos which may at first sound too leisurely to ears accustomed to the frenetic pace chosen by some rival versions. Occasionally, he is a little too slow as, for instance, in the opening chorus of Part Four but for the most part he directs a performance free from intrusive mannerisms which bedevil too many performances of baroque music today. The treble, Hans Buchhierl and the alto, Andreas Stein, are outstanding, and the tenor Theo Altmeyer and the bass, Barry McDaniel, are hardly less impressive. With its ingenuousness, its spirit of innocent joy and in its simple but sensitive response to the music this performance comes closer than most to the contemplative heart of Bach's Christmas masterpiece.

Additional recommendations ...
Soloists; Vienna Boys' Choir; Chorus Viennensis; Vienna Concentus Musicus/ Nikolaus Harnoncourt. Teldec 9031-77610-2 — ⠌ ② 2h 35m 12/86 Ⓑ ✐
Soloists; Monteverdi Choir; English Baroque Soloists/John Eliot Gardiner. Archiv Produktion 423 232-2AH — ⠌ ② 2h 20m DDD 12/87 Ⓑ ✐
Soloists; Munich Bach Choir and Orchestra/Karl Richter. Archiv Produktion 427 236-2AX3 — ⠌ ③ 2h 44m ADD 3/89 Ⓑ ✐
Soloists; Ghent Collegium Vocale Chorus and Orchestra/Philippe Herreweghe. Virgin Classics Veritas VCD7 59530-2 — ⠌ ② 2h 30m DDD 12/89 Ⓑ ✐
Soloists; Frankfurt Vocal Ensemble; Cologne Concerto/Ralf Otto. Capriccio 60 025-2 — ⠌ ② 2h 21m DDD 4/92 Ⓑ ✐

Further listening ...

Trio Sonatas — D minor, BWV1036; C major, BWV1037; G major, BWV1038; G major, BWV1039. **London Baroque.** Harmonia Mundi HMC90 1173 (6/86).

Sacred Cantatas, Volumes. 1-41. **Soloists; Choruses; Vienna Concentus Musicus/Nikolaus Harnoncourt; Leonhardt Consort/Gustav Leonhardt.** *1: Nos. 1-4,* 2292-42497-2; *2:*

Nos. 5-8, 2292-42498-2; *3: Nos. 9-11,* 2292-42499-2; *4: Nos. 12-14, 16,* 2292-42500-2; *5: Nos. 17-20,* 2292-42501-2 (all reviewed in *Gramophone*, 9/85); *6: Nos. 21-23,* 2292-42502-2; *7: Nos. 24-27,* 2292-42503-2; *8: Nos. 28-30,* 2292-42504-2 (all reviewed 1/86); *9: Nos. 31-34,* 2292-42505-2; *10: Nos. 35-38,* 2292-42506-2; *11: Nos. 39-42,* 2292-42556-2; *12: Nos. 43-46,* 2292-42599-2; *13: Nos. 47-50,* 2292-42560-2 (all reviewed 1/88); *14: Nos. 51, 52, 54-56,* 2292-42422-2; *15: Nos. 57-60,* 2292-42423-2·(all reviewed 11/88); *16: Nos. 61-64,* 2292-42465-2; *17: Nos. 65-68,* 2292-42571-2 (all reviewed 2/89); *18: Nos. 69, 69a-72,* 2292-42572-2; *19: Nos. 73-75,* 2292-42573-2; *20: Nos. 76-79,* 2292-42576-2 (all reviewed 9/89); *21: Nos. 80-83,* 2292-42577-2; *22: Nos. 84-90,* 2292-42578-2; *23: Nos. 91-94,* 2292-42582-2; *24: Nos. 95-98,* 2292-42583-2; *25: Nos. 99-102,* 2292-42584-2 (all reviewed 12/89); *26: Nos. 103-106,* 2292-42602-2; *27: Nos. 107-110,* 2292-42603-2; *28: Nos. 111-114,* 2292-42606-2; *29: Nos. 115-117, 119,* 2292-42608-2 (all reviewed 2/90); *30: Nos. 120-123,* 2292-42609-2; *31: Nos. 124-127,* 2292-42615-2; *32: Nos. 128-131,* 2292-42617-2; *33: Nos. 132-135,* 2292-42618-2 (all reviewed 3/90); *34: Nos. 136-139,* 2292-42619-2; *35: Nos. 140, 143, 144-146,* 2292-42630-2; *36: Nos. 147-151,* 2292-42631-2 (2/86); *37: Nos. 152-156,* 2292-42632-2 (4/86); *38: Nos. 157-159, 161-163,* 2292-42633-2 (4/87); *39: Nos. 164-169,* 2292-42634-2 (9/87); *40: Nos. 170-174,* 2292-426635-2 (1/88); *41: Nos. 175-179,* 2292-42428-2 (10/88).

Musicalisches Gesangbuch, BWV439-507 — excerpts[a]. Clavier-Ubung, Part 3, BWV669-89, "Orgelmesse". [a]**Peter Schreier** (ten); [a]**Jaap ter Linden** (vc); **Ton Koopman** (org). Philips 434 083-2PH (4/93).

Complete Organ Works:
Marie-Claire Alain — Erato 2292-45732-2 (parts 1-4).
Kevin Boyer — *Volume 1* (reviewed above). *Volume 2*, Nimbus NI5289.
Michel Chapuis — Auvidis Valois V4425 (1-4). *Also available separately.*
Hans Fagius — *Volume 1*, BIS CD235/6 (11/86). *Volume 2*, BIS CD308/9. *Volume 3*, BIS CD329/30. *Volume 4*, BIS CD343/4 (10/91). *Volume 5*, BIS CD379/80. *Volume 6*, BIS CD397/8. *Volume 7*, BIS CD439/40 (10/91). *Volume 8*, BIS CD443/4. *Volume 9*, BIS CD445 (10/91).
Bernard Foccroulle — *Volume 4*, Ricercar RIC015030. *Volume 5*, Ricercar RIC064042 (3/90). *Volume 6*, Ricercar RIC085068 (10/91). *Volume 7*, Ricercar RIC086069 (10/91).
Peter Hurford — *Volume 1*, Decca Ovation 421 337-2DM3 (2/90). *Volume 2*, Decca Ovation 421 341-2DM3. *Volumes 3 and 4* (reviewed above).
André Isoir — Calliope CAL9703/17 (*Volumes 1-5*). *Volume 6*, CCAL9708. *Volume 7*, CAL9709. *Volume 8*, CAL9710 (8/89). *Volume 9*, CAL9711 (4/88). *Volume 10*, CAL9712. *Volume 12*, CAL9714. *Volume 13*, CAL9715. *Volume 14*, CAL9716. *Volume 15*, CAL9717.
Ton Koopman — *Volume 1*, Novalis 150 005-2 (4/88). *Volume 2*, Novalis 150 020-2. *Volume 3* (reviewed above). *Volume 4*, Novalis 150 052-2 (10/91). *Volume 5*, Novalis 150 066-2.

Easter Oratorio, BWV249[a]. Cantata No. 4, Christ lag in Todesbanden[b]. **Emily Van Evera** (sop); **Caroline Trevor** (contr); **Charles Daniels** (ten); [a]**Peter Kooy**, [b]**David Thomas** (basses); **Taverner Consort and Players/Andrew Parrott**. Virgin Classics VC5 45011-2 (7/94).

Wilhelm Friedemann Bach

German 1710-1784

New review

W.F. Bach. SINFONIAS. **C.P.E. Bach Chamber Orchestra/Hartmut Haenchen.** Berlin Classics BC1098-2. Recorded in 1993.
D major, F64. D minor, F65. F major, "Dissonance", F67. F major, F88. D major, F91. G major, F92. Suite in G minor, BWV1070 (attrib.).

Ih 5m DDD 5/94

These works illustrate a composer whose distinctive originality and vitality have been less generally recognized than those of his younger brother Carl Philipp Emanuel, but who also inherited some of his illustrious father's contrapuntal skill. W.F. Bach's propensity for the wind is also exemplified in the cheerful F64 — prominent horns in the first movement, two flutes again in the *Andante* — and F91, the sinfonia to an Ascension cantata with triumphant trumpets and oboes. The exuberant finale to F64 is a joy, as is the skittish *Allegro* of F67, whose opening *Vivace* is full of angularities and unexpected phrase-shapes. The chamber orchestra named after Friedemann's brother plays throughout with splendid alertness and brio: it employs modern instruments, but with an awareness of eighteenth-century style. The recording was made in the bright acoustic of the Jesus-Christus Kirche in Dahlem.

Heinrich Baermann
German 1784-1847

Suggested listening ...

Quintet in E flat major, Op. 23 — Adagio. *Coupled with* **Brahms.** Clarinet Quintet in B minor, Op. 115. **Mozart.** Clarinet Quintet in A major, K581. **Alfred Boskovsky** (cl); **Vienna Octet.** Decca Ovation 417 643-2DM (9/88).

Tadeusz Baird
Polish 1928-1981

Suggested listening ...

Voices from Afar[a]. Goethe-Briefe[b]. Scene[c]. Canzona[d]. [a]**Jerzy Artysz,** [b]**Andrzej Hioski** (bars); [c]**Klaus Storck** (vc); [c]**Helga Storck** (hp); [a]**Warsaw National Philharmonic Symphony Orchestra/Witold Rowicki;** [c]**Katowice Radio Symphony Orchestra/Wojciech Michniewski;** [d]**Cracow Radio and Television Chorus and Orchestra;** [d]**Polish National Symphony Orchestra/Jan Krenz.** Olympia OCD388 (9/93).

Sir Edward Bairstow
British 1874-1946

New review
Bairstow. CHORAL WORKS. **York Minster Choir/Philip Moore** with **John Scott Whiteley** (org). Priory PRCD365. Played on the organ of York Minster Cathedral, York, UK. Blessed City, heavenly Salem. The Lamentation. Jesu, the very thought of Thee. Lord, Thou has been our refuge. Let all mortal flesh keep silence. Lord, I call upon Thee. When Israel came out of Egypt. Jesu, grant me this I pray. Save us, O Lord. If the Lord had not helped me. A Blessed Virgin's Cradle Song. Evening Service in D major.

Ih 2m DDD 6/93

"The Lord is the strength of my countenance": hearing Bairstow's vigorous setting of the line one thinks of the strength of *his* countenance. It was, as legends tell and Francis Jackson's vivid introductory note partly confirms, one that put the fear of the Lord into a great many in his time. The wonder is that his music is characteristically so sweet-tempered, soft and tender in its touch. He could, of course, bring out the trumpets, quicken the pace and fret the Minster's echoes into a delirium of mimicry. But what seems most personal and individual in his music is the quiet mysticism of *Let all mortal flesh keep silence*, the modestly exercised skill of *Jesu, grant me this I pray* and the comfortable, judiciously sugared melodic and harmonic idiom of *Save us, O Lord*. The recital has an authenticity of place, coming from the great building where the composer did so much of his life's work, from 1913 till his death in 1946. The organ on which he must have played these very works is the one heard now, its bountiful resources imaginatively employed. The choir, under Philip Moore, has a particularly fine complement of trebles and sings with sensitivity and, when required, considerable power.

Further listening ...

Prelude in C major. Evening Song. Scherzo in A flat major. Nocturne. Prelude on "Vexilla Regis". Elegy. Toccata and Prelude on "Pange Lingua". Meditation. Three Short Preludes. Legend. Organ Sonata in E flat major. **Francis Jackson** (org). Mirabilis MRCD902 (4/91).

Key to symbols

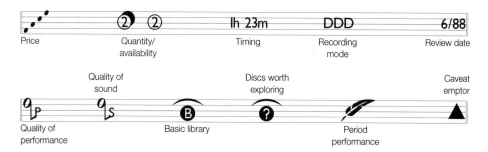

Price	Quantity/ availability	Timing	Recording mode	Review date
Quality of sound		Discs worth exploring		Caveat emptor
Quality of performance	Basic library		Period performance	

Mily Balakirev

Russian 1837-1910

New review

Balakirev. Piano Concertos — No. 1 in F sharp major, Op. 1; No. 2 in E flat major, Op. posth.
Rimsky-Korsakov. Piano Concerto in C sharp minor, Op. 30. **Malcolm Binns** (pf); **English Northern Philharmonia/David Lloyd-Jones.** Hyperion CDA66640.

1h 1m DDD 7/93

'Op. 1' and 'Op. posth.' says a lot about Balakirev's two piano concertos. The First is a single movement only, composed at the age of 18 and massively indebted to the Chopin concertos. The Second was begun not long after, in 1861, but abandoned after the first movement; he was only persuaded to write the other movements down near the end of his life. At his death in 1910 the finale had to be completed by Lyapunov, which may be partly why it sounds so splendidly rambunctious, so close in places, to Gershwin. The concerto was certainly worth the efforts of all concerned; the first movement's fugal episodes and the slow movement's tinges of Russian Orthodox gloom stay in the mind, compensating for Balakirev's occasional recourse to inflating and over-decorating short sub-phrases. The First Concerto, too, has little flashes of individuality which keep you listening despite the obvious naïvety and derivative quality of the material. The Rimsky-Korsakov has come and goes from the catalogue over the years. It is in effect more of a folk-song fantasia than a concerto, but there is much post-Liszt-and-Griegian charm, as well as a striking foretaste of Rachmaninov's *Paganini* Rhapsody (Paganini's famous opening motif coincidentally also begins the second strain of Rimsky's chosen theme). These three works make an excellent programme, then. And Malcolm Binns, though not the most sparkling of soloists, plays with commendable solidity. The quality of the English Northern Philharmonia's contribution is high, and all in all this is an admirably conceived and executed disc.

Additional recommendation ...
No. 1[a]. **Rimsky-Korsakov.** *Piano Concerto*[b]. **Medtner.** *Piano Concerto No. 1 in C minor, Op. 33*[a]. **Igor Zhukov** (pf); **USSR TV and Radio Large Orchestra/[a]Alexander Dmitriev; [b]Gennadi Rozhdestvensky.** Mezhdunarodnaya Kniga MK417087 (*See review under Medtner; refer to the Index to Reviews*) — 1h 2m ADD 2/94

Further listening ...

Symphony No. 2 in D minor. Tamara — symphonic poem. Overture on the themes of three Russian songs. **Philharmonia Orchestra/Evgeni Svetlanov.** Hyperion CDA66586 (9/92).

Michael William Balfe

Suggested listening ...

THE BOHEMIAN GIRL. **Soloists; Radio Telefis Eireann Philharmonic Choir; National Symphony Orchestra of Ireland/Richard Bonynge.** Argo 433 324-2ZH2 (8/92).

Sir Granville Bantock

Bantock. Pagan Symphony. Fifine at the Fair. Two Heroic Ballads. **Royal Philharmonic Orchestra/Vernon Handley.** Hyperion CDA66630. Recorded in 1992.

lh 20m   DDD   3/93

Granville Bantock was a man born at the wrong time. He wrote colourful, hedonistic late-romantic music well into the second quarter of the twentieth century, and has been neglected for many years as an anachronism. At times he recalls Strauss, at others Bax, but if he lacks that personal utterance that would stamp every page with his name and no other, there's plenty of compensation in his sheer craftsmanship. With some composers that word means a worthy but rather dull demonstration of technical facility, but Bantock has the gift of communicating his own pleasure in his craft. He will take a scale, twist it, bend it slightly, and we are not only delighted by the fine melody that he has made (and there are many of them) but also by the cleverness of the process. This could lead to mere garrulousness, an endless succession of pretty tricks, but Bantock's resource also ensures that the impulse of the two big pieces here (and they are both very big, single movement structures lasting half-an-hour) never flags. His scoring is particularly beautiful, sumptuous yet clean throughout, with many ingeniously original sonorities that work perfectly in such fine performances as these. The recordings are clear and spacious.

Further listening ...

Celtic Symphony. Tone Poems 5 — The Witch of Atlas. The Sea Reivers. Hebridean Symphony. **Royal Philharmonic Orchestra/Vernon Handley.** Hyperion CDA66450 (5/91).

Samuel Barber

Barber. Cello Concerto, Op. 22.
Britten. Symphony for Cello and Orchestra, Op. 68. **Yo-Yo Ma** (vc); **Baltimore Symphony Orchestra/David Zinman.** CBS Masterworks CD44900.

lh 2m   DDD   6/89

This recording is highly recommended. The acoustic is warm, balance ideal and there is sufficient resonance. On this evidence, the Baltimore is a splendid orchestra, responding alertly and intelligently to David Zinman's very positive interpretation. How enterprising, too, to record two works which are not in the main repertoire of cello concertos, excellent though they are. Barber's dates from 1945 and has something of the late-romanticism of the Violin Concerto, but with a more classical approach. It makes large demands on the virtuosity of the soloist, which are met with apparent ease and relish by Yo-Yo Ma. Britten's Cello Symphony is more problematical. Its predominantly dark and brooding mood, with a savage *scherzo* followed by an almost jaunty finale, disconcerts some listeners, but the clue lies in the dedication to Rostropovich, for the music seems also to be an act of homage to the composer's friend Shostakovich and emulates the Russian master's ability to combine the tragic and the bizarre within one framework. Once the listener has penetrated the rather forbidding outer shell of this work, the rewards are great. Ma and Zinman obviously agree on the music's stature, for this is a compelling performance.

Barber. Essays for orchestra — No. 1, Op. 12; No. 2, Op. 17; No. 3, Op. 47.
Ives. Symphony No. 1. **Detroit Symphony Orchestra/Neeme Järvi.** Chandos CHAN9053.
Recorded in 1991.

·· **Ih 10m DDD 3/92**

This issue comes with a booklet celebrating Neeme Järvi's 100th disc for Chandos and a
remarkable joint achievement by this conductor and company. Järvi's wide-ranging sympathies
are proved yet again in the music of these two American composers, but there is a paradox here
in that it is the innovator Ives who is the more conventional and the conservative Barber who
challenges the ear. The explanation is that Ives's First Symphony is a graduation work from his
years at Yale University, representing a compromise between his natural boldness and the
discipline that he grudgingly accepted from his teacher Horatio Parker. The result is romantically
expansive, often fascinating and occasionally beautiful, with influences including Brahms and
Dvořák (there are echoes of the *New World* Symphony in the slow movement) but also a bold
homespun element in places suggesting the Ivesian innovations that were yet to come. Samuel
Barber seemed unhappy with the symphony as a form, writing a one-movement First Symphony
in 1936 and eventually destroying all but one movement of his wartime Second (1944). Instead
he wrote three impressive *Essays for orchestra* that have been called "surrogate symphonies" and of
which No. 3 was his final work before his death. Each has a sequence of moods and tempos, the
First Essay being partly elegiac (recalling his *Adagio for Strings*), the Second having some vigorously
busy music and the Third being the most enigmatic. While none of these works sound especially
American, the performances are convincing and the recording offers rich sound.

Barber. Adagio for Strings, Op. 11.
Copland. Appalachian Spring — suite.
Gershwin. Rhapsody in Blue. **Los Angeles Philharmonic Orchestra/Leonard Bernstein**
(pf). DG 431 048-2GBE. Recorded live in Davies Symphony Hall, San Francisco in 1982.

·· **54m DDD** Ⓑ

This disc shows Bernstein on home ground: American music played by an American orchestra. It
captures, too, the most enduring elements of his music-making — the ryhthmic vitality and the
sense of poise that he could so winningly embrace in music with a strong melody. This is
Bernstein at his most engaging, his piano-playing as impressive as always, his feeling for the ebb
and flow of this most elusive music beautifully judged. The 'big-band' version of the piece is
used but with such a vital response from soloist and orchestra alike — the sense of real interplay
between the musicians is almost palpable. Copland's lyrical *Appalachian Spring* is gloriously
unfolded, the tempos are nicely judged and the Los Angeles orchestra clearly revels in the
melodic weave of the piece. Similarly, the serene *Adagio* by Barber finds the strings rapt,
unhurried and poised, the tempo dangerously slow but carried along by the commitment of the
inspirational conductor. The live recordings are well handled, with virtually no evidence of the
audience to be heard.

Additional recommendations ...
Adagio for Strings. **Janáček** *(arr. Tognetti). String Quartet No. 1, "Kreutzer Sonata".* **Walton.**
Sonata for Strings. **Australian Chamber Orchestra/Richard Tognetti.** Sony Classical
SK48252 — ·· 55m DDD 8/92 Ⓑ
Adagio for Strings. Medea's Meditation and Dance of Vengeance, Op. 23. **Elgar.** *Introduction and
Allegro for String Quartet and String Orchestra, Op. 47.* **Tchaikovsky.** *Serenade in C, Op. 48.*
Boston Symphony Orchestra/Charles Munch. RCA Victor Gold Seal 09026 61424-2 —
·· Ih Im ADD 9/93 Ⓑ

Barber. Symphony No. 1, Op. 9. The School for Scandal Overture, Op. 5.
Beach. Symphony in E minor, Op. 32, "Gaelic". **Detroit Symphony Orchestra/Neeme
Järvi.** Chandos CHAN8958. Recorded in 1991.

·· **Ih 12m DDD 10/91**

Amy Beach (or Mrs H.H.A. Beach, as she was known professionally in her lifetime) was born in
Henniker, New Hampshire in 1867. By all accounts she was a prodigiously talented youngster
— she could sing 40 tunes by the age of two, and at four she was composing small pieces for

the piano. She made her 'official' début as a pianist at the age of 16 playing Chopin's Rondo in E flat and Moscheles's G minor Piano Concerto, but after her marriage to a noted Boston surgeon in 1885 she abandoned her concert career and devoted her time exclusively to composition. The *Gaelic* Symphony (her only work in the genre) dates from 1896. Like Dvořák's *New World* Symphony, which had received its American première just a few years earlier, it draws its inspiration from folk material; though Beach's sources are drawn not from native America but rather from her Gaelic forebears. The writing reveals a remarkable degree of craftsmanship and maturity, and although the music contains perhaps more imitation than originality (Brahms, Tchaikovsky and Parry spring to mind) there is nevertheless plenty of enjoyment to be had from this fresh and engaging work. Barber's First Symphony made a welcome return after a protracted absence from the catalogue. Slatkin's account (listed below) might in some ways be more satisfactory as his orchestra seems more comfortable, and the American conductor clearly has an innate grasp of the music's style. This one-movement, highly compact work deserves to be much better known as it contains some of Barber's most invigorating and memorable material. Stylistically it finds allegiance with the post-romanticism of symphonies such as Walton's First and Howard Hanson's Second (*Romantic*). The disc also includes Barber's equally engaging Overture to *The School for Scandal*. Committed performances.

Additional recommendations ...
School for Scandal Overture. Symphony No. 2, Op. 19. Music for a Scene from Shelley, Op. 7. Essay No. 1. Adagio for Strings. **New Zealand Symphony Orchestra/Andrew Schenck.** Stradivari SCD8012 — .•⁺ 1h 6m DDD 8/89
No. 1ᵃ. Piano Concerto, Op. 38ᵇ. Souvenirs, Op. 28ᶜ. ᵇᶜ**John Browning** (pf); ᵃᵇ**St Louis Symphony Orchestra/Leonard Slatkin** (ᶜpf). RCA Victor Red Seal RD60732 — .•⁺ 1h 10m DDD 11/91
No. 1. Adagio for Strings. Essays for Orchestra, Opp. 12 and 17. Music for a scene from Shelley, Op. 7. The School for Scandal Overture. **Baltimore Symphony Orchestra/David Zinman.** Argo 436 288-2ZH — .•⁺ 1h 4m DDD 1/93 ℗

New review
Barber. String Quartet, Op. 11.
Britten. String Quartet No. 2 in C major, Op. 36.
Takemitsu. A Way A Lone. **Tokyo Quartet** (Peter Oundjian, Kikuei Ikeda, vns; Kazuhide Isomura, va; Sadao Harada, vc). RCA Victor Red Seal 09026 61387-2. Recorded in 1992.

.•⁺ **1h 1m DDD 2/94**

Three very different minds grappling with the intricacies of four-way musical dialogue. Takemitsu, a habitual aesthete wandering in the thick of sensual Bergian textures; Barber, a compelling New World Romantic revelling among memories of Dvořák and, perhaps, Nielsen; and then Britten, a bold, incandescent voice in prime condition, proclaiming during the year (1945) that also witnessed *Peter Grimes* and *The Holy Sonnets of John Donne*. All are summoned among the sonorous ranks of the Tokyo Quartet for performances that combine rigour, warmth and textual acuity. It's a compelling mix, the standard of playing is uniformly high, the record-ing pleasingly full-bodied and the programme itself well chosen. This and the CD listed below are the result of very different programming concepts: the Tokyos offering "the responses of three composers to the challenge of tradition", the Emersons, a conspectus on American quartet writing in the first half of the century. Which makes a choice relatively easy and the chances of disappointment correspondingly remote.

Additional recommendation ...
String Quartet. **Ives.** *String Quartets — No. 1, "From the Salvation Army"; No. 2. A set of three short pieces — Scherzo, "Holding Your Own".* **Emerson Quartet.** DG 435 864-2GH — .•⁺ 1h 5m DDD 4/93

New review
Barber. Ballade, Op. 46. Excursions, Op. 20. Nocturne, Op. 33. Piano Sonata, Op. 26. Souvenirs, Op. 28. **Eric Parkin** (pf). Chandos CHAN9177. Recorded in 1992.

.•⁺ **1h 3m DDD 10/93** ℗

This is not quite the Complete Works for Solo Piano, as claimed in the title, nor is it "the entire output for solo piano, save for a single childhood essay" as stated in the booklet. This is the
complete published piano music, apart from *Three Sketches*, and there are quite a lot of unpublished

pieces. None of this matters when the playing is as polished and sympathetic as Parkin's. He responds wonderfully to the nostalgic melancholia of Barber. The ballet score, *Souvenirs*, is available in the orchestral and piano-duet versions, but this solo piano treatment is just as engaging. Parkin knows exactly how to present this side of Barber and his treatment of the *Four Excursions* based on different popular idioms is equally convincing. A performer as well versed as Parkin in British post-romantics such as Ireland and Bax finds home ground again in Barber's *Nocturne* and the late *Ballade*. In Barber's classic, the Sonata, Parkin is in competition with several other recordings including Horowitz's (listed below), Peter Lawson's and Joanna MacGregor's (both reviewed elsewhere in this *Guide*; refer to the Index to Reviews.) Parkin treats the work lyrically and never forces us to regard the finale, especially, as a hard-hitting block-buster in the way that so many young pianists do. He is transparent in the scherzo; sings in the *Adagio*; and the final fugue subject has exactly the catchy, swinging quality that many players miss. At times there is a lack of brilliance, which the rather dull recording emphasizes, but this is a winning anthology of this major American romantic.

Additional recommendation ...

Piano Sonata. **Prokofiev.** *Piano Sonata No. 7.* **Kabalevsky.** *Piano Sonata No. 3 in F major, Op. 46. with music by* **Fauré, Prokofiev** *and* **Poulenc. Vladimir Horowitz** (pf). RCA Victor Gold Seal mono/stereo GD60377 — .ᐧ 1h 5m ADD 7/94 ꭅₚ ▲

New review

Barber. SONGS. [a]**Cheryl Studer** (sop); [b]**Thomas Hampson** (bar); [c]**John Browning** (pf); [d]**Emerson Quartet** (Eugene Drucker; Philip Setzer, vns; Lawrence Dutton, va; David Finckel, vc). DG 435 867-2GH2. Notes and texts included.
A Slumber Song of the Madonna[ac]. There's Nae Lark[bc]. Love at the door[bc]. Serenades[bc]. Love's Caution[ac]. Night Wanderers[bc]. Oh that so sweet imprisonment[ac]. Strings in the Earth and Air[bc]. The Beggar's song[bc]. In the dark pinewood[bc]. Three Songs, Op. 2[bc]. Three Songs, Op. 10[abc], Four Songs, Op. 13[ac]. Dover Beach, Op. 3[bd], Two Songs, Op. 18[ac]. Nuvoletta, Op. 25[ac]. Mélodies passagères, Op. 27[bc]. Hermit Songs, Op. 29[ac]. Despite and Still, Op. 41[bc]. Three Songs, Op. 45[bc].

.ᐧ ② 1h 50m DDD 5/94 ꭅₚ

Sung in chronological order these songs are almost an autobiography and the set provides a compelling argument for regarding Barber's songs as his art at its most complete. There's hardly a weak song in the collection. Hampson brings to this music a remarkable range of expression and colour, a subtle use of words and a conviction that not a few of these songs are masterpieces. Studer has a slightly cooler approach, but often provides the vocal glamour, the ability to sketch long curves and floated high notes, that Barber (singer himself and connoisseur of singing) so often demanded. And John Browning, to whose virtuosity Barber tailored his Piano Concerto, sounds not only like a man who has yearned to accompany these singers in these songs for a long while, but like a considerable accompanist indeed, matching Hampson's dynamic range and expressive flexibility and Studer's seamless line with resourceful sympathy. The recorded sound is flawless.

Additional recommendations ...

Three Songs, Op. 2. Three Songs, Op. 10. Four Songs, Op. 13. Two Songs, Op. 18. Nuvoletta. Hermit Songs. Despite and Still. **Roberta Alexander** (sop); **Tan Crone** (pf). Etcetera KTC1055 — .ᐧ 1h 1m DDD 9/88

Knoxville: Summer of 1915. Dover Beach. Hermit Songs. Andromache's Farewell, Op. 39. **Soloists; Juilliard Quartet; Dumbarton Oaks Orchestra/William Strickland; New York Philharmonic Orchestra/Thomas Schippers.** CBS Masterworks Portrait CD46727 — .ᐧ 51m AAD 10/91 ▲

Knoxville. Andromache's Farewell. ANTONY AND CLEOPATRA — *Give me some music. Orchestrated Songs* — *I hear an Army, Op. 10 No. 3; Sure on this Shining Night, Op. 13 No. 3. Nocturne, Op. 13 No. 4.* VANESSA — *Must the winter come so soon?.* **Roberta Alexander** (sop); **Netherlands Philharmonic Orchestra/Edo de Waart.** Etcetera KTC1145 — .ᐧ 1h 1m DDD 6/93 ꭅₚ

Further listening ...

Piano Concerto[a]. Medea — Media's Meditation and Dance of Vengeance. Adagio for Strings. [a]**Tedd Joselson** (pf); **London Symphony Orchestra/Andrew Schenck.** ASV CDDCA534 (6/86).

Prayers of Kierkegaard, Op. 30. The lovers, Op. 43. **Sarah Reese** (sop); **Dale Duesing** (bar); **Chicago Symphony Chorus and Orchestra/Andrew Schenck.** Koch International Classics 37125-2 (3/92).

Agnus Dei, Op. 11. *Coupled with* **Bernstein.** Chichester Psalms[a]. **Copland.** In the Beginning[b]. Four Motets. [a]**Dominic Martelli** (treb); [b]**Catherine Denley** (mez); [a]**Rachel Masters** (hp); [a]**Gary Kettel** (perc); [a]**Thomas Trotter** (org); **Corydon Singers/Matthew Best.** Hyperion CDA66219 (9/87).

A HAND OF BRIDGE[ae]. Essay for orchestra No. 2, Op. 17[e]. Music for a Scene from Shelley, Op. 7[e]. A Stopwatch and an Ordnance map, Op. 15[be]. Serenade for String Orchestra, Op. 1[e]. Adagio for Strings, Op. 11[d]. Let Down the Bars, O Death![c]. [a]**Patricia Neway** (sop) Geraldine; [a]**Eunice Alberts** (contr) Sally; [a]**William Lewis** (ten) Bill; [a]**Philip Maero** (bar) David; [b]**Robert De Cormier Chorale;** [c]**Washington DC Cathedral Choir;** [d]**Zagreb Soloists/Antonio Janigro;** [e]**Symphony of the Air, New York/Vladimir Golschmann.** Vanguard Classics 084016 71 (8/92)

Reincarnations, Op. 16. The Virgin Martyrs, Op. 8. A Stopwatch and an Ordnance map, Op. 15[a]. Agnus Dei, Op. 11. ANTONY AND CLEOPATRA — On the death of Antony; On the death of Cleopatra[b]. Twelfth Night, Op. 41 No. 1. The Monk and his Cat, Op. 29 No. 8[b]. Four Songs, Op. 13 — No. 1, A nun takes the veil; No. 3, Sure on this shining night. Let Down the Bars, O Death, Op. 8 No. 2. To be sung on the water, Op. 42 No. 2. VANESSA, Op. 32 — Under the Willow Tree[b]. **Cambridge University Chamber Choir/Timothy Brown** with [a]**Timothy Palmer** (timp); [b]**Thomas Adès** (pf). Gamut Classics GAMCD535 (11/93).

Key to symbols

Price	Quantity/ availability	Timing	Recording mode	Review date
	② ②	1h 23m	DDD	6/88

Wayne Barlow

American 1912-

Suggested listening ...

Barlow. The Winter's Past. *Coupled with* **Bloom.** Requiem. Narrative. **Corigliano.** Aria. **Wilder.** Concerto for Oboe, String Orchestra and Percussion. Piece for Oboe and Improvisatory Percussion[a]. **Humbert Lucarelli** (ob); [a]**Mark Wood** (perc); **Brooklyn Philharmonic Orchestra/Michael Barrett.** Koch International Clasics 37187-2 (7/94). *See Review under Wilder; refer to the Index to Reviews.*

John Barry

British 1933-

Suggested listening ...

MOVIOLA — *Film Scores:* Out of Africa; Midnight Cowboy; Body Heat; Somewhere in Time; Mary, Queen of Scots; Born Free; Dances with Wolves; Chaplin; The Cotton Club; Walkabout; Frances; On Her Majesty's Secret Service — We have all the time in the world. Moviola. **Royal Philharmonic Orchestra/John Barry.** Epic 472 490-2.

THE CLASSIC JOHN BARRY — *Film Scores:* Zulu; Out of Africa; Midnight Cowboy; The Last Valley; Eleanor and Franklin; Hanover Street; Born Free; Chaplin; Dances with Wolves; Raise the Titanic; Indecent Proposal; The Persuaders; Robin and Marian; Body Heat; Somewhere in Time; The Lion in Winter. **City of Prague Philharmonic Orchestra/Nic Raine.** Silva Screen FILMCD141.

Lionel Bart

Suggested listening ...

OLIVER! **Soloists; National Symphony Orchestra/John Owen Edwards.** TER Classics CDTER1184 (10/92).

Béla Bartók

New review

Bartók. Piano Concertos — No. 1, Sz83; No. 2, Sz95; No. 3, Sz119. **Peter Donohoe** (pf); **City of Birmingham Symphony Orchestra/Simon Rattle.** EMI CDC7 54871-2. Recorded 1990-92.

· **1h 17m DDD 11/93** ⁹ₚ Ⓑ

Making Bartók's First Piano Concerto sound fun must have taken some doing, but Donohoe and Rattle have certainly managed it. The recording blends the instrument in among the orchestra, so that Rattle's sensitivity to nuance, Donohoe's lightness of touch and the accommodating acoustic of Birmingham's Symphony Hall transform what we frequently hear as an angular confrontation into something genuinely palatable. The Second Concerto, in this impressively urgent account, could hold its own in any company, even though there are one or two passages where articulation momentarily falters. The rest is either pungent or evocative: the second movement's 'night music' *Adagio* sections are beautifully sustained and the finale has terrific *élan.* Taken overall, this is a marvellous trio of performances and serves as a fresh reminder of just how great these works are. Its most serious rival is the vintage Géza Anda/Ferenc Fricsay recording (listed below).

Additional recommendations ...
Nos. 1 and 2. **Maurizio Pollini** (pf); **Chicago Symphony Orchestra/Claudio Abbado.** DG 415 371-2GH — ·· 52m ADD 9/86 ⁹ₚ Ⓑ
Nos. 1 and 2. Music for Strings, Percussion and Celesta. Rhapsody for Piano and Orchestra. Scherzo for Piano and Orchestra. **Zoltán Kocsis** (pf); **Budapest Festival Orchestra/Iván Fischer.** Philips 416 831-2PH3 — ·· ③ 2h 37m 1/88 Ⓑ
Nos. 1-3. Concerto for Orchestra, Sz116ᵃ. Rhapsody for Piano and Orchestra, Op. 1ᵇ. **Géza Anda** (pf); **Berlin RIAS Symphony Orchestra/Ferenc Fricsay.** DG Dokumente 427 410-2GDO2 — ·· ② 2h 19m ADD 5/89 ⁹ₚ Ⓑ ▲
Nos. 1-3ᵃ. **Stephen Kovacevich** (pf); ᵃ**London Symphony Orchestra; BBC Symphony Orchestra/Sir Colin Davis.** Philips Silver Line 426 660-2PSL — ·· 1h 17m ADD 5/91 Ⓑ

New review

Bartók. Viola Concerto, Sz120ᵃ. Music for Strings, Percussion and Celesta, Sz106ᵇ. ᵃ**Wolfram Christ** (va); **Berlin Philharmonic Orchestra/Seiji Ozawa.** DG 437 993-2GH. Item marked ᵃ recorded in 1989, ᵇ recorded live in 1992.

· **52m DDD 4/94** ⁹ₚ

The performing edition of this affecting but uncompleted Viola Concerto takes obvious heed of Bartók's other 'late' works: yet Tibor Serly's 'completion' relates a strongly individual brand of musical poetry, not least via the lonely *più dolce* passage for viola and bassoons (4'02") and the sinister *Lento parlando* (12'25") that precedes the slow movement. The *Adagio religioso* visits an unruffled calm parallel to that in the Third Piano Concerto's similarly named centre-piece, while the finale achieves a lilting, 'folksy' sense of release. Wolfram Christ and Seiji Ozawa take a fairly gentle view though they offer us manifold interpretative insights and Christ's instrument has the textural warmth of seasoned mahogany. Neither the performance nor the (clean but close) recording can be found wanting: both do justice to the music's subtle but pensive sense of tonal fantasy. This recording of the *Music for Strings, Percussion and Celesta* has pin-point definition, a rich bass and a startlingly realistic piano sound. It is a compelling performance and a worthy coupling for the most wholly recommendable version of the Viola Concerto currently available.

Bartók. Violin Concertos — No. 1, Sz36[a]; No. 2, Sz112[b]. **Kyung-Wha Chung** (vn); [a]**Chicago Symphony Orchestra;** [b]**London Philharmonic Orchestra/Sir Georg Solti.** Decca Ovation 425 015-2DM. Item marked [a] from 411 804-1DH (10/84), [b] SXL6212 (4/78). Item marked [a] recorded in 1984, [b] 1977.

59m ADD/DDD 2/91

New review

Bartók. Violin Concerto No. 2, Sz112. Rhapsodies — No. 1, Sz87; No. 2, Sz90. **Kyoko Takezawa** (vn); **London Symphony Orchestra/Michael Tilson Thomas.** RCA Victor Red Seal 09026 61675-2. Recorded 1992-93.

1h 3m DDD 12/93

New review

Bartók. Violin Concerto No. 2, Sz112. Rhapsodies — No. 1, Sz87; No. 2, Sz90. **Kyung-Wha Chung** (vn); **City of Birmingham Symphony Orchestra/Simon Rattle.** EMI CDC7 54211-2. Recorded in 1990.

59m DDD 6/94

Long gone are the times when Bartók was thought of as an arch-modernist incapable of writing a melody and the young Yehudi Menuhin was considered daring in championing his Violin Concerto. Today this work is listed as his second in this form, but four decades ago it stood alone because the composer had suppressed an earlier one dating from 1908, or more precisely reshaped it into another work called *Two Portraits*. When this earlier piece was finally published in its original form some 30 years ago, it became his First Concerto and the more familiar one of 1938 his Second. The First was inspired by a beloved woman friend, but it does not by any means wear its heart on its sleeve, being a complex and edgy work to which Kyung-Wha Chung brings a passionate lyricism. Her conductor Sir Georg Solti is the composer's compatriot and was actually his piano pupil as well, so that he too knows how to make this music breathe and sing. Chung and Solti are equally at home in the more obviously colourful and dramatic Second Concerto, giving it all the range, expressive force and occasional violence, driving momentum and sheer Hungarian charm that one could desire. The London Philharmonic Orchestra play as if inspired and the recordings (in two locations, seven years apart) are subtle yet lit with the right brilliance. Kyoko Takezawa's reading of the Second has a tonal bloom and sense of purpose that place it securely among the best available versions, while Michael Tilson Thomas and the London Symphony follow her every move, etching orchestral detail — and this score is particularly rich in incident — with obvious care and considerable imagination. The *Rhapsodies*, too, are crisply turned, and the recording well balanced.

It is rare indeed to encounter a concerto recording where the critical honours can be evenly distributed, but the EMI recording really does suggest a strong team spirit. Heard purely for its own sake, Chung's playing is sinewy, agile and occasionally a mite brittle: phrasing is always judicious, but tone production is generally less physically engaging than Takezawa's. Yet one soon realizes that every passage has been carefully thought through — the opening sequence, for example, which Chung traces as a continuous line of monologue. However, it is when soloist and conductor grapple in dialogue that the sparks really start to fly. Rattle and his players make the very most of Bartók's orchestral commentary: instrumental interplay is always alert, rhythms are keenly focused and his way of cushioning Chung, palpably convincing. The well-matched *Rhapsody* recordings are, again, revealing. The solo line is nicely attenuated, and the overall approach one of fine-tuned improvisation. Detail is legion (note the way solo violin and woodwinds intertwine at the beginning of the Second *Rhapsody*'s second movement) and Rattle compounds the rhapsodic idea by shaping his phrases with imaginatively applied rubato. So, it's a strong recommendation, with the sole proviso that Takezawa has a rather more ingratiating tonal profile than Kyung-Wha Chung. However, Chung is certainly a more probing Bartókian than she was at the time of her recording under Solti; and her poignantly expressed intelligence will doubtless prove a durable virtue.

Additional recommendations ...
Nos. 1 and 2. **Nell Gotkovsky** (vn); **National Philharmonic Orchestra/Charles Gerhardt.** Pyramid PYR13486 — ⠌ 1h DDD 3/87 Ⓑ
No. 2. Sonata for Solo Violin, Sz117ᵃ. ᵃ**Christian Tetzlaff** (vn); **London Philharmonic Orchestra/Michael Gielen.** Virgin Classics VC7 59062-2 — ⠌ 1h 3m DDD 11/91 Ⓑ
No. 2. Moret. En rêve. **Anne-Sophie Mutter** (vn); **Boston Symphony Orchestra/Seiji Ozawa.** DG 431 626-2GH — ⠌ 58m DDD 11/91 Ⓑ
Nos. 1 and 2. **Gerhard Hertzel** (vn); **Hungarian State Symphony Orchestra/Iván Fischer.** Nimbus NI5333 — ⠌ 1h 3m DDD 7/93 Ⓑ
No. 2ᵃ. Sonata for Solo Violin, Sz117. **Bruch.** *Violin Concerto No. 1 in G minor, Op. 26ᵃ.* **Mendelssohn.** *Violin Concerto in E minor, Op. 64ᵇ.* **Tchaikovsky.** *Violin Concerto in D major, Op. 35ᵇ.* **Ivry Gitlis** (vn); **Vienna Pro Musica Orchestra/**ᵃ**Jascha Horenstein,** ᵇ**Hans Swarowsky.** Vox Legends mono CDX2 5505 — ⠄ ② 2h 39m ADD 11/93 Ⓑ ▲
No. 2ᶜ. Piano Concertos Nos. 1-3ᵃᵇ. Concerto for Orchestraᵈ. ᶜ**Henryk Szeryng** (vn); ᵃᵇ**Stephen Kovacevich** (pf). ᵃ**London Symphony Orchestra;** ᵇ**BBC Symphony Orchestra/Sir Colin Davis;** ᶜᵈ**Concertgebouw Orchestra/Bernard Haitink.** Philips Duo 438 812-2PM2 — ⠌ ② 2h 31m ADD 2/94 ᵠₚ Ⓑ
Rhapsody No. 1ᵇ. Contrasts, Sz111ᵇ (with Benny Goodman, cl). **Bloch.** *Baal Shemᵃ.* **Debussy.** *Sonata for Violin and Pianoᵃ.* **Ives.** *Violin Sonata No. 4, "Children's Day at the Camp Meeting"ᵃ.* **Schubert.** *Sonatina for Violin and Piano in D major, D384ᵃ.* **Joseph Szigeti** (vn); ᵃ**Andor Foldes,** ᵇ**Béla Bartók** (pfs). Biddulph mono LAB070/71 *(see review in the Collections section; refer to the Index to Reviews)* — ⠌ ② 2h 9m ADD ▲ ᵠₚ

New review
Bartók. Concerto for Orchestra, Sz116. Four Pieces, Sz51. **Chicago Symphony Orchestra/ Pierre Boulez.** DG 437 826-2GH.

⠌ 1h DDD 3/94 Ⓑ

New review
Bartók. Concerto for Orchestra, Sz116ᵃ. Music for Strings, Percussion and Celesta, Sz106ᵇ. Hungarian Sketches, Sz97ᵇ. **Chicago Symphony Orchestra/Fritz Reiner.** RCA Victor Living Stereo 09026 61504-2. Items marked ᵃ from VICS1110 (12/65), ᵇ VICS1160 (1/66)

⠌ 1h 16m DDD 3/94 Ⓑ ▲

The four lavish canvases that make up Bartók's *Pieces* are virtually as much a 'concerto for orchestra' as the better-known masterpiece so named. The first is a steamy re-enactment of Bluebeard's shadowy castle, ripe to bursting-point with extravagant orchestration and magnificently conveyed here, although brass and high strings are occasionally a mite brittle. The *Scherzo* is a garish burlesque, all savagery and ritual masks, with seething brass trills, pounding ostinatos and startling contrasts in metre and dynamics. The third is a sort of extended *valse triste*, scant consolation perhaps after the *Scherzo*'s violence, but prophetic of the Straussian *Marcia funèbre* that ends the set. Boulez unleashes these mammoth effusions without taming them: his orchestra confronts Bartók's searing climaxes head-on, and DG's engineers brook no compromise. Boulez delivers a relatively conservative interpretation of the *Concerto for Orchestra*; it is a good, clear-headed reading, generally well played but his disc is recommendable mainly for the *Four Pieces* which is one of the best versions available. If you really want to test the mettle of Boulez's *Concerto for Orchestra*, then Reiner's is a good place to start. Both recordings were made in Chicago's Orchestra Hall: Boulez's at the end of 1992, Reiner's in October 1955 (not that spot-check sampling would reveal the age difference — quite the contrary). RCA's sound reportage of the score's quieter moments has uncanny realism and if the climaxes are occasionally reined in, the sheer fervour of Reiner's direction more than compensates. The "Pair Play" is a very brisk 6'26", the finale taut and agile: compare the movement's opening in both versions and Reiner's greater precision and control is immediately apparent. The couplings, too, are excellent: a *Music for Strings, Percussion and Celesta* that goes all out for smooth transitions and fleet execution, and a stylishly turned set of *Hungarian Sketches*. RCA's remastering is a revelation.

Additional recommendations ...
Concerto for Orchestra. **Lutoslawski.** *Concerto for Orchestra.* **Cleveland Orchestra/Christoph von Dohnányi.** Decca 425 694-2DH — .•ʼ lh 6m DDD 3/90 Ⓑ
Concerto for Orchestra[a]. *Dance Suite, Sz77. Two Portraits, Sz37. Mikrokosmos — From the diary of a fly.* [a]**London Symphony Orchestra; Philharmonia Hungarica/Antál Dorati.** Mercury 432 017-2MM — .•ʼ lh 12m ADD 11/91 Ⓑ ▲
Concerto for Orchestra[a]. *The miraculous mandarin, Sz73 — suite*[b]. [a]**Boston Symphony Orchestra/Rafael Kubelík;** [b]**Boston Symphony Orchestra/Seiji Ozawa.** DG 437 247-2GGA — .•ʼ 58m ADD 11/93 Ⓑ
Concerto for Orchestra. **Enescu.** *Romanian Rhapsodies, Op. 11 — No. 1 in A major; No. 2 in D major.* **Royal Scottish Orchestra/Neeme Järvi.** Chandos CHAN8947 — .•ʼ lh 6m DDD 2/92 Ⓑ
Concerto for Orchestra. **Mussorgsky.** *Pictures at an exhibition.* **Chicago Symphony Orchestra/Sir Georg Solti.** Decca 417 754-2DM — .•ʼ lh 9m DDD Ⓑ

New review

Bartók. The wooden prince, Sz60. Cantata profana, Sz94[a]. [a]**John Aler** (ten); [a]**John Tomlinson** (bass); **Chicago Symphony** [a]**Chorus and Orchestra/Pierre Boulez.** DG 435 863-2GH.

.•ʼ lh 13m DDD 3/93 ⁹ₚ ⁹ₛ

Bartók's parable of fathers, sons and fleeing the nest, his 1930 *Cantata profana* is a mesmerizing, symmetrically designed masterpiece, where words and music are forged into an action-packed 18 minutes. Boulez provides what is by far the best studio recording the work has ever had and truly state-of-the-art in terms of sound. Boulez is able to command a shimmering, hushed *pp* yet the battle-hardy *Allegro molto* with its hectoring syncopations and warlike percussion is full of grit and muscle. John Aler is wonderfully adroit with Bartók's high-flying solo tenor line, John Tomlinson sounds like an authentic Magyar, and the Chicago Symphony Chorus egg the proceedings on with tireless zeal. Turn then to *The wooden prince* and you confront the final flowering of Bartók's post-romantic phase; it's an effulgent, exotic piece, full of wistful, melancholy wind solos (clarinet and saxophone figure prominently) and billowing, heavily-scored climaxes. How astonishing to reflect that it was written *after* the composer's trail-blazing opera, *Bluebeard's Castle.* Again, the soft music is wonderfully atmospheric: the *ppp* muted violins in the Prelude have a ghostly pallor that is so typical of this orchestra's quiet string playing, yet when all are engaged at full throttle, the effect is shattering. Detail is legion throughout: the basses, brass and drums have immense presence.

Additional recommendation ...
The wooden prince. *Hungarian sketches, Sz97.* **Philharmonia Orchestra/Neeme Järvi.** Chandos CHAN8895 — .•ʼ lh 6m DDD 10/91

Bartók. The miraculous mandarin, Sz73 — ballet[a].
L. Weiner. Suite on Hungarian Folk-tunes, Op. 18. [a]**London Voices; Philharmonia Orchestra/Neeme Järvi.** Chandos CHAN9029. Recorded in 1990.

.•ʼ lh 2m DDD 3/92 ⁹ₚ ⁹ₛ

It is scarcely surprising that *The miraculous mandarin* failed to reach the stage for some years after it was composed, for the plot concerns three ruffians who force a girl into luring men from the street up to a shabby garret where they rob them. Bartók's music matches the savagery of the subject, with wild pounding rhythms and jagged outbursts. Järvi is flexible in the early scenes which are slow and characteristically drawn, bringing, at times a welcome touch of humanity to the score. And the benefit of this holding back of tempo is felt immediately the Mandarin's passion explodes and he begins his frenzied pursuit of the girl; not one opportunity is missed to deliver the violence of the succeeding scenes (suffocation, stabbing and electrocution) with a graphic impact that renders the visual element completely unnecessary. Chandos are on hand to supply wide-screened sound that is literally stunning. Weiner's *Suite* comprises four short tone poems which draw on phonographic collections of original Hungarian folk-music. But there the parallels with his contemporary, Bartók, cease. The idiom is most definitely nineteenth rather than twentieth century, and the orchestration has a Respighian richness and colour. On this showing Järvi and the Philharmonia must surely be born, bred and proud Hungarians.

Additional recommendations ...
Music for Strings, Percussion and Celesta, Sz106. Divertimento, Sz113. The miraculous mandarin — suite. **Chicago Symphony Orchestra/Sir Georg Solti.** Decca 430 352-2DH — .•˙ lh 9m DDD 5/91 ꝗₚ ꝗₛ
The miraculous mandarin[a]. Two portraits, Sz37. Divertimento, Sz113. **Montreal Symphony** [a]**Chorus and Orchestra/Charles Dutoit.** Decca 436 210-2DH — .•˙ lh 8m DDD 3/94 ꝗₛ

New review
Bartók. CHAMBER WORKS. **Susanne Stanzeleit** (vn); **Gusztáv Fenyö** (pf). ASV CDDCA883.
Rhapsody No. 2, Sz89. 15 Hungarian Peasant Songs, Sz71 (trans. cpsr and Országh). Piano Sonatine, Sz55 (trans. Gertler). Hungarian Folktunes, Sz66 (trans. Szigeti). Violin Sonata No. 1, Sz75.

.•˙ **lh 9m DDD 6/94**

Central to Stanzeleit's programme is a trio of folk-inspired miniatures, the most unusual being André Gertler's skilful re-working of the piano *Sonatine*. The *Hungarian Peasant Songs* and *Folktunes* are again derived from piano pieces, yet their soulful melodies sound with especial eloquence as presented here. However, their trump card is an exceptionally imaginative and mercifully tenderized account of the hard-headed First Violin Sonata, a work that too often sounds blatantly confrontational. Here there is mystery as well as power, although readers weaned on Oistrakh and Bauer or Kremer and Argerich (listed below) might crave rather more in the way of raw aggression. Yet this performance somehow makes more sense of the score's many dramatic contrasts, especially in the outer movements. The *Adagio*, too, sounds intensely personal and draws far closer than usual to the introspective world of the Second Sonata. Stanzeleit and Fenyö convince by virtue of their flexibility and mutual perception, and are well-recorded.

Additional recommendations ...
Violin Sonata. *Janáček.* Violin Sonata (1914-21). *Messiaen.* Theme and Variations. **Gidon Kremer** (vn); **Martha Argerich** (pf). DG 427 351-2GH — .•˙ 57m DDD 1/91
Violin Sonatas — No. 1[a]; No. 2, Sz76[b]. For Children, Sz42 (trans. Szigeti)[c] — No. 28, Parlando; No. 18, Andante non molto; No. 42, Allegro vivace; No. 33, Andante sostenuto; No. 38. [ac]**David Oistrakh,** [b]**Gidon Kremer** (vns); [ac]**Frida Bauer,** [b]**Oleg Maisenberg** (pfs). Praga PR250038 — .•˙ lh ADD 10/93

Bartók. CHAMBER WORKS. [a]**Michael Collins** (cl); **Krysia Osostowicz** (vn); [b]**Susan Tomes** (pf). Hyperion CDA66415. Recorded in 1990.
Contrasts, Sz111[ab]. Rhapsodies — No. 1, Sz86; No. 2, Sz89[b]. Romanian folk-dances, Sz56 (arr. Székely)[b]. Solo Violin Sonata, Sz117 (original version).

.•˙ **lh 12m DDD 4/91**

Unusually for a composer who wrote so much fine chamber music Bartók was not himself a string player. But he did enjoy close artistic understanding with a succession of prominent violin virtuosos, including the Hungarians Jelly d'Arányi, Joseph Szigeti and Zoltán Székely, and, towards the end of his life, Yehudi Menuhin. It was Menuhin who commissioned the Sonata for solo violin, but Bartók died before he could hear him play it — Menuhin was unhappy with the occasional passages in quarter-tones and the composer had reserved judgement on his proposal to omit them. It was Menuhin's edition which was later printed and which has been most often played and recorded; but Krysia Osostowicz returns to the original and, more importantly, plays the whole work with intelligence, imaginative flair and consummate skill. The Sonata is the most substantial work on this disc, but the rest of the programme is no less thoughtfully prepared or idiomatically delivered. There is the additional attraction of an extremely well balanced and natural-sounding recording. As a complement to the string quartets, which are at the very heart of Bartók's output, this is a most recommendable disc.

Additional recommendation ...
Solo Violin Sonata. Rhapsody No. 1. Violin Sonata No. 2, Sz76. Romanian Folk Dances, Sz56. **Susanne Stanzeleit** (vn); **Gustáv Fenyö** (pf). ASV CDDCA852 — .•˙ lh 4m DDD 6/93

Bartók. STRING QUARTETS. **Emerson Quartet** (Eugene Drucker, Philip Setzer, vns; Lawrence Dutton, va; David Finckel, vc). DG 423 657-2GH2. Recorded in 1988.
No. 1 in A minor; No. 2 in A minor; No. 3 in C sharp minor; No. 4 in C major; No. 5 in B flat major; No. 6 in D major.

② 2h 29m DDD 12/88

It has long been recognized that this series of string quartets written over three decades has been one of the major contributions to Western music. The Emerson Quartet does not play them all the same way, for as its first violinist Eugene Drucker rightly says, "each has its own style". The Quartet has a fine unanimity and is equally good in the tense melodic lines and harmony of slower movements and the infectious rhythmic drive of quicker ones; and it also copes extremely well with Bartók's frequent changes of dynamics, texture and tempo. Here is not only striking virtuosity — to be convinced, listen to the wildly exciting *Allegro molto* finale of No. 4 — and yet great subtlety too. The recording is excellent, with good detail yet without harshness. Where most Bartók cycles take three discs, here 149 minutes are accommodated on two CDs. One readily concurs with the critic who called this "one of the most exciting chamber music recordings of recent years".

Additional recommendations ...
Nos. 1-6. **Végh Quartet.** Astrée Auvidis. *Nos. 1 and 2:* E7717. *Nos. 3 and 4:* E7718. *Nos. 5 and 6:* E7719 — ③ 57m 38m 60m DDD 3/87
Nos. 1-6. **Lindsay Quartet.** ASV CDDCS301 — ③ 2h 43m DDD 3/89
Nos. 3-5. **Chilingirian Quartet.** Chandos CHAN8634 — 1h 8m DDD 6/89

New review
Bartók. PIANO WORKS, Volume 1. **Zoltán Kocsis.** Philips 434 104-2PH. Recorded 1991.
14 Bagatelles, Sz38. Two Elegies, Sz41. Sonatine, Sz55. Six Romanian Folk Dances, Sz56. Three Hungarian Folk Tunes, Sz66.

54m DDD 1/94

Bartók himself admitted that his *Bagatelles* (1908) were largely experimental, and indeed at least half-a-dozen of them could easily have fallen from a jazz-pianist's copybook (Nos. 7, 11 and 12, particularly), their sensual harmonies and capricious rhythmic computations prophetic of so much that was to happen in that world. Debussy, too, is much in evidence (No. 3), as is Bartók's love of folk-song (Nos. 4 and 5). The *Elegies* would sit nicely among the shorter works of Busoni. These virtuosic effusions recall the moon-flecked world of late Liszt, albeit flushed with a Hungarian rather than a gipsy complexion. Folk-song proper informs Kocsis's last three selections: the familiar *Six Romanian Folk Dances*, the cheerful and ingenious *Sonatine* and the relatively dense *Hungarian Folk Tunes*, Sz66 — the last bringing us to the far edge of the Great War. It's a cliffhanger of a finale, and has us eager for more. Kocsis's readings are absolutely on target. A peach of a disc.

New review
Bartók. DUKE BLUEBEARD'S CASTLE[a]. **Olga Szönyi** (sop) Judith; **Mihály Székely** (bass) Bluebeard.
Berg. WOZZECK — excerpts[b]. **Helga Pilarczyk** (sop); **London Symphony Orchestra/ Antál Dorati.** Mercury Living Presence 434 325-2MM. Item marked [a] from AMS16140 (6/63), [b] AMS16117 (10/62).

1h 13m ADD 7/93

Dorati's high opinion of *Bluebeard's Castle* informs his interpretation: a taut, keenly accented affair, where atmosphere takes second place to precision and directness of utterance. The LSO winds relish the tart, spicy texture of Bartók's writing; the strings, too — although Mercury's engineering fails to capture their full lustre. Mihály Székely studied the leading role with the composer, and his idiomatic inflexions are always evident. Olga Szönyi is equally compelling, but vocally rather thin and unsteady. This is probably the spiciest *Bluebeard* around and compares favourably with the more sophisticated approach favoured by Sawallisch (listed below). Add Dorati's wonderfully sensitive *Wozzeck* excerpts (with an involving Helga Pilarczyk as Marie) and you have a most desirable bargain.

Additional recommendation ...
Soloists; Bavarian State Orchestra/Wolfgang Sawallisch. DG 20th Century Classics 423
236-2GC — .•' 58m ADD 9/88

Further listening ...

Sonata for Two Pianos and Percussion, Sz110[a]. Suite for Two Pianos, Sz115a. **Jean-François
Heisser, Georges Pludermacher** (pfs); [a]**Guy-Joel Cipriani,** [a]**Gérard Perotin** (perc).
Erato 2292-45861-2 (4/93).

44 Duos for Two Violins, Sz98. **Sándor Végh, Albert Lysy** (vns). Astrée Auvidis E7720 (3/88).

For Children, Sz42 — 85 Pieces for Piano. Mikrokosmos, Sz107 — progressive pieces for piano
in six volumes (complete, Books 1-6). **Dezsö Ránki** (pf). Teldec 9031-76139-2 (three-CD set,
10/92).

Five Songs, Sz61[a]. Five Songs, Sz63[a]. Hungarian Folksongs, Sz64 — Black is the earth; My God,
my God; Wives, let me be one of your company; So much sorrow; If I climb the rocky
mountains. Five Songs, Sz61 (orch. Kodály)[b]. Five Hungarian Folksongs, Sz101[b]. **Júlia Hamari**
(contr); [a]**Ilona Prunyi** (pf); [b]**Hungarian State Orchestra/János Kovacs.** Hungaroton
HCD31535 (7/93).

Sir Arnold Bax

British 1883-1953

New review
Bax. Festival Overture[a]. Christmas Eve on the Mountains[b]. Dance of Wild Irravel[c]. Paean[c].
Nympholept[d]. Tintagel[e]. [abcd]**London Philharmonic Orchestra,** [e]**Ulster Orchestra/Bryden
Thomson.** Chandos CHAN9168. Items marked [a] from CHAN8586 (7/88), [b]CHAN8480 (2/87),
[c]CHAN8454 (12/86), [d]ABRD1203 (5/87), [e]ABRD1091 (1/84).

.•' **1h 16m DDD 2/94**

A useful compilation of pieces that first appeared mostly as fillers to Bryden Thomson's complete
recording of the Bax symphonies. Useful, that is, for those who've bought that cycle in its boxed-
set format from which the fillers have been removed or simply those who are beginning to explore
Bax but would rather not start with a symphony. The latter group will find the purest Bax, of
course, in *Tintagel*, and a sumptuous reading it receives, but also in *Nympholept* — alluring wood
magic of a kind Bax made peculiarly his own, here ravishingly scored. *Christmas Eve* is a less
expected side of him, a moving vision of radiant peace descending upon a troubled Ireland. It just
occasionally stumbles into his two besetting sins: sheer density of sound and a certain repetitiveness
of rhythm — but Bax's Irish vein is strong within it, so is a powerful solemnity. *Dance of Wild
Irravel* is Bax's *La valse*; altogether too close to its model, you might think, until you realize that
Bax's delirious waltz fantasy precedes Ravel's by a good few years (and even Ravel didn't manage
a brazen side-long wink at Tchaikovsky amid the Viennese glitter). *Paean* is a deafening piece of
pomp and circumstance for an enormous orchestra, redeemed by its exuberance and its brevity.
The *Festival Overture* is exactly what its name suggests, but just when you think festivity is wearing
a touch thin, a moment of truly Baxian wildness or a vintage Bax tune will lift it from among his
occasional works into one of his characteristic ones. Thomson had a pretty well unerring instinct
for Bax's elusive, glintingly changing moods — and both playing and recorded sound are first-class.

Bax. Symphonies — No. 1 in E flat major[a]; No. 7[b]. **London Philharmonic
Orchestra/**[a]**Myer Fredman,** [b]**Raymond Leppard.** Lyrita SRCD232. Item marked [a] from
SRCS53 (8/71), [b] SRCS83 (11/75).

.•' **1h 18m ADD 12/92**

Few English composers have expressed such intense and fiercely passionate emotions as Bax has
in the first two movements of his First Symphony. Such rage and grief as can be found there

seem to suggest a psycho-drama being played out, and when we learn that at the time of its composition (1921) Bax may still have been coming to terms with the aftermath of the Great War, the loss of friends in the Easter Rising in Ireland and the irretrievable breakdown of his marriage, it is tempting to imagine that the symphony is indeed exercising some kind of personal exorcism on these events. Bax himself, however, was always reluctant to admit the existence of such a 'programme' behind the symphony, and in many ways he was probably right to do so. Whatever personal experiences Bax had poured into it, the end result is unquestionably a powerful, cogent symphony of universal appeal. The Seventh and last of Bax's symphonies makes an intelligent and well contrasted coupling. The first movement, though not without tension and some storm-tossed passages (very much a Baxian seascape this) has a prevailing mood of hope and expectation — as though embarking on some adventurous seaward journey to new lands, whilst the second movement finds Bax in wistful 'legendary' mood so evocative of the early tone-poems. The last movement begins by echoing the optimism of the first movement, but finally gives way, in the long and beautiful epilogue, to a mood of autumnal nostalgia and sad farewell. These are classic Lyrita recordings, with exceptionally fine performances from Fredman and Leppard and superb digital transfers.

Bax. Symphony No. 3 in C major. Four Orchestral Sketches — Dance of Wild Irravel. Paean. **London Philharmonic Orchestra/Bryden Thomson.** Chandos CHAN8454.

59m DDD 12/86

Bax's Third Symphony has a long and gravely beautiful epilogue, one of the most magical things he ever wrote: a noble processional with a disturbing, motionless glitter at its centre and, just before the very end, a sudden bitter chill. It is pure Bax, and will haunt you for days. We may associate some of the Symphony with the lonely sands and the shining sea of Morar in Invernessshire (where the work was written), the impassioned string music that rises from that sea in the centre of the slow movement with deep emotion, the war-like dance of the finale with conflict or war and the frequent violent intercuttings of lyricism and darkness with what we know about Bax's temperament. But it is harder to explain in programmatic terms why lyric can become dark or vigour become brooding within startlingly few bars, why that epilogue seems so inevitable, why the Symphony for all its wild juxtapositions does not sound like a random sequence of vivid memories and passionate exclamations. That it is a real symphony after all, powered by purely musical imperatives, is suggested by this finely paced and tautly controlled performance, one of the finest in Thomson's Bax cycle. The enjoyable racket of *Paean* and the glittering colour of *Irravel* respond no less gratefully to the sumptuousness of the recording.

Further listening ...

Cello Concerto[a]. Northern Ballad No. 3 — Prelude for a Solemn Occasion. Cortège. Mediterranean. Overture to a Picaresque Comedy. [a]**Raphael Wallfisch** (vc); **London Philharmonic Orchestra/Bryden Thomson.** Chandos CHAN8494 (11/87).

Violin Concerto. Legend. Romantic Overture. Golden Eagle — incidental music. [a]**Lydia Mordkovitch** (vn); **London Philharmonic Orchestra/Bryden Thomson.** Chandos CHAN9003 (4/92).

On the sea-shore (ed./orch. Parlett). *Coupled with* **Bridge.** The Sea. **Britten.** PETER GRIMES — Four Sea Interludes; Passacaglia. **Ulster Orchestra/Vernon Handley.** Chandos CHAN8473 (3/87).

Northern Ballad No. 1[a]. Mediterranean[a]. The Garden of Fand[a]. Tintagel[a]. November Woods[b]. **London Philharmonic Orchestra/Sir Adrian Boult.** Lyrita SRCD231 (9/92).

Spring Fire. Symphonic Scherzo. Northern Ballad No. 2. **Royal Philharmonic Orchestra/ Vernon Handley.** Chandos CHAN8464 (9/86).

Winter Legends. Saga Fragment. **Margaret Fingerhut** (pf); **London Philharmonic Orchestra/Bryden Thomson.** Chandos CHAN8484 (2/87).

Two Russian Tone Pictures — Nocturne, "May Night in the Ukraine"; Gopak, "National Dance". The Maiden with the Daffodil — Idyll. The Princess's Rose Garden — Nocturne. Apple Blossom Time. On a May Evening. O Dame get up and bake your pies — Variations on a North Country Christmas carol. Nereid. Sleepy Head. A romance. Burlesque. **Eric Parkin** (pf). Chandos CHAN8732 (7/90).

This worldes joie. Mater ora filium. Five Greek Folk-Songs. I sing of a maiden. *Coupled with* **Howells.** Two Madrigals. Long, long ago. The summer is coming. Take him, earth, for cherishing. **Finzi Singers/Paul Spicer.** Chandos CHAN9139 (6/93).

Enchanted Summer[a]. Walsinghame[b]. Fatherland[c]. [a]**Anne Williams-King,** [ab]**Lynore McWhirter** (sops); [bc]**Martyn Hill** (ten); **Brighton Festival Chorus; Royal Philharmonic Orchestra/Vernon Handley.** Chandos CHAN8625 (10/89).

Oliver Twist — excerpts. Malta GC — suite. The Sound Barrier — Rhapsody for Orchestra. **Royal Philharmonic Orchestra/Kenneth Alwyn.** ASV White Line CDWHL2058.

Oboe Quintet. *Coupled with* **Bliss.** Oboe Quintet. **Britten.** Phantasy for Oboe Quartet, Op. 2. **Pamela Woods** (ob); **Audubon Quartet.** Telarc CD80205 (10/89).

François Bazin
French 1816-1878

New review

Bazin. LE VOYAGE EN CHINE[a]. **Claudine Collart** (sop) Marie; **Michel Sénéchal** (ten) Henri de Kernoisan; **Lina Dachary** (sop) Berthe; **André Balbon** (bar) Pompéry; **Annette Martineau** (sngr) Madame Pompéry; **Gaston Rey** (bar) Alidor de Rosenville; **René Lenoty** (ten) Maurice Freval; **Duvaleix** (ten) Bonneteau.
MAITRE PATHELIN[b]. **Christiane Harbell** (sop) Guillemette; **Monique Stiot** (mez) Bobinette; **Linda Felder** (sop) Angélique; **Bernard Plantey** (bass) M. Pathelin; **Gérard Friedmann** (ten) Charlot; **Michel Jarry** (sngr) Josseaume; **Joseph Peyron** (ten) Le Bailli; **Michel Hamel** (ten) Aignelet; **French Radio Lyric Chorus and Orchestra/**[a]**Marcel Cariven,** [b]**Jean Brebion.** Musidisc Gaieté Lyrique 202552. Item marked [a] recorded during a broadcast performance in 1968, [b] 1971.

② 2h 6m ADD 4/94 ❓

François Bazin's greatest success, *Le Voyage en Chine* (1865) is a typical farce of mistaken identities, young lovers, and worthy gentlemen embarrassed by taps that won't turn off. The trip to China never takes place, since the ship stays anchored at Cherbourg. If one heard the music 'blind' one might guess that it was by Offenbach, with its occasional parodies — "Ah! Italie!" sighs one of the heroines, an obvious musical reference to *Les troyens*, which had been given at the Théâtre Lyrique a year or so before. There is a splendid ensemble, "Quel temps effroyable", which sounds as if it might have influenced the end of Act 1 of *La vie parisienne*. Michel Sénéchal as a hapless suitor and Lina Dachary as the younger of the two daughters trying to find a husband, lead the cast. It is a joy to hear the French language spoken and sung with such ease. Few of these singers achieved fame but they all carry the piece off with authority, and Marcel Cariven keeps the whole soufflé just *à point.*

Amy Beach
American 1867-1944

Suggested listening ...

Piano Concerto in C sharp minor, Op. 45[a]. *Coupled with* **MacDowell.** Piano Concerto No. 2 in D minor, Op. 23[b]. [a]**Mary Louise Boehm,** [b]**Eugene List** (pfs); **Westphalian Symphony Orchestra/Siegfried Landau.** Vox 115718-2 (5/93).

Symphony in E minor, Op. 32, "Gaelic". *Coupled with* **Barber.** Symphony No. 1, Op. 9. The School for Scandal Overture, Op. 5. **Detroit Symphony Orchestra/Neeme Järvi.** Chandos CHAN8958 (10/91). *See review under Barber; refer to the Index to Reviews.*

Piano Trio in A minor, Op. 150. *Coupled with* **Ives.** Trio. **Bloch.** Three Nocturnes. **Copland.** Vitebsk (Study on a Jewish theme). **Cowell.** Trio. **Hartley Piano Trio.** Gamut Classics GAMCD536 (6/94). *See review in the Collections section; refer to the Index to Reviews.*

David Bedford
British 1937-

Suggested listening ...

Song of the White Horse[a]. Star Clusters, Nebulae and Places in Devon[b]. [a]**Soloists;** [a]**Queen's College Choir;** [a]**Nash Ensemble/Stuart Bedford;** [b]**London Philharmonic Chorus;** [b]**London Philharmonic Orchestra Brass/John Alldis.** Voiceprint VP110CD.

Ludwig van Beethoven
German 1770-1827

New review

Beethoven. Violin Concerto in D major, Op. 61. Two Romances — No. 1 in G major, Op. 40; No. 2 in F major, Op. 50. **Gidon Kremer** (vn); **Chamber Orchestra of Europe/Nikolaus Harnoncourt.** Teldec 9031-74881-2. Recorded live in 1992.

57m DDD 12/93

Gidon Kremer offers one of his most commanding performances, both polished and full of flair, magnetically spontaneous from first to last. Rarely do you hear such consistently pure tone in this work and the orchestral writing too is superbly realized, with magical sounds in the slow movement in particular. It has become customary to treat the long first movement as expansively as possible — Chung and Perlman provide outstanding examples — but Kremer takes a much more urgent view and after his thoughtful and dedicated, slightly understated reading of the slow movement, he and Harnoncourt round the performance off magically with a finale that skips along the more infectiously thanks to light, clean articulation and textures. Traditional performances seem heavyweight by comparison. The controversial point for some will be the cadenza in the first movement where he uses a transcription of the big cadenza which Beethoven wrote for his piano arrangement of the work. However, this is altogether one of the most refreshing versions of the concerto ever committed to record, backed up by crisp unsentimental readings of the two *Romances*.

Additional recommendations ...
Violin Concerto. **Itzhak Perlman** (vn); **Philharmonia Orchestra/Carlo Maria Giulini.** EMI CDC7 47002-2 — 44m DDD 2/84
Violin Concerto. **Erich Gruenberg** (vn); **New Philharmonia Orchestra/Jascha Horenstein.** Chandos Premium CHAN6521 — 58m DDD 1/85
Violin Concerto. **Brahms.** *Violin Concerto in D major, Op. 77.* **Jascha Heifetz** (vn); **Boston Symphony Orchestra/Charles Munch.** RCA RD85402 — ADD 10/87
Violin Concerto[a]. **Mendelssohn.** *Violin Concerto in E minor, Op. 64*[b]. **Yehudi Menuhin** (vn); [a]**Philharmonia Orchestra;** [b]**Berlin Philharmonic Orchestra/Wilhelm Furtwängler.** EMI Références CDH7 69799-2 — lh llm ADD 10/89 ▲
Violin Concerto. Two Romances. **Itzhak Perlman** (vn); **Berlin Philharmonic Orchestra/ Daniel Barenboim.** EMI CDC7 49567-2 — lh lm DDD 11/89
Violin Concerto. Two Romances[a]. **Arthur Grumiaux** (vn); **New Philharmonia Orchestra/ Alceo Galliera;** [a]**Concertgebouw Orchestra/Bernard Haitink.** Philips Concert Classics 426 064-2PCC — 57m ADD 11/89 ▲
Piano Concerto in D major, Op. 61 (transcribed by the composer from the Violin Concerto)[a]. *Two Romances*[b]. [a]**Daniel Barenboim** (pf); [b]**Pinchas Zukerman** (vn); [a]**English Chamber**

Orchestra, [b]London Philharmonic Orchestra/Daniel Barenboim. DG Galleria 429 179-2GGA — ·· lh lm ADD 4/90 Ⓑ

Violin Concerto. Egmont, Op. 84 — Overture[a]. **Herman Krebbers** (vn); **Concertgebouw Orchestra; [a]London Philharmonic Orchestra/Bernard Haitink.** Philips Concert Classics 422 971-2PCC — ·· 54m ADD 3/91 ꟼp Ⓑ

*Violin Concerto. **Bruch.** Violin Concerto No. 1 in G minor, Op. 26*[a]. **Kyung Wha Chung** (vn); **Royal Concertgebouw Orchestra; [a]London Philharmonic Orchestra/Klaus Tennstedt.** EMI CDC7 54072-2 — ·· lh 10m DDD 6/92 Ⓑ

Violin Concerto. Piano Sonata No. 10 in G major, Op. 96[a]. [a]**Marc Neikrug** (pf); **Pinchas Zukerman** (vn); **Los Angeles Philharmonic Orchestra/Zubin Mehta.** RCA Victor 09026-61219-2 — ·· lh 13m DDD 11/92 ꟼp Ⓑ

Violin Concerto. Romance No. 2. **Oscar Shumsky** (vn); **Philharmonia Orchestra/Andrew Davis.** ASV Quicksilva CDQS6080 — ·· 54m ADD 12/92 ꟼp Ⓑ

Violin Concerto. Two Romances. **Stephanie Chase** (vn); **Hanover Band/Roy Goodman.** Cala CACD1013 — ·· 55m DDD 12/93 Ⓑ

Violin Concerto. Two Romances. **Dmitri Sitkovetsky** (vn); **Academy of St Martin in the Fields/Sir Neville Marriner.** Virgin Classics VC5 45001-2 — ·· lh 2m DDD 3/94 ꟼp Ⓑ

*Violin Concerto. **Sibelius.** Violin Concerto in D minor, Op. 47.* **David Oistrakh** (vn); **Stockholm Festival Orchestra/Sixten Ehrling.** Testament mono SBT1032 — ·· lh 15m ADD 7/94 ꟼp Ⓑ ▲

New review

Beethoven. Triple Concerto, Op. 56[a]. Choral Fantasia in C minor, Op. 80[b]. **Beaux Arts Trio** ([a]Ida Kavafian, vn; [a]Peter Wiley, vc; Menahem Pressler, pf); [b]**Mid-German Radio Chorus; Leipzig Gewandhaus Orchestra/Kurt Masur.** Philips 438 005-2PH. Recorded in 1992.

·· 52m DDD 6/94 ꟼp Ⓑ

Kurt Masur has rarely conducted more electrifying Beethoven performances on disc. The opening tutti of the concerto establishes a speed markedly faster than usual, and if the three soloists modify it slightly, the characteristic which marks this performance is its urgency. But there is no feeling of breathlessness, simply exhilaration. The evenness and clarity of Pressler's articulation in scales and passagework is a delight. As for the brief central meditation, led — like most main themes in this work — by the cello, it flows very warmly and naturally, with Peter Wiley just as rich and positive an artist as Pressler. This now stands as one of the very finest versions of a work which at last looks like being appreciated, not as a rarity, but as an important pillar of the Beethoven canon. The *Choral Fantasia* is hardly likely to establish itself in a comparable niche, but this performance is most persuasive. The variations on the corny main theme are regularly pointed with engaging wit, not just by Pressler but by the wind soloists, and the brass sound is glorious. It is rather like having the choral finale of the Ninth anticipated with tongue-in-cheek. Balances are always difficult, not just in this work but notoriously in the Triple Concerto. The soloists are well-focused and the orchestral sound is warm and full.

Additional recommendations ...
Triple Concerto[a]. *Choral Fantasia*[b]. [a]**Christian Funke** (vn); [a]**Jürnjakob Timm** (vc); [a]**Peter Rösel,** [b]**Jörg-Peter Weigle** (pfs); [b]**Leipzig Radio Chorus; Dresden Philharmonic Orchestra/Herbert Kegel.** Capriccio 10 150 — ·· 54m DDD 9/87 Ⓑ

Triple Concerto. Piano Sonata No. 17 in D minor, Op. 31 No. 2, "Tempest". **Sviatoslav Richter** (pf); **David Oistrakh** (vn); **Mstislav Rostropovich** (vc); **Berlin Philharmonic Orchestra/Herbert von Karajan.** EMI Studio CDM7 69032-2 — ·· lh ADD 4/88 Ⓑ

Triple Concerto[a]. *Brahms. Double Concerto in A minor, Op. 102*[b]. [a]**Rudolf Serkin** (pf); [a]**Jaime Laredo,** [b]**Isaac Stern** (vns); [a]**Leslie Parnas,** [b]**Leonard Rose** (vcs); [a]**Marlboro Festival Orchestra/Alexander Schneider;** [b]**Philadelphia Orchestra/Eugene Ormandy.** Sony Portrait MK44842 — ·· lh 11m ADD 11/89 Ⓑ

Triple Concerto[a]. *Brahms. Double Concerto in A minor, Op. 102*[b]. [ab]**David Oistrakh** (vn), [ab]**Mstislav Rostropovich** (vc); [b]**Sviatoslav Richter** (pf); [a]**Berlin Philharmonic Orchestra/Herbert von Karajan;** [b]**Cleveland Orchestra/George Szell.** EMI Studio Plus CDM7 64744-2 — ·· lh 10m ADD 7/93 ꟼp Ⓑ

Beethoven. PIANO CONCERTOS. **Maurizio Pollini** (pf); **Berlin Philharmonic Orchestra/Claudio Abbado.** DG 439 770-2GH3. Recorded at performances in the Philharmonie, Berlin in December 1992 (Nos. 1-4) and January 1993 (No. 5).
No. 1 in C major, Op. 15; No. 2 in B flat major, Op. 19; No. 3 in C minor, Op. 37; No. 4 in G major, Op. 58; No. 5 in E flat major, "Emperor", Op. 73.

③ 2h 54m DDD 6/94 — ℗ Ⓑ

Whilst Gilels was alive, Pollini was one of the heirs apparent; now that Gilels is gone he is king — in Beethoven, at least. There may be more individual and idiosyncratic interpreters of the music but there is none whose command, at best, is sovereign. The Fourth Concerto has a keenly felt sense of the evolving drama, and a slow movement where the dialogue between piano and orchestra is spellbinding in its intensity. Maybe Pollini is not yet entirely reconciled to Beethoven's prankish first concerto, the Concerto No. 2 in B flat. In the outer movements, he can seem brusque: ill-at-ease with Beethoven in his rumbustious, amorous, Hooray Henry mood. By contrast, the performance of the Third is a joy from start to finish. Abbado and Pollini are hand-in-glove, which gives this cycle a cohesiveness which Pollini's previous set (1/89) with Böhm and Jochum rather obviously lacked, though the Berliners don't play the first movement of the *Emperor* Concerto as commandingly as Böhm and the Vienna Philharmonic on the earlier recording. But the slow movement goes well, and the finale is more jovial than before. Musically, though, there are evident gains — in these live recordings — moments where the tension is palpable in a way that it rarely is in the recording studio. The sound is full-bodied and immediate, with applauses, a few squeaks, bumps and ill-timed coughs.

Additional recommendations ...
Nos. 1-5. **Steven Lubin** (fp); **Academy of Ancient Music/Christopher Hogwood.** L'Oiseau-Lyre Florilegium 421 408-2OH3 — ③ 2h 44m DDD 5/88 ℗ Ⓑ ✍
Nos. 1-5. **Murray Perahia** (pf); **Concertgebouw Orchestra/Bernard Haitink.** CBS Masterworks CD44575. *The Gramophone Award-winning disc containing Nos. 3 and 4 are available separately and are reviewed in full below* — ③ 2h 58m DDD 1/89 ℗ Ⓑ
Nos. 1-5. **Claudio Arrau** (pf); **Staatskapelle Dresden/Sir Colin Davis.** Philips 422 149-2PH3 — ③ 3h 9m DDD 1/89 ℗ Ⓑ
Nos. 1-5. *Choral Fantasia in C minor, Op. 80ª.* **Cleveland ªChorus and Orchestra/Vladimir Ashkenazy** (pf). Decca 421 718-2DH3 — ③ 3h 19m DDD 3/89 ℗ Ⓑ
Nos. 1-5. *Choral Fantasiaª.* **Daniel Barenboim** (pf); ª**John Alldis Choir; New Philharmonia Orchestra/Otto Klemperer.** EMI CMS7 63360-2 — ③ 3h 31m ADD 3/90 ℗ Ⓑ
Nos. 1-5. *Rondos, Op. 51.* **Wilhelm Kempff** (pf); **Berlin Philharmonic Orchestra/Paul van Kempen.** DG Dokumente mono 435 744-2GDO3 — ③ 3h 9m ADD 4/93 ℗ Ⓑ ▲

Beethoven. Piano Concertos — No. 1 in C major, Op. 15ª; No. 2 in B flat major, Op. 19ᵇ. **Wilhelm Kempff** (pf); **Berlin Philharmonic Orchestra/Ferdinand Leitner.** DG Galleria 419 856-2GGA. Item marked ª from SLPM138774 (6/62), ᵇ SLPM138775 (9/62).

1h 5m ADD 9/88 — ℗ Ⓑ

The Second Piano Concerto was in fact written before the First, and recent research suggests that an initial version of the so-called Second Concerto dates back to Beethoven's teenage years. If the Second Concerto inevitably reflects eighteenth-century classical style, it has Beethoven's familiar drive and energy and a radical use of form and technique. The First Concerto pre-dates the revolutionary *Eroica* Symphony by some eight years and still shows classical influences, but it is on a larger scale than the Second Concerto, and has greater powers of invention. Kempff's recording of these two works dates from the early 1960s, but the sound quality is pleasingly open and full-bodied, so that the soloist's pearly, immaculate tone quality is heard to good effect. Kempff and Leitner enjoy what is obviously a close rapport and their aristocratic, Olympian but poetic music-making suits both works admirably.

Additional recommendations ...
Nos. 1 and 2. **Martha Argerich** (pf); **Philharmonia Orchestra/Giuseppe Sinopoli.** DG 415 682-2GH — 1h 5m DDD 9/86 Ⓑ
Nos. 1 and 2. **Murray Perahia** (pf); **Concertgebouw Orchestra/Bernard Haitink.** CBS CD42177 — 1h 10m DDD 4/87 Ⓑ

Beethoven. Piano Concertos — No. 3 in C minor, Op. 37; No. 4 in G major, Op. 58.
Murray Perahia (pf); **Concertgebouw Orchestra/Bernard Haitink.** CBS Masterworks
CD39814. From IM39814 (7/86).

˙∙ Ih I0m DDD I0/86

This is an outstanding disc, containing two of the finest Beethoven performances to appear in
recent years. In both works one feels that there is no conscious striving to interpret the music,
rather that Perahia is allowing it simply to flow through him — an illusion, of course, but one
which he is able to sustain with almost miraculous consistency. But the honours do not belong
solely to Perahia: the contributions of Haitink and the Concertgebouw cannot be praised too
highly, and the extraordinary sense of rapport and shared purpose that exist between these two
fine musical minds is perhaps the most impressive aspect of the performances. The recordings,
made by Decca engineers, are unusually sensitive, both to the sound of the piano and to the
need for an overall balance that is homogeneous and clearly detailed.

Additional recommendations …
Vladimir Ashkenazy (pf); **Chicago Symphony Orchestra/Sir Georg Solti.** Decca
Ovation 417 740-2DM — ˙∙ Ih IIm ADD 5/88 Ⓑ ▲
Melvyn Tan (fp); **London Classical Players/Roger Norrington.** EMI CDC7 49815-2 —
˙∙ Ih 5m DDD II/89 Ⓑ ✎
Stephen Kovacevich (pf); **BBC Symphony Orchestra/Sir Colin Davis.** Philips Concert
Classics 426 062-2PCC — ∙ Ih 9m ADD 12/89 Ⓑ

Beethoven. Piano Concerto No. 5 in E flat major, Op. 73, "Emperor". **Claudio Arrau** (pf);
Staatskapelle Dresden/Sir Colin Davis. Philips 416 215-2PH. From 416 215-1PH (4/86).

˙∙ 4Im DDD 8/86

By the time he wrote his Fifth Concerto, Beethoven was too deaf to continue playing in public
and though he was still only 39 years old he wrote no more concertos. So the *Emperor* has a
particular heroic quality, as if the composer was making a final, defiant contribution to a
medium in which he could no longer physically participate. Arrau's is a highly personal and
obviously deeply considered reading which appears to have gained in depth and insight over the
years. The *Adagio* and *Rondo* come over particularly well: the slow movement sounds very
relaxed, but there is actually considerable tension in Arrau's playing, as when he arrives at the
astonishing transitional passage from which the finale suddenly erupts; it's as if a store of
accumulated energy were suddenly translated into action, though once again there's a wonderful
leisurely quality here, for all the purposefulness of the playing. Davis and the orchestra provide
firm and dynamic support in a recording whose aural perspective is entirely plausible.

Additional recommendations …
No. 5. Piano Sonata No. 32 in C minor, Op. 111. **Wilhelm Kempff** (pf); **Berlin Philharmonic
Orchestra/Ferdinand Leitner.** DG Galleria 419 468-2GGA — ˙∙ Ih 3m ADD 12/87 Ⓑ
No. 5. Piano Sonata in E major, Op. 109. **Stephen Kovacevich** (pf); **BBC Symphony
Orchestra/Sir Colin Davies.** Philips Concert Classics 422 482-2PCC — ∙ 59m ADD 12/89 Ⓑ
No. 5. **Arturo Benedetti Michelangeli** (pf); **Vienna Symphony Orchestra/Carlo Maria
Giulini.** DG 419 249-2GH — ˙∙ 42m ADD 2/88 Ⓑ
No. 5. Choral Fantasia in C minor, Op. 80[a]. **Melvyn Tan** (fp); [a]**Schütz Choir of London;
London Classical Players/Roger Norrington.** EMI Reflexe CDC7 49965-2 — ˙∙ 52m DDD
4/90 Ⓑ ✎
No. 5. Triple Concerto in C major, Op. 56[a]. **Leon Fleisher** (pf); **Cleveland Orchestra/George
Szell;** [a]**Eugene Istomin** (pf); [a]**Isaac Stern** (vn); [a]**Leonard Rose** (vc); [a]**Philadelphia
Orchestra/Eugene Ormandy.** Sony Classics Essential Classics MK46549 — ˙∙ Ih 14m ADD
8/91 Ⓑ
No. 5. Choral Fantasia[a]. **Alfred Brendel** (pf); **London Philharmonic** [a]**Choir and
Orchestra/Bernard Haitink.** Philips Insignia 434 148-2PM — ˙∙ Ih Im ADD 7/92 Ⓑ

Beethoven. SYMPHONIES. [a]**Charlotte Margiono** (sop); [a]**Birgit Remmert** (mez); [a]**Rudolf
Schasching** (ten); [a]**Robert Holl** (bass); [a]**Arnold Schoenberg Choir; Chamber Orchestra
of Europe/Nikolaus Harnoncourt.** Teldec 2292-46452-2. Recorded 1990-91.

No. 1 in C major, Op. 21. No. 2 in D major, Op. 36. No. 3 in E flat major, Op. 55, "Eroica". No. 4 in B flat major, Op. 60. No. 5 in C minor, Op. 67. No. 6 in F major, Op. 68, "Pastoral". No. 7 in A major, Op. 92. No. 8 in F major, Op. 93. No. 9 in D minor, Op. 125, "Choral"[a].

⑤ 5h 58m DDD 11/91 q_P q_S Ⓑ

Brimful of intrepid character and interpretative incident, Nikolaus Harnoncourt and the splendid Chamber Orchestra of Europe give us what is surely the most stimulating Beethoven symphony cycle of recent times. As Harnoncourt himself states in a lively interview for the accompanying booklet to this set: "It has always been my conviction that music is not there to soothe people's nerves ... but rather to open their eyes, to give them a good shaking, even to frighten them". So it transpires that there's a re-creative daring about his conducting — in essence an embracement of recent scholarly developments and Harnoncourt's own pungent sense of characterization — which is consistently illuminating, thus leaving the listener with the uncanny sensation that he or she is in fact encountering this great music for the very first time. In all of this Harnoncourt is backed to the hilt by some superbly responsive, miraculously assured playing from the COE: their personable, unforced assimilation of Harnoncourt's specific demands (complete with period-style lean-textured strings and bracingly cutting brass and timpani), allied to this conductor's intimate knowledge of the inner workings of these scores, make for wonderfully fresh, punchy results. In this respect Symphonies Nos. 6-8 in particular prove immensely rewarding, but the *Eroica* and (especially) the Fourth, too, are little short of superb. In sum, it's a cycle which excitingly reaffirms the life-enhancing mastery of Beethoven's vision for the 1990s and into the next century beyond: a more thought-provoking, unimpeachably eloquent achievement one does not expect to encounter for many moons to come.

Additional recommendations ...

Nos. 1-9. Overtures — Coriolan, Op. 62; Leonore No. 3, Op. 72b; Fidelio, Op. 72c; Egmont, Op. 84. **Leipzig Gewandhaus Orchestra/Kurt Masur.** Philips 416 274-2PH6 — ⑥ 6h 38m ADD 2/86 q_P Ⓑ

Nos. 1-9. Egmont Overture. **Royal Concertgebouw Orchestra/Bernard Haitink.** Philips 416 822-2PH6 — ⑥ 6h 5m DDD 6/88 q_P Ⓑ

Nos. 1-9. Overtures — Die Geschöpfe des Prometheus, Op. 43. Coriolan. Egmont. **London Classical Players/Roger Norrington.** EMI Reflexe CDS7 49852-2 — ⑥ 5h 53m DDD 11/89 q_P Ⓑ

Nos. 1-9. **Berlin Philharmonic Orchestra/Herbert von Karajan.** DG 429 036-2GX5 — ⑤ 5h 32m ADD 1/90 q_P Ⓑ

Nos. 1-9. Overture — Leonore No. 3, Op. 62a. **NBC Symphony Orchestra/Arturo Toscanini.** RCA Gold Seal mono GD60324 — ⑤ 5h 37m ADD 5/90 q_P Ⓑ ▲

Nos. 1-9. **Leipzig Radio Chorus; Leipzig Gewandhaus Orchestra/Kurt Masur.** Philips 426 290-2PH5 (*also available separately*): Nos. 1 and 5: 426 782-2PH (*reviewed below*); Nos. 2 and 7: 432 994-2PH; Nos. 3 and 8: 434 913-2PH; Nos. 4 and 6: 434 919-2PH; No. 9: 432 995-2PH — ⑤ 1h 3m 1h 13m 1h 16m 1h 17m 1h 6m DDD 5/93 q_P Ⓑ

Overtures[a] — Coriolan; Egmont; König Stefan; Die Geschöpfe des Prometheus; Fidelio; Leonora No. 1, Op. 138; Leonora No. 2, Op. 72a; Leonora No. 3. The Consecration of the House, Op. 124. Namensfreier, Op. 115. Die Ruinen von Athen, Op. 113. 12 Menuets, WoO7[b]. 12 German Dances, WoO8[b]. 12 Contredanses, WoO14[b]. [a]**Leipzig Gewandhaus Orchestra/Kurt Masur;** [b]**Academy of St Martin in the Fields/Sir Neville Marriner.** Philips Duo — 438 702-2PM2 — ② 2h 33m ADD 5/94 Ⓑ

Beethoven. Symphonies — No. 1 in C major, Op. 21; No. 5 in C minor, Op. 67. **Leipzig Gewandhaus Orchestra/Kurt Masur.** Philips 426 782-2PH. Recorded in 1987-89.

1h 3m DDD 7/90 q_P Ⓑ

So many loud partisan claims are made about Beethoven performances these days that you must use the instruments of the composer's own time, or that it's hopeless trying to equal past giants like Furtwängler, Toscanini or Klemperer — that it's very refreshing indeed to discover a conductor who pursues his own course, and argues for it so convincingly. Kurt Masur always gives the impression of having gone back to the score and thought it all through afresh. He not only adopts the recent innovation of restoring the scherzo-trio repeat in No. 5, he shows deep understanding of how this affects the finale's thunderous self-assertion. And while he avoids the old-fashioned wallowing of a Leonard Bernstein, the *Andantes* of both symphonies show that classicism doesn't mean coldness; far from it and the dancing energy of the First Symphony's *Scherzo* and finale make some revered older versions sound stodgy. There is a slight snag: the recording in the Fifth Symphony pushes the trumpets and drums back and the piccolo in the finale isn't the glittering presence it should be, but don't let that put you off buying these refreshing and authoritative Beethoven performances.

Additional recommendations ...
Nos. 1 and 4. Egmont Overture. **Berlin Philharmonic Orchestra/Herbert von Karajan.** DG Galleria 419 048-2GGA — ⠂⠄ 1h 4m ADD 4/88 ᶠₚ Ⓑ
Nos. 1 and 6. **London Classical Players/Roger Norrington.** EMI Reflexe CDC7 49746-2 — ⠂⠄ 1h 6m DDD 9/88 ᶠₚ Ⓑ ✓
Nos. 1 and 2. **Cleveland Orchestra/Christoph von Dohnányi.** Telarc CD80187 — ⠂⠄ 59m DDD 6/89 ᶠₚ Ⓑ
Nos. 1 and 6. **Vienna Philharmonic Orchestra/Hans Schmidt-Isserstedt.** Decca 433 622-2DH — ⠂⠄ 55m ADD 3/90 Ⓑ
Nos. 1 and 4. **Vienna Philharmonic Orchestra/Karl Böhm.** DG Resonance 429 152-2GR — ⠂⠄ 1h 4m ADD 4/90 ᶠₚ Ⓑ

Beethoven. Symphonies — No. 2 in D major, Op. 36; No. 4 in B flat major, Op. 60. **North German Radio Symphony Orchestra/Günter Wand.** RCA Victor Red Seal RD60058. Recorded in 1988.

⠂⠄ 1h 8m DDD 9/89 ᶠₚ ᶠₛ Ⓑ

Seldom has Beethoven's Second Symphony sounded as fresh, dynamic or persuasive as this. The work occupies a transitional place in the symphonic line as begun by Mozart and Haydn; on the one hand it forms the climax of that line, on the other it looks forward to new beginnings. Günter Wand's stance clearly leans towards those new beginnings, with a reading that is more 'Beethovian' in approach than most, highlighting the fingerprints of his future symphonic style. The Fourth Symphony has always tended to be eclipsed by the towering edifices of the Third and Fifth Symphonies, but the Fourth takes stock, and with the maturity gained in the writing of the Third, looks back once more in an act of homage to the triumphs of the past. Wand's performances are inspired; he is a conductor who never imposes his own ego and never does anything for the sake of effect, resulting in performances that are honest, direct and unpretentious. His tempos are superbly judged; brisk, but not hurried, allowing the pristine articulation of the strings to come shining through (this needs to be heard to be believed; orchestral playing such as this is rare indeed). The orchestral balance is ideal, with woodwind textures nicely integrated into the orchestral sound, and this is supported by the excellent recorded sound which approaches demonstration quality. A very fine issue indeed.

Additional recommendations ...
Nos. 4 and 5. **London Symphony Orchestra/Wyn Morris.** Pickwick IMP Classics PCD869 — ⠂⠄ 1h 7m DDD 11/87 Ⓑ
Nos. 2 and 4. **Philharmonia Orchestra/Otto Klemperer.** EMI Studio CDM7 63355-2 — ⠂⠄ 1h 13m ADD 8/90 ᶠₚ Ⓑ ▲

Beethoven. Symphony No. 3 in E flat major, Op. 55, "Eroica"[a]. Overture — Leonora No. 3, Op. 72a[b]. **North German Radio Symphony Orchestra/Günter Wand.** RCA Victor RD60755. Recorded live in [a] 1989, [b] June 1990.

⠂⠄ 1h 5m DDD 10/91 ᶠₚ Ⓑ

Günter Wand's live performance of the *Eroica* represents a worthy alternative to Klemperer's 1955 landmark recording. In many ways Wand stands as a legitimate successor to Klemperer as one of the holders of the great Teutonic tradition of interpreting Beethoven in terms of struggle and triumph. Certainly he launches into the symphony with tremendous vigour and power and he sustains these characteristics throughout. Following an opening movement in which the tension never relaxes at all, Wand leads a reading of the Funeral March which is deeply felt but without self-indulgence. The scherzo and trio provide well-pointed relief prior to an epic reading of the triumphant final movement, which carries all before it. The fill-up, an equally powerful reading of the *Leonora* Overture No. 3, precedes the performance of the *Eroica* and acts as an excellent curtain-raiser and introduction to Wand's interpretative style: genuine and powerful and wholly without self-indulgence. The North German Radio recording is excellent, capturing the involved atmosphere of a live performance without any of the distractions normally encountered. Highly recommended.

Additional recommendations ...
No. 3. Die Geschöpfe des Prometheus. **London Classical Players/Roger Norrington.** EMI Reflexe CDC7 49101-2 — ⸱⸱* 49m DDD 4/89 ⁹ₚ Ⓑ ✎
No. 3. Egmont Overture. **Staatskapelle Dresden/Sir Colin Davis.** Philips 434 120-2PH — ⸱⸱*
1h 5m DDD 3/93 ⁹ₚ Ⓑ

Beethoven. Symphony No. 5 in C minor, Op. 67. **Vienna Philharmonic Orchestra/ Carlos Kleiber.** DG 415 861-2GH. From 2530 516 (6/75).

⸱⸱*   **33m ADD II/85**   ⁹ₚ   Ⓑ

Rarely, if ever, has the spirit of revolutionary turbulence been better expressed in music than in the first movement of the Fifth Symphony; and no musical transformation is more likely to lift the spirits than the transition from scherzo to finale over which Beethoven laboured so hard and pondered so long. Even if our century cannot always share Beethoven's unshakeable sense of optimism, the visionary goal he proposes is one which we abandon at our peril. The trouble with the Fifth Symphony is that it is, for all its apparent familiarity, a brute of a piece to conduct. The opening bars have unseated many a conductor, and it must be admitted that even Carlos Kleiber comes perilously close to allowing the famous motto to be played as a fast triplet. Thereafter, he barely puts a foot wrong. There are many other distinguished interpreters of this symphony but Kleiber's reading has an electricity, a sense of urgency and fresh discovery which puts it in a class of its own. The DG recording is rather dry and immediate, but the lean texturing is an aspect of Kleiber's radicalism without which the reading would not be the astounding thing it is. The timing of 33 minutes is short measure, but when the performance is of this revealing quality, the duration of the experience is of relatively little importance.

Additional recommendations ...
Nos. 5 and 7. **Concertgebouw Orchestra/Bernard Haitink.** Philips 420 540-2PH — ⸱⸱*
1h 12m DDD 10/87 ⁹ₚ Ⓑ
Nos. 5 and 7. **Philharmonia Orchestra/Vladimir Ashkenazy.** Decca Ovation 430 701-2DM
— ⸱⸱* 1h 17m DDD 8/91 ⁹ₚ Ⓑ
Nos. 5 and 6. **Vienna Philharmonic Orchestra/Karl Böhm.** *Overtures* — *Egmont; Name-Day, Op. 115; The Consecration of the House, Op. 124* (**Orchestre Lamoureux, Paris/Igor Markevitch**); *Die Ruinen von Athen, Op. 113* (**Bavarian Radio Symphony Orchestra/ Eugen Jochum**). DG Compact Classics 413 144-2GW2 — ⸱⸱ ② 1h 54m ADD 12/91 ⁹ₚ Ⓑ ▲
Nos. 5 and 7. **Philharmonia Orchestra/Otto Klemperer.** EMI mono CDM7 63868-2 — ⸱⸱*
1h 14m ADD 4/92 ⁹ₚ Ⓑ
Nos. 5 and 7. **Royal Liverpool Philharmonic Orchestra/Sir Charles Mackerras.** EMI Eminence CD-EMX2212 — ⸱⸱* 1h 8m DDD 12/93 Ⓑ

New review
Beethoven. Symphonies — No. 5 in C minor, Op. 67; No. 6 in F major, Op. 68, "Pastoral". **North German Radio Symphony Orchestra/Günter Wand.** RCA Victor Red Seal 09026 61930-2. Recorded at performances in the Musikhalle, Hamburg, Germany in 1992.

⸱⸱*   **1h 19m DDD 5/94**   ⁹ₚ   Ⓑ

New review
Beethoven. Symphony No. 6 in F major, Op. 68, "Pastoral". Overtures — Coriolan, Op. 62; Egmont, Op. 84. **La Scala Philharmonic Orchestra/Carlo Maria Giulini.** Sony Classical SK53974.

⸱⸱*   **1h 5m DDD 5/94**   ⁹ₚ   Ⓑ

To judge from this live performance of the Fifth Symphony, Wand has the trick of keeping something back for the performance itself; a remarkable skill in repertory as familiar as this after so much detailed preparation. In matters of rhythm and phrasing and the balancing of lines,

Wand is difficult to fault. Indeed, you will hear things in these performances — from the basses and bassoons, and, in the Fifth Symphony, from the trombones — which are all too often glossed over. Apart from a curiously measured *Scherzo*, the Fifth Symphony goes exceptionally well. The first movement is not over-driven, yet the finale has real *élan*, the reading, for want of a better word, suddenly and surprisingly rather Furtwänglerish. In the *Pastoral* Symphony it is Wand's exemplary account of the Scene by the Brook that most obviously stands out. Here he has the knack of marrying the music's necessary forward movement with the murmurous beauty of its inner detailing. Wand's *Pastoral* gives profound pleasure

As, in its very different way, does Giulini's, his third recording of the Symphony and, by some distance, his finest. Superbly sustained and expressively moulded, this is a performance in which every sentence is gloriously phrased and where individual string lines are always richly distinct; not a note is extraneous to Beethoven's purpose. The whole performance is wonderfully at odds with the hell-for-leather spirit of an agnostic age. It is, in the end, a deeply *spiritual* performance of a work which was conceived by Beethoven, first and last, as an essentially spiritual experience. The disc begins with a profoundly satisfying *Coriolan* Overture and the dramatic opening of the *Egmont* Overture is played with a near-ideal blend of trenchancy and *espressivo* intensity. As for the coda, the so-called 'Victory Symphony', few have brought out as vividly as Giulini its musical and moral sure-footedness.

Additional recommendations ...
Nos. 5 and 6. **Concertgebouw Orchestra/Erich Kleiber.** Decca mono 417 637-2DH — ⠠⠶
1h 13m ADD 9/87 ♀ℙ ⓑ ▲
Egmont. Der Geschöpfe des Prometheus. Fidelio. Die Ruinen von Athen. Coriolan. Leonore Nos. 1 and 3.
Bavarian Radio Symphony Orchestra/Sir Colin Davis. CBS Masterworks CD44790 —
⠠⠶ 1h 3m DDD 9/89 ♀ℙ ⓑ
Nos. 1 and 6. **Chicago Symphony Orchestra/Fritz Reiner.** RCA GD60002 — ⠠⠶ 1h 4m ADD
9/90 ♀ℙ ⓑ

Beethoven. Symphony No. 6 in F major, Op. 68, "Pastoral"ª. ORCHESTRAL WORKS.
ᶜ**Birgit Nilsson** (sop); ᵃᵇᶜ**Philharmonia Orchestra;** ᵈ**New Philharmonia Orchestra/Otto Klemperer.** EMI Studio CDM7 63358-2. Items marked ª from SAX2260 (10/58), ᵇᶜ 33CX1575 (11/58), ᵈ HMV SXDW3032 (6/77). Recorded in 1957.
Egmont, Op. 84 — Overtureᵇ; Die Trommel gerühretᵇ; Freudvoll und leidvollᶜ; Klärchens Tod bezeichnendᵇ. Der Geschöpfe des Prometheus, Op. 43 — Overtureᵈ.

⠠⠶ 1h 9m ADD 8/90 ♀ℙ ⓑ ▲

Klemperer's most revered Beethoven recordings date from the middle and late 1950s. In its day, his account of the *Pastoral* was notorious for the slow *Scherzo* — "it's a Ländler" — he is said to have retorted grumpily — but once again the performance as a whole offers a wonderful example of Klemperer's ability to sustain dramatic interest within generously conceived spaces. The result is an overwhelming sense of vital but unhurrying reflection. The *Egmont* numbers on this disc are also very fine. Birgit Nilsson is wonderfully fresh in the two arias, and the rarely recorded "Klärchens Tod bezeichnend" is very affecting. As for the famous overture, Klemperer's account is steadily paced, and as cogent and gauntly explicit a reading of this symphonic music-drama as any on disc. It is a reading of great power and nobility in which nothing is overdone; in this respect the coda is a particular success.

Additional recommendation ...
Nos. 1 and 6. **Chicago Symphony Orchestra/Fritz Reiner.** RCA GD60002 — ⠠⠶ 1h 4m
ADD 9/90 ♀ℙ ⓑ
Nos. 6 and 8. **London Philharmonic Orchestra/Klaus Tennstedt.** EMI CDD7 63891-2 —
⠠⠶ 1h 9m DDD 7/91

Beethoven. Symphony No. 7 in A major, Op. 92. **Vienna Philharmonic Orchestra/ Carlos Kleiber.** DG 415 862-2GH. From 2530 706 (9/76).

⠠⠶ 39m ADD 2/86 ♀ₛ ⓑ

This may also seem short measure but as pointed out when discussing Kleiber's recording of the Fifth, the duration must be seen to be of relatively little importance. Kleiber's performance fairly bristles with electricity, but at all times one is aware of a tight control which never lets the exuberance get out of hand; moreover, he shows a scrupulous regard for the composer's instructions: all repeats are observed (to thrilling effect in the scherzo and finale) and tempo relationships are carefully calculated. It is Kleiber's feeling for the overall shape of each movement that is most impressive: how else could there be such a powerful sense of cumulative excitement in the finale? The recording is pre-digital, but it hardly seems to matter when given such a high-quality CD transfer.

Additional recommendations ...
Nos. 7 and 8. **Academy of Ancient Music/Christopher Hogwood.** L'Oiseau-Lyre Florilegium 425 695-2OH — ⋰ lh 3m DDD 2/90 ⁹ₚ Ⓑ ✒
Nos. 7 and 8. **London Symphony Orchestra/Wyn Morris.** Pickwick IMP Classics PCD918 — ⋰ lh 6m DDD 2/90 Ⓑ
No. 7. **Haydn.** *Symphony No. 101 in D major, "Clock".* **Mendelssohn.** *A Midsummer Night's Dream — incidental music, Op. 61: Scherzo.* **New York Philharmonic Orchestra/Arturo Toscanini.** RCA Gold Seal mono GD60316 — ⋰ lh 6m ADD ll/92 ⁹ₚ Ⓑ ▲

Key to symbols

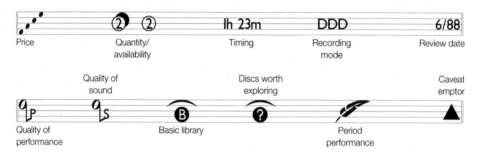

Price	Quantity/availability	Timing	Recording mode	Review date
⋰	② ②	lh 23m	DDD	6/88

	Quality of sound		Discs worth exploring		Caveat emptor
⁹ₚ	⁹ₛ	Ⓑ	❓	✒	▲
Quality of performance		Basic library		Period performance	

New review
Beethoven. Symphonies — No. 8 in F major; No. 2 in D major. **London Classical Players/ Roger Norrington.** EMI CDC7 47698-2.

⋰ 59m DDD 3/87   ⁹ₚ Ⓑ ✒

This is an exceptionally exciting recording and can stand comparison with the best we have had on record on modern instruments during the past 35 or so years. These particular works suit Norrington's temperament and musicological preoccupations unusually well. The D major Symphony is a joy from start to finish, while Norrington treats the F major as though it was specially written for him in an electrifying performance which challenges all his predecessors. Norrington learnt conducting in the opera house. Though he conducts Beethoven's music with the verve of a young man who has just discovered it for the first time, at the time of this recording he was 53 and an experienced musician with the kind of control over rhythm and argument which was always the hallmark of the very best of operatically trained musicians. His way with Beethoven is mapped out in his own insert-note where he states as his aim the recapturing of much of "the exhilaration and sheer disturbance that his music certainly generated in his day". Norrington achieves this not by the imposition on the music of some world view but by taking up its immediate intellectual and physical challenges. He is not unduly preoccupied by matters of orchestral size (44 players are listed on the insert-note) but sound interests him a good deal. Throughout these two performances the contributions of horns, trumpets and drums most rivet the attention; by contrast, the woodwinds have, to modern ears, an almost rustic charm, a *naïf* quality which technology and sophisticated playing techniques have to some extent obliterated. What really fascinates Norrington, though, is rhythm and pulse and their deter-mining agencies: eighteenth-century performing styles, instrumental articulacy (most notably, bowing methods), and Beethoven's own metronome markings. He strives to get as near to the metronome as is humanly possible consistent with instrumental clarity. He plays the Eighth Symphony's third movement as a quick dance and makes excellent sense of crotchet=126, a marking often regarded as being beyond the pale. The second movement is spot on: as witty and exact a reading as you are likely to hear. The recordings are warm and vivid and generally well balanced.

Beethoven. Symphony No. 9 in D minor, Op. 125, "Choral". **Anna Tomowa-Sintow** (sop); **Agnes Baltsa** (mez); **Peter Schreier** (ten); **José van Dam** (bass-bar); **Vienna Singverein; Berlin Philharmonic Orchestra/Herbert von Karajan.** DG Galleria 415 832-2GGA. Text and translation included. From 2740 172 (10/77). Recorded in 1976.

Ih 7m ADD 4/87

New review

Beethoven. Symphony No. 9 in D minor, Op. 125, "Choral". **Alessandra Marc** (sop); **Iris Vermillion** (mez); **Siegfried Jerusalem** (ten); **Falk Struckmann** (bar); **Berlin State Opera Chorus; Berlin Staatskapelle/Daniel Barenboim.** Erato 4509-94353-2. Text and translation included.

Ih 14m DDD 7/94

All collections need Beethoven's *Choral* Symphony as one of the works at the very core of the nineteenth-century romantic movement. Within its remarkable span, Beethoven celebrates both the breadth and power of man's conception of his position in relation to the Universe; his sense of spirituality — especially in the great slow movement — and in the finale the essential life-enhancing optimism emerges, which makes human existence philosophically possible against all odds. Karajan lived alongside the Beethoven symphonies throughout his long and very distinguished recording career, and he recorded the Ninth three times in stereo. Sadly the most recent digital version, in spite of glorious playing in the *Adagio*, is flawed, but both analogue versions are very impressive indeed. His 1976 version is the best of the three. The slow movement has great intensity, and the finale brings a surge of incandescent energy and exuberance which is hard to resist. All four soloists are excellent individually and they also make a good team. The reading as a whole has the inevitability of greatness and the recording is vivid, full and clear. At mid-price this is very recommendable indeed.

Barenboim's is an important recording in that it re-establishes — in its own way and with a telling eloquence that is specially its own — that the Ninth is a work of the new romanticism, a prophetic work that cannot be adequately dealt with by so-called 'authenticists' desirous of tethering it either to the letter of the written text or to performance practice in Beethoven's own lifetime. The literalists and authenticists have had some powerful advocates on record — Toscanini, not easily gainsaid, and, for the authenticists, Norrington. Barenboim's Ninth starts deep in the *Urwald*, far away, wreathed in the mists of time. Yet it is a measure of his mastery that the reading never appears to meander or hold fire. On the contrary, the development and recapitulation blaze quietly, from within. 'Quietly' because the Erato recording, made in Berlin's Jesus-Christus Kirche, is rather soft-grained. Important solo voicings, human or instrumental, are neither obscured nor specifically 'lit'. In the finale, words sound clearly enough whilst at the same time being part of the performance's general euphony. The extreme inwardness of Barenboim's reading at key points — the symphony's opening bars, most of the slow move-ment, the very slow *molto pianissimo* start of the first instrumental statement of the "Joy" theme — is complemented by considerable ebullience in the *Scherzo* and in the later stages of the finale. The soloists are generally reliable, the choir first-rate, the orchestra more than adequate to the considerable task in hand.

Additional recommendations ...
No. 9. Coriolan Overture. **Gundula Janowitz** (sop); **Hilde Rössi-Majdan** (mez); **Waldemar Kmentt** (ten); **Walter Berry** (bass); **Vienna Singverein; Berlin Philharmonic Orchestra/Herbert von Karajan.** DG 435 095-2GCE — .*' DDD ᑫₚ ⓑ
No. 9. **Anna Tomowa-Sintow** (sop); **Annelies Burmeister** (mez); **Peter Schreier** (ten); **Theo Adam** (bass); **Dresden Philharmonic Children's Choir; Berlin and Leipzig Radio Choruses; Leipzig Gewandhaus Orchestra/Kurt Masur.** Philips Silver Line 420 701-2PSL — .*' Ih 9m 12/87 ᑫₚ ⓑ
No. 9. **Yvonne Kenny** (sop); **Sarah Walker** (mez); **Patrick Power** (ten); **Petteri Salomaa** (bass); **Schütz Choir; London Classical Players/Roger Norrington.** EMI CDC7 49221 — .*' 10/87 DDD ᑫₚ ⓑ ✍
No. 9. **Arleen Auger** (sop); **Catherine Robbin** (mez); **Anthony Rolfe Johnson** (ten); **Gregory Reinhart** (bass); **London Symphony Chorus; Academy of Ancient Music/Christopher Hogwood.** L'Oiseau-Lyre 425 517-2OH — .*' Ih 3m DDD 11/89 ᑫₚ ⓑ ✍

No. 9. **Aase Nordmo-Lövberg** (sop); **Christa Ludwig** (mez); **Waldemar Kmentt** (ten); **Hans Hotter** (bass); **Philharmonia Chorus and Orchestra/Otto Klemperer.** EMI Studio CDM7 63359-2 — .•ʼ Ih 12m ADD 8/90 ⁹ₚ Ⓑ ▲

No. 9. **Brigitte Poschner-Klebel** (sop); **Margareta Hintermeier** (contr); **Robert Tear** (ten); **Robert Lloyd** (bass); **Vienna Singakademie; Vienna Symphony Orchestra/Eliahu Inbal.** Denon CO-76646 — .•ʼ Ih 8m DDD 3/91 ⁹ₚ Ⓑ

No. 9. **Joan Rodgers** (sop); **Della Jones** (mez); **Peter Bronder** (ten); **Bryn Terfel** (bass); **Royal Liverpool Philharmonic Choir and Orchestra/Sir Charles Mackerras.** EMI Eminence CD-EMX2186 — .•ʼ Ih Im DDD 12/91 ⁹ₚ Ⓑ

No. 9. **Tilla Briem** (sop); **Elisabeth Höngen** (contr); **Peter Anders** (ten); **Rudolf Watzke** (bass); **Bruno Kittel Choir; Berlin Philharmonic Orchestra/Wilhelm Furtwängler.** Music and Arts mono CD-653 — .•ʼ Ih 14m ADD 5/94 ⁹ₚ Ⓑ ▲

New review

Beethoven. Egmont — incidental music, Op. 84. Symphony No. 5 in C minor, Op. 67. **Sylvia McNair** (sop); **Will Quadflieg** (narr); **New York Philharmonic Orchestra/Kurt Masur.** Teldec 9031-77313-2. Recorded in 1992.

.•ʼ **Ih 15m DDD 1/94**

This gives us a chance (rare on record) to hear all the music Beethoven wrote for Goethe's *Egmont*. Lamoral, Count of Egmont, a middle-aged paterfamilias (he sired 11 children), liberal-minded, open-hearted and a brilliant general, was a hero worthy of the oppressed people of The Netherlands. Which explains why the Duke of Alva, the sinister agent of the Spanish *imperium*, had him executed in Brussels in 1568. In Beethoven's *Egmont* Overture the execution is grimly delineated with a scything two-note drop on the violins followed by silence. Masur's reading of the *Egmont* Overture is in the Klemperer/Szell mould with sensible gearing of tempos and a notable absence of sentimentality or rant. He also has a superbly articulate soloist in Sylvia McNair. His new account of the Fifth Symphony has a degree of gutsiness and electricity you won't find in his civilized but rather sedate 1975 Leipzig performance and Masur now joins those who believe, with a good deal of contemporary evidence on their side, that Beethoven wanted the scherzo and Trio to be repeated. In his earlier recording, he observed neither the repeat of the scherzo and Trio, nor the repeat of the finale's exposition. Now he observes both. The recording, like Masur's performances, is splendidly positive

---

New review

Beethoven. Septet in E flat major, Op. 20. Sextet in E flat major, Op. 81*b*. **Vienna Chamber Ensemble.** Denon CO-75373. Recorded in 1992.

.•ʼ **57m DDD 11/93**   ⁹ₚ

Beethoven's Septet is a charming work whose importance lies not only in its consolidation of its composer's style before its composition in 1799/1800 but also in its anticipation of his further development as a composer. Moreover, its scoring for clarinet, bassoon, horn and strings and its divertimento structure offer music which is exquisite both in form and textural diversity. The present performance by the Vienna Chamber Ensemble is distinguished by interpretative and acoustical refinement which is sensational. The ensemble is ideally matched and the phrasing is elegantly shaped. Clarinettist Norbert Täubl achieves a wonderful smoothness of line, and his playing in the second movement, in particular, sounds heavenly. The Sextet's classical balance and charm, designed to delight the aristocratic audiences of the time, are winningly caught by this Viennese group.

Additional recommendations ...
Septet. **Mendelssohn.** Octet in E flat major, Op. 20*b*. Members of the **Vienna Octet.** Decca 421 093-2DM — .•ʼ Ih 14m ADD 5/88 ▲
Septet. Sextet. **Gaudier Ensemble.** Hyperion CDA66513 — .•ʼ 57m DDD 7/92
Septet. String Quintet in C major, Op. 29. **Hausmusik.** EMI Reflexe CDC6 54656-2 — .•ʼ Ih 12m DDD 6/93

New review

Beethoven. String Quartets — Op. 18, Nos. 1-6; F major, H34 (transcribed from Piano Sonata in F major, Op. 14, No. 1). String Quintet in C major, Op. 29. ªᵃ**Tokyo Quartet**

(Peter Oundjan, Kikuei Ikeda, vns; Kazuhide Isomura, va; Sadao Harada, vc) with **Pinchas Zukerman** (va). RCA Victor Red Seal 09026 61284-2.
Op. 18 — No. 1 in F major; No. 2 in G major; No. 3 in D major; No. 4 in C minor; No. 5 in A major; No. 6 in B flat major.

③ 3h 24m DDD 9/93

It is doubtful whether quartet playing comes much better than this. These performers relate to the sensibility of the period, a world in which horse-driven vehicles and candlelight were the norm rather than jet engines and striplighting. The *Scherzo* of the F major is ideal in this respect. The first movement, too, is beautifully paced and sweet toned but they judge the tempo and the character of the slow movement equally well. But then, thoroughout this set, the playing is unfailingly alive, sensitive and poised. The recordings are very natural with plenty of air round the image; the A major is slightly closer (and at a higher level) than its companions. Given its stature the C major String Quintet is grievously neglected both in the concert-hall and on CD, and is as well played as any one of its all too few rivals on disc.

Additional recommendations ...
Complete Quartets: Op. 18 Nos. 1-6. No. 7 in F major, Op. 59 No. 1, "Rasumovsky". No. 8 in E minor, Op. 59 No. 2, "Rasumovsky". No. 9 in C major, Op. 59 No. 3, "Rasumovsky". No. 10 in E flat major, Op. 74, "Harp". No. 11 in F minor, Op. 95, "Serioso". No. 12 in E flat major, Op. 127. No. 13 in B flat major, Op. 130. No. 14 in C sharp minor, Op. 131. No. 15 in A minor, Op. 132. No. 16 in F major, Op. 135. **Talich Quartet.** Calliope CAL9633/9 — ⑦ 8h 22m AAD 1/89
Nos. 1-6. **Quartetto Italiano.** Philips 426 046-2PM3 — ③ 2h 43m ADD 2/90
Nos. 1-6. **Smithson Quartet.** Deutsche Harmonia Mundi RD77029 — ⑦ 2h 39m DDD 4/90
Nos. 3, 4 and 6. **New Budapest Quartet.** Hyperion CDA66402 — 1h 15m DDD 10/90
Nos. 1, 3, 4, 10, 12, 13 and 14. **Alban Berg Quartet.** EMI CDS7 54587-2 — ④ 4h 2m DDD 10/92
Nos. 2, 5, 6, 8, 9, 11, 15 and 16. Grosse Fuge. **Alban Berg Quartet.** EMI CDS7 54592-2 — ④ 4h 19m DDD 10/92

Beethoven. String Quartet No. 7 in F major, Op. 59 No. 1, "Rasumovsky". String Quintet in C major, Op. 29[a]. **Medici Quartet** (Paul Robertson, David Matthews, vns; Ivo-Jan van der Werff, va; Anthony Lewis, vc); [a]**Simon Rowland-Jones** (va). Nimbus NI5207. Recorded in 1989.

1h 14m DDD 3/90

Beethoven. String Quartets — No. 7 in F major, Op. 59 No. 1, "Rasumovsky"; No. 8 in E minor, Op. 59 No. 2, "Rasumovsky"; No. 9 in C major, Op. 59 No. 3, "Rasumovsky". **Lindsay Quartet** (Peter Cropper, Ronald Birks, vns; Roger Bigley, va; Bernard Gregor-Smith, vc). ASV CDDS207. From CDDCA554 (1/89).

1h 11m DDD

In the few years that separate the Op. 18 from the Op. 59 quartets, Beethoven's world was shattered by the oncoming approach of deafness and the threat of growing isolation. The Op. 59 consequently inhabit a totally different plane, one in which the boundaries of sensibility had been extended in much the same way as the map of Europe was being redrawn. Each of the three quartets alludes to a Russian theme by way of compliment to Count Rasumovsky, who had commissioned the set. The immediate impression the F major Quartet conveys is of great space, breadth and vision; this is to the quartet what the *Eroica* is to the symphony. The neglect of Beethoven's C major Quintet is unaccountable for it is a rewarding and remarkable score, written only a year before the First Symphony. At one time the presto finale earned it the nickname "Der Sturm", doubtless on account of the similarity, or rather anticipation of the storm in the *Pastoral* Symphony. The Medici Quartet with Simon Rowland-Jones give an eminently faithful and musical reading, free from any egocentric posturing. Tempos are sensible and the performance has all the spontaneity of live music-making: nothing is glamorized, yet there is no lack of polish. The first *Rasumovsky*, on the other hand, is not quite as successful: it is well played and there are some felicitous touches of phrasing and colour. Their first movement is on the fast side — not unacceptably so, but the slow movement is far too brisk and this may pose problems for some collectors. All the same the String Quintet alone is worth the price of the disc.

Although the Lindsays may be rivalled (and even surpassed) in some of their insights by the Végh and the Talich, taken by and large, they are second to none and superior to most. In each movement of the E minor they find the *tempo giusto* and all that they do as a result has the ring of complete conviction. The development and reprise of the first movement are repeated as well as the exposition and how imaginatively they play it too! The *pp* markings are scrupulously observed but are not obtrusively pasted on as they are in some sets. The C major is not quite in the same class though the opening has real mystery and awe and some listeners might legitimately feel that the whole movement could do with a little more momentum. On the other hand, they move the second movement on rather too smartly. Yet how splendidly they convey the pent-up torrent of energy unleashed in this fugal onrush. Even if it does not command quite the same elevation of feeling or quality of inspiration that distinguishes their F major and E minor quartets, it is still pretty impressive.

Additional recommendations ...

Nos. 8 and 9. **Végh Quartet.** Auvidis Valois V4404 — .••' lh llm ADD 4/88 ⁹ₚ

Nos. 7 and 8. **Budapest Quartet.** Sony Classical Essential Classics MK46545 — .•• lh l0m ADD 8/91 ▲

Nos. 7-11. **Quartetto Italiano.** Philips 420 797-2PM3 — .•• ③ 2h 45m ADD 2/90 ⁹ₚ

Nos. 12-16. Grosse Fuge in B flat major, Op. 133. **Quartetto Italiano.** Philips 426 050-2PM4 — .•• ④ 3h 36m ADD 2/90 ⁹ₚ

Nos. 7-9 and 11. **Tokyo Quartet.** RCA Victor Red Seal RD60462 — .••' ③ 2h 50m DDD 3/92 ⁹ₚ

Nos. 7-9. **Brandis Quartet.** Nimbus NI5382 — .••' lh l2m DDD 6/94

Beethoven. String Quartets — No. 11 in F minor, Op. 95, "Serioso"[a]; No. 15 in A minor, Op. 132[b]. **Végh Quartet** (Sándor Végh, Sándor Zöldy, vns; Georges Janzer, va; Paul Szabó, vc). Auvidis Valois V4406. Item marked [a] from Telefunken EX6 35041 (8/76); [b] EX6 35040 (10/74).

.••' lh 8m ADD 4/88   ⁹ₚ

Beethoven. String Quartets — No. 15 in A minor, Op. 132[a]; No. 16 in F major, Op. 135[b]. **Talich Quartet** (Petr Messiereur, Jan Kvapil, vns; Jan Talich, va; Evzen Rattai, vc). Calliope CAL9639. Item marked [a] from CAL1639, (6/80), [b] CAL1640 (6/80).

.••' lh 8m ADD 12/86

After the expansive canvas of the Op. 59 Quartets and the *Eroica*, Beethoven's F minor Quartet, Op. 95, displays musical thinking of the utmost compression. The first movement is a highly concentrated sonata design, which encompasses in its four minutes almost as much drama as a full-scale opera. With it comes one of the greatest masterpieces of his last years, the A minor, Op. 132. The isolation wrought first by his deafness and secondly, by the change in fashion of which he complained in the early 1820s, forced Beethoven in on himself. Opus 132 with its other-worldly *Heiliger Dankgesang*, written on his recovery from an illness, is music neither of the 1820s nor of Vienna, it belongs to that art which transcends time and place. Though other performances may be technically more perfect, these are interpretations that come closer to the spirit of this great music than any other on CD. Collectors need have no doubts as to the depth and intelligence of the Talich Quartet's readings for they bring a total dedication to this music: their performances are innocent of artifice and completely selfless. There is no attempt to impress the listener with their own virtuosity or to draw attention to themselves in any way. The recordings are eminently faithful and natural, not 'hi-fi' or overbright but the overall effect is thoroughly pleasing.

Beethoven. STRING QUARTETS. **Végh Quartet** (Sándor Végh, Sándor Zöldy, vns; Georges Janzer, va; Paul Szabó, vc). Auvidis Valois V4405, V4408. Items marked [a] from Telefunken EX6 35041 (8/76), [b] Telefunken SKA25113T/1-4 (10/74).

V4405 — No. 10 in E flat major, Op. 74, "Harp"[a]; No. 12 in E flat major, Op. 127[b]. *V4408* — No. 14 in C sharp minor, Op. 131[b]; No. 16 in F major, Op. 135[b].

.••' ② lh llm lh 6m ADD 6/87   ⁹ₚ

Beethoven (orch. Mitropoulos/Bernstein). String Quartets — No. 14 in C sharp minor, Op. 131[a]; No. 16 in F major, Op. 135[b]. **Vienna Philharmonic Orchestra/Leonard**

Bernstein. DG 435 779-2GH. Item marked [a] recorded in 1977, from 2531 077 (1/80), [b] 1989, new to UK.

◆◆ 1h 17m ADD/DDD 11/92

Beethoven stepped both outside and beyond his period nowhere more so than in the late quartets and the last five piano sonatas. The Op. 127 has been called Beethoven's "crowning monument to lyricism", whilst the Op. 131 is more inward-looking. Every ensemble brings a different set of insights to this great music so that it is not possible to hail any single quartet as offering the whole truth — yet these are as near to the whole truth as we are ever likely to come. The Végh give us music-making that has a profundity and spirituality that completely outweigh any tiny blemishes of intonation or ensemble. One does not get the feeling of four professional quartet players performing publicly for an audience but four thoughtful musicians sharing their thoughts about this music in the privacy of their own home. They bring us closer to this music than do any of their high-powered rivals.

Fifty or so years ago, there was something of a vogue for performing Beethoven's late quartets (either *in toto* or just selected movements) with a full complement of orchestral strings. In 1936, the young Leonard Bernstein, then an undergraduate at Harvard, heard Dmitri Mitropoulos present Beethoven's great Op. 131 with the strings of the Boston Symphony, later recalling: "I went out of my mind and have been ever since". Any understandable reservations one might have about the prospect of hearing such profoundly intimate music thus transformed are swept into insignificance by the huge eloquence of these live performances, both of which feature playing of extraordinary accomplishment and dedication from the incomparable VPO string section. Small wonder, then, that Bernstein himself rated the account of Op. 131 as the culmination of his long-standing relationship with this distinguished orchestra.

Beethoven. String Quartets — No. 13 in B flat major, Op. 130[a]; No. 8 in E minor, Op. 59 No. 2, "Rasumovsky"[b]. **Talich Quartet** (Petr Messiereur, Jan Kvapil, vns; Jan Talich, va; Evzen Rattai, vc). Calliope CAL9637. Item marked [a] from CAL1637/40, [b] CAL1634/6.

◆◆ 1h 13m ADD 3/87

The Beethoven quartets are one of the greatest musical expressions of the human spirit and they must be represented in any collection. The advantage of this Talich recording is that it couples a masterpiece from Beethoven's middle period, the great E minor Quartet, with one of the greatest of his last years. The B flat was the third of the late quartets to be composed and at its first performance in 1826 its last movement, the *Grosse Fuge*, baffled his contemporaries. Later that same year, he substituted the present finale, publishing the *Grosse Fuge* separately. The Talich Quartet have a no less impressive technical command than other ensembles but theirs are essentially private performances, which one is privileged to overhear rather than the over-projected 'public' accounts we so often hear on record nowadays. At 73 minutes this is marvellous value too.

New review
Beethoven. Piano Trio in B flat major, Op. 97, "Archduke". Allegretto in E flat major, Hess 48. Variations in G major on "Ich bin der Schneider Kakadu", Op. 121*a*. **Solomon Trio** (Rodney Friend, vn; Timothy Hugh, vc; Yonty Solomon, pf). Pickwick IMP Masters MCD69.

◆◆ 1h 6m DDD 3/94

This is a discerning, warmly felt performance of the *Achduke* that takes you close to the heart of the matter, most notably in the slow movement. Without loss of flow, the Soloman Trio allow themselves to bask in its serenity, avoiding over-excitability in the triplet variation. In the coda they make you keenly aware that Beethoven enters regions of the sublime. They are also mellow in response to the tautly sprung vitality of the *Scherzo* and finale, not least in their accentuation. The ear is caught by Timothy Hugh's gloriously ripe cello — and the supremely eloquent role Beethoven gives it in this work. Enjoyable too is Solomon's searching intensity in the *Kakadu* Variations. The disc ends with the comparatively unfamiliar brief *Allegretto* in E flat, not published until 1955. Even if not of high-gloss brightness, there is not a trace of hardness in the wholly acceptable recorded sound.

Additional recommendation ...
"*Archduke*". No. 4 in B flat major, Op. 11. **Alexander Schneider** (vn); **Pablo Casals** (vc); **Eugene Istomin** (pf). Sony Classical Casals Edition mono SMK58990 — ◆◆ 1h 5m ADD 5/94 ▲

Beethoven. Piano Trios — E flat major, Op. 1 No. 1; B flat major, Op. 97, "Archduke".
Trio Zingara (Elizabeth Layton, vn; Felix Schmidt, vc; Annette Cole, pf). Collins Classics
1057-2.

:: 1h 13m DDD 5/90 $\quad$ 9p

The young Trio Zingara's performance of Beethoven's great *Archduke* Trio is one of the most
impressive versions in the current catalogue. It's a performance that flows, sometimes slowly
and thoughtfully, sometimes with elegant quickness. Despite a slightly hesitant start, the *Andante*
third movement grows steadily in intensity, and its quietly rippling fourth variation is revealed as
the heart of the work. Impressive too is the way Trio Zingara manage the transition to the
genial finale: all too often this can seem like a let-down — not here. The early E flat Trio
makes a fine foil for the *Archduke*, and Zingara wisely don't try to find intimations of later
profundity here, but then neither is there any twee 'classicizing' — the tone seems just right
throughout. Balancing a grand piano with two solo strings is a nightmare for any recording
producer, but the Collins team seem to have got it about right: the strings are clearly audible,
the piano doesn't sound over-restrained. One minor word of warning though: the insert note
refers to the wrong E flat trio — Op. 70/2, instead of Op. 1/1.

Additional recommendations ...
Complete Piano Trios. Variations Op. 121a. Variations, Op. 44. Allegretto in E flat major. **Vladimir
Ashkenazy** (pf); **Itzhak Perlman** (vn); **Lynn Harrell** (vc). EMI EX290834-3 — :: ④
4h 17m DDD 3/87
Complete Piano Trios. Variations Op. 121a. Variations, Op. 44. Allegretto in E flat major. **Borodin
Trio.** Chandos CHAN8352/5 — :: ④ 4h 31m DDD 7/87
"Archduke". Variations in G major on Müller's "Ich bin der Schneider Kakudü", Op. 121a. **Robinson
Trio.** Pickwick IMP Classics PCD874 — :: 1h 3m DDD 1/88
"Ghost"ᵃ. **Schubert.** *Piano Quintet in A major, D667, "Trout"ᵇ.* ᵇ**Samuel Rhodes** (va); ᵇ**Georg
Hörtnagel** (db); ᵃ**Beaux Arts Trio.** Philips Silver Line Classics 420 716-2PSL — :: 1h 2m ADD 6/88
*Op. 1 Nos. 1-3. "Ghost". "Archduke". Variations in G major on Müller's "Ich bin der Schneider Kakadu".
14 Variations in E flat major, Op. 44. Allegretto in E flat major, Hess 48.* **Pinchas Zukerman** (vn);
Jacqueline du Pré (vc); **Daniel Barenboim** (pf). EMI Studio CMS7 63124-2 — :: ③
3h 50m ADD 8/89
"Archduke". "Ghost". **Henryk Szeryng** (vn); **Pierre Fournier** (vc); **Wilhelm Kempff** (pf). DG
429 712-2GGA — :: 1h 11m ADD 9/90
Op. 1 — Nos. 1 and 3. Variations in E flat major on an original theme, Op. 44. **Castle Trio.** Virgin
Classics VC7 59590-2 — :: 1h 16 DDD 4/91 ✍
"Archduke". B flat major, WoO39. Variations in G major on Müller's "Ich bin der Schneider Kakadu".
Castle Trio. Virgin Classics Veritas VC7 59044-2 — :: 1h 7m DDD 3/92 ✍
*Op. 1, Nos. 1-3. B flat major, Op. 11. D major after Symphony No. 2, Op. 36. E flat major, Op. 44.
E flat major, Op. 38 (after Septet, Op. 20). "Ghost". E flat major, Op. 70 No. 2. "Archduke". G major,
Op. 121a. E flat major, WoO38. B flat major, WoO39. Trio-movement in E flat major, Hess 48.* **Beaux
Arts Trio.** Philips 432 381-2PM5 — :: ⑤ 5h 59m ADD/DDD 3/92
*"Archduke"ᵇ. Op. 1, No. 3ᵃ. "Ghost"ᶜ. Cello Sonatas — F major, Op. 5, No. 1ᵈ; G minor, Op. 5 No. 2ᵉ;
F major, Op. 17ᵍ; C major, Op. 102, No. 1ᶠ.* ᵃᵇᶜ**Sándor Vegh.** (vn); **Pablo Casals** (vc); ᶜ**Karl
Engel,** ᵃᵇᵉᶠᵍ**Mieczyslaw Horszowski,** ᵈ**Wilhelm Kempf** (pfs). Philips 438 520-2PM3 — ::
③ 3h 20m ADD 3/94 9p
E flat major, Op. 1 No. 1. G major, Op. 1 No. 2. **Stuttgart Piano Trio.** Naxos 8 550946 — .
1h 3m DDD 7/94
*C minor, Op. 1 No. 3. E flat major, WoO38. E flat major, Op. 44. Trio-movement in E flat major, Hess
No. 48.* **Stuttgart Piano Trio.** Naxos 8 550947 — . 1h DDD 7/94

Key to symbols

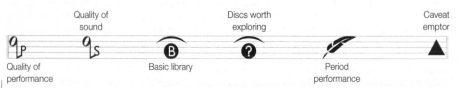

Quality of sound	Discs worth exploring	Caveat emptor
Quality of performance	Basic library	Period performance

Beethoven. STRING TRIOS. **Itzhak Perlman** (vn); **Pinchas Zukerman** (va); **Lynn Harrell** (vc). EMI CDS7 54198-2. Recorded live 1989-90.
String Trios: E flat major, Op. 3; Op. 9 — No. 1 in G major; No. 2 in D major; No. 3 in C minor. Serenade in D major, Op. 8.

② 2h 23m DDD 2/93

Beethoven. String Trios, Op. 9 — No. 1 in G major; No. 2 in D major; No. 3 in C minor. **Archibudelli** (Vera Beths, vn; Jürgen Kussmaul, va; Anner Bylsma, vc). Sony Classical Vivarte SK48190. Recorded in 1991.

1h 8m DDD 9/92

Whereas the last of Beethoven's six Piano Trios, the *Archduke*, was not written until he was 41, all five of his String Trios date from his twenties, with the six-movement E flat Trio, Op. 3 appearing in 1792, to be followed by the *Serenade* in D, Op. 8, some five years later. But after banishing all such eighteenth-century entertainment connotations in his three next classically designed, four-movement String Trios (Op. 9) of 1798, he thereafter preferred to write not for three but rather, four strings in what grew into a legendary, life-long cycle of string quartets. The double-stopping in the noble slow movement of the high-powered C minor String Trio already portends pursuit of richer textures. So it is essentially the artist as a young man that we meet on the EMI set, and what a revelation of youthful genius they offer in imaginative range. Recorded live in New York, the playing is eloquent testimony to that little extra piquancy and boldness of characterization that an audience can draw from artists even as studio-friendly as Perlman, Zukerman and Harrell — perhaps all the more fresh in their approach because not in daily harness as an ensemble. Tone is splendidly vibrant. And incidentally they score over their also excellent, but less succulently reproduced DG rivals (listed below), by including the arresting extra trio Beethoven subsequently provided for the *Scherzo* of the G major Trio.

A group with "a special love for historical stringed instruments" is how Archibudelli is described, as might be gleaned from their name (an Italian compilation of bows and strings) plus the fact that Anner Bylsma plays a 1835 Gianfrancesco Pressenda cello, Vera Bath a 1727 Stradivari violin and Jürgen Kussmaul a 1785 William Forster viola. But though striving for a special period quality of sound they are anything but antiquarian in their approach to these works, all of them striking enough to have placed Beethoven among the immortals even if he had written nothing else. With their brisk tempo, strong dynamic contrast and piquant accentuation, they leave no doubt of the urgency inherent in the key of C minor for this composer. The other two Trios in major keys are equally imaginatively characterized and contrasted. Some listeners might even feel they are over-volatile in their response to every detailed innuendo, at the expense of firmly drawn, classical line. But their relish of the music wins the day. Once or twice busy figuration in the lower strings emerge a bit bottom-heavy. The recording is true to life.

Additional recommendation ...
As EMI. **Anne-Sophie Mutter** (vn); **Bruno Giuranna** (va); **Mstislav Rostropovich** (vc). DG 427 687-2GH2 — ② 2h 19m DDD 7/89
E flat major. Serenade in D major, Op. 8. **L'Archibudelli.** Sony Classical Vivarte SK53961 —
1h 11m DDD 5/94

Beethoven. Cello Sonatas, Op. 5 — No. 1 in F major; No. 2 in G minor. 12 Variations in F major on "Ein Mädchen oder Weibchen" from "Die Zauberflöte", Op. 66. Seven Variations in E flat major on Mozart's "Bei Männern, welche Liebe fühlen" from "Die Zauberflöte", WoO46. **Mischa Maisky** (vc); **Martha Argerich** (pf). DG 431 801-2GH.

1h 6m DDD 2/92

Beethoven wrote five cello sonatas in all, and this disc, which concentrates on his earlier music for the instrument, has Nos. 1 and 2 (which date from 1796) flanked by two melodious sets of variations on themes from Mozart's *Die Zauberflöte* ("The Magic Flute"). This makes for an attractive programme that is on the light and playful side. The playing of Mischa Maisky and Martha Argerich is so vivid that we feel no monotony even though the *Ein Mädchen oder Weibchen* Variations (which are a bit conventional but make for very pleasant listening) and the First Sonata are in the same key of F major. Above all, it has a freshness that reminds us that we are listening to a young man's music. Maisky's cello tone has plenty of glow and warmth, and Argerich is a sensitive partner, her piano being placed a little backwardly but for that reason never threatening to overpower the cello as might otherwise happen with this gifted and passionate artist. Here, in sum, is impeccable ensemble, agility and wit, together with the broader style of utterance that we require in the slower music of the two sonatas. The special strength of the whole disc is that it conveys an infectious feeling of sheer enjoyment that was undoubtedly felt by Beethoven himself and then communicates in turn to the artists and, finally, ourselves as listeners.

Additional recommendations ...

Nos. 1 and 2. No. 3 in A major, Op. 69. No. 4 in C major, Op. 102 No. 1. No. 5 in D major, Op. 102 No. 2. **Mstislav Rostropovich** (vc); **Sviatoslav Richter** (pf). Philips 412 256-2PH2 — .•* ② lh 49m ADD l/85

Nos. 1-5. Seven Variations in E flat major on Mozart's "Bei Männern, welche Liebe fühlen" from "Die Zauberflöte". 12 Variations in F major on "Ein Mädchen oder Weibchen" from "Die Zauberflöte". Variations on Handel's "See the conqu'ring hero comes" from "Judas Maccabaeus". **Pierre Fournier** (vc); **Friedrich Gulda** (pf). DG Dokumente 437 352-2GDO2 — .•* ② 2h 19m ADD 6/93

Nos. 1ᵃ, 2ᵇ and 4ᶜ. F major Op. 17ᵈ. Piano Trios — B flat major, Op. 1 No. 3ᵉ; E flat major, Op. 70ᶜ; "Archduke"ᵇ. ᵇᶜᵉ**Sándor Vegh.** (vn); **Pablo Casals** (vc); ᶜ**Karl Engel,** ᵃᵇᵉᶠᵍ**Mieczyslaw Horszowski,** ᵃ**Wilhelm Kempf** (pfs). Philips 438 520-2PM3 — .•* ③ 3h 20m ADD 3/94 𝄞ₚ

Nos. 1-5. Seven Variations in E flat major on Mozart's "Bei Männern, welche Liebe fühlen" from "Die Zauberflöte". 12 Variations in F major on "Ein Mädchen oder Weibchen" from "Die Zauberflöte". **Pablo Casals** (vc); **Rudolf Serkin** (pf). Sony Classical Casals Edition mono SMK58985 — .•* ② 2h 28m ADD 5/94 ▲

Beethoven. COMPLETE VIOLIN SONATAS. **Itzhak Perlman** (vn); **Vladimir Ashkenazy** (pf). Decca Ovation 421 453-2DM4.
No. 1 in D major, Op. 12 No. 1 (from SXL6790, 7/77); No. 2 in A major, Op. 12 No. 2 (SXL6632, 2/75); No. 3 in E flat major, Op. 12 No. 3 (SXL6789, 12/76); No. 4 in A minor, Op. 23; No. 5 in F major, Op. 24, "Spring" (both from SXL6736, 7/76); No. 6 in A major, Op. 30 No. 1; No. 7 in C minor, Op. 30 No. 2 (both from SXL6791, 12/77); No. 8 in G major, Op. 30 No. 3 (SXL6789); No. 9 in A major, Op. 47, "Kreutzer" (SXL6632); No. 10 in G major, Op. 96 (SXL6790).

.•* ④ 3h 59m ADD l/89   𝄞ₚ Ⓑ

Although Beethoven designated these works as "for piano and violin", following Mozart's example, it is unlikely that he thought of the piano as leading the proceedings, or the violin either, for that matter: both instruments are equal partners and in that sense this is true chamber music. These are artists of the first rank and there is much pleasure to be derived from this set. Such an imaginative musician as Ashkenazy brings great subtlety to these works composed by a supreme pianist-composer. And the better the pianist is in this musc, the better does the violinist play. Discernment is matched by spontaneity and the whole series is remarkably fine, while their celebrated performance of the *Kreutzer* Sonata (listed under the next review) has quite superb eloquence and vitality. The recording boasts unusually truthful violin sound capturing all the colour of Perlman's playing — and that is saying something. Ashkenazy's vivid attack is always faithful to the Beethoven idiom.

Additional recommendations ...

Complete Violin Sonatas. **Sir Yehudi Menuhin** (vn); **Wilhelm Kempff** (pf). DG 415 874-2GCM4 — .•* ④ 4h 32m ADD 6/87 𝄞ₚ Ⓑ

Complete Violin Sonatas. **Arthur Grumiaux** (vn); **Clara Haskil** (pf). Philips Legendary Classics mono 422 140-2PLC3 — .•* ③ 3h 34m ADD l/89 𝄞ₚ Ⓑ ▲

Beethoven. Violin Sonatas — No. 5 in F major, Op. 24, "Spring"; No. 8 in G major, Op. 30 No. 3; No. 9 in A major, Op. 47, "Kreuzer". **Pinchas Zukerman** (vn); **Daniel Barenboim** (pf). EMI Studio Plus CDM7 64631-2. Recorded in 1971-73.

.•* lh 18m ADD 3/93   Ⓑ

This generously filled mid-price disc is a winner, for although the recordings date from the early 1970s, the sound has come up well in its digital transfer. The only reservation is that

Barenboim's piano in the *Spring* Sonata seems more closely balanced than Zukerman's violin: we can hear every detail of the violin part; it is only the balance which gives grounds for doubt, and one soon gets used to it. There is no doubt, though, about the quality of the performances of these three works, of which the ones with nicknames are deservedly the most popular among the ten that Beethoven wrote for these instruments. Zukerman and Barenboim do not hurry the music or force it expressively, so that all sounds natural. Not only that, their playing is also in scale and even intimate, as chamber music should be — in contrast to the over-projected performances offered by some of today's players. This, of course, is ideal for listening in one's own living room, in other words in much the same circumstances as prevailed when these works were written. We might like the Minuet middle movement of the G major Sonata to dance along a bit more freely, but such is the elegance of the playing that we are persuaded of the viability of the tempo, at least on this occasion, and it does bring a good contrast with the rapid (but unrushed) finale that follows. The performance of the *Kreutzer* Sonata is as noble as the music itself, something which one guesses will be the case as soon as one hears Zukerman's aristocratic delivery of the difficult double-stopped opening, played with impeccable intonation. This is not the most fiery account of the first movement and finale, but its warmth is still tempered by authority, and the variation-form slow movement is beautifully shaped.

Additional recommendations ...
Nos. 5 and 9. **Itzhak Perlman** (vn); **Vladimir Ashkenazy** (pf). Decca 410 554-2DH — .•'
1h 2m ADD 11/83 Ⓑ
Nos. 5 and 9. **Thomas Zehetmair** (vn); **Malcolm Frager** (fp). Teldec Digital Experience 9031-75856-2 — .•' 59m DDD 6/92 Ⓑ 🖊
Nos. 5, 9 and 10. **Zino Francescatti** (vn); **Robert Casadesus** (pf). Sony Classical Essential Classics MK46342 — .•' 1h 16m ADD 3/91 Ⓑ ▲
Nos. 5 and 9. **Takako Nishizaki** (vn); **Jenö Jandó** (pf). Naxos 8 550283-2 — .• 56m DDD 3/91 Ⓑ
Nos. 8-10. **Jascha Heifetz** (vn); **Emmanuel Bay** (pf). RCA Victor Gold Seal mono GD87706 — .•' 1h 12m ADD 11/88 Ⓑ ▲

Beethoven. VARIATIONS.
Schumann. Etudes symphoniques, Opp. 13 and posth. **Alfred Brendel** (pf). Philips 432 093-2PH. Recorded in 1990.
Variations — Six in F major on an Original Theme, Op. 34; Five in D major on "Rule Britannia", WoO79; Six in G major on "Nel cor più non mi sento" from Paisiello's "La mollinara", WoO70.

.•' 59m DDD 3/92

Throughout his life Beethoven was scarcely less drawn to variations than sonata form. Brendel includes the early Paisiello set as an example of the inherited classical tradition, but clearly enjoys himself most in the surprises of the composer's early thirties. "Worked out in quite a new manner" was Beethoven's own description of his Op. 34, in which he changes tempo, time-signature and even key for each successive number. In the *Rule Britannia* set we're not only given a "stylization of the sea in its various ruffles and wind speeds" but also racy humour, for "Beethoven treats the imperial folk-song with a broad wink" as Brendel himself puts it in insert-notes as stimulating and fresh as his own playing. The disc's main interest nevertheless centres in Schumann's *Etudes symphoniques* (or *Etudes en forme de variations* as he renamed his later revision) in a performance including the five posthumously published Eusebius-like variations rejected by the composer from both versions. Admitting to no longer being able to do without them ("since it is their inclusion that makes Schumann's Op. 13 one of his finest compositions") Brendel in fact inserts them so judiciously and imparts so splendid a romantic fervour and continuity to the performance as a whole that all doubts about defiance of Schumann's own wishes are silenced — at least temporarily! Made at The Maltings, Snape, the recording is wholly truthful.

Additional recommendations ...
Variations, Op. 34. 15 Variations and a Fugue on an Original Theme in E flat major, Op. 35, "Eroica". Rondos, Op. 51 — No. 1 in C major; No. 2 in G major. Bagatelle in A minor, WoO59, "Fur Elise". **Louis Lortie** (pf). Chandos CHAN8616 — .•' 58m DDD 10/90
Variations, Op. 34. Six Variations, WoO70. 15 Variations and a Fugue. 32 Variations on an Original Theme in C minor, WoO80. **Jenö Jandó** (pf). Naxos 8 550676 — .• 54m DDD 9/93

Six Variations, Op. 34 (same recording as reviewed above). Piano Sonata No. 12 in A flat major, Op. 26. **Mozart.** *Piano Sonata No. 11 in A major, K331/300i. Nine Variations in D major on a minuet by J. P. Duport, K573.* **Alfred Brendel** (pf). Philips Insignia 436 306-2PM — .•ʼ Ih 8m ADD/DDD
10/93

New review
Beethoven. Six Variations in F major on an Original Theme, Op. 34[a]. Six Variations in D major, Op. 76. 15 Variations and a Fugue on an Original Theme in E flat major, Op. 35, "Eroica"[a].
Chopin. Four Scherzos[b] — No. 1 in B minor, Op. 20; No. 2 in B flat minor, Op. 31; No. 3 in C sharp minor, Op. 39; No. 4 in E major, Op. 54.
Schumann. Etudes symphoniques, Opp. 13 and posth[a]. Bunte Blätter, Op. 99[b]. **Sviatoslav Richter.** Olympia OCD339[a] and OCD338[b]. Recorded by Eurodisc 1970-77.

.•ʼ ② Ih I7m Ih I5m ADD 4/94   𝄞 p

Remarkably well-recorded considering the source, one performance after another here is so memorable as to rank among the best versions around of the piece in question. There is such richness in the Beethoven Variations that it seems pointless and unfair to highlight any one in particular. Nevertheless, the *Eroica* Variations end with Richter playing most pianists under the table. He is not usually thought of as a very credible Chopin player, and yet he strides through the four *Scherzos* with an abundance of technique and deftly coloured textures that make this version a definite front-runner. His Schumann, on the other hand, has always been dazzling, because he has a temperament that convincingly responds to the extreme swings in mood. The reading of the *Etudes symphoniques* is an overwhelming experience. The fourth of the supplementary variations emerges as an exotic lament of ravishing beauty and the pianist's very large hands enable him to attack the chords of the finale with ferocious confidence. Well-chosen and excellent in sound, these performances should not be missed.

Beethoven. THE BEETHOVEN BROADWOOD FORTEPIANO. **Melvyn Tan** (fp). EMI CDC7 54526-2. Recorded in 1992.
Seven Bagatelles, Op. 33. 11 Bagatelles, Op. 119. Fantasia in G minor, Op. 77. Seven Variations in C major on "God save the King", WoO78. Five Variations in D major on "Rule Britannia", WoO79.

.•ʼ Ih IIm DDD I2/92   𝄞 p 🖋

A collector's piece, this, and primarily because of the fortepiano itself — none other than Beethoven's own six-octave Broadwood (then the world's most 'modern' keyboard) presented to him by its renowned English manufacturers in 1817. Much the worse for wear it was subsequently acquired by Liszt, who in his turn passed it on to the Hungarian National Museum where only two years ago it was restored (by the American-born David Winston) to a playable condition. Entrusted with it on a brief tour, Melvyn Tan recorded this recital in May 1992, at Forde Abbey in Dorset. Nothing in his discerningly chosen programme better demonstrates what warmth, strength, range and bravura can be drawn from it than the wholly unpredictable, improvisatory G minor *Fantasia,* which but for its date (1809) might be thought to have been written for that very purpose. In view of the instrument's country of origin it was a happy thought to begin and end with the pungent *God save the King* and *Rule Britannia,* both of 1803. The main musical substance nevertheless comes in the Bagatelles, miniatures yes, but as revealing of the composer's kaleidoscopic daily mood-changes as the pages of a diary. Characteristically, Tan slightly hurries one or two slower numbers which need more time to sing or speak, and just now and again he adds to the music's in-built caprice with a few little rhythmic idiosyn-crasies of his own. But his playing remains a constant delight for its spontaneity, colour and spirit. The recording cannot be faulted.

Beethoven. 33 Variations on a Waltz by Diabelli, Op. 120. **Alfred Brendel** (pf). Philips 426 232-2PH. Recorded in 1988.

.•ʼ 53m DDD 8/90   Ⓑ 𝄞 p

Beethoven's *Diabelli Variations* respond better to pianists who think between the notes than to
those who take them at face value. Alfred Brendel's achievement is twofold: on the one hand he

produces a refined, beautifully integrated body of tone, while on the other, he manages to quietly underline the very different character of each individual variation while keeping a watchful eye on the structural 'long view'. The result is a consistently compelling trip through one of Beethoven's most testing obstacle courses, and by the time we reach the far end — a satisfied, almost tongue-in-cheek *Tempo di minuetto moderato* — we doubly appreciate everything that went before. This is wholly magnificent music: playful, angry, profound, searching (Variations 29-31), sublime (try Variation 24, the Fughetta, more beautifully played here than anywhere else on disc) and cumulatively immense. It's also one of the most far-reaching of Beethoven's late works (although sketches for it date from as early as 1819), and is often prophetic of Liszt, Schumann, and even the music of our own century in its harmonic boldness. The recording is close but clear, and my only regret is that Brendel's own fascinating study on the work — which is printed in the booklet in French, German and Italian — is not printed in English, although William Kinderman's essay (included in the place of Brendel's) is both useful and informative.

Additional recommendations …

Diabelli Variations. **Stephen Kovacevich** (pf). Philips Concert Classics 422 969-2PCC — .• 54m ADD 8/90 Ⓑ

Diabelli Variations. 11 Bagatelles, Op. 119. **Rudolf Serkin** (pf). CBS Masterworks Portrait CD44837 — .•˙ lh 6m ADD 8/90 Ⓑ

Diabelli Variations. Two Variations on an Original Theme in C minor, WoO80. **Benjamin Frith** (pf). ASV CDDCA715 — .•˙ lh lm DDD ll/91 Ⓑ

Diabelli Variations. Piano Sonata No. 31 in A flat major, Op. 110. Coupled with music by **C. P. E. Bach, Bach, Chopin, Mozart** *and* **Schubert.** **Mieczyslaw Horszowski** (pf). Pearl GEMMCDS9979 — .•˙ ② 2h 35m ADD 12/93 ⁹ₚ

New review

Beethoven. COMPLETE PIANO SONATAS. **Richard Goode.** Elektra Nonesuch 7559-79328-2. Items marked [a] from 7559-79213-2 (4/92), [b] 979 212-2 (9/90), [c] 979 211-2 (9/89). Remainder new to UK.
No. 1 in F minor, Op. 2 No. 1; No. 2 in A major, Op. 2 No. 2; No. 3 in C major, Op. 2 No. 3; No. 4 in E flat major, Op. 7; No. 5 in C minor, Op. 10 No. 1[a]; No. 6 in F major, Op. 10 No. 2[a]; No. 7 in D major, Op. 10 No. 3[a]; No. 8 in C minor, Op. 13, "Pathétique"; No. 9 in E major, Op. 14 No. 1; No. 10 in G major, Op. 14 No. 2; No. 11 in B flat major, Op. 22; No. 12 in A flat major, Op. 26; No. 13 in E flat major, Op. 27 No. 1, "quasi una fantasia"; No. 14 in C sharp minor, Op. 27 No. 2, "Moonlight"; No. 15 in D major, Op. 28, "Pastoral"; No. 16 in G major, Op. 31 No. 1[b]; No. 17 in D minor, Op. 31 No. 2, "Tempest"[b]; No. 18 in E flat major, Op. 31 No. 3[b]; No. 19 in G minor, Op. 49 No. 1; No. 20 in G major, Op. 49 No. 2; No. 21 in C minor, Op. 53, "Waldstein"; No. 22 in F major, Op. 54; No. 23 in F minor, Op. 57, "Appassionata"; No. 24 in F sharp major, Op. 78; No. 25 in G major, Op. 79; No. 26 in E flat major, Op. 81a, "Les adieux"; No. 27 in E minor, Op. 90; No. 28 in A major, Op. 101[c]; No. 29 in B flat major, Op. 106, "Hammerklavier"[c]; No. 30 in E major, Op. 109[c]; No. 31 in A flat major, Op. 110[c]; No. 32 in C minor, Op. 111[c].

.•˙ ⑩⑩ l0h 8m DDD 3/94   ⁹ₚ ⁹ₛ Ⓑ

Rather like Mieczyslaw Horszowski, who was one of his mentors, Goode as a soloist has for many years been hiding his light under a bushel. If you already know him in this capacity, that is likely to be through his broadcasts. For until the last few years he has been active principally as an ensemble player, in chamber music, a field in which he excels — as Horszowski and Goode's other mentor at the Curtis Institute, Rudolf Serkin, did. He is American and his reputation in the USA is considerable, but in the UK his currently listed recordings, on Nonesuch and RCA, are still few, and mostly of chamber music. All this by way of preamble because there is nothing whatsoever about him in the Nonesuch booklet. Whoever commissioned the long essay for the booklet from Michael Steinberg did the set a fine service. The production and engineering are credited to Max Wilcox and his expertise and care leaves one with little to quibble with. The sound and microphone balances rates from good to very good and they're pretty consistent over the ten CDs. The lower end of the dynamic range is very well defined, perhaps better than the other. In the first movement of the *Hammerklavier* Sonata and the *Scherzo* of the A flat Sonata, Op. 110, Wilcox hasn't been completely successful in dissuading Goode from stamping on the pedal, but this Serkinesque habit is not obtrusive elsewhere. There is some unevenness of achievement in Goode's playing but the level, in general, is wonderfully high, with no lapses from grace. Everything demands assessment in the company of the best there is. The interpretation of the A major Sonata, Op. 101 is one of the finest ever put on record. Reservations? You may have a doubt as to whether the playing in this sonata or that represents everything Goode is capable of: sometimes he disappoints, slightly, by appearing to hold back from the listener — through temperamental reserve? — the boldness and fullness of communciation the greatest players achieve. One might say that, for all their insight and illumination, some of the performances lack the final leap and a degree of transcendence. In the first movement of the A flat, Op. 110 Goode sounds as if he's trying too hard. Yet he is marvellous later in the sonata, at the close of the reprise of the *Arioso*, taking the listener through the 'heartbeat' chords into the inversion of the Fugue and by way of the difficult transition (which gave Beethoven much trouble) to the serentiy and triumph of the final pages with a sureness and quality of imagination that are exceptional. If this isn't Beethoven interpretation of the highest class it is impossible to say what is. One might prefer an even stiller slow movement of the *Hammerklavier* Sonata, but that and a few other small regrets are probably attributable to the business of record making. Consideration of that enormous span of slow music in the *Hammerklavier* brings to mind the great 'set-piece' slow movements of the early sonatas as well: in Op. 2 Nos. 2 and 3, Op. 7, Op. 10 Nos. 1 and 3. Those processional, inward, even monumental and ineluctable qualities which they share demand intense concentration on both sides of the microphone and Goode makes them eloquent, even though they could smile a little more. In Op. 14 No. 2 in G he is delicious — perfect. There is abundant wit, as he plays it, in the first movement of Op. 10 No. 2 in F too. A quality often to be observed in Goode is allure. Maybe that is why his playing is so very likeable: the finish of his playing, technical and musical, is immaculate but on top of that he is exciting. His sound always makes you listen. His feeling for it and for fine gradations of sound from one end of his wide dynamic range to the other are those of a virtuoso and inform everything he does. And when he's more obviously on virtuoso territory, as in the *Waldstein* and *Appassionata*, he responds to their demands for brilliance and thrilling projection as to the manner born. One is reminded that this man had five years of Russian-school training; he really can play. Well, brilliance in Beethoven is commonly met with. One could say that sheer musical competence, of Richard Goode's order, is harder to come by. He is constantly inside the music, not on the outside looking in, and what a lively, cultivated, lucid and stimulating guide he is. There is nothing diffident or half-hearted about the way he makes this cycle of Beethoven resound wonderfully, the earlier sonatas appearing as no less masterly or characteristic of their composer than the later. Time, and other opinions, will be needed before one can rank this set in relations to all the others, though it is undoubtedly an important one, superior to many, and will last. How gratifying that a musician-pianist who has avoided being hoovered up by anyone's publicity machine and has been quietly getting better these past 30 years should now float to the top.

Additional recommendations ...
Complete Piano Sonatas. **Alfred Brendel.** Philips 412 575-2PH11 — .·' ①① 10h 59m ADD 1/85 Ⓑ
Complete Piano Sonatas. **Daniel Barenboim.** EMI CZS7 62863-2 — .· ①① 11h 27m ADD 10/90 Ⓑ
Complete Piano Sonatas. **Wilhelm Kempff.** DG 429 306-2GX9 — .· ⑨ 9h 54m ADD 3/91 ⁹ₚ Ⓑ
Complete Piano Sonatas. **Artur Schnabel.** EMI Références mono CHS7 63765-2 — .·' ⑧ 10h 5m ADD 7/91 Ⓑ
Complete Piano Sonatas. Piano Variations. **Claudio Arrau.** Philips 432 301-2PM11 — .·' ①① 12h 19m ADD 1/92 Ⓑ
Nos. 1, 5, 6, 9, 10, 13, 14, 15 and 25. **Alfred Brendel** (pf). Vox Box 115772-2 — .· ② 2h 25m ADD 9/93 Ⓑ
Nos. 8, 14 and 23. **Daniel Barenboim.** EMI CDC7 47345-2 — .·' 1h 2m ADD 9/86 Ⓑ
Nos. 8, 14, 15 and 24. **Wilhelm Kempff** (pf). DG Galleria 415 834-2GGA — .·' ADD 1h 8/87 Ⓑ
Nos. 14, 21 and 23. **Vladimir Ashkenazy** (pf). Decca Ovation 417 732-2DM — .·' 1h 6m ADD 12/87 Ⓑ
Nos. 17, 18 and 26. **Murray Perahia** (pf). CBS Masterworks CD43419 — .·' 1h 1m DDD 2/88 Ⓑ
Nos. 28-32. **Maurizio Pollini** (pf). DG 419 199-2GH2 — .·' ② 2h 6m DDD 12/86 Ⓑ

Jenö Jandó's excellent complete super-bargain set of the sonatas are available on Naxos on two sets comprising five CDs each (8 505002 and 8 505003). They are also available on ten separate CDs, the details of which follow (the volume numbers do not indicate the numerical order of the sonatas).

(Vol. 3) *Nos. 1-3*. Naxos 8 550150 — . lh 7m DDD 12/90 Ⓑ
(Vol. 5) *Nos. 5, 6, 7 and 25*. Naxos 8 550161 — . lh 3m DDD 12/90 Ⓑ
(Vol. 8) *Nos. 4, 13, 19, 20 and 22*. Naxos 8 550167 — . lh 8m DDD 12/90 Ⓑ
(Vol. 6) *Nos. 9, 10, 24, 27 and 28*. Naxos 8 550162 — . lh 12m DDD 12/90 Ⓑ
(Vol. 1) *Nos. 8, 14 and 23*. Naxos 8 550045 — . 56m DDD 2/91 Ⓑ
(Vol. 10). *Nos. 15 and 33-38*. Naxos 8 550255 — . lh 9m DDD 2/91 Ⓑ
(Vol. 2) *Nos. 17, 21 and 26*. Naxos 8 550054 — . lh 3m DDD 2/91 Ⓑ
(Vol. 7) *Nos. 12, 16 and 18*. Naxos 8 550166 — . lh 4m DDD 6/91 Ⓑ
(Vol. 9) *Nos. 11 and 29*. Naxos 8 550234 — . lh 4m DDD 6/91 Ⓑ
(Vol. 4) *Nos. 30, 31 and 32*. Naxos 8 550151 — . lh 4m DDD 6/91 Ⓑ

Beethoven. Piano Sonatas — No. 1 in F minor, Op. 2 No. 1; No. 2 in A major, Op. 2 No. 2; No. 3 in C major, Op. 2 No. 3. **Melvyn Tan** (fp). EMI Reflexe CDC7 54657-2. Recorded in 1992.

| lh 13m DDD 5/93 Ⓑ |

Only after launching his Beethoven cycle with three of the most popular middle period sonatas (the *Waldstein*, *Appassionata* and *Les Adieux*) and following them with the three of Op. 31 and Op. 10 does Melvyn Tan allow us to hear how the great series of 32 actually began. As with previous releases in the cycle he plays not Beethoven's recently restored Broadwood but a Derek Adlam fortepiano modelled on an early nineteenth-century instrument of Anton Walter. And nothing better reveals the richness and variety of sonority he draws from it, in the very favourable recording venue of Forde Abbey in Dorset, than the *Adagio* of Op. 2 No. 3. If his tempo here might be thought just a little too fast to convey the full impact of Beethoven's plunge from the home key of C into the brave new world of E, the other two slow movements are judiciously paced, with a splendid inexorability of rhythmic tread in the *Largo appassionato* of Op. 2 No. 2 in A. For the rest he captures the 25-year-old composer's exploratory *élan* with an imaginative freshness and vitality all his own, only occasionally causing a raised eyebrow when underlining *sforzando* markings with a momentary disruption of pulse.

Additional recommendation ...
Nos. 1-3. **John O'Conor** (pf). Telarc CD80214 — .⁰ lh 7m DDD 9/90 Ⓑ

Beethoven. Piano Sonatas — No. 5 in C minor, Op. 10 No. 1; No. 6 in F major, Op. 10 No. 2; No. 7 in D major, Op. 10 No. 3. **Louis Lortie** (pf). Chandos CHAN9101. Recorded in 1991.

| 56m DDD 3/93 Ⓑ |

Written in his late twenties, Beethoven's three piano sonatas of Op. 10 point firmly forward towards romanticism in their sheer energy, drama and pathos, the latter quality being clearly exemplified in the *Largo e mesto* movement of the final D major work, with which Beethoven himself moved listeners to tears. In this famous slow movement, the Quebec-born pianist Louis Lortie does not let the music sink under excessive weight and solemnity (he takes less than eight minutes here where one British pianist on record requires more than 11), but is none the less powerfully expressive and moving. In general, this fine young artist brings a splendid crispness and energy to all three of these pieces, to say nothing of the dexterity he gives us in the *Presto* finale of the F major Sonata. He can be unusually forceful and brusque tonally, and although he never quite pushes his piano beyond what it will accept without protest, there are places where he gets dangerously close to that point. However, elsewhere his playing also shows the sensitiv-ity of his ear, while even in quick and vigorous outer movements, such as those of the C minor work which comes first in the set, he will sometimes linger tellingly over an expressive detail so that the music never becomes merely well-drilled and indeed has a real feeling of spontaneity. Thus vitality and eloquence go hand-in-hand in these performances, and gives them much freshness. The sound of Lortie's modern grand may at first seem brittle and reverberant in the space of this large concert-hall, but the ear does become accustomed to it and one may well feel that it suits these early Beethoven sonatas better than the more cushioned and enclosed studio sound that we often hear.

Additional recommendation ...
Nos. 5-7 and 25. **Melvyn Tan** (fp). EMI CDC7 54207-2 — .⁰ lh 5m DDD 6/92 Ⓑ

New review

Beethoven. PIANO SONATAS. **Alfred Brendel** Philips Duo 438 730-2PM2. Recorded 1970-77.
No. 8 in C minor, Op. 13, "Pathétique". No. 14 in C sharp minor, Op. 27 No. 2, "Moonlight". No. 15 in D major, Op. 28, "Pastoral". No. 17 in D minor, Op. 31 No. 2, "Tempest". No. 21 in C major, Op. 53, "Waldstein". No. 23 in F minor, Op. 57, "Appassionata". No. 26 in E flat major, Op. 81*a*, "Les Adieux".

2h 32m ADD 4/94

This reissue, containing seven of Beethoven's most popular named sonatas admirably played by Alfred Brendel, is in every way an outstanding bargain, well worth obtaining, even if duplication is involved. All the performances are authoritative and offer consistently distinguished playing, while the recording is very realistic indeed. The *Tempest* resonates in the memory and the central movements of the *Pastoral* are most beautifully shaped. The *Pathétique, Moonlight* and *Appassionata* all bring deeply satisfying readings that are compellingly conceived and freshly executed. This set can be recommended without any reservations whatsoever.

Additional recommendations ...
Nos. 21, 23 and 26. **Emil Gilels** (pf). DG 419 162-2GH — ADD 8/86
Nos. 21 and 31. **Stephen Kovacevich.** EMI CDC7 54896-2 — 53m DDD 2/94
Nos. 21, 23 and 27. **Barry Douglas.** RCA Victor Red Seal 09026 61280-2 — 1h 6m DDD 6/94
Nos. 30, 31 and 32. **Vladimir Feltsman.** Music Masters 67098-2 — 1h 6m DDD 6/94
Nos. 14, 21 and 23. **Vladimir Horowitz.** Sony Classical SK53467 — 1h 4m ADD 7/94

New review

Beethoven. Piano Sonatas — No. 9 in E major, Op. 14 No. 1[a]; No. 11 in B flat major, Op. 22[b]; No. 12 in A flat major, Op. 26; No. 27 in E minor, Op. 90.
Haydn. Keyboard Sonatas — No. 39 in D major, HobXVI/24; No. 62 in E flat major, HobXVI/52.
Weber. Piano Sonata No. 3 in D minor, J206. **Sviatoslav Richter** (pf). Philips 438 617-2PH2. Item marked [a] from SAL3457 (9/64), [b] SAL3456 (9/64), remainder new to UK.

② **2h 11m ADD/DDD**

Richter's greatness is due partly to his limitless artistic and technical ability and partly to his extraordinarily wide range of repertoire. His unique capacity to surprise derives from a profound understanding of musical processes, and his concerts are events in a continuous sequence of musical discovery. In Haydn's E flat Piano Sonata, Richter's extreme sensitivity to detail produces a captivating performance of great delicacy and charm. Haydn's D major Sonata provides further evidence of Richter's wholly unselfconscious approach: the opening movement is expressed with transparent clarity; the *cantabile Adagio* is beautifully judged, and the finale has an engaging ethnic gait. He recorded Beethoven's Piano Sonatas, Op. 14 No. 1 and Op. 22 in 1963 and, though there is a noticeably drier quality to the sound, the performances have retained a remarkable freshness of resonance. The dramatic intensity of the E major work, for example, is heightened by Richter's tendency to controversial extremes of tempo in both directions. Specifically, Richter rejects the *Allegretto* marking for the second movement in favour of a speed that is closer to *Adagio* to which the finale provides a scintillating conclusion. His wide dynamic and expressive range in both of these sonatas creates effects that are quite simply miraculous. The versions of the Sonatas, Op. 26 and Op. 90 are new digital recordings, but there are no signs that Richter has lost any of his interpretative power or originality. His command of broad structural relationships is as assured as ever, as is his scrupulous attention to the music's harmonic and motivic detail. His comprehensive exploitation of the music's intrinsic possibilities generates great energy and pace as a means of intensifying its natural warmth and expressiveness. The set concludes with a startling performance of Weber's Third Piano Sonata. The first movement, marked *Allegro feroce*, contrasts a powerfully driven opening with music of simple melodic charm which, after a richly diverse variation slow movement, culminates in a bravura finale of breathtaking virtuosity. As is so often the case with Richter's performances, then, these are landmarks in piano playing which no lover of piano music should be without.

Additional recommendations ...
| Nos. 27, 28 and 32. **Stephen Kovacevich.** EMI CDC7 54599-2 — 1h DDD 10/92

Beethoven. Piano Sonatas — No. 17 in D minor, Op. 31 No. 2, "Tempest"; No. 18 in E flat major, Op. 31 No. 3; No. 26 in E flat major, Op. 81*a*, "Les Adieux". **Murray Perahia** (pf). CBS Masterworks CD42319.

Ih Im DDD 2/88

"I am by no means satisfied with my works hitherto, and I intend to make a fresh start", so Beethoven is reputed to have remarked before embarking on the three sonatas comprising his Op. 31 in 1802. Ominous symptoms of deafness were already overshadowing his private life, as the flanking movements of the D minor Sonata betray even if feeling runs too deep to ruffle the tranquil surface of the central *Adagio*. Perahia's texture is crystalline (with skilful half-pedalling in the problematical recitatives in the opening movement of the D minor work) and even amidst the *con fuoco* of the E flat Sonata's finale rhythm is held on a tautly controlled rein. Whereas these two sonatas were studio recordings, the venue for *Les Adieux* was a warmer, more reverberant concert hall. Here we rightly meet a more impressionably romantic Perahia making every passing innuendo wholly his own in response to Beethoven's overtly expressed sadness, yearning and joy at the departure from — and return to — Vienna at the time of the Napoleonic invasion. Ingratiating in tone throughout a wide dynamic range, perfectly propor-tioned and finally excitingly brilliant, this performance has with good reason been widely hailed as "one of the most complete realizations of this work that has appeared in recent years".

Additional recommendations ...
Nos. 16-18. **Alfred Brendel.** Philips 438 134-2PH — **Ih 12m DDD 7/93**
Nos. 17, 25 and 28. **Bruno-Leonardo Gelber.** Denon CO-75245 — **54m DDD 1/94**

New review
Beethoven. Piano Sonatas — No. 21 in C major, Op. 53, "Waldstein"; No. 24 in F sharp major, Op. 78; No. 31 in A flat major, Op. 110. **Stephen Kovacevich** (pf). EMI CDC7 54896-2. Recorded in 1992.

53m DDD 2/94

Few pianists today — not Brendel, not Ashkenazy, not Serkin — can free themselves of self-awareness enough to find the tender simplicity of the opening *Moderato cantabile* of Beethoven's Op. 110. Kovacevich can, and he goes on to fill each moment of figuration and trilling with light. His finale has a mesmeric inwardness generated by the seemingly infinite nuances he can find in a single repeated note. A steadiness of purpose in the *Arioso* leads naturally into the quiet self-assurance of the effortless building of the Fuga. The coupling — with the little Op. 78 and the *Waldstein* — makes for a sensitively built recital in its own right. Again, Kovacevich's skill at drawing the listener in marks the Op. 78 Sonata, with its effervescent figurework and spontan-eous major-minor changes. The same nimble fingerwork, over a thrumming bass, makes the *Waldstein* positively tingle with life: Kovacevich's joy in the physical excitement and momentum of the writing is equalled by his strength in delineating the song at its heart.

Additional recommendation ...
Nos. 21, 23 and 26. **Melvyn Tan** (fp). EMI Reflexe CDC7 49330-2 — **Ih 3m DDD 5/88**

Beethoven. Piano Sonata No. 29 in B flat major, Op. 106, "Hammerklavier". **Emil Gilels** (pf). DG 410 527-2GH. From 410 527-1GH (12/83).

49m DDD 2/84

The great Soviet pianist Emil Gilels died in 1986, not many months before his seventieth birthday, and left behind him a major legacy of recorded performances. This account of the *Hammerklavier* is a fine memorial. The work is very long and exceedingly taxing technically and the pianist must plumb its often turbulent emotional depth, not least in the enormous 20-minute slow movement which requires deep concentration from player and listener alike. After the recording was made in 1983, the pianist told his producer: "I feel that the weight has been lifted, but I feel very empty." Gilels manages to give it more tonal beauty and warmth than most pianists, without any loss of strength or momentum. His is measured and beautiful playing, and finely recorded too.

Additional recommendations ...
Nos. 27-29. **John O'Conor.** Telarc CD80335 — .·'' lh l3m DDD 8/93 ⓑ
Nos. 28 and 29. **Mieczyslaw Horszowski.** Relief CR911021 — .·'' lh 5m ADD 12/93 ꟼₚ ▲ ⓑ
Nos. 28 and 29. **Vladimir Ashkenazy** (pf). Decca 436 735-2DH — .·'' 66m DDD 4/94 ꟼₚ ⓑ

Beethoven. PIANO SONATAS. **Maurizio Pollini** (pf). DG 429 569/70-2GH. From 419
199-2GH2 (12/86). Recorded 1975-77.
429 569-2GH — No. 28 in A major, Op. 101; No. 29 in B flat major, Op. 106,
"Hammerklavier". *429 570-2GH* — No. 30 in E major, Op. 109; No. 31 in A flat major,
Op. 110; No. 32 in C minor, Op. 111.

.·'' ② lh 3m lh 2 AAD 7/90   ꟼₚ ⓑ

If Beethoven's 32 piano sonatas may be likened to a range of foothills and mountains, then these
five sonatas are the last lofty pinnacles, difficult of access but offering great rewards to both
pianist and listener. No library is complete without them. Pollini's playing must be praised for
its interpretative mastery as well as its exemplary keyboard skill. These are prizewinning issues
which have been widely admired, not least for the magnificent last sonata of all, Op. 111, and
the recordings hardly show their age.

Additional recommendations ...
Nos. 30-32. **John O'Conor.** Telarc CD80261 — .·'' lh 5m DDD 11/92 ⓑ
Nos. 27-32. **Solomon.** EMI Références mono/stereo CHS7 64708-2 — .·'' ② 2h 2lm ADD 7/93
ꟼₚ ▲
Nos. 27-32. **Alfred Brendel.** Philips Duo 438 374-2PM2 — .·'' ② 2h 28m ADD 8/93 ꟼₚ ⓑ

Beethoven. LIEDER[a].
Brahms. LIEDER. **Dietrich Fischer-Dieskau** (bar); **Jörg Demus** (pf). DG 415 189-2GH.
Text and translations included. Items marked [a] from SLPM139216/18 (2/67), [b] SLPM138644
(10/61), [c] SLPM138011 (5/59).
Beethoven: An die ferne Geliebte. Op 98. Adelaide, Op. 46. Zärtliche Liebe, WoO123.
L'amante impaziente, Op. 82 Nos. 3 and 4. In questa tomba oscura, WoO133. Maigesang,
Op. 52 No. 4. Es war einmal ein König, Op. 75 No. 3. **Brahms:** Vier ernste Gesänge,
Op. 121[b]. O wüsst' ich doch den Weg zurück, Op. 63 No. 8[c]. Auf dem Kirchhofe, Op. 105
No. 4[c]. Alte Liebe, Op. 72 No. 1[c]. Verzagen, Op. 72 No. 4[c]. Nachklang, Op. 59 No. 4[c].
Feldeinsamkeit, Op. 86 No. 2[c].

.·'' lh llm ADD 9/85   ▲

Beethoven's small oeuvre of songs is rich and varied. The six songs of *An die ferne Geliebte* follow the
unrequited lover's reflections on his beloved, with the piano weaving its way between the individual
songs setting the mood and gently assisting the narrative; indeed, it even has the last word. Fischer-
Dieskau's intelligent and intense delivery are assisted by his warm tone and easy legato. He adds
Beethoven's great song *Adelaide* and, among others, three Italian settings, lightening the tone and raising
the spirits for the second half of the programme. Brahms's *Vier ernste Gesänge*, drawn from the image-
laden texts of the Old Testament, reflect on man's fate in the great order of life and more particularly
on death. The songs have a solemn character and settle in the lower register of the baritone's vocal
range, a range that finds a particularly appropriate tone-colour in Fischer-Dieskau's expressive voice.
The remainder of the recital draws on similarly severe songs, making for a well-devised programme
with a consistent theme. Jörg Demus accompanies sensitively and the elderly recordings sound well.

Beethoven. Mass in C major, Op. 86[a]. Ah perfido!, Op. 65[b]. Meeresstille und glückliche
Fahrt, Op. 112[c]. [ab]**Charlotte Margiono** (sop); [a]**Catherine Robbin** (mez); [a]**William
Kendall** (ten); [a]**Alistair Miles** (bass); [ac]**Monteverdi Choir; Orchestre Révolutionnaire
et Romantique/John Eliot Gardiner.** Archiv Produktion 435 391-2AH. Texts and
translations included. Items marked [a] recorded in 1989, [b] 1991.

.·'' lh 2m DDD 11/92   ✍

The distinctive genius of this Mass would have been recognized much more widely if it had not
been overshadowed by the supreme masterpiece, the *Missa solemnis*. That was written in 1820,

and the C major Mass dates from 1808, so that not surprisingly it has a freshness of spirit about it as well as an innovative challenge caught in Beethoven's words to his publishers: "I believe I have treated the text as it has seldom been treated before". One feature that startled his contemporaries was a responsiveness to words, almost as though as to a dramatic text. Another is the characteristic unpredictability, a quality well brought out in this recording. Gardiner came to it in the studio *after* the *Missa solemnis*, in which his way of making familiar things new had almost limitless scope. It is manifest here too: details of the score repeatedly spring to a life which has specific character and purpose in it. The rhythms dance in the fine orchestral playing, and the Monteverdi Choir have always had the happy knack of making their discipline sound like spontaneity, and vice versa. There is also an excellent performance by Charlotte Margiono of the dramatic *scena, Ah perfido!*, marked equally by variety of expression and beauty of tone. The choral *Meeresstille* ("Sea-calm") has been used before now as a fill-up: a marvellously descriptive piece, imaginatively performed here and recorded with a finely-achieved balance between chorus and orchestra.

Additional recommendation ...
Mass, Op. 86. Mass in D major, Op. 123, "Missa Solemnis". **Soloists; London Symphony Chorus and Orchestra/Sir Colin Davis.** Philips Duo 438 362-2PM2 — .ᐧ ② 2h 16m ADD 8/93 ⁹ₚ ⑧

Beethoven. Mass in D major, Op. 123, "Missa solemnis". **Charlotte Margiono** (sop); **Catherine Robbin** (mez); **William Kendall** (ten); **Alastair Miles** (bass); **Monteverdi Choir; English Baroque Soloists/John Eliot Gardiner.** Archiv Produktion 429 779-2AH. Text and translation included. Recorded in 1989.

.ᐧ Ih I2m DDD 3/9I   ⑧ 🖊

Beethoven. Mass in D major, Op. 123, "Missa solemnis". **Cheryl Studer, Jessye Norman** (sops); **Plácido Domingo** (ten) **Kurt Moll** (bass); **Leipzig Radio Chorus; Swedish Radio Chorus; Eric Ericson Chamber Choir; Vienna Philharmonic Orchestra/James Levine.** DG 435 770-2GH2. Text and translation included. Recorded in 1991.

.ᐧ ② Ih 23m DDD II/92   ⁹ₚ ⑧

Beethoven. Mass in D major, Op. 123, "Missa solemnis". **Eva Mei** (sop); **Marjana Lipovšek** (mez); **Anthony Rolfe Johnson** (ten); **Robert Holl** (bass); **Arnold Schöenberg Choir; Chamber Orchestra of Europe/Nikolaus Harnoncourt.** Teldec 9031-74884-2. Text and translation included. Recorded in 1992.

.ᐧ ② Ih 2Im DDD 4/93   ⁹ₚ ⑧ 🖊

The *Missa solemnis* is generally agreed to be one of the supreme masterpieces of the nineteenth century, but attempts to record a genuinely great performance have over many years run into difficulties. Usually the greatness itself is flawed, perhaps in the quality of the solo singers or in some particular passages where the conductor's approach is too idiosyncratic or momentarily not up to the challenge of Beethoven's inspiration (an example is Klemperer's heavy-handedness in the fugues). The strain upon the choir, especially its sopranos, is notorious; similarly the technical problems of balance by producer and engineers. But suddenly in the last three years there have appeared three recordings, all of which rank with the best as performances, and at least two of which can be recommended as recorded sound. The version under John Eliot Gardiner came first, and it remains a very probable first choice. It combines discipline and spontaneous creativity, the rhythms are magically alive and the intricate texture of sound is made wonderfully clear. The great fugues of the *Gloria* and *Credo* achieve at the right points their proper Dionysiac sense of exalted liberation. These are qualities which the Levine recording shares, but the means are sharply contrasted. Gardiner uses a choir of 36 and an orchestra of 60 playing on period instruments, aiming at a "leaner and fitter" sound. Levine has the traditional large forces of singers and players. Gardiner's soloists are admirable but they are not 'names', whereas Levine has a quartet that constitutes what the record's promoters claimed as "the most luxurious of our time". That may create more suspicion than confidence, for singers who are at home in *Aida* do not necessarily fit the bill in the *Missa solemnis*. These four, however, sing magnificently and their opulence of tone proves a genuine enrichment. In some respects, Harnoncourt's performance is still finer. Though he, like Levine, is working in the Grosses Festspielhaus at Salzburg and is recorded live, his performance has the greater clarity, partly because of the forces used: his period timpani, for instance, do not boom like Levine's later ones. Then, in comparison with Gardiner, Harnoncourt's way sometimes has more humanity about it: the march of his *Credo*, for instance, is less military than Gardiner's. The drawback is in the quality of recorded sound, which lacks the bloom of Levine's and the sharp immediacy of the Gardiner, which, to that extent and in their contrasting ways, may be found preferable.

Additional recommendations ...
Missa solemnis. Mass, Op. 86. **Soloists; New Philharmonia Chorus; London Philharmonic Orchestra/Carlo Maria Giulini.** EMI CZS7 62693-2 — ·*' ② 2h 17m ADD
Missa solemnis. **Soloists; Vienna Singverein; Berlin Philharmonic Orchestra/Herbert von Karajan.** DG 419 166-2GH2 — ·*' ② 2h 2lm DDD 10/86 Ⓑ
Missa solemnis. **Soloists; Atlanta Symphony Chorus and Orchestra/Robert Shaw.** Telarc CD80150 — ·*' ② 2h 19m DDD 11/88 Ⓑ
Missa solemnis[a]. *Choral Fantasia in C minor, Op. 80*[b]. **Soloists; [a]New Philharmonia Chorus; [b]John Alldis Choir; New Philharmonia Orchestra/Otto Klemperer.** EMI CMS7 69538-2 — ·*' ② lh 40m ADD 12/88 ⁹ₚ Ⓑ
Missa solemnis. **Verdi.** *Quattro pezzi sacri.* **Soloists; Chicago Symphony Chorus and Orchestra/Sir Georg Solti.** Decca 425 844-2DM2 — ·*' ② 2h 2m ADD 7/90 Ⓑ
Missa solemnis. Mass in C major, Op. 86. **Soloists; London Symphony Chorus and Orchestra/Sir Colin Davis.** Philips Duo 438 362-2PM2 — ·*' ② 2h 16m ADD 8/93 ⁹ₚ Ⓑ
Missa solemnis. **Soloists; Chicago Symphony Chorus and Orchestra/Daniel Barenboim.** Erato 4509-91731-2 — ·*' lh 24m DDD 6/94 ⁹ₚ Ⓑ

Beethoven. FIDELIO. **Christa Ludwig** (mez) Leonore; **Jon Vickers** (ten) Florestan; **Walter Berry** (bass) Don Pizarro; **Gottlob Frick** (bass) Rocco; **Ingeborg Hallstein** (sop) Marzelline; **Gerhard Unger** (ten) Jacquino; **Franz Crass** (bass) Don Fernando; **Kurt Wehofschitz** (ten) First Prisoner; **Raymond Wolansky** (bar) Second Prisoner; **Philharmonia Chorus and Orchestra/Otto Klemperer.** EMI CMS7 69324-2. Notes, text and translation included. From Columbia SAX2451/3 (6/62). Recorded in 1962.

·*' ② 2h 8m ADD 1/90 ⁹ₚ Ⓑ

Fidelio teems with emotional overtones and from the arresting nature of the Overture, through the eloquence of the quartet, through the mounting tension of the prison scene to the moment of release when the wrongly imprisoned Florestan is freed, Beethoven unerringly finds the right music for his subject. Klemperer's set has been a classic since it first appeared on LP way back in 1962. The performance draws its strength from his conducting: he shapes the whole work with a granite-like strength and a sense of forward movement that is unerring, while paying very deliberate attention to instrumental detail, particularly as regards the contribution of the woodwind. With the authoritative help of producer Walter Legge, the balance between voices and orchestra is faultlessly managed. The cumulative effect of the whole reading is something to wonder at and shows great dedication on all sides. Most remarkable among the singers is the soul and intensity of Christa Ludwig's Leonore. In her dialogue as much as in her singing she conveys the single-minded conviction in her mission of rescuing her beleaguered and much-loved husband. Phrase after phrase is given a frisson that has the ring of truth to it. As her Florestan, Jon Vickers conveys the anguish of his predicament. One or two moments of exaggeration apart this is another memorable assumption. Walter Berry, as Pizarro, suggests a small man given too much power. Gottlob Frick is a warm, touching Rocco, Ingeborg Hallstein a fresh, eager Marzelline, Gerhard Unger a youthful Jacquino, Franz Crass a noble Don Fernando. This is a set that should be in any worthwhile collection of opera. ·

Additional recommendations ...
Fidelio. **Soloists; Vienna State Opera Chorus; Vienna Philharmonic Orchestra/ Leonard Bernstein.** DG 419 436-2GH2 — ·*' ② 2h 15m ADD 6/87 ⁹ₚ Ⓑ
Fidelio. **Soloists; Chorus of the Deutsche Oper, Berlin; Berlin Philharmonic Orchestra/Herbert von Karajan.** EMI CMS7 69290-2 — ·*' ② lh 59m ADD 4/88 Ⓑ
Fidelio. **Soloists; Dresden State Opera Chorus; Staatskapelle Dresden/Bernard Haitink.** Philips 426 308-2PH2 — ·*' ② 2h 13m ADD 1/91 Ⓑ
Fidelio. **Soloists; Chorus; NBC Symphony Orchestra/Arturo Toscanini.** RCA Victor Gold Seal mono GD60273 — ·*' ② lh 52m ADD 10/92 Ⓑ ▲
Fidelio. Leonore Overture No. 3, Op. 72[a]. **Soloists; Bavarian State Opera Chorus; Bavarian State Orchestra; [a]Berlin Philharmonic Orchestra/Ferenc Fricsay.** DG Dokumente 437 345-2GDO2 — ·*' ② 2h 8m ADD 5/93 Ⓑ ▲

Fidelio. **Soloists; Vienna State Opera Chorus; Vienna Philharmonic Orchestra/ Wilhelm Furtwängler.** EMI Références mono CHS7 64496-2 — $\cdot{}^\bullet$ ② 2h 13m ADD 5/93 Ⓑ ▲
Fidelio. **Soloists; Vienna State Opera Chorus; Vienna Philharmonic Orchestra/ Wilhelm Furtwängler.** EMI Festspieldokumente mono CHS7 64901-2— $\cdot{}^\bullet$ ② 2h 30m ADD 12/93 ⁹ₚ Ⓑ ▲

Further listening ...

Quintet in E flat major for Piano and Wind, Op. 16. *Coupled with* **Mozart.** Quintet in E flat major for Piano and Wind, K452. **Murray Perahia** (pf); members of the **English Chamber Orchestra.** CBS Masterworks CD42099 (12/86).

Duets, WoO27 — No. 1 in C major[a]. Trio in G major, WoO37[b]. Serenade in D major, Op. 25[c]. **Susan Milan** (fl); [ab]**Sergio Azzolini** (bn); [c]**Levon Chilingirian** (vn); [c]**Louise Williams** (va); [b]**Ian Brown** (pf). Chandos CHAN9108 (4/93).

Clarinet Trio in B flat major, Op. 11. *Coupled with* **Brahms.** Clarinet Trio in A minor, Op. 114. **Musicfest Trio.** Pickwick IMP Classics PCD959 (11/91).

Vincenzo Bellini

Italian 1801-183

New review

Bellini. I CAPULETI ED I MONTECCHI — Eccomi in lieta vesta ... Oh! quante volte. La sonnambula[a] — Oh! se una volta sola ... Ah! non credea mirarti ... Ah! non giunge. **Donizetti.** DON PASQUALE — Quel guardo il cavaliere ... So anch'io la virtu magica. LINDA DI CHAMOUNIX — Ah! tardai troppo ... o luce di quest' anima. **Rossini.** TANCREDI[b] — Gran Dio! Deh! tu proteggi ... Giusto Dio. IL VIAGGIO A REIMS[b] — Partir, oh ciel! desio. **Kathleen Battle** (sop); [a]**Randi Stene** (contr); [a]**Richard Croft** (ten); [a]**Mark S. Doss** (bass); [b]**Ambrosian Opera Chorus; London Philharmonic Orchestra/Bruno Campanella.** DG 435 866-2GH. Texts and translations included. Recorded in 1991.

$\cdot{}^\bullet$ 56m DDD 12/93   ⁹ₚ

All here is exquisitely performed. The first note of Juliet's solo in *I Capuleti ed i Montecchi* with its sure placing and gentle swell prepares for a sequence of delights ending with the cadenza in which the voice is heard in sad isolation, as is the girl. Just enough variation is introduced, and for the rest the beauties of tone and of Bellini's melody, sensitively supported by the orchestra, are amply sufficient. Much the same could be said about much of the recital. To some extent the closing scene from *La sonnambula* wants more vivacity and stronger projection as it develops into joy. Yet the aria itself is beautifully sung, and indeed there is high accomplishment throughout. The *Tancredi* solo sparkles, with its scales and staccatos in brilliant order. Norina in *Don Pasquale* has a genuine gaiety and Linda of Chamounix sings her song of happiness with blissful virtuosity. The work of chorus and supporting soloists is all up to standard.

Bellini. IL PIRATA. **Piero Cappuccilli** (bar) Ernesto; **Montserrat Caballé** (sop) Imogene; **Bernabé Martí** (ten) Gualtiero; **Giuseppe Baratti** (ten) Itulbo; **Ruggero Raimondi** (bass) Goffredo; **Flora Raffanelli** (sop) Adele; **Rome RAI Chorus and Orchestra/Gianandrea Gavazzeni.** EMI CMS7 64169-2. Notes, text and translation included. From HMV SLS953 (9/71). Recorded in 1970.

$\cdot{}^\bullet$ ② 2h 22m ADD 2/93

Bellini's third opera had its première in 1827, in the heyday of Rossini whose influence is clearly discernible. Where the composer's own special qualities find best scope is often in the duets and ensembles, some of which rise to the needs of the dramatic situation with great power and beauty. The story tells of Gualtiero and his pirate band shipwrecked and thrown on the mercy·of the noble lady Imogene who turns out to be the lost love of Gualtiero and subsequently married through cruel necessity to Ernesto. There is also a role for a hermit

(Goffredo), so everybody is well provided, and the scenario yields many a dire event, signalled in the English translation by cries such as "What a moment to arrive!". In 1971 when the recording itself first arrived it was more of a novelty in kind than it is now and was warmly welcomed, both for the opportunity to hear an operatic rarity and for the singing of Montserrat Caballé, then at the height of her powers. She does indeed give a lovely performance, unmatched however by Bernabé Martí, who at least deserves credit for grappling with such a daunting role, or Piero Cappuccilli, who is simply dull. Fine singing comes from the young Raimondi as the hermit, and the Rome chorus and orchestra respond well to Gavazzeni's often inspired conducting.

Bellini. NORMA. **Maria Callas** (sop) Norma; **Ebe Stignani** (mez) Adalgisa; **Mario Filippeschi** (ten) Pollione; **Nicola Rossi-Lemeni** (bass) Orovesco; **Paolo Caroli** (ten) Flavio; **Rina Cavallari** (sop) Clotilde; **Chorus and Orchestra of La Scala, Milan/Tullio Serafin.** EMI mono CDS7 47304-8. Notes, text and translation included. From Columbia mono 33CX1179/80 (11/54). Recorded in 1954.

③ 2h 40m ADD 3/86

Norma may be considered the most potent of Bellini's operas, both in terms of its subject — the secret love of a Druid priestess for a Roman general — and its musical content. It has some of the most eloquent music ever written for the soprano voice and two duets that show Bellini's gift for liquid melody. The title-role has always been coveted by dramatic sopranos, but there have been few in the history of the opera who have completely fulfilled its considerable vocal and histrionic demands: in recent times the leading exponent has been Maria Callas. The mono recording comes up sounding remarkably forward and immediate on CD, and it captures Callas's commanding and moving assumption of the title part, the vocal line etched with deep feeling, the treatment of the recitative enlivening the text. Stignani is a worthy partner whilst Filippeschi is rough but quite effective. Serafin knew better than anyone since how to mould a Bellinian line to best effect.

Additional recommendations ...
Soloists; London Symphony Chorus and Orchestra/Richard Bonynge. Decca 425 488-2DM3 — ⠴ ③ 2h 5lm ADD ꝙₚ
Soloists; Chorus and Orchestra of La Scala, Milan/Tullio Serafin. EMI CMS7 63000-2 — ⠴ ③ 2h 4lm ADD 7/89 ꝙₚ
Highlights from the above recording are also available separately. Details are as follows: Casta diva; Va, crudele; O rimembranza; O non tremare; Introduction, Act 2; Mira, o Norma; Guerra, guerra; In mia man' alfin tu sei; Taci, ne ascolta appena. EMI CDM7 63091-2 — ⠴ lh 4m ADD 7/89 ꝙₚ

Bellini. LA SONNAMBULA. **Maria Callas** (sop) Amina; **Nicola Monti** (ten) Elvino; **Nicola Zaccaria** (bass) Count Rodolfo; **Fiorenza Cossotto** (Mez) Teresa; **Eugenia Ratti** (sop) Lisa; **Giuseppe Morresi** (bass) Alessio; **Franco Ricciardi** (ten) Notary. **Chorus and Orchestra of La Scala, Milan/Antonino Votto.** EMI mono CDS7 47378-8. Notes text and translation included. From Columbia 33CX51469, 33CX1470/1 (10/57). Recorded in 1957.

② 2h lm ADD 9/86

Dramatically this opera is a tepid little mix which might be subtitled *The mistakes of a night* if that did not suggest something more amusing than what actually takes place. Musically, the promise of a brilliant finale keeps most people in their seats until the end, and there are half-a-dozen charming, sometimes exquisite items on the way. But it is all a little insubstantial, and much depends upon the performance, especially that of the soprano. The name of Maria Callas is sufficient to guarantee that there will be a particular interest in the work of the heroine. As usual, her individuality is apparent from the moment of her arrival. Immediately a character is established, not an insipid little miss but a woman in whom lurks a potential for tragedy. This is the pattern throughout and much has exceptional beauty of voice and spirit. Nicola Monti has all the sweetness of the traditional lyric tenor; the pity is that what might have been a most elegant performance is marred by the intrusion of unwanted aspirates. Nicola Zaccaria sings the bass aria gracefully, and carrying off her small role with distinction is Fiorenza Cossotto, at the start of her career. The orchestral playing is neat, the conducting sensible and the recording clear.

Additional recommendation ...
Soloists; London Opera Chorus; National Philharmonic Orchestra/Richard Bonynge. Decca 417 424-2DH2 — .·· ② 2h 21m DDD 4/87

Bellini. I PURITANI. **Montserrat Caballé** (sop) Elvira; **Alfredo Kraus** (ten) Arturo; **Matteo Manuguerra** (bar) Riccardo; **Agostino Ferrin** (bass) Giorgio; **Júlia Hamari** (mez) Enrichetta; **Stefan Elenkov** (bass) Gualtiero; **Dennis O'Neill** (ten) Bruno; **Ambrosian Opera Chorus; Philharmonia Orchestra/Riccardo Muti.** EMI CMS7 69663-2. Notes, text and translation included. From SLS5201 (1/81). Recorded in 1979.

.·· ③ 2h 52m ADD 4/89

Bellini's opera of the English Civil War is probably his most readily attractive score, for its moods encompass a gaiety unknown to *Norma* and the writing is much more robust than *La sonnambula*. As in all of his work, a great deal depends upon the singers and it is to them that one normally looks first. Here, however, Riccardo Muti is in charge, a conductor with strong ideas about what may be allowed the singers by way of traditional license: on the whole he keeps a tight rein but compensates by taking slow speeds so that the melodies may never pass by with their beauties unobserved. The refinement is notable in the introduction to the bass aria near the start of Act 2, and there is no lack of strength and rhythmic excitement in the surging melody of the Finale to Act 1. The performance also benefits from particularly alert choral work by the Ambrosians, and from imaginative production. The spotlight is on the singers even so. As the sorely tried heroine Caballé is ideal as long as nothing too strenuous arises to put pressure on her exceptionally lovely voice. Her ethereal tones have a fine effect in the off-stage prayer, and her "Qui la voce" is deeply felt as well as beautifully sung. Kraus is perhaps the best tenor of recent times in this repertoire and there is nearly always a personal character about his singing that gives it distinction. This is a quality somewhat lacking in the baritone, Matteo Manuguerra; all the same there is some good solid tone and he makes an honest job of his cadenzas.

Additional recommendations ...
Soloists; Chorus and Orchestra of La Scala, Milan/Tullio Serafin. EMI mono CDS7 47308-8 — .·· ② 2h 22m ADD 4/89 ▲
Soloists; Chorus and Orchestra of the Teatro Massimo, Catania/Richard Bonynge. Nuova Era 6842/44 — .·· ③ 2h 30m DDD 10/91

Georg Benda

Bohemian 1722-1795

New review
Benda. LIEDER AND FORTEPIANO WORKS. [a]**Emma Kirkby** (sop); [b]**Rufus Müller** (ten); **Timothy Roberts** (fp). Hyperion CDA66649. Texts and translations included. Recorded 1993. Du, kleine Blondine, bezauberst ja schon![b]. Du fehlest mir[a]. Venus, wenn du willst mich rühren[a]. Cephalus und Aurore[a]. Philint ist still, und fliehet die Schönen[b]. Philint stand jüngst vor Babets Thur[b]. Ich liebte nur Ismenen[b]. Mein Thyrsis! dürft ich dir doch sagen[a]. Belise starb, und sprach im Scheiden[a]. Lieber Amor, leihe mir[b]. Mein Geliebter hat versprochen[a]. Faulheit, itze will ich dir[b]. Ein trunkner Dichter leerte[b]. Mir Armen, den des Fiebers Kraft[b]. Von nun an, O Liebe, verlass' ich dein Reich[b]. Das Andenken[a]. Piano Sonatinas — No. 3 in A minor; No. 9 in A minor; No. 16 in G minor; No. 21 in F major; No. 29 in E flat major; No. 32 in A major.

.·· 1h 3m DDD 1/94

The musical fare on this disc is by and large, generously endowed with pleasing melodies, The keyboard pieces are *galant* in manner but without the extremes of temperament explored by Benda's older contemporary, C.P.E. Bach. Timothy Roberts presents a strong case for exploring them in his affectionate and appropriately sensitive approach. The songs and the cantata perhaps make a more enduring impression. There is plenty of character in Benda's melodies, some of which are poignantly affecting. Emma Kirkby captures the spirit of the pieces to perfection, producing a warm, clear-focused tone complemented by a reassuringly secure technique. The remaining songs are sung by Rufus Müller, who matches Kirkby in expression, clear tonal projection, and characterful singing. The recorded sound is pleasingly intimate and the booklet well documented.

Paul Ben-Haim

Suggested listening ...

Violin Concerto. *Coupled with* **Castelnuovo-Tedesco.** Violin Concerto No. 2, Op. 66, "I profeti". **Itzhak Perlman** (vn); **Israel Philharmonic Orchestra/Zubin Mehta.** EMI CDC7 54296-2 (5/93).

George Benjamin

Suggested listening ...

At first light[a]. Ringed by the flat horizon[b]. A Mind of Winter[c]. [c]**Penelope Walmsley-Clark** (sop); [a]**Gareth Hulse** (ob); [b]**Ross Pople** (vc); [c]**P. Archibald** (cl); [ac]**London Sinfonietta/ George Benjamin;** [b]**BBC Symphony Orchestra/Mark Elder.** Nimbus NI5075.

Antara. *Coupled with* **Boulez.** Dérive. Memoriale[a]. **J. Harvey.** Song Offerings[b]. [b]**Penelope Walmsley-Clark** (sop); [a]**Sebastian Bell** (fl); **London Sinfonietta/George Benjamin.** Nimbus NI5167 (10/89).

Piano Sonata. **George Benjamin.** Nimbus NI1415 (CD single).

Richard Rodney Bennett

New review
Bennett. Guitar Concerto[a].
Arnold. Guitar Concerto, Op. 67[b].
Rodrigo. Concierto de Aranjuez[c]. **Julian Bream** (gtr); **Melos Ensemble/**[c]**Sir Colin Davis.** RCA Julian Bream Edition 09026 61598-2. Item marked [a] recorded in 1972, [b] 1959, [c] 1963.

1h 2m ADD 6/94

Sir Malcolm Arnold's Concerto was written for Julian Bream in 1957. Bream made his record in partnership with the composer — directing the Melos Ensemble — two years later and the results are in every way definitive. The recording was made for RCA by Decca engineers and is beautifully balanced and strikingly warm and atmospheric. The couplings include Bream's first stereo recording of the Rodrigo *Concierto de Aranjuez* with Sir Colin Davis in charge of the accompaniment and Richard Rodney Bennett's Guitar Concerto, written in 1970 and also dedicated to Bream. Its imaginative variety of texture, lustrous and transparent, consistently titillates the ear. The performance, like that of the Arnold, is definitive and the 1972 recording is excellent. Bream has since recorded both the Arnold and the Rodrigo for EMI with Simon Rattle (reviewed under Arnold; refer to the Index to Reviews), although the earlier disc is by no means superseded.

Further listening ...

Saxophone Concerto. *Coupled with* **Debussy.** Rapsodie. **Glazunov.** Saxophone Concerto in E flat major, Op. 109. **Heath.** Out of the Cool. **Ibert.** Concertino da camera. **Villa-Lobos.** Fantasia. **John Harle** (sax); **Academy of St Martin in the Fields/Sir Neville Marriner.** EMI CDC7 54301-2 (1/92). *See review in the Collections section; refer to the Index to Reviews.*

Alban Berg

Berg. Violin Concerto.
Rihm. Gesungene Zeit. **Anne-Sophie Mutter** (vn); **Chicago Symphony Orchestra/James Levine.** DG 437 093-2GH. Recorded in 1992.

52m DDD I/93

Berg. Violin Concerto[a].
Janáček. Violin Concerto, "Pilgrimage of the soul"[a].
Hartmann. Concerto funebre[b]. **Thomas Zehetmair** (vn/[b]dir); [a]**Philharmonia Orchestra/Heinz Holliger;** [b]**Deutsche Kammerphilharmonie.** Teldec 2292-46449-2. Recorded 1990-91.

Ih DDD 3/93

One of the very few 12-note pieces to have retained a place in the repertory, Berg's Violin Concerto is in fact a work on many levels. Behind the complex intellectual facade of the construction is a poignant sense of loss, ostensibly for Alma Mahler's daughter, Manon Gropius, but also for Berg's own youth; and behind that is a thoroughly disconcerting mixture of styles which resists interpretation as straightforward Romantic consolation. Not that performers need to go out of their way to project these layers; given a soloist as comprehensively equipped as Anne-Sophie Mutter and orchestral support as vivid as the Chicago Symphony's they simply cannot fail to register. This then makes a fine demonstration-quality recording alternative to the even more idiomatically insightful historic version of Krasner and Webern. And in their less flamboyant but equally persuasive way, Zehetmair and Holliger are very much in the same class; the Teldec recording is not quite so brightly lit as DG's, but if anything it is more realistically balanced. In other words, choice can safely be left to the couplings; in which respect honours are again fairly even. In recent years Mutter has made a point of seeking out effective new *concertante* pieces as couplings to established repertoire concertos. The latest of these, by the 40-year-old German composer Wolfgang Rihm, is more or less in a historical line from Berg and his fellow-expressionists. *Gesungene Zeit* means "Time Chanted", and the music reflects the mystical implications of the title. It steers clear of the extremes of avant-garde hermeticism and post-modernist opportunism and should prove rewarding to anyone who can take Berg in their stride and is curious to discover what lies beyond. Zehetmair's choice is adventurous in a different way. Janáček's 12-minute Concerto, recently reconstructed from the fragmentary state in which he abandoned it in 1926, is related to his opera *From the House of the Dead*. Not a major addition to the repertory, it nevertheless has enough authentic late-Janáčekian passion to merit occasional performances. No less worthy of preservation is the 1959 Concerto by the Webern-pupil Karl Amadeus Hartmann. This is an energetic and assertive work, rather like radically intellectualized Prokofiev; performances and recording are again fine.

Additional recommendations ...
Violin Concerto. **Stravinsky.** *Violin Concerto in D minor.* **Itzhak Perlman** (vn); **Boston Symphony Orchestra/Seiji Ozawa.** DG 413 725-2GH — .•" 48m ADD 12/84 ⁹ₚ
Violin Concerto[a]. **Stravinsky.** *Violin Concerto*[b]. **Arthur Grumiaux** (vn); **Concertgebouw Orchestra/**[a]**Igor Markevitch,** [b]**Ernest Bour.** Philips Legendary Classics 422 136-2PLC —
.•" 45m ADD 10/88 ⁹ₚ
Violin Concerto[a]. *Lyric Suite*[b]. [a]**Louis Krasner** (vn); [b]**Galimir Quartet;** [a]**BBC Symphony Orchestra/Anton Webern.** Testament SBT1004 — .•" 57m ADD 6/91 ⁹ₚ ▲

New review
Berg. String Quartet, Op. 3.
Liszt. Am Grabe Richard Wagners, S135[a].
Webern. Five Movements, Op. 5. **Kronos Quartet** (David Harrington, John Sherba, vns; Hank Dutt, va; Joan Jeanrenaud, vc); [a]**Marcella deCray** (hp); [a]**Aki Takahashi** (pf). Elektra Nonesuch (special price) 7559-79318-2.

33m DDD I/94

Liszt's tender memorial, scored for piano, harp and string quartet, *Am Grabe Richard Wagners*, leaves no intimation of what is to follow — a whirlwind of a string quartet, rich in dramatic

contrasts yet uncompromising in its expressionist zeal. The Kronos Quartet make effective play
with Berg's more sensuous stylistic elements and engage a lusty pooled tone for its many
coruscating climaxes. A real *tour de force*. The recording, too, is revealing of inner detail both for
Berg and Webern, the latter displaying his strategic dynamism to full advantage — especially in
the 'ejector-scherzo' (third movement), all 38 seconds of it. Presentation and annotation are
wholly up to scratch, so if you're at all hesitant about edging beyond the entrance to the Second
Viennese School, then this short-play, inexpensive, beautifully performed programme will serve
to facilitate easy admission. You won't regret having taken the plunge.

Berg. Piano Sonata, Op. 1.
Liszt. Piano Works.
Webern. Variations, Op. 27. **Barry Douglas** (pf). RCA Victor Red Seal 09026 61221-2.
Recorded in 1991.
Liszt. Piano Sonata in B minor, S178. Nuages gris, S199. R.W. — Venezia, S201. Schlaflos,
Frage und Antwort, S203. Elegie No. 2, S197.

1h 1m   DDD   12/92

Liszt's Piano Sonata leads something of a double life in the musical world. First of all it is a
calling card for virtually every young virtuoso seeking to make a big impression; secondly it is
recognized as one of the great path-breaking achievements in terms of compositional innovation,
since its four-movements-in-one structure is a source of inspiration for the early works of
Schoenberg. Even more strikingly, the near-atonal intensity of the late piano works prepares for
the harmonic explorations of Schoenberg, Berg and Webern. So Barry Douglas has been
extremely astute in planning this recital. Berg's single-movement Sonata shares its home tonality
with the Liszt Sonata and its main motif with that of *Nuages gris*, while the Webern *Variations*
show the distant consequences of essentially the same line of thought. The outstanding
performance is of the Berg, where Douglas is more responsive to the expressive ebb and flow
than any current rival. His Liszt Sonata does not approach the heights of a Zimerman or a
Brendel, but it is still an impressive achievement and the other works give much satisfaction too.
The warm acoustic of Watford Town Hall lends a welcome glow to the recorded sound.

Additional recommendation ...
Piano Sonata, Op. 1. **Krenek.** *Piano Sonatas — No. 2, Op. 59; No. 3, Op. 92 No. 4.* **Webern.**
Variations, Op. 27. **Marcelo Bratke** (pf). Olympia OCD431 *(reviewed under Krenek; refer to the
Index to Reviews)* — 57m DDD 4/94

New review
Berg. Seven Early Songs.
Korngold. LIEDER.
R. Strauss. LIEDER. **Anne Sofie von Otter** (mez); **Bengt Forsberg** (pf). DG 437
515-2GH. Texts and translations included.
Korngold: Liebesbriefchen, Op. 9 No. 4; Sterbelied, Op. 14 No. 1; Gefasster Abschied,
Op. 14 No. 4; Drei Lieder, Op. 18; Glückwunsch, Op. 38 No. 1; Alt-spanisch, Op. 38 No. 3;
Sonett für Wien, Op. 41. **R. Strauss:** Wie sollten wir geheim sie halten, Op. 19 No. 4; Ich
trage meine Minne, Op. 32 No. 1; Der Rosenband, Op. 36 No. 1; Hat gesagt — bleibt's nicht
dabei, Op. 36 No. 3; Meinem Kinde, Op. 37 No. 3; Befreit, Op. 39 No. 4; Die sieben Siegel,
Op. 46 No. 3.

1h 4m   DDD   6/94

The chosen Strauss songs here are characteristically gentle and affectionate, a mood in which von
Otter is often at her best. Not that, having captured a mood, she is content to let it lie dully
over as much as a verse or a line. In *Der Rosenband* she is always sensitive to the modulations; in
Ich trage meine Minne the voice darkens with the change of tonality in verse two; in *Wie sollten wir
geheim sie halten* she captures the subdued excitement of the opening as she does the frank
exultation of the close. For lightness of touch, the Op. 38 songs endear themselves among the
Korngold group: *Glückwunsch* has an unaffected, comfortable way with it (a little adaptation could
turn it neatly into Roger Quilter or even Jerome Kern), and *Alt-spanisch* (with its reminiscence
of "On yonder hill there stands a maiden") is a charmer. At the centre of the recital are the
Seven Early Songs of Alban Berg. The first, "Nacht", which is also the longest and most readily

memorable, is taken rather more slowly than usual, but gaining in its subtler evocations of the mists and then the silvered mountain paths. Von Otter's draining the voice of all vibrato also helps create the sense of watchful stillness, just as in the sixth song, "Liebesode", it makes for an almost other-worldly dreaminess, deepening to a full-bodied passion as the rose scent is borne to the love-bed. Always the mezzo-soprano voice is resourcefully used, able to colour deeply at such points, to float a pure head-tone in "Traumgekrönt" or launch a radiant high A in "Die Nachtigall".

Berg. WOZZECK. **Franz Grundheber** (bar) Wozzeck; **Hildegard Behrens** (sop) Marie; **Heinz Zednik** (ten) Captain; **Aage Haugland** (bass) Doctor; **Philip Langridge** (ten) Andres; **Walter Raffeiner** (ten) Drum-Major; **Anna Gonda** (mez) Margret; **Alfred Sramek** (bass) First Apprentice; **Alexander Maly** (bar) Second Apprentice; **Peter Jelosits** (ten) Idiot; **Vienna Boys' Choir; Vienna State Opera Chorus; Vienna Philharmonic Orchestra/ Claudio Abbado.** DG 423 587-2GH2. Notes, text and translation included. Recorded live in 1987.

② 1h 29m DDD 2/89

A live recording, in every sense of the word. The cast is uniformly excellent, with Grundheber, good both at the wretched pathos of Wozzeck's predicament and his helpless bitterness, and Behrens as an outstandingly intelligent and involving Marie, even the occasional touch of strain in her voice heightening her characterization. The Vienna Philharmonic respond superbly to Abbado's ferociously close-to-the-edge direction. It is a live recording with a bit of a difference, mark you: the perspectives are those of a theatre, not a recording studio. The orchestra is laid out as it would be in an opera house pit and the movement of singers on stage means that voices are occasionally overwhelmed. The result is effective: the crowded inn-scenes, the arrival and departure of the military band, the sense of characters actually reacting to each other, not to a microphone, makes for a grippingly theatrical experience. Audiences no longer think of *Wozzeck* as a 'difficult' work, but recordings have sometimes treated it as one, with a clinical precision either to the performance or the recorded perspective. This version has a raw urgency, a sense of bitter protest and angry pity that are quite compelling and uncomfortably eloquent.

Additional recommendations ...
Wozzeck. **Soloists; Chorus and Orchestra of the Deutsche Oper, Berlin/Karl Böhm.** *Lulu (two-act version).* **Soloists; Chorus and Orchestra of the Deutsche Oper, Berlin/Karl Böhm.** DG 435 705-2GX3 — ③ ADD 3h 37m 1/93

Wozzeck. **Soloists; Vienna State Opera Chorus.** *Schoenberg.* *Erwartung, Op. 17.* **Anja Silja** (sop); **Vienna Philharmonic Orchestra/Christoph von Dohnányi.** Decca 417 348-2DH2 — ② 2h 3m DDD 2/89

Berg. LULU (orchestration of Act 3 completed by Friedrich Cerha). **Teresa Stratas** (sop) Lulu; **Franz Mazura** (bar) Dr Schön, Jack; **Kenneth Riegel** (ten) Alwa; **Yvonne Minton** (mez) Countess Geschwitz; **Robert Tear** (ten) The Painter, A Negro; **Toni Blankenheim** (bar) Schigolch, Professor of Medicine, The Police Officer; **Gerd Nienstedt** (bass) An Animaltamer, Rodrigo; **Helmut Pampuch** (ten) The Prince, The Manservant, The Marquis; **Jules Bastin** (bass) The Theatre Manager, The Banker; **Hanna Schwarz** (mez) A Dresser in the theatre, High School Boy, A Groom; **Jane Manning** (sop) A 15-year-old girl; **Ursula Boese** (mez) Her Mother; **Anna Ringart** (mez) A Ldy Artist; **Claude Meloni** (bar) A Journalist; **Pierre-Yves Le Maigat** (bass) A Manservant; **Paris Opéra Orchestra/Pierre Boulez.** DG 415 489-2GH3. Notes, text and translation included. From 2740 213 (10/79).

③ 2h 52m ADD 11/86

Now here's a masterpiece that fulfils all the requirements needed for a commercial smash hit — it's sexy, violent, cunning, sophisticated, hopelessly complicated and leaves you emotionally drained. *Lulu* was Berg's second opera and easily matches his first — *Wozzeck* — for pathos and dramatic impact. The meaningful but gloriously over-the-top story-line, after two tragedies by Frank Wedekind, deserves acknowledgement. Lulu, mistress of Dr Schön, is married to a medical professor. An artist also has the hots for her, but just as his passion gets interestingly out of hand, her husband walks in, catches them approaching the act and dies of shock. She marries the artist, who learns about Dr Schön and kills himself; then she marries the jealous Dr

Schön, and eventually kills *him*. Smuggled out of prison by an adoring lesbian, she sets up home in Paris with Schön's son, gets blackmailed and ends up in London as one of Jack the Ripper's victims! And that's not the half of it — but we'll spare you the rest. What matters is that Berg's music is magnificent, romantic enough to engage the passions of listeners normally repelled by 12-tone music, and cerebral enough to keep eggheads fully employed. It's opulent yet subtle (saxophone and piano lend the score a hint of jazz-tinted decadence), with countless telling thematic inter-relations and much vivid tonal character-painting. Berg left it incomplete (only 390 of the Third Act's 1,326 bars were orchestrated by him), but Friedrich Cerha's painstaking reconstruction is a major achievement, especially considering the complicated web of Berg's musical tapestry. This particular recording first opened our ears to the 'real' Lulu in 1979, and has transferred extremely well to CD. The booklet contains a superb essay by Boulez which in itself is enough to stimulate the interest of a potential listener. Performance-wise, it is highly distinguished. Teresa Stratas is an insinuating yet vulnerable Lulu, Yvonne Minton a sensuous Gräfin Geschwitz and Robert Tear an ardent artist. Dr Schön is tellingly portrayed by Franz Mazura (who also turns up as Jack the Ripper), Kenneth Riegel is highly creditable as Schön's son and that Boulez himself is both watchful of detail and responsive to the drama, hardly needs saying. It's not an easy listen, but it'll certainly keep you on your toes for a stimulating, even exasperating evening.

Further listening ...

Lulu Suite[a]. Three Orchestral Pieces, Op. 6. Altenberg Lieder, Op. 4[a]. [a]**Dame Margaret Price** (sop); **London Symphony Orchestra/Claudio Abbado.** DG 20th Century Classics 423 238-2GC (8/88).

Erik Bergman

Finnish 1911-

Suggested listening ...

Nox, Op. 65. Bim Bam Boom, Op. 80. (The Birds) Fåglarna, Op. 56a. Hathor Suite, Op. 70. **Penelope Walmsley-Clark** (sop); **Stephen Varcoe** (bar); **John Potter** (ten); **New London Chamber Choir; Endymion Ensemble/James Wood.** Chandos CHAN8478 (1/88).

Auch so (myös näin). Came a letter (Det kom ett brev). Dreams. Four Gallow Songs (Galgenlieder). Hathor Suite. The Lasses (Tyttöset). My tree is the stone-pine (Mitt träd är pinjen). Rain (Regn). Samothrake. The Single Moment (Den enda studen). Such an evening (En såda kväll). Watercolour (Akvarell). **Finnish Chamber Choir/Eric-Olof Söderström.** Finlandia FACD371 (12/89).

THE SINGING TREE. **Soloists; Dominante Choir; Tapiola Chamber Choir; Finnish National Opera Orchestra/Ulf Söderblom.** Ondine ODE794-2D (5/93).

Luciano Berio

Italian 1925-

Suggested listening ...

Sinfonia[a]. Eindrücke. [a]**Regis Pasquier** (vn); [a]**New Swingle Singers; French National Orchestra/Pierre Boulez.** Erato 2292-45228-2 (7/88).

Sequenza XI. *Coupled with* **Britten.** Nocturnal after John Dowland, Op. 70. **Brouwer.** La Espiral Eterna. **Takemitsu:** All in Twilight. **Torres.** Mil y una caras. **Yocoh.** Sakura. **Eduardo Fernández** (gtr). Decca 433 076-2DH (7/93). *See review in the Collections section; refer to the Index to Reviews.*

Formazioni. 11 Folk Songs[a]. Sinfonia[b]. [a]**Jard van Nes** (mez); [b]**Electric Phoenix; Royal Concertgebouw Orchestra/Riccardo Chailly.** Decca 425 832-2DH (8/90).

Coro for Voices and Instruments. **Cologne Radio Chorus and Symphony Orchestra/Luciano Berio.** DG 20th Century Classics 423 902-2GC (10/88).

Laborintus II. **Soloists; Chorale Expérimentale; Ensemble Musique Vivante/Luciano Berio.** Harmonia Mundi Musique d'Abord HMA190 764 (12/87).

Sir Lennox Berkeley British 1903-1989

New review

Berkeley. ORCHESTRAL WORKS. **London Philharmonic Orchestra/Sir Lennox Berkeley.** Lyrita SRCD226. Items marked [a] from SRCS74 (9/75), [b] SRCS57 (10/72), [c] SRCS50 (6/71).
Serenade, Op. 12[a]. Divertimento in B flat major, Op. 18[a]. Partita, Op. 66[a]. Sinfonia concertante, Op. 84 — Canzonetta[a] (with Roger Winfield, ob). Symphony No. 3, Op. 74[b].
Berkeley/Britten: Mont Juic, Op. 9[c].

1h 14m ADD 3/93

A certain stiffness in execution pervades all the interpretations here, but there is also an unvarnished directness and strength, a kind of rugged authenticity which uniquely and mysteriously springs from composer performances. So although one will have heard more sophisticated and subtle readings of the popular *Serenade* and *Divertimento*, Berkeley conveys in both works a sense of 'this is what the music is, and this is how it is played', and in very convincing fashion. The later *Partita* seems a less attractive and effective work, but it was shrewd of Berkeley to include the Canzonetta from his *Sinfonia concertante*, since it contains a delicious melody which should be the signature tune of a popular television series if it hasn't been already. The Berkeley/Britten collaboration in putting together the suite of Catalan folk-tunes which make up *Mont Juic* was a simple division of labour, for Berkeley composed the first two movements and Britten wrote the last two. The short, concentrated, one-movement Third Symphony is by far the most serious work played here, and is a very impressive composition indeed. Berkeley's tough, rugged performance does it full justice. The 1970s recordings have been quite well transferred.

New review

Berkeley. PIANO WORKS. **Raphael Terroni,** [a]**Norman Beedie** (pfs). British Music Society BMS416CD.
Piano Sonata, Op. 20. Six Preludes, Op. 23. Five Short Pieces, Op. 4. Palm Court Waltz, Op. 81 No. 2[a]. Sonatina for Piano Duet, Op. 39[a]. Theme and Variations, Op. 73[a].

58m DDD 3/94

This is some of the finest British piano music of the century. If you find Bax turgid, Ireland too sweet, Tippett gawky or repetitive, Britten and Walton virtually non-existent in the solo repertoire, then Sir Lennox Berkeley's consistently melodic piano writing should be a real discovery. Both Terroni and Headington (listed below) really understand the Berkeley style: the latter pianist was Berkeley's first pupil at the Academy. The outer movements of the Sonata demand a special feeling for flow to give quite diverse material continuity. Both Terroni and Headington achieve this. Terroni's finale is excellent, and the overwhelming impression confirms Malcolm Williamson's description: "a flawless masterpiece". There are real delights, too, in the rest of Terroni's offering. His *Six Preludes* are just right, musically dedicated and unidiosyncratic. The *Five Short Pieces* are a microcosm of Berkeley's style in the 1930s, as are the *Preludes* for the 1940s. Terroni gauges them beautifully — the balance of melody and accompaniment in No. 4 is sheer perfection. And his duo with Norman Beedie is everything one could ask for in the *Sonatina* and *Theme and Variations*, exquisite piano duets in the great tradition of Schubert, Fauré or Satie.

Additional recommendation ...

Piano Sonata. Six Preludes. Five Short Pieces. Three Pieces, Op. 2. Polka, Op. 5a. Three Mazurkas, Op. 32 No. 1. Paysage (1944). Improvisation on a Theme of Falla, Op. 55 No. 2. Mazurka, Op. 101 No. 2. **Christopher Headington** (pf). Kingdom KCLCD2012 — .•' lh lm DDD 6/89

Michael Berkeley
British 1948-

New review

M. Berkeley. Clarinet Concerto[a]. Pere du doux repos[b]. Flighting[c]. [ac]**Emma Johnson** (cl); [b]**Henry Herford** (bar); [a]**Northern Sinfonia/Sian Edwards.** ASV (Special Price) CDDCB1101. Notes, text and translation included.

27m DDD 2/94

Michael Berkeley's Clarinet Concerto, written for Emma Johnson in 1991, represents a new generation of this always-accessible composer's music. Over its 20-minute, single-movement span, it delves into searchingly painful emotions, directly inspired by the sufferings of Rudyard Kipling as a boy, the subject of the opera, *Baa Baa Black Sheep*, which Berkeley was writing at the time. Though there is a high proportion of stratospheric shrieking reminiscent of the expressionist style of Harrison Birtwistle and Peter Maxwell Davies in the 1960s, and lyricism is at a premium, the clear structure of the piece leads the ear on. The two other, much briefer, simpler works on the disc are what the composer himself regards as "fitting pendants", bringing out further the lyrical side of Emma Johnson, though this programme does not present the easy ride many will expect from this soloist and this composer. The players of the Northern Sinfonia under Sian Edwards provide dedicated accompaniment in the concerto, and the recording presents the piece with clarity and warmth.

Irving Berlin
American 1888-1989

Suggested listening ...

ANNIE GET YOUR GUN. **Soloists; Ambrosian Chorus; London Sinfonietta/John McGlinn.** EMI CDC7 54206-2 (11/91).

Hector Berlioz
French 1803-1869

Berlioz. Harold in Italy, Op. 14[a]. Tristia, Op. 18[b]. Les troyens à Carthage — Act 2, Prelude[c]. [a]**Nobuko Imai** (va); [b]**John Alldis Choir; London Symphony Orchestra/Sir Colin Davis.** Philips 416 431-2PH. Texts and translations included. Item marked [a] from 9500 026 (3/76), [b] 9500 944 (6/83), [c] SAL3788 (3/70).

.•' lh 10m ADD 12/86

Berlioz was much influenced by the British romantic poet, Byron, and his travels in Italy — where he went in 1831 as the winner of the Prix de Rome — led him to conceive a big orchestral work based on one of Byron's most popular works, *Childe Harold's Pilgrimage*. Like Berlioz's earlier *Symphonie fantastique*, *Harold in Italy* was not only a programme work but brilliantly unconventional and imaginative in its structure and argument. A commission from the great virtuoso, Paganini, led him to conceive a big viola concerto, but the idea of a Byronic symphony got in the way of that. Though there is an important viola solo in the symphony as we know it — richly and warmly played on this recording by Nobuko Imai — it is far from being the vehicle for solo display that Paganini was wanting. Sir Colin Davis's 1975 perform-ance, beautifully transferred to CD, emphasizes the symphonic strength of the writing without losing the bite of the story-telling. The shorter works are also all valuable in illustrating Berlioz's extraordinary imagination. Excellent sound on all the different vintage recordings.

Additional recommendations ...
Harold in Italy. **Yuri Bashmet** (va); **Frankfurt Radio Symphony Orchestra/Eliahu Inbal.**
Denon CO-73207 — .•'' 40m DDD 12/89
Harold in Italy (arr. Liszt)[a]. **Liszt.** *Romance oubliée, S132*[a]. *Hymne à Sainte Cécile (Gounod), S491. Le Moine (Meyerbeer), S416. Festmarsch zu Schillers Jähriger Geburtsfeier (Meyerbeer), S549.* **Leslie Howard** (pf); [a]**Paul Coletti** (va). Hyperion CDA66683 — .•'' 1h 13m DDD 11/93 ℗

New review
Berlioz. ORCHESTRAL WORKS.
Saint-Saëns. Le rouet d'Omphale in A major, Op. 31[c]. **Boston Symphony Orchestra/Charles Munch.** RCA Victor Gold Seal 09026-61400-2. Items marked [a] from SB2125 (10/61), [b] LDS6098 (10/62), [c] SB2041 (9/59). Recorded 1957-61.
Le carnaval romain, Op. 9[a]. Béatrice et Bénédict — Overture[a]. Le corsaire, Op. 21[a]. Les troyens — Royal Hunt and Storm[a]. Benvenuto Cellini — Overture[a]. Roméo et Juliette, Op. 17 — Queen Mab scherzo[b].

.•'' **1h 1m ADD 11/93** ▲

This particular Berlioz concert has long enjoyed classic status. Munch secures an electrifying response from his great Boston orchestra, whose playing is virtuosic and tender by turns. Highlights include truly exhilarating renderings of *Le corsaire* and *Benvenuto Cellini* as well as a quite riveting Royal Hunt and Storm, which attains a breathtaking poetry in the horn-led moments of repose. The bonus item, Saint-Saëns's colourful tone-poem, *Le rouet d'Omphale*, is also superbly managed here: its central climax has surely never sounded more gripping. Recordings are a bit thin in the treble, but not enough to take the shine off what is an irresistible mid-price anthology.

Berlioz. Symphonie fantastique, Op. 14. **Vienna Philharmonic Orchestra/Sir Colin Davis.** Philips 432 151-2PH. Recorded in 1990.

.•'' **56m DDD 5/92**

Sir Colin Davis's third Philips recording of the *Symphonie fantastique* benefits, like its two predecessors (with the London Symphony and Royal Concertgebouw Orchestras, respectively), from the specific tonal properties of its orchestra — which, in this case, means a rich textural bloom to the strings, creamy woodwinds and powerful, though never coarse or ungainly, brass. Davis has the VPO responding to him with absolute naturalness: barlines may as well not exist, and subtle rubato nudges salient passages with just the right degree of expressive emphasis. Repeats are observed in the first and fourth moments, while the second includes the rarely-heard solo cornet part which Berlioz added later and the fifth has tubular bells rather than electronic sound-alikes. The recording has immense impact, capturing as it does the orchestra's sweet violin tone, even at *pianissimo* and less, while allowing full impact at climaxes. The timpani, in particular, have great presence. As a composition, the *Symphonie fantastique* is a notoriously difficult synthesis of classical and romantic elements, a real stylistic crossroads. But Davis has the measure of its parts and fully undertands its musical tensions; his is the nearest we have to a thorough, all-embracing oveview, and it is to be enthusiastically recommended.

Additional recommendations ...
Symphonie fantastique. **London Classical Players/Roger Norrington.** EMI Reflexe CDC7 49541-2 — .•'' 53m DDD 4/89 ℗ Ⓑ ✦
Symphonie fantastique[a]. *Overtures* — King Lear, Op. 4[b]. Le carnaval romain, Op. 9[c]. [a]**French Radio National Orchestra,** [b]**Royal Philharmonic Orchestra,** [c]**London Philharmonic Orchestra/Sir Thomas Beecham.** EMI Beecham Edition mono CDM7 64032-2 — .•'' 1h 11m ADD 8/92 Ⓑ ▲
Symphonie fantastique. **Orchestre Révolutionnaire et Romantique/John Eliot Gardiner.** Philips 434 402-2PH — .•'' 53m DDD 6/93 ℗ Ⓑ ✦
Symphonie fantastique. Overtures — Le carnaval romain, Op. 9; Le corsaire, Op. 21. LA DAMNATION DE FAUST — Hungarian March. LES TROYENS — Trojan March. **Detroit Symphony Orchestra/Paul Paray.** Mercury 434 328-2MM — .•'' 1h 13m ADD 9/93 ℗ Ⓑ

Berlioz. ORCHESTRAL AND VOCAL WORKS. [b]**Sheila Armstrong** (sop); [b]**Josephine Veasey** (mez); [b]**Frank Patterson** (ten); [b]**John Shirley-Quirk** (bar); **London Symphony Orchestra/Sir Colin Davis**. Philips Insignia 438 307-2PM. Items marked [a] from SAL3573 (10/66), [b] 6500 009 (6/70), [c] SAL3695/6 (12/68), [d] 6700 121 (5/79).
Le carnaval romain, Op. 9[a]. Les nuits d'été, Op. 7[b]. Roméo et Juliette, Op. 17 — Love scene; Queen Mab scherzo[c]. Béatrice et Bénédict — Overture[d].

lh l3m   ADD   7/93

In the late 1960s the LSO was a superb orchestra, Davis was at his peak as a Berlioz interpreter and Philips's recording technique was in a golden period — the sound in all these performances is still of demonstration quality evincing warmth depth and clarity. All these splendid characteristics were channelled into the company's memorable Berlioz cycle. Davis's ear for, and affinity with, the composer is there to be heard in every bar and strand of these readings. Particularly notable is his gift for sustaining those seemingly endless passages of melody — as in the *Roméo et Juliette* love scene, his ability to conjure up, with all his youthful enthusiasm, the bravura of Berlioz's writing, as in the *Béatrice et Bénédict* Overture, and his understanding of the importance of Berlioz's wind writing to which he gives due prominence everywhere but perhaps most pertinently in *Les nuits d'été*. That work receives a performance, in most respects, unrivalled elsewhere. The choice of four singers precisely to fulfil the composer's wishes as regards type of voice and therefore key distribution gives this performance a unique value, and the casting could hardly be bettered. This is a version all Berliozians must have, even if they'll regret the absence of texts and translations. For anyone not yet introduced to the many pleasures of Berlioz's music this would form an ideal introduction.

Berlioz. SONGS. [a]**Brigitte Fournier** (sop); [b]**Diana Montague**, [c]**Catherine Robbin** (mezs); [d]**Howard Crook** (ten); [e]**Gilles Cachemaille** (bar); **Lyon Opéra Orchestra/John Eliot Gardiner**. Erato MusiFrance 2292-45517-2. Texts and translations included. Recorded in 1989.
Le jeune pâtre breton, Op. 13 No. 4[d]. La captive, Op. 12[c]. Le chasseur danois, Op. 19 No. 6[e]. Zaïde, Op. 19 No. 1[a]. La belle voyageuse, Op. 2 No. 4[b]. Les nuits d'été, Op. 7 — Villanelle[d]; Le spectre de la rose[c]; Sur les lagunnes[e]; Absence[b]; Au cimetière[d]; L'île inconnue[b]. Aubade[d]. Tristia, Op. 18 — No. 2, La mort d'Ophélie[c].

lh 5m   DDD   2/91

As noted in the review above, Berlioz intended the songs in his cycle *Les nuits d'été* to be assigned to different types of singers. This excellent issue fulfils his wishes, and each of the performers has been carefully chosen to fit his or her particular offering. In turn, Montague, Robbin, Crook and Cachemaille ideally catches the mood and feeling of his or her piece, and each has the kind of tone that seems perfectly suited to Berlioz's idiom. In support, Gardiner finds just the right tempo for each song, never indulging in the over-deliberate speed that can kill the slower songs with kindness. He and his orchestra play Berlioz's wonderfully atmospheric accompaniments with beauty and sensitivity. To add to one's pleasure there is a generous selection of Berlioz's other songs with orchestra, equally well interpreted. Robbin's account of the marvellous *La captive*, the very essence of this composer's brand of romanticism, is a particular joy.

Additional recommendations ...
Les nuits d'été[a]. **Ravel.** *Shéhérazade*[a]. **Debussy.** *Trois chansons de Bilitis*[b]. **Poulenc.** *Banalities — Chansons d'Orkenise; Hôtel. La courte paille — Le carafon; La reine de coeur. Chansons villageoises — Les gars qui vont à la fête. Deux poémes de Louis Aragon.* **Régine Crespin** (sop); [b]**John Wustman** (pf); [a]**Suisse Romande Orchestra/Ernest Ansermet.** Decca 417 813-2DH — **lh 8m   ADD** 11/88
Les nuits d'été. **Duparc.** *Chanson triste. La manoir de Rosemonde. L'invitation au voyage. Soupir. Phidylé. La vie anterieure. Sérénade florentine.* **Bernadette Greevy** (mez); **Ulster Orchestra/Yan Pascal Tortelier.** Chandos CHAN8735 — **56m   DDD** 1/90

Berlioz. Messe Solennelle (also includes revised version of Resurrexit). **Donna Brown** (sop); **Jean-Luc Viala** (ten); **Gilles Cachemaille** (bar); **Monteverdi Choir; Orchestre**

Révolutionnaire et Romantique/John Eliot Gardiner. Philips 442 137-2PH. Text and translation included. Recorded at a performance in Westminster Cathedral, London in 1993.

♪ 1h 1m DDD 4/94 ⓟ

The reappearance of Berlioz's lost Mass of 1824 is the most exciting musical discovery of modern times. Why did Berlioz abandon the work? Only the *Resurrexit* was retained, though it was rewritten: both versions are included here. Some of it, but not much, is dull, some is awkward, but the best of the work is superb: among this one may count the *Incarnatus*, the *O Salutaris* and the lovely *Agnus Dei*. The latter was too good to lose, and survives in another form in the *Te Deum*. So do other ideas: it is at first disconcerting to hear the chorus singing "Laudamus te, benedicamus te" to the Carnival music from *Benvenuto Cellini*, more so than to hear the slow movement of the *Symphonie fantastique* in the beautiful *Gratias*. Once these and other associations are overcome, the work coheres remarkably well. Yet perhaps it did not do so well enough for Berlioz, and perhaps he was dissatisfied with the conjunction of some rather academic music with ideas that were too original, indeed too beautiful, to make a satisfying whole. All the same, no wonder the precocious 20-year-old was embraced after the first performance by his teacher, old Le Sueur, with the promise that he would be a great composer. Who knows whether he might have been made to think twice about abandoning the work had he heard a performance such as this, almost certainly more perceptive and assured than he would have got from the Opéra orchestra in 1825? His far-seeing imagination, especially with extraordinary textures and conjunctions of novel ideas, is now understood better than it could have been then. This applies to the wonderful Monteverdi Choir (their sopranos never sounding better), to an orchestra including serpent, ophicleide and the nobly dragon-headed buccin, and above all to Gardiner himself. This is a record of a great musical event, not to be missed.

Berlioz. Grande messe des morts[a]. Symphonie funèbre et triomphale[b]. [a]**Ronald Dowd** (ten); [b]**Dennis Wick** (tb); [a]**Wandsworth School Boys' Choir**; [b]**John Alldis Choir**; **London Symphony Chorus**[a] **and Orchestra/Sir Colin Davis.** Philips 416 283-2PH2. Notes, texts and translations included. Item marked [a] from 6700 019 (9/70), [b] SAL3788 (3/70).

♪ ② 2h 7m ADD 4/86

Berlioz's Requiem is not a liturgical work, any more than the *Symphonie funèbre* is really for the concert hall; but both are pieces of high originality, composed as ceremonials for the fallen, and standing as two of the noblest musical monuments to the French ideal of a *gloire*. The Requiem is most famous for its apocalyptic moment when, after screwing the key up stage by stage, Berlioz's four brass bands blaze forth "at the round earth's imagin'd corners"; this has challenged the engineers of various companies, but the Philips recording for Colin Davis remains as fine as any, not least since Davis directs the bands with such a strong sense of character. He also gives the troubled rhythms of the *Lacrymosa* a stronger, more disturbing emphasis than any other conductor, and time and again finds out the expressive counterpoint, the emphatic rhythm, the telling few notes within the texture, that reveal so much about Berlioz's intentions. The notorious flute and trombone chords of the *Hostias* work admirably. Ronald Dowd is a little strained in the *Sanctus*, but the whole performance continues to stand the test of time and of other competing versions. The same is true of the *Symphonie funèbre et triomphale*, which moves at a magisterial tread and is given a recording that does well by its difficult textures. A fine coupling of two remarkable works.

Additional recommendation ...
Grande messe[a]. Te Deum, Op. 22[b]. [a]**Stuart Burrows** (ten); [b]**Jean Dupouy** (ten); [b]**Jean Guillou** (org); [a]**French Radio Chorus**; [b]**Paris Orchestra Chorus**; [b]**Paris Enfante Choir**; [b]**Maîtrise de la Résurrection**; [a]**French National Orchestra**; [a]**French Radio Philharmonic Orchestra/Leonard Bernstein**; [b]**Paris Orchestra/Daniel Barenboim.** CBS Maestro CD46461 — ♪ ② 2h 7m ADD 9/91

Berlioz. Roméo et Juliette — dramatic symphony, Op. 16. **Patricia Kern** (contr); **Robert Tear** (ten); **John Shirley-Quirk** (bar); **John Alldis Choir; London Symphony Chorus**

and Orchestra/Sir Colin Davis. Philips 416 962-2PH2. Notes, text and translation included. From SAL3695/6 (12/68). Recorded in 1968.

⟨♪ ② lh 37m ADD 6/88 ⟩

Berlioz's 'dramatic symphony' of 1839 is a prime example of early and full-blooded romanticism. The impulsive young composer adored Shakespeare and here he took the English playwright's celebrated love story and set it to music, not as an opera but a symphony with voices, partly because he felt that the language of instrumental music was "richer, more varied and free of limitations and ... incomparably more powerful". This music is, nevertheless, sometimes inspired and sometimes simply naïve, but always spontaneous and Sir Colin Davis, a great Berlioz champion, plays it as if he believed passionately and urgently in every note. He is well supported by his three vocal soloists and the London Symphony Chorus and Orchestra plus the John Alldis Choir, and although the recording is now over 27 years old it does not show its age to any significant extent and indeed may be regarded as a classic Berlioz performance although the total length of 97 minutes for two full-priced discs is not generous by CD standards.

Additional recommendations ...
Roméo et Juliette[a]. *Les nuits d'été, Op. 7*. **Anne Sofie von Otter** (mez); [a]**Philip Langridge** (ten); [a]**James Morris** (bass); [a]**Berlin RIAS Chamber Choir;** [a]**Ernst Senff Chorus; Berlin Philharmonic Orchestra/James Levine.** DG 427 665-2GH2 — ♪ ② lh 43m DDD 8/90
Roméo et Juliette[a]. *Franck.* *Le Chasseur maudit*[b]. *Rédemption — Morceau symphonique*[b]. *Nocturne*[c]. [a]**Yvonne Minton,** [c]**Christa Ludwig** (mezs); [a]**Francisco Araiza** (ten); [a]**Jules Bastin** (bass); [a]**Orchestre de Paris Chorus;** [abc]**Orchestre de Paris/Daniel Barenboim.** DG Galleria 437 244-2GGA2 — ♪ ② 2h 9m ADD 1/93

Berlioz. L'enfance du Christ, Op. 25. **Robert Tear** (ten) Narrator; **David Wilson-Johnson** (bar) Herod; **Ann Murray** (mez) Mary; **Thomas Allen** (bar) Joseph; **Matthew Best** (bass) Ishmaelite Father; **Gerald Finley** (bar) Polydorus; **William Kendall** (ten) Centurion; **Choir of King's College, Cambridge; Royal Philharmonic Orchestra/Stephen Cleobury.** EMI CDS7 49935-2. Notes, text and translation included. Recorded in 1989.

⟨♪ ② lh 37m DDD 12/90 ⟩

The Choir of King's College, Cambridge has made this splendid recording of *L'enfance du Christ* with a strong, well-chosen all-English cast. The important role of Narrator falls to Robert Tear, who assumes it with warmth and sympathy and a good sense of the drama as it unfolds. David Wilson-Johnson makes a superb Herod, tortured and anguished in his mind before delivering his half-demented sentence of death upon the Holy Innocents. Ann Murray, as Mary, is tender and gentle, particularly in the quiet, idyllic stable scene. Thomas Allen portrays a convincing Joseph, firm and decisive in his singing, well able to face up to his responsibilities as head of the Holy Family. Matthew Best sings a rich and heart-warming welcome to them on their arrival in Egypt. The King's Choir, amply assisted by the chapel acoustics, are able to make the choir of angelic voices sound truly other-worldly, their repeated "Hosannas" fading gently upwards and away into the fan-vaulting — like clouds of incense — with magical effect. The acoustics also play an important part at the close of the oratorio, enabling the choir to bring it almost inevitably to its breathtaking conclusion of peace and quiet contemplation. Even if you've never heard any of this music before, except the famous "Shepherds' farewell" chorus, this really is compulsory listening!

Additional recommendations ...
L'enfance du Christ. **Soloists; Monteverdi Choir; Lyons Opera Orchestra/John Eliot Gardiner.** Erato 2292-45275-2 — ♪ ② lh 36m DDD 1/88 ♪ 🏅
L'enfance du Christ[a]. *Tristia, Op. 18 — excerpts*[b]. *Sara la baigneuse, Op. 11*[b]. *La mort de Cléopâtre*[b]. [a]**Soloists;** [ab]**St Anthony Singers;** [b]**English Chamber Orchestra,** [a]**Goldsbrough Orchestra, Sir Colin Davis.** Decca 425 445-2DM2 — ♪ ② 2h 22m ADD ♪

Berlioz. La damnation de Faust. **Nicolai Gedda** (ten) Faust; **Jules Bastin** (bass) Méphistophélès; **Josephine Veasey** (mez) Marguérite; **Richard Van Allan** (bass) Brander; **Gillian Knight** (mez) Celestial Voice; **Wandsworth School Boys' Choir; Ambrosian**

Singers; London Symphony Chorus and Orchestra/Sir Colin Davis. Philips 416 395-2PH2. Notes, text and translation included. From 6703 042 (1/74). Recorded in 1973.

② 2h 11m ADD 1/87

Sir Colin Davis's performance of *La damnation* reveals the colour and excitement of a work that has never found a true home in the opera house. None of Berlioz's other scores surpasses it in the subtle and telling use of detail, from the whole orchestra in full cry to the subtly judged chamber music combinations and to details of instrumental choice (as when the husky viola for Marguérite's touching little song about the bereft King of Thule yields to the mournful cor anglais for her abandonment by Faust). Davis's performance has the grandeur and excitement of Berlioz's vision of romantic man compassing his own damnation by being led to test and reject the consolations maliciously offered by Méphistophélès. No other conductor has made the "Hungarian March" turn so chillingly from its brave panoply to a menacing emptiness. The sylphs and will-o'-the-wisps flit and hover delicately. The transformation from the raucous boozers in Auerbach's cellar to Faust's dream of love on the banks of the Elbe is beautifully done, as the hurtling pace slows and the textures soften, Méphistophélès's sweet melodic line betrayed by the snarling brass accompaniment. The arrival of CD gave an extra edge to all this vivid and expressive detail. The singers are very much within this fine and faithful concept of the work. Gedda is an incomparably elegant, noble Faust, whose very gentleness is turned against him by the cold, sneering, ironic Méphistophélès of Jules Bastin. Josephine Veasey is a touching Marguérite who is not afraid to be simple; and Richard Van Allan knocks off a jovial Brander. Chorus and orchestra clearly enjoy the whole occasion, and rise to it.

Additional recommendation ...
Soloists; Cologne Radio Chorus; Stuttgart Radio Chorus; North German Radio Chorus, Hamburg; Frankfurt Radio Symphony Orchestra/Eliahu Inbal. Denon CO-77200/01 — ② 2h 7m DDD 7/91

Berlioz. BEATRICE ET BENEDICT. **Susan Graham** (sop) Béatrice; **Jean-Luc Viala** (ten) Bénédict; **Sylvia McNair** (sop) Héro; **Catherine Robbin** (mez) Ursule; **Gilles Cachemaille** (bar) Claudio; **Gabriel Bacquier** (bar) Somarone; **Vincent Le Texier** (bass) Don Pedro; **Philippe Magnant** (spkr) Léonato; **Lyon Opera Chorus and Orchestra/John Nelson.** Erato MusiFrance 2292-45773-2. Notes, text and translation included. Recorded in 1991.

② 1h 51m DDD 6/92

We have to note that the title is not a French version of *Much Ado about Nothing*, but that it takes the two principal characters of Shakespeare's play and constructs an opera around them. The comedy centres on the trick which is played upon the protagonists by their friends, producing love out of apparent antipathy. Much of the charm lies in the more incidental matters of choruses, dances, the magical "Nocturne" duet for Béatrice and Héro, and the curious addition of the character Somarone, a music-master who rehearses the choir in one of his own compositions. There is also a good deal of spoken dialogue, the present recording having more of it than did its closest rival, a version made in 1977 with Sir Colin Davis conducting and Dame Janet Baker and Robert Tear in the title-roles (see below). Perhaps surprisingly, the extra dialogue is a point in favour of the new set, for it is done very effectively by good French actors and it makes for a more cohesive, Shakespearian entertainment. John Nelson secures a well-pointed performance of the score, comparing well with Davis's, and with excellent playing by the Lyon Orchestra. Susan Graham and Jean-Luc Viala are attractively vivid and nimble in style, and Sylvia McNair makes a lovely impression in Héro's big solo. The veteran Gabriel Bacquier plays the music-master with genuine panache and without overmuch clownage. There is good work by the supporting cast and the chorus and the recording is finely produced and well recorded.

Additional recommendation ...
Soloists; John Alldis Choir; London Symphony Orchestra/Sir Colin Davis. Philips 416 952-2PH2 — ② 1h 38m DDD 9/87

Berlioz. LES TROYENS. **Jon Vickers** (ten) Aeneas; **Josephine Veasey** (mez) Dido; **Berit Lindholm** (sop) Cassandra; **Peter Glossop** (bar) Corebus, Ghost of Corebus; **Heather Begg** (sop) Anna; **Roger Soyer** (bar) Narbal, Spirit of Hector; **Anne Howells** (mez) Ascanius;

Anthony Raffell (bass) Panthus; **Ian Partridge** (ten) Iopas; **Pierre Thau** (bass) Priam, Mercury, a Trojan soldier; **Elizabeth Bainbridge** (mez) Hecuba, Ghost of Cassandra; **Ryland Davies** (ten) Hylas; **David Lennox** (ten) Helenus; **Raimund Herincx** (bass) Ghost of Priam, First Sentry; **Dennis Wicks** (bar) Ghost of Hector, Second Sentry, Greek Chieftain; **Wandsworth School Boys' Choir; Royal Opera House, Covent Garden Chorus and Orchestra/Sir Colin Davis.** Philips 416 432-2PH4. Notes, text and translation included. From 6709 002 (5/70). Recorded in 1969.

④ 4h 1m ADD 12/86

One of the largest canvases in the whole genre of opera, *Les troyens* was for long considered unperformable. Yet it is no longer than some of Wagner's scores and certainly no more difficult to encompass in one evening. That has been proved conclusively in a succession of productions at Covent Garden, this one recorded not actually 'live' but immediately after stage performances. Sir Colin Davis, the leading Berlioz conductor of the day, fired his forces to give the kind of reading that could only have emerged from experience of the work in the opera house. He is fully aware of the epic quality of the story and no one else has quite so successfully conveyed the score's dramatic stature, its nobility and its tragic consequences. There are many splendid performances on this set, but in the end it is the sense of a team effort, of a cast, chorus and orchestra utterly devoted to the task in hand that is so boldly declared. The recording matches the quality of the music-making.

Additional recommendation ...

Act 5, scenes 2 and 3[c]. *Les nuits d'été*, Op. 7[a]. *La mort de Cléopâtre*[b]. **Dame Janet Baker** (mez); [c]**Bernadette Greevy** (contr); [c]**Keith Erwen** (ten); [c]**Gwynne Howell** (bass); [c]**Ambrosian Opera Chorus;** [a]**New Philharmonia Orchestra/Sir John Barbirolli;** [bc]**London Symphony Orchestra/Sir Alexander Gibson.** EMI Studio CDM7 69544-2 — 1h 18m ADD 11/88 Ⓑ

Further listening ...

Rêverie et caprice, Op. 8. *Coupled with* **Lalo.** Symphonie espagnole, Op. 21. **Itzhak Perlman** (vn); **Orchestre de Paris/Daniel Barenboim.** DG 400 032-2GH (3/83).

BENVENUTO CELLINI. **Soloists; Royal Opera House Chorus, Covent Garden; BBC Symphony Orchestra/Sir Colin Davis.** Philips 416 955-2PH3 (1/89).

Baronet Lord Berners
British 1883-1950

Suggested listening ...

Berners. The Triumph of Neptune[a] — Schottische; Hornpipe; Polka; Harlequinade; Dance of the Fairy Princess; Intermezzo; Apotheosis of Neptune. *Coupled with* **Bantock.** Fifine at the Fair[b]. **Bax.** The Garden of Fand[b]. [a]**Robert Alva** (bar); [a]**London Philharmonic Orchestra,** [b]**Royal Philharmonic Orchestra/Sir Thomas Beecham.** EMI Beecham Edition mono CDM7 63405-2 (6/92).

Elmer Bernstein
American 1922-

Suggested listening ...

The Great Escape — *film score.* **orchestra/Elmer Bernstein.** Intrada MAF7025D (5/93).

Kings Go Forth. Some Came Running — *Original film soundtracks.* Cloud Nine CNS5004 (5/93).

The Age of Innocence — *Original film soundtrack.* Epic 474576-2.

The Magnificent Seven — *film score.* **The Phoenix Symphony/James Sedares.** Koch International 37222-2.

Leonard Bernstein

American 1918-1990

Bernstein. ORCHESTRAL WORKS. **New York Philharmonic Orchestra/Leonard Bernstein.** CBS Maestro CD44773. Items marked [a] from 72405 (5/66), [b] Philips SBBL652 (2/62). Candide — Overture[a]. West Side Story — Symphonic dances[b]. On the Town — Three Dance Episodes[a]. On the Waterfront — Symphonic Suite[b].

·•* 55m ADD 2/91   *♩ₚ*

Broadway and Hollywood form a backcloth to all the music on this disc. A maniacally driven Overture to Bernstein's third Broadway musical, *Candide*, sets the style from the outset with the conductor intent on squeezing every last ounce from both his music and players. The orchestra can sound hard-pressed at times and details get smudged, especially so in the cavernous acoustic, but the dazzling zest of this approach is totally winning and, when the music does relax into more tender moments, the pathos is overwhelming. In the Symphonic dances from *West Side Story*, few orchestras could better the NYPO's intuitive feel for the dance rhythms and cross accents, the rampaging Latin percussion barrage, the screaming trumpet writing, or the theatre-pit instrumental balance. The "Three Dance Episodes" from Bernstein's first musical, *On the Town*, are more overtly eclectic, with hints of Gershwin alongside allusions to Stravinsky, whilst the magnificent score for the film, *On the Waterfront*, finds Bernstein inventively complementing the highlights and deep shadows of Elia Kazan's visual style, and the savagery of the plot. As his own best interpreter, Bernstein goes straight for the key features of all these scores and inspires his orchestra to produce its best.

Bernstein. Songfest[a]. Chichester Psalms[b]. [a]**Clamma Dale** (sop); [a]**Rosalind Elias,** [a]**Nancy Williams** (mezs); [a]**Neil Rosenshein** (ten); [a]**John Reardon** (bar); [a]**Donald Gramm** (bass); [b]soloist from the **Vienna Boys' Choir;** [b]**Vienna Jeunesse Choir;** [a]**National Symphony Orchestra of Washington,** [b]**Israel Philharmonic Orchestra/Leonard Bernstein.** DG 415 965-2GH. Texts and, where appropriate, translations included. Item marked [a] from 2531 044 (11/78), [b] 2709 077 (9/78). Recorded in 1977.

·•* 1h 2m ADD 5/86

"I, too, am America", is the message of Leonard Bernstein's orchestral song-cycle *Songfest*. The subject of the work is the American artist's emotional, spiritual and intellectual response to life in an essentially Puritan society, and, more specifically, to the eclecticism of American society and its many problems of social integration (blacks, women, homosexuals and expatriates). As expected from a composer/conductor equally at home on Broadway or in Vienna's Musikverein, the styles range widely. The scoring is colourful, occasionally pungent, always tuneful. Bernstein's soloists are well chosen and sing with feeling. This vivid live recording of the *Chichester Psalms* offers the full orchestral version and the performers all give their utmost.

New review
Bernstein. ON THE TOWN. **Frederica von Stade** (mez) Claire; **Tyne Daly** (sngr) Hildy; **Marie McLaughlin** (sop) Ivy; **Thomas Hampson** (bass) Gabey; **Kurt Ollmann** (bar) Chip; **David Garrison** (sngr) Ozzie; **Samuel Ramey** (bass) Pitkin; **Evelyn Lear** (sop) Madame Dilly; **Cleo Laine** (sngr) Nightclub singer; **London Voices; London Symphony Orchestra/Michael Tilson Thomas.** DG 437 516-2GH. Notes and text included. Recorded in 1992.

·•* 1h 15m DDD 10/93   *♩ₚ*

On the Town is a peach of a show, a show which positively hums along on the heat of its inspiration, a show rejoicing in the race of time, but regretful of its passing, a show which lovingly encapsulates those transitory moments seized and then lost amidst the impatient, pulsating heart and soul of the lonely city — the Big Apple. On two amazing nights Michael Tilson Thomas and this starry cast brought New York City to the Barbican in London. Recording this semi-staged performance live must have been a living nightmare for DG's engineers, but one wonders if they might not have pulled off a more up-front balance for the voices. Only Cleo Laine gets to be really intimate with her bluesy nightclub song "Ain't got no tears left". You'll hang on every breath Laine takes. Many of the notes are threadbare, but who needs the notes when you've got instincts like hers. As to the major roles there are happily no grave misjudgements in casting such as marred the composer's by now infamous *West Side Story* on this label. Mind you, you know you're in big-league production when you get Samuel Ramey delivering (gloriously) the Brooklyn Navy Yard Workers' ode to morning "I feel like I'm not out of bed yet". And Ramey was an inspired choice for Clare's monumentally boring boyfriend, Pitkin. His "Song", a masterpiece of arch formality, is very funny indeed. In performance, Tyne Daly's cab-driving Hildy knocked 'em in the aisles with her huggable personality, and the three sailors, Gabey, Chip, Ozzie — Thomas Hampson, Kurt Ollmann, David Garrison — are just perfect. Not only are they well-matched vocally, but you could put them on any stage and never look back. Hampson's two big numbers — "Lonely Town" and "Lucky to be Me" — are handsomely sung with careful avoidance of that peculiarly 'operatic' articulation. The real heroes of this dizzy enterprise are Tilson Thomas and the London Symphony Orchestra, every last player a character, an individual. John Harle's soaring, throaty sax and rhythms are so hot, tight and idiomatic that you'd never credit this wasn't an American band. The playing here is stunning, there's no other word.

New review

Bernstein. WEST SIDE STORY. **Tinuke Olafimihan** Maria; **Paul Manuel** Tony; **Caroline O'Connor** Anita; **Sally Burgess** Off-stage voice; **Nicholas Warnford** Riff; **Julie Paton** Rosalia; **Elinor Stephenson** Consuela; **Nicole Carty** Francisca; **Kieran Daniels** Action; **Mark Michaels** Diesel; **Adrian Sarple** Baby John; **Adrian Edmeads** A-rab; **Garry Stevens** Snowboy; **Nick Ferranti** Bernardo; **chorus and National Symphony Orchestra/John Owen Edwards.** TER CDTER2 1197. Recorded in 1993.

② 1h 4lm DDD 2/94

To cap the composer's own recording of *West Side Story,* even given his controversial casting of opera stars, is something of an achievement. The set starts with the major advantage of being inspired by a production at the Haymarket, Leicester, so many of the cast are really inside their roles. They have youth on their side, too. Paul Manuel from that company may not have a large voice, but his sympathetic portrayal of Tony, both in his solos and duets with Maria, makes one feel that he identifies totally with the part. Moreover, the way in which he can float a high note, as at the end of the alternative film version of "Something's coming" puts him on a par with Carreras (for Bernstein). His Maria, Tinuke Olafimihan, is a gem. Her ability to interact with him and to express the laughter and the tragedy of the heroine is very real. At the heart of the "Somewhere" ballet, Sally Burgess voices the lovers' plea for peace with a magnificent rendition of its famous soaring tune. Nicholas Warnford as leader of the Jets gives no less than his rival in the tricky "Cool" sequence and Jet song. John Owen Edwards directs Bernstein's score as if he believes in every note of it. Moreover, he has imparted to his players the very pulse that sets this music ticking.

Additional recommendation ...
Dame Kiri Te Kanawa (sop); **José Carreras** (ten); **Tatiana Troyanos** (mez); **Kurt Ollmann** (bar); composite chorus and orchestra from 'on and off' Broadway/**Leonard Bernstein** with **Marilyn Horne** (mez). DG 415 253-2GH2 — ② 1h 38m DDD 4/85

Bernstein. CANDIDE (1988 final version). **Jerry Hadley** (ten) Candide; **June Anderson** (sop) Cunegonde; **Adolph Green** (ten) Dr Pangloss, Martin; **Christa Ludwig** (mez) Old lady; **Nicolai Gedda** (ten) Governor, Vanderdendur, Ragotski; **Della Jones** (mez) Paquette; **Kurt Ollmann** (bar) Maximilian, Captain, Jesuit father; **Neil Jenkins** (ten) Merchant, Inquisitor, Prince Charles Edward; **Richard Suart** (bass) Junkman, Inquisitor, King Hermann Augustus; **John Treleaven** (ten) Alchemist, Inquisitor, Sultan Achmet, Crook; **Lindsay Benson** (bar) Doctor, Inquisitor, King Stanislaus; **Clive Bayley** (bar) Bear-Keeper, Inquisitor,

Tsar Ivan; **London Symphony Chorus and Orchestra/Leonard Bernstein.** DG 429 734-2GH2. Notes and text included.

> ⓶ 1h 52m DDD 8/91

Here it is — all of it — musical comedy, grand opera, operetta, satire, melodrama, all rolled into one. We can thank John Mauceri for much of the restoration work: his 1988 Scottish Opera production was the spur for this recording and prompted exhaustive reappraisal. Numbers like "We Are Women", "Martin's Laughing Song" and "Nothing More Than This" have rarely been heard, if at all. The last mentioned, Candide's 'aria of disillusionment', is one of the enduring glories of the score, reinstated where Bernstein always wanted it (but where no producer would have it), near the very end of the show. Bernstein called it his "Puccini aria", and that it is — bitter-sweet, long-breathed, supported, enriched and ennobled by its inspiring string counterpoint. And this is but one of many forgotten gems. It was an inspiration on someone's part (probably Bernstein's) to persuade the great and versatile Christa Ludwig and Nicolai Gedda (in his sixties and still hurling out the top Bs) to fill the principal character roles. To say they do so ripely is to do them scant justice. Bernstein's old sparring partner Adolph Green braves the tongue-twisting and many-hatted Dr Pangloss with his own highly individual form of *sprechstimme*, Jerry Hadley sings the title role most beautifully, *con amore*, and June Anderson has all the notes, and more, for the faithless, air-headed Cunegonde. It is just a pity that someone didn't tell her that discretion is the better part of comedy. "Glitter and Be Gay" is much funnier for being played straighter, odd as it may sound. Otherwise, the supporting roles are all well taken and the London Symphony Chorus have a field-day in each of their collective guises. Having waited so long to commit every last note (or thereabouts) of his cherished score to disc, there are moments here where Bernstein seems almost reluctant to move on. His tempos are measured, to say the least, the score fleshier now in every respect: even that raciest of Overtures has now acquired a more deliberate gait, a more opulent tone. But Bernstein would be Bernstein, and there are moments where one is more than grateful for his indulgence: the grandiose chorales, the panoramic orchestrascapes (sumptuously recorded), and of course, that thrilling finale — the best of all possible Bernstein anthems at the slowest of all possible speeds — and why not (prepare to hold your breath at the choral *a capella*). It's true, perhaps, that somewhere in the midst of this glossy package there is a more modest show trying to get out, but let's not look gift horses in the mouth.

Additional recommendation ...
(Revised 1982 version). **Soloists; New York City Opera Chorus and Orchestra/John Mauceri.** New World NW340/41-2 — ⓶ 1h 33m DDD 10/86

Further listening ...

Candide — Overture. Symphony No. 2, "The Age of Anxiety"[a]. Fancy Free — ballet[b]. [b]**Billie Holiday** (sngr); [a]**Jeffrey Kahane** (pf); **Bournemouth Symphony Orchestra/Andrew Litton.** Virgin Classics VC7 59038-2 (9/91).

Serenade after Plato's Symposium. Fancy Free — ballet. **Gidon Kremer** (vn); **Israel Philharmonic Orchestra/Leonard Bernstein.** DG 423 583-2GH (1/89).

Clarinet Sonata[a]. *Coupled with* **Gershwin** (arr. Heifetz, trans. Ma)[b]. Three Preludes. **Ives.** Trio for Violin, Clarinet and Piano[c]. **Kirchner.** Triptych[d]. **Yo-Yo Ma** (vc); [c]**Ronan Lefkowitz,** [d]**Lynn Chang** (vns); [ab]**Jeffrey Kahane,** [c]**Gilbert Kalish** (pfs). Sony Classical SK53126 (4/94). *See review in the Collections section; refer to the Index to Reviews.*

Symphony No. 1, "Jeremiah"[a]. Songfest[b]. Anniversaries — In Memoriam: Nathalie Koussevitzky[c]. [b]**Linda Hohenfeld** (sop); [a]**Nan Merriman,** [b]**Wendy White,** [b]**Patricia Spence** (mezs); [b]**Walter Planté** (ten); [b]**Vernon Hartman** (bar); [b]**John Cheek** (bass); [ab]**St Louis Symphony Orchestra/**[a]**Leonard Bernstein,** [b]**Leonard Slatkin** ([c]pf). RCA Victor Red Seal [a]mono/[b]stereo 09026 61581-2 (6/94).

ON THE TOWN. TROUBLE IN TAHITI. On the Town — Three Dance Episodes. Candide — Overture. Fancy Free. West Side Story — Symphonic Dances. On the Waterfront — Symphonic Suite. Facsimile choreographic essay. **Soloists; Columbia Wind Ensemble; New**

York Philharmonic Orchestra/Leonard Bernstein. Sony Classical Portrait CD47154 (3-CD set) (5/92).

A QUIET PLACE. Soloists; Austrian Radio Symphony Orchestra/Leonard Bernstein. DG 419 761-2GH2 (10/87).

WEST SIDE STORY. *Original film soundtrack.* Sony CD48211.

WONDERFUL TOWN. **Original TV cast.** Sony Broadway CD48021.

Franz Adolf Berwald
Swedish 1796-1868

New review

Berwald. ORCHESTRAL WORKS. [a]**Arve Tellefsen** (vn); [b]**Marian Migdal** (pf); **Royal Philharmonic Orchestra/Ulf Björlin.** EMI Matrix CDM5 65073-2. From HMV SLS5014 (10/77). The Queen of Golconda — Overture. Piano Concerto in D major[b]. The Festival of the Bayadères. Violin Concerto in C sharp minor, Op. 2[a]. Serious and joyful fancies.

Ih 9m ADD 6/94

Apart from the four symphonies, little of Berwald's music is much heard. He is an unfailingly intelligent and original figure and his neglect is our loss. The lightly scored Violin Concerto (1820), an early piece, is slight but charming, particularly when it is played as beautifully and elegantly as it is here by Arve Tellefsen. Its spirit is not far removed from Spohr or Weber. The Piano Concerto, from the other end of his career, is a curious piece in that the soloist plays without any relief or pause. Some of the writing is Chopinesque but there is much that is quite individual. *The Queen of Golconda* Overture (1864) is certainly a captivating overture and in a just world ought to be a repertory piece. *The Festival of the Bayadères* and *Serious and joyful fancies* are both vintage pieces dating from the same period as the symphonies. Ulf Björlin gets good results from the RPO and gives good support to both soloists. The disc is well recorded.

Berwald. SYMPHONIES. **Gothenburg Symphony Orchestra/Neeme Järvi.** DG 415 502-2GH2.
No. 1 in G minor, "Sinfonie sérieuse"; No. 2 in D major, "Sinfonie capricieuse"; No. 3 in C major, "Sinfonie singulière"; No. 4 in E flat major.

② Ih 5Im DDD 12/85

Franz Berwald is certainly not an everyday name and his discovery was a twentieth-century phenomenon. His best music is fresh, original and appealing, and a refreshing change from the more familiar symphonies of Mendelssohn and Schumann. The *Singulière,* composed in 1845, had its first performance in 1905. The opening is simple in technique but provides a rich germ for development. The *Sinfonie capricieuse* has momentary whiffs of Mendelssohn but, as with all of Berwald's music, parallels are not made easily. The smiling world of the last symphony, the E flat, finds Berwald in light-hearted mood, proffering a particularly charming and classical *Scherzo.* Järvi's advocacy of these works is totally committed and the Gothenburg Symphony Orchestra play splendidly with some fine wind articulation. The recording is well-detailed and crisp.

Additional recommendation ...
Nos. 3 and 4. **London Symphony Orchestra/Sixten Ehrling.** Bluebell ABCD037 — ·⸫
57m ADD 8/92
Nos. 1 and 2. **San Francisco Symphony Orchestra/Herbert Blomstedt.** Decca 436 597-2DH — ·⸫ Ih 3m DDD 1/94

Further listening ...

Piano Quintet No. 1 in C minor. Piano Trios — No. 1 in E flat major; No. 3 in D minor.
Stefan Lindgren (pf); **Berwald Quartet.** Musica Sveciae MSCD521 (10/93).

String Quartets — [ab]No. 2 in A minor; [c]No. 3 in E flat major. [a]**Skåne Quartet;** [b]**Ericson Quartet;** [c]**Kyndel Quartet.** Caprice CAP21506.

Antonio Bibalo

Norwegian/Italian 1922-

Suggested listening ...

Sinfonia notturna. Sonatina 2A, Astrale. Autumnale. **Soloists; Norwegian Wind Quintet; Bergen Philharmonic Orchestra/Karsten Andersen.** Aurora NCD-B4943.

Heinrich Biber

Bohemian 1644-1704

Biber. Mystery Sonatas. **John Holloway** (vn); **Davitt Moroney** (org/hpd); **Tragicomedia** (Stephen Stubbs, lte/chitarrone; Erin Headley, va da gamba/lirone; Andrew Lawrence-King, hp/regal). Virgin Classics Veritas VCD7 59551-2.

② 2h 11m DDD 5/91

Biber was among the most talented musicians of the late seventeenth century. He was a renowned violinist and his compositions, above all for the violin, are technically advanced and strikingly individual. The 15 *Mystery Sonatas* with their additional *Passacaglia* for unaccompanied violin were written in about 1678 and dedicated to Biber's employer, the Archbishop of Salzburg. Each Sonata is inspired by a section of the Rosary devotion of the Catholic Church which offered a system of meditation on 15 Mysteries from the lives of Jesus and His mother. The music is not, strictly speaking, programmatic though often vividly illustrative of events which took place in the life of Christ. All but two of the 16 pieces require *scordatura* or retuning of the violin strings; in this way Biber not only facilitated some of the fingerings but also achieved sounds otherwise unavailable to him. The Sonatas are disposed into three groups of five: Joyful, Sorrowful and Glorious Mysteries whose contrasting states are affectingly evoked in music ranging from a spirit reflecting South German baroque exuberance to one of profound contemplation. John Holloway plays with imaginative sensibility and he is supported by a first-rate continuo group whose instruments include baroque lute, chitarrone, viola da gamba, a 15-string lirone, double harp and regal.

Additional recommendation ...
Cologne Musica Antiqua/Reinhard Goebel (vn). Archiv Produktion 431 656-2AH2 —
② 1h 54m DDD 10/91

New review
Biber. Requiem in F minor.
Valls. Missa Scala Aretina. **Sandrine Piau, Mieke van der Sluis** (sops); **Bouke Lettinga, David Cordier** (altos); **John Elwes** (ten); **Harry van der Kamp** (bass); **Netherlands Bach Society Choir and Baroque Orchestra/Gustav Leonhardt.** Deutsche Harmonia Mundi 05472 77277-2. Texts and translations included.

1h 1m DDD 8/93

Gustav Leonhardt has chosen here two works of outstanding originality. Fransisco Valls, choirmaster at Barcelona Cathedral, wrote his *Missa Scala Aretina* in 1702 for performance in the Cathedral. It is a richly scored piece disposed into four distinct sound bodies or choirs. One of these contains the solo voices (soprano, alto, tenor), two others are larger vocal ensembles of different sizes while the fourth is instrumental, consisting of strings with additional oboes, trumpets and a colourful continuo group including harp. Leonhardt brings a vital sense of occasion to the performance, injecting it with passion and evidently revelling in its rich and varied sonorities. Of the five sections of Biber's F minor Requiem (1692), the "Dies irae" is the most extended and allows for several beautifully wrought passages for the soloists. But the "Offertorium" is hardly less expressive and here Biber makes an additional contrast by casting the movement in C minor; his lean and despairing harmonies are arresting in conjuring up vivid images of man's frail condition and mortality. In short, this is a fascinating disc containing pieces of starkly contrasting outlook. The Valls is full of little, and not so little, harmonic surprises which tease the senses, the Biber a contemplative, profound work of dark and serene beauty. Recorded sound is appropriately spacious and the booklet contains an informative essay with texts and translations.

New review

Biber. Requiem in F minor[a]. Ballettae a 4 violettae. Battalia a 10 in D major. Serenada in C major, "Der Nachtwächter"[b]. Sonata a 6 in B major, "Die Pauern Kirchfahrt genandt". **[a]Catherine Bott, [a]Tessa Bonner** (sops); **[a]Christopher Robson** (alto); **[a]John Mark Ainsley** (ten); **[a]Michael George, [b]Simon Grant** (basses); **New London Consort/Philip Pickett.** L'Oiseau-Lyre 436 460-2OH. Text and translation included.

Ih 6m DDD 6/94

The layout of Salzburg Cathedral, where Biber was Kapellmeister in the last two decades of the seventeenth century, and the very large number of singers and instrumentalists available to him, made possible spatial polychoral effects similar to those in Venice a century earlier at St Mark's; and for this recording of Biber's F minor Requiem Philip Pickett has disposed his forces — five solo singers plus organ continuo in one group, two violins and three violas plus organ continuo in another facing the first, and between them a ripieno chorus with three sackbuts, violone and organ — in such a way as to suggest the original positioning. The work's richly sombre colours are expressively deployed, and all the words are invested with significance. The Requiem is a noble work, and the present fine performance is very highly recommended. Biber's illustrative penchant is even more clearly exemplified here by some programmatic string works. He was far from being unique in writing quasi-realistic music in the representation of a battle but he was perhaps the only one to anticipate Charles Ives (in the "Dissolute company of musketeers" movement) by a cacophonous hurly-burly of folk-tunes played simultaneously, regardless of each other: the suite also contains loud snapped-string bass pizzicatos (for cannon shots), *col legno* effects and, in the "March", a papered bass. An utterly charming suite of *balletti* completes an attractive disc.

Further listening ...

Trumpet music — Sonata à 7. Sonata pro tabula. Sonata VII à 5. Sonata à 3. Sonata à 6. Sonata I à 8. Sonata Sancti Polycarpi à 9. *Coupled with* **Schmelzer***:* Trumpet music — Sonata con arie zu der kaiserlichen Serenada. Sonata à 7 flauti. Balletto di spiritelli. Sonata I à 8. Balletto di centauri, ninfe e salvatici. **New London Consort/Philip Pickett.** L'Oiseau-Lyre 425 834-2OH (9/91).

William Billings
American 1746-1800

Suggested listening ...

The New-England Psalm-Singer. The Singing Master's Assistant. The Psalm-Singer's Amusement. The Suffolk Harmony. The Continental Harmony. The Lord is ris'n indeed. **His Majesties Clerkes/Paul Hillier.** Harmonia Mundi HMU90 7048 (10/92).

Gilles Binchois
French c.1400-1460

Suggested listening ...

"Triste plaisir et douleureuse joye" — Rondos and Ballades. *Coupled with* **Dufay.** Rondeaux, Ballades and Lamentations. **Ensemble Gilles Binchois/Dominique Vellard.** Virgin Classics Veritas VC7 59043-2.

Sir Harrison Birtwistle

New review

Birtwistle. The Triumph of Time. Gawain's Journey. **Philharmonia Orchestra/Elgar Howarth.** Collins Classics 1387-2. Recorded in 1993.

· 55m DDD 7/93   𝕢ₚ 𝕢s

Gawain's Journey offers a substantial set of extracts from Sir Harrison Birtwistle's opera *Gawain* (vocal lines allotted to instruments) which forms a convincing whole and reinforces the impression that this is one of the weightiest dramatic scores of this or any other age. It has the immediate, unmediated forcefulness so typical of Birtwistle. It may verge on the unremitting, but there's no mistaking the visceral theatrical power. In no sense is *The Triumph of Time* operatic, but its structure and material (which Birtwistle linked to the Bruegel engraving) is vividly dramatic, the sure-footed skill and economy of its gradual accumulation of tension and density still unsurpassed in Birtwistle's output — this triumphant return to the catalogue of a 1970s masterwork is cause for jubilation.

New review

Birtwistle. Melencolia I[a]. Ritual Fragment. Meridian[b]. [b]**Mary King** (mez); [a]**Antony Pay** (cl); [b]**Michael Thompson** (hn); [b]**Christopher van Kampen** (vc); [a]**Helen Tunstall** (hp); [b]**London Sinfonietta Voices; London Sinfonietta/Oliver Knussen.** NMC NMCD009. Text included.

· 1h 3m DDD 8/93

In Birtwistle the combination of powerful idiosyncrasy with finely developed musical craft results in something forceful and sharply memorable, whether you like it or not. There are also, occasionally, touches of modernist mannerism or dryness. The main work on this disc, *Melencolia I*, doesn't completely dodge that charge, and yet the dark, opulent, sinister atmosphere lingers like the memory of a disturbing dream, with the clarinet soloist as perhaps the central figure — sometimes trying to make sense of what it hears, sometimes protesting violently. With it go the short, incisive, high-action *Ritual Fragment* and *Meridian* — vocal, but instrumentally-led, and like the equally spacious *Melencolia I* a work that seems to open a world of its own. Standards in playing and reproduction are generally on a very high level.

Birtwistle. PUNCH AND JUDY. **Stephen Roberts** (bar) Punch; **Jan DeGaetani** (mez) Judy, Fortune-teller; **Phyllis Bryn-Julson** (sop) Pretty Polly, Witch; **Philip Langridge** (ten) Lawyer; **David Wilson-Johnson** (bar) Choregos, Jack Ketch; **John Tomlinson** (bass) Doctor; **London Sinfonietta/David Atherton.** Etcetera KTC2014. Notes and text included. From Decca Headline HEAD24/5 (9/80).

· ② 1h 43m ADD 12/89   𝕢ₚ

In *Punch and Judy* Sir Harrison Birtwistle and his inspired librettist Stephen Pruslin succeeded in giving characters normally presented as simple caricatures an almost mythic power and substance. As opera *Punch and Judy* may owe more to such Stravinskian fables as *Renard* than to the great lyric tragedies of the Monteverdi/Wagner tradition, yet even in *Punch and Judy* the music is most memorable in moments of reflection — sinister, poignant, or both. Though different performers have presented the work brilliantly in the theatre since this recording was made, it is hard to imagine a more effective account of the opera on disc. The singers are expert and well contrasted, with none of the ranting and approximation that this kind of expressionistic vocal writing often elicits. Moreover, the London Sinfonietta are at their most responsive, as well they might be given the outstandingly musical direction of David Atherton, who conducted the opera's première at Aldeburgh in 1968. The analogue recording may sound a trifle shallow by the latest standards, but it leaves you in no doubt as to the brilliance and resourcefulness of Birtwistle's vocal and instrumental design.

Further listening ...

Carmen Arcadiae Mechanicae Perpetuum. Silbury Air. Secret Theatre. **London Sinfonietta/ Elgar Howarth.** Etcetera KTC1052 (4/88).

For O, for O, the Hobby-horse is Forgot[a]. Refrains and Choruses[b]. Verses for Ensembles. [b]**Netherlands Wind Ensemble;** [a]**The Hague Percussion Ensemble/James Wood.** Etcetera KTC1130 (7/92).

Endless Parade[a]. *Coupled with* **Blake Watkins.** Trumpet Concerto. **Maxwell Davies.** Trumpet Concerto. **Håkan Hardenberger** (tpt); [a]**Paul Patrick** (vib); **BBC Philharmonic Orchestra/Elgar Howarth.** Philips 432 075-2PH (6/91).

Cesare Andrea Bixio

Italian 1898-1978

Suggested listening ...

Mamma. Vivere. Parlami d'amore, Mariù. La mia canzone al vento, with a selection of Italian songs. **Luciano Pavarotti** (ten); **Andrea Griminelli** (fte); **Chorus and Orchestra/Henry Mancini.** Decca 411 959-2DH (8/84).

Georges Bizet

French 1838-1875

Bizet. Symphony in C major[a]. L'Arlésienne — Suite No. 1[b]; Suite No. 2 (arr. Guiraud)[b]. [a]**French Radio National Symphony Orchestra,** [b]**Royal Philharmonic Orchestra/Sir Thomas Beecham.** EMI CDC7 47794-2. Item marked [a] from ASD388 (4/61), recorded in 1959 [b] ASD252 (2/59), recorded in 1956.

| .•' | lh 5m ADD II/87 | | 9ₚ ⑧ ▲ |

Bizet's only symphony was written within the space of a month just after his seventeenth birthday. It is an easy piece to listen to, fairly light-weight and with a hint of the mature composer-to-be in a long and beautiful oboe solo. But it has many conventional, immature features too, and needs special advocacy in performance. Beecham had a genius for making second-rate works seem masterpieces and his recording has tremendous flair, imagination and affection. From the incidental music for *L'Arlésienne* Bizet salvaged four pieces and re-orchestrated them for full orchestra in the form of what we know now as Suite No. 1. After his death Bizet's friend Ernest Guiraud re-scored four more numbers to make up Suite No. 2. The music has a marvellous sense of colour and atmosphere and Bizet's inspired invention reaches great heights of expression. It is difficult to imagine a more inspired, more sympathetic and beautifully played performance, for Beecham makes the music live and breathe in a way that is head and shoulders above any other conductor. The recordings were made in 1959 and 1956 respectively but both sound rich and clear.

Additional recommendations ...
Symphony. Jeux d'enfants — petite suite. **Debussy.** Danse sacrée et danse profane. **Vera Badings** (hp); **Concertgebouw Orchestra/Bernard Haitink.** Philips 416 437-2PH — .•' 50m ADD 10/86 9ₚ ⑧
L'Arlésienne — Suites. Carmen — Suites Nos. 1 and 2. **Montreal Symphony Orchestra/ Charles Dutoit.** Decca 417 839-2DH — .•' lh 13m DDD 6/88 9ₚ 9ₛ ⑧
Symphony. **Britten.** Simple Symphony, Op. 4. **Prokofiev.** Symphony No. 1 in D major, Op. 25, "Classical". **Orpheus Chamber Orchestra.** DG 423 624-2GH — .•' lh 4m DDD 1/89 9ₚ ⑧
L'Arlésienne — Suites. Carmen — Suite. Jeux d'enfants. **Orchestre de la Bastille/Myung-Whun Chung.** DG 431 778-2GH — .•' lh 9m DDD 11/91 ⑧
Symphony. **Ravel.** Ma mère l'oye. **Scottish Chamber Orchestra/Jukka-Pekka Saraste.** Virgin Classics Virgo VJ7 59657-2 — . lh 4m DDD 12/91 ⑧
Symphony. L'Arlésienne — Suites. **Lyon National Orchestra/Emmanuel Krivine.** Denon CO-75471 — .•' lh 10m DDD 2/94 ⑧

Bizet. CARMEN. **Julia Migenes** (mez) Carmen; **Plácido Domingo** (ten) Don José; **Faith Esham** (sop) Micaëla; **Ruggero Raimondi** (bass) Escamillo; **Lilian Watson** (sop) Frasquita;

Susan Daniel (mez) Mercédès; **Jean-Philippe Lafont** (bar) Dancairo; **Gérard Garino** (ten) Remendado; **François Le Roux** (bar) Moralès; **John Paul Bogart** (bass) Zuniga; **French Radio Chorus; French Radio Children's Chorus; French National Orchestra/Lorin Maazel.** Erato 2292-45207-2. Notes, text and translation included. From NUM75113 (3/84).

③ 2h 31m DDD 9/85 ⁹ₚ ⓑ

With some justification, *Carmen* is reckoned to be the world's most popular opera. Its score is irresistible, its dramatic realism riveting, its sense of *milieu* unerring, though it has to be remembered that the work was not an immediate triumph. Too many recordings have blown up the work to proportions beyond its author's intentions but here Maazel adopts a brisk, lightweight approach that seems to come close to what Bizet wanted. Similarly Julia Migenes approaches the title part in an immediate, vivid way, exuding the gipsy's allure in a performance that suggests Carmen's fierce temper and smouldering eroticism, and she develops the character intelligently into the fatalistic person of the card scene and finale. Her singing isn't convention-ally smooth but it is compelling from start to finish. Plácido Domingo has made the part of Don José very much his own, and here he sings with unstinting involvement and a good deal of finesse. Ruggero Raimondi is a macho Toreador though Faith Esham is a somewhat pallid Micaëla.

Additional recommendations ...
Soloists; Les Petits Chanteurs de Versailles; French National Radio Chorus and Orchestra/Sir Thomas Beecham. EMI CDS7 49240-2 — ③ 2h 41m ADD 6/88 ⁹ₚ ⓑ ▲
Soloists; Ambrosian Singers; London Symphony Orchestra/Claudio Abbado. DG 419 636-2GH3 — ③ 2h 37m 2/88 ⁹ₚ ⓑ
Soloists; Radio France Maîtrise and Chorus; French National Orchestra/Seiji Ozawa. Philips 422 366-2PH3 — ③ 2h 39m DDD 8/89 ⁹ₚ ⓑ
Soloists; Manhattan Opera Chorus; Metropolitan Opera Children's Chorus and Orchestra/Leonard Bernstein. DG 427 440-2GX3 — ③ 2h 40m ADD 9/91 ⁹ₚ ⓑ
Soloists; René Duclos Choir; Jean Pesneaud Children's Choir; Paris Opera Orchestra/Georges Prêtre. EMI CDS7 54368-2 — ② 2h 26m ADD 5/92 ⁹ₚ ⓑ

Bizet. LES PECHEURS DE PERLES. **Barbara Hendricks** (sop) Leïla; **John Aler** (ten) Nadir; **Gino Quilico** (bar) Zurga; **Jean-Philippe Courtis** (bass) Nourabad; **Chorus and Orchestra of the Capitole, Toulouse/Michel Plasson.** EMI CDS7 49837-2. Notes, text and translation included.

② 2h 7m DDD 1/90

Let a tenor and a baritone signify that they are willing to oblige with a duet, and the cry will go up for *The Pearl Fishers*. It's highly unlikely that many of the company present will know what the duet is about — it recalls the past, proclaims eternal friendship and nearly ends up in a quarrel — but the melody and the sound of two fine voices blending in its harmonies will be quite sufficient. In fact there is much more to the opera than the duet, or even than the three or four solos which are sometimes sung in isolation; and the EMI recording goes further than previous versions in giving a complete account of a score remarkable for its unity as well as for the attractiveness of individual numbers. It is a lyrical opera, and the voices need to be young and graceful. Barbara Hendricks and John Aler certainly fulfil those requirements, she with a light, silvery timbre, he with a high tenor admirably suited to the tessitura of his solos. The third main character, the baritone whose role is central to the drama, assumes his rightful place here: Gino Quilico brings genuine distinction to the part, and his aria in Act 3 is one of the highlights. Though Plasson's direction at first is rather square, the performance grows in responsiveness act by act. It is a pity that the accompanying notes are not stronger in textual detail, for the full score given here stimulates interest in its history. One of the changes made in the original score of 1863 concerns the celebrated duet itself, the first version of which is given in an appendix. It ends in a style that one would swear owed much to the 'friendship' duet in Verdi's *Don Carlos* — except that Bizet came first.

Additional recommendation ...
Soloists; Paris Opéra Chorus and Orchestra/Georges Prêtre. Classics for Pleasure CD-CFPD4721 — ② 1h 44m ADD 10/91

Further listening ...

Jeux d'enfants — petite suite. *Coupled with* **Ravel.** Ma mère l'oye — ballet. **Saint-Saëns.** Le carnaval des animaux[a]. [a]**Julian Jacobson,** [a]**Nigel Hutchinson** (pfs); members of **London Symphony Orchestra/Barry Wordsworth.** Pickwick IMP Classics PCD932 (4/90).

DJAMILEH. **Soloists; Bavarian Radio Chorus; Munich Radio Orchestra/Lamberto Gardelli.** Orfeo C174881A (4/89).

Michel Blavet

French 1700-1768

Suggested listening ...

Flute Sonatas: Op. 2 — No. 1 in E minor; Op. 9 — No. 7 in G major. *Coupled with* **Blavet.** Sonata in D minor, "La Vibray", Op. 2 No. 2. **Rameau.** Pièces de Clavecin en Concerts—Cinquième Concert. **M. La Barre.** Sonate L'inconnuë in G major, Book 2 No. 9. **Hotteterre.** Airs et Brunettes. **Rachel Brown** (fl); **Mark Caudle** (viol); **James Johnstone** (hpd). Chandos Chaconne CHAN0544 (2/94). *See review in the Collections section; refer to the Index to Reviews.*

Flute Sonatas: Op. 2 — No. 2 in D minor; No. 4 in G minor, "La lumague"; No. 5 in D major, "Lachauvet". Op. 3 — No. 2 in B minor; No. 6 in D major. **Masahiro Arita** (fl); **Wieland Kuijken** (bass viol); **Chiyoko Arita** (hpd). Denon Aliare CO-79550 (9/92).

Sir Arthur Bliss

British 1891-1975

Bliss. Music for Strings. Pastoral: Lie Strewn the White Flocks[a]. [a]**Della Jones** (mez); [a]**Sinfonia Chorus; Northern Sinfonia/Richard Hickox.** Chandos CHAN8886. Text included. Recorded in 1990.

1h 1m   DDD   7/91

Surely *the* disc with which to start a Bliss collection. Here is a pairing of two of the composer's very strongest works in sensitive, ideally disciplined accounts from the ever-responsive Northern Sinfonia under Richard Hickox. Brimful of fine invention as well as the most swaggeringly idiomatic (and technically demanding) writing, Bliss's athletic *Music for Strings* is a mightily impressive achievement: its enviable fluency and consummately argued progress mark it out as another in the long line of superb string works British composers have produced this century. It was first performed in 1935 at the Salzburg Festival by the strings of the Vienna Philharmonic (no less) under Sir Adrian Boult; suffice to report, Hickox draws playing of splendidly full-blooded tone and unanimous skill from his Tyneside group that would not disgrace even the string section of that same great orchestra. The classically-inspired idyll *Pastoral: Lie Strewn the White Flocks* dates from seven years earlier and constitutes perhaps the first fully characteristic example of Bliss's mature style. It's a most beguiling song-cycle, limpidly scored for small choir, mezzo-soprano, flute, strings and timpani, and some of the individual numbers are hauntingly lovely, not least that ravishing setting of Robert Nichols's "The Pigeon Song" (with Della Jones a touchingly tender soloist). A valuable coupling, then, complemented by ideally warm-toned, transparent Chandos sonics throughout.

Further listening ...

Piano Concerto, Op. 58[a]. March, Op. 99, "Homage to a Great Man". [a]**Philip Fowke** (pf); **Royal Liverpool Philharmonic Orchestra/David Atherton.** Unicorn-Kanchana Souvenir UKCD2029 (8/90).

Cello Concerto[a]. The Enchantress[b]. Hymn to Apollo. [b]**Linda Finnie** (mez); [a]**Raphael Wallfisch** (vc); **Ulster Orchestra/Vernon Handley.** Chandos CHAN8818 (7/91).

String Quartets — No. 1 in B flat major; No. 2. **Delmé Quartet.** Hyperion CDA66178 (11/89).

Miniature Scherzo. Sonata. The Rout Trot. Study. Suite. Triptych. *Coupled with* **Bach** (arr. Bliss): Das alte Jahr vergangen ist BWV614. **Philip Fowke** (pf). Chandos CHAN8979 (1/92).

Checkmate — suite. *Coupled with* **Lambert.** Horoscope — suite. **Walton.** Façade — Suites Nos. 1 and 2. **English Northern Philharmonia/David Lloyd-Jones.** Hyperion CDA66436 (3/91).

Morning Heroes[a]. Investiture Antiphonal Fanfares[b]. Prayer of St Francis of Assisi[c]. [a]**Brian Blessed** (narr); [ac]**East London Chorus; [a]Harlow Chorus; [a]East Hertfordshire Chorus; [ab]London Philharmonic Orchestra/Michael Kibblewhite.** Cala CACD1010 (2/93).

Marc Blitzstein
American 1905-1964

Suggested listening ...

REGINA. **Soloists; Scottish Opera Chorus and Orchestra/John Mauceri.** Decca 433 812-2DH2 (3/93).

Ernest Bloch
Swiss/American 1880-1959

Bloch. Symphony in C sharp minor. Schelomo[a]. [a]**Torleif Thedéen** (vc); **Malmö Symphony Orchestra/Lev Markiz.** BIS CD576. Recorded in 1990.

`Ih 18m  DDD  5/93`

Ernest Bloch's early symphony is an endearing and at times impressive showcase for a young composer (he was 23) endowed by nature and nurture with all the gifts save individuality (though there are hints in the later movements that that too is on the way). He can write impressively strong, expansive melodies, develop them with real ingenuity and build them into monumental climaxes. Climax-building, indeed, is what young Bloch seems most interested in at this stage of his career, that and a love for all the rich contrasts of colour and texture that a big orchestra, imaginatively used, can provide. He is so very good at his craft, so adept at pulling out still more stops when you thought there could hardly be any left, so sheerly and likeably clever that one is scarcely ever made impatient by the occasional feeling that this or that movement could have ended two or three minutes earlier. It's a pleasure, too, to listen for fulfilled echoes of that youthful exuberance in the mature 'biblical rhapsody' *Schelomo*. Just as Lev Markiz adroitly avoids any impression of over-padded grossness in the symphony, so he and his fine soloist find more than richly embroidered oriental voluptuousness in this portrait of King Solomon; there is gravity and even poignancy to the music as well, and Thedéen's subtle variety of tone colour gives the work shadow and delicacy as well as richness. Typically BIS reproduce a truthful aural equivalent of the modern concert hall experience.

Additional recommendation ...
Schelomo. Concerti grossiNos. 1 and 2. **Georges Miquelle** (vc); **Eastman Rochester Orchestra/Howard Hanson.** Mercury 432 718-2MM — `Ih 3m  ADD  II/91`

Further listening ...

Concerto grosso No. 1[a]. *Coupled with* **Barber.** Adagio for strings, Op. 11. **Grieg.** Holberg Suite, Op. 40. **Puccini.** Crisantemi (arr. string orchestra). [a]**Irit Rob** (pf); **Israel Chamber Orchestra/Yoav Talmi.** Chandos CHAN8593 (8/88).

America — epic rhapsody. **American Concert Choir; Symphony of the Air/Leopold Stokowski.** Vanguard Classics 08.8014.71.

Piano Quintets Nos. 1 and 2. **American Chamber Players.** Koch International 37041-2.

Three Nocturnes. *Coupled with* **Beach.** Piano Trio in A minor, Op. 150. **Ives.** Trio.
Copland. Vitebsk (Study on a Jewish theme). **Cowell.** Trio.**Hartley Piano Trio.** Gamut
Classics GAMCD536 (6/94). *See review in the Collections section; refer to the Index to Reviews.*

Baal Shem[a]. *Coupled with* **Bartók.** Rhapsody No. 1, Sz86[b]. Contrasts, Sz111[b] (with Benny
Goodman, cl). **Debussy.** Violin Sonata[a]. **Ives.** Violin Sonata No. 4, "Children's Day at the
Camp Meeting"[a]. **Schubert:** Violin Sonatina, D384[a]. Also includes works by **Bach, Brahms,
Corelli, Debussy, Dvořák, Falla, Hubay, Kodály, Lalo, Milhaud, Mussorgsky**
and **Schubert.** Joseph Szigeti (vn); [a]**Andor Foldes,** [b]**Béla Bartók** (pfs). Biddulph mono
LAB070/71. *See review in the Collections section; refer to the Index to Reviews.*

Robert Bloom
American 1908-

Suggested listening ...

Requiem. Narrative. *Coupled with* **Barlow.** The Winter's Past. **Corigliano.** Aria. **Wilder.**
Concerto for Oboe, String Orchestra and Percussion. Piece for Oboe and Improvisatory
Percussion[a]. **Humbert Lucarelli** (ob); [a]**Mark Wood** (perc); **Brooklyn Philharmonic
Orchestra/ Michael Barrett.** Koch International Clasics 37187-2 (7/94). *See Review under
Wilder; refer to the Index to Reviews.*

John Blow
British 1649-1708

New review

Blow. AWAKE, MY LYRE. **Red Byrd** (Suzie LeBlanc, Geraldine McGreevy, sops; Charles
Daniels, John Potter, tens; Richard Wistreich, bass); [a]**The Parley of Instruments** (Judy
Tarling, Theresa Caudle, vns; Mark Caudle, bass viol; Fred Jacobs, theorbo; Peter Holman,
hpd/org). Hyperion CDA66658. Texts and translations included. Recorded in 1993.
Awake, my lyre. Salvator mundi. Stay, gentle Echo. Poor Celadon, he sighs in vain. St
Cecilia's Day Ode, "Begin the song" — Music's the cordial of a troubled heart. Go, perjur'd
man. Help, Father Abraham. Chloe found Amintas. Whilst on Septimnius's panting breast.
Gloria patri, qui creavit nos. Paratum cor meum. Sing ye Muses. Sonata in A[a]. Ground in G
minor[a].

1h 10m DDD 1/94

The performances match the scholarship of their preparation. The voices are also well-
matched, the sopranos with one rather brighter, the other rather more mellow. Of the
tenors, Charles Daniels copes skilfully with the high tessitura of *Poor Celadon* and John
Potter dramatizes Dives in the burning lake so well that we are entirely on his side against
the implacable Father Abraham. The instrumentalists also contribute valuably, the violins
playing in the G minor Ground on fine William Baker fiddles of 1683, the very ones which
may have been used on Blow's visits to Oxford. This delightful record ends with an
Epilogue, *Sing, ye Muses,* adapted by the composer from his wedding ode, *Bring, shepherds,
bring the kids and lambs* which we must hope is a treat that lies ahead in the English
Orpheus's schedule.

New review

Blow. FAIREST WORK OF HAPPY NATURE. **John Mark Ainsley** (ten); **Paula
Chateauneuf** (theorbo/gtr); **Timothy Roberts** ([a]spinet/[b]hpd/[c]org). Hyperion CDA66646.
Texts included. Recorded in 1993
Songs — No more the dear, lovely nymph's no more. The Self-banished. Lovely Selina, innocent
and free. O turn not those fine eyes away. Fairest work of happy nature. Flavia grown old. O

that mine eyes would melt into a flood. O mighty God, who sit'st on high. Sabina has a thousand charms. O all the torments, all the cares. The Queen's Epicedium, "No, Lesbia, no, you ask in vain". *Solo keyboard* — A Choice Collection of Lessons[a]: Suite No. 1 in D minor; Suite No. 3 in A minor. Prelude in G major[a]. Morlake Ground[a]. Grounds: G minor[a]; C major[b]. Voluntary in G minor[c].

Ih I3m DDD I0/93

Dr Burney thought that Blow's melody was "either of a Scots cast, or of a languid kind, that excites no other sensation than fatigue and drowsiness". Towards the end of the first song here, *No more the dear, lovely nymph's no more*, one suspects that he may not have been far wrong. Then comes *The Self-banished*, Waller's graceful verses gracefully set, the style plainer and not languorous at all. Later, *Flavia grown old* has a fluid vocal line unlike either of these. *O mighty God* develops in a pictorial manner, Purcellian yet with a flavour of its own. The Elegy on the death of Queen Mary involves a variety of vocal styles, and indeed it is evident that Blow had a great deal that was neither languid nor 'Scots'. It is perhaps a pity that Dr Burney could not have heard these performances. John Mark Ainsley sings with pure, firm tone, sensitive to every modulation of sense and harmony, and clearly having considerable reserves of both power and passion, and the accompaniments, by theorbo and organ, spinet, harpsichord or guitar, have flavour and are finely played. This collection is full of interest, rich in its varied pleasures and in the high standard of recording and performance.

New review
Blow. VENUS AND ADONIS. **Catherine Bott** (sop) Venus; **Michael George** (bass) Adonis; **Libby Crabtree** (sop) Cupid; **Julia Gooding** (sop) Shepherdess, Grace 1; **Andrew King** (ten) Shepherd 1; **Simon Grant** (bass) Shepherd 2, Huntsman 3, Grace 3; **Christopher Robson** (alto) Shepherd 3, Huntsman 1, Grace 2; **Paul Agnew** (ten) Huntsman 2; **Westminster Abbey School Choristers; New London Consort/Philip Pickett.**
L'Oiseau-Lyre 440 220-2OH. Notes and text included.

57m DDD 7/94

This recording reveals Blow's opera (and lamentably one of only two real 'all-sung' dramas to emerge from England in the Restoration period), to be a work of rare quality and pathos with Philip Pickett at his most luminous. Whilst Charles Medlam and London Baroque (listed below) take a robust and homespun view of the overture, Pickett has his listener mentally prepared from the outset for the opera's solemn denouement. The noble and eloquent opening (with some minor ensemble infelicities) sets the scene in more ways than one since Pickett is not content to see the Prologue's traditional machinations undermine the cultivated expression he believes this work merits. Consequently, the introduction of *Venus and Adonis* emerges sumptuously from Blow's skilful preparations, notably in the beautifully sung chorus refrain "In these sweet groves" and an ethereal Act Tune of three recorders which delivers the doomed lovers to their first intimate exchanges. Catherine Bott is the most telling and sensual Venus imaginable, her singing always captivating in its tonal variety and emotional nuance. Her relationship with Adonis is never mannered but tense and simmering, and in its chilling realism allows the listener to experience the brutal psychology of an anonymous adaptation. (Story line: Venus insists that Adonis goes hunting and the former suffers incessant grief when he meets his match with an Aedalian boar.) Michael George, as Adonis, plays his part thoughtfully in the striking immediacy of the tragedy, elegantly shaping his lines with a prescient tinge of melancholy before he is led in wounded at the start of Act 3.

Additional recommendation ...
Soloists; Chorus; London Baroque/Charles Medlam. Harmonia Mundi Musique d'abord
HMA190 1276 — **50m DDD 9/88**

Luigi Boccherini   *Italian 1743-1805*

New review
Boccherini. SYMPHONIES, Volumes 3-6. **German Chamber Academy, Neuss/Johannes Goritzki.** CPO CPO999 173/6-2. Recorded 1990-93.

CPO999 173-2 — Op. 12: No. 4 in D minor, G506; No. 5 in B flat major, G507; No. 6 in A major, G508. *CPO999 174-2* — Op. 21: No. 1 in B flat major, G493; No. 2 in E flat major, G494; No. 3 in C major, G495; No. 4 in D major, G496; No. 5 in B flat major, G497. *CPO999 175-2* — Op. 21: No. 6 in A major, G498. Op. 35: No. 1 in D major, G509; No. 2 in E flat major, G510; No. 3 in A major, G511. *CPO999 176-2* — Op. 35: No. 4 in F major, G512; No. 5 in E flat major, G513; No. 6 in B flat major, G514. Op. 37: No. 1 in C major, G515.

④ **55m 1h 1m 49m 52m DDD 1/94**

Boccherini is deserving of proper exploration. Although the chief riches lie in the chamber music, at the moment it seems to be the symphonies that are principally being explored. In one sense, Boccherini is at his most conventional in his symphonies, yet he is still unconventional in much of his thematic material and his handling of it. Listen, for example, to the first movement of Vol. 4 here, in Op. 21 No. 1, with its curious silent pauses, its explosive tuttis and its treatment of little figurative patterns, or to the elliptical idea that begins Op. 21 No. 4 — a movement which goes on to show Boccherini at his most brilliant and witty with its sharply contrasted themes. The finest and most entertaining of all is possibly Op. 21 No. 3. This symphony goes on to a slow movement with two solo violins, a delightful and gently pathetic serenade, and to a finale that might be described, if this isn't a contradiction, as tastefully rumbustious. Try this symphony if you are considering the set, and you will certainly buy it. Boccherini's music is just as often, in its slow movement, run through with a tone of delicate pathos and Boccherini offers a splendid variety in minuets, which provide several of the finales in these three-movement works. Johannes Goritzki, himself a cellist, is clearly sympathetic to Boccherini. He executes the quick movements with plenty of life though in some of the slow ones he is apt to dawdle. Still, these remain very attractive and sympathetic interpretations of appealing music.

Additional recommendation ...
Op. 12: Nos. 4 and 6; Op. 21: No. 6. **London Festival Orchestra/Ross Pople.** Hyperion CDA66236 — **54m DDD 9/87**

Boccherini. CELLO CONCERTOS. David Geringas (vc); **Orchestra da Camera di Padova e del Veneto/Bruno Giuranna.** Claves CD50-8814/16.
No. 1 in E flat major, G474; No. 2 in A major, G475; No. 3 in D major, G476; No. 4 in C major, G477; No. 5 in D major, G478; No. 6 in D major, G479; No. 7 in G major, G480; No. 8 in C major, G481; No. 9 in B flat major, G482; No. 10 in D major, G483; No. 11 in G major, G573; No. 12 in E flat major.

③ **3h 24m DDD 7/89**

New review
Boccherini. CELLO CONCERTOS[a]. [b]Marta Almajano (sop); **Limoges Baroque Ensemble/Christophe Coin** (vc). Astrée Auvidis E8517. Recorded in 1993.
No. 3 in D major, G476; No. 7 in G major, G480; No. 9 in B flat major, G482. Concert aria — Se d'un amor tiranno, G557[b].

1h 2m DDD 4/94

"Boccherini: 12 Concerti per il Violoncello" proclaims the cover, a little ambitiously, perhaps — for Boccherini probably didn't compose that many. David Geringas has had to exercise a little ingenuity to reach this figure (two of the concertos are almost certainly spurious), but it was probably worth the effort, and his set is a thoroughly enjoyable one in its undemanding way. His intonation is virtually perfect, even high up on the A string, his passage-work is clean, his rhythms are crisp, and he produces (not using a period instrument) a light but pleasingly resonant tone. Listen in particular to the slow movements (such as those of G477 or G483) for eloquence and neatly timed detail. Geringas provides his own cadenzas, including one that quotes Mozart. A very pleasing release. The recording quality and balance are exemplary.

Christophe Coin throws off in the deftest fashion the typical Boccherinian filigree figuration, the little ornamental flourishes perfectly placed and timed, the numerous stratospheric excursions above the treble stave sweet-toned and delicate. And with it he shows a command of Boccherini's style, affectionately graceful, sometimes with a faintly quizzical air. The tone of Coin's instrument is light and translucent, and with this small orchestra the sound in the solos, which are anyway lightly accompanied, is particularly sweet: in the first movement of G482 (the concerto known from the Grützmacher version) the unassuming handling of the virtuoso writing has a special kind of charm and the rather grander manner called for in the D major work G476 is also very happily caught, not without a hint of the romantic at times, for Coin is no austere stylist. The aria that completes his disc is a large-scale duet for cello, in its full concerto manner, and soprano; the lines are full of eloquent appoggiaturas and there is some beguiling duetting for the voice and the instrument. Marta Almajano has a big, clear top register and plenty of drama to her singing.

Additional recommendations ...
Nos. 1-12. **Julius Berger** (vc); **South-West German Chamber Orchestra/Vladislav Czarnecki.** EBS EBS6058 — .•ʹ ③ 3h 3lm DDD 9/92
Nos 7 and 9[b]. *Sonatas*[a] — *C minor, G2b; G major, G5; A major, G6.* **Steven Isserlis** (vc); [a]**Maggie Cole** (hpd); [b]**Ostrobothnian Chamber Orchestra/Juha Kangas.** Virgin Classics VC7 59015-2 — .•ʹ lh lm DDD 7/92 𝑞ₚ 𝑞ₛ

Key to symbols

Quality of sound   Discs worth exploring   Caveat emptor

Quality of performance   Basic library   Period performance

New review
Boccherini. String Sextets, Op. 23 — No. 1 in E flat major, G454; No. 2 in B flat major, G455; No. 5 in D major, G458. **Ensemble 415** (Chiara Banchini, Enrico Gatti, vns; Emilio Moreno, Wim ten Have, vas; Rolf Dieltiens, Hendrike ter Brugge, vcs). Harmonia Mundi HMC90 1478.

.•ʹ **58m DDD 6/94** 𝑞ₚ

These are quite extraordinarily beautiful pieces, rich in sound, mostly contemplative in mood. The first in particular has much slow-moving music, enlivened in the opening movement by sudden outbursts and passages with rapid figuration, but the *Larghetto* enters into those realms of melancholy that seem to be very personal to Boccherini. Lastly there is a minuet with three trios, the last of them *minore* and with cello writing that is both eloquent and florid. All the minuets here are unorthodox in some way — that of No. 2 is a sustained, inward piece, that of No. 5 full of D minor pathos expressed in imitative contrapuntal writing but with a trio full of dance-like rhythms. No. 2 is also graced with a witty and brilliant finale, No. 5 with an opening *Grave* for muted strings including some remarkable and highly expressive decorative writing. This disc is full of beautiful, fine-drawn, sensitive playing, very much alert to Boccherini's mercurial moods. Period instruments and restrained use of vibrato give a welcome airiness to the textures.

New review
Boccherini. Piano Quintets, Op. 56 — No. 1 in E minor, G407; No. 2 in F major, G408; No. 5 in D major, G411. **Patrick Cohen** (pf); **Quatuor Mosaïques** (Erich Höbarth, Andrea Bischof, vns; Anita Mitterer, va; Christophe Coin, vc). Astrée Auvidis E8518. Recorded 1993.

.•ʹ **lh lOm DDD 4/94** 𝑞ₚ

These artists do not treat Boccherini as a Dresden-china composer, all delicacy and exquisiteness, though there is a good deal of that; they treat this music pretty robustly — as of course they can, using period instruments. The opening movement here of the E minor Quintet exemplifies this: it starts with the most gentle of *pianissimos*, but the dynamic range is very wide, with ebullient tuttis and long crescendos during those typical passages where Boccherini uses ostinato figures with slowly shifting harmony and builds up a formidable degree of tension. In this particular movement, too, he does extraordinarily ingenious things with scales: you would never imagine they could be so expressive, indeed so varied in their expressive significance. G411 abjures the usual movement scheme in favour of a grandiose *Andante* to start with, followed by a minuet, then a repeat of part of the *Andante* leading to a brilliant and jolly march, and last a fascinating, beautifully textured and ultimately very exciting set of variations. It is hard to imagine performances better than these: the rhythms springy, full of subtle details of timing, alert to the faintest hints of shifts in the music's expressive sense, and finely polished and balanced, with touches of real virtuosity. They are excellently recorded.

Boccherini. String Quintets, Op. 11 — No. 4 in F minor, G274; No. 5 in E major, G275; No. 6 in D major, G276. **Smithsonian Chamber Players** (Marilyn MacDonald, Jorie Garrigue, vns; Anthony Martin, va; Anner Bylsma, Kenneth Slowik, vcs). Deutsche Harmonia Mundi RD77159.

Ih 7m DDD 4/92

Boccherini was a virtuoso cellist and often played together with a family string quartet in Madrid and the experience was obviously a very pleasant one, for he wrote 100 quintets for two violins, viola and two cellos. He was never at a loss for ideas: the quintets are richly varied in form and texture, the latter enhanced by Boccherini's intimate knowledge of the techniques and sound-qualities of the bowed-string instruments. Many of us know the famous Minuet — but how many are familiar with the work from which it comes? The Quintet in E, the fifth of the six Quintets of his Op. 11 (1775), of which it is the third movement, is one of those in this recording. The bucolic Quintet in D, *dello l'ucceleria*, ("The aviary") is a cyclic work with bird-song, shepherd's pipes and hunting sounds. If Boccherini was, as Giuseppe Pupo described him, "the wife of Haydn", his music has the charm, grace and poise of the best wives, and there is nothing wrong with that"! The Smithsonian Players, using original Stradivarius instruments (1688-1787), play like good Italians, which none of them is, and are superbly recorded in this irresistibly attractive album.

New review
Boccherini. STRING QUINTETS. **Petersen Quartet** (Conrad Muck, Gernot Süssmuth, vns; Friedemann Weigle, va; Hans-Jakob Eschenburg, vc); **Ulrich Knorzer** (va); **Guido Schiefen** (vc). Capriccio 10 452. Recorded in 1992.
Op. 13, No. 4 in D minor, G280. Op. 31, No. 2 in G major, G326. Op. 60, No. 3 in A major, G393. Op. 62, No. 5 in D major, G401.

Ih IIm DDD 4/94

New review
Boccherini STRING QUINTETS[a]. **Mayumi Seiler, Silvia Walch** (vns); [ab]**Diemut Poppen** (va); [ab]**Richard Lester**, [a]**Howard Penny** (vcs). Capriccio 10 453. Recorded in 1993.
Op. 30, No. 6 in C major, "La musica notturna delle strade di Madrid", G324. Op. 36, No. 6 in F major, "Quintetto dello Scacciapensiero", G336. String Quartet in G major, Op. 44, No. 4, "La Tiranna", G223[b]. Duet for Two Violins in E flat major, "La bona notte", G62.

49m DDD 4/94

New review
Boccherini. QUINTETS FOR OBOE AND STRINGS. **Lajos Lencsés** (ob); **Parisii Quartet** (Thierry Brodard, Jean-Michel Berrette, vns; Dominique Lobet, va; Jean-Philippe Martignoni, vc). Capriccio 10 454.
No. 1 in G major. No. 2 in F major. No. 3 in D major. No. 4 in A major. No. 5 in E flat major. No. 6 in D minor.

Ih 2m DDD 4/94

Boccherini's originality is vividly apparent in the Quintet, G324, written in 1780 when he was firmly ensconced in Madrid. Solemn chords on the cello represent the bell of the Ave Maria and guitar-like pizzicatos pervade much of the night-music that follows — he rearranged the final *ritirata* to end his Guitar Quintet, G453; the cellists are asked to hold their instruments across their knees, like guitars on 10 453. It is coupled with three other titled works. Most of Boccherini's numerous string quintets were scored with one viola and two cellos (an innovation) and the last of that genre was written in 1795. There followed 12 quintets with two violas

(1797-9), reworkings of piano quintets, and finally 12 more original works (1801-2). Two of these quintets, G393 and G401, are included in the programme of 10 452. To the natural grace, sweetness, charm and ingenuity, all abundant in his music, may be added superb craftsmanship, unexcelled knowledge of the capabilities of bowed strings, and acute sensitivity to instrumental colour — evident in the variety of his textures as well as in the 'special effects'. The concept of quintets for oboe or flute with string quartet was another Boccherini 'first'. He referred in a letter to the "extraordinary sweetness" of tone of his oboist friend Gaspar Barli, who probably played these quintets; he would have been no less pleased with that of Lajos Lencsés, as he would also by the sweetly shaped and finely recorded performances by the Parisii Quartet — and those on the other two discs. All three discs are warmly recommended.

New review

Boccherini. CELLO SONATAS. **Anner Bylsma,** [abdef]**Kenneth Slowik** (vcs); [bce]**Bob van Asperen** (fp). Sony Classical Vivarte SK53362.
No. 2 in C minor, G2[a]; No. 8 in B flat major, G8[b]; No. 9 in F major, G9[c]; No. 10 in E flat major, G10[d]; No. 9 in G major, G15[e]. Six Fugues, G73 — No. 2 in F major; No. 3 in B flat major; No. 5 in A major[f].

1h 17m DDD 3/94

Anner Bylsma is a tremendous enthusiast. He plays these five sonatas with a quite extraordinary rhythmic vitality; his articulation is as sharp and precise as can be imagined, and his rhythms, though by no means inflexible, are tough and firmly sprung. In the slow movements he achieves a good deal of intensity. The actual sound is rather different from what we are used to in this music, or any eighteenth-century cello repertory. Bylsma produces an incisive, rather wiry and resonant cello tone, supported here by fortepiano (in three of the five sonatas) and a second cello (in four of them); the combination of all three gives quite a rich sound, though not an indistinct one, for the fortepiano is light and clear — but with only the two cellos there is no sense of harmonies missing in the middle, because of the ring of the instruments.

Further listening ...

Guitar Quintets — No. 1 in D minor, G445; No. 2 in E major, G446; No. 3 in B flat major, G447; No. 4 in D major, G448; No. 5 in D major, G449; No. 6 in G major, G450; No. 7 in E minor, G451; No. 9 in in C major, "La ritrata di Madrid", G453. **Pepe Romero** (gtr); **Academy of St Martin in the Fields Ensemble.** Philips 438 769-2PM2 (4/94).

Guitar Quintets — No. 5 in D major, G449[a]; No. 7 in E minor, G451[b]. String Quintet in A major, G308 (Op. 20 No. 2)[c]. [ab]**David Starobin** (gtr); **Pina Carmirelli,** [a]**Joseph Genualdi,** [b]**Philip Setzer,** [c]**Michaela Paetsch** (vns); [ab]**Philipp Naegele,** [c]**Toby Hoffman** (vas); [a]**Marcy Rosen,** [b]**Peter Wiley,** [c]**Ramon Bolipata,** [c]**Gary Hoffman** (vcs). Sony Classical SBK47298 (9/92).

Piano Quintets, Op. 57 — No. 2 in B flat major, G414; No. 3 in E minor, G415; No. 6 in C major, G418. **Patrick Cohen** (fp); **Mosaïques Quartet.** Astrée Auvidis E8721 (12/92).

BOCCHERINI EDITION, Volumes 1-5. **Soloists; Petersen Quartet; New Berlin Chamber Orchestra/Michael Erxleben** (vn). Capriccio (5/93) available as follows: *Volume 1* — 10 450: String Sextets, Op. 23 — No. 1 in E flat major, G454; No. 3 in E major, G456; No. 4 in F minor, G457; No. 6 in F major, G459. *Volume 2* — 10 456: Sextets (Divertimentos), Op. 16 — No. 1 in D major, G461; No. 4 in E flat major, G464; No. 5 in A major, G465; No. 6 in C major, G466. *Volume 3* — 10 457: Symphonies, Op. 37 — No. 1 in C major, G515; No. 3 in D minor, G517; No. 4 in A major, G518. *Volume 4* — 10 458: Symphonies — C minor, Op. 41, G519; D major, Op. 42, G520; D major, Op. 43, G521; D minor, Op. 45, G522. *Volume 5* — 10 451: String Quartets — D major, Op. 15 No. 1, G177; G minor, Op. 24 No. 6, G194; A major, Op. 39, G213; F major, Op. 64 No. 1, G248.

Stabat mater, G532 (1781 version)[a]. String Quintet in C minor, G328 (Op. 31 No. 4). [a]**Agnès Mellon** (sop); **Ensemble 415.** Harmonia Mundi HMC90 1378 (9/92).

Léon Boëllmann

Suggested listening ...

Piano Quartet in F minor, Op. 10[a]. Piano Trio in G major, Op. 19. **Béla Bánfalvi** (vn); [a]**János Fejérvári** (va); **Károly Botvay** (vc); **Ilona Prunyi** (pf). Marco Polo 8 223524 (11/93).

Deuxième Suite, Op. 27. 12 Pièces, Op. 16. Suite gothique, Op. 25. **Patrice Caire** (org). REM Editions REM311053 (7/89).

Georg Böhm

New review
Böhm. KEYBOARD WORKS. **Gustav Leonhardt** (hpd/[a]clavichord). Sony Classical Vivarte SK53114.
Suites — C minor[a]; D major; E flat major; F minor[a]. Prelude, Fugue and Postlude in G minor. Capriccio in D major. Wer nur den lieben Gott lässt walten. Ach wie nichtig, ach wie flüchtig.

 1h 3m   DDD   9/93

The late-baroque composer, Georg Böhm, was one of the leading German organists of his day and his craft is brilliantly reflected in this disc of his keyboard music. At the heart of the recital are two chorale *partite* on the famous Lutheran hymns, *Wer nur den lieben Gott lässt walten* and *Ach wie nichtig, ach wie flüchtig*. These consist of sets of seven and eight variations, respectively, and are intended for harpsichord rather than organ. Leonhardt's beautifully spoken account of the variations, clear-textured, eloquently phrased and animated in delivery, is one of the greatest delights in the recital; but throughout the recital you cannot fail to admire the sheer nobility of statement and the refinement of his taste. These are qualities, admittedly, which you find to a greater or lesser extent in all Leonhardt's work but when they are placed at the service of music with which he seems to have a close personal affinity then the performances enter the realms of magic. The disc is admirably recorded and well documented.

François Boïeldieu

Suggested listening ...

LES VOITURES VERSEES — opéra-comique. **Soloists; French Radio Lyric Orchestra/Jean Brebion.** Musidisc 20152-2 (3/92).

Arrigo Boito

New review
Boito. MEFISTOFELE. **Cesare Siepi** (bass) Mefistofele; **Mario del Monaco** (ten) Faust; **Renata Tebaldi** (sop) Margherita; **Floriana Cavalli** (sop) Elena; **Lucia Danieli** (mez) Marta, Pantalis; **Piero De Palma** (ten) Wagner, Nereo; **Chorus and Orchestra of the Santa Cecilia Academy/Tullio Serafin.** Decca Grand Opera 440 054-2DMO2. Notes, text and translation included. From SXL2094/6 (6/59). Recorded in 1958.

 ② 2h 21m   ADD   4/94

This recording has in Siepi a real Italian bass with a fine sense of line and a genuine enjoyment
of Boito's words. Phrases that are often merely snarled are here truly sung, and Siepi's is the

only devil to suggest in the quartet that he is trying to seduce Martha, and that he will very probably succeed. There is incisiveness and grain there, too, to add menace to his suavity. Tebaldi gives one of the best accounts of "L'altra notte" on record, strongly sung and very touching in its suggestion of grieving guilt. Del Monaco sings "Dai campi, dai prati" without the slightest acknowledgement of its poetry, but the splendour of the sound and his instinctive feeling for legato have their own allure, and they give nobility to his finely phrased "Giunto sul passo estremo". The recording doesn't allow Serafin to make a sonic spectacular of the outer scenes, but his care for Boito's often rather old-fashioned *cantabile,* his quirky rhythms and orchestral colours is scrupulous throughout.

Alexander Borodin
Russian 1833-1887

Borodin. ORCHESTRAL WORKS. [a]**Torgny Sporsén** (bass); **Gothenburg Symphony** [a]**Chorus and Orchestra/Neeme Järvi.** DG 435 757-2GH2. Items marked [b] from 429 984-2GH (3/91), others new to UK. Recorded 1989-91.
Symphonies — No. 1 in E flat major; No. 2 in B minor; No. 3 in A minor. Prince Igor — Overture; Dance of the Polovtsian Maidens; Polovtsian Dances[ab]. String Quartet No. 2 in D major — Notturno (orch. N. Tcherepnin). In the Steppes of Central Asia[b]. Petite Suite (orch. Glazunov).

② 2h 28m DDD 9/92

While it is possible to imagine performances of even greater power and finesse in this strangely unfashionable repertoire, Järvi's Borodin set is by far the best to have appeared in recent years. The extravagant lay-out means we get not just the symphonies but a rich supplement of orchestral works, including even the *Petite Suite* as arranged by Glazunov. Another rarity, Nikolay Tcherepnin's orchestration of the famous *Notturno* will astonish those familiar with the chaste original: Tcherepnin transforms it into an exotic Scriabin-like tableau, almost as remote from Borodin as its kitschy *Kismet* mutation. The more recognizable *Steppes* are negotiated with ample eloquence and the *Prince Igor* excerpts score by including a brief contribution from the great Khan himself, reminding us of the music's original operatic context. The main works are equally persuasive. The First Symphony emerges here as far more than a dry-run for the Second. Järvi plays the music for all its worth, with DG's big, resonant sound serving to boost the symphonic credentials of the piece. The unfinished Third is also tougher and more dramatic than usual, no mere pastoral reverie in Järvi's interventionist view. The Second Symphony is rather different, suitably epic and yet unusually long-drawn and thoughtful. Thus, the *Scherzo* is bubbling but sensibly articulate, while the *Andante* is daringly broad with a superbly sensitive horn solo.

Additional recommendations ...
No. 2. In the Steppes of Central Asia. Prince Igor — Overture; March; Dance of the Polovtsian Maidens; Polovtsian Dances. **John Alldis Choir; National Philharmonic Orchestra/Loris Tjeknavorian.** RCA Victor Silver Seal VD60535 — . Ih 4m ADD 8/77
Nos. 1-3. **CSR Symphony Orchestra, Bratislava/Stephen Gunzenhauser.** Naxos 8 550238 — . Ih 16m DDD 8/91 ⁹ₚ
No. 2. Stravinsky. Petrushka. **Concertgebouw Orchestra/Kyrill Kondrashin.** Philips Collector Series 438 280-2PM — . Ih 2m ADD 9/93 ⁹ₚ

Borodin. String Quartets — No. 1 in A major; No. 2 in D major. **Borodin Quartet** (Mikhail Kopelman, Andrei Abramenkov, vns; Dmitri Shebalin, va; Valentin Berlinsky, vc). EMI CDC7 47795-2. From EMI Melodiya ASD4100 (3/82).

Ih 6m DDD 5/88

These quartets are delightful music, and they are played here by the aptly-named Borodin Quartet with a conviction and authority that in no way inhibits panache, spontaneity and sheer charm. Doubtless the most popular music of Borodin and the other members of the Russian 'Five' will always be their colourful orchestral and stage music, but no CD collector should ignore these chamber works. Their style derives from a mid-nineteenth-century Russian tradition of spending happy hours in music-making at home and also from the refreshing musical springs of folk-song. This performance offers not only first-rate playing from artists who 'have the music in their blood' but also a warm and convincing recorded sound.

Additional recommendations ...
As above. **Talich Quartet.** Calliope CAL9202 — .•' 57m DDD 5/88 ℗
No. 2[a]*.* **Shostakovich.** *String Quartet No. 8 in C minor, Op. 110*[a]*.* **Tchaikovsky.** *String Quartet No. 1 in D major, Op.11*[b]*.* [a]**Borodin Quartet;** [b]**Gabrieli Quartet.** Decca 425 541-2DM — .•'
1h 16m ADD 5/90 ℗

Borodin. PRINCE IGOR. **Boris Martinovich** (bar) Igor; **Nicolai Ghiuselev** (bass) Galitsky; **Nicolai Ghiaurov** (bass) Konchak; **Kaludi Kaludov** (ten) Vladimir; **Angel Petkov** (ten) Eroshka; **Stoil Georgiev** (bass) Skula; **Mincho Popov** (ten) Ovlur; **Stefka Evstatiev** (sop) Yaroslavna; **Alexandrina Milcheva** (contr) Konchakovna; **Elena Stoyanova** (sop) Nurse, Polovtsian Girl; **Sofia National Opera Chorus; Sofia Festival Orchestra/Emil Tchakarov.** Sony Classical SK44878. Notes, text and translation included.

.•' ③ 3h 30m DDD 6/90 ℗

Borodin's limited time to devote to composition meant that many of his works often took years to complete. *Prince Igor* was no exception; even after 18 years of work it remained unfinished at his death in 1887, and it was finally completed by Rimsky-Korsakov and Glazunov. Borodin's main problem with *Prince Igor* was the daunting task of turning what was principally an undramatic subject into a convincing stage work. In many ways he never really succeeded in this and the end result comes over more as a series of epic scenes rather than a musical drama. Despite this, however, one is nevertheless left with an impression of a rounded whole, and it contains some of Borodin's most poignant and moving music, rich in oriental imagery and full of vitality. Tchakarov conducts a performance that is both vigorous and refined, and there are some excellent performances from the principal singers too — Boris Martinovich makes a particularly strong Igor and Nicolai Ghiuselev and Nicolai Ghiaurov in the roles of Prince Galitsky and the Polovtsian Khan Konchak deserve special mention also. This Sony issue is a particularly welcome addition to the catalogue as it represents the only *complete* version of the opera on disc.

Additional recommendation ...
Prince Igor (Act 3 omitted). Songs — Those people; Song of the dark forest; From my tears; The queen of the sea; The beauty no loves me; The magic garden; Arabian melody; The Fishermaiden; Listen to my song, little friend; The sleeping princess; Arrogance; The sea; Why art thou so early, dawn? There is poison in my songs; The false note; For the shores of thy far native land. . **Boris Christoff** (bass) Galitsky, Konchak; **Soloists; Chorus and Orchestra of the National Opera Theatre, Sofia/Jerzy Semkov;** [b]**Lamoureux Concerts Orchestra/Georges Tzipine.** EMI Studio CMS7 63386-2 — .•' ③ 3h 23m ADD 6/90

Dmitry Bortnyansky

Ukrainian 1751-1825

New review
Bortnyansky. Te Deum.
Plainchant Seventeenth-century Russian Liturgy. **Moscow Patriarchal Choir/Anatoly Grindenko.** Opus 111 OPS30-79. Recorded in 1992.

.•' 1h 3m DDD 4/94

This anthology is made up of chants from the Vigil Service (that is, Vespers and Matins) and a shorter selection from the Liturgy of St John Chrysostom. A chronological span of something over a century is covered, and various repertoires of chant can therefore be demonstrated, including seventeenth-century *znamenny* monody and polyphony of both earlier and later periods. There are also a number of hauntingly beautiful examples of *demiestvienny* chant, which employs the drone. It is all too easy to sing this kind of music, with its extremely unpredictable harmonic sequences and dissonant parallel intervals, loudly and aggressively; but in fact its true qualities only manifest themselves when it is sung, as here, quietly and without exaggeration, projecting the words. The Patriarchal Choir regularly sings these texts, if not precisely this music, as part of liturgical celebrations, and their knowledge of the liturgical context pays enormous dividends in the subtlety and flexibility which characterize their singing. They are also perfectly in tune, and there is no Russian 'operatic vibrato'. Unfortunately, no texts are provided.

Rutland Boughton

British 1878-1960

Suggested listening ...

Symphony No. 3 in B minor. Oboe Concerto No. 1. **Sarah Francis** (ob); **Royal Philharmonic Orchestra/Vernon Handley.** Hyperion CDA66343 (1/90).

THE IMMORTAL HOUR. **Soloists; George Mitchell Choir; English Chamber Orchestra/Alan G. Melville.** Hyperion CDA66101/2 (8/87).

Lili Boulanger

French 1893-1918

Suggested listening ...

Les sirènes. Renouveau. Hymne au soleil. Soir sur la plaine. Dans l'immense tristesse. Attente. Reflets. Le retour. *Coupled with* ***Mendelssohn-Hensel.*** Gartenlieder, Op. 3. Nachtreigen; *C. Schumann.* Three Geibel Part-songs. **Christine Friedek** (sop); **Mitsuko Shirai, Regine Böhm** (mezs); **Bernhard Gärtner** (ten); **Hartmut Höll, Sabine Eberspächer** (pfs); **Heidelberg Madrigal Choir/Gerald Kegelmann.** Bayer BR100041 (4/90).

Pierre Boulez

French 1925-

Boulez. Rituel (1974-75). Messagesquisse (1976). Notations 1-4 (1978). **Orchestre de Paris/Daniel Barenboim.** Erato 2292-45493-2.

41m DDD 10/90

Obviously enough, this disc wins no prizes for length. It is nevertheless important in several significant respects. Only rarely do we have the chance to hear Boulez's music, not only under a conductor other than the composer, but a conductor whose whole artistic background is so different to Boulez's own. Barenboim clearly has his own point of view, and the technical skill to realize it convincingly with a first-class French orchestra. Boulez himself now tends to underline the public ceremonial of *Rituel* (a tribute to the Italian composer and conductor Bruno Maderna), whereas Barenboim, restraining the cumulative clangour of the music's dialogues between the implacable reiterations of gongs and tamtams and the seven other instrumental groups, preserves more of the intimacy of personal regret and loss. *Rituel* is unusual for Boulez in the clear-cut logic of its gradually evolving form, and Barenboim does well to convey that logic without making the whole design seem too predictable for its own good. He is equally attentive to the need to balance striking details with a feeling for overall shape in the shorter but no less personal structures of *Notations* and *Messagesquisse*. The recording is outstanding in its spaciousness and tonal range.

Boulez. Pli selon pli. **Phyllis Bryn-Julson** (sop); **BBC Symphony Orchestra/Pierre Boulez.** Erato 2292-45376-2. From NUM75050 (5/83).

1h 8m DDD 3/89

Pli selon pli (1957-62) is one of the great pillars of post-war musical modernism. If that proclamation merely makes it sound forbidding, then it could scarcely be less appropriate.

'Pillar' it may be, but as exciting in its moment-to-moment shifts of colour and contour, and as compelling in its command of large-scale dramatic design as anything composed since the great years of Schoenberg and Stravinsky. Easy, no: enthralling and rewarding — yes. This is no grand, single-minded work in the great Germanic symphonic tradition, but a sequence of distinct yet balanced responses to aspects of the great symbolist poet Mallarmé. In this, his second recording of the piece, Boulez is prepared to let the music expand and resonate, the two large orchestral tapestries enclosing three "Improvisations", smaller-scale vocal movements in which the authority and expressiveness of Phyllis Bryn-Julson is heard to great advantage. The sound is brilliantly wide-ranging and well-balanced, and while the contrast between delicacy and almost delirious density embodied in *Pli selon pli* does take some getting used to, to miss it is to miss one of modern music's most original masterworks.

Further listening ...

Structures pour deux pianos. **Alfons Kontarsky, Aloys Kontarsky** (pfs). Wergo WER6011-2 (6/93).

Flute Sonatine[a]. Piano Sonata No. 1[b]. Dérive[c]. Mémoriale (... explosante-fixe ... originel)[d]. Dialogue de l'ombre double[e]. Cummings ist der Dichter[f]. [ad]**Sophie Cherrier** (fl); [e]**Alain Damiens** (cl); [ab]**Pierre-Laurent Aimard** (pf); [e]**Andrew Gerzo** (musical assistant); [f]**BBC Singers**; [cdf]**Ensemble Intercontemporain/Pierre Boulez.** Erato 2292-45648-2 (2/92).

Rituel in memoriam Bruno Maderna[a]. Eclat/Multiples[b]. [a]**BBC Symphony Orchestra,** [b]**Ensemble Intercontemporain/Pierre Boulez.** Sony Classical SK45839 (8/90).

Le visage nuptial[a]. Le soleil des eaux[b]. Figures, Doubles, Prismes. [ab]**Phyllis Bryn-Julson** (sop); [a]**Elizabeth Laurence** (mez); [ab]**BBC Singers; BBC Symphony Orchestra/Pierre Boulez.** Erato 2292-45494-2 (12/90).

Guillaume Bouzignac

before 1592-after 1641

New review

Bouzignac. MOTETS. **Les Pages de la Chapelle; Orlando Gibbons Viol Ensemble; Les Arts Florissants Chorus and Instrumental Ensemble/William Christie.** Harmonia Mundi HMC90 1471.
Ecce festivitas amoris. Ecce homo. Unus ex vobis. In pace in idipsum. Ha, plange, filia Jerusalem. Vulnerasti cor meum. Alleluya, Venite amici. Flos in floris tempore. O mors, ero mors tua. Clamant clavi. Ecce aurora. Dum silentium. Jubilate Deo. Salve Jesus piissime. Ave Maria. Tota pulchra es. Te Deum.

1h 3m DDD 6/94

If, by any chance, you should think that with another disc of French seventeenth-century church music from Les Arts Florissants you know what to expect, think again. Bouzignac is quite definitely, quite splendidly, different. Try *Unus ex vobis* on your friends and see if they can tell what century it comes from, let alone what country (its lugubrious dialogue between Christ and his disciples actually sounds more like something from the Russian Orthodox Church). This is music that abandons itself to its text in as absolute and direct a way as you are ever likely to encounter in the baroque period, and the results are sometimes gripping, sometimes haunting, and sometimes both. But that is not all. Bouzignac knew his counterpoint; he could write in joyous, celebratory vein, rather like a lightfooted Gabrieli (*Jubilate Deo*); and there is also music of aching beauty — *In pace in idipsum* should be enough to melt anyone into their chair. Christie marries an acute sense of drama to a sensitivity to words and to the music's lyrical qualities. He uses boy sopranos, and though their singing is hardly in the polished Arts Florissants mould, it does square nicely with this music's straightforward mode of communication.

William Boyce

New review

Boyce. Eight Symphonies, Op. 2. **Academy of Ancient Music/Christopher Hogwood.** L'Oiseau-Lyre 436 761-2OH. Recorded in 1992.

1h 1m DDD 4/94

The Boyce *Eight Symphonys* (as he himself spelt the title) are one of the treasures of English eighteenth-century music, cheerful, unassuming and confident, full of good tunes, and typically English in style — their quirky lines, their refusal to follow the regular procedures, their mixture of baroque and classical features, with their fugues declining to remain fugal, their very un-French French overtures: all this is part of their particular charm. Hogwood catches the eccentric character of the music well and gives a great deal of attention to the textural depth of the music and its inner detail. All the fugal movements go well, done with vitality and a feeling for their logic.

Boyce. SELECT ANTHEMS. **New College Choir, Oxford/Edward Higginbottom** with [a]**Gary Cooper** (org). CRD CRD3483. Texts included. Recorded in 1991.
O where shall widom be found? Wherewithal shall a young man. I have surely built thee an house. O praise the Lord. Turn thee unto me. O give thanks. By the waters of Babylon. The Lord is King be the people never so impatient. Voluntaries[a] — Nos. 1, 4 and 7.

1h 16m DDD 10/92

Boyce was a younger contemporary of Handel and one of England's most gifted baroque composers. Nowadays Boyce is remembered chiefly for his Symphonies but in his own time he was highly regarded for his vocal music. Five of the pieces on this disc are verse anthems which essentially belong to the tradition established by Restoration composers in the previous century. Three others are full anthems consisting of outer choral movements framing one for a smaller group of voices. Additionally, the programme includes three organ solos from Boyce's *Ten Voluntaries for Organ and Harpsichord*. The authenticity of some of these has been questioned but they sound well in the present context. The choir of New College, Oxford under Edward Higginbottom's direction is on characteristically strong form with carefully balanced vocal strands, clear textures, secure pitch and a pleasing radiance in the upper voices. The verse anthem, *I have surely built thee an house* comes over splendidly, providing the listener with a satisfying account of a fine piece. No less impressive is *By the waters of Babylon* in which Boyce's skill in the marriage of words with music is especially affecting. In this piece Higginbottom brings lucidity to the vocal ensemble while suffusing the whole with a soft radiance.

Further listening ...

Solomon — serenata. **Bronwen Mills** (sop) She; **Howard Crook** (ten) He; **The Parley of Instruments/Roy Goodman.** Hyperion CDA66378 (11/90).

Johannes Brahms

Brahms. Piano Concertos[a] — Nos. 1 and 2. Fantasias, Op. 116[b]. **Emil Gilels** (pf); [a]**Berlin Philharmonic Orchestra/Eugen Jochum.** DG 419 158-2GH2. Items marked [a] from 2707 064 (12/72), [b] 2530 655 (7/76). Items marked [a] recorded in 1972, [b] 1975.

② 2h 6m ADD 9/86

Emil Gilels was an ideal Brahms interpreter and his account of the two concertos with Eugen Jochum, another great Brahmsian, is one of the inspired classics of the gramophone. The youthful, leonine First Concerto and the expansive, lyrical Second were both played for the first time by Brahms himself, and it would be difficult to imagine any performances coming closer to the spirit of his music than these. They should not be missed and their value is further enhanced by the addition of the autumnal Fantasias, Op. 116. The recording, too, is natural and has plenty of concert hall ambience and an ideal balance between soloist and orchestra. This set cannot be too strongly recommended. We now also have them available separately at mid-price (see listings below).

Additional recommendations …

No. 1. **Claudio Arrau** (pf); **Concertgebouw Orchestra/Bernard Haitink.** Philips Silver Line 420 702-2PSL — .⁃' 53m ADD 11/87 ⁹ₚ Ⓑ

No. 1. **Alfred Brendel** (pf); **Berlin Philharmonic Orchestra/Claudio Abbado.** Philips 420 071-2PH — .⁃' 49m DDD 11/87 ⁹ₚ Ⓑ

No. 2. ***Beethoven.*** *Piano Sonata No. 23 in F minor, Op. 57, "Appassionata".* **Sviatoslav Richter** (pf); **Chicago Symphony Orchestra/Erich Leinsdorf.** RCA Papillon GD86518 — .⁃' 1h 11m ADD 5/88 ⁹ₚ Ⓑ

No. 1ª. *Variations on a Theme by Haydn, Op. 56aᵇ.* **Daniel Barenboim** (pf); ᵃ**Philharmonia Orchestra,** ᵇ**Vienna Philharmonic Orchestra/Sir John Barbirolli.** EMI Studio CDM7 63536-2 — .⁃' 1h 10m ADD 11/90 ⁹ₚ Ⓑ

No. 1. *Four Ballades, Op. 10.* **Emil Gilels** (pf); **Berlin Philharmonic Orchestra/Eugen Jochum.** DG Brahms Edition 431 595-2GCE (*coupled with No. 2 and reviewed above*) — .⁃' 1h 17m ADD 8/91 ⁹ₚ Ⓑ

No. 1ª. *Zwei Gesänge, Op. 91ᵇ.* **Stephen Kovacevich** (pf); ᵇ**Ann Murray** (mez); ᵇ**Nobuko Imai** (va); ᵃ**London Philharmonic Orchestra/Wolfgang Sawallisch.** EMI CDC7 54578-2 — .⁃' 59m DDD 10/92 ⁹ₚ Ⓑ

No. 2ª. *Academic Festival Overture, Op. 80ᵇ. Tragic Overture, Op. 81ᵇ.* **Daniel Barenboim** (pf); ᵃ**Philharmonia Orchestra,** ᵇ**Vienna Philharmonic Orchestra/Sir John Barbirolli.** EMI Studio CDM7 63537-2 — .⁃' 1h 16m ADD 11/90 ⁹ₚ Ⓑ

No. 2. **Alfred Brendel** (pf); **Berlin Philharmonic Orchestra/Claudio Abbado.** Philips 432 975-2PH — .⁃' 49m DDD 6/92 ⁹ₚ Ⓑ

No. 2. *Fantasias.* **Emil Gilels** (pf); **Berlin Philharmonic Orchestra/Eugen Jochum.** DG Galleria 435 588-2GGA (*coupled with No. 1 and reviewed above*) — .⁃' 1h 14m ADD 9/92 ⁹ₚ Ⓑ

Brahms. Violin Concerto in D major, Op. 77.
Sibelius. Violin Concerto in D minor, Op. 47. **Tasmin Little** (vn); **Royal Liverpool Philharmonic Orchestra/Vernon Handley.** EMI Eminence CD-EMX2203. Recorded 1991.

.⁃' 1h 12m DDD 2/93	⁹ₚ Ⓑ

New review

Brahms. Violin Concerto in D major, Op. 77.
Schumann. Violin Concerto in D minor, Op. posth. **Takayoshi Wanami** (vn); **London Philharmonic Orchestra/Adrian Leaper.** Pickwick IMP Classics PCD1062. Recorded 1992.

.⁃' 1h 11m DDD 4/94	Ⓑ

Tasmin Little admits that she prefers not to commit her interpretations to disc until she has "something to say and the means with which to say it". That is certainly the case with the Brahms Concerto, a clear, considered reading (much aided in the slow movement by Jonathan Small's excellent oboe solo), quite without mannerism and beautifully accompanied by Vernon Handley and the Royal Liverpool Philharmonic. The Sibelius has even more character, and here Little adds to an impressive roster of the work's many great female interpreters (Neveu, Wicks, Bustabo, Ignatius, etc). Handley is an impressive Sibelian whose feel for the idiom is apparent in every bar, and both recordings are excellent. As a coupling the two performances are irresistible. It says much for the brilliance and concentration of the Japanese violinist, Takayoshi Wanami in the Brahms that even in direct comparison with the best available performances his claims are still impressive. In the tutti Adrian Leaper draws bright, intense playing from the LPO, leading to a strong, positive first entry from the soloist. Wanami's coloration is not always ideally pure, even if his intonation is at all times secure, whether on or above the stave. At a noticeably fast speed, clearly keeping the feeling of *Allegro non troppo*, the movement is held cleanly together, with the simple lyricism of the *tranquillo* coda most beautifully phrased, if not at a hushed *pianissimo*. Again, in the central *Adagio* Wanami adopts a flowing speed, naturally songful, while with very clean passagework and with full, vivid orchestral recording, the finale has all the bite and swagger needed in a Hungarian dance. After this it is a pity that Wanami is let down by the orchestra in the still relatively rare Schumann concerto. His feeling for this difficult work is plain throughout, not least in the lovely slow interlude of the second movement, but after a lacklustre account of the opening tutti, the LPO never recaptures the bite of its playing in the Brahms. However, at mid-price, one might simply regard the Schumann as a generous makeweight for a highly enjoyable account of the Brahms.

Additional recommendations ...
Violin Concerto. **Mendelssohn.** *Violin Concerto in E minor, Op. 64.* **Xue-Wei** (vn); **London Philharmonic Orchestra/Ivor Bolton.** ASV CDDCA748 — .·' lh 7m DDD 4/91 Ⓑ
Violin Concerto. **Itzhak Perlman** (vn); **Berlin Philharmonic Orchestra/Daniel Barenboim.** EMI CDC7 54580-2 — .·' 40m DDD 2/93 Ⓑ
Violin Concerto. **Tchaikovsky.** *Violin Concerto in D major, Op. 35.* **Jascha Heifetz** (vn); **Chicago Symphony Orchestra/Fritz Reiner.** RCA Living Stereo 09026 61495-2 — .·' lh 4m ADD 4/93 Ⓑ ▲

Brahms. Double Concerto in A minor, Op. 102[a]. Piano Quartet No. 3 in C minor, Op. 60[b]. **Isaac Stern** (vn); [b]**Jaime Laredo** (va); **Yo-Yo Ma** (vc); [b]**Emmanuel Ax** (pf); [a]**Chicago Symphony Orchestra/Claudio Abbado.** CBS Masterworks CD42387.

.·' **lh 8m DDD 6/88**

The grave, declamatory utterances at the beginning of the Double Concerto tell us much about the nature of what will follow. They can also reveal a great deal about the two soloists who enter in turn with solo cadenzas separated by thematic orchestral material. Perhaps surprisingly it is the much younger man, Yo-Yo Ma, who brings out most strongly the noble gravity of the composer's inspiration, while the relatively veteran Isaac Stern is more melodious and spontaneous-sounding. The music's steady but unhurried paragraphs are very well handled by Claudio Abbado and the excellent Chicago Symphony Orchestra is responsive and pretty faithfully balanced with the soloists. This is a performance to satisfy rather than to thrill, perhaps, but satisfy it does. The recording is rich and rather reverberant, notably in orchestral tuttis. The powerful C minor Piano Quartet is also well played and provides a substantial partner to the concerto. Apparently Brahms once said that it had the mood of a man thinking of suicide, but one hastens to say that it is nothing like as gloomy as that would suggest.

Additional recommendation ...
Double Concerto[b]. **Beethoven.** *Triple Concerto in C major, Op. 56*[a]. [a]**Rudolf Serkin** (pf); [a]**Jaime Laredo,** [b]**Isaac Stern** (vns); [a]**Leslie Parnas,** [b]**Leonard Rose** (vcs); [a]**Marlboro Festival Orchestra/Alexander Schneider;** [b]**Philadelphia Orchestra/Eugene Ormandy.** Sony Portrait MK44842 — .·' lh llm ADD ll/89 ▲

Brahms. Serenades — No. 1 in D major, Op. 11; No. 2 in A major, Op. 16. **West German Sinfonia/Dirk Joeres.** Pickwick IMP Classics PCD1024. Recorded in 1992.

.·' **lh 19m DDD 5/93**

If the term serenade suggests something which is open-hearted and uncomplicated then Brahms's two compositions in this form follow classical conventions up to a point. Each work has an appealing geniality and mellow warmth, but Brahms had a perpetually serious side to his nature, and there's always a nearby cloud threatening to move over the sun. Such mixed characteristics are particularly evident in the Second Serenade, which is scored without violins, and lacks the brightness which upper strings bring to orchestral textures. It is no easy task for a conductor to balance the opposing elements in either work, but Dirk Joeres manages this very successfully. He has at his disposal a very fine body of players, who are given clear, high-quality recordings. In the faster, more outgoing sections of each score he points the rhythms very skilfully, and he shapes the slower, more inward movements in a highly sympathetic, attentive fashion. Even the First Serenade's long *Adagio no troppo* movement, which so easily loses direction, is kept on course through Joeres's subtle use of phrase and pulse.

Brahms. ORCHESTRAL AND VOCAL WORKS. **NBC Symphony Orchestra/Arturo Toscanini.** RCA Gold Seal mono GD60325. Texts and translations included.
Symphonies — No. 1 in C minor, Op. 68 (from HMV ALP1012, 11/52); No. 2 in D major, Op. 73 (ALP1013, 11/52); No. 3 in F major, Op. 90 (ALP1166, 10/54); No. 4 in E minor,

Op. 98 (ALP1029, 6/53). Double Concerto in A minor, Op. 102 (with Mischa Mischakoff, vn; Frank Miller, vc. RB16066, 7/58). Variations on a Theme by Haydn, Op. 56*a* (ALP1204, 12/54). Tragic Overture, Op. 81 (VCM3, 4/67). Academic Festival Overture, Op. 80 (VCM3, 4/67). *Hungarian Dances* — No. 1 in G minor; No. 17 in F sharp minor; No. 20 in E minor; No. 21 in E minor (ALP1235, 5/55). Gesang der Parzen, Op. 89 (Robert Shaw Chorale. AT125, 4/74). Liebeslieder-Walzer, Op. 52 (Chorus; Artur Balsam, Joseph Kahn, pfs. Recorded in 1948. New to UK).

④ 4h 27m ADD 5/90

Despite many reissues, technical tinkerings, and critical re-evaluations, the recordings of the great Italian maestro Arturo Toscanini still stand head and shoulders above those which have the unenviable task of rivalling his genius as conductor and interpreter. This generous Brahms set is an excellent example of why Toscanini's recordings are still essential. The readings of the four symphonies must stand as benchmarks against which others are compared, and generally are found wanting. Toscanini's command of this music is total: his sense of architecture is unfailing, his control of tempos and rubato are masterly, and his ability to persuade the NBC Symphony Orchestra to play with extraordinary dynamic variety and tonal beauty is proof of his genius. In addition to the symphonies the set contains a fiery performance of the Double Concerto with the orchestra's principals as eloquent, if occasionally overshadowed, soloists and excellent readings of the essential shorter works of Brahms: the *Haydn Variations, Academic* and *Tragic* Overtures and *Hungarian Dances.* And to round off the set there are good, if not perfect, performances of two choral works, the rarely performed *Song of the Fates* and the *Liebeslieder Waltzes,* Op. 52. The transfer to CD of the original tapes has been handled particularly well: the worst tonal excesses have been successfully tamed, and there is a fine sense of balance throughout (the recordings range from 1948 to 1963). With such a giant as Toscanini recommendation really becomes superfluous. Suffice it to say that these recordings are testimony to the genius of one of the greatest conductors this century has ever known.

Additional recommendation ...
Hungarian Dances. **Dvořák.** *Symphonic Variations, B70. Czech Suite, B93.* **North German Radio Symphony Orchestra/John Eliot Gardiner.** DG 437 506-2GH — •• 1h 2m DDD 6/93

Brahms. Symphony No. 1 in C minor, Op. 68. Gesang der Parzen, Op. 89[a]. [a]**Berlin Radio Chorus; Berlin Philharmonic Orchestra/Claudio Abbado.** DG 431 790-2GH. Recorded in 1990.

58m DDD 10/91

Brahms. Symphony No. 1 in C minor, Op. 68[a].
Wagner. Siegfried Idyll[bc]. Siegfried — Siegfried's horn-call[c]. [c]**Dennis Brain** (hn); [ab]**Philharmonia Orchestra/Guido Cantelli.** Testament mono SBT1012. Item marked [a] from HMV ALP1152 (7/54), [b] HMV DB9746/7 (4/52), [c] HMV C3622 (11/47). Recorded 1947-53.

1h 2m ADD 2/93

Claudio Abbado's 1990 recording of Brahms's First Symphony achieves the sort of musical and sonic impact that Karajan's first DG version did in the mid-1960s. That too was with the Berlin Philharmonic, a rich, grandly imposing performance that sung and stamped, culminating in a massively jubilant finale. Abbado's tempos are generally broad — his first movement (without its repeat) is as boldly emphatic as Klemperer's — but he never stints on affection, and few would find fault with his warm, lyrical handling of the beautiful *Andante,* 'sostenuto', indeed! Abbado ventures between the score's little nooks and crannies (in that respect at least, he's Karajan's superior), highlighting small details without impeding the music's flow or weakening the performance's overall structure. When the finale breaks from *Più Andante* to *Allegro non troppo, ma con brio* (not *too* fast, but with plenty of spirit), Abbado really goes for the burn, very much as Furtwängler did before him. It's a truly inspired reading, grand but never grandiose; appreciative of Brahms's thick-set orchestration, but never stodgy. The fill-up is of enormous import, and opens with one of the composer's most inspired musical gestures: a bold, burgeoning *Maestoso,* anticipating the words "The gods should be feared/by the human race ...". *Gesang der Parzen,* or "Song of the Fates" is a setting of a particularly unsettling poem by Goethe, one that warns how the uplifted have particular reason to fear the gods, those who "turn their beneficent eyes away from whole races." Abbado surely sensed the terrible truth of that prophesy, and his reading of Op. 89 breathes a deeply disquieting air. Cantelli conducts an interpretation of the Symphony which is free of any idiosyncrasy. Yet there is an extraordinary electricity in his conducting, a sense of concentration and conviction which lifts the performance into one of the greatest ever set down on record. The fiery young Italian makes the vintage Philharmonia play in an inspired fashion, and the 1953 mono recording is very acceptable. A slightly edgy string sound betrays the 1951 origin of the *Siegfried Idyll* recording, but the performance has a tenderness, warmth and eloquence which has never been surpassed. Dennis Brain's exuberant horn-call completes a very desirable Testament disc.

Additional recommendations ...

Nos. 1-4. **North German Radio Symphony Orchestra/Günter Wand.** RCA GD60085 —
.·' ③ 2h 38m ADD Ⓑ

Nos. 1-4. Variations on a Theme by Haydn, Op. 56a, "St Antoni". Academic Festival Overture, Op. 80. Hungarian Dances Nos. 17-21. Tragic Overture, Op. 81. **Cleveland Orchestra/George Szell.** Sony Classical SK48398 — .· ③ 3h 34m ADD Ⓑ

Nos. 1-4. Tragic Overture. Academic Festival Overture. **Chicago Symphony Orchestra/Sir Georg Solti.** Decca 430 799-2DC4 — .·' ④ 3h 19m ADD 4/92 Ⓑ

No. 1. Academic Festival Overture. **Concertgebouw Orchestra/Riccardo Chailly.** Decca 421 295-2DH — .·' 59m DDD 9/88 ⁹ₚ Ⓑ

No. 1. Tragic Overture. Academic Festival Overture. **Philharmonia Orchestra/Otto Klemperer.** EMI Studio CDM7 69651-2 — .·' 1h 7m ADD 1/90 ⁹ₚ Ⓑ

No. 1. **Schumann.** *Overture, Scherzo and Finale, Op. 52.* **Berlin Philharmonic Orchestra/ Herbert von Karajan.** DG Privilege 431 161-2GR — .· 1h 3m ADD 8/91 ⁹ₚ Ⓑ

No. 1. Variations on a Theme by Haydn. **London Classical Players/Roger Norrington.** EMI CDC7 54286-2 — .·' 1h 1m DDD 10/91 ⁹ₚ Ⓑ ✍

No. 1. Serenade No. 2 in A major, Op. 16. **NBC Symphony Orchestra/Arturo Toscanini.** RCA GD60277 — .·' 1h 11m ADD 11/92 Ⓑ

No. 1. **Royal Liverpool Philharmonic Orchestra/Marek Janowski.** ASV Quicksilva CDQS6101 — . 46m DDD 9/93 Ⓑ

Brahms. Symphony No. 2 in D major, Op. 73. Tragic Overture, Op. 81. **Boston Symphony Orchestra/Bernard Haitink.** Philips 432 094-2PH. Recorded in 1990.

.·' **1h 2m DDD 10/92** ⁹ₚ Ⓑ

Brahms. Symphony No. 2 in D major, Op. 73. Academic Festival Overture, Op. 80. **New York Philharmonic Orchestra/Kurt Masur.** Teldec 9031-77291-2. Recorded in 1992.

.·' **50m DDD 5/93** ⁹ₚ Ⓑ

Brahms's Second Symphony is the warmest, most lyrical of the four, and on the Philips disc it receives a performance which brings out those qualities to the full. Haitink's reading is very straightforward and unselfconscious: he allows the first movement to blossom attractively, but he ensures that this process is achieved within a string framework — one is always aware that detail has its secure place within the musical argument. The second movement's basic pulse is on the slow side, but Haitink's affectionate, watchful conducting ensures that the music flows naturally. The third movement is brought to life quite gently too, but accents are light and rhythms are sharp enough to ensure that the mood is still outgoing. In the finale Haitink sets a fast initial tempo, but he allows the music to breathe through the use of subtle inflexions and changes of pulse. There's plenty of excitement, but nothing is too hectic. In the Overture Haitink's basic tempo is quite measured, but again accents are sharp, and the score's dramatic element is well brought out. Throughout both works the playing of the Boston Symphony Orchestra is superlative, and the recording is excellent, with just a slight reservation that there is an occasional moment of slightly acid string tone.

Masur also brings warmth and affection to the Symphony. In the first movement he maintains a strong sense of line, and paces the music more objectively and straightforwardly than Haitink. The structure is clearer, but there's also a natural, unforced lyricism. The *Adagio* has a natural ebb and flow, and once again Masur makes the listener aware of the music's shape and argument very clearly. After a neatly pointed *Allegretto* the finale is given a beautifully balanced, strongly argued reading which eschews superficial excitement, but satisfies through the feeling of a symphonic argument brought to a logical conclusion. To sum up, Haitink caresses the music with more subjective warmth than Masur, whose reading by no means lacks affection, but is more architectural and objective. The New York Philharmonic responds to its musical director with highly sensitive, very accomplished playing, and Teldec's attractively warm but clearly recorded disc is completed by a genial, uplifting *Academic Festival Overture*.

Additional recommendations ...
No. 2. Alto Rhapsody, Op. 53[a]. [a]**Christa Ludwig** (mez); [a]**Philharmonia Chorus; Philharmonia Orchestra/Otto Klemperer.** EMI Studio CDM7 69650-2 — .·´ 51m ADD 1/90 ꝗₚ Ⓑ
No. 2. Alto Rhapsody[a]. [a]**Marjana Lipovšek** (contr); [a]**Ernst Senff Choir; Berlin Philharmonic Orchestra/Claudio Abbado.** DG 427 643-2GH — .·´ 1h DDD 2/90 ꝗₚ Ⓑ
No. 2. Academic Festival Overture. **Columbia Symphony Orchestra/Bruno Walter.** CBS Maestro CD44870 — .·´ 51m ADD 7/90 Ⓑ ▲
No. 2. Webern. Im Sommerwind. **Royal Concertgebouw Orchestra/Riccardo Chailly.** Decca 430 324-2DH — .·´ 56m DDD 12/90 Ⓑ
No. 2. **Vienna Philharmonic Orchestra/Carlo Maria Giulini.** DG 435 348-2GH — .·´ 47m DDD 5/92 Ⓑ
No. 2. Tchaikovsky. Piano Concerto No. 1 in B flat minor, Op. 23. **Vladimir Horowitz** (pf); **NBC Symphony Orchestra/Arturo Toscanini.** RCA Victor Gold Seal GD60319 — .·´ 1h 14m ADD 9/93 Ⓑ ▲
No. 2. **Royal Liverpool Philharmonic Orchestra/Marek Janowski.** ASV Quicksilva CDQS6102 — ₎ 58m DDD 11/93 Ⓑ
No. 2. Tragic Overture, Op. 81. **London Classical Players/Roger Norrington.** EMI Reflexe CDC7 54875-2 — .·´ 55m DDD 12/93 ꝗₚ Ⓑ ✒

Brahms. Symphony No. 3 in F major, Op. 90. Tragic Overture, Op. 81. Schicksalslied, Op. 54[a]. [a]**Ernst-Senff Choir; Berlin Philharmonic Orchestra/Claudio Abbado.** DG 429 765-2GH.

.·´ 1h 8m DDD 1/91   ꝗₚ Ⓑ

New review
Brahms. Symphony No. 3 in F major, Op. 90.
Schoenberg. Chamber Symphony No. 1, Op. 9. **Royal Concertgebouw Orchestra/ Riccardo Chailly.** Decca 436 466-2DH.

.·´ 58m DDD 9/93   ꝗₛ Ⓑ

Abbado's disc is gloriously programmed for straight-through listening. He gets off to a cracking start with an urgently impassioned *Tragic Overture* in which the credentials of the Berlin Philharmonic to make a richly idiomatic, Brahmsian sound — already well accepted — are substantially reaffirmed. A wide-eyed, breathtaking account of the *Schicksalslied* ("Song of Destiny") follows to provide sound contrast before the wonders of the Third Symphony are freshly explored. This is a reading of the Symphony to be savoured; it is underpinned throughout by a rhythmic vitality which binds the four movements together with a forward thrust, making the end inevitable right from the opening bars. Even in the moments of repose and, especially, the warmly-felt *Andante*, Abbado never lets the music forget its ultimate goal. Despite this, there are many moments of wonderful solo and orchestral playing along the way in which there is time to delight, and Abbado seems to bring out that affable, Bohemian-woods, Dvořák-like element in Brahms's music to a peculiar degree in this performance. The Symphony is recorded with a particular richness and some may find the heady waltz of the third movement done too lushly, emphasized by Abbado's lingering tempo. Nevertheless, this is splendid stuff, and not to be missed.

Chailly's No. 3 is a very likeable, impressive reading which just seems to lose confidence in itself from time to time. The recording is outstanding, as is the playing of the full orchestra. Chailly's account of the first movement is well-conceived, although lacking a certain natural flow. The basic tempo is ideal, there is plenty of spirit and expression, but the music seems slightly ill at ease with itself. Matters improve greatly in the second movement, which moves forward calmly and easily, with plenty of natural warmth. Only an occasional awkwardness in the phrasing disturbs an otherwise almost ideal account of the third movement, and the finale is very impressively managed throughout. Although Abbado and Walter on CBS/Sony at mid-price remain the top recommended versions, this disc is very desirable, perhaps mainly for the coupling. Schoenberg's *Chamber Symphony* dates from an early stage in his development, and shows tonality under severe pressure and in fact cracking apart under the composer's assault. This feeling of pressure, of music somehow fighting to get out, is something which needs to be brought out strongly in performance, and Chailly succeeds brilliantly in conveying the score's wild intensity. He drives the music very hard, chooses fast, almost hectic tempos, and gets superbly committed playing from his 15 orchestral soloists. The influence of the older composer is apparent not only in the work's few quieter passages, which are shaped very beautifully by Chailly, but in certain rhythmic characteristics, which sound rather like Brahms caught up in a nightmare. The ensemble must be a brute to balance successfully, but the engineers have succeeded brilliantly.

Additional recommendations ...
No. 3. Variations on a Theme by Haydn. **Columbia Symphony Orchestra/Bruno Walter.** CBS Masterworks CD42531 — .·* 52m ADD 9/86 ⁹ₚ Ⓑ ▲
No. 3. Serenade No. 1 in D major, Op. 11. **Belgian Radio and Television Philharmonic Orchestra, Brussels/Alexander Rahbari.** Naxos 8 550280 — ₌ 1h 17m DDD 1/92 Ⓑ
No. 3. Alto Rhapsody, Op. 53[a]. [a]**Dunja Vejzovic** (mez); [a]**Houston Symphony Male Chorus; Houston Symphony Orchestra/Christoph Eschenbach.** Virgin Classics VC5 45006-2 — .·* 54m DDD 6/94 Ⓑ

Brahms. Symphony No. 4 in E minor, Op. 98. **Vienna Philharmonic Orchestra/Carlos Kleiber.** DG 400 037-2GH. From 2532 003 (4/81).

.·* 39m DDD 9/85	Ⓑ

Carlos Kleiber's reading of Brahms's Fourth Symphony is highly individual and thought-provoking but those listeners who know Kleiber from his thrilling recordings of Beethoven's Fifth and Seventh Symphonies and are expecting similarly uncompromising, high-tension performances with enormous muscular energy are in for a surprise! His reading certainly has plenty of muscle, but he shows considerable patience and generosity in his handling of Brahms's long, constantly developing melodic lines. Sound is generally good, though the bass may need assistance on some equipment.

Additional recommendations ...
No. 4. Variations on a Theme by Haydn. **Chicago Symphony Orchestra/Sir Georg Solti.** Decca 430 440-2DM — .·* 1h 2m ADD 4/92 Ⓑ
No. 4. Variations on a Theme by Haydn. **Hallé Orchestra/James Loughran.** Classics for Pleasure CD-CFP4614 — .· 59m ADD 3/93 Ⓑ

Brahms. String Sextets — No. 1 in B flat major, Op. 18; No. 2 in G major, Op. 36. **Raphael Ensemble** (James Clarke, Elizabeth Wexler, vns; Sally Beamish, Roger Tapping, vas; Andrea Hess, Rhydian Shaxson, vcs). Hyperion CDA66276.

.·* 1h 14m DDD 1/89	⁹ₚ

New review
Brahms. String Sextets — No. 1 in B flat major, Op. 18; No. 2 in G major, Op. 36. **Academy of St Martin in the Fields Chamber Ensemble** (Kenneth Sillito, Malcolm Latchem, vns; Robert Smissen, Stephen Tees, vas; Stephen Orton, Roger Smith, vcs). Chandos CHAN9151.

.·* 1h 18m DDD 8/93	⁹ₛ

Completed after the First Piano Concerto, but still comparatively early works, the Sextets are typified by lush textures, ardent emotion, and wonderfully memorable melodic lines. The first is the warmer, more heart-on-the-sleeve piece, balancing with complete naturalness a splendidly lyrical first movement, an urgent, dark set of intricate variations, a lively rustic dance of a *Scherzo*, and a placidly flowing finale. The Second Sextet inhabits at first a more mysterious world of half-shadows, occasionally rent by glorious moments of sunlight. The finale, however, casts off doubt and ends with affirmation. Both works are very susceptible to differing modes of interpretation, and the Raphael Ensemble has established very distinctive views of each, allowing the richness of the texture its head without obscuring the lines, and selecting characteristically distinct tone qualities to typify the two works. The recording is clear and analytic without robbing the sound of its warmth and depth. Altogether an impressive recording début for this ensemble.

At once the Chandos issue impresses with a particularly beautiful quality of sound, to match playing which is also of a very high standard. As the opening movement of the First Sextet develops, an attractive quality of relaxed warmth is very much in evidence. The expression seems perhaps a little applied from without, rather than springing naturally from the music itself, but a very satisfying account of the movement is still made manifest. The second movement variations unfold pleasantly, but here the musical characterization is not quite as sharp as it might be, and a slightly strenuous quality is present in the *Scherzo*. The finale is however played in an appealingly graceful, warm-hearted fashion. In the Second Sextet the first movement is again expressive in a slightly calculated fashion but the second movement *Scherzo* is delicately and beautifully played. The succeeding *Adagio* doesn't quite flow as easily as it might, and in the finale the ASMF players adopt a slightly restrained manner. High standards indeed were set by the Raphael Ensemble and any newcomer faces a stiff challenge. The Chandos performances are very good, and in two respects they improve on the Hyperion disc, for in the First Sextet the ASMF Chamber Ensemble play the first movement exposition repeat omitted by the Raphael Ensemble, and Chandos's recording is more mellow and pleasing to the ear. Nevertheless, the Hyperion players show a quite extraordinary sensitivity and flair, and their response to each other and to the music itself is inspired in a manner rarely achieved on record.

Additional recommendations ...
No. 1[a]. Piano Trio No. 1 in B major, Op. 8[b]. **Isaac Stern**, [a]**Alexander Schneider** (vns); [a]**Milton Katims**, [a]**Milton Thomas** (vas); **Pablo Casals**, [a]**Madeline Foley** (vcs); [b]**Dame Myra Hess** (pf). Sony Classical Casals Edition mono SMK58994 — .∙∙ 1h 17m ADD 5/94 **9**ᵖ ▲

Brahms. Clarinet Quintet in B minor, Op. 115[a].
Mozart. Clarinet Quintet in A major, K581[b]. **Gervase de Peyer** (cl); Members of the **Melos Ensemble** (Emanuel Hurwitz, Ivor McMahon, vns; Cecil Aronowitz, va; Terence Weill, vc). EMI CDM7 63116-2. Item marked [a] from ASD620 (3/65), [b] ASD605 (9/64).

.∙∙ **1h 5m   ADD   11/89**   **9**ᵖ

There can be few who hear the opening to Brahms's Clarinet Quintet who fail to succumb to the main subject's tender and haunting melancholy — surely one of Brahms's most poignant utterances and certainly one guaranteed to send tingles down the spine. Gervase de Peyer's warm, full-bodied tone and liquid playing is a delight to the ear, and the autumnal beauty of the work is captured particularly well in this affectionate and thoughtful performance. Unlike the Mozart Quintet, which treats the clarinet very much as a concertante instrument, Brahms integrates the clarinet into the overall texture, skilfully blending and juxtaposing the characteristic timbre with that of the strings into an homogeneous whole, a quality that comes over exceptionally well in this performance. The Mozart Quintet makes an ideal contrast to the autumnal glow of the Brahms, and receives an equally fine and engaging performance, if perhaps lacking just that extra bit of magic that makes the Brahms so irresistible. The Melos Ensemble convey the work's geniality and freshness from beginning to end, and the slow movement is imbued with great serenity and beauty. The 1964 recordings have retained a remarkable freshness, and are both naturally balanced and beautifully clear. At mid-price this reissue should not be missed.

Additional recommendations ...
Clarinet Quintet. Clarinet Trio in A minor, Op. 114. **Thea King** (cl); **Gabrieli Quartet; Karina Georgian** (vc); **Clifford Benson** (pf). Hyperion CDA66107 — .∙∙ 1h 5m DDD 2/87
Clarinet Quintet[a]. Clarinet Trio[ab]. **József Balogh** (cl); [a]**Csaba Onczay** (vc); [b]**Danubius Quartet.** [a]**Jenö Jandó** (pf). Naxos 8 550391 — .∙ 59m DDD 9/93

Brahms. Piano Quintet in F minor, Op. 34. **Maurizio Pollini** (pf); **Quartetto Italiano** (Paolo Borciani, Elisa Pegreffi, vns; Dino Asciolla, va; Franco Rossi, vc). DG 419 673-2GH. From 2531 197 (9/80).

.∙∙ **43m   AAD   6/87**   **9**ᵖ

This work was originally composed as a string quintet with two cellos. Brahms's influential friend Joseph Joachim then subjected the composition to a good deal of criticism, and Brahms took this to heart so much that he converted the quintet into a sonata for two pianos. As this version also was not well received Brahms turned to another friend, Clara Schumann, and as a result of her advice the work emerged in a third form, for piano quintet. This powerfully argued work gives little indication of its varied origins. The long first movement has a particularly strong yet highly romantic vein of expression, and in their performance Pollini and his colleagues bring out particularly well its stormy, dramatic nature. In the slow movement the performers bring a certain restless, questing quality to Brahms's rich lyricism and the *Scherzo*, perhaps the most inventive movement, is quickly and urgently expressed. The rondo-finale is a very substantial movement in its own right and is given its full weight by the five excellent players. The recording is clear and very immediate.

Additional recommendations ...
Piano Quintet. **Schumann.** *Piano Quintet in E flat major, Op. 44.* **Jenö Jandó** (pf); **Kodály Quartet.** Naxos 8 550406 — . lh 7m DDD 2/91
Piano Quintet[a]. *String Quartet No. 3 in B flat major, Op. 67.* [a]**Piers Lane** (pf); **Budapest Quartet.** Hyperion CDA66632 — .⋰ lh 18m DDD 4/93

Brahms. Piano Quartets — No. 1 in G minor, Op. 25; No. 2 in A major, Op. 26; No. 3 in C minor, Op. 60. **Isaac Stern** (vn); **Jaime Laredo** (va); **Yo-Yo Ma** (vc); **Emanuel Ax** (pf). Sony Classical SK45846.

.⋰ ② 2h 8m DDD 3/91 ⑨ₚ

These three piano quartets belong to the middle of Brahms's life. They have all the power and lyricism that we associate with his music, as well as the fine craftsmanship that he acquired when young and, with the high standards he set himself, demonstrated in every work thereafter. The mood of the music is again Brahmsian in that alongside a wealth of melodic and harmonic invention there are some shadows: all we know of Brahms's life suggests that he was never a happy man. But if this is reflected in the music, and especially the C minor Quartet, we can recognize the strength of intellect and will that keeps all in proportion so that there is no overt soul-bearing. These quartets are big pieces which often employ a grand manner, though less so in No. 2 than the others. For this reason, the present performances with their exuberant sweep are particularly telling, and although no detail is missed the players offer an overall strength. Top soloists in their own right, they combine their individual gifts with the ability to play as a well integrated team. The recording is close but not overwhelmingly so. Only the booklet, with notes in four languages, mars at least some copies of this issue, for it has some blank pages and details of the movements are missing, as are parts of the English and Italian notes.

Additional recommendations ...
Nos. 1 and 3. **Domus.** Virgin Classics VC7 59248-2 — .⋰ lh 16m DDD 6/88
No. 2. **Mahler.** *Movement for piano quartet.* **Domus.** Virgin Classics VC7 59144-2 — .⋰ lh lm DDD 1/89
No. 1. Variations and Fugue on a Theme by Handel, Op. 24 (orch. Rubbra). **London Symphony Orchestra/Neeme Järvi.** Chandos CHAN 8825 — .⋰ lh 11m DDD 2/91

New review
Brahms. String Quartets — No. 1 in C minor, Op. 51 No. 1; No. 2 in A minor, Op. 51 No. 2; No. 3 in B flat major, Op. 67. **Alban Berg Quartet** (Günter Pichler, Gerhard Schulz, vns; Thomas Kakuska, va; Valentin Erben, vc). EMI CDS7 54829-2. Recorded 1991-92.

.⋰ ② lh 42m DDD 2/94 ⑨ₚ

All three works emerge not only with the technical fluency and finish for which this Viennese team have long been renowned but also with quite exceptional immediacy and vividness. The first and last movements of No. 1 spring at you with all the drama Brahms invariably drew from C minor. Yet the music's cajoling lyricism is very lovingly cherished too. The players' wide dynamic range is faithfully reproduced right down to the most intimate confidence — and of course the ensuing *Romanze*, very tenderly and delicately interwoven, brings still stronger proof of their awareness of the eloquence of *pianissimo* in all its variations of colour and character. In No. 3 they at once capture its carefree rustic verve with their bold dynamic contrasts and relish of the composer's rhythmic teasing, and in the second Quartet tonal production is no less clear and true even if just a shade less vibrant and lustrous. Maybe this impression can be attributed to the players' desire to convey the work's retreat into a more elusive, wistful world, a world they evoke with such effortless fluency, fluidity and grace in the opening *Allegro non troppo*. Strongly recommended for anyone wanting a keen-edged reminder of this composer's warm and vulnerable romantic heart.

Additional recommendations ...
Nos. 1-3. **Takács Quartet.** Decca 425 526-2DH — ••* lh 6m DDD 9/90 ⁹ₚ
Nos. 2 and 3. **Orlando Quartet** . Ottavo OTRC68819 — ••* lh l5m DDD 6/90 ⁹ₚ
Nos. 1 and 2. **New Budapest Quartet.** Hyperion CDA66651 — ••* lh 7m DDD 4/93
No. 3. Piano Quintet in F minor, Op. 34ᵃ. ᵃ**Piers Lane** (pf); **Budapest Quartet.** Hyperion CDA66632 — ••* lh l8m DDD 4/93

Brahms. Cello Sonatas — No. 1 in E minor, Op. 38; No. 2 in F major, Op. 99. **Steven Isserlis** (vc); **Peter Evans** (pf). Hyperion CDA66159. From A66159 (10/85).

| ••* 50m DDD 4/86 | ⁹ₚ |

Brahms worked on his Cello Sonata No. 1 over a period of three years, from 1862 to 1865. Originally the work included an *Adagio*, but this was destroyed by the composer before publication, and as a result we have a three-movement sonata consisting of a somewhat dark-hued, questing *Allegro non troppo*, a central *Allegretto quasi menuetto*, which has a slight eighteenth-century pastiche flavour, and a bold, tautly argued *Allegro* finale. The F major Sonata of 1886 is a bigger work in every way. It was one of three chamber works written during a summer stay in Switzerland, and the glorious scenery stimulated Brahms to compose in a warm, open-hearted fashion. Steven Isserlis plays throughout both works with an impressive tone-quality and an immaculate technique. Though his sympathy for the music is everywhere evident, he does lack the last ounce of interpretative insight. But with fine playing from the pianist Peter Evans, and a very good, natural sounding recording, this is a disc which will give much pleasure.

Additional recommendations ...
Nos. 1 and 2. **Mstislav Rostropovich** (vc); **Rudolf Serkin** (pf). DG 410 510-2GH — ••* 58m DDD 9/83 ⁹ₚ
Nos. 1 and 2. **Lynn Harrell** (vc); **Vladimir Ashkenazy** (pf). Decca 414 558-2DH — ••* 52m ADD l0/85 ⁹ₚ
Nos. 1 and 2. Violin Sonata No. 3 in D minor, Op. 108 (trans. cello). **Yo-Yo Ma** (vc); **Emanuel Ax** (pf). Sony Classical SK48191 — ••* lh l5m DDD ll/92 ⁹ₚ
Nos. 1 and 2. **Pieter Wispelwey** (vc); **Paul Komen** (pf). Channel Classics CCS5493 — ••* 53m DDD l/94 ✒

Brahms. Piano Triosᵃ — No. 1 in B major, Op. 8; No. 2 in C major, Op. 87; No. 3 in C minor, Op. 101.
Mendelssohn. Piano Trio No. 1 in D minor, Op 49ᵇ.
Schubert. Piano Trios — No. 1 in B flat major, D898ᶜ; No. 2 in E flat major, D929ᵈ. **Isaac Stern** (vn); **Leonard Rose** (vc); **Eugene Istomin** (pf). Sony Classical SK46425. Items marked ᵃ from CBS SBRG72596/7 (1/68), ᵇ 73667 (9/68), ᶜ SBRG72344 (10/65), ᵈ 72858 (1/73). Recorded 1964-66.

| ••* ③ 3h l9m ADD 5/9l | ⁹ₚ |

Brahms's three published piano trios, which are among his greatest chamber works, combine the resonant lyricism that was such a distinctive aspect of his mature style with an engaging sense of mystery and, in the faster movements, a muscular ruggedness. The Op. 8 Trio (substantially revised from an earlier version) is the most expansively romantic, whereas the other two are more elusively argued, tightly constructed and less willing to reveal their secrets at a first hearing. The Stern/Rose/Istomin set of the trios was recorded in 1964-6, when America was producing a veritable plethora of great chamber music recordings. Isaac Stern was at the very height of his powers, producing a warm, strong body of tone and phrasing with endless reserves of imagination, while Leonard Rose achieved parallel distinction on cello, and Eugene Istomin — ever under-rated in Britain — leavened the mix with clean, thoughtful pianism. The overall blend is one of secure and perceptive musicianship, captured in sound that, although subject to some exaggerated channel separation, emerges on CD with far more warmth and presence than it did on LP. But that's not all Sony offer us: in addition to the Brahms, we're given Schubert's two great Trios and the first, and more immediately appealing, of Mendelssohn's two. These recordings date from roughly the same period as the Brahms set and are similarly direct, considered and sonically fresh.

Additional recommendations ...
Nos. 1-3; A major, Op. posth. (attrib. Brahms). **Beaux Arts Trio.** Philips Duo 438 365-2PM2 — 〰 ② lh 59m DDD 1/88
*No. 1. **Ives.** Piano Trio.* **Trio Fontenay.** Teldec 2292-44924-2 — 〰 57m DDD 4/90 ℚ𝓈
*No. 2. **Dvořák.** Piano Trio No. 1 in B flat major, B51.* **Trio Fontenay.** Teldec 2292-44177-2 — 〰 lh 4m DDD 2/90 ℚ𝓅 ℚ𝓈
Nos. 1-3; A major, Op. posth; Horn Trio E flat major, Op. 40[c]; Clarinet Trio A minor, Op. 114[c]. **Odeon Trio;** [c]**Rainer Moog** (va). Capriccio 10 633 — 〰 ③ 2h 55m DDD 7/93
Nos. 1-3[a]; A major, Op. posth. Horn Trio in E flat major, Op. 40[b]. Clarinet Trio, in A minor, Op. 114[c]. [ad]**Beaux Arts Trio;** [c]**George Pieterson** (cl); [b]**Francis Orval** (hn); [b]**Arthur Grumiaux** (vn); [b]**Gyorgy Sebok** (pf). Philips Duo 438 365-2PM2 — 〰 ② 2h 10m ADD 8/93
No. 1[a]. String Sextet No. 1 in B major, Op. 18[b]. **Isaac Stern,** [b]**Alexander Schneider** (vns); [b]**Milton Katims,** [b]**Milton Thomas** (vas); **Pablo Casals,** [b]**Madeline Foley** (vcs); [a]**Dame Myra Hess** (pf). Sony Classical Casals Edition mono SMK58994 — 〰 lh 17m ADD 5/94 ℚ𝓅 ▲

Brahms. Horn Trio in E flat major, Op. 40[a].
Franck. Violin Sonata in A major. **Itzhak Perlman** (vn); [a]**Barry Tuckwell** (hn); **Vladimir Ashkenazy** (pf). Decca 414 128-2DH. From SXL6408 (5/69).

〰 56m AAD 4/85 ℚ𝓅

Anyone who thinks of chamber music as predominantly an intellectual medium should easily be persuaded otherwise by these two mellow works of the late nineteenth century. Brahms is the more classically shaped of the two, while the third movement of the Franck Sonata is a "recitative-fantasia" whose quiet eloquence seems more than a little to foreshadow Debussy. Here, as in the strictly canonic theme of the finale, Franck shows us that even baroque techniques can be turned with no apparent effort to romantic ends. In the Brahms Horn Trio, Perlman and Ashkenazy are joined by another virtuoso in the person of Barry Tuckwell; but it is not their dazzling technical command that we notice so much as their musicianly subtlety. In the rich textures of this work we are reminded of the composer's inspiration by the beauty of the Black Forest and also of his grief at the recent loss of his beloved mother. The combination of these three instruments is rare to say the least, but the engineer has balanced them satisfactorily.

Additional recommendations ...
Horn Trio[a]. **Beethoven.** *Sonata for horn and piano in F major, Op. 17.* **Krufft.** *Sonata for horn and piano in F major.* **Lowell Greer** (hn); [a]**Stephanie Chase** (vn); **Steven Lubin** (pf). Harmonia Mundi HMU90 7037 — 〰 lh 5m DDD 9/92
Horn Trio[a]. **Franck.** *Violin Sonata.* **Schumann.** *Adagio and Allegro, Op. 70[a].* **Saint-Saëns.** *Romance, Op. 67[a].* **Itzhak Perlman** (vn); [a]**Barry Tuckwell** (hn); **Vladimir Ashkenazy** (pf). Decca 433 695-2DM (*the first two works on this disc are the same recordings reviewed above*) — 〰 lh 13m ADD 9/92 ℚ𝓅
Horn Trio[a]. **Schumann.** *Andante and Variations[b]. Adagio and Allegro, Op. 70.* **Radovan Vlatkovic** (hn); [a]**Hans Maile** (vn); [b]**George Donderer,** [b]**Mathias Donderer** (vcs); **Vladimir Ashkenazy,** [b]**Vovka Ashkenazy** (pfs). Decca 433 850-2DH — 〰 56m DDD 10/93

New review
Brahms. Clarinet Sonatas, Op. 120 — No. 1 in F minor; No. 2 in E flat major.
Schumann. Fantasiestücke, Op. 73. **Franklin Cohen** (cl); **Vladimir Ashkenazy** (pf). Decca 430 149-2DH.

〰 52m DDD 10/93 ℚ𝓈

All music-lovers know well that inspiration for Brahms's two clarinet sonatas came from the playing of Richard Mühlfeld, principal clarinettist of the Meiningen Court Orchestra, just at a moment in later life when Brahms might otherwise have laid down his pen. But on this disc it is not so much the wind instrument's song that captures your ear as the rich textural variety of the piano writing — and this, of course, thanks to Ashkenazy's super-sensitive tonal colouring as well as inexhaustible vitality of every kind. Without sacrifice of strength there is always a translucency of keyboard sound, ensuring that no detail of craftsmanly cunning is ever obscured, or equally no note from his partner. Ensemble between the two players cannot be faulted in matters of timing and balance. However, in temperament one feels that whereas for Ashkenazy Brahms, at heart, remains the vulnerable romantic of earlier days, for Cohen he is the mid-nineteenth-century's middle-aged upholder of classical purity and restraint, of avoidance of all untoward extemes including dynamic contrast. Schumann's three *Fantasiestücke* of 1849 make lesser demands: they date from his brief recourse to miniatures, in politically disturbed times, between loftier projects. These pieces might have benefited from more personal inflexion of phrasing from Cohen, and not least in rather stronger leanings on first-beat heart-tugs to squeeze out the nostalgia underlying all three. Full marks to Decca's recording engineers for quality of sound.

Additional recommendations ...
Clarinet Sonatas. **Thea King** (cl); **Clifford Benson** (pf). Hyperion CDA66202 — ⸬ 43m DDD 10/87
Clarinet Sonatas. **Gervase de Peyer** (cl); **Gwenneth Pryor** (pf). Chandos CHAN8563 — ⸬ 43m DDD 3/88
Clarinet Sonatas. **Weber.** *Grand duo concertant, J204.* **Paul Meyer** (cl); **François-René Duchable** (pf). Erato 2292-45480-2 — ⸬ 1h 6m DDD 9/90

New review
Brahms. 21 Hungarian Dances. 16 Waltzes, Op. 39. **Yaara Tal, Andreas Groethuysen** (pf duet). Sony Classical SK53285. Recorded in 1992.

⸬ 1h 8m DDD 4/94

These duettists offer excellent ensemble, a crisp and convincing idea of the music they play, and above all an invigorating zest and zip. In the Waltzes some tempos are quicker than usual, but at no time do these artists hurry us, and their elegant and perfectly synchronized rubato is a delight throughout, as is their dynamic range, texture, phrasing and pedalling. The *Hungarian Dances* are no less enjoyable, being infectiously alert and sparkling and offering vigour without coarseness. The duettists' chosen piano is a fine one in good condition and Sony's recording is clear and spacious.

Brahms. Viola Sonatas, Op. 120 — No. 1 in F minor; No. 2 in E flat major.
Joachim. Variations on an Original Theme in E major, Op. 10. **Rivka Golani** (va); **Konstantin Bogino** (pf). Conifer CDCF199. Recorded in 1991.

⸬ 1h 11m DDD 9/92

The Brahms Viola Sonatas belong to the last years of his life and were originally written for clarinet. But the composer always saw them as alternatively for viola and this version goes further than just transposing notes as necessary: for example, some figuration is different, there is double-stopping, and sometimes the viola even plays where the clarinet does not. Rivka Golani brings plenty of tonal flexibility to the music and demonstrates her understanding of Brahms's autumnal style, with its smouldering passions and hints of regret. So does her pianist Konstantin Bogino. The recording successfully balances the two players and instruments, and if the piano bass has a heavyish sound, that suits the music quite well. Golani comes across here as an essentially serious artist, which is perhaps right, although she might have brought more pace to the opening *Allegro appassionato* of the F minor Sonata and more of a smile to its *grazioso* third movement. She is also a little deliberate in the two *allegro* movements in the E flat major Sonata although its finale has fine vigour. But in compensation she offers much tonal beauty. Joachim was a friend of Brahms and the first interpreter of his Violin Concerto, and his Variations are here recorded for the first time. Their style suggests something between Schumann and Elgar and no very strong individuality emerges, but he wrote beautifully for the instrument and Golani's playing is as refined and expressive as one could wish for.

Additional recommendations ...
Viola Sonatas[a]. *Trio in A minor for viola, cello and piano, Op. 114*[b]. [ab]**Yuri Bashmet** (va); [b]**Valentin Berlinsky** (vc); [ab]**Mikhail Muntyan** (pf). Olympia OCD175 — ⸬ 1h 7m DDD 5/88

Viola Sonatas. **Schumann.** *Märchenbilder, Op. 113.* **Lars Anders Tomter** (va); **Leif Ove Andsnes** (pf). Virgin Classics VC7 59309-2 — ..·˙ lh DDD ll/93

Brahms. Violin Sonatas — No. 1 in G major, Op. 78; No. 2 in A major, Op. 100; No. 3 in D minor, Op. 108. **Josef Suk** (vn); **Julius Katchen** (pf). Decca Ovation 421 092-2DM. From SXL6321 (1/68).

..·˙ lh 8m ADD 5/88 ⁹ₚ

Brahms. Violin Sonatas — No. 1 in G major, Op. 78; No. 2 in A major, Op. 100; No. 3 in D minor, Op. 108. **Augustin Dumay** (vn); **Maria-João Pires** (pf). DG 435 800-2GH.

..·˙ lh l2m DDD 3/93 ⁹ₚ

Brahms was 45 when he began to work on the first of these sonatas and he completed the final one some ten years later. These products of his mature genius are certainly the greatest works written in this form since Beethoven's. Though they are lovingly crafted and have a predominant air of lyricism, there is great variety of melody and of mood. The invention always sounds spontaneously conceived and they fit the CD format like a kid glove. Suk's control over nuance is magical whilst Katchen has a complete understanding of the style. In every way these are performances that truly deserve to be labelled as classics and the naturally vivid recorded sound brings them to life with magnificent immediacy. Collectors who seek a fully digital version of these sonatas, although coming at full price, will do well to consider the much more recent one by Augustin Dumay and Maria-João Pires. Again, these works, which could not have fitted on to a single disc in the days of LP, do so comfortably on CD and make a splendid triptych. Like Suk and Katchen, these younger artists recognize that, for all its technical challenges and occasional fiery outbursts, this is still predominant-ly lyrical music; and although they miss no special points and offer much interpretative refinement, their delivery is pleasingly unfussy, with the degree of simplicity and directness that was always characteristic of this composer. Though each sonata is finely performed, the G major, with its expansive eloquence, suits Dumay and Pires especially well. Some collectors will wish that they had brought a little more momentum to the A major Sonata, but there is an adequate *Sturm und Drang* content in the D minor which is the most dramatic of the three works, and as with Suk and Katchen, both artists are of distinction and at no time does the piano merely accompany. The recording is a good one, although ideally the piano sound could have a touch more immediacy.

Additional recommendations ...
Sonatas. **Itzhak Perlman** (vn); **Vladimir Ashkenazy** (pf). EMI CDC7 47403-2 — ..·˙ lh l0m DDD 2/87 ⁹ₚ
Sonatas. **Krysia Osostowicz** (vn); **Susan Tomes** (pf). Hyperion CDA66465 — ..·˙ lh 8m DDD ll/91
Sonatas. Scherzo in C minor. **Pierre Amoyal** (vn); **Pascal Rogé** (pf). Decca 430 555-2DH — ..·˙ lh l5m DDD ll/91
Sonatas — Nos. 1, 2[a] and 3[b]. **Gioconda De Vito** (vn); [a]**Edwin Fischer,** [b]**Tito Aprea** (pfs). Testament mono SBT1024 — ..·˙ lh llm ADD 12/93 ⁹ₚ ▲
No. 1[a]. Violin Concerto in D major, Op. 77[b]. [a]**Isaac Stern, Pincas Zukerman** (vns); [b]**Paris Orchestra/Daniel Barenboim** ([a]pf). DG Classikon 439 405-2GCL — ..· lh l0m ADD 1/94

New review
Brahms. PIANO WORKS. **Gerhard Oppitz.** Eurodisc RD69245 (five-CD set; also available separately as detailed below).
RD69246 — Piano Sonata No. 1 in C major, Op. 1. Four Piano Pieces, Op. 119. Variations and Fugue on a Theme by Handel, Op. 24. *RD69247* — Four Ballades, Op. 10. Variations on an Original Theme, Op. 21 No. 1. Variations on a Hungarian Song, Op. 21 No. 2. Six Piano Pieces, Op. 118. *RD69248* — Three Intermezzos, Op. 117. Piano Sonata No. 2 in F sharp minor, Op. 2. Eight Piano Pieces, Op. 76. *RD69249* — Two Rhapsodies, Op. 79. Scherzo in E flat minor, Op. 4. Seven Fantasias, Op. 116. Variations on a Theme by Paganini, Op. 35. *RD69250* — Variations on a Theme by Robert Schumann, Op. 9. 16 Waltzes, Op. 39. Piano Sonata No. 3 in F minor, Op. 5.

..·˙ ⑤ lh l4m lh l3m lh l3m lh l6m lh l6m DDD 10/90

Aaron Copland once called Fauré "the French Brahms", and we can find the same reticent warmth, harmonic subtlety and pianistic refinement, together with the ability to say much in little, in a Brahms intermezzo as we do in one of his nocturnes. But the comparison falls away as soon as we turn to Brahms's earlier piano music, and it's worth remembering that most of his solo pieces are either early or late — there's nothing save for the Eight Pieces, Op. 76 and the Two Rhapsodies, Op. 79, in the three decades and 80 opus numbers between the *Paganini* Variations in 1863 and the Fantasias, Op. 116, in 1892. There's also a marked contrast between the fire of the young Brahms writing big virtuoso pieces and the mellower emotions that a man nearing the end of his life expressed in fewer (but no less telling) notes. In the three sonatas, all written before the composer reached 21, Gerald Oppitz convinces us at once in the big gestures over the whole keyboard that characterize the opening of each, yet he is a gentle giant, too, in the tender moments that invariably follow by the next page. We are in safe interpretative hands, for Oppitz is at one with the ebb-and-flow of tempo and tone, while pedalling (not always easy in this music) is convincing too. He also manages the sometimes naïve figuration well, as in the trio in the *Scherzo* of the First Sonata. His technical command is excellent. The other two sonatas have the same strength and high seriousness. He takes a predictably stern view of the E flat minor Scherzo and the Ballades, Op. 10, although perhaps the *Handel* Variations and the other variation sets could have done with a little more fantasy and playfulness. However, the taxing *Paganini* Variations have sureness and strength. Oppitz is also pretty well at home in the late music. The sorrowful B minor and E flat minor Intermezzos are compelling, though the former is taken slower than usual, as are the First and Third Intermezzos of Op. 117. This serious artist sometimes fails to lighten his heart enough, e.g. in the B minor Capriccio, Op. 76 and the C major Intermezzo, Op. 119, with its markings of *grazioso, giocoso* and *leggiero*. Nevertheless, the pianist is so good at conveying the Brahmsian dour or questioning seriousness that with that one reservation, no collector getting these CDs will be disappointed. Not quite everything is here — there are studies and other smaller items that have not yet entered the concert repertory.

Additional recommendation ...
Julius Katchen. Decca 430 053-2DM6 — ⌁ ⑥ 6h 28m ADD 2/91

Brahms. PIANO WORKS. **Murray Perahia.** Sony Classical SK47181.
Piano Sonata No. 3. Capriccio in B minor, Op. 76 No. 2. Intermezzo in E flat minor, Op. 118 No. 6. Two Rhapsodies, Op. 79 — No. 1 in B minor. Four Piano Pieces, Op. 119 — No. 4 in E flat major.

— ⌁ 1h DDD 10/91 ... ⑨ P Ⓑ

Brahms composed his three piano sonatas early in life, completing the Third during his important friendship with Robert Schumann. It is a work of colossal scale and dimension, possessing a grandeur that seems to cry out for comparison with Beethoven's last compositions. Murray Perahia leads the field in his performance of this masterwork but Kocsis, Ashkenazy and the super-bargain Biret should also give great satisfaction to collectors who savour different approaches. Perahia's playing is riper and less youthfully impetuous and ardent, yet this too yields its rewards and makes him all the more capable of encompassing the many changes from virtuoso vigour to quiet lyricism in the first movement. He reminds us that Brahms was naturally introspective even when he was 20 and writing a virtuoso, leonine work such as this one — yet such is his pianistic intelligence and sensitivity that he does so without sacrificing vigour and forward movement, essential qualities in this big five-movement work. Needless to say, he is in his element in the songful twilight musings of the *Andante* and Intermezzo, but the big *Scherzo* and fleet finale (with a whirling, triumphant coda) are just as effective. The other four pieces are also satisfying, with tremendous vigour in the Rhapsody and all the brooding drama one could wish for in the tragic E flat minor Intermezzo. The recorded sound is faithful and enjoyable in all sound levels and textures — and that last word reminds me to praise his finely judged use of the sustaining pedal, so important in this composer.

Additional recommendations ...
Piano Sonata No. 3. **Zoltán Kocsis.** Hungaroton HCD12601 — ⌁ 40m DDD 1/85 Ⓑ
Piano Sonata No. 3. Variations and Fugue on a Theme by Handel, Op. 24. **Vladimir Ashkenazy** (pf). Decca 430 771-2DH — ⌁ 1h 4m DDD 7/92 Ⓑ

| *Piano Sonata No. 3. Four Ballades, Op. 10.* **Idil Biret** (pf). Naxos 8 550352 — ⌁ 1h 3m DDD 12/92 Ⓑ

Brahms. Four Ballades, Op. 10. Variations and Fugue on a Theme by Handel, Op. 24. Two Rhapsodies, Op. 79 — No. 1 in B minor; No. 2 in G minor. **Pascal Rogé** (pf). Decca 433 849-2DH. Recorded in 1991.

Ih 8m DDD 4/93

We may still think of Pascal Rogé as a young pianist, but this Paris-born artist passed his fortieth birthday four years ago and has in fact recorded Brahms's Handel Variations before, back in the 1970s. Clearly this work means much to him, and he brings the right clean and crisp baroque quality to the theme itself and to those of the succeeding variations which call for it, while opening out into a richer romanticism as and when Brahms demands. As regards tone and tempo, he avoids extremes as the *Variations* progress and his civilized playing style, which includes an admirably judged use of the sustaining pedal, is matched by a refined recording that in the bigger passages offers weight without harshness. In the two *Rhapsodies*, Rogé again gives us both strength and sensitivity, for, here as elsewhere, he understands that Brahms's northern dourness, central though it is to his music and its performance, was always tempered by gentleness and tenderness. The interpretative challenge for the pianist is perhaps greater in the Four *Ballades*, early works that are predominantly quiet and introspective although No. 1, based on a grim Scottish ballad, is a powerful tone-poem and No. 3 is a quirky, scherzo-like piece. Here, too, Rogé blends sternness with affection and these are likeable performances, refreshingly eschewing the heavy and ultimately self-conscious profundity that some German pianists bring to this repertory. Warmly recommended.

Additional recommendations ...

Ballades. **Schubert.** *Piano Sonata in A minor, D537.* **Arturo Benedetti Michelangeli** (pf). DG 400 043-2GH — 48m ADD 3/83 Ⓑ

Ballades. Variations and Fugue. Variations on a Theme by Schumann, Op. 9. **Jorge Federico Osorio** (pf). ASV CDDCA616 — Ih 8m DDD 11/88 ⁹ₛ Ⓑ

Ballades. **Weber.** *Piano Sonata No. 2 in A flat major, J199.* **Alfred Brendel** (pf). Philips 426 439-2PH — 53m DDD 6/91 Ⓑ

Variations and Fugue. **Reger.** *Variations and Fugue on a Theme by Telemann, Op. 134.* **Jorge Bolet** (pf). Decca Ovation 417 791-2DM — 59m ADD 2/90 ⁹ₚ Ⓑ

Variations and Fugue. Rhapsodies. Six Piano Pieces, Op. 118. **Emanuel Ax** (pf). Sony Classical SK48046 — Ih 8m DDD 10/92 Ⓑ

Brahms. Two Rhapsodies, Op. 79 — No. 1 in B minor; No. 2 in G minor. 16 Waltzes, Op. 39. Six Piano Pieces, Op. 118. **Stephen Kovacevich** (pf). Philips 420 750-2PH. From 6514 229 (4/83).

53m DDD 4/88

Brahms. 16 Waltzes, Op. 39. Eight Piano Pieces, Op. 76. Two Rhapsodies, Op. 79 — No. 1 in B minor; No. 2 in G minor. **Mikhail Rudy** (pf). EMI CDC7 54233-2. Recorded 1991-92.

59m DDD 5/93

The Op. 79 *Rhapsodies* have been described as the "most temperamental" of all Brahms's later keyboard works. It would certainly be hard to imagine more vehement performances than those given by Kovacevich, thanks to his robust tone, trenchant attack and urgent tempos — perhaps even a shade too fast for the *Molto passionato, ma non troppo allegro* of the Second. But the pleading second subject of No. 1 in B minor brings all the requisite lyrical contrast. The Waltzes, too, have their tenderer moments of *Ländler*-like sentiment and charm. However, they emerge faster and more excitable than usual, as if Kovacevich were trying to remind us of Brahms's old love of Hungary no less than his new love of Vienna. "It is wonderful how he combines passion and tenderness in the smallest of spaces" was Clara Schumann's comment on the miniatures and the phrase fits Kovacevich's warmly responsive account of the Op. 118 set just as well. The piano is faithfully and fearlessly reproduced in what sounds like a ripely reverberant venue. Mikhail Rudy's account of the Two *Rhapsodies* and the 16 Waltzes makes a pleasing alternative to Stephen Kovacevich's disc. For a start, the younger pianist has been exceptionally well recorded in the Salle Wagram in Paris, and he also plays a fine instrument that is in perfect condition. Of course that is not all: Rudy brings great character to the Eight

Pieces, Op 76, with each one fully (but not exaggeratedly) characterized, not least in matters of texture, dynamics and pedalling. Similarly, this pianist effortlessly encompasses the blend of passion and gentler poetry that we find in the *Rhapsodies*. As for the Waltzes, this golden chain of Viennese melody and lilting charm comes across with affection and panache, as well as idiomatic rubato, not least in the famous A flat major Waltz which is the penultimate number. Repeats, too, are never mechanical, but often reveal something subtly new about the music which we could not have with a single playing. Finally, the frequent difficulty of Brahms's idiosyncratic piano writing, both here and in the other pieces, presents no more than a pleasing challenge to this intelligent and sensitive artist and all proceeds fluently, though never in a routine way.

Additional recommendations ...
Two Rhapsodies. Three Intermezzos, Op. 117. Six Piano Pieces. Four Piano Pieces, Op. 119. **Radu Lupu**. Decca 417 599-2DH —.•' lh llm ADD 8/87 ℗ Ⓑ
Two Rhapsodies. Three Intermezzos. Theme and Variations in D minor. Variations on a Theme by Paganini, Op. 35. **François-René Duchable**. Erato 2292-45477-2 — .•' lh 3m DDD 3/91 Ⓑ

Brahms. CHORAL WORKS. [a]**Jard van Nes** (mez); **San Francisco Symphony Chorus and Orchestra/Herbert Blomstedt.** Decca 430 281-2DH. Texts and translations included. Gesang der Parzen, Op. 89. Nänie, Op. 82. Schicksalslied, Op. 54. Begräbnisgesang, Op. 13. Alto Rhapsody, Op. 53[a].

.•' lh 3m DDD 8/90 ℗

Brahms is such a familiar figure that it is salutary to be reminded that one area of his work, choral music, remains mostly unknown to collectors save for the *German Requiem* and *Alto Rhapsody*. This is a pity, for this composer who was also a distinguished choral conductor drew some of his finest inspiration from this medium. This issue includes the *Rhapsody*, warmly and movingly sung by Jard van Nes, but its importance lies in the fact that it also does much to give us a better knowledge of other big pieces too. Don't be put off by the sombre subject matter — including *Begräbnisgesang*, "A Song of the Fates" (a tremendous piece), another work about fate itself and not one but two funeral hymns! — but listen instead to thrilling choral singing and orchestral playing under the direction of a conductor who believes passionately in the music. "Plenty of strength, light and drama" is what *Gramophone*'s critic found in this programme when it first came out, and to that one would add that the San Francisco Symphony Chorus sing the German texts with complete conviction. If this music makes us regret that Brahms wrote no opera, we may at least feel that here is something not far short of it even though it was not intended for the stage; to see this, listen only to the *Schicksalslied* which is the first work performed. A good recording complements the quality of performance, though ideally the choral textures could be clearer.

Additional recommendations ...
Marienlieder, Op. 22. Schicksalslied. Alto Rhapsody[a]. Nänie. Gesang der Parzen. [a]**Nathalie Stutzmann** (contr); **Bavarian Radio Chorus and Symphony Orchestra/Sir Colin Davis.** RCA Victor Red Seal 09026 61201-2 — .•' lh 7m DDD 5/93
Triumphlied, Op. 55. Schicksalslied. Nänie. Alto Rhapsody[a]. [a]**Brigitte Fassbaender** (mez); **Prague Philharmonic Choir; Czech Philharmonic Orchestra/Giuseppe Sinopoli.** DG Galleria 435 066-2GGA — .•' lh l0m DDD ll/91

New review
Brahms. Liebeslieder, Op. 52. Neue Liebeslieder, Op. 65. Three Quartets, Op. 64. **Edith Mathis** (sop); **Brigitte Fassbaender** (mez); **Peter Schreier** (ten); **Dietrich Fischer-Dieskau** (bar); **Karl Engel, Wolfgang Sawallisch** (pf, four hands). DG 423 133-2GH. Texts and translations included. From 2740 280 (6/83).

.•' 55m DDD 12/88

These delightful works will be eagerly snapped up by lovers of these seemingly simple but, in fact, quite complex settings for one, two or four voices. The performances are thoroughly idiomatic, both as regards the singers and pianists, with full value given to the words and their meaning. It is not merely a question of fine singing, which with this quartet one may more or less take for granted: the subtlety and charm of the interpretations makes what can all too often be a dreary sequence of three-four numbers into a poetic response to the nature of the waltz. There is an intelligent give-and-take between the soloists, so that voices move in and out of the limelight, as the skilful recording allows, and an extra dimension of the music is disclosed here that is too often obscured. The immediate sound is here a great advantage. This is a very worthwhile and welcome reissue of a most attractive individual record.

New review

Brahms. LIEDER. **Dame Margaret Price** (sop); **Graham Johnson** (pf). RCA Victor Red Seal 09026 60901-2. Notes, texts and translations included. Recorded in 1992.
Op. 96 — No. 1, Der Tod, das ist die kühle Nacht; No. 3, Es schauen die Blumen; No. 4, Meerfahrt. Op. 85 — No. 1, Sommerabend; No. 2, Mondenschein. Es liebt sich so lieblich im Lenze!, Op. 71 No. 1. Op. 14 — No. 1, Vor dem Fenster; No. 2, Vom vernundeten Knaben; No. 7, Ständchen; No. 8, Sehnsucht. Mädchenfluch, Op. 69 No. 9. Klage, Op. 105 No. 3. Op. 148 — No. 4, Gold überwiegt die Liebe; No. 6, Vergangen ist mir Glück und Heil. Op. 84 — No. 4, Vergebliches Ständchen; No. 5, Spannung. Deutsche Volkslieder, WoO33 — No. 6, Da unten in Tale; No. 15, Schwesterlein, Schwesterlein; No. 37, Du mein einzig Licht. Op. 97 — Dort in den Weiden, No. 4. Zigeunerlieder, Op. 103 — No. 1, He, Zigeuner, greife; No. 2, Hochgetürmte Rimaflut; No. 3, Wisst ihr, wann mein Kindchen; No. 4, Leiber Gott, du weisst; No. 5, Brauner Bursche führt zum Tanze; No. 6, Röslein dreie in der Reihe; No. 7, Kommt dir manchmal; No. 11, Rote Abendwoken ziehn.

lh lm   DDD   5/94

With Graham Johnson to devise intelligent, logical programmes, Dame Margaret Price and himself to interpret them, a remarkable unanimity of thought and confidence of manner is being achieved, the delights there for the taking. Here we begin with six contrasted settings of Heine, all reasonably familiar songs, each given with a nice balance between breadth of phrasing and warmth of feeling. The account of *Mondenschein* fully realizes its autumnal melancholy in phrases that seem to linger endlessly in the air. The judicious choice of *Volkslieder* settings once more indicates Brahms's deep understanding of the originals and just how to clothe them in appropriate harmonies, as in the antique Dorian mode of *Sehnsucht* and *Vergangen ist mir Glück und Heil*, both sung and played here with an exquisite sense of longing. Finally, the partnership lavish a winningly uninhibited *élan* on the *Zigeunerlieder*. If we are occasionally aware of a momentary strain on Price's present resources, we are consoled by the passionate spontaneity of the results. The recording is ideally balanced, intimate yet open.

Key to symbols

Price	Quantity/ availability	Timing	Recording mode	Review date
	② ②	lh 23m	DDD	6/88

Brahms. LIEDER. **Thomas Allen** (bar); **Geoffrey Parsons** (pf). Virgin Classics VC7 59593-2. Texts and translations included.
Wir wandelten, Op. 96 No. 2. Der Gang zum Liebchen, Op. 48 No. 1. Komm bald, Op. 97 No. 5. Salamander, Op. 107 No. 2. Nachtigall, Op. 97 No. 1. Serenade, Op. 70 No. 3. Geheimnis, Op. 71 No. 3. Von waldbekränzter Höhe, Op. 57 No. 1. Dein blaues Auge hält so still, Op. 59 No. 8. Wie bist du, meine Königin, Op. 32 No. 9. Junge Lieder I, Op. 63 No. 5. Die Kränze, Op. 46 No. 1. Sah dem edlen Bildnis, Op. 46 No. 2. An die Nachtigall, Op. 46 No. 4. Die Schale der Vergessenheit, Op. 46 No. 3. In Waldeseinsamkeit, Op. 85 No. 6. Wiegenlied, Op. 49 No. 4. Sonntag, Op. 47 No. 3. Heimweh II, Op. 63 No. 8. Minnelied, Op. 71 No. 5. Feldeinsamkeit, Op. 86 No. 2. Ständchen, Op. 106 No. 1. Von ewiger Liebe, Op. 43 No. 1. Die Mainacht, Op. 43 No. 2. Botschaft, Op. 47 No. 1.

lh 2m   DDD   9/90

Brahms's songs are, on the whole, intimate, one-to-one statements. They rarely approach the nature of public announcements and thus only occasionally explore extreme loudness:

they are ideally suited to home listening. The darkening timbre of Thomas Allen's voice makes it increasingly suited to Brahms, and his characteristic, though far from common, qualities of heroic breath control and vital, lissom phrasing compound his affinity with this music. The songs make best use of the distinctive parts of his range and this, wedded to Allen's innate musicianship, sets a solid foundation for an engrossing recital. Geoffrey Parsons picks up these features and mirrors them in the searching piano parts, bringing light and shade, clarity and mist to support the voice. The recital as a whole is well thought out: the songs have clear, unifying links in terms of mood and gesture, but there is enough variety here to retain interest throughout. A pleasantly close recording of the voice emphasizes subtleties of tonal shading, and the more subdued setting of the piano allows it to make its effect without overpowering the singer. This is a disc to delight both novice and seasoned listener alike.

New review

Brahms. LIEDER. **Robert Holl** (bass-bar); **András Schiff** (pf). Decca 433 182-2DH. Texts and translations included.
Die Mainacht, Op. 43 No. 2. An die Nachtigall, Op. 46 No. 4. Botschaft, Op. 47 No. 1. Wiegenlied, Op. 49 No. 4. O wüsst, ich doch den Weg zurück, Op. 63 No. 8. Es liebt sich so lieblich im Lenze!, Op. 71 No. 1. O kühler Wald, Op. 72 No. 3. Verzagen, Op. 72 No. 4. Sommerabend, Op. 85 No. 1. Mondenschein, Op. 85 No. 2. Feldeinsamkeit, Op. 86 No. 2. Der Tod, das ist die kühle Nacht, Op. 96 No. 1. Es schauen die Blumen, Op. 96 No. 3. Meerfahrt, Op. 96 No. 4. Auf dem Kirchhofe, Op. 105 No. 4. Ständchen, Op. 106 No. 1. Meine Lieder, Op. 106 No. 4. Vier ernste Gesänge, Op. 121.

Ih IIm   DDD   6/93

Holl brings to Brahms's Lieder a full understanding of the import of the poems. He enunciates the text with the utmost care in accenting words and then places them on a stream of warm bass-baritone tone. He brings the full weight of his voice to bear on grand pieces such as *Auf dem Kirchhofe*, plumbs the depths of feeling of *Mondenschein* and *Meerfahrt*, yet can also fine down his voluminous voice to the delicate half-voice called for by *Feldeinsamkeit* and *Wiegenlied*, and find the lighter touch called for by *Ständchen* and *Botschaft*. Finally he broaches the challenge of the *Vier ernste Gesänge* with due recognition of their grave and often depressing message, most notably in "Ich wandte mich", arguably the greatest song Brahms ever wrote. Holl is supported by Schiff's positive playing and the recording is up to Decca's high standards.

Brahms. LIEDER. **Anne Sofie von Otter** (mez); **Bengt Forsberg** (pf). DG 429 727-2GH. Texts and translations included.
Zigeunerlieder, Op. 103 — No. 1-7 and 11. Dort in den Weiden, Op. 97 No. 4. Vergebliches Ständchen, Op. 84 No. 4. Die Mainacht, Op. 43 No. 2. Ach, wende diesen Blick, Op. 57 No. 4. O kühler Wald, Op. 72 No. 3. Von ewiger Liebe, Op. 43 No. 1. Junge Lieder I, Op. 63 No. 5. Wie rafft' ich mich auf in der Nacht, Op. 32 No. 1. Unbewegte laue Luft, Op. 57 No. 8. Heimweh II, Op. 63 No. 8. Mädchenlied, Op. 107 No. 5. Ständchen, Op. 106 No. 1. Sonntag, Op. 47 No. 3. Wiegenlied, Op. 49 No. 4. Zwei Gesänge, Op. 91 (with Nils-Erik Sparf, va).

Ih Im   DDD   4/91   P

Many of the Lieder here are but meagrely represented in current catalogues, so that this recital is all the more welcome, particularly in view of the perceptive musicality of both singer and pianist. They show a fine free (but unanimous!) flexibility in the *Zigeunerlieder*, with a dashing "Brauner Bursche" and "Röslein dreie" and a passionate "Rote Abendwolken"; but there is also lightness, happy in "Wisst ihr, wann mein Kindchen", troubled in "Lieber Gott, du weisst"; and Otter's coolly tender tone in "Kommt dir manchmal in den Sinn" touches the heart. Also deeply moving are the profound yearning and the loving but anxious lullaby in the two songs with viola obbligato (most sensitively played). Elsewhere, connoisseurs of vocal technique will admire Otter's command of colour and legato line in the gravity of *O kühler Wald*, the stillness of *Die Mainacht* and the intensity of *Von ewiger Liebe*, and her lovely *mezza voce* in the *Wiegenlied* and the partly repressed fervour of *Unbewegte laue Luft*; but to any listener her remarkable control, her responsiveness to words and, not least, the sheer beauty of her voice make this a most rewarding disc, aided as she is by Forsberg's characterful playing.

Brahms. Ein deutsches Requiem, Op. 45. **Dame Elisabeth Schwarzkopf** (sop); **Dietrich Fischer-Dieskau** (bar); **Philharmonia Chorus and Orchestra/Otto Klemperer.** EMI CDC7 47238-2. Notes, text and translation included. From Columbia SAX2430/31 (2/62).

Ih 9m ADD 6/87

Brahms. Ein deutsches Requiem, Op. 45. **Charlotte Margiono** (sop); **Rodney Gilfry** (bar); **Monteverdi Choir; Orchestre Révolutionnaire et Romantique/John Eliot Gardiner.** Philips 432 140-2PH. Text and translation included.

Ih 6m DDD 4/91

Brahms's *German Requiem*, a work of great concentration and spiritual intensity, is, rather surprisingly, the creation of a man barely 30 years old. He turned for his text not to the liturgical Mass but to the German translations of the Old Testament. It is decidedly *not* a Requiem of 'fire and brimstone' overshadowed by the Day of Wrath; instead it is a work for those who mourn, those who remain in sorrow ("As one whom his mother comforteth, so I will comfort you", sings the soprano in a soaring hymn of grief-assuaging beauty). The texture is sinuous and Brahms employs the orchestra with great delicacy as well as enormous muscular energy. Klemperer's reading of this mighty work has long been famous: rugged, at times surprisingly fleet and with a juggernaut power. The superb Philharmonia are joined by their excellent Chorus and two magnificent soloists — Elisabeth Schwarzkopf offering comfort in an endless stream of pure tone and Fischer-Dieskau, still unequalled, singing with total absorption. A great performance, beautifully enhanced on CD.

The pungency of a small chorus and the incisive edge provided by the orchestra of period instruments, the Orchestre Révolutionnaire et Romantique, makes for a fresh reappraisal of a work that can all too often sound turgid and dull. Gardiner has written of the work's radiance, optimism and full-bloodedness and he instils these characteristics into his performance. The reduced forces employed mean that great subtlety can be drawn out of the score — words are meticulously cared for, dynamic nuances observed and, above all, strong and secure attack ensure a genuine intensity of expression. The soloists are good too, with the young American baritone Rodney Gilfry quite outstanding, offering firm, warm and beautifully rounded tone throughout. Charlotte Margiono, set a little far back in the aural perspective, is a sweet and suitably conciliatory soprano soloist. For anyone who has in the past found Brahms's *Ein deutsches Requiem* difficult to come to terms with then this pioneering period instrument set is probably the one to win the most converts.

Additional recommendations ...
Ein deutsches Requiem. **Felicity Lott** (sop); **David Wilson-Johnson** (bar); **London Symphony Chorus and Orchestra/Richard Hickox.** Chandos CHAN8942 — Ih 14m DDD 1/92

Ein deutsches Requiem[a]. *Begräbnisgesang, Op. 13.* [a]**Lynne Dawson** (sop); [a]**Olaf Bär** (bar); **Schütz Choir of London; London Classical Players/Roger Norrington.** EMI Reflexe CDC7 54658-2 — Ih 8m DDD 4/93

Ein deutsches Requiem. **Angela Maria Blasi** (sop); **Bryn Terfel** (bass-bar); **Bavarian Radio Chorus and Symphony Orchestra/Sir Colin Davis.** RCA Victor Red Seal 09026 60868 — Ih 13m DDD 5/93

Walter Braunfels
German 1882-1954

Braunfels. VERKUNDIGUNG. **Siegmund Nimsgern** (bass-bar) Andreas Gradherz; **Claudia Rüggeberg** (sngr) The mother; **Andrea Trauboth** (sop) Violaine; **Chieko Shirasaka-Teratani** (sop) Mara; **John Bröcheler** (bass) Jakobäus; **Christer Bladin** (ten) Peter von Ulm; **Christian Brüggemann** (sngr) Peter's assistant; **Akemi Kajiyama** (sngr) Angel; **Stefan Sevenich** (sngr) Labourer; **Barbara Dommer** (spkr) A woman; **Rolf-Dieter Krüll** (spkr) Mayor of Rothenstein; **Cologne Symphony Chorus and Orchestra/Dennis Russell**

Davies. EMI CDS5 55104-2. Notes and text included. Recorded at a performance in the Philharmonie, Cologne in 1992.

② 2h 12m DDD 7/94

In the period between the two world wars, Walter Braunfels was among the most widely performed of all living opera composers. He fell foul of the Nazis, and little was heard of him again until after their fall from power. *Verkündigung* ("Annunciation") was written between 1934 and 1937, presumably in full knowledge that it had no foreseeable prospect of performance, and it was not staged until 1948. It is not an opera, but a mystery play, the action proceeding in almost free-standing emblematic tableaux, with few narrative links between them, all the characters being more symbolic than three-dimensional. It tells the story of a woman, Violaine, who is moved by pity to kiss a leper. She contracts leprosy herself, heals the leper she had embraced, brings the child born to her evil sister Mara and her own former fiancé back from the dead, and dies forgiving the ex-fiancé who could never quite bring himself to believe that her kiss to the leper was no more than an act of saintly compassion. What might be difficult for some listeners (though it must be stressed that Braunfels's language is amply melodious and harmonically straightforward), is the fact that the drama proceeds on an almost exclusively spiritual level. Moments of insight and mystical vision are dramatized, more everyday events, such as there are, are not. It places something of a premium on the listener's response to the story. A note in the booklet explains that all the characters represent earthly reactions to heavenly forces. An unsympathetic listener may find Mara's 'wickedness' bafflingly unmotivated, her father's action selfish and may side with the downtrodden and unconsidered mother, may even find the incessant sweetness and light of Violaine cloying. When her jealous fiancé curses her for her apparent infidelity she exclaims, radiantly, "I am not accursed, I am the gentle, the gentle Violaine"; when he discovers she has given her engagement ring to the leper as well, to help pay for the cathedral he is building, her response is "I am more than a ring; I am a great treasure". The music is often radiant, often touching in the sincerity of its belief in tonality and the workings of the Holy Ghost; one can readily imagine it becoming a sort of cult piece among some listeners, while others are bound to find it, like some really virtuous and spiritual people, a touch boring. A third group, those who simply cannot accept a eulogy of redemptive suffering and a concluding cry of praise to death, may even find it repulsive. What no one can deny is a curious and individual voice, individual even in its Catholic reliance on the sanctified authority of tradition. Nor could anyone claim that this fine performance sells the work short in any way: the singing is admirable throughout, Andrea Trauboth in especially beautiful voice, and Davies conducts with real conviction. The live recording has only a few minor fluffs to mar it.

Havergal Brian
British 1876-1972

Brian. Symphony No. 1, "Gothic". **Eva Jenisová** (sop); **Dagmar Pecková** (contr); **Vladimir Dolezal** (ten); **Peter Mikuláš** (bass); **Slovak Philharmonic Choir; Slovak National Theatre Opera Chorus; Slovak Folk Ensemble Chorus; Lucnica Chorus; Bratislava Chamber Choir; Bratislava Children's Choir; Youth Echo Choir; Czechoslovak Radio Symphony Orchestra, Bratislava; Slovak Philharmonic Orchestra/Ondrej Lenárd.** Marco Polo 8 223280/1. Text and translation included. Recorded in 1989.

② 1h 4m DDD 7/90

Left unperformed for 30-odd years and unrecorded for a further 40, the legendary *Gothic* makes superhuman demands of its performers: a passage where four four-part choirs sing in four adjacent keys simultaneously; another in which the music is designed to 'rotate' before the listener's ears, through a semicircle of four choirs and four brass bands. This first-ever recorded performance is amazingly good: such prodigies of choral virtuosity can only have been achieved at the cost of months of preparation (the spacious recording is a remarkable achievement, too). It is a performance also of radiant enthusiasm: everyone involved seems gripped, intent on communicating a true vision. For the work is visionary: a vision of an age of faith, the age that produced the complex majesty of the gothic cathedrals. The vision is that of a modern man, seeing gothic through the expressive resources of the intervening centuries; seeing, too, that the age of faith was also an age gripped with fear of judgement, wracked by guilt. All that is present in, and justification for, the symphony's vast structure. Huge, multi-part choruses to represent sorrowing, panic-stricken, jubilant humanity not as a monolithic mass but as individuals in all their variety. An enormous orchestra is employed (sextuple woodwind, octuple brass) to support this choral weight and also to provide a range of sonorities as wide as the contrasts, from brilliant windows to deep shadow, from massive piers to delicate tracery, of Lichfield Cathedral, a visit to which as a young man so moved Brian that it became one of the formative events of his life. There are flaws in the vision: the first movement has something of hesitancy to it, the eloquence of the choral pages sometimes stammers. But the tremendous second movement, with its Berliozian grandeur of utterance, is a genuine masterpiece, and the tripartite choral finale often reaches a comparably lofty nobility. And this was Havergal Brian's *first* symphony!

Further listening ...

8 223447: Symphonies — No. 4, "The Song of Victory"[a]; No. 12[b]. *8 223481*[c]: Symphonies — No. 17; No. 32 in A flat major. In Memoriam. Festal dance. [a]**Jana Valásková** (sop); [a]**Slovak Philharmonic Chorus; **[a]**Brno Philharmonic Chorus; **[a]**Cantus Choir; **[a]**Slovak Opera Chorus; **[a]**Youth Echo Choir; **[ab]**Bratislava Radio Symphony Orchestra/**[c]**Ireland National Symphony Orchestra/Adrian Leaper.** Marco Polo 8 223447/8 223481 (2/93).

Symphonies Nos. 7 and 31. Comedy Overture—The Tinker's Wedding. **Royal Liverpool Philharmonic Orchestra/Sir Charles Mackerras.** EMI British Composers CDM7 64717-2 (9/93).

Frank Bridge

British 1879-1941

Bridge. Oration — Concerto elegiaco, H180.
Britten. Cello Symphony, Op. 68. **Steven Isserlis** (vc); **City of London Sinfonia/Richard Hickox.** EMI CDM7 63909-2. From CDC7 49716-2 (5/88).

Ih 8m   DDD   2/92

Steven Isserlis's decision to couple these two English masterpieces on one disc was a particularly intelligent one: not only because Frank Bridge was one of Britten's most influential teachers and mentors, but also because both works reflect, in their different ways, the two composers' strong pacifist beliefs and their deep concern at man's inhumanity to man. *Oration* (subtitled *Concerto elegiaco*) dates from 1930 and is both an explicit outcry against the futility of war and a vast lament for the many friends and colleagues that Bridge had lost as a result of the Great War. Indeed, throughout its 30-minute span the work is constantly haunted by images of war — sometimes in mocking parody (as in the central march section, or the martial fanfares that erupt violently into orchestral climaxes), and sometimes in sombre, grief-stricken episodes of moving intensity. Isserlis gives us an exceptionally fine performance that fully captures the intensity and vision of this richly rewarding and shamefully neglected masterpiece. Britten's own masterpiece in the idiom — the Cello Symphony — was composed some 30 years later, but the influence of *Oration* can be clearly discerned both in its emotional content (if perhaps less overtly displayed than in the former) and in the similar way that it eschews the conventions of a formal concerto. Again both soloist and conductor deserve the highest praise for a performance that matches the profundity and vision of the music. Well recorded.

Bridge. Cello Sonata in D minor, H125. Four Short Pieces, H104 — Meditation; Spring song.
Debussy. Cello Sonata.
E. Dohnányi. Cello Sonata in B flat minor, Op. 8. **Bernard Gregor-Smith** (vc); **Yolande Wrigley** (pf). ASV CDDCA796.

Ih 8m   DDD   9/92

The centrepiece of this superb recital disc from Bernard Gregor-Smith (long-standing cellist of the Lindsay Quartet) and the pianist Yolande Wrigley is the sumptuously expansive Sonata in B flat minor by Ernö Dohnányi. This vital and often heroic work dates from 1899, and despite its obvious lyric and virtuoso appeal, it has yet to attain any real foothold in the regular repertoire.

It is lavishly conceived, owing much to the Lisztian pattern of juxtaposing virtuoso material with passages of affecting lyricism. Gregor-Smith's performance could scarcely be more persuasive or rewarding; his dextrous, fine-toned playing should do much to ensure that this splendid Sonata gains wider acceptance. This excellent husband and wife team are also heard to advantage in the Debussy Cello Sonata, never easy to bring off with its *commedia dell'arte* transparency and specialized effects. Gregor-Smith plays with refinement and tremendous *élan* in the finale particularly, and this is certainly a reading of great distinction. He is an ardent and confident exponent of the Bridge items too, and there have been few finer recorded versions of the Cello Sonata in D minor: a personal testament of grief and outrage following the atrocities of the First World War. Its broad paragraphs and obviously questioning language dictates, to a large extent, the most natural performing approach here. This is a most moving and dignified reading of another sadly undervalued composition. Gregor-Smith and Wrigley are splendid throughout this disc; their skills are eloquently supported by interpretations of unusual insight and perception, and they have been faithfully served by clear yet never unduly brilliant recorded sound.

Further listening ...

Elegy, H47. Scherzetto, H19. *Coupled with* **Ireland.** Cello Sonata in G minor; **Stanford.** Cello Sonata No. 2 in D minor, Op. 39. **Julian Lloyd-Webber** (vc); **John McCabe** (pf). ASV CDDCA807 (2/93).

Phantasm. *Coupled with* **Ireland.** Piano Concerto; **Walton.** Sinfonia concertante (original version). **Kathryn Stott** (pf); **Royal Philharmonic Orchestra/Vernon Handley.** Conifer CDCF175 (1/90).

A Sea Idyll, H54*a*. Capriccios — No. 1 in A minor, H52; No. 2 in F sharp minor, H54*b*. Three poems — Ecstasy, H112*b*. The Hour Glass, H148. Piano Sonata, H160. Vignettes de Marseille, H166. **Kathryn Stott** (pf). Conifer CDCF186 (9/91).

Benjamin Britten (Lord Britten of Aldeburgh)   *British 1913-1976*

Britten. Piano Concerto, Op. 13[a]. Violin Concerto, Op. 15[b]. [b]**Mark Lubotsky** (vn); [a]**Sviatoslav Richter** (pf); **English Chamber Orchestra/Benjamin Britten.** Decca London 417 308-2LM. From SXL6512 (8/71).

| ♪ Ih 7m ADD 10/89 | ♀♪ |

Just after Britten's performances were released on LP in 1971, the composer admitted with some pride that Sviatoslav Richter had learned his Piano Concerto "entirely off his own bat", and had revealed a Russianness that was in the score. Britten was attracted to Shostakovich during the late 1930s, when it was written, and the bravado, brittleness and flashy virtuosity of the writing, in the march-like finale most of all, at first caused many people (including Lennox Berkeley, to whom it is dedicated) to be wary of it, even to think it somehow outside the composer's style. Now we know his music better, it is easier to accept, particularly in this sparkling yet sensitive performance. The Violin Concerto dates from the following year, 1939, when Britten was in Canada, and it too has its self-conscious virtuosity, but it is its rich nostalgic lyricism which strikes to the heart and the quiet elegiac ending is unforgettable. Compared to Richter in the other work, Mark Lubotsky is not always the master of its hair-raising difficulties, notably in the scherzo, which has passages of double artificial harmonics that even Heifetz wanted simplified before he would play it (Britten refused), but this is still a lovely account. Fine recordings, made in The Maltings at Snape.

Additional recommendations ...
Piano Concerto[a]. Violin Concerto[b]. [a]**Joanna MacGregor** (pf); [b]**Lorrainse McAslan** (vn); **English Chamber Orchestra/Steuart Bedford.** Collins Classics 1301-2 — ♪ Ih 6m DDD 9/92 ♀♪

Violin Concerto[a]. Canadian Carnival, Op. 19. **Britten/Berkeley.** Mont Juic, Op. 12. [a]**Lorraine McAslan** (vn); **English Chamber Orchestra/Steuart Bedford.** Collins Classics 1123-2 —

♪ 58m DDD 12/90 ♀♪ ♀♪

Piano Concerto. **Copland.** *Piano Concerto.* **Gillian Lin** (pf); **Melbourne Symphony Orchestra/John Hopkins.** Chandos Collect CHAN6580 — .•' 5lm ADD 3/93

New review
Britten. Sinfonia da Requiem, Op. 20. Four Sea Interludes, Op. 33*a*. Passacaglia, Op. 33*b*. The Young Person's Guide to the Orchestra, Op. 34.
Purcell (arr. Britten). Chaconne in G minor, Z730. **London Philharmonic Orchestra/ Leonard Slatkin.** RCA Victor Red Seal 09026 61226-2. Recorded in 1989.

.•' lh 8m ADD 3/94   𝄞P 𝄞S Ⓑ

New review
Britten. Four Sea Interludes, Op. 33*a*. Johnson over Jordan. The Young Person's Guide to the Orchestra, Op. 34. Suite on English Folk Tunes (A time there was ...), Op. 90. **Bournemouth Symphony Orchestra/Richard Hickox.** Chandos CHAN9221. Recorded in 1993.

.•' lh 7m DDD 3/94   𝄞P Ⓑ

Both Slatkin and Hickox turn in alert, fresh-faced readings of the *Young Person's Guide*. When it comes to the *Grimes* Interludes, they could hardly view the music more differently. The American concentrates on meticulous refinement, with radiantly airy textures throughout: the results are more coolly detached than we are used to hearing and often strikingly beautiful, but the comparative lack of physical impact in the "Storm" will not be to all tastes. As the very opening of "Dawn" reveals, Hickox adopts a more tenderly expressive manner than Slatkin and there's no gainsaying the greater elemental fury of Hickox's "Storm"; however, his two middle tableaux are perhaps rather less memorable. Overall, Slatkin's account remains the more eventful; and he offers a bonus in the shape of a lucid and refined account of the "Passacaglia" from the same opera. Brittenites will find much to savour in the remainder of both concerts. Hickox enterprisingly gives us Paul Hindmarsh's enjoyable suite compiled from the incidental music for J.B. Priestley's 1939 morality play, *Johnson over Jordan*. Even more welcome is the *Suite on English Folk Tunes*, Britten's final orchestral work, full of the most bracing invention and intensely poignant to boot. The vigour, snap and discipline of this Bournemouth performance are utterly commendable; equally, Hickox sees to it that the wistful concluding "Lord Melbourne" touches to the very marrow. From Slatkin there's a most eloquent rendering of the Purcell *Chaconne* — Britten's loving realization can rarely have sounded more beguiling. However, the major attraction here is the *Sinfonia da Requiem*. This could hardly start more promisingly, with fearsome timpani blows and balefully growling tuba. Again, what immediately impresses is the focus and sheen of the orchestral playing, and in the concluding "Requiem aeternam" Slatkin transmits a soothing, consolatory glow that many will find deeply moving.

Britten. Cello Symphony, Op. 68[a]. Sinfonia da Requiem, Op. 20[b]. Cantata misericordium, Op. 69[c]. [a]**Mstislav Rostropovich** (vc); [c]**Sir Peter Pears** (ten); [c]**Dietrich Fischer-Dieskau** (bar); [c]**London Symphony Chorus and Orchestra,** [a]**English Chamber Orchestra,** [b]**New Philharmonia Orchestra/Benjamin Britten.** Decca London 425 100-2LM. Text and translation included. Item marked [a] from SXL6138 (12/64), [bc] SXL6175 (9/65).

.•' lh l5m ADD 9/89   𝄞P Ⓑ

This mid-price disc offers two of Britten's finest works, the *Cello Symphony* and the *Sinfonia da Requiem*. The latter was written in 1940 and is one of the composer's most powerful orchestral works, harnessing opposing forces in a frighteningly intense way. From the opening drumbeat the *Sinfonia* employs sonata form in a dramatically powerful way, though the tone is never fierce or savage; it has an implacable tread and momentum. The central movement, "Dies irae", however, has a real sense of fury, satirical in its biting comment — the flutter-tongued wind writing rattling its defiance. The closing "Requiem aeternam" is a movement of restrained beauty. On this recording from 1964 the New Philharmonia play superbly. The Cello Symphony, written in 1963 as part of a series for the great Russian cellist Mstislav Rostropovich, was the first major sonata-form work written since the *Sinfonia*. The idea of a struggle between soloist and orchestra, implicit in the traditional concerto, has no part here; it is a conversation between the two. Rostropovich plays with a depth of feeling that has never quite been equalled in other recordings and the playing of the ECO has great bite. The recording too is extraordinarily fine for its years. The *Cantata misericordium*, one of Britten's lesser known works, was written in 1962 as a commission from the Red Cross. It takes the story of the Good Samaritan and is scored for tenor and baritone soloists, chorus, string quartet and orchestra. It is a universal plea for charity and here receives a powerful reading. This is a must for any collector of Britten's music.

Additional recommendations ...
Sinfonia da Requiem. The Young Person's Guide to the Orchestra, Op. 34. PETER GRIMES — Four Sea Interludes; Passacaglia. **Royal Liverpool Philharmonic Orchestra/Libor Pešek.** Virgin Classics VC7 59550-2 — .•' lh 3m DDD 4/90 ᴼₚ ᴼₛ Ⓑ
Cello Symphony. **Bridge.** *Oration — Concerto elegiaco, H180.* **Steven Isserlis** (vc); **City of London Sinfonia/Richard Hickox.** EMI CDM7 63909-2 — .•' lh 8m DDD 2/92 ᴼₚ Ⓑ

Britten. The Young Person's Guide to the Orchestra, Op. 34ᵃ. Simple Symphony, Op. 4ᵇ. Variations on a Theme of Frank Bridge, Op. 10ᶜ. ᵃ**London Symphony Orchestra;** ᵇᶜ**English Chamber Orchestra/Benjamin Britten.** Decca 417 509-2DH. Item marked ᵃ from SXL6110 (9/64), ᵇ SXL6405 (6/69), ᶜ SXL6316 (11/67).

.•' **lh lm ADD 1/87** ᴼₚ Ⓑ

Britten's *Young Person's Guide to the Orchestra,* adapted from a theme by Purcell, came about through a film which would demonstrate to children the instruments of the orchestra. Britten's performance of his *Young Person's Guide* wisely omits the now rather dated text. He adopts quick tempos that must be demanding even for the LSO players, along with more spacious ones for the more introspective sections. This is beautiful playing, with all kinds of memorable touches. Britten's own childhood music is also here, in the shape of the delightfully fresh *Simple Symphony.* This fine CD then ends with more variations, the young composer's tribute to his teacher Frank Bridge. It is marvellous music, of astonishing wit and often intensely serious too, and the composer's own performance with the ECO is uniquely authoritative.

Additional recommendations ...
Simple Symphony. **Bizet.** *Symphony in C major.* **Prokofiev.** *Symphony No. 1 in D major, Op. 25, "Classical".* **Orpheus Chamber Orchestra.** DG 423 624-2GH — .•' lh 4m DDD 1/89 ᴼₚ Ⓑ
The Young Person's Guide to the Orchestra. Cello Symphony, Op. 68ᵃ. PETER GRIMES — Four Sea Interludes, Op. 33a. **Pärt.** *Cantus in memory of Benjamin Britten.* ᵃ**Truls Mørk** (vc); **Bergen Philharmonic Orchestra/Neeme Järvi.** BIS CD420 — .•' lh 15m DDD 6/89 Ⓑ
The Young Person's Guide to the Orchestra. Variations on a Theme of Frank Bridge. PETER GRIMES — Four Sea Interludes; Passacaglia. **BBC Symphony Orchestra/Andrew Davis.** Teldec British Line 9031-73126-2 — .•' lh 8m DDD 8/91 Ⓑ
Simple Symphony. Variations on a theme of Frank Bridge. Prelude and Fugue for String Orchestra, Op. 29. **Bournemouth Sinfonietta/Ronald Thomas.** Chandos Collect CHAN6592 — .•' 51m ADD 11/93 Ⓑ

Britten. String Quartet No. 3, Op. 94.
Tippett. String Quartet No. 4 (1978). **Lindsay Quartet** (Peter Cropper, Ronald Birks, vns; Robin Ireland, va; Bernard Gregor-Smith, vc). ASV CDDCA608.

.•' **53m DDD 5/88** ᴼₚ ᴼₛ

Neither Britten nor Tippett had written a string quartet for over 30 years when they returned to the medium in the 1970s. Both composed a masterpiece. In Britten's case there was the poignancy of its being the last major work he completed, yet there is no sign of declining powers in a work that pays homage to Shostakovich as well as to the special qualities of the Amadeus Quartet for whom it was written. The Lindsay Quartet's interpretation is very different; it is emotionally more intense and one can rarely be unaware of the shadow over the score, with its thematic references to Britten's last opera, *Death in Venice.* The last movement, a Passacaglia from which all passion has been drained to leave a serene air of resignation, is played very slowly. Tippett's Fourth Quartet has a lyrical and impassioned slow movement at its core and the predominant impression is one of energy and vigour. The music has such abundance that it seems to be bursting the confines of the medium and it is no surprise to learn that Tippett authorized an arrangement for string orchestra, not that the Lindsays sound at all strained by this vibrant score. The playing is masterful and the recording is admirably clear.

Additional recommendations ...
No. 2 in C major, Op. 36. No. 3. **Alberni Quartet.** CRD CRD3395 — 55m ADD 3/89
Nos. 2 and 3. **Britten Quartet.** Collins Classics 1025-2 — lh 4m DDD 12/90

New review
Britten. BLUES AND CABARET SONGS.
Porter. SONGS[a]. [a]**Jill Gomez** (sop); [a]**Martin Jones** (pf); [b]**Instrumental Ensemble** (David Roach, cl/sax; Graham Ashton, tpt; Beverley Davison, vn; Chris Lawrence, db; John Constable, pf; Gregory Knowles, perc). Unicorn-Kanchana DKPCD9138. Texts included.
Britten: Four Cabaret songs[a]. When you're feeling like expressing your affection[a]. On this Island — As it is, plenty[a]. Blues (arr. Runswick)[b] — The Spider and the Fly; Blues; The clock on the wall; Boogie-Woogie. *Porter:* Paris — Let's do it. Gay Divorce — Night and Day. Leave it to Me — My heart belongs to daddy. Miss Otis Regrets. Nymph Errant — The Physician.

52m DDD 9/93

Britten's cabaret songs were written for the singing actress Hedli Anderson; there were more than four, but these are the only ones to have seen publication so far. The texts by Auden are full of the spirit that William Coldstream described, writing about one of Anderson's performances, "teaching of carefree lucidity and the non-avoidance of banality". *When you're feeling like expressing your affection* which is published and performed here for the first time is one of the results of Auden and Britten's work for the GPO in the 1930s. Apart from the references to "any telephone kiosk" and "Press button A" it would still serve well as an encouragement to make use of the telephone. "As it is, plenty", the last song from *On this Island*, being also in the ironic popular-music style, rounds off the group nicely. Jill Gomez's performances are perfect in every nuance, her beautiful tone, clear diction and just hinted-at irony, never overdoing it, give the songs the exact weight they need. The Cole Porter encores and Daryl Runswick's arrangements of four *Blues* by Britten complete a quite delicious record.

New review
Britten. A Spring Symphony, Op. 44[a]. Cantata Academica, Op. 62[b]. Hymn to St Cecilia, Op. 27c. [ab]**Jennifer Vyvyan** (sop); [a]**Norma Procter,** [b]**Helen Watts** (contrs); [ab]**Sir Peter Pears** (ten); [b]**Owen Brannigan** (bass); [a]**Emanuel School Boys' Choir;** [a]**Chorus and Orchestra of the Royal Opera House, Covent Garden/Benjamin Britten; London Symphony** [bc]**Chorus and** [b]**Orchestra/George Malcolm.** Decca London 436 396-2LM. Texts and translation included. Item marked [a] from SXL2264 (5/61), [bc] L'Oiseau-Lyre SOL60037 (10/61). Recorded in 1960.

lh 14m ADD 9/93

Britten's performance of the *Spring Symphony* fairly leaps out of one's speakers, and the 1960 sound is as crisp and alive as the performance and the work itself. In the last two pieces George Malcolm's direction is as vivid as Britten's elsewhere. The *Cantata Academica* (1959) is one of Britten's happiest pieces, bubbling over with warmth, jollity and good fellowship. Indeed the Latin title is only one of mock-solemnity. Try "Tema seriale con fuga" to hear how this composer could make living music out of the most perniciously academic device of our troubled century. Further high points are Owen Brannigan's marvellously pompous bass aria and the boisterous "Canone ed ostinato". The performance of the *Hymn to St Cecilia* is skilful, idiomatic and touching.

Britten. Serenade for tenor, horn and strings, Op. 31[a]. Les illuminations, Op. 18[b]. Nocturne, Op. 60[c]. [abc]**Sir Peter Pears** (ten); [c]**Alexander Murray** (fl); [c]**Roger Lord** (cor ang); [c]**Gervase de Peyer** (cl); [c]**William Waterhouse** (bn); [ac]**Barry Tuckwell** (hn); [c]**Dennis Blyth** (timp); [c]**Osian Ellis** (hp); [ac]strings of the **London Symphony Orchestra,** [b]**English Chamber Orchestra/**[abc]**Benjamin Britten.** Decca 417 153-2DH. Texts included. Item marked [a] from SXL6110 (9/64), [b] SXL6316 (11/67), [c] SXL2189 (5/60). Recorded 1959-66.

lh 13m ADD 8/86 ▲

No instrument was more important to Britten than the human voice and, inspired by the musicianship and superb vocal craftsmanship of his closest friend, he produced an unbroken stream of vocal works of a quality akin to those of Purcell. Three of his most haunting vocal pieces are featured on this wonderful CD. The performances date from between 1959 and 1966 with Pears in penetratingly musical form, even if the voice itself was by now a little thin and occasionally unsteady. The ECO and LSO are superb in every way and of course Britten was his own ideal interpreter. The recordings are vintage Decca and excellent for their time.

Additional recommendation ...
Les illuminations[a]. *Simple Symphony, Op. 4. Phaedra, Op. 93*[a]. [a]**Christiane Eda-Pierre** (sop); **Jean-Walter Audoli Instrumental Ensemble/Jean-Walter Audoli.** Arion ARN68035 — ⋰•′ 56m DDD 6/89 **q**s

Britten. SACRED CHORAL MUSIC. [a]**Sioned Williams** (hp); **Westminster Cathedral Choir/David Hill** with [b]**James O'Donnell** (org). Hyperion CDA66220. From A66220 (12/86). Texts included.
A Ceremony of Carols, Op. 28[a]. Missa brevis in D major, Op. 63[b]. A Hymn to the Virgin. A Hymn of St Columba[b]. Jubilate Deo in E flat major[b]. Deus in adjutorum meum.

⋰•′ 49m DDD 2/88 **q**s

A Ceremony of Carols sets nine medieval and sixteenth-century poems between the "Hodie" of the plainsong Vespers. The sole accompanying instrument is a harp, but given the right acoustic, sensitive attention to the words and fine rhythmic control the piece has a remarkable richness and depth. The Westminster Cathedral Choir perform this work beautifully; diction is immaculate and the acoustic halo surrounding the voices gives a festive glow to the performance. A fascinating *Jubilate* and *A Hymn to the Virgin*, whilst lacking the invention and subtlety of *A Ceremony*, intrigue with some particularly felicitous use of harmony and rhythm. *Deus in adjutorum meum* employs the choir without accompaniment and has an initial purity that gradually builds up in texture as the psalm (No. 70) gathers momentum. The *Missa brevis* was written for this very choir and George Malcolm's nurturing of a tonal brightness in the choir allowed Britten to use the voices in a more flexibile and instrumental manner than usual. The effect is glorious. St Columba founded the monastery on the Scottish island of Iona and Britten's hymn sets his simple and forthright prayer with deceptive simplicity and directness. The choir sing this music beautifully and the recording is first rate.

Additional recommendations ...
Hymn to St Cecilia, Op. 27. Sacred and Profane, Op. 91. Rejoice in the Lamb, Op. 30. A Ceremony of Carols. **Soloists; Vasari Singers/Jeremy Backhouse.** EMI Eminence CD-EMX2204 — ⋰•′ 1h 6m DDD 5/93
Missa Brevis[c]. *Festival Te Deum, Op. 32*[c]. *Jubilate Deo in C major. Hymn to St Peter, Op. 56*[ac]. *A Hymn to the Virgin. A Hymn of St Columba*[c]. *Sweet was the Song the Virgin sang. A New Year Carol*[b]. *A Shepherd's Carol. A Ceremony of Carols*[b]. **The Sixteen/Harry Christophers** with [a]**Sioned Williams** (hp); [b]**Stephen Westrop** (pf); [c]**Margaret Phillips** (org). Collins Classics 1370-2 — ⋰•′ 1h 1m DDD 7/93

Britten. Saint Nicolas, Op. 42[a]. Rejoice in the Lamb, Op. 30[b]. [a]**David Hemmings,** [b]**Michael Hartnett** (trebs); [b]**Jonathan Steele** (alto); [a]**Sir Peter Pears,** [b]**Philip Todd** (tens); [b]**Donald Francke** (bass); [a]**Girls' Choir of Sir John Leman School, Beccles;** [a]**Boys' Choir of Ipswich School Preparatory Department;** [b]**Purcell Singers;** [a]**Aldeburgh Festival Choir and Orchestra/Benjamin Britten** with [a]**Ralph Downes,** [b]**George Malcolm** (orgs). Decca London mono 425 714-2LM. Texts included. Item marked [a] from LXT5060 (7/55), recorded in 1955; [b] LXT5416 (5/58), recorded in 1957.

⋰•′ 1h 4m ADD 9/90 ▲

This disc is a further example of Decca's wisdom in transferring to CD its historic collection of Britten/Pears performances of the former's music; and, incidentally, it shows how extremely good the recordings were in the first place. The performance of the cantata *Rejoice in the Lamb*, composed just after Britten returned to England from America during the war, was made in 1957 and remains unsurpassed. The mood of the work's touching setting of Christopher Smart's innocent but soul-searching poem is perfectly caught by the performers, who include George Malcolm as the organist. Britten's writing for the organ here is full of invention, whether he is illustrating Smart's cat Jeoffry "wreathing his body seven times round with elegant quickness" or the "great personal valour" of the mouse who defies Jeoffry. The Purcell Singers, impeccable in clarity of diction, and the soloists, are first-rate. *Saint Nicolas* was recorded even earlier, in Aldeburgh Church in 1955. The treble soloist is David Hemmings who had created Miles in *The Turn of the Screw* the previous year, and Pears sings the role he had created at the first Aldeburgh Festival in 1948. This disc is indispensable for the quality of the performance and as documentary evidence of the standard of the festival in its early years.

Britten. War Requiem, Op. 66[a]. Sinfonia da Requiem, Op. 20. Ballad of Heroes, Op. 14[b]. [a]**Heather Harper** (sop); [a]**Philip Langridge**, [b]**Martyn Hill** (tens); [a]**John Shirley-Quirk** (bar); [a]**St Paul's Cathedral Choir; London Symphony** [ab]**Chorus and Orchestra/ Richard Hickox.** Chandos CHAN8983/4. Texts and translations included.

② 2h 5m DDD 11/91

Britten's *War Requiem* is the composer's most public statement of his pacifism. The work is cast in six movements and calls for massive forces: full chorus, soprano soloist and full orchestra evoke mourning, supplication and guilty apprehension; boys' voices with chamber organ, the passive calm of a liturgy which points beyond death; tenor and baritone soloists with chamber orchestra, the passionate outcry of the doomed victims of war. The most recent challenger to the composer's classic Decca version offers up-to-date recording, excellently managed to suggest the various perspectives of the vast work, and possibly the most convincing execution of the choral writing to date under the direction of a conductor, Richard Hickox, who is a past master at obtaining the best from a choir in terms of dynamic contrast and vocal emphasis. Add to that his empathy with all that the work has to say and you have a cogent reason for acquiring this version even before you come to the excellent work of the soloists. In her recording swan song, Harper at last commits to disc a part she created. It is right that her special accents and impeccable shaping of the soprano's contribution have been preserved for posterity. Shirley-Quirk, always closely associated with the piece, sings the three baritone solos and duets with rugged strength and dedicated intensity. He is matched by Langridge's compelling and insightful reading, with his notes and words more dramatic than Pears's approach. The inclusion of two additional pieces, neither of them short, gives this version an added advantage even if the *Ballad of Heroes* is one of Britten's slighter works.

Additional recommendations ...
War Requiem. **Soloists; Christ Church Cathedral Choir, Oxford; City of Birmingham Symphony Chorus and Orchestra/Simon Rattle.** EMI CDS7 47034-8 — ② DDD 12/84 Ⓑ
War Requiem. **Soloists; Bach Choir; Highgate School Choir; London Symphony Chorus; Melos Ensemble; London Symphony Orchestra/Benjamin Britten.** Decca 414 383-2DH2 — ② 1h 21m ADD 4/85 Ⓑ
War Requiem. **Soloists; Atlanta Symphony Chorus and Orchestra/Robert Shaw.** Telarc CD80157 — ② 1h 23m DDD 12/89 Ⓑ
War Requiem. **Soloists; Monteverdi Choir; Tölz Boys' Choir; North German Radio Chorus and Symphony Orchestra/John Eliot Gardiner.** DG 437 801-2GH2 — ② 1h 23m DDD 11/93 Ⓑ

Britten. PETER GRIMES. **Sir Peter Pears** (ten) Peter Grimes; **Claire Watson** (sop) Ellen Orford; **James Pease** (bass) Captain Balstrode; **Jean Watson** (contr) Auntie; **Raymond Nilsson** (ten) Bob Boles; **Owen Brannigan** (bass) Swallow; **Lauris Elms** (mez) Mrs Sedley; **Sir Geraint Evans** (bar) Ned Keene; **John Lanigan** (ten) Rector; **David Kelly** (bass) Hobson; **Marion Studholme** (sop) First Niece; **Iris Kells** (sop) Second Niece; **Chorus and Orchestra of the Royal Opera House, Covent Garden/Benjamin Britten.** Decca 414 577-2DH3. Notes and text included. From SXL2150/52 (10/59). Recorded in 1958.

② 2h 22m ADD 4/86

The Decca set has long been regarded as the definitive recording which, in 1958, introduced the opera to many listeners and one which has never been superseded in its refinement or insight. Britten's conducting, lithe, lucid and as inexorable as "the tide that waits for no man", reveals his work as the complex, ambiguous drama that it is. Sir Peter Pears, in the title-role which was written for him, brings unsurpassed detail of nuance to Grimes's words while never losing sight of the essential plainness of the man's speech. The rest of the cast form a vivid portrait gallery. The recording is as live and clear as if it had been made yesterday and takes the listener right on to the stage. The bustle of activity and sound effects realize nicely Britten's own masterly painting of dramatic foreground and background.

Additional recommendations ...

Soloists; Chorus and Orchestra of the Royal Opera House, Covent Garden/Sir Colin Davis. Philips 432 578-2PM2 — .•° ② 2h 26m ADD 11/91 ꟼₚ Ⓑ

Soloists; Chorus and Orchestra of the Royal Opera House, Covent Garden/Bernard Haitink. EMI CDS7 54832-2 — .•° ② 2h 25m DDD 7/93 ꟼₚ ꟼₛ Ⓑ

New review

Britten. THE RAPE OF LUCRETIA (abridged)[a]. **Nancy Evans** (mez) Lucretia; **Sir Peter Pears** (ten) Male Chorus; **Joan Cross** (sop) Female Chorus; **Frederick Sharp** (bar) Tarquinius; **Norman Lumsden** (bass) Collatinus; **Denis Dowling** (bar) Junius; **Margaret Ritchie** (sop) Lucia; **Flora Nielsen** (contr) Bianca; **English Opera Group Chamber Orchestra/Sir Reginald Goodall.**

PETER GRIMES[b] — Whatever you say ... Let her among you without fault; Now the Great Bear and Pleiades; Interlude III ... Glitter of waves ... Wherefore I pray and beseech you ... O all ye works of the Lord; In dreams I've built myself some kindlier home; Embroidery in childhood; Interlude VI ... Grimes! ... Steady! There you are!.

Folk-song Arrangements — Voici le printemps[c]; Fileuse[c]; Quand j'étais chez mon père[c] (all prev. unpub. 1943); Le roi s'en va-t'en chasse[c]; La belle est au jardin d'amour[c] (both from Decca M568, 9/44); The Salley Gardens[d]; Little Sir William[d]; Oliver Cromwell[d] (all from M555, 5/44); The Bonny Earl o' Moray[d] (1945); The ash grove[d] (1944); Quand j'étais chez mon père[d] (sung in English. 1945. All new to UK); There's none to soothe[d]; Sweet Polly Oliver[d] (M678. 1946); Le roi s'en va-t'en chasse[d] (Eng. RLS748, 6/80. 1950); The plough boy[d]; The foggy foggy dew[d]; Come you not from Newcastle?[d] (HMV DA1873, 1/48); O waly waly[d] (DA2032, 4/53). [b]**Joan Cross**, [c]**Sophie Wyss** (sops); [bd]**Sir Peter Pears**, [b]**Tom Culbert** (tens); [cd]**Benjamin Britten** (pf); [b]**BBC Theatre Chorus**; [b]**Orchestra of the Royal Opera House, Covent Garden/Sir Reginald Goodall.** EMI British Composers mono CMS7 64727-2. Notes and texts included. Item marked [a] from HMV C3699/706 (3/48 and one previously unpublished 78rpm side. Recorded 1947), [b]HMV RLS707 (11/72 and three prev. unpub. 78rpm sides. 1948).

.•° ② 2h 36m ADD 2/94   ꟼₚ ▲

Here are performances by creator artists of the utmost importance. In *The Rape of Lucretia* Evans is infinitely moving, both in the timbre of her lovely mezzo and in her verbal accents — the simplicity of her Orchid aria would melt the hardest heart. Frederick Sharp is a fiery, priapic Tarquinius. Best of all are the Choruses of Cross and Pears, still unrivalled in their roles, revelling in the colourful imagery of Ronald Duncan's libretto. Pears is magnificent both in the Ride to Rome and the *Sprechgesang* of Tarquinius's stealthy approach to Lucretia's chamber. Equally, in *Peter Grimes*, nobody, not even Pears in the complete 1958 Decca set (listed below), sung with such beauty of tone and such consummate mastery in welding voice to words, every accentuation subtly placed, to achieve a searingly truthful portrayal, and the Ellen/Grimes confrontation in Act 2 and Grimes's mad scene in Act 3 are both quite heartrendingly done. Goodall shows his empathy with and command of both scores. The orchestral playing isn't always as exact as one might wish, but the spirit of the orchestral contribution is all it should be. As a substantial bonus we have all the folk-song arrangements that Pears and Britten recorded on 78s for both Decca and EMI. As throughout this issue, Pears is in glorious voice and these performances surpass the repetitions set down for LP. A 'must' for any lover of Britten's music and a reissue that shows as much care and dedication in preparation as is evinced by the performers themselves. An exhilarating, pioneering period in British music is here suitably chronicled.

Additional recommendation ...

THE RAPE OF LUCRETIA[a]. Phaedra, Op. 93[b]. **Soloists; English Chamber Orchestra/ [a]Benjamin Britten, [b]Steuart Bedford.** Decca London 425 666-2LH2 — .•° ② 2h 4m ADD

Britten. GLORIANA. **Josephine Barstow** (sop) Queen Elizabeth I; **Philip Langridge** (ten) Earl of Essex; **Della Jones** (mez) Lady Essex; **Jonathan Summers** (bar) Lord Mountjoy; **Alan Opie** (bar) Sir Robert Cecil; **Yvonne Kenny** (sop) Penelope; **Richard Van Allan** (bass) Sir Walter Raleigh; **Bryn Terfel** (bass-bar) Henry Cuffe; **Janice Watson** (sop) Lady-in-waiting; **Willard White** (bass) Blind ballad-singer; **John Shirley-Quirk** (bar) Recorder of Norwich; **John Mark Ainsley** (ten) Spirit of the Masque; **Peter Hoare** (ten) Master of Ceremonies; **Welsh National Opera Chorus and Orchestra/Sir Charles Mackerras.** Argo 440 213-2ZHO2. Notes and text included.

♪ ② 2h 28m DDD 7/93

Four decades on from the ill-fated première of Britten's Coronation opera where, instead of the staid pageant expected by the bejewelled and stiff audience assembled for a royal gala, they were given an intimate study of the ageing Queen's torment as she copes with the conflict of private emotions in the midst of public pomp, *Gloriana* has now at last been given a complete recording on CD. Sir Charles Mackerras presents it here with the utmost conviction, drawing together the motivic strands of the score into a unified, coherent whole (not an altogether easy task), apprec-iating the contrast of the public and private scenes, exposing the raw sinews of the writing for the two principal characters, and drawing superb playing from his own WNO Orchestra. Josephine Barstow crowns her career with her Gloriana, commanding the opera by her vocal presence, her imposing, vibrant tone, her vital treatment of the text, and her attention to detail. Philip Langridge projects all the vehement impetuosity of Essex but also, in the famous lute songs, the poetic ardour of the handsome if unruly Earl. There is much discerning interpretation elsewhere and the recording is worthy of the performance. Any small reservations are as nothing before the triumph of the achievement as a whole.

Britten. THE TURN OF THE SCREW. **Philip Langridge** (ten) Prologue, Quint; **Felicity Lott** (sop) Governess; **Sam Pay** (treb) Miles; **Eileen Hulse** (sop) Flora; **Phyllis Cannan** (mez) Mrs Grose; **Nadine Secunde** (sop) Miss Jessel; **Aldeburgh Festival Ensemble/Steuart Bedford.** Collins Classics 7030-2. Notes and text included.

♪ ② 1h 46m DDD 6/94

Arguably the tautest, most compact of all his scores for the stage, this version comes with a fascinating essay by Donald Mitchell, and letters from the composer revealing that, as a youth in 1932, Britten heard a dramatized version of James's story on the wireless and described it as "eerie and scary", adjectives that apply even more strongly to his own setting of 22 years later. Mitchell explains that the music discloses the Governess and Quint as two sides of the same character: "The Governess/Quint symbiosis (and its musical realisation) has its roots precisely in the pursuit of power, power to possess Miles ...". Consciously or not, that struggle, once you are aware of it, is very much present in the forceful, histrionic portrayal of the roles here by Felicity Lott and Philip Langridge, coming to a climax in the final confrontation where the tension is almost unbearable in such a lifelike, big-scale recording. Both bring all their long stage experience to bear on giving character and verbal enlightenment to their roles. Steuart Bedford (who paces the work to within a minute of Britten's own timing) and his players have the advantage over the composer and his hand-picked ensemble in the ability of modern recording to open up the score and also subject it to the minutest scrutiny so that one is amazed again not only at the intricate skill with which it is woven but also by its extraordinary aptness in fitting individual instruments to evoke a mood, a situation, a place. The supporting singers offer arresting interpretations. Those who have lived with and loved the original version over 40 years are not going to let affection for it dim, but the new set is happily in the true tradition of the piece, and deserves a high placing among all the other recent performances of Britten's operas. The work itself will surely capture the imagination of any newcomer who hasn't yet been made aware of its greatness.

Additional recommendation ...
Soloists; English Opera Group Orchestra/Benjamin Britten. Decca London mono 425 672-2LH2 — ♪ ② 1h 45m ADD 5/90 ▲

Further listening ...

The Prince of the Pagodas, Op. 57. **London Sinfonietta/Oliver Knussen.** Virgin Classics VCD7 59578-2 (7/90).

Nocturnal after John Dowland, Op. 70. *Coupled with* **Schafer.** Le cri de Merlin; **Tippett.** The blue guitar. **Norbert Kraft** (gtr). Chandos CHAN8784 (1/90).

Antiphon, Op. 56*b*[b]. Te Deum in C major[b]. A Wedding Anthem, Op. 46[b]. Rejoice in the Lamb, Op. 30[b]. The Sycamore tree. The Ballad of Little Musgrave and Lady Barnard[a]. Advance Democracy. Sacred and Profane, Op. 91. **The Sixteen/Harry Christophers** with [a]**Stephen Westrop** (pf); [b]**Margaret Phillips** (org). Collins Classics 1343-2 (6/93).

Deus in adjutorium meum[f]. Chorale on an old French carol[f]. Cantata misericordium, Op. 69[bdfg]. *Coupled with* **Finzi.** Requiem da camera[acdfg]. **Holst.** Psalms, H117 — No. 86[aefg]; No. 148[efg]. [a]**Alison Barlow** (sop); [b]**John Mark Ainsley** (ten); [c]**David Hoult,** [d]**Stephen Varcoe** (bars); [e]**John Alley** (org); [f]**Britten Singers;** [g]**City of London Sinfonia/Richard Hickox.** Chandos CHAN8997 (3/92).

PAUL BUNYAN. **Soloists; Plymouth Music Series Chorus and Orchestra/Philip Brunelle.** Virgin Classics VC7 59249-2 (8/88).

ALBERT HERRING. **Soloists; English Chamber Orchestra/Benjamin Britten.** Decca London 421 849-2LH2 (6/89).

THE LITTLE SWEEP[a]. CHILDREN'S CRUSADE, Op. 82[c]. Gemini Variations, Op. 73[b]. [a]**Soloists;** [a]**Alleyn's School Choir;** [a]**English Opera Group Orchestra/Benjamin Britten.** [b]**Gabriel Jeney** (vn/pf); [b]**Zoltán Jeney** (fl/pf). [c]**Soloists;** [c]**Wandsworth School Boys' Choir; chamber ensemble/Russell Burgess, Benjamin Britten.** Decca London [a]mono/[bc]stereo 436 393-2LM (11/93).

BILLY BUDD. The Holy Sonnets of John Donne, Op. 35. Songs and Proverbs of William Blake, Op. 74. **Soloists; Ambrosian Opera Chorus; London Symphony Orchestra/Benjamin Britten.** Decca 417 428-2LH3 (6/89).

NOYE'S FLUDDE[a]. THE GOLDEN VANITY, Op. 78[b]. [ab]**Soloists;** [b]**Benjamin Britten** (pf); [a]**English Opera Group Orchestra; An East Suffolk Children's Orchestra/Norman Del Mar.** [b]**Wandsworth School Boys' Choir/Russell Burgess.** Decca London 436 397-2LM (11/93).

A MIDSUMMER NIGHT'S DREAM. **Soloists; Choirs of Downside and Emanuel Schools; London Symphony Orchestra/Benjamin Britten.** Decca London 425 663-2LH2 (5/90).

CURLEW RIVER. **Soloists; English Opera Group/Benjamin Britten** and **Viola Tunnard.** Decca London 421 858-2LM (9/89).

THE BURNING FIERY FURNACE. **Soloists; English Opera Group/Benjamin Britten.** Decca 414 663-2LM (10/90).

THE PRODIGAL SON. **Soloists; English Opera Group/Benjamin Britten.** Decca 425 713-2LM (9/90).

OWEN WINGRAVE[a]. Six Hölderlin fragments, Op. 61[b]. The Poet's Echo, Op. 76[c]. [a]**Soloists;** [a]**Wandsworth School Boys' Choir; English Chamber Orchestra/Benjamin Britten.** [b]**Sir Peter Pears** (ten); [c]**Galina Vishnevskaya** (sop); [b]**Benjamin Britten;** [c]**Mstislav Rostropovich** (pfs). Decca London 433 200-2LHO2 (11/93).

DEATH IN VENICE. **Soloists; English Opera Group Chorus; English Chamber Orchestra/Steuart Bedford.** Decca London 425 669-2LH2 (5/90).

František Brixi

Suggested listening ...

Organ Concertos — No. 2 in D major; No. 4 in C major; No. 5 in C major. **Jan Hora** (org);
Prague Chamber Orchestra/František Vajnar. Supraphon 10 3029-2 (9/92).

Max Bruch

New review
Bruch. Violin Concerto No. 1 in G minor, Op. 26.
Mendelssohn. Violin Concerto in E minor, Op. 64. **Maxim Vengerov** (vn); **Leipzig
Gewandhaus Orchestra/Kurt Masur.** Teldec 4509-90875-2. Recorded in 1993.

5lm DDD 4/94

As one might expect with Mendelssohn's own orchestra, the Leipzig Gewandhaus, under Kurt
Masur, there is a freshness and clarity in the Mendelssohn which ideally matches the soloist's
playing, at once felt and expressive but clean and direct, with articulation of diamond precision and
fine tonal shading. If anyone has ever thought this work at all sentimental, this shatters any such
idea, and characteristically Masur encourages a flowing speed in the central *Andante*, which brings
out the songfulness of the main theme. It is consistent with this approach that in his expressiveness
Vengerov is more inclined to press ahead than to hold back, so that with a dashingly fast speed for
the finale one is left breathless at the end. The slow movement of the Bruch gains from being
taken at a flowing speed and Vengerov finds a rare depth of expressiveness, which makes the
movement a meditation rather than simply a lyrical interlude. With outstanding recorded sound,
warm yet clear and detailed, there is now no more recommendable disc of this favourite coupling.

Additional recommendations ...
Violin Concerto. **Mendelssohn.** *Violin Concerto.* **Anne-Sophie Mutter** (vn); **Berlin
Philharmonic Orchestra/Herbert von Karajan.** DG 400 031-2GH — 57m DDD 3/83
Violin Concerto. **Mendelssohn.** *Violin Concerto.* **Scottish Chamber Orchestra/Jaime Laredo**
(vn). Pickwick IMP Red Label PCD829 — 53m DDD 1/87
Violin Concerto. Scottish Fantasy, Op. 46. **Cho-Liang Lin** (vn); **Chicago Symphony
Orchestra/Leonard Slatkin.** CBS Masterworks CD42315 — 53m DDD 7/87
Violin Concerto. **Mendelssohn.** *Violin Concerto.* **Joshua Bell** (vn); **Academy of St Martin in
the Fields/Sir Neville Marriner.** Decca 421 145-2DH — 54m DDD 5/88
Violin Concerto. **Mendelssohn.** *Violin Concerto.* **Schubert.** *Rondo in A major, D438.* **Nigel
Kennedy** (vn); **English Chamber Orchestra/Jeffrey Tate.** EMI CDC7 49663-2 —
1h 11m DDD 1/89
Violin Concerto. **Dvořák.** *Violin Concerto in A minor, Op. 53.* **Tasmin Little** (vn); **Royal
Liverpool Philharmonic Orchestra/Vernon Handley.** Classics for Pleasure CD-CFP4566
— 1h DDD 7/90
Violin Concerto. **Mendelssohn.** *Violin Concerto.* **Nathan Milstein** (vn); **Philharmonia
Orchestra/Leon Barzin.** Classics for Pleasure CD-CFP4374 — 48m ADD
Violin Concerto[c]. **Mendelssohn.** *Violin Concerto[b].* **Sarasate.** *Introduction et Tarantelle, Op. 43[a].*
Kreisler. *Liebesfreud[a].* **Cho-Liang Lin** (vn); [a]**Sandra Rivers** (pf); [b]**Philharmonia
Orchestra/Michael Tilson Thomas;** [c]**Chicago Symphony Orchestra/Leonard Slatkin.**
CBS Masterworks CD44902 — 1h 1m DDD 3/91
*Complete Works for Violin and Orchestra: Violin Concertos — No. 1; No. 2 in D minor, Op. 44; No. 3
in D minor, Op. 58. Adagio Appassionato, Op. 57. Romance, Op. 42. Scottish Fantasy[a]. Konzertstück,
Op. 84. Serenade, Op. 75. In Memoriam, Op. 65.* [a]**Elizabeth Unger** (hp); **Salvatore Accardo**
(vn); **Leipzig Gewandhaus Orchestra/Kurt Masur.** Philips Silver Line 432 282-2PSL3 —
③ 3h 34m ADD 7/91
Violin Concerto. Scottish Fantasy. **Lalo.** *Symphonie espagnole, Op. 21.* **Anne Akiko Meyers** (vn);
Royal Philharmonic Orchestra/Jesús López-Cobos. RCA Victor Red Seal RD60942 —
1h DDD 9/92

Bruch. Double Piano Concerto, Op. 88*a*.
Mendelssohn. Double Piano Concerto in E major. **Katia and Marielle Labèque** (pfs);
Philharmonia Orchestra/Semyon Bychkov. Philips 432 095-2PH. Recorded in 1990.

> •‧• **lh lm DDD 7/93**

Bruch's Double Piano Concerto will probably confound your expectations. It starts in an
uncompromisingly solemn mood: dark, thick-textured and fugal, and with more than a suggestion of
Busoni trailing in its wake. The second movement is healthily energetic, while the melodic richness
and full-throated romanticism of the *Adagio* are fairly typical of the Max Bruch we all know and love
so well. The Labèques indulge both its burgeoning romanticism and its considerable virtuoso
demands, while Bychkov directs a big, warm-textured accompaniment. Mendelssohn's E major
Double Piano Concerto is one of a pair that he composed during his early teens. Beethoven was an
obvious model (his *Emperor* Concerto in particular), but the music is quintessentially Mendelssohnian
none the less, with an abundance of sunny melodies and much dexterous solo writing. The
Labèques never stint on brilliance and the Philharmonia is on good form. The recording copes well.

Bruch. Symphonies — No. 1 in E flat major, Op. 28; No. 2 in F minor, Op. 36; No. 3 in
E major, Op. 51. **Cologne Gürzenich Orchestra/James Conlon.** EMI CDS5 55046-2.
Recorded 1992-93.

> •‧• ② **lh 43m DDD 4/94**

Bruch's three symphonies are works whose rather reticent melodic style, at times dense scoring
and formal stiffness, need affectionate help if their genuine qualities are to emerge and outweigh
their flaws. Carefully handled there is real romantic charm (and some agreeably brusque
sturdiness) to the first movement of the Third Symphony; its *Adagio* has sonorous solemnity and
an ardent climax, and its *Scherzo* some fire. The Second Symphony, its over-extended finale apart,
is stronger still. Conlon and his Cologne players cannot always disguise passages of awkwardly
coarse scoring, but their sound, though full, is lean and that is in itself an advantage. Conlon is
also more likely than Masur (listed below) to relax into Bruch's genial melodies, to linger and
shape them with affectionate rubato. For some tastes Masur's urgency will compensate for his at
times lumbering massiveness of sound. Although *longueurs* are obvious in both conductors' hands,
Conlon seems the more concerned to persuade us not to mind them. For anyone wanting all the
symphonies of this neglected but likeable composer his set is a pretty safe recommendation.

Additional recommendation:

Nos. 1-3. Swedish Dances, Op. 63. **Leipzig Gewandhaus Orchestra/Kurt Masur.** Philips 420
932-2PH2 — •‧• ② lh 45m DDD 3/89

Further listening ...

Clarinet and Viola Concerto in E minor, Op. 88[a]. *Coupled with* **Crusell.** Introduction, Theme
and Variations on a Swedish air, Op. 12[b]; **Mendelssohn.** Two Concert Pieces[c] — F major,
Op. 113; D minor, Op. 114. [abc]**Thea King** (cl); [a]**Nobuko Imai** (va); [c]**Georgina Dobrée**
(basset-hn); **London Symphony Orchestra/Alun Francis.** Hyperion CDA66022 (1/88).

String Quartets — No. 1 in C minor, Op. 9; No. 2 in E major, Op. 10. **Academica
Quartet.** Dynamic CDS29 (5/94).

Anton Bruckner
Austrian 1824-1896

Bruckner. SYMPHONIES. **Berlin Philharmonic Orchestra/Herbert von Karajan.** DG
Karajan Symphony Edition 429 648-2GSE9. Recorded 1974-1981.
No. 1 in C minor (Linz version)[b]; No. 2 in C minor (ed. Nowak[b]. Both from 2740 264, 6/82);
No. 3 in D minor (1889 version, ed. Nowak[b]. 2532 007, 7/81); No. 4 in E flat major,

"Romantic"[a] (2530 674, 10/76); No. 5 in B flat major[a] (2702 101, 10/78); No. 6 in A major[a] (2531 295, 11/80); No. 7 in E major[a] (2707 102, 4/78); No. 8 in C minor (ed. Haas[a]. 2707 085, 5/76); No. 9 in D minor[a] (2530 828, 6/77).

⑨ 8h 40m ADD/DDD 3/91

It is often said that the essence of good Bruckner conducting is a firm grasp of structure. In fact that's only a half-truth. Of course one must understand how Bruckner's massive statements and counterstatements are fused together, but a performance that was nothing but architecture would be a pretty depressing experience. Karajan's understanding of the slow but powerful currents that flow beneath the surfaces of symphonies like the Fifth or Nos. 7-9 has never been bettered, but at the same time he shows how much more there is to be reckoned with: strong emotions, a deep poetic sensitivity (a Bruckner symphony can evoke landscapes as vividly as Mahler or Vaughan Williams) and a gift for singing melody that at times rivals even Schubert. It hardly needs saying that there's no such thing as a perfect record cycle, and this collection of the numbered Bruckner symphonies (unfortunately Karajan never recorded "No. 0") has its weaknesses. The early First and Second Symphonies can be a little heavy-footed and, as with so many Bruckner sets, there's a suspicion that more time might have been spent getting to know the fine but elusive Sixth — and there's an irritating throwback to the days of corrupt Bruckner editions in the first big crescendo of the Fourth Symphony (high swooping violins — nasty!) — but none of these performances is without its major insights, and in the best of them — particularly Nos. 3, 5, 7, 8 and 9 — those who haven't stopped their ears to Karajan will find that whatever else he may have been, there was a side to him that could only be described as 'visionary'. As for the recordings: climaxes can sound a touch overblown in some of the earlier symphonies, but on the whole the image is well-focused and atmospheric. A valuable set, and a landmark in the history of Bruckner recording.

Additional recommendations ...
No. 2 (ed. Nowak). **Berlin Philharmonic Orchestra/Herbert von Karajan.** DG 415 988-2GH — ... Ih Im ADD 2/87
Nos. 1, 4 and 7-9 — **Berlin Philharmonic Orchestra;** *Nos. 2, 3, 5 and 6* — **Bavarian Radio Symphony Orchestra/Eugen Jochum.** DG 429 079-2GX9 — ... ⑨ 9h 12m ADD 2/90
Nos. 1-9. **Cologne Radio Symphony Orchestra/Günter Wand.** Deutsche Harmonia Mundi Editio Classica GD60075 — ... ①⓪ 9h 19m ADD/DDD 2/90
No. 2. **Chicago Symphony Orchestra/Sir Georg Solti.** Decca 436 844-2DH — ... 56m DDD 8/93

Key to symbols

Price	Quantity/availability	Timing	Recording mode	Review date
	② ②	Ih 23m	DDD	6/88

Bruckner. Symphony No. 0 in D minor, "Die Nullte" (rev. 1869). Overture in G minor. **Berlin Radio Symphony Orchestra/Riccardo Chailly.** Decca 421 593-2DH.

58m DDD I/90

It should be remembered that Bruckner wrote all his symphonies (including this one) after he was 40, indeed the bulk of *Die Nullte* that we encounter here was written after his official No. 1, and can be regarded as the progenitor of much that was to come in Bruckner's symphonic output: many of the motives can be found in later symphonies, the obvious example being the opening ostinato which later provided the underlay to the opening of the Third Symphony. Chailly's thoroughly convincing performance takes a fairly spacious view of the work, with much emphasis on nobility, poise and dynamic shaping. And if at times he comes dangerously close to sentimentality in the Andante, in the end it is his feeling of serenity and warmth that win us over. This is superbly contrasted with the exuberance and urgency that he conveys in the dance-like Scherzo. At times the strings have a tendency to sound a little thin in the trio section, but this is more than compensated for in the lyrical and graceful playing of the Berlin

RSO. The Overture in G minor, dating from 1862, makes a welcome filler and receives a similarly warm and persuasive performance. The recording is warm and well balanced.

Bruckner. Symphony No. 1 in C minor (1866 version)[a]. Te Deum[b]. [a]**Jessye Norman** (sop); [b]**Yvonne Minton** (mez); [b]**David Rendall** (ten); [b]**Samuel Ramey** (bass); **Chicago Symphony** [b]**Chorus and Orchestra/Daniel Barenboim.** DG Galleria 435 068-2GGA. Text and translation included. Item marked [a] from 2740 253 (10/81), [b] 2741 007 (10/81). Recorded 1980-81.

Ih 10m DDD 12/91

A Schubertian grace informs the first part of Bruckner's mighty First Symphony and this quality abounds in Barenboim's outstanding performance. His attention to detail and rhythmic accuracy, coupled with the Chicago Symphony Orchestra at their most brilliant and incisive, produces a fiery account of the work. Barenboim may lack the sweep and architectural control of Karajan but he brings a compensating wit and enthusiasm to the score — his view of the delightful scherzo, for example, is deft and appropriately capricious. The rousing finale rips along as Barenboim and his orchestra pile on the power. To further enhance this mid-price recording, Barenboim's urgent, heroic and gloriously spontaneous version of the *Te Deum* is the substantial coupling. The superb diction, dynamic discipline and overall alertness of the Chicago Symphony Chorus brings refreshing vigour to this potentially turgid work. The soloists make a superb team, blending in with the glittering array of choral and orchestral colours. The 1981 recordings shine with rich, full-bodied balance. All in all, this is a Brucknerian bargain not to be missed.

Bruckner. Symphony No. 3 in D minor (1889 version). **Vienna Philharmonic Orchestra/ Karl Böhm.** Decca Ovation 425 032-2DM. From SXL6505 (10/71). Recorded in 1970.

57m ADD 3/93

Karl Böhm's impressive account of Bruckner's Third Symphony re-emerges with startling clarity and body on this mid-price Ovation CD. Sonically speaking, of course, this was a peak period for the Decca technicians, and the exemplary focus and spectacular dynamic range of this Sofiensaal production really does take the breath away. As on Böhm's indispensable companion CD of the *Romantic* (listed under No. 4), the VPO respond splendidly throughout (Bruckner's rustic trio section is inimitably Viennese in its earthy gait), though, perhaps inevitably, there isn't quite the same degree of electricity or concentration on show here that this conductor was later to achieve in that legendary traversal of the Fourth. At the price, though, this is undoubtedly worth investigating and must now be considered one of the front-runners. Incidentally, DG could do us all a great favour and transfer to the Privilege label Eugen Jochum's superb 1967 Munich account of this wonderful work (at present only available as part of a nine-CD set, details of which are listed above) — now, that really *would* sweep the board!

Additional recommendations ...
(original version, 1873). **Frankfurt Radio Symphony Orchestra/Eliahu Inbal.** Teldec 2292-42961-2 — .•ˑ DDD 1/86
(1877 version). **Vienna Philharmonic Orchestra/Bernard Haitink.** Philips 422 411-2PH — .•ˑ Ih 2m DDD 3/91

New review
Bruckner. Symphony No. 4 in E flat major, "Romantic". **Hallé Orchestra/Stanislaw Skrowaczewski.** Pickwick IMP Classics PCD1059.

Ih 9m DDD 3/94

New review
Bruckner. Symphony No. 4 in E flat major, "Romantic". **Berlin Philharmonic Orchestra/ Daniel Barenboim.** Teldec 9031-73272-2.

Ih 8m DDD 3/94

Skrowaczewski's is a remarkable performance — fiery and true, rightly denying even lip-service to the symphony's misleadingly sentimental nickname. In fact, it is about ten minutes into the first movement that the performance's real stature is finally manifest. This is the great modulating chorale, one of the most inspired passages in all Bruckner, and their profoundly beautiful aftermath. Böhm and the Vienna Philharmonic (listed below) are superb here; but, if anything, under Skrowaczewski the tension is ever higher, the Hallé brass playing even more exalted. Throughout the Hallé performance, horns, violas and cellos play supremely well. This is important in the finale where the lyrical subjects are all-important. Since Barenboim first recorded the Fourth Symphony in Chicago in 1972 he has broadened his interpretation whilst at the same time creating an even more compelling sense of a great organic symphonic utterance. The finale, in particular, is now wonderfully evolved, the whole thing so organically of a piece one fails to notice the occasional bit of otiose detailing left in the works by Bruckner. The slow movement is also further deepened. What in Chicago was a serene meditation has now become a profound act of spiritual indwelling. The Teldec engineers favour a fairly warm sound, apt to the cultured Berlin playing. Pickwick, by contrast, favour a sound that is keener and more immediate, equally apt to the performance in hand.

Additional recommendations …

No. 4. **Philharmonia Orchestra/Otto Klemperer.** EMI Studio CDM7 69127-2 — ⠶ lh lm
ADD 12/88 ⁹ₚ Ⓑ

No. 4. **Vienna Philharmonic Orchestra/Claudio Abbado.** DG 431 719-2GH — ⠶ lh 9m
DDD 4/91 ⁹ₚ Ⓑ

No. 4. **Staatskapelle Dresden/Herbert Blomstedt.** Denon C37-7126 — ⠶ lh 7m DDD 2/85 Ⓑ

No. 4 (Original version). **Frankfurt Radio Symphony Orchestra/Eliahu Inbal.** Teldec
Digital Experience 9031 77597-2 — ⠶ lh 8m DDD 12/92 ⁹ₚ Ⓑ

No. 4. **Vienna Philharmonic Orchestra/Karl Böhm.** Decca Ovation 425 036-2DM — ⠶
lh 8m ADD 3/93 ⁹ₚ Ⓑ

Nos. 4[a] *and 7*[b]. [a]**Hamburg Philharmonic Orchestra,** [b]**Vienna Philharmonic
Orchestra/Eugene Jochum.** Dante Lys mono LYS007/8 — ⠶ ② 2h 7m ADD 7/93 Ⓑ ▲

New review

Bruckner. Symphony No. 5 in B flat major. **Cleveland Orchestra/Christoph von
Dohnányi.** Decca 433 318-2DH. Recorded in 1991.

⠶ lh 14m DDD 8/93	⁹ₚ Ⓑ

Rarely can Bruckner's Fifth Symphony have seemed as gaunt, as dramatic, as fiercely concentrated as here. Rarely, too, do you hear a Bruckner performance more physically exciting than this; yet the source of the excitement is not in the tempos as such. In the finale, for example, Dohnányi takes a relatively measured view of the music. The *Allegro moderato* is perfectly judged, neither too lumbering nor too quick; but its effect is made electric by the skilful way Dohnányi holds successive subjects within the gravitational pull of that enunciatory pulse. Dohnányi binds the fabric of the symphony together with hoops of finely tempered steel. Yet, at the same time, the whole thing exults and blazes. What we have here is the Cleveland Orchestra at its exacting best and Decca's recording is clean and analytical. This is a uniquely exciting reading.

Additional recommendations …

No. 5 (orig. version); No. 1 (1866 version). **Berlin Philharmonic Orchestra/Herbert von
Karajan.** DG 415 985-2GH2 — ⠶ ② 2h 12m ADD/DDD 6/87 ⁹ₚ Ⓑ

No. 5. Te Deum[a]. [a]**Karita Mattila** (sop); [a]**Susanne Mentzer** (mez); [a]**Vinson Cole** (ten);
[a]**Robert Holl** (bass); [a]**Bavarian Radio Chorus; Vienna Philharmonic Orchestra/
Bernard Haitink.** Philips 422 342-2PH2 — ⠶ ② lh 40m DDD 11/89 ⁹ₚ ⁹ₛ Ⓑ

No. 5. **Berlin Philharmonic Orchestra/Daniel Barenboim.** Teldec 9031-73271-2 — ⠶
lh 12m DDD 3/93 ⁹ₚ ⁹ₛ Ⓑ

No. 5. **Royal Concertgebouw Orchestra/Riccardo Chailly.** Decca 433 819-2DH — ⠶
lh 15m DDD 11/93 Ⓑ

Bruckner (ed. Haas). Symphony No. 6 in A major. **New Philharmonia Orchestra/Otto
Klemperer.** EMI Studio CDM7 63351-2. From Columbia SAX2582 (9/65). Recorded in 1964.

⠶ 55m ADD 3/90	⁹ₚ

No Brucknerian will want to be without Klemperer's legendary performance, indeed it has long been regarded as perhaps the finest recorded interpretation of this symphony. Part of

Klemperer's success lies in his unerring ability to project the symphony's architectural and organic content through Bruckner's ever changing terrain. His vigorous and resolute approach is apparent from the outset, where the opening ostinato string figure, crisp and rhythmically assured, tell us that this is no routine performance. His handling of Bruckner's frequent *fortissimo* 'blaze ups' is always dramatic, exhilarating and sonorous, whilst never destroying the beautifully clear and lucid textures he achieves throughout the symphony. The adagio is one of Bruckner's most sublime creations. Klemperer's choice of tempo may seem fast here, but is entirely justified by the resulting sense of momentum and forward drive: and you will be hard pressed to find a better rendering of the tender and expansive second theme as it burgeons out of the sombre introduction. The Scherzo, with its incessant bass and cello ostinato tread is given a subtle and evocative reading, building the tension superbly before resolving into the haunting and mysterious trio section with its Tristanesque horn calls. The recording, made in the Kingsway Hall in 1964, is excellent.

Additional recommendations ...
Berlin Philharmonic Orchestra/Herbert von Karajan. DG 419 194-2GH — .·´ 58m ADD 4/87
North German Radio Symphony Orchestra/Günter Wand. RCA Victor Red Seal RD60061 — .·´ 55m DDD 2/91

Bruckner. Symphony No. 7. **Staatskapelle Dresden/Herbert Blomstedt.** Denon C37-7286. Recorded in 1980.

| .·´ 1h 8m DDD 8/86 | 9ᵖ 9ₛ Ⓑ |

Bruckner's gloriously long-breathed Seventh Symphony is, of all his works, the one most indebted to the music of Wagner. Although the Third was dedicated to this composer, it is the Seventh which is closer in spirit and tonal colour to that of Wagner. Bruckner worked on this symphony for some two years, and after a play-through on two pianos in Vienna, it received its first performance in Leipzig late in 1884 under the baton of the great Artur Nikisch. The symphony is constructed in the usual four movements, the *Adagio* second movement being the powerful core of the work — a long, richly-scored meditation that carries solemn, even funereal overtones. Herbert Blomstedt's performance of this great work is glorious — well judged, beautifully played and with just the right blend of eloquence and tension. The recording is excellent.

Additional recommendations ...
Berlin Philharmonic Orchestra/Herbert von Karajan. EMI Studio CDM7 69923-2 — .·´ 1h 8m ADD 6/89 9ᵖ Ⓑ
Vienna Philharmonic Orchestra/Herbert von Karajan. DG 429 226-2GH — .·´ 1h 6m DDD 5/90 9ᵖ Ⓑ
Cleveland Orchestra/Christoph von Dohnányi. Decca 430 841-2DH — .·´ 1h 4m DDD 10/92 9ᵖ Ⓑ
Staatskapelle Dresden/Giuseppe Sinopoli. DG 435 786-2GH — .·´ 1h 5m DDD 9/93 Ⓑ
Vienna Philharmonic Orchestra/Claudio Abbado. DG 437 518-2GH — .·´ 1h 4m DDD 5/94 Ⓑ

Bruckner. Symphony No. 8 in C minor. **Vienna Philharmonic Orchestra/Herbert von Karajan.** DG 427 611-2GH2. Recorded in 1988.

| .·´ ② 1h 23m DDD 10/89 | 9ᵖ 9ₛ Ⓑ |

As if by some strange act of providence, great conductors have often been remembered by the immediate posthumous release of some fine and representative recording. With Karajan it is the Eighth Symphony of Bruckner, perhaps the symphony he loved and revered above all others. It is the sense of the music being in the hearts and minds and collective unconscious of Karajan and every one of the 100 and more players of the Vienna Philharmonic that gives this performances its particular charisma and appeal. It is a wonderful reading, every bit as authoritative as its many predecessors and every bit as well played but somehow more profound, more humane, more lovable if that is a permissible attribute of an interpretation of this Everest among symphonies. The end of the work, always astonishing and uplifting, is especially fine here and very moving. Fortunately, it has been recorded with plenty of weight and space and warmth and clarity, with the additional benefit of the added vibrancy of the Viennese playing. The sessions were obviously sufficiently happy for there to shine through moments of spontaneous power and eloquence that were commonplace in the concert hall in Karajan's later years, but which recordings can't always be relied upon to catch.

Additional recommendations ...
No. 8. **Vienna Philharmonic Orchestra/Carlo Maria Giulini.** DG 415 124-2GH2 — ⨀ DDD 7/85 Ⓑ
No. 8. *Wagner.* *Siegfried Idyll.* **Royal Concertgebouw Orchestra/Bernard Haitink.**
Philips 412 465-2PH2 — ⨀ 1h 44m DDD 7/86 Ⓑ

Bruckner. Symphony No. 9 in D minor. **Berlin Philharmonic Orchestra/Herbert von Karajan.** DG 419 083-2GH. From 2530 828 (6/77). Recorded in 1976.

⟶ 1h 2m ADD 9/86   Ⓑ

Karajan's 1976 recording has long been something of a classic, capturing the conductor and the Berlin Philharmonic on top form. From the opening of the titanic first movement to the final grinding dissonance of the lofty *Adagio* Karajan's control of phrase lengths, tempo and rhythmic swing are gloriously apparent. Compared with many more recent accounts of this solemn work, Karajan's beautifully recorded performance seems refreshingly urgent, cohesive and properly threatening. Exceptionally vivid, it was sometimes difficult to tame on LP, but the CD version gives unalloyed pleasure.

Additional recommendations ...
Cleveland Orchestra/Christoph von Dohnányi. Decca 425 405-2DH — 58m DDD 6/89 Ⓑ
Vienna Philharmonic Orchestra/Carlo Maria Giulini. DG 427 345-2GH — 1h 8m DDD 8/89 Ⓑ
Berlin Philharmonic Orchestra/Daniel Barenboim. Teldec 9031 72140-2 — 1h 3m DDD 10/91 Ⓑ
Vienna Philharmonic Orchestra/Herbert von Karajan. DG 435 326-2GWP — ADD 2/92 Ⓑ

New review
Bruckner. Mass No. 1 in D minor. Te Deum in C major. **Joan Rodgers** (sop); **Catherine Wyn-Rogers** (contr); **Keith Lewis** (ten); **Alastair Miles** (bass); **Corydon Singers and Orchestra/Matthew Best** with **James O'Donnell** (org). Hyperion CDA66650. Texts and translations included. Recorded in 1993.

⟶ 1h 7m DDD 11/93

Earth-shaking is the only way to describe Bruckner's great *Te Deum* — literally as well as metaphorically with, on this disc, the thundering Westminster Cathedral organ (superimposed sensitively). The considerably enlarged Corydon Singers sing with consummate skill, rooting out all the subtleties and nuances of Bruckner's magnificent score yet always faithful to Matthew Best's thrusting, athletic direction. It is followed with a performance of the D minor Mass of extraordinary power and strength. From the dazzling orchestral colour and the electrically charged climaxes piling in one on top of the other, to the opulent writing for voices encompassing a vast array of human emotions, Bruckner's debt to Wagner is everywhere apparent. This is very much Bruckner the symphonist — the orchestra certainly dominates the work — and this orchestra produces playing of the very highest calibre.

Bruckner. SACRED CHORAL WORKS. [a]**Anne-Marie Owens** (mez); [b]**City of Birmingham Symphony Chorus;** [c]**Birmingham Symphony Orchestra Wind Ensemble/**[d]**Simon Halsey.** Conifer CDCF192. Texts and translations included.
Mass No. 2 in E minor[bcd]. Afferentur regi[bcd]. Ave Maria (1861)[bd]. Ave Maria (1882, with Peter King, org)[a]. Ecce sacerdos magnus[bcd]. Locus iste[bd]. Aequali for three trombones, No. 1 and 2[c].

⟶ 1h 4m DDD 1/91

Bruckner's religious works require for their full realization an elusive combination of classical restraint and romantic fervour. In this excellent recording by the City of Birmingham Symphony

Chorus and Wind Ensemble this style is captured perfectly. Under conductor Simon Halsey the chorus's finely tuned singing and rich tone is ideally suited both to the E minor Mass of 1866 and the four brief but intense motets which provide an excellent makeweight. The CBSO Wind Ensemble's accompaniment in the Mass, and solo playing in the two *Aequali* for three trombones, is well-balanced and sonorous, qualities which are also shared by Conifer's atmospheric recorded sound. These choral works display a more personal side to Bruckner's character than the mighty symphonies, and so help to round out in a unique way the musical portrait of this great composer. Thus this finely prepared CD, completed by the first-ever recording of the *Ave Maria,* is an essential complement to the more well-known, and more public, works.

Additional recommendation ...
Mass No. 2. Libera me in F minor (Colin Sheen, Roger Brenner, Philip Brown, tbns). *Aequali for three trombones, Nos. 1 and 2* (Sheen, Brenner, Brown). **Corydon Singers; English Chamber Orchestra Wind Ensemble/Matthew Best.** Hyperion CDA66177 — .·˙ 53m DDD 9/86 ⁹ₚ ⁹ₛ

Bruckner. Mass No. 3 in F minor. Psalm 150 in C major. **Juliet Booth** (sop); **Jean Rigby** (mez); **John Mark Ainsley** (ten); **Gwynne Howell** (bass); **Corydon Singers and Orchestra/Matthew Best.** Hyperion CDA66599. Texts and translations included. Recorded in 1992.

.·˙ **1h 8m DDD 3/93** ⁹ₚ

Bruckner, the devout Catholic who poured his very soul into his devotional, liturgical choral pieces often seems a very different being from Bruckner, the composer of gargantuan, almost self-indulgent symphonies rich in luscious orchestral colour and sensuous harmony. Where the two combine the result can be something almost other-worldly. The F minor Mass is certainly his finest choral work, if not the finest music he ever created. The intensity of religious feeling is heightened rather than diminished by the sumptuous orchestral support, and the soaring melodies and opulent harmonies are somehow purified and enriched by the devotional character of these familiar texts. Here is a performance which by understating the music's abundant richness gives tremendous point to the inner conviction of Bruckner's faith. This orchestra, brought together for this recording but sounding as if they have been playing this music all their days, plays with commendable discretion balancing admirably with a relatively small choral body. As with everything the Corydon Singers and Matthew Best turn their hands to, it is an impeccable performance, infused with real artistry and sensitive musicianship. Enhanced by the glorious solo voices from a high-powered team this is a CD of rare depth and conviction.

Key to symbols

Gramophone
Awards winners

Gramophone
Editor's choice

Nicolaus Bruhns

German 1665-1697

Suggested listening ...

Cantatas. Organ Works — Preludes and Fugues: No. 1 in E minor; No. 2 in E minor; G major; G minor. Nun komm der Heiden Heiland. **Greta de Reyghere, Jill Feldman** (sops); **James Bowman** (alto); **Guy de Mey, Ian Honeyman** (tens); **Max van Egmond** (bass); **Bernard Foccroulle** (org); **Ricercar Consort.** Ricercar RIC048035/7 (1/90).

Organ Works — Praeludia: E minor No. 1; E minor, No. 2; G major; G minor. Nun komm, der Heiden Heiland. *Coupled with* **Buxtehude.** Auf meinen lieben Gott, BuxWV179; Gott der Vater wohn uns bei, BuxWV190; Nun komm, der Heiden Heiland, BuxWV211; Nimm von uns, herr du treuer Gott, BuxWV207; Puer natus in Bethlehem, BuxWV217; Von Gott will ich nicht lassen, BuxWV220/1 **Piet Kee** (org). Chandos Chaconne CHAN0539 (10/93).

Antoine Brumel

French c.1460-c.1515

Brumel. Missa "Et ecce terrae motus". Lamentations. Magnificat Secundi toni. **The Tallis Scholars/Peter Phillips.** Gimell CDGIM026. Texts and translations included.

lh 13m   DDD   9/92

Antoine Brumel was one of the French members of the great Franco-Flemish school of composers which flourished during the fifteenth and sixteenth centuries. His 12-part *Earthquake Mass* is one of the most glorious, if little-known products of this school — a work of colossal power whose rhythmic complexities and virtuoso vocal writing are exceptionally demanding. It is a great tribute to the excellent Tallis Scholars and their fine conductor Peter Phillips that their performance of this masterpiece leaves nothing to be desired. The choir enters fully into the spirit of this visionary work — balancing vocal ecstasy with musical discipline in equal parts. The recording was made in the warm but clear acoustic of the parish church of Salle in Norfolk, an ideal setting for music of this period. The most sympathetic recorded sound captures perfectly the atmosphere of this location. Two more restrained works by Brumel, a set of *Lamentations* and a *Magnificat*, complete a disc of great interest. The comparison of the *Earthquake Mass* with another work of great complexity, Thomas Tallis's 40-part motet *Spem in alium*, is unavoidable. For those who enjoy the grandeur of such choral music performed in a completely authentic style this disc can be strongly recommended.

Additional recommendation:
Missa "Et ecce terrae motus". Dies irae. **Huelgas Ensemble/Paul van Nevel.** Sony Classical Vivarte SK46348 — lh 7m DDD 5/91

New review
Brumel. Missa "Berzerette savoyenne". Laudate Dominum de caelis. Sicut lilium inter spinas. Heth: Cogitavit Dominus. Lauda Sion Salvatorem.
Josquin Desprez. Bergerette savoyenne. **Chanticleer.** Chanticleer Records CR-8805. Texts and translations included.

lh 13m DDD 7/94

Avid listeners to Renaissance music who know Brumel's glorious Mass *Et ecce terrae motus* (reviewed above), should be drawn to take an interest in this anthology of some of his other sacred works. Brumel, like many other composers around 1500, has been overshadowed by that of Josquin. The more one hears of that generation the more one is convinced that it was a true golden age of polyphony with a range of composers who can fully match the High Renaissance painters and architects of those years. But such a view is hard to reach from the printed page alone: until more of this music is available in decent recordings its artistic richness will remain hidden. To listen to this issue is yet another experience of astonishment at the sheer quality of the music. Brumel's Mass *Berzerette savoyenne* is a lucid and gripping work. It is difficult to understand how it was possible for a composer to have based a Mass on a piece like Josquin's shepherdess-seduction song; but Brumel certainly hides nothing. In the *Kyrie* the melody is clearly presented in the top line; later it is in the tenor, but always unmistakably audible, despite the range of crystalline motivic devices that surround it in the other voices. Each movement contains an apparently inexhaustible repertory of new ideas; and the final *Agnus Dei* has a series of almost unbelievable repetitions (in the old days one would suspect that the needle had got stuck in a groove), which bring this unusually witty work to a surprising close. As a piece of devotional music, it raises questions; but as pure music it is wonderfully satisfying. The men of Chanticleer manage to keep exactly the right balance of serenity and lightness of touch in the Mass: they succeed marvellously (which is not the case in their rough opening performance of the Josquin chanson). Of the motets, the tiny *Sicut lilium* and the thick-textured *Heth: Cogitavit*

Dominus sound particularly good. Hearing this record will open your ears to a new dimension of Renaissance music.

Gavin Bryars

New review

Bryars. Jesus' Blood never failed me yet. **Tom Waits** (sngr); **Hampton Quartet** (Regis Inadiorio, Richard Henrickson, vns; Richard Maximoff, va; John Reed, vc); **chorus; orchestra/Michael Riesman.** Point Music 438 823-2PTH.

Ih 15m DDD 10/93

Jesus' Blood never failed me yet is built on the idea of untainted religious conviction: the fragile, trusting voice of a tramp, recorded solo then converted into a tape-loop and treated to a seamless, slowly evolving harmonic accompaniment. The first phase of the work's evolution climaxed in a recording made for Brian Eno's Obscure label back in 1975, but *Jesus' Blood never failed me yet* didn't really appeal beyond a relatively small band of initiates. It has taken CD, superior media coverage and the now widely accepted, variously 'minimalist' musical languages of Philip Glass (the current recording's executive producer), Reich, even Górecki, to pave the way for a wider acceptance of Bryars's masterpiece. For the first 25 minutes of the re-make, Bryars keeps his design very much as it was: the old man alone, backed first by a quietly supportive string quintet, then by winds, brass and pizzicato guitar. However, we're *en route* not for 25, but nearly 75 minutes of continuous music, and the succeeding sections greatly expand on the relatively modest textures of Bryars's original, and the real difference between the old and the new reveals itself in the last 21 or so minutes of the revision, where the grainy voice of Tom Waits casually enters into a posthumous duet (the tramp had died years before), the folksy 'pro' set alongside the tramp's private, restrained musings. Ultimately, Waits is the only voice that survives. As the work gradually draws towards its high-reaching, ethereal close and Waits himself wanders into the aural distance, an idea suddenly dawns: the old man may have died, but his faith lives on. The effect is ultimately poignant, a fitting conclusion to a beautiful work, minimalist in its basic musical language, but universal in its message and impact.

Further listening ...

Prologue. String Quartet No. 1, "Between the National and the Bristol". First Viennese Dance. Epilogue. **Pascal Pongy** (hn); **Charles Fullbrook, Gavin Bryars** (perc); **Arditti Quartet.** ECM New Series 8829 484-2 (3/87).

Incipit Vita Nova[a]. Glorious Hill[b]. Four Elements[c]. Sub Rosa[d]. [a]**Hilliard Ensemble;** [a]**Annemarie Dreyer** (vn); [a]**Ulrike Lachner** (va); [a]**Rebecca Firth** (vc); [c]**Chamber Ensemble;** [d]**Gavin Bryars Ensemble.** ECM New Series 445 351-2 (5/94).

Norbert Burgmüller

Symphony No. 2 in D major. *Coupled with* **Schumann.** Symphony No. 4 in D minor, Op. 120. **Berlin Radio Symphony Orchestra/Georg Schmöhe.** Koch Schwann Musica Mundi 311010 (11/89).

Geoffrey Burgon

Suggested listening ...

Magnificat. Nunc dimittis. Two hymns to Mary. This world from. But have been found again. Short Mass. At the round earth's imagined corners. A prayer to the Trinity. Laudate Dominum.

Michael Laird (tpt); **Jeremy Suter** (org); **Chichester Cathedral Choir/Alan Thurlow.**
Hyperion CDA66123 (9/84).

Television Scores — Brideshead Revisited; Testament of Youth; Bleak House; Tinker, Tailor,
Soldier, Spy[a]; The Chronicles of Narnia. [a]**Lesley Garrett** (sop); **Philharmonia Orchestra/
Geoffrey Burgon.** Silva Screen FILMCD117 (5/93).

Ferruccio Busoni

Italian/German 1866-1924

New review

Busoni. Piano Concerto, Op. 39. **Garrick Ohlsson** (pf); Men's voices of the **Cleveland
Orchestra Chorus; Cleveland Orchestra/Christoph von Dohnányi.** Telarc CD80207.
Recorded in 1989.

1h 12m DDD 4/90

Busoni's Concerto is a thundering vehicle for virtuosity and one doubts while listening to this
whether the concerto has ever been played so outstandingly, from the conductor and his players
as well as the soloist. The second scherzo is so infectiously exciting that one feels tempted to
cheat and play it all over again before proceeding to the finale, and the enormous central
movement has a formidable sense of scale and pacing, to which Ohlsson's sonorous pianism is a
bonus as well as a contributing factor. The orchestral sound is outstandingly beautiful and
transparent and the piano (Ohlsson uses a Bösendorfer) produces crags of grandiose tone
without ever seeming to approach its limit or giving any impression that the engineers have
helped it.

New review

Busoni. ORCHESTRAL WORKS. [a]**Jean-Claude Gérard** (fl); [b]**Ulf Rodenhäuser** (cl);
Berlin Radio Symphony Orchestra/Gerd Albrecht. Capriccio 10 479.
Turandot — Suite, Op. 41. Nocturne symphonique, Op. 43. Rondo arlecchinesco, Op. 46.
Divertimento for Flute and Orchestra, Op. 52[a]. Two Studies from "Doktor Faust", Op. 51.
Concertino for Clarinet and Small Orchestra, Op. 48[b]. Tanzwalzer, Op. 53.

1h 16m DDD 6/94

Here is a good cross-section of orchestral and *concertante* works displaying the various styles and
techniques that Busoni adopted in the latter part of his life. Gerd Albrecht is an ideal interpreter
with a highly instinctive feel for Busoni's uniquely personal sound-world. A prime example is
the *Nocturne symphonique* (one of the composer's many studies for *Doktor Faust*) where he
admirably succeeds in conveying the eerie, amorphous atmosphere of this strange orchestral
study, and this is also true of the other *Faust* Studies, "Sarabande" and "Cortège". The two
concertante works — the *Divertimento* for flute and orchestra and the *Concertino* for clarinet and
small orchestra — reveal Busoni the neo-classicist (though the 'darker' Busoni is never far below
the surface). The enigmatic *Tanzwalzer* (Busoni's homage to Johann Strauss II), with its strange
and disquieting Mahlerian overtones, brings to a conclusion an exceptionally authoritative and
well-recorded disc.

Additional recommendation ...
Concertino for Clarinet and Small Orchestra. **Copland.** *Concerto for Clarinet and String Orchestra with
Harp and Piano.* **Mozart.** *Clarinet Concerto in A major, K622.* **Paul Meyer** (cl); **English
Chamber Orchestra/David Zinman.** Denon CO-75289 (*see review under Copland; refer to the
Index to Reviews*) — 56m DDD 11/93

New review

Busoni. Turandot – Suite, Op. 41.
Casella. Paganiniana, Op. 65.
Martucci. Nocturne in G flat major, Op. 70 No. 1. Novelletta, Op. 82 No. 2. Giga, Op. 61

No. 3. **La Scala Philharmonic Orchestra, Milan/Riccardo Muti.** Sony Classical SK53280. Recorded in 1992.

⠿ **59m DDD 4/94** ⓠℙ

Riccardo Muti takes time out here to present some of the lesser known, rarely heard orchestral scores of his fellow countrymen, and a superbly played, enjoyable concert it is too. Proceedings commence with a fine and spirited performance of Alfredo Casella's divertimento *Paganiniana* – not a great piece by any means but a work possessing plenty of charm and humour nevertheless; the outer movements are a bit of a romp (very *opera buffa*) and must have been as much fun to write as they clearly are for the La Scala Philharmonic to play. The tone and temperature rise a few degrees in Martucci's gorgeously lyrical *Nocturne*, Op. 70 No. 1 – a sort of Mahler-meets-Puccini-meets-Respighi love song – and this is nicely contrasted with the affable if somewhat lightweight musings of his *Novelletta* and *Giga*. The high point of the disc, though, must surely be Muti's account of Busoni's *Turandot* Suite, Op. 41, the work that, after several tinkerings, finally ended up forming the basis of his 1917 opera. The recording is exceptionally clear and well focused, if at times a little dry.

Busoni. Fantasia contrappuntistica[a]. Fantasia nach J. S. Bach[a]. Toccata[b]. **John Ogdon** (pf). Continuum CCD1006. Items marked [a] from Altarus AIR-2-9074 (10/88), [b] new to UK.

⠿ **1h AAD 7/89** ⓠₛ ⑦

Busoni's *Fantasia contrappuntistica* is of legendary difficulty, density and length and pianists seem very reluctant to learn it. Ogdon plays it with consummate virtuosity, clarity and sustained concentration, and alongside the technical assurance there is a firm intellectual grasp of Busoni's prodigious structure and a lofty eloquence in expressing his faith. It is a formidable feat of musicianship as well as pianism. The two other pieces are more personal; many may find them even more moving. The *Fantasia nach J.S. Bach* is freer in structure than the *Fantasia contrap-puntistica* and with its dedication to his father's memory it is as though Busoni has chosen particularly beloved and appropriate pages for his tribute, adding his own meditations on them. The very late *Toccata* is a resurgence of the Faustian vein that runs throughout Busoni's work, but now dark and pessimistic. The three works add up to a sort of triple self-portrait and Ogdon characterizes them finely. Busoni's piano-writing demands a huge range of sonority as well as endurance and sheer dexterity; in these performances (and this superb recording) Busoni's piano is rendered full-size.

New review

Busoni. ARLECCHINO. **Ernst Theo Richter** (bar) Arlecchino; **Susanne Mentzer** (mez) Colombina; **Thomas Mohr** (bar) Ser Matteo del Sarto; **Wolfgang Holzmair** (bar) Abbate Cospicuo; **Philippe Huttenlocher** (bar) Dottor Bombasto; **Stefan Dahlberg** (ten) Leandro. TURANDOT. **Mechtild Gessendorf** (sop) Turandot; **Stefan Dahlberg** (ten) Kalaf; **Franz-Josef Selig** (bass) Altoum; **Gabriele Sima** (sop) Adelma; **Falk Struckmann** (bar) Barak; **Anne-Marie Rodde** (sop) Queen Mother; **Markus Schäfer** (ten) Truffaldino; **Michael Kraus** (ten) Pantalone; **Wolfgang Holzmair** (bar) Tartaglia; **Chorus and Orchestra of the Opéra de Lyon/Kent Nagano.** Virgin Classics VCD7 59313-2 Notes, texts and translations included. Recorded 1991-92.

⠿ ② **2h 17m DDD 11/93** ⓠℙ ⓠₛ

Arlecchino and *Turandot* were intended as an evening's double-bill. Musically *Arlecchino* is by far the superior and evenly inspired of the two. It also demands a good deal more from the listener both musically and intellectually. Though superficially a simple and straightforward tale of the rakish exploits of the hero/rogue Arlecchino, the opera contains a good deal of philosophical debate on the human condition — particularly the less attractive side of human nature. An interesting feature of the opera is the purely spoken role of Arlecchino, which serves the two-fold purpose of creating a bridge between audience and action as well as emphasizing his vital, disruptive force over the other characters. The opera must surely take its place as a major landmark in Busoni's output. Musically (and indeed philosophically) there is much that foreshadows his crowning achievement — begun around the same time but unfinished at his death in 1924 — *Doktor Faust*. One could not wish for a finer, more persuasive modern recording. Ernst Theo Richter's spoken Arlecchino is outstanding — a performance of irresistible magnetism — and Thomas Mohr provides a fine account of the much put upon Matteo, but the opera is strongly cast throughout, and the orchestral playing from the Lyon Opéra Orchestra is quite superb, with Kent Nagano displaying his skill at finding the perfect dramatic pace whilst eliciting exceptionally elegant performances from his players. *Turandot* contains a good deal of fine music. As a representation of Carlo Gozzi's original fable however, it is much more faithful (and closer in spirit) than Puccini's masterpiece. The Capriccio recording (listed below) has much to commend it though Linda Plech's interpretation of the title-role is a little weak beside Mechthild Gessendorf's magnificent performance for Virgin. The Berlin Radio Symphony Orchestra respond with some stunningly inspired playing for Albrecht but Nagano's players are not far behind in their involvement and commitment to the score. The Virgin recording, as in *Arlecchino*, is well balanced and spacious and the set is crowned with an informative and lavish booklet.

Additional recommendation ...
Turandot. **Soloists; Berlin RIAS Chamber Choir; Berlin Radio Symphony Orchestra/ Gerd Albrecht.** Capriccio 60 039 — ⠠⠄ lh 14m DDD 11/93

Further listening ...

Violin Concerto in D major, Op. 35*a*[a]. Violin Sonata No. 2 in E minor, Op. 36*a*[b]. [ab]**Joseph Szigeti** (vn); [b]**Mieczyslaw Horszowski** (pf); [a]**Little Orchestra Society/Thomas Scherman.** Sony Classical mono SK52537 (5/93).

Violin Sonatas — No. 1 in E minor, Op. 29; No. 2 in E minor, Op. 36*a*. **Lydia Mordkovitch** (vn); **Victoria Postnikova** (pf). Chandos CHAN8868.

DOKTOR FAUST. **Soloists; Bavarian Radio Chorus and Symphony Orchestra/ Ferdinand Leitner.** DG 20th Century Classics 427 413-2GC3 (8/89).

Sylvano Bussotti
Italian 1931-

The Rara Requiem[a]. Bergkristall. Lorenzaccio Symphony[b]. [a]**Soloists; Chorus of the Saabrücken Conservatory; Saabrücken Radio Symphony Orchestra/Gianpiero Taverna;** [b]**North German Radio Symphony Orchestra/Guiseppe Sinopoli.** DG 437 739-2GC.

George Butterworth
British 1885-1916

New review
Butterworth. A Shropshire Lad. Two English Idylls. The banks of green willow. **Coleridge-Taylor.** Ballade in A minor, Op. 33. Symphonic Variations on an African Air, Op. 63.
MacCunn. The land of the mountain and the flood, Op. 3. **Royal Liverpool Philharmonic Orchestra/Grant Llewellyn.** Argo 436 401-2ZH.

⠠⠄ lh 8m DDD 6/93

Grant Llewellyn's Butterworth is a model of sensitivity and poise and how tellingly he manages to convey the vulnerable poignancy behind this engaging music. The misty introduction to *A Shropshire Lad* is beautifully evocative, with scrupulously observed dynamics whilst the central portion brings just the right amount of pulse-quickening passion. Samuel Coleridge-Taylor completed his *Ballade* in 1898, the same year as the first scene of his once widely popular cantata *The Song of Hiawatha*. It's an enjoyable essay, full of effective orchestral bluster, but in no way distinctive — only the touchingly sweet secondary melody lingers in the memory. The *Symphonic Variations on an African Air* of 1906, on the other hand, show far greater imaginative scope. The African air in question is the resonant black spiritual *I'm troubled in mind*, and Argo's booklet-annotator rightly cites Delius's *Appalachia* as a kindred creation. Under Llewellyn, Hamish MacCunn's delightful Victorian concert overture, *The land of the mountain and the flood*, also receives crisp yet affectionate treatment, its 'big' tune most stirringly attended to. Argo's production is vivid and well-lit. A lovely collection.

Dietrich Buxtehude

Danish 1637-1707

Buxtehude. ORGAN WORKS. **Ton Koopman.** Novalis 150 048-2. Played on the Arp-Schnitger organ of St Ludgeri's, Norden.
Prelude and Ciacona in C major, BuxWV137. Eine feste Burg ist unser Gott, BuxWV184. Passacaglia in D minor, BuxWV161. Nun komm, der Heiden Heiland, BuxWV211. In dulci jubilo, BuxWV197. Fuga in C major, BuxWV174. Puer natus in Bethlehem, BuxWV217. Prelude in D major, BuxWV139. Nun lob, mein Seel, den Herren, BuxWV212. Prelude in G minor, BuxWV163. Wie schön leuchtet der Moregenstern, BuxWV223. Prelude in G minor, BuxWV149.

57m DDD 6/90

A most welcome by-product of the CD revolution has been the generous exposure given to those composers whose music, if not their names, has been familiar only to those with specialized interest. For readers of potted histories of music Buxtehude will be known primarily as the man whose organ playing was considered sufficiently impressive for the young J.S. Bach to walk 400 miles to hear. But as for his music, even organists are largely unaware of the vast amount he wrote for that instrument. Yet there are those who would claim that, had it not been for the towering genius of Bach, Buxtehude would today be considered as one of the 'great' composers of the baroque age. Those of an inquisitive disposition who would like a representative cross-section of Buxtehude's organ music on a single disc will find this one ideal. From the big, flamboyant, virtuoso works (such as the Prelude in G minor) to the delightful miniatures which had a particularly strong influence on the young Bach (including a frivolous Gigue Fugue) here is Buxtehude on top form. Ton Koopman gives them all sturdy, no-nonsense performances on a full-blooded, earthy instrument dating from Buxtehude's time, and the recording has great presence.

Further listening ...

Trio Sonatas — C major, BuxWV266; G major, BuxWV271; B flat major, BuxWV273. *Coupled with* **Pachelbel.** Suite in G major. Musicalische Ergotzung — Suite No. 4 in E minor. Aria con variazoni in A major. Canon and Gigue in D major. **Cologne Musica Antiqua/Reinhard Goebel.** Archiv Produktion Galleria 427 118-2AGA (6/89).

Organ Works — Ach Gott und Herr, BuxWV177. Ach Herr mich armen Sünder, BuxWV178. Canzona in C major, BuxWV166. Canzonetta in C major, BuxWV167. Canzonetta in D minor, BuxWV168. Canzonetta in E minor, BuxWV168. Ciacona in C minor, BuxWV159. Jesus Christus, unser Heiland, BuxWV198. Komm, heiliiger Geist, Herre Gott, BuxWV199. Komm heiliger Geist, Herre Gott, BuxWV200. Prelude and Fugue in F major, BuxWV144. Prelude and Fugue in F major, BuxWV145. Prelude and Fugue in F sharp minor, BuxWV146. Prelude and Fugue in G minor, BuxWV150. Te Deum laudamus, Phrygian, BuxWV218. **Michel Chapuis** (org). Auvidis Valois V4431 (12/89).

Cantatas — Herr, ich lasse dich nicht, BuxWV36. Wo ist doch mei Freund geblieben, "Dialogus inter Christum et fidelium animam", BuxWV111. Nichts soll uns scheiden, BuxWV77. Ich halte es dafür, BuxWV48. Ich suchte des Nachtes, BuxWV50. Das neugeborne Kinderleine, BuxWV13. **Greta de Reyghere, Agnès Mellon** (sops); **Henri Ledroit** (alto); **Guy de Mey** (ten); **Max van Egmond** (bass); **Ricercar Consort.** Ricercar RIC041016 (1/90).

William Byrd

British 1543-1623

New review

Byrd. My Ladye Nevells Booke. **Christopher Hogwood** (hpd/virg/org). L'Oiseau-Lyre 430 484-2OM3. From D29D4 (1/77). Recorded 1974-75.

 ③ 3h 12m ADD 11/93

This set contains the 42 keyboard pieces — ranging from variation sets to pavans and galliards, and from contrapuntal fantasias to the descriptive sequence *The Battell* — which Byrd selected for a beautifully copied manuscript collection in 1591. At the time he recorded it, Hogwood was still better known as a harpsichordist than as a conductor, and his performances here, though rarely spectacular, remind us that he was a sensitive interpreter with a sound basic touch. The fast passages all come off well, and Hogwood draws consistently pleasing tone from his four instruments (all modern copies): a mellow, deep-toned virginal; two harpsichords, one bright and resonantly Flemish, the other spikily Italian; and a rather straightforward-sounding chamber organ. This is a welcome project that seems unlikely to be repeated for quite a while, if ever.

Byrd. Mass for five voices. Mass for four voices. Mass for three voices. Motet — Ave verum corpus a 4. **The Tallis Scholars/Peter Phillips.** Gimell CDGIM345. From BYRD345 (5/84).

 1h 7m DDD 3/86 ⓠs Ⓑ

Byrd was a fervently committed Roman Catholic and he helped enormously to enrich the music of the English Church. His Mass settings were made for the many recusant Catholic worshippers who held services in private. They were published between 1593 and 1595 and are creations of great feeling. The contrapuntal writing has a much closer texture and fibre than the Masses of Palestrina and there is an austerity and rigour that is allowed to blossom and expand with the text. The beautifully restrained and mellow recording, made in Merton College Chapel, Oxford, fully captures the measure of the music and restores the awe and mystery of music that familiarity has sometimes dimmed.

Additional recommendations ...

Masses. **Winchester Cathedral Choir/David Hill.** Argo 430 164-2ZH — 1h 6m DDD 12/90 Ⓑ

Mass for five voices. Mass Propers for the Feast of All Saints. Motets. **Christ Church Cathedral Choir, Oxford/Stephen Darlington** Nimbus NI5237 — 52m DDD 12/90 Ⓑ

Masses. Anglican Music — The Great Service. O Lord, make thy servant. O God, the proud are risen against me. Sing joyfully unto God our strength. **The Tallis Scholars/Peter Phillips.** Gimell CDGIM343/4 — ② 2h 12m DDD 7/93 ⓠs Ⓑ

Mass for five voices. Mass for four voices. Infelix ego. **Oxford Camerata/Jeremy Summerly.** Naxos 8 550574 — 1h 5m DDD 7/93 Ⓑ

Byrd. GRADUALIA — THE MARIAN MASSES. **William Byrd Choir/Gavin Turner.** Hyperion CDA66451. Texts and translations included. Recorded in 1990.
Mass Propers — Feasts of the Purification of the BVM, the Nativity of the BVM, the Annunciation of the BVM, the Assumption of the BVM; Votive Masses of the BVM: Advent, Christmas to the Purification, Purification to Easter, Easter to Pentecost and Pentecost to Advent.

 1h 20m DDD 11/91

For sheer productivity and versatility William Byrd is unrivalled among Tudor composers, and much of his impressive output is still poorly represented in the catalogue. This useful recording explores one of those shadowy corners: *Gradualia*, the cycle of motets Byrd composed for English Roman Catholics to sing in their clandestine services. He began the project soon after writing the three Masses (which date from the mid 1590s), and took ten years to bring it to completion. Like so much of Byrd's late music, the *Gradualia* motets are compact and economical in expression: miniature masterpieces that glow with the warmth of the composer's personal religious convictions, and miraculously balance exquisite musical design with the most intelligent word-setting. Their chamber-music scale is nicely captured in these performances by the William Byrd Choir, headed by a superb team of five solo voices.

Everything on the disc belongs to feasts of the Blessed Virgin, many of which share texts with one another. Byrd economized by setting each text once only, and to play them in their correct liturgical order the various tracks of the CD have to be pre-selected. This is great fun to do; but the disc also makes perfectly satisfying listening when played straight through from start to finish.

Further listening ...

Keyboard Works: Fantasias — No. 2 in C major; No. 2 in G major. Pavans and Galliards — No. 2 in F major, "Ph. Tregian"; No. 2 in G major; No. 3 in G minor. The Carman's Whistle; The Woods so Wild; Walsingham; All in a garden green. The Queen's Alman. The Bells. Ut re mi fa sol la. La volta — No. 1 in G major. **Ursula Duetschler** (hpd). Claves CD50-9001 (10/90).

Keyboard Works: My Lady Nevell's Ground. O mistress mine I must. John must come kiss me now. Passamezzo Pavan and Galliard. The Carman's Whistle. Walsingham. Hugh Ashton's Ground. Fortune my foe. Sellinger's Round. **Elaine Thornburgh** (hpd). Koch International Classics 37057-2 (4/92).

The Great Service: Morning Service — Venite; Te Deum; Benedictus; Creed. Evening Service — Magnificat; Nunc dimittis. Anthems — O God, the proud are risen against me; O Lord make thy servants. Sing joyfully unto God our strength. **The Tallis Scholars/Peter Phillips.** Gimell CDGIM011 (6/87).

Motets: In resurrectione tua. Aspice Domine de sede. Vide Domine afflictionem. Domine tu iurasti. Vigilate. Domine secundum multitudinem. Tristitia et anxietas. Ne irascaris Domine. O quam gloriosum. **New College Choir, Oxford/Edward Higginbottom.** CRD CRD3420 (12/91).

John Cage

American 1912-1992

New review

Cage. CHAMBER WORKS. **The Barton Workshop.** Etcetera KTC3002. Recorded in 1992. Concert for Piano and Orchestra. Atlas eclipticalis. Hymnkus. Solos for Voice — Nos. 22 and 79. Imitations II. Music for six. Sonata for Clarinet. Five. Totem ancestor. A Valentine out of Season. Sonata for Two Voices. Seven².

③ 3h 3lm DDD 12/93 ❓

A bumper load of Cage on three 70-minute CDs from the enterprising Etcetera label. The Barton Workshop, founded in 1989 and led by James Fulkerson, is an international group specializing in experimental music. The first CD starts with *Atlas eclipticalis*. This is of chamber-orchestra proportions and shares starry characteristics with other performances on a different scale. The *Concert for Piano and Orchestra*, by comparison, is a comedy with swirling *glissandos* and attacks of instrumental hiccups. The Sonata for solo clarinet (1933) ought to be a classic, like Stravinsky's *Three Pieces*. The prepared piano pieces, *Totem ancestor* and *A Valentine out of Season*, provide welcome contrast and are recognizably typical of Cage's rhythmic vitality in every bar. The novelties, and first recordings, are some of Cage's more recent works. *Five* (1988) — named after the number of players employed — is unexpectedly euphonious, sustained and beautiful. *Seven²* (1990) is more of a test at over 50 minutes. It consists of long ethereal silences out of which soft single notes are caressed into life. If a player has more than one note in succession, this is an event! The result, in these long pieces, is predictably static and at a meditational pace. All is well managed and recorded here. *Hymnkus* (1986) has the same qualities, punctuated with breathy sounds from (presumably) the flute. The whole set is not the most immediately accessible Cage. But it is a carefully assembled representation of almost 60 years of Cage's creative activity played with exemplary dedication born of understanding and sympathy.

New review

Cage. String Quartet in four parts. Music for four. **Arditti Quartet** (Irvine Arditti, David Alberman, vns; Levine Andrade, va; Rohan de Saram, vc). Mode Records mode27. Recorded in 1989.

50m DDD 12/93

Which is John Cage's catchiest tune? In the last movement of his String Quartet (1950), with the players using no vibrato throughout and a modal melodic line passed from instrument to instrument, the result has a distinctly medieval and cheerful sound. Cage said he was gifted with a sunny disposition! The work seems to arise naturally from Cage's involvement with the timeless disengagement of Zen Buddhism and the intimate objectivity of Erik Satie, especially his *Socrate*. But the result is entirely Cage and completely convincing, a classic in the quartet repertoire. When the performers are as dedicated and experienced as the Arditti, everything falls into place. Each of the four movements, reflecting the seasons, is based on a different texture, with the third one practically static: then the last one is an abrupt contrast. Contrast is not a feature of *Music for four* (1989). The pace is slow and meditational: the sounds almost consistently sustained. Part 1 and Part 2 are simply two different readings of the same material, with the players' parts exchanged. Everything sounds magical and is cleanly recorded.

Cage. Sonatas and Interludes for prepared piano. **Gérard Frémy** (prepared pf). Etcetera KTC2001. From ETC2001 (12/83).

1h 10m DDD 9/88

John Cage made two major discoveries when he invented the 'prepared piano' in 1946. The first was that to insert nuts, bolts, rubber wedges and bits of plastic between the strings of a piano does not make it sound hideously nasty but, if done with care and precision, turns it into an orchestra of delicately chiming, bright, fragile and gamelan-like sounds. The second discovery was that this 'new' instrument had to be treated with great subtlety. The result is the most mysteriously lucid score he has ever written, a sequence of quiet rituals and arabesque gestures, of silences in which hazes of resonance die away. Transparent textures and low dynamic levels predominate, but the work is by no means incidentless. There is a fairly clear progress from the briefer, quieter, more hesitant earlier Sonatas to the bigger and more dramatic gestures of Sonatas 9 to 12. To hear the Sonatas and Interludes complete and in sequence, at least once in a while, is a wonderfully ear-cleansing experience, a demonstration of how potent, beautiful and startlingly fresh the simplest of musical events can be. The discovery led Cage into an entranced contemplation of the sounds around us that we cannot accept as 'music', and these pieces raise questions about how we listen and how we hear that will not go away. Frémy's absorbed and absorbing performance has the composer's approval and the transparent clarity of the recording is ideal.

Further listening ...

Etudes Australes. **Grete Sultan** (pf). Wergo WER6152-2 (7/93).

Atlas eclipticalis. **Eberhard Blum** (fls). Hat Hut Now Series ARTCD6111 (12/93).

A flower[ad]. Mirakus[a]. Eight Whiskus[a]. The Wonderful Widow of Eighteen Springs[ad]. Nowth Upon Nacht[ad]. Sonnekus[f]. Forever and Sunsmell[ace]. Solo for Voice 49[a]. Solo for Voice 52[b]. Solo for Voice 67[a]. Music for Two (by One)[a]. **Joan La Barbara** ([a]voc/[b]perc); [c]**Scott Evans** (perc); **William Winant** ([d]pf/[e]perc); [f]**Leonard Stein** (pf). New Albion NA035CD (9/91).

The Perilous Night (1944)[a]. Four walls (1944)[b]. [b]**Joan La Barbara** (sop); **Margaret Leng Tan** ([a]prepared pf; [b]pf). New Albion NA037CD (1/91).

Etudes borealis. 26'1.1449". Concert for Piano and Orchestra — solo for cello. Variations — I-III. A Dip in the Lake. Lecture on nothing. **Frances-Marie Uitti** (vc, voice, various instruments). Etcetera KTC2016 (3/92).

Raffaele Calace

Italian 1863-1934

Suggested listening ...

Works for Mandolin — Danza Spagnola, Op. 105[a]. Mattino d'autunno, Op. 164[a]. Concerto a plettro, Op. 155[a]. Impressionismo, "Momento lirico", Op. 145[b]. Intermezzo, "Mesto pensiero", Op. 146[b]. Suite[b] — Pavana, Op. 54; Bolero, Op. 26; Mazurka, Op. 41; Tarantella, Op. 18. Impressioni Orientali, Op. 132[b]. [a]**Raffaele Calace Quintet;** [b]**Brescia Mandolin and Guitar Orchestra/Claudio Mandonico.** Fonè 91FO2 (12/93).

Antonio Caldara

Italian c.1670-1736

Suggested listening ...

Cantatas[a]: Medea in Corinto. Soffri, mio caro Alcino. D'improvviso. Vicino a un rivoletto. 12 Suonate da camera, Op. 2 — No. 3 in D major. 12 Suonate a 3, Op. 1 — No. 5 in E minor. [a]**Gérard Lesne** (alto); **Il Seminario Musicale.** Virgin Classics Veritas VC7 59058-2 (11/91).

Madrigals — Fra pioggie, nevi e gelo. Dell'uom la vita. Fugge di Lot a moglie. Vedi co'l crine sciolto. Là su morbide. De piacari. *Cantatas* — Lungi dall'idol mio. Il Dario. La forriera del giorno. Stella ria. Il Gelsomino. **Wren Baroque Soloists/Martin Elliott.** Unicorn-Kanchana DKPCD9130 (2/93).

Thomas Campion

British 1567-1620

Suggested listening ...

Ayres—Beauty, since you so much desire. Love me or not. Your faire lookes. Never love unlesse you can. O never to be moved. The sypres curten of the night is spread. Awake thou spring of speaking grace. Come you pretty false-ey'd wanton. So tyr'd are all my thoughts. Fire, fire. Pin'd I am and like to dye. Author of light. See where she flies. Faire if you expect admiring. Shall I come sweet love to thee? It fell on a sommers daie. Kinde are her answers. Beauty is but a painted hell. Sweet exclude me not. Are you what your faire lookes expresse? I care not for these ladies. Never weather-beaten saile. **Drew Minter** (alto); **Paul O'Dette** (lte). Harmonia Mundi HMU90 7023 (6/91).

André Campra

French 1660-1744

Campra. IDOMENEE. **Bernard Deletré** (bass) Idoménée; **Sandrine Piau** (sop) Electre; **Monique Zanetti** (sop) Ilione; **Jean-Paul Fouchécourt** (bass) Idamante; **Marie Boyer** (mez) Venus; **Jérôme Correas** (bass) Eole, Neptune, Jealousy, Nemesis; **Richard Dugay** (ten) Arcas; **Jean-Claude Sarragosse** (bass) Arbas, Protée; **Mary Saint-Palais** (sop) Cretan Girl; **Anne Pichard** (sop) First Shepherd; **Anne Mopin** (sop) Second Shepherd, Trojan Girl; **Les Arts Florissants Chorus and Orchestra/William Christie.** Harmonia Mundi HMC90 1396/8. Notes, text and translation included. Recorded in 1991.

③ 2h 46m DDD 9/92

André Campra was one of the leading lights on the French musical scene between Lully's death in 1687 and Rameau's operatic début in 1733. He was a pioneer of opéra-ballet and wrote a significant corpus of sacred music and several successful *tragédies en musiques*. One of these was *Idoménée* which was first staged in 1712 and revived in 1731 in a reworked version. This later version has been chosen by William Christie for his recording. Campra's librettist was Antoine Danchet whose text was later to serve as a prime source for Mozart's *opera seria, Idomeneo*. Campra's score is an attractive one with few weak moments and the same may be said of Danchet's adaptation of Crébillon's contemporaneous play of the same name. Campra shows much skill in his writing for the human voice and a greater degree of sympathy, perhaps, than some of his fellow French composers. There are passages of finely sustained dialogue, notably between Idoménée and his son Idamante (Act 2, Scene 4), and Idoménée and Priam's daughter, Ilione. The instrumental writing, which plays a prominent part in the texture throughout the opera is also very effective; Act 3, for instance, contains a captivating sailors' dance for piccolos, drums and strings. Here is an opera which quickly proves itself deserving of the loving attention paid it by Christie and Les Arts Florissants. Supple choruses, colourful divertissements and a profusion of beguiling airs sung by a strong cast of soloists set the seal on a fine issue.

Further listening ...

Messe de Requiem. **Elisabeth Baudry, Monique Zanetti** (sops); **Josep Benet** (alto); **John Elwes** (ten); **Stephen Varcoe** (bar); **La Chapelle Royale Chorus and Orchestra/ Philippe Herreweghe.** Harmonia Mundi HMC90 1251 (9/87).

TANCREDE. **Soloists; The Sixteen; Grande Ecurie et la Chambre du Roy/Jean-Claude Malgoire.** Erato Musifrance 2292-45001-2 (6/90).

Joseph Canteloube
French 1879-1957

Suggested listening ...

Chants d'Auvergne — La pastoura al camps. Baïlèro. L'ïo dè rotso; Ound' onorèn gorda? Obal, din lou limouzi. Pastourelle. L'Antouèno. La pastrouletta è lo chibaliè. La delaïssádo. N'aï pas iéu de mîo. Lo calhé. Lo fiolairé. Passo pel prat. Lou boussu. Brezairola. Malurous qu'o uno fenno. **Dame Kiri Te Kanawa** (sop); **English Chamber Orchestra/Jeffrey Tate.** Decca 410 004-2DH (7/83).

André Caplet
French 1878-1925

New review
Caplet. Le masque de la mort rouge[a].
Debussy (ed. Allende-Blin). La chute de la maison Usher[b].
Schmitt. Le palais hanté, Op. 49. [b]**Christine Barbaux** (sop); [b]**François Le Roux** (bar); [b]**Pierre-Yves Le Maigat** (bass-bar); [b]**Jean-Philippe Lafont** (bar); [a]**Frédérique Cambreling** (hp); **Monte-Carlo Philharmonic Orchestra/Georges Prêtre.** EMI L'Esprit Français CDM7 64687-2. From HMV EL270158-1 (4/85).

52m DDD 4/85

The Symphonic study based on *The Masque of the Red Death* by Debussy's great friend and helper, André Caplet is very striking and inventive. The virtuoso solo part is handled with assurance and sensitivity (and is very cleanly recorded), and the strings, though not always at ease in the very high register, successfully evoke the work's mysterious and febrile atmosphere: there is a heart-stopping moment when terrifying rappings precede the striking of midnight, enveloped in a haze of ghostly harmonies. In the Debussy Georges Prêtre is out to make our flesh creep. The prose and poetry of Edgar Allan Poe made a sensational impact on French writers and musicians. Debussy toyed for some 15 years with plans for two Poe operas. For *The fall of the house of Usher* he completed 21 pages in vocal score and left another 25 scattered pages of sketches. These were all collated and scored in perceptively Debussyan style by Juan Allende-Blin: the results exude a sombre dread. It is largely athematic save for Lady Madeline's offstage song and for the very opening of the Prelude, which is an echo from Debussy's string quartet. The song referred to, incidentally, is a setting of *The haunted palace*, the poem on which Schmitt's early (1905) study is based. Its language is more conventional, but its rich dark colouring, nervy rhythms and final brute strength make it worth reviving in this context. Altogether a valuable reissue, although unfortunately lacking the full texts which accompanied the original LP.

Further listening ...

Conte fantastique[a]. Two Divertissements[b]. Les prières[c]. Two Sonnets[d]. Septet[e]. [ce]**Sharon Coste,** [de]**Sandrine Piau** (sops); [e]**Sylvie Deguy** (mez); [abcd]**Laurence Cabel** (hp); [ace]**Musique Oblique Ensemble.** Harmonia Mundi HMC90 1417 (2/93).

Key to symbols

| Quality of sound | | Discs worth exploring | | | Caveat emptor |

Quality of performance   Basic library   Period performance

Manuel Cardoso
Portuguese 1566-1650

Suggested listening ...

Requiem. Non mortui. Sitivit anima mea. Mulier quae erat. Nos autem gloriari. Magnificat Secundi Toni a 5. **The Tallis Scholars/Peter Phillips.** Gimell CDGIM021 (10/90).

Giacomo Carissimi
Italian 1605-1674

Suggested listening ...

Oratorios — Jepthe; Judicium Salomonis; Jonas. **Gabrieli Consort and Players/Paul McCreesh** (bass vn). Meridian CDE84132 (7/87).

John Alden Carpenter
American 1876-1951

Suggested listening ...

Piano Sonata No. 1 in G minor. Diversions. Nocturne. Polonaise américaine. Impromptu. Tango américain. Minuet. Litle Dancer. Little Indian. Twilight Reverie. Danza. **Denver Oldham** (pf). New World NW328/9-2 (7/88).

Teresa Carreño
Venezuelan 1853-1917

Suggested listening ...

String Quartet in B minor[bc]. *Coupled with* **C. Schumann.** Piano Trio in G minor, Op. 17[a]. **Beach.** Piano Trio in A minor, Op. 150[a]. **Tailleferre.** Sonata for Violin and Piano No. 1[bd]. **Boulanger.** Pièces — Nocturne; Cortège[bd]. **Mendelssohn-Hensel.** Piano Trio in G minor,

Op. 11ª. *Chaminade.* Piano Trio No. 1 in G minor, Op. 11ª. ª**Macalester Trio;** ᵇ**Joseph Roche,** ᶜ**Robert Zelnick** (vns); ᶜ**Tamas Strasser** (va); ᶜ**Camilla Heller** (vc); ᵈ**Paul Freed** (pf). Vox Box 115845-2. *See review in the Collections section; refer to the Index to Reviews.*

Elliott Carter

American 1908-

Carter. Concerto for Orchestra. Three Occasions for Orchestra. Violin Concertoª. ª**Ole Böhn** (vn); **London Sinfonietta/Oliver Knussen.** Virgin Classics VC7 59271-2.

Ih 3m DDD 7/92

This disc is a first-class *recording*, the sound doing as much as is technically possible to ensure that the multiple, superimposed strata of Elliott Carter's characteristically complex textures are spaced and focused to make maximum aural sense. But there is also first-class music-making to be heard here. It would be an exaggeration to say that Oliver Knussen and the London Sinfonietta play Carter's *Concerto for orchestra* (1969) as effortlessly as if it were Mozart: but the effort it takes to get this music right, and to convey its full measure of exhilarating drama, has been transformed into a marvellously positive reading of the score. Comparison with Leonard Bernstein's LP recording of the *Concerto* with the New York Philharmonic Orchestra for CBS, first issued in 1973 (currently unavailable), gives graphic evidence of how far Carter interpretation has advanced in two decades. The more recent *Occasions for orchestra* are no less characterful: music of celebration and lament showing that the originality and intensity of Carter's vision have not faded as he moves into his eighties. The Violin Concerto (1990) may not be on the same high level of inspiration as the other works on this disc but it is still an absorbing demonstration of how to 'Carterize' the solo instrument's essential lyricism and capacity for fantasy, while ensuring that it remains bracingly at odds with the orchestra.

Further listening ...

Piano Concertoª. Variations for Orchestra. ª**Ursula Oppens** (pf); **Cincinnati Symphony Orchestra/Michael Gielen.** New World NW347-2 (4/87).

String Quartets. KTC1065: No. 1; No. 4. *KTC1066:* No. 2; No. 3. Elegy. **Arditti Quartet.** Etcetera KTC1065/6 (5/89).

Robert Carver

British c.1490-1550

Suggested listening ...

Missa Dum sacrum mysterium. O bone Jesu. Gaude flore virginali. **Cappella Nova/Alan Tavener.** ASV Gaudeamus CDGAU124 (10/91).

Missa L'Homme armé. Mass for Six Voices. **Cappella Nova/Alan Tavener.** ASV Gaudeamus CDGAU126 (10/91).

Missa Fera pessima. Missa Pater creator omnium. **Cappella Nova/Alan Tavener.** ASV Gaudeamus CDGAU127 (5/92).

Pablo Casals

Spanish 1876-1973

Suggested listening ...

Sacred Choral Music — Nigra sum. Tota pulchra es. Cançó a la verge. Rosari. O vos omnes. Eucaristica. Recordare, virgo mater. Oració a la verge de Montserrat. Salve regina. **Montserrat Escolania/Ireneu Segarra.** Koch-Schwann Musica Sacra 313062 (1/92).

Alfredo Casella

Italian 1883-1947

Suggested listening ...

Paganiniana, Op. 65. *Coupled with* **Busoni.** Turandot – Suite, Op. 41. **Martucci.** Nocturne in G flat major, Op. 70 No. 1. Novelletta, Op. 82 No. 2. Giga, Op. 61 No. 3. **La Scala Philharmonic Orchestra, Milan/Riccardo Muti.** Sony Classical SK53280 (4/94). *See review under Busoni; refer to the Index to Reviews.*

John Casken

British 1949-

Suggested listening ...

Cello Concerto. **Northern Sinfonia/Heinrich Schiff** (vc). Collins 20th Century Plus 2006-2 (6/93).

GOLEM. **Soloists; Music Projects London/Richard Bernas.** Virgin Classics VCD7 59028-2 (8/91).

Mario Castelnuovo-Tedesco

Italian/American 1895-1968

New review

Castelnuovo-Tedesco. Guitar Concerto No. 1 in D major, Op. 99.
Rodrigo. Concierto de Aranjuez.
Villa-Lobos. Guitar Concerto. **Norbert Kraft** (gtr); **Northern Chamber Orchestra/ Nicholas Ward.** Naxos 8 550729. Recorded in 1992.

Ih DDD 4/94

The time has long passed when it was possible to point to any one recording of any of these concertos (the Rodrigo in particular) as 'The Best'; as with players, one can only discern a 'top bracket' within which choice depends finally on personal preference — or allegiance to one's favourite performer, or indeed with the other works on the disc. Norbert Kraft's accounts of these concertos takes its place therein. In this recording Kraft is placed forwardly enough for every detail to be heard, but not to create an impression of artificiality. The Northern Chamber Orchestra plays with freshness and are alert to every detail and the beautifully clear recording catches it faithfully.

Additional recommendation ...

No. 1; No. 2 in C major, Op. 160. Concerto for Two Guitars, Op. 201. **Kazuhito Yamashita, Naoko Yamashita** (gtrs); **London Philharmonic Orchestra/Leonard Slatkin.** RCA Victor Red Seal RD60355 — Ih 8m DDD 12/90

Further listening ...

Violin Concerto No. 2, "I profeti". *Coupled with* **Ferguson.** Violin Sonata No. 1, Op. 2; **Françaix.** String Trio in C major; **K. Khachaturian.** Violin Sonata in G minor, Op. 1. **Jascha Heifetz** (vn); **Joseph de Pasquale** (va); **Gregor Piatigorsky** (vc); **Lilian Steuber** (pf); **Los Angeles Philharmonic Orchestra/Alfred Wallenstein.** RCA Victor Gold Seal GD87872 (9/90).

The Divan of Moses-ibn-Ezra, Op. 207[a]. Variazioni à travers les siècles, Op. 71. Tre Preludi Mediterranei, Op. 176. [a]**Roberta Alexander** (sop); **Dick Hoogeveen** (gtr). Etcetera KTC1150 (4/94).

Alfredo Catalani

Italian 1854-1893

Suggested listening ...

**LA WALLY. Soloists; Turin Lyric Chorus; Monte Carlo National Opera Orchestra/
Fausto Cleva.** Decca 425 417-2DM2 (2/90).

Emmanuel Chabrier

French 1841-1894

Chabrier. ORCHESTRAL WORKS.
Roussel. Suite in F major, Op. 33. **Detroit Symphony Orchestra/Paul Paray.** Mercury
434 303-2MM. Recorded 1957-60.
España. Suite pastorale. Joyeuse marche. Bourrée fantasque. Le Roi malgré lui — Fête
polonaise; Danse slave. Gwendoline — Overture.

.•ʻ Ih 8m ADD

An irresistible confection. Paray's classic Chabrier collection radiates a truly life-enhancing
spontaneity, an all-too-rare commodity in this day and age. His *España* has to be one of the
most twinklingly good-humoured ever committed to disc — an account overflowing with
rhythmic panache and unbuttoned exuberance — whilst the adorable *Suite pastorale* has rarely
sounded so fresh-faced and sheerly disarming, even though Paray's very swift "Sous bois" does
admittedly take some getting use to. Both the swaggering "Fête polonaise" and "Danse slave"
from *Le Roi malgré lui* are despatched with memorable theatrical charisma and huge gusto,
qualities which extend to a blistering rendition of the remarkable, almost feverish overture to
Gwendoline. But Paray reserves perhaps his finest achievement for the uproarious *Joyeuse marche*
and *Bourrée fantasque* (an astonishingly quick-witted, vital conception). Throughout, the Detroit
SO respond with irrepressible spirit and characteristic Gallic poise, and the Mercury
engineering continues to astonish in its intrepidly wide range of dynamic and full-blooded
brilliance (just sample those wonderfully hefty bass-drum thwacks towards the end of *España*).
All this and Roussel's bustling, neo-classical *Suite* too! An unmissable CD and make no
mistake.

Additional recommendation ...
España. Suite pastorale. **Dukas.** *L'apprenti sorcier. La péri.* **Ulster Orchestra/Yan Pascal
Tortelier.** Chandos CHAN8852 — .•ʻ 57m DDD 2/91 ⁹ₛ

Chabrier. Bourrée fantasque. Impromptu in C major. Dix pièces pittoresques. **Richard
McMahon** (pf). Pianissimo PP10792. From Oriana ONA0002 (9/84). Recorded in 1982.

.•ʻ 52m DDD 8/92

Gaiety and sentiment, allied to a certain formality, sit at the heart of Chabrier's charming and
largely neglected piano *oeuvre*. Various of the *Dix pièces pittoresques* are more familiar in their
orchestral guise, but they work even better as piano pieces: the celebrated "Idylle", with its
balletic staccato accompaniment and wistful melodic line, is on a par with late Brahms, while
the joyous "Scherzo-valse" trips around the corners of your memory long after it has left the
keys. Other notable movements include an atmospheric "Sous bois" and a consolatory,
somewhat Schumanesque Improvisation. But were one to single out a highlight on this
rewarding CD, it would unquestionably be the *Bourrée fantasque*, a miraculous six-minute tone-
poem, rich in contrasts and harbouring one of Chabrier's inimitable, long-breathed melodies. In
this instance, Felix Mottl's orchestration also has a special magic, but the original is just as
appealing in its own way. As with the "Scherzo-valse", Richard McMahon takes on the work
with manly resolve, yet remains sensitive to its poetry. Elsewhere, he negotiates the music's
myriad interpretative stumbling blocks (elegance is called for as well as considerable reserves of
virtuosity) with great facility, and his instrument is clearly, albeit rather dryly, recorded.
Anyone seeking a full understanding of late nineteenth-century French piano music will have to
hear this disc.

Further listening ...

L'ETOILE — *opéra bouffe*. **Soloists; Lyon Opera Chorus and Orchestra/John Eliot Gardiner.** EMI CDS7 47889-8 (8/88).

LE ROI MALGRE LUI — *opéra-comique*. **Soloists; French Radio Chorus; French Radio New Philharmonic Orchestra/Charles Dutoit.** Erato 2292-45792-2.

UNE EDUCATION MANQUEE — *operetta*. **Soloists;.orchestra/Charles Bruck.** LE ROI MALGRE LUI — Hélas, à l'esclavage. Chanson pour Jeanne. L'île heureuse. GWENDOLINE — Blonde aux yeux de pervenche. Ballade des gros dindons. Pastorale des cochons roses. **Christiane Castelli** (sop); **Hélène Boschi** (pf). Le Chant du Monde mono LDC278 1068 (8/92).

Jacques Champion de Chambonnières
French 1601-1672

Suggested listening ...

Harpsichord Suites[a] — C major; G major; A major; D major. *Coupled with d'Anglebert.* Tombeau de M. de Chambonnières. **Skip Sempé** (hpd) with [a]**Brian Feehan** (theorbo). Deutsche Harmonia Mundi 05472 77210-2 (4/93).

Cécile Chaminade
French 1857-1944

Suggested listening ...

Piano Trio No. 1 in G minor, Op. 11[a]. *Coupled with Carreño.* String Quartet in B minor[bc]. **C. Schumann.** Piano Trio in G minor, Op. 17[a]. **Beach.** Piano Trio in A minor, Op. 150[a]. **Tailleferre.** Sonata for Violin and Piano No. 1[bd]. **Boulanger.** Pièces — Nocturne; Cortège[bd]. **Mendelssohn-Hensel.** Piano Trio in G minor, Op. 11[a]. [a]**Macalester Trio;** [b]**Joseph Roche,** [c]**Robert Zelnick** (vns); [c]**Tamas Strasser** (va); [c]**Camilla Heller** (vc); [d]**Paul Freed** (pf). Vox Box 115845-2. *See review in the Collections section; refer to the Index to Reviews.*

Gustave Charpentier
French 1860-1956

Suggested listening ...

LOUISE. **Soloists; Ambrosian Opera Chorus; New Philharmonia Orchestra/Georges Prêtre.** Sony Classical S2K46429 (6/91).

Marc-Antoine Charpentier
French 1643-1704

Charpentier. SACRED CHORAL WORKS: Canticum ad Beatam Virginem Mariam. **Le Concert des Nations/Jordi Savall.** Astrée Auvidis E8713. Texts and translations included. Canticum in honorem Beatae Virginis Mariae inter homines et angelos, H400. Prélude a 3, H509. Pour la conception de la Vierge, H313. Nativité de la Vierge, H309. Prélude pour Salve regina a 3, H23a. Salve regina a 3, H23. Pour la fête de l'Epiphanie, H395. Prélude pour le

Magnificat a 4, H533. Magnificat a 4, H80. Stabat mater pour des religieuses, H15. Litanies de la vierge, H83.

Ih 15m   DDD   2/90

The music on this disc is a skilful compilation of disparate pieces by Charpentier all connected with Marian devotion. The two most extended works are the *Canticum in honorem Beatae Virginis Mariae* and the *Litanies de la vierge*; the first is intimate yet ardent in expression and takes the form of a dialogue between man and angels. Charpentier was a master of small-scale dramatic forms such as these and Jordi Savall brings passion and a lively sense of theatre to this one. The *Litanies* are more contemplative, sometimes profoundly so, but they are not without a quiet radiance and Savall convincingly explores their expressive vocabulary. Hardly less appealing is the beautiful *Stabat mater pour des religieuses*, written for soprano soloist with unison soprano chorus. Charpentier may well have composed it for the nuns of the convent of Port Royal, though Savall in fact uses male voices for the refrains retaining the soprano for the serene and ethereal solos. The remaining pieces are more modestly conceived but extremely effective in this thoughtfully constructed context. Savall creates a marvellous sense of occasion, bringing the music to life with Mediterranean verve. Lively continuo realizations, in which a theorbo plays a prominent part, are a constant delight as indeed is so much else in this captivating performance. Small vocal and instrumental insecurities matter little when interpretative skill is on such a level as this. Faithful and vibrant recorded sound set the seal on a distinguished project.

Charpentier. LE MALADE IMAGINAIRE. **Isabelle Poulenard, Jill Feldman** (sops); **Guillemette Laurens** (mez); **Gilles Ragon** (ten); **Michel Verschaeve, Bernard Deletré, Jean-Louis Bindi, Jean-Paul Fouchécourt** (basses); **Les Musiciens du Louvre/Marc Minkowski.** Erato MusiFrance 2292-45002-2. Notes, text and translation included. Recorded in 1988.

Ih 13m   DDD   6/90

Comédie-ballet was a dramatic form developed by Molière in which music played both an integral and incidental part. Lully was his earliest collaborator but, following a quarrel Molière turned to Charpentier to provide music. *Le malade imaginaire*, first performed in 1673, was the playwright's last *comédie-ballet* and the one to which Charpentier made his most substantial contribution. Here it is the medical profession which comes under Molière's merciless scrutiny with a hypochondriac, his deceitful wife and doctors who know everything about disease except the cure of it. This recording omits the spoken dialogue but includes almost all of Charpentier's music; and delightful it is, too, in its engaging variety of airs and dances. The orchestra is colourful, consisting of flutes, recorders, oboes and strings together with some surprising sounds in the third of three *intermèdes* which follow the prologue. Here, besides castanets, drums and tambourines, Charpentier calls for apothecary's mortars, once cast in a bell foundry and for this recording lent by a Paris antiquarian: such is the lure of authenticity these days! Marc Minkowski, Les Musiciens du Louvre and a strong ensemble of solo voices combine to give a refreshingly unbuttoned performance of the music, little of which has previously been available to record collectors. The recording is excellent.

Additional recommendation ...
Soloists; Les Arts Florissants Chorus and Orchestra/William Christie. Harmonia Mundi HMC90 1336 — .·*   Ih 19m DDD 4/91
Included with this CD is a complementary CD (41m) containing Charpentier's "'O' Anthems for Advent", H36-43; "In nativatem Domini nostri Jesus Christi canticum", H414; "Noëls dur les instruments", H534.

Charpentier. MEDEE. **Jill Feldman** (sop) Médée; **Gilles Ragon** (ten) Jason; **Agnès Mellon** (sop) Creuse; **Jacques Bona** (bass) Créon; **Sophie Boulin** (sop) Nérine; **Philippe Contor** (bass) Oronte; **Les Arts Florissants Chorus and Orchestra/William Christie.** Harmonia Mundi HMC90 1139/41. Notes, text and translation included. From HM1139/41 (11/84).

③   3h 2m   AAD   3/85

Médée is Charpentier's dramatic masterpiece in the conventional French baroque form of a prologue and five acts and was first performed in 1693. Thomas Corneille based his libretto on the story of the sorceress Medea as told by Euripides and the opera begins after the arrival of Jason and Medea at Corinth in the "Argo"; thus the adventure of the Golden Fleece has already taken place. Charpentier's music is well able to rise to the occasion and does so with chilling effect in the memorable witchcraft scenes of Act 3. Jill Feldman's Medea contains many layers of expressive subtlety and her command of French declamation is impressive. Agnès Mellon is affecting as the innocent and sincere Creuse and Gilles Ragon is an articulate and suitably complacent Jason. The chorus and orchestra of Les Arts Florissants have their rough patches but William Christie directs a thrilling performance of a work representing one of the finest achievements of French baroque musical drama. The recording was made in a lively and sympathetic acoustic but you will need a magnifying glass to read the libretto.

Further listening ...

Quatuor anni tempestatis, H335-8. *Psalms* — Quemadmodum desiderat cervus, H174. Nisi Dominus, H231. Notus in Judea, H179. **Françoise Semellaz, Noémi Rime** (sops); **Bernard Délétré** (bass); **Le Parlement de Musique/Martin Gester.** Opus 111 OPS30-9005 (9/91).

Magnificat pour le Port Royal, H81[abde]. Messe pour le Port Royal, H5[abcde]. O clementissime Domine Jesu, H256[abe]. Dixit Dominus pour le Port Royal[abdf]. Laudate Dominum pour le Port Royal, H227[abdf]. Stabat mater pour les religieuses, H15[bdf]. *Raison:* Pièces d'orgue[d]. [a]**Greta de Reyghere,** [b]**Isabelle Poulenard,** [b]**Jill Feldman** (sops); [c]**Ludwig van Gijsegem** (ten); [d]**Capella Ricercar/Jerome Léjeune** with [e]**Bernard Foccroulle,** [f]**Benoit Mernier** (orgs). Ricercar RIC052034 (1/89).

Office de ténèbres — Incipit oratio Jeremiae, H95. Leçons de ténèbres — Manum suam, H92; Ego vir videns, H93. Responsories — Eram quasi agnus, H116; O Juda, H119; O vos omnes, H134. Miserere, H157. **Le Parlement de Musique/Martin Gester** (org, hpd). Opus 111 OPS55-9119 (9/92).

ACTEON. **Dominique Visse** (alto) Actéon; **Agnès Mellon** (sop) Diane; **Guillemette Laurens** (mez) Junon; **Jill Feldman** (sop) Arthébuze; **Françoise Paut** (sop) Hyale; **Les Arts Florissants Vocal and Instrumental Ensemble/William Christie.** Harmonia Mundi Musique d'abord HMA190 1095 (5/83).

Ernest Chausson
French 1855-1899

Chausson. Poème de l'amour et de la mer, Op. 19[a]. Poème, Op. 25[b].
Fauré. Pelléas et Mélisande — Suite, Op. 80. Pavane, Op. 50[c]. [a]**Linda Finnie** (contr); [c]**Renaissance Singers; Ulster Orchestra/Yan Pascal Tortelier** ([b]vn). Chandos CHAN8952. Texts and translations included. Recorded 1989-90.

 Ih 9m DDD 12/91

Belfast's Ulster Hall may seem an unlikely source for nearly 70 minutes worth of demure *fin de siècle* melancholia, but the Chandos engineers have secured just that from Yan Pascal Tortelier and the Ulster Orchestra, who show just how convincing they can sound in this refined and evocative music by Chausson and Fauré. They are joined by Linda Finnie in a voluptuous and often tenderly seductive reading of Chausson's *Poème de l'amour et de la mer* — a performance of clarity and winning understatement. The rich, dark-hued violin tone of Yan Pascal Tortelier, in the enigmatic *Poème* by Chausson, is an ideal foil to Finnie's crystalline vocalization of the earlier work, and the accompaniment of both soloists reveals the Ulster Orchestra to be as sympathetic and sensitive to their needs as one could possibly wish in this music. Fauré, like Debussy, Sibelius and even Schoenberg, perceived the musical possibilities of Maeterlinck's symbolist play *Pelléas et Mélisande*, and Tortelier and his orchestra offer a memorable performance of the suite from Fauré's complete incidental music of 1898. Again, a degree of reticence and under-statement allows the elusive simplicity of expression to come to the fore, particularly in the contributions of the Ulster wind players. The orchestra are joined by the Renaissance Singers in the popular *Pavane* although it has to be said that the actual text by Robert de Montesquiou makes little impression here. With first-class sound and affecting, richly idiomatic performances, however, this admirable recording could hardly be more inviting.

Further listening ...

Symphony in B flat major, Op. 20[a]. Poème, Op. 25[b]. *Coupled with* **Saint-Saëns.** Introduction and Rondo capriccioso, Op. 28[b]. [b]**David Oistrakh** (vn); **Boston Symphony Orchestra/ Charles Munch.** RCA Gold Seal GD60683.

LE ROI ARTHUS. **Soloists; French Radio Chorus and New Philharmonic Orchestra/ Armin Jordan.** Erato Libretto 2292-45407-2 (10/91).

Carlos Chávez (Y Ramírez)

Mexican 1899-1978

Suggested listening ...

Sinfonia de Antigona[a]. Symphony No. 4, "Sinfonia romantica"[a]. *Coupled with* **Revueltas.** Caminos[b]. Musica para charlar[b]. Ventanas[b]. [a]**Royal Philharmonic Orchestra,** [b]**Mexican State Philharmonic Orchestra/Enrique Bátiz.** ASV CDDCA653 (8/89).

Sinfonía India. *Coupled with* **Copland.** Danzón cubano. **Roldán.** Suite from "La Rebambaramba". Rítmica V. **Revueltas.** Sensemayá. **García Caturla.** Tres danzas cubanas. **Piazzolla.** Tangazo. **Ginastera.** Suite from "Estancia". **New World Symphony/Michael Tilson Thomas.** Argo 436 737-2ZH. *See review in the Collections section; refer to the Index to Reviews.*

Luigi Cherubini

Italian 1760-1842

New review
Cherubini. OVERTURES. **Academy of St Martin in the Fields/Sir Neville Marriner.** EMI CDC7 54438-2.
Eliza. Médée. L'hôtellerie portugaise. Les deux journées. Anacréon. Faniska. les abencérages. Concert Overture.

· · lh 7m DDD 9/92

Cherubini's overtures were once quite popular concert items and they still occasionally surface individually on records, though rather less often in concert. And the opera house, alas, hardly knows anything now by this master of *opéra-comique*. So it was a good idea for Sir Neville Marriner to put together the present anthology, which gives an impressive idea of Cherubini's strengths even if we can also readily perceive some of the weaknesses. The latter include a certain caution in developing what are time and again bold, arresting ideas, dramatically presented. Berlioz, the composer of *Les troyens*, had no occasion to be so scornful: he gained much from Cherubini, and ought to have admired the graceful classicism of *Anacréon*, with its light, airy Greek atmosphere, tinged with a Watteau-like eroticism, its storm, and its happy ending as (in the opera) Eros, or Cupid, himself is revealed as the mysterious visitor. *Eliza* is another excellent overture, making much use of a charming pastoral theme from later in the opera, and agreeably characterizing the Swiss mountain setting. *Les abencérages* is a lively, cleverly composed piece, very imaginatively orchestrated, as is the nimble overture to *L'hôtellerie portugaise,* a one-act comedy of amorous mistakes and intrigues. It is a pity to dislodge *Lodoïska*, the obvious absentee from this set, in favour of the rather grandiose *Concert Overture* written for the London Philharmonic Society in 1815; but *Faniska,* also a Resuce Opera, provides another energetic and colourful overture. *Médée* and *Les deux journées* are likely to be a little more familiar, but are very welcome. The players respond intelligently to Marriner, shaping the melodies carefully and charging with a will into Cherubini's powerful tuttis. The recording is lucid, sensitive to the variety and colour of Cherubini's orchestration.

Further listening ...

Mass in D minor[a], "Messe solennelle". *Coupled with* **Haydn.** Mass in C major, "Missa in tempore belli", HobXXII/9[b]. [ab]**Soloists; Stuttgart Gächinger Kantorei;** [a]**Stuttgart Bach-Collegium;** [b]**Stuttgart Chamber Orchestra/Helmuth Rilling.** Hänssler 98 981 (two discs) (5/93).

Fryderyk Chopin

Polish 1810-1849

Chopin. Piano Concertos — No. 1 in E minor, Op. 11; No. 2 in F minor, Op. 21. **Murray Perahia** (pf); **Israel Philharmonic Orchestra/Zubin Mehta.** Sony Classical SK44922. Recorded live in 1989.

♪ Ih I6m DDD 6/90 — 9ₚ Ⓑ

Warm applause from the audience is not the only pointer to the fact that Perahia's are live concert recordings. The playing itself is full of that "inspirational heat-of-the-moment" long known to mean more to Perahia than mere streamlined studio correctness. The miracle is the way his urgency of feeling finds an outlet in playing of such super-sensitive finesse. Nearly always he favours slightly faster tempo than many of his rivals on disc, giving the first movements of both works a strong sense of direction in response to their *risoluto* markings. Mehta and the Israel Philharmonic might even be thought over-resolute, at the cost of a measure of the music's aristocratic elegance. But tonal balance is good, and progressively in each work a close-tuned partnership is achieved. Both rapt slow movements are sung with an exquisite tonal purity as well as embellished with magical delicacy. Their contrasting middle sections nevertheless bring eruptions of burning intensity. The dance-inspired finales have a scintillating lightness and charm recalling Perahia, the fingertip magician, in Mendelssohn. Even if not in the five-star class, the recorded sound is the equal of anything to be heard in rival CD versions of these two endearing reminders of the young Chopin's last year in Warsaw before leaving his homeland for ever.

Additional recommendations ...

No. 1. **Liszt.** *Piano Concerto No. 1 in E flat major, G124.* **Martha Argerich** (pf). **London Symphony Orchestra/Claudio Abbado.** DG 415 061-2GH — ♪ 55m ADD 4/85 Ⓑ

Nos. 1 and 2. **Krystian Zimerman** (pf). **Los Angeles Philharmonic Orchestra/Carlo Maria Giulini.** DG 415 970-2GH — ♪ Ih I2m ADD 9/86 9ₚ Ⓑ

No. 2[a]. **Tchaikovsky.** *Piano Concerto No. 1 in B flat minor, Op. 23*[b]. **Vladimir Ashkenazy** (pf); **London Symphony Orchestra/**[a]**David Zinman,** [b]**Lorin Maazel.** Decca Ovation 417 750-2DM — ♪ Ih 6m ADD 1/89 Ⓑ

No. 1[a]. No. 2[b]. **Tamás Vásáry** (pf). **Berlin Philharmonic Orchestra/**[a]**Jerszy Semkow,** [b]**János Kulka.** DG Privilege 429 515-2GR — ♪ Ih I5m ADD 6/90 9ₚ Ⓑ

Nos. 1 and 2. Concerto Rondo in F major, Op. 14, "Krakowiak". Variations in B flat major on "Là ci darem la mano", Op. 2. Andante spianato and Grande Polonaise brillante in E flat major, Op. 22. Fantaisie-impromptu in C sharp minor, Op. 66. Barcarolle in F sharp major, Op. 60. Nocturnes — No. 2 in E flat major, Op. 9 No. 2; No. 5 in F sharp major, Op. 15 No. 2. Waltzes — No. 7 in C sharp minor, Op. 64 No. 2; No. 9 in A flat major, Op. 69 No. 1. Prelude in D flat major, Op. 28 No. 15. Ballade No. 3 in A flat major, Op. 47. Fantaisie in F minor, Op. 49. **Claudio Arrau** (pf); **London Philharmonic Orchestra/Eliahu Inbal.** Philips 426 147-2PS3 — ③ 3h 5m ADD 6/90 Ⓑ

No. 1. Fantasia on Polish Airs, Op. 13. Andante spianato and Grande polonaise brillante in E flat major, Op. 22. **Idil Biret** (pf). **Czecho-Slovak State Philharmonic Orchestra, Košice/Robert Stankovsky.** Naxos 8 550368 — Ih I4m DDD 4/92 Ⓑ

No. 2. Variations on "Là ci darem le mano", Op. 2. Concerto Rondo in F major, Op. 14, "Krakowiak". **Idil Biret** (pf). **Czecho-Slovak State Philharmonic Orchestra, Košice/Robert Stankovsky.** Naxos 8 550369 — Ih 7m DDD 4/92 Ⓑ

Nos. 1 and 2. Waltz in C sharp minor, Op. 64 No. 2. Nocturnes — Nos. 1-19. **Artur Rubinstein** (pf); **London Symphony Orchestra/Sir John Barbirolli.** EMI Références mono CHS7 64491-2 — ② 2h 41m ADD 7/93 9ₚ Ⓑ ▲

Nos. 1 and 2. **Nikolai Demidenko** (pf); **Philharmonia Orchestra/Heinrich Schiff.** Hyperion CDA66647 — ♪ Ih I3m DDD II/93 Ⓑ

Chopin. PIANO WORKS. **Maurizio Pollini;** [a]**Philharmonia Orchestra/Paul Kletzki.**
EMI Studio Plus CDM7 64354-2. Item marked [a] from ASD370 (11/60), [b] ASD2577 (8/70).
Piano Concerto No. 1 in E minor, Op. 11[a]. Ballade in G minor, Op. 23[b]. Nocturnes, Op. 15
— No. 1 in F major[b]; No. 2 in F sharp minor[b]. Nocturnes, Op. 27 — No. 1 in C sharp
minor; No. 2 in D flat major. Polonaise No. 6 in A flat major, Op. 53, "Heroic"[b].

•* 1h 13m   ADD   11/92

This disc is a classic. The concerto was recorded shortly after the 18-year-old pianist's victory at
the Warsaw competition in 1959. Nowadays we might expect a wider dynamic range to allow
greater power in the first movement's tuttis, but in all other respects the recording completely
belies its age, with a near perfect balance between soloist and orchestra. This is, of course, very
much Pollini's disc, just as the First Concerto is very much the soloist's show, but effacing as
the accompaniment is, Pollini's keyboard miracles of poetry and refinement could not have been
achieved without one of the most characterful and responsive accounts of that accompaniment
ever committed to tape. The expressive range of the Philharmonia on top form under Kletzki is
at once, and continuously, exceptional, as is the accord between soloist and conductor in matters
of phrasing and shading. The solo items, recorded in 1968, are a further reminder of Pollini's
effortless bravura and aristocratic poise.

New review
Chopin. PIANO WORKS. **Evgeni Kissin.** RCA Victor Red Seal 09026 60445-2. Recorded at
performances in Carnegie Hall, New York in 1993.
Fantasie in F minor, Op. 49. Waltzes — No. 2 in A flat major, Op. 34 No. 1; No. 3 in
A minor, Op. 34 No. 2; No. 5 in A flat major, Op. 42. Polonaise No. 5 in F sharp minor,
Op. 44. Nocturnes — No. 1 in C sharp minor, Op. 27 No. 1; No. 2 in D flat major, Op. 27
No. 2; No. 10 in A flat major, Op. 32 No. 2. Scherzo No. 2 in B flat minor, Op. 31.

•* 1h 7m   DDD   5/94

Evgeni Kissin's playing at 21 (which he was when these performances were recorded) quite
easily outmatches that of the young Ashkenazy and Pollini — and most particularly in terms of
the maturity of his musicianship. The programme launches off with a reading of the great F
minor *Fantasie*, which, though a bit measured, is integrated to perfection. The power and
determination of the performance certainly make one sit up and listen, but at the same time it
would be difficult not to be moved by the heartfelt lyricism of the melodic passages. Although
Kissin may be a little unsmiling in the three waltzes, at least he has admirable sophistication in
being able to work in detail from the accompaniments so as to add interest to the interpretations. His control in the tricky A flat, Op. 42 is quite amazing. Of all the items on the CD,
however, the *Nocturne* in C sharp minor is the jewel. This reading is amongst the most darkly
imaginative and pianistically refined on disc. The release is rounded off by a powerfully glittering
performance of the Second *Scherzo*.

Chopin. PIANO WORKS. Volume 8. **Vladimir Ashkenazy.** Decca 410 122-2DH. From 410
122-1DH (7/84).
Mazurkas, Op. 30 — No. 1 in C minor; No. 2 in B minor; No. 3 in D flat major; No. 4 in
C sharp minor. Op. 33 — No. 1 in G sharp minor; No. 2 in D major; No. 3 in C major;
No. 4 in B minor. *Nocturnes,* Op. 32 — No. 9 in B major; No. 10 in A flat major; No. 20 in
C minor, Op. posth. Impromptu No. 1 in A flat major, Op. 29. Largo in E flat major,
Op. posth. Scherzo No. 2 in B flat minor, Op. 31. Waltz in F major, Op. 34 No. 3. Variation
No. 6 in E major, "Hexameron".

•* 52m   DDD   7/84

Though Ashkenazy's decision to offer a mix of genres on a disc instead of a chronological
sequence may be questioned, the result is probably more satisfactory for listening, since one has
here a real recital of varied music. It ranges from the extrovert brilliance of the B flat minor
Scherzo and the F major *Grande valse brillante*, Op. 34 No. 3, through the elegantly wistful 'salon'
mood of the A flat major Nocturne and the surprisingly varied and dramatic Mazurkas, to mere
chips from the composer's workbench like the *Largo* in E flat major and the C minor Nocturne
which were both unpublished until 1938. Ashkenazy's affinity with Chopin in all his moods is the
justification for such a complete survey as this and only very occasionally might one feel a need

for even more mystery and spontaneity. As for the sound-quality, it is bright but very faithful and never approaches harshness even in the most powerful passages. This is a noble recording.

New review
Chopin. PIANO WORKS. **Seta Tanyel.** Collins Classics 1330-2.
Preludes Nos. 1-24, Op. 28. Scherzo No. 2 in B flat minor, Op. 31. Mazurkas — No. 13 in A minor, Op. 17 No. 4; No. 15 in C major, Op. 24 No. 2; No. 25 in B minor, Op. 33 No. 4. Polonaise No. 5 in F sharp minor, Op. 44.

Ih 9m DDD 4/94

Avoiding all overtly self-conscious point-making in pursuit of expression, Seta Tanyel gets to the heart of the matter with a stylish simplicity. And how beautifully she makes the piano sing within a sound-world that is wholly Chopinesque in its translucency. That said, there is certainly no lack of strength, either of motivation or sheer tonal weight, as the more demonstratively disturbed of the 24 Preludes make very clear. However stormy the outburst or complex the figuration she nevertheless always manages to reveal a hidden melodic thread. Slower numbers carry their weight of sentiment without being allowed to drag. Nothing in the first half of the recital is more pleasing than the three *Mazurkas*. Each tells its own personal tale while — with a spring-like tonal delicacy and freshness — never allowing you to forget its origin in the dance. In the flanking B minor *Scherzo* and F sharp minor *Polonaise*, darker undertones of disquiet and defiance are conveyed with an urgent nervous energy far more telling than bombast. And what beguiling *cantabile* she draws from her instrument in the gracious mazurka-like trio of the Polonaise. The Abbey Road reproduction is pleasing enough.

Additional recommendations ...
24 Preludes. Prelude in A flat. Piano Sonatas — No. 1 in C minor, Op. 4; No. 2 in B flat minor, Op. 35; No. 3 in B minor, Op. 58. Rondos — C minor, Op. 1; F major, "à la mazur", Op. 5. Four Ballades. Introduction and Rondo in C minor/E flat major, Op. 16. Rondo in C major, Op. 73. **Garrick Ohlsson.** *Arabesque Z6628/30 — ⑶ Ih 18m Ih 6m Ih 4m DDD 10/93 ♀ₚ Ⓑ*
Preludes: Nos. 1-24; No. 25 in C sharp minor, Op. 45; No. 26 in A flat major. Op. posth. Spring, Op. 74 No. 2. Allegretto and Mazur. Two Bourées. Ecossaise, Op. 72 No. 3. Three Ecossaises, WN27. Boléro in C major, Op. 19. Contredanse in G flat major. Galop marquis in A flat major. Allegretto in F sharp minor. Feuille d'album in E major. Cantabile in B flat major. Fugue in A minor. **Cyprien Katsaris.** Sony Classical SK53355 — *♪ Ih 9m DDD 10/93 ♀ₚ Ⓑ*

Chopin. PIANO WORKS. **Peter Katin.** Olympia OCD254.
Nocturnes: Op. 9 — No. 1 in B flat minor; No. 2 in E flat major; No. 3 in B major. Op. 15 — No. 1 in F major; No. 2 in F sharp major; No. 3 in G minor. Op. 27 — No. 1 in C sharp minor; No. 2 in D flat major. Op. 32 — No. 1 in B major; No. 2 in A flat major; C minor. Op. 37 — No. 1 in G minor; No. 2 in G major. Op. 48 — No. 1 in C minor; No. 2 in F sharp minor. Op. 55 — No. 1 in F minor; No. 2 in E flat major. Op. 62 — No. 1 in B major; No. 2 in E major. No. 19 in E minor, Op. 72 No. 1; No. 20 in C sharp minor, Op. posth. *Impromptus* — No. 1 in A flat major, Op. 29; No. 2 in F sharp major, Op. 35; No. 3 in G flat major, Op. 51. Fantaisie-impromptu in C sharp minor, Op. 66.

⑵ 2h 20m DDD 12/89

Here at medium price are 140 minutes of great piano music finely played. Katin is a quietly persuasive artist rather than a virtuoso and he brings an entirely appropriate sense of intimacy to this Chopin recital of nocturnes and impromptus. The approach is chronological and complete, so that in the nocturnes the E minor and the *Lento con gran espressione* in C sharp minor come first, although they were published posthumously, and we also hear the rarely played C minor (without opus number) which only came to light in 1937, a century after its composition. Rubato is used freely but tastefully and melodies really sing, so that a good balance is achieved between emotional richness and the fastidiousness that was also part of Chopin's musical nature. The impromptus are well done too, with the famous *Fantaisie-impromptu* played according to a manuscript source and so with rather fewer ornaments than usual. The recording was made in an Oslo church with a fine acoustic and an instrument that the pianist finds "exceptionally sympathetic", as the booklet tells us and his own programme notes are almost as poetic as the music itself, as when he writes of the E flat major Nocturne, Op. 55/2, that "a coda of sheer magic seems to descend from a height and passes into infinity" — which is not purple prose but a statement demonstrably true of the music and the performance.

Additional recommendations ...
Complete Nocturnes. **Livia Rév.** Hyperion CDA66341/2 — ,·•' lh 52m DDD 2/90 Ⓑ
Three Impromptus. Fantaisie-impromptu. Barcarolle in F sharp major, Op. 60. Piano Sonata No. 3 in B minor, Op. 58. **Howard Shelley.** Chandos CHAN9175 — ,·•' 57m DDD 11/93 Ⓑ
Complete Nocturnes. Fantaisie-impromptu in C sharp minor, Op. 66. Barcarolle in F sharp major, Op. 60. **Kathryn Stott.** Unicorn-Kanchana DKPCD9147/8 — ,·•' ② 2h 4m DDD 7/94 ♀ₚ Ⓑ

Chopin. PIANO WORKS. **Nikolai Demidenko.** Hyperion CDA66514. Recorded 1989-90. Introduction and Variations in E major on a German air ("Der Schweizerbub"). *Scherzos* — No. 1 in B minor, Op. 20; No. 2 in B flat minor, Op. 31; No. 3 in C sharp minor, Op. 39; No. 4 in E major, Op. 54. Variations in B flat major on "Là ci darem la mano", Op. 2.

,·•' **lh 3m DDD 1/92**

"Off with your hats, gentlemen — a genius" were the percipient words of the 21-year-old Schumann on first discovering the *Là ci darem* Variations composed by Chopin when still only 17. Though well represented as originally conceived for piano and orchestra, it was left to the young Russian, Nikolai Demidenko to introduce the work to the CD catalogue as recast for solo piano. Serving as a grand finale to a recital opening with Chopin's still earlier, charmingly innocent *Swiss Boy* Variations, Demidenko's performance confirms him as a pianist of outstanding imagina-tive vitality as well as technical brilliance, moreover a player really able to make the piano sing throughout a wide and varied tonal range. The main musical tests nevertheless come in the four *Scherzos*, where again he surmounts all hurdles with effortless ease and poetic grace while extracting the loveliest sound from his instrument. But Chopin devotees should be warned that in making this music wholly his own he is sometimes a little idiosyncratically self-indulgent, notably in matters of lyrical relaxation, though also in No. 1, in choosing to remove the sting from Chopin's challenging opening chords. He is very well recorded.

Additional recommendation ...
Scherzos Nos. 1-4. **Schumann.** *Bunte Blätter, Op. 99.* **Sviatoslav Richter.** Olympia OCD338 *(See review under Beethoven; refer to the Index to Reviews)* — ,·•' lh 15m ADD 4/94 ♀ₚ

Chopin. PIANO WORKS. **Nikolai Demidenko.** Hyperion CDA66597. Recorded in 1992. *Polonaises* — No. 7 in A flat major, Op. 61, "Polonaise-fantaisie"; No. 12 in G flat major; No. 13 in G minor; No. 14 in B flat major; No. 15 in A flat major; No. 16 in G sharp minor. Bolero in A minor, Op. 19. Allegro de concert, Op. 46. Berceuse in D flat major, Op. 57. Tarantelle in A flat major, Op. 43.

,·•' **lh 6m DDD 11/92** ♀ₚ Ⓑ

Nikolai Demidenko's first Chopin recital for Hyperion (see above) coloured familiarity with novelty, coupling the four *Scherzos* with lesser known sets of *Variations*. Here he takes such enterprise a stage further, alternating Chopin's earliest *Polonaises* (elegant and scintillating juvenilia) with mature examples of his poetic genius, and with the *Bolero* and *Tarantelle* as racy and exotic additions. Even more importantly, Demidenko's playing, while maintaining its former finesse and precision, is altogether more poised, less arbitrary in its musical thinking. The *Allegro de concert* may be among the most daunting examples of Chopin's virtuosity — some of its more outrageous demands suggest the influence of his next door neighbour, the reclusive and quixotic Charles-Valentin Alkan — but for Demidenko such difficulties hardly exist; the greater the challenge the cooler and more nonchalant the response. The *Polonaise-fantaisie* and *Berceuse*, too, are both given with great individuality, challenging convention in one detail after another yet remaining meticulously close to the score. Such exceptional lucidity and clarity of line combine with recordings of the finest quality to make further discs from this source eagerly anticipated occasions.

Chopin. PIANO WORKS. **Artur Rubinstein.** EMI Références mono CHS7 64697-2. Recorded 1928-39.
Waltz No. 2 in A flat major, Op. 34 No. 1 (from HMV DB1168, 2/30). Mazurkas Nos. 1-51 (DB3802/8, 9/39 and DB3839/45, 2/42). Four Scherzos (DB1915/8, 11/33). Barcarolle in

F sharp major, Op. 60 (DB1161, 8/28). Berceuse in D flat major, Op. 57 (DB2149, 7/34). Polonaises Nos. 1-7 (DB2493/6, 7/36 and DB2497/9, 8/36). Andante spianato and Grand polonaise in E flat major, Op. 22 (DB2499/500, 8/36).

③ 3h 53m ADD 10/93

Artur Rubinstein is popularly remembered as Chopin's genial, sparkling elder statesman; but, up until now, only seasoned collectors have been aware of his many pre-war recordings — where "aristocratic poise" (Rubinstein's best-known interpretative attribute) went hand-in-hand with impulsiveness, spontaneity and dazzling virtuosity. To compare these 1932-5 versions of the *Scherzos* and Polonaises with Rubinstein's wise, elegant (and extremely musical) post-war recordings for RCA is to pit "emotion recollected in tranquillity" against the hot-headed impact of immediate experience. There's less of a contrast with the Mazurkas, although — again — these first recordings (Rubinstein made two subsequent sets) have that extra degree of 'lift' and tension. Readers will of course ask themselves whether transfers from old 78s really can deliver as much musical pleasure as modern recordings. But in this case, so-called 'surface noise' is never intrusive and the quality of the playing is so exceptional that the mono sound and relative lack of dynamic range soon cease to pose a problem.

Chopin. PIANO WORKS. **Martha Argerich.** DG Galleria 415 836-2GGA.
Preludes Nos. 1-24, Op. 28. *Preludes* — No. 25 in C sharp minor, Op. 45; No. 26 in A flat major, Op. posth. (all from 2530 721, 2/78). Barcarolle in F sharp major, Op. 60 (SLPM138672, 1/68). Polonaise No. 6 in A flat major, Op. 53 (SLPM139317, 5/68). Scherzo No. 2 in B flat minor, Op. 31 (2530 530, 6/75).

1h 2m ADD 4/88

Professor Zurawlew, the founder of the Chopin Competition in Warsaw was once asked which one of the prizewinners he would pick as having been his favourite. Looking back over the period 1927-75, the answer came back immediately: "Martha Argerich". This CD could explain why. There are very few recordings of the 24 Preludes that have such a perfect combination of temperamental virtuosity and compelling artistic insight. Argerich has the technical equipment to do whatever she wishes with the music. Whether it is in the haunting, dark melancholy of No. 2 in A minor or the lightning turmoil of No. 16 in B flat minor, she is profoundly impressive. It is these sharp changes of mood that make the performance scintillatingly unpredictable. In the *Barcarolle* there is no relaxed base on which the melodies of the right hand are constructed, as is conventional, but more the piece emerges as a stormy odyssey through life, with moments of visionary awareness. Argerich, it must be said, is on firmer ground in the *Polonaise*, where her power and technical security reign triumphant. The CD ends with a rippling and yet slightly aggressive reading of the second Scherzo. This is very much the playing of a pianist who lives in the 'fast lane' of life. The sound quality is a bit reverberant, an effect heightened by the fact that Argerich has a tendency to over-pedal.

Chopin. PIANO WORKS. **Krystian Zimerman.** DG 423 090-2GH.
Ballades — No. 1 in G minor, Op. 23; No. 2 in F major, Op. 38; No. 3 in A flat major, Op. 47; No. 4 in F minor, Op. 52. Barcarolle in F sharp major, Op. 60. Fantasie in F minor, Op. 49.

1h DDD 10/88

Chopin's choice of the previously unused literary title of "ballade" for the four great works with which this recital begins suggests that they may well have been inspired by tales of his country's past. Certainly Krystian Zimerman, a Pole himself, unfolds all four with a rare appreciation of their freely self-evolving narrative style, almost as if he were composing the music himself while going along. His timing here and there might be thought a little self-indulgent in its lingerings but he never rushes his fences. The overall impression left by his playing is one of uncommon expansiveness, upheld by a splendidly full, warm, rich recording. Despite his very slow tempo in the F minor Fantasie he still manages to suggest that patriotic fires were very much aflame in the composer at the time. The *Barcarolle* is as seductively sensuous as it is passionate.

Additional recommendations ...

Ballades. Piano Sonata No. 2 in B flat minor, Op. 35. **Andrei Gavrilov.** DG 435 622-2GH — ･ﾟ

Ballades. Barcarolle. Berceuse. Fantasie. **Alexeï Lubimov** (fp). Erato 2292-45990-2 — ⁘ 1h 3m
DDD 7/93 Ⓑ ✏

Ballades. Piano Sonata No. 3. **Nikolai Demidenko.** Hyperion CDA66577 — ⁘ 1h 1m DDD 11/93
ᵠₛ Ⓑ

New review
Chopin. WALTZES. **Jean-Bernard Pommier.** Erato 4509-92887-2. Recorded in 1993.
No. 1 in E flat major, Op. 18. No. 2 in A flat major, Op. 34 No. 1. No. 3 in A minor,
Op. 34 No. 2. No. 4 in F major, Op. 34 No. 3. No. 5 in A flat major, Op. 42. No. 6 in
D flat major, Op. 64 No. 1. No. 7 in C sharp minor, Op. 64 No. 2. No. 8 in A flat major,
Op. 64 No. 3. No. 9 in A flat major, Op. 69 No. 1. No. 10 in E minor, Op. 69 No. 2.
No. 11 in G flat major, Op. 70 No. 1. No. 12 in F minor, Op. 70 No. 2. No. 13 in D flat
major, Op. 70 No. 3. No. 14 in E minor, Op. posth. No. 15 in E major, Op. posth. No. 16 in
A flat major, Op. posth. No. 17 in E flat major, Op. posth. No. 18 in E flat major, Op. posth.
No. 19 in A minor, Op. posth.

⁘ **57m DDD 3/94** Ⓑ

This pianist has given long and careful thought as to what aspect of the composer he feels these
waltzes should reveal: while recognizing them as "fashionable" Chopin, he never allows his fingers
just to trip their way along. The result is never less than pleasing for judicious choice of tempo, for
several stimulating textual variants taken from original manuscripts, and a general surefootedness.
Perhaps the disc doesn't haunt the memory in quite the same way as several CD reissues, some
less costly, of legendary waltzers of yore. Of these, the one with whom Pommier has least in
common is the mercurial, light-fingered Lipatti, someone too loved by the gods to have time for
second thoughts about some questionably breathless tempos or swiftness of internal vacillations of
mood, but who so miraculously conveyed the "rapture and poignancy of first sensations". Maybe
Pommier more often looked to Rubinstein's finely integrated last recording of these waltzes —
though without wholly achieving the eloquent simplicity of phrasing and naturalness of rubato of
that artist in later days — or indeed his life-long fingertip magic. But the trenchancy with which
the French pianist makes his every point is undeniably impressive. Full, clear-toned recording.

Additional recommendations ...
Nos. 1-14. **Artur Rubinstein.** RCA RD89564 — ADD ᵠₚ ▲
Nos. 1-14. Mazurka No. 32 in C sharp minor, Op. 50 No. 3. Barcarolle in F sharp major, Op. 60.
Nocturne No. 8 in D flat major, Op. 27 No. 2. **Dinu Lipatti.** EMI Références mono CDH7
69802-2 — ⁘ 1h 5m ADD 7/89 ᵠₚ ▲

Chopin. Etudes, Opp. 10 and 25. **Maurizio Pollini.** DG 413 794-2GH. From 2530 291
(11/72).

⁘ **56m ADD 5/85** ᵠₚ Ⓑ

The 24 *Etudes* of Chopin's Opp. 10 and 25, although dating from his twenties, remain among
the most perfect specimens of the genre ever known, with all technical challenges — and they
are formidable — dissolved into the purest poetry. With his own transcendental technique (and
there are few living pianists who can rival it) Pollini makes you unaware that problems even
exist — as for instance in Op. 10 No. 10 in A flat, where the listener is swept along in an
effortless stream of melody. The first and last of the same set in C major and C minor have an
imperious strength and drive, likewise the last three impassioned outpourings of Op. 25.
Lifelong dislike of a heart worn on the sleeve makes him less than intimately confiding in more
personal contexts such as No. 3 in E and No. 6 in E flat minor from Op. 10, or the nostalgic
middle section of No. 5 in E minor and the searing No. 7 in C sharp minor from Op. 25. Like
the playing, so the recording itself could profitably be a little warmer from time to time, but it
is a princely disc all the same, which all keyboard *aficionados* will covet.

Additional recommendations ...
Etudes. **Vladimir Ashkenazy.** Decca 414 127-2DH — ⁘ DDD 1/85 ᵠₚ Ⓑ
Etudes. Trois nouvelles études, Op. posth. **Boris Berezovsky** (pf). Teldec 9031-73129-2 — ⁘
1h 8m DDD 4/92 ᵠₚ Ⓑ
Etudes. **John Bingham.** Meridian CDE84221 — ⁘ 1h 7m DDD 5/93 ᵠₚ Ⓑ

Chopin. Piano Sonata No. 2 in B flat minor, Op. 35[a]. 12 Etudes, Op. 25[b]. **Grigory Sokolov.** Opus 111 OPS30-83. Item marked [a] recorded at a performance in the Salle Gaveau, Paris in 1992; [b] Glinka Chapel, St Petersburg in 1985.

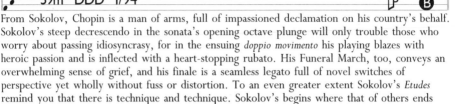

From Sokolov, Chopin is a man of arms, full of impassioned declamation on his country's behalf. Sokolov's steep decrescendo in the sonata's opening octave plunge will only trouble those who worry about passing idiosyncrasy, for in the ensuing *doppio movimento* his playing blazes with heroic passion and is inflected with a heart-stopping rubato. His Funeral March, too, conveys an overwhelming sense of grief, and his finale is a seamless legato full of novel switches of perspective yet wholly without fuss or distortion. To an even greater extent Sokolov's *Etudes* remind you that there is technique and technique. Sokolov's begins where that of others ends and his pulverizing strength in the magnificent last three studies is truly overwhelming; even Richter and Gilels at their height would find this a hard act to follow. Accompanying gasps and intakes of breath are added testimony to the immense effort of interpretation and few discs have captured more vividly a truly great pianist live and on the wing. The recordings — when you stop to notice them — are more than adequate.

Chopin. Piano Sonatas — No. 2 in B flat minor, Op. 35; No. 3 in B minor, Op. 58. **Maurizio Pollini.** DG 415 346-2GH.

These two magnificent romantic sonatas are Chopin's longest works for solo piano. The passion of the B flat minor Sonata is evident throughout, as is its compression (despite the overall length) — for example, the urgent first subject of its first movement is omitted in the recapitulation. As for its mysterious finale, once likened to "a pursuit in utter darkness", it puzzled Chopin's contemporaries but now seems totally right. The B minor Sonata is more glowing and spacious, with a wonderful *Largo* third movement, but its finale is even more exhilarating than that of the B flat minor, and on a bigger scale. Pollini plays this music with overwhelming power and depth of feeling; the expressive intensity is rightly often disturbing. Magisterial technique is evident throughout and the recording is sharp-edged but thrilling.

Additional recommendations ...

Nos. 2 and 3. Fantaisie in F minor, Op. 49. **Artur Rubinstein.** RCA Red Seal RD89812 — *1h 1m ADD 2/87*

Nos. 2 and 3. **Murray Perahia.** CBS CD76242 — *50m ADD 3/89*

Nos. 2 and 3. No. 1 in C minor, Op. 4. Etudes, Op. 10 — No. 6 in E flat minor. Etudes, Op. 25 — No. 3 in F major; No. 4 in A minor; No. 10 in B minor; No. 11 in A minor. Mazurkas, Op. 17 — No. 1 in B flat major; No. 2 in E minor; No. 3 in A flat major; No. 4 in A minor. **Leif Ove Andsnes.** Virgin Classics Duo VCK7 59072-2 — *② 1h 51m DDD 6/92*

Further listening ...

Rondo in C minor, Op. 1. Rondo "à la Mazur" in F major, Op. 5. Introduction and Rondo in C minor/E flat major, Op. 16. Rondo in C major, Op. 73. *Mazurkas, Op. posth.* — G major; B flat major; C major; A flat major; D major. Introduction and Variations in E major on "Der Schweizerbub". Introduction and Variations in B flat major on a theme from Hérold's "Ludovic", Op. 12. Souvenir de Paganini (Variations in A major). Variations No. 6 in E major on a March from Bellini's "I Puritani". Introduction, Theme and Variations (with Martin Sauer, pf). **Idil Biret** (pf). Naxos 8 550508 (5/93).

Preludes Nos. 1-26. Three Impromptus. Fantaisie-impromptu in C sharp minor, Op. 66. Waltzes Nos. 1-19. Four Ballades. Barcarolle in F sharp major, Op. 60. Fantasie in F minor, Op. 49. Four Scherzos. Polonaises — No. 7 in A flat major, Op. 61, "Polonaise-fantaisie". Nocturnes Nos. 1-21. **Claudio Arrau** (pf). Philips 422 038-2PH6 (6-disc set).

Complete Piano Works. **Vladimir Ashkenazy.** Decca 421 185-2DH13 (13-disc set).

Johannes Ciconia

Suggested listening ...

Amor por ti sempre. Caçando un giorno. O Padua, sidus praeclarum. Regina gloriosa. Aler m'en veus. Io crido amor. O rosa bella. Poy che morir. Ben che va dui donna. Le ray au soleyl (three versions). Pertrum Marcello Venetum/O petre antistes inclite. Chi nel servir antico. Per quella strada. Una panthera. Gli atti col dançar. Sus une fontayne. O Petre, Christe discipule. Doctorem principem/Melodia suavissima/Vir mitis. O virum omnimoda/O Lux et decus/O beate Nicholae. **Project Ars Nova Ensemble.** New Albion NA048CD (5/93).

Key to symbols

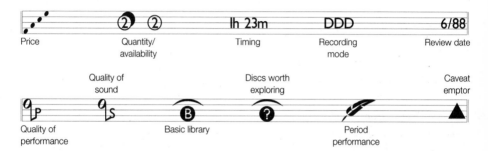

| Price | Quantity/
availability | Timing | Recording
mode | Review date |

Quality of sound — Discs worth exploring — Caveat emptor

Quality of performance — Basic library — Period performance

Francesco Cilea

Cilea. ADRIANA LECOUVREUR. **Renata Scotto** (sop) Adriana Lecouvreur; **Plácido Domingo** (ten) Maurizio; **Sherrill Milnes** (bar) Michonnet; **Elena Obraztsova** (mez) Princesse de Bouillon; **Giancarlo Luccardi** (bass) Prince de Bouillon; **Florindo Andreolli** (ten) Abbe de Chazeuil; **Lillian Watson** (sop) Jouvenot; **Ann Murray** (mez) Dangeville; **Paul Crook** (ten) Poisson; Major-domo; **Paul Hudson** (bass) Quinault; **Ambrosian Opera Chorus; Philharmonia Orchestra/James Levine.** CBS CD79310. Notes, text and translation included. From 79310 (6/78). Recorded in 1977.

Adriana Lecouvreur is an archetypal prima donna vehicle. Look at the plot coldly, without reference to the music, and it is costumed hokum of an improbability that takes the breath away (of course there's jealousy, of course there's a death-scene, but what do you say to a bunch of poisoned violets as a murder weapon?). Even with the music, even allowing that Cilea was a much shrewder man of the theatre and a much more able musician than his detractors can bear to allow, it is still ... well, hokum with some damned good tunes. But Cilea wrote his opera in the full knowledge that an essential five per cent of its appeal would be added by the prima donna. Not with faultless vocalism, though that's a prerequisite too, but with the sort of allure of vocal personality that elsewhere would be called "star quality". With that extra five per cent, arguments about the artifice of the plot and the occasional thinness of the score fall away as the irrelevancies that they are. And you can tell very soon whether the soprano in question has that quality: after Cilea's brief but evocative scene-setting (telling us that we're back-stage at the Comédie Française in the eighteenth century, a world of glamour and intrigue), she enters, a prima donna portraying a prima donna, and tells us, to a sumptuous melody, that star though she is she's but the humble handmaid of her art. If you are not moved despite yourself, despite the obvious artifice (is it Adriana or the soprano herself speaking?) proceed no further; either this opera or this performance is not for you. Scotto has that magic quality, in abundance. That Domingo is an ardent hero, Milnes a touching elderly admirer, Obraztsova a baleful rival and Levine an enthusiastic exponent of the subtleties and ingenuities of a composer often despised for having written prima donna vehicles is all bonus, making this a performance that you can return to again and again. But the centre of its allure, its *raison d'être*, is Renata Scotto, glamour personified. Her entrance is electrifying, her death moving and everything between is more than life-size.

Domenico Cimarosa

New review

Cimarosa. IL MATRIMONIO SEGRETO. **Arleen Auger** (sop) Carolina; **Julia Varady** (sop) Elisetta; **Dietrich Fischer-Dieskau** (bar) Geronimo; **Júlia Hamari** (contr) Fidalma; **Ryland Davies** (ten) Paolino; **Alberto Rinaldi** (bar) Count Robinson; **English Chamber Orchestra/Daniel Barenboim.** DG 437 696-2GX3. Text and translation included. From 2709 069 (9/77).

③ 2h 45m ADD 8/93

The music may not have the more adventurous harmony or contrapuntal dexterity of Mozart (whose opening of the *Zauberflöte* Overture only four months earlier Cimarosa must almost certainly have cribbed), but it abounds in delightfully fresh melodic invention and rhythmic vitality — its bubbling patter-work too is worthy of Rossini at his best. Together with its construction, with as many ensembles as solo arias and with skilfully planned finales, and its scoring, primarily aimed at supporting the singers but giving the orchestra some independent interest, it marks not merely an expert craftsman but a composer of distinction whose wide popularity at the time is understandable. Barenboim makes the music dance along with the utmost sparkle, and he is fortunate in having a splendid cast, in whom it is almost invidious to praise Ryland Davies (with free tone-production, fine breath-control and native-sounding Italian) and the silver-voiced Arleen Auger as the young couple at the centre of the plot. But Alberto Rinaldi also brings a real sense of character to the blustering Count Robinson (was this personage intended as a dig at the British?), who sets his heart on the clandestinely married Caroline and ends up, most improbably, marrying her shrewish elder sister whom he had previously declared he would rather die than wed; and Julia Varady gives a stunning performance of that character's big florid aria in the last act. An issue not to be missed.

Mikolajus Ciurlionis

Suggested listening ...

Symphonic poems — The sea; In the forest. Five Preludes for String Orchestra. **Slovak Philharmonic Orchestra/Juozas Domarkas.** Marco Polo 8 223323 (6/91).

Rebecca Clarke

New review

R. Clarke. Sonata for Viola and Piano[a].
Maconchy. Five Sketches for Viola.
Shostakovich. Sonata for Viola and Piano, Op. 147[a]. **Philip Dukes** (va); [a]**Sophia Rahman** (pf). Gamut Classics GAMCD537. Recorded in 1992.

lh 9m DDD 4/94

These are big pieces, all three of them, and they receive imposingly big performances. All the readings are acutely aware, as were all three composers, that although a capacity for delicately shadowed lyricism and plaintiveness are among the features that distinguish the viola from the violin, others no less important include a throaty eloquence and an ability to sketch large gestures in firm, grainy lines. Rebecca Clarke's fine Sonata says as much at its outset, with a bold flourish of fifths. It is marked, that opening movement, *impetuoso*: 'impetuous' indeed, but the work lives up to its opening in impetus as well: the ideas, strong even when they are rhapsodic or lyrical, are subjected throughout to genuine, searching development. Maconchy's *Sketches* are big, too, despite their brevity, as though restriction of means had prompted a laconic concentration of utterance. The Shostakovich Sonata, his last work, with its intensely moving finale "in memory of the great Beethoven", responds very well to such big-scaled playing, but it also demands great seriousness, concentration and an ability to fine down richness of tone to a ghostly pallor. This performance has the work's measure, which is saying a great deal. A most welcome and impressive début recital.

Further listening ...

Vocal and Chamber Works — June Twilight[ac]. A Dream[ac]. The Cherry Blossom Wand[ac]. The Cloths of Heaven[ac]. Shy one[ac]. The Seal Man[ac]. Down by the Salley Gardens[ac]. Infant Joy[ac]. Lethe[ac]. Tiger tiger[ac]. Tears[ac]. God made a tree[ac]. Come, oh come, my Life's Delight[ac]. Greeting[ac]. The Donkey[ac]. Cradle Song[ac]. Eight o'clock[ac]. Psalm of David when he was in the wilderness of Judah[ac]. The Aspidistra[ac]. Three Old English Songs[ab]. Three Irish Country Songs[ab]. Midsummer Moon[bc]. Chinese Puzzle[bc]. Lullaby[bc]. [a]**Patricia Wright** (sop); [b]**Jonathan Rees** (vn); [c]**Kathron Sturrock** (pf). Gamut Classics GAMCD534 (5/93).

Clemens non Papa

French/Flemish c.1510-c.1556

Suggested listening ...

Missa Pastores quidnam vidistis. *Motets* — Pastores quidnam vidistis; Tribulationes civitatum; Pater peccavi; Ego flos campi. **The Tallis Scholars/Peter Phillips.** Gimell CDGIM013 (12/87).

Muzio Clementi

Italian/British 1752-1832

New review

Clementi. KEYBOARD SONATAS. **Maria Tipo** (pf). EMI CDC7 54766-2. Recorded 1992. G minor, Op. 8 No. 1. F minor, Op. 13 No. 6. F sharp minor, Op. 25 No. 5. D major, Op. 40 No. 3. Batti, batti (after the aria from Mozart's "Don Giovanni").

lh 13m DDD 2/94

Peter Katin (listed below) uses a fortepiano but Maria Tipo makes an equally compelling case for the modern piano in a programme which shows both Clementi's broad talent for invention and expressive variety, and the extent of his output as a composer over some 40 years. In the case of the F minor Sonata, the greater dynamic range of the modern instrument increases the music's dramatic impact over Katin's authentic instrument version. The F sharp minor Sonata, Op. 25 No. 5 provides an especially telling example of the differences between the two instruments. The lyrical expressiveness and richness of Clementi's harmonic language are particularly well suited to the modern piano's greater ability to sustain sound, but the double thirds, which are a feature of this piece's finale, have a more appealing lightness in the fortepiano version. The recorded piano sound is immensely satisfying.

Additional recommendation ...

F minor; F sharp minor; G minor, Op. 7 No. 3; B flat major, Op. 24 No. 2; D major, Op. 25 No. 6. **Peter Katin** (fp). Athene ATHCD4 — lh 15m DDD 12/93

Further listening ...

Symphonies, Op. 18 — No. 1 in B flat major; No. 2 in D major. Minuetto pastorale in D major. Piano Concerto in C major. **Pietro Spada** (pf). **Philharmonia Orchestra/ Francesco D'Avalos.** ASV CDDCA802 (2/93).

Symphonies — No. 1 in C major; No. 3 in G major, "Great National Symphony". Overture in C major. **Philharmonia Orchestra/Francesco D'Avalos.** ASV CDDCA803 (2/93).

Symphonies — No. 2 in D major; No. 4 in D major. Overture in D major. **Philharmonia Orchestra/Francesco D'Avalos.** ASV CDDCA804 (2/93). *These three recordings are also available as part of a three-disc mid-price set* (ASV CDDCS322).

Key to symbols

Price	Quantity/ availability	Timing	Recording mode	Review date
	② ②	1h 23m	DDD	6/88

Louis-Nicolas Clérambault

French 1676-1749

Suggested listening ...

Cantatas — Orphée; Médée. *Harpsichord Suites* — No. 1 in C major; No. 2 in C minor. **Rachel Yakar** (sop); **Wilbert Hazelzet** (fl); **Reinhard Goebel** (vn); **Charles Medlam** (va da gamba); **Alan Curtis, Kenneth Gilbert** (hpds). Archiv Produktion Collectio Argenta 437 085-2AT (1/93).

Cantatas — Orphée; Zéphire et Flore; Léandre et Héro. Sonata, "La Magnifique". **Julianne Baird** (sop); **Music's Re-creation.** Meridian CDE84182 (1/91).

Eric Coates

British 1886-1957

Coates. ORCHESTRAL WORKS. [a]**Royal Liverpool Philharmonic Orchestra/Sir Charles Groves**; [b]**London Symphony Orchestra/Sir Charles Mackerras**; [c]**City of Birmingham Symphony Orchestra/Reginald Kilbey.** Classics for Pleasure CD-CFPD4456. From CFPD414456-3 (11/86). Recorded 1956-71.
Saxo-Rhapsody. Wood Nymphs. Music Everywhere (Rediffusion March). From Meadow to Mayfair. The Dam Busters — march ([a] all from Columbia TWO226, 12/68); London. Cinderella — phantasy. London Again ([a] TWO321, 12/70). The Merrymakers — Miniature Overture. Summer Days — At the dance. By the Sleepy Lagoon. The Three Men — Man from the sea. The Three Bears — Phantasy ([b] CFP40279, 3/78). Calling all Workers — March. The Three Elizabeths ([c] TWO361, 12/71).

	②	2h 9m	ADD	9/89		B	▲

Eric Coates reached a vast public through the use of his music as signature tunes for radio programmes such as "In Town Tonight" ("Knightsbridge" from the *London Suite*), "Music While You Work" (*Calling all Workers*) and "Desert Island Discs" (*By the Sleepy Lagoon*). The cinema furthered the cause with the huge success of *The Dam Busters* march. There is much more to his music, though, than mere hit themes. Suites such as *London, London Again, From Meadow to Mayfair* and *The Three Elizabeths* offer a wealth of delights and are all the better for the juxtaposition of their contrasted movements. The two tone-poems for children, *Cinderella* and *The Three Bears* are splendidly apt pieces of programme music — simple to follow, ever charming, never trite. The miniature overture *The Merrymakers* and the elegant waltz "At the dance" (from the suite *Summer Days* are other superb pieces of light music, whilst the *Saxo-Rhapsody* shows Coates in somewhat more serious mood. Throughout there is a rich vein of melody, and an elegance and grace of orchestration that makes this music to listen to over and over again with ever increasing admiration. The three conductors and orchestras featured adopt a no-nonsense approach that modestly suggests that his music should not be lingered over, never taken too seriously.

Considering that the Mackerras items were first issued in 1956 (the rest being from 1968-71), the sound is of astonishingly good and remarkably uniform quality. This is a veritable feast of delightful music and, at its low price, a remarkable bargain.

Coates. The Seven Dwarfs. The Jester at the Wedding. Four Centuries. **East of England Orchestra/Malcolm Nabarro.** ASV White Line CDWHL2075.

`lh 7m DDD 8/93`

Nabarro treads ground virtually ignored in recent times. The *Four Centuries* suite has not been recorded since 1953. Yet the real rarity is *The Seven Dwarfs*, the themes of which were reused for *The Enchanted Garden*, but which has never been heard in its original form and orchestration since shortly after its creation as a ballet for the 1930 revue *Charlot's Masquerade*. The results may not be the very best of Coates; but even Coates a little below his most inventive still means music that is highly tuneful, elegantly constructed and beautifully orchestrated. The "Dance of the Orange Blossoms" from *The Jester at the Wedding* is justly celebrated, and the fifth movement ("The Princess") is an especially delightful piece in more restrained vein. In the *Four Centuries* suite, Nabarro brings out the contrasting dance styles of the various centuries and gives an extra vigour to the closing twentieth-century movement, complete with saxophones and syncopated effects. This is a must not only for Coates enthusiasts but for all lovers of quality light music.

Samuel Coleridge-Taylor

British 1875-1912

Coleridge-Taylor. Scenes from "The Song of Hiawatha". **Helen Field** (sop); **Arthur Davies** (ten); **Bryn Terfel** (bar); **Welsh National Opera Chorus and Orchestra/Kenneth Alwyn.** Argo 430 356-2ZH2. Notes and text included. Recorded in 1990.

`② lh 59m DDD 9/91`

Hiawatha's best days probably lie irrevocably in the past when the choral societies kept its publishers going with orders for copies and every year at the Albert Hall the tribes would gather for a performance in costume under Great Chief Malcolm Sargent. This new recording is at the very least an honourable reminder of those times, with choral forces that make it very clear why it was so beloved of choirs throughout the land, and orchestral playing that brings out the attractions of rhythm and colour that are also characteristic. There is an appropriately limpid, sparkling Laughing Waters in Helen Field, Arthur Davies sings the famous "Onaway, awake beloved" in fine lyrical style and Bryn Terfel makes a splendidly dramatic impression as he laments the death of Minnehaha. In short, it is a fully worthy performance under Kenneth Alwyn, and the recording is fine too. A question mark still hangs over the work itself. So often it seems to be on the verge of adventurous exploration and then to withdraw so as to remain within sound of the matinée teacups. Yet it has a genuine impulse behind it, and at times (particularly in Hiawatha's farewell) it generates emotion which one can well imagine might be almost alarmingly powerful on a grand occasion in the Albert Hall, if rather less so on an evening with the compact disc player at home.

Further listening ...

Ballade in A minor, Op. 33. Symphonic Variations on an African Air, Op. 63. *Coupled with* **Butterworth.** A Shropshire Lad. Two English Idylls. The banks of green willow. **MacCunn.** The land of the mountain and the flood, Op. 3. **Royal Liverpool Philharmonic Orchestra/Grant Llewellyn.** Argo 436 401-2ZH (6/93). *Reviewed under Butterworth; refer to the Index to Reviews.*

Petite suite de concert, Op. 77[d]. Ballade in D minor, Op. 4[bd]. 24 Negro Melodies, Op. 59[d] — Take Nabandji; Going Up; Deep River; Run, Mary, run; Sometimes I feel like a motherless child; The Bamboula. Clarinet Quintet in F sharp minor, Op. 10[ac]. [a]**Harold Wright** (cl); [b]**Michael**

Ludwig (vn); ᶜ**Hawthorne Quartet** (Ronan Lefkowitz, Si-Jing Huang, vns; Mark Ludwig, va; Sato Knudson, vc); ᵈ**Virginia Eskin** (pf). Koch International Classics 37056-2 (10/92).

Loÿset Compère

French c.1445-1518

New review

Compère. SACRED AND SECULAR VOCAL WORKS. **Orlando Consort** (Robert Harre-Jones, alto; Charles Daniels, Angus Smith, tens; Donald Greig, bar). Metronome METCD1002. Texts and translations included.
Omnium bonorum plena. Se j'ay parlé. Seray je vostre mieulx amée. Ave Maria, gratia plena. Alons fere nos barbes. Ne vous hastez pas. Asperges me, Domine. Che fa la ramacina. Scaramella fa la galla. Missa in Nativitate, "Deus Noster Jesu Christie".

⸱•⸱ 58m DDD 6/94

The generation born around 1450 spawned a marvellous muchness of cosmopolitan, inventive and versatile musicians. Loÿset Compère's surname may be freely translated as 'crony', which fits the composer's musical personality very nicely. Far from the intellectual preoccupations of Josquin or the existential *Angst* of La Rue, Compère typifies a less self-conscious idiom of straightforward formal schemes and easily remembered melodies. His versatility is evident from the sheer variety of musical types represented here: *Seray je vostre mieulx amée* embodies the courtly love tradition at its most lyrical, while the naughty *Se j'ay parlé* and the frankly obscene *Alons fere nos barbes* are clear forerunners of the Parisian chanson of a generation or two later. But an ecstatic tone is not beyond Compère's reach: *Asperges me, Domine* is most moving. The Orlandos are at their best in this kind of melody-driven polyphony: phrasing and dynamic variations are sensitively and skilfully managed, tempos are well judged and the sound quality is admirable.

Aaron Copland

American 1900-1990

New review

Copland. Concerto for Clarinet and String Orchestra with Harp and Piano.
Busoni. Concertino for Clarinet and Small Orchestra, Op. 48.
Mozart. Clarinet Concerto in A major, K622. **Paul Meyer** (cl); **English Chamber Orchestra/David Zinman.** Denon CO-75289.

⸱•⸱ 56m DDD 11/93

One of Paul Meyer's most distinctive qualities as a clarinettist is the smoothness of his tone at all dynamic levels, together with his ability to initiate a soft note with a scarcely audible beginning and to let it die away until it loses itself almost inaudibly. This betokens, of course, immense technical control, and it is impressively displayed on this record; the variety of the tone is less remarkable. So the long, cool phrases at the start of Copland's Concerto are beautifully poised, and the rare atmosphere is sustained as by almost no other player, perhaps not even Benny Goodman. Goodman, for whom the work was written and who gave encouragement to Meyer, naturally had the swing manner as no one else did (once he had got round the technical difficulties, which seem to have rattled him). Meyer plays brightly, and this is a very fresh and pleasant performance. With Busoni's odd, eclectic *Concertino*, Meyer does his best to make sense of the welter of half-allusions and shifts in manner. It is not his fault if the piece remains somewhat unfocused. These two works will probably guide listeners in their choice rather than Mozart's Concerto, which has of course been recorded by pretty well every modern clarinettist of note. Meyer keeps it cool, fairly near the surface. He does not respond to the darker elements in the development of the first movement, nor to the tensions that clutch at the centre of the *Adagio*. He is at his best in the cheerful insouciance he brings to the finale.

Additional recommendation ...
Clarinet Concerto[a]. Connotations. El salón México. Music for the Theatre. [a]**Stanley Drucker** (cl); **New**
York Philharmonic Orchestra/Leonard Bernstein. DG 431 672-2GH — ⸱•⸱ 1h 14m DDD 8/91

Copland. ORCHESTRAL WORKS. **Detroit Symphony Orchestra/Antál Dorati.** Decca Ovation 430 705-2DM. Items marked [a] from SXDL7547 (10/82), [b] 414 457-2DH (6/86). Recorded 1981-84.
El salón México[a]. Dance Symphony[a]. Fanfare for the Common Man[a]. Rodeo — Four Dance Episodes[a]. Appalachian Spring — suite[b].

1h 14m DDD 8/91   Ⓑ

This glorious disc shows how well Antál Dorati assimilated the music of Aaron Copland. The big-boned swagger of "Buckaroo Holiday" from *Rodeo* with its vision of open spaces and clear blue skies is established straightaway in Dorati's performance with keen rhythmic drive and fine orchestral articulation. The "Hoe Down" is properly exciting while the other two dance episodes are wonderfully expressive. In the 1945 suite of *Appalachian Spring* Dorati secures marvellous phrasing and dynamics but tends to understate the poetic elements of the score. Decca's sound quality is exemplary and is of demonstration standard in *Fanfare for the Common Man*, as it is in the enjoyable curtain-raiser, the sturdy, big-hearted *El salón México*. Dorati's vast experience as an interpreter of Stravinsky and Bartók pays fine dividends in Copland's gruesome *Dance Symphony*, music inspired by the vampire film fantasy, *Nosferatu*. This survey of Copland's most popular orchestral works is a welcome addition to the mid-price catalogue.

Additional recommendation ...
El salón México[c]. Danzón cubano[e]. An Outdoor Overture[e]. Quiet City[e]. Our Town[e]. Las agachadas[c]. Fanfare for the Common Man[e]. Lincoln Portrait[be]. Appalachian Spring — suite[e]. Rodeo — four dance episodes[e]. Billy the Kid — orchestral suite[e]. Music for Movies[d]. Letter from Home[e]. John Henry[e]. Symphony No. 3[d]. Clarinet Concerto[af]. [a]**Benny Goodman** (cl); [b]**Henry Fonda** (narr); [c]**New England Conservatory Chorus;** [d]**New Philharmonia Orchestra;** [e]**London Symphony Orchestra;** [f]**Columbia Symphony Orchestra/Aaron Copland.** Sony Classical M3K46559 — ③ 3h 46m ADD 7/91 b
Appalachian Spring (orig. version). Music for the Theatre. Quiet City. Three Latin American Sketches. **St Paul Chamber Orchestra/Hugh Wolff.** Teldec 2292-46314-2 — 1h 16m DDD 7/91 ⁹ₛ Ⓑ
Appalachian Spring. Billy the Kid — Suite. Rodeo. Fanfare for the Common Man. **New York Philharmonic Orchestra/Leonard Bernstein.** Sony Classical Bernstein Royal Edition SMK47543 — 1h 3m ADD 5/93 Ⓑ

Copland. ORCHESTRAL WORKS.
R. Harris. American Creed. When Johnny comes marching home. [a]**James Earl Jones** (spkr); **Seattle** [b]**Chorale and Symphony Orchestra/Gerard Schwarz.** Delos DE3140. Texts included. Recorded in 1992.
Copland: Fanfare for the Common Man. Lincoln Portrait[a]. Canticle of Freedom[b]. An Outdoor Overture.

1h 1m DDD 5/93

Recordings of Copland's music are legion, but not many are as well done as this and few are as imaginatively coupled. The familiar *Fanfare for the Common Man* makes an obvious enough prelude, followed by the rousing *Lincoln Portrait* but the *Canticle of Freedom*, not otherwise available on record, is something of a Copland discovery: strong, stirring and simple of outline. The lively *Outdoor Overture* reminds us how close wide open spaces are to the American idea of freedom, and this is taken up in the splendid *American Creed* of Roy Harris, which evokes the freedom to dream and the freedom to build as fundamentals: cues, respectively, for one of Harris's nobly plangent melodies and for a grandiose display of his contrapuntal skill. Even the overture on *When Johnny comes marching home* is more than a filler: finding contrasting characters within a single melody was another of Harris's gifts. The orchestra and choir are on excellent form, and Schwarz is as good at distilling Copland's and Harris's quiet lyricism as he is their pages of sonorous grandeur. James Earl Jones brings an actor's care to the projection and expression of Lincoln's words, in a work that is too often used as a vehicle by less vocally gifted politicians. He effortlessly dwarfs the orchestra, even when hardly raising his voice: the only flaw on an otherwise clear and natural recording.

Copland. SONGS. **Roberta Alexander** (sop); **Roger Vignoles** (pf). Etcetera KTC1100. Texts included. Recorded in 1990.

A Summer Vacation. Alone. My heart is in the East. Night. Old American Songs, Sets 1 and 2. Old Poem. Pastorale. Poet's Song. 12 Poems of Emily Dickinson.

1h 12m DDD 3/92

It's a joy to have one of the greatest song-cycles to an English text back in the record catalogue — and performed by such a polished team as Alexander and Vignoles. The *12 Poems of Emily Dickinson* (1950) come from Copland's finest period — after the acknowledged successes of the three folk ballets and before he began to take on aspects of serial technique, after which he composed less and less. The cycle is a wonderful match between America's great New England nineteenth-century poet and one of her greatest composers. Warm lyricism, drama, and a continuously sensitive response to the poems make this work a landmark comparable to the best of Britten's cycles. The texts (the edited versions available at the time) are provided for all the songs. The performances, in a few details, are not quite flawless but Alexander has grown in stature and vocal control since her earliest recordings. Just as delightful, if not more so, are the early Copland songs — wistful, sad, nostalgic and beautifully wrought in every way. They demonstrate an instinctive musicianship of the highest order even before Copland went to study with Boulanger in Paris. And they get superb performances worthy of the finest Lieder. The *Old American Songs* are simply some of Copland's favourite tunes, some of which he used in other works and which he often performed himself as pianist or conductor. Alexander has plenty of zip, Vignoles is perhaps a little staid, but these songs complete an excellent and well-recorded vocal anthology.

Copland. THE TENDER LAND. **Elisabeth Comeaux** (sop) Laurie; **Janis Hardy** (mez) Ma Moss; **Maria Jette** (sop) Beth; **LeRoy Lehr** (bass) Grandpa Moss; **Dan Dressen** (ten) Martin; **James Bohn** (bar) Top; **Vern Sutton** (ten) Mr Splinters; **Agnes Smuda** (sop) Mrs Splinters; **Merle Fristad** (bass) Mr Jenks; **Sue Herber** (mez) Mrs Jenks; **Chorus and Orchestra of The Plymouth Music Series, Minnesota/Philip Brunelle.** Virgin Classics VCD7 59253-2. Notes and text included.

② 1h 47m DDD 8/90

Aaron Copland was a father figure of American music, and Leonard Bernstein expressed a lifelong admiration when he called him "the best we have". Yet though a generation separates them, *The Tender Land* had its première in 1954 just three years before *West Side Story*. Both opened in New York, but while Bernstein's piece is set there and portrays a violent urban America, Copland's belongs to the wide Midwest and the quiet of a farming home. It was written for young singers and has a wonderful freshness, a clean 'plainness' which Copland compared to that of his ballet *Appalachian Spring*. The story tells how the young girl Laurie Moss falls in love with Martin, a travelling harvester who visits her mother's farm, and after being left by him still decides to leave home and make her own way in the world. It has been criticized as undramatic, and its partly spoken dialogue and small cast have also gone against it — Copland later wryly called opera "la forme fatale" and never wrote another — but whatever its viability on stage, on record it provides a satisfying experience and this Minnesota performance has just the right flavour, offering simplicity and sensitivity without affectation. The conductor is himself a Midwesterner who writes that his young cast "have their roots in this particular soil" which is the heartland of America. The recording is every bit as fresh as the music.

Further listening ...

Piano Concerto. *Coupled with* **Britten.** Piano Concerto. **Gillian Lin** (pf); **Melbourne Symphony Orchestra/John Hopkins.** Chandos Collect CHAN6580 (3/93).

Symphony No. 3. Music for a Great City. **Saint Louis Symphony Orchestra/Leonard Slatkin.** RCA Victor Red Seal RD60149 (2/91).

Arcangelo Corelli

Italian 1653-1713

Corelli. 12 Concerti grossi, Op. 6. **The English Concert/Trevor Pinnock.** Archiv Produktion 423 626-2AH2.

No. 1 in D major; No. 2 in F major; No. 3 in C minor; No. 4 in D major; No. 5 in B flat major; No. 6 in F major; No. 7 in D major; No. 8 in G minor; No. 9 in F major; No. 10 in C major; No. 11 in B flat major; No. 12 in F major.

② 2h 10m DDD 1/89

In his working life of about 40 years Corelli must have produced a great deal of orchestral music, yet the 12 Concerti grossi, Op. 6 form the bulk of what is known to have survived. Their original forms are mostly lost but we know that those in which they were published in Amsterdam by Estienne Roger had been carefully polished and revised by the composer — and that they were assembled from movements that had been written at various times. The first eight are in *da chiesa* form, the last four in *da camera* form — without and with named dance movements respectively, and the number of their movements varies from four to seven. Each features the interplay of a group of soloists, the *concertino* (two violins and a cello) and the orchestra, the *ripieno*, the size of which Corelli stated to be flexible. These are masterpieces of their genre, one that was later developed by, notably, Bach and Handel, and they are rich in variety. The scores leaves scope for embellishment, not least in cadential and lining passages, and the players of The English Concert take full advantage of them. Regarding the overall performances, suffice it to say that this recording won a *Gramophone* Award in 1990.

Additional recommendations ...
La Petite Bande/Sigiswald Kuijken. Deutsche Harmonia Editio Classica GD77007 — ② 2h 16m ADD 9/90
Academy of Saint Martin in the Fields/Sir Neville Marriner. Decca Serenata 430 560-2DM2 — ② 2h 7m ADD 2/92
Ensemble 415/Chiara Banchini (vn); **Jesper Christensen** (hpd). Harmonia Mundi HMC90 1406/7 — 2h 27m DDD 6/92
Guildhall String Ensemble/Robert Salter (vn). RCA Victor Red Seal RD60071 — ② 2h 8m DDD 9/91
Nos. 1, 3, 7, 8, 9 and 11. **Tafelmusik Baroque Orchestra/Jean Lamon** (vn). Deutsche Harmonia Mundi RD77908 — 1h 6m DDD 12/89
Brandenburg Consort/Roy Goodman. Hyperion CDA66741/2 — ② 2h 18m DDD 9/93

Corelli. TRIO SONATAS. [c]**Jakob Lindberg** (theorbo); **Purcell Quartet** (Catherine Mackintosh, [a]**Elizabeth Wallfisch,** [b]**Catherine Weiss,** vns; Richard Boothby, vc); **Robert Wooley** ([a]hpd/[b]org). Chandos Chaconne CHAN0526. Recorded (Op. 3) 1990, (Op. 4) 1992. 12 Trio Sonatas, Op. 3[a] — F major; D major[c]; B flat major; B minor; D minor[c]; G major. 12 Trio Sonatas, Op. 4[b] — C major; G minor; A major; D major; A minor; E major.

1h 16m DDD 12/92

Corelli's chamber music was reprinted 84 times during his lifetime and 31 more during the rest of the eighteenth century, a record that most composers would find enviable even today. The Sonatas of Op. 3 are *da chiesa*, those of Op. 4 are *da camera* (with dance-titled movements); the recording contains the first six of each set — the remaining ones are on another disc (Chandos CHAN0532), should you (as is probable) be tempted to add them to your collection. They are small gems: most have four movements and their durations range from five-and-a-half to seven-and-a-half minutes, within which they pack a wealth of invention, pure beauty and variety of pace and mood. Surviving evidence suggests that they were played at a much lower pitch than today's standard, the lower string tension adding warmth and opulence to the sound. Catherine Mackintosh takes full advantage of the works' opportunities for pliant phrasing and added embellishments; Elizabeth Wallfisch 'converses' with her in her own characteristic way, whilst Catherine Weiss (Wallfisch's replacement in Op. 4) follows her example more closely. The Purcell Quartet's oneness of thought and timing in these landmark works is a joy to hear and the recording is superb in all respects.

Additional recommendation ...
12 Trio Sonatas, Op. 1. 12 Trio Sonatas, Op. 2. 12 Trio Sonatas, Op. 3. 12 Trio Sonatas, Op. 4. 12 Violin Sonatas, Op. 5. Violin Sonatas — A major; D major (3); A minor. 12 Concerti grossi, Op. 6. Sinfonia in D minor. Sonata a quattro in D major. Fuga a quattro in D major. 6 Trio Sonatas, Op. posth. — A major; D major (3); G minor (2). Sonata a quattro in G minor. **Bizantina Accademia/ Carlo Chiarappa.** Europa Musica 350 202 — ⑨ 9h 56m DDD 5/91

Further listening ...

Concerto grosso in G minor, Op. 6 No. 8, "Christmas Concerto". *Coupled with* **A. Scarlatti.**
O di Betlemme altera povertà[a]. **Vivaldi.** Gloria in D major, RV589[b]. [ab]**Nancy Argenta,**
[b]**Jennifer Smith** (sops); [b]**Catherine Wyn-Rogers** (contr); [b]**The English Concert Choir;**
The English Concert/Trevor Pinnock. Archiv Produktion 437 834-2AH (3/94). *See review
under A. Scarlatti; refer to the Index to Reviews.*

John Corigliano

American 1938-

New review
Corigliano. Violin Sonata. MUSIC FOR VIOLIN AND PIANO. **Maria Bachmann** (vn); **Jon
Klibonoff** (pf). Catalyst 09026 61824-2. Recorded in 1993.
Pärt: Fratres. *Moravec:* Violin Sonata. *Glinsky:* Toccata-Scherzo. *Messiaen:* Quatuor pour
la fin du temps — Louange à l'Eternité de Jésus.

lh 9m DDD 12/93

Here's a double-barrelled surprise: gripping new music for violin and piano and a performing
style that revisits a sweet-scented immediacy more typical of previous generations. Maria
Bachmann has a bright, winsome tone and a heart-warming interpretative manner. The works
that particularly suit her are Corigliano's 1963 Violin Sonata and the two pieces that were
written with her in mind, Albert Glinsky's Toccata-Scherzo and Paul Moravec's Sonata. Of the
latter two, the Glinsky is the more memorable — a sort of Sarasate for the 1990s, its lyrical
centre-piece flanked by brilliant outer sections. The Corigliano harbours the kind of juicy
'tunes' that modern players search for in vain but hardly ever find in contemporary music. The
Lento is strikingly memorable, whereas elsewhere Corigliano demands all the tricks of the
fiddler's trade — harmonics, pizzicatos, sul ponticello and so on, all couched in an appealing
musical context that might best be described as Stravinsky-cum-Samuel Barber. Messiaen
himself said of his "Praise to the Immortality of Jesus" that it "specifically addresses the second
aspect of Jesus, namely His human aspect, the Word that has become flesh, resurrected
immortal to give Him life." And it's as well to bear that in mind when listening to Bachmann's
unusually sensuous performance. Bachmann receives sympathetic support from Jon Klibonoff
and both are nicely recorded.

Further listening ...

Symphony No. 1. **Chicago Symphony Orchestra/Daniel Barenboim.** Erato 2292-45601-2
(7/91).

Clarinet Concerto[a]. *Coupled with* **Barber.** Third Essay for Orchestra, Op. 47. [a]**Stanley
Drucker** (cl); **New York Philharmonic Orchestra/Zubin Mehta.** New World NW309-2
(5/88).

Oboe Concerto[a]. Three Irish Folk-song Settings[b] — The Salley Gardens; The Foggy, Foggy dew;
She moved thro' the fair. Poem in October[c]. [bc]**Robert White** (ten); [b]**Ransom Wilson,**
[c]**Thomas Nyfenger** (fls); [ac]**Humbert Lucarelli** (ob); [c]**Joseph Rabbai** (cl); [c]**American
Quartet/Maurice Peress** (hpd); [a]**American Symphony Orchestra/Kazuyoshi Akiyama.**
RCA Victor Gold Seal GD60395 (5/91).

Aria. *Coupled with* **Barlow.** The Winter's Past. **Bloom.** Requiem. Narrative. **Wilder.**
Concerto for Oboe, String Orchestra and Percussion. Piece for Oboe and Improvisatory
Percussion[a]. **Humbert Lucarelli** (ob); [a]**Mark Wood** (perc); **Brooklyn Philharmonic
Orchestra/ Michael Barrett.** Koch International Classics 37187-2 (7/94). *See Review under
Wilder; refer to the Index to Reviews.*

Carl August Cornelius

Suggested listening ...

Stabat mater. Requiem. **Soloists; Cannes-Provence-Alpes-Côte d'Azur Chorus and Orchestra/Michel Piquemal.** Harmonia Mundi HMC90 5206 (4/90).

William Cornysh

Suggested listening ...

Salve regina. Ave Maria, mater Dei. Gaude virgo mater Christi. Magnificat. Ah, Robin. Adieu, adieu, my heartes lust. Adieu courage. Woefully arrayed. Stabat mater. **The Tallis Scholars/ Peter Phillips.** Gimell CDGIM014 (4/89).

Ave Maria, mater Dei. *Coupled with* **Davy.** O Domine caeli terraeque. A myn hart remembir the well. A blessid Jhesu. **Lambe.** Stella caeli. **Wilkinson.** Credo in Deum/Jesus autem. Salve regina. **The Sixteen/Harry Christophers.** Collins Classics 1342-2 (7/93). *See review in the Collections section; refer to the Index to Reviews.*

Napoléon Coste

New review
Coste. GUITAR WORKS.
Sor. GUITAR WORKS. **Raphaëlla Smits** (gtr). Accent ACC29182D.
Coste: Pièces originales, Op. 53 — No. 1, Reverie. Morceaux episodiques, Op. 23 — No. 7, Les soirées d'Auteuil. Grande sérénade, Op. 30. *Sor:* Introduction and Variations on a theme by Mozart, Op. 9. Fantasia élégiaque in C minor, Op. 59. Etudes — Op. 6 No. 11; Op. 31 No. 12; Op. 35 No. 22.

Ih Im DDD 8/93

There are other currently available recordings of all but one (Op. 31 No. 12) of the works by Sor, but none that takes clear precedence over these by Raphaëlla Smits. The sum total of her attention to detail, sensitivity, controlled use of rubato, expressive vibrato, purity of tone and crystal-clear delivery is one which is matched by very few. Sor stood on the threshold of romanticism, Coste stepped over it enthusiastically. His music, radically different from that of Sor, often deals in overtly poetic images and abounds in gestural cadenzas: in various respects, both technical and musical, he stood between Sor and Tárrega — and was arguably more harmonically adventurous than either. These performances are of the utmost refinement, character and authority, and are superbly recorded.

François Couperin

New review
F. Couperin. Pièces de violes. Les goûts-réunis[a] — Douzième Concert in A major; Troisième Concert in G major. **Wieland Kuijken,** [a]**Kaori Uemura** (va da gambas); **Robert Kohnen** (hpd). Accent ACC9288D.

58m DDD 4/94

Couperin composed his first and only pieces for bass viol and figured bass towards the end of his life. They were published in two suites in 1728 by which time a magnificent French tradition in virtuoso bass viol composition was drawing to a close. Kuijken adopts a brisk tempo and a rhetorical approach to the wonderfully expressive Préludes with which Couperin begins each of the two Suites. An important deciding factor in choosing any performance of these suites is the extent to which sensibilities are aroused by the melancholy "Pompe funèbre" (Suite No. 2), Couperin's immortal contribution to the French musical-poetic *tombeau* and Kuijken does not disappoint. He impresses with his vital playing of the enigmatically titled "La Chemise blanche" of the same suite and readers will further be attracted by the inclusion of two suites from Couperin's *Les goûts réunis* (1724). An excellent performance with a slightly reverberant acoustic.

F. Couperin. HARPSICHORD WORKS. **Kenneth Gilbert.** Harmonia Mundi Musique d'abord HMA190 351/60 (two triple- and two double-disc sets).
HMA 190 351/3 (2h 32m) — Premier livre de clavecin: *Ordres* — 1 (from RCA LSB4067, 9/72); 2 (LSB4077, 2/73); 3 and 4 (LSB4087, 5/73); 5 (LSB4098, 8/73). HMA190 354/6 (3h 11m) — Deuxième livre de clavecin: *Ordres* — 6 and 7 (RCA LHL1 5048, 1/75); 8. L'art de toucher le clavecin (LHL1 5049, 1/75). *Ordres* — 9 and 10 (LHL1 5050, 2/75); 11 and 12 (LHL1 5051, 2/75). HMA190 357/8 (2h 30m) — Troisième livre de clavecin: *Ordres* — 13 (new to UK); 14 to 19 (all from RCA SER5720/23, 4/75). HMA190 359/60 (2h 32m) — Quatrième livre de clavecin: *Ordres* — 20 to 27 (LHL4 5096, 12/75).

④ ADD 10/89

Couperin's solo harpsichord music, collected in four volumes and published between 1713 and 1730, represents one of the highest peaks of baroque keyboard repertory. Its elusive and, indeed allusive style, however, frequently gets the better of would-be performers and it is doubtless partly for this reason that only five complete versions of this music have been issued commercially. Kenneth Gilbert has long been acknowledged a master of French baroque interpretation and his performance of Couperin's 27 *Ordres* — the word implies something between a suite and an anthology — though now 25 years old, has not been surpassed. Indeed, it is no mean tribute to his informed approach that these interpretations strike today's audiences as being as stylish as when they were first issued in 1971. Gilbert scrupulously adheres to aspects of performance by which the composer himself set such store. Couperin was precise about ornamentation and related matters and Gilbert is meticulous in his observance of them. Unequal rhythms are applied discerningly but with a natural ease that variously brings out the nobility, the grandeur, and the tenderness of the music. There is, in short, a wonderful variety of affects to be found in these pieces and Gilbert seldom if ever disappoints us in his feeling for them. From among the most infinite delights to be found in this impressive and satisfying project we may, perhaps, mention the *Ordres* Nos. 6, 7, 8 and 26 in their entirety, and the exquisitely shaped seventh prelude from *L'art de toucher le clavecin* are outstanding examples of Gilbert's artistry. Small technical deficiencies in the remastering appear almost negligible in the face of so much that is rewarding. These are performances to treasure for a lifetime.

Additional recommendations ...
L'art de toucher le clavecin: Préludes — C *major;* D *minor;* G *minor;* B *flat major;* F *minor;* A *major.*
Premier livre: Troisième ordre — *Allemande La ténébreuse; Courantes I and II; Sarabande La lugubre;*
L'espagnolète; Chaconne La favorite. Cinquième ordre — *Sarabande La dangereuse; Les ordes. Dieuxième*
livre: Sixième ordre — *Les baricades mistérieuses. Huitième ordre* — *La Raphaéle; Allemande L'Ausoniène;*
Courantes I and II. Sarabande L'unique; Gavotte; Rondeau; Gigue; Passacaille. Troisième livre: Quinzième
ordre — *Le dodo ou L'amour au berçeau. Quatrième livre: Vingt-troisième ordre* — *L'arlequine.*
Vingtquatrième ordre — *Les vieux seigneurs.* **Skip Sempé.** Deutsche Harmonia Mundi RD77219 —
.·′ 1h 12m DDD 1/91 ⁹ₚ ✎
Troisième livre de clavecin. Quartre concerts royaux. **Christopher Rousset, Blandine Rannou**
(hpds). Harmonia Mundi HMC90 1442/4 — .·′ ③ 3h 33m DDD 9/93 ⁹ₚ ✎
Troisième livre de clavecin. **Olivier Baumont, Davitt Moroney** (hpds). Erato MusiFrance 4509-
92859-2 — .·′ ② 2h 14m DDD 2/94 ⁹ₚ ✎

F. Couperin. Trois leçons de ténèbres[a]. Motet — Victoria! Christo resurgenti. **Judith Nelson** [a]**Emma Kirkby** (sops); **Jane Ryan** (va da gamba); **Christopher Hogwood**

(chamber org). L'Oiseau-Lyre 430 283-2OH. Notes, texts and translations included. From DSLO536 (6/78). Recorded in 1977.

43m ADD 12/91

Couperin's three *Leçons de ténèbres*, dating from the second decade of the eighteenth century, are masterly examples of a peculiarly French sacred musical idiom. Sung during Holy Week, their texts are drawn from the *Lamentations of Jeremiah* interspersed with ornamental melismatic phrases inspired by ritualistic Hebrew letters. The subtle blend of Italian monody with French court air, which characterizes Couperin's *Leçons* and those of his predecessor Charpentier, seems to have been appearing both at court and wider afield. Several recordings of these beautiful pieces have been made and the competition is very strong. That being said, the lightly articulated and fresh-sounding performances of the sopranos Emma Kirkby and Judith Nelson have lost little or nothing of their charm over the intervening years. Nelson sings the first *Leçon* and Kirkby the second, by the way. These are cooler readings than some others and, one might perhaps say, more *da chiesa* in their approach than other sensuous performances. It is well recorded and includes the radiant Easter motet, *Victoria! Christo resurgenti*. Attention to stylistic details is a major feature here; the continuo realizations are discreet, tasteful and assured.

Additional recommendation ...
As above. Magnificat. **Mieke van der Sluis** (sop); **Guillemette Laurens** (mez); **Pascal Monteilhet** (lute); **Marianne Muller** (va da gamba); **Laurence Boulay** (hpd, org). Erato Musifrance 2292-45012-2 — lh lm DDD 8/90

Further listening ...

H/CD8613 — Messe à l'usage ordinaire des paroisses[a]. *Plainchant:* Liturgy for Easter Day (Ensemble Organum/Marcel Pérès). *H/CD8615* — Messe pour les couvents de religieux et religieuses. *Coupled with* **Du Mage.** Livre d'orgue[b]. **Jean-Charles Ablitzer** (org). Harmonic Records H/CD8613 and H/CD8615 (9/91).

Louis Couperin
French c.1626-1661

Suggested listening ...

Harpsichord Suites. Pavanne in F sharp minor. Prelude and Chaconne in G minor; Two Pieces in B flat major. Three Pieces in G minor. Four Pieces in G major. **Davitt Moroney** (hpd). Harmonia Mundi Musique d'abord HMA190 1124/7 (4/90).

Sir Noël Coward
British 1899-1973

Suggested listening ...

BITTER SWEET — *operetta.* **Soloists; New Sadler's Wells Opera Chorus and Orchestra/ Michael Reed.** That's Entertainment Records CDTER2 1160 (11/89).

Sir Frederic Cowen
British 1852-1935

Suggested listening ...

Symphony No. 3 in C minor, "Scandinavian". Indian Rhapsody. The Butterfly's Ball. **Košice State Philharmonic Orchestra/Adrian Leaper.** Marco Polo 8 223273 (2/91).

Paul Creston

Suggested listening ...

Symphony No. 3, Op. 48, "Three Mysteries". Invocation and Dance, Op. 58. Out of the Cradle. Partita for Flute, Violin and String Orchestra, Op. 12. **Iikka Talvi** (vn); **Scott Goff** (fl); **Seattle Symphony Orchestra, Gerald Schwarz.** Delos DE3114 (12/92).

William Croft

New review
Croft. Te Deum and Jubliate in D major. Musica sacra — Rejoice in the Lord, O ye righteous; The Burial Service. **St Paul's Cathedral Choir; Parley of Instruments/John Scott.** Hyperion CDA66606. Texts included.

Ih 12m   DDD   4/93

Modesty in the music of triumph, restraint in that of loss and grief, a decent moderation in all things: Croft's compositions represent much that was best in the age. He was a pupil of John Blow, whom he succeeded as organist at Westminster Abbey and as Master of the Chapel Royal, receiving an additional £80 per annum for teaching the children to read, write and do their sums. The *Te Deum* and *Jubilate*, thought to be written in celebration of Malplaquet, clearly have Purcell's settings in mind, but are rather more deliberately sustained, the sections developing their material more systematically. *Rejoice in the Lord* has a sprightly opening chorus (did Sullivan's mind jig along to it as he set Gilbert's "We thanked our lucky stars we were hardy British tars" in *Ruddigore*?). *The Burial Service*, with its more than merely respectful inclusion of Purcell's "Thou knowest, Lord", fully deserves its honoured place in traditional Anglican services, with the final "Amen" bringing the single relaxation of the severe features, the intertwining of rose and scythe in a chaste and simple eighteenth-century memorial-stone. Choir, soloists and players all do good work, and the none-too-easy processes of balancing the various groups in the acoustic of St Paul's have been judiciously worked out.

William Crotch

Suggested listening ...

Organ Concerto No. 2 in A major. Overture in G major. Sinfonias — E flat major; F major. **Andrew Lumsden** (org); **Milton Keynes Chamber Orchestra/Hilary Davan Wetton.** Unicorn-Kanchana DKPCD9126 (1/93).

George Crumb

Suggested listening ...

Five Pieces. Gnomic Variations. Makrokosmos I. **Jeffrey Jacob** (pf). Centaur CRC2050 (4/91).

Black Angels: Thirteen images from the Dark Land. *Coupled with* **Schubert.** String Quartet in D minor, "Death and the Maiden", D810. **Brodsky Quartet.** Teldec 9031-76260-2 (9/93).

Bernhard Crusell

Crusell. Clarinet Concerto No. 1 in E flat major, Op. 1.
L. Koželuch. Clarinet Concerto in E flat major.
Krommer. Clarinet Concerto in E flat major, Op. 36. **Emma Johnson** (cl); **Royal Philharmonic Orchestra/Günther Herbig.** ASV CDDCA763.

․ᐟ lh 7m DDD 9/91

The idiom of Stockholm-based composer Bernhard Crusell embraces elements of Mozart, Spohr, Weber, Rossini and even Beethoven. But in the hands of the young woodwind virtuoso, Emma Johnson, his music has a personality all its own. Here she turns her attention to his First Clarinet Concerto which is full of engaging ideas. The slow movement is beautifully done and in the finale the soloist is at her very best — full of impulsive charm and swagger. Although the Koželuch concerto, a recent discovery, seems less distinctive, the slow movement of the Krommer is undeniably affecting and its finale bounces along in fine style. Emma Johnson plays throughout with a winning spontaneity and the RPO, arguably just a shade tubby of timbre for such music, back her up with distinction. The generous acoustic is effectively caught.

Additional recommendation ...
Clarinet Concertos — No. 1; No. *2* in F minor, Op. 5; No. 3 in B flat major, Op. 11. **Orchestra of the Age of Enlightenment/Anthony Pay** (cl). Virgin Classics Veritas VC7 59287-2 — *․ᐟ*
lh 12m DDD 12/93 *⌕*

Frederic Curzon

Suggested listening ...

The·Boulevardier. Punchinello. In Málaga. Salterello[a]. Dance of an Ostracised Imp. Capricante. Galavant. Pasquinade. Simonetta. Cascade. Le Peinata. Robin Hood. Bravada. [a]**Silvia Capova** (pf); **Bratislava Radio Symphony Orchestra/Adrian Leaper.** Marco Polo British Light Music 8 223425 (6/93).

Carl Czerny

Suggested listening ...

Fantasie in F minor, Op. 226. Grande Sonate in F minor, Op. 178. Grande Sonate brillante in C minor, Op. 10. Ouverture characteristique et brillante in B minor, Op. 54. **Yaara Tal, Andreas Groethuysen** (pf, four hands). Sony Classical SK45936 (5/91).

Franz Danzi

Suggested listening ...

Flute Concertos — No. 1 in G major, Op. 30; No. 2 in D minor, Op. 31; No. 3 in D minor, Op. 42; No. 4 in D major, Op. 43. **András Adorján** (fl); **Munich Chamber Orchestra/ Hans Stadlmair.** Orfeo C003812H (8/88).

William Levi Dawson

American 1899-

Suggested listening ...

Dawson. Negro Folk Symphony. *Coupled with* **Ellington.** Harlem. **W.G. Still.** Symphony No. 2 in G minor, "Song of a New Race". **Detroit Symphony Orchestra/Neeme Järvi.** Chandos CHAN9226 (3/94). *See review under Still; refer to the Index to Reviews.*

Claude Debussy

French 1862-1918

New review

Debussy. ORCHESTRAL WORKS. **Concertgebouw Orchestra/[a]Eduard van Beinum, Bernard Haitink.** Philips Duo 438 742-2PM2. Items marked [a] from SABL130 (2/60), [b] 9500 509 (5/79), [c] 9500 674 (11/80), [d] 9500 359 (4/78).
Berceuse héroïque[a]. Images[b]. Danse sacrée et danse profane (with Vera Badings, hp)[b]. Jeux[c]. Nocturnes[c]. Marche écossaise sur un thème populaire[d]. Prélude à l'après-midi d'un faune[d]. La mer[d]. Première rapsodie (George Pieterson, cl)[d].

② 2h 2lm ADD 3/94

Philips have repackaged Haitink's late-1970s recordings on two CDs for the price of one. Space has also been found for Debussy's last orchestral work, the short *Berceuse héroïque* conducted by Eduard van Beinum (in excellent 1957 stereo). In every respect this package is a genuine bargain. In *La Mer*, like the 1964 Karajan on DG Galleria, there is a concern for refinement and fluidity of gesture, for a subtle illumination of texture; and both display a colourist's knowledge and use of an individually apt variety of orchestral tone and timbre. It is the wind playing that you remember in Haitink's *Images*: the melancholy and disconsolate oboe d'amore in "Gigues"; and from "Ibéria", the gorgeous oboe solo in "Les parfums de la nuit", and the carousing clarinets and raucous trumpets in the succeeding holiday festivities. And here, as elsewhere in the set, the Concertgebouw acoustic plays a vital role: after its wide open spaces, EMI's sound for Rattle (see below) suggests only an empty hall. Haitink's *Jeux*, though not as slow, or as naughty as Rattle's, is slower and freer than average, and possessed of a near miraculous precision, definition and delicacy. The jewel in this set, for many, will be the *Nocturnes*, principally for the purity of the strings in "Nuages"; the dazzling richness and majesty of the central procession in "Fêtes"; and the cool beauty and composure of "Sirènes". It is in this last movement where interpretation and balance differ most widely, with Solti (see below) opting for a voluptuous presence for the ladies' chorus, and Haitink an ethereal distance. With Haitink, there may be passages where you are unsure if they are singing or not, but the effect is quite as magical as the entry of the offstage choir in "Neptune" from *The Planets*.

Additional recommendations ...
La mer. Prélude à l'après-midi d'un faune. Jeux — poème dansé. **London Philharmonic Orchestra/Serge Baudo.** EMI Eminence CD-EMX9502 — 52m DDD 10/87
La mer. Prélude à l'après-midi d'un faune. **Ravel.** Daphnis et Chloé — Suite No. 2[a]. Boléro. **Berlin Philharmonic Orchestra/Herbert von Karajan.** DG Galleria 427 250-2GGA — lh 4m ADD 7/89
Jeux. Images. Musiques pour le Roi Lear. **City of Birmingham Symphony Orchestra/Simon Rattle.** EMI CDC7 49947-2 — lh 2m DDD 3/90
La mer. Prélude à l'après-midi d'un faune. Jeux. Le martyre de Saint Sébastien. **Montreal Symphony Orchestra/Charles Dutoit.** Decca 430 240-2DH — lh l5m DDD 2/91
Nocturnes[a]. Prélude à l'après-midi d'un faune. La mer. [a]womens' voices of the Chicago Symphony Chorus; **Chicago Symphony Orchestra/Sir Georg Solti.** Decca 436 468-2DH 55m DDD 10/92
Nocturnes — Nuages; Fêtes. Prélude à l'après-midi d'un faune. Le martyre de Saint Sébastien — symphonic fragments. La mer. **Philharmonia Orchestra/Guido Cantelli.** Testament mono SBT1011 — lh 7m ADD 10/92 ▲
La mer. Prélude à l'après-midi d'un faune. Nocturnes. **Orchestre de Paris/Daniel Barenboim.**

DG Classikon 439 407-2GCL — lh 2m ADD/DDD 1/94

La mer. Nocturnes. Prélude à l'après-midi d'un faune. Danse. **Philadelphia Orchestra/Eugene Ormandy.** Sony Classical SBK53256 — .⸱ Ih 5m ADD 3/94 ꝗ⟍p Ⓑ

La mer. Prélude à l'après-midi d'un faune.. Jeux. Rapsodie[a]. *Suite bergamasque — Clair de lune. Petite Suite — Menuet.* [a]**Robert Gugholz** (cl); **Suisse Romande Orchestra/Ernest Ansermet.** Decca 433 711-2DM — .⸱ Ih 14m ADD Ⓑ

Debussy. Khamma. Jeux. Printemps. Prélude à l'après-midi d'un faune. **Finnish Radio Symphony Orchestra/Jukka-Pekka Saraste.** Virgin Classics VC5 45018-2. Recorded 1991.

.⸱ Ih DDD 4/94   ꝗ⟍p

The familiar and the unfamiliar. In the latter category are works from the beginning and end of Debussy's output: the early "Suite Symphonique" *Printemps* in an orchestration by Henri Busser (Debussy's own had been destroyed in a fire at the book-binders), and the "Anglo-Egyptian Ballet" *Khamma* completed in 1913 to a commission from Maud Allen, an English dancer (an Isadora Duncan figure), and orchestrated by Charles Koechlin. Saraste's *Printemps* is not as distinguished as the spectacularly recorded 1962 Munch but the first movement is faster than usual and appealingly fresh and the second movement expresses, more than most, "the joy of being born into some new life". Saraste's *Prélude* joins an increasing number of recordings that dream for a mere nine minutes. His *Jeux* is also one of the most animated and mobile on disc. *Khamma* is unfairly neglected. Debussy himself declared that the work's exoticism occasioned "the most recent discoveries of harmonic chemistry". For a full appreciation of the ballet, a synopsis is essential; fortunately Virgin Classics include one; equally fortunately Saraste responds to the dramatic needs of the piece, and is decently recorded.

Additional recommendations ...
Printemps. Prélude à l'après-midi d'un faune. La mer. Nocturnes — Nuages; Fêtes. **Boston Symphony Orchestra/Charles Munch.** RCA Papillon GD86719 — .⸱ Ih 2m ADD 7/88

Debussy. La boîte a joujoux — ballet. Prélude à l'après-midi d'un faune. Jeux. **London Symphony Orchestra/Michael Tilson Thomas.** Sony Classical SK48231. Recorded 1991.

.⸱ Ih 3m DDD II/92   ꝗ⟍s

"Something to amuse the children, nothing more" wrote Debussy about his ballet score for *La boîte à joujoux* (mostly written in 1913, but completed after his death by André Caplet). The children would have been a lot more amused by the goings-on of the occupants of Tilson Thomas's toy box had Sony provided a decent synopsis, but his characterization, storytelling and evocation of atmosphere are so vivid that foreknowledge of events is almost unnecessary. Strictly adult entertainment is provided by this languorous *Prélude*, with particularly lovely, long-breathed playing from the LSO's principal flute; and the suspect shenanigans of *Jeux*, where Tilson Thomas eschews some of Haitink's miraculous acuity of rhythm and texture (reviewed above), and Rattle's rich romanticism (listed above), in favour of greater urgency and spontaneity. Recorded levels are higher for the *Prélude* than the rest of the programme, but this disc is superbly engineered: the sound has both a fine bloom and a tactile presence.

Debussy. Images — Ibéria.
Ravel. Rapsodie espagnole. Pavane pour une infante défunte. Valses nobles et sentimentales. Alborada del gracioso. **Chicago Symphony Orchestra/Fritz Reiner.** RCA Gold Seal GD60179. Recorded 1956-57.

.⸱ Ih 8m ADD I/90   ꝗ⟍p

These performances are seldom less than mesmeric. The extremes of tempo and dynamics are exploited to the full in the Spanish night/day pieces: has any other conductor managed the gradual transition from *Ibéria*'s "perfumes of the night" to the gathering brilliance of the succeeding morning's holiday festivities, with such a delicate, yet precisely focused tracery of sounds? This is the very stuff of a waking dream. And the disc opens with what has to be the slowest, most languid account of the "Prélude" from the *Rapsodie espagnole* ever recorded; the resulting total concentration of the players on their conductor for control of rhythm and dynamics can be felt in every bar; it's not just a musical stunt, it creates a unique tension and atmosphere. Just listen to the finesse of the playing throughout, particularly the percussion, and marvel at how Reiner balances the textures in even the most riotous outbursts of the *Rapsodie*'s explosive "Feria". And the sound? Normally this *Guide* carries caveats for discs recorded in the mid-1950s, and audio boffins might nod their heads at a minuscule degree of tape saturation and hiss, but it is difficult to think of any modern recording that renders the spectacle, colour and refinement of these scores with more clarity and atmosphere.

New review
Debussy. String Quartet in G minor, Op. 10.
Ravel. String Quartet in F major.
Webern. String Quartet (1905). **Hagen Quartet** (Lukas Hagen, Rainer Schmidt, vns; Veronika Hagen, va; Clemens Hagen, vc). DG 437 836-2GH.

Ih 10m DDD 6/94

The first movement of the Debussy is taken fastish, but its passionate urgency convinces and it is not forced tonally or tempo-wise. Indeed, the playing is beautifully polished, and this fine ensemble also fully understand the emotional world of the music, the slow movement (again more flowing than usual) offering an acid test which they pass easily. The finale is thrilling. In the Ravel, the playing is sensitive and skilful. Webern's one-movement Quartet was inspired by a painting entitled "Evolving, Being, Passing Away", and the music begins with a motif akin to Beethoven's "Muss es sein?" figure in his String Quartet, Op. 135. The scenario here is predictable: youthfully Germanic heart-searching and struggle, but with little that is memorable, and ultimately somewhat constipated. Still, this performance is persuasive, and the work deserves to be heard when played as well as this. The recording deserves praise: the sound is excellent, not least for viola and cello.

Additional recommendations …
Melos Quartet. DG 419 750-2GH — .•* 53m ADD 10/87 ⁹ₚ Ⓑ
Quartetto Italiano. Philips Silver Line 420 894-2PSL — .•* 57m ADD 10/88 ⁹ₚ Ⓑ
Chilingirian Quartet. EMI Eminence CD-EMX2156 — .•* 55m DDD 3/91 Ⓑ
LaSalle Quartet. DG Galleria 435 589-2GGA — .•* 52m ADD 9/92 Ⓑ
Carmina Quartet. Denon CO-75164 — .•* 53m DDD 3/93 ⁹ₚ Ⓑ
Debussy. Ravel. Dutilleux. *String Quartet, "Ainsi la Nuit".* **Juilliard Quartet.** Sony Classical SK52554 — .•* Ih 14m DDD 3/94 ⁹ₚ Ⓑ

Debussy. Violin Sonata in G minor[a]. Sonata for Flute, Viola and Harp[b].
Franck. Violin Sonata in A major[a].
Ravel. Introduction and Allegro[b]. [a]**Kyung Wha Chung** (vn); [b]**Osian Ellis** (hp); [a]**Radu Lupu** (pf); [b]**Melos Ensemble.** Decca 421 154-2DM. Items marked [a] from SXL6944 (9/80), [b] SOL60048 (9/62). Items marked [a] recorded in 1977, [b] 1962.

.•* Ih 7m ADD 1/89

This must be one of the best CD bargains around, with three masterpieces from the French tradition in excellent performances that have won the status of recording classics. Kyung Wha Chung and Radu Lupu are a fine duo who capture and convey the delicacy and poetry of the Franck Sonata as well as its rapturous grandeur, and never can the strict canonic treatment of the great tune in the finale have sounded more spontaneous and joyful. They are no less successful in the different world of the elusive Sonata which was Debussy's last work, with its smiles through tears and, in the finale, its echoes of a Neapolitan tarantella. The 1977 recording is beautifully balanced, with a natural sound given to both the violin and piano. The Melos Ensemble recorded the Ravel *Introduction and Allegro* 15 years before, but here too the recording is a fine one for which no allowances have to be made even by ears accustomed to good digital sound; as for the work itself, this has an ethereal beauty that is nothing short of magical and Osian Ellis and his colleagues give it the most skilful and loving performance. To talk about this disc as one for every collection savours of cliché, but anyone who does not have it may safely be urged to make its acquisition.

Additional recommendations ...
Violin Sonata. Sonata for Flute, Viola and Harp. Syrinx. Cello Sonata. Première Rapsodie for Clarinet and Piano. Petite pièce for Clarinet and Piano. **Athena Ensemble.** Chandos CHAN8385 — ⠴ 55m ADD 5/87 ⓑ
Violin Sonata[a]. Cello Sonata[b]. Syrinx[c]. Sonata for Flute, Viola and Harp[d]. [cd]**Roger Bourdin** (fl); [a]**Arthur Grumiaux** (vn); [d]**Colette Lequien** (va); [b]**Maurice Gendron** (vc); [d]**Annie Challan** (hp); [a]**István Hajdu**, [b]**Jean Françaix** (pfs). Philips Musica da Camera 422 839-2PC — ⠴ 45m ADD 10/89 ⁹ₚ ⓑ
Violin Sonata. Sonata for Flute, Viola and Harp. Syrinx. Cello Sonata. Chansons de Bilitis. **Nash Ensemble/Lionel Friend.** Virgin Classics VC7 59604-2 — ⠴ 1h 8m DDD 4/91 ⁹ₚ ⓑ
Violin Sonata. **Franck.** *Violin Sonata in A major.* **Fauré.** *Violin Sonata No. 1 in A major, Op. 13.* **Maurice Hasson** (vn); **Christian Ivaldi** (pf). Pickwick IMP Masters MCD37 — ⠴ 1h 7m DDD 6/92 ⓑ
Violin Sonata. **Lekeu.** *Violin Sonata in G major.* **Schubert.** *Sonatinas — D major, D384; A minor, D385; G minor, D408. Violin Sonata in A major, D574.* **Kreisler.** *Liebeslied. Liebesfreud. Schön Rosmarin. Caprice viennois. Tambourin chinois.* **Tartini** *(arr. Kreisler). Sonata in G minor, "Devil's Trill".* **Corelli** *(arr. Castagnone). Sonata in D minor, "La Follia", Op. 5 No. 12.* **Vitali** *(arr. Grumiaux). Ciacona in G minor.* **Veracini** *(arr. Castagnone). Sonata in A major, Op. 1 No. 7.* **Paganini.** *Le Streghe, Op. 8. I palpiti, Op. 13.* **Arthur Grumiaux** (vn); **Riccardo Castagnone** (pf). Philips The Early Years mono 438 516-2PM3 — ⠴ ③ 3h 16m ADD 11/93 ⁹ₚ ▲

Debussy. Cello Sonata[a].
Schubert. Sonata in A minor, D821, "Arpeggione"[b].
Schumann. Fünf Stücke im Volkston, Op. 102[a]. **Mstislav Rostropovich** (vc); **Benjamin Britten** (pf). Decca 417 833-2DH. Items marked [a] from SXL6426 (10/70), [b] SXL2298 (1/62).

⠴ **59m ADD 9/87** ⁹ₚ ⓑ

Britten was supremely gifted as conductor and pianist and here we hear him interpreting the music of others. The bewildering concentration of mood and imagery in Debussy's avowedly classical temperamental 15-minute Sonata presents special challenges to the players and its subtleties reveal themselves only after many hearings. Britten and Rostropovich bring to it and the other works a depth of understanding which is quite extraordinary. The Schubert Sonata is an engaging work, whilst the five Schumann pieces have a rustic simplicity and strength which these performers turn entirely to Schumann's advantage. Certainly a collector's item, this CD ought to be part of every chamber music collection. The analogue recordings have transferred extremely well.

Additional recommendations ...
Cello Sonata. **Martin.** *Ballade.* **Poulenc.** *Cello Sonata.* **William Conway** (vc); **Peter Evans** (pf). Linn Records CKD002 — ⠴ 51m DDD 11/91 ⁹ₚ ⓑ
Cello Sonata. **Bridge.** *Cello Sonata in D minor, H125. Four Short Pieces, H104 — Meditation; Spring song.* **E. Dohnányi.** *Cello Sonata in B flat minor, Op. 8.* **Bernard Gregor-Smith** (vc); **Yolande Wrigley** (pf). ASV CDDCA796 — ⠴ 1h 8m DDD 9/92 ⁹ₚ ⓑ

New review
Debussy. Préludes, Books 1 and 2. **Krystian Zimerman** (pf). DG 435 773-2GH2.

⠴ ② 1h 24m DDD 3/94 ⁹ₚ ⁹ₛ ⓑ

Two discs, retailing at a high mid price and playing for a total of 84 minutes? The playing and the recording had better be in the luxury class. Fortunately they are. Zimerman is the very model of a modern virtuoso. His overrriding aim is vivid projection of character. His quasi-orchestral range of dynamic and attack, based on close attention to textual detail (there are countless felicities in his observation of phrase-markings) and maximum clarity of articulation, is the means to that end. As a result, he draws out the many connections in this music with the romantic tradition, especially in pianistic *tours de force* such as "Les collines d'Anacapri", "Ce qu'a vu le vent d'Ouest" and "Feux d'artifice", which are treated to a dazzling Lisztian *élan*. The instrument he has selected is itself something of a star and DG's recording combines opulence with razor-sharp clarity. At the other extreme Zimerman displays an exquisite refinement of touch that makes the quieter pieces both evocative and touching. Such sensitively conceived and wonderfully executed Debussy playing stands, at the very least, on a level with a classic recording such as Gieseking's, or a comparably idiomatic modern one such as Martino Tirimo's.

Additional recommendations ...
Préludes. **Walter Gieseking.** EMI Références mono CDH7 61004-2 — .·* lh l0m ADD 4/88 ⁹ₚ ▲ Ⓑ
Préludes. **Martino Tirimo.** IMP Masters MCD16 — .·* lh l8m DDD 2/91 ⁹ₚ Ⓑ
Préludes. Images — *Sets 1 and 2. Estampes.* **Claudio Arrau.** Philips 432 304-2PM2 — .·* ②
2h l4m ADD 2/92 ⁹ₚ Ⓑ
Préludes. Deux Arabesques. Children's Corner. Estampes. Images, Sets 1 and 2. Mazurka, L'île joyeuse.
Pour le piano. **Werner Haas**. Philips Duo 438-718-2PM2 — .·* ② 2h 37m ADD 4/94 Ⓑ

Key to symbols

**Gramophone
Awards winners**

**Gramophone
Editor's choice**

Debussy. Suite bergamasque. Images oubliées. Pour le piano. Estampes. **Zoltán Kocsis.** Philips 412 118-2PH.

.·* **55m DDD 4/85**   ⁹ₚ Ⓑ

Debussy. PIANO WORKS. **Zoltán Kocsis.** Philips 422 404-2PH. Recorded in 1988. Images, Sets 1 and 2. D'un cahier d'esquisses. L'isle joyeuse. Deux arabesques. Hommage à Haydn. Rêverie. Page d'album. Berceuse héroïque.

.·* **lh 2m DDD 2/90**   ⁹ₚ ⁹ₛ Ⓑ

Three decades ago you could have counted on the fingers of one hand the performers who really had the measure of Debussy's piano style. Today there are many, but even so the Hungarian pianist Zoltán Kocsis stands out as especially idiomatic. On the first disc here, he plays four earlyish sets of pieces of which all but the *Suite bergamasque* are in the composer's favourite triptych form that he also used in *La mer*. The most 'classical' of them are the oddly titled *Pour le piano*, in which the Prelude echoes Bach's keyboard writing, and the *Suite bergamasque* with its eighteenth-century dances, but even in the latter work we find the composer's popular "Clair de lune" memorably impressionistic in its evocation of moonlight. In the *Estampes*, the last pieces played, he displayed a still more fully developed impressionism in musical pictures of the Far East, Moorish Spain and lastly a mysteriously rainswept urban garden. The rarity here is the *Images oubliées*, pieces dating from 1894 that Debussy left unpublished, doubtless because he reworked material from them in the *Estampes* and very obviously in the Sarabande of *Pour le piano*, but they are in their own right and here we can compare the different treatments of the similar ideas. The second recital is also a revealing portrait of the composer, its items discerningly offsetting the familiar with the less-known. It also brings playing not only of exceptional finesse, but at times of exceptional brilliance and fire. The main work is of course *Images*, its two sets completed in 1905 and 1907 respectively, by which time the composer was already master of that impressionistic style of keyboard writing so different from anything known before. For superfine sensitivity to details of textural shading Kocsis is at his most spellbinding in the first two numbers of the second set, "Cloches à travers les feuilles" and "Et la lune descend sur le temple qui fût". He is equally successful in reminding us of Debussy's wish to "forget that the piano has hammers" in the atmospheric washes of sound that he conjures (through his pedalling no less than his fingers) in *D'un cahier d'esquisses*. The sharp, clear daylight world of *L'isle joyeuse* reveals a Kocsis exulting in his own virtuosity and strength as he also does in the last piece of each set of *Images*, and even in the second of the two familiar, early *Arabesques*, neither of them mere vapid drawing-room charmers here. The recording is first rate. Both discs are highly recommendable. Zoltán Kocsis brings refinement and brilliance to all this music and the piano sound is exceptionally rich and faithful.

Additional recommendation ...
Images, Sets 1 and 2. Berceuse héroïque. Mazurka. La plus que lente. Masques. Elégie. La petit nègre. Page d'album. Morceau de concours. Hommage à Haydn. D'un cahier d'esquisses. Children's Corner. **Martino Tirimo** (pf). Pickwick IMP Masters MCD32 — .·' 1h 17m DDD 10/92 b

Debussy. Etudes, Books 1 and 2. **Mitsuko Uchida** (pf). Philips 422 412-2PH. Recorded in 1989.

.·' **47m DDD 7/90** q̣ₚ q̣ₛ

Near the beginning of his career, Debussy's *Prélude à l'après-midi d'un faune* (1894) opened the door (so it is often said) for modern music. His late works, including three chamber sonatas and the set of 12 piano studies (1915), opened another door, through which perhaps only he could have stepped. But his death from cancer in 1918 at the age of 56 put paid to that prospect. The harmonic language and continuity of the *Studies* is elusive even by Debussy's standards, and it takes an artist of rare gifts to play them 'from within', at the same time as negotiating their finger-knotting intricacies. Mitsuko Uchida is such an artist. On first hearing perhaps rather hyperactive, her playing wins you over by its bravura and sheer relish, eventually disarming criticism altogether. This is not just the finest-ever recorded version of the *Studies*; it is also one of the finest examples of recorded piano playing in modern times, matched by sound quality of outstanding clarity and ambient warmth.

Additional recommendations ...
Etudes, Books 1 and 2. Pour le piano. **Gordon Fergus-Thompson** (pf). ASV CDDCA703 — .·' 1h 2m DDD 7/90
Etudes. Estampes. L'isle joyeuse. **Martino Tirimo.** IMP Masters MCD14 — .·' 1h 11m DDD 10/90 q̣ₚ

Debussy. Le martyre de Saint-Sébastien. **Sylvia McNair** (sop); **Ann Murray** (mez); **Nathalie Stutzmann** (contr); **Leslie Caron** (narr); **London Symphony Chorus and Orchestra/Michael Tilson Thomas.** Sony Classical SK48240. Text and translation included. Recorded in 1991.

.·' **1h 6m DDD 3/93**

"Archers aim closely, I am the target; whoever wounds me the most deeply, loves me the most. From the depths I call forth your terrible love ... again ... again! ...AGAIN!" cries the Saint in ecstasy. What Oscar Wilde did to the story of Salome, so the Italian writer D'Annunzio did to the story of Saint Sebastian (a young Roman officer ordered to be killed by his own archers because of his sympathy for persecuted Christians). This was the first modern recording, not of the complete play (which lasted five hours!), but of an intelligent and effective reduction of the written text using the Saint as narrator, and incorporating all of an hour's worth of Debussy's incidental music. And it must be called a triumph. Leslie Caron's Saint is quietly intense and a model of restraint; Sylvia McNair's *vox coelestis* is just that, a gift from God; and the chorus and orchestra respond with total conviction to what is evidently, from Tilson Thomas, direction with a mission. The sheer sorcery of Debussy's music, as strongly imbued as his *Pélleas* with Wagner's *Parsifal*, benefits enormously from the acoustic of, appropriately, All Saints' Church in Tooting, London.

Additional recommendation ...
Le martyre de Saint-Sébastien. Ibéria. **Boston Symphony Orchestra/Charles Munch.** RCA GD60684 — .·' 1h 13m ADD ▲

Debussy. La damoiselle élue[a]. Prélude à l'après-midi d'un faune. Images — No. 2, Ibéria. [a]**Maria Ewing** (sop) Damoiselle; [a]**Brigitte Balleys** (contr) Narrator; **London Symphony** [a]**Chorus and Orchestra/Claudio Abbado.** DG 423 103-2GH. Text and translation included.

.·' **49m DDD 3/88** q̣ₛ

La damoiselle élue is scored for soprano, women's chorus and orchestra and sets verses from Dante Gabriel Rossetti's *The Blessed Damozel*. It is cast into four short movements and owes a clear debt to Wagner's *Parsifal*. The *Prélude à l'après-midi d'un faune* was Debussy's first real masterpiece and this evocation of Mallarmé's poem introduced a whole palette of new, supremely beautiful sounds, combining them into a musical structure both concise and subtly complex. Once heard it can never be forgotten. "Ibéria" is the central component of the orchestral set of *Images* and its three movements employ the rhythms and harmonies of Spanish music to conjure up a perfect picture of the Spanish/Mediterranean climate in its various moods. A fine Debussyan, Abbado penetrates to the heart of all these works and is given fine orchestral support throughout. Maria Ewing is an impressive Damoiselle and the women of the LSO chorus are in excellent voice. The recording is most successful, with good atmosphere and clarity.

Debussy. PELLEAS ET MELISANDE. **Eric Tappy** (ten) Pelléas; **Rachel Yakar** (sop) Mélisande; **Philippe Huttenlocher** (bar) Golaud; **Jocelyne Taillon** (mez) Geneviève; **Colette Alliot-Lugaz** (sop) Yniold; **François Loup** (bass) Arkel; **Michel Brodard** (bass) Doctor, Shepherd; **Monte-Carlo National Opera Orchestra/Armin Jordan.** Erato Libretto 2292-45684-2. Notes, text and translation included. From STU71296 (10/80). Recorded in 1979.

> ③ 2h 40m ADD 12/91

Maeterlinck's play was the inspiration for Debussy's sole masterpiece in the operatic genre. *Pelléas et Mélisande* tells of a medieval princess who falls in love with her husband Golaud's younger half-brother Pelléas, who is then killed by Golaud before Mélisande herself dies in childbirth. The story has a Wagnerian parallel in *Tristan und Isolde*, but the music is very different, being more restrained on the surface while suggesting no less powerful passions beneath. No modern performances have really succeeded in replacing the classic versions conducted by Roger Desormière (not currently available) and Ernest Ansermet, both of which preserve a tradition of performing this elusive piece that has since been lost. Armin Jordan's performance at once conjures up and then sustains the strange half-lit world of Maeterlinck's tale. Despite the title, in some ways the chief role is that of Golaud, and Philippe Huttenlocher, who is a superb singer-actor, makes us believe in and feel for him. Rachel Yakar is mysterious, delicate and wholly feminine as Mélisande — indeed, sometimes maddeningly so, for in her passivity and reluctance to explain herself she positively invites Golaud's jealous suspicions. The role of Pelléas can be sung either by a high baritone or by a tenor: again it is the latter and Eric Tappy therefore sounds all the more youthful and innocent compared with the dark baritone quality of Golaud (he's supposed to be 20 years younger). The other principals have less to do but are also satisfying, not least the bass François Loup as the kindly old king, Arkel. The orchestra under Armin Jordan play as if inspired and the clear recording allows every word to be heard, which is what Debussy wanted but is hard to achieve in the theatre. One gladly agrees with the original *Gramophone* review which found this performance "profoundly moving" and it offers us a considerable and very agreeable mid-price bargain.

Additional recommendations ...
Soloists; Montreal Symphony Chorus and Orchestra/Charles Dutoit. Decca 430 502-2DH2 — ② 2h 31m DDD 3/91
Soloists; Vienna State Opera Chorus; Vienna Philharmonic Orchestra/Claudio Abbado. DG 435 344-2GH2 — ② 2h 28m DDD 3/92
Soloists; Suisse Romande Orchestra/Ernest Ansermet. Decca Historic mono 425 965-2DM2 — ② 2h 28m ADD 4/93 ▲

Further listening ...

Music for Two Pianos — En blanc et noir[a]. Petite Suite[a]. Six épigraphes antiques[a]. Lindaraja[a]. Marche écossaise[a]. Ballade slave. Berceuse héroïque. Danse. Danse Bohémienne. Etudes, books 1 and 2. D'un cahier d'esquisses. Hommage à Haydn. Masques. Nocturne. Le petit nègre. La plus que lente. Rêverie. Suite bergamasque. Valse romantique. **Werner Haas,** [a]**Noël Lee** (pfs). Philips Duo 438 721-2PM2 (4/94).

Mélodies — L'âme évaporée. Ariettes oubliées. Beau soir. Les cloches. Fêtes galantes, Sets 1 and 2. Mandoline. Musique. Noël des enfants qui n'ont plus de maison. Nuit d'étoiles. Proses lyriques. **Claudette LeBlanc** (sop); **Valerie Tryon** (pf). Unicorn-Kanchana DKPCD9133 (4/93).

Mélodies — Jane. Caprice. Rondeau. Aimons-nous et dormons. La fille aux cheveux de lin. Calmes dans le demi-jour. Sept poèmes de Banville. Proses lyriques. Trois Poèmes de Stéphane Mallarmé. **Anne-Marie Rodde** (sop); **Noël Lee** (pf). Etcetera KTC1048 (4/88).

Ariettes oubliées. Cinq poèmes de Charles Baudelaire. Chansons de Bilitis. *Coupled with* **Ravel.** Histoires naturelles. **Nathalie Stutzmann** (contr); **Cathérine Collard** (pf). RCA Victor Red Seal RD60899 (7/92).

Lex van Delden

The Netherlands 1919-

New review

van Delden. Concerto for Two String Orchestras, Op. 71[a]. Piccolo Concerto, Op. 67[b]. Musica sinfonica, Op. 93[c]. Sinfonia No. 3, "Facets", Op. 45[d]. **Concertgebouw Orchestra/ [ab]Eugen Jochum, [c]Bernard Haitink, [d]George Szell.** Etcetera [ac]stereo/[bd]mono KTC1156. Item marked [a] recorded at a performance in the Concertgebouw, Amsterdam in 1968, [b] 1964, [c] 1969, [d] 1957.

1h 3m   ADD   3/94

Lex van Delden is an unfamiliar name to the majority of professional musicians, let alone the average record buyer in this country. In The Netherlands van Delden's name is more widely known and, judging by the calibre of the conductors featured in these late 1950s and 1960s radio broadcasts, a highly respected name at that. The four works presented here date from the mid-1950s to the late-1960s and reveal either a preoccupation with variation techniques, or an interest in realizing acoustic effects by means of two separately arranged ensembles. The Concerto for Two String Orchestras, Op. 71 (1961) is an example of the latter, and a minor masterpiece awaiting discovery. The contrasting movements are muscular, sinewy and contrapuntal in character and share something in common with the sound-world of Tippett's Double Concerto. The *Piccolo Concerto* ('little' concerto) possesses an altogether more neo-classical (Stravinskian) sound-world. The exhilarating *Musica sinfonica* of 1967 is brimming with colourful incident (soaring string lines over angular, rhythmic brass and woodwind textures) and subtle instrumental sonorities. As one would expect, the performances under Haitink, Jochum and Szell are all of the highest calibre, and the live radio recordings (some mono) have come up well.

Michel Delalande

French 1657-1726

Delalande. Dies irae, S31. Miserere mei Deus secundum, S27. **Linda Perillo, Patrizia Kwella** (sops); **Howard Crook** (alto); **Herve Lamy** (ten); **Peter Harvey** (bass); **Chorus and Orchestra of La Chapelle Royale/Philippe Herreweghe.** Harmonia Mundi HMC90 1352. Recorded in 1990.

1h 2m   DDD   12/91

Grands motets are sacred compositions for solo voices and chorus with instruments which epitomize an aspect of courtly life at Versailles during the reign of Louis XIV, the 'Sun King'. Delalande and his older contemporary Charpentier in their very different ways brought the *grand motet* to an expressive peak. The two works on this disc are especially fine examples of Delalande's skill in this sphere of composition. The *Dies irae* contains some wonderfully descriptive movements from among which we might single out the declamatory "Tuba mirum" whose music breathes the air of the opera house, and the chromatic, tenderly affecting "Lacrimosa". The *Miserere* continues a prevailing C minor tonality and, like the *Dies irae* is a grief-laden utterance. Philippe Herreweghe and the Choir of La Chapelle Royale give fervent performances and there are strong contributions above all from Howard Crook and Linda Perillo. The recording is clear and spacious and the accompanying booklet contains full texts with translations.

Further listening ...

Sinfonies pour les soupers du Roi. **La Symphonie du Marais/Hugo Reyne.** Harmonia Mundi HMC90 1337/40 (four-disc set, 7/91).

Te Deum, S32. Super flumina. Confitebor tibi, Domine. **Véronique Gens, Sandrine Piau, Arlette Steyer** (sops); **Jean-Paul Fouchécourt, François Piolino** (tens); **Jérôme Corréas** (bass); **Les Arts Florissants/William Christie.** Harmonia Mundi HMC90 1351 (7/91).

Petits Motets — Miserere a voix seule. Vanum est vobis ante lucem. Miserator et misericors. Cantique quatrième. *Coupled with* **Lemaire.** Assumpta est Maria; *Morin.* Regina coeli. **Soloists; Les Arts Florissants Chorus and Orchestra/William Christie.** Harmonia Mundi HMC90 1416 (4/93).

Leo Delibes

French 1836-1891

Delibes. Sylvia — ballet[a]. Coppélia — ballet[b]. [a]**London Symphony Orchestra/Anatole Fistoulari;** [b]**Minneapolis Symphony Orchestra/Antál Dorati.** Mercury Living Presence 434 313-2MM3. Items marked [a] from MMA11036/7 (8/59), [b] MMA11000/1 (2/59). Recorded 1957-58.

③ 2h 53m ADD 3/93

It is really is astonishing that, in recordings some 38 years old, brass and percussion can burst forth with such vividness, or that instrumental detail can be as clear and faithful as they are here — in *Sylvia* especially. Nor, of course, do the attractions of this coupling by any means stop there. These have always been highly regarded performances of two of the most attractively tuneful ballets ever composed. *Coppélia* may be that bit more consistently inventive than its successor, but both repay hearing in full. Moreover, both conductors here had a great deal of experience in, and feeling for, the style of these ballets. As a result, both extract playing that is for the most part gracious and brilliant in turn, only occasionally lacking the final degree of finesse. In such passages as Fistoulari's vigorous "Les Chasseresses" or Dorati's "Musique des Automates" one can scarcely fail to be won over. It is only fair to warn you that the recording of *Sylvia* is not absolutely complete, since it lacks the "Pas des esclaves" and "Variation-Valse" from the Act 3 *Divertissement*. On its own terms, though, this coupling represents a most compelling offering.

Additional recommendation ...
Sylvia[a]. **Massenet.** LE CID — *ballet music*[b]. [a]**New Philharmonia Orchestra,** [b]**National Philharmonic Orchestra/Richard Bonynge.** Decca Ovation 425 475-2DM2. ② lh 58m ADD 1/90 ▲

New review

Delibes. Coppélia. **Orchestra of the Opéra de Lyon/Kent Nagano.** Erato 4509-91730-2. Recorded in 1993.

② lh 39m DDD 5/94

Though the text played absolutely complete may be straightforward Delibes, the interpretation instantly announces itself as being anything but straightforward. Every phrase, every accent, every nuance seems to be newly considered, without ever losing the feel for the action that is taking place on the stage. Where Bonynge tends to achieve effect by pushing the music to extremes, the overriding impression here is of the rightness and naturalness of Nagano's whole reading. The rare quality of the performance is evident at once from the way the music lights up at the *cantando* section in the twelfth bar of the Prelude. Later, in Act 2, the Boléro has a rare dash and brio, while the opening March of Act 3 has a similarly compelling onward momentum. The sequence of speciality dances that makes up most of the final Act is delightfully turned, with a quite heavenly viola solo in "La Paix" and a thrilling final Galop. It is unfortunate that the recording is extravagantly spread over two CDs, but anyone who loves this music should make a point of hearing Nagano's outstanding reading.

Additional recommendations:
National Philharmonic Orchestra/Richard Bonynge. Decca 414 502-2DH2 — ⚫
Ih 32m DDD 12/86
Orchestra of the Royal Opera House, Covent Garden/Mark Ermler. Royal Opera
House ROH006 — Ih 14m DDD 7/93

Delibes. LAKME. **Dame Joan Sutherland** (sop) Lakmé; **Alain Vanzo** (ten) Gérald;
Gabriel Bacquier (bar) Nilakantha; **Jane Berbié** (sop) Mallika; **Claud Calès** (bar) Frederick;
Gwenyth Annear (sop) Ellen; **Josephte Clément** (sop) Rose; **Monica Sinclair** (contr) Miss
Benson; **Emile Belcourt** (ten) Hadji; **Monte-Carlo Opera Chorus; Monte-Carlo
National Opera Orchestra/Richard Bonynge.** Decca Grand Opera 425 485-2DM2.
Synopsis, text and translation included. From SET387/9 (5/69). Recorded in 1967.

② 2h 18m ADD 12/89

Like Pinkerton in *Madama Butterfly* (but not a cad like him), the British officer Gérald has
succumbed to the exotic charm of the East: in particular, though engaged to a high-born English
girl, he has become infatuated with the Brahmin priestess Lakmé, who returns his love, despite
the fact that her father is bitterly hostile to the British and is plotting against them. A tragic
outcome (with the help of a poisonous plant) is predictable: you might call this a Plain Tale
from the Raj. This recording of Delibes's opera, though nearly 28 years old, still sounds fresh
and clean. In Alain Vanzo it has a near-ideal lyric tenor hero; Gabriel Bacquier is suitably dark-
hued as Lakmé's vengeful father; and in the title-role Joan Sutherland produces strikingly
beautiful tone and seemingly effortless precision in florid passages (as in that famous showpiece
the "Bell song"). Her words, however, are difficult to make out, owing to her weak consonants
— a rare failing of hers, but one which her admirers have learnt to tolerate. In all other
respects this is a very recommendable issue (especially at medium price).

Further listening ...

La Source, ou Naila — ballet. *Coupled with* **Drigo.** The Magic Flute — ballet. **Orchestra of
the Royal Opera House, Covent Garden/Richard Bonynge.** Decca 421 431-2DH2
(9/90).

LE ROI L'A DIT[a]. L'OMELETTE A LA FOLLEMBUCHE[b] — excerpts. LE SERPENT A
PLUMES[c] — excerpts. [abc]**Soloists; French Radio Lyric** [a]**Chorus and** [abc]**Orchestra/**[a]**André
Girard;** [bc]**Jean Brebion.** Musidisc Gaieté-Lyrique [a]mono/[bc]stereo 20239-2 (11/93).

Frederick Delius

British 1862-1934

Delius. ORCHESTRAL WORKS. [a]**Tasmin Little** (vn); **Welsh National Opera
Orchestra/Sir Charles Mackerras.** Argo 433 704-2ZH. Recorded 1990-1991.
Violin Concerto[a]. Two Aquarelles (arr. Fenby). On hearing the first cuckoo in Spring. Summer
Night on the River. Fennimore and Gerda Intermezzo (arr. Fenby). Irmelin Prelude. Dance
Rhapsodies Nos. 1 and 2.

Ih 15m DDD 7/92

This disc of the Violin Concerto should be played to friends who are not committed Delians; it
is sure to persuade them that this concerto merits the same devotion as those by Elgar and
Walton. Tasmin Little has the edge over Ralph Holmes (but only just) in coping with the work's
technical difficulties; and under Mackerras's purposeful guidance, and with greater contrasts of
pace between the various sections of its one movement form, the piece behaves more like a
conventional concerto. If a certain amount of dream-like atmosphere is shed in the work's
opening section in favour of classical rigour and vigour, at the heart of this account is the central

accompanied cadenza: a minor miracle of flowing improvisation, with Mackerras and Little more freely rhapsodic than previous partnerships, and as twins in the seamless unfolding of the musical line. Argo's sound is very immediate, with a believable balance between soloist and orchestra, and excellent handling of the (albeit very few) orchestral climaxes. To the many shorter pieces that make up this disc's generous duration, only Beecham has brought a comparable feeling for texture and atmosphere. *Summer Night on the River*, in particular, is remarkable for its Debussian delicacy and the chamber-like intimacy of its sonorities.

Additional recommendations ...
Violin Concerto. Suite. Légende. **Ralph Holmes** (vn); **Royal Philharmonic Orchestra/Vernon Handley.** Unicorn-Kanchana DKPCD9040 — .•˙ 53m DDD 9/85 ⁹ₚ
Violin Concerto[b]. *Dance Rhapsody No. 1*[a]. *A song of the high hills*[c]. *Paa Vidderne*[d]. [c]**Freda Hart** (sop); [c]**Leslie Jones** (ten); [b]**Jean Pougnet** (vn); [c]**Luton Choral Society; Royal Philharmonic Orchestra/Sir Thomas Beecham.** EMI Beecham Edition mono CDM7 64054-2 — .•˙ 1h 13m ADD 9/92 ⁹ₚ ▲

Delius. North Country Sketches. Brigg Fair — An English Rhapsody. In a Summer Garden. A Village Romeo and Juliet — Walk to the Paradise Garden. **Welsh National Opera Orchestra/Sir Charles Mackerras.** Argo 430 202-2ZH. Recorded in 1989.

.•˙ **1h 8m   DDD   12/90** ⁹ₚ

After *The Walk to the Paradise Garden*, written in 1906, there were for Delius many real gardens of paradise to which Wagner was less readily admitted: *Brigg Fair* (1907), which Delius called "An English Rhapsody", begins with early morning mists and birdsong leading to variations on the Lincolnshire folk-song of the title. *In a Summer Garden* (1908) incorporates the sensations of Delius's own garden at Grez-sur-Loing outside Paris into perhaps his most intimate, exquisite improvisation; and the *North Country Sketches* (1913-14) paint the seasons and moods of the Yorkshire Moors around his birthplace. These quintessential Delian contemplations require, and here receive, lucidity of texture, a keen response to the moments of quietude, freedom from barlines, and animation for the 'wildlife'. With sound that is generally close and dry, Mackerras's Delius may for some, be wanting in *fin de siècle* opulence and 'impressionist' mist, but the effect is never clinical. This is a Delius disc of striking individuality; one that invites you to listen to music that is so often just heard.

Additional recommendation ...
North Country Sketches. Florida — suite. **Ulster Orchestra/Vernon Handley.** Chandos CHAN8413 — .•˙ 1h 7m DDD 12/86 ⁹ₛ

Delius. Paris: The Song of a Great City. Double Concerto[ab]. Cello Concerto[b]. [a]**Tasmin Little** (vn); [b]**Raphael Wallfisch** (vc); **Royal Liverpool Philharmonic Orchestra/Sir Charles Mackerras.** EMI Eminence CD-EMX2185. Recorded in 1991.

.•˙ **1h 4m   DDD   3/92** ⁹ₚ

Paris is an extravagant nocturnal impression of the city where "Le grand anglais", as Delius was known to his friends (who included Gaugin and Eduard Munch) spent a decade of his life, during which he developed, as Eric Fenby put it, "a painter's sense of orchestral colour". Premièred in 1901, it shows Delius relishing the full palette of his Staussian-sized orchestra to conjure an intoxicating merry-go-round of the city's night-life. Mackerras's performance is very physical, propelling the dancing to wild, whirling climaxes, and his balance engineers place us firmly among the excitement. In the Cello Concerto, a personal favourite of Delius's, Raphael Wallfisch and Mackerras seek out the contrasts inherent in the score, and, for the first time on disc, its pervasive dreaminess is offset by faster decorative passages, and a genuine playfulness. In short, it dances as well as sings. They are joined by Tasmin Little for an account of the Double Concerto that has never before received teamwork of such confidence, security and unanimity of purpose. This Eminence disc is an essential acquisition for all Delians, especially at the modest asking price.

Additional recommendation ...
Paris. Life's Dance. Dance Rhapsody No. 1. Piano Concerto[a]. [a]**Philip Fowke** (pf); **Royal Philharmonic Orchestra/Norman Del Mar.** Unicorn-Kanchana DKPCD9108 — .•˙ 1h 17m DDD 3/92 ⁹ₚ

Delius. ORCHESTRAL WORKS. **BBC Symphony Orchestra/Andrew Davis.** Teldec
British Line 4509-90845-2. Recorded in 1992.
Brigg Fair. In a Summer Garden. Paris: The Song of a Great City. On hearing the first cuckoo
in Spring. Summer Night on the River. A Village Romeo and Juliet — Walk to the Paradise
Garden.

Ih 17m DDD I/94

This *Brigg Fair* is unique. What a lovely surprise to hear real London sparrows sharing the air
space of St Augustine's Church with Delius's translated Lincolnshire larks (flute and clarinet) in
the opening minutes of the work, albeit much more distantly. Very effective too are those
almost still pools of string sound (early morning mists?), given the extended boundaries of this
acoustic, and the familiar warmth and depth of tone Davis draws from the orchestra's strings. In
the final magnificently broad climax (pealing bells, for once, very clear), you cannot fail to be
impressed by the depth, coherence and articulacy of the sound — hallmarks, indeed, of the
entire disc. Davis's strings come into their own in the *Walk to the Paradise Garden*. For *In a
Summer Garden*, Davis mutes his strings more often than Delius asks; but the reading's delicacy of
texture and hazy, suffusing warmth are difficult to resist. And it will please those who don't
respond to the more animated Mackerras freshening up of the score (listed below). As no other
Delius disc has an identical programme, and very few such a generously extended one, this disc
is the best of its kind currently available for those wanting state-of-the-art sound and wishing to
start a Delius investigation; it will also bring many moments of joy and illumination to seasoned
Delians.

Additional recommendations ...
Brigg Fair. In a Summer Garden. Eventyr. A Song of Summer. **Hallé Orchestra/Vernon Handley.**
Classics for Pleasure CD-CFP4568 — 56m DDD 8/90

Delius. THE FENBY LEGACY. **Royal Philharmonic Orchestra/Eric Fenby.** Unicorn-
Kanchana DKPCD9008/9. Texts included. From DKP9008/09 (10/81).
Songs of Farewell (with Ambrosian Singers). Idyll (Felicity Lott, sop; Thomas Allen, bar).
Fantastic Dance. A Song of Summer. Cynara (Allen). Irmelin Prelude. A Late Lark (Anthony
Rolfe Johnson, ten). La calinda (arr. Fenby). Caprice and Elegy (Julian Lloyd Webber, vc). Two
Aquarelles (arr. Fenby). Fennimore and Gerda Intermezzo (arr. Fenby. New to UK).

(2) Ih 45m DDD 12/87

It was Fenby's visit to the home of Delius in rural France that re-established the stricken
composer's link with the outside world. Fenby became Delius's amanuensis and the tangible
results of his French visit are offered here on a pair of CDs which make a perfect supplement
to Beecham's EMI set (listed above). The *Irmelin* Prelude is the most famous but the most
important are the more ambitious and equally evocative *Song of Summer*, and the *Songs of
Farewell* set to words from his favourite American poet, Walt Whitman. The characteristically
opaque choral textures tend to obscure the words at times, but this is of relatively small
importance for Delius was mainly concerned with the sounds and colours of intertwining his
ambitious chorus and equally large orchestra. The *Idyll* is an ardent love duet and its erotic
element is in no doubt. The other orchestral pieces are characteristically appealing Delian
miniatures, played with passionately romantic feeling and a real sense of ecstasy by the RPO;
while in the choral music Fenby achieves the richest colours and wonderfully hushed
pianissimos.

Delius. Sea Drift[a]. Songs of Sunset[b]. Songs of Farewell. [b]**Sally Burgess** (mez); [ab]**Bryn Terfel**
(bass-bar); **Waynflete Singers; Southern Voices; Bournemouth Symphony Chorus and
Orchestra/Richard Hickox.** Chandos CHAN9214. Texts included.

Ih 17m DDD II/93

Sea Drift is a sublime conjunction of Whitman's poetry and Delius's music describing love, loss
and unhappy resignation, with the sea (as Christopher Palmer puts it) as "symbol and agent of
parting". Written in 1903-4 (the same years as Debussy's *La mer*), it is surely Delius's

masterpiece; right from the swaying opening bars its spell is enduring and hypnotic. Hickox in his second recording of the work now gives us the finest recorded post-Beecham *Sea Drift*. The shaping of the opening falling woodwind figures at a slow tempo more than usually (and very beautifully) portends the sad turn of events; and the climax is broad and superbly co-ordinated. Terfel's bar-by-bar characterization (and glorious voice), conveys the full expressive range of the role from impassioned appeal to gentle call without artifice; and the choral singing from Hampshire's finest is superb. The whole is recorded with warmth, spaciousness, depth and clarity. If Hickox's Sally Burgess is taxed a little by the high notes in the *Songs of Sunset*, Hickox is greatly to be preferred to Fenby (see below) in the *Songs of Farewell*, where Fenby's chorus have difficulty with some of his broad tempos — there's a lot more life in Hickox's last three songs, particularly the "Old Sailor" of the final song. Strongly recommended.

Additional recommendations ...
Sea Drift[a]. *Florida — Suite.* [a]**Thomas Hampson** (bar); **Welsh National Opera** [a]**Chorus and Orchestra/Sir Charles Mackerras.** Argo 430 206-2ZH — .•' 1h 3m DDD 12/91
Sea Drift[a]. *A Village Romeo and Juliet.* [a]**Gordon Clinton** (bar); **Soloists; chorus; Royal Philharmonic Orchestra/Sir Thomas Beecham.** EMI Beecham Edition mono CMS7 64386-2 — .•' ② 2h 4m ADD 11/92 ꝙP ▲
Songs of Sunset (with Maureen Forrester, contr; John Cameron, bar; Beecham Choral Society). *Over the Hills and Far Away. Sleigh Ride. Irmelin Prelude. Dance Rhapsody No. 2. Summer Evening. Brigg Fair. On hearing the first cuckoo in Spring. Summer Night on the River. A Song before Sunrise. Marche Caprice. Florida — Suite. Fennimore and Gerda — Intermezzo.* **Royal Philharmonic Orchestra/Sir Thomas Beecham.** EMI CDS7 47509-8 — .•' 6/87

Delius. ORCHESTRAL SONGS. [a]**Felicity Lott** (sop); [b]**Sarah Walker** (mez); [c]**Anthony Rolfe Johnson** (ten); [d]**Ambrosian Singers; Royal Philharmonic Orchestra/Eric Fenby.** Unicorn-Kanchana DKPCD9029. Notes and texts included. From DKP9029 (12/84). Recorded in 1983.
A song of the high hills[d]. *Twilight fancies*[b]. *Wine roses*[b]. *The bird's story*[a]. *Let springtime come*[a]. *Il pleure dans mon coeur*[c]. *Le ciel est, par dessus le toit*[a]. *La lune blanche*[c]. *To Daffodils*[b]. *I-Brasil*[c].

.•' **56m DDD 3/85** ꝙP ꝙS

A song of the high hills is one of Delius's most original masterpieces. Scored for a large orchestra and chorus it evokes with extraordinary power and beauty the grandeur and the spirit of nature. Eight of the nine songs with orchestra were scored by the composer himself, and *To Daffodils* was orchestrated by Eric Fenby. They all reflect in one manner or another Delius's favourite theme of the transience of love. The soloists are admirable, but Sarah Walker's three contributions are particularly perceptive. Fenby and the RPO accompany with total understanding and the recording is superlative.

Additional recommendation ...
Twilight Fancies[bd]. *The Violet*[ad]. *In the Seraglio Garden*[ad]. *Silken Shoes*[cd]. *Autumn*[bd]. *Sweet Venevil*[ad]. *Irmelin Rose*[ad]. *Let Springtime Come*[bd]. *Il pleure dans mon coeur*[cd]. *Le ciel est pardessus le toit*[ad]. *La lune blanche*[cd]. *Chanson d'automne*[ad]. *Avant que tu ne t'en ailles*[ad]. *To Daffodils*[bd]. *So sweet is she*[cd]. *I-Brasil*[cd]. *Three Preludes*[e]. *Zum Carnival — polka*[e]. [a]**Felicity Lott** (sop); [b]**Sarah Walker** (mez); [c]**Anthony Rolfe Johnson** (ten); [d]**Eric Fenby,** [e]**Eric Parkin** (pfs). Unicorn-Kanchana Souvenir UKCD2041 — .•' 51m DDD 10/91 ꝙP

Further listening ...

A Mass of Life[a]. *Songs of Sunset*[b]. *Arabesque*[c]. [abc]**Soloists;** [a]**London Philharmonic Choir,** [bc]**Liverpool Philharmonic Choir;** [a]**London Philharmonic Orchestra,** [bc]**Royal Liverpool Philharmonic Orchestra/Sir Charles Groves.** EMI CMS7 64218-2 (two-disc set).

A VILLAGE ROMEO AND JULIET. **Soloists; Arnold Schönberg Choir; Austrian Radio Symphony Orchestra/Sir Charles Mackerras.** Argo 430 275-2ZH2 (12/90).

Edison Denisov

Suggested listening ...

Chamber Music for Viola, Harpsichord and Strings[a]. Concerto for Two Violas, Harpsichord and String Orchestra[b]. Epitaph. [a]**Nabuko Imai, Petra Vahle** (vas); **Annelie de Man** (hpd); **Amsterdam Neuw Sinfonietta/Lev Markiz.** BIS CD518 (9/92).

David Del Tredici

American 1937-

Suggested listening ...

Steps[a] (1990). Haddock's Eyes[b] (1985). [b]**David Tel Tredici** (pf); [b]**Susan Naruki** (sop); [b]**Claire Bloom** (narr); [a]**New York Philharmonic Orchestra;** [b]**New York Philharmonic Ensemble/Zubin Mehta.** New World 80390-2.

François Devienne

French 1759-1803

Suggested listening ...

Oboe Sonatas — G minor, Op. 23 No. 3; C major, Op. 71 No. 3; G major, Op. 71 No. 1; D minor, Op. 71 No. 2. **Peter Bree** (ob); **Roderick Shaw** (fp). Etcetera KTC1106 (12/91).

Frédéric Devreese

The Netherlands 1929-

Suggested listening ...

Piano Concertos Nos. 2, 3 and 4. **Daniel Blumenthal** (pf); **Belgian Radio and Television Orchestra/Frédéric Devreese.** Marco Polo 8 223505 (11/93).

David Diamond

American 1915-

New review

Diamond. Symphony No. 1. The Enormous Room. Violin Concerto No. 2[a]. [a]**Ilkka Talvi** (vn); **Seattle Symphony Orchestra/Gerard Schwarz.** Delos DE3119. Recorded 1991-92.

1h 11m DDD 1/94

David Diamond of the 1940s — eager, impressionable, modal. Fresh from Boulanger in Paris, the First Symphony vaults from the launch pad with a confident three-note motif: it's sharp, it's versatile, and the treatment is propulsive, the spring of ambition in every step. Diamond works his material with a sure and disciplined hand. There is a very real sense in which this music is out to prove itself, yet time and again invention does transcend technique. In the finale the keynote motif turns regal proclamation and a real hat-in-the-air *allegro* conveys a feeling of "now I can do anything". 'Anything' soon included a Violin Concerto with Waltonian impulse and an effusive line in lyric invention. A kind of hyperactive vocalise, barely pausing to draw breath and energetically exploited here by Ilkka Talvi. Clearly the composer of this piece would thrive on free fantasy. And did, in 1948, with *The Enormous*

Room, an atmospheric tone-poem, with its commanding, well-made orchestral sonorities that takes an almost Delian delight in rhapsody. It sounds gorgeous in this rich, deeply rooted performance and recording.

Further listening ...

Symphonies Nos. 2 and 4[a]. Concerto for Small Orchestra[a]. [a]**Seattle Symphony Orchestra;** [b]**New York Chamber Symphony Orchestra/Gerald Schwarz.** Delos DE3093 (4/91).

Symphony No. 3[c]. Romeo and Juliet[b]. Psalm[c]. Kaddish[ac]. [a]**János Starker** (vc); [b]**New York Chamber Symphony Orchestra,** [c]**Seattle Symphony Orchestra/Gerard Schwarz.** Delos DE3103 (4/93).

Peter Dickinson
British 1934-

Suggested listening ...

Mass of the Apocalypse. Outcry. The Unicorns. **Soloists; London Consort Choir; City of London Sinfonia/Nicholas Cleobury; Solna Brass/Lars-Gunnar Björklund.** Conifer CDCF167 (5/89).

Alphons Diepenbrock
Dutch 1862-1921

Suggested listening ...

The Birds — Overture. Suites — Marsyas; Electra. Hymne for violin and orchestra. **Emmy Verhey** (vn); **The Hague Residentie Orchestra/Hans Vonk.** Chandos CHAN8821 (8/90).

Hymnen an die Nacht No. 2, Muss immer der Morgen wiederkommen. Die Nacht. Im grossen Schweigen. Wenige wissen das Geheimnis der Liebe. **Linda Finnie** (contr); **Christopher Homberger** (ten); **Robert Holl** (bass); **The Hague Residentie Orchestra/Hans Vonk.** Chandos CHAN8878 (4/91).

James Dillon
British 1950-

Suggested listening ...

East 11th St NY10003. La femme invisible. Windows and Canopies. **Music Projects London/ Richard Bernas.** NMC NMCD004 (9/92).

Stephen Dodgson
British 1924-

Suggested listening ...

Concerto for Flute and Strings[a]. Last of the Leaves[b]. Duo Concerto[c]. [b]**Michael George** (bass); [a]**Robert Stallman** (fl); [b]**John Bradbury** (cl); [c]**Anthea Gifford** (gtr); **Northern Sinfonia/ Ronald Zollman.** Biddulph LAW013 (7/94).

Ernö Dohnányi

Dohnányi. Piano Concertos — No. 1 in E minor, Op. 5; No. 2 in B minor, Op. 42. **Martin Roscoe** (pf); **BBC Scottish Symphony Orchestra/Fedor Glushchenko.** Hyperion CDA66684. Recorded in 1993.

| · · · 1h 15m DDD 5/94 | ♀ₚ |

This coupling provides a salutary reminder of two of Dohnányi's most substantial if sadly neglected works. Both concertos — separated by 50 years, but mildly rather than radically different in their musical language — burgeon with heartfelt melody and high-flying pianistics. And if Dohnányi hardly provides anything so important as a bridge between Liszt and Bartók, his alternation of dark and scintillating ideas is accomplished with an easy and professional aplomb. The Second Concerto's crisply accented finale in whirling and nationalistic duple time is notably attractive. Martin Roscoe's superbly authoritative performances are majestic and glittering as required, and his survival of his recessed placing in relation to the orchestra is doubly to his credit. Fedor Glushchenko's partnership is excellent and, overall, the recordings are of high quality.

Further listening ...

Konzertstück for Cello and Orchestra, Op. 12. *Coupled with* **Dvořák.** Cello Concerto in B minor, B191. **Raphael Wallfisch** (vc); **London Symphony Orchestra/Sir Charles Mackerras.** Chandos CHAN8662 (5/89).

Piano Quintet No. 1 in C minor, Op. 1. String Quartet No. 2 in D flat major, Op. 15. **Wolfgang Manz** (pf); **Gabrieli Quartet.** Chandos CHAN8718 (5/89).

Cello Sonata in B flat minor, Op. 8. *Coupled with* **Bridge.** Cello Sonata in D minor, H125. Four Short Pieces, H104 — Meditation; Spring song. **Debussy.** Cello Sonata. **Bernard Gregor-Smith** (vc); **Yolande Wrigley** (pf). ASV CDDCA796. *See review under Bridge; refer to the Index to Reviews.*

Gaetano Donizetti

Donizetti. ANNA BOLENA. **Maria Callas** (sop) Anna Bolena; **Nicola Rossi-Lemeni** (bass) Enrico VIII; **Giulietta Simionato** (mez) Giovanna Seymour; **Gianni Raimondi** (ten) Riccardo Percy; **Plinio Clabassi** (bass) Rochefort; **Gabriella Carturan** (mez) Smeton; **Luigi Rumbo** (ten) Hervey; **Chorus and Orchestra of La Scala, Milan/Gianandrea Gavazzeni.** EMI mono CMS7 64941-2. Notes, text and translation included. Recorded at a performance in La Scala, Milan in 1957.

| · · · ② 2h 20m ADD 1/94 | ♀ₚ ▲ |

Here Callas gives one of her finest performances. The first impression is essentially a vocal one, in the sense of the sheer beauty of sound, for recording reveals it to be so much better focused than Simionato's. Then, in the first solo, "Come innocente giovane", addressing Jane Seymour, she is so clean in the cut of the voice and the style of its usage, delicate in her *fioritura*, often exquisite in her shading, that anyone, ignorant of the Callas legend, would know immediately that this is an artist of patrician status. There are marvellous incidental moments, and magnificent crescendos, into, for instance, "per pietà delmio spavento" and "segnata è la mia sorte", culminating in the Tower scene. The singers at her side hardly measure up. Even so, the great ensembles still prove worthy of the event, and the recording, which is clear without harshness or other distortion, conveys the special quality of this memorable evening at the opera with remarkable vividness and fidelity.

Donizetti. L'ELISIR D'AMORE. **Mariella Devia** (sop) Adina; **Roberto Alagna** (ten) Nemorino; **Pietro Spagnoli** (bar) Belcore; **Bruno Praticò** (bar) Dulcamara; **Francesca Provvisionato** (mez) Giannetta; **Tallis Chamber Choir; English Chamber Orchestra/ Marcello Viotti.** Erato 4509-91701-2. Notes, text and translation included.

② 2h 9m DDD 6/93

A modern and completely recommendable set of this delightful piece, country cousin to *Don Pasquale*, was badly needed — and here it is. It is a delight from start to finish, making one fall in love again with this delightful comedy of pastoral life. The plot is a variant of the much used theme of the fake love potion. Here the potion is supplied by the charlatan Doctor Dulcamara to the shy young Nemorino to help him win the love of Adina. Roberto Alagna, disciple of Pavarotti, sings Nemorino with all his mentor's charm and a rather lighter tone appropriate to the role. He also evinces just the right sense of vulnerability and false bravado that lies at the heart of Nemorino's predicament. Here is a tenor with a great future if only he stays with roles within his range. He is partnered by Mariella Devia who has every characteristic needed for the role of Adina. With a fine sense of buoyant rhythm, she sings fleetly and uses the coloratura to enhance her reading. She can spin a long, elegiac line where that is needed, and her pure yet full tone blends well with that of her colleagues. She also suggests all Adina's high spirits and flirtatious nature. The other principals, though not as amusing in their interpretations as some of their more experienced predecessors, enter into the ensemble feeling of the performance. All are helped by the lively but controlled conducting of Viotti and by the ideal recording.

Additional recommendations ...
Soloists; Ambrosian Opera Chorus; English Chamber Orchestra/Richard Bonynge. Decca 414 461-2DH2 — ② 2h 21m ADD 6/86
Soloists; Turin Radio Symphony Chorus and Orchestra/Claudio Scimone. Philips 412 714-2PH2 — ② 2h 7m DDD 6/86
Soloists; Chorus and Orchestra of the Metropolitan Opera, New York/James Levine. DG 429 744-2GH2 — ② 1h 59m DDD 2/91
Soloists; Chorus and Orchestra of La Scala, Milan/Tullio Serafin. Classics for Pleasure CD-CFPD4733 — ② 1h 51m ADD 5/94

Donizetti. LUCIA DI LAMMERMOOR. **Cheryl Studer** (sop) Lucia; **Plácido Domingo** (ten) Edgardo; **Juan Pons** (bar) Enrico; **Samuel Ramey** (bass) Raimondo; **Jennifer Larmore** (mez) Alisa; **Fernando de la Mora** (ten) Arturo; **Anthony Laciura** (ten) Normanno; **Ambrosian Opera Chorus; London Symphony Orchestra/Ion Marin.** DG 435 309-2GH2. Notes, text and translation included. Recorded in 1990.

② 2h 18m DDD 4/93

With 12 recordings currently available, *Lucia di Lammermoor*, once regarded as *passé*, appears to be in remarkably good health. Not so long ago it was dismissed as little more than a convenient vehicle for the latest coloratura soprano, who could enjoy a double success, first in the Fountain Scene where she would be applauded on entry and then able to warm up for the celebrated Mad Scene, which was the real culmination of the evening even to the extent (in Melba's day, for instance) of finishing the opera on Lucia's final high note and eliminating the tenor's big scene which is to follow. Nowadays, while the opera is still a *tour de force* for the soprano, the tenor shares the honours and the whole thing is much more of a company production. Its likely hero is Donizetti himself, whose music has strengths of many kinds, including expert and evocative orchestration. Recordings by Callas and Sutherland are generally respected as permanent classics of the gramophone, but recent versions deserve consideration, and this one, with Studer and Domingo in the leading roles, is certainly fit as a whole to stand alongside its eminent predecessors. It does so principally on its comparative merit as an overall performance and recording. The fine deep colours of the orchestra, the sturdy dramatic cohesion and well-wrought climaxes, are well brought out; passages traditionally omitted are in place (and deserve to be). The role of Lucia's confidante is sung with distinction by Jennifer Larmore, and though Juan Pons could do with more bite to his tone and Samuel Ramey with more expressiveness in his vocal acting these have their strengths too. Studer combines beautiful tone, technical accomplishment and touching pathos. Details include an extended cadenza in the Mad Scene, which ends on a not too exposed high E flat (D being the ceiling elsewhere). Domingo triumphantly overcomes the difficulties such a role must pose at this stage of his career: Edgardo di Ravenswood in this recording is as firmly at the centre of the opera as is its eponymous heroine.

Additional recommendations ...
Soloists; Royal Opera House Chorus and Orchestra, Covent Garden/Richard Bonynge. Decca 410 193-2DH3 — .·' ③ 2h 20m ADD 11/85 ⁹ₚ Ⓑ
Soloists; Maggio Musicale Fiorentino Chorus and Orchestra/Tullio Serafin. EMI mono CMS7 69980-2 — .·' ② 1h 51m ADD 10/89 ⁹ₚ ▲ Ⓑ
Soloists; Ambrosian Opera Chorus; New Philharmonia Orchestra/Jesús López-Cobos. Philips 426 563-2PM2 — .·' ② 2h 23m ADD 1/91 ⁹ₚ Ⓑ
Soloists; Chorus of La Scala, Milan; Berlin RIAS Symphony Orchestra/Herbert von Karajan. EMI mono CMS7 63631-2 — .·' ② 1h 59m ADD 2/91 ⁹ₚ ▲ Ⓑ
Soloists; Ambrosian Singers; London Symphony Orchestra/Richard Bonynge. Teldec 9031-72306-2 — .·' ② 2h 23m DDD 11/92 ⁹ₚ Ⓑ

Donizetti. DON PASQUALE. **Sesto Bruscantini** (bar) Don Pasquale; **Mirella Freni** (sop) Norina; **Leo Nucci** (bar) Dr Malatesta; **Gösta Winbergh** (ten) Ernesto; **Guido Fabbris** (ten) Notary; **Ambrosian Opera Chorus; Philharmonia Orchestra/Riccardo Muti.** EMI CDS7 47068-2. Notes, text and translation included. From SLS143436 (4/84). Recorded 1982.

.·' ② 2h 3m DDD 8/88

In this delightful opera Donizetti's inspiration is unfaltering, and he manages to combine sentiment and comedy in equal proportions. The somewhat hard-hearted treatment of old Pasquale's weakness for the lovely Norina, and the ruse she and Malatesta play on him are eventually dissolved in the triumph of love over cynicism. Riccardo Muti is a stickler for fidelity to the score, playing it complete and insisting on his cast singing the written notes and nothing else. Donizetti blossoms under such loving treatment. It is a reading, brisk and unvarnished, that demands one's attention throughout, and the playing of the Philharmonia is splendidly vital. As Pasquale, Bruscantini sings with the benefit of long experience in defining line and words. Leo Nucci sings a smiling, resourceful Malatesta, at once Pasquale's friend and the author of the trick played on him. Gösta Winbergh is an accurate and fluent Ernesto, and Mirella Freni, the Norina, delivers her difficult aria with all her old sense of flirtatious fun: but when the joke has gone too far, she finds just the plaintive tone to express Norina's doubts and regret.

Additional recommendation ...
Soloists; Lyon Opera Chorus and Orchestra/Gabriele Ferro. Erato 2292-45487-2 — .·' ② 2h DDD 11/90

Further listening ...

Italian Songs — Canto d'Ugolino; L'amor funesto; Il trovatore in caricatura; Spirito di Dio benefico; Viva il matrimonio. *French Songs* — Le renégat; Noé, scène du Deluge; Le départ pour la chasse; Un coeur pour abri; Le hart (chant diabolique). **Ian Caddy** (bass-bar); **Melvyn Tan** (fp). Meridian CDE84183 (4/90).

UGO, CONTE DI PARIGI. **Soloists; Geoffrey Mitchell Choir; New Philharmonia Orchestra/Alun Francis.** Opera Rara ORC1 (12/90).

EMILIA DI LIVERPOOL. L'EREMITAGGIO DI LIWERPOOL. **Soloists; Geoffrey Mitchell Choir; Philharmonia Orchestra/David Parry.** Opera Rara ORC8 (5/92).

IMELDA DE' LAMBERTAZZI. **Soloists; Chorus and Orchestra of Swiss-Italian Radio and Television/Marc Andreae.** Nuova Era 6778/9 (10/91).

LUCREZIA BORGIA. **Soloists; RCA Italiana Opera Chorus and Orchestra/Jonel Perlea.** RCA Victor Gold Seal GD86642 (9/90).

MARIA STUARDA. **Soloists; Bologna Teatro Communale Chorus and Orchestra/ Richard Bonynge.** Decca 425 410-2DM2 (9/90).

L'ASSEDIO DI CALAIS. **Soloists; Geoffrey Mitchell Choir; Philharmonia Orchestra/ David Parry.** Opera Rara ORC9 (7/91).

GIANNI DI PARIGI. **Soloists; Chorus and Orchestra of RAI, Milan/Carlo Felice Cillario.** Nuova Era 6752/3 (10/91).

LA FILLE DU REGIMENT. **Chorus; Chorus and Orchestra of the Royal Opera House, Covent Garden/Richard Bonynge.** Decca 414 520-2DH2 (11/86).

LA FAVORITA. **Soloists; Slovak Philharmonic Chorus; Italian International Opera Orchestra/Fabio Luisi.** Nuova Era 6823/4 (10/91).

MARIA PADILLA. **Soloists; Geoffrey Mitchell Choir; London Symphony Orchestra/ Alun Francis.** Opera Rara ORC6 (2/93).

POLIUTO. **Soloists; Vienna Singakademie Chorus; Vienna Symphony Orchestra/Oleg Caetani.** CBS Masterworks CD44821 (3/90).

John Dowland

British c.1563-1626

New review

Dowland. Lachrimae, or Seaven Teares. **Christopher Wilson** (lte); **Fretwork** (Wendy Gillespie, Richard Campbell, Julia Hodgson, William Hunt, Richard Boothby, viols). Virgin Classics Veritas VC5 45005-2. From VC7 90795-2 (11/89) and VC7 91117-2 (3/91).

⟨ lh   DDD   7/94 ⟩

Did Dowland ever expect this collection to be played in its entirety, at one sitting? If so, in what order? Whatever your own 'answers' to these unanswerable questions may be, you can (if you feel strongly about it) easily impose them on any of the various integral versions on CD. Fretwork's reissue presents them as an entirety, with the dances in their original published order — the whole book 'as is'. The performances are laudable in their characterization (of the pavans in particular), discreet embellishment of the dances, clarity of detail (the product of pleasantly dry string sound and acoustic) and overall balance, in which the lute is neither backgrounded nor obtrusive. Christopher Wilson adds a firmly propulsive edge to the dances. This is the best available version of Dowland's monumental work, graced with Peter Holman's splendid notes and blessed with superbly engineered recording. The recording by The Parley of Instruments Renaissance Violin Consort is also recommended, being the only one to avail itself of Dowland's "or Violons" option; Holman directs the proceedings — you can't keep a good man down!

Additional recommendation ...
Lachrimae[b]. Captain Digorie Piper his Pavan[b]. The King of Denmarke his Galliard, P40[a]. Moritz, Landgrave of Hessen-Kassel: Pavan[a]. [a]**Paul O'Dette** (lte); [b]**The Parley of Instruments Renaissance Violin Consort/Peter Holman.** Hyperion CDA66637 — lh 9m DDD 8/93

New review

Dowland. The First Booke of Songes or Ayres. **Rufus Müller** (ten); **Christopher Wilson** (lte). ASV Gaudeamus CDGAU135 Texts included.

⟨ lh 14m   DDD   10/93 ⟩

The fresh balletic quality of Dowland's masterful First Booke of Songes is sweetly caught here. Rufus Müller is unquestionably a natural in this repertoire, capable of bringing acute observations to these deceptively hard pieces. His singing is infused with an individuality and clear-sightedness which rules out any timbral monotony. Although he is prone to force the point in matters of detail, his soft-grained tone and unfussy style allows the imagination to revel in the artifice and poignancy of all but the odd song in which he sits slightly below pitch. The songs are generally shaped wistfully and in gems like *His goulden locks* the rounded middle

register produces his most cultured and beautiful sounds, discreetly decorated and sensitively accompanied by Christopher Wilson. There are indeed many accomplished moments but none more so than the clearly enunciated and ravishingly etched *Go cristall teares*. Strongly recommended.

Additional recommendation ...
The First Booke of Songes — *Awake sweet loue thou art returned; Can she excuse my wrongs; All ye whom Loue; Deare if you change. The Second Booke of Songs* — *Sorow sorow stay, lend true repentant teares; Dye not before thy day; Mourne, mourne; Wofull heart; Now cease my wandering eyes. The Third and Last Booke of Songs* — *Behold a wonder heare; The lowest trees; Me, me and none but me; Farewell too faire. A Pilgrimes Solace* — *Stay time a while thy flying; Shall I strive with words to move; Thou mighty God. Instrumental works* — *Semper Dowland semper dolens, P9; Mr Dowland's Midnight, P99; Earle of Darby, his Galliard, P44a. Mistris Winter's Jumpe, P55.* **Emma Kirkby** (sop); **Anthony Rooley** (lute/orpharion). Virgin Classics Veritas VC7 90768-2 — ⨎ 58m DDD 4/90 ♩ₚ

Dowland. The Second Booke of Songes. **The Consort of Musicke/Anthony Rooley** (lte). L'Oiseau-Lyre 425 889-2OH. Texts included. From DSLO528/9 (9/77). Recorded in 1976.

⨎ **1h 10m   ADD   8/91**

This recording originally appeared in 1977 as part of Florilegium's complete Dowland cycle. The "Second Booke of Songes" dates from 1600 and contains two of Dowland's most famous compositions *Flow my teares* and *I saw my Lady weepe*, though here these are presented unusually (and not entirely convincingly) as vocal duets. In fact there is a surprisingly wide variety of vocal and instrumental combinations throughout the disc, from consort song to four-part vocal to the more familiar sound of solo voice and lute, all of which were suggested as performance possibilities by Dowland himself. It is partly as a result of this that the recording retains its freshness in spite of its age, but it would be wrong to ignore the contribution made by the intelligent and sensitive singing of Emma Kirkby and Martyn Hill, both of whom sound completely in their element.

Patrick Doyle
British 20th Century

Suggested listening ...

Henry V — *original film soundtrack.* **City of Birmingham Symphony Orchestra/Simon Rattle.** EMI CDC7 49919-2 (2/90).

Riccardo Drigo
Italian 1846-1930

Suggested listening ...

The Magic Flute — ballet. *Coupled with* **Delibes.** La Source, ou Naila — ballet. **Orchestra of the Royal Opera House, Covent Garden/Richard Bonynge.** Decca 421 431-2DH2 (9/90).

Henri Du Mont
French 1610-1684

New review
Du Mont. MOTETS EN DIALOGUE. **Les Talens Lyriques** (Sandrine Piau, sop; Marie Boyer, mez; Mark Padmore, alto; François Piolino, Stephan van Dyck, tens; Paul Gerimon, bass; Florence Malgoire, Alain Petit, vns; Kaori Uemura, bass viol)/**Christophe Rousset** ([a]org/[b]hpd). FNAC Music 592098. Texts and translations included.

Allemande grave in D minor[a]. Litanies de la vierge. Symphonia à 3 in C minor. Allemande à 3 in G minor. Dialogus angeli et peccatoris. Allemande en tablature in A minor[a]. Pavane à 3 in D minor. Sarabande à 3 in D minor. Echo in lectulo meo. Allemande sur les Anches[a]. In Te Domine. Dialogus de anima. Pavane in D minor[b].

Ih 13m   DDD   9/93

Henry Du Mont was an organist and composer who held a succession of important court appointments in France during the third quarter of the seventeenth century. This attractive release happily mixes motets for solo voices and continuo with some of the instrumental pieces Du Mont liked to include in his published collections, some of them for keyboard and some of them for two violins and continuo. The result is a sort of sacred concert, a pleasingly contrasted programme which invites 73 minutes' listening more readily than a whole disc of motets would have done. All the motets are in some degree in dialogue form, giving Du Mont the chance to exercise his skills in dramatic vocal writing. The singers and players of Les Talens Lyriques, too, rise to the challenge and turn in boldly expressive performances. Christophe Rousset explains in the insert-note that for this recording all the musicians were placed together in the relatively confined space of the organ loft rather than the open body of the church itself, and the result is a good rapport between singers and players, with the proximity of the organ inspiring, of necessity, a more outgoing vocal style. Perhaps not everyone will like it, but it certainly has more fire in its belly than the slightly distanced and impersonal 'churchy' style of performance this sort of music often gets. The string pieces are less extrovert, but they receive alert performances, while Rousset's solo organ and harpsichord playing is characteristically assured.

Guillaume Dufay   *French c.1400-1474*

Suggested listening ...

Triste plaisir et douleureuse joye — Rondeaux, Ballades and Lamentations. *Coupled with* **Binchois.** Rondeaux and Ballades. **Ensemble Gilles Binchois/Dominique Vellard.** Virgin Classics Veritas VC7 59043-2.

François Dufault   *French c.1600?-1670*

Suggested listening ...

Suites — A minor; C major; G minor (three); C minor; D major; . Pavane in E minor. **Pascal Monteilhet** (lte). FNAC Music 592267 (3/94).

Paul Dukas   *French 1865-1935*

New review
Dukas. Symphony in C major. Polyeucte — overture. **BBC Philharmonic Orchestra/Yan Pascal Tortelier.** Chandos CHAN9225.

56m   DDD   6/94

Before *L'Apprenti sorcier* (there is an excellent version of this work reviewed in the Collections section; refer to the Index to Reviews), the tradition Dukas was following was that of Franck, and he was also heavily influenced by the Wagnerianism then holding French composers in thrall. Both models can be discerned in the overture *Polyeucte*: nevertheless, and despite extensive Wagnerian use of the brass, there is a clarity (even delicacy in the third of its five sections) and an imaginative sense of colour which are individual to him. The finely crafted Symphony composed four years later, in 1896 — daringly in C major at a time when tonality was undergoing such general buffeting — shows Dukas as essentially a classicist, although the middle section of the central movement reveals that Nature romanticism had not passed him by. The eloquent performance here gives the vigorous first movement a splendid *élan* (and a terrific ending) while also luxuriating in the Franckian secondary subjects, there is lovely warm, lyrical playing and sensitive nuance in the second movement, and the finale (even more Franckian in its harmonic thinking) bubbles over with nervous energy. Exemplary recording quality.

Further listening ...

La Péri — ballet. L'Apprenti sorcier. *Coupled with* **Debussy.** La boîte à joujoux — ballet. **Suisse Romande Orchestra/Ernest Ansermet.** Decca 433 714-2DM.

Variations, Interlude and Finale on a theme by Rameau. Prélude élégiaque. La plainte, au loin, du faune. Piano Sonata in E flat minor. **Margaret Fingerhut** (pf). Chandos CHAN8765 (1/90).

ARIANE ET BARBE-BLEUE. **Soloists; French Radio Chorus; French Radio New Philharmonic Orchestra/Armin Jordan.** Erato Libretto 2292-45663-2 (9/91).

Marie Eugène Duparc
French 1848-1933

New review

Duparc. MELODIES. **José van Dam** (bass-bar); [a]**Florence Bonnafous** (sop); **Maciej Pikulski** (pf). Forlane UCD16692. Texts and translations included. Recorded in 1993.
L'Invitation au voyage. Sérénade florentine. La Vague et la cloche. Extase. Phidylé. Le Manoir de Rosemonde. Lamento. Testament. Chanson triste. Elégie. Soupir. La Vie antérieure. Le Galop. Sérénade. Au pays où se fait la guerre[a]. Romance de Mignon[a]. La Fuite[a].

Ih 7m   DDD   I/94

These songs may justly be held to represent the peak of development of the French *mélodie* in their sensitivity, intensity, scope of expression and unfaltering taste. Influences may be seen of his teacher César Franck in his emotionalism and chromatic texture, of Gounod in the rippling piano part of a song like *Chanson triste*, and particularly of Wagner in the harmonic colouring of *Soupir* and the almost Tristanesque *Extase*; but it has been well observed that the sinister drama of *Le Manoir de Rosemonde*, with its insistent rhythm, is worthy of Hugo Wolf, and that the bleak tints of *Lamento* show some foreshadowing of Ravel's *Le gibet*. Despite all this, however, Duparc is very much an individual genius; and the breadth of his stylistic range, from the passionate lyricism of *L'Invitation au voyage* or the haunting sensuousness of *Phidylé* to the simple heartbreak of *Au pays où se fait la guerre*, makes any *intégrale* of his songs of riveting interest. Particularly so when sung with such imaginative insight, commitment and verbal intensity as by José van Dam here. He is expertly partnered by a responsively musical young Polish accompanist, Maciej Pikulski.

Jacques Duphly
French 1715-1789

New review

Duphly. PIECES DE CLAVECIN. **Mario Raskin** (hpd). Pierre Verany PV793021.
Livre I — Allemande in D minor; Courante in D minor; La Damanzy; Allemande in C minor; La Boucon; La larare; Rondeau. *Livre II* — La Félix; La Lanza; La d'Héricourt. *Livre III* — La Forqueray; Médée; Les Grâces. *Livre IV* — La de Vaucanson; La Porthouin.

Ih I6m   DDD   3/94

In nearly all his pieces, Duphly presents two contrasting images — the bold and brazen virtuoso, and the wistful dreamer. The one exploits the compass of the harpsichord with scales and dense chords while the other enchants with delicately voiced textures. Only occasionally, as in pieces such as the fiercely passionate "Médée", or the elegant "Les Grâces", does one mood prevail. Nimbly shifting back and forth between these extremes within pieces (as, for example in "La larare" or "La d'Héricourt") and between them presents a formidable challenge to any performer. Mario Raskin plays warmly and musically, even in the bravura passages. His tempos are sensible and his command of Duphly's ornamentation sure. This CD is wonderfully recorded.

Further listening ...

Harpsichord Solos — La de Redemond. La du Buq. *Coupled with* **Leclair.** Violin Sonatas — A minor, Op. 5 No. 7; A major, Op. 9 No. 4. **Mondonville.** Violin Sonata in G major, Op. 3 No. 5. **Guillemain.** Violin Sonata in A major, Op. 1 No. 4. *Harpsichord Solos* — **J-B. Forqueray.** La Morangis ou La Plissay. **Simon Standage** (vn); **Lars Ulrik Mortensen** (hpd). Chandos CHAN0531 (6/93). *See review under Leclair; refer to the Index to Reviews.*

Marcel Dupré

French 1886-1971

Suggested listening ...

Prelude and Fugue in A flat major, Op. 36 No. 2. Evocation, Op. 37. Six antiennes pour le temps de Noël, Op. 48. Psalm XVIII, Op. 47. Choral and Fugue, Op. 57. **Jeremy Filsell** (org). Gamut Classics GAMCD530 (5/92).

Preludes and Fugues, Op. 7. *Coupled with* **Alain.** Intermezzo. Litanies, Op. 79. **Franck.** Prélude, Fugue et Variation in B minor, Op. 18. Fantaisie in A major. **Tournemire.** Petite rapsodie improvisée. Cantilène Improvisée. Improvisation sur le Te Deum. **Jane Watts** (org). Priory PRCD286 (9/90).

Maurice Duruflé

French 1902-1986

New review

Duruflé. Prélude et Fugue sur le nom d'Alain, Op. 7[c]. Requiem, Op. 9[c]. Quatre Motets sur des thèmes grégoriens, Op. 10[b].
Fauré. Requiem[a]. Cantique de Jean Racine, Op. 11[a]. Messe basse[b].
Poulenc. Mass in G major[d]. Salve Regina[d]. Exultate Deo[d]. Litanies à la vierge noire[d]. **Jonathon Bond, Andrew Brunt, Robert King** (trebs); **Benjamin Luxon** (bar); **Christopher Keyte** (bass); **St John's College Choir, Cambridge; Academy of St Martin in the Fields/George Guest** with **Stephen Cleobury** (org). Double Decca 436 486-2DF2. Items marked [a] from Argo ZRG841 (4/76), [b] ZRG662 (2/71), [c] ZRG787 (5/75), [d] ZRG883 (6/78).

② 2h 29m ADD 7/94

Here is (practically) two-and-a-half hours of bliss. They are recordings to set aside for the time when, as the prayer says, "the busy world is hushed". The two discs would make an excellent present and it would be necessary to buy a second copy (for yourself) while about it. Asked to characterize Fauré's and Duruflé's Requiems as compared with others, we might suggest words such as 'delicate', 'restrained', 'meditative', 'undramatic'; but that last would be a mistake. These performances certainly do not go out of their way to 'be' dramatic or anything else other than faithful to the music but one is struck by the power exercised by those rare moments that rise to a *forte* and above. In Fauré the orchestral crescendo introducing the baritone soloist has the effectiveness of a spotlight brought up gradually upon a motionless figure on stage; the entry of brass in the *Sanctus* has breadth and majesty incommensurate with its scoring and duration; the brief orchestral climax of the *Lux aeterna* looms imposingly like the front of a great cathedral. Duruflé too is dramatic, but in the way that (say) Westminster Cathedral is dramatic, with stillness and space, and the light of candles amid a brooding darkness. The choir is surely at its best, the trebles with their fine, clear-cut, distinctive tone, the tenors (so important in the Fauré) graceful and refined without being precious, the altos exceptionally good, and only the basses just occasionally and briefly plummy or obtrusive in some way. The Poulenc works further test a choir's virtuosity yet in the extremely difficult Mass, the choir seems secure, and in the *Salve Regina* they catch the necessary tenderness. Of the treble soloists, Andrew Brunt sings most beautifully in the *Messe basse*, while Jonathon Bond's high, well-floated tones have ethereal effect in the *Agnus Dei* of Poulenc's Mass in G. Christopher Keyte dramatizes almost too convincingly in Duruflé's "tremens factus", and Benjamin Luxon, his production less even, builds finely in Fauré's *Libera me*. Stephen Cleobury, the organist throughout, contributes an admirably played solo written by Duruflé as a tribute to the young organist Jehan Alain, killed early in the war. These recordings have a vividness, certainly in the choral sound, that modern recordings generally lack.

Additional recommendation ...
Requiem, Op. 9ª. Quatre Motets. ª**Ann Murray** (mez); ª**Thomas Allen** (bar); **Corydon Singers;** ª**English Chamber Orchestra/Matthew Best** with ª**Thomas Trotter** (org). Hyperion CDA66191 — .·' 5lm DDD 4/87 ⁹ₚ

Further listening ...

Prélude sur l'introit de l'Epiphanie. Prélude et Fugue sur le nom d'Alain, Op. 7. Suite, Op. 5. Scherzo, Op. 2. Prélude, Adagio et Choral Varié sur le "Veni creator spiritus", Op. 4 (with the men's voices of St Paul's Cathedral Choir). Fugue sur le carillon des heures de la Cathédrale de Soissons, Op. 12. **John Scott** (org). Hyperion CDA66368 (1/91).

Jan Ladislav Dussek

Bohemian 1760-1812

Suggested listening ...

Piano Sonatas — C major, Op. 9 No. 2; G minor, Op. 10 No. 2. Three Sonatas, Op. 35. **Geoffrey Govier** (pf). Olympia Explorer OCD430 (9/93).

Henri Dutilleux

French 1916-

New review
Dutilleux. Symphonies — No. 1; No. 2, "Le double". **BBC Philharmonic Orchestra/Yan Pascal Tortelier.** Chandos CHAN9194.

.·' 1h DDD 11/93   ⁹ₚ ⁹ₛ

This pair of relatively early works by Henri Dutilleux, completed in 1951 and 1959 respectively, show him poised to inherit the Honegger/Martinů strand of the symphonic tradition. Yet, while an almost Simpsonian *élan* in the first movement of No. 2 promises a rich vein for further exploration, the Stravinskian strategies of the finale, ending with a virtual recomposition of the chorale that concludes the *Symphonies of Wind Instruments*, reveals a more modernist tendency, and leads away from the well-made, tonally-resolving symphony altogether. With their broad thematic vistas and persuasive adaptations of traditional forms, Dutilleux's symphonies offer considerable rewards to interpreters and listeners alike. Yan Pascal Tortelier and the BBC Philharmonic allow the music all the space it needs in strongly characterized, rhythmically well-sprung performances with uniformly excellent solo playing in No. 2, and the Chandos sound is rich and natural.

Dutilleux. Mystère de l'instant[a]. Métaboles[b]. Timbres, Espace, mouvement[b]. [a]**Zurich Collegium Musicum/Paul Sacher;** [b]**French National Orchestra/Mstislav Rostropovich.** Erato MusiFrance 2292-45626-2. Item marked [a] recorded in 1990, [b] 1982.

46m ADD/DDD 8/92

Métaboles was written in 1964 for the fortieth anniversary of the Cleveland Orchestra, and is dedicated to its conductor, George Szell. The work is in five sections, each showing off different sections of the orchestra until the fifth, which alone involves the whole ensemble. Szell had trained the Cleveland Orchestra into a virtuoso instrument, and Dutilleux's score, if structurally somewhat threadbare, reflects the composer's exotic taste for colour and sonority to great effect. If the French National Orchestra is not quite in the Cleveland league it gives a convincing account of the work under Rostropovich's direction. *Timbres, Espace, mouvement* was in fact commissioned by Rostropovich in 1978 for his Washington National Symphony Orchestra. Van Gogh's painting, "The Starry Night" was the source of inspiration, and once more Dutilleux paints his response in vivid sound colours. The work is in two sections, and the unusual scoring is for lower strings only, woodwind, brass and metallic percussion. Rostropovich leads a pungent, brightly lit performance. Paul Sacher commissioned *Mystère de l'instant* in 1989 for his Zurich Collegium Musicum. Once more Dutilleux creates magical sonorities from a smaller ensemble of strings, cymbalum and timbales, but his score, cast in ten short sections which are played continuously, is this time more inward-looking, and has greater substance. Sacher's sensitive, masterly direction gives great pleasure. Recordings throughout the disc are first-rate and it is only to be regretted that the playing time is so short.

Additional recommendation ...
Métaboles. Timbres, espace, mouvement (rev. 1991). Symphony No. 2, "Le double". **Orchestre de Paris/Semyon Bychkov.** Philips 438 008-2PH — **1h 3m DDD 5/94**

Further listening ...

Cello Concerto, "Tout un monde lointain" *Coupled with* **Agopov.** Cello Concerto, "Tres Viae" Op. 10. **Arto Noras** (vc); **Finnish Radio Symphony Orchestra/Jukka-Pekka Saraste.** Finlandia FACD401 (10/92).

Symphony No. 1. Timbres, espaces, mouvement. **Orchestre National de Lyon/Serge Baudo.** Harmonia Mundi HMC90 5159 (3/87).

Antonin Dvořák
Czechoslovakian 1841-1904

New review

Dvořák. Cello Concerto in B minor, B191[a]. Silent woods, B173[b]. Rondo in G minor, B171[b]. Slavonic Dance in A flat major, B147 No. 8[b]. **Heinrich Schiff** (vc); [a]**Vienna Philharmonic Orchestra/André Previn** ([b]pf). Philips 434 914-2PH.

54m DDD 9/93

Schiff's cello is recorded in a more natural balance than is common in this concerto, so that the solo instrument's first entry does not give the impression of a super-cello, as most recordings do, but the concentration and tension bear witness to the scale and power of the interpretation. When it comes to the great second subject melody Schiff's hushed *pianissimo* is ravishingly gentle, and unlike almost every rival he avoids drawing the tempo out, observing Dvořák's *In tempo* marking at a very marginally broader speed. The result has a touching simplicity and tenderness. André Previn is a fresh and understanding partner, pointing rhythms even more crisply, and the Vienna Philharmonic brings out the Slavonic tang in the score. The bright detailed recording helps, with the Vienna horns — so important in this work from the opening tutti on — sounding glorious. Schiff's flowing speed in the slow movement again brings out the freshness of folk-based ideas. Only in the finale does the balance of the cello mean that the result is less biting. Few versions come near to matching this. The coupling is apt. These are not the usual orchestral arrangements but have Previn as a sparkling piano accompanist.

Additional recommendations ...

Cello Concerto. **Tchaikovsky.** *Variations on a Rococo theme, Op. 33.* **Mstislav Rostropovich** (vc); **Berlin Philharmonic Orchestra/Herbert von Karajan.** DG 413 819-2GH — .⋅⋅ lh ADD 3/85 ⁹ₚ Ⓑ

Cello Concerto[a]. **Elgar.** *Cello Concerto in E minor, Op. 85*[b]. **Heinrich Schiff** (vc); [a]**Concert-gebouw Orchestra/Sir Colin Davis;** [b]**Staatskapelle, Dresden/Sir Neville Marriner.** Philips 412 880-2PH — .⋅⋅ 2/86 Ⓑ

Cello Concerto. **Schubert.** *Sonata in A major, D821, "Arpeggione".* **Lynn Harrell** (vc); **London Symphony Orchestra/James Levine.** RCA Papillon GD86531 — .⋅⋅ lh 7m ADD 11/87 Ⓑ

Cello Concerto[a]. **Bloch.** *Schelomo*[b]. **Bruch.** *Kol Nidrei, Op. 47*[c]. **Pierre Fournier** (vc); [ab]**Berlin Philharmonic Orchestra/**[a]**George Szell,** [b]**Alfred Wallenstein,** [c]**Jean Martinon.** DG Privilege 429 155-2GR — .⋅ lh llm ADD 5/90 Ⓑ

Cello Concerto (Berlin Philharmonic Orchestra/Lorin Maazel). **Elgar.** *Cello Concerto in E minor, Op. 85* (London Symphony Orchestra/André Previn). **Haydn.** *Cello Concerto in D major, HobVIIb/2* (English Chamber Orchestra). **Saint-Saëns.** *Cello Concerto No. 1 in A minor, Op. 33* (French National Orchestra/Lorin Maazel). **Schumann.** *Cello Concerto in A minor, Op. 129* (Bavarian Radio Symphony Orchestra/Sir Colin Davis). **Yo-Yo Ma** (vc). CBS Masterworks CD44562 — .⋅⋅ ② DDD/ADD 2h 20m 5/90 Ⓑ

Cello Concerto[a]. **Bruch.** *Kol Nidrei*[b]. **Elgar.** *Cello Concerto in E minor, Op. 85*[c]. **Pablo Casals** (vc); [a]**Czech Philharmonic Orchestra/George Szell;** [b]**London Symphony Orchesta/Sir Landon Ronald;** [c]**BBC Symphony Orchestra/Sir Adrian Boult.** EMI Références mono CDH7 63498-2 — .⋅⋅ lh l5m ADD 8/90 ⁹ₚ Ⓑ ▲

Cello Concerto. **Elgar.** *Cello Concerto.* **Maria Kliegel** (vc); **Royal Philharmonic Orchestra/ Michael Halász.** Naxos 8 550503 — , lh l3m DDD 9/92 Ⓑ

Cello Concerto[a]. **Saint-Saëns.** *Cello Concerto No. 1 in A minor, Op. 33*[b]. *Le carnaval des animaux — Le cygne*[c]. **Fauré.** *Elégie, Op. 24*[d]. *Berceuse, Op. 16*[d]. **Debussy.** *Rêverie*[d]. **Ravel.** *Pièce en forme de habanera*[d]. **Pierre Fournier** (vc); [d]**Ernest Lush,** [c]**Gerald Moore** (pfs); **Philharmonia Orchestra/**[a]**Rafael Kubelík,** [b]**Walter Susskind.** Testament mono SBT1016 — .⋅⋅ lh l7m ADD 7/93 ⁹ₚ Ⓑ

Cello Concerto[a]. *Piano Concerto in G minor*[b]. [a]**Mstislav Rostropovich** (vc); [b]**František Maxián** (pf); **Czech Philharmonic Orchestra/Václav Talich.** Supraphon Historical mono 11 1901-2 — .⋅⋅ lh l7m ADD 3/94 ⁹ₚ Ⓑ ▲

Dvořák. *Violin Concerto in A minor, B108. Romance in F minor, B39.* **Kyung Wha Chung** (vn); **Philadelphia Orchestra/Riccardo Muti.** EMI CDC7 49858-2.

.⋅⋅ 47m DDD 11/89 ⁹ₚ Ⓑ

Considering the popularity of his Cello Concerto, Dvořák's Violin Concerto has never quite caught on with the general public. But a top class performance can convince us that the neglect is unfair. Kyung Wha Chung plays the concerto with the right blend of simplicity and brilliance, Slavonic warmth and folk-like quality, and the Philadelphia Orchestra under Riccardo Muti give her the right kind of support, unobtrusive enough to make us forget that the orchestral writing is not Dvořák at his most instrumentally imaginative, yet positive enough to provide more than just a discreet background. Ultimately, we probably enjoy the concerto most for its Bohemian lilt, a quality we feel in the violin's very first entry and that is present again in ample measure in the rondo finale — a movement of unfailingly dancing rhythm and considerable charm that here receives a sparkling performance. The delicately scored Romance in F minor that completes the programme is a slightly earlier work than the Violin Concerto and, it has been said, suggests a leisurely walk through the Bohemian countryside with someone who knows it well. The recorded sound is well defined and faithful, capturing Chung's fine tonal palette.

Additional recommendations ...

Violin Concerto[a]. **Sibelius.** *Violin Concerto in D minor, Op. 47*[b]. **Salvatore Accardo** (vn); [a]**Concertgebouw Orchestra,** [b]**London Symphony Orchestra/Sir Colin Davis.** Philips Silver Line 420 895-2PSL — .⋅⋅ lh 8m ADD 10/88 ⁹ₚ Ⓑ

Violin Concerto. **Suk.** *Fantasy, Op. 24.* **Josef Suk** (vn); **Czech Philharmonic Orchestra/ Karel Ančerl.** Supraphon Crystal Collection 11 0601-2 — .⋅ 56m ADD 9/89 Ⓑ

Violin Concerto[a]. *Romance in F minor*[a]. *Carnival Overture.* **Midori** (vn); **New York Philharmonic Orchestra/Zubin Mehta.** CBS Masterwoks CD44923 — .⋅⋅ 53m DDD 11/89 Ⓑ

Violin Concerto. **Glazunov.** *Violin Concerto in A minor, Op. 83.* **Frank Peter Zimmermann** (vn); **London Philharmonic Orchestra/Franz Welser-Möst.** EMI CDC7 54872-2 — ⠂⠄•
52m DDD 3/94 Ⓑ

Violin Concerto. **Lalo.** *Symphonie espagnole, Op. 21.* **Christian Tetzlaff** (vn); **Czech Philharmonic Orchestra/Libor Pešek.** Virgin Classics VC5 45022 2 *(See review under Lalo; refer to the Index to reviews)* — ⠂⠄• 1h 3m DDD 7/94 ⑨ₚ Ⓑ

Dvořák. Piano Concerto in G minor, B63[a].
Schumann. Introduction and Allegro appassionato, Op. 92. **András Schiff** (pf); **Vienna Philharmonic Orchestra/Christoph von Dohnányi.** Decca 417 802-2DH. Item marked [a] recorded at a performance in the Musikverein, Vienna in 1986.

⠂⠄• 53m DDD 1/89   ⑨ₚ ⑨ₛ

It seems extraordinary that the Piano Concerto is not all that well known. For a long time it was thought unpianistic, but András Schiff gives a fresh and agile account of what is a delightful score. He is very well partnered by Dohnányi and the Vienna Philharmonic Orchestra, and the playing is singularly sure for a live performance. The music is unmistakably Dvořák's, though in this relatively early work we do not find the consistently Bohemian flavour that is actually stronger in his later music. Schumann wrote his *Introduction* while under the literary influence of Byron's dramatic poem *Manfred* with its tormented hero. Here is another relatively neglected piece, but it has considerable atmosphere and is once again persuasively performed. Clear yet spacious recording in both works.

Additional recommendation ...
Piano Concerto[a]. *Cello Concerto*[b]. [a]**František Maxián** (pf); [b]**Mstislav Rostropovich** (vc); **Czech Philharmonic Orchestra/Václav Talich.** Supraphon Historical mono 11 1901-2 —
⠂⠄• 1h 17m ADD 3/94 ⑨ₚ Ⓑ ▲

Dvořák. OVERTURES AND SYMPHONIC POEMS. **Bavarian Radio Symphony Orchestra/Rafael Kubelík.** DG Galleria 435 074-2GGA2. Items marked [a] from 2530 593 (12/75), [b] 2530 785 (2/78), [c] 2530 712 (11/76), [d] 2530 713 (11/76). Recorded 1973-76.
Overtures and Symphonic Poems — My home, B125a[a]. Hussite, B132[b]. In nature's realm, B168[b]. Carnival, B169[b]. Othello, B174[b]. The water goblin, B195[c]. The noon witch, B196[c]. The golden spinning-wheel, B197[d]. The wild dove, B198[d]. Symphonic Variations, B70[c].

⠂⠄• ② 2h 37m ADD 11/91

Writing about Richard Strauss's *Don Juan*, Tovey remarked that "programme music ... either coheres as music or it does not". Perhaps Dvořák's symphonic poems have never attained the popularity of those by Richard Strauss because there are a few too many seams in his musical narrative. Equally, the gruesome local folk ballads on which they are based (and which Dvořák gleefully brings to life) afforded him less range for depth of human characterization. But there are lots of good reasons to value them. There's his inimitable stream of heart-easing melody, and alongside the obvious debt to Liszt and Wagner, their harmonic boldness and magical instrumental effects look forward to Suk, Martinů and Janáček. Indeed, in the central section of *The golden spinning-wheel*, where the wheel and assorted paraphernalia are offered to the false queen in return for the various dismembered portions of the heroine's body, the repeated patterns on muted strings sound like pure Janáček. And the exquisite closing pages of *The wild dove* could be the best thing Martinů ever wrote. Also written when Dvořák was at the height of his power (in the 1890s), these two mid-priced discs offer the chance to hear his three concert overtures — *In nature's realm, Carnival* and *Othello* — as he originally conceived them: a thematically linked three movement 'symphonic' work on the theme of nature, life and love. The earlier and no less worthy *Symphonic Variations* and *My home* and *Hussite* overtures complete a set that would be fine value in terms of minutes for your money even if the performances were mediocre. As it is you won't find a finer account at any price. Knowing when to keep this music on the move is the secret of Kubelík's success, but the mobility is always marked by freshness of spirit rather than plain drive. The whole set is informed with his burning belief in the value of the music and his experience is drawing precisely what he wants from his own Bavarian players. DG's mid-seventies recordings project this with clarity and coherence and need fear nothing from more recent digital contenders.

Additional recommendation ...
In nature's realm. Carnival. Othello. My home. Vanda. **BBC Philharmonic Orchestra/Stephen Gunzenhauser.** Naxos 8 550600 — . 57m DDD 10/93

Dvořák. SLAVONIC DANCES. **Bavarian Radio Symphony Orchestra/Rafael Kubelík.**
DG Galleria 419 056-2GGA. Items marked [a] from 2530 466 (11/75), [b] 2530 593 (11/75).
B83[a] — No. 1 in C major; No. 2 in E minor; No. 3 in A flat major; No. 4 in F major; No. 5 in A major; No. 6 in D major; No. 7 in C minor; No. 8 in G major. *B147*[b] — No. 1 in B major; No. 2 in E minor; No. 3 in F major; No. 4 in D flat major; No. 5 in B flat minor; No. 6 in B flat major; No. 7 in C major; No. 8 in A flat major.

· 1h 10m ADD 8/87 Ⓟ

Dvořák wrote his first set of eight *Slavonic Dances* in 1878 at the request of his publisher. They were originally cast in piano duet form, but the composer almost immediately scored them for orchestra. They achieved a great success and a further set of eight were requested. Dvořák initially doubted his ability to repeat the prescription, and it was not until 1886 that he produced a second set of eight dances. Again they were originally written for piano duet and then orchestrated, and again they proved to be very popular. Kubelík's recording was made at a time when he was head of the Bavarian Radio Symphony Orchestra. As a musician steeped in the romantic traditions of his native Czechoslovakia he managed to persuade his orchestra to play Czech music almost to the manner born. His performances of the dances are brilliant, very vivacious, and highly idiomatic. The recording is very clear but slightly lacking in depth and atmosphere.

Additional recommendations ...
Slavonic Dances. **Rheineland-Pfalz State Philharmonic Orchestra/Leif Segerstam.** BIS CD425 — · 1h 18m DDD 7/89 Ⓟ
Slavonic Dances. Carnival — Overture, B169. **Czech Philharmonic Orchestra/Václav Talich.**
Slavonic Dances. Music and Arts mono CD-658 — · 1h 15m AAD 6/92 Ⓟ ▲
Cleveland Orchestra/George Szell. Sony Classical Essential Classics MK48161 — · 1h 14m ADD 11/92 Ⓟ

Dvořák. Serenade in D minor, B77. Slavonic Dance No. 7 in C major, B147 (arr. Clements).
Krommer. Partita in E flat major, Op. 45[a].
Mysliveček. Octet in E flat major. [a]**Charles Kavalovski,** [a]**Scott Brubaker** (hns); **New York Harmonie Ensemble/Steven Richman.** Music and Arts CD-691. Recorded live in 1990.

· 59m DDD 8/92

There's some really high-class wind-playing on this delightful CD; indeed, the performance of the Dvořák Wind *Serenade* is one the finest around, brimful of affectionate vigour and pungent character. This is followed by an idiomatic arrangement of the same composer's C major *Slavonic Dance* (No. 7 from the second set) — again despatched with agreeably earthy panache. Apparently, the members of the Harmonie Ensemble are drawn from the cream of New York's major orchestras, which would account for the technical excellence and first-rate musicianship on show. Two enjoyable Czech rarities comprise the remainder: the E flat Octet by Josef Mysliviček (1737-81) possesses a truly Mozartian grace and delicacy, whilst the Partita of Franz Krommer (1759-1831) (one of three comprising his Op. 45 and first published in 1803) is a concerto for two horns in all but name — bouquets here for the two solo players (Charles Kavalovski and Scott Brubaker) who deal superbly with Krommer's fiendishly demanding writing. Annotations are most helpful, and the recording, made in a New York church during a live concert (though you would never guess it — off-stage noises are virtually non-existent), has ideal warmth and blend, though more of the rasp of double-bass in the Dvořák *Serenade* would have been preferable.

Additional recommendation ...
Serenades — B77; E major, B52. **Academy of St Martin in the Fields/Sir Neville Marriner.** Philips 400 020-2PH — · 51m DDD 4/83

Dvořák. COMPLETE SYMPHONIES AND ORCHESTRAL WORKS. **London Symphony Orchestra/István Kertész.** Decca 430 046-2DC6. Recorded 1963-66.
Symphonies — No. 1 in C minor, B9, "The Bells of Zlonice" (from SXL6288, 10/67); No. 2 in B flat major, B12 (SXL6289, 9/67); No. 3 in E flat major, B34 (SXL6290, 5/67); No. 4 in D minor, B41 (SXL6257, 4/67); No. 5 in F major, B54 (SXL6273, 3/67); No. 6 in D major, B112 (SXL6253, 11/66); No. 7 in D minor, B141; No. 8 in G major, B163 (SXL6044, 7/63); No. 9 in E minor, B178, "From the New World" (SXL6291, 11/67). Scherzo capriccioso, B131 (SXL6348, 7/63). *Overtures* — In nature's realm, B168 (SXL6290, 5/67); Carnival, B169 (SXL6253, 11/66); My home, B125a (SXL6273, 3/67).

⑥ 7h 11m ADD 4/92   **♩♪**

István Kertész recorded the Dvořák symphonies during the mid-1960s and his integral cycle was quick to achieve classic status, with his exhilarating and vital account of the Eighth Symphony (the first to be recorded in February 1963) rapidly becoming a special landmark in the catalogue. The original LPs, with their distinctive Breughel reproduction sleeves are now collectors' items in their own right, but these magnificent interpretations became available again in 1992, in glitteringly refined digitally remastered sound, and it is a tribute to the memory of this tragically short-lived conductor that this cycle continues to set the standard by which all others are judged. Kertész was the first conductor to attract serious collectors to the early Dvořák symphonies which, even today are not performed as often as they should be; and his jubilant advocacy of the unfamiliar First Symphony, composed in the composer's twenty-fourth year, has never been superseded. This work offers surprising insights into the development of Dvořák's mature style, as does the Second Symphony. Kertész shows that Symphonies Nos. 3 and 4 have much more earthy resilience than many commentators might have us believe, insisting that Dvořák's preoccupation with the music of Wagner and Liszt had reached its zenith during this period. The challenging rhetoric of the Fourth has never found a more glorious resolution than here, with Kertész drawing playing of gripping intensity from the London Symphony Orchestra. The Fifth Symphony, and to a still greater extent, its glorious successor, Symphony No. 6, both reveal Dvořák's clear affinity with the music of Brahms. Kertész's superb reading of the Sixth, however, shows just how individual and naturally expressive this underrated work actually is, whilst the playing in the great climax of the opening movement and the vigorous final peroration remains tremendously exciting, even almost 30 years after the recording first appeared. In the great final trilogy, Kertész triumphs nobly with the craggy resilience of the Seventh Symphony, and his buoyant ardour brings a dynamic thrust and momentum to the Eighth Symphony, whereas his *New World* is by turns indomitable and searchingly lyrical. The six-disc set also offers assertive and brilliant readings of the Overtures *Carnival, In nature's realm* and the rarely heard *My home*, together with a lucid and heroic account of the *Scherzo capriccioso*. These definitive performances have been skilfully reprocessed, the sound is astonishingly good, even by modern standards, and the playing of the London Symphony Orchestra is often daringly brilliant under the charismatic direction of one of this century's late-lamented masters of the podium.

Additional recommendations ...
Symphonies Nos. 1-9[a]. Scherzo capriccioso, B131[b]. Carnival[b]. The wild dove, B198[b]. [a]**Berlin Philharmonic Orchestra;** [b]**Bavrian Radio Symphony Orchestra/Rafael Kubelík.** DG 423 120-2GX6 — .·' ⑥ 7h 5m ADD 10/88
Symphonies Nos. 1-9. Carnival. My home. Othello, B174. Hussite, B132. **London Symphony Orchestra/Witold Rowicki.** Philips 432 602-2PM6 — .·' ⑥ 7h 9m ADD 4/92
No. 1. The Hero's Song, B199. **Scottish National Orchestra/Neeme Järvi.** Chandos CHAN8597 — .·' 1h 14m DDD 4/89
No. 2. Slavonic Rhapsody in A flat major, B86 No. 3. **Scottish National Orchestra/Neeme Järvi.** Chandos CHAN8589 — .·' 1h 1m DDD 7/88
No. 3. Carnival. Symphonic Variations, B70. **Scottish National Orchestra/Neeme Järvi.** Chandos CHAN8575 — .·' 1h 3m DDD 5/88
No. 4. Ten Biblical Songs, B185[a]. [a]**Brian Rayner Cook** (bar); **Scottish National Orchestra/ Neeme Järvi.** Chandos CHAN8608 — .·' 1h 8m DDD 12/88

Dvořák. Symphony No. 5 in F major, B54. Othello, B174. Scherzo capriccioso, B131. **Oslo Philharmonic Orchestra/Mariss Jansons.** EMI CDC7 49995-2. Recorded in 1989.

.·' 1h 4m DDD 7/90   **♩♪**

Of all the romantic composers, it is probably Dvořák who best evokes a sunlit, unspoiled and relatively untroubled picture of nineteenth-century country life. Light and warmth radiate from his Fifth Symphony, composed in just six weeks of the year 1875 when he was in his early thirties. It has been called his "Pastoral Symphony", and it is easy to see why, especially in a performance as fresh and sunny as this one. Mariss Jansons brings out all the expressiveness and heart of the music without exaggerating the good spirits and playful humour that are so characteristic of the composer, and one would single out for praise the fine wind playing of the Oslo Philharmonic Orchestra (and not least its golden-toned horns) were it not for the fact that the strings are no less satisfying. The lyrical *Andante con moto* brings out the fine interplay of the instrumental writing, the bouncy *Scherzo* is uninhibited without going over the top and the exciting finale has plenty of momentum. The other two pieces are also nicely done, the *Scherzo capriccioso* having both lilt and vigour and the rarely played *Othello* Overture (a late work) being a suitably dramatic response to Shakespeare's tragedy. The recording is warm and clear.

Additional recommendation ...
No. 5. The water goblin, B195. **Scottish National Orchestra/Neeme Järvi.** Chandos CHAN8552 — .·'' lh lm DDD 12/87

Dvořák. Symphony No. 6 in D major, B112.
Janáček. Taras Bulba. **Cleveland Orchestra/Christoph von Dohnányi.** Decca 430 204-2DH. Recorded in 1989.

.·'' lh 6m DDD 7/91   ⁹ₚ

With its obvious echoes of Brahms's Second Symphony, the Sixth Symphony is a work which, for all its pastoral overtones, gains from refined playing, and quite apart from the imaculate ensemble, the Cleveland violins play ethereally, as in the melody at the start of the slow movement. Dohnányi does not miss the earthy qualities of the writing either, and the impact of the performance is greatly enhanced by the fullness and weight of the recording. This is altogether a superb account. There is also the bonus of an unusual makeweight, *Taras Bulba*. The account here is very Viennese in style and warmly expressive against its opulent background. However, if Janáček is your first priority, then Mackerras's version, coupled with the *Sinfonietta* (refer to the Index to Reviews) is the obvious choice, for he charcterfully persuades his truly Viennese musicians to sound more like Czechs, playing brilliantly with a sharp attack very apt for the composer's music. But those who want a radiant account of the Dvořák will find comparable joy in the characterful Janáček rhapsody.

Additional recommendations ...
No. 6. The noon witch, B196. **Scottish National Orchestra/Neeme Järvi.** Chandos CHAN8530 — .·'' 56m DDD 11/87
No. 6. The wild dove, B198. **Czech Philharmonic Orchestra/Jiří Bělohlávek.** Chandos CHAN9170 — .·'' lh 3m DDD 11/93 ⁹ₚ

Dvořák. Symphonies — No. 7 in D minor, B141; No. 8 in G major, B163. **Oslo Philharmonic Orchestra/Mariss Jansons.** EMI CDC7 54663-2. Recorded in 1992.

.·'' lh 14m DDD 6/93   ⁹ₚ Ⓑ

Dvořák. Symphonies — No. 7 in D minor, B141; No. 9 in E minor, B178, "From the New World". **London Philharmonic Orchestra/Sir Charles Mackerras.** EMI Eminence CD-EMX2202. Recorded in 1991.

.·'' lh 19m DDD 2/93   ⁹ₚ Ⓑ

Mariss Jansons's popular pairing makes most agreeable listening. With clean-cut playing from the fine Oslo orchestra and natural, unexaggerated sonics, these are engagingly alive, refreshingly energetic readings, if not quite as warm-hearted or openly affectionate as some Dvořákians might like. Jansons's sophisticated sense of texture impresses throughout, however, and the outer movements of No. 8 in particular emerge with genuinely vivid freshness. True, in terms of irrefutable symphonic strength both these interpretations fall some way short of Sir Colin Davis's magnificent achievement with the Concertgebouw (listed below and now coupled with No. 9 and available on a two-CD set), but Jansons's clean-heeled direction brings with it a certain endearing spontaneity and rhythmic resilience that will undoubtedly give pleasure. Sir Charles Mackerras's long-standing authority in the Czech repertoire is of course well-known by now, so his thoughts are not to be dismissed lightly, especially when, at nearly 80 minutes, Nos. 7 and 9 make a terrifically generous pairing. In the tragic Seventh, Mackerras concentrates largely on the more endearingly lyrical side of Dvořák's invention; in this respect both inner movements are particularly memorable in their open-hearted grace and charm. However, those who (rightly) crave a greater degree of intensity and symphonic rigour in the two great flanking outer movements (such as one encounters with rival interpreters like Kubelík, Rowicki, Sir Colin Davis or Dorati, all either listed or reviewed in this section) will perhaps come away not quite so satisfied. Similarly, this *New World* is an affectingly unfussy traversal. The slow movement glows ravishingly at an exceptionally broad tempo, and in the finale Mackerras draws Dvořák's structural threads together with undemonstrative cogency. Overall, this is undoubtedly a fine account, if not quite as winningly spontaneous an experience as Kubelík's famous BPO recording for DG or Barbirolli's inspirational Hallé performance on EMI Phoenixa. With all that, Mackerras's are still warmly affectionate readings, superbly played and resplendently recorded. At mid-price the value is obvious.

Additional recommendations ...
Nos. 7-9. Symphonic Variations, B70. **Royal Concertgebouw Orchestra/Sir Colin Davis.** Philips Duo 438 347-2PM2 — .·' ② 2h 19m ADD 8/93 ♩ₚ Ⓑ
Nos. 7 and 9. **Hallé Orchestra/Sir John Barbirolli.** EMI Phoenixa CDM7 63774-2 — .·' Ih I6m ADD 2/91 ♩ₚ Ⓑ ▲
Nos. 7 and 8. **Cleveland Orchestra/Christoph von Dohnányi.** Decca Ovation 430 728-2DM — .·' Ih I3m DDD 12/91 ♩ₚ Ⓑ
London Symphony Orchestra/Antál Dorati. Mercury 434 312-2MM — .·' Ih IIm ADD ♩ₚ Ⓑ
No. 8. Scherzo capriccioso. Legends, Op. 59 Nos. 4, 6 and 7. **Hallé Orchestra/Sir John Barbirolli.** EMI Phoenixa CDM7 64193-2 — .·' Ih Im ADD 6/92 ♩ₚ Ⓑ ▲
No. 8. The golden spinning-wheel. **Philharmonia Orchestra/Eliahu Inbal.** Teldec 9031-72305-2 — .·' Ih 5m DDD II/92 ♩ₚ Ⓑ
No. 8[a]. Carnival[b]. The wild dove[b]. **[a]Berlin Philharmonic Orchestra; [b]Bavarian Radio Symphony Orchestra/Rafael Kubelík.** DG Privilege 429 518-2GR — .· Ih 4m ADD ♩ₚ Ⓑ
Nos. 7-9[a]. Symphonic Variations, B70[b]. **[a]Concertgebouw Orchestra; [b]London Symphony Orchestra/Sir Colin Davis.** Philips Duo 438 347-2PM2 — .·' ② 2h 19m ADD 8/93 ♩ₚ ♩ₛ Ⓑ

[New review]
Dvořák. Symphony No. 8 in G major, B163. Symphonic Variations, B70. **London Philharmonic Orchestra/Sir Charles Mackerras.** EMI Eminence CD-EMX2216.
.·' Ih DDD 4/94 ♩ₚ Ⓑ

This is an unmissable account of the Eighth Symphony. Mackerras realizes all the score's indications of shading, pointing and phrasing, or to put it another way, all its elegance and bittersweet ambiguity. In this, amongst the listed comparisons above, he has no peers. He has a spirited and willing LPO in the palm of his guiding, illuminating hand. Articulation and emphases are consistently light, and not only in the energetic tuttis. In the flute solo some 40 seconds into the first movement the LPO principal, without disturbing the tranquillity of the scene, animates the solo to suggest birdsong (all the solo and ensemble flute work on the Mackerras disc is outstanding). It is this wide range of pictoral suggestion and emotion, and an orchestra audibly fired up by the occasion, that mark Mackerras's performance of the Symphony as an example of great Dvořák conducting. Has anybody, one wonders, made as much of the contrast between the joyous pealing of bells and fanfares that end the first appearance of the slow movement's second subject, and the abrupt hush for its chorale-like conclusion, as if the traveller has suddenly entered the dark interior of a church and encountered a solemn procession. And revelation follows revelation: you can't fail to notice the tension as the *pianopianissimo* strings prepare for the anguished transformation of the movement's opening theme. Mackerras relaxes in the *Symphonic Variations* but keeps the work flowing along and gives as fine a performance of this work as you are likely to hear. The Eminence sound for Mackerras (from London's Henry Wood Hall), is immediate and lively, with a wider dynamic range.

Dvořák. Symphony No. 9 in E minor, B178, "From the New World"[a]. American Suite[b]. **[a]Vienna Philharmonic Orchestra/Kirill Kondrashin; [b]Royal Philharmonic Orches-**

tra/Antál Dorati. Decca 430 702-2DM. Item marked [a] from SXDL7510 (7/80), [b] 410 735-2DH2 (3/85). Recorded 1979-83.

․ **Ih 3m DDD 8/91**

Kondrashin's *New World* caused something of a sensation when originally transferred to CD. Here was a supreme example of the clear advantages of the new medium over the old and the metaphor of a veil being drawn back between listener and performers could almost be extended to a curtain: the impact and definition of the sound is quite remarkable and the acoustic of the Sofiensaal in Vienna are presented as quite ideal for this score. The upper strings have brilliance without edginess, the brass — with characteristically bright VPO trumpets — has fine sonority as well as great presence, the bass is firm, full and rich and the ambience brings luminosity and bloom to the woodwind without clouding.

Additional recommendations …
No. 9. **Cleveland Orchestra/Christoph von Dohnányi.** Decca 414 421-2DH — **․** 4lm DDD 1/87 🄱
No. 9. Symphonic Variations. **London Philharmonic Orchestra/Zdenek Macal.** Classics for Pleasure CD-CFP9006 — **․** Ih 6m DDD 9/87 🄱
No. 9. Carnival Overture, B169. Scherzo capriccioso. **London Symphony Orchestra/István Kertész.** Decca Ovation 417 724-2DM — **․** Ih 5m ADD 12/87 🄱

Dvořák. String Sextet in A major, B80[a].
Martinů. Serenade No. 2. String Sextet[a]. **Academy of St Martin in the Fields Chamber Ensemble** (Kenneth Sillito, Malcolm Latchem, vns; Robert Smissen, [a]Stephen Tees, vas; [a]Stephen Orton, [a]Roger Smith, vcs). Chandos CHAN8771. Recorded in 1989.

․ **50m DDD 5/90**

There is little which links the music of Dvořák and Martinů except a common Czech background, but the ASMF Chamber Ensemble respond well to both composers' styles and the result is a highly enjoyable, well-contrasted programme. Martinů's smart metropolitan 1930s style is encapsulated in the brief, but rather trifling *Serenade*. The Sextet is a longer and a more substantial work, still written in a busy, neoclassical style and effective in its way. These two works inspire an alert, spick-and-span response in the ASMF players. Their style in the warmly romantic Dvořák work is appropriate, too. In the first movement their tempo variations are quite marked, and the playing is highly expressive. The second movement *Dumka* has effectively strong accents and is followed by a fast, exhilarating third movement *Furiant*. The finale comprises a set of variations, each episode of which is vividly characterized in this performance. The recording was made in a church, but fortunately the acoustic is generous without having unwanted resonances and the balance is good.

Additional recommendations …
String Sextet. String Quintet in E flat major, B180. **Raphael Ensemble.** Hyperion CDA66308 — **․** Ih 5m DDD 8/89
String Sextet. String Quintet. **Josef Suk** (va); [a]**Josef Chuchro** (vc); **Smetana Quartet.** Supraphon 11 1469-2 — **․** Ih 8m DDD 10/93

Dvořák. Piano Quintet in A major, B155[a].
Franck. Piano Quintet in F minor[b]. **Sir Clifford Curzon** (pf); **Vienna Philharmonic Quartet** (Willi Boskovsky, Otto Strasser, vns; Rudolf Streng, va; [a]Robert Scheiwein, [b]Emanuel Brabec, vcs). Decca 421 153-2DM. Item marked [a] from SXL6043 (6/63), [b] SXL2278 (9/61). Item marked [a] recorded in 1962, [b] 1960.

․ **Ih 9m ADD 4/90**

New review
Dvořák. Piano Quintet in A major, B155.
Martinů. Piano Quintet No. 2. **Peter Frankl** (pf); **Lindsay Quartet** (Peter Cropper, Ronald Birks, vns; Robin Ireland, va; Bernard Gregor-Smith, vc). ASV CDDCA889.

․ **Ih 10m DDD 6/94** 🄱

The first disc contains two self-recommending accounts dating from the 1960s that long enjoyed classic status. An aristocrat of the keyboard, Curzon gives commanding accounts of both works, and his Viennese partners offer playing of great finesse and subtlety. The Dvořák is among his most endearing and captivating scores, and the Franck belongs to that master's most impassioned utterances. The quintets are separated by barely a decade (the Dvořák comes from 1887, the Franck from 1879), and it would be difficult to improve on these performances. Both are standard classics and belong in every basic collection: together in such fine performances and at such a reasonable price they offer outstanding value. The Decca sound, always very good, is as fresh and powerful as the music itself. One of the most successful aspects of Frankl and the Lindsays' performance of Dvořák's Quintet is their sensitivity to the tempo contrasts which are a central part of the work's expressive language. There is also a very intelligent interplay, in the scherzo, between the various levels of texture for which Dvořák asks: around the piano melody run at various stages a warm cello theme but also a dancing, almost edgy, fantastic violin figure that sets it off. This is most sensitively and intelligently done, and the point has been no less well grasped by the engineers. The textures in Martinů's Quintet are more difficult to clarify, and less well contrasted; but the players make the most of the contrasts between the dark opening, the grave *Adagio* and the somewhat insistent finale.

Dvořák. String Quintets — G major, B49[a]; E flat major, B180[b]. Intermezzo in B major, B49[c].
Chilingirian Quartet (Levon Chilingirian, Mark Butler, vns; Louise Williams, va; Philip De Groote, vc); [b]**Simon Rowland-Jones** (va); [ac]**Duncan McTier** (db). Chandos CHAN9046. Recorded 1990-91.

⠶ **1h 9m DDD 11/92**

Dating from 1875 (a particularly productive year for the composer), Dvořák's G major String Quintet is a thoroughly engaging affair, winning first prize in a competition for new chamber works organized by the Prague Artistic Circle. Originally in five movements, Dvořák subsequently removed the "Intermezzo" second movement, revising and publishing it separately eight years later as the haunting *Nocturne* for string orchestra. Enterprisingly, this Chandos disc includes that "Intermezzo" in its original string quintet garb. The E flat Quintet from 1893, on the other hand, is a wholly mature masterpiece. Completed in just over two months during Dvořák's American sojourn, it replaces the double-bass of the earlier Quintet with the infinitely more subtle option of a second viola. Brimful of the most delightfully fresh, tuneful invention, the score also shares many melodic and harmonic traits with the popular *American* Quartet — its immediate predecessor. The Chilingirian Quartet, ideally abetted by double-bassist Duncan McTier and violist Simon Rowland-Jones, are enthusiastic, big-hearted proponents of all this lovely material, and the excellent Chandos recording offers both a realistic perspective and beguiling warmth.

Additional recommendations ...
String Quintet in E flat major, B180[a]. Terzetto. Bagatelles. [a]**Patrick Ireland** (va); **Lindsay Quartet.** ASV CDDCA806 — ⠶ 1h 9m DDD 9/93 ⑨ₚ
String Quintet in G major[a]. Intermezzo[a]. String Sextet in A major, B80[b]. **Panocha Quartet;** [b]**Josef Kluson** (va); [b]**Michal Kaňka** (vc); [a]**Pavel Nejtek** (db). Supraphon 11 1461-2 — ⠶ 1h 11m DDD 5/94 ⑨ₚ

Dvořák. String Quartet No. 12 in F major, B179, "American". Cypresses, B152 — Nos. 1, 2, 5, 9 and 11.
Kodály. String Quartet No. 2, Op. 10. **Hagen Quartet** (Lukas Hagen, Annette Bik, vns; Veronika Hagen, va; Clemens Hagen, vc). DG 419 601-2GH.

⠶ **1h 1m DDD 5/87**   ⑨ₚ Ⓑ

Dvořák. String Quartet No. 12 in F major, B179, "American"[a].
Schubert. String Quartet No. 14 in D minor, D810, "Death and the Maiden"[b].
Borodin. String Quartet No. 2 in D major — Notturno[a]. **Quartetto Italiano** (Paolo Borciani, Elisa Pegreffi, vns; Piero Farulli, va; Franco Rossi, vc). Philips Silver Line 420 876-2PSL. Items marked [a] from SAL3618 (8/67), [b]SAL3708 (5/69). Item marked [a] recorded in 1968, [b] 1965.

⠶ **1h 15m ADD 3/89**   Ⓑ

Surely no work in the string quartet repertoire expresses so much contentment and joy as
Dvořák's *American* Quartet. The Hagen Quartet penetrate the work's style, with its dance-like

rhythms and open-hearted, folksy melodies, very successfully and they produce an attractively full-bodied tone-quality. With Kodály's brief Quartet No. 2 we enter a very different world. As in Dvořák's quartet there is a folk-music influence, but here it is the music of Kodály's native Hungary, which by its very nature is more introspective. The Hagen Quartet again capture the work's nationalistic flavour very adroitly. Dvořák's youthful *Cypresses* were originally voice and piano settings of poems which reflected the composer's love for a singer and are played with an affecting simplicity and warmth. The recording is a little too cavernous, but not so much as to spoil the enjoyment afforded by this excellent disc. Philips give us another cherishable coupling of two of the finest quartets in the repertoire. The Quartetto Italiano bring to the Schubert, with its drama and passion so close to the surface, great panache and involvement. The singing theme of the second movement receives a grave intensity that is all too elusive. Similarly the *American* is given exactly the right quality of nostalgia and ease that the work requires. The charming finale, one of Dvořák's most enchanting movements, is given a real folk-like sense of fun. As a bonus the Quartet play the celebrated *Notturno* slow movement from Borodin's Second Quartet; charming though it is it really deserves to be heard in context (refer to the Index to Reviews for a complete recording). The 1960s recordings sound well.

Additional recommendations ...
String Quartets — *No. 1 in A major, B8. No. 2 in B flat major, B17. No. 3 in D major, B18. No. 4 in E minor, B19. No. 5 in F minor, B37. No. 6 in A minor, B40. No. 7 in A minor, B45. No. 8 in E major, B57. No. 9 in D minor, B75. No. 10 in E flat major, B92. No. 11 in C major, B121. No. 12. No. 13 in G major, B192. No. 14 in A flat major, B193. F major, B120 (Fragment). Cypresses, B152. Quartettsatz. Two Waltzes, B105.* **Prague Quartet.** DG 429 193-2GCM9 — .ᐟ ⑨ 9h 49m ADD 8/90 ⁹ₚ Ⓑ*

No. 12. **Barber.** *String Quartet, Op. 11.* **Glass.** *String Quartet No. 1.* **Duke Quartet.** Collins Classics 1386-2 — .ᐟ 1h 1m DDD 1/94 Ⓑ

New review
Dvořák. Piano Trios — No. 1 in B flat major, B51; No. 2 in G minor, B56. **Borodin Trio** (Rotislav Dubinsky, vn; Yuli Turovsky, vc; Luba Edlina, pf). Chandos CHAN9172. Recorded in 1992.

.ᐟ   1h 15m   DDD   11/93

Of Dvořák's six piano trios, only four survive, and only two are at all familiar to most listeners. These here are the other two, written in 1875 and 1876 when he was in his mid-thirties. They are delightful works, even if they cannot match the quality of the F minor Trio and the *Dumky*; and are given splendid advocacy by the Borodin Trio, who sense their quality while not overstating claims. That is to say, the players do not try to milk the fine slow movements for more emotion than they actually contain, and by playing them with sensitivity and a light touch manage to draw the most from them. The two scherzos are similarly given a lively spring but not any kind of forced hilarity: they are in fact quite gentle movements. Luba Edlina opens the B flat Trio with a beautifully delicate exposition of the melody arpeggiated in a manner instantly recognizable as by Dvořák. These are attractive works, attractively played.

Additional recommendation ...
No. 1. **Brahms.** *Piano Trio No. 2 in C major, Op. 87.* **Trio Fontenay.** Teldec 2292-44177-2 — .ᐟ 1h 4m DDD 2/90 ⁹ₚ ⁹ₛ

Dvořák. Piano Trios — No. 3 in F minor, B130; No. 4 in E minor, B166, "Dumky". **Barcelona Trio** (Gerard Claret, vn; Lluís Claret, vc; Albert G. Attenelle, pf). Harmonia Mundi HMC90 1404. Recorded in 1991.

.ᐟ   1h 10m   DDD   11/92   ⁹ₚ   Ⓑ

Whereas the current edition of *The Classical Catalogue* (1994, No. 2) lists some 20 different versions of the *Dumky* Trio, there are only ten of its F minor forerunner which dates from nine years earlier. Obviously collectors prefer their Dvořák in national dress. The richly romantic F minor work comes primarily as a reminder of Dvořák's profound admiration for Brahms, who so gallantly championed his cause to the publisher, Simrock, when life was still an uphill struggle. The Barcelona Trio play it with loving care for textural detail while at the same time effortlessly sustaining tension throughout each movement's larger span. The *Dumky* was the last of his piano trios, written in 1891 at the age of 50. Before leaving for America the following year he and the violinist, Ferdinand Lachner, and the cellist, Hanuš Wihan, undertook a farewell concert tour of some 40 towns in his beloved Bohemia and Moravia with the *Dumky* always their central work. The sharp alternations of melancholy and dance-like gaiety giving this folk-genre its special character are met with splendid intensity and abandon by the Barcelona team. Their own temperament, coupled with the openness of the recorded sound, gives this disc pride of place among recent rivals.

Additional recommendation ...
No. 4. **Schumann.** *Piano Trio No. 1 in D minor, Op. 63.* **Oslo Trio.** Victoria VCD19020 — .··
1h 2m DDD 10/91 ♀ₚ ⑧

New review
Dvořák. VOCAL WORKS.
Janáček. Moravian folk poetry in songs — Nosegay; The Forester; A Letter; Wounded Head.
Martinů. Seven Songs on one page. **Gabriela Beňačková** (sop); **Rudolf Firkušný** (pf).
RCA Victor Red Seal 09026 60823-2. Texts and translations included. Recorded in 1991.
Dvořák: Love Songs, B160 — When thy sweet glances; Death reigns; I know that on my love; Never will love lead us. Seven Gipsy Melodies, B104. In Folk Tone, B146. Biblical Songs, B185 — I will sing a new song; By the rivers of Babylon; O sing unto the Lord.

.·· **1h 2m DDD 1/94** ♀ₚ

Here is a record of great and rare beauty: rare, that is, in the nature of the repertoire, in the distinguished quality of the two artists individually, and in the good fortune of their collaboration. The only complete recording of Dvořák's *Gipsy Melodies* is listed below. Of the Janáček and Martinů there is nothing else in the current edition of *The Classical Catalogue*, and they certainly deserve to be known: Martinů's *Songs on one page* have a simplicity that is never banal, and something of the same fastidiousness is present in Janáček's *Moravian Songs*, never over-written but always rich in restrained feeling. Restraint is also a remarkable feature of Firkušný's playing. Throughout, the percussive element, or even any suggestion of the concert-grand, is kept to a minimum. Instead, the dance rhythms are wonderfully light-footed, the murmurings of tenderness, loss and consolation all voiced with an affectionate gentleness. Beňačková, in most lovely voice, preserves an unbroken singing-line. With unflawed tone she lifts her voice with perfect accuracy in the broad intervals of Dvořák's *Love Songs* and in the octave leaps of "A Letter" in the Janáček group.

Additional recommendation ...
Seven Gipsy Melodies. **Schumann.** *Frauenliebe und -leben, Op. 42.* **Mendelssohn.** *Duets, Op. 63*[a] — No. 1, Ich woll't meine Lieb; No. 3, Gruss; No. 5, Volkslied. Abendlied[a]. **Marilyn Horne,** [a]**Frederica von Stade** (mezs); **Martin Katz** (pf). RCA Victor Red Seal 09026 61681-2 — .·· 49m DDD 3/93

Dvořák. Stabat mater[a]. Psalm 149. [a]**Lívia Aghová** (sop); [a]**Marga Schiml** (contr); [a]**Aldo Baldin** (ten); [a]**Luděk Vele** (bass); [a]**Prague Children's Choir; Prague Philharmonic Choir; Czech Philharmonic Orchestra/Jiří Bělohlávek.** Chandos CHAN8985/6. Notes, texts and translations included.

.·· ② **1h 36m DDD 2/92**

The *Stabat mater* is a thirteenth-century Christian poem in Latin describing the Virgin Mary standing at the foot of the Cross. It has been set to music by many Catholic composers from Palestrina to Penderecki, and Dvořák's version, first heard in Prague in 1880, soon went on to other countries including Britain, where it had a number of cathedral performances and one in the Royal Albert Hall in London in 1884 that was conducted by the composer himself and used a choir of over 800 singers — "the impression of such a mighty body was indeed enchanting", he wrote. Its ten sections are well laid out for the different vocal and instrumental forces and so avoid the monotony which might seem inherent in a contemplative and deeply sombre text. This performance was recorded by Chandos with Czech forces in Prague Castle, and in it we feel the full dignity and drama of the work, an oratorio in all but name. The four solo singers convey genuine fervour and one feels that their sound, which is quite unlike that of British singers, must be akin to what the composer originally imagined. If they are a touch operatic, that doesn't sound misplaced and they perform well together, as in the second verse quartet "Quis est home". The choral singing is no less impressive, and indeed the whole performance under Bělohlávek gets the balance right between reverent simplicity and intensity of feeling. Psalm 149 is a setting of "Sing unto the Lord a new song" for chorus and orchestra and its celebratory mood provides a fine complement to the other work.

Additional recommendation …
Stabat mater. Ten Legends, Op. 59[a]. **Soloists; Bavarian Radio Chorus and Symphony Orchestra, [a]English Chamber Orchestra/Rafael Kubelík.** DG 423 919-2GGA2 — ⁚⁚ ②
2h 8m ADD 9/90

Further listening …

Piano Quartets — No. 1 in D major, B53; No. 2 in E flat major, B162. **Domus.** Hyperion CDA66287 (3/89).

16 Slavonic Dances — Piano Duet, B78 and B145. **Artur Balsam, Gena Raps** (pf, four hands). Arabesque Z6559 (3/87).

Moravian Duets, B50, B60, B62 and B69. **Kühn Mixed Chorus/Pavel Kühn** with **Stanislav Bogunia** (pf). Supraphon 10 4093-2 (1/90).

Requiem, B165[a]. *Coupled with* **Kodály.** Psalmus Hungaricus, Op. 13[b]. Hymn of Zrinyi[c]. **Soloists; [a]Ambrosian Singers; [b]Wandsworth School Boys' Choir; [bc]Brighton Festival Chorus; [ab]London Symphony Orchestra/István Kertész, [c]László Heltay.** Decca Ovation 421 810-2DM2 (5/89).

RUSALKA. **Soloists; Prague Philharmonic Chorus; Czech Philharmonic Orchestra/ Václav Neumann.** Supraphon 10 13641-2 (7/86).

DIMITRIJ. **Soloists; Prague Radio Chorus; Czech Philharmonic Chorus and Orchestra/Gerd Albrecht.** Supraphon 11 1259-2 (3/93).

Key to symbols

⁚⁚	② ②	lh 23m	DDD	6/88
Price	Quantity/ availability	Timing	Recording mode	Review date

Sir George Dyson

British 1883-1964

Suggested listening …

Concerto da camera. Concerto da chiesa. Concerto leggiero[a]. [a]**Eric Parkin** (pf); **City of London Sinfonia/Richard Hickox.** Chandos CHAN9076 (8/93).

Three Rhapsodies. *Coupled with* **Howells.** String Quartet No. 3, "In Gloucestershire" (1923). **Divertimenti.** Hyperion CDA66139 (6/89).

Choral and Instrumental Works — The Blacksmiths. The Canterbury Pilgrims — Suite. To Music. Quo Vadis — Nocturne. Song on May Morning. A Spring Garland. Three Rustic Songs. A Summer Day — Suite. **Soloists; Royal College of Music Chamber Choir; Royal Philharmonic Orchestra/Sir David Willcocks.** Unicorn-Kanchana DKPCD9061 (8/88).

Werner Egk
German 1901-1983

Suggested listening ...

PEER GYNT. **Soloists; Bavarian Radio Chorus; Munich Radio Orchestra/Heinz Wallberg.** Orfeo C005822H (10/89).

Hanns Eisler
German 1898-1962

Suggested listening ...

Lieder and Songs — Spruch 1939. In die Stadte kam ich. An die Uberlebenden. Uber die Dauer des Exils. Zufluchtsstätte. Elegie 1939. An den Schlaf. An den kleinen Radioapparat. In den Weiden. Frühling. Auf der Flucht. Uber den Selbstmord. Gedenktafel für 4000 Soldaten, die im Krieg gegen Norwegen versenkt wurden. Spruch. Hotelzimmer 1942. Die Maske des Bösen. Despite these miseries. The only thing. Die letzte Elegie. unter den grünen Pfefferbäumen. Die Stadt ist nach den Engeln genannt. Jeden Morgen, mein Brot zu verdienen. Diese Stadt hat mich belehrt. In den Hügeln wird Gold gefunden. In der Frühe. Erinnerung an Eichendorff und Schumann. An die Hoffnung. Andenken. Elegie 1943. Die Landschaft des Exils. Verfehlte Liebe. Monolog des Horatio. **Dietrich Fischer-Dieskau** (bar); **Aribert Reimann** (pf). Teldec 2292-43676-2 (7/89).

Edward Elgar
British 1857-1934

Elgar. Cello Concerto in E minor, Op. 85[a]. Sea Pictures, Op. 37[b]. [a]**Jacqueline du Pré** (vc); [b]**Dame Janet Baker** (mez); **London Symphony Orchestra/Sir John Barbirolli.** EMI CMS7 69707-2. From CDC7 47329-2 (5/86). Recorded in 1965.

ₒ∙° 1h 10m ADD 3/89

This is a classic recording, offering two performances by soloists at the turning point of their careers. Jacqueline du Pré's performance of the Elgar Concerto is extraordinarily complete: the cello sings, cries almost, with burning force in its upper registers; *pianissimos* barely whisper; pizzicatos ring with muted passion; those moments of palpitating *spiccato* bowing convey more than is almost imaginable. The LSO perform as if inspired; hardly surprising given Barbirolli's magical accompaniment. Dame Janet Baker's *Sea Pictures* are no less masterly. The young voice is gloriously rich but agile, her diction superb whilst some of the exquisite floated high notes simply defy description. The 1965 sound is quite spectacular; its very immediacy and vividness grabs one at the outset and doesn't let go.

Additional recommendations ...
Cello Concerto. **Bloch.** Schelomo. **Steven Isserlis** (vc); **London Symphony Orchestra/ Richard Hickox.** Virgin Classics VC7 59511-2 — ∙° 51m DDD 7/89 ⁹ₚ ⁹ₛ Ⓑ
Cello Concerto[a]. Violin Concerto in B minor, Op. 61[b]. [a]**Beatrice Harrison** (vc); [b]**Sir Yehudi Menuhin** (vn); [a]**New Symphony Orchestra,** [b]**London Symphony Orchestra/Sir Edward Elgar.** EMI Great Recordings of the Century mono CDH7 69786-2 — ∙° 1h 15m AAD 11/89 ⁹ₚ Ⓑ ▲
Cello Concerto[a]. **Tchaikovsky.** Fantasia on a theme by Thomas Tallis. Fantasia on "Greensleeves" (arr. Greaves). [a]**Felix Schmidt** (vc); **London Symphony Orchestra/Rafael Frühbeck de Burgos.** Pickwick IMP Classics PCD930 — ∙° 49m DDD 1/90 Ⓑ
Cello Concerto (London Symphony Orchestra/André Previn). **Dvořák.** Cello Concerto in B minor, B191 (Berlin Philharmonic Orchestra/Lorin Maazel). **Haydn.** Cello Concerto in D major, HobVIIb/2 (English Chamber Orchestra). **Saint-Saëns.** Cello Concerto No. 1 in A minor, Op. 33 (French National Orchestra/Lorin Maazel). **Schumann.** Cello Concerto in A minor, Op. 129 (Bavarian Radio Symphony Orchestra/Sir Colin Davis). **Yo-Yo Ma** (vc). CBS Masterworks

| CD44562 — ∙° ② DDD/ADD 2h 20m 5/90 Ⓑ

Cello Concerto. **Tchaikovsky.** Variations on a Rococo Theme, Op. 33. **Mischa Maisky** (vc); **Philharmonia Orchestra/Giuseppe Sinopoli.** DG 431 685-2GH — .·' 47m DDD 7/91 Ⓑ
Cello Concerto[a]. The Dream of Gerontius, Op. 38[b]. [a]**Paul Tortelier** (vc); [b]**Soloists;** [b]**Huddersfield Choral Society;** [b]**BBC Symphony Orchestra;** [a]**Liverpool Philharmonic Orchestra/Sir Malcolm Sargent.** Testament mono SBT2025 — .·' ② 2h ADD 2/94 ⁹ₚ Ⓑ ▲
Cello Concerto. Violin Concerto[b]. **Lynn Harrell** (vc); [b]**Kyung-Wha Chung** (vn); **Cleveland Orchestra/Lorin Maazel;** [b]**London Philharmonic Orchestra/Sir Georg Solti.** Decca 440 319-2DWO — .·' 1h 18m ADD 4/94 Ⓑ
Cello Concerto[a]. **Milhaud.** Cello Concerto No. 1, Op. 136[b]. **Respighi.** Adagio con variazioni[a]. [a]**Mstislav Rostropovich** (vc); [a]**Moscow Philharmonic Orchestra;** [b]**USSR TV and Radio Large Orchestra/Gennadi Rozhdestvensky.** Russian Disc RDCD11104 — .·' 52m ADD 7/94 ⁹ₚ Ⓑ

Elgar. Violin Concerto in B minor, Op. 61. **Nigel Kennedy** (vn); **London Philharmonic Orchestra/Vernon Handley.** EMI Eminence CD-EMX2058. From EMX412058-1 (12/84). Recorded in 1984.

.·' 45m DDD 12/84 ⁹ₚ ⁹ₛ Ⓑ

Even after the success of his First Symphony, Elgar's self-doubt persisted and caused his creative instincts to look inward. He could identify with his own instrument, the violin, as his own lonely voice pitted against an orchestra which might represent the forces of the outside world. Usually a concerto consisted of a big first movement, then a lyrical slow movement and a lighter finale: Elgar's finale, which balanced the first movement in weight, was unique, and at first the 45-minute-long work daunted all but the bravest soloists. Nigel Kennedy's technique is such that the work's formidable difficulties hold no terrors for him; his playing is first and foremost immaculate in its execution, and it is complemented by Handley's sensitive accompaniment. But it is more than that. He has a pure silvery tone-quality which is a joy to hear; his response to Elgar's vision is unfailingly sympathetic and understanding, and his projection of it is fresh and stimulating. The natural concert-hall sound is excellent in quality, with important orchestral detail always registering clearly.

Additional recommendations ...
Violin Concerto[a]. **Walton.** Violin Concerto[b]. **Jascha Heifetz** (vn); [a]**London Symphony Orchestra/Sir Malcolm Sargent;** [b]**Philharmonia Orchestra/Sir William Walton.** RCA Victor Gold Seal mono GD87966 — .·' 1h 10m ADD 3/89 ⁹ₚ Ⓑ ▲
Violin Concerto[a]. Cello Concerto[b]. [a]**Sir Yehudi Menuhin** (vn); [b]**Beatrice Harrison** (vc); [a]**London Symphony Orchestra,** [b]**New Symphony Orchestra/Sir Edward Elgar.** EMI Great Recordings of the Century mono CDH7 69786-2 — .·' 1h 15m AAD 11/89 ⁹ₚ Ⓑ ▲
Violin Concerto. Cockaigne Overture, Op. 40. **Dong-Suk Kang** (vn); **Polish National Radio Symphony Orchestra/Adrian Leaper.** Naxos 8 550489 — . 1h 1m DDD 4/92 ⁹ₚ Ⓑ
Violin Concerto. Violin Sonata in E minor, Op.82[b]. **Hugh Bean** (vn); [b]**David Parkhouse** (pf); **Royal Liverpool Philharmonic Orchestra/Sir Charles Groves.** Classics for Pleasure CD-CFP4632 — .· 1h 15m ADD 9/93 Ⓑ

Elgar. Variations on an original theme, Op. 36, "Enigma"[a]. Falstaff — Symphonic Study, Op. 68[b]. [a]**Philharmonia Orchestra;** [b]**Hallé Orchestra/Sir John Barbirolli.** EMI Studio CDM7 69185-2. Item marked [a] from ASD548 (11/63), recorded in 1962, [b] ASD610-11 (12/64), recorded in 1964.

.·' 1h 5m ADD 11/88 ⁹ₚ Ⓑ

Elgar. Variations on an Original Theme, Op. 36, "Enigma"[a]. Pomp and Circumstance Marches, Op. 39[b]. [a]**London Symphony Orchestra,** [b]**London Philharmonic Orchestra/Sir Adrian Boult.** EMI CDM7 64015-2. Item marked [a] from HMV ASD2750 (11/71), recorded in 1970, [b] ASD3388 (10/77), recorded in 1976.

.·' 55m ADD 4/92 ⁹ₚ Ⓑ

The first EMI disc restored to the catalogue at a very reasonable price two key Elgar recordings of works which Sir John Barbirolli made very much his own. Barbirolli brought a flair and ripeness of feeling to the *Enigma* with which Elgar himself would surely have identified. Everything about his performance seems exactly right. The very opening theme is phrased with an appealing combination of warmth and subtlety, and variation after variation has a special kind of individuality, whilst for the finale Barbirolli draws all the threads together most satisfyingly. *Falstaff* is a continuous, closely integrated structure and again Barbirolli's response to the music's scenic characterization is magical while he controls the overall piece, with its many changes of mood, with a naturally understanding flair. The original recordings perhaps sounded more sumptuous but on CD there is more refined detail and greater range and impact to the sound.

As one might expect, Sir Adrian Boult's 1970 recording of the *Enigma* Variations offers similar riches to those of Barbirolli with the additional bonus of a slightly superior recorded sound. Boult's account has authority, freshness and a beautiful sense of spontaneity so that each variation emerges from the preceding one with a natural feeling of flow and progression. There is warmth and affection too coupled with an air of nobility and poise, and at all times the listener is acutely aware that this is a performance by a great conductor who has lived a lifetime with the music. One need only sample the passionate stirrings of Variation One (the composer's wife), the athletic and boisterous "Troyte" variation, or the autumnal, elegiac glow that Boult brings to the famous "Nimrod" variation to realize that this is a very special document indeed. The LSO, on top form, play with superlative skill and poetry and the excellent recording has been exceptionally well transferred to CD. The *Pomp and Circumstance* Marches, recorded six years later with the London Philharmonic Orchestra, are invigoratingly fresh and direct — indeed the performances are so full of energy and good humour that it is hard to believe that Boult was in his late eighties at the time of recording! A classic.

Additional recommendations ...
"Enigma" Variations. Pomp and Circumstance Marches. **Royal Philharmonic Orchestra/Norman Del Mar.** DG Galleria 429 713-2GGA — .·' 58m ADD 9/90 Ⓑ
"Enigma" Variations. Cockaigne Overture, Op. 40. Serenade for Strings. Salut d'amour, Op. 12. **Baltimore Symphony Orchestra/David Zinman.** Telarc CD80192 — .·' 1h 2m DDD 10/90 Ⓑ
"Enigma" Variations. Serenade for Strings in E minor, Op. 20. In the South, Op. 50, "Alassio". **Philharmonia Orchestra/Giuseppe Sinopoli.** DG 423 679-2GH — .·' 1h 12m DDD 10/90 Ⓑ
Falstaff[a]. *Cockaigne Overture*[a]. *The Crown of India*[a]. *"Enigma" Variations*[a]. *Serenade for Strings*[b]. *Pomp and Circumstance Marches Nos. 1-5*[a]. *Imperial March*[a]. [a]**London Philharmonic Orchestra;** [b]**English Chamber Orchestra/Daniel Barenboim.** CBS Maestro CD46465 — .·' ② 2h 40m ADD 9/91 Ⓑ
"Enigma" Variations. Cockaigne Overture, Op. 40. Serenade for Strings. Introduction and Allegro, Op. 47. **BBC Symphony Orchestra/Andrew Davis.** Teldec British Line 9031-73279-2 — .·' 1h 14m DDD 3/92 Ⓑ
"Enigma" Variations. Froissart, Op. 19. Cello Concerto[a]. [a]**Robert Cohen** (vc); **Royal Philharmonic Orchestra/Sir Charles Mackerras.** Argo 436 545-2ZH — .·' 1h 17m DDD 6/93 Ⓑ

Elgar. Falstaff — Symphonic Study, Op. 68[a]. Cockaigne Overture, Op. 40[a]. Introduction and Allegro, Op. 47[b]. **London Philharmonic Orchestra/Vernon Handley.** Classics for Pleasure CD-CfP4617. Items marked [a] from CFP403131 (7/79), recorded in 1978, [b] EMI Eminence EMX412011 (8/83), recorded in 1983.

.· 1h 8m ADD 6/93 　　　　　　　　　　　　　　　　　　　　Ⓠ/p

One of the triumphs of the Classics for Pleasure catalogue, Vernon Handley's magnificent account of *Falstaff* has at last made it onto CD. Superbly played by the LPO and given ripely resonant sound (if now with just a fraction less body than on the original LP), Handley's achievement is considerable, evincing such a hugely impressive alliance of invincible symphonic thrust and warm-hearted characterization as to make his a version worthy of comparison with the very finest on disc. Barbirolli (reviewed elsewhere in this section), Barenboim (CBS Maestro CD46465, 9/91), Solti and most notably Elgar himself (listed under Symphony No. 1) have all given of their best in this masterpiece: Handley now joins their company. To the original vinyl coupling of *Cockaigne* (another swaggering display, incidentally), CfP have added Handley's disciplined, if somewhat less inspired *Introduction and Allegro*: digitally recorded, this sounds rather less beguiling than its analogue companions. No matter, this is an unmissable prospect overall, and a formidable bargain to boot.

Additional recommendations ...
Falstaff[a]. *"Enigma" Variations*[b]. [a]**Chicago Symphony Orchestra,** [b]**London Philharmonic Orchestra/Sir Georg Solti.** Decca London 425 155-2LM — .·' 1h 4m ADD 12/89

Introduction and Allegro[a]. *Serenade for Strings in E minor, Op. 20*[b]. *Pomp and Circumstance Marches Nos. 1 and 4*[c]. *"Enigma" Variations — Nimrod*[d]. *The Dream of Gerontius — Praise to the Holiest in the height*[ae]. *Salut d'amour*[f]. *There is sweet music*[g]. [a]**English Chamber Orchestra/**[ae]**Benjamin Britten;** [b]**Academy of St Martin in the Fields/Sir Neville Marriner;** [cde]**London Symphony Orchestra/Sir Arthur Bliss;** [d]**Pierre Monteux;** [e]**Sir Peter Pears** (ten); [e]**Yvonne Minton** (sop); [f]**Kyung-Wha Chung** (vn); [f]**Philip Moll** (pf); [g]**Louis Halsey Singers.** Decca 430 094-2DWO — *⁂* Ih 6m ADD 6/91

Cockaigne Overture. Introduction and Allegro. Serenade for Strings. "Enigma" Variations. **BBC Symphony Orchestra/Andrew Davis.** Teldec British Line 9031-73279-2 — *⁂* Ih 14m DDD 3/92

Introduction and Allegro. **Barber.** *Adagio for Strings. Medea's Meditation and Dance of Vengeance, Op. 23.* **Tchaikovsky.** *Serenade in C major, Op. 48.* **Boston Symphony Orchestra/Charles Munch.** RCA Victor Gold Seal 09026 61424-2 — *⁂* Ih Im ADD 9/93

Elgar. Symphony No. 1 in A flat major, Op. 55. In the South, Op. 50, "Alassio". **London Philharmonic Orchestra/Leonard Slatkin.** RCA Victor Red Seal RD60380.

⁂ Ih 14m DDD 6/91

Elgar's First Symphony was one of those rare pieces of music that seemed to attain full stature and admiration from the very first public hearing. At its première in Manchester in 1908 it caused a sensation, and Elgar was received by the audience very much in the same way that the pop stars of today are. The previous successes of the *Enigma* Variations, *Gerontius* and the masterly *Introduction and Allegro* had created high hopes in the public's mind for what they felt would be the first truly great English Symphony, and they were not disappointed. Its popularity has never waned and it still holds a special place in the affections of the public today. Leonard Slatkin is a conductor whose passion for British music has become something of a crusade, and a listener hearing him play Elgar's First Symphony without knowing the artists could well think that this was a performance under a conductor such as Sir Adrian Boult. But good music knows no bounds (after all, you don't have to be Austrian to play Mozart!) and Slatkin's understanding of this composer is abundantly clear throughout. There is no trace of sentimentality in the mighty first movement, for here is real grandeur and not just grandiose utterance while the noble sadness of the coda has special beauty. The other movements are hardly less fine, for the richly textured *Adagio* is most eloquently done and the finale is thrilling. Elgar's massive though subtle scoring can present problems for engineers; here they are magnificently solved and the sound is rich yet detailed with excellent bass. The Overture *In the South* which begins the disc is brilliantly vivid and dramatic.

Additional recommendations ...
No. 1. Serenade for Strings. Chanson de nuit, Op. 15 No. 1. Chanson de matin, Op. 15 No. 2.
London Philharmonic Orchestra/Sir Adrian Boult. EMI British Composers CDM7 64013-2 — *⁂* Ih 9m ADD (B)
No. 1. **Royal Philharmonic Orchestra/André Previn.** Philips 416 612-2PH — *⁂* 52m DDD 6/86 (B)
No. 1. **London Philharmonic Orchestra/Vernon Handley.** Classics for Pleasure CD-CFP9018 — *⁂* 52m ADD 8/88 (B)
No. 1. Cockaigne Overture. **London Philharmonic Orchestra/Sir Georg Solti.** Decca London 421 387-2LM — *⁂* Ih 3m ADD 8/89 (B)
No. 1. Pomp and Circumstance Marches, Op. 39 — No. 1 in D major; No. 3 in C minor; No. 4 in G major. **BBC Symphony Orchestra/Andrew Davis.** Teldec British Line 9031-73278-2 — *⁂* Ih IIm DDD 1/92 ⁹ₛ (B)
Nos. 1 and 2[a]. *Falstaff*[a]. *The Dream of Gerontius*[ab] — excerpts. *The Music Makers*[a] — excerpts. *Civic Fanfare*[a]. **Anonymous** (arr. Elgar). *The National Anthem*[a]. [ab]**Soloists;** [a]**London Symphony Orchestra,** [b]**Royal Albert Hall Orchestra/Sir Edward Elgar.** EMI mono CDS7 54560-2 — *⁂* ③ 3h 3Im ADD 6/92 (B) ▲
No. 1. Pomp and Circumstance Marches — No. 1; No. 2 in A minor. **Baltimore Symphony Orchestra/David Zinman.** Telarc CD80310 — *⁂* Ih 2m DDD 11/92 (B)
No. 1. Cockaigne Overture. **London Symphony Orchestra/Jeffrey Tate.** EMI CDC7 54414-2 — *⁂* Ih 12m DDD 1/93 (B)

Elgar. Symphony No. 2 in E flat major, Op. 63. In the South; Op. 50, "Alassio". **BBC Symphony Orchestra/Andrew Davis.** Teldec 9031-74888-2. Recorded in 1992.

.•˙ 1h 10m DDD 11/92   ♀ₚ Ⓑ

New review

Elgar. Symphony No. 2 in E flat major, Op. 63[a]. Serenade for Strings in E minor, Op. 20[b]. [a]**Hallé Orchestra/James Loughran;** [b]**Academy of St Martin in the Fields/Sir Neville Marriner.** ASV Quicksilva CDQS6087. Item marked [a] from WEA Enigma K535904 (11/79), [b]DCA518 (5/83).

.• 1h 10m ADD/DDD 8/93   ♀ₚ Ⓑ

In what is unquestionably his finest achievement on record to date, Andrew Davis penetrates right to the dark inner core of this great symphony. In the opening *Allegro vivace e nobilmente*, for example, how well he and his acutely responsive players gauge the varying moods of Elgar's glorious inspiration: be it in the exhilarating surge of that leaping introductory paragraph or the spectral, twilight world at the heart of this wonderful movement, no one is found wanting. In fact, Davis's unerring structural sense never once deserts him, and the BBC Symphony Orchestra simply play their hearts out for their music director. Above all, though, it's in the many more reflective moments that Davis proves himself an outstandingly perceptive Elgarian, uncovering a vein of intimate anguish that touches to the very marrow; in this respect, his account of the slow movement is quite heart-rendingly poignant (just listen to those BBC strings at the final climax!) — undoubtedly the finest since Boult's incomparable 1944 performance with this very same orchestra — whilst the radiant sunset of the symphony's coda glows with luminous beauty. Prefaced by an equally idiomatic, stirring *In the South* (and aided throughout by some sumptuously natural engineering), this is an Elgar Second to set beside the very greatest. In every way a treasurable release.

ASV's super-budget reissue is surely well worth anyone's money. The Hallé for James Loughran respond with commendable, sure-footed discipline and their playing lacks nothing in whole-hearted application or fervour. Loughran's view is a spacious one, yet its cumulative power is undeniable (the work's crowning climax in the finale hits home with magnificent inevitability) and his structural grasp of the whole is most impressive. Only in the uneasy half-lights of the first movement's development is there any unwelcome slackening of tension. For the rest, few Elgarians could fail to be moved by the gentle perception of Loughran's thoughtful conducting. A fine achievement. The recording has impressive clarity, though a little more ambient warmth would not have gone amiss. Marriner's efficient, somewhat stiff account of the Serenade adds nothing to our knowledge of this lovely music; the digital recording here is a trifle hard-edged. For the symphony alone, though, this release represents quite a bargain.

Additional recommendations ...
No. 2. *Cockaigne Overture.* **London Philharmonic Orchestra/Sir Adrian Boult.** EMI CDM7 64014-2 — .•˙ 1h 8m ADD ♀ₚ Ⓑ ▲
No. 2. **London Philharmonic Orchestra/Vernon Handley.** Classics for Pleasure CD-CFP4544 — .• 54m ADD 10/88 Ⓑ
No. 2. *In the South.* **London Philharmonic Orchestra/Sir Georg Solti.** Decca 436 150-2DSP — .•˙ 1h 12m ADD 8/89 Ⓑ
No. 2. *Serenade for Strings.* **London Philharmonic Orchestra/Leonard Slatkin.** RCA RD60072 — .•˙ 1h 7m DDD 8/89 ♀ₚ Ⓑ

Elgar. MUSIC FOR STRINGS. [a]**José-Luis Garcia, [a]Mary Eade** (vns); [a]**Quentin Ballardie** (va); [a]**Olga Hegedus** (vc); **English Chamber Orchestra/Sir Yehudi Menuhin.** Arabesque Z6563. From ABQ6563 (1/87).
Introduction and Allegro, Op. 47[a]. Chanson de nuit, Op. 15 No. 1 (arr. Fraser). Chanson de matin, Op. 15 No. 2 (arr. Fraser). Three Characteristic Pieces — No. 1, Mazurka, Op. 10. Serenade for Strings in E minor, Op. 20. Salut d'amour, Op. 12 (arr. Fraser). Elegy, Op. 58.

.•˙ 45m DDD 6/87

Elgar's pieces for string orchestra contain some of his greatest music and certainly the *Introduction and Allegro*, *Serenade* and *Elegy* included in this delightful programme embody quintessential Elgar. Sir Yehudi Menuhin's readings dig deep into the hearts of these works, drawing out the nostalgia and inner tragedy that underpins even some of the most seemingly high-spirited of

Elgar's music. The lighter pieces allow relief from the intensity of the major works, thus making that intensity all the more effective. The English Chamber Orchestra is more than capable of providing first-rate soloists from its own ranks, and the quartet extracted for the *Introduction and Allegro* is suitably virtuosic. Both performers and engineers have produced an ideal integration of this solo group with the main string body, and the generally effervescent sound suits the celebratory nature of the piece.

Additional recommendation ...
Violin Sonata in E minor, Op. 82. Six Very Easy Melodious Exercises in the First Position, Op. 22. Salut d'amour (with Steven Isserlis, vc). Mot d'amour, Op. 13. In the South — Canto popolare (In Moonlight). Sospiri, Op. 70. Chanson de nuit. Chanson de matin. **Nigel Kennedy** (vn); **Peter Pettinger** (pf). Chandos CHAN8380 — .·' 55m DDD 8/85 ᵠₚ

New review
Elgar. The Light of Life (Lux Christi), Op. 29. **Judith Howarth** (sop); **Linda Finnie** (mez); **Arthur Davies** (ten); **John Shirley-Quirk** (bar); **London Symphony Chorus and Orchestra/Richard Hickox.** Chandos CHAN9208. Text included. Recorded in 1993.

.·' 1h 3m DDD 5/94 ᵠₛ

Hickox's Elgarian credentials are immediately established in the glorious orchestral "Meditation", where his conducting demonstrates a noble flexibility, sensitivity to dynamic nuance and feeling for climax. Equally the engineering, sumptuous yet detailed, comes close to the ideal. The LSO and Chorus contribute to proceedings in exemplary, disciplined fashion. As The Blind Man, Arthur Davies could hardly be more ardent, but his slightly tremulous timbre will not be to all tastes. John Shirley-Quirk, so eloquent and firm-toned a Jesus for Groves back in 1980 (listed below), now shows signs of unsteadiness in the same part. On the other hand, Linda Finnie and Judith Howarth make a creditable showing. Hickox's reading excels in precisely the areas where the Groves was deficient, and vice versa. If you already have the Groves reissue, hang on to it, for it is by no means outclassed by the Hickox. However, for anyone coming to this underrated score for the first time, Hickox's must now be the preferred version.

Additional recommendations ...
Soloists; Liverpool Philharmonic Choir; Royal Liverpool Philharmonic Orchestra/ Sir Charles Groves. EMI British Composers CDM7 64732-2 — .·' 1h 4m ADD 5/93
The Light of Life — Meditation. The Apostles[a]. [a]**Sheila Armstrong** (sop); [a]**Helen Watts** (contr); [a]**Robert Tear** (ten); [a]**Benjamin Luxon, John Carol Case** (bars); [a]**Clifford Grant** (bass); [a]**London Philharmonic Choir;** [a]**Downe House School Choir; London Philharmonic Orchestra/Sir Adrian Boult.** EMI CMS7 64206-2 — .·' ② 2h 7m ADD

Elgar. The Dream of Gerontius, Op. 38[a]. The Music Makers, Op. 69[b]. [b]**Dame Janet Baker** (mez); [a]**Helen Watts** (contr); [a]**Nicolai Gedda** (ten); [a]**Robert Lloyd** (bass); [a]**John Alldis Choir;** [ab]**London Philharmonic Choir;** [a]**New Philharmonia Orchestra;** [b]**London Philharmonic Orchestra/Sir Adrian Boult.** EMI CDS7 47208-8. Notes and texts included. Items marked [a] from SLS987 (5/76), recorded in 1975, [b] ASD2311 (5/67), recorded in 1966.

.·' ② 2h 16m ADD 1/87 Ⓑ

Elgar's best-known oratorio is the nearest he ever came to writing an opera. The story of the anguished Gerontius in his death throes and his momentary vision of Heaven was set by Elgar in the most graphic terms, and the principals are like characters in music-drama. Throughout most of its history Sir Adrian Boult was a renowned interpreter of the work, but it was only late in his life that he came to record it. The results were both worth waiting for and rewarding in their own right, capturing its intensity of emotion while never allowing the structure to weaken through too much affection. Nicolai Gedda may not be the ideal interpreter of the title-role, but Boult persuaded him to catch something of its fervour. Helen Watts's Angel was in the best tradition of singing that sympathetic part — warm but firm — whilst Robert Lloyd is heard to strong effect in both bass roles. The London Philharmonic Choir and the New Philharmonia sing and play at their collective best. The spacious recording is a fine match for the calibre of the reading.

Additional recommendations ...

The Dream of Gerontius[a]. **Holst.** *The Hymn of Jesus, Op. 37*[b]. [a]**Yvonne Minton** (mez); [a]**Sir Peter Pears** (ten); [a]**John Shirley-Quirk** (bar); [a]**Choir of King's College, Cambridge;** [a]**London Symphony Chorus and Orchestra/Benjamin Britten;** [b]**BBC Chorus and Symphony Orchestra/Sir Adrian Boult.** Decca London 421 381-2LM2 — .·' ② 1h 53m ADD 5/89 Ⓑ

The Dream of Gerontius[a]. *Sea Pictures, Op. 37*[b]. **Dame Janet Baker** (mez); [a]**Richard Lewis** (ten); [a]**Kim Borg** (bass); [a]**Hallé Choir;** [a]**Sheffield Philharmonic Chorus;** [a]**Ambrosian Singers;** [b]**London Symphony Orchestra,** [a]**Hallé Orchestra/Sir John Barbirolli.** EMI Studio CMS7 63185-2 — .·' ② 2h 2m ADD 12/89 Ⓑ

The Dream of Gerontius. **Walton.** *Belshazzar's Feast.* **Soloists; Huddersfield Choral Society; Liverpool Philharmonic Orchestra/Sir Malcolm Sargent.** EMI Great Recordings of the Century mono CHS7 63376-2 — .·' ② 2h 9m ADD 6/90 Ⓑ ▲

The Dream of Gerontius[a]. *Organ Sonata No. 1 in G major, Op. 28 (orch. Jacob).* [a]**Soloists;** [a]**Huddersfield Choral Society; Liverpool Philharmonic** [a]**Choir and Orchestra/ Vernon Handley.** EMI Eminence CD-EMXD2500 — .·' ② 1h 59m DDD 10/93 Ⓑ

Elgar. *The Dream of Gerontius, Op. 38*[a]. *Cello Concerto in E minor, Op. 85*[b]. [a]**Gladys Ripley** (contr); [a]**Heddle Nash** (ten); [a]**Dennis Noble** (bar); [a]**Norman Walker** (bass); [b]**Paul Tortelier** (vc); [a]**Huddersfield Choral Society;** [b]**BBC Symphony Orchestra,** [a]**Liverpool Philharmonic Orchestra/Sir Malcolm Sargent.** Testament mono SBT2025. Text included. Item marked [a] from HMV C3435/46 (6/45), [b] HMV BLP1043 (4/54).

.·' ② 2h ADD 2/94 9p Ⓑ ▲

This pioneering set of *Gerontius* has come up newly minted in these superbly engineered transfers taken from 78rpm masters. That only enhances the incandescence and fervour of the reading itself, in virtually all respects the most convincing the work has received. Sargent's conducting, influenced by Elgar's, is direct, vital and urgently crafted with an inborn feeling for the work's ebb and flow and an overall picture that comprehends the piece's spiritual meaning while realizing its dramatic leanness and force. Heddle Nash's Gerontius is unrivalled in its conviction and inwardness. He was encouraged by Elgar in 1930 to take the part and sang it under the composer's baton in 1932 to his satisfaction. By 1945 the work was in Nash's being; he sang it from memory and had mastered every facet of interpreting it. Such phrases as "Mary pray for me", "Novissima hora est" and "My soul is in my hand, I have no fear" come from and go to the heart. "Take me away" is like a searing cry of pain from the depth of the singer's soul. Gladys Ripley is a natural and communicative Angel throughout, her flexible and appealing tone always a pleasure to hear. The Liverpool Philharmonic lives up to its reputation at the time as the country's leading orchestra (in particular the sonorous string section) and the Huddersfield Choral Society sing as though their lives depended on the outcome. Tortelier's Cello Concerto presents the classical approach as compared with the romantic one of Du Pré, and is the best of Tortelier's readings of the work on disc, with his tone and phrasing at their firmest and most telling. A considered and unaffected reading among the best ever committed to disc.

Further listening ...

The Wand of Youth — Suites Nos. 1 and 2, Opp. 1*a* and 1*b*. *The Starlight Express, Op. 78* — O children, open your arms to me[b]; There's a fairy that hides[b]; I'm everywhere[a]; Wake up, you little night winds[b]; O stars, shine brightly![a]; We shall meet the morning spiders[a]; My old tunes[b]; O, think beauty[a]; Dustman, Laughter, Tramp and busy Sweep[ab]. *Dream Children, Op. 43.* [a]**Alison Hagley** (sop); [b]**Bryn Terfel** (bass-bar); **Welsh National Opera Orchestra/Sir Charles Mackerras.** Argo 433 214-2ZH (10/92).

THE ELGAR EDITION, Volume 1. **London Symphony Orchestra, Royal Albert Hall Orchestra/Sir Edward Elgar.** EMI Elgar Edition mono CDS7 54560-2 (6/92).

THE ELGAR EDITION, Volume 2. **Sir Yehudi Menuhin** (vn); **London Symphony Orchestra, Royal Albert Hall Orchestra, New Symphony Orchestra, London Philharmonic Orchestra/Sir Edward Elgar.** EMI Elgar Edition mono CDS7 54564-2 (2/93).

THE ELGAR EDITION, Volume 3. **Sir Edward Elgar** (pf); **London Philharmonic Orchestra; Royal Albert Hall Orchestra; London Symphony Orchestra; New Symphony Orchestra; BBC Symphony Orchestra/Sir Edward Elgar, Lawrence Collingwood, Sir Landon Ronald. New Light Symphony Orchestra/J. Ainslie Murray. Light Symphony Orchestra/Haydn Wood.** EMI Elgar Edition mono CDS7 54568-2 (8/93).

String Quartet in E minor, Op. 83. *Coupled with* **Walton.** String Quartet in A minor. **Britten Quartet.** Collins Classics 1280-2 (7/92).

Caractacus, Op. 35[a]. Severn Suite, Op. 87a. [a]**Judith Howarth** (mez); [a]**Arthur Davies** (ten); [a]**David Wilson-Johnson** (bar); [a]**Stephen Roberts** (bar); [a]**Alistair Miles** (bass); **London Symphony** [a]**Chorus and Orchestra/Richard Hickox.** Chandos CHAN9156/7 (2/93).

Sea Pictures, Op. 37. The Music Makers, Op. 69. **Linda Finnie** (contr); **London Philharmonic** [a]**Choir and Orchestra/Bryden Thomson.** Chandos CHAN9022 (3/92).

Coronation Ode, Op. 44[a]. The Spirit of England, Op. 80[b]. [ab]**Teresa Cahill** (sop); [a]**Anne Collins** (contr); [a]**Anthony Rolfe Johnson** (ten); [a]**Gwynne Howell** (bass); **Scottish National Chorus and Orchestra/Sir Alexander Gibson.** Chandos Collect CHAN6574 (11/92).

The Apostles. **Soloists; London Symphony Chorus; London Symphony Orchestra/ Richard Hickox.** Chandos CHAN8875/6 (12/90).

Duke Ellington
American 1899-1974

Suggested listening ...

Mainly Black (Black, brown and beige) — Suite. *Coupled with* **Bartók.** Sonata for Solo Violin. **Nigel Kennedy** (vn); **Alec Dankworth** (db). EMI CDC7 47621-2 (5/87).

The River — Suite. *Coupled with* **Still.** Afro-American Symphony. **Detroit Symphony Orchestra/Neeme Järvi.** Chandos CHAN9154 (4/93).

Harlem. *Coupled with* **Still.** Symphony No. 2 in G minor, "Song of a New Race". **Dawson.** Negro Folk Symphony. **Detroit Symphony Orchestra/Neeme Järvi.** Chandos CHAN9226 (3/94). *See review under Still; refer to the Index to Reviews.*

Maurice Emmanuel
French 1862-1938

New review
Emmanuel. Symphonies[a] — No. 1 in A major, Op. 18; No. 2 in A major, "Bretonne", Op. 25. Le poème du Rhône[b]. **Rhenish Philharmonic Orchestra/**[a]**James Lockhart,** [b]**Gilles Nopre.** Marco Polo 8 223507.

56m DDD 3/94

Maurice Emmanuel was born three months before Debussy and later his pupils included Messiaen. Emmanuel does not have the distinctive imaginative world of either composer, but the symphonies are subtle and attractive works, very intelligently written, drawing creatively on the modal studies. The methods are not in familiar symphonic cast, and the Second Symphony (which lasts under 17 minutes) comes close to being more of a Breton symphonic suite in nature; *Le poème du Rhône* derives from a Mistral novel. The French insert-note makes a passionate plea for Emmanuel as the most scandalously neglected of French composers, and even if this appears extreme there is certainly a case for taking him seriously. These careful, clear performances should help us to do that.

Juan del Encina

Suggested listening ...

Romances — Una sañosa porfía. Qu'es de ti, desconsolado?. Mortal tristura me dieron (instrumental version). Triste España sin ventura. *Villancicos* — Levanta, Pascual, levanta. Amor con fortuna. Fata la parte. Ay triste, que vengo. Cucú, cucú, cucucú. A tal perdida tan triste. Quedate, Carillo, adios (instrumental version). Si abrá en este baldres. El que rigue y el regido. Mas vale trocar. Oy comamos y bebamos. Tragedia — Despierta, despierta tus fuerças, Pegaso (recited). **Hespèrion XX/Jordi Savall.** Astrée Auvidis E8707 (2/92).

Mi libertad en sosiego. Los sospiros no sosiegan. *Coupled with* **Peñalosa.** Por las sierras de Madrid. Ne reminiscaris, Domine. Precor te, Domine. Sancta Maria. **Mena.** Yo creo que n'os dió Dios. La bella malmaridada. **Enrique.** Mi querer tanto vos quiere. **Anonymous.** Pase el agoa, ma Julieta. Harto de tanta porfía. Dindirín, dindirín. Ave, Virgo, gratia plena. Dentro en el vergel. Entra Mayo y sale Abril. *Instrumental works* — **Narváez.** Fantasía II tono; Fantasía III tono. Paseávase el rey moro. **Fernández Palero.** Paseávase el rey moro. **Milán.** Fantasías 10, 12 and 18. **Segni.** Tiento. **Anonymous.** A la villa voy. **Gothic Voices/Christopher Page** with **Christopher Wilson** (vihuela) and **Andrew Lawrence-King** (hp). Hyperion CDA66653 (2/94). *See review in the Collections section; refer to the Index to Reviews.*

George Enescu

New review
Enescu. Symphonies — No. 1 in E flat major, Op. 13; No. 2 in A major, Op. 17. **Monte-Carlo Philharmonic Orchestra/Lawrence Foster.** EMI CDC7 54763-2.

1h 18m   DDD   9/93

Brahmsian in colour the First Symphony may very well be, but the rhythmic vigour of its outer movements is quite unlike Brahms. Wagner? Well, any 24-year-old in 1905 writing a slow movement with moments of romantic yearning to it may be permitted to veer towards *Tristan*. Strauss may be the first name that springs to mind when listening to the Second Symphony, but by then Enescu's orchestration, highly individual and of remarkable refinement, had matured: 'Strauss', here, is merely a metaphor for richness of incident and colour. There is a flavour of Rachmaninov to the Second Symphony's slow movement, and an apparent kinship with Mahler, audible in the tense, martial finale, an apparent reaction to the outbreak of the First World War. Apart from the vividly imaginative orchestration, amazingly assured even in the First Symphony, Enescu's own voice is heard most clearly in his extremely detailed and complex working (which demands close attention from the listener; foreground and background, development and embellishment are in constant flux) of what is often basically bold and clear-cut melodic material. The symphonies are accomplished, immaculately crafted, and add up to distinctly more than the sum of their sometimes only apparent influences. Lawrence Foster's direction is brilliantly successful in ensuring that the wood is not obscured by all its luxuriant foliage; the recording is natural but very clear.

Enescu. Violin Sonatas — No. 2 in F minor, Op. 6; No. 3 in A minor, Op. 25, "dans le caractère populaire roumain". Violin Sonata Movement, "Torso". **Adelina Oprean** (vn); **Justin Oprean** (pf). Hyperion CDA66484. Recorded in 1991.

1h 4m   DDD   2/92

Enescu's First Violin Sonata, written when he was 16, is said to be immature and derivative: the Second Sonata, composed two years later in 1899, is an impressive achievement for an 18-year-old. It's true that there are still Brahmsian elements, and the work is also clearly influenced by Fauré, who was then Enescu's teacher, but the three movements are well-contrasted, and the quality of invention is high. The *Torso* Sonata dates from 1911, when Enescu's style was in a state of transition. Only one movement of this work survives, and it is a long, somewhat sprawling but impassioned statement. It would seem that Enescu abandoned the composition, but it deserves much more than oblivion. In his fascinating and highly individual Third Sonata Enescu invests the work with a Romanian folk flavour, and the style of country folk-fiddlers is imitated, but all the material is of his own invention. Adelina Oprean is a highly accomplished artist, as is her brother Justin. Together they produce performances which are rich in character and highly idiomatic — both players were born and brought up in Romania, and they understand Enescu's music to perfection. The recordings are excellent.

Additional recommendation ...

No. 3[a]. **Chausson.** *Poème, Op. 25[b]. Also includes works[a] by* **Beethoven, Corelli, D'Ambrosio, Handel, Kreisler, Pugnani** *and Wagner, recorded 1924-1929.* [a]**Sir Yehudi Menuhin,** [b]**George Enescu** (vns); [a]**Hepzibah Menuhin,** [b]**Sanford Schlüssel** (pfs). Biddulph mono LAB066 — .•˙ 1h 20m ADD 6/93 ⁹ₚ ▲

Further listening ...

String Octet in C major, Op. 7[a]. *Coupled with* **Shostakovich.** Two Pieces, Op. 11[a]. **R. Strauss.** Capriccio — Sextet. **Academy of St Martin in the Fields Chamber Ensemble.** Chandos CHAN9131 (5/93).

String Quartets, Op. 22 — No. 1 in E flat major; No. 2 in G major. **Voces Quartet.** Olympia Explorer OCD413 (5/92).

Christian Erbach

German 1570/73-1653

Suggested listening ...

Sacerdotes Dei[acd]. Canzona secundi toni[c]. Hic est sacerdos[acd]. Fantasia sub Elevatione[c]. Toccata octavi toni[d]. Posuisti Domine[acd]. La Paglia[bc]. *Coupled with* **Hassler.** Canzon duodecimi toni[bcd]. Cantate Domino canticum novum[abcde]. Toccata in G[d]. Canzon noni toni[bcd]. O sacrum convivium[acd]. Domine Dominus noster[abcde]. **Lassus.** Missa Bell'Amfitrit' altera[abcd]. [a]**Westminster Cathedral Choir;** [b]**His Majesties Sagbutts and Cornetts/James O'Donnell** with [c]**Timothy Roberts,** [d]**Iain Simcock,** [e]**Iris Schöllhorn** (orgs). Hyperion CDA66688 (6/94). *See review under Lassus; refer to the Index to Reviews.*

Manuel de Falla

Spanish 1876-1946

Falla. El sombrero de tres picos[a]. Harpsichord Concerto[b]. [a]**Maria Lluisa Muntada** (sop); [b]**Jaime Martin** (fl); [b]**Manuel Angulo** (ob); [b]**Joan-Enric Lluna** (cl); [b]**Santiago Juan** (vn); [b]**Jorge Pozas** (vc); [b]**Tony Millan** (hpd); [a]**Spanish National Youth Orchestra/Edmon Colomer.** Auvidis Valois V4642. Recorded in 1989.

.•˙ 56m DDD 9/92

Falla's *El sombrero de tres picos* ("The three-cornered hat") started life as a 'mimed farce', but Diaghilev then persuaded the composer to revise and enlarge it as a one-act ballet for his company which had its première in London in 1919. Besides the orchestra, it features a soprano solo warning wives to resist temptation and cries of "Olé" from men's voices representing a bullring crowd. Much of the score consists of dances such as the fandango and seguidillas, while the finale is a jota. This performance by Maria Lluisa Muntada and the Spanish National Youth Orchestra, playing under the direction of their founder Edmon Colomer, brings to us all the vivid colours, intense melodies and vigorous rhythms that together evoke that southernmost province of Spain which is Andalusia. These artists clearly love and understand this music and they bring tremendous gusto to the famous "Miller's Dance" (the longest single number) with its chunky chords getting louder and faster. The Harpsichord Concerto, completed in 1926, shows us another side of Falla and was among the first twentieth-century compositions for the instrument. It is less obviously Spanish in style and instead more neo-classical — indeed, Stravinsky was probably the chief model — although we may detect an Iberian element in its directness and even toughness. With just five instruments playing alongside the soloist, it is really a chamber work, but the writing is so powerful that the composer's title is doubtless justified. Here, too, the playing is fine and the recording of both these works is full-blooded and atmospheric.

Additional recommendation …

El sombrero de tres picos. El amor brujo — ballet[b]. **Colette Boky** (sop); [b]**Huguette Tourangeau** (mez); **Montreal Symphony Orchestra/Charles Dutoit.** Decca 410 008-2DH — .·´ lh 2m DDD 8/83 ᑫₚ ᑫₛ

Siete canciones populares españolas[a]. *El amor brujo*[a] — *Canción del fuego fátuo. Soneto a Córdoba. Harpsichord Concerto*[e]. **Granados.** *Goyescas — No. 7, El pelele*[c]. *Danzas españolas, Op. 37*[c] — *No. 7, Valenciana; No. 10, Danza triste.* **Mompou**[d]. *Scènes d'enfants — No. 5, Jeunes filles au jardin. Suburbis — No. 1, El carrer, el guitarrista i el vell cavall. Cançons i dansas — Nos. 5-8. Paisajes — No. 1, La fuente y la campana.* **Nin**[b]. *Cantos populares españolas — No. 3, Tonada de la niña perdida; No. 4, Montañesa; No. 6, Malagueña; No. 7, Granadina; No. 19, Canto Andaluz; No. 20, Polo.* [a]**Maria Barrientos,** [b]**Ninon Vallin** (sops); [c]**Enrique Granados,** [d]**Federico Mompou,** [b]**Joaquin Nin** (pfs); **Manuel de Falla** ([a]pf/[e]hpd); [e]**instrumental ensemble.** EMI Composers in Person mono CDC7 54836-2 (*See review in the collections section; refer to the Index to Reviews*) — .·´ lh l8m ADD ll/93 ▲

New review

Falla. El sombrero de tres picos[a]. Noches en los jardines de España[b]. [a]**Ann Murray** (mez); [b]**Tzimon Barto** (pf); **Academy of St Martin in the Fields/Sir Neville Marriner.** EMI CDC5 55049-2. Text and translation included. Recorded 1992-93.

.·´ lh 3m DDD 5/94 ᑫₚ

The impressionist *Noches en los jardines de España* ("Nights in the gardens of Spain") owes so much to Debussy — its original title of *Nocturnes*, its structure, harmony and orchestration — while *El sombrero de tres picos* combines incisiveness, folk rhythms and harmonies and more than a touch of neo-classicism. These performances are captivating. The proper proportions of piano and orchestra in *Nights* are exceptionally well realized. In the first movement Tzimon Barto's lucid and delicate passagework aptly suggests the cool plashing of the fountains in the Generalife, and later his reiterated notes evoke the thrumming of a guitar: the reminiscences of the flamenco melismata in the last movement are truly poetic. Marriner exactly matches (as few do) the atmosphere of the "Dance in the distance" and is suitably boisterous in the finale. A performance to cherish, admirably recorded. The colours of *The three-cornered hat* glow in southern sunshine, the rhythmic sections are crisply pungent, the seductive playfulness in the music for the miller's wife is well brought out. Overall, however, it is Marriner's dramatic sense and feeling for continuity, plus first-class orchestral playing, that makes this disc so persuasive.

Falla. Noches en los jardines de España[a].
Gerhard. Alegrías.
E. Halffter. Rapsodia portuguesa[a]. [a]**Guillermo Gonzalez** (pf); **Tenerife Symphony Orchestra/Victor Pablo Pérez.** Etcetera KTC1095. Recorded in 1989.

.·´ 57m DDD 7/92

Etcetera have come up with a clever and enterprising programme, Falla's sultry *Noches en los jardines de España* serving very much as the artistic prime mover — especially of Ernesto Halffter's evocative *Portuguese Rhapsody* (written in 1940, revised in 1951). As to the performances, you need only sample Falla's "En el Generalife" on track 1 — say, from 9'27" to the end of the movement — to get the gist of the whole: an enthusiastic body of players that draws together as the music climaxes, and then reduces its pooled tone to an eerie whisper, as per the dictates of the score. The soloist, Guillermo Gonzalez, displays a sensitive touch as well as impressive timing, and the latter quality is crucial for the closing pages of the Falla. The recording itself is relatively close-miked, yet although we remain in closest proximity to the piano, the orchestra is always perfectly clear. The winds have a 'reedy' sound, very characteristic of Spanish orchestras; the strings are sweet but slim (as opposed to thin) in tone, the brass imposing (the horns don just a hint of vibrato) and the piano timbre clean and realistic, especially in the treble. Brass and keyboard emerge with considerable presence in Falla's third movement. Halffter's endearingly atmospheric and aptly-titled *Rhapsody* has considerable charm and a disarming gracefulness that would serve well in the context of an evening concert, either as an appetizer or a dessert; programming it, say, before or after Ravel's complete *Daphnis et Chloé* would set it off to its best advantage. But the real hit of the disc is Roberto Gerhard's spicy *Alegrías,* premièred in Birmingham in 1943 under Stanford Robinson and jam-packed with humour and irony: if you want to end the day with a smile, then put on the second movement, "Farruca-Jaleo" — eight minutes' worth of Milhaud-style high spirits (and don't be temporarily misled by a mischievous quotation from Chopin's "Funeral March"!).

Falla. El amor brujo — Ballet (complete)[a]. Noches en los jardines de España[b].
Rodrigo. Concierto de Aranjuez[c]. [c]**Carlos Bonnell** (gtr); [b]**Alicia de Larrocha** (pf); [ac]**Montreal Symphony Orchestra/Charles Dutoit;** [b]**London Philharmonic Orchestra/ Frühbeck de Burgos.** Decca Ovation 430 703-2DM. Item marked [a] from SXDL7560 (7/83), [b] 410 289-2DH (10/84), [c] SXDL7525 (7/81). Recorded 1980-83.

lh llm   DDD   8/91

New review

Falla. El amor brujo — Ballet (1915 version)[a]. Siete canciones populares españolas (orch. Berio). **Alicia Nafé** (mez); [a]**Silvia Aguilar,** [a]**Antonio Belda Egea** (narrs); **Lausanne Chamber Orchestra/Jesús Lopez-Cobos.** Denon CO-75339. Notes, texts and translations included. Recorded in 1992.

44m   DDD   10/93

Decca's hugely enjoyable disc of Spanish music includes Rodrigo's most famous work, the *Concierto de Aranjuez* which has never lost its popularity since its Barcelona première in 1940 and here Carlos Bonnell imparts a wistful, intimate feeling to the work, aided by a thoughtful accompaniment from Charles Dutoit's stylish Montreal Orchestra. The famous string tune in the *Adagio* enjoys a fulsome rendition. Dutoit's beautifully played interpretation of *El amor brujo* captures the wide range of emotions that this fiery, mysterious piece requires and his performance of the famous "Ritual Fire Dance" must be among the best in the catalogue. A cooler mood is captured in *Nights in the gardens of Spain* with Alicia de Larrocha as the distinguished soloist. Her smooth, effortless playing matches the mood of the piece exactly and de Burgos's accompaniment with the London Philharmonic is equally sympathetic, with ripe tone colour and careful dynamics. Those unfamiliar with these great Spanish works will be hard pressed to find a better introduction than this superbly recorded disc.

The second disc here provides an opportunity to hear the original 1915 version of *El amor brujo* and the coupling, though stingy, is attractive. Berio's 1978 orchestration of the *Siete canciones* is stylish, the sort of thing that Falla might have done himself had it occurred to him (it uses, in fact, almost exactly the same orchestra that Falla chose for the more familiar 1925 revision of *El amor brujo*). In the *gitaneria* version of *El amor brujo* Nafé must be actress as well as singer, and in the latter role as much folk-singer as concert artist (the central role of Candelas was written for a famous gipsy dancer, Pastora Imperio). She's first-class in all respects, bending notes slightly and expressively, using the quiet and subtle end of her voice as well as its considerable reserves of throaty pungency. Among the alternatives are the Swiss mezzo Martha Senn and the Carme Ensemble, similarly coupled (though Senn uses the original, piano accompanied *Siete canciones*, and there are a couple of minor piano pieces as fill-ups) — excellent though the conductor, Luis Izquierdo, he has not quite Lopez-Cobos's fire. Nor has Nicholas Cleobury, but his coupling, for anyone interested in Falla first editions, is the most desirable of all — *El Corregidor y la Molinera,* the fascinating 'original' of *El sombrero de tres picos,* and both his soloists (Clare Powell as Candelas, Jill Gomez as the *molinera*) are good.

Additional recommendations …
El amor brujo[a]. El corregidor y la molinera[b]. [b]**Jill Gomez** (sop); [a]**Claire Powell** (mez); **Aquarius/Nicholas Cleobury.** Virgins Classics VC7 90790-2 — **lh 15m   DDD   1/90**
El amor brujo[ac]. Siete canciones populares españolas[ab]. Serenata[b]. Serenata andaluza[b]. [a]**Martha Senn** (mez); [b]**Maria Rosa Bodini** (pf); [c]**Carme Ensemble/Luis Izquierdo.** Nuova Era 6809 —
57m   DDD   5/90

Falla. EL RETABLO DE MAESE PEDRO[a]. **Matthew Best** (bass) Don Quijote; **Adrian Thompson** (ten) Maese Pedro; **Samuel Linay** (treb) El Trujamán; **Maggie Cole** (hpd). *Milhaud.* LES MALHEURS D'ORPHEE[b]. **Malcolm Walker** (bar) Orphée; **Anna Steiger** (sop) Eurydice; **Paul Harrhy** (ten) Maréchal, Le sanglier; **Patrick Donnelly** (bass) Le charron; **Matthew Best** (bass) Le vannier, L'ours; **Gaynor Morgan** (sop) Le renard, La soeur Jumelle; **Patricia Bardon** (sop) Le loup, La soeur Ainée; **Susan Bickley** (mez) Le soeur Cadette. *Stravinsky.* RENARD[c]. **Hugh Hetherington, Paul Harrhy** (tens); **Patrick Donnelly, Nicolas Cavallier** (basses); **Christopher Bradley** (cimbalom) [abc]**Matrix Ensemble/Robert Ziegler.** ASV CDDCA758. Texts and translations included.

· 1h 17m DDD 7/91

Three complete operas on one disc lasting 77 minutes must be good value, and especially so when they are important works from the first quarter of this century. One thing they have in common is that all were commissioned by the American-born Princess de Polignac, a patroness of music who exercised considerable flair in her choice of gifted artists in a Paris that was then full of them. The performances here by Robert Ziegler and his Matrix Ensemble are full of flair and his chosen singers for the three works (who include the convincingly Spanish boy treble Samuel Linay as El Trujamán in the Falla) sound at home in Spanish, French and Russian in turn. As presented here, Falla's puppet-opera is full of Iberian colour and verve, and although Milhaud's piece on the Orpheus legend is not so striking or dramatic it still has beauty and is elegantly and expressively sung and played. But the best music is still to come in Stravinsky's magnificently earthy and vivid 'barnyard fable' *Renard*, not a long work but a dazzling one, where this performance of great panache simply bursts out of one's loudspeakers to transport us instantly to a farmyard of old Russia. There's excellent cimbalom playing here from Christopher Bradley. The libretto of all three works is usefully provided in the booklet, together with an English translation. The recording is first class, being both immediate and atmospheric.

Further listening ...

LA VIDA BREVE. **Soloists; Ambrosian Opera Chorus; London Symphony Orchestra/Garcia Navarro.** DG 435 851-2GH (10/92).

Robert Farnon

Canadian/British 1917-

Suggested listening ...

Portrait of a Flirt. How Beautiful is Night. Melody Fair. A la Claire Fontaine. Peanut Polka. In a Calm. Gateway to the West. Jumping Bean. Pictures in the Fire. Little Miss Molly. Colditz March. A Star Is Born. Westminster Waltz. Manhattan Playboy. Lake in the Woods. Derby Day. State Occasion. **Bratislava Radio Symphony Orchestra/Adrian Leaper.** Marco Polo 8 233401 (9/92).

Gabriel Fauré

French 1845-1924

Fauré. ORCHESTRAL WORKS. [a]**Lorraine Hunt** (sop); [b]**Jules Eskin** (vc); [c]**Tanglewood Festival Chorus; Boston Symphony Orchestra/Seiji Ozawa.** DG 423 089-2GH. Text and translation included where appropriate. Recorded in 1986.
Pelléas et Mélisande, Op. 80 (with Chanson de Mélisande — orch. Koechlin)[a]. Three Songs, Op. 7 — Après un rêve (arr. vc/orch. Dubenskij)[b]. Pavane, Op. 50[c]. Elégie, Op. 24[b]. Dolly Suite, Op. 56 (orch. Rabaud).

· 56m DDD 1/88

Fauré's music for Maeterlinck's play *Pelléas et Mélisande* was commissioned by Mrs Patrick Campbell and to the usual four movement suite Ozawa has added the "Chanson de Mélisande", superbly sung here by Lorraine Hunt. Ozawa conducts a sensitive, sympathetic account of the score, and Jules Eskin plays beautifully in both the arrangement of the early song, *Après un rêve* and the *Elégie*, which survived from an abandoned cello sonata. The grave *Pavane* is performed here in the choral version of 1901. *Dolly* began life as a piano duet, but was later orchestrated by the composer and conductor Henri Rabaud. Ozawa gives a pleasing account of this delightful score and the recording is excellent.

Additional recommendation ...
Pelléas et Mélisande. Pavane[a]. **Chausson.** *Poème de l'amour et de la mer, Op. 19*[b]. *Poème, Op. 25*[c].
[b]**Linda Finnie** (mez); [a]**Renaissance Singrs; Ulster Orchestra/Paul Tortelier** ([c]vn).
Chandos CHAN8952 *(reviewed under Chausson; refer to the Index to Reviews)* — ●·'' 1h 9m DDD 12/91 **9**ₛ

Fauré. Piano Quartets — No. 1 in C minor, Op. 15; No. 2 in G minor, Op. 45. **Domus** (Krysia Osostowicz, vn; Robin Ireland, va; Timothy Hugh, vc; Susan Tomes, pf). Hyperion CDA66166. From A66166 (10/86).

●·'' **1h 2m DDD 10/86** **9**ₚ

The First Piano Quartet reveals Fauré's debt to an earlier generation of composers, particularly Mendelssohn. Yet already it has the refined sensuality, the elegance and the craftsmanship which were always to be hallmarks of his style and it is a thoroughly assured, highly enjoyable work which could come from no other composer's pen. The Second Quartet is a more complex, darker work, but much less ready to yield its secrets. The comparatively agitated, quicksilver scherzo impresses at once, however, and repeated hearings of the complete work reveal it to possess considerable poetry and stature. Just occasionally one could wish that the members of Domus had a slightly more aristocratic, commanding approach to these scores, but overall the achievement is highly impressive, for their playing is both idiomatic and technically impeccable. The recording has an appropriately intimate feel to it and is faithful and well-balanced.

Additional recommendations ...
Piano Quartets. Piano Quintets — No. 1 in C minor, Op. 89; No. 2 in D minor, Op. 115. String Quartet in E minor, Op. 121. **Jean-Philippe Collard** (pf); **Augustin Dumay** (vn); **Bruno Pasquier** (va); **Frédéric Lodéon** (vc); **Michel Debost** (fl); **Parrenin Quartet.** EMI Rouge et Noir CMS7 62548-2 — ●·'' ② 2h 37m ADD 5/89 **9**ₚ
No. 1[a]. *Piano Trio in D minor, Op. 120.* **Beaux Arts Trio;** [a]**Kim Kashkashian** (va). Philips 422 350-2PH — ●·'' 53m DDD 6/90 **9**ₚ
Piano Quartets. **Isaac Stern** (vn); **Jaime Laredo** (va); **Yo-Yo Ma** (vc) **Emanuel Ax** (pf). Sony Classical SK48066 — ●·'' 1h 7m DDD 9/93 **9**ₚ
Piano Quartets. **Los Angeles Piano Quartet.** Pickwick IMP Masters MCD66 — ●·'' 1h 6m DDD 10/93

Fauré. Violin Sonatas — No. 1 in A major, Op. 13[a]; No. 2 in E minor, Op. 108[a].
Franck. Violin Sonata in A major[b]. **Arthur Grumiaux** (vn); [a]**Paul Crossley,** [b]**György Sebok** (pfs). Philips Musica da Camera 426 384-2PC. Items marked [a] from 9500 534 (7/79), recorded in 1977, [b] 9500 568 (10/80), recorded in 1978.

●·'' **1h 13m ADD 7/90** **9**ₚ

Fauré was only 31, and on the crest of his first great love affair, when writing his radiantly lyrical A major Violin Sonata. But curiously he allowed four decades to elapse before following it up with the E minor Sonata, by which time deafness, no less than the dark background of war, had drawn him into a more recondite world of his own. As portraits of the composer in youth and full artistic maturity the two works make an ideal coupling. But here, as a bonus, we are also given César Franck's one and only Violin Sonata, written when he was 64, bringing the playing time to the very generous total of almost an hour-and-a-quarter. It would be hard to find any two artists closer to Fauré's own heart than the intimately attuned Grumiaux and Crossley. Their original LP was immediately hailed as the best available way back in 1979. And despite fine newcomers in recent years this mellow CD transfer still triumphs over all the catalogue's rivals. An unerring sense of style goes hand in hand with very beautiful, finely nuanced tone and an immediacy of expression suggesting joyous new discovery. Even if Sebok's piano emerges a little more plummy than Crossley's, the Franck Sonata, too, appeals through its warmth of heart. | 277

Additional recommendation ...

Nos. 1 and 2. **Krysia Osostowicz** (vc); **Susan Tomes** (pf). Hyperion CDA66277 — ❯❯ 50m
DDD II/88

Fauré. PIANO WORKS. **Albert Ferber** (pf). Saga Classics EC3397-2. Recorded 1974-79.
Nine Préludes, Op. 103. 13 Nocturnes — No. 1 in E flat minor, Op. 33 No. 1; No. 3 in
A flat major, Op. 33 No. 3; No. 4 in E flat major, Op. 36; No. 6 in D flat major, Op. 63;
No. 13 in B minor, Op. 119. Five Impromptus — No. 3 in A flat major, Op. 34. Eight Pièces
brèves — No. 1, Capriccio; No. 4, Adagietto; No. 5, Improvisation. Three Romances sans
paroles, Op. 17 — No. 3, Andante moderato. Thème et Variations in C sharp minor, Op. 73.

❯❯ 5lm DDD 3/94   𝄐P

Albert Ferber ("one of our very greatest pianists" proclaimed *Gramophone*) was among the least
known and most distinguished names on the Saga roster. The quality of his playing can be
sampled in this reissue of a first-rate anthology of Fauré's piano music, including the *Thème et
Variations*, a 15-minute work with an immediately attractive basic idea which is embellished and
transmuted with felicitous ingenuity, yet always remains there in profile. Ferber plays most
imaginatively, as he does the nine *Préludes*, music which does not immediately reveal its secrets
but certainly does so with familiarity. The shorter pieces are also expertly played. Good, not too
immediate recording, which suits this repertoire.

Fauré. CHANSONS, Volume 2. **Sarah Walker** (mez); **Malcolm Martineau** (pf). CRD
CRD3477. Texts and translations included.
La papillon et la fleur, Op. 1 No. 1. Op. 3 — No. 1, Seule!; No. 2, Sérénade toscane.
L'absent, Op. 5 No. 3. Op. 8 — No. 1, Au bord de l'eau; No. 3, Ici-bas. Op. 10 — No. 1,
Puisqu'ici-bas; No. 2, Tarentelle. La fée aux chansons, Op. 27 No. 2. Op. 39 — No. 2, Fleur
jetée; No. 3, Le Pays des rêves; No. 4, Les Roses d'Ispahan. Nocturne, Op. 43 No. 2. Clair de
lune, Op. 46 No. 2. Op. 51 — No. 1, Larmes; No. 2, Au cimetière. Arpège, Op. 76 No. 2.
Accompagnement, Op. 85 No. 3. Le plus doux chemin, Op. 87 No. 1. Le don silencieux,
Op. 92. Chanson, Op. 94. C'est la paix!, Op. 114. Vocalise-étude. Pelleas et Mélisande —
Chanson de Mélisande.

❯❯ lh 8m DDD 8/93

Starting with an early song, and a charmer, *Le papillon et la fleur* has the young Fauré with (so it
seems) a head full of Schubert, as the piano enters with a ripple of *Die Forelle* and waltzes away
into something more like *Seligkeit*. Here, that rather crusty quality in Sarah Walker's louder
tones is something of a liability. Still, if this is the initial reaction it is not one that prevails for
long. It is hard to imagine the *Nocturne* and *Au bord de l'eau* more beautifully sung, the first
entering a very private world, the second catching perfectly the relaxed, reflective mood, and
both benefiting from the softened, warmed tone of the singer and her excellent accompanist.
The programme follows no chronological order. This has the advantage that the best-known
songs can be distributed fairly evenly, with *Clair de lune*, *Les roses d'Ispahan* and *Aurore* mingled
here with some from the 1870s and others that extend into the twentieth century. These include
the frank emotion of the postwar *C'est la paix!* and *Le don silencieux* which Sarah Walker sings so
affectionately to the haunting accompaniment of those wistfully unfulfilled harmonies. Most
haunting of all, perhaps, is Mélisande's song, in English, written for Mrs Patrick Campbell and
the London production of 1889.

Additional recommendation ...

*Op. 1 — No. 1, Le papillon et la fleur; No. 2, Mai. Op. 2 — No. 1, Dans les ruines d'une abbaye;
No. 2, Les matelots. Op. 3 — No. 1, Seule!; No. 2, Sérénade toscane. Op. 4 — No. 1, La chanson du
pêcheur; No. 2, Lydia. Op. 5 — No. 1, Chant d'automne; No. 2, Rêve d'amour; No. 3, L'absent. Op. 6
— No. 1, Aubade; No. 2, Tristesse; No. 3, Sylvie. Op. 7 — No. 1, Après un rêve; No. 2, Hymne; No.
3, Barcarolle. Op. 8 — No. 1, Au bord de l'eau; No. 2, La rançon; No. 3, Ici-bas!. Op. 10 — No. 1,
Puisqu'ici-bas; No. 2, Tarantelle. Op. 18 — No. 1, Nell; No. 2, Le voyageur; No. 3, Automne. Poèmes
d'un jour, Op. 21. Op. 23 — No. 1, Les berceaux; No. 2, Notre amour; No. 3, Le secret. Op. 27 —
No. 1, Chanson d'amour; No. 2, La fée aux chansons. Op. 39 — No. 1, Aurore; No. 2, Fleur jetée;*

No. 3, Le Pays des rêves; No. 4, Les Roses d'Ispahan. Op. 43 — No. 1, Noël; No. 2, Nocturne. Op. 46 — No. 1, Les présents; No. 2, Clair de lune. Op. 51 — No. 1, Larmes; No. 2, Au cimetière; No. 3, Spleen; No. 4, La rose. Shylock — Suite. Op. 57 — No. 1, Chanson; No. 2, Madrigal. Cinq mélodies de Venise, Op. 58. La bonne chanson, Op. 61. Pleurs d'or, Op. 72. Op. 76 — No. 1, Le parfum impérissable; No. 2, Arpège. Op. 83 — No. 1, Prison; No. 2, Soir. Op. 85 — No. 1, Dans la forêt de septembre; No. 2, La fleur qui a sur l'eau; No. 3, Accompagnement. Op. 87 — No. 1, Le plux doux chemin; No. 2, Le ramier. Le don silencieux, Op. 92. Chanson, Op. 94. La chanson d'Eve, Op. 95. Le jardin clos, Op. 106. Mirages, Op. 113. C'est la paix!, Op. 114. L'horizon chimérique, Op. 118. L'aurore, Op. posth. En prière. Sérénade du bourgeois gentilhomme. Pelléas et Mélisande — Chanson de Mélisande. Vocalise-étude. **Elly Ameling** (sop); **Gérard Souzay** (bar); **Dalton Baldwin** (pf). EMI L'Esprit Français CMS7 64079-2 (4/92).

New review

Fauré. Requiem[a]. Pavane, Op. 50. [a]**Robert Chilcott** (treb); [a]**John Carol Case** (bar); [a]**King's College Choir Cambridge; New Philharmonia Orchestra/Sir David Willcocks.** EMI CDM7 64715-2. Text and translation included. From HMV ASD2358 (3/68).

.·' 42m ADD 7/93

This is the Fauré Requiem to come home to. Its original reviewer in *Gramophone* was Alec Robertson, who declared that it had provided him with a very rare professional experience, the chance "to describe a recording as near as can be to absolute perfection from start to finish". A quarter of a century has passed, and the catalogue now has 29 other recordings currently available: many are fine, but this one has still not been overtaken on its own ground. The textual dimension of course is new since then, and if an earlier version of the score is wanted, the smaller orchestra being in some ways preferable, then the recording by King's under Cleobury or the Cambridge Singers under the text's editor, John Rutter might be tried instead. But for what we used to mean by the Fauré Requiem in days when ignorance (of textual complications) was bliss, then this is still the best. Willcocks neither sentimentalizes nor hurries; the choir (especially in respect of its tenors) is on top form; Robert Chilcott sings the *Pie Jesu* with the most touchingly beautiful purity and control, and John Carol Case brings to his solos a style that exactly matches that of the famous choir. If anything, time has enhanced appreciation, for the recorded sound compares so favourably, giving due prominence to the choir and obtaining an immediacy of sound that these days is exceptional. The only matter for regret is that the *Pavane* was not performed in its choral version, but as it is such an exquisite composition in either form the regret is short lived.

Additional recommendations ...

Requiem (original version, ed. Rutter). Motets — Ave verum corpus; Tantum ergo; Ave Maria; Maria, Mater gratiae. Cantique de Jean Racine, Op. 11 (orch. Rutter). Messe basse. **Soloists; Cambridge Singers; City of London Sinfonietta/John Rutter.** Collegium COLCD109 — .·' 1h 3m ADD/DDD 1/89 Ⓑ

Requiem, Op. 48 (original 1894 version)[a]. *Fauré/Messager.* Messe des Pêcheurs de Villerville[b]. [a]**Agnès Mellon** (sop); [a]**Peter Kooy** (bar); [b]**Jean-Philippe Audoli** (vn); [a]**Leo van Doeselaar** (org); **Petits Chanteurs de Saint-Louis; Paris Chapelle Royale Chorus; Musique Oblique Ensemble/Philippe Herreweghe.** Harmonia Mundi HMC90 1292 — .·' 56m DDD 4/89 Ⓑ

Requiem[a]. *Duruflé.* Requiem, Op. 9[b]. [b]**Richard Eteson** (treb); [b]**Ann Murray** (sop); [b]**Olaf Bär** (bar); **King's College Choir, Cambridge; English Chamber Orchestra/Stephen Cleobury.** EMI CDC7 49880-2 — .·' 1h 3m DDD 12/89 Ⓑ

Requiem (revised version). Cantique de Jean Racine, Op. 11. Messe basse. *Poulenc.* Mass in G major. Salve Regina. **Soloists; Academy of St Martin in the Fields; Choir of St John's College, Cambridge/George Guest.** Decca Ovation 430 360-2DM — .·' 1h 14m ADD 9/91 Ⓑ

Further listening ...

Cello Sonatas — No. 1 in D minor, Op. 109; No. 2 in G minor, Op. 117. Sicilienne, Op. 78. Elégie, Op. 24. Romance in A major, Op. 69. Berceuse, Op. 16. Three Songs, Op. 7 — Après un rêve. **Lowri Blake** (vc); **Caroline Palmer** (pf). Etcetera KTC1153 (6/94).

Barcarolles Nos. 1-13. **Paul Crossley** (pf). CRD CRD3422 (6/88).

Nocturnes Nos. 1-7. **Paul Crossley** (pf). CRD CRD3406 (6/88).

Nocturnes Nos. 8-13. 8 Pièces brèves, Op. 84. **Paul Crossley** (pf). CRD CRD3407 (6/88).

PENELOPE — *drama lyrique*. **Soloists; Jean Laforge Vocal Ensemble; Monte-Carlo Philharmonic Orchestra/Charles Dutoit.** Erato Libretto 2292-45405-2 (4/92).

Robert Fayrfax

British 1464-1521

Suggested listening ...

Missa Albanus. Aeternae laudis lilium. **The Sixteen/Harry Christophers.** Hyperion CDA66073 (12/89).

Morton Feldman

American 1926-1987

New review
Feldman. Quintet for Piano and Strings. **Kronos Quartet** (David Harrington, John Sherba, vns; Hank Dutt, va; Joan Jeanrenaud, vc); **Aki Takahashi** (pf). Elektra Nonesuch 7559-79320-2. Recorded in 1991.

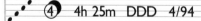 lh 20m DDD 2/94

Lasting just under 80 minutes, the Piano Quintet is — for late Feldman — a medium-length piece, exquisitely imagined through these instruments and changing its routines just enough to avoid monotony. Feldman liked quiet sounds to seem sourceless and would have agreed with Ad Reinhardt, the abstract painter, who wanted "art as art and as nothing else ... purer and emptier, more absolute and more exclusive". The auditory scenario of the Piano Quintet is simple. A rising piano figure leaves sustained sounds hanging in the strings: the gesture is consistent, but the details continually vary. This is what the listener hangs on to and it remains absorbing. The piano's rising figures get much slower towards the end: finally, it is the piano that has the last few wisps of sound. This seems an ideal interpretation, easy to live with and in exactly the right recorded ambience. The Feldman experience *par excellence*.

New review
Feldman. For Philip Guston. **Eberhard Blum** (fls); **Nils Vigeland** (pf/celesta); **Jan Williams** (perc). Hat Hut Now Series ARTCD4-6104. Recorded in 1991.

④ 4h 25m DDD 4/94

Feldman enthusiasts are here tested with the full treatment: *For Philip Guston* lasts over four hours and is, like much of Feldman, in a slow processional and meditative tempo. The mood is an exploration of stillness comparable to some of the apparently empty expanses of the 1950s and 1960s New York abstract expressionist painters, or the plays of Becket. Feldman particularly admired Guston, as well as Rothko and De Kooning. The music can evoke those almost lunar landscapes, but it really sets its own scene without depending on associations. Its isolation and lack of projection in conventional terms stem perhaps from the Rosicrucian ritual music of Satie, whose late cantata, *Socrate*, Feldman idolized. The result is music almost consistently poignant and surprisingly sustained against all odds over a seemingly endless time-scale. This is beautiful music to live with, either as a consolation in one's immediate environment or for more detailed listening chapter by chapter. It needed to be recorded.

Feldman. For Christian Wolff. **Eberhard Blum** (fl); **Nils Vigeland** (pf/celesta). Hat Hut Hat Now Series ARTCD3-6120.

③ 3h 22m DDD 7/94

Two of the dedicated players who were involved in the première of *For Philip Guston* have now gone on to record *For Christian Wolff* (1986). The whole work takes up three CDs lasting well over three hours. It starts with the flute and piano quietly pecking away at isolated notes, without agreeing on pitches. There is something particularly suited to Feldman in the naked quality of flute and piano (doubled with celesta) as the textures slowly unfold: his instruments are always fastidiously chosen. You can check the work's progress by using the CD index points provided, which are not formal divisions in any way. Just as Feldman wanted his sounds to be 'sourceless' so his forms are formless in any conventional sense, and his integrity tangible. As with Cage you don't have to listen from start to finish: portions can be sampled or used as background music, conditioning the environment as a calming influence. In any case there is nothing quite like Feldman, played in the right spirit and, as here, well recorded.

Howard Ferguson
Northern Irish 1908-

Suggested listening ...

Overture for an Occasion, Op. 16. Partita, Op. 5a. Two Ballads, Op. 1[a]. The Dream of the Rood, Op. 16[b]. [a]**Brian Rayner Cook** (bar); [b]**Anne Dawson** (sop); **London Symphony** [ab]**Chorus and Orchestra/Richard Hickox.** Chandos CHAN9082 (4/93).

Violin Sonata No. 1, Op. 2. *Coupled with* **Castelnuovo-Tedesco.** Violin Concerto No. 2, "I profeti"; *Françaix.* String Trio in C major; *K. Khachaturian.* Violin Sonata in G minor, Op. 1. **Jascha Heifetz** (vn); **Joseph de Pasquale** (va); **Gregor Piatigorsky** (vc); **Lilian Steuber** (pf); **Los Angeles Philharmonic Orchestra/Alfred Wallenstein.** RCA Victor Gold Seal mono GD87872 (9/90).

Piano Sonata in F minor, Op. 8. Partita for Two Pianos, Op. 5b[a]. **Howard Shelley,** [a]**Hilary Macnamara** (pfs). Hyperion CDA66130 (1/91).

Zdeněk Fibich
Bohemian 1850-1900

Fibich. Sonata in B flat major, Op. 28.
Goetz. Sonata in G minor, Op. 17.
Moscheles. Grande Sonate in E flat major, Op. 47. **Anthony Goldstone, Caroline Clemmow** (pf duet). Meridian CDE84237.

1h 7m DDD 7/93

All three sonatas in this superbly enterprising recital explore, in radically different ways, the potential and achievement of the duet form. Moscheles's *Grande Sonate* is grand indeed, enlivening an outwardly conventional virtuosity with wit and ingenuity. A favourite of Chopin's, its *Andante* and finale in particular contain a super-abundance of ideas paraded by Anthony Goldstone and Caroline Clemmow (a dazzling husband and wife team) with an irresistible relish and sparkle. You enter another poetic world when you turn to Fibich's contribution. Here, all extrovert, concert-hall brio is banished to make way for an almost Fauréan subtly and ambiguity though throughout Fibich (a pupil of Moscheles) shows a harmonic piquancy peculiarly his own. The Goetz Sonata's romantic declamation often suggests Mendelssohn at his most urgent and least urbane, a quality caught with rare focus and concentration by Goldstone and Clemmow. But all their performances are exemplary in their commitment, sensitivity and *joie de vivre*. The recordings are spacious and resonant.

Further listening ...

Symphonies — No. 2 in E flat major, Op. 38; No. 3 in E minor, Op. 53. **Brno State Philharmonic Orchestra/Jiří Bělohlávek.** Supraphon CO-1256 (2/88).

SARKA. **Soloists; Janáček Opera Chorus; Brno State Philharmonic Orchestra/Jan Stych.** Supraphon CO-1746/8 (10/88).

John Field
Irish 1782-1837

New review
Field. NOCTURNES. **Roberto Mamou** (pf). Pavane ADW7110.
No. 1 in E flat major, H24. No. 2 in C minor, H25. No. 3 in A flat major, H26. No. 4 in A major, H36. No. 5 in B flat major, H37. No. 6 in F major, H40. No. 7 in C major, H45. No. 8 in A major, H14*E*. No. 9 in E flat major, H30. No. 10 in E minor, H46*B*. No. 11 in E flat major, H56*A*. No. 12 in G major, H58*D*. No. 13 in D minor, H59. No. 14 in C major. No. 15 in C major, H61.

Ih 4m DDD 8/93

New review
Field. NOCTURNES. **Joanna Leach** (fp). Athene ATHCD1.
No. 1 in E flat major, H24. No. 2 in C minor, H25. No. 3 in A flat major, H26. No. 4 in A major, H36. No. 5 in B flat major, H37. No. 6 in F major, H40. No. 7 in C major, H45. No. 8 in A major, H14*E*. No. 9 in E flat major, H30. No. 10 in E minor, H46*B*. No. 11 in E flat major, H56*A*. No. 12 in G major, H58*D*. No. 13 in D minor, H59. No. 14 in C major. No. 15 in C major, H61. No. 16 in F major, H62*A*.

Ih I6m DDD I0/93

Liszt was among the first to celebrate Field's quality, finding in the *Nocturnes*, "the morn of life ... before the radiant freshness of emotion was over-clouded by the shadow of reflection", very much a world of innocence rather than experience. Chopin, too, admired Field, locating in his predecessor an ideal foundation for his own *Nocturnes*; works smouldering with an altogether different voltage and range. The Tunisian-born pianist Roberto Mamou achieves an often exemplary middle course between drama and understatement and he stresses Field's closeness to, rather than his remoteness from, Chopin. The recordings are satisfactory and although the last two *Nocturnes* are omitted this is an appealing issue. Joanna Leach forfeits only the last *Nocturne*. She performs on square pianos by Stodart, Broadwood and Thomas D'Almaine dating from 1823 to 1835 and, most persuasively, suggests an intimacy and transparency hard to parallel on more modern, brilliant and forceful instruments. The ear is quickly attuned to the sound, to the radically different pedalling Leach refers to in her excellent notes, and to a cloudy but appropriate and often hypnotic resonance. Melody and accompaniment (at the very heart of this music) are more closely entwined than on today's instruments, offering a greater sense of Field's harmonic subtlety. There are some extraneous noises, inseparable from period instruments, but so far from distracting attention they somehow add to the potent atmosphere of these performances. A fascinating pair of issues.

Further listening ...

Piano Concertos — No. 1 in E flat major, H27; No. 2 in A flat major, H31; No. 3 in E flat major, H32; No. 4 in E flat major, H28; No. 5 in C major, H39, "L'incendie par l'orage"; No. 6 in C major, H49; No. 7 in C minor, H58. **John O'Conor** (pf); **New Irish Chamber Orchestra/Janos Furst.** Onyx ONYX CD101/3 (three-disc set).

Piano Sonatas — E flat major, H8 No. 1; A major, H8 No. 2; C minor, H8 No. 3; B major, H17. *Nocturnes* — No. 3 in A flat major, H26; No. 7 in C major, H45; No. 17 in E major, H54*A*. **John O'Conor** (pf). Telarc CD80290 (11/92).

Irving Fine

American 1914-1962

Fine. Blue Towers. Diversions for Orchestra. Music for Piano (orch. Spiegelman). Toccata concertante. Symphony. **Moscow Radio Symphony Orchestra/Joel Spiegelman.** Delos DE3139.

•·* Ih 2m DDD 7/94

Composer, scholar and conductor, Irving Fine was one of the most gifted products of Boston musical life in the 1940s. His music is distinguished by a certain fastidiousness and sound craftsmanship, yet there is an attractive lyrical impulse, too, as well as an ever-impressive economy of thought and texture. The present representative selection is lucidly conducted by Joel Spiegelman, one of Fine's pupils when he was Professor of Music at Brandeis University and a close personal friend of the composer. Stravinsky is most assuredly the principal guiding light behind the bustling, neo-classical *Toccata concertante* from 1947, the earliest work on this disc. Composed the same year, *Music for Piano* is an engagingly pithy four-movement suite containing many an echo of Fine's colleague, Copland. Both the rousing *Blue Towers* (1959) and winsome *Diversions for Orchestra* (1960) show Fine at his most immediately communicative; indeed, the latter piece is a real peach. Finally, Delos give us the Symphony (1962): dedicated to Charles Munch and the Boston Symphony Orchestra, it shows Fine embracing serial techniques whilst retaining his own strongly personal voice. A substantial, ambitious utterance, it benefits, as do all the works gathered here, from some lively, highly responsive playing from the Moscow Radio Symphony Orchestra. The recorded sound is excellent.

Michael Finnissy

British 1946-

Suggested listening ...

English Country-Tunes. **Michael Finnissy** (pf). Etcetera KTC1091 (12/90).

Catana — Nine Instruments[a]. String Trio[b]. Contretänze — Six Instruments[c]. [a]**Uroboros Ensemble/Michael Finnissy;** [b]**Gagliano Trio;** [c]**Exposé Ensemble.** Etcetera KTC1096 (2/92).

Gerald Finzi

British 1901-1956

Finzi. ORCHESTRAL WORKS. [a]**Alan Hacker** (cl); **English String Orchestra/William Boughton.** Nimbus NI5101. Recorded in 1987.
Love's Labour's Lost — Suite, Op. 28. Clarinet Concerto in C minor, Op. 31[a.] Prelude in F minor, Op. 25. Romance in E flat major, Op. 11.

•·* Ih 5m DDD 12/88

There are several other Finzi issues available which include the Clarinet Concerto. Alan Hacker, however, encompasses all his colleagues' virtues, providing special insights and revelling in the brilliant writing. He also adds something extra — an almost mystical realization of the music's poetic vision which is deeply moving. This is in spite of the fact that the string-playing sometimes lacks polish and precision. Finzi wrote incidental music for a BBC production of *Love's Labour's Lost* and expanded it for a later open-air production. It is tuneful, graceful music, but one cannot feel that the stage was Finzi's world. The disc is completed by two interesting early pieces for strings, the *Prelude* and *Romance*, both wholly characteristic of the composer and very well played.

Additional recommendation ...
Clarinet Concerto[a]. Five bagatelles, Op. 23[b]. **Stanford.** Clarinet Concerto in A minor, Op. 80[a]. Three Intermezzos, Op. 13[b]. **Emma Johnson** (cl); [b]**Malcolm Martineau** (pf); [a]**Royal Philharmonic Orchestra/Sir Charles Groves.** ASV CDDCA787 — •·* Ih 14m DDD 6/92

New review
Finzi. Intimations of Immortality, Op. 29[a]. Grand Fantasia and Toccata in D minor, Op. 38[b].
[a]**Philip Langridge** (ten); [b]**Philip Fowke** (pf); [a]**Liverpool Philharmonic Choir; Royal Liverpool Philharmonic Orchestra/Richard Hickox.** EMI Digital Classics CDM7 64620-2. From CDC7 49913-2 (2/90). Text included. Recorded in 1988.

/• **lh lm DDD l0/93**

At the beginning of Finzi's setting of Wordsworth's *Ode on the Intimations of Immortality*, which is both eclectic and very Elgarian in feeling, Finzi makes his romantic intentions quite clear in the lovely, evocative orchestral introduction which sets the scene for the first poem, "There was a time when meadows, grove and stream". This is definitely in the pastoral tradition of English song setting, yet with injections of choral passion echoing the dedication of the soloist. Philip Langridge is absolutely committed, although it must be conceded that his ardour leads to an almost uncontrolled vibrato at times. However, in moments of repose the lyrical line is very appealing. This involved and involving performance conducted by Richard Hickox is very rewarding and the choral recording is as spacious as it is brilliant. The coupling is another fascinatingly eclectic piece, this time for piano and orchestra. The opening *Grand Fantasia* is more than neo-baroque; it is an unashamed extension of Bach, and very well written too. The *Toccata* which follows brings a good-natured *vigoroso* fugato idea in a similar style. It is commandingly played by Philip Fowke and Richard Hickox is again a sympathetic partner.

New review
Finzi (arr. Ferguson). Interlude in A minor, Op. 21.
Howells. Oboe Sonata.
Patterson. Duologue. **Nicholas Daniel** (ob); **Julius Drake** (pf). Léman Classics LC44801. From Pearl SHE591.

/• **50m DDD l0/93** **q|p**

This is a most interesting and rewarding recital, devoted to English pieces for oboe and piano that deserve to be better known. The earliest of them, the *Interlude* for oboe and string quartet composed by Finzi between 1932 and 1936, is a big, impassioned piece, lasting over 12 minutes, in a skilful arrangement for oboe and piano made in 1981 by his close friend Howard Ferguson. The real discovery is the Sonata by Herbert Howells, composed in 1943 and only now being published. Its four movements are: a ruminative, long-breathed, Prologue; a rhapsodic, lyrical *Lento*; a nimble, quirky *Scherzo*; and an expansive Epilogue. These two fine works, both of them in very much the same tradition, are separated on the CD by Paul Patterson's brilliant, virtuosic Duologue, first performed in 1984. It comprises a brilliant, toccata-like first movement, an eloquent *Adagio*, and a dashing finale. Nicholas Daniel, who has already done so much to champion new music for his instrument by English composers, together with Julius Drake, plays all three works absolutely marvellously, and they are given a vivid recording.

Finzi. CHORAL WORKS. **Finzi Singers/Paul Spicer** with [a]**Harry Bicket** (org). Chandos CHAN8936. Texts included. Recorded in 1990.
All this night, Op. 33. Let us now praise famous men, Op. 35[a]. Lo, the full, final sacrifice, Op. 26[a]. Magnificat, Op. 36[a]. Seven Part-songs, Op. 17. Though did'st delight my eyes, Op. 32. Three Anthems, Op. 27[a]. Three Short Elegies, Op. 5[a]. White-flowering days, Op. 37.

/• **lh l9m DDD 9/91**

Finzi is no composer to look to for the musical counterpart of a quick fix — and how he would have abhorred that expression. To the patient spirit of the listener who seeks music in which the fastidious limitation of its means is itself some guarantee of the depth of its purposes, he will always be rewarding. This is true of all the works collected here. Some, such as the first and last, *God is gone up* and *Lo, the full, final sacrifice*, are relatively well-known, which is not to say that they will necessarily prove the most satisfying. There are some fine shorter pieces including the unaccompanied *Seven Poems of Bridges* and the *Three Drummond Elegies* that delight as word-settings. "White-flowering days", to words by Edmund Blunden, comes from *A Garland for the Queen*, the Coronation gift of ten composers in 1953, none happier than this in catching the fresh hopefulness of the time. Best of all perhaps is the *Magnificat*, which also had its first British
performance in that year. It is heard here in its original version with organ, beautifully played on

this disc and providing a more spiritual association than is found in the orchestral accompaniment added later. The Finzi Singers are sensitive, assured and accurate; their tone is uniformly good, and they convey a sense of personal involvement in the music. The qualities of recorded sound and presentation are well up to the rest.

Further listening ...

Cello Concerto, Op. 40. *Coupled with* **Leighton.** Veris gratia — suite, Op. 9[a]. **Rafael Wallfisch** (vc); [a]**George Caird** (ob); **Royal Liverpool Philharmonic Orchestra/Vernon Handley.** Chandos CHAN8471 (10/86).

Key to symbols

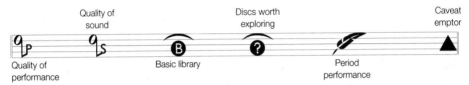

| Quality of sound | Discs worth exploring | Caveat emptor |

Quality of performance   Basic library   Period performance

Gioseffo-Hectore Fiocco
Italian/South Netherlands 1703-1741

Suggested listening ...

Pièces de clavecin, Op. 1. **Ton Koopman** (hpd). Astrée Auvidis E7731 (3/90).

Johann Fischer
German c.1670-1746

Suggested listening ...

Harpsichord Suites — Musicalischer Parnassus: D minor, "Uranie"; F major, "Euterpe"; C major, "Clio"; in E minor, "Erato". Les pièces de clavecin, Op. 2 — Suite in D major. **Gilbert Rowland** (hpd). Keyboard Records KGR1043 (7/93).

Graham Fitkin
British 1963-

 New review

Fitkin. Hook[a]. Mesh[b]. Stub[c]. Cud[d]. [a]**Bash Ensemble;** [b]**Icebreaker;** [c]**Delta Saxophone Quartet;** [d]**John Harle Band/Graham Fitkin.** Argo 440 216-2ZH. Recorded in 1992.

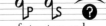 42m DDD 10/93

The sheer enjoyment and fizzing vitality of these pieces often push matters of structure and development into the background. Fitkin himself, though, places considerable emphasis on structural detail, with every bar, dynamic nuance and rhythmic gear change governed by strict mathematical procedures. The resulting musical experiences, however, have spontaneity and immediate appeal in abundance. Also to be savoured here are the considerable talents of the featured ensembles: the Bash Ensemble (rototoms and marimbas) in the jazzy/tribal poundings of *Hook;* Icebreaker's *tour de force* performance of the glittering virtuosic and adrenalin-pumping *Mesh* (breathtaking!), and the Delta Saxophone Quartet's brilliantly articulated performance of the syncopated gyrations of *Stub.* The final work, *Cud,* and the earliest of Fitkin's pieces represented here, is tremendous fun — a shamelessly catchy homage (or send up) to the world of big-band jazz. Originally written for the Cleveland Youth Jazz Orchestra, it is here performed with great panache and flair (not to mention consummate artistry) by the John Harle Band. Recording and production are exemplary.

Friedrich von Flotow
German 1812-1883

Suggested listening ...

MARTHA. **Soloists; Bavarian Radio Chorus; Munich Radio Orchestra/Heinz Wallberg.** Eurodisc 352 878 (2/89).

Josef Foerster
Bohemian 1859-1951

Suggested listening ...

From Shakespeare, Op. 76[a]. Cyrano de Bergerac, Op. 55[b]. [a]**Prague Symphony Orchestra;** [b]**Czech Philharmonic Orchestra/Václav Smetáček.** Campion RRCD1319 (11/93).

Wind Quintet in D major, Op. 95. *Coupled with* **Haas.** Wind Quinet, Op. 10. *Janáček.* Mládí[a]. **Aulos Wind Quintet;** [a]**Kurt Berger** (bass cl). Koch Schwann Musica Mundi 310051 (6/93).

Antoine Forqueray
French 1671-1745

Suggested listening ...

Pièces de Viole — Allemande La Laborde[a]. La Cottin. La Portugaise[a]. La Forqueray. La Régente[a]. La Marella. Sarabande La d'Aubonne. La Ferrand[a]. La Couperin. Chaconne La Buisson[a]. Le Leclair. La Rameau. Jupiter[a]. [a]**Jay Bernfield** (va da gamba); **Skip Sempé** (hpd). Deutsche Harmonia Mundi RD77262 (5/92).

John Foulds
British 1880-1939

Suggested listening ...

Dynamic Triptych, Op. 88. *Coupled with* **Vaughan Williams.** Piano Concerto in C major. **Howard Shelley** (pf); **Royal Philharmonic Orchestra/Vernon Handley.** Lyrita SRCD211 (3/93).

Jean Françaix
French 1912-

Suggested listening ...

String Trio in C major. *Coupled with* **Castelnuovo-Tedesco.** Violin Concerto No. 2, "I profeti"; **Ferguson.** Violin Sonata No. 1, Op. 2; **K. Khachaturian.** Violin Sonata in

G minor, Op. 1. **Jascha Heifetz** (vn); **Joseph de Pasquale** (va); **Gregor Piatigorsky** (vc); **Lilian Steuber** (pf); **Los Angeles Philharmonic Orchestra/Alfred Wallenstein.** RCA Victor Gold Seal GD87872 (9/90).

Alberto Franchetti

Italian 1860-1942

Suggested listening ...

CRISTOFORO COLOMBO. **Soloists; Hungarian Radio Chorus; Frankfurt Radio Symphony Orchestra/Marcello Viotti.** Koch Schwann 310302 (7/92).

Cesar Franck

Belgian/French 1822-1890

Franck. Symphony in D minor.
d'Indy. Symphonie sur un chant montagnard français, Op. 25[a]. [a]**Jean-Yves Thibaudet** (pf); **Montreal Symphony Orchestra/Charles Dutoit.** Decca 430 278-2DH. Recorded in 1989.

Ih 7m DDD I/92

These two French masterpieces of the 1880s complement each other perfectly. The Franck, drawing its inspiration from the other side of the Alps, is very much in the Austro-German symphonic tradition. Its language calls to mind the vaulted splendours and gothic interiors of many a Bruckner Symphony. d'Indy's Symphony, in reality more of a piano concerto, is based on a folk-song he heard whilst holidaying in the Cévennes mountains. Definitely outdoors music this, and far more recognizably French; indeed, with its echoes of Berlioz to its pre-echoes of Debussy and even 'Les Six', it occupies a central position in a century of French music. Dutoit's elegant, flowing way with the Franck (marvellously refined *espressivo* playing from the Montreal violins, and shining, incisive brass) is ideal for those who shy away from the Brucknerian monumentalism of the work; and Jean-Yves Thibaudet's eloquent solo playing in the d'Indy is matched by exquisitely drawn instrumental solos from within the orchestra. Decca's spacious Montreal sound, too, proves just as apt for the organ-like timbres of the Franck, as for the fresh air and wide horizons of the d'Indy.

Additional recommendations ...
Symphony in D minor[a]. **Berlioz.** *Béatrice et Bénédict — Overture*[b]. **d'Indy.** *Symphonie sur un chant montagnard français*[c]. [c]**Nicole Henriot-Schweitzer** (pf); [bc]**Boston Symphony Orchestra/ Charles Munch;** [a]**Chicago Symphony Orchestra/Pierre Monteux.** RCA Victor Papillon GD86805 — Ih 12m ADD 3/89 ▲
Symphony in D minor. Symphonic Variations[a]. [a]**Rudolf Firkušný** (pf); **Royal Philharmonic Orchestra/Claus Peter Flor.** RCA Victor Red Seal RD60146 — Ih DDD 8/90
Symphony in D minor. **Lalo.** Symphony in G minor. **French Radio National Orchestra/Sir Thomas Beecham.** EMI CDM7 63396-2 — Ih 6m ADD 9/92
Symphony in D minor. Symphonic Variations[a]. Prélude, Choral et Fugue[b]. [a]**Philippe Entremont, Pascal Devoyon** (pfs); **Orchestra National de l'ORTF/Jean Martinon.** Erato Bonsai 4509-92871-2 — Ih 15m ADD 12/93

Franck. Symphonic Variations, Op. 46[b].
Grieg. Piano Concerto in A minor, Op. 16[a].
Schumann. Piano Concerto in A minor, Op. 54[c]. [ab]**Sir Clifford Curzon,** [c]**Friedrich Gulda** (pfs); [a]**London Symphony Orchestra/Øivin Fjeldstad;** [b]**London Philharmonic Orchestra/Sir Adrian Boult;** [c]**Vienna Philharmonic Orchestra/Volkmar Andreae.**

Decca Headline Classics 433 628-2DSP. Item marked [a] from LW5350 (7/59), [b] SXL2173 (1/60), [c] LXT5280 (5/57).

⏺ 1h 16m ADD 1/92   𝄽ₚ   Ⓑ   ▲

Since the advent of the LP the Grieg and Schumann concertos have been ideally paired and here we have Sir Clifford Curzon's classic account of the Grieg from 1959 where he is most sympathetically and idiomatically accompanied by Øivin Fjeldstad and the London Symphony Orchestra. Curzon was at his finest in romantic piano concertos, and his playing achieves an exceptional balance between poetry and strength. This is a performance which clearly stakes a claim for the concerto as a work of genius. These same characteristics are also to the fore in the recording of the Franck *Symphonic Variations*, this time with Sir Adrian Boult conducting. This is probably the finest performance of this popular work on CD: imaginative and romantic with a perfect sense of style, and excellent rapport between conductor and soloist. As if these riches were not enough, and at bargain price, the Decca CD is rounded off with another extremely masterly reading of the Schumann Concerto by Friedrich Gulda, this time dating from 1956 and with Volkmar Andreae leading the Vienna Philharmonic. This reading is absolutely in the centre of the authentic romantic style: it is both extremely personal and authoritative. Decca's recorded sound for all three performances is more than acceptable, with true piano tone throughout. This is probably one of the finest bargain issues currently available.

Additional recommendation ...
Symphonic Variations[a]. *Violin Sonata in A major (trans. Delsart)*[b]. *Piano Quintet in F minor*[c]. **Pascal Rogé** (pf); [c]**Richard Friedman, Steven Smith** (vns); [c]**Christopher Wellington** (va); [a]**London Festival Orchestra/Ross Pople** ([bc]vc). ASV CDDCA769 — .ᐟᐟ 1h 19m DDD 11/91 Ⓑ

Franck. Violin Sonata in A major.
Szymanowski. Mythes, Op. 30. King Roger (trans. Kochański). Kurpian Song (trans. Kochanski). **Kaja Danczowska** (vn); **Krystian Zimerman** (pf). DG Galleria 431 469-2GGA. From 2531 330 (6/81). Recorded in 1980.

.ᐟᐟ 58m ADD 8/91   𝄽ₚ

Franck's Sonata, with its yearning romantic nature, makes a good foil for Szymanowski's rather wild, rhapsodic invention. Kaja Danczowska, a pupil of Eugenia Uminska and David Oistrakh, shows a fine technique, a beautiful tone-quality, and plenty of temperament on this very well-recorded disc. In the Franck, Zimerman is a mite too reticent, though he plays beautifully and impeccably, but Danczowska captures Franck's changing moods perfectly and brings a not at all inappropriate Polish fervour to the three quicker movements. The third movement, *Recitativo-Fantasia,* is finely characterized, too, with its more thoughtful, inward episodes sympathetically explored. (Kyung Wha Chung's and Radu Lupu's classic version is reviewed under Debussy; refer to the Index to Reviews.) The best known of Szymanowski's three shortish *Mythes* is the first, "La fontaine d'Arethuse", which has often been played on its own. It has an exotic, other worldly beauty which is very well realized by Danczowska, with Zimerman here a more positive, purposeful partner. The second piece, "Narcisse", inhabits a similar world, but "Dryades et Pan" is quite daring for 1915, with its use of quarter-tones. These pieces, and the effective transcriptions, are vividly brought to life by Szymanowski's two compatriots.

Additional recommendation ...
Violin Sonata. **Brahms.** *Horn Trio in E flat major, Op. 40*[a]. **Itzhak Perlman** (vn); [a]**Barry Tuckwell** (hn); **Vladimir Ashkenazy** (pf). Decca 414 128-2DH — .ᐟᐟ 56m AAD 4/85 𝄽ₚ

Franck. ORGAN WORKS. **Michael Murray.** Telarc CD80234. Played on the Cavaillé-Coll organ of Saint Sernin Basilica, Toulouse. Recorded in 1989.
Fantaisie in A major. Cantabile in B major. Pièce Héroïque in B minor. Fantaisie in C major. Grande Pièce Symphonique. Prélude, Fugue et variation. Pastorale. Prière in C sharp minor. Final in B flat major. Chorales — No. 1 in E major; No. 2 in B minor; No. 3 in A minor.

.ᐟᐟ ② 2h 29m DDD 7/90   𝄽ₚ 𝄽ₛ 🖎

Although Franck wrote a great many small pieces for organ it was with these 12 (the 'master-

works' as the disc styles them) that he established an organ music tradition which French composers to this day have followed. Michael Murray is entirely respectful of tradition. There is about his performances something akin to reverence. He is completely faithful to the finest detail of the score, and the authenticity of these performances is underlined by being recorded on an instrument contemporaneous (just) with Franck and still in virtually unaltered shape; this was the kind of organ sound that inspired Franck to write these pieces. Authentic and respectful as they are, Murray's performances are beautifully played. Like most American organists he seems to have a natural gift for direct communication; a gift wholeheartedly supported by Telarc's exceptionally fine recording.

Franck. Prélude, Choral et Fugue.
Liszt. PIANO WORKS. **Murray Perahia** (pf). Sony Classical SK47180. Recorded 1990-91.
Mephisto Waltz No. 1, S514. Années de pèlerinage, première année, S160, "Suisse" — Aubord d'une source; deuxième année, S161, "Italie" — Sonetto 104 del Petrarca. Two Concert Studies, S145. Rhapsodie espagnole, S254.

Ih DDD 10/91

Having surprised many of his admirers by launching the second half of his earlier, much-praised "Aldeburgh Recital" (Sony Classical SK46437, 4/91) with a *Hungarian Rhapsody* by Liszt, Murray Perahia now leaves us in no doubt that his encounter with this composer was no mere passing flirtation in the course of an ever-widening exploration of the romantic repertory. 'Aristocratic' is the adjective that first comes to mind in describing his approach. It is Liszt playing of quite exceptional finesse, ravishing in pellucid sonority, delicately glistening (like frost on every individual blade of grass in early morning winter sunshine) in sleight-of-hand, yet not lacking strength in the bolder climaxes of a bravura piece such as the concluding *Rhapsodie espagnole*. Only in the *Mephisto Waltz* is there just a slight suspicion of caution on the dance-floor and chasteness in the "lascivious, caressing dreams of love". Franck's *Prélude, Choral et Fugue* in its turn has a simplicity and dignity, free of all arrogance or bluster very much Perahia's own. Predictably his unfailing textural clarity is a major asset — not least in the contrapuntal cunning of the fugue. Recorded mainly at The Maltings, Snape, but in part at the Royce Hall in Los Angeles, the sound *per se* is first-class throughout.

Additional recommendation ...
Prélude, Choral et Fugue. Prélude, Aria et Final. Symphonic Variations[b]. **Jorge Bolet** (pf); **Royal Concertgebouw Orchestra/Riccardo Chailly.** Decca 421 714-2DH — Ih 2m DDD 9/89

Further listening ...

Piano Concerto No. 2 in B minor, Op. 11. Variations brillantes sur la ronde favorite de Gustave III, Op. 8. **Jean-Claude Vanden Eynden** (pf); **RTBF New Symphony Orchestra/Edgar Doneux.** Koch Schwann Musica Mundi 311 111G1 (3/90).

Le Chasseur maudit. Les Eolides. Psyché — symphonic poem. **Basle Symphony Orchestra/ Armin Jordan.** Erato 2292-45552-2 (7/86).

Piano Quintet in F minor. *Coupled with* **Dvořák.** Piano Quintet in A major, B155. **Sir Clifford Curzon** (pf); **Vienna Philharmonic Quartet.** Decca 421 153-2DM (4/90). *See review under Dvořák; refer to the Index to Reviews.*

Les Béatitudes. **Soloists; Stuttgart Gächinger Kantorei and Radio Symphony Orchestra/Helmuth Rilling.** Hänssler 98 964 (7/91).

Le Chasseur maudit. Rédemption — Morceau symphonique. Nocturne. Coupled with *Berlioz.* Roméo et Juliette[a]. [a]**Yvonne Minton, Christa Ludwig** (mezs); [a]**Francisco Araiza** (ten); [a]**Jules Bastin** (bass); [a]**Orchestre de Paris Chorus; Orchestre de Paris/Daniel Barenboim.** DG Galleria 437 244-2GGA2 (1/93).

Benjamin Frankel

American 1906-1973

New review

Frankel. Symphonies — No. 1, Op. 33; No. 5, Op. 67. May Day Overture, Op. 22.
Queensland Symphony Orchestra/Werner Andreas Albert. CPO CPO999 240-2.

53m DDD 7/94

The two symphonies on this disc demonstrate that Frankel's inexplicable neglect has been our loss. Neglect because of rumours that he was a serialist and therefore probably tuneless and rebarbative (you could well find yourself whistling tunes from these Symphonies for days)? He seems, if the overture *May Day* is anything to go by (it precedes all of his eight symphonies), to have been a natural, indeed an abundantly fertile melodist who felt the need for some sort of discipline on his inventiveness stronger than that of conventional nineteenth-century symphonic form. He found it in a highly personal adaptation of serialism, an adaptation designed to retain a strong sense of key and indeed of melody, but to use the elements of melody with great economy and rigour. Already those very nouns may suggest aridity, but they shouldn't: Haydn, after all, very often did much the same thing. They do not sound like Haydn, these symphonies, nor in the least like Schoenberg. In their openness of texture they are reminiscent of Copland or Martinů, in the rather alfresco geniality of the opening movement of No. 5 of Nielsen, once or twice, fleetingly, of Mahler. The performances are first-class and so are the recordings.

Girolamo Frescobaldi

Italian 1583-1643

Suggested listening ...

Capriccio V sopra la Bassa fiammenga[d]. Canzon prima[a]. *Coupled with* **Conforti.** Ricercar del quarto tono[d]. **Merula.** La Lusignuola[a]. **R. Johnson II.** The Temporiser a 4[a]. **Byrd.** Sermone blando a 3, BE17/23[a]. **Anonymous.** Istampita, "Tre fontane"[a.] Prince Edward's Paven[c]. The Queine of Ingland's Paven[c]. **Bach.** The Art of Fugue, BWV1080 — Contrapunctus I[b]. Fugue in G major, BWV550[b]. Brandenburg Concerto No. 3 in G major, BWV1048 — Allegro. **Sweelinck.** Mein junges Leben hat ein End'[b]. **Palestrina.** Lamentationum Hieremiae prophetae[d]. **Trabaci.** Canzon francesa terza[d]. **Aston.** Hugh Ashton's Maske[c]. **Taverner.** In nomine a 4[c]. **Shott.** Aan de Amsterdamse Grachten (new to UK). **Amsterdam Loeki Stardust Quartet** (Daniel Brüggen, Bertho Driever, Paul Leenhouts, Karel van Steenhoven, recs). L'Oiseau-Lyre 440 207-2OM. *See review in the Collections section; refer to the Index to Reviews.*

Hugo Friedhofer

American 1902-1981

Suggested listening ...

The Young Lions; This Earth is Mine — *Original film soundtracks.* Varèse Sarabande VSD2-5403 (10/93).

Johann Jacob Froberger

German 1616-1667

Suggested listening ...

Harpsichord Suites — I in E minor; II in A minor; III in G minor; IV; V in D major; VI in C major. Lamentation sur la mort sa Majesté Impérial, Ferdinand III for harpsichord. **Kenneth Gilbert** (hpd). Archiv Produktion 437 080-2AT (1/93).

Walter Frye

Suggested listening ...

Missa "Flos Regalis". Trinitatis dies. Salve virgo mater pya. O florens rosa. Ave regina celorum (two settings). Sospitati dedit. Tout a par moy. So ys emprentid. Myn hertis lust. Alas, alas is my chief song. **The Hilliard Ensemble.** ECM New Series 437 684-2 (6/93).

Robert Fuchs

Fuchs. Clarinet Quintet in E flat major, Op. 102.
Romberg. Quintet in E flat major, Op. 57ª.
Stanford. Two Fantasy Pieces. **Thea King** (cl); **Britten Quartet** (Peter Manning, vn; Keith Pascoe, vn/ªva; Peter Lale, va; Andrew Shulman, vc). Hyperion CDA66479. Recorded in 1991.

Ih 20m DDD 7/92

Though the clarinet is a beautiful instrument that was admired by several composers from Mozart onwards, its solo repertory is small and we cannot afford to neglect any part of it, particularly as there are many fine players, among whom Thea King stands out as one of the finest. None of these three composers can claim to be among the musical greats, but each wrote sympathetically for the instrument and this sensitively played and well recorded disc makes for pleasing listening. It should win friends for Andreas Romberg (a contemporary of Beethoven and not the Romberg who composed *The Desert Song*), and the turn-of-the-century composers Robert Fuchs and Sir Charles Villiers Stanford — not least if we also gratefully remember two men for teaching, between them, Mahler, Sibelius, Vaughan Williams and Holst. Romberg's Quintet is fluent and unfailingly agreeable, if not more than that: listening to it, and not least the outer sections of the minuet second movement (the trio is more personal), one is reminded of Mozart in a genial yet elegant mood, and Romberg surely knew that composer's Clarinet Quintet and Concerto. Fuchs's work, written in 1917 when he was 70 and first performed at a concert to mark the occasion, is romantic in an almost Schubertian way although it was composed after the radical works of Stravinsky and Schoenberg had shaken the musical world. But we need not disagree with Brahms, who once said, "Fuchs is a splendid musician: all's so refined, skilled and delightfully inventive that we can always enjoy what we hear". The Two *Fantasy Pieces* by Stanford have similar civilized qualities plus occasional attractive touches of Irishness and complete a valuable and very enjoyable programme.

Further listening ...

Cello Sonatas — No. 1 in D minor, Op. 29; No. 2 in E flat minor, Op. 83. Fantasiestücke, Op. 78. **Nancy Green** (vc); **Caroline Palmer** (pf). Biddulph LAW005 (4/93).

Piano Sonatas — No. 1 in G flat major, Op. 19; No. 2 in G minor, Op. 88. **Daniel Blumenthal** (pf). Marco Polo 8 223377 (6/93).

Giovanni Gabrieli

Suggested listening ...

Sacrae symphoniae — Canzon duodecemi toni a 10; Sonata piano e forte alla quarta bassa a 8; Canzon noni toni a 12; Canzon septimi e octavi toni a 12; Canzon primi toni a 8. *Canzoni e sonata* — Sonata XVIII a 14; Sonata XIX a 15; Canzon VII a 7; Canzon X a 8; Canzon XV a 10; Canzon XVI a 12; Canzon XII a 8; Sonata XX a 22. Canzon La Spiritata a 4. *Coupled with*

A. Gabrieli. Ricercar del duodecimi tono (1589). **Viadana.** Sinfonias a 8 — La Bergamasca; La Padovanna. **Frescobaldi.** Canzon terzadecima detta la Bianchina a 4. **Wallace Collection/Simon Wright.** Nimbus NI5236 (11/90).

Niels Gade

Danish 1817-1890

Gade. Elf-shot, Op. 30[a]. Echoes from Ossian, Op. 1[b]. Five Songs, Op. 13[c]. [a]**Eve Johansson** (sop); [a]**Anne Gjevang** (mez); [a]**Poul Elming** (ten); [a]**Danish National Radio Choir;** [c]**Danish National Radio Chamber Choir/Stefan Parkman;** [ab]**Danish National Radio Symphony Orchestra/Dmitri Kitaienko.** Chandos CHAN9075. Texts and translations included. Recorded 1991-92.

1h 17m   DDD   11/92

Gade was Denmark's leading nineteenth-century composer and *Elverskud*, variously translated as *The Fairy Spell, The Elf-King's Daughter* or, as on this CD, *Elf-shot* is generally thought to be his finest work. It is much indebted to Mendelssohn's *Die erste Walpurgisnacht* and its text is based on a medieval Danish ballad, the story of Lord Oluf, enticed to his death by the elfins on his wedding night. In *A Short History of Scandinavian Music* (Faber, 1963), John Horton went so far as to say that it "contains some of the most beautiful orchestral writing of the romantic period in any country", and it is difficult not to succumb to its charm and grace, particularly the opening of the second half which evokes the moonlit world of the Fairy Hill. Like Mendelssohn, Gade rarely betrays any hint of tragedy; the symphonies are equally sunny and equable, and the same holds true of *Elf-shot,* which comes from the year after the Fifth Symphony (for piano and orchestra). The soloists are excellent even if Anne Gjevang's vibrato may be just a little too wide for some tastes; the orchestral playing under Dmitri Kitaienko is highly responsive and sympathetic. This CD comes with Gade's very first opus, the overture *Echoes from Ossian* which together with the First Symphony brought him to the attention of Mendelssohn. It has a particularly appealing second subject. The Five Songs, Op. 13, are also delightful. They are beautifully fashioned and there is a pleasing freshness and grace that is absolutely captivating.

Further listening ...

Symphonies — No. 1 in C minor, Op. 5; No. 2 in E major, Op. 10. **Copenhagen Collegium Musicum/Michael Schøwandt.** Marco Polo Dacapo DCCD9201 (5/94).

Symphonies — No. 2 in E major, Op. 10; No. 7 in F major, Op. 45. **Stockholm Sinfonietta/Neeme Järvi.** BIS CD355 (12/87).

Symphonies — No. 3 in A minor, Op. 15; No. 4 in B flat major, Op. 20. **Stockholm Sinfonietta/Neeme Järvi.** BIS CD338 (7/87).

Symphonies — No. 4 in B flat major, Op. 20; No. 6 in G minor, Op. 32. **Copenhagen Collegium Musicum/Michael Schøwandt.** Marco Polo Dacapo DCCD9202 (5/94).

Symphonies — No. 5 in D minor, Op. 25[a]; No. 6 in G minor, Op. 32. [a]**Roland Pöntinen** (pf); **Stockholm Sinfonietta/Neeme Järvi.** BIS CD356 (12/87).

Phillipe Gaubert

French 1879-1941

Gaubert. COMPLETE WORKS FOR FLUTE AND PIANO. **Susan Milan** (fl); **Ian Brown** (pf). Chandos CHAN8981/2. Items marked [a] from CHAN8609 (11/88), recorded in 1988, others recorded in 1991.

Sonata. Madrigal. Deux esquisses. Fantaisie[a]. Romance. Flute Sonatas — No. 2; No. 3. Sicilienne. Berceuse. Suite. Nocturne et Allegro scherzando[a]. Romance. Sonatine. Sur l'eau. Ballade.

② 2h DDD 11/91

This integral recording of the complete works for flute and piano by Philippe Gaubert commemorates the fiftieth anniversary of the death of one of the seminal figures in the history of modern flute playing. Although still revered as co-author (with Paul Taffanel) of a famous tutorial for the instrument, the majority of Gaubert's enchanting compositions will be largely unfamiliar. Fortunately, his music could hardly find more convincing advocacy than in the hands of Susan Milan and Ian Brown. Listening to these works, one cannot avoid wondering about the remainder of Gaubert's large output, which included operas, ballet scores, a symphony, several concertos, and much chamber music, all of which now seems to be forgotten. Gaubert's three sonatas are lithe, lyrical and affable, although essentially traditional in concept, but the real joys of this set are the various salon miniatures, ranging from the *Madrigal* of 1908 to such delights as *Sur l'eau* and the delectable *Sicilienne* and *Berceuse*. The *Suite* of 1921 is thoughtfully and tastefully cast, with the final "Scherzo-Valse" being particularly memorable. The playing is sparkling and witty, with the mellifluous tone of Susan Milan a lasting pleasure throughout. She is ably supported by the pianist, Ian Brown, and the recordings are beyond criticism. Strongly recommended.

John Gay
British 1685-1732

New review

Gay (arr. Britten). THE BEGGAR'S OPERA. **Ann Murray** (mez) Polly; **Philip Langridge** (ten) Macheath; **Yvonne Kenny** (sop) Lucy; **John Rawnsley** (bar) Lockit; **Robert Lloyd** (bass) Peachum; **Anne Collins** (contr) Mrs Peachum; **Nuala Willis** (mez) Mrs Trapes; **Christopher Gillett** (ten) Filch; **Declan Mulholland** (sngr) Beggar; **Aldeburgh Festival Choir and Orchestra/Steuart Bedford.** Argo 436 850-2ZHO2. Notes and text included. Recorded in 1992.

② 1h 48m DDD 9/93

"Not a 'sport' among Britten's operas but an integral part of the totality of theatrical work, from *Paul Bunyan* to *Death in Venice*": Donald Mitchell puts the claim well, and this first recording supports it all the way. *The Beggar's Opera* was Britten's new work for the English Opera Group in 1948 but it has had less than its due. Everything here is well set-up to make amends. The 12 players forming the chamber orchestra are excellent individually and they respond sensitively to Steuart Bedford's direction. The singer-actors are expertly assisted, and Michael Woolcock's production is vivid without being obtrusive. At the very least, the speech causes no embarrassment; at best it is spirited, and the full-fathom-five depth of Robert Lloyd's Peachum gives profound pleasure. The singing is probably as good as it should be; in many of the numbers, character matters more than beauty of tone. But it is to Britten's score that one has to return when making a recommendation. *The Beggar's Opera* can also be obtained on records in very different forms. The starry version under Richard Bonynge (listed below) is more entertaining, but the gloss is thick and the enrichment of musical interest, when it occurs, scarcely stretches the imagination. Britten's work is of a different order altogether. It is not mere cleverness, though the sheer ingenuities of rhythm, counterpoint, harmony and orchestration keep the ear fully occupied and delighted. Much more, the process is one of absorption and re-creation, sometimes fierce or poignant, sometimes magical in its loveliness (the use of the chorus in "Cease your funning", for example). The marvel is that the tunes themselves, so far from rejecting Britten's treatment as the body might reject a transplant, seem to find themselves in their element. The recording fills a gap in respect of Gay's masterpiece as surely as it fills another in the Britten *oeuvre*.

Additional recommendation ...
Soloists; London Voices; National Philharmonic Orchestra/Richard Bonynge. Decca 430 066-2DH2 — **②** 2h 5m DDD 5/91

Francesco Geminiani

Italian 1687-1762

Geminiani. Concerti grossi, Op. 2. Concerti grossi after Corelli's Op. 5 — No. 3 in C major; No. 5 in G minor. **Tafelmusik/Jeanne Lamon.** Sony Classical Vivarte SK48043. Recorded in 1990.
Op. 2 — No. 1 in C minor; No. 2 in C minor; No. 3 in D minor; No. 4 in D major; No. 5 in D minor; No. 6 in A major.

59m DDD II/92

Imagine the scene. The year is 1715 and Francesco Geminiani is playing his violin for King George I, accompanied on the harpsichord by none other than Handel. But Geminiani had not always enjoyed the absolute favour of his colleagues; it is said that in Italy complaints were voiced regarding his excessive use of rubato — a very unexpected phenomenon, especially when seen in the light of our own attitudes to period performance. So, he left his workplace in Naples (where he was Concert Master), came to London — his new 'base', so to speak — and additionally went on to work in Dublin and Paris. The individual works in Geminiani's concerto-style Op. 2 set are forged in the *sonata da chiesa* (slow-fast-slow-fast) format and contain much beautiful music, especially where, in chordal passages, there is an overlapping of string lines. The faster movements set out on dancing feet — an aspect of the music that Tafelmusik indulges with obvious relish — and the slower ones have a mildly sensuous character. Nowhere, however, will you find as much as a hint of the wayward rubato about which Geminiani's colleagues complained! Similar positive qualities apply to the performances of the two Corelli violin sonata transcriptions, the second of which is particularly appealing. The recordings, too, are warm and immediate, with plenty of space around them and impressive definition.

Geminiani. Concerti grossi, Op. 3. **Bern Camerata/Thomas Füri.** Novalis 150 083-2. Recorded in 1991.
No. 1 in D major. No. 2 in G minor. No. 3 in E minor. No. 4 in D minor. No. 5 in B flat major. No. 6 in E minor.

52m DDD I/93

Geminiani's six Concertos, Op. 3, in Dr Burney's words "established his character, and placed him at the head of all the masters then living" — no small tribute to a composer working at a time when Vivaldi and Handel were still around. The earliest version of Geminiani's Op. 3 appeared in 1733 but between then and 1755 or thereabouts the composer made substantial revisions, and it is the later text which has been chosen by Camerata Bern. This talented ensemble of modern instrumentalists respond stylishly and with infectious enthusiasm to these concertos. Geminiani's art was a versatile one — harmonically bold on occasion, and invariably entertaining; there is an easy blend of virtuosity with simpler gestures which are contained, above all in the many short but beautifully modulating slow movements. A distinctive feature present in all of them is his solo or *concertino* group which, unlike those of Corelli or Handel, for instance, includes a viola in addition to the customary trio of two violins and cello. Strong but sensitive playing throughout which reveals many of the subtleties of Geminiani's music. The recording is clear and ideally resonant.

Roberto Gerhard

Spanish/British 1896-1970

Suggested listening ...

Don Quixote. Pedrelliana (En memoria). Albada, Interludi i Dansa. **Tenerife Symphony Orchestra/Victor Pablo Pérez.** Auvidis Valois V4660 (10/92).

Alegrías. *Coupled with* **Falla.** Noches en los jardines de España[a]; **E. Halffter.** Rapsodia portuguesa[a]. [a]**Guillermo Gonzalez** (pf); **Tenerife Symphony Orchestra/Victor Pablo Pérez.** Etcetera KTC1095 (7/92). *See review under Falla; refer to the Index to Reviews.*

Sir Edward German

Suggested listening ...

Nell Gwyn — Overture; Country Dance; Pastoral Dance; Merry-maker's Dance; Gipsy Suite. Henry VIII — Shepherds's Dance; Torch Dance; Morris Dance. The Conqueror — Berceuse. Romeo and Juliet — Pavane; Nocturne; Pastorale. Tom Jones — Waltz Song (arr. Tomlinson). Merrie England — Hornpipe; Minuet; Rustic Dance; Jig. **Bratislava Radio Symphony Orchestra/Adrian Leaper.** Marco Polo British Light Music 8 223419 (6/93).

George Gershwin

Gershwin. Piano Concerto in F major. Rhapsody in Blue. Second Rhapsody. **Howard Shelley** (pf); **Philharmonia Orchestra/Yan Pascal Tortelier.** Chandos CHAN9092. Recorded in 1992.

.·ʾ lh 4m DDD 3/93

It is only in recent years that Gershwin's *Second Rhapsody* has emerged from the shadows to take its place beside the vastly successful earlier essay, *Rhapsody in Blue*. With hindsight it is difficult to see how such a likeably attractive, inventive piece should have languished in comparative obscurity for so long. It is probably a better work overall than the Piano Concerto, whose first movement is just a minute or two too long for the basic material used. The combination of a British pianist and orchestra with a French conductor in very American works may seem unpromising, but all concerned enter the fray with great skill and aplomb. It can't be every day that the Philharmonia plays this kind of repertoire, but its players seem to be enjoying themselves immensely, and there is a delicious feeling of spontaneity and exuberance throughout all three performances. Shelley plays with great freedom and brilliance, and with Tortelier in sympathetic support, he gives a particularly sensitive performance of the Piano Concerto's deeply-felt middle *Adagio* movement. The recording quality matches the performances in being fresh, immediate and very attractive to the ear.

Additional recommendations ...
Piano Concerto. Rhapsody in Blue[a]. An American in Paris. Variations on "I got rhythm". [a]**Earl Wild** (pf); **Boston Pops Orchestra/Arthur Fiedler.** RCA Papillon GD86519 — .·ʾ lh 10m ADD 11/87 Ⓑ
Piano Concerto. **Ravel.** *Piano Concerto in G major.* **Bournemouth Symphony Orchestra/ Andrew Litton** (pf). Virgin Classics VJ7 59693-2 — .·ʾ 57m DDD 9/90 Ⓑ
Piano Concerto[a]. Rhapsody in Blue. An American in Paris. [a]**Joanna MacGregor** (pf); **London Symphony Orchestra/Carl Davis.** Collins Classics 1139-2 — .·ʾ lh 5m DDD 11/91 Ⓑ

Gershwin. An American in Paris[a]. Rhapsody in Blue[b]. [a]**Columbia Symphony Orchestra;** [b]**New York Philharmonic Orchestra/Leonard Bernstein** (pf[a]). CBS Maestro CD42611. From Philips SABL160 (10/60).

.·ʾ 35m ADD 11/90

Bernstein conducted and played the music of Gershwin with the same naturalness as he brought to his own music. Here, *An American in Paris* swings by with an instinctive sense of its origins in popular and film music; no stilted rhythms or four-squareness delay the work's progress, and where ripe schmaltz is wanted, ripe schmaltz is what we get, devoid of all embarrassment. *Rhapsody in Blue* is playful and teasing, constantly daring us to try to categorize its style, and then confounding our conclusions. Although the solo passages from individual players are beautifully taken, both orchestras pull together magnificently to capture the authentic flavour of Gershwin's idiom, and Bernstein pushes them to transcend the printed score. His own playing in the *Rhapsody* is tantalizingly unpredictable. The recording is clear and bright, perhaps a touch hard-edged, and a little of the richness of the original LP issue might have been preferred by some, especially as the editing is now made more obvious. The only major criticism would be of the stingy overall timing of the disc — but with these performances quality compensates.

Gershwin. PORGY AND BESS. **Willard White** (bass) Porgy; **Cynthia Haymon** (sop) Bess; **Harolyn Blackwell** (sop) Clara; **Cynthia Clarey** (sop) Serena; **Damon Evans** (bar) Sportin' Life; **Marietta Simpson** (mez) Maria; **Gregg Baker** (bar) Crown; **Glyndebourne Chorus; London Philharmonic Orchestra/Simon Rattle.** EMI CDS7 49568-2. Notes and text included. Recorded in 1988.

③ 3h 9m DDD 6/89

The company, orchestra and conductor from the outstanding 1986 Glyndebourne production recreate once more a very real sense of Gershwin's 'Catfish Row' community on EMI's complete recording. Such is the atmosphere and theatricality of this recording, we might easily be back on the Glyndebourne stage; you can positively smell the drama in the key scenes. From the very first bar it's clear just how instinctively attuned Simon Rattle and this orchestra are to every aspect of a multi-faceted score. The cast, too, are so *right*, so much a part of their roles, and so well integrated into the whole, that one almost takes the excellence of their contributions for granted. Here is one beautiful voice after another, beginning in style with Harolyn Blackwell's radiant "Summertime", which at Rattle's gorgeously lazy tempo, is just about as beguiling as one could wish. Willard White conveys both the simple honesty and inner-strength of Porgy without milking the sentiment and Haymon's passionately sung Bess will go wherever a little flattery and encouragement take her. As Sportin' Life, Damon Evans not only relishes the burlesque elements of the role but he really *sings* what's written a lot more than is customary. But the entire cast deliver throughout with all the unstinting fervour of a Sunday revivalist meeting. Sample for yourself the final moments of the piece — "Oh Lawd, I'm on my way" — if that doesn't stir you, nothing will.

Additional recommendations ...
Soloists; Cleveland Chorus and Orchestra/Lorin Maazel. Decca 414 559-2DH3 — ③ DDD

Excerpts. **Soloists; RCA Victor Chorus and Orchestra/Skitch Henderson.** RCA Victor Gold Seal GD85234 — 48m ADD 4/89

Further listening ...

Piano Transcriptions (arr. Wild) — Fantasy on "Porgy and Bess". Improvisation in the form of a Theme and Three Variations on "Someone to watch over me". Seven Virtuoso Etudes: I got rhythm; Lady be good; Liza; Embraceable you; Somebody loves me; Fascinatin' rhythm; The man I love. **Earl Wild.** Chesky CD32 (10/90).

Film Music: Overture — Gershwin in Hollywood. Delicious — New York Rhapsody[c]. Shall we dance — Walking the dog; I've got beginner's luck[ab]; Slap that bass[b]; They all laughed[a]; Let's call the whole thing off[ab]; Watch your step. A damsel in distress — A foggy day[b]; Nice work if you can get it[b]; An American in London. The Goldwyn follies[a] — Love walked in; Love is here to stay. The shocking Miss Pilgrim — For you, for me, for evermore[ab]. [a]**Patti Austin,** [b]**Gregory Hines** (singers); [c]**Wayne Marshall** (pf); **Hollywood Bowl Orchestra/John Mauceri.** Philips 434 274-2PH (5/92).

GIRL CRAZY. Cast includes **Lorna Luft, David Carroll, Judy Blazer, Frank Gorshin, David Garrison, Vicki Lewis, chorus and orchestra/John Mauceri.** Elektra Nonesuch 7559-79250-2. Notes and text included (2/91).

LADY, BE GOOD. **Soloists; chorus and orchestra/Eric Stern.**. Elektra Nonesuch 7559-79308-2 (7/93).

STRIKE UP THE BAND. **Soloists; chorus and orchestra/John Mauceri.** Elektra Nonesuch 7559-79273-2 (1/92).

Key to symbols

	②	②	1h 23m	DDD	6/88
Price	Quantity/ availability		Timing	Recording mode	Review date

Carlo Gesualdo

Gesualdo. Responsoria et alia ad Officium Hebdonadae Sanctae spectantia. Benedictus. Miserere. **The Hilliard Ensemble.** ECM New Series 843 867-2. Texts and translations included. Recorded in 1990.

② 2h 4m DDD 3/92

To many, Gesualdo is known above all for the *crime passionnel* which left his wife and her lover impaled on the same sword, but the notion that his highly-charged music is the product of a tortured and unstable mind is, no doubt, over-romanticized. The exaggeratedly chromatic melodies and daring harmonic style of his late music were fully in keeping with the experimental madrigal school of the late sixteenth century. That said, Gesualdo's setting of the Responds for the Tenebrae of Holy Week is surely one of the most intense and disturbing works of the entire period. The complex service of Tenebrae is made up of the two offices, Matins and Lauds. Within Matins come the 27 responsories that were the inspiration for Gesualdo's music, in addition to which he set the "Miserere" and "Benedictus" from Lauds. At the beginning of the service the church is illuminated with candles, but these are extinguished one by one, hence the name *tenebrae* (darkness). It is significant that Gesualdo chose the most dramatic service of the church year, and one that is concerned with betrayal and death. The Hilliard Ensemble has not missed one ounce of the profundity of this music, and their performance is one of those rare artistic achievements that combines a heartfelt emotional response with faultless technical control. Their phrases are perfectly shaped and directed, and while it is virtually impossible to single out one particular contribution, David Beaven's ideally focused bass line should not go unmentioned. The recording is excellent and every detail of the individual voices can be heard. Texts and translations are included, together with an extract from Hildesheimer's *Tynset*, but some explanatory notes would have been helpful.

Additional recommendation ...
Responsoria et alia ad Officium Hebdonadae Sanctae spectantia — excerpts. Marian Motets — Ave, dulcissima Maria; Precibus et meritis beatae Mariae; Ave, regina coelorum; Maria, mater gratiae. **The Tallis Scholars/Peter Phillips.** Gimell CDGIM015 — 52m DDD 12/87

Further listening ...

Madrigals — Ahi, disperata vita. Sospirava il mio cor. O malnati messaggi. Non t'amo, o voce ingrata. Luci serene e chiare. Sparge la morte al mio Signor nel viso. Arde il mio cor. Occhi del mio cor vita. Mercè grido piangendo. Asciugate i begli ochi. Se la mia morte brami. Io parto. Ardita Zanzaretta. Ardo per te, mio bene. *Instrumental items* — Canzon francese. Io tacerò. Corrente, amanti. **Les Arts Florissants Vocal and Instrumental Ensembles/William Christie.** Harmonia Mundi HMC90 1268 (10/88).

Orlando Gibbons

Gibbons. MUSIC FOR PRINCE CHARLES.
Lupo. MUSIC FOR PRINCE CHARLES. **The Parley of Instruments/Peter Holman.** Hyperion CDA66395. Recorded in 1990.
Gibbons: Two Fantasias a 4. 9 Fantasias a 3. Galliard a 3. **Lupo:** Fantasy-Airs a 3 — Nos. 16, 17 and 20. Fantasy-Airs a 4 — Nos. 5-7, 11 and 12. Fantasies a 4 — Nos. 4 and 9.

59m DDD 9/91

Don't be put off by the rather forbidding titles: the terms "fantasia" and "fantasy-air" in fact conceal a wonderful mixture of the most varied music — by turns passionate, lively, languid and elegant. Peter Holman and his excellent Parley of Instruments have put together a programme which gives a snap-shot of music at the beginning of the English baroque. The composers represented are two of the most eminent English musicians of the seventeenth century: Orlando Gibbons and Thomas Lupo. Both worked in the service of King Charles I during his years as the

Prince of Wales, and this collection represents the type of music the Prince's household musicians wrote for him to play. Charles was a keen patron of the arts and his musical tastes were adventurous: these pieces all include parts for the violin — then a relative newcomer to the English musical scene. Beautifully-judged — and recorded — performances capture the warmth and wit of this music.

Further listening ...

Canticles — Magnificat; Nunc dimittis, "Short Service"; Magnificat; Nunc dimittis, "Second Service". *Full Anthems* — Almighty and Everlasting God; Lift up your heads; Hosanna to the Son of David. *Verse Anthems*[a] — This is the record of John; See, see, the Word is incarnate; O Thou, the central orb. *Hymns and Songs of the Church* — Now shall the praises of the Lord be sung; O Lord of Hosts; A song of joy unto the Lord we sing; Come, kiss me with those lips of thine. *Organ works* — Voluntary; Fantasia for double organ; Fantasia. **King's College Choir, Cambridge/Philip Ledger** with **John Butt** (org) and [a]**London Early Music Group.** ASV Gaudeamus CDGAU123 (4/86).

Second Service (ed. Higginbottom) — Te Deum Laudamus; Jubilate Deo; Magnificat; Nunc dimittis. Full Anthems — O clap your hands; O Lord, in Thy wrath rebuke me not. *Verse Anthems* — O God, the king of glory; Glorious and powerful God; Sing unto the Lord; See, see, the Word is incarnate. *Organ works*[a] — Fantasia of four parts; A Fancy in A major; Fantasia for double organ. **New College Choir, Oxford/Edward Higginbottom** with [a]**David Burchell** (org). CRD CRD3451 (12/88).

Full Anthems — Hosanna to the Son of David; I am the resurrection; O clap your hands; O Lord, how do my woes increase; O Lord, I lift my heart to thee; O Lord, in thy wrath rebuke me not. Verse Anthems — Lord, we beseech thee, pour thy grace; Praise the Lord, O my soul; See, see, the Word is incarnate; Sing unto the Lord, o ye saints. *Hymns and Songs of the Church* — Come, kiss me with those lips of thine; How sad and solitary now; Lord, I will sing to Thee; Lord, thy answer I did hear; Now in the Lord my heart doth pleasure take; Now shall the praises of the Lord; O Lord of Hosts and God of Israel; O my love, how comely now; Sing praises Is'rel to the Lord; Song of joy unto the Lord we sing; The beauty, Israel, is gone; When one among the Twelve there was; Who's this, that leaning on her friend. Preces and Psalm 145. **The Clerkes of Oxenford/David Wulstan.** Calliope CAL9611 (12/89).

Alberto Ginastera
Argentinian 1916-1983

Ginastera. Harp Concerto, Op. 25[a].
Glière. Harp Concerto, Op. 74[a]. Concerto for Coloratura Soprano and Orchestra, Op. 82[b].
[b]**Eileen Hulse** (sop); [a]**Rachel Masters** (hp); **City of London Sinfonia/Richard Hickox.**
Chandos CHAN9094. Recorded in 1992.

1h 5m DDD 2/93   **?**

Glière was among the comparatively few front-rank Russian composers who stayed on in their homeland after the 1917 Revolution. The music he composed there adopted a middle-of-the-road conservative style which helped him to steer clear of the more viscous controversies of the 1920s and 1930s. The Concertos for harp and coloratura sorano date from 1938 and 1942 respectively and are unashamedly ingratiating, high-grade mood-music, here played and recorded in a manner that those with a sweet tooth should find absolutely irresistible. The Harp Concerto by the Argentinian Alberto Ginastera is made of sterner stuff, but only slightly — it's Bartókian acerbities are tempered by an engaging Latin American swing. Once again the performance is crisp and bouncy, although in this instance the reverberant recording takes something of the edge off the rhythmic bite.

New review
Ginastera. Cello Sonata, Op. 49[a]. Pampeana No. 2, Op. 21[a]. Triste, Op. 10 No. 2 (trans. Fournier)[a]. Danzas argentinas, Op. 2. Pequeña danza, Op. 8 No. 1. 12 American Preludes,

Op. 12. Piano Sonata No. 1, Op. 22. [a]**Aurora Natola-Ginastera** (vc); **Alberto Portugheis** (pf). ASV CDDCA865.

∴ 1h 18m DDD 10/93

Ginastera's two cello concertos and fantastically difficult cello sonata were written for his wife Aurora Natola, whom he had first met in 1950 when the young virtuoso had won a Buenos Aires award playing his *Pampeana* No. 2. That is a rhapsodic showpiece with several solo cadenzas (beautifully shaped here), and features strongly rhythmic ostinatos of nationalist colouring: similar violently accented repetitive rhythms characterize most of the earlier works for piano here and Alberto Portugheis is brilliantly fiery in all of these, but equally he brings seductive nuances to the languid second Argentine dance, a sensitivity matched by Natola in the affecting short *Triste*. The principal works on this disc are the two sonatas. That for piano (1952) shows some stylistic development in its ghostly flitting scherzo and desolate *Adagio*. Portugheis's reading is suitably intense and, where required, ferociously rhythmic. He has a splendid duo partner in the much later and exceptionally demanding Cello Sonata(1979), the most remarkable movement of which is the palindromic *Presto*, full of bizarre effects that seem to reflect Ginastera's enthusiasm for the paintings of Paul Klee. Outstandingly good recorded quality.

Umberto Giordano

Italian 1867-1948

Giordano. ANDREA CHENIER. **Luciano Pavarotti** (ten) Andrea Chenier; **Leo Nucci** (bar) Gerard; **Montserrat Caballé** (sop) Maddalena; **Kathleen Kuhlmann** (mez) Bersi; **Astrid Varnay** (sop) Countess di Coigny; **Christa Ludwig** (mez) Madelon; **Tom Krause** (bar) Roucher; **Hugues Cuénod** (ten) Fleville; **Neil Howlett** (bar) Fouquier-Tinville, Major-domo; **Giorgio Tadeo** (bass) Mathieu; **Piero De Palma** (ten) Incredible; **Florindo Andreolli** (ten) Abate; **Giuseppe Morresi** (bass) Schmidt; **Ralph Hamer** (bass) Dumas; **Welsh National Opera Chorus; National Philharmonic Orchestra/Riccardo Chailly.** Decca 410 117-2DH2. Notes, text and translation included. From 411 117-1DH3 (11/84). Recorded 1982-84.

∴ ② 1h 47m DDD 2/85

Andrea Chenier, set at the start of the French Revolution, is a potent blend of the social and the emotional. The three main characters, the aristocratic Maddalena, the idealistic poet Chenier and the fiercely republican Gerard, are caught up in a triangle that pits love against conscience, independence against society. The opera has many well-known set numbers and high on any list of favourites must be Chenier's so-called *Improviso* in Act 1 where he bursts out in a spontaneous poem on the power of love, or Maddalena's glorious and moving "La mamma morta" in the Third Act where she describes how her mother gave up her life to save her. Giordano had a real theatrical flair for the 'big moment' and he paces the work masterfully. The tunes seem to flow endlessly from his pen and the characters have real flesh and blood. The cast is strong, with Caballé and Pavarotti making a powerful central pair. Riccardo Chailly conducts the excellent National Philharmonic with flair and feeling and the whole opera is beautifully recorded.

Additional recommendation ...
Soloists; John Alldis Choir; National Philharmonic Orchestra/James Levine. RCA GD82046 — ∴ ② 1h 54m ADD 9/89

Giordano. FEDORA[a]. **Magda Olivero** (sop) Fedora; **Mario del Monaco** (ten) Loris; **Tito Gobbi** (bar) de Siriex; **Leonardo Monreale** (bass) Lorek, Nicola; **Lucia Cappellino** (sop) Olga; **Virgilio Carbonari** (bass) Borov; **Silvio Maionica** (bass) Grech; **Piero de Palma** (ten) Rouvel; **Peter Binder** (bar) Kiril; **Dame Kiri Te Kanawa** (sop) Dmitri; **Riccardo Cassinelli** (ten) Desire; **Athos Cesarini** (ten) Sergio; **Pascal Rogé** (pf) Boleslao Lazinski; **Monte-Carlo Opera Chorus and Orchestra/Lamberto Gardelli.**
Zandonai. FRANCESCA DA RIMINI — excerpts[b]. [c]**Magda Oliviero** (sop) Francesca; [d]**Mario del Monaco** (ten) Paolo; [e]**Annamaria Gasparini** (mez) Biancofiore; [f]**Virgilio Carbonari** (bass) Man-at-arms; [g]**Athos Cesarini** (ten) Archer; **Monte-Carlo Opera Orchestra/Nicola Rescigno.** Decca Grand Opera 433 033-2DM2. Notes, texts and translations included. Item marked [a] from SET435/6 (3/70), [b] SET422 (1/70). Recorded 1969. | 299

Francesca da Rimini: Act 2 — E ancora sgombro il campo del comune? ... Date il segno, Paolo, date ... Un'erba io m'avea, per sanare ... Onta et orrore sopra[cdfg]. Act 3 — No, Smadragedi, no! ... Paolo, datemi pace! ... Ah la parola chi i miei occhi incontrano[cd]. Act 4 — Ora andate ... E così, vada s'è pur mio destino[cde].

② 2h 12m ADD 3/92

Today the name 'Fedora' may suggest a type of hat rather than an opera, but although Giordano was overshadowed by his contemporary Puccini he was a successful composer. *Fedora* is based on a play by Victorien Sardou, the French dramatist whose *La Tosca* provided Puccini with a plot. It is set in the nineteenth century and variously in St Petersburg, Paris and Switzerland, and tells of the tragic love between the Russian Count Loris Ipanov and the Princess Fedora Romazov (Romanov), but to go into further detail of the plot, which disposes of various characters in turn and ends with the heroine herself taking poison, would take up too much space and one admires the booklet writer who has managed to produce a synopsis. *Fedora* has some Trivial Pursuits claim to be the first opera to feature bicycles in the plot! The music is richly textured orchestrally and finely written for the voices, and this recording made in 1969 is notable for the singing of Magda Olivero and Mario del Monaco, who despite being in their mid-fifties bring tremendous verve, vocal resource and dramatic skill to their roles. Tito Gobbi has less to do as the diplomat de Siriex, but gives him character, and another plus is the playing of Pascal Rogé, who performs the non-singing role of the Polish pianist and spy Boleslao Lazinski in Act 2 who, while performing, eavesdrops on a dialogue between Loris and Fedora. This exchange is a marvellous example of verismo writing and singing, and so is their final scene with her death. The set opens with excerpts from another opera, Zandonai's *Francesca da Rimini* with the same two excellent principals. The recordings are as clear and fresh-sounding as they were on the original releases.

Mauro Giuliani
Italian 1781-1829

Giuliani. GUITAR WORKS. **David Starobin.** Bridge BCD9029. Recorded in 1990.
Choix de mes Fleurs chéries, Op. 46 — Le Jasmin; Le Rosmarin; La Rose. Etude in E minor, Op. 100 No. 13. Grande Ouverture, Op. 61. Leçons Progressives, Op. 51 Nos. 3, 7 and 14. Minuetto, Op. 73 No. 9. Preludes, Op. 83 Nos. 5 and 6. Rondeaux Progressives, Op. 14 Nos. 1 and 5. Six Variations, Op. 20. Variazioni sulla Cavatina favorita, "De calma oh ciel", Op. 101.

48m DDD 3/92

Giuliani was born and died in Italy, in between which he lived for many years in Vienna, where he achieved great success in salon-music circles with his guitar virtuosity and counted many distinguished musicians amongst his friends and colleagues. He was in a sense the rival of Sor for the guitar's nineteenth-century crown but the two were 'chalk and cheese'. Giuliani the more volatile, ebullient and (as a composer) loquacious — with over 200 works as against Sor's less than 70. Giuliani's incessant desire to please his public (and to make much-needed money in the process) led to the presence of much treadmill dross amongst the gold of his best works, a thing that has contributed to his chronic undervaluation. David Starobin, playing a nineteenth-century guitar, greatly helps to redress the balance in his unfailingly musical and technically fluent playing of a selection of Giuliani's best works. Some testify to Giuliani's contribution to the student literature, the titles of others reflect the salon tastes at which they were aimed; all show that, when he took the trouble, Giuliani could be charming, polished and ingenious, all at the same time. This is a disc to charm the ear without bruising the emotions, in the nicest possible way.

Further listening ...

CD411 — Duo for flute and guitar. Gran duetto concertante, Op. 52. Grand duo concertant, Op. 85. 12 Ländler samt Coda, Op. 75. Duetinno facile, Op. 77. *CD413* — Grand Pot-pourri, Op. 126. Grand Potpourri, Op. 53. Pièces faciles et agréables, Op. 74. Potpourri tiré de l'Opéra Tancredi, Op. 76. Six Variations, Op. 81. **Mikael Helasvuo** (fl); **Jukka Savijoki** (gtr). BIS CD411 and CD413 (1/91).

Philip Glass

Glass. Itaipúa. The Canyon. **Atlanta Symphony ᵃChorus and Orchestra/Robert Shaw.** Sony Classical SK46352.

·ᵉ **56m DDD ll/93**

The idea of spacious natural vistas has always been central to the work of Philip Glass. *Itaipú* and *The Canyon* are the second and third of his "portraits of nature". *Itaipú* is located on the Paraná River, which in turn forms the border between Brazil and Paraguay. It is the location of a massive hydro-electric dam with individual generators large enough to house a full symphony orchestra. So it's little wonder that *Itaipú* provided Glass with instant inspiration. The score itself is divided into four separate sections and calls on substantial orchestral and choral forces. The hub of the work — "The Dam" itself — is in the third movement, where from 6'05" onwards, brass and winds abet a pounding ostinato and a series of modulations redolent of such scenically aware late-romantics as Sibelius, Bruckner and Roy Harris. It's one of the most arresting passages in Glass's output and gives a vivid impression of the dam's overwhelming physical presence. *The Canyon* is purely orchestral, much shorter, less heavily scored than *Itaipú*, and utilizes a large array of percussion, which Glass exploits with his usual ear for nuance. The recordings are cleanly balanced, the performances neat. Recommended, especially to those not normally 'behind Glass'.

Glass. HYDROGEN JUKEBOX. **Allen Ginsberg** (narr); **Vocal Ensemble** (Elizabeth Futral, Michele Eaton, sops; Mary Ann Hart, mez; Richard Fracker, ten; Gregory Purnhagen, Nathaniel Watson, bars); **Carol Wincenc** (fl); **Andrew Sterman** (sax/bass cl); **Richard Peck** (sax); **Frank Cassara, James Pugliese** (perc); **Philip Glass** (pf)/**Martin Goldray** (keybds). Elektra Nonesuch 7559-79286-2. Texts included. Recorded 1992-93.

·ᵉ **lh l3m DDD l/94**

This is 'standard' Glass through and through, vital, rhythmically pungent and — in this instance — hauntingly supportive of a writer whom Norman Mailer once described as "himself a United States of America, teaming, sprawling, uneven ..." — Allen Ginsberg. So what exactly is on offer? Well, among much else, there's a highly percussive, multi-denominational protest about Middle Eastern tensions, a "happy birthday" for a much-loved friend, a kaleidoscopic, trans-American journey, a heart-felt indictment of modern man's relative soullessness (from "Howl" — Ginsberg's most famous single poem), a visit to a "Cabin in the Woods", a wishful pilgrimage in search of gay love and, to end, a simple, six-part *a cappella* chorus on the death of Ginsberg's father. Neither chamber opera nor musical, song cycle nor pop 'concept' album, *Hydrogen Jukebox* is all of these plus a useful resumé of insights, revelations and misconceptions that helped father the thinking of an entire generation. And that it succeeds without the aid of pop nostalgia says something both for the strength of Ginsberg's poetry and the suggestive power of Glass's music. Recording, performance and presentation (with full texts included) are state-of-the-art.

Further listening ...

String Quartet No. 1. *Coupled with* **Barber.** String Quartet, Op. 11. **Dvořák.** String Quartet No. 12 in F major, B179. **Duke Quartet.** Collins Classics 1386-2 (1/94).

"Low" Symphony. **Brooklyn Philharmonic Orchestra/Dennis Russell Davies.** Point Music 438 150-2PTH (5/93).

Metamorphosis. Mad rush. Wichita vortex sutra. **Philip Glass** (pf). CBS CD45576 (3/90).

AKHNATEN. **Soloists; Stuttgart State Opera Chorus and Orchestra/Dennis Russell Davies.** CBS Masterworks CD42457 (2/88).

ANIMA MUNDI. **Jeannie Gagné, Dora Ohrenstein** (sops); **Patricia Dunham, Linda November** (mezzos); **David Düsing, David Frye** (tens); **Alexander Blachly, Bruce Rodgers** (bars); **orchestra/Michael Riesman.** Elektra Nonesuch 7559-79329-2 (1/94).

EINSTEIN ON THE BEACH. **Soloists; Philip Glass Ensemble/Michael Riesman.** CBS CD38875 (9/86).

SATYAGRAHA. **NYC Opera Chorus and Orchestra/Christopher Keene.** CBS CD39672 (9/86).

Alexander Glazunov
Russian 1865-1936

Glazunov. Violin Concerto in A minor, Op. 82[a].
Prokofiev. Violin Concerto No. 2 in G minor, Op. 63[b].
Sibelius. Violin Concerto in D major, Op. 47[c]. **Jascha Heifetz** (vn); [a]**RCA Victor Symphony Orchestra/Walter Hendl;** [b]**Boston Symphony Orchestra/Charles Münch;** [c]**Chicago Symphony Orchestra/Walter Hendl.** RCA Red Seal RD87019. Items marked [ab] from GL89833 (9/86), [c] GL89832 (9/86).

lh 9m ADD 10/86

Here are three great concertos on one CD, all of them classics which have never been equalled, let alone surpassed. Heifetz made the première recording of all three concertos in the 1930s and his interpretations have particular authority. The recordings here were all issued in the early 1960s and in their digital refurbishment sound remarkably good. Heifetz's golden tone shines more brightly than ever and his technical virtuosity and profound musicianship remain dazzling. The performances can only be described as stunning and they remain an indispensable part of any collection.

Additional recommendations ...
Violin Concerto[a]. The Seasons — ballet, Op. 67. [a]**Oscar Shumsky** (vn); **Scottish National Orchestra/Neeme Järvi.** Chandos CHAN8596 — 57m DDD 3/89
Violin Concerto[a]. *Prokofiev. Violin Concerto No. 1 in D major, Op. 19[a]. Shchedrin. Stihira.* [a]**Anne-Sophie Mutter** (vn); **Washington National Symphony Orchestra/Mstislav Rostropovich.** Erato 2292-45343-2 — lh 4m DDD 3/89
Violin Concerto. *Shostakovich. Violin Concerto No. 1 in A minor, Op. 99.* **Itzhak Perlman** (vn); **Israel Philharmonic Orchestra/Zubin Mehta.** EMI CDC7 49814-2 — 55m DDD 1/90
Violin Concerto. *Dvořák. Violin Concerto in A minor, B108.* **Frank Peter Zimmermann** (vn); **London Philharmonic Orchestra/Franz Welser-Möst.** EMI CDC7 54872-2 — 52m DDD 3/94
Violin Concerto[b]. *Mazurka-Oberek[c]. Chausson. Poème, Op. 25[a]. Ravel. Tzigane[a]. Kabalevsky.* Violin Concerto[d]. **David Oistrakh** (vn); [a]**Moscow State Symphony Orchestra/Kyrill Kondrashin;** USSR State Orchestra/[b]**Kondrashin,** [d]**Dmitry Kabalevsky;** [c]**USSR Radio Symphony Orchestra/Gabril Yudin.** Monitor Collectors Series mono MCD72073 (*see review in the Collections section; refer to the Index to Reviews*) — lh 12m AAD

Glazunov. The seasons — ballet, Op. 67.
Tchaikovsky. The Nutcracker — ballet, Op. 71[a]. [a]**Finchley Children's Music Group; Royal Philharmonic Orchestra/Vladimir Ashkenazy.** Decca 433 000-2DH2. Recorded 1989-90.

② **2h llm DDD 4/92**

One cannot think of a happier coupling than Glazunov's complete *Seasons* — perhaps his finest and most successful score — with Tchaikovsky's *Nutcracker*. Glazunov's delightful ballet, with even the winter's "Frost", "Hail", "Ice" and "Snow", glamorously presented, and the bitterness of a Russian winter quite forgotten are, like the scenario of the *Nutcracker*, part of a child's fantasy world, for Tchaikovsky too, in Act 2, has a wintry fairy scene and a delectable "Waltz of the snowflakes" (featuring children's wordless chorus). Glazunov's twinklingly dainty scoring of the picturesque snowy characters is contrasted with the glowing summer warmth of the "Waltz of the cornflowers and poppies", and the vigorously thrusting tune (perhaps the most memorable theme he ever wrote) of the Autumn "Bacchanale". Tchaikovsky's ballet opens with a children's Christmas party with the guests arriving, presents distributed and family dancing, in which everyone joins. Ashkenazy captures the atmosphere very engagingly; then night falls, the church clock outside strikes midnight and the magic begins. The drama of the spectacular mock battle between good and evil, the children's journey through the pine forest (to one of Tchaikovsky's most ravishing tunes) and the famous multi-coloured characteristic dances of the Act 2 Divertis-sement are all beautifully played by the RPO. There is much finesse and sparkle, and the lightest and most graceful rhythmic touch from Ashkenazy: the conductor's affection for the score and his feeling for Tchaikovsky's multi-hued orchestral palette is a constant delight to the ear. Yet the big *Pas de deux* brings a climax of Russian fervour. The recording is properly expansive here; made at Walthamstow, it sets everything within a glowing acoustic ambience. *The seasons* was recorded in Watford Town Hall, and again the ear is seduced by the aural richness and the glowing woodwind detail. The one minor drawback is that in the *Nutcracker* the cueing is not generous and the action not precisely related to the narrative detail. But in every other respect this is marvellous entertainment.

Additional recommendation ...
The Seasons. Scènes de Ballet in A major, Op. 52. **Minnesota Orchestra/Edo de Waart.** Telarc CD80347 — .•˙ Ih 6m DDD 12/93

Glazunov. SYMPHONIES. **USSR Ministry of Culture State Symphony Orchestra/ Gennadi Rozhdestvensky.** Olympia OCD100/1.
OCD100 — No. 1 in E major, Op. 5, "Slavyanskaya"; No. 7 in F major, Op. 77, "Pastoral'naya".
OCD101 — No. 4 in E flat major, Op. 48; No. 5 in B flat major, Op. 55.

.•˙ ② Ih 10m Ih 10m ADD 8/86 ⁹ₚ ❓

It is always easy to underestimate the Glazunov symphonies. There is no doubt that this set of performances from Rozhdestvensky and the splendid orchestra, give them a 'new look'. There is a sophistication in the playing to match the elegance of Glazunov's often highly engaging wind scoring — especially in the scherzos, always Glazunov's best movements — but there is a commitment and vitality too, which makes all the music spring readily to life. In Rozhdest-vensky's hands the fine *Adagio* of No. 1 sounds remarkably mature while the *Andante* movements of Nos. 5 and 7 are romantically expansive in a very appealing way. The Fourth Symphony is a highly inventive piece throughout and held together by a moto theme; and the better-known Fifth does not disappoint when the presentation is so persuasive. On both discs the recording is brightly lit without being too brittle, and has plenty of fullness too. For anyone looking for new nineteenth-century symphonies to explore, this would be a good place to start.

Additional recommendations ...
Nos. 1 and 5. **Bavarian Radio Symphony Orchestra/Neeme Järvi.** Orfeo C093101A —
.•˙ Ih 6m DDD 9/87
No. 8 in E flat major, Op. 83. Ouverture solennelle, Op. 73. Wedding procession, Op. 21. **Bavarian Radio Symphony Orchestra/Neeme Järvi.** Orfeo C093201A — .•˙ 56m DDD 1987
No. 2 in F sharp minor, Op. 16. Concert Waltz No. 1 in D major, Op. 47. **Bamberg Symphony Orchestra/Neeme Järvi.** Orfeo C148101A — .•˙ 50m DDD II/90
Nos. 4 and 7. **Bamberg Symphony Orchestra/Neeme Järvi.** Orfeo C148201A — .•˙ Ih 6m DDD II/90
No. 6 in C minor, Op. 58. Lyric Poem, Op. 12. **Bamberg Symphony Orchestra/Neeme Järvi.** Orfeo C157201A — .•˙ 53m DDD II/90
No. 3 in D major, Op. 33. Concert Waltz No. 2 in F major, Op. 51. **Bamberg Symphony Orchestra/Neeme Järvi.** Orfeo C157201A — .•˙ 47m DDD II/90

New review
Glazunov. PIANO MUSIC, Volume 1. **Tatyana Franová** (pf). Marco Polo 8 223151.
Suite on the name "Sacha", Op. 2. Two Pieces, Op. 22. Waltzes on the Theme "Sabela",

Op. 23. Three Etudes, Op. 31. Petite Valse, Op. 36. Nocturne, Op. 37. Grande valse de concert in E flat major, Op. 41. Three Miniatures, Op. 42. Prelude and Two Mazurkas, Op. 25.

.⁛ **1h 9m DDD 7/93** ❓

Glazunov may have possessed a fundamentally conservative nature but, as this first volume in Tatyana Franová's complete cycle of the piano music shows, he had all sorts of delectable, cosmopolitan as well as ultra-Russian tricks up his sleeve. In the dazzling *Valse Allegro* from the *Suite on the name "Sacha"* there is more than a touch of Saint-Saëns's glitter and urbanity; of a *Valse en forme d'étude*, so to speak. All lovers of virtuoso *bonnes bouches* will fall for this, rejoicing in whirling cross-accentuation and page after page of flashing intricacy. Other favourites will surely include the *Grande valse de concert* (which Moiseiwitsch used to play with such matchless elegance), alive with all of Glazunov's balletic charm and complete with a whirl-away coda guaranteed to leave even the most skilled ballroom dancer breathless. The *Three Etudes* are similarly attractive, their succulent melodic life elaborated with style and ingenuity. Such conversational brio is less evident in the two Mazurkas — an indigenous genre if ever there was one — and it has to be said that much of the playing, particularly in the more reflective numbers, is proficient rather than ardently committed. Nevertheless, Franová can certainly get around, and although the recordings are hardly flattering there are enough gems scattered throughout to provide a field day for seekers of unusual encores.

Additional recommendation ...

Piano Sonatas — No. 1 in B flat minor, Op. 74; No. 2 in E flat major, Op. 75. Three Etudes, Op. 31. Grand valse de concert. **Massimilliano Damerini** (pf). Etcetera KTC1118 — .⁛ 1h 15m DDD 2/93 ❓

Further listening ...

Violin Concerto in A minor, Op. 82[a]. Piano Concerto No. 2 in B major, Op. 100[b]. Saxophone Concerto in E flat major, Op. 109[c]. [a]**Sergei Stadler** (vn); [b]**Dmitri Alexeev** (pf); [c]**Lev Mikhailov** (sax); [a]**Leningrad Philharmonic Orchestra/Vladimir Ponkin**; [b]**USSR Radio Symphony Orchestra/Yuri Nikolaevsky**; [c]**USSR Radio Symphony Orchestra Soloists Ensemble/Alexander Korneiev.** Olympia OCD165 (2/90).

From the middle ages, Op. 79. Scènes de ballet, Op. 52. *Coupled with* **Liadov.** A musical snuffbox, Op. 31. **Scottish National Orchestra/Neeme Järvi.** Chandos CHAN8804 (10/90).

Chant du ménéstrel, Op. 71. *Coupled with* **Kabalevsky.** Cello Concerto No. 2. in C major, Op. 77. **Khachaturian.** Cello Concerto. **Raphael Wallfisch** (vc); **London Philharmonic Orchestra/Bryden Thomson.** Chandos CHAN8579 (6/88).

The sea — fantasy, Op. 28. Spring, Op. 34. *Coupled with* **Kalinnikov.** Symphony No. 1 in G minor. **Scottish National Orchestra/Neeme Järvi.** Chandos CHAN8611 (10/88).

Reyngol'd Glière

Russian 1875-1956

New review

Glière. Symphony No. 1 in E flat major, Op. 8. The Red Poppy — Ballet Suite, Op. 70. **BBC Philharmonic Orchestra/Sir Edward Downes.** Chandos CHAN9160.

.⁛ **1h 1m DDD 7/93**

Glière's First Symphony is no better or worse than one might expect of a gifted, well-taught 25-year-old Russian in 1900. The first movement works its Borodin-derived material to death, the 5/4 scherzo is more than a touch mechanical, and good, clean fun is about the most the finale aspires to. But anyone who has invested in the Second and Third Symphonies in this cycle (which really *are* worth hearing) will want to add the First, if only to see where Glière's musical roots were. *The Red Poppy* was the Soviet Union's first 'successful' ballet (it appeared in 1927), and if its material now sounds rather 'by the yard' it does at least include the splendidly uninhibited Russian Sailors' Dance, based on the famous "Little Apple" folksong, as a crowd-pleasing finale. It also has a few unexpected reminders of the Wagner-cum-Rachmaninov style Glière more or less had to abandon after the Revolution.

Glière. Symphony No. 3 in B minor, Op. 42, "Il'ya Mouromets". **Royal Philharmonic Orchestra/Harold Farberman.** Unicorn-Kanchana Souvenir UKCD2014/5. From PCM500-1 (8/79). Recorded in 1978.

② 1h 33m DDD 3/89

What happened to the Russian symphony between Tchaikovsky and Shostakovich? Scriabin and Rachmaninov were active of course, plus the solidly respectable Glazunov. But there was another distinctive voice, one whose interest lay in blending the heroic-saga tone of Borodin with the orchestral opulence of Wagner. This was Reyngol'd Glière, and his Third Symphony of 1912 is his undoubted masterpiece. It is a supremely late-romantic technicolour score, extreme but never uncontrolled in its excess, and always directed towards vividness of narrative rather than self-display. Now usually performed without the once-standard cuts, its four movements are fairly protracted, the more so when taken at exceptionally spacious tempos as they are here by Harold Farberman (other more recent uncut recordings have clocked in at single-CD duration). But the spaciousness proves the making of the piece, giving the dimensions a truly epic feel and developing an unstoppable slow momentum. The recording quality no longer quite seems to justify the 'demonstration-class' praise originally accorded it, but it is still impressive enough.

Additional recommendations ...

No. 3. **BBC Philharmonic Orchestra/Sir Edward Downes.** Chandos CHAN9041 — 1h 18m DDD 5/92

No. 3. **Czech Radio Symphony Orchestra/Donald Johanos.** Naxos 8 550858 — 1h 16m DDD 2/94

No. 3. *Loeffler.* A Pagan Poem, Op. 14[a]. [a]**Houston Symphony Orchestra;** [b]**Leopold Stokowski Symphony Orchestra/Leopold Stokowski.** EMI Matrix CDM5 65074-2 — 1h 2m ADD 7/94 ▲

Further listening ...

Symphony No. 2 in C minor, Op. 25. The Zaporozhy Cossacks, Op. 64. **BBC Philharmonic Orchestra/Sir Edward Downes.** Chandos CHAN9071 (7/92).

Concerto for Coloratura Soprano, Op. 82[a]. Harp Concerto, Op. 74[b]. *Coupled with* **Ginastera.** Harp Concerto, Op. 25[b]. [a]**Eileen Hulse** (sop); [b]**Rachel Masters** (hp); **City of London Sinfonia/Richard Hickox.** Chandos CHAN9094. *See review under Ginastera; refer to the Index to Reviews.*

Mikhail Ivanovich Glinka
Russian 1804-1857

Suggested listening ...

A LIFE FOR THE TSAR. **Soloists; Sofia National Opera Chorus and Festival Orchestra/Emil Tchakarov.** Sony Classical SK46487 (9/91).

Albert Glinsky
American 1952-

Suggested listening ...

Toccata-Scherzo. *Coupled with* **Corigliano.** Violin Sonata. **Pärt.** Fratres. **Moravec.** Violin Sonata. **Messiaen.** Quatuor pour la fin du temps — Louange à l'Eternité de Jésus. **Maria**

Bachmann (vn); **Jon Klibonoff** (pf). Catalyst 09026 61824-2 (12/93). *See review under Corigliano; refer to the Index to Reviews.*

Christoph Gluck

Bohemian 1714-1787

New review

Gluck. ORFEO ED EURIDICE. **Derek Lee Ragin** (alto) Orfeo; **Sylvia McNair** (sop) Euridice; **Cyndia Sieden** (sop) Amore; **Monteverdi Choir; English Baroque Soloists/ John Eliot Gardiner.** Philips 434 093-2PH2. Notes, text and translation included. Recorded in 1991.

② 1h 29m DDD 2/94

This new version of *Orfeo*, played on period instruments and following the original text, has a degree of spiritual force to which other recordings scarcely aspire, and that is to the credit primarily of the conductor, John Eliot Gardiner. It begins with a taut, almost explosive account of the overture, moves to a deeply sombre opening chorus and then a *ballo* of intense expressiveness, finely and carefully moulded phrases (but plenty of air between them) and a lovely translucent orchestral sound. Every one of the numerous dances in this set, in fact, is the subject of thoughtful musical characterization, shapely execution and refined timing of detail. Derek Lee Ragin excels himself as Orpheus; the sound is often very beautiful, the phrasing quite extraordinarily supple and responsive for a counter-tenor voice. Eurydice is sung clearly and truly, and with due passion, by Sylvia McNair — she delivers "Che fiero momento" and some of the recitative, with considerable force — and the casting of Cyndia Sieden, with her rather pert, forward voice, as Amore is very successful. This is, as a total interpretation of the work, more penetrating than any other in the catalogue.

Additional recommendations ...
Orfeo ed Euridice. **Soloists; Ghent Collegium Vocale; La Petite Bande/Sigiswald Kuijken.** Accent ACC48223/4D — ② 1h 46m ADD 1/90
Orfeo ed Euridice. Orphée et Eurydice — *Air de furies; Ballet des ombres heureuses; Air vif; Menuet; Chaconne.* **Soloists; Berlin Radio Chorus; Carl Philipp Emanuel Bach Chamber Orchestra/Hartmut Haenchen.** Capriccio 60 008-2 — ② 1h 54m DDD 1/90
Orfeo ed Euridice. **Soloists; Stuttgart Chamber Choir; Tafelmusik/Frieder Bernius.** Sony Classical Vivarte SX2K48040 — ② 1h 23m DDD 8/92
Orphée et Euridice. **Soloists; Robert Blanchard Vocal Ensemble; Lamoureux Orchestra/Hans Rosbaud.** Philips Opera Collector mono 434 784-2PM2 — ② 1h 55m ADD 5/93 ▲
Orphée et Euridice. **Soloists; Glyndebourne Chorus; London Philharmonic Orchestra/Raymond Leppard.** Erato Libretto 2292-45864-2 — ② 2h 7m DDD 5/93

Gluck. IPHIGENIE EN AULIDE. **Lynne Dawson** (sop) Iphigénie; **José van Dam** (bass) Agamemnon; **Anne Sofie von Otter** (mez) Clytemnestre; **John Aler** (ten) Achille; **Bernard Deletré** (bass) Patrocle; **Gilles Cachemaille** (bass) Calchas; **René Schirrer** (bass) Arcas; **Guillemette Laurens** (mez) Diane; **Ann Monoyios** (sop) First Greek woman, Slave; **Isabelle Eschenbrenner** (sop) Second Greek woman; **Monteverdi Choir; Lyon Opéra Orchestra/ John Eliot Gardiner.** Erato 2292-45003-2. Notes, text and translation included. Recorded in 1987.

② 2h 12m DDD 6/90

Gluck's first reform opera for Paris has tended to be overshadowed by his other *Iphigénie*, the *Tauride* one. But it does contain some superb things, of which perhaps the finest are the great monologues for Agamemnon. On this recording, José van Dam starts a little coolly; but this only adds force to his big moment at the end of the second act where he tussles with himself over the sacrifice of his daughter and — contemplating her death and the screams of the vengeful Eumenides — decides to flout the gods and face the consequences. To this he rises in noble fashion, fully conveying the agonies Agamemnon suffers. The cast in general is strong. Lynne Dawson brings depth of expressive feeling to all she does and her Iphigénie, marked by a slightly grainy sound and much intensity, is very moving. John Aler's Achille too is very fine, touching off the lover and the hero with equal success, singing both with ardour and vitality.

There is great force too in the singing of Anne Sofie von Otter as Clytemnestre, especially in her outburst "Ma fille!" as she imagines her daughter on the sacrificial altar. John Eliot Gardiner's Monteverdi Choir sing with polish, perhaps seeming a little genteel for a crowd of angry Greek soldiers baying for Iphigénie's blood. But Gardiner gives a duly urgent account of the score, pressing it forward eagerly and keeping the tension at a high level even in the dance music. A period-instrument orchestra might have added a certain edge and vitality but this performance wants nothing in authority or drama and can be securely recommended.

Additional recommendation ...
Soloists; Chorus and Orchestra of La Scala, Milan/Riccardo Muti. Sony Classical S2K52492 — .·' ② 1h 57m DDD ♀ₚ

Further listening ...

LE CINESI — *opera-serenade*. **Kaaren Erickson** (sop) Sivene; **Alexandrina Milcheva** (contr) Lisinga; **Marga Schiml** (contr) Tangia; **Thomas Moser** (ten) Silango; **Munich Radio Orchestra/Lamberto Gardelli.** Orfeo C178891A (1/90).

DON JUAN. SEMIRAMIS. **Tafelmusik/Bruno Weil.** Sony Classical SK53119 (10/93).

PARIDE ED ELENA. **Soloists; La Stagione Vocal Ensemble; La Statione/Michael Schneider.** Capriccio 60 027-2 (6/93).

ALCESTE. **Soloists; Bavarian Radio Chorus; Bavarian Radio Symphony Orchestra/ Serge Baudo.** Orfeo C027823F (6/87).

IPHIGENIE EN TAURIDE. **Soloists; Monteverdi Choir; Lyon Opera Orchestra/John Eliot Gardiner.** Philips 416 148-2PH2 (6/86).

Leopold Godowsky

Polish/American 1870-1938

Suggested listening ...

Grand Sonata in E minor. **Geoffrey Douglas Madge** (pf). Dante PSG890-7.

3 Studies on Chopin Etudes — Nos. 1-25. **Geoffrey Douglas Madge** (pf). Dante PSG8903/4

53 Studies on Chopin Etudes — Nos. 26-48. **Geoffrey Douglas Madge** (pf). Dante PSG8905/6.

Triakontameron (30 moods and scenes in triple time). **Geoffrey Douglas Madge** (pf). Dante PSG9009.

Piano Transcriptions: Passacaglia. Triakontameron — Alt Wien. *Coupled with* **Schubert.** Die schöne Müllerin, D795 — Das Wandern; Ungeduld. Winterreise, D911 — Gute Nacht. Rosamunde — Ballet Music. Moments musicaux, D780 — No. 3 in F minor. **Weber.** Invitation to the dance, J260. **J. Strauss II.** Kunstlerleben, Op. 316. **Rian De Waal.** Hyperion CDA66496 (3/92).

Alexander Goehr

British 1932-

Goehr. Sing, Ariel, Op. 51[a]. The Mouse Metamorphosed into a Maid, Op. 54. **Lucy Shelton,** [a]**Eileen Hulse,** [a]**Sarah Leonard** (sops); [a]**Ensemble** (David White, bass cl/sax; John Wallace,

tpt; Marcia Crayford, vn/va; Chi-Chi Nwanoku, db; Ian Brown, pf)/**Oliver Knussen**.
Unicorn-Kanchana DKPCD9129. Texts included.

lh 5m   DDD   9/93

Frank Kermode's text for the song-cycle *Sing, Ariel* is an achievement in itself: fragments of
Auden, Shakespeare, Yeats, Pound, Hardy, Wallace Stevens and more, so artfully drawn
together that they constantly throw new lights on each other, and at the heart, a fine piece of
late Larkin — gloomy, growingly apprehensive and then, at the climax, a breathtaking
surprise. Line after line seems rich in musical possibilities. In other words, it's a gift for a
composer. So what does the recipient of this gift, Alexander Goehr, make of it? The answer
comes as rather a surprise in these times of instant-access new music: Goehr's *Sing, Ariel* is a
piece of almost bewildering richness, like a garden that offers too many paths and shifting
perspectives to be comprehended in one round trip. But it's precisely that which draws the
ear back — that, and the sheer beauty of some passages. So often in contemporary vocal
works the voice writing is the least memorable facet. But in *Sing, Ariel* soprano phrases fix
themselves in the memory — the core of the expression, and of the melodic writing, is there.
The performers must take their share of the credit. Lucy Shelton responds to expressive
nuances and the rise and fall of the phrases as though she'd been immersed in *Sing, Ariel* for
years, and the instrumentalists under Oliver Knussen respond like a single, sensitive
accompanist. Shelton shines again in the unaccompanied *The Mouse Metamorphosed into a Maid*
— not as repeatable as *Sing, Ariel*, perhaps, but still a *tour de force* of singing and writing.
Excellent recordings.

Key to symbols

Quality of sound	Discs worth exploring	Caveat emptor

Quality of performance   Basic library   Period performance

New review
Goehr. The Death of Moses, Op. 53. **Sarah Leonard** (sop); **Michael Chance** (alto);
Gautam Rangarajan (ten); **Stephen Richardson** (bar); **Paul Robinson** (bass); **Sawston
Village College Chamber Choir; Cambridge University Musical Society Chorus;
instrumental ensemble/Stephen Cleobury.** Unicorn-Kanchana DKPCD9146. Text
included. Recorded in 1993.

55m   DDD   9/93

To Alexander Goehr, the Jewish Patriarch's refusal to die symbolizes his people's determined
survival through the violence of the ages, culminating in the Holocaust. Goehr's musical
response to the selected Hebrew verse narratives is highly original — not *personal* though, for
this is a work in which personal involvement in the romantic sense is minimal. The argument is
ritualized, the expression restrained, the harmonic/melodic language modal, though not tonal.
The sound world is a kind of electronic age Monteverdi — saxophones in place of cornets,
flutes, trombones, and a fascinating re-realization of the lute-saturated continuo sound of
Monteverdi's operas: electronic organ, harp, bass guitar. Its hieratic, expressively restrained
manner recalls late Stravinsky, though with touches of Schoenberg here and there. But this is no
remnant of new music long past. Formalized, even cool though it may sometimes seem, *The
Death of Moses* can be eloquent, the word-setting highly sensitive. Performances are generally
impressive. This is a courageous issue; it is unlikely to be another Górecki Third Symphony, but
is it only the easily accessible countries that are worth visiting?

Further listening ...

Metamorphosis/Dance, Op. 36. Romanza, Op. 24[a]. [a]**Moray Welsh** (vc); **Royal Liverpool
Philharmonic Orchestra/David Atherton.** Unicorn-Kanchana Souvenir UKCD2039 (7/91).

... a musical offering (J. S. B. 1985) ..., Op. 46. Behold the Sun, Op. 44*a*[a]. Lyric Pieces, Op. 35. Sinfonia, Op. 42. [a]**Jeanine Thames** (sop); [a]**James Holland** (vib); **London Sinfonietta/Oliver Knussen.** Unicorn-Kanchana DKPCD9102 (11/91).

Hermann Goetz

German 1840-1876

Suggested listening ...

Sonata in G minor, Op. 17. *Coupled with* **Fibich.** Sonata in B flat major, Op. 28. *Moscheles.* Grande Sonate in E flat major, Op. 47. **Anthony Goldstone, Caroline Clemmow** (pf duet). Meridian CDE84237 (7/93). *See review under Fibich; refer to the Index to Reviews.*

Károly Goldmark

Austrian/Hungarian 1830-1915

Suggested listening ...

Violin Concerto No. 1 in A minor, Op. 28[a]. *Coupled with* **Paganini.** Violin Concerto No. 1 in E flat major, Op. 6[b]. [a]**Alberto Kocsis,** [b]**Mária Bálint** (vns); [a]**Savaria Symphony Orchestra/János Petró;** [b]**Budapest Symphony Orchestra/György Lehel.** Hungaroton White Label HRC162 (3/94).

Rustic Wedding Symphony, Op. 26. Sakuntula Overture, Op. 13. **Royal Philharmonic Orchestra/Yondani Butt.** ASV CDDCA791 (5/92).

DIE KONIGIN VON SABA. **Soloists; Hungarian State Orchestra/Adám Fischer.** Hungaroton HCD12179/81 (6/86).

Berthold Goldschmidt

German 1903-

New review

Goldschmidt. DER GEWALTIGE HAHNREI[a]. Mediterranean Songs[b]. [a]**Roberta Alexander** (sop) Stella; [a]**Robert Wörle** (ten) Bruno; [a]**Michael Kraus** (ten) Petrus; [a]**Claudio Otelli** (bar) Ochsenhirt; [a]**Helen Lawrence** (sop) Mémé; [a]**Martin Petzold** (ten) Estrugo; [a]**Erich Wottrich** (ten) Young Man; [a]**Marita Posselt** (sop) Cornelie; [a]**Christiane Berggold** (mez) Florence; [a]**Franz-Josef Kapellmann** (bass) Gendarme; [a]**Berlin Radio Chorus;** [a]**Berlin Deutsches Symphony Orchestra;** [b]**John Mark Ainsley** (ten); [b]**Leipzig Gewandhaus Orchestra/Lothar Zagrosek.** Decca Entartete Musik 440 850-2DHO2. Notes, texts and translations included.

② 2h 5m DDD 3/94

There are two causes for rejoicing here. Firstly that Berthold Goldschmidt's *Der gewaltige Hahnrei* ("The magnificent cuckold") has been rediscovered at last; after its successful première in Mannheim in 1932, it and its composer's career were victims of the rise of the Nazis. Secondly and more importantly, the opera is masterly. In its vivid characterization, its dramatic use of pungent orchestral colour and sinewy counterpoint and its gripping narrative thrust it is an achievement all the more remarkable for a first opera by a composer then in his twenties. The central character, Bruno, is a man so jealous of his submissive, adoring wife that he compels her to commit adultery and ends by forcing her into the arms of a would-be rapist. Goldschmidt's language is tonal but bony; those who know the music of his teacher Schreker may hear echoes of it; others may detect an occasional kinship (scarcely attributable to influence) with Weill, Shostakovich or Prokofiev. But it is undoubtedly a personal voice, and the assurance of his style is almost as impressive a feature of this opera as its swift-moving, murderously ironic dramaturgy.

So often when a work of real quality is rediscovered one has to make a few apologies for the performance. Not in this case. Alexander sings her heart out as the cruelly treated Stella, and as a result quite avoids the risk that she will appear a mere faceless victim. Wörle, very properly a Loge rather than a Siegfried, acts shrewdly as well as singing incisively. It is a tribute as much to Goldschmidt as to the singers to say that even in quite brief roles they all make very positive contributions to the drama. Each of them is there for a purpose, and so is the pithily characterful music given to each of them. The concise economy of this opera is one of the reasons for its power. The *Mediterranean Songs* date from nearly 30 years later, and for those encountering Goldschmidt's music for the first time they will be an encouraging indication that three decades of neglect had not soured his lyricism. They are rich and delicate, eloquent evocations of the Mediterranean world, scored with great refinement and with vocal lines of a grateful amplitude. Ainsley sings them beautifully, with care for words (Goldschmidt sets English as eloquently as he does German) as well as smoothness of line. Zagrosek is throughout a powerful advocate for Goldschmidt's music, sensitive to its poignancy (the end of the opera is quite haunting) as well as its formidable strength. A major rediscovery, and all those involved seem urgently convinced of it.

Further listening ...

String Quartets[a] — No. 2; No. 3. Belsatzar[d]. Letzte Kapitel[bcd]. [a]**Mandelring Quartet;** [b]**Jörg Gottschick** (narr); [c]**Alan Marks** (pf); [d]**Berlin Ars Nova Ensemble/Peter Schwarz.** Largo 5115 (11/91).

Jerry Goldsmith

American 1929-

Suggested listening ...

Legend — *original film soundtrack.* **National Philharmonic Orchestra/Jerry Goldsmith.** Silva Screen FILMCD045 (5/93).

Rudy — *original film soundtrack.* Varèse Sarabande VSD5446 (6/94).

Lionheart — *original film soundtrack.* Varèse Sarabande VSD5484.

Nicolas Gombert

Flanders c.1495-c.1560

Suggested listening ...

Music from the Court of Charles V — Missa Tempore paschali. Regina caeli. In te Domine speravi. Media vita. Tous les regretz. Je prens congie. Magnificat Secundi toni. **Huelgas Ensemble/ Paul van Nevel.** Sony Classical Vivarte SK48249 (4/93).

Henryk Górecki

Polish 1933-

New review

Górecki. Symphony No. 2, "Copernican", Op. 31[a]. Beatus vir, Op. 38. [a]**Emese Soós** (sop); **Tamás Altorjay** (bar); **Bartók Chorus; Fricsay Symphonic Orchestra/Tamás Pál.** Stradivarius STR33324.

53m DDD 7/94

There can be no doubt that Górecki's *Copernican Symphony* — one of his first 'reductionist' works — is far nearer the world of the now-ubiquitous Third than to the more obviously 'modernist' (that is, Lutoslawski-inspired) First. Not that you'd guess from the Symphony's opening, a dense, grey, insistently forceful onslaught, pounding on the walls of the Universe with big drums and impenetrable tone clusters. That's more or less the story of the first movement; but then the quiet, low-lying second (about "the sun, the moon and the stars") summons familiar, signalling piano chords and a harmonic language that anticipates the serene sensuality of the Third Symphony's second and third movements. Resting finally in A flat, the Second Symphony makes resourceful use of soprano, baritone and chorus. The performance itself seems fairly committed and the recording is texturally warm although revealing occasional instances of suspect tuning. *Beatus vir* is one of Górecki's most accessible scores. It starts dramatically in C minor — the initial shock almost matches that of the *Copernican*'s opening sequence — then summons a baritone soloist for a chant-like vocal line set to a warm, slowly pulsating accompaniment. Although Nikita Storojev (the soloist on the disc listed below) has the surer vocal technique, with a far better focused recording, Tamás Altorjay's more lyrical voice better suits the role of priestly commentator. Again, the sound is pleasantly warm. A valuable and rewarding coupling.

Additional recommendation ...
Old Polish music, Op. 24[a]. Totus tuus, Op. 60[b]. Beatus vir[c]. [c]**Nikita Storojev** (bass); [bc]**Prague Philharmonic Choir,** [ac]**Czech Philharmonic Orchestra/John Nelson.** Argo 436 835-2ZH — .•' lh 8m DDD 4/93

Górecki. Symphony No. 3, "Symphony of Sorrowful Songs", Op. 36. **Dawn Upshaw** (sop); **London Sinfonietta/David Zinman.** Elektra Nonesuch 7559-79282-2. Recorded in 1991.

.•' 54m DDD 4/93

Górecki's Third Symphony has become legend. Composed over 16 years ago it has always had its champions and admirers within the contemporary music world, but in 1993 it found a new audience of undreamt-of proportions. A few weeks after its release, this Elektra Nonesuch release not only entered the classical top-ten charts, but was also riding high in the UK Pop Album charts. With sales figures exceeding 300,000 it has since become the biggest selling disc of music by a contemporary classical composer. The Symphony, subtitled *Symphony of Sorrowful Songs* was composed during a period when Górecki's musical style was undergoing a radical change from avant-garde serialism to a more accessible style firmly anchored to tonal traditions. The Symphony's three elegiac movements (or 'songs') form a triptych of laments for all the innocent victims of World War Two and are a reflection upon man's inhumanity to man in general, and as such it has become one of the most moving artistic documents of our time. The songs — including a poignant setting of an inscription scratched by a girl prisoner on the wall of her cell in a Gestapo prison — are beautifully and ethereally sung by Dawn Upshaw, and David Zinman and the London Sinfonietta provide an intense and committed performance of the shimmering orchestral writing. The whole venture is supported by an excellent recording.

Additional recommendation ...
No. 3[b]. Three Pieces in Old Style[a]. [b]**Stefania Woytowicz** (sop); [a]**Warsaw Chamber Orchestra/Karol Teutsch;** [b]**Berlin Radio Symphony Orchestra/Wlodzimierz Kamirski.** Koch Schwann Musica Mundi 311041 — .•' 55m ADD 4/93

Further listening ...

Epitafium, Op. 12[ab]. Scontri, Op. 17[b]. Genesis II: Canti strumentali, Op. 19 No. 2[b]. Refrain, Op. 21[b]. Old Polish music, Op. 24[c]. [a]**Polish National Philharmonic Choir;** [b]**Polish National Symphony Orchestra, Katowice/Jan Krenz;** [c]**Polish National Philharmonic Orchestra, Warsaw/Andrzej Markowski.** Olympia OCD385 (4/93).

Key to symbols

Price	Quantity/availability	Timing	Recording mode	Review date
.•'	② ②	lh 23m	DDD	6/88

Louis Moreau Gottschalk

American 1829-1869

New review

PIANO WORKS, Volumes 1 and 2. [a]**Eugene List,** [b]**Cary Lewis,** [c]**Joseph Werner,** [d]**Reid Nibley** (pfs); [e]**Utah Symphony Orchestra/Maurice Abravanel.** Vanguard Classics 08.4050/1.71. Recorded 1956-62.

08.4050.71[a] — Le Banjo, RO22. The Dying Poet, RO75. Souvenir de Porto Rico, RO250. Le Bananier, RO21. Ojos Criollos, RO185. Bamboula, RO20. The maiden's blush, RO141. The last hope, RO133. Suis-moi!, RO253. Pasquinade, RO189. La Savane, RO232. Tournament Galop, RO264. *08.4051.71* — La jota aragonesa, RO130[ab]. Souvenir d'Andalousie, RO242[ac]. La gallina, RO100[ac]. Orfa, RO186[ab]. Marche de nuit, RO151[ac]. Printemps d'amour, RO214[ab]. Radieuse, RO217[ac]. Réponds-moi, RO225[ab]. Tremolo, RO265[ab]. L'etincelle, RO80[ac]. Ses yeux, RO234[ac]. The Union, RO269[ab] (arr. Liszt). Grande tarantelle, RO259[de] (arr. Hershykay). Symphony No. 1, RO255, "La nuit des tropiques"[e].

② 56m 1h 17m ADD 5/93

This is a real discovery, especially in the solo piano disc (Vol. 1). Not new performances either but Eugene List's pioneering recordings from the late 1950s which did so much to bring Gottschalk to a wider public. The old Vanguard LPs come up splendidly and if the sound is a little thin that, as it turns out, must have been exactly what attracted Gottschalk to his own favourite Chickering instruments. How refreshing to have Gottschalk played without exaggeration as he intended! A good test of a Gottschalk pianist is the syncopated masterpiece *Souvenir de Porto Rico*. List is spectacular at the climax with effortless octaves and he understands the shape of the piece — a march emerging from the distance and finally disappearing again. List's poise in *The last hope*, where the introduction anticipates the advanced harmonies of *Tristan*, is exemplary and never merely sentimental. Gottschalk's solo pieces are consistently satisfying, full of colour and atmosphere both in the earliest works like *La Savane* and the latest, like the satirical *Pasquinade*. Volume 2 of this set consists mostly of vivid arrangements for piano duet or two pianos made in exactly the right spirit by List and his colleagues. Gottschalk's homophonic style adapts easily so that the sound suggests the mechanically filled-out piano rolls of a later generation. *La galina* ("The Hen") is enchanting, including the *accelerando* ending, but *The Union* benefits less from the double act with some rather unnecessary realistic drum effects added, when the original alone was uncanny. The enchanting two-movement oddity, *A night in the tropics*, presumably incomplete, recalls Berlioz in the *Andante* and the ensuing samba anticipates Milhaud. Altogether these two CDs show how good these Gottschalk revival performances were but, sadly, how long it has taken for such immediately attractive music to enter the standard repertoire.

Charles François Gounod

French 1818-1893

New review

Gounod. SONGS. [a]**Felicity Lott** (sop); [b]**Ann Murray** (mez); [c]**Anthony Rolfe Johnson** (ten); **Graham Johnson** (pf). Hyperion CDA66801/02. Texts and translations included.
Où voulez-vous aller?[a]. Le soir[a]. Venise[a]. Ave Maria[b]. Sérénade[b]. Chanson de printemps[a]. Au rossignol[b]. Ce que je suis sans toi[a]. Envoi de fleurs[a]. La pâquerette[b]. Boléro[b]. Mignon[a]. Rêverie[a]. Ma belle amie est morte[b]. Loin du pays[b]. Clos ta paupière[a]. Prière[b]. L'absent[a]. Le temps des roses[a]. Biondina[c]. The Worker[c]. A lay of the early spring[c]. My true love hath my heart[b]. Oh happy home! Oh blessed flower![c]. The fountain mingles with the river[a]. Maid of Athens[c]. Beware![a]. The Arrow and the Song[b]. Ilala: stances à la mémoire de Livingston[c]. If thou art sleeping, maiden[c].

② 2h 16m DDD 3/94

This well-filled two-CD set is surely the most wide-ranging single issue ever devoted to Gounod's *mélodies*. The first of the discs confirms the commonly held view of Gounod. Almost without exception the songs are pleasing and sentimental, a sweetly-scented posy of hymns to flowers, of reveries and serenades. The selection includes two settings of poems that Berlioz had used in *Les nuits d'été*, plumbing the depths of the poetry, where Gounod is content to skim across the surface. Arranged in chronological order, the songs show how little Gounod's music deepened, but also how evergreen was his inspiration in melody and harmony. To turn to the second disc is to have all one's prejudices overturned. This comprises non-French settings, for which Gounod dons first Italian garb for the song-cycle *Biondina*, and then English for a group of ten songs written during his stay in London in the 1870s. The Italian cycle is a delight. It would be impossible to guess the composer, as Gounod exchanges his customary flowing themes and rippling arpeggios for an ardent, Tosti-like vocal line over dry staccato chords. Anthony Rolfe Johnson catches its mix of sunny lyricism and Gallic sensitivity to perfection. The English songs are even more unusual, ranging from the Victorian ballad style of *The Worker* to a bizarre musical tribute to Livingstone, entitled *Ilala*. All three singers are on their best form here, with Rolfe Johnson bringing an air of intimate seductiveness to Byron's *Maid of Athens*.

New review

Gounod. FAUST. **Jerry Hadley** (ten) Faust; **Cecilia Gasdia** (sop) Marguerite; **Samuel Ramey** (bass) Méphistophélès; **Alexander Agache** (bar) Valentin; **Susanne Mentzer** (mez) Siébel; **Brigitte Fassbaender** (mez) Marthe; **Philippe Fourcade** (bass) Wagner; **Welsh National Opera Chorus and Orchestra/Carlo Rizzi.** Teldec 4509-90872-2. Notes, text and translation included.

③ 3h 31m DDD 7/94 — Ⓑ

Where Gounod is at his most inspired this version of his most popular work is more than commendable. Most notable are the solos for Marguerite and Faust, the Garden scene, the vignette in Marguerite's room that used to be regularly cut, and the Prison scene (considerably extended by the restoration of passages cut — presumably — before the première: we are in controversial Oeser territory). Following the Oeser Edition means unusual variants and an alteration in the placing (later) of the Church scene. These are questionable decisions but not serious enough to cause a problem when making a choice of versions. The ballet music is rightly consigned to an appendix. The tender, sweet-toned and idiomatically French singing and style of Gasdia and Hadley quite exceed expectations in these days of homogenized and uniform interpretation. These two principals step outside those predictable parameters to give us readings of high individuality, favouring their grateful music with delicately etched line, varied dynamics and real involvement in their characters' predicaments — Faust's vain search for the elixir of renewal, Marguerite for the ideal man. Both their happiness and later remorse are eloquently expressed. Gasdia gives a well-nigh faultless performance — light-hearted, elated in the Jewel song, ardent in the Garden duet, ecstatic in the bedtime solo that follows, ineffably sad in her "Il ne revient pas". How can this exquisite solo have ever been omitted, we think, when Gasdia moves us so deeply? She is no less touching when she has lost her reason. Subtle timbres, poised high notes inform all her singing. Hadley, with the ideal weight of voice for Faust, has done nothing better. "Je t'aime" at the first meeting with Marguerite is whispered in wonder. In the love duet he sings to her as a gentle lover, never bawling, caressing his music, and Gasdia replies in kind. The good news continues with Mentzer. She sings both Siébel's regular solos with vibrant, properly virile tone, the quick vibrato attractive. It's a real coup to have Fassbaender as Marthe, making so much of little. Ramey is the one singer to give a standardized performance. His Méphisto is as soundly and resolutely sung as one would expect from this sturdy bass, but it doesn't have the Francophone smoothness and subtlety of other interpretations. The only drawback is the often lax conducting. Rizzi conducts an often alarmingly slow account of the score and in compensation the more exciting passages are given rather too much verve. However, he is always aware of the sensuous nature of Gounod's scoring and the WNO Chorus and Orchestra are excellent. A choice between this and Plasson for a modern recording must rest on one or other singer. Haunted by the plaintive timbre of Gasdia and the artistry of Hadley one is persuaded that this is the version to have. The recording is by and large open, full of presence and well balanced.

Additional recommendations ...
Soloists; Paris Opéra Chorus and Orchestra/André Cluytens. EMI CMS7 69983-2 —
③ 2h 51m ADD 7/89 ▲ Ⓑ
Faust — Ballet Music[a]. Coupled with **Delibes.** *Coppélia — Ballet Suite*[b]. *Sylvia — Ballet Suite*[b].
[a]**Budapest Philharmonic Orchestra/János Sándor;** [b]**Berlin Radio Symphony Orchestra/Heinz Fricke.** Capriccio 15 616 — 57m DDD 5/90 Ⓑ
Richard Leech (ten) Faust; **Cheryl Studer** (sop) Marguerite; **José van Dam** (bass-bar)

Méphistophélès; **Thomas Hampson** (bass) Valentin; **Martine Mahé** (mez) Siebel; **Nadine Denize** (sop) Marthe; **Marc Barrard** (bar) Wagner; **French Army Chorus; Toulouse Capitole Choir and Orchestra/Michel Plasson.** EMI CDS7 54228-2 — .·' ③ 3h 24m DDD 12/91 Ⓑ

Faust (sung in English)[a]. *Faust — Ballet Music*[b]: *Les nubiennes; Adagio (includes an introduction by Beecham).* [a]**Soloists;** [a]**BBC Choir;** [a]**symphony orchestra;** [b]**London Philharmonic Orchestra/**[ab]**Sir Thomas Beecham,** [a]**Clarence Raybould.** Dutton Laboratories mono 2CDAX2001 — .·' ② 2h 18m ADD 5/94 Ⓑ ▲

Further listening ...

Symphony No. 1 in D major. Petite symphonie. *Coupled with* **Bizet** (ed. Hogwood). L'Arlésienne — excerpts. **Saint Paul Chamber Orchestra/Christopher Hogwood.** Decca 430 231-2DH (7/91).

Mors et Vita. **Barbara Hendricks** (sop); **Nadine Denize** (mez); **John Aler** (ten); **José van Dam** (bass-bar); **Orféon Donostiarra; Toulouse Capitole Orchestra/ Michel Plasson.** EMI CDS7 54459-2 (2/93).

SAPPHO. **Soloists; Saint-Etienne Lyric Chorus and Nouvel Orchestra/Patrick Fournillier.** Koch Schwann 313112 (7/94).

Louis Théodore Gouvy
French 1819-1898

New review

Gouvy. Morceaux, Op. 59 — No. 1, Prelude; No. 2, Caprice. Sonatas — D minor, Op. 36; C minor, Op. 49; F major, Op. 51. Impromptu, Op. 83 No. 5. Scherzo, Op. 77 No. 1. Aubade, Op. 77 No. 2. **Yaara Tal, Andreas Groethuysen** (pfs). Sony Classical SK53110. Recorded in 1992.

.·' Ih I7m DDD 10/93 ❓

The piano duet team of Yaara Tal and Andreas Groethuysen have resurrected an entirely forgotten French/German composer of the nineteenth century, who turns out to have been a master in writing for this idiom. The best of these pieces are without doubt equal in calibre to much of the accepted repertoire. As the booklet points out, Gouvy was no romantic and the works here, classical in conception, belong to the world of Schubert. A heavily touched-up photograph of the composer gives the impression of austerity, something that is not borne out in the music. True, his grasp of structure is very assured, but Gouvy comes across more as a very gentle person with a colourful imagination, at times reminiscent of Dvořák. Many of his ideas are off-beat, his modulations individual and sophisticated. The three sonatas, curiously enough, have motivic links. Gouvy never wastes notes and is a master of four-hand texture. Tal and Groethuysen play the music with such a fantastic degree of ensemble that one is oblivious of there being two performers involved. Recorded sound is exemplary.

Percy Grainger
American/Australian 1882-1961

New review

Grainger. PIANO MUSIC FOR FOUR HANDS, Volumes 2 and 3. **Penelope Thwaites, John Lavender** (pfs). Pearl SHECD9623/31. Recorded 1989-91.
SHECD9623 — Children's March (Over the hills and far away), RMTB4. Shepherd's Hey, BFMS16. Hill Song No. 1. Handel in the Strand, RMTB2. Harvest Hymn. The Widow's Party, KS7. The Lonely Desert Man Sees the Tents of the Happy Tribes. The Rival Brothers. Warriors II. Two Musical Relics of My Mother. Let's Dance Gay in Green Meadow, FI. Blithe bells.

Pritteling, Pratteling, Pretty Poll Parrot. *SHECD9631* — Rondo. Crew of the Long Dragon. Fantasy on George Gershwin's "Porgy and Bess". Ye Banks and Braes, BFMS32. Tiger-Tiger, KS4/JBC9. Walking Tune, RMTB3. **C. Scott:** Three Symphonic Dances. **Delius:** A Dance Rhapsody No. 1, RTVI/18. **Grieg:** Knut Lurasens Halling II. **Addinsell:** Festival. **Le Jeune:** La Bel'aronde. **Gershwin:** Girl Crazy — Embraceable you (all trans. Grainger).

(2) 1h 6m 1h 18m DDD 1/94

The first volume of this series (listed below) brought many surprising successes. There, as here, Grainger's 'dishings-up' of his music for keyboard is often more satisfying than the better-known orchestral versions. Quite frequently his arrangements for two pianists are his last thoughts about music that has often gone through as many as half a dozen rethinkings already, so Vol. 2 of this highly accomplished series is something more than an anthology of pieces that many Graingerites will already have. *Shepherd's Hey*, for example, is equipped with a particularly exuberant new coda, and the bafflingly titled *Pritteling, Pratteling, Pretty Poll Parrot* turns out to be our old friend the *Gumsuckers' March* with an entirely new middle section and some affectionate sidelong glances at (apparently) Erik Satie. There is literally new music as well, most substantially *Warriors II*, which turns out to have rather little connection with the strange 'imaginary ballet' that we might now call *Warriors I*. Reconstructed from Grainger's sketches by no fewer than four hands it turns out to be one of his stronger pieces: ardently melodious, at times very close to Rachmaninov, big gestured and with more urgency than some of his works of this length. Volume 3 contains shorter original Grainger compositions and a number of his transcriptions. These latter are fascinating in their combination of scrupulous fidelity and creative rethinking for an entirely different medium. You wouldn't think that a transcription, even for *two* pianos, of Delius's First *Dance Rhapsody* could possibly work. In fact, it works so well, revealing in the process quite a few of the constituents of Delius's style, that some may prefer Grainger's version to the original. In the *Porgy and Bess* Fantasy he treats the tunes with loving respect, but as a pianist can't help seeing different ways of presenting them: the very big gestures surrounding "My man's gone now"; a searching little prelude to "It ain't necessarily so" implying all sorts of interesting things Grainger could have done with that slithery little tune if he weren't obliged to play it straight — which he then does, with sparkling enjoyment.

Additional recommendation ...
Vol. 1 — *In a Nutshell. Spoon River. When the world was young. Molly on the Shore. Hill Song No. 2. Country Gardens. Mowgli's song against people. Eastern Intermezzo. English waltz. The Wraith of Odin. Always bright and merry. The Duke of Marlborough's Fanfare. A Lincolnshire Posy.* **Penelope Thwaites, John Lavender** (pfs). Pearl SHECD9611 — 1h 17m DDD 10/89

Further listening ...

Youthful Suite — Rustic dance; Eastern intermezzo. Blithe bells (free ramble on a theme by Bach, "Sheep may safely graze"). Spoon River. My Robin is to the Greenwood Gone. Green Bushes. Country Gardens (orch. Schmid). Mock Morris. Youthful Rapture[a]. Shepherd's Hey. Walking Tune. Molly on the shore. Handel in the Strand (orch. Wood). **Philip Martin** (pf); [a]**Moray Welsh** (vc); **Bournemouth Sinfonietta/Kenneth Montgomery.** Chandos Collect CHAN6542 (2/92).

The Warriors. Hill-Song No. 1. Irish Tune from County Derry, BFMS20. Hill-Song No. 2. Danish Folk-Music Suite. **Traditional Chinese** (harmonized Yasser, arr. Grainger, orch. Sculthorpe): Beautiful fresh flower. **Melbourne Symphony Orchestra/Geoffrey Simon.** Koch International Classics 37003-2 (11/90).

Danish Folk-Music Suite — The Power of Love; The Nightingale and the two Sisters; Jutish Medley. One More Day, my John. Knight and Shepherd's Daughter. Near Woodstock Town. Country Gardens. Sussex Mummer's Christmas Carol. Shepherd's Hey. To a Nordic Princess. Love at first sight. Over the Hills and far away. Bridal Lullaby. Handel in the Strand. Colonial Song. Paraphrase on the Waltz of the Flowers from Tchaikovsky's "The Nutcracker". **Fauré** (arr. Grainger): Nell, Op. 18 No. 1. **Dowland** (arr. Grainger): Now, O now, I needs must part. **Penelope Thwaites** (pf). Unicorn-Kanchana DKPCD9127 (3/93).

Enrique Granados

Spanish 1867-1916

Granados. Goyescas — Suite for Piano. **Alicia de Larrocha** (pf). Decca 411 958-2DH. From SXL6785 (12/77). Recorded in 1976.

.•´ 57m ADD 3/89   ♀ₚ

The Granados *Goyescas* are profoundly Spanish in feeling, but the folk influence is more of court music than of the flamenco or *cante hondo* styles which reflect gipsy and Moorish influence. This set of seven pieces was given its first performance by the composer in 1911, and his own exceptional ability as a pianist is evident in its consistently elaborate textures. That performance took place in Barcelona, and as Granados's compatriot and a native of that very city Alicia de Larrocha fully understands this music in its richly varied moods; a fact which tells in interpretations that have a compelling conviction and drive. Thus, she can dance enchantingly in such a piece as "El Fandango de candil", while in the celebrated "Maiden and the nightingale", No. 4 of the set, we listen to a wonderful outpouring of Mediterranean emotion, all the more moving for its avoidance of excessive rubato and over-pedalling. A splendid disc of one of the twentieth century's piano masterpieces, which was atmospherically recorded in the former Decca studios in West Hampstead in 1976 and has transferred well to CD.

Additional recommendation ...

Goyescas — No. 7, El pelele[c]. Danzas españolas, Op. 37[c] — No. 7, Valenciana; No. 10, Danza triste. **Falla.** Siete canciones populares españolas[a]. El amor brujo[a] — Canción del fuego fátuo. Soneto a Córdoba. Harpsichord Concerto[e]. **Mompou**[d]. Scènes d'enfants — No. 5, Jeunes filles au jardin. Suburbis — No. 1, El carrer, el guitarrista i el vell cavall. Cançons i dansas — Nos. 5-8. Paisajes — No. 1, La fuente y la campana. **Nin**[b]. Cantos populares españolas — No. 3, Tonada de la niña perdida; No. 4, Montañesa; No. 6, Malagueña; No. 7, Granadina; No. 19, Canto Andaluz; No. 20, Polo. [a]**Maria Barrientos,** [b]**Ninon Vallin** (sops); [c]**Enrique Granados,** [d]**Federico Mompou,** [b]**Joaquin Nin** (pfs); **Manuel de Falla** ([a]pf/[c]hpd); [e]**instrumental ensemble.** EMI Composers in Person mono CDC7 54836-2 (*See review in the Collections section; refer to the Index to Reviews*) — .•´ lh 18m ADD 11/93 ▲

Further listening ...

Seven Valses poéticos (trans. Williams). *Coupled with* **Albéniz.** Iberia[a] (arr. Gray) — El Albaicín; Triana; Rondeña. **Rodrigo.** Invocación y Danza. En los trigales. *Anonymous* (arr. Llobet). Ten Catalan Folk-songs — Cançó del Lladre; El testament d'Amelia; La filadora; El mestre; La nit de Nadal; L'hereu Riera; Lo fill del Ré; La Pastoreta; El Noi de la Mare. **John Williams** (gtr); [a]**London Symphony Orchestra/Paul Daniels.** Sony Classical SK48480 (7/92).

12 Danzas españolas, Op. 37. **Alicia de Larrocha** (pf). Decca 414 557-2DH (10/85).

Carl Heinrich Graun

German 1703/4-1759

Suggested listening ...

MONTEZUMA. **Soloists; Cantica Nova Chamber Choir; Neuss German Chamber Academy/Johannes Goritzki.** Capriccio 60 032-2 (7/93).

Alexandr Grechaninov

Russian/American 1864-1956

Suggested listening ...

Piano Trios — No. 1 in C minor, Op. 38; No. 2 in G major, Op. 128. **Viktor Simčisko** (vn); **Jura Alexander** (vc); **Daniela Ruso** (pf). Marco Polo 8 223416 (6/93).

Edvard Grieg

New review

Grieg. Piano Concerto in A minor, Op. 16.
Schumann. Piano Concerto in A minor, Op. 54. **Murray Perahia** (pf); **Bavarian Radio Symphony Orchestra/Sir Colin Davis.** CBS CD44899. Recorded at performances in the Philharmonie Gasteig, Munich in 1987 and 1988.

⟪♪ lh DDD 5/89 ᴼₚ

Although ready to enlarge on attendant hazards, Murray Perahia (in an interview in *Gramophone* in May 1987), admitted to a delight in the "inspirational heat-of-the-moment" of a live recording. There are, however, no claps, coughs or shuffles to confirm the presence of an audience. Of the two works it is the Grieg that is better served by the immediacy and warmth of his response, whether through rhythmic bite in livelier dance tempo or total surrender to lyrical nostalgia elsewhere. Never is there the slightest sacrifice of his customary artistic sensitivity or keyboard finesse. It is delightful to discover that someone so dedicated to Mozart, Beethoven and the light-fingered Mendelssohn in the concerto field could so patently revel in Grieg's unabashed sentiment and bravura too. His Scumann is no less ardent. In the spirited finale, as throughout the Grieg, any collector would be just as happy with this performance as that of the long and much praised (and now sadly unavailable) Stephen Bishop-Kovacevich for Philips. Davis, needless to say, goes all the way in both works to uphold Perhahia in his open-hearted point-making, and the Bavarian Radio Symphony Orchestra give him all he asks of them.

Additional recommendations ...
As above. **Radu Lupu** (pf); **London Symphony Orchestra/André Previn.** Decca Ovation 417 728-2DM — ⟪♪ lh lm ADD 12/87 ᴼₚ Ⓑ
As above. **Pascal Devoyon** (pf); **London Philharmonic Orchestra/Jerzy Maksymiuk.** Classics for Pleasure CD-CFP4574 — ⟪♪ lh 3m DDD 2/91 ᴼₚ Ⓑ
Grieg[a]. **Schumann**[c]. **Franck.** *Symphonic Variations*[b]. [ab]**Sir Clifford Curzon,** [c]**Friedrich Gulda** (pfs); [a]**London Symphony Orchestra/Øivin Fjeldstad;** [b]**London Philharmonic Orchestra/Sir Adrian Boult;** [c]**Vienna Philharmonic Orchestra/Volkmar Andreae.** Decca Headline Classics 433 628-2DSP *(see review under Franck; refer to the Index to Reviews)* — ⟪♪ lh 16m ADD 1/92 ᴼₚ Ⓑ ▲
As above. **Lars Vogt** (pf); **City of Birmingham Symphony Orchestra/Simon Rattle.** EMI CDC7 54746-2 — ⟪♪ lh 2m DDD 1/93 ᴼₚ Ⓑ
Grieg *(orig. version)*[a]. *Larvik's Polka, CW102*[a]. *23 Short Pieces, CW105*[a]. [a]**Love Derwinger** (pf); **Norrköping Symphony Orchestra/Jun'ichi Hirokami.** BIS CD619 — ⟪♪ lh 2m DDD 9/93 ᴼₚ

New review
Grieg. ORCHESTRAL WORKS. [b]**Stephen Kovacevich,** [d]**Zoltán Kocsis** (pfs); [ac]**English Chamber Orchestra;** [c]**Philharmonia Orchestra/Raymond Leppard;** [b]**BBC Symphony Orchestra/Sir Colin Davis.** Philips Duo 438 380-2PM2.
Piano Concerto in A minor, Op. 16 (6500 166, 3/72)[b]. *Peer Gynt* — Suites Nos. 1 and 2 (from 9500 106, 11/76)[a]. Lyric Suite, Op. 54 (9500 748, 12/80)[c]. Holberg Suite, Op. 40 (9500 748)[c]. Lyric Pieces — Book 1, Op. 12; Book 3, Op. 13 (recorded 1981, new to UK)[d]. Symphonic Dances, Op. 64 (6514 203, 4/83)[e].

② ⟪♪ 2h 35m ADD 8/93 ᴼₚ

This mid-price package is ideal for anyone wanting a single issue representing Grieg's best-known music. It includes what is for many people the outstanding account of the Piano Concerto — although there are others of nearly equal distinction (see above). Raymond Leppard's perform-ances with the ECO of Grieg's suites of incidental music to *Peer Gynt* have an affectionate refinement matched by the recording. However, both "Morning" and "In the Hall of the Mountain King" fail to take off, the latter lacking sheer physical excitement until near the end, although the playing has great finesse — as it also has in "Solveig's Song", with the ECO violins on excellent form. No complaints about Leppard's *Lyric Suite* (originally piano music), *Holberg Suite* and the less familiar *Symphonic Dances*. Besides all this, Zoltán Kocsis gives us 14 of the *Lyric Pieces*, miniatures for solo piano which are charmingly done.

Grieg. Norwegian Dances, Op. 35. Lyric Suite, Op. 54. Symphonic Dances, Op. 64.
Gothenburg Symphony Orchestra/Neeme Järvi. DG 419 431-2GH.

`.·'  1h 8m  DDD  1/87` 🔘

Grieg's music has that rare quality of eternal youth: however often one hears it, its complexion
retains its bloom, the smile its radiance and the youthful sparkle remains undimmed. Though he
is essentially a miniaturist, who absorbed the speech rhythms and inflections of Norwegian folk
melody into his bloodstream, Grieg's world is well defined. Both the *Norwegian Dances* and the
Symphonic Dances were originally piano duets, which Grieg subsequently scored: Järvi conducts
both with enthusiasm and sensitivity. In the *Lyric Suite* he restores "Klokkeklang" (Bell-ringing),
which Grieg omitted from the final score: it is remarkably atmospheric and evocative, and serves
to show how forward-looking Grieg became in his late years. The recording is exceptionally fine
and of wide dynamic range; the sound is very natural and the perspective true to life.

Additional recommendations ...
*Norwegian Dances. Old Norwegian Romance with Variations, Op. 51. In Autumn, Op. 11. Lyric Pieces,
Op. 43 — No. 5, "Erotik".* **Svendsen.** *Two Icelandic Melodies.* **Iceland Symphony Orchestra/
Petri Sakari.** Chandos CHAN9028 — .·' 1h 6m DDD 8/92
*Symphonic Dances. Sigurd Jorsalfar, Op. 56. Peer Gynt — Solvejg's Song[a]; Solvejg's Cradle Song[a]. Six
Romances, Op. 39 — From Monte Pincio[a]. A swan, Op. 25[a]. Spring, Op. 33[a]. Norway, Op. 58 —
Henrik Wergeland[a].* [a]**Solveig Kringleborn** (sop); **Royal Stockholm Philharmonic
Orchestra/Gennadi Rozdestvensky.** Chandos CHAN9113 — .·' 1h 13m DDD 3/93 🔘

Grieg. ORCHESTRAL WORKS. [a]**Ilse Hollweg** (sop); [a]**Beecham Choral Society;
Royal Philharmonic Orchestra/Sir Thomas Beecham.** EMI Studio Plus CDM7 64751-2.
Items marked [a] from HMV ASD258 (1/59), [b] HMV ASD518 (4/63), [cd] Columbia 22CX1363
(9/56). Recorded 1956-57.
Peer Gynt — The Bridal March passes by; Prelude; In the Hall of the Mountain King; Solveig's
Song; Prelude; Arab Dance; Anitra's Dance; Prelude; Solveig's Cradle Song[a]. Symphonic
Dances, Op. 64 — Allegretto grazioso[b]. In Autumn, Op. 11[c]. Old Norwegian Romance with
Variations, Op. 51[d].

`.·'  1h 16m  ADD` Ⓑ ▲

Grieg's incidental music was an important integral part of Ibsen's *Peer Gynt* and from this score Grieg
later extracted the two familiar suites. This recording of excerpts from *Peer Gynt* goes back to 1957
but still sounds well and is most stylishly played. He included the best known ("Anitra's Dance" is a
delicate gem here) together with "Solveig's Song" and "Solveig's Cradle Song". Sir Thomas uses Ilse
Hollweg to advantage, her voice suggesting the innocence of the virtuous and faithful peasant
heroine. There is also an effective use of the choral voices which are almost inevitably omitted in
ordinary performances of the two well-known orchestral suites: the male chorus of trolls in the "Hall
of the Mountain King" are thrilling, and the women in the "Arab Dance" are charming. The other
two pieces are well worth having too; *Symphonic Dances* is a later, freshly pastoral work, while the
overture *In Autumn* is an orchestral second version of an early piece for piano duet. This reissue is
further enhanced by the first release in stereo of the *Old Norwegian Romance*.

Additional recommendations ...
Peer Gynt — complete. Sigurd Jorsalfar — incidental music, Op. 22. **Soloists; Gösta Ohlin's Vocal
Ensemble; Pro Musica Chamber Choir; Gothenburg Symphony Orchestra/Neeme
Järvi.** DG 423 079-2GH2 — .·' ② 2h 4m DDD 2/88 Ⓑ
Peer Gynt — excerpts. **Soloists; San Francisco Symphony Chorus and Orchestra/Herbert
Blomstedt.** Decca 425 448-2DH — .·' 1h 13m DDD 3/90 Ⓑ
Peer Gynt Suites — No. 1, Op. 46; No. 2, Op. 55. Land Sighting, Op. 31[a]. Olav Trygvason, Op. 50[b].
[b]**Randi Stene** (mez); [b]**Anne Gjevang** (contr); [ab]**Håkan Hagegård** (bar); [ab]**Gothenburg
Symphony Chorus; Gothenburg Symphony Orchestra/Neeme Järvi.** DG Grieg Edition
437 523-2GH — .·' 1h 13m DDD 6/93 🔘 Ⓑ

`New review`
Grieg. String Quartets — No. 1 in G minor, Op. 27; No. 2 in F major, CW146.
Schumann. String Quartet No. 1 in A minor, Op. 41 No. 1. **Petersen Quartet** (Conrad

Muck, Gernot Süssmuth, vns; Friedemann Weigle, va; Hans-Jakob Eschenburg, vc). Capriccio 10 476. Recorded in 1993.

⠶ 1h 15m DDD 1/94 ♩P

New review
Grieg. String Quartet No. 1 in G minor, Op. 27.
Mendelssohn. String Quartet No. 2 in A minor, Op. 13. **Shanghai Quartet** (WeiGang Li, HongGang Li, vns; Zheng Wang, va; James Wilson, vc). Delos DE3153.

⠶ 1h 4m DDD 6/94 ♩P

Since Grieg owed much to Schumann, coupling their quartets seems a good idea. These G minor and A minor Quartets were written when the composers were in their thirties, but Grieg was a few years older. Yet it is his work that sounds more youthfully passionate, while the Schumann is a rather self-conscious homage to his friend Mendelssohn and classical models. These German players invest the Grieg G minor Quartet with *gravitas* and are skilful in linking together the disparate sections of its structure. Their recording has a very natural balance and an impressively wide dynamic range with real *pianissimo*; it also copes well with Grieg's forceful, semi-orchestral string writing. The whole performance has vigour and tenderness in good proportion, and a truly Scandinavian feeling. The unfinished F major Quartet is another sensitively moulded performance and the work sounds no more incomplete than Schubert's *Unfinished* Symphony. The Schumann is no less enjoyable; the artists are fully inside his idiom and make a consistently beautiful and meaningful sound. The youthful Shanghai Quartet's brightly-lit account of the Mendelssohn suggests a rich store of interpretative potential. Theirs is a sizzling, multicoloured performance. The Grieg coupling is, if anything, even finer, with an *Allegro molto* first movement that truly is *ed agitato*, a warming *Romanze* and a superbly characterized *Intermezzo*. It is arguably the most compelling performance of this endearing score since the original Budapest Quartet's trail-blazing HMV 78s from 1937. It is richly (if rather cavernously) recorded.

Additional recommendation ...
No. 1. **Schumann.** String Quartet No. 1 in A major, Op. 41. **English Quartet.** Unicorn-Kanchana DKPCD9092 — ⠶ 1h 6m DDD 3/92

New review
Grieg. Violin Sonatas — No. 1 in F major, Op. 8; No. 2 in G major, Op. 13; No. 3 in C minor, Op. 45. **Augustin Dumay** (vn); **Maria-João Pires** (pf). DG 437 525-2GH.

⠶ 1h 10m DDD 9/93

Grieg's violin sonatas span his creative life, the first two dating from his early twenties, before his Piano Concerto, and the Third Sonata of 1887 belonging to the last decade of his life. Augustin Dumay brings to this music a youthful *seigneur*, manifest in the impetuosity, charm and command of his playing. He and Maria-João Pires are at their considerable best in the G major Sonata, with its vivid first movement, lilting *Allegretto* and triumphant finale — whose conclusion they lift to the skies. The recording does full justice to Dumay's silky and resourceful tone. Pires is rightly an equal partner, and both artists bring an infectiously fresh response to the music. The finale of the C minor Sonata, music that anticipates Sibelius in its urgency and elemental force, is compellingly played.

New review
Grieg. PIANO WORKS. **Leif Ove Andsnes** (pf). Virgin Classics VC7 59300-2.
Piano Sonata in E minor, Op. 7. Poetic tone-pictures, Op. 3 — Nos. 4, 5 and 6. Album Leaves, Op. 28 — No. 1 in A flat major; No. 4 in C sharp minor. Agitato. Lyric Pieces — Book 3, Op. 43; Book 5, Op. 54.

⠶ 1h 12m DDD 6/93

Andsnes was 22 when he recorded Grieg's Sonata — exactly the composer's age when he wrote it. Despite the heroic opening, Andsnes does not save the first movement from sounding repetitive. It is the two inner movements that display real character and imagination and the pianist rises to the occasion in both. The finale is stunningly played. He is to be heard at his very best in the *Lyric Pieces*, Op. 43, which is the most familiar set of all. One relishes the glinting colours in "Butterfly", the simple heartfelt yearnings of "Solitary Wanderer" and the delightful twittering energy of the "Little Bird". This is a pianist with sufficient insight and subtlety not to feel the need to prettify the music. This well-crafted CD has pleasant piano sound, not over-close in impact.

Grieg. LYRIC PIECES — excerpts. **Emil Gilels** (pf). DG 419 749-2GH. From 2530 476 (3/75).
Arietta, Op. 12 No. 1. Berceuse, Op. 38 No. 1. Butterfly, Op. 43 No. 1. Solitary Traveller, Op. 43 No. 2. Album-leaf, Op. 47 No. 2. Melody, Op. 47 No. 3. Norwegian Dance, "Halling", Op. 47 No. 4. Nocturne, Op. 54 No. 4. Scherzo, Op. 54 No. 5. Homesickness, Op. 57 No. 6. Brooklet, Op. 62 No. 4. Homeward, Op. 62 No. 6. In ballad vein, Op. 65 No. 5. Grandmother's minuet, Op. 68 No. 2. At your feet, Op. 68 No. 3. Cradlesong, Op. 68 No. 5. Once upon a time, Op. 71 No. 1. Puck, Op. 71 No. 3. Gone, Op. 71 No. 6. Remembrances, Op. 71 No. 7.

> 56m ADD 10/87

This record is something of a gramophone classic. The great Russian pianist Emil Gilels, an artist of staggering technical accomplishment and intellectual power, here turns his attention to Grieg's charming miniatures. He brings the same insight and concentration to these apparent trifles as he did to towering masterpieces of the classic repertoire. The programme proceeds chronologically and one can appreciate the gradual but marked development in Grieg's harmonic and expressive language — from the folk-song inspired early works to the more progressive and adventurous later ones. Gilels's fingerwork is exquisite and the sense of total involvement with the music almost religious in feeling. This is a wonderful recording: pianistic perfection.

New review
Grieg. SONGS, Volumes 1 and 2. **Håkan Hagegård** (bar); **Warren Jones** (pf). RCA Victor Red Seal 09026 61518/61629-2. Texts and translations included. Recorded in 1992.
09026 61518-2 — Melodies of the Heart, Op. 5. Nine Songs, Op. 18. Six Songs, Op. 25. The Mountain Thrall, Op. 32. Last Spring, Op. 33 No. 2. Rocking on Gentle Waves, Op. 49 No. 2. Henrik Wergeland, Op. 58 No. 3. *09026 61629-2* — Four Songs and Ballads, Op. 9. Four Songs, Op. 21. Five Songs, Op. 26. Six Songs, Op. 39. Reminiscences from Mountain and Fjord, Op. 44.

> ② 1h 7m 1h 8m DDD 2/94

Håkan Hagegård is the ideal male singer for Grieg's songs, singing with marvellously fresh, firm tone. Warren Jones is an excellent partner, and the recording keeps voice and piano happily in balance. The two records are issued separately, and, though the programmes are arranged broadly in chronological order, each includes early and late compositions so that either of them can offer a fairly representative conspectus. Volume 1 begins with Op. 5, *Melodies of the Heart*, settings of poems by Hans Andersen. A crisp rhythm in the piano part of the first, "Two brown eyes", matches the clean, bright focus of the voice, and in the third song, the famous "I love thee", both artists catch the affectionate impulsiveness without mawkish indulgence. The *Nine Songs*, Op. 18 are attractive though less striking than the Op. 25 set of six, which begins with "Fiddlers", an eerie song, almost a Norwegian "Doppelgänger". It also includes the Ibsen setting, "A swan", which is among the loveliest of all. "Våren" (better known as the second of the *Elegiac Melodies* for strings) suits the singer beautifully, a saddened tone colouring the voice till the verse's climax which opens out in superb vocal health. Then with the second volume we are back to Op. 9, ending with the *Reminiscences from Mountain and Fjord*, Op. 44, the fine, responsive settings of Holger Drachmann's lyrical ballads about the local girls and his conviction that "in the hills there is no sin".

Additional recommendation ...
Six Songs with Orchestra[a]. *The First Meeting, Op. 21 No. 1*[a]. *The Mountain Thrall*[b]. *Before a Southern Convent, Op. 20*[c]. *Bergliot, Op. 42*[d]. [ac]**Barbara Bonney** (sop); [ac]**Randi Stone** (mez); [ab]**Håkan Hagegård** (bar); [d]**Rut Tellefsen** (narr); [c]**Gothenburg Symphony Chorus and Orchestra/Neeme Järvi**. DG Grieg Edition 437 519-2GH — ∴ 1h 1m DDD 6/93 ⁹ₚ

Grieg. SONGS. **Anne Sofie von Otter** (mez); **Bengt Forsberg** (pf). DG Grieg Anniversary Edition 437 521-2GH. Texts and translations included. Recorded in 1992.
Haugtussa, Op. 67. Two brown eyes, Op. 5 No. 1. I love but thee, Op. 5 No. 3. A swan, Op. 25 No. 2. With a waterlily, Op. 25 No. 4. Hope, Op. 26 No. 1. Spring, Op. 33 No. 2. Beside the stream, Op. 33 No. 5. From Monte Pincio, Op. 39 No. 1. Six Songs, Op. 48. Spring showers, Op. 49 No. 6. While I wait, Op. 60 No. 3. Farmyard Song, Op. 61 No. 3.

♪ ♪ **lh 8m   DDD   6/93**   ♪ₚ

With performances like this, Grieg in his celebratory year emerged as a first-rank composer in this genre. Anne Sofie von Otter is at the peak of her powers, glorying in this repertoire which she obviously loves and knows intimately. Take the *Haugtussa* cycle, which Grieg considered his greatest achievement in this sphere of writing. Von Otter projects her imagination of the visionary herd-girl with absolute conviction. She is no less successful in the German settings that follow. The sad depths of *One day, my thought* from Six Songs, Op. 48 also set memorably by Wolf in his *Spanish Songbook*, the hopelessness of Goethe's *The time of roses* (Op. 48 No. 5), a setting of great beauty are encompassed with unfettered ease, but so are the lighter pleasures of *Lauf der Welt.* Even the familiar *A dream* (Op. 48 No. 6) emerges as new in von Otter's daringly big-boned reading. Throughout, her readings are immeasurably enhanced by the imaginative playing by Bengt Forsberg. They breathe fresh life into *A swan* and in the almost as familiar *With a waterlily,* another superb Ibsen setting, the questing spirit expressed in the music is marvellous-ly captured by the performers. And there are more pleasures to come. A superb account of *Hope,* a wistful, sweetly voiced and played account of *Spring,* the charming, teasing *While I wait* and a deeply poetic reading of the justly renowned *From Monte Pincio* are just three more definitive interpretations. This should be regarded as a 'must' for any collector of songs, indeed a collector of any kind.

Additional recommendation ...
Haugtussa. Seven Children's Songs, Op. 61. Songs from Haugtussa, CW149 — The sparrow; Veslemoy's wandering; Veslemoy's longing; Cow call; The haying; Condemned. Clara's song from "The proposal at Helgoland", CW115. Posthumous Songs, Volume 1 — I love you dear. The Princess. Posthumous Songs, Volume 2 — Sigh. Occasional Songs, CW129 — Morning Prayer. **Marianne Hirsti** (sop); **Knut Skram** (bar); **Rudolf Jansen** (pf). Victoria Grieg Edition VCD19040 — ♪ ♪ lh l6m DDD 2/94 ♪ₚ

Further listening ...

Funeral March in memory of Rikard Nordraak. In Autumn, Op. 11. Old Norwegian Romance with Variations, Op. 51. Symphony in C minor. **Gothenberg Symphony Orchestra/Neeme Järvi.** DG 427 321-2GH (6/89).

Holberg Suite, Op. 40. *Coupled with* **Barber.** Adagio for Strings, Op. 11. **Bloch.** Concerto grosso No. 1ª. **Puccini.** Crisantemi (arr. string orchestra). ªIrit Rob (pf); **Israel Chamber Orchestra/Yoav Talmi.** Chandos CHAN8593 (8/88).

Lyric Pieces — Book 5, Op. 54; Book 6, Op. 57; Book 7, Op. 62. **Peter Katin** (pf). Unicorn-Kanchana Souvenir UKCD2034 (11/90).

Lyric Pieces — Book 8, Op. 65; Book 9, Op. 68; Book 10, Op. 71. **Peter Katin** (pf). Unicorn-Kanchana Souvenir UKCD2035 (2/91).

Violin Sonatas — No. 1 in F major, Op. 8; No. 2 in G major, Op. 13; No. 3 in C minor, Op. 45. **Rodrigue Milosi** (vn); **Noël Lee** (pf). Adda 581028 (1/90).

Key to symbols

Quality of sound		Discs worth exploring		Caveat emptor
♪ₚ ♪ₛ	Ⓑ	❓	🖋	▲
Quality of performance	Basic library		Period performance	

Francis Grier

Grier. A Sequence for the Ascension. **Rodolfus Choir/Ralph Allwood** with **Francis Grier** (org). Herald HAVPCD158.

lh 7m   DDD   7/93

"The Rodolfus Choir consists of young people who have attended one or more of the Eton Choral Courses. Many are choral scholars, some are still at school." Reading that before listening to this disc may conjure up preconceptions which will be immediately shattered by the stunning display of unison singing in the opening "Introit"; first the men, then the women and finally both float through Grier's quasi-Medieval chant with each phrase, syllable and every tiny inflexion perfectly blended. Perhaps their relative lack of experience accounts for a total willingness to submit to Ralph Allwood's exemplary direction. Solo voices, both sung and spoken (for Grier's *Sequence* includes three Biblical readings) are drawn from the ranks of the choir and are, without exception, splendid, while the recording has pleasing warmth and atmosphere. Grier's intention was to produce a sequence of choral items, organ solos and readings within the framework of a service but with the "unity of a single composer's work". His style is so eclectic, ranging from Taverner to Tavener, that any stylistic unity seems purely superficial. Never mind, this is a beautiful work given a truly memorable performance.

Charles Griffes

Griffes. Piano Sonata in F sharp minor.
Ives. Piano Sonata No. 1.
Sessions. Piano Sonata No. 2. **Peter Lawson** (pf). Virgin Classics VC7 59316-2. Recorded in 1991.

lh 12m   DDD   2/94

Critical praise greeted Peter Lawson's first volume of American piano sonatas (reviewed in the Collections section; refer to the Index to Reviews) which contains Barber, Carter, Copland and the *Three-page Sonata* by Ives. It says much about the standing of the American piano sonata in the instrument's twentieth-century repertory that there are now so many fine recordings on offer. With this second record, too, Lawson has plenty of competition and, once again, he is well ahead. The Griffes Sonata is the composer's late masterpiece. Landes made an impressive case for this work and, like Lawson, has absolutely no technical problems. However, the way Lawson controls the soft textures which appear like oases between outbursts of passion is preferable; and the passacaglia texture in the final section is admirably paced. There is strong competition in the Ives from Joanna MacGregor. Lawson, too, is outstanding. He manages the same frenzy with greater control and gets the epic moments, such as the last movement, absolutely right. Even in the Sessions there is tough competition — from Barry David Salwen on an all-Sessions CD. Once again, there is not much to choose between two excellent perform-ances with similar qualities of fidelity to the composer's intentions. What a great achievement to record two CDs of major sonatas and come up with virtually the best available performance of every one! Whatever can we expect from Vol. 3?

Additional recommendations ...
Griffes. Piano Sonata. Fantasy Pieces, Op. 6 —Barcarolle; Notturno; Scherzo. Three Tone-Pictures, Op. 5. **Macdowell.** Piano Sonata No. 4 in E minor, Op. 59, "Keltic". **Garah Landes** (pf). Koch International Classics 37045-2 — **lh 6m   DDD   7/91**
Ives. Piano Sonata. **Barber.** Piano Sonata in E flat major, Op. 26. Excursions, Op. 20. **Joanna MacGregor** (pf). Collins Classics 1107-2 (reviewed under Ives; refer to the Index to Reviews) — **lh 8m   DDD   3/92**
Sessions. Piano Sonatas Nos. 1-3. Pages from a Diary. Five Pieces. Waltz. **Barry David Salwen** (pf). Koch International Classics 37106-2 — **lh 14m   DDD   12/92**

Further listening ...

Songs — Am Kreuzweg wird begraben. An den Wind. Auf geheimem Waldespfade. Auf ihrem Grab. Das ist ein Brausen und Heulen. Das sterbende Kind. Elfe. Meeres Stille. Mein Herz ist wie die dunkle Nacht. Mit schwarzen Segeln. Des Müden Abendlied. Nachtlied. So halt' ich endlich dich umfangen. Der träumende See. Wo ich bin, mich rings umdunkelt. Wohl lag ich einst in Gram und Schmerz. Zwei Könige sassen auf Orkadal. *Coupled with* **Ives.** Du bist wie eine Blume. Feldeinsamkeit. Frühlingslied. Gruss. Ich grolle nicht. Ilmenau. Marie. Minnelied. Rosamunde. Rosenzweige. Ton. Weil' auf mir. Widmung. Wiegenlied; *MacDowell:* Drei Lieder, Op. 11. Zwei Leider, Op. 12. **Thomas Hampson** (bar); **Armen Guzelimian** (pf). Teldec 9031-72168-2.

Ferde Grofé
American 1892-1972

Suggested listening ...

Grand Canyon Suite. *Coupled with* **Gershwin.** Porgy and Bess —A Symphonic Picture. **Detroit Symphony Orchestra/Antál Dorati.** Decca Ovation 430 712-2DM (8/91).

Nicolas de Grigny
French 1672-1703

New review
Grigny. Premier Livre d'Orgue[a]. [b]**Delphine Collot,** [b]**Emmanuelle Gall,** [b]**Françoise Masset** (sops); [b]**Sophie Vatillon** (bass viol); [a]**Sagittarius Vocal Ensemble;** [a]**André Isoir** (org). Erato 4509-91722-2. Recorded in 1992.
Charpentier. O salutaris hostia, H261[b]. *Lully.* Domine salvum[b].

② 2h 11m DDD 10/93

Nicolas de Grigny was a contemporary of François Couperin and, in the sphere of organ music, the equal of his much better known compatriot. Grigny's *Premier Livre d'Orgue* — he didn't in fact produce another — was pubished in 1699 and contains an organ Mass and paraphrases on five Gregorian hymns. The concept of the 'organ mass' goes back to early Renaissance times and consists of versets for organ solo in place of sections of the Ordinary and Proper of the Mass, but alternating with sections of sung plainchant. The late seventeenth century was the richest period in the history of French organ masses and Grigny's is one of the very finest of them. André Isoir plays an organ by Jean Boizard in the church of St Michel-en-Thiérache. In Grigny's *Livre d'Orgue* it is the five-strand textures in six of the fugues which most consistently underline the splendour of this instrument; but individual colours are hardly less striking especially the beautiful recorder-like quality of the flutes, heard to advantage in the *Sanctus* of the Mass. The inclusion of two very short motets by Charpentier and Lully which are sung at the close of the *Sanctus* and of the *Agnus Dei*, respectively, follow a common practice of the period. Isoir is more rhythmic than some of his fellow organists and he has a feeling both for the inherent nobility of the music and the conventions which bring it to life. The contributions by the Sagittarius Vocal Ensemble are enjoyable with a rough edge to the singing and a feeling of spontaneity, too. Both the motets are attractively sung. A fine recording.

Carlos Guastavino
Argentinian 1912-

New review
Guastavino. PIANO WORKS. [a]**Hector Moreno,** [b]**Norberto Capelli** (pfs). Marco Polo 8 223462. Recorded in 1992.

Romance del Plata[ab]. Three Romances[ab]. Bailecito[ab]. Gato[ab]. Llanura[ab]. Se equivocó la paloma[ab]. La Siesta[a]. Las Presencias[b].

Ih 6m DDD 5/94

Here, surely, is an excellent answer to that elusive Christmas or birthday present for a friend who loves music, provided it is not too highbrow. Not everything is equally inspired but none of these works is ever less than enjoyable, with melodically grateful ideas, sometimes rising to starry declamation, lavishly treated and embroidered. Guastavino wears his Argentinian colours lightly but unmistakably, though there is a near Fauréan modulatory ease and cunning in the *Romance del Plata*'s opening *Allegro*, its mood of bittersweet regret resolved in a busy tarantella finish. "Baile" from the *Three Romances* cocks a snook at its own sentiment and *Llanura*, after a reflective start, whirls us away in a dizzying concert waltz. The performances are sympathetic but be warned, the recordings are somewhat airless and close.

New review

Guastavino. SONGS. **Ulises Espaillat** (ten); **Pablo Zinger** (pf). New Albion NA058CD. Texts and translations included. Recorded in 1992.
Cuatro Canciones Argentinas. Cuatro Canciones Coloniales. Piececitos. Cita. Se equivocó la paloma. Siete Canciones. La rosa y el sauce. Pueblito, mi pueblo.

49m DDD 1/94

The songs of Guastavino have tunes that can be remembered and hummed, verse structure with beginning and end, and sentiments that are often frankly nostalgic. The writing for voice is that of a composer who sings in imagination as he writes, and so it lies comfortably, encouraging expressiveness without recourse to modernist extremes of vocal range or anti-vocal intervals and dynamics. Ulises Espaillat, a tenor from the Dominican Republic, takes due advantage: we hear a voice which can spend quite a high proportion of the time singing pleasantly at a *mezzo forte* in the upper-middle register where his tone is at its most attractive. He catches the dreamy, midday atmosphere of *Cita*, the affectionate longing of *Pueblito, mi pueblo* and makes a lovely effect in that most haunting of songs, *Se equivocó la paloma*. He is well accompanied by Pablo Zinger, and the recorded sound is clear and well-balanced.

Sofia Gubaidulina

Russian 1931-

Gubaidulina. String Quartet No. 2.
Kurtág. String Quartet No. 1, Op. 1. Hommage à Milhály András, Op. 13. Officium breve in memoriam Andreae Szervánzky, Op. 28.
Lutoslawski. String Quartet. **Arditti Quartet** (Irvine Arditti, David Alberman, vns; Levine Andrade, va; Rohan de Saram, vc). Disques Montaigne 789007. Recorded in 1990.

Ih 12m DDD 4/92

Recent political developments ensure that Sofia Gubaidulina's country of birth is given in the notes, not as Russia, but as the Tatar Autonomous People's Republic. Autonomy — the need for a personal tone of voice — is a quality all three of these eastern European composers well understand. Lutoslawski's quartet (1964) came at a crucial time in his development, as the first work to relate his new technique of aleatory counterpoint (in which the pitches but not necessarily the rhythms are prescribed) to a traditional, abstract genre. Compared to the best of his later works the quartet is perhaps too long-drawn-out, but this highly expressive and strongly disciplined performance makes an excellent case for it. Alongside the Lutoslawski the three works by György Kurtág sound remarkably intense and concentrated, yet with a lyricism that prevents their evident austerity from growing merely arid, and which makes the reference to a tonal melody in the *Officium breve* seem natural as well as touching. The world of consonant harmony is also evoked by Gubaidulina, not as an expression of regret for the irretrievable past but as a way of extending her own essentially modern language. There is a special sense of personal certainty and confidence about all the music on this well-recorded disc. It needs no special pleading, but the commanding authority of the Arditti Quartet's performance is still something to marvel at.

Further listening ...

Symphony "Stimmen ... Verstummen". Stufen. **Royal Stockholm Philharmonic Orchestra/ Gennadi Rozhdestvensy.** Chandos CHAN9183 (8/93).

Concerto for Bassoon and Low Strings[a]. Concordanza. Detto II[b]. [a]**Harri Ahmas** (bn); [b]**Ilkka Pälli** (vc); **Lahti Chamber Ensemble/Osmo Vänskä.** BIS CD636 (6/94).

Offertorium[a]. Hommage à T.S. Eliot[b]. [b]**Christine Whittlesey** (sop); [a]**Gidon Kremer,** [b]**Isabelle van Keulen** (vns); [b]**Tabea Zimmermann** (va); [b]**David Geringas** (vc); [b]**Alois Posch** (db); [b]**Eduard Brunner** (cl); [b]**Klaus Thunemann** (bn); [b]**Radovan Vlatkovič** (hn); [a]**Boston Symphony Orchestra/Charles Dutoit.** DG 427 336-2GH (9/89).

Francisco Guerrero

Spanish 1528-1599

Suggested listening ...

Sacra Cantiones. **La Cappella Reial de Catalunya; Hespèrion XX/Jordi Savall.** Astrée Auvidis E8766 (10/93).

Jean-Adam Guilain

French fl. 1702-39

New review

Guilain. Pièces d'orgue pour le Magnificat.
Marchand. Pièces choisies pour l'orgue — Premier Livre. **François Espinasse** (org). Sony Classical SK57489. Played on the Holy Trinity organ of the Abbey Church of Ottobeuren, Germany.

`.·´ lh 12m  DDD  7/94`   **9** p **9** s ✍

This famous German instrument is so beautifully designed and tonally opulent that it would sound ideal in just about any music, but here it is shown to speak French with thoroughly convincing accents, meeting the detailed and specific registration demands of both Guilain and Marchand without hesitation. This rich, immensely varied yet utterly authentic sound-world has been splendidly recorded, the instrument placed a little distantly but with an ideal balance between clarity and the abbey's atmospheric acoustic backdrop. François Espinasse has clearly identified the unique stylistic characteristics of both Marchand and Guilain and his performances do much to enrich our perception not only of the whole period but of these two important composers in particular. Undoubtedly these are performances of considerable authority, stylistically persuasive and musically compelling, but, even more importably, there is something in Espinasse's warmly communicative approach which brings this music vividly to life. He has performed an important service to two composers whom organists too often pigeon-hole as second-division Couperin or Clérambault.

Louis-Gabriel Guillemain

French 1705-1770

Suggested listening ...

Violin Sonata in A major, Op. 1 No. 4. *Coupled with* **Leclair.** Violin Sonatas — A minor, Op. 5 No. 7; A major, Op. 9 No. 4. **Mondonville.** Violin Sonata in G major, Op. 3 No. 5. *Harpsichord Solos* — **Duphly.** La de Redemond. La du Buq. **J-B. Forqueray.** La Morangis ou La Plissay. **Simon Standage** (vn); **Lars Ulrik Mortensen** (hpd). Chandos CHAN0531 (6/93). *See review under Leclair; refer to the Index to Reviews.*

Ivor Gurney

British 1890-1937

Suggested listening ...

Five Preludes — No. 1 in F sharp major; No. 2 in A minor; No. 3 in D flat major; No. 4 in F sharp major; No. 5 in D major. *Preludes* — C major; C minor; D flat major; F sharp major. *Nocturnes* — A flat major; B major. Revery. To E. M. H.: A birthday present from Ivor. A picture. *Coupled with* **Elgar.** Concerto Allegro. Skizze. In Smyrna. Adieu. **Alan Gravill** (pf). Gamut Classics GAMCD516 (3/91).

The Western Playland[b]. Ludlow and Teme[a]. *Coupled with* **Vaughan Williams.** On Wenlock Edge[a]. [a]**Adrian Thompson** (ten); [b]**Stephen Varcoe** (bar); **Iain Burnside** (pf); **Delmé Quartet.** Hyperion CDA66385 (9/90).

Pavel Haas

Czechoslovakian 1899-1944

New review

P. Haas. String Quartets — No. 2, "From the Monkey Mountains", Op. 7; No. 3, Op. 15. **Krása.** String Quartet. **Hawthorne Quartet** (Ronan Lefkowitz, Si-Jing Huang, vns; Mark Ludwig, va; Sato Knudsen, vc). Decca 440 853-2DH.

Ih 16m   DDD   3/94   ⁹p ⁹s

Pavel Haas and Hans Krása were both born in Czechoslovakia in 1899; both were influenced by the modern movement, including neo-classicism, jazz and 'the new tonality', and both entered Theresienstadt in 1941 to travel to their deaths (on the same day) three years later in the gas chambers of Auschwitz. Of all Janáček's pupils it was Haas who absorbed rather than merely imitated his ideas. Something of the master's aphoristic, questing manner remains, but other than that the Quartet represents the mature Haas. An air of tension pervades the three-movements, alternating passages of lyricism with tightly intertwining parts of harmonic complexity. Krása's Quartet also reveals a voice of exceptional talent. As a product of his studies with Zemlinsky its harmonic world leans more towards *fin de siècle* Vienna than his native homeland. The central movement contains a marvellous section of burlesque (very boulevardier in allure) on a theme from the overture to Smetana's *The Bartered Bride*, whilst the slow finale opens up a magical, almost mystical, twilight world that Zemlinsky himself would have been proud to have penned. Excellent performances and superb recording.

Further listening ...

Wind Quintet, Op. 10. *Coupled with* **Foerster.** Wind Quintet in D major, Op. 95. **Janáček.** Mládi[a]. **Aulos Wind Quintet;** [a]**Kurt Berger** (bass cl). Koch Schwann Musica Mundi 310051 (6/93).

Alois Hába

Czechoslovakian 1893-1973

Suggested listening ...

THE MOTHER. **Soloists; Prague National Theatre Chorus and Orchestra/Jiří Jirouš.** Supraphon 10 8258-2 (11/94).

Patrick Hadley

New review

Hadley. The Trees so High[a].
Sainton. The Island. [a]**David Wilson-Johnson** (bar); **Philharmonia** [a]**Chorus and Orchestra/Matthias Bamert.** Chandos CHAN9181 Text included. Recorded in 1992.

52m DDD 10/93

There's a powerful, brooding melancholy pervading every bar of Patrick Hadley's 1931 symphonic ballad, *The Trees so High*; indeed, the music conveys a wistful, often disturbing intensity unusual for an English work of the period. The kindly presence of Vaughan Williams dominates Hadley's musical landscape, whilst much of the tricky high *divisi* string writing betrays the influence of Delius's *Song of the High Hills*. Matthias Bamert directs sensitively, securing a cultivated orchestral and choral response, and this new Chandos production has fine bloom and detail. According to Philip Sainton, *The Island* (1942) "depicts, in orchestral colours, the impression made upon me by a lovely seascape where fir trees come down to the rocks in Spring, Summer and Winter". Baxian territory, this: Sainton's expert orchestration shimmers enticingly and there's no lack of memor-able invention throughout (the trumpet calls at the start are indeed striking), even if things tend to sprawl a bit uncomfortably in the later stages. No matter, this is headily evocative stuff, and Anglophiles everywhere will surely want to add this sumptuous-sounding CD to their collections.

Johann Christian Haeffner

New review

Haeffner. ELECTRA. **Hillevi Martinpelto** (sop) Electra; **Peter Mattei** (bar) Orest; **Helle Hinz** (sop) Klytemnestra; **Mikael Samuelson** (bar) Aegisth; **Klas Hedlund** (ten) Pilad; **Stig Tysklind** (bass) Arcas; **Alf Häggstam** (bass) High Priest; **Christina Högman** (sop) Ismene; **Stockholm Radio Chorus; Drottningholm Baroque Ensemble/Thomas Schuback.** Caprice CAP22030. Notes, text and translation included.

② 1h 28m DDD 7/94

Haeffner studied in Leipzig, and after conducting in Frankfurt and Hamburg moved to Stockholm, where he eventually rose from singing coach and occasional viola player in the Royal Opera to become (still aged only 36) its Musical Director. Eight years earlier, he had been commissioned to write his first opera for the queen's nameday. This was *Electra*, given in Drottningholm in July 1787; it was written to a Swedish translation of a French libretto after Sophocles that had already been used by Jean-Baptiste Lemoyne. Haeffner was even more heavily influenced by Gluck (whom he idolized) than his slightly older French contemporary; and the colourful orchestration (especially his use of trombones), the declamatory recitative, and indeed the shaping of some scenes, clearly reveal that admiration. Of special interest, too, is his employment of leitmotifs, which begins with the programmatic overture depicting Electra's thirst for Orest to avenge their father's murder, and the intervention of the Furies. Various cuts have been made here, particularly of choruses, and Act 3 is compressed. Except in that part there is little stage action, so that all emphasis falls on the music itself; and from the very outset, where the Furies are urging Orest on (only to pursue him at the end of the opera) Haeffner shows a powerful dramatic sense. Much of the plot is played in a continually inventive, highly expressive orchestrally accompanied recitative that constantly flowers into arioso; and there are effective homophonic choruses, orchestral processionals and, at the close, an exciting mime for the Furies. Thomas Schuback drives the work along with an unremitting instinct for its tension, securing crisp playing from the orchestra and well-drilled vigorous singing from the chorus; and he is fortunate in having at his disposal a cast so uniformly excellent, bringing clarity and meaning to every word and expressive nuance to every phrase. The whole adds up to one of the most stimulating operatic discoveries of 1994. Gluck would surely have been proud to acknowledge Haeffner's *Electra*.

Georg Haentzschel

German 1907-1992

Suggested listening ...

Film Scores: Via Mala. Annelie. Münchhausen. Robinson soll nicht sterben. Emil und die Detektive. Meine Kinder und ich. Hotel Adlon. **Cologne Radio Orchestra/Emmerich Smola.** Capriccio 10 400.

Reynaldo Hahn

Venezuelan-French 1875-1947

Suggested listening ...

Premières Valses. Le rossignol éperdu — excerpts. **Catherine Joly** (pf). Accord 20054-2 (5/90).

MOZART — *musical comedy.* **Soloists; French Radio Lyric Orchestra/Pierre-Michel Le Conte.** Musidisc 20137-2 (3/92).

Ernesto Halffter

Spanish/Mexican 1905-1989

Suggested listening ...

Rapsodia portuguesa[a]. *Coupled with* **Falla.** Noches en los jardines de España[a]. **Gerhard.** Alegrías. [a]**Guillermo Gonzalez** (pf); **Tenerife Symphony Orchestra/Victor Pablo Pérez.** Etcetera KTC1095 (7/92). *See review under Falla; refer to the Index to Reviews.*

George Frederic Handel

German-British 1685-1759

Handel. ORGAN CONCERTOS. **Ton Koopman** (org); **Amsterdam Baroque Orchestra.** Erato Emerald 2292-45613-2.
Op. 4 — No. 2 in B flat major; No. 4 in F major; No. 6 in B flat major. Op. 7 — No. 8 in A major; No. 10 in D minor; No. 11 in G minor.

Ih 18m   DDD   II/91

Handel's highly acclaimed skill as a virtuoso organist was a significant factor in attracting audiences. His organ concertos are rich in catchy tunes, with some of the long *allegros* sailing along with unstoppable momentum. But there are great treasures in the slow movements too — the *Andante* from Op. 4 No. 4 is full of colour and the solo part performs wonders of invention over a simple foundation of chords while the Menuet and Gavotte from Op. 7 No. 11 have great charm and elegance. Handel adapted several of these Concertos from other works — Op. 4 No. 5 comes from a recorder sonata and Op. 4 No. 6 was originally for harp — but the universality of the writing means that everything seems entirely at home in this context, especially given such compelling performances as here. Ton Koopman leads his performances from the organ stool, giving his disc a real feeling of intimacy which makes ideal home listening. He indulges in some thoroughly convincing improvisations at points where Handel too would have given free rein to his skills as a virtuoso organist.

Additional recommendation ...

Op. 4 — *No. 1 in G minor; No. 2; No. 3 in G minor; No. 4; No. 5 in F major; No. 6. No. 14 in A major, HWV296.* **Simon Preston** (org); **The English Concert/Trevor Pinnock.** Archiv Produktion 413 465-2AH2 — Ih 30m DDD 12/84

New review

Handel. Concerti grossi, Op. 3. **Tafelmusik/Jeanne Lamon.** Sony Classical Vivarte SK52553.

••	lh DDD 7/93			♀ₚ ♀ₛ	Ⓑ	✒

This is a fine issue impressive both for its stylistic fluency and its infectious response to Handel's music which could not conceivably disappoint anyone. Tafelmusik play only the six concertos of which Handel's authorship is undisputed. Goodman (listed below) further included the Concerto in F major (No. 4B), which, though not by Handel, is an attractive piece in its own right. Having said that, it is the Sony version which, in respect of finesse and vitality, has the edge over all the competition. Where Tafelmusik scores is in the sheer virtuosity of its playing and the easy grace-fulness of its phrasing. Strong accents are not over emphasized and, though vigorous, there is nothing aggressive in this approach to the music. Tafelmusik includes a plucked string instrument among its continuo colloquium; they have large reinforcements at the top and bottom of the string texture and the performances have great radiance. The disc is beautifully recorded and lucidly documented.

Additional recommendations ...
English Baroque Soloists/John Eliot Gardiner. Erato 2292-45981-2 — •• lh Ⓑ ✒
The English Concert/Trevor Pinnock (hpd). Archiv Produktion 413 727-2AH — •• 57m
DDD 3/85 Ⓑ ✒
Handel and Haydn Society/Christopher Hogwood. L'Oiseau-Lyre 421 729-2OH — ••
lh lm DDD 6/89 Ⓑ ✒
Brandenburg Consort/Roy Goodman. Hyperion CDA66633 — •• lh l7m DDD 6/93 Ⓑ ✒

Key to symbols

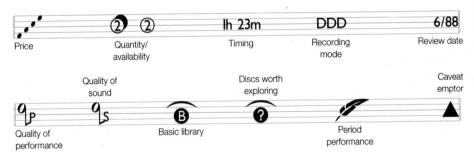

Price	Quantity/ availability	Timing	Recording mode	Review date
•• ② ②		lh 23m	DDD	6/88

Quality of sound		Discs worth exploring		Caveat emptor
♀ₚ ♀ₛ Ⓑ	Quality of performance	? Basic library	✒	▲ Period performance

Handel. Concerti grossi, Op. 6. **The English Concert/Trevor Pinnock.** Archiv Produktion 410 897/9-2AH. From 2742 002 (11/82).
410 897-2AH — No. 1 in G major; No. 2 in F major; No. 3 in E minor; No. 4 in A minor. *410 898-2AH* — No. 5 in D major; No. 6 in G minor; No. 7 in B flat major; No. 8 in C minor. *410 899-2AH* — No. 9 in F major; No. 10 in D minor; No. 11 in A major; No. 12 in B minor.

••	③	42m lh lm 58m	DDD	5/84 6/85 8/85	Ⓑ	✒

Handel's 12 *Concerti grossi*, Op. 6 have from four to six movements and are mostly in *da chiesa* form, i.e. without dance movements. They were written within one month in the autumn of 1739 (an average of two movements per day!) and when a great composer is thus carried on the tide of urgent inspiration it usually shows, as it does here in the flow of felicitous invention and memorable tune-smithing. The range of musical idioms used throughout is impressive and to them all Handel imparts his own indelible and unmistakable stamp. Trevor Pinnock's account contains much that is satisfying: polished ensemble, effectively judged tempos, a natural feeling for phrase, and a buoyancy of spirit which serves Handel's own robust musical language very well. Crisp attack, a judicious application of appoggiaturas and tasteful embellishment further enhance these lively performances. Pinnock varies the continuo colour by using organ and harpsichord and also includes Handel's autograph (though not printed) oboe parts for Concertos Nos. 1, 2, 5 and 6; where they occur a bassoon is sensibly added to fulfil the customary three-part wind texture of the period. Recorded sound is clear and captures the warm sonorities of the instruments.

Additional recommendations ...

Nos. 1-12. **Guildhall String Ensemble.** RCA Victor Red Seal. *RD87895 — Nos. 1-4.*
RD87907 — Nos. 5-8. RD87921 — Nos. 9-12 — .⠂' ③ 44m 1h 56m DDD 2/90 Ⓑ
Nos. 1-6. **Boston Baroque/Martin Pearlman.** Telarc CD80253 — .⠂' 1h 16m DDD 10/92 Ⓑ ✒
Nos. 1-12. Concerto grosso in C major, HWV318, "Alexander's Feast". **Collegium Aureum.** Deutsche
Harmonia Mundi 05472 77267-2 — .⠂' ③ 3h 8m ADD 2/93 Ⓑ ✒

New review

Handel. The Water Music, HWV348-50. Music for the Royal Fireworks, HWV351. **Le
Concert des Nations/Jordi Savall.** Astrée Auvidis E8512.

.⠂' 1h 14m DDD 3/94   ♩ℙ Ⓑ ✒

New review

Handel. The Water Music, HWV348-50. **English Baroque Soloists/John Eliot
Gardiner.** Philips 434 122-2PH.

.⠂' 53m DDD 5/93   ♩ℙ Ⓑ ✒

New review

Handel. The Water Music, HWV348-50. **Amsterdam Baroque Orchestra/Ton
Koopman.** Erato 4509-91716-2.

.⠂' 56m DDD   ♩ℙ Ⓑ ✒

Of the period-instrument couplings of these two 'elemental' suites, Savall's must be placed at
or near the top of the list. It is, however, strange that, though the booklet-notes
acknowledge that the *Water Music* falls into "three suites" and that the Suite in G major was
probably played during supper, the recorded performance ends with that in F major
(described as "Suite II") preceded by the rest ("Suite I") — neither the published nor the
'logical' order. The 74-minute duration of the disc does not allow the movements from the
earlier Concerto in F to be included. There is the familiar re-titling and juggling with the
order of movements, so that, *inter alia*, the "Coro" in Suite III becomes "Menuet I" and is
followed by the Menuet in G major ("Menuet II"). By now we should be used to such
manipulations, and those who like to follow the score will be grateful that they do not
extend to the *Royal Fireworks Music*. What splendid performances these are though, spirited,
clean-edged and elegantly embellished — by a solo trumpet in the *Adagio* of the Ouverture
of the *Fireworks Music*, where the preceding section is repeated as marked. The orchestral
force is substantial, and the comparatively high-level recording and generous acoustic give a
deliberate sense of being close to the performers — just as, on the Thames, King George III
may have been in a barge adjacent to the musicians — rather than of hearing them from the
riverside. Should the order of play disturb you it will be worth the trouble to programme
your player to recognize your preferred one.
    Gardiner presents the three suites of the *Water Music* in what seems to be their logical
order. He does not add to existing confusion by giving names to undesignated movements,
but here the final "This Air to be played 3 times over" becomes a Bourrée. No matter
though, it ends the proceedings in a blaze of glory. This is as 'festive' a performance as has
ever been committed to disc, with well-chosen tempos, alert rhythms, fine style, tasteful and
thoughtfully placed embellishment, and topped in the outer suites with incisive brass —
bright, sharp-edged but never coarse. The recording is whistle-clean and meticulously
balanced, and the 'outdoor' suites sound appropriately spacious. This will be a hard act to
follow and another is the one by Amsterdam Baroque with Ton Koopman. He also places the
three Suites in logical rather than printed order, and they are liberally and attractively
embellished in appropriate places. The playing is superb. Where Gardiner and Koopman
differ importantly is in weight: whilst it was reported that about 50 musicians were
employed in Handel's original performance, Gardiner settles for 42 and Koopman for a mere
20. Koopman's is thus a chamber performance, aimed at presenting the music with clarity,
and with an acoustic that makes no effort to re-create the spaciousness of the 'great
outdoors' in the F and D major Suites. Thus the two latter versions are complementary
rather than competitive, and all three are worthy of a place in a CD collection. If, however,
you insist on having a coupling with the *Fireworks Music* and aren't devoted to period
instruments, then the conductorless Orpheus Chamber Orchestra recording will serve you
well enough.

Additional recommendations ...
Water Music. **Simon Standage, Elizabeth Wilcock** (vns); **The English Concert/Trevor Pinnock** (hpd). Archiv Produktion 410 525-2AH — .·* 54m DDD 2/84 Ⓑ ✍
Water Music. Music for the Royal Fireworks. **Academy of Ancient Music/Christopher Hogwood.** L'Oiseau-Lyre 400 059-2OH — .·* 3/83 ⁹ₚ Ⓑ ✍
Music for the Royal Fireworks. Concerti a due cori — *No. 2 in F major; No. 3 in F major.* **The English Concert/Trevor Pinnock.** Archiv Produktion 415 129-2AH — .·* 54m DDD 8/85 ⁹ₛ Ⓑ ✍
Music for the Royal Fireworks. Coronation Anthems[a] — *Zadok the priest; The King shall rejoice; My heart is inditing; Let thy hand be strengthened.* [a]**New College Choir, Oxford; King's Consort/ Robert King.** Hyperion CDA66350 — .·* 57m DDD 12/89 Ⓑ ✍
Water Music. Music for the Royal Fireworks. **Orpheus Chamber Orchestra.** DG 435 390-2GH — .·* 1h 6m DDD 11/92 Ⓑ
Music for the Royal Fireworks. Solomon — *Arrival of the Queen of Sheba. Concerto grosso in C major, "Alexander's Feast". Organ Concerto No. 6 in B flat major, Op. 4. Suite in D major, "Water piece".* **La Stravaganza/Andrew Manze.** Denon Aliare CO-79943 — .·* 58m DDD 3/93 Ⓑ ✍

Handel. TRIO SONATAS. **London Baroque** (Ingrid Seifert, Richard Gwilt, vns; Charles Medlam, vc; Richard Egarr, hpd). Harmonia Mundi HMC90 1379 and 1389. Recorded in 1991. *HMC90 1379* — Op. 2: No. 1 in B minor; No. 2 in G minor; No. 3 in B flat major; No. 4 in F major; No. 5 in G minor; No. 6 in G minor. *HMC90 1389* — Op. 5: No. 1 in A major; No. 2 in D major; No. 3 in E minor; No. 4 in G major; No. 5 in G minor; No. 6 in F major; No. 7 in B flat major.

.·* ② 58m 1h 9m DDD 4/93

Handel's publisher, Walsh, printed the six Trio Sonatas, Op. 2 in about 1730, following them up in 1739 with seven further trios which he published as the composer's Op. 5. In each set Handel offered a choice of melody instruments though the writing suggests that he had violins foremost in mind. This is the way in which all 13 sonatas are played on these two separately available discs and the decision is a good one. The performances by London Baroque are poised, well-shaped and susceptible to the subtle nuances of Handel's part-writing. Ingrid Seifert and Richard Gwilt are partners of long standing and their even dialogue, sometimes grave, sometimes lively and at other times playful, serves the music effectively. Tempos are well-judged and phrases are eloquently shaped and articulately spoken. In all this the violinists are sympathetically supported by the continuo players who make their own vital contribution to clear textures and overall balance. Recorded sound is appropriately intimate, serving the sound character of the instruments themselves and evoking a chamber music ambience. The music, it hardly need be said, maintains a high level of craftsmanship and interest which will surely delight listeners.

New review
Handel. FLUTE SONATAS. **Barthold Kuijken** (fl); **Wieland Kuijken** (va da gamba); **Robert Kohnen** (hpd). Accent ACC9180D.
No. 1 in E minor, HWV359*b*; No. 2 in G major, HWV363*b*; No. 3 in B minor, HWV367*b*; No. 4 in A minor, HWV374; No. 5 in E minor, HWV375; No. 6 in B minor, HWV376; No. 7 in D major, HWV378; No. 8 in E minor, HWV379.

.·* 1h 13m DDD 11/93   ⁹ₚ

In this recording of solo flute sonatas Barthold Kuijken plays pieces unquestionably by Handel as well as others over which doubt concerning his authorship has been cast in varying degrees. Three of the Sonatas (HWV359*b*, 363*b* and 367*b*) were published as Part of Handel's Op. 1 by Walsh in about 1730. Three others (HWV374-6) were published in a collection of pieces by various composers at about the same time. The remaining two (HWV378 and 379) have been preserved in manuscript. HWV378, though attributed to Johann Sigmund Weiss, brother of the celebrated lutenist — his name appears on the manuscript — is now thought to be the product of Handel's pen. HWV379 is an oddity in that it consists of a somewhat haphazard compilation and rearrangement of movements from other of Handel's solo sonatas. Certainly not all of the pieces here were conceived for transverse flute — there are earlier versions of HWV363*b* and 367*b*, for example, for oboe and treble recorder, respectively; but we can well imagine that in Handel's day most, if not all, of these delightful sonatas were regarded among instrumentalists as more-or-less common property. Barthold Kuijken, with his eldest brother Wieland and Robert Kohnen, gives characteristically graceful and stylish performances of the music. Kuijken is skilful in matters of ornamentation and is often adventurous, though invariably within the bounds of good taste. Dance movements are brisk and sprightly though he is careful to preserve their poise, and phrases are crisply articulated. This is of especial benefit to movements such as the lively *Vivace* of the B minor Sonata (HWV367b) which can proceed rather aimlessly when too legato an approach is favoured; and the virtuosity of these players pays off in the *Presto (Furioso)* movement that follows. In short, a delightful disc which should please both Handelians and most lovers of Baroque chamber music.

Handel. KEYBOARD SUITES, HWV426-33. **Colin Tilney** (hpd). Archiv Produktion Galleria 427 170-2AGA2. Items marked [a] from 2533 169 (2/75), [b] 2533 168 (2/75). Recorded 1973.
No. 1 in A major[a]; No. 2 in F major[b]; No. 3 in D minor[a]; No. 4 in E minor[b]; No. 5 in E major[b]; No. 5a — Air and Variations, "The Harmonious Blacksmith"; No. 6 in F sharp minor[a]; No. 7 in G minor[a]; No. 8 in F minor[b].

② 1h 58m ADD 8/91

Handel published his eight harpsichord suites in 1720 though he had written much of the music earlier in his life. One of the many striking features of these pieces is that of variety. Handel's terms of reference were wide and cosmopolitan and the harpsichord suites contain many contrasting ingredients ranging from well sustained imitative part-writing on the one hand to simpler airs and dances on the other. These two aspects of Handel's art find a happy and celebrated conjunction in the Air and Variations affectionately known as *The Harmonious Blacksmith*. The music, displaying elements of French, Italian and German styles, reflects Handel's own cosmopolitan nature and tastes. Many readers may be as surprised to find how much of this music is unfamiliar to them as they will be delighted by its ceaseless invention and affecting idiom. Colin Tilney is a persuasive interpreter of this repertory, bringing a muscular strength to Handel's often complex part-writing while never complicating simpler musical ideas with misplaced rhetoric or exaggerated gestures. Preludes with their strongly improvisatory character are given just the right amount of rhythmic freedom even if *The Harmonious Blacksmith* air, though tastefully ornamented, is a shade lacking in conviviality. Tilney plays two especially fine instruments made in Hamburg during the early years of the eighteenth century. The recorded sound is sympathetic.

Additional recommendations ...
Scott Ross (hpd). Erato 2292-45452-2 — ② 1h 52m DDD 2/90
Nos. 5, 5a and 7. **D. Scarlatti.** *Keyboard Sonatas* — *G major, Kk2; D minor, Kk9; C minor, Kk11; G major, Kk14; E minor, Kk15; E major, Kk20; D major, Kk21; D major, Kk23; A major, Kk24.*
Martin Souter (hpd). Isis ISISCD001 — 1h 15m DDD 3/93
Nos. 1-5. **Martin Souter** (hpd). Isis ISISCD003 — 1h 19m DDD 7/93

Handel. Dixit Dominus, HWV232[a]. Nisi Dominus, HWV238[b]. Salve Regina, HWV241[c].
[ac]**Arleen Auger,** [a]**Lynne Dawson** (sops); [ab]**Diana Montague** (mez); [a]**Leigh Nixon,** [b]**John Mark Ainsley** (tens); [ab]**Simon Birchall** (bass); **Choir and Orchestra of Westminster Abbey/Simon Preston.** Archiv Produktion 423 594-2AH. Texts and translations included.

56m DDD 2/89

Although *Dixit Dominus* is the earliest surviving large scale work by Handel (he was only 22 at the time of its composition in 1707) it displays a remarkable degree of competence and invention and also looks forward to the mature style to come. The vocal writing for both chorus and soloists is extremely ornate and embellished and requires a considerable amount of expertise and flair in order to do full justice to the music. Fortunately, Simon Preston and his team possess all the necessary requirements — indeed, this is one of the most energetic, exhilarating and purposeful performances of this work ever recorded. One need only single out the rhythmically incisive performances of the opening "Dixit Dominus Domineo meo" or the "Judicabit in nationibus" and the superbly crisp and articulate performances from the Orchestra of Westminster Abbey to realize that it is a very special recording indeed. The well thought out coupling of *Nisi Dominus* and *Salve Regina* are no less impressive, with the latter offering the listener another chance to sample the beautiful solo contributions of Arleen Auger. The recorded sound is also outstandingly fine. A delightful disc.

Dixit Dominus. Coronation Anthems — Zadok the priest; The King shall rejoice; My heart is inditing; Let thy hand be strengthened. **Soloists; Monteverdi Choir; Monteverdi Orchestra/John Eliot Gardiner.** Erato 2292-45136-2 — ⁖ ADD

Handel. Aci, Galatea e Polifemo[a]. Recorder Sonatas[b] — F major, HWV369; C major, HWV365; G major (trans. F major), HWV358. **Emma Kirkby** (sop) Aci; **Carolyn Watkinson** (contr) Galatea; **David Thomas** (bass) Polifemo; [b]**Michel Piquet** (rec); [b]**John Toll** (hpd); **London Baroque/Charles Medlam** ([b]vc). Harmonia Mundi HMC90 1253/4. Notes, text and translation included. Item marked [a] new to UK, [b] from HMC1190/91 (9/86).

⁖ ② **1h 46m DDD II/87** ✒

Handel's English pastoral *Acis and Galatea* has always been one of his most popular works, but not many of its admirers are aware that he had written a completely different treatment of the same story ten years earlier (when he was 23) for a ducal wedding in Naples. In this version modern ears need to adjust to Acis (a young shepherd lad) being represented by a soprano (originally a castrato), while the nymph Galatea is a contralto. The work is full of invention and instrumental colour, and there are several memorably beautiful items in the score, such as the opening duet (with the lovers' voices intertwining), and above all Acis's dying farewell after the jealous giant Polyphemus has crushed him under a huge rock. To suggest the giant's vast size Handel employed a prodigious vocal range of two-and-a-half octaves, which has proved the chief obstacle to performances of the work, here receiving a very enjoyable first recording. All three singers are excellent and so is the technical quality.

Handel. Acis and Galatea. **Norma Burrowes** (sop) Galatea; **Anthony Rolfe Johnson** (ten) Acis; **Martyn Hill** (ten) Damon; **Willard White** (bass) Polyphemus; **Paul Elliot** (ten); **English Baroque Soloists/John Eliot Gardiner.** Archiv Produktion 423 406-2AH2. Notes, text and translation included. From 2708 038 (9/78). Recorded in 1978.

⁖ ② **1h 35m ADD 8/88** ♩ₚ ✒

John Eliot Gardiner made this recording of Handel's masque during the late 1970s when the revival of period instruments was still in a comparatively early stage. Listeners may detect weaknesses both in intonation and in ensemble from time to time but, nevertheless, Gardiner's performance is lively and stylistically assured. He paces the work dramatically revealing nuances both in the text and in the music. The solo team is a strong one and there are especially fine contributions from Norma Burrowes and Anthony Rolfe Johnson. This is an enjoyable performance of an enchanting work.

Acis and Galatea. Look down, harmonious Saint, "The Praise of Harmony", HWV124. **Soloists; King's Consort/Robert King.** Hyperion CDA66361/2 — ⁖ ② 1h 46m DDD 6/90 ♩ₚ ✒
Acis and Galatea (arr. Mozart). **Soloists; Handel and Haydn Society Chorus and Orchestra/Christopher Hogwood.** L'Oiseau-Lyre 430 538-2OH2 — ⁖ ② 1h 36m DDD 7/92 ✒
Acis and Galatea. **Soloists; St Anthony Singers; Philomusica of London/Sir Adrian Boult.** Decca 436 227-2DM2 — ⁖ ② ADD ♩ₚ

New review
Handel. Deborah. **Yvonne Kenny, Susan Gritton** (sops); **Catherine Denley** (mez); **James Bowman** (alto); **Michael George** (bass); **New College Choir, Oxford; Salisbury Cathedral Choristers; King's Consort/Robert King.** Hyperion CDA66841/2. Text included. Recorded in 1993.

⁖ ② **2h 20m DDD 2/94** ♩ₚ

Deborah, written in 1733, occupies an honoured place in the canon of Handel's oratorios as the first composed for the entertainment of London theatre audiences. It is also a compound of numerous earlier works, including the Chandos and Coronation Anthems, the *Brockes Passion* and the *Ode for the Birthday of Queen Anne*, and in putting *Deborah* together in this manner, Handel was less successful than he usually was in creating a unified work — though the librettist and indeed the Bible itself have to be assigned some of the blame. It is, however, eminently worth revival, and this recording, the first on CD, is warmly welcome. It begins with an overture different from the one usually heard: a fine, stirring D major trumpety piece, with a concluding minuet that was to find a place in the *Fireworks* Music. There are some noble choruses, several of which are in five or even eight voices, giving Handel the opportunity for grand effects. In *Deborah*, the chief interest rests with the choruses. Here they are very well sung by forces from Salisbury Cathedral and New College, Oxford, 32 trebles, eight countertenors, six tenors and eight basses, who produce a lot more sound than you might expect. Robert King's control of this group and the polish he imparts to the choral singing, with its clearly projected lines and its firmness of tone is admirable as is Michael George's warm and resonant contribution as Abinoam and Catherine Denley's firm, direct and stylish singing of the music of the unfortunate Sisera. The orchestral playing is polished; the recorded sound is more reverberant than might be ideal.

Handel. Alexander's Feast[a]. Concerto Grosso in C major, HWV318, "Alexander's Feast". [a]**Donna Brown** (sop); [a]**Carolyn Watkinson** (contr); [a]**Ashley Stafford** (alto); [a]**Nigel Robson** (ten); [a]**Stephen Varcoe** (bar); [a]**Monteverdi Choir, English Baroque Soloists/ John Eliot Gardiner.** Philips 422 053-2PH2. Text included. Recorded live in 1987.

── ② lh 38m DDD II/88 ──

Alexander's Feast was the first work Handel had set by a major English poet (Dryden) and it was also the first time he allotted the principal male part to a tenor instead of the castrato heroes of his Italian operas. These two factors, combined with much fine music, scored with great brilliance and imagination, ensured the immediate success of *Alexander's Feast*. It is strange that nowadays it is seldom performed so this recording would have been very welcome even had it not been so full of vitality and so stylishly performed (though perhaps with more sophisticated detail than the eighteenth century would have managed). The Monteverdi Choir and the soloists are all Gardiner regulars, though the pure-voiced Canadian soprano Donna Brown is a fairly recent (and welcome) acquisition; and the English Baroque Soloists have ample opportunities to shine — especially the violins, although the natural horns' lusty entry in the bucolic "Bacchus, ever fair and young" is exhilarating.

Additional recommendation ...
Alexander's Feast. Harp Concerto in B flat major, HWV294. Organ Concerto in G minor/major, HWV289.
Soloists; Tragicomedia; The Sixteen Choir and Orchestra/Harry Christophers.
Collins Classics 7016-2 — ② lh 56m DDD 10/91

Handel. Saul. **Lynne Dawson, Donna Brown** (sops); **Derek Lee Ragin** (alto); **John Mark Ainsley, Neil Mackie, Philip Salmon, Philip Slane** (tens); **Alastair Miles, Richard Savage** (basses); **Monteverdi Choir; English Baroque Soloists/John Eliot Gardiner.** Philips 426 265-2PH3. Recorded live in 1989.

── ③ 2h 39m DDD 8/91 ──

Saul is considered by many to be one of the most arresting music dramas in the English language, even though it is officially classed as an oratorio. In it Handel explores in some psychological depth the motivations of his characters, most notably that of the eponymous anti-hero, whose tantrums caused by envy and his searching for supernatural intervention are all vividly delineated; as is the friendship of David and Jonathan and the different characters of Saul's daughters, Merab and Michal. In yet another compelling performance of Handel under his baton, John Eliot Gardiner — in this live recording made at the Göttingen Handel Festival in Germany — fulfils every aspect of this varied and adventurous score, eliciting execution of refined and biting calibre from his choir and orchestra. The young British bass Alastair Miles captures Saul in all his moods. John Mark Ainsley and Derek Lee Ragin are both affecting as Jonathan and David; so are Lynne Dawson and Donna Brown as Michal and Merab. There are a few cuts, but they aren't grievous enough to prevent a firm recommendation.

Handel. Israel in Egypt. **Nancy Argenta, Emily Van Evera** (sops); **Timothy Wilson** (alto); **Anthony Rolfe Johnson** (ten); **David Thomas, Jeremy White** (basses); **Taverner Choir and Players/Andrew Parrott.** EMI CDS7 54018-2. Text included. Recorded in 1989.

② 2h 15m DDD 2/91

If anyone needs to assure themselves as to whether the English choral tradition is alive and well, they need only buy this CD. *Israel in Egypt*, of all Handel's works, is the choral one *par excellence* — so much so, in fact, that it was something of a failure in Handel's own time because solo singing was much preferred to choral by the audiences. Andrew Parrott gives a complete performance of the work, in its original form: that is to say, prefaced by the noble funeral anthem for Queen Caroline, as adapted by Handel to serve as a song of mourning by the captive Israelites. This first part is predominantly slow, grave music, powerfully elegiac; the Taverner Choir show themselves, in what is testing music to sing, firm and clean of line, well focused and strongly sustained. The chorus have their chances to be more energetic in the second part, with the famous and vivid Plague choruses — in which the orchestra too play their part in the pictorial effects, with the fiddles illustrating in turn frogs, flies and hailstones. And last, in the third part, there is a generous supply of the stirring C major music in which Handel has the Israelites give their thanks to God, in some degree symbolizing the English giving thanks for the Hanoverian monarchy and the Protestant succession. Be that as it may, the effect is splendid. The solo work is first-rate, too, with Nancy Argenta radiant in Miriam's music in the final scene and distinguished contributions too from David Thomas and Anthony Rolfe Johnson.

Handel. Messiah. **Judith Nelson, Emma Kirkby** (sops); **Carolyn Watkinson** (contr); **Paul Elliott** (ten); **David Thomas** (bass); **Christ Church Cathedral Choir, Oxford; Academy of Ancient Music/Christopher Hogwood.** L'Oiseau-Lyre Florilegium 430 488-2OH2. Notes and text included. From D189D3 (4/80). Recorded in 1979.

② 2h 17m ADD 7/84 Ⓑ

Christopher Hogwood's recording of *Messiah* was first issued on LP in 1980. Four years later it was successfully transferred to three CDs. Now, with the advance of technology the three-disc package has been supplanted by this two-disc box retaining the full texts of the original. Hogwood's version of *Messiah* conforms with a Foundling Hospital performance in 1754, directed by the composer himself. A significant difference between this recording and most others is the use of boys' treble voices in the choir as opposed to women's. That is what Handel wanted and it is this feature of the interpretation which, perhaps more than any other makes it appealing. In contrast again with many alternative versions this one dispenses with the solo counter-tenor, the contralto Carolyn Watkinson singing the music often allotted to the other. She is excellent and a considerable adornment to the set. Only the Academy of Ancient Music is likely to cause occasional disappointment with playing that falls short of ideal in matters of tuning and ensemble. The acoustic is a shade reverberant but the performance comes close to the heart of the music and remains a satisfying interpretation.

Additional recommendations ...
Soloists; Royal Philhrmonic Chorus and Orchestra/Sir Thomas Beecham. RCA Red Seal 09026-61266-2 — ③ 2h 41m ADD Ⓑ ▲
Messiah (arr. Mozart). **Soloists; Austrian Radio Chorus and Orchestra/Sir Charles Mackerras.** Archiv Produktion Galleria 427 173-2AGA2 — ② 2h 26m ADD 11/90
Soloists; Collegium Musicum 90 Chorus; Collegium Musicum 90/Richard Hickox. Chandos Chaconne CHAN0522/3 — ② 2h 21m DDD 3/92 Ⓑ
Soloists; The Sixteen; Amsterdam Baroque Orchestra/Ton Koopman. Erato 2292-45960-2 — ② 2h 20m DDD 3/93 Ⓑ
The Scholars Baroque Ensemble/David van Asch (bass). Naxos 8 550667/8 — ② 2h 41m DDD 4/93 Ⓑ

Handel. Semele. **Kathleen Battle** (sop) Semele; **Marilyn Horne** (mez) Juno, Ino; **John Aler** (ten) Jupiter; **Michael Chance** (alto) Athamas; **Samuel Ramey** (bass) Cadmus, Somnus; **Neil Mackie** (ten) Apollo; **Sylvia McNair** (sop) Iris; **Mark S. Doss** (bar) Priest; **Ambrosian**

Opera Chorus; English Chamber Orchestra/John Nelson. DG 435 782-2GH3. Text included.

③ 2h 55m DDD 6/93

Nelson opens out the serious cuts in Handel's dramatic oratorio (which Gardiner makes). On disc what matters above all is the quality of the music rather than the supposed effectiveness on stage, and hearing the extra numbers that Nelson includes makes it almost unthinkable ever again to do without them. Nelson, for all his use of modern instruments, has learnt most of the essential lessons of period performance, whether double-dotting, ornamentation or light, crisp articulation. As Semele, Kathleen Battle is sensuous as well as silvery, knowingly innocent in her self-regard and stylish in coping with elaborate divisions. Her cadenzas and extra ornamentations on *da capos* are spectacular, with attack consistently clean. As the fire-snorting Juno, Marilyn Horne is superb, rich, full of flair and wonderfully agile. As Ino she aptly modifies her tone. Samuel Ramey who doubles the role of Cadmus, Semele's father, with that of Somnus, is first rate, the *buffo* element in the role of Somnus delightfully sketched in. The chorus is excellent, adding to the impact of a masterly opera that on record has never fully had its due. The full-ranging recording provides some convincing sound-effects of thunder and the like.

Additional recommendation ...
Soloists; Monteverdi Choir; English Baroque Soloists/John Eliot Gardiner. Erato Libretto 2292-45982-2 — ② 2h 34m ADD 6/93

Handel. Theodora. **Lorraine Hunt** (sop) Theodora; **Jennifer Lane** (mez) Irene; **Drew Minter** (alto) Didymus; **Jeffrey Thomas** (ten) Septimus; **Nigel Rogers** (ten) Messenger; **David Thomas** (bass) Valens; **California University, Berkeley Chamber Chorus; Philharmonia Baroque Orchestra/Nicholas McGegan.** Harmonia Mundi HMU90 7060/2. Text included. Recorded in 1991.

③ 2h 50m DDD 10/92

"The Jews will not come to it ... because it is a Christian story, and the ladies will not come to it because it is a virtuous one" wrote Handel somewhat bitterly after the unfavourable reception of his sublime late oratorio, *Theodora*. If contemporary audiences were put off by its theme of martyrdom, we should be grateful that the self-righteous piety of Morell's libretto inspired some of Handel's finest music, complete for the first time on record with the added bonus of both the original and revised versions of "Symphony of Soft Musick". And at last it has a recording which can be wholeheartedly recommended. David Thomas as Valens, the Roman governor, opens the proceedings with a firm and resolute tone and later gives the bloodthirsty "Racks, gibbets, sword and fire" much menace. Lorraine Hunt was an inspired choice for the taxing title-role: the top notes of "Angels ever bright and fair" are celestially floated, while she finds great intensity in "With darkness deep", the emotional centre of the work. Drew Minter gives a mellifluous and characterful account of Didymus, a Roman officer recently converted to Christianity who attempts to save Theodora. Listen to their duet, "To Thee, Thou glorious Son" to hear how winningly they blend their voices. Praise too for Jeffrey Thomas as Septimius, particularly in his elegant ornamentation in the virtuoso aria "Dread the fruits of Christian folly", only occasionally showing strain in the wide leaps in "From virtue springs". Jennifer Lane is also impressive as Irene (described in the libretto simply as "A Christian") — despite being burdened with some of Morell's most trite utterances: "True Happiness is only found, where Grace and Truth and Love Abound, And pure religion feeds the Flame". This is perhaps Nicholas McGegan's best Handel recording yet. He has at his command a highly skilled orchestra, chooses tempos which are unfailingly apt, supporting and giving weight to the vocal lines. Praise too, for the excellent University of California Chamber Chorus, well schooled by their director John Butt. Harmonia Mundi have provided an informative booklet with a full libretto in three languages and an illuminating introductory essay from McGegan himself.

Additional recommendations ...
Soloists; Amor Artis Chorale; English Chamber Orchestra/Johannes Somary. Vanguard Classics 08.4075.72 — 2h 32m ② ADD
Soloists; Vienna Concentus Musicus/Nikolaus Harnoncourt. Teldec 2292-46447-2 —
② 2h 11m DDD 8/91

Handel. OPERA ARIAS. **Nathalie Stutzmann** (contr); **Hanover Band/Roy Goodman.** RCA Victor Red Seal 09026 61205-2. Texts and translations included. Recorded in 1991. ORLANDO — Fammi combattere; Ah stigie larve! ... Già latra Cerbero ... Ma la Furia ... Vaghe pupille. ACI, GALATEA E POLIFEMO — Qui l'augel di pianta. RINALDO — Cara sposa, amante cara. GIULIO CESARE — Va tacito e nascosto; Se in fiorito ameno prato. FLORIDANTE — Bramo te sola; Se dolce m'era già. PARTENOPE — Furibondo spira il vento. RADAMISTO — Ombra cara di mia sposa.

⊙ 1h 9m DDD 3/93

The richness and variety of Nathalie Stutzmann's vocal expression, and her deep understanding of music that is all too often performed with a dispassionate reverence, belie her youth. Yet that youth is of use, for the proclamations of love in many of these arias are not conveyed here with matronly recollection but immediate passion. It has to be said that RCA have served her well, for the recording engineers have found that sweet microphone spot for her to enable her qualities to cut through the recording process — and those qualities are many and well worth preserving on disc. The repertoire that makes up this programme, though not ideally documented in the insert-notes, is wide ranging, including a number of items intended for castratos; many items require both a fine bel canto and technical agility. "Ah Stigie larve! ... Vaghe pupille" from Act 2 of *Orlando* is a case in point, and ideally illustrates just how well Stutzmann can cope with both these extreme demands. The Hanover Band give her a spirited accompaniment, packed with fine solo work, more of which should be acknowledged in the notes.

New review
Handel. TESEO. **Eirian James** (mez) Teseo; **Julia Gooding** (sop) Agilea; **Della Jones** (mez) Medea: **Derek Lee Ragin** (alto) Egeo; **Catherine Napoli** (sop) Clizia; Jeffrey Gall (alto) Arcane; **François Bazola** (bar) Sacerdote di Minerva; **Les Musiciens du Louvre/ Marc Minkowski**. Erato 2292-45806-2. Texts and translations included.

⊙ ② 2h 28m DDD 3/93   🄯 P

Teseo was Handel's third opera for London, given at the beginning of 1713. Exceptionally, its libretto was based on a French original, written by Quinault for Lully; it is a spectacular piece, in five acts, with Medea (after the events of *Médée*) and Theseus (before the events of *Hippolyte* or the Ariadne operas) as its central characters. It is Medea who, as slighted lover and jealous sorceress, provides the principal musical thrills; but the score is, in any case, an unusually rich and inventive one, with much colourful orchestral writing even before she turns up at the beginning of Act 2. When she does, she introduces herself with a *Largo* aria. "Dolce riposo", of a kind unique to Handel in its depth of poetic feeling, with a vocal line full of bold leaps above throbbing strings and an oboe obbligato; but, lest we should think her docile, Medea hints at her true colours in the ensuing C minor aria, and by the end of the act she is singing furious recitative and fiery, incisive lines — real sorceress music. Her biggest scene comes at the start of the final act, a *Presto* vengeance aria, packed with raging rapid semiquavers. Handel scored the opera for a more varied orchestra than usual; there are recorders, flutes, oboes, bassoons and trumpets called for. The arias themselves tend to be rather shorter than usual for Handel. The work needs first-rate singing, and by and large receives it here. The role of Medea falls to Della Jones, a singer with a superb technique and a remarkable ability to identify with the role; she truly lives Medea's part and brings to it great resources of spirit and technique. Except when asked, or allowed, to play too fast, too loudly or too coarsely, the Musiciens du Louvre are an impressive group, with an outstanding first oboist and some very capable violinists. Several numbers are accompanied with only a continuo instrument, to good effect. The recitative always moves well, and appoggiatures are duly observed.

New review
Handel. RADAMISTO. **Ralf Popken** (alto) Radamisto; **Juliana Gondek** (sop) Zenobia; **Lisa Saffer** (sop) Polissena; **Dana Hanchard** (sop) Tigrane; **Monika Frimmer** (sop) Fraarte; **Michael Dean** (bass-bar) Tiridate; **Nicolas Cavallier** (bass) Farasmane; **Freiburg Baroque Orchestra/ Nicholas McGegan** (hpd). Harmonia Mundi HMU90 7111/3. Notes, text and translation included.

⊙ ③ 3h 10m DDD 6/94   🄯 P 🎗

Radamisto was Handel's first opera for the Royal Academy of Music, the company set up in 1719 under his musical directorship to put London opera on a secure basis (as optimistic a notion then as now). It is a tale of dynastic doings in post-classical Thrace, with King Tiridate of Armenia forsaking his wife Polissena because he becomes enamoured of Zenobia, Radamisto's queen; Radamisto and Zenobia go through various trials, but "after various Accidents, it comes to pass, that he recovers both Her and his Kingdom". It is easy enough to poke fun at plots such as these, but the score of *Radamisto*, one of Handel's richest, is its justification. Handel certainly knew how to 'wow' the London audiences on these big occasions. In the Second Act particularly, one arresting number follows another; Radamisto's "Ombra cara", which has been claimed (not without justice) as the finest aria Handel ever wrote, falls early in the act, and towards the end there is a wonderful sequence, chiefly of minor-key numbers, as the emotional tensions mount, culminating in a duet for the apparently doomed lovers. The Third Act, although dramatically less powerful, is also full of colourful and characterful music, including a noble quartet which Handel clearly remembered 30 years later when composing *Jephtha*. This performance is the best by far we have had from Nicholas McGegan. Any Handelian will relish the constantly alert playing, the strong dramatic pacing and the weight given to the orchestral textures, and he has the benefit of an excellent cast.

Handel. FLAVIO. **Jeffrey Gall** (alto) Flavio; **Derek Lee Ragin** (alto) Guido; **Lena Lootens** (sop) Emilia; **Bernarda Fink** (contr) Teodata; **Christina Högman** (sop) Vitige; **Gianpaolo Fagotto** (ten) Ugone; **Ulrich Messthaler** (bass) Lotario; **Ensemble 415/René Jacobs.** Harmonia Mundi HMC90 1312/3. Notes, text and translation included. Recorded in 1989.

② 2h 36m DDD 7/90

Flavio is one of the most delectable of Handel's operas. Although it comes from his 'heroic' period, it is not at all in the heroic mould but rather an ironic tragedy with a good many comic elements. Does that sound confusing? — well, so it is, for you never know quite where you are when King Flavio of Lombardy starts falling in love with the wrong woman, for although this starts as an amusing idle fancy it develops into something near-tragic, since he imperils everyone else's happiness, ultimately causing the death of one counsellor and the dishonour of another. The delicately drawn amorous feeling is like nothing else in Handel, and in its subtle growth towards real passion and grief is handled with consummate skill. The opera, in short, is full of fine and exceptionally varied music, and it is enhanced here by a performance under René Jacobs that, although it takes a number of modest liberties, catches the moods of the music surely and attractively, with shapely, alert and refined playing from the admirable Ensemble 415. And the cast is strong. The central roles, composed for two of Handel's greatest singers, Cuzzoni and Senesino, eighteenth-century superstars, are done by Lena Lootens, a delightfully natural and expressive soprano with a firm, clear technique, and the counter-tenor Derek Lee Ragin, who dispatches his brilliant music with aplomb and excels in the final aria, a superb minor-key expression of passion. The singers also include Bernarda Fink as the lightly amorous Teodata and Christina Högman, both fiery and subtle in the music for her lover, and the capable Jeffrey Gall as the wayward monarch. Altogether a highly enjoyable set, not flawless but certainly among the best ever Handel opera recordings.

Handel. GIULIO CESARE. **Jennifer Larmore** (mez) Giulio Cesare; **Barbara Schlick** (sop) Cleopatra; **Bernarda Fink** (mez) Cornelia; **Marianne Rørholm** (mez) Sextus; **Derek Lee Ragin** (alto) Ptolemy; **Furio Zanasi** (bass) Achillas; **Olivier Lallouette** (bar) Curio; **Dominique Visse** (alto) Nirenus; **Concerto Cologne/René Jacobs.** Harmonia Mundi HMC90 1385/7. Notes, text and translation included. Recorded in 1991.

④ 4h 4m DDD 4/92

Handel's greatest heroic opera sports no fewer than eight principal characters and one of the largest orchestras he ever used. Undoubtedly this, and the singing of Francesca Cuzzoni (Cleopatra) and Senesino (Caesar), helped to launch *Giulio Cesare* into enduring popularity that it enjoys to this day. But it is primarily the quality of the music, with barely a weak number in four hours of entertainment, that has made it such a favourite choice with musicians and audiences. Surprisingly, this is the only complete performance on period instruments currently available, an immediate advantage in giving extra 'bite' to the many moments of high drama without threatening to drown the singers in *forte* passages. This performance is a particularly fine one with an excellent cast; Caesar, originally sung by a castrato, is here taken by the young mezzo, Jennifer Larmore. She brings weight and a sense of integrity to the role (which surely couldn't be matched by a counter-tenor), seemingly untroubled by the demands of the final triumphant aria, "Qual torrente". Occasionally her vibrato becomes intrusive, particularly near the beginning of the opera, but that is a minor quibble in a performance of this stature. Handel could just as well have called his opera *Cleopatra* as it is she who is the pivotal element in the drama, a role taken here by Barbara Schlick. One of Handel's most vividly developed characters, Schlick represents this many faceted woman with acuity and imagination, ranging from the haunting pathos of "Piangerò", where she occasionally seems stretched on the top notes, to the exuberant virtuosity of "Da tempeste" in the final act. If Cleopatra represents strength in a woman, then Cornelia is surely the tragic figure, at the mercy of events. Her first aria, "Priva son", here taken very slowly, shows Bernarda Fink to be more than equal to the role, admirable in her steady tone and dignity of character. Derek Lee Ragin's treacherous Ptolemy is also memorable, venom and fire injected into his agile voice. A first-rate cast is supported by René Jacobs and Concerto Cologne on fine form, though the continuo line is sometimes less than ideally clear. The excellent recording completes one's pleasure in a momentous issue.

Additional recommendation ...
Sung in English. **Soloists; English National Opera Chorus and Orchestra/Sir Charles Mackerras.** EMI CMS7 69760-2 — .·' ③ 3h 3m DDD 5/89 ⁹ₚ

Further listening ...

Chandos Anthems, Volume 4 — The Lord is my light, HWV255; Let God arise, HWV256. **Lynne Dawson** (sop); **Ian Partridge** (ten); **The Sixteen Chorus and Orchestra/Harry Christophers.** Chandos Chaconne CHAN0509 (7/90).

Italian Duets — A miravi io son intento; Conservate, raddoppiate; Fronda leggiera e mobile; Langue, geme e sospira; Nò, di voi non vuo fidarmi; Se tu non lasci amore; Sono liete, fortunate; Tanti strali al sen. Troppo crudo. **Gillian Fisher** (sop); **James Bowman** (alto); **The King's Consort/Robert King.** Hyperion CDA66440 (4/91).

Occhi mei, che faceste?[abc]. Udite il mio consiglio[abc]. Quel fior che all'alba ride[abc]. Violin Sonata in G minor, HWV364b[bc]. Harpsichord Suite in F minor, HWV433[c]. [a]**Julianne Baird** (sop); [b]**John Dornenburg** (va da gamba); [c]**Malcolm Proud** (hpd). Meridian CDE84189 (12/91).

Cantatas[a] — Splende l'alba in oriente. La Lucrezia. Mi palpita il cor. Carco sempre di gloria. Trio Sonata, Op. 5 No. 4. [a]**Gérard Lesne** (alto); **Il Seminario Musicale.** Virgin Classics VC7 59059-2 (12/91).

Arias for Montagnana — Acis and Galatea — Avampo ... Ferito son d'Amore. Athalia — Ah, canst thou but prove me! Deborah — Barak, my son ... Awake the ardour; They ardours warm ... Swift inundation; Tears, such as tender fathers shed. Esther — I'll hear no more ... Pluck root and branch; Turn not, O Queen; How art thou fall'n. Ezio — Perchè tanto tormento? ... Se un bell'ardire; Folle è colui ... Nasce al bosco; Che indegno! ... Già risonar. Orlando — Mira, prendi l'essempio! ... Lascia Amor; Impari ognun da Orlando ... O voi, del mio poter ... Sorge infausta una procella. Sosarme — Addio, principe scrupoloso ... Fra l'ombre e gli orrori; Quanto più Melo ... Sento il core; Tanto s'eseguirà ... Tiene Giove. Tolomeo, re di egitto — Piangi pur. **David Thomas** (bass); **Philharmonia Baroque Orchestra/Nicholas McGegan.** Harmonia Mundi HMU90 7016 (8/90).

Clori, Tirsi e Fileno, HWV96 — *dramatic cantata.* **Soloists; Philharmonia Baroque Orchestra/ Nicholas McGegan.** Harmonia Mundi HMU90 7045 (2/93).

La Resurrezione — *oratorio.* **Soloists; Amsterdam Baroque Orchestra/Ton Koopman.** Erato 2292-45617-2 (7/91).

Athalia — *oratorio.* **Soloists; New College Choir, Oxford; Academy of Ancient Music/Christopher Hogwood.** L'Oiseau-Lyre 417 126-2OH2 (2/87).

L'Allegro, il Penseroso ed il Moderato — *oratorio.* **Soloists; Monteverdi Choir; English Baroque Soloists/John Eliot Gardiner.** Erato 2292 45377-2 (7/85).

Hercules — *oratorio.* **Soloists; Monteverdi Choir; English Baroque Soloists/John Eliot Gardiner.** Archiv Produktion 423 137-2AH3 (1/88).

Belshazzar — *oratorio.* **Soloists; The English Concert Choir; The English Concert/ Trevor Pinnock.** Archiv Produktion 431 793-2AH3 (10/91).

Judas Maccabaeus — *oratorio.* **Soloists; New College Choir, Oxford; The King's Consort/Robert King.** Hyperion CDA66641 (12/92).

Joshua — *oratorio.* **Soloists; New College Choir, Oxford; The King's Consort/Robert King.** Hyperion CDA66461/2 (7/91).

Solomon — *oratorio.* **Soloists; Monteverdi Choir; English Baroque Soloists/John Eliot Gardiner.** Philips 412 612-2PH2 (12/85).

Susanna — *oratorio.* **Soloists; Chamber Chorus of the University of California, Berkeley; Philharmonia Baroque Orchestra/Nicholas McGegan.** Harmonia Mundi HMU90 7030/2 (10/90).

Jephtha — *oratorio.* **Soloists; Monteverdi Choir; English Baroque Soloists/John Eliot Gardiner.** Philips 422 351-2PH3 (6/89).

AGRIPPINA. **Soloists; Cappella Savaria/Nicholas McGegan.** Harmonia Mundi HMU90 7063/5 (3/93).

AMADIGI DI GAULA. **Soloists; Les Musiciens du Louvre/Marc Minkowski.** Erato 2292-45490-2 (9/91).

FLORIDANTE (abridged). **Soloists; Tafelmusik Baroque Orchestra/Alan Curtis.** CBC Records SMCD5110 (1/93).

MUZIO SCEVOLA (Act 3). *Coupled with* **Bononcini.** MUZIO SCEVOLA (Act 2) — Overture; Dolce pensier; E pure in mezzo all'armi; Si, t'ama, o cara; Mutio Scevola — Pupille amate; Come, quando alle mie pene. **Soloists; Brewer Baroque Chamber Orchestra/Rudolph Palmer.** Newport Classic Premier NPD85540 (3/93).

OTTONE. **Soloists; Freiburg Baroque Orchestra/Nicholas McGegan.** Harmonia Mundi HMU90 7073/5 (3/93).

TAMERLANO. **Soloists; English Baroque Soloist/John Eliot Gardiner.** Erato 2292-45408-2.

RODELINDA. **Soloists; La Stagione/Michael Schneider.** Deutsche Harmonia Mundi RD77192 (1/93).

ALESSANDRO. **Soloists; La Petite Bande/Sigiswald Kuijken.** Deutsche Harmonia Mundi Editio Classica GD77110 (2/91).

PARTENOPE. **Soloists; La Petite Bande/Sigiswald Kuijken.** Deutsche Harmonia Mundi Editio Classica GDD77109 (2/91).

ORLANDO. **Soloists; Academy of Ancient Music/Christopher Hogwood.** L'Oiseau-Lyre 430 845-2OH3 (8/91).

ALCINA. **Soloists; Opera Stage Chorus; City of London Baroque Sinfonia/Richard Hickox.** EMI CDS7 49771-2 (11/88).

ATALANTA. **Soloists; Savaria Vocal Ensemble; Capella Savaria/Nicholas McGegan.** Hungaroton HCD12612/14-2 (3/86).

ALCESTE. COMUS. **Soloists; Academy of Ancient Music/Christopher Hogwood.** L'Oiseau-Lyre Florilegium 421 479-2OH (3/89).

Howard Hanson

Suggested listening ...

Piano Concerto, Op. 36[a]. Symphonies — No. 5, Op. 43, "Sinfonia Sacra"; No. 7, "A Sea Symphony"[b]. Mosaics. [a]**Carol Rosenberger** (pf); [b]**Seattle Symphony Chorale and Orchestra/Gerard Schwarz.** Delos DE3130 (3/93).

John H. Harbison

New review

Harbison. String Quartet No. 2.
Schuller. String Quartet No. 3.
Wernick. String Quartet No. 4. **Emerson Quartet** (Eugene Drucker, Philip Setzer, vns; Lawrence Dutton, va; David Finckel, vc). DG 437 537-2GH. Recorded 1991-2.

1h 8m DDD 11/93

Of these three American composers, John Harbison is now making the most headway in the British catalogue. One can see why Harbison is found attractive. His works are grateful to play and easy to listen to, especially when heard alongside the Schuller and Wernick pieces. Richard Wernick's two-movement Quartet No. 4 from 1990 seems commendably taut after the Harbison. The first scherzo in the second movement is an oblique homage to Dvořák and some of the arioso writing is transcendentally calm. Gunther Schuller is a brilliantly gifted musician in many capacities and is well qualified to bring together various musical traditions. He rarely does so in his concert music, although there are different levels within this quartet — intriguingly a G minor snippet that Beethoven wrote in an English woman's autograph album crops up in the finale at 2'26". But the long *Canzona*, the central slow movement, is unusually passionate. The Emerson Quartet serve all three composers with characteristically magnificent dedication — and are well recorded too.

Further listening ...

Oboe Concerto[a]. Symphony No. 2. *Coupled with* **Sessions.** Symphony No. 2. [a]**William Bennett** (ob); **San Francisco Symphony Orchestra/Herbert Blomstedt.** Decca 443 376-2DH (7/94). *See review under Sessions; refer to the Index to Reviews.*

Roy Harris

Harris. Symphony No. 3.
Schuman. Symphony No. 3. **New York Philharmonic Orchestra/Leonard Bernstein.**
DG 419 780-2GH. Recorded at a performance in the Avery Fisher Hall, New York in 1985.

51m DDD 11/87

If you already know music by Gershwin and Copland and wish to explore the work of other American composers then these two symphonies provide the ideal opportunity. Harris's short Third Symphony of 1939 is in one continuous movement, which however falls into five sections — Tragic, Lyric, Pastoral, Fugue-Dramatic and Dramatic-Tragic. The style is austere without being in the least forbidding; the musical arguments are terse but easy to follow, the orchestral sound solid but not opaque. When first performed the symphony was an instant critical and popular success, as was Schuman's Third Symphony when premièred two years later. Harris's influence on his slightly younger colleague is apparent, but Schuman has a rather more brilliant orchestral style and the mood of the work, cast in two movements, each of which has two connected sections, is a little more outgoing. The New York Philharmonic has this kind of music in its bones, and it gives superlative performances under its former chief conductor, whose sympathy and insight into the music of his older contemporaries has always been notable. The recordings are superlative.

Further listening ...

American Creed. When Johnny comes marching home. *Coupled with* **Copland.** Fanfare for the Common Man. Lincoln Portrait[a]. Canticle of Freedom[b]. An Outdoor Overture. [a]**James Earl Jones** (spkr); **Seattle** [b]**Chorale and Symphony Orchestra/Gerard Schwarz.** Delos DE3140 (5/93). *See review under Copland; refer to the Index to Reviews.*

Lou Harrison

American 1917-

New review

L. Harrison. Harp Suite[a]. Serenade[ac]. Perilous Chapel[cd]. Fugue[ce]. Song of Quetzalcoatl[ce]. May Rain[bc]. [b]**John Duykers** (ten); [a]**David Tanenbaum** (gtr); [b]**Julie Steinberg** (pf); [c]**William Winant** (perc); [d]**San Francisco Contemporary Music Players** (Barbara Chaffe, fl; Steve Harrison, vc; Doug Rioth, hp)/**Stephen Mosko;** [e]**Percussion Ensemble** (Daniel Kennedy, David Rosenthal, Todd Manley, perc). New Albion NA055CD.

⏺ **54m DDD 2/94** ❓

Lou Harrison composes as if he were discovering the simplest materials for the first time. This 1940s anticipation of minimalism can be fresh: it can also be naïve. The anthology has lots of accessible guitar music which is virtually unknown and there is much scope in *Perilous Chapel* and the colourful ensemble pieces which follow. *Perilous Chapel's* first movement, "Prelude", begins with a flute ostinato straight from Satie. The arrival of the harp at 1'21" provides an atmosphere of Debussian luxury. There is a bongo drum background to the flute and cello in the next movement and the final "Alleluia" goes round in circles of modal serenity. Harrison's hallmark is an immediacy regardless of style. The Fugue, opening and closing with the sound of the flexatone (or musical saw), is a surprise, with an enchanting plethora of gongs and bells echoing Partch or early Cage, with whom Harrison collaborated. The rhythmic, dry percussion is another original touch in the instrumental piece called *Song of Quetzalcoatl*, the Mexican deity. The only actual song in this collection is *May Rain*, a simple setting of a poem by Elsa Gidlaw, where the accompanying piano is tuned to a special intonation system.

Further listening ...

Symphony No. 2, "Elegiac". *Coupled with* **Hovhaness.** Symphony No. 2, "Mysterious mountain", Op. 132. Lousadzak, Op. 48[a]. [a]**Keith Jarrett** (pf); **American Composers Orchestra/Dennis Russell Davies.** MusicMasters 7021-2. *See review under Hovhaness; refer to the Index to Reviews.*

Mass (to St Anthony). *Coupled with* **Pärt.** Berliner Messe[a]. **LeaAnne DenBeste** (sop); **Laura Crockett** (mez); [a]**David Vanderwal** (ten); [a]**Karl Blume** (bass); [a]**Marianne Lewis** (org); **Oregon Repertory Singers/Gilbert Seeley.** Koch International Classics 37177-2 (4/94).

Key to symbols

| Gramophone Awards winners | Gramophone Editor's choice |

Karl Amadeus Hartmann

German 1905-1963

Hartmann. SYMPHONIES. Gesangszene (1963)[b]. [a]**Doris Soffel** (contr); [b]**Dietrich Fischer-Dieskau** (bar); **Bavarian Radio Symphony Orchestra/**[c]**Fritz Rieger,** [d]**Rafael Kubelík,** [e]**Ferdinand Leitner,** [f]**Zdenek Macal.** Wergo WER60187-50. From WER60086 (6/81). Symphonies — No. 1[ac]; No. 2 — Adagio[d]; No. 3[e]; No. 4[d]; No. 5[d]; No. 6[d]; No. 7 (1957-8)[f]; No. 8[d].

④ 3h 45m ADD 5/90

Stravinsky once remarked that Alban Berg was "synthetic, in the best sense" — the same could perhaps be said about Hartmann. In the 1930s he was beginning to establish a reputation, but was forced to withdraw himself and his works from public musical life as a known opponent of the Nazi regime. During the war he destroyed or radically revised most of his output up till then, and these eight symphonies (five of which are based on, or are revisions of, earlier works) appeared between 1946 and his death in 1963. Together they show his broad sympathies with the twentieth-century masters. As Hartmann chose to write symphonies, he had to be mindful of the enormity of the tradition that preceded him, and you can hear the presence of Bruckner in the monumental sense of structure, of Reger in the densely chromatic counterpoint and an intense, tortured lyricism derived from Berg. There is a tribute to the neo-classical Stravinsky in the Fifth Symphony, and more than a hint of Bartók in the irresistible momentum of the fugues that conclude the Sixth. Mahler is present in the Whitman settings of the First Symphony, significantly entitled *Attempt at a Requiem*; also, in the upheavals of the first movement of the Eighth, the crisis near the end of the *Adagio* of Mahler's Tenth is vividly recalled (sustained high trumpet, screaming violins). The spectral Funeral March in Webern's *Pieces*, Op. 6 haunts sections of the First, Third and Eighth Symphonies. Whether, with Hartmann's synthesis of his models, he managed to forge a demonstrably personal idiom is open to question. What is indisputable is the power of Hartmann's music to communicate, and its capacity to fascinate as sheer sound. On the debit side, not all the vigorously contrapuntal sections of the later works avoid sounding academic. The dates of these live recordings are not given, but they are all naturally balanced, with excellent clarity — Hartmann's torrents of tuned percussion are thrillingly captured. The Bavarian Radio Symphony Orchestra play with polish and evident conviction. Recommended to anyone interested in the development of the symphony in our century.

Additional recommendation ...

No. 4. **Messiaen.** *Et exspecto resurrectionem mortuorum.* **Bamberg Symphony Orchestra/Ingo Metzmacher.** EMI CDC7 54916-2 — 1h 3m DDD 4/94 9s

Hartmann. Symphony No. 2, "Adagio". Gesangsszene to words from Jean Giraudoux's "Sodom and Gomorrah"[a]. Sinfonia Tragica. [a]**Siegmund Nimsgern** (bar); **Bamberg Symphony Orchestra/Karl Anton Rickenbacher.** Koch Schwann 312952. Recorded 1992.

1h 4m DDD 5/94 9p

New recordings of the music of Karl Amadeus Hartmann are long overdue, not because of any inadequacies in the pioneering Wergo set (reviewed above), but because the music itself demands them. If honours are even in the Second Symphony, in *Gesangssezene* (1961-3) Rickenbacher definitely has the edge, securing a tauter performance without sacrificing clarity. Nimsgern excels as an even more full-blooded soloist than Fischer-Dieskau (for whom the work was written). Hartmann died with the last nine lines unset, although the final two were intended to be spoken; here Nimsgern's heavier delivery makes for a more fitting close. Hartmann buffs will want this disc for the première recording of the *Sinfonia Tragica* (1940, rev. 1943), one of Hartmann's most impressive early works. Koch Schwann's clear, natural recordings are complemented by excellent notes.

Further listening ...

Piano Sonata, "27 April 1945". Piano Sonatine. Zwei kleine Suiten. Jazz-Toccata und Fuge. **Siegfried Mauser** (pf). Virgin Classics VC7 59017-2 (8/91).

Sir Herbert Hamilton Harty

Irish 1879-1941

New review

Harty. A John Field Suite. In Ireland.
Handel. Water Music (trans. Harty).
Traditional. The Londonderry Air — Folksong (trans. Harty). **Ulster Orchestra/Bryden Thomson.** Chandos Collect CHAN6583. Recorded 1979-83.

· · 50m ADD/DDD II/93

A warm welcome must be extended to this reissue — not least for the highly sympathetic performance of Sir Hamilton Harty's *A John Field Suite*. The opening "Polka" and the closing *Rondo* ("Midi") are real lollipops, and the chosen "Nocturne" is quite lovely, too. Also offered here is Harty's own scoring of his suite from Handel's *Water Music*, another arrangement famous in the 78 era, and how enjoyable it is: full of colour and vitality, with all thoughts of acerbic 'authentic' violins banished in the famous serene "Air" and the equally appealing *Andante espressivo*. If you have a soft spot for this Handel/Harty arrangement, it has never been more winningly presented on disc. To complete the programme, we are given an arrangement of the *Londonderry Air*, plus Harty's own whimsical lightweight fantasy for flute, harp and orchestra, *In Ireland*. Most delectable and digitally recorded. The rest of the programme is in excellent analogue sound.

Further listening ...

Ode to a Nightingale. The Children of Lir. **Heather Harper** (sop); **Ulster Orchestra/ Bryden Thomson.** Chandos CHAN8387 (10/87).

Piano Concerto in B minor[a]. In Ireland — Fantasy for Flute, Harp and Orchestra[b]. With the Wild Geese. [a]**Malcolm Binns** (pf); [b]**Claude Fleming** (fte); [b]**Denise Kelly** (hp); **Ulster Orchestra/Bryden Thomson.** Chandos CHAN8321 (4/85).

An Irish Symphony. A Comedy Overture. **Ulster Orchestra/Bryden Thomson.** Chandos CHAN8314 (9/84).

Jonathan Harvey

British 1939-

New review

J. Harvey. CELLO WORKS. **Frances-Marie Uitti** (vc); [a]**Jonathan Harvey** (electronics); [b]**Emilia Romagna "Toscanini" Symphony Orchestra/José Roman Encinar.** Etcetera KTC1148. Item marked [c] recorded at a performance at the Teatro Farnese, Parma in 1991. Cello Concerto[bc]. Curve with Plateaux. Ricercare una melodia[a]. Three Sketches. Philia's Dream[a].

· · 58m DDD 7/93

Jonathan Harvey applies the metaphor of a journey through life to his Cello Concerto (1990). It achieves an extremely successful balance between richness of detail and clarity of outline, and while it appears to be much more concerned with the often turbulent progress of the journey than with its ultimate, blissful goal, the music is fully equal to the essentially spiritual context within which Harvey seeks to place it. It is also — for those of more secular predispositions — a brilliant display piece superbly realized in this live but confident and polished performance. A comparable metaphor serves for *Curve with Plateaux* (1982), which travels from depths to heights, then reverses the process, reaching an explicitly funereal conclusion. The journeys charted by the other works on the disc are perhaps best described as excursions into the heart and soul of the cello. The disc is technically exemplary, a celebration alike of Harvey's musical imagination and the outstanding interpretative gifts of Frances-Marie Uitti.

Further listening ...

Bhakti for Chamber Ensemble and Quadraphonic Tape. **Spectrum/Guy Protheroe.** NMC NMCD001 (9/89).

From Silence[a]. Natajara[b]. Ritual Melodies[c]. [a]**Karol Bennett** (voc); [b]**Harrie Starreveld** (fl/picc); [a]**Lucy Chapman Stoltzman** (vn); [a]**Michael Thompson** (hn); [a]**Dean Anderson** (perc); [b]**René Eckhardt** (pf); [a]**Kathleen Supove,** [a]**John MacDonald,** [a]**Diana Dabby** (electric keyboards); [ac]**David Atherton** (tape op); [ac]**Brent Koeppel,** [ac]**Ken Malsky,** [ac]**Philip Sohn** (computer/tape ops)/**Barry Vercoe.** Bridge BCD9031 (11/92).

Song Offerings. *Coupled with* **G. Benjamin.** Antara. *Boulez.* Dérive. Memoriale. **Penelope Walmsley-Clark** (sop); **Sebastian Bell** (fl); **London Sinfonietta/George Benjamin.** Nimbus NI5167 (10/89).

Johann Hasse

German 1699-1783

New review

Hasse. PIRAMO E TISBE. **Barbara Schlick** (sop) Piramo; **Suzanne Gari** (sop) Tisbe; **Michel Lecocq** (ten) Father; **Capella Clementina/Helmut Müller-Brühl.** Koch Schwann 310882. Recorded in 1984.

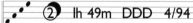

When Hasse (who had been a pupil of Alessandro Scarlatti) wrote *Piramo e Tisbe* in 1768, he already had over 70 stage works to his credit and had long been the most famous opera composer in Europe. The story of this two-act *intermezzo tragico* is familiar from its parody in Shakespeare's *A Midsummer Night's Dream*, though besides the two ill-starred lovers there is a part for Thisbe's father, who at the end, discovering that they have both (in fatal misunderstandings) taken their own lives, also stabs himself as being responsible. In Hasse's setting a number of features at once capture the attention — the vigour of his melodic invention, the richness of the harmony, the very prominent role allotted to the orchestral wind, the strongly contrasting middle sections of *da capo* arias, the expressive, characterful and dramatic accompanied recitatives, and particularly the fluid continuity, so unlike the closed forms of the older *opera seria*. The role of Pyramus was cast by Hasse as a breeches part (not for a castrato), and it is not always easy to distinguish between the two soprano voices in the regrettable absence of a printed libretto. Both ladies, however, are admirable and the Capella Clementina gives first-rate partnership. Müller-Brühl not only seems unerring in his choice of tempos but keeps the work flowing forward with a well-judged sense of its drama. A most distinguished issue.

Further listening ...

Flute Concerto in G major[b]. *Coupled with* ***Agrell.*** Flute Concerto in D major[a]. *Scheibe.* Flute Concertos — A major[a]; D major[b]. [a]**Maria Bania,** [b]**Irene Spranger** (fls); **Concerto Cophenhagen/Andrew Manze.** Chandos Chaconne CHAN0535 (6/93).

La conversione di Sant' Agostino. **Soloists; Berlin RIAS Chamber Choir; Berlin Ancient Music Academy/Marcus Creed.** Capriccio 10 389/90 (7/93).

Requiem in C major[a]. Miserere in E minor. **Greta de Reyghere** (sop); **Susanna Moncayo von Hase** (contr); [a]**Ian Honeyman** (ten); **Dirk Snellings** (bass); **Il Fondamento Chorus and Orchestra/Paul Dombrecht.** Opus 111 OPS30-80 (11/93).

Hans Johann Leo Hassler

German 1564-1612

New review

Hassler. Missa I super Dixit Maria. Ad Dominum cum tribularer. O admirabile commercium. Usquequo, Domine. Domine Deus, Israel. Vater unser in Himmelreich.

Lechner. Si bona suscepimus. **Chapelle Royale European Vocal Ensemble/Philippe Herreweghe.** Harmonia Mundi HMC90 1401. Texts and translations included. Recorded 1991.

1h 7m DDD 10/93

Hassler's *Missa I super Dixit Maria*, though far from representing the best of his work, is the perfect vehicle for displaying the dark and splendid sonority of the Chapelle Royale Ensemble. The group takes hold of the music by the scruff of its neck, and gives as convincing a perform-ance as one could wish for; the precision and rich glow of the sound are perfect for Hassler's restrained homophony. The Latin motets and the impressive *Vater unser in Himmelreich* cycle are more polyphonic, but it is not simply because of this that they outshine the Mass — rather, Hassler here seems to be giving much fuller rein to his imagination and responding musically to the texts. Lechner's motet *Si bona suscepimus* is similarly expansive and resourceful. In champion-ing such obscure repertoire, Philippe Herreweghe and Harmonia Mundi might be thought to be taking a risk, but with performances of this calibre there is no cause for concern.

Further listening ...

Canzon duodecimi toni[bcd]. Cantate Domino canticum novum[abcde]. Toccata in G[d]. Canzon noni toni[bcd]. O sacrum convivium[acd]. Domine Dominus noster[abcde]. *Coupled with* **Erbach.** Sacerdotes Dei[acd]. Canzona secundi toni[c]. Hic est sacerdos[acd]. Fantasia sub Elevatione[c]. Toccata octavi toni[d]. Posuisti Domine[acd]. La Paglia[bc]. **Lassus.** Missa Bell'Amfitrit' altera[abcd]. [a]**West-minster Cathedral Choir;** [b]**His Majesties Sagbutts and Cornetts/James O'Donnell** with [c]**Timothy Roberts,** [d]**Iain Simcock,** [e]**Iris Schöllhorn** (orgs). Hyperion CDA66688 (6/94). *See review under Lassus; refer to the Index to Reviews.*

Joseph Haydn

Austrian 1732-1809

Haydn. Cello Concertos — C major, HobVII*b*/1; D major, HobVII*b*/2.
A. Kraft. Cello Concerto in C major, Op. 4. **Anner Bylsma** (bar vc); **Tafelmusik/Jeanne Lamon.** Deutsche Harmonia Mundi RD77757. Recorded in 1989.

1h 7m DDD 9/91

At best, an 'authentic' performance can only aspire to return to the spirit, rather than the letter of the period it strives to recreate, and yet the fine Dutch cellist Anner Bylsma comes as near as anyone to convincing us that this is indeed the way Haydn might have wished these sunny, yet highly sophisticated concertos to be played. Haydn composed these works for the virtuoso cellist of the Esterházy court orchestra, Anton Kraft, and the bold and adventurous solo writing reflects his fabled technical prowess and musical sensitivity. Bylsma offers a lithe, yet scrupulously classical and poised account of the C major Concerto, with a romantically inflected central *adagio* followed by a dashingly brilliant, yet suitably witty finale. His rapid passagework in higher registers is astonishing, while he reveals the stately dignity of the D major work (long attributed to Kraft) in a cultured and attractively proportioned reading of rich intensity and variety. Bylsma includes his own revisions of period cadenzas, which are never less than apposite, and deftly executed. The real discovery here, though, is the Cello Concerto by Kraft himself, which combines the expected brilliant pyrotechnics with some effective melodic writing, in a work which anticipates the styles developed during the early nineteenth century. In fact, Kraft advised Beethoven on the cello part of his Triple Concerto, and his compositions exercised great influence on the genesis of modern cello technique. Bylsma is superbly supported by the excellent Canadian ensemble, Tafelmusik, and the recording is first rate. A revealing, and often stunningly played collection — highly recommended to all cello enthusiasts.

Additional recommendations ...
Cello Concerto in D major (English Chamber Orchestra). **Dvořák.** Cello Concerto in B minor, B191 (Berlin Philharmonic Orchestra/Lorin Maazel). **Elgar.** Cello Concerto in E minor, Op. 85 (London Symphony Orchestra/André Previn). **Saint-Saëns.** Cello Concerto No. 1 in A minor, Op. 33 (French National Orchestra/Lorin Maazel). **Schumann.** Cello Concerto in A minor, Op. 129

(Bavarian Radio Symphony Orchestra/Sir Colin Davis). **Yo-Yo Ma** (vc). CBS Masterworks
CD44562 — .•˙ ② 2h 20m DDD/ADD 5/90

As Haydn[ab]. *Violin Concertos*[c] — *C major, HobVIIa/1; A major, HobVIIa/3; G major, HobVIIa/4.*
Double Concerto for Violin and Harpsichord in F major, HobXVIII/6[ac]. [a]**Christine Walevska** (vc);
English Chamber Orchestra/[b]**Edo de Waart,** [c]**Salvatore Accardo** (vn). Philips Duo 438
797-2PM2 — .•˙ ② 2h 22m ADD 4/94

As Haydn. **Truls Mørk** (vc); **Norwegian Chamber Orchestra/Iona Brown.** Virgin Classics
VC5 45014-2 — .•˙ 50m DDD 6/94

Haydn. Keyboard Concertos — F major, HobXVIII/3; G major, HobXVIII/4; D major,
HobXVIII/11. **Franz Liszt Chamber Orchestra/Emanuel Ax** (pf). Sony Classical SK48383.
.•˙ **59m DDD 5/93** ⁹|ₚ

Mozart's unique achievement in his 27 piano concertos has tended to overshadow the more
modestly scored, less overtly virtuoso works by Haydn and only the D major Concerto is at all
well known today. Whilst none of the three works recorded here could claim to add to the
development of the form in the way that those of Mozart did, all three possess great charm:
take for example the *Largo cantabile* of the early F major work to hear Haydn's melodic gift at its
most endearing. The *Presto* finale of the same concerto recalls some of his later piano sonatas in
its juxtaposition of knockabout comedy and theatrical minor-key drama. The G major,
supposedly written for the blind pianist, composer and singer Maria Theresia von Paradis boasts
an extended *Grave* slow movement. But it is the D major with its larger orchestra (horns and
oboes added to strings) that works best and the *Rondo all'Ungarese* finale with its myriad key
changes and sparkling good humour is predictably the highlight of the disc. Emanuel Ax
(directing from the keyboard) gives performances of the utmost finesse and affection: if any
performance were to help to restore the fortunes of these works then this is surely it. His
playing throughout is deeply felt: graceful in the slow movements and dexterous in the outer
ones. In addition, he plays his own charming cadenzas in the F and G major works. Sony's
sound is spacious, with the piano forwardly placed and the notes are adequate, though no
biographical information is included.

Haydn. Trumpet Concerto in E flat major, HobVIIe/1[a]. Cello Concerto in D major,
HobVIIb/2[b]. Violin Concerto No. 1 in C major, HobVII[c]. [c]**Cho-Liang Lin** (vn); [b]**Yo-Yo Ma**
(vc); [a]**Wynton Marsalis** (tpt); [a]**National Philharmonic Orchestra/Raymond Leppard;**
[b]**English Chamber Orchestra/José Luis Garcia;** [c]**Minnesota Orchestra/Sir Neville
Marriner.** CBS Masterworks CD39310. From IM39310 (1/85).
.•˙ **59m DDD 1/86** ⁹|ₚ Ⓑ

This compilation of three Haydn concertos has a different soloist and orchestra for each. The
young American trumpeter Wynton Marsalis has all the fluency one could wish for and an
instrument allowing a full three octaves (E flat — E flat) to be displayed in his own cadenza to
the first movement. Although this is an efficient performance, it in no way approaches the class of
the next one. The cellist Yo-Yo Ma is very different as a performer: though equally a master of
his instrument, and indeed a virtuoso who seems incapable of producing an ugly sound or playing
out of tune, one feels a deep emotional involvement in all he does. Also, the recording in this D
major Cello Concerto is unusually faithful in blending the cello well into the ensemble without
ever covering it. Ma is supported by the excellent English Chamber Orchestra and the qualities of
integration and ensemble under their leader's direction are all that one could wish for. In the C
major Violin Concerto the skilful Cho-Liang Lin has the benefit of a most sympathetic conductor
in Sir Neville Marriner, but he cannot match Ma's subtlety and commitment.

Additional recommendations ...
Trumpet Concerto[a]. *Cello Concerto in C major, HobVIIb/1*[b]. *Horn Concertos*[c] — *No. 1 in D major,*
HobVIId/3; No. 2 in D major, HobVIId/4. [a]**Håkan Hardenberger** (tpt); [b]**Heinrich Schiff** (vc);
[c]**Hermann Baumann** (hn); **Academy of St Martin in the Fields/**[ab]**Sir Neville Marriner,**
[c]**Iona Brown.** Philips Laser Line Classics 432 060-2PM — .•˙ 1h 10m DDD 2/91 ⁹|ₚ Ⓑ
Trumpet Concerto[a]. *Oboe Concerto in C major, HobVIIg/C1*[b]. *Keyboard Concerto in D major,*
HobXVIII/11[c]. [a]**Mark Bennett** (tpt); [b]**Paul Goodwin** (ob); **The English Concert/Trevor
Pinnock** ([c]hpd). Archiv Produktion 431 678-2AH — .•˙ 56m DDD 9/92 ⁹|ₚ Ⓑ

New review

Haydn. Violin Concertos — A major, HobVIIa/3; C major, HobVIIa/1; G major, HobVIIa/4; F major, HobXVIII/6[a]. **Rainer Kussmaul** (vn); [a]**Robert Hill** (hpd); **Amsterdam Bach Soloists.** Olympia OCD428.

⏺ **1h 11m   DDD   6/94**

The first thing one notices about this disc is the attractive sound, rounded yet detailed; the second is that the playing of the orchestra is stylish; last but not least, Rainer Kussmaul produces a lovely sound on what sounds like an excellent instrument, and phrases gracefully: altogether this is most enjoyable Haydn playing. The three violin concertos and the Concerto for violin and keyboard in F, HobXVIII/6, are all relatively early, dating from about 1765-70, but that does not mean that they lack interest. Far from it: Haydn always wrote sympathetically for the instrument and the invention is also strong. Thus the Concerto in A, which begins this programme, is both sunny and charming, lacking a real slow movement (the middle one is marked *Adagio* but is on the busy side) but with a dashing yet melodious finale. The other music is no less likeable, and the performances have an infectiously happy swing to them. The harpsichordist Robert Hill is discreetly supportive in the three works where that is his role, but rightly a co-soloist in the F major Concerto. In this work he is placed a little backwardly, but otherwise the recording is well balanced with a pleasingly full bass.

Haydn. SYMPHONIES. **Philharmonia Hungarica/Antál Dorati.** Decca 430 100-2DM32. Also available as eight four-disc sets. Recorded 1969-73.
425 900-2DM4 (4h 30m) — Nos. 1-16. *425 905-2DM4* (4h 34m) — Nos. 17-33. *425 910-2DM4* (4h 43m) — Nos. 34-47. *425 915-2DM4* (4h 33m) — Nos. 48-59. *425 920-2DM4* (4h 11m) — Nos. 60-71. *425 925-2DM4* (4h 29m) — Nos. 72-83. *425 930-2DM4* (4h 46m) — Nos. 84-95. *425 935-2DM4* (4h 46m) — Nos. 96-104. Symphony "A" in B flat major. Symphony "B" in B flat major. Sinfonia concertante in B flat major, HobI/105.

⏺ ③② **36h 31m   ADD   6/91**   🔊P

Though there are now two period-instrument Haydn cycles underway (from Goodman on Hyperion and Hogwood on L'Oiseau-Lyre), this pioneering modern-instrument cycle recorded by Antál Dorati and his band of Hungarian exiles between 1969 and 1973 is always going to be a hard act to follow. When first issued on LP Dorati's performances won almost universal praise for their style and verve, their eager and imaginative engagement with the music's astonishing, protean inventiveness. And in their very overdue CD incarnation, in eight sets of four discs each, they still have little to fear from most of the competition. Remarkably, in such an extended project, there is hardly a whiff of routine: time and again the orchestra seems to play out of its skin for Dorati, the strings sweet-toned and luminous, the wind deft and resourceful, savouring to the full the wit and whimsy of Hadyn's writing. And though one might have reservations about this or that symphony, Dorati's actual interpretations are often exemplary, combining rhythmic resilience and a splendid overall sweep with an unusual care for detail.

Aficionados of period performances may feel that the strings, especially in the earlier symphonies, are too numerous and too liberal with vibrato. But the buoyancy of Dorati's rhythms and the crispness of the strings' articulation constantly preclude any suggestion of undue opulence. Most of the early symphonies (in which Dorati uses a discreetly balanced harpsichord continuo) are captivatingly done: *Allegros* dance and leap and slow movements are shaped with finesse and affection. Listen, for instance, to the beautiful neo-baroque D minor *Andante* in No. 4, or the grave *siciliano* in No. 12, a particularly appealing, warm-textured work. And in the second box, containing Nos. 17-33, Dorati brings a characteristic breadth and intensity of line to the opening *Adagios* of No. 21 (a notably mature and eloquent movement, this) and No. 22, the so-called *Philosopher*. The famous *Hornsignal*, No. 31, is also irresistibly done, with rollicking, ripe-toned horns; and practically the only disappointment in the first two boxes is the *Lamentatione*, No. 26, where both the tragic first movement and the quizzical final minuet are too smooth and sluggish.

A number of the minuets in the middle-period symphonies (those written between the late 1760s and the early 1780s) are also distinctly leisurely, lacking Dorati's usual rhythmic spring — cases in point are those in Nos. 43, 52 and 49 (the last funereally slow). And one or two of the passionate minor-keyed symphonies, especially Nos. 39 and 52, are, like No. 26, wanting in fire and dramatic thrust. But in many of these works of Haydn's first full maturity (several still virtually unknown) Dorati gives penetrating, shrewdly judged performances. Highlights among the rarer symphonies include No. 41, with its pealing trumpets and high horns (stunningly played), the expansive No. 42, done with real breadth and grandeur, and the subtle, lyrical No. 64, whose sublime *Largo* is sustained at the slowest possible tempo. In one or two works (notably the large-scale D major, No. 61, and the so-called *Laudon*, No. 69), Dorati might seem too frothy and frolicsome. And just occasionally (as in the outrageous six-movement *Il Distratto*, No. 60) he can underplay the earthy, rumbustious side of Haydn's complex musical personality.

Two of the most desirable boxes of all are those containing Symphonies Nos. 72-83 and 84-95 — though some collectors may find it inconvenient that both the "Paris" and the "London" sets are split between boxes. Most of the pre-Paris symphonies are still underrated: but works like Nos. 76, 77 and 81 reveal a new, almost Mozartian suavity of manner and a sophistication of thematic development influenced by the Op. 33 String Quartets, while the two minor-keyed symphonies, Nos. 78 and 80, have notably powerful, concentrated first movements. If Dorati is a shade too comfortable in No. 80 he is superb elsewhere on these discs. Though the competition from rival performances continually hots up, he can more than hold his own in the "Paris" set: listen to the mingled grace and strength he brings to Nos. 85 and 87, with their clear, gleaming textures, or his dramatic urgency in the first movement of the misleadingly named *La Poule*, No. 83.

As for the "London" Symphonies, Dorati's readings are as detailed and attentive as any on the market, though at times he can underestimate the music's boldness, grandeur and dangerous wit. This is partly a question of tempos (some distinctly on the slow side) and accent, but also of the variable prominence accorded the brass and timpani — in several works, notably Nos. 94, 96 and, most seriously, the flamboyant, aggressive Nos. 97 and 100, these instruments are too recessed to make their full dramatic effect. Elsewhere, though, the balance is more satisfying: and in symphonies like Nos. 93, 103 and 104 Dorati combines power, incisiveness and symphonic breadth with an unusual sensitivity to the lyrical poignancy which underlies much of Haydn's later music.

The recordings, outstanding in their day, still sound pretty impressive, with a fine spaciousness and bloom, even if the violins can acquire a touch of glare above the stave. All in all, a magnificent, life-enhancing series that has contributed vastly to our deeper understanding of Haydn's genius over the last two decades. Whatever integral cycles may appear in the future, Dorati's will stand as one of the gramophone's grandest achievements.

Additional recommendations ...
No. 13 in D major. No. 14 in A major. No. 15 in D major. No. 16 in B flat major.. **Hanover Band/Roy Goodman.** Hyperion CDA66534 — .·' lh 14m DDD 3/94 ⁹ₚ 🖋
No. 41 in C major. No. 48 in C major, "Maria Theresia". No. 65 in A major. **The English Consort/Trevor Pinnock.** Archiv Produktion 429 399-2AH — .·' 58m DDD 7/90 🖋
No. 45 in F sharp minor, "Farewell". No. 48. No. 102 in B flat major. **Capella Istropolitana/Barry Wordsworth.** Naxos 8 550382 — . lh 13m DDD 9/91
Nos. 48. No. 49 in F minor, "La passione". No. 50 in C major. **Hanover Band/Roy Goodman.** Hyperion CDA66531 — .·' lh 17m DDD 7/93 🖋
No. 49. **Schubert.** *Symphony No. 5 in B flat major, D485.* **St John's Smith Square Orchestra/John Lubbock.** Pickwick IMP Classics PCD819 — .· 53m DDD 1/86
No. 85 in B flat major, "La reine". No. 86 in D major. No. 87 in A major. **Orchestra of the Age of Enlightenment/Sigiswald Kuijken.** Virgin Classics Veritas VC7 59557-2 — .·' lh 19m DDD 5/90 ⁹ₚ 🖋
No. 91 in E flat major. No. 92 in G major, "Oxford". **Concertgebouw Orchestra/Sir Colin Davis.** Philips 410 390-2PH — .·' 51m DDD 4/85 ⁹ₚ ⁹ₛ

New review
Haydn. EARLY SYMPHONIES. **Academy of Ancient Music/Christopher Hogwood.**
L'Oiseau-Lyre 436 428-2OH3. Recorded 1990-91.
No. 1 in D major. No. 2 in C major. No. 4 in D major. No. 5 in A major. No. 10 in D major. No. 11 in E flat major. No. 18 in G major. No. 27 in G major. No. 32 in C major. No. 37 in C major. No. 107 in B flat major.

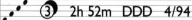 .·' ③ 2h 52m DDD 4/94 ⁹ₚ 🖋

These very early symphonies, composed before Haydn moved to the Eszterházy court in 1761, may all too easily blur together in the mind: driving *allegros*, long on physical energy but short on memorable ideas, sparse-textured 'walking' *andantes* and breezy *buffo* finales. Superficially the opening movements of the three D major works, Nos. 1, 4 and 10, and many of the finales throughout this set can seem virtually interchangeable. But even here there is more variety than you might at first suspect; and there is a world of difference between, say, the opening movement of No. 1, all quivering nervous energy, and that of No. 2, with its surprising amplitude and contrapuntal weight. If some of the slow movements are dull and arid, there is a melancholy, neo-baroque D minor *Andante* in No. 4 and a delicately expressive *Adagio, ma non troppo* in No. 32, probably the first in Haydn's long line of ceremonial C major symphonies with trumpets and timpani. But the two richest slow movements, both in texture and expression, stand at the head of works cast in church-sonata form (a sequence of slow, fast, minuet, fast): that in No. 5, with its high-lying *concertante* writing for horns; and the noble, processional *Adagio cantabile* of No. 11, whose eloquent violin writing foreshadows the well-known *Adagio* of No. 44. Hogwood's performances are pretty persuasive: crisp, precise, lightly and elegantly articulated, rhythmically spruce and almost invariably well-tuned. Compared with the rival period-instrument versions from Goodman and the Hanover Band, Hogwood and the Academy are generally rather broader and more poised in quick movements, with more gracious, shapely phrasing and in several of the slow movements, Hogwood finds more in the music than Goodman, phrasing more considerately, with greater sensitivity to harmonic flux. Hogwood also has fuller presentation and slightly clearer, less reverberant recorded sound.

Additional recommendations:
Nos. 1-5. **Hanover Band/Roy Goodman** (hpd). Hyperion CDA66524 — .·· lh 12m DDD 3/92 ዋ
No. 9 in C major; Nos. 10 and 11; No. 12 in E major. **Hanover Band/Roy Goodman.** Hyperion CDA66529 — .·· lh 9m DDD 12/92
No. 17 in F major; No. 18; No. 19 in D major; No. 20 in C major; No. 21 in A major. **Hanover Band/Roy Goodman.** Hyperion CDA66533 — .·· lh 19m DDD 12/93

Haydn. Symphonies — No. 6 in D major, "Le matin"; No. 7 in C major, "Le midi"; No. 8 in G major, "Le soir". **The English Concert/Trevor Pinnock** (hpd). Archiv Produktion 423 098-2AH.

.·· **lh 5m   DDD   1/88**

These symphonies represent the times of day; *Le matin* portrays the sunrise, and there is a storm in *Le soir*, but otherwise there is not a lot that could be called programmatic. But Haydn did take the opportunity to give his new colleagues in the princely band something interesting to do, for there are numerous solos here, not only for the wind instruments but for the section leaders — listen especially to the *Adagio* of No. 6, with solo violin and prominent flutes and cello, a delectable piece of writing. Inventively, the music is uneven; the concerto-like style was not wholly harmonious with Haydn's symphonic thinking. But there is plenty of spirited and cheerful music here, and that is well caught in these vivacious performances by Trevor Pinnock and his band, with their brisk tempos and light textures; the playing is duly agile, and the period instruments give a bright edge to the sound.

Additional recommendations ...
Nos. 6-8. **Hanover Band/Roy Goodman.** Hyperion CDA66523 — .·· lh 9m DDD 12/91
Nos. 6-8; No. 9 in C major; No. 12 in E major; No. 13 in D major; No. 16 in B flat major; No. 40 in F major; No. 72 in D major. **Academy of Ancient Music/Christopher Hogwood.** L'Oiseau-Lyre 433 661-2OH3 — .·· ③ 3h 9m DDD 6/93

New review
Haydn. Symphonies — No. 17 in F major; No. 18 in G major; No. 19 in D major; No. 20 in C major; No. 21 in A major. **Hanover Band/Roy Goodman.** Hyperion CDA66533. Recorded in 1993.

.·· **lh 19m   DDD   12/93**

The symphonies numbered 17-20 were among Haydn's very first; and while none is especially riveting in its invention they are all compact in design, with lean, economical orchestration and a characteristically high quota of nervous energy. The most colourful and ambitious work in this group, and the only one in four movements, is the ceremonial C major, No. 20 with its panoply of trumpets, timpani and horns. Symphony No. 21, the final work on the disc, dates from several years later (1764) and sounds it: the ideas in the fast movements are more striking in themselves and more tautly developed, while the opening *Adagio* is perhaps the most lyrically intense movement in all Haydn's early symphonies. Goodman allows the *Adagio* plenty of space, shaping the music sympathetically, with a firm sense of harmonic direction. Faster movements are rhythmically vital yet never over-driven, with Haydn's contrasts of colour and dynamics vividly realized (thrilling brass sonorities in No. 20). The minuets in Nos. 20 and 21 are neatly phrased, light on their feet (you may initially be thrown by that in No. 21, which opens exactly like the minuet in *Eine kleine Nachtmusik*). Delightful performances, stylish, spirited and deftly executed. Recording, documentation and playing time are all up to the standards set by other issues in the series.

Haydn. SYMPHONIES. **Academy of Ancient Music/Christopher Hogwood.** L'Oiseau-Lyre 430 082-2OH3. Recorded 1988-89.
No. 21 in A major; No. 22 in E flat major, "The Philosopher"; No. 23 in G major; No. 24 in D major; No. 28 in A major; No. 29 in E major; No. 30 in C major, "Alleluja"; No. 31 in D major, "Hornsignal"; No. 34 in D minor.

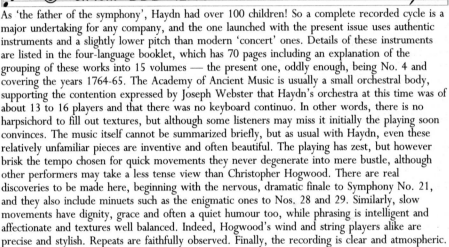

③ 3h 10m DDD 12/90

As 'the father of the symphony', Haydn had over 100 children! So a complete recorded cycle is a major undertaking for any company, and the one launched with the present issue uses authentic instruments and a slightly lower pitch than modern 'concert' ones. Details of these instruments are listed in the four-language booklet, which has 70 pages including an explanation of the grouping of these works into 15 volumes — the present one, oddly enough, being No. 4 and covering the years 1764-65. The Academy of Ancient Music is usually a small orchestral body, supporting the contention expressed by Joseph Webster that Haydn's orchestra at this time was of about 13 to 16 players and that there was no keyboard continuo. In other words, there is no harpsichord to fill out textures, but although some listeners may miss it initially the playing soon convinces. The music itself cannot be summarized briefly, but as usual with Haydn, even these relatively unfamiliar pieces are inventive and often beautiful. The playing has zest, but however brisk the tempo chosen for quick movements they never degenerate into mere bustle, although other performers may take a less tense view than Christopher Hogwood. There are real discoveries to be made here, beginning with the nervous, dramatic finale to Symphony No. 21, and they also include minuets such as the enigmatic ones to Nos. 28 and 29. Similarly, slow movements have dignity, grace and often a quiet humour too, while phrasing is intelligent and affectionate and textures well balanced. Indeed, Hogwood's wind and string players alike are precise and stylish. Repeats are faithfully observed. Finally, the recording is clear and atmospheric.

Additional recommendation ...
No. 31. Horn Concerto No. 1 in D major, HobVIId/3. **M. Haydn.** *Horn Concerto in D major.*
Anthony Halstead (natural hn); **Hanover Band/Roy Goodman.** Nimbus NI5190 —
lh lm DDD II/89

Haydn. Symphonies — No. 26 in D minor, "Lamentatione"; No. 52 in C minor; No. 53 in D major, "L'Impériale". **La Petite Bande/Sigiswald Kuijken.** Virgin Classics Veritas VC7 59148-2.

lh 2m DDD 3/89

This period instrument coupling contains some sprightly and imaginative playing. Symphony No. 26, is sub-titled *Lamentatione* and the nickname alludes to Haydn's use of Gregorian chant in the first two movements. The C minor Symphony No. 52 is a dramatic work, vividly capturing a mood of restless, brooding expectancy. Symphony No. 53, *L'Impériale*, has a glorious confidence and authority to it; the title, scholars suppose, refers to the Empress Maria Theresa. It has an air of sophistication and nobility worthy of Austria's great ruler and receives a vivid and accomplished recording. The sound throughout is warm and ingratiating.

Additional recommendation ...
No. 26; No. 35 in B flat major; No. 49 in F minor, "La Passione". **Northern Chamber Orchestra/Nicholas Ward.** Naxos 8 550721 — , 55m DDD I/94

Haydn. Symphonies — No. 30 in C major, "Alleluia"; No. 53 in D major, "Imperial"; No. 69 in C major, "Loudon". **Vienna Concentus Musicus/Nikolaus Harnoncourt.** Teldec Das Alte Werk 9031-76460-2. Recorded in 1990.

1h 7m DDD 6/93

Three brilliant, extrovert pieces here, with much festive trumpeting and drumming in the two C major symphonies. More, in fact, than Haydn would have expected, since Harnoncourt has added his own trumpet and timpani parts for No. 30 (1765). Whatever the purists might think, the augmented scoring is undeniably effective, enhancing the symphony's celebratory spirit (the nickname, incidentally, comes from the use of the Easter Alleluia plainchant in the first movement); and Harnoncourt and his brilliant period-intrument orchestra give a splendidly vivid, sharp-edged performance. The other symphonies both date from the mid- to late-1770s, and combine ceremonial grandeur with the tuneful, popular manner that Haydn was beginning to cultivate around this time. No. 53, obscurely nicknamed *Imperial* in the early nineteenth century, was among the most spectacular international successes of the composer's career, mainly on account of its *Andante* variations. Harnoncourt is perhaps a touch over-sophisticated here; and the aristocratic minuet is taken at a vehement one-in-a-bar, necessitating a violent deceleration for the trio. But the splendid opening movement is played with verve and flair, while the curious, dullish-looking *Capriccio* which Haydn substituted for the original finale leaps right off the page at Harnoncourt's cracking pace. No. 69, dedicated to the Austrian Field Marshal Laudon (or Loudon), is perhaps one of Haydn's less fetching symphonies, at least until the finale, with its surprisingly violent C minor centrepiece. But Harnoncourt's powerful rhythmic drive and sense of colour (thrilling impact from brass and timpani) make out an unusually strong case for the work. The Teldec recording is spacious and reverberant, but rarely at the expense of clarity.

Haydn. SYMPHONIES. **The English Concert/Trevor Pinnock.** Archiv Produktion 429 756-2AH. Recorded in 1989.
No. 42 in D major; No. 44 in E minor, "Trauer"; No. 46 in B major.

1h 3m DDD 9/90

These are inspiriting performances of three of Haydn's greatest symphonies from the so-called *Sturm und Drang* years of the early 1770s. Storm and stress is most evident in the *Trauer* ("Mourning"), whose outer movements push the contemporary musical language to new limits of violent intensity; the nickname, incidentally, derives from the sublime *Adagio*, which Haydn is said to have wanted played at his funeral. Symphony No. 46 is probably the only eighteenth-century symphony in the key of B major. And with the outlandish tonality go extremes of expression: the first movement is astonishingly tense and dark-hued for a work of this period in the major key, while the finale is Haydn at his most bizarrely humorous. The other work on the disc, No. 42, is a real rarity, and may well come as a revelation to many. Both the first and second movements have an expansiveness and a harmonic breadth new in Haydn's symphonic music; and the finale is a delightful early example of the racy, popular style which colours so many of his later symphonies. Using an orchestra of around 20 players, as Haydn himself would have done, Pinnock gives vital, characterful readings, with a blend of sophistication and earthiness ideally suited to the composer. The string playing is supple and sweet-toned — no wire-wool associations here — and the expertly played oboes and horns cut through pungently in the tuttis. Outer movements are boldly projected, their often exceptional rhythmic and harmonic tension powerfully controlled. All three slow movements are done with finesse and a beautiful sense of line (none of the exaggerated 'squeezed' phrasing favoured in some authentic performances), though the *Adagio* of No. 44 has a slightly too easy, *grazioso* feel. More controversial are the minuets, taken very smartly indeed, with a loss of dignity and grandeur in Nos. 42 and 46. But these truthfully recorded performances can be recommended to anyone who is not ideologically opposed to period instruments.

Additional recommendations ...
No. 44. **Mozart.** *Symphony No. 40 in G minor, K550.* **St John's Smith Square Orchestra/ John Lubbock.** Pickwick IMP Red Label PCD820 — 55m DDD 8/86
No. 42; No. 43 *in E flat major, "Mercury"; No. 44.* **Hanover Band/Roy Goodman.** Hyperion CDA66530 — 1h 19m DDD 2/93
No. 41 *in C major; Nos. 42-3.* **Tafelmusik/Bruno Weil.** Sony Classical Vivarte SK48370 —

No. 44; No. 51 in B flat major; No. 52 in C minor. **Tafelmusik/Bruno Weil.** Sony Classical Vivarte SK48371 — .·˙ 1h 2m DDD 4/93 ✒

Haydn. Symphonies — No. 60 in C major, "Il distratto"; No. 91 in E flat major. Armida — Overture. **Orpheus Chamber Orchestra.** DG 437 783-2GH. Recorded in 1992.

.·˙ **54m DDD 12/93**

The Orpheus Chamber Orchestra combine a rare precision of ensemble and a minute attention to rhythmic detail with a vivid sense of character, an infectious delight in the wit and sheer unpredictability of the composer's invention. Throughout you get a real sense of the players listening closely to one another, like true chamber musicians. They clearly relish the drolerie, waywardness and manic energy of the six-movement *Il distratto*, though they never overplay the moments of slapstick humour. In No. 91, with its far richer woodwind scoring, the marvellous opening *Allegro* is rhythmically crisp and elegantly phrased, contrapuntal detail ideally lucid, the tonally fluid second subject shaped with a nice touch of flexibility. There are witty and poetic touches of timing, too. Only the finale brings reservations, with the players' virtuosity tempting them to a headlong speed: one that leaves little room for warmth or subtlety — both Dorati in his complete cycle and Kuijken's period-instrument version find richer meaning in this movement. Still, the powerful overture to Haydn's last Esterházy opera, sandwiched between the symphonies, receives a compelling, high-voltage reading. The outstanding quality of the performances is complemented by an exemplary recording, clear, natural and immediate.

Additional recommendation ...
No. 90 in C major; No. 91. **La Petite Bande/Sigiswald Kuijken.** Virgin Classics Veritas VC7 59599-2 — .·˙ 58m DDD 2/91 ꝗₚ ✒

Haydn. Symphonies — No. 82 in C major, "L'ours"; No. 83 in G minor, "La poule"; No. 84 in E flat major. **Hanover Band/Roy Goodman** (hpd). Hyperion CDA66527. Recorded 1991.

.·˙ **1h 19m DDD 10/92** ꝗₚ ✒

Written in 1785-6 for the ample forces of the Concert de la Loge Olympique, Haydn's *Paris* symphonies were his grandest and most imposing works in the form to date. The first three in the published order receive bristling, high-voltage performances from Goodman and his period band. No. 82, in particular, is thrillingly done, its magnificent opening movement combining lucidity of detail with a splendid sweep and a sheer brazen brilliance: the C alto horns slash through the texture and the hard-stick timpani crack like gunfire. Goodman's minuet has a fine lordly swagger (and some characteristically delicate, precisely articulated woodwind playing in the trio), while his finale, fast, taut, sharply accented, is full of shrewdly observed instrumental detail. The other two symphonies here are hardly less exhilarating. The outer movements of No. 84, perhaps the least fêted of the *Paris* set, are crisply done, eager, light and transparent of texture, with sharply defined wind detail. The minuet is lusty of gait and accent, while Goodman's briskish tempo imparts an easy sway to the beautiful 6/8 *Andante* Variations. In the vehement opening movement of the misleadingly named *La poule*, No. 83, Goodman's fierce tempo can seem more than a touch hectic; but against this the Hanover Band turn the minuet into an irresistible bucolic waltz and give an unusually piquant, sharply articulated reading of the finale. As usual in this series, Goodman is generous with repeats; and his harpsichord continuo is propulsive and forwardly balanced. The recording is a touch resonant, but never at the expense of clarity. This is by far the most exciting instalment in Hyperion's Haydn Edition and is an essential acquisition for all Haydn lovers.

Additional recommendations ...
Nos. 82 and 83. **Concertgebouw Orchestra/Sir Colin Davis.** Philips 420 688-2PH — .·˙ 52m DDD 2/88 ꝗₚ ꝗₛ
Nos. 82-84. **Orchestra of the Age of Enlightenment/Sigiswald Kuijken.** Virgin Classics Veritas VC7 59537-2 — .·˙ 1h 18m DDD 2/90 ✒
Nos. 82-86. **Montreal Sinfonietta/Charles Dutoit.** Decca 436 739-2DH2 — .·˙ ② 2h 26m DDD 6/93

Haydn. Symphonies — No. 90 in C major; No. 93 in D major. **Orchestra of the Eighteenth Century/Frans Brüggen.** Philips 422 022-2PH. Recorded in 1987.

> ♪ **5lm DDD 5/88**

These performances are of a calibre which deserve to be noticed. Amongst the many delights of this recording are the mellow sound and warm textures of the wind instruments and the generally high level of technical expertise with which they are played. Haydn's wind writing is usually interesting, sometimes witty and, especially in the case of the horns, often extremely difficult to play. These fine players surmount most of the difficulties with an admirable degree of self-assurance and Brüggen's direction is always lively. Lovers of Haydn's music should find much that is rewarding in this issue.

Haydn. LONDON SYMPHONIES. **Concertgebouw Orchestra/Sir Colin Davis.** Philips Silver Line Classics 432 286-2PSL4. Recorded 1975-81.
No. 93 in D major; No. 94 in G major, "The Surprise" (both from 6514 192, 1/83); No. 95 in C minor (6514 074, 1/82); No. 96 in D major, "The Miracle" (6725 010, 6/82); No. 97 in C major (6514 074); No. 98 in B flat major (9500 678, 12/80); No. 99 in E flat major (9500 139, 4/77); No. 100 in G major, "Military" (9500 510, 3/79); No. 101 in D major, "The Clock" (9500 679, 7/81); No. 102 in B flat major (9500 679); No. 103 in E flat major, "Drumroll" (9500 303, 7/78); No. 104 in D major, "London" (9500 510).

> ♪ ④ **5h 4m ADD/DDD 7/92** ♩p ♩s Ⓑ

A superb achievement all round — indeed, it's nigh on impossible to imagine better 'big-band' Haydn than one encounters here on these four exceedingly well-filled CDs. Sir Colin Davis's direction has exemplary sparkle (try the superb opening movement of the *Miracle* Symphony) and sensitivity (witness his eloquent moulding of No. 98's great *Adagio*). Minuets are never allowed to plod, outer movements have an ideal combination of infectious zip and real poise, and the humour (a commodity, of course, that is never absent for too long in Haydn's music) is always conveyed with a genial twinkle in the eye. Quite marvellous, wonderfully unanimous playing from the great Amsterdam Orchestra, too (the woodwind contributions are particularly distinguished), with never a trace of routine to betray the six-year recording span of this critically acclaimed project. The Philips engineering, whether analogue or digital, is of the very highest quality throughout, offering a totally natural perspective, gloriously full-bodied tone and consistently sparkling textures within the sumptuous Concertgebouw acoustic. Invest in this set: it will yield enormous rewards for many years to come.

Additional recommendations ...
No. 68 in B flat major. Nos. 93-104. **Royal Concertgebouw Orchestra/Nikolaus Harnoncourt.** Teldec 4509-92628-2 — ♪ ⑥ 5h lm DDD 4/94 Ⓑ
No. 92 in G major, "Oxford". No. 104. **English Sinfonia/Sir Charles Groves.** Pickwick IMP Classics PCD916 — ♪ 55m DDD 6/89 ♩p Ⓑ
Nos. 93-95. **Hanover Band/Roy Goodman.** Hyperion CDA66532 — ♪ lh 6m DDD 8/93 ♩p ✍ Ⓑ
Nos. 93-95. **La Petite Bande/Sigiswald Kuijken.** Deutsche Harmonia Mundi 05472 77275-2 — ♪ lh 6m DDD 10/93 ♩p Ⓑ ✍
Nos. 93-104. **London Philhrmonic Orchestra/Sir Georg Solti.** Decca Ovation 436 290-2DM6 — ♪ ⑥ 5h 7m DDD 3/93 ♩p Ⓑ
Nos. 93-98. **Royal Philharmonic Orchestra/Sir Thomas Beecham.** EMI Beecham Edition mono CMS7 64389-2 — ♪ ② 2h 16m ADD 9/93 Ⓑ ▲
Nos. 99-104. **Royal Philharmonic Orchestra/Sir Thomas Beecham.** EMI Beecham Edition CMS7 64066-2 — ♪ ② 2h 36m ADD 9/92 ♩p Ⓑ ▲
Nos. 103 and 104. **London Classical Players/Roger Norrington.** EMI CDC5 55002-2 — ♪ 55m DDD 7/94 Ⓑ ✍

Haydn. Symphonies — No. 100 in G major, "Military"; No. 104 in D major, "London". **Orchestra of the Eighteenth Century/Frans Brüggen.** Philips 434 096-2PH. Recorded live in 1990.

> ♪ **54m DDD 6/93**

Brüggen and his crack period orchestra give arresting, strongly characterized performances here of two favourite Haydn symphonies. Though the crashing, jangling 'Turkish' instruments (triangle, cymbals and bass drum) in the *Military* are allowed their head, Brüggen's reading consistently stresses the work's drama, boldness and symphonic strength. The Beethovenian development of the first movement, for instance, is built with tremendous power and logic, while the finale's darting wit can scorch and sting, with articulation of virtuoso precision and point from both strings and wind. Brüggen's tempo in the *Allegretto* is on the leisurely side, though this movement gains especially from the distinctive, soft-hued timbres of the period woodwind. The live recording (minimal audience participation) under-balances the timpani and the bass drum, but is otherwise excellent. Curiously, timpani are far better defined in No. 104, where they register with exciting physical impact. After a massive, brooding slow introduction, Brüggen gives plenty of space to the first-movement *Allegro*, phrasing the lyrical music warmly (the slight astringency of the orchestra's violins softened by a touch of vibrato) and bringing an acutely judged cumulative intensity to the development. The minor-keyed eruption in the *Andante* is unusually disquieting, horns and trumpets grinding balefully; and despite the occasional rhythmic vagary, both the minuet and the finale are gloriously incisive and articulate, with Brüggen inspiring the orchestra to playing of incandescent intensity in the finale's closing pages. Even those normally resistant to period instruments should sample these charismatic, superbly executed performances.

Additional recommendation ...
Concertgebouw Orchestra/Sir Colin Davis. Philips 411 449-2PH — .·′ 54m ADD 10/84 Ⓑ

Haydn. STRING QUARTETS, Op. 20. **Mosaïques Quartet** (Erich Höbarth, Andrea Bischof, vns; Anita Mitterer, va; Christophe Coin, vc). Astrée Auvidis E8784 (as a two-disc set). Recorded in 1990. *Please note that they are also available separately as detailed below.* *E8785* — No. 1 in E flat major; No. 5 in F minor; No. 6 in A major. *E8786* — No. 2 in C major; No. 3 in G minor; No. 4 in D major.

.·′ ② **2h 27m DDD 5/93** ᵠₚ Ⓑ ✒

Haydn was 40 when he completed his set of Op. 20 String Quartets in 1772. They therefore date from the composer's so-called *Sturm und Drang* period, though Haydn's increasingly frequent use of the more dramatic and 'serious' minor mode in these pieces can perhaps be attributed just as much to the fruitful influence of the three operatic projects he had been working on just a few years previously between 1766 and 1769. Moreover, these quartets also reveal a greater preoccupation with counterpoint than any of his music to that date, and the great fugal finales of Nos. 2, 5 and 6 clearly herald the arrival of the consummate craftsman so overwhelmingly displayed in the mature quartets to come. Incidentally, the Op. 20 set's nickname *Sun* derives from the illustration on the handsome title-page of the Hummel edition of this music, at the top of which peers out the sun-god's head. Admirable though the Salomon Quartet's readings are (listed below), they are surpassed by those of the superb Quatuor Mosaïques on Astrée Auvidis. These wonderfully flexible performances display an altogether breathtaking refinement, sensitivity and illumination. Indeed, in terms of expressive subtlety, imaginative intensity and sheer depth of feeling, the Mosaïques' achievement in these marvellous works is unmatched in the present catalogue and it is difficult to foresee it being surpassed for some considerable time to come. A stunning set in every way, with vividly realistic engineering to match.

Additional recommendations ...
No. 2. Op. 50: No. 1 in B flat major. Op. 76: No. 2 in D minor. **Lindsay Quartet.** ASV CDDCA622 — .·′ 1h 3m DDD 9/88 ᵠₚ Ⓑ
Nos. 1-3. **Salomon Quartet.** Hyperion CDA66621 — .·′ 1h 15m DDD 2/93 ᵠₚ Ⓑ ✒
Nos. 4-6. **Salomon Quartet.** Hyperion CDA66623 — .·′ 1h 18m DDD 2/93 ᵠₚ Ⓑ ✒

New review
Haydn. STRING QUARTETS, Op. 33. **Salomon Quartet** (Simon Standage, Micaela Comberti, vns; Trevor Jones, va; Jennifer Ward Clarke, vc). Hyperion CDA66681/2. *CDA66681* — No. 1 in B minor; No. 2 in E flat major, "The Joke"; No. 3 in C major, "The Bird". *CDA66682* — No. 4 in B flat major; No. 5 in G major, "How do you do?"; No. 6 in D major. String Quartet in D minor, Op. 42.

.·′ ② **1h 8m 1h 12m DDD 9/93** Ⓑ ✒

Written, according to Haydn himself, "in a completely new and special style", the so-called 'Russian' quartets were among his most influential works, and had a decisive effect on the six quartets Mozart dedicated to the older composer. Mozart doubtless appreciated the exhilarating formal freedom of Op. 33, its air of relaxed, witty conversation and its fusion of elaborate developmental techniques with a tuneful, popular manner — all manifestations of the 'new and special style' advertised by Haydn. Many of the movements adopt a racy, jocular tone, notably several of the scherzos which the composer substitutes for minuets, and the finales of Nos. 2, 3 and 4 (No. 2 ends with Haydn's most outrageous piece of comic deception, hence the work's nickname). But sophisticated playfulness is far from the whole picture: No. 1 in B minor is an astringent, sinewy piece, its first movement foreshadowing Beethoven in its rigorous, far-reaching investigation of tonal ambiguity; and each of the slow movements is unusually eloquent, ranging from the pungent, chromatically inflected *Andante* of No. 1 to the tragic, quasi-operatic G minor aria in No. 5. The Salomon Quartet give positive, strongly projected performances of this music, clean and crisp of attack, virile of rhythm and Hyperion's recording is clear, full and immediate.

Additional recommendations ...
Nos. 1-6. **Festetics Quartet.** Quintana QUI90 3002/3 — ⠂⠂ ② 2h 20m DDD 8/92 Ⓑ
Nos. 1-3. Op. 1: No. 3 in D major. **Weller Quartet.** Decca 433 691-2DM — ⠂⠂ Ih IIm ADD 9/92 Ⓑ
Nos. 4-6. Op. 103 in D minor (unfinished). **Weller Quartet.** Decca 433 692-2DM — ⠂⠂ Ih I3m ADD 9/92 Ⓑ

Haydn. STRING QUARTETS, Op. 54. **Lindsay Quartet** (Peter Cropper, Robin Ireland, vns; Ronald Birks, va; Bernard Gregor-Smith, vc). ASV CDDCA582.
No. 1 in G major. No. 2 in C major. No. 3 in E major.

⠂⠂ Ih 6m DDD 8/87   q_P q_S Ⓑ

All three quartets are in the usual four-movement form but with many surprises: in No. 1, the false recapitulation in the first movement, the dark modulations in the following sonata-form *Allegretto* and the Hungarian-gipsy flavour (anticipated in the Minuet) and mischievousness of the final Rondo. Number 2 has a rhapsodic fiddler in its second movement, a nostalgic Minuet with an extraordinarily anguished Trio, and an *Adagio* finale in which a *Presto* section turns out to be no more than an episode. A notable feature of No. 3 is its tenary-form *Largo cantabile*, the centre of which is more like a mini-concerto for the first violin; 'Scotch snaps' pervade the Minuet, and pedal points the finale. The performances (and the recording) are superb, marked by unanimity, fine tone, suppleness of phrasing, and acute dynamic shaping; in the second movement of No. 1 there are hushed passages whose homogeneity and quality of sound is quite remarkable. Even more remarkable would be the Haydn lover who found this recording resistible.

Additional recommendations ...
No. 2. Op. 64: No. 5 in D major, "The Lark". **Gabrieli Quartet.** Chandos CHAN8531 — ⠂⠂ 39m DDD II/87 Ⓑ
Nos. 1-3. Op. 55: No. 1 in A major; No. 2 in F minor, "Razor"; No. 3 in B flat major. **Amadeus Quartet.** DG 437 134-2GX2 — ⠂⠂ ② 2h Im ADD 2/93 Ⓑ

New review
Haydn. STRING QUARTETS, Op. 64. **Kodály Quartet** (Attila Falvay, Tamás Szabo, vns; Gábor Fias, va; János Devich, vc). Naxos 8 550673/4. Recorded in 1992.
8 550673. — No. 1 in C major; No. 2 in B minor; No. 3 in B flat major. *8 550674* — No. 4 in G major; No. 5 in D major, "The Lark"; No. 6 in E flat major.

② Ih 4m Ih 5m DDD I/94   q_P Ⓑ

Like Handel, Haydn remains a victim of his own prodigality. And most of his 70-odd quartets, Op. 64, are still underexposed both in the concert-hall and on disc. The exception is the so-called *Lark*, whose soaring opening melody and *moto perpetuo* finale have made it perhaps the most immediately fetching of all Haydn's quartets. But No. 6 in E flat (Haydn's homage to Mozart's K428?) is at least as fine, with its intimate and intensely argued opening movement, its poignant, exquisitely textured *Andante* and a finale full of instrumental fooling and insouciant contrapuntal virtuosity. Of the other works, No. 2 in B minor is one of

Haydn's most astringent pieces, from its tonally deceptive opening to the mordant, unsettling humour of the finale. Quartets Nos. 3 and 4 return to a more familiar vein of sociable wit. Both are endlessly subtle and surprising in their arguments, with *cantabile* slow movements of peculiar candour and eloquence. Quartet No. 1 in C, is certainly the plainest in its thematic ideas. However, it is an absorbing, immensely sophisticated piece. The Kodaly's wonderfully civilized playing, mellow and lyrical, is far removed from the highly-strung brilliance cultivated by many modern quartets. Ensemble and intonation are first-class, tempos generally spacious, with broad, natural and beautifully matched phrasing. The recording, made in a Budapest church, is resonant and less intimate than is ideal in this music. Even so, not even the most casual lover of Haydn's quartets will regret spending a tenner on this pair of discs.

Haydn. STRING QUARTETS, Opp. 71 and 74. **Kodály Quartet** (Attila Falvay, Tamás Szabo, vns; Gábor Fias, va; János Devich, vc). Naxos 8 550394 and 8 550396. Recorded 1989.
8 550394 — Op. 71: No. 1 in B flat major, No. 2 in D major; No. 3 in E flat major.
8 550396 — Op. 74: No. 1 in C major; No. 2 in F major; No. 3 in G minor, "The Rider".

② lh 2m lh 3m DDD 2/91   ⁹ₚ ⁹ₛ Ⓑ

The enterprising Kodály Quartet are working their way through the middle and late Haydn Quartets and, rightly, taking their time about it. They rehearse together privately, and then every so often turn up at the Hungaroton Studios in Rottenbiller with a new group ready to record. They play with self-evident joy in the music and an easy immaculateness of ensemble, which comes from familiarity with each other's company. There is never a hint of routine and the intercommunication is matched by enormous care for detail and clean ensemble. In short they play as one, and project this wonderful music with enormous dedication. Just sample the elegant *Andante* with variations which form the slow movement of Op. 71 No. 3, or the witty Menuet which follows, or any of the consistently inspired Op. 74 set. The hushed intensity of playing in the *Largo assai* of Op. 74 No. 3 is unforgettable. The recordings are wholly natural and balanced within a well-judged acoustic; the sound is of the highest quality and documenta-tion is excellent. At their modest price this pair of CDs is irresistible.

Additional recommendations ...
Op. 74: Nos. 2 and 3. **Salomon Quartet.** Hyperion CDA66124 — ⠎ AAD 3/87 ⁹ₚ Ⓑ
Op. 71 No. 3; Op. 74 No. 1. **Salomon Quartet.** Hyperion CDA66098 — ⠎ 59m AAD 12/87 ⁹ₚ Ⓑ

Haydn. STRING QUARTETS, Op. 76. **Takács Quartet** (Gábor Takács-Nagy, Károly Schranz, vns; Gábor Omai, va; András Fejér, vc). Decca 425 467-2DH. Recorded in 1988.
No. 4 in B flat major, "Sunrise". No. 5 in D major, "Fifths". No. 6 in E flat major, "Fantasia".

⠎ lh 8m DDD 1/90   ⁹ₚ Ⓑ

In these three quartets from a set of six published in 1797, one can only be delighted by the sheer invention that Haydn showed in his sixties. This youthful Hungarian ensemble bring to this music a freshness that does not inhibit them from the necessary underlining of this or that point. The *Sunrise* Quartet is invigorating in the first movement and lyrically broad in the Adagio, and the syncopated minuet and lilting finale are no less delightful. The D major Quartet starts with an Allegretto suggesting a set of variations but then moves into a section in new keys before ending with a brisk coda. The slow movement's *cantabile e mesto* marking is fully realized, as is the major-minor contrast of the minuet and the playful Presto finale, which begins with an unmistakable joke of six bars that sound more like the end of a movement. The third of these quartets begins with variations that culminate in a fugato; the slow movement (called a fantasia) is another original, and this is followed by a witty scherzo and a finale in which scale fragments participate in a game of dizzy contrapuntal complexity. The recording, made in a London church, is immediate yet atmospheric, although with a touch of glare that tone controls will tame.

Additional recommendation ...
Eder Quartet. Teldec Digital Experience 9031 77602-2 — ⠎ lh 2m DDD 12/92 ⁹ₚ Ⓑ

Haydn. STRING QUARTETS, Opp. 77 and 103. **Mosaïques Quartet** (Erich Höbarth, Andrea Bischof, vns; Anita Mitterer, va; Christophe Coin, vc). Astrée Auvidis E8799. Op. 77: No. 1 in G major; No. 2 in F major. Op. 103: D minor (unfinished).

lh 2m   DDD   2/90

Anyone who thinks that period-instrument performance means austerity and coolness should listen to this disc. Here is a group of youngish French players, using instruments of the kind Haydn would have heard, played (as far as we can know) in a style he would have been familiar with: the result is a disc full of expressive warmth and vigour. The opening of Op. 77 No. 1 is done duly gracefully, but with a sturdy underlying rhythm and the Scherzo is as crisp and alive as one could ask for. Then the first movement of the F major work is very beautifully done, with many sensitive details; and the lovely second movement is happily leisurely, so that the players have ample room for manoeuvre and the leader makes much of his opportunities for delicate playing in the filigree-like high music. The players show a real grasp of the structure and they know when to illuminate the key moments, with a touch of extra deliberation or a little additional weight of tone. These performances, clearly recorded, are competitive ones not merely within the protected world of 'early music' but in the bigger, 'real' world too!

New review

Haydn. Seven Last Words, Op. 51. **Lindsay Quartet** (Peter Cropper, Ronald Birks, vns; Robin Ireland, va; Bernard Gregor-Smith, vc). ASV CDDCA853.

lh llm   DDD   6/93

This performance by the Lindsay Quartet is magical and it confirms them as something a bit more special than just the finest British quartet. There are few quartets who could sustain these seven slow movements, each lasting about ten minutes, and yet give them such variety of intensity, colour and mood. Haydn revealed himself as a visionary composer in the way he set about creating these seven miniature tone-poems for string quartet. The work is divided into nine sections comprising the seven slow movements each describing one of the final utterances of Christ on the Cross together with a slow introduction and a final *Presto con tutta la forza* which depicts the earthquake which occurred when "the veil of the temple was rent in twain".

Seven Last Words. String Quartet in D minor, Op. 103 (Unfinished). **Kodály Quartet.** Naxos 8 550346 — . lh 4m DDD 2/91

Haydn. PIANO TRIOS. **Beaux Arts Trio** (Isidore Cohen, vn; Bernard Greenhouse, vc; Menahem Pressler, pf). Philips 432 061-2PM9. Recorded 1970-79.
G major, HobXV/25. F sharp minor, HobXV/26. C major, HobXV/27 (all from 6500 023, 6/71). E flat major, HobXV/29. E flat major, HobXV/30. E flat major, HobXV/31 (all from 6500 400, 3/73). C major, HobXV/21. D minor, HobXV/23. D major, HobXV/24. E major, HobXV/28 (all from 6500 401, 3/73). A major, HobXV/18. G minor, HobXV/19. E flat major, HobXV/22 (all from 6500 521, 6/74). B flat major, HobXV/20. G major, HobXV/32 (both from 6500 522, 11/73). G minor, HobXV/1. F major, HobXV/37. F major, HobXV/39. G major, HobXV/41. C major, HobXV/C1 (all from 6768 077). A flat major, HobXV/14. G major, HobXV/15 (both from 9500 034, 11/76). C minor, HobXV/13, D major, HobXV/16. F major, HobXV/17 (all from 9500 035, 2/77). G major, HobXIV/6. F major, HobXV/6. B flat major, HobXV/8. G major, XVI/6 (all from 9500 325, 3/78). F major, HobXV/2 (9500 325, 3/78). D major, HobXV/7. A major, HobXV/9. E minor, HobXV/12 (all from 9500 326, 8/77). G major, HobXV/5. E flat major, HobXV/10. E flat major, HobXV/f1 (all from 9500 327, 2/78). F minor, HobXV/11. E flat major, HobXV/36. C major, HobXIV/C1. D major, Hobdeest (all from 9500 472, 7/79). E major, HobXV/34. A major, HobXV/35. B flat major, HobXV/38. F major, HobXV/40 (all from 9500 473, 6/79).

⑨   6h 34m   ADD   7/92

Far more than Mozart's, Haydn's trios are essentially accompanied keyboard sonatas, with the cello wedded to the keyboard bass almost throughout; this lack of cello independence has deterred many groups from investigating their undoubted musical riches. Not, fortunately, the Beaux Arts, whose acclaimed complete cycle accumulated by stealth during the 1970s (when it was finally completed it received almost universal accolades, including *Gramophone's* Record of the Year Award) and has now reappeared on nine mid-price discs. A dozen of the works date from the 1760s, or even earlier (which for a late developer like Haydn meant pre-puberty), and offer little more than rococo charm, though the G minor (No. 1 in Hoboken's catalogue), with its neo-baroque severity, is a notable exception. But the majority of the trios date from the 1780s and 1790s and contain some of Haydn's most imaginative, lyrical and harmonically adventurous music. Two outstanding works from the 1780s are the E minor, No. 12, with its passionate, closely worked opening *Allegro*, and No. 14 in A flat, with its exquisitely tender *Adagio* in a remote E major that leads without a break into one of Haydn's most hilariously quixotic finales.

The 14 magnificent trios of the 1790s range from relaxed, intimate pieces like the E flat, No. 29, through the sombre, almost tragic F sharp minor, No. 26, to the C major, No. 27, unsurpassed in the whole series for its intellectual and virtuoso brilliance. Finest of all, perhaps, are the E major, No. 28, with its radiant outer movements (wonderfully fanciful, delicate textures here) and its astonishing central E minor *passacaglia*; and the E flat, No. 30, with its noble, lyrically expansive first movement, its deep-toned, often richly chromatic *Andante* and its glorious German-dance finale. The Beaux Arts's playing throughout is vital, refined, and sharply responsive to the music's teeming richness and variety. The early trios were conceived for harpsichord, though such is the deftness and delicacy of Menahem Pressler's touch here that there is no question of the music being overpowered by the modern Steinway; and among individual delights in the group's performances of these early works mention should be made of their gentle, affectionate way with the central minuets, underlining their dual function as dances and surrogate slow movements. In the later trios they catch beautifully the leisurely, almost improvisatory feel of many of the opening movements, and bring a ruminative intensity, and a wonderful quality of soft playing to the great slow movements, while the finales have immense brio, wit and virtuosity, with ideally clean, crisp articulation from Pressler. Occasionally in the earlier works the Beaux Arts sound a touch over-sophisticated for this guileless music — the opening violin solo in No. 2 is a case in point. And there are a few disappointments in the later trios — the first movement of the great F sharp minor, No. 26, sounds too lightweight, even skittish while, conversely, in the *passacaglia* of No. 28 they take a surprisingly ponderous view of Haydn's *Allegretto*. But there's a feast of superlative, little-known music here, most of the playing is extraordinarily felicitous, and the recording has Philips's customary warmth and refinement. £70 or so may seem a lot to fork out all at once, but no one is likely to regret the investment — this is a set that will last a lifetime.

New review

Haydn. PIANO TRIOS. **Erich Höbarth** (vn); **Christophe Coin** (vc); **Patrick Cohen** (fp). Harmonia Mundi HMC90 1400. Recorded in 1992.
C major, HobXV/21. E flat major, HobXV/22. D minor, HobXV/23.

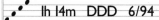 1h 2m DDD 9/93

Of the three works here, No. 21 is a generally lightweight, uncomplicated piece, with bucolic bagpipe effects in the gigue-like opening movement, an *Andante* built on a *Romanze*-type melody such as Mozart often favoured in his later music and a racy final *Presto*, a more compact counter-part to the finales in several of the "Salomon" Symphonies. The D minor, No. 23, opening with a set of variations on Haydn's favourite plan of alternating minor and major themes, has a richly ornamented *Adagio ma non troppo* with a rhapsodic, almost improvisatory feel (a type of Haydn slow movement only found in these late trios) and a wiry, syncopated finale full of teasing cross-rhythms. Finest of the three works, though, is the E flat, No. 22, all of whose movements show Haydn's harmonic thinking at its most subtle and exploratory, above all, the haunting, pre-Schubertian G major *Poco Adagio*. The performances from Patrick Cohen and his string colleagues are technically assured (string intonation well-nigh perfect throughout) and strongly character-ized, with a wide spectrum of tone colour and dynamics; and the relatively light sonorities of period instruments make for consistently lucid textures. They are vividly recorded.

New review

Haydn. PIANO TRIOS. **Vera Beths** (vn); **Anner Bylsma** (vc); **Robert Levin** (fp). Sony Classical Vivarte SK53120.
C major, HobXV/27. E major, HobXV/28. E flat major, HobXV/29. E flat major, HobXV/30.

1h 14m DDD 6/94

These are truly magnificent pieces, full of ideas of startling originality, and conceived on a grand scale — not simply long (though No. 42 certainly is that) but composed with a remarkable spaciousness to their ideas and their working-out. These performances do them ample justice, with their very brilliant and stylish pianism and a beautifully held instrumental balance (which, incidentally, gives the lie to the old notion that Haydn's cello parts are routine stuff: clearly Bylsma doesn't see them that way). Robert Levin, using a McNulty copy of a 1780 piano by J.A. Stein, produces playing of great vitality and delightful crispness, and puts across powerfully the intellectual force and the argumentative character of the music. Outstandingly keen and vital musicianship, excellently recorded.

Haydn. PIANO WORKS. **Alfred Brendel** (pf). Philips 416 643-2PH4. Booklet included.
Sonatas — C minor, HobXVI/20; E flat major, HobXVI/49 (both from 9500 774, 8/81); E minor, HobXVI/34; B minor, HobXVI/32; D major, Hob XVI/42 (412 228-1PH, 8/85); C major, HobXVI/48; D major, HobXVI/51; C major, Hob XVI/50 (6514 317, 11/83); E flat major, HobXVI/52; G major, HobXVI/40; D major, HobXVI/37 (416 365-1PH, 12/86). Fantasia in C major, HobXVI/4. Adagio in F major, HobXVI/9 (412 228-1PH, 8/85). Andante with variations in F minor, Hob XVI/6 (416 365-1PH, 12/86).

④ 52m 55m 37m 1h 1m ADD/DDD 3/87

The Sonatas collected in this set are some magnificent creations wonderfully well played by Alfred Brendel. Within the order and scale of these works Haydn explores a rich diversity of musical languages, a wit and broadness of expression that quickly repays attentive listening. It is the capriciousness as much as the poetry that Brendel so perfectly attends to; his playing, ever alive to the vitality and subtleties, makes these discs such a delight. The sophistication innate in the simple dance rhythms, the rusticity that emerges, but above all, the sheer *joie de vivre* are gladly embraced. Brendel shows in this music what makes a merely technically accomplished player a truly great one — his continual illumination of the musical ideas through intense study pays huge dividends. The recording quality varies enormously between the various works and though the close acoustic on some of the later discs could be faulted for allowing one to hear too much of the keyboard action, it certainly brings one into vivid contact with the music.

New review
Haydn. PIANO WORKS. **Andreas Staier** (fp). Deutsche Harmonia Mundi 05472 77285-2. Recorded in 1992.
Sonatas — D major, HobXVI/33; E minor, HobXVI/34. *Variations* — E flat major, HobXVII/3; F minor, HobXVII/6; G major, on "Gott erhalte den Kaiser".

1h 12m DDD 2/94

Staier is a player of immense technical and imaginative flair; using a beautiful, even-toned copy of a Walter fortepiano he brings to this shrewdly contrasted programme a rare sense of creative involvement, relishing to the full the music's wit, passion and fantasy. The Variations in E flat based on the minuet from the Quartet Op. 9 No. 2, are of the off-the-peg rococo-decorative type that tends to look pretty unpromising on paper. But the sheer inventiveness of Staier's playing easily overcomes any potential monotony. Of the two sonatas here the earlier is the D major, dating from the early to mid-1770s. The lightweight outer movements, gaining more than most from the fortepiano's clarity of texture, are spruce and puckish, with Staier palpably savouring every quirk in Haydn's argument. The relatively familiar E minor Sonata of *c.*1780 has a magnificent, driving opening movement, which Staier attacks with tigerish energy and a characteristically wide dynamic range. If you still doubt that performances on the fortepiano can rival those on a modern Steinway in colour, excitement and passion, then this is the disc to convert you although the recording is more closely miked than some might prefer.

New review
Haydn. PIANO WORKS. **Jenö Jandó** (pf). Naxos 8 550657.
Sonatas — E flat major, HobXVI/49; C major, HobXVI/50; D major, HobXVI/51; E flat major, HobXVI/52.

1h 2m DDD 6/94

The keyboard sonatas which Haydn originally intended for piano, such as the four considered here, show the composer's exploration of the instrument's capacity for greater dynamic variation. Jandó is sensitively responsive to the relationship between motif and dynamics which is particularly evident in the E flat and D major Sonatas, Nos. 59 and 61 respectively. Aided by clear recorded sound, Jandó's satisfying warmth in the lyrical passages provides an effective dramatic contrast to his crisp, positive approach in the livelier music. Jandó's glittering technique has a high profile in the other two sonatas in the programme. Pletnev's recordings (listed below) of the same pieces are no less impressive technically but, in the C major Sonata, No. 60, he takes more liberties than Jandó does. However, Pletnev's charm lies in the sheer musical personality of his playing and, in matters of articulation and shaping of thematic material, his performances leave a deep and lasting impression. Jandó's stylistically well-turned readings are less controversial, but they lack nothing in excitement. Sample the finale of the E flat Sonata, No. 62, where the wealth of expressive detail at an extremely fast tempo is breathtaking.

Additional recommendations ...
C minor, HobXVI/20. HobXVI/50. HobXVI/52. **Mikhail Pletnev.** Virgin Classics VC7 59258-2
— .•⁚ lh 7m DDD ll/89
F major, HobXVI/23; G major, HobXVI/27; C major, HobXVI/35; D major, HobXVI/37; E minor,
HobXVI/34; G major, HobXVI/40; C major, HobXVI/48; HobXVI/50; HobXVI/52. **Michèle**
Boegner (pf). Erato 2292-45705-2 — .•⁚ ⊙ 2h 5m DDD ll/92
G minor, HobXVI/44; C minor, HobXVI/20; D major, HobXVI/42. Variations in F minor, HobXVII/6.
Andrew Wilde (pf). Collins Quest 3017-2— .•⁚ lh 9m DDD ll/92
D major, HobXVI/24; A major, XVI/26; F major, XVI/29; C major, HobXVI/35; C sharp minor,
HobXVI/36. **Julia Cload** (pf). Meridian CDE84210 — .•⁚ lh l7m DDD 3/93

New review
Haydn. Masses — No. 6 in G major, "Missa Sancti Nicolai", HobXXII/6; No. 12 in B flat major, "Theresienmesse", HobXXII/12. **Nancy Argenta** (sop); **Catherine Robbin** (mez); **Michael Schade** (ten); **Alastair Miles** (bass); **The English Concert Choir; The English Concert/Trevor Pinnock.** Archiv Produktion 437 807-2AH. Texts and translations included. Recorded in 1992.

.•⁚ lh l2m DDD l/94

Happy in the coupling as in the performance, both Masses are radiant with energy, the *Sancti Nicolai* serene in its bliss, the *Theresienmesse* adding splendour and expansiveness. The G major Mass, with its shortened texts for *Gloria* and *Credo*, has a pastoral tint, anticipating early in the December of 1772 the adoration of the shepherds in the Christmas to come: courtly shepherds, one might think, with a sanctity that is not at all averse to the tribute of a good tune and a dancing rhythm. When gaiety gives way to gravity, as in the *Agnus Dei*, there is no sense that the one is more or less profound than the other; the joy 'matters' quite as much as the 'serious-ness', and it is to joy that the Mass returns in its "Dona nobis pacem". The *Theresienmesse* of 1799, a masterpiece on a larger scale, exhilarates in its vitality of invention and is effortlessly graceful in its formal control. These are the qualities most emphasized in performance here. The rhythms have a fine spring to them, a sense of bodily zest as of mental illumination. The *allegro* movements go a shade faster than usual, a little more urgent in manner than in the recording under Sir George Guest. The soloists, an admirable quartet, are placed well forward, and the orchestra claims more of the listener's attention than does the choir.

Additional recommendation ...
No. 12. **M. Haydn.** *Ave regina caelorum.* **Mozart.** *Ave verum corpus, K618.* **Soloists; Choir of St John's College, Cambridge; Academy of St Martin in the Fields/George Guest.** Decca Ovation 430 159-2DM — .•⁚ 56m ADD 6/91

Haydn. Mass No. 11 in D minor, "Nelson"ᵃ. Te Deum in C major, HobXXIIIc/2. ᵃ**Felicity Lott** (sop); ᵃ**Carolyn Watkinson** (contr); ᵃ**Maldwyn Davies** (ten); ᵃ**David Wilson-Johnson** (bar); **The English Concert and Choir/Trevor Pinnock.** Archiv Produktion 423 097-2AH. Texts and translations included.

.•⁚ 50m ADD 2/88

The British Admiral had ousted the Napoleonic fleet at the Battle of the Nile just as Haydn was in the middle of writing his *Nelson* Mass. Although the news could not have reached him until after its completion, Haydn's awareness of the international situation was expressed in the work's subtitle, "Missa in Augustiis", or "Mass in times of fear". With its rattle of timpani, its pungent trumpet calls, and its highly-strung harmonic structure, there is no work of Haydn's which cries out so loudly for recording on period instruments; and it is the distinctive sonority and charged tempos of this performance which sets it apart from its competitors. The dry, hard timpani and long trumpets bite into the dissonance of the opening *Kyrie*, and the near vibrato-less string playing is mordant and urgent. The fast-slow-fast triptych of the *Gloria* is set out in nervously contrasted speeds, and the *Credo* bounces with affirmation. Just as the choral singing is meticulously balanced with instrumental inflection, so the soloists have been chosen to highlight the colours in Pinnock's palette. This is an unusually exciting recording.

Additional recommendation ...
No. 11[a]. **Mozart.** *Mass in C major, K317*[b]. **Soloists;** [a]**London Symphony Chorus,** [b]**Choir of King's College, Cambridge;** [a]**City of London Sinfonia/Richard Hickox;** [b]**English Chamber Orchestra/Stephen Cleobury.** Decca Ovation 436 470-2DM — .·* lh 7m DDD 5/93

Haydn. Die Jahreszeiten. **Barbara Bonney** (sop); **Anthony Rolfe Johnson** (ten); **Andreas Schmidt** (bar); **Monteverdi Choir; English Baroque Soloists/John Eliot Gardiner.** Archiv Produktion 431 818-2AH2. Text and translation included. Recorded in 1990.

.·* ② 2h 7m DDD 5/92   ⁹P ✒

The comparative unpopularity of Haydn's *The Seasons* when considered against his other great oratorio *Die Schöpfung* ("The Creation"), is understandable perhaps, but it is not really all that well deserved. Less exalted its subject and libretto may be, but its depiction of the progress of the year amid the scenes and occupations of the Austrian countryside drew from its composer — then in his late sixties — music of unfailing invention, benign warmth and constant musical-pictoral delights. It is charming music written with great affection, and as such it is not only quintessentially Haydnesque, but also virtually guaranteed to raise a smile. As usual, John Eliot Gardiner and his forces turn in disciplined, meticulously professional performances. This is not one of those massive readings currently favoured even by period practitioners for Haydn's oratorios, though the orchestra is slightly larger — and consequently a tiny bit less lucid — than the sort you might nowadays find playing a classical symphony. The choir, however, performs with great clarity and accuracy, and brings, too, an enjoyable sense of characterization to its various corporate roles, be they drunken revellers, improbably noisy hunters, homely fireside spinners, or whatever. The soloists all perform with notable poise and intelligence: Barbara Bonney's voice is pure and even, Anthony Rolfe Johnson sounds entirely at ease with the music, and Andreas Schmidt is gentle-voiced but certainly not lacking in substance. Perhaps in the end this is a performance that just lacks that last inch of necessary warmth to make it unbeatable, but it's a first-rate recommendation none the less.

Additional recommendations ...
Angela Maria Blasi (sop); **Josef Protschka** (ten); **Robert Holl** (bass); **Arnold Schönberg Choir; Vienna Symphony Orchestra/Nikolaus Harnoncourt.** Teldec 2292-42699-2— .·* ② 2h 25m DDD 2/88
Ileana Cotrubas (sop); **Werner Krenn** (ten); **Hans Sotin** (bass); **Brighton Festival Chorus; Royal Philharmonic Orchestra/Antál Dorati.** Decca 425 708-2DM2 — .·* 2h 22m ADD 9/90 ⁹P ⁹S
Edith Mathis (sop); **Siegfried Jerusalem** (ten); **Dietrich Fischer-Dieskau** (bar); **Chorus and Academy of St Martin in the Fields/Sir Neville Marriner.** Philips Duo 438 715-2PM2 — .·* ② 2h 14m ADD 6/94

Haydn. Die Schöpfung (sung in English). **Emma Kirkby** (sop); **Anthony Rolfe Johnson** (ten); **Michael George** (bass); **Choir of New College, Oxford; Academy of Ancient Music Chorus and Orchestra/Christopher Hogwood.** L'Oiseau-Lyre 430 397-2OH2. Text included. Recorded in 1990.

.·* ② lh 39m DDD 3/91   ⁹P Ⓑ ✒

Haydn. Die Schöpfung. **Gundula Janowitz** (sop); **Fritz Wunderlich, Werner Krenn** (tens); **Dietrich Fischer-Dieskau** (bar); **Walter Berry** (bass); **Christa Ludwig** (alto)

Vienna Singverein; Berlin Philharmonic Orchestra/Herbert von Karajan. DG Galleria
435 077-2GGA2. Text and translation included. From 2707 044 (10/69). Recorded 1966-69.

⏺ ② 1h 49m ADD 12/91 ⑨ₚ Ⓑ

The claims to historical authenticity made on behalf of Hogwood's performance of Haydn's
oratorio *Die Schöpfung* ("The Creation"), are diffuse and overstated, but that need not worry the
listener overmuch, for what counts is the performance itself. It is the second to have been
recorded using period instruments but the first to use Peter Brown's new performing edition
based on appropriate sources. The Academy of Ancient Music fields an orchestra expanded to
115 players together with the Choir of New College, Oxford and a strong solo vocal group. The
results are mostly satisfying and the performance greatly enhanced by a sympathetic recorded
balance which captures the distinctive character of period instruments. When Haydn published
the first edition, it included both German and English texts and it would seem probable that he
intended one or other to be sung according to the nationality of the audience. This version is
sung in English, a feature that many listeners will find illuminating. All in all this is an
enterprising project which has largely succeeded in achieving its aim as outlined by the Director
of the performance, Christopher Hogwood "to recapture in sound, scale and text the
performances conducted by the composer". The booklet contains full texts in four languages and
an informative essay.

Herbert von Karajan's 1966 version of *Die Schöpfung* is something of a classic and probably
one of the best recordings ever made of this joyous work. In the depiction of the chaos Karajan
immediately set the atmosphere with a massive luminous tone quality from the Berlin
Philharmonic, sustained fermatas and fortissimos like ocean breakers. The choir's mighty
outburst in "and there was light" almost takes the roof off and the elegant accompaniment to the
ensuing arias are a continuous delight. But the main glory of this recording are the soloists
including Fritz Wunderlich as a brilliantly mercurial Uriel. This performance is a superb
monument to the tenor whose tragically premature death occurred before the sessions were
completed. Only the recitatives were left unrecorded and Werner Krenn made an excellent
substitute. Walter Berry's narration of Haydn's pre-Darwinian evolution is buoyant while
Gundula Janowitz's creamy soprano is a pleasure throughout. DG's recording sounds pleasantly
fresh and well-balanced.

Additional recommendations ...
(Sung in English). **Soloists; King's College Choir, Cambridge; Academy of St Martin in
the Fields/Sir David Willcocks.** EMI Studio CMS7 69894-2 — ⏺ ② 1h 47m ADD 2/89 ⑨ₚ Ⓑ
(Highlights). **Soloists; Chicago Symphony Chorus and Orchestra/Sir Georg Solti.** Decca
Ovation 430 739-2DM — ⏺ 1h 10m DDD 8/92 ⑨ₚ Ⓑ

New review

Haydn. ARMIDA. **Jessye Norman** (sop) Armida; **Claes Hakon Ahnsjö** (ten) Rinaldo;
Norma Burrowes (sop) Zelmira; **Samuel Ramey** (bass) Idreno; **Robin Leggate** (ten)
Ubaldo; **Anthony Rolfe Johnson** (ten) Clotarco. Philips 432 438-2PH2. From 6769 021
(9/79).

⏺ ② 2h 20m ADD 6/93

Armida, widely considered Haydn's finest opera, is based on a familiar literary classic adopted
for opera by numerous other composers: what is surprising is that in his setting Haydn reverted
to *opera seria* style, with no *buffo* characters, very few ensembles and extensive *secco* recitatives.
Dramatic action is minimal: for three acts Rinaldo lingers under the spell of the enchantress
Armida despite all the efforts of fellow-Crusaders to recall him to his mission. The work's
static nature, however, casts the emphasis on its musical qualities, and in this regard *Armida* is
of the highest standard. The enchantress herself, personified by the redoubtable Jessye Norman,
has the widest range of emotions to portray, from tenderness to rage; Ahnsjö as Rinaldo
produces a fine legato and very accurate florid passagework, but his low register rather lets him
down; Ramey shows laudable firmness and flexibility; and Burrowes's fresh youthful charm is
very appealing. Another strength is the alert orchestral playing. The most notable features of
the opera are three long through-composed sequences and imaginative scoring: the scene in the
magic forest, where Rinaldo at last, to Armida's fury, breaks free from her spell, is masterly,
and in itself is sufficient to compel a revision of the too common neglect of Haydn as an
operatic composer.

Further listening ...

String Quartets — Op. 1: No. 5 in E flat major; No. 6 in C major. Op. 2: No. 1 in A major; No. 2 in E major. **Kodály Quartet.** Naxos 8 550399.

Divertimentos — A minor/major, HobX/3; G major, HobX/5; D major, HobX/10; G major, HobX/12. **Ricercar Consort.** Ricercar RIC067050 (9/91).

The Seven Last Words of Our Saviour on the Cross. **Soloists; Arnold Schönberg Choir; Vienna Concentus Musicus/Nikolaus Harnoncourt.** Teldec Das Alte Werk 2292-46458-2 (5/92).

Arianna a Naxos. *English Canzonettas* — A pastoral song. Despair. Fidelity. The mermaid's song. O tuneful voice. Piercing eyes. Pleasing pain. Sailor's song. She never told her love. The spirit's song. The wanderer. **Carolyn Watkinson** (mez); **Glen Wilson** (fp). Virgin Classics Veritas VC7 59033-2 (1/92).

Stabat mater. **Patricia Rozario** (sop); **Catherine Robbin** (mez); **Anthony Rolfe Johnson** (ten); **Cornelius Hauptmann** (bass); **The English Concert and Choir/Trevor Pinnock.** Archiv Produktion 429 733-2AH (9/90).

L'ANIMA DEL FILOSOFO. **Soloists; Netherlands Chamber Choir; La Stagione/Michael Schneider.** Deutsche Harmonia Mundi RD77229 (4/92).

ESTERHAZA OPERA CYCLE. — L'INFEDLTÀ DELUSA *(432 413-2PH2)*; L'INCONTRO IMPROVVISO — excerpts *(432 416-2PH3)*; IL MONDO DELLA LUNA — excerpts *(432 420-2PH3)*; LA VERA COSTANZA *(432 424-2PH2)*; L'ISOLA DISABITATA *(432 427-2PH2)*; LA DEFELTÀ PREMIATA *(432 430-2PH3)*; ORLANDO PALADINO *(432 434-2PH3)*; ARMIDA *(432 438-2PH2)*. **Soloists; Lausanne Chamber Orchestra/Antál Dorati.** Philips 438 167-2PH20 (20 discs, also available separately as indicated above [6/93]).

Key to symbols

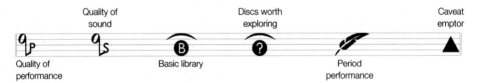

Quality of sound   Discs worth exploring   Caveat emptor

Quality of performance   Basic library   Period performance

Michael Haydn

Austrian 1737-1806

Suggested listening ...

Violin Concerto in B flat major, P53[a]. Clarinet Concerto in D major, P54[b]. Concerto for Harpsichord and Viola in C major, P55[c]. **Soloists;** [ac]**Oradea Philharmonic Orchestra/ Ervin Acél;** [b]**Quodlibet Musicum Chamber Orchestra/Aurelian Octav Popa** (cl). Olympia OCD406 (10/90).

Romanze in A flat major. *Coupled with **Mozart.*** Horn Quintet in E flat major, K407/K386c[b]. *Haydn.* Divertimento a tre in E flat major, HobIV/5. *Beethoven.* Sextet in E flat major, Op. 81b[a]. *Reicha.* Horn Quintet, Op. 106[c].**Hermann Baumann,** [a]**Vladimir Dshambasov** (hns); **Gewandhaus Quartet;** [b]**Olaf Hallmann** (va); [c]**Christian Ockert** (db). Philips 426 440-2PH (9/93). *See review in the Collections section; refer to the Index to Reviews.*

Missa Sancti Aloysii, MH257. Missa sub titulo Sancti Leopoldi, MH837. Vesperae pro festo Sanctissimae innocentium, MH548. **Trinity College Choir, Cambridge; ensemble/Richard Marlow.** Conifer CDCF220 (2/94).

Christopher Headington

Headington. Violin Concerto.
R. Strauss. Violin Concerto, Op. 8. **Xue-Wei** (vn); **London Philharmonic Orchestra/ Jane Glover.** ASV CDDCA780.

 1h 3m DDD 12/91

Xue-Wei's penetrating and intuitive realization of Christopher Headington's Violin Concerto, written in 1959, commands great admiration for this significant modern concerto, dedicated to the late Ralph Holmes, which in many respects inherits the lyric mantle of the great masterworks for the violin composed earlier in the century by Elgar and Walton. Xue-Wei also reminds the listener of the work's darker aspect, especially during the opening paragraphs of the concerto, where an affinity with the Walton Concerto is apparent. The central *Vivace* movement again has something of Walton's caustic wit, but the Headington concerto is searching and original in concept, without being overtly heroic or virtuosic. The lyrical potential of the solo writing is gloriously revealed by Xue-Wei, whose playing is superb, particularly in the lucid six-variation finale, which leads to a hushed and deeply-felt conclusion. The Violin Concerto by Richard Strauss is very much in the traditionally romantic virtuoso vein of Wieniawski and Vieuxtemps, and although an early work it displays great pointers in the direction of Strauss's mature heroism. Xue-Wei's playing is volatile, affectionate and involving, while his rare tonal finesse has an evocative Heifetzian lustre which is always compelling. He is admirably supported throughout by the London Philharmonic, under Jane Glover, and ASV capture every nuance of the performance in the ample acoustic of London's Henry Wood Hall. The interpretation of the Headington concerto alone could well acquire classic status, and this is a disc which deserves to be heard by all who have an affinity with violin music of the twentieth century.

Further listening ...

Ballade-Image. Cinquanta. *Coupled with* **Britten.** Holiday Diary; **Delius.** Three Preludes; **Elgar.** Adieu. In Smyrna. Serenade; **Ireland.** The Island Spell; **Moeran.** Summer Valley; **Patterson.** A Tunnel of Time, Op. 66. **Christopher Headington** (pf). Kingdom KCLCD2017 (11/90).

Johann David Heinichen

Suggested listening ...

Concertos — C major, S211; G major: S213; S214, "Darmstadt"; S214, "Venezia"; S215; S217; F major: S226; S231; S232; S233; S234; S235. Serenata di Moritzburg in F major, S204. Sonata in A major, S208. Concerto Movement in C minor, S240. **Cologne Musica Antiqua/ Reinhard Goebel.** Archiv Produktion 437 549-2AH2 (5/93).

Peter Heise

New review

Heise. DROT OG MARSK. **Poul Elming** (ten) King Erik; **Bent Norup** (bar) Stig Andersen; **Eva Johansson** (sop) Ingeborg; **Kurt Westi** (ten) Rane Johnsen; **Christian Christiansen** (bass) Count Jakob; **Aage Haugland** (bass) Jens Grand; **Ole Hedegaard** (ten) Arved Bengtsen; **Inge Nielsen** (sop) Aase; **Ronnie Johansen** (bass) Herald; **Danish National Radio Choir; Danish National Radio Symphony Orchestra/Michael Schønwandt.** Chandos CHAN9143/5. Notes, text and translation included.

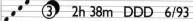 ③ 2h 38m DDD 6/93

There is a lot to be said for Nordic charm and *Drot og Marsk* ("King and Marshall"), despite its tragic plot, possesses this in abundance. As with so much Scandinavian painting of the period, suffused by that crystal-clear light so redolent of Northern Europe, this opera (completed in 1877) breathes that special air made familiar by the scores of Grieg, Svendsen and Nielsen. Peter Heise is an important figure in Danish music, forming the essential link between Niels Gade and Carl Nielsen. In *Drot og Marsk* one can hear in many passages the manner from which sprang the Nielsen of *Maskarade* and *Springtime in Funen* (though towards the end of Heise's final act there is one brief, astonishing pre-echo of the Hindemith of *Mathis der Maler*). Heise remained relatively free of Wagner's influence, learning rather from Verdi and his conflation of song-like lyricism within large-scale structures is most impressive. The all-Danish cast distinguish themselves, particularly Poul Elming and Bent Norup in the title-roles and Michael Schønwandt proves to be in complete command of this wonderful score. Heise's premature death at the age of 49 and probably with his best work still to come was a great loss. Not until Nielsen arrived on the scene was a comparable figure active.

Heneker, David/John Taylor

British 1906-

Suggested listening ...

CHARLIE GIRL. **Original 1986 London revival cast.** First Night OCRCD9.

George Martin Adolf von Henselt

German 1814-1889

New review

Henselt. Piano Concert in F minor, Op. 16. Variations de concert, Op. 11, on "Quand je quittai la Normandie" from Meyerbeer's "Robert le Diable".
Alkan. Concerti da camera, Op. 10 — No. 1 in A minor; No. 2 in C sharp minor. **Marc-André Hamelin** (pf); **BBC Scottish Symphony Orchestra/Martyn Brabbins.** Hyperion CDA66717.

lh 10m DDD 8/94

Much of the credit for this disc must go to the phenomenal playing and superb musicianship of Marc-André Hamelin (whose account of the staggeringly difficult Henselt Concerto is quite breathtaking) but plaudits must also go to the imaginative programming and excellent accompanying booklet-notes. The main work of the disc, both in terms of quality and length, is of course the above-mentioned Henselt F minor Concerto, which, although once an active participant in the repertoire of most top league pianists during the late nineteenth century (at least those sufficiently technically equipped to approach it), dropped out of sight in the early part of this century until revived by those 'champions of the forgotten', Raymond Lewenthal and Michael Ponti. As a concerto it is particularly 'giving' to the listener and very unforgiving to the pianist, as the extreme technical difficulties are concealed in such a way that they become almost transparent to the ear — which probably accounts for its disappearance from the repertoire. Rubinstein once recounted that "I procured the concerto and his *études*, but after working on them for a few days I realised it was a waste of time, for they were based on an abnormal formation of the hand. In this respect Henselt, like Paganini, was a freak." Musically the concerto owes allegiance to Chopin (in the *Larghetto*) and Thalberg and Mendelssohn in the outer movements, but generally the overall Henseltian style has its own peculiar flavour which should win many friends through Hamelin's highly persuasive and thoroughly committed performance. The slightly earlier *Variations de concert* (on a theme from Meyerbeer's *Robert le Diable*) is admittedly slighter fare but is nevertheless an attractive and enjoyable work which hails from the same stable as Chopin's *Là ci darem* Variations. The remainder of the disc consists of two 'mini' concertos by Henselt's exact contemporary and fellow 'reticent' Charles-Valentin Alkan (Henselt, like Alkan, gave very few public concerts due to stage-fright that bordered on the pathological). The two early *Concerti da camera* (the only surviving *concertante* pieces by Alkan) are not, it has to be said, 'major' Alkan works, but they are original in invention and full of melodic appeal, with more than a hint or two of the Alkan of later years. Hamelin, who has already proved himself a formidable Alkan exponent with his outstanding recording of the *Concerto for solo piano* (see review under Alkan; refer to the Index to Reviews), delivers them with astonishing dexterity and panache and, as in the Henselt pieces, he is given equally committed support from the BBC Scottish Symphony Orchestra under the direction of Martyn Brabbins. A thoroughly enjoyable disc, well worth exploring.

Further listening ...

Ballade in B flat major, Op. 31. Grande Valse, Op. 30, "L'aurore boréale". Impromptus — B flat minor, Op. 34; B minor, Op. 37; C minor, Op. 7; F minor, Op. 17. Introduction and Variations on a theme by Donizetti, Op. 1. Pensée fugitive, Op. 8. Rondo serioso. Scherzo in B minor, Op. 9. Toccatina in C minor, Op. 25. Valse mélancolique, Op. 36. **Rudiger Steinfatt** (pf). Koch Schwann 310023.

Hans Werner Henze

German 1926-

New review

Henze. Symphony No. 7. Barcarola. **City of Birmingham Symphony Orchestra/Simon Rattle.** EMI CDC7 54762-2. Recorded live in 1992.

Ih   DDD   II/93

This is a most important and overdue issue. Henze's Seventh adopts a recognizably Beethovenian model, although the music's point of departure may lie more immediately in the symphonies of Karl Amadeus Hartmann. Henze states in the notes that the Seventh is "a German symphony, and it deals with matters German". One of these is the poet Friedrich Hölderlin, whose sufferings in an asylum and late poem *Hälfte des Lebens* ("Half of Life") inspired respectively the Scherzo and finale; what lies behind the intense and complex threnody of the towering second — and longest — movement is not divulged. This repertoire is not normally associated with Simon Rattle or the Birmingham band but there is no lack of knowledge or commitment evident in the playing. Particularly impressive are the climaxes to the first and last movements, both superbly prepared and flawless in execution. The many delicate passages in which both the symphony and the earlier *Barcarola* (1979) abound are rendered equally impressively and the excellent recording does full justice to these eruptive scores. All in all, a tremendous achievement.

Further listening ...

Symphonies — Nos. 1-5[a]; No. 6[b]. [a]**Berlin Philharmonic Orchestra;** [b]**London Symphony Orchestra/Hans Werner Henze.** DG 20th Century Classics 429 854-2GC2 (12/90).

String Quartets Nos. 1-5. **Arditti Quartet.** Wergo WER60114/5-50 (3/90).

El Cimarrón. **Paul Yoder** (bar); **Michael Faust** (fl); **Reinbert Evers** (gtr); **Mircea Ardeleanu** (perc). Koch Schwann Musica Mundi 314030 (1/92).

BOULEVARD SOLITUDE. **Soloists; Epalinges Children's Chorus; Lausanne Opera Chorus; Orchestre des Rencontres Musicales/Ivan Anguelov.** Cascavelle 1000 Series VEL1006 (12/92).

DIE BASSARIDEN. **Soloists; Berlin Radio Chamber Choir; South German Radio Choir; Berlin Radio Symphony Orchestra/Gerd Albrecht.** Koch Schwann Musica Mundi 314006 (10/91).

THE ENGLISH CAT. **Soloists; Parnassus Orchestra/Markus Stenz.** Wergo WER6204-2 (12/92).

Victor Herbert

American 1859-1924

Suggested listening ...

Cello Concertos — No. 1 in D major, Op. 8; No. 2 in E minor, Op. 30. Five Pieces for Cello and Strings (trans. Dennison) — Yesterthoughts; Pensée amoureuse; Punchinello; Ghazel; The Mountain Brook. **Lynn Harrell** (vc); **Academy of St Martin in the Fields/Sir Neville Marriner.** Decca 417 672-2DH (10/88).

Jerry Herman

American 1933-

Suggested listening ...

LA CAGE AUX FOLLES. **Original Broadway cast.** RCA Red Seal BD84824 (3/87).

MACK AND MABEL. **Original Broadway cast.** MCA MCLD19089.

Louis Hérold

French 1791-1833

New review
Hérold (arr. Lanchbery). La fille mal gardée — excerpts. **Orchestra of the Royal Opera House, Covent Garden/John Lanchbery.** Decca Ovation 430 196-2DM. From SXL2313 (8/62). Recorded in 1962.

·· 51m ADD 1/94

The Royal Ballet's *La fille mal gardée* remains a source of perpetual delight, not least for the music that John Lanchbery arranged largely from Hérold's patchwork score for the 1828 version. The Clog dance is the obvious highlight of the score; but there are felicitous moments throughout, with snatches of Rossini, Donizetti *et al* cropping up all over the place. This recording is the original one that Lanchbery conducted when the ballet proved such a success in the Royal Ballet's repertoire in 1960. More recently he has recorded the score complete (listed below); and ballet lovers will doubtless consider this fuller version essential. However, others will undoubtedly find that the complete score rather outstays its welcome by comparison with this constantly uplifting selection. At medium price and wearing its 30-odd years lightly, it makes a most compelling recommendation.

Additional recommendation ...
La fille mal gardée — ballet[a]. **Lecocq** (arr. G. Jacob). *Mam'zelle Angot* — ballet[b]. [a]**Orchestra of the Royal Opera House, Covent Garden/John Lanchbery;** [b]**National Philharmonic Orchestra/Richard Bonynge.** Decca Ovation 430 849-2DM2 — ·· ② 2h 14m DDD 12/91

Bernard Herrmann

American 1911-1975

New review
Herrmann. The Devil and Daniel Webster — Suite. Silent Noon. For the Fallen. Currier and Ives Suite. **New Zealand Symphony Orchestra/James Sedares.** Koch International Classics 37224-2.

·· 51m DDD 6/94

The popular 20-minute suite from *The Devil and Daniel Webster* was assembled shortly after the film's score won its Oscar in 1942, and throughout the five movements Herrmann treats several

New England folk-tunes to his own special brand of orchestral wizardry. The score is both a gentle, sepia-tinted portrait of rustic Americana and a wickedly endearing account of Mr Scratch's devilish interventions. *Silent Noon* is a warm if rather meandering romantic idyll clearly influenced by Delius. Far more characteristic is the 1943 berceuse *For the Fallen*, a brief, but poignant lament for the soldiers killed in action. The star items of the disc, though, are the five vibrant dance episodes that make up the *Currier and Ives Suite* (1935). As well as bringing to life the painter's beautifully detailed engravings with a sparkling, generous humour that would rarely surface in Herrmann's later works, the Suite also possesses the elegant period flavour that would colour the scores for *Citizen Kane, The Magnificent Ambersons* as well as *Daniel Webster*. James Sedares and the NZSO are on top form and the sound is pleasantly warm and full-bodied.

New review
Herrmann. Symphony No. 1[a]. The Fantasticks[b]. [b]**Gillian Humphreys** (sop); [b]**Meriel Dickinson** (mez); [b]**John Amis** (ten); [b]**Michael Rippon** (bass); [b]**Thames Chamber Choir; National Philharmonic Orchestra/Bernard Herrmann.** Unicorn-Kanchana Souvenir UKCD2063. Texts included. Items marked [a] from RHS331 (2/76), [b]RHS340 (9/76). Recorded 1974-75.

•• lh 5m ADD I/94

Unicorn-Kanchana's reissue gives a welcome new lease of life for the composer's recording of his enjoyable Symphony (1941). Herrmann and the National Philharmonic Orchestra bring a great epic feel to bear (and the orchestral playing has none of the hint of scramble that sometimes marred James Sedares's excellent Phoenix Symphony Orchestra version, listed below). As a coupling Sedares offers a reliable, if not really distinctive rendering of Schuman's *New England Triptych*; Herrmann gives us more Herrmann: the song-cycle, *The Fantasticks*. Based on texts by the Elizabethan poet Nicolas Breton, these are five most evocative, consistently imaginative settings, given here with disarming commitment if not always complete technical assurance. Decent sound.

Additional recommendation ...
No. 1. **Schuman.** *New England Triptych.* **Phoenix Symphony Orchestra/James Sedares.** Koch International Classics 37135-2 — •• 52m DDD 9/92

Further listening ...

Film Scores: The Day the Earth Stood Still; Fahrenheit 451; Journey to the Centre of the Earth; The Seventh Voyage of Sinbad. **National Philharmonic Orchestra/Bernard Herrmann.** Decca 421 266-2DA (11/89).

Film Scores: On Dangerous Ground — The death hunt. Citizen Kane — Suite[a]. Beneath the 12-Mile Reef — Suite. Hangover Square — Concerto macabre[b]. White Witch Doctor — Suite. [a]**Dame Kiri Te Kanawa** (sop); [b]**Joaquin Achucarro** (pf); **National Phlharmonic Orchestra/Charles Gerhardt.** RCA Victor GD80707 (11/91).

Vertigo — *Original film soundtrack.* **Sinfonia of London/Muir Mathieson.** Mercury 422 106-2MM (3/90).

Film Scores: Citizen Kane. The Devil and Daniel Webster. The Man Who Knew Too Much (Arthur Benjamin). Psycho. The Wrong Man. Vertigo. North by Northwest. The Bride Wore Black. Fahrenheit 451. Taxi Driver. **Royal Philharmonic Orchestra/Elmer Bernstein.** Milan 14081-2 (3/94).

Welles Raises Kane — suite[a]. The Devil and Daniel Webster — suite[a]. Obsession — film score[b]. [a]**London Philharmonic Orchestra;** [b]**National Philharmonic Orchestra/Bernard Herrmann.** Unicorn-Kanchana UKCD2065.

WUTHERING HEIGHTS. **Soloists; Elizabethan Singers; Pro Arte Orchestra/Bernard Herrmann.** Unicorn-Kanchana UKCD2050/2 (8/93).

Hildegard of Bingen

German 1098-1179

Suggested listening ...

A FEATHER ON THE BREATH OF GOD — Columba aspexit. Ave, generosa. O ignis spiritus. O Jerusalem. O Euchari. O viridissima virga. O presul vere civitatis. O Ecclesia. **Gothic Voices/Christopher Page** with **Doreen Muskett** (symphony); **Robert White** (reed drones). Hyperion CDA66039 (7/85).

O magne Pater. O aeterne Deus. Ave generosa. O frondens virga. O felix anima. Ave Maria, o auctrix vitae. O quam mirabilis. O virtus sapientiae. O vis aeternitatis. *Coupled with **Abelard.*** Planctus David. O quanta qualia; ***Anonymous.*** Promat chorus hodie. Annus novus in gaudio. Fulget dies celebris. **Augsburg Early Music Ensemble.** Christophorus Musica Practica CHR74584 (3/93).

Ordo Virtutum. **Sequentia Medieval Music Ensemble.** Deutsche Harmonia Mundi Editio Classica GD77051 (1/84).

Paul Hindemith

German 1895-1963

Hindemith. Cello Concerto[a]. The Four Temperaments[b]. [a]**Raphael Wallfisch** (vc); [b]**Howard Shelley** (pf); **BBC Philharmonic Orchestra/Yan Pascal Tortelier.** Chandos CHAN9124. Recorded in 1992.

52m DDD 3/93

These two concertos, both from Hindemith's maturity (1940), make a good pairing. The outwardly conventional Cello Concerto contrasts a relatively small voice (the cello) which carries the work's lyrical message, with a large orchestra used initially for active statements delivered with great power. Hindemith's plan would seem to be to slowly reconcile these apparently contradictory modes of address. *The Four Temperaments* is a concerto for piano and string orchestra, a much more evenly balanced combination, using theme and variations form to integrate and relate the contrasted 'humours'; the old jibe that Hindemith's variations should have been called "Four Equal Temperaments" is not too wide of the mark, and Hindemith's treatment of his material would appear to argue that all temperaments, whatever the dominant disposition, are closely related. His portraiture, in fact, reveals characterization of great depth and dimension. Performances are superbly accomplished, indeed this is the finest of many currently available recordings of *The Four Temperaments*. And Chandos have resisted the temptation, which must be considerable, to move in on the soloist in the Cello Concerto. The sound is open and spacious.

Hindemith. Violin Concerto[a]. Symphonic Metamorphosis on Themes of Carl Maria von Weber[b]. Mathis der Maler — Symphony[c]. [a]**David Oistrakh** (vn); [ab]**London Symphony Orchestra/**[a]**Paul Hindemith,** [b]**Claudio Abbado;** [c]**Suisse Romande Orchestra/Paul Kletzki.** Decca Enterprise 433 081-2DM. Item marked [a] from SXL6035 (2/63), recorded in 1962, [b] SXL6398 (5/69), [c] SXL6445 (12/70), both recorded in 1968.

Ih I7m ADD 9/92

Hindemithians who can afford to be choosy about the *Mathis der Maler* Symphony and the *Symphonic Metamorphosis* will immediately recognize the superiority of the full-price Blomstedt readings (reviewed below). Consistently spectacular 1960s Decca sound adds allure to the merely proficient performances on offer here. What makes this medium-priced disc indispensable is the 30 minute Violin Concerto with Oistrakh at his legendary best and the composer conducting. The late Deryck Cooke, in his original *Gramophone* review, wrote of Oistrakh as "superbly poised and eloquent ... and as performed here the Concerto shows that behind Hindemith's stony neo-classical facade beats a romantic German heart". Listening to this recording it's hard to understand the Concerto's relative neglect — strange indeed are the tides of fashion — but easy to imagine current star violinists finding Oistrakh's an impossible act to follow. The 1962 sound gives Oistrakh a discreet dominance, and the engineers flatten out the slow movement's central climax, but thankfully no other allowances need be made for this preservation of a classic recording.

Additional recommendation ...
Symphonic Metamorphosis. **Weber.** *Overtures — Euryanthe; Der Freischütz; Oberon; Der Beherrscher der Geister. Turandot — Overture; March.* **Philharmonia Orchestra/Neeme Järvi.** Chandos CHAN8766 — .⦁⠂' lh lm DDD 1/90 ⁹ₚ

Hindemith. Mathis der Maler — Symphony. Trauermusik[a]. Symphonic Metamorphosis on Themes of Carl Maria von Weber. [a]**Geraldine Walther** (va); **San Francisco Symphony Orchestra/Herbert Blomstedt.** Decca 421 523-2DH. Recorded in 1987.

.⦁⠂' **55m   DDD   10/88**   ⁹ₚ

The charge sometimes levelled against Hindemith of being dry and cerebral utterly collapses in the face of Blomstedt's disc. Masterly craftsmanship and virtuosity there is in plenty; but the powerful emotions of *Mathis der Maler* and the festive high spirits of the *Symphonic Metamorphosis* could not be denied except by those who wilfully close their ears. Each of the three movements of the *Mathis* symphony is based on a panel of Grünewald's great Isenheim altar. The eventual glorious illumination of "The angels" folk-tune, the poignant slow movement and the blazing triumphant Allelujas after the desperate struggle with the demons in the finale have a searing intensity in this performance, which also presents Hindemith's elaborate web of counterpoints with the utmost lucidity. For brilliant and joyously ebullient orchestral writing few works can match that based on Weber's piano duets and his *Turandot* overture: here the San Francisco woodwind and brass have a field day. In addition, this warmly recommended disc contains a heartfelt performance of the touching elegy on the death of King George V which Hindemith wrote overnight in 1936.

Additional recommendations ...
Mathis der Maler. **Stravinsky.** *Jeu de cartes.* **Berlin Philharmonic Orchestra/Paul Hindemith.** Teldec 9031-76440-2 — .⦁⠂' 46m ADD ▲
Mathis der Maler. Symphonic Metamorphosis. Konzertmusik for Strings and Brass, Op. 50. **Israel Philharmonic Orchestra/Leonard Bernstein.** DG 429 404-2GH — .⦁⠂' lh 7m DDD 5/91 ⁹ₚ
Symphonic Metamorphosis. Symphony in E flat major. Konzertmusik for Strings and Brass, Op. 50. **New York Philharmonic Orchestra/Leonard Bernstein.** Sony Classical Bernstein Royal Edition SMK47566 — .⦁⠂' lh 10m ADD 5/93

New review
Hindemith. HINDEMITH PLAYS AND CONDUCTS HINDEMITH. [a]**Louis Cahuzac** (cl); [b]**Dennis Brain** (hn); [c]**Szymon Goldberg** (vn); [d]**Emanuel Feuermann** (vc); [e]**Philharmonia Orchestra/Paul Hindemith** ([f]va). EMI Composers in Person mono/[e]stereo CDS5 55032-2. Recorded 1934-56.
Sonata for Solo Viola, Op. 25 No. 1[f] (from German Columbia LW10/12). Scherzo for Viola and Cello[df] (LW12. Both recorded 1934). String Trio No. 2[cdf] (Columbia LX311/13, 8/34). Nobilissima Visione[e] (EG291173-2, 4/87). Clarinet Concerto[ae] (Columbia 33CX1533, 5/58). Symphonia serena[e] (33CX1676, 12/59; both stereo, appears for first time). Horn Concerto[be] (HMV HLS7001, 3/72). Concert Music, Op. 50[e] (EG291173-2).

.⦁⠂' ② **2h 37m   ADD   5/94**   ⁹ₚ ▲

As a young man Hindemith played the viola professionally and is an excellent advocate of his own Solo Viola Sonata, a work of considerable emotional depth. The orchestral items (all from 1956 sessions) include the Clarinet Concerto, with the veteran Louis Cahuzac a beautifully clear-toned soloist, the *Symphonia serena*, Dennis Brain's unique, unmatchable account of the Horn Concerto, and superlatively played performances of the masterly *Nobilissima Visione* suite and the *Concert Music* for brass and strings, all in excellent stereo for the era. Common to all the interpretations here is that very special directness of expression which is a unique feature of composer recordings. Hindemith's clear, practical approach as a performer in a way reflects the symmetry and logic of his own music. What is striking, however, is the degree of emotion that he also finds in it.

Hindemith. Nobilissima visione — Suite. Der Schwanendreher (Concerto after Folk-songs)[a]. Konzertmusik for strings and brass, Op. 50. [a]**Geraldine Walther** (va); **San Francisco Symphony Orchestra/Herbert Blomstedt.** Decca 433 809-2DH. Recorded 1989-91.

⠪⠆ Ih 7m DDD 4/93 ⠀⠀⠀⠀⠀⠀⠀⠀⠀⠀⠀⠀⠀⠀⠀⠀⠀⠀⠀⠀⠀ **⁹ₚ ❓**

This is the second of Blomstedt's Hindemith discs and, like his first of *Mathis der Maler*, in a class of its own. Here are three Hindemith masterpieces which demonstrate the diversity of his output, and mark a progression from his interest in unusual instrumental combinations; the bold and exuberant *Konzertmusik* for strings and brass of 1931, *Der Schwanendreher* of 1935 (literally "The Swanturner", he who turns the swans on the spit), in effect a concerto for viola and small orchestra and the suite from his 1938 ballet music *Nobilissima visione*, a piece depicting the life of St Francis of Assisi, and inspired by the Giotto frescoes in the church of Santa Croce in Florence. Blomstedt seems to have an instinct for pacing and 'weighting' Hindemith's music, and each piece has its own dimensions and gestures finely considered and realized. No finer performances of any of these works have, or are likely to appear, and Decca's sound is either intimate, or grandly spectacular, as the music demands.

Hindemith. KAMMERMUSIK. [c]**Konstanty Kulka** (vn); [d]**Kim Kashkashian** (va); [e]**Norbert Blume** (va d'amore); [b]**Lynn Harrell** (vc); [a]**Ronald Brautigam** (pf); [f]**Leo van Doeselaar** (org); **Royal Concertgebouw Orchestra/Riccardo Chailly.** Decca 433 816-2DH2. Recorded in 1990. Kammermusik No. 1, Op. 24 No. 1. Kleine Kammermusik No. 1 for wind quintet, Op. 24 No. 2. Kammermusik — No. 2[a]; No. 3, Op. 36 No. 2[b]; No. 4, Op. 36 No. 3[c]; No. 5, Op. 36 No. 4[d]; No. 6, Op. 46 No. 1[e]; No. 7, Op. 46 No. 2[f].

⠪⠆ ② 2h I8m DDD II/92 ⠀⠀⠀⠀⠀⠀⠀⠀⠀⠀⠀⠀⠀⠀⠀⠀⠀⠀ **⁹ₚ ⁹ₛ**

Even were the performances and recordings not outstanding (and they most certainly are) this would be an extremely valuable set. Hindemith's series of *Chamber Music* began in 1921 as an iconoclastic response to the hyper-intense emotionalism of German music over the previous 15 years (somewhat loosely termed Expressionism). It continued until 1927, at which point he began to rationalize both the harmonic and the expressive foundations of his style (and arguably lost as much as he gained). This, then, is neo-classicism with a German accent and as such it was to be a vital force in sweeping away the cobwebs of musty late romanticism; Walton, Prokofiev, Shostakovich and Britten were among those who, however indirectly, would feel the benefit. The music is also immensely enjoyable in its own right. Hindemith cheekily throws together disparate idioms, ideas spiral off with unselfconscious abandon, and sheer force of personality is all that guards against total anarchy. All this is done with more than half an eye on the performers' own enjoyment of recreation, and the fine array of artists assembled by Chailly savour every detail. Recording quality is exemplary.

New review

Hindemith. Octet.
Prokofiev. Overture on Hebrew Themes in C minor, Op. 34[a]. Quintet in G minor, Op. 39. **Berlin Soloists**; [a]**Elena Bashkirova** (pf). Teldec 9031-73400-2.

⠪⠆ 58m DDD 6/93 ⠀⠀⠀⠀⠀⠀⠀⠀⠀⠀⠀⠀⠀⠀⠀⠀⠀⠀⠀⠀⠀⠀⠀⠀⠀⠀⠀ **⁹ₚ**

This intriguing disc brings together two of Prokofiev's early chamber works and Hindemith's last. The earlier of the two Prokofiev pieces, the *Overture on Hebrew Themes* for piano, string quartet and clarinet (1919), is an attractive, rather sad little work (he made a version for small orchestra in 1934). The Quintet for oboe, clarinet, violin, viola and double-bass (1924) has six well-contrasted movements, whose often spikey (but by no means unmelodic) character owes much to Stravinsky and Les Six. Hindemith wrote his Octet for clarinet, bassoon, horn, violin, two violas, cello and double-bass in 1957-8 for the Berlin Philharmonic Octet, for whose benefit he quoted, in the fourth of its five movements, a popular tune from Berlin. There are allusions to classical models, a compact set of variations, and in the finale, a fugue and three dances (waltz, polka and galop). It is not, perhaps, one of his most immediately ingratiating works, but it will repay closer acquaintance. The Berlin Soloists play all three works marvellously, and are

| beautifully recorded.

Further listening ...

Orchestral Works — *999 005-2*[a] — Lustige Sinfonietta, Op. 4. Rag Time ("well-tempered"). Symphonische Tänze. *999 006-2*[a] — Das Nusch-Nuschi — dance suite, Op. 20. Konzertmusik for strings and brass, Op. 50. Symphony, "Die Harmonie der Welt". *999 078-2*[b] — Theme and Variations, "The Four Temperaments". Piano Concerto. [b]**Siegfried Mauser** (pf); [a]**Queensland Symphony Orchestra,** [b]**Frankfurt Radio Symphony Orchestra/Werner Andreas Albert.** CPO 999 005-2, 999 006-2, 999 078-2 (12/91).

Organ Sonatas Nos. 1-3. Coupled with **Reger.** Prelude in D minor, Op. 65 No. 7. Aus tiefer Not schrei ich zu dir, Op. 67 No. 3. Intermezzo in F minor, Op. 129 No. 7. Introduction and Passacaglia in D minor, Op. posth. **Piet Kee** (org). Chandos CHAN9097 (12/92).

When Lilacs Last in the Door-yard Bloom'd (Requiem for those we love). **Jan DeGaetani** (mez); **William Stone** (bar); **Atlanta Symphony Chorus and Orchestra/Robert Shaw.** Telarc CD80132 (7/87).

CARDILLAC. **Soloists; Cologne Radio Chorus and Symphony Orchestra/Joseph Keilberth.** MATHIS DER MALER[b] — excerpts. **Soloists; Berlin Radio Symphony Orchestra/Leopold Ludwig.** DG 20th Century Classics 431 741-2GC2 (12/91).

Alun Hoddinott

British 1929-

New review

Hoddinott. Piano Sonatas — No. 1, Op. 17; No. 2, Op. 27; No. 3, Op. 40; No. 4, Op. 49; No. 5, Op. 57. **Martin Jones.** Nimbus NI5369. Recorded in 1992.

Ih Im DDD 12/93 ❓

Alun Hoddinott isn't a pianist himself, but he has written (so far) three concertos for the instrument and 11 sonatas. Something obviously draws him back to the piano again and again. The value of a complete recording of his sonatas in chronological order, of which this is the first of two volumes, is that it demonstrates why. A continued fascination with the variety of the instrument's sonority, for a start. One might call it a quasi-orchestral use of the piano, except that his keyboard writing, though often taxing, is highly idiomatic, indeed pianistic. Dramatic contrasts of colour and texture have always been a feature of his style, and as these works follow each other you can hear ideas in one sonata prompting further explorations in the next. Other likeable features of these sonatas include the fact that such apparently recondite formal processes as palindrome always make perfect musical sense, and a very precise knowledge of when to stop. Hoddinott knows that some ideas gain impact from compression rather than expansion. That's one reason, no doubt, why these five short sonatas make such a satisfying programme. Jones's performances have just the sort of bold brilliance that they need, and the recording conveys this well.

Further listening ...

Passagio, Op. 94. The Heaventree of Stars, Op. 102[a]. Doubles, Op. 106[b]. Start Children, Op. 135. [a]**Hu Kun** (vn); [b]**David Cowley** (ob); [b]**Rosalie Armstrong** (hpd); **BBC Welsh Symphony Orchestra/Tadaaki Otaka.** Nimbus NI5357 (7/93).

Ernst Theodor Amadeus Hoffmann

German 1776-1822

New review

E.T.A. Hoffmann. UNDINE. **Krisztina Laki** (sop) Undine; **Roland Hermann** (bar) Huldbrand von Ringstetten; **Hans Franzen** (bass) Fisherman; **Elisabeth Glauser** (contr)

Fisherman's Wife; **Mani Mekler** (sop) Berthalda; **Karl Ridderbusch** (bass) Kühleborn; **Ulrich Ress** (ten) Duke; **Dora Koschak** (mez) Duchess; **Heikki Orama** (bar) Heilmann; **St Hedwig's Cathedral Choir, Berlin; Berlin Radio Symphony Orchestra/Roland Bader.** Koch Schwann 31092-2. Notes, text and translation included. Recorded in 1982.

③ 2h 39m DDD 10/93

This recording is a very welcome chance to hear the musical masterpiece of one of the great figures of the romantic movement. Weber's words of 1816 about the German operatic ideal have often been quoted: "a self-sufficient work of art in which every feature and every contribution by the related arts are moulded together in a certain way and dissolve, to form a new world". His example was *Undine*, which he went on to praise for its truth and urgency and for its absorption of separate numbers into a swiftly moving drama. Fouqué's tale (and libretto) is the familiar one of the water-spirit who weds a human but must suffer for abandoning her element. It is one of the many legends — Rusalka, Melusine, the Donauweibchen — that caught the romantic imagination in times when Nature was to be embraced anew in the aftermath of the Age of Reason. Hoffmann's orchestral originalities are on the whole well caught by a recording that is somewhat resonant and tends to favour the strings. The strange introduction of Heilmann, the holy man, to a pacing double bass obbligato, just comes off; Undine's appearance in the waterfall shimmers ravishingly; the Liebestod (opera's first use of the word), to woodwind phrases recalling the lovely Act 3 introduction, is very touching. Roland Bader directs a performance that responds well to the work's energy. One of the great strengths is the choral singing, which is rightly given prominence as having a functional role greater than much previous German opera and Krisztina Laki makes a touching Undine.

Antony Holborne
British fl. 1584-1602

Suggested listening ...

Pavans, Galliards, Almaines and other Short Aeirs — The Choise. The widowes myte. Heres paternus. Muy linda. Infernum. Pardizo. The Sighes. The night watch. As it fell on a holie Eve. Heigh ho holiday. Spero. Last will and testament. Posthuma. The Honie-suckle. The Fairie-round. Almayne. Three Pavans. Seven Galliards. *Solo Pieces* — Almaine. Fantasia. Prelude. Quadro Pavan. Lullaby. The maydens of the Countrey. The Spanish Pavane. A Jyg. **Dowland Consort/Jakob Lindberg.** BIS CD469 (4/92).

Joseph Holbrooke
British 1878-1958

New review

Holbrooke. Ulalume, Op. 35. Bronwen — Overture. The Bells, Op. 50 — Prelude. The Raven, Op. 25. Byron, Op. 39[a]. [a]**Slovak Philharmonic Choir; Bratislava Radio Symphony Orchestra/Adrian Leaper.** Marco Polo 8 223446. Recorded in 1992.

lh 9m DDD 11/93

Joseph Holbrooke was one of the great hopes of British music in the early years of the century; but by the time of his death in 1958 his music was seldom performed. He gained much inspiration from Edgar Allen Poe, whose writings inspired three of the works here. Like Poe, Holbrooke enjoyed conflict and confrontation, and the prevailing tone of the music here is of dark brooding. Holbrooke was uniformly praised for the mastery of his orchestration and the boldness of his harmonies; but his penchant for huge forces and unusual orchestral instruments (including concertinas and sarrusophones) meant he was not always taken seriously. It was with The Raven in 1900 that Holbrooke first made his mark; perhaps, though, it is the orchestral prelude to his cantata *The Bells* that most grabs the attention. From the Ravelian opening to the grand climax in which massed bells ring out it is impressive stuff.

Trevor Hold

New review
Hold. Kemp's Nine Daies Wonder. The Lilford Owl. Kaleidoscopes. **Peter Jacobs** (pf). Continuum CCD1066.

Ih I7m DDD I0/93

Trevor Hold is a man of many parts: a composer and a poet, who has spent much of his life teaching in universities. The three suites for piano on this disc were all inspired by extra-musical associations and they cover a period of 20 years in Hold's compositional life. The inspiration for *Kemp's Nine Daies Wonder* (1970) was the account of Will Kemp's celebrated Morris-dance from London to Norwich in 1599. Hold has composed a dance for each day of the journey "with echoes of popular songs and dances of the last fifty years". There is much in Hold's music that will remind the listener of Britten and this is especially evident in *The Lilford Owl* composed in 1977. It's a collection of ten delightful settings of British folk-tunes "lovingly and reverently dedicated to the memories of Edward Grieg and Percy Grainger". The last suite, *Kaleidoscopes*, was composed in 1989 and is dedicated to Peter Jacobs who plays it with real affection. The six movements that make up the suite are based on the sestina, an old Italian verse form. However, this needn't worry the listener who should simply sit back and enjoy the fine craftsmanship and eminent listenability of Trevor Hold's music.

Lee Holdridge

Suggested listening ...

El Pueblo del Sol — *Original film soundtrack.* **London Symphony Orchestra/Lee Holdridge.** Bay Cities BCD1031 (10/92).

Heinz Holliger

New review
Holliger. Scardanelli-Zyklus. [cd]**Aurèle Nicolet** (fl); [a]**London Voices/Terry Edwards**; [bde]**Ensemble Modern/Heinz Holliger**. ECM New Series 437 441-2. Texts and translations included.
Die Jahreszeiten[a]. Ubungen zu Scardanelli[b]. (t)air(e)[c]. Turm-Musik — excerpts[d]. Ostinato funebre[e].

② 2h I9m DDD 7/93

Heinz Holliger's brilliance as an oboist has long tended to overshadow his achievements as a composer, so it is all the more important to declare that the *Scardanelli Cycle* is a major work by one of the most prodigiously gifted musicians of our time. Scardanelli is one of the names with which Hölderlin signed the poems of his madness. The poems, named after the seasons, are not in themselves crazy, but they are obsessive, and it is their search for intensity of expression through economy of materials which Holliger has so imaginatively matched. As a committed modernist of the electro-acoustic generation he knows how to explore the complex components of apparently simple sounds. At his best Holliger attains a poised gravity worthy of the texts. The Hölderlin settings — *The Seasons* — are interspersed with various instrumental pieces: *Scardanelli Exercises* for small orchestra: *(t)air(e)* for flute: excerpts from *Tower Music* for flute, orchestra and tape: and — the most recent composition — *Ostinato funebre* for orchestra. The performance brings together Terry Edwards's outstanding team of British singers, the leading German contemporary music ensemble, and the formidably versatile Aurèle Nicolet, with superb results. The recording achieves an excellent balance between clarity and atmosphere.

Robin Holloway

British 1943-

New review
Holloway. Second Concerto for Orchestra, Op. 40. **BBC Symphony Orchestra/Oliver Knussen.** NMC (Special price) NMCD015. Recorded in 1993.

34m DDD 5/94

It was a visit to North Africa during 1977-8 that launched Robin Holloway on his *Second Concerto for Orchestra*. The extremes of contrast, he tells us, haunted him and were soon demanding to be turned into music. At the same time, the experience seems to have set him off on a more enigmatic, private voyage through his, and our musical past. We hear a few particularly aching bars from Act 2 of *Tristan* and rather more of Chopin's F sharp major *Barcarolle*; *Arrivederci Roma* reaches a breathtaking, brash Honegger/Messiaen apotheosis, while a strange, broken tune on muted trombone metamorphoses neatly into Parry's *Jerusalem*. It's bewildering, but gripping at the same time. Holloway doesn't just quote — his allusions or clear references emerge from the musical fabric, and then return to fertilize it again. And what gorgeous, vibrant, bewitching fabric it is. Holloway can swerve from lush, late romanticism to strident modernism and back again with the alarming quickness of an opium dream; but as with any really revelatory dream, the more you probe it, the more lucid it seems. Oliver Knussen's triumph in pulling it all together, and then shaping and shading it so lovingly, is just one of the technically miraculous aspects of this disc; another is that the production team have somehow turned BBC Maida Vale Studio No. 1 into a fine, spacious acoustic, with teeming details beautifully focused. It adds up to a fascinating disc that deserves the widest possible hearing.

Vagn Holmboe

Danish 1909-

New review
Holmboe. String Quartets — No. 1, Op. 46; No. 3, Op. 48; No. 4, Op. 63. **Kontra Quartet** (Anton Kontra, Boris Samsing, vns; Peter Fabricius, va; Morten Zeuthen, vc). Marco Polo Dacapo DCCD9203.

1h 16m DDD 6/94

Holmboe's impact is not always immediate: he relies on the cumulative effect of a work rather than on isolated details of colour and textures. Among Nordic symphonists there are few that are as masterful, as searching or as profound. His first three quartets were all written in quick succession in 1949, the year before the Seventh Symphony, which the closing bars of the first movement of the First Quartet foreshadow. The Fourth belongs to 1953-4 and is a highly concentrated and compelling piece. At the present time Holmboe's output numbers no fewer than 20 string quartets and not only are they finer than any other Nordic cycle, including that of Hilding Rosenberg, they are without question the finest since those of Nielsen and Stenhammar. Those who admire the Shostakovich and Simpson quartets will warm to them. The Kontra Quartet play all these works with splendid eloquence and the engineering is exemplary.

Further listening ...

Symphonies — No. 4, Op. 29, "Sinfonia sacra"[a]; No. 5, Op. 35. [a]**Jutland Opera Choir; Aarhus Symphony Orchestra/Owain Arwel Hughes.** BIS CD572 (6/93).

Symphonies — No. 6, Op. 43; No. 7, Op. 50. **Aarhus Symphony Orchestra/Owain Arwel Hughes.** BIS CD573 (6/93).

Gustav Holst

British 1874-1934

Holst. ORCHESTRAL WORKS. [ab]**London Philharmonic Orchestra, [c]London Symphony Orchestra/Sir Adrian Boult.** Lyrita SRCD222. Items marked [a] from SRCS56 (5/72), [b] SRCS37 (10/68), [c] SRCS50 (6/71).

Beni Mora, H107[a]. A Fugal Overture, H151[b]. Hammersmith, H178[a]. Japanese Suite, H126[c.] Scherzo, H192[a]. A Somerset Rhapsody, H87[a]

·• 1h 2m ADD 7/92

Here's another classic Boult anthology from Lyrita, and unquestionably one of this enterprising company's finest CDs to date. Opening in fine style with a roistering account of the *Fugal Overture*, this indispensable all-Holst concert also includes the haunting *Somerset Rhapsody* (framed by a ravishingly atmospheric oboe d'amore contribution), the riotously colourful "Oriental Suite" entitled *Beni Mora*, the engaging *Japanese Suite*, as well as the very late, bracing *Scherzo* (all that the composer left us of a projected symphony). But the highlight of the collection has to be that utterly magical nocturnal evocation *Hammersmith*: heard here in its full orchestral dress, it's one of Holst's most sublimely personal utterances and an undoubted masterpiece. These uniquely authoritative, radiantly played performances all show Sir Adrian at the height of his considerable powers, and the remastered Lyrita recordings continue to sound, for the most part, quite superb. In a word: unmissable.

Holst. The Planets, H125 — Mars. Venus. Mercury. Jupiter. Saturn. Uranus. Neptune. Women's voices of the **Montreal Symphony Chorus; Montreal Symphony Orchestra/ Charles Dutoit.** Decca 417 553-2DH. Recorded in 1986.

·• 53m DDD 4/87

Holst's brilliantly coloured orchestral suite, *The Planets*, is undoubtedly his most famous work and its success is surely deserved. The musical characterization is as striking as its originality of conception: the association of "Saturn" with old age, for instance, is as unexpected as it is perceptive. Bax introduced Holst to astrology and while he wrote the music he became fascinated with horoscopes, so it is the astrological associations that are paramount, although the linking of "Mars" (with its enormously powerful 5/4 rhythms) and war also reflects the time of composition. Throughout, the work's invention is as memorable as its vivid orchestration is full of infinite detail. No recording can reveal it all but this one comes the closest to doing so. Dutoit's individual performance is in a long line of outstanding recordings.

Additional recommendations ...
The Planets. **Berlin RIAS Chamber Choir; Berlin Philharmonic Orchestra/Herbert von Karajan.** DG 400 028-2GH — ·• 52m DDD 7/83 ℗ Ⓑ
The Planets. **Geoffrey Mitchell Choir; London Philharmonic Orchestra/Sir Adrian Boult.** EMI Studio CDM7 69045-2 — ·• 49m ADD 5/88 ℗ Ⓑ
The Planets. The Perfect Fool — *ballet music.* **Royal Liverpool Philharmonic Chorus and Orchestra/Sir Charles Mackerras.** Virgin Classics Virgo VJ7 59645-2 — . 1h DDD 12/91 ℗ Ⓑ
The Planets. **King's College Choir, Cambridge; Royal Philharmonic Orchestra/James Judd.** Denon CO-75076 — ·• 50m DDD 3/93 ℗ Ⓑ
The Planets. Egdon Heath. The Perfect Fool. **London Philharmonic Orchestra/ Sir Adrian Boult.** Decca 425 152-2DM — ·• 1h 13m ADD 4/94 ℗ Ⓑ
The Planets, H125[a]. St Paul's Suite, H118. [a]**Ambrosian Singers; Royal Philharmonic Orchestra/Vernon Handley.** Tring International TRP007 — . 1h 2m DDD 6/94 Ⓑ

New review
Holst. PARTSONGS. [a]**David Theodore** (ob); [b]**Robert Truman** (vc); [c]**Sioned Williams** (hp); **Holst Singers/Stephen Layton.** Hyperion CDA66705.
Ave Maria, H49. Of one that is so fair, H130. Lullay my liking, H129. Bring us in good ale, H131. Diverus and Lazarus, H137. This have I done for my true love, H128. Songs from The Princess, H80-81. O Spiritual Pilgrim, H188. Welsh Folk Songs, H183 — No. 9, My sweetheart's like Venus. Eastern Pictures, H112[c]. Light Leaves Whisper, H20. In Youth is Pleasure, H76. Choral Folk Songs, H136. Carols, H91[ab]. Jesu, thou the Virgin-born, H82.

·• 1h 11m DDD 6/94

For an object lesson in economy of means look no further than the magical setting of "Terly Terlow" accompanied by oboe and cello. The richness of this music belies such meagre resources. Part-songs, of which this single disc can only offer a representative selection, were in many ways central to Holst's output. The earliest dates from 1896, the latest (Holst's last choral composition *O Spiritual Pilgrim*) from 1933. During this period he passed from being a student, a touring orchestral musician and a girls' school teacher into the realms of international acclaim as the composer of *The Planets*. The styles and influences are as multifarious as were the choirs and singers for whom the songs were written. The Holst Singers' beautifully pure sound easily moulds itself to the character of each song, while Stephen Layton's unfussy, tightly controlled direction keeps everything perfectly in proportion.

Holst. CHORAL MUSIC. **Holst Singers and** [a]**Orchestra/Hilary Davan Wetton.** Hyperion CDA66329. Texts included. Recorded in 1988.
Two psalms, H117[a]. Six choruses, H186[a]. The evening watch, H159. Seven Partsongs, H162[a]. Nunc dimittis, H127.

1h 5m DDD 1/90

It is incomprehensible that so much of Holst's wonderful music for chorus should still remain comparatively unknown to the general listening public. Hyperion must be particularly commended on the care and attention that have obviously been devoted to the fine recording and production here. Hilary Davan Wetton took on the mantle of Director of Music at St Paul's Girls' School in Hammersmith, the position held by Holst himself from 1905 until his death in 1934, and the spirit of the venue seems to suffuse both the performances and the recording. Featuring a chorus and orchestra dedicated to Holst's music, these readings capture exactly the sonorities that the composer implies in his scores and the spiritual world that the works inhabit. It is perhaps invidious to single out from a programme of such consistent quality a couple of items of particular merit, but the two short unaccompanied pieces for eight-part choir, *The evening watch* and the appropriately concluding *Nunc dimittis* are both outstanding and worthy of special attention.

Holst. The Cloud Messenger, Op. 30[a]. The Hymn of Jesus, Op. 37. [a]**Della Jones** (mez); **London Symphony Chorus and Orchestra/Richard Hickox.** Chandos CHAN8901. Texts included. Recorded in 1990.

1h 6m DDD 5/91

When this CD was first released, the great talking point was *The Cloud Messenger*, a 43-minute work of considerable imaginative power, virtually forgotten since its disastrous première under the baton of Holst himself in 1913. It shows the composer already working on an epic scale — something which casts light on the subsequent eruption of *The Planets*. It is marvellous to have the work on disc, though it is, as you might expect, uneven. Those who admire the ascetic rigour of Holst's later music may share the reservations of Imogen Holst and find the score disappointingly 'backward'. There are certainly echoes of Vaughan Williams's *A Sea Symphony* and several older models. On the other hand, the glittering approach to the sacred city on Mount Kailasa and the stylized orientalism of the climactic dance are new to British music; another world, the world of "Venus", is foreshadowed in the closing pages. The text is Holst's own translation from the Sanskrit. Hickox's expansive account of the familiar *Hymn of Jesus* is more than a mere filler. One of the few incontrovertible masterpieces in Holst's output, it has never received a better performance on disc, although the impressively grand acoustics of London's St Jude's impart a certain warm imprecision — the choral singing itself is splendidly crisp — which can blunt the impact of Holst's acerbic harmonies.

Additional recommendation ...
The Hymn of Jesus[a]. **Elgar.** The Dream of Gerontius[b]. [b]**Yvonne Minton** (mez); [b]**Sir Peter Pears** (ten); [b]**John Shirley-Quirk** (bar); [b]**Choir of King's College, Cambridge;** [b]**London Symphony Chorus and Orchestra/Benjamin Britten;** [a]**BBC Chorus and Symphony Orchestra/Sir Adrian Boult.** Decca London 421 381-2LM2 — .·' ② 1h 53m ADD 5/89

Further listening ...

Two songs without words, H88[a]. Concerto for Two Violins, H175[b]. The Golden Goose, H163 — Ballet Music[a]. Capriccio for Orchestra, H185[a] (ed. I. Holst). A Fugal Concerto, H152[c]. A

Moorside Suite, H173 — Nocturne[c]. Lyric Movement, H191[d]. Brook Green Suite, H190[d].
[c]**William Bennett** (fl); [c]**Peter Graeme** (ob); [b]**Emanuel Hurwitz**, [b]**Kenneth Sillito** (vns);
[d]**Cecil Aronowitz** (va); **English Chamber Orchestra/Imogen Holst.** Lyrita SRCD223
(4/93).

A Winter Idyll, H31[c]. The Cotswolds, Symphony in F major, H47 — Elegy in memoriam
William Morris[c]. A Song of the Night, H74[ac]. Indra, H66[c]. Invocation for Cello and Orchestra,
H75[bc]. SITA — Act 3, Interlude (ed. C. Matthews)[c]. Dances from "The Morning of the Year",
H164 (ed. C. Matthews)[c]. The Lure, H149 (ed. C. Matthews and I. Holst)[d]. [a]**Lorraine
McAslan** (vn); [b]**Alexander Baillie** (vc); [c]**London Philharmonic Orchestra;** [d]**London
Symphony Orchestra/David Atherton.** Lyrita SRCD209 (6/93).

Piano Quintet in A minor H11[b]. Wind Quintet in A flat major, H67[a]. *Coupled with* **Jacob.**
Sextet, Op. 3[ab]. **Elysian Wind Quintet;** [b]**Anthony Goldstone** (pf). Chandos CHAN9077
(10/92).

Simon Holt
British 1958-

Suggested listening ...

. . . Era madrugada. Canciones[a]. Shadow realm. Sparrow night[b]. [a]**Fiona Kimm** (mez); [b]**Gareth
Hulse** (ob); **Nash Ensemble/Lionel Friend.** NMC NMCD008 (5/93)

Iver Holter
Norwegian 1850-1941

New review
Holter. String Quartets — No. 1 in E flat major, Op. 1; No. 2 in G major, Op. 18.
Norwegian Quartet (Harald Aadland, Mette Elisabeth Steen, vns; Oddbjørn Bauer, va; Merete
Olsen Carr, vc). NKF NKFCD50027-2. Recorded 1991-92.

♪ **56m DDD 11/93** ❓

Iver Holter was one of the most distinguished of a whole generation of Norwegian composers
whose reputations have been eclipsed by the international acclaim accorded to Grieg and Svendsen.
There seems to be little in his music to suggest a particularly Norwegian — or even Scandinavian
— flavour and, although much influenced by Svendsen, Holter's works adhere to solid Central
European models. Despite the apparent closeness in opus number, Holter's two string quartets
were composed over three decades apart. The First from 1876 is an extrovert apprentice work,
full of affable joviality if overlong for its material. The more mature composer of 1910 was able to
strike a better balance between form and content in the Second Quartet; indeed, No. 2 is a
splendid work of considerable attainment and its hitherto near-total neglect was most unjust.
Happily, this recording should go a long way towards putting matters right: the Norwegian Quartet
plays with commendable commitment and NKF's recording is a model of clarity. Very enjoyable.

Arthur Honegger
French/Swiss 1892-1955

Honegger. ORCHESTRAL WORKS. **Bavarian Radio Symphony Orchestra/Charles
Dutoit.** Erato 2292-45242-2. From NUM75254 (4/86). Recorded in 1985.
Symphony No. 1. Pastorale d'été. Three symphonic movements — Pacific 231; Rugby; No. 3.

♪ **55m DDD 12/86** ❓

Honegger's First Symphony is a highly impressive work, concisely and effectively constructed in
what might be generally described as a neoclassical style; and the scoring is attractive and skilful.

His evocation of dawn on a summer's day in *Pastorale d'été*, scored for small orchestra with exquisite, quiet beauty, is surely a miniature masterpiece, and both *Pacific 231* (1924) and *Rugby* (1928) are brilliantly contrived essays in imaginative scoring and the use of cross-rhythms. Honegger was distressed by a critical notion that he was trying to imitate the sound of a steam locomotive and specific moves in a game of rugby: he insisted that the two scores conveyed only a general impression of a train journey and the atmosphere of Colombes stadium. So offended was he that he called the third companion piece merely *Mouvement symphonique No. 3*, but it is a little less effective than its two bedfellows. These vigorous performances are excellent.

Additional recommendations ...
Le tempête — Prélude. Pastorale d'été. Horace victorieux. Pacfic 231; Rugby. La traversée des Andes. Le vol sur l'Atlantique. **Toulouse Capitole Orchestra/Michel Plasson.** DG 435 438-2GH — .ᐧ' lh 5m DDD 9/93
Pastorale d'été[a]. *Cello Concerto*[b]. **Poulenc.** *Trois mouvements perpétuels*[c]. *Trio for Oboe, Bassoon and Piano*[d]. *Deux novelettes*[c]. *Nocturnes*[f] — *No. 1 in C major; No. 2 in A major; No. 4 in C minor. Improvisations*[g] — *No. 2 in A flat major; No. 5 in A minor; No. 9 in D major; No. 10 in F major. Aubade for Piano and 18 Instruments*[h]. [d]**Roger Lamorlette** (ob); [d]**Gustave Dhérin** (bn); [b]**Maurice Maréchal** (vc); [cdefgh]**Francis Poulenc** (pf); [b]**Paris Conservatoire Orchestra;** [a]**symphony orchestra/Arthur Honegger;** [h]**Walther Straram Concerts Orchestra/ Walther Straram.** EMI Composers in Person mono CDC5 55036-2 — .ᐧ' lh 16m ADD 6/94 ▲

Honegger. Symphonies — No. 2; No. 3, "Liturgique". **Berlin Philharmonic Orchestra/ Herbert von Karajan.** DG 20th Century Classics 423 242-2GC. From 2530 068 (7/73). Recorded in 1969.

.ᐧ' **59m ADD 6/88**   ♩ₚ

New review

Honegger. Symphonies — No. 2; No. 3, "Liturgique". Pacific 231. **Oslo Philharmonic Orchestra/Mariss Jansons.** EMI CDC5 55122-2.

.ᐧ' **lh 6m DDD 7/94**   ♩ₚ ♩ₛ

This classic Karajan recording is unlikely to be surpassed. The Second Symphony is a powerfully atmospheric piece written during the grim years of the German occupation. It is a searching, thoughtful piece, appropriately dark in colouring which eventually breaks into the light with its chorale melody played on the trumpet. The *Liturgique* is a powerhouse of energy and its slow movement is among Honegger's most glorious inspirations. The playing of the Berlin Philharmonic is sumptuous in tone, vibrant with energy and encompasses an enormously wide range of dynamics and colour. One can only marvel at the quality of sound they achieve in both the beautiful slow movements and their virtuosity in the finale of No. 3. Astonishing performances and an indispensable disc for all lovers of modern music. Though the commanding heights continue to be dominated by Karajan, Mariss Jansons and the Oslo Philharmonic face the challenge head on by coupling the two together and rise magnificent-ly to the occasion. Indeed this is arguably their best record to date. The Second is concentrated and intense, with attention being given to every nuance of phrasing and dynamics, and every detail falling naturally into place. The Oslo strings produce a highly responsive and sumptuous sonority, subtle in blending and homogeneous in tone. The *Symphonie Liturgique* is no less concentrated and powerful, emotion being refined and disciplined. Nothing is over-projected; the various strands in the orchestral texture are beautifully balanced and phrases eloquently yet effortlessly shaped. There is no question of its compelling mastery and moreover its white-heat is generated without any of the hysteria this score can at times excite. Indeed, one is reminded of a phrase by the French critic, Bernard Gavoty in a letter to Karajan which spoke of him "transcending emotions and imparting to them that furnace heat that makes a work of genius give off light if brought to the desired temperature": this performance has that same incandescence. Jansons's account of the two symphonies are unquestionably the best to have appeared since Karajan's and has the advantage of quite outstanding recorded sound, with plenty of presence, bite and definition. The *Pacific 231* completes the disc and makes a splendid bonus.

Additional recommendations ...
No. 2. **Milhaud.** *Suite provençal, Op. 152b.* **Boston Symphony Orchestra/Charles Munch.**
| RCA GD60685 — .ᐧ' lh I7m ADD ♩ₚ ▲

No. 2; No. 4, "Deliciae basiliensis". Pastorale d'été. Prélude, arioso et fugue (on BACH). **Lausanne Chamber Orchestra/Jesús López-Cobos.** Virgin Classics VC7 59064-2 — ,··' lh 3m DDD 6/92 ♩ₚ

Nos. 2 and 4. **Bavarian Radio Symphony Orchestra/Charles Dutoit.** Erato 2292-45247-2 — ,··' 54m DDD

No. 2; No. 5, "di tre re". **Milhaud.** *Suite Provençale, Op. 152*[b]. *La création du monde, Op. 81*[b]. **Boston Symphony Orchestra/Charles Munch.** RCA GD60685 — ,··' lh 16m ADD ▲

Nos. 3 and 5. **Danish National Radio Symphony Orchestra/Neeme Järvi.** Chandos CHAN9176 — ,··' 57m DDD 9/93

No. 2. **R. Strauss.** *Metamorphosen.* **Webern** *(trans. Schwarz) Langsamer Satz.* **Seattle Symphony Orchestra Strings/Gerard Schwarz.** Delos DE3121 — ,··' lh llm DDD 4/94 ♩ₚ

Nos. 3 and 5. Pastorale d'été. Chant de joie. Pacific 231. **Czech Philharmonic Orchestra/Serge Baudo.** Supraphon 11 0667-2 — ,··' lh llm ADD ▲

Key to symbols

Price	Quantity/ availability	Timing	Recording mode	Review date
,··'	② ②	lh 23m	DDD	6/88

	Quality of sound	Discs worth exploring		Caveat emptor
	♩ₚ ♩ₛ Ⓑ	❓	✒	▲
Quality of performance		Basic library	Period performance	

Honegger. Jeanne d'Arc au bûcher. **Françoise Pollet, Michèle Command** (sops); **Nathalie Stutzman** (contr); **John Aler** (ten); **Marthe Keller, Georges Wilson, Pierre-Marie Escourrou, Paola Lenzi** (narrs); **Chorus and Children's Voices of French Radio; French National Orchestra/Seiji Ozawa.** DG 429 412-2GH. Text and translations included. Recorded live in 1989.

,··' lh 9m DDD 4/91   ♩ₚ ♩ₛ ❓

Honegger described *Joan of Arc at the stake* as a "dramatic oratorio", but it is a work almost impossible to categorize, the two chief characters — Joan and Brother Dominc — being speak-ing parts, but with a chorus (now commenting on, now involved in, the action), a children's chorus, and a curiously constituted orchestra including saxophones instead of horns, two pianos and, most notably, an ondes martenot which, with its banshee shriek, bloodcurdling-ly reinforces the climax as Joan breaks her earthly chains. The action is partly realistic, partly symbolic, unfolding in quasi-cinematic flashbacks. The musical techniques and styles employed by Honegger are extraordinarily varied, with humming and shouting besides singing, and with elements of polyphony, folk-song, baroque dances and jazz rhythms; yet all is fused together in a remarkable way to produce a work of gripping power and, in the final scenes, almost intolerable emotional intensity: the beatific *envoi* "Greater love hath no man ..." is a passage that catches the throat and haunts the mind for long afterwards. Ozawa fully captured the work's dramatic forces in this public performance, which has been skilfully served by the recording engineers; Marthe Keller vividly portrays Joan's bewilderment, fervour and agony, John Aler makes a swaggering Procus, and Françoise Pollet is radiant-voiced as the Virgin. Even more than *Le roi David*, this is Honegger's masterpiece.

Further listening ...

Crime et Châtiment — Suite[a]. Le Déserteur ou Je t'attendrai. Farinet ou L'Or dans la Montagne — Suite. le Grand Barrage. L'Idée. [a]**Jacques Tchamkerten** (ondes martenot); **Bratislava Radio Symphony Orchestra/Adriano.** Marco Polo 8 223466 (6/94).

Le Roi David[a]. Symphonic movements — No. 3. Le tempête — Prélude. [a]**Soloists; [a]Prague Philharmonic Chorus; Czech Philharmonic Orchestra/Serge Baudo.** Supraphon CO1412/13 (6/88).

Les misérables — *film score.* **Bratislava Radio Symphony Orchestra/Adriano.** Marco Polo 8 223181 (3/91).

Alan Hovhaness

Hovhaness. Symphony No. 2, "Mysterious mountain", Op. 132. Lousadzak, Op. 48[a]. **L. Harrison.** Symphony No. 2, "Elegiac". [a]**Keith Jarrett** (pf); **American Composers Orchestra/Dennis Russell Davies.** MusicMasters 7021-2.

 1h 7m DDD 5/93

An exemplary, enterprising pairing. The American composers Alan Hovhaness and Lou Harrison have much in common: both are based on the musically unfashionable West Coast (Hovhaness in Seattle, Harrison in Santa Cruz); both have remained relative outsiders, untouched by contemporary fads; both share a passionate preoccupation with exotic musical cultures — Hovhaness with that of his ancestral Armenia, Harrison with the Indonesian gamelan tradition; and the chosen idioms of both tend to exude an overwhelming sense of meditative ecstasy which seems to be very much in vogue at the present time. Certainly, there's no denying the potent spell of much of the quasi-improvisatory piano writing in Hovhaness's *Lousadzak*; similarly, the trance-like string euphony which dominates the same composer's Second Symphony (*Mysterious mountain*) from 1955 is oddly compelling. Harrison's own Second Symphony (*Elegiac*) is perhaps the most substantial offering of the present trio, though: some three decades in gestation, this is an impressive, five-movement edifice finally completed in 1975 and bearing a dedication to the memory of Serge and Natalie Koussevitzky. Spiritual and serene, this is music of considerable resonance and power, and Harrison's wholly distinctive, often deliciously piquant sound-world draws the listener ineluctably in. Do try and hear this superbly performed and recorded release: given the current interest in the likes of Górecki, Pärt and Tavener, it could well, with proper exposure, become another contemporary cult classic.

Additional recommendation ...
"*Mysterious mountain* ". Prayer of St Gregory, Op. 62b. Prelude and Quadruple Fugue, Op. 128. And God Created Great Whales, Op. 229 No. 1. Alleluia and Fugue, Op. 40b. Celestial Fantasy, Op. 44. **Seattle Symphony Orchestra/Gerard Schwarz.** Delos DE3157 — .•˙ 1h 3m DDD 7/94

Hovhaness. Symphonies — No. 22, "City of Light", Op. 236[a]; No. 50, "Mount St Helens", Op. 360[b]. **Seattle Symphony Orchestra/[a]Alan Hovhaness; [b]Gerard Schwarz.** Delos DE3137. Recorded in 1992.

.•˙ 1h 1m DDD 12/93

A beguiling lyrical impulse informs the first two movements of the *Mount St Helens* Symphony from 1983. The second, entitled "Spirit Lake", is particularly affecting. Insistent, strangely Sibelian pizzicatos form a background against which lonely woodwind sing out their expressive runes (on this evidence, Hovhaness's identification with nature is potent). After a gentle introduction, the last movement, "Volcano", erupts with a vengeance. The pounding central portion achieves a frightening momentum, and Hovhaness's sense of orchestral spectacle produces some often thrilling sounds — no wonder the symphony went down so well with the public at its Seattle première. Granted, the coupling from 1971, *City of Light* (No. 22), is rather less interesting, yet both middle movements do possess a certain homespun charm. The composer directs here, and very competently too, though he doesn't quite draw playing of the same refulgent tonal richness from the splendid Seattle orchestra that Schwarz manages in the later work.

Hovhaness. Symphonies — No. 39, Op. 321[a]; No. 46, "To the Green Mountains", Op. 347. **Traditional.** (arr. Kim Hee-jo) Milyang Arirang. [a]**Michael Long** (gtr); **KBS Symphony Orchestra Vakhtang Jordania.** Koch International Classics 37208-2.

·•ʹ **1h 13m DDD** ⁹ₚ

The record companies, it seems, have caught the Hovhaness bug, and, make no mistake, there are plenty more symphonies where these came from. Both 'symphonies' inhabit a serenely modal, non-Western world, where melody and atmosphere take precedence over any traditional 'working out' of material one would expect to find in a piece designated thus. Too much of this music could quickly expose its relative dearth of emotional variety, but, taken individually, these works have the power to intrigue and entrance in equal measure (for the time being, at least); certainly, one can readily understand the composer's growing cult status. These are quite excellent, full-toned performances from the KBS (Korean Broadcasting System) Symphony Orchestra under their Georgian Principal Guest Conductor, Vakhtang Jordania, and guitarist Michael Long contributes admirably in the Symphony No. 39. Moreover, the recording leaves little to be desired. Hovhaness fans (and one suspects their numbers are growing daily) need not hesitate.

Hovhaness. CHAMBER WORKS. [a]**Chris Gekker** (tpt); **Manhattan Chamber Orchestra/Richard Auldon Clark.** Koch International Classics 37221-2. Mountains and Rivers without End, Op. 225. Symphony No. 6, "The Celestial Gate", Op. 173. Prayer of St Gregory, Op. 62*b*[a]. Haroutiun, Op. 71 — Aria[a]. Return and Rebuild the Desolate Places, Op. 213[a].

·•ʹ **1h 3m DDD 7/94**

In *Mountains and Rivers without End* (1968), sliding solo trombone writing alternates with passages of canonic woodwind bird-song and exotic, percussion-laden promises of the Orient (the work was, in fact, originally inspired by a Korean landscape painting). Quite what it all adds up to is anybody's guess, but presumably that is all part of the intrigue. Hovhaness's beautifully judged string-writing lends an enchanting serenity to both the *Prayer of St Gregory* and *Haroutiun* ("Resurrection"), whilst the Sixth Symphony contains perhaps the most consistently memorable melodic material of all the works gathered here; certainly, it possesses a spiritual glow and sense of enchantment to which many will readily warm. The disc concludes with *Return and Rebuild the Desolate Places*, a ten-minute concerto for trumpet and wind band. Again, the scoring is deceptively assured, with some hauntingly luminous woodwind sonorities. These are all immaculately-turned, highly responsive performances from the Manhattan Chamber Orchestra, Richard Auldon Clark and Chris Gekker (with his astonishingly poised solo trumpet contributions). The recording is beautifully transparent.

Herbert Howells
British 1892-1983

Howells. Piano Quartet in A minor, Op. 21[a]. Phantasy Quartet, Op. 25. Rhapsodic Quintet, Op. 31[b]. [b]**Michael Collins** (cl); **Lyric Quartet** (Patricia Calnan, Harriet Davies, vns; Nick Barr, va; David Daniels, vc); [a]**Andrew West** (pf). Metier MSVCD92003. Recorded in 1992.

·•ʹ **52m DDD 10/93**

Herbert Howells wrote a brief note about his Piano Quartet, slightly defensively justifying his having written such an effusion of untroubled lyricism in 1916, when many of his contemporaries and friends were facing death. However, the abiding impression of the work is not of evanescent nature poetry, still less a redolence of cowpats, but a wonderfully sturdy and forthright lyricism. The slightly later *Phantasy Quartet* has rather more of elegy to it, and a further development is heard in the immediately post-war *Rhapsodic Quintet*. The lyricism here is more subdued, the energy more angular, as though Howells were deliberately taming the fecundity of his invention and making his ideas really work for their living; the variety of their development is all the more striking for this. The performances have just the qualities one hopes for: the sense of a group of young performers delightedly discovering that these neglected works are not in the least dusty or faded, but strong, urgent and brilliantly crafted is palpable throughout. Good sound, too, despite a very slightly boxy piano.

New review

Howells. Violin Sonatas — No. 1, Op. 18; No. 2, Op. 26; No. 3, Op. 38. Cradle Song, Op. 9 No. 1. Three Pieces, Op. 28. **Paul Barritt** (vn); **Catherine Edwards** (pf). Hyperion CDA66665.

⏱ 1h 13m DDD 3/94

Howells had just turned 30 when he wrote the latest work in this collection. We expect ample lyricism, vigorous energy and formal ingenuity and we're not disappointed. We also expect from these as yet untroubled years untroubled geniality, but the Second Violin Sonata almost shockingly contradicts this. It is a work of dark, intense eloquence, grandly confident in its big gestures; there is not a trace of the elegiac to it, but not a trace either of rhapsody or pastoral. The First Sonata is often very lovely, once or twice a little too fertile to be focused, the Third is a fascinating interplay of gentle lyricism and bold vigour, but in the Second you can hear in much more than embryo form the mature symphony, quartet and concerto that Howells never wrote. First-rate playing and a clean but not antiseptic recording.

New review

Howells. Lambert's Clavichord, Op. 41. Howells' Clavichord, Books 1 and 2. **John McCabe** (pf). Hyperion CDA66689.

⏱ 1h 19m DDD 8/94

Clavichord music played on the piano? Howells published these pieces as "for clavichord or piano", as it happens, but one wonders whether they could ever sound better on the older instrument than they do here. No, Thurston Dart, the dedicatee of one of the most searching pieces in Book 1 of *Howells' Clavichord*, had it just about right when he wrote to the composer "the pieces sound *at least as good* on the pfte.(!!)". Thirty-two shortish clavichord pieces, whatever they're played on, ought to be much too much of a good thing at a single sitting. You may well find, however, that you will wolf them down and be disappointed at the end that there aren't more of them. They quite delightfully mingle delicate pastiche, pure Howells and at times touching, at times witty homages "to my friends pictured (or at all events affectionately saluted) within". The pastiche and the pure Howells are sometimes singularly difficult to disentangle (Howells always said that he was a Tudor composer born out of his time, "straying about in this 20th century"), and occasionally Howells and Giles Farnaby jointly merge into Fauré or even Poulenc. Howells is at his Howells-est in, as you would expect, "H. H. His Fancy", a serious lyrical fugue with precisely judged but surprising harmonies; also in "Lord Sandwich's Dreame", Howells's lyricism at its purest, shaded with his characteristic reticent melancholy. Some of the homages are still more striking: the quietly grand, deeply felt "Ralph's Pavane", a lovingly grateful tribute to Vaughan Williams, or the moving "Finzi's Rest", written the day after Gerald Finzi died and having the skill and the modesty to mourn him with a melody that in its grace and serenity might be one of his own (though the harmonies again are Howells's own tributes). They are enchanting pieces, all of them. McCabe obviously loves these pieces dearly, and although he realizes that some of them (the eloquent "Samuels' Air", for example, or the grandly dignified "De la Mare's Pavane") invite quite big tone and expansive gesture he never overstates any of them. Both the instrument used (a less than full-sized grand piano) and the acoustic emphasize this: we might be in McCabe's own music-room. A lovely collection. Reserve it for your desert island.

Howells. Requiem (1936)[a]. Take him, earth, for cherishing (1963).
Vaughan Williams. Mass in G minor (1922)[b]. Te Deum in G major (1928)[c]. [a]**Mary Seers** (sop); [ab]**Michael Chance** (alto); [ab]**Philip Salmon** (ten); [ab]**Jonathan Best** (bass); **Corydon**

Singers/Matthew Best with ^c**Thomas Trotter** (org). Hyperion CDA66076. Texts included. From A66076 (8/83).

.:' **1h AAD 10/87**

Vaughan Williams's unaccompanied Mass in G minor manages to combine the common manner of Elizabethan liturgical music with those elements of his own folk-music heritage that make his music so distinctive, and in so doing arrives at something quite individual and new. The work falls into five movements and its mood is one of heartfelt, if restrained, rejoicing. Herbert Howells wrote his unaccompanied Requiem in 1936, a year after the death of his only son. The work was not released in his lifetime but was reconstructed and published in 1980 from his manuscripts. It is a most hauntingly beautiful work of an obviously intensely personal nature. *Take him, earth, for cherishing* was composed to commemorate the assassination of President John F. Kennedy. The text is an English translation by Helen Waddell of Prudentius's fourth-century poem, *Hymnus circa Exsequias Defuncti*. Again it demonstrates the great strength of Howells's choral writing, with a clear outline and aptly affecting yet unimposing harmonic twists. The Corydon Singers give marvellous performances of these works and the sound is very fine indeed. An hour of the finest English choral music and not to be missed.

Additional recommendation ...
Requiem. A Sequence for St Michael. The House of the Mind. **Vaughan Williams.** *Prayer to the Father of Heaven. A Vision of Aeroplanes. Lord, Thou has been our Refuge.* **Finzi Singers/Paul Spicer** with **Harry Bickett** (org). Chandos CHAN9019 — .:' 1h 7m DDD 5/92

Further listening ...

Collegium regale — canticles. Six Pieces for Organ — No. 3, Master Tallis's Testament^a. Like as the hart. Behold, O God our defender. Psalm-Preludes, Set 2 — No. 1, De profundis^a. Take him, earth, for cherishing. St Paul's — Canticles. ^a**Christopher Dearnley** (org); **St Paul's Cathedral Choir, London/John Scott.** Hyperion CDA66260 (9/88).

Piano Concerto No. 2 in C minor^a. Three Dances, Op. 7^b. Concerto for Strings. ^a**Kathryn Stott** (pf); ^b**Malcolm Stewart** (vn); **Royal Liverpool Philharmonic Orchestra/Vernon Handley.** Hyperion CDA66610 (3/93).

Sonata for Oboe and Piano. *Coupled with* **Finzi** (arr. Ferguson). Interlude in A minor, Op. 21. **Patterson.** Duologue. **Nicholas Daniel** (ob); **Julius Drake** (pf). Léman Classics LC44801 (10/93). *See review under Finzi; refer to the Index to Reviews.*

Mass in the Dorian Mode. Salve regina. O salutaris Hostia. Sweetest of sweets. Come, my soul. Let all the world in every corner sing. Nunc dimittis. Regina caeli. *Coupled with* **Stevens.** Mass for double choir. **Finzi Singers/Paul Spicer.** Chandos CHAN9021 (12/92).

Hymnus Paradisi^a. An English Mass. ^a**Julie Kennard** (sop); ^a**John Mark Ainsley** (ten); **Royal Liverpool Philharmonic Choir and Orchestra/Vernon Handley.** Hyperion CDA66488 (5/92).

Johann Hummel

Austrian 1778-1837

Hummel. Piano Concertos — A minor, Op. 85; B minor, Op. 89. **Stephen Hough** (pf); **English Chamber Orchestra/Bryden Thomson.** Chandos CHAN8507.

.:' **1h 6m DDD 4/87**

This is a staggering disc of Hummel's piano concertos played by Stephen Hough. The most obvious comparison is with the piano concertos of Chopin, but whereas those works rely on the grace and panache of the piano line to redeem an often lacklustre orchestral role, the Hummel works have finely conceived orchestral writing and certainly no shortage of original ideas. The piano part is formidable, combining virtuosity of a very high order indeed with a vigour and athleticism that does much to redress Hummel's somewhat tarnished reputation. The A minor is probably the better known of the two works here, with a thrilling rondo finale, but the B minor is no less inventive with some breathtaking writing in the piano's upper registers. This disc makes strong demands to be heard: inventive and exciting music, a masterly contribution from Stephen Hough, fine orchestral support from the ever sympathetic ECO under Bryden Thomson and, last but not least, a magnificent Chandos recording.

Further listening ...

Trumpet Concerto in E flat major. *Coupled with* **Jolivet.** Concertino for Trumpet, Piano and Strings[a]. **Tomasi.** Trumpet Concerto. **Haydn.** Trumpet Concerto in E flat major, HobVIIe/1. **Sergei Nakariakov** (tpt); [a]**Alexander Markovich** (pf); **Lausanne Chamber Orchestra/ Jésus López-Cobos.** Teldec 4509-90846-2 (10/93). *See review in the Collections section; refer to the Index to Reviews.*

Piano Quintet in E flat major, Op. 87. *Coupled with* **Schubert.** Piano Quintet in A major, D667, "Trout". **Schubert Ensemble of London.** Hyperion Helios CDH88010 (6/90).

Piano Trios — E flat major, Op.12; F major, Op. 22; G major, Op. 35; G major, Op. 65; E major, Op. 83; E flat major, Op. 93; E flat major, Op. 96. **Parnassus Trio.** Dabringhaus und Grimm L3307/08 (6/93).

Englebert Humperdinck

German 1854-1921

New review

Humperdinck. HÄNSEL UND GRETEL. **Ann Murray** (mez) Hänsel; **Edita Gruberová** (sop) Gretel; **Dame Gwyneth Jones** (sop) Mother; **Franz Grundheber** (bar) Father; **Barbara Bonney** (sop) Sandman; **Christiane Oelze** (sop) Dew Fairy; **Christa Ludwig** (mez) Witch; **Staatskapelle Dresden/Sir Colin Davis.** Philips 438 013-2PH2. Notes, text and translation included. Recorded in 1992.

② lh 43m 10/93

Sir Colin Davis has rarely conducted a more glowing opera performance on record than this. It is his inspired direction, beautifully paced, as though captured live, which above all compels attention. His performance has an emotional thrust that has less to do with beautiful singing and playing than with deeper, more tender feelings. On balance the Karajan and Pritchard versions are all more beautifully, more immaculately sung, but thanks to Davis's understanding and a recorded sound that is both warmly atmospheric and full of presence, with extreme *pianissimos* refined and clear, the magic of this score comes home more involvingly than has been known since the 1953 Karajan set in the days of early mono LPs. Though in sheer beauty neither Gruberová nor Murray can quite match their rivals, the contrast of timbre between the bright, sometimes edgy quality of Gruberová and the plainer sound of Murray is always very clearly defined, and their brilliant characterization and feeling for words seal that sharp distinction. Dame Gwyneth Jones could not be more positive as the mother, cutting through all textures, the pitching always perfectly clear and defined. Predictably Ludwig gives a similarly positive and characterful performance as the Witch. More than most rivals her sinister inflexions are totally convincing and spontaneous-sounding, a naturally larger-than-life figure who puts over both the melodramatic and the comic moments with superb timing. The recording has plenty of bloom on voices and orchestra, without the blurring of inner lines that marks the Pritchard but the new Philips conveys a sense of presence, with vivid detail captured.

Additional recommendations ...
Soloists; Loughton High School for Girls and Bancroft's School Choirs; Philharmonia Orchestra/Herbert von Karajan. EMI mono CMS7 69293-2 — ② lh 48m ADD 4/88 ▲

Soloists; Cologne Opera Children's Chorus; Cologne Gurzenich Orchestra/Sir John Pritchard. CBS Masterworks CD79217 — ② lh 48m ADD ll/88

Further listening …

DER BLAUE VOGEL — Der Weinachtstraum; Sternenreigen. DORNROSCHEN — Vorspiel; Ballade; Irrfahrten; Dornenschloss; Festklänge. HANSEL UND GRETEL — Overture. KONIGSKINDER — Concert Overture; Hellafest und Kinderreigen; Verdorben-Gestorben … Spielmanns letzter Gesang. **Bamberg Symphony Orchestra/Karl Anton Rickenbacher.** Virgin Classics VC7 59067-2 (6/92).

William Yeates Hurlstone

British 1876-1906

Suggested listening …

Variations on an original theme. The Magic Mirror Suite. Variations on a Hungarian air. **London Philharmonic Orchestra/Nicholas Braithwaite.** Lyrita SRCD208 (4/93).

Jacques Ibert

French 1890-1962

New review
Ibert. ORCHESTRAL WORKS. [a]**Timothy Hutchins** (fl); **Montreal Symphony Orchestra/Charles Dutoit.** Decca 440 332-2DH. Recorded in 1992.
Bacchanale. Bostoniana. Escales. Concerto for Flute and Orchestra[a]. Louisville Concerto. Suite Symphonique, "Paris". Hommage à Mozart.

> **· ·** **lh l9m   DDD   6/94**   **q** p

Ibert has never had his due as a serious composer, even in France. This is a pity, for his music is superbly crafted and of a life affirming quality rare in our century, even more positive (though no less witty) than that of Poulenc. Each of these pieces is stylish and finely scored; further-more, Charles Dutoit and his superb Montreal orchestra perform with skill and panache (as does Timothy Hutchins in the Concerto), while the recording is all that one could ask, encompassing every delicate texture or exciting burst of sound. Thus *Escales* (1922) has rarely sounded so deliciously Mediterranean and North African. But the real treasure here is the unfamiliar music, which takes us up to the composer's unfinished Second Symphony 40 years later, written for the Boston Symphony and existing only as a single movement, posthumously entitled *Bostoniana*. As its names suggests, the *Louisville Concerto* (1953) was also written for an American orchestra, but *Paris* (1932) is a six-movement symphonic suite that the composer made from his music to a play by Jules Romains with the curious name of *Donogoo-Tonka*. Finally, *Hommage à Mozart* (not a pastiche) was commissioned as a tribute for the bicentenary of Mozart's birth. Recommended to all save gloom merchants.

Ibert. Divertissement.
Milhaud. Le boeuf sur le toit, Op. 58. La création du monde, Op. 81.
Poulenc. Les biches — Suite. **Ulster Orchestra/Yan Pascal Tortelier.** Chandos CHAN9023. Recorded in 1991.

> **· ·** **lh 8m   DDD   9/92**   **q** p

Here is 1920s French music directed by a conductor who is completely in the spirit of it, and plenty of spirit there is, too. Except for Ibert's *Divertissement*, this is ballet music, and that work too originated in the theatre as incidental music for Eugène Labiche's farce *The Italian Straw Hat*. Poulenc's suite from *Les biches*, written for Diaghilev's ballet company and first heard in Monte Carlo, is unfailingly fresh and bouncy and stylishly played here although Chandos's warm recording, good though it is, takes some edge off the trumpet tone; the genial nature of it all makes us forget that it is a unique mix of eighteenth-century *galanterie*, Tchaikovskian lilt and Poulenc's own inimitable street-Parisian sophistication and charm. As for Ibert's piece, this is uproariously funny in an unbuttoned way, and the gorgeously vulgar trombone in the Waltz and

387

frantic police whistle in the finale are calculated to make you laugh out loud. Milhaud's *Le boeuf sur le toit* also has Parisian chic and was originally a kind of music-hall piece, composed to a scenario by Cocteau. It was while attending a performance of it in London in 1920 that the composer first heard the American jazz orchestra that, together with a later experience of new Orleans jazzmen playing "from the darkest corners of the Negro soul" (as he later expressed it) that prompted him to compose his masterly ballet, *La création du monde*, in which a deep-rooted African voice seems to speak through western instruments. Tortelier and his orchestra understand this strangely powerful music no less than the other pieces. This is a most desirable disc.

Additional recommendation ...

Divertissement. **Ravel.** *Le tombeau de Couperin.* **Debussy.** *Danse sacrée et danse profane*[a]. **Fauré.** *Dolly Suite, Op. 56.* [a]**Osian Ellis** (hp); **Academy of St Martin in the Fields/Sir Neville Marriner.** ASV CDDCA517 — .•' lh ADD 2/85

Further listening ...

Film Suites — Macbeth; Golgotha[b]. Don Quichotte — Chanson de Sancho[a]. Chanson de Don Quichotte[a]. [a]**Henry Kiichli** (bass); [b]**Jacques Tchamkerten** (ondes martenot); **Bratislava Radio Symphony Orchestra/Adriano.** Marco Polo 8 223287 (3/91).

Sigismondo d'India

Italian c.1582-1629

Suggested listening ...

Il Terzo Libro de Madrigali a cinque voci. **Consort of Musicke/Anthony Rooley.** Deutsche Harmonia Mundi RD77119 (11/88).

Vincent d'Indy

French 1851-1931

New review

d'Indy. Symphony No. 3, "de bello gallico", Op. 70. Saugefleurie, Op. 21. Souvenirs, Op. 62. **Strasbourg Philharmonic Orchestra/Theodore Guschlbauer.** Auvidis Valois V4686. Recorded in 1992.

.•' lh l2m DDD 9/93

The real find here is *Souvenirs* (1906), a haunting, imaginatively scored tone-poem that starts with what sounds like a ghostly premonition of Shostakovich's Eleventh Symphony, then proceeds to varieties of chromatic lyricism that recall the Debussy of *Pelléas* and the lone Symphony of Ernest Chausson. The Third Symphony, a highly inventive commentary on aspects of the Great War, suggests a specific programme and is an ambiguous, loosely constructed piece that effectively extends one's limited experience of its composer. Theodore Guschlbauer's broadly sympathetic readings are more appreciative of the music's *lent et calm* than its *vif et agité*. Still, it's a gripping programme and essential listening for all incurable romantics.

Further listening ...

Symphonie sur un chant montagnard français, Op. 25[a]. *Coupled with* **Franck.** Symphony in D minor. [a]**Jean-Yves Thibaudet** (pf); **Montreal Symphony Orchestra/Charles Dutoit.** Decca 430 278-2DH (1/92). *See review under Franck; refer to the Index to Reviews.*

String Quartets — No. 1 in D major, Op. 35; No. 2 in E major, Op. 45. **Kodály Quartet.**
Marco Polo 8 223140 (10/91).

John Ireland

Ireland. ORCHESTRAL WORKS. **London Symphony Orchestra/Richard Hickox.** Chandos CHAN8994. Recorded 1990-91.
Scherzo and Cortège (arr. G. Bush). Tritons --- Symphonic Prelude. The Forgotten Rite — Prelude. Satyricon — Overture. The Overlanders — Suite from the film (arr. Mackerras).

lh 2m DDD 2/92

Ireland's fluent and approachable orchestral style found its voice in two quite distinct areas, both of which are represented in this recording. The evocative musical imagery of the symphonic prelude *Tritons* typifies Ireland's descriptive essence, sharing the same impressionistic influence of Debussy and Ravel with the *Forgotten Rite* Prelude. Described by the composer as "an evocation of the mystical and occult forces of nature", this is possibly the finest of Ireland's large-scale compositions, and it is splendidly realized here. The concert overture *Satyricon*, Ireland's final orchestral work, juxtaposes brilliant and vigorous material with a reflective central clarinet discourse. These expansive canvases are framed by characteristic examples of Ireland's radio and film scores. Geoffrey Bush, a former student of the composer, has arranged the *Scherzo and Cortège* from surviving sketches for incidental music written for a 1942 BBC production of *Julius Caesar*. The suite from the 1946 Ealing Studios film *The Overlanders* was compiled by Sir Charles Mackerras from original orchestrations by Ernest Irving. This colourful suite is utilitarian, reflecting the obvious needs of the production, but the music is of high quality. Richard Hickox secures forthright and dedicated playing from the LSO, in a rich and characteristically reverber-ant Chandos recording. As an introduction to John Ireland's orchestral works, this disc can be strongly recommended to all devotees of British music.

Further listening ...

Piano Concerto. *Coupled with* **Bridge.** Phantasm. **Walton.** Sinfonia concertante (original version). **Kathryn Stott** (pf); **Royal Philharmonic Orchestra/Vernon Handley.** Conifer CDCF175 (1/90).

Cello Sonata in G minor[a]. *Coupled with* **Bridge.** Elegy, H47[a]. Scherzetto, H19[b]. **Stanford.** Cello Sonata No. 2 in D minor, Op. 39[b]. **Julian Lloyd Webber** (vc); **John McCabe** (pf). ASV CDDCA807 (2/93).

Decorations. The Almond Tree. Four Preludes. Rhapsody. The Towing-Path. Merry Andrew. Summer Evening. Piano Sonata in E minor. **Eric Parkin** (pf). Chandos CHAN9056 (8/92).

Key to symbols

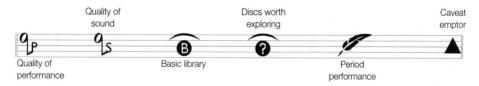

| Quality of sound | Discs worth exploring | Caveat emptor |

| Quality of performance | Basic library | Period performance |

Heinrich Isaac

Suggested listening ...

Missa de Apostolis a 6. Optime pastor. Regina caeli laetare. Resurexi et adhuc tecum sum. Tota pulchra es. Virgo prudentissima a 6. **The Tallis Scholars/Peter Phillips.** Gimell CDGIM023 (10/91).

Charles Ives

Ives. ORCHESTRAL WORKS. **New York Philharmonic Orchestra/Leonard Bernstein.**
DG 429 220-2GH. Recorded 1987-88.
Symphony No. 2. The Gong on the Hook and Ladder. Tone Roads — No. 1. A set of 3 Short
Pieces — Largo cantabile, Hymn. Hallowe'en. Central Park in the Dark. The Unanswered Question.

lh 8m   DDD   8/90

Although Bernstein thought of Ives as a primitive composer, these recordings reveal that he had
an undeniably deep affinity for, and understanding of, Ives's music. The Second Symphony
(written in 1902 and first performed in 1951) is a gloriously beautiful work, still strongly rooted
in the nineteenth century yet showing those clear signs of Ives's individual voice that are largely
missing from the charming but lightweight First Symphony. Bernstein brings out all its richness
and warmth without wallowing in its romantic elements, and he handles with utter conviction
the multi-textures and the allusions to popular tunes and snatches from Bach, Brahms and
Dvořák, to name but a few. The standard of playing he exacts from the NYPO, both here and
in the disc's series of technically demanding shorter pieces, is remarkably high with the depth of
string tone at a premium — and the engineers retain this to a degree unusual in a live
recording. Altogether an essential disc for any collection.

Additional recommendations ...
The Unanswered Question (orig. and rev. versions)[a]. Central Park in the Dark. A Symphony: New England
Holidays[b]. **[a]Adolph Herseth** (tpt); **Chicago Symphony [b]Chorus and Orchestra/Michael
Tilson Thomas.** CBS Masterworks CD42381 — **lh 3m DDD 10/88**
*Central Park in the Dark. The Unanswered Question. Orchestral Set No. 1 — Three Places in New
England. March No. 3, with My Old Kentucky Home. Fugue in four keys, on The Shining Shore.
Symphony No. 3, "The Camp Meeting".* **St Louis Symphony Orchestra/Leonard Slatkin.** RCA
Victor Red Seal 09026 61222-2 — **lh 3m DDD 4/93**

Ives. Symphonies — Nos. 1 and 4 (including original hymn settings). **Chicago Symphony
Orchestra/Michael Tilson Thomas.** Sony Classical SK44939.

lh l7m   DDD   2/91

It could be worth asking a musical friend to listen to the start of Ives's First Symphony here and
(presuming he or she doesn't already know the work) then to identify the composer. It seems
almost impossible that anyone would get the answer right, for this tuneful, vigorous music hardly
suggests the wild-eyed 'ornery crittur' and iconoclast represented to many listeners by much of
Ives's later music; Dvořák, Mahler and Nielsen all flash through the mind, which is significant
because all three drew their deepest inspiration from folk music, as did Ives himself. The
explanation is that this is an early work written in 1898 as an exercise for music graduation at
Yale; but make no mistake, it shows that this composer in his twenties knew a good deal about
symphonic writing and (as the slow second movement, complete with Dvořákian cor anglais,
demonstrates) about writing melodies as well. The Fourth Symphony with all its wild and wilful
complexities is another matter, for the good tunes (which are sometimes those of hymns and
Gospel songs) are interwoven with astonishing boldness into a score of daunting individuality and
complexity. This disc also includes some of these hymn tunes in their original form with voices
with one, however, *Beulah Land*, being an organ solo played on a modern instrument that sounds
splendidly authentic. The conductor Michael Tilson Thomas has a proven affinity with Ives's
music, and these authoritative performances have a touching strength, while the recording too
does justice to some of the most challenging music ever to come out of America.

Additional recommendation ...
No. 4. **John Alldis Choir; London Philharmonic Orchestra/José Serebrier.** Chandos
CHAN8397 — **33m ADD 1/86**

New review
Ives. String Quartets — No. 1, "From the Salvation Army"; No. 2. A set of three short pieces
— Scherzo, "Holding Your Own".

Barber. String Quartet, Op. 11. **Emerson Quartet** (Eugene Drucker, Philip Setzer, vns; Lawrence Dutton, va; David Finckel, vc). DG 435 864-2GH. Recorded 1990-91.

1h 5m DDD 4/93

The First Ives Quartet assembles an affectionate archive of religious forms of musical expression ranging from mystical intensity to almost ecstatic fervour. This is vintage early Ives and wears well. The Emersons have everything under control. Ives's Second Quartet (1913) is wildly different. With the first movement called "Discussions" and the second "Arguments" there is free scope for all Ives's photographic realism with textures as violent as middle-period Bartók later on. The last movement, "The Call of the Mountains", has a real chill when it opens largely without vibrato: and it climaxes resoundingly on "Nearer my God", linking this peroration to the last movement of the Fourth Symphony. The *Scherzo* is a rarity — a brief comic study in rhythmic juxtapositions with the occasional diatonic tune sticking out of the mêlée. The CD is completed with Barber's early Quartet (1936) famous for its *Adagio*, heard here as the soft centre between the two *allegro* movements which were its original packaging. Another fine performance, well recorded, in a most welcome release.

New review
Ives. CHAMBER WORKS. **Mondriaan Quartet** (Jan Erik Van Regteren Altena, Edwin Blankensteijn, vns; [a]Annette Bergman, [b]Prunella Pacey, vas; Eduard Van Regteren Altena, vc); [d]**Quirijn Van Regteren Altena** (db); [c]**Fred Oldenburg** (pf). Etcetera KTC1169. Recorded 1988-92.
A Set of Three Short Pieces[acd]. String Quartet No. 2[b]. Largo risoluto No. 2, Op. 13[ac]. Halloween, Op. 11[ac]. Intermezzo[a]. In re con moto et al, Op. 20[ac].

54m DDD 3/94

Most of Ives's exploratory ear-stretchers for piano quintet are new to the British catalogue. These pieces are really ingenious games with notes; punch-ups with pitch, extraordinary for the first decade of the century. The *Largo risoluto No. 2* has the strings in one key and the piano in another, with the piano played loud against soft strings the first time and the roles reversed the second. The String Quartet No. 2 — a realistic representation of players arguing with each other — has the viola desperately holding on to *Nearer my God to Thee* in double-stopping against odds, and the whole quartet quoting the Westminster chimes with the viola again just out of step and in the wrong key before they return to shape the final climax. All Ives's party tricks come off with an infectious enjoyment that we can share now, although they got him into trouble at the time. And he could also be sweetly conventional, as in the *Intermezzo* from 1897, which sounds like early Delius. So, a splendid collection of characteristic Ives, played with understanding throughout.

Ives. Piano Sonata No. 1.
Barber. Piano Sonata in E flat major, Op. 26. Excursions, Op. 20. **Joanna MacGregor** (pf). Collins Classics 1107-2.

1h 8m DDD 3/92

There are other fine recordings of the Barber Sonata, including Peter Lawson's which is reviewed in the "Collections" section of this book (refer to the Index to Reviews) and Eric Parker's reviewed under Barber. It is a work which has attracted well-equipped players right from the start. MacGregor stands up well, but the greater attraction is her Ives Sonata No. 1, which ought to sweep the board on both sides of the Atlantic now. The work, which waited 45 years for a first performance, is just as characteristic of Ives as the Second Sonata, and in some ways its mixture of hymn-tunes and ragtime makes a more coherent impact. The ragtime aspects are based on what Ives heard improvised or played that way himself: he went to a lot of trouble to catch the difference between playing the dots and swinging away. This informality is superbly caught by MacGregor, who risks all in truly Ivesian fashion in one or two places. She thoroughly understands the driving rhythms as well as the transcendental calm. By comparison anything by Barber is more polite. But the four *Excursions* come off well and show a different approach to popular idioms — more that of a tourist than an insider. But both composers know how to make use of sonata structure in these two American classics, vividly played and recorded.

Further listening ...

Symphony No. 3, "The camp meeting". Second Orchestral Set. **Royal Concertgebouw Chorus and Orchestra/Michael Tilson Thomas.** CBS Masterworks CDCD46440.

Trio for Violin, Clarinet and Piano[c]. *Coupled with* **Bernstein** (trans. Ma). Clarinet Sonata[a]. **Gershwin** (arr. Heifetz, trans. Ma)[b]. Three Preludes. **Kirchner.** Triptych[d]. **Yo-Yo Ma** (vc); [c]**Ronan Lefkowitz,** [d]**Lynn Chang** (vns); [ab]**Jeffrey Kahane,** [c]**Gilbert Kalish** (pfs). Sony Classical SK53126 (4/94). *See review in the Collections section; refer to the Index to Reviews.*

Violin Sonata No. 4, "Children's Day at the Camp Meeting"[a]. *Coupled with* **Bartók.** Rhapsody No. 1, Sz86[b]. Contrasts, Sz111[b] (with Benny Goodman, cl). **Bloch.** Baal Shem[a]. **Debussy.** Violin Sonata in G minor[a]. **Schubert.** Violin Sonatina in D major, D384[a]. Also includes works by **Bach, Brahms, Corelli, Debussy, Dvořák, Falla, Hubay, Kodály, Lalo, Milhaud, Mussorgsky** and **Schubert. Joseph Szigeti** (vn); [a]**Andor Foldes,** [b]**Béla Bartók** (pfs). Biddulph mono LAB070/71. *See review in the Collections section; refer to the Index to Reviews.*

Piano Sonata No. 2, "Concord, Mass., 1840-60". *Coupled with* **M. Wright.** Piano Sonata. **Marc-André Hamelin** (pf). New World NW378-2 (9/89).

Leos Janáček
Czechoslovakian 1854-1928

Janáček. Sinfonietta, Op. 60[a]. Taras Bulba — Rhapsody for Orchestra[a]. **Shostakovich.** The Age of Gold — Suite, Op. 22a[b]. [a]**Vienna Philharmonic Orchestra/ Sir Charles Mackerras;** [b]**London Philharmonic Orchestra/Bernard Haitink.** Decca Ovation 430 727-2DM. Item marked [a] from 410 138-2DH (11/83), recorded in 1980, [b] D213D2 (11/80), recorded in 1979.

.ᵃ 1h 6m DDD 12/91 ᵍₛ

The Janáček items have long been a favourite coupling and in these thoroughly idiomatic performances the effect is spectacular. Of course these are far more than just orchestral show-pieces. Both works were fired by patriotic fervour — Taras Bulba by Czechoslovakia's struggle towards independence, the *Sinfonietta* by the city of Brno, the composer's adopted home town. Both works display a deep-seated passion for the basic elements of music and yield unpreceden-ted levels of excitement. To get the most out of *Taras Bulba* you really need all its gory programmatic details (of battles, betrayal, torture and murder) to hand. The *Sinfonietta* needs no such props; its impact is as irresistible and physically direct as a massive adrenalin injection. If the listener is to revel in this music a corresponding sense of abandon in the playing is even more important than precision. The Vienna Philharmonic supplies a good measure of both and Sir Charles Mackerras's commitment and understanding are second to none, while the high-level recording captures every detail in vivid close-up. Bernard Haitink's highly disciplined if somewhat straitlaced LPO account of Shostakovich's *Age of Gold* suite is the coupling.

Additional recommendations ...
Sinfonietta. **Smetana.** *Symphonic Poems — Má vlast; Richard III; Walenstein's camp. Haakon Jarl. Carnival in Prague.* **Bavarian Radio Symphony Orchestra/Rafael Kubelík.** DG Galleria 437 254-2GGA — .ᵃ 1h 11m ADD 1/93
Sinfonietta. The Danube — Symphony[a]. Violin Concerto, "Pilgrimage of the Soul"[b]. Schluk und Jau. [a]**Karolina Dvořáková** (sop); [b]**Ivan Zenaty** (vn); **Brno State Philharmonic Orchestra/ František Jílek.** Supraphon 11 1522-2 — .ᵃ 1h 3m DDD 9/93

Janáček. String Quartets[a] — No. 1, "Kreutzer Sonata"; No. 2, "Intimate Letters". Along an overgrown path — Suite No. 1[b]. [b]**Radoslav Kvapil** (pf); [a]**Talich Quartet** (Petr Messiereur,

Jan Kvapil, vns; Jan Talich, va; Evzen Rattai, vc). Calliope CAL9699. Items marked [a] from CAL1699 (1/86), [b] CAL9206 (8/88).

Ih 13m   DDD   4/89

Janáček's two string quartets stand with those of Bartók, Debussy and Ravel among the supreme masterpieces of the medium, composed during the first half of this century. Both are relatively late works: the *Kreutzer* Sonata dates from 1923 and was inspired by Tolstoy's tragic short story of the same title, depicting a women's disappointment in love both inside and outside marriage. Janáček translates the emotions of Tolstoy's story into music of intense passion. Even more immediate and personal is the Second Quartet entitled *Intimate Letters*, inspired by Janáček's infatuation at the age of 64 for his young pupil Kamila Slösslova. He poured into this quartet all his feelings for her: doubt, release, joy and despair are all graphically portrayed in Janáček's eliptical music. Inference and statement paradoxically give the quartet a wholeness which eludes other more forthright works. The Talich Quartet portray these two similar psycho-dramas with total commitment and devotion. The immense technical difficulties with which Janáček confronts his performers are set aside by the white heat of emotion clearly felt both by performers and composer. The insight of these readings fortunately even overcomes a recording perhaps too dry for Janáček's highly exposed string writing. As a bonus, Radoslav Kvapil gives an idiomatic reading of the first suite from *Along an overgrown path*, written between 1901 and 1908, and marked by the death of his daughter Olga in 1903. These short piano pieces display in embryo many of the stylistic features which were later to reappear in the two quartets. Again the performance is wholly authentic and committed, allowing Janáček's exceptional creativity to shine through without compromise. Again a rather dry recording.

Additional recommendations ...
Quartets. **Dvořák.** *Cypresses, B152.* **Lindsay Quartet.** ASV CDDCA749 — Ih I5m DDD II/9I
Quartets. **Dvořák.** *String Quartet No. 10 in E flat major, B92.* **Vanbrugh Quartet.** Collins Classics 1381-2 — Ih I3m DDD 4/94

Janáček. PIANO WORKS. **Rudolf Firkušný.** DG 20th Century Classics 429 857-2GC. From 2707 055 (6/72). Recorded in 1971.
Piano Sonata 1.X.1905, "From the street". Along an overgrown path. In the mists. Thema con variazioni, "Zdenka".

Ih 19m   ADD   3/9I

Janáček's only piano sonata has a history almost as dramatic as the events which inspired it. Its subtitle, *From the Street* commemorates a student demonstration in which a 20-year-old worker was killed, an event which so outraged Janáček that he wrote a three movement sonata as an expression of his feelings. Before the première in 1906 he burnt the third movement and after a private performance in Prague he threw the remaining movements into a river. It is only thanks to the pianist, Ludmil Tučkova, who had copied out the first two movements, that the work survives. The underlying theme of Firkušný's approach to this work (who may claim historical authenticity as he studied with Janáček) is anger, turning the first movement into a defiant roar of fury whilst the slow movement has an inherent restlessness, bitterness never far below the surface. Much of the same characteristics can be found in the other works — *Along an overgrown path* and the masterly *In the mists* although he occasionally overloads these delicate little pieces with dramatic power. The early Theme and Variations are conventionally romantic but impeccably played. This disc represents playing of the highest class with full notes and tracking details.

Additional recommendations ...
Piano Sonata. Along an overgrown path — Suite No. 1. In the mists. **Josef Páleníček** (pf). Supraphon 10 1481-2 — 54m ADD 3/92

Janáček. Glagolitic Mass[a]. Sinfonietta, Op. 60[b]. [a]**Felicity Palmer** (sop); [a]**Ameral Gunson** (mez); [a]**John Mitchinson** (ten); [a]**Malcolm King** (bass); [a]**Jane Parker-Smith** (org); [a]**City of Birmingham Chorus and Orchestra,** [b]**Philharmonia Orchestra/Simon Rattle.** EMI

CDC7 47504-2. Text and translation included. Item marked [a] from ASD4066 (5/82), recorded in 1981, [b] ASD143522-1 (10/83), recorded in 1982, .

Ih 2m DDD 10/88

"I am not an old man, and I am not a believer — until I see for myself." Thus Janáček replied angrily to a critic after the première of his *Glagolitic* Mass. This is a gritty, masterful perform-ance of a jagged, uncomfortable masterpiece. Its unusual title stems from the script of the ancient Slavonic text (Glagol) which Janáček set to music. Rattle's is a full-blooded, urgent view of the work, with particularly fine solo contributions from Felicity Palmer and John Mitchinson. That the language is an unfamiliar one is occasionally evident in the chorus, though they, like the orchestra, give totally committed performances under Rattle's inspired leadership. Also included on this disc is the *Sinfonietta* (originally entitled "Military Sinfonietta", reflecting in the brass-heavy scoring of the work). It is as much a study in orchestration as form with the melody of the fourth movement appearing unaltered no less than 14 times, changed only in orchestral colour. It is brilliantly played here, with the 12 trumpets coming up gleaming in the final climax. An enticing proposition!

Additional recommendation ...
Glagolitic Mass[a]. *Sinfonietta*. [a]**Soloists; London Symphony Chorus and Orchestra/Michael Tilson Thomas.** Sony Classical CD47182 — .·ʼ Ih l0m DDD 9/92

Janáček. JENUFA. **Elisabeth Söderström** (sop) Jenůfa; **Wieslaw Ochman** (ten) Laca; **Eva Randová** (mez) Kostelnička; **Petr Dvorskü** (ten) Steva; **Lucia Popp** (sop) Karolka; **Marie Mrazová** (contr) Stařenka; **Václav Zitek** (bar) Stárek; **Dalibor Jedlička** (bass) Rychtar; **Ivana Mixová** (mez) Rychtarka; **Vera Soukopová** (mez) Pastuchyňa, Tetka; **Jindra Pokorná** (mez) Barena; **Jana Janasová** (sop) Jano; **Vienna State Opera Chorus; Vienna Philharmonic Orchestra/Sir Charles Mackerras.** Decca 414 483-2DH2. From D276D3 (9/83). Recorded in 1982.

② 2h 10m DDD 12/85

Janáček's first operatic masterpiece is a towering work which blends searing intensity with heart-stopping lyricism. It tells of Jenůfa and the appalling treatment she receives as she is caught between the man she loves and one who eventually comes to love her. But dominating the story is the Kostelnička, a figure of huge strength, pride and inner resource who rules Jenůfa's life and ultimately kills her baby. Eva Randová's characterization of the role of the Kostelnička is frightening in its intensity but also has a very human core. The two men are well cast and act as fine foils to Elisabeth Söderström's deeply impressive Jenůfa. The Vienna Philharmonic play beautifully and Mackerras directs magnificently. The recording is all one could wish for and the booklet is a mine of informed scholarship.

Janáček. KATA KABANOVA[a]. Capriccio[b]. Concertino[b]. **Elisabeth Söderström** (sop) Kátá; **Petr Dvorský** (ten) Boris; **Naděžda Kniplová** (contr) Kabanicha; **Vladimír Krejčík** (ten) Tichon; **Libuše Márová** (mez) Varvara; **Dalibor Jedlička** (bass) Dikoj; **Zdeněk Svehla** (ten) Kudrjáš; **Jaroslav Souček** (bar) Kuligin; **Jitka Pavlová** (sop) Glaša; **Gertrude Jahn** (mez) Fekluša; **Vienna State Opera Chorus; Vienna Philharmonic Orchestra/Sir Charles Mackerras.** [b]**Paul Crossley** (pf); [b]**London Sinfonietta/David Atherton.** Decca 421 852-2DH2. Notes, text and translation included. Item marked [a] from D51D2 (10/77), recorded in 1976, [b] D223D5 (4/81), recorded in 1978.

② 2h 20m ADD 10/89

With *Kátá Kabanová* in 1919, Janáček embarked on the four operatic masterpieces that would occupy him for the remaining nine years of his life, and Decca in 1976 on their now classic series of Janáček opera recordings with Sir Charles Mackerras. Unlike the other three late operas, *Kátá Kabanová*'s story *is* one you would expect to see on the opera stage: Kátá, a free spirit, is imprisoned by marriage into, and domicile with, a family in a provincial Russian town on the Volga. The family is manipulated by her mother-in-law, a widow whose sole, obsessive concern is her status (familial and social). The only son (Kátá's husband) is understandably spineless, and Kátá looks for escape in love. She finds the love, but true escape only in suicide. Janáček focuses on his heroine, giving her at least two of the most moving scenes in opera: the first where, to music of shimmering, seraphic beauty she describes her childhood imagination given free rein by pillars of sunlight streaming through the dome in church; and the second in the last scene where, after her confession of adultery, she concludes that "not even God's own sunlight" gives her pleasure any more. Söderström has the intelligence and a voice which guarantees *total* credibility (how often can you claim that of an operatic portrayal?); and of the superb all-Czech supporting cast one might only have wished for a slightly younger-sounding sister-in-law. Mackerras persuades from the Vienna Philharmonic their very finest ensemble and tone; and Decca, true to their best operatic traditions, reproduce the whole with clarity, atmosphere, ideal perspectives and discernible stage movement — only a detectable levelling of the score's few extreme *fortissimos* points to the recording's vintage. Decca add the late chamber concertos, both excellently performed and engineered, and equally essential Janáček.

Additional recommendation ...
Soloists; Prague National Theatre Chorus and Orchestra/Jaroslav Krombholc.
Supraphon 10 8016-2 — .•⁚ ② 1h 30m ADD 11/93 ℗

Janáček. THE CUNNING LITTLE VIXEN. The Cunning Little Vixen — orchestral suite (arr. V. Talich)[a]. **Lucia Popp** (sop) Vixen, Young vixen; **Dalibor Jedlička** (bass) Forester; **Eva Randová** (mez) Fox; **Eva Zikmundová** (mez) Forester's wife, Owl; **Vladimir Krejčik** (ten) Schoolmaster, Gnat; **Richard Novák** (ten) Priest, Badger **Václav Zítek** (bar) Harašta; **Beno Blachut** (ten) Pásek; **Ivana Mixová** (mez) Pásek's wife, Woodpecker, Hen; **Libuše Marová** (contr) Dog; **Gertrude Jahn** (mez) Cock, Jay; **Eva Hríbiková** (sop) Frantik; **Zuzana Hudecová** (sop) Pepik; **Peter Saray** (treb) Frog, Grasshopper; **Miriam Ondrášková** (sop) Cricket; **Vienna State Opera Chorus; Bratislava Children's Choir; Vienna Philharmonic Orchestra/Sir Charles Mackerras.** Decca 417 129-2DH2. Notes, text and translation included. From D257D2 (5/82). Item marked [a] new to UK. Recorded in 1981.

.•⁚ ② 1h 49m DDD 11/86   ℗ ℗s

Janáček used the most unlikely material for his operas. For *The Cunning Little Vixen* his source was a newspaper series of drawings, with accompanying text, about the adventures of a vixen cub and her escape from the gamekeeper who raised her. The music is a fascinating blend of vocal and orchestral sound — at times ludicrously romantic, at others raw and violent. Sir Charles Mackerras's Czech training has given him a rare insight into Janáček's music and he presents a version faithful to the composer's individual requirements. In the title-role, Lucia Popp gives full weight to the text while displaying all the richness and beauty of her voice. There is a well-chosen supporting cast of largely Czech singers, with the Vienna Philharmonic to add the ultimate touch of orchestral refinement. Decca's sound is of demonstration quality, bringing out all the violent detail of Janáček's exciting vocal and orchestral effects.

Additional recommendation ...
The Cunning Little Vixen (sung in English)[a]. *Taras Bulba*[b]. **Soloists; [a]Chorus and Orchestra of the Royal Opera House, Covent Garden, [b]Philharmonic Orchestra/Simon Rattle.**
EMI CDS7 54212-2 — .•⁚ ② 2h DDD 3/92

New review
Janáček. SARKA. **Alena Nováková** (sop) Sárka; **Antonín Jurečka** (ten) Ctirad; **František Kunc** (bar) Přemysl; **Josef Válka** (ten) Lumír; **Brno Radio Symphony Chorus and Orchestra/Břetislav Bakala.** Multisonic mono 310154-2. From a 1953 broadcast.

.•⁚ 1h 3m ADD 6/94   ℗ ❓ ▲

This is a thrilling discovery, both in terms of work and performance. *Sárka* is the first of Janáček's operas, written in 1887-8, twice revised, latterly in 1924-5 when it belatedly received its première. It carries forward the story told in *Libuše* by Smetana, who used the legend in Part 3 of *Má vlast*. The action is succinct but the music is full of wonderful incident, culminating in a superb Act 3 ensemble. It seems, both in compositional style, melodic cut and musical development, full of pre-echoes of what was to come. While obviously influenced by Smetana, it is quite recognizably Janáček's work, and nobody else's. The vocal writing is as grateful as that in *Jenůfa* for strong, dramatically inclined singers. In this splendid broadcast of 1953 it receives its due. Nováková is wholly capable of conveying the dedicated, visionary quality of the

Brünnhilde-like Sárka, while Jurečka is in the best tradition of Czech tenors and fills Ctirad's taxing role with vibrant, soaring tones. But perhaps the true hero of the performance is Bakala, one of Janáček's earliest and best advocates. He and his Brno orchestra disclose the full beauty and power of a score that we ought to hear live, if only in concert form.

Further listening ...

The diary of one who disappeared[a]. String Quartet No. 1, "Kreutzer Sonata"[b]. [a]**Clara Wirz** (mez); [a]**Peter Keller** (ten); [a]**Lucerne Singers/Mario Venzago** (pf); [b]**Doležal Quartet.** Accord 22031-2 (4/90).

OSUD (sung in English). **Soloists; Welsh National Opera Chorus and Orchestra/Sir Charles Mackerras.** EMI CDC7 49993-2 (9/90).

THE MAKROPOULOS AFFAIR. Lachian Dances[a]. **Soloists; Vienna State Opera Chorus; Vienna Philharmonic Orchestra/Sir Charles Mackerras;** [a]**London Philharmonic Orchestra/François Huybrechts.** Decca 430 372-2DH2 (10/91).

FROM THE HOUSE OF THE DEAD. Mládi[a]. Nursery rhymes[b]. **Soloists; Vienna State Opera Chorus; Vienna Philharmonic Orchestra/Sir Charles Mackerras;** [c]**London Sinfonietta Chorus;** [ab]**London Sinfonietta/David Atherton.** Decca 430 375-2DH2 (10/91).

Clément Janequin

French c.1485-1558

Suggested listening ...

Chansons — Le chant des oiseaux. Toutes les nuictz. J'atens le temps. Il estoit une fillette. Ung jour Colin. O doulx regard, o parler. Or sus vous dormez trop (L'alouette). Quand contrement verras. Hellas mon Dieu, ton ire. Ma·peine n'est pas grande. O mal d'aymer. Herbes et fleurs. A ce joly moys. Assouvy suis. Quelqu'un me disoit l'aultre jour. M'y levay par ung matin. M'ayme a eu de Dieu. Le chant du rossignol. Las on peult juger (arr. Morlaye). L'aveuglé dieu qui partout vole (arr. Alberto da Ripa). **Ensemble Clément Janequin.** Harmonia Mundi HMC90 1099 (8/85).

John Jenkins

British 1592-1678

Jenkins. Two Pavans. 11 Fantasias. Two In Nomines. **Hespèrion XX** (Jordi Savall, Eunice Brandao, Sergi Casademunt, Imke David, Laurence Bonnal, Paolo Pandolfo, Lorenz Duftschmid, viols); **Michel Behringer** (org). Astrée Auvidis E8724. Recorded in 1990.

1h 13m DDD 2/92

John Jenkins was, according to many sources of his day, a man whose music and personality were held in the highest esteem. Roger North, his student, describes him as an "accomplisht ingenious person, and so well behaved ... and wheerever he went was always welcome and courted to stay". That his music is arguably the most congenial and classically poised of his day is perhaps no coincidence. These six-part works reveal a master of counterpoint with a rare gift for melodic shape and outstanding pacing. Most of them are almost certainly works of the late Jacobean age, written when Jenkins was supposedly still perfecting his art. Judging by the effervescent and lyrical playing of these fantasias, Jordi Savall and Hespèrion XX treat them as works of an established composer in full flight; and who would doubt them on the evidence of the complete six-part music (one spurious *fantasia* is omitted) with its feast of noble, richly textured and variegated pieces. Understated though Jenkins's language is, Savall is attracted to the idea of impassioned and brooding melody; in this respect a very English type of music is flavoured with continental traits. The sound is dark and full though with the outermost parts illuminated to make a more penetrating and unequal ensemble. This works well in the profoundly-felt chordal sections ("Bell Pavan") but will irritate those who understand this music to be a secret discourse of ideas tossed about in a democratic manner. Savall and his group engage in conversation but light-hearted banter is definitely out of order and Savall himself is clearly the chairman. Approached more openly than English performances of similar music, these magisterial works have been firmly taken out of the parochial closet to smoulder in the hands of foreigners. An indigenous tradition maybe, but cultured playing of this sort makes one wonder whether environment is really the issue.

Further listening ...

Fantasia-Suites in four parts — F major; C major; E minor; A minor; F major; D major. *Airs for lyra consort* — C major, "The Six Bells"; G major. **The Parley of Instruments/Peter Holman.** Hyperion CDA66604 (12/92).

Joseph Joachim
Austrian/Hungarian 1831-1907

Suggested listening ...

Violin Concerto in Hungarian Style, Op. 11[a]. *Overtures* — Hamlet, Op. 4; Henry IV, Op. 7. [a]**Elmar Oliveira** (vn); **London Philharmonic Orchestra/Leon Botstein.** Pickwick IMP Masters MCD27 (8/91).

Variations on an Original Theme in E major, Op. 10. *Coupled with* **Brahms.** Viola Sonatas, Op. 120 — No. 1 in F minor; No. 2 in E flat major. **Rivka Golani** (va); **Konstantin Bogino** (pf). Conifer CDCF199 (9/92). *See review under Brahms; refer to the Index to Reviews.*

Robert Johnson II
British c.1583-1633

New review
R. Johnson. Shakespeare's Lutenist. [a]**Emma Kirkby** (sop); [b]**David Thomas** (bass); **Anthony Rooley** (lte). Virgin Classics Veritas VC7 59321-2. Texts included. Recorded 1991. Where the bee sucks[ab]. Hark, hark! the lark[a]. Come hither, you that love[a]. As I walked forth[a]. Woods, rocks and mountains[a]. 'Tis late and cold[b]. O let us howl[b]. Arm, arm![b]. Come away, Hecate[ab]. Charon, oh Charon[a]. Away delights[a]. Come, heavy sleep[a]. Care-charming sleep[a]. Full fathom five[b]. Have you seen the bright lily grow?[b]. Adieu, fond love[b]. Come away, thou lady gay[ab]. Tell me dearest[ab]. *Lute solo:* Fantasia. Pavan. Galliard. Three almans. Corant.

1h 7m DDD 4/94

Robert Johnson's reputation in his own time was comparable with that of Dowland, but though his also rested heavily on his songs and lute works he wrote far fewer of either. With this recording about 80 per cent of Johnson's songs are now available, and we are unlikely to be disturbed by their removal from their original contexts. Kirkby is superbly expressive in her solo items, effortlessly agile in *Hark, hark! the lark*, and contemptuously mocking in *Come away, thou lady gay*, giving her seducer a hard time. Thomas snarls with mock menace in *Come away, Hecate* — Kirkby, the 'airy spirit', calls from a microphonic distance — and is as stentorian in *Arm, arm!*, as he is sensitive in *Full fathom five* and *Have you seen the bright lily grow?*. Rooley delivers the lute solos confidently. In short, a magnificent (and clearly recorded) tribute to a composer who has received rather less attention than he deserves.

Andre Jolivet

Suggested listening ...

Concertino for Trumpet, Piano and Strings[a]. *Coupled with* **Hummel.** Trumpet Concerto in E flat major. **Tomasi.** Trumpet Concerto. **Haydn.** Trumpet Concerto in E flat major, HobVIIe/1. **Sergei Nakariakov** (tpt); [a]**Alexander Markovich** (pf); **Lausanne Chamber Orchestra/Jésus López-Cobos.** Teldec 4509-90846-2 (10/93). *See review in the Collections section; refer to the Index to Reviews.*

Chant de Linos[a]. Flute Sonata[b]. *Coupled with* **Koechlin.** Sonata for Piano and Flute, Op. 52[c]. Quintet, Op. 156, "Primavera"[d]. **Philippe Racine** (fl); [ad]**Robert Zimansky** (vn); [ad]**Monika Clemann** (va); [ad]**Curdin Coray** (vc); [ad]**Xenia Schindler** (hp); [bc]**Daniel Cholette** (pf). Claves CD50-9003 (10/90).

Joseph Jongen

Jongen. Symphonie concertante, Op. 81[a]. Suite, Op. 48[b]. Allegro appassionato, Op. 79[b]. [a]**Hubert Schoonbroodt** (org); [b]**Therese-Marie Gilissen** (va); [a]**Liège Symphony Orchestra/René Defossez;** [b]**RTBF Symphony Orchestra/Brian Priestman.** Koch Schwann 315 012. Recorded 1975-85.

> ♪ **1h 10m DDD 8/92** ❓

Jongen's *Symphonie concertante* is a spectacular showpiece for organ and large orchestra, full of thrilling effects, unforgettable tunes, spine-tingling climaxes and flashes of great beauty. Written in 1926 its rare performances today belie its sheer crowd-pulling potential, so it's very good to have the work readily available on CD. Having said that it should be pointed out that while this is a perfectly acceptable recording, it's neither the only one nor the best (see below for details of the Telarc recording which is very much in the demonstration class). No, what makes this a "Good CD" are the two works for viola and orchestra. The viola is pretty well starved of worthwhile concert repertory yet here is some wonderful music (especially the ravishing "Poème élégiaque" from the *Suite*) which has been allowed to wallow in obscurity for the best part of a century. Hopefully this disc will change all that. Therese-Marie Gilissen puts her all into this music, summoning up a vast array of emotions in the *Suite* and producing the kind of virtuoso playing in the *Allegro appassionato* more usually associated with the violin.

Additional recommendation ...
Symphonie. **Franck.** *Fantaisie in A major. Pastorale, Op. 19.* **Michael Murray** (org); **San Francisco Symphony Orchestra/Edo de Waart.** Telarc CD80096 — ♪ 56m DDD 3/85 ❓

New review
Jongen. ORGAN WORKS, Volume 1. **John Scott Whiteley** (org). Priory PRCD324. Played on the organs of York Minster, Notre Dame de Laeken, Brussels and St Jude's Church, Detroit. Recorded 1989-91.
Pièce pour Grand Orgue. Two Pieces, Op. 53. Pieces, Op. 5 — No. 1, Andante cantabile; No. 2, Pastorale; No. 4, Offertoire; No. 5, Communion. Prélude et Fugue, Op. 121. Elégie. Cantilene. Papillons noirs, Op. 69 No. 11. Two Pieces, Op. 47. Petite Pièce. Petit Prélude. Toccata, Op. 104.

> ♪ **1h 11m DDD 7/93**

John Scott Whiteley plays with total commitment, presenting a thoroughly compelling case for this largely underrated composer. An added attraction is his vast dissertation which has been crammed into the booklet. But the music's the thing and while novice organists will probably already have encountered the charming *Petite Pièce* and *Chant de Mai*, and more experienced players should know the bittersweet *Menuet-Scherzo* and Toccata in D flat, much here will be unfamiliar. Very distinctive is the sparkling *Prélude et Fugue* of 1943 while his fertile imagination is amply displayed in the more impressionistic Op. 47 pieces and in Whiteley's own transcription of the virtuoso piano piece *Papillons noirs*. The use of three different organs is puzzling: it's somewhat disconcerting to go straight from the throaty roar of the Detroit instrument to the swirling and mystic mists surrounding the Brussels organ (an instrument which Jongen himself played) and thence to York where we seem to hear almost as much blower as pipe.

Scott Joplin
American 1868-1917

Suggested listening ...

Maple Leaf Rag. Original Rags. Swipesy. Peacherine Rag. The Easy Winners. Sunflower Slow Drag. The Entertainer. Elite Syncopations. The Strenuous Life. A Breeze from Alabama. Palm Leaf Rag. Something Doing. Weeping Willow. The Chrysanthemum. The Cascades. The Sycamore. **Dick Hyman** (pf). RCA Victor Gold Seal GD87993 (10/89).

TREEMONISHA. **Soloists; Houston Grand Opera Chorus and Orchestra/Gunther Schuller.** DG 435 709-2GX2 (8/92).

Josquin Desprez
French c.1440-1521

Josquin Desprez. Missa Ave maris stella. MOTETS AND CHANSONS. **Taverner Consort and Choir/Andrew Parrott.** EMI Reflexe CDC7 54659-2. Texts and translations included. Recorded in 1992.
Motets — Illibata Dei virgo nutrix. Gaude virgo, mater Christi. Salve regina. In te Domine speravi (with Andrew Lawrence-King, hp). Plaine de dueil. Que vous madame. Regretz sans fin. Adieu mes amours. Je n'ose plus (both with Andrew Lawrence-King). *Anonymous:* Ave maris stella.

1h 17m DDD 5/93

The customary glittering, steely sound of the Taverner Consort and Choir is here altered by the unexpected presence of counter-tenors, in an impressive programme of seldom-heard and seldom-recorded Josquin. The panorama it gives of Josquin's mastery of various techniques is fascinating: nobody could miss the contrast between *Illibata Dei virgo nutrix* and *Gaude virgo, mater Christi*. They are equally impressive, perfect examples of Josquin's contrapuntal and harmonic skill, and yet significantly different in their technical procedures and utterly different in the impression they make. Similarly, the *Missa Ave maris stella*, which stands midway between the earlier Mass settings and later works such as the *Missa Pange lingua*, offers points of comparison and contrast both because of its musical magnificence and because of its relative unfamiliarity. The performances are commensurate with the music, and though it is often a risk for an English group to record French-texted works (especially when experiments in pronunciation are involved), the *chansons* recorded here are also delightful. Altogether a provocative collection.

Additional recommendation ...
Missa Ave maris stella. Monstra te esse matrem (Ave maris stella). Salve regina. Gaude virgo, mater Christi. Alma Redemptoris mater. Ave regina celorum. Vultum tuum deprecabuntur. **A Sei Voci/Bernard Fabre-Garrus.** Astrée Auvidis E8507 — 1h 3m DDD 2/94 ⁹ₚ

Josquin Desprez. Missa L'homme armé super voces musicales. Missa L'homme armé sexti toni. *Anonymous.* L'homme armé. **The Tallis Scholars/Peter Phillips.** Gimell CDGIM019. Text and translation included.

1h 14m DDD 7/89

Towards the end of the Middle Ages it became customary to use popular secular melodies instead of the usual plainchant themes as the basis for composing polyphonic Masses. One such was the fifteenth-century melody *L'homme armé* ("Beware of the armed man"), a melody that may have originated as a crusader song. These settings would provide endless opportunities for a composer to demonstrate his contrapuntal skills. In the first of Josquin's two settings, *Super voces musicales*, he uses the tune over and over again, beginning each time on successive ascending degrees of the six-note scale *Ut Re Mi Fa Sol La*, so that it rises higher and higher as the Mass progresses. Sometimes the melody appears back to front from half way through the piece on to the end. In the *Sexti toni* Mass the tune is transposed so that F rather than G is the final note. The listener's enjoyment is in no way lessened by all this contrapuntal ingenuity. The music flows along with unsurpassed ease and beauty, displaying that unique quality of seeming inevitability which characterizes all great music. It is well matched by the expertise and enthusiasm of The Tallis Scholars and their first-class recording engineers.

Further listening ...

Missa Pange lingua. Missa La sol fa re mi. **The Tallis Scholars/Peter Phillips.** Gimell CDGIM009 (3/87).

Missa Hercules dux Ferrarie. La déploration de Johannes Ockeghem, "Nymphes des bois". *Coupled with **La Rue.*** Missa pro defunctis. **New London Chamber Choir/James Wood.** Amon Ra CDSAR24 (3/87).

Missa Pange Lingua. Vultum tuum deprecabuntur. Planxit autem David. **Westminster Cathedral Choir/James O'Donnell.** Hyperion CDA66614 (4/93).

Dmitry Kabalevsky
Russian 1904-1987

Suggested listening ...

Cello Concerto No. 1 in G minor, Op. 49. *Coupled with **Shostakovich.*** Cello Concerto No. 1 in E flat major, Op. 107. **Yo-Yo Ma** (vc); **Philadelphia Orchestra/Eugene Ormandy.** CBS CD37840 (5/85).

Cello Concerto No. 2. in C major, Op. 77. *Coupled with **Glazunov.*** Chant du ménéstrel, Op. 71; ***Khachaturian.*** Cello Concerto. **Raphael Wallfisch** (vc); **London Philharmonic Orchestra/Bryden Thomson.** Chandos CHAN8579 (6/88).

Violin Concerto[d]. *Coupled with **Chausson.*** Poème, Op. 25[a]. ***Ravel.*** Tzigane[a]. ***Glazunov.*** Violin Concerto[b]. Mazurka-Oberek[c]. **David Oistrakh** (vn); [a]**Moscow State Symphony Orchestra/Kyrill Kondrashin; USSR State Orchestra/**[b]**Kondrashin,** [d]**Dmitry Kabalevsky;** [c]**USSR Radio Symphony Orchestra/Gabril Yudin.** Monitor Collectors Series mono MCD72073. *See review in the Collections section; refer to the Index to Reviews.*

Piano Sonata No. 3, Op. 46. *Coupled with **Prokofiev:*** Piano Sonata No. 7 in B flat major, Op. 83. Toccata, Op. 11. ***Poulenc:*** Presto in B flat major. ***Barber:*** Piano Sonata, Op. 26. ***Fauré:*** Nocturne No. 13 in B minor, Op. 119[a]. **Vladimir Horowitz** (pf). RCA Gold Seal mono/[a]stereo GD60377 (6/92). *See review in the Collections section; refer to the Index to Reviews.*

Vaasily Sergeyevich Kalinnikov
Russian 1866-1901

Suggested listening ...

Symphony No. 1 in G minor. *Coupled with **Glazunov.*** The sea — Fantasy, Op. 28. Spring, Op. 34. **Scottish National Orchestra/Neeme Järvi.** Chandos CHAN8611 (10/88).

Symphony No. 2 in A major. Tsar Boris — Overture. The cedar and the palm. **Scottish National Orchestra/Neeme Järvi.** Chandos CHAN8805 (6/90).

Imre Kalmán

Suggested listening ...

Gräfin Mariza — *operetta: excerpts.* **Soloists; New Sadlers Wells Opera Chorus and Orchestra/Barry Wordsworth.** TER Classics CDTED1007.

Giya Kancheli

Suggested listening ...

Symphonies Nos. 3[a] and 6[b]. [a]**Gamlet Gonashvili** (ten); [b]**Archil Kharadze,** [b]**Giya Chaduneli** (vas); **Georgia State Symphony Orchestra/Dzansug Kakhidze.** Olympia Explorer OCD401 (9/90).

Symphonies — No. 4, "In Commemoration of Michaelangelo" (1975); No. 5 (1976). **Georgia State Symphony Orchestra/Dzansug Kakhidze.** Olympia OCD403 (4/91).

Liturgy for Viola and Orchestra, "Mourned by the Wind"[a]. *Coupled with* **Schnittke.** Viola Concerto[b]. **Kim Kashkashian** (va); [a]**Bonn Beethovenhalle Orchestra,** [b]**Saarbrücken Radio Symphony Orchestra/Dennis Russell Davies.** ECM New Series 437 199-2 (4/93).

Nikolai Karetnikov

Suggested listening ...

Till Eulenspiegel. **Soloists; Chorus; Soviet Cinema Orchestra/Emin Khatchaturian, Valery Poliansky.** CDM Russian Season LDC288 029/30 (7/92).

Sigfrid Karg-Elert

New review

Karg-Elert. Stimmen der Nacht, Op. 142 No. 1. Four diverse Pieces, Op. 75.
Bach. Trio Sonata No. 5 in C major, BWV529.
Reger. Chorale Fantasia, "Wie schön leucht' uns der Morgen-stern", Op. 40 No. 1. **Graham Barber** (org). Priory PRCD315. Played on the Klais Organ of Altenberg Cathedral.

Ih Ilm   DDD   II/93

For the incurable organ-buff the chance to hear this wonderful instrument put through its paces by a player with an ever-alert ear for scintillating aural effects will provide ample justification for buying this disc. Here he is indulging in another programme of heavyweight Germaniana with only a bit of Bach to sugar the pill. One must admire Graham Barber's perseverance in giving us as committed and persuasive performances as anyone could realistically expect. Barber launches straight into Reger's monumental *Chorale Fantasia* which, like all Reger, has its moments; a truly magical one here when the chorale melody first appears (2'04"). The trouble is there's a further 15 minutes to wade through: sometimes it can seem longer. It doesn't even have the attraction of the ever-changing colours of Karg-Elert's music. *Stimmen der Nacht* seems long-drawn-out but does come as a welcome relief after the self-indulgent excesses of Reger, and one cannot fail to like the Op. 75 pieces, one of which is a joyful improvisation on *In dulci jubilo* which positively reeks of Christmas spirit. Barber finds some gorgeous sounds yet keeps the music flowing uninterruptedly in spite of Karg-Elert's frequent and complex registration demands.

Reinhard Keiser

German 1674-1739

Suggested listening ...

MASAGNIELLO FURIOSO. **Soloists; Bremen Vocal Ensemble for Ancient Music; Fiori Musicali/Thomas Albert.** CPO CPO999 110-2 (11/93).

David Kellner

German c.1670-1748

Suggested listening ...

Auserlesene Lauten-Stücke. **Stephen Stubbs** (lte). CPO CPO999 097-2 (9/93).

Jerome Kern

American 1885-1945

New review

Kern. JEROME KERN TREASURY. [a]**Rebecca Luker** (sngr); [b]**Jeanne Lehman** (sop); [c]**Lydia Mila** (sngr); [d]**Hugh Panaro** (sngr); [e]**George Dvorsky** (ten); [f]**Thomas Hampson** (bar); [g]**London Sinfonietta Chorus; London Sinfonietta/John McGlinn.** EMI CDC7 54883-2. Texts included. Recorded in 1992.
The Red Petticoat — The Ragtime Restaurant[adg]. Very Good Eddie — Babes in the Wood[ad]. Love o' Mike — Drift with me[ae]. Have a Heart — I'm so busy[ae]. Oh Boy! — Till the clouds roll by[ad]. Zip Goes a Million — Whip-poor-will[be]. She's a Good Fellow — The Bullfrog Patrol[abg]. Dear Sir — I want to be there[ae]; Wishing-well scene[ae]. The Cat and the Fiddle — She didn't say "Yes"[b]; Every little while[be]. Music in the Air — In Egern of the Tegern See[b]; The song is you[f]. Roberta — Smoke gets in your eyes[b]. High, Wide and Handsome — The folks who live on the hill[f]. Very Warm for May — Harlem Boogie-Woogie; Heaven in my arms[abcdeg]. The last time I saw Paris[f].

1h 19m   DDD   4/94

A quick glance at these titles points up the familiarity of the post-*Show Boat* songs of the 1930s in comparison with those recorded here from 1912 to 1924, of which "Till the clouds roll by" alone has found popularity. With the exception of "The Ragtime Restaurant", a timely reminder that Berlin didn't have the monopoly on that craze, these early songs inhabit a world of expression that Kern made peculiarly his own both in the sentiments they express and in his musical settings. Included here is the "Wishing-well scene" from *Dear Sir* that foreshadows the composition of *Show Boat* three years later. In the later songs, it is instructive to be reminded that a song like "The folks who live on the hill" was composed with a lolloping rhythmic background not at all like the popular version by Peggy Lee. Thomas Hampson brings his powerful baritone to this ballad and gives a sensitive account of *Last time I saw Paris*, and the other soloists have never given better of themselves than here. In common with their conductor, they have an instinct and a rapport for Kern's infectious musical world that is matched by the warmth of this recording that enables all the many varied touches in the orchestrations to gleam brightly. This treasury deserves to become a classic of the music-theatre discography.

Additional recommendation ...
High, Wide and Handsome — The folks who live on the hill. You Were Never Lovelier — I'm old
fashioned. Swing Time — The way you look tonight; A fine romance. Music in the Air — The song is
you. Roberta — Yesterdays; Smoke gets in your eyes. Lady be good. The last time I saw Paris. Very Warm
for May — All the things you are. Show Boat — Can't help lovin' dat man; Bill. Cover Girl — Long
ago and far away. Centennial Summer — All through the day. Sally — Look for the silver lining. **Dame**
Kiri Te Kanawa (sop); **London Sinfonietta/Jonathan Tunick.** EMI CDC7 54527-2 —
·.·' 45m DDD 7/93 ⁹ₚ

Kern. SHOW BOAT. Cast includes **Teresa Stratas, Frederica von Stade, Jerry Hadley,**
Bruce Hubbard, Karla Burns; Ambrosian Chorus; London Sinfonietta/John
McGlinn. EMI CDS7 49108-2. Notes and text included. Recorded in 1987.

·.·' ③ 3h 42m DDD 11/88 ⁹ₚ ⁹ₛ

This three-CD *Show Boat* is a remarkable, inspired achievement that is far from being an example
of a musical swamped by the misguided use of operatic voices. *Show Boat* was composed on a
large scale for singers of accomplishments far above those we often hear in the theatre today, and
here it is given its due. "Make believe", "Ol' man river", "Can't help lovin' dat man", "Why do I
love you?" and "You are love" have been sung by countless singers over the years, but in beauty
and style the performances here can surely never have been rivalled. The love duets between
Frederica von Stade and Jerry Hadley are stunningly beautiful and Bruce Hubbard's firm, honeyed
baritone has absolutely nothing to fear from comparisons with Paul Robeson. Teresa Stratas's
"Can't help lovin' dat man" is quite ravishing. But the success of this set is due above all to the
enthusiasm and dedication of its conductor, John McGlinn. His avowed aim has been to include
all the music Kern wrote for the piece over the years for various stage and film productions.
Much of this appears in a lengthy and fascinating appendix; but the main text itself includes not
only full-length versions of numbers traditionally much shortened but other magnificent items
dropped during try-outs and only rediscovered in a Warner Brothers warehouse in 1982. Not
least he has restored the original orchestrations of Robert Russell Bennett. The London
Sinfonietta clearly revels in them, not least the jazz-flavoured elements of the final Act. The
Ambrosian Chorus, too, has a field day in the rousing choral numbers. Bright, spacious recorded
sound helps to make this a quite magnificent, quite irresistibly enjoyable achievement.

Additional recommendation ...
Soloists; National Symphony Orchestra.John Owen Edwards. TER Classics
CDTER21199 — ·.·' ② 1h 35m DDD 6/94 ⁹ₚ

Albert Ketèlbey

British 1875-1959

New review
Ketèlbey. ORCHESTRAL AND CHORAL WORKS. [a]**Slovak Philharmonic Male Chorus;**
Bratislava Radio Symphony Orchestra/Adrian Leaper. Marco Polo 8 223442. Recorded
in 1992.
In a Monastery Garden[a]. The Adventurers. Chal Romano — Descriptive Overture. Suite
romantique. Caprice pianistique. The Clock and the Dresden Figures. Cockney Suite — No. 3,
At the Palais de Danse; No. 5, Bank Holiday. In the Moonlight. Wedgwood Blue. Bells across
the meadows. Phantom melody. In a Persian Market[a].

·.·' 1h 14m DDD 4/94 ⁹ₚ

New review
Ketèlby. ORCHESTRAL AND CHORAL WORKS.
Luigini. Ballet égyptien, Op. 12 — Suite[c]. [d]**Jean Temperley** (mez); [e]**Vernon Midgley**
(ten); [f]**Leslie Pearson** (pf); [a]**Ambrosian Singers;** [b]**Philharmonia Orchestra/John**
Lanchbery; [c]**Royal Philharmonic Orchestra/Anatole Fistoulari.** Classics for Pleasure
CD-CFP4637. Items marked [abdef] recorded in 1977, [c] 1958.
Bells across the meadows[b]. Chal Romano — Descriptive Overture[b]. The Clock and the Dresden
Figures[bf]. In a Chinese Temple Garden[ab]. In a Monastery Garden[ab]. In a Persian Market[ab]. In the

403

Moonlight (Sous la lune) — Poetic Intermezzo[b]. In the Mystic Land of Egypt[abe]. Sanctuary of the Heart — Méditation religieuse[abd].

lh 9m ADD 3/94

The favourites are played with grace and sensitivity on the Marco Polo disc but we also get the opportunity to hear some of Ketèlbey's unjustly overshadowed compositions. And what delights there are! Over-exposure to Ketèlbey's more stereotyped, highly perfumed compositions has disguised what varied and inventive music he composed. We know the charms of *The Clock and the Dresden Figures* and *In the Moonlight*, the invigorating open-air spirit of *Chal Romano* from the Lanchbery collection. However, surely nobody would want to be without the equally invigorating overture *The Adventurers*, the elegant *Suite romantique*, the sparkling *Caprice pianistique* and the jaunty *Wedgwood Blue* — and what a pity we are restricted to just two movements of the *Cockney Suite*. With playing, conducting and recording of a high standard, this is a collection that demands to be heard. The Classics for Pleasure reissue gives us a captivating and indispensable budget-price Ketèlbey collection with the Philharmonia Orchestra playing with great style and hugely enjoying themselves. The Ambrosian Singers provide additional atmosphere in *In a Monastery Garden*, *In a Persian Market*, *In a Chinese Temple Garden* and *In the Mystic Land of Egypt*, and ensure the sentimental opulence of *Sanctuary of the Heart*. Ketèlbey programmes don't come much better than this. To make it even more enticing, CfP have added the superb 1958 RPO/Anatole Fistoulari recording of Luigini's *Ballet égyptien*. Like the Ketèlbey pieces it is a tuneful suite and has been in and out of the catalogue seemingly since the dawn of time, but has certainly never been better played than it is here. This CD also benefits from exceptionally informative notes.

Aram Khachaturian

Russian 1903-1978

New review

Khachaturian. The Widow of Valencia — Suite. Gayaneh — Suite No. 2.
Tjeknavorian. Danses fantastiques. **Armenian Philharmonic Orchestra/Loris Tjeknavorian.** ASV CDDCA884.

lh 5m DDD 3/94

Khachaturian's *The Widow of Valencia* is an early work (1940), yet already reveals the composer's fund of good tunes. He admitted its lack of authentic Spanishness and while the "Introduction" opens with flashing southern Mediterranean gusto, it soon makes way for a sultry Armenian melody of best local vintage. However, why worry? Altogether this is a most winning suite, without a dull bar, piquantly scored and brilliantly presented by an orchestra who are completely at home and clearly enjoying themselves. They also give us another suite, comprising six indelible numbers — for the most part little known — from Khachaturian's masterpiece, *Gayaneh*. Tjeknavorian's own *Danses fantastiques* frequently burst with energy and the gentler dances have that Armenian flavour so familiar in *Gayaneh*. Brilliant playing in glittering yet spacious sound.

Additional recommendation ...
Masquerade — Waltz; Nocturne; Mazurka. *Violin Concerto in D minor*[a]. *Gayaneh* — Sabre Dance; Ayesha's Dance; Dance of the Rose Maidens; Lullaby; Lezghinka; Gayaneh's Adagio; Lyrical duo; Dance of the old people. [a]**David Oistrakh** (vn); **Philharmonia Orchestra/Aram Khachaturian.** EMI Composers in Person mono CDC5 55035-2 — lh 19m ADD 6/94 ▲

Further listening ...

Trio. *Coupled with* **Kokai.** Quartettino. **Prokofiev.** Overture on Hebrew Themes in C minor, Op. 34. Quintet in G minor, Op. 39. **Walter Boeykens Ensemble.** Harmonia Mundi HMC90 1419 (6/93).

Violin Concerto in D minor. *Coupled with* **Kabalevsky.** Violin Concerto in C major, Op. 48. **Lydia Mordkovitch** (vn); **Royal Scottish National Orchestra/Neeme Järvi.** Chandos CHAN8918 (3/91).

Spartacus — Ballet Suite No. 1: Variations of Aegina and Bacchanalia; Dance of the Gaditanian Maidens and Victory of Spartacus; Ballet Suite No. 2: Adagio of Spartacus and Phrygia. Gayaneh — excerpts. Masquerade — Incidental Music to Lermontov's play. **London Symphony Orchestra/Stanley Black.** Decca Weekend 417 062-2DC (3/90).

Karen Khachaturian

USSR 1920-

Suggested listening ...

Violin Sonata in G minor, Op. 1. *Coupled with* **Castelnuovo-Tedesco.** Violin Concerto No. 2, "I profeti". **Ferguson.** Violin Sonata No. 1, Op. 2. **Français.** String Trio in C major. **Jascha Heifetz** (vn); **Joseph de Pasquale** (va); **Gregor Piatigorsky** (vc); **Lilian Steuber** (pf); **Los Angeles Philharmonic Orchestra/Alfred Wallenstein.** RCA Victor Gold Seal GD87872 (9/90).

Theodor Kirchner

German 1823-1903-

Suggested listening ...

Triptych[d]. *Coupled with* **Ives.** Trio for Violin, Clarinet and Piano[c]. **Bernstein** (trans. Ma). Clarinet Sonata[a]. **Gershwin** (arr. Heifetz, trans. Ma)[b]. Three Preludes. **Yo-Yo Ma** (vc); [c]**Ronan Lefkowitz**, [d]**Lynn Chang** (vns); [ab]**Jeffrey Kahane**, [c]**Gilbert Kalish** (pfs). Sony Classical SK53126 (4/94). *See review in the Collections section; refer to the Index to Reviews.*

Gideon Klein

Czechoslovakian 1919-1945

Klein. String Trio. Fantasie a Fuga. Piano Sonata[a]. String Quartet, Op. 2.
Ullmann. String Quartet No. 3, Op. 43. **Hawthorne Quartet** (Roman Lefkowitz, Si Jing Huang, vns; Mark Ludwig, va; Sato Knudsen, vc); [a]**Virginia Eskin** (pf). Channel Classics CCS1691. Recorded in 1991.

 ••• 1h 8m DDD 12/91

This CD is devoted to music by two Jewish musicians incarcerated in the Theresienstadt ghetto camp established by the Nazis in November 1941. On the evidence of the works recorded here, Gideon Klein and Viktor Ullmann were substantial figures whose music needs no special pleading. In stylistic terms, Ullman is perhaps the more predictable of the two. His Third Quartet shows him remaining true to Schoenbergian expressionism within a tonal context. Klein, deported to the camp at the age of 21, was by all accounts an astonishingly accomplished musician. His own music shows unmistakable signs of potential greatness even if the major influences — including Schoenberg, Janáček and Bartók — are not fully assimilated within a definitive creative profile. The bravely invigorating String Trio, completed only nine days before Klein's disappearance, receives a magnificent performance from members of the Hawthorne Quartet, a group drawn from the Boston Symphony Orchestra. Virginia Eskin gives a powerful account of the hard-hitting Piano Sonata, humming along discreetly as she plays. Channel Classics deserve high praise for these ideally balanced recordings which document a form of spiritual resistance of an isolated and terrorized community which we can barely begin to comprehend.

New review
Klein. Fantasie a Fuga[a]. Trio for Violin, Viola and Cello[b]. Piano Sonata[c]. First Sin[d]. Two Madrigals[e]. Czech and Russian Folksongs[f]. [d]**Karel Kožušnik** (ten); [c]**Allan Sternfield** (pf); [ab]**The Group for New Music** (Ora Shiran, Carmela Leiman, vns; Michael Kugel, va; Felix

Nemirovsky, vc); [ef]**Prague Philharmonic Choir/Pavel Kühn.** Koch International Classics 37230-2. Texts and translations included. Recorded in 1992.

♪ 5lm DDD

This collection focuses exclusively on works composed by Klein during his imprisonment. He had at one stage hoped to study at the Royal Academy in London but he produced a remarkable body of work in the few months left to him. There are unresolved tensions between the Schoenbergian and the Nationalistic in his evolving idiom, the Piano Sonata looking one way, the String Trio the other. Both are near-masterpieces. In the chamber works, the members of the Israeli Group for New Music are marginally less polished than the Hawthornes, less preoccupied with carefully matched tone and artful nuancing. In the Piano Sonata, Allan Sternfield is extremely effective, more moderate than the supercharged almost-thumping of Virginia Eskin (reviewed above). By taking the outer movements rather faster than the competition, he gives them an attractive toccata-like quality, throwing the expressive content of the *Adagio* into greater relief. New to CD, the choral works include two *Madrigals*, amazingly chromatic and complex if they were indeed composed for camp perform-ance, and some more accessible folk-song settings. This disc is concerned as much to record the spiritual resistance as to rehabilitate the scores themselves. Accordingly the notes are unusually full and include a wealth of documentary material, not least a striking colour portrait of the composer. The recording quality is good.

Key to symbols

♪   ②   ②   lh 23m   DDD   6/88

Price	Quantity/ availability	Timing	Recording mode	Review date

	Quality of sound		Discs worth exploring		Caveat emptor

♪P   ♪S   Ⓑ   ❓   ✒   ▲

Quality of performance		Basic library		Period performance	

Oliver Knussen

British 1952-

New review

Knussen. Songs without Voices, Op. 26[d]. Whitman Settings, Op. 25[bc]. Hums and songs of Winnie-the-Pooh, Op. 6[ad]. Piano Variations, Op. 24[c]. Four Late Poems and an Epigram of Rainer Maria Rilke, Op. 23[a]. Sonya's Lullaby, Op. 16[c]. Océan de terre, Op. 10[bd]. [a]**Lisa Saffer,** [b]**Lucy Shelton** (sops); [c]**Peter Serkin** (pf); [d]**Lincoln Center Chamber Music Society/Oliver Knussen.** Virgin Classics VC7 59308-2. Texts and translations included. Recorded in 1992.

♪ lh l6m DDD 10/93   ♪P

If Ravel had been an expressionist, living now, this is the music he might have been writing. The early *Océan de terre*, a setting of Apollinaire, still has traces of the strenuousness which Knussen needed to exorcize in order to free his personal voice. But all the rest is sheer delight. Even the potential whimsy of *Hums and songs* is transcended by the quality of the musical thought, summed up in the poignant concluding "Cloud Piece". If the later works suggest that Knussen might be a miniaturist from now on, there can be little sense of loss when so much richness results. The boldly sculpted Piano Variations, the tellingly concentrated Rilke monodies, the Whitman settings that brilliantly elucidate the poet's tricky rhetoric, the *Songs without Voices* whose pulsating inventiveness is matched by cool formal discipline — all are realized with uncommon finesse and conviction. The recordings have both clarity and character, while the performances are as exuberant and polished as one would expect with the composer

| at hand.

Further listening ...

Symphonies — No. 2, Op. 7[a]; No. 3, Op. 18[b]. Trumpets, Op. 12[c]. Coursing, Op. 17[e].
Cantata, Op. 15[d]. Ophelia Dances, Book 1, Op. 18[b]. [a]**Elaine Barry,** [c]**Linda Hirst** (sops);
[c]**Michael Collins,** [c]**Edward Pillinger,** [c]**Ian Mitchell** (clarinets); [d]**Nash Ensemble;**
[b]**Philharmonia Orchestra/Michael Tilson Thomas;** [ae]**London Sinfonietta/Oliver
Knussen.** Unicorn-Kanchana Souvenir UKCD2010 (9/88).

WHERE THE WILD THINGS ARE. **Soloists; London Sinfonietta/Oliver Knussen.**
Unicorn-Kanchana DKPCD9044 (9/85).

Zoltán Kodály

Hungarian 1882-1967

Kodály. Psalmus Hungaricus, Op. 13[a]. Missa Brevis[b]. Pange Lingua[c]. Psalm 114[d]. [a]**Lajos
Kozma,** [b]**Ian Caley** (tens); [ab]**Elizabeth Gale,** [b]**Sally Le Sage,** [b]**Hannah Francis** (sops);
[b]**Alfreda Hodgson** (contr); [b]**Michael Rippon** (bass); [bc]**Christopher Bowers-Broadbent,**
[d]**Gillian Weir** (orgs); [abcd]**Brighton Festival Chorus/László Heltay;** [a]**London Symphony
Orchestra/István Kertész.** Decca Enterprise 433 080-2DM. Item marked [a] recorded in 1970,
[b] 1975, [c] 1976, [d] 1977.

∴ Ih l0m ADD 8/92

Kodály composed his stirring and masterly *Psalmus Hungaricus* in response to a commission to
celebrate the fiftieth anniversary of the union of Buda, Pest and Obuda to form the city of
Budapest. Fellow composer Dohnányi led the hugely successful first performance on
November 19th, 1923 (also on the programme that evening was the première of Bartók's
wonderful *Dance Suite* — what a concert that must have been!). István Kertész's 1970
account of this choral masterpiece is one of his most fervently inspired achievements on
record and the Brighton Festival Chorus (trained by László Heltay) produce a thrillingly
idiomatic sonority. Heltay himself takes over at the helm for the remaining items: the
wartime *Missa Brevis* is easily the most substantial of these, beautifully conceived for the idiom
and framed by an organ-only *Introitus* and a postlude, *Ite, missa est. Pange lingua* dates from
1928 (though Kodály added the prelude for organ three years later), and it's a wonderfully
heartfelt setting of St Thomas Aquinas's eponymous hymn; and Decca also give us the brief,
touchingly direct setting of *Psalm 114*, composed in 1952. Apart from this last offering (set
down in Guildford Cathedral), London's Kingsway Hall was the venue for all this material,
and its ideal acoustical properties are heard to superb advantage in these recordings: *Psalmus
Hungaricus*, in particular, sounds magnificent — the work of that incomparable engineer
Kenneth Wilkinson. Given the consistent excellence of this idiomatic music-making (one is
reminded that Heltay was a pupil and close friend of the composer), this represents a
marvellous mid-price compilation.

Additional recommendation ...
Psalmus Hungaricus, Op. 13[a]. Hymn of Zrinyi[b]. **Dvořák.** *Requiem, B165[c].* **Soloists;** [c]**Ambrosian
Singers;** [a]**Wandsworth School Boys' Choir;** [ab]**Brighton Festival Chorus;** [ac]**London
Symphony Orchestra/István Kertész,** [b]**László Heltay.** Decca Ovation 421 810-2DM2 —
∴ ② 2h 17m ADD 5/89

Further listening ...

String Quartet No. 2, Op. 10. *Coupled with* **Dvořák.** String Quartet No. 12 in F major, B179,
"American". Cypresses, B152 — Nos. 1, 2, 5, 9 and 11. **Hagen Quartet.** DG 419 601-2GH
(5/87). *See review under Dvořák; refer to the Index to Reviews.*

Háry János Suite[a]. Concerto for Orchestra[b]. Summer Evening[b]. [a]**Berlin Radio Symphony
Orchestra/Ferenc Fricsay;** [b]**Budapest Philharmonic Orchestra/Zoltán Kodály.** DG
Dokumente 427 408-2GDO (5/89).

Dances from Marosszék. Dances from Galánta. *Coupled with* **Bartók.** Divertimento, Sz113. Romanian folk dances, Sz68. **Saint Paul Chamber Orchestra/Hugh Wolff.** Teldec 9031-73134-2 (5/94).

Seven Pieces, Op. 11. *Coupled with* **Liszt.** Csárdás macabre, S224. **Dohnányi.** Gavotte and Musette. **Bartók** (trans. cpsr.): Dance Suite, Sz77. **Weiner.** Three Hungarian Rural Dances. **Kurtág.** Plays and Games for Piano, Book 3 — excerpts. **Szöllösy.** Paesaggio con morti. **Peter Frankl** (pf). ASV CDDCA860 (6/93). *See review in the Collections section; refer to the Index to Reviews.*

Charles Koechlin

French 1867-1950

Koechlin. Le livre de la jungle. [a]**Iris Vermillion** (mez); [a]**Johan Botha** (ten); [a]**Ralf Lukas** (bass); [a]**Berlin Radio Chamber Choir; Berlin Radio Symphony Orchestra/David Zinman.** RCA Victor Red Seal (Special Price) 09026 61955-2. Texts and translations included. Recorded in 1993.
Poèmes, Op. 18[a]. La course de printemps, Op. 95. La méditation de Purun Bhagat, Op. 159. La loi de la Jungle, Op. 175. Les Bandar-Log, Op. 176.

② 1h 30m DDD 6/94   𝄞 P ❓

For 40 years, from his mid-thirties onwards, Koechlin, when he wasn't day-dreaming about goddesses of the cinema screen, was obsessed with Kipling's two *Jungle Books*. This eventually materialized in a large canvas of four symphonic poems, preceded by three songs (with chorus) that he then orchestrated. The complete sequence, called *The Jungle Book*, appears for the first time on the present disc; the Marco Polo disc (listed below) contains only the orchestral works. RCA's inclusion of the Op. 18 songs necessitates spreading to two discs, (though priced as a single disc): nevertheless the first song, the lushly scored "Seal lullaby" (the only movement not sited in the Indian rain forest) is so seductively beautiful that it would be a pity to miss it, especially as well sung as it is by Iris Vermillion. Of the symphonic poems, only *The Bandar-Log* is at all known here. The title refers to the noisy, empty-headed race of monkeys — "self-satisfied mimics whose only goal is to follow the fashions of the day" — which gives Koechlin an opportunity to pillory parallelism, dodecaphony and the sterile 'Back to Bach' movement then topical (in a fugato with each voice in a different key), all in a dazzlingly virtuoso piece of scoring for a huge orchestra. Much the longest of the orchestral pieces is *The spring running*, another virtuoso score, which falls into four sections — mysticism as spring slowly stirs in the forest, Mowgli's urge finally to leave the animal companions with whom he has lived and return to mankind, the painful following of unsettling "new trails" and "time of new talk" (another metaphor for the world of musical composition), and night falling again (mainly an immensely long monodic line over a pedal-note). Do not miss these remarkable scores, which reveal a distinctly individual and boldly forward-looking mind with a wide stylistic vocabulary (generally atonal), great dramatic sense and a stunning technical command. The orchestra rises fully to the occasion and the sound is clear and vivid.

Additional recommendation ...
Rheinland-Pfalz Philharmonic Orchestra/Leif Segerstam. Marco Polo 8 223484 — .·'
1h 13m DDD 6/94

Further listening ...

14 Chants, Op. 157/2[c]. Premier album de Lilian, Op. 139[ac]. Second album de Lilian, Op. 149[c] — Sérénade à l'étoile errante; Swimming; Les jeux du clown; Le voyage chimérique. Morceau de lecture, Op. 218[c]. Sonata for piano and flute, Op. 52[c]. Sonata for two flutes, Op. 75[b]. [a]**Jayne West** (sop); **Fenwick Smith,** [b]**Leone Buyse** (fls); [c]**Martin Amlin** (pf). Hyperion CDA66414 (10/90).

Sonata for Piano and Flute, Op. 52[c]. Quintet, Op. 156, "Primavera"[d]. *Coupled with* **Jolivet.** Chant de Linos[a]. Flute Sonata[b]. **Philippe Racine** (fl); [ad]**Robert Zimansky** (vn); [ad]**Monika**

Clemann (va); [ad]**Curdin Coray** (vc); [ad]**Xenia Schindler** (hp); [bc]**Daniel Cholette** (pf).
Claves CD50-9003 (10/90).

Joonas Kokkonen

Finnish 1921-

Suggested listening ...

Cello Concerto[a]. Symphonic Sketches. Symphony No. 4. [a]**Torleif Thedéen** (vc); **Lahti
Symphony Orchestra/Osmo Vänskä.** BIS CD468 (12/91).

Erich Wolfgang Korngold

Austrian/Hungarian 1897-1957

Korngold. Violin Concerto, Op. 35[a].
Rózsa. Violin Concerto, Op. 24[b]. Tema con variazioni, Op. 29a[c].
Waxman. Fantasy on Bizet's "Carmen"[d]. **Jascha Heifetz** (vn); [c]**Gregor Piatigorsky** (vc);
[c]**Chamber Orchestra,** [a]**Los Angeles Philharmonic Orchestra/Alfred Wallenstein;**
[b]**Dallas Symphony Orchestra/Walter Hendl;** [d]**RCA Victor Symphony Orchestra/
Donald Voorhees.** RCA Gold Seal [ad]mono/[bc]stereo GD87963. Item marked [a] from HMV
ALP1233 (12/55), [b] SB6605 (4/65), [cd] new to UK. Recorded 1946-63.

.• **lh l0m   ADD   4/89**

Heifetz's legendary recording of the Korngold Concerto serves a double purpose: as an effective
introduction to Korngold's seductive musical style, and as the best possible example of Heifetz's
violin artistry. The work itself was written at the suggestion of Bronislaw Huberman, but it was
Heifetz who gave the première in 1947. It calls on material that Korngold had also used in three
of his film scores (he was at the time composing for Hollywood), although the way he welds the
themes into a three-movement structure is masterly enough to suggest that the concerto came to
him 'of a piece'. The very opening would be enough to seduce most listeners, unless — that is
— they have an aversion to the film music of the period. Miklós Rózsa's Concerto has its roots
in the composer's Hungarian soil, and echoes of Bartók are rarely absent. But whereas Korngold's
score is taken from movie music, Rózsa's (or parts of it) became a film score — namely, *The
Private Life of Sherlock Holmes.* Rózsa's self-possessed, skilfully written "Tema con Variazoni" was
taken, in 1962, from a much larger work then in progress, but Heifetz and Piatigorsky play it in
a reduced orchestration. As to the *Carmen Fantasy* by Franz Waxman (another notable film
composer), its luscious tunes and frightening technical challenges were written with the great
violinist very much in mind. It's a stunning piece of playing, and wears its 48 years lightly. The
other recordings sound far better, and the Rózsa items are in stereo. Marvellous stuff!

Korngold. Baby Serenade, Op. 24[a]. Cello Concerto, Op. 37[b]. Symphonic Serenade, Op. 39[c].
[b]**Julius Berger** (vc); **North West German Philharmonic Orchestra/Werner Andreas
Albert.** CPO 999 077-2. Item marked [a] recorded in 1989, [b] 1991, [c] 1990.

.• **lh 6m   DDD/ADD   l0/91**

All of Korngold's music to a greater or lesser degree has similar characteristics: virtuoso
orchestration which always surprises and delights, memorable lyricism which combines optimism
and regret in similar quantities (a quality shared with his beloved Johann Strauss) and rhythmic
dynamism which creates tremendous forward motion. The 1928 *Baby Serenade* was written to
mark the birth of his second son George who later repaid the compliment by initiating the
renaissance of his father's music in the 1960s and 1970s. With a breezy banjo and three vigorous
saxophones there is more than a hint of America and jazz in this entertaining piece. The Cello
Concerto, which receives a committed performance of the solo part from Julius Berger, is a
reworking of the music for a major Bette Davis vehicle of 1946 entitled *Deception.* Like all his
film music it is both memorable and atmospheric — indeed a miniature masterpiece of only 16
minutes in length. The Symphonic Serenade was premièred by no less than Wilhelm Furtwängler

and the Vienna Philharmonic in December 1950; but despite its similarity in mood to Richard Strauss's *Metamorphosen*, it failed to establish itself in the repertoire. Werner Andreas Albert's well prepared and sympathetic reading makes up for this extraordinary situation. Highly recommended.

New review

Korngold. Symphony in F sharp major, Op. 40. Abschiedlieder, Op. 14ᵃ. ᵃ**Linda Finnie** (mez); **BBC Philharmonic Orchestra/Sir Edward Downes.** Chandos CHAN9171.

Ih 8m DDD 9/93

Newcomers to Korngold's music who have dipped their toes into the waters of *Das Wunder der Heliane* and found the temperature a little too hot and headily intoxicating might do well to explore the orchestral version of the beautiful *Abschiedlieder* songs. Though there is much that is operatic here, musically they fall more within the gravitational orbit of Mahler than the opulent excesses of his operas. Linda Finnie gives rapt and majestic performances of considerable insight and conviction. The sparse, percussive opening of the symphony and the stridently defiant stance of the material seem a world apart from the warmth and chromatic richness of the songs, despite the fact that Mahlerian undertones can be heard here too. It is one of Korngold's most crucial compositions — an exposé of the man if you like, and an exposé which, despite a tragically nostalgic slow movement, reveals a bold and powerfully optimistic spirit. Downes and the BBC Philharmonic's performance is all one could wish for. In their hands the sombre, tragic *Adagio* becomes pure melt-down as climax upon inexorable climax culminate in a passage of almost unbearable intensity. Chandos have complemented inspirational music-making with inspirational recorded sound.

Additional recommendation ...
Symphony. Theme and Variations, Op. 42. Straussiana. **North West German Philharmonic Orchestra/Werner Andreas Albert.** CPO 999 146-2 — Ih 8m DDD/ADD 10/91

Korngold. DAS WUNDER DER HELIANE. **Anna Tomowa-Sintow** (sop) Heliane; **Hartmut Welker** (bar) Ruler; **John David de Haan** (ten) Stranger; **Reinhild Runkel** (contr) Messenger; **René Pape** (bass) Porter; **Nicolai Gedda** (ten) Blind Judge; **Martin Petzold** (ten) Young Man; **Berlin Radio Chorus; Berlin Radio Symphony Orchestra/John Mauceri.** Decca 436 636-2DH3. Notes, text and translation included.

③ 2h 48m DDD 4/93

This recording — part of Decca's ongoing Entartete Musik series — marks the rediscovery of a major operatic masterpiece of the 1920s, and certainly the rediscovery of one of the most ravishing, opulently orchestrated and complex scores of the period. *Das Wunder der Heliane* was the fourth of Korngold's five magnificent contributions to the genre, and was considered by the composer to be his finest achievement. The plot, based on the play *Die Heilige* by Hans Kaltneker, concerns the strange mystical — non-physical — union between Heliane (wife of the tyrant Ruler) and a character known only as The Stranger who has been imprisoned and condemned to death by Ruler. When their love is discovered, Heliane and The Stranger are put on trial, during which Heliane sings the memorable aria "Ich ging zu ihm" ("I went to him who is to die tomorrow") in her own defence. After an ecstatic duet The Stranger stabs himself. Heliane proves her innocence by miraculously bringing him back to life, but she is stabbed to death by her husband in a fit of jealousy. Heliane is brought to life by The Stranger, and after a tender duet the lovers finally depart this life into the realm of Eternal Love. The opera was premièred in 1927, but despite enjoying a certain success with its audiences it failed to establish itself in the repertoire and disappeared completely after 1930. Reasons for its neglect are numerous and complex (it was labelled 'degenerate' by the Nazis and banned, and it also became embroiled in a musical and artistic battle with Krenek's opera *Jonny spielt auf* which was premièred in the same year) and these are discussed in depth in the excellent booklet-notes. The orchestral writing is lush and harmonically complex (almost bitonal in places) and plays throughout the opera like a vast symphonic poem, and indeed the enormous orchestral and vocal forces required for performance may well have been a contributing factor in its demise. *Das Wunder der Heliane*, however, could not have wished for a more persuasive and triumphant reappraisal than this recording. Anna Tomowa-Sintow is a moving, compassionate Heliane, John David de Haan an ardent and suitably mysterious Stranger, and Hartmut Welker a strong and menacing Ruler. John Mauceri conducts the RSO Berlin with passion, commitment and bravura, and the recording, made in Jesus-Christus-Kirche, Dahlem is excellent. *Heliane* may turn out to be one of the most important and significant opera recordings this decade.

Further listening ...

String Sextet in D major, Op. 10. *Coupled with* **Schoenberg.** Verklärte Nacht. **Raphael Ensemble.** Hyperion CDA66425 (1/91).

The Adventures of Robin Hood — *film score.* **Utah Symphony Orchestra/Varujan Kojian.** That's Entertainment CDTER1066 (3/87).

Cello Concerto in C major, Op. 37[a]. *Film scores:* The Private Lives of Elizabeth and Essex — Overture; The Prince and the Pauper — Suite; Anthony Adverse — In the forest; The Sea Wolf — Suite; Deception. Another Dawn — Night scene; Of Human Bondage — Suite. [a]**Francisco Gabarro** (vc); **National Philharmonic Orchestra/Charles Gerhardt.** RCA Victor GD80185 (11/91).

Tomorrow, Op. 33 — Tone Poem[a]. *Film scores:* The Adventures of Robin Hood — Prologue; Duel, Victory and Epilogue. Anthony Adverse — No father, no mother, no name. Between Two Worlds — Main Title; Mother and Son. Captain Blood — Overture. Deception — Overture. Devotion — Death of Emily Brontë. Escape me never — Main Title; Venice; March; Love Scene; Finale. Juarez — Carlotta. Kings Row — Main Title. Of Human Bondage — Nora. The Sea Hawk[b] — Main Title; Reunion; End Title. [a]**Norma Procter** (contr); [ab]**Ambrosian Singers; National Philharmonic Orchestra/Charles Gerhardt.** RCA GD60863.

KING'S ROW — excerpts. **National Philharmonic Orchestra/Charles Gerhardt.** That's Entertainment VCD47203.

DIE TOTE STADT. **Soloists; Tolz Boys' Choir; Bavarian Radio Chorus; Munich Radio Orchestra/Erich Leinsdorf.** RCA Opera Series GD87767 (11/89).

VIOLANTA. **Soloists; Bavarian Radio Chorus; Munich Radio Orchestra/Marek Janowski.** CBS CD79229 (9/89).

Leopold Koželuch

Bohemian/Austrian 1747-1818

Suggested listening ...

Clarinet Concerto in E flat major. *Coupled with* **Crusell.** Clarinet Concerto No. 1 in E flat major, Op. 1. **Krommer.** Clarinet Concerto in E flat major, Op. 36. **Emma Johnson** (cl); **Royal Philharmonic Orchestra/Günther Herbig.** ASV CDDCA763 (9/91). *See review under Crusell; refer to the Index to Reviews.*

Anton Kraft

Bohemian 1749-1820

Suggested listening ...

Cello Concerto in C major, Op. 4. *Coupled with* **Haydn.** Cello Concertos — C major, HobVIIb/1; D major, HobVIIb/2. **Anner Bylsma** (bar vc); **Tafelmusik/Jeanne Lamon.** Deutsche Harmonia Mundi RD77757 (9/91). *See review under Haydn; refer to the Index to Reviews.*

Timpani Concerto[a]. Piano Concerto[b]. Veils and Variations[c]. Evening Voluntaries[d]. [cd]**Jeff von der Schmidt** (hn); [b]**Mona Golabek** (pf); [a]**Thomas Akins** (timp); [ab]**Alabama Symphony Orchestra/Paul Polivnick;** [c]**Berkeley Symphony Orchestra/Kent Nagano.** Harmonia Mundi HMU90 7106 (2/94).

Hans Krása

Czechoslovakian 1899-1944

Suggested listening …

String Quartet. *Coupled with* **Haas.** String Quartets — No. 2, "From the Monkey Mountain", Op. 7; No. 3, Op. 15. **Hawthorne Quartet.** Decca 440 853-2DH (3/94). *See review under Haas; refer to the Index to Reviews.*

BRUNDIBAR[a]. *Coupled with* **Domazlicky.** Eight Czech Songs, Op. 17[b]. [a]**Soloists;** [b]**Disman Radio Children's Choir and Orchestra/Joža Karas.** Channel Classics CCS5193 (8/93).

Joseph Martin Kraus

Swedish 1756-1792

New review
Kraus. SYMPHONIES. **Concerto Cologne.** Capriccio 10 430. Recorded in 1992.
Sinfonia con fugato per la chiesa. Symphony in C major. Symphonie funèbre in C minor.
Sinfonia in C sharp minor.

 Ih Ilm DDD 9/93

The first volume of Concerto Cologne's Kraus symphony survey contains four works, one of which is a fine Symphony in C minor. This disc contains four more symphonies including Kraus's first version of the aforementioned C minor piece, now in C sharp minor with two horns rather than the four of the revised version, with flutes rather than oboes, one viola strand as opposed to two, and a pair of minuets omitted from the three movement revision. The remainder of this volume consists of a Symphony in D major written in 1789 for the opening of parliament in Stockholm Cathedral, a C major Symphony and, finest of all, the C minor *Symphonie funèbre.* This last-mentioned piece was composed for the funeral of Gustavus III who had been assassinated at a masked ball in March 1792 (the event provided the plot for Verdi's opera). Concerto Cologne is on sparkling form — accomplished orchestral playing with unfailingly secure and warm-sounding woodwind texture.

Johann Krebs

German 1713-1780

Suggested listening …

Fantasia à giusto Italiano. Fantasia sopra Wer nur den lieben Gott lässt walten. Fugue in B flat major on B-A-C-H. Herr Gott disch loben alle wir. Herzlich lieb hab ich dich, o Herr. Preludes and Fugues — C major; D major. Trios — D minor; E flat major. Wir glauben all an einen Gott. Zeuch ein zu deinen Toren. **Graham Barber** (org). ASV Gaudeamus CDGAU125 (10/91).

Fritz Kreisler

Austrian 1875-1962

Suggested listening …

Schön Rosmarin. Liebeslied. Liebesfreud. *Coupled with* **Tchaikovsky.** Méditation, Op. 42 No. 1. Valse-Scherzo, Op. 34. Mélodie, Op. 42 No. 3. **Dvořák.** Violin Sonata in G major, B183.

Schubert. Violin Sonatina in G major, B183. **Vera Vaidman** (vn); **Emanuel Krasovsky** (pf). Pickwick CDI PWK1137 (6/90). *See review in the Collections section; refer to the Index to Reviews.*

Liebesfreud[a]. *Coupled with* **Mendelssohn:** Violin Concerto in E minor, Op. 64[b]. **Bruch:** Violin Concerto No. 1 in G minor, Op. 26[c]. **Sarasate:** Introduction et Tarantelle, Op. 43. **Cho-Liang Lin** (vn); [a]**Sandra Rivers** (pf); [b]**Philharmonia Orchestra/Michael Tilson Thomas;** [c]**Chicago Symphony Orchestra/Leonard Slatkin.** CBS Masterworks CD44902 (3/91).

Original Compositions and Arrangements — works by **Kreisler** and arrangements of works by *Bach, Brandl, Dvořák, Falla, Glazunov, Heuberger, Poldini, Rimsky-Korsakov, Schubert, Scott Tchaikovsky* and *Weber.* **Fritz Kreisler** (vn) with various artists. EMI Références mono CDH7 64701-2 (12/93).

Key to symbols

Price	Quantity/ availability	Timing	Recording mode	Review date
	② ②	1h 23m	DDD	6/88

Ernst Krenek

Austrian/American 1900-1991

New review
Krenek. Piano Sonatas — No. 2, Op. 59; No. 3, Op. 92 No. 4.
Berg. Piano Sonata, Op. 1.
Webern. Variations, Op. 27. **Marcelo Bratke** (pf). Olympia OCD431. Recorded in 1993.

57m DDD 4/94

Ernst Krenek's ambivalence towards the Second Viennese School can be clearly heard in the two piano sonatas recorded here. Before No. 2, which dates from 1928, he had been critical of the 12-note method, thereby alienating himself from Schoenberg and his disciples. And this sonata is an intriguing blend of a very unGermanic eclecticism (taking in influences from Debussy, Tchaikovskian romanticism, Les Six and jazz) and Schoenbergian strictness. The Third Sonata, by contrast, is more unified along Hindemithian lines, with flights of contrapuntal and textural fantasy which makes one think that the piece must have been somewhere at the back of Tippett's mind when he was composing *his* Third Sonata. The 33-year-old Brazilian Marcelo Bratke gives exemplary performances of both works, finding plentiful light and shade beneath their austere surfaces. His Berg Sonata and Webern Variations are also beautifully thought out. Berg's densely-woven counterpoint is sensitively clarified; the opening may be unduly languid and the pacing as a whole may be rather too uniform, but not even Barry Douglas's rather more suave approach is more illuminating of Berg's overwrought expressive world. Bratke's Webern could perhaps be freer and he does not quite cross all the t's and dot the i's in the fast second variation; here it is Douglas who comes closer to the heart of the matter. But Bratke's remains a distinguished account, and the Krenek coupling should attract collectors who already have finer accounts of the Liszt Sonata than Douglas's. Bratke is well recorded. The disc comes complete with a sleeve-note written in fluent pseudish, an endangered language comparatively rarely sighted since its heyday in the 1950s and 1960s when it bred in the sheltered climes of mid-European summer festivals.

Additional recommendation ...
Berg. *Piano Sonata.* **Webern.** *Variations.* **Liszt.** *Piano Sonata in B minor, S178. Nuages gris, S199. R.W. — Venezia, S201. Schlaflos, Frage und Antwort, S203. Elegie No. 2, S197.* **Barry Douglas** (pf). RCA Victor Red Seal 09026 61221-2 *(reviewed under Berg; refer to the Index to Reviews)* — 1h 1m DDD 12/92

Krenek. JONNY SPIELT AUF. **Krister St Hill** (bar) Jonny; **Heinz Kruse** (ten) Max; **Alessandra Marc** (sop) Anita; **Michael Kraus** (bar) Daniello; **Martina Posselt** (sop) Yvonne; **Dieter Scholz** (bass) Manager; **Diter Schwartner** (ten) Hotel Manager; **Martin Petzold** (sngr) Station Announcer, First Policeman; **Matthias Weichert** (sngr) Second Policeman; **Erwin Noack** (sngr) Third Policeman; **Leipzig Opera Chorus; Chinchilla; Leipzig Gewandhaus Orchestra/Lothar Zagrosek.** Decca 436 631-2DH2. Notes, text and translation included. Recorded in 1991.

② 2h 11m DDD 4/93

This is the 'jazz opera' that made Krenek's name and fortune, playing to enthusiastic audiences in every opera house in Germany until the rise of Nazism branded it "degenerate music" and cast it into half a century of oblivion. With the appeal of the jazz element in the music went a staging full of sensational effects (a motor-car on stage; a scene in which all the theatre's fire alarms are set off; in another, set halfway up a mountain, music is relayed from the public address system of a hotel in the valley below) and a sort of 'double plot' intended to blow a blast of fresh air from the New World through the stuffy culture of the Old. In one plot Jonny, a black jazz fiddler, steals a valuable violin from a famous virtuoso and ultimately uses it to send the whole cast dancing off to America and freedom. In the other, Max, a composer so obsessed with the icy perfection of his art that he cannot come to terms with the real world (Krenek's own self-portrait?) finds love and the power to control his own destiny. Apart from the excellent cast (Marc, in gorgeous voice as Max's 'muse' Anita, and St Hill as a genially amoral Jonny are especially good) the great quality of this performance is that the subtle and often beautiful lines of Max's music and his duet scenes with Anita are projected with as much flair as the more obviously stage-stealing moments. Jonny's 'theme-song' (a sort of blues), the catchy tango duet and the uproarious final scene, the cheerful incursion into the orchestra of flexatone and swanee whistle — all these are hugely enjoyable, but in the opera's 'other' world a real composer, Krenek himself as much as Max, is finding his own voice, one that's bound to make you wonder why we've heard so little of his 12 subsequent operas.

Conradin Kreutzer

German 1780-1849

New review

Kreutzer. DAS NACHTLAGER IN GRANADA. **Hermann Prey** (bar) Huntsman; **Regina Klepper** (sop) Gabriele; **Michael Pabst** (ten) Gomez; **Wolf Matthias Friedrich** (bar) Vasco; **Cornelius Hauptmann** (bass) Pedro; **Martin Blasius** (bass) Ambrosio; **Cologne Radio Chorus and Symphony Orchestra/Helmuth Froschauer.** Capriccio 60 029. Notes, text and translation included. Recorded in 1992.

② 1h 39m DDD 1/94 ❓

Conradin Kreutzer's most famous opera used to turn up in pre-war German repertories (it has even been recorded), and contemporary journals suggest the hold it had on the German and even the wider European public from its première in 1834. The plot, after a play by Weber's *Freischütz* librettist Friedrich Kind, is set in sixteenth-century Granada. A huntsman strays into a valley, where he is promptly smitten by the charms of Gabriele. She gently rejects him, for she is in love with Gomez and is also being pursued by Vasco. The huntsman is found the night's shelter which provides the work's title, where his dreams of Gabriele's charms are interrupted first by her arrival to warn him of treachery and then by the jealous Vasco and some shepherds, intent on murder. He foils them, and when a retinue of other huntsmen arrives, he is revealed as the benevolent Prince Regent who can, not without ruefulness, bless the lovers' union. Kreutzer sets this naïve story to music that draws on recitative and some more continuous arioso to link the arias and ensembles. Essentially, though, it is a 'number' opera, with at its best a good sense of cumulative drama. The example of Weber was not lost on Kreutzer. Hermann Prey is the lynchpin of the performance, authoritative but also touching as he lies awake in the ruins of the old Moorish castle that dominates the valley, reflecting on the beauty of the night and of Gabriele. The orchestra plays admirably for Helmut Froschauer, who judges extremely well the pace, weight and colour of an interesting score.

Franz Krommer

Bohemian 1759-1831

New review
Krommer. Symphonies — No. 2 in D major, Op. 40; No. 4 in C minor, Op. 102. **London Mozart Players/Matthias Bamert.** Chandos CHAN9275. Recorded in 1993.

58m DDD 7/94

Franz Krommer is František Kramář, one of the most gifted of the Bohemians who made a career in Vienna in the latter years of the eighteenth century. These two symphonies reflect that world, one glorified by the genius of Mozart but also dignified by the music of many lesser composers. They are fine works, carrying with them something of the Haydn of the *Sturm und Drang* symphonies, something of Mozart's romantic anticipations, even a touch of Beethoven's energy. The Second Symphony opens on a magnificent slow introduction that comes very close to being justified by the powerful succeeding *Allegro vivace*. There is a graceful *Adagio* and a scherzoid Minuet that includes a Viennese waltz trio of the utmost charm. The C minor No. 4 is a rather more sombre work, more ambitious and indeed perhaps a touch too much so for its complete success. Nevertheless, these are well-made, inventive and impressive symphonies which should give a lot of pleasure. The performances take the works very seriously, making out the best case for them as works too substantial to deserve neglect because of the composer's comparatively modest reputation. The playing is excellent, the recording full and well-balanced.

Further listening ...

Clarinet Concerto in E flat major, Op. 36. *Coupled with* **Crusell.** Clarinet Concerto No. 1 in E flat major, Op. 1. **Koželuch.** Clarinet Concerto in E flat major. **Emma Johnson** (cl); **Royal Philharmonic Orchestra/Günther Herbig.** ASV CDDCA763 (9/91). *See review under Crusell; refer to the Index to Reviews.*

Nikolaus von Krufft

Austrian 1779-1818

Suggested listening ...

Sonata for Horn and Piano in F major. *Coupled with* **Brahms.** Horn Trio in E flat major, Op. 40[a]. **Beethoven.** Sonata for Horn and Piano in F major, Op. 17. **Lowell Greer** (hn); [a]**Stephanie Chase** (vn); **Steven Lubin** (pf). Harmonia Mundi HMU90 7037 (9/92).

Daniel Kuhlau

German/Danish 1786-1832

Suggested listening ...

The elf's hill — Suite[a]. *Overtures* — Lulu; The triplet brothers from Damascus; The robber's castle; William Shakespeare. **Odense Symphony Orchestra/[a]Othmar Maga, Eduard Serov.** Unicorn-Kanchana DKPCD9132 (5/93).

György Kurtág

Romanian 1926-

New review
Kurtág. Messages of the late Miss R. V. Troussova, Op. 17[a]. ... Quasi una Fantasia ..., Op. 27[b]. Scenes from a Novel, Op. 19[c]. [a]**Rosemary Hardy**, [c]**Christine Whittlesey** (sops); [c]**Mathias Tacke** (vn); [c]**Thomas Fichter** (db); [c]**Márta Fábián** (cimbalom); [b]**Hermann**

Kretzschmar (pf); [ab]**Ensemble Modern/Peter Eötvös.** Sony Classical SK53290. Texts and translations included. Recorded 1990-92.

•♪• 55m DDD 12/93 ⊘

At last — an all-Kurtág CD that celebrates the full substance and power of his music. The *Troussova* cycle, still Kurtág's most familiar score, is well performed by a vibrant Rosemary Hardy, with Peter Eötvös and his players bringing out the score's varied colours and imaginative instrumental effects. Kurtág is at his most expressionistic and also his most lyrical here. The later *Scenes from a Novel* has a comparable obsessiveness in its exploration of feminine frustration and resignation but, with only violin, double bass and cimbalom supporting the voice, the emotional range is more restricted, the music often more personal, yet also more explicitly allusive, not least to Kurtág's Bartókian heritage. The performance grips from start to finish. … *Quasi una Fantasia* … (1987-8) is the most recent work included. Its four short movements for piano and assorted instruments, including prominent mouth organs and an extraordinary timpani part, turn its (apparently accidental) Beethovenian connection into a remarkable exploration of extremes. Caliban and Prospero are mentioned in the insert-notes, but no extra-musical props are needed to mediate the impact of this absorbing score, which can veer from simple, sustained scale figures to extreme fragmentation without loss of coherence. The recordings are appropriately vivid.

Further listening …

String Quartet No. 1, Op. 1. Hommage à Milhály András, Op. 13. Officium breve in memoriam Andreae Szervánszky, Op. 28. *Coupled with* **Gubaidulina.** String Quartet No. 2. **Lutoslawski.** String Quartet. **Arditti Quartet** . Disques Montaigne 789007 (4/92). *See review under Gubaidulina; refer to the Index to Reviews.*

Key to symbols

**Gramophone
Awards winners**

**Gramophone
Editor's choice**

Pierre de La Rue

Flanders c.1460-1518

Suggested listening …

Missa "L'homme armé". Missa pro defunctis. **Ensemble Clément Janequin** with **Yvon Repérant** (org). Harmonia Mundi HMC90 1296 (9/89).

Missa pro defunctis. *Coupled with* ***Josquin Desprez.*** Missa Hercules dux Ferrarie. La déploration de Johannes Ockeghem, "Nymphes des bois". **New London Chamber Choir/ James Wood.** Amon Ra CDSAR24 (3/87).

Edouard Lalo

French 1823-1892

New review
Lalo. Cello Concerto in D minor.
Massenet. Fantaisie.

Saint-Saëns. Cello Concerto No. 1 in A minor, Op. 33. **Sophie Rolland** (vc); **BBC Philharmonic Orchestra/Gilbert Varga.** ASV CDDCA867. Recorded 1992-93.

· •˙ **1h 5m DDD 12/93** 𝄽ₚ 𝄽ₛ

Sophie Rolland's performance of the Lalo Concerto is surely as fine as any recorded. It opens with great character, thanks to Gilbert Varga's strong accompaniment, and the solo playing is wonderfully songful. But Rolland is heard at her very finest as she plays her introduction to the finale with commanding improvisatory spontaneity. The orchestra bursts in splendidly and she shows her technical mettle with some lovely bouncing bowing in the attractive closing Rondo. The Saint-Saëns Concerto brings similar felicities. Massenet's *Fantaisie* opens dramatically and is rhythmically vital, flowing onwards boldly to produce a winningly sentimental yearning melody which the soloist clearly relishes. A cadenza then leads to a charming, very French Gavotte (which has a flavour of *Manon*) and the piece ends jubilantly. It really is a find, and it could hardly be presented more persuasively. The balance is as near perfect as one could wish, the orchestral sound detailed, yet attractively full and resonant, and the cello placed in excellent perspective.

Additional recommendations ...
Cello Concerto. **Bruch.** *Kol Nidrei, Op. 47.* **Saint-Saëns.** *Cello Concerto.* **Matt Haimovitz** (vc); **Chicago Symphony Orchestra/James Levine.** DG 427 323-2GH — · •˙ 59m DDD 6/89
Cello Concerto. **Saint-Saëns.** *Cello Concerto[b].* **Schumann.** *Cello Concerto No. 1 in A minor, Op. 129[a].* **János Starker** (vc); **London Symphony Orchestra/[a]Stanislaw Skrowaczewski, [b]Antál Dorati.** Mercury 432 010-2MM — · •˙ 1h 5m ADD 4/92 𝄽ₚ

New review
Lalo. Symphonie espagnole, Op. 21.
Dvořák. Violin Concerto in A minor, B108. **Christian Tetzlaff** (vn); **Czech Philharmonic Orchestra/Libor Pešek.** Virgin Classics VC5 45022-2.

· •˙ **1h 3m DDD 7/94** 𝄽ₚ

This is a unique and generous coupling and if Virgin Classics' decision to record Tetzlaff in Prague was dictated by the obvious advantage in having Dvořák's compatriots accompanying in his Violin Concerto, the Czech Philharmonic's playing under Pešek proves just as idiomatic in the Spanish dance rhythms of Lalo as in Czech dances, with crisp ensemble and rhythm deliciously sprung. What is especially remarkable about Tetzlaff's performances of the *Symphonie espagnole* as well as the Violin Concerto, is the quicksilver lightness of the passagework, which brings out the element of fantasy; in that he is helped by a recording balance which does not spotlight the soloist as sharply as in most other versions. In both works, each more episodic than most and hard to hold together, Tetzlaff's concentration makes for a sense of spontaneity, leading one on just as magnetically as, for example, Perlman in his more obviously weighty, more vibrato-laden readings of both pieces. Tetzlaff's sense of fantasy consistently marks him out, so that with delectable pointing of rhythm and phrase he makes the Lalo more subtly winning than it often is, less of a mere barnstorming showpiece, helped by the extra transparency of textures.

Additional recommendations ...
Symphonie espagnole. **Saint-Saëns.** *Introduction and Rondo capriccioso, Op. 28.* **Vieuxtemps.** *Violin Concerto No. 5 in A minor, Op. 37.* **Shlomo Mintz** (vn); **Israel Philharmonic Orchestra/Zubin Mehta.** DG 427 676-2GH — · •˙ 1h DDD 3/92 Ⓑ
Symphonie espagnole. **Bruch.** *Scottish Fantasy, Op. 46.* **Anne Akiko Meyers** (vn); **Royal Philharmonic Orchestra/Jesús López-Cobos.** RCA Victor Red Seal RD60942 — · •˙ 1h DDD 9/92
Symphonie espagnole[a]. **Ravel.** *Tzigane[a].* **Sibelius.** *Violin Concerto in D minor, Op. 47[b].* **Itzhak Perlman** (vn); **[a]London Symphony Orchestra/André Previn, [b]Boston Symphony Orchestra/Erich Leinsdorf.** RCA Gold Seal Masters Collection 07863 56520-2 — · •˙ 1h 12m ADD 7/93 Ⓑ
Symphonie espagnole[a]. *Cello Concerto[b].* **Saint-Saëns.** *Violin Concerto No. 1[a].* **[a]Kyung-Wha Chung** (vn); **[b]Lynn Harrell** (vc); **[a]Montreal Symphony Orchestra/Charles Dutoit; [b]Berlin Radio Symphony Orchestra/Riccardo Chailly.** Decca 436 483-2DM — · •˙ 1h 14m DDD 2/94 𝄽ₚ Ⓑ

Further listening ...

Symphony in G minor. *Coupled with* **Franck.** Symphony in D minor. **French Radio National Orchestra/Sir Thomas Beecham.** EMI CDM7 63396-2 (9/92).

Constant Lambert

British 1905-1951

Suggested listening ...

Rio Grande[a]. Summer's Last Will and Testament[b]. Aubade héroïque. [a]**Sally Burgess** (mez); [b]**William Shimell** (bar); [a]**Jack Gibbons** (pf); [a]**Opera North Chorus;** [b]**Leeds Festival Chorus; English Northern Philharmonia/ David Lloyd-Jones.** Hyperion CDA66565 (6/92).

John Lampe

British c.1703-1751

Suggested listening ...

Britannia — Welcome Mars[a]. Dione — Pretty warblers[a]. *Coupled with* **Arne.** Comus — By the rushy-fringed bank; Brightest Lady; Thrice upon thy Finger's Tip[a]. Rosamond — Rise, Glory, rise[a]. The Tempest — Ariel's song[a]. **Handel.** Ariodante — Neghittosi or voi che fate?[a]. Alcina — Credete al mio dolore; Tornami a vagheggiar[a]. Alexander's Feast — War, he sung, is toil and trouble[a]. L'Allegro, il penseroso ed il moderato — Sweet bird[a]. Saul — Capricious man[a]. Overture, Allessandro Severo, HWVAnh13. Hornpipe in D major, HWV356. March in D major, HWV345. [a]**Emma Kirkby** (sop); **Academy of Ancient Music/Christopher Hogwood.** L'Oiseau-Lyre 436 132-2OH (7/93). *See review under Arne; refer to the Index to Reviews.*

John Lanchbery

British 1923-

Suggested listening ...

The Tales of Beatrix Potter — *film score.* **Royal Opera House Orchestra, Covent Garden/ John Lanchbery.** EMI CDC7 54537-2.

Burton Lane

American 1912-

Suggested listening ...

The Burton Lane Songbook. **Michael Feinstein** (bar); **Burton Lane** (pf). Elektra Nonesuch. 7559-79285-2 (6/94).

Craig Sellar Lang

British 1891-1971

Suggested listening ...

Tuba tune. *Coupled with* **Whitlock.** Hymn Preludes — Darwall's 148th; Song 13. **Howells.** Three Psalm-Preludes (Set 1), Op. 32. **Elgar.** Organ Sonata No. 1 in G major, Op. 28.

Vaughan Williams. Three Preludes on Welsh Hymn Tunes — Rhosymedre. *Cocker.* Tuba tune. **Gareth Green** (org). Naxos 8 550582 (3/93). *See review in the Collections section; refer to the Index to Reviews.*

Rued Langgaard

Danish 1893-1952

Langgaard. Symphonies — No. 4, "Fall of the Leaf"; No. 5, "Steppelands"; No. 6, "Heavens Asunder". **Danish National Radio Symphony Orchestra/Neeme Järvi.** Chandos CHAN9064. Recorded in 1991.

 1h 3m   DDD   12/92

This reclusive Dane (pronounced Ruth Langor, should you want to rave about him to your friends) was either a visionary mystic or wildly nutty, depending on your point of view. Unfortunately for Langgaard, the Danes had already embraced Carl Nielsen as their country's answer to Sibelius; and in any case these three Langgaard symphonies seldom display the much valued Scandinavian symphonic virtues of coherence and far-sighted evolution. Indeed Robert Layton, in his original *Gramophone* review, referred to the effect of the Fifth and Sixth as "overwhelmingly episodic". But what astonishing episodes! The Fourth Symphony's "Leaf-fall" is a Danish, foreshortened but distinctly apocalyptic, *Alpine Symphony* with quite as much Wagner along the way as Richard Strauss (it opens with exactly the same brass chord as *Götterdämmerung*); it is thrilling nature music, with moments of wild, flying energy contrasted with episodes of almost Delian contemplation and atmosphere. The Fifth is more ordered and shows that, for all Langgaard's jealousy of Nielsen, in his Rondo theme for the work, he was quite content to powerfully imitate him. And the Sixth's cosmic conflicts recall Bruckner and Charles Ives. That's enough influences to be going on with; you can enjoy spotting many more for yourself. None of them detract from these communications of an extraordinary imagination. As to the performances, suffice it to say that the Danish orchestra sound entirely at home, and Järvi has never been more in his element. And Chandos, even by their own standards, have never produced more spectacular sound.

Orlando Lassus

Franco/Flemish 1532-1594

New review

Lassus. Missa Bell'Amfitrit' altera[abcd].
Erbach. CHORAL AND INSTRUMENTAL WORKS.
Hassler. CHORAL AND INSTRUMENTAL WORKS. [a]**Westminster Cathedral Choir;** [b]**His Majesties Sagbutts and Cornetts/James O'Donnell** with [c]**Timothy Roberts,** [d]**Iain Simcock,** [e]**Iris Schöllhorn** (orgs). Hyperion CDA66688. Texts and translations included. Recorded in 1993.
Erbach. Sacerdotes Dei[acd]. Canzona secundi toni[c]. Hic est sacerdos[acd]. Fantasia sub Elevatione[c]. Toccata octavi toni[d]. Posuisti Domine[acd]. La Paglia[bc]. *Hassler.* Canzon duodecimi toni[bcd]. Cantate Domino canticum novum[abcde]. Toccata in G[d]. Canzon noni toni[bcd]. O sacrum convivium[acd]. Domine Dominus noster[abcde].

 1h 3m   DDD   6/94

In this elegant and imaginative contribution to the four hundredth anniversary of the death of Lassus, the music of the "divine Orlando" (as the French poet Ronsard called him) is heard alongside works by his younger contemporaries. The chosen setting is not the Bavarian ducal chapel at Munich, but Augsburg Cathedral round the turn of the sixteenth century. Both the Protestant Hans Leo Hassler and the Catholic Christian Erbach worked in that city and are audibly indebted to the Venetian school: their choral works, organ toccatas and instrumental canzonas adhere to the patterns set by the Gabrielis. The programme presents the music in its liturgical context: the movements of Lassus's *Bell'Amfitrit'* Mass are interspersed with polychoral and instrumental pieces. In most of the vocal works (including the Mass) the choir are doubled by a wind band and no fewer than three organs. Everything is stylishly done: the wind-band pieces are especially gorgeous and balance the movements of the Mass very nicely indeed. Voices and instruments blend very satisfyingly in the acoustic of Westminster Cathedral, and the discreet ornamentation from the wind band further enhances the sense of occasion.

Additional recommendation ...

Missa Bell'Amfitrit altera. Tui sunt coeli. **Caldara.** *Crucifixus.* **A. Gabrieli.** *De profundis clamavi.*
Frescobaldi. *Fiori musicali, Op. 12 — Toccata cromatica per l'Elevatione; Toccata per l'Elevationea.*
Cavalli. *Salve Regina.* **Monteverdi.** *Domine, ne in furore.* **G. Gabrieli.** *Hodie completi sunt.*
The Sixteen/Harry Christophers with [a]**Laurence Cummings** (org). Collins Classics 1360-2 *(see review in the Collections section; refer to the Index to Reviews)* — .•˙˙ 57m DDD 10/93 ℗

Further listening ...

Libro de villanelle, moresche, et altre canzoni — excerpts. Chansons. Chansons (arr. for lute).
Eric Belloq (lte); **Ensemble Clément Janequin.** Harmonia Mundi HMC90 1391 (2/93).

Lamentationes Hieremiae a 5. **La Chapelle Royale European Ensemble/Philippe Herreweghe.** Harmonia Mundi HMC90 1299 (12/89).

Missa Osculetur me. *Motets* — Osculetur me; Hodie completi sunt; Timor et tremor; Alma Redemptoris mater a 8; Salve regina mater a 8; Ave regina caelorum Il a 6; Regina coeli a 7.
The Tallis Scholars/Peter Phillips. Gimell CDGIM018 (7/89).

Missa Qual donna attende à gloriosa fama. Tristis est anima mea. Exaltabo te Domine a 4.
Psalmi Davidis poenitentiales — De profundis. Missa Venatorum. *Coupled with* **de Rore.** Qual donna à gloriosa fama. **Christ Church Cathedral Choir, Oxford/Stephen Darlington.** Nimbus NI5150 (4/89).

Prophetiae Sibyllarum. **Cantus Cölln/Konrad Junghänel.** Deutsche Harmonia Mundi 05472 77304-2 (7/94).

Antonio Lauro
Venezuelan 1917-1986

Suggested listening ...

Suite Venezolana. Carora. El Marabino. Variaciones sobre un Tema Infantil Venezolano. Cuatro Valses Venezolanos. Sonata. Tripitco. Maria Luisa. Angostura. **Jesus Castro Balbi** (gtr).
Etcetera KTC1110 (11/91).

William Lawes
British 1602-1645

New review
W. Lawes. Eight Fantasia-Suites — G minor; G major; A minor; C major; D minor; D major; D minor; D major. **London Baroque** (Ingrid Seifert, Richard Gwilt, vns; Charles Medlam, bass viol; Richard Egarr, hpd). Harmonia Mundi HMC90 1423. Recorded in 1992.

.•˙˙ 1h 13m DDD 6/93

New review
W. Lawes. Eight Fantasia-Suites — G minor; G major; A minor; C major; D minor; D major; D minor; D major. **Purcell Quartet** (Catherine Mackintosh, Catherine Weiss, vns;

Richard Boothby, bass viol; Robert Woolley, org). Chandos Chaconne CHAN0552. Recorded in 1992.

♩ 1h 7m   DDD   5/94

William Lawes was by all evidence as charming and endearing as he was talented, and accordingly much mourned by both his brother Henry and his liege, Charles I, in whose service in battle he died. He was admired as a composer of both vocal and instrumental music, of which the latter is marked for his experiments with form and ensemble texture. Until now, only individual works from his various sets of consort music (in two to six parts) have been recorded. We are now provided with two recordings of the entire set of eight fantasia-suites for two violins, bass viol and organ, which by their scale and the independence of their parts are among his most idiomatic and forward-looking works. This is consort music with a difference. The Purcell Quartet's instruments — later seventeenth-century violins and reproduction viol and organ — cannot strictly be considered period instruments specific to this repertory, though neither are those used by London Baroque. Their choice of pitch is distinctly higher and probably more 'modern' than that used by London Baroque; certainly they produce a brighter sound, with less chiaroscuro, which because of their generally faster tempos is also more virile. To its credit, the music flourishes in both guises. Richard Boothby's bowing articulation, even more than that of Charles Medlam, reflects his familiarity through Fretwork with the subtleties of the English consort repertory. The violin playing of Catherine Mackintosh and Catherine Weiss is polished and spirited. They emphasize the linear quality of the music, bringing Lawes's particular kind of chromaticism and the concluding *rallentandos* (known as 'drags') into sharp relief. However much one may muse about the probable original circumstances of this music, thoughtful performances as different as these by the Purcell Quartet and London Baroque serve to remind us of the power of the interpreter.

Key to symbols

② ②		1h 23m	DDD	6/88
Price	Quantity/ availability	Timing	Recording mode	Review date

Quality of sound		Discs worth exploring	Caveat emptor

♩P	♩S Ⓑ	❓	▲
Quality of performance	Basic library	Period performance	

Ludwig Lebrun
German 1752-1790

Suggested listening ...

Oboe Concerto No. 1 in D minor. *Coupled with* **C.P.E. Bach.** Oboe Concerto in E flat major, H468. ***Mozart.*** Oboe Concerto in C major, K314/285d. **Paul Goodwin** (ob); **The English Concert/Trevor Pinnock.** Archiv Produktion 431 821-2AH (7/91).

Leonhard Lechner
Austrian/German 1553-1606

Suggested listening ...

Si bona suscepimus. *Coupled with* ***Hassler.*** Missa I super Dixit Maria. Ad Dominum cum tribularer. O admirabile commercium. Usquequo, Domine. Domine Deus, Israel. Vater unser in Himmelreich. **Chapelle Royale European Vocal Ensemble/Philippe Herreweghe.** Harmonia Mundi HMC90 1401 (10/93). *See review under Hassler; refer to the Index to Reviews.*

Jean-Marie Leclair

French 1697-1764

New review

Leclair. TRIO SONATAS, Op. 4. **Purcell Quartet** (Catherine Mackintosh, Catherine Weiss, vns; Richard Boothby, va da gamba; Robert Woolley, hpd). Chandos Chaconne CHAN0536. Recorded in 1992.
No. 1 in D minor; No. 2 in B flat major; No. 3 in D minor; No. 4 in F major; No. 5 in G minor; No. 6 in A major.

lh 16m DDD 7/93

Hats off to the Purcell Quartet for introducing to us the Op. 4 Trio Sonatas (1731-3) of Jean-Marie Leclair *l'aîné*. These must be the finest French examples of their genre after Couperin's *Les Nations* (published in 1726) and represent not only another step in the integration of the Italian style into French music (called by Couperin "les goûts-réunis") but a bridge between baroque and classical musical textures. They are composed with panache and aplomb, exhibiting a rich imagination, vitality and wit. Each sonata is differently weighted with regard to old and new styles, and French and Italian elements. The Purcell Quartet bring off all of these stylistic elements with their usual spiritedness and precision. These are trio sonatas that will delight lovers of eighteenth-century chamber music, especially when so tastefully performed as here.

New review

Leclair. Violin Sonatas — A minor, Op. 5 No. 7; A major, Op. 9 No. 4. **Simon Standage** (vn); [a]**Lars Ulrik Mortensen** (hpd). Chandos Chaconne CHAN0531. Recorded in 1992.
Harpsichord solos — [a]***Duphly:*** La de Redemond. La du Buq. ***J-B. Forqueray:*** La Morangis ou La Plissay.***Mondonville:*** Violin Sonata in G major, Op. 3 No. 5. ***Guillemain:*** Violin Sonata in A major, Op. 1 No. 4.

lh 8m DDD 6/93

From the beginning of the eighteenth century and during the minority of Louis XV, there was a great flowering of chamber music and, in particular, violin sonatas and harpsichord suites. These are not, however, works for amateurs. They are fiendishly demanding and all the more exciting for being so. Simon Standage has never been diffident, but as he matures he plays more beautifully. The sonatas of Leclair and Guillemain admirably suit Standage. The Leclair sonatas are packed with wonderful arching phrases, intricately wrought ornamentation and unexpected chromatic twists. They are essentially happy works. Lars Ulrik Mortensen's performance is no less impressive, weaving exquisite textures beneath and, as in the Mondonville sonata, around the violin part, subtly picking up on all the composers' nuances and tricks, all the while offering just the right support to the violin. As a soloist, Mortensen delivers equally fascinating performances by developing a rich palette of instrumental colour on the Blanchet copy made by David Rubio.

Further listening ...

Flute Sonatas: ACC58435D — Op. 1: No. 2 in C major. Op. 2: No. 1 in E minor; No. 3 in C major; No. 5 in G major. *ACC58436D* — Op. 1: No. 6 in E minor. Op. 2: No. 8 in D minor; No. 11 in B minor. Op. 9: No. 2 in E minor; No. 7 in G major. **Barthold Kuijken** (fl); **Wieland Kuijken** (va da gamba); **Robert Kohnen** (hpd). Accent ACC58435/6D (2/86).

Ouvertures et Sonates en trio, Op. 13. **Les Talens Lyriques/Christophe Rousset** (hpd). FNAC Music 592100 (9/93).

Trio Sonatas — No. 1 in E minor, Op. 2; No. 7 in G major, Op. 9. *Coupled with* **Blavet.** Trio Sonata No. 2 in D minor, "La Vibray", Op. 2. **Rameau.** Pièces de clavecin en concerts — Cinquième concert. **M. La Barre.** Sonate l'inconnuë in G major, Book 2 No. 9. **Hotteterre.** Airs et Brunettes. **Rachel Brown** (fl); **Mark Caudle** (viol); **James Johnstone** (hpd). Chandos Chaconne CHAN0544 (2/94). *See review in the Collections section; refer to the Index to Reviews.*

SCYLLA ET GLAUCUS. **Soloists; Monteverdi Choir; English Baroque Soloists/John Eliot Gardiner.** Erato 2292-45277-2 (4/88).

Alexandre Charles Lecocq

French 1832-1918

Suggested listening ...

Mam'zelle Angot — Ballet[a]. *Coupled with **Hérold.*** La fille mal gardée — Ballet (arr. Lanchbery)[b]. [a]**National Philharmonic Orchestra/Richard Bonynge;** [b]**Orchestra of the Royal Opera House, Covent Garden/John Lanchbery.** Decca Ovation 430 849-2DM2 (12/91).

Le Jour et la Nuit — *Operetta*[a]. Rose Mousse — *Musical Comedy*[b]. [a]**National Philharmonic Orchestra/Richard Bonynge;** [b]**French Radio Lyric Orchestra/Jean-Claude Hartemann.** Musidic 20136-2 (3/92).

Michel Legrand

French 1932-

Suggested listening ...

MAGIC — THE MUSIC OF MICHEL LEGRAND. *Songs include* His eyes, her eyes; I will say goodbye; magic; The windmills of your eyes; Little boy lost; What are you doing the rest of your life? **Dame Kiri Te Kanawa** (sop); **Ambrosian Singers; London Studio Orchestra/ Michel Legrand.** Teldec 9031-73285-2 (11/92).

Franz Lehár

Austrian/Hungarian 1870-1948

Lehár. DIE LUSTIGE WITWE. **Josef Knapp** (bar) Baron Mirko Zeta; **Hanny Steffek** (sop) Valencienne; **Eberhard Waechter** (bar) Graf Danilo Danilowitsch; **Elisabeth Schwarzkopf** (sop) Hanna Glawari; **Nicolai Gedda** (ten) Camille Rosillon; **Kurt Equiluz** (ten) Vicomte Cascada; **Hans Strohbauer** (ten) Raoul de St Brioche; **Franz Böheim** (buffo) Njegus; **Philharmonia Chorus and Orchestra/Lovro von Matačic.** EMI CDS7 47178-8. Notes, text and translation included. From Columbia SAN101/2 (5/63). Recorded in 1962.

② **1h 20m   AAD   4/86**   **Ⓑ**

The Merry Widow contains some marvellous melodies and although versions have come and gone none have ever managed to oust the classic 1962 recording with Elisabeth Schwarzkopf. She is a merry widow without equal, conveying with her rich and alluring voice the ebullience and glamour of the character as in no other recording. EMI's preference for a baritone (rather than tenor) Danilo in successive recordings has not always been successful, but here Eberhard Waechter encompasses the role without difficulty and gives a rousing portrayal of the playboy embassy *attaché*. As the second couple, Nicolai Gedda is in typically radiant voice, whilst Hanny Steffek makes a charming and vibrant Valencienne. Josef Knapp is a spirited ambassador. If von Matačic's tempos are at times a little on the fast side, this is fully justified by the extra excitement achieved. At the same time there are moments of tenderness, as in the beautifully paced "Vilja" song, which comes off to perfection with Schwarzkopf's beautifully held final note. The contribution of the "Königliche-Pontevedrinische Hof-Tamburrizzakapelle" to provide authentic Balkan atmosphere at Hanna's party is just one of the delightful touches of Walter Legge's production that go to make this a very special recording. The pity is that the score is given less than absolutely complete and that the CD changeover comes in the middle of Act 2. However, the artistry and sheer enjoyment of the recording are unmatched. It is one of those occasions when everything seems to come off perfectly.

Additional recommendations ...

Soloists; BBC Chorus; Philharmonia/Otto Ackermann. EMI mono CDH7 69520-2 — .·'
1h 12m ADD 11/88 ⁹ₚ Ⓑ ▲

Excerpts. **Soloists; Berlin Deutsche Opera Chorus; Berlin Symphony Orchestra/Robert Stolz.** Eurodisc 258 372 — .·' 48m 4/88 ⁹ₚ Ⓑ

Further listening ...

Der Graf von Luxemburg — *Operetta: excerpts.* **Soloists; Günther Arndt Choir; Berlin Symphony Orchestra/Robert Stolz.** Eurodisc 258 358 (4/88).

Die Zarewitsch — *Operetta: excerpts.* **Berlin Deutsche Opera Chorus; Berlin Symphony Orchestra/Robert Stolz.** Eurodisc 258 357 (4/88).

Paganini — *Operetta: excerpts.* **Soloists; Günther Arndt Choir; Berlin Symphony Orchestra/Robert Stolz.** Eurodisc 258 359 (4/88).

Der Land des Lächelns — *Operetta.* **Soloists; Günther Arndt Choir; Berlin Symphony Orchestra/Robert Stolz.** Eurodisc 258 373 (4/88).

GIUDITTA — *Opera: excerpts.* **Soloists; Günther Arndt Choir; Berlin Symphony Orchestra/Werner Schmidt-Boelcke.** Eurodisc 258 374 (4/88).

Key to symbols

Price	Quantity/ availability	Timing	Recording mode	Review date
.·'	② ②	1h 23m	DDD	6/88

Kenneth Leighton

British 1929-1988

Leighton. CATHEDRAL MUSIC. [a]**Neil Mackie** (ten); **St Paul's Cathedral Choir/John Scott** with **Andrew Lucas** (org). Hyperion CDA66489. Texts included. Recorded in 1991.
Te Deum laudamus. Missa brevis, Op. 5. Crucifixus pro nobis, Op. 38[a·] Second Service, Op. 62. An Evening Hymn. Let all the world in every corner sing. *Traditional* (arr. Leighton): Lully, lulla (Coventry carol).

.·' 1h 14m DDD 12/92

Though church music — the sound of choir and organ, the 'feel' of church as a place for music-making — was part of the air Kenneth Leighton breathed, he was no narrow product or insular exponent of the system. His technical facility as a composer was phenomenal, but 'facile' is one of the last words that could be used of his compositions. They have nothing of the standardized modernism of innocuous discords and brightly quirky rhythms; rather, his work often has a certain bleakness. His structures, like his ideas, are strong, yet quite frequently one feels that "Naught for your comfort" could be the motto. The cantata *Crucifixus pro nobis* is the major work here, to words by the early seventeenth-century poet Patrick Carey, with Phineas Fletcher's *Drop, drop, slow tears* for the final movement. The performance is a fine one, with Neil Mackie as the excellent soloist and with subtle playing of the organ part by Andrew Lucas. The St Paul's choristers, who have made several notable recordings under John Scott, cope expertly throughout, especially in the *Missa brevis* written in 1968 for Liverpool Cathedral. They are also sensitive in their care for words, and the somewhat chilly text of Sir Thomas Browne's *Evening Hymn* comes over with a clarity that also does credit to Hyperion's production team.

Additional recommendation ...
Crucifixus pro nobis[a]. Second Service[a]. Give me wings of faith[a]. O sacrum convivium. Solus ad victimam[a]. **Howells:** Chichester Service[a]. A Hymn for St Cecilia[a]. Salve regina. O salutaris hostia. My eyes for beauty pine[a]. Like as the hart[a]. **Queen's College Choir, Oxford/Matthew Owens** with

[a]**David Went** (org). ASV CDDCA851 (*see review in the Collections section; refer to the Index to Reviews*) — .·'· lh 14m DDD 5/93

Further listening ...

Fantasy on an American Hymn Tune, Op. 70[a]. Alleluia Pascha Nostrum, Op. 85[b]. Variations, Op. 30. Piano Sonata, Op. 64. [a]**Janet Hilton** (cl); [ab]**Raphael Wallfisch** (vc); **Peter Wallfisch** (pf). Chandos CHAN9132 (5/93).

Guillaume Lekeu

Belgian 1870-1894

Suggested listening ...

Andromède[a]. Les burgraves — Introduction symphonique. [a]**Dinah Bryant** (sop); [a]**Zeger Vandersteene** (ten); [a]**Philippe Huttenlocher** (bar); [a]**Jules Bastin** (bass); [a]**Namur Symphonic Chorus; Liège Philharmonic Orchestra/Pierre Bartholomée.** Ricercar Secondo RIS099083 (10/92).

Violin Sonata in G major. *Coupled with* **Debussy.** Violin Sonata in G minor. **Ravel.** Violin Sonata, Op. posth. **Jean-Jacques Kantorow** (vn); **Jacques Rouvier** (pf). Denon CO72718 (8/89).

Leonardo Leo

Italian 1694-1744

Suggested listening ...

Concerto in D major for Four Violins and Strings. *Coupled with* **Torelli:** Concerto in E minor for four Violins and Strings. **Mossi:** Concertos, Op. 4 — No. 12 in G minor. **Valentini:** Concerti grossi, Op. 7 — No. 11 in A minor. **Locatelli:** Introduttioni Teatrali and Concerti, Op. 4 — No. 12 in F major. **Cologne Musica Antiqua/Reinhard Goebel.** Archiv Produktion 435 393-2AH (9/92). *See review in the Collections section; refer to the Index to Reviews.*

Ruggero Leoncavallo

Italian 1858-1919

Leoncavallo. PAGLIACCI[a]. **Carlo Bergonzi** (ten) Canio; **Joan Carlyle** (sop) Nedda; **Giuseppe Taddei** (bar) Tonio; **Rolando Panerai** (bar) Silvio; **Ugo Benelli** (ten) Beppe; . *Mascagni.* CAVALLERIA RUSTICANA[a]. **Fiorenza Cossotto** (mez) Santuzza; **Adriane Martino** (mez) Lola; **Carlo Bergonzi** (ten) Turiddu; **Giangiacomo Guelfi** (bar) Alfio; **Maria Gracia Allegri** (contr) Lucia; **Chorus and Orchestra of La Scala, Milan/Herbert von Karajan.**
OPERA INTERMEZZOS. **Berlin Philharmonic Orchestra/Herbert von Karajan.** DG 419 257-2GH3. Notes, texts and translations included. Items marked [a] from SLPM139205/07 (10/66), [b] SLPM139031 (6/69), both recorded in 1965.
Verdi: LA TRAVIATA — Prelude, Act 3. *Puccini*: MANON LESCAUT — Intermezzo. SUOR ANGELICA — Intermezzo. *Schmidt*: NOTRE DAME — Intermezzo. *Massenet*: THAIS — Meditátion (with Michel Schwalbé, vn). *Giordano*: FEDORA — Intermezzo. *Cilea*: ADRIANA LECOUVREUR — Intermezzo. *Wolf-Ferrari:* I GIOIELLO DELLA MADONNA — Intermezzo. *Mascagni:* L'AMICO FRITZ — Intermezzo.

.·'· ③ 3h 18m ADD 10/87 Ⓑ

Cav and Pag as they are usually known have been bedfellows for many years. Lasting for about 75 minutes each, they have some similarities. Both works concern the passions, jealousies and hatred of two tightly-knit communities — the inhabitants of a Sicilian town and the players in a travelling troupe of actors. *Cavalleria rusticana* ("Rustic chivalry") concerns the triangular relationship of mother, son and his rejected lover. Played against a rich musical tapestry, sumptuously orchestrated, the action is played out during the course of an Easter day. Bergonzi is a stylish, ardent Turiddu whose virile charms glitter in his every phrase and Fiorenza Cossotto makes a thrilling Santuzza motivated and driven by a palpable conviction; her contribution to the well-known Easter hymn scene is gripping. But the real hero of the opera is Karajan, whose direction of this powerful work is magnificent. Conviction and insight also instil *Pagliacci* with excitement and real drama. A troupe of actors arrive to give a performance of a *commedia dell'arte* play. The illustration of real love, life and hatred is portrayed in the interplay of Tonio, Silvio, Nedda and her husband Canio. As the two rivals, Bergonzi and Taddei are superb. Taddei's sinister, hunch-backed clown, gently forcing the play-within-the-play closer to reality until it finally bursts out violently is a masterly assumption, and Karajan controls the slow build-up of tension with a grasp that few conductors could hope to equal. The Scala forces respond wholeheartedly and the 1965 recording sounds well. The third disc is filled by a selection of very rich, very soft-centred opera intermezzos.

Additional recommendations ...
Pagliacci[a]/*Cavalleria*[b]. **Soloists; [a]London Voices; [a]Finchley Children's Music Group; [b]London Opera Chorus; [ab]National Philharmonic Orchestra/[a]Giuseppe Patanè; [b]Gianandrea Gavazzeni.** Decca 414 590-2DH2 — ⠶ ② 2h 23m ADD 1/89 Ⓑ
Pagliacci/*Cavalleria*. **Soloists; Ambrosian Opera Chorus; Philharmonia Orchestra/ Riccardo Muti.** EMI CMS7 63650-2 — ⠶ ② 2h 30m ADD 3/91 Ⓑ
Pagliacci. **Soloists; Slovak Philharmonic Chorus; Bratislava Radio Symphony Orchestra/Alexander Ráhbari.** Naxos 8 660021 — . 1h 10m DDD 4/93 Ⓑ

Franciszek Lessel
Polish c.1780-1838

Piano Concerto in C major, Op. 14[ab]. Adagio et rondeau à la polonaise, Op. 9[b]. Variations, Op. 15 — No. 1, on a Ukrainian song, "Jichaw kozak zza Dunaju"; No 2, in A minor. [b]**Jerzy Sterczynski** (pf); [b]**Silesian Philharmonic Orchestra/Jerzy Salwarowski.** Le Chant du Monde LDC278 1092 (10/93).

Anatoli Liadov
Russian 1855-1914

Liadov. ORCHESTRAL WORKS. **Slovak Philharmonic Orchestra/Stephen Gunzenhauser.** Marco Polo 8 220348.
Baba-Yaga, Op. 56. Intermezzo in B flat major, Op. 8 No. 1. Pro starinu — Ballade in D major, Op. 21b. The enchanted lake, Op. 62. Village scene by the inn — Mazurka, Op. 19. Nénie, Op. 67. Polonaise, Op. 49. Polonaise in D major, Op. 55. Kikimora, Op. 63. From the Apocalypse, Op. 66.

⠶ **58m DDD 10/86** ❓

Liadov was a superb miniaturist and as a professor of composition at the St Petersburg Conservatory he had an interestingly potent influence on the music of his younger contemporaries. His finest works are jewel-like in the depth and luminosity of colour they embody and the finesse with which they are worked. His short tone-poem, *The enchanted lake*, immediately establishes in a few delicate strokes the dank mystery of his subject; *Baba-Yaga* conjures up in only three minutes the menace of the mythical witch in flight; *Kikimora*, so well admired by Stravinsky, summons from out of hushed menace the demon wife of the house spirit, Domovoi. Listening to Liadov's works in succession highlights his problem with more protracted formal structures, but a programme such as this one is worth dipping into for the choice morsel or two. Each of these performances drives straight to the heart of the mood Liadov has in mind and the recording more than adequately captures the sparkle and solidity of the orchestral sound. For anyone interested in Liadov or the flowering of late-romanticism in music, this disc is well worth sampling.

Ingvar Lidholm

New review

Lidholm. Greetings from an Old World. Toccata e Canto. Kontakion. Ritornell. **Royal Stockholm Philharmonic Orchestra/Gennadi Rozhdestvensky.** Chandos CHAN9231. Recorded 1991-93.

> ·· **lh 3m DDD 3/94** **q**[s]

Since the death in 1985 of his former teacher, Hilding Rosenberg, Ingvar Lidholm (b. 1921) has been the dominant figure amongst Swedish composers. The programme ranges across four decades of his career, covering a diversity of styles: early neo-classicism (*Toccata e Canto*), aggressive modernism (*Ritornell*) and the mature synthesis of the lyrical with the radical (*Greetings, Kontakion*). In *Greetings from an Old World* (1976) and *Kontakion,* Lidholm gradually unveils the pre-existing melodies, that serve as the musical basis for each work. In *Kontakion* the source is the Byzantine/Orthodox hymn for the dead. Unsurprisingly, *Kontakion* struck a deep and emotive chord in Russian audiences, but non-Orthodox listeners have also responded keenly, especially to the moving closing pages, as passionate and fervent as Pärt but without the numbing repetition. The opening of *Toccata e Canto* has an invigorating, American brashness to it, but British listeners may be struck more by uncanny pre-echoes of Rubbra and Simpson in the elegiac *Canto*. The disc concludes in exuberant — and heavily percussive — fashion with *Ritornell* (1954), a tribute to the virtuosity of composer and performers. Excellent recordings.

New review

Lidholm. A DREAM PLAY. **Hillevi Martinpelto** (sop) Daughter; **Håkan Hagegård** (bar) Officer; **Ingrid Tobiasson** (contr) Stage-Door Keeper; **Sten Wahlund** (bar) Advocate; **Curt Applegren** (bass) Poet; **Lars Kullenbo** (ten) Bill-Poster, Dean of Theology; **Arild Helleland** (ten) Schoolmaster, Dean of Law; **Anders Bergström** (bar) Glazier, Blind man; **Staffan Sandlund** (bass) Chancellor; **Henrik Westberg** (bar) Dean of Philosophy; **Rolf Cederlöf** (bass) Policeman, Dean of Medicine; **Nina Stemme** (sop) Victoria, She; **Carl Unander-Scharin** (ten) He; **Harriet Andersson** (spkr) Kristin; **Adolf Frederik Boys' and Girls' Choirs; Stockholm Royal Choir and Orchestra/Kjell Ingebretsen.** Caprice CAP22029. Notes, text and translation included. Recorded 1992-93.

> ·· ② **2h 17m ADD 9/93** **q**[p]

Something of the semi-religious character as well as the internal processes of *Kontakion* (Lidholm's best known orchestral work reviewed above) surface in his first full-length stage opera, *A Dream Play*, which makes use of, amongst other things, an old medieval hymn (*Rex caeli, domine maris*) and two motets for unaccompanied chorus from the early 1980s. The text is from Strindberg, whose writings have inspired Lidholm throughout his career. The first thing that strikes one about this new opera, after the solemn, opening brass chords, is the glorious writing for the chorus, which must rank as amongst the finest committed to an opera this century. The style of Lidholm's music in this work is a little hard to place: somewhere between Hindemith, Berg and the Aulis Sallinen of *The King goes forth to France* will give a very general indication of its nature. For much of its length the music is beautiful, yet beneath its dream-like exterior, darker, nightmarish forces lurk. Caprice's recording is a model of clarity and the performance is extremely fine; invidious as it is to pick out individuals from such an excellent team, Hillevi Martinpelto as Indra's daughter and Håkan Hagegård as the long-suffering Officer are splendid.

Gyorgy Ligeti

New review

Ligeti. Cello Concerto[a]. Piano Concerto[b]. Chamber Concerto. [a]**Miklós Perényi** (vc); [b]**Ueli Wiget** (pf); **Ensemble Modern/Peter Eötvös.** Sony Classical SK58945. Recorded in 1990.

> ·· **57m DDD 6/94**

The Cello Concerto (1966) and the Chamber Concerto for 13 instrumentalists (1970) are exemplary demonstrations of that Ligetian kind of process music in which schemes which might appear mechanical in the abstract are brought to life by a beguiling flexibility of rhythm and colour. For any movement which seems too long or unvaried (the second movement of the Chamber Concerto?) there is a compensating freshness and vitality (the same work's finale), and these performances bubble with elegance and virtuosity. In this context the Piano Concerto (1988) certainly doesn't suggest a completely new start. Yet Ligeti's renewed delight in pattern-making promotes ever more complex textures, and an unusually wide frame of reference is established when the Nancarrow-like dance of the first movement is followed by an austere lament — the perfect antidote to the ebullient activity that surrounds it. It is persuasively performed here, and recorded with a fidelity that brings Ueli Wiget's remarkable range of touch and nuance into the clearest focus.

Ligeti. String Quartet No. 1.
Lutoslawski. String Quartet.
Schnittke. Kanon in memoriam I. Stravinsky. **Hagen Quartet** (Lukas Hagen, Rainer Schmidt, vns; Veronika Hagen, va; Clemens Hagen, vc). DG 431 686-2GH. Recorded in 1990.

54m DDD 9/91

You won't find Ligeti and Lutoslawski subscribing to the conventional view of the string quartet as requiring four 'symphonic' movements. Ligeti's extended single movement has 17 kaleidoscopically-interacting sub-sections, and Lutoslawski's two main sections are also mosaic-like in form, with a wide variety of different ideas emerging and, on occasion, conflicting. Both quartets — not least because they are superbly imagined for the medium, and finely played on this disc — make fascinating listening, and Ligeti's subtitle ("Nocturnal Metamorphoses") would not be wholly inappropriate for the Lutoslawski as well. There's a dark quality, many rustlings and flickerings, which Ligeti balances against a more fantastic, sardonic tone, and which Lutoslawski leads into both highly dramatic and poignantly lyrical regions. The Ligeti is an early work, beholden to Bartók but bursting with its own very definite ideas about both form and content. The Lutoslawski is more mature, less adventurous, but far from cautious either. With Schnittke's austere, grief-stricken tribute to Stravinsky as a bonus, and with admirably natural yet spacious recorded sound, this is a disc which anyone sceptical about the rewards of modern chamber music can approach with confidence.

Further listening ...

Continuum[a]. Ten Pieces for Wind Quintet[d]. Artikulation[e]. Glissandi[f]. Two Studies for Organ[b]. Volumina[c]. [a]**Antoinette Vischer** (hpd); [b]**Zsigmond Sathmáry**, [c]**Karl-Erik Welin** (orgs); [d]**South-West German Radio Wind Quintet;** [ef]**Cologne Radio Studio for Electronic Music.** Wergo WER60161-50 (11/89).

Melodien[a]. Concerto for Flute and Oboe[b]. Chamber Concerto[c]. Ten Pieces for Wind Quintet[d]. [b]**Aurèle Nicolet** (fl); [b]**Heinz Holliger** (ob); [d]**Vienna Wind Soloists;** [abc]**London Sinfonietta/David Atherton.** Decca Enterprise 425 623-2DM (8/90).

Chamber Concerto[b]. Ramifications (versions for String Orchestra[d] and Solo Strings[c]). Lux aeterna[a]. Atmosphères[d]. [a]**Stuttgart Schola Cantorum/Clytus Gottwald;** [b]**Vienna Die Reihe Ensemble/Friedrich Cerha;** [c]**Saar Radio Chamber Orchestra/Antonio Janigro;** [d]**South West German Radio Symphony Orchestra/Ernest Bour.** Wergo WER60162-50 (10/89).

LE GRAND MACABRE. **Soloists; Austrian Radio Chorus; Arnold Schönberg Choir; Gumpoldskirchner Spartzen; Austrian Radio Symphony Orchestra/Elgar Howarth.** Wergo WER6170-2 (12/91).

Douglas Lilburn

New Zealand 1915-

New review
Lilburn. Symphonies — No. 1[a]; No. 2[b]; No. 3[c]. **New Zealand Symphony Orchestra/** [ac]**John Hopkins,** [b]**Ashley Heenan.** Kiwi-Pacific Records CDSLD-90. Item marked [a] new to

UK, recorded in 1975; [b] from Jerusalem ATD8203 (3/83), recorded in 1982; [c] Oryx ORYX1900 (2/70), recorded in 1968.

1h 14m ADD 3/94 ❓

Now here's a find! The three symphonies of New Zealand's elder statesman of music, Douglas Lilburn are all works of substance and no little potential for popular appeal. Readers with a penchant for Sibelius, Barber, Nielsen and Vaughan Williams will find this music very appetizing. Even on first hearing, it is clear that Lilburn has a natural talent for symphonic form and his material evolves with a quiet, dignified purpose which commands respect. True, stylistic echoes are legion, especially in the First Symphony (1947). The Second of four years later is a far more mature utterance: its four movements are beautifully crafted and the whole symphony evinces a genuine feel for nature and sense of atmosphere, an antipodean counterpart, if you like, to Sibelius's Sixth or Tubin's Fourth. But it is the single-movement Third from 1960 that shows Lilburn at his most challenging. This is a notably terse piece in five interlinked sections, uncompromisingly gritty in idiom. It certainly packs a wealth of incident into its 14-and-a-half minute duration. These performances are warm-hearted, consistently involving and very decently engineered.

Thomas Linley

British 1756-1778

Suggested listening ...

Ode on the Spirits of Shakespeare. **Lorna Anderson, Julia Gooding** (sops); **Richard Wistreich** (bass); **The Parley of Instruments Choir; The Parley of Instruments/Paul Nicholson.** Hyperion CDA66613 (5/93).

Franz Liszt

Hungarian 1811-1886

Liszt. Piano Concertos — No. 1 in E flat major, S124[b]; No. 2 in A major, S125[b]. **Beethoven.** Cello Sonata in G minor, Op. 5 No. 2[a]. **Sviatoslav Richter** (pf); [a]**Mstislav Rostropovich** (vc); [b]**London Symphony Orchestra/Kyrill Kondrashin.** Philips Insignia 434 163-2PM. Item marked [a] from SAL3453/4 (2/64), recorded in 1962, [b] SABL207 (5/62), recorded in 1961.

1h 7m ADD 9/92 ♪P Ⓑ

At the height of his powers, as he was in the early 1960s shortly after his first appearance in the West, Richter at the piano was an awe-inspiring phenomenon. His recording of the Liszt Concertos was instantly recognized as a classic. Not only was it breathtaking in its pianistic command, it had Kyrill Kondrashin galvanizing the London Symphony Orchestra into something far more vital than mere accompaniment. The opening bars of the E flat Concerto throw down the gauntlet in such a way as to make the soloist's heroics sound motivated as they hardly ever do, and sparks fly between piano and orchestra throughout both works. Admittedly the record-ing now sounds slightly constricted, but that detracts hardly at all from the cumulative intensity of the performances. And with a rock-solid account of the Beethoven G minor Sonata added for good measure this medium-price issue is clearly one not to be missed.

Additional recommendations ...
Piano Concertos. Totentanz, S126. **Alfred Brendel** (pf); **London Philharmonic Orchestra/ Bernard Haitink.** Philips Silverline 426 637-2PSL — ♪ 56m ADD 11/90 Ⓑ
Piano Concertos. Totentanz. **Krystian Zimerman** (pf); **Boston Symphony Orchestra/Seiji Ozawa.** DG 423 571-2GH — ♪ 56m DDD 11/88 ♪P Ⓑ
No. 1[a]. Piano Sonata in B minor[a]. Hungarian Rhapsody No. 6[a]. Les jeux d'eau à la Villa d'Este[b]. Vallée d'Oberman. [a]**Martha Argerich,** [b]**Lazar Berman** (pfs); [a]**London Symphony Orchestra/ Claudio Abbado.** DG 439 409-2GCL — ♪ 1h 12m ADD 1/94 ♪P Ⓑ

Liszt. A Dante Symphony, S109[a]. Années de pèlerinage — deuxième année: Italie, S161 — No. 7, Après une lecture du Dante — Fantasia Quasi Sonata[b]. [a]**Berlin Radio Women's Chorus;** [a]**Berlin Philharmonic Orchestra/Daniel Barenboim** ([b]pf). Teldec 9031-77340-2. Item marked [a] recorded at a performance in the Schauspielhaus, Berlin in 1992.

Ih 7m DDD 7/94

This disc proves conclusively that the *Dante Symphony* (a contemporary of the *Faust Symphony*) is no longer one that needs its apologists. Tone, full and rounded, firm and true, and rock-steady pacing elevate the Symphony's opening ("Abandon all hope, ye who enter here") beyond its all too familiar resemblance to a third-rate horror-film soundtrack. As the Symphony progresses, together with the countless examples of Berlin tone and artistry filling out, refining or shaping gestures in often revelatory ways, you become aware of Barenboim's skill in maintaining the large-scale tension he has created. And that is a very real achievement. As for the final choral Magnificat, if Liszt owed Wagner a debt of gratitude for persuading him to conclude the Symphony with the "noble and softly soaring" bars that precede a more noisily affirmative appended coda, in Barenboim's Magnificat (and much else in the Symphony), it is Wagner's debt to Liszt that is more readily apparent; the Parsifalian radiance of these final pages is unmistak-able. More importantly, for once they sound convincingly conclusive. The Sonata was recorded with the kind of risk-taking abandon and occasionally less than perfect execution that you might expect from a live event. Improvisatory, impulsive and full of extreme contrasts, Barenboim's *Dante* Sonata is vividly pictorial (with almost orchestral colourings). In the best Lisztian tradition, the instrument itself (closely miked and widely spaced) sounds larger than life. This is, in a word, riveting. The recording of the Symphony is spacious, focused and expertly balanced.

Liszt. A Faust Symphony, G108. **Kenneth Riegel** (ten); **Tanglewood Festival Chorus; Boston Symphony Orchestra/Leonard Bernstein.** DG Galleria 431 470-2GGA. From 2707 100 (4/78). Recorded in 1976.

Ih I7m ADD 8/9I

Goethe's *Faust* provided a source of inspiration for numerous symphonic, operatic, literary and stage works and, indeed, its influence is hardly diminished even in the late twentieth century. With its heroic and undeniably visionary qualities, it is hardly surprising that many romantic composers seized upon Goethe's text and the work offers a huge range of interpretative possibilities. A mystical and philosophical Faust is revealed by Bernstein in his performance with the Boston Symphony Orchestra. He adds the extra dimensions of real musical perception and true dramatic mastery to Liszt's concoction of sinister diablerie. The 1977 DG sound is excellent in its remastered form and has the added attraction of being mid-price.

Additional recommendations ...
Alexander Young (ten); **Beecham Choral Society; Royal Philharmonic Orchestra/Sir Thomas Beecham.** EMI CDM7 63371-2 — Ih I0m ADD 2/88 ▲
Gösta Winbergh (ten); **Westminster Choir College Male Chorus; Philadelphia Orchestra/Riccardo Muti.** EMI CDC7 49062-2 — Ih I7m DDD I0/9I
Charles Bressler (ten); **New York Choral Art Society; New York Philharmonic Orchestra/Leonard Bernstein.** Sony Classical Royal Edition SMK47570 — Ih I2m ADD 5/93

Liszt. COMPLETE SYMPHONIC POEMS, Volumes 1 and 2. **London Philharmonic Orchestra/Bernard Haitink.** Philips 438 751/4-2PM2 (two sets of two discs. Recorded 1968-71.
438 751-2PM2 — Ce qu'on entend sur la montagne, S95 (from 6500 189, 1/72). Tasso, S96. Les Préludes, S97. Orpheus, S98 (SAL3750, 12/69). Prometheus, S99. Festklänge, S101 (6709 005, 9/72). Mazeppa, S100 (6500 046, 8/71). *438 754-2PM2* — Héroïde funèbre, S102. Die Ideale, S106. Mephisto Waltz No. 1, "Der Tanz in der Dorfschenke", S110 No. 2 (from 6709

005, 9/72). Hungaria, S103. Hamlet, S104 (6500 046, 8/71). Hunnenschlacht, S105. Von der Wiege bis zum Grabe, S107 (6500 189, 1/72).

.·ᵉ ② ② 2h 7m 2h 11m ADD 𝄞ₚ

The 12 'numbered' symphonic poems date from Liszt's rich maturity (the first, *Ce qu'on entend sur la montagne*, was composed during the late 1840s) with the lean, near-expressionist *Von der Wiege bis zum Grabe* ("From the Cradle to the Grave") following on after a period of some 25 years. Initial orchestration was invariably undertaken by Joachim Raff, although the composer himself always had the final say. When, in the early 1970s, Bernard Haitink galvanized the LPO into re-enacting these symphonic dramas, he had the field more or less to himself. Then, some years later, Kurt Masur taped the cycle in Leipzig, an excellent, warmly recorded excursion, not quite as intense as Haitink's — but only four of the poems and the Second *Mephisto Waltz* are currently available on EMI's Studio Plus label (listed below). Haitink's readings have an abundance of personality. In *Héroïde funèbre*, for example, his dangerously slow tempo exceeds Liszt's prescribed timing by some seven minutes: it is a terrifying vision, superbly sustained and beautifully played. He also copes manfully with the more explosive aspects of *Hamlet, Prometheus* and *Hunnenschlacht* (which he paces more securely than any other rival, past or present), and his way with the scores' many reflective episodes is entirely winning. Elsewhere, he sorts through the complexities of Liszt's colourful orchestration with a cool head and a warm heart, etching the frequent examples of 'nature music' much as he does Wagner's and keeping abreast of each tone-poem's narrative trail. True, some of Liszt's *marcatos, impetuosos, appassionatos* and *agitatos* are occasionally brought to heel, but then others aren't — and we have Liszt's blessing for flexibility in what he himself terms "the degree of sympathy" that conductors employ for his work. What matters is that Haitink has us enter Liszt's world direct, rather than through the distorting mirror of the conductor's own ego. It is a volatile sequence, yes, and not without its *longueurs*, but it remains an essential musical confrontation for all students of the romantic orchestra and an accurate pointer to where Tchaikovsky, Smetana and countless others found significant musical sustenance. With excellent sound and commonsense documentation, these two sets will provide hours of aural adventure.

Additional recommendation ...
Tasso. Les Préludes. Orpheus. Mazeppa. Mephisto Waltz No. 2, S111. **Leipzig Gewandhaus Orchestra/Kurt Masur.** EMI Studio Plus CDM7 64850-2 — .·ᵉ ADD

Liszt. PIANO WORKS. **Alfred Brendel.** Philips 410 040-2PH. From 6514 147 (11/82). Piano Sonata in B minor, S178. Légendes, S175 — St François d'Assise: la prédication aux oiseaux; St François de Paule marchant sur les flots. La lugubre gondola Nos. 1 and 2, S200/1-2.

.·ᵉ 1h 2m DDD 10/83 𝄞ₚ Ⓑ

Liszt's Piano Sonata is one of the monuments of the romantic period and is the only sonata which the greatest pianist of musical history wrote for his instrument. It is in one long movement that has its component parts contained within a mighty sonata structure. Unfortunately it is also a work that has often been misunderstood and when treated chiefly as a virtuoso warhorse and vehicle for self-display the Sonata loses its dignity and poise. Alfred Brendel has lived with this music for decades, and his love and understanding of it are evident. Technically it is not flawless, but the blend of the various qualities needed — power, dignity, dexterity, sheer excitement, charm and above all structural cohesion is admirable. The two *St Francis* Legends and the funereal *Gondola* pieces are more than a fill-up and enhance this fine disc, revealing as they do other aspects of the composer.

Additional recommendations ...
Piano Sonata. Piano Concerto No. 1 in E flat major (with orchestra/David Brockman). *Années de pèlerinage, deuxième année, "Italie" — Sonnetto 104 del Petrarca. Rapsodie espagnole. Two Concert Studies — No. 2, Gnomenreigen (two performances). Harmonies poétiques et religieuses — No. 7, Funérailles. Hungarian Rhapsody No. 12 in C sharp minor.* **Gounod** (trans. Liszt): *Faust — Waltz.* **Simon Barere.** APR CDAPR7007 — .·ᵉ ② 1h 33 ADD 11/89 𝄞ₚ Ⓑ ▲
Piano Sonata. Nuages gris, S199. Unstern: sinistre, disastro, S208. La lugubre gondola No. 1. R. W. — Venezia, S201. **Maurizio Pollini.** DG 427 322-2GH — .·ᵉ 46m DDD 7/90 Ⓑ
Piano Sonata. **Schubert.** *Piano Sonata in B flat major, D960.* **Annie Fischer.** Hungaroton HCD31494 — .·ᵉ 1h 7m ADD 7/92 Ⓑ ▲

Piano Sonata. Two Légendes, S175. Scherzo and March, S177. **Nikolai Demidenko.** Hyperion CDA66616 — .·˙ 1h 7m DDD 2/93 ⁹ₚ Ⓑ

Piano Sonata. Hungarian Rhapsody No. 6 in D flat major, S244. **Brahms.** *Two Rhapsodies, Op. 79.* **Schumann.** *Piano Sonata No. 2 in G minor, Op. 22.* **Martha Argerich.** DG Galleria 437 252-2GGA — .·˙ 1h 4m ADD 2/93 ⁹ₚ Ⓑ

Piano Sonata. **Schubert.** *Piano Sonata in D major, D850*ᵇ. **Emil Gilels.** RCA Victor Living Stereo 09026 61614-2 — .·˙ 1h 11m ADD 4/94 ⁹ₚ

New review

Liszt. Années de pèlerinage — première année, Suisse, S160; deuxième année, Italie, S161; troisième année, S163. Venezia e Napoli, S162. **Lazar Berman** (pf). DG 437 206-2GX3. Recorded in 1977.

.·˙ ③ 2h 56m ADD 11/93   ⁹ₚ

Liszt's three volumes of *Années de pèlerinage* are rarely recorded complete, largely because many pianists remain baffled by the dark-hued prophecy and romanticism of the third and final book. So it is particularly gratifying to welcome Lazar Berman's superb DG recordings back into the catalogue. Berman's resource here is remarkable and his performance of the entire book is hauntingly inward and sympathetic to both the radiance of "Les jeux d'eau à la Villa d'Este" and to Liszt's truly dark night of the soul (*lamentoso, doloroso* and so on), and to his desolating lack of spiritual solace elsewhere. He is hardly less persuasive in the first two books. "Chapelle de Guillaume Tell" is a true celebration of Switzerland's republican hero with alpine horns ringing through the mountains, while in "Au lac de Wallenstadt" Berman's gently undulating traversal is truly *pianissimo* and *dolcissimo egualamente*. His "Orage" is predictably breathtaking, and in the gloomy Byronic "Vallée d'Obermann" the severest critic will find himself mesmerized by Berman's free-wheeling eloquence. The 1977 recordings have been finely remastered.

Additional recommendation ...
Deuxième année. **Michael Dalberto.** Denon CO-75500 — .·˙ 1h 11m DDD 2/94

New review

Liszt. PIANO WORKS, Volume 21. **Leslie Howard.** Hyperion CDA66661/2. Recorded 1991-92.
Soirées musicales, S424. Soirées italiennes, S411. Nuits d'été à Pausilippe, S399. Tre sonetti del Petraca, S158. Venezia e Napoli, S159. La serenata e L'orgia (Grande fantaisie sur des motifs des Soirées musicales), S422. La pastorella dell'Alpi e Li marinari (Deuxième fantaisie sur des motifs des Soirées musicales), S423.

.·˙ ② 2h 37m DDD 7/93

The two discs comprising Vol. 21 of Howard's mammoth cycle remind us of the young Liszt's love affair with Italy, the spotlight now falling primarily — though not exclusively — on frolics with Rossini, Mercadante and Donizetti in lighter, lyrical vein. The special interest of the two original sets of pieces included, i.e. the three *Sonetti del Petrarca* and the four *Venezia e Napoli*, is that Howard introduces them as first written (*c.*1839 and 1840 respectively) before Liszt's characteristically painstaking later revisions. There is much to enjoy in the playing itself, especially in simpler contexts when gondolas glide through calm waters, or lovers dream, or shepherds dance. Melody, so important throughout, is nicely sung. And whether in filigree delicacy or exuberant zest (as in excitable Venetian regattas) Howard invariably relishes Liszt's ear-catching ornamentation.

New review

Liszt PIANO WORKS, Volume 25. **Leslie Howard.** Hyperion CDA66694. Recorded 1992-93.
Cantico di San Francesco — Preludio per il Cantico del Sol, S499a. Cantico del sol di San Francesco, S499. Von der Wiege bis zum Grabe, S512. O sacrum convivium, S674a (two versions). Salve Regina, S669 No. 1. Ave maris stella, S669 No. 2. Gebet, S265. Ora pro nobis,

S262. Resignazione, S187*b*. Il m'aimait tant, S533. Romance, "O pourquoi donc", S169. Ich liebe dich, S546*a*. Die Zelle in Nonnenswerth, S534.

1h 17m DDD 5/94

Transcriptions? Yes, in the case of the four Liszt songs — including the hauntingly nostalgic *Die Zelle in Nonnenswerth* — with which the disc ends. For the rest, this volume of Howard's mammoth cycle goes to rarities and the emphasis is on "the more sober and serious side of Liszt's character, whether in sacred or secular mood", as Howard puts it in his valuable booklet-notes. The piano version of the then 70-year-old composer's last symphonic poem, *Von der Wiege bis zum Grabe*, is of the greatest interest. Howard meets the challenge of the central struggle with a telling starkness, and plays the two sparsely-noted outer movements with a mesmeric simplicity. Obviously these 77 minutes of predominantly private music are not likely to make the disc one of the cycle's best-sellers. But in its testimony to Howard the musician behind Howard the pianist it is as choice as anything he has yet given us and the same goes for the recording.

New review

Liszt. Harmonies poétiques et religieuses, S173. **Hugh Tinney** (pf). Meridian CDE84240.

1h 18m DDD 7/93

Although containing such important pieces as the "Bénédiction de Dieu dans la solitude" and "Funérailles", the *Harmonies poétiques et religieuses* of 1847-52 are hardly familiar Liszt. There are ten numbers in all, varying in length from three to 16 minutes, and they just manage to fit on to a CD. This is the composer at his most self-indulgent; a man obsessed with his own religious experience. Demands on the interpreter, naturally, are considerable. Much of the time he has to respond to a lofty cerebral notion of spirituality that can sound ridiculously inflated when expressed at the piano. The Dublin-born Hugh Tinney is judicious at all times. He approaches the music with due weight — and a compelling range of pianistic sonorities to match. The instrument has not been recorded very closely and an effective sense of space and grandeur has been achieved. Whilst maybe not reaching the highest level of interpretative insight, Tinney's version carries a definite recommendation. There are always details in his pianism to be admired. Some listeners may take a moment or two to acclimatize to the Yamaha grand — it is a piano with a lot of overtones — but overall the sound is extremely lifelike.

Additional recommendation ...

Harmonies poétiques et religieuses. Venezia e Napoli. Années de pèlerinage, Troisième année, S163 — No. 4, Les jeux d'eaux à la Villa d'Este. Ballade No. 2 in B minor, S171. **Jorge Bolet.** Decca 411 803-2DH — 58m DDD 12/85

Liszt. PIANO WORKS, Volume 15 — SONG TRANSCRIPTIONS. **Leslie Howard.** Hyperion CDA66481/2. Recorded in 1990.
Beethoven: Adelaïde, S466. Sechs geistliche Lieder, S467. An die ferne Geliebte, S469. Lieder von Goethe, S468. **Mendelssohn:** Lieder, S547. **Dessauer:** Lieder, S485. **Franz:** Er ist gekommen in Sturm und Regen, S488. Lieder, S489. **Rubinstein:** Two songs, S554. **Schumann:** Lieder von Robert und Clara Schumann, S569. Provenzalisches Lied, S570. Two songs, S567. Frühlingsnacht, S568. Widmung, S566.

② **1h 27m DDD 4/92**

Few composers have ever shown a more insatiable interest in the music of others than Liszt, or devoted more time to transcribing it for the piano. In this radio-cum-gramophonic age, such activity might even be deemed time wasted. But in Liszt's day it was a godsend for music-lovers and composers alike, and all praise to Leslie Howard for including it in his mammoth pilgrimage through the composer's complete keyboard works. Here, he plays 60 of Liszt's 100 or so song transcriptions, including several by the lesser-known Dessauer, Franz and (as composers) Anton Rubinstein and Clara Schumann, alongside Beethoven, Mendelssohn and Robert Schumann. The selection at once reveals Liszt's variety of approach as a transcriber no less than his unpredic-tability of choice. Sometimes, as most notably in Beethoven's concert aria, *Adelaïde*, the keyboard virtuoso takes over: he links its two sections with a concerto-like cadenza as well as carrying bravura into an amplified coda. Mendelssohn's *On wings of song* brings imitative subtleties all his own, while the fullness of heart of Schumann's *Dedication* and *Spring Night* is likewise allowed to expand and overflow. But after the dazzling pyrotechnics of many of his operatic arrangements, the surprise here is the self-effacing simplicity of so much included. The five songs from Schumann's *Liederalbum für die Jugend* are literal enough to be played by young children. Even his later (1880) fantasy-type transcriptions of Rubinstein's exotic *The Asra* has the same potent economy of means, characterizing his own original keyboard music in advancing years. Howard responds keenly to mood and atmosphere, and never fails, pianistically, to emphasize the 'singer' in each song — in response to the actual verbal text that Liszt was nearly always conscientious enough to write into his scores. The recording is clean and true.

New review

Liszt. OPERA TRANSCRIPTIONS. **Jean-Yves Thibaudet** (pf). Decca 436 736-2DH. Recorded in 1992.
RIGOLETTO (Verdi) — Paraphrase, S434. LUCIA ET PARISINA (Donizetti) — Valse à capriccio, S401. FAUST (Gounod) — Waltz, S407. EUGENE ONEGIN (Tchaikovsky) — Polonaise, S429. DER FLIEGENDE HOLLANDER (Wagner) — Spinning Chorus, S440. TANNHAUSER (Wagner) — Rezitativ und Romanze, S444. LOHENGRIN (Wagner) — Verweis an Elsa, S446. TRISTAN UND ISOLDE (Wagner) — Liebestod, S447. LE NOZZE DI FIGARO (Mozart) — Fantasia, S697.

lh 9m DDD 2/94

Surely no major composer ever did more to propagate the music of others than Liszt. But he was also a legendary virtuoso, not easily allowing himself to forget his own dazzling fingers in his innumerable transcriptions. In this operatic selection Jean-Yves Thibaudet artfully contrasts five of the more demonstrative kind with four in which faithfulness to the original text was Liszt's main concern — these latter, significantly, drawn from the music of his formidable son-in-law to be, Richard Wagner. The filigree delicacy of Thibaudet's effortlessly brilliant finger-work is very impressive, not least in the decorative flights of the first three Verdi, Donizetti and Gounod numbers. Sometimes it suggests the trickles of scintillating fairy lights in the sky after the bursting of a rocket, sometimes the liquidity of water itself though still with each note retaining its own pinpoint glisten. In the earlier Wagner items Thibaudet matches Wagner's comparative simplicity with a similar concern for the unadorned truth, again, with his light pedalling, drawing sounds of ear-catching translucency from the keyboard's upper reaches. He finds the full, close-woven intensity of the "Liebestod" harder to sustain but the piece is finely shaped as a whole. The recital ends heartily with the less frequently heard *Figaro* Fantasia completed in 1912 by no less a man than Busoni.

LISZT AT THE THEATRE. Leslie Howard (pf). Hyperion CDA66575. Recorded in 1991.
Capriccio alla turca from "Die Ruinen von Athen", S388. March from "Die Ruinen von Athen", S388a. Fantasie über "Die Ruinen von Athen", S389. Wedding March and Dance of the Elves from "A Midsummer Night's Dream", S410. Einsam bin ich, nicht alleine from "La Preciosa", S453. Incidental music to Hebbel's "Nibelungen" and Goethe's "Faust", S496. Symphonisches Zwischensiel zu Calderons schauspiel "Uber allen Zauber Liebe", S497. Pastorale from choruses to Herder's "Prometheus Bound", S508.

lh 18m DDD 3/93

After two volumes of "Liszt at the Opera" in his mammoth cycle, Leslie Howard now introduces us to "Liszt at the Theatre", i.e. as transcriber-paraphraser of incidental music written for various stage productions by Beethoven, Weber, Mendelssohn, Lassen — and even an excerpt from what he himself produced for Herder's *Prometheus Bound*. Best-known, of course, is Mendelssohn's *Midsummer Night's Dream* inspired "Wedding March" and "Dance of the Elves", miraculously merged in the course of Liszt's transcription. The "Turkish March" from Beethoven's *The Ruins of Athens* is familiar enough too, though it's not every day of the week that we can compare Liszt's first, succinctly piquant transcription with his two extended and elaborated later versions, as Howard allows us to do here. The 'mystery' composer of the five is Liszt's protégé (and ultimately his successor at Weimar), the Danish-born, Belgian-naturalized Eduard Lassen, at his best in his Wagner-influenced music for Hebbel and Calderon, but on this showing no match for Goethe's *Faust*. As always Howard meets diabolical technical challenges with commendable *sang-froid*, and the recording maintains Hyperion's customary fidelity.

Liszt. ORGAN WORKS.
Reubke. Sonata on the 94th Psalm. **Thomas Trotter** (org). Argo 430 244-2ZH. Played on the organ of the Münster zur Schönen Unsrer Lieben Frau, Ingolstadt, Germany. Recorded in 1989.
Liszt: Prelude and Fugue on the name B-A-C-H, S260. Gebet, S265 (arr. Gottschalg). Orpheus S98 (arr. Schaab). Prometheus, S99 (trans. Guillou).

⏐ ·•⁺ 1h 13m DDD 2/91 ⏐ 𝄪 S

This is a spectacular organ record, made on a big modern instrument in the very resonant acoustic of the Church of Our Lady, at Ingolstadt in Germany, which Thomas Trotter plays with great flair. The music is no less spectacular, belonging as it does to the nineteenth century and a full-blooded romantic tradition. The longest piece is the Reubke Sonata, music by a composer who died at 24 and is virtually unknown except to organists, and even to them by just this one work. It is a mighty one-movement sonata which reflects the influence of his teacher Liszt, to whom he went in 1856 shortly after the older man completed his great Piano Sonata, and was inspired by the powerful text of *Psalm* No. 94, which calls for God's judgement upon the wicked. Liszt himself is represented here by another work of surging strength, the *Prelude and Fugue* on the letters of the name Bach (the notes B flat, A, C, B natural), which make for a tightly chromatic motif yielding great harmonic and contrapuntal possibilities, not least in the fugue. This work begins the recital, and is followed by the same composer's serene tone poem in praise of music which he called *Orpheus*. Then comes the Reubke, and the other Liszt items follow it and thus make a sort of triptych with the longest work (the Sonata) as the centrepiece. Though two of the Liszt pieces are transcriptions rather than original organ works, they are effective in this form.

New review
Liszt. ROMANTIC SONGS. **Thomas Hampson** (bar); **Geoffrey Parsons** (pf). EMI CDC5 55047-2. Texts and translations included.
Liszt: Die Vätergruft, S281. Go not, happy day, S335. Es rauschen die Winde, S294. Ihr Auge, S310. Uber allen Gipfeln ist Ruh, S306. Am Rhein, in schönen Strome, S272. Es muss ein Wunderbares sein, S314. Vergiftet sind meine Lieder, S289. La Tombe et la rose, S285. Comment, dissaient-ils, S276. Oh! quand je dors, S282. *Wagner:* Mignonne. Tout n'est qu'images fugitives. Les Deux grenadiers. Faust Lieder, Op. 5 — No. 4, Es war einmal ein König; No. 5, Was machst du mir. Der Tannenbaum. *Berlioz:* Mélodies Irlande, Op. 2 — No. 1, Le Coucher du soleil, revêrie; No. 4, La Belle voyageuse; No. 7, L'origine de la harpe; No. 8, Adieu, Bessy; No. 9, Elégie en prose.

⏐ ·•⁺ 1h 17m DDD 5/94 ⏐ 𝄪 P

An enterprising programme introduces us to Hampson the scholar as well as the singer. In a long introductory note, of which he was the co-author, Hampson seeks to provide the social and artistic background against which Berlioz, Wagner and Liszt should be viewed and to reveal the links between these three adventurous spirits — a valuable exercise, although it is undertaken with a rather lofty tone. To some extent that spills over into the performances. Hampson makes heavy work of his Berlioz songs, taken from *Irlande,* possibly because he is trying to make them seem more substantial than they really are. He is on stronger ground in the Wagner songs and "Les Deux grenadiers", the most ambitious of them, is given a bold and dramatic performance. For his Liszt group Hampson wisely mixes some well-known songs among the rarities. The singing is of de luxe quality, a warm and romantic baritone voice shaping luxurious phrases, enhanced by Geoffrey Parsons's rich sonorities at the piano. *Oh! quand je dors*, his last song, is guaranteed to send the listener away wanting more.

Liszt. LIEDER. **Brigitte Fassbaender** (mez); **Jean-Yves Thibaudet** (pf). Decca 430 512-2DH. Texts and translations included. Recorded in 1990.
O lieb', so lang du lieben kannst, S298. Freudvoll und leidvoll, S280. Mignons Lied, I, S275. Es war ein König in Thule, I, S278. Uber allen Gipfeln ist Ruh, S306. Der du von dem Himmel bist, S279. Ich möchte hingehn, S296. Und wir dachten der Toten, S338. Lasst mich ruhen, S317. Blume und Duft, S324. Du bist wie eine Blume, S287. Im Rhein, im schönen Strome,

S272. Was Liebe sei, S288. Hohe Liebe, S307. Einst, S332. Wieder möcht ich dir begegnen, S322. Ihr Auge, S310. Dei drei Zigeuner, S320.

58m DDD 9/92

The mysteriously widespread idea of Liszt as a piano virtuoso *par excellence* but short on depth is nowhere in his output given the lie more than in his Lieder. These intense, beautiful settings have in many cases been selected by Fassbaender from several different revisions by the composer, and generally she has chosen the pithiest, most emotionally concentrated incarnation. The amount of revision Liszt chose to give the songs may be some suggestion of their significance to him; the operative word, Fassbaender suggests in her loving and illuminating introduction is 'fervour'. Her singing bears this out to its fullest extent: the opening song of the disc, *O lieb', so lang du lieben kannst* (better known in its piano version as the third *Liebestraume*) sets the tone for all that follows including settings of such well-known poems as *Du bist wie eine Blume* and *Im Rhein, im schönen Strome* performed with unshakeable conviction, deep passion and the most glorious tone. Jean-Yves Thibaudet's piano playing glistens and glows around Fassbaender's voice and he sails happily through the most demanding moments such as the disc's final song *Dei drei Zigeuner*. The recorded sound is superb and the interpretations probably as near to definitive as one could hope to find.

Further listening ...

Fantasia on Hungarian Folk-themes, S123[a]. Mazeppa, S100. Les préludes, S97. Mephisto Waltz No. 2, S111. Hungarian Rhapsodies, S359: Nos. 2, 4 and 5. Tasso, lamento e trionfo, S96. [a]**Shura Cherkassky** (pf); **Berlin Philharmonic Orchestra/Herbert von Karajan.** DG 415 967-2GH2 (9/86).

Hungarian Rhapsodies, S244 — Nos. 1-19: No. 1 in C sharp minor; No. 2 in C sharp minor; No. 3 in B flat major; No. 4 in E flat major; No. 5 in E minor, "Héroïde-Elégiaque"; No. 6 in D flat major; No. 7 in D minor; No. 8 in F sharp minor, "Capriccio"; No. 9 in E flat major, "Carnival in Pest"; No. 10 in E major; No. 11 in A minor; No. 12 in C sharp minor; No. 13 in A minor; No. 14 in F minor; No. 15 in A minor, "Rákóczy"; No. 16 in A minor, "For the Munkascy festivities in Budapest"; No. 17 in D minor; No. 18 in F sharp minor, "On the occasion of the Hungarian Exposition in Budapest"; No. 19 in D minor. **Roberto Szidon** (pf). DG Galleria 423 925-2GGA2 (3/89).

Années de pèlerinage, première année, S160, "Suisse". **Jorge Bolet** (pf). Decca 410 160-2DH (12/84).

Années de pèlerinage, deuxième année, S161, "Italie". **Jorge Bolet** (pf). Decca 410 161-2DH (7/85).

12 Transcendental Studies, S139. **Claudio Arrau** (pf). Philips 416 458-2PH (6/86).

Prelude and Fugue on the name B-A-C-H, S260. Evocation à la Chapelle Sixtine, S658. Variations on "Weinen, Klagen, Sorgen, Zagen", S673. Fantasia and Fugue on "Ad nos, ad salutarem undam", S259. **Gunther Kaunzinger** (org). Novalis 150 069-2 (2/91).

Beethoven Symphonies, S464. **Leslie Howard** (pf). Hyperion CDA66671/5 (9/93).

Romance oubliée, S132[a]. *Coupled with* **Berlioz.** Harold in Italy[a]. **Gounod.** Hymne à Sainte Cécile, S491. **Meyerbeer.** Le Moine, S416. Festmarsch zu Schillers Jähriger Geburtsfeier, S549. **Leslie Howard** (pf); [a]**Paul Coletti** (va). Hyperion CDA66683 (11/93).

Variations on a Waltz by Diabelli, S147. Waltz in A major, S208a. Variations on a Theme from Méhul's "Joseph", S147a. Eight Variations, S148. Variations brillantes on a Theme by Rossini, S149. Impromptu brillant on themes by Rossini and Spontini, S150. Allegro di bravura, S151. Rondi di bravura, S152. Etude en douze exercices, S136. Scherzo in G minor, S153. Hungarian Recruiting Dances (Zum Andenken), S241. Waltz in E flat major, S209a. Galop de bal, S220. Marche hongroise in E flat minor, S233b. Klavierstücke in A flat major, S189a. Liebesträume No. 2, "Gestorben war ich", S192a. Berceuse, S174. Feuille d'Album (Albumblatt) in E major,

S164. Feuille d'Album in A minor, S167. Feuilles d'Album in A flat major, S165. Apparitions, S155. **Leslie Howard** (pf). Hyperion CDA66771/2 (7/94).

Missa choralis, S10ª. Via crucis, S53[b]. [b]**Donna Brown** (sop); [b]**Eliane Tantcheff** (mez); [b]**Marie-Claude Alary** (contr); [b]**Régis Oudot** (ten); [b]**Michel Piquemal** (bar); [ab]**Vocal Audite Nova de Paris Ensemble/Jean Sourisse** with [ab]**Marie-Claire Alain** (org). Erato 2292-45350-2 (10/92).

Key to symbols

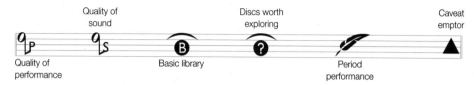

Quality of sound   Discs worth exploring   Caveat emptor

Quality of performance   Basic library   Period performance

George Lloyd
British 1913-

New review

G. Lloyd. A Symphonic Mass. **Brighton Festival Chorus; Bournemouth Symphony Orchestra/George Lloyd.** Albany TROY100-2. Text and translation included. Recorded in 1993.

lh lm   DDD   12/93

It is a joy to come across such a powerful expression of faith — in humanity as well as God — written in our own time that utterly eschews barbed wire and avant-garde self-consciousness, producing writing which is real and genuinely inspired. The music is immediately communicative, deeply felt and without a single facile bar. Although, of course, there is much else besides, the structure has at its core a principal motif, a real tune, which continually re-creates itself throughout the work at key moments. Lloyd has told us that he chose the piece's title carefully, for while he uses the Latin text of the Mass, his working is designedly non-liturgical in conception. This is arguably one of the finest pieces of English choral writing of the twentieth century. Listening to it in the composer's electrically intense performance, so realistically reproduced, is a very moving experience.

Further listening ...

Piano Concerto No. 3. **Kathryn Stott** (pf); **BBC Philharmonic Orchestra/George Lloyd.** Albany TROY019-2 (3/90).

Symphonies — No. 6ª; No. 10, "November Journeys"[b]. John Socman — Overtureª. [b]**BBC Philharmonic Brass;** [a]**BBC Philharmonic Orchestra/George Lloyd.** Albany TROY015-2 (8/89).

Sir Andrew Lloyd Webber
British 1948-

Suggested listening ...

JESUS CHRIST SUPERSTAR. **Various artists.** First Night Records ENCORECD7 (10/92).

THE PHANTOM OF THE OPERA. **Original London cast.** Polydor 831 273-2 (7/87).

SUNSET BOULEVARD. **Original London cast.** Polydor 519 767-2.

Duarte Lôbo

Lôbo. Missa Pro defunctis a 6. Missa Vox clamantis. **The Tallis Scholars/Peter Phillips.** Gimell CDGIM028. Texts and translations included.

Ih 6m DDD 3/93

The Portuguese composer Duarte Lôbo was the leading musician of his country during the first half of the seventeenth century. Heavily influenced by the music of the Spaniard, Victoria, Lôbo's music is an interesting development of the late Renaissance style, to which Lôbo brought both originality and austere expression. The two works on this disc are excellent examples of his music, with the Requiem representing the more creative side of Lôbo's character. Written for six parts this is a sonorous and inventive masterpiece, with a considerable sense of the baroque about it. By contrast the Mass is rather more reserved: written also for six voices it has a noble, restrained character, which still holds the listener's attention throughout. The performances by The Tallis Scholars under Peter Phillips are excellent: intonation is perfect, and Phillips's control of phrasing, tempos and dynamics is masterly throughout. Aided by an excellent ecclesiastical acoustic, the recording is warm without being muddy: both clarity and perspective of sound are exemplary. While Lôbo is unlikely to be a composer whose works command a large following, he was clearly a master in his own right, and this fine recording goes a long way in both establishing and justifying his reputation.

Pietro Locatelli

Suggested listening ...

Introduttioni Teatrali and Concerti, Op. 4 — No. 12 in F major. *Coupled with* **Leo.** Concerto in D major for Four Violins and Strings. *Torelli:* Concerto in E minor for Four Violins and Strings. *Mossi:* Concertos, Op. 4 — No. 12 in G minor. *Valentini:* Concerti grossi, Op. 7 — No. 11 in A minor. **Cologne Musica Antiqua/Reinhard Goebel.** Archiv Produktion 435 393-2AH (9/92). *See review in the Collections section; refer to the Index to Reviews.*

12 Flute Sonatas, Op. 2. **Stephen Preston** (fl); **Anthony Pleeth** (vc); **Christopher Hogwood** (hpd). L'Oiseau Lyre 436 191-2OH2 (6/93).

Matthew Locke

New review
Locke. The Tempest[a]. Musick for His Majesty's Sackbutts and Cornetts[b].
Purcell. Abdelazar, Z570[c] — Incidental Music. [a]**Judith Nelson,** [a]**Emma Kirkby,** [a]**Prudence Lloyd,** [c]**Joy Roberts** (sops); [a]**Martyn Hill,** [a]**Rogers Covey-Crump,** [a]**Richard Morton,** [a]**Alan Byers** (tens); [a]**David Thomas** (bass); [b]**Michael Laird Cornett and Sackbut Ensemble; Academy of Ancient Music/Christopher Hogwood.** L'Oiseau-Lyre 433 191-2OH. Texts included. Items marked [ab] from DSLO507 (7/77), [c] DSLO504 (6/76). Recorded in 1974.

Ih 5m ADD 4/94

The music of *The Tempest* is a collaborative effort of composers chosen by Thomas Shadwell, the playwright, to adorn his adaptation of Davenant and Dryden's own revision of Shakespeare's play seven years earlier. The most distinguished among them is Locke. He was responsible for the fine instrumental music including the remarkable 'curtain tune' which menacingly and savagely depicts the storm, complete with performance directions and dynamics. Despite the variable quality of the music, this important recording from 1977 is welcome. It remains the only 'complete' version of this work on disc. The performances are not as technically assured as you would expect from the Academy of Ancient Music today but there is no shortage of spirit. The same can be said for the singers whose inconsistency is outweighed by a type of characterization which is not so easy to create in these relatively unpioneering times. Locke's *Musick for His Majesty's Sackbutts and Cornetts* and Purcell's incidental music from *Abdelazar* provide the fillers.

Further listening ...

Sacred Choral Music — Descende caelo cincta sororibus (The Oxford Ode). How doth the city sit solitary. Super flumina Babylonis. O be joyful in the Lord, all ye lands. Audi, Domine, clamantes ad te. Lord let me know mine end. Jesu auctor clementie. Be Thou exalted, Lord. **Choir of New College, Oxford; The Parley of Instruments/Edward Higginbottom** with **Peter Holman** (org). Hyperion CDA66373 (9/91).

Charles Martin Loeffler
French/American 1861-1935

New review

Loeffler. Two Rhapsodies[a].
Nielsen. Wind Quintet, FS100[b].
Prokofiev. Quintet in G minor, Op. 39[c]. **Chamber Music Northwest** ([b]Ransom Wilson, fl; Allan Vogel, ob; [b]Julie Feves, bn; [b]David Jolley, hn; [c]Pamela Frank, vn; [a]Paul Neubauer, [c]Steven Tenenbom, vas; [a]Irma Vallecillo, pf)/**David Shifrin** ([c]cl). Delos DE3136. Recorded in 1992.

1h 11m DDD 12/93

Charles Martin Loeffler, Nielsen's close contemporary, was for many years assistant Concert Master of the Boston Symphony Orchestra. His *Rhapsodies*, once stigmatized as "decadent", are reworkings of two songs to texts by Maurice Rollinat. There is a whiff of Debussy in the second *Rhapsody* to perk up the superior salon idiom which prevails in the first. Both are performed here with great delicacy of feeling and evident concern for balance. Prokofiev's Quintet, by contrast, is one of his more exploratory, chromatic scores, although the influence of the Stravinsky *L'histoire du soldat* is not difficult to detect. Despite the presence of familiar soloists in Chamber Music Northwest, the emphasis is on ensemble polish and well-matched tone rather than individualistic display. The 'individual' v. 'collective' aspect of the Nielsen is in fact a little underplayed, and it is certainly the case that other performers have found darker clouds in the *Praeludium* which precedes the finale. This is limpid, comfortable, ultimately slightly under-characterized Nielsen, beautifully played and most sensitively recorded. There are helpful notes provided and, it has to be said, a notably garish cover.

Frank Loesser
American 1910-1969

Suggested listening ...

GUYS AND DOLLS. **Original 1992 Broadway revival cast.** RCA Victor 09026-61317-2 (10/92).

THE MOST HAPPY FELLA. **Original Broadway cast.** Sony Broadway SK48010 (5/93).

Theo Loevendie
Dutch 1930-

Suggested listening ...

Venus and Adonis[d]. Strides[c]. Six Turkish Folk Poems[ad]. Music for Flute and Piano[b]. NAIMA[bd] — A man of life upright; As fast as thou shalt wane. Back Bay Bicinium[d]. [a]**Rosemary Hardy**

(sop); [b]**Jard van Nes** (mez); [c]**John Snijders** (pf); [d]**Nieuw Ensemble/Ed Spanjaard.**
Etcetera KTC1097 (12/91).

Frederick Loewe

German/American 1901-1988

Suggested listening ...

BRIGADOON. **Soloists; Ambrosian Chorus; London Sinfonietta/John McGlinn.** EMI
CDC7 54481-2 (1/93).

Simon Lole

British 1957-

New review

Lole. CHORAL WORKS. **St Mary Collegiate Church Choir, Warwick/Simon Lole** with
Kevin Bowyer (org). Regent REGCD107. Notes and texts included. Recorded in 1992.
This is the Day. The St David's Service. Angels. Vesper Responsory. The St Nicholas Service.
An Evening Hymn. I will lift up mine eyes. O God the Holy Spirit. The Father's Love. Shall we
not love thee, Mother dear?. I got me Flowers. The St Mary's Service. Love Eternal.
Traditional (arr. Lole): Mary's Child. Morning Star. Child of the Manger. The Journey.
Jesus, good above all other.

⠶ 52m DDD 3/94

A world-class organist and a top-notch recording would be wasted if neither the choirs nor the
music were worth hearing on disc. As it is, both manifestly are. Simon Lole is a gifted choir trainer.
The Warwick girls' choir is tonally rather hard-edged but tautly disciplined and readily responsive.
The boys' voices are full-blooded, nicely-blended and possess an impressive expressive range. Best
of all are the men, who display the kind of musical and vocal maturity often lacking from even the
best cathedral and college choirs. As a composer Lole's style can best be described as 'comfortable
anglicanism'. There are fluffy carol arrangements with Rutteresque accompaniments (including an
enchanting *Jesus, good above all other*), well-crafted and eminently singable congregational services, a
fluent Evening Service for girls' voices, and two beautifully sinuous tunes, *The Journey* and Lole's
only published piece *The Father's Love*. A rewarding disc for all lovers of church music.

Albert Lortzing

German 1801-1851

Suggested listening ...

UNDINE. **Soloists; Cologne Radio Chorus and Orchestra/Kurt Eichhorn.** Capriccio
60 017-2 (3/91).

Arthur Lourié

Russian 1892-1966

New review

Lourié. Concerto da camera[a]. A Little Chamber Music[a]. Little Gidding[c]. [c]**Kenneth Riegel**
(ten); [a]**Gidon Kremer**, [b]**Thomas Klug** (vns); **Deutsche Kammerphilharmonie.** DG 437
788-2GH. Texts and translations included. Recorded in 1992.

⠶ 55m DDD 2/94

The accompanying notes describe Arthur Lourié as one of the 'great unknowns' of twentieth-
century music. In Russia before the Easter Revolution he was a futurist, but he failed to

return to Russia after a trip to Western Europe in 1922 and made his home in Paris (his family were of French extraction). *A Little Chamber Music*, the first work Lourié wrote in the West, has a rather heavy neo-classicism that already betrays his closeness to Stravinsky, but it is also unexpectedly Shostakovich-like in its irony. A reference to the *Dies irae* undercuts any expectation of Parisian flippancy; a solemn chorale develops; the music returns to its starting point. Odd, disjointed, but interesting. The *Concerto da camera*, 20 years later and from Lourié's American years, is odd too: a six-movement, somewhat neo-baroque concerto that only behaves as concertos should in the finale. There is a clever juggling with short motives that at one point hints at minimalism but there are longer, stronger melodic lines as well, and they take over entirely in the impassioned, elegiac finale. The roughly contemporary setting of extracts from T.S. Eliot's "Little Gidding" was written not long after the poem was published, and indicates how rapidly Lourié recognized a kindred spirit in the Christian conservative Eliot. The performances could hardly be bettered — Kremer is in his glint-eyed, button-holing, genius-discovering mood, Riegel in excellent voice — and the recording is first-class.

Hermann Løvenskjold
Danish 1815-1870

Suggested listening ...

La Sylphide — ballet. **Royal Danish Orchestra/David Garforth.** Chandos Collect CHAN6546 (4/92)

Nicholas Ludford
British c.1485-1557

Suggested listening ...

Missa Videte miraculum. Ave cuius conceptio. **The Cardinall's Musick/Andrew Carwood.** ASV Gaudeamus CDGAU131 (7/93).

Alexandre Luigini
French 1850-1906

Suggested listening ...

Ballet égyptien, Op. 12 — Suite. *Coupled with* **Ketèlby.** Bells across the meadows. Chal Romano — Descriptive Overture. The Clock and the Dresden Figures. In a Chinese Temple Garden. In a Monastery Garden. In a Persian Market. In the Moonlight (Sous la lune) — Poetic Intermezzo. In the Mystic Land of Egypt. Sanctuary of the Heart — Méditation religieuse. **Soloists; Ambrosian Singers; Philharmonia Orchestra/John Lanchbery; Royal Philharmonic Orchestra/Anatole Fistoulari.** Classics for Pleasure CD-CFP4637 (3/94). *See review under Ketèlbey; refer to the Index to Reviews.*

Jean-Baptiste Lully
Italian-French 1632-1687

New review

Lully. ARMIDE. **Guillemette Laurens** (mez) Armide; **Howard Crook** (ten) Renaud; **Véronique Gens** (sop) Fame, Phenice, Melisse, Shepherdess; **Noémi Rime** (sop) Wisdom, Sidonie, Lucinde, Naiad; **Bernard Delétré** (bass) Hidraot, Ubalde; **Gilles Ragon** (ten) Danish Knight, Fortunate Lover; **John Hancock** (bar) Artemidore, Hate; **Luc Coadou** (bass) Aronte;

Collegium Vocale; La Chapelle Royale Chorus and Orchestra/Philippe Herreweghe. Harmonia Mundi HMC90 1456/7. Notes, text and translation included.

② 2h 36m DDD 8/93

Armide was the last of the *tragédies en musique* in which Lully and his trusty Quinault collaborated — Gluck was to use the same *livret* some 90 years later. Armide, a sorceress and a warrior, has won a victory over the Crusaders; but one of the Christian knights, Renaud (Rinaldo) — the bravest of them all — though held captive, remains unconquered in spirit and impervious to her charms. At last two knights rescue Renaud by breaking Armide's spell with a magic shield. Her palace collapses and she flies away in a winged chariot. Herreweghe and his expert groups of singers and players give a pleasingly rounded account of Lully's accomplished and often strikingly beautiful score. The casting of Guillemette Laurens in the title-role was an inspired choice. She is notably skilful in the art of declamation, is gifted with a sharp ear for detail and has a lively feeling for musical gesture. Howard Crook's Renaud is lightly articulated and tonally well-focused and the remaining soloists make a very impressive showing, too. A must for opera-lovers and Francophiles.

Lully. ATYS. *Prologue* — **Bernard Deletré** (bass) Le Temps; **Monique Zanetti** (sop) Flore; **Jean-Paul Fouchécourt** (bass), **Gilles Ragon** (ten) Zephirs; **Arlette Steyer** (sop) Melpomene; **Agnès Mellon** (sop) Iris. *Tragédie-lyrique* — **Guy de Mey** (ten) Atys; **Agnès Mellon** (sop) Sangaride; **Guillemette Laurens** (mez) Cybèle; **Françoise Semellaz** (sop) Doris; **Jacques Bona** (bass) Idas; **Noémi Rime** (sop) Mélisse; **Jean-François Gardeil** (bass) Célénus; **Gilles Ragon** (ten) Le sommeil; **Jean-Paul Fouchécourt** (ten) Morphée, Trio; **Bernard Deletré** (bass) Phobétor, Sangar; **Michel Laplénie** (ten) Phantase; **Stephan Maciejewski** (bass) Un songe funeste; **Isabelle Desrochers** (sop) Trio; **Véronique Gens** (sop) Trio; **Les Arts Florissants Chorus and Orchestra/William Christie.** Harmonia Mundi HMC90 1257/9. Notes, text and translation included.

③ 2h 50m DDD 7/87

Once upon a time Lully's melodies were the property of the common people. Not so today when, apart from occasional revivals and broadcasts, his operas are largely forgotten. *Atys* is reputed to have been Louis XIV's favourite opera and here William Christie and a fine line-up of soloists bring the work to life in a most compelling way. There are some beautiful choruses and ensembles through-out the opera which should make wide and immediate appeal; but it is in the Third Act where Lully treats his audience to a *sommeil* or sleep scene that much of the most arresting and original music is contained. Recorded sound is effective and the booklet contains the full libretto.

Further listening ...

Divertissements. **Guillemette Laurens** (mez); **Capriccio Stravagante/Skip Sempé.** Deutsche Harmonia Mundi RD77218 (1/91).

Harpsichord Works (trans. d'Anglebert). **Kenneth Gilbert.** Harmonia Mundi HMC90 1267 (4/88).

Le bourgeois gentilhomme — Incidental Music. *Coupled with* **Campra.** L'Europe galante — Ballet Suite. **Soloists; Tölz Boys' Choir; La Petite Bande/Gustav Leonhardt.** Deutsche Harmonia Mundi Editio Classica GD77059 (2/91).

ALCESTE. **Soloists; Sagittarius Vocal Ensemble; La Grande Ecurie et La Chambre du Roy/Jean-Claude Malgoire.** Disques Montaigne 782012 (4/93).

Hans Christian Lumbye
Danish 1810-1874

New review
Lumbye. WALTZES, GALOPS AND POLKAS. **Danish National Radio Symphony Orchestra/Gennadi Rozhdestvensky.** Chandos CHAN9209. Recorded in 1993.

Amélie. Britta. Champagne, Op. 14. Columbine. Concert. Copenhagen Steam Railway Galop. The Guard of Amager — Final Galop. Mon salut à Petersburg. Napoli — Final Galop. Petersburg Champagne. Petersburg. Pictures from a Dream. Polonaise with cornet solo. Queen Louise's Waltz. Salute to August Bournonville.

1h 8m   DDD   2/94

The career of Hans Christian Lumbye makes a fascinating story. Starting as a trumpeter in the Danish dragoon guards, he became the leader of an orchestra intent on matching what an Austrian band had been achieving in Copenhagen in 1839 with the waltzes and galops of Lanner and Johann Strauss senior. Lumbye's own waltzes and galops written for the newly-opened Tivoli Gardens in Copenhagen brought him instant success. In 1844 he extended his experience in visits to Paris and Vienna, but for the rest of his life, knowing his own forte, he was content to base himself at the Tivoli. Yet in 1850 he took five months leave, and paid a summer visit to St Petersburg, writing several pieces specially for the occasion. Aptly, a distinguished Russian conductor of today, Gennadi Rozhdestvensky, offers three of those St Petersburg items in his programme with the Danish National Radio Symphony Orchestra, including a *St Petersburg Polka* with a vaguely Slavonic-sounding main theme in the minor mode. Also a march, *Salute to St Petersburg*, which he dedicated to the Tsar, but which was in fact adapted from a March for the Danish Civil Guard, written two years earlier. The collection ends with a St Petersburg *Champagne Galop*, which like the piece which gives the disc its title, "Champagne Galop", begins with popping corks and also includes a xylophone episode, suggesting a tune played on bottles. Rozhdestvensky is marvellous at bringing out the fun of all this, continually making you smile. Lumbye favourites in the selection include the *Copenhagen Steam Railway Galop*, with its train imitations, as well as the *Britta* Polka, while other items like the Concert Polka for two violins and the Polonaise with cornet solo are also made memorable by Rozhdestvensky's sly moulding and pointing. The recording is atmospheric.

David Lumsdaine
Australian 1931-

Suggested listening ...

Aria for Edward John Eyre[a]. What shall I sing[b]. [a]**Jane Manning,** [b]**Mary Wiegold** (sops); [a]**John Baddeley,** [a]**John Rye** (narrs); **Gemini/**[a]**Elgar Howarth.** NMC NMC007 (6/93).

Thomas Lupo
British c.1598-1628

Suggested listening ...

Fantasy-Airs a 3 — Nos. 16, 17 and 20. Fantasy-Airs a 4 — Nos. 5-7, 11 and 12. Fantasies a 4 — Nos. 4 and 9. *Coupled with* **Gibbons:** Two Fantasias a 4. 9 Fantasias a 3. Galliard a 3. **The Parley of Instruments/Peter Holman.** Hyperion CDA66395 (9/91).

Witold Lutoslawski
Polish 1913-

New review

Lutoslawski. Concerto for Orchestra. Symphony No. 3. **Chicago Symphony Orchestra/ Daniel Barenboim.** Erato 4509-91711-2. Recorded at performances in the Orchestra Hall, Chicago in 1992.

58m   DDD   8/93

Lutoslawski's Third Symphony was commissioned by the Chicago SO and first performed by them under Sir Georg Solti in 1983, but only nine years later did the orchestra record the work. None of the versions made in the interim can equal Barenboim's blend of refined detail and cumulative power, and the Erato recording is also more faithful to the dynamics marked in the score. The *Concerto for Orchestra*, completed almost 30 years before the symphony, is comparatively conservative in style, but it has ample substance to match its panache. It also remains a formidable challenge to an orchestra. As with the symphony, Barenboim's strength is the large-scale creation and sustaining of tension, and the Erato recording contains the heavy climaxes without draining them of clarity or impact.

Lutoslawski. Paganini Variations.
Rachmaninov. Rhapsody on a Theme of Paganini, Op. 43.
Shostakovich. Concerto in C minor for piano, trumpet and strings, Op. 35[a]. **Peter Jablonski** (pf); [a]**Raymond Simmons** (tpt); **Royal Philharmonic Orchestra/Vladimir Ashkenazy.** Decca 436 239-2DH. Recorded in 1991.

55m DDD 12/92

Among Peter Jablonski's credentials are, apparently, having been voted best jazz drummer in Sweden at the age of seven. You can see how such a talent might come in handy for the Shostakovich, as riotous a succession of high and low styles as has ever successfully cohabited in one concerto. Jablonski is in fact a little on the cool side here, but his level-headed approach never misses the idiomatic point, and trumpeter Raymond Simmons is an accomplished partner. Rachmaninov's *Rhapsody* was actually composed one year after the Shostakovich in 1934, and it would not be forcing a point to detect interesting similarities in approach behind their obviously disparate surfaces. Here Jablonski does not quite convince at moments of emotional extreme, though there is certainly nothing in his interpretation to cause offence, and orchestral support from the RPO and Ashkenazy is first-rate. But the gem on this disc is undoubtedly the Lutoslawski. This 1978 arrangement of the familiar 1941 two-piano *Paganini Variations* is masterly in its orchestration and the high jinks of the original are genuinely enhanced by the change of palette, as they are by the panache and verve of the performance. A demonstration quality recording from Decca.

Lutoslawski. Partita for Violin, Orchestra and Obbligato Solo Piano (1985)[a]. Chain 2 for Violin and Orchestra (1984)[b].
Stravinsky. Violin Concerto in D major[c]. **Anne-Sophie Mutter** (vn); [a]**Phillip Moll** (pf); [ab]**BBC Symphony Orchestra/Witold Lutoslawski;** [c]**Philharmonia Orchestra/Paul Sacher.** DG 423 696-2GH.

56m DDD 2/89

This disc contains some spellbinding violin playing in a splendidly lifelike recording, and it's a bonus that the music, while unquestionably 'modern', needs no special pleading: its appeal is instantaneous and long-lasting. Anne-Sophie Mutter demonstrates that she can equal the best in a modern classic — the Stravinsky Concerto — and also act as an ideal, committed advocate for newer works not previously recorded. The Stravinsky is one of his liveliest neoclassical pieces, though to employ that label is, as usual, to underline its rough-and-ready relevance to a style that uses Bach as a springboard for an entirely individual and unambiguously modern idiom. Nor is it all 'sewing-machine' rhythms and pungently orchestrated dissonances. There is lyricism, charm, and above all humour: and no change of mood is too fleeting to escape the razor-sharp responses of this soloist and her alert accompanists, authoritatively guided by the veteran Paul Sacher. Lutoslawski's music has strongly individual qualities that have made him perhaps the most approachable of all contemporary composers. This enthralling collaboration between senior composer and youthful virtuoso is not to be missed.

Further listening ...

Paroles tissées[a]. Cello Concerto[b]. Postlude I[bc]. Livre pour Orchestre[d]. [a]**Louis Devos** (ten); [b]**Roman Jablónski** (vc); [b]**Katowice Radio Symphony Orchestra;** [ad]**Warsaw National Philharmonic Orchestra;** [cd]**Jan Krenz;** [ab]**Witold Lutoslawski.** Polskie Nagrania Muza PNCD042 (9/90).

Venetian games[a]. Trois Poèmes d'Henri Michaux[b]. Symphony No. 2[c]. [b]**Cracow Polish Radio Choir**; [ac]**Warsaw National Philharmonic Orchestra/**[a]**Witold Rowicki**, [c]**Witold Lutoslawski**; [b]**Katowice Radio Symphony Orchestra/Jan Krenz.** Polskie Nagrania Muza PNCD041 (9/90).

Preludes and Fugues for 13 Solo Strings[a]. Mi-parti[a]. Novelette[b]. [a]**Polish Chamber Orchestra/Witold Lutoslawski**; [b]**Junge Deutsche Philharmonie/Heinz Holliger.** Polskie Nagrania Muza PNCD043 (9/90).

Piano Concerto[a]. Chain 3. Novelette. [a]**Krystian Zimerman** (pf); **BBC Symphony Orchestra/Witold Lutoslawski.** DG 431 664-2GH (4/92).

Agnes Elisabeth Lutyens
British 1906-1983

New review

Lutyens. VOCAL AND CHAMBER WORKS. [a]**Jane Manning** (sop); [b]**Jane's Minstrels/ Roger Montgomery.** NMC NMCD011. Notes, texts and translations included. Recorded in 1992.
Chamber Concerto No. 1, Op. 8 No. 1[b]. The Valley of Hatsu-Se, Op. 62[ab]. Six Tempi, Op. 42[b] Lament of Isis on the Death of Osiris[a]. Triolet I, Op. 160[a]. Triolet II, Op. 160[b]. Requiescat, "in memoriam Igor Stravinsky"[ab].

Ih 6m DDD 10/93

Serialism for Elizabeth Lutyens was no dogma or easy route to 'modernity' but a refining process, and with it she distilled a very individual voice. It is salutary and in a way thrilling to set her First Chamber Concerto of 1940 in the context of its age: who else in Britain at that time was capable of such elegant rigour, channelling such an intense lyricism? It is — or should be — a landmark of recent British music. The *Six Tempi* are its lineal descendant of nearly 20 years later: still more pared-down, 'late serial' in their bare economy but all of them radiating out from the tenderly haunting funeral march at their centre and all rooted in a lyricism which we can now recognize as Lutyens's own: no wonder this piece prompted, at an unexpected meeting with Stravinsky, an embrace and a cry of "This is the sort of music that I like!". Moving in another way are the two late *Triolets*, each composed when the pain of arthritis made writing an ordeal: 'miniatures' in which the craft of a lifetime is used to draw big images with the fewest possible notes. The performances are eloquently phrased, amply expressive, refined of sound: the recording is clean and natural. One can think of a dozen other Lutyens compositions that would be welcome on CD, but this collection has been very shrewdly compiled to represent her at her best.

Sergey Lyapunov
Russian 1859-1924

New review

Lyapunov. Symphony No. 1 in B minor, Op. 12. Ballada in C sharp minor, Op. 2. **Moscow State Symphony Orchestra/Fedor Glushchenko.** Olympia OCD519. Recorded in 1993.

58m DDD 11/93

Sergei Lyapunov's output includes two symphonies which can be ranged alongside those of Glazunov, Glière and his teacher Taneyev as characteristic products of Russia's pre-revolution 'Silver Age'. The presiding spirits in the First Symphony are Borodin and Tchaikovsky, and the warmth of Lyapunov's lyrical invention at times brings him into coincidental proximity with Elgar. The same qualities may be found in the *Ballada*, which despite the misleading opus number actually postdates the symphony. The recording manages to combine the recessed spaciousness of the classic Soviet recordings of the 1960s and 1970s with a cleanness and clarity they rarely achieved (some edits remain clearly audible, however). Much the same could be said of the playing — excellently prepared, generous in expression yet retaining the best features of the national tradition. Fans of the non-hysterical tendency in Russian music will find much to enjoy here.

Further listening ...

Transcendental Studies — No. 1 in F sharp major, "Berceuse"; No. 2 in D sharp minor, "Rondes des fantômes"; No. 3 in B major, "Carillon"; No. 4 in G sharp minor, "Terek"; No. 5 in E major, "Nuit d'été"; No. 6 in C sharp minor, "Tempête"; No. 7 in A major, "Idylle"; No. 8 in F sharp minor, "Chant épique"; No. 9 in D major, "Harpes éoliennes"; No. 10 in B minor, "Lesghinka"; No. 11 in G major, "Rondes des Sylphes"; No. 12 in E minor, "Elégie en mémoire de François Liszt". **Malcolm Binns** (pf). Pearl SHECD9624 (5/92).

Hamish MacCunn
British 1868-1916

Suggested listening ...

The land of the mountain and the flood, Op. 3. *Coupled with* **Butterworth.** A Shropshire Lad. Two English Idylls. The banks of green willow. **Coleridge-Taylor.** Ballade in A minor, Op. 33. Symphonic Variations on an African Air, Op. 63. **Royal Liverpool Philharmonic Orchestra/Grant Llewellyn.** Argo 436 401-2ZH (6/93). *See review under Butterworth; refer to the Index to Reviews.*

Edward MacDowell
American 1860-1908

Suggested listening ...

Piano Concerto No. 2 in D minor, Op. 23[a]. Woodland Sketches, Op. 51 — No. 1, To a Wild Rose[b]. *Coupled with* **Schumann.** Piano Concerto in A minor, Op. 54[c]. **Van Cliburn** (pf); **Chicago Symphony Orchestra/[a]Walter Hendl, [c]Fritz Reiner.** RCA Victor Van Cliburn Collection GD60420 (10/91).

James MacMillan
Scottish 1959-

New review

MacMillan. Veni, veni, Emmanuel[a]. After the tryst[b]. "...as others see us..."[c]. Three Dawn Rituals[c]. Untold[c]. [a]**Evelyn Glennie** (perc); [b]**Ruth Crouch** (vn); [b]**Peter Evans** (pf); [ac]**Scottish Chamber Orchestra/[a]Jukka-Pekka Saraste.** [c]**James MacMillan.** Catalyst 09026 61916-2. Recorded in 1992.

Ih 8m DDD 9/93

The composer's dedication, strongly motivated by his devout Catholicism and his equally passionate Left-wing stance, invariably colours what he writes, making us share not his precise beliefs but the spiritual intensity that goes with them. As with both Górecki and Tavener there is a physical, even sensual impact in the music alongside the spiritual, but the difference with MacMillan is that he cannot be accused in any way of dabbling in minimalism. In *Veni, veni, Emmanuel* he has written a concerto for percussion that in its energy as well as its colour consistently reflects not just the virtuosity of Evelyn Glennie, for whom it was written, but her charismatic personality, which has directly sparked off his dramatic flair. Taking the Advent plainsong of the title as his basis, he reflects in his continuous 26-minutes sequence the theological implications behind the period between Advent and Easter. *After the tryst* is a brief meditation for violin and piano on the same song-melody which MacMillan used in his big orchestral work *The tryst*. *Untold* is a lyrical slow movement for wind quintet with a haunting Irish flavour, and *Three Dawn Rituals* is an adaptation for conventional ensemble of music originally written for Javanese instruments, three sharply contrasted pieces which use many of the techniques developed in *Veni, veni, Emmanuel*. Those techniques are apparent again, using plentiful percussion, in the biggest of the fill-up works, the six movements of "…as others see us…". They are all inspired by portraits of celebrated Englishmen contained in the National Portrait Gallery in Scotland. In each, MacMillan displays his gift for writing with sharp ingenuity, characterizing each subject strikingly, to make this a colourful, attractive suite, with various musical allusions from Tudor music to jazz, adding piquancy. Strong, positive performances, with first-rate, atmospheric sound — this is an outstanding issue.

New review

MacMillan. The Confession of Isobel Gowdie. Tryst. **BBC Scottish Symphony Orchestra/Jerzy Maksymiuk.** Koch-Schwann 310502.

· 54m DDD 10/92

This time the publicity doesn't exaggerate. The première of *The Confession of Isobel Gowdie* at the 1990 Proms was a "spectacular triumph" — nothing less — and this with an audience drawn largely (one presumes) by Beethoven's Fourth Symphony and Sibelius's Violin Concerto. But success can fade with alarming rapidity. What matters now is that years later, away from the uplift of that extraordinary reception, *The Confession of Isobel Gowdie* tells its story as stirringly as ever. If MacMillan's programme (the martyrdom of a Scottish Catholic 'witch') seems over-pictorial, no problem; the progression from rapt modal string threnody (complete with keening *glissandos*) through mounting violence to the re-emergence and transformation of the modal lament is as easy to follow as the 'narrative' of a Mahler symphony — and the after-effect isn't all that dissimilar. Others may be bothered by undisguised echoes of other composers: Copland, Messiaen, Stravinsky, Ives, the famous single-note crescendo from Berg's *Wozzeck* … but the fact that they are undisguised is part of their strength — that and the way they are so obviously drawn into the argument. Of course the quality of the performance matters, and Maksymiuk and his orchestra give the kind of penetrating performance which (usually) only comes from long involvement. *Tryst* too emerges well: the forces may be smaller, but the head-on confrontation of violence with calmer, more humane sounds again generates a compelling musical drama, and the ending, though less spectacular than Isobel Gowdie's final one-tone immolation, works both as an imaginative conclusion and a challenge to go back and dig deeper. Away with caution! Give this a try.

Guillaume de Machaut

French c.1300-1377

Machaut. Messe de Nostre Dame. Je ne cesse de prier (lai "de la fonteinne"). Ma fin est mon commencement. **Hilliard Ensemble/Paul Hillier.** Hyperion CDA66358. Texts and translations included.

· 54m DDD 2/90

Machaut's *Messe de Nostre Dame* is the earliest known setting of the Ordinary Mass by a single composer though we cannot be certain either that Machaut wrote it at one time or even that he initially intended to bring its six movements together. Paul Hillier avoids a full reconstruc-tion: his deference to 'authenticity' restricts itself to the usage of fourteenth-century French pronunciation of the Latin. His ensemble sing two to a part, with prominent counter-tenors. It is arguable whether the group sings the chant at too fast a tempo but they are smooth and flexible and the performance as a whole is fluid and light in texture. Also included are two of Machaut's French compositions. The wonderful *Lai "de la fonteinne"* is admirably sung by three tenors and is pure delight — food for the heart as well as the intellect. The more familiar *Ma fin est mon commencement*, with its retrograde canon, is a final happy addition to this admirable disc.

Additional recommendation …
Messe de Nostre Dame. **Ensemble Gilles Binchois/Dominique Vellard.** Harmonic Records H/CD8931 — · 56m DDD

Further listening ...

Songs — Dame, de qui toute ma joie vient. Foy porter, honneur garder. Dame, je sui cilz/Fins cuers doulz. Tuit mi penser. Dame, mon cuer en vous temaint. Dame a qui m'ottri. Biauté qui toutes autres pere. Je vivroie liement. Rose, liz. Dame, a vous sans retollir. Amours me fait desirer. Douce dame jolie. Felix virgo/Inviolata/Ad te suspiramus. **Gothic Voices/ Christopher Page.** Hyperion CDA66087 (1/84).

French Songs and Motets — Dame, je suis cilz/Fins cuer. Trop plus/Biauté paree/Je ne suis. Tres bonne et belle. Se mesdisans. Dame, je vueil endurer. *Coupled with* **Pycard:** Gloria. **Solage:** Le basile. **Anonymous:** Pour vous servir. Puis que l'aloe ne fine. Jour a jour la vie. Combien que j'aye (two versions). Marticius qui fu. Renouveler me feïst. Fist on dame. Il me convient guerpir. Le ior. En la maison Dedalus. La grant biaute. En esperent. Ay las! quant je pans. **Gothic Voices/Christopher Page.** Hyperion CDA66619 (6/93). *See review in the Collections section; refer to the Index to Reviews.*

Elizabeth Maconchy

British 1907-

Suggested listening ...

Concertinos — Nos. 1 and 2. *Coupled with* **Arnold.** Clarinet Concertos — No. 1, Op. 20; No. 2, Op. 115. You know what sailors are — Scherzetto. **Britten.** Movement for Clarinet and Orchestra. **Thea King** (cl); **English Chamber Orchestra/Barry Wordsworth.** Hyperion CDA66634 (12/93). *See review under Arnold; refer to the Index to Reviews.*

String Quartets Nos. 1-4. **Hanson Quartet.** Unicorn-Kanchana DKPCD9080 (11/89).

String Quartets — Nos. 5-8. **Bingham Quartet.** Unicorn-Kanchana DKPCD9081 (6/90).

String Quartets — Nos. 9-12; No. 13, "Quartetto Corto". **Mistry Quartet.** Unicorn-Kanchana DKPCD9082 (2/91).

Five Sketches for Viola. *Coupled with* **R. Clarke.** Sonata for Viola and Piano[a]. **Shostakovich.** Sonata for Viola and Piano, Op. 147[a]. **Philip Dukes** (va); [a]**Sophia Rahman** (pf). Gamut Classics GAMCD537 (4/94). *See review under Clarke; refer to the Index to Reviews.*

Bruno Maderna

Italian 1920-1973

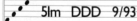

Maderna. SATYRICON. **Paul Sperry** (ten) Trimalchio, Habinnas; **Aurio Tomicich** (bass) Niceros, Eumolpus; **Liliana Oliveri** (sop) Criside; **Milagr Vargas** (contr) Fortunata; **Divertimento Ensemble/Sandro Gorli.** Salabert Actuels SCD9101. Recorded in 1991.

5lm DDD 9/93

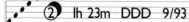

Maderna. HYPERION. **Penelope Walmsley-Clark** (sop); **Bruno Ganz** (spkr); **Jacques Zoon** (fl); **Les Jeunes Soloists Vocal Ensemble; Asko Ensemble/Peter Eötvös.** Disques Montaigne 782014. Notes, text and translation included. Recorded live in 1992.

② 1h 23m DDD 9/93

This pair of works promises a study in musico-dramatic extremes: *Satyricon* (1971-3), after Petronius, is a comedy, centering on the cynical chancer Trimalchio: *Hyperion* (1959-69), after Hölderlin, is a serious meditation on human aspiration and disillusion. Neither is conventionally operatic, neither is more than partly successful, yet the study — thanks to the intermittent power of Maderna's music — proves a fascinating one. That musical power is most fully displayed in *Hyperion*. Characteristically, Maderna left it in a fragmentary state, but even so Peter Eötvös's version may be too fragmented for its own good. However, this is scarcely a crippling flaw, given that most of the score is not vocal at all, and can be related to *Hyperion*'s dramatic theme only by an associative leap of imagination in which the music's moods are heard to reflect the (silent) protagonist's, the solo instruments — primarily the flute — standing for a character who is most directly represented in passages of spoken text. Maderna's tendency to 'set' large amounts of pure prose as a melodramatic mixture of speech and song is even more evident in *Satyricon*, whose longest episode, the gripping tale of the Widow of Ephesus, has an impact to which the text itself contributes at least as much as the music. The sardonic tone of *Satyricon* is generally well-matched by Maderna's light-fingered recourse to parody and quotation, and the performers — especially Paul Sperry as a streetwise New Yorker of a Trimalchio — enter into the spirit of things. The performance of *Hyperion* is no less accomplished, and whatever doubts one has about the work as a dramatic treatment of Hölderlin's noble text, there is some memorable music, especially in the third of the "Dimension"; the second and third of the "Entropia" pieces, and, above all, in the gravely simple setting of the "Song of Fate" — so different from Brahms. The recording of *Satyricon* is rather starved of atmosphere: that of *Hyperion* is excellent.

Leevi Madetoja
Finnish 1897-1947

Madetoja. Symphonies — No. 1 in F major, Op. 29; No. 2 in E flat major, Op. 35. **Iceland Symphony Orchestra/Petri Sakari.** Chandos CHAN9115. Recorded in 1992.

Ih 7m DDD I/93

Leevi Madetoja briefly studied with Sibelius, though his musical idiom also reflects the influence of Strauss, Reger and the Russian post-nationalists such as Glazunov — and there are strong Gallic touches too. Both symphonies (the Second dates from 1916-18) evince a strong sense of purpose and a feeling for proportion that is striking. As a conductor Madetoja championed such French post-romantic as Vincent d'Indy, with whom he had hoped to study, the impressionist masters and such contemporary masters as Szymanowski and Janáček. His music is conventionally post-nationalist in feeling but is distinguished by a certain rigour and clarity. His debt to Sibelius is considerable and the slow movement of the Second Symphony at one point even anticipates *Tapiola*. Although he is not a composer of the first order, Madetoja is a sensitive and cultured creator with a refined technique and engaging manner. Petri Sakari gets excellent results from the Icelandic orchestra and the recording is completely natural and lifelike.

Albéric Magnard
French 1865-1914

Suggested listening ...

Violin Sonata in G major, Op. 13. Three Piano Pieces, Op. 1. En Dieu mon espérance. Cello Sonata in A major, Op. 20. Promenades, Op. 7. Piano and Wind Quintet in D minor, Op. 8. Piano Trio in F minor, Op. 18. Six poèmes, Op. 3. Quatre poèmes, Op. 15. A Henriette. Suite dans le style ancien in G minor, Op. 2. String Quartet in E minor, Op. 16. **Soloists; Artis Quartet.** Accord 20075-2 (3/90).

Gustav Mahler
Austrian 1860-1911

Mahler. SYMPHONIES. **Bavarian Radio Symphony Orchestra/Rafael Kubelík.** DG 429 042-2GX10. Recorded 1967-70.
Symphonies — No. 1 (from SLPM139331, 5/68); No. 2, "Resurrection" (Edith Mathis, sop; Norma Procter, contr; Bavarian Radio Chorus. 139332/3, 4/70); No. 3 (Marjorie Thomas,

contr; Tölz Boys' Choir; Bavarian Rad. Chor. SLPM139337/8, 9/68); No. 4 (Elsie Morison, sop. SLPM139339, 12/68); No. 5 (2720 033, 10/71); No. 6 (139341/2, 11/69); No. 7 (2720 033); No. 8 (Martina Arroyo, Erna Spoorenberg, Mathis, sops; Júlia Hamari, Procter, contrs; Donald Grobe, ten; Dietrich Fischer-Dieskau, bar; Franz Crass, bass; Regensburg Cathedral Boys' Choir; Munich Motet Choir; Bavarian Rad. Chor; North German Radio Chorus; West German Radio Chorus, 2720 033); No. 9 (SLPM139 345/6, 12/67); No. 10 — Adagio (139341/2).

① ⑩ 10h 51m ADD 5/90 ⁹ℙ Ⓑ

There are hundreds of recordings of Mahler's symphonies listed in the current *Classical Catalogue*, so anyone approaching them for the first time is faced with the daunting problem of which versions to acquire. This reissue may well be something of a solution. Here we have a distinguished and highly commendable cycle of the symphonies at bargain price that provides an excellent opportunity for the newcomer to explore the symphonies at a relatively low cost. Kubelík's cycle is still one of the most completely satisfying on disc. There is a breadth and consistency of vision in these interpretations, that comes only from a conductor who has a deep understanding and a long association with this music. The most successful performances are perhaps Symphonies Nos. 1, 4, 5, 7 and 9. The First, notable for its fresh, youthful account and clearly defined textures, is still one of the finest versions available. The Fourth is equally as impressive, with lively tempos and excellent orchestral playing. There is a strong sense of direction and structural unity in this performance and Elsie Morison's warm and poetic performance in the finale is a real delight. Kubelík's reading of Symphonies Nos. 5 and 7 have not always met with the credit that they deserve. The Fifth is a very individual performance, though certainly not lacking in intensity or power. Kubelík avoids dwelling too much on the tragic elements in the first movement of the Seventh and instead tries to build out of the devastation of the Sixth Symphony's finale. The Ninth is a very strong performance indeed, with great clarity of detail and a strong sense of architecture. It would of course be foolish to suggest that Kubelík's cycle is without flaws — the Second Symphony, although not without intensity, lacks perhaps the drama and spirituality of, say, Klemperer or Rattle and the same could be said of the Third. The Eighth is a fine performance superbly recorded and with some excellent singing from the soloists, but is ultimately outclassed by the superb award-winning Tennstedt recording (reviewed further on). The recordings are all clear, spacious and naturally balanced and were recorded in the warm and resonant acoustic of the Munich Herkulessaal between 1967 and 1971. A considerable bargain.

Additional recommendations ...
Nos. 1-9. Lieder aus "Des Knaben Wunderhorn". Das klagende Lied — Der Spielmann; Hochzeitstuck. Lieder eines fahrenden Gesellen. Kindertotenlieder. **Soloists; Collegium Musicum Amstelodam-ense; Amsterdam Toonkunst Choir; Amsterdam Stem des Volks Choir; St Willibrord and Pius X Children's Choir; Netherlands Radio Chorus; St Willibrord's Boys' Choir; Concertgebouw Orchestra/Bernard Haitink.** Philips 434 053-2PM15 — .·' ①⑤ 13h 53m ADD/DDD 12/92 Ⓑ
Nos. 1-9. No. 10 — Adagio. **Soloists; Brooklyn Boys' Choir; Vienna Boys' Choir; Westminster Choir; New York Choral Artists; Vienna Singverein; Vienna State Opera Chorus; New York Philharmonic Orchestra, Royal Concertgebouw Orchestra, Vienna Philharmonic Orchestra/Leonard Bernstein.** DG 435 162-2GX13 — .·' ①③ 12h 44m ADD/DDD 2/92 Ⓑ
Nos. 1-9. **Soloists; Chicago Chorus and Symphony Orchestra/Sir Georg Solti.** Decca 430 804-2DC10 — .· ①⑩ 11h 12m DDD/ADD 4/92 Ⓑ
Nos. 1-9. No. 10 — Adagio. **Soloists; Southend Boys's Choir; Tiffin Boys' School Choir; London Philharmonic Choir and Orchestra/Klaus Tennstedt.** EMI Mahler Edition available as follows:
Nos. 1-4: CMS7 64471-2 — .·' ④ 4h 55m ADD/DDD 4/93 Ⓑ
Nos. 6-8: CMS7 64476-2 — .·' ④ 4h 14m ADD/DDD 4/93 Ⓑ
Nos. 5, 9 and 10 — Adagio: CMS7 64481-2 — .·' ③ 3h 9m ADD/DDD 4/93 Ⓑ

Mahler. Symphony No. 1. **Berlin Philharmonic Orchestra/Claudio Abbado.** DG 431 769-2GH. Recorded live in 1989.

.·' 55m DDD 10/91 ⁹ℙ Ⓑ

While Bernstein's vision of this symphony is intense, with every corner of the work stamped with his personality, Abbado directs a technically immaculate account. Combined with his own particular insight this performance conveys more a sense of Mahler's sound world rather than, as previously, Mahler and Bernstein's. The playing of the BPO combined with the extraordinarily vivid and well balanced recording takes the performance of this work into a new league. Perhaps orchestras are only now fully able to realize Mahler's music in the way that they have been able to with, for instance, Beethoven's for years. There is here a confidence, familiarity and precision that is most unusual and deeply impressive. Added to its technical perfection is Abbado's assured control of tempos, phrasing and dynamics. These define very strongly both the character and atmosphere of each movement which are much more clearly delineated than has usually been the case in the past. The overall result is a major symphonic work at last coming into true focus: both weaknesses, such as its episodic nature, and strengths, its tremendous originality and character, stand fully revealed. Warts and all, this is an outburst of young musical genius fully realized by another, interpretative, genius.

Additional recommendations ...

No. 1. **London Symphony Orchestra/Sir Georg Solti.** Decca 417 701-2DM — .·' DDD ⁹ₚ ⓐ
No. 1. **Frankfurt Radio Symphony Orchestra/Eliahu Inbal.** Denon C37-7537 — .·' 55m DDD 12/85 ⁹ₚ ⓑ
No. 1. **Berlin Philharmonic Orchestra/Bernard Haitink.** Philips 420 936-2PH — .·' 57m DDD 10/88 ⁹ₚ ⓑ
No. 1. **Concertgebouw Orchestra/Leonard Bernstein.** DG 431 036-2GBE — .·' 56m DDD 3/89 ⁹ₚ ⓑ
No. 1. **London Symphony Orchestra/Jascha Horenstein.** Unicorn-Kanchana Souvenir UKCD2012 — .·' 57m ADD 4/89 ⓑ
No. 1. *Lieder eines fahrenden Gesellen.* **Bavarian Radio Symphony Orchestra/Rafael Kubelík.** DG 3D Classics 429 157-2GR — .· 1h 6m ADD 2/90 ⓑ
No. 1. **Chicago Symphony Orchestra/Klaus Tennstedt.** EMI CDC7 54217-2 — .·' 1h 1m DDD 11/91 ⁹ₚ ⓑ
No. 1. **Royal Liverpool Philharmonic Orchestra/Sir Charles Mackerras.** EMI Eminence CD-EMX2197 — .·' 54m DDD 12/92 ⓑ
No. 1. *Blumine.* **City of Birmingham Symphony Orchestra/Simon Rattle.** EMI CDC7 54647-2 — .·' 1h 5m DDD 12/92 ⓑ
No. 1. *Blumine.* **Danish National Radio Symphony Orchestra/Leif Segerstam.** Chandos CHAN9242 — .·' 1h 7m DDD 3/94 ⓑ

Mahler. Symphony No. 2, "Resurrection". **Arleen Auger** (sop); **Dame Janet Baker** (mez); **City of Birmingham Symphony Chorus and Orchestra/Simon Rattle.** EMI CDS7 47962-8. Text and translation included. From EX270598-3 (10/87).

.·' ② 1h 26m DDD 12/87   ⁹ₚ ⁹ₛ ⓑ

New review

Mahler. Symphony No. 2, "Resurrection". **Cheryl Studer** (sop); **Waltraud Meier** (mez); **Arnold Schoenberg Choir; Vienna Philharmonic Orchestra/Claudio Abbado.** DG 439 953-2GH2. Recorded live in the Musikverein, Vienna in 1992.

.·' ② 1h 27m DDD 5/94   ⁹ₚ ⁹ₛ ⓑ

The folk-poems from *Des knaben Wunderhorn*, with their complex mixture of moods and strong ironic edge, formed the basis of Mahler's inspiration for the Second Symphony. It is a work of huge scope, emotionally as well as physically taxing, and from Rattle it receives a performance that remarkably rekindles the feeling of a live performance with a quite breathtaking immediacy. The CBSO play magnificently and Rattle's attention to the letter of the score never hinders his overall vision of this masterpiece. The recording is superb. As has often been suggested in these pages, a live performance should have a headstart in tapping the vital component of spiritual uplift. Abbado presents the score directly with the maximum clarity and precision. In this he is assisted by playing of astounding accuracy and beauty of tone, captured in a recording of (impractically?) wide dynamic range and exquisite detail. Rattle's more radical rethink is not on the agenda; neither is his slow and deliberate treatment of the curious staccato nose-dive at the end of the first movement. Abbado's funeral march is relatively contained, the quiet passages very atmospheric. The deft, restrained manner works well enough in the inner movements, especially the *Andante moderato*. He launches into the third movement *Scherzo* with the audience restive (elsewhere they are pleasingly inaudible); there follows charm but perhaps insufficient sense of threat. The "Urlicht" is again on the cool side, though Waltraud Meier, beautifully controlling her legato while conscientiously projecting to a real public in a large hall, is suddenly impassioned at "Ich bin von Gott". The massive finale, conceived here on the very grandest scale, goes well but not quite well enough: the choir is backwardly balanced and does not efface memories of the Philharmonia Chorus for Klemperer or the City of Birmingham chorus for Rattle. More seriously, there are some agogic touches which impede the natural flow. However, as a document of a great occasion, the Abbado set stands up very well indeed.

Additional recommendations ...
Gabriela Beňačková (sop); Eva Randová (mez); **Czech Philharmonic Chorus and Orchestra/Václav Neumann.** Supraphon Gems 2SUP0020 — .·• 1h 15m 12/87 Ⓑ
Benita Valente (sop); **Maureen Forrester** (mez); **Ardwyn Singers; BBC Welsh Chorus; Cardiff Polyphonic Choir; Dyfed Choir; London Symphony Chorus and Orchestra/ Gilbert Kaplan.** Pickwick IMP Classics DPCD910 — .·• ② 1h 23m DDD 1/89 Ⓑ
Barbara Hendricks (sop); **Christa Ludwig** (mez); **Westminster Choir; New York Philharmonic Orchestra/Leonard Bernstein.** DG 423 395-2GH2 — .·• ② 1h 34m DDD 7/88 ᵠₚ Ⓑ
Elisabeth Schwarzkopf (sop); **Hilde Rössl-Majdan** (mez); **Philharmonia Chorus and Orchestra/Otto Klemperer.** EMI Studio CDM7 69662-2 — .·• 1h 19m ADD 1/90 ᵠₚ Ⓑ

Mahler. Symphony No. 3. **Norma Procter** (contr); **Wandsworth School Boys' Choir; Ambrosian Singers; London Symphony Orchestra/Jascha Horenstein.** Unicorn-Kanchana Souvenir UKCD2006/7. Text and translation included. From RHS302/03 (12/70).

.·• ② 1h 37m ADD 11/88 ᵠₚ Ⓑ

Every now and again, along comes a Mahler *performance* that no serious collector can afford to be without. Horenstein's interpretation of the Third Symphony is an outstanding example and its reissue on CD at mid-price is a major addition to the Mahler discography. No other conductor has surpassed Horenstein in his total grasp of every facet of the enormous score. Even though the LSO strings of the day were not as powerful as they later became, they play with suppleness and a really tense sound, especially appropriate in the kaleidoscopic first movement, where changes of tempo and mood reflect the ever-changing face of nature. Horenstein gives the posthorn solo to a flügelhorn, a successful experiment. His light touch in the middle movements is admirable, and Norma Procter is a steady soloist in "O Mensch! Gib acht!", with the Wandsworth School Boys' Choir bimm-bamming as if they were all Austrian-born! Then comes the *Adagio* finale, its intensity and ecstasy sustained by Horenstein without dragging the tempo. The recording is not as full and rich in dynamic range as some made more recently, but it is still a classic.

Additional recommendations ...
No. 3ᵃ. Four Rückert Liederᵇ. Seven Lieder und Gesänge aus der Jugendzeitᵇ. ᵃ**Martha Lipton** (mez); ᵇ**Dietrich Fischer-Dieskau** (bar); ᵃwomens' chorus of the **Schola Cantorum;** ᵃ**Boys' Choir of the Transfiguration;** ᵃ**New York Philharmonic Orchestra/Leonard Bernstein** (pfᵇ). CBS Masterworks CD42196 — .·• 2h 22m 12/86 ᵠₚ Ⓑ
No. 3ᵃ. Das klagende Liedᵇ. ᵇ**Heather Harper** (sop); ᵃ**Maureen Forrester,** ᵇ**Norma Procter** (contrs); ᵇ**Werner Hollweg** (ten); ᵃ**St Willibrord Church Boys' Choir, Amsterdam;** ᵃwomens' voices of the **Netherlands Radio Chorus; Concertgebouw Orchestra/Bernard Haitink.** Philips 420 113-2PH2 — .·• ② 2h 13m ADD 11/88 ᵠₚ Ⓑ
No. 3. **Jessye Norman** (sop); **Vienna Boys' Choir; Vienna State Opera Concert Choir; Vienna Philharmonic Orchestra/Claudio Abbado.** DG 410 715-2GH2 — .·• ② 1h 43m DDD 11/88 ᵠₚ Ⓑ
No. 3. **Christa Ludwig** (mez); **Brooklyn Boys' Chorus; New York Choral Artists; New York Philharmonic Orchestra/Leonard Bernstein.** DG 427 328-2GH2 — .·• ② 1h 46m DDD 6/89 ᵠₚ Ⓑ

Mahler. Symphony No. 4 in G major. **Kathleen Battle** (sop); **Vienna Philharmonic Orchestra/Lorin Maazel.** Sony Classical SK39072. From IM39072 (3/85). Recorded 1983.

.·• 1h 1m DDD 1/86 ᵠₚ Ⓑ

"With sincere and serene expression" says Mahler's footnote in the finale — "absolutely without parody!" And that is exactly how Lorin Maazel, Kathleen Battle and the Vienna Philharmonic

Orchestra respond to this music: the grotesqueries of the scherzo are nicely underplayed; the darker outbursts of the slow movement are not overloaded with *Angst*; and there is nothing wry or sentimentally nostalgic about "Die himmlischen Freuden". Instead, there is warmth, tenderness and, especially in the closing movement, a kind of heart-easing simplicity, enhanced by the purity and uncloying sweetness of Kathleen Battle's singing. The recording is warm-toned and beautifully balanced and the dynamic range is impressive, though never unrealistic.

Additional recommendations ...
Helmut Wittek (treb); **Concertgebouw Orchestra/Leonard Bernstein.** DG 423 607-2GH — .·⸱ 57m DDD 8/88 ⁹ₚ Ⓑ
Judith Raskin (sop); **Cleveland Orchestra/George Szell.** CBS Maestro CD44713 — .·⸱ 58m ADD 11/88 Ⓑ
Felicity Lott (sop); **London Philharmonic Orchestra/Franz Welser-Möst.** EMI Eminence CD-EMX2139 — .·⸱ 1h 3m DDD 12/88 ⁹ₚ Ⓑ
Barbara Hendricks (sop); **Los Angeles Philharmonic Orchestra/Esa-Pekka Salonen.** Sony Classical SK48380 — .·⸱ 58m DDD 8/92 ⁹ₚ Ⓑ
Dawn Upshaw (sop); **Cleveland Orchestra/Christoph von Dohnányi.** Decca 440 315-2DH — .·⸱ 57m DDD 4/94 Ⓑ

New review
Mahler. Symphony No. 5 in C sharp minor. **Berlin Philharmonic Orchestra/Claudio Abbado.** DG 437 789-2GH. Recorded live in the Philharmonie, Berlin in 1993.

.·⸱ 1h 9m DDD 12/93   ⁹ₚ Ⓑ

The *Adagietto* is suddenly, almost imperceptibly, there. It is the hallmark of any great performance of the symphony, and Abbado is in amongst the very select few as these magical bars materialize. It might even be the most beautiful, the most subtly inflected account of the movement we have yet heard on disc; the breathless *pianopianissimo* to a barely grazed *glissando* towards the close is out of this world. So too the huge central *Scherzo*, another of those testing movements separating natural Mahlerians from the would-bes. The key here is patience — respect for space, silence, atmosphere. Not even Bernstein (also DG) quite matches Abbado's relish of the finale's airborne fantasy (how commonly this movement is driven to distraction): it's that delicate balance between tip-toeing sweetness and light and inherently rugged, foot-stomping good humour. He is right inside the spirit and sound of this score, much freer and less calculating over detail than he can sometimes be. In the eye of the second movement storm is an extraordinary passage for shell-shocked cellos over rolling timpani: it's rather like the *Adagietto*; only a select few get through to the subtext. Abbado is one.

Additional recommendations ...
Czech Philharmonic Orchestra/Václav Neumann. Supraphon Gems 2SUP0021 — .⸱ 1h 10m 12/87 Ⓑ
Vienna Philharmonic Orchestra/Leonard Bernstein. DG 423 608-2GH — .·⸱ 1h 15m DDD 8/88 ⁹ₚ Ⓑ
New Philharmonia Orchestra/Sir John Barbirolli. EMI CDM7 64749-2 — .·⸱ 1h 14m ADD 11/88 Ⓑ
Cleveland Orchestra/Christoph von Dohnányi. Decca 425 438-2DH — .·⸱ 1h 5m DDD 6/89 Ⓑ
Royal Liverpool Philharmonic Orchestra/Sir Charles Mackerras. EMI EMinence CD-EMX2164 — .·⸱ 1h 10m DDD 3/91

Mahler. Symphony No. 6. Kindertotenlieder[a]. [a]**Thomas Hampson** (bar); **Vienna Philharmonic Orchestra/Leonard Bernstein.** DG 427 697-2GH2. Recorded live in 1988.

.·⸱ ② 1h 55m DDD 1/90   ⁹ₚ Ⓑ

Mahler's tragic Sixth Symphony digs more profoundly into the nature of man and Fate than any of his earlier works, closing in desolation, a beat on the bass drum, a coffin lid closing. Bernstein's reading was a live recording at a concert, with all the electricity of such an occasion, and the Vienna Philharmonic Orchestra respond to the conductor's dark vision of Mahler's score with tremendous bravura. Fortunately, the achingly tender slow movement brings some relief, but with the enormous finale lasting over 30 minutes we must witness a resumption of a battle to the death and the final outcome. The coupling is a logical one, for the *Kindertotenlieder* takes up the theme of death yet again. But it is in a totally different, quieter way: these beautiful songs express a parent's grief over the loss of a child, and although some prefer a woman's voice, the sensitive Thomas Hampson makes a good case here for a male singer. The recording of both works is so good that one would not know it was made 'live', particularly as the applause is omitted.

Additional recommendations ...
No. 6. *Five Rückert Lieder*[a]. [a]**Christa Ludwig** (mez); **Berlin Philharmonic Orchestra/ Herbert von Karajan.** DG 415 099-2GH2 — .·˙ ② 1h 42m ADD 4/85 ♀ₚ Ⓑ
No. 6[a]. No. 8[b]. **Soloists; Leeds Festival Chorus; London Symphony Chorus; Orpington Junior Singers; Highgate School Boys' Choir; Finchley Childrens' Music Group;** [a]**New York Philharmonic Orchestra,** [b]**London Symphony Orchestra/Leonard Bernstein.** CBS CD42199 — .·˙ ③ 2h 39m DDD 12/86 ♀ₚ Ⓑ
No. 6. *Five Rückert Lieder*[a]. [a]**Hanna Schwarz** (mez); **Chicago Symphony Orchestra/Claudio Abbado.** DG Galleria 423 928-2GGA2 — .·˙ ② 1h 44m ADD/DDD 3/89 Ⓑ
No. 6. **City of Birmingham Symphony Orchestra/Simon Rattle.** EMI CDS7 54047-2 — .·˙ ② 1h 26m DDD 11/90 ♀ₚ ♀ₛ Ⓑ

Mahler. Symphony No. 7. **New York Philharmonic Orchestra/Leonard Bernstein.** DG 419 211-2GH2.

.·˙ ② 1h 23m DDD 12/86   ♀ₚ Ⓑ

This is Mahler's most orchestrally glamorous symphony. After the "roars" of nature in the first movement, there are three night pieces — two full of old world romance that frame a central, almost 'expressionist' nightmare — leading to an emphatically daylight finale; an euphoric, nay, distinctly manic collage where Wagner's *Meistersingers* rub shoulders with Lehar's *Merry Widow*. Arguments will probably rage forever as to whether Bernstein is the only conductor to properly understand and communicate Mahler's language, or whether he hijacked Mahler as the perfect vehicle for his own hyper-emotive brand of music-making. The fact remains that in few other performances of the Seventh do you encounter so complete a realization of Mahler's claim for this Symphony that "with me all the instruments sing, even the brass and kettledrums" (just listen to the woodwind in the fourth bar!); such a wide-ranging mix of the old *and* the new in the central night music (often conducted with too much or too little awareness that, say, Berg's *Wozzeck* was just around the corner); and last but far from least, a conductor that makes long-term sense of the merry-go-round finale. The New York Philharmonic give their all, and DG produce a dry, but very articulate Mahler sound.

Additional recommendations ...
No. 7. **Frankfurt Radio Symphony Orchestra/Eliahu Inbal.** Denon CO-1553/4 — .·˙ ② 1h 18m 8/87 ♀ₚ Ⓑ
No. 7. *Kindertotenlieder*[a]. [a]**Jessye Norman** (sop); **Boston Symphony Orchestra/Seiji Ozawa.** Philips 426 249-2PH2 — .·˙ ② 1h 46m DDD 5/91 ♀ₚ Ⓑ
No. 7. **City of Birmingham Symphony Orchestra/Simon Rattle.** EMI CDC7 54344-2 — .·˙ 1h 17m DDD 9/92 ♀ₚ Ⓑ

Mahler. Symphony No. 8. **Elizabeth Connell, Edith Wiens, Felicity Lott** (sops); **Trudeliese Schmidt, Nadine Denize** (contrs); **Richard Versalle** (ten); **Jorma Hynninen** (bar); **Hans Sotin** (bass); **Tiffin Boys' School Choir; London Philharmonic Choir and Orchestra/Klaus Tennstedt.** EMI CDS7 47625-8. Notes, text and translation included. From EX270474-3 (3/87). Recorded in 1986.

.·˙ ② 1h 22m DDD 5/87   ♀ₚ Ⓑ

Mahler's extravagantly monumental Eighth Symphony, often known as the *Symphony of a Thousand*, is the Mahler symphony that raises doubts in even his most devoted of admirers. Its epic dimensions, staggering vision and sheer profligacy of forces required make it a 'difficult work'. Given a great live performance it will sway even the hardest of hearts; given a perform- ance like Tennstedt's, reproduced with all the advantages of CD, home-listeners, too, can be mightily impressed (and so, given the forces involved, will most of the neighbourhood!) — the sheer volume of sound at the climax is quite overwhelming. The work seeks to parallel the Christian's faith in the power of the Holy Spirit with the redeeming power of love for mankind and Tennstedt's performance leaves no doubt that he believes totally in Mahler's creation. It has a rapt, almost intimate, quality that makes this reading all the more moving. The soloists are excellent and the choruses sing with great conviction.

Additional recommendation ...

Soloists; Vienna State Opera Chorus; Vienna Singverein; Vienna Boys Choir; Chicago Symphony Orchestra/Sir Georg Solti. Decca 414 493-2DH2 — .·' 10/85 ♀ₚ Ⓑ

Mahler. Symphony No. 9. **Berlin Philharmonic Orchestra/Herbert von Karajan.** DG 410 726-2GH2. Recorded live in 1982.

.·' ② Ih 25m DDD 7/84   ♀ₚ Ⓑ

New review

Mahler. Symphony No. 9. **South-West German Radio Symphony Orchestra/Michael Gielen.** Intercord Gielen Edition INT860 913.

.·' Ih 19m DDD 2/94   ♀ₚ Ⓑ

Mahler's Ninth is a death-haunted work, but is filled, as Bruno Walter remarked, "with a sanctified feeling of departure". Rarely has this Symphony been shaped with such understanding and played with such selfless virtuosity as it was by Karajan and the Berlin Philharmonic in a legendary series of concerts in 1982. The performance is electric and intense, yet Karajan — ever the enigmatic blend of fire and ice — has the measure of the symphony's spiritual coolness. Karajan had previously made a fine studio recording of the Ninth but this later concert performance is purer, deeper, and even more dauntingly intense. The recording has great clarity and a thrilling sense of actuality; no symphony in the repertoire benefits more than this one from the absolute quietness that CD allows. When the history of twentieth-century music-making comes to be written this performance will be seen as one of its proudest landmarks.

One-disc Ninths are not exactly commonplace but, with both Walter's celebrated, notably hard-pressed, 1938 recording and Barbirolli's 1964 Berlin version in the running, the field is not short of distinguished contenders. It is to Michael Gielen's credit that he is by no means outclassed. The strength of his reading lies above all in the analytical clarity he brings to the complex polyphonic writing of the third and, more especially, the first movement. Here, within an essentially 'straight' conception, he creates both a convincing sense of momentum and brings off the sudden mood swings without which the music can seem becalmed. The finale is the real problem: the emotional apex of the work in Barbirolli's passionate and driven performance, it has no such function here. Throughout, the pace can seem a notch too swift, although, since Barbirolli is sometimes faster, the impression must have more to do with a lack of flexibility. While Gielen is perfectly fluent, there isn't really enough bite to his strings. No apologies are offered for judging this exceptionally lucid performance by the very highest standards. If you want an account of the first movement that really shows you what's going on there, Gielen is well worth considering, perhaps as a supplement to a more conventional, two-pack recom-mendation, the first choice for which remains Karajan's more richly upholstered live account. Down in Baden-Baden, the playing is less resplendent but no less precisely honed: Gielen has been chief conductor there since 1986. There is a fierce intelligence about his interpretation which compels respect without pummelling the deepest reaches of the soul.

Additional recommendations ...

No. 9. Kindertotenlieder[a]. [a]**Hermann Prey** (bar); **Concertgebouw Orchestra/Bernard Haitink.** Philips 416 466-2PH2 — .·' ② ADD 5/86 ♀ₚ ♀ₛ Ⓑ

No. 9. No. 10 — Adagio. **Vienna Philharmonic Orchestra/Lorin Maazel.** CBS Masterworks CD39721 — .·' ② Ih 51m DDD 10/86 ♀ₚ Ⓑ

No. 9. No. 10 — Adagio. **Frankfurt Radio Symphony Orchestra/Eliahu Inbal.** Denon CO-1566/7 — .·' ② Ih 44m DDD 1/88 ♀ₚ Ⓑ

No. 9. **Vienna Philharmonic Orchestra/Bruno Walter.** EMI Références mono CDH7 63029-2 — .·' Ih 10m ADD 8/89 ♀ₚ Ⓑ ▲

No. 9. **Berlin Philharmonic Orchestra/Sir John Barbirolli.** EMI Studio CDM7 63115-2 — .·' Ih 18m ADD 11/89 ♀ₚ Ⓑ

No. 9[a]. **Wagner.** *Siegfried Idyll*[b]. [a]**New Philharmonia Orchestra;** [b]**Philharmonia Orchestra/Otto Klemperer.** EMI Studio CMS7 63277-2 — .·' ② 1h 45m ADD 1/90 9ₚ Ⓑ
No. 9. **Berlin Philharmonic Orchestra/Leonard Bernstein.** DG 435 378-2GH2 — .·' ②
1h 22m ADD 5/92 9ₚ Ⓑ

Mahler (ed. Cooke). Symphony No. 10. **Bournemouth Symphony Orchestra/Simon Rattle.** EMI CDC7 54406-2. From HMV SLS5206 (12/80).

.·' 1h 16m DDD 5/92   9ₚ Ⓑ

Rattle's superb interpretation of Cooke's performing version of the Tenth Symphony now sweeps the board. His achievement is in a special class, empowering the music with such emotional clout that you forget the scholarly debates. There are in fact several adjustments to Schirmer's published score which Rattle explained in the splendid booklet which accompanied the original LP issue. Unfortunately, this has not been included with this CD reissue. One example of his innovatory approach is his merging of the drum stroke which ends the fourth movement with the one which triggers the fifth; furthermore the opening pages of the finale are truly awesome here. Tempos are unfailingly appropriate and the Bournemouth band is second to none. This is music-making of extraordinary fervour, with excellent sound. It is altogether an essential purchase.

Additional recommendations ...
(Ed. Cooke). **Schoenberg.** *Verklärte Nacht, Op. 4.* **Berlin Radio Symphony Orchestra/Riccardo Chailly.** Decca 421 182-2DH2 — .·' ② 1h 50m DDD 3/88 Ⓑ
(Ed. Cooke). **Frankfurt Radio Symphony Orchestra/Eliahu Inbal.** Denon CO-75129 —
.·' 1h 11m DDD 4/93 Ⓑ

Key to symbols

.·'	② ②	1h 23m	DDD	6/88
Price	Quantity/ availability	Timing	Recording mode	Review date

New review
Mahler Plays Mahler. The 1905 Welte-Mignon Piano Rolls. Pickwick Golden Legacy of Recorded Sound GLRS101. Texts and translations included. Recorded in 1992.
Symphonies — No. 4 in G major: Fourth movement (two versions: with and without Yvonne Kenny, sop); No. 5 in C sharp minor: Trauermarsch. Lieder eines fahrenden Gesellen — Ging heut' Morgen übers Feld (two versions: with and without Claudine Carlson, mez). Lieder und Gesänge — Ich ging mit Lust durch einen grünen Wald (two versions: with and without Carlson). Also includes "Remembering Mahler", an oral history with the voices of Alfred Sendry, Victor Fuchs, Richard Lert, Klaus Pringsheim, Herman Martonne, Franz Kuchynka, Alois Reiser, Benjamin Kohon, Herbert Borodkin and Anna Mahler.

.·' 1h 6m DDD 12/93   9ₚ ⑦

This really is a historic 'Historic' CD. In November 1905 Mahler made four piano rolls for M. Welte & Söhne in Leipzig, piano rolls that properly reproduced can give us an incredibly accurate and detailed impression of how Mahler played the music. (At least, how he played it in piano transcription. Sadly there are no recordings whatsoever of Mahler the conductor.)
Under the supervision of that indefatigable Mahlerian Gilbert Kaplan, we now have what are probably the definitive reproductions. At last, we really can have Mahler the pianist as our house-guest. Interpretatively, the play-throughs have an interest that is enormous — there is no doubting the exhilaration and sweetness of his way with the Fourth Symphony's finale, or the authority and daunting power of his playing of the first movement of the Fifth Symphony. Playing three of the recordings straight, then playing them again with the voice added is also a nice idea. No doubt Yvonne Kenny's agent is even now revising her biography to include Gustav Mahler as one of the artists with whom she has successfully collaborated. Finally, there is a bonus which is alone worth the price of the CD. In the early 1960s Los Angeles musicologist

William Malloch tracked down and recorded a group of musicians all of whom had played under Mahler, mainly in New York. He also recorded Mahler's daughter, Anna — an old lady of enormous charm who provides her own riveting short memoir. The result is an absorbing warts-and-all profile of Mahler the man, musician and conductor.

Mahler. Das Lied von der Erde. **Agnes Baltsa** (mez); **Klaus König** (ten); **London Philharmonic Orchestra/Klaus Tennstedt.** EMI CDC7 54603-2. Text and translation included. Recorded 1982-84.

> ⸫ **lh 7m DDD 2/93** ♩ₚ Ⓑ

For some unaccountable reason, this version of Mahler's masterpiece was left to languish in EMI's vaults for almost ten years. When it finally saw the light of day, it was revealed as by far the most convincing version in recent times, given by one of the most committed Mahler exponents ever. Tennstedt penetrates to the heart of every aspect of the soul-searching work. Without any sign of self-indulgence he gives it a searing, emotion-draining performance faithfully supported by the superb work of the London Philharmonic which rivals and, in most cases, surpasses the readings of the work by other great orchestras. Their work would be set at naught were it not for the lifelike and wide-ranging recording (produced by John Willan). Baltsa might seem an unlikely candidate for this piece but her clean line, her nourishing overtones, her direct but eloquent phrasing fulfil almost all its demands. König, a true Heldentenor but one with lightness and sensitivity needed for the middle of his three songs, makes an honest and positive soloist. The alternative recommendations all have much to offer, especially the classic Walter, a truly inspired and dedicated interpretation by one of Mahler's earliest advocates. Walter and Klemperer have, by a small margin, the better soloist but neither is recorded or played with more conviction than the new EMI. At mid-price Fritz Reiner's interpretation presents a fitting alternative and in some ways Barenboim's is the most compelling and spontaneous of recent recordings. Although Meier and Jerusalem give the impression of not having lived quite long enough with this music, the sheer beauty of the sound is outstanding. The première Teldec recording of the composer's own piano version also provides us with a valuable insight into Mahler's creative processes. As the informative booklet-notes point out this is not just a piano transcription of the orchestral score but a valid performing version in its own right. Any doubts one may have about the validity or necessity for such a recording are soon dispelled by the commitment and persuasiveness of the performances by Fassbaender, Moser and Katsaris.

Additional recommendations ...
Kathleen Ferrier (contr); **Julius Patzak** (ten); **Vienna Philharmonic Orchestra/Bruno Walter.** Decca 414 194-2DH — ⸫ ADD 1/85 ♩ₚ Ⓑ ▲
Christa Ludwig (mez); **Fritz Wunderlich** (ten); **Philharmonia Orchestra, New Philharmonia Orchestra/Otto Klemperer.** EMI CDC7 47231-2 — ⸫ lh 4m ADD 12/85 ♩ₚ Ⓑ
Maureen Forrester (contr); **Richard Lewis** (ten); **Chicago Symphony Orchestra/Fritz Reiner.** RCA Victor Gold Seal GD60178 — ⸫ lh 3m ADD 10/91 ♩ₚ Ⓑ
Brigitte Fassbaender (mez); **Thomas Moser** (ten); **Cyprien Katsaris** (pf). Teldec 2292-46276-2 — ⸫ lh lm DDD 6/90 ♩ₚ ⊚
Waltraud Meier (mez); **Siegfried Jerusalem** (ten); **Chicago Symphony Orchestra/ Daniel Barenboim.** Erato 2292-45624-2 — ⸫ lh DDD 4/92 ♩ₚ Ⓑ

New review
Mahler. Lieder aus "Des Knaben Wunderhorn". **Jard van Nes** (contr); **John Bröcheler** (bass); **Arnhem Philharmonic Orchestra/Roberto Benzi.** Ottavo OTRC79238. Texts included. Recorded in 1992.

> ⸫ **55m DDD 2/94** ♩ₚ

Jard van Nes is a natural for Mahler, both from the vocal and interpretative point of view. Particularly admirable is the fresh, spontaneous way in which she approaches her contributions, free from both the long shadow of past performance or awe before such familiar songs. She catches ideally the folk-like charm of "Rheinlegendchen" and "Wer hat dies Liedlein erdacht?". She is also appropriately earthy in "Das irdische Leben", then marvellously tender as the distant lover in "Des Schildwache Nachtlied". Her unadorned mastery of word and tone cannot be too highly praised — listen to the *keck* delivery of "Verlor'ne Muh": just right — and she crowns her performance with her grave utterance in "Urlicht". Bröcheler is among the best, characterizing "Lob des hohen Verstandes" with enthusiastic vivacity and revelling in St Antony's sermon. Benzi and his orchestra never make the mistake of some more noted performers of over-egging the pudding. Although the detail is all clearly projected and keenly played, in a perfectly balanced recording, the music is kept on the move, never sentimentalized.

Additional recommendation ...

Dame Elisabeth Schwarzkopf (sop); **Dietrich Fischer-Dieskau** (bar); **London Symphony Orchestra/George Szell.** EMI CDC7 47277-2 — .•' 48m ADD II/88
No. 2, Verlorne Müh; No. 7, Rheinlegendchen; No. 9, Wo die schönen Trompeten blasen; No. 10, Lob des hohen Verstands. Lieder und Gesang — No. 1, Frühlingsmorgen. No. 2, Erinnerung. No. 4, Serenade aus Don Juan. No. 5, Phantasie aus Don Juan No. 7, Ich ging mit Lust durch einen grünen Wald. No. 8, Aus! Aus!. Coupled with **Wolf.** *Heiss mich nicht reden (Mignon I). Nur wer die Sehnsucht (Mignon II). So lasst mich scheinen (Mignon III). Kennst du das Land (Mignon). Frühling übers Jahr. Frage nicht. Die Spröde. Der Schäfer. Gesang Weylas.* **Anne Sofie von Otter** (mez); **Ralf Gothóni** (pf). DG 423 666-2GH — .•' 59m DDD 6/89 **q**p

---

Mahler. Das klagende Lied (complete version including "Waldmärchen"). **Susan Dunn** (sop); **Markus Baur** (alto); **Brigitte Fassbaender** (mez); **Werner Hollweg** (ten); **Andreas Schmidt** (bar); **Städtischer Musikverein Düsseldorf; Berlin Radio Symphony Orchestra/Riccardo Chailly.** Decca 425 719-2DH. Text and translation included. Recorded in 1989.

.•' **Ih 4m DDD 2/92**   **q**p **q**s

Even the musically acute listener would be unlikely to realize that *Das klagende Lied* is the work of a teenager. Mahler's first significant work is as self-assured as anything he was to write in later life. Indeed enthusiastic Mahlerians will recognize here passages which crop up in other works, most notably the Second Symphony. Those same enthusiastic Mahlerians might not recognize much of this recording, however, since only two movements of *Klagende Lied* are usually performed: the 30-minute first movement is considered too rambling. But no one could possibly arrive at that conclusion from this tautly directly, electrifying performance, and it contains some wonderfully imaginative music, including some delightful forest murmurs, which it seems tragic to miss out. For this movement alone this CD is a must for any Mahler fan, but more than that this is a spectacular recording of a one-in-a-million performance. The soloists, choir and orchestra achieve near perfection under Chailly's inspired direction, and the decision to substitute for the marvellous Brigitte Fassbaender a boy alto (Markus Baur) to represent the disembodied voice of the dead brother is a stroke of pure genius. His weird, unnatural voice provide a moment of sheer spine-tingling drama.

Additional recommendations ...

Soloists; Shin-Yuh Kai Chorus; Philharmonia Orchestra/Giuseppe Sinopoli. DG 435 382-2GH — .•' Ih 5m DDD 8/92
Soloists; Bath Festival Chorus; Waynflete Singers; Bournemouth Symphony Orchestra/Richard Hickox. Chandos CHAN9247 — .•' Ih IIm DDD 5/94

Mahler. Kindertotenlieder[a]. Rückert Lieder[b]. Lieder eines fahrenden Gesellen[a]. **Dame Janet Baker** (mez); [a]**Hallé Orchestra**; [b]**New Philharmonia Orchestra/Sir John Barbirolli.** EMI CDC7 47793-2. Texts and translations included. Items marked [a] from ASD2338 (2/68), [b] ASD2518/19 (12/69).

.•' ③ **Ih 5m ADD 12/87**   **q**p **B**

New review

Mahler. Kindertotenlieder. Rückert-Lieder. Lieder eines fahrenden Gesellen. Lieder aus Des Knaben Wunderhorn — Das irdische Leben; Des Antonius von Padua Fischpredigt; Urlicht. **Brigitte Fassbaender** (mez); **Deutsches Symphony Orchestra, Berlin/Riccardo Chailly.** Decca 425 790-2DH. Texts and translations included. Recorded 1988-89.

.•' **Ih IIm DDD 4/94**   **q**p **B**

The songs of the *Lieder eines fahrenden Gesellen* ("Songs of a Wayfarer") are directly quoted from Mahler's First Symphony and the same fresh, springtime atmosphere is shared by both works. The orchestration has great textural clarity and lightness of touch. The *Kindertotenlieder*, more chromatically expressive than the earlier work, tap into a darker, more psychologically complex vein in Mahler's spiritual and emotional make-up. The *Rückert Lieder* are not a song cycle as such but gather in their romantic awareness and response to the beauties of the poetry a unity and shape that acts to bind them. Together, Baker and Barbirolli reach a transcendental awareness of Mahler's inner musings. Barbirolli draws from the Hallé playing of great delicacy and precision and establishes a clear case for having this CD in your collection.

Fassbaender's emotionally charged way of singing is ideally matched to Mahler yet she is just as able — as in St Anthony's Sermon from the *Knaben Wunderhorn* — to smile and sing gently, wittily. It is the dramatic declamation, however, as at "Herr über Tod und Leben" in "Um Mitternacht" from the *Rückert-Lieder*, that the true flavour of her singing is caught. Throughout the *Fahrenden Gesellen* it is the immediacy, fearlessness of attack and her particular intensity, that makes the readings so arresting. The swiftish speeds throughout make sure sentimentality is kept at bay; so does Chailly's and the orchestra's biting precision and light touch. Similar characteristics inform a deeply eloquent interpretation of *Kindertotenlieder*. Right from the start the world-weary tone and verbal illumination in the first song catch at the heart and suggest palpably the sense of personal responsibility for the children's deaths on the part of the protagonist. Baker/Barbirolli, still surprisingly at full price, with the singer in lovely voice, must be a 'safer' recommendation than the more daring Fassbaender, but with up-to-date recording and even more songs included the new disc is an inviting proposition — and a searing experience.

Additional recommendations ...
Catherine Robbin (mez); **Kitchener-Waterloo Symphony Orchestra/Raffi Armenian.** CBC Records SMCD5098 — .•ʻ 55m DDD 5/92 ℗ Ⓑ
Andreas Schmidt (bar); **Cincinnati Symphony Orchestra/Jésus López-Cobos.** Telarc CD80269 — .•ʻ 56m DDD 5/93 ℗ Ⓑ

Gian Francesco Malipiero

Italian 1882-1973

New review
Malipiero. SYMPHONIES. **Moscow Symphony Orchestra/Antonio de Almeida.** Marco Polo 8 223602/4. Recorded in 1993.
8 223602 — No. 3, "delle campane"; No. 4, "in memoriam". Sinfonia del mare. *8 223603* — No. 1, "in quattro tempi, come le quattro stagioni"; No. 2, "elegiaca". Sinfonia del silenzio e de la morte. *8 223604* — No. 7, "delle canzoni". Sinfonia in un tempo. Sinfonia per Antigenida.

.•ʻ ③ 1h 12m 1h 18m 1h 9m DDD 4/94

Malipiero's symphonies are 'symphonies' in no conventional sense: they eschew all the ground-rules of the Austro-German tradition save (usually) division into four movements. He was trying, undoubtedly, to find an extended orchestral form more in tune with the Italian genius as he understood it, but also to accommodate his own restlessly fertile imagination. To him sonata form was as unnecessary (why develop or transform a theme when a dozen new ones are clamouring to be written down?) as it was theoretically antipathetic. He used instead an almost instinctive process of varied embellishment, striking juxtaposition and rhythmic propulsion, often passing in a single movement through many variants of a basic mood, a lyrical or aggressive incidental idea being used to calm or crush the music by way of coda. His symphonies are sets of kindred pieces rather than arguments that build to something greater than the sum of their parts. Even so, the best of them are oddly gripping and although this selection of nine has troughs as well as peaks, the survey it offers is an intriguing one. There are movements that could easily have ended a couple of minutes earlier (or later) than they do, and others that rather disconcertingly stop just when you thought they were about to take off. De Almeida has a shrewd grasp of what one might call the 'Malipiero sound'. The orchestral playing is decent and the recording clean, if not especially atmospheric.

Further listening ...

String Quartets — No. 1, "Rispetti e strambotti"; No. 2, "Stornelli e ballate"; No. 3, "Cantari alla madrigalesca"; No. 4; No. 5, "dei capricci"; No. 6, "L'arca di Noè"; No. 7; No. 8, "per Elisabetta". **Orpheus Quartet.** ASV CDDCD457 (2/92).

Sette Invenzioni. Quattro Invenzioni, "La festa degli indolenti". IL FINTO ARLECCHINO — Symphonic fragments. Vivaldiana. **Veneto Philharmonic Orchestra/Peter Maag.** Marco Polo 8 223397 (9/93).

Henry Mancini

American 1924-1994

Suggested listening ...

Film Scores: The Pink Panther; Charade; Hatari!; Breakfast at Tiffany's. **Henry Mancini and his Orchestra.** RCA Victor RD85938.

MANCINI IN SURROUND — *Film Scores:* The White Dawn — Arctic whale hunt. Mommie Dearest. Frenzy. Monster Movie Music Suite. Fear — Casey's theme. The Man Who Loved Women — Little boys. The Prisoner of Zenda — Suite. Nightwing. Without a clue — excerpts. Sunset — Suite. **The Mancini Pops Orchestra/Henry Mancini.** RCA Victor RD60471 (5/91).

Marin Marais

French 1656-1728

New review

Marais: Tombeau pour M. de Sainte-Colombe[a]. **Philippe Pierlot,** [a]**Sophie Watillon,** [b]**Rainer Zipperling** (vas da gamba); [a]**Rolf Lislevand** (theorbo). Ricercar RIC118100. Recorded in 1992.
Du Buisson III: Troisième Suite in A minor. *Machy:* Pièces de viole — Suite in G major; Suite in D minor. *Sainte-Colombe le fils:* Tombeau pour M. de Sainte-Colombe le père. Fantaisie en Rondeau. *Sainte-Colombe:* Tombeau les regrets[b].

· 52m DDD 2/94

A new generation of viol players are recording the music of Sainte-Colombe and Marin Marais, inspired by the success of the film *Tous les matins du monde*. Pierlot in this recording of viol music from the era of Sainte-Colombe proves himself an important interpreter of the French style. His sound, small and grainy as reproduced here, does take a bit of getting used to. However, it is ultimately very satisfying, for these are intimate performances, with all the delicacy and contemplativeness one imagines might have embodied Marais's performances before Louis XIV. By seeming to play softly Pierlot compels you to listen to his sublime musical discourse in Marais's *Tombeau pour M. de Sainte-Colombe*. So at ease with time is he that your heartbeat slows. While including such popular works as the *Tombeau* and Sainte-Colombe's *Les regrets* (which fades away at the end of the CD rather like a pop music track), he also introduces CD listeners to the solo viol music of Du Buisson III and Sainte-Colombe *le fils*, whose own extended and tortuous *Tombeau pour M. de Sainte-Colombe le père*, with its strikingly reminiscent dialogue section two-thirds of the way through and its virtuoso figuration, deserves to be better known.

Marais. ALCYONE. **Jennifer Smith** (sop) Alcyone; **Gilles Ragon** (ten) Ceyx; **Philippe Huttenlocher** (bar) Pélée; **Vincent Le Texier** (bass-bar) Pan, Phorbas; **Sophie Boulin** (sop) Ismène, First Sailor; **Bernard Delétré** (bass) Tmole, High Priest, Neptune; **Jean-Paul Fouchécourt** (alto) Morpheus; **Véronique Gens** (sop) Second Sailor, Priestess; **Les Musiciens du Louvre/Marc Minkowski.** Erato MusiFrance 2292-45522-2. Notes, text and translation included. Recorded in 1990.

· ② 2h 34m DDD 4/92

Today, Marin Marais is remembered almost entirely for his legacy of music for the bass viol. But in his own day Marais was recognized as a talented opera composer, too. *Alcyone*, first performed in 1706, was his dramatic *chef d'oeuvre* and held the stage at intervals for more than half a century. Though he followed in Lully's footsteps, Marais spoke with a voice of his own and nowhere is this more apparent than in *Alcyone*, which contains in its Fourth Act one of the great moments in French opera literature — a tempest, judged so successful by his contemporaries that not only was it performed as a separate item at court, at the express command of the king, but also found its way into a revival of a Lully opera early in the eighteenth century. The plot centres on the thwarted love of Alcyone for Ceyx, a *tragédie* which moves, however, to a happy ending. Marais's music explores a wide range of emotions. Catchy instrumental pieces — the sailors' dance in Act 3 is especially captivating — supple choruses and touching airs abound, several foreshadowing Rameau in their colourful orchestration. The mainly strong cast is headed by the soprano, Jennifer Smith, in the title role, with lively performances by Sophie Boulin as Ismène, Phorbas's partner in crime, and Gilles Ragon as Ceyx. Minkowski directs with stylish conviction and a good sense of pace. A few rough edges count for little where so much else is enlightened. The vivid recording comes with full texts and translations.

Further listening …

Pièces en trio — Suites: C major; B flat major; G minor; F major; E minor; G minor. **Quadro Hotteterre.** Teldec 9031-77617-2.

Pièces en Trio — Suites: B flat major; C minor; E minor. Suite d'un goût étranger — La rêveuse; Le badinage. **Ensemble Fitzwilliam.** Auvidis Valois V4638 (11/92).

Pièces de Viole, Troisième Livre — Suites: E minor; D major; G major. **Jordi Savall** (va da gamba); **Hopkinson Smith** (theorbo); **Ton Koopman** (hpd). Astrée Auvidis E8761 (12/92).

Pièces de Viole, Quatrième Livre: Suite d'un goût étranger — Marche Tartare; La Tartarine and Double; Les festes champêtre; Le toubillon; Le labyrinthe; L'arabesque; Allemande la superbe; La rêveuse; Marche; Gigue; Le badinage. **Jordi Savall** (va da gamba); **Ton Koopman** (hpd); **Hopkinson Smith** (baroque gtr, theorbo). Astrée Auvidis E7727 (9/88).

Pièces de Viole, Cinquième Livre — Suites: G minor; E minor/major. Le tableau de l'opération de la taille. Le tombeau pour Marais le cadet. **Jordi Savall** (bass viol); **Hopkinson Smith** (theorbo); **Ton Koopman** (hpd) with **Jean-Michael Damian** (spkr). Astrée Auvidis E7708 (2/88).

La gamme et autres Morceaux de Simphonies — La gamme en forme d'un petit opéra; Sonate à la mariesienne; Saint-Geneviève du Mont. **Boston Musum Trio.** Centaur CRC2129

Alessandro Marcello

Italian 1684-1750

Suggested listening …

Oboe Concerto in D minor. *Coupled with* **Vivaldi.** Trio Sonata in D minor, RV63, "La folia". Flautino Concerto in C major, RV443. Amor hai vinto, RV651. Nulla in mundo pax, RV630. **Soloists; Academy of Ancient Music/Christopher Hogwood.** L'Oiseau-Lyre 421 655-2OH (9/89).

Louis Marchand

French 1669-1732

Suggested listening …

Pièces Choisies pour l'Orgue — Premier Livre. *Coupled with* **Guilain.** Pièces d'Orgue pour le Magnificat. **François Espinasse** (org). Sony Classical SK57489 (7/94). *See review under Guilain; refer to the Index to Reviews.*

Luca Marenzio

New review

Marenzio. BACI SOAVI E CARI. **The Consort of Musicke** (Emma Kirkby, Evelyn Tubb, sops; Mary Nichols, mez; Andrew King, Rufus Müller, tens; Alan Ewing, bass)/**Anthony Rooley.** Musica Oscura 070992. Texts and translations included. Recorded 1987-88.

Il primo libro de madrigali (5vv) — Dolorosi martir, fieri tormenti; Liquide perle Amor da gli occhi sparse. Il secondo libro de madrigali (5vv) — O voi che sospirate a miglior note. Il quinto libro de madrigali (5vv) — Due rose fresche, e colte in Paradiso. Madrigali ... libro primo (4-6vv) — O fere stelle homai datemi pace; Piango che Amor con disusato oltraggio. Il quinto libro de madrigali (6vv) — Baci soavi e cari. Il sesto libro de madrigali (6vv) — Se quel dolor che va inanzi al morire.

Ih 3m DDD I/94

There is more to Marenzio than simply providing models for England's short-lived flirtation with madrigals. He was a composer whose wide-ranging qualities earned him the reputation of being a master of fresh and lucid texts, as well as the more serious and anguished style of the mannerists. This recording contains examples of both in a well-judged and diverse cross-section of Marenzio's work. The First Book of 1580 is represented at the outset with *Liquide perle*, a pearl indeed with its outstanding motivic control and perfectly worked contrasts. The Consort of Musicke respond acutely to textual mood shifts, stroking and colouring the phrases with abandon and always constantly aware of the subtle impact of dynamics. Roundness of tone and the sweet (and bittersweet) response to a paragraph is beautifully caught in the deeply felt *O voi che sospirate* and that catalogue of kissing techniques, *Baci soavi e cari*, the latter acting as the title to the disc. It is an endless madrigal given the limitations of the topic but entertainingly sung here. *Se quel dolor* from the Sixth Book is an intensely profound work in ten sections which crowns the disc in a number of respects. It is a half-hour of vivid preparation for death in which Marenzio stalks from one idea to the next, disfiguring conventional musical language with deft chromaticisms, dissonance and nervous, unstable melodic fragments. The Consort turn in a performance of remarkable quality, movingly paced and immaculately blended. A fine achievement and not to be missed.

Biagio Marini

Suggested listening ...

Concerto terzo delle musiche da camera, Op. 16. **The Consort of Musicke/Anthony Rooley.** Musica Oscura 070994 (3/94).

Frank Martin

Martin. Concerto for Seven Wind Instruments, Percussion and String Orchestra. Polyptique[a]. Etudes. [a]**Marieke Blankestijn** (vn); **Chamber Orchestra of Europe/Thierry Fischer.** DG 435 383-2GH.

Ih 6m DDD 6/92

This is a disc of exceptional excellence. These three pieces have all been recorded before but never as well — and they have certainly never been better played! In the concerto the virtuosity and sophistication of the wind of the Chamber Orchestra of Europe is so effortless and their accents far lighter in touch than their rivals. Their playing has real delicacy and clarity of articulation and the slow movement for once really sounds as it is marked, mysterious and yet elegant, while the muted strings have a lightness of sonority and colour which greatly enhances the atmosphere. The artistry of the strings is everywhere in evidence in the Etudes and they quite outclass other performances in their sensitivity of response and range of colour. The

Polyptique for violin and two string orchestras dates from the last year of Martin's life, when he was 83. It was inspired by a polyptych, a set of very small panels that Martin saw in Sienna representing various episodes in the Passion. The work is inward-looking and powerfully searching, and is played with great beauty and purity of tone, and rapt concentration by Marieke Blankestijn and the Chamber Orchestra of Europe. The recording is one of the best from this (or any other) source. It is completely natural, truthful in timbre and has remarkable clarity and presence. The perspective is very musically judged and both producer and engineer deserve a special mention for the refinement and quality of the sound they have captured.

Additional recommendations ...
Concerto for Seven Wind Instruments. Petite Symphonie Concertante. Etudes for String Orchestra. **Suisse Romande Orchestra/Ernest Ansermet.** Decca Enterprise 430 003-2DM — .·ʼ 58m ADD 12/90 ꞯₚ
Concerto for Seven Wind Instruments. Petite Symphonie Concertante[a]. Sechs Monologe aus "Jedermann"[b]. [b]**Gilles Cachemaille** (bar); [a]**Eva Guibentif** (hp); **Christiane Jaccottet** (hpd); [a]**Ursula Riuttimann** (pf); **Suisse Romande Orchestra/Armin Jordan.** Erato 2292-45694-2 — .·ʼ 1h 2m DDD 11/91
Concerto for Seven Wind Instruments. Erasmi Monumentum. Etudes for String Orchestra. **London Philharmonic Orchestra/Matthias Bamert.** Chandos CHAN9283 — .·ʼ 1h 7m DDD 7/94 ꞯₛ

Martin. Three Danses[bcf]. Petite complainte[be]. Pièce brève[abd].
Martinů. Concerto for Oboe and Small Orchestra[bf].
Honegger. Concerto da camera[acf]. Petite Suite, H89[ace]. Antigone[bcd]. [a]**Aurèle Nicolet** (fl); **Heinz Holliger** ([b]ob/[c]cor ang); [d]**Ursula Holliger** (hp); [e]**John Constable** (pf); [f]**Academy of St Martin in the Fields/Sir Neville Marriner.** Philips 434 105-2PH. Recorded in 1991.
.·ʼ 1h 4m DDD 9/93 ꞯₚ

Anyone prepared to explore some unusual twentieth-century repertory of the less *outré* kind may safely be advised to try this fine Philips issue. It is a splendid disc, with some music that is new to the catalogue, including all three works by Martin. It is played with skill, panache and idiomatic insight by fine soloists and one of the world's best chamber orchestras, and to add to that, the music itself is rewarding. It is played very persuasively, and the recording is refined yet with ample presence. Heinz Holliger is one of the world's greatest oboists, and in his hands the instrument is infinitely flexible. If that were all, of course, we would still lack something, but in fact he understands all this music and presents it with both authority and charm. During the course of the seven works here, he is variously joined by his harpist wife Ursula Holliger, the flautist Aurèle Nicolet, and pianist John Constable. He also plays the cor anglais in the three Honegger works and makes us wish that one heard this lovely instrument more often as a soloist. All the artists play with finesse and the orchestra under Marriner is on top form even in this relatively unfamiliar music.

Martin. Golgotha[a]. Mass for Double Chorus[b]. [a]**Wally Staempfli** (sop); [a]**Marie-Lise de Montmollin** (mez); [a]**Eric Tappy** (ten); [a]**Pierre Mollet**, [a]**Philippe Huttenlocher** (bars); [a]**Lausanne University Choir;** [a] **Robert Faller Choir and Symphony Orchestra/Robert Faller** with **André Luy** (org); [b]**Midi Chamber Choir/Denis Martin.** Erato 2292-45779-2. Item marked [a] recorded in 1968, [b] 1990. Texts and translations included. Recorded in 1968.
.·ʼ ② 1h 53m ADD/DDD 10/92

Shortly after the war Martin saw *The Three Crosses* of Rembrandt and it was this that triggered the composition of *Golgotha* which occupied him for the following three years (1945-8). It is one of his major works and can claim the distinction of being the first major *Passion* since Bach. Martin wrote that his intention was to "make the sacred tragedy come to life again before our eyes", and in contradistinction to Bach, the narrative passes freely between the various soloists and the body of the choir. Apart from his debt to Bach and Mussorgsky, his musical language has an affinity at a profound level with the Debussy of *Pelléas*, particularly in the glowing final section, "La Resurrection". *Golgotha* is a work of sustained eloquence, power and dignity, and the conviction of this 1968 performance under Robert Faller communicates effectively and impressively. *Golgotha* is an inspired and inspiring work, very well played and recorded, and there is only one other representation in *The Classical Catalogue*. The Mass for unaccompanied double chorus, on the other hand, is a work whose beauties are gaining wider recognition and it is now well represented in the catalogue. This version, however, can hold its own with the best.

Additional recommendation ...
Mass for Double Chorus. **Poulenc.** *Mass in G major. Quatre petites prières de Saint François d'Assise. Salve regina.* **Christ Church Cathedral Choir, Oxford/Stephen Darlington.** Nimbus NI5197 — .··' 59m DDD 12/89 ꟼₚ

Further listening ...

Pavane couleur du temps[a]. *Piano Quintet*[b]. *String Trio*[c]. *Trio sur des mélodies populaires irlandaises*[d]. **Zurich Chamber Ensemble** (Brenton Langbein, [ab]Andreas Pfenninger, vns; [a]Cornel Anderes, [bc]Jürg Dähler, vas; Raffaele Altwegg, [a]Luciano Pezzani, vcs); [bd]**Hanni Schmid-Wyss** (pf). Jecklin Disco JD646-2 (10/91).

Petite symphonie concertante[a]. *Maria-Triptychon*[b]. *Passacaglia* (transc. comp.)[c]. [b]**Irmgaard Seefried** (sop); [b]**Wolfgang Schneiderhan** (vn); [a]**Eva Hunziker** (hp); [a]**Germaine Vaucher-Clerc** (clavecin); [a]**Doris Rossiaud** (pf); [ab]**Suisse Romande Orchestra;** [c]**Berlin Philharmonic Orchestra/Frank Martin.** Jecklin Disco mono JD645-2 (10/91).

Requiem. **Elisabeth Speiser** (sop); **Ria Bollen** (contr); **Eric Tappy** (ten); **Peter Lagger** (bass); **Lausanne Women's Chorus; Union Chorale; Ars Laeta Vocal Ensemble; Suisse Romande Orchestra/Frank Martin.** Jecklin Disco JD631-2 (1/90).

Vicente Martín y Soler
Spanish 1754-1806

Suggested listening ...

UNA COSA RARA. **Soloists; La Capella Reial de Catalunya; Le Concert des Nations/ Jordi Savall.** Astrée Auvidis E8760 (2/92).

Bohuslav Martinů
Czech 1890-1959

Martinů. Cello Concertos — No. 1; No. 2. Cello Concertino. **Raphael Wallfisch** (vc); **Czech Philharmonic Orchestra/Jiří Bělohlávek.** Chandos CHAN9015. Recorded in 1991.
.··' **1h 16m DDD 4/92**

Following his centenary year in 1990, Bohuslav Martinů has been returning to favour, although, as the composer of almost 30 concerto-type works, he cannot always escape the charge of flatulent note-spinning that attaches itself to such fertility. On the present disc, his unique imaginative vision is most obvious in the Cello Concerto No. 1. The central slow movement in particular finds Martinů at his best, a deeply moving threnody with a potent nostalgic quality which will be instantly recognizable to admirers of the later symphonies. There is an improvisatory freedom about the Second Concerto which makes it harder to grasp and the thematic material has rather too much in common with other, better scores. The much earlier *Concertino* is in Martinů's playful, more overtly neoclassical vein. You may notice some vamp-until-ready eighteenth-century scrubbing in the concertos, but here the younger composer is preoccupied with the lighter aspects of the style. There's a Stravinskian wit and elegance about the writing and the chamber scoring reflects both the fashionable trends and the economic constraints of life in 1920s Paris. In the First Concerto, Raphael Wallfisch is rather backwardly balanced *vis-à-vis* the Czech Philharmonic, whose regular conductor, Jiří Bělohlávek, is of course totally inside this music. At the same time, the resonant Spanish Hall of Prague Castle provides an agreeable ambient glow which does not mask too much detail. Make no mistake: this is a most attractive proposition for those already familiar with the idiom. Adventurous beginners should perhaps start elsewhere.

Martinů. Double Concerto for Two String Orchestras, Piano and Timpani[a]. Sinfonietta giocosa[b]. Rhapsody-Concerto for Viola and Orchestra[c.] [c]**Rivka Golani** (va); [a]**Jiří Skovajska,** [b]**Dennis Hennig** (pfs); [a]**Brno State Philharmonic Orchestra,** [b]**Australian Chamber Orchestra/Sir Charles Mackerras;** [c]**Berne Symphony Orchestra/Peter Maag.** Conifer CDCF210. Item marked [a] from CDCF202 (3/92), recorded in 1990, [b] CDCF170 (8/89), recorded in 1988, [c] CDCF146 (10/88), recorded in 1986.

.•* **lh l3m   DDD   9/92**

This is as good an entry point into Martinů's world as any. The *Rhapsody-Concerto* (1952) is one of the most lyrical and affecting of his later works and Rivka Golani's account is all the more moving for being completely unaffected and straightforward as, indeed, are Peter Maag and the Berne orchestra whose natural, unforced eloquence are equally persuasive. The *Double Concerto* (1938) was composed as the war-clouds were gathering in Europe, and is a power-house of dark, propulsive energy. Mackerras and the Brno orchestra maintain the right kind of tension and sense of momentum. The lightness and high spirits of the *Sinfonietta giocosa* never fails to amaze, considering the anxious circumstances under which it was composed (Martinů was living in Vichy France and desperately trying to escape from the Nazis). Sir Charles and his pianist, Dennis Hennig, turn in a good performance though by comparison with the *Double Concerto*, the recording is a shade synthetic in perspective with little back-to-front depth. None the less, this provides a well-balanced portrait of a composer who is at long last coming into his own, as evidenced by the number of recordings under review and listed here.

Key to symbols

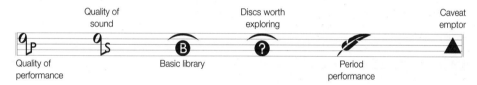

Martinů. SYMPHONIES. **Bamberg Symphony Orchestra/Neeme Järvi.** BIS CD362, BIS CD363 and BIS CD402.
CD362 — Nos. 1 and 2. *CD363* — Nos. 3 and 4. *CD402* — Nos. 5 and 6.

.•* ③ **lh lm   lh 3m   59m   DDD   9/87   12/88** 𝄐ₛ

Martinů began composing at the age of ten and later studied and lived in Paris, America and Switzerland. Despite his travels he remained a quintessentially Czech composer and his music is imbued with the melodic shapes and rhythms of the folk-music of his native homeland. The six symphonies were written during Martinů's years in America and in all of them he uses a large orchestra with distinctive groupings of instruments which give them a very personal and unmistakable timbre. The rhythmic verve of his highly syncopated fast movements is very infectious, indeed unforgettable, and his slow movements are often deeply expressive, most potently, perhaps, in that of the Third Symphony which is imbued with the tragedy of war. The Bamberg orchestra play marvellously and with great verve for Järvi, whose excellently judged tempos help propel the music forward most effectively. His understanding of the basic thrust of Martinů's structures is very impressive and he projects the music with great clarity. The BIS recordings are beautifully clear, with plenty of ambience surrounding the orchestra, a fine sense of scale and effortless handling of the wide dynamic range Martinů calls for. Enthusiastically recommended.

Additional recommendations ...
No. 4. Field Mass[a]. *Memorial to Lidice.* [a]**Ivan Kusnjer** (bar); **Czech Philharmonic** [a]**Chorus and Orchestra/Jiří Bělohlávek.** Chandos CHAN9138 — .•* lh 5m DDD 5/93
Nos. 3 and 4. **Royal Scottish National Orchestra/Bryden Thomson.** Chandos CHAN8917
— .•* lh DDD 6/91

Memorial to Lidice. Symphony No. 5. Les fresques de Piero della Francesca[a]. **Czech Philharmonic Orchestra/Karel Ančerl.** Supraphon Historical mono/[a]stereo 11 1931-2 — ‥• Ih 17m AAD 3/93 ⁹ₚ ▲

New review
Martinů. Three Czech Dances. Borová. 12 Esquisses. Four Mouvements. Les ritournelles. Windows on the garden. **Radoslav Kvapil** (pf). Unicorn-Kanchana DKPCD9140. Recorded in 1991.

‥• Ih 13m DDD 12/93

There are 36 pieces here, played chronologically, from the 'early' *Three Czech Dances* of 1926 to the *Windows on the garden* of 12 years later (Op. 270!), and to leap across 32 cueing bands from the first of the *Czech Dances* to the first of the *Windows* is a fascinating indication of how far Martinů's style had developed in the interim. In 1926 he writes like a modern, even a modern Parisian Smetana, well aware of Stravinsky and so exuberantly full of ideas that he packs enough of them into this three-minute dance to furnish a sonata. The *Windows* are warmly happy music, with a serenity tinged with nostalgia that is wholly characteristic of the mature Martinů. *En route* between the two we hear him lending an interested ear to Milhaud, discovering kinships between Moravian dances and the proto-jazz of Gottschalk and, in the second of the *Esquisses*, borrowing enough of ragtime to come within an ace of *Tea for two*. Kvapil plays these pieces like someone who knows their context in the whole of Martinů's huge output. Illuminating as well as entertaining, in short, and very naturally recorded.

New review
Martinů. The Opening of the Wells[a]. Legend of the Smoke from Potato Fires[b]. Mikeš of the Mountains[c]. **Milada Cejková** (sop); [a]**Agáta Cakrtová,** [b]**Marie Mrázová** (contrs); [c]**Vladimír Doležal** (ten); [ab]**Ivan Kusnjer** (bar); [a]**Petr Haničinec** (spkr); [b]**Jiří Stivín** (rec); [b]**Vlastimil Mareš** (cl); [b]**Petr Duda** (hn); [b]**Milan Bláha** (accordion); [ac]**Petr Messiereur,** [ac]**Jan Kvapil** (vn); [ac]**Jan Talich** (va); [ac]**Stanislav Bogunia** (pf); **Kühn Chorus/Pavel Kühn.** Supraphon 11 0767-2. Translations included. Recorded in 1988.

‥• Ih 3m DDD 5/94

New review
Martinů. Echec au Roi[a]. The Revolt. [a]**Vladimír Olexa** (spkr); [a]**Kateřina Kachlíkova** (contr); **Prague Symphony Orchestra/Jiří Bělohlávek.** Supraphon 11 1415-2. Recorded in 1987.

‥• 45m DDD 5/94

In the 1950s Martinů wrote four little cantatas that looked back to his earliest origins. Three of them are recorded here, and a touching group they make. The first uses a narrator; all have chorus, solo singers and a varied instrumental group. These sharp, bright sounds conjure up the folk music and the legends, tales and rituals of Bohemia where Martinů grew up. They pick up the quick rhythms of Bohemian folk music and the raw edge of folk bands, recreating in much simpler fashion the atmosphere that was invoked with genius by Stravinsky in *The Wedding*. They are touching, clever, and not in the least sentimental: Martinů was a countryman. But it was the urban sophisticate who turned this sharp ear upon the music he heard in Paris in the 1920s and 1930s for the two ballets on the second record. *Echec au Roi* (1930) allows Martinů plenty of scope for jazzy pastiche: there is a blues, plenty of jazz, quotations of fanfares, and an *ouverture espagnole* that is not so much a Spanish Overture as an allusion to the Ruy Lopez opening in chess. In *The Revolt* (1925), to a text by the composer, the action is pretty surreal, and ends in a call for a general strike which brings out conservatories and instrument makers, drives critics to suicide and Stravinsky off to a Pacific island. There is plenty of occasion for pastiche again, pleasantly in a Night Club scene and a Music Hall foxtrot. Matters are returned to normal by Inspiration. It is all very smart.

Martinů. JULIETTA. **Maria Tauberová** (sop) Julietta; **Ivo Zidek** (ten) Michel; **Antonín Zlesák** (ten) Police Officer, Postman, Forest Warden; **Zdeněk Otava** (bar) Man with the Helmet; **Václav Bednář** (bass) Man in the Window; **Ivana Mixová** (mez) Small Arab;

Vladimir Jedenáctik (bas) Old Arab; **Jaroslava Procházková** (mez) Bird-Seller; **Ludmila Hanzalíková** (mez) Fishmonger; **Jaroslav Horáček** (bass) Old Man Youth; **Karel Kalaš** (bass) Grandfather; **Milada Cadikovičová** (contr) Grandmother; **Stěpánka Jelinková** (sngr) Old Lady; **Věra Soukupová** (mez) Fortune-Teller; **Jindřich Jindrák** (bar) Souvenir Seller; **Jaroslav Veverka** (bass) Old Sailor; **Zdeněk Svehla** (ten) Young Sailor; **Marcela Lemariová** (mez) Errand-Boy; **Karel Berman** (bass) Beggar; **Dalibor Jedlička** (bass) Convict; **Jaroslav Střiška** (ten) Engine Driver; **Bohumír Lalák** (bass) Night Watchman; **Prague National Theatre Chorus and Orchestra/Jaroslav Krombholc.** Supraphon 10 8176-2. Notes, text and translation included. From SUAST50611/3 (8/73). Recorded in 1964.

③ 2h 25m ADD 6/93

Julietta is Martinů's most magical score, a 'dream book' indeed (the opera's subtitle), set in a land where all the people are amnesiacs, where even imaginary memories are treasured and where falsehood is as real as truth. A young man comes to this country in search of a girl he may once have met there (or did he dream her?). He finds her, but does she really recognize him, or find in him a comforting illusion? He loses her again, and returns to the 'real' world where the only hope of continuing his search for her is to remain in the unreal world of the insane for the rest of his life. But everything in that dream-world is more alluringly real, if also much more surreally strange, than in our reality. The subject immediately appealed to Martinů. As an expatriate and inveterate traveller he identified with the young man. As one whose dearest reality was his magic childhood, suspended above the world in the room at the top of a tower which was his family's home, a childhood around which he had woven a tissue of half-remembered idyll, he felt at home in that land where dreams, reality and imagination can hardly be distinguished. And he knew how to conjure up dreams and half-memories so vividly that we almost recognize them as our own. A fragment of dance-melody, the sound of an accordion, a song that you could swear you have known all your life — and in a flash Martinů's imaginary world (as oddly matter-of-fact and realistic, despite its strangeness, as a painting by Magritte) is there in front of you. It and its inhabitants are so real that a single hearing of this mysteriously poetic opera can haunt you for days. This classic recording could hardly be bettered with Ivo Zidek an ideal exponent of the central role, not a weak link in the rest of the large cast, and Jaroslav Krombholc an outstandingly sensitive conductor. The recording still sounds very good indeed.

Further listening ...

The parables. Estampes. Overture. La rhapsodie, "Allegro symphonique". **Czech Philharmonic Orchestra/Jiří Bělohlávek.** Supraphon 10 4140-2 (6/91).

String Sextet. Three Madrigals[a]. *Coupled with* **Schulhoff.** String Sextet. **Raphael Ensemble.** Hyperion CDA66516 (7/92).

Nonet. Trio in F major. La Rêvue de Cuisine. **The Dartington Ensemble.** Hyperion CDA66084.

The Epic of Gilgamesh. **Eva Depoltová** (sop); **Stefan Margita** (ten); **Ivan Kusnjer** (bar); **Ludek Vele** (bass); **Milan Karpíšek** (spkr); **Slovak Philharmonic Choir; Slovak Philharmonic Orchestra/Zdeněk Košler.** Marco Polo 8 223316 (4/91).

Giuseppe Martucci

Italian 1856-1909

Suggested listening ...

Piano Concerto No. 2 in B flat minor, Op. 66[a]. Canzonetta, Op. 55 No. 1. Tempo di gavotta, Op. 55 No. 2. Giga, Op. 61 No. 3. Serenata, Op. 57 No. 1. Minuetto, Op. 57 No. 2. Momento musicale, Op. 57 No. 3. [a]**Francesco Caramiello** (pf); **Philharmonia Orchestra/ Francesco d'Avalos.** ASV CDDCA691 (7/90).

Symphony No. 1 in D minor, Op. 75. Novelletta, Op. 82 No. 2. Notturno, Op. 70 No. 1. Tarantella, Op. 44 No. 6. **Philharmonia Orchestra/Francesco d'Avalos.** ASV CDDCA675 (12/89).

Symphony No. 2 in F major, Op. 81. Andante in B flat major, Op. 69 No. 2ᵃ. Colore orientale, Op. 44 No. 3. ᵃ**George Ives** (vc); **Philharmonia Orchestra/Francesco d'Avalos.** ASV CDDCA689 (5/90).

Nocturne in G flat major, Op. 70 No. 1. Novelletta, Op. 82 No. 2. Giga, Op. 61 No. 3. *Coupled with* **Busoni.** Turandot – Suite, Op. 41. **Casella.** Paganiniana, Op. 65. **La Scala Philharmonic Orchestra, Milan/Riccardo Muti.** Sony Classical SK53280 (4/94). *See review under Busoni; refer to the Index to Reviews.*

Key to symbols

Quality of sound	Discs worth exploring	Caveat emptor
Quality of performance	Basic library	Period performance

Pietro Mascagni

Italian 1863-1945

Suggested listening ...

CAVALLERIA RUSTICANA — *See review and listings under Leoncavallo; refer to the Index to Reviews.*

IRIS. **Soloists; Bavarian Radio Chorus; Munich Radio Orchestra/Giuseppe Patanè.** CBS Masterworks CD45526 (9/89).

Jules Massenet

French 1842-1912

Massenet. CHERUBIN. **Frederica von Stade** (mez) Chérubin; **Samuel Ramey** (bass) Jacoppo; **June Anderson** (sop) L'Ensoleillad; **Dawn Upshaw** (sop) Nina; **Jean-Marc Ivaldi** (bar) Count; **Hélène Garetti** (sop) Countess; **Michel Trempont** (ten) Baron; **Brigitte Balleys** (contr) Baroness; **Michel Sénéchal** (ten) Duke; **Claes Hakon Ahnsjö** (ten) Ricardo; **Armand Arapian** (ten) Innkeeper; **Rainer Scholze** (bass) Officer; **Bavarian State Opera Chorus; Munich Radio Orchestra/Pinchas Steinberg.** RCA Victor Red Seal 09026-60593-2. Notes, text and translation included. Recorded in 1991.

② 1h 55m DDD 12/92

Massenet is best known for his operatic heroines, who include Manon and Thaïs, but here, in a late opera which he called a *comédie chantée,* the protagonist is a boy of 17, the Cherubino of Mozart's *The Marriage of Figaro.* But as in Mozart, Cherubino is played by a woman singer, and this gives a special eloquence to the role. A little of the Beaumarchais play that inspired Mozart's opera still survives, in that we are still in Seville and the Count and Countess still live there along with Chérubin himself. But otherwise there is little resemblance and Massenet's opera, based on a later play, makes the flirtatious youth the centre of the action and takes a roman-ticized view of the emotions with which the story deals. This opera stands or falls by its central character — Frederica von Stade makes Chérubin as believable as we can hope to expect, and her first entrance (with the words "I'm drunk!" — though only with happiness) has exactly the right ebullience. Both vocally and as an actress, she is equal to the role and evidently enjoys it, and RCA have assembled a supporting cast who are also in sympathy with Massenet's score. Two other roles are those of Nina, who loves Chérubin faithfully and finally wins him, and the dancer L'Ensoleillad: they are well played by Dawn Upshaw and June Anderson. Among the men, Jean-Marc Ivaldi is an imperious Count and Samuel Ramey is suitably weighty in the bass role of the 'philosopher' who is the wayward youth's moral tutor and who finally persuades him to enter a world of adult responsibility. The scene in which this happens, at the end, is movingly written, and the whole opera, without the cuts sometimes made in the theatre, is strongly and sympathetically presented by the singers and orchestra under Pinchas Steinberg. The recording, made in a Munich studio, is clear and spacious.

Massenet. DON QUICHOTTE[a]. Scènes alsaciennes.[b]. **Nicolai Ghiaurov** (bass) Don Quichotte; **Régine Crespin** (sop) Dulcinée; **Gabriel Bacquier** (bar) Sancho Panza; **Michèle Command** (sop) Pedro; **Annick Duterte** (sop) Garcias; **Peyo Garazzi** (ten) Rodriguez; **Jean-Marie Fremeau** (ten) Juan; **Suisse Romande Chorus and Orchestra/Kazimierz Kord;** [b]**National Philharmonic Orchestra/Richard Bonynge.** Decca 430 636-2DM2. Notes, text and translation included. Item marked [a] from D156D3 (11/79), [b] SXL6827 (12/77). Recorded in 1978.

② 2h 13m ADD 4/92

Massenet's operas are patchily represented in the catalogue, and this heroic comedy, which was his last big success (in 1910, when he was 67) is most welcome. People who think of him as only a salon composer, lacking the vigour and depth of a Berlioz or a Debussy, should listen to the start of Act 1, set in a Spanish town square at fiesta time; the opening music bursts out of the loudspeakers like that of Verdi's *Otello*, although here the mood is joyous, with tremendous rhythmic verve and gusto. In fact, this opera is closer to Verdi's *Falstaff*, with the same admixture of gentler serious moments amidst the comic bustle and intrigue, and of course, here again the central character is a comic yet lovable figure. The recording, made by a British team in Geneva in 1978, still sounds well although orchestral detail could be clearer. As for the performance by mainly Swiss forces under Kazimierz Kord, and with a Bulgarian bass in the title role (written for Chaliapin), one can only praise it for its idiomatic realization of a 'Spanish' opera by a gifted French composer for the theatre. Though Régine Crespin may be too mature vocally for Dulcinée, the object of the elderly Don Quixote's adoration, she sings splendidly and few will find this a serious weakness. Nicolai Ghiaurov rightly makes Quixote himself a real person, touching and dignified as well as comic, and Gabriel Bacquier gives a rounded portrayal of his servant Sancho Panza, so that Quixote's death scene in the company of his old friend is particularly strong. The booklet provides a synopsis plus the French text and a translation. This is a fine mid-price issue, and the lively and tuneful *Scènes alsaciennes* with a British orchestra under Richard Bonynge make a fine fill-up.

Additional recommendation ...
Soloists; Toulouse Capitole Chorus and Orchestra/Michel Plasson. EMI CDS7 54767-2
— ② 1h 55m DDD 12/93

Further listening ...

Fantaisie. *Coupled with* **Lalo.** Cello Concerto in D minor. **Saint-Saëns.** Cello Concerto No. 1 in A minor, Op. 33. **Sophie Rolland** (vc); **BBC Philharmonic Orchestra/Gilbert Varga.** ASV CDDCA867 (12/93). *See review under Lalo; refer to the Index to Reviews.*

Orchestral Suites — 2292-45858-2: No. 3, "Scènes dramatiques"; No. 6, "Scènes de féerie". La Vierge — Le dernier sommeil de la Vierge. 2292-45859-2: No. 4, "Scènes pittoresques"; No. 7, "Scènes alsaciennes". Don Quichotte — Interludes. **Monte-Carlo Opera Orchestra/John Eliot Gardiner.** Erato 2292-45858/9-2 (2/93).

LE ROI DE LAHORE. **Soloists; London Voices; National Philharmonic Orchestra/ Richard Bonynge.** Decca Grand Opera 433 851-2DMO2 (2/93).

WERTHER. **Soloists; Children's Choir; Royal Opera House Orchestra, Covent Garden/Sir Colin Davis.** Philips 416 654-2PH2 (2/87).

LE CID. **Soloists; Byrne Camp Chorale; New York Opera Orchestra/Eve Queler.** CBS CD79300 (2/90).

THAIS. **Soloists; French Radio Lyric Chorus and Orchestra/Albert Wolff.** Le Chant du Monde LDC278 895/6.

William Mathias
British 1934-1992

Suggested listening ...

Fanfare. Processional. Invocations, Op. 35. Fantasy, Op. 78. Berceuse, Op. 95 No. 3. Jubilate, Op. 67 No. 2. Antiphonies, Op. 88 No. 2. Fenestra. Recessional, Op. 96 No. 4. Chorale. **John Scott** (org). Nimbus NI5367 (6/93).

Church, Choral and Organ Works — I will celebrate. O how amiable, Op. 90 No. 3. Rex Gloriae — Four Latin Motets, Op. 83. Missa Aedis Christi, Op. 92. Jesus College Service, Op. 53. A Grace, Op 89 No. 3. Ave Rex, Op. 45. As truly as God is our Father. Let the people praise Thee, O God, Op. 87. Fantasy for organ, Op. 78 — No. 2, Canzonetta. **Simon Lawford** (org); **Christ Church Cathedral Choir/Stephen Darlington.** Nimbus NI5243 (9/90).

Nicola Matteis
Italian/British d. 1707 or later

Suggested listening ...

Ayres for the Violin — Book 1: Sonata in C minor[bc]. Book 2: Suite in G minor[a]. Book 4: Suites — A major[ab]; D minor[ab]; E minor[ab]. Sonata in C major[ab]. **Arcadian Academy/Nicholas McGegan** (hpd/[c]org). Harmonia Mundi HMU90 7067 (9/92).

Nicholas Maw
British 1935-

Suggested listening ...

Odyssey. **City of Birmingham Symphony Orchestra/Simon Rattle.** EMI CDS7 54277-2 (9/91).

Sir Peter Maxwell Davies
British 1934-

Maxwell Davies. Symphony No. 4[a]. Trumpet Concerto[b]. [b]**John Wallace** (tpt); [a]**Scottish Chamber Orchestra/Sir Peter Maxwell Davies.** Collins Classics 1181-2.

⏱ **lh l3m DDD 6/91** ❓

Sir Peter Maxwell Davies has survived the transition from *enfant terrible* to *éminence grise* with equanimity — perhaps because he was always less 'terrible' than he seemed, and is still far from seriously 'grise'. From his earliest works to his most recent — the Trumpet Concerto and Fourth Symphony date from the late 1980s — he has used his delight in system-building to generate ambitious and complex structures that vibrate with no less complex but utterly uninhibited emotions. The Concerto is the immediately accessible of the two: the nature of the solo instrument, and Maxwell Davies's willingness not to jettison all the conventions of the concerto genre see to that. The work was written for John Wallace, and while it would be wrong to say that he makes light of its difficulties — at times you could swear that only a flautist could get round such florid writing — he succeeds brilliantly in demonstrating that the difficulties serve musical ends. The Symphony has less immediately arresting ideas, but when the music is savoured, returned to, and allowed time to weave its spells, its rewards become progressively more apparent. These recordings capture the composer's own highly-charged readings with commendable fidelity.

Additional recommendation ...

Trumpet Concerto. **Birtwistle.** Endless Parade[a]. **Blake Watkins.** Trumpet Concerto. **Håkan Hardenberger** (tpt); [a]**Paul Patrick** (vib); **BBC Philharmonic Orchestra/Elgar Howarth.** Philips 432 075-2PH — .ᐧᐧ Ih 19m DDD 6/91 ❼

Maxwell Davies. Strathclyde Concertos — No. 3[a]; No. 4[b]. [a]**Randall Cook** (hn); [b]**Lewis Morrison** (cl); [a]**Peter Franks** (tpt); **Scottish Chamber Orchestra/Sir Peter Maxwell Davies.** Collins Classics 1239-2. Recorded in 1991.

.ᐧᐧ Ih Im DDD 10/92

Sir Peter Maxwell Davies's plan to write a sequence of no fewer than ten *Strathclyde* Concertos for the principals of the Scottish Chamber Orchestra is turning into a research project into the nature of the concerto, the relationship between soloist and orchestra. His solo parts are always satisfying, even virtuoso, but the orchestra seldom adopts an accompanying or antagonistic role. In the double concerto for trumpet and horn, for example, the flutes and strings also play a very important part, with material of their own that the soloists hardly touch, but the effect is to emphasize the 'flute-ness' of the flutes and the 'string-ness' of the strings: they become, in effect, co-soloists themselves. Maxwell Davies is also interested of course, in this concerto, in the 'trumpet-ness' and 'horn-ness' of his two principal soloists, and in the beautiful slow movement they dramatize this by eventually exchanging functions, the trumpet becoming lyrical, the horn martial. One of the functions of the clarinet, in its concerto, is to point up the sober beauty, the 'un-clarinet-ness', of the textures against which its cool solo line moves; it has an especially fruitful relationship with that section of the orchestra with which it is in greatest contrast, the low strings. Both works require intent listening; both reward it with readily perceptible formal ingenuity (the way in which the clarinet concerto's main theme is only gradually revealed as a haunting folk-song is especially absorbing) and a fascinating interplay of instrumental character. Both concertos are vividly performed and very cleanly recorded.

New review
Maxwell Davies. Strathclyde Concertos — No. 5 for Violin, Viola and String Orchestra[a]; No. 6 for Flute and Orchestra[b]. [b]**David Nicholson** (fl); [a]**James Clark** (vn); [a]**Catherine Marwood** (va); **Scottish Chamber Orchestra/Sir Peter Maxwell Davies.** Collins Classics 1303-2. Recorded in 1993.

.ᐧᐧ 59m DDD 5/94

Each of these concertos has a sort of programme which provides useful signposts as well as an intriguing puzzle to solve. In the Fifth Concerto Maxwell Davies's material includes a sixteenth-century two-part song and a fragment of a Haydn overture. In the Sixth a simple, folk-like theme recurs in various transformations, suggested by a Brueghel painting of children's games. In both concertos, though, the nature of the solo instruments is at least as important as the programme in determining the work's sound-world. Apart from the avowed subtexts, you feel that there must be others: the flute in No. 6 is audibly trying out lyrical partners, finding perhaps its most satisfying relationship with the clarinet in the concerto's beautiful slow coda. And in No. 5 the two disparate pieces of pre-existing material are surely not the only kinships with the past; for instance, of whom does a finale beginning in Bulgarian dance-rhythm remind you? In formal ingenuity, too, both concertos repay repeated listening; both are extremely well played and cleanly, carefully recorded.

Further listening ...

"A Celebration of Scotland". An Orkney Wedding, with Sunrise. Kinloche, his Fantasie[b]. Seven Songs Home[a]. Yesnaby Ground[c]. Dances from "The Two Fiddlers"[b]. Jimmack the Postie[b].

Farewell to Stromness[c]. Lullaby for Lucy[a]. Renaissance Scottish Dances[b]. [a]**St Mary's Music School Choir;** [b]**Scottish Chamber Orchestra/Sir Peter Maxwell Davies** ([c]pf). Unicorn-Kanchana DKPCD9070 (12/88).

Solstice of Light[a]. Five Carols[b]. Hymn to the Word of God[c]. [ac]**Neil Mackie** (ten); [a]**Christopher Hughes** (org); **King's College Choir, Cambridge/Stephen Cleobury.** Argo 436 119-2ZH (2/93).

Miss Donnithorne's Maggot[a]. Eight Songs for a Mad King[b]. [a]**Mary Thomas** (sop); [b]**Julius Eastman** (bar); **The Fires of London/Sir Peter Maxwell Davies.** Unicorn-Kanchana DKPCD9052 (3/88).

Ave maris stella. Image, Reflection, Shadow[a]. Runes from a Holy Island[b]. [a]**Gregory Knowles** (cimbalom); **The Fires of London/**[b]**Sir Peter Maxwell Davies.** Unicorn-Kanchana Souvenir UKCD2038 (3/91).

The Martyrdom of St Magnus. **Soloists; Scottish Chamber Opera Ensemble/Michael Rafferty.** Unicorn-Kanchana DKPCD9100 (3/91).

Black Pentecost[a]. Stone Litany. **Della Jones** (mez); [a]**David Wilson-Johnson** (bar); **BBC Philharmonic Orchestra/Sir Peter Maxwell Davies.** Collins Classics 1366-2 (8/93).

Billy Mayerl

British 1902-1959

New review

Mayerl. PIANO MUSIC, Volume 3. **Eric Parkin.** Chandos CHAN9141. Recorded in 1991. Filigree. Three Miniatures in syncopation, Op. 76. Siberian lament. In my Garden: Summertime. Three Japanese Pictures, Op. 25 — A Temple in Kyoto; The Cherry Dance. Beguine Impromptu. The Big Top. The Legends of King Arthur — The Sword Excalibur; Guinevere. Honky-tonk. In my Garden: Autumntime. Romanesque. Four insect Oddities. Leprechaun's Leap.

1h 9m   DDD   9/93

There is no pianist better equipped to carry the Billy Mayerl revival forward than Eric Parkin and this latest volume is further justification. He employs the strict rhythm arising from dance music which the composer often specifies; he understands the piano style — lyrical but fairly dry; and he plays with real musicianship without apology for music which makes friends through being easy on the ear. He is particularly winning in the two suites called *In my Garden*, which were intended for amateurs to play. "Meadowsweet" is a perfect example of the genre. This is the domestic music of the inter-war period, called "The Long Weekend" by Robert Graves, and it's as English as the poetry of Betjeman. Parkin, with his rare understanding of Bax, Bridge and Ireland, can place pieces like *Filigree* and *Siberian lament* (in spite of its title!) into their English tradition.

Further listening ...

Four Aces Suite — No. 1, Ace of Clubs; No. 4, Ace of Spades. Mistletoe. Autumn crocus. Hollyhock. White heather. Three Dances in Syncopation, Op. 73. Sweet William. Parade of the Sandwich-Board Men. Hop-O'-My-Thumb. Jill all alone. Aquarium Suite. *Coupled with* ***Mayerl/Croom-Johnson:*** Bats in the Belfry. Green tulips. **Eric Parkin** (pf). Chandos CHAN8848 (11/90).

The Legends of King Arthur — Prelude; Merlin the Wizard; Lady of the Lake; The Passing of Arthur. Almond Blossom. April's Fool. The Harp of the Winds. Marigold. Railroad Rhythm. Shallow Waters. From a Spanish Lattice. Song of the Fir Tree. Nimble-Fingered Gentleman. Evening Primrose. Four Aces — Ace of Diamonds; Ace of Hearts. The Joker. **Eric Parkin** (pf). Chandos CHAN8560 (6/88).

Domenico Mazzocchi *Italian 1592-1665*

Suggested listening ...

Misereris omnium, Domine[ac]. Gaudebunt labia mea[ade]. Peccantem me quotidie[abe]. Jesu, dulcis memoria[ade]. Dialogo della Cantica. Vide, Domine, afflictionem nostram. Dialogo di Lazaro. Dialogo della Maddalena. Dialogo dell'Apocalisse. Lamento di David. Concilio de' Farisei. [a]**Maria Cristina Kiehr**, [b]**Barbara Borden** (sops); [c]**Andreas Scholl** (alto); [d]**Gerd Türk** (ten); [e]**Ulrich Messthaler** (bass); **Netherlands Chamber Choir; Lucia Swarts** (vc); **Karl-Ernst Schröder** (theorbo); **Christophe Rousset** (org/hpd)/**René Jacobs.** Harmonia Mundi HMC90 1357 (2/92).

Sir John McEwen *Scottish 1868-1948*

Suggested listening ...

Three Border Ballads. **London Philharmonic Orchestra/Alasdair Mitchell.** Chandos CHAN9241 (3/94).

Nikolay Medtner *Russian 1880-1951*

New review

Medtner. Piano Concerto No. 1 in C minor, Op. 33[a].
Balakirev. Piano Concerto No. 1 in F sharp major, Op. 1[a].
Rimsky-Korsakov. Piano Concerto in C sharp minor, Op. 30[b]. **Igor Zhukov** (pf); **USSR TV and Radio Large Orchestra**/[a]**Alexander Dmitriev**; [b]**Gennadi Rozhdestvensky.** Mezhdunarodnaya Kniga MK417087. Recorded 1968-73.

⸱•⸱ lh 2m ADD 2/94 | **P**

In these performances Igor Zhukov's colossal, straight-from-the-shoulder technique and his full, saturated, all-Russian sonority are overwhelming, particularly in the Medtner, the principal work on this recital of single-movement concertos. The ghosts of Brahms and Schumann, albeit in ultra-virtuoso form, haunt Medtner's romantic epic, yet from the opening warlike stance to a later (*tranquillo*) memory of happier times, the writing pulses with passion and integrity. In such hands all stale notions of Medtner's supposed conservatism vanish into oblivion. Zhukov's brilliance is equally electrifying in the Balakirev and Rimsky-Korsakov concertos, the former wheeling decorously and obsessively round a single idea, the latter an exuberant Lisztian rhapsody with a strong Russian flavour (it is surely far more attractive than either of the Liszt concertos). There is delicacy, too, in Zhukov's performances and the opening of the Rimsky is beautifully idiomatic, with a rare sense of romantic wonder, while Balakirev's Chopinesque tracery is spun off with great affection. The recordings have come up impressively and these are unquestionably the finest versions of all three concertos.

Medtner. Piano Concertos — No. 2 in C minor, Op. 50; No. 3 in E minor, Op. 60. **Nikolai Demidenko** (pf); **BBC Scottish Symphony Orchestra/Jerzy Maksymiuk.** Hyperion CDA66580. Recorded in 1991.

⸱•⸱ lh 14m DDD 4/92 | **P**

New review

Medtner. ORCHESTRAL WORKS. **Nikolay Medtner** (pf); [ab]**Philharmonia Orchestra/ Issay Dobrowen.** Testament mono SBT1027. Item marked [a] from HMV DB6559/63 (2/48), [b] DB6718/22 (8/48), [c] DB6563, [d] DB6564 (both 2/48). Recorded in 1947.

473

Piano Concertos — No. 2 in C minor, Op. 50[a]; No. 3 in E minor, Op. 60[b]. Arabesque in A minor, Op. 7 No. 2[c]. Fairy Tale in F minor, Op. 26 No. 3[d].

⟩• Ih I7m ADD 4/94 ○p ▲

Hyperion's splendid disc is given a fine recording, good orchestral playing from a Scottish orchestra under a Polish conductor and, above all, truly coruscating and poetic playing from the brilliant young Russian pianist Nikolai Demidenko. It also did a splendid rehabilitation job for Nikolay Medtner who is steadily coming in from the cold after half a century of neglect. He was a contemporary and friend of Rachmaninov who settled in Britain in the 1930s, and like Rachmaninov (to whom the Second Concerto is dedicated and who returned the compliment with his own Fourth) he was an excellent pianist. But while the other composer became immensely popular, Medtner languished in obscurity, regarded (if thought about at all) as an inferior imitation of Rachmaninov who wrote gushing music that was strong on gestures but weak on substance. The fact is that he can be diffuse (not to say long-winded) and grandiose, and memorable tunes are in short supply, so that his music needs to be played well to come off. But when it is there's much to enjoy and the strong Russian flavour of the ornate writing is evident, as is the composer's masterly understanding of the piano. Listening to the composer himself in the Second's first *molto cantabile a tempo, ma expressivo* or the Third's *dolce cantabile* is to be made doubly aware of his haunting and bittersweet lyricism. The streaming figuration in the Second Concerto's *Romanza* is spun off with deceptive ease, a reminder that while Medtner despised obvious pyrotechnics he was a superlative pianist. So here, surely, is an ideal complement to Demidenko's hypnotically fiery and articulate accounts. Two exquisitely played encores are included (the ambiguous poetry of the A minor *Arabesque* could be by no other composer), and the 1947 recordings have been superbly remastered.

New review
Medtner. Violin Sonatas — No. 1 in B minor, Op. 21; No. 2 in G major, Op. 44; No. 3 in E minor, "Epica", Op. 57. Three Nocturnes, Op. 16. Canzonas and Danzas, Op. 43.
Alexander Shirinsky (vn); **Dmitri Galynin** (pf). Mezhdunarodnaya Kniga MK417109. Recorded in 1992.

⟩• ② Ih 2Im DDD II/93

One can easily see why the second and third sonatas have remained neglected for so long — expansive and taxingly virtuosic they require enormous stamina and dedication from both performers. Shirinsky and Galynin have both, and provide excellent introductions to these rarely heard works. The music itself abounds in unfettered lyricism and rhapsodic passion. The First Sonata is perhaps the most immediately engaging of the three, with its Fauréesque charm in the first movement, its attractive *Chanson de Matin*-like second movement and festive finale. The remaining items, the three Nocturnes, Op. 16 and Two *Canzonas with Dances*, Op. 43, reveal a much more compact and concise side to Medtner's style, but like the sonatas seem to have failed to gain a foothold in the violin repertoire. Quite why this should be is a mystery, for the poetic, lyrical *Nocturnes* would make a welcome addition to any recital, as would the gentle, unassuming charm of the character pieces, Op. 43. Good recorded sound, if perhaps a little over resonant in places.

New review
Medtner. PIANO WORKS. **Nikolai Demidenko.** Hyperion CDA66636. Recorded in 1992. Forgotten Melodies, Op. 38 — Sonata reminiscenza; Canzona serenata. Sonaten-Triade, Op. 11 — Sonata elegia. Forgotten Melodies, Op. 39 — Canzona matinata; Sonata tragica. Scazka (Fairy Tale) in B flat minor, Op. 20 No. 1. Theme and Variations in C sharp minor, Op. 55. Dithyramb in E flat major, Op. 10 No. 2.

⟩• Ih IIm DDD 9/93 ○p ○s

From the first bar of the gently lyrical *Canzona serenata*, you instinctively know that the following 71 minutes are going to be special indeed — and they are. The first thing that impresses is Demidenko's diaphonous tone, his bell-like *cantabile* and his ability to probe deep below the surface of the music. As the recital progresses the next thing to become obvious is the natural sense of flow. This is achieved (be it conscious or not) with the placement of each piece in a harmonic scheme. There are other connections made too, such as the thematic interrelationship between the two canzonas and sonatas, as for example the *Canzona matinata* echoing the *Sonata elegia* of some 16 years earlier before proffering, in the central section, the gorgeous Interludium section of the following Sonata tragica. Logically presented, as they are here, all these inter-connections and *déjà vu* episodes amount to a thoroughly absorbing and intelligent presentation of Medtner's music and creative psyche, allowing the listener a fuller and more rounded appreciation of the composer than is normally presented. With the help of the luminous acoustics of The Maltings, Snape, Hyperion have produced a truly remarkable piano sound full of warmth and intimacy, which can only be described as the next best thing to being there.

Henryk Melcer-Szczawinski

Polish 1869-1928

New review

Melcer-Szczawinski. Piano Concerto No. 1 in E minor[b].
Paderewski. Piano Concerto in A minor, Op. 17[a]. [a]**Piotr Paleczny,** [b]**Michael Ponti** (pfs);
[a]**Polish National Radio Symphony Orchestra;** [b]**Warsaw National Philharmonic Orchestra/Tadeusz Strugala.** Olympia OCD398. Item marked [a] recorded in 1982, [b] 1992.

· · 1h 3m DDD 7/94

Subtitled "Two Leschetizky Pupils" this dazzling coupling will be snapped up by all lovers of the romantic piano concerto at its most lush and scintillating. Not that Paderewski and Melcer-Szczawinski are similar composers. From the first bar the latter makes it clear that he has ambitions above and beyond Paderewski's more amiable and domestic charm, and the gauntlet he throws down is taken up with a vengeance by Michael Ponti. Ponti, who has possibly learnt more notes than any other pianist in history, can penetrate even the densest orchestral thicket (Reger is prominent among several other more conventional influences) and his thunder-and-lightning brio when Melcer-Szczawinski roars his passions to the heavens (10'50") is dazzlingly apt. Piotr Paleczny, a pianist much acclaimed in his native Poland but too little known here, is hardly less successful in Paderewski's sugar-and-spice Concerto in A minor. His playing is wonderfully musical and engaging. His way with the central *Nocturne* in particular, would melt a heart of stone, and his handling of Paderewski's decorative flights suggests the most delicate poetic sensibility. The orchestral contributions are more than adequate (with enthusiastic squeaks from the woodwind egging everyone on in Paderewski's finale), and although the recordings range from average to impressive, the performances are exemplary. Certainly, lovers of swashbuckling extravaganza need look no further than the Melcer-Szczawinski Concerto.

Felix Mendelssohn

German 1809-1847

New review

Mendelssohn. Piano Concertos — No. 1 in G minor, Op. 25; No. 2 in D minor, Op. 40. Capriccio brillant in B minor, Op. 22. **London Mozart Players/Howard Shelley** (pf). Chandos CHAN9215.

· · 55m DDD 4/94

New review

Mendelssohn. Piano Concertos — No. 1 in G minor, Op. 25; No. 2 in D minor, Op. 40. Capriccio brillant in B minor, Op. 22. Rondo brillant in E flat, Op. 29. **Benjamin Frith** (pf); **Košice State Philharmonic Orchestra/Robert Stankovsky.** Naxos 8 550681. Recorded in 1992.

| 1h 10m DDD 4/94

The piano concertos were composed when Mendelssohn was still in his twenties. Benjamin Frith, playing with a full symphony orchestra under Robert Stankovsky, includes two of the composer's three single-movement works for piano and orchestra as bonus on his super-bargain-price disc. Howard Shelley contents himself with just the familiar *Capriccio brillant* as an extra, and prefers to direct the London Mozart Players himself on a full-price issue some 15 minutes shorter. The difference in playing time is not just due to Shelley's omission of the *Rondo brillant*. Always he prefers a livelier tempo for the flanking movements of both concertos, particularly their scintillating finales. Mendelssohn himself liked to play that of the G minor work "as fast as possible provided that the notes can be heard", and that's exactly what Shelley does — quickening an already electrifying introductory *presto* into a *molto allegro e vivace* of irrepressible youthful *joie de vivre*. Both here and in this concerto's opening *Molto allegro con fuoco*, Frith and his Slovakian colleagues emerge just a little more middle-aged in their caution. Nor do they arrest attention with Shelley's immediacy and urgency in the opening *Allegro appassionato* of the D minor work. In the finale, however, their refusal to rush allows fuller appreciation of its craftsmanly cunning. While in its way a virtuoso *tour de force*, Shelley's tempo here is fast enough to sound gabbled. As for the slow movements, both pianists open one's ears anew to their beauties. From both of them the *Andante* of the earlier work, in particular, would melt the heart of the proverbial stone. But if forced to make a choice it would have to be the slightly older, maturer Shelley for the effortless continuity of his shapely phrasing and the closeness of the orchestral response. With his slower spread chords and more expansive melodic line in the introduction, plus springier rhythms in the ensuing fun and games, Shelley does just that little bit more for the engaging *Capriccio brillant* too. But that said, Frith is willing to challenge metronome tyranny with an occasional touch of caprice. He is also keenly aware of the music as well as the notes in the less often heard *Rondo brillant*. As for recording, the Chandos brings you better balance between keyboard and orchestra, and by and large a more truthful quality of sound. But at its modest price the Naxos disc remains a bargain on every count.

Additional recommendations ...
Nos. 1 and 2. Prelude and Fugue in E major/minor, Op. 35 No. 1. Variations sérieuses in D minor,
Op. 54. Andante and Rondo capriccioso, Op. 14. **Murray Perahia;** [a]**Academy of St Martin in**
the Fields/Sir Neville Marriner. CBS Masterworks CD42401 — .⸳'' 1h 10m ADD/DDD 11/87 ⁹ₚ
Nos. 1 and 2[a]*. Piano Concerto in A minor*[b]*.* **Cyprien Katsaris (pf);** [a]**Leipzig Gewandhaus**
Orchestra/Kurt Masur; [b]**Liszt Chamber Orchestra/János Rolla.** Teldec Digital
Experience 9031 75860-2 — .⸳'' 1h 10m DDD 6/92

Mendelssohn. Violin Concertos — E minor, Op. 64; D minor. **Viktoria Mullova (vn);**
Academy of St Martin in the Fields/Sir Neville Marriner. Philips 432 077-2PH.
Recorded in 1990.

.⸳'' **50m DDD 5/91** ⁹ₚ Ⓑ

Since the competition is strong to say the least, new accounts of 'the' Mendelssohn Violin Concerto have to be rather special to make their way in the catalogue, but that of Viktoria Mullova and the ASMF under Sir Neville Marriner falls into the category of distinguished additions. The deliberate mention of the orchestra and conductor here is because this work is emphatically not a show-piece for a soloist in the way that Paganini's or Wieniawski's violin concertos are. Instead it offers a real dialogue with orchestra although there are plenty of opportunities for violin virtuosity as well. Mullova's sweet and somehow youthful tone is beautifully matched here by Marriner and his orchestra, which in turn does not sound so big as to overwhelm the often intimate character of the music. The recording helps, too, with its natural balance between the soloist and the orchestral body. The reference above to this E minor work as 'the' Mendelssohn Violin Concerto is because after his death it was found that as a boy of 13 he also composed the one in D minor which here makes a useful coupling. Of course it shows the influence of classical models, including Mozart, but the slow movement has an attractive warmth and the finale a zest and drive that owes something to gipsy music. Maybe in less than expert hands it could sound ordinary, but not when it is done as stylishly as here.

Additional recommendations ...
E minor. **Bruch.** *Violin Concerto No. 1 in G minor, Op. 26.* **Anne-Sophie Mutter (vn); Berlin**
Philharmonic Orchestra/Herbert von Karajan. DG 400 031-2GH — .⸳'' 57m DDD 3/83 Ⓑ
E minor. **Bruch.** *Violin Concerto.* **Scottish Chamber Orchestra/Jaime Laredo (vn).** Pickwick
IMP Red Label PCD829 — .⸳'' 53m DDD 1/87 Ⓑ
E minor. **Bruch.** *Violin Concerto.* **Schubert.** *Rondo in A major, D438.* **Nigel Kennedy (vn);**
English Chamber Orchestra/Jeffrey Tate. EMI CDC7 49663-2 — .⸳'' 1h 11m DDD 1/89 ⁹ₚ Ⓑ
D minor. *Violin and Piano Concerto in D minor.* **Gidon Kremer (vn); Martha Argerich (pf).** DG

| 427 338-2GH — .⸳'' 59m DDD 9/89

Violin Concerto[a]. **Beethoven.** *Violin Concerto in D major, Op. 61*[b]. **Yehudi Menuhin** (vn); [a]**Berlin Philharmonic Orchestra,** [b]**Philharmonia Orchestra/Wilhelm Furtwängler.** EMI Références mono CDH7 69799-2 — *.·'* lh llm ADD 10/89 𝄞p Ⓑ ▲

E minor[b]. **Bruch.** *Violin Concerto*[c]. **Kreisler.** *Liebesfreud*[a]. **Sarasate.** *Introduction et Tarantelle, Op. 43*[a]. **Cho-Liang Lin** (vn); [a]**Sandra Rivers** (pf); [b]**Philharmonia Orchestra/Michael Tilson Thomas;** [c]**Chicago Symphony Orchestra/Leonard Slatkin.** CBS Masterworks CD44902 — *.·'* lh lm DDD 3/91 Ⓑ

E minor[b]. **Bruch.** *Violin Concerto*[b]. [a]**Miklós Szenthelý,** [b]**Emmy Verhey** (vns); [a]**Budapest Philharmonic Orchestra/János Sándor;** [b]**Budapest Symphony Orchestra/Arpád Joó.** LaserLight 15 615 — *.·* 52m DDD 3/91 Ⓑ

E minor. **Brahms.** *Violin Concerto in D major, Op. 77.* **Xue-Wei** (vn); **London Philharmonic Orchestra/Ivor Bolton.** ASV CDDCA748 — *.·'* lh 7m DDD 4/91 Ⓑ

E minor[a]. *Symphony No. 4 in A major, Op. 90, "Italian". The Hebrides, Op. 26, "Fingal's Cave".* [a]**Pinchas Zukerman** (vn); **New York Philharmonic Orchestra/Leonard Bernstein.** Sony Classical The Royal Edition SMK47592 — *.·'* lh l3m DDD 8/93 Ⓑ

E minor. **Prokofiev.** *Violin Concerto No. 2 in G minor, Op. 63.* **Itzhak Perlman** (vn); **Chicago Symphony Orchestra/Daniel Barenboim.** Erato 4509-91732-2 — *.·'* 53m DDD 1/94 Ⓑ

Key to symbols

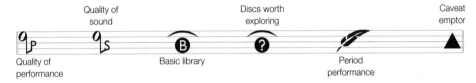

| Quality of sound | | Discs worth exploring | | | Caveat emptor |

| 𝄞p | 𝄞s | Ⓑ | ❓ | ✒ | ▲ |

| Quality of performance | | Basic library | | Period performance | |

Mendelssohn. STRING SYMPHONIES. **London Festival Orchestra/Ross Pople.** Hyperion CDA66561/3. Items marked [a] from CDA66196 (6/87), [b] CDA66318 (11/89), others new to UK. Recorded 1985-90.
No. 1 in C major. No. 2 in D major. No. 3 in E minor. No. 4 in C minor. No. 5 in B flat major[b]. No. 6 in E flat major. No. 7 in D minor[b]. No. 8 in D major[b]. No. 9 in C minor[a]. No. 10 in B minor[a]. No. 11 in F major. No. 12 in G minor[a].

.· ③ 3h 23m DDD 12/91

"Mendelssohn — twelve years old — promises much": this prophetic entry made by Beethoven in one of his conversation books, shortly after his first encounter with the young genius, is certainly vindicated in the astonishing cycle of 12 symphonies for string orchestra. These youthful works chart the composer's mastery of symphonic genre and total command of formal classicism over a period of barely two years, and Ross Pople is eager to communicate his own tangible sense of wonderment and deepening incredulity throughout this excellent integral cycle. Whilst Pople himself confirms this ongoing revelation in his performances, Hyperion have ensured that the layout of the discs conform to the chronology of the works themselves. Symphonies Nos. 1 and 2 were evidently compositional studies directed by Mendelssohn's private tutor, Zelter, but they have charm and true melodic interest, whereas No. 3 clearly owes much to the turbulence of Haydn's *Sturm-und-drang-Periode*. The spirit of the high baroque is revealed in the Handelian *Grave* introduction to Symphony No. 4, whilst its successor is evidently something of a fusion of baroque and early classical styles. The central works of the cycle reveal a greater sense of assurance and individuality, but as Pople avidly demonstrates, they have a growing emotional impetus and architectural potency also. Equally, the influence of other composers is diminishing as the later symphonies assume a traditional four-movement form, of increasing complexity and cohesion, and Pople directs a memorably vigorous account of Symphony No. 8, with its astonishing *Scherzo* and ingenious double fugue. If one senses more than ever the forward looking innovation of the last three symphonies, then this is as much a tribute to the sheer excellence of these performances as to the actual resources of the music itself, for Pople conveys all the joy and wonderment of each fresh discovery, and the London Festival Orchestra clearly share in his delight as they unfold the true genius of these extraordinary works. Very highly recommended.

Additional recommendations ...

Nos. 1-6. **English String Orchestra/William Boughton.** Nimbus NI5141 — .⁚ lh DDD 3/89

Nos. 7, 8 and 10. **English String Orchestra/William Boughton.** Nimbus NI5142 — .⁚
52m DDD 3/89

Nos. 9, 11 and 12. **English String Orchestra/William Boughton.** Nimbus NI5143 — .⁚
lh llm DDD 3/89

Nos. 8, 9 and 10. **Orpheus Chamber Orchestra.** DG 437 528-2GH — .⁚ 58m DDD 8/93

New review

Mendelssohn. String Symphonies — No. 2 in D major; No. 3 in E minor; No. 9 in C major; No. 10 in B minor. **Nieuw Sinfonietta, Amsterdam/Lev Markiz.** BIS CD643. Recorded in 1993.

.⁚ lh DDD 6/94

These very pleasant works demand little of performers other than a certain rhythmic buoyancy in the quicker music, and sympathetic warmth in the slow movements. These qualities are very well supplied by Lev Markiz and his admirable players throughout this disc, and the recording is certainly very impressive in possessing both clarity and tonal opulence within an ideally balanced acoustic. BIS's issue is subtitled "The Complete String Symphonies —Volume 1", so we may expect two more CDs to make up a set. This will rival the existing complete surveys by Ross Pople and William Boughton. Nimbus's set, available on three separate discs, but coupled differently from the sequence listed above, suffers a little from occasional lapses in the playing and an over-reverberant recording acoustic. Hyperion's performances (reviewed above) are only available as a complete set: here the quality of recording is not quite so strikingly good as the engineering on BIS's new issue. Those who just wish to sample the string symphonies should investigate this new BIS disc, and they will still have the option of completing the survey in due course if they so wish.

Mendelssohn. Symphonies — No. 1 in C minor, Op. 11; No. 5 in D major, Op. 107, "Reformation". **Bamberg Symphony Orchestra/Claus Peter Flor.** RCA Victor Red Seal 09026-60391-2. Recorded in 1990.

.⁚ 58m DDD

As a companion CD from RCA of assorted Mendelssohn overtures has already demonstrated (reviewed below), Leipzig-born Claus Peter Flor is an outstandingly sympathetic interpreter of this particular figure. Here, then, is a pair of most enjoyable readings, not as bracingly dynamic as some (Sawallisch, listed below, in his marvellous New Philharmonia account for Philips of the *Reformation* undoubtedly brought more thrust to the opening *Allegro con fuoco*), but always engagingly affectionate. Certainly, Flor's wholly winning presentation of the *Reformation*'s lovely, tripping *Scherzo* is an absolute delight, and here as elsewhere the Bamberg SO's response combines a most agreeably homogeneous tone-production with no little discipline. Warm, if not ideally focused recording to match. For some, this music-making may be a mite *too* relaxed and cosily 'old world'; however, Flor's comparatively laid back manner is easy to enjoy, and his thoughtful interpretations are by no means lacking in guile, character or fresh-faced charm.

Additional recommendations ...

No. 1; No. 2 in B flat major, Op. 52, "Lobgesang" (with Elizabeth Connell, Karita Mattila, sops; Hans-Peter Blochwitz, ten)*; No. 3 in A minor, Op. 56, "Scottish"; No. 4 in A major, Op. 90, "Italian"; No. 5. Overtures — The Hebrides, Op. 26, "Fingal's Cave"; A Midsummer Night's Dream, Op. 21. The Fair Melusina, Op. 32. Octet in E flat major, Op. 20 — Scherzo.* **London Symphony Orchestra/Claudio Abbado.** DG 415 353-2GH4 — .⁚ ④ 4h 5m DDD 1/86

Symphonies Nos. 1-5. **New Philharmonia Orchestra/Wolfgang Sawallisch.** Philips 432 598-2PB3 — .⁚ ③ 3h 14m ADD 8/91

Symphonies Nos. 1-5. **Berlin Philharmonic Orchestra/Herbert von Karajan.** DG 429 664-2GSE3 — .⁚ ③ 3h 22m ADD 8/91

Nos. 1 and 5. **Milton Keynes Chamber Orchestra/Hilary Davan Wetton.** Unicorn-Kanchana DKPCD9117 — .⁚ lh 3m DDD 2/93

Nos. 1 and 5. The Hebrides. **Philharmonia Orchestra/Walter Weller.** Chandos CHAN9099

— .⁚ lh 15m DDD 2/93

Mendelssohn. Symphony No. 2 in B flat major, Op. 52, "Hymn of Praise". **Barbara Bonney, Edith Wiens** (sops); **Peter Schreier** (ten); **Leipzig Radio Choir; Leipzig Gewandhaus Orchestra/Kurt Masur.** Teldec 2292-44178-2. Text and translation included. Recorded in 1988.

59m DDD 4/90

In this memorable performance of one of Mendelssohn's lesser-known but highly rewarding symphonies, Kurt Masur carries forward a tradition of music-making of which Mendelssohn was himself a part, through his conducting of the Leipzig Gewandhaus Orchestra. The *Hymn of Praise* stands under the shade of Beethoven's *Choral* Symphony, with its considerable length and choral and solo contributions, both here extremely well delivered, but it does not reach similar heights of sublimity. What it does possess is an unassuming lyricism, vitality and elegance throughout that is highly attractive. Popular with choral societies during the last century, this is an interesting part of Mendelssohn's symphonic canon. Masur's performance is perfectly attuned to the work's character, the orchestral playing is excellent with an assured sense of style, and the recording is spacious. Well worth investigating.

Additional recommendation ...
Cynthia Haymon, Alison Hagley (sops); **Peter Straka** (ten); **Philharmonia Chorus and Orchestra/Walter Weller.** Chandos CHAN8995 — 1h 13m DDD 5/92

Mendelssohn. Symphonies — No. 3 in A minor, Op. 56, "Scottish"[a]; No. 4 in A major, Op. 90, "Italian"[b]. **San Francisco Symphony Orchestra/Herbert Blomstedt.** Decca 433 811-2DH. Item marked [a] recorded in 1989, [b] 1991.

1h 7m DDD 4/93

Recent years have seen a number of competitive releases of this popular coupling, not least a treasurable Teldec CD featuring Nikolaus Harnoncourt at the helm of the remarkably responsive Chamber Orchestra of Europe, full of that conductor's special brand of re-creative insight. Enter Herbert Blomstedt and his splendid San Francisco orchestra, in matters of interpretation more traditionally solid and less daring than that Teldec partnership, perhaps, but with considerable virtues of their own. Blomstedt's *Scottish* impresses most by dint of its joyous vigour (outer movements go with a will), rhythmic bounce (perky, personable winds and razor-sharp strings in the *Scherzo*) and unaffected eloquence (as in his affectionately flowing yet never short-winded conception of the third movement *Adagio*). This new *Italian*, too, is first-rate. Under Blomstedt the opening *Allegro vivace* positively fizzes along, aided by some quite beautifully sprung string playing, whilst the *Saltarello* finale is articulated with real panache. The middle movements are perhaps marginally less memorable, though again the irreproachably stylish orchestral response yields much pleasure. Although the symphonies were actually set down some 17 months apart, Decca's admirably consistent sound-picture possesses the exemplary clarity and sheen we have now come to expect from this particular source. No one can go far wrong with this disc.

Additional recommendations ...
Nos. 4 and 5. **London Symphony Orchestra/Claudio Abbado.** DG 415 974-2GH — DDD 9/86
Nos. 3 and 4. **Orchestra of St John's, Smith Square/John Lubbock.** ASV Quicksilva QS6004 — 1h 11m ADD 12/87
Nos. 3 and 4. **Leipzig Gewandhaus Orchestra/Kurt Masur.** Teldec 2292-43463-2 — 1h 7m DDD 11/88
Nos. 3 and 4. Die erste Walpurgisnacht[a]. [a]**Christine Cairns** (mez); [a]**Jon Garrison** (ten); [a]**Tom Krause** (bar); **Cleveland Orchestra and** [a]**Chorus/Christoph von Dohnányi.** Telarc CD80184 — 1h 7m DDD 3/89
Nos. 3 and 4. **London Symphony Orchestra/Claudio Abbado.** DG 3D-Classics 427 810-2GDC — 1h 11m DDD 2/90
Chamber Orchestra of Europe/Nikolaus Harnoncourt. Teldec 9031-72308-2 — 1h 9m DDD 5/92
Nos. 4 and 5. A Midsummer Night's Dream[b] — *Scherzo. Octet in E flat major, Op. 20 — Scherzo.* **NBC Symphony Orchestra/Arturo Toscanini.** RCA Gold Seal mono GD60284 — 1h 4m ADD 6/92

No. 4ª. *Overture — The Hebrides*, Op. 26ª. *A Midsummer Night's Dream*[b] *— Overture; Scherzo; Nocturne; Wedding March.* [a]**Israel Philharmonic Orchestra;** [b]**Bavarian Radio Symphony Orchestra/Leonard Bernstein.** DG Classikon 439 411-2GCL — .•' lh 7m ADD 3/94 ℗ Ⓑ
Nos. 3 and 4. **Leipzig Gewandhaus Orchestra/Kurt Masur.** Teldec Digital Experience 4509-92148-2 — .•' lh 7m DDD 4/94 Ⓑ

Mendelssohn. Symphony No. 5 in D major, Op. 107, "Reformation"ª.
Schumann. Symphony No. 3 in E flat major, Op. 97, "Rhenish"[b]. **Berlin Philharmonic Orchestra/Herbert von Karajan.** DG Galleria 419 870-2GGA. Item marked ª from 2720 068 (12/73), [b] 2720 046 (9/72).

.•' lh 9m ADD 4/88

This is just the sort of repertoire at which Karajan excels; his Schumann is strongly characterized, firmly driven and beautifully shaped and his Mendelssohn often achieves a delicacy of touch that belies the size of orchestra employed. Karajan's set of the Schumann symphonies made in 1971 was a notable success and the *Rhenish* speaks for them all. Here the powerful thrust of the work is gorgeously conveyed by the Berlin strings and the spontaneity of the music-making is striking. The Mendelssohn makes an ideal companion, since in scale the *Reformation* embraces wide vistas and far horizons. Laden with references to Protestant worship, Mendelssohn paints a picture of security and solidity achieved over many years and much struggle. Karajan maybe overemphasizes the epic qualities of the work but the playing of the orchestra is superb. The recordings have 'dried-out' a little in the transfer, but still sound well.

Additional recommendation ...
No. 5. Die erste Walpurgisnacht, Op. 60ª. [a]**Jean Rigby** (mez); [a]**Robert Tear** (ten); [a]**Anthony Michaels-Moore** (bar); [a]**Richard Van Allan** (bass); **Philharmonia** [a]**Chorus and Orchestra/Francesco d'Avalos.** Pickwick IMP Masters MCD68 — .•' lh lm DDD 3/94 ℗

Mendelssohn. OVERTURES. **Bamberg Symphony Orchestra/Claus Peter Flor.** RCA Victor Red Seal RD87905. Recorded 1987-88.
Die Hochzeit des Camacho, Op. 10. A Midsummer Night's Dream, Op. 21 (from RD87764, 10/88). Meeresstille und glückliche Fahrt, Op. 27. Ruy Blas, Op. 95. Athalie, Op. 74. The Hebrides, Op. 26, "Fingal's Cave".

.•' 59m DDD 1/89   ℗ ℗s

Die Hochzeit des Camacho ("The Marriage of Camacho") Overture was written in 1825, two years before the masterly evocation of *A Midsummer Night's Dream*, with its gossamer fairies, robust mortals and pervading romanticism, and already demonstrates the teenage composer's enormous musical facility and organizational skills, together with the high quality of his invention. *Meeresstille und glückliche Fahrt* ("Calm sea and prosperous voyage" of 1828) anticipates *The Hebrides* of a year later, and celebrates an ocean voyage on a sailing ship. *Ruy Blas* is a jolly, slightly melodramatic, but agreeably tuneful piece and *Athalie* is also attractive in its melodic ideas. *Fingal's Cave* with its beauty and dramatic portrayal of Scottish seascapes matches the Shakespearian overture in its melodic inspiration (the opening phrase is hauntingly unforgettable) and shows comparable skill in its vivid orchestration. Flor directs wonderfully sympathetic and spontaneous performances, with the Bamberg Symphony Orchestra playing gloriously. There is abundant energy and radiant lyrical beauty in the playing and each piece is unerringly paced and shaped. The glowing recording gives a wonderful bloom to the orchestral textures without preventing a realistic definition. There has never been a collection of Mendelssohn's overtures to match this and it will give enormous pleasure in every respect.

Mendelssohn. A Midsummer Night's Dream — incidental music, Opp. 21 and 61. **Edith Wiens** (sop); **Christiane Oertel** (mez); **Friedhelm Eberle** (spkr); **Leipzig Radio Chorus; Leipzig Gewandhaus Orchestra/Kurt Masur.** Teldec 2292-46323-2. Text and translation included. Recorded in 1990.

.•' lh 3m DDD 5/92   Ⓑ

To have a recording of Mendelssohn's incidental music with linking dialogue is an advantage, for the shorter pieces in particular make more of an impact when performed in the appropriate dramatic context. Teldec's recording was made in conjunction with a concert performance. Friedhelm Eberle speaks his lines in German, but no matter, for the insert notes contain Shakespeare's original English text set alongside the German translation. Of more concern is the fact that Eberle takes all the parts, occasionally going into falsetto for female roles. Edith Wiens and Christiane Oertel both sing their brief parts very capably, and in German, and the choral and orchestral contributions are first-rate. Masur's conception of the score is a little more serious and a little tougher than usual, but there is a good deal of personality in his conducting, and plenty of poetic expression. He takes the *Scherzo* a little more slowly than is the norm, but there is still a lightness of touch: the "Wedding March", by contrast, goes at a cheerfully fast pace. Throughout the performance, in fact, textures are kept very clear, and rhythms are appropriately light-footed. The recording quality is fully up to today's best standards.

Additional recommendations ...
Lillian Watson (sop); **Delia Wallis** (mez); **Finchley Childrens' Music Group; London Symphony Orchestra/André Previn.** EMI CDC7 47163-2 — .•' 58m DDD 9/86 Ⓑ
Lucia Popp (sop); **Marjana Lipovšek** (mez); **Bamberg Symphony Chorus and Orchestra/Claus Peter Flor.** RCA Victor Red Seal RD87764 — .•' 47m DDD 10/88 Ⓑ
Edith Wiens (sop); **Sarah Walker** (mez); **London Philharmonic Choir and Orchestra/ Andrew Litton.** Classics for Pleasure CD-CFP4593 — .• 50m DDD 9/92 Ⓑ
A Midsummer Night's Dream[a]. *Die schöne Melusine — Overture, Op. 32.* [a]**Judith Howarth** (sop); [a]**Jean Rigby** (mez); [a]**Bach Choir; Philharmonia Orchestra/Francesco d'Avalos.** Pickwick IMP Masters MCD78 — .•' 1h 3m DDD 7/94 Ⓑ

New review
Mendelssohn. A Midsummer Night's Dream — incidental music, Opp. 21 and 61: Overture; Scherzo; Intermezzo; Dance of the clowns. The Hebrides, "Fingal's Cave", Op. 26. Die schöne Melusine, Op. 32. **Suisse Romande Orchestra/Armin Jordan.** Erato 4509-91734-2. Recorded in 1993.

.•' **52m DDD 5/94** Ⓑ

Armin Jordan is a Mendelssohn conductor of exceptional sensitivity and insight. In the six numbers from *A Midsummer Night's Dream* he gets delicate, alert playing, and the way in which he allows the music to express its own very particular qualities of innocence, joy and exuberance is very appealing. *The Hebrides* is given a leisurely, warm, very romantic and highly expressive reading. Still more in *Die schöne Melusine* Jordan shows that he is not afraid to indulge in old-fashioned fluctuations of tempo, reminiscent of Furtwängler, and there is an almost Beecham like quality in the elegance of Jordan's phrasing. Those who want *A Midsummer Night's Dream* complete can invest in the Masur (reviewed above) with every confidence. Those who require only the better-known items need look no further than here.

Mendelssohn. Octet in E flat major, Op. 20. String Quintet No. 2 in B flat major, Op. 87. **Academy of St Martin in the Fields Chamber Ensemble.** Philips 420 400-2PH. From 9500 616 (3/80). Recorded in 1978.

.•' **1h 3m ADD 11/87** Ⓑ

Mendelssohn was as remarkable a prodigy as Mozart and one can only speculate with sadness what marvels he might have left us had he lived longer. Had death claimed him at 20 we would still have this glorious Octet, a work of unforced lyricism and a seemingly endless stream of melody. The Academy Chamber Ensemble, all fine soloists in their own right, admirably illus-trate the benefits of working regularly as an ensemble for they play with uncommon sympathy. The string quintet is a work of greater fervour and passion than the Octet but it is characterized by the same melodiousness and unfettered lyricism with plenty of opportunities for virtuoso playing, which are well taken. The recordings, made in 1978, give a pleasant and warm sheen to the string colour of the ensemble.

Additional recommendations ...
Octet. String Symphonies — No. 6 in E flat major; No. 10 in B minor. **I Solisti Italiani.** Denon CO-73185 — .•' 58m DDD 4/90 Ⓑ
Octet. String Quintet No. 1 in A major, Op. 18[a]. **Hausmusik.** EMI CDC7 49958-2 — .•' 1h 3m DDD 9/90 Ⓑ 🖋

Mendelssohn. STRING QUARTETS. **Melos Quartet** (Wilhelm Melcher, Gerhard Voss, vns; Hermann Voss, va; Peter Buck, vc). DG 415 883-2GCM3. From 2740 267 (11/82). Recorded 1976-81.
E flat major (1823); No. 1 in E flat major, Op. 12; No. 2 in A minor, Op. 13; No. 3 in D major, Op. 44 No. 1; No. 4 in E minor, Op. 44 No. 2; No. 5 in E flat major, Op. 44 No. 3; No. 6 in F minor, Op. 80. Andante, Scherzo, Capriccio and Fugue, Op. 81 Nos. 1-2.

③ **3h 19m ADD 12/87**

The familiar and misleading cliché of Mendelssohn as the cheerful chappie of early romanticism vanishes at the sound of the F minor Quartet, Op. 80. Here is the intensity, anguish and anger that everyone thought Mendelssohn incapable of. His beloved sister Fanny died in May 1847 (his own death was merely months away), and the ensuing summer saw him leave Berlin for Switzerland, where he began to "write music very industriously". And what remarkable music it is. Right from the opening *Allegro assai* one senses trouble afoot, an unfamiliar restlessness mixed in with the more familiar busyness. Furthermore the second movement is surely the most fervent and punishing that Mendelssohn ever wrote — wild, insistent and unmistakably tragic in tone. This gradual intensification and darkening that occurs throughout Mendelssohn's quartet cycle makes it a most revealing guide to his creative development. But of course much of the earlier music is in fact profoundly 'Mendelssohnian' in the accepted sense of that term: fresh, dynamic, light-textured, beautifully crafted and full of amiable melodic invention. The very early E flat Quartet, Op. posth (composed when Mendelssohn was only 14), although fashioned very much in the style of Haydn and Mozart, points towards imminent developments — a song-like A minor Quartet, already taking its lead from late Beethoven in the same key, the E flat, Op. 12, with its delightful Canzonetta (once popular as a separate 'encore') and the eventful Op. 44 set, three of Mendelssohn's most concentrated full-scale works. And DG also add the four separate pieces, Op. 81, thus treating us to the entire Mendelssohn string quartet canon (the chronology of which, incidentally, is very much at odds with that suggested by the published opus numbers). The Melos Quartet comes up trumps with a really superb set of performances — technically immaculate, transparent in tone and full of enthusiasm. The recordings, too, although analogue, report their playing with great presence and clarity.

Additional recommendations ...
E flat major (1823). Nos. 1-6. Andante, Scherzo, Capriccio and Fugue, Op. 81 Nos. 1-4. **Bartholdy Quartet.** Acantai 43 075 — ③ 3h 15m ADD 12/89
Nos. 1 and 2. **Gabrieli Quartet.** Chandos CHAN8827 — 59m DDD 1/92
Nos. 2 and 6. **Carmina Quartet.** Denon CO-79527 — 53m DDD 3/92
E flat major (1823). No. 2. **Coull Quartet.** Hyperion CDA66579 — 1h 20m DDD 11/92
Nos. 1-6. **Cherubini Quartet.** EMI CDS7 54514-2 — ③ 2h 5m DDD 8/93
Nos. 1-6. Four Pieces for String Quartet, Op. 81 — Andante in E major; Scherzo in A minor; Capriccio in E minor; Fugue in A flat major. **Coull Quartet.** Hyperion CDS44051/3 — ③ 3h 42m DDD 6/94

Mendelssohn. WORKS FOR CELLO AND PIANO. **Lynn Harrell** (vc); **Bruno Canino** (pf). Decca 430 198-2DH. Recorded in 1989.
Cello Sonatas — No. 1 in B flat major, Op. 45; No. 2 in D major, Op. 58. Variations concertantes, Op. 17. Songs without words — Op. 19 No. 1; Op. 109.

1h 7m DDD 10/92

Lynn Harrell's Mendelssohn is bold and hugely compelling; his are full-blooded and overtly dramatic accounts of works which, in the wrong hands, can seem distinctly passive. His partner, Bruno Canino, an accompanist of rare perception, is superb throughout, matching Harell's flair and fantasy with his own specialized musical insight. Mendelssohn wrote his First Sonata in 1838, intending it for his brother Paul, a capable amateur cellist and wealthy financier. Its dignity and breadth impressed Schumann, who considered it to be "a Sonata for the most refined family circle, best enjoyed after some poems by Goethe or Lord Byron". In fact, Mendelssohn's model was the grandest of Beethoven's sonatas, the one in A major, Op. 69; and the similarities of scale and purpose are especially telling in this wonderful performance from Harrell and Canino. The Sonata in D major is more public in utterance, and more assuredly brilliant in form and content. Harrell's playing is nobly ardent, polished, and yet responsive to the structural needs of the music with an insight only rarely encountered. Bruno Canino constantly excels too; the precision and

grace of his playing is never more evident than in the chorale episode of the *Adagio*. This is an unsurpassable performance, strong on musical sensitivity as well as sheer dynamism, and certainly very hard to resist! This disc also includes a lucid and enjoyable reading of Mendelssohn's earliest compositions for the medium, the *Variations concertantes*. Predictable economies of scale have been made here, giving the performance a more obviously episodic feel as each section is glowingly characterized. Harrell is evidently in winning mood; his playing has an effortless grace and finesse, also much in evidence in the two *Songs without words*, which complete the disc. With first-class Decca sound and performances of absolute distinction, this is a compulsory purchase.

Mendelssohn. ORGAN WORKS, Volume 1. **Peter Planyavsky.** Motette CD11271. Played on the organ of the Church of St Augustin, Perchtoldsdorf, Germany. Recorded in 1988.
Sonatas, Op. 65 — No. 1 in F minor; No. 2 in C minor. Fugue in D minor. Chorale variations on "Wie gross ist des Allmächt'gen Güte". Andante in D major. Trio in F major. Prelude and Fugue in G major. Andante with variations. Allegro in D minor/major.

1h 9m DDD 10/92

"Mendelssohn is, without doubt, the greatest organist who has ever performed in London." So claimed a *Musical Times* review of 1837. Mendelssohn actually performed more often as an organist in England than he did in his native Germany, and it was for the English market that he wrote his organ music; six great Sonatas, three Preludes and Fugues and a handful of smaller individual works. Peter Planyavsky is making the first-ever comprehensive recordings of Mendelssohn's organ music and it's hard to think of anyone better suited. Planyavsky is himself one of the handful of present-day organists who has a world-wide reputation as a great player and a noted composer and one can't avoid drawing parallels between his career and Mendelssohn's. His playing has the real stamp of authority and, in the nicest possible way, a sense of evangelical zeal. The finale of the First Sonata comes across as a virtuoso *tour de force*, the last two movements of the Second have wonderful majesty and power while the smaller pieces (including a delightful *Andante with variations*) are played with genuine affection. The recording is crisp and well-balanced and the organ suits the music admirably.

New review
Mendelssohn. PIANO SONATAS. **Frederic Chiu.** Harmonia Mundi HMU90 7117. Recorded in 1993.
Piano Sonatas — E major, Op. 6; G minor, Op. 105; B flat major, Op. 106. Andante and Rondo capriccioso in E major, Op. 14.

1h 7m DDD 5/94

The three piano sonatas, while hardly audacious, are much less conventional than expected. The gently cascading figure at the close of the E major Sonata's *Allegretto* makes a magical reappearance in the *Adagio*, a movement which moves via recitatives to a serene *Andante* before an exhilaratingly busy finale. The G minor Sonata has a startlingly taut argument for a 12-year-old composer, its central *Adagio* alive with experimental rather than tentative ideas, its finale a gloriously urgent scamper. The B flat Sonata mischievously apes both Beethoven's *Hammerklavier* and *Moonlight* Sonatas before opting for gentler ambitions. Bright and ceremonial, the opening *Allegro vivace* finally recedes in a distant, fairy-tale fanfare showing, like the reminiscence which closes the E major Sonata, that Mendelssohn often resolves even his most hyperactive ideas in a haunting peace and tranquility. Frederic Chiu hardly erases memories of Murray Perahia (reviewed below) in the E major Sonata, where his Minuet is clipped rather than elegantly pointed yet his affection and dexterity are never in doubt. But all these performances are sufficiently stylish to survive the cramped sound.

Mendelssohn. PIANO WORKS. **Murray Perahia.** CBS Masterworks CD37838. From IM37838 (5/85).
Piano Sonata in E major, Op. 6. Prelude and Fugue in E minor/major, Op. 35 No. 1. Variations sérieuses in D minor, Op. 54. Andante and Rondo capriccioso in E minor, Op. 14.

50m DDD 5/85

This is a beautifully controlled and very welcome glimpse of a side of Mendelssohn rarely encountered in the concert-hall. Perahia's exquisitely fleet finger-work and finely controlled pianism matches the weight of the music ideally. The four pieces represented here are not of equal stature but there are certainly some fine things. The *Variations sérieuses* is Mendelssohn's best-known work for the piano — as the title might imply there is a darker, maybe even melancholy flavour to the theme and the subsequent variations have real substance. Here and in the other works, particularly the delightful *Rondo capriccioso*, Perahia's performance overlooks nothing in mood or atmosphere.

New review

Mendelssohn. LIEDER. **Dietrich Fischer-Dieskau** (bar); **Wolfgang Sawallisch** (pf). EMI CMS7 64827-2. Texts included. From HMV SLS805 (7/72). Recorded in 1970.
Op. 8 — No. 4, Erntelied; No. 8, And'res Maienlied. Op. 9 — No. 6, Scheidend. Op. 19*a* — No. 1, Frühlingslied; No. 2, Das erste Veilchen; No. 3, Winterlied; No. 4, Neue Liebe; No. 5, Gruss; No. 6, Reiselied. Op. 34 — No. 1, Minnelied; No. 2, Auf Flügeln des Gesanges; No. 3, Frühlingslied; No. 6, Reiselied. Op. 47 — No. 1, Minnelied; No. 2, Morgengruss; No. 3, Frühlingslied; No. 4, Volkslied; No. 6, Bei der Wiege. Op. 57 — No. 1, Altdeutsches Lied; No. 2, Hirtenlied; No. 4, O Jugend; No. 5, Venetianisches Gondellied; No. 6, Wanderlied. Op. 71 — No. 1, Tröstung; No. 3, An die Entfernte; No. 4, Schilflied; No. 5, Auf der Wanderschaft; No. 6, Nachtlied. Op. 84 — No. 1, Da lieg' ich unter den Bäumen; No. 3, Jagdlied. Op. 86 — No. 1, Es lauschte das Laub; No. 4, Allnächtlich im Traume; No. 5, Der Mond. Op. 99 — No. 1, Erster Verlust; No. 5, Wenn sich zwei Herzen Scheiden. Op. posth — Das Waldschloss; Pagenlied; Der Blumenkranz; Warnung vor dem Rhein; Schlafloser Augen Leuchte.

(2) 1h 35m ADD 12/93

Mendelssohn's Lieder offer a challenge all their own, and Fischer-Dieskau takes it up with characteristic alacrity. As the majority of these songs are primarily accompanied melody, with little inherent teasing out or biting on the words, the singer is presented with a comparatively empty stage for his recreative imagination to design and pace. There are passing moments (in the Op. 47 *Morgengrüss*, for example) when the simplicity and ingenuousness of Mendelssohn's settings seems to frustrate Fischer-Dieskau. These moments, though, are rare. His voice, here in its prime, can draw on an extraordinarily wide palette of colour within the legato of the most timeworn strophic song. Both Fischer-Dieskau and Sawallisch, whose light-filled piano playing shows his real sympathy and understanding for this composer, know just when to move into the salon with Mendelssohn. The four Lenau settings and the little drama of mortality offered in *Das erste Veilchen* are recreated with a perfectly-scaled sense of fleeting ardour and melancholy. Best of all, perhaps, are those little vignettes of the dark mythology of the German folk-soul, those diabolic night rides into the forest which find Mendelssohn at his witchy best, and Fischer-Dieskau at his most virtuosic. This revelatory boxed set comes with gracefully detailed notes by Philip Radcliffe, full song texts but no translations.

Additional recommendation ...
Scheidend. Frühlingslied. Winterlied. Neue liebe. Gruss. Auf Flügeln des Gesanges. Reiselied. Das Waldschloss. Pagenlied. Morgengrüss. Frühlingslied. Volkslied. Bei der Wiege. Venetianisches Gondellied. An die Entferne. Schilflied. Herbstlied, Op. 84 No. 2. Allnächtlich im Traume. Der Mond. Lieblingsplätzchen, Op. 99 No. 3. **Wolfgang Holzmair** (bar); **Anna Wagner** (pf). Harmonia Mundi 93368 —
53m ADD 7/91

Mendelssohn. LIEDER. **Barbara Bonney** (sop); **Geoffrey Parsons** (pf). Teldec 2292-44946-2. Texts and translations included. Recorded in 1991.
Op. 8 — No. 8, And'res Maienlied; No. 10, Romanze. *Op. 9* — No. 1, Frage; No. 5, Im Herbst; No. 7, Sehnsucht; No. 8, Frühlingsglaube; No. 9, Ferne; No. 10, Verlust; No. 12, Die Nonne. *Op. 19a* — No. 3, Winterlied; No. 4, Neue Liebe. *Op. 34* — No. 2, Auf Flügeln des Gesanges; No. 3, Frühlingslied; No. 4, Suleika; No. 5, Sonntagslied. *Op. 47* — No. 3, Frühlingslied; No. 5, Der Blumenstrauss; No. 6, Bei der Wiege. *Op. 57* — No. 3, Suleika. *Op. 71* — No. 2, Frühlingslied; No. 6, Nachtlied. *Op. 86* — No. 3, Die Liebende schreibt; No. 5, Der Mond. *Op. 99* — No. 1, Erster Verlust; No. 5, Wenn sich zwei Herzen Scheiden; No. 6, Es weiss und rät es doch keiner. Pagenlied, Op. posth.

1h DDD 2/93

The charm of these songs lies in their simple style and almost endless stream of delightful melody. Unlike other Lieder composers Mendelssohn avoided blatant word-painting or vivid characterizations and certainly the most satisfying songs here tend to be settings of texts which do not on the surface of it offer much scope for musical expression. But while this disc may not give us the very best of Mendelssohn, or indeed the finest examples of nineteenth-century Lied, the singing of Barbara Bonney makes this a CD not to be missed. Here is a rare example of a singer caught on record at the very height of her technical and artistic powers, able to exercise seemingly effortless vocal control in portraying the subtle colours and understated moods of each songs. The partnership with that ever-sensitive accompanist Geoffrey Parsons is inspired. Listen to how Bonney seems to float ethereally above the rippling piano figures in that most famous of all Mendelssohn songs, *Auf Flügeln des Gesanges* ("On wings of song") — a performance which can surely never have been bettered on record. An interesting footnote is that three of these songs are by Fanny Mendelssohn but have by convention always been ascribed to her brother.

New review

Mendelssohn. LIEDER. **Dame Margaret Price** (sop); **Graham Johnson** (pf). Hyperion CDA66666. Texts and translations included. Recorded in 1993.
Lieder, Op. 8 — No. 7, Maienlied; No. 8, And'res Maienlied, Op. 9 — No. 1, Frage; No. 2, Geständnis; No. 8, Frühlingsglaube; Op 19*a* — No. 4, Neue Liebe; No. 5, Gruss; Op. 34 — No. 2, Auf Flügeln des Gesanges; No. 3, Frühlingslied; No. 4, Suleika; Op. 47 — No. 1, Minnelied; No. 4, Volkslied; Op. 57 — No. 3, Suleika; No. 6, Wanderlied; Op. 71 — No. 4, Schilflied; No. 6, Nachtlied; Op. 86 — No. 3, Die Liebende schreibt; No. 5, Der Mond; Op. 99 — No. 1, Erster Verlust; No. 6, Es weiss und rät es doch keiner. Op. posth. — Mädchens Klage; Das Waldschloss. Romances (Byron) — There be none of beauty's daughters; Sun of the sleepless.

59m DDD 3/94

This recital wholly dispels any lingering doubts there may be about Mendelssohn as a composer of Lieder. He surpassed even Schubert and Brahms in his understanding of Heine's *Die Liebende schreibt*. At the heart of the recital are the settings of Goethe. Besides *Die Liebende schreibt* the pair include the poignant *Erster Verlust* and the two Suleika settings, neither quite a match for Schubert's inspired versions but valid in their own right, particularly when sung with Price's uninhibited, Lehmannesque ardour. Another facet of the performances, a free-ranging *Schwung*, can be heard in *Frühlingslied* and the familiar *Neue Liebe*. The real discoveries here are the two Byron settings uncovered by Johnson. Mendelssohn understood and knew how to set English and the accentuations here are wholly idiomatic. The recording has great presence. Both singer and pianist are in the room with us, anxious and able to please.

Mendelssohn. Elijah. **Helen Donath, Kerstin Klein** (sops); **Jard van Nes** (contr); **Donald George** (ten); **Alistair Miles** (bass); **Leipzig Radio Chorus; Israel Philharmonic Orchestra/Kurt Masur.** Teldec 9031-73131-2. Text and translation included. Recorded live in 1991.

(2) 1h 50m DDD 5/93

New review

Mendelssohn. Elijah (sung in German). **Soile Isokoski, Delphine Collot** (sops); **Monica Groop** (mez); **John Mark Ainsley** (ten); **Petteri Salomaa** (bass); **Collegium Vocale; La Chapelle Royale Choir and Orchestra; Champs Elysées Orchestra/Philippe Herreweghe.** Harmonia Mundi HMC90 1463/4. Text and translation included. Recorded live in 1993.

(2) 2h 7m DDD 11/93

Masur's is a compelling account of a much maligned work. Once the staple of every choral society throughout the land, its popularity declined at the same time as did other things deemed Victorian. Masur has the advantage of the Leipzig Radio Chorus, who are steeped in the work's tradition and sing their varying roles as though their lives depended on it. With predominantly fast tempos, he directs them and the equally vital Israel Philharmonic with unflagging energy, and contrasts the forces of good and evil with operatic ideas about characterization. In consequence the work sounds new-minted. Alastair Miles is by turns a fiery and tormented Elijah, keen with his word-painting and alive to most of the nuances of his part. Jard van Nes intones the alto's famous solos with feeling but rightly avoids sentimentality. Helen Donath defies the years in bringing fresh tone and open-hearted feeling to the soprano role. Only the uningratiating tenor soloist mars an unqualified recommendation for this splendidly prepared and produced recording. It is a worthy successor to the tried and true Sawallisch who employed an antecedent of the same choir. That is available on the Philips mid-price Duo label; though less well recorded than the Teldec, it remains one of the excellent alternatives, a compelling interpretation with soloists just that bit more convincing than Masur's.

The first performance of this oratorio in Birmingham is said to have been given by a choir and orchestra of 400 (Masur's is also superbly large-scale). Herreweghe has little more than a quarter of that number. In the earlier numbers of the first part in his performance it is easy to feel that his reading is too small in scale and anonymous, and the vocal forces do not seem entirely idiomatic with their German. Gradually one is won over by the sheer *beauty* of the reading expressed in choral singing of the utmost accuracy and refinement and by orchestral playing in which every strand is clear. Because the choir is not large, Mendelssohn's subtlety of instrumentation is heard as never before. The harmonic clashes in the chorus "Wehe ihn" in Part 2 and the quite lovely account of the Angels' Trio a little later, followed by the ethereal singing in the chorus "Siehe, der Hüter Israels schläft", and the succeeding solos and choruses, create an impression of ideal execution and perfect balance that even the splendid Masur and Sawallisch versions don't quite match. The soloists are happily on a par with the choir and orchestra. Salomaa may make a little too much of his consonants and rolled 'r's, but he is a deeply expressive, vital and exact Elijah, a more youthful prophet than usual and none the worse for that. Isokoski singing is radiantly attractive and she makes an urgent Widow. John Mark Ainsley is a great improvement on his Teldec counterpart, and produces fine-grained, confident singing, but lacks something — who doesn't? — of Schreier's presence and acuity of diction for Sawallisch. Monica Groop is a euphonious, fluent alto soloist. Special praise too for Delphine Collot for her Youth and her contributions to the solo ensembles, each one of which is beautifully sung. The recording is warm and properly balanced between choir and orchestra. It matches the flowing, unsentimental yet always sensitive conducting of Herreweghe, who ensures that the interpretation is all of a piece. In consequence this is a version that must lie alongside the best as a recommendation.

Additional recommendations ...
(*Sung in English*). **Soloists; Academy of St Martin in the Fields Chorus and Orchestra/ Sir Neville Marriner.** Philips 432 984-2PH2 — .·' ⓥ 2h 7m DDD 10/92
Soloists; Leipzig Radio Chorus; Leipzig Gewandhaus Orchestra/Wolfgang Sawallisch. Philips Duo 438 368-2PM2 — .·' ② 2h 11m ADD 8/93 ⓠp

Further listening ...

Piano Duets — Piano Trio No. 2 in C minor, Op. 66. Variations in B flat major, Op. 83*a*. Andante and Allegro brillant in A major, Op. 92. *Coupled with* **Mendelssohn-Hensel.** Three pieces for Piano Duet. **Yaara Tal, Andreas Groethuysen** (pf/duet). Sony Classical CD48494 (6/93).

Piano Trios — No. 1 in D minor, Op. 49; No. 2 in C minor, Op. 66. **Solomon Trio.** Pickwick Masters MCD46 (12/92).

Violin Sonatas — F minor, Op. 4; F major. **Shlomo Mintz** (vn); **Paul Ostrovsky** (pf). DG 419 244-2GH (8/87).

Songs without Words. Kinderstücke, Op. 72. **Daniel Barenboim** (pf). DG 423 931-2GGA2.

Fanny Mendelssohn-Hensel

German 1805-1847

Suggested listening ...

Piano Trio in G minor, Op. 11*a*. *Coupled with* **Beach.** Piano Trio in A major, Op. 150*a*.
Carreño. String Quartet in B minor[bc]. **C. Schumann.** Piano Trio in G minor, Op. 17*a*.

Tailleferre. Sonata for Violin and Piano No. 1[bd]. **Boulanger.** Pièces — Nocturne; Cortège[bd]. **Chaminade.** Piano Trio No. 1 in G minor, Op. 11[a]. [a]**Macalester Trio;** [b]**Joseph Roche,** [c]**Robert Zelnick** (vns); [c]**Tamas Strasser** (va); [c]**Camilla Heller** (vc); [d]**Paul Freed** (pf). Vox Box 115845-2. *See review in the Collections section; refer to the Index to Reviews.*

Saverio Mercadante

Italian 1795-1870

New review
Mercadante Flute Concertos — D major; E minor; E major. **James Galway** (fl); **I Solisti Veneti/Claudio Scimone.** RCA Victor Red Seal 09026 61447-2. From RD87703. Recorded in 1987.

1h 2m DDD 4/94

Given that the flute and the soprano voice share the attributes of flexibility and tonal purity, it is hardly surprising that it should enter the mind of a composer of some 60 operas and a player of the flute, as Mercadante was, to write a few flute concertos; despite their classical form, they sound like winsome, extended showcases for agile divas in libretto-less operas. Galway's disc offers three of Mercadante's six flute concertos, each of which consists of three 'instrumental operatic scenes', to which you might pass a few pleasant evenings writing your own libretti. Though Irena Grafenauer's version of the E minor work is rather more subtly nuanced, Galway plays with his accustomed silver-tongued panache and has the co-operation of I Solisti Veneti and the recording engineers at their best.

Additional recommendation ...

E minor. **Mozart.** *Flute Concerto No. 2 in D major, K314/285d.* **Stamitz.** *Flute Concerto in G major.* **Irena Grafenauer** (fl); **Academy of St Martin in the Fields/Sir Neville Marriner.** Philips 426 318-2PH — 1h DDD 1/91

Aarre Merikanto

Finland 1893-1958

Suggested listening ...

Fantasy[a]. Notturno[b]. Pan[a]. Symphonic Study[a]. **Finnish Radio Symphony Orchestra/**[a]**Leif Segerstam,** [b]**Jukka-Pekka Saraste.** Finlandia FACD349 (7/88).

Tarquinio Merula

Italian 1594/5-1665

New review
Merula. VOCAL WORKS. **Montserrat Figueras** (sop); **Jean-Pierre Canihac** (cornet); **Lorenz Duftschmid** (vn); [b]**Andrew Lawrence-King** (hp); **Rolf Lislevand** (theorbo/baroque gtr); **Jordi Savall** (va da gamba); [a]**Ton Koopman** (hpd). Astrée Auvidis E8503. Texts and translations included. Recorded in 1992.
Madrigali, libro secondo, Op. 10 — Aria di Ciaccona, "Su la cetra amorosa". Curtio precipitato, libro secondo, Op. 13 — Folle è ben che si crede; Chi vuol ch'io m'inamori; Un bambin chi va alla scola; Quando gli uccelli portaranno i zoccoli; Sentirete una canzonetta; Menti lingua bugiarda; Ho ch'è tempo di dormire. Capriccio cromatico[a]. Toccata del secondo tono[b].

56m DDD 1/94

Tarquinio Merula is barely represented in the catalogue except as a composer of distinctive instrumental music. This release shows that Merula's secular vocal style is if anything even more interesting. The 1638 book of solo songs, from which most of this disc is taken, is an expressive and ingenious collection which displays amongst other things Merula's mature handling of

Monteverdi's *stile concitato* and a highly attractive treatment of popular songs. Figueras's approach in the intricate and colourful melodic strands of the 'concerted' pieces is impetuous but effectively paced too. The result is at times little short of spellbinding: *Su la cetra amorosa* is executed with all the considerable virtuosity, energy and emotional intensity it deserves, complemented moreover by an exciting and fluent dialogue with a solo cornett. Also impressive is her ability to judge the fine line between comedy and despair in *Quando gli uccelli portaranno i zoccoli* ("When birds wear clogs"), where Merula's slightly bizarre sense of humour and a proven sense of irony are exhibited to the full. Ensemble can be a little ropey, but the overall richness of musical timbre and freedom of expression is what ultimately prevails. Well worth investigating.

André Charles Messager
French 1853-1929

New review

Messager. MONSIEUR BEAUCAIRE. **Willy Clément** (bar) Monsieur Beaucaire; **Lina Dachary** (sop) Lady Mary Carlisle; **Nicole Broissin** (sop) Lady Lucy; **René Lenoty** (ten) Molyneux; **Lucien Lovano** (bass) Winterset; **Henri Bedex** (sngr) Nash; **Jacques Pruvost** (bar) Bantinson; **Georges Foix** (sngr) Townbrake; **Marcel Enot** (sngr) Rakell; **André Balbon** (bar) Captain Badger; **Gilbert Moryn** (sngr) Mirepoix; **French Radio Lyric Chorus and Orchestra/Jules Gressier.** Musidisc Gaieté-Lyrique mono 20241-2. Recorded at a broadcast performance in 1958.

② 1h 37m AAD 11/93 ▲

Beaucaire is all about disguise, prince as barber, and the work revolves around mistaken identity. It was first written for production in England but is best known in its 1925 French version. Hearing the whole work complete as in this Gaieté-Lyrique issue, taken from a 1958 radio production, it is enhanced considerably. The way the numbers, whether light-hearted duets, choruses or romantic love songs, grow out of the plot makes Messager's achievement in welding eighteenth-century pastiche to contemporary popular style all the more impressive. Jules Gressier directs the performance with just the right pace, while Willy Clément in the main part and Lina Dachary, the resident prima donna in the Radio Lyric studio, are both completely at home in the dialogue and sing the famous numbers with passion.

Further listening ...

Les deux pigeons. **Orchestra of Welsh National Opera/Richard Bonynge.** Decca 433 700-2DH (10/93).

Olivier Messiaen
French 1908-1992

New review

Messiaen. Quatuor pour la fin du temps.
Krauze. Quatuor pour la Naissance. **David Campbell** (cl); **Madeline Mitchell** (vn); **Christopher van Kampen** (vc); **Joanna MacGregor** (pf). Collins Classics 1393-2. Recorded in 1993.

1h 5m DDD 6/94

An all-star team for this performance of Messiaen's extraordinary quartet, a team which manages to outdo all its rivals in tonal warmth and intensity of feeling. Christopher van Kampen is supreme, and significantly slower than anyone else, in the fifth movement's ecstatically sweet hymn. Both van Kampen and Madeleine Mitchell are helped by a recording of almost extravagant depth and range — never has the second section of the second movement sounded so unartificially distant — and Mitchell leads the work to its sumptuously ethereal apotheosis with a winning blend of poise and fervour. The competition is left sounding almost dull by comparison. The advantages of modern recording are especially evident in the first movement, where Joanna MacGregor achieves a veiled smoothness which is at the opposite extreme from the 'granitic' vehemence she delivers elsewhere. In these passages, MacGregor's Steinway threatens to shatter your speakers, but the impact is never inappropriately over-the-top in this least churchy of religious compositions. David Campbell's trumpet-like clarinet fits in well with the overriding, even overwhelming emotional force of this new account. The Teldec group (listed below) may please listeners seeking a less vibrantly dramatic reading. Collins add a work for the same combination as the Messiaen by the Polish-born composer Zygmunt Krauze (b. 1938). Written to mark the birth of his son in 1985, it is rather characterless, at least in this company. Krauze is not the only composer of his generation to have become stranded between the increasing promptings of nostalgia and the modern propensity for tough talking. The piece has its moments — an edgily serene ending, for example — but it still seems longer than its actual 17 and a bit minutes.

Additional recommendations ...

Quatuor pour la fin du temps. **Tashi.** RCA Victor Gold Seal GD87835 — .•' 47m ADD 4/89 ◌ₚ

Quatuor pour la fin du temps[a]. *Le merle noir*[b]. [b]**Karlheinz Zöller** (fl); [a]**Erich Gruenberg** (vn); [a]**Gervase de Peyer** (cl); [a]**Anthony Pleeth** (vc); [a]**Michel Béroff**, [b]**Aloys Kontarsky** (pfs). EMI CDM7 63947-2 — .•' 51m ADD 3/92 ◌ₚ

Quatuor pour la fin du temps. **Eduard Brunner** (cl); **Trio Fontenay.** Teldec 9031-73239-2 — .•' 44m DDD 12/92 ◌ₚ

Messiaen. Turangalîla-symphonie[a]. Quatuor pour la fin du temps[b]. [b]**Saschko Gawriloff** (vn); [b]**Siegfried Palm** (vc); [b]**Hans Deinzer** (cl); [b]**Aloys Kontarsky**, **Peter Donohoe** (pfs); [a]**Tristan Murail** (ondes martenot); [a]**City of Birmingham Symphony Orchestra/Simon Rattle.** EMI CDS7 47463-8. Item marked [b] from Deutsche Harmonia Mundi 065 99711 (8/79).

.•' ② 2h 10m DDD/ADD 12/87

No longer a rarity in the concert-hall, Messiaen's epic hymn to life and love has been lucky on record too, with Rattle's performance staying just ahead of the pack. Messiaen's luxuriant scoring presents a challenge for the engineers as much as the players and the EMI team come through with flying colours. Tristan Murail's ondes martenot is carefully balanced here — evocative and velvety, neither reduced to inaudibility nor over-miked to produce an ear-rending screech. Peter Donohoe's piano obbligato is similarly integrated into the orchestral tapestry yet provides just the right kind of decorative intervention. Rattle is at his best in the work's more robust moments like the jazzy fifth movement and the many rhythmic passages which recall Stravinsky's *Le Sacre*. But those unfamiliar with Messiaen's extraordinary score should perhaps start with the central slow movement, the beautiful *Jardin du sommeil d'amour*, exquisitely done by the Birmingham team. Unlike at least one rival account, this *Turangalîla* spills on to a second CD, which leaves room for a distinguished *Quatuor pour la fin du temps* as a makeweight. The music-making here lacks the youthful spontaneity of the main work, but is notable for an unusually slow and sustained performance of the movement with cello solo.

Additional recommendations ...

Turangalîla-symphonie[a]. **Lutoslawski.** *Symphony No. 3*[b]. *Les espaces du sommeil*[c]. [bc]**Soloists;** [a]**Philharmonic Orchestra,** [bc]**Los Angeles Philharmonic Orchestra/Esa-Pekka Salonen.** CBS Masterworks CD42271 — .•' ② 2h 5m DDD 6/87

Turangalîla-symphonie. **Soloists; Royal Concertgebouw Orchestra/Riccardo Chailly.** Decca 436 626-2DH — .•' 1h 17m DDD 11/93 ◌ₚ ◌ₛ

New review

Messiaen. Eclairs sur L'Au-Delà. **Polish Radio National Symphony Orchestra, Katowice/Antoni Wit.** Jade JADC099. Recorded live in 1993.

.•' 1h 3m DDD 6/94 ◌ₚ

Eclairs sur L'Au-Delà ("Illuminations of the Beyond") was Olivier Messiaen's last major work. It is almost a summary, musical and spiritual, of the preoccupations of his preceding 60 years but, inspiritingly enough, shows him delightedly discovering not only new birds but also entrancingly new sounds: he has not made such startling use before of the contrabass clarinet (in the huge and complex eighth movement, which culminates in a Great Messiaen Tune of sonorous nobility), nor employed (to evoke the Lyrebird) such vertiginous leaps between sections of the orchestra. In one way, then, it is a series of nostalgic revisits. In the fourth movement, for example, there's a sort of two-minute summary of the extremely dense counterpoint of *Chronochromie*; the sixth recalls the "Dance of fury for the seven trumpets" in the *Quartet for the end of time*. But there's also a touching sense of Messiaen in his eighties preparing to contemplate the beyond. In the ninth of the 11 movements he writes his last birdsong piece, no fewer that 25 birds impersonated simultaneously by 18 woodwind instruments: the image is of Christ as the Tree of Life, the birds are the souls of the blessed, and of course they are all singing at once. He then considers "The path to the invisible", and if we were expecting a rapt meditation we do not know Messiaen: it is a clamorous and insistent piece, one of his great angular toccatas, expressing the very difficulty of keeping to that path. And finally, most movingly, one of his almost motionless, beginningless and endless string chorales, "Christ, Light of Paradise". This live recording has remarkably few signs of how very difficult a piece it is to play. The recording is pleasantly spacious, the audience only makes its presence felt by a certain amount of coughing between movements; it is, in short, the sort of 'première recording' in which one can safely concentrate on the music.

New review

Messiaen. Pièce pour le tombeau de Paul Dukas. Fantaisie burlesque. Rondeau. Six Petites esquisses d'oiseaux. Visions de l'Amen[a]. **Peter Hill, [a]Benjamin Frith** (pfs). Unicorn-Kanchana DKPCD9144. Recorded 1984-92.

lh 19m DDD 6/94

The fifth and final volume of Peter Hill's Messiaen survey includes the *Visions de l'Amen*, although they are not for solo piano. They include some of Messiaen's grandest solemnities, at least one of his Great Tunes (the chorale in the last movement, skirting perilously but so satisfyingly the very edge of a deep abyss with a warning notice of "Beware: Gounod") and, in their frequent pages of frank virtuosity, the earliest of his passionate tributes to the pianism and the personality of Yvonne Loriod. No less touching in this regard are the six "little sketches" of birds, Messiaen's last solo keyboard work, coaxed out of him by Loriod when the tired Old Master was ready to declare his life's work over: they are archetypal but distilled Messiaen, florid and lovely arabesques, shimmering colours, crystalline chords. Even the three very early pieces, from long before Messiaen became a musical ornithologist, are well worth having: the finely-carved gravestone for Dukas is already characteristic in its hieratic gravity, and if the two others are anything but characteristic it's agreeable to find Messiaen wearing tap-shoes and a straw hat in the jaunty *Fantaisie burlesque* and demonstrating in the *Rondeau* that at one stage of his youth he could write pretty but quite empty virtuoso salon pieces. However, the *Visions de l'Amen* are the disc's *raison d'être*, and it's good to hear that, in Benjamin Frith, Hill has a duo partner as responsive to Messiaen's demands for subtlety of colour and delicacy of texture as he is himself. As ever in this series Hill is supported by a recording of satisfyingly huge range: at the end of the third movement and elsewhere you will hear a genuine *pppp*, while the reverberation from the magnificent final chord of "Amen de la Consommation" takes a full minute to fade to silence.

Messiaen. Vingt regards sur l'enfant-Jésus. **Peter Hill** (pf). Unicorn-Kanchana DKPCD9122/3. Recorded in 1991.

② 2h 22m DDD 9/92

Messiaen's huge 1944 cycle of *20 Contemplations of the Child Jesus* is as much a challenge to the adventurous pianist of the late twentieth century as Liszt's *Transcendental Studies* were to previous generations (and continue to be). And Liszt is parent not only to the fearsome pyrotechnics of the piano writing but to the spiritual aspect of the music as well — compare Messiaen's "Contemplations by the Father" (No. 1) with Liszt's "Bénédiction de Dieu dans la Solitude" from his *Harmonies poétiques et religieuses*. Peter Hill is neither by technique or temperament a card-carrying Lisztian. But he does command an unusual range of subtle colours, and his agility and attention to detail cannot be faulted. So while his performances may not sweep the listener off his feet, they do present the music very much as a set of Contemplations. Similarly the distinctive tone-quality of the Fazioli instrument — a little bland, but capable of the most exquisite quiet shadings — is a perfectly valid alternative to the familiar Steinway sound. Recording quality, as throughout this Unicorn-Kanchana series, is exemplary in its clarity and unobtrusive radiance.

Additional recommendations ...
Vingt regards. **John Ogdon** (pf). Decca Enterprise 430 343-2DM — .· ② 2h 7m ADD 12/91
Vingt regards. **Mélisande Chauveau** (pf). Forlane UCD16709/10 — .· ② 2h 20m DDD 7/94

Messiaen. La nativité du Seigneur[a]. Le banquet céleste[b]. **Jennifer Bate** (org). Unicorn-Kanchana DKPCD9005. Played on the organ of Beauvais Cathedral. Item marked [a] from DKP9005 (6/82), [b] DKP9018 (2/83).

.· **1h 2m   DDD   2/88** 🎵 s

La nativité du Seigneur comprises nine meditations on themes associated with the birth of the Lord. Messiaen's unique use of registration gives these pieces an extraordinarily wide range of colour and emotional potency and in Jennifer Bate's hands (and feet) it finds one of its most persuasive and capable advocates. Bate was much admired by the composer and is so far the only organist to have recorded his complete works for the instrument. *Le banquet céleste* was Messiaen's first published work for the organ and is a magical, very slow-moving meditation on a verse from St John's Gospel (VI, 56). The very faithful recording captures both the organ and the large acoustic of Beauvais Cathedral to marvellous effect.

Messiaen. Méditations sur le mystère de la Sainte Trinité. **Hans-Ola Ericsson** (org). BIS CD464. Played on the Grönlund organ of Luleå Cathedral, Sweden.

.· **1h 18m   DDD   3/92**

At the time of his death Messiaen could point to tangible evidence of international stature as a composer of organ music. Several recordings of his organ works were either complete or in the throes of completion including this one from the 35-year-old Swedish organist, Hans-Ola Ericsson. Using the organ of Luleå Cathedral, an instrument which had to be modified in order to be more faithful to Messiaen's score, Ericsson shows a consistently strong command of both the technical and inspirational aspects of this unique body of organ music. Dating from 1969 the principal strands of Messiaen's diverse sources of musical inspiration coalesce in this remarkable work. Precisely annotated birdsong perches happily alongside Greek and Indian rhythms, but the central element throughout is plainsong; Messiaen may have been strongly influenced by exotic elements, but his profound faith and firm Catholic background remained his principal channel of expression. Ericsson's performance is clean, precise and flawless in its technical delivery although, perhaps, Messiaen's mystic vision might seem just a little too sharply focused.

Additional recommendation ...
Méditations. L'Ascension. Messe de la Pentecôte. **Jennifer Bate** (org). Unicorn-Kanchana DKPCD9024/5 — .· ② 2h 14m DDD 5/89

Messiaen. Livre du Saint Sacrement. **Jennifer Bate** (org). Unicorn-Kanchana DKPCD9067/8. Recorded on the organ of L'Eglise de la Sainte-Trinité, Paris.

.· ② **2h 9m   DDD   10/87** 🎵 P

The crowning achievement of Messiaen's unique cycle of music for the organ, the *Livre du Saint Sacrement* is also his largest work for the instrument. It is an intensely personal score based on the cornerstone of his faith, the Blessed Sacrament, and spans a wide range of emotions from hushed, private communion to the truly apocalyptic. Jennifer Bate gave the British première of the work in 1986, following which Messiaen invited her to record it using his own organ at the Trinity Church in Paris. He was on hand throughout the sessions as he so often was. The recording is a model of clarity and it is hard to imagine the complex and often very subtle textures of this music being better conveyed. This is a magnificent achievement and should be heard by all who profess an interest in the music of our time.

Messiaen. L'Ascension. Apparition de l'église éternelle. Diptyque. Messe de la Pentecôte. **Thomas Trotter** (org). Decca 436 400-2DH. Played on the organ of the Eglise-Collégiale Saint-Pierre de Douai, France. Recorded in 1991.

Ih 15m DDD 9/93

Even if the shelf is buckling under the weight of Messiaen recordings this one just has to be included. Trotter proves to be in the top rank of Messiaen interpreters. Both the vision and language of *Messe de la Pentecôte* are remote and too often performers fight shy of such musical intensity by concentrating on dazzling registration or displays of technical bravado. Not so Trotter whose sensitivity and self-control are never in doubt, not least at the spiritual and emotional climax of the work, "Communion". There's nothing remotely silly or contrived about the birdsong element here — it seems a natural and musical expression of joy and peace: which is what we all know Messiaen intended but which so rarely works in performance. The choice of instrument is inspired. Its warm colours glow like sunlight seen through a stained glass window down the length of a dark, incense-laden nave. Perhaps the action noise can be a little distracting at first but this is quickly forgotten in these intense and deeply moving performances.

Additional recommendation ...

L'Ascension. Le banquet céleste. Apparition de l'église éternelle. Diptyque. **Hans-Ola Ericsson.** BIS CD409 — ⁙ Ih 4m DDD 9/89

Messiaen. Trois petites liturgies de la Présence Divine[a]. Cinq Rechants[b]. O sacrum convivium[c]. [a]**Cynthia Miller** (ondes martenot); [a]**Rolf Hind** (pf); [a]**London Sinfonietta** [a]**Chorus and** [bc]**Voices;** [a]**London Sinfonietta/Terry Edwards.** Virgin Classics VC7 59051-2. Notes, texts and translations included.

Ih DDD II/91

Even if, as Messiaen himself insisted, he was pre-eminently a 'theological' composer, dedicated to celebrating the divine presence in his music, that music often seems to embrace the sensuous as wholeheartedly as the spiritual. Indeed, one suspects that anyone listening to the *Trois petites liturgies de la Présence Divine* in ignorance of the content of the text would assume that the chanted phrases and opulent consonances of the all-female chorus, coupled with the swooning tonal quality of the ondes martenot, which is so prominent in the instrumental accompaniment, were hymning an essentially physical union after the manner of Stravinsky's *Les Noces*. In *Cinq Rechants* the secularity is more explicit, though hidden to a degree within Messiaen's own rather surrealistic texts. Here the musical focus is even more directly on the voices, now unaccompanied, and the panache and polish of the London Sinfonietta Chorus are remarkably well sustained. For the ultimate in refined control of a slow moving, quiet choral texture, the short motet *O sacrum convivium* is the ideal foil to the larger, more dramatic compositions, and the recordings are exemplary in ensuring that each vocal strand is clear without any artificial spotlighting.

Further listening ...

Cantéyodjayâ[a]. Visions de l'Amen[b]. **Yvonne Loriod,** [b]**Olivier Messiaen** (pfs). Adès 13233-2 (6/92).

Catalogue d'oiseaux — *Book 1:* Le Chocard des Alpes; Le Loriot; Le Merle bleu. *Book 2:* Le Traquet Stapazin. *Book 3:* Le Chouette Hulotte; L'Alouette Lulu. **Peter Hill** (pf). Unicorn-Kanchana DKPCD9062 (5/88).

Catalogue d'oiseaux — *Books 4-6.* **Peter Hill** (pf). Unicorn-Kanchana DKPCD9075 (9/89).

Catalogue d'oiseaux — *Book 7.* La Fauvette des jardins. **Peter Hill** (pf). Unicorn-Kanchana DKPCD9090 (8/90).

La nativité du Seigneur[a]. La Transfiguration de Notre Seigneur Jésus-Christ. **Soloists; Westminster Symphonic Choir; Washington National Symphony Orchestra/Antál Dorati.** Decca Enterprise 425 616-2DM2 (9/90).

Giacomo Meyerbeer

New review
***Meyerbeer*. DINORAH. Deborah Cook** (sop) Dinorah; **Christian du Plessis** (bar)
Hoël; **Alexander Oliver** (ten) Corentin; **Della Jones** (mez) Goatherd; **Marilyn Hill
Smith** (sop) Goatgirl; **Roderick Earle** (bass) Huntsman; **Ian Caley** (ten) Reaper;
Geoffrey Mitchell Choir; Philharmonia Orchestra/James Judd. Opera Rara
ORC005. Notes, text and translation included. From OR5 (8/80). Recorded in 1979.

③ 2h 3lm ADD 4/94

The day after its première at the Opéra-Comique, Meyerbeer wrote to his wife to say that
everybody, including the Emperor and Empress, seemed to have liked his opera but that with a
Paris first-night you could never really be sure. In the event, success pursued it till the taste for
such things lapsed. There is nothing second-rate about the singing here, simply that it lacks star-
quality (which does not necessarily mean big names). Deborah Cook is fluent and likeable in the
title-role; Christian du Plessis competent in his (the grief-stricken ending of his aria having fine
effect); and Alexander Oliver, an excellent comedian, brings a happy touch to the simple but not
entirely witless Corentin. Della Jones does admirably in her supporting role, and the Geoffrey
Mitchell Choir sing as well as ever. The orchestral playing is of a quality that makes appreciation
of Meyerbeer's scoring no problem at all, and James Judd conducts without too much of the
modern maestro's rigidity. As always in Opera Rara's record productions, the presentation is
exemplary, and recorded sound, if afflicted in this outdoor opera with distinctly indoor resonance,
is clear and well-balanced. The opera itself is hampered by an awkward plot (involving, for one
thing, almost as much retrospective narration as *The Ring*), but the music has a genuine lyric
charm. More than that, its strands are skilfully interwoven, with a delightful ending. Meyerbeer
and his librettists planned originally a short opera in three scenes; if they had had their way it
might have been a masterpiece.

Further listening ...

Komm!. Der Garten des Herzens. Lied des venezianischen Gondoliers. Hör' ich das Liedchen
klingen. Die Rose, die Lilie, die Taube. Sie und ich. Menschenfeindlich. Chant des moissonneurs
vendéens. La barque légère. La chanson de Maître Floh. Sicilienne. La poète mourant. *Coupled
with **Rossini**.* Au chevet d'un mourant. La lazzarone. La chanson du bébé. La gita in gondola. Il
rimprovero. Ave Maria. L'ultimo ricordo. **Thomas Hampson** (bar); **Geoffrey Parsons** (pf).
EMI CDC7 54436-2 (4/92).

LES HUGUENOTS. **Soloists; Montpellier Opera Chorus and Orchestra/Cyril
Diederich.** Erato 2292-45027-2 (9/90).

Nikolay Miaskovsky

New review
***Miaskovsky*.** Symphonies — No. 5 in D major, Op. 18^a; No. 9 in E minor, Op. 28^b.
BBC Philharmonic Orchestra/Sir Edward Downes. Marco Polo 8 223499. Recorded
in 1992.

lh 13m DDD 7/94

Here are two symphonies highly contrasting in musical language, yet stamped with the same
gentle probing spirit that was always Miaskovsky's hallmark. The Fifth (of 1918) he once
dubbed his "Quiet" Symphony, and it is indeed predominantly restful and spacious; yet there
is also a troubled chromatic fugato in the first movement (the fugato in Shostakovich's Fourth
is its rebellious cousin), and the Borodin-in-heavy-boots finale has as many shadows as bright
spots. By contrast the Ninth (of 1927) is anxious and unsure of its footing, continually
looking inward to its own subconscious. It conveys a sense of being profoundly hurt and yet

alive; it constantly eludes one's emotional grasp at the same time as fascinating the ear by its Slavonic Twilight style — Rachmaninov as reheard by Bax, perhaps; it is also one of Miaskovsky's most highly wrought compositions, especially in its sonata-form scherzo. This is the Ninth's première recording and is admirably served by the BBC Philharmonic and Sir Edward Downes. Their performance of the Fifth could have been marginally less refined, marginally more urgent and passionate. The recording is a little recessed and muddy but the Ninth, recorded in a different location, sounds better. Overall this is a distinguished addition to Marco Polo's invaluable crusades on behalf of deserving, lesser-known corners of the orchestral repertoire.

Further listening ...

Cello Concerto in C minor, Op. 66. *Coupled with* **Shostakovich.** The Limpid Stream, Op. 39 — Adagio. **Tchaikovsky.** Variations on a Rococo Theme in A minor, Op. 33. Nocturne, Op. 19 No. 4. **Julian Lloyd Webber** (vc); **London Symphony Orchestra/Maxim Shostakovich.** Philips 434 106-2PH (5/92).

Violin Concerto in D minor, Op. 44[a]. Symphony No. 22 in B minor, Op. 54[b]. [a]**Grigori Feigin** (vn); [a]**USSR Radio Symphony Orchestra/Alexander Dmitriev;** [b]**USSR Symphony Orchestra/Yevgeni Svetlanov.** Olympia OCD134 (2/88).

Symphonies — No. 1 in C minor, Op. 3[a]; No. 19 in E flat major, Op. 46[b]. [a]**USSR Ministry of Culture Symphony Orchestra/Gennadi Rozhdestvensky;** [b]**Russian State Brass Orchestra/Nikolai Sergeyev.** Russian Disc RDCD11007 (3/94).

Piano Sonatas — No. 1 in D minor, Op. 6; No. 2 in F sharp minor, Op. 13; No. 3 in C minor, Op. 19; No. 6 in A flat major, Op. 64 No. 2. **Murray McLachlan** (pf). Olympia OCD214 (12/88).

Piano Sonatas — No. 4 in C minor, Op. 27; No. 5 in B major, Op. 64 No. 1. Sonatine in E minor, Op. 57. Prelude, Op. 58. **Murray McLachlan** (pf). Olympia OCD217 (3/89).

Luis de Milán

Spanish c.1500-c.1561

Suggested listening ...

Libro de musica de vihuela de mano, "El maestro" — excerpts. **Hopkinson Smith** (vihuela). Astrée Auvidis E7748 (5/91).

Darius Milhaud

French 1892-1974

Milhaud. Harp Concerto, Op. 323[a]. Le boeuf sur le toit, Op. 58. La création du monde, Op. 81. [a]**Frédérique Cambreling** (hp); **Lyon Opéra Orchestra/Kent Nagano.** Erato MusiFrance 2292-45820-2. Recorded in 1992.

59m DDD 2/93

Here is music to delight, with performances to match. Milhaud's ballet *Le boeuf sur le toit* was written for Jean Cocteau in 1919 and is set in an American bar during the Prohibition period (forbidding the manufacture and sale of alcohol) that was then just beginning. Some performances of this vivid French score lay the humour on too thick, but this one under Kent Nagano has more Gallic taste and sophistication and the playing is above all musicianly, while the more uproarious moments come over all the more effectively for this very reason. The playing by the accomplished Lyon orchestra is excellent, not least the wind players who have plenty to do. Written four years later, *La création du monde* was one of the first works by a European composer to take its inspiration from African folklore and the raw black jazz that Milhaud heard in New Orleans. This ballet on the creation myth ends with a mating dance and the whole work is powerfully and darkly sensual. Nagano and his French orchestra bring out all the character of this music and take the jazz fugue in Scene 1 more urgently than usual, to excellent effect. The Harp Concerto dates from 1953, three decades further on into Milhaud's career, and inevitably it has a brighter character, though here, too, there is some jazz influence, though of a far gentler kind. Frédérique Cambreling is a fine player and the radiant good spirits that emerge by the finale are typical of this uneven but nearly always fascinating composer who composed no less than 25 concertos in all.

Additional recommendations ...
Le boeuf sur le toit. Le carnaval d'Aix, Op. 83b[a]. *Le carnaval de Londres, Op. 172. L'Apothéose de Molière, Op. 286.* [a]**Jack Gibbons** (pf); **New London Orchestra/Ronald Corp.** Hyperion CDA66594 — .•˙ lh 17m DDD 12/92
Le boeuf sur le toit. La création du monde[b]. *Scaramouche, Op. 165b*[a]. *Saudades do Brasil, Op. 67. Suite provençale, Op. 152b.* **Marcelle Meyer** (pf); **Concerts Arts Orchestra; Champs Elysées Theatre Orchestra/Darius Milhaud**[a]. EMI Composers in Person [a]mono CDC7 54604-2 — .•˙ lh 17m ADD 4/93 ▲
Le boeuf sur le toit. La création du monde. Trois opéras-minute. Piano Concerto No. 1[a]. *La fête de la musique, Op. 159.* [a]**Marguerite Long** (pf); **Darius Milhaud** (pf/cond) various artists. EPM Classical Collector mono 150 122 — .•˙ ③ ADD 4h 16m 9/93 ⁹ₚ

New review
Milhaud. ORCHESTRAL WORKS. **Claude Helffer** (pf); **French National Orchestra/ David Robertson.** Erato MusiFrance 2292-45992-2. Recorded 1991-92.
Le Carnaval d'Aix, Op. 83b. Piano Concertos — No. 1, Op. 127; No. 4, Op. 294. Five Etudes, Op. 63. Ballade, Op. 61.

.•˙ **lh 8m DDD 6/93**

Of the five *concertante* works — out of the nearly 50 (!) Milhaud wrote — on the present disc, *Le Carnaval d'Aix* is availably differently coupled (listed above). Not too far from it in style, as in date, is the 1920 *Ballade*, beginning with chords of piled-up fifths; its rhythms and procedures recall his still earlier *Saudades do Brasil*. But that same year also found Milhaud plunging deep into polytonality of the most acerbic and chaotic kind in the five *Etudes* for piano and small orchestra and after that there's no holding Milhaud's zest for pungent polytonality. The First Concerto (1933) has an elegantly frivolous first movement, a note-spinning central barcarolle and an acid, hectically gay finale: the virtuosic Fourth (1949), rarely played because of its ferocious difficulty, with acres of double octaves, is burdened with grossly overloaded textures and an excessively long and arid slow movement. Claude Helffer battles valiantly with the ungrateful myriads of notes so plausibly and wholeheartedly that a very occasional smudge is easily forgivable, and the orchestra hangs on doggedly throughout.

Further listening ...

Cello Concerto No. 1, Op. 136[b]. *Coupled with* **Elgar.** Cello Concerto in E minor, Op. 85[a].
Respighi. Adagio con variazioni[a]. [a]**Mstislav Rostropovich** (vc); [a]**Moscow Philharmonic Orchestra;** [b]**USSR TV and Radio Large Orchestra/Gennadi Rozhdestvensky.** Russian Disc RDCD11104 (7/94).

Little Symphonies and Little Operas — No. 1, Op. 43, "Le printemps"; No. 2, Op. 49, "Pastorale"; No. 3, Op. 71, "Serenade"; No. 4, Op. 74, "Dixtuour"; No. 5, Op. 75; No. 6, Op. 79. L'enlèvement d'Europe. L'abandon d'Ariane. La deliverance de Thésée. **Capella Cracoviensis/ Karl Anton Rickenbacher.** Koch Schwann 311392 (5/93).

Pacem in terris, Op. 404[a]. L'homme et son désir[b]. [ab]**Soloists;** [a]**Utah University Chorus; Utah Symphony Orchestra/Maurice Abravanel.** Vanguard Classics 08.9070.71 (11/93).

Léon Minkus

Czechoslovakian or Polish 1826-1917

New review

Minkus (orch. Lanchbery). La Bayadère. **English Chamber Orchestra/Richard Bonynge.** Decca 436 917-2DH2. Recorded in 1992.

② lh 54m DDD 7/94 ⓆP ⓆS

Anyone who knows the "Pas de deux" from Minkus's *Don Quixote*, to which the ice-skater, the late John Curry, gave wider currency, will know his power to write rousing, tuneful music. This is one of the very best of all the delightful ballet recordings that Richard Bonynge has brought us over a period of some 30 years. Marius Petipa's ballet *La Bayadère* was first presented at the Maryinsky Theatre, St Petersburg, in 1877, eight years after *Don Quixote*. It panders to the idealized vision of the Orient that exerted such a lingering fascination on the nineteenth-century romantics, centring its plot on the *bayadère* who emerged from a Hindu temple to perform her ritual dance before retreating into its mysterious shadows. The highlight of Minkus's ballet score is the Shades scene, which Nureyev revived in London in 1963. Natalia Makarova revived the entire ballet in New York in 1980, and then in 1989 staged it with the Royal Ballet. The Paris Opéra's 1991 staging was Nureyev's final offering. Now here is this splendid recording. It is, one may note, attributed to Minkus/Lanchbery, and without doubt John Lanchbery's colourful and masterly orchestration contributes much to the ultimate effect. Since certain numbers are described as original Pavolova material, perhaps not all the music is even by Minkus. But, when the result is as enjoyable as this, who cares? Delight follows upon delight — perhaps never highly memorable, but always diverting, alternately engaging, alternately exciting, always tuneful and instantly enjoyable. It is exhilaratingly tuneful, lovingly played and brilliantly recorded.

Key to symbols

② ② lh 23m DDD 6/88

Price	Quantity/ availability	Timing	Recording mode	Review date

	Quality of sound		Discs worth exploring		Caveat emptor

ⓆP ⓆS Ⓑ ❓ ▲

Quality of performance		Basic library		Period performance	

Ernest Moeran

British 1894-1950

New review

Moeran. Serenade in G major. Sinfonietta.
Finzi. The Fall of the Leaf. New Year Music, Op. 7. **Northern Sinfonia/Richard Hickox.** EMI British Composers CDM7 64721-2. From CDC7 49912-2 (2/90). Recorded in 1988.

lh 2m DDD

Moeran's *Serenade* from 1948 (his last orchestral piece) makes a delightful impression here. Hickox gives us Moeran's score in its published six-movement form, whereas Handley restores the two numbers (a gorgeous "Intermezzo" and rather less distinctive "Forlana") which Novello decided to drop shortly after the work's Proms première. Of the two performances, Hickox's is the more boisterous and good-humoured, Handley's the more graceful and affectionate: suffice to say, both are required listening for all Moeranites. In the *Sinfonietta*, Hickox is acutely responsive to the chimerical mood-changes of the central Theme and Variations. Both Finzi offerings are presented with the utmost sensitivity, especially the wistful *New Year Music*, whose stately tread is so poignantly suggestive of the march of time and man's own mortality. Rich, resonant recording, with an occasional hint of strain in some tuttis.

Additional recommendation ...
Serenade. Nocturne[a]. ***Warlock.*** *Serenade for Strings. Capriol Suite.* [a]**Hugh Mackey** (bar); [a]**Renaissance Singers; Ulster Orchestra/Vernon Handley.** Chandos CHAN8808 — .⸫
54m DDD 3/91

New review
Moeran. Songs of Springtime. Phyllida and Corydon.
Warlock. A Cornish Carol. I saw a fair maiden. Benedicamus Domino. The full heart. The rich cavalcade. Corpus Christi. All the flowers of the Spring. As dew in Aprylle. Bethlehem Down. A Cornish Christmas Carol. **Finzi Singers/Paul Spicer.** Chandos CHAN9182. Texts included. Recorded in 1992.

.⸫ **lh l6m DDD l0/93**

The Peter Warlock we all know and love from the evergreen *Capriol Suite* and the boisterous songs seems a world away from the introverted and intense artist of these unaccompanied choral carols. Perhaps Warlock's real genius was an ability to create profound expression in short musical structures, but even the more outgoing pieces — the joyful *Benedicamus Domino* and the Cornish Christmas Carol with its gentle hint at "The First Nowell" — have an artistic integrity which raises them high above the level of the syrup of modern day carol settings. Given performances as openly sincere and sensitive as these few could remain unmoved. In the two Moeran madrigal suites there is an indefinable Englishness — the result of a deep awareness of tradition and love of the countryside. Again the innate musicality of the Finzi Singers pays handsome dividends; these warm-toned, richly expressive voices seem to capture the very essence of this uniquely lovely music.

Further listening ...

Cello Concerto. Sinfonietta. **Bournemouth Sinfonietta/Norman Del Mar.** Chandos CHAN8456 (9/87).

Violin Concerto[a]. Lonely Waters. Whythorne's Shadow. [a]**Lydia Mordkovitch** (vn); **Ulster Orchestra/Vernon Handley.** Chandos CHAN8807 (9/90).

Symphony in G minor. Overture to a Masque. **Ulster Orchestra/Vernon Handley.** Chandos CHAN8577 (4/88).

Johann Molter

German 1696-1765

Suggested listening ...

Trumpet Concertos in D major Nos. 1-3. Concertos for Two Trumpets Nos. 1, 2, 4 and 5. **Guy Touvron, Guy Messler** (tpts); **Württemberg Chamber Orchestra/Jörg Faerber.** RCA Victor Red Seal 09026 61200-2 (5/93).

Federico Mompou

Spanish 1893-1987

New review
Mompou. Los Improperios[a]. Combat del somni[b]. Suburbis (orch. Rosenthal). Scènes d'enfants (orch. Tansman). [ab]**Virgínia Parramon** (sop); [a]**Jerzy Artysz** (bar); [a]**Valencia Choir; Teatre**

Lliure Chamber Orchestra, Barcelona/Josep Pons. Harmonia Mundi HMC90 1482. Texts included. Recorded in 1993.

· ·⸍ 58m DDD 4/94

The usual image (a true one) of Mompou is of a quiet, retiring composer of exquisite miniatures for piano or for voice. Not until he had reached the age of 70 did he write for the orchestra, and then only in the present *Improperia* (from the liturgy for Good Friday). This issue has a very good solo baritone, a well-trained and fresh-sounding choir and clean orchestral sound. It is a moving performance of a work of deep commitment, exhibiting more passion and drama than is usually associated with Mompou. Harmonically it is, at times, reminiscent of Poulenc (who was an admirer of his), especially in the curiously jaunty ritornello in "Ego propter te" and in the beatific close-harmony female chorus in the final antiphon, which after an exultant climax dies away with repeated calls of "Domine!". The orchestrations by other hands of two of his early piano suites are undeniably effective, but they decidedly change the music's character.

Additional recommendation ...

Scènes d'enfants[d] — *No. 5, jeunes filles au jardin. Suburbis*[d] — *No. 1, El carrer, el guitarrista i el vell cavall. Cançons i dansas*[d] — *Nos. 5-8. Paisajes*[d] — *No. 1, La fuente y la campana.* **Falla.** *Siete canciones populares españolas*[a]. *El amor brujo*[a] — *Canción del fuego fátuo. Soneto a Córdoba. Harpsichord Concerto*[e]. **Granados.** *Goyescas — No. 7, El pelele*[c]. *Danzas españolas, Op. 37*[c] — *No. 7, Valenciana; No. 10, Danza triste.* **Nin**[b]. *Cantos populares españolas — No. 3, Tonada de la niña perdida; No. 4, Montañesa; No. 6, Malagueña; No. 7, Granadina; No. 19, Canto Andaluz; No. 20, Polo.* [a]**Maria Barrientos,** [b]**Ninon Vallin** (sops); [c]**Enrique Granados,** [d]**Federico Mompou,** [b]**Joaquin Nin** (pfs); **Manuel de Falla** ([a]pf/[e]hpd); [e]**instrumental ensemble.** EMI Composers in Person mono CDC7 54836-2 *(See review in the collections section; refer to the Index to Reviews)* — **·⸍** 1h 18m ADD 11/93 ▲

Jean-Joseph de Mondonville

French 1711-1772

Suggested listening ...

Violin Sonata in G major, Op. 3 No. 5. *Coupled with* **Leclair.** Violin Sonatas — A minor, Op. 5 No. 7; A major, Op. 9 No. 4. **Guillemain.** Violin Sonata in A major, Op. 1 No. 4. Harpsichord Solos — **Duphly.** La de Redemond. La du Buq. **J-B. Forqueray.** La Morangis ou La Plissay. **Simon Standage** (vn); **Lars Ulrik Mortensen** (hpd). Chandos Chaconne CHAN0531 (6/93). *See review under Leclair; refer to the Index to Reviews.*

TITON ET L'AURORE. **Soloists; Françoise Herr Vocal Ensemble; Les Musiciens du Louvre/Marc Minkowski.** Erato MusiFrance 2292-45715-2 (10/92).

Stanislaw Moniuszko

Polish 1819-1872

Suggested listening ...

Overtures — Paria[a]. THE COUNTESS[b]. Verbum nobile[c]. HALKA[d] — Overture; Mazur. THE RAFTSMAN[d]. The fairy tale[d]. Polonaise de concert in A major[d]. [abc]**Polish National Radio Symphony Orchestra, Katowice/**[ac]**Grzegorz Fitelberg,** [b]**Jan Krenz;** [d]**National Philharmonic Orchestra, Warsaw/Witold Rowicki.** Olympia OCD386 (8/93).

Meredith Monk

American 1943-

Suggested listening ...

ATLAS. **Soloists; Orchestra/Wayne Hankin.** ECM New Series 437 773-2 (10/93).

Michel Pignolet de Montéclair

Montéclair. Jephté. **Jacques Bona** (bass-bar) Jephté; **Sophie Daneman** (sop) Iphise; **Claire Brua** (sop) Almaise, Vénus; **Nicolas Rivenq** (bass) Phinée, Apollon; **Mark Padmore** (ten) Ammon; **Bernard Loonen** (ten) Abdon; **Jean-Claude Sarragosse** (bass) Abner; **Sylviane Pitour** (sop) Polhymnie, Israelite; **Sylvie Colas** (sop) Terpsichore; **Mary Saint-Palais** (sop) Woman of Maspha, Shepherdess, Truth. **François Bazola** (bass) Man of Maspha; **Patrick Foucher** (ten) A Hebrew; **Anne Pichard** (sop) Elise; **Les Arts Florissants Chorus and Orchestra/William Christie.** Harmonia Mundi HMC90 1424/5. Notes, text and translation included. Recorded in 1992.

② 2h 30m DDD 1/93

Growing acquaintance with the operas of Lully, Charpentier and Rameau has led to an increasing curiosity about the works of fellow compatriots: composers whom we have long suspected might have something more to say than we have been led to believe. It is clear from the opening bars of *Jephté* that Montéclair's dramatic instincts are embedded in the finest French traditions of opera. Writing at a time when the 'giants' were either dead or yet to influence the stage (Rameau's *Hippolyte et Aricie* was performed a year after *Jephté,* in 1733), Montéclair has been historically judged as an operatic footnote between Lully and Rameau. On the evidence of this fine *tragédie lyrique* opinions of French opera in the early eighteenth century need to be seriously revised. *Jephté* is a full-scale work which deservedly had a considerable following in its day. The plot is an entertaining conflation of a fiery, action-packed Old Testament story with a tale of romance running simultaneously. Jephté returns from exile to defend Israel from Ammon, vowing that he will not permit himself to see his wife or daughter until he has defeated him, and that he will sacrifice the first person he sees after conquering the enemy. Ammon is spared but falls in love with Iphisa, Jephté's daughter. Iphisa is the unfortunate soul whom her father first notices, her grief compounded by the guilt of loving Jephté's enemy. A thunderbolt removes Ammon permanently and Iphisa's life is spared. Far-fetched certainly, but like Handel, Montéclair has the resource to elevate standard emotions in a convincing and inventive manner. William Christie is as alert to the possibilities of colour as the composer himself, pacing the narrative with momentum and extreme sensitivity to nuance. All the singers, without exception, are well-groomed for the delicacies of the style and vocally they make a pleasantly contrasting team. The choir are not as exact as the outstanding instrumental group but they are exciting and always alive to theatricality. Many moments to savour then: try Iphisa's haunting and sensual scene at the beginning of Act 4 evoking memories of Charpentier's *Médée* (and Christie's recording too) or instrumental vignettes, such as the enchanting *Air* in Act 2, which anticipates Rameau. Every effort should be made to get acquainted with this spellbinding masterpiece.

Claudio Monteverdi

New review
Monteverdi. Il Combattimento di Tancredi e Clorinda[a]. Il ballo della ingrate[b]. Tempro la cetra[c]. Tirsi e Clori[d]. [ab]**Barbara Borden,** [bd]**Suzie LeBlanc** (sops); [b]**Päivi Järviö** (mez); [cd]**John Potter,** [a]**Douglas Naswari** (tens); [a]**Cesare Righetti** (bar); [b]**Harry van der Kamp** (bass); **Tragicomedia/Stephen Stubbs** (lte). Teldec Das Alte Werk 4509-90798-2. Texts and translations included. Recorded in 1992.

1h 16m DDD 10/93

The *Combattimento* was premièred at the Venice Carnival of 1624. It is a crucial work in Monteverdi's output, partly because it is virtually the only clue we have of his approach to music for dramatic performance between the two Mantuan operas and the two late Venetian ones. Moreover, the style that he so comprehensively introduces, the *genere concitato*, was closely bound up with his general thinking on the subject of musical rhythm, merely one aspect of his lifelong concern with the ability of music to portray the full range of human experience. In other words, it is something of an oddity. As if to emphasize the narrative element, Monteverdi uses a deliberately narrow vocal range, leaving all expressiveness, even pictorial effects, to the accompaniment. Tragicomedia, directed by Stephen Stubbs, offers a rich and at times rather fussy interpretation of the unprecedentedly full orchestral palate, but in Cesare Righetti Stubbs has the advantage of a native-singing Italian narrator with a full, clear, firm and at times operatic voice. The disc is interestingly completed with Monteverdi's surviving *balli* including the *Ballo delle ingrate*. The latter is superbly done; nicely resonant accompaniment, a good sense of the theatrical nature of the piece, and some fine singing particularly from Harry van der Kamp's plummy and agile Pluto. This is without doubt the best version available of this work.

Additional recommendations ...
Il Combattimento di Tancredi e Clorinda. Il ballo della ingrate. Altri canti d'amor. Volgendo il ciel. **Red Byrd; The Parley of Instruments/Peter Holman.** Hyperion CDA66475 — .⁚' lh 9m DDD 9/92 🖙

Il Combattimento di Tancredi e Clorinda. Madrigals — Ardo, avvampo, mi struggo; Mentre vaga Angioletta ogn'anima; Con che soavita; O come sei gentile, caro augellino; Tu dormi? Ah crudo core; Eri già tutta mia; Quel sguardo sdegnosetto; Zefiro torna; Presso un fiume tranquillo. **Les Arts Florissants/William Christie.** Harmonia Mundi HMC90 1426 — .⁚' 59m DDD 10/93

Il Combattimento di Tancredi e Clorinda. Madrigali guerrieri et amorosi[a] *— Ogni amante e guerrier; Lamento della ninfa, "Non havea Febo ancora"; Mentre vaga Angioletta ogn'anima.* [a]**Soloists; Vienna Concentus Musicus/Nikolaus Harnoncourt.** Teldec Das Alte Werk 4509-92181-2 — .⁚' 53m DDD 2/94 ⁹ₚ 🖙

Il ballo del ingrate. Lamento d'Arianna. **Soloists; Alfred Deller Consort.** Vanguard Classics 08.2030.71 — .⁚' lh lm ADD 4/94

New review
Monteverdi. Il quarto libro de madrigali. **Concerto Italiano/Rinaldo Alessandrini.** Opus 111 OPS30-81. Texts and translations included. Recorded in 1993.

.⁚' **lh 2m DDD 12/93**   ⁹ₚ ⁹ₛ

Monteverdi's Fourth Book, first published in 1603, is a wide-ranging collection of pieces written during the previous ten years. Originally written for performance before a select audience by an ensemble of professional virtuoso singers, these madrigals, many of which are set to the sensuous, emotional and epigrammatic verses of Guarini and Tasso, demonstrate Monteverdi's seemingly inexhaustible ability to unite words and music in expressively effective ways. A complete and profound understanding of textual nuance is, then, central to any successful performance and here the Concerto Italiano begins with an obvious and considerable advantage over any group of non-Italians. Some of the finest madrigals in the Fourth Book are those involving direct speech, which allowed Monteverdi to make full use of the court *virtuosi*, famed for their abilities to combine clear declamation with dramatic gestures and subtle shadings of dynamics and speed. In general the Concerto Italiano have taken the combined messages of music and history to heart; these are performances infused with a flexible approach to tempo and strong projection of text geared to a determination to allow each detail of the words to speak with due force. The singing style itself is muscular without losing its ability to move into a gentler mood, the vocal balance good, the overall sound rich in its lower registers and bright and clear in the upper ones. At its best this record is simply without equal.

Additional recommendation:
The Consort of Musicke/Anthony Rooley. L'Oiseau-Lyre 414 148-2OH — .⁚' 55m DDD 2/87

New review
Monteverdi. L'ORFEO. **Nigel Rogers** (ten) Orfeo; **Patrizia Kwella** (sop) Euridice; **Emma Kirkby** (sop) Music; **Jennifer Smith** (sop) Proserpina; **Helena Afonso** (sop) Nymph; **Catherine Denley** (mez) Hope; **Guillemette Laurens** (mez) Messenger; **Mario Bolognesi** (ten) Apollo, Shepherd I; **Rogers Covey-Crump** (ten) Shepherd II; **John Potter** (ten) Shepherd III; **Stephen Varcoe** (bar) Shepherd IV, Pluto; **David Thomas** (bass) Charon; **Terry Edwards** (bass) Spirit; **Geoffrey Shaw** (bass) Spirit; **Chiaroscuro; London Cornett and Sackbutt Ensemble/Theresa Caudle; London Baroque/Charles Medlam.**

EMI CMS7 64947-2. From HMV EX270131/3 (5/85). Notes, text and translation included. Recorded in 1983.

⠂⠄ ② lh 44m DDD 4/94

The printed score of *L'Orfeo*, the only source that has come down to us, is often unclear about details of instrumentation. Medlam's innovatory and minimalist approach, which essentially saw the work as a chamber opera, has been highly influential, not least on Philip Pickett (listed below) whose own recent full-price recording starts from the same position, but reaches rather different conclusions about how instruments should be deployed. In this respect Medlam's interpretation is less interested in the possibility of there being a symbolic system at work, and throws the weight more comprehensively on the voices. And, despite some roughness of intonation from David Thomas, there is some fine singing on this version, notably from Emma Kirkby, lyrically rhetorical in the Prologue, and above all, from Nigel Rogers. In the end it is "Possente spirto" that makes or breaks a performance and Rogers, here at the top of his form, produces an unforgettable reading, beautifully paced and with breathtaking control of the passagework. For that alone this reissue is worth having, but there are many other good things too, all subsumed in a dramatically effective approach marked by a strong sense of style and characterization.

Additional recommendations ...
Soloists; Munich Capella Antiqua; Vienna Concentus Musicus/Nikolaus Harnoncourt. Teldec Das Alte Werk 2292-42494-2 — ⠂⠄ ② lh 48m ADD 7/85
Soloists; New London Consort/Philip Pickett. L'Oiseau-Lyre 433 545-2OH2 — ⠂⠄ ② lh 48m DDD 2/93

Monteverdi. IL RITORNO D'ULISSE IN PATRIA. **Christoph Prégardien** (ten) Ulisse; **Bernarda Fink** (contr) Penelope; **Christina Högmann** (sop) Telemaco, Siren; **Martyn Hill** (ten) Eumete; **Jocelyne Taillon** (mez) Ericlea; **Dominique Visse** (alto) Pisandro, Human Fragility; **Mark Tucker** (ten) Anfinomo; **David Thomas** (bass) Antinoo; **Guy de Mey** (ten) Iro; **Faridah Subrata** (mez) Melanto; **Jörg Dürmüller** (ten) Eurimaco; **Lorraine Hunt** (sop) Minerva, Fortune; **Michael Schopper** (bass) Nettuno, Time; **Olivier Lallouette** (bass) Giove; **Claron McFadden** (sop) Giunone; **Martina Bovet** (sop) Siren, Love; **Concerto Vocale/René Jacobs.** Harmonia Mundi HMC90 1427/9. Notes, text and translation included. Recorded in 1992.

⠂⠄ ③ 2h 59m DDD 3/93

The only surviving manuscript score of this major musical drama, preserved in Vienna, presents an incomplete version of three acts. For this recording, René Jacobs has, within the spirit of seventeeth-century music-making, added more music by Monteverdi and others to expand the work to a satisfying five-act structure suggested by some surviving librettos. He has also considerably expanded the scoring, very much enlivening the instrumental palette that Monteverdi would have had available to him for his original production in Vienna in 1641. For some, this will rule this recording out of consideration. However, the result, even though weakly argued for in the insert-notes, is so powerful and effective that it is to be hoped that most would not be prey to such reservations. The extensive cast, led by Christoph Prégardien in the title role, is excellently chosen, not only for vocal quality but also for a convincing awareness of Monteverdi's idiom. Without that, the performance could have seemed tame, and that is nowhere better exemplified than in Act 1, Scene 7 where Ulysses awakes, wondering where he is and what is to happen to him. Prégardien here manages to convey as much depth of feeling as a Pagliaccio yet stays clearly within the bounds of Monteverdi's expressive style. The result is a *tour de force*, one of the many within this production. The adept instrumental contribution certainly helps to maintain variety throughout the work, and an accompaniment suited to the sentiments expressed by the vocalists is always possible with these resources. Ultimately, this production is very much one for our time. It presents a practical solution to the problems of performing music of another age — this realization was, in fact, for a 1992 Montpellier production — and one that turns out to be inspired, moving and totally compelling.

Additional recommendation ...
Soloists; Vienna Concentus Musicus/Nikolaus Harnoncourt. Teldec Das Alte Werk 2292-42496-2 — ⠂⠄ ③ 3h l3m ADD

Further listening ...

Vespro della Beata Vergine (ed Parrott/Keyte). **Taverner Consort; Taverner Choir; Taverner Players/Andrew Parrott.** EMI CDS7 47078-8 (10/85).

Altri canti d'amor. Il Combattimento di Tancredi e Clorinda[abc]. Volgendo il ciel. Il Ballo delle ingrate. **Red Byrd; The Parley of Instruments/Peter Holman.** Hyperion CDA66475 (9/92).

Madrigals, Book 5. **Consort of Musicke/Anthony Rooley.** L'Oiseau-Lyre 410 291-2OH (11/89).

Motets — Dixit Dominus a 8; Confitebor tibi, Domine a 3; Beatus vir a 6; Laudate pueri a 5; Laudate Dominum a 5; Deus tuorum militum a 3; Magnificat a 8 (ed. Parrott); Jubilet tota civitas a 1; Salve Regina a 3. **Soloists; Taverner Consort, Choir and Players/Andrew Parrott.** EMI CDC7 47016-2 (3/85).

Motets — Gloria in excelsis Deo a 7; Chi vol che m'innamori; O ciechi il tanto affaticar; Confitebor tibi, Domine a 5; E questa vita un lampo; Beatus vir a 6; Adoramus te, Christe a 6; Confitebor tibi, Domine a 1; Laudate Dominum a 1. **Les Arts Florissants Vocal and Instrumental Ensemble/William Christie.** Harmonia Mundi HMC90 1250 (7/87).

Motets — Dixit Dominus. Laetanie della beata vergine. Laetatus sum. Lauda, Jerusalem. Laudate pueri, Dominum. Nisi Dominus. Beatus vir. Memento et omnis mansuetudinis. Adoramus te, Christe. Christe, adoramus te. Cantate Domino. Domine, ne in furore. **Trinity College Choir, Cambridge/Richard Marlow.** Conifer CDCF212 (11/92).

Mass of Thanksgiving. Ab aeterno ordinata sum. Salve Regina a 2. *Coupled with* **Fantini.** Intrada, Toccata e Sonata Imperiale I. Sonata Imperiale II e Intrada. **Scarani.** Sonata a 3. **Rovetta.** Credo a 7 (Et in spiritum sanctum). **Usper.** Sonata a 8. **Marini.** Canzon quarta. Plainsong Chant for the Feast of S. Maria della salute. **Soloists; Taverner Consort, Choir and Players/Andrew Parrott.** EMI Reflexe CDS7 49876-2 (11/89).

L'INCORONAZIONE DI POPPEA. **Soloists; Vienna Concentus Musicus/Nikolaus Harnoncourt.** Teldec Das Alte Werk 2292-42547-2 (9/86).

Cristóbal de Morales

Spanish c.1500-1553

Morales. Missa "Queramus cum pastoribus". Andreas Christi famulus. Sancta Maria, succurre miseris. Clamabat autem mulier. O sacrum convivium. Regina coeli.
Mouton. Queramus cum pastoribus. **Westminster Cathedral Choir/James O'Donnell.** Hyperion CDA66635. Texts and translations included. Recorded in 1992.

Ih 5m   DDD

In the *Missa Queramus cum pastoribus* the *divisi* basses of Westminster provide the ideal counter-weight to the warm forthright tone of the boys. James O'Donnell adopts generally unhurried tempos that allow the counterpoint to unfold with seamless ease, but the choral sound is of such intensity and focus that the ear is constantly arrested. At its most punchy, as in the "Osannas", this could become wearing, but in the more sustained movements it is just what is needed to bring the music alive. Parts of this recording have an almost tactile quality and these occur precisely where the tactus is at its most spacious. Westminster Cathedral Choir supplement their Mass, preceded by the Mouton motet on which it is based, with five marvellous motets by Morales, of which the simplest but perhaps the most effective is *Sancta Maria, succurre miseris*. The *Regina coeli*, with its running quaver figures, could have done with a little more lightness of touch, but what a thrilling sound this choir makes when in full cry.

Further listening ...

Missa Pro defunctis a 5. Officium defunctorum a 5. **La Capella Reial de Catalunya;
Hespèrion XX/Jordi Savall.** Astrée Auvidis E8765.

Robert Moran

American 1937-

Suggested listening ...

Three Dances. *Coupled with* **D. Lang.** Face so pale. **Volans.** Kneeling Dance. **Reich.** Four
Organs. **Piano Circus.** Argo 440 294-2ZH (1/94).

DESERT OF ROSES — Arias, Interludes and Inventions (Movement 1; I can go? I can go to my
father?; Movement 3; Look into my eyes; Movement 5[a]). Open Veins[b]. Ten Miles high over
Albania[c]. [a]**Jayne West** (sop); [b]**Alexander Balanescu** (vn); [c]**Mario Falco** (hp); [ab]**Piano
Circus/**[a]**Craig Smith;** [bc]**Robert Moran.** Argo 436 128-2ZH (8/92).

Paul Moravec

American 1957-

Suggested listening ...

Violin Sonata. *Coupled with* **Corigliano.** Violin Sonata. **Glinsky.** Toccata-Scherzo. **Pärt.**
Fratres. **Messiaen.** Quatuor pour la fin du temps — Louange à l'Eternité de Jésus. **Maria
Bachmann** (vn); **Jon Klibonoff** (pf). Catalyst 09026 61824-2 (12/93). *See review under
Corigliano; refer to the Index to Reviews.*

Thomas Morley

British 1557-1602

Morley. JOYNE HANDS. **Red Byrd; Musicians of Swanne Alley/Paul O'Dette; Lyle
Nordstrom.** Virgin Classics Veritas VC7 59032-2. Texts included.
Morley: Joyne hands. A lieta vita. O griefe, even on the bud. Our bonny bootes could toote it.
Pavan (arr. Cutting). Galliard. Sleepe slumbr'ring eyes. Thirsis and Milla Sacred End Pavin (arr.
Rosseter). Galliard to Sacred End (arr. Baxter). Pavin and Galliard. A painted tale. Faire in a
morne. Sayd I that Amarillis. Now is the gentle season. Harke; Alleluia cheerely. Hard by a
cristall fountaine. Now is the month of maying (arr. Rosseter). **P. Philips:** Philips Paven and
Galliard. **Conversi:** Sola soletta (arr.? Morley). **Strogers:** In Nomine Pavin and Galliard.
Anonymous: O mistresse mine (vocal and consort versions). La Coranto (all arr.? Morley).
Monsieurs Almaine. My Lord of Oxenfordes March.

1h 12m DDD 1/92

Thomas Morley was a central figure in English renaissance music, a composer of the first
rank, an arranger of his own and other people's music, and a publisher who greatly helped to
spread the gospel of Italian style on these shores. His major contribution to instrumental
music was his two books (1599 and 1611) of "Lessons" for that most English of bands, the
'broken consort', an ingenious and flexible combination of blown, bowed and plucked
instruments (here the Musicians of Swanne Alley) which grew out of the Elizabethan theatre.
The music of the "Lessons" was of both instrumental and vocal origin and included only one
arrangement known to be by Morley, that which gives this album its title. His books of vocal
music (again mostly by others) were numerous and it is in these that his helping hand to
Italian music was strongest. The traffic was two-way: Morley's music, including some of the
lute solos in this recording, was also arranged and published by others. When the Musicians
of Swanne Alley play in concert you can see that they are enjoying themselves; on record

you can *hear* it just as easily, and this recording is no exception. Very little of the music is to be had in any other recording, and hearing it you may well wonder why. These magnificent performances are a worthy tribute to the multi-faceted work of a man of no small importance.

Jerome Moross

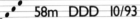

Moross. Symphony No. 1. The Last Judgement. Variations on a Waltz. **London Symphony Orchestra/JoAnn Falletta.** Koch International Classics 37188-2. Recorded in 1993.

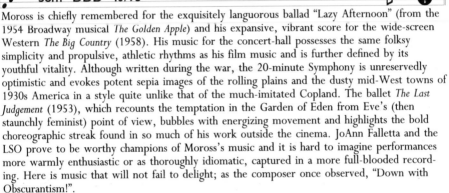

58m DDD 10/93

Moross is chiefly remembered for the exquisitely languorous ballad "Lazy Afternoon" (from the 1954 Broadway musical *The Golden Apple*) and his expansive, vibrant score for the wide-screen Western *The Big Country* (1958). His music for the concert-hall possesses the same folksy simplicity and propulsive, athletic rhythms as his film music and is further defined by its youthful vitality. Although written during the war, the 20-minute Symphony is unreservedly optimistic and evokes potent sepia images of the rolling plains and the dusty mid-West towns of 1930s America in a style quite unlike that of the much-imitated Copland. The ballet *The Last Judgement* (1953), which recounts the temptation in the Garden of Eden from Eve's (then staunchly feminist) point of view, bubbles with energizing movement and highlights the bold choreographic streak found in so much of his work outside the cinema. JoAnn Falletta and the LSO prove to be worthy champions of Moross's music and it is hard to imagine performances more warmly enthusiastic or as thoroughly idiomatic, captured in a more full-blooded recording. Here is music that will not fail to delight; as the composer once observed, "Down with Obscurantism!".

Further listening ...

The Big Country — *film score.* **Philharmonia Orchestra/Tony Bremner.** Silva Screen FILMCD030 (5/89).

Key to symbols

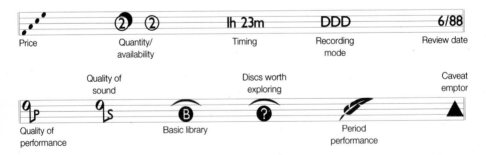

②	②	Ih 23m	DDD	6/88
Price	Quantity/ availability	Timing	Recording mode	Review date

Quality of sound		Discs worth exploring		Caveat emptor
Quality of performance	Basic library		Period performance	

Ignaz Moscheles

Suggested listening ...

Grande Sonate in E flat major, Op. 47. *Coupled with* **Fibich.** Sonata in B flat major, Op. 28. **Goetz.** Sonata in G minor, Op. 17. **Anthony Goldstone, Caroline Clemmow** (pf duet). Meridian CDE84237 (7/93). *See review under Fibich; refer to the Index to Reviews.*

Moritz Moszkowski

German 1854-1925

Suggested listening ...

Piano Concerto in E major, Op. 59. *Coupled with* **Paderewski.** Piano Concerto in A minor, Op. 17. **Piers Lane** (pf); **BBC Scottish Symphony Orchestra/Jerzy Maksymiuk.** Hyperion CDA66452 (2/92).

Jean-Joseph Mouret

French 1682-1738

Suggested listening ...

LES AMOURS DE RAGONDE. **Soloists; Les Musiciens du Louvre/Marc Minkowski.** Erato MusiFrance 2292-45823-2 (12/92).

Leopold Mozart

German/Austrian 1719-1787

Suggested listening ...

Trumpet Concerto in D major. *Coupled with* **Hummel.** Trumpet Concerto in E major. **M. Haydn.** Concertos for Trumpet and Strings — C major; D major. **J. Haydn.** Trumpet Concerto in E flat major, HobVIIe/1. **Reinhold Friedrich** (tpt); **Academy of St Martin in the Fields/Sir Neville Marriner.** Capriccio 10 436 (6/93).

Wolfgang Amadeus Mozart

Austrian 1756-1791

Mozart. Sinfonia Concertante in E flat major, K364/320d[a]. Concertone in C major for Two Violins, Oboe, Cello and Orchestra, K190/186E[b]. **Cho-Liang Lin** (vn); **Jaime Laredo** ([b]vn/[a]va); **English Chamber Orchestra/Raymond Leppard.** Sony Classical SK47693. Recorded in 1991.

1h DDD 6/92

Cho-Liang Lin's Mozart concerto cycle has been quite the best to have appeared in recent years: he possesses great beauty of tone and purity of style. His accounts of the *Sinfonia Concertante* in E flat and the *Concertone* in C, with Jaime Laredo and the English Chamber Orchestra under Raymond Leppard are performances of great quality. They possess all the spontaneity and warmth of live music-making with the perfection of the studio. Both Lin and Laredo bring to this music an aristocratic finesse and a magic that put the listener wholly under their spell. The slow movement of the *Sinfonia Concertante* shows a marvellous interplay between these distinguished artists and has both depth and eloquence. Excellent, well-balanced recordings too.

Additional recommendations ...
As Sony. **Itzhak Perlman** (vn); **Pinchas Zukerman** (va, vn); **Chaim Jouval** (ob); **Marcel Bergman** (vc); **Israel Philharmonic Orchestra/Zubin Mehta.** DG 415 486-2GH —
1h DDD 12/85
Sinfonias Concertante — K364/320d; E flat major, KAnh9/C14.01/297b[a]. **Todd Phillips** (vn); **Maureen Gallagher** (va); [a]**Stephen Taylor** (ob); [a]**David Singer** (cl); [a]**Steven Dibner** (bn); [a]**William Purvis** (hn); **Orpheus Chamber Orchestra.** DG 429 784-2GH — 1h 3m
DDD 4/91

Mozart. Clarinet Concerto in A major, K622[a]. Clarinet Quintet in A major, K581[b]. **Thea King** (basset cl); [b]**Gabrieli String Quartet** (Kenneth Sillito, Brendan O'Reilly, vns; Ian Jewel, va; Keith Harvey, vc); [a]**English Chamber Orchestra/Jeffrey Tate.** Hyperion CDA66199. From A66199 (3/86).

•.•' Ih 4m DDD 9/86   Ⓑ

New review

Mozart. Clarinet Concerto in A major, K622[a].
Spohr. Clarinet Concerto No. 1 in C minor, Op. 26.
Weber. Clarinet Concerto No. 2 in E flat major, J118. **Ernst Ottensamer** (cl, [a]basset cl); **Vienna Philharmonic Orchestra/Sir Colin Davis.** Philips 438 868-2PH. Recorded 1992.

•.•' Ih 12m DDD 6/94   ⓟ Ⓑ

The two works on the Hyperion disc are representative of Mozart's clarinet writing at its most inspired; however, the instrument for which they were written differed in several respects from the modern clarinet, the most important being its extended bass range. Modern editions of both the Concerto and the Quintet have adjusted the solo part to suit today's clarinets, but Thea King reverts as far as possible to the original texts, and her playing is both sensitive and intelligent. Jeffrey Tate and the ECO accompany with subtlety and discretion in the Concerto, and the Gabrielli Quartet achieve a fine sense of rapport with King in the Quintet. Both recordings are clear and naturally balanced, with just enough distance between soloist and listener.

Ernst Ottensamer is a virtuoso with a real sense of style, that is to say a musician with an instinct for the difference between the contained romanticism of Mozart's concerto and the overt but differing romanticism of Spohr and Weber. His tone is rich and warm, with a beautiful depth in the lower registers of the basset clarinet in the Mozart, but also a brilliance that has a bit of a wicked glint to it in Weber's finale compared to the dancing ease of Mozart's. Mozart's *Adagio* is beautifully judged in tempo, a song with a seamless line, while Weber's *Romanza* is taken quite differently, like a wordless operatic aria. Spohr's short *Adagio*, a touchingly simple, direct piece, is charmingly delivered, and elsewhere Ottensamer listens with a careful ear to the woodwind and other lines which in this work intermingle so subtly: he is an old Philharmoniker who shows a proper attention to his colleagues. He is given close, sympathetic support by orchestra and conductor. One of Davis's particular qualities is his ear for the telling simplicities in Mozart, so that here a plain arpeggio springs to life with the clarinet's melody, or a set of repeated notes has a sense of direction towards a cadence. Anyone acquiring this record should enjoy taking special note of just how musically the 'accompaniment' is all done. The Vienna Philharmonic respond with complete understanding, and the recording engineers have missed nothing. Ottensamer's beautiful performances deserve no less.

Additional recommendations ...
Clarinet Concerto[a]. *Flute and Harp Concerto in C major, K299/297c*[b]. [a]**Emma Johnson** (cl); [b]**William Bennett** (fl); [b]**Osian Ellis** (hp); **English Chamber Orchestra/Raymond Leppard.** ASV CDDCA532 — •.•' 54m DDD Ⓑ
Clarinet Concerto. Oboe Concerto in C major, K314/285. **Antony Pay** (basset cl); **Michael Piguet** (ob); **Academy of Ancient Music/Christopher Hogwood** (fp, hpd). L'Oiseau-Lyre 414 339-2OH — •.•' 47m DDD 5/86 ✍ Ⓑ
Clarinet Concerto. Oboe Concerto. **Jack Brymer** (cl); **Neil Black** (ob); **Academy of St Martin in the Fields/Sir Neville Marriner.** Philips 416 483-2PH — •.•' 50m ADD 10/88 Ⓑ
Clarinet Quintet. Oboe Quartet. Horn Quintet. **Anthony Pay** (cl); **Neil Black** (ob); **Timothy Brown** (hn); **Academy of St Martin in the Fields Chamber Ensemble.** Philips Musica da Camera 422 833-2PC — •.•' Ih 9m ADD 10/89 Ⓑ
Clarinet Concerto. Bassoon Concerto in B flat major, K191/186e. Sonata in B flat major for Bassoon and Cello, K292. **Karl Leister** (cl); **Klaus Thunemann** (bn); **Stephen Orton** (vc); **Academy of St Martin in the Fields/Sir Neville Marriner.** Philips 422 390-2PH — •.•' 55m DDD 3/90 Ⓑ
Clarinet Concerto[b]. *Oboe Concerto*[c]. *Bassoon Concerto*[g]. *Flute and Harp Concerto*[ah]. *Flute Concerto in G major, K313*[a]. *Horn Concertos — D major, K412/386b*[e]; *E flat major, K417*[f]; *E flat major, K447*[f]; *E flat major, K495*[e]. *Andante for Flute and Orchestra in C major, K315/284e. Sinfonia Concertante in E flat major, KAnh9/297B*[bf]. [b]**Susan Palma** (fl); [b]**Stephen Taylor**, [c]**Randall Wolfgang** (obs); [b]**David Singer** (cl); [d]**Charles Neidich** (basset cl); [b]**Steven Dibner**, [g]**Frank Morelli** (bns); [e]**David Jolley**, [f]**William Purvis** (hns); [h]**Nancy Allen** (hp); **Orpheus Chamber Orchestra.** DG 431 665-2GX3 — •.• ③ 3h 33m DDD 7/91 Ⓑ

Clarinet Concerto[a]. *Oboe Concerto*[b]. *Bassoon Concerto*[d]. [a]**Jacques Lancelot** (cl); [b]**Pierre Pierlot** (ob); [c]**Paul Hongne** (bn); [a]**English Chamber Orchestra/Jean-Pierre Rampal**; [b]**Jean-François Paillard Chamber Orchestra/Jean-François Paillard**; [c]**Bamberg Symphony Orchestra/Theodore Guschlbauer.** Erato Bonsai 2292-45937-2 — .•' lh 7m ADD 6/93 Ⓑ
Clarinet Concerto[a]. **Spohr.** *Clarinet Concerto No. 1*[b]. **Weber.** *Clarinet Concerto No. 2*[b]. **Gervase de Peyer** (cl); **London Symphony Orchestra/**[a]**Peter Maag,** [b]**Sir Colin Davis.** Decca Serenata 433 727-2DM — .•' lh 12m ADD 7/93 Ⓑ
Clarinet Concerto[a]. *Bassoon Concerto*[b]. *Oboe Concerto*[c]. [a]**Michele Carulli** (cl); [b]**Sergio Azzolini** (bn); [c]**Alessandro Baccini** (ob); **European Community Chamber Orchestra/Eivind Aadland.** Pickwick IMP Classics PCD 1054 — .•' lh 7m DDD 12/93 Ⓑ
Clarinet Quintet. Divertimento in D major, K136. **Thea King** (cl); **Aeolian Quartet.** Saga EC3387-2 — .•' 5lm ADD 3/94 ⁹ₚ Ⓑ

Mozart. Flute Concerto No. 1 in G major, K313/285c. Andante in C major, K315/285e. Flute and Harp Concerto in C major, K299/297c[a]. **Susan Palma** (fl); [a]**Nancy Allen** (hp); **Orpheus Chamber Orchestra.** DG 427 677-2GH. Recorded in 1988.

.•' **58m DDD 3/90**   ⁹ₚ

Mozart described the flute as "an instrument I cannot bear" in 1778 before composing his G major Flute Concerto for the Dutch amateur Ferdinand DeJean. However, he was incapable of writing poor music and this is a work of much charm and some depth that comes up with admirable freshness in this performance by Susan Palma. She is a remarkably gifted player and a member of the no less skilled Orpheus Chamber Orchestra, a conductorless ensemble of 24 players who shape the music with unfailing skill and unanimity so that everything is alert, lithe and yet sensitive. Palma's tone is liquid and bright, and she offers fine tonal nuances too, while her cadenzas are no less well imagined. The Concerto for Flute and Harp, written for another amateur player (the Count de Guines) to play with his harpist daughter, combines these two beautiful instruments to celestial effect; again the soloists are highly skilled and beyond that, they are perfectly matched. Palma is as delightful as in the other work and the spacious *Andante* in C major that separates the two concertos, while Nancy Allen makes an exquisite sound and also articulates more clearly than many other harpists in this work. The balance between the soloists and the orchestra is natural and the recording from New York's State University has a very pleasing sound.

Additional recommendations ...
As DG. *Bassoon Concerto in B flat major, K191/186a.* **Soloists; Academy of Ancient Music/ Christopher Hogwood.** L'Oiseau-Lyre 417 622-2OH — .•' lh 14m DDD 5/88 ✍
Flute Concertos — No. 1; No. 2 in D major, K314/285d. Flute and Harp Concerto. Andante. Rondo in D major for Flute and Orchestra, K373 (arr. Galway). Divertimento in D major, K334 — Menuetto (arr. Galway). Serenade in G major, K525, "Eine kleine Nachtmusik". **Marisa Robles** (hp); **Chamber Orchestra of Europe/James Galway** (fl). RCA Red Seal RD87861 — .•' ② lh 49m DDD 7/89
As DG. **Irena Grafenauer** (fl); **Maria Graf** (hp); **Academy of St Martin in the Fields/Sir Neville Marriner.** Philips 422 339-2PH — .•' 58m DDD 7/89

New review
Mozart. HORN CONCERTOS. Rondo for Horn and Orchestra in E flat major, K371 (rev. Levin). **Ab Koster** (hn); **Tafelmusik/Bruno Weil.** Sony Classical Vivarte SK53369. Recorded 1992-93.
No. 1 in D major, K412/386b (rev. Levin); No. 2 in E flat major, K417; No. 3 in E flat major, K447; No. 4 in E flat major K495.

.•' **lh 4m DDD 2/94**   ⁹ₚ Ⓑ ✍

This recording of the horn concertos differs from previous ones in its treatment of the incomplete works, the Rondo K371 and the fourth of the concertos (that is, the one formerly reckoned as No. 1), K412. For these, the American Mozartian Robert Levin has provided new orchestration — in the case of K371 incorporating, of course, the 60-bar passage that came to light when a missing leaf was found in 1990, and for K412 jettisoning the Süssmayr completion of the Rondo and working, in more Mozartian fashion, from the surviving fragment. Levin is a properly unobtrusive editor and has done a tactful job on the music, though there are three or four passages in K371 and one or two in K412 where one feels that Mozart would have done it slightly differently. The concertos are taken almost in chronological order: K371, K417, then K447 preceding K495 although it is actually later, and lastly K412. Ab Koster is a very accomplished player on the natural horn, with a sure hand technique (needed to obtain the notes not in the harmonic series); the stopped notes are often very lightly coloured, though sometimes Koster uses hand stopping to emphasize a chromatic or unexpected note. He plays quite coolly, with occasional touches of wit (which Mozart often invites), with some delicacy of timing, and often gracefully — for example in the *Romance* of K447, the finest of the slow movements. His broad phrasing in the first movement of that concerto is most appealing; there is a pleasant spaciousness to his playing throughout. He supplies good cadenzas of his own; the one in K447 seems to take note of the resemblance between the secondary theme of the movement and that of the Piano Concerto, K467. Tafelmusik produce a pleasantly luminous string texture, although their conductor sometimes seems to overlook interesting harmonic events that might merit being drawn to the listener's attention.

Additional recommendations ...

Horn Concertos. **English Chamber Orchestra/Barry Tuckwell** (hn). Decca 410 284-2DH — .•'` 52m DDD 9/85 `⁹ₚ` Ⓑ

Horn Concertos. **Dennis Brain** (hn); **Philharmonia Orchestra/Herbert von Karajan.** EMI Références mono CDH7 61013-2 — .•'` 55m ADD 2/88 `⁹ₚ` Ⓑ ▲

Horn Concertos. Fragment. **Anthony Halstead** (natural hn); **Hanover Band/Roy Goodman.** Nimbus NI5104 — .•'` 55m DDD 8/88 `⁹ₚ` Ⓑ ✐

Horn Concertos. **Alan Civil** (hn); **Royal Philharmonic Orchestra/Rudolf Kempe.** EMI Eminence CD-EMX2004 — .•` 59m ADD 1/89 Ⓑ

Horn Concertos. Rondo (cpted Tuckwell). **Barry Tuckwell** (hn); **Academy of St Martin in the Fields/Sir Neville Marriner.** EMI Studio CDM7 69569-2 — .•` 1h ADD 1/89 `⁹ₚ` Ⓑ

Horn Concertos. Rondos — K371 (cpted Greer); D major, K514 (cpted Jeurissen). **Lowell Greer** (natural hn); **Philharmonia Baroque Orchestra/Nicholas McGegan.** Harmonia Mundi HMU90 7012 — .•'` 1h 2m AAD 3/89 Ⓑ ✐

Mozart. Oboe Concerto in C major, K314/285.
R. Strauss. Oboe Concerto in D major. **Douglas Boyd** (ob); **Chamber Orchestra of Europe/Paavo Berglund.** ASV CDCOE808. From COE808 (7/87).

.•'` 44m DDD 11/87

This coupling links two of the most delightful oboe concertos ever written. Mozart's sprightly and buoyant work invests the instrument with a chirpy, bird-like fleetness encouraging the interplay of lively rhythm and elegant poise. Boyd's reading of this evergreen work captures its freshness and spontaneity beautifully. If the Mozart portrays the sprightly side of the instrument's make-up the Strauss illustrates its languorous ease and tonal voluptuousness. Again Boyd allows himself the freedom and breadth he needs for his glowing interpretation; he handles the arching melodies of the opening movement and the witty staccato of the last with equal skill. Nicely recorded.

Additional recommendations ...

Oboe Concerto. Clarinet Concerto in A major, K622. **Michael Piguet** (ob); **Antony Pay** (basset cl); **Academy of Ancient Music/Christopher Hogwood** (fp, hpd). L'Oiseau-Lyre 414 339-2OH — .•'` DDD 5/86 ✐

Oboe Concerto. Clarinet Concerto. **Neil Black** (ob); **Jack Brymer** (cl); **Academy of St Martin in the Fields/Sir Neville Marriner.** Philips 416 483-2PH — .•'` 50m ADD 10/88

Mozart. PIANO CONCERTOS. **English Chamber Orchestra/Daniel Barenboim** (pf). EMI CZS7 62825-2. Recorded 1967-74.
No. 1 in F major, K37; No. 2 in B flat major, K39; No. 3 in D major, K40; No. 4 in G major, K41 (all from SLS5031, 1/76); No. 5 in D major, K175 (ASD2484, 11/69); No. 6 in B flat major, K238 (ASD3032, 11/74); No. 8 in C major, K246 (ASD3033, 1/75); No. 9 in E flat major, K271, "Jeunehomme" (ASD2484); No. 11 in F major, K413/387a (ASD2999, 9/74); No. 12 in A major, K414/385p (ASD2956, 2/74); No. 13 in C major, K415/387b (ASD2357, 4/68); No. 14 in E flat major, K449; No. 15 in B flat major, K450 (both ASD2434, 11/68);

No. 16 in D major, K451 (ASD2999); No. 17 in G major, K453 (ASD2357); No. 18 in B flat major, K456 (ASD2887, 7/73); No. 19 in F major, K459 (ASD2956); No. 20 in D minor, K466 (ASD2318, 7/67); No. 21 in C major, K467 (ASD2465, 2/69); No. 22 in E flat major, K482 (ASD2838, 11/72); No. 23 in A major, K488 (ASD2318); No. 24 in C minor, K491 (ASD2887); No. 25 in C major, K503 (ASD3033); No. 26 in D major, K537, "Coronation" (ASD3032); No. 27 in B flat major, K595 (ASD2465). Rondo in D major, K382 (ASD2838).

⟨1⟩⟨0⟩ llh lm ADD 6/90

Here are all 27 of Mozart's piano concertos plus the D major Rondo, K382, on ten medium-priced discs giving a total of 11 hours' listening. The skills of Daniel Barenboim and the English Chamber Orchestra in this repertory are well proven, and his account of these concertos, directed from the keyboard, is spacious and satisfying. This artist has always been a master of clean exposition and structure, and from the early Concertos to the late masterpieces such as Nos. 21, 24 and 27 he is a sure guide with a full awareness of Mozart's inventive and expressive range. Sometimes one may feel that he allows a rather romantic self-indulgence to creep in, and in the more dramatic music (e.g. in the D minor and C minor concertos) he may be thought to be too powerfully Beethovenian and, incidentally, he uses a Beethoven cadenza, as arranged by Edwin Fischer, in the first movement of the first of these. Ideally, too, we might prefer a smaller body of strings than was used in these performances from the late 1960s and early 1970s. But these are only small reservations, given the high overall standard, and certainly this is a major achievement. The recordings sound well, with mellow piano tone and good balance.

Additional recommendations ...
Nos. 1-27. Rondos — D major, K382; A major, K386. Three Concertos after J.C. Bach, K107 — D major; G major; E flat major. **Schröter.** *Concerto in C major, Op. 3 No. 3.* **English Chamber Orchestra/Murray Perahia** (pf). CBS Masterworks CD42055 — .·' ⟨1⟩⟨3⟩ ADD 4/86
Nos. 5-27. Double Piano Concertos — F major, K242, "Lodron"; E flat major, K365/316a. Rondos — D major, K382; A major, K386. **Alfred Brendel** (pf); **Academy of St Martin in the Fields/ Sir Neville Marriner.** Philips 412 856-2PH10 — .·' ⟨1⟩⟨0⟩ ADD/DDD 4/86
Nos. 1-27. **Salzburg Mozarteum Orchestra/Géza Anda** (pf). DG 429 001-2GX10 — .·' ⟨1⟩⟨0⟩ 10h 10m ADD 6/90
Nos. 1-27. Concertos after J.C. Bach, K107 — D major; G major; E flat major. Double Piano Concertos — K242; K365/316a. Concerto in F major for Three Pianos, K242, "Lodron". Rondos — K382; A major, K386. **Alfred Brendel, Imogen Cooper, Katia** and **Marielle Labèque** (pfs); **Ingrid Haebler** (fp); **Academy of St Martin in the Fields/Sir Neville Marriner; Berlin Philharmonic Orchestra/Semyon Bychkov** (pf); **Vienna Capella Academica/Eduard Melkus; Amsterdam Baroque Orchestra/Ton Koopman** (hpd). Philips Mozart Edition 422 507-2PME12 — .·' ⟨1⟩⟨2⟩ 12h 35m ADD/DDD 5/91
Nos. 5 and 8. Rondos — K382; K386. **Malcolm Bilson** (fp); **English Baroque Soloists/John Eliot Gardiner.** Archiv Produktion 415 990-2AH — .·' lh DDD 6/87 ✓
Nos. 8 and 11. Rondo, K386. **András Schiff** (pf); **Salzburgh Mozarteum Camerata Academica/Sándor Vegh.** Decca 433 042-2DH — .·' 55m DDD 5/93
Nos. 9 and 21. **English Chamber Orchestra/Murray Perahia** (pf). CBS Masterworks CD34562 — .·' 59m DDD 6/87
Nos. 14 and 27. **London Mozart Players/Howard Shelley** (pf). Chandos CHAN9137 — .·' 55m DDD 6/93 ⁹ₚ
Nos. 18 and 25. **Rudolf Firkušný** (pf); **South-West German Radio Symphony Orchestra/Ernest Bour.** Intercord Classical Creations INT820 548 — . lh lm DDD 7/94
Nos. 21, 22, 23, 24, 26 and 27. Double Piano Concerto in E flat major, K365. **Robert Casadesus, Gaby Casadesus** (pfs); **Cleveland Orchestra, Columbia Symphony Orchestra/George Szell;** [a]**Philadelphia Orchestra/Eugene Ormandy.** Sony Legendary Interpretations MK46519 — .·' ⟨3⟩ 3h 15m ADD 9/92 Ⓑ ▲
Nos. 21 and 23. **Rudolf Serkin** (pf); **London Symphony Orchestra/Claudio Abbado.** DG 410 068-2GH — .·' DDD 9/83 Ⓑ
Nos. 21 and 24. **City of London Sinfonia/Howard Shelley.** Pickwick IMP Red Label PCD832 — . lh DDD 1/87 Ⓑ
Nos. 21 and 24. **Robert Casadesus** (pf); **Cleveland Orchestra/George Szell.** CD42594 — .·' 57m ADD 2/90 Ⓑ
Nos. 21 and 25. **Stephen Kovacevich** (pf); **London Symphony Orchestra/Sir Colin Davis.** Philips Concert Classics 426 077-2PC — . 59m ADD 2/90 ⁹ₚ Ⓑ

No. 21. Tchaikovsky. *Piano Concerto No. 2 in G major, Op. 44.* **Emil Gilels** (pf); **USSR Symphony Orchestra/Kyrill Kondrashin.** Mezhdunarodnaya Kniga MK417106 — .·*' lh 3m
AAD 5/93 ⒷⒷ ▲

No. 22ᵃ. *Double Piano Concerto, K365/316aᵇ.* ᵃ**Philharmonia Orchestra/Vladimir Ashkenazy** (ᵃᵇpf); ᵇ**English Chamber Orchestra/Daniel Barenboim** (ᵇpf). Decca 421 036-2DH — .·*'
lh 2m ADD 1/89 Ⓑ

Nos. 25 and 26. Malcolm Bilson (fp); **English Baroque Soloists/John Eliot Gardiner.**
Archiv Produktion 423 119-2AH — .·*' lh lm DDD 7/88 ✍

Mozart. Piano Concertos — No. 9 in E flat major, K271; No. 17 in G major, K453.
London Mozart Players/Howard Shelley (pf). Chandos CHAN9068. Recorded in 1991.

.·*' lh lm DDD 11/92 ⒬ₚ

Howard Shelley has already proved himself to be an excellent performer in the Mozart piano concertos, and the present disc only reinforces that view. The performance of the E flat major Concerto, in which the piano unconventionally enters very near the start instead of waiting throughout a lengthy orchestral exposition, is warm, gentle and vigorous as the music requires. As for the partnership between the soloist and the orchestra, it is ideal: Shelley has often worked as a soloist-cum-director with this fine body of players, and their rapport is evident. Perhaps most important of all in Mozart's music, the pianist achieves distinction without mannerism; the music sounds above all natural and unforced, not least in the beautiful central *Andantino* in C minor and the buoyant finale, which is unconventional in incorporating a Watteau-like rococo minuet. The G major Concerto also demonstrates the skill and sensitivity of these artists. Chandos's recording also deserves praise: it was made in a London church and manages to be both clear and atmospheric, with the piano tone (a modern piano but played in scale with the music) perfectly caught with a good overall balance. Indeed, the disc is so pleasing as a whole that one is aware that the musicians, the producer Ralph Couzens and the sound engineers have to be a happy team with the kind of mutual respect and trust that make for good teamwork.

Additional recommendations ...
Nos. 8 and 9. Mitsuko Uchida (pf); **English Chamber Orchestra/Jeffrey Tate.** Philips 432 086-2PH — .·*' 55m DDD 7/92
Nos. 9 and 13. András Schiff (pf); **Salzburg Mozarteum Camerata Academica/Sándor Végh.** Decca 425 466-2DH — .·*' 59m DDD 7/90
Nos. 9 and 17. Berlin Philharmonic Orchestra/Daniel Barenboim (pf). Teldec 9031-73128-2 — .·*' lh 3m DDD 11/92
Nos. 9 and 24. Rudolf Firkušný (pf); **South-West German Radio Symphony Orchestra/ Ernest Bour.** Intercord Classical Creations INT820 547 — . lh lm DDD 7/94
Nos. 9 and 27. Jenö Jandó (pf); **Concentus Hungaricus/András Ligeti.** Naxos 8 550203 — . 58m DDD 10/90
Nos. 16 and 17. Malcolm Bilson (fp); **English Baroque Soloists; John Eliot Gardiner.** Archiv Produktion 415 525-2AH — .·*' 54m DDD 2/87 ✍
Nos. 17 and 21. Philharmonia Orchestra/Vladimir Ashkenazy (pf). Decca 411 947-2DH — .·*' lh lm DDD 12/85 Ⓑ
Nos. 17 and 18. Jenö Jandó (pf); **Concentus Hungaricus/Mátyás Antal.** Naxos 8 550205 — . 57m DDD 10/90

New review
Mozart. Piano Concertos — No. 12 in A major, K414/K385p; No. 19 in F major, K459.
London Mozart Players/Howard Shelley (pf). Chandos CHAN9256. Recorded in 1993.

.·*' 52m DDD 6/94

These are clear and stylish readings. The playing of both the soloist-director and the London Mozart Players is assured, relaxed and unfailingly enjoyable, allowing the music to unfold very naturally. Shelley demonstrates his fine judgement of that very important matter, tempo, and textures are also well served; the recording gives quite a bold sound to his modern piano, but its overall immediacy and warmth are not excessive and the balance is just right. Phrasing is another area deserving praise: Shelley and his expert team manage to shape the music gracefully without falling into the slightly mannered delivery which can affect other artists in this repertory. Finally, cadenzas have the right balance of freedom and formality. Perhaps the two 'slow' movements here — the quotes are because that of K414 is an *Andante* and K459's is an *Allegretto* — are richer in style than will suit many tastes: they do not sound authentic in period-performance terms, but then this is another kind of performance and perfectly convincing. The excellent recordings earn a tribute to the Chandos team.

Additional recommendations ...
Nos. 12 and 14. **Louis Lortie** (pf); **I Musici de Monteal/Yuli Turovsky.** Chandos CHAN8455 — .⠶ 48m DDD 1/87
Nos. 12 and 15. **Mozartian Players/Steven Lubin** (fp). Arabesque Z6552 — .⠶ 48m DDD 3/87
Nos. 18 and 19. **Malcolm Bilson** (fp); **English Baroque Soloists; John Eliot Gardiner.** Archiv Produktion 415 111-2AH — .⠶ DDD 6/86
Nos. 19 and 27. **András Schiff** (pf); **Salzburg Mozarteum Camerata Academica/Sándor Végh.** Decca 421 259-2DH — .⠶ 59m DDD 3/89 ⑨ₚ Ⓑ

Mozart. Piano Concertos — No. 15 in B flat major, K450; No. 16 in D major, K451. **András Schiff** (pf); **Salzburg Mozarteum Camerata Academica/Sándor Végh.** Decca 433 374-2DH. Recorded in 1990.

.⠶ 48m DDD 10/92 ⑨ₚ

This is another valuable disc in the Mozart piano concerto series which András Schiff and Sándor Végh have been recording, unhurriedly, for Decca. Their B flat major Concerto is glowing and graceful, with Végh and his Salzburg orchestra providing Schiff with a characterful yet always attentive partnership. Maybe the pianist makes the first movement a touch winsome, with mannered little gusts of sound in places, but his interpretation is all of a piece and convincing, even if one would not necessarily always want to hear the music played this way. As always, too, one must admire the way in which he can use a Bösendorfer to produce tone, articulation and phrasing which suit this music conceived for an earlier and less powerful keyboard instrument. In the gentle middle movement, it sounds as if he is using the soft pedal, which may be wrong stylistically but has its own kind of beauty; this movement is sensitively played (also by the flautist Irena Grafenhauer and the oboist Heinz Holliger) and the hunting-type finale has both high spirits and delicacy. The Concerto in D major is a more virile piece, with trumpets and timpani (not used in K450) giving the first movement a touch of the military (or mock-military). The artists bring this out without overdoing it, so that we get elegance as well as energy. The slow movement and good-natured rondo finale also go well, although Schiff's normally impeccable articulation is momentarily less than clear at one point early in the latter. But that is just one tiny passage in a performance that is assured and satisfying. The recording of both concertos has fine presence.

Additional recommendations ...
Nos. 15 and 16. **English Chamber Orchestra/Murray Perahia** (pf). CBS Masterworks CD37824 — .⠶ 50m DDD ⑨ₚ ⑨ₛ
Nos. 14-16. **English Chamber Orchestra/Daniel Barenboim** (pf). EMI Studio CDM7 69124-2 — .⠶ 1h 14m ADD 12/88
Nos. 16 and 20. **Rudolf Firkušný** (pf); **South-West German Radio Symphony Orchestra/Ernest Bour.** Intercord Classical Creations INT820 546 — . 54m DDD 7/94

Mozart. PIANO CONCERTOS. **English Chamber Orchestra/Murray Perahia** (pf). CBS Masterworks CD42241 and CD42243. Items marked [a] from 76651 (4/78), [b] 76731 (5/80), [c] 76481 (5/76).
CD42241 — No. 20 in D minor, K466[a]; No. 27 in B flat major, K595[b]. *CD42243* — No. 11 in F major, K413[a]; No. 12 in A major, K414/385p[b]; No. 14 in E flat major, K449[c].

.⠶ ② 2h 3m 1h 10m ADD/DDD 9/87 Ⓑ

These discs happily epitomize some of the best qualities of the complete Perahia/ECO set. Always intelligent, always sensitive to both the overt and less obvious nuances of this music, Perahia is firstly a true pianist, never forcing the instrument beyond its limits in order to express the ideas, always maintaining a well-projected singing touch. The superb ECO reflect his integrity and empathy without having to follow slavishly every detail of his articulation or phrasing. K414 and K413 are charming and typically novel for their time, but do not break new ground in quite the way that K449 does. Here, Mozart's success in the theatre may have suggested a more dramatic presentation and working of ideas for this instrumental genre. K595 is a work pervaded by a serenity of acceptance that underlies its wistfulness. Mozart had less than a year to live, and the mounting depression of his life had already worn him down, yet there is still a sort of quiet joy in this music. The vast range of styles, emotions, and forms that these few works encompass are evocatively celebrated in these performances, and admirably captured in civilized recordings.

Additional recommendations ...

Nos. 12 and 20. Rondo in D major, K382. **Evgeni Kissin** (pf); **Moscow Virtuosi/Vladimir Spivakov.** RCA Victor Red Seal 09026 60400-2 — .·· 1h 7m DDD 2/93 Ⓑ

Nos. 12 and 21. **Beethoven.** *32 Variations in C minor, WoO80.* **Radu Lupu** (pf). **English Chamber Orchestra/Uri Segal.** Decca Ovation 417 773-2DM — .·· 1h 4m ADD 1/89 Ⓑ

Nos. 13 and 20. **Jenö Jandó** (pf); **Concentus Hungaricus/András Ligeti.** Naxos 8 550117 — . 54m DDD 10/90

Nos. 12, 14 and 21. **Jenö Jandó** (pf); **Concentus Hungaricus/András Ligeti.** Naxos 8 550202 — . 1h 11m DDD 10/90

Nos. 20 and 21. **Mitsuko Uchida** (pf); **English Chamber Orchestra/Jeffrey Tate.** Philips 416 381-2PH — .·· 1h 2m DDD 7/86 Ⓑ

Nos. 20 and 21. **Malcolm Bilson** (fp); **English Baroque Soloists/John Eliot Gardiner.** Archiv Produktion 419 609-2AH — .·· 58m DDD 1/88 Ⓑ ✎

Nos. 20 and 27. **Sir Clifford Curzon** (pf); **English Chamber Orchestra/Benjamin Britten.** Decca 417 288-2DH — .·· 1h 5m ADD 10/86 Ⓑ

Nos. 20 and 21. **Berlin Philharmonic Orchestra/Daniel Barenboim** (pf). Teldec 9031-75710-2 — 1h 1m DDD 11/92 Ⓑ

Nos. 26 and 27. **Mitsuko Uchida** (pf); **English Chamber Orchestra/Jeffrey Tate.** Philips 420 951-2PH — .·· 1h 5m DDD 11/88 Ⓑ

Mozart. Piano Concertos — No. 20 in D minor, K466; No. 23 in A major, K488. **Melvyn Tan** (fp); **London Classical Players/Roger Norrington.** EMI CDC7 54366-2. Recorded in 1991.

.·· 54m DDD 11/92 Ⓑ ✎

This A major Concerto is among the most popular of all Mozart's piano concertos, perhaps because its predominantly sunny mood is effectively contrasted with the hauntingly beautiful minor-key slow movement. Collectors who already have more than one version may see no need for another, but such is the persuasiveness of this performance on period instruments by Tan and Norrington that their disc is tempting. As always in Mozart, one must balance energy and sweetness, and this is well achieved in the flowing first movement, first by Norrington's orchestra and then by the fortepianist with his first entry, quieter than one expects but with adequate authority. If Tan's instrument sounds small against the orchestra, we may remember that Mozart's did, too, and no significant detail of the piano part is covered although in places one wonders if it will be. The fortepiano sound may also convert people who dislike honkytonk varieties: this is a sweet, clear sound whose expressive range fits and serves the music. Tan's view of the *Adagio* is quite purposeful, with an unselfconscious expressiveness and his playing here (with a few tasteful extra ornaments) has rightly been called "fluent and fragrant". The D minor Piano Concerto offers an example of *Sturm und Drang*, particularly in the outer movements. Tan's fortepiano is arguably less appropriate here and one may wish at first for the fuller sound of a modern piano. But one is soon convinced, for after all, Mozart didn't write for a modern grand and the power of the solo instrument is not just a matter of decibels. Tan's own cadenza for the first movement is another plus, suiting the music better than the one by Beethoven that we often hear.

Additional recommendations ...

Nos. 22 and 23. **Mitsuko Uchida** (pf); **English Chamber Orchestra/Jeffrey Tate.** Philips 420 187-2PH — .·· 1h 2m DDD 8/87 Ⓑ

Nos. 22 and 23. **Malcolm Bilson** (fp); **English Baroque Soloists/John Eliot Gardiner.**

| Archiv Produktion 423 595-2AH — .·· 1h DDD 3/89 Ⓑ

Nos. 22 and 23. **Berlin Philharmonic Orchestra/Daniel Barenboim** (pf). Teldec 9031-75711-2 — .•· 1h 3m DDD 11/92 ⓑ
Nos. 23 and 27. **Alfred Brendel** (pf); **Academy of St Martin in the Fields/Sir Neville Marriner.** Philips Silver Line 420 487-2PM — .•· 55m ADD 6/87 ⓑ

New review

Mozart. Piano Concerto No. 20 in D minor, K466[a]. Symphony No. 38 in D major, K504, "Prague"[b]. Serenade in G major, K525, "Eine kleine Nachtmusik", [c]. Three German Dances, K605[d]. **Vienna Philharmonic Orchestra/Bruno Walter** ([a]pf). Pearl mono GEMMCD9940. Item marked [a] from HMV DB3273/6 (10/38), [b] DB3112/14, [c] DB3075/6, [d]HMV DA1570, 9/37).

.•· 1h 12m AAD 3/94

Bruno Walter was an accomplished pianist, and his solo work in Mozart's D minor Concerto is full of personality. The first movement cadenza by Reinecke is boring, but otherwise there's much to enjoy in this romantic and subjective interpretation. The VPO plays beautifully both here and in the other Mozart works. The *Prague* Symphony has lots of muscle as well as grace and elegance. If a romantic approach to *Eine kleine Nachtmusik* is sought by the listener then Walter's affectionate interpretations will surely give great pleasure, and the little *German Dances* are charmingly played. Pearl have used commercial pressings for their issue, and a certain amount of surface noise is present. Colin Attwell has reproduced the original sound-quality very faithfully and straightforwardly, and his transfers are much kinder to the ears than most others from this period.

Mozart. Piano Concertos[a] — No. 23 in A major, K488; No. 24 in C minor, K491.
Schubert. Impromptus[b] — G flat major, D899; A flat major, D899. **Sir Clifford Curzon** (pf); **London Symphony Orchestra/István Kertész.** Decca 430 497-2DWO. Items marked [a] from SXL6354 (11/68), recorded in 1968, [b] SXL6135 (11/64), recorded in 1964.

.•· 1h 9m ADD 10/91

These two piano concertos succeed one another in Mozart's catalogue but could hardly be more different, the A major being a sunny work (at least in its outer movements) and the C minor one of storm and distress. Thus the coupling is attractive. Attentively partnered by his conductor and orchestra, Sir Clifford Curzon takes a serene, unusually spacious view of the first movement of the A major which allows every detail to tell and yet does not lose sight of the whole. The lovely *Adagio* (in F sharp minor, the only instance of Mozart using this key) is not beautified tonally but its slight understatement makes it all the more poignant, and the bustling finale is all of a piece with the rest of the interpretation in being distinctly unhurried. The performance of the C minor Concerto is again typical of this fine pianist in that nothing is exaggerated and no 'effects' are sought: what we have instead is quietly artistic and sensitive playing, much less urgent and dramatic than some other performances but equally satisfying in its own way; predictably, the oasis of calm that is the slow movement has a quiet simplicity. The two Schubert impromptus make an unusual fill-up, but receive attractive performances, though the sound has a good deal of background hiss. In the concertos, the piano sound could have more brilliance and the orchestral violins are somewhat whiskery; but this need not be a major consideration when the performances are of this quality.

Additional recommendations ...
Nos. 22 and 24. **English Chamber Orchestra/Murray Perahia.** CBS Masterworks CD42242 — .•· 1h 7m 8/87 ⓑ
Nos. 23 and 24. **Wilhlem Kempff** (pf); **Bamberg Symphony Orchestra/Ferdinand Leitner.** DG Galleria 423 885-2GGA — .•· 56m ADD 12/88 ⓑ
Nos. 23 and 24. **Jenö Jandó** (pf); **Concentus Hungaricus/Mátyás Antal.** Naxos 8 550204 — .•· 1h 3m DDD 10/90 ⓑ
Nos. 24 and 27. **Malcolm Bilson** (fp); **English Baroque Soloists/John Eliot Gardiner.** Archiv Produktion 427 652-2AH — .•· 1h 3m DDD 2/90 ⓑ

Mozart. Double Piano Concertos[a] — E flat major, K365/316a; F major, K242, "Lodron". Andante and Variations in G major, K501. Fantasia in F minor, K608 (arr. Busoni). **Murray**

Perahia, Radu Lupu (pfs); [a]**English Chamber Orchestra.** Sony Classical SK44915. Recorded 1988-90.

> ♪ **1h 2m DDD 10/91**

Since each of the pianists on this disc is a fine Mozartian, it will attract many collectors, who should not be disappointed despite a couple of reservations listed below. The recording of the two concertos derives from a packed-out concert at The Maltings, Snape, during the 1988 Aldeburgh Festival and has a live immediacy, but the microphone placing does not allow a spacious sound. The playing itself is also immediate, and in the famous Concerto for two pianos there is a consistent feeling of energy in the outer movements. Less expectedly, we note it also in the central *Adagio*, which could have been more restfully done, particularly as the piano tone is close and full throughout. But there it is, the performance is all of a piece and its vigour certainly does not exclude grace, while the English Chamber Orchestra play with its customary skill. The less memorable *Lodron* Concerto was originally a triple piano concerto written for Countess Lodron and her two daughters and is here done in the composer's own duo transcription. The other two pieces on the disc were recorded a year later in London's Abbey Road Studio No. 1 and are skilfully done, but the beautiful and dramatic F minor *Fantasia* for mechanical organ loses much in Busoni's tubby arrangement for two pianos, particularly as Perahia and Lupu choose a deliberate tempo for the outer sections. However, the G major *Andante and Variations* for piano duet, presented here in a somewhat restrained performance, are both graceful and attractive.

Additional recommendations ...
Double Piano Concerto, K365/316a[a]. *Piano Concerto No. 22*[b]. [b]**Philharmonia Orchestra/ Vladimir Ashkenazy** ([ab]pf); [a]**English Chamber Orchestra/ Daniel Barenboim** ([b]pf). Decca 421 036-2DH — ♪ **1h 2m ADD 1/89**

Mozart. VIOLIN CONCERTOS. [a]**Richard Morgan** (ob); [b]**Henryk Szeryng,** [c]**Gérard Poulet** (vns); [d]**Nobuko Imai** (va); [e]**Norman Jones,** [f]**Stephen Orton** (vcs); [g]**Howard Shelley** (pf); [b]**New Philharmonia/Sir Alexander Gibson;** [h]**Academy of St Martin in the Fields/Iona Brown** (vn). Philips Mozart Edition 422 508-2PME4. Recorded 1966-70. *Violin Concertos*[b] — No. 1 in B flat major, K207; No. 2 in D major, K211; No. 3 in G major, K216; No. 4 in D major, K218 (all from 6706 011-1/4, 10/70); No. 5 in A major, K219; D major, K271a/271i (both from SAL3588, 2/67). *Rondos*[b] — B flat major, K269/261a; C major, K373 (6707 011-1/4). Concertone in C major, K190/186E (6707 011-1/4)[abce]. Adagio in E major, K261 (6500 036, 1/72)[b]. Sinfonia Concertante in E flat major, K364/320d[dh]. Keyboard and Violin Concerto in D major, KAnh56/315f[gh]. Sinfonia Concertante in A major, KAnh104/320e[dfh] (all new to UK).

> ♪ ④ **4h 25m ADD/DDD 6/91** Ⓑ

Leaving aside works of doubtful authenticity, there are five Mozart violin concertos. They belong to his late teenage years in Salzburg and were composed in 1775. They have always been overshadowed by the piano concertos which, of course, are not only five times as numerous but also span the composer's whole career and include many mature masterpieces. While this is understandable, it would be a pity to miss out on these violin works which are surprisingly refreshing, youthful works of great charm. They agreeably reflect their creator's love and understanding of an instrument which he himself played more than capably. It is believed that his father Leopold, who was an authority on violin playing as well as a performer, may have encouraged him to compose them and then play them himself. It seems likely that Mozart did play them, at least for his own pleasure. The concertos have much in common with Mozart's cassations, divertimentos and serenades, which also highlight the solo violin and have other concerto-like elements in them. But their lightweight means of expression in no way diminishes their long-term appeal, for Mozart filled them to the brim with wonderful ideas. Henryk Szeryng has a relaxed way with these works and the orchestral contribution from the New Philharmonia under Sir Alexander Gibson is alert yet sensitive. Szeryng's tone is unfailingly beautiful with a sweetness that is greatly appealing. His evident affection for these works makes for pleasing listening and the vivid and witty 'Turkish' episode in the finale of No. 5 has great spirit. This disc also includes the 'doubtful' but agreeable solo Concerto in D major, K271a, together with a rather laid-back account of the *Sinfonia concertante* with Iona Brown and Nobuko Imai as the soloists (beautifully matched and blending). In addition we have the reconstructions of the incomplete projected Concerto for keyboard and violin and the single-movement *Sinfonia concertante* in A major for string trio and orchestra. The quality of the recordings is quite satisfying and at mid-price this compilation is very good value indeed.

Additional recommendations ...

Nos. 1-5. Adagio in E major, K261. Rondos — C major, K373; B flat major, K269/261a. **Itzhak Perlman** (vn); **Vienna Philharmonic Orchestra/James Levine.** DG 419 184-2GH3 — ⋰'
③ 2h 18m DDD 12/86 Ⓑ

Nos. 1 and 2. Rondo, K269/261a. **Jean-Jacques Kantorow** (vn); **Netherlands Chamber Orchestra/Leopold Hager.** Denon C37-7506 — ⋰' 47m DDD 12/86 Ⓑ

Nos. 3 and 5. Adagio, K261. **Cho-Liang Lin** (vn); **English Chamber Orchestra/Raymond Leppard.** CBS Masterworks CD42364 — ⋰' 1h 2m DDD 12/87 Ⓑ

Concertos Nos. 3, 4 and 5. **Christian Altenburger** (vn); **German Bach Soloists/Helmut Winscherman.** LaserLight 15 525 — ⋰ 1h 15m DDD 5/90 Ⓑ

No. 1. Adagio, K261. Sinfonia Concertante in E flat major, K364/320d[a]. **Anne-Sophie Mutter** (vn); [a]**Bruno Giuranna** (va); **Academy of St Martin in the Fields/Sir Neville Marriner.** EMI CDC7 54302-2 — ⋰' 59m DDD 1/92 Ⓑ

Concertos Nos. 1-5. Adagio, K261. Rondos — K269/261a; K373. **Simon Standage** (vn); **Academy of Ancient Music/Christopher Hogwood.** L'Oiseau-Lyre 433 045-2OH2 — ⋰' ② 2h 8m DDD 4/92 Ⓑ ✒

Nos. 1-5. **Andrea Cappelletti** (vn); **European Community Chamber Orchestra/Eivind Aaland.** Koch Schwann Musica Mundi 311164 — ⋰' ② 2h 3m DDD 5/92 Ⓑ

Nos. 2 and 4. Sinfonia Concertante, K364/320d[a]. [a]**Josef Suk** (vn); **Academy of St Martin in the Fields/Iona Brown** (vn). Argo 433 171-2DM — ⋰ 1h 14m ADD/DDD 5/92 Ⓑ

Nos. 1, 3 and 5. **Academy of St Martin in the Fields/Iona Brown** (vn). Argo 433 170-2DM — ⋰ 1h 10m ADD/DDD 5/92 Ⓑ

Nos. 3 and 5. **Frank Peter Zimmermann** (vn); **Württemberg Chamber Orchestra/Jörg Faerber.** EMI CDD7 64288-2 — ⋰ 1h 19m DDD 9/92 Ⓑ

Nos. 1-5[a]. *Rondo, K373*[b]. *Adagio, K261*[b]. *Sinfonia Concertante, K364/320d*[c]. **Arthur Grumiaux** (vn); [c]**Arrigo Pelliccia** (va); [a]**London Symphony Orchestra/Sir Colin Davis;** [b]**New Philharmonia Orchestra/Raymond Leppard.** Philips Duo 438 323-2PM2 — ⋰' ② 2h 33m ADD 9/93 Ⓑ

Nos. 3 and 5. Sinfonia Concertante, K364/320d[a]. **Stephanie Chase** (vn); [a]**Roger Chase** (va); **Hanover Band/Roy Goodman.** Cala CACD1014 — ⋰' ② 1h 22m DDD 12/93 Ⓑ ✒

Mozart. Serenade No. 7 in D major, K250/248b, "Haffner". March in D major, K249, "Haffner". **Orchestra of the Eighteenth Century/Frans Brüggen.** Philips 432 997-2PH. Recorded in 1991.

⋰' 55m DDD 3/93 ✒

Mozart's *Haffner* Serenade could rightly be considered all things to all men. It has the breadth of a fully-fledged symphony, the soloistic charisma of a violin concerto, the intimacy of chamber music and the celebratory ring of a work written for a specific occasion — which was, in this particular case, the wedding of Elisabeth Haffner, daughter of a wealthy banker and Burgomaster of Salzburg, to Franz Xaver Späth. The so-called *Haffner* Symphony — which Mozart pared down to symphonic proportions from a six-movement serenade — was written for another personage of the same name, and is not musically related to K250. The haughty March in D serves as a splendid overture and sets the tone for the main work's varied eight movements, the fourth of which, a *concertante* Rondo, was transcribed and popularized as a violin solo by Fritz Kreisler (who made a memorable recording of it). Frans Brüggen's recording on period instruments is pure joy. With keenly inflected phrasing, swift tempos, a relatively warm sonority and an abundance of enthusiasm from the players, it leaps into action and maintains a feeling of spontaneity from start to finish. Lucy van Dael (the Orchestra of the Eighteenth Century's concert master) despatches her solos with great agility, and the recording, made at the Anton Philipzaal, The Hague, is splendidly alive. There's a fascinating footnote to the production, too: Frans Brüggen dispenses with cellos and fills the gap between viola and bass with horns. The reasons? In Mozart's time, it was customary to play open-air music (which this is) standing up; furthermore, it was considered ill-mannered to stay seated if higher-ranking persons were standing. So the exchange of horns for cellos is both historically acceptable and aesthetically pleasing.

Additional recommendations ...

Serenade. March. **Pavlo Beznosiuk** (vn); **Amsterdam Baroque/Ton Koopman.** Erato 2292-45436-2 — .ᐧ' 1h 4m DDD 2/90

Complete Edition, Volume 3 — Serenades, Marches and Cassations for Orchestra. Serenades: No. 3 in D major, K185/167a; No. 4 in D major, K203/189b; No. 5 in D major, K204/231a; No. 6 in D major, K239, "Serenata notturna"; No. 7; No. 9 in D major, K320, "Posthorn"; No. 13 in G major, K525, "Eine kleine Nachtmusik". *Marches:* D major, K62; D major, K189/167b; D major, K215/213b; D major, K237/189c; K249; D major, K335/320a No. 1; D major, K335/320a No. 2. *Cassations:* G major, K63; B flat major, K99/63a; D major, K100/62a. Divertimento in D major, K131. Notturno in D major, K286/269a. Galimathias musicum, K32. **Soloists; Academy of St Martin in the Fields/Sir Neville Marriner.** Philips Mozart Edition 422 503-2PME7 — .ᐧ' ⑦ 6h 44m DDD 12/90

New review

Mozart. Serenade No. 10 in B flat major for 13 Wind Instruments, K361/K370a, "Gran Partita". **Sabine Meyer Wind Ensemble.** EMI CDC7 54457-2.

.ᐧ' **47m DDD 7/93**

There are already numerous excellent recordings of this work, and here's another, which for sheer technical accomplishment is at least as good as the best of them. Sabine Meyer's ensemble (she of course plays first clarinet) is marvellously warm and euphonious, and there is not a single note in the whole work that is even marginally off pitch. What perhaps might be missing is any strong feeling about the music. In this very beautiful and very exact performance — the accents, for example, are done with absolute precision, the timing and the weight unfalteringly the same every time — there doesn't seem to be a lot of room for individual expression. The second minuet is taken rather quickly, much faster than the first, and one wonders if that is right; Mozart marked it *Allegretto*, which could well be taken to imply slower, rather than faster, than the norm. The bassoon playing in the middle section is impeccable, shapely as well as virtuoso. There is much fine playing in the variations too — each has a separate track, incidentally— though Sabine Meyer's usually perfect clarinet fails to speak promptly at one point in Variation No. 3 (a retake would have been justified). In sum, however, a very fine if slightly impersonal performance.

Additional recommendations ...

Serenade. **Chamber Orchestra of Europe Wind Soloists/Alexander Schneider.** ASV CDCOE804 — .ᐧ' 52m DDD 4/87 ⁹ₚ Ⓑ
Serenade. **Academy of St Martin in the Fields Wind Ensemble/Sir Neville Marriner.** Philips 412 726-2PH — .ᐧ' 49m DDD 5/87 ⁹ₚ Ⓑ
Orpheus Chamber Orchestra. DG 423 061-2GH — .ᐧ' 51m DDD 1/88 ⁹ₚ Ⓑ
Serenade. Divertimento in F major, K213. **Scottish National Orchestra Wind Ensemble/ Paavo Järvi.** Chandos CHAN8553 — .ᐧ' 59m DDD 5/88 Ⓑ
Serenade. **Orchestra of the Eighteenth Century/Frans Brüggen.** Philips 422 338-2PH — .ᐧ' 51m DDD 4/89 ⁹ₚ Ⓑ
Serenade. **Amadeus Winds/Christopher Hogwood.** L'Oiseau-Lyre 421 437-2OH — .ᐧ' 47m DDD 4/89 ⁹ₚ Ⓑ
Serenade. **Hungarian State Opera Wind Ensemble/Ervin Lukács.** Hungaroton White Label HRC076 — . 51m ADD 10/90 Ⓑ

Mozart. Serenades — No. 11 in E flat major, K375; No. 12 in C minor, K388/384a. **Orpheus Chamber Orchestra.** DG 431 683-2GH. Recorded in 1990.

.ᐧ' **48m DDD 9/91** ⁹ₚ

These two big pieces for wind instruments are well-contrasted although they share the same title. Indeed, the use of a minor key for the four-movement K388 tells us at once that it is no ordinary serenade and certainly not just music for casual entertainment — in fact it is quite stormy in character, and the DG booklet notes go so far as to call it "dramatic and sombre". Why Mozart called it a serenade we do not know: but at any rate it has a tense first movement and a terse finale in variation form, and in between them a minuet with some ingenious counterpoint for oboes and bassoon. As for the E flat major Serenade, K373, this has delicacy as well as expressive qualities (the *Adagio* is notably eloquent), and the finale really dances. Few artists or orchestral bodies who regularly contribute to the record catalogue can claim an unbroken record of success, but the Orpheus is among them. The oboes, clarinets, bassoons and horns of this fine ensemble blend together so well that one's only regret may be the feeling that Mozart himself can never have heard such sensitive playing of this music, and the recording in a New York location is no less worthy of it.

Additional recommendation ...
Wind soloists of the **Chamber Orchestra of Europe/Alexander Schneider.** ASV CDCOE802 — ‥ 47m DDD 5/88 ⁹ₚ

Mozart. Serenade No. 13 in G major, "Eine kleine Nachtmusik". Divertimentos — E flat major, K252/240*a*; D major, K131. **Orpheus Chamber Orchestra.** DG 419 192-2GH.

‥ lh 4m DDD 12/86 ⁹ₚ Ⓑ

There are many worthy recorded performances of Mozart's most famous Serenade, the one that is now universally called *Eine kleine Nachtmusik,* but this one by the string section of the Orpheus Chamber Orchestra has qualities of refinement and alertness, even enthusiasm, that make it rather special. These players clearly enjoy the music, but bring to it a delightful precision as well as the necessary *joie de vivre* and spontaneity, and each of the four movements is beautifully shaped and characterized, so that this very familiar music comes up as fresh as anyone could wish for. The two early divertimentos which accompany the serenade provide a pleasing complement and contrast. Each has a different instrumentation, the one in D (written when Mozart was 16, but sounding more mature) being for flute, oboe, bassoon, four horns and strings while the one in E flat is for just six instruments, these being pairs of oboes, bassoons and horns. Here, too, the Orpheus players are of the highest calibre both technically and artistically and their sound is well captured, as is that of the strings in *Eine kleine Nachtmusik.*

Additional recommendations ...
Eine kleine Nacthmusik. Serenade No. 6 in D major, "Serenata notturna", K239. **Elgar.** *Serenade for Strings in E minor, Op. 20.* **Grieg.** *Holberg Suite, Op. 40.* **Serenata of London.** Pickwick IMP Classics PCD861 — ‥ lh 5m DDD 11/87 Ⓑ
Eine kleine Nachtmusik. Divertimentos — K252/240a; K131. **Berlin Philharmonic Orchestra/ Herbert von Karajan.** DG Mozart Masterpieces 429 805-2GMM — ‥ lh lm ADD 8/90 Ⓑ
Eine kleine Nachtmusik. Serenata notturno. Divertimentos for Strings (Salzburg Symphonies) — No. 1 in D major, K136/125a; No. 2 in B flat major, K137/125b; No. 3 in F major, K138/125c. **I Musici.** Philips Laser Line Classics 432 055-2PM — ‥ lh 4m DDD 2/91 ⁹ₚ Ⓑ
Eine kleine Nachtmusik. Serenata notturna. Notturno in D major, K286/269a. Ein musikalischer Spass, K522. **Vienna Mozart Ensemble/Willi Boskovsky.** Decca Serenata 430 259-2DM — ‥ lh 9m ADD 7/91 ⁹ₚ Ⓑ
Eine kleine Nachtmusik. Overtures — Idomeneo; Die Entführung aus dem Serail; Der Schauspieldirektor; Le nozze di Figaro; Don Giovanni; Così fan tutte; La clemenza di Tito; Die Zauberflöte. **Tafelmusik/ Bruno Weil.** Sony Classical Vivarte SK46695 — ‥ lh DDD 5/92 ⁹ₚ ⁹ₛ Ⓑ ✎
Eine kleine Nachtmusik. **Tchaikovsky.** *Symphony No. 5 in E minor, Op. 64.* **Vienna Philharmonic Orchestra/David Oistrakh.** Orfeo C302921B — ‥ lh 7m ADD 6/93 Ⓑ

Mozart. Divertimentos — B flat major, K287/271*h*; D major, K205/167*a*. **Salzburg Mozarteum Camerata Academica/Sándor Végh.** Capriccio 10 271.

‥ 59m DDD 11/89 ⁹ₚ

Mozart's Divertimento, K287 is a six-movement work cast on quite a large scale, and is scored for two violins, viola, two horns and bass, a combination which presents some difficulties of balance. One solution is to use a full orchestral string section, as did Toscanini and Karajan in their recordings, but this can bring its own problems, for Mozart demands playing of virtuoso standard in this score, and anything less than this is ruthlessly exposed. Sandor Végh's smallish string band is of high quality, and has a pleasantly rounded tone quality. The engineers have managed to contrive a satisfactory balance which sounds not at all unnatural, and the sound quality itself is very good. Végh directs an attractive, neatly-pointed performance of the work, one which steers a middle course between objective classicism and expressive warmth. The

Divertimento, K205, has five movements, but none lasts longer than five minutes, and the work is much shorter and more modest than K287. Scoring in this case is for violin, viola, two horns, bassoon and bass, to provide another difficult but well resolved problem for the engineers. Végh directs another characterful, delightful performance, to round off a very desirable disc.

Additional recommendations ...
K287. F major, K247. **Berne Camerata.** Novalis 150 040-2 — .·*˙ lh 5m DDD 3/90
K205ᵃ; D major, K334/320bᵇ. *March in D major, K290/167abᵃ.* **Franz Liszt Chamber Orchestra/ᵃJános Rolla, ᵇFrigyes Sándor.** Hungaroton White Label HRC080 — .· lh 7m ADD 5/90
Complete Edition, Volume 4 — Divertimentos and Marches. Divertimentos: E flat major, K113; D major, K136/125a; B flat major, K137/125b; F major, K138/125c; K205/167a; F major, K247; D major, K251; K287/271h; D major, K334/320b. *Marches:* F major, K248; D major, K290/167ab; D major, K445/320c. Serenade in G major, K525, "Eine kleine Nachtmusik". Ein musikalischer Spass, K522. **Academy of St Martin in the Fields/Sir Neville Marriner.** Philips Mozart Edition 422 504-2PME5 — .·*˙ ⑤ 4h 3lm DDD 12/90

Mozart. Cassations — G major, K63, "Final-Musik"; B flat major, K99/63a; D major, K100/62a. **Salzburg Chamber Orchestra/Harald Nerat.** Naxos 8 550609. Recorded 1992.
· lh 7m DDD 4/93

Look at the Köchel numbers here and you will rightly guess that these pieces all represent the boy Mozart. Indeed, all of them date from the summer of 1769, when he was just 13 years old. But unlike some of his early music, these pieces are more than just the fluent doodling of a boy wonder and so this disc is well worth investigating. Thus the *Allegro* second movement of the Cassation in G major has genuinely buoyant invention and attractive textures in which two horns stand out, and this attractive movement is followed by a charming little *Andante* in which a plucked-string accompaniment complements a graceful and witty tune. One's praise for this Cassation (the word implies outdoor entertainment music) is matched by enjoyment of the performance. Harald Nerat is a viola player in the famous Salzburg Mozarteum Orchestra, and his experience is evident in the playing of the Chamber Orchestra of the city that was Mozart's birthplace. It has qualities of poise, affection and vitality in the right proportions, and deserves to make friends for this orchestra and conductor. We also hear stylish solo violin playing from Georg Hölscher in the slow fifth movement. The other two cassations are also good value, and although the one in B flat major is less striking than the one discussed above, the one in D major is splendidly vivid. Here we have trumpets and flutes as well as the oboes, horns and strings of the other cassations, and there are attractive wind solos. The recording is excellent, with a pleasing bloom on the string sound, and altogether this is a fine issue which at super-bargain price should not be missed by collectors looking for some different Mozart.

Additional recommendation ...
K63. K99/63a. Adagio and Fugue in C minor, K546. **Salzburg Mozarteum Camerata Academica/Sándor Végh.** Capriccio 10 192 — .·*˙ 5lm DDD 3/88

Mozart. ORCHESTRAL WORKS. ᵃArvid Engegard (vn); **Salzburg Mozarteum Camerata Academica/Sándor Végh.** Capriccio 10 302. Recorded 1988-89.
Serenade No. 3 in D major, K185/167aᵃ. March in D major, K189/167b. Five Contretanze, K609. Notturno in D major, K286/269a.
.·*˙ lh 6m DDD 10/91 ⁹P

The main work here is the big Serenade, K185, commissioned by the Antretter family of Salzburg and first performed in August 1773 to celebrate the end of the university year. Like other works of its kind it incorporates a miniature two-movement violin concerto within a loose symphonic framework: an *Andante* designed to display the instrument's powers of cantilena, and a brisk *contredanse* with plenty of opportunities for ear-catching virtuosity. There is also a violin solo in the glum D minor trio of the second minuet. But perhaps the finest movements are the sensuous A major *Andante grazioso*, with its *concertante* writing for flutes and horns, and the rollicking 6/8 finale, preceded by an unexpectedly searching *Adagio* introduction. The

performance by Végh and his hand-picked Salzburg players is affectionate, rhythmically alive and beautifully detailed, with an imaginative, subtly coloured solo violin contribution from Arvid Engegard. The tempo and specific character of each movement is shrewdly judged: the two minuets, for example, are vividly differentiated, the first properly swaggering, with a nice lilt in the trio, the second spruce and quick-witted. Only in the finale is Végh arguably too leisurely, though here too the style and rhythmic lift of the playing are infectious. Végh follows the serenade with deft, colourful readings of five contredanses from Mozart's last year and a beguiling performance of the *Notturno* for four orchestras, exquisitely imagined open-air music, with its multiple echoes fading into the summer night. All in all a delectable disc, offering a varied concert of Mozart's lighter music performed with exceptional flair and finesse. The recording, too, is outstandingly vivid, with the spatial effects in the *Notturno* beautifully managed.

Mozart. ORCHESTRAL WORKS. **Orpheus Chamber Orchestra.** DG 429 783-2GH. Recorded in 1989.
Ein musikalischer Spass, K522. *Contredanses* — C major, K587, "Der Sieg vom Helden Koburg"; D major, K534, "Das Donnerwetter"; C major, K535, "La Bataille"; G major, K610, "Les filles malicieuses"; E flat major, K607/605a, "Il trionfo delle donne". Gallimathias musicum, K32. *German Dances* — K567; K605; C major, K611, "Die Leyerer". March in D major, K335 No. 1.

1h 9m   DDD   4/91

After all the Mozart with which we were bombarded during his bicentenary year, it is a mark of his greatness that an issue such as this comes up with an incomparably engaging freshness. The celebrated *Musikalischer Spass* ("Musical Joke") which begins the disc is never so crudely funny that it wears thin, but make no mistake, the jokes are there in just about every passage, whether they are parodying third-rate music or wobbly playing, and oddly enough sound still more amusing when the performance is as stylishly flexible as this one by the conductorless Orpheus Chamber Orchestra. One of the tunes here (that of the finale on track four) is that of the BBC's *Horse of the Year* programme — and what a good tune it is, even at the umpteenth repetition as the hapless composer finds himself unable to stop. The rest of this programme is no less delightful and includes miniature pieces supposedly describing a thunderstorm, a battle, a hurdy-gurdy man and a sleigh-ride (with piccolo and sleigh-bells). There is also a *Gallimathias musicum*, a ballet suite of dainty little dances averaging less than a minute in length, which Mozart is supposed to have written at the age of ten. Whatever the case this CD, subtitled "A Little Light Music", provides proof of his genius, though differently from his acknowledged masterpieces. The recording is as refined as anyone could wish yet has plenty of impact.

New review
Mozart. EARLY SYMPHONIES **The English Concert/Trevor Pinnock.** Archiv Produktion 437 792-2AH4. Recorded in 1992.
No. 1 in E flat major, K16; No. 4 in D major, K19; No. 5 in B flat major, K22; No. 6 in F major, K43; No. 7 in D major, K45; No. 7*a* in G major, "Alte Lambach", K45*a*/KAnh221; No. 8 in D major, K48; No. 9 in C major, K73; No. 10 in G major, K74; No. 11 in D major, K84/K73*q*; No. 12 in G major, K110/K75*b*; No. 13 in F major, K112; No. 14 in A major, K114; No. 15 in G major, K124; No. 42 in F major, K75; No. 43 in F major, K76/K42*a*; No. 44 in D major, K81/K731; No. 45 in D major, K95/K73*n*; No. 46 in C major, K96/K111*b*; No. 47 in D major, K97/K73*m*; No. 55 in B flat major, K45*b*; F major, KAnh223/K19*a*; B flat major, K74*g*/KAnh216/C11.03.

④   4h 57m   DDD   11/93

Pinnock's Mozart symphony cycle is only the second to use period instruments, and the performances on these four discs are outstandingly vital and stylish, making the most persuasive case for this music. Hogwood's pioneering period cycle from the early 1980s, with its revelations of articulation and sonority, is often exciting, but suffers from intermittent roughness of execution and an often stiff, austere approach to the slow movements. In both these respects Pinnock and The English Concert are far preferable, reflecting the advance in all facets of period performance in the intervening decade. The string sound is recognizably 'authentic' in its bright edge and restrained use of vibrato, but is altogether smoother, sweeter and more subtly coloured than on the Hogwood discs. Ensemble is more polished, tuning (especially of the oboes) far more precise. And Pinnock is not only more elegant and affectionate in the slow movements, but often shapes the *Allegros* more purposefully, with more considered phrasing and surer long-term control. The first contains six works (Köchel Nos. 16, 19, 19*a*, 22, 43 and 45*a*) written between 1764, when Mozart was eight, and late 1767, just before his twelfth birthday. Though the invention here is often rudimentary, Mozart already reveals himself as a precocious musical mimic, adeptly manipulating the clichés of the contemporary *galant* style. Textures are, as always, ideally transparent, and violins divided on opposite sides so that the many antiphonal passages make their proper effect. The second disc covers the years 1768-70, and begins with Mozart's first symphony with trumpets and drums, K45, unremarkable in its actual ideas but shrewdly laid out for maximum orchestral brilliance. Most of the works on the third disc were written on Mozart's first two Italian journeys, in the spring and summer of 1770 and the autumn of 1771; and they are distinctly Italianate in their harmonic and textural simplicity and easy *buffo* brilliance. Not surprisingly, the final disc, with five symphonies from 1771 and early 1772, contains the most consistently memorable music in this set. Finest of all these symphonies is the very Viennese K114 in A major, a key that invariably drew something out of the ordinary from Mozart. The first movement, with its luminous textures (high horns complemented by flutes rather than oboes), has a particularly expressive second theme in imitation, shaped by Pinnock with a vocal eloquence. This superb set, recorded with truthful immediacy, becomes the prime recommendation for these juvenile symphonies.

Additional recommendations ...

Complete Edition, Volume 1 — Early Symphonies: No. 1 in E flat major, K16; No. 4 in D major, K19; F major, KAnh223/19*a*; No. 5 in B flat major, K22; No. 6 in F major, K43; No. 7 in D major, K45; G major, Kdeest, "Neue Lambacher" (attrib. L. Mozart); No. 7*a* in G major, KAnh221/45*a*, "Alte Lambacher"; (No. 55) in B flat major, KAnh214/45*b*; No. 8 in D major, K48; No. 9 in C major, K73; No. 10 in G major, K74; (No. 42) in F major, K75; (No. 43) in F major, K76/42*a*; (No. 44) in D major, K81/73*l*; No. 11 in D major, K84/73*q*; (No. 45) in D major, K95/73*n*; (No. 46) in C major, K96/111*b*; (No. 47) in D major, K97/73*m*; No. 12 in G major, K110/75*b*; No. 13 in F major, K112; No. 14 in A major, K114 (with additional alternative minuet); No. 15 in G major, K124; No. 16 in C major, K128; No. 17 in G major, K129; No. 18 in F major, K130; No. 19 in E flat major, K132 (with additional alternative slow movement); No. 20 in D major, K133; (No. 50) in D major, K141*a* (K161 and K163); (No. 48) in D major, K111*a* (K111 and K120); (No. 51) in D major, K207*a* (K196 and K121); (No. 52) in C major, K213*c* (K208 and K102). Minuet in A major, K61*g* No. 1. **Academy of St Martin in the Fields/Sir Neville Marriner.** Philips Mozart Edition 422 501-2PME6 — .·' ⑥ 6h 39m ADD/DDD 12/90

Complete Edition, Volume 2 — Middle and Late Symphonies: No. 21 in A major, K134; No. 22 in C major, K162; No. 23 in D major, K181/162*b*; No. 24 in B flat major, K182/173*dA*; No. 25 in G minor, K183/173*dB*; No. 26 in E flat major, K184/161*a*; No. 27 in G major, K199/161*b*; No. 28 in C major, K200/189*k*; No. 29 in A major, K201/186*a*; No. 30 in D major, K202/186*b*; No. 31 in D major, K297/300*a*, "Paris" (with additional alternative slow movement); No. 32 in G major, K318; No. 33 in B flat major, K319; No. 34 in C major, K338; No. 35 in D major, K385, "Haffner"; No. 36 in C major, K425, "Linz"; No. 38 in D major, K504, "Prague"; No. 39 in E flat major, K453; No. 40 in G minor, K550; No. 41 in C major, K551, "Jupiter". Minuet in C major, K409/383*f*. Adagio maestoso in G major, K444/425*a*. **Academy of St Martin in the Fields/Sir Neville Marriner.** Philips Mozart Edition 422 502-2PME6 — .·' ⑥ 6h 42m ADD 12/90

CD80256 — No. 1 in E flat major, K16; F major, K19a; No. 4 in D major, K19; No. 5 in B flat major, K22; No. 6 in F major, K43; B flat major, KAhn214/45b; No. 7 in D major, K45. CD80272 — No. 8 in D major, K48; No. 9 in C major, K73/75a; D major, K731/81; D major, K73m/97; D major, K75n/95; D major, K73n/95; D major, K73q/84. CD80273 — No. 10 in G major, K74/73p; C major, K111b/96; F major, K75; G major, K75b/110; No. 13 in F major, K112. **Prague Chamber Orchestra/Sir Charles Mackerras.** Telarc CD80256, CD80272/3 — .·'' ③ 1h 13m 1h 1m 58m DDD 11/91

8 550113 (1h 5m): No. 25 in G minor, K183/173dB; No. 32 in G major, K318; No. 41 in C major, K551, "Jupiter". 8 550119 (1h 9m): No. 29 in A major, K201/186a; No. 30 in D major, K202/186b; No. 38 in D major, K504, "Prague". 8 550164 (1h 1m): No. 28 in C major, K200/189k; No. 31 in D major, K297/300a, "Paris"; No. 40 in G minor, K550. 8 550186 (1h 2m): No. 34 in C major, K338; No. 35 in D major, K385, "Haffner"; No. 39 in E flat major, K543. 8 550264 (1h 5m): No. 27 in G major, K199/161b; No. 33 in B flat major, K319; No. 36 in C major, K425, "Linz". 8 550299 (1h 2m): No. 40 in G minor, K550; No. 41 in C major, K551, "Jupiter". **Capella Istropolitana/Barry Wordsworth.** Naxos (as numbered above) — . ⑥

Nos. 21, 23, 24 and 27. **Amsterdam Baroque Orchestra/Ton Koopman.** Erato 2292-45544-2 — .·'' 53m DDD 2/91 ✍

Nos. 31, 33 and 34. **Prague Chamber Orchestra/Sir Charles Mackerras.** Telarc CD80190 — .·'' 1h 5m DDD 3/90

Mozart. SYMPHONIES. **Amsterdam Baroque Orchestra/Ton Koopman.** Erato 2292-45714-2. Recorded 1990-91.
No. 17 in G major, K129; No. 18 in F major, K130; No. 19 in E flat major, K132; No. 22 in C major, K162; No. 32 in G major, K318.

.·'' **1h 9m DDD 8/92** ♩P ✍

Except for No. 32, all the works here date from 1772-3, Mozart's most prolific period as a symphonist. Symphonies K129 and K162 are in three movements only, the former a bustling, lightly scored piece, elegantly and wittily developed, the latter a more brilliant, ceremonial C major work. Symphonies K130 and K132 both include a minuet (both trios, curiously, have an archaic, quasi-modal flavour) and feature a quartet of horns. Incidentally, Mozart composed alternative slow movements for K132, both recorded here so you can programme your own version; the original *Andante* opens with a Gregorian plainsong melody, and later quotes a medieval German carol — some private joke may be intended here. With his brilliant period-instrument band, Koopman gives readings of immense flair and verve. Faster movements are fiery and inspiriting, with sharp dynamic contrasts, yet always allow space for telling expressive detail and the lithe, springing bass lines ensure that the minuets and the jig finales truly dance. Slow movements tend to be more leisurely than in most period performances, and are shaped with finesse and a keen ear for Mozart's subtleties of texture. But the most arresting feature of these performances are the pungent, colourful sonorities Koopman draws from his Amsterdam players: in both K130 and K132 the four horns, superlatively played, cut through the texture with thrilling effect, while the raw, rasping horns and trumpets and the incisive, crisply articulated strings lift the apparently conventional outer movements of K162 right off the page. Here and there Koopman's phrasing can sound a bit precious; and some may feel that the string section is too slender for K318, with its rich scoring and Mannheim-inspired orchestral effects. But these are uncommonly stylish, physically exciting performances, spaciously and transparently recorded; and they could well come as a revelation to those who still resist period instruments.

Additional recommendation ...
No. 18. No. 19. No. 20 in D major, K133; No. 21 in A major, K134; No. 22; No. 23 in D major, K181/162b; No. 24 in B flat major, K182/173dA; D major, K135; (No. 50) in D major, K141a/161-3; No. 26 in E flat major, K161a/184; No. 27 in G major, K199/161b. **Academy of Ancient Music/Jaap Schröder** (vn) with **Christopher Hogwood** (hpd). L'Oiseau-Lyre 417 592-2OH3 — .·'' ③ 2h 56m DDD 10/87 ✍

Mozart. SYMPHONIES. **The English Concert/Trevor Pinnock** (hpd). Archiv Produktion 431 679-2AH. Recorded in 1990.
No. 25 in G minor, K183/173dB; No. 26 in E flat major, K184/161a; No. 29 in A major, K201/186a.

.·'' **53m DDD 7/91** ✍

The bicentenary year brought so many Mozart issues (and reissues) that there is a danger that with its passing some of them may quickly be forgotten. However, this one has enough personality to keep its place in the catalogue, and that quality comes across instantly at the start of Symphony No. 26, which is played first. Admittedly the marking is *molto presto*, but even so the listener may be startled by the brisk pace and the near-aggressive vigour of this sound. This is a performance with period instruments (note the veiled string tone in quiet passages), yet there is also something modern about the spotless efficiency of it all and one wonders whether Mozart heard or intended performances like this and if Trevor Pinnock's penchant for pace and sheer energy is sometimes excessive. Set aside that doubt, however, and one must admire the polish and ensemble of this playing, and make no mistake, there is sensitivity too, as the *Andante* shows. This miniature symphony lasts less than nine minutes and its three movements are played without a break. Predictably, Pinnock brings out all the "storm and stress" drama of the G minor Symphony, but there is mystery too in the strangely gliding slow movement and the quiet start of the finale. The elegantly genial A major is nicely shaped, too, and only in the finale might one wish for more space for the music to sound. A vivid and well balanced recording complements this expert playing.

Additional recommendation ...
No. 24 in B flat major, K182/173dA. No. 26. No. 27 in G major, K199/161b. No. 30 in D major, K202/186b. **Prague Chamber Orchestra/Sir Charles Mackerras.** Telarc CD80186 — ,·˙
58m DDD 8/89

Mozart. Symphonies — No. 25 in G minor, K183/173*d*B; No. 28 in C major, K200/189*k*; No. 29 in A major, K201/186*a*. **Prague Chamber Orchestra/Sir Charles Mackerras.** Telarc CD80165.

,·˙ **1h 18m   DDD   9/88**

Here are three symphonies from Mozart's late teens, written in his native Salzburg, in crisply articulated performances. The first of them is a *Sturm und Drang* piece in a key that the composer reserved for moods of agitation. Mackerras takes the orchestra through the big opening *Allegro con brio* of No. 25 with drive and passion, although it is unlikely that Mozart would have expected a Salzburg orchestra in the 1770s to play as fast as this skilful body of Czech players. The gentle *Andante* comes therefore as a relief, though here too Mackerras keeps a firm rhythmic grasp on the music, and indeed a taut metrical aspect is a feature of all three symphonies as played here, so that minuets dance briskly and purposefully and finales bustle. However, the sunlit warmth of the beautiful A major Symphony, No. 29, comes through and the bracing view of the other two symphonies is a legitimate one, though giving little or nothing in the direction of expressive lingering, much less towards sentimental indulgence. The Prague Chamber Orchestra is an expert ensemble, not over-large for this style of music and the recording is admirably clear although a little reverberant. A well-filled disc.

Additional recommendations ...
No. 27 in G major, K199/161b; No. 28; No. 34 in C major, K338. **English Sinfonia/Sir Charles Groves.** Pickwick IMP Classics PCD933 — ,·˙ 1h 3m DDD 3/90
Nos. 28 and 29. No. 35 in D major, K385, "Haffner". **Berlin Philharmonic Orchestra/ Claudio Abbado.** Sony Classical SK48063 — ,·˙ 1h 14m DDD 3/92 Ⓑ
No. 29; No. 33 in B flat major, K319. **English Baroque Soloists/John Eliot Gardiner.** Philips 412 736-2PH — ,·˙ 44m DDD 8/86 Ⓑ ✎
No. 29. No. 35 in D major, K385, "Haffner". No. 40 in G minor, K550. **Academy of St Martin in the Fields/Sir Neville Marriner.** Philips Silver Line 420 486-2PM — ,·˙ 1h 10m DDD 6/87 Ⓑ
No. 29. No. 32 in G major, K318; No. 33. **English Sinfonia/Sir Charles Groves.** Pickwick IMP Classics PCD922 — ,·˙ 1h 1m DDD 11/91 Ⓑ

New review
Mozart. SYMPHONIES. Academy of St Martin in the Fields/Sir Neville Marriner. EMI Digital Twins CZS7 67564-2. Items marked [a] from CDC7 49864-2 (12/89), [b] CDC7 49073-2 (3/88), [c] EL270401-1 (12/86).
No. 28 in C major, K200/K189*k*[a]; No. 29 in A major, K201/K186*a*[a]; No. 30 in D major, K202/K186*b*[b]; No. 40 in G minor, K550[b]; No. 41 in C major, K551, "Jupiter"[c].

,·˙ ② **2h 7m   DDD   6/93**   ⁹[P] Ⓑ

These are cultured and sensitive readings, beautifully prepared and snappily executed; they do not boast the multifarious points of detail that some rivals underline so effectively, but then Marriner is not that sort of conductor. Heard without reference to alternatives, these are deeply satisfying performances and will provide an admirable introduction for those who have yet to discover these wonderful works. Finding an interpretative Mean has its advantages, and Marriner's discreet middle course does indeed pay some rewarding dividends. Firstly, there's the matter of blending textures which, in the G minor especially, adds warmth to the music's inbuilt pensiveness. There's also the important repeat in the first section of the *Jupiter's* finale, although a give-away studio noise proves it to be a re-run of the take for the exposition. The acoustic is generous, airy and accommodating, which is especially helpful for the woodwinds.

| Symphony No. 28 is given a sprightly reading, with the welcome addition of the first movement

repeat. Marriner keeps No. 30's affecting *Andantino* sensibly *con moto*, and proves admirably adept at delineating the intertwining string lines in the first movement of No. 29.

Mozart. Symphonies — No. 35 in D major, K385, "Haffner"[a]; No. 36 in C major, K425, "Linz"[a]. Rondo in B flat major, K269[b]. [a]**Bavarian Radio Symphony Orchestra/Rafael Kubelík;** [b]**Saint Paul Chamber Orchestra/Pinchas Zukerman** (vn). CBS Masterworks CD44647.

⟐ **57m DDD 9/89** Ⓑ

These are very satisfying accounts of the *Linz* and *Haffner* Symphonies. Kubelík's ability to project a strong sense of architecture and formal balance is remarkable, and this is reflected on the small scale too, with melodic phrases beautifully shaped and refined. The outer movements of both works are consistently well paced with plenty of rhythmic drive, vitality and drama, with Kubelík never allowing his grip on the symphonic argument to falter or slacken. His unfussy approach in the *Andante* of the *Haffner* allows the pastoral freshness of this movement to surface with ease, and in the *Menuetto* much is made of the contrast between loud and soft, emphasizing the Haydnesque qualities of this movement. The Bavarian orchestra respond well to Kubelík's approach with playing that is warm, full-toned and very assured. The disc also contains an extra bonus in the shape of the *Rondo* in B flat, originally written as an alternative finale to the Violin Concerto No. 1, K207, and is played here in a very attractive performance. The recorded sound has warmth and presence.

Additional recommendations ...

No. 32; No. 33 in B flat major, K319; D major ("Posthorn Serenade"), K320; No. 34 in C major, K338. Nos. 35 with March in D major, K385a (K408 No. 2) and 36. (No. 52) in C major, K213c (K208 and K102); D major (Serenade), K248b (K250); **Academy of Ancient Music/Jaap Schröder** (vn) with **Christopher Hogwood** (hpd). L'Oiseau-Lyre 421 104-2OH3 — ⟐ ③ 3h 6m ADD 4/88 Ⓑ ✍

No. 32 in G major, K318; Nos. 35 and 36. **Scottish Chamber Orchestra/Jukka-Pekka Saraste.** Virgin Classics Virgo VJ7 59679-2 — ⟐ 1h 9m DDD 6/88 Ⓑ

Nos. 34 and 35. No. 39 in E flat major, K453. **London Mozart Players/Jane Glover.** ASV CDDCA615 — ⟐ 1h 14m DDD 7/88 Ⓑ

Nos. 32; Nos. 35 and 36. **English Baroque Soloists/John Eliot Gardiner.** Philips 422 419-2PH — ⟐ 1h 13m DDD 9/89 Ⓑ ✍

Nos. 35 and 36, No. 38 in D major, K504, "Prague". No. 39. No. 40 in G minor, K550. No. 41 in C major, K551, "Jupiter". **Columbia Symphony Orchestra/Bruno Walter.** CBS Maestro CD45676 — ⟐ ② 2h 34m ADD 7/90 Ⓑ

Mozart. Symphonies — No. 36 in C major, K425, "Linz"; No. 38 in D major, K504, "Prague". **Prague Chamber Orchestra/Sir Charles Mackerras.** Telarc CD80148.

⟐ **1h 6m DDD 10/87** Ⓑ

Mozart wrote his *Linz* Symphony in great haste (five days to be precise), but needless to say there is little evidence of haste in the music itself, except perhaps that the first movement has all the exuberance of a composer writing on the wing of inspiration. The slow movement with its siciliano rhythm certainly has no lack of serenity, although it has drama too. The *Prague* Symphony was written only three years later, yet Mozart's symphonic style had matured and the work is altogether more ambitious and substantial. A glorious spaciousness surrounds Sir Charles's performances. The recording venue is reverberant, yet there is no loss of detail, and the fullness of the sound helps to add weight to climaxes without going beyond the bounds of volume that Mozart might have expected. Sir Charles captures the joy and high spirits that these symphonies embody without in any way undermining their greatness. This vivacity is emphasized by the east-European sound of the Prague Chamber Orchestra, with the out-of-doors timbre of its winds which provides a pleasing contrast both with those of the standard British and Germanic orchestras and specialist, authentic ensembles. Mackerras does, however, adopt some aspects of the modern approach to Mozart performance: he includes harpsichord continuo, his minuets are taken trippingly, one-to-a-bar, and he prefers bowing that is crisper, more detached, and pointed. Phrasing and articulation are taken with a natural grace and without overemphasis, dynamics being graded to provide drama at the right moments. The very rightness of the result is recommendation enough.

Additional recommendations ...

No. 31 in D major, K300a, "Paris" (first and second versions). No. 35 in D major, K385, "Haffner" (second version). No. 38. No. 39 in E flat major, K543. No. 40 in G minor, K550 (first version). No. 41 in C major, K551, "Jupiter". **Academy of Ancient Music/Jaap Schröder** (vn) with **Christopher Hogwood** (hpd). L'Oiseau-Lyre 421 085-2OH3 — ⏺ ③ 3h 11m DDD 9/88 ⌁

Nos. 31 and 38. **English Sinfonia/Sir Charles Groves.** Pickwick IMP Classics PCD892 — ⏺ 55m DDD 9/88 ⓆP

No. 38. *Le Nozze di Figaro — Overture.* **Orchestra of the Eighteenth Century/Franz Brüggen.** Philips 426 231-2PH — ⏺ 42m DDD 2/90 Ⓑ ⌁

Nos. 38 and 39. **Bavarian Radio Symphony Orchestra/Rafael Kubelík.** CBS CD44648 — ⏺ 56m DDD 2/90 Ⓑ

Nos. 38 and 39. **Sinfonia Varsovia/Sir Yehudi Menuhin.** Virgin Classics VC7 59561-2 — ⏺ 56m DDD 3/90 Ⓑ

Nos. 38 and 39. **English Baroque Soloists/John Eliot Gardiner.** Philips 426 283-2PH — ⏺ 1h 6m DDD 2/91 Ⓑ ⌁

No. 39. ***Beethoven.*** *Symphony No. 2 in D major, Op. 36.* **Orchestra of the Eighteenth Century/Frans Brüggen.** Philips 422 389-2PH — ⏺ 1h 3m DDD 6/89 Ⓑ

Key to symbols

Price	Quantity/ availability	Timing	Recording mode	Review date
⏺	② ②	1h 23m	DDD	6/88

Mozart. Symphonies — No. 40 in G minor, K550; No. 41 in C major, K551, "Jupiter". **English Chamber Orchestra/Jeffrey Tate.** EMI CDC7 47147-2. From EL270154-1 (2/85).

⏺ **1h 4m DDD 7/85** Ⓑ

Jeffrey Tate's approach to both these works is fresh and vigorous and, while he has obviously laboured long and hard over these scores, there isn't the faintest suggestion of contrivance or self-conscious novelty-seeking. His lucid articulation and attention to detail give the music a distinctive textural clarity. There is a monumental quality about these interpretations but this by no means precludes expressive intimacy, for human interest is there too. Just listening to this sportive, yet exultant performance of the finale of the *Jupiter*, with its dazzling contrapuntal devices, the listener is prompted to recall that Mozart's greatness lay so much in his ability to rise above his personal misery to create music that, whilst profoundly meaningful, could still retain a strong element of childlike playfulness. The playing of the English Chamber Orchestra is a constant delight, and the recording is admirably clear and realistically balanced.

Additional recommendations ...

No. 40. ***Beethoven.*** *Symphony No. 1 in C major, Op. 21.* **Orchestra of the Eighteenth Century/Frans Brüggen.** Philips 416 329-2PH — ⏺ DDD 7/86 Ⓑ ⌁

No. 40. ***Haydn.*** *No. 44 in E minor, "Trauer".* **St John's Smith Square Orchestra/John Lubbock.** Pickwick IMP Red Label PCD820 — ⏺ DDD 8/86 Ⓑ

Nos. 40 and 41. **Prague Chamber Orchestra/Sir Charles Mackerras.** Telarc CD80139 — ⏺ 1h 11m DDD 5/87 Ⓑ

No. 41. ***Beethoven.*** *Symphony No. 2 in D major, Op. 36.* **Royal Philharmonic Orchestra/ Sir Thomas Beecham.** EMI Studio CDM7 69811-2 — ⏺ 1h 2m ADD 2/89 Ⓑ ▲

Nos. 40 and 41. **Bavarian Radio Symphony Orchestra/Rafael Kubelík.** CBS Masterworks CD44649 — ⏺ 58m DDD 9/89 Ⓑ

Nos. 40 and 41. **Sinfonia Varsovia/Sir Yehudi Menuhin.** Virgin Classics VC7 59564-2 — ⏺ 58m DDD 3/90 Ⓑ

Nos. 40 and 41. **Cleveland Orchestra/George Szell.** CBS Maestro CD42538 — ⏺ 53m ADD 5/90 Ⓑ ▲

No. 40. *Eine kleine Nachtmusik.* ***Haydn.*** *Cello Concerto in D major.* **Lynn Harrell** (vc); **Academy of St Martin in the Fields/Sir Neville Marriner.** EMI CDM7 64448-2 — ⏺ 1h 5m ADD

Nos. 40 and 41. **English Baroque Soloists/John Eliot Gardiner.** Philips 426 315-2PH —
.·' Ih I5m DDD II/92 Ⓑ ✐

Mozart. COMPLETE EDITION, Volume 14 — PIANO QUINTET, QUARTETS, TRIOS, etc. [a]**Aurèle Nicolet** (fl); [ac]**Heinz Holliger** (ob); [a]**Eduard Brunner,** [b]**Jack Brymer** (cls); [a]**Hermann Baumann** (hn); [a]**Klaus Thunemann** (bn); [cd]**Bruno Hoffmann** (glass harmonica); [b]**Patrick Ireland,** [c]**Karl Schouten,** [e]**Bruno Giuranna** (vas); [c]**Jean Decroos** (vc); [ef]**Beaux Arts Trio** (Isidore Cohen, vn; Bernard Greenhouse, vc; Menahem Pressler, pf); [a]**Alfred Brendel,** [b]**Stephen Kovacevich** (pfs). Philips Mozart Edition 422 514-2PME5. Quintet in E flat major for Piano and Wind, K452[a] (from 420 182-2PH, 8/87). Clarinet Trio in E flat major, K498, "Kegelstatt"[b] (6500 073, 2/71). Adagio and Rondo in C minor, K617[c] (9500 397, 5/78). Adagio in C major, K356/617a[d]. Piano Quartets[e] — No. 1 in G minor, K478; No. 2 in E flat major, K493 (both from 410 391-1PH, 10/84). Piano Trios[f] — B flat major, K254; D minor, K442 (cpted. Stadler and Marguerre); G major, K496; B flat major, K502; E major, K542; C major, K548; G major, K564 (all from 422 079-2PH3, 11/88).

.·' Ⓢ **4h 34m ADD/DDD 9/91**

These recordings come from different locations and dates, ranging from 1969 to 1987. Four discs out of the five offer the two piano quartets and seven piano trios, played by the Beaux Arts Trio who are joined in the quartets by the viola player Bruno Giuranna; these are clearly the centrepiece of the issue and the playing of this fine ensemble is strongly characterful yet thoughtful. These are alert, direct and yet refined performances and earn only praise, although the recording in Philips's favoured Swiss location of La-Chaux-de-Fonds could have placed a little more distance between the players and the listener (we also hear the odd intake of breath). But otherwise this clear sound suits the music, and Menahem Pressler's piano tone is well captured. The D minor Trio which ends the series is not wholly authentic, being mainly Maximilian Stadler's compilation from existing material found by Mozart's widow Constanze after his death. Before we come to the piano quartets and piano trios, the first disc also has important works in fine performances in which Alfred Brendel and Heinz Holliger are just two of the artists involved (the Quintet for piano and wind was among the composer's favourite works). The first disc also offers two pieces featuring the ravishing sound of the glass harmonica (musical glasses), which is played by its leading exponent, Bruno Hoffmann, and the solo *Adagio* in C major is quite ethereally beautiful if rather closely recorded. This unique instrument is usefully described and illustrated in the booklet.

Additional recommendations ...
Piano Quartets Nos. 1 and 2. **Malcolm Bilson** (fp); **Elizabeth Wilcock** (vn); **Jan Schlapp** (va); **Timothy Mason** (vc). Archiv Produktion 423 404-2AH — .·' Ih Im DDD 3/89 ✐
Piano Quartets Nos. 1 and 2. **Mozartean Players.** Harmonia Mundi HMU90 7018 — .·' Ih 4m DDD 3/91
Piano Trios — K496; K502; K542; K548; K564. Divertimento in B flat major, K254. **Trio Fontenay.** Teldec 2292-46439-2 — .·' Ⓩ 2h 9m DDD II/91
Piano Trios — K496, K502, K542, K548, K564. Divertimento, K254. **Mozartean Players.** Harmonia Mundi HMU90 7033/4 — .·' Ⓩ 2h 16m DDD 8/93 ⁹ₚ ✐

Mozart. COMPLETE EDITION, Volume 11 — STRING QUINTETS. **Arthur Grumiaux, Arpad Gérecz** (vns); **Georges Janzer, Max Lesueur** (vas); **Eva Czako** (vc). Philips Mozart Edition 422 511-2PME3. From 6747 107 (1/76). Recorded in 1973. B flat major, K174; C minor, K406/516b; C major, K515; G minor, K516; D major, K593; E flat major, K614.

.·' Ⓩ **2h 50m ADD 9/91** ⁹ₚ

Of the six works which comprise Mozart's complete *oeuvre* for string quintet, that in B flat major, K174, is an early composition, written at the age of 17. It is a well-made, enjoyable work, but not a great deal more than that. The C minor work, K406, is an arrangement by Mozart of his Serenade for six wind instruments, K398. It is difficult not to feel that the original is more effective, since the music seems to sit a little uncomfortably on string instruments. But the remaining four works, written in the last four years of Mozart's life, are a different matter. The last string quintets from Mozart's pen were extraordinary works, and the addition of the second viola seems to have encouraged him to still greater heights. It has been suggested that Mozart wrote K515 and K516 to show King Friedrich Wilhelm II of Prussia that he was a better composer of string quintets than Boccherini, whom the King had retained as chamber music composer to his court. There was no response, so he offered these two quintets for sale with the K406 arrangement to make up the usual set of three. K593 and K614 were written in the last year of his life. Arthur Grumiaux and his colleagues recorded their survey in 1973. Refinement is perhaps the word that first comes to mind in discussing these performances, which are affectionate yet controlled by a cool, intelligent sensitivity. The recordings have been well transferred, the quality is warm and expansive and Grumiaux's tone, in particular, is a delight to the ear but all the playing is alert and stylish. In all, this Philips release is one to earn a strong recommendation, offering as it does Mozart playing of fine quality allied to very decent sound.

Additional recommendations ...
K515. K593. **Simon Whistler** (va); **Salomon Quartet.** Hyperion CDA66431 — .⁚' lh 6m DDD
11/91 🖋

K516. K614. **Simon Whistler** (va); **Salomon Quartet.** Hyperion CDA66432 — .⁚' lh 4m DDD
11/91 🖋

New review
Mozart. String Quintets — D major, K593; E flat major, K614. **Hausmusik** (Monica Huggett; Pavlo Beznosiuk, vns; Roger Chase; Simon Whistler, vas; Richard Lester, vc). EMI Reflexe CDC7 54876-2.

.⁚' 58m DDD 2/94 ‎ ◌S 🖋

The particular quality of the textures in Mozart's late chamber music makes it good material for players on period instruments with light bows. Indeed one of the chief pleasures that this CD has to offer lies in the clarity of the sound and the readiness with which the ear can pick up the subtleties. Listen, for example, to those dotted-rhythm frolickings in the first movement of the D major work, and then the pseudo-horncall passages that follow; Monica Huggett's deft bow-work in the finale makes it especially alive and clear. The E flat Quintet too benefits, perhaps still more: this isn't one of Mozart's deepest works, but it does have some extraordinary sonorities, demanding rapid and light bowing, and on modern instruments the sound is apt to thicken and grow heavier than Mozart probably intended. Some of the quicksilvery effects in the second-subject material are quite remarkable here. There are, however, some moments at which these performances don't seem to go much below the surface of the music. Time and again in these late works Mozart builds towards an expressive climax by repetition, varied in some way, of an idea or a series of ideas, and these players rarely seem to permit themselves to let the music intensify at such moments. However, throughout the performances the players listen carefully to each other and produce some nice touches of timing. The first-movement second repeats here are particularly welcome, by the way, as they incorporate subtle extra musical links which are lost in the generality of performances. Attractive and fascinating listening, then, if not the most searching performances, expressively speaking. The recording is a model of clarity.

Mozart. COMPLETE EDITION, Volume 12 — STRING QUARTETS. **Quartetto Italiano** (Paolo Borciani, Elisa Pegreffi, vns; Piero Farulli, va; Franco Rossi, vc). Philips Mozart Edition 422 512-2PME8. Recorded 1966-73.
G major, K80/73f; D major, K155/134a; G major, K156/134b (with additional original Adagio); C major, K157 (all from 6500 142, 12/71); F major, K158; B flat major, K159; E flat major, K160/159a; F major, K168 (6500 172, 12/72); A major, K169; C major, K170; E flat major, K171; B flat major, K172; D minor, K173 (6747 097, 9/74); G major, K387; D minor, K421/417b (SAL3632, 10/67); E flat major, K428/421b; B flat major, K458, "Hunt" (SAL3633, 10/67); A major, K464; C major, K465, "Dissonance" (SAL3634, 10/67); D major, K499; D major, K575 (6500 241, 7/72); B flat major, K589; F major, K590 (6500 225, 7/73).

.⁚' ⑧ 7h 54m ADD 8/91 ‎ ◌P

These are classic performances which have won praise ever since they began to appear back in 1967. Admittedly, a little allowance has to be made for the sound since the recordings date from between 1966 and 1973. For example, it is a touch heavy and close in the 1966 recording of the D minor Quartet that is one of the wonderful set of six that Mozart dedicated to Haydn.

In a way, this accords to some extent with the playing of the Quartetto Italiano, which is at times rather earnest — and in the first movement of this work, rather deliberate in its pace. But these are really the only criticisms of a generally splendid issue, and the innate seriousness of these fine Italian artists is almost always a plus feature: indeed, they bring an overall intelligence, refinement and, above all, range of interpretative values to this often superb and always attractive music. As for quality of ensemble, they are impeccable. This is undeniably still the best general survey of Mozart's string quartets available, and at mid-price the eight discs represent a safe investment that should yield many years of pleasure.

Additional recommendations ...
K499; K575. **Chilingirian Quartet.** CRD CRD3427 — ⠶ 53m DDD 2/87
K421/417b; K465. **Salomon Quartet.** Hyperion CDA66170 — ⠶ lh 3m DAD 4/87
K421/417b; K387. **Bartók Quartet.** Hungaroton White Label HRC129 — ⠶ 59m ADD 10/89
K575; K590. **Salomon Quartet.** Hyperion CDA66355 — ⠶ lh lm DDD 4/91 🪶
K80/73f; K155/134a; K156/134b; K157; K158; K159; K160/159a; K168; K169; K170; K171;
K172; K173. Divertimentos — D major, K136/125a; B flat major, K137/125b; F major, K138/125c.
Hagen Quartet. DG 431 645-2GH3 — ⠶ ③ 3h 36m DDD 6/91
K136-8. K465. **Eder Quartet.** Naxos 8 550543 — ⠄ lh 6m DDD 9/93
K160/159a. K169. K168. K589. **Eder Quartet.** Naxos 8 550544 — ⠄ lh 7m DDD 9/93

Mozart. STRING QUARTETS. **Chilingirian Quartet** (Levon Chilingirian, Mark Butler, vns; Nicholas Logie, va; Philip de Groote, vc). CRD CRD3362/4. From CRD1062/4 (12/80). Recorded in 1979.
CRD3362 — G major, K387; D minor, K421/417b. *CRD3363* — E flat major, K428/421b; B flat major, K458, "Hunt". *CRD3364* — A major, K464; C major, K465, "Dissonance".

⠶ ③ 59m 56m lh 8m ADD 9/90

Mozart. STRING QUARTETS. **Mosaïques Quartet** (Erich Höbarth, Andrea Bischof, vns; Anita Mitterer, va; Christophe Coin, vc). Astrée Auvidis E8748. Recorded in 1991.
A major, K464; C major, K465, "Dissonance".

⠶ lh l6m DDD 8/92 🪶

Though the Chilingirians may yield to quartets like the Melos and the Alban Berg in sheer virtuosity, their performances of these six inexhaustible works represent some of the most thoughtful, naturally expressive Mozart playing in the catalogue. Unlike some of their more high-powered rivals their manner is essentially private, devoid of both surface gloss and self-conscious point-making. Tempos tend to be rather slower than average, especially in the outer movements of the *Hunt* and the *Dissonance* and in some of the minuets. But any lack of bite and brio is more than offset by their breadth of phrase and unusual care for inner detail. The A major, Beethoven's favourite among Mozart's quartets, is especially successful, done with a gentle, luminous intensity, the minuet spare and absorbed, the variations shaped with a real sense of cumulative growth. If the 6/8 *Andantes* of K421 and K428 are a touch too deliberate (the latter hardly *con moto* as Mozart asks), the Chilingirian's profound reflective tenderness, here and in the other slow movements, brings its own rewards. The quality of the interpretations is matched by that of the recordings, which is intimate, truthful and rounded, with the four instruments nicely separated.

Using period instruments, the Mosaïques offer searching, richly imagined interpretations of the final two "Haydn" quartets. The first movement of the A major, the most chromatic, elusive and densely argued of Mozart's quartets, is done with grace and a subtle rhythmic fluidity; but the Mosaïques's reading has an underlying urgency: *fortes* are robustly physical, climaxes powerfully clinched, the development's counterpoint and cross-rhythms sharply etched. Their minuet is taut and disquieting, and they bring a real cumulative intensity to the *Andante* variations, with the cello's faintly ominous drumbeat towards the close building to a disturbing climax. The Mosaïques are equally compelling in the more worldly, sociable atmosphere of the C major. The outer movements have a fine sweep and an athletic, unaggressive brilliance, with a marvellous clarity and detail of articulation from Erich Höbarth in rapid semiquaver passages. And in the *Andante* the Mosaïques's breadth and tenderness of line, their discreet, telling use of vibrato and their care for the fine details of Mozart's part-writing make for an exceptional performance, as moving as any of the more overtly expressive readings on modern instruments. The recording gives a vivid immediacy to each of the instruments, not least to Christophe Coin's rich, gutty cello.

K458. K465. **Alban Berg Quartet.** Teldec 2292-43037-2 — ⠠⠶ 57m ADD 7/86
As CRD. **Melos Quartet.** DG 415 870-2GCM3 — ⠠⠶ ③ 2h 5lm ADD 6/87

New review

Mozart. FLUTE QUARTETS. **Australia Ensemble** (Geoffrey Collins, fl; David Nuttall, ob; Dene Olding, vn; Irina Morozova, va; Julian Smiles, vc). Tall Poppies TP029. Recorded 1992. D major, K285; G major, K285*a*; C major, K285*b*/KAnh171; A major, K298. Oboe Quartet in F major, K370/K368*b*.

⠠⠶ **1h 5m DDD 7/94** 🄀ₚ

Despite the composer's open declarations of dislike for the flute which appear in his correspondence, there is no evidence that they affected the music. In this new issue of the flute quartets, the Australia Ensemble embrace the music's carefree, buoyant mood wholeheartedly. Their mix of youthful enthusiasm and disciplined ensemble is particularly well suited to this music, and an incisively edged tone-quality gives their performances added impact. They are at their best in the exuberant, faster music, as in the light-hearted expression of, say, the finale of K285, the first movement of K285*b*, or the wittily parodic finale of K298. However, in slower, lyrical passages, such as the slow movement of the D major Quartet, K285, or the second movement of the C major Quartet, K285*b*, they deny some of the music's possibilities for contrast. Here, the tonal purity of Bennett and the Grumiaux Trio, or the extremely sensuous melodiousness of Galway and the Tokyo Quartet seem more successful. Galway's disc includes his own version for flute of the Oboe Quartet, K370; here it is played in its original scoring. Galway's arrangement is wholly convincing, but Nuttall's fine oboe playing makes an eloquent case for Mozart's original scoring. These bold, forthright performances from the Australia Ensemble will have a wide appeal.

Flute Quartets. **William Bennett** (fl); **Grumiaux Trio.** Philips Musica da Camera 422 835-2PC — ⠠⠶ 49m ADD 10/89 🄀ₚ
Flute Quartets. Oboe Quartet[a]. Clarinet Quintet in A major, K581[b]. Horn Quintet in E flat major, K407/386c[c]. [a]**Lothar Koch** (ob); [b]**Gervase de Peyer** (cl); [c]**Gerd Seifert** (hn); **Amadeus Quartet.** DG 437 137-2GCM2 — ⠠⠶ ② 1h 55m ADD 2/93 🄀ₚ
Flute Quartets. Oboe Quartet (arr. Galway)[a]. [a]**James Galway** (fl); **Tokyo Quartet.** RCA Victor Red Seal 09026 60442-2 — ⠠⠶ 1h 9m DDD 6/93 🄀ₚ

Mozart. Divertimento in E flat major for String Trio, K563[a]. Six Preludes and Fugues (after Bach), K404*a*[b] — No. 1 in D minor; No. 2 in G minor; No. 3 in F major. **Grumiaux Trio** (Arthur Grumiaux, vn; Georges Janzer, va; Eva Czako, vc). Philips 416 485-2PH. Item marked [a] from SAL3664 (8/68), [b] 6500 605 (5/75). Recorded 1967-73.

⠠⠶ **1h 2m ADD 11/87**

There cannot be many major works by great composers that are undoubted masterpieces and yet remain still relatively little known, but Mozart's Divertimento for string trio is certainly one of them. The late Arthur Grumiaux leads his Trio in a very skilful and sensitive performance, and they bring out the tragic power of the *Andante* in a way that cannot fail to impress and move a sympathetic listener. This is a work that all who love Mozart should know, and this performance is persuasive and very well recorded, so that one would not guess that the date of the sessions was 1967. The three Preludes followed by Fugues in three contrapuntal parts were recorded in 1973 and while not personal in the obvious sense they have a special interest of their own for students of this composer.

Divertimento. Duos for Violin and Viola — G major, K423; B flat major, K424. **Dénes Kovács** (vn); **Géza Németh** (va); **Ede Banda** (vc). Hungaroton White Label HRC072 — ⠄⠶ 1h 13m ADD 5/90
Divertimento. Six Preludes and Fugues (after Bach), K404a — No. 1 in D minor; No. 2 in G minor; No. 3 in F major; No. 6 in F minor. **L'Archibudelli Trio.** Sony Classical Vivarte MK46497 — ⠄⠶ 1h 3m DDD ✍

Mozart. COMPLETE EDITION, Volume 18 — PIANO VARIATIONS, RONDOS, etc.
[a]**Ingrid Haebler,** [b]**Mitsuko Uchida** (pfs); [c]**Ton Koopman** (hpd). Philips Mozart Edition 422 518-2PME5.

Variations — G major, K24[a]; D major, K25[a]; C major, K179/189*a*[a]; G major, K180/173*c*[a]; C major, K264/315*d*[a]; C major, K265/300*e*[a]; F major, K352/374*ca*[a]; E flat major, K353/300*f*[a]; E flat major, K354/299*a*[a]; F major, K398/416*e*[a]; G major, K455[a] (all from 6747 380, 6/79); A major, K460/454*a*[c] (new to UK); B flat major, K500[a]; D major, K573[a]; F major, K613[a] (6747 380). *Minuets* — F major, K1*d*[c]; G major/C major, K1/1*e*/1*f*[c]; F major, K2[c]; F major, K4[c]; F major, K5[c]; D major, K94/73*h*[c]; D major, K355/576*b*[b] (all new to UK). Fantasia in D minor, K397/385*g*[b] (412 123-1PH, 7/84). *Rondos* — D major, K485[b] (420 185-2PH, 7/87); A minor, K511[b] (412 122-1PH, 11/84). Adagio in B minor, K540[b]. Gigue in G major, K574[b] (both from 412 616-1PH, 4/85). Klavierstück in F major, K33*B*[c]. Capriccio in C major, K395/300*g*[c]. March No. 1 in C major, K408/383*e*[c]. Prelude and Fugue in C major, K394/383*a*[c]. *Allegros* — C major, K1*b*[c]; F major, K1*c*[c]; B flat major, K3[c]; C major, K5*a*[c]; G minor, K312/590*d*[c]; B flat major, K400/372*a* (cpted Stadler)[c]. Suite in C major, K399/385*i*[c]. Kleine Trauermarsch in C minor, K453*a*[c]. Andante in C major, K1*a*[c]. Fugue in G minor, K401/375*e*[c] (with Tini Mathot, hpd. All new to UK).

⑤ 4h 34m ADD/DDD 10/91

These five mid-price discs offer music of fine and often superb quality in a convenient format. The piano was Mozart's own instrument (though he also played the violin) and he composed much music for it besides the sonatas and concertos. Of the three artists here, two are generally fine and satisfying, though the third is more controversial. Ingrid Haebler was recorded back in 1975, but the piano sound is good and little tape background remains, and her performances of the variation sets, which take up the first three discs, are delicate without cuteness, effortlessly encompassing the music's wide range of moods. Mitsuko Uchida, on the fourth disc, performs individual pieces including the two rondos and the beautiful *Adagio* in B minor (the only piece Mozart wrote in this key) in a highly refined manner, a touch over-sophisticated perhaps but still beautiful and expressive and taking full, unashamed advantage of the sound of a modern grand. By contrast, Ton Koopman's disc of minuets and other miscellaneous things is played on a harpsichord at a semitone below modern concert pitch and offers a recording of such immediacy that some listeners will regard it as too bright. Koopman puts gusto into everything he does, but not always to good effect. However, even if grace is in short supply in his performances, they undeniably offer ample personality and such reservations as one may have about his playing should not affect the desirability of the set as a whole.

Additional recommendation ...
Variations — *K265/300e; K455. Andante in F major, K616. Rondo, K511. Adagio in C major, K356/617a. Minuet in D major, K355/576b. Gigue in G major, K574. Adagio in B minor, K540.*
András Schiff. Decca 421 369-2DH — 1h 12m DDD 10/88

New review
Mozart. SONATAS FOR KEYBOARD AND VIOLIN, K6-15 and K26-31. **Gérard Poulet** (vn); **Blandine Verlet** (hpd). Philips Duo 438 803-2PM2. From 4422 515-2PME7 (9/91). Recorded in 1975.
No. 1 in C major. No. 2 in D major. No. 3 in B flat major. No. 4 in G major. No. 5 in B flat major. No. 6 in G major. No. 7 in A major. No. 8 in F major. No. 9 in C major. No. 10 in B flat major. No. 11 in E flat major. No. 12 in G major. No. 13 in C major. No. 14 in D major. No. 15 in F major. No. 16 in B flat major.

② 2h 15m ADD 4/94

The early keyboard and violin sonatas include the boy composer's first works to appear in print: K6-9 were composed during his five-month Paris stay of 1763-4; K10-15 followed in 1765, when the Mozarts resided in London's Belgravia for over a year. The Sonatas, K26-31 appeared a month or two later when the family moved to The Hague. The precociously lively invention is consistently ear-catching, especially in the spunky violin part in the *allegros* and the often graceful lyrical writing. Even if the keyboard dominates the musical partnership, the violinist is always contributing attractive comments. The performances here are very well played, being vital and fresh, and very spontaneous sounding; moreover, they are well balanced and naturally recorded. There is much to intrigue here and many of these miniature works are extremely rewarding in their simplicity and direct melodic appeal.

Mozart. SONATAS FOR KEYBOARD AND VIOLIN. **Szymon Goldberg** (vn); **Radu Lupu** (pf). Decca 430 306-2DM4. From 13BB 207/12 (11/75).
C major, K296; G major, K301/293a; E flat major, K302/293b; C major, K303/293c; E minor, K304/300c; A major, K305/293d; D major, K306/300l; F major, K376/374d; F major, K377/374e; B flat major, K378/317d; G major, K379/373a; E flat major, K380/374f; B flat major, K454; E flat major, K481; A major, K526; F major, K547.

④ 4h 42m ADD 9/91

New review

Mozart. SONATAS FOR KEYBOARD AND VIOLIN. **Chiara Banchini** (vn); **Temenuschka Vesselinova** (pf). Harmonia Mundi HMC90 1466/7. Recorded in 1993.
G major, K301/293a; E flat major, K302/K293b; C major, K303/K293c; E minor, K304/K300c; A major, K305/K293d; D major, K306/K300l. Variations in G on "La bergère Célimène", K359/K374a. Variations in G minor on "Hélas, j'ai perdu mon amant", K360/K374b.

② 1h 50m DDD 5/94

The Decca set of the violin sonatas has acquired something like classic status since it was released on six vinyl discs in 1975. On four mid-price CDs, it represents fine value. Szymon Goldberg and Radu Lupu make an excellent partnership, for the inherent vigour of the violinist's playing is tempered by the innate warmth of the pianist in such a way that their various qualities appear to advantage according to the nature of each sonata as well as individual movements. In other words, Lupu is still there as a personality in his own right, which is as it should be when one remembers that, strictly speaking, these are sonatas designated as "for piano and violin" but he is never over-assertive. There's much to enjoy here, such as the agreeable quiet charm with which the artists handle the finale of the two-movement Sonata in G major, K301, and the elegance of the finale in the late A major Sonata, K526, one of the finest of all as well as the most challengingly difficult. But similar examples of their empathy abound in the 42 movements (and 16 sonatas) that are played, and even if some collectors may feel that the minuets in K303 and K377 are a touch too dreamy, this is a most desirable set, clearly yet warmly recorded.

The performances on the Harmonia Mundi disc are not quite the kind you might expect from period specialists. They are not at all 'objective', careful, small-scale or self-conscious but, on the contrary, full-blooded, spirited, eager to make the most of the music. They bring out the variety in this group of sonatas as strongly as any performance available. The appealing E flat work, K302, is tellingly done, its *Andante grazioso* second movement in particular, with the melancholy tone of its principal theme accentuated by the deliberate tempo, the intensity, and the care with which the varying textures are characterized. The last sonata, K306, is the only one in three movements, and these players make it clear that they regard it as a bigger piece in every sense, the opening movement done with glitter and spirit, the *Andante cantabile* taken slowly and allowed considerable weight and the finale not so much elegant and humorous, as it is apt to be, but again duly serious and substantial. The recording is excellent.

Additional recommendation ...
K481, K526 and K547. **Szymon Goldberg** (vn); **Radu Lupu** (pf). Decca 425 420-2DM *(part of the four-disc set reviewed above)* — 1h 2m ADD 10/89

Mozart. SONATAS AND VARIATIONS FOR KEYBOARD AND VIOLIN. **Yuuko Shiokawa** (vn); **András Schiff** (fp). Decca 436 547-2DH. Recorded in 1992.
Sonatas — E minor, K304/300c; G major, K379/373a; C major, K403/385c; B flat major, K454. Variations in G minor on "Hélas, j'ai perdu mon amant", K360/374b.

1h 11m DDD 3/93

What immediately makes this record special is the instruments used. The violin that Yuuko Shiokawa plays once belonged to Mozart's sister Nannerl and is currently on display in the house in Salzburg where the composer was born. As for the fortepiano, which is also in the Mozart Museum, according to tradition it was the composer's own and was played by him in the last years of his life. Finally, the recording has been made in the actual room where he was born. Given these facts, it is easy to feel that that the sounds we hear are as close as we are likely to get to the ones that Mozart himself imagined and listened to two centuries ago. And beyond this, there is a warmth about the playing of the two artists that surely reflects circumstances which must have made them feel privileged and excited. The three sonatas have been well chosen, for the G major and E minor (the only one of the violin sonatas that is in a minor key) in different ways suggest the imaginative vigour and occasional stressfulness of the young musician whose Salzburg background first inspired and then frustrated him while the B flat Sonata, although composed when he was still under 30, comes from his noble maturity and sounds like it. The Variations in G minor, on a French folksong, are less familiar, but attractively wistful and played with elegance. Overall, these performances have both energy and subtlety. For an example of the latter, witness Schiff's quiet, silvery introduction to the *Minuet* second movement of the E minor Sonata. It must be admitted, however, that after this Shiokawa enters rather too boldly, and if one has a reservation about the playing it is that the violin is often a little loud relative to the keyboard, a matter partly of recording but not entirely so. The two instruments are tuned about a semitone below normal concert pitch.

Key to symbols

Price	Quantity/availability	Timing	Recording mode	Review date
	② ②	lh 23m	DDD	6/88

	Quality of sound		Discs worth exploring		Caveat emptor

Quality of performance		Basic library		Period performance	
♀P ♀S		Ⓑ	?		▲

Mozart. Double Piano Sonata in D major, K448/375a.
Schubert. Fantasia in F minor, D940. **Murray Perahia, Radu Lupu** (pfs). CBS Masterworks CD39511. From IM39511 (3/86). Recorded in 1984.

42m	ADD	10/86	♀P

One of the highlights of concert-going at Snape in the 1980s was to hear Lupu and Perahia, two of the greatest pianists of our era, performing together as one, and yet retaining their own, very individual identities. This disc is a happy reminder of that experience; it was recorded live at The Maltings and it captures exactly that peculiarly characterful, wayward acoustic that has been the bane of so many recording engineers. Having an audience present makes the job infinitely simpler, yet the task is still not an easy one. The performances that are so admirably conveyed here are not of the conventional block-buster type. Neither of these pianists has made tickets to their recitals as difficult to grasp as the Grail by producing virtuosic histrionics. Perfect tone control, total dedication to the inner life of the music, satisfying originality of vision, and a beguiling spontaneity have made their solo performances special; together they show themselves to be selfless chamber musicians of the highest order, capable of lifting already great music to a higher plain. Despite the warm tone of the instruments and ambience, their Mozart is totally classical in ethos, their Schubert divinely other-worldly. One of the desert island's life-sustaining Eight.

Additional recommendations ...
Double Piano Sonatas — *K448/375a; C major, K19d; D major, K381/123a; B flat major, K358/186c; G major, K357/497a; F major, K497. C major, K521. Andante and Variations in G major, K501. Adagio and Allegro in F minor, K594. Fantasia in F minor, K608. Fugues* — *C minor, K426; G minor, K401.* **Güher** and **Süher Pekinel.** Teldec 2292-46014-2 — ③ 2h 5lm DDD 6/92
K448/375a. Andante and Variations in G major, K501. **Schubert.** *Fantasie in F minor, D940.* **Louis Lortie, Hélène Mercier** (pfs). Chandos CHAN9162 — 50m DDD 7/93

Mozart. KEYBOARD WORKS. [a]**Bernard Foccroulle** (org); [b]**Luc Devos** (pf); [c]**Dennis James** (glass harmonica); **Guy Penson** ([d]hpd/[e]clav/[f]tangent pf). Ricercar RIC105081. Recorded in 1991.
Andante in B flat major, K15ii[a]. *Piano Piece in F major, K33b*[a]. *Allegro in G major, K72a*[a].
Andante in C major, K1a[e]. *Allegros* — *C major, K1b*[e]; *F major, K1c*[e]. *Minuets* — *F major, K1d*[e]; 531

G major, K1/1e[e]; C major, K1f[f]; F major, K2[d]. Allegro in B flat major, K3[d]. *Minuets* —
F major, K4[d]; F major, K5[d]; C major, K9a[d]. Londoner Notenskizzenbuch — K15a, K15m[e].
Minuets — C major, K61g/ii[d]; D major, K94/73h[d]. Eight Minuets, K315a[f]. Allegro in G minor,
K312/590d[d]. Capriccio in C major, K395/300g[f]. Fugue in G minor, K401/375e[a]. Prelude and
Fugue in C major, K394/383a[b]. March in C major, K408/1[b]. *Fantasias* — C minor, K396/385f[b];
D minor, K397/385g[b]. Suite in the style of Handel in C major, K399/385i[d]. Allegro in B flat
major, K400/372a[b]. Kleiner Traurermarsch in C minor, K453a[b]. Fantasia in C minor, K475[b].
Rondo in D major, K485[b]. Six German Dances, K509[b]. Rondo in A minor, K511[b]. Adagio in
B minor, K540[b]. Allegro and Allegretto in F major, KAnh135/547a[b]. Minuet in D major,
K355/567b[b]. Andantino (theme with variations) in E flat major, K236[b]. Gigue in G major,
K574[a]. Andante fur eine Walze in eine kleine Orgel in F major, K616[a]. Adagio and Rondo in
C minor, K617[c].

③ 2h 55m DDD 12/92

Here are the odds-and-ends of Mozart's vast output for keyboard — the pieces which don't
easily fit on to CDs devoted to more significant works (like the piano sonatas and sets of
variations). Ricercar have taken the "lump them all together" approach and the result is not
only immensely fascinating but this whole three-CD package makes a thoroughly rewarding
listening experience in spite of its somewhat piecemeal appearance. There are six different
keyboard instruments involved including the peculiar glass harmonica, which isn't strictly
speaking a keyboard instrument at all but basically a set of tuned wine-glasses carefully
recreated by Dennis James from contemporary accounts of the instrument for which Mozart
wrote the *Allegro and Rondo* in C minor. But Mozart didn't always specify which instrument a
piece was intended to be played on and a certain amount of guesswork has been involved in
distributing music to instrument for these recordings. However, even if the *Allegro* in G (K72a)
seems more likely to have been written for clavichord, and the Minuets of K315a were
probably intended to be orchestrated at some later date, their performance here on a charming
sweet-toned Dutch organ and the *Tantgentenflügel* (a tangent piano) respectively works well.
Each disc is designed to give a varied selection both of pieces and instruments, and the playing
and recordings are exemplary. For the most part the music is simple, charming but
unexceptional, the real joy of these discs being to hear it played on instruments which would
have been entirely familiar to Mozart's ears.

Mozart. COMPLETE EDITION, Volume 17 — COMPLETE PIANO SONATAS. **Mitsuko
Uchida** (pf). Philips Mozart Edition 422 517-2PME5.
C major, K279/189d (from 412 617-1PH, 1/86); F major, K280/189e; B flat major,
K281/189f; E flat major, K282/189g; G major, K283/189h (all from 420 186-2PH, 4/88);
D major, K284/205b (420 185-1PH, 7/87); C major, K309/284b; A minor, K310/300d; D
major, K311/284c (412 174-1PH, 4/86); C major, K330/300h (412 616-1PH, 4/85); A major,
K331/300i; F major, K332/300k (412 123-1PH, 7/84); B flat major, K333/315c (412 616-
1PH); C minor, K457 (412 617-1PH); F major, K533/494; C major, K545 (412 122-1PH,
11/84); B flat major, K570 (420 185-1PH); D major, K576 (420 617-1PH). Fantasia in
C minor, K475 (412 617-1PH).

⑤ 5h 25m DDD 9/91 P Ⓑ

By common consent, Mitsuko Uchida is among the leading Mozart pianists of today, and her
recorded series of the piano sonatas won critical acclaim as it appeared and finally *Gramophone*
Awards in 1989 and 1991. Here are all the sonatas, plus the Fantasia in C minor, K475,
which is in some ways a companion piece to the sonata in the same key, K457. This is
unfailingly clean, crisp and elegant playing, that avoids anything like a romanticized view of
the early sonatas such as the delightfully fresh G major, K283. On the other hand, Uchida
responds with the necessary passion to the forceful, not to say *Angst*-ridden, A minor Sonata,
K310. Indeed, her complete series is a remarkably fine achievement, comparable with her
account of the piano concertos. The recordings were produced by Erik Smith in the Henry
Wood Hall in London and offer excellent piano sound; thus an unqualified recommendation is
in order for what must be one of the most valuable volumes in Philips's Complete Mozart
Edition. Do not be put off by critics who suggest that these sonatas are less interesting than
some other Mozart compositions, for they are fine pieces written for an instrument that he
himself played and loved.

Additional recommendations ...

Complete Sonatas. Fantasia, K475. **Maria João Pires.** DG 431 760-2GH6 — .⸰•ʼ ⑥ 6h 37m DDD
2/92 Ⓑ

Complete Sonatas. Fantasia, K475. **András Schiff.** Decca 430 333-2DM5 — .⸰•ʼ ⑤ 5h 21m ADD
2/92 Ⓑ

Complete Sonatas. Fantasias — D minor, K397/385g; K475. **Lili Kraus.** Sony Classical SM4K47222
— .⸰•ʼ ④ 5h 2m ADD Ⓑ

Complete Sonatas. Fantasia in C minor, K475. **Christoph Eschenbach.** DG 419 445-2GX5 — .⸰•ʼ ⑤ 5h 39m
ADD 3/94 Ⓑ

K280/189e. K281/189f. K282/189g. K283/189h. **Mitsuko Uchida.** Philips 420 186-1PH (*part
of the 5-disc set reviewed above*) — .⸰•ʼ 54m DDD 4/88 ⁹ₚ Ⓑ

K280/189e. K281/189f. K283/189h. K311/284c. K330/300h. K331/300i. **Malcolm Bilson**
(fp). Hungaroton HCD31009/10 — .⸰•ʼ ② 1h 56m DDD 12/89 Ⓑ ✍

K310/300d. K331/300i. K533/494. **Murray Perahia** (pf). Sony Classical SK48233 — .⸰•ʼ 1h 4m
DDD 12/92 Ⓑ

K281/189f. K282/189g. K533/494. **Maria-João Pires** (pf). DG 437 546-2GH — .⸰•ʼ 1h 2m
DDD 7/93 Ⓑ

K331/300i. Duport Variations, K573. **Beethoven.** *Piano Sonata No. 12 in A flat major, Op. 26. Six
Variations in F major, Op. 34.* **Alfred Brendel.** Philips Insignia 436 306-2PM — .⸰•ʼ 1h 8m ADD
10/93 ⁹ₚ Ⓑ

New review

Mozart. Piano Sonatas — G major, K283/189*h*; D major, K284/205*b*; C major, K330/300*h*.
Maria-João Pires (pf). DG 437 791-2GH.

.⸰•ʼ 1h 13m DDD 3/94

Maria-João Pires presents these sonatas with clear yet lightly pedalled textures and an overall
directness that still allows room for tonal and rhythmic flexibility — which, generally speaking,
is not overdone. Largely, her playing seems to let the music speak for itself, although of course
just offering the notes is not enough and what we here appreciate is the art that conceals art.
However, one might question the occasional detail: for example, less than a minute into the
G major Sonata, Pires's longish trill on the D preceding the second subject is questionable,
which gives us a bar with four beats in it instead of three. The *Andante* of the same work begins
with repeated Cs that seem too emphatically staccato, and its central section is a little over-
dramatized. The dance movement called *Rondeau en Polonaise* in K284 is on the slow side, though
it still holds together, and the variation-form finale varies considerably in pace. Pires consistently
observes repeats, including the second halves of movements (thus we get virtually every note of
K283 twice), as is indicated. These are clear, commendable performances that give pleasure, and
the kind of grace that Pires brings to this music, in which other pianists can sound a touch
severe, is most appealing. The recording is pleasing and admirably faithful.

New review

Mozart. Mass in C major, "Credo", K257. Litaniae de venerabili altaris sacramento, K243.
Angela Maria Blasi (sop); **Elisabeth von Magnus** (contr); **Deon van der Walt** (ten);
Alistair Miles (bass); **Arnold Schoenberg Choir; Vienna Concentus Musicus/Nikolaus
Harnoncourt.** Teldec Das Alte Werk 9031-72304-2. Notes, texts and translations included.
Recorded in 1991.

.⸰•ʼ 1h 1m DDD 6/93

The *Litaniae de venerabili altaris sacramento* of 1775 has powerful claims to be reckoned the finest
of Mozart's church works before the C minor Mass and Requiem; but it has never quite had the
recognition it deserves. Or the performance: until now, that is. It is clearly a deeply felt work,
from the grave, warm opening of the "Kyrie", through the imposing "Verbum caro factum" and
the graceful "Hostia" that succeeds it, the "Tremendum" with its almost Verdian menace and the
appealing "Dulcissum convivium" (a soprano aria with soft textures supplied by flutes and
bassoons), the highly original "Viaticum" and the resourcefully and lengthily developed "Pignus"
to the "Agnus", a beautiful soprano aria with solo writing for flute, oboe and cello. The
performance here under Nikolaus Harnoncourt rightly sees no need to apologize for the stylistic
diversity of the work. The issue is made still more attractive by the inclusion of a Mass setting

of the same year, one of Mozart's most inventive and original in its textures and its treatment of words. Altogether a very attractive record.

New review

Mozart. Mass in C major, "Coronation", K317. Vesperae solennes de confessore in C major, K339. Epistle Sonata in C major, K278/K271e[a]. **Emma Kirkby** (sop); **Catherine Robbin** (mez); **John Mark Ainsley** (ten); **Michael George** (bass); **Winchester Cathedral Choir; Winchester Quiristers; Academy of Ancient Music/Christopher Hogwood** with [a]**Alastair Ross** (org). L'Oiseau-Lyre 436 585-2OH. Texts and translations included. Recorded in 1990.

54m DDD 4/93

It is difficult to think of any recording of Mozart's church music that so happily captures its character — the particular mixture of confidence, jubilation and contemplation — as this one. Christopher Hogwood's unfussy direction, his broad phrasing, his lively but generally unhurried tempos and his happy details of timing serve splendidly in the *Coronation Mass*, the finest of Mozart's completed mass settings; the solemnity of the *Kyrie*, the fine swing of the *Gloria* and the energy of the Credo, with due pause for its rapt moment at the "Et incarnatus", all these come over with due effect. Arguably the "Osanna" is rather quick, but its jubilance is splendid. And the sweetness of the *Benedictus* is ravishing. Not more so, however, than the *Agnus*, for there, at a decidedly slow tempo, Hogwood allows Emma Kirkby to make the most of this very sensuous music, which she duly most beautifully does. The soloists are altogether an excellent team, with two refined voices in the middle and Michael George a firm and sturdy bass. The inclusion of the K278 Epistle Sonata is a happy notion. The *Vesperae solennes de confessore* is a setting of the five vesper psalms and the *Magnificat*, made in 1780, a year after the Mass, for some church feast in Salzburg. With admirable singing from the choir, a fresh-voiced group whose boys have a fine bright ring, and a spacious recording with exceptionally good stereo separation that properly conveys the ecclesiastical ambience, this is a disc to treasure.

Additional recommendation ...
K317[a]. C minor, "Great", K427/417d[b]. D minor, "Requiem", K626[c]. **Soloists;** [ac]**John Alldis Choir; London Symphony** [b]**Chorus and** [ab]**Orchestra,** [c]**BBC Symphony Orchestra/Sir Colin Davis.** Philips Duo 438 800-2PM2 — ② 2h 15m ADD 3/94

Mozart (ed. Maunder). Mass in C minor, K427/417a. **Arleen Auger, Lynne Dawson** (sops); **John Mark Ainsley** (ten); **David Thomas** (bass); **Winchester Cathedral Choir; Winchester College Quiristers; Academy of Ancient Music/Christopher Hogwood.** L'Oiseau-Lyre Florilegium 425 528-2OH. Text and translation included. Recorded in 1988.

51m DDD 7/90

Mozart left unfinished the work that ought to have been the choral masterpiece of his early Viennese years but there is enough of it to make up nearly an hour's music — music that is sometimes sombre, sometimes florid, sometimes jubilant. Christopher Hogwood avoids any charge of emotional detachment in his steady and powerful opening *Kyrie*, monumental in feeling, dark in tone; and he brings ample energy to the big, bustling choruses of the *Gloria* — and its long closing fugue is finely sustained. The clarity and ring of the boys' voices serve him well in these numbers. There is a strong solo team, headed by the late Arleen Auger in radiant, glowing voice and, as usual, singing with refined taste; Lynne Dawson joins her in the duets, John Mark Ainsley too in the trio. But this is essentially a "soprano mass" — Mozart wrote it, after all, with the voice of his new wife (and perhaps thoughts of the much superior one of her sister Aloysia) in his mind — and Auger, her voice happily stealing in for the first time in the lovely "Christe", excels in the florid and expressive music of the "Et incarnatus" (where Richard Maunder has supplied fuller string parts than usual, perhaps fuller than Mozart would have done had he finished the work). Hogwood directs with his usual spirit and clarity.

Additional recommendations ...
Mass in C minor. **Soloists; Monteverdi Choir; English Baroque Soloists/John Eliot Gardiner.** Philips 420 210-2PH — 54m DDD 5/88

Mass in C minor. **Beethoven.** *Missa solemnis.* **Soloists; Atlanta Symphony Chorus and Orchestra/Robert Shaw.** Telarc CD80150 — ⚫ ② 2h 19m DDD 11/88
Mass in C minor. **Soloists; Berlin Radio Chorus; Berlin Philharmonic Orchestra/ Claudio Abbado.** Sony Classical SK46671 — ⚫ 53m DDD 10/91 ⁹ₚ

Mozart (cptd Süssmayr). Mass in D minor, K626, "Requiem". **Sylvia McNair** (sop); **Carolyn Watkinson** (contr); **Francisco Araiza** (ten); **Robert Lloyd** (bass); **Chorus and Academy of St Martin in the Fields/Sir Neville Marriner.** Philips 432 087-2PH. Text and translation included. Recorded in 1990.

⚫ 50m DDD 12/91   ⁹ₚ Ⓑ

Alongside those old musical teasers, "Who wrote Haydn's *Toy* Symphony?" (Leopold Mozart) and "Who wrote Purcell's Trumpet Voluntary?" (Jeremiah Clarke) can be added "Who wrote Mozart's Requiem?". Mozart's pupil Süssmayr was responsible for much of the work as most modern audiences would recognize it, but exactly how much was Mozart's, how much Süssmayr's, and how much anybody else's is anyone's guess. But performers don't seem unduly perturbed by this masterpiece's less than certain provenance, and there is no shortage of first-rate CD versions. Sir Neville Marriner's interpretation stands out as one of towering authority with a nobility and emotional impact few performances outside the concert-hall could expect to muster. From the stately opening "Requiem aeternam" to the Requiem's emotional climax, the "Agnus Dei", Marriner's musicians produce superlative performances. The chorus is remarkably well disciplined (just listen to the beautifully incisive singing with its dramatic dynamic contrasts in the "Domine Jesu"), and from the soloists Robert Lloyd's resonant "Tuba mirum" is a stunning contribution to a disc of exceptional quality.

Additional recommendations ...
Requiem. Kyrie in D minor K341. **Soloists; Monteverdi Choir; English Baroque Soloists/ John Eliot Gardiner.** Philips 420 197-2PH — ⚫ 54m DDD 11/87 Ⓑ ✍
Requiem. **Soloists; St John's College Choir, Cambridge; English Chamber Orchestra/ George Guest.** Chandos CHAN8574 — ⚫ 54m DDD 2/88 Ⓑ
Requiem. **Soloists; John Alldis Choir; BBC Symphony Orchestra/Sir Colin Davis.** Philips Silver Line 420 353-2PM — ⚫ 54m ADD 2/88 Ⓑ
Requiem. **Soloists; Northern Sinfonia and Chorus/Richard Hickox.** Virgin Classics Virgo VJ7 59648-2 — ⚫ 47m DDD 12/91 ⁹ₚ Ⓑ
Requiem (ed. Druce). Ave verum corpus, K618. Maurerische Trauermusik, K477/479. **Soloists; Schütz Choir of London; Schütz Consort; London Classical Players/Roger Norrington.** EMI CDC7 54525-2 — ⚫ 58m DDD 11/92 ⁹ₚ ❼ ✍

[New review]
Mozart. La Betulia liberata, K118. **Lynda Russell, Catherine Trogu Röhrich, Sabina Macculi** (sops); **Gloria Banditelli** (contr); **Ernesto Palacio** (ten); **Petteri Salomaa** (bass); **Padua Centro Musica Antica Choir; Venice and Padua Chamber Orchestra/Peter Maag.** Denon CO-79945/6. Text and translation included. Recorded in 1991.

⚫ ② 2h 26m DDD 5/94

Mozart composed his oratorio *Betulia liberata* on a commission from a nobleman in Padua in 1771, but what happened to it then remains a mystery. It concentrates on the religious message and the states of mind of the characters — the Israelites in besieged Bethulia, whose want of faith is the subject of much discussion and exhortation. Judith's courage and faith, of course, lead her to decapitate the Assyrian general, an event described in a telling narration in accompanied recitative, in some respects the highpoint of the work, delivered with a halo of string sound (like the words of Christ in Bach's Passions) that imparts a remarkable visionary quality to the music. Indeed, much of the work has this quality. Whether or not the Paduans gave *Betulia* in 1771, they did in 1991, and this recording follows from a bicentenary performance. It is assured and strongly felt. Peter Maag's tempos tend to be on the slow side but the error is probably in the right direction, for it does help to put across the *gravitas* of the work. Gloria Banditelli's Judith is a poised interpretation, supported by firm and even tone and some intensity of manner.

Mozart. Thamos, König in Aegypten. **Alastair Miles** (bass); **Monteverdi Choir; English Baroque Soloists/John Eliot Gardiner.** Archiv Produktion 437 556-2AH. Recorded 1991.

54m DDD 2/94

Composed in the late 1770s Mozart's choruses and entr'actes for the Gebler play, *Thamos, König in Aegypten*, his sole incidental dramatic music, are much less well known than they deserve to be. Of the four entr'actes the first is fiery and full of powerful gestures; the second represents the characters of the noble King Thamos and the treacherous Pheron (the play is set in Egypt, at the Heliopolis shrine to the sun, but there any resemblance to *Die Zauberflöte* ends); then comes one in a stormy G minor leading to a more docile B flat, originally (though happily not here) to be heard against spoken words; and lastly there is a passionate movement in D minor (ending in the major). There are three choruses, the first two of which exist in alternative versions, of which Gardiner slightly oddly includes the earlier in the main text and the later, rather more richly worked, versions in the appendix. The third incorporates a fine bass solo in the later version (decisively sung here by Alastair Miles) but in the earlier there is only an orchestral piece, more effective than musically interesting. Gardiner directs in vivid fashion, with precise articulation, electricity in the rhythms, powerful accents and a wide dynamic range. Mozart wrote prominent wind parts and Gardiner makes sure they ring through the textures. His tempos are fast: the D minor entr'acte has you on the edge of your seat. The choral singing is first-rate and the tone of ritual and grandeur in the big choruses is finely caught.

Mozart. LIEDER. **Peter Schreier** (ten); **András Schiff** (pf). Decca 430 514-2DH. Texts and translations included. Recorded in 1990.
Dans un bois solitaire, K308/295b. Die Zufriedenheit, K349. Komm, liebe Zither, K351/367b. Ich würd'auf meinem Pfad, K390/340c. Lied zur Gesellenreise, K468. Der Zauberer, K472. Die Zufriedenheit, K473. Die betrogene Welt, K474. Das veilchen, K476. Lied der Freiheit, K506. Die Alte, K517. Der Verschweigung, K518. Das Lied der Trennung, K519. Als Luise die Breife, K520. Abendempfindung, K523. An Chloe, K524. Das Traumbild, K530. Das kleine Spinnerin, K531. Sehnsucht nach dem Frühling, K596. Frühlingsanfang, K597. Eine kleine deutsche Kantate, K619.

1h 10m DDD 8/92

Two songs in this collection bear the title *Die Zufriedenheit* ("Contentment") and that word virtually sums up this disc of 21 songs. It is wholly satisfying in every way, not something that can be said of any recordings but the very best. The Lieder range from the popular and often-heard songs such as *An Chloe* ("To Chloe") and *Abendempfindung* ("Thoughts at eventide") to the devoutness of the masonic-like Cantata, K619, *Die ihr des unermesslichen Weltalls Schopfer ehrt* ("You who honour the Creator of the infinite Universe"). Peter Schreier and András Schiff offer a range of expression which swings effortlessly between the calm, profound qualities of the Masonic settings and the charm and subtlety of the narrative or allegorical songs. Throughout, the performers tenderly convey Mozart's lightness of touch, keeping the emotions balanced on the fine thread between longing, objectivity, irony and the deep, childlike directness of *Sehnsucht nach dem Frühling* ("Longing for Spring") — on which the last movement of Mozart's last piano concerto is based. Schreier and Schiff are an equal partnership from start to finish. Schreier's full, deep tenor can characterize *Die Alte* ("The old woman") with a nasal nastiness or infuse some of the other songs with real anguish. Schiff's playing is glorious, embodying emotional essences within the simplest accompaniment figuration or dazzling with the lightness and vividness of his touch in the quasi-pizzicato in *Komm, liebe Zither* ("Come, my dear Zither").

Mozart. ARIAS. **Cecilia Bartoli** (mez); [a]**András Schiff** (pf); **Peter Schmidtl** ([b]basset cl and [c]basset hn); **Vienna Chamber Orchestra/György Fischer.** Decca 430 513-2DH. Texts and translations included. Recorded 1989-90.
LE NOZZE DI FIGARO — Non so più; Voi che sapete; Giunse alfin il momento ... Deh vieni.
COSI FAN TUTTE — E'amore un ladroncello. DON GIOVANNI — Vedrai, carino. LA
CLEMENZA DI TITO — Parto, parto[b]; Deh, per questo; Ecco il punto, o Vitellia ... Non piu

di fiori[c]. Concert Arias — Chi sa, chi sa, qual sia, K582; Alma grande e nobil core, K578; Ch'io mi scordi di te?, K505[a].

58m DDD 12/91

Mozart wrote some of his most appealing music for the mezzo-soprano voice with the roles of Cherubino and Susanna in *Le nozze di Figaro*, Dorabella in *Così fan tutte* and Zerlina in *Don Giovanni* each boasting at least one memorable aria. Alongside these this disc includes a handful of concert arias including *Ch'io mi scordi di te?* which was written for the farewell performance of the great mezzo Nancy Storace with Mozart himself playing the concertante piano role. Here with as innate an interpreter of Mozart's piano writing as András Schiff and a voice so remarkably self-assured as Cecilia Bartoli's the electricity of that first, historic performance seems almost to be recreated. And, here as elsewhere, György Fischer directs the splendid Vienna Chamber Orchestra with disarming sensitivity while the recording is wonderfully warm and vibrant. Cecilia Bartoli boasts a voice of quite extraordinary charm and unassuming virtuosity: her vocal characterizations would be the envy of the finest actresses and her intuitive singing is in itself a sheer delight. But she also brings to these arias a conviction and understanding of the subtleties of the language which only a native Italian could. Listen to the subtle nuances of "Voi che sapete", the depth of understanding behind Dorabella's seemingly frivolous "E'amore un ladroncello"; these are not mere performances, but interpretations which penetrate to the very soul of the music. No Mozart lover should be without this CD.

Additional recommendation ...
COSI FAN TUTTE — Temerari! ... Come scoglio. LA CLEMENZA DI TITO — Non più di fiori. DON GIOVANNI — In quali eccessi ... Mi tradì quell'alma ingrata. DIE ENTFUHRUNG AUS DEM SERAIL — Marten aller Arten. IDOMENEO — Oh smanie! ... D'Oreste e d'Aiace. LE NOZZE DI FIGARO — E Susanna non vien! ... Dove sono i bei momenti; Porgi, amor. DIE ZAUBERFLOTE — O zittre nicht ... Zum Leiden bin ich auserkoren; Der Hölle Rache; Ach, ich fühl's. **Cheryl Studer** (sop); **Academy of St Martin in the Fields/Sir Neville Marriner.** Philips 426 721-2PH — ⠢ 55m DDD 5/91 ⁹ₚ

Mozart. LE NOZZE DI FIGARO. **Sesto Bruscantini** (bar) Figaro; **Graziella Sciutti** (sop) Susanna; **Franco Calabrese** (bass) Count Almaviva; **Sena Jurinac** (sop) Countess Almaviva; **Risë Stevens** (mez) Cherubino; **Monica Sinclair** (contr) Marcellina; **Ian Wallace** (bass) Bartolo; **Hugues Cuénod** (ten) Don Basilio; **Daniel McCoshan** (ten) Don Curzio; **Gwyn Griffiths** (bar) Antonio; **Jeanette Sinclair** (sop) Barbarina; **Glyndebourne Festival Chorus and Orchestra/Vittorio Gui.** Classics for Pleasure CD-CFPD4724. From HMV ALP1312/15 (1/56). Recorded in 1955.

② 2h 38m ADD 9/91 ⁹ₚ Ⓑ ▲

Le nozze di Figaro ("The marriage of Figaro") is comically inventive (though subtly spiked with irony), musically fleet and theatrically well-nigh perfect. The plot revolves around the domestic arrangements of the Count and Countess and their servants Figaro and Susanna, and more specifically around the male/female struggle in the household. Plots involving disguise and much hiding lead effortlessly through this most enchanting of operas to a rousing chorus when, in true Mozartian style, the world is restored to rights and everyone is just that bit chastened and a little wiser. This set is an outright bargain. Although the performance hasn't quite the dramatic drive or vocal glamour of the others listed below it has a lively, intimate ambience deriving from performances at Glyndebourne and boasts the loveliest of all Countesses in Jurinac and a vitally idiomatic Figaro in Bruscantini. The recording is more than adequate. The impecunious newcomer should hurry to catch this set while it's available — such reissues have the habit of not lasting long in the catalogue.

Additional recommendations ...
Soloists; London Opera Chorus; London Philharmonic Orchestra/Sir Georg Solti. Decca 410 150-2DH3 — ⠢ ③ 2h 49m 4/84 ⁹ₚ Ⓑ
Soloists; Glyndebourne Chorus; London Philharmonic Orchestra/Bernard Haitink with **Martin Isepp** (hpd). EMI CDS7 49753-2 — ⠢ ③ 2h 58 DDD 7/88 ⁹ₚ Ⓑ
Soloists; Chorus and Orchestra of the Drottningholm Court Theatre/Arnold Ostman with **Mark Tatlow** (hpd cont). L'Oiseau-Lyre 421 333-2OH3 — ⠢ ③ 3h 6m DDD 12/88 ⁹ₚ Ⓑ ✍
Soloists; Vienna State Opera Chorus; Vienna Philharmonic Orchestra/Erich Kleiber. Decca Grand Opera Series 417 315-2DM3 — ⠢ ③ 2h 52m ADD 2/90 ⁹ₚ Ⓑ ▲

Mozart. DON GIOVANNI. **Eberhard Waechter** (bar) Don Giovanni; **Dame Joan
Sutherland** (sop) Donna Anna; **Dame Elisabeth Schwarzkopf** (sop) Donna Elvira;
Graziella Sciutti (sop) Zerlina; **Luigi Alva** (ten) Don Ottavio; **Giuseppe Taddei** (bar)
Leporello; **Piero Cappuccilli** (bar) Masetto; **Gottlob Frick** (bass) Commendatore;
Philharmonia Chorus and Orchestra/Carlo Maria Giulini. EMI CDS7 47260-8. Notes,
texts and translation included. From Columbia SAX2369/72 (2/61).

> ③ 2h 42m ADD 12/87 ⑨ₚ Ⓑ ▲

Although this set is more than 30 years old, none of its successors is as skilled in capturing the
piece's drama so unerringly. It has always been most recommendable and he captures all the
work's most dramatic characteristics, faithfully supported by the superb Philharmonia forces of
that time. At this stage of Giulini's career, he was a direct, lithe conductor, alert to every turn
in the story and he projects the nervous tension of the piece ideally while never forcing the pace,
as can so easily happen. Then he had one of the most apt casts ever assembled for the piece.
Waechter's Giovanni combines the demonic with the seductive in just the right proportions,
Taddei is a high-profile Leporello, who relishes the text and sings with lots of 'face'. Elvira was
always one of Schwarzkopf's most successful roles: here she delivers the role with tremendous
intensity. Sutherland's Anna isn't quite so full of character but it is magnificently sung. Alva is a
graceful Ottavio. Sciutti's charming Zerlina, Cappuccilli's strong and Italianate Masetto and
Frick's granite Commendatore are all very much in the picture. The recording still sounds well.

Additional recommendations ...
**Soloists; Glyndebourne Festival Chorus; London Philharmonic Orchestra/ Bernard
Haitink.** EMI CDS7 47037-8 — ③ 2h 52m DDD 12/84 ⑨ₚ Ⓑ
Soloists; Vienna State Opera Chorus; Vienna Philharmonic Orchestra/Joseph Krips.
Decca 411 626-2DM3 — ③ 2h 46m ADD 9/89 Ⓑ
Soloists; Drottningholm Theatre Chorus and Orchestra/Arnold Ostman. L'Oiseau-
Lyre 425 943-2OH3 — ③ 2h 51m DDD 12/90 ⑨ₚ Ⓑ ✒
**Soloists; Vienna State Opera Chorus; Vienna Philharmonic Orchestra/Wilhelm
Furtwängler.** EMI Références mono CHS7 63860-2 — ③ 3h 2m ADD 7/91 ⑨ₚ Ⓑ ▲
**Soloists; Chorus and Orchestra of the Royal Opera House, Covent Garden/Sir Colin
Davis.** Philips Mozart Edition 422 541-2PME3 — ③ 2h 44m ADD 1/92 ⑨ₚ Ⓑ
Soloists; Schütz Choir of London; London Classical Players/Roger Norrington. EMI
CDS7 54859-2 — ③ 3h 15m DDD 10/93 ⑨ₚ Ⓑ ✒

Mozart. COSI FAN TUTTE. **Dame Elisabeth Schwarzkopf** (sop) Fiordiligi; **Christa
Ludwig** (mez) Dorabella; **Hanny Steffek** (sop) Despina; **Alfredo Kraus** (ten) Ferrando;
Giuseppe Taddei (bar) Guglielmo; **Walter Berry** (bass) Don Alfonso; **Philharmonia
Chorus and Orchestra/Karl Böhm.** EMI CMS7 69330-2. Notes, text and translation
included. From SAN103/6 (5/63). Recorded in 1962.

> ③ 2h 45m ADD 11/88 ⑨ₚ Ⓑ

New review

Mozart. COSI FAN TUTTE. **Amanda Roocroft** (sop) Fiordiligi; **Rosa Mannion** (sop)
Dorabella; **Eirian James** (mez) Despina; **Rainer Trost** (ten) Ferrando; **Rodney Gilfry** (bar)
Guglielmo; **Carlos Feller** (bass) Don Alfonso; **Monteverdi Choir; English Baroque
Soloists/John Eliot Gardiner.** Archiv Produktion 437 829-2AH3. Recorded at a performance
in the Teatro Comunale, Ferrara in June, 1992.

> ③ 2h 14m DDD 2/94 ⑨ₚ Ⓑ ✒

New review

Mozart. COSI FAN TUTTE. **Soile Isokoski** (sop) Fiordiligi; **Monica Groop** (mez)
Dorabella; **Nancy Argenta** (sop) Despina; **Markus Schäfer** (ten) Ferrando; **Per Vollestad**
(bar) Guglielmo; **Huub Claessens** (bass) Don Alfonso; **La Petite Bande and Chorus/
Sigiswald Kuijken.** Accent ACC9296/8D. Notes, text and translation included. Recorded at a
performance in the Franz Liszt Conservatory, Budapest in October 1992.

> ③ 3h 1m DDD 2/94 ⑨ₚ Ⓑ ✒

Così fan tutte is the most balanced and probing of all Mozart's operas, formally faultless, musically
inspired from start to finish, emotinally a matter of endless fascination and, in the second act,

profoundly moving. It has been very lucky on disc, and besides this delightful set there have been several other memorable recordings. However, Böhm's cast could hardly be bettered, even in one's dreams. The two sisters are gloriously sung — Schwarzkopf and Ludwig bring their immeasurable talents as Lieder singers to this sparkling score and overlay them with a rare comic touch. Add to that the stylish singing of Alfredo Kraus and Giuseppe Taddei and the central quartet is unimpeachable. Walter Berry's Don Alfonso is characterful and Hanny Steffek is quite superb as Despina. The pacing of this endlessly intriguing work is immaculate. The emotional control of the characterization is masterly and Böhm's totally idiomatic response to the music is arguably without peer. However, two modern recordings, using period instruments, do offer stimulating alternative views.

Gardiner's is a *Così* with a heart, and a heart in the right place. It comes from a stage performance given in the Teatro Comunale at Ferrara — the city from which, of course, the sisters in the story hail — in 1992. The vitality and the communicativeness of the recitative is one result of recording a live performance; it is flexible, conversational and lively, as it ought to be, and the Italian pronunciation is remarkably good considering there isn't a single Italian in the cast. Amanda Roocroft makes a capable Fiordiligi, with a big, spacious "Come scoglio", and shows real depth of feeling in what is a very beautiful account of "Per pietà"; her tone is bright and forward. Rosa Mannion, as Dorabella, acts effectively with her voice in "Smanie implacabili" and is full of life in her Act 2 aria. The Guglielmo, Rodney Gilfry, is quite outstanding for his light, warm and flexible baritone, gently seductive in Act 1, showing real brilliance and precision of articulation in "Donne mie". Eirian James's Despina is another delight, spirited, sexy and rich-toned, and full of charm without any of the silliness some Despinas show. Period instruments notwithstanding, this is a fairly traditional performance. Gardiner often uses quite generous rubato to highlight the shape of a phrase, and he is alert, as always, to how the orchestral writing can underline the sense.

The Kuijken, another live recording, is lighter in mood than Gardiner's. Nearly all the tempos are quicker and there is more sense of spontaneity. Mozart very rarely wrote dynamic or accentuation marks into his singers' parts; the singers were expected to learn their music from a repetiteur (or Mozart himself) and take their cues from what they heard in performance. Gardiner has his singers follow, meticulously, the orchestral dynamics; Kuijken leaves them, more or less, to sing with what they hear. This is a symptomatic difference: one performance is highly wrought, the other freer and more natural. The sisters in the Kuijken version are excellently done by Soile Isokoski, even in voice and with an attractive ring, and Monica Groop, again a pleasing and even voice intelligently and musically used. Their duets are both very appealing, with a happy sense in "Prenderò quel brunettino" that they might be getting up to a little mischief. The Alfonso here, Huub Claessens, more baritone than bass, is particularly successful in the recitative, which here again is done with much care for its meaning. A pleasing and lively *Così*, it would be a good recording with which to get to know the opera, whereas the Gardiner is a connoisseur's performance, subtle and sophisticated, and communicating important things about the opera.

Additional recommendations ...

Soloists; Chorus and Orchestra of the Drottningholm Court Theatre/Arnold Ostman. L'Oiseau-Lyre 414 316-2OH3 — .·* ③ ADD 7/86 ⁹ₚ Ⓑ ✍

Soloists; Glyndebourne Chorus; London Philharmonic Orchestra/Bernard Haitink with **Martin Isepp** (hpd). EMI CDS7 47727-2 — .·* ③ 3h 6m DDD 7/87 ⁹ₚ Ⓑ

Soloists; Philharmonia Chorus and Orchestra/Herbert von Karajan. EMI Références mono CHS7 69635-2 — .·* ③ 2h 37m ADD 12/88 Ⓑ

Soloists; Ambrosian Opera Chorus; Academy of St Martin in the Fields/Sir Neville Marriner. Philips 422 381-2PH3 — .·* ③ 3h 11m DDD 11/90 ⁹ₚ Ⓑ

Soloists; Royal Concertgebouw Orchestra/Nikolaus Harnoncourt. Teldec 9031-71381-2 — .·* ③ 3h 17m DDD 11/91 ⁹ₚ Ⓑ

Soloists; Chorus and Orchestra of the Royal Opera House, Covent Garden/Sir Colin Davis. Philips Mozart Edition 422 542-2PME3 — .·* ③ 3h 3m ADD 1/92 Ⓑ

Soloists; Edinburgh Festival Chorus; Scottish Chamber Orchestra/Sir Charles Mackerras. Telarc CD80360 — .·* ③ 3h 8m DDD 4/94 Ⓑ

Excerpts. **Soloists; Glyndebourne Festival Orchestra/Fritz Busch; Philharmonia Orchestra/Walter Susskind.** Testament mono SBT1040 — .·* 1h 13m ADD 6/94 Ⓑ ▲

Mozart. IDOMENEO. **Anthony Rolfe Johnson** (ten) Idomeneo; **Anne Sofie von Otter** (mez) Idamante; **Sylvia McNair** (sop) Ilia; **Hillevi Martinpelto** (sop) Elettra; **Nigel Robson** (ten) Arbace; **Glenn Winslade** (ten) High Priest; **Cornelius Hauptmann** (bass) Oracle;

Monteverdi Choir; English Baroque Soloists/John Eliot Gardiner. Archiv Produktion
431 674-2AH3. Notes, text and translation included. Recorded in 1990.

③ 3h 31m DDD 6/91

This is unquestionably the most vital and authentic account of the opera to date on disc. We
have here what was given at the work's first performance in Munich plus, in appendices, what
Mozart wanted, or was forced, to cut before that première and the alternative versions of
certain passages, so that various combinations of the piece can be programmed by the listener.
Gardiner's direct, dramatic conducting catches ideally the agony of Idomeneo's terrible
predicament — forced to sacrifice his son because of an unwise row. This torment of the soul is
also entirely conveyed by Anthony Rolfe Johnson in the title role to which Anne Sofie von
Otter's moving Idamante is an apt foil. Sylvia McNair is a diaphanous, pure-voiced Ilia, Hillevi
Martinpelto a properly fiery, sharp-edged Elettra. With dedicated support from his own choir
and orchestra, who have obviously benefited from a long period of preparation, Gardiner
matches the stature of this noble *opera seria*. The recording catches the excitement which all who
heard the live performances will recall.

Additional recommendations ...
Soloists; Zurich Opera House Chorus and Mozart Orchestra/Nikolaus Harnoncourt.
Teldec 2292-42600-2 — ③ ADD 3/86
Soloists; Leipzig Radio Choir; Staatskapelle Dresden/Karl Böhm. DG 429 864-2GX3
— 2h 50m ADD 12/90
Soloists; Bavarian Radio Chorus and Orchestra/Sir Colin Davis. Philips Mozart Edition
422 537-2PME3 — ③ 4h 2m DDD 12/91

Mozart. DIE ENTFUHRUNG AUS DEM SERAIL. **Lynne Dawson** (sop) Konstanze;
Marianne Hirsti (sop) Blonde; **Uwe Heilmann** (ten) Belmonte; **Wilfrid Gahmlich** (ten)
Pedrillo; **Gunther von Kannen** (bass) Osmin; **Wolfgang Hinze** (spkr) Bassa Selim;
Academy of Ancient Music Chorus and Orchestra/Christopher Hogwood. L'Oiseau-
Lyre 430 339-2OH2. Notes, text and translation included. Recorded in 1990.

② 2h 24m DDD 11/91

This is the first recording of Mozart's delectable harem *Singspiel* to use period instruments, and
very persuasive it is too. Hogwood's direction is fresh and unfussy, high on comic energy but
always allowing his cast ample room for manoeuvre. If the string sound is sparer and dustier
than with some other period groups, Mozart's wonderful, sometimes exotic scoring for wind in
this opera has never been more tellingly realized, from the piping, piercing piccolo in the
overture and the 'Turkish' numbers to the rasping brass in the Act One finale and the dark,
nutty basset-horns in Konstanze's sorrowful *Traurigkeit*. Hogwood uses a fortepiano continuo,
following the composer's own practice; and his musical text is absolutely complete, restoring the
optional cuts Mozart made in several arias, and including for good measure a little march in Act
One that has only recently come to light. Though other recordings have fielded starrier casts,
Hogwood's singers are aptly and appealingly youthful, and characterize their roles with flair.
Pride of place goes to Uwe Heilmann's elegant, ardent Belmonte, a Mozartian of real
distinction, with plenty of sap in the voice and a honeyed *mezza voce*. His Konstanze is Lynne
Dawson, less grand and impassioned than some exponents of the role but singing with grace,
warmth and all the agility Mozart demands; and she and Heilmann bring a rare poignancy to
their final duet. Marianne Hirsti makes a delicious, quick-witted Blonde, Wilfrid Gahmlich a
likeable Pedrillo, though his intonation falters in the romance, "Im Mohrenland". And though
others have brought a juicier, more rotund bass to the plum role of Osmin, Gunther von
Kannen has ample weight for Mozart's subterranean writing, articulates vividly and relishes the
gleeful malice of "Ach, wie will ich triumphieren". The dialogue is delivered naturally by the
singers themselves (many other recordings bus in actors for this, thereby causing a frequent
sense of culture shock), while Wolfgang Hinze brings nobility and some pathos to the spoken
role of the Bassa Selim. Altogether a fetching, colourful and involving reading of this most
lovable of Mozart's operas, captured in a clear, crisp, if slightly dry, recording.

Additional recommendations ...
Soloists; Zurich Opera House Chorus and Orchestra/Nikolaus Harnoncourt. Teldec

2292-42643-2 — ③ 2h 15m DDD 5/88

Soloists; Leipzig Radio Choir; Staatskapellle Dresden/Karl Böhm. DG 429 868-2GX2
— .·˙ ② 2h llm ADD 12/90

Soloists; Vienna State Opera Chorus; Vienna Symphony Orchestra/Bruno Weil. Sony
Classical SK48053 — .·˙ ② 2h 3m DDD 5/92

Mozart. LA CLEMENZA DI TITO. **Anthony Rolfe Johnson** (ten) Tito; **Julia Varady**
(sop) Vitellia; **Anne Sofie von Otter** (mez) Sesto; **Catherine Robbin** (mez) Annio; **Sylvia
McNair** (sop) Servilia; **Cornelius Hauptmann** (bass) Publio; **Monteverdi Choir; English
Baroque Soloists/John Eliot Gardiner.** Archiv Produktion 431 806-2AH2. Notes, text
and translation included. Recorded in June 1991.

.·˙ ② lh 58m DDD 12/91 ⑨ℙ ✐

This matches the twin recording of the *Gramophone* award-winning *Idomeneo* as an almost ideal
interpretation of *opera seria*. There is nothing marmoreal or static about Gardiner's reading which
suggests a taut and vivid drama unfolding before the listener, enhanced by a sense of an occasion
and of an ensemble dedicated to the work in hand. Tempos are keenly judged and related
unerringly to each other. The playing of the period instruments is disciplined, phrasing keen and
well pointed. Rolfe Johnson makes a convincingly sensitive, clement Emperor who dispatches his
runs with imperial finesse. Beside him, von Otter is superb in her taxing arias, using her runs to
expressive purpose. Their rapport is heartening. Varady makes a bitingly vengeful and jealous
Vitellia, also sensual and eventually remorseful. Sylvia McNair is a sweet-voiced, slightly bland
Servilia, Catherine Robbin a stylistically and vocally secure Annio. The recitatives (by Süssmayr)
are substantially cut, probably an advantage in a recording.

Additional recommendations ...
Soloists; Leipzig Radio Choir; Staatskapelle Dresden/Karl Böhm. DG 429 878-2GX2
— .·˙ ② 2h 20m ADD 12/90

**Soloists; Chorus and Orchestra of the Royal Opera House, Covent Garden/Sir Colin
Davis.** Philips Mozart Edition 422 544-2PME2 — .·˙ ② 2h 8m ADD 4/92

New review
Mozart. DIE ZAUBERFLOTE. **Barbara Bonney** (sop) Pamina; **Sumi Jo** (sop) Queen of
Night; **Kurt Streit** (ten) Tamino; **Gilles Cachemaille** (bar) Papageno; **Kristin Sigmundsson**
(bass) Sarastro; **Håkan Hagegård** (bar) Speaker; **Martin Petzold** (ten) Monostatos; **Lilian
Watson** (sop) Papagena; **Ruth Ziesak** (sop), **Pia Hansen, Iris Vermillion** (mezzos) First,
Second and Third Ladies; **Dennis Naseband, Kai Suzuki, Simon Schnorr** (trebs) First,
Second and Third Boys; **Robert Worle** (ten), **Petteri Salomaa** (bass) First and Second Armed
Men; **Herbert Lippert** (ten), **Oliver Widmer** (bar) First and Second Priests; **Drottning-
holm Court Theatre Chorus and Orchestra/Arnold Oestman.** L'Oiseau-Lyre 440 085-
2OHO2. Notes, text and translation included. Recorded in 1992.

.·˙ ② 2h 36m DDD 2/94 ⑨ℙ ⑨ₛ Ⓑ ✐

Buoyant, unportentous, intimate, wondrous are fitting epithets for Oestman's conducting,
with tempos that are consistently related one with another. Singers, players and engineers
contribute to the sense of a spontaneous and joyous reading created in the same mood as
Oestman's other sets of Mozart operas, and so designed to lift the most downtrodden spirit
— and isn't that what this unique work should achieve? Throughout, the approach is new-
minted. Too often period-instrument performances can seem didactic and/or etiolated or too
keen to make a point. Here the translucent and light textures, the smart speeds, the elating
rhythms create an intimate and immediate experience that speaks directly to listeners at
home, takes them into its confidence. Once drawn in, he or she must be enchanted by its
magic. Barbara Bonney as Pamina sings with finely poised tone and immaculate phrasing.
Kurt Streit's silvery tenor, beautifully even delivery and sense of wonder at articulating the
text make him an ideal Tamino. Cachemaille manages neatly to balance comedy and
poignancy in portraying a childlike yet paradoxically virile Papageno. Sumi Jo, as Queen of
Night has already recorded the part under Solti but she justifies her reappearance by her
accomplishments in her arias, accommodating Oestman's spirited approach. At the other end
of the vocal scale, Sigmundsson is a paragon of a Sarastro. The spoken text is as full as on
any version but it is taken so briskly that its length seems wholly justified. In sum the life-

enhancing delights of this new Oestman set offer the nearest to perfection one can expect in an imperfect world.

Additional recommendations ...

Soloists; Bavarian Radio Chorus and Symphony Orchestra/Bernard Haitink. EMI CDS7 47951-8 — .⁙ ③ 2h 39m DDD 3/88 Ⓑ

Soloists; Favres Solisten Vereinigung; Berlin Philharmonic Orchestra/Sir Thomas Beecham. Pearl mono GEMMCDS9371 — .⁙ ② 2h 10m AAD 3/90 Ⓑ ▲

Soloists; Vienna Boys' Choir; Vienna State Opera Concert Choir; Vienna Philharmonic Orchestra/Sir Georg Solti. Decca 433 210-2DH2 — .⁙ ② 2h 32m DDD 10/91 ⁹ₚ Ⓑ

Soloists; Schütz Choir of London; London Classical Players/Roger Norrington. EMI Reflexe CDS7 54287-2 — .⁙ ② 2h 19m DDD 11/91 Ⓑ ✍

Soloists; Scottish Chamber Chorus and Orchestra/Sir Charles Mackerras. Telarc CD80302 — .⁙ ② 2h 33m DDD 12/91 Ⓑ

Soloists; Dresden Kreuzchor; Leipzig Radio Chorus; Staatskapelle Dresden/Sir Colin Davis. Philips Mozart Edition 422 543-2PME3 — .⁙ ③ 2h 42m DDD 4/92 Ⓑ

Soloists; Hungarian Festival Chorus; Budapest Failoni Orchestra/Michael Halász. Naxos Opera Classics 8 660030/31 — . ② 2h 29m DDD 7/94 Ⓑ

Further listening ...

Dances, Marches and Overtures — Five Minuets, K461/448a[b]. *Contredanses*[b] — Six, K462/448b; D major, K534, "Das Donnerwetter"; C major, K535, "La Bataille"; C major, K587, "Der Sieg vom Helden Koburg"; Two, K603. Two Minuets with Contredanses (Quadrilles), K463[b]. *German Dances*[b] — Six, K509; Six, K600; Three, K605. *Marches*[b] — D major, K52; D major, K189/167b; C major, K214; D major, K215/213b; D major, K237/189c; F major, K248; D major, K249; Two in D major, K335/320a; C major, K408 No. 1/383e; D major, K408 No. 2/385a; C major, K408 No. 3/383F; D major, K445/320c. *Overtures*[a] — DIE ZAUBERFLOTE; LE NOZZE DI FIGARO; ASCANIO IN ALBA; IDOMENEO; DER SCHAUS-PIELDIREKTOR; COSI FAN TUTTE; DIE ENTFUHRUNG AUS DEM SERAIL; LA FINTA GIARDINIERA; LUCIO SILLA; LA CLEMENZA DI TITO; DON GIOVANNI. IDOMENEO — Marches[b]: Nos. 8, 14 and 25. LE NOZZE DI FIGARO: March[b]: No. 23. [a]**Staatskapelle Dresden/Hans Vonk;** [b]**Salzburg Mozarteum Orchestra/Hans Graf.** Capriccio 10 809 (three-disc set, 10/91).

Symphonies after Serenades — D major: K100/62a; K185/167a; K203/198b; K204/213a; K250/248b; K320. **Tafelmusik/Bruno Weil.** Sony Classical SK47260 (12/92).

17 Church Sonatas. **Ian Watson** (org); **Classical Orchestra of the King's Consort/Robert King** (org). Hyperion CDA66377 (11/90).

Masonic music — Lobegesang auf die feierliche Johannisloge, K148[ae]. Dir, Seele des Weltalls, K429/K468a[acf]. Lied zur Gesellenreise, K468[ae]. Die Maurerfreude, K471[acf]. Maurerische Trauermusik, K477[f]. Zerfliesset heut', geliebte Brüder, K483[acd]. Ihr unsre neuen Leiter, K484[acd]. Die ihr des unermesslichen Weltalls, K619[ae]. Laut verkünde unsre Freude, K623[abcf]. Lasst uns mit geschlungnen Händen, K623a[cd]. [a]**Werner Krenn** (ten); [b]**Tom Krause** (bar); [c]**Edinburgh Festival Chorus; György Fischer** ([d]org/[e]pf); [f]**London Symphony Orchestra/István Kertész.** Decca Serenata 425 722-2DM (11/90).

APOLLO ET HYACINTHUS — COMPLETE EDITION. **Soloists; Salzburg Chamber Choir; Salzburg Mozarteum Orchestra/Leopold Hager.** Philips Mozart Edition 422 526-2PME2 (11/91).

LA FINTA SEMPLICE — COMPLETE EDITION. **Soloists; C.P.E. Bach Chamber Orchestra/Peter Schreier.** Philips Mozart Edition 422 528-2PME2 (11/91).

MITRIDATE — *opera seria*. **Soloists; Salzburg Mozarteum Orchestra/Leopold Hager.** Philips Mozart Edition 422 529-2PME3 (2/92).

LUCIO SILLA — *opera seria*. **Soloists; Arnold Schönberg Choir; Vienna Concentus Musicus/Nikolaus Harnoncourt.** Teldec 2292-44928 (3/91).

LA FINTA GIARDINIERA — *opera buffa.* **Soloists; Salzburg Mozarteum Orchestra/ Leopold Hager.** Philips Mozart Edition 422 533-2PME3 (5/92).

IL RE PASTORE — *serenata.* **Soloists; London Symphony Orchestra/Sir Colin Davis.** Philips Mozart Edition 422 535-2PME2 (4/92).

Henri Mulet

French 1878-1967

Suggested listening ...

Carillon-sortie in D major. *Coupled with* **Alain.** Litanies, Op. 79. **Sibelius** (arr. H. Fricker). Finlandia, Op. 26. **Sløgedal.** Variations on a Norwegian Folk Tune. **Lindberg.** Organ Sonata in G minor, Op. 23 — Alla Sarabanda; Allegro con brio. **Mozart.** Orgelstück (Fantasia) für eine Uhr, K608. **Lefébure-Wély.** Marche. **Nielsen.** Commotio, FS155. **Elgar.** Pomp and Circumstance March in G major, Op. 39 No. 4. **Christopher Herrick** (org). Hyperion CDA66676. *See review in the Collections section; refer to the Index to Reviews.*

Modest Mussorgsky

Russian 1839-1881

Mussorgsky. Pictures at an Exhibition (orch. Ravel). A night on the Bare Mountain (arr. Rimsky-Korsakov).
Ravel. Valses nobles et sentimentales. **New York Philharmonic Orchestra/Giuseppe Sinopoli.** DG 429 785-2GH.

⸫ 1h 7m DDD 5/91

Sinopoli's recording of *Pictures at an Exhibition* has great panache and is full of subtle detail and sharply characterized performances. Of course none of this would be possible without the marvellous virtuosity of the New York Philharmonic, whose brass section play with a wonderful larger-than-life sonority (just what's needed in this colourful extravaganza) and whose woodwind section produce playing of considerable delicacy and finesse, as for example in "Tuileries" and the "Ballet of the Unhatched Chicks". Sinopoli clearly revels in the drama of this work and this is nowhere more noticeable than in his sinister readings of "Catacombs" and "Baba-Yaga". *A night on the Bare Mountain* is no less impressive, where again the flair and dazzling virtuosity of the NYPO have an almost overwhelming impact. Less successful are Ravel's *Valses nobles et sentimentales* which are perhaps a little too idiosyncratic for an individual recommendation despite some superb performances and moments of great beauty. The sound is beautifully balanced and engineered.

Additional recommendations ...
Pictures at an Exhibition. A night on the Bare Mountain. **Cleveland Orchestra/Lorin Maazel.** Telarc CD80042 — ⸫ 41m DDD 11/84 ⁹ₛ Ⓑ
Pictures at an Exhibition (orig. piano version)[a]. *Pictures at an Exhibition (orch. Ashkenazy)*[b].
[b]**Philharmonia Orchestra/Vladimir Ashkenazy** ([a]pf). Decca 414 386-2DH. — ⸫ 1h 7m DDD 5/86 Ⓑ
Pictures at an Exhibition (orig. piano version). Gopaks. Souvenirs d'enfance — No. 2. *First punishment (Nurse shuts me in a dark room). Intermezzo in modo classico. Ein Kinderscherz. Une larme. Au village.* **Mario Papadopoulos** (pf). Helicon CDHLR143-2 — ⸫ 59m DDD 1/89
Pictures at an Exhibition. **Stravinsky.** *Petrushka*[a]. [a]**Leslie Howard** (pf); **London Symphony Orchestra/Claudio Abbado.** DG 423 901-2GH — ⸫ 1h 8m DDD 3/89 Ⓑ
Pictures at an Exhibition. A night on the Bare Mountain. KHOVANSHCHINA — *Prelude.* **Oslo Philharmonic Orchestra/Mariss Jansons.** EMI CDC7 49797-2 — ⸫ 49m DDD 1/90 Ⓑ
Pictures at an Exhibition (original piano version). **Tchaikovsky** (arr. Pletnev). *The Sleeping Beauty, Op. 66* — excerpts. **Mikhail Pletnev** (pf). Virgin Classics VC7 59611-2 — ⸫ 1h 4m DDD 4/91 ⁹ₛ Ⓑ
Pictures at an Exhibition (arr. Howarth)[a]. **Saint-Saëns.** *Le carnaval des animaux (arr. Reeve)*[b]. **Philip Jones Brass Ensemble/**[a]**Elgar Howarth,** [b]**Philip Jones.** Decca Ovation 425 022-2DM —
⸫ 58m ADD/DDD 6/91 Ⓑ

Pictures at an Exhibition (arr. Howarth). A night on the Bare Mountain (arr. Wiltshire). **Khachaturian.** *Spartacus — Adagio of Spartacus and Phrygia (arr. Wiltshire).* **Wallace Collection/John Wallace.** Collins Classics 1227-2 — ,•⁗ 53m DDD 6/91 Ⓑ

Pictures at an Exhibition. A night on the Bare Mountain. **Borodin.** *In central Asia. PRINCE IGOR — Polovtsian Dances.* **Slovak Philharmonic Orchestra/Daniel Nazareth.** Naxos 8 550051 — ,• 1h 8m DDD 7/91 Ⓑ

Pictures at an Exhibition. KHOVANSHCHINA — symphonic excerpts. **Rotterdam Philharmonic Orchestra/James Conlon.** Erato 2292-45596-2 — ,•⁗ 49m DDD 8/91 Ⓑ

Pictures at an Exhibition. A night on the Bare Mountain. KHOVANSHCHINA — Prelude. **Atlanta Symphony Orchestra/Yoel Levi.** Telarc CD80296 — ,•⁗ 50m DDD 4/92 ⁹s Ⓑ

Pictures at an Exhibition (orig. piano version). **Stravinsky.** *Three movements from "Petrushka".* **Tchaikovsky.** *Dumka: Russian rustic scene in C minor, Op. 59.* **Yefim Bronfman** (pf). Sony Classical SK46481 — ,•⁗ 56m DDD 1/92 ⁹p Ⓑ

Pictures at an Exhibition. **Respighi.** *The Pines of Rome. The Fountains of Rome.* **Chicago Symphony Orchestra/Fritz Reiner.** RCA Victor Gold Seal 09026 61401-2 — ,•⁗ 1h 10m ADD 8/93 ⁹p Ⓑ

Pictures at an Exhibition. **Stravinsky.** *The Rite of Spring.* **New York Metropolitan Opera Orchestra/James Levine.** DG 437 531-2GH — ,•⁗ 1h 7m DDD 11/93 Ⓑ

Pictures at an Exhibition (arr. Leonard)[a]. *A night on the Bare Mountain (orch. Rimsky-Korsakov). SOROCHINSKY FAIR — Gopak (orch. Liadov). Pictures from the Crimea (orch. Goehr). KHOVANSHCHINA — Prelude (orch. Stokowski). From my tears (orch. Kindler). Scherzo in B flat major (orch. Rimsky-Korsakov).* [a]**Tamás Ungár** (pf). **Philharmonia Orchestra/Geoffrey Simon.** Cala CACD1012 — ,•⁗ 1h 17m DDD 11/93 ⁹p Ⓑ

New review

Mussorgsky. ORCHESTRAL AND CHORAL WORKS. [a]**Zehava Gal** (contr); **London Symphony** [b]**Chorus and Orchestra/Claudio Abbado.** RCA Gold Seal Master Series 09026 61354-2. From RL31540 (2/81). Recorded in 1980.
KHOVANSHCHINA — Prelude; Galitsin's journey (Introduction, Act 4). Joshua[ab]. SALAMMBO — Chorus of priestesses[b]. Scherzo in B flat major. The destruction of Sennacherib[b]. St John's Night on the Bare Mountain. OEDIPUS IN ATHENS — Chorus of people in the temple[b]. Triumphal march, "The capture of Kars".

,•⁗ 54m ADD 6/93

This is a well-merited reissue of some Mussorgsky rarities by one of his most intelligent and forceful modern champions, Claudio Abbado. Four of them (orchestrated by the indefatigable Rimsky-Korsakov) are real collectors' items — an entrancing priestesses' chorus from Act 4 of *Salammbô* (they seem to have a drop of Polovtsian blood in their veins), a vehement chorus, *Joshua*, also originating in *Salammbô* and with a languorous middle section, *The destruction of Sennacherib*, and a less distinguished temple chorus which is all that survives of *Oedipus in Athens*. The original version of *St John's Night on the Bare Mountain* is terrifying.

New review

Mussorgsky (orch. Rozhdestvensky). THE MARRIAGE[a]. **Vladimir Khrulev** (bar) Podkolesin; **Alexandre Podbolotov** (ten) Kochkarev; **Loudmila Kolmakova** (mez) Fiokla Ivanovna; **Vladimir Ribasenko** (bass) Stepan; **USSR Ministry of Culture Symphony Orchestra/Gennadi Rozhdestvensky.**
Rimsky-Korsakov. MOZART AND SALIERI[b]. **Alexander Fedin** (ten) Mozart; **Evgeny Nesterenko** (bass) Salieri; **Sergei Girshenko** (vn); **Vera Chasovennaya** (pf); **Bolshoi Theatre Orchestra/Mark Ermler.** Olympia OCD145. Notes, texts and translations included. Item marked [a] recorded in 1986, [b] 1982.

,•⁗ 1h 16m DDD 9/93

Composed in 1868 *The Marriage* is Mussorgsky's most *outré* composition, a document of calculatedly experimental 'realism' from which *Boris Godunov*, begun in the same year, marks a certain retreat (though a retreat to a more artistically satisfying position, it has to be said). The work was abandoned as a one-act fragment in piano score only and Gennadi Rozhdestvensky is the latest in a succession of orchestrators. If his scoring occasionally sounds like a cross between Janáček and an accompaniment to cartoon comedy, it should be remembered that Mussorgsky's music is itself far ahead of its time. No *aficionado* of Russian opera can afford not to know this extraordinary work. Rimsky-Korsakov's *Mozart and Salieri* is no *Amadeus*, except insofar as its basic premise is the same well-known fiction of the poisoning — Pushkin's text ends with a Requiem-obsessed Mozart going to lie down, having quaffed the draught prepared by Salieri. Rimsky-Korsakov set it word for word in a blend of arioso and recitative. The score weaves quotations from *Don Giovanni, Le nozze di Figaro* and the Requiem into a texture which is otherwise frank pastiche. Probably not even the most ardent Rimsky-admirer would claim the work as one of his finest; but in its proto-neo-classical outlook and its radical attitude to word-setting it is certainly of no mean historical interest.

Mussorgsky. KHOVANSHCHINA. **Aage Haugland** (bass) Ivan Khovansky; **Vladimir Atlantov** (ten) Andrey Khovansky; **Vladimir Popov** (ten) Golitsin; **Anatolij Kotscherga** (bar) Shaklovity; **Paata Burchuladze** (bass) Dosifey; **Marjana Lipovšek** (contr) Marfa; **Brigitte Poschner-Klebel** (sop) Susanna; **Heinz Zednik** (ten) Scribe; **Joanna Borowska** (sop) Emma; **Wilfried Gahmlich** (ten) Kouzka; **Vienna Boys' Choir; Slovak Philharmonic Choir; Vienna State Opera Chorus and Orchestra/Claudio Abbado.** DG 429 758-2GH3. Recorded in 1989. Notes, text and translation included.

③ 2h 51m DDD 11/90

The booklet essay with this issue suggests that, like Dostoevsky's novels, Mussorgsky's music constantly poses a question to his Russian compatriots: "What are the causes of our country's continuing calamities, and why does the state crush all that is good?". Anyone who follows today's news from Russia and then experiences this opera will understand what is meant, and while we observe with sympathy we seem no nearer than the citizens of that great, tormented country to finding solutions for its endemic problems. However, Mussorgsky was not the least of those Russian musicians who found lasting beauty in her history and he expressed it in a powerfully dramatic idiom that drew on folk-music and had both epic qualities and deep humanity as well as an occasional gentleness. There is also an element here of Russian church music, since *Khovanshchina* has a political and religious theme and is set in the 1680s at the time of Peter the Great's accession. Since the work was unfinished when Mussorgsky died, performances always involve conjectural work, and the version here — which works convincing-ly — is mostly that of Shostakovich with the choral ending that Stravinsky devised using Mussorgsky's music. The cast in this live recording is not one of star opera singers, but they are fully inside the drama and the music, as is the chorus and the orchestra under Abbado, and the result is deeply and compellingly atmospheric. The booklet has the Russian text and a translation as well as informative essays on the music.

Additional recommendations ...
Soloists; Kirov Theatre Chorus and Orchestra/Valery Gergiev. Philips 432 147-2PH3
— ③ 3h 16m DDD 6/92
KHOVANSHCHINA — Prelude; Galitsin's journey (Introduction, Act 4). Joshua[ab]. SALAMMBO — Chorus of priestesses[b]. Scherzo in B flat major. The destruction of Sennacherib[b]. St John's Night on the Bare Mountain. OEDIPUS IN ATHENS — Chorus of people in the temple[b]. Triumphal march, "The capture of Kars". [a]**Zehava Gal** (contr); **London Symphony** [b]**Chorus and Orchestra/Claudio Abbado.** RCA Gold Seal Master Series 09026 61354-2 — 54m ADD 6/93

New review
Mussorgsky. BORIS GODUNOV. **Anatoly Kotcherga** (bass) Boris; **Sergei Larin** (ten) Grigory; **Marjana Lipovšek** (mez) Marina; **Samuel Ramey** (bass) Pimen; **Gleb Nikolsky** (bass) Varlaam; **Philip Langridge** (ten) Shuisky; **Helmut Wildhaber** (ten) Missail; **Sergei Leiferkus** (bar) Rangoni; **Liliana Nichiteanu** (mez) Feodor; **Valentina Valente** (sop) Xenia; **Yevgenia Gorokhovskaya** (mez) Nurse; **Eléna Zaremba** (mez) Hostess; **Alexander Fedin** (ten) Simpleton; **Albert Shagidullin** (bar) Shchelkolov; **Wojciech Drabowicz** (ten) Mitukha, Krushchov; **Slovak Philharmonic Chorus; Berlin Radio Chorus; Tölz Boys' Choir; Berlin Philharmonic Orchestra/Claudio Abbado.** Sony Classical S3K58977. Notes, text and translation included.

③ 3h 20m DDD 5/94

Nobody has been more diligent than Abbado in seeking the truth about this vast canvas. Here we have the latest fruits of his efforts. He plays the definitive 1872-4 version, adding scenes, including the complete one in Pimen's cell and the St Basil's scene from 1869. His is a taut, tense reading, grand, virtuosic, at times hard-driven, favouring extremes of speed and dynamics. The orchestra is very much in the foreground, sounding more emphatic than would ever be the case in the opera house. Kotcherga has a superb voice, firmly produced throughout an extensive register. His is a Boris avoiding conventional melodrama and concerned to show the loving father. The ambitious lovers are well represented. Indeed, Larin is quite the best Grigory yet on disc, sounding at once youthful, heroic and ardent, and quite free of tenor mannerisms. Lipovšek characterizes Marina forcefully: we are well aware of the scheming Princess's powers of wheeler-dealing and of erotic persuasion. The recording is of demonstration standard: most potent in the way it captures the incisive and pointed singing of the combined choruses in their various guises. Here all is vividly brought before us by conductor and producer in the wide panorama predicated by Mussorgsky's all-enveloping vision.

Additional recommendations ...
Soloists; Spring Studio Children's Chorus; USSR TV and Radio Large Chorus and Symphony Orchestra/Vladimir Fedoseyev. Philips 412 281-2PH3 — .·' ③ 3h 18m ADD 3/85
Soloists; Bodra Smyana Representative Children's Choir; Sofia National Opera and Festival Orchestra/Emil Tchakarov. Sony Classical CD45763 — .·' ③ 3h 30m DDD 4/92

Key to symbols

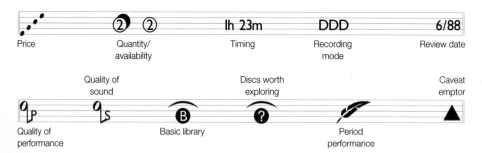

Price	Quantity/availability	Timing	Recording mode	Review date

Quality of sound — Discs worth exploring — Caveat emptor

Quality of performance — Basic library — Period performance

Josef Mysliveček

Bohemian 1737-1781

Suggested listening ...

IL BELLEROFONTE. **Soloists; Czech Philharmonic Chorus; Prague Chamber Orchestra/Zoltán Peskó.** Supraphon 11 0006-2 (3/92).

Conlon Nancarrow

Mexican 1912-

New review

Nancarrow. Studies for Player Piano (arr. Mikhashoff) — Nos. 1, 2, 3c, 5, 6, 7, 9, 12, 14, 18, 19. Tango? (arr. Mikhashoff). Toccata (arr. Mikhashoff). Piece No. 2. Trio. Sarabande and Scherzo. **Ensemble Modern/Ingo Metzmacher.** RCA Victor Red Seal 09026 61180-2. Recorded in 1992.

.·' Ih 13m DDD II/93 ❓

It's a curious comment on the state of American music in the late 1930s that one of its most adventurous spirits was effectively banished to Mexico City where his only creative outlet was composing for the player piano. If anything is likely to convince anyone who doubts that Nancarrow is one of the great rhythmic innovators in twentieth-century music — a rhythmic genius in fact — it's this splendid collection from Ensemble Modern. Through these performances we can get to know Nancarrow's earliest works such as the *Sarabande and Scherzo* from 1930, a perky piece of neo-classicism with the positive enjoyment of superimposed independent rhythmic entities that characterizes almost all of Nancarrow. All his music is well made and is mathematical in the sense that Bach or Webern are — or like architects who need to make the right calculations for their buildings to stay up. Nancarrow also achieves apparent spontaneity, reflecting his early jazz connections, but unlike a lot of jazz there is nothing superfluous. He has the energy of some minimalist composers, but better focus and no sprawl. An unexpected feature here is the inclusion of arrangements of player piano *Studies* made by Mikhashoff for this mixed ensemble and authorized by the composer, who apparently had instruments in mind in some cases. A most refreshing release, vividly played and recorded — from all points of view essential Nancarrow.

Further listening ...

Songs and Dances of Death. *Coupled with* **Rimsky-Korsakov.** SADKO — The paragon of cities; Beautiful city! KASHCHEY THE IMMORTAL — In this, night's darkest hour. SNOW MAIDEN (second version) — Under the warm blue sea. THE TSAR'S BRIDE — Still the beauty haunts my mind. **Borodin.** PRINCE IGOR — No sleep, no rest. **Rubinstein.** THE DEMON — Do not weep, my child; On the airy ocean; I am he whom you called. NERO — Vindex's Epithalamium: I sing to you, Hymen divine! **Rachmaninov.** ALEKO — Aleko's cavatina. **Dmitri Hvorostovsky** (bar); **Kirov Theatre Orchestra/Valery Gergiev.** Philips 438 872-2PH (5/94). *See review in the Collections section; refer to the Index to Reviews.*

Studies for Player Piano — Nos. 42, 45*a*, 45*b*, 45*c*, 48*a*, 48*b*, 48*c*, 49*a*, 49*b*, 49*c*. Wergo 60165-50 (8/89).

Ernesto Nazareth

Brazilian 1863-1934

Suggested listening ...

Apanhei-tecavaquinho. Cavaquinho. Vitorioso. Odeon. Nove de Julho. Labirinto. Guerreiro. Plangente. Cubanos. Fon-Fon! *Coupled with* **Scott.** Evergreen Rag. Modesty Rag. Peace and Plenty Rag. Troubadour Rag. **Lamb.** Ragtime Nightingale. American Beauty Rag. Bohemia Rag. Topliner Rag. **Joshua Rifkin** (pf). Decca 425 225-2DH (4/92).

Alfred Newman

American 1900-1970

Suggested listening ...

Film Scores: 20th Century-Fox fanfare. Street scene. Captain from Castile — Pedro and Catana. Conquest[a]. Wuthering Heights — Cathy. Down to the Sea in Ships — Hornpipe. The Song of Bernadette — Prelude; The vision[b]. The Bravados — main title. Anastasia — main title. Airport — main title. The Robe — Suite[ab]. [a]**Grenadier Guards Band;** [b]**Ambrosian Singers; National Philharmonic Orchestra/Charles Gerhardt.** RCA Victor GD80184 (10/90).

Airport — *original film soundtrack.* Varèse Sarabande VSD5436.

Anastasia — *original film soundtrack.* Varèse Sarabande VSD5422.

How Green Was My Valley — *original film soundtrack.* Fox 07822 11008-2.

The Robe — *original film soundtrack.* Fox 07822 11011-2.

Carl Nielsen

New review

Nielsen. Clarinet Concerto, FS129[a]. Pan and Syrinx, FS87. Love and the Poet — Allegretto con brio. Little Suite in A minor, FS6. [a]**Walter Boeykens** (cl); **Beethoven Academy/Jan Caeyers.** Harmonia Mundi HMC90 1489. Recorded 1985-89.

54m DDD 6/94

There have been plenty of recommendable recordings of Nielsen's concerto masterpiece in recent years, but this one is something special. You sense it in the opening theme on the lower strings, which strikes that paradoxical and immensely appealing Nielsenesque balance between grace and clumsiness, something that often eludes conductors. And you find it confirmed in the lyricism and poetry with which Walter Boeykens invests the solo part. This is above all a dignified, caring and musicianly performance. For some tastes that may mean that it fractionally underplays the bellicose outbursts to which the main protagonist is prone. Yet there is no shortage of boisterous *élan* and virtuosity, and the regretful returns to even-temperedness are properly touching. *Pan and Syrinx* (1918) is an intriguing curiosity — a compelling instance of the experimental idiom Nielsen favoured in his comparatively rare forays into programme music, and shot through with Sibelian influences. The overture from *Love and the Poet* is a late piece — four-and-a-half minutes of intense musings on musical images from Nielsen's last and most far-out symphony, the *Sinfonia semplice*. Like these, the genial *Little Suite*, from the other end of Nielsen's career, has immense care lavished on every detail of articulation, phrasing and balance. The acoustic may be on the borders of over-reverberant; but for most ears, it will surely be an entirely positive feature of an outstandingly rewarding disc.

Additional recommendations ...
Concertos — Clarinet, *FS129*[b]; Flute, *FS119*[a]; Violin, *FS61*[c]. [a]**Patrick Gallois** (fl); [b]**Olle Schill** (cl); [c]**Dong-Suk Kang** (vn); **Gothenburg Symphony Orchestra/Myung-Whun Chung.** BIS CD616 — **1h 19m DDD 7/93**
Flute Concerto[a]. *Clarinet Concerto*[b]. *Rhapsody Overture: an imaginary trip to the Faroe Islands, FS123.* SAUL AND DAVID—Prelude to Act 2. *Springtime in Funen (Fynsk Forår), FS96*[c]. [c]**Asa Bäverstam,** [c]**Linnéa Ekdahl** (sops); [c]**Andreas Thors** (treb); [c]**Kjell Magnus Sandvé** (ten); [c]**Per Høyer** (bar); [a]**Per Flemström** (fl); [b]**Håken Rosengren** (cl); [c]**Swedish Boys' Choir;** [c]**Swedish Radio Choir; Swedish Radio Symphony Orchestra/Esa-Pekka Salonen.** Sony Classical SK53276 — **1h 15m DDD 4/94**

Nielsen. Violin Concerto, FS61[a].
Sibelius. Violin Concerto in D minor, Op. 47[b]. **Cho-Liang Lin** (vn); [a]**Swedish Radio Symphony Orchestra,** [b]**Philharmonia Orchestra/Esa-Pekka Salonen.** CBS Masterworks CD44548. Recorded 1987-88.

1h 9m DDD 1/89

Nielsen. Violin Concerto, FS61[a]. Flute Concerto, FS119[b]. Clarinet Concerto, FS129[c]. [d]**Toke Lund Christiansen** (fl); **Niels Thomsen** (cl); [a]**Kim Sjøgren** (vn); **Danish National Radio Symphony Orchestra/Michael Schønwandt.** Chandos CHAN8894. Recorded in 1990.

1h 20m DDD 4/91

Oddly enough no one has previously recorded the two greatest Nordic violin concertos on one disc and the result on the CBS disc is a triumphant success. This was the best recording of the Sibelius Concerto to have appeared for more than a decade and probably the best ever of the Nielsen. Cho-Liang Lin brings an apparently effortless virtuosity to both concertos. He produces a wonderfully clean and silvery sonority and there is no lack of aristocratic finesse. Only half-a-dozen years separate the two concertos, yet they breathe a totally different air. Lin's perfect intonation and tonal purity excite admiration and throughout them both there is a strong sense of line from beginning to end. Esa-Pekka Salonen gets excellent playing from the Philharmonia Orchestra in the Sibelius and almost equally good results from the Swedish Radio Symphony Orchestra. This should take its place among the classic concerto recordings of the century. The well-filled Chandos CD brings all three concertos together: the Violin Concerto comes from the period of the Third Symphony and the two wind concertos were written after the Sixth during the last years of his life. Nielsen planned to write five concertos, one for each member of the Copenhagen Wind Quintet. Kim Sjøgren may not command the purity of tone of Cho-Liang Lin but he has the inestimable advantage of totally idiomatic orchestral support: Michael Schønwandt has an instinctive feeling for this music — and this shows throughout the whole disc. The perspective between soloist and orchestra is well-judged (Sjøgren is never larger than life) and so is the internal balance. In the Flute Concerto, which veers from Gallic wit to moments of great poetic feeling, Toke Lund Christiansen is an excellent soloist. He has no want of brilliance or authority and his performance also has plenty of character. Niels Thomsen's account of the Clarinet Concerto is one of the very finest now before the public. If there is any music from another planet, this is it! There is no attempt to beautify the score nor to overstate it: every dynamic nuance and expressive marking is observed by both the soloist and conductor. Thomsen plays as if his very being is at stake and Michael Schønwandt secures playing of great imaginative intensity from the Danish Radio Orchestra.

Additional recommendation ...
Flute Concerto[a]. *Clarinet Concerto*[b]. **Hindemith.** *Violin Concerto*[c]. [a]**Julius Baker** (fl); [b]**Stanley Drucker** (cl); [c]**Isaac Stern** (vn); **New York Philharmonic Orchestra/Leonard Bernstein.** Sony Classical Bernstein Royal Edition SMK47599 — .·' lh l3m ADD 7/93

Nielsen. Symphonies — No. 1 in G minor, FS16; No. 6, "Sinfonia semplice", FS116. **San Francisco Symphony Orchestra/Herbert Blomstedt.** Decca 425 607-2DH. Recorded in 1989.

.·' lh 7m DDD 8/90   9p 9s

Nielsen always nurtured a special affection for his First Symphony — and rightly so, for its language is natural and unaffected. It has great spontaneity of feeling and a Dvořákian warmth and freshness. Blomstedt's recording is one of the best to have appeared for some years. It is vital, beautifully shaped and generally faithful to both the spirit and the letter of the score. The recording, too, is very fine: the sound has plenty of room to expand, there is a very good relationship between the various sections of the orchestra and a realistic perspective. Blomstedt gives a powerful account of the Sixth, too, with plenty of intensity and an appreciation of its extraordinary vision. It is by far the most challenging of the cycle and inhabits a very different world from early Nielsen. The intervening years had seen the cataclysmic events of the First World War and Nielsen himself was suffering increasingly from ill health. Blomstedt and the fine San Fransisco orchestra convey the powerful nervous tension of the first movement and the depth of the third, the *Proposta seria*. He is splendidly served by Decca's recording team.

Additional recommendations ...
No. 1. Flute Concerto[a]. *An imaginary trip to the Faroe Islands — Rhapsody Overture, FS123.* [a]**Patrick Gallois** (fl); **Gothenburg Symphony Orchestra/Myung-Whun Chung.** BIS CD454 — .·' lh 3m DDD 8/90 9s
No. 1. No. 2 in B minor, "The four temperaments", FS29. **Royal Scottish Orchestra/Bryden Thomson.** Chandos CHAN8880 — .·' lh 3m DDD 6/92 9p
Nos. 1-6. **Gothenburg Symphony Orchestra/Neeme Järvi.** DG 437 507-2GH3 — .·' ③ 3h 22m DDD 12/93

Nielsen. Symphonies — No. 2, FS29, "The Four Temperaments"; No. 3, FS60, "Sinfonia espansiva"[a]. [a]**Nancy Wait Fromm** (sop); [a]**Kevin McMillan** (bar); **San Francisco Symphony Orchestra/Herbert Blomstedt.** Decca 430 280-2DH.

.·' lh 7m DDD 8/90   9p 9s

This disc couples two of Nielsen's most genial symphonies, both of which come from the earliest part of the century, in performances of the very first order. The Second (1902), inspired by the portrayal of *The Four Temperaments* (Choleric, Phlegmatic, Melancholic, Sanguine) that he had seen in a country inn, has splendid concentration and fire and, as always, from the right pace stems the right character. Moreover the orchestra sounds inspired, for there is a genuine excitement about their playing. Indeed Blomstedt's accounts are by far the most satisfying to have appeared for some time. The Third *Espansiva*, is even more personal in utterance than *The Four Temperaments*, for during the intervening years Nielsen had come much further along the road of self-discovery. His melodic lines are bolder, the musical paragraphs longer and his handling of form more assured. It is a glorious and richly inventive score whose pastoral slow movement includes a part for two wordless voices. Blomstedt gives us an affirmative, powerful reading and in the slow movement, the soprano produces the required ethereal effect. The Decca sound is very detailed and full-bodied, and in the best traditions of the company. Blomstedt's *Espansiva* has greater depth than most rival accounts; the actual sound has that glowing radiance that characterizes Nielsen, and the tempo, the underlying current on which this music is borne, is expertly judged — and nowhere better than in the finale. Blomstedt is an experienced guide in this repertoire and this shows, while his orchestra play with refreshing enthusiasm.

Additional recommendation ...
No. 2. *Aladdin* — *Suite for Orchestra, Op. 34.* **Gothenburg Symphony Orchestra/Myung-Whun Chung.** BIS CD247 — .·'' 56m DDD 5/84

Nielsen. Symphonies — No. 3, FS60, "Sinfonia espansiva"[a]; No. 5, FS97. [a]**Catherine Bott** (sop); [a]**Stephen Roberts** (bar); **Royal Scottish Orchestra/Bryden Thomson.** Chandos CHAN9067. Recorded in 1991.

.·'' 1h 11m DDD 2/93   9ₚ

Bryden Thomson and the Royal Scottish Orchestra give fresh and direct readings of the *Espansiva* and the Fifth which are eminently satisfying. At no point are we aware of the conductor interposing himself between composer and listener, and one can sense an evident enthusiasm on the part of the players. This is Nielsen plain and unadorned without any frills. Thomson has a very good feeling for Nielsen's tempos and his account of the finale feels just right. All in all, a splendidly sane performance with good singing from the fine soloists in the slow movement. The Fifth Symphony is another unaffected and straightforward performance that has a great deal going for it — not least the beautiful clarinet playing in the coda, and the thoroughly committed second movement. One is, perhaps, more aware of the beat in the first movement than in Blomstedt's Decca account (reviewed above) and it rarely seems to float or sound disembodied as it does with him. However, Thomson gets very spirited playing from all departments of the orchestra and the recordings are very good and present, even if the sound lacks the transparency Decca achieved for Blomstedt. These are eminently enjoyable, ardent performances that can hold their head high amongst any competition.

Additional recommendations ...
No. 3. *Clarinet Concerto, FS129*[a]. *MASKARADE* — *Overture.* **Pia Raanoja** (sop); **Knut Skram** (bar); [a]**Olle Schill** (cl); **Gothenburg Symphony Orchestra/Myung-Whun Chung.** BIS CD321 — .·'' 1h 8m DDD 8/86
Nos. 3 and 5. **New York Philharmonic Orchestra/Leonard Bernstein.** Sony Classical Bernstein Royal Edition SMK47958 — .·'' 1h 11m ADD 7/93

Nielsen. Symphonies — No. 4, FS76, "Inextinguishable"; No. 5, FS97. **San Francisco Symphony Orchestra/Herbert Blomstedt.** Decca 421 524-2DH.

.·'' 1h 12m DDD 10/88   9ₚ   9ₛ

Nielsen. Symphonies — No. 4, FS76, "Inextinguishable"; No. 6, FS116, "Sinfonia semplice". **Royal Scottish National Orchestra/Bryden Thomson.** Chandos CHAN9047. Recorded in 1991.

.·'' 1h 10m DDD 3/93   9ₚ   9ₛ

These are two of Nielsen's most popular and deeply characteristic symphonies. Blomstedt's are good performances that can hold their own with any in the current catalogue, and as recordings they surpass the competition. The Fourth Symphony occupied Nielsen between 1914 and early 1916 and reveals a level of violence new to his art. The landscape is harsher; the melodic lines soar in a more anguished and intense fashion (in the case of the remarkable slow movement, "like the eagle riding on the wind", to use the composer's own graphic simile). Blomstedt's opening has splendid fire: this must sound as if galaxies are forming and he is not frightened of letting things rip. The finale with its exhilarating dialogue between the two timpanists comes off splendidly. The Fifth Symphony of 1922 is impressive, too: it starts perfectly and has just the right glacial atmosphere. The climax and the desolate clarinet peroration into which it dissolves are well handled. The recording balance could not be improved upon: the woodwind are decently recessed (though clarinet keys are audible at times), there is an almost ideal relationship between the various sections of the orchestra and a thoroughly realistic overall perspective. Blomstedt has a good rapport with his players who sound in excellent shape and respond to these scores as to the manner born.

Bryden Thomson's accounts of the Fourth and Sixth calls to mind the ardent intensity of the pioneering Danish recordings (no longer available) by Launy Gróndahl and Thomas Jensen such are their fire. The orchestra play as if their lives depend on it and the underlying violence of No. 4 makes a powerful impact, both at the opening and in the finale. But his Sixth is arguably the very finest version of the work on disc, notwithstanding the cultured and splendidly recorded account by Herbert Blomstedt (reviewed with the First Symphony). Thomson strikes exactly the right tempo for the first movement nor has the problematic "Humoreske" ever made better sense. He takes it at a steadier pace than most rival conductors, so that its questioning spirit registers. The third movement, the "Proposta seria", is both eloquent and searching. Even in a strongly competitive field this splendidly recorded Chandos account brings one closer to this extraordinary work than any other.

Additional recommendations ...
Nos. 4 and 5. *MASKARADE* — *Overture.* **BBC Symphony Orchestra/Andrew Davis.** Virgin Classics VC7 59618-2 ⸫ 1h 14m DDD 4/91 Ⓑ
Nos. 3 and 6. **Royal Danish Orchestra/Paavo Berglund.** RCA Victor Red Seal RD60427 — ⸫ 1h 8m DDD 4/92 Ⓑ

New review
Nielsen. String Quartets — No. 1 in G minor, FS4; No. 2 in F minor, FS11; No. 3 in E flat major, FS23 (Op. 14); No. 4 in F major, FS36. Movements for String Quartet, FS3c. **Danish Quartet** (Tim Frederiksen, Arne Balk-Møller, vns; Claus Myrup, va; H. Brendstrup, vc). Kontrapunkt 32150/1.

⸫ ② 2h 18m DDD 10/93

Nielsen composed two quartets and a string quintet during his student years. There was a gap of eight years between the F minor Quartet and the Third, in E flat, Op. 14 (FS23) during which Nielsen had written his First Symphony, and another eight before the F major, Op. 44 (FS36) saw the light of day. By this time he had written his opera, *Saul and David* and the best part of *Maskarade* as well as the Second Symphony. The Danish Quartet do not have the thrust or, perhaps, the finish of the Kontra Quartet on BIS, but they are very sensitive to dynamic nuance, phrase more imaginatively, and are generally speaking more involving. Of course, the F major Quartet goes deeper than the Third. There is a grace, an effortless fluency and a marvellous control of pace. Ideas come and go just when you feel they should; yet its learning and mastery is worn lightly. Though the earlier quartets are not such perfect works of art, they are nevertheless always endearing. The Danish Quartet is completely inside this music and is totally persuasive. In spite of the closely balanced recording this set gives real pleasure and can be recommended with enthusiasm.

Additional recommendation ...
Nos. 1-4. *String Quintet in G major, FS5[a]. At the bier of a young artist, FS58[b].* **Kontra Quartet;** [a]**Philipp Naegele** (va); [b]**Jan Johannsson** (db). BIS CD503/04 — ⸫ ② 2h 30m DDD 4/92

New review
Nielsen. Aladdin. **Mette Ejsing** (contr); **Guido Paevatalu** (bar); **Danish National Radio Chamber Choir; Danish National Radio Symphony Orchestra/Gennadi Rozhdestvensky.** Chandos CHAN9135. Text and translation included. Recorded in 1992.

⸫ 1h 19m DDD 5/93

So far Nielsen's music to Adam Oehlenschläger's *Aladdin* has been known only from the seven-movement suite. However, the suite only comprises about 20 minutes of music, which is little more than a quarter of Nielsen's original score. *Aladdin* comes from 1917-18, and was commissioned for a particularly lavish production of the play at the Royal Theatre in Copenhagen. More than half the music consists of orchestral interludes to accompany processions and dances, most of which come in the Third Act. Many are delightful and endearing, and once heard difficult to get out of one's head. Robert Simpson summed the work up in his Nielsen monograph: "The market-square in Isfahan where four orchestras play in four different tempi suggesting marvellously the clashing colours, movements and sounds of an eastern market-place in undoubtedly the most striking and original part of the music. Some of it is not very interesting (the rather commonplace Blackamoors' Dance, for instance) but most is intensely perceptive and colourful." It is full of characteristic Nielsenesque touches, and although it is not the composer at his very best, it offers many irresistible delights. Performance and recording are superb.

Further listening ...

Wind Quintet. *Coupled with* **Loeffler.** Two Rhapsodies. **Prokoviev.** Quintet in G minor, Op. 39. **Chamber Music Northwest.** Delos DE3136 (12/93).

Wind Quintet, FS100[a]. Fantasy Piece for Clarinet and Piano, FS3h[b]. Fantasy Pieces for Oboe and Piano, FS8[c]. Canto serioso for Horn and Piano, FS132[d]. Serenata in vano, FS68[e]. The Mother, FS94 — The fog is lifting[f]; The children are playing[g]; Faith and Hope are playing[h]. Allegretto for Two Recorders, FS157[i]. [a]**Bergen Wind Quintet** (Gro Sandvik, fl[fgh], rec[i]; [c]Steinar Hannevold, ob; [be]Lars Kristian Holm Brynildsen, cl; [de]Vidar Olsen, hn; Per Hannevold, bn[e], rec[i]); [f]**Turid Kniejski** (hp); [h]**Lars Anders Tomter** (va); [e]**Sally Guenther** (vc); [e]**Torbjorn Eide** (db); [bcd]**Lief Ove Andsnes** (pf). BIS CD428 (9/89).

Commotio, FS155. *Coupled with* **Alain.** Litanies, Op. 79. **Mulet.** Carillon-sortie in D major. **Sibelius** (arr. H. Fricker). Finlandia, Op. 26. **Sløgedal.** Variations on a Norwegian Folk Tune. **Lindberg.** Organ Sonata in G minor, Op. 23 — Alla Sarabanda; Allegro con brio. **Mozart.** Orgelstück (Fantasia) für eine Uhr, K608. **Lefébure-Wély.** Marche. **Elgar.** Pomp and Circumstance March in G major, Op. 39 No. 4. **Christopher Herrick** (org). Hyperion CDA66676. *See review in the Collections section; refer to the Index to Reviews.*

SAUL AND DAVID. **Soloists; Danish National Radio Choir and Symphony Orchestra/Neeme Järvi.** Chandos CHAN8911/12 (3/91).

Luigi Nono

Italian 1924-1990

New review

Nono. Il canto sospeso[a].
Mahler. Kindertotenlieder[b]. Rückert-Lieder — Ich bin der Welt abhanden gekommen[b]. [a]**Susanne Lothar,** [a]**Bruno Ganz** (spkrs); [a]**Barbara Bonney** (sop); [a]**Susanne Otto** (mez); [b]**Marjana Lipovšek** (contr); [a]**Marek Torzewski** (ten); [a]**Berlin Radio Chorus; Berlin Philharmonic Orchestra/Claudio Abbado.** Sony Classical SK53360. Recorded at performances in the Philharmonie, Berlin in 1992.

1h 10m DDD 10/93

Three years on from the re-unification of Berlin, the promise of *Freiheit* looks distinctly hollow, undermined by resurgent nationalism, rampant consumerism, xenophobia, racism and fear. The mood of the present programme (edited together from individual concerts) is therefore very different. Nono's *Il canto sospeso* is a key work of the European avant-garde, one in which serial processes and Communist ideology are brought together in a dramatically compelling memorial to the victims of Fascism and this performance is unlikely to be bettered for a long time. Under Abbado, the playing is as tight and stylish as might be expected from these forces: choral singing is unprecedentedly secure and Barbara Bonney is especially radiant. Less welcome for repeated listening are the interpolated readings, by Bruno Ganz and Susanne Lothar, of the letters from which Nono builds his cantata, the last dispatches of members of the Resistance condemned to death. Nono's texts include many painful messages from children to parents — they too might have been subtitled *Kindertotenlieder* — and Mahler's familiar Rückert verses are lent a new resonance from the very first. Marjana Lipovšek sings with long, resonant and well-balanced phrases and a dark, solemn manner. The 20-bit technology does not entirely offset the drawbacks of live recording in the Philharmonie, but the results are perfectly acceptable. Despite reservations, strongly recommended.

Arne Nordheim

Norwegian 1931-

Suggested listening ...

Tenebrae[a]. Magma. [a]**Truls Mørk** (vc); **Oslo Philharmonic Orchestra/Yoav Talmi.** Aurora ACD4966 (12/92).

Ib Nørholm

Danish 1931-

Suggested listening ...

Violin Concerto, Op. 60[a]. Cello Concerto, Op. 108[b]. [a]**Kishiko Suzumi** (vn); [b]**Erling Blöndal Bengtsson** (vc); **Aalborg Symphony Orchestra/Tamás Vetö.** Kontrapunkt 32099 (9/93).

Symphonies — No. 1, Op. 10; No. 3, "Day's Nightmare", Op. 57. **Odense Symphony Orchestra/Eduard Serov.** Kontrapunkt 32132 (9/93).

Symphonies — No. 6, "Moralities, or There may be many miles to the nearest spider", Op. 85[a]. No. 8, "Faith and Longing", Op. 114[b]. [a]**Majken Bjerno** (sop); [ab]**Per Høyer** (bar); [a]**Uffe Henriksen**, [a]**Ulla Seel** (narrs); **Odense Symphony Orchestra/Edward Serov.** Kontrapunkt 32162 (2/94).

Symphonies — No. 7, "Ecliptic Instincts", Op. 88; No. 9, "The Sun Garden in Three Shades of Light", Op. 116. **Odense Symphony Orchestra/Eduard Serov.** Kontrapunkt 32112 (9/93).

Alex North

American 1910-1991

Suggested listening ...

2001 — *film score.* **National Philharmonic Orchestra/Jerry Goldsmith.** Varèse Sarabande VSD5400 (3/94).

Vítezslav Novák

Bohemian 1870-1949

New review
Novák. Slovak Suite, Op. 32[a].
Janáček. Taras Bulba[b]. THE CUNNING LITTLE VIXEN — Suite[b]. **Czech Philharmonic Orchestra/Václav Talich.** Supraphon Historical mono 11 1905-2. Item marked [a] recorded in 1953, new to UK; [b] from LPV266 (8/58), recorded 1953-54.

•• 1h 11m AAD 1/94 ▲

The Novák is unmitigated delight. Talich's wonderful conception has the requisite tangy affection and lithe, rhythmic punch, but he locates and taps into a vein of tangible, old-world nostalgia that is extremely moving. If you don't already know this lovely score, immediate investigation is recommended for you are unlikely to ever hear a better performance than this. Talich's *Taras Bulba* is imposing. Aided by playing of brazen fervour, his reading has a rare dignity, culminating in an apotheosis of grandeur and majesty and the battle scenes of the first two tableaux possess thrilling snap and vigour. The orchestral suite from *The Cunning Little Vixen* was compiled by Talich himself in 1937. Not all Janáčekians will approve of the great conductor's 'sensualizing' of the original instrumentation, but its sense of enchantment and magical atmosphere remain utterly intoxicating.

Additional recommendation ...
Slovak Suite[a]. *Eternal Longing, Op. 33*[b]. *In the Tatra Mountains, Op. 26*[a]. [a]**Brno State Philharmonic Orchestra,** [b]**Czech Philharmonic Orchestra/Karel Sejna.** Supraphon Crystal Collection 11 0682-2 — .•˙ 1h 5m ADD 6/93

Further listening ...

Pan — Tone-poem, Op. 43. **Slovak Philharmonic Orchestra/Zdenek Bílek.** Marco Polo 8 223325 (10/91).

Michael Nyman

British 1944-

Suggested listening ...

The Piano Concerto[a]. MGV (Musique a Grande Vitesse)[b]. [a]**Kathryn Stott** (pf); [a]**Royal Liverpool Philharmonic Orchestra;** [b]**Michael Nyman Band and Orchestra/Michael Nyman.** Argo 443 382-2ZH.

String Quartets Nos. 1-3. **Balanescu Quartet.** Argo 433 093-2ZH (8/91).

Prospero's Books (music from the film by Peter Greenaway). **Sarah Leonard, Ute Lemper, Marie Angel** (sops); **Deborah Conway** (sngr); **Michael Nyman Band/Michael Nyman.** Decca 425 224-2DH (11/91).

THE MAN WHO MISTOOK HIS WIFE FOR A HAT. **Soloists; Nyman Band/Michael Nyman** (pf). CBS CD44669 (11/88).

Knut Nystedt

Norwegian 1915-

Suggested listening ...

Chamber and Vocal Works — Lucis creator optime, Op. 58[a]. Pia memoria, Op. 65[b]. Rhapsody in Green, Op. 82[c]. 19 Motets[d]. [a]**Erna Skaug** (sop); [a]**Olav Eriksen** (bar); [c]**Norwegian Brass Quintet;** [d]**Bergen Cathedral Choir/Magnar Mangersnes;** [a]**Norwegian Soloists Choir;** [a]**Oslo Philharmonic Orchestra,** [b]**Brass Ensemble**/[ab]**Knut Nystedt** with [d]**Tor Grønn** (org). Aurora ACD4971 (5/93).

Johannes Ockeghem

Flanders c.1410-1497

New review
Ockeghem. Missa Ecce ancilla Domini. Intemerata Dei mater. Ave Maria.
Josquin Desprez. Déploration sur la mort de Johannes Ockeghem, "Nymphes des bois".

Obrecht. Salve regina. **The Clerks' Group/Edward Wickham.** Proud Sound PROUCD133. Texts and translations included. Recorded in 1993.

・・ Ih 4m DDD I0/93 ⁹P

This is the finest Ockeghem disc available, and there are very few recordings of fifteenth-century polyphony to match it. This astonishing music poses a considerable challenge in performance. With formal and stylistic conventions being flouted at every turn, matters of phrasing and pacing acquire a crucial importance, and much depends on the performers' ability to render local details intelligently. That is what makes this recording so special. *Missa Ecce ancilla*, though one of Ockeghem's most impressive Mass-cycles, is hardly an obvious choice for an ensemble making its recording début, but the Clerks' Group have absorbed Ockeghem's idiom to an extent that has scarcely been achieved hitherto, and command the technical means to match: balance and richness of tone, registral security and dynamic flexibility are all spot on. As a result, one makes sense of details which seemed baffling in previous recordings. Better still, such moments acquire the dramatic impact that is their ultimate justification. It is a joy to hear such an intelligent reading delivered with such confidence.

New review
Ockeghem. Requiem. **Les Pages de la Chapelle; Organum Ensemble/Marcel Pérès.** Harmonia Mundi HMC90 1441. Text and translation included. Recorded in 1992.

・・ 55m DDD 2/94

Marcel Pérès brings his own colour to what will always remain the strangest piece by one of music's most puzzling composers. Mainly he works at about a fourth below modern pitch, keeps all the singing unusually quiet and chooses fairly sprightly tempos. In general this works extremely well, with the cheerful and occasionally slap-happy voices of the Ensemble Organum bringing an attractive dash of *élan* to what would otherwise be intolerably lugubrious. Pérès makes the occasional strange decision: he returns to the manuscript with some bizarre results; he also changes pitch standard by a fourth for the middle section of the Tract. There is also his decision to add on a couple of movements from the much later Requiem of Divitis at the end, so entirely different in sound as to startle the ear and adds boy trebles for the first of the Divitis movements. Most of the intervening chants are sung by Pérès himself in a kind of muezzin style (big upward *glissandos* on the consonants and oriental ornaments on various notes), which adds to the solemnity of the event. In all, this is a fascinating and challenging record.

Further listening ...

Complete Secular Music — Ma bouche rit. La despourveue. D'un autre amer. Quant ce viendra. Il ne m'en chault plus. Presque trainsi. Ma maistresse. Les desleaux. Mort tu as navre. Quant de vous. Au travail suis. Prenez sur moi. Fors seulement l'actente. L'autre d'antan. S'elle m'amera. O rosa bella. Tant fuz gentement. Je n'ay dueil. Malheur me bat. Se vostre cuer. Qu'es mi vida. Qu'es mi vida (original version by Johannes Cornago). Je n'ay dueil. Ce n'est pas jeu. Resjois toy. Departez vous. Ung aultre l'a. Autre Venus. Baissiez moi. Fors seulement contre ce. **The Medieval Ensemble of London/Peter Davies, Timothy Davies.** L'Oiseau-Lyre 436 194-2OH2 (9/93).

Jacques Offenbach

German/French 1819-1880

New review
Offenbach (arr. M. Rosenthal). Gaîté parisienne — ballet.
Rossini (arr./orch. Respighi). La boutique fantasque — ballet. **Boston Pops Orchestra/ Arthur Fiedler.** RCA Living Stereo 09026 61847-2. Recorded 1954-56.

・・ Ih 4m ADD 2/94 ⁹P

Arthur Fiedler and the Boston Pops, for so long the guardians of traditional concert-hall light music in America, never made a better stereo recording than the amazing early (1954) complete

Offenbach/Rosenthal *Gaîté parisienne* ballet score. It scintillates with effervescence and vitality, has just the right degree of brash vulgarity, yet the richly embracing acoustics of Symphony Hall ensure that the entry of the great "Barcarolle" has warmth as well as allure. This transfer makes the very most of the outstanding mastertape. The coupling comprises some 27 minutes (almost all the best music) from the hardly less delectable Rossini/Respighi *La boutique fantasque* also brightly and atmospherically played and again given first-class sound from two years later. A real collector's item, not to be missed by anyone who cares about the history of stereo reproduction and also for the sheer *joie de vivre* of the music.

Key to symbols

Price	Quantity/ availability	Timing	Recording mode	Review date
	② ②	1h 23m	DDD	6/88

Quality of sound		Discs worth exploring		Caveat emptor
Quality of performance	Basic library	Ⓑ	？	Period performance	▲

Offenbach. CHRISTOPHER COLUMBUS. **Maurice Arthur** (ten) Christopher Columbus; **Joy Roberts** (sop) Beatriz; **Johanna Peters** (mez) Rosa Columbus; **Lissa Gray** (sop) Fleurette Columbus; **Marilyn Hill Smith** (sop) Gretel Columbus; **Christian du Plessis** (bar) Luis de Torres; **Alan Opie** (bar) Chief of Police; **Anna Dawson** (sop) Queen Isabella; **Alec Bregonzi** (ten) King Ferdinand; **Clive Harré** (bar) Tourist; **John Duxbury** (ten) Waiter; **Rosemary Ashe** (sop) Princess Minnehaha Columbus, Esperanza; **Celia Kite** (sop) Carmelita; **Kathleen Smales** (mez) Manuela; **Amilia Dixey** (mez) Valencia; **Geoffrey Mitchell Choir; London Mozart Players/Alun Francis.** Opera Rara ORC2. Notes and text included. From OR2 (8/78). Recorded in 1977.

	②	2h 4m ADD	4/93	

You will look in vain for *Christopher Columbus* in lists of Offenbach's works. It was put together by Opera Rara for the 1976 American bicentenary celebrations, using a totally new book allied to music from a variety of Offenbach works. But not without reason has it been described as "the best Offenbach opera Offenbach never wrote". It is an absolutely hilarious piece, right from the opening chorus, in which the young ladies of Córdoba express their boredom at having nothing to do but snap their castanets and shout "Olé!" through to the marvellously inventive conclusion. The lyrics are quite brilliant, and the racy melodies, whose sources are all listed in the accompanying libretto, are all the better for being generally unfamiliar. If the whole doesn't sound quite like an authentic Offenbach piece, it is only for the very good reason that it largely forswears dialogue and the lead-ins to numbers in favour of the big juicy tunes. One should not look to a performance of a work such as this for mere purity of vocal sound, so much as for ability to put a number across. In this respect, with singers and singing actors of the quality of Marilyn Hill Smith, Johanna Peters, Anna Dawson and Alec Bregonzi supporting Maurice Arthur in the title-role, it would be difficult to imagine the piece performed with greater skill or relish. If you want a CD set for sheer uninhibited enjoyment, this should be it.

Further listening ...

Gaîté parisienne — ballet. *Coupled with* **Gounod.** Faust — ballet music. **Montreal Symphony Orchestra/Charles Dutoit.** Decca Ovation 430 718-2DM (8/91).

LA BELLE HELENE. **Soloists; Toulouse Capitol Chorus and Orchestra/Michel Plasson.** EMI CDS7 47157-8 (9/86).

ORPHEE AUX ENFERS — *operetta*. **Soloists; Les Petits Chanteurs à la Croix Potencée; Toulouse Capitole Chorus and Orchestra/Michel Plasson.** EMI CDS7 49647-2 (1/89).

LA PERICHOLE. **Soloists; Rhine Opera Chorus; Strasbourg Philharmonic Orchestra/ Alain Lombard.** Erato Libretto 2292-45686-2 (5/92).

LES CONTES D'HOFFMANN. **Soloists; Lausanne Pro Arte Chorus; Du Brassus Chorus; Suisse Romande Chorus and Orchestra/Richard Bonynge.** Decca 417 363-2DH2 (11/86).

Julián Orbón
Cuban 1925-1991

Suggested listening ...

Concerto grosso[a]. *Coupled with* **Ginastera.** Pampeana No. 3. **Revueltas.** Redes. Sensemayá. [a]**Latin American Quartet**; **Simón Bolívar Symphony Orchestra, Venezuela/Eduardo Mata.** Dorian DOR90178 (11/93). *See review under Ginastera; refer to the Index to Reviews.*

Carl Orff
German 1895-1982

New review

Orff. Carmina burana. **Sumi Jo** (sop); **Jochen Kowalski** (alto); **Boje Skovhus** (bar); **Southend Boys' Choir; London Philharmonic Choir and Orchestra/Zubin Mehta.** Teldec 9031-74886-2. Texts and translations included.

Ih DDD 2/94

This is a lively, enjoyable performance with excellent contributions from all concerned. The unison choral singing of the "Veris leta facies" is balanced by the vigour of men and boys alike at the joyous "Ecce gratum" and there is good control of light and shade in the "Floret silva". Boje Skovhus is suitably vociferous in the Tavern scene with a vibrant response from the orchestral percussion and chorus, and plenty of energy later in the "Tempus est iocundum" (where the boys are pubescently throaty). Sumi Jo makes an attractive "Girl in the red shift", and her strong swelling line and later moment of submission (with a lovely scale up to a *pianissimo* climax) suggests a rather knowing virgin. The choral "Ave formosissima" is then exultantly broad in its praise of her beauty. The resonant acoustic encompasses the climaxes spectacularly, even if the *sotto voce* choral singing seems at times a little distanced. There is plentiful percussion (the timps at the opening are splendidly incisive and the splashes of tam-tam equally colourful). Overall, with such a well balanced recording this is an enjoyably impressive *Carmina burana*. Blomstedt's Decca version has just as much character. His performance positively erupts with energy and the Decca sound is very much demonstration-worthy. Ozawa, too, on Philips has an exuberant freshness, while at mid price Ormandy's splendid Philadelphia version (reissued on Sony) is gloriously, resonantly memorable — one of this conductor's very finest records.

Additional recommendations ...
Soloists; St Clement Danes Grammar School Boys' Choir; London Symphony Chorus and Orchestra/André Previn. EMI CDC7 47411-2 — Ih 3m DDD 12/86
Soloists; Schöneberger Boys' Choir; Deutsche Oper Chorus and Orchestra, Berlin/ Eugen Jochum. DG Galleria 423 886-2GGA — 56m ADD 11/88
Soloists; Shinyukai Choir; Berlin Cathedral Boys' Choir; Berlin Philharmonic Orchestra/Seiji Ozawa. Philips 422 363-2PH — Ih DDD 7/89
Soloists; San Francisco Girls' Chorus; San Francisco Boys' Chorus; San Francisco Symphony Chorus and Orchestra/Herbert Blomstedt. Decca 430 509-2DH — 59m DDD 12/91
Soloists; Rutgers University Choir; Philadelphia Orchestra/Eugene Ormandy. Sony Classical SK47668 — 58m ADD

Further listening ...

Catulli carmina. *Coupled with* **Stravinsky.** Les noces. **Soloists/Wolfgang Schäfer.** Koch Schwann Musica Mundi 314021 (7/91).

De temporum fine comoedia — *symbolic drama.* **Soloists; Cologne Radio Chorus; Tölz Boys' Choir; Berlin RIAS Chamber Chorus; Cologne Radio Symphony Orchestra/ Herbert von Karajan.** DG 20th Century Classics 429 859-2GC.

DIE KLUGE; DER MOND. **Soloists; Rudolf Kiermeyer Children's Choir; Bavarian Radio Chorus; Munich Radio Orchestra/Kurt Eichhorn.** Eurodisc GD69069 (3/91).

ANTIGONE. **Soloists; Bavarian Radio Chorus and Symphony Orchestra/Ferdinand Leitner.** DG 20th Century Classics 437 721-2GC3 (8/93).

Leo Ornstein

Russian/American 1892-

Suggested listening ...

Cello Sonata, Op. 52. *Coupled with* **Foss.** Capriccio. **Barber.** Cello Sonata, Op. 6. **Yehuda Hanani** (vc); **Michelle Levin** (pf). Koch International Classics 37070-2 (10/93).

Johann Pachelbel

German 1653-1706

New review

Pachelbel. MOTETS.
J. Christoph Bach. Fürchte dich nicht. Der Gerechte, ob er gleich zu zeitlich stirbt. Ich lasse dich nicht.
J.M. Bach. Halt, was du hast. Fürchtet euch nicht. **Cantus Cölln/Konrad Junghänel.**
Deutsche Harmonia Mundi 05472 77305-2. Texts and translations included. Recorded in 1993.
Motets — auchzet dem Herrn. Nun Danket alle Gott. Exsurgat Deus. Tröste uns Gott. Magnificat. Der Herr ist König und herrlich geschmückt. Gott ist unser Zuversicht. Paratum cor meum Deus. Der Herr ist König. Singet dem Herrn. Jauchzet Gott, alle Lände.

Ih 4m DDD 7/94

At the moment, Pachelbel is represented in the catalogue by 'that' canon and by organ music, with scarcely a hint of his vocal works, which in his lifetime were equally prized. Listening to this immensely engaging disc of ten of his motets for double choir from the last two decades of the seventeenth century (recorded for the first time) and a four-part Magnificat, one is grateful indeed that this superb vocal ensemble (with one voice to a part) has made the effort to redress the balance. Almost the first thing to strike one about these motets is their melodic charm: phrases are tossed back and forth antiphonally between the two choirs (the effect greatly enhanced here by widely separated stereo placing), but there is relatively little real polyphony except for an occasional fugato and the interweaving of chorales into the texture in *Nun danket alle Gott* and *Gott ist unser Zuversicht* (which incorporates "Ein' feste Burg"). The Johann Christoph introduced here with two five-part funeral motets and an eight-part piece is not, as might have been expected, Pachelbel's pupil, Johann Sebastian's eldest brother, but his uncle (there were, confusingly, no fewer than five Johann Christophs in the family). He too introduces chorales, though against a texture less melodically, more harmonically orientated. His younger brother Johann Michael's eight-part motets are simpler in structure, with less antiphonal treatment: *Fürchtet euch nicht* (a Christmas motet) includes a lengthy strophic treatment of "Jesu meine Freude". The singing of the Cantus Cölln is a sheer pleasure to hear.

Further listening ...

Suite in G major. Musicalische Ergotzung — Suite No. 4 in E minor. Aria con variazoni in A major. Canon and Gigue in D major. *Coupled with* **Buxtehude.** *Trio Sonatas* — C major, BuxWV266; G major, BuxWV271; B flat major, BuxWV273. **Cologne Musica Antiqua/ Reinhard Goebel.** Archiv Produktion Galleria 427 118-2AGA (6/89).

Ignacy Paderewski

Polish 1860-1941

Suggested listening ...

Piano Concerto in A minor, Op. 17[a]. *Coupled with* **Melcer-Szczawinski.** Piano Concerto No. 1 in E minor[b]. [a]**Piotr Paleczny,** [b]**Michael Ponti** (pfs); [a]**Polish National Radio Symphony Orchestra;** [b]**Warsaw National Philharmonic Orchestra/Tadeusz Strugala.** Olympia OCD398 (7/84). *See review under Melcer-Szczawinski; refer to the Index to Reviews.*

Nicolò Paganini

Italian 1782-1840

Paganini. Violin Concertos — No. 1 in D major, Op. 6; No. 2 in B minor, Op. 7, "La campanella". **Salvatore Accardo** (vn); **London Philharmonic Orchestra/Charles Dutoit.** DG 415 378-2GH. From 2740 121 (11/75).

$\cdot\cdot$ **lh 9m ADD 2/87**

Paganini's violin music was at one time thought quite inaccessible to lesser mortals among the violin-playing fraternity, but as standards of technique have improved master technicians are now able to do justice to such works as these concertos. Salvatore Accardo is certainly among them, and we can judge his skill as early as the opening violin solo of the First Concerto. This is typical of the style, with its authoritative and rhetorical gestures and use of the whole instrumental compass, but so is the second theme which in its refinement and songlike nature demands (and here receives) another kind of virtuosity expressed through a command of tone, texture and articulation. Dutoit and the London Philharmonic Orchestra have a mainly subordinate role, certainly when the soloist is playing, but they fulfil it well and follow Accardo through the kind of rhythmic flexibilities which are accepted performing style in this music and which for all we know were used by the virtuoso performer-composer himself. The 1975 recording is faithful and does justice to the all-important soloist.

Additional recommendations ...
No. 1. **Wieniawski.** *Violin Concerto No. 2 in D minor, Op. 22.* **Mark Kaplan** (vn); **London Symphony Orchestra/Mitch Miller.** Arabesque Z6597 — $\cdot\cdot$ **57m DDD 7/89** Ⓑ
No. 1. **Vieuxtemps.** *Violin Concerto No. 5 in A minor, Op. 37.* **Viktoria Mullova** (vn); **Academy of St Martin in the Fields/Sir Neville Marriner.** Philips 422 332-2PH — $\cdot\cdot$ **55m 10/89** ᵠP Ⓑ
No. 1. **Saint-Saëns.** *Violin Concerto No. 3 in B minor, Op. 61[a].* **Zino Francescatti** (vn); **Philadelphia Orchestra/Eugene Ormandy.** CBS Masterworks Portrait mono CD46728 — $\cdot\cdot$ **5lm ADD 12/91** ᵠP Ⓑ ▲
Nos. 1 and 2. **Auvergne Orchestra/Jean-Jacques Kantorow** (vn). Denon CO-77611 — $\cdot\cdot$ **lh DDD 4/92** ᵠP Ⓑ
Nos. 1 and 2. **Ilya Kaler** (vn); **Polish National Radio Symphony Orchestra/Stephen Gunzenhauser.** Naxos 8 550649 — **.** **lh 7m DDD 12/93** ᵠP Ⓑ
No. 1[a]. **Goldmark.** *Violin Concerto No. 1 in A minor, Op. 28[b].* [b]**Alberto Kocsis,** [a]**Maria Bálint** (vns); [b]**Savaria Symphony Orchestra/János Petró.** [a]**Budapest Symphony Orchestra/ György Lehel.** Hungaroton White Label HRC162 — **.** **lh lm ADD 3/94** Ⓑ

Paganini. CHAMBER MUSIC. **Gil Shaham** (vn); **Göran Söllscher** (gtr). DG 437 837-2GH. Recorded in 1992.
Sonata Concertata in A major, Op. 61. Six Sonatas for Guitar and Violin, Op. 3 — No. 1 in A major; No. 4 in A minor; No. 6 in E minor. Grand Sonata for Violin and Guitar in A major, Op. posth. Centone di Sonate, Op. 64 — No. 2 in D major; No. 4 in A major. Cantabile in D major, Op. 17. Sonata a preghiera (arr. Hannibal). Moto perpetuo in C major (Allegro di concert), Op. 11.

Ih Im DDD 4/94

Paganini wrote a great deal of guitar music both with and without the violin, bringing together the two instruments he played so well. Paganini played these works with the guitarist/violinist Luigi Legnani who, it is said, finally protested that he always had the easy guitar parts, whilst Paganini enjoyed the violinistic limelight. However, when Paganini produced his *Grand Sonata* and gave the violin part to Legnani the roles were doubly reversed; the violin plays such a minor role that it is usually omitted from performances. As a violinist was to hand he plays his part here, from which you may judge what is (not) lost when it is omitted. The guitar parts in the Six Sonatas, Op. 3 are of student level — Segovia refused many invitations to play them — and could benefit from revision, as those in Opp. 11 and 17, adapted from the original piano parts, firmly suggest. The *Sonata Concertata* finds the two instruments on a more even playing field, with the guitar often leading the way. Polished and expressive performances, clearly recorded, well annotated, and welcome.

Paganini. 24 Caprices, Op. 1. **Itzhak Perlman** (vn). EMI CDC7 47171-2. From SLS832 (6/72).

Ih I2m ADD 7/88

This electrifying music with its dare-devil virtuosity has long remained the pinnacle of violin technique, and they encapsulate the essence of the composer's style. For a long time it was considered virtually unthinkable that a violinist should be able to play the complete set; even in recent years only a handful have produced truly successful results. Itzhak Perlman has one strength in this music that is all-important, other than a sovereign technique — he is incapable of playing with an ugly tone. He has such variety in his bowing that the timbre of the instrument is never monotonous. The notes of the music are despatched with a forthright confidence and fearless abandon that are ideal. The frequent double-stopping passages hold no fear for him. Listen to the fire of No. 5 in A minor and the way in which Perlman copes with the extremely difficult turns in No. 14 in E flat; this is a master at work. The set rounds off with the famous A minor Caprice, which inspired Liszt, Brahms and Rachmaninov, amongst others, to adapt it in various guises for the piano.

Additional recommendations ...
Midori (vn). CBS Masterworks CD44944 — Ih I7m DDD 3/90
Frank Peter Zimmermann (vn). EMI CDC7 47644-2 — Ih I4m ADD I/88
Leonidas Kavacos (vn). Dynamic CDS66 — Ih I7m DDD 9/93
Michael Rabin (vn). EMI CDM7 64560-2 — Ih 9m ADD 9/93
Ilya Kaler (vn). Naxos 8 550717 — Ih I9m DDD 9/93

Giovanni Palestrina

Italian c.1525/6-1594

Palestrina. THE PALESTRINA 400 COLLECTION. **The Tallis Scholars/Peter Phillips.** Gimell CDGIMB400. Items marked [a] from 1585-01 (11/81), [b]1585-03 (4/83), [c]CfP CFP40339 (10/80), [d]CDGIM008 (1/87), [e]CDGIM020 (9/90). Recorded 1980-89.
Palestrina: Missa Benedicta es[a]. Missa Nigra sum[b]. Missa Papae Marcelli[c]. Missa brevis[d]. Missa Nasce la gioia mia[d]. Missa Assumpta est Maria[e]. Missa Sicut lilium inter spinas[e]. Nigra sum[b]. Assumpta est Maria[e]. Sicut lilium inter spinas I[e]. *Anonymous:* Benedicta es[a]. Assumpta est

Maria in caelum[e]. *Josquin Desprez:* Benedicta es, celorum regina[a]. *Lheritier:* Nigra sum[b]. *Primavera:* Nasce la gioia mia[d].

④ 4h 9m ADD/DDD 1/94

From the 100-plus Masses that he could have recorded, Peter Phillips has chosen so shrewdly that the selection here offered appears as comprehensive a cross-section of Palestrina's achievement as you could possibly wish in the space of four hours. The Palestrina enthusiast, converted perhaps by The Tallis Scholars' recording of the *Missa Papae Marcelli* (reviewed below) will very likely have bought all these performances as they appeared. But does the non-specialist need more than a couple of Palestrina Masses to represent the composer? Would not seven of them prove ... well, not to put too fine a point upon it, a bit same-y? The answers are an emphatic 'yes' and a firm 'no' respectively. The variety of texture and audible technique among these Mass settings is quite remarkable. Among the seven Masses collected here, a profound development takes place between the massive sonority of the *Missa Benedicta es*, audibly both Palestrina's homage to, and his measuring of himself against, his great predecessor Josquin Desprez (Josquin's motet and its plainchant base are included, to make the point crystal-clear), and the division of the voices in the *Missa Assumpta est Maria* into two dissimilar, antiphonal choirs, projecting and dramatizing the text with urgent force as well as beauty. The music is most beautifully but not too beautifully sung. Balance, intonation, chording and clarity of texture are all immaculate, but the performances respond to the changes of emotional temperature between the Masses also; they are expressively sung, in the best sense of that word. The recordings, in ample but not obscuring acoustics, are very fine.

Palestrina. Missa Papae Marcelli. Tu es Petrus. ITALIAN SACRED CHORAL WORKS. **Westminster Abbey Choir/Simon Preston.** Archiv Produktion 415 517-2AH. Texts and translations included.
Allegri: Miserere. *Anerio:* Venite ad me omnes. *Nanino:* Haec dies. *Giovannelli:* Jubilate Deo.

59m DDD 5/86

Palestrina. Missa Papae Marcelli.
Allegri. Miserere[a].
W. Mundy. Vox patris caelestis. [a]**Alison Stamp** (sop); **The Tallis Scholars/Peter Phillips.** Gimell CDGIM339. From Classics for Pleasure CFP40339 (10/80).

1h 9m ADD 7/86

To listen to Simon Preston's disc is to enjoy a feast of sacred choral music composed by members of the well-known school of eminent Roman musicians of the sixteenth and early seventeenth centuries. Palestrina heads the list with his *Missa papae marcelli*, but no less famous is the Allegri *Miserere*, which is performed here with a musical understanding and penetration that is comparatively rare. The alternating *Falsobordone* verses excel in richness, and those of the semi-chorus, admirably distanced from the main choir, float across and upwards with an ethereal quality of amazing beauty and magic. The Choir of Westminster Abbey find plenty of scope to display their varied musical skills in the Mass itself, the psalm, and the four motets, and particularly enjoyable is the precision and crispness of the rhythm in Giovannelli's *Jubilate*, and also the careful balance and fullness of the sound in Anerio's *Venite ad me*. The highlight of the Gimell disc is Allegri's *Miserere*. Peter Phillips has used the natural acoustics of Merton College Chapel, adding a note of variety which relieves the repetitious nature of the long penitential psalm: what a simple idea it was to space the singers so that those with the low-lying verses were near the microphone and the others half-way down the chapel, with Alison Stamp's high C rising pure and clear above distant hushed voices! *Vox patris caelestis* is an imaginative and cleverly-designed motet for the Assumption of the Virgin, dating from the mid-sixteenth-century Catholic revival and based on texts from the *Song of songs*. The music rises to an ecstatic climax at the words "Veni, veni ...", with two high trebles at the top of their range crowning the rich harmonies of the lower voices. In marked contrast to such exuberance, the *Missa papae marcelli*, dating from the same period, represents a sober, lapidary style. The declamatory speech-rhythms are admirably rendered and the performance is notable for its moments of intense, if restrained, emotion. Highly recommended.

Additional recommendation ...
Missa Aeterna Christi munera. Sicut cervus. Super flumina Babylonis a 4. Vidi turbam magnam. Quae est ista. Duo ubera tua. Nigra sum, sed formosa. Surge, amica mea. Magnificat Primi Toni. **Anonymous.**

Aeterna *Christi munera*. **Westminster Cathedral Choir/James O'Donnell.** Hyperion CDA66490 — .·˙ lh 7m DDD 🖋

Palestrina. SACRED CHORAL WORKS. **Westminster Cathedral Choir/James O'Donnell.** Hyperion CDA66316. Texts and translations included. Recorded in 1988. *Masses* — Viri Galilaei; O Rex gloriae. *Motets* — Viri Galilaei; O Rex gloriae.

.·˙ lh 8m DDD l/90 🖋

This is music in which Westminster Cathedral Choir excel: their response to the richly reverberant acoustic is warm and generous; they perform with the ease and freedom of kinship — a far cry from the studied perfection of many other choirs. Each motet is heard before its reworking as a Mass. The six-part scoring of *Viri Galilaei* (two trebles, alto, two tenors and bass) invites a variety of combinations and textures, culminating in the joyful cascading Alleluias at the end of Part I and the jubilant ascending series in Part II. In the Mass the mood changes from triumph to quiet pleading — a change partly due to revised scoring: the two alto parts beneath the single treble produce a more subdued sound. The Choir clearly relishes this exploration of the deeper sonorities: in the *Creed* one entire section is entrusted to the four lowest voices. The four-part motet *O Rex gloriae* is lithe and fast-moving. The corresponding Mass, largely syllabic in style, gives the Choir the chance to demonstrate their superb command of phrasing and accen-tuation: the Latin comes over with intelligibility and subtlety. Listen, also, to the wonderful solo boys' trio in the "Crucifixus", and for the carefully crafted canons in the *Benedictus* and the *Agnus Dei*.

Further listening ...

Missa Dum complerentur. *Motets* — Super flumina Babylonis; Exsulate Deo; Sicut cervus; O bone Jesu, exaudi me a 8; Dum complerentur a 6. **Christ Church Cathedral Choir, Oxford/Stephen Darlington.** Nimbus NI5100 (11/88).

Motets — Stabat mater a 8. Hodie beata virgo. Senex puerum portabat. Magnificat a 8. Litaniae de Beata Vergine Mariae I a 8. *Coupled with Allegri.* Miserere mei. **Roy Goodman** (treb); **King's College Choir, Cambridge/Sir David Willcocks.** Decca Ovation 421 147-2DM (5/89). *See review under Allegri; refer to the Index to Reviews.*

Masses — Assumpta est Maria; Sicut lilium inter spinas. *Motets* — Assumpta est Maria a 6; Sicut lilium inter spinas I. *Coupled with Plainchant.* Assumpta est Maria. **The Tallis Scholars/Peter Phillips.** Gimell CDGIM020 (9/90).

Selim Palmgren

Finland 1878-1951

Suggested listening ...

Piano Concertos — No. 2, Op. 33; No. 3, Op. 41; No. 5 in A major, Op. 99. **Soloists; Turku Philharmonic Orchestra/Jacques Mercier.** Finlandia FACD379.

Giovanni Pandolfi

fl. 1660-1669

New review

Pandolfi. CHAMBER WORKS. **Andrew Manze** (vn); [a]**Richard Egarr** (hpd); **Fred Jacobs** (theorbo). Channel Classics CCS5894. Recorded in 1992.
Sonatas per chiesa e camera, Op. 3 — No. 2, La Cesta in A minor; No. 4, La Castella in D major; No. 5, La Clemente in E minor; No. 6, La Sabbatina in C major. Sonatas for Violin

and Continuo, Op. 4 — No. 1, La Bernabea in E minor; No. 4, La Biancuccia in D minor; No. 6, La Vinciolina in D minor. *Anonymous:* Harpsichord Suites[a] — C major; D minor; A major.

Ih 8m DDD 7/94

The existence of Giovanni Antonio Pandolfi Mealli (to give him his full name) is known only from a single mention in the Innsbruck court archives for 1660 and one surviving copy of two volumes of violin sonatas (each containing six works) published there in the same year. Let it be said at once that these sonatas are remarkably interesting discoveries, often chromatically bold, rhapsodic and full of vitality. Several of the seven presented here include among their move-ments (which surely should have been itemized!) a ground bass; of these the most striking is that of Op. 3 No. 2, which is strongly Purcellian (as is the opening of Op. 4 No. 4). Manze plays the sonatas brilliantly, with great verve in fast sections, expressively in reflective ones, and throughout with effectively contrasted dynamics and copious stylish embellishments. He is alertly accompanied by Fred Jacobs and Richard Egarr, who contributes three very worthwhile suites which may possibly be by one Christian Flor. Though composed at much the same time as the Pandolfi, they are totally different in style, very French with their sequence of firmly structured, liberally ornamented dance movements plus, in the case of the C and A major suites, un-measured preludes. They add to the hearty recommendation already earned by this excellently recorded disc.

Sir Andrzej Panufnik

Polish/British 1914-1991

New review

Panufnik. String Quartets — No. 1; No. 2, "Messages"; No. 3. Song to the Virgin Mary[a]. String Sextet[a]. **Chilingirian Quartet** (Levon Chilingirian, Charles Stewart, vns; Simon Rowland, va; Philip de Groote, vc); [a]**Roger Chase** (va); [a]**Stephen Orton** (vc). Conifer CDCF218. Recorded in 1993.

Ih 12m DDD 12/93

While the Second Quartet (1980) recalls the outdoor nocturnals of Bartók and Szymanowski, the First (1976) — opens with urgent, strongly differentiated chatter and then switches to luminous, long-breathed lines; subdued, shifting and rising to an ethereal height. The Third Quartet (1991) serves as a concentrated résumé of Panufnik's quartet style. The *Song to the Virgin Mary* was transcribed from an *a cappella* choral piece of the same name and conjures up something of Dvořák's steadfast, simple piety. "Trains of Thought" was inspired by the hypnotic rhythm of wheels on a track and the thoughts suggested by them; it is based on a three-note cell, "constantly rotated and frequently transposed and reflected". But the effect is more like a dream one might have of the train floating off the tracks and careering up into the firmament: the rhythm remains gently insistent, the harmonic language subtle and suggestive. The Chilingirian Quartet perform well, the sound is excellent and the notes are both appetizing and informative. A most engaging release.

Further listening ...

Symphony No. 9, "Sinfonia della Speranza". Piano Concerto[a]. [a]**Ewa Poblocka** (pf); **London Symphony Orchestra/Sir Andrzej Panufnik.** Conifer CDCF206 (5/92).

Sinfonia sacra[a]. Arbor cosmica[b]. [a]**Royal Concertgebouw Orchestra;** [b]**New York Chamber Symphony/Sir Andrzej Panufnik.** Elektra Nonesuch 7559-79228-2 (5/91).

Sir Hubert Parry

British 1848-1918

Parry. ORCHESTRAL WORKS. **London Philharmonic Orchestra/Matthias Bamert.** Chandos (four discs, as detailed below, available separately). Recorded 1990-92.

CHAN9062 (53m) — Symphony No. 1 in G minor. Concertstück in G minor. *CHAN8961* (52m) — Symphony No. 2 in F major, "Cambridge". Symphonic Variations. *CHAN8896* (1h16m) — Symphonies: No. 3 in C major, "English"; No. 4 in E minor. *CHAN8955* (57m) — Symphony No. 5 in B minor, "Symphonic Fantasia 1912". From Death to Life. Elegy for Brahms.

7/92 10/91 1/91 9/91 DDD

Written in its composer's thirty-second year, Parry's First Symphony witnessed the realization of several decades of aspiration and dedication toward this grandest of musical objectives. Despite its obvious Germanic, and more specifically Brahmsian affiliations, the symphony reflects much of the comfortable optimism of the Victorian era. Even so, there's little in the way of Gothic excess, and not a trace of inflated jingoism here. The symphony is ably constructed and tastefully orchestrated, with several of its most powerful statements returning in the finale. Matthias Bamert's performance is assured and totally committed, as he makes out the strongest possible case for the work from its very opening bars. He also includes an ardently reasoned account of Parry's *Concertstück* in G minor, hardly music of the calibre of the Symphony, but worth hearing, none the less. This is a revelatory issue and it is difficult to imagine these triumphant offerings being superseded for a very long time to come. The same forces score another important first with their fine recordings of the *Cambridge* Symphony and the *Symphonic Variations*. This disc also offers some surprises, for it seems incredible that this music has remained virtually unknown for the best part of a century! The Second Symphony has no particular link with Cambridge, save for the fact that it received its première there in 1883. Bamert and the LPO offer a revelatory performance here in which the real qualities of the music are allowed to shine through any reverential backward glances at the works of Brahms, Dvořák and Schumann. Parry was enthusiastic, however, about Dvořák's *Symphonic Variations* and Brahms's *Haydn* Variations, and followed the example of both in his own set for orchestra. The London Philharmonic are captured here on vibrant form and the Chandos sound is especially full-bodied and resonant.

The discovery on the third disc is the Fourth Symphony, first performed (conducted by Hans Richter) in 1889, revised in 1910, performed twice in its new version and then forgotten for nearly 80 years. It is a deeply personal work, almost confessional in its repressed passion. The first movement (16 minutes) is on an immense scale, covering an emotional range comparable with Elgar's Second (which it preceded). The Third Symphony is more conventional, an English equivalent of Schumann's *Rhenish*. Its sunny exuberance and the lightness of the scoring make it highly attractive. Performance and recording are both admirable. Parry's Fifth Symphony dates from 1912 and like so much of his output this substantial work reveals the composer's enduring devotion to the music of Brahms. However, Parry was fascinated by the idea of writing a programmatic symphony, in the Lisztian mould, and thus each of the four linked movements have titles which relate strongly to his personal ethical outlook. The finale, entitled "Now" culminates with an expansive review of material from earlier in the work, and here it is clearly a sense of confidence and affirmation, expressed in grandiose Edwardian musical rhetoric, which concludes Parry's symphonic cycle. The remaining movements, "Stress", "Love" and "Play" also serve to remind us of the clear romantic origins of this splendid and inexplicably neglected British symphony. Also included on this disc are two shorter, although no less weighty Parry rarities, and the Symphonic Poem *From Death to Life* shares much common ground with the Fifth Symphony, at least in terms of its general subject matter. The London Philharmonic again respond with tremendous conviction and brilliance. In conclusion, all these recordings are highly recommended.

Further listening ...

Nonet in B flat major (ed J. Dibble). *Coupled with* **Stanford.** Serenade (Nonet) in F major, Op. 95. **Capricorn.** Hyperion CDA66291 (9/89).

Violin Sonata in D major. 12 Short Pieces. Fantasie-sonata in B minor. **Erich Gruenberg** (vn); **Roger Vignoles** (pf). Hyperion CDA66157 (9/91).

The Soul's Ransom — Sinfonia Sacra[a]. Choric song from Tennyson's "The Lotos Eaters". **Della Jones** (mez); [a]**David Wilson-Johnson** (bar); **London Philharmonic Choir and Orchestra/Matthias Bamert.** Chandos CHAN8990 (1/92).

Blest pair of sirens. I was glad (orch. Jacob). Jerusalem (orch. Elgar). Judith — Long since in Egypt's plenteous land. *Coupled with* **Bairstow.** Blessed city, heavenly Salem. **Elgar.** Give unto the Lord, Op. 74. Great is the Lord, Op. 67. O hearken Thou. **Hadley.** My beloved spake. **Stanford.** Evening Service in B flat major, Op. 10. Te Deum in B flat major. **Winchester Cathedral Choir; Waynflete Singers; Bournemouth Symphony Orchestra/David Hill** with **Timothy Byram-Wigfield** (org). Argo 430 836-2ZH (4/92).

Arvo Pärt

Estonian 1935-

New review

Pärt. CHAMBER AND ORCHESTRAL WORKS. [a]**Tasmin Little** (vn); [b]**Martin Roscoe** (pf); [c]**Bournemouth Sinfonietta/Richard Studt** ([d]vn). EMI Eminence CD-EMX2221. Recorded in 1993.
Fratres[ab]. Cantus in memory of Benjamin Britten[c]. Summa[c]. Spiegel im Spiegel[ab]. Festina lente[c]. Tabula Rasa[abcd].

⠂ Ih 4m DDD 6/94

Fratres comes bounding in on a breathless, arpeggiated violin crescendo that stops suddenly in mid-air, revealing — in its immediate aftermath, and beyond a masterful piano chord — music that is both harmonically powerful and profoundly peaceful. Tasmin Little is as adept at realizing the score's ecstatic sense of ritual. The *Cantus in memory of Benjamin Britten* and *Festina lente* are two sublime inhabitants of the one world, both of which operate at three simultaneous speeds: the one, a weeping veil of cascading A minor scales, the other a simple shared melody where individual strands entwine around each other. The *Cantus* is prompted by a distantly chiming bell, then falls across the ear like a tonal shroud, gradually gaining in intensity before settling, at length, on a single chord. *Summa*, on the other hand, is a sonorous and largely effective transcription of Pärt's *Creed* for four voices, one of his most striking creations — especially the second movement "Silentium", where the presiding chimes of a prepared piano set the atmosphere, and the whole gradually descends to a static duet for cello and bass. It's the perfect "Stressbuster" although the first movement ("Ludus") is one of Pärt's most consistently motoric creations. This admirably recorded programme allows Pärt's bell-like creations to resonate freely within a generous acoustic. The sum effect is one of immediate spirituality. Studt and Little convey a feeling of presence, of excited discovery that will surely win this fine composer many new friends.

Additional recommendation ...
Fratres. **Corigliano.** *Violin Sonata.* **Moravec.** *Violin Sonata.* **Glinsky.** *Toccata-Scherzo.*
Messiaen. *Quatuor pour la fin du temps — Louange à l'Eternité de Jésus.* **Maria Bachmann** (vn); **Jon Klibonoff** (pf). Catalyst 09026 61824-2 (*See review under Corigliano; refer to the Index to Reviews*) — ⠂ Ih 9m DDD 12/93 ℗

New review

Pärt. Te Deum[a]. Silouans Song, "My soul yearns after the Lord ... "[a]. Magnificat. Berliner Messe[a]. **Estonian Philharmonic Chamber Choir;** [a]**Tallinn Chamber Orchestra/Tonu Kaljuste.** ECM New Series 439 162-2. Texts and translations included. Recorded in 1993.

⠂ Ih 6m DDD II/93 ℗

Pärt's *Te Deum* sets the standard liturgical text to a wide range of nuances, shades and dynamics; brief string interludes provide heart-rending wordless commentaries, and the work's closing pages provide a serenely moving affirmation of holiness. Although relatively static in its musical narrative, Pärt's *Te Deum* is both mesmerizing and enriching. *Silouans Song* (1991), an eloquent study for strings, is as reliant on silence as on sonority. It is again austere and chant-like, although its dramatic interpolations approximate a sort of sacral protest. The brief *Magnificat* for *a cappella* choir (1989) positively showers multi-coloured resonances. However, the *Te Deum*'s closest rival — in terms of substance and appeal — is surely the 25-minute *Berliner Messe* (1990-2). Here again Pärt employs the simplest means to achieve the most magical ends: "Veni Sancte Spiritus" weaves a luminous thread of melodic activity either side of a constant, mid-voice drone, while the weighted phrases of the *Sanctus* take breath among seraphic string chords. And how wonderful the gradual darkening of the closing *Agnus Dei*, where tenors initially answer sopranos and an almost imperceptible mellowing softens the work's final moments. Beautiful sounds, these — gripping yet remote, communicative yet deeply personal in their contemplative aura, while the all-round standard of presentation — performance, engineering, documentation — serves Pärt as devotedly as Pärt serves the Divine Image.

New review
Pärt. Fratres.
Tubin. String Quartet. Piano Quartet in C sharp minor[a]. Elegy.
Tüür. String Quartet. **Tallinn Quartet** (Urmas Vulp, Toomas Nestor, vns; Viljar Kuusk, va; Teet Järvi, vc); [a]**Love Derwinger** (pf). BIS CD574. Recorded in 1992.

1h 7m	DDD	1/94

Arvo Pärt's *Fratres* exists in various arrangements. The quartet version is possibly the eeriest, with the second violinist's held fifth serving as a backdrop for a ghostly chain of repetitions on the one three-bar theme. Erkki-Sven Tüür's String Quartet is an audible relation to Pärt — at least in terms of its ethereal harmonic language. Tüür was born in 1959 in Hiiumaa and subsequently absorbed popularist and modernist influences, including rock music, atonality and minimalism. Eduard Tubin is far better known, although the works recorded here are quite unfamiliar — which, in the case of the short but touching *Elegy*, is a pity. Tubin's early Piano Quartet (1930) is cast in a single 15-minute movement and bears a resemblance to the late chamber music of Gabriel Fauré, both as musical drama and in the upwardly spiralling progress of its harmonies. The late String Quartet (1979) is a fairly animated piece that recalls the earlier Shostakovich quartets and — in its combination of folkiness and rhythmic animation — the Second Quartet of Prokofiev. All five works are strongly projected by the Tallinn Quartet (with Love Derwinger in the Tubin Piano Quartet), beautifully recorded, informatively annotated and usefully representative of a varied and absorbing musical heritage that deserves wider exposure than it has so far received.

Further listening ...

Cello Concerto, "Pro et contra"[a]. Perpetuum mobile, Op. 10. Symphonies — No. 1, "Polyphonic"; No. 2; No. 3. [a]**Frans Helmerson** (vc); **Bamberg Symphony Orchestra/ Neeme Järvi.** BIS CD434 (9/89).

Passio Domini nostri Jesu Christi secundum Johannem. **Michael George** (bass); **John Potter** (ten; **Hilliard Ensemble; Western Wind Chamber Choir/Paul Hillier.** ECM New Series 837 109-2 (2/89).

Miserere[a]. Festina lente[b]. Sarah was ninety years old[c]. [a]**Western Wind Choir;** [ac]**Hilliard Ensemble/Paul Hillier;** [b]**Bonn Beethovenhalle Orchestra/Dennis Russell Davies.** ECM New Series 847 539-2 (1/92).

Key to symbols

	② ②	1h 23m	DDD	6/88
Price	Quantity/ availability	Timing	Recording mode	Review date

Paul Patterson

British 1947-

Suggested listening ...

Duologue. *Coupled with* **Finzi** (arr. Ferguson). Interlude in A minor, Op. 21. **Howells.** Sonata for Oboe and Piano. **Nicholas Daniel** (ob); **Julius Drake** (pf). Léman Classics LC44801 (10/93). *See review under Finzi; refer to the Index to Reviews.*

Francisco de Peñalosa

New review

Peñalosa. Missa Ave Maria peregrina. Missa nunca fue pena mayor. Sacris solemnüs. **Westminster Cathedral Choir/James O'Donnell.** Hyperion CDA66629. Texts and translations included.

`•• 1h 7m  DDD  6/93`

Francisco de Peñalosa was the best of his generation at the courts of Ferdinand and Isabella, and the nearest the Iberian peninsula came to rivalling Josquin in his own lifetime. On this disc we have one of the best choirs in the world for this kind of polyphony, Richard Runciman Terry (director of the choir, 1902-24) having established a tradition for performing the works of sixteenth-century Spanish composers that has been preserved ever since. Their many more recent recordings of this repertory have been much and justly acclaimed, and this is another feather in their cap. Maybe Peñalosa's polyphony was intended to flow a little more freely, especially in the *Kyrie* and *Sanctus* of the Marian Mass. This apart, there are some marvellous moments: the excitement of the triple section at "Cum sancto spiritu" in the *Gloria* of the *Missa Ave Maria*, with its upward leaping basses; the intensity of the sustained passages in the *Credos* of both Masses; the contemplative tone of the *Agnus dei* movements and so on. Unmissable.

Further listening ...

Por las sierras de Madrid. Ne reminiscaris, Domine. Precor te, Domine. Sancta Maria. *Coupled with* **Encina.** Mi libertad en sosiego. Los sospiros no sosiegan. **Mena.** Yo creo que n'os dió Dios. La bella malmaridada. **Enrique.** Mi querer tanto vos quiere. **Anonymous.** Pase el agoa, ma Julieta. Harto de tanta porfia. Dindirín, dindirín. Ave, Virgo, gratia plena. Dentro en el vergel. Entra Mayo y sale Abril. *Instrumental works —* **Narváez.** Fantasía II tono; Fantasía III tono. Paseávase el rey moro. **Fernández Palero.** Paseávase el rey moro. **Milán.** Fantasías 10, 12 and 18. **Segni.** Tiento. **Anonymous.** A la villa voy. **Gothic Voices/Christopher Page** with **Christopher Wilson** (vihuela) and **Andrew Lawrence-King** (hp). Hyperion CDA66653 (2/94). *See review in the Collections section; refer to the Index to Reviews.*

Motets — Inter vestibulum et altare. Tribularer, si nescirem. Ne reminiscaris, Domine. Versa est in luctum. Domine, secundum actum meum. Adore te, Domine Jesus Christe. Ave, verum corpus natum. Nigra sum, sed formosa. Sancta Maria. Unica est colomba mea. Ave, vera caro Christi. Ave, vere sanguis Domini. In passione positus. Precor te, Domine Jesu Christe. Pater noster. Ave Regina caelorum. Sancta Mater, istud agas. O Domina sanctissima. Emendemus in melius. Deus, qui manus tuas. Domine Iesu Christe, qui neminem. Transeunte Domino Jesu. **Pro Cantione Antiqua/Bruno Turner.** Hyperion CDA66574 (7/92).

Krzysztof Penderecki

New review

Penderecki. ORCHESTRAL AND VOCAL WORKS. [e]**Wanda Wilkomirska** (vn); [f]**Cracow Philharmonic Chorus;** [bcdefgh]**Polish National Radio Symphony Orchestra,** [a]**London Symphony Orchestra/Krzysztof Penderecki.** EMI Matrix CDM5 65077-2. Items marked [a] from HMV EMD5507 (1/74), [bdfh] EMD5529 (6/76), [ceg] HMV SLS850 (8/74). Recorded 1972-75.
Anaklasis[a]. Threnody for the victims of Hiroshima[b]. Fonogrammi[c]. De natura sonoris I[d]. Capriccio[e]. Canticum canticorum Salomonis[f]. De natura sonoris II[g]. Dream of Jacob[h].

`•• 1h 15m  ADD`

Krzysztof Penderecki's creative heyday (1950s-70s) prompted a release of dramatic aural ingenuity the like of which had not been heard before and has rarely been heard since. Works such as the *St Luke Passion*, the *Dies irae* and, most especially, the *Threnody for the victims of Hiroshima* featured on this CD, delve deep within the recesses of collective memory, often triggering disturbing nightmare images. Even that master musical psychologist Alban Berg could hardly have approximated the *Threnody*'s chamber of horror — the blinding light of its opening bars, the aural swerve as trees bend and houses shatter, the jittery aftermath as fall-out spreads its poisonous message, and the myriad gestures and effects that amount to a terrifying experience. No other twentieth-century instrumental work quite equals the *Threnody* for graphic impact and no other composer has provided the victims of Hiroshima and Nagasaki with such a dramatic or telling memorial. The trouble is that the *Threnody* accounts for just 9'55" on a 75'25" CD — so what of the rest? Penderecki's invariable preference for slow motion, dense tonal clusters, roaring sonorities (*De natura sonoris II* rises to a deafening primeval groan), wailing vocalizations and sundry instrumental effects (tapping and screeching), not to mention a virtual absence of melody and definable rhythm, make for a pretty draining listening session. One wonders whether the musical metaphors that Penderecki used during this phase of his career are actually capable of expressing anything brighter than *Angst*, terror, fear, disorientation and — very occasionally — black humour. If they do it is difficult to discern, and yet it is a fascinating sound-world for all that, and the *Threnody* is surely its most profound justification. The recordings report all with merciless clarity.

Further listening ...

St Luke Passion (Passio et mors Domini nostri Jesu Christi secundum Lucam). **Soloists; Cracow Boys' Choir; Warsaw National Philharmonic Chorus; Polish Radio National Symphony Orchestra/Krzysztof Penderecki.** Argo 430 328-2ZH (3/91).

Polish Requiem. **Soloists; North German Radio Chorus; Bavarian Radio Chorus; North German Radio Symphony Orchestra/Penderecki.** DG 429 720-2GH2 (3/91).

Ernst Pepping
German 1901-1981

Suggested listening ...

Concerto No. 2. Four Fugues. Partita No. 1, "Ach wie flüchtig". Wie schön leuchtet der Morgenstern. **Wolfgang Stockmeier** (org). CPO CPO999 039-2 (7/91).

Giovanni Pergolesi
Italian 1710-1736

New review

Pergolesi. Salve Regina in A minor[a]. Salve Regina in C minor[a].
Leo. Salve Regina in F major[a].
Gallo. Trio Sonatas — G major; B flat major. [a]**Barbara Schlick** (sop); **Europa Galante** (Fabrizio Cipriani, vn; Robert Ferrentino Brown, va; Maurizio Naddeo, vc; Rinaldo Alessandrini, org; Pascal Monteilhet, theorbo)/**Fabio Biondi** (vn). Opus 111 OPS30-88. Texts and translations included. Recorded in 1993.

· 59m DDD 4/94

An interesting idea, to compare settings of the compline's Marian antiphon by two composers of much the same period, both connected with the royal court of Naples. Of Pergolesi's two for soprano — he also wrote another *Salve Regina* for alto — that in C minor (don't believe the disc case, which thinks it's in C major) is by far the more intense. The very opening of the C minor, with its yearning suspensions and dark-hued chromaticisms, immediately sets an emotional atmosphere which the blander A minor setting does not try to match; but both works are admirable examples of the baroque style. Surprisingly, the attractive *Salve Regina* by Leonardo Leo, who was almost a generation older than Pergolesi, is a lot more galant than baroque with elaborately florid vocal writing of an almost operatic nature. (Leo did, after all, write some 60 operas!) Barbara Schlick brings to all three works a great deal of involvement, expressive and clean singing and, in the Leo, beautifully placed high coloratura. The strings, theorbo and organ are excellent partners; and on their own, in a pleasingly warm acoustic, play with engaging verve and neatness two agreeable little trio sonatas once attributed to Pergolesi but now thought to be by one Domenico Gallo. The fact that the strings are not 'period' instruments should deter no one except stern purists.

Pergolesi. Stabat mater[a]. Salve regina in C minor. **Emma Kirkby** (sop); [a]**James Bowman** (alto); **Academy of Ancient Music/Christopher Hogwood.** L'Oiseau-Lyre Florilegium 425 692-2OH. Texts and translations included.

52m DDD 2/90 ⁹ₚ 🖋

Pergolesi's *Stabat mater*, written in the last few months of his brief life, enjoyed a huge popularity throughout the eighteenth century. But modern performances often misrepresent its nature, either through over-romanticizing it or by transforming it into a choral work. None of these are qualities overlooked in this affecting performance, for Emma Kirkby and James Bowman are well-versed in the stylistic conventions of baroque and early classical music — and their voices afford a pleasing partnership. Both revel in Pergolesi's sensuous vocal writing, phrasing the music effectively and executing the ornaments with an easy grace. Singers and instrumentalists alike attach importance to sonority, discovering a wealth of beguiling effects in Pergolesi's part writing. In the *Salve regina* in C minor Emma Kirkby gives a compelling performance, pure in tone, expressive and poignant, and she is sympathetically supported by the string ensemble. The recording is pleasantly resonant and does justice to Pergolesi's translucent textures. Full texts are included.

Additional recommendation ...
Stabat mater[ab]. *Salve regina*[a]. *In coelestibus regnis*[b]. [a]**Gillian Fisher** (sop); [b]**Michael Chance** (alto); **King's Consort/Robert King.** Hyperion CDA66294 — 54m DDD 11/88 ⁹ₚ ⁹ₛ 🖋

Pergolesi. LA SERVA PADRONA. **Maddalena Bonifaccio** (sop) Serpina; **Siegmund Nimsgern** (bass-bar) Uberto; **Collegium Aureum/Franzjosef Maier** (vn). Deutsche Harmonia Mundi RD77184. Text included. From 1C 065 99749 (3/80). Recorded in 1969.

49m ADD 9/92

It was a performance in Paris in 1752 of Pergolesi's celebrated intermezzo *La serva padrona* which sparked off that celebrated pamphleteer squabble, the "Querelle des Bouffons". It was a confrontation between supporters of Italian music and supporters of the French, in which the king and queen took opposing sides. Convincing performances of Pergolesi's comic domestic 'contretemps' are few and far between but this version, recorded in the late 1960s, is certainly one of them. Maddalena Bonifaccio as the scheming servant-girl Serpina and Siegmund Nimsgern as her vain, foolish and elderly employer play their roles to the hilt, but thankfully not beyond it as many others have done. The leader and director of the Collegium Aureum, Franzjosef Maier sets mostly ideal tempos for the arias and, of even greater importance to the drama, keeps the recitative moving at a brisk pace and in a lively conversational way. Listeners, though, may be irritated by the absence of any translation of the Italian libretto, though a clearly argued synopsis *is* provided in translation. The mid- to late-1960s and early 1970s were the heyday of the Collegium Aureum and many of their recordings dating from this period are withstanding the passage of time well. Recorded sound is of a comparably high level.

George Perle
American 1915-

Suggested listening ...

Wind Quintets — No. 1, Op. 37; No. 2, Op. 41; Nos. 3 and 4. **Dorian Quintet; Julie Landsman** (hn). New World NW359-2 (10/88).

Pérotin

French c.1160-c.1225

Suggested listening ...

Viderunt omnes. Alleluia, Posui adiutorium. Dum sigillum summi Patris. Alleluia, Nativitas. Beata viscera. Sederunt principes. *Coupled with* **Anonymous Twelfth Century:** Veni creator spiritus. O Maria virginei. Isias cecinit. **Hilliard Ensemble/Paul Hillier** (bar). ECM New Series 837 751-2 (2/90).

Allan Pettersson

Swedish 1911-1980

New review

Pettersson. Symphonies Nos. 7 and 11. **Norrköping Symphony Orchestra/Leif Segerstam.** BIS CD580. Recorded in 1992.

Ih I0m   DDD   4/94

Most of Pettersson's major works are constructed as large, unified movements (although he was an accomplished miniaturist) and Nos. 7 and 11, respectively 46 and 24 minutes in length, are no exceptions. The former in some ways is unrepresentative of the composer; the obsessiveness of mood and hectoring tone are present, especially in the *Angst*-ridden first and third spans, but the range of expression is much wider than in most of his other works. Composed in 1967-8, it has a unique atmosphere, both haunting and haunted, which will stay with you for a long time. His melodic genius is confirmed in the long and heartfelt central threnody, as well as by the beautiful quiet coda, truly music to "soften the crying of a child"; its delivery by the Norrköping players has just the right amount of detachment. Segerstam's tempos permit the work to breathe and resonate not unlike Mahler. The Eleventh Symphony (1974) is less combative in tone, although it has its moments, and is not on the same elevated plane as the Seventh. As usual from BIS, the recording quality is first-rate, allowing both the devastating power and delicate fine detail of these scores to emerge equally well.

Hans Pfitzner

German 1869-1949

New review

Pfitzner. Cello Concertos — G major, Op. 42; A minor, Op. 52; A minor, Op. posth. **David Geringas** (vc); **Bamberg Symphony Orchestra/Werner Andreas Albert.** CPO CPO999 135-2. Recorded in 1992.

Ih   DDD   4/94

In his Op. 52 Cello Concerto of 1943 Pfitzner seems to rejoice in the constraints of an anti-modernist romanticism which excludes any associations with a manner much more progressive than that of Schumann. The technical strengths of Pfitzner's early style are clear in the concerto of 1888 (rediscovered in 1975), written when the composer was only 19. The work brims with confidence and potential. Nearly half a century later, in the single-movement G major Concerto of 1935, Pfitzner's shunning of overt psychological conflict is securely in place. Somehow, nevertheless, this carefully restricted territory still makes for a distinctive musical experience. These performances, efficiently recorded, manage to find that core of personality that prevents the music from lapsing into passive introversion. David Geringas is a cellist of distinction, and Werner Andreas Albert and the Bamberg orchestra provide committed support.

New review

Pfitzner. PALESTRINA. **Nicolai Gedda** (ten) Palestrina; **Dietrich Fischer-Dieskau** (bar) Borromeo; **Gerd Nienstedt** (bass) Master of Ceremonies; **Karl Ridderbusch** (bass) Christoph Madruscht, Pope Pius IV; **Bernd Weikl** (bar) Morone; **Herbert Steinbach** (ten) Novagerio;

Helen Donath (sop) Ighino; **Brigitte Fassbaender** (mez) Silla; **Renate Freyer** (contr)
Lukrezia; **Victor von Halem** (bass) Cardinal of Lorraine; **John van Kesteren** (ten) Abdisu;
Peter Meven (bass) Anton Brus; **Hermann Prey** (bar) Count Luna; **Friedrich Lenz** (ten)
Bishop of Budoja; **Adalbert Kraus** (ten) Theophilus; **Franz Mazura** (bass) Avosmediano;
Tölz Boys' Choir; Bavarian Radio Chorus and Symphony Orchestra/Rafael Kubelík.
DG 20th Century Classics 427 417-2GC3. Notes, text and translation included. From 2711 013
(2/74).

③ 3h 26m ADD 7/89 ♩♩P

Pfitzner. PALESTRINA. **Peter Schreier** (ten) Palestrina; **Siegfried Lorenz** (bar) Borromeo;
Ekkehard Wlaschiha (bass) Master of Ceremonies; **Fritz Hübner** (bass) Christoph
Madruscht; **Hans-Joachim Ketelsen** (bar) Morone; **Peter-Jürgen Schmidt** (ten) Novagerio;
Carola Nossek (sop) Ighino; **Rosemarie Lang** (contr) Silla; **Uta Priew** (contr) Lukrezia;
Hermann Christian Polster (bass) Pope Pius IV; **Reiner Süss** (bar) Cardinal of Lorraine;
Henno Garduhn (ten) Abdisu; **Horst Reeh** (bass) Anton Brus; **Günther Leib** (bass) Count
Luna; **Günther Kurth** (ten) Bishop of Budoja; **Joachim Arndt** (ten) Theophilus; **Bernd
Zettisch** (bar) Avosmediano; **Chorus of the Deutsche Oper, Berlin; Staatskapelle
Berlin/Otmar Suitner.** Berlin Classics 0310 001. Recorded at performances in the
Schauspielhaus, Berlin in June 1986 (Acts 1 and 3) and January 1988 (Act 2). Notes, text and
translation included.

③ 3h 23m DDD ♩♩P ♩♩S

Rafael Kubelík's magnificent, sumptuously cast DG recording of *Palestrina* is an almost impossible
act to follow, indeed it's hard to imagine such an extravagance of vocal riches being encountered
in a German opera recording nowadays: Brigitte Fassbaender ardently impulsive in the brief role
of Palestrina's pupil Silla, Helen Donath pure-voiced and touching as his son Ighino (neither of
these is matched in the new recording), and an absolute constellation of superb basses and
baritones, often doubling quite small parts: Karl Ridderbusch, Bernd Weikl, Hermann Prey,
Franz Mazura, with at their head Dietrich Fischer-Dieskau as a surely unsurpassable Borromeo:
dangerously powerful, intensely concerned and in magnificent voice. And those are just the
'secondary' roles! The newer recording simply cannot match that richness. Siegfried Lorenz, for
example, an intelligent and refined singer, conveys much of Borromeo's earnestness but he is
too light of voice to present him as formidably authoritative. One or two other singers have
worn or ill-focused voices, but there is a sharply etched Novagerio, that subtle ecclesiastical
Loge, from Peter-Jürgen Schmidt, and Henno Garduhn is an appropriately weird Abdisu, his
voice breaking into falsetto as the ancient Patriarch of Assyria tremulously greets his brethren at
the Council of Trent. As a more substantial plus, this recording of a concert performance
features singers nearly all of whom had sung their roles in a stage production not long before.
The sense of genuine issues being hotly debated by real characters makes the whole of the
difficult Second Act quite gripping. Inevitable comparisons aside, the attempt at a new recording
needed to be made, not least because Peter Schreier was obviously born to sing the title-role.
He is as much the Palestrina of our day as Nicolai Gedda (for Kubelík) was of his. Schreier sings
with great intelligence, deep expression and care for words, and with the slightly piercing,
fundamentally German tenor sound for which the role was surely conceived. Pfitzner's text is
one of the finest librettos ever written, and Schreier's quiet singing in particular gives the
impression that the beauty of the words and their portrayal of Palestrina's dignity and suffering
are more important to him than concern for his own voice. The most moving passages in the
role all need this Lieder singer's art more than they need vocal glamour, and at such moments
Schreier's subtlety is more affecting even than Gedda's beautiful but less detailed reading. Otmar
Suitner is obviously a Pfitzner conductor of experience and great sympathy. The orchestral and
choral detail, the complex balances in many crucial scenes, are quite superbly handled, and if at
times the result lacks a touch or two of Kubelík's urgency or his marvellous ear for the lucid
radiance of this wonderful score, Suitner's is a most distinguished performance. The new account
has the edge in terms of recording. There is just a hint of rawness to the 20-year-old DG sound
in the fuller passages, and it doesn't have the dynamic range of the new version. Suitner's
performance was recorded in a concert-hall, with the chorus seated well above the orchestra,
and this is splendidly effective in the 'angelic dictation' scene at the end of Act 1; the sense of
space around the musicians is excellent throughout. For Kubelík's visionary quality, though, as
well as for his casting, his recording is arguably the first choice. But Suitner, Schreier and the
modern recording's powerful sense of a real stage performance make it a very close-run thing.

Further listening ...

Piano Concerto in E flat major, Op. 31. **Volker Banfield** (pf); **Munich Philharmonic Orchestra/Werner Andras Albert.** CPO CPO999 045-2.

Violin Concerto in B minor, Op. 34. Duo for Violin, Cello and Orchestra, Op. 43. Scherzo in C minor. **Saschko Gawriloff** (vn); **Julius Berger** (vc); **Bamberg Symphony Orchestra/ Werner Andreas Albert.** CPO CPO999 079-2 (5/91).

Das Fest auf Solhaug — Three Preludes. Kleine Symphonie in G major, Op. 44. Symphony in C major, Op. 46. **Bamberg Symphony Orchestra/Werner Andreas Albert.** CPO CPO999 080-2 (5/91).

Peter Philips

British 1560/1-1628

Suggested listening ...

Consort Music — Pavan and Galliard Pavan. Paget Pavan and Galliard. Aria del Gran Duca. Galliard. Bassano Galliard. Morley Pavan and Galliard. Bassano Pavan and Galliard. Dolorosa Pavan and Galliard. Alman Tregian. Balla d'Amore. Pavan and Galliard in F major. Aria. Passamezzo Pavan. **The Parley of Instruments.** Hyperion CDA66240 (1/89).

Astor Piazzolla

Argentinian 1921-1992

Suggested listening ...

Five Tango Sensations for String Quartet and bandoneon. **Astor Piazzolla** (bandoneon); **Kronos Quartet.** Elektra Nonesuch 7559-79254-2.

Histoire du Tango[ab]. Five Pieces[b]. Six Etudes tanguistiques[a]. [a]**Mikael Helasvuo** (fl); [b]**Jukka Savijoki** (gtr). Ondine ODE781-2 (12/92).

Wenzel Pichl

New review

Pichl. Symphonies – D major, "Mars"; B flat major, Op. 1 No. 5; D major, Op. 17. Symphonie Concertante in D major, "Apollo", Op. 6. **Oradea Philharmonic Orchestra/ Romeo Rimbu.** Olympia Explorer Series OCD434. Recorded in 1993.

 1h 9m DDD 5/94

Wenzel Pichel – or, to use the name he was born with, Václav Pichl – was one of the most prolific composers of the classical era. His style is distinctive but not easy to describe. He favours rather full and rich orchestral scoring; themes that tend to be brief, but avoid cliché by their individual turns of phrase; and a harmonic palette considerably more adventurous than that of most minor composers. There are quite a lot of oddities: solemn *maestoso* introductions (notably in the work subtitled *Apollo*, truly glowing), ingeniously devised themes made from quite modest material, rhythms that confound expectation, and real poetry to some of the slow music. It is not great music, of course. But it is salutary for us, whose classical diet rarely goes beyond the two great masters, to hear something by a minor figure that isn't just Haydn or Mozart, but has quite a sharp flavour of its own. The Oradea Philharmonic is not specially accomplished. However, the spirit is good and the solo work is very capable.

Daniel Pinkham

American 1923

Pinkham. Christmas Cantata[a]. Advent Cantata[b]. Wedding Cantata[c]. Introduction, Nocturne and Rondo[d]. String Quartet[e]. [d]**William Buonocore** (mndl); [d]**John Curtis** (gtr); [b]**Carol Baum** (hp); [c]**Barbara Bruns** (pf); [b]**Ariel Wind Quintet**; [e]**Boston Composers Quartet** (Clayton Hoener, Mark Beaulieu, vns; Scott Woolweaver, va; Andrew Mark, vc); [a]**Lennox Brass**; [abc]**Boston Cecilia/Donald Teeters** with [a]**James David Christie** (org). Koch International Classics 37180-2. Texts and translations included. Recorded in 1992.

 1h 7m DDD 1/94

After initial studies with Piston, Barber, Honegger and Nadia Boulanger (amongst others) Daniel Pinkham (a native New Englander) has led a distinguished musical career. As both the *Christmas Cantata* in 1957, and *Wedding Cantata* (1956) readily show, Pinkham writes gratefully for the choral medium, whilst the accompanying brass sonorities in the former reveal his indebtedness to the motets of Gabrieli and Schütz; indeed, hearing this engaging piece, it's not hard to understand why performances of it have become a Christmas institution in Boston over the years. The *Advent Cantata* (1991) is enhanced by some engagingly piquant scoring for the accompanying ensemble of wind quintet and harp. Koch International's enterprising showcase also features two purely abstract items: the *Introduction, Nocturne and Rondo* for mandolin and guitar duo from 1984 and the 1990 String Quartet — the latter is a particularly impressive achievement, its progress both purposeful and dignified. Given exemplary performances and truthful recording, this is a thoroughly likeable release and one well worth exploring.

Key to symbols

② ② 1h 23m DDD 6/88

Price	Quantity/ availability	Timing	Recording mode	Review date

Walter Piston

American 1894-1976

Piston. The Incredible Flutist — Suite[a]. Fantasy for English Horn, Harp and Strings[b]. Suite for Orchestra. Concerto for String Quartet, Wind Instruments and Percussion[c]. Psalm and Prayer of David[d]. [a]**Scott Goff** (fl); [b]**Glen Danielson** (hn); [b]**Theresa Elder Wunrow** (hp); [c]**Juilliard Quartet** (Robert Mann, Joel Smirnoff, vns; Samuel Rhodes, va; Joel Krosnick, vc); **Seattle Symphony** [d]**Chorale and Orchestra/Gerard Schwarz.** Delos DE3126. Recorded 1991-92.

 1h 8m DDD 2/94

Piston's most lovable score is in fine fettle here. The circus comes and goes with panache, cheering crowds and obbligato dog right on cue. Schwarz's flutist fixes you with his limpid tone. But it will always be the score with the Tango. Schwarz goes with the flow, the sway of the melody, but it can never linger long enough. The *Fantasy* enters darkened Elysian fields — Piston's lyricism sits well with this distinctive voice of sorrow and regret. We can trace their kinship right back to the composer's first published work — the orchestral *Suite* of 1929. At its heart is a long and intense pastorale: the cor anglais is there at the inception. Framing it, motoric syncopations carry us first to a kind of drive-by the blues with bar-room piano and Grappelli violin. The finale is essentially a fugal work-out: high-tech Hindemith. Cut to 1976 and Piston's very last work, the *Concerto*. Ten eventful minutes in which the imperative is once again pitted against the contemplative. The mixing of timbres is masterly, a fleck of woodwind or a brush of tambourine or antique cymbal speaking volumes. But at the centre of gravity is the Juilliard Quartet, moving in mysterious ways, leading on to a closing viola solo — another dark voice posing both unanswered question and valediction. In fact, the last words uttered here are those of the *Psalm and Prayer of David* — a rare vocal setting for Piston, and as such, refreshingly open, unhackneyed, unhieratical. Performance and recording values make the strongest possible case for the musical goods.

Piston. Symphony No. 6. The Incredible Flutist — Suite. Three New England Sketches. **St Louis Symphony Orchestra/Leonard Slatkin.** RCA Victor Red Seal RD60798. Recorded 1989-90.

57m DDD 1/92

The Incredible Flutist's title is perhaps misleading, for there is no solo flute part, and in fact the score consists of a series of short, attractive dance movements. The original music was written for a 1938 ballet: two years later Piston used about half the material for a concert suite which soon became quite popular. The *Three New England Sketches* date from 1959. They comprise "Seaside", a mostly peaceful, evocative essay, "Summer Evening", a wispy, delicate scherzo and "Mountains", whose very grand, portentous outer sections surround a central episode of busy counterpoint. Piston's Sixth Symphony is generally regarded as his best. Written in 1955, it is typically direct in expression, and has no programme. The first movement is very American in its suggestion of wide-open space and in its rhythmic irregularities. A quicksilver scherzo forms the second movement, and then a serene *Adagio* is followed by a cheerful finale, with strident brass, rushing strings, and bubbling woodwind. Leonard Slatkin always conducts music of his own country with great sympathy and insight, as he does here. His orchestra has exactly the right timbre, which is important in American repertoire of this kind, and the engineering is very good.

Further listening ...

Symphony No. 2. *Coupled with* **Ruggles.** Sun-treader. **Schuman.** Violin Concerto[a]. [a]**Paul Zukofsky** (vn); **Boston Symphony Orchestra/Michael Tilson Thomas.** DG 20th Century Classics 429 860-2GC (1/91).

John Playford I

Suggested listening ...

The English Dancing Master — Country Dance Collection. Musick's Delight on the Cithren, Restored and Refined — Collection for the Cithren. Musick's Recreation on the Lyra Viol. **Broadside Band/Jeremy Barlow.** Amon Ra CD-SAR28 (3/88).

Manuel Ponce

Suggested listening ...

Sonatina meridional. Thème varié et finale. Sonata III. Variations and Fugue on "La Folia de España". **Timo Korhonen** (gtr). Ondine ODE770-2 (7/92).

Amilcare Ponchielli

Ponchielli. LA GIOCONDA. **Maria Callas** (sop) La Gioconda; **Fiorenza Cossotto** (mez) Laure Adorno; **Pier Miranda Ferraro** (ten) Enzo Grimaldo; **Piero Cappuccilli** (bar) Barnaba; **Ivo Vinco** (bass) Alvise Badoero; **Irene Companeez** (contr) La Cieca; **Leonardo Monreale** (bass) Zuane; **Carlo Forte** (bass) A Singer, Pilot; **Renato Ercolani** (ten) Isepo,

First Distant Voice; **Aldo Biffi** (bass) Second Distant Voice; **Bonaldo Giaiotti** (bass) Barnabotto; **Chorus and Orchestra of La Scala, Milan/Antonio Votto.** EMI mono CDS7 49518-2. Notes, text and translation included. From Columbia SAX2359/61 (11/60). Recorded in 1959.

③ 2h 47m DDD 2/88 ▲

Ponchielli's old warhorse has had a bad press in recent times, which seems strange in view of its melodic profusion, his unerring adumbration of Gioconda's unhappy predicament and of the sensual relationship between Enzo and Laura. But it does need large-scale and involved singing — just what it receives here on this now historic set. Nobody could fail to be caught up in its conviction. Callas was in good and fearless voice when it was made, with the role's emotions perhaps enhanced by the traumas of her own life at the time. Here her strengths in declaiming recitative, her moulding of line, her response to the text are all at their most arresting. Indeed she turns what can be a maudlin act into true tragedy. Ferraro's stentorian ebullience is most welcome. Cossotto is a vital, seductive Laura. Cappuccilli gives the odious spy and lecher Barnaba a threatening, sinister profile, whilst Vinco is a suitably implacable Alvise. Votto did nothing better than this set, bringing out the subtlety of the Verdi-inspired scoring and the charm of the "Dance of the Hours" ballet. The recording sounds excellent for its age.

Additional recommendations ...
Soloists; London Opera Chorus; Finchley Children's Music Group; National Philharmonic Orchestra/Bruno Bartoletti. Decca 414 349-2DH3 — ③ 1h 1m ADD 7/85
Soloists; Chorus and Orchestra of the Accademia di Santa Cecilia, Rome/Lamberto Gardelli. Decca Grand Opera 430 042-2DM3 — ③ 2h 35m ADD ♀♭
Soloists; Maggio Musicale Fiorentino Chorus and Orchestra/Gianandrea Gavazzeni. Decca Grand Opera 433 770-2DMO2 — ② 2h 30m ADD 9/93 ▲

Cole Porter
American 1891-1964

Suggested listening ...

Paris — Let's do it. Gay Divorce — Night and Day. Leave it to Me — My heart belongs to daddy. Miss Otis Regrets. Nymph Errant — The Physician. *Coupled with* **Britten:** Four Cabaret songs[a]. When you're feeling like expressing your affection[a]. On this Island — As it is, plenty[a]. Blues (arr. Runswick)[b] — The Spider and the Fly; Blues; The clock on the wall; Boogie-Woogie. [a]**Jill Gomez** (sop); [a]**Martin Jones** (pf); [b]**Instrumental Ensemble.** Unicorn-Kanchana DKPCD9138 (9/93). *See review under Britten; refer to the Index to Reviews.*

KIRI SINGS PORTER: Born to Dance — I've got you under my skin. Broadway Melody of 1940 — I concentrate on you. Can-Can — I love Paris; It's all right with me. Gay Divorce — Night and Day; After you. High Society — True Love. Jubilee — Just one of those things. Kiss me, Kate — So in Love am I. Paris — Let's Misbehave; Don't look at me that way. Red, Hot and Blue — Ridin' high. Rosalie — In the still of the night. Seven Lively Arts — Ev'ry time we say goodbye. Something to shout about — You'd be so nice to come to. **Dame Kiri Te Kanawa** (sop); **New World Philharmonic/Peter Matz.** EMI CDC5 55050-2 (7/94).

ANYTHING GOES. **Soloists; Ambrosian Chorus; London Symphony Orchestra/John McGlinn.** EMI CDC7 49848-2 (12/89).

Francis Poulenc
French 1899-1963

Poulenc. CONCERTOS AND ORCHESTRAL WORKS. [e]**Aimée van de Wiele** (hpd); [f]**Francis Poulenc,** [f]**Jacques Février** (pfs); [a]**Ambrosian Singers;** [ab]**Philharmonia Orchestra,** [c]**Orchestre de Paris,** [d]**Paris Conservatoire Orchestra/Georges Prêtre.** EMI Rouge et Noir CZS7 62690-2. Recorded 1962-80.

Les Biches[a]. Bucolique[b]. Pastourelle[b]. Matelote provençale[b] (all from ASD4067, 9/81). Les Mariés de la Tour Eiffel[c] — Discours; La baigneuse de Trouville. Suite française, d'après Claude Gervaise[c] (all from ASD2450, 6/69). Les animaux modèles[d] (ASD2316, 7/67). Sinfonietta[c]. Marches et un intermède[c] (both from ASD2450, 6/69). Concert champêtre[de]. Double Piano Concerto in E minor[df] (both from ASD517, 4/63).

.•' ② 2h 36m ADD/DDD 3/92

Now here's a bargain not to be missed — over two-and-a-half hours of the inimitably frothy art of Francis Poulenc crammed on to just two CDs. The highlight has to be Georges Prêtre's marvellous 1980 recording of the complete *Les Biches* ballet music: with the Philharmonia on sparkling form and a suitably lusty contribution from the Ambrosian Singers, it makes for deliciously inconsequential entertainment. This item, as well as a trio of shorter purely orchestral offerings (the graceful *Pastourelle*, cheeky *Matelote provençale* and sublimely haunting *Bucolique: Hommage à Marguerite Long*), are captured here in a stunningly vivid Abbey Road recording — unquestionably one of EMI's very finest early digital efforts. In fact, Prêtre directs proceedings with no little flair throughout, though the robust response of the two Paris-based groups may come as something of a shock after the silky refinement of our own Philharmonia. Vintage accounts of the winsomely skittish *Concert champêtre* (with harpsichordist Aimée van de Wiele) and elegant Concerto for two pianos (featuring Jacques Février and the composer himself) are joined by lively readings of the engagingly anachronistic *Suite française*, *Sinfonietta* and the rarely-heard wartime ballet *Les Animaux modèles*. This last item suffers most from orchestral imprecision (and is rather dully engineered into the bargain), though Poulenc's actual music is well worthy of further investigation: both outer tableaux ("Le petit jour" and "Le repos de midi") are supremely touching in their wistful nobility. In sum, an irresistible package — and it's at mid-price, too!

Additional recommendation ...
Gloria[a]. Piano Concerto[b]. Les biches — Ballet Suite[c]. [a]**Norma Burrowes** (sop); [b]**Cristina Ortiz** (pf); **City of Birmingham Symphony Orchestra and** [a]**Chorus/Louis Frémaux.** EMI CDM7 69644-2 — .•' 1h 2m ADD 1/89

New review
Poulenc. Piano Concerto[a]. Double Piano Concerto in D minor[b]. Organ Concerto in G minor[c]. [ab]**Pascal Rogé,** [b]**Sylviane Deferne** (pf); [c]**Peter Hurford** (org); **Philharmonia Orchestra/ Charles Dutoit.** Decca 436 546-2DH. Recorded in 1992.

.•' 1h DDD 12/93   ⊙P

The Piano Concerto has the right blend of melodic and textural richness, wit and warmth in the hands of performers who understand the music well enough to bring out all its felicitous detail without exaggeration. The mood of its expansive first movement is more tender than usual here, with its incisive wit and spiky Stravinskian instrumentation being correspondingly less in evidence. But the music can take this approach, and the climaxes are not underplayed, while the ecstatically chorale-like music towards the end of the movement is done to perfection. In the gentle *Andante con moto*, Rogé and Dutoit are in their element, but here again the powerful passages also make their impact, while the romp of a finale has the right *joie de vivre*. The Double Piano Concerto comes over with great vivacity, with Deferne and Rogé (playing second piano) skilfully unanimous and crisply recorded. The Organ Concerto, recorded in St Alban's Cathedral, is also successful; Peter Hurford's mastery in Bach serves him well in its more darkly baroque aspects, but he is equally idiomatic in the uninhibitedly bouncy passages.

Additional recommendations ...
Organ Concerto[a]. **Saint-Saëns.** Symphony No. 3 in C minor, Op. 78, "Organ"[b]. **George Malcolm,** [b]**Anita Priest** (orgs); [a]**Academy of St Martin in the Fields/Iona Brown;** [b]**Los Angeles Philharmonic Orchestra/Zubin Mehta.** Decca Ovation 417 725-2DM — .•' 56m ADD 12/87
Double Piano Concerto[a]. Piano Concerto. Aubade. **François-René Duchable,** [a]**Jean-Philippe Collard** (pfs); **Rotterdam Philharmonic Orchestra/James Conlon.** Erato 2292-45232-2 — .•' 59m DDD 9/88
Organ Concerto[a]. Concert champêtre[b]. Piano Concerto[c]. [a]**Gillian Weir** (org); [b]**Maggie Cole** (hpd); [c]**Jean-Bernard Pommier** (pf); **City of London Sinfonia/Richard Hickox.** Virgin Classics
| VC7 59540-2 — .•' 1h 10m DDD 4/90

Organ Concerto[a]. *Concert champêtre*[b]. *Gloria*[c]. **George Malcolm** ([a]org/[b]hpd); [ab]**Academy of St Martin in the Fields/Iona Brown**; [c]**Sylvia Greenberg** (sop); [c]**Lausanne Pro Arte Chorus**; [c]**Suisse Romande Chorus and Orchestra/Jesús López-Cobos.** Decca Enterprise 425 627-2DM — .•' ⑨ 1h 13m ADD/DDD 7/90

Double Piano Concerto[a]. *Sonata for Piano Duet. Capriccio. L'embarquement pour Cythère. Elégie.* **Milhaud.** *Scaramouche.* **Katia and Marielle Labèque** (pfs); [a]**Boston Symphony Orchestra/Seiji Ozawa.** Philips 426 284-2PH — .•' 50m DDD 8/91

Key to symbols

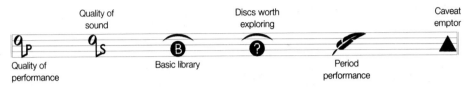

Quality of sound	Discs worth exploring	Caveat emptor

Quality of performance   Basic library   Period performance

Poulenc. PIANO WORKS. **Pascal Rogé.** Decca 417 438-2DH. Recorded in 1986.
Les soirées de Nazelles. Deux Novelettes — No. 1 in C major; No. 2 in B flat minor. Novelette "sur un thème de M de Falla". Pastourelle (arr. pf). Trois Mouvements Perpétuels. Valse. 15 Improvisations — No. 1 in B minor; No. 2 in A flat major; No. 3 in B minor; No. 6 in B flat major; No. 7 in C major; No. 8 in A minor; No. 12 in E flat major, "Hommage à Schubert"; No. 13 in A minor; No. 15 in C minor, "Hommage à Edith Piaf". Trois Pièces.

.•' 1h 7m DDD 7/87   ⑨

Poulenc. PIANO WORKS. **Pascal Rogé.** Decca 425 862-2DH. Recorded in 1989.
Humoresque. Nocturnes. Suite in C. Thème varié. 15 Improvisations — No. 4 in A flat major; No. 5 in A minor; No. 9 in D major; No. 10 in F major, "Eloge des gammes"; No. 11 in G minor; No. 14 in D flat major. Two Intermezzos. Intermezzo in A flat major. Villageoises. Presto in B flat major.

.•' 1h 3m DDD 4/91   ⑨

These beautifully recorded and generously filled discs offer a rich diversity of Poulenc's output. On the first disc, the masterly *Soirées de Nazelles* were improvised during the early 1930s at a country house in Nazelles as a memento of convivial evenings spent together with friends. It paints a series of charming portraits — elegant, witty and refined. The *Trois mouvements perpétuels* are, like so many of the works represented here, lighthearted and brief, improvisatory in flavour and executed with a rippling vitality. The *Improvisations* constantly offer up echoes of the piano concertos with their infectious rhythmic drive — the "Hommage à Schubert" is a tartly classical miniature in three-time played with just the right amount of nonchalant ease by Pascal Rogé. The "Hommage à Edith Piaf" is a lyrical and touching tribute — obviously deeply felt.

The *Humoresque* which opens the second recital is open-air and open-hearted in style, yet songlike too in its melodic richness. The simplicity of this music is deceptive, as is that of the warmly caressing C major Nocturne that follows, for both pieces need subtle phrasing, rubato and the kind of textures only obtainable through the most refined use of the sustaining pedal. Rogé has these skills, and he is also fortunate in having an excellent piano at his disposal as well as a location (the Salle Wagram in Paris) that gives the sound the right amount of reverberation. There are many delights in this music and the way it is played here: to mention just one, listen to the masterly way that the composer and pianist together gradually bring around the flowing freshness of the C major Nocturne towards the deeply poignant feeling of the close. Both discs hold the listener's attention effortlessly from one piece to the next, and though suitable for any time of day they make perfect late-night listening. They should especially delight, and to some extent reassure, anyone who deplores the absence of charm and sheer romantic feeling in much of our century's music.

Additional recommendations ...
Suite in C. Les biches — Adagietto. Trois mouvements perpétuels. Les soirées de Nazelles. Intermezzo No. 3 in A flat major. Valse-improvisation sur le nom de Bach. Trois pièces. Badinage. Napoli. **Eric Parkin** (pf). Chandos CHAN8637 — .•' 59m DDD 10/88

Humoresque. Deux novelettes. Novelette "sur un thème de M de Falla". Villageoises. 15 Improvisations.
Intermezzos — No. 1 in C major; No. 2 in D flat major. Suite française. Presto. Mélancolie. Thème varié.
Eric Parkin (pf). Chandos CHAN8847 — .•˙ 1h 12m DDD 12/90

Poulenc. CHORAL WORKS. **Trinity College Choir, Cambridge/Richard Marlow.**
Conifer CDCF151. Texts and translations included.
Mass in G major. Quatre motets pour le temps de Noël. Quatre petites prières de Saint François
d'Assise. Quatre motets pour un temps de pénitence. Laudes de Saint Antoine de Padoue. Salve
regina. Ave verum corpus. Exultate Deo.

.•˙ 1h 10m DDD 10/88   9p

The lusciously chromatic harmony of the Mass in G major can easily cloy but the bright,
radiant textures of the singing of the Trinity College Choir avoids this entirely. Readers
unfamiliar with this work will be surprised how potent it is. The *Ave verum corpus* for high
high voices is quite exquisite and in the St Francis *Prières* Marlow is assured and musically
aware. The choir does, however, produce occasional curious French pronunication, with
some very odd mute "e"s. An interesting personal sidelight on these graceful and expressive
pieces for male voices is revealed by the dedication to Frère Jérome of Champfleury "in
memory of his grandfather, my uncle Camille Poulenc". The interpretation of the Penitential
Motets is very dramatic and the short motet *Salve regina* is graceful and serene. Caution
needs to be taken not to listen to too many of these works — virtually entirely
homophonic, and nearly all characterized by Poulenc's special brand of tartly sweet
harmonies — one after the other. The performances, with fine balance, expressive dynamic
shadings, pure intonation, intelligent phrasing and excellent enunication, are very
impressive. Marlow, of course, is operating on home ground, in the almost ideal acoustics
of Trinity College Chapel in Cambridge. The accompanying notes are interesting and
informative.

Additional recommendations ...
Gloria[ab]. Salve regina. Ave verum corpus. Exultate Deo. Litanies à la Vierge Noire[b]. Quatre motets pour un
temps de pénitence[c]. Quatre motets pour le temps de Noël. [a]**Donna Deam**, [c]**Mary Seers** (sops);
Cambridge Singers; [b]**City of London Sinfonia/John Rutter.** Collegium COLCD108 —
.•˙ 1h 7m DDD 10/88
Mass. Quatre petites prières. Salve regina. **Martin.** Mass for double chorus. **Christ Church**
Cathedral Choir, Oxford/Stephen Darlington. Nimbus NI5197 — .•˙ 59m DDD 12/89 9p
Mass[a]. Quatre motets pour le temps de Noël. Quatre motets pour un temps de pénitence. Quatre petites
prières de Saint François d'Assise[b]. [a]**Donna Carter** (sop); [b]**Christopher Cock** (ten); **Robert**
Shaw Festival Singers/Robert Shaw. Telarc CD80236 — .•˙ 52m DDD 10/90 9p
Mass[d]. Salve Regina. **Fauré.** Requiem (revised version)[a]. Cantique de Jean Racine, Op. 11[b]. Messe
basse[c]. [ad]**Jonathon Bond** (treb); [c]**Andrew Brunt** (treb); [a]**Benjamin Luxon** (bar);
[abc]**Stephen Cleobury** (org); [a]**Academy of St Martin in the Fields; Choir of St John's**
College, Cambridge/George Guest. Decca Ovation 430 360-2DM — .•˙ 1h 14m ADD 9/91
Mass[a]. Petites prières de Saint François d'Assise. Motets pour un temps de pénitence[b]. Motets pour le temps
de Noël. Salve Regina. Exultate Deo. Litanies à la vierge noire[c]. [a]**Mark Kennedy**, [b]**Eamonn**
O'Dwyer (trebs); **Westminster Cathedral Choir/James O'Donnell, with** [c]**Ian Simcock**
(org). Hyperion CDA66664 — .•˙ 1h 10m DDD 6/94

New review
Poulenc. DIALOGUES DES CARMELITES. **Catherine Dubosc** (sop) Blanche de la Force;
Rachel Yakar (sop) Madame Lidoine; **Rita Gorr** (mez) Madame de Croissy; **Brigitte**
Fournier (sop) Soeur Constance; **Martine Dupuy** (mez) Mère Marie; **José van Dam** (bass-
bar) Marquis de la Force; **Jean-Luc Viala** (ten) Chevalier de la Force; **Michel Sénéchal** (ten)
L'Aumônier; **François Le Roux** (bar) Le geôlier; **Lyon Opéra Chorus and Orchestra/**
Kent Nagano. Virgin Classics VCD7 59227-2. Notes, text and translation included.

.•˙ ② 2h 32m DDD 9/92   9p

Once more in a work out of the ordinary (following that given to them in 1990 for
Prokofiev's *Love for Three Oranges*) the dedication of Kent Nagano and his Opéra de Lyon
forces resulted in the 1993 *Gramophone* Record Award for best opera recording. Poulenc's chef

d'oeuvre is one of the few operas written since Wozzeck that has survived in the repertory — and deservedly so. It is written from, and goes to, the heart, not in any extrovert or openly histrionic way but by virtue of its ability to explore the world of a troubled band of Carmelite nuns at the height of the terrors caused by the French Revolution, and do so in an utterly individual manner. Poulenc unerringly enters into their psyches as they face their fatal destiny. Nagano responds keenly to the sombre, elevated mood and intensity of Poulenc's writing and unfailingly delineates the characters of the principals as they face their everyday martyrdom. The magisterial authority of Martine Dupuy's Mère Marie, the agony of Rita Gorr's Old Prioress, the inner torment of Catherine Dubosc's Sister Blanche, the restraint of Rachel Yakar's Madame Lidoine, the eager charm of Brigitte Fournier's Sister Constance are only the leading players in a distribution that is admirable in almost every respect. The score is for once given complete. The recording is atmospheric and suggests stage action without exaggeration.

New review
Poulenc. LA VOIX HUMAINE. **Françoise Pollet** (sop) La Femme; **Lille National Orchestra/Jean-Claude Casadesus.** Harmonia Mundi HMC90 1474. Notes, text and translation included. Recorded in 1993.

· 46m DDD 7/94

Auteuil 04 virgule 7 is on the line again. But one shouldn't make jokes. Poor woman, the situation is real and dreadful, with Cocteau's script never betraying itself into the cheapness which lies waiting, available at the drop of a word or a receiver, and with the music capturing mood, pace and development in such sympathy with the text that one marvels both were not written by the same man. It conjures up the image of her agonized one-sided conversation, over a maddeningly frustrating telephone line, as a woman driven suicidal by her lover's desertion for another woman. Imagination, of course, can do much on its own, as it certainly did with the original singer, Denise Duval, and also with Julia Migenes whose recording on Erato (listed below), skilfully judged and varied, provides a genuine dramatic experience. This new version is more of a *musical* experience. Françoise Pollet has a warmer, richer voice than the others, and in passages of sad indulgence this enriches the score, adds to the musical pleasure and perhaps increases feeling for the woman *as* a woman rather than as a nervous-system. The high C ("je devenais folle") brings a marvellous sense of release, partly because of its extremity amid so much middle-register deep velvet tone. But the little shifts of pathos, the woeful little efforts at brightness, the sense of 'catching' words from the other end of the line, these are muted, turned into something too monochromatic. The orchestral playing is fine and brings constantly appreciating relish for that morbid sweetness at which Poulenc is so expert.

Additional recommendation ...
Julia Migenes (sop); **French National Orchestra/Georges Prêtre.** Erato 2292-45651-2
— · 45m DDD 9/91

Further listening ...

Sonata for Clarinet and Piano. Sonata for Clarinet and Bassoon. Trio for Oboe, Bassoon and piano. Sonata for Two Clarinets. Sonata for Oboe and Piano. **Ozi Wind Trio; Jacques Di Donato** (cl); **Kun Woo Paik** (pf). Adda 590042 (9/92).

Banalites[b] — Chansons d'Orkenise; Hôtel. La courte paille[b] — Le carafon; La reine de coeur. Chansons villageoises[b] — Les gars qui vont à la fête. Deux poèmes de Louis Aragon[b]. *Coupled with* **Berlioz.** Les nuits d'été[a]. **Ravel.** Shéhérazade[a]. **Debussy.** Trois chansons de Bilitis[b]. **Régine Crespin** (sop); [b]**John Wustman** (pf); [a]**Suisse Romande Orchestra/Ernest Ansermet.** Decca 417 813-2DH (11/88).

Le travail du peintre. Chansons gaillardes. Tel jour, telle nuit. Cinq Poèmes d'Eluard. **Bernard Kruysen** (bar); **Noël Lee** (pf). Arion ARN68258 (3/94).

Michael Praetorius

German 1571-1621

Praetorius. Terpsichore — excerpts. **New London Consort/Philip Pickett.** L'Oiseau-Lyre Florilegium 414 633-2OH.

·.·   5lm   DDD   11/86   ♀ᴘ   **❓**   🖋

For the full range of late Renaissance instruments, impressively played and brimming over with good humour, this is unquestionably the finest disc in the catalogue. Schryari, racketts, crumhorns, sorduns, theorboes, archlutes, viols, regal: all these and lots more, played by some of Britain's finest exponents and recorded with dazzling clarity. Moreover, should you be at all unsure about the difference between the sound of a shawm and a rauschpfeife, you will find all the instruments used carefully itemized for each of the 31 different dances presented here. And the insert reproduces the pictures of these instruments that Praetorius himself published in his massive *Syntagma musicum.* The dances themselves are chosen from over 300 that Praetorius published in his *Terpsichore* of 1612. They are the perfect vehicle for this array of machinery. Pickett and his musicians go to work on them with considerable verve and the result fairly fizzles.

Further listening ...

Magnificat per omnes versus. Aus tiefer Not à 4. Der Tag vertreibt die finster Nacht. Venite exultemus Domino. Maria Magdalena. Peccavi fateor. Psalm 116. **Huelgas Ensemble/Paul van Nevel.** Sony Classical Vivarte SK48039.

Sergey Prokofiev

Russian 1891-1953

Prokofiev. PIANO CONCERTOS. **Vladimir Ashkenazy** (pf); **London Symphony Orchestra/André Previn.** Decca 425 570-2DM2. From 15BB 218 (10/75). Recorded 1974-75.
No. 1 in D flat major, Op. 10. No. 2 in G minor, Op. 16. No. 3 in C major, Op. 26. No. 4 in B flat major, Op. 53, "for the left hand". No. 5 in G major, Op. 55.

·.·   ②   2h 6m   ADD   3/90   ♀ᴘ   **Ⓑ**

While it's true that the Prokofiev piano concertos are an uneven body of work, there's enough imaginative fire and pianistic brilliance to hold the attention even in the weakest of them; the best, by common consent, Nos. 1, 3 and 4 have stood the test of time very well. As indeed have these Decca recordings. The set first appeared in 1975, but the sound is fresher than many contemporary digital issues, and Ashkenazy has rarely played better. Other pianists have matched his brilliance and energy in, say, the Third Concerto, but very few have kept up such a sure balance of fire and poetry. The astonishingly inflated bravura of the Second Concerto's opening movement is kept shapely and purposeful and even the out-of-tune piano doesn't spoil the effect too much. And the youthful First has the insouciance and zest its 22-year-old composer plainly intended. Newcomers to the concertos should start with No. 3: so many facets of Prokofiev's genius (including that wonderfully piquant lyricism) are here, and Ashkenazy shows how they all take their place as part of a kind of fantastic story. But there are rewards everywhere, and the effort involved in finding them is small. Why hesitate?

Additional recommendations ...
Nos. 1-5. Overture on Hebrew themes, Op. 34[a]. Visions fugitives, Op. 22. **Michel Béroff** (pf); [a]**Michel Portal** (cl); [a]**Parrenin Quartet; Leipzig Gewandhaus Orchestra/Kurt Masur.** EMI CMS7 62542-2 — ·.· ② 2h 28m ADD 7/89 ♀ᴘ Ⓑ
Nos. 1-5. **Kun Woo Paik** (pf); **Polish National Radio Symphony Orchestra/Antoni Wit.** Naxos 8 550565 (*Nos. 2 and 5*); 8 550566 (*Nos. 1, 3 and 4*) — , ② 57m 1h 12m DDD 11/92 Ⓑ
Nos. 1-5. **Vladimir Krainev** (pf); **Frankfurt Radio Symphony Orchestra/Dmitri Kitaienko.** Teldec 9031-73257-2 — ·.· ② 2h 3m DDD 7/93 ♀ᴘ Ⓑ
No. 4. **Reger.** Piano Concerto in F minor, Op. 114. **Rudolf Serkin** (pf); **Philadelphia Orchestra/Eugene Ormandy.** CBS Masterworks Portrait CD46452 — ·.· 1h 2m ADD 12/91

New review

Prokofiev. Piano Concertos — No. 1 in D flat major, Op. 10; No. 3 in C major, Op. 26; No. 5 in G minor, Op. 55. **Yefim Bronfman** (pf); **Israel Philharmonic Orchestra/Zubin Mehta.** Sony Classical SK52483. Recorded in 1991.

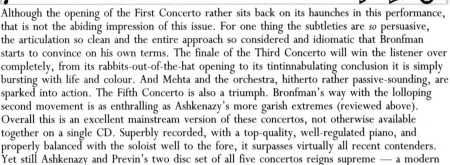

1h 6m DDD 12/93

Although the opening of the First Concerto rather sits back on its haunches in this performance, that is not the abiding impression of this issue. For one thing the subtleties are *so* persuasive, the articulation so clean and the entire approach so considered and idiomatic that Bronfman starts to convince on his own terms. The finale of the Third Concerto will win the listener over completely, from its rabbits-out-of-the-hat opening to its tintinnabulating conclusion it is simply bursting with life and colour. And Mehta and the orchestra, hitherto rather passive-sounding, are sparked into action. The Fifth Concerto is also a triumph. Bronfman's way with the lolloping second movement is as enthralling as Ashkenazy's more garish extremes (reviewed above). Overall this is an excellent mainstream version of these concertos, not otherwise available together on a single CD. Superbly recorded, with a top-quality, well-regulated piano, and properly balanced with the soloist well to the fore, it surpasses virtually all recent contenders. Yet still Ashkenazy and Previn's two disc set of all five concertos reigns supreme — a modern classic worthy of the name.

Additional recommendations ...
Nos. 1, 4 and 5. **Boris Berman** (pf); **Royal Concertgebouw Orchestra/Neeme Järvi.** Chandos CHAN8791 — 1h 4m DDD 10/90
Nos. 1 and 3. Piano Sonata No. 7 in B flat major, Op. 83. **Mari Kodama** (pf); **Philharmonia Orchestra/Kent Nagano.** ASV CDDCA786 — 1h 4m DDD 4/92
No. 3[a]. Violin Concerto No. 1 in D major, Op. 19[b]. Lieutenant Kijé — Suite, Op. 60[b]. [a]**Martha Argerich** (pf); [b]**Shlomo Mintz** (vn); [a]**Berlin Philharmonic Orchestra;** [b]**Chicago Symphony Orchestra/Claudio Abbado.** DG Classikon 439 413-2GCL — 1h 9m ADD/DDD 1/94

New review

Prokofiev. Piano Concerto No. 3 in C major, Op. 26. Toccata in C major, Op. 11.
Rachmaninov. Piano Concerto No. 1 in F sharp minor, Op. 1.
Pinto. Three Scenes from Childhood. **Byron Janis** (pf); **Moscow Philharmonic Orchestra/Kyrill Kondrashin.** Mercury 434 333-2MM. Recorded in 1962.

1h 9m ADD 7/94

Many would consider this Mercury reissue to be the finest record to emerge from that company's visit to Moscow in 1962, where they went to make the first Western-engineered recordings of the Soviet era. Byron Janis accompanied the American team to join Kyrill Kondrashin and the Moscow Philharmonic in two quite remarkable concerto performances, in which soloist, conductor and orchestra consistently strike sparks off each other. The Prokofiev Third Piano Concerto is an unforgettable mix of Russian lyricism, in which powerful pianistic bravura is spiced with wit — especially in the slow movement theme and variations. In the coupled Rachmaninov Concerto No. 1 the solo playing is of Horowitz calibre: scintillating in the finale, the work's warmth fully conveyed. Don't miss this, even if it involves duplication. To fill out the disc some solo piano 'encores' have been added, including the Prokofiev *Toccata*, Op. 11 and an engaging suite called *Three scenes from Childhood* by the virtually unknown Octavio Pinto (1890-1950). The recording, crystal clear, yet full and never clinical, is another brilliant example of Mercury's engineering expertise.

Prokofiev. Piano Concerto No. 5 in G major, Op. 55[a].
Rachmaninov. Piano Concerto No. 2 in C minor, Op. 18[b]. **Sviatoslav Richter** (pf); **Warsaw Philharmonic Orchestra/[a]Witold Rowicki, [b]Stanislaw Wislocki.** DG 415 119-2GH. Item marked [a] from 138075 (3/60), [b] 138076 (1/60). Recorded in 1959.

58m ADD 6/85

Prokofiev was to find no more dedicated an advocate for his keyboard works than Richter. So how good that this artist's now legendary account of the Fifth Piano Concerto has been granted a new lease of life on CD. Although it has never enjoyed the popularity of Prokofiev's Nos. 1 and 3, here, however, attention is riveted from first note to last. Richter delights in the music's rhythmic vitality and bite, its melodic and harmonic unpredictability. Both piano and orchestra are so clearly and vividly reproduced that it is difficult to believe that the recording is 35 years old. Though betraying its age slightly more, notably in the sound of the keyboard itself, Rachmaninov's No. 2 is no less gripping. Not all of Richter's tempos conform to the score's suggested metronome markings, but his intensity is rivalled only by his breathtaking virtuosity. Never could the work's opening theme sound more laden, more deeply and darkly Russian.

Prokofiev. Violin Concertos — No. 1 in D major, Op. 19[a]; No. 2 in G minor, Op. 63[a]. **Stravinsky.** Violin Concerto in D major. **Kyung-Wha Chung** (vn); **London Symphony Orchestra/André Previn.** Decca Ovation 425 003-2DM. Items marked [a] from SXL6773 (3/77), [b] SXL6601 (5/73). Recorded 1972-75.

1h 12m ADD 7/90

This is Chung at her most compelling, never deliberately attention seeking, yet riveting attention from the first bar. Her deft mastery of the solo sword-play in the First Concerto's *Scherzo* defies criticism, yet it is the contemplative moments one remembers most of all: the very start of the First Concerto, for example, with tone of extraordinary delicacy and finesse; and the withdrawn, initially almost whispered delivery of the opening melody of the Second Concerto's slow movement. The LSO were audibly inspired by the example and by the time the Prokofiev concertos were made, Previn was already a proven Prokofievian and Chung's most frequent partner on disc. The Stravinsky was an earlier collaboration. The concerto is in Stravinsky's most diamond-edged neo-classical manner. It finds Chung at her most incisive and high spirited, and Previn relishing the sonorities and the syncopations.

Additional recommendations ...

Nos. 1 and 2. **Shlomo Mintz** (vn); **Chicago Symphony Orchestra/Claudio Abbado.** DG 410 524-2GH — DDD 4/84

Nos. 1 and 2. **Itzhak Perlman** (vn); **BBC Symphony Orchestra/Gennadi Rozhdestvensky.** EMI CDC7 47025-2 — DDD 9/84

No. 2[a]. **Glazunov.** *Violin Concerto in A minor, Op. 82[b].* **Sibelius.** *Violin Concerto in D major, Op. 47[c].* **Jascha Heifetz** (vn); [b]**RCA Victor Symphony Orchestra/Walter Hendl;** [a]**Boston Symphony Orchestra/Charles Münch;** [c]**Chicago Symphony Orchestra/ Walter Hendl.** RCA Red Seal RD87019 (*see review under Glazunov; refer to the Index to Reviews*) — 1h 9m ADD 10/86 ▲

No. 2. **Shostakovich.** *Violin Concerto No. 1 in A minor, Op. 99.* **Viktoria Mullova** (vn); **Royal Philharmonic Orchestra/André Previn.** Philips 422 364-2PH — 1h DDD 6/89

No. 1[a]. Piano Concerto No. 3 in C major, Op. 26[b]. [a]**Shlomo Mintz** (vn); [b]**Martha Argerich** (pf); [a]**Chicago Symphony Orchestra;** [b]**Berlin Philharmonic Orchestra/Claudio Abbado.** DG Classikon 439 413-2GCL — 1h 9m ADD/DDD 1/94

Nos. 1 and 2[a]. THE LOVE FOR THREE ORANGES — Les ridicules; Scène infernale; Marche; Scherzo; Le Prince et la Princesse; La fruite. [a]**Joshua Bell** (vn); **Montreal Symphony Orchestra/Charles Dutoit.** Decca 440 331-2DH — 1h 5m DDD 1/94

New review

Prokofiev. Symphony-Concerto (Sinfonia Concertante) for Cello and Orchestra in E minor, Op. 125[a]. Concertino for Cello and Orchestra in G minor, Op. 132[b]. **Lynn Harrell** (vc); **Royal Philharmonic Orchestra/Vladimir Ashkenazy.** Decca 436 233-2DH. Item marked [a] recorded in 1989, [b] 1991.

58m DDD 5/94

The *Symphony-Concerto* or *Sinfonia Concertante* as it is called on this disc, is Prokofiev's overhaul of his earlier Cello Concerto, made in the last two years of his life in collaboration with Rostropovich. The balance of the work was radically changed: he expanded the role of the orchestra (hence the new title), reorganized the themes and even wrote some new ones. Vladimir Ashkenazy draws playing of much character from the RPO, captures the humour of the variation movement (far more effectively than Ozawa) and brings out the sardonic, demonic side of the middle movement. There is also some pretty dazzling playing from Lynn Harrell.

Ashkenazy keeps a firm grip on proceedings and conveys an obvious enthusiasm for this piece, and the much slighter makeweight. Prokofiev had been inspired by his collaboration with Rostropovich to embark on another piece, the *Concertino* for Cello and Orchestra, Op. 132, which he had nearly completed at his death. It was put into its present shape and orchestrated by Rostropovich and Kabalevsky. The recording is excellent in every way but benefits from a slightly higher level setting than usual.

Additional recommendations ...
Symphony-Concerto. **Shostakovich.** *Cello Concerto No. 1 in E flat major, Op. 107.* **Mstislav Rostropovich** (vc); **London Symphony Orchestra/Seiji Ozawa.** Erato 2292-45332-2 — .•˙ 1h 3m DDD 1/89
Symphony-Concerto. **Tchaikovsky.** *Variations on a Rococo Theme for Cello and Orchestra, Op. 33. Andante cantabile for Cello and Strings.* **Yo-Yo Ma** (vc); **Pittsburgh Symphony Orchestra/Lorin Maazel.** Sony Classical SK48382 — .•˙ 1h 8m DDD 11/92 ℗ ♊s

Prokofiev. ORCHESTRAL WORKS. [a]**Sting** (narr); [b]**Stefan Vladar** (pf); **Chamber Orchestra of Europe/Claudio Abbado.** DG 429 396-2GH. Recorded 1986-90.
Peter and the wolf, Op. 67[a]. Symphony No. 1 in D major, Op. 25, "Classical". March in B flat minor, Op. 99. Overture on Hebrew Themes, Op. 34*bis*[b].

.•˙ **50m DDD 4/91** ♊℗ Ⓑ

Abbado and the multi-talented Sting offer a lively and beautifully crafted account of Prokofiev's ever popular *Peter and the wolf*. The choice of Sting as narrator is clearly aimed at a younger audience who would otherwise never give this delightful work a second glance. Any fears that the original freshness of Prokofiev's creation may be lost in favour of a less formal approach are soon dispelled — Sting is an effective and intelligent storyteller capable of capturing the imagination of adults and children alike, and there is never a feeling of contrivance or mere gimmickry. The orchestral playing is a real delight too; sharply characterized and performed with great affection. The *Overture on Hebrew Themes* is more commonly heard in its drier, more acerbic version for clarinet, piano and string quartet, but makes a welcome and refreshing appearance on this disc in Prokofiev's own arrangement for small orchestra. Abbado's elegant and graceful reading of the *Classical* Symphony is one of the finest in the catalogue, and is particularly notable for its beautifully shaped phrasing, clarity of inner detail and crisp articulation.

Additional recommendations ...
Peter and the wolf[a]. **Britten.** *The Young Person's Guide to the Orchestra, Op. 34. GLORIANA — Courtly dances.* **Royal Philharmonic Orchestra/André Previn** ([a]narr). Telarc CD80126 — .•˙ 55m DDD 10/87 Ⓑ
Peter and the wolf[a]. **Saint-Saëns.** *Le carnaval des animaux*[b]. **Mozart.** *Serenade No. 13 in G major, "Eine kleine Nachtmusik".* [a]**Sir John Gielgud** (narr); [b]**Anton Nel, Keith Snell** (pfs); **Academy of London/Richard Stamp.** Virgin Classics VC7 59533-2 — .•˙ 1h 7m DDD 9/89 Ⓑ
Peter and the wolf[a]. Symphony No. 1 in D major, Op. 25, "Classical"[b]. Lieutenant Kijé Suite, Op. 60[c]. THE LOVE FOR THREE ORANGES — Suite[d]. [a]**Sir Ralph Richardson** (narr); [b]**London Symphony Orchestra/Sir Malcolm Sargent;** [c]**Paris Conservatoire Orchestra/Sir Adrian Boult;** [d]**London Philharmonic Orchestra/Walter Weller** Decca Headline Classics 433 612-2DSP — .• 1h 16m ADD 1/92 Ⓑ

Prokofiev. WAR AND PEACE — Symphonic Suite (arr. Palmer). Summer night, Op. 123. Russian Overture, Op. 72. **Philharmonia Orchestra/Neeme Järvi.** Chandos CHAN9096. Recorded in 1991.

.•˙ **1h 4m DDD 3/93** ♊s

This issue comes to us thanks not only to Chandos, Neeme Järvi and the Philharmonia but also to that intelligent and selfless musician Christopher Palmer, who in providing us with a symphonic suite from the opera *War and Peace* does Prokofiev the same kind of service as he has already performed in the case of his *Ivan the Terrible* film music, also recorded for Chandos by the same conductor and orchestra. The music taken here from *War and Peace* is vintage Prokofiev, unmistakable in its personal language — direct yet never conventional — and its sheer individuality of orchestral sound. Here is the epic power that is proper to his treatment of

Tolstoy's great novel, as well as a lighter dance music style that shows him as the compatriot of Tchaikovsky and the fine ballet composer that he was. The finale of this immensely colourful triptych portrays the retreat from Moscow of Napoleon's defeated French troops in all its agony (from their point of view) and triumph (from that of the Russian forces who harry them unmercifully). *Summer night is* Prokofiev's own concert suite from another opera called *Betrothal in a Monastery,* a love story which perhaps had its parallel in the composer's own life, since at the time of writing it he was about to leave his wife for another woman whom he later married. This is no longer epic music, but it is no less Russian in its quiet yet rich sensuality, and most of all in the movement called "Dreams". The *Russian Overture* is earlier, written shortly after the composer's return to the Soviet Union after his years of self-imposed exile following the Revolution. The original version of 1936 had an enormous orchestra with quadruple woodwind; Prokofiev reduced this in his revision of the following year which is played here, but even as it stands the score is demandingly brilliant and powerful, abounding in vitality and the quirky humour that is unique to this composer. Järvi and the Philharmonia play this music with tremendous panache and Chandos's recording is outstanding.

Prokofiev. Cinderella, Op. 87 — Ballet Suite: excerpts[a]. Romeo and Juliet, Op. 64 — Ballet: excerpts[b]. [a]**Royal Philharmonic Orchestra/Robert Irving;** [b]**Philharmonia Orchestra/Efrem Kurtz.** EMI Eminence CD-EMX2194. Items marked [a] recorded in 1957, [b] 1963.

Ih 4m ADD 12/92 ⬥ Ⓑ ▲

Although Prokofiev's two greatest ballets share certain stylistic characteristics, they inhabit very different worlds. As well as being musically the more substantial, *Romeo and Juliet* (1936) has the ambitious sweep of a major symphony, whereas *Cinderella* (1941) constitutes — as is appropriate to its subject matter — more a succession of colourful, fantasy-filled miniatures. Of the two, it is also the one that perhaps gains more in concert from being trimmed down into a sequence of carefully chosen excerpts. On this excellent reissue, *Romeo* is represented by seven items, most of them very well known ("Montagues and Capulets" especially); these excellently refurbished 1963 Philharmonia recordings under Efrem Kurtz are delicately pointed, if just a little lacking in drama — especially in the predominantly propulsive "Death of Tybalt". *Cinderella,* however, is played with more imagination than is often the case on disc, and has the added advantage of superb instrumental solos from Sir Thomas Beecham's Royal Philharmonic Orchestra. Robert Irving phrases with sensitivity and a vivid sense of theatre: rarely has "Midnight" (which is slightly cut in this recording) sounded so musical, its doleful, descending brass motives registering as *melody,* which they rarely do elsewhere. Again, the sound is excellent; in fact, these 1957 Kingsway Hall sessions sound, if anything, even cleaner and more realistic than their 1963 Abbey Road coupling. A real delight.

Additional recommendations ...
Cinderella — Suite (arr. Slatkin). **St Louis Symphony Orchestra/Leonard Slatkin.** RCA Red Seal RD85321 — ⬥ DDD 3/86 ⁹ₛ Ⓑ
Romeo and Juliet — excerpts. **Philharmonia Orchestra/Claus Peter Flor.** RCA Victor Red Seal 09026 61388-2 — ⬥ 58m DDD 10/93 ⁹ₚ Ⓑ
Romeo and Juliet — excerpts. **Royal Liverpool Philharmonic Orchestra/Libor Pešek.** Virgin Classics VC7 59278-2 — ⬥ Ih IIm DDD 10/93 ⁹ₚ ⁹ₛ Ⓑ

Prokofiev. Romeo and Juliet, Op. 64 — Ballet Suites Nos. 1-3: excerpts. Chout, Op. 21 — ballet suite. **London Symphony Orchestra/Claudio Abbado.** Decca Ovation 425 027-2DM. From SXL6286 (5/67).

54m ADD 6/91 ⬥ Ⓑ

It was an excellent idea to couple nine items from the familiar *Romeo and Juliet* ballet score with a similar sequence from the unjustly neglected *Chout* — the blackly comic tale of a village trickster, the Buffoon of the alternative title. *Romeo and Juliet* is more popular than ever these days, but Abbado's mid-1960s selection — less predictable than most — retains its freshness and appeal; only his sluggish *Dance of the girls with lilies* lacks something in charm. The sound is pretty good, the brass very immediate. While *Chout* has that rather sadistic plot — and the audiences of 1921 had ultra-modern cubist sets, costumes and choreography to object to — its

neglect seems unaccountable today, given the quality of the music. Here, Prokofiev was clearly inspired by Stravinsky's *Petrushka*. Even if there remains some loosely-written connective tissue, there is also a fund of melodic invention that could only have come from the younger man. The orchestration glitters throughout, sharp-edged and totally distinctive. Decca's analogue recording remains impressive with the scintillating textures clearly defined.

Additional recommendations ...
Romeo and Juliet — *Suites Nos. 1 and 2: excerpts.* **Cleveland Orchestra/Yoel Levi.** Telarc
CD80089 — .⦁' 50m DDD 2/87 **⑨ₛ ⑧**
Romeo and Juliet — *Suites Nos. 1 and 2.* **Oslo Philharmonic Orchestra/Mariss Jansons.** EMI
CDC7 49289-2 — .⦁' 59m DDD 5/89 **⑧**
Romeo and Juliet — *Suites Nos.1-3*[a]. **Mussorgsky.** *A night on the Bare Mountain*[b]. [a]**Minneapolis
Symphony Orchestra/Stanislav Skrowaczewski;** [b]**London Symphony Orchestra/
Antal Dorati.** Mercury Living Presence 432 004-2MM — .⦁' 1h 7m ADD 3/91 **⑧**
Romeo and Juliet — *Suites Nos. 1-3.* **Royal Scottish National Orchestra/Neeme Järvi.**
Chandos CHAN8940 — .⦁' 1h 18m DDD 9/91 **⑧**
Romeo and Juliet — *Suites Nos.1-3: excerpts.* **Czecho-Slovak State Philharmonic Orchestra,
Košice/Andrew Mogrelia.** Naxos 8 550380 — . 55m DDD 9/91 **⑧**
Romeo and Juliet — *Suites Nos.1-3.* **Suisse Romande Orchestra/Armin Jordan.** Erato 2292-
45817-2 — .⦁' 1h 16m DDD 7/93 **⑧**

Prokofiev. Romeo and Juliet, Op. 64 — ballet: excerpts. **Montreal Symphony
Orchestra/Charles Dutoit.** Decca 430 279-2DH. Recorded in 1989.
Introduction; Romeo; The street awakens; Morning Dance; The Quarrel; The Fight; The Prince
gives his order; Juliet, as a young girl; Arrival of the guests; Mask; Dance of the Knights;
Romeo and Juliet; Folk Dance; Friar Laurence; Dance; Tybalt and Mercutio fight; Mercutio dies;
Romeo decides to avenge Mercutio's death; Romeo fights Tybalt; Introduction to Act 3; The
last farewell; Dance of the girls with the lilies; Juliet's funeral; Death of Juliet.

.⦁' **1h 15m DDD 9/91** **⑨ₛ ⑧**

The melodic invention, always consistently inspired, the harmonic flavour, often pungent, and
the individual and brilliantly colourful orchestration of *Romeo and Juliet* bring the ear constant
diversity and stimulation. Charles Dutoit's 1991 recording is extremely attractive: by judicious
selection he compresses the epic span of the ballet into 24 separate items from the original
score. The playing of the Montreal Symphony Orchestra is spectacular with very fleet strings and
brass playing of imposing weight and tragic pungency. Dutoit's interpretation is highly theatrical:
the lighter excerpts from the score are pointed and witty, while the more romantic elements are
given full expression and the variety of Shakespeare's and Prokofiev's dramatic vision is most
expertly recreated by Dutoit. The recording is top class, not only expertly balanced but
capturing the wide dynamic range and finesse of the splendidly virtuoso Montreal orchestra.

Additional recommendations ...
Complete ballet. **Cleveland Orchestra/Lorin Maazel.** Decca 417 510-2DH2 — .⦁' **②** 2h 21m
ADD 2/87 **⑧**
Excerpts. **Berlin Philharmonic Orchestra/Esa-Pekka Salonen.** CBS Masterworks CD42662
— .⦁' 56m DDD 8/88 **⑧**

Prokofiev. COMPLETE SYMPHONIES. **Royal Scottish National Orchestra/Neeme
Järvi.** Chandos CHAN8931/4.
No. 1 in D major, Op. 25, "Classical" (from CHAN8400, 3/86); No. 2 in D minor, Op. 40
(CHAN8368, 10/85); No. 3 in C minor, Op. 44; No. 4 in C major, Op. 47 (original 1930
version, both from CHAN8401, 5/86); No. 4 in C major, Op. 112 (revised 1947 version, from
CHAN8400, 3/86); No. 5 in B flat major, Op. 100 (CHAN8450, 7/86); No. 6 in E flat minor,
Op. 111 (CHAN8359, 7/85); No. 7 in C sharp minor, Op. 131 (CHAN8442, 7/86).

.⦁' **④ 4h 20m DDD** **⑨ₚ ⑧**

Prokofiev was not a natural symphoniest. Albeit successful in emulating Haydn in the *Classical*
Symphony, the Sixth Symphony is his only undisputed integrated symphonic structure (and an
epic-tragic utterance as intense as any by Shostakovich). It has been suggested that his
symphonies all have a sense of some unstaged scenario, and the Third and Fourth (and to a

lesser extent, the Seventh) Symphonies actually rework material from his music for the stage. The Fourth (in both versions) in particular fails to convince as a symphony owing to the profusion and individuality of its often strikingly beautiful thematic ideas — it's a real patchwork quilt of a piece. Enter Neeme Järvi, nothing if not a man of the theatre, to give maximum dramatic intensity and character to all Prokofiev's ideas, whether they add up symphonically or not; capable of overawing his Scottish forces into playing of aerial lightness and easeful lyricism in the *Classical* Symphony, and pulling no punches where Prokofiev's inspiration (as in the Second and Third Symphonies) is at is most strident, violent and hysterical. Make no mistake, though, these are also readings of real stature: where there is symphonic 'line', Järvi unerringly finds it. Drawbacks? Some may feel the need for a deeper pile of string sound, particularly in the Fifth Symphony; and these typically spacious Chandos productions do not always ensure adequate projection for the woodwind (e.g. some of the quiet, lyrical woodwind lines in the Fourth Symphony), but more often than not one cannot faile to be impressed by the coherence and co-ordination, both musically and technically, of some of this century's most fabulous and fraught orchestral essays. As a cycle, this is unlikely to be challenged for some time.

Additional recommendations ...

No. 1. **Bizet.** *Symphony in C major.* **Britten.** *Simple Symphony, Op. 4.* **Orpheus Chamber Orchestra.** DG 423 624-2GH — .·* 1h 4m DDD 1/89 ꝙₚ Ⓑ

Nos. 1 and 3. **Philadelphia Orchestra/Riccardo Muti.** Philips 432 992-2PH — .·* 49m DDD 2/93 ꝙₚ ꝙₛ Ⓑ

No. 1. No. 4 (revised 1947 version). **Scottish National Orchestra/Neeme Järvi.** Chandos CHAN8400 — .·* 52m DDD 3/86 ꝙₚ Ⓑ

Nos. 1 and 7. *THE LOVE FOR THREE ORANGES — Suite, Op. 33a*[b]. **Philharmonia Orchestra/Nicolai Malko.** Classics for Pleasure CD-CFP4523 — .· 57m ADD ꝙₚ Ⓑ ▲

Nos. 1 and 5. **Los Angeles Philharmonic Orchestra/André Previn.** Philips 420 172-2PH — .·* 58m DDD 11/87 ꝙₚ Ⓑ

Nos. 1 and 5. **Berlin Philharmonic Orchestra/Herbert von Karajan.** DG Galleria 437 253-2GGA — .·* 1h 11m ADD 1/93 ꝙₚ Ⓑ

Nos. 1[a] and 5[b]. [a]**London Philharmonic Orchestra,** [b]**Saint Louis Symphony Orchestra/ Leonard Slatkin** RCA Masters Collection 09026 61350-2 — .·* 57m DDD 3/93 Ⓑ

No. 1. Peter and the wolf, Op. 67[a]. March in B flat major, Op. 99. Overture on Hebrew Themes, Op. 34bis[b]. [a]**Sting** (narr); [b]**Stefan Vladar** (pf); **Chamber Orchestra of Europe/Claudio Abbado.** DG 429 396-2GH (*reviewed earlier in this section*) — .·* 50m DDD 4/91 ꝙₚ Ⓑ

No. 2. Romeo and Juliet, Op. 64 — Suite No. 1. **Scottish National Orchestra/Neeme Järvi.** Chandos CHAN8368 — .·* 1h 1m DDD 10/85 ꝙₛ

No. 6. Waltz Suite, Op. 110 — Nos. 1, 5 and 6. **Scottish National Orchestra/Neeme Järvi.** Chandos CHAN8359 — .·* 57m DDD 7/85 ꝙₚ ꝙₛ

No. 6. **Stravinsky.** *Petrushka (1911 version).* **Leningrad Philharmonic Orchestra/Evgeny Mravinsky.** Multisonic Russian Treasure mono 310189-2 — .·* 1h 16m ADD 6/93 ꝙₚ ▲

No. 7. Sinfonietta in A major, Op. 48. **Scottish National Orchestra/Neeme Järvi.** Chandos CHAN8442 — .·* 51m DDD 7/86

New review

Prokofiev. Symphonies — No. 3 in C minor, Op. 44; No. 4 in C major, Opp. 47/112. **Berlin Philharmonic Orchestra/Seiji Ozawa.** DG 437 838-2GH. Recorded 1990-92.

.·* 1h 18m DDD ꝙₚ

A mere glance at the full score of Prokofiev's Third Symphony is enough to induce a migraine. Virtually every page reveals many more details than any listener could hope to hear, either in concert or on disc: it really is a brute of a piece, a rowdy eruption pushed to the very limits of propriety. Which, in a sense, makes Seiji Ozawa's attempts at musical riot control especially rewarding: one is almost grateful for his careful charting of significant counterpoint (especially in the work's opening moments), his way of stalking the anguished first movement development and keeping the ensuing revolution tidily under control. Turn to Kondrashin (listed below), and the shields are down, the violent aggressors given full reign (which, I'm sure, is precisely what Prokofiev intended), yet Ozawa's acknowledgement of the score's more *espressivo* elements makes for some tender revelations; the *Scherzo* (with its slithery 12-part string writing) is as shockingly reptilian as any on disc. The Third is of course a re-working of music from

Prokofiev's opera *The Fiery Angel*, whereas the 1947 revision (and expansion) of the Fourth is a second symphonic exploitation of music from his ballet, *The Prodigal Son*. Here Ozawa's warmth, energy and relative decorum pay high dividends. The first movement's *Allegro eroica* has great cut and vigour and the huge, almost desperate central climax (complete with fiercely clapping wood blocks) is truly its crowning glory. The one disappointment is a *Moderato, quasi allegretto* third movement that sounds sluggish and uninvolving. The last movement, though, is excellent, with a deft, punchy coda and plenty of power for the concluding *Moderato, brioso*. This is generally more refined — but less spontaneous — than Järvi's (reviewed above). Ozawa's Fourth is now top of the league, but the Third is marginally better served by Muti (listed below) and Kondrashin, the latter being live and an essential purchase for anyone wishing to understand this provocative but endlessly fascinating phase in Prokofiev's creative development.

Additional recommendations ...
No. 3. No. 4 (original 1930 version). **Scottish National Orchestra/Neeme Järvi.** Chandos CHAN8401 — .·' 59m DDD 5/86 ᵠₚ
No. 3. **Shostakovich.** *Symphony No. 9 in E flat major, Op. 70.* **Concertgebouw Orchestra/ Kyrill Kondrashin.** Philips Collector Series 438 284-2PM — .·' 58m ADD 9/93 ᵠₚ

| New review |

Prokofiev. Symphony No. 5 in B flat major, Op. 100. Scythian Suite, Op. 20. **City of Birmingham Symphony Orchestra/Simon Rattle.** EMI CDC7 54577-2. Recorded 1992.
.·' 1h 4m DDD 6/93   ᵠₚ ᵠₛ

A Prokofiev Fifth as vibrant, intelligent and meticulously prepared as you'd expect from this partnership. In the mighty opening movement, there's real mystery about those fairy-tale slumberings at the start of the development, and how naturally Rattle quickens the pulse during the pages which follow, the sense of expectancy and adventure palpably conveyed. Come the coda, and Rattle's expertly-graduated dynamics ensure a riveting succession of spectacular climaxes. Here, too, EMI's impressive Birmingham Symphony Hall production opens out magnificently. Rattle's scherzo is a marvellously quick-witted conception, the slow movement etched with genuine tenderness and bustling good humour reigns supreme in the admirably spirited finale. The coupling is a pretty stunning *Scythian Suite*, combining foundation-threatening pagan spectacle and heart-stopping beauty in ideal equilibrium. A terrific display, excitingly engineered.

Prokofiev. String Quartets — No. 1 in B minor, Op. 50; No. 2 in F major, Op. 92. **American Quartet** (Mitchell Stern, Laurie Carney, vns; Daniel Avshalomov, va; David Geber, vc). Olympia OCD340. Recorded in 1982.
.·' 50m ADD 2/90

Prokofiev's wider popularity has never extended to his chamber music. Of his two quartets, the Second is by far the better-known and comes from the war years when Prokofiev was evacuated to the Caucasus, where he made a study of the musical folklore of Kabarda — indeed, it is sometimes known as the "Kabardinian" Quartet. Although the material is folk-derived, it is completely absorbed into Prokofiev's own melodic bloodstream and doesn't sound in the least bit 'folksy'. The second movement quotes a Kabardinian love song of great lyrical beauty, and at one point in the slow movement, the accompaniment imitates a Caucasian stringed instrument, the kamancha. It is a work of real quality which has the astringent flavouring and poetic flair that characterizes Prokofiev at his best. Although the First Quartet, written at the behest of the Library of Congress in 1930, is not so immediately appealing it, too, is a work of substance which grows on the listener. Prokofiev's friend and colleague, Nikolay Miaskovsky, who composed 13 string quartets and more than twice as many symphonies, particularly admired the last movement, and encouraged Prokofiev to score it for full strings. The American Quartet communicate conviction and belief in this music: theirs is a persuasive account, sensitive and yet full-blooded, and they are very well recorded.

Additional recommendation ...
Nos. 1 and 2. Overture on Hebrew Themes in C minor, Op. 34[a]. **Coull Quartet;** [a]**Angela Malsbury** (cl); [a]**David Petitt** (pf). Hyperion CDA66573 — .·' 57m DDD 9/92

Prokofiev. Violin Sonatas — No. 1 in F minor, Op. 80; No. 2 in D major, Op. 94*a*. **Shlomo Mintz** (vn); **Yefim Bronfman** (pf). DG 423 575-2GH. Recorded in 1987.

56m DDD 2/89

Both Prokofiev sonatas are wartime pieces; both follow the classical four-movement plan and both must be numbered among Prokofiev's very finest achievements. There the similarities end, for the First is declamatory, agonized and predominantly introspective, whereas the Second, originally for flute and piano, is untroubled, intimate and consoling. This essential difference in character presents a challenge which not all duos have risen to. Mintz and Bronfman have got right to the heart of the matter, however, and if their First Sonata is still marginally the finer that is only because it is on a truly rare level of insight. Both players deploy a wide range of colour and accent, superbly captured in a bright but not over-reverberant acoustic, and they are united in their nuanced response to Prokofiev's lyricism and motoric drive. In the extraordinary first movement coda of the First Sonata, they create an atmosphere of almost hypnotic numbness, and it is a pity that one terrible edit breaks the spell here (the violin tone changes abruptly in mid-bar). But that is the only serious defect in what is a truly outstanding recital.

Key to symbols

Price	Quantity/ availability	Timing	Recording mode	Review date
	② ②	lh 23m	DDD	6/88

Prokofiev. PIANO SONATAS, Volume 1. **Murray McLachlan.** Olympia OCD255. Piano Sonatas — No. 1 in F minor, Op. 1; No. 4 in C minor, Op. 29; No. 5 in C major (revised version), Op. 135; No. 9 in C major, Op. 103; No. 10 in E minor, Op. 137.

lh 10m DDD 3/90

The first volume of Murray McLachlan's complete survey of the Prokofiev Piano Sonatas contains some very fine performances indeed. A suitably bold and youthfully exuberant account of the romantic First Sonata Op. 1 is followed by a particularly thoughtful and probing reading of the introverted and less frequently heard Fourth Sonata — the slow movement is especially intense and poetic. Indeed, one of McLachlan's strengths, both here and in the other sonatas on this disc, is his ability to bring out the poetry and lyricism of these pieces that so often get overlooked by pianists in favour of the more abrasive and dissonant aspects. The Fifth Sonata (again most persuasively handled) is heard here in its revised version of 1953, which used to be the accepted version among pianists but which is now taking something of a back seat in favour of the original 1938 version. However, the real gem of the disc lies in McLachlan's performance of the much underrated Ninth Sonata. Richter (to whom it was dedicated) described it as "intimately chamber in character, concealing riches which are not immediately obvious to the eye". Performed as it is here, with a great deal of poetry and insight, the concealed riches become more readily apparent and one is left wondering why the sonata has remained neglected for so long. The disc concludes with the tiny fragment (a mere 27 bars) that would have become the Tenth Sonata had Prokofiev's lived to complete it. Excellent sleeve notes from Murray McLachlan.

Additional recommendations ...
No. 1. Gavotte No. 4 from "Hamlet", Op. 77bis. Three Pieces, Op. 96. Sonatinas, Op. 54 — No. 1 in E minor; No. 2 in G major. Four Pieces, Op. 4. **Buxtehude** *(arr. Prokofiev). Organ Prelude and Fugue in D minor.* **Boris Berman.** Chandos CHAN9017 — 57m DDD 11/92
Piano Sonata No. 3 in A minor, Op. 28. Three Pensées, Op. 62. Three Pieces from "Cinderella", Op. 95. Ten Pieces, Op. 12. **Boris Berman.** Chandos 9069 — 56m DDD 11/92
No. 1. No. 8 in B flat major, Op. 84. Four Pieces, Op. 3. Three Pieces, Op. 59. The tales of an old grandmother, Op. 31. **Oleg Marshev.** Danacord DACOCD392 — lh 4m DDD 1/94

Prokofiev. PIANO WORKS. **Barry Douglas.** RCA Victor Red Seal RD60779. Recorded in 1991.

Piano Sonatas — No. 2 in D minor, Op. 14; No. 7 in B flat major, Op. 83. The Love for Three Oranges, Op. 33*ter* — March. Ten Pieces from "Cinderella", Op. 97 — No. 10, Waltz. Six Pieces from "Cinderella", Op. 102 — No. 4, Amoroso. Three Pieces, Op. 96 — No. 1, Waltz from "War and Peace".

56m DDD 3/92

Prokofiev. PIANO WORKS. Tedd Joselson. Olympia OCD453. Recorded in 1991. Ten Pieces from "Romeo and Juliet", Op. 75. Ten Pieces from "Cinderella", Op. 97. The Love for Three Oranges, Op. 33*ter* — March; Scherzo.

1h 2m DDD 10/92

There has often been a tendency with Prokofiev's piano music for pianists to overplay the percussive, steely qualities of the piano writing at the expense of the lyrical aspects. Barry Douglas, however, attains the perfect blend — muscular and athletic where power and agility are called for, but ever alert to the lyricism which lies beneath the surface. The Second Sonata is a prime example. Douglas has the full measure of this youthful, energetic masterpiece, and one feels that he has fully assimilated this piece before committing it to disc. The first movement with its restless oscillation between expressive melody and ruminative figuration is thoughtfully fashioned, and the knockabout scherzo and fleet-footed energetic finale are delivered with much vigour and flair. The Seventh Sonata (the central work of Prokofiev's "War Trilogy") is impressive too, with Douglas fully in command of its bristling difficulties. As for the rest of the disc, Douglas offers some of the less frequently heard piano transcriptions, of which the delirious 'love' Waltz from *Cinderella* and the March from *The Love for Three Oranges* crave particular attention. The recording is beautifully engineered and balanced.

Crisp, clean finger-work and a fine sense of rhythmic buoyancy can also be found on the very recommendable Olympia disc featuring the American pianist Tedd Joselson. Joselson made a considerable impact in 1976 with his recording of Prokofiev's Sonatas Nos. 2 and 8 (no longer available), and his special empathy with this composer can be heard further in his readings of Prokofiev's own transcriptions from the ballets *Cinderella* and *Romeo and Juliet*. Both collections contain some of the composer's most delightful and engaging numbers: from the charming character portrait "Juliet as a young girl" (brilliantly characterized here by Joselson) and the famous "Montagues and "Capulets" found in *Romeo and Juliet*, to the capricious "Grasshoppers and Dragonflies" and miniature "Four Seasons" suite from *Cinderella*. Joselson displays a keen talent for story-telling and atmosphere throughout, and has been exceptionally well served with a clear and vivid recording.

Additional recommendations ...
No. 7. Toccata, Op. 11. **Poulenc.** *Presto in B flat major.* **Barber.** *Piano Sonata, Op. 26.* **Kabalevsky.** *Piano Sonata No. 3, Op. 46.* **Fauré.** *Nocturne No. 13 in B minor, Op. 119*[a]. **Vladimir Horowitz.** RCA Gold Seal mono/[a]stereo GD60377 *(see review in the Collections section; refer to the Index to Reviews)* — 1h 5m ADD 6/92 ▲
No. 2. Dumka. Three Pièces, Op. 59. Six Pieces from "Cinderella", Op. 102. Waltzes Suite (Schubert). **Boris Berman.** Chandos CHAN9119 — 1h 5m DDD 4/93
Nos. 2 and 7. Visions fugitives. **Laurent Cabasso.** Auvidis Valois V4655 — 58m DDD 11/92

New review

Prokofiev. Piano Sonatas — No. 6 in A major, Op. 82; No. 7 in B flat major, Op. 83. Dumka. Visions fugitives, Op. 22. **Oleg Marshev** (pf). Danacord DACOCD391. Recorded in 1991.

1h 14 DDD 1/94

Oleg Marshev is a charismatic performer whose dynamic, full-throated volcanic approach (though he is certainly not afraid to allow lyricism into the music when called upon to do so), provides great involvement for the listener. This, Volume One of his complete survey, opens with a commanding, virtuosic performance of the Sixth Sonata which simply teems with detail and subtle nuance. The second movement *Allegretto* is delivered with tremendous flair and élan in the outer sections, and the phlegmatic third movement is beautifully paced and crafted. Marshev unleashes the full power of his formidable armoury in the tumultuous finale, where in the closing bars he almost hits boiling-point in terms of sheer virtuosity; his performance may not quite reach those of Kissin or Pogorelich but it is certainly a recording that anyone would be happy to live with. In contrast, the early *Dumka* is given a beautifully poised and effortless reading, and the same can be said of Marshev's extremely fine account of the *Visions fugitives*, which can be added to the growing throng of commendable recordings in the catalogue. Marshev concludes the first volume with a stunning account of the Seventh Sonata, which approaches Pollini's classic recording for its breadth of vision, dynamic control and sheer virtuosity; pianistically it has all one could wish for — superb rhythmic impetus, tremendous force, wonderful phrasing and in the slower, more reflective moments beautiful tonal control and expressive nuance. The fearsome, toccata finale can only be compared to Pollini's scorching reading for its accuracy and heart-pounding excitement. The recording is full bodied.

Additional recommendations ...
No. 6. **Ravel.** *Gaspard de la nuit.* **Ivo Pogorelich** (pf). DG 413 363-2GH — .⋅•' 52m DDD 11/84 ⁹ₚ
No. 7. **Boulez.** *Piano Sonata No. 2.* **Stravinsky.** *Three movements from "Petrushka".* **Webern.**
Variations for piano, Op. 27. **Maurizio Pollini.** DG 419 202-2GH — .⋅•' 1h 9m ADD 11/86 ⁹ₚ
No. 6. *Etude in C minor, Op. 2 No. 3.* **Chopin.** *Waltz in C sharp minor, Op. 64 No. 2.* **Liszt.**
Etude d'exécution transcendante in F minor, S139 No. 10, "Appassionata". Liebestraum No. 3, S541.
Rhapsodie espagnole, S254. **Schumann.** *Etudes symphoniques, Op. 13. Theme and Variations on the*
name "Abegg", Op. 1. **Schumann/Liszt.** *Widmung, S566.* **Evgeni Kissin.** RCA Victor Red Seal
RD60443 *(see review in the Collections section; refer to the Index to Reviews)* — .⋅•' ② 1h 43m DDD 3/91 ⁹ₚ

Prokofiev. Piano Sonata No. 8 in B flat major, Op. 84[a]. Visions fugitives, Op. 22 — Nos. 3, 6 and 9[a].
Debussy. Estampes[b]. Préludes, Book 1[b] — Voiles; Le vent dans la plaine; Les collines d'Anacapri.
Scriabin. Piano Sonata No. 5 in F sharp major, Op. 53[b]. **Sviatoslav Richter** (pf). DG Dokumente 423 573-2GDO. Items marked [a] from SLPM138950 (8/65), [b] SLPM138849 (4/63). Recorded in 1963.

⸻ .⋅•' 1h 7m ADD 9/88 ⁹ₚ ⸻

Richter has long been acclaimed as one of the most dedicated champions of Prokofiev's keyboard music, with the Eighth Sonata always particularly close to his heart. It would certainly be hard to imagine a more profoundly and intensely experienced performance than the one we get here, or one of greater keyboard mastery. After the yearning introspection of the temperamental opening movement and the *Andante*'s evocation of a more gracious past, the rhythmic tension and sheer might of sonority he conjures in the finale make it easy to understand why the composer's biographer, I.V. Nestyev, suspected some underlying programme culminating in "heroic troops resolutely marching ahead, ready to crush anything in their path". In the uniquely Prokofievian fantasy of the three brief *Visions fugitives* he is wholly bewitching. As for the Fifth Sonata of Scriabin, his impetuous start at once reveals his understanding of its manic extremities of mood. For just these Russian performances alone, this excellently refurbished disc can be hailed as a collector's piece. And as a bonus there is Debussy too, with infinite subtleties of tonal shading to heighten atmospheric evocation.

Additional recommendation ...
Visions fugitives, Op. 22. **Scriabin.** *Piano Sonatas — No. 2 in G sharp minor, Op. 19, "Sonata-*
fantasy"; No. 9 in F major, Op. 68, "Messe noire". Etudes — F sharp minor, Op. 8 No. 2; B major, Op.
8 No. 4; E major, Op. 8 No. 5; F sharp major, Op. 42 No. 3; F sharp major, Op. 42 No. 4; F minor,
Op. 42 No. 7. Four Pieces, Op. 51. Vers la flamme, Op. 72. **Nikolai Demidenko** (pf). Conifer
CDCF204 — .⋅•' 1h 13m DDD 8/91 ⁹ₚ

Prokofiev. THE LOVE FOR THREE ORANGES (sung in French). **Gabriel Bacquier** (bar)
King of Clubs; **Jean-Luc Viala** (ten) Prince; **Hélène Perraguin** (mez) Princess Clarissa;
Vincent Le Texier (bass-bar) Leandro; **Georges Gautier** (ten) Truffaldino; **Didier Henry**
(bar) Pantaloon, Farfarello, Master of Ceremonies; **Gregory Reinhart** (bass) Tchelio; **Michèle**
Lagrange (sop) Fata Morgana; **Consuelo Caroli** (mez) Linetta; **Brigitte Fournier** (sop)
Nicoletta; **Catherine Dubosc** (sop) Ninetta; **Jules Bastin** (bass) Cook; **Béatrice Uria**

Monzon (mez) Smeraldina; **Chorus and Orchestra of Lyon Opéra/Kent Nagano.** Virgin Classics VCD7 59566-2. Notes, text and translation included.

② Ih 42m DDD 12/89

This is a wonderfully zany story about a prince whose hypochondriac melancholy is lifted only at the sight of a malevolent witch tumbling over, in revenge for which she casts on him a love-spell for three oranges: in the ensuing complications he encounters an ogre's gigantic cook who goes all gooey at the sight of a pretty ribbon, princesses inside two of the oranges die of oppressive desert heat, and the third is saved only by the intervention of various groups of 'spectators' who argue with each other on the stage. The music's brittle vivacity matches that of the plot, and though there are no set-pieces for the singers and there is practically no thematic development — the famous orchestral March and Scherzo are the only passages that reappear — the effervescent score is most engaging. The performance, conducted by the musical director of the Lyon Opéra, is full of zest, with lively orchestral playing and a cast that contains several outstanding members and not a single weak one; and the recording is extremely good. Those desirous of so doing can delve into the work's symbolism and identify the objects of its satire — principally Stanislavsky's naturalistic Moscow Arts Theatre: others can simply accept this as a thoroughly enjoyable romp.

Prokofiev. WAR AND PEACE. **Lajos Miller** (bar) Prince Andrei Bolkonsky; **Galina Vishnevskaya** (sop) Natasha Rostova; **Katherine Ciesinski** (mez) Sonya; **Maria Paunova** (mez) Maria Akhrosimova; **Dimiter Petkov** (bass) Count Ilya Rostov; **Wieslaw Ochman** (ten) Count Pytor Bezukhov; **Stefania Toczyska** (mez) Helena Bezukhova; **Nicolai Gedda** (ten) Anatol Kuragin; **Vladimir de Kanel** (bass-bar) Dolokhov; **Mira Zakai** (contr); Princess Maria Bolkonsky; **Malcolm Smith** (bass) Colonel Vasska Denisov; **Nicola Ghiuselev** (bass) Marshal Mikhail Kutuzov; **Eduard Tumagian** (bar) Napoleon Bonaparte; **Radio France Chorus; French National Orchestra/Mstislav Rostropovich.** Erato Libretto 2292-45331-2. Notes, text and translation included. From ECD75480 (1/89). Recorded in 1986.

④ 4h 7m DDD 4/92

Over four hours long, 72 characters, 13 scene changes: is it any wonder that Prokofiev's *War and Peace*, adapted from Tolstoy's famously epic novel, has had few performances and even fewer forays into the recording studio? At the front of the booklet Rostropovich recalls how, as Prokofiev lay dying, he reiterated one wish, that Rostropovich should make this opera known to the world. It comes as no surprise, then, to find a deeply committed performance from both soloists (only 45 of them due to some adroit doubling), chorus and orchestra. Prokofiev adapted the novel into seven 'peace' and six 'war' tableaux, thus sustaining drama through contrast throughout its Wagnerian length. With few exceptions the multinational cast sing in good Russian and among them Lajos Miller is particularly affecting as Prince Andrei, pleasingly ardent in his opening moonlit aria. The central female role of Natasha is taken by Galina Vishnevskaya. She sang the role in the 1959 première and inevitably no longer sounds like an innocent 16 year old. Unfortunately, problems are compounded by a hardness in her tone and a lack of attention to detail in some of the quieter sections — particularly in her exchanges with Helena where the asides sound like part of the normal conversation. Stefania Toczyska as the treacherous Helena makes a great impression, as does Katherine Ciesinski as Natasha's confidante, Sonya. Of the men, Nicolai Gedda as Prince Anatol sings with character and great style and Eduard Tumagian is a suitably heroic and steadfast Napoleon. An added attraction of the recording are the sound effects, particularly in the war scenes, convincing but never overly obtrusive. Good translations are provided in three languages, crowning a laudable achievement.

Further listening ...

Cantata for the 20th Anniversary of the October Revolution, Op. 74[a]. The tale of the stone flower — excerpts. [a]**Gennadi Rozhdestvensky** (spkr); **Philharmonia** [a]**Chorus and Orchestra/Neeme Järvi.** Chandos CHAN9095 (3/93).

Cello Sonata in C major, Op. 119. *Coupled with* **Shostakovich.** Cello Sonata in D minor, Op. 40. Moderato for Cello and Piano. **Lynn Harrell** (vc); **Vladimir Ashkenazy** (pf). Decca 421 774-2DH (3/90). *See review under Shostakovich; refer to the Index to Reviews.*

Flute Sonata in D major, Op. 94. *Coupled with* **Poulenc.** Flute Sonata. **E. Burton.** Flute
Sonatina. **Fauré.** Morceau de lecture. **Martinů.** Flute Sonata No. 1. **Jennifer Stinton** (fl);
Scott Mitchell (pf). Collins Classics 1103-2 (12/91).

Alexander Nevsky. Ivan the Terrible, Op. 116 (ed. Lankester). **Soloists; New London
Children's Choir; London Symphony Chorus and Orchestra/Mstislav Rostropovich.**
Sony Classical CD48387 (4/93).

THE FIERY ANGEL. **Soloists; Ohlin Vocal Ensemble; Gothenburg Pro Musica
Chamber Choir; Gothenburg Symphony Orchestra/Neeme Järvi.** DG 431 669-2GH2
(7/91).

Giacomo Puccini

Italian 1858-1924

New review

Puccini. MANON LESCAUT. **Mirella Freni** (sop) Manon Lescaut; **Luciano Pavarotti** (ten)
Des Grieux; **Dwayne Croft** (bar) Lescaut; **Giuseppe Taddei** (bar) Geronte; **Ramon Vargas**
(ten) Edmondo; **Cecilia Bartoli** (mez) Singer; **Federico Davia** (bass) Innkeeper, Captain;
Anthony Laciura (ten) Dancing Master; **Paul Groves** (ten) Lamplighter; **James Courtney**
(bass) Sergeant; **Chorus and Orchestra of the Metropolitan Opera/James Levine.**
Decca 440 200-2DHO2. Notes, text and translation included. Recorded in 1992.

② 2h DDD 11/93

With Luciano Pavarotti as a powerful Des Grieux, James Levine conducts a comparably big-
boned performance of *Manon Lescaut*, bringing out the red-blooded drama of Puccini's first
big success, while not ignoring its warmth and tender poetry in exceptionally full, vivid
sound with the voices well in front of the orchestra. In the title-role Freni's performance
culminates in an account of the big Act 4 aria, more involving and passionate than any of the
others on the versions listed below with the voice showing no signs of wear, and with her
sudden change of face at the words "terra di pace" ("a land of peace") bringing a magical
lightening of tone. That aria makes a thrilling climax, when too often this act can seem a
letdown. In this as in so much else, Levine conveys the tensions and atmosphere of a stage
performance in a way that owes much to his experience at the Metropolitan. More
completely than the other versions, each with very great merits, it avoids the feeling of a
studio performance. Reactions to Pavarotti as Des Grieux will differ widely. The closeness of
balance means that in volume his singing rarely drops below *mezzo forte*, but there is little
harm in having so passionate a portrait of Des Grieux as Pavarotti's. Needless to say, the
hero's big emotional climaxes in each of the first three acts come over at full force. The rest
of the cast is strong too, with Dwayne Croft a magnificent Lescaut who, as well as singing
with rich, firm tone, brings out the character's wry humour. Many collectors will count this
a clear first choice among current versions. For the sheer power of Puccinian drama, vividly
conveyed, it will be hard to beat.

Additional recommendations ...
**Soloists; Chorus of the Royal Opera House, Covent Garden; Philharmonia
Orchestra/Giuseppe Sinopoli.** DG 413 893-2GH2 — ② DDD 3/85
Soloists; Chorus and Orchestra of La Scala, Milan/Tullio Serafin. EMI mono CDS7
47393-8 — ② 2h ADD 9/86 ▲
**Soloists; Jack Gregoor Choir; Belgian Radio and TV Philharmonic Chorus and
Orchestra/Alexander Rahbari.** Naxos 8 660019/20 — ② 2h 6m DDD 12/92

Puccini. LA BOHEME. **Jussi Björling** (ten) Rodolfo; **Victoria de los Angeles** (sop) Mimì;
Robert Merrill (bar) Marcello; **Lucine Amara** (sop) Musetta; **John Reardon** (bar)
Schaunard; **Giorgio Tozzi** (bass) Colline; **Fernando Corena** (bass) Benoit, Alcindoro;
William Nahr (ten) Parpignol; **Thomas Powell** (bar) Customs Official; **George del Monte**
(bar) Sergeant; **Columbus Boychoir; RCA Victor Chorus and Orchestra/Sir Thomas**

Beecham. EMI mono CDS7 47235-8. Notes, text and translation included. From ALP1409/10 (1/57).

⏺ ② Ih 48m ADD 6/87   𝒒ₚ Ⓑ ▲

To recommend a 37-year-old mono recording of *La bohème* over all the more glamorously star-studded and sumptuously recorded versions that have appeared since may seem perverse, but the Beecham version is a true classic which has never been surpassed. This intimate opera is not about two superstars showing off how loudly they can sing their top Cs, but about a poverty-stricken poet's love for a mortally-ill seamstress. De los Angeles's infinitely-touching Mimì and Björling's poetic, ardent Rodolfo are backed by consistently fine and characterful ensemble work making this the most realistic version ever recorded. The recording of course shows its age, but this is scarcely noticeable as page after page of the score come freshly alive again: not a *tour de force* of vocalism, not a sequence of famous arias with bits of dialogue between but a lyric tragedy of wrenching pathos and truth.

Additional recommendations ...
Soloists; Chorus and Orchestra of La Scala, Milan/Antonino Votto. EMI mono CDS7 47475-2 — ⏺ ② Ih 46m ADD II/87 𝒒ₚ Ⓑ ▲
Soloists; Schöneberger Boys' Choir; Berlin German Opera Chorus; Berlin Philharmonic Orchestra/Herbert von Karajan. Decca 421 049-2DH2 — ⏺ ② Ih 50m ADD II/87 𝒒ₚ Ⓑ

Puccini. TOSCA. **Maria Callas** (sop) Floria Tosca; **Giuseppe di Stefano** (ten) Mario Cavaradossi; **Tito Gobbi** (bar) Baron Scarpia; **Franco Calabrese** (bass) Cesare Angelotti; **Angelo Mercuriali** (ten) Spoletta; **Melchiorre Luise** (bass) Sacristan; **Dario Caselli** (bass) Sciarrone, Gaoler; **Alvaro Cordova** (treb) Shepherd Boy; **Chorus and Orchestra of La Scala, Milan/Victor de Sabata.** EMI mono CDS7 47175-8. Notes, text and translation included. From Columbia 33CX1094/5 (12/53). Recorded in 1953.

⏺ ② Ih 48m ADD 9/85   𝒒ₚ Ⓑ ▲

In the course of *Tosca*'s history there have been many notable interpreters, but few have been able to encompass so unerringly the love, jealousy and eventual courage of Tosca as well as Maria Callas. Her resinous, sensuous tone, her wonderful diction, and her inborn passion filled every phrase of the score with special and individual meaning. In 1953 she was in her early prime, the tone seldom prey to those uneasy moments on high that marred her later recordings, and with the vital, vivid conducting of Victor de Sabata, her performance has rightly attained classic status. Giuseppe di Stefano is the ardent Cavaradossi, his tone forward and vibrant in that way peculiar to Italians. Tito Gobbi's cynical, snarling Scarpia, aristocratic in manner, vicious in meaning, remains unique in that part on record. The mono recording stands up well to the test of time.

Additional recommendations ...
Soloists; Vienna State Opera Chorus; Vienna Philharmonic Orchestra/Herbert von Karajan. Decca Grand Opera 421 670-2DM2 — ⏺ ② Ih 54m ADD I/89 𝒒ₚ Ⓑ
Soloists; Paris Opéra Chorus and Conservatoire Orchestra/Georges Prêtre. EMI CMS7 69974-2 — ⏺ ② Ih 52m DDD 8/89 Ⓑ
Soloists; Slovak Philharmonic Chorus; Czecho-Slovak Radio Symphony Orchestra, Bratislava/Alexander Rahbari. Naxos 8 660001/2 — ● ② Ih 56m DDD 10/91 Ⓑ
Soloists; Chorus and Orchestra of the Royal Opera House, Covent Garden/Sir Colin Davis. Philips Duo 438 359-2PM2 — ⏺ ② Ih 58m ADD 8/93 Ⓑ

Puccini. MADAMA BUTTERFLY. **Renata Scotto** (sop) Madama Butterfly; **Carlo Bergonzi** (ten) Pinkerton; **Rolando Panerai** (bar) Sharpless; **Anna di Stasio** (mez) Suzuki; **Piero De Palma** (ten) Goro; **Giuseppe Morresi** (ten) Prince Yamadori; **Silvana Padoan** (mez) Kate Pinkerton; **Paolo Montarsolo** (bass) The Bonze; **Mario Rinaudo** (bass) Commissioner; **Rome Opera House Chorus and Orchestra/Sir John Barbirolli.** EMI CMS7 69654-2. Notes, text and translation included. From SAN184/6 (9/67). Recorded in 1966.

⏺ ② 2h 22m ADD 5/89   𝒒ₚ Ⓑ

This is not quite the best sung *Butterfly* available but Barbirolli ensures that it is the most richly and enjoyably Italianate. Italian opera was in his blood and as a cellist at Covent Garden, playing under Puccini's direction, and as a conductor whose formative years were spent in the theatre (his Covent Garden début was in this very opera), Barbirolli's pleasure in returning to the world of opera is audible throughout this recording. The rapport between him and the Italian orchestra is close and affectionate; it is a heartwarming performance, subtle and supple in the pacing of the love duet, urgently passionate in the great outbursts. Scotto is a touching Butterfly, with all the tiny and crucial details of characterization delicately moulded. There have been more dashing Pinkertons than Bergonzi, but not many who have so effectively combined suavity of sound with neatness of phrasing and good taste. Panerai is a first-class Sharpless and di Stasio a sympathetic Suzuki; there are no weak links elsewhere, and the recording is decent enough for its date, if a bit narrow in perspective and with the singers rather forwardly placed. Barbirolli's *Butterfly* has several distinguished rivals on CD, but for a performance that will remind you of the first time you fell in love with this opera it has permanent value and great eloquence.

Additional recommendations ...
Soloists; Vienna State Opera Chorus; Vienna Philharmonic Orchestra/Herbert von Karajan. Decca 417 577-2DH3 — .·' ③ 2h 25m ADD 6/87 ⁹ₚ Ⓑ
Soloists; Chorus and Orchestra of La Scala, Milan/Herbert von Karajan. EMI mono CDS7 47959-8 — .·' ② 2h 19 ADD 10/87 ⁹ₚ Ⓑ ▲
Soloists; Rome Opera Chorus and Orchestra/Gabriele Santini. EMI Studio CMS7 63634-2 — .·' ② 2h 17m ADD 3/91 ⁹ₚ Ⓑ
Soloists; Slovak Philharmonic Chorus; Czecho-Slovak Radio Symphony Orchestra, Bratislava/Alexander Rahbari. Naxos 8 660015/6 — . 2h 21m DDD 5/92 Ⓑ

Puccini. LA FANCIULLA DEL WEST. **Carol Neblett** (sop) Minnie; **Plácido Domingo** (ten) Dick Johnson; **Sherrill Milnes** (bar) Jack Rance; **Francis Egerton** (ten) Nick; **Robert Lloyd** (bass) Ashby; **Gwynne Howell** (bass) Jake Wallace; **Paul Hudson** (bass) Billy Jackrabbit; **Anne Wilkens** (sop) Wowkle; **Chorus and Orchestra of the Royal Opera House, Covent Garden/Zubin Mehta.** DG 419 640-2GH2. Notes, text and translation included. From 2709 078 (9/78). Recorded in 1977.

.·' ② 2h 10m ADD 11/87 ⁹ₚ

This opera depicts the triangular relationship between Minnie, the saloon owner and 'mother' to the entire town of gold miners, Jack Rance, the sheriff and Dick Johnson (alias Ramerrez), a bandit leader. The music is highly developed in Puccini's seamless lyrical style, the arias for the main characters emerge from the texture and return to it effortlessly. The vocal colours are strongly polarized with the cast being all male except for one travesti role and Minnie herself. The score bristles with robust melody as well as delicate scoring, betraying a masterly hand at work. Carol Neblett is a strong Minnie, vocally distinctive and well characterized, whilst Plácido Domingo and Sherrill Milnes make a good pair of suitors for the spunky little lady. Zubin Mehta conducts with real sympathy for the idiom and the orchestra respond well.

Additional recommendations ...
Soloists; Santa Cecilia Academy Chorus and Orchestra, Rome/Franco Capuana. Decca Grand Opera 421 595-2DM2 — .·' ② 2h 13m ADD 1/89 ▲
Soloists; Hungarian Radio Chorus; Frankfurt Radio Symphony Orchestra/Marcello Viotti. Sine Qua Non 39820212 — .·' ② 2h 5m DDD 1/94

New review
Puccini. IL TABARRO[a]. **Tito Gobbi** (bar) Michele; **Margaret Mas** (sop) Giorgetta; **Giacinto Prandelli** (ten) Luigi; **Piero De Palma** (ten) Tinca; **Plinio Clabassi** (bas) Talpa; **Miriam Pirazzini** (mez) Frugola.
SUOR ANGELICA[b]. **Victoria de los Angeles** (sop) Suor Angelica; **Fedora Barbieri** (mez) Princess; **Mina Doro** (mez) Abbess, Mistress of the novices; **Corinna Vozza** (mez) Sister Monitor; **Lidia Marimpietri** (sop) Suor Genovieffa, Almoner Sister I; **Santa Chissari** (sop) Suor Osmina, Almoner Sister II, Novice; **Anna Marcangeli** (sop) Suor Dolcina; **Teresa Cantarini** (mez) Infirmary Sister; **Silvia Bertona** (sop) Lay Sister I; **Maria Huder** (mez) Lay Sister II.
GIANNI SCHICCHI[c]. **Tito Gobbi** (bar) Gianni Schicchi; **Victoria de los Angeles** (sop) Lauretta; **Carlo del Monte** (ten) Rinuccio; **Anna Maria Canali** (Zita); **Adelio Zagonara** (ten)

Gherardo; **Lidia Marimpietri** (sop) Nella; **Claudio Cornoldi** (ten) Gherardino; **Saturno Meletti** (bass) Betto di Signa; **Paolo Montarsolo** (bass) Simone; **Fernando Valentini** (bar) Marco; **Giuliana Raymondi** (sop) La Cieca; **Rome Opera Chorus; Rome Opera Orchestra/**[a]**Vincenzo Bellezza,** [b]**Tullio Serafin,** [c]**Gabriele Santini.** EMI mono/[c]stereo CMS7 64165-2. Texts and translations included. Item marked [a] from HMV ALP1355 (5/56), [b] ALP1577 (6/58), [c] ASD295 (12/59).

③ 2h 4lm ADD 6/93 **P ▲**

Unless you insist on the most up-to-date recorded sound, or on buying the individual operas of Puccini's trilogy separately (and that, regrettably, is becoming harder to do these days; most available recordings come as indivisible boxed sets) this is the classic *Trittico*, and the obvious first recommendation. Gobbi's blackly authoritative but pitiful Michele in *Il Tabarro* and his genially authoritative Schicchi (the two outer panels of the triptych *do* match, in an odd sort of way) have seldom been equalled, let alone surpassed. De los Angeles's Angelica is more purely and movingly sung than any other on record, and her Lauretta in *Gianni Schicchi* is enchanting. Could it be said, even so, that *Il Tabarro* is the weak link in this trilogy? It is a three-hander, surely, and neither the soprano nor the tenor are quite in Gobbi's league? Mas is a bit plummy and mezzoish, true, but the slight implication this gives that Giorgetta's liaison with the young stevedore Luigi is her last chance at escape from a hateful life and a marriage that has soured adds an extra twinge of pain to a plot in which all three principals are victims. And in this context Prandelli's slightly strenuous rawness of tone characterizes Luigi rather well. In *Gianni Schicchi*, Carlo del Monte as Rinuccio also looks like under-casting but in fact he's one of the few tenors who've recorded the part who sounds convincingly young, and his ardent praise of Florence and the 'new men' who are reinvigorating the city is proudly sung. Here, too, Gobbi is surrounded by a constellation of pungent character actors, and de los Angeles in *Suor Angelica* is teamed with a charmingly girlish, impulsive Genovieffa and with Fedora Barbieri's rigidly implacable Princess (is there another parallel here, with the stiff-necked Zita, 'La Vecchia', in *Gianni Schicchi?*). With generally very stylish conducting throughout (only Belezza in *Il Tabarro* is a touch staid, and he omits nearly all of Puccini's off-stage sound effects) only the rather elderly recordings might be seen as a drawback. EMI boldly label the whole set 'stereo', but both *Il Tabarro* and *Suor Angelica* sound like minimally 'processed' mono: a touch congested in fuller pasages, a hint of fizzy brightness here and there but nothing that's not abundantly worth putting up with for such performances as these.

Additional recommendation ...
Suor Angelica. **Soloists; Hungarian State Opera Chorus and Orchestra/Lamberto Gardelli.** Hungaroton HCD12490-2 — **52m** DDD

Puccini. TURANDOT. **Dame Joan Sutherland** (sop) Princess Turandot; **Luciano Pavarotti** (ten) Calaf; **Montserrat Caballé** (sop) Liù; **Tom Krause** (bar) Ping; **Pier Francesco Poli** (ten) Pang, Prince of Persia; **Piero De Palma** (ten) Pong; **Sir Peter Pears** (ten) Emperor Altoum; **Nicolai Ghiaurov** (bass) Timur; **Sabin Markov** (bar) Mandarin; **Wandsworth School Boys' Choir; John Alldis Choir; London Philharmonic Orchestra/Zubin Mehta.** Decca 414 274-2DH2. From SET561 (9/73). Notes, text and translation included.

② lh 57m ADD 5/85 **P Ⓑ**

Turandot is a psychologically complex work fusing appalling sadism with self-sacrificing devotion. The icy Princess of China has agreed to marry any man of royal blood who can solve three riddles she has posed. If he fails his head will roll. Calaf, the son of the exiled Tartar king Timur, answers all the questions easily and when Turandot hesitates to accept him, magnanimously offers her a riddle in return — "What is his name?". Liù, Calaf's faithful slave-girl, is tortured but rather than reveal his identity kills herself. Turandot finally capitulates, announcing that his name is Love. Dame Joan Sutherland's assumption of the title role is statuesque, combining regal poise with a more human warmth, whilst Montserrat Caballé is a touchingly sympathetic Liù, skilfully steering the character away from any hint of the mawkish. Pavarotti's Calaf is a heroic figure in splendid voice and the chorus is handled with great power, baying for blood at one minute, enraptured with Liù's nobility at the next. Mehta conducts with great passion and a natural feel for Puccini's wonderfully tempestuous drama. Well recorded.

Additional recommendations ...

Soloists; Chorus and Orchestra of La Scala, Milan/Tullio Serafin. EMI CDS7 47971-2
— .⁛ ② 1h 58m ADD 11/87 ⓑ ▲
Soloists; Rome Opera Chorus and Orchestra/Francesco Molinari-Pradelli. EMI CMS7
69327-2 — .⁛ ② 1h 52m ADD ⁹ₚ ⓑ ▲

Further listening ...

Messe di Gloria in A flat major[a]. *Coupled with* **Mozart.** Vesperae solennes de confessore —
Laudate Dominum[b]. [a]**Soloists;** [b]**Dame Kiri Te Kanawa** (sop); [a]**West German Radio
Chorus;** [b]**London Symphony Chorus;** [a]**Frankfurt Radio Symphony Orchestra/Eliahu
Inbal;** [b]**London Symphony Orchestra/Sir Colin Davis.** Philips 434 170-2PM (1/93).

LE VILLI. **Soloists; Ambrosian Opera Chorus; National Philharmonic Orchestra/
Lorin Maazel.** CBS Masterworks CD768890 (5/88).

EDGAR. **Soloists; New York Schola Cantorum; New York City Opera Children's
Chorus; New York Opera Orchestra/Eve Queler.** CBS CD79213 (10/89).

LA RONDINE. **Soloists; Ambrosian Opera Chorus; London Symphony Orchestra/
Lorin Maazel.** CBS CD37852 (10/85).

Maximo Diego Pujol

Suggested listening ...

Tristango en vos. Preludio tristón. Candombe en mi. *Coupled with* **Tippett.** The blue guitar.
Villa-Lobos. Five Preludes. **Delerue.** Mosaïque. **Giorginakis.** Four Greek images.
Fampas. Greek Dances Nos. 1 and 3. **Eleftheria Kotzia** (gt). Pearl SHECD9609 (6/89).

Henry Purcell

New review

Purcell. COMPLETE ANTHEMS AND SERVICES, Volume 5. [a]**Nicholas Witcomb,** [b]**Mark
Kennedy,** [c]**Jerome Finnis,** [d]**Philip Hallchurch,** [e]**Eamonn O'Dwyer** (trebs); [f]**Susan
Gritton** (sop); [g]**James Bowman** (alto); [h]**Rogers Covey-Crump,** [i]**Charles Daniels,** [j]**Paul
Agnew** (tens); [k]**Michael George** (bass); [l]**Robert Evans** (bass); **New College Choir,
Oxford;** [m]**King's Consort Choir; King's Consort/Robert King.** Hyperion CDA66656.
Texts included. Recorded 1992-93.
Lord, rebuke me not, Z40[bdm]. With sick and famish'd eyes, Z200[i]. How long, great God,
Z189[a]. Awake, and with attention hear, Z181[k]. O God, thou art my God, Z35[achik]. We sing to
him whose wisdom form'd the ear, Z199[f]. Praise the Lord, O my soul and all that is within me,
Z47[achilk]. O, I'm sick of life, Z140[hi]. O God, the King of glory, Z34. Job's Curse, "Let the
night perish", Z191[fk]. When on my sick bed I languish, Z144[hi]. The Bell Anthem, "Rejoice in
the Lord alway", Z49[gik].

.⁛ 1h 11m DDD 2/94 ⁹ₚ

It is difficult to understand how there could be *any* music by England's greatest composer that
has never found its way on to disc, let alone that there could be so much. For rectifying this
situation King deserves our gratitude. This volume includes a few familiar works: *O God, thou art
my God* (well-known at least for its final section's later adaptation as the hymn-tune "Westminster
Abbey") and *Rejoice in the Lord alway*, the so-called Bell Anthem, the latter with the use of
theorbos on the descending basslines of the 'prelude' greatly enhancing its bell effects. *Awake,
and with attention hear* is an imposing bass song which, with quite a few words to get through,

perhaps unavoidably seems a touch overlong, but as usual Purcell's treatment of text is a marvel and Michael George's singing rock solid; *How long, great God* moves involvingly from despair to hope and is well sung by one of the series's star boys, Nicholas Witcomb; while the verse anthem *Praise the Lord, O my soul and all that is within me* is sunny and rich. There is also another fine performance in the gloomy *Job's Curse* from soprano Susan Gritton, who sounds like quite a find.

New review

Purcell. COMPLETE ANTHEMS AND SERVICES, Volume 7. [dfgi]**Mark Kennedy,** [dg]**Eamonn O'Dwyer,** [fg]**James Goodman** (trebs); [e]**Susan Gritton** (sop); [fg]**James Bowman,** [g]**Nigel Short** (altos); [bcdi]**Rogers Covey-Crump,** [bcfghi]**Charles Daniels,** [g]**Mark Milhofer** (tens); [bcdfghi]**Michael George,** [g]**Robert Evans** (basses); [b]**New College Choir, Oxford;** [acfi]**King's Consort Choir; King's Consort/Robert King.** Hyperion CDA66677. Recorded in 1993.

I was glad when they said unto me[a]. I was glad when they said unto me, Z19[b]. O consider my adversity, Z32[c]. Beati omnes qui timent Dominum, Z131[d]. In the black dismal dungeon of despair, Z190[e]. Save me, O God, Z51[f]. Morning and Evening Service in B flat, Z230 — Te Deum; Jubilate[g]. Thy Way, O God, is Holy, Z60[h]. Funeral Sentences for the death of Queen Mary II[i] — Drum Processional; March and Canzona in C minor, Z860; Man that is born of Woman, Z27; In the midst of Life, Z17*b*; Thou know'st Lord, Z58*b*; Thou know'st Lord, Z58*c*.

Ih 10m DDD 6/94 **P**

This recording is made up predominantly of anthems, devotional songs and a morning service (a functional, though not perfunctory, setting of the *Te Deum* and *Jubilate*) most of which disclose the range and quality of the composer's sacred *oeuvre* near its best. Of the two settings of *I was glad*, the first was, until not long ago, thought to be the work of John Blow. This full anthem more than whets our appetite with its agreeable tonal and melodic twists; when the *Gloria* arrives, we are assured that this is vintage Purcell by the sensitive pacing as much as an exquisite contrapuntal denouement. The earlier setting is more poignant. Opening with a string symphony in the spirit of a Locke consort, the music blossoms into a deliciously Elysian melodic fabric. Good sense is made of the overall shape and the soloists are, as ever, excellent. *Beati omnes* is a positive gem; this may well have been written for the composer's wedding. Of the small-scale pieces, *In the black dismal dungeon* is the real masterpiece and it is delivered astutely by the secure and musicianly voice of Susan Gritton. Finally to the funeral pieces. Here we have an ominous procession from the Guild of Ancient Fifes and Drums and the first appearance of four 'flatt' trumpets — as opposed to two plus two sackbuts; the effect of this subtle timbral change makes extraordinary sense of the music, engendering a new grandeur and uncompromising clarity as would have befitted such an occasion. The vocal performances are earthy and impassioned.

Purcell. THEATRE MUSIC. **Joy Roberts, Judith Nelson, Emma Kirkby, Elizabeth Lane, Prudence Lloyd** (sops); **James Bowman** (alto); **Martyn Hill, Paul Elliott, Alan Byers, Peter Bamber, Rogers Covey-Crump, Julian Pike** (tens); **David Thomas, Christopher Keyte, Geoffrey Shaw, Michael George** (basses); **Taverner Choir; Academy of Ancient Music/Christopher Hogwood** (hpd). L'Oiseau-Lyre 425 893-2OM6. Texts included.

Abdelazar, Z570. Distressed Innocence, Z577. The Married Beau, Z603. The Gordian Knot Unty'd, Z597 (all from DSLO504, 6/76). Sir Anthony Love, Z588. Bonduca, Z574. Circe, Z575 (DSLO527, 2/78). The Virtuous Wife, Z611. The Old Bachelor, Z607. Overture in G minor, Z770. Amphitryon, Z572 (DSLO55Q, 12/79). The Comical History of Don Quixote, Z578 (DSLO534, 11/78). The Double Dealer, Z592. The Richmond Heiress, Z608. The Rival Sisters, Z609. Henry the Second, King of England Z580. Tyrannic Love, Z613 (DSLO561, 4/81). Overture in G minor, Z772. Theodosius, Z606. The Libertine, Z600. The Massacre of Paris, Z604. Oedipus, Z583 (DSLO590, 3/82). Overture in D minor, Z771. The History of King Richard II, Z581. Sir Barnaby Whigg, Z589. Sophonisba, Z590. The English Lawyer, Z594. A Fool's Preferement, Z571. The Indian Emperor, Z598. The Knight of Malta, Z599. Why, my Daphne, why complaining?, Z525. The Wifes' Excuse, Z612. Cleomenes, Z576. Regulus, Z586. The Marriage-hater Match'd, Z602 (414 173-1OH, 7/85). Love Triumphant, Z582. Rule a Wife and have a Wife, Z587. The Female Virtuosos, Z596. Epsom Wells, Z579. The Maid's Last Prayer, Z601. Aureng-Zebe, Z573. The Canterbury Guests, Z591. The Fatal

Marriage, Z595. The Spanish Friar, Z610. Pausanias, Z585. The Mock Marriage, Z605. Oroonoko, Z584 (414 174-1OH, 9/85). Pavans — A major, Z748; A minor, Z749; B flat major, Z750; G minor, Z751; G minor, Z752. Trio Sonata for Violin, Bass Viol and Organ, Z780. Chaconne in G minor, Z730 (DSLO514, 10/77).

⑥ 6h 54m ADD/DDD 4/91

This six-CD anthology of vocal and instrumental music by Purcell is as rich and rewarding in its variety as it is indispensable to our picture of Purcell. Although Restoration England continued to take an interest in theatre music from abroad towards the end of the seventeenth century she began to develop staged musical entertainments along hybrid lines of her own. Most of the music contained here dates from the last six years of Purcell's life when plays, from Shakespeare to Shadwell were seldom staged without songs, instrumental interludes and dances. Purcell's legacy to the Restoration stage contains jewels of almost priceless worth and these are lovingly burnished by Christopher Hogwood, the Academy of Ancient Music and an excellent group of vocalists; choruses are imaginatively sung by the Taverner Choir under Andrew Parrott's direction. It would be difficult to isolate any particular songs and dances from such a vast treasure-trove but few may be able to resist Emma Kirkby's saucy "Lads and Lasses, blithe and gay" (*Don Quixote*), Martyn Hill's "Thus to a ripe, consenting maid" (*The Old Bachelor*), the ravishing trio "With this sacred charming wand" (*Don Quixote*) or the "Scotch tune" from *Amphitryon*. Performances are lively and stylish if not always polished but that, one suspects, is as authentic a touch as anything else here. The booklet contains texts of all the songs and the discs are pleasantly recorded.

Additional recommendations ...
Abdelazer — Suite. Timon of Athens, Z632 — No. 1, Overture; No. 20, Curtain tune. The Gordion Knot Unty'd — Suite. Bonduca — Suite. The Virtuous Wife — Suite. Chaconne. **The Parley of Instruments/Peter Holman.** Hyperion CDA66212 — .•' 57m DDD 9/87 ⁹ₚ
Fantasia upon a Ground in D major/F major/Z731. Ten Sonatas in Four Parts — No. 6 in G minor, Z801. Pavans — Z748; Z749; Z750; Z751; Z752. Chaconne. 12 Sonnatas of Three Parts — E minor, Z796; D major, Z801. Overtures — Z771; Z772. Swiftere Isis, swifter flow, Z336 — Overture in G major. Suite in G major, Z770. **London Baroque.** Harmonia Mundi HMC90 1327 — .•' 1h 4m DDD 10/90

New review
Purcell. Music for the Funeral of Queen Mary. [a]**Winchester Cathedral Choir;** [b]**Hilary Brooks** (vc); [c]**Baroque Brass of London;** [d]**The Brandenburg Consort/David Hill** ([e]org) with **David Dunnett** (org). Argo 436 833-2ZH. Texts included. Recorded in 1992.
March and Canzona in C minor, Z860[c]. Funeral Sentences for the death of Queen Mary II[a]. The Bell Anthem, "Rejoice in the Lord alway", Z49[ad]. Remember not, Lord, our offences, Z50[a]. Give sentence with me, O Lord, Z12[a]. Jehova, quam multi sunt hostes mei, Z135[ab]. O, I'm sick of life, Z140[a]. My beloved spake, Z28[ad]. Hear my prayer, O Lord, Z15[a]. O God, thou art my God, Z35[ab]. Voluntaries[e] — No. 1 in C major, Z717; No. 4 in G major, Z720.

1h 6m DDD 6/94

David Hill is a master of long-breathed melody and sustained intensity and he brings to Purcell's anthems a breadth of vision inspired by the time-span of earlier genres. Indeed, it is the range of anthems skilfully chosen from amongst Purcell's finest church music which distinguishes this disc as much as the funeral pieces. *Jehova, quam multi sunt hostes mei* is particularly effective, exemplifying not only Hill's astute pacing but also his vigorous sense of the dramatic declamatory style which Purcell must have gleaned from continental sources. The open-throated treble sound is equally appropriate and characterizes the vocal colouring of almost all the works. The soloists for the verse anthems are drawn both from the ranks of the choir and a pool of professional soloists. Between them they shape the music with spirit and eloquence as can be relished in the abundant fruits of *My beloved spake*. The strings of The Brandenburg Consort balance the buoyant vocal style here with sparkling rhythmic exchanges. Winchester benefits from that fragility and loneliness which a solo treble can give to "In the midst of life", especially in a gothic acoustic. The Baroque Brass of London capture the doleful strains with finesse and make wonderful musical sense of the Canzona. The same players on 'flat' trumpets reappear on all current versions. There is good reason for this: only the truly dedicated are prepared to spend hours practising an instrument which splits notes as soon as you look at it, for a complete repertoire lasting no more than ten minutes.

Purcell. ODES AND WELCOME SONGS, Volumes 6-8. **Gillian Fisher, Mary Seers, Susan Hamilton, Tessa Bonner** (sops); **James Bowman, Nigel Short, Michael Chance** (altos); **Mark Padmore, Andrew Tusa, Rogers Covey-Crump, Charles Daniels, John Mark Ainsley** (tens); **Michael George, Robert Evans** (basses); **New College Choir, Oxford; King's Consort/Robert King.** Hyperion CDA66494, CDA66587 and CDA66598. Texts included. Recorded in 1991.
CDA66494 — Love's goddess sure was blind, Z331. Raise, raise the voice, Z334. Laudate Ceciliam, Z329. From those serene and rapturous joys, Z326. *CDA66587* — Of old, when heroes thought it base, Z333. Swifter, Isis, swifter flow, Z336. What, what shall be done on behalf of the man?, Z341. *CDA66598* — Come ye sons of art, away, Z323. Welcome, viceregent of the mighty king, Z340. Why, why are all the Muses mute?, Z343.

③ 1h 8m 1h 6m 1h 8m DDD 3/93

These three CDs represent the final instalments in Hyperion's complete recording of Purcell's Odes and Welcome Songs. Purcell composed a number of these celebratory works between 1680 and 1695, and 24 survive. They were written for a considerable range of events: most of them for royal birthdays, of King James II and Queen Mary, but also for a royal wedding, educational celebrations, and the 'Yorkshire Feast' of 1689. This cornucopia of wonderful music has largely been ignored, and Hyperion's edition is to be warmly welcomed, not only for bringing to the catalogue such magnificent music, but also for the extremely sympathetic and musical performances by the King's Consort under the direction of Robert King. Of all the works on these discs, probably the most well-known is *Come ye sons of art, away* written for Queen Mary in 1694 (Volume 8). This joyous work contains some of Purcell's most ebullient music, typified by the duet for two counter-tenors, "Sound the trumpet". Like all of the works in the set this is surrounded by a well contrasted group of solos and duets for individual voices, instrumental interludes, and the occasional chorus. Less famous, but equally full of Restoration pomp and ceremony is the Yorkshire Feast song (Volume 7). Like many of the odes, the text for this is second-rate, ostensibly telling the story of York from the Roman occupation to the seventeenth century. However, this is merely the pretext for a splendidly varied set of vocal and instrumental items, the climax of which might be more fitting for a coronation than for a dinner of Yorkshire worthies! Volume 6 contains four of the least well-known if no less rich and varied odes, two of which are dedicated to the patron saint of music, St Cecilia. While composed for slightly smaller forces than the more ceremonial odes, these contain music which is equally jaunty and exhilarating. Throughout all three volumes the most striking fact is Purcell's extraordinary inventiveness, and his incredible facility at word setting: even the most lame texts come alive in his hands, and the variety of expression throughout is astonishing. That such fine music should have lain unrecognized and unplayed for so long is cause for some amazement, but no less rejoicing that at last it has been restored in such understanding performances. Robert King's direction is always sensitive to both the broad span and individual nuances of Purcell's kaleidoscopic writing for voice and instruments. The King's Consort play with great understanding throughout and has clearly wholly absorbed the often elusive style of this music, in which many influences, most notably those from France, are combined. The vocal soloists are uniformly excellent, but special mention must be made of the ravishing soprano Gillian Fisher, and the versatile counter-tenor James Bowman. Hyperion's recordings throughout are without fault, achieving both excellent internal balance and appropriate atmosphere and perspective.

New review
Purcell. SONGS AND AIRS. **Nancy Argenta** (sop); [a]**Nigel North** (lte/gtr); [b]**Richard Boothby** (va da gamba); [c]**Paul Nicholson** (hpd/org). Virgin Classics Veritas VC7 59324-2. Texts included. Recorded in 1992.
O Solitude! my sweetest choice, Z406[a]. Not all my torments can your pity move, Z400[ac]. Stript of their green our groves appear, Z444[abc]. The Blessed Virgin's Expostulation — Tell me, some pitying Angel, Z196[abc]. If music be the food of love, Z379/1[bc]. The fatal hour comes on apace, Z421[a]. The Queen's Epicedium — Incassum, Lesbia, rogas, Z383[ac]. Cupid, the slyest rogue alive, Z367[abc]. Bess of Bedlam — From silent shades, Z370[abc]. An Evening Hymn on a Ground — Now that the sun hath veiled his light, Z193[c]. O Solitude! my sweetest choice, Z406[b]. Tyrannic Love — Ah! how sweet it is to love[bc]. The Fairy Queen — Hark! the echoing air[abc]. Pausanias — Sweeter than roses[ab]. The Tempest — Dear pretty youth[ab]. The Comical History of Don Quixote — From rosy bow'rs[abc]. Sophonisba — Beneath the poplar's shadow[ab]. The

Indian Queen — I attempt from love's sickness[c]. The History of Dioclesian — Let us dance, let us sing[abc]. King Arthur — Fairest isle[a].

1h 14m DDD 6/94

Here we can delight in one of the best recordings of Purcell's songs (mainly taken from *Orpheus Britannicus*) to have emerged in recent times and arguably the most literary-sensitive accounts since Alfred Deller. Nancy Argenta proves that declamatory and strophic songs (and many sub-genres in between) can be negotiated in the same recital with supreme technical finesse, profound understanding of the texts and the type of inventive nuances which enhance the implied conceits of an extraordinary range of songs. Moreover, she has the technical and temperamental control to explore the expressive gamut, from impish and deliberately impersonal no-nonsense texts (such as "Stript of their green", where the singer's rolling spontaneity is just what is called for) to the impulsive gestures and psychological tensions in "Tell me, some pitying Angel" and "From rosy bow'rs". The former is an especially fine portrayal with its sustained organ continuo commentating alongside sundry plucks (always astutely gauged by Nigel North, Richard Boothby and Paul Nicholson) whilst Argenta delivers the Virgin's touching and anxious expostulation with a rare understanding and empathy. Sheer technical bravura, however, is what performances of these songs too frequently lack and the quality of pitching (notoriously awkward leaps abound) and tuning sets this disc in a class of its own; only very occasionally does shrillness or a rather lifeless vibrato detract from an otherwise exquisite release — one which should sit on the shelves of all those who need convincing that Purcell's solo vocal music of this ilk is anything but a glorious testament to the human voice.

New review

Purcell. DIDO AND AENEAS. **Catherine Bott** (sop) Dido; **John Mark Ainsley** (ten) Aeneas; **Emma Kirkby** (sop) Belinda; **David Thomas** (bass) Sorceress; **Elizabeth Priday** (sop) First Witch; **Sara Stowe** (sop) Second Witch; **Julianne Baird** (sop) Second Woman; **Daniel Lochmann** (treb) First Sailor; **Michael Chance** (alto) Spirit; **Academy of Ancient Music Chorus and Orchestra/Christopher Hogwood.** L'Oiseau-Lyre 436 992-2OH. Notes and text included. Recorded in 1992.

52m DDD 7/94

Luxury casting here. Emma Kirkby (whose Dido, for Parrott, remains one of the finest on record) sings Belinda; David Thomas (whose Aeneas, on the same recording, was outstanding) sings the Sorceress; Michael Chance takes the tiny part of the Spirit, thereby putting its moment into centre stage as the gloriously conceived turning-point of the story. A few innovations, too. We have had all kinds of Sorceress on record but following the arguments that the Sorceress could be a man, Hogwood opts for David Thomas, who offers perhaps the most eloquent version so far. He gives full value to the words and the music. Less convincing, perhaps, is the use of a boy for the sailor's song; despite direct and spirited singing, its text is so inappropriate for a boy as to make the decision seem quite wrong. Much more successful is the use of the Drottningholm wind-machines, in all their wonderful variety, to interpret the various stage-instructions and give the entire performance a real sense of verisimilitude. Catherine Bott is a fine Dido, even-voiced across the range and powerfully expressive if occasionally a touch free with the rhythms. John Mark Ainsley easily stands as the finest Aeneas since David Thomas. This is a very difficult role to handle dramatically, because its moods change so fast; and Ainsley handles all this with heartbreaking ease. This is a classic interpretation. So too is Hogwood's reading of the score, with his faultless sense of the right speed and the right rhythm as well as his ability to see the moment when everything must be interrupted to give space to the drama.

Additional recommendations ...
Soloists; The English Concert and Choir/Trevor Pinnock. Archiv Produktion 427 624-2AH — 54m DDD 10/89
Soloists; St Anthony Singers; English Chamber Orchestra/Anthony Lewis. Decca Serenata 425 720-2DM — 53m ADD 12/90
Soloists; Hamburg Monteverdi Choir; Hamburg NDR Chamber Orchestra/Sir Charles Mackerras. Archiv Produktion 431 121-2AGA — 1h 3m ADD 12/90
Soloists; English Chamber Choir and Orchestra/Raymond Leppard. Erato Libretto 2292-45263-2 — 56m ADD 11/91

Soloists; Taverner Choir and Players/Andrew Parrott. Chandos Chaconne CHAN0521
— .·' 56m DDD 11/91 ✍

Soloists; St James's Singers and Baroque Players/Ivor Bolton. Teldec Das Alte Werk
4509-91191-2 — .·' 58m DDD 9/93 ✍

Purcell. THE FAIRY QUEEN. **Gillian Fisher, Lorna Anderson** (sops); **Ann Murray**
(mez); **Michael Chance** (alto); **John Mark Ainsley, Ian Partridge** (tens); **Richard Suart,
Michael George** (basses); **The Sixteen Choir and Orchestra/Harry Christophers.**
Collins Classics 7013-2. Text included. Recorded in 1990.

.·' ② 2h 13m DDD 4/92 ✍

As we reach the Purcell tercentenary, it seems more and more likely that it will be his stage
works — in particular his four semi-operas in which extended musical set-pieces or masques are
mixed with substantial dialogue — that will emerge most strongly from the inevitable
reassessments of the true masterpieces that they are. And of these, it is perhaps *The Fairy Queen*
that stands the best chance of catching the public's imagination, not only because of its superb
music but also on account of its foundation in such a well-loved part of England's literary
heritage as *A Midsummer Night's Dream*. Much has been made of the liberties taken by Purcell's
anonymous librettist for this work, but no one who has heard the music could deny that the
composer conjures just as truthfully as Shakespeare the pains and pleasures of love, the
interludes of low comedy, and the magical atmosphere of the fairy wood. Harry Christophers
has assembled a strong cast for this recording. With singers like Gillian Fisher, Michael Chance,
John Mark Ainsley and Ian Partridge aboard, things are hardly likely to go far astray, while the
contribution of the always excellent Sixteen Choir means, too, that this is a performance without
any serious weakness. The orchestra, it's true, could sound more committed at times, while Ann
Murray seems a little out of place in this particular company (though there's certainly nothing
wrong with her singing as such); but in general there is a refreshing lightness, an authentic
Englishness, to this recording that serves the music well. Perhaps the highlight is the gentle
Second Act Masque which lulls the eponymous Titania to sleep, but also highly enjoyable are the
comic scenes, such as the one in which a drunken poet suffers an uncomfortable encounter with
some fairies. This is not a recording which has everything — it lacks sheer splendour for one
thing — but of those available it perhaps comes closest to the ideal.

Additional recommendations ...
Soloists; Monteverdi Choir; English Baroque Soloists/John Eliot Gardiner. Archiv
Produktion 419 221-2AH2 — .·' ② 2h 18m DDD 8/87 ✍
Soloists; Les Arts Florissants/William Christie. Harmonia Mundi HMC90 1308/9 — .·'
② 2h 8m DDD 1/90 ✍
Soloists; Ambrosian Opera Chorus; English Chamber Orchestra/Benjamin Britten.
Decca Serenata 433 163-2DM2 — .·' ② 1h 36m ADD 5/92
The Scholars Baroque Ensemble. Naxos 8 550660/1 — . ② 2h 9m DDD 7/94

Further listening ...

Organ Works — Four Voluntaries, Z717-20. Verse in F major, Z716. A Choice Collection of
Lessons: March in C major, ZT687; Chaconne in G minor, ZT680; Trumpet Tune in C major,
"Cibell", ZT678; Trumpet Tune in C major, ZT698. Ground in Gamut in G major, Z645.
Ground in C minor, TD221. Voluntary in A major on the Old Hundredth, Z721. Trumpet
Voluntary in D major. *Coupled with* **Blow.** Six Voluntaries. **Locke.** Seven Voluntaries from
Melothesia. **John Butt** (org). Harmonia Mundi HMU90 7103 (6/94).

Suites — The Fairy Queen; Dido and Aeneas; King Arthur; Abdelazer; Chaconne in G minor,
Z730. **Freiburg Baroque Orchestra/Thomas Hengelbrock.** Deutsche Harmonia Mundi
RD77231 (3/92).

Ten Sonatas in Four Parts, Z802-11 — No. 3 in A minor; No. 4 in D minor; No. 5 in G minor;
No. 6 in G minor; No. 7 in G major; No. 8 in G minor (with two variant movements); No. 9 in F
major; No. 10 in D major. Organ Voluntaries, Z717-20 — No. 2 in D minor; No. 4 in G major.
Prelude for Solo Violin in G minor, ZN773. **Purcell Quartet.** Chandos CHAN8763 (12/89).

Songs from Orpheus Britannicus: The Rival Sisters, Z609 — Calia has a thousand charms. Fly swift, ye hours, Z369. Gentle shepherds, you that know, Z464. Aureng-Zebe, Z573 — I see, she flies me. Pausanias, Z585 — Sweeter than roses. I came, I saw, and was undone, Z375. If music be the food of love, Z379/3. Bess of Bedlam, "From silent shades", Z370. Timon of Athens, Z632 — Love in their little veins. The Comical History of Don Quioxte, Z578 — From rosy bow'rs. King Arthur, Z628 — Fairest isle. Tyrannic Love, Z613 — Ah! how sweet it is to love. The Fatal hour comes on apace, Z421. O Solitude! my sweetest choice, Z406. The history of Dioclesian, Z627 — Since from my dear Astrea's sight. Bonduca, Z574 — O lead me to some peaceful gloom. The Fairy Queen, Z629 — Thrice happy lovers. *Solo Harpsichord:* The Second Part of Musick's Handmaid — A New Ground in E minor, Z T682. Ground in D minor, Z D222. Hornpipe in D minor, "Round O", Z T684. A Choice Collection of Lessons — Chaconne in G minor, Z T680. **Agnès Mellon** (sop); **Wieland Kuijken** (va da gamba); **Christophe Rousset** (hpd). Astrée Auvidis E8757 (9/93).

Complete Anthems and Services, Volume 3 — Blow up the trumpet in Sion, Z10. The Lord is king, be the people never so impatient, Z53. Begin the song, and strike the living lyre, Z183. Thy word is a lantern unto my feet, Z61. Tell me, some pitying Angel, Z196. Hear my prayer, O Lord, Z15. Lord, I can suffer Thy rebukes, Z136. O Lord our governor, Z39. Remember not, Lord, our offences, Z50. Hosanna to the highest, Z187. O God, thou hast cast us out, Z36. **Soloists; King's Consort Choir; King's Consort/Robert King.** Hyperion CDA66623 (4/93).

Anthems, Instrumental Music and Songs. **Soloists; King's College Choir, Cambridge/Sir David Willcocks; Leonhardt Consort/Gustav Leonhardt; Brüggen Consort/Frans Brüggen.** Teldec 9031-77608-2 (9/93).

KING ARTHUR — *semi-opera.* **Soloists; Monteverdi Choir; English Baroque Soloists/ John Eliot Gardiner.** Erato 2292-45211-2 (7/86).

THE INDIAN QUEEN — *semi-opera.* **Soloists; Deller Choir; The King's Music/Alfred Deller.** Harmonia Mundi HMC90 243 (8/87).

Key to symbols

Price	Quantity/ availability	Timing	Recording mode	Review date
♪	② ②	lh 23m	DDD	6/88

Johann Quantz

German 1697-1773

Suggested listening ...

Flute Concertos — C major; D major, "pour Potsdam"; G major; G minor. **James Galway** (fl); **Württemberg Chamber Orchestra/Jörg Faerber.** RCA Victor Red Seal RD60247 (11/91).

Roger Quilter

British 1877-1953

Suggested listening ...

Songs — Three Songs, Op. 3 — No. 1, Love's Philosophy; No. 2, Now Sleeps the Crimson Petal. At Close of Day. Three Shakespeare Songs, Op. 6. To Julia, Op. 8. Four Songs, Op. 14.

Seven Elizabethan Lyrics, Op. 12. Three Songs of William Blake, Op. 20. Go, Lovely Rose, Op. 24 No. 3. Arab Love Song, Op. 25 No. 4. Music, When Soft Voices Die, Op. 25 No. 5. In the Bud of the Morning-o, Op. 25 No. 6. I Arise from Dreams of Thee, Op. 29. **Benjamin Luxon** (bar); **David Willison** (pf). Chandos CHAN8782 (3/90).

Sergey Rachmaninov

Russian/American 1873-1943

New review

Rachmaninov. THE COMPLETE RECORDINGS. [a]**Fritz Kreisler** (vn); [b]**Sergey Rachmaninov** (pf); **Philadelphia Orchestra/**[c]**Leopold Stokowski,** [d]**Eugene Ormandy,** [e]**Sergey Rachmaninov.** RCA Victor Gold Seal mono 09026 61265-2.
Rachmaninov. Piano Concertos[b] — No. 1 in F sharp minor, Op. 1[d]; No. 2 in C minor, Op. 18[c]; No. 3 in D minor, Op. 30[d]; No. 4 in G minor, Op. 40[d]. Rhapsody on a Theme of Paganini, Op. 43[bc]. The isle of the dead, Op. 29[e]. Vocalise, Op. 34 No. 14[e]. Symphony No. 3 in A minor, Op. 44[e]. *Solo piano works*[b] — Daisies. Nine Etudes-tableaux, Op. 33 — No. 2 in C major; No. 7 in E flat major. Nine Etudes-tableaux, Op. 39 — No. 6 in A minor. Lilacs (two versions, recorded in 1923 and 1942). Six Moments musicaux, Op. 16 — Allegretto. Five Morceaux de fantaisie, Op. 3 — No. 5, Sérénade in B flat minor. Seven Morceaux de salon, Op. 10 — No. 5, Humoresque in G major. Oriental Sketch in B flat major. Polka de W.R. (three versions, recorded in 1919, 1921 and 1928). *24 Preludes* — C sharp minor, Op. 3 No. 2 (three versions, recorded in 1919, 1921 and 1928); G minor, Op. 23 No. 5; G flat major, Op. 23 No. 10; E major, Op. 32 No. 3; G major, Op. 32 No. 5; F minor, Op. 32 No. 6; G sharp minor, Op. 32 No. 12. **Beethoven.** Violin Sonata No. 8 in G major, Op. 30 No. 3[ab]. 32 Variations on an original theme in C minor, WoO80[b]. **Schubert.** Violin Sonata in A major (Duo), D574[ab]. **Grieg.** Violin Sonata No. 3 in C minor, Op. 45[ab]. **Schumann.** Carnaval, Op. 9[b]. **Chopin.** Piano Sonata No. 2 in B flat minor, Op. 35[b]. *Also includes solo piano works by* **Bach, Beethoven, Bizet, Borodin, Chopin, Daquin, Debussy, Dohnányi, Gluck, Grieg, Handel, Henselt, Kreisler, Liszt, Mendelssohn, Moszkowski, Mozart, Mussorgsky, Paderewski, Rimsky-Korsakov, Saint-Saëns, D. Scarlatti, Schubert, Schumann, Scriabin, J. Strauss II** and *Tchaikovsky.*

⁙ ①⑩ l0h 40m ADD 3/93 ⁹ₚ ▲

Here, on RCA's superbly remastered ten-disc set, is awe-inspiring and scintillating confirmation of Rachmaninov's greatness; as composer, pianist, chamber musician and conductor. Controversy over his stature as a composer may live on in the dustier corners of academia, but today once confident assertions that his music would never last, that it lacked the regenerative force of true tragedy or that it was, in essence, little more than a precursor of Hollywood, have been triumphantly erased. Works such as the Second Symphony, the Third Piano Concerto and the Second Piano Sonata are played without the once acceptable and debilitating cuts so sadly sanctioned by the composer, and innovative as well as traditional elements in Rachmaninov's writing are celebrated. What is indisputable, however, is Rachmaninov's quality as a pianist. Alternatively teasing and granitic in other composer's music (his way with Schumann's *Carnaval* and Chopin's Second Sonata, to name but two, will always incite argument) his performances of his own works are, quite simply, inimitable, imbued with a brio and aristocracy entirely his own. The most immediately appealing include all four concertos and the Paganini *Rhapsody*, Handel's *Harmonious Blacksmith* Variations (pure pianistic sorcery) and Rachmaninov's own second *Moment musical* and *Mélodie*, Op. 3 No. 2; the former of a mind-bending virtuosity, the latter aglow with the *cantabile* and rubato of another, far-off age. But everything is absorbing, nothing without interest. These recordings blazen out Rachmaninov's stature both as creator and re-creator in every golden bar.

Additional recommendations ...
Nos. 1-4. Rhapsody on a Theme of Paganini. **Rafael Orozco** (pf); **Royal Philharmonic Orchestra/Edo de Waart.** Philips 438 326-2PM2 — ⁙ ② 2h 30m ADD
Nos. 1-4. Rhapsody on a Theme of Paganini. **Earl Wild** (pf); **Royal Philharmonic Orchestra/Jascha Horenstein.** Chandos CHAN8521/2 — ⁙ ② 2h 14m ADD 9/87
No. 4 in G minor, Op. 40. **Ravel.** *Piano Concerto in G major.* **Arturo Benedetti Michelangeli** (pf); **Philharmonia Orchestra/Ettore Gracis.** EMI CDC7 49326-2 — ⁙ 47m ADD 9/88 ⁹ₚ ▲

Nos. 1-4. **Vladimir Ashkenazy** (pf); **Concertgebouw Orchestra/Bernard Haitink.** Decca
421 590-2DH2 — .•' ② 2h 14m DDD 4/89

Nos. 1-4. **Vladimir Ashkenazy** (pf); **London Symphony Orchestra/André Previn.** Decca
425 576-2DM2 — .•' ② 2h 15m ADD 3/90

Nos. 1 and 4. **Vladimir Ashkenazy** (pf); **London Symphony Orchestra/André Previn.**
Decca 425 004-2DM — .•' 55m ADD 7/90

Nos. 1-4. Rhapsody on a Theme of Paganini. **Howard Shelley** (pf); **Royal Scottish National
Orchestra/Bryden Thomson.** Chandos CHAN8882/3 — .•' ② 2h 34m DDD 4/91

Rachmaninov. Piano Concerto No. 1 in F sharp minor, Op. 1[a]. Rhapsody on a Theme of
Paganini, Op. 43[b]. **Vladimir Ashkenazy** (pf); [a]**Concertgebouw Orchestra,** [b]**Philharmonia
Orchestra/Bernard Haitink.** Decca 417 613-2DH.

.•' **52m DDD 12/87**   ᑫₚ

Showpiece that it is, with its lush romantic harmonies and contrasting vigorous panache, the First
Concerto has much to commend it in purely musical terms and although its debts are clear
enough (most notably perhaps to Rimsky-Korsakov), it stands on its own two feet as far as
invention, overall design and musical construction are concerned. The *Paganini* Rhapsody is one
of the composer's finest works and arguably the most purely inventive set of variations to be
based on Paganini's catchy tune ever written. The wealth of musical invention it suggested to
Rachmaninov is truly bewildering and his control over what can in lesser hands become a rather
laboured formal scheme is masterly indeed. Ashkenazy gives superb performances of both works
and the Concertgebouw and the Philharmonia are in every way the perfect foils under Bernard
Haitink's sympathetic direction. There is weight, delicacy, colour, energy and repose in equal
measure here and it is all conveyed by a full-bodied and detailed recording.

Additional recommendations ...
No. 1. **Prokofiev.** *Piano Concerto No. 3 in C major, Op. 26. Toccata in C major, Op. 11.* **Pinto.**
Three Scenes from Childhood. **Byron Janis** (pf); **Moscow Philharmonic Orchestra/Kyrill
Kondrashin.** Mercury 434 333-2MM (*see review under Prokofiev; refer to the Index to Reviews*) —
.•' 1h 9m ADD 7/94 ᑫₚ

Rachmaninov. Piano Concerto No. 2 in C minor, Op. 18. Rhapsody on a Theme of
Paganini, Op. 43. **Vladimir Ashkenazy** (pf); **London Symphony Orchestra/André
Previn.** Decca Ovation 417 702-2DH. From SXLF6565/7 (9/72).

.•' **58m ADD 7/87**   Ⓑ

Rachmaninov. Piano Concerto No. 3 in D minor, Op. 30[a]. PRELUDES[b]. **Vladimir
Ashkenazy** (pf); [a]**London Symphony Orchestra/André Previn.** Decca Ovation 417 764-
2DM. Item marked [a] from SXLF6565/7 (9/72), recorded in 1971, [b] 5BB 221/2 (2/76),
recorded 1974-75.
24 Preludes — C sharp minor, Op. 3 No. 2; B flat major, Op. 23 No. 2; G minor, Op. 23
No. 5; B minor, Op. 32 No. 10; D flat major, Op. 32 No. 13.

.•' **1h 10m ADD 10/88**   Ⓑ

The C minor Concerto of Rachmaninov symbolizes romanticism at its ripest. Its combination of
poetry and sensuous warmth with languorously memorable melodic lines balanced by exhilarating
pianistic brilliance happily avoids any suggestion of sentimentality. The simple chordal
introduction from the soloist ushers in one of the composer's most luscious tunes, yet the slow
movement develops even greater ardour in its melodic contour, and the composer holds back a
further haunting expressive idea to bring lyrical contrast to the scintillating finale. Ashkenazy's
1972 performance with Previn is a superb mid-price bargain, coupled with an exhilarating
performance of the *Rhapsody on a Theme of Paganini*, where the famous Variation No. 18
blossoms with passionate fervour. The Concerto is no less involving, the first movement building
to an engulfing climax, the *Adagio* radiantly beautiful, perhaps the finest on disc. The recording
represents Decca vintage analogue sound at its best and the remastering is extremely successful,
rich, well balanced and vivid. Ashkenazy's recording of the Third Concerto complements the
composer's own (listed below). It is more conspicuously expressive, more heroic and more
yielding by turns; it is uncut, includes the more massive of the first movement cadenzas, and it

enjoys a full-blooded modern recording. There is a tendency to bang away when the chords are coming thick and fast and to overdo expressive lingerings; also, Previn's accompaniment is fine but not outstandingly idiomatic. But these points do not outweigh the advantages of what, especially at mid-price, is one of the top recommendations for this concerto. A selection of five of Rachmaninov's most popular Preludes enhances the attractions of the disc.

Additional recommendations ...
No. 2[a]. **Prokofiev.** *Piano Concerto No. 5 in G major, Op. 55*[b]. **Sviatoslav Richter** (pf); **Warsaw Philharmonic Orchestra/**[a]**Stanislaw Wislocki;** [b]**Witold Rowicki.** DG 415 119-2GH *(see review under Prokofiev; refer to the Index to Reviews)* — ⠰ 58m ADD 6/85 🎵ₚ Ⓑ ▲
No. 2. *Rhapsody on a Theme of Paganini.* **Philip Fowke** (pf); **Royal Philharmonic Orchestra/ Yuri Temirkanov.** EMI Eminence CD-EMX9509 — ⠰ 59m DDD 10/87 Ⓑ
No. 2[ab]. **Tchaikovsky.** *Piano Concerto No. 1 in B flat minor, Op. 23*[ac]. [a]**Van Cliburn** (pf); [b]**Chicago Symphony Orchestra/Fritz Reiner;** [c]**RCA Victor Symphony Orchestra/ Kyril Kondrashin.** RCA RD85912 — ⠰ 1h 9m ADD 1/88 🎵ₚ Ⓑ
Nos. 2[a] and 3[b]. **Sergei Rachmaninov** (pf); **Philadelphia Orchestra/**[a]**Leopold Stokowski;** [b]**Eugene Ormandy.** RCA Red Seal mono RD85997 — ⠰ 1h 6m ADD 10/88 🎵ₚ Ⓑ ▲
No. 2. *Rhapsody on a Theme of Paganini.* **Jenö Jandó** (pf); **Budapest Symphony Orchestra/György Lehel.** Naxos 8 550117 — . 58m DDD 10/90 Ⓑ
Nos. 2 and 3. **Earl Wild** (pf); **Royal Philharmonic Orchestra/Jascha Horenstein.** Chandos Collect CHAN6507 — ⠰ 1h 6m ADD 2/91 🎵ₚ Ⓑ
No. 3. **Saint-Saëns.** *No. 2 in G minor, Op. 2.* **Shostakovich.** *Prelude and Fugue in D major, Op. 87.* **Emil Gilels** (pf); **Paris Conservatoire Orchestra/André Cluytens.** Testament mono SBT1029 *(see review under Saint-Saëns; refer to the Index to Reviews)* — ⠰ 1h 5m ADD 2/94 🎵ₚ Ⓑ ▲
No. 3[a]. *Piano Sonata No. 2 in B flat minor, Op. 36.* **Vladimir Horowitz** (pf); [a]**RCA Victor Symphony Orchestra/Fritz Reiner.** RCA Victor Gold Seal GD87754 — ⠰ 1h 11m ADD 7/94 🎵ₚ Ⓑ

Rachmaninov. SYMPHONIES. ORCHESTRAL WORKS. **London Symphony Orchestra/ André Previn.** EMI CMS7 64530-2. Items marked [a] from ASD3259 (9/76), [b] ASD3284 (12/76), [c] ASD3369 (8/77). Recorded 1974-76.
Symphonies — No. 1 in D minor, Op. 13; No. 2 in E minor, Op. 27; No. 3 in A minor, Op. 44[c]. Symphonic Dances, Op. 45[a]. The isle of the dead, Op. 29[a]. Vocalise, Op. 34 No. 14[b] (arr. composer). Aleko[c] — Intermezzo; Gipsy Girls' Dance.

⠰ ③ **3h 47m ADD 10/93** 🎵ₚ

Rachmaninov's three symphonies reflect three very different phases in his creative development: the first (1895) is a stormy synthesis of contemporary trends in Russian symphonic music, the Second (1906-7), an epic study in Tchaikovskian opulence, and the third (1935-6) a seemingly unstoppable stream of original ideas and impressions. The Second was the first to gain wide acceptance, and for good reason. It shares both the key and general mood of Tchaikovsky's Fifth. Cast in E minor, its initial gloom ultimately turns to triumph, and the Symphony includes enough glorious melodies to keep Hollywood happy for decades. The First Symphony had a difficult birth, largely through the incompetent musical midwifery of Alexander Glazunov whose conducting of the work's première apparently left much to be desired. It is, however, an immensely promising piece and although undeniably the product of its times, prophetic not only of the mature Rachmaninov, but of other Northern voices, including — occasionally — the mature Sibelius. Both the Third Symphony and its near-contemporary, the *Symphonic Dances* find Rachmaninov indulging a fruitful stream of musical consciousness, recalling motives and ideas from earlier compositions, yet allowing gusts of fresh air to enliven and rejuvenate his style. Both works have yet to receive their full due in the concert-hall, although the strongly evocative *Isle of the dead* is more securely embedded in the repertory. What with these and a trio of warming shorter pieces, André Previn's mid-1970s LSO package makes for an excellent mid-price bargain package. The performances are entirely sympathetic, avoiding familiar interpretative extremes such as slickness, bombast and emotional indulgence. Previn shows particular under-standing of the Third Symphony, the *Symphonic Dances* and *The isle of the dead,* works that represent Rachmaninov at his most innovative and assured. The Second Symphony is played without cuts (not invariably the case, even today) and Christopher Bishop's recordings are generous in tone and revealing of detail, especially among the woodwinds.

Additional recommendations …

Nos. 1-3. Youth Symphony. **Concertgebouw Orchestra/Vladimir Ashkenazy.** Decca 421 065-2DM3 — ⸲ ③ 2h 30m DDD 12/87 ♩ₚ

No. 1. The isle of the dead. **Royal Philharmonic Orchestra/Andrew Litton.** Virgin Classics VC7 59547-2 — ⸲ Ih 7m DDD 5/90 ♩ₚ

Nos. 1-3. Vocalise. **Philadelphia Orchestra/Eugene Ormandy.** CBS Maestro CD45678 — ⸲ ② 2h 17m ADD 8/90 ♩ₚ

Nos. 1-3. The isle of the dead. Symphonic Dances. Vocalise. **Royal Philharmonic Orchestra/ Andrew Litton.** Virgin Classics VC7 90831-2 — ⸲ ③ 3h 34m DDD 10/93 ♩ₚ ♩ₛ

No. 1. The isle of the dead. **Concertgebouw Orchestra/Vladimir Ashkenazy.** Decca Ovation 436 479-2DM — ⸲ Ih 3m DDD 2/94 ♩ₚ

New review

Rachmaninov. Symphony No. 2 in E minor, Op. 27. The Rock, Op. 7. **Russian National Orchestra/Mikhail Pletnev.** DG 439 888-2GH. Recorded in 1993.

⸲ **Ih 4m DDD 6/94** ♩ₚ

Mikhail Pletnev's achievement is to make us hear the music afresh: a performance characterized by relatively discreet emotionalism, strong forward momentum and a fanatical preoccupation with clarity of articulation. When there is no Slavic wobble, it scarcely matters that his winds display an individuality which once or twice fails to transcend mere rawness — so much the better in this music! The strings, forceful and husky (with separated violin desks) are beyond reproach. The most remarkable playing comes in the finale, often bringing to mind the orchestra's staggering display in the third movement of Tchaikovsky's *Pathétique* (see review under Tchaikovsky; refer to the Index to Reviews). The lyrical effusions are superbly characterized without undermining the sense of inexorability, the climaxes not just powerful but affecting too. The closing pages bring a rush of adrenalin of the kind rarely experienced live, let alone in the studio. This is great music-making, the rubato always there when required, the long phrases immaculately tailored yet always sounding spontaneous. DG's unexpected coupling is *The Rock*, an early, rather bitty piece which is however very deftly scored and intriguingly Scriabinesque in places. In Pletnev's hands, the central climax is surprisingly powerful, with just a hint of the buzz-saw in the brass playing. The fabulous delicacy elsewhere is alone worth the price of admission.

Additional recommendations …

No. 2. **Concertgebouw Orchestra/Vladimir Ashkenazy.** Decca 400 081-2DH — ⸲ 55m 3/83 DDD ♩ₚ

No. 2. **London Symphony Orchestra/Gennadi Rozhdestvensky.** Pickwick IMP Classics PCD904 — ⸲ Ih 6m DDD 1/89 ♩ₚ

No. 2. Vocalise, Op. 34 No. 14. **Royal Philharmonic Orchestra/Andrew Litton.** Virgin Classics VC7 59548-2 — ⸲ Ih 10m DDD 5/90 ♩ₚ

No. 2. **Orchestre de Paris/Semyon Bychkov.** Philips 432 101-2PH — ⸲ 58m DDD 9/91 ♩ₚ ♩ₛ

No. 2. Vocalise. **BBC Welsh Symphony Orchestra/Tadaaki Otaka.** Nimbus NI5322 — ⸲ Ih 6m DDD 5/92

No. 2. Vocalise[a]. [a]**Sylvia McNair** (sop); **Baltimore Symphony Orchestra/David Zinman.** Telarc CD80312 — ⸲ Ih 8m DDD 10/92 ♩ₚ

New review

Rachmaninov. Symphony No. 3 in A minor, Op. 44. Symphonic Dances, Op. 45. **St Petersburg Philharmonic Orchestra/Mariss Jansons.** EMI CDC7 54877-2. Recorded in 1992.

⸲ **Ih 12m DDD 12/93** ♩ₚ

This is one of the more distinguished Rachmaninov issues of recent years. While no Rachmaninov Third unfolds as inexorably as Previn's (reviewed above), it is refreshing to hear the opening 'motto' theme played perfectly in tune by an orchestra on even more dazzling form than the LSO, and Jansons unearths such exquisite details of sonority and texture that criticism is all but silenced. There have been more haunting, more fundamentally pessimistic accounts, but none with such an ear for Rachmaninov's sometimes risky orchestral effects. The *Symphonic Dances* are even more impressive. The insinuating waltz movement is irresistible, very free with idiomatic-sounding rubato, while the dynamic outer portions of the finale are superbly articulated, dazzling in the closing stages. EMI's close-miking of instrumental lines may inhibit the sort of tonal blend implied by Rachmaninov's scoring, but the distinctive heft and huskiness of Mravinsky's string section is not betrayed. In its lush, extrovert way, this disc is unbeatable.

Additional recommendations ...
No. 3. **Shostakovich.** *Symphony No. 6 in B minor, Op. 54[b].* **London Symphony Orchestra/ André Previn.** EMI Studio CDM7 69564-2 — .•˙ lh l5m ADD 12/88
No. 3. *Symphonic Dances, Op. 45.* **Royal Philharmonic Orchestra/Andrew Litton.** Virgin Classics VC7 59549-2 — .•˙ lh l8m DDD 5/90 ꟼₚ
No. 3. *The isle of the dead, Op. 29. Vocalise, Op. 34 No. 14 (arr. composer).* **Philadelphia Orchestra/Sergey Rachmaninov.** Pearl GEMMCD9414 — .•˙ 59m AAD ▲
No. 3. *The isle of the dead.* **BBC Welsh Symphony Orchestra/Tadaaki Otaka.** Nimbus NI5344 — .•˙ lh 4m DDD 4/93
No. 3. *Symphonic Dances, Op. 45.* **Concertgebouw Orchestra/Vladimir Ashkenazy.** Decca Ovation 436 481-2DM — .•˙ lh l6m DDD 2/94 ꟼₚ ꟼₛ

New review
Rachmaninov. Cello Sonata in G minor, Op. 19.
R. Strauss. Cello Sonata in F major, Op. 6. **Anne Gastinel** (vc); **Pierre-Laurent Aimard** (pf). Auvidis Valois V4692. Recorded in 1993.

.•˙ lh DDD 12/93

Rich in a sub-Brahmsian romanticism, Strauss's youthful Cello Sonata demonstrates little of the flair that one finds in the Serenade for 13 Wind Instruments, or the First Horn Concerto, both of which date from the same period. But the finale is tuneful and appealing in a lightweight manner. The Rachmaninov is quite another matter. Gastinel and Aimard work so well together, are both such proficient and sympathetic players, that this emerges as a performance with real dramatic impact. Gastinel's phrasing is always natural-sounding. Her tone is very Gallic in being crystal-clear and a tiny bit nasal. In the *Andante* slow movement the duo hold the long, broad lines of the music with absolute assurance. Her intonation is faultless; he is incapable of making an ugly sound. One waits until the last movement to hear the darker side emerge, and yet here Aimard never resorts to melodrama for effect. The recording is good.

New review
Rachmaninov. COMPLETE SOLO PIANO MUSIC. **Howard Shelley.** Hyperion CDS44041/8. From CDA66081, CDA66082, CDA66184, CDA66047, CDA66009 (all 10/88), CDA66198 (9/87), CDA66091 (8/88) and CDA66486 (3/92).
Variations on a Theme of Chopin, Op. 22. Variations on a Theme of Corelli, Op. 42. Mélodie in E major, Op. 3 No. 3. Piano Sonatas — No. 1 in D minor, Op. 28; No. 2 in B flat minor, Op. 36 (orig. version); No. 2 in B flat minor, Op. 36 (rev. version). Ten Preludes, Op. 23. 13 Preludes, Op. 32. Prelude in D minor (1917). Prelude in F major (1891). Morceaux de fantaisie, Op. 3. Morceau de fantaisie in G minor (1899). Song without words in D minor (?1887). Pièce in D minor (1917). Fughetta in F major (1899). Fragments in A flat major (1917). Oriental Sketch in B flat major (1917). Three Nocturnes — No. 1 in F sharp minor (1887); No. 2 in F major (1887); No. 3 in C minor (1887). Quatre Pièces (?1887) — Romance in F sharp minor; Prélude in E flat minor; Mélodie in E major; Gavotte in D major. 17 Etudes-tableaux, Opp. 33 and 39. *Transcriptions* — **Rimsky-Korsakov.** THE TALE OF TSAR SALTAN — The flight of the bumble-bee. **Kreisler.** Liebesleid. Liebesfreud. **Bizet.** L'Arlésienne suite No. 1 — Menuet. **Schubert.** Die schöne Müllerin, D957 — Wohin? **Mussorgsky.** SOROCHINSKY FAIR — Gopak. **Bach.** Solo Violin Partita No. 3 in E major, BWV1006 — Preludio, Gavotte, Gigue. **Rachmaninov.** Daisies, Op. 38 No. 3. Lilacs, Op. 21 No. 5. Vocalise, Op. 34 No. 14 (arr. Kocsis). **Mendelssohn.** A Midsummer Night's Dream, Op. 61 — Scherzo. **Behr.** Lachtäubchen, Op. 303 (pubd. as Polka de VR). **Tchaikovsky.** Cradle Song, Op. 16 No. 1.

.•˙ ⑧ 7h 29m DDD 3/94 ꟼₚ

This Hyperion set is a significant testament to Howard Shelley's artistry. Pianistically impeccable, he understands what Rachmaninov was about. The original piano works span some 45 years of the composer's life. The earliest pieces here, the *Nocturnes*, strangely owe allegiance neither to Field nor Chopin, but are very much in the mid-to-late nineteenth-century Russian salon style. The Third, in C minor, has nothing whatever to do with its title. Nicely written too, but still uncharacteristic, are four pieces from 1888, which amply demonstrate that from his early teens the composer had something individual to say. The *Mélodie* in E (not to be confused with that from Op. 3) is memorable for its hypnotic use of piano tone. Hyperion's recording quality can be heard at its very best here; there is real bloom and colour. Written shortly after his First Piano Concerto in the early 1890s, the *Morceaux de fantaisie*, Op. 3 bring us to familiar Rachmaninov. The ubiquitous Prelude in C sharp minor is the second number but Shelley tries to do too much with it; he is more effective in the *Sérénade* with its Spanish overtones. In the E flat minor *Moments musicaux*, Op. 16 one feels that he is able to master Rachmaninov's swirling accompaniments idiomatically. In Variation No. 15 of the seldom-heard *Variations on a Theme of Chopin* (the theme is the Prelude in C minor from Op. 28) Shelley succeeds in bringing the notes to life, getting his fingers around the fleet *scherzando* writing. The first set of Preludes is, of course, mainstream repertoire and, as such, easier to assess. In the warmly expressive D major Prelude he lends the piece a strong Brahmsian feel and it emerges as very well focused, especially since the voices are so subtly separated. He manages to transform the C minor into a restless mood picture. Moving on to the First Sonata Shelley achieves a symphonic stature. This is a piece that is conventionally dismissed as being unwieldy; he convinces one otherwise and allows it to be seen in conjunction more with the composer's orchestral writing. Within a couple of years Rachmaninov was at the height of his powers and shortly after the Third Concerto he wrote the Op. 32 Preludes. Shelley is able to conjure up an exquisite, shimmering moonlit scene for the G major, but he is not as monumentally impressive in the B minor. However, with him it is always the music that dictates the course of the interpretation. In the two sets of *Etudes-tableaux* he excels as he does too in the Second Sonata. He draws together the disparate elements of the finale with terrific mastery and shows himself entirely the equal of the 'Horowitz clones' in matters of technique. In the *Corelli* Variations he is not quite in tune with the scope of the work but is outstanding in the transcriptions, if a little straight-faced. The recorded sound is never less than serviceable and is sometimes excellent.

Additional recommendations ...
24 Preludes. Piano Sonata No. 2. **Vladimir Ashkenazy** (pf). Decca 414 417-2DH2 — .·' ②
1h 46m ADD 11/85 ⁹ₚ
24 Preludes — B flat major, Op. 23 No. 2; G minor, Op. 23 No. 5; C minor, Op. 23 No. 7; C major, Op. 32 No. 1; B flat minor, Op. 32 No. 2. *Tchaikovsky*. Piano Concerto No. 1 in B flat minor.
Sviatoslav Richter (pf); **Vienna Symphony Orchestra/Herbert von Karajan.** DG Galleria 419 068-2GGA — .·' 50m ADD 8/87
Piano Sonata No. 2. Morceau de fantaisie. Song without words. Pièce in D minor. Fughetta. Fragments. Oriental Sketch. Three Nocturnes. Quatre Pièces — Romance; Prélude; Mélodie; Gavotte. **Howard Shelley** (pf). Hyperion CDA66198 (reviewed above) — .·' 59m DDD 9/87 ⁹ₚ
24 Preludes. **Peter Katin** (pf). Olympia OCD110 — .· ② 1h 20m ADD 10/87
24 Preludes — C sharp minor, Op. 3 No. 2; B flat major, Op. 23 No. 2; G minor, Op. 23 No. 5; B minor, Op. 32 No. 10; D flat major, Op. 32 No. 13. Piano Concerto No. 3 in D minor, Op. 30.
Vladimir Ashkenazy (pf); **London Symphony Orchestra/André Previn.** Decca Ovation 417 764-2DM — .·' 1h 10m ADD 10/88
Preludes, Op. 23. Morceaux de fantaisie. **Howard Shelley** (pf). Hyperion CDA66081 (reviewed above) — .·' 1h ADD 10/88 ⁹ₚ
Preludes, Op. 32. Preludes — F major; D minor. **Howard Shelley** (pf). Hyperion CDA66082 — .·' 48m ADD 10/88 ⁹ₚ
Piano Sonatas — No. 1; No. 2 (original version). **Gordon Fergus-Thompson** (pf). Kingdom KCLCD2007 — .·' 1h 13m DDD 6/89
The bells. Three Russian Songs, Op. 41. **Concertgebouw Chorus and Orchestra/Vladimir Ashkenazy.** Decca Ovation 436 482-2DM — .·' 50m DDD 2/94 ⁹ₚ
Variations on a Theme of Chopin. Piano Sonata No. 1. **Boris Berezovsky** (pf). Teldec 4509-90890-2 — .·' 1h 6m DDD 7/94

New review
Rachmaninov. PIANO WORKS. **Dmitri Alexeev** (pf). Virgin Classics VCD7 59289-2.
Recorded 1987-89.

24 Preludes, Opp. 23 and 32. Prelude in D minor. Morceaux de fantaisie, Op. 3. Lilacs. Daisies. Mélodie in E major. Oriental Sketch in B flat major. Moments musicaux, Op. 16.

② 2h 18m DDD 5/94

Alexeev's all-Russian mastery has seldom been heard to such advantage and his technical force and authority throughout are unarguable. True, he hardly wears his heart on his sleeve in the quixotic minuet of Op. 23 No. 3, is less than poetically yielding in the Chopinesque tracery of Op. 23 No. 4. He does, however, capture the Slavonic malaise of No. 1 with rare insight and his punishing weight and rhetoric in Op. 23 Nos. 2 or 7 will make even the most sanguine listener's pulse beat faster. He unleashes the central build-up of Op. 32 No. 7 with the impact of a Siberian whirlwind and time and again his icy, determinedly unsentimental approach gives added strength and focus to the composer's brilliant fury. Alexeev is more convincing in the more vertiginous numbers from the *Moments musicaux*, in Nos. 2, 4 and 6 rather than in the opening rhythmic play of No. 1 where he sounds altogether too literal and austere. Yet you only have to hear his way of making even *Polichinelle*'s well-worn phrases come up as fresh as paint or his trenchancy in *Oriental Sketch* to realize that you are in the presence of a master pianist. The recordings are of demonstration quality and the accompanying essay mirrors the rare toughness and integrity of these performances; the essential nobility of Rachmaninov's genius.

New review
Rachmaninov. ETUDES-TABLEAUX AND PRELUDES. **Sviatslav Richter.** Olympia OCD334/7. Items marked [a] recorded in 1983, others 1971.
Etudes-tableaux: Op. 33[a] — No. 5 in D minor (new to UK. 1983), No. 6 in E flat minor, No. 9 in C sharp minor (610 075, 10/84); Op. 39 — No. 1 in C minor, No. 2 in A minor, No. 3 in F sharp minor, No. 4 in B minor, No. 7 in C minor, No. 9 in D major (all 610 075). *Preludes:* Op. 23 — No. 1 in F sharp minor, No. 2 in B flat major, No. 4 in D major, No. 5 in G minor, No. 7 in C minor, No. 8 in A flat major; Op. 32 — No. 1 in C major, No. 2 in B flat minor, No. 6 in F minor, No. 7 in F major, No. 9 in A major, No. 10 in B minor, No. 12 in G sharp minor (all new to UK. 1971).

1h 14m DDD/ADD 1/94

As in previous volumes in this valuable series, sound-quality is on the dry side. But Richter's is the sort of playing which positively benefits from close analytical scrutiny, and serious collectors of piano recordings should need no further encouragement. Recorded between 1971 and 1983 they show a Richter in transition. Still in evidence is the prime-of-life virtuoso who burst on to the Western scene in the 1960s; but increasingly taking over is the uncompromising, ascetic philosopher-pianist of the 1980s. Metaphysics in Rachmaninov? Certainly. And not just the apparently superhuman fingerwork in the E flat minor *Etude-tableau* or the first C minor of Op. 39. What comes across is something beyond expression. It is an overriding fatalism, a sense of the immense sadness of Russia, broken only by moments of heroic resistance. The Preludes are more resonantly recorded, with a rather disappointing tubby bass. If you can live with that there is a quite unique Rachmaninov to be heard here — a brave, noble spirit, expressed in piano writing of an unquenchable fervour and orchestral solidity.

New review
Rachmaninov. PIANO WORKS.
Scriabin. PIANO WORKS.
Tchaikovsky. Piano Sonata in C sharp minor, Op. 80. **Beate Berthold** (pf). EMI CDC7 54550-2. Recorded in 1991.
Rachmaninov. Preludes — F major; D minor. Morceau de fantaisie in G minor. Polka de W. R. **Scriabin.** Poème tragique in B flat major, Op. 34. Trois Pièces, Op. 2. Fantasie in B minor, Op. 28.

1h DDD 7/93

Tchaikovsky's early C sharp minor Sonata is hardly a model of lucidity yet his many engaging ideas are presented by Berthold with such vividness and propagandist zeal that they almost erase one's sense of token organization as well as the ghostly presence of Schumann, albeit Slavonically transformed. Only purists will resist the *Andante*'s starry ebb and flow; her novel perspective is gloriously fresh and vital. She is no less ardently committed to Rachmaninov's F major Prelude (a heart-easing reminder of the composer's early happiness at Ivanovka, his family's country estate) and in the *Morceau de fantaisie* and the D minor Prelude she suggests a most graphic sense of turbulence and hallucination. Her *Polka*, too, is brilliantly engaging and her Scriabin blazes with a true sense of the composer's incandescence. Excellent recording.

Rachmaninov. The bells, Op. 35[a]. Vocalise, Op. 34 No. 14[b].
Tchaikovsky. Romeo and Juliet (orch. Taneyev) — duet[ac]. Festival Coronation March in D major. [abc]**Suzanne Murphy** (sop); [ab]**Keith Lewis** (ten); [a]**David Wilson-Johnson** (bar); **Scottish National** [a]**Chorus and Orchestra/Neeme Järvi.** Chandos CHAN8476. Notes and English texts included.

Ih 3m DDD 2/87

Rachmaninov had grown up in a land where different kinds of church bells were often heard, and their sound evoked in him vivid childhood memories. Edgar Allan Poe's evocation of four human states and their bell connotations seemed to Rachmaninov an ideal basis for a four-part choral symphony. This is well realized by Järvi, though perhaps the urgency of the "Loud Alarum Bells" could be expressed more vehemently. The soloists are not ideal, but a rich, atmospheric recording provides a suitable vehicle for some lusty though well-disciplined choral singing. *Vocalise* is reasonably well sung, as is the Tchaikovsky *Romeo and Juliet* duet. After Tchaikovsky's death Taneyev discovered and then put together sketches for the operatic duet recorded here: no doubt he was aided by the fact that the duet re-uses material from the Fantasy overture. *The Festival Coronation March* was written to celebrate the 1883 crowning of Tsar Alexander III.

Additional recommendation ...
The bells[a]. **Prokofiev.** *Alexander Nevsky*[b]. [a]**Sheila Armstrong** (sop); [a]**Anna Reynolds** (mez); [a]**Robert Tear** (ten); [a]**John Shirley-Quirk** (bar); **London Symphony Chorus and Orchestra/André Previn.** EMI Studio CDM7 63114-2 — ... Ih 18m ADD 10/89 ◖p

Further listening ...

Vespers, Op. 37. **Corydon Singers/Matthew Best.** Hyperion CDA66460 (7/91).

Six Songs, Op. 4 — No. 1, Oh no, I beg you, forsake me not; No. 3, In the silence of the secret night; No. 4, Sing not to me, beautiful maiden. *Six Songs, Op. 8* — No. 5, The dream. *12 Songs, Op. 14* — No. 9, She is as lovely as the noon. *12 Songs, Op. 21* —No. 6, Fragment from Musset. *15 Songs, Op. 26* — No. 2, He took all from me; No. 6, Christ is risen; No. 13, When yesterday we met. *Coupled with* **Tchaikovsky.** *Six Songs, Op. 6* — No. 4, A tear trembles; No. 6, None but the lonely heart. *Six Songs, Op. 25* — No. 1, Reconciliation. *Six Songs, Op. 28* — No. 6, The fearful minute. *Six Songs, Op. 38* — No. 1, Don Juan's Serenade. *12 Songs, Op. 60* — No. 4, The nightingale; No. 11, Exploit. *Six Songs, Op. 63* — No. 2, I opened the window. *Six Songs, Op. 73* — No. 6, Again, as before, alone. **Dmitri Hvorostovsky** (bar); **Oleg Boshniakovich** (pf). Philips 432 119-2PH (10/91).

Joseph Raff

Swiss/German 1822-1882

Suggested listening ...

Symphonies — No. 3 in F major, "Im Walde", Op. 153; No. 4 in G minor, Op. 167. **Milton Keynes City Orchestra/Hilary Davan Wetton.** Hyperion CDA66628 (9/93).

Symphonies — No. 8 in A major, Op. 205, "Frühlingsklänge"; No. 9 in E minor, Op. 208, "Im Sommer". **Košice State Philharmonic Orchestra/Urs Schneider.** Marco Polo 8 223362 (11/92).

Priaulx Rainier

Suggested listening ...

String Quartet[a]. Quanta[b]. String Trio[b]. Ploërmel[c]. [a]**Edinburgh Quartet** (Miles Baster, Peter Markham, vns; Michael Beeston, va; Mark Bailey, vc); [b]**Redcliffe Ensemble;** [c]**Royal Northern College of Music Wind Ensemble/Timothy Reynish.** Redcliffe Recordings RR007 (11/92).

Thomas Rajna

Suggested listening ...

Harp Concerto[a]. Piano Concerto No. 2[b]. [a]**Moya Wright** (hp); [b]**Thomas Rajna** (pf); **South African National Symphony Orchestra/Allan Stephenson.** Claremont CDGSE1526 (11/93).

Stěpán Rak

Suggested listening ...

Guitar Works — First Love. Hiroshima. Danza Mauretana. Cry of the guitar. Hora/Czardas. Remembering Prague. The Czech Chorale. Pavanne. **Stěpán Rak** (gtr). Chandos CHAN8622 (9/88).

David Raksin

Suggested listening ...

Film Scores — Laura. Forever Amber — Suite. The Bad and the Beautiful — Suite. **New Philharmonia Orchestra/David Raksin.** RCA Victor GD81490 (6/90).

Jean-Philippe Rameau

New review
Rameau. Pièces de clavecin en concerts. **Catherine Mackintosh** (vn); **Laurence Dreyfus** (va da gamba); **Ketil Haugsand** (hpd). Simax PSC1095. Recorded in 1992.

Ih 9m   DDD   6/94

These miniatures are not merely crafted with superlative skill but also reflect an astonishingly wide spectrum of moods, lovingly evoked, and without exception born of sustained musical talent of a very high order. But, like many such products of genius, their realization proves elusive, that is, perhaps until now. The reason is not hard to find, for these players address themselves to two considerations of primary importance in bringing the music to life: texture and rhetoric, to which a third, gesture, is closely related. Although Rameau himself went to some pains to demonstrate the propriety of playing these pieces as harpsichord solos, they are essentially ensemble music. Each movement of the five suites contains a fully written out harpsichord part with additional parts for violin or flute, bass viol or second violin. In this recording violin and bass viol are preferred throughout. Phrases are articulated with clarity and each piece, be it dance or miniature portrait, is given a distinctive, well-delineated character. Everything, in short, is graceful in movement, refined in sentiment and infused with delicacy or robust vigour as the occasion demands. Clear and resonant recorded sound.

Additional recommendations ...
Pièces de clavecin en concerts. **Masahiro Arita** (fl); **Natsumi Wakamatsu** (vn); **Wieland Kuijken** (va da gamba); **Chiyoko Arita** (hpd). Denon Aliare CO-79045 — .·*·* lh 8m DDD 10/92
Pièces de clavecin en concerts. **Ryo Terakado** (vn); **Kaori Uemura** (va da gamba); **Christophe Rousset** (hpd). Harmonia Mundi HMC90 1418 — .·*·* lh 14m DDD 4/93 ℗
Pièces de clavecin en concerts — Cinquième concert. **Leclair.** *Sonatas — E minor, Op. 2 No. 1; G major, Op. 9 No. 7.* **Blavet.** *Sonata in D minor, "La Vibray", Op. 2 No. 2.* **M. La Barre.** *Sonate l'inconnuë in G major, Book 2 No. 9.* **Hotteterre.** *Airs et Brunettes.* **Rachel Brown** (fl); **Mark Caudle** (viol); **James Johnstone** (hpd). Chandos Chaconne CHAN0544 — .·*·* lh 11m DDD 2/94 ℗

Rameau. HARPSICHORD WORKS. **Christophe Rousset** (hpds). L'Oiseau-Lyre 425 886-2OH2. Recorded in 1989.
Premier livre de pièces de clavecin. Pièces de clavecin en concerts. Nouvelles suites de pièces de clavecin. Les petits marteaux de M Rameau. La Dauphine.

.·*·* ② 2h 9m DDD 12/91 ℗

This recording of Rameau's solo harpsichord music outdistances most of the competition. Rousset does not include everything that Rameau wrote for the instrument but he does play all the music contained in the principal collections of 1706, 1724 and *c.*1728 as well as *La Dauphine.* Rousset's phrasing is graceful and clearly articulated, the inflexions gently spoken and the rhythmic pulse all that one might wish for. Tempos are, for the most part, well-judged and the playing admirably attentive to detail and delightfully animated. Only occasionally does Rousset perhaps just miss the mark with speeds that are uncomfortably brisk and lacking that choreo-graphic poise which is such a vital ingredient in French baroque music. But he is at his strongest is irresistible and this is how we find him in "Les niais de Sologne" and its variations, the reflective "L'entretien des Muses", the animated "Les cyclopes", "La poule", "L'enharmonique" and the dazzling A minor Gavotte and variations. In these and in many other of the pieces, too, Rousset's impeccable taste and seemingly effortless virtuosity provide the listener with constant and intense delight. The quality of the recording is ideal as are the two instruments which Rousset has chosen to play.

Additional recommendations ...
Nouvelles suites de pièces de clavecin — A minor. Pièces de clavècin — Suite in E minor. **Trevor Pinnock.** CRD CRD3310 — .·*·* 52m ADD 8/88 ℗
Premier livre de pièces de clavecin — Suite in A minor. La Dauphine. Cinq pièces pour clavecin seull. Pièces de clavecin en concerts. La pantomime. **Trevor Pinnock.** CRD CRD3320 — .·*·* 43m ADD 8/88 ℗
Pièces de clavecin — Suite in D minor/major. Nouvelles suites de pièces de clavecin — G major/minor. **Trevor Pinnock.** CRD CRD3330 — .·*·* 52m ADD 8/88 ℗
L'enharmonique. L'Egyptienne. La Dauphine. **D'Anglebert.** *Pièces de Clavecin – Suite in G minor; Tombeau de M. de Chambonnières.* **F. Couperin.** *L'Art de toucher le clavecin – Prélude in D minor. Livre de clavecin, Deuxième ordre – Seconde Courante; Sarabande, "La Prude"; Les Idées heureuses; La Voluptueuse.* **Forqueray.** *La Rameau; La Boisson; La Sylva; Jupiter.* **Sophie Yates.** Chandos Chaconne CHAN0545 (*See review in the Collections section; refer to the Index to Reviews*) — .·*·* lh 11m DDD 11/93

New review
Rameau. CASTOR ET POLLUX. **Howard Crook** (ten) Castor; **Jérôme Corréas** (bass) Pollux; **Agnès Mellon** (sop) Télaïre; **Veronique Gens** (sop) Phebe; **René Schirrer** (bar) Mars; Jupiter; **Sandrine Piau** (sop) Venus, Happy Spirit, Planet; **Mark Padmore** (ten) Love, High Priest; **Claire Brua** (sop) Minerve; **Sophie Daneman** (sop) Follower of Hebe; Celestial Pleasure; **Adrian Brand** (ten) Athlete I; **Jean-Claude Sarragosse** (bass) Athlete II; **Les Arts**

Florissants and Orchestra/William Christie. Harmonia Mundi HMC90 1435/7. Notes, text and translation included. Recorded in 1992.

③ 2h 53m DDD 7/93

Castor et Pollux was Rameau's second *tragédie en musique*. Its first performance took place in October 1737 but the opera was greeted with only moderate enthusiasm. It was only with the composer's thoroughly revised version of 1754 that the opera enjoyed the popularity that it unquestionably deserved. The revision tautened a drama which had never been weak but it dispensed with a very beautiful Prologue. Christie and Les Arts Florissants perform Rameau's first version complete with its Prologue. The librettist, Pierre-Joseph Bernard, was one of the ablest writers with whom Rameau collaborated and his text for *Castor et Pollux* has been regarded by some as the best in the history of eighteenth-century French opera. Bernard focuses on the fraternal love of the 'heavenly twins' and specifically on the generosity with which Pollux renounces his immortality so that Castor may be restored to life. Christie's production was staged at Aix-en-Provence in the summer of 1991 and recorded by Harmonia Mundi a year later. This performance, more than that of Nikolaus Harnoncourt on Teldec (listed below), realizes the element of tragedy, above all in the First Act, and Christie's singers sound altogether more at home with French declamation than Harnoncourt's cast. A very beautiful score, affectionately and perceptively interpreted that will afford deep and lasting pleasure.

Additional recommendation ...
Soloists; Stockholm Chamber Choir; Vienna Concentus Musicus/Nikolaus Harnoncourt. Teldec Das Alte Werk 2292-42510-2 — ③ 2h 46m ADD 7/87

Rameau. LES INDES GALANTES — *Prologue:* **Claron McFadden** (sop) Hébé; **Jérôme Corréas** (bar) Bellone; **Isabelle Poulenard** (sop) L'Amour. *Le Turc généreux:* **Nicolas Rivenq** (bass) Osman; **Miriam Ruggieri** (sop) Emilie; **Howard Crook** (ten) Valère. *Les Incas du Pérou:* **Bernard Delétré** (bass) Huascar; **Poulenard** (Phanie); **Jean-Paul Fouchécourt** (ten) Carlos. *Les fleurs:* **Fouchécourt** (Tacmas); **Corréas** (Ali); **Sandrine Piau** (sop) Zaïre; **Noémi Rime** (sop) Fatime. *Les sauvages:* **Rivenq** (Adario); **Crook** (Damon); **Delétré** (Don Alvar); **McFadden** (Zima); **Les Arts Florissants/William Christie.** Harmonia Mundi HMC90 1367/9. Notes, text and translation included.

③ 3h 23m DDD 2/91

Les Indes galantes was Rameau's first *opéra-ballet*. He completed it in 1735 when it was performed at the Académie Royale in Paris. *Opéra-ballet* usually consisted of a prologue and anything between three and five entrées or acts. There was no continuously developing plot but instead various sections might be linked by a general theme, often hinted at in the title. Such is the case with *Les indes galantes* whose linking themes derives from a contemporary taste for the exotic and the unknown. Following a prologue come four entrées, "Le Turc généreux", "Les Incas du Pérou", "Les fleurs" and "Les sauvages". William Christie and Les Arts Florissants give a characteristically warm-blooded performance of one of Rameau's most approachable and endearing stage works. Christie's control of diverse forces — his orchestra consists of some 46 players — his dramatic pacing of the music, his recognition of Rameau's uniquely distinctive instrumental palette and his feeling for gesture and rhythm contribute towards making this a lively and satisfying performance. The choir is alert and well-disciplined and the orchestra a worthy partner in respect of clear textures and technical finesse; this can be readily appreciated in the splendid, spaciously laid out and tautly constructed orchestral Chaconne which concludes the work. The booklet contains full texts in French, English and German and the music is recorded in a sympathetic acoustic.

Additional recommendation ...
LES INDES GALANTES — *Suite*[a]. DARDANUS — *Suite*[b]. **Collegium Aureum/**[a]**Gustav Leonhardt,** [b]**Reinhard Peters.** Deutsche Harmonia Mundi Editio Classica 05472 77269-2 — 1h 10m ADD 8/93

New review
Rameau. PYGMALION[a]. Le temple de la gloire — Airs gays; Ramages. [a]**Jean-Paul Fouchécourt** (ten) Pigmalion; [a]**Nicole Fournié** (sop) Céphise; [a]**Sandrine Piau** (sop) Statue;

[a]**Greta de Reyghere** (sop) Amour; **Le Concert Spirituel Orchestra/Hervé Niquet.**
FNAC Music 592196. Notes, texts and translations included. Recorded in 1992.

.•' **5lm DDD 10/93**

Readers so far intimidated by the much larger canvases and weightier content of *tragédie en musique* may find this music, vigorous and tender in turn, an alluring introduction to the composer's beguiling art. The story of *Pygmalion* (1748) concerns the sculptor Pygmalion who falls in love with a statue he has created. Aphrodite brings the statue to life whereupon, to Pygmalion's delight it reciprocates his affection. Love's triumph is celebrated with dances and a virtuoso tenor ariette, one of Rameau's many salutes to the Italian opera aria, and the work concludes with a rousing *contredanse*. This is all musically entertaining stuff in which Rameau probes a wide range of emotional states, ranging from the tender scene between a rapt Pygmalion and the Statue, to the sparkling ariette "Règne, Amour, fais briller tes flammes" which Fouchécourt dispatches fluently and articulately. Fouchécourt proves himself an ardent Pygmalion and Sandrine Piau, an alluring Statue. Greta de Reyghere and Nicole Fournié complete a strong solo cast and Le Concert Spirituel under Niquet plays well. An enjoyable, often affecting *Pygmalion* which can confidently be recommended.

Additional recommendations ...
Pygmalion. **Soloists; Paris Chapelle Royale Chorus; La Petite Bande/Gustav Leonhardt.**
Deutsche Harmonia Mundi Editio Classica GD77143 — .•' 47m ADD 7/90
Pygmalion. Nélée et Myrthis. **Soloists; Les Arts Florissants Chorus and Orchestra/William Christie.** Harmonia Mundi HMC90 1381 — .•' lh l8m DDD 7/92 ✒

Further listening ....

Hippolyte et Aricie — Orchestral Suite. **La Petite Bande/Sigiswald Kuijken.** Deutsche Harmonia Mundi Editio Classica GD77009 (7/90).

Abaris (Les Boréades) — *tragédie lyrique:* Orchestral Suite. Dardanus — *tragédie en musique.* **Eighteenth Century Orchestra/Frans Brüggen.** Philips 420 240-2PH (11/87).

PLATEE. **Soloists; Françoise Herr Vocal Ensemble; Musiciens du Louvre/Marc Minkowski.** Erato MusiFrance 2292-45028-2 (9/90).

ZOROASTRE. **Soloists; Ghent Collegium Vocale; La Petite Bande/Sigiswald Kuijken.** Deutsche Harmonia Mundi Editio Classica GD77144 (7/90).

LES PALADINS — Suite. **Orchestra of the Age of Enlightenment/Gustav Leonhardt.** Philips 432 968-2PH (9/92).

Maurice Ravel

French 1875-1937

Ravel. PIANO CONCERTOS AND ORCHESTRAL WORKS. [a]**Pascal Rogé** (pf); **Montreal Symphony Chorus and Orchestra/Charles Dutoit.** Decca Ovation 421 458-2DM4. Boléro. Alborada del gracioso. Rapsodie espagnole. La valse (all from SXDL7559, 9/82). Ma mère l'oye — Ballet. Pavane pour une infante défunte. Le tombeau de Couperin. Valses nobles et sentimentales (all from 410 254-1DH, 8/84). Piano Concerto in G major[a]. Piano Concerto for the Left Hand[a]. Menuet antique. Une barque sur l'océan. Fanfare from "L'Eventail de Jeanne" (all from SXDL7592, 8/83). Daphnis et Chloé — Ballet (from SXDL7526, 6/81).

.•' ④ 3h 50m DDD ꟼ P Ⓑ

Ravel's orchestral music, during the eight-year span of this *Guide*, has had more than its fair share of claimants for an entry. Yet in every edition, three of these four discs have consistently remained top recommendations (the fourth disc was, and still is, equally worthy of inclusion, and is listed below), and Decca have conveniently gathered together their four discs (in their
| original format) into this mid-price box. The survey turns out to be not absolutely complete, as

Dutoit omitted the early *Shéhérazade* Overture (not a serious loss) and the violin work *Tzigane*, but there is, to date, no comparably comprehensive set of Ravel's orchestral music. It is, of course, possible to build a satisfying Ravel library from different sources, but that would bring unavoidable duplication of repertoire. Yet collections like this one, however convenient and financially attractive, are rarely consistent in quality. This is that rare case: not one of these recordings is seriously outclassed, either interpretatively or sonically. Dutoit and his Montreal orchestra are superb stylists; Ravel was just as much of a musical magpie as Stravinsky, with few historical, contemporary, or popular styles remaining exempt from a sophisticated Ravelian transformation (in some works they rub shoulders, for example, the *Valses nobles et sentimentales*). Dutoit ensures that the styles register, but without labouring the point — the result is always pure Ravel. There is also a consistent elegance, both of execution and expression, though Dutoit has a cunning (or sixth sense) in knowing when to let the players off the leash, and by how much (the G major Piano Concerto abounds in examples). A balletic stance goes hand in hand with rare departures from Ravel's suggestions of pace; for example, the languorous *Rapsodie espagnole* "Prélude" is kept on its toes (even this atmospheric nocturne is a slow dance), and the virtuosity of his orchestra allows him to take the mercurial "Prélude" to *Le tombeau de Couperin* at Ravel's marking, without loss of composure. One radical departure from the score is his slow tempo for the strings' melody as we enter the "Jardin féerique" in *Ma mère l'oye*, but even the most fastidious Ravelian will surely succumb to the rapt beauty of the result. Ravel, the time traveller, from the childhood, fairy-tale world of *Ma mère l'oye* to *Le tombeau de Couperin*'s homage to the French baroque, also benefits from an acoustic setting where space can add an extra dimension, a depth for, say, the horn fanfares at the "once upon a time" start of *Ma mère l'oye* or the last post resonances that the trumpet imparts in the Trio of *Le tombeau*'s Minuet. St Eustache in Montreal has just such an acoustic, and nowhere is it put to better use than in *Daphnis*, where the perspective laid out by the different planes draws you in and envelops you. Unlike so many recordings made in churches these days, there's no blurring of detail, or ungainly weight in *fortissimos*; and microphone placement gives a discreet presence to all that glitters. The only possible causes for concern may be the gremlin in the machine that brings some momentary (and hardly serious) distortion near the end of *Boléro*; and there is a general, prudent tailoring of extreme *fortissimos* (compared to Rattle's recordings, for example), but many will regard that as an attribute. No, even after all this time, Dutoit's Ravel firmly remains *the* reference.

Additional recommendations ...
Piano Concerto in G major[a]. Piano Concerto for the Left Hand[a]. Menuet antique. Une barque sur l'océan. Fanfare from "L'éventail de Jeanne". [a]Pascal **Rogé** (pf); **Montreal Symphony Orchestra/ Charles Dutoit**. Decca 410 230-2DH — .·* 57m DDD 3/84 Ⓑ
Piano Concerto in G major. Gaspard de la nuit. Sonatine. **Martha Argerich** (pf); **Berlin Philharmonic Orchestra/Claudio Abbado**. DG Galleria 419 062-2GGA — .·* 54m ADD 12/87 ⁹ₚ Ⓑ
Piano Concerto in G major. *Rachmaninov*. Piano Concerto No. 4 in G minor, Op. 40. **Arturo Benedetti Michelangeli** (pf); **Philharmonia Orchestra/Ettore Gracis**. EMI CDC7 49326-2 — .·* 47m ADD 9/88 ⁹ₚ Ⓑ ▲
Piano Concerto in G major[a]. Piano Concerto for the Left Hand[b]. Fanfare for "L'éventail de Jeanne". Menuet antique. Le Tombeau de Couperin. [a]**Martha Argerich**, [b]**Michel Béroff** (pfs); **London Symphony Orchestra/Claudio Abbado**. DG 423 665-2GH — .·* 1h 5m DDD 2/89 ⁹ₚ Ⓑ
Piano Concerto in G major. Piano Concerto for the Left Hand. **Louis Lortie** (pf); **London Symphony Orchestra/Rafael Frühbeck de Burgos**. Chandos CHAN8773 — .·* 57m DDD 1/90 Ⓑ

Ravel. VOCAL AND ORCHESTRAL WORKS. [a]**Maria Ewing** (mez); **City of Birmingham Symphony Orchestra/Simon Rattle**. EMI CDC7 54204-2. Text and translation included. Recorded in 1989.
Fanfare pour "L'éventail de Jeanne". Shéhérazade[a]. Alborada del gracioso. Miroirs — La vallée des cloches (arr. Grainger). Ma mère l'oye. La valse.

.·* **1h 15m DDD 8/91** ⁹ₚ Ⓑ

A paean of British critical praise greets almost every new issue from this team with monotonous regularity, so it is gratifying, in this instance, to note *Diapason*'s (the French contemporary to *Gramophone*) reviewer finding Rattle's *Ma mère l'oye* of a "striking delicacy" and "releasing an indescribable emotion" (apologies to Rémy Louis for a wholly inadequate translation). In the past there have been instances of Rattle's intensive preparation for setting down a much loved masterpiece precluding spontaneity in the end result. Not here. Along with the customary refinement and revelation of texture, there is a sense of Rattle gauging the very individual fantasy worlds of this varied programme with uncanny precision: an aptly childlike wonder for *Ma mère l'oye*'s fairy tale illustrations; the decadence and decay that drive *La valse* to its inevitable doom; and the sensual allure of the Orient in *Shéhérazade* providing a vibrant backdrop for soprano Maria Ewing's intimate confessions. Space does not permit enthusing about the three shorter items that make up this indispensable (and generously filled) disc, recorded with stunning realism. Try it for yourself and marvel at the astonishing range of Ravel's imagination.

Additional recommendations ...
Shéhérazade[a]. *Vocalise en forme de habanera (orch. Hoerée)*[a]. *Alborada del gracioso. Boléro. La valse. Pavane pour une infante défunte.* [a]**Arleen Auger** (sop); **Philharmonia Orchestra/Libor Pešek.** Virgin Classics VC7 59235-2 — ·· 1h 4m DDD 3/93 ᵠₚ Ⓑ
Ma mère l'oye. Pavane pour une infante défunte. Le tombeau de Couperin. Valses nobles et sentimentales. **Montreal Symphony Orchestra/Charles Dutoit.** Decca 410 254-2DH — ·· 1h 7m DDD 11/84 ᵠₚ Ⓑ
Ma mère l'oye. **Debussy.** *La boîte à joujoux — ballet.* **Ulster Orchestra/Yan Pascal Tortelier.** Chandos CHAN8711 — ·· 57m DDD 9/89 ᵠₚ Ⓑ
Ma mère l'oye. **Bizet.** *Symphony in C major.* **Scottish Chamber Orchestra/Jukka-Pekka Saraste.** Virgin Classics Virgo VJ7 59657-2 — . 1h 4m DDD 12/91 Ⓑ

Ravel. *Daphnis et Chloé — ballet*[a]. *Rapsodie espagnole*[b]. *Pavane pour une infante défunte*[b]. [a]**Chorus of the Royal Opera House, Covent Garden; London Symphony Orchestra/ Pierre Monteux.** Decca Historic 425 956-2DM. Item marked [a] from SXL2164 (12/59), recorded in 1959, [b] SXL2312 (7/62), recorded in 1961.

·· 1h 14m ADD 5/90 ᵠₚ Ⓑ ▲

New review
Ravel. *Daphnis et Chloé.* **New England Conservatory Choir; Boston Symphony Orchestra/Charles Munch.** RCA Victor Living Stereo 09026 61846-2. From VICS1297 (12/70). Recorded in 1955.

·· 54m ADD 3/94 ᵠₚ Ⓑ ▲

Diaghilev's ballet *Daphnis et Chloé*, based on a pastoral romance by the ancient Greek poet Longus, was first produced in June 1912, with Nijinsky and Karsavina in the title roles and choreography by Mikhail Fokine. Pierre Monteux conducted the first performance, and 47 years later he recorded his peerless interpretation for Decca. Though the Second Suite from the ballet is familiar to concert-goers and makes an effective piece in its own right, the full score, with wordless chorus, conveys still greater atmosphere and magic. No work of more sheer sensual beauty exists in the entire orchestral repertoire, and Monteux was its perfect interpreter. He conducts with a wonderful sense of clarity and balance: every important detail tells, and there is refinement of expression, yet inner strength too. The LSO play with superlative poetry and skill, and the chorus is magnificent in its tonal blend and colour. The *Rapsodie espagnole* and *Pavane* are also given ideal performances, and the recordings show off Decca's exceedingly high standards during the late 1950s and early 1960s. Another landmark *Daphnis*, Munch's with the Boston Symphony Orchestra made in stereo, sounds equally astonishing in RCA's transfer (available with or without the mono Roussel coupling, listed below). Robert Layton, writing in *Gramophone*, and comparing Monteux with Munch "succumbed more readily to the heady intoxication, the dazzling richness of colour and virtuosity" of the Munch. Both Monteux and Munch (along with Ansermet and more recently Dutoit) understood the dangers of extremes and excessive lingering in this score; of sentiment turning into syrup and Ravel's "Choreographic Symphony" (his own term) falling apart. It should be noted that, though their recordings balance Ravel's complex score more skilfully and imaginatively than most modern contenders, the score's huge range of dynamics (almost overwhelming in the recent recordings from Rattle and Nagano, listed below) could not be fully realized by the technology of the time.

Additional recommendations ...
Daphnis et Chloé. **Montreal Symphony Chorus and Orchestra/Charles Dutoit.** Decca 400 055-2DH — ·· 56m DDD 3/83 ᵠₚ ᵠₛ Ⓑ

Daphnis et Chloé — Suite No. 2. Boléro. **Debussy.** *La mer. Prélude à l'après-midi d'un faune.* **Berlin Philharmonic Orchestra/Herbert von Karajan.** DG Galleria 427 250-2GGA — .·` 1h 4m ADD 7/89 ᛩₚ Ⓑ

Daphnis et Chloé[a]. **Roussel.** *Bacchus et Ariane — Ballet Suite No. 2*[b]. [a]**New England Conservatory Choir;** [a]**Alumni Chorus; Boston Symphony Orchestra/Charles Munch.** RCA Victor Gold Seal [a]stereo/[b]mono GD60469 — .·` 1h 11m ADD 12/91 ᛩₚ Ⓑ ▲

Daphnis et Chloé. Boléro. **City of Birmingham Symphony Orchestra/Simon Rattle.** EMI CDC7 54303-2 — .·` 1h 14m DDD 6/92 ᛩₚ ᛩₛ Ⓑ

Daphnis et Chloé. Rapsodie espagnole. Alborada del gracioso. Pavane pour une infante défunte. Le tombeau de Couperin. Valses nobles et sentimentales. Ma mère l'oye. **Geneva Motet Choir; Suisse Romande Orchestra/Ernest Ansermet.** Decca 425 997-2DM2 — .·` ② 2h 16m ADD 9/92 ᛩₚ Ⓑ ▲

Daphnis et Chloé. **London Symphony Chorus and Orchestra/Kent Nagano.** Erato 4509-91712-2 — .·` 58m DDD 7/93 ᛩₚ Ⓑ

Ravel. ORCHESTRAL WORKS. **Chicago Symphony Orchestra/Daniel Barenboim.** Erato 2292-45766-2. Recorded in 1991.
Daphnis et Chloé — Suite No. 2. Rapsodie espagnole. Pavane pour une infante défunte. Alborada del gracioso. Boléro.

.·` 1h 3m DDD 12/92   ᛩₚ ᛩₛ

Some are undoubtedly going to find Barenboim's Ravel too (at times, self-consciously) beautiful. But make no mistake, this is a real showcase disc for Chicago and its new director. The flute solo in the "Pantomime" from *Daphnis* must be the slowest on disc, but this is unmistakably "un air mélancholique" as the drama demands; and the sustaining of the alto flute at the end of the solo, though unmarked, is sheer sorcery. Flutes are prominent in the Erato balance throughout *Daphnis*, as is the entire woodwind section as they reel and squeal in the final "Danse générale". Barenboim has grouped the remaining four items into "a kind of Spanish symphony", and sees to it that the many guitar-like effects (plucked strings) of these scores are picked out. Fritz Reiner, a famous predecessor in Chicago, is recalled in the very slow and atmospheric "Prélude" from the *Rapsodie espagnole*, though Reiner wouldn't have allowed the single lapse of ensemble in its last movement "Feria" (at 3'42") to pass. Elsewhere there is brilliance and precision aplenty, and the selective miking favoured by the engineers rarely impedes a rendering of the full orchestra with a natural spread and good depth.

Ravel. *Alborada del gracioso. Rapsodie espagnole. La valse. Boléro.* **Montreal Symphony Orchestra/Charles Dutoit.** Decca 410 010-2DH. From SXDL7559 (9/82). Recorded 1982.

.·` 51m DDD 8/83   ᛩₛ Ⓑ

Ravel's *Boléro* is now so popular and universally familiar that it is easy to forget its originality. Dutoit plays it magnetically as a steady, remorseless crescendo and its power and marvellous command of orchestral colour are freshly revealed. The glittering *Alborada del gracioso* and the sensuous and exciting *Rapsodie espagnole* readily demonstrate the special feeling French composers had for the Spanish idiom, with diaphanous textures to capture the sultry quality of the Mediterranean evening and offset the sparkle of the Flamenco dance rhythms. *La valse* begins in the mists and expands to a breathtaking climax with a vision of countless dancing couples whirling round in an intoxicating infinity of space; then cruelly and abruptly the imagery disintegrates into silence. This CD is a model of its kind while the music-making combines a feeling for spectacle with the utmost refinement of detail.

Additional recommendations ...
Alborada del gracioso. Rapsodie espagnole. Valses nobles et sentimentales. Pavane pour une infante défunte. **Debussy.** *Images.* **Chicago Symphony Orchestra/Fritz Reiner.** RCA GD60179 — .·` 1h 8m ADD 1/90 ᛩₚ Ⓑ ▲

Alborada del gracioso. Rapsodie espagnole. La valse. Pavane pour une infante défunte. Le tombeau de Couperin. **Ibert.** *Escales.* **Detroit Symphony Orchestra/Paul Paray.** Mercury Living Presence 432 003-2MM — .·` 1h 7m ADD 4/91 Ⓑ ▲

Alborada del gracioso. Boléro. La valse. **Debussy.** *La mer. Prélude à l'après-midi d'un faune.* **Orchestre de Paris/Herbert von Karajan.** EMI CDM7 64357-2 — .·` 1h 15m ADD 11/92 Ⓑ

New review

Ravel. Violin Sonata[a]. Trois poèmes de Stéphane Mallarmé[b]. Chansons madécasses[c]. Piano Trio[d]. [bc]**Sarah Walker** (mez); [ad]**Marcia Crayford** (vn); [ad]**Christopher van Kampen** (vc); [d]**Ian Brown** (pf); [bc]**Nash Ensemble/Lionel Friend.** Virgin Classics VC5 45016-2. Texts and translations included. Recorded in 1990.

lh l0m DDD 6/94 **Ⓠ**ₚ

The Nash Ensemble have recorded all four of these works before. In the first movement of the Trio the players show an immense gain in subtlety and depth of involvement. Everything is finely balanced, with needle-sharp staccatos from the piano (a 'bravo' to Ian Brown!). The *Passacaille* has great breadth and a tragic glow and the finale emerges with great clarity and, initially, delicacy and clean climaxes. This is a most impressive performance. From the luscious harmonies and romantic atmosphere of the Trio to the more cerebral, starkly 'stripped down' Duo Sonata eight years later (over which Ravel agonized for two years) is as big a stylistic leap as can be imagined, but Marcia Crayford and Christopher van Kampen have a good under-standing of the Sonata's uncompromising idiom, and here give it an even greater degree of commitment than before: Ravel would have approved of their bite and meticulous observance of his markings in the fantastic scherzo, the contrast they provide in an expressive third movement, and the mordant humour they bring to the grotesqueries of the finale. If there is slightly less enthusiasm about the other works here, it is absolutely no reflection on Sarah Walker's seductive voice, sensitive control of nuance and intelligent use of words, nor of the Nash players' admirable contribution: the Mallarmé songs are full of delicate half-lights, the Madagascan aptly veer between exotic eroticism and fierce outrage. However, the vocal line, which carries the words on which the atmosphere of the music depends, must surely stand out a little from the texture — in fact, Ravel himself said of the Madagascan songs that they were "a kind of quartet in which the voice has the principal instrumental part" — and here it is, for the most part, too discreetly placed in respect to the very clear instrumental detail. Considerable artistry not quite shown to its best advantage.

Additional recommendations ...

Violin Sonata. **Prokofiev.** *Violin Sonata No. 2 in D major, Op. 94a.* **Stravinsky.** *Divertimento.* **Viktoria Mullova** (vn); **Bruno Canino** (pf). Philips 426 254-2PH — ⟩ lh lm DDD 8/90 Ⓠₚ
Piano Trio. **Debussy.** *Premier Trio in G major.* **Fauré.** *Piano Trio in D minor, Op. 120.* **Solomon Trio.** Pickwick IMP Masters MCD41 — ⟩ lh 8m DDD 7/92

Ravel. String Quartet in F major.
Vaughan Williams. On Wenlock Edge[ab]. String Quartet No. 1 in G minor. [a]**Philip Langridge** (ten); [b]**Howard Shelley** (pf); **Britten Quartet** (Peter Manning, Keith Pascoe, vns; Peter Lale, va; Andrew Shulman, vc). EMI CDC7 54346-2. Recorded 1990-91.

lh l8m DDD 2/92 **Ⓠ**ₚ **Ⓠ**ₛ

This outstanding disc from the Britten Quartet brings together several works which share far more in common than one might at first imagine. Vaughan Williams spent a short study vacation in Paris during 1908 hoping, on his own admission, to acquire "a little French polish" from Ravel, who himself took part in the French première of his student's song cycle, *On Wenlock Edge*. Ravel's String Quartet receives a provocative, and yet totally convincing reading from the Britten Quartet, who choose to dwell upon the polarization of tonal and melodic content in this work to a greater degree than any of their rivals on disc, all of whom offer the more usual coupling in the shape of the Debussy Quartet. *On Wenlock Edge*, a setting of six poems selected from A.E. Housman's set of 63 poems, *A Shropshire Lad*, is heard here in a quite exceptional performance from the tenor, Philip Langridge, joined by pianist Howard Shelley and the Britten Quartet. Langridge recognizes the irony and understatement of Housman's verse, whilst exploiting its more sinister undertones with searching skill, as he does in the uncanny dialogue between the living and the dead, in "Is my team ploughing", bringing chilly pallor to his delivery of the opening stanza in particular. It would be difficult to match the communicative power of this performance even in the concert-hall. The Brittens also excel in a crystalline and devoted account of Vaughan Williams's underrated G minor Quartet, which sounds more than usually weighty and musically coherent in this fluid and sharply perceived reading. The technical aspects of the playing are second to none, while its added sensitivity contributes to an involving and frequently moving musical experience. The recorded sound is brilliant and immediate, and this disc is a clear triumph from every conceivable viewpoint!

Additional recommendations ...

String Quartet. **Debussy.** *String Quartet in G minor, Op. 10.* **Melos Quartet.** DG 419 750-2GH
— .·´ 53m DDD 10/87 ꝗₚ

String Quartet. **Debussy.** *String Quartet.* **Quartetto Italiano.** Philips Silver Line 420 894-2PSL
— .·´ 57m ADD 10/88 ꝗₚ

String Quartet. **Debussy.** *String Quartet.* **Dvořák.** *String Quartet No. 12 in F major, Op. 96,*
"American". **Bartók Quartet.** Hungaroton White Label HRC122 — . 1h 14m ADD 1/90

String Quartet. **Debussy.** *String Quartet.* **La Salle Quartet.** DG Galleria 435 589-2GGA — .·´
52m ADD 9/92 ꝗₚ

Ravel. COMPLETE PIANO WORKS. **Jean-Yves Thibaudet.** Decca 433 515-2DH2.
Recorded in 1991.
Sérénade grotesque. Menuet antique. Pavane pour une infante défunte. Jeux d'eau. Sonatine.
Miroirs. Gaspard de la nuit. Menuet sur le nom de Haydn. Valses nobles et sentimentales.
Prélude. A la manière de Borodine. A la manière de Chabrier. Le tombeau de Couperin.

.·´ ② 2h 10m DDD 11/92   ꝗₚ ꝗₛ Ⓑ

Jean-Yves Thibaudet could hardly have chosen better for his first Decca solo album. Blessed
with an innate musical elegance and quick-silver technique he compels one to reassess Ravel's
elusive genius at every point; his sophisticated mix of archaism and modernity, of *tendresse* and
malevolence. Few pianists have played "Scarbo" from *Gaspard de la nuit* with such immaculate
dexterity or evoked his will-o'-the-wisp antics — now you see him, now you don't — with
such luminous tone or pianistic cunning. His poetic delicacy is no less remarkable in Ravel's
more amiable creations, in, for example, "La Vallée des cloches" from *Miroirs* or in the dawn
freshness of the "Prélude" from *Le tombeau de Couperin*. And if you want a sense of his range,
his capacity to capture Ravel's idiom in all its multi-faceted glory, then follow the *Sérénade
grotesque* (an early example of Ravel's Hispanism) with the A minor *Prélude*, written for a Paris
Conservatoire sight-reading test yet characterized by rare subtlety and transparency. Above all
Thibaudet is sensitive to writing as fastidiously wrought as the finest jewellery. The recordings
are of demonstration quality and so this two-disc set is a treasurable addition to the catalogue.

Additional recommendations ...
Miroirs. Jeux. Pavane. Gaspard. **Vlado Perlemuter.** Nimbus NIM5005 — .·´ 59m AAD 1/84 ꝗₚ Ⓑ
Gaspard. **Prokofiev.** *Piano Sonata No. 6 in A major, Op. 82.* **Ivo Pogorelich.** DG 413 363-2GH
— .·´ 52m DDD 11/84 ꝗₚ Ⓑ
Gaspard. Pavane. Valses nobles. **Vladimir Ashkenazy.** Decca 410 255-2DH — .·´ ADD 6/85 ꝗₚ Ⓑ
Gaspard. Sonatine. Piano Concerto in G major[a]. **Martha Argerich;** [a]**Berlin Philharmonic
Orchestra/Claudio Abbado.** DG Galleria 419 062-2GGA — .·´ 54m ADD 12/87 ꝗₚ Ⓑ
Le tombeau — Toccata. Coupled with works by **Debussy, Liszt** *and* **Scriabin. Emil Gilels.**
Olympia mono OCD166 — .·´ 1h 12m AAD 12/88 ꝗₚ Ⓑ ▲
Pavane. Le tombeau de Couperin. Sérénade. Jeux. Valses nobles. La valse. **Louis Lortie.** Chandos
CHAN8620 — .·´ 1h 6m DDD 5/89 ꝗₚ Ⓑ
*Gaspard. Menuet antique. Menuet sur le nom de Haydn. A la manière de Borodine. A la manière de
Chabrier. Prélude. Miroirs. Sonatine.* **Louis Lortie.** Chandos CHAN8647 — .·´ 1h 14m DDD 10/89 ꝗₚ Ⓑ
Miroirs — Alborada del gracioso. Coupled with works by **Brahms, Chopin, Enescu** *and* **Liszt.**
Dinu Lipatti. EMI Références mono CDH7 63038-2 — .·´ 1h 6m ADD 11/89 ꝗₚ Ⓑ ▲
Gaspard. Jeux. Le Tombeau de Couperin. Valses nobles. **Gordon Fergus-Thompson.** ASV
CDDCA805 — .·´ 1h 12m DDD 12/92 ꝗₚ Ⓑ

New review
Ravel. PIANO WORKS, Volume 2. **Gordon Fergus-Thompson** (pf). ASV CDDCA809.
A la manière de Borodine. A la manière de Chabrier. Menuet antique. Menuet sur le nom de
Haydn. Miroirs. Pavane pour une infante défunte. Prélude. Sérénade grotesque. Sonatine.

.·´ 1h 8m DDD 10/93   ꝗₚ Ⓑ

With this recital Gordon Fergus-Thompson confirms his calibre and status as a distinguished,
most individual Francophile. Time and again the listener is enveloped in a sensuous, richly
nuanced and coloured world that is the polar opposite of a classic French clarity of line and
argument. Indeed, Fergus-Thompson's rubato at the start of the *Sonatine*'s "Menuet" or his

insinuating way with, say, *A la manière de Borodine* will make some listeners feel positively light-headed. Such lavish affection is hard to resist and in "Une barque sur l'océan" (*Miroirs*) he evokes Ravel's marinescape (his own miniature *La mer*) with a vivid and haunting sense of indolence and hyperactivity; the very essence of Mediterranean poetry. The flashing repeated notes and double-note *glissandos* of *Miroirs*'s "Alborada" have been more fluently negotiated yet even here Fergus-Thompson is right at the heart of Ravel's beloved Hispanicism, and in the remoter reaches of "Oiseaux tristes" and "La vallée des cloches" his playing has a symbolic calm far removed from merely local colour or appeal. You might like to hear an opposing view of *Miroirs* from Thibaudet (reviewed above) in a less idiosyncratic but no less beguiling performance. But for a true and haunting sense of romance beneath Ravel's inscrutable surface, Gordon Fergus-Thompson is your man.

Ravel. Shéhérazade[a]. Deux mélodies hébraïques[a]. Trois poèmes de Stéphane Mallarmé[a].
Berlioz. Les nuits d'été, Op. 7[b]. **Suzanne Danco** (sop); [a]**Suisse Romande Orchestra/ Ernest Ansermet**; [b]**Cincinnati Symphony Orchestra/Thor Johnson.** Decca 425 988-2DH. Notes, text and translation included. Items marked [a] from LXT5031 (7/55), recorded in 1954, [b] LXT2605 (10/51), recorded in 1951.

Ih ADD

Though the *Guide* lists recommendations of more modern recordings of the Berlioz *Nuits d'été* and the Ravel *Shéhérazade* songs, space had to be found for this disc. Suzanne Danco not only possessed a soprano voice of unique shining purity, but every song bears witness to the beauty and clarity of diction, her natural ease with the language; and, above all, as the booklet writer remarks, to "her striving for the correct style and appropriate expression". Arguably the *Shéhérazade* songs respond to her innocent enthusiasm and sensitive colouring rather more than to Maria Ewing's overtly voluptuous relish (reviewed earlier in this section); and it's hard to believe that the Mallarmé settings, with their obscure but tantalizing imagery, are so difficult to perform, such is Danco's complete surety of pitch and line. The sound, from the early 1950s (stereo, excepting the Mallarmé settings and Berlioz songs), is orchestrally thin, but with a good dynamic range. Crucially, the voice itself is reproduced with full tone, a lovely bloom and crystalline clarity.

Additional recommendations ...
Shéhérazade[a]. **Berlioz.** *Les nuits d'été*. **Debussy.** *Trois chansons de Bilitis*[b]. **Poulenc.** *Banalities*[b] — *Chansons d'Orkenise; Hôtel. La courte paille*[b] — *Le carafon; La reine de coeur. Chansons villageoises*[b] — *Les gars qui vont à la fête. Deux poèmes de Louis Aragon*[b]. **Régine Crespin** (sop); [b]**John Wustman** (pf); [a]**Suisse Romande Orchestra/Ernest Ansermet.** Decca 417 813-2DH (*see review in the Collections section; refer to the Index to Reviews*) — Ih 8m ADD 11/88

Ravel. L'ENFANT ET LES SORTILEGES. **Françoise Ogéas** (sop) Child; **Jeanine Collard** (contr) Mother, Chinese cup, Dragonfly; **Jane Berbié** (sop) Sofa, She Cat, Squirrel, Shepherd; **Sylvaine Gilma** (sop) Fire, Princess, Nightingale; **Colette Herzog** (sop) Bat, Little Owl, Shepherdess; **Heinz Rehfuss** (bar) Armchair, Tree; **Camille Maurane** (bar) Grandfather Clock, Tom Cat; **Michel Sénéchal** (ten) Teapot, Little Old Man (Mr Arithmetic), Frog; **Chorus and Children's Voices of French Radio; French Radio National Orchestra/ Lorin Maazel.** DG 423 718-2GH. Notes, text and translation included. From SLPM138675 (6/61). Recorded in 1960.

43m ADD 3/89

This is a Desert Island Disc if ever there was one. Every musical and verbal point in Ravel's brilliantly ingenious, deliciously witty and entirely enchanting score is brought out by a well-nigh perfect cast, backed by first class orchestral playing; and the recording is as vivid as anyone could wish. The story is that of a petulant brat who breaks the china, pulls the cat's tail, pricks the pet squirrel with a pen-nib, puts the fire out by upsetting the kettle on it, tears the wallpaper and his books and snaps off the pendulum of the grandfather clock — only to find that all these come to life and turn on him. Their anger is appeased only when he tends the squirrel's paw; and finally the naughty child, having seen the error of his ways, falls tearfully into his mother's arms. Everyone will have their own favourite passages but the last pages of the opera, in particular, are hauntingly beautiful. An absolute gem of a disc.

Further listening ...

Boléro. Introduction and Allegro. La valse. Ma mère l'oye. Rapsodie espagnole. **Louis Lortie, Hélène Mercier** (pfs). Chandos CHAN8905 (3/91).

L'HEURE ESPAGNOLE. **Soloists; French Radio National Orchestra/Lorin Maazel.** DG 423 719-2GH (3/89).

Thomas Ravenscroft

British c.1582-c.1635

Suggested listening ...

A Round of three Country dances in one. A wooing Song of a Yeoman of Kents Sonne. Browning Madame. The crowning of Belphebe. The Cryers Song of Cheape-Side. Laboravi in gemitu meo. The Marriage of the Frogge and the Mouse. Martin said to his man. Musing mine owne selfe all alone. Ne laeteris inimica mea. Of all the birds that ever I see. There were three ravens. Three blinde Mice. To morrow the Fox will come to towne. Wee be Souldiers three. The wooing of Hodge and Malkyn. Yonder comes a courteous knight. Instrumental works — Fancy No. 1. Fantasia No. 4. Viol Fancy a 5. **Consort of Musicke/Anthony Rooley.** Virgin Classics Veritas VC7 59035-2 (8/91).

Alan Rawsthorne

British 1905-1971

Suggested listening ...

Piano Concerto No. 2. Concerto for Piano, Strings and Percussion No. 1. Double Piano Concerto[a]. **Geoffrey Tozer,** [a]**Tamara-Anna Cislowski** (pfs); **London Philharmonic Orchestra/Matthias Bamert.** Chandos CHAN9125 (4/93).

Jean-Féry Rebel

French 1661-1747

New review

Rebel. Les élémens. Les caractères de la danse. Le tombeau de Monsieur de Lully. **Les Musiciens du Louvre/Marc Minkowski.** Erato 2292-45974-2. Recorded in 1992.

48m DDD 11/93

Jean-Féry Rebel, a contemporary of Couperin, was among those composers who lent real distinction to the comparatively unsung period of French baroque music between Lully's death and the full flowering of Rameau's genius. In *Les élémens* (1737) the composer, in accordance with intellectual trends of the time, evokes Nature in many of its movements; and at times it is quite startlingly vivid as you will hear at once in the harmonically confused opening measures of the overture. Each element is allotted its own distinctive character, Earth recognizable by its tied bass notes, Water by upward and downward scale passages on the flutes, Air by reiterated piccolo trills and Fire by brilliant upper string passagework. The second of the suites on this delightful disc, like *Les élémens*, has both a programmatic and choreographic purpose. *Les caractères de la danse* (1715) consists of a compendium of some of the most popular dances of the time, skilfully interlocked to form a single unit. Third on the disc is a touching and beautifully written three-part sonata *Le tombeau de Monsieur de Lully*. Italian and French manners interweave rewardingly in this heartfelt lament for Louis XIV's redoubtable "surintendant de la musique". Here and throughout the programme the performances are first-rate. All is well documented and superbly recorded. A splendid achievement and a 'must' for all who love music of this period.

Max Reger

Reger. Four Symphonic Poems after Arnold Böcklin, Op. 128. Variations and Fugue on a Theme of J.A. Hiller, Op. 100. **Royal Concertgebouw Orchestra/Neeme Järvi.** Chandos CHAN8794. Recorded in 1989.

Ih 7m DDD 3/90

New review

Reger. Variations and Fugue on a Theme of Beethoven, Op. 86. Eine Ballettsuite in D major, Op. 130. Four Symphonic Poems after Arnold Böcklin, Op. 128. **Norrköping Symphony Orchestra/Leif Segerstam.** BIS CD601. Recorded in 1993.

Ih 12m DDD 6/94

Mention of Reger's name in 'informed' circles is likely to produce a conditioned reflex: "Fugue!". In his day he was the central figure of the 'Back to Bach' movement, but he was also a romantic who relished all the expressive potential of the enormous post-Wagnerian orchestra. Then came the slender acerbities of the next generation of neo-classicists, and Reger's backward glances were deemed inflated and in shocking taste. Until relatively recently he has proved largely unexportable from his native Germany. Chandos, not surprisingly, exploit the open spaces of the Amsterdam Concertgebouw, forsaking some of the healthy transparency of the Davis disc (listed below) for an extra spatial dimension; a more sumptuous glow. With Järvi's instinct for pacing in late romantic music, and his great orchestra's evident delight in the copious riches of the discovery, for the *Hiller* Variations, this disc is very tempting. Anyone who warms to Vaughan Williams's *Tallis Fantasia* will immediately respond to the "Hermit playing the violin", the first of the four *Böcklin* tone-poems; Debussy's "Jeux de vagues" from *La mer* was obviously in Reger's mind for the second poem "At play in the waves"; and the "Isle of the dead" is Reger's no less doom- and gloom-laden response to the painting that so captured Rachmaninov's imagination. The final painting, "Bacchanal", was described as a Munich beer festival in Roman costume — an entirely fitting description for Reger's setting of it!

Segerstam's disc is well programmed to show off the contrasting sides of orchestral Reger: firstly, the familiar champion of absolute music and the German tradition in the Variations; secondly, in *Eine Ballettsuite*, the unlikely purveyor of a relatively lightly scored *divertissement* of six dance or character portraits "for musical epicures"; and finally, in the *Böcklin* Poems, one who succumbed to the lure of programme music and 'impressionist' colour and timbre. Maybe the epicurean pleasures of *Eine Ballettsuite* are savoured by Sir Colin Davis with a little more humour, and, as recorded, brighter timbres, but Segerstam's Swedish orchestra in every way match Davis's Bavarians' evident love for the music (the oboe and cello solos in Segerstam's "Pierrot et Pierette" are exquisite). In both the first and third *Böcklin* Poems Segerstam is closer to Reger's metronome markings than the faster, more freewheeling Järvi. Segerstam is also, throughout the Poems, more acutely responsive to the extremes — and the minutest gradations in between — of both pace and dynamics. For the first and third poems (and parts of the second) this means that you are now aware just how much of this music dwells in the regions of *pianissimo* and beyond, and also how fine an impressionist Reger was. In the Poems, Järvi, it has to be said, has the advantage of a great orchestra, rather than a very good one, and a more accommodating acoustic. BIS give Segerstam another of their textbook recordings, that is to say: an ears only, halfway back in an average size, modern concert-hall experience (levels are lower for the *Böcklin* Poems).

Additional recommendations ...
Hiller Variations. Eine Ballettsuite, Op. 130. **Bavarian Radio Symphony Orchestra/Sir Colin Davis.** Orfeo CO90841A — 59m DDD 4/87 🔊
Hiller Variations. **Zemlinsky.** *Gesänge nach Maeterlinck, Op. 13*[a]. [a]**Hedwig Fassbender** (mez); **Czech Philharmonic Orchestra/Václav Neumann.** Supraphon 11 1811-2 — Ih DDD 7/93 🔊

Further listening ...

Piano Concerto, Op. 114. **Gerhard Oppitz** (pf); **Bamberg Symphony Orchestra/Horst Stein.** Koch Schwann 311058.

Variations and Fugue on a Theme of Mozart, Op. 132. *Coupled with* **Hindemith.** Symphonic Metamorphosis on Themes of Carl Maria von Weber. **Bavarian Radio Symphony Orchestra/Sir Colin Davis.** Philips 422 347-2PH (9/90).

Violin Sonatas — No. 6 in E minor, Op. 122; No. 7 in C minor, Op. 139. **Hansheinz Schneeberger** (vn); **Jean-Jacques Dünki** (pf). Jecklin Disco JD649-2 (5/93).

Variations and Fugue on a Theme by Telemann, Op. 134. *Coupled with* **Brahms.** Variations and Fugue. **Jorge Bolet** (pf). Decca Ovation 417 791-2DM (2/90).

Latin Requiem, Op. 145*a*. Requiem, Op. 144*b*. **Soloists; North German Radio Chorus and Symphony Orchestra/Roland Bader.** Koch Schwann 313004.

Key to symbols

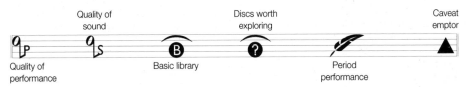

Quality of sound   Discs worth exploring   Caveat emptor

Quality of performance   Basic library   Period performance

Steve Reich

American 1936-

Reich. Different Trains[a]. Electric Counterpoint[b]. [a]**Kronos Quartet** (David Harrington, John Sherba, vns; Hank Dutt, va; Joan Jeanrenaud, vc); [b]**Pat Metheny** (gtr). Elektra Nonesuch 7559-79176-2.

42m   DDD   6/89

The name 'minimalist' clings to Steve Reich, but in fact there's little that can be called minimal in works of the richness and comparative complexity of *Octet* or *The Desert Music*, where all that's left of his earlier style is a taste for pulsating rhythms, short-term circular repetitions and a sonorous harmoniousness. *Different Trains* also combines strong ideas with superb craftsmanship, and it is carried out with total confidence. The programme is autobiographical: Reich evokes his long childhood train journeys across America in the aftermath of the Second World War, and ponders on the parallel but enforced train journeys undertaken by Jewish refugees in Europe. A tinge of melancholy darkens the otherwise excited mood of music, which draws most of its imagery from the driving motor-rhythms of steam trains, constantly punctuated by the evocative sound of whistles, and scraps of recorded interviews. *Different Trains* is given an exemplary reading by the Kronos Quartet, and it is nicely complemented by Pat Metheny's performance of the short *Electric Counterpoint* for live and multi-tracked acoustic guitars.

Further listening ...

The desert music. **Brooklyn Philharmonic Chorus and Orchestra/Michael Tilson Thomas** with **Steve Reich.** Elektra Nonesuch 7559-79101-2 (6/86).

Drumming. Six Pianos. Music for Mallet Instruments, Voices and Organs. **Steve Reich and Musicians.** DG 20th Century Classics 427 428-2GC2 (9/89).

Four Organs. *Coupled with* **Moran.** Three Dances. **D. Lang.** Face so pale. **Volans.** Kneeling Dance. **Piano Circus.** Argo 440 294-2ZH (1/94).

The Four Sections[a]. Music for Mallet Instruments, Voices and Organ[b]. [b]**Steve Reich and Musicians;** [a]**London Symphony Orchestra/Michael Tilson Thomas.** Elektra Nonesuch 7559-79220-2 (6/91).

Tehillim (Psalms) for Women's Voices and Instruments. **Vocal Ensemble, Instrumental Ensemble George/Manahan.** ECM New Series 827 411-2.

Antoine-Joseph Reicha

Bohemian/French 1770-1836

Suggested listening ...

Cello Quintets — No. 1 in A major; No. 2 in F major; No. 3 in E major. **Anner Bylsma** (vc); **L'Archibudelli.** Sony Classical Vivarte SK53118 (10/93).

Horn Quintet, Op. 106[c]. *Coupled with **M. Haydn.*** Romanze in A flat major. ***Mozart.*** Horn Quintet in E flat major, K407/K386c[b]. ***Haydn.*** Divertimento a tre in E flat major, HobIV/5. ***Beethoven.*** Sextet in E flat major, Op. 81b[a]. **Hermann Baumann,** [a]**Vladimir Dshambasov** (hns); **Gewandhaus Quartet;** [b]**Olaf Hallmann** (va); [c]**Christian Ockert** (db). Philips 426 440-2PH (9/93). *See review in the Collections section; refer to the Index to Reviews.*

Ottorino Respighi

Italian 1879-1936

New review
Respighi. Concerto gregoriano[a]. Poema autunnale. Ballata delle gnomidi. [a]**Lydia Mordkovitch** (vn); **BBC Philharmonic Orchestra/Sir Edward Downes.** Chandos CHAN9232. Recorded in 1993.

·• Ih 4m DDD 4/94

Respighi set great store by the *Concerto gregoriano* and was distressed by its failure with critics and public. It is quite easy to understand both his attitude and theirs. If he wanted, which may well have been the case, to write a concerto rooted in an ancient past yet not an obviously derivative pastiche; if he felt that flamboyantly violinistic gesture would be out of place in such a work, then he may be said to have succeeded on both counts. Yet to call a concerto 'Gregorian' but approach no closer to genuine chant than a sort of wistful modality risks offending those with a taste for 'early music', while to harmonize and score the result so richly and beautifully is to provide an obvious setting for a virtuosity that never arrives. It has a lyrical serenity that is attractive, however, as is its insistence that the solo instrument is fundamentally a singer, not an acrobat. The *Poema autunnale* has rather more to satisfy the fiddle-fancier and a good deal for those to whom the name Respighi promises orchestral opulence. The colourful and vociferous *Ballata delle gnomidi*, offering approximately equal measures of luscious bacchanale, grotesque scherzo and sumptuous dawn-music, is the nearest thing here to the popular Respighi of the Roman pictures.

Additional recommendations ...
Ballata delle gnomidi. Adagio con variazioni[a]. Trittico botticelliano. Suite in G major for Strings and Organ[b]. [a]**Alexander Baillie** (vc); [b]**Leslie Pearson** (org); **Philharmonia Orchestra/ Geoffrey Simon.** Cala CACD1007 — **·•** Ih 9m DDD 3/93
*Poema autunnale[a]. Suite in G major[b]. Il tramonto[c]. **Menotti.** Cantilena e scherzo[d].* [c]**Christopher Trakas** (bar); [a]**Igor Gruppman** (vn); [b]**Hollace C. Koman** (org); [d]**Marian Rian Hays** (hp); [c]**Quartetto di Venezia;** [abd]**San Diego Chamber Orchestra/Donald Barra.** Koch International Classics 37215-2 — **·•** Ih 3m DDD 7/94

New review
Respighi. Sinfonia drammatica. **BBC Philharmonic Orchestra/Sir Edward Downes.** Chandos CHAN9213.

·• Ih DDD 1/94

To luxuriate in this piece as an hour of sumptuous textures and gigantic crescendos without
worrying too much about its status as a major symphonic statement would be the obvious

conclusion, were it not for two factors, both very clear in this outstandingly sympathetic reading, which seem to point in opposite directions. On the one hand it sounds scarcely like the familiar Respighi at all; puzzlingly, since his orchestral mastery is already mature and *Fountains of Rome* was written barely two years later. If this is in any sense a disappointment the emotional temperature of the symphony, on the whole dark, indeed dramatic, with many moments of tension and unease, is striking as an element of Respighi's personality that was only intermittently heard again, in the best of his operas. Is it a reaction to the darkness of the times (it was completed just before the outbreak of the First World War)? Whatever the impetus, it gives the symphony urgency at moments when it needs it, and a sense that Respighi, for all his indebtedness to others and his riskily distended structure, is engaged in something more earnest than mere orchestral self-indulgence. This is a stunning performance, intensely responsive to the work's emotional core; it is most magnificently played and sumptuously recorded, and has such conviction to it that the indulgent smile ("poor old Respighi! Pretending to be a symphonist!") is quite often wiped from one's face.

New review

Respighi. Symphonic Poems — Pines of Rome. Fountains of Rome. Roman Festivals. **Montreal Symphony Orchestra/Charles Dutoit.** Decca 410 145-2DH. From SXDL7591 (9/83).

⠂⠄ lh DDD ll/83 ⁹ₚ ⁹ₛ Ⓑ

Respighi's three orchestral showpieces inspired by Rome have often been dismissed as merely musical picture postcards, but in ripely committed performances like Dutoit's, stunningly recorded, there are few works to match them in showing off the glories of a modern orchestra in full cry. Dutoit's performance is as brilliant as any, but he also finds a vein of warm expres-siveness in the writing as well as rhythmic point, so adding to the vividness of atmosphere. The atmospheric central movements of *Pines* have such a lovely radiance that one is not a bit surprised the nightingale feels the need to respond to the beauty of the evening. Similarly, the picturesque *Fountains* all spring to watery life, with detail beautifully observed and naturally revealed by the recording. In *Roman Festivals*, which can often merely sound noisy, there is a nice balance between pictorial vividness and brashness. There is an unsurpassed edge of brilliance in this recording, emphasized by the microphone placing of the Decca engineers, and the acoustics of St Eustache, Montreal combine glitter and translucence.

Additional recommendations ...
Pines of Rome. Fountains of Rome. Roman Festivals. **Philadelphia Orchestra/Riccardo Muti.** EMI CDC7 47316-2 — ⠂⠄ 3/86 ⁹ₚ Ⓑ
Pines of Rome. Fountains of Rome. Gli uccelli. **London Symphony Orchestra/István Kertész.** Decca Weekend 425 507-2DC — ⠄ 56m ADD 4/90 ⁹ₚ Ⓑ
Pines of Rome. Fountains of Rome. Roman Festivals. **NBC Symphony Orchestra/Arturo Toscanini.** RCA Gold Seal mono GD60262 — ⠂⠄ lh ADD 1/91 ⁹ₚ Ⓑ ▲
Pines of Rome. Fountains of Rome. Roman Festivals. **Philadelphia Orchestra/Eugene Ormandy.** RCA Silver Seal VD60486 — ⠄ lh 2m ADD 2/91 ⁹ₚ Ⓑ
Pines of Rome. Fountains of Rome. Roman Festivals. **Academy of St Martin in the Fields/Sir Neville Marriner.** Philips 432 133-2PH — ⠂⠄ lh 4m DDD 4/92 ⁹ₚ Ⓑ
Pines of Rome; Fountains of Rome; Roman Festivals. **Royal Philharmonic Orchestra/Enrique Bátiz.** Naxos 8 550539 — ⠄ lh lm DDD 8/92 ⁹ₚ Ⓑ
Pines of Rome. Fountains of Rome. **Mussorgsky.** *Pictures at an Exhibition.* **Fritz Reiner.** RCA 09026 61401-2 — ⠄ lh 10m ADD 8/93 ⁹ₚ Ⓑ ▲
Pines of Rome. Fountains of Rome. Roman Festivals. **London Philharmonic Orchestra/Carlo Rizzi.** Teldec 9031-76263-2. — ⠂⠄ lh 8m DDD 9/93 Ⓑ
Pines of Rome. Roman Festivals. **Verdi.** *The Four Seasons* — *Ballet.* **Cleveland Orchestra/Lorin Maazel.** Decca 425 052-2DM — ⠂⠄ lh 16m ADD ll/93 ⁹ₚ Ⓑ

New review

Respighi. Church Windows. Brazilian Impressions. Roman Festivals. **Cincinnati Symphony Orchestra/Jesús López-Cobos.** Telarc CD80356. Recorded in 1993.

⠂⠄ lh llm DDD 7/94 ⁹ₚ ⁹ₛ

The conventional coupling of *Pines, Fountains* and *Festivals* makes sense, of course. They are seen as the 'essential' Respighi, and one could easily argue that neither *Church Windows* nor *Brazilian*

Impressions is quite as successful (and that *Festivals* is the weakest of the Roman trilogy anyway). The only answer to that, López-Cobos seems to suggest, is to take the music perfectly seriously and pay scrupulous attention not just to its potential for sonorous spectacle but to its wealth of beautifully crafted detail. The gong at the end of the second movement of *Church Windows* is magnificently resonant, as is the organ in the finale, and the work is given an extra inch or two of stature by sensitive handling of those moments that need but don't always get delicacy. He pays such care to character and detail in "Butantan", that creepy depiction of a snake-farm in *Brazilian Impressions*, that you can not only recapture the real, crawling horror that Respighi experienced there, but discover in the music also a queer sort of Debussian grace as well. And as for *Roman Festivals*, well, what's wrong with 20-odd minutes of wide-screen spectacular once in a while? But if every colour is precisely rendered, the quiet passages are affectionately turned as they are here (and it's surprising how much of this score is quiet), what skill there is to be found in it, what a gift for immaculately precise instrumental detail. With that sort of handling all three pieces sound quite worthy of sharing shelf space with *Pines* and *Fountains*. The recording is spectacular and the orchestral playing is in the luxury class.

New review
Respighi. Gli uccelli. Antiche danze ed arie per liuto — Suites Nos. 1 and 3. Trittico botticelliano. **Orpheus Chamber Orchestra.** DG 437 533-2GH. Recorded in 1991.

Ih 9m DDD 7/93

This is astonishing playing. To do without a conductor when performing Respighi might seem an easier task than in an authentic masterpiece, but these suites require so much care over details of phrasing, colour, balance and articulation that not a few skilled conductors have failed to distil their freshness and charm unalloyed. But there are no conducted performances that excel these in their immaculate care over texture, delicacy of nuance and precision of tuning. Nor do they lack character, by any means: the orchestra's method of rehearsal, democracy tempered by the authority of a leader elected for each work, seems to have ensured a pretty well ideal balance between unanimity and soloistic individuality. If you add an infectious sense of enjoyment (not least, in these purist times, the not quite respectable enjoyment of Respighi's hand-colouring of his monochrome originals) and solo playing of great refinement, it becomes hard to imagine how these readings could be improved on. The recording is as transparent as one could wish. If this *Guide* was in the habit of awarding stars, this would get three out of three, plus a rosette.

Additional recommendations ...
Gli uccelli. Trittico botticelliano. Il tramonto[a]. Adagio con variazioni[b]. [a]**Linda Finnie** (contr); [b]**Raphael Wallfisch** (vc); **Bournemouth Sinfonietta/Tamás Vásáry.** Chandos CHAN8913 — Ih 5m DDD 3/92
Gli uccelli. Antiche danze ed arie per liuto — Suites Nos. 1 and 3. Trittico botticelliano. **Orpheus Chamber Orchestra.** DG 437 533-2GH — Ih 9m DDD 7/93

Respighi. Violin Sonata in B minor.
R. Strauss. Violin Sonata in E flat major, Op. 18. **Kyung-Wha Chung** (vn); **Krystian Zimerman** (pf). DG 427 617-2GH. Recorded in 1988.

52m DDD 2/90

This is wonderful violin playing, as richly romantic as both works often demand, but with a wide range of colour to underline the subtleties and the varying tones of voice that both employ. To add to the coupling's appeal, Kyung-Wha Chung's pianist is a musician of exceptional subtlety who is clearly as intent as she is to demonstrate that both sonatas deserve a position much closer to the centre of the repertory than they have so far been given. In the Strauss in particular they succeed eloquently. It is often described as the last work of his apprentice years, but in this performance the mature Strauss steps out from the shadow of Brahms so often and so proudly that its stature as his 'real' Op. 1 seems confirmed. The Respighi is a lesser piece, no doubt, but its melodies and its rhapsodic manner are attractive, and Chung's warm response to Respighi's idiomatic way with the instrument (he was a violinist himself) is infectious. Good and natural-sounding balance between violin and piano is not easy to achieve, but the recording here, significantly helped by Zimerman's combination of poetry and alert responsiveness, is outstandingly successful.

Additional recommendation …
Violin Sonata. **Franck.** *Violin Sonata.* **Poulenc.** *Violin Sonata.* **Josef Suk** (vn); **Josef Hála** (pf).
Supraphon 11 0710-2 — .ᐧᐧᐧ 1h 10m ADD 5/90

Respighi. Aretusa[a]. Il tramonto[a]. Lauda per la natività del Signore[b]. Trittico botticelliano.
[b]**Patricia Rozario** (sop); [a]**Dame Janet Baker,** [b]**Louise Winter** (mezs); [b]**Lynton Atkinson**
(ten); [b]**Richard Hickox Singers; City of London Sinfonia/Richard Hickox.** Collins
Classics 1349-2. Texts and translations included. Recorded in 1991.

.ᐧᐧᐧ 1h 12m DDD 9/92   ♩**P**

Attention is probably attracted towards this disc in the first place by Dame Janet Baker's presence
on it. *Aretusa* and *Il tramonto* are also set to translations of poems by Shelley: colourful works with
a wide range of expression, stimulating just that kind of boldness and generosity of utterance in
which Dame Janet is expert. She is in fine voice here, and at the end of *Il tramonto* ("the tomb of
the dead self") her tone is stern, strong and dark, intensely personal. Even so, going to the disc
initially for these tone-poems for solo voice and orchestra, one may still eventually be most glad
of the purchase for its introduction to the choral *Lauda per la natività del Signore*. This was written
in the late 1920s and is a most lovely work. It has solo parts for Mary, the Angel and a shepherd
(all well taken), but the great joy lies in the choral and orchestral writing, rich and imaginative,
its medievalism shot through with delight in the idiom. The better-known *Trittico botticelliano* is
highly enjoyable too, and all are fine in performance and recorded sound.

New review
Respighi. SEMIRAMA. **Eva Marton** (sop) Semirama; **Veronika Kincses** (sop) Susiana;
Lando Bartolini (ten) Merodach; **Lajos Miller** (bar) Falasar; **László Polgár** (bass) Ormus;
Tamás Clementis (bass) Satibara; **Hungarian Radio and Television Chorus; Hungarian
State Orchestra/Lamberto Gardelli.** Hungaroton HCD31197/8. Notes, text and translation
included. Recorded in 1990.

.ᐧᐧᐧ ② 2h 23m DDD 7/93

Semirama pre-dates any of Respighi's more familiar works by several years; it was his first major
critical success, completed when he was 31. The morning after the first performance an Italian
critic described it as "the first grand opera in the Italian repertory to be written in the Straussian
style". Straussian it certainly is in its orchestral richness; it has Strauss's complexion, you might
say, if not quite enough of his vigour, despite a plot of *Salome*-like gaminess (the ruthless
Babylonian Queen Semirama seduces her serving-maid's lover; only in the nick of time is it
revealed that he is her son). More rarely the opera is Debussyan, even Delian in colour, and
there are hints as well in some of the declamatory passages of the years Respighi had spent
working and studying in Russia. More startling when one considers the date of the opera (1910)
are the distinct, at times quite uncanny, apparent kinships with Puccini's *Turandot*. It would
be ten years before Puccini even began to consider that subject, and he can't have heard
Respighi's opera. One notices these things before one starts recognizing characteristic Respighian
fingerprints; even at 31 his style was not yet fully formed. Its constituents are all there —
sumptuous orchestral writing, grateful Italianate line, atmospheric evocation — but as yet they
are not really unified. Respighi's archaizing vein, seeking roots in a pre-romantic Italian past, is
as yet hardly present. For the lack of it he resorts to orientalisms learned from Rimsky-Korsakov
and others, but they tap shallower dramatic soil than the conjurings of a mysterious past in his
later operas. Marton is in fine voice, excitingly full, authoritative and yet able to yield to
lyricism and Gardelli conducts with a real feeling of excited discovery, and with a fine ear for
delicate texture as well as sympathy with his singers. The forward balance of the singers aside,
the recording is excellent.

Further listening …

Adagio con variazioni[a]. *Coupled with* **Elgar.** Cello Concerto in E minor, Op. 85[a]. **Milhaud.**
Cello Concerto No. 1, Op. 136[b]. [a]**Mstislav Rostropovich** (vc); [a]**Moscow Philharmonic
Orchestra;** [b]**USSR TV and Radio Large Orchestra/Gennadi Rozhdestvensky.** Russian
Disc RDCD11104 (7/94).

LA FIAMMA. **Soloists; Hungarian Radio and Television Chorus; Hungarian State Orchestra/Lamberto Gardelli.** Hungaroton HCD12591/3 (12/85).

Key to symbols

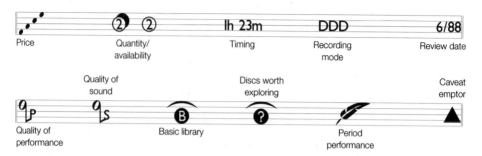

| Price | Quantity/ availability | Timing | Recording mode | Review date |

Quality of sound — Discs worth exploring — Caveat emptor

Quality of performance — Basic library — Period performance

Julius Reubke

German 1834-1858

New review

Reubke. Sonata on the 94th Psalm in C minor.
Schumann. Six Fugues on B-A-C-H, Op. 60. **Kevin Bowyer** (org). Nimbus NI5361. Played on the Marcussen organ of Odense Cathedral, Denmark. Recorded in 1992.

59m DDD 2/94

Reubke's Sonata's vivid musical imagery depicting verses from one of the most menacing of psalms ("O God, to whom vengeance belongeth") is the epitome of romantic organ music at its most lavish. Setting this great gothic edifice beside Schumann's taut, strictly disciplined Fugues is an inspired piece of programme-building from Kevin Bowyer. His performance of the Schumann reinforces the view that the pieces were primarily intended for organ. There is nothing remotely pianistic about this playing; the organ's sustaining powers come into their own as Bowyer skilfully traces the contrapuntal lines and his registration scheme is cleverly contrived to present the six fugues as a single cyclic whole. In the Reubke Bowyer understates the drama to chilling effect. The central *Adagio* ("the multitude of sorrows in my heart") is all the more tragic for its absence of sentimentality, while the strong, confident Fugue ("God is the strength of confidence") never forgets the horrible viciousness of the psalm's closing lines: "He shall destroy them in their own malice". Spine-tingling stuff.

Silvestre Revueltas

Mexican 1899-1940

Suggested listening ...

String Quartets — No. 1; No. 2, "Agaves"; No. 3; No. 4, "Musica de Feria". **Latin-American Quartet.** New Albion NA062CD (6/94).

Caminos[b]. Musica para charlar[b]. Ventanas[b]. *Coupled with* **Chávez.** Sinfonia de Antigona[a]. Symphony No. 4, "Sinfonia romantica"[a]. [a]**Royal Philharmonic Orchestra,** [b]**Mexican State Philharmonic Orchestra/Enrique Bátiz.** ASV CDDCA653 (8/89).

Sensemayá. *Coupled with* **Chávez.** Sinfonía India. **Copland.** Danzón cubano. **Roldán.** Suite from "La Rebambaramba". Rítmica V. **García Caturla.** Tres danzas cubanas. **Piazzolla.** Tangazo. **Ginastera.** Suite from "Estancia". **New World Symphony/Michael Tilson Thomas.** Argo 436 737-2ZH (6/93). *See review in the Collections section; refer to the Index to Reviews.*

Emil Nikolaus von Rezniček

Suggested listening ...

Symphonies — No. 3 in D major; No. 4 in F minor. **Philharmonia Hungarica/Gordon Wright.** Koch Schwann 312032.

Joseph Rheinberger

Suggested listening ...

Organ Concertos — No. 1 in F major, Op. 137; No. 2 in G minor, Op. 177. **Andreas Juffinger** (org); **Berlin Radio Symphony Orchestra/Hartmut Haenchen.** Capriccio 10336.

Wolfgang Rihm

Suggested listening ...

Gesungene Zeit. *Coupled with* **Berg.** Violin Concerto. **Anne-Sophie Mutter** (vn); **Chicago Symphony Orchestra/James Levine.** DG 437 093-2GH (1/93). *See review under Berg; refer to the Index to Reviews.*

Nicolay Rimsky-Korsakov

Rimsky-Korsakov. Scheherazade, Op. 35. Capriccio espagnol, Op. 34. **London Symphony Orchestra/Sir Charles Mackerras.** Telarc CD80208. Recorded in 1990.

1h DDD 10/90

Sir Charles Mackerras throws himself into this music with expressive abandon, but allies it to control so that every effect is realized and the London Symphony Orchestra play this familiar music as if they were discovering it afresh. Together they produce performances that are both vivid and thoughtful, while the solo violin in *Scheherazade*, who represents the young queen whose storytelling skills prolong and finally save her life in the court of the cruel Sultan Shahriar (portrayed by powerful brass), is seductively and elegantly played by Kees Hulsmann, not least at the wonderfully peaceful end to the whole work. The finale featuring a storm and shipwreck is superbly done, the wind and brass bringing one to the edge of one's seat and reminding us that Rimsky-Korsakov served in the Russian Navy and well knew the beauty and danger of the sea. This sensuous and thrilling work needs spectacular yet detailed sound, and that is what it gets here, the 1990 recording in Walthamstow Town Hall being highly successful and giving us a CD that many collectors will choose to use as a demonstration disc to impress their friends. The performance and recording of the *Capriccio espagnol* is no less of a success, and this issue is worth every penny of its price.

Additional recommendations ...
Scheherazade. **Debussy.** La mer. **Chicago Symphony Orchestra/Fritz Reiner.** RCA GD60875 — .⸱ 1h 9m ADD Ⓑ ▲
Scheherazade. **Tchaikovsky.** Capriccio italien. **Philharmonia Orchestra/Paul Kletzki.** Classics for Pleasure CD-CFP4341 — . 1h m ADD ⁹ₚ Ⓑ
Scheherazade. **Borodin.** PRINCE IGOR — *Polovtsian Dances*[a]. [a]**Beecham Choral Society; Royal Philharmonic Orchestra/Sir Thomas Beecham.** EMI CDC7 47717-2. — .⸱ 58m ADD 9/87 ⁹ₚ Ⓑ ▲

Scheherazade[a]. **Mussorgsky.** *A night on the Bare Mountain (orig. version)*[b]. [b]**Rodney Friend** (vn); **London Philharmonic Orchestra/**[a]**David Lloyd-Jones,** [b]**Bernard Haitink.** Philips Silverline 420 898-2PSL — .·' Ih ADD 3/90 ⁹ₚ Ⓑ

Scheherazade. **Ravel.** *Boléro.* **London Philharmonic Orchestra/Andrew Litton.** Virgin Classics Virgo VJ7 91470 — . Ih 4m DDD 12/91 ⁹ₚ Ⓑ

Scheherazade. **Prokofiev.** *Lieutenant Kijé — Suite, Op. 60.* **London Philharmonic Orchestra/ Takuo Yuasa.** EMI Eminence EMX2214 — .·' Ih 8m DDD 12/93 ⁹ₚ ⁹ₛ Ⓑ

Scheherazade. Russian Easter Festival Overture, Op. 36. **Vienna Philharmonic Orchestra/Seiji Ozawa.** Philips 438 941-2PH — .·' 58m DDD 6/94 Ⓑ

Scheherazade. THE TALE OF TSAR SALTAN, Op. 57 — Tsar's farewell and departure; Tsarina in a barrel at sea; The three wonders. **Philharmonia Orchestra/Enrique Bátiz.** Naxos 8 550726 — . Ih Im DDD 6/94 ⁹ₚ Ⓑ

Rimsky-Korsakov. SYMPHONIES AND ORCHESTRAL WORKS. **Gothenburg Symphony Orchestra/Neeme Järvi.** DG 423 604-2GH2.
Symphonies — No. 1 in E minor, Op. 1; No. 2 (Symphonic Suite), Op. 9, "Antar"; No. 3 in C major, Op. 32. Russian Easter Festival Overture, Op. 36. Capriccio espagnol, Op. 34.

.·' ② 2h 5m DDD 2/89

No one is going to claim Rimsky's First and Third Symphonies to be neglected masterpieces. He came to refer to his First (partly written whilst the young naval officer was on duty!) as a "disgraceful composition", and along with the other two symphonies, it was subjected to extensive revision by the later learned master of musical technique. As the equally learned, entertaining and informative essay accompanying this set points out, the opening of the symphony could have been a trial run for the opening of Schumann's Fourth (and a very fine one, too!). It's the beautifully lyrical second theme which reminds us that Rimsky was reared in the country and had the early advantage of a good soaking in folk-song. Though the debt to Glinka is obvious, to our ears classical concerns seem uppermost throughout, and the music is free from anything that could be called exoticism. Not so the Second. Rimsky was a member of the 'Mighty Five', a group of composers (including Mussorgsky, Balakirev and Borodin) sworn to the nationalist cause, professing horror at anything tinged with German academicism and ever searching for subjects on which they could lavish a preference for orchestral colour above form. Rimsky's *Antar* combined these ideals, and more. Our hero of the title is allocated a Berliozian *idée fixe*, an oriental location (the desert of Sham) and the joys of vengeance, power and love from the grateful fairy Gul-Nazar as a gift for saving her from a winged monster. It is, in every way, an antecedent of *Sheherazade* and, after hearing Järvi's rich and eloquently descriptive account, one wonders why it has never attained anything like the same popularity. His Third Symphony reverts to a more academic manner. In 1871 he was invited to join the theory and composition faculty at the St Petersburg Conservatory and, in Tchaikovsky's words, "from contempt of schooling he had turned all at once to the cult of musical technique". Despite a paucity of truly memorable ideas, it is a symphony to admire for its construction and light-as-air orchestration. The set is completed with urgent, vibrant accounts of the *Capriccio espagnol* and the *Russian Easter Festival Overture*, quite the most colourful and exciting versions on disc, and they confirm that the less familiar symphonies could not be in better hands. DG's engineers resist the temptation to glamorize the music and offer a lucid and spacious panorama of sound.

Additional recommendation ...
Russian Easter Festival Overture. Capriccio espagnol. **Borodin.** *In Central Asia.* PRINCE IGOR — *Polovtsian Dances*[ab]. **Tchaikovsky.** *1812 Overture, Op. 49*[bc]. *Marche slave, Op. 31.* [a]**Torgny Sporsén** (bass); [b]**Gothenburg Symphony Brass Band; Gothenburg Symphony** [b]**Chorus and Orchestra/Neeme Järvi.** DG 429 984-2GH — .·' Ih 16m DDD 3/91

New review
Rimsky-Korsakov. THE TSAR'S BRIDE. **Pyotr Gluboky** (bass) Sobakin; **Ekaterina Kudriavchenko** (sop) Marfa; **Vladislav Verestnikov** (bar) Grigory Gryaznoy; **Nikolai Nizinenko** (bass) Skuratov; **Arkady Mishenkin** (ten) Ivan Lykov; **Nina Terentieva** (mez) Lyubasha; **Vladimir Kudriashov** (ten) Bomelius; **Irina Udalova** (sop) Saburova; **Elena Okolycheva** (contr) Duniasha; **Tatiana Pechuria** (mez) Petrovna; **Vladislav Pashinsky** (bass) Driver; **Nina Larionova** (mez) Servant; **Yury Markelov** (ten) Boy; **Sveshnikov**

Russian Academy Choir; Bolshoi Theatre Orchestra/Andrey Tchistiakov. CdM Russian
Season LDC288 056/7. Notes and English text included. Recorded in 1992.

② 2h 26m DDD 8/93

The Tsar's Bride comes roughly half way in the list of Rimsky-Korsakov's operas (a complicated
list, due to various revisions and differing versions). Though there have been Russian-language
productions in America and Britain, it has not really caught on in the West. Though there
should be a welcome for this new recording (there have been at least two others), one can see
why. The story is awkward, turning on the search by the Tsar in question, Ivan the Terrible, for
a wife. He chooses Marfa, betrothed to Ivan Lykov but also loved by Grigory Gryaznoy, who in
turn is trying to discard his impassioned lover Lyubasha in favour of Marfa. There is a sinister
German doctor, Bomelius, who supplies poisons and also love potions: confusion and substitu-
tion here lead to Marfa's madness and her final eerie song. Tchaikovsky is the most potent
influence on the work. It is cast in separate but linked numbers, and draws in part on the kind
of elegant, song-like melodic line of which Tchaikovsky was such a great master. Some of the
duets are quite close in manner to those in *Eugene Onegin*. Yet there is also a strong folk
influence: Marfa's beautiful aria in Act 2 scene 2 owes much to the Russian predilection for
developing a melody out of varied repetition of a single idea. Rimsky-Korsakov was very familiar
with the manner, as his own collection of national songs alone goes to show. The aria is
tenderly sung by Ekaterina Kudriavchenko, who handles with great sensitivity this portrayal of
a figure familiar from many Russian novels and operas, the suffering heroine. Lyubasha is
potently sung by Nina Terentieva, somewhat in the charged manner of another Marfa, that of
Mussorgsky's *Khovanshchina*. She suggests banked fires of passion, sings her unaccompanied song
caressingly, and rounds with both dignity and rage on the slimy Bomelius (Vladimir Kudriashov)
even as she consents to his advances for the sake of his potions, snarling at him the word
"nemets": translated by the libretto as "monster", it is the ordinary Russian word for "German",
but carries with it the older, contemptuous meaning, "dumb". Arkady Mishenkin tenorizes
fluently as Ivan Lykov, not a very grateful part. Gryaznoy's opening aria is also a difficult one,
for Rimsky-Korsakov gives him a melodic line that presents him as a character of some
sympathy, if we do not know that he is regretting that he is now getting too old for the rapes
he used to enjoy so much and is casting his eyes on the innocent Marfa instead of his mistress
Lyubasha. Vladislav Verestnikov rightly handles this with a kind of blunt strength that does not
give away too much. Later, he suggests an increasing and destructive tension, while also a
certain magnificence. The chorus consists chiefly of oprichniks, Ivan the Terrible's dreaded
private army which was, really, the ancestors of the KGB. They might have been characterized
more menacingly, with more sense of the brutalizing effect of their comradeship; and the
orchestral playing, too, while graceful and responsive, is a little lacking in character and is not
always ideally synchronized with the singers. Andrey Tchistiakov is better in the more lyrical
sections, but he paces the music well and does not over-discipline the work. It is one very well
worth hearing, especially as recordings of Rimsky-Korsakov's operas, apart from the most
famous, are not that easy to come by. The booklet provides essays and synopses in French,
German and English, the text only in French and English.

Further listening …

Piano Concerto in C sharp minor, Op. 30[b]. *Coupled with* **Balakirev.** Piano Concerto No. 1 in
F sharp major, Op. 1[a]. **Medtner.** Piano Concerto No. 1 in C minor, Op. 33[a]. **Igor Zhukov**
(pf); **USSR TV and Radio Large Orchestra/[a]Alexander Dmitriev; [b]Gennadi
Rozhdestvensky.** Mezhdunarodnaya Kniga MK417087 (2/94). *See reviews under Balakirev and
Medtner; refer to the Index to Reviews.*

Orchestral Suites — THE GOLDEN COCKEREL; THE TALE OF TSAR SALTAN; CHRISTMAS
EVE. **Armenian Philharmonic Orchestra/Loris Tjeknavorian.** ASV CDDCA772 (9/92).

SADKO — The paragon of cities; Beautiful city! KASHCHEY THE IMMORTAL — In this,
night's darkest hour. SNOW MAIDEN (second version) — Under the warm blue sea. THE
TSAR'S BRIDE — Still the beauty haunts my mind. *Coupled with* **Mussorgsky.** Songs and
Dances of Death. **Borodin.** PRINCE IGOR — No sleep, no rest. **Rubinstein.** THE
DEMON — Do not weep, my child; On the airy ocean; I am he whom you called. NERO —
Vindex's Epithalamium: I sing to you, Hymen divine! **Rachmaninov.** ALEKO — Aleko's

cavatina. **Dmitri Hvorostovsky** (bar); **Kirov Theatre Orchestra/Valery Gergiev.** Philips 438 872-2PH (5/94). *See review in the Collections section; refer to the Index to Reviews.*

MOZART AND SALIERI. **Soloists; Bolshoi Theatre Orchestra/Mark Ermler.** *Coupled with **Mussorgsky*** (orch. Rozhdestvensky). THE MARRIAGE. **Soloists; USSR Ministry of Culture Symphony Orchestra/Gennadi Rozhdestvensky.** Olympia OCD145 (9/93). *See review under Mussorgsky; refer to the Index to Reviews.*

Richard Rodgers

American 1902-1979

Suggested listening ...

Overtures — Oklahoma!. Allegro. South Pacific. The King and I. Me and Juliet. Pipe Dream. Cinderella. Flower Drum Song. Carousel — Waltz. State Fair — Suite. The Sound of Music — Entr'acte. **Hollywood Bowl Orchestra/John Mauceri.** Philips 434 127-2PH (9/92).

Victory at Sea — *television score.* **RCA Victor Symphony Orchestra/Robert Russell Bennett.** RCA Victor 09026 60963-2.

Carousel — *original film soundtrack.* EMI Angel ZDM7 64692-2.

Oklahoma! — *original film soundtrack.* EMI Angel ZDM7 64691-2.

South Pacific — *original film soundtrack.* RCA ND83681 (12/89).

THE RODGERS AND HAMMERSTEIN SONGBOOK. *Selections* — Oklahoma!. Carousel. South Pacific. The King and I. Cinderella. Flower Drum Song. The Sound of Music. **Original Broadway casts, etc.** Sony Broadway CD53331.

THE BOYS FROM SYRACUSE. **Soloists; orchestra/Lehman Engel.** Sony Broadway CD53329.

THE KING AND I. **Soloists; Hollywood Bowl Orchestra/John Mauceri.** Philips 438 007-2PH (10/92).

ON YOUR TOES. **Original 1983 Broadway revival cast.** That's Entertainment CDTER1063 (10/83).

CAROUSEL. **Original 1993 London cast.** First Night CASTCD40 (5/94).

Joaquin Rodrigo

Spanish 1901-

Rodrigo. Concierto de Aranjuez. Fantasía para un gentilhombre. **John Williams** (gtr); **Philharmonia Orchestra/Louis Frémaux.** CBS Masterworks CD37848. From IM37848 (7/84).

53m DDD 7/85

The *Concierto de Aranjuez* is a romantic work whose success remains unparalleled. Rodrigo's recipe for both works on this recording is to express his reverence for past traditions in terms of his own, neoclassical musical language — lush tunes and harmonies, some courtly formality and a soupçon of mischievous spikiness. The *Fantasía* (the *Gentilhombre* is Segovia) pays its respects also to a great guitarist of the seventeenth century, Gaspar Sanz, some of whose themes are winsomely reworked by Rodrigo. Both works call for a high degree of virtuosity but difficulties present no problem to John Williams, who brings to both pieces the proper blend of expressive-ness and poise. To describe a recording as 'vivid' has become a cliché but in this case it is inevitable.

Additional recommendations ...
Concierto de Aranjuez. Fantasía para un gentilhombre. **Villa-Lobos.** Guitar Concerto. **Göran Söllscher** (gtr); **Orpheus Chamber Orchestra.** DG 429 232-2GH — .·ʼ lh 5m DDD 6/90 Ⓑ
Concierto de Aranjuez. Fantasía para un gentilhombre. **Walton.** Five Bagatelles (arr. Russ).
Christopher Parkening (gtr); **Royal Philharmonic Orchestra/Andrew Litton.** EMI CDC7 54665-2 — .·ʼ 59m DDD 9/93 ꝗₚ Ⓑ
Concierto de Aranjuez[a]. Fantasia para un gentilhombre[b]. Tres piezas españolas. Invocacíon y danza. **Julian Bream** (gtr); [a]**Chamber Orchestra of Europe/John Eliot Gardiner;** [b]**RCA Victor Chamber Orchestra/Leo Brouwer.** RCA Gold Seal 09026 61611-2 — .·ʼ lh 9m DDD 2/94 ꝗₚ Ⓑ

Further listening ...

Concierto serenata[a]. Concierto de Aranjuez[b]. *Coupled with* **Casteldnuovo-Tedesco.** Guitar Concerto No. 1[c]. [a]**Nicanor Zabaleta** (hp); [bc]**S. Behrend** (gtr); [a]**Berlin Radio Symphony Orchestra/Ernst Märzendorfer;** [bc]**Berlin Philharmonic Orchestra/Reinhard Peters.** DG 427 214-2GR.

Concierto pastoral. *Coupled with* **Khachaturian** (arr. Gallois). Flute Concerto in D minor. **Patrick Gallois** (fl); **Philharmonia Orchestra/Ion Marin.** DG 435 767-2GH (10/92).

Suite. Preludio al gallo mañanero. Zarabanda lejana. Pastorale. Bagatela. Serenata española. Sonada de adiós (Hommage à Paul Dukas). Tres Danzas de España. Danza de la Amapola. Tres Evocaciones. Preludio de Añoranza. Cinco Sonatas de Castilla con Toccata a modo de pregón. Berceuse de printemps. Berceuse d'automne. Air de Ballet sur le nom d'une Jeune Fille. El Album de Cecilia (Seis Piezas para manos pequeñas). A l'ombre de Torre Bermeja. Cuatro Piezas. Cuatro Estampas andaluzas. Cinco Piezas infantiles[a]. Sonatiuna para dos Munecas[a]. Gran Marcha de los Subsecretarios[a]. Atardecer[a]. **Gregory Allen,** [a]**Anton Nel** (pfs). Bridge BCD9027 (7/92).

Johan Helmich Roman
Swedish 1694-1758

Suggested listening ...

Suites — D major, "Lilla Drottningholmsmusiquen"; G minor, "Sjukmans musiquen". Piante amiche[a]. [a]**Pia-Maria Nilsson** (sop); **Stockholm Nationalmuseum Chamber Orchestra/ Claude Génetay.** Musica Sveciae MSCD417 (1/93).

Andreas Romberg
German 1767-1821

Suggested listening ...

Quintet in E flat major, Op. 57[a]. *Coupled with* **Fuchs.** Clarinet Quintet in E flat major, Op. 102. **Stanford.** Two Fantasy Pieces. **Thea King** (cl); **Britten Quartet.** Hyperion CDA66479 (7/92). *See review under Fuchs; refer to the Index to Reviews.*

Sigmund Romberg
Hungarian/American 1887-1951

Suggested listening ...

THE STUDENT PRINCE (Romberg/Donelly). **Soloists; Ambrosian Chorus; Philharmonia Orchestra/John Owen Edwards.** TER Classics CDTER2 1172 (3/91).

Cipriano de Rore

New review

Rore. MADRIGALS. **The Consort of Musicke** (Emma Kirkby, Evelyn Tubb, sops; Mary Nichols, mez; Andrew King, Paul Agnew, tens; Alan Ewing, bass)/**Anthony Rooley.** Musica Oscura 070991. Texts and translations included. Recorded in 1991.

Il quinto libro de madrigali. Le vive fiamme — Alma real, se come fida stella; Alma Susanna; Amor che t'ho fatt'io; Di l'estrem' orizonte; Fera gentil; Vaghi pensieri. O voi che sotto.

56m DDD 1/94

Cipriano de Rore's understanding of the emotional potential of the madrigal was explored in both four- and five-part scorings. The four-part pieces are generally lighter-veined but the imagery and expressive range is no less detailed than the intensely wrought five-part madrigals, and in many ways they are more representative of the compendium of skills which were to blossom with Monteverdi and his contemporaries. This is an imaginative first step in The Consort of Musicke's latest departure of 'encircling' Monteverdi with music by his predecessors and contemporaries, and they have rightly considered it irrelevant that Monteverdi was minus two years old when Rore died, since it is clear that Monteverdi sought much inspiration from his rich musical inheritance. Impressive as ever is the uniform breathing, the purring ensemble, even in works with speech rhythms which require extreme discipline to make them sound spontaneous. The mock piety of the darker-scored works is greatly assisted by the singers' subtlety of accentuation. Less persuasive is the way The Consort imposes rhetorical formulae on Rore's relatively abstract style (in this book anyway). That said, there are, as you would expect, many fine things here, including a stunning *Vaghi pensieri* and *O santo fior felice*, the latter all but releasing the sweet scent of Rore's blest and happy flower.

New review

Rore. Missa Praeter rerum seriem. Motets — Infelix ego; Parce mihi; Ave regina; Descendi in hortum meum.
Josquin Desprez. Praeter rerum seriem. **The Tallis Scholars/Peter Phillips.** Gimell CDGIM029. Texts and translations included.

1h 12m DDD 6/94

This record begins with a magisterially concentrated and evocative account of one of Josquin's most inspired and tightly-constructed motets, the six-voice *Praeter rerum seriem*. This in turn is the starting-point for Rore's Mass — which takes as its cue Josquin's antiphonal approach — wherein the song on which the Mass is based is passed from the upper to the lower voices in succession. Rore, whose piece is in one sense an act of homage to Josquin was, if briefly, Josquin's successor at the d'Este court at Ferrara. It is in this context that Rore's work is an act of homage in a second sense, since to Josquin's already rich texture Rore adds an additional soprano part, while the first alto voice carries throughout a *cantus firmus* to the text "Hercules secundus dux Ferrarie quartus vivit et vivet". Around this structural scaffolding the remaining voices weave an endlessly inventive sequence of carefully-worked motives reminiscent of Josquin's original. This performance is characterized by great sensitivity to textual inflexion and to the many moments of exquisite bonding of words and music. Nevertheless, in the end it is Peter Phillips's ability to control the overall architecture of the music, as well as its detail, that provides the basis for a reading of such conviction; his direction, combined with The Tallis Scholars's strongly-focused singing and well-balanced ensemble, results in a gripping performance of rare beauty, intelligence and power. No less fine is the group of four motets that completes the recording, and which reveals Rore as one of the greatest and last exponents of the Franco-Flemish tradition.

Ned Rorem

Suggested listening ...

Winter pages[a]. Bright music[b]. [b]**Marya Martin** (fl); [a]**Todd Palmer** (cl); [a]**Frank Morelli** (bn); **Ida** and [b]**Ani Kavafian** (vns); **Fred Sherry** (vc); [a]**Charles Wadsworth**, [b]**André-Michel Schub** (pfs). New World 80416-2 (10/92).

Hilding Rosenberg

Swedish 1892-1985

Suggested listening ...

Symphony No. 4, "The Revelation of St John". **Håkan Hagegård** (bar); **Swedish Radio Choir; Pro Musica Choir; Rilke Ensembe; Gothenburg Symphony Orchestra/Sixten Ehrling.** Caprice CAP21429 (5/93).

Orpheus in Town. Sinfonia Concertante. Violin Concerto No. 1, Op. 22. Suite in D major, Op. 13 — Pastorale. Symphonies — No. 3; No. 4, "The Revelation of St John": Fragments; No. 5, "Ortågardsmästern". The Holy Night. **Soloists; Swedish Radio Choir, Stockholm Chamber Choir, Radiojänst Symphony Orchestra, Stockholm Concert Society Orchestra, Radiotjänst Entertainment Orchestra, Swedish Radio Orchestra/Hilding Rosenberg.** Caprice Collector's Classics mono CAP21510 (three-CD set, recorded from broadcast performances between 1940-49, 5/93).

Johann Rosenmüller

German 1619-1684

New review

Rosenmüller. Sacri Concerti — Beatus vir qui timet Dominum. Magnificat. Benedicam Dominum. De profundis clamavi. Confitebor. Gloria in excelsis Deo. **Cantus Cölln** (Johanna Koslowsky, Maria Cristina Kiehre, sops; David Cordier, alto; Gerd Türk, Wilfried Jochens, tens; Stephan Schreckenberger, bass)/**Konrad Junghänel** (lte). Deutsche Harmonia Mundi 05472 77181-2. Texts and translations included. Recorded in 1991.

⸬ **Ih I4m DDD 6/93**

Mid-baroque German sacred music, indeed German baroque music in general, still suffers from a condition which fails to provide just recognition for a number of 'lesser' masters between Schütz and Bach. Johann Rosenmüller may not quite be Germany's equivalent of Corelli, Purcell or Charpentier but he was regarded in his lifetime as a composer to be reckoned with, and judging by the music on this disc, it is not hard to understand Rosenmüller's popularity. Deft organizational skills and melodic charm are effortlessly combined with fluent counterpoint and exciting rhythmic exclamations. Cantus Cölln are a tight-knit group of consort singers with a capacity for extolling Rosenmüller's qualities vividly and persuasively. Each of the six *Sacri Concerti* reveals singing of notable discipline and an attractive, controlled blend. Indeed, this is an enterprising (and generously filled) recording from Cantus Cöln whose work is unveiling many hidden gems. Strongly recommended.

Antonio Rosetti

Bohemian c.1750-1792

Suggested listening ...

Horn Concertos — E major, K3:42; E major, K3:44; E flat major, K3:39. **English Chamber Orchestra/Barry Tuckwell** (hn). Classics for Pleasure CD-CFP4578 (8/91).

Luigi Rossi

Italian c.1597-1653

Rossi. ORFEO. **Agnès Mellon** (sop) Orfeo; **Monique Zanetti** (sop) Euridice; **Dominique Favat** (mez) Nutrice, Bacco; **Sandrine Piau** (sop) Aristeo; **Nicholas Isherwood** (bass) Satiro; **Caroline Pelon** (sop) Amore; **Noémi Rime** (sop) Venere, Vittoria; **Jean-Paul**

Fouchécourt (ten) Vecchia, Giove; **Jérôme Corréas** (bar) Endimione; **Marie Boyer** (mez) Giunone; **Cécile Eloir** (mez) Gelosia; **Bernard Deletré** (bass) Augure, Plutone; **Benoît Thivel** (alto) Apollo, Mercurio; **Jean-Marc Salzmann** (bar) Caronte, Momo; **Donatienne Michel-Dansac** (sop) Proserpina; **Beatrice Malleret** (sop) Himeneo; **Les Arts Florissants/ William Christie.** Harmonia Mundi HMC90 1358/60. Notes, text and translation included. Recorded in 1990.

③ 3h 39m DDD 3/92

Luigi Rossi spent most of his career in Rome, but in 1646 he was invited by Cardinal Mazarin to the Parisian Court. Shortly after he arrived, and while he was working on his second opera *Orfeo*, he received the tragic news of his wife's death in Italy. Small wonder, then, that he produced such profound and affecting music for the subject of this opera. Francesco Buti's libretto consists of three acts, with a prologue and postlude in praise of Louis XIV — dramatically, quite inapposite. Buti supplemented the mythological characters with a host of minor roles, many of them comic figures to lighten the mood. With these resources, Rossi was able to intersperse the recitatives and arias with ensembles, choruses, and dance music, no doubt to appeal to French taste. This recording is most welcome, not just because it is the only one available, but more because it is so impeccably performed. William Christie achieves the finest musical precision as well as giving a powerful dramatic thrust to the whole. He has a crack orchestra, with some admirably fleet cornetts and very polished continuo playing. Of the soloists, Agnès Mellon handles the title role beautifully, and her interpretation of "Lagrime, dove sete?", which Orfeo sings on hearing of Euridice's death, is particularly moving. What emotive and perfectly crafted music this is; and how deeply Rossi must have felt it. Monique Zanetti is appropriately sweet-toned as Euridice — very poised in her death scene; and Sandrine Piau's interpretation of the complex character of Aristeo is particularly admirable. One or two of the minor roles are not so strong, and Buti's interpolations do tend to interrupt the dramatic thread, but these are insignificant quibbles. It is an absolutely first-rate recording of a work which deserves to be better known.

Further listening …

Le Canterine Romane. **Tragicomedia.** Teldec Das Alte Werke 4509-90799-2 (10/93).

Gioachino Rossini

Italian 1792-1868

Rossini. OVERTURES. **Chicago Symphony Orchestra/Fritz Reiner.** RCA GD60387. From SB2075 (7/60). Recorded in 1958.
GUILLAUME TELL; LA SCALA DI SETA; IL SIGNOR BRUSCHINO; IL BARBIERE DI SIVIGLIA. LA GAZZA LADRA; LA CENERENTOLA.

47m ADD 9/90

This is one of the most famous of all collections featuring this sparkling repertoire. By the time of this recording, Fritz Reiner had built the Chicago Symphony into one of the world's greatest ensembles, and its swaggering yet supremely flexible virtuosity is heard to superb effect on this survey. Not that these accounts are in any sense over-driven or that Rossini's music is used merely as an excuse for high-powered orchestral display; far from it: Reiner's direction possesses elegance, genial high-spirits and (at times) an almost Beechamesque wit — sample, say, the pointed woodwind dialogue in the scintillating reading of *La Cenerentola* to hear this. In fact, the only regret one could possibly have about this simply marvellous music-making is that, with a total duration of just under 47 minutes there isn't more of it! Despite some (inevitable) residual hiss, the RCA transfer engineers have worked wonders with these elderly tapes, producing a far more full-blooded, transparent sound-picture than one would have thought possible. At mid-price, this is unmissable. Buy it!

Additional recommendations …
TANCREDI. L'ITALIANA IN ALGERI. L'INGANNO FELICE. LA SCALA DI SETA. IL BARBIERE DI SIVIGLIA. IL SIGNOR BRUSCHINO. LA CAMBIALE DI MATRIMONIO. IL TURCO IN ITALIA.
Orpheus Chamber Orchestra. DG 415 363-2GH — 52m DDD 10/85

LA SCALA DI SETA. IL SIGNOR BRUSCHINO. L'ITALIANA IN ALGERI. IL BARBIERE DI SIVIGLIA. LA GAZZA LADRA. SEMIRAMIDE. GUILLAUME TELL. **London Classical Players/Roger Norrington.** EMI Reflexe CDC7 54091-2 — .·′ 1h DDD 4/91 ᑫₚ Ⓑ ✏
Complete Overtures — *LA CAMBRIALE DI MATRIMONIO. LA SCALA DI SETA. IL BARBIERE DI SIVIGLIA. TANCREDI. L'ITALIANA IN ALGERI. IL SIGNOR BRUSCHINO. IL TURCO IN ITALIA. L'INGANNO FELICE. GUILLAUME TELL. SEMIRAMIDE. LE SIÈGE DE CORINTHE. LA CENERENTOLA. LA GAZZA LADRA. IL VIAGGIO A REIMS. MAOMETTO II. RICCIARDO E ZORIADE. OTELLO. ARMIDA. ERMIONE. TORVALDO E DORLISKA. BIANCA E FALLIERO. DEMETRIO E POLIBIO. EUDARDO E CRISTINA. EDIPO A COLONO. Sinfonia al Conventello. Sinfonia di Bologna.*
Academy of St Martin in the Fields/Sir Neville Marriner. Philips 434 016-2PM3 — .·′ ③ 3h 29m ADD 10/92 ᑫₚ Ⓑ

Rossini. SONATE A QUATTRO. **Serenata of London** (Barry Wilde, Clive Lander, vns; Roger Smith, vc; Michael Brittain, db). ASV CDDCA767.
No. 1 in G major; No. 2 in A major; No. 3 in C major; No. 4 in B flat major; No. 5 in E flat major; No. 6 in D major.

.·′ 1h 18m DDD 10/91

Rossini's six string sonatas are usually heard performed by a string orchestra, although they were in fact composed for a quartet of two violins, cello and double bass. This issue, which gives us for the first time on CD the original instrumentation, is therefore most welcome. The sonatas, which display amazing musical dexterity and assurance may date from 1804, when Rossini was only 12. The world of eighteenth-century opera is never far away, with the first violin frequently taking the role of soprano soloists, particularly in the slow movements. Written for Rossini's friend Agostino Triosso, who was a keen double bass player, the sonata's bass parts are full of wit and suavity. The performances by the Serenata of London are full of elegance and polish. Rossini's youthful high spirits are always to the fore and some of the fearsome string writing clearly holds no terrors for the members of this group. ASV's resonant recording adds the final touch of satisfaction to a most welcome recording.

Additional recommendations ...
Nos. 1-6. **Academy of St Martin in the Fields/Sir Neville Marriner.** Decca 430 563-2DM2 — .·′ ② 1h 52m ADD
Nos. 1-6. **Elizabeth Wallfisch, Marshall Marcus** (vns); **Richard Tunnicliffe** (vc); **Chi-Chi Nwanoku** (db). Hyperion CDA66595 — .·′ 1h 20m DDD 10/92
Nos. 1, 3 and 6. Variations in C major[a]. Variazoni a più instrumenti obbligati in F major[a]. Serenata in E flat major. [a]**Dmitri Ashkenazy** (cl); **Bologna Teatro Communale Orchestra/Riccardo Chailly.** Decca 433 701-2DH — .·′ 1h 13m DDD 2/93
Nos. 1-6. **Kremlin Chamber Orchestra/Mischa Rachlevsky.** Claves CD50-9222 — .·′ 1h 19m DDD 11/93 ᑫₚ

New review
Rossini. PECHES DE VIEILLESSE. **Maryse Castets** (sop); **Mechthild Georg** (mez); **Jean-Luc Maurette** (ten); **Michel Brodard** (bar); **Raimund Nolte** (bass); **Elzbieta Kalvelage** (pf); **Marcel Jorand** (perc); **Chorus Musicus/Christoph Spering** (harm). Opus 111 OPS30-70. Text and translations included. Recorded in 1992.
Book 2, "Album français"; Book 3, "Morceaux réservés" — Chant funèbre à Meyerbeer; Les amants de Séville; Ave Maria; Le chant des titans.

.·′ 1h 14m DDD 7/93 ᑫₚ

This is a very collectable CD. In the first place, it gives us not some arbitrary and ill-matched selection from Rossini's *Péchés de vieillesse*, but a charming gallimaufry of pieces that make up the *Album français*, plus four striking items from Rossini's *Morceaux réservés*. For the most part, it is Gallic music played and sung with in an authentic Gallic style. And that includes a splendid period Erard piano, expertly played by Elzbieta Kalvelage. There is also an Alexandre harmonium joining the piano in Rossini's exquisite *pastorale* "La Nuit de Noël" and in a spirited orchestra-less rendering of his strangely belligerent "Le chant des titans". The disc begins with the firefly brilliance of the *a cappella* "Toast pour le nouvel an" and ends with an exquisite short "Requiem". On the way, we have the desperate brilliance of "Roméo", a musical soliloquy

Berlioz might have been proud to own. Flirtatiousness and pathos sit side by side in "La grande Coquette" and the famous tenor and baritone duo "Un sou". And if that seems too lachrymose, relief is at hand in the form of a charming musical sorbet, "Chanson de Zora". Each of the soloists seems to be a natural Rossinian and Christoph Spering's Chorus Musicus are stylish and disciplined in the five choral pieces.

Rossini. Stabat mater. **Helen Field** (sop); **Della Jones** (mez); **Arthur Davies** (ten); **Roderick Earle** (bass); **London Symphony Chorus; City of London Sinfonia/Richard Hickox.** Chandos CHAN8780. Text and translation included. Recorded in 1989.

⏺ **59m DDD 3/90** ... ⁹ₚ ⁹ₛ Ⓑ

This used to be a ripe nineteenth-century favourite, and many a proudly-bound vocal score at present languishing in a pile of second-hand music would testify to a time when its owner felt enabled, with its help, to combine the pleasure of church-going with the duty of attendance at the opera. The words are those of Jacapone da Todi's sacred poem, but Rossini's music is dramatic, exciting and sometimes almost indecently tuneful. Certainly the soloists have to be recruited from the opera company; the soprano who launches out into the "Inflammatus" must be generously supplied with high Cs as well as the power to shoot them over the heads of full choir and orchestra, while the tenor at one alarming moment is asked for a top D flat and has to ring out the melody of his "Cujus animam" with tone to match the trumpets which introduce it. In all four soloists, grace and technical accomplishment are as important as range and power; they must also have the taste and discipline to work harmoniously as a quartet. In this recording they certainly do that, and neither are they lacking in range or technique; if there is a limitation it is rather in richness of tone and in the heroic quality which the solos mentioned above ideally need. Even so, individually and collectively, they compare well with most of their competitors on record, and the choral and orchestral work under Hickox is outstanding.

Additional recommendations ...
Soloists; Philharmonia Chorus and Orchestra/Carlo Maria Giulini. DG 410 034-2GH — ⏺ 1h 5m DDD 9/83 ⁹ₚ Ⓑ
Soloists; London Symphony Chorus and Orchestra/István Kertész. Decca Ovation 417 766-2DM — ⏺ 54m ADD 7/89 Ⓑ
Soloists; Bavarian Radio Chorus and Symphony Orchestra/Semyon Bychkov. Philips 426 312-2Ph — ⏺ 1h 5m DDD 3/91 ⁹ₚ Ⓑ

Rossini. Petite messe solennelle. **Helen Field** (sop); **Anne-Marie Owens** (mez); **Edmund Barham** (ten); **John Tomlinson** (bass); **David Nettle, Richard Markham** (pfs); **Peter King** (harmonium); **City of Birmingham Symphony Orchestra Chorus/Simon Halsey.** Conifer CDCF184. Text and translation included. Recorded in 1989.

⏺ **1h 18m DDD 10/90** ⁹ₚ ⁹ₛ

Of Rossini's later works, none has won such affection from the general listening public as the *Petite messe solennelle*. He called it "the final sin of my old age" and, as with the other of his *pêches de vieillesse*, he declined to have it published. Editions issued in 1869, the year after his death, failed to retain his original scoring and contained numerous inaccuracies, yet these have been the basis of most subsequent recordings of the work. This disc presents the mass in a revelatory new Oxford University Press edition by Nancy Fleming, using two pianos in addition to a fine, French harmonium. That alone would mark it out for prime consideration, even if the reading were only passable, but here we have the bonus of dedicated, heartfelt performances from all involved. Above all, the scale of the work is finely captured — it was intended for chamber performance and both writing and scoring reflect the intimacy of Rossini's ideas. Much praise must go to Simon Halsey for so clearly establishing the parameters for this performance, and to the recording engineers for making it all seem so convincing. The whole issue establishes a new benchmark for assessing recordings of this work.

Rossini. HEROINES. **Cecilia Bartoli** (mez); [a]**Chorus and Orchestra of the Teatro La Fenice, Venice/Ion Martin.** Decca 436 075-2DH. Recorded in 1991. Texts and translations included.

ZELMIRA — Riedi al soglio[a]. Le nozze di Teti e di Peleo — Ah, non potrian reistere.
MAOMETTO II — Ah! che invan su questo ciglio; Giusto ciel, in tal periglio[a]. LA DONNA
DEL LAGO — Tanti affetti in tal momento[a]. ELISABETTA, REGINA D'INGHILTERRA —
Quant' è grato all'alma mia[a]; Fellon, la penna avrai[a]. SEMIRAMIDE — Serenai vaghirai ... Bel
raggio lusinghier[a].

59m DDD 2/92

This sparkling disc brings together a collection of arias composed by Rossini for one of the great
prima donnas of the nineteenth century, who was also his wife, Isabella Colbran. It is tempting
to wonder whether even she had a voice to match that of Cecilia Bartoli, one of the most
luscious, most exciting voices in opera. All those dazzling chromatic runs, leaps, cadenzas and
cascading coloraturas are handled with consummate ease. Throughout, Bartoli sounds as if she's
enjoying the music; there is always an engaging smile in the voice, although she is properly
imperious in the extracts from *Elisabetta* and disarmingly simple in the prayerful "Giusto ciel, in
tal periglio" ("Righteous heaven in such danger") from *Maometto II*. The orchestral and choral
forces bring a delightful intimacy to the proceedings, with some cheeky woodwind solos and
fruity brass passages. The recording, produced at the Teatro La Fenice by Decca veteran
Christopher Raeburn, favours the voices but gives it just enough distance to accommodate high
Cs and astounding A flats at the bottom of the range. The orchestral perspective is changeable
but satisfactory. For Rossini and Bartoli fans alike, this disc is a must.

New review

Rossini. IL SIGNOR BRUSCHINO. **Samuel Ramey** (bass) Gaudenzio; **Claudio Desderi**
(bar) Bruschino padre; **Kathleen Battle** (sop) Sofia; **Frank Lopardo** (ten) Florville; **Michele
Pertusi** (bass) Filiberto; **Jennifer Larmore** (mez) Marianna; **Octavio Arévalo** (ten)
Bruschino figlio, Commissario; **English Chamber Orchestra/Ion Marin.** DG 435 865-2GH.
Notes, text and translation included. Recorded in 1991.

1h 16m DDD 12/93

Witty and sentimental but also at times hair-raisingly cruel, *Il Signor Bruschino* is the last, and
arguably the best, of the one-acters Rossini wrote for the tiny Teatro San Moisè in Venice
between 1810 and January 1813. These early *farse* can get by on tolerably good singing. What
they absolutely can't do without is first-rate conducting — and, on record, clear, sharply
defined orchestral sound. Choosing between the conducting of DG's Ion Marin and Claves's
Marcello Viotti isn't all that difficult. Marin is far more vital; and what a cast there is on DG
— a cast so expert and experienced they can't fail to bring the score wonderfully to life.
Central to the whole enterprise is the Bruschino of Desderi, a superbly rounded portrait of a
man who, despite the sweltering heat and the machinations of everyone around him, finally
gives as good as he gets. Ramey's portrait of Gaudenzio is masterly, acted with relish and richly
sung. Battle gives a ravishing account of Sofia's aria "Ah!, donate il caro sposo" with its cor
anglais colourings. This *Bruschino* is probably the one to have. Whatever reservations one may
occasionally have about the conducting and the focus of the recording, it is difficult to imagine a
better-cast account.

Additional recommendations:
Soloists; Turin Philharmonic Orchestra/Marcello Viotti. Claves CD50-8904/5 —
② 1h 24m DDD 10/89
Soloists; Warsaw Chamber Opera Orchestra/Jacek Kaspszyk. Pavane ADW7158 —
1h 12m DDD 5/93

Rossini. IL TURCO IN ITALIA. **Simone Alaimo** (bar) Selim; **Sumi Jo** (sop) Fiorilla;
Enrico Fissore (bar) Geronio; **Raúl Giménez** (ten) Narciso; **Susanne Mentzer** (mez) Zaida;
Peter Bronder (ten) Albazar; **Alessandro Corbelli** (bar) Prosdocimo; **Ambrosian Opera
Chorus; Academy of St Martin in the Fields/Sir Neville Marriner.** Philips 434 128-
2PH2. Notes, text and translation included. Recorded in 1991.

② 2h 34m DDD 12/92

The audience at the première of *Il turco in Italia*, given in 1814 at La Scala in Milan, presumed
(wrongly) that Rossini was recycling material for what was essentially *L'italiana in Algeri* in

another guise. The notion has stuck with the opera, and its reputation has not been helped by the fact that Rossini delegated much of the work on the *secco* recitative and arias. In fact, and in contrast to *L'italiana*, *Il turco* is a surprisingly searching piece of psychological drama, given the seemingly trivial and prejudiced nature of its subject matter, and it very much benefits from the insight that repeated listening on CD, with commentary and translation, can supply. It depends for its effect on ensembles, rather than finding its dramatic and emotional heart in the solo arias and so, inevitably, the chief star of this performance must be Sir Neville Marriner, as the skilful development of the drama rests chiefly in his hands. The soloists are generally first rate. Although Sumi Jo is not perhaps as forceful or acerbic a Fiorilla as Caballé or Callas in their recordings of this work, she is nevertheless a highly skilled performer who makes her entrance with delicate phrasing and sweet tone. Alaimo, Corbelli and Fissore bring a particularly distinguished solidity to the casting. Captured in a clean, unfussy recording, the result is enthralling. Typically for a Rossini opera, recording *Il turco* has not been without its problems of deciding which version of the text to use. This issue scores heavily because it finds a happy balance of theatrical necessity and authenticity. The opera's music that is not by Rossini has been pruned and the result added to in order to develop the dramatic pacing. But in the end it is the overall quality of this performance that carries the day.

Additional recommendations ...
Soloists; Chorus and Orchestra of La Scala, Milan/Gianandrea Gavazzeni. EMI mono CDS7 49344-8 — .·˙ ② lh 53m ADD 12/87 ⁹ₚ ▲
Soloists; Ambrosian Opera Chorus; National Philharmonia Orchestra/Riccardo Chailly. CBS Masterworks CD37859 — .·˙ ② 2h 26m DDD 9/89

<u>New review</u>
Rossini. IL BARBIERE DI SIVIGLIA. **Roberto Servile** (bar) Figaro; **Sonia Ganassi** (mez) Rosina; **Ramon Vargas** (ten) Almaviva; **Angelo Romero** (bar) Doctor Bartolo; **Franco de Grandis** (bass) Don Basilio; **Ingrid Kertesi** (sop) Berta; **Kázmér Sarkany** (bass) Fiorello; **Hungarian Radio Chorus; Failoni Chamber Orchestra, Budapest/Will Humburg.** Naxos 8 660027/9. Notes and text included.

③ 2h 38m DDD 3/94 ⁹ₚ Ⓑ

Not everyone will approve, but there are ways in which this super-budget recording of *Il barbiere di Siviglia* puts to shame just about every other version of the opera there has yet been. Those it may not please are specialist vocal collectors for whom *Il barbiere* is primarily a repository of vocal test pieces, a kind of musical Badminton. If, on the other hand, you regard *Il barbiere* (Rossini, ex-Beaumarchais) as a gloriously subversive music drama — vibrant, scurrilous, unstoppably vital — then the new set is guaranteed to give a great deal of pleasure. 'Performance' is the key word here. Humburg is described in the Naxos booklet as "Conductor and Recitative Director"; and for once the recitatives really are part of the larger drama. The result is a meticulously produced, often very funny, brilliantly integrated performance that you will almost certainly find yourself listening to as a stage play — rather than an opera with eminently missable (often arbitrarily abbreviated) recitatives. With a virtually all-Italian cast, the results are a revelation. The erotic allure of the duet "Dunque io son" is striking, arising as it does here out of the brilliantly played teasing of Rosina by Figaro about her new admirer. Similarly, Don Basilio's Calumny aria, superbly sung by Franco de Grandis, a black-browed bass from Turin who was singing for Karajan, Muti and Abbado while still in his twenties. This takes on added character and colour from the massive sense of panic created by de Grandis and the admirable Dr Bartolo of Angelo Romero when Basilio comes in with news of Almaviva's arrival in town. The Overture is done with evident relish, the playing of the Failoni Chamber Orchestra (a group from within the Hungarian State Opera Orchestra) nothing if not articulate. Aided by a clear, forward recording, a *sine qua non* with musical comedy, the cast communicates the Rossini/ Sterbini text — solo arias, ensembles, recitatives—with tremendous relish. They are never hustled by Humburg, nor are they spared: the *stretta* of the Act 1 finale is a model of hyper-tension and clarity. It would have been nice to have an English version of the libretto, but you can't have everything at rock-bottom prices and Naxos do provide an excellent track-by-track synopsis. Super-Scrooges might complain that 158 minutes of music could have been shoe-horned on to two CDs, but three CDs is a fair deal for a complete *Il barbiere*, and the layout is first-rate. This *Il barbiere* jumps to the top of the pile in a single leap. As operatic pole-vaulters, this puts Naxos in the Olympic class

Additional recommendations ...

Soloists; Ambrosian Opera Chorus; Academy of St Martin in the Fields/Sir Neville Marriner with **Nicholas Kraemer** (fp). Philips 411 058-2PH3 — ·.·' ③ 2h 27m DDD 4/84 ⁹ₚ Ⓑ

Soloists; Philharmonia Chorus and Orchestra/Alceo Galliera. EMI CDS7 47634-8 — ·.·' ② 2h 10m ADD 6/87 ⁹ₚ Ⓑ ▲

Soloists; Chorus and Orchestra of La Scala, Milan/Riccardo Chailly. CBS Masterworks CD37862 — ·.·' ③ 2h 35m DDD 9/88 Ⓑ

Soloists; Chorus and Orchestra of the Teatro Communale, Bologna/Giuseppe Patanè. Decca 425 520-2DH3 — ·.·' ③ 2h 41m DDD 9/89 Ⓑ

Soloists; Glyndebourne Festival Chorus; Royal Philharmonic Orchestra/Vittorio Gui. EMI Rossini Edition CMS7 64162-2 — ·.·' ② 2h 21m ADD 5/92 ⁹ₚ Ⓑ

Soloists; Chorus of the Teatro La Fenice, Venice; Chamber Orchestra of Europe/Claudio Abbado. DG 435 763-2GH — ·.·' ③ 2h 35m DDD 12/92 Ⓑ

Soloists; Chorus; Orchestra della Toscana/Gianluigi Gelmetti. EMI CDS7 54863-2 — ·.·' ③ 2h 20m DDD 11/93 ⁹ₚ Ⓑ

Rossini. L'ITALIANA IN ALGERI. **Marilyn Horne** (mez) Isabella; **Ernesto Palacio** (ten) Lindoro; **Domenico Trimarchi** (bar) Taddeo; **Samuel Ramey** (bass) Mustafà; **Kathleen Battle** (sop) Elvira; **Clara Foti** (mez) Zulma; **Nicola Zaccaria** (bass) Haly; **Prague Philharmonic Chorus; I Solisti Veneti/Claudio Scimone.** Erato Libretto 2292-45404-2. Notes and text included. From STU7 1394 (3/81). Recorded in 1980.

·.·' ② **2h 20m ADD 1/92**

Written within the space of a month during the spring of 1813, and with help from another anonymous hand, Rossini's *L'italiana in Algeri* was an early success, and one which went on to receive many performances during the nineteenth century, with an increasingly corrupt text. A complete reconstruction was undertaken by Azio Corghi and published in 1981; this recording uses this new edition which corresponds most closely to what was actually performed in Venice in 1813. *L'italiana* is one of Rossini's wittiest operas, featuring as did a number of his most successful works a bewitching central character, in this case Isabella, who makes fun of her various suitors, with the opera ending with a happy escape with her beloved, Lindoro, a typical *tenorino* role. This fine recording on Erato has plenty of vocal polish. Scimone's biggest asset is Marilyn Horne as Isabella: possibly the finest Rossini singer of her generation and a veteran in this particular role, she sings Rossini's demanding music with great virtuosity and polish. Her liquid tone and artful phrasing ensure that she is a continuous pleasure to listen to. She is strongly supported by the rest of the cast: Kathleen Battle is a beguiling Elvira, Domenico Trimarchi a most humorous Taddeo, and Samuel Ramey a sonorous Bey of Algiers — Isabella's opponent and pursuer. Ernesto Palacio's Lindoro, however, has patches of white tone and is correct rather than inspiring. Scimone's conducting is likewise efficient if at times slightly lacking in sparkle. It is, however, guaranteed to give considerable pleasure.

Rossini. LA CENERENTOLA. **Teresa Berganza** (mez) Angelina; **Luigi Alva** (ten) Don Ramiro; **Renato Capecchi** (bar) Dandini; **Paolo Montarsolo** (bar) Don Magnifico; **Margherita Guglielmi** (sop) Clorinda; **Laura Zannini** (contr) Tisbe; **Ugo Trama** (bass) Alidoro; **Scottish Opera Chorus; London Symphony Orchestra/Claudio Abbado.** DG 423 861-2GH2. Notes, text and translation included. From 2709 039 (6/72). Recorded 1971.

·.·' ② **2h 24m ADD 9/86** ⁹ₚ Ⓑ

Rossini's Cinderella is a fairy-tale without a fairy, but no less bewitching for the absence of a magic wand. In fact the replacement of the winged godmother with the philanthropic Alidoro, a close friend and adviser of our prince, Don Ramiro, plus the lack of any glass slippers and the presence of a particularly unsympathetic father character, makes the whole story more plausible. *La Cenerentola*, Angelina, is more spunky than the average pantomime Cinders, not too meek to complain about her treatment or to beg to be allowed to go to the ball. She herself gives Don Ramiro one of her pair of bracelets, charging him to find the owner of the matching ornament and thus taking in hand the control of her own destiny. Along the way, Don Ramiro and his valet Dandini change places, leading to plenty of satisfyingly operatic confusion and difficult situations. This recording, when originally transferred to CD, was spread across three discs, but it has now been comfortably fitted into two. It gives a sparkling rendition of the score with a lovely light touch and well-judged tempos from Abbado and the London Symphony Orchestra and virtuoso vocal requirements are fully met by the cast. The chief delight is Teresa Berganza's Angelina, gloriously creamy in tone and as warm as she is precise. The supporting cast is full of character, with Luigi Alva a princely Don Ramiro, Margherita Guglielmi and Laura Zannini an affected and fussy pair of sisters, and Renato Capecchi as Dandini, gleeful and mischievous as he takes on being prince for a day. Although the recording was made in 1972 it has survived its technological transfers more than usually well.

Additional recommendations ...
Soloists; West German Radio Choir; Cappella Coloniensis/Gabriele Ferro. Sony Classical S2K46433 — .·' ② 2h 28m ADD 6/91 ⁹ₚ Ⓑ
Soloists; Glyndebourne Festival Chorus and Orchestra/Vittorio Gui. EMI Rossini Edition mono CMS7 64183-2 — .·' ② 1h 57m ADD 5/92 ⁹ₚ Ⓑ ▲
Soloists; Chorus and Orchestra of the Maggio Musicale, Florence/Oliviero de Fabritiis. Decca Grand Opera 433 030-2DM2 — .·' ② 2h 25m ADD 5/92 ⁹ₚ Ⓑ
Soloists; Bologna Teatro Communale Chorus and Orchestra/Riccardo Chailly. Decca 436 902-2DHO2 — .·' ② 2h 28m DDD 11/93 ⁹ₛ Ⓑ

Rossini. SEMIRAMIDE. **Dame Joan Sutherland** (sop) Semiramide; **Marilyn Horne** (mez) Arsace; **Joseph Rouleau** (bass) Assur; **John Serge** (ten) Idreno; **Patricia Clark** (sop) Azema; **Spiro Malas** (bass) Oroe; **Michael Langdon** (bass) Ghost of Nino; **Leslie Fryson** (ten) Mitrane; **Ambrosian Opera Chorus; London Symphony Orchestra/Richard Bonynge.** Decca 425 481-2DM3. Notes, text and translation included. From SET317/19 (10/66). Recorded in 1966.

.·' ③ 2h 48m ADD 2/90 — ⁹ₚ

Wagner thought it represented all that was bad about Italian opera and Kobbe's *Complete Opera Book* proclaimed that it had had its day — but then added what looked like second thoughts, saying that "were a soprano and contralto to appear in conjunction in the firmament the opera might be successfully revived". That was exactly what happened in the 1960s, when both Sutherland and Horne were in superlative voice and, with Richard Bonynge, were taking a prominent part in the reintroduction of so many nineteenth-century operas which the world thought it had outgrown. This recording brought a good deal of enlightenment in its time. For one thing, here was vocal music of such 'impossible' difficulty being sung with brilliance by the two principal women and with considerable skill by the men, less well-known as they were. Then it brought to many listeners the discovery that, so far from being a mere show-piece, the opera contained ensembles that possessed quite compelling dramatic intensity. People who had heard of the duet "Giorno d'orroré" (invariably encored in Victorian times) were surprised to find it remarkably unshowy and even expressive of the ambiguous feelings of mother and son in their extraordinary predicament. It will probably be a long time before this recording is superseded, admirably vivid as it is in sound, finely conducted and magnificently sung.

New review
Rossini. IL VIAGGIO A REIMS. **Sylvia McNair** (sop) Corinna; **Cheryl Studer** (sop) Madama Cortese; **Luciana Serra** (sop) Contessa di Folleville; **Lucia Valentini Terrani** (mez) Marchesa Melibea; **Raúl Giménez** (ten) Cavalier Belfiore; **William Matteuzzi** (ten) Conte di Libenskof; **Samuel Ramey** (bass) Lord Sidney; **Ruggero Raimondi** (bass) Don Profondo; **Enzo Dara** (bar) Barone di Trombonok; **Giorgio Surian** (bar) Don Prudenzio; **Lucio Gallo** (bar) Don Alvaro; **Berlin Radio Chorus; Berlin Philharmonic Orchestra/Claudio Abbado.** Sony Classical S2K53336. Notes, text and translation included. Recorded live in 1992.

.·' ② 2h 15m DDD 12/93 — ⁹ₚ ⁹ₛ

The rediscovery of Rossini's dazzling, sophisticated coronation entertainment *Il viaggio a Reims* was one of the musical highlights of the 1980s; and it was Abbado's DG recording that brought the work to the public at large (it was voted *Gramophone*'s Record of the Year in 1986). No one who already has the DG recording need feel compelled to go out and buy the Sony. After all, the music is the same, and so are no fewer than six of the 11 principal singers. Of the singers who are repeating their roles, both Ramey and Dara now surpass their already superb earlier performances. Dara has transformed the aria in which Baron Trombonok catalogues national foibles. What was previously more or less a straight recitation is now a miracle of subversive inflexion, with Abbado and the Berlin players adding wonderful new colours that seem to lie dormant in the earlier recording. When it comes to new singers, the Sony set has its weaknesses. Not Gallo. His Don Alvaro is less cumbersome than Nucci's on DG. Nor perhaps Serra as the fashion-crazed young French widow. But for Count Libenskof DG's Francisco Araiza is far more in command of the role than William Matteuzzi. On balance, though, new collectors will be better off with the new Sony, and it is better recorded.

Additional recommendation ...
Soloists; Prague Philharmonic Chorus; Chamber Orchestra of Europe/Claudio Abbado. DG 415 498-2GH2 — .·ʼ ③ 2h 16m DDD 1/86 ⁹ₚ ⁹ₛ

Rossini. GUILLAUME TELL. **Gabriel Bacquier** (bar) Guillaume Tell; **Montserrat Caballé** (sop) Mathilde; **Nicolai Gedda** (ten) Arnold; **Kolos Kovacs** (bass) Walter Furst; **Gwynne Howell** (bass) Melcthal; **Mady Mesplé** (sop) Jemmy; **Jocelyne Taillon** (mez) Hedwige; **Louis Hendrikx** (bass) Gessler; **Charles Burles** (ten) Fisherman; **Ricardo Cassinelli** (ten) Rudolph; **Nicholas Christou** (bar) Leuthold; **Ambrosian Opera Chorus; Royal Philharmonic Orchestra/Lamberto Gardelli.** EMI CMS7 69951-2. Notes and text included. From SLS970 (11/73). Recorded in 1972.

.·ʼ ④ **3h 58m ADD 3/89**

Rossini's last opera was not only his grandest but also the very epitome of operatic grandeur. In length alone it involves a formidable commitment, but more fundamental are the span of the scenes, the amplitude of the forces employed and the range of mood and feeling from simple rustic happiness to a passionate affirmation of liberty hard-won in the face of cruelty and personal loss. Near the end of the whole epic work, as the sky clears, literally and figuratively, there comes a passage of inspired sublimity, with an effect worthy of *Fidelio*; it also is built with Rossini's favourite device of the crescendo, but having its excitement now transfigured and ennobled, so that even if Rossini had composed more operas one feels he could hardly have gone beyond this. Though frequently given in Italian, it was written to a French text and the language gives a strong initial advantage to this recording over its notable rivals. Among the principals Bacquier is a dignified, elderly-sounding Tell, Caballé a tender yet patrician Mathilde, Gedda a lyrical Arnold who fortifies his voice manfully for the heroic passages. Gardelli conducts with control and flexibility; the orchestral playing and chorus work are alike admirable, as are the clarity and sense of presence in the recorded sound.

Further listening ...

Messa di gloria. **Sumi Jo** (sop); **Ann Murray** (mez); **Raúl Giménez, Francisco Araiza** (tens); **Samuel Ramey** (bass); **Academy of St Martin in the Fields Chorus and Orchestra/Sir Neville Marriner.** Philips 434 132-2PH (12/92).

Piano Works — Danse sibérienne. Péchés de vieillesse, Book 5 — Thème naïf et variations idem. Péchés de vieillesse, Book 6 — Une caresse à ma femme; Barcarolle in E flat major; Un petit train de plaisir. Péchés de vieillesse, Book 7 — Petite valse, "L'huile de Ricin". Péchés de vieillesse, Book 9 — Marche et réminiscences pour mon dernier voyage. Péchés de vieillesse, Book 10 — Petit caprice (style Offenbach). Petite promenade de Passy à Courbevoie. **Helge Antoni** (pf). Etcetera KTC1107 (11/91).

Giovanna d'Arco. *Songs* — Ariette à l'ancienne. Beltà crudele. Canzonetta spagnuola. Il risentimento. Il trovatore. L'âme délaissée. L'Orpheline du Tyrol. La Grande Coquette. La légende de Marguerite. La pastorella. La regate veneziana. Mi lagnerò. Nizza. **Cecilia Bartoli** (mez); **Charles Spencer** (pf). Decca 430 518-2DH (4/91).

L'OCCASIONE FA IL LADRO. **Soloists; English Chamber Orchestra/Marcello Viotti.** Claves CD50-9208/9 (5/93).

LA PIETRA DEL PARAGONE. **Soloists; New York Clarion Concerts Chorus and Orchestra/Newell Jenkins.** Vanguard Classics 08903173 (12/92).

OTELLO. **Soloists; Ambrosian Opera Chorus; Philharmonia Orchestra/Jesús López-Cobos.** Philips 432 456-2PM2 (12/92).

ARMIDA. **Soloists; Ambrosian Opera Chorus; I Solisti Veneti/Claudio Scimone.** Europa Musica 350211 (12/91).

LA GAZZA LADRA. **Soloists; Prague Philharmonic Choir; Turin Radio Symphony Orchestra/Gianluigi Gelmetti.** Sony Classical MK45850 (10/90).

MOSE IN EGITTO. **Soloists; Ambrosian Opera Chorus; Philharmonia Orchestra/ Claudio Scimone.** Philips 420 109-2PM2 (12/92).

LA DONNA DEL LAGO. **Soloists; Prague Philharmonic Chorus; Chamber Orchestra of Europe/Maurizio Pollini.** CBS Masterworks CD39311 (8/88).

LE COMTE ORY. **Soloists; Chorus and Orchestra of Lyon Opera/John Eliot Gardiner.** Philips 422 406-2PH2 (10/89).

Nino Rota

Italian 1911-1979

New review

Rota. FILM MUSIC. **Monte-Carlo Philharmonic Orchestra/Gianluigi Gelmetti.** EMI CDC7 54528-2. Recorded in 1991.
War and Peace — Introduction; Natasha's Waltz; La rosa di Novgorod; Finale. Il gattopardo — Allegro maestoso; Allegro impetuoso; Sostenuto appassionato. La strada — Country wedding; The three musicians and the "Madman" on the tightrope; Rumba. The circus — The jugglers; Zampano's anger; Zampano kills the "Madman"; The last show in the snow; Zampano alone and in tears. Waterloo — Andante eroico: Tempo di Valzer; Andante con moto: Alla marcia.

Ih   DDD   3/93

Refined musicians have been known to splutter with rage at the mention of Nino Rota's name because of the use to which he put Bruckner's Seventh in Visconti's movie *Senso*. This disc is something of an oddity, in that it contains layers of adaptation. The movements from Rota's score for King Vidor's lumbering *War and Peace* were made for a concert in London in the 1970s, and have had some extra passages taken from the film and tacked on to make this recorded sequence. Then *La strada* is not the film score, but a ballet that Rota composed some years after the film. Having done his utmost with Bruckner, Rota used one of his own symphonies as the basis for the music for Visconti's *The Leopard*. A melody winding under the opening suggests some great Verdi aria — the jump from this lush romanticism to the merry vaudeville sounds at the opening of *La strada* is a leap not only into the twentieth century, but into a more recognizable Rota score. *La strada* was considered by many to be Fellini's masterpiece, and he provided the scenario for Rota's ballet which was given at La Scala in 1966. People with but a passing interest in film music should not be put off by this record's title, for the *Strada* ballet is much more than an ephemeral suite from a movie. With much sparer orchestration and unshackled from the demands imposed upon a composer by the editor's stop-watch, *La strada* is one of the best Rota scores on record. Attractive though his pastiche music is for the big historical blockbusters that make up the rest of this disc, Rota was at his most characterful in the neo-realistic world of Fellini's modern satires.

Further listening ...

THE SYMPHONIC FELLINI/ROTA — *Film Scores:* Lo Sceicco Bianco. I Vitelloni. La Strada. Il Bidone. Le Notte di Cabiria. La Dolce Vita. Boccaccio '70. Otto e Mezzo. Giulietta degli Spiriti. Fellini Satyricon. I Clowns. Roma. Amarcord. Casanova. Prova d'orchestra. **Czech Symphony Orchestra/Derek Wadsworth.** Silva Screen FILMCD129 (10/93).

Hans Rott

Suggested listening ...

Symphony in E major. **Cincinnati Philharmonic Orchestra/Gerhard Samuel.** Hyperion CDA66366 (12/89).

Albert Roussel

Roussel. Symphonies — No. 1 in D minor, Op. 7, "Le poème de la forêt"; No. 3 in G minor, Op. 42. **French National Orchestra/Charles Dutoit.** Erato 2292-45254-2. From NUM75283 (2/87).

`59m DDD 6/87`

Roussel's First Symphony is not a symphony in the usual sense at all, but more a cycle of four tone-poems. When the first of these, "Soir d'été", was performed Roussel did not envisage any further seasonal depictions of nature, but after "Renouveau" was written it was quickly followed by "Forêt d'hiver" and "Faunes et Dryades" — this last piece having autumnal connotations to complete Roussel's own 'Four Seasons'. The completed Symphony was Roussel's first major orchestral work, and although it is more romantic than his later works it already has characteristic fingerprints in his use of the orchestra. The Third Symphony is a very outgoing work in conventional four movement form, with characteristic 'motor' rhythms, and breezy, rather terse melodies — except in the *Scherzo*, which almost has the air of a jaunty popular song. Dutoit's performances are quite admirable in their clarity and understanding of Roussel's contrasted styles. The orchestra have just the right timbre and the recording is superb.

Roussel. Symphonies — No. 2 in B flat major, Op. 23; No. 4 in A major, Op. 53. **French National Orchestra/Charles Dutoit.** Erato 2292-45253-2.

`1h DDD 6/87`

This disc couples one of Roussel's most often-played symphonies with one of his least. The Fourth Symphony is a late work written only a few years before his death, and is a delightful score, the product of a richly-stocked imagination. It has a dark and powerful slow movement, a most infectiously engaging scherzo and a captivating finale. The Second Symphony is a rarity. It is abundantly resourceful and full of colour, and the scoring is refined and opulent. Dutoit gets playing of great vitality from this great French orchestra, dynamic markings are scrupulously observed but it is not just the letter but the spirit of the score that is well served. The Erato engineers do full justice to the dark and richly-detailed orchestral textures and the sound is particularly imposing in the definition of the bottom end of the register. Not to be missed.

Roussel. La Festin de l'arraigneé — ballet[a]. Symphonies[b] — No. 3 in G minor, Op. 42; No. 4 in A major, Op. 53. **Suisse Romande Orchestra/Ernest Ansermet.** Decca Ovation 433 719-2DM. From LXT5234 (1/57). Item marked [a] recorded in 1954, [b] 1956.

`1h 15m ADD`

Roussel. Symphonies — No. 3 in G minor, Op. 42; No. 4 in A major, Op. 53. **Lamoureux Concerts/Charles Munch.** Erato 2292-45687-2. From ERA9515 (7/78). Recorded in 1965.

`48m ADD`

Nobody would choose these recordings for glamorous orchestral tone or state of the art sound. But the narrow frequency range of the Erato recording in no way detracts from the power and sweep of Charles Munch's readings of Roussel's two finest symphonies. Both works date from the 1930s and under Munch their almost irreconcilable moods of mechanistic power, dark disquiet, brief oases of calm and cheerful indifference are fully explored and yet add up to a convincing whole. Ernest Ansermet wrote of Roussel that "his melodies pass from one instrument to another, crossing a variety of orchestral textures, where they risk being lost". In Ansermet's recordings of the symphonies, which date from 1956, he ensures that nothing is lost. The textual clarity and rhythmic precision, enduring hallmarks of his best recordings, are invaluable for getting to grips with Roussel's methods and from there to his message. Hallmarks that are just as vital for the minimal detailing and delicacy of Roussel's earlier (1913) ballet *La Festin de l'arraigneé* ("The Spider's Banquet"), a generous addition to Ansermet's disc.

Further listening ...

Bacchus et Ariane — ballet. **Orchestre de Paris/Charles Dutoit.** Erato 2292-45278-2 (9/88).

Bacchus et Ariane — Ballet Suite No. 2[b]. *Coupled with* **Ravel.** Daphnis et Chloé[a]. [a]**New England Conservatory Chorus; [a]Alumni Chorus; Boston Symphony Orchestra/ Charles Munch.** RCA Victor Gold Seal [a]stereo/[b]mono GD60469 (12/91).

Joseph-Nicolas-Pancrace Royer
French c.1705-1755

New review
Royer. Pièces de clavecin. La Chasse de Zaïde. **Christophe Rousset** (hpd). L'Oiseau-Lyre 436 127-2OH. Recorded in 1991.

59m DDD 9/93

Pancrace Royer was a more prominent figure in French musical life than the comparative unfamiliarity of his name nowadays would suggest. He was an imaginative director of the Concert Spirituel, leader for several years of the Opéra orchestra, and a successful composer for the stage. His ballet-héroïque, *Zaïde* (1739) was especially popular and was still being performed in the 1760s. *La Chasse de Zaïde* is the composer's own harpsichord arrangement of a "symphonie" in the opera and, in this new recital, Christophe Rousset appends it to the pieces of the 1746 publication. Royer's music is not on a level with that of Rameau, his illustrious older contemporary, but it is neither dull or predictable; and it sometimes recalls Rameau's idiom, especially in the more delicately wrought pieces such as the wistful "La Zaïde" which hints at the latter's "Les Tendres Plaintes". Royer could be quite an adventurous harmonist — another quality which he shared with Rameau — and he proves this in a wild piece, "Le Vertigo", full of extravagant gestures and excitement generated by vigorously repeated chordal passages, *tirades*, rhythmic interruptions and so forth. Indeed, its distinctly improvisatory character foreshadows C.P.E. Bach. Rousset responds to these extremes of temperament with passion on the one hand and sensibility on the other. The beautifully recorded, fine sounding harpsichord is a 1751 instrument by the Parisian maker, Hemsch.

Miklós Rózsa
Hungarian/American 1907-

New review
Rózsa. ORCHESTRAL WORKS. **New Zealand Symphony Orchestra/James Sedares.** Koch International Classics 37191-2. Recorded in 1992.
Theme, Variations and Finale, Op. 13*a*. Hungarian Nocturne, Op. 28. Three Hungarian Sketches, Op. 14. Overture to a Symphony Concert, Op. 26*a*.

57m DDD 9/93

The fervent Magyar rhythms that captivated Rózsa during his upbringing in Hungary spice almost every bar of his music for both concert-hall and screen, but strikingly so in his early non-film work. The *Theme, Variations and Finale* from 1933 was inspired by a wistful melody that came to him after leaving his family and homeland for Paris. Tightly structured and bustling with youthful energy, it illustrates perfectly how Rózsa's rhapsodic intensity and flair for dramatic shading would soon lead to a remarkable career in Hollywood (Variation No. 4 could have come straight from one of the many *films noirs* he later scored during the 1940s). Similarly flavourful and just as vigorously rhythmic are the *Three Hungarian Sketches* (1938), whilst the balmy, moonlit *Hungarian Nocturne* (1964), reminiscent of his impressionistic score for *Lust for Life*, is the composer's attempt "to recapture the rare beauty of the nights on our estate in rural Hungary". The composition of the turbulent Overture coincided with the Hungarian revolution in 1957. Sedares and the NZSO are remarkably intuitive and, in the composer's own words "combine passion with discipline in exactly the way my music demands". Add to this a clean, full-bodied recording and no further endorsement is required.

New review
Rózsa. Symphony in Three Movements, Op. 6a. The Vintner's Daughter, Op. 23a. **New Zealand Symphony Orchestra/James Sedares.** Koch International Classics 37244-2. Recorded in 1993.

· · ♪ 56m DDD 6/94 ♀ₚ

Written in 1930, when the composer was 23, Rózsa deemed the Symphony a failure, and after several attempts to pare down its length he eventually cast it aside completely. However, in 1993 with the aid of Christopher Palmer, the surviving portions of his manuscript were dusted off once again and edited into the 39-minute work premièred here. The ambitious structure and expansive canvas used for the volatile 19-minute opening movement is particularly impressive, with Rózsa fusing two memorable themes (one vigorously heroic, the other strongly nostalgic) into a compelling, well-argued piece that possesses the direct intensity and emotion of his film scores, and could well stand on its own. The second movement is a misty, reflective *andante* for strings, whilst the energetic finale is charged with the furious dancing rhythms so redolent of Rózsa's beloved Hungary. *The Vintner's Daughter* (1953) makes a lovely and revealing companion. Here the youthful zeal and bold, dramatic gestures that define the Symphony have matured into a sensitive command of orchestral colour. Through 12 enchanting variations, each one more beguiling than the last, Rózsa illuminates Juste Olivier's nineteenth-century poem in delicate, sun-bleached shades, crowning the piece with a nocturne liberally sprinkled with stardust. James Sedares and the NZSO prove exemplary interpreters of this composer's music. Rózsa himself endorses the "fire and passion" they undoubtedly bring to the Symphony (aided by warm and beefy sound), but their eloquent shading of the 12 variations also deserves the highest praise.

Further listening ...

Film Scores — The Red House — Suite[a]; The Thief of Bagdad — The love of the princess; The Lost Weekend — Suite; The Four Feathers — Sunstroke/River journey; Double Indemnity — Mrs Dietrichson/The conspiracy; Knights of the Round Table — Hawks in flight; The Jungle Book — Song of the jungle[a]; Spellbound — The dream sequence, The mountain lodge; Ivanhoe — Overture. [a]**Ambrosian Singers; National Philharmonic Orchestra/Charles Gerhardt.** RCA Victor GD80911 (5/91).

Lust for Life — Suite. Background to Violence — Suite. **Frankenland State Symphony Orchestra/Miklós Rózsa.** Varèse Sarabande VSD5405 (10/93).

Edmund Rubbra

British 1901-1986

New review
Rubbra. String Quartet No. 2 in E flat major.
Tate. String Quartet in F major.
P. Wishart. String Quartet No. 3 in A major. **English Quartet** (Diana Cummings, Keith Lewis, vns; Luciano Iorio, va; Geoffrey Thomas, vc). Tremula TREM102-2. Recorded in 1992.

· · ♪ 1h 9m DDD 12/93 ♀ₚ ♀ₛ

The word 'masterpiece' may apply to the Rubbra, to its first and third movements at least, those in which he most overtly evokes Beethoven but also most demonstrates his own individuality. Two of Rubbra's other characteristics, at least as important, are a lyrical fantasy that adds grace to the sobriety of his first *allegro*, and a noble melodic breadth that makes the slow *Cavatina* resonate in the memory for days. Wishart's piece is not of this stature, but it is 'well-made' in the good rather than the patronizing sense of that word; its craftsmanship is satisfying, not arid. Phyllis Tate's most accomplished works come mostly from a little later, but the second movement of this piece, in which a wistful tune and a fragment of ostinato suggest a lyrical intermezzo but are then built to music of considerable power and intensity, and the third, which similarly hints (it is marked *grazioso*) at a quite gentle, English ('feminine', even?) scherzo, before launching with great vigour into music of Shostakovich-like ferocity, are characteristic. The performances of all three works are first-rate, the recording exemplary.

Further listening …

Violin Concerto, Op. 103[a]. [a]**Carl Pini** (vn); [b]**Geoffrey Tozer** (pf); **Melbourne Symphony Orchestra/David Measham.** *Coupled with* **Ireland.** Piano Concerto in E flat major[b]. Unicorn-Kanchana DKPCD9056 (1/87).

Symphonies — No. 2 in D major, Op. 45[a]; No. 7 in C major, Op. 88[b]. Festival Overture, Op. 62[c]. [ac]**New Philharmonia Orchestra/Vernon Handley;** [b]**London Philharmonic Orchestra/Sir Adrian Boult.** Lyrita SRCD235 (12/92).

Symphonies — No. 3, Op. 49; No. 4, Op. 53. A Tribute, Op. 56. Resurgam — Overture, Op. 149. **Philharmonia Orchestra/Norman Del Mar.** Lyrita SRCD202 (11/90).

Symphonies — No. 6, Op. 80[a]; No. 8, Op. 132, "Hommage à Teilhard de Chardin". Soliloquy, Op. 57[b]. [b]**Rohan de Saram** (vc); [b]**London Symphony Orchestra/Vernon Handley;** [a]**Philharmonia Orchestra/Norman Del Mar.** Lyrita SRCD234 (10/92).

Symphony No. 10, "Sinfonia da camera", Op. 145. Improvisations on Virginal Pieces by Giles Farnaby, Op. 50. A Tribute, Op. 56. **Bournemouth Sinfonietta/Hans-Hubert Schönzeler.** Chandos CHAN6599 (11/93).

Anton Rubinstein

Russian 1829-1894

Suggested listening …

Piano Concertos — No. 1 in E major, Op. 25; No. 2 in F major, Op. 35. **Joseph Banowetz** (pf); **Košice State Philharmonic Orchestra/Alfred Walter.** Marco Polo 8 223456 (7/93).

Piano Concertos — No. 3 in G major, Op. 45; No. 4 in D minor, Op. 70. **Joseph Banowetz** (pf); **Košice State Philharmonic Orchestra/Robert Stankovsky.** Marco Polo 8 223382.

Violin Concerto in G major, Op. 46[a]. Don Quixote — Musical picture after Cervantes, Op. 46. [a]**Takako Nishizaki** (vn); **Slovak Philharmonic Orchestra/Michael Halász.** Marco Polo 8 220359.

Symphony No. 2 in C major, Op. 42, "Ocean". **Slovak Philharmonic Orchestra/Stephen Gunzenhauser.** Marco Polo 8 220449 (11/87).

THE DEMON — Do not weep, my child; On the airy ocean; I am he whom you called. NERO — Vindex's Epithalamium: I sing to you, Hymen divine! *Coupled with* **Rimsky-Korsakov.** SADKO — The paragon of cities; Beautiful city! KASHCHEY THE IMMORTAL — In this, night's darkest hour. SNOW MAIDEN (second version) — Under the warm blue sea. THE TSAR'S BRIDE — Still the beauty haunts my mind. **Mussorgsky.** Songs and Dances of Death. **Borodin.** PRINCE·IGOR — No sleep, no rest. **Rachmaninov.** ALEKO — Aleko's cavatina. **Dmitri Hvorostovsky** (bar); **Kirov Theatre Orchestra/Valery Gergiev.** Philips 438 872-2PH (5/94). *See review in the Collections section; refer to the Index to Reviews.*

Poul Ruders

Suggested listening ...

String Quartets — No. 2; No. 3, "Motet". *Coupled with* **Abrahamsen.** String Quartets Nos. 1 and 2. **Kontra Quartet.** Da Capo DCCD9006.

Corpus Cum Figuris[a]. Manhattan Abstraction[b]. Thus Saw Saint John[c]. [a]**Ensemble Intercontemporain/Peter Eötvös;** [bc]**Danish Radio Symphony Orchestra/**[b]**Michael Schønwandt;** [c]**Oliver Knussen.** Point Records PCD5084.

Violin Concerto No. 1[a]. Concerto for clarinet and twin-orchestra[b]. Drama-Trilogy — Cello Concerto, "Polydrama"[c]. [a]**Rebecca Hirsch** (vn); [b]**Niels Thomsen** (cl); [c]**Morten Zeuthen** (vc); **Odense Symphony Orchestra/Tamás Vetö.** Unicorn-Kanchana DKPCD9114 (4/92).

Psalmodies[a]. Vox in Rama[b]. Nightshade[c]. [a]**David Starobin** (gtr); [a]**Speculum Musicae/David Palma;** [bc]**Capricorn/**[c]**Oliver Knussen.** Bridge BCD9037 (5/93).

Gong. Symphony, "Himmelhoch Jauchzend — zum Tode Betrübt". Thus saw St John. **Danish National Symphony Orchestra/Leif Segerstam.** Chandos CHAN9179 (10/93).

Key to symbols

**Gramophone
Awards winners**

**Gramophone
Editor's choice**

Carl Ruggles

Suggested listening ...

Sun-treader[b]. *Coupled with* **Piston.** Symphony No. 2[a]. **Schuman.** Violin Concerto[c]. [c]**Paul Zukofsky** (vn); **Boston Symphony Orchestra/Michael Tilson Thomas.** DG 20th Century Classics 429 860-2GC (1/91).

John Rutter

New review

Rutter. Five Traditional Songs.
Vaughan Williams. Five English Folksongs. **Cambridge Singers; City of London Sinfonia/John Rutter.** Collegium COLCD120. Texts included.
Traditional (arr. Rutter): I know where I'm going. Down by the sally gardens. The bold grenadier. The keel row. The cuckoo. She's like the swallow. Willow song. The willow tree. The miller of Dee. O can ye sew cushions? Afton water. The sprig of thyme. She moved through the fair (arr. Runswick). The lark in the clear air (arr. Carter).

lh 6m   DDD   ll/93

Pleasure in singing is almost the *raison d'être* of this disc. John Rutter not only provides those of us over 30 with a healthy dollop of nostalgia, but gives these songs a whole new lease of life in some characteristically scrumptuous arrangements. He is not attempting to follow in the footsteps of the great folk-song arrangers (he pays tribute to this tradition by including Vaughan Williams's *Five English Folksongs*). His arrangements belong more to the light music tradition; what Messrs Binge, Coates and Tomlinson achieved with orchestral colours Rutter finds primarily through vocal ones — and it's significant that the very finest arrangements here (including a ravishing "Golden Slumbers") are unaccompanied. To this end he is supported beyond all dreams by this outstanding group of singers. This is a lovely disc.

Further listening ...

Fancies[a]. Suite antique[b]. Five Childhood Lyrics[c]. When icicles hang[a]. [b]**Duke Dobing** (fl); [b]**Wayne Marshall** (hpd); [ac]**Cambridge Singers;** [ab]**City of London Sinfonia/John Rutter.** Collegium COLCD117 (3/93).

Gloria for chorus and orchestra. *Anthems* — All things bright and beautiful; The Lord bless you and keep you; The Lord is my shepherd; O clap your hands; Open thou mine eyes; Praise ye the Lord; A Prayer of St Patrick. **Cambridge Singers; Philip Jones Brass Ensemble/John Rutter.** Collegium COLCD100 (6/87).

Requiem. I will lift up mine eyes — Psalm 121. **Caroline Ashton, Donna Deam** (sops); **Cambridge Singers; City of London Sinfonia/John Rutter.** Collegium COLCD103 (11/86).

Terje Rypdal

Norwegian 1947-

Suggested listening ...

Q.E.D., Op. 52. Largo, Op. 55. **Terje Rypdal** (electric gtr); **Borealis Ensemble/Christian Eggen.** ECM 513 374-2 (8/93).

Kaija Saariaho

Finnish 1952-

New review
Saariaho. Du cristal[a]. ... à la fumée[b]. Nymphea, "Jardin secret III"[c]. [b]**Petri Alanko** (alto fl); [b]**Anssi Karttunen** (vc); [c]**Kronos Quartet** (David Harrington, John Sherba, vns; Hank Dutt, va; Joan Jeanrenaud, vc); [ab]**Los Angeles Philharmonic Orchestra/Esa-Pekka Salonen.** Ondine ODE804-2. Recorded 1990-92.

57m DDD 10/93

California, where *Du cristal* was composed, is a long way from Finland, especially if you have broken your journey at IRCAM: but much that is most distinctive in Kaija Saariaho's music is the result of an unmistakably Nordic intensity in fruitful conjunction with the technical resources and poetic stimuli she found in Boulez's Paris bunker. *Nymphea* (1987) — French for the white water-lily — might promise pastel-shaded neo-impressionism, yet the way in which the quartet interacts with and escapes from the electronic penumbra creates tension and drama, in elaborate textures whose flowing contours develop sharper edges from time to time. Similar qualities appear on a much larger canvas in the orchestral works (1989-90), which play together for more than 37 minutes. There is a special sense of mystery, with eerily quiet harmonies hinting at archaic consonances, which is powerful and haunting. Performances and recordings serve the composer well.

Camille Saint-Saëns

Saint-Saëns. Cello Concerto No. 1 in A minor, Op. 33[a]. Violin Concerto No. 3 in B minor, Op. 61[b]. Piano Concerto No. 2 in G minor, Op. 22[c]. [a]**Yo-Yo Ma** (vc); [b]**Cho-Liang Lin** (vn); [c]**Cécile Licad** (pf); [a]**Orchestre National de France/Lorin Maazel**; [b]**Philharmonia Orchestra/Michael Tilson Thomas**; [c]**London Philharmonic Orchestra/André Previn.** CBS Digital Masters CD46506. Item marked [a] from 35949 (5/81), [b] 35007 (6/84), [c] IM39153 (1/85). Recorded 1980-83.

1h 12m DDD 7/91

The concertos of Saint-Saëns are expert vehicles for subtle virtuosity, and the First Cello Concerto — which the composer completed in 1872 — is possibly the most fluent of them all. However, Saint-Saëns found the technical means of the instrument so restrictive that he vowed never to write another one, a vow he failed to keep. With an ardent, swirling *Allegro non troppo* as a prelude, a delicate *Allegretto* at its core and the cyclic return of important first movement material (supplemented by one of Saint-Saëns's most heartfelt melodies), the First Cello Concerto is a pleasing, symmetrical design, full of engaging music. The G minor Piano Concerto — the second of five — was written in 1868 in just over a fortnight; it starts out with overtly grand designs before settling to relative urbanity, while its sunny central *Scherzo* is delectably light and frothy. Incidentally, this appealing pattern of grave, commanding introductions followed by comparatively light-hearted argument is a formula that Francis Poulenc went on to develop with consummate artistry. The warmly melodic Third Violin Concerto is the longest piece in the programme, though its tunes and textures are no less appealing. A passionate and outgoing piece, it was written in 1880 for Sarasate and is full of engaging, colourfully contrasted music. Of the performances gathered here, the Lin/Tilson Thomas recording of the Violin Concerto is the most distinctive, with superb solo playing and a buoyant, balletic orchestral accompaniment under Tilson Thomas. Yo-Yo Ma offers a highly personable reading of the Cello Concerto, strongly supported by Maazel, and if Cécile Licad lacks the aristocratic poise of, say, a Rubinstein or a Ciccolini, her playing is never less than vital, and Previn offers her excellent support. A generous, well played collection, admirably recorded.

Additional recommendations ...

Piano Concerto No. 2[a]. **Falla.** *Nights in the gardens of Spain*[a]. *El amor brujo. Ritual Fire Dance (arr. Rubinstein).* **Franck.** *Symphonic Variations, Op. 46*[b]. **Prokofiev.** *The Love for Three Oranges — March.* **Artur Rubinstein** (pf); [a]**Philadelphia Orchestra/Eugene Ormandy**; [b]**Symphony Orchestra of the Air/Alfred Wallenstein.** RCA Red Seal RD85666 — **1h 3m ADD 10/87**

Cello Concerto No. 1. **Bruch.** *Kol Nidrei, Op. 47.* **Lalo.** *Cello Concerto in D minor.* **Matt Haimovitz** (vc); **Chicago Symphony Orchestra/James Levine.** DG 427 323-2GH — **59m DDD 6/89**

Cello Concerto No. 1. **Fauré.** *Elégie in C minor, Op. 24.* **Lalo.** *Cello Concerto.* **Heinrich Schiff** (vc); **New Philharmonia Orchestra/Sir Charles Mackerras.** DG Privilege 431 166-2GR. — **53m ADD 8/91** ℗

Cello Concerto No. 1[a]. **Lalo.** *Cello Concerto*[b]. **Schumann.** *Cello Concerto No. 1 in A minor, Op. 129*[b]. **János Starker** (vc); **London Symphony Orchestra/**[a]**Antal Dorati,** [b]**Stanislaw Skrowaczewski.** Mercury 432 010-2MM — **1h 5m ADD 4/92** ℗

Cello Concerto No. 1. **Lalo.** *Cello Concerto.* **Massenet.** *Fantaisie.* **Sophie Rolland** (vc); **BBC Philharmonic Orchestra/Gilbert Varga.** ASV CDDCA867 (*reviewed under Lalo; refer to the Index to Reviews*) — **1h 5m DDD 12/93** ℗ ℗s

Cello Concerto No. 1. Le Carnaval des animaux — The swan[a]. *Romance in F major, Op. 36*[b]. *Romance in D major, Op. 51*[b]. *Cello Sonata No. 1 in C minor, Op. 32*[b]. *Chant saphique in D major, Op. 91*[b]. *Gavotte in G minor, Op. posth*[b]. *Allegro Appassionato in B minor, Op. 43*[b]. *Priére, Op. 158*[c]. **Steven Isserlis** (vc); **Dudley Moore,** [b]**Pascal Devoyon** (pfs); [c]**Francis Grier** (org); **London Symphony Orchestra/Michael Tilson Thomas.** RCA Victor Red Seal 09026 61678-2 — **59m DDD 12/93**

Saint-Saëns. Piano Concerto No. 2 in G minor, Op. 22[b].
Rachmaninov. Piano Concerto No. 3 in D minor, Op. 30[a].
Shostakovich. Prelude and Fugue in D major, Op. 87 No. 5[c]. **Emil Gilels** (pf); [ab]**Paris**

Conservatoire Orchestra/André Cluytens. Testament mono SBT1029. Item marked [a] from Columbia 33CX1323 (1/56), [b] 33CX1217 (3/55), [c] 33CX1364 (9/56). Recorded 1954-56.

1h 5m   ADD   2/94

Gilels (1916-85) was a true king of pianists and these Paris and New York based recordings can only strengthen and confirm his legendary status. Here, once more, is that superlative musicianship, that magisterial technique and, above all, that unforgettable sonority; rich and sumptuous at every level. What breadth and distinction he brings to the first movement of the Saint-Saëns, from his fulmination in the central octave uproar to his uncanny stillness in the final pages. High jinks are reserved for the second and third movements, the former tossed off with a teasing lightness, the latter's whirling measures with infinite brio. An approximate swipe at the *Scherzo*'s flashing double-note flourish, a false entry and a wrong turning five minutes into the finale offer amusing evidence of Gilels's high-wire act; this performance was, after all, recorded before today's obsession with a gleaming and artificial perfection. No performance of this concerto (the one that goes from Bach to Offenbach) is more 'live', and it is small wonder that Claudio Arrau included it among his desert island favourites. Gilels's Rachmaninov is altogether more temperate yet, once more, this is among the few truly great performances of this work. His tempo is cool and rapid, and maintained with scintillating ease through even the most formidable intricacy. The cadenza — the finer and more transparent of the two — billows and recedes in superbly musical style and the climax is of awe-inspiring grandeur and the central *scherzando* in the finale is as luminous as it is vivacious. The finale's *meno mosso* variation is excluded (a beautiful passage that Gilels would doubtless have reinstated in our more generous and enlightened times) and, it has to be said, Cluytens's partnership is distant and run of the mill. But the recordings hardly show their age in such admirably smooth transfers. Gilels's 'encore', Shostakovich's piquant Prelude and Fugue No. 5 shines like a brilliant shaft of light after the Rachmaninov. The performance is, again, perfection, entirely justifying Artur Rubinstein's comment after hearing him play in Russia: "If that boy comes to the West, I shall have to shut up shop".

Key to symbols

| Quality of sound | | Discs worth exploring | | | Caveat emptor |

Quality of performance · Basic library · Period performance

Saint-Saëns. PIANO CONCERTOS. **Pascal Rogé** (pf); [a]**Philharmonia Orchestra,** [b]**Royal Philharmonic Orchestra,** [c]**London Philharmonic Orchestra/Charles Dutoit.** Decca 417 351-2DH2. From D244D3 (10/81).

No. 1 in D major, Op. 17[a]; No. 2 in G minor, Op. 22[b]; No. 3 in E flat major, Op. 29[c]; No. 4 in C minor, Op. 44[a]; No. 5 in F major, Op. 103, "Egyptian"[b].

2h 21m   ADD   12/86

Saint-Saëns's First Concerto was written when the composer was 23 years old, and it is a sunny, youthful, happy work conventionally cast in the traditional three-movement form. A decade later he wrote the Second Concerto in a period of only three weeks. This concerto begins in a mood of high seriousness rather in the style of a Bach organ prelude; then this stern mood gives way to a jolly fleet-footed scherzo and a *presto* finale: it is an uneven work, though the most popular of the five concertos. The Third Concerto is perhaps the least interesting work, whilst the Fourth is the best of the five. It is in effect a one-movement work cast in three ingeniously crafted sections. Saint-Saëns wrote his last, the *Egyptian*, in 1896 to mark his 50 years as a concert artist. Mirroring the sights and sounds of a country he loved, this is another brilliant work. Pascal Rogé has a very secure, exuberant sense of rhythm, which is vital in these works, as is his immaculate, pearly technique. Dutoit is a particularly sensitive accompanist and persuades all three orchestras to play with that lean brilliance which the concertos demand. The recordings are true and well-balanced.

Additional recommendations ...
Additional recommendations ...
Nos. 1-5. **Aldo Ciccolini** (pf); **Orchestre de Paris/Serge Baudo.** EMI Rouge et Noir
CMS7 69443-2 — .· ② 2h 18m ADD 3/92
Nos. 2 and 4. **Idil Biret** (pf); **Philharmonia Orchestra/James Loughran.** Naxos 8 550334
— .· 55m DDD 12/90

Saint-Saëns. Violin Concerto No. 3 in B minor, Op. 61.
Wieniawski. Violin Concerto No. 2 in D minor, Op. 22. **Julian Rachlin** (vn); **Israel
Philharmonic Orchestra/Zubin Mehta.** Sony Classical SK48373. Recorded in 1991.

.· **52m DDD 12/92**

Saint-Saëns's expansive Third Violin Concerto has the rare distinction of providing a showcase
for virtuosos without compromising purely musical values. In terms of thematic material and
orchestration, it has all the gracefulness and restraint of a classical concerto (as well it might,
given its composer's admiration for Beethoven), but, additionally, it manages to find space for
passion (first movement) and tenderness (second), as well as encourage a highly musical brand
of technical display (third). Written for Sarasate in the early 1880s, the Concerto has long
attracted the attention of leading players, yet has still to achieve the popularity of Saint-Saëns's
more celebrated shorter works for violin and orchestra, his *Havanaise* and *Introduction and Rondo
capriccioso*. Tchaikovsky was much taken with Henryk Wieniawski's Second Concerto (1862), a
less ambitious piece than the Saint-Saëns but one that, over the years, has proved more
popular. A great violinist himself, Wieniawski knew how to challenge his interpreters with
devilishly difficult passage-work and gorgeous melodies (such as we encounter at the heart of
this D minor Concerto), and it is a pleasure to encounter a young player who so fully
understands its idiom. Lithuanian-born Julian Rachlin has a smooth, velvety tone and a lightning
left hand; his playing has something of the cultured refinement of the late Nathan Milstein, yet
it has its own personality and on this particular CD enjoys the added advantage of superb
accompaniments, beautifully recorded. Incidentally, in the Wieniawski, the orchestral tutti
passages are played complete — a bonus that you won't find on either of Jascha Heifetz's
classic recordings!

Additional recommendations ...
Violin Concerto No. 3. **Lalo.** *Symphonie espagnole, Op. 21.* **Itzhak Perlman** (vn); **Paris
Orchestra/Daniel Barenboim.** DG 429 977-2GDC — .·' ADD 3/84
Violin Concerto No. 3. **Wieniawski.** *Violin Concerto No. 2.* **Bruch.** *Violin Concerto No. 2 in
D minor, Op. 44.* **Conus.** *Violin Concerto in E minor.* **Tchaikovsky.** *Sérénade mélancolique in B
minor, Op. 26*[a]. **Jascha Heifetz** (vn); **RCA Victor Symphony Orchestra/Izler Solomon;**
[a]**Los Angeles Philharmonic Orchestra/Alfred Wallenstein.** RCA Victor Gold Seal mono
GD60927 — .·' 1h 6m ADD 11/92 ⁹ₚ ▲

Saint-Saëns. ORCHESTRAL WORKS. [a]**Kyung-Wha Chung** (vn); [a]**Royal Philharmonic
Orchestra, Philharmonia Orchestra/Charles Dutoit.** Decca 425 021-2DM.
Danse macabre in G minor, Op. 40. Phaéton in C major, Op. 39. Le rouet d'Omphale in
A major, Op. 31. La Jeunesse d'Hercule in E flat major, Op. 50. Marche héroïque in E flat
major, Op. 34. Introduction and Rondo capriccioso in A minor, Op. 28[a]. Havanaise in E major,
Op. 3[a].

.· **1h 6m ADD**   ⁹ₚ

It's enough to make you weep — at the age of three, Saint-Saëns wrote his first tune, analysed
Mozart's *Don Giovanni* from the full score when he was five, and at ten claimed he could play all
of Beethoven's 32 piano sonatas from memory. There is some consolation in the fact that,
according to a contemporary, physically "he strangely resembled a parrot", and perhaps even his
early brilliance was a curse rather than a blessing, as he regressed from being a bold innovator to
becoming a dusty reactionary. In his thirties (in the 1870s) he was at the forefront of the
Lisztian avant-garde. To Liszt's invention, the 'symphonic poem' (Saint-Saëns was the first
Frenchman to attempt the genre, with César Franck hard on his heels), he brought a typically
French concision, elegance and grace. Charles Dutoit currently has few peers in this kind of
music; here is playing of dramatic flair and classical refinement that exactly matches Saint-Saëns
intention and invention. Decca's sound has depth, brilliance and richness.

Additional recommendation …

Introduction and Rondo capriccioso. Havanaise. **Paganini.** *Violin Concerto No. 1 in D major, Op. 6.* **Waxman.** *Carmen Fantasy.* **Maxim Vengerov** (vn); **Israel Philharmonic Orchestra/ Zubin Mehta.** Teldec 9031-73266-2 — .ᐟ 1h 3m DDD 5/92

Saint-Saëns. SYMPHONIES. [a]**Bernard Gavoty** (org); **Orchestre National de l'ORTF/ Jean Martinon.** EMI CZS7 62643-2. Recorded 1972-75.
A major; F major, "Urbs Roma"; No. 1 in E flat major, Op. 2; No. 2 in A minor, Op. 55; No. 3 in C minor, Op. 78, "Organ"[a].

.ᐟ ② 2h 36m ADD 5/91

Saint-Saëns's four early symphonies have rather tended to be eclipsed by the popularity of his much later *Organ* Symphony. It's easy to see why the latter, with its rich invention, its colour and its immediate melodic appeal has managed to cast an enduring spell over its audiences, but there is much to be enjoyed in the earlier symphonies too. The A major dates from 1850 when Saint-Saëns was just 15 years old and is a particularly attractive and charming work despite its debt to Mendelssohn and Mozart. The Symphony in F major of 1856 was the winning entry in a competition organized by the Societé Sainte-Cécile of Bordeaux but was immediately suppressed by the composer after its second performance. The pressures of writing for a competition no doubt contribute to its more mannered style but it nevertheless contains some impressive moments, not least the enjoyable set of variations that form the final movement. The Symphony No. 1 proper was in fact written three years before the *Urbs Roma* and shares the same youthful freshness of the A major, only here the influences are closer to Schumann and Berlioz. The Second Symphony reveals the fully mature voice of Saint-Saëns and in recent years has achieved a certain amount of popularity which is almost certainly due in part to this particularly fine recording. Inevitably we arrive at the *Organ* Symphony, and if you don't already have a recording then you could do a lot worse than this marvellously colourful and flamboyant performance. Indeed, the performances throughout this generous set are persuasive and exemplary. A real bargain and well worth investigating.

Saint-Saëns. Symphony No. 3 in C minor, Op. 78, "Organ"[a]. Le Carnaval des animaux[b]. [a]**Peter Hurford** (org); [b]**Pascal Rogé**, [b]**Christina Ortiz** (pfs); [a]**Montreal Symphony Orchestra**, [b]**London Sinfonietta/Charles Dutoit.** Decca Ovation 430 720-2DM.

.ᐟ 58m DDD 12/91   q[p] q[s] Ⓑ

New review

Saint-Saëns. Symphony No. 3 in C minor, Op. 78, "Organ"[a].
Debussy. La mer[b].
Ibert. Escales[b]. [a]**Berj Zamkochian** (org); **Boston Symphony Orchestra/Charles Munch.** RCA Living Stereo 09026 61500-2. Item marked [a] recorded in 1959, [b] 1956.

.ᐟ 1h 13m ADD 4/93   q[p] Ⓑ ▲

Let's face it, 'motto' themes and their transformations rarely produce good singable tunes. This Symphony uses a unifying motto theme, but it is fertile enough to produce two unforgettable melodies: the sensuous, arching string cantilena in the slow movement, and the grandly striding theme of the finale (so singable it was even borrowed for a pop chart-topping hit in the 1970s). In 1886 Saint-Saëns poured his considerable experience as an unequalled virtuoso of the organ, piano and practitioner of Lisztian unifying techniques into his *Organ* Symphony; it instantly put the French Symphony on the map, and provided a model for Franck and many others. With its capacity for grand spectacle (aside from the organ and a large orchestra, its scoring includes two pianos) it has suffered inflationary tendencies from both conductors and recording engineers. Dutoit's (and Decca's) achievement is the restoration of its energy and vitality. The private and affectionate portraits in the 'zoological fantasy', *The Carnival of the animals,* benefit from more intimate though no less spectacular sound, and a direct approach that avoids obvious clowning.

   The famous Charles Munch recording of this Symphony was made in Symphony Hall, Boston. To get round the problems of the hall resonance the RCA engineers moved many of the seats from the body of the hall so that the orchestra could spread out, while the organ (situated behind the stage) was miked separately. The result was a wonderfully rich, sumptuous sound which at the same time achieved internal clarity — one notices that in the

Scherzo and the filigree passages for piano in the introduction to the finale. However, it is the spectacular moments that one remembrs: the rich bonding of organ and strings in the *Poco adagio* and the full-blooded organ entry from Berj Zamkochian in the finale. Munch's superb reading moves forward with a powerful lyrical impulse in a single sweep from the first note to the last. To make this issue even more enticing Munch's 1956 versions of Debussy's *La mer* and Ibert's *Escales* ("Port of call") have been included. There is some marvellous playing in both, especially from the lustrous Boston violins. Here, however, the original recordings were more closely balanced and the effect is less rich, the dynamic range less wide. Yet the adrenalin runs high in both performances and the picturesque imagery of *Escales* is vividly conveyed.

Additional recommendations ...

No. 3. **Daniel Chorzempa** (org); **Berne Symphony Orchestra/Peter Maag.** Pickwick IMP Red Label PCD847 — ,·ʼ 37m DDD 4/87 Ⓑ

No. 3ᵃ. SAMSON ET DALILA — *Bacchanale*ᵇ. *Le déluge* — *Prélude*ᵇ. *Danse macabre*ᵇ. ᵃ**Gaston Litaize** (org); ᵃ**Chicago Symphony Orchestra,** ᵇ**Orchestre de Paris/Daniel Barenboim.** DG Galleria 415 847-2GGA — ,·ʼ 56m DDD 4/87 ꝗₚ Ⓑ

No. 3. **Dukas.** *L'apprenti sorcier.* **Simon Preston** (org); **Berlin Philharmonic Orchestra/ James Levine.** DG 419 617-2GH — ,·ʼ 47m DDD 8/87 ꝗₚ Ⓑ

No. 3ᵃ. **Poulenc.** *Organ Concerto*ᵇ. ᵃ**George Malcolm,** ᵇ**Anita Priest** (orgs); ᵃ**Academy of St Martin in the Fields/Iona Brown;** ᵇ**Los Angeles Philharmonic Orchestra/Zubin Mehta.** Decca Ovation 417 725-2DM — ,·ʼ 56m ADD 12/87 Ⓑ

No. 3ᵃ. **Poulenc.** *Organ Concerto*ᵃ. **Franck.** *Le Chasseur Maudit.* ᵃ**Berj Zamkochian** (org); **Boston Symphony Orchestra/Charles Munch.** RCA Red Seal RD85720 — ,·ʼ 1h 11m ADD 2/88 Ⓑ

*Le Carnaval des animaux*ᵃ. **Bizet.** *Jeux d'enfants.* **Ravel.** *Ma mère l'oye.* ᵃ**Julian Jacobson,** ᵃ**Nigel Hutchinson** (pfs); members of **London Symphony Orchestra/Barry Wordsworth.** Pickwick IMP Classics PCD932 — ,·ʼ 1h 3m DDD 4/90 Ⓑ

*Le Carnaval des animaux (arr. Reeve)*ᵃ. **Mussorgsky.** *Pictures at an Exhibition (arr. Howarth)*ᵇ. **Philip Jones Brass Ensemble/**ᵃ**Philip Jones,** ᵇ**Elgar Howarth.** Decca Ovation 425 022-2DM — ,·ʼ 58m ADD/DDD 6/91 Ⓑ

No. 3ᵃ. Phaeton, Op. 39. ᵃ**Michael Murray** (org); **Royal Philharmonic Orchestra/ Christian Badea.** Telarc CD80274 — ,·ʼ 46m DDD 12/91 ꝗₛ Ⓑ

No. 3ᵃ. **Paray.** *Mass for the 500th Anniversary of the Death of Joan of Arc*ᵇ. ᵃ**Marcel Dupré** (org); ᵇ**Soloists;** ᵇ**Rackham Symphony Choir; Detroit Symphony Orchestra/Charles Dutoit, Paul Paray.** Mercury Living Presence 432 719-2MM — ,·ʼ 1h 13m ADD 9/92 Ⓑ

Saint-Saëns. SAMSON ET DALILA. **Plácido Domingo** (ten) Samson; **Waltraud Meier** (mez) Dalila; **Alain Fondary** (bar) Priest; **Jean-Philippe Courtis** (bass) Abimelech; **Samuel Ramey** (bass) Old Hebrew; **Christian Papis** (ten) Messenger; **Daniel Galvez-Vallejo** (ten), **François Harismendy** (bass) First and Second Philistines; **Chorus and Orchestra of the Bastille Opera, Paris/Myung-Whun Chung.** EMI CDS7 54470-2. Notes, text and translation included.

,·ʼ ② 2h 4m DDD 2/93 ꝗₚ

Surviving the shafts of Bernard Shaw, bans by the Lord Chamberlain, and cries of "oratorio" from New York pundits, this impressive, subtly composed work continues to hold the attention of the opera-going public whenever and wherever it is performed, mainly because of its discreet combination of the pagan and the religious, the exotic and the erotic. Within a framework of the struggle between the Jews and Philistines, Delilah's overpowering sexuality and her dark soul are magnificently portrayed as are the proud, sensual and eventually tragic sides of Samson, while the High Priest is a vengeful, preening, frustrated figure. Their well-defined characters are depicted against a background of splendidly written choruses for Jews and Philistines. Here, at last, we have a modern version worthy of the piece, largely owing to Chung's understanding of tempo relationships, the refinement of the composer's orchestration and the energy of the pagan sections. Meier may not have the ideally voluptuous tone called for by Delilah's music but she does suggest her seductive powers and equivocal nature, singing in good French. Domingo has been *the* Samson of the day delivering Samson's defiance and love with equal aplomb if without the particular insights of great French tenors of the past. Being French and a splendid baritone, Fondary is an ideal High Priest. The recording is exemplary.

Additional recommendations ...

Soloists; Bavarian Radio Symphony Chorus and Orchestra/Sir Colin Davis. Philips
426 243-2PH2 — .·˙ ② 2h 3m DDD 1/91

Soloists; Chorus and Orchestra de Paris/Daniel Barenboim. DG 413 297-2GX2 — .·˙
② 2h 6m ADD 11/91

Further listening ...

HENRY VIII. **Soloists; Rouen Théâtre des Arts Chorus; French Lyrique Orchestra/
Alain Guingal.** Le Chant du Monde LDC278 1038/5 (4/93).

Key to symbols

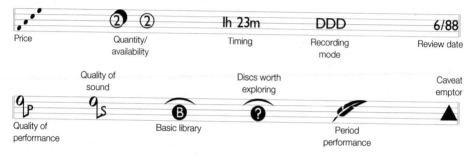

Price	Quantity/availability	Timing	Recording mode	Review date
	Quality of sound		Discs worth exploring	Caveat emptor
Quality of performance		Basic library		Period performance

Sieur de Sainte-Colombe

French 1691-1701

New review

Sainte-Colombe. Concerts a Deux Violes Esgales, Volumes 1 and 2. **Jordi Savall, Wieland
Kuijken** (bass viols). Astrée Auvidis E7729/8743. Item marked [a] from Telefunken 6 42123
(2/78). Volume marked [a] recorded in 1976, [b] 1992.
E7729[a] — No. 27, Bourrasque; No. 41, Le retour; No. 44, Tombeau les regrets; No. 48, La
raporté; No. 54, La dubois. *E8743* — No. 3, Le tendre, No. 8, La conférence; No. 42, Dalain;
No. 51, La rougeville; No. 67, Le figuré.

.·˙ ② 53m 6lm AAD/DDD 11/93

When the complete works of the mysterious Sieur de Sainte-Colombe were published in 1973,
few viol players had even heard of him. In 1976 Savall and Kuijken recorded five of the concerts
and then five more in 1992, in the wake of the success of the film *Tous les matins du monde,* for
which Savall provided the soundtrack. There is a tremendous difference of character between the
performances. The earlier recording now seems to have an air of gruff perfunctoriness about its
pacing, as if the players were somehow ill at ease. But we have in the second recording a series
of refined virtuoso dialogues. The rapport between players and with the music is sublime:
elegiac in the extended passages of echoes in *La conférence,* wonderfully seductive in *Le tendre*
(used in the film) and almost able to make time stand still in *La rougeville.* Gone is the tension
one senses in the earlier recording, replaced by an unrivalled rapport that will be truly satisfying
to those who have avidly followed their musical development during the intervening years.

Philip Sainton

British 1891-1967

Suggested listening ...

The Island. *Coupled with* **Hadley.** The Trees so High[a]. [a]**David Wilson-Johnson** (bar);
Philharmonia [a]**Chorus and Orchestra/Matthias Bamert.** Chandos CHAN9181 (10/93).

Antonio Salieri

Suggested listening ...

AXUR, RE D'ORMUS. **Soloists; Guido d'Arezzo Choir; Russian Philharmonic Orchestra/René Clemencic.** Nuova Era 6852/4 (12/90).

Aulis Sallinen

New review
Sallinen. ORCHESTRAL WORKS. [a]**Eeva Koskinen** (vn); [b]**Torleif Thedéen** (vc); **Tapiola Sinfonietta/Osmo Vänskä.** BIS CD560. Recorded in 1992.
Variations for Orchestra, Op. 8. Violin Concerto, Op. 18[a]. Some aspects of Peltoniemi Hintrik's funeral march, Op. 19[b]. The nocturnal dances of Don Juanquixote, Op. 58.

Ih 3m   DDD   6/93

Sallinen's operas and symphonies have stolen the limelight in recent years at the expense of other works fully worthy of attention as this well-played and well-recorded disc proves. Whereas the Variations (1963) are somewhat anonymous if deftly written, the Violin Concerto (1968) is an altogether maturer work, unusually sombre for so bright a solo instrument. The Third String Quartet (1969), subtitled *Some aspects of Peltoniemi Hintrik's funeral march* has, thanks to the Kronos Quartet's advocacy, become one of Sallinen's most heard works. This arrangement for string orchestra dates from 1981. *The nocturnal dances of Don Juanquixote* is an extended fantasia for cello and strings, the title being the only parody of Strauss (although a solo violin enters late as Sancho Panza-leporello!). Sallinen is fond of playing games and all is never as it seems: one can almost hear the collective thud of critics' jaws falling open at this Arnold-like spoof, yet there are darker moments too: bravo to Sallinen and BIS for this intriguing issue.

Further listening ...

Shadows, Op. 52. Cello Concerto, Op. 44[a]. Symphony No. 4, Op. 49. [a]**Arto Noras** (vc); **Helsinki Philharmonic Orchestra/Okko Kamu.** Finlandia FACD346 (6/86).

THE HORSEMAN. **Soloists; Savonlinna Opera Festival Chorus and Orchestra/Ulf Söderblom.** Finlandia FACD101 (12/91).

THE RED LINE. **Soloists; Finnish National Chorus and Orchestra/Okko Kamu.** Finlandia FACD102 (12/91).

Giuseppe Sammartini

Giovanni Battista Sammartini

New review
G. Sammartini. Sonata for Flute and Continuo in E minor. Solos for Flute, Violin or Oboe and Continuo, Op. 13 — No. 1 in G major; No. 4 in G major. Sonatas for Recorder and Continuo — F minor; G major. Recorded in 1992.
G.B. Sammartini. Sonata for Cello and Continuo in B flat major, Op. 4 No. 2. Sonata for Harpsichord in A major. Sonata No. 6 for Organ in C major. **Cologne Camerata** (Michel

Schneider, rec; Karl Kaiser, fl; Hans-Peter Westermann, ob; Rainer Zipperling, Nicholas Selo, vcs; Sabine Bauer, hpd/org). Deutsche Harmonia Mundi 05472 77283-2.

Ih 4m DDD 10/93

Giuseppe, the elder of the two brothers, was a celebrated oboist who came to London in the 1720s and who played in many of Handel's opera productions. He is represented here by two recorder sonatas, two flute sonatas and an oboe sonata. Giovanni Battista Sammartini's contribution consists of two keyboard sonatas, one for organ, the other for harpsichord and a Sonata in B flat for cello and continuo. The younger brother was the more forward-looking of the two in matters of style and his music reflects the changes in musical idiom taking place on the continent in the second quarter of the eighteenth century. New and old, so to speak, are clearly differentiated in the juxtaposition of the entirely 'baroque' oboe sonata of Giuseppe, on the one hand, and the 'galant' cello sonata of Giovanni Battista, on the other. These are the strongest pieces in a programme which contains little that is either routine or predictable. An entertaining recital, thoughtfully constructed and imaginatively performed. Fine recorded sound.

Further listening ...

G. Sammartini. Concerto in G major. *Coupled with* **Romano.** Concerto in G major. **Cecere.** Concerto in A major. **Alberti.** Concerto in F major, "Con sordini". **Jean-Pierre Rampal** (fl); **I Solisti Veneti/Claudio Scimone.** Sony Classical SK47228 (2/92). *See review in the Collections section; refer to the Index to Reviews.*

Pablo Sarasate

Spanish 1844-1908

Suggested listening ...

Zigeunerweisen, Op. 20. *Coupled with* **Saint-Saëns.** Introduction and Rondo capriccioso, Op. 28. **Massenet.** THAIS — Méditation. **Chausson.** Poème, Op. 25. **Ysaÿe.** Caprice d'après l'etude en forme de valse de Saint-Saëns. **Ravel.** Tzigane. **Joshua Bell** (vn); **Royal Philharmonic Orchestra/Andrew Litton.** Decca 433 519-2DH (1/92). *See review in the Collections section; refer to the Index to Reviews.*

Danzas españolas, Op. 22 No. 1 (Romanze andaluza). *Coupled with* **Glazunov.** Violin Concerto in A minor, Op. 82. **Tchaikovsky** (arr. Glazunov). Souvenir d'un lieu cher, Op. 42. **Chausson.** Poème, Op. 25. **Saint-Saëns** (trans. Ysaÿe). Caprice en forme de valse, Op. 52. **Hideko Udagawa** (vn); **London Philharmonic Orchestra/Kenneth Klein.** Pickwick IMP Classics PCD966 (3/92).

Erik Satie

French 1866-1925

Satie. BALLET AND ORCHESTRAL TRANSCRIPTIONS. **New London Orchestra/ Ronald Corp.** Hyperion CDA66365. Recorded in 1989.
Parade. Gymnopédies — Nos. 1 and 3 (orch. Debussy); No. 2 (orch. Corp). Mercure. Three Gnossiennes (orch. Corp). Rêlache.

Ih 6m DDD 2/90

In 1918, the year after Diaghilev's Russian Ballet staged Satie's *Parade* in Paris, Poulenc wrote that "to me, Satie's *Parade* is to Paris what *Petrushka* is to St Petersburg" (André Gide, however, commented on its poverty-stricken pretentiousness). Satie was thenceforth adopted as the spiritual father of "Les Six", whose ideal was the marriage of serious music with jazz, vaudeville, and the circus. Those who only know Satie from his early *Gymnopédies* and *Gnossiennes* — take

heed: *Parade* shuffles along its apparently aimless, deadpan and wicked way with interjections from typewriters, lottery wheels, pistols and sirens. What does it all mean? Ronald Corp could be accused of retaining a slightly stiff upper lip, but there may well be a seriousness of purpose behind Satie's balletic miniatures. Certainly, there is little here of the uproarious debunking of some of "Les Six". His orchestrations of the *Gnossiennes* and the remaining *Gymnopédie* are idiomatic, and his performances of all six have the requisite cool beauty. Hyperion's sound is spacious and natural.

Satie. PIANO WORKS. **Anne Queffélec.** Virgin Classics VC7 90754-2.
Six Gnossiennes. Véritables préludes flasques (pour un chien). Vieux séquins et vieilles cuirasses. Chapitres tournés en tous sens. Trois Gymnopédies. Embryons desséchés. Je te veux valse. Sonatine bureaucratique. Heures séculaires et instantanées. Le Picadilly. Avant-dernières pensées. Sports et divertissements.

··•' **1h 16m DDD 5/89** ⒷⒷ

Satie. PIANO WORKS. **Pascal Rogé** (pf). Decca 410 220-2DH. From 410 220-1DH (6/84). Recorded in 1983.
Trois Gymnopédies. Je te veux valse. Quatre préludes flasques. Prélude en tapisserie. Nocturne No. 4. Vieux séquins et vieilles cuirasses. Embryons desséchés. Six Gnossiennes. Sonatine bureaucratique. Le Picadilly.

··•' **1h 1m DDD 5/89** Ⓑ

Satie. PIANO WORKS. **Peter Dickinson.** Conifer CDCF512. From CDCF183 (12/90).
Chapitres tournés en tous sens. Croquis et agaceries d'un gros bonhomme en bois. Je te veux valse. Le Picadilly. Pièces froides. Le piège de Méduse. Poudre d'or. Trois préludes du fils des étoiles. Prélude en tapisserie. Sonatine bureaucratique. Sports et divertissements. Trois Gymnopédies. Véritables préludes flasques (pour un chien). Vexations.

··•' **1h 17m DDD 5/93** Ⓑ

Satie is a composer who defies description. His piano music has the same quirky originality as his life and his love of flying in the face of convention are crystallized in these fascinating miniatures. Anne Queffélec has made an excellent selection of Satie piano music starting with the famous and well-loved *Gnossiennes* and also including the *Gymnopédies*, works of a chaste almost ritualistic stillness. Also included are the wicked *Véritables préludes flasques (pour un chien)* containing his celebrated parody of Chopin's funeral march, credited typically à la Satie as a quotation "from the famous mazurka by Schubert". The programme ends with the whimsical and charming *Sports et divertissements* played with just the right air of mock seriousness. The recorded quality is good. It is a hard-hearted and humourless listener who cannot respond to the often childlike charm and evident warm and guileless heart of this very individual composer. Pascal Rogé plays these short pieces with the right kind of (again one must use the word) childlike gravity and sensuousness and the 1983 recording made in London's Kingsway Hall is excellent. Peter Dickinson also succeeds admirably in his selection; the gravity and/or humour of these pieces is perfectly caught and conveyed, and as regards the latter quality the slightly understated playing in, say, *Le piège de Méduse* is right for this enigmatic composer. The three *Gymnopédies* provide a good test of Satie performance as well as being his most popular work, and Peter Dickinson is dead on target in his blend of gravity, sadness and tenderness — one almost writes "suppressed tenderness", given that their rarely understood titles evokes ceremonial dances of ancient Sparta performed by naked boys. There's also charm in plenty in the *café-concert* waltzes called *Poudre d'or* and *Je te veux*, and though not distinguished as music they have a fetching Gallic variety of schmaltz, while the Rosicrucian music of *Le fils des étoiles* is impressively serious. The recording has piano sound that is immediate yet well textured.

Additional recommendations ...
Six Gnossiennes. Avant-dernières pensées. Première pensée Rose + Croix. Trois préludes du fils des étoiles. Chapitres tournés en tous sens. Trois Gymnopédies. Le Piège de Méduse. Rêverie du pauvre. Je te veux valse. Prélude de la Porte héroïque du ciel. **John Lenehan.** Earthsounds CDEEASM003 — ··•' 1h 3m DDD 5/93 Ⓑ
Croquis et agaceries d'un gros bonhomme en bois. Trois descriptions automatiques. Trois valses du précieux dégoûté. Petite ouverture à danser. Valse-ballet. Fantaisie-valse. Les pantins dansent. Caresse. Danse de travers. Deux pièces froides. Première pensée Rosé + Croix. Prélude de la Porte heroïque du ciel. Passacaille. Prélude en tapisserie. Poudre d'or. Trois morceaux en forme de poire[a]. La belle excentrique. **Anne Queffélec,** [a]**Cathérine Collard** (pfs). Virgin Classics VC7 59296-2— ··•' 1h 12m DDD 8/93 Ⓑ

Avant-dernières pensées. Caresse. Chapitres tournés en tous sens. Trois Gymnopédies. Jack-in-the-box. Six Pieces. Trois Préludes flasques. Deux Rêveries nocturnes. Sonatine bureaucratique. Sports et divertissements. **Michel Legrand.** Erato 4509-92857-2 — ⸬ 54m DDD 12/93 ℗ Ⓑ

Robert Saxton

British 1953-

Suggested listening ...

Concerto for Orchestra[a]. The Sentinel of the Rainbow[b]. The Ring of Eternity[a]. Chamber Symphony: The Circles of Light[b]. [a]**BBC Symphony Orchestra,** [b]**London Sinfonietta/ Oliver Knussen.** EMI CDC7 49915-2 (4/90).

Violin Concerto[a]. I will awake the dawn[b]. In the beginning[c]. [a]**Tasmin Little** (vn); [b]**BBC Singers/John Poole;** [ac]**BBC Symphony Orchestra/Matthias Bamert.** Collins Classics 1283-2 (4/92).

Alessandro Scarlatti

Italian 1660-1725

New review
A. Scarlatti. O di Betlemme altera povertà[a].
Corelli. Concerto grosso in G minor, Op. 6 No. 8, "Christmas Concerto".
Vivaldi. Gloria in D major, RV589[b]. [ab]**Nancy Argenta,** [b]**Jennifer Smith** (sops); [b]**Catherine Wyn-Rogers** (contr); [b]**The English Concert Choir; The English Concert/ Trevor Pinnock.** Archiv Produktion 437 834-2AH. Texts and translations included.

⸬ 1h 1m DDD 3/94

Pinnock's English Concert have recorded the Corelli previously, but here the listener is struck by the calmly solemn *Grave*, the welcome presence of a theorbo in the continuo, the gently contrasted dynamics and the reverentially tender Pastorale. The charm of the Scarlatti, which also contains a joyous first aria and a more substantial second with expressive chromaticisms, is heightened by Nancy Argenta's pure voice. In terms of vibrato, there is some disparity between her and the other two soloists in the Vivaldi *Gloria*, but all three are good, and if the small (18-voice) chorus is not tonally outstanding, it is efficient and the clarity of its words is excellent. Highlights of the performance are the spring-heeled orchestral opening, the hushed tension that Pinnock secures in "Et in terra pax", the lightness of the "Laudamus te" duet and Paul Goodwin's oboe obbligato in "Domine Deus". The recordings deserve the highest commendation for capturing a warm resonance while preserving admirable clarity.

Further listening ...

Cain overo Il Primo Omicidio — *oratorio.* **Concerto Italiano; L'Europa Galante/Fabio Biondi.** Opus 111 OPS30-75/6.

Il sonno. Clori e Mirtillo. Marc'Antonio e Cleopatra. Doralbo e Niso. **Gradiva Ensemble.** Adès 20217-2 (9/93).

Variations on "La folia"[a]. Cantatas[b] — Correa nel seno amato; Già lusingato appieno. [b]**Lynne Dawson** (sop); **Purcell Quartet.** Hyperion CDA66254 (3/90).

Agar et Ismaele esiliati (Ishmael). Sonatas for Recorder and Strings — C minor; A minor[a]. **Soloists;** [a]**Elissa Berardi** (rec); **Brewer Chamber Orchestra/Rudolph Palmer.** Newport Classics Premier NPD85558 (7/94).

Domenico Scarlatti

Italian 1685-1757

D. Scarlatti. KEYBOARD SONATAS.
Soler. KEYBOARD SONATAS. **Virginia Black** (hpd). United Recordings 88005-2.
D. Scarlatti: A minor, Kk7. C minor, Kk84. F minor, Kk185. F minor, Kk187. E flat major, Kk193. A major, Kk208. D major, Kk491. D major, Kk492. *Soler:* No. 36 in C minor. No. 72 in F minor. No. 88 in D flat major. No. 119 in B flat major. Fandango.

58m DDD 8/94

This highly recommendable disc is particularly exhilarating, even among a multitude of Scarlatti recordings. Thought has been given to the order of the sonatas selected, so as to provide a smooth key-sequence as well as contrasts of mood and pace. Black starts off in fine style with the sturdy Kk491 Sonata, complete with trumpet tuckets: she shows that it is perfectly possible to maintain strict time without any danger of sounding mechanical. On the other hand, her slight flexibility for expressive purposes in Kk208 is judged to a nicety. There is joyousness in Kk492, with its quasi-guitar thrummings and rushing scales, and noisy high spirits in Kk187; the exuberant vivacity of Kk7 really needed to be seen — not to check that there was no cheating in the perversely lengthy cross-handed sections (for who could not trust Virginia Black), but to enjoy the left-hand leaps, as we do the sixths and thirds of Kk84. The chosen sonatas by Scarlatti's disciple Soler are equally pleasurable. The chattering repeated notes of No. 88 and the right-hand leaps of tenths in No. 119 are entirely in the tradition of his mentor: the modulations in the second half of No. 36 and No. 119 point to Soler's special interest in that subject. (By an unfortunate mis-reading, this latter is billed as *Allegro arioso* instead of *Allegro airoso*, which is a very different thing.) The only disappointment in the disc is the amazing and spectacular *Fandango* (which may or may not be by Soler, but is remarkable whoever wrote it): not only does Virginia Black make numerous cuts in this, but her small inflexions of pace undermine the relentlessly cumulative drive of the dance rhythm. No details are given of the harpsichord employed, but it is a fine instrument with a magnificently rich tone.

D. Scarlatti. KEYBOARD SONATAS, Volume 2. **Andreas Staier** (hpd). Deutsche Harmonia Mundi 05472-77274-2. Recorded in 1991.
D minor, Kk64; B minor, Kk87; D major, Kk96; C major, Kk132; C major, Kk133; A minor, Kk175; B flat major, Kk202; D minor, Kk213; D major, Kk214; E minor, Kk263; E major, Kk264; D major, Kk277; D major, Kk278; C major, Kk420; C major, Kk421; C major, Kk460; C major, Kk461.

1h 11m DDD 3/93

D. Scarlatti. KEYBOARD SONATAS. **Ivo Pogorelich** (pf). DG 435 855-2GH.
D minor, Kk1; G minor, Kk8; D minor, Kk9; C minor, Kk11; G major, Kk13; E major, Kk20; B minor, Kk87; E minor, Kk98; D major, Kk119; E major, Kk135; C major, Kk159; E major, Kk380; G minor, Kk450; C major, Kk487; B flat major, Kk529.

1h DDD 1/93

These two first-rate issues epitomize the two extremes of approach to recording Scarlatti sonatas shown in the recommended list below. Though both are brilliantly and sympathetically recorded, the resulting sounds could not be more different. Staier uses a modern harpsichord, constructed according to traditional principles, that is mild-mannered and deliciously expressive, and his playing reflects this with supple articulation and well-chosen ornament — though he also injects an invigorating degree of sparkle and zest into a number of the pieces. His programme of mainly not-so-well-known sonatas (with over 550 of these single-movement works to choose from, such a choice is not problematic) provides insight into the more intimate aspects of Scarlatti's art, through works in which the composer is less intent on novelty and show for their own sakes — though, for our delight, he never completely avoids these qualities. Pogorelich has gone for much better-known sonatas and, of course, uses a modern grand piano, but makes his effect time and again through restraint: dynamics are within eighteenth-century bounds, textures are kept crisply open, and speeds are consistently on the slow side; expression, though deeply felt and effective, is achieved through suggestion. But he also allows the fine tonal gradation and dynamic shading of the modern piano to add to the expressive range of this music. Staier is revolutionary in his 'authentic' approach, Pogorelich 'conservative' in his less authentic choice of instrument, yet both succeed in revealing the true voice of the composer through the sheer quality of their playing.

Additional recommendations ...

A major, Kk113; E major, Kk380; E major, Kk381; D minor, Kk213; D major, Kk119; D minor, Kk120; C major, Kk501; C major, Kk502; F minor, Kk466; G major, Kk146; F sharp major, Kk318; F sharp major, Kk319; A major, Kk24. **Virginia Black** (hpd). CRD CRD3442 — ⠶⠶ 1h DDD 6/87 🗗

G major, Kk124; C minor, Kk99; G major, Kk201; B minor, Kk87; E major, Kk46; C major, Kk95; F minor/major, Kk204a; D major, Kk490; D major, Kk491; D major, Kk492; G major, Kk520; G major, Kk521; C major, Kk513. **Trevor Pinnock** (hpd). CRD CRD3368 — ⠶⠶ 1h 1m DDD 12/86 🗗

D minor, Kk9; E major, Kk46; E minor, Kk98; C minor, Kk129; A major, Kk208; A major, Kk209; B flat major, Kk360; B flat major, Kk361; G major, Kk454; G major, Kk455; C major, Kk514; C major, Kk515. **Gilbert Rowland** (hpd). Keyboard Records KGR1025CD — ⠶⠶ 51m DAD 10/89 🗗

D major, Kk33; A major, Kk39; A minor, Kk54; G major, Kk55; D major, Kk96; G major, Kk146; E major, Kk162; E minor, Kk198; A major, Kk322; E major, kk380; G major, Kk455; F minor, Kk466; E flat major, Kk474; F minor, Kk481; D major, Kk491; F major, Kk525; E major, Kk531. **Vladimir Horowitz** (pf). CBS Masterworks CD42410 — ⠶⠶ 1h 1m AAD 5/89

D minor, Kk52; A major, Kk211; A major, Kk212; B flat major, Kk248; B flat major, Kk249; B major, Kk261; B major, Kk262; E minor, Kk263; E major, Kk264; F sharp major, Kk318; F sharp major, Kk319; G minor, Kk347; G major, Kk348; D major, Kk416; D minor, kk417; D major, kk490; D major, Kk491; D major, Kk492. **Elaine Thornburgh** (hpd). Koch International Classics 37014-2 — ⠶⠶ 1h 12m DDD 10/91 🗗

G minor, Kk108; D major, Kk118; D major, Kk119; D minor, Kk141; E minor, Kk198; E minor, Kk203; G major, Kk454; G major, Kk455; D major, Kk490; D major, Kk491; D major, Kk492; C major, Kk501; C major, Kk502; D minor, Kk516; D minor, Kk517; F major, Kk518; F minor, Kk519. **Andreas Staier** (hpd). Deutsche Harmonia Mundi RD77224 — ⠶⠶ 1h 10m DDD 2/92 🗗

24 Keyboard Sonatas. **Wanda Landowska** (hpd). EMI Références mono CDH7 64934-2 — ⠶⠶ 1h 9m ADD 8/94 ⁹ₚ ▲

18 Keyboard Sonatas. **Vladimir Horowitz** (pf). Sony Classical SK53460 — ⠶⠶ 1h 12m ADD 7/94

Further listening ...

Stabat mater[a]. *Coupled with* **Esteves.** Mass for Eight Voices. [a]**Elisabeth Hermans** (sop); [a]**Jan Van Elsaker** (ten); **Currende Vocal Ensemble/Erik Van Nevel** with **Jacques Van Der Meer** (va da gamba); **Lidewij Scheifes** (vc); **Herman Stinders** (org). Accent ACC9069D (5/92).

Cantatas — Scritte con falso inganno. Tinte a note di sangue. O qual meco Nice cangiata. Dir vorrei. **Kate Eckersley** (sop); **Fiori Musicali/Penelope Rapson** (hpd). Unicorn-Kanchana DKPCD9119 (5/92).

Giacinto Scelsi

Italian 1905-1988

Suggested listening ...

Aion. Pfhat[a]. Konx-Om-Pax[a]. **Cracow Radio and Television** [a]**Chorus and Symphony Orchestra/Jürg Wyttenbach.** Accord 20040-2 (8/90).

Chukrum. Hurqualia. Hymnos. **Cracow Radio and Television Orchestra/Wyttenbach.** Accord 20111-2.

String Quartets Nos. 1-5. String Trio. Khoom[a]. [a]**Michiko Hirayama** (sop); [a]**Frank Lloyd** (hn); [a]**Maurizio Ben Omar** (perc); **Arditti Quartet/**[a]**Aldo Brizzi.** Salabert Actuels SCD8904/05 (9/90).

Trilogia. Ko-Tha. **Frances-Marie Uitti** (vc). Etcetera KTC1136 (11/92).

Piano Suites — No. 8, "Bot-Ba" (Tibet); No. 9, "Ttai" (Paix). **Werner Bärtschi** (pf). Accord 20080-2.

Franx Xaver Scharwenka
Polish 1850-1924

Suggested listening ...

Piano Concerto No. 1 in B flat minor, Op. 32. *Coupled with* **Chopin.** Piano Concerto No. 1 in E minor, Op. 11. **Seta Tanyel** (pf); **Philharmonia Orchestra/Yuri Simonov.** Collins Classics 1263-2.

Five Polish Dances, Op. 3. Piano Sonata No. 1 in C sharp minor, Op. 6. First Polonaise, Op. 12. Impromptu, Op. 17. Valse-Caprice, Op. 31. Polonaise, Op. 42. Eglantine Waltz, Op. 84. **Seta Tanyel** (pf). Collins Classics 1325-2 (9/92).

Peter Schat
Dutch 1935-

Suggested listening ...

The Heavens, Op. 37. **Royal Concertgebouw Orchestra/Riccardo Chailly.** NM Classics NM92033 (7/94).

Johann Scheibe
German 1708-1776

Suggested listening ...

Concertos for Flute and Strings — A major[a]; D major[b]. *Coupled with* **Agrell.** Concerto for Flute and Strings in D major[a]. **Hasse.** Concerto for Flute and Strings in G major[b]. [a]**Maria Bania,** [b]**Irene Spranger** (fls); **Concerto Cophenhagen/Andrew Manze.** Chandos Chaconne CHAN0535 (6/93).

Johann Hermann Schein
German 1586-1630

Suggested listening ...

Vocal Works — O Amarilli zart. Aurora schön mit ihrem Haar. Frischauf, ihr Klosterbrüder mein. Ringstum mich schwebet Trauerigkeit. Als Filli schön und fromm. In Filli schönen Augelein. O Scheiden, o bitter Scheiden. Unlängst dem blinden Gröttelein. Wie kommst's, o zarte Filli mein. Kickehihi, kakakanei. Cupido blind, das Venuskind. Wenn Filli ihre Liebesstrahl. O Amarilli, schönste Zier. Heulen und schmerzlichs Weinen. All wilden Tier im grünen Wald. O Venus und Cupido blind. Amor, das liebe Räuberlein. O seidene Härelein. Ihr Brüder, lieben Brüder mein. Mirtillo hat ein Schäfelein. Die Vöglein singen. Mein Schifflein lief im wilden Meer. **Cantus Cölln/Konrad Junghänel.** Deutsche Harmonia Mundi RD77088 (10/90).

Johann Schelle

German 1648-1701

New review

Schelle. CHORAL WORKS. [a]**La Capella Ducale** (Gundula Anders, Mona Spägele, sops; Andreas Scholl, alto; Wilfried Jochens, ten; Harry van der Kamp, bass); **Musica Fiata, Cologne/Roland Wilson.** Deutsche Harmonia Mundi 05472 77298-2. Texts and translations included. Recorded in 1993.
Actus musicus auf Weyh-Nachten[a]. Vom Himmel kam der Engel Schar[a]. Uns ist ein Kind geboren[a]. Ach mein herzliebes Jesulein[a]. Machet die Tore weit[a]. Nun komm der Heiden Heiland.

Ih   DDD   5/94

Johann Schelle was Bach's predecessor-but-one as Thomaskantor at Leipzig and among the composers who played a part in the development of the Lutheran sacred cantata. One of the greatest attractions of his music is the colourful way in which he deploys instruments to effect striking textual illustration. There is a freshness in Schelle's writing which reflects a stylistically exciting time in German music as composers eagerly embraced new ideas from abroad and began to integrate them with Lutheran hymnody. Most of the music on this splendid disc is inspired by and, indeed indissolubly linked with, a handful of the greatest German Advent and Christmas hymns. The most highly developed piece on the disc is *Actus musicus auf Weyh-Nachten* which shows the influence of his teacher, Schütz. The work is in three unequal parts and is further broken up into sections of recitative, hymns treated in a variety of ways, and three short but very attractive instrumental 'sonatas', the second of which, a captivating "Sonatina pastorella" quoting *In dulci jubilo* and raucously played by two Rauschpfeiffen is happily repeated in Part 3. A satisfying disc which explores largely unfamiliar repertory in an invigorating way.

Johann Heinrich Schmelzer

Austrian c.1620/23-1680

Suggested listening ...

Trumpet Music — Sonata con arie zu der kaiserlichen Serenada. Sonata à 7 flauti. Balletto di spiritelli. Sonata I à 8. Balletto di centauri, ninfe e salvatici. *Coupled with* **Biber.** Trumpet Music — Sonata à 7. Sonata pro tabula. Sonata VII à 5. Sonata à 3. Sonata à 6. Sonata I à 8. Sonata Sancti Polycarpi à 9. **New London Consort/Philip Pickett.** L'Oiseau-Lyre 425 834-2OH (9/91).

Balletto in G major, "Fechtschule". Polonische Sackpfeiffen in G major. *Coupled with* **Biber.** Sonata in B flat major, "Die Bauern-Kirchfartt genandt". Battalia in D major. Serenade in C major, "Nightwatchman's Call". Sonata in A major, "La Pastorella". Sonata jucunda in D major (attrib). Sonata in G major, "Campanarum" (attrib). **J.J. Walther.** Sonata in G major, "Imitatione del Cuccu". **Cologne Musica Antiqua/Reinhard Goebel.** Archiv Produktion 429 230-2AH (1/91).

Sonatas — Lamento sopra la morte Ferdinandi III; Sonata a tre violini. Sonata a tre; Sonata a tre "Lanterly"; Duodena selectarum sonatarum — No. 9. *Coupled with* **Muffat.** Sonata for Violin and Basso Continuo. Armonico tributo — Five Sonatas: No. 5. **London Baroque/Charles Medlam.** Harmonia Mundi HMC90 1220 (11/87).

Franz Schmidt

Czechoslovakian/Austrian 1874-1939

Schmidt. Symphony No. 2 in E flat major. **Chicago Symphony Orchestra/Neeme Järvi.** Chandos CHAN8779. Recorded live in 1989.

47m   DDD   3/90

Franz Schmidt, a Czech-born Viennese, was a cellist in the Vienna Philharmonic under Mahler,
and an exact contemporary of Schoenberg, but you'd be hard put in his four symphonies to find

any evidence of Mahler's world-embracing concept of the late romantic symphony, or of Schoenberg's negation of it. The Second Symphony was completed in 1913 and, as one biographer put it, "on the eve of the international war, in which the Danube monarchy was defeated, Schmidt erected to that monarchy a monument in music". It's not difficult to hear the Danube itself in the Symphony's flowing opening pages, but on the whole this is absolute music in the symphonic tradition of Brahms and Bruckner, with Czech woodwind colourings and a Straussian opulence. Järvi restores a cut sometimes made in the reprise of the *Scherzo*, and keeps the music moving purposefully forward. The Chandos engineers take a little while to find the correct levels for this live taping, made in Orchestra Hall, Chicago, but as with his Third Symphony, once you have found the right replay level, the sound is satisfyingly full, bright and airy.

Further listening ...

Chaconne in C sharp minor. *Coupled with* **Stanford.** Fantasia and Toccata in D minor, Op. 57. **Reger.** Five Easy Preludes and Fugues, Op. 56 — No. 1 in E major. **Shostakovich.** Lady Macbeth of the Mtsensk district — Passacaglia. **Ravanello.** Theme and Variations in B minor. **Keith John** (org). Priory PRCD370 (11/92). *See review in the Collections Section; refer to the Index to Reviews.*

NOTRE DAME. **Soloists; Choir of St Hedwig's Cathedral, Berlin; Berlin RIAS Chamber Choir; Berlin Radio Symphony Orchestra/Christof Perick.** Capriccio 10 248/9 (5/89).

Florent Schmitt

French 1870-1958

New review

Schmitt. Salammbô, Op. 76. **French Army Chorus; National Orchestra of the Ile de France/Jacques Mercier.** Accord 20359-2. Recorded in 1991.

· · · 56m DDD 6/94

When the producer and director of the 1925 silent film of Flaubert's *Salammbô* asked Florent Schmitt to provide a two-hour score for it, they may well have had in mind, besides his acknowledged reputation as a creator of exotic, opulently barbaric scores (*La tragédie de Salomé*, *Les Dionysiaques* and the saxophone *Légende*, for example), his extraordinary facility: he already had to his credit a vast output of large-scale works conceived and elaborated with the utmost seriousness and skill. Schmitt thought well enough of his score, after well-deserved oblivion had fallen on the film, to extract three orchestral suites from it. The story offered plenty of opportunity for colour and the music demonstrates Schmitt's mastery in handling a very large orchestra and his imaginative creation of atmosphere. It is a matter of regret that none of these three sumptuous scores is in the repertoire of any of our major orchestras; but the splendid performance here by the Ile de France orchestra could well act as a stimulus to their adoption. Cordially recommended to all those with an appreciation of virtuoso orchestral writing and playing.

New review

Schmitt. La tragédie de Salomé. **Marie-Paule Fayt** (sop); **Rhineland-Pfalz State Philharmonic Orchestra/Patrick Davin.** Marco Polo 8 223448. Recorded in 1991.

· · · 59m DDD 12/93

This is a real rarity. We have had recordings of the large-orchestra suite from *La tragédie de Salomé* before but here, apparently for the first time, is the complete ballet which runs to twice the length of the suite and calls for only a chamber orchestra (the theatre couldn't accommodate more). Schmitt's virtuosity in drawing rich sonorities and a voluptuous, barbaric atmosphere from it is astonishing. Unlike the treatments of the biblical story by Strauss or Massenet, in the scenario here there is no question of Salome being in love with John the Baptist. Schmitt composed a well-structured score of exotic and sensual colour that includes broad lyrical episodes as well as vividly orgiastic sections. Compared to the suite for full orchestra, these lose nothing in impact or impressiveness by the smaller forces employed — indeed, the music gains in clarity and pungency thereby. It is not surprising that Stravinsky, to whom the work was dedicated, described it as "one of the greatest masterpieces of modern music". The performance, and the recording, are deserving of the highest commendation. A notable issue.

Artur Schnabel

German 1882-1951

Suggested listening ...

Symphony No. 2. **Royal Philharmonic Orchestra/Paul Zukofsky.** Musical Observations CP2104 (9/92).

Alfred Schnittke

Russian 1934-

Schnittke. Cello Concerto No. 1.
Schumann. Cello Concerto in A minor, Op. 129. **Natalia Gutman** (vc); **London Philharmonic Orchestra/Kurt Masur.** EMI CDC7 54443-2. Recorded in 1991.

Ih 5m DDD 8/92

One suspects that no composer since Mahler has been more predisposed to translate personal crises into music than Alfred Schnittke, and the concerto provides him with an ideal medium for the synthesis of feeling and thought, the triumph of the individual over potentially tragic circumstances. This composition seems to gain a stronger identity and greater conviction as it proceeds, and the remarkable final movement, written after one of Schnittke's bouts of serious illness in 1985, carries the work into a visionary world where ideas representative of vulnerability and victory engage in a battle royal. Without a recording as carefully and cleanly balanced as this one the music could sound incoherent and congested: without a performance as skilfully placed and sensitively projected as this, the work could come across as self-indulgent and even hysterical. Given that the concerto was written for Natalia Gutman you might expect her account to emphasize emotional involvement. Fortunately, she is also able to stand back and convey its sense of formal stability without over-indulging the expressive details, and she receives admirable support from Masur and the LPO. The Schumann is a worthwhile coupling in that it reminds us that romanticism has a gentler, less barnstorming side to it.

Schnittke. Concerto Grosso No. 1[a]. Quasi una sonata[b]. Moz-Art à la Haydn[c]. [ac]**Tatiana Grindenko** (vn); **Yuri Smirnov** ([a]hpd/[a]prep pf/[b]pf); **Chamber Orchestra of Europe/** [a]**Heinrich Schiff,** [bc]**Gidon Kremer** ([a]vn). DG 429 413-2GH. Recorded live in 1988.

Ih 2m DDD 9/90

For a single representative of Alfred Schnittke's work you could choose nothing better than the first *Concerto Grosso* of 1977. Here are the psychedelic mélanges of baroque and modern, the drastic juxtapositions of pseudo-Vivaldi with pseudo-Berg, producing an effect at once aurally exciting and spiritually disturbing. The piece has been recorded several times over, but never with the panache of Gidon Kremer and friends and never with the vivid immediacy of this live DG recording (in fact the solo violins are rather too closely miked for comfort, but that's only a tiny drawback). *Quasi una sonata* was originally composed in 1968 for violin and piano and it was something of a breakthrough piece for Schnittke as he emerged from what he called "the puberty rites of serialism", letting his imagination run riot for the first time. No-one could call it a disciplined piece, but if that worries you, you should leave Schnittke alone anyway. The transcription for solo violin and string orchestra is an ingenious one and Kremer again supplies all the requisite agonized intensity. *Moz-Art à la Haydn* is a very slight piece of work, and it really depends on visual theatricality to make its effect. Still, it complements the other two pieces well enough, and the disc as a whole makes an excellent introduction to a composer currently enjoying an enormous vogue.

New review
Schnittke. Symphony No. 1. **Ben Kallenberg** (vn); **Ake Lännerholm** (tbn); **Carl-Axel Dominique** (pf); **Royal Stockholm Philharmonic Orchestra/Leif Segerstam.** BIS CD577. Recorded in 1992.

1h 12m DDD 11/93

The First Symphony is at one and the same time a symphony, in its four-movement layout, and an anti-symphony in its musical content, including as it does theatrical entrances and exits for the orchestra at either end, a full-scale unnotated free-jazz improvisation (from around four minutes into the quasi-scherzo second movement), and a panoply of Western avant-garde-isms from collage à la Berio *Sinfonia* to post-Webernian 12-note *cantus firmus* writing. This is not so much a "what if?" piece as a "what the hell!" one. If you are a traditionalist looking for the epitome of everything you hate about contemporary music, you need look no further (but then do seek out Schnittke's latest symphony, the Fifth, to see how inspiring his subsequent re-engagement with traditional values has been). But if Schnittke only responded to the surface of Western avant-gardism, rather as Prokofiev only responded to the surface of Stravinsky's *Rite of Spring*, he nevertheless connected up that response to an agonized world-view all his own. Segerstam keeps a firm grasp on every aspect of this colossal, overwhelming and infuriating orchestral extravaganza, while the recording, despite reproducing at a lowish level, lets us hear the music's teeming strands and layers.

New review
Schnittke. Quasi una sonata[a]. Piano Trio[b]. Piano Sonata No. 2[c]. [ab]**Mark Lubotsky** (vn); [bc]**Irina Schnittke** (pf); [a]**English Chamber Orchestra/Mstislav Rostropovich** ([b]vc). Sony Classical SK53271. Recorded in 1992.

1h 3m DDD 4/94

The opening bars of Schnittke's *Quasi una sonata* grab you by the throat here and the rest of the piece never lets go. Being one of the earliest examples of Schnittke's polystylistic manner, its raw, agonized inspiration and marvellous sense of dramatic timing make it one of his most durable works. Mark Lubotsky's playing is spellbinding. The orchestration of the piano part, dating from 1986, also works extremely well. The Second Piano Sonata (1990) was written for, and is here marvellously played by, the composer's wife. Like so many of Schnittke's recent works it largely avoids the Gothic horror effects which made so much of his earlier output immediately appealing. All the same, the fake-Brahms-cum-Franck siciliano which underpins the last of the three movements is a haunting idea. The 1992 Piano Trio is another reworking, this time of the String Trio of 1985, of which yet another version, probably the most striking of all, is Yuri Bashmet's for string orchestra (listed under *Further Listening*). The chilling eruptions and dumbstruck responses come across well enough in the piano trio medium, and like everything on the disc it is played with intensity and dedication. Beautiful recorded sound, too.

Schnittke. String Quartet No. 3. Piano Quintet[a].
Mahler/Schnittke. Piano Quartet[a]. **Borodin Quartet** (Mikhail Kopelman, Andrei Abramenkov, vns; Dmitri Shebalin, va; Valentin Berlinsky, vc); [a]**Ludmilla Berlinsky** (pf). Virgin Classics VC7 59040-2. Recorded in 1990.

1h 6m DDD 12/91

Schnittke's chamber music does not have the high public profile of some of his symphonies and concertos, but in many ways it is more fastidiously composed and it certainly makes for equally rewarding listening at home. The Piano Quintet is the outstanding feature of this disc. Predominantly slow and mournful (it is dedicated to the memory of the composer's mother) and with a haunting waltz on the notes of the BACH monogram, it is here played with compelling intensity, especially by the pianist Ludmilla Berlinsky, daughter of the Borodin Quartet's cellist. The Piano Quartet is a conflation of the 16-year-old Mahler's first movement with his incomplete second movement in Schnittke's own paraphrase — another haunting experience, beautifully played and recorded. Less satisfying as a performance, because slightly glossed over, is the Third Quartet; but this is perhaps the finest and undoubtedly the most often performed of Schnittke's chamber works, and as a whole the disc can be warmly recommended to those looking for a representative sample of Schnittke rather than a comprehensive library.

Additional recommendation ...
String Quartets Nos. 1-3. **Tale Quartet.** BIS CD467 — 1h 2m DDD 7/90

Further listening ...

Minnesang. Choir Concerto. **Danish National Radio Choir/Stefan Parkman.** Chandos CHAN9126 (2/93).

Concerti grossi — No. 3; No. 4/Symphony No. 5. **Royal Concertgebouw Orchestra/ Riccardo Chailly.** Decca 430 698-2DH (2/92).

Concerto grosso No. 5[a]. *Coupled with* **Glass.** Violin Concerto. **Gidon Kremer** (vn); [a]**Rainer Keuschnig** (invisible pf); **Vienna Philharmonic Orchestra/Christoph von Dohnányi.** DG 437 091-2GH (10/93).

Viola Concerto[a]. Trio Sonata (arr. Bashmet)[b]. [a]**London Symphony Orchestra/Mstislav Rostropovich;** [b]**Moscow Soloists/Yuri Bashmet** ([a]va). RCA Victor Red Seal RD60446 (2/92).

Piano Sonata. *Coupled with* **Stravinsky.** Piano Sonata. Serenade in A. Piano-rag-music. **Boris Berman** (pf). Chandos CHAN8962 (10/91).

Johann Schobert

Silesian c.1735-1767

New review
Schobert. Four Trio Sonatas for Harpsichord, Violin and Cello, Op. 16. **Concerto Rococo** (Alice Piérot, vn; Paul Carlioz, vc; Jean-Patrice Brosse, hpd). Pierre Verany PV791042. Recorded in 1990.

 57m DDD 6/94

The main appeal of Schobert's music lies in its wide emotional range and the rich variety of its forms and textures. Mozart warmly admired his work and the skilled musical invention in the four trios on this disc makes it easy to see why. These are period instrument performances, using lower pitch, and the matching of mood and theme to the characteristics of the keys in which they are written makes an immediate impact. Contrast the deeply felt *Andante poco adagio* first movement of the second Trio in C minor with the much brighter opening *Andante* of the third Trio in D major. Alert phrasing combined with freshness and spontaneity from the Concerto Rococo contributes effectively to interpretations which capture the individual character of each piece. They respond with appropriate robustness to the bold, direct expression of the First Trio, while the greater emotional intensity of the C minor Trio's opening movement is engagingly contrasted with cheerfulness and wit in both its Minuet and final *Allegro*. In addition to their vivid characterization, this group also exploits the textural variety of these pieces. In the finale of the D major Trio, for example, they produce a remarkably full, orchestral sound, while they achieve an affecting intimacy in the fluid expression of the F major Trio's opening *Andante*. With clear, naturally balanced recorded sound this issue offers music which deserves to be better known.

Othmar Schoeck

Swiss 1886-1957

Suggested listening ...

Concerto quasi una fantasia, Op. 21[a]. PENTHESILEA — Suite (arr. Delfs). [a]**Bettina Boller** (vn); **Swiss Youth Symphony Orchestra/Andras Delfs.** Claves CD50-9201 (2/93).

Arnold Schoenberg

Schoenberg. Verklärte Nacht, Op. 4 (arr. string orch.). Variations for Orchestra, Op. 31. **Berlin Philharmonic Orchestra/Herbert von Karajan.** DG 415 326-2GH. From 2711 014 (3/75).

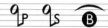

.•° **52m ADD 3/86** q_p **Ⓑ**

Schoenberg. Verklärte Nacht, Op. 4 (arr. string orch.).
R. Strauss. Metamorphosen for 23 solo strings, AV142.
Wagner. Siegfried Idyll. **Sinfonia Varsovia/Emmanuel Krivine.** Denon CO-79442. Recorded in 1990.

.•° **lh 14m DDD 10/92** q_p q_s **Ⓑ**

The decadence of German culture in the 1920s and 1930s is already very apparent in the saturated romanticism of *Verklärte Nacht* (1899), the most lusciously sentient work ever conceived for a string group. By comparison the *Variations for Orchestra* comes at the peak of the composer's atonal period and is perhaps the most impressive and imaginative demonstration of the possibilities of this compositional method. Thus the two works on this CD are pivotal in Schoenberg's career and Karajan and the Berlin Philharmonic make the very best case for both works. It is impossible not to respond to the sensuality of *Verklärte Nacht* in their hands, while the challenging *Variations* also make a profound impression. The recording matches the intensity of the playing brilliantly. The stimulating Denon issue embraces three works which are as ideally matched as one could wish for. The performances verge on the miraculous; Krivine's visionary direction summons up playing of exultant intensity from the Polish orchestra. *Verklärte Nacht* has seldom sounded so moving; with Krivine, the transformation from aspiration to absolution is magical. His nobly compelling *Metamorphosen* charges each strand of Strauss's valedictory essay with tangible dismay and regret, as quotations from *Tristan* and Beethoven's *Eroica* lament the passing of a once great culture. An ardent yet naturally paced account of Wagner's *Siegfried Idyll* recalls that sense of sanctified joy which filled the Villa Triebschen on Christmas morning in 1870, as this musical birthday offering was heard for the first time. Krivine's spiritual empathy with these works combined with the outstanding orchestral playing and exemplary recorded sound make this a disc to covet.

Additional recommendations ...
Verklärte Nacht. **Mahler.** *Symphony No. 10.* **Berlin Radio Symphony Orchestra/Riccardo Chailly.** Decca 421 182-2DH — *.•°* ② lh 50m DDD 3/88 Ⓑ
Verklärte Nacht. Variations for Orchestra. Pelleas und Melisande, Op. 5 — Symphonic Poem. **Berg.** *Three Pieces for String Orchestra.* **Webern.** *Passacaglia, Op. 1. Five Movements, Op. 5. Six Pieces for Orchestra, Op. 6. Symphony, Op. 21.* **Berlin Philharmonic Orchestra/Herbert von Karajan.** DG 427 424-2GC3 — *.•°* ③ 3h lm ADD 9/89 Ⓑ
Variations for Orchestra. Cello Concerto in D major. Five Orchestral Pieces, Op. 16. Modern Psalm. **Soloists/Bratislava Philharmonic Choir; South-West German Radio Symphony Orchestra/Michael Gielen.** Wergo WER60185-50 — *.•°* lh DDD 10/90 Ⓑ
Verklärte Nacht. **R. Strauss.** *Metamorphosen, AV142.* **Wagner.** *Siegfried Idyll.* **Berlin Philharmonic Orchestra/James Levine.** DG 435 883-2GH — *.•°* lh 19m DDD 8/93 Ⓑ
The original version of *Verklärte Nacht* is reviewed further on in this section.

Schoenberg. Variations for Orchestra, Op. 31. Pelleas und Melisande, Op. 5. **Chicago Symphony Orchestra/Pierre Boulez.** Erato 2292-45827-2. Recorded in 1991.

.•° **lh 2m DDD 4/93** q_p

The two faces of Schoenberg could scarcely be more starkly juxtaposed than they are on this superbly performed and magnificently recorded disc — Boulez and the CSO at their formidable best. *Pelleas und Melisande* can be taken not only as Schoenberg's 'answer' to Debussy's opera (also based on Maeterlinck's play) but as his challenge to Richard Strauss's supremacy as a composer of symphonic poems. It is indeed an intensely symphonic score in Schoenberg's early, late-romantic vein, with an elaborate single-movement structure and a subtle network of thematic cross-references. Yet none of this is an end in itself, and the music is as gripping and immediate a representation of a tragic love story as anything in the German romantic tradition.

To move from this to the abstraction of the 12-note Variations, Op. 31 may threaten extreme anticlimax. Yet from the delicate introduction of the work's shapely theme to the turbulent good-humour of the extended finale Schoenberg proves that his new compositional method did not drain his musical language of expressive vitality. The elaborate counterpoint may not make for easy listening, but the combination of exuberance and emotion is irresistible — at least in a performance like this.

Additional recommendation ...
Pelleas und Melisande. **Webern.** *Passacaglia for Orchestra, Op. 1.* **Scottish National Orchestra/ Matthias Bamert.** Chandos CHAN8619 — .·' 54m DDD 10/88 ⑨ₚ

Schoenberg. Chamber Symphonies — No. 1, Op. 9; No. 2, Op. 38. Verklärte Nacht, Op. 4 (arr. string orch). **Orpheus Chamber Orchestra.** DG 429 233-2GH. Recorded in 1989.

.·' Ih 9m DDD 7/90   ⑨ₚ ⑨ₛ Ⓑ

In the late twentieth century there's increasing evidence that the early twentieth century's most radical music is becoming so easy to perform that it may at last be losing its terrors for listeners as well as players. This can only be welcomed, provided that performances do not become bland and mechanical, and the conductorless Orpheus Chamber Orchestra triumphantly demonstrate how to combine fluency with intensity. If you like your Schoenberg effortful — to feel that the players are conquering almost insuperable odds — these recordings may not be for you. But if you like spontaneity of expression that is never an end in itself, and communicates Schoenberg's powerfully coherent forms and textures as well as his abundant emotionalism, you should not hesitate. The DG disc is the first to place Schoenberg's two Chamber Symphonies alongside *Verklärte Nacht.* The First Chamber Symphony shows Schoenberg transforming himself from late-romantic into expressionist, while in the Second the recent American immigrant, in the 1930s, looks back to his romantic roots and forges a new, almost classical style. With superb sound, this is a landmark in recordings of twentieth-century music.

Additional recommendation ...
Symphony No. 1. Pierrot lunaire, Op. 21[a]. [a]**Marianne Pousseur** (sop); **Musique Oblique Ensemble/Philippe Herreweghe.** Harmonia Mundi HMC90 1390 — .·' 58m DDD 8/92 Ⓑ

New review
Schoenberg. Verklärte Nacht, Op. 4[a] (orig. version).
Schubert. String Quintet in C major, D956[b]. [a]**Alvin Dinkin** (va); **Kurt Reher** (vc); **Hollywood Quartet** (Felix Slatkin, Paul Shure, vns; Paul Robyn, va; Eleanor Aller, vc). Testament mono SBT1031. Item marked [a] from Capitol CCL7507 (4/51), [b]Capitol CTL7011 (1/52). Item marked [a] recorded in 1950, [b] 1951.

.·' Ih 13m ADD 4/94   ⑨ₚ ▲

This was the first ever recording of *Verklärte Nacht* in its original sextet form and it remains unsurpassed. When it was first reviewed in *Gramophone*, Lionel Salter wrote of it as being "beautifully played with the most careful attention to details of dynamics and phrasing, with unfailing finesse, with consistently sympathetic tone, and, most important, with a firm sense of the basic structure". The Schubert too fully deserves its classic status. The tranquillity of the slow movement has never been conveyed with greater nobility or more perfect control. The Hollywood Quartet made music for the sheer love of it and as a relaxation from their duties in the film-studio orchestras, for which they were conspicuously overqualified. They have incomparable ensemble and blend; and their impeccable technical address and consummate tonal refinement silence criticism. The transfers could not be better.

New review
Schoenberg. Das Buch der hängenden Gärten, Op. 15.
Debussy. SONGS.
R. Strauss. SONGS. **Julie Kaufmann** (sop); **Irwin Gage** (pf). Orfeo C305931A. Texts and translations included. Recorded in 1992.

Debussy. Pantomime. Clair de lune. Pierrot. Apparition. Mandoline. **R. Strauss.**

Wasserrose, Op. 22 No. 4. Glückes genug, Op. 37 No. 1. Lieder, Op. 68 — No. 2, Ich wollt'
ein Sträusslein binden; No. 3, Säusle, liebe Myrthe; No. 4, Als mir dein Lied erklang; No. 5,
Amor. Kleine Lieder, Op. 69 — No. 4, Waldesfahrt; No. 5, Schlechtes Wetter. Malven. Wir
beide wollen springen, AV90.

Ih 12m DDD 2/94

Julie Kaufmann, the young American soprano, sounds entirely at home in the Lieder that make
up the greater part of this disc. The voice is sweet and pure, but the programme enticingly
decadent. In the Schoenberg cycle, the major work on the disc, encouraged by Irwin Gage's
helpful accompaniments, she enunciates the words urgently to create the right feeling of
heightened emotion for these highly expressive songs. The cycle's emotional climax draws from
her singing of full dramatic strength. The Strauss songs come mostly from late in his output,
when he asked his sopranos to negotiate florid acrobatics high on a vocal trapeze wire.
Kaufmann is unfailingly assured and delicate in them. In a live recital she would need to project
her personality more, especially in the five Debussy songs, which are too demure (Pierrot and
Harlequin are lively characters). However, Kaufmann is verbally incisive and her balance of
poetry and intensity are nearly ideal.

Schoenberg. Gurrelieder. **Susan Dunn** (sop); **Brigitte Fassbaender** (mez); **Siegfried
Jerusalem, Peter Haage** (tens); **Hermann Becht** (bass); **Hans Hotter** (narr); **St
Hedwig's Cathedral Choir, Berlin; Dusseldorf Musikverin Chorus; Berlin Radio
Symphony Orchestra/Riccardo Chailly.** Decca 430 321-2DH2. Text and translation
included. Recorded in 1985.

② Ih 41m DDD 3/91   **P**

"Every morning after sunrise, King Waldemar would have a realization of the renewing power of
nature, and would feel the love of Tove within the outward beauty of Nature's colour and form"
(thus said Leopold Stokowski, who made the first-ever recording of *Gurrelieder*). This vast cantata,
here more than ever experienced as a direct descendant of Wagnerian music-drama, was for the
turn-of-the-century musical scene in general, more the ultimate gorgeous sunset. Schoenberg
started work on it in 1899, the same year as his *Verklärte Nacht*, but delayed its completion for
over a decade, by which time some of his more innovatory masterpieces were already behind
him. Schoenberg's forces are, to put it mildly, extravagant. As well as the six soloists and two
choruses, the orchestra sports such luxuries as four piccolos, ten horns and a percussion battery
that includes iron chains; and so complex are some of the textures that, to achieve a satisfactory
balance, a near miracle is required of conductor and recording engineers. Decca have never been
mean with miracles where large scale forces are concerned and this set is no exception. Chailly
and Decca's give us a superbly theatrical presentation of the score. The casting of the soloists is
near ideal. Susan Dunn's Tove has youth, freshness and purity on her side. So exquisitely does
she float her lines that you readily sympathize with King Waldemar's rage at her demise.
Siegfried Jerusalem has the occasional rough moment but few previous Waldemars on disc have
possessed his heroic ringing tones and range of expression. And Decca make sure that their
trump card, the inimitable Hans Hotter as the speaker in "The wild hunt of the summer wind",
is so tangibly projected that we miss not one single vowel or consonant of his increasing
animation and excitement at that final approaching sunrise.

Additional recommendation ...
Soloists; Tanglewood Festival Chorus; Boston Symphony Orchestra/Seiji Ozawa.
Philips 412 511-2PH2 — **②** Ih 51m ADD 3/85

New review
Schoenberg. ERWARTUNG. Brettl-Lieder (Cabaret Songs)[a]. **Jessye Norman** (sop);
Metropolitan Opera Orchestra, New York/James Levine ([a]pf). Philips 426 261-2PH.
Texts and translations included. Recorded 1989-90.

Ih 2m DDD 9/93

Not many discs of Schoenberg are as welcoming as this. The neurotic tensions behind *Erwartung*
can be painful. The nightmare story might come from a Freudian case-history, with the central
character, lost in a wood, finding the dead body of her lover. Norman and Levine bring great

warmth, intensity, range of expression and sheer beauty to this score. He draws ravishing sounds from the Metropolitan Opera Orchestra. One is reminded not just of *Verklärte Nacht*, but the closing scenes of Berg's *Wozzeck*, and even in places Debussy's *Pelléas et Mélisande*. The contrasted coupling helps to heighten the impact of *Erwartung*. Schoenberg wrote these songs in 1901, when living in Berlin, for the Uber-Brettl cabaret theatre. Levine at the piano proves a sparkling partner, understanding the cabaret style, and Norman projects her personality as masterfully as a latterday Marlene Dietrich. The extra item, *Nachtwandler* ("Night Wanderer"), is also a delight: piccolo, trumpet and side-drum join the piano in military style, with syncopated fanfares pointing jaunty rhythms.

New review

Schoenberg. MOSES UND ARON. **Günter Reich** (spkr) Moses; **Louis Devos** (ten) Aron; **Werner Mann** (bass) Priest; **Eva Csapó** (sop) Young girl; **Elfride Obrowsky** (contr) Invalid woman; **Roger Lucas** (ten) Young man, Naked youth; **Richard Salter** (bar) Another man; **Ladislav Illavsky** (bar) Ephraimite; **Vienna Boys' Choir; Austrian Radio Chorus; Austrian Radio Symphony Orchestra/Michael Gielen.** Philips 438 667-2PM2. Notes, text and translation included. From 6700 084 (1/75). Recorded in 1974.

② 1h 38m ADD 4/94

Gielen's account of *Moses und Aron* has a raw intensity which Schoenberg himself might have found overdone – too purely 'operatic'. The Philips sound is larger than life, the voices (especially Moses) grafted on to a close yet remarkably vivid orchestral tapestry. The Austrian Radio orchestra squeezes the last drop of expressionist exoticism out of the "Dance round the Gold Calf", and no one who likes the idea of linking Schoenberg with Puccini, and who enjoys thinking of the more sadistic aspects of *Moses und Aron* in terms of a kind of 12-note *Turandot*, will want to be without this fiery reading. With Boulez (see below) you get more sense of the war between ideas and actions which lies at the heart of the drama. Günter Reich is the Moses in both recordings, and the degree of histrionic projection in his performances reflects the different attitudes of the conductors. Both Arons – Richard Cassilly (Boulez) and Louis Devos – convey the strength as well as the seductiveness of Moses's *alter ego* with considerable success. For the rest, no performance of this opera could survive with an inadequate chorus, or with weak links in the smaller roles. Boulez's team is musically admirable, yet Gielen's chorus sounds that much more at home in the pithy abstractions of Schoenberg's German text.

Additional recommendation ...
Soloists; **BBC Singers; Orpheus Boys' Choir; BBC Symphony Orchestra/Pierre Boulez.** Sony Classical SM2K48456 — ② 2h 1m ADD 12/93

Further listening ...

Piano Concerto, Op. 42. *Coupled with* **Schumann.** Piano Concerto in A minor, Op. 54. **Maurizio Pollini** (pf); **Berlin Philharmonic Orchestra/Claudio Abbado.** DG 427 771-2GH (7/90).

Choral Works — Friede auf Erden, Op. 13; Kol nidre, Op. 39; Drei Volkslieder, Op. 49. *Zwei Kanons* — Wenn der schwer Gedrückte klagt; O dass der Sinnen doch so viele sind!. *Drei Volkslieder* — Es gingen zwei Gespielen gut; Herzlieblich Lieb, durch Scheiden; Schein uns, du liebe Sonne. Vier Stücke, Op. 27. Drei Satiren, Op. 28. Sechs Stücke, Op. 35. Dreimal tausen Jahre, Op. 50*a*. De profundis (Psalm 130), Op. 50*b*. Modern Psalm (Der erste Psalm), Op. 50*c*. A Survivor from Warsaw, Op. 46. **John Shirley-Quirk, Günter Reich** (narrs); **BBC Singers; BBC Chorus and Symphony Orchestra; London Sinfonietta/Pierre Boulez.** Sony Classical S2K44571 (8/90).

Three Piano Pieces, Op. 11. Six Little Piano Pieces, Op. 19. Five Piano Pieces, Op. 23. Piano Suite, Op. 25. Piano Pieces, Opp. 33*a* and 33*b*. **Maurizio Pollini.** DG 20th Century Classics 423 249-2GC (6/88).

Pierrot lunaire, Op. 21[a]. *Coupled with* **Webern.** Concerto, Op. 24. [a]**Jane Manning** (sop); **Nash Ensemble/Simon Rattle.** Chandos Collect CHAN6534 (8/92).

Paul Schoenfield

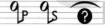

New review
Schoenfield. Four Parables[a]. Vaudeville[b]. Klezmer Rondos[c]. [c]**Carol Wincenc** (fl); [b]**Wolfgang Basch** (piccolo tpt); [a]**Jeffrey Kahane** (pf); **New World Symphony/John Nelson.** Argo 440 212-2ZH. Recorded in 1992.

Ih 12m   DDD   6/94

Paul Schoenfield's existentialist response to a 70-year-old murderer's release from prison prompts a wildly diverting, madcap tone-poem that opens amongst pensive, dank shadows and suddenly flies into dizzy, high spirited confusion — a sort of Gershwin-cum-Shostakovich, complete with sliding brass, high-hat cymbals and tam-tam. This is the first of Schoenfield's hugely enjoyable *Four Parables*: 'slices of life' etched with a combination of wry humour and pathos. *Vaudeville* takes its cue from Schumann's versicoloured brand of thematic transformation (as displayed in *Carnaval*), with piccolo trumpet and clarinet taking centre stage. As in the *Klezmer Rondos*, Jewish folk-style music has a spot to itself, whereas elsewhere, Schoenfield's roll-call of effects includes the sentimental ballad, hectic dancing and a hilarious send-up of Mahler's Second Symphony as the "Sketches" swing into "Carmen Rivera". The *Rondos* themselves are perhaps the most 'mainstream' items on the CD, with telling but well-integrated side-glances at Bartók, Stravinsky, Weill and Bernstein. Here, as elsewhere, you leave his work with a party-bag full of good tunes and the meaningful recollection of his own guiding aphorism, that "Life is tantamount to a burlesque show". So, sit back — and *enjoy*, as they say. Which barely leaves enough room to pay adequate tribute to the performers, all of them first-rate. The sound, by the way, is superb. A real tonic!

Key to symbols

	Quality of sound		Discs worth exploring		Caveat emptor
Quality of performance		Basic library		Period performance	

Claude-Michel Schönberg

Suggested listening ...

LES MISERABLES. **Original London cast.** First Night ENCORECD1 (3/87).

Franz Schreker

Suggested listening ...

Chamber Symphony[a]. Prelude to a Drama[a]. Valse lente[b]. Die Ferne Klang — Night Interlude[b]. **Berlin Radio Symphony Orchestra/[a]Michael Gielen, [b]Karl Anton Rickenbacher.** Koch Schwann 311078 (11/88).

DER FERNE KLANG. **Soloists; Berlin RIAS Chamber Chorus; Berlin Radio Chorus and Symphony Orchestra/Gerd Albrecht.** Capriccio 60 024-2 (12/91).

DIE GEZEICHNETEN. **Soloists; Dutch Radio Philharmonic Chorus and Orchestra/ Edo de Waart.** Marco Polo 8 223328/30 (12/91).

Franz Schubert

Austrian 1797-1828

Schubert. SYMPHONIES. **Royal Concertgebouw Orchestra/Nikolaus Harnoncourt.**
Teldec 4509-91184-2. Recorded at performances in the Concertgebouw, Amsterdam in 1992.
No. 1 in D major, D82. No. 2 in B flat major, D125. No. 3 in D major, D200. No. 4 in
C minor, "Tragic", D417. No. 5 in B flat major, D485. No. 6 in C major, D589. No. 8 in
B minor, "Unfinished"', D759. No. 9 in C major, "Great", D944.

④ 4h 44m DDD 12/93

Harnoncourt, like Abbado on DG (listed below), has researched Schubert's own manuscripts, and
corrected many unauthentic amendments that found their way into the printed editions of the
symphonies, such as the eight bars later added to the Fourth Symphony's first movement exposition;
but the differences between Harnoncourt's interpretative Schubert and Abbado's are startling. The
Ninth's finale, unlike Abbado's, a whirling, spinning *vivace* — is borne aloft on astonishingly precise
articulation of its rhythms and accents, and a springy delivery of the triplets. Characteristics, of
course, one has come to expect from an Harnoncourt performance. Still, what a joy to hear this
Allegro, and those of most of the earlier symphonies, seized with such bright and light-toned
enthusiasm. Here is urgent, virile and vehement playing, never over-forceful, over-emphatic or
burdened with excessive weight. What came as a surprise was the consistent drawing out of these
scores' potential for sadness and restlessness. Harnoncourt does not set apart the first six
symphonies as merely diverting, unlike Abbado (out-and-out charm is seldom part of Harnoncourt's
Schubertian vocabulary): their bittersweet ambiguities and apparent affectations of anxiety here
acquire a greater significance, and the cycle, as a whole, a greater continuity. Up to a point, the
darker, more serious Schubert that emerges here, derives from the type of sound Harnoncourt
fashions from his orchestra; not least, the lean string tone and incisive brass. And maybe, up to a
point, from the corrections: Harnoncourt refers to the manuscripts as often being "harsher and
more abrupt in tone [than the printed editions], juxtaposing extreme dynamic contrasts", though
you can't help feeling that contrasts in general have been given a helping hand. Trios are mostly
much slower than the urgent minuets/scherzos that frame them (with pauses in between the two).
And Schubert's less vigorous moments are very noticeable as such, and are inflected with varying
degrees of melancholy — it is uncanny how the string playing, in particular, often suggests a feeling
of isolation (along with the sparing vibrato is an equally sparing use of that enlivening facility:
staccato). The *Unfinished* Symphony's first movement is a stark, harrowing experience (yet it remains
a well-tempered musical one: gestures are never exaggerated); the opening is as cold as the grave
itself; the second subject knows its song is short-lived. In both movements, the elucidation and
balance of texture can only be described as masterly: just listen to the trombones casting shadows in
both codas. This, then, is as seriously pondered, coherent and penetrating a view of the complete
cycle as we have had. Whether or not you feel Harnoncourt focuses too much on Schubert's darker
side, you have to marvel at his ability to realize his vision. The recorded sound offers that inimitable
Concertgebouw blend of the utmost clarity and wide open spaces.

Additional recommendations ...
Nos. 1-6. No. 7 in E major, D729. Nos. 8 and 9. No. 10 in D major, D936A (realized Newbould).
Symphonic fragments — D major, D615 (orch. Newbould); D major, D708A (completed and orch.
Newbould). **Academy of St Martin in the Fields/Sir Neville Marriner.** Philips 412 176-
2PH6 — .·' ⑥ DDD 3/85 ⁹ₚ
No. 1 in B minor; Ballet Music No. 2 in G major. **Cologne Radio Symphony Orchestra/
Günter Wand.** RCA GD60096 — .·' ⑤ 4h 27m ADD/DDD 2/89
Nos. 1-6, 8 and 9. **Chamber Orchestra of Europe/Claudio Abbado.** DG 423 651-2GH5
— .·'' ⑤ 5h 20m DDD 2/89 ⁹ₚ ⁹ₛ
Nos. 1-6, 8 and 9. **Hanover Band/Roy Goodman.** Nimbus NI5270 — .·' ④ 4h 20m DDD 3/91 🖈
Nos. 1 and 2. **Chamber Orchestra of Europe/Claudio Abbado.** DG 423 652-2GH — .·''
59m DDD 9/89 ⁹ₚ
Nos. 1 and 4. **Hanover Band/Roy Goodman.** Nimbus NI5198 — .·' 59m DDD 7/90 🖈
Nos. 1 and 5. Overtures — D major, D590, "In the Italian Style"; "Des Teufels Lustschloss", D84.
English Sinfonia/Sir Charles Groves. Pickwick IMP Classics PCD944 — .·' 1h 18m DDD 11/91 Ⓑ
Nos. 1-6, 8 and 9. Rosamunde — Incidental Music, D797: Entr'acte No. 3 in B flat major; Ballet Music
Nos. 1-9. Rosamunde — Overture Die Zauberharfe; Ballets — B minor; G major. **Vienna Philhar-**
monic Orchestra/Riccardo Muti. EMI CMS7 64873-2 — .·' ④ 4h 55m DDD 5/94 ⁹ₚ

Schubert. Symphony — No. 3 in D major, D200[a]; No. 5 in B flat major, D485[a]; No. 6 in C major, D589[b]. **Royal Philharmonic Orchestra/Sir Thomas Beecham.** EMI Studio CDM7 69750-2. Items marked [a] from HMV ASD345 (6/60), [b] Columbia 33CX1363 (9/56).

·•⁰ 1h 18m ADD 8/90　　　　　　　　　　　　　**⁹ₚ Ⓑ ▲**

Beecham was well into his seventies when he made these recordings with the Royal Philharmonic, the orchestra he had founded in 1946. His lightness of touch, his delight in the beauty of the sound he was summoning, the directness of his approach to melody, and his general high spirits will all dominate our memory of these performances. But listening again, we may be reminded that Beecham could equally well dig deep into the darker moments of these works. Schubert's elation was rarely untroubled and the joy is often compounded by its contrast with pathos — Beecham had that balance off to a tee. It should be noted that he does not take all the marked repeats and he doctored some passages he considered over-repetitive. However, these recordings may also serve as a reminder of the wonderful heights of musicianship that his players achieved, as in the Trio of the Third Symphony's *Minuet*, where a simple waltz-like duet between oboe and bassoon attains greatness by the shapeliness, ease and poignancy of its execution. Despite some signs of age, these recordings still preserve the brilliance of their readings and the tonal quality of this orchestra. Altogether, a disc to lift the heaviest of spirits.

Additional recommendations ...

Nos. 3 and 8. **Vienna Philharmonic Orchestra/Carlos Kleiber.** DG 415 601-2GH — ·•⁰
46m ADD 12/85 ⁹ₚ Ⓑ

Nos. 3 and 8. **London Sinfonia/Richard Hickox.** Pickwick IMP Red Label PCD848 — ·•
49m DDD 4/87 Ⓑ

Nos. 3 and 4. **Chamber Orchestra of Europe/Claudio Abbado.** DG 423 653-2GH — ·•⁰
58m DDD 9/89 ⁹ₚ

Nos. 3 and 5. **Hanover Band/Roy Goodman.** Nimbus NI5172 — ·•⁰ 58m DDD 7/89 Ⓑ ✏

Nos. 3 and 5. Overture in C major in the Italian style, D591. **Northern Sinfonia/Heinrich Schiff.** Chandos CHAN9136 — ·•⁰ 59m DDD 6/93 ⁹ₚ Ⓑ

No. 3. **Schumann.** *Symphony No. 3 in E flat major, "Rhenish", Op. 97.* **North German Radio Symphony Orchestra/Günter Wand.** RCA Victor Red Seal 09026 61876-2 — ·•⁰ 56m DDD 2/94 ⁹ₚ

Schubert. Symphonies — No. 5 in B flat major, D485;[a] No. 8 in B minor, D759, "Unfinished"[b]. [a]**Columbia Symphony Orchestra,** [b]**New York Philharmonic Orchestra/ Bruno Walter.** CBS Masterworks CD42048. From Philips SABL209 (2/62).

·•⁰ 53m ADD 9/86　　　　　　　　　　　　　**⁹ₚ Ⓑ**

Those readers who never heard Bruno Walter should be warned not to expect his Schubert to be above all, exciting. Not that it is ever dull; but exciting in the way some modern interpreters have made our ears used to, it is not. There have been more impressive climaxes — since these records first appeared — that showed more electrifying attack and, above all, that settled for more exciting speeds; the second movement of the *Unfinished*, for example, is a real slow movement rather than an *Andante con moto* as is marked. But what Walter does give us is musical Schubert above all and a warmth that suits the composer admirably and most satisfyingly; also, he insists that all the main lines should sing. Nor is he concerned with such things as repeats, which he regarded as purely a convention of the times — unlike the modern fashion, especially for recordings, which regards the observance of every one as obligatory, irrespective of the demands of commonsense. He does observe just one in these symphonies, the quite short one marked soon after the start of No. 5. In suggesting that you should take Walter for what he was, rather than be disappointed because he is not like Beecham, say, suffice it to say that his recordings are guaranteed to be always warm and affectionate, often not hurried or specious as some of today's are, with some glorious playing of every kind. There are whole acres of superb *pp*; and listen to the horn calls in the second movement of the *Unfinished*, the two dynamic markings, *pp* and *ppp* clearly differentiated. His control over the music is notable in that the emotional response is never, ever allowed to become sentimental. It is as strong as is his control over the players. Recordings are pretty good though not so clear as one could hope for, on occasion.

Additional recommendations ...

Nos. 5 and 6. Overture in D major in the Italian style, D591. **Stockholm Sinfonietta/Neeme Järvi.** BIS CD387 — ⸫ 1h 12m DDD 9/88 Ⓑ

Nos. 5 and 6. **Chamber Orchestra of Europe/Claudio Abbado.** DG 423 654-2GH — ⸫ 1h 1m DDD 9/89 🄀ₚ Ⓑ

Nos. 5 and 8. **Royal Concertgebouw Orchestra/Leonard Bernstein.** DG 427 645-2GH — ⸫ 57m DDD 1/90 Ⓑ

Nos. 5 and 8. **Vienna Philharmonic Orchestra/Sir Georg Solti.** Decca 430 439-2DM — ⸫ 59m DDD 5/91 Ⓑ

No. 5. **Mendelssohn.** *Symphony No. 4 in A major, Op. 90, "Italian".* **Orchestra of the Eighteenth Century/Frans Brüggen.** Philips 432 123-2PH — ⸫ 56m DDD 12/91 🖋 Ⓑ

Nos. 5 and 8. Rosamunde, D797 — Entr'acte in B minor; Ballet Music No. 2 in G major. **Orchestra of the Age of Enlightenment/Sir Charles Mackerras.** Virgin Classics Veritas VC7 59273-2 — ⸫ 1h 14m DDD 12/92 Ⓑ 🖋

Schubert. Symphony No. 8 in B minor, D759, "Unfinished".
Schumann. Symphony No. 4 in D minor, Op. 120. **North German Radio Symphony Orchestra/Günter Wand.** RCA Victor Red Seal RD60826. Recorded live in 1991.

⸫ **57m DDD 5/92** Ⓑ

Wand's is a traditionally unhurried unfolding of Schubert's *Unfinished*, and one which does not exploit its troubled lyrical expanses, bar by bar, for the utmost drama. Perceptible deviations from his well maintained pulse give heightened expressiveness to crucial moments in the 'symphonic' drama, such as the fearful start of the first movement's development section, and the second movement's haunting central transition. But the quality here that is most easy to recognize, and just as impossible to analyse, is its spirituality. The live origins may help to explain this, as they do a few trifling imprecisions in the playing. His Schumann Fourth has impressive cumulative power; something the composer obviously intended with all four movements linked and sharing common themes. Wand's purposeful manner does not preclude many individual touches early in the work (the *Romanze* is darkly coloured and beautifully phrased), but as Schumann's thematic unity in continuity becomes more established, so Wand tightens his grip: the finale's introductory "darkness to dawn", for example, is here no interpolated episode, but an amassing of energies already in the air. The sound is full, deep and natural.

Additional recommendations ...

No. 8. **Schumann.** *Symphony No. 3 in E flat major, Op. 97, "Rhenish".* **Concertgebouw Orchestra/Leonard Bernstein.** DG 431 042-2GBE — ⸫ DDD Ⓑ

No. 8. **Mendelssohn.** *Symphony No. 4 in A major, Op. 90, "Italian".* **Giuseppe Sinopoli.** DG 410 862-2GH — ⸫ DDD 4/84 Ⓑ

No. 8ᵃ. **Schumann.** *Symphony No. 3ᵇ.* ᵃ**Philharmonia Orchestra/Giuseppe Sinopoli;** ᵇ**Los Angeles Philharmonic Orchestra/Carlo Maria Giulini.** DG 3D Classics 427 818-2GDC — ⸫ 1h 3m DDD 4/90 🄀ₚ Ⓑ

New review
Schubert. Symphony No. 9 in C major, D944, "Great". **North German Radio Symphony Orchestra/Günter Wand.** RCA Victor Red Seal RD60978. Recorded live in 1991.

⸫ **53m DDD 1/92** 🄀ₚ Ⓑ

A "heart-breaking show of spirit in adversity" is how Tovey describes the solitary oboe at the start of the Symphony's second movement, and by the end of the *Andante* here the spirit seems irredeemably shattered. Your attention is drawn to the significance of the foreboding 'tolling bell' transition (bar 148, 5'45") by a slowing of pace. And it *is* a significant passage, of that there can be no doubt, as its relative stillness becomes much more pervasive in the latter half of the movement; and its repeated warning horn notes are transformed, at the central climax, into hammering fanfares. One wonders initially if its significance needed pointing out in this manner and whether Wand's slackenings and hastenings of tempo generally throughout the symphony draw attention to themselves because we are now familiar with the more firmly maintained pulses of other versions. However, his long term management of his different tempos is often marvellous, particularly in the first movement, where the two-in-a-bar introduction leads (without an *accelerando*) to a slightly faster main *Allegro*. These variations of tempo are, of course, part of the process that is continually probing the surface of the score and beneath it to explore the contrasts of emotion, at the same time as exploring the symphony's structural possibilities. Put simply you sense a heightened awareness of what this music is capable of expressing bar by bar and over longer spans. Recorded live with great richness, presence and spaciousness, this may be a *Great* C major that doesn't have *all* the answers, but it adventures further than most, and that, surely, is in keeping with the spirit of the work.

Additional recommendations ...

No. 9. **Vienna Philharmonic Orchestra/Sir Georg Solti.** Decca 430 747-2DM — .⁚ 55m DDD 3/83 ⁹ₚ Ⓑ

No. 9. **Staatskapelle Dresden/Karl Böhm.** DG Galleria 419 484-2GA — .⁚ 50m DDD 12/87 Ⓑ

No. 9. **Orchestra of the Age of Enlightenment/Sir Charles Mackerras.** Virgin Classics VC7 59669-2 — .⁚ 1h DDD 6/88 Ⓑ ✧

No. 9. **Royal Concertgebouw Orchestra/Leonard Bernstein.** DG 427 646-2GH — .⁚ 50m DDD 1/90 Ⓑ

No. 9. Mendelssohn. *No. 4 in A major, Op. 90, "Italian".* **Berlin Philharmonic Orchestra/ Klaus Tennstedt.** EMI CDD7 64085-2 — .⁚ 1h 17m DDD 1/92 ⁹ₚ Ⓑ

New review

Schubert. Octet in F major, D803. Minuet and Finale in F major, D72[a]. **Vienna Octet; [a]Vienna Wind Soloists.** Decca 430 516-2DH.

.⁚ **1h 12m DDD 2/93** ────────────────────────── Ⓑ

This is a very pleasing account of Schubert's Octet for three wind and five strings including double-bass, with warm and bassy sound to match. The music itself is, of course, on a big scale. With the exposition repeat in the first movement observed, it takes nearly nine minutes to reach the development section and the movement takes 15 minutes in all, with five movements still to come. But the tempo of this *Allegro* is well chosen, being brisk yet unhurried, and the affectionate quality of the interpretation as a whole is never in any doubt. Indeed, the adjective that keeps coming to one's mind is 'Viennese', which is appropriate for the music and the players: the golden horn tone, liquid clarinet and sweet but slightly 'slidy' lead violin are all part of that incomparable style. The scherzo is delightfully poised and sprung, and one would have to be an austere listener to fail to respond to the *Andante* with seven variations which, once again, is played with the repeats as written. The dramatic and somewhat orchestral slow introduction to the finale leads well into the busy *Allegro* that is the main part of the movement, which also comes over effectively. The other work on this disc is most attractive and is played very stylishly here by a wind octet.

Additional recommendations ...

Octet. **Academy of Ancient Music Chamber Ensemble.** L'Oiseau-Lyre Florilegium 425 519-2OH — .⁚ 1h DDD 5/90 Ⓑ ✧

Octet. **Gaudier Ensemble.** ASV CDDCA694 — .⁚ 1h 4m DDD 5/90 Ⓑ

Octet. **Walter Boeykens Ensemble.** Harmonia Mundi HMC90 1440 — .⁚ 1h 4m DDD 8/93 Ⓑ

Octet. **Budapest Schubert Ensemble.** Naxos 8 550389 — . 1h 8m DDD 8/93 Ⓑ

Octet. **Berlin Soloists.** Teldec Digital Experience 4509-91448-2 — .⁚ 1h 3m DDD 11/93 Ⓑ

Schubert. String Quintet in C, D956. **Mstislav Rostropovich** (vc); **Emerson Quartet** (Eugene Drucker, Philip Setzer, vns; Lawrence Dutton, va; David Finckel, vc) DG 431 792-2GH. Recorded live in 1990.

.⁚ **53m DDD 9/92** ──────────────────────────── Ⓑ

Arguably the finest of Schubert's late chamber works, the String Quintet, like the *Unfinished* and *Great* C major symphonies, had to wait some years after his death for its first performance. Many consider it to be the finest of his late works, with its virtually perfect fusion of compositional technique and artistic balance, its natural marriage of rhythmic and harmonic subtlety. Unlike Mozart, who added a second viola to give the basic string quartet texture a more mellow centre, Schubert employs the extra weight of a second cello, though he gives it free rein to explore its exceptionally wide compass. The Emerson Quartet are joined in this performance by none other than Mstislav Rostropovich, a partnership of persuasive integrity, steeped in the kind of mutual understanding that one would expect of such a meeting of minds; this is a marvellously well structured performance, conceived very much as a whole across its long, 53-minute span. The recording serves well enough; it is very clear and well laid out across the sound stage, but perhaps a little too closely focused and, as a result, a shade over-bright.

Additional recommendations ...
String Quintet. **Heinrich Schiff** (vc); **Alban Berg Quartet**. EMI CDC7 47018-2 — .·ˑ
DDD 8/84 Ⓑ
String Quintet. **Douglas Cummings** (vc); **Lindsay Quartet**. ASV CDDCA537 — .·ˑ DDD
9/85 Ⓑ
String Quintet. **Yo-Yo Ma** (vc); **Cleveland Quartet**. CBS Masterworks CD39134 — .·ˑ 54m
DDD 8/86 Ⓑ
String Quintet. **Bruno Schrecker** (vc); **Aeolian Quartet**. Saga Classics SCD9011 — .·ˑ 54m
ADD 4/92 ꝙₚ Ⓑ ▲
String Quintet[a]. *String Quartet No. 12 in C minor, D703, "Quartettsatz"*. **Takács Quartet;** [a]**Miklos Perényi** (vc). Decca 436 324-2DH — .·ˑ 1h 4m DDD 6/93 Ⓑ
String Quintet. **Wenn-Sinn Yang** (vc); **Brandis Quartet**. Nimbus NI5313 — .·ˑ 54m DDD 6/93 Ⓑ
String Quintet[a]. *String Quartet No. 8 in B flat major, D112*. **Medici Quartet;** [a]**Melissa Phelps** (vc). Medici-Whitehall MQCD9002 — .·ˑ 1h 17m DDD 10/93 ꝙₚ Ⓑ
String Quintet[a]. *Symphony No. 5 in B flat major, D485*[b]. [a]**Isaac Stern,** [a]**Alexander Schneider** (vns); [a]**Milton Katims** (va); [a]**Paul Tortelier** (vc); [b]**Prades Festival Orchestra/Pablo Casals** ([a]vc). Sony Classical Casals Edition mono SMK58992 — .·ˑ 1h 16m ADD 5/94 Ⓑ

Schubert. Piano Quintet in A major, D667, "Trout"[a]. String Quartet No. 14 in D minor, D810, "Death and the Maiden"[b]. [a]**Sir Clifford Curzon** (pf); [a]members of the **Vienna Octet** (Willi Boskovsky, vn; Gunther Breitenbach, va; Nikolaus Hübner, vc; Johann Krump, db); [b]**Vienna Philharmonic Quartet** (Willi Boskovsky, Otto Strasser, vns; Rudolf Streng, va; Robert Scheiwein, vc). Decca 417 459-2DM. Item marked [a] from SXL2110 (6/59), recorded in 1957, [b] SXL6092 (5/64), recorded in 1963.

.·ˑ **1h 11m ADD 6/88** Ⓑ ▲

Schubert composed the *Trout* Quintet in his early twenties for a group of amateur musicians in the town of Steyr in Upper Austria, which lies upon the River Enns which was then noted for its fine fishing and keen fishermen. The Quintet was certainly tailored for special circumstances, but like all great occasional music it stands as strongly as ever today, with its freshly bubbling invention and sunny melodiousness. Willi Boskovsky's gentle and cultured mind is very much responsible for the success of these performances of Schubert's two best-known chamber works. In the delectable *Trout* Quintet there is real unanimity of vision between the players, as well as an immaculate attention to the details of the scoring. Clifford Curzon's part in the performance is memorable especially for his quiet playing — the atmosphere is magical in such moments. Everywhere there is a great awareness of the delicacy and refinement of Schubert's inventiveness. The *Death and the Maiden* Quartet is no less successful. Schubert's strikingly powerful harmonies, together with a sustained feeling of intensity, all go to heighten the urgency of the first movement. Despite this, string textures are generally kept light and feathery. In the *Andante* all is subtly understated and although a mood of tragedy is always lurking in the background, never is it thrown at the listener. Boskovsky's understanding of the music is very acute and the performance cannot fail to satisfy even the most demanding. These are two vintage recordings and in the quartet the quality of sound is quite remarkable.

Additional recommendations ...
Piano Quintet. **Alfred Brendel** (pf); **James van Denmark** (db); **Cleveland Quartet**. Philips
400 078-2PH — .·ˑ ADD 3/83 ꝙₚ Ⓑ
Piano Quintet. **Clemens Hagen** (vn); **Veronika Hagen** (va); **Lukas Hagen** (vc); **Alois
Posch** (db); **András Schiff** (pf). Decca 411 975-2DH — .·ˑ 44m DDD 4/85 ꝙₚ Ⓑ
Piano Quintet. *Der Hirt auf dem Felsen, D965*[b]. [b]**Felicity Lott** (sop); **Nash Ensemble**. Pickwick
IMP Classics PCD868 — .·ˑ 57m DDD 12/87 Ⓑ
Piano Quintet[a]. **Beethoven.** *Piano Trio No. 5 in D major, Op. 70 No. 1, "Ghost"*[b]. **Beaux Arts
Trio;** [a]**Georg Hörtnagel** (db); [b]**Samuel Rhodes** (va). Philips Silver Line Classics 420 716-
2PSL — .·ˑ 1h 2m ADD 6/88 Ⓑ

Piano Quintet. String Trios[a] — B flat major, D471; B flat major, D581. **Ingrid Haebler** (pf); **Jacques Cazauran** (db); [a]**Grumiaux Trio**. Philips Musica da Camera 422 838-2PC — .·˙ lh 3m ADD 10/89 Ⓑ

Piano Quintet. **Hummel.** *Piano Quintet in E flat major, Op. 87.* **Schubert Ensemble of London.** Hyperion Helios CDH88010 — .·˙ lh lm DDD 6/90 Ⓑ

Piano Quintet[a]. *Adagio and Rondo Concertante in F major, D487.* **Jenö Jandó** (pf); **Kodály Quartet;** [a]**István Tóth** (db). Naxos 8 550658 — ˌ 53m DDD 4/93 Ⓑ

Piano Quintet[b]. *Lieder*[a] — *Die Forelle, D550; Am Strome, D539; Auf dem see, D543; Erlafsee, D586; An eine Quelle, D530; Der Jüngling am Bache, D192; Der Schiffer, D536.* [a]**John Mark Ainsley** (ten); [b]**Steven Lubin** (fp); [b]**Academy of Ancient Music Chamber Ensemble.** L'Oiseau-Lyre 433 848-2OH — .·˙ lh DDD 9/93 𝄞ₚ Ⓑ ✍

Piano Quintet[a]. *Quartet in G major, D96*[b]. [b]**Wolfgang Schulz** (fl); [a]**Georg Hetzel** (vn); [ab]**Wolfram Christ** (va); [ab]**Georg Faust** (vc); [a]**Alois Posch** (db); [b]**Göran Söllscher** (gtr); [a]**James Levine** (pf). DG 431 783-2GH — .·˙ lh 5m DDD 1/94 Ⓑ

Key to symbols

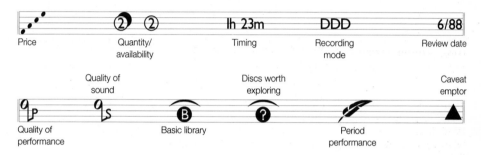

| Price | Quantity/ availability | Timing | Recording mode | Review date |
| | | | | |

| | Quality of sound | | Discs worth exploring | | Caveat emptor |

| Quality of performance | | Basic library | | | Period performance | |

Schubert. STRING QUARTETS. **Melos Quartet** (Wilhelm Melcher, Gerhard Voss, vns; Hermann Voss, va; Peter Buck, vc). Harmonia Mundi HMC90 1408/9. String Quartets — No. 12 in C minor, D703, "Quartettsatz"[b]; No. 13 in A minor, D804[a]; No. 14 in D minor, D810, "Death and the Maiden"[a]; No. 15 in G major, D887[b]. Items marked [a] recorded 1989, [b] 1991.

.·˙ ② 2h 14m DDD 12/92 ——————— 𝄞ₚ Ⓑ

These quartets belong to the years 1820-26 and thus the last decade of Schubert's short life. As the violent *fortissimo* attack of the D minor reminds us right away, they don't make for comfortable listening: there's plenty of passion and tension here, and even an occasional alarming outburst such as occurs in the *Andante un poco moto* of the G major Quartet. Yet since this is still Schubert's music, there's also melodic richness. In fact one often senses a dramatic contrast between Viennese *Gemütlichkeit* and something like terror or pain, maybe even the thought of approaching death which we know haunted the already ill composer. The Melos Quartet have played this music in public over a period of years and bring authority as well as insight to the performance of the three late quartets and the earlier but no less compelling *Quartettsatz* in C minor. Thus, the big first movement of *Death and the Maiden* has both vigour in the fiery first subject and gentleness in the lilting second, while the coda smoulders impressively before bursting into flames. There is a hushed beauty in the famous slow movement, based on the song which gave its name to the work, while the final *Presto* has all the urgency of an Erl King-like pursuit. The Melos are equally at home in the radiantly melodious yet sorrowful A minor Quartet and the dramatic and enigmatic G major Quartet. These are performances of distinction, and the recording is truthful, with a natural degree of resonance.

Additional recommendations ...
No. 14. **Beethoven.** *String Quartet in E flat major, Op. 74, "Harp".* **Brodsky Quartet.** Pickwick IMP Red Label PCD831 — ˌ lh l0m DDD 1/87 Ⓑ

Nos. 12 and 14. **Lindsay Quartet.** ASV CDDCA560 — .·˙ 52m DDD 3/87 Ⓑ

Nos. 14 and 15. **Busch Quartet.** EMI Références mono CDH7 69795-2 — .·˙ lh l3m ADD 5/89 𝄞ₚ Ⓑ ▲

No. 13 (trans. Mahler). No. 14 (trans. Liszt CO). **Franz Liszt Chamber Orchestra/János Rolla.** Quintana QUI90 3025 — ⁣.·•ʼ 56m DDD 3/92 ꟼₚ Ⓑ
No. 2 in C major, D32. No. 14. **Artis Quartet.** Sony Classical SK52582 — ⁣.·•ʼ 59m DDD 6/93 Ⓑ
Nos. 13 and 14. **Takács Quartet.** Decca 436 843-2DH — ⁣.·•ʼ 1h 15m DDD 12/93 Ⓑ

New review

Schubert. PIANO TRIOS. STRING TRIOS. ªBeaux Arts Trio (Menahem Pressler, pf; Daniel Guilet, vn; Bernard Greenhouse, vc); ᵇGrumiaux Trio (Arthur Grumiaux, vn; Georges Janzer, va, Eva Czako, vc). Philips Duo 438 700-2PM2. Items marked ª recorded in 1966, ᵇ 1969. Piano Triosª — B flat major, D28 (Sonata in one movement); No. 1 in B flat major, D898; No. 2 in E flat major, D929. Notturno in E flat major, D897ª. String Triosᵇ — B flat major, D471; B flat major, D581.

.·•ʼ ② 2h 7m ADD 4/94 ꟼₚ

These performances are polished, yet the many solo contributions from each of the players emerge with a strong personality. The Beaux Arts cellist brings lovely phrasing and a true simplicity of line, so right for Schubert — memorably in the lovely slow movement melody of the Trio No. 2 in E flat. In addition to the great piano trios (B flat, D898 and E flat, D929) the set includes the extremely personable, very early Sonata in B flat, D28, where the lyrical line already has the unmistakable character of its young composer. Also included is the *Notturno*, D897, a raptly emotive short piece played here with a remarkable depth of feeling that recalls the gentle intensity of the glorious slow movement of the String Quintet. The recording is naturally balanced, although a little dry in the treble. Of the two rarer string trios, also early works, the four-movement Trio, D581 is totally infectious, with that quality of innocence that makes Schubert's music stand apart. Given such persuasive advocacy, and vivid recording, both pieces cannot fail to give the listener great pleasure.

Additional recommendations ...
No. 1. **Borodin Trio.** Chandos CHAN8308 — ⁣.·•ʼ 43m DDD 3/84
No. 2 in E flat major, D929. **Borodin Trio.** Chandos CHAN8324 — ⁣.·•ʼ DDD 11/84
Nos. 1 and 2. **Brahms.** Piano Trios — No. 1 in B major, Op. 8; No. 2 in C major, Op. 87; No. 3 in C minor, Op. 101. **Mendelssohn.** Piano Trio No. 1 in D minor, Op. 49. **Isaac Stern** (vn); **Leonard Rose** (vc); **Eugene Istomin** (pf). Sony Classical SK46425 — ⁣.·• ③ 3h 19m ADD 5/91 ꟼₚ
B flat major, D28; Nos. 1 and 2. Notturno. **Trio Zingara.** Collins Classics 1215-2 — ⁣.·•ʼ 1h 1m DDD 10/91
No. 2. Piano Trio in B flat major, D28. **Castle Trio.** Virgin Classics Veritas VC7 59303-2 — ⁣.·•ʼ 58m DDD 11/93 ✍

Schubert. Violin Sonata in A major (Duo), D574. Rondo brillant in B minor, D895. Fantasy in C major, D934. **Gidon Kremer** (vn); **Valery Afanassiev** (pf). DG 431 654-2GH. Recorded in 1990.

.·•ʼ 1h 7m DDD 3/92 ꟼₚ ꟼₛ

Few indeed are the recital discs which can offer the listener such unalloyed pleasure as this gloriously played and generously conceived Schubert recording from Gidon Kremer and Valery Afanassiev. Rarer yet by far, though, are releases capable of generating the kind of communicative ambience more normally revealed by the intimacy of live music making. The very opening bars of Afanassiev's piano introduction at the start of the *Duo* in A major, D574, with its restrained yet expectant dignity of utterance would mesmerize the heart of the sternest critic, whilst Kremer exhibits charm, wit, understatement and sheer delight in this work. The B minor Rondo and the magnificent Fantasy in C major were written a decade after the *Duo* and were both intended to display the talents of the composer's friend, the Czech violinist, Josef Slavic, who had settled in Vienna during 1826. Neither work found favour at the time, and quite possibly the dark premonitions of the Rondo, whose emotional sympathies recalled those of the *Unfinished* Symphony, were inappropriate for Viennese popular tastes. However, although Kremer's approach avoids mere rhetoric here, this superb recording is surely crowned by a magisterial performance of the C major Fantasy. This account combines bravura, elegance and a deep affinity with the Schubertian genre, captured with splendid realism by a recording which is technically beyond criticism.

Additional recommendations ...
Violin Sonatas — D major, D384; A minor, D385; G minor, D408; D574. **Raphaël Oleg** (vn);
Théodore Paraskivesco (pf). Denon CO-75027 — .·*ᐟ* lh llm DDD 3/93
Violin Sonatas — D384. D385. D408; D574. **Gidon Kremer** (vn); **Oleg Maisenberg** (pf). DG
437 092-2GH — .·*ᐟ* lh 2m DDD 4/93
Violin Sonata, D574. **Schumann.** *Fantasiestücke, Op. 73. Funf Stücke im Volkston, Op. 102.* **Maria**
Kliegel (vc); **Kristin Merscher** (pf). Naxos 8 550654 — . lh 8m DDD 7/93
Fantasy in C major, D934[a]*. Rondo brillant*[b]*.* **Raphael Oleg** ([a]vn/[b]va); **Gerard Wyss** (pf). Denon
CO-75636 — .·*ᐟ* lh 6m DDD 7/94

Schubert. Piano Sonata in A minor, D821, "Arpeggione". WORKS FOR VIOLA AND
PIANO. **Yuri Bashmet** (va); **Mikhail Muntian** (pf). RCA Victor Red Seal RD60112.
Recorded in 1989.
Schumann: *Märchen-bilder, Op. 113. Adagio and Allegro, Op. 70.* **Bruch:** *Kol nidrei,
Op. 47.* **Enescu:** *Konzertstück.*

.·*ᐟ* **lh l3m   DDD   12/90**   **⁹ₚ**

The booklet tells us that Yuri Bashmet, aged 38 at the time of this recording, had already 30 new
works for the viola dedicated to him. Perhaps thanks should go to this Russian artist, with his
glorious tone, and his closely attuned pianist, Mikhail Muntian, for enriching the CD catalogue
with Georges Enescu's rarely heard *Konzertstück*, written in Paris in the composer's impressionable
early twenties, and played here with intuitive understanding of its fantasy and lyrical rapture. Like
that work, the four miniatures of Schumann's *Märchenbilder* of 1851 were also inspired by the
viola itself, whereas Schumann's *Adagio and Allegro*, Bruch's *Kol nidrei* (based on one of the oldest
and best-known synagogue melodies) and Schubert's charming A minor Sonata were originally
written for valve-horn, cello and the now obsolete arpeggione respec-tively. But with his wide
range of colour and his "speaking" phrasing Bashmet makes them all entirely his own, only
causing the occasional raised eyebrow with slower tempos for slow numbers (such as Schumann's
lullaby-like Op. 113, No. 4 and the *Adagio* of Schubert's Sonata) than could be enjoyed from
players without his own fine-spun, intimately nuanced line. Strongly recommended.

Additional recommendations ...
Sonata, D821. **Debussy.** *Cello Sonata.* **Schumann.** *Fünf Stücke im Volkston, Op. 102.* **Mstislav**
Rostropovich (vc); **Benjamin Britten** (pf). Decca 417 833-2DH *(reviewed under Debussy; refer
to the Index to Reviews)* — .·*ᐟ* 59m ADD 9/87 ⁹ₚ
(All trans. Stallman). Sonata, D821. Violin Sonatina in G minor, D408. Fantasy in C major, D934.
Robert Stallman (fl); **Erika Nickrenz** (pf). ASV CDDCA742 — .·*ᐟ* lh 9m DDD 4/92 ⁹ₚ
Sonata, D821. **Schumann.** *Fantasiestücke, Op. 73. Fünf Stücke im Volkston. Adagio and Allegro in
A flat major, Op. 70.* **Mendelssohn.** *Variations Concertantes, Op. 17. Song without words in D major,
Op. 109.* **Friedrich-Jürgen Sellheim** (vc); **Eckart Sellheim** (pf). Sony Classical Essential
Classics MK48171 — . lh 12m ADD 10/92 ⁹ₚ

Schubert. Impromptus — D899; D935. **Murray Perahia** (pf). CBS Masterworks CD37291.
From 37291 (1/84).

.·*ᐟ* **lh 3m   DDD   4/85**   **⁹ₚ   Ⓑ**

Though an able pianist, Schubert was not a concert-giving virtuoso out to conquer an
international public with largescale bravura works. The music-making he most enjoyed was at
informal parties in the homes of music-loving friends, hence the very large number of miniatures
— with the *Impromptus* among them — that flowed unceasingly from his pen. Whereas so much
of what he wrote was never published in his lifetime, he had the satisfaction of seeing all eight
Impromptus in print the year before he died. And their popularity has never waned, as the
quickest glance at any catalogue at once makes clear. Inevitably Murray Perahia has strong rivals
all equally deserving of a place in this *Guide*. His own version nevertheless constantly enchants
with its pellucid tone and spontaneous spring-like freshness. Note the rippling lightness of the
triplets in No. 2 in E flat and the pinpoint clarity of his semiquaver articulation in No. 4 in A
flat in the first set, likewise the dancing lilt he brings to the variations of No. 3 in B flat and his
respect for the *scherzando* expressively qualifying the *allegro* in No. 4 in F minor in the second
set. None are 'overloaded'. The recording is no less pleasing.

Additional recommendations ...

D899. D935. **Alfred Brendel** (pf). Philips 420 840-2PM — .·' Ih 2m DDD 4/84 Ⓑ

D899. D935. **Radu Lupu** (pf). Decca 411 711-2DH — .·' DDD 10/84 Ⓑ

D899. D935. **Alfred Brendel** (pf). Philips 422 237-2PH — .·' Ih Im DDD 10/89 Ⓑ

D899. D935. **Krystian Zimerman** (pf). DG 423 612-2GH — .·' Ih 5m DDD 5/91 Ⓑ

D899. *Six Moments musicaux, D780. Ungarische Melodie in B minor, D817. Six Deutsche Tänze, D820. Grazer Galopp, D925.* **András Schiff** (pf). Decca 430 425-2DH — .·' Ih IIm DDD 11/92 Ⓑ

D899. D935. **Edwin Fischer** (pf). Dante Historical Piano Collection mono HPC006 — .·' 53m ADD 5/93 Ⓑ ▲

D935. *D946. Allegretto in C minor, D915. 12 Ländler, D790.* **András Schiff.** Decca 425 638-2DH — .·' Ih 14m DDD 7/90 Ⓑ

Schubert. PIANO WORKS. **Sviatoslav Richter** (pf). Olympia OCD286/8. Recorded live in 1979.
OCD286 — Piano Sonatas: B major, D575; F minor, D625. Six Moments musicaux, D780 — No. 1 in C major; No. 3 in F minor; No. 6 in A flat major. *OCD288* — Piano Sonatas: A major, D664; A minor, D784. Impromptus, D899 — No. 2 in E flat major; No. 4 in A flat major. *OCD287* — **Chopin.** Preludes, Op. 28 — No. 2 in A minor; No. 4 in E minor; No. 5 in D major; No. 6 in B minor; No. 7 in A major; No. 8 in F sharp minor; No. 9 in E major; No. 10 in C sharp minor; No. 11 in B major; No. 13 in F sharp major; No. 19 in E flat major; No. 21 in B flat major; No. 23 in F major. **Schumann.** Novelletten, Op. 21 — No. 2 in D major; No. 4 in D major; No. 8 in F sharp minor. Fantasiestücke, Op. 12 — In der Nacht; Traumes-Wirren.

.·' ③ Ih 5m Ih 3m 50m DDD 10/92   ⁹ₚ

Richter's dislike for studio recording can be frustrating — some of his most stupendous performances can only be heard on unofficial tapes of almost unlistenable quality; and when in the mid-1980s the record companies finally started recording his concerts in a big way something of the edge had already gone off his formerly unassailable mastery. But these 1979 Tokyo performances have the best of most worlds. The sound is drier and closer than usual. That suits the monumentality of the playing, which itself marks the beginning of Richter's ultra-austere late manner without betraying the least technical discomfort. The Chopin Preludes are perhaps uninvitingly plain, for all their consummate pianism. But the Schumann *Novelettes* on the same disc are uncannily insightful, and "Traumes-Wirren" is quite breathtaking. Both Schubert compilations demonstrate a philosophical approach to this composer which some listeners may find an acquired taste. Richter shuns surface beauty and charm and instead follows the music to elevated realms of reflection. Slow movements are profoundly inward and meditative, fast ones crackle with energy, and the rapt attention of the audience tells you as much about the atmosphere generated as the wild applause and raucous bravos which conclude some of the finest piano recordings ever reviewed.

Additional recommendations ...

A major, D664. Fantasy in C major, "Wanderer", D760. Works by **Beethoven, Berg, Schumann** and **Prokofiev.** Sviatoslav Richter (pf). EMI CMS7 64429-2 — .·' ④ 4h 33m ADD 3/93 ⁹ₚ

D571, D840 and D845. **András Schiff** (pf). Decca 440 305-2DH — .·' Ih IIm DDD 12/93 ⁹ₚ

D566, D784 and D850. **András Schiff** (pf). Decca 440 306-2DH — .·' Ih 15m DDD 12/93 ⁹ₚ

D575, D840 and D894. **Sviatoslav Richter** (pf). Philips 438 483-2PH2 — .·' ② Ih 57m DDD 7/94 ⁹ₚ

New review
Schubert. Piano Sonatas — A flat major, D557; B major, D575; G major, D894. **András Schiff** (pf). Decca 440 307-2DH. Recorded in 1992.

.·' Ih 16m DDD 6/94   ⁹ₚ

Schubert's piano music from András Schiff always lifts the spirits, and this time quite a bit higher than most comparable available versions. Typically, he chooses his favourite Bösendorfer Imperial with its Viennese accent and writes in an introduction to the notes of its Schubertian sensitivity to tone-quality, particularly in the softest dynamics. Schiff cites the opening of the G major Sonata, D894 as an example and, indeed, this movement, which the composer originally called a

Fantasy, has a gentle luminosity about it. Schiff's approach to the vast first movement more closely resembles Lupu's (reviewed further on) in its meditative, long-sighted qualities; but Schiff again triumphs, in coaxing both a wider and a more finely controlled tone palette out of his instrument. Schiff's greatest achievement here, though, is his organic view of the inner and outer worlds of this sonata. As in the song, "Der Lindenbaum" (from *Winterreise*), images of both tender dream and harsh reality seem to shape the piece. Schiff makes them seem simply different sides of the same persona. One flows into and out of another, with the dark concentration of rhythm in the eye of the storm never compromising the original impulse of the music. In the last movement, Schiff outdoes Lupu in the dance of constantly shifting weights and measures, lights and half-lights which dapple the rondo's returns. Schiff seems to play through the childlike ears and eyes of Schubert himself. This outstanding performance of D894 is nicely balanced by a deliciously understated D557, the most classically conceived of all Schubert's sonatas, and by the more adventurous D575. Here, Schiff continues to exploit the qualifying *ma non troppo* of the opening *Allegro* to create a sense of a plethora of ideas and energies being held back within an unquiet serenity. If the slow movement is a little over-deliberate, the finale again seems to be constantly surprising itself with the new ideas which sing out as if they had only just been imagined.

New review

Schubert. Piano Sonatas in A major — D664; D959. **Elisabeth Leonskaja** (pf). Teldec 9031-74865-2.

Ih IIm DDD 10/93

In the earlier of the two A major sonatas, Leonskaja's pursuit of depth maybe robs it of just a little of its effortless lyrical flow, of its smiling youthful freshness and grace, but her lively tempo and crisp, crystalline articulation in the finale come as a welcome reminder that the composer was still only 22. For the 'big' A major Sonata the world had to wait another nine years — by which time Schubert had only a few more months to live. After a boldly assertive launching Leonskaja at once makes you aware of the first movement's deeper and sometimes darker undertones. Some listeners might feel that she over-relaxes tension in her very personal response to the music's more intimate innuendos, but how well the mystery she draws from the coda prepares you for things-to-come in the *Andante*. This she plays meditatively, in a spirit of resigned desolation (except of course for its central outburst of panic). The *Scherzo* is crisply sprung, and the finale both lyrical and (when required) strong. Above a certain level there's a touch of steel in the recorded sound, but softer tone is pleasing enough.

Additional recommendation ...
D664; D959; C minor, D958; B flat major, D960. Impromptus, D899. Allegretto in C minor, D915.
Claudio Arrau (pf). Philips Arrau Edition 432 307-2PM3 — ⫶ ③ 3h 3m ADD 5/92

Schubert. Piano Sonata in B flat major, D960. Fantasy in C major, D760, "Wanderer". **Alfred Brendel** (pf). Philips 422 062-2PH.

58m DDD 1/90

Brendel meets Schubert on his own ground, exulting in the *con fuoco* panache of the earlier work, and just as keenly revealing the 'other-worldliness' of Schubert's farewell. For immediacy of response, it would be hard to name any player more aware of Schubert's own impression-ability — the impressionability of a composer who died young enough to have known only "the poignancy and rapture of first sensations". Some might feel that Brendel's reaction to the mood of the moment at times results in over-elasticity of pulse, as in his drastic slowings-down for the lyrical second subject in the *Wanderer*'s first movement. But never mind. Whatever he does is done with enough conviction to make you feel, at the moment of listening, that there could be no other way. The recording is both rich and clear.

Additional recommendations ...
Fantasy. **Schumann.** *Fantasia in C major, Op. 17.* **Murray Perahia** (pf). CBS Masterworks CD42124 —⫶ 52m DDD 12/86 Ⓑ
Fantasy. Piano Sonata in A minor, D845. **Maurizio Pollini** (pf). DG 419 672-2GH — ⫶ 58m DDD 8/87 Ⓑ

Piano Sonata. Fantasy. **Alfred Brendel** (pf). Philips Silver Line 420 644-2PM — ⠂⠄ 57m ADD 8/87 ⁹ₚ Ⓑ

Piano Sonata. Impromptu in A flat major, D935 No. 2. Six Moments musicaux, D780. **Sir Clifford Curzon** (pf). Decca 417 642-2DH — ⠂⠄ 1h 10m ADD 8/87 ⁹ₚ Ⓑ

Piano Sonata. Allegretto in C minor, D915. Impromptus, D946. **Maurizio Pollini.** DG 427 326-2GH — ⠂⠄ 1h 11m DDD 5/89 ⁹ₚ Ⓑ

New review

Schubert. Piano Sonatas – C minor, D958[a]; A major, D959[b]; B flat major, D960[c]. Three Impromptus, D946[d]. **Alfred Brendel** (pf). Philips Duo 438 703-2PM2. Item marked [a] from 6500 415 (3/73), [b] 6500 284 (4/73), [c] 6500 285 (11/72), [d] 6500 928 (9/75). Recorded 1971-74.

⠂⠄ ② 2h 8m ADD 5/94 ⁹ₚ

Schubert and Brendel are repackaged once again in a compilation which concentrates the ear and mind particularly enrichingly. Brendel himself wrote, of the C minor Sonata, that "the leading character in this tragedy is being chased and cornered, and looks in vain for a way of escape". The insistent rhythmic movement which can irritate in some of Brendel's playing, here expresses entirely appropriately the unnerving sense of disquiet which pervades the whole work. In the A major Sonata, Brendel allows himself to follow Schubert's own flights of fancy and sweet digressions, moulding them with an unmistakably firm sense of ultimate purpose and direction. The slow movement's song is held back by its own halting, tolling second beat, only to be released into the nonchalant virtuosity of the *Scherzo*. This is a virtuosity of placing and timing, and it characterizes, too, the slow movement of the B flat Sonata, surely one of the most beautiful performances of this movement on disc. The entire sonata, indeed, has a rare sense of emotional and intellectual coherence. The *Impromptus* show Brendel apparently having fun.

Additional recommendation ...
D959 and A minor, D537. **Laurent Cabasso** (pf). Auvidis Valois V4630 — ⠂⠄ 1h 4m DDD 4/91 Ⓑ

Key to symbols

Price	Quantity/availability	Timing	Recording mode	Review date
⠂⠄	② ②	1h 23m	DDD	6/88

Schubert. Piano Sonata in C minor, D958. Impromptus, D899. Deutsche Tänze, D783. **Imogen Cooper** (pf). Ottavo OTRC78923. Recorded in 1989.

⠂⠄ 1h 10m DDD 2/92

This is in fact the last of Imogen Cooper's six-disc cycle of the piano music of Schubert's last six years, a cycle launched in 1988 hard on the heels of similar cycles given on the concert platform in both London and Amsterdam. Like its predecessors, it confirms her as a Schubert player of exceptional style and finesse. Intuitively perceptive phrasing and a willingness to let the music sing within a wholly Schubertian sound-world are prime virtues. And though (like her erstwhile mentor, Alfred Brendel) she is no slave to the metronome when contrasting first and second subjects in sonata expositions, she still makes the music her own without the self-consciously mannered kind of interpretation heard from one or two more recent rivals in this strongly competitive field. Her urgent yet poised performance of the late C minor Sonata certainly confirms her admission (in a 1988 *Gramophone* interview) that the comparatively clinical atmosphere of an audience-less recording venue worries her not at all. In London's Henry Wood Hall her Yamaha is as clearly and truthfully reproduced (save for a slight suspicion of pedal-haze in the sonata's demonically driven finale) as most else in the series. The *Impromptus* reveal an acutely sensitive response to Schubert's dynamic subtleties and surprises of key, while the 16 *German Dances* tell their own simple Viennese tale without any suggestion of applied make-up.

Additional recommendation ...
D958. D960. **Jenö Jandó** (pf). Naxos 8 550475 — *.* lh 9m DDD

Schubert. Piano Sonata in A minor, D845. Impromptus, D946. **Alfred Brendel** (pf). Philips
422 075-2PH.

.• lh lm DDD l0/89 ⁹ₚ

Schubert. Piano Sonatas — A minor, D845[a]; G major, D894[b]. **Radu Lupu** (pf). Decca 417
640-2DH. Item marked [a] from SXL6931 (12/79), [b] SXL6741 (5/76).

.• lh l4m ADD 6/87 ⁹ₚ

Though love of the music alone, as pianists know, is not enough to master these pieces, it is
essential, and in this big A minor Sonata (a key that was somehow especially important to
Schubert) Brendel presents us with a drama that is no less tense for being predominantly
expressed in terms of shapely melody. There is a flexibility in this playing that reminds us of the
pianist's own comment that in such music "we feel not masters but victims of the situation": he
allows us plenty of time to savour detail without ever losing sight of the overall shape of the
music, and the long first movement and finale carry us compellingly forwards, as does the
scherzo with its urgent energy, while the *Andante* second movement, too, has the right kind of
spaciousness. In the *Impromptus* which date from the composer's last months, Brendel is no less
responsive and imaginative. Richly sonorous digital recording in a German location complements
the distinction of the playing on this fine disc. Radu Lupu also understands Schubert's style as do
few others and the way in which he is able to project this essentially private world is
outstanding. His tone is unfailingly clear, and this adds substantially to the lucidity of the
readings. The simplicity of the opening themes of the A minor Sonata is a marvel of eloquence
and when it is reset in the development section of the first movement one is amazed to hear
Lupu transforming it into something far more urgent and full of pathos. The G major Sonata
again fires Lupu's imagination and in the Minuet third movement he uses a considerable amount
of rubato for the dance; its solid rhythmic pulse is an ideal foil to offset the extraordinary
transitions of the finale that follows. The recorded sound does full justice to the colour of the
pianist's tone.

Additional recommendations ...
*Piano Sonatas — D845; E major, D157. Valses sentimentales, D779 — No. 1 in C major; No. 3 in
G major; No. 5 in B flat major; No. 7 in G minor; No. 13 in A major; No. 14 in D major; No. 19 in
A flat major; No. 21 in E flat major; No. 24 in G minor; No. 28 in E flat major; No. 30 in C major;
No. 34 in A flat major. Waltz in A flat major, D978.* **Michel Dalberto** (pf). Denon CO-73787
— *.•* lh 7m DDD 4/90
Piano Sonatas — D894; A minor, D784. 12 Waltzes, D145. **Vladimir Ashkenazy** (pf). Decca
Ovation 425 017-2DM — *.•* lh l4m ADD 8/90 ⁹ₚ

Schubert. Piano Sonatas — D major, D850; A minor, D784. **Alfred Brendel** (pf). Philips
422 063-2PH.

.• lh 3m DDD ll/88

There is an extraordinary amount of highly experimental writing in Schubert's piano sonatas.
The essence of their structure is the contrasting of big heroic ideas with tender and inner
thoughts; the first impresses the listener, the second woos him. The two works on this CD are
in some ways on a varying scale. The D major lasts for 40 minutes, the A minor for around
23. However, it is the latter that contains the most symphonically inspired writing — it sounds
as if it could easily be transposed for orchestra. Alfred Brendel presents the composer not so
much as the master of Lieder-writing, but more as a man thinking in large forms. Although
there are wonderful quiet moments when intimate asides are conveyed with an imaginative
sensitivity one remembers more the urgency and the power behind the notes. The A minor,
with its frequently recurring themes, is almost obsessive in character whilst the big D major
Sonata is rather lighter in mood, especially in the outer movements. The recorded sound is
very faithful to the pianist's tone, whilst generally avoiding that insistent quality that can mar
his loudest playing.

Additional recommendations …

Piano Sonata — *D784. Six Moments musicaux, D780. Scherzos, D593.* **Maria João Pires** (pf). DG 427 769-2GH — ⠶⠶ 1h 3m DDD 2/90

Piano Sonatas — *D784; A minor, D845; G major, D894; A major, D959.* **Trudelies Leonhardt** (fp). Jecklin J4420/1-2 — ⠶⠶ ② 2h 21m ADD 11/91 ✔

D784. D157 in E major. D959 in A major. **Radu Lupu** (pf). Decca Ovation 425 033-2DM — ⠶⠶ 1h 13m ADD 2/92

New review

Schubert. SACRED WORKS, Volumes 1 and 2. [abcdh]**Lucia Popp,** [abefgh]**Helen Donath,** [h]**Maria Venuti** (sops); [acdef]**Brigitte Fassbaender** (mez); [abcd]**Adolf Dallapozza,** [a]**Peter Schreier,** [ef]**Francisco Araiza,** [gh]**Josef Protschka,** [h]**Robert Tear** (tens); **Dietrich Fischer-Dieskau** (bar); **Bavarian Radio Chorus; Bavarian Radio Symphony Orchestra/ Wolfgang Sawallisch.** EMI Sawallisch Edition CMS7 64778-2 and CMS7 64783-2 (four and three disc sets. Texts and translations included. From HMV SLS5220 (2/82), SLS5254 (2/83), SLS5278 (5/83) and SLS143607-3 (3/84). Recorded 1981-83.
CMS7 64778-2 — Masses: No. 1 in F major, D105[a]; No. 2 in G major, D167[b]; No. 3 in B flat major, D324[c]; No. 4 in C major, D452[d]; No. 5 in A flat major, D678[e]; No. 6 in E flat major, D950[f]. Stabat mater, D383[g]. Also contains six other short works. *CMS7 64783-2* — Lazarus, D689[h]. Deutsche Messe, D872. Also contains 20 other short works.

⠶⠶ ④ ③ 4h 57m 3h 37m ADD/DDD ⓠp

Schubert's sacred choral works seem very much the poor relation in an output comprising undoubted masterpieces of vocal, piano, chamber and orchestral music. Yet he wrote more than enough, as EMI shows us, to fill seven CDs. There are seven Masses, ranging from the plain *Deutsche Messe* (D872) to the majestic B flat major (D324), an intense *Stabat mater* and the tantalizingly incomplete oratorio *Lazarus*, not to mention a host of smaller pieces and fragments. Quantity doesn't necessarily imply quality, even where Schubert is concerned. Certainly not even Schubert's greatest advocates would describe everything he wrote for the Church as a masterpiece. But there can never be any doubting the sincerity of Schubert's intentions and given sensitive, well-conceived performances, his unquenchable gift for melodic invention and ability to write instantly attractive music overrides any technical shortcomings. Such are Sawallisch's performances. His clear sense of direction, his natural feel for the line and his unpretentious approach never fail to reveal the inherent beauty in almost everything Schubert wrote. The Bavarian Radio Chorus, with their rich, vibrant tone, show a consistent level of technical accomplishment, following Sawallisch's naturally shaped lines and beautifully moulded hairpin dynamics with a wholly natural flow. Similarly, with such accomplished Schubertians as Lucia Popp, Robert Tear and Fischer-Dieskau one can expect some memorable performances; and Tear's sublimely controlled opening aria sets the scene for a performance of *Lazarus* almost overburdened with sublime artistry. The highlight of these discs is the deliciously delicate trio between Popp, Adolf Dallapozza and Dietrich Fischer-Dieskau, supported by some extraordinarily elegant orchestral playing, in the *Benedictus* of D167: this is real desert island fodder. Sawallisch impresses in maintaining so consistent an approach and producing performances of exemplary musicianship, even in works of less than uniform quality themselves. The recordings are first rate, with the older analogue transfers coming up unusually well. A treat for all devout Schubertians.

Schubert. LIEDER, Volumes 1-3. **Dietrich Fischer-Dieskau** (bar); **Gerald Moore** (pf). DG 437 214-2GX21. Volumes also available separately, as detailed below. Recorded 1966-72. *437 215-2GX9* (Volume 1: nine discs: 6h 44m): 234 Lieder, written between 1811 and 1817 (from 2720 022, 12/70). *437 225-2GX9* (Volume 2: nine discs: 6h 35m): 171 Lieder, written between 1817 and 1828 (from 643547/58, 1/70). *437 235-2GX3* (Volume 3: three discs: 3h 4m): Die schöne Müllerin, D795. Winterreise, D911. Schwanengesang, D957 (2720 059, 1/73).

⠶ ② ① 24h 23m ADD 3/93 ⓠp

Twenty-one discs at under £100 bringing together two of this century's greatest Lieder interpreters — it sounds like a recipe for success, as indeed it is, fulfilling the highest expectations. The recordings were made when Dietrich Fischer-Dieskau was at his peak and

Gerald Moore could draw on a lifetime's experience and love of this repertoire. Though the set makes no claims to completeness (in the way that Graham Johnson's Schubert series on Hyperion does), most of the songs for male voice are included here. The use of a single singer and pianist gives the set a unity that allows the listener to gasp anew at the composer's wide-ranging inspiration and imagination. Fischer-Dieskau brings a unique understanding, an elegant line and a diction that renders the text clear without resort to the written texts. If occasionally he imparts an unnecessary weightiness to the lighter songs, this quibble is as nothing when his historic achievement is taken as a whole. And though he made many recordings of the song cycles these are perhaps the finest, with Moore the ideal partner. Try for example, the bleakness of "Ihr Bild" from *Schwanengesang* or the hallucinatory happiness of "Der Lindenbaum" from *Winterreise*. The songs themselves are basically in chronological order (but with the three song cycles collected together in the final box). It is unfortunate there is no index — trying to find individual songs can be frustrating. It should also be added that the translations are distinctly quirky in places; better to use Richard Wigmore's excellent book *Schubert: The Complete Song Texts* (Gollancz: 1988) if you have a copy to hand. This is undoubtedly one of the greatest bargains in the *Guide*. Buy, without fear of disappointment.

Additional recommendations ...
Die Forelle, D550. An Sylvia, D891. Heidenröslein, D257. Du bist die Ruh, D776. Der Musensohn,
D764. An die Musik, D547. Auf dem Wasser zu singen, D774. Sei mir gegrüsst, D741. Litanei, D343.
Die junge Nonne, D828. Ave Maria, D839. Im Frühling, D882. Gretchen am Spinnrade, D118. Nacht
und Traüme, D827. Ganymed, D544. Mignon und der Harfner, D877. Seligkeit, D433. **Felicity Lott**
(sop); **Graham Johnson** (pf). Pickwick IMP Classics PCD898 — .•⁺ 1h 5m DDD 10/88 ᵠₚ
Abendbilder, D650. Abschied, D475. Am Grabe Anselmos, D504. An mein Herz, D860. Beim Winde,
D669. Frühlingsglaube, D686. Ganymed, D544. Strophe aus Die Götter Griechenlands, D677. Gretchen
am Spinnrade, D118. Heimliches Lieben, D922. Im Abendrot, D799. Der Knabe, D692. Lachen und
Weinen, D777. Lied der Anne Lyle, D830. Nachtstück, D672. Die Rose, D745. Schlaflied, D527.
Sehnsucht, D879. Der Wanderer an den Mond, D870. Wanderers Nachtlied, D224. Der Winterabend,
D938. **Elisabeth Speiser** (sop); **John Buttrick** (pf). Jecklin Disco JD630-2 — .•⁺ 1h 15m ADD 2/91
Am See, D746. Auf dem Wasser zu singen, D774. Auflösung, D807. Der Fluss, D693. Die Forelle, D550.
Ganymed, D544. Die Gebüsche, D646. Im Abendrot, D799. Im Frühling, D882. Klage der Ceres, D323.
Das Lied im Grünen, D917. Nacht und Träume, D827. Die Rose, D745. Die Vögel, D691. Wehmut,
D772. **Cheryl Studer** (sop); **Irwin Gage** (pf). DG 431 773-2GH — .•⁺ 1h 5m DDD 10/91 ᵠₚ
Heimliches Lieben, D922. Minnelied, D429. Die abgeblühte Linde, D514. Der Musensohn, D764.
Schumann: *Frauenliebe und -leben, Op. 42.* **Brahms:** *Die Mainacht, Op. 43 No. 2. Das Mädchen*
spricht, Op. 107 No. 3. Nachtigall, Op. 97 No. 1. Von ewiger Liebe, Op. 43 No. **Dame Janet**
Baker (mez); **Martin Isepp** (pf). Saga Classics SCD9001 *(reviewed in the Collections section; refer*
to the Index to Reviews) — .•⁺ 47m AAD 3/92
Seligkeit, D433. Frühlingsglaube, D686. Das Lied im Grunen, D917. Lachen und Weinen, D777. Der
Jüngling an der Quelle, D300. Auf dem Wasser zu singen, D774. Die junge Nonne, D828. Die
Verschworenen (Der hausliche Krieg) — Ich schleiche bang und still[a]. *Claudine von Villa Bella — Liebe*
schwarmt auf allen Wegen. Der Einsame, D800. Nacht und Träume, D827. Die Mutter Erde, D788. Der
Hirt auf dem Felsen, D965[a]. *Fischerweise, D881. Heidenröslein, D257. An Silvia, D891. Liebhaber in*
allen Gestalten, D558. An die Musik, D547. **Edith Wiens** (sop); [a]**Joaquin Valdepeñas** (cl);
Rudolf Jansen (pf). CBC Records Musica Viva MVCD1053— .•⁺ 1h 6m DDD 5/93

New review
Schubert. LIEDER. **Christoph Prégardien** (ten); **Andreas Staier** (fp). Deutsche Harmonia
Mundi 05472 77296-2. Texts and translations included. Recorded in 1993.
Schiller Lieder — Die Bürgschaft, D246; Hoffnung, D637; Hektors Abschied, D312; An Emma,
D113; Des Mädchens Klage, D191; Gruppe aus dem Tartarus, D583; Der Pilgrim, D794; Der
Alpenjäger, D588; Leichenfantasie, D7; Die Götter Griechenlands, D677; Sehnsucht, D636.

.•⁺ 1h 14m DDD 1/94

In *Die Götter Griechenlands*, Prégardien encompasses all the most compelling aspects of such notable tenor interpreters of Lieder as Patzak, Pears and Schreier. The plangent timbre is perfect for this elegiac lament, the legato ideal, the phraseology touching. Because this is perhaps Schubert's most telling setting of Schiller, to whose poetry the disc is devoted, it heads the many reasons for buying it. The performance of a quite different song, the ballad *Die Bürgschaft*, is another as here Prégardien brings to bear quite different attributes — a darker tone, a powerful sense of the song's drama and an innate feeling for the pulse of this long but ultimately rewarding piece. Over and above that the singer makes every word tell. The same is true of the jejune but entertaining *Leichenfantasie*. All the other songs, even the more intractable ones, are interpreted with the high intelligence and sense of style one would expect. Staier is both an alert and persuasive player, but once or twice, such as in *Der Pilgrim*, one longs for the softer timbre of a modern instrument, in preference to the fortepiano. The recording is first-rate.

New review

Schubert. LIEDER, Volume 18. **Peter Schreier** (ten); **Graham Johnson** (pf). Hyperion CDJ33018. Texts and translations included.
Das Finden, D219. Die Nacht, D358. An den Schlaf, D477. Blumenlied, D431. Auf den Tod einer Nachtigall, D399. Erntelied, D434. An die Harmonie, D394. Das Heimweh, D456. Abendlied, D499. An die Entfernte, D765. Drang in die Ferne, D770. Das Heimweh, D851. Auf der Bruck, D853. Um Mitternacht, D862. Die Blume und der Quell, D874 (cpted. R. Van Hoorickx). Der liebliche Stern, D861. Tiefes Lied (Im Jänner 1817), D876. Im Walde, D834. Im Frühling, D882. Lebensmut, D883. Über Wildemann, D884. Am mein Herz, D860.

·· **1h 16m DDD 7/93**

New review

Schubert. LIEDER, Volume 21. **Edith Mathis** (sop); **Graham Johnson** (pf). Hyperion CDJ33021. Texts and translations included.
Schlaflied D527. Sehnsucht, D516. Liebe, D522. Die Forelle, D550. Nur wer die Liebe kennt, D513a. Flug der Zeit, D515. Trost, D523. Die Abgeblühte Linde, D514. Das Lied vom Reifen, D532. An eine Quelle, D530. An die Musik, D547. Der Schäfer und der Reiter, D517. Hänflings Liebeswerbung, D552. Schweizerlied, D559. Liebhaber in allen Gestalten, D558. Abschied, D578. Erlafsee, D586. Lied eines Kindes, D596. Evangelium Johannis, D607. Lob der Tränen, D711. Grablied für die Mutter, D616. Der Blumenbrief, D622. Blondel zu Marien, D626. Vom Mitleiden Mariä, D632.

·· **1h 5m DDD 8/94**

Volume 18 is a superlative issue from Peter Schreier, the foremost interpreter of Lieder still active, indeed one of the greatest singers of songs in the history of recording. The passing of time seems hardly to have touched the peculiar beauty of his timbre, and his skill in the treatment of words is, of course, as gratifying as ever. Johnson has chosen this collection with emphasis on the composer's strophic songs. And Johnson seems himself to have been inspired by his singer to surpass even his own high standards. Schreier's invigorating and pointed sense of rhythm is aptly seconded at the piano throughout. So much included here is unjustly neglected — or seems so when performed with such dedication and understanding. The paradox of intensity within simplicity of *Die Nacht*, one of two Uz settings here, the gentle harmonies of the other, *An den Schlaf*, the inspired juxta-positions of the two Hölty settings, *Auf den Tod einer Nachtigall* and *Erntelied*, showing Schubert's gifts in perceiving sadness (elegiac A minor) in the first, and joy in the second, the strange Wolfian harmonies of *Das Heimweh* — these are some unexpected pleasures. Throughout, the faithful, well-balanced recording is happily supportive of the disc.

What riches are to be found in Volume 21 in a recital that is, by any yardstick, a profoundly satisfying one. Like the sopranos of a certain age who have already contributed to this series — Ameling and Popp (listed below) — Mathis brings a lifetime's experience of singing Lieder to her contribution to this invaluable and unique series and an intensity of expression allowed only to those with deep knowledge of the genre. As is only right for a senior interpreter, Johnson has given to Mathis some of the most inspired and moving of all Schubert's songs. Then the musical marriage of the performers seems one made in heaven. Rarely in the Edition have the two artists concerned appeared to have had such an instinctive rapport or pierced so effortlessly to the soul of the music in hand: they sing and play as though they had been partners for years, Mathis's strong, concentrated tone underpinned by Johnson's limpid, pointed playing. To add still further to the disc's many qualities, it may be the best engineered to date with the voice and instrument ideally balanced in a very present acoustic — marvellous! Particular attention should be drawn to the poised naturalness in *Schlaflied*, passionate conviction in the seldom-heard *Liebe*, inwardness in *Trost*, serene beauty in *An eine Quelle*, effervescent lightness in *Hänflings Liebeswerbung*, peasant earthiness in *Schweitzerlied*, B minor poignancy in *Abschied*. And that's only half of it.

Listen for the tears and consolation ideally mixed by composer and interpreters in *Lob der*

Tränen, the easeful sadness of *Erlafsee*, and the melancholic musings of Blondel. Then, in those two great favourites, *Die Forelle* and *An die Musik* we have readings to challenge the very best from the past. Buy, buy.

Additional recommendations ...
Volume 1. *Der Jüngling am Bache, D30. Thekla, D73. Schäfers Klagelied, D121 (first version). Nähe des Geliebten, D162 (second version). Meerestille, D216. Amalia, D195. Die Erwartung, D159 (second version). Wandrers Nachtlied, D224. Der Fischer, D225 (second version). Erster Verlust, D226. Wonne der Wehmut, D260. An den Mond, D296. Das Geheimnis, D250. Lied, D284. Der Flüchtling, D402. An den Frühling, D587 (second version). Der Alpenjäger, D588 (second version). Der Pilgrim, D794. Sehnsucht, D636 (second version).* **Dame Janet Baker** (mez); **Graham Johnson.** Hyperion CDJ33001 —
.•' Ih 10m DDD 10/88 ᵠₚ
Volume 6. *Die Nacht, D534 (completed by Anton Diabelli). Jagdlied, D521 (with chorus). Abendstern, D806. Abends unter der Linde, D235. Abends unter der Linde, D237. Der Knabe in der Wiege, D579. Abendlied für die Entfernte, D856. Willkommen und Abschied, D767. Vor meiner Wiege, D927. Der Vater mit dem Kind, D906. Des Fischers Liebesglück, D933. Die Sterne, D939. Alinde, D904. An die Laute, D905. Zur guten Nacht, D903 (chorus).* **Anthony Rolfe Johnson** (ten); **Graham Johnson.** Hyperion CDJ33006 — .•' Ih 13m DDD 6/90 ᵠₚ
Volume 7. *Minona, D152. Der Jüngling am Bache, D192. Stimme der Liebe, D187. Naturgenuss, D188. Des Mädchens Klage, D191. Die Sterbende, D186. An den Mond, D193. An die Nachtigall, D196. Die Liebe (Klärchens Lied), D210. Meeresstille, D215a. Idens Nachtgesang, D227. Von Ida, D228. Das Sehnen, D231. Die Spinnerin, D247. Wer kauft Liebesgötter?, D261. An den Frühling, D283. Das Rosenband, D280. Liane, D298. Idens Schwanenlied, D317. Luisens Antwort, D319. Mein Gruss an den Mai, D305. Mignon, D321. Sehnsucht, D310 (two versions).* **Elly Ameling** (sop); **Graham Johnson.** Hyperion CDJ33007 — .•' Ih 11m DDD 8/90 ᵠₚ
Volume 8. *An den Mond, D259. Romanze, D114. Stimme der Liebe, D418. Die Sommernacht, D289. Die frühen Gräber, D290. Die Mondnacht, D238. An den Mond in einer Herbstnacht, D614. Die Nonne, D208. An Chloen, D462. Hochzeit-Lied, D463. In der Mitternacht, D464. Trauer der Liebe, D465. Die Perle, D466. Abendlied der Fürstin, D495. Wiegenlied, D498. Ständchen, D920 (with chorus). Bertas Lied in der Nacht, D653. Der Erlkönig, D328.* **Sarah Walker** (mez); **Graham Johnson.** Hyperion CDJ33008 — .•' Ih 12m DDD 10/90 ᵠₚ
Volume 10. *Der Sänger, D149. Auf einen Kirchhof, D151. Am Flusse, D160. An Mignon, D161. Vergebliche Liebe, D177. An die Apfelbäume, wo ich Julien erblickte, D197. Seufzer, D198. Auf den Tod einer Nachtigall, D201. Der Liebende, D207. Adelwold und Emma, D211. Der Traum, D213. Die Laube, D214. Der Weiberfreund, D271. Labetrank der Liebe, D302. An die Geliebte, D303. Harfenspieler I, D325.* **Martyn Hill** (ten); **Graham Johnson.** Hyperion CDJ33010 — .•' Ih 14m DDD 5/91 ᵠₚ
Volume 11. *An den Tod, D518. Auf dem Wasser zu singen, D774. Auflösung, D807. Aus Heliopolis I, D753. Aus Heliopolis II, D754. Dithyrambe, D801. Elysium, D584. Der Geistertanz, D116. Der König in Thule, D367. Lied des Orpheus, D474. Nachtstück, D672. Schwanengesang, D744. Seligkeit, D433. So lasst mich scheinen, D727. Thekla, D595. Der Tod und das Mädchen, D531. Verklärung, D59. Vollendung, D989. Das Zügenglöcklein, D871.* **Brigitte Fassbaender** (mez); **Graham Johnson.** Hyperion CDJ33011 — .•' Ih 5m DDD 8/91 ᵠₚ
Volume 14. *An die Leier, D737. Amphiaraos, D166. Gruppe aus dem Tartarus, D396. Gruppe aus dem Tartarus, D583. Hippolits Lied, D890. Memnon, D541. Fragment aus dem Aeschylus, D450. Philoktet, D540. Uraniens Flucht, D554. Hektors Abschied, D312. Antigone und Oedip, D542 (both with Marie McLaughlin, sop). Lied eines Schiffers an die Dioskuren, D360. Orest auf Tauris, D548. Der entsühnte Orest, D699. Der zürnenden Diana, D707. Freiwilliges Versinken, D700. Die Götter Griechenlands, D677.* **Thomas Hampson** (bar); **Graham Johnson.** Hyperion CDJ33014 — .•' Ih 20m DDD 4/92 ᵠₚ
Volume 15. *An die untergehende Sonne, D457. Der Mondabend, D141. Klage an den Mond, D436. Die Mainacht, D194. Der Unglückliche, D713. An die Sonne, D270. Der Morgenkuss, D264. Kolmas Klage, D217. Ins stille Land, D403. Gondelfahrer, D808. Der Winterabend, D938. Der Wanderer an den Mond, D870. Im Freien, D880. Am Fenster, D878. Der blinde Knabe, D833. Die junge Nonne, D828.* **Dame Margaret Price** (sop); **Graham Johnson** (pf). Hyperion CDJ33015 — .•' Ih 12m DDD 2/93 ᵠₚ
Volume 16. *Leichenfantasie, D7. Laura am Klavier, D388. Die Entzückung an Laura — first version, D390, second version (completed van Hoorickx), D577. An die Freude, D189. An Emma, D113. Das Mädchen aus der Fremde, D117. Das Geheimnis, D793. Die Bürgschaft, D246. Der Jüngling am Bache, D638. Die vier Weltalter, D391. Sehnsucht, D52. Der Pilgrim, D794.* **Thomas Allen** (bar); **Graham Johnson** (pf). Hyperion CDJ33016 — .•' Ih 18m DDD 3/93 ᵠₚ
Volume 17. *Lied (Mutter geht durch ihre kammern), D373. Lodas Gespenst, D150. Klage, D371. Lorma, D376. Der Herbstabend, D405. Die Einsiedelei, D393. Der Herbstnacht, D404. Lied in der Abwesenheit,*

D416. Frühlingslied, D398. Winterlied, D401. Minnelied, D429. Aus Diego Manazares (Ilmerine), D458. Pflicht und Liebe, D467. An den Mond, D468. Litanei auf das Fest aller Seelen, D343. Geheimnis (An Franz Schubert), D491. Am Grabe Anselmos, D504. An die Nachtigall, D497. Klage um Ali Bey, D496a. Phidile, D500. Herbstlied, D502. Lebenslied, D508. Lieden der Trennung, D509. An mein Klavier, D342. **Lucia Popp** (sop); **Graham Johnson** (pf). Hyperion CDJ33017 — `.·'` lh llm DDD 6/93

New review

Schubert. LIEDER. **Elly Ameling** (sop); [a]**Dalton Baldwin**, [b]**Rudolf Jansen** (pfs). Philips The Early Years 438 528-2PM4. Texts included. Recorded 1972-84.

Im Abendrot, D799. Die Sterne, D939. Nacht und Träume, D827. Der liebliche Stern, D861. Der Vollmond strahlt, D797 No. 3b. Der Einsame, D800. Schlaflied, D527. An Silvia, D891. Das Mädchen, D652. Minnelied, D429. Die Liebe hat gelogen, D751. Du liebst mich nicht, D756. An die Laute, D905. Der Blumenbrief, D622. Die Männer sind méchant, D866 No. 3. Seligkeit, D433 (all from [a]6500 704, 1/76). Nachtviolen, D752. Du bist die Ruh, D776 (both from [a]9500 350, 6/78). Das Lied im Grünen, D917. Der Schmetterling, D633. An die Nachtigall, D497. An die Nachtigall, D196. Der Wachtelschlag, D742. Im Freien, D880. Die Vögel, D691. Fischerweise, D881. Die Gebüsche, D646. Im Haine, D738 ([a]6500 706, 10/75). Kennst du das Land, D321. Nur wer die Sehnsucht kennt, D877 No. 4. Heiss mich nicht reden, D877 No. 2. So lasst mich scheinen, D877 No. 3. Die Liebende schreibt, D673. Nähe des Geliebten, D162. Heidenröslein, D257. Liebhaber in allen Gestalten, D558 (6500 515, 7/74). Die junge Nonne, D828. Der König in Thule, D367. Gretchen am Spinnrade, D118. Gretchens Bitte, D564. Szene aus Goethes Faust, D126 (with Meinard Kraak, ten; chorus and org). Suleika I, D720. Suleika II, D717. Raste Kreiger!, D837. Jäger, ruhe von der Jagd, D838. Ave Maria, D839 ([a]9500 169, 4/78). An die Musik, D547. Schwestergrüss, D762. Sei mir gegrüsst, D741. Die Blumensprache, D519. An den Mond, D296. Abendbilder, D650. Frühlingssehnsucht, D957 No. 3. Erster Verlust, D226. Nachthymne, D687. Die Sterne, D684. Der Knabe, D692. Wiegenlied, D498. Berthas Lied in der Nacht, D653 ([a]6514 298, 6/83). Ganymed, D544. Die Götter Griechenlands, D677. Der Musensohn, D764. Fülle der Liebe, D854. Sprache der Liebe, D410. Schwanengesang, D744. An den Tod, D518. Die Forelle, D550. Am Bach im Frühling, D361. Auf dem Wasser zu singen, D774. Der Schiffer, D694. An die Entfernte, D765. Sehnsucht, D516. An die untergehende Sonne, D457. Abendröte, D690 ([b]416 294-2PH, 8/87).

`.·'` ④ 4h 20m ADD/DDD 4/94 `q` `p`

The first *Im Abendrot* (the Lappe setting) introduces the smiling Ameling of 1973, her voice basking in the images of golden shafts of light, and rapt in an easeful legato. In the shorter vowels and pulsing pianistic light of *Die Sterne*, she still finds serenity, just as in *Der Einsame* the poet's solitude is sensed at the heart of a tingling, sentient world. The expressive subtlety of these performances comes from an unique fusion of response between Ameling and Baldwin during this period. In the second disc, their creative empathy is turned to Schubert's settings of Goethe. Ameling focuses on the vulnerability and childlike eagerness of Mignon, missing, perhaps, the nervous feverishness which lies just below the surface of these songs, and which Wolf was to exploit to the full. After one of the most perfectly scaled performances of *Heidenröslein* on disc, Ameling and Baldwin turn to Goethe's Gretchen and Suleika, and to Scott's Ellen. Gretchen's searing vision at the spinning-wheel is answered by the rarely heard *Szene aus Goethes Faust* in which Ameling finds herself in the company of an anonymous and very spooky *Böser Geist*, as well as a ghostly choir who seem piped in from another planet. Seven years later, Ameling turns to a still stranger spirit world. The third disc, recorded in 1982, includes the lunar beauty of Schubert's Bruchmann setting, *Schwestergrüss*, articulated by a voice bleached of any colour. It is almost impossible to detect any sense of ageing in the voice here. Characterized by songs which search out the most elusive of soul moods, this third recital reveals Ameling's soprano at its most finely nuanced, in songs such as *Abendbilder* and the Novalis *Nachthymne*. In the final disc, at the age of 50, Ameling took on the challenge of some of Schubert's most visionary songs: facing Schiller's Greek gods, Goethe's *Ganymed*, Schlegel's *Der Schiffer* and moving through Mayrhofer's longing to Schlegel's final sunset. These songs stretch the voice and the mind to its very limits, yet Ameling's artistry seems to grow with the music itself. Collectors should probably be warned that the set includes full texts but no translations. In the end, though, Ameling's singing renders them all but redundant.

Additional recommendation ...
Der Hirt auf dem Felsen, D965 (with Hans Deinzer, cl). Seligkeit, D433. Gretchen am Spinnrad, D118. Du liebst mich nicht, D756. Heimliches Lieben, D922. Im Frühling, D882. Die Vögel, D691. Der

Jüngling an der Quelle, D300. Der Musensohn, D764. **Schumann.** *Myrthen, Op. 25 Widmung; Der Nussbaum. Aufträge, Op. 77 No. 5. Sehnsucht, Op. 51 No. 1. Frage, Op. 35 No. 9. Mein schöner Stern, Op. 101 No. 4. Lieder Album für die Jugend, Op. 79 — Schmetterling; Käuzlein; Der Sandmann; Marienwürmchen; Er ists's; Schneeglöckchen. Erstes Grün, Op. 35 No. 4. Die Sennin, Op. 90 No. 4. Sehnsucht nach der Waldgegend, Op. 35 No. 5. Jasminenstrauch, Op. 27 No. 4. Liederkreis, Op. 39 — Waldesgespräch. Loreley, Op. 53 No. 2. Die Meerfee, Op. 125 No. 1.* **Elly Ameling** (sop); **Jörg Demus** (fp). Deutsche Harmonia Mundi Editio Classica GD77085 — .•ʹ lh 9m ADD 5/90 ꟼ ✒*

Schubert. LIEDER. **Per Vollestad** (bar); **Sigmund Hjelset** (pf). Simax PSC1071. Texts and translations included.
Der Einsame, D800. Der Kreuzzug, D932. Der Pilgrim, D794. Abendstern, D806. Der Wanderer an den Mond, D870. Sei mir gegrüsst, D741. Im Frühling, D882. Der Blumenbrief, D622. Wie Ulfru fischt, D525. Fischerweise, D881. Des Fischers Liebesglück, D933. Im Walde, D834. Das Weinen, D926. Du bist die Ruh, D776. An den Mond, D193. An die Laute, D905. Hoffnung, D637. Wiedersehen, D855. Lied des gefangenen Jägers, D843. Normans Gesang, D846.

.•ʹ **lh llm DDD 9/92**

There is no doubt about it: the young Norwegian, Per Vollestad, is certainly a singer to watch. His baritone is rich and warm, occasionally reminiscent of Fischer-Dieskau. This selection of Schubert Lieder is perhaps on balance rather sombre, with *Im Frühling* and *An die Laute* providing some limited sunny moments; and the approach taken by Vollestad and the sensitive accompaniment of Sigmund Hjelset is generally serious in the extreme. While the singing and playing is always deeply felt and beautiful in tone, occasionally the coloration seems limited; it would be nice to hear more of the understated, flowing Schubertian *innigkeit* in place of this mostly extrovert approach, through which *Du bist die Ruh* in particular falls prey to far too much rubato. This is more about musical imagination than anything else; for example, the imagery of *Des Fischers Liebesglück* offers far more scope for expressive variety and vision than this rather matter-of-fact interpretation suggests. Nevertheless, interpretations can only deepen with age and experience and there are many moments of both beauty and tenderness here: in *Hoffnung* and *An den Mond*, to name but two. *Sei mir gegrüsst* is particularly heartfelt, from both singer and pianist. Even if you're collecting the Hyperion set don't overlook this very rewarding achievement from an artist still at the start of his career.

Key to symbols

.•ʹ   ② ②   lh 23m   DDD   6/88

| Price | Quantity/ availability | Timing | Recording mode | Review date |

Schubert. LIEDER. **Simon Keenlyside** (bar); **Malcolm Martineau** (pf). EMI Eminence CD-EMX2224. Texts and translations included.
Der Einsame, D800. Ständchen, D889. An Silvia, D891. Der Jüngling an der Quelle, D300. Lied eines Schiffers, D360. Gruppe aus dem Tartarus, D583. Die Götter Griechenlands, D677. Im Walde, D708. Der Wanderer an den Mond, D870. Freiwilliges Versinken, D700. Himmelsfunken, D651. Prometheus, D674. Gondelfahrer, D808. Die Sterne, D939. Auf der Bruck, D853. Heidenröslein, D257. Im Haine, D738. Nachtviolen, D752. Bei dir allein, D866/2. Du bist die Ruh, D776.

.•ʹ **lh llm DDD 8/94**   ꟼ

Simon Keenlyside is the best baritone singer and interpreter of Schubert this country has ever had and is fully the equal of such Austro-German coevals as Holzmair and Schmidt. Hyperbole? Anyone who hears this enriching recital will not think so. Keenlyside has just about all the attributes needed by a Schubert interpreter: a magnificent tone, firm and natural, rounded throughout an extensive register, an inborn sense of line, perfect German, and in addition to all that an instinctive intelligence that carries him confidently through his long and taxing programme with hardly a phrase that could be bettered in terms of colour or word-painting. You can sit back without a qualm knowing that he will have the reserves and the trenchancy of purpose to conquer such Everests of the Schubert repertory as *Prometheus* and *Gruppe aus dem Tartarus* where his vocal means are fully equal to the defiance the songs proclaim. *Auf der Bruck* is filled with the ongoing energy Schubert calls for. Then there's the thoughtfulness to fulfil the demands of such a philosophical and forward-looking song as *Freiwilliges Versinken*, the sense of questing romanticism for *Im Walde*. Among the reflective pieces, *Die Götter Griechenlands* is notable for plangent feeling and tone — just right. *Gondelfahrer*, that marvellous evocation of bells heard at night, is full of nocturnal mystery. *Heidenröslein* is delicate in its subtle timbres and smiling tone; so is *Die Sterne* while *Bei dir allein* has a Fischer-Dieskau enthusiasm. And the recital is crowned by the final offering, *Du bist die Ruh*, where the voice opens out in its full beauty. These successes make the one or two failures mystifying. They come at the start of the disc so perhaps the performers weren't yet into their stride. *Der Einsame* plods at an unduly slow tempo. *Ständchen* lacks airiness, Martineau's foursquare accompanying thereabouts doesn't help. Later he provides many inspired moments (try *Im Haine*, where he so charmingly supports the baritone's *mezzo voce*), and he never overeggs the pudding in the heavier songs. The recording is ideally balanced and judged but the texts and translations have been carelessly read. However, any trifling drawbacks don't prevent an outright recommendation for this well chosen and absorbing mid-price disc.

Schubert. LIEDER. **Peter Schreier** (ten); **András Schiff** (pf). Decca 425 612-2DH. Texts and translations included. Recorded in 1989.
Schwanengesang, D957. Herbst, D945. Der Wanderer an den Mond, D870. Am Fenster, D878. Bei dir allein, D866 No. 2.

> **1h 3m DDD 6/90**

Schubert. LIEDER. **Brigitte Fassbaender** (mez); **Aribert Reimann** (pf). DG 429 766-2GH. Texts and translations included. Recorded 1989-91.
Schwanengesang, D957. Sehnsucht, D879. Der Wanderer an den Mond, D870. Wiegenlied, D867. Am Fenster, D878. Herbst, D945.

> **1h 8m DDD 6/92**

Though *Schwanengesang* is not a song-cycle but a collection of Schubert's last (or 'swan') songs by their first publisher, it is generally felt to form a satisfying sequence, with a unity of style if not of theme or mood. This is certainly not weakened by the addition on the Decca disc of the four last songs which were originally omitted, all of them settings of poems by Johann Seidl. Seidl is one of the three poets whose work Schubert used in these frequently sombre songs and it is strange to think that all concerned in their creation were young men, none of the poets being older than Schubert. The listener can scarcely be unaware of a shadow or sometimes an almost unearthly radiance over even the happiest (such as "Die Taubenpost", the last of all) and that is particularly true when the performers themselves have such sensitive awareness as here. Peter Schreier is responsive to every shade of meaning in music and text; graceful and charming in "Das Fischermädchen", flawlessly lyrical in "Am Meer", he will sometimes risk an almost frightening raw-boned cry as in the anguish of "Der Atlas" and "Der Doppelgänger". András Schiff's playing is a miracle of combined strength and delicacy, specific insight and general rightness. One of the great Lieder recordings, and not merely of recent years.

Fassbaender and Reimann offer something equally compelling but rather different in their account of *Schwanengesang*. Fassbaender's interpretation, idiosyncratic in every respect, pierces to the heart of the bleak songs with performances as daring and challenging as the playing of her partner. More than anyone, these two artists catch the fleeting moods of these mini-dramas, and their searing originality of concept. Even the lighter songs have a special individuality of utterance. This is a starkly immediate interpretation that leaves the listener shattered. The extra Seidl settings, rarely performed, are all worth hearing. The true lover of Lieder will need to have both these notable partnerships, superb in their own, searching ways.

Additional recommendations ...
Schwanengesang. **Bryn Terfel** (bass-bar); **Malcolm Martineau** (pf). Sain SCDC4035 — .·˙
57m DDD 5/92 ⁹ₚ

Schwanengesang. Die schöne Müllerin, D795. Winterreise, D911. **Dietrich Fischer-Dieskau** (bar); **Gerald Moore** (pf). DG 437 235-2GX3 *(reviewed above)* — .· ③ 3h 4m ADD 3/93 ⁹ₚ

Schubert. Die schöne Müllerin, D795. **Peter Schreier** (ten); **András Schiff** (pf). Decca 430 414-2DH. Texts and translations included. Recorded in 1989.

> Ih 3m DDD 5/91

Schubert. Die schöne Müllerin, D795. **Christoph Prégardien** (ten); **Andreas Staier** (fp). Deutsche Harmonia Mundi 05472 77273-2. Texts and translations included.

> Ih DDD 12/92

Schubert. Die schöne Müllerin, D795. **Wolfgang Holzmair** (bar); **Jörg Demus** (pf). Preiser 93337. Recorded in 1984.

> Ih 8m ADD 3/89

The 20 songs of *Die schöne Müllerin* portray a Wordsworthian world of heightened emotion in the pantheistic riverside setting of the miller. The poet, Wilhelm Müller, tells of solitary longings, jealousies, fears and hopes as the river rushes by, driving the mill-wheel and refreshing the natural world. Schreier's partnership with a notable Schubert pianist, András Schiff, surpasses all its predecessors and should be part of any worthwhile collection of Lieder. With his plangent tone, now more disciplined than ever, allied to his poignant and finely accented treatment of the text, Schreier gives moving expression to the youth's love and loss, nowhere more so than in his colloquy with the stream, "Der Müller und der Bach". Everything in his reading has been carefully thought through yet the result sounds wholly spontaneous and natural. To his role Schiff brings an inquiring mind, deft and pliant fingers and an innate feeling for Schubertian phraseology. He probes as deep into the music's meaning, perhaps deeper than any before him yet without giving the accompaniment undue prominence or calling attention to the piano. More than anything, it is as a unified concept that this reading achieves its greatness. It is recorded with an ideal balance between voice and piano, in a sympathetic acoustic.

It is possible to approach the cycle in a simpler way than Schreier's, emphasizing the youthful, ingenuous character of the sad protagonist. This is the way adopted by Prégardien in his finely shaped, understated version. It is a reading that is instinctively shaped and felt, the tenor suggesting the boy's vulnerability to perfection. It is neither as broadly conceived nor as romantic as the Schreier, and the straightforward character is emphasized by strict tempos and a fortepiano accompanist, the instrument finely and sympathetically played by Staier. If you prefer a baritone in the cycle, the recommendation must be for Holzmair's 1984 performance which first revealed this singer's gifts as a Lieder singer of sensitivity and one, who like Prégardien, catches the youth's joy and inner suffering through a natural feeling for word and phrase. His light tone and instinctive way with the text are immediately appealing and with Demus as a faultless partner, this version never fails to make its mark.

Additional recommendations ...
Die schöne Müllerin. **Dietrich Fischer-Dieskau** (bar); **Gerald Moore** (pf). DG 415 186-2GH — Ih 2m ADD 9/85
Die schöne Müllerin. **Josef Protschka** (ten); **Helmut Deutsch** (pf). Capriccio 10 082 — Ih 6m DDD 6/87
Die schöne Müllerin. **Olaf Bär** (bar); **Geoffrey Parsons** (pf). EMI CDC7 47947-2 — Ih 5m DDD 8/87
Die schöne Müllerin. **Siegfried Lorenz** (bar); **Norman Shetler** (pf). Capriccio 10 220 — Ih 8m DDD 5/90
Die schöne Müllerin. **Beethoven.** An die ferne Geliebte, Op. 98. **Gerhard Hüsch** (bar); **Hanns Udo Müller** (pf). Preiser Lebendige Vergangenheit mono 89202 — ② 2h 17m AAD 12/92 ▲
Die schöne Müllerin. Schwanengesang, D957 — Die Taubenpost. Der Einsame, D800. An die Laute, D905. **Sir Peter Pears** (ten); **Benjamin Britten** (pf). Decca 436 201-2DM — Ih 13m ADD 8/93

New review
Schubert. Winterreise, D911. **Peter Schreier** (ten); **András Schiff** (pf). Decca 436 122-2DH. Text and translation included. Recorded in 1991.

> Ih 12m DDD 5/94

Winterreise can lay claim to be the great song cycle ever written. It chronicles the sad, numbing journey of a forsaken lover, recalling past happiness, anguishing over his present plight, commenting on how the snow-clad scenery reflects or enhances his mood. Schreier himself, in his note in the booklet, refers to the unique density and spiritual concentration of the songs; that, and their hallucinatory nature, inform this riveting performance from start to finish, nowhere more so than in "Wasserflut" and "Einsamkeit". The latter is a paradigm of the whole searing, almost unbearable experience. If you can tolerate it you will be engaged and surely moved by the whole. In this song, Schreier leans into the words and notes of "Ach, das die Luft so ruhig!" suggesting the cry of a desperate, tormented soul — as does the emphatic enunciation of the single word "Bergstroms" earlier, in "Irricht". Also arresting is the curiously daring way Schreier asks the question at the end of "Die Post", as if it were a spontaneous afterthought. These make the moments of calm and repose all the more eerie. The sad delicacy of Schiff's playing at the start of "Frühlingstraum" sets the scene of the imagined May to perfection, and the flowing lift of his left hand in "Täuschung" is as deceptively friendly as the light described by the singer. "Das Wirtshaus" is all false resignation: voice and piano tell us of the man's tired emptiness. Anger and defiance, as in the earlier performance, are registered in raw, chilling tone and phraseology. Then, in the pair's revelatory way, they draw attention anew to the originality of concept of "Letzte Hoffnung". The final songs taken simply, speak beautifully of acceptance. Among tenor versions, this is now the preferred choice, benefiting from the warm yet clear acoustic of the recording. Viewing the whole scene, it matches Fassbaender in its unbridled involvement. Fischer-Dieskau is still there as another kind of benchmark for those who prefer a lower, more amenable voice in this cycle.

Additional recommendations ...
Winterreise. Piano Sonata in C major, D840, "Reliquie". **Peter Schreier** (ten); **Sviatoslav Richter** (pf). Philips 416 289-2PH2 — ⚪ ② 2h 3m ADD/DDD 3/86 ♪ₚ Ⓑ
Winterreise. **Dietrich Fischer-Dieskau** (bar); **Alfred Brendel** (pf). Philips 411 463-2PH — ⚪ 1h 10m DDD 12/86 ♪ₚ Ⓑ
Winterreise. **Robert Holl** (bass-bar); **Konrad Richter** (pf). Preiser 93317 — ⚪ 1h 12m ADD 8/89 ♪ₚ Ⓑ
Winterreise. **Olaf Bär** (bar); **Geoffrey Parsons** (pf). EMI CDC7 49334-2 — ⚪ 1h 15m DDD 11/89 ♪ₚ Ⓑ
Winterreise. **Brigitte Fassbaender** (mez); **Aribert Reimann** (pf). EMI CDC7 49846-2 — ⚪ 1h 10m DDD 7/90 ♪ₚ Ⓑ
Winterreise. **Sir Peter Pears** (ten); **Benjamin Britten** (pf). Decca 417 473-2DM — ⚪ 1h 13m ADD 10/91 ♪ₚ Ⓑ
Winterreise. **Andreas Schmidt** (bar); **Rudolf Jansen** (pf). DG 435 384-2DG — ⚪ 1h 12m DDD 3/92 ♪ₚ Ⓑ
Winterreise. **Max van Egmond** (bar); **Jos van Immerseel** (fp). Channel Classics CCS0190 — ⚪ 1h 7m DDD 3/92 ♪ₚ Ⓑ 🖊

Schubert. Masses — G major, D167[a]; E flat major, D950[b]. [a]**Dawn Upshaw**, [b]**Benita Valente** (sops); [b]**Marietta Simpson** (mez); [a]**David Gordon**, [b]**Jon Humphrey**, [b]**Glenn Siebert** (tens); [a]**William Stone** [b]**Myron Myers** (bars); **Atlanta Symphony Chamber Chorus; Atlanta Symphony Chorus and Orchestra/Robert Shaw.** Telarc CD80212. Text and translation included. Recorded 1988-89.

⚪ **1h 18m DDD 9/90**

Schubert's second Mass, D167, was written in six days during 1815 when he was 18. This small-scale, tuneful work, given only a light accompaniment of strings and organ, conformed closely with what was expected of Schubert by his teacher, Salieri, and has many moments of simple charm, expressive of a simple faith. The Mass in E flat was completed, along with *Tantum Ergo* and the *Offertorium*, in the autumn of 1828, the year of Schubert's death, and is clearly the work of a composer at the height of his powers, intent on extending the boundaries of expression whilst still having to retain some of the conventions of formal liturgical structure. The accompaniment here is for the full orchestra of the time, minus flutes, and the dramatic impact of these resources is exploited to the full. Yet more than this, it is the revolutionary harmonic ideas that single this Mass out for special note, orchestral colours emphasizing the drastic shifts and subtle slides. The composer's faith had, by this time, become more individual, less conformist, and there are hints in this work of that reassessment. Robert Shaw and his Atlanta forces set the two works in stark contrast, underlining the individual qualities of each. The choral singing is of a high order and there is an underlying detachment in their approach that fits well with the intended use of this music; operatic emotion would hardly have been in keeping.

Additional recommendations ...

D950. Soloists; Vienna State Opera Concerto Choir; Vienna Philharmonic Orchestra/Claudio Abbado. DG 423 088-2GH — *..* 57m DDD 8/88

D950. Soloists; Suisse Romande Chamber Choir; Lausanne Pro Arte Choir; Suisse Romande Orchestra/Armin Jordan. Erato 2292-45300-2 — *..* 54m DDD 8/88

D167. *Salve regina in A major, D676.* **Haydn.** *Missa brevis Sancti Joannis de Deo, "Kleine Orgelmesse". Flute-clock pieces, HobXIX — Nos. 6, 9, 15, 20 and 32.* **Soloists; Haydn Society Chorus and Orchestra/Denis McCaldin.** Meridian Duo DUOCD89003 — *..* 55m AAD 2/90

Further listening ...

Sonata for Piano Duet in C major, "Grand Duo", D812. Eight Variations in A flat major, D813. Grande Marche in E flat major, D819 No. 1. **Isabel Beyer, Harvey Dagul** (pfs). Four Hands Music FHMD893 (6/94).

FIERRABRAS. **Soloists; Arnold Schönberg Choir; Chamber Orchestra of Europe/ Claudio Abbado.** DG 427 341-2GH2 (10/90).

Gunther Schuller

American 1925-

Suggested listening ...

String Quartet No. 3. *Coupled with* **Harbison.** String Quartet No. 2. **Wernick.** String Quartet No. 4. **Emerson Quartet.** DG 437 537-2GH (11/93). *See review under Harbison; refer to the Index to Reviews.*

Suite. *Coupled with* **Barber.** Summer Music, Op. 31. **Beach.** Pastorale. **Fine.** Partita. **Harbison.** Quintet for Wind. **Villa-Lobos.** Quinteto em forma de chôros. **Reykjavik Wind Quintet.** Chandos CHAN9174 (11/93). *See review in the Collections section; refer to the Index to Reviews.*

William Schuman

American 1910-1992

New review

Schuman. New England Triptych. Symphony for Strings. (Symphony No. 5). Judith. **Ives** (orch. Schuman). Variations on "America". **Seattle Symphony Orchestra/Gerard Schwarz.** Delos DE3115.

.. **1h 4m DDD 7/93**

This record was completed before Schuman died and when he heard some of it on a cassette he wrote: "The performance has so many superlative elements that I would do the overall excellence of the rendition an injustice by citing the special places that appeal particularly to this composer's soul ...". This may seem to disarm criticism but one can see what Schuman meant. He must have been particularly pleased to have a modern performance of his ballet *Judith*. Its bloodthirsty subject from the Apocrypha brings out many facets of Schuman's resourceful and dynamic personality at its most serious. There are dramatic moments but also areas of melodic power (after 18'20") which are particularly characteristic of Schuman and sound like nobody else. His Fifth Symphony (1943) must be one of the most successful American works for string orchestra this century. Schwarz's performance is effective enough and it fills a gap in the catalogue for Schuman on both sides of the Atlantic. The Americana side of Schuman comes in the popular *New England Triptych* based on three choral pieces by the eccentric pioneer William Billings (1746–1800). When Schuman wrote *New England Triptych* in 1956, Billings was less recognized, and Schuman was linking up with part of his own New England heritage. But in 1963, when he orchestrated Ives's *Variations on America* (the tune is the same as *God save the*

Queen) Ives was beginning to reach his special position in American music. This is a brilliantly witty transformation of the organ work Ives wrote in his teens and performed himself. Perhaps as a result the Ives is more often played by organists now. Its zest matches the exuberance of Schuman throughout his busy career and it makes a fun start to this recorded tribute.

Additional recommendation ...
American Festival Overture. New England Triptych. Symphony No. 10, "American Muse". **Ives** *(orch. Schuman). Variations on "America".* **St Louis Symphony Orchestra/Leonard Slatkin.** RCA Victor Red Seal 09026 61282-2 — .•' lh 7m DDD 5/93

Further listening ...

Symphony No. 3. *Coupled with* **Harris.** Symphony No. 3. **New York Philharmonic Orchestra/Leonard Bernstein.** DG 419 780-2GH (11/87). *See review under Harris; refer to the Index to Reviews.*

Clara Schumann

German 1819-1896

Suggested listening ...

Sonata in G minor. Romance in B minor. Impromptu in E major. Romance in A minor. Scherzo in D minor, Op. 10 Deuxième Scherzo in C minor, Op. 14. Präludium in F minor. Soirées musicales, Op. 6. Etude in A flat major. Geburtstagmarsch in E flat major. Three Preludes and Fugues, Op. 19. Variations on a Theme of Robert Schumann Op. 20. Three Romances, Op. 11. Nine Caprices en forme de valse, Op. 2. Souvenir de Vienne, Op. 9. Valses romantiques, Op. 4. Variations de concert sur la cavatine du Pirate de Bellini, Op. 8. Four Polonaises, Op. 1. Four Pièces caracteristiques, Op. 5. Four Pièces fugitives, Op. 15. Three Fugues on Themes of Bach. Three Romances, Op. 21. **Josef de Beenhouwer** (pf). Partridge PART9293-2 (1/93).

Piano Trio in G minor, Op. 17[a]. *Coupled with* **Beach.** Piano Trio in A minor, Op. 150[a]. **Carreño.** String Quartet in B minor[bc]. **Mendelssohn-Hensel.** Piano Trio in G minor, Op. 11[a]. **Tailleferre.** Sonata for Violin and Piano No. 1[bd]. **Boulanger.** Pièces — Nocturne; Cortège[bd]. **Chaminade.** Piano Trio No. 1 in G minor, Op. 11[a]. [a]**Macalester Trio;** [b]**Joseph Roche,** [c]**Robert Zelnick** (vns); [c]**Tamas Strasser** (va); [c]**Camilla Heller** (vc); [d]**Paul Freed** (pf). Vox Box 115845-2. *See review in the Collections section; refer to the Index to Reviews.*

Robert Schumann

German 1810-1856

New review
Schumann. CONCERTOS. [d]**Gerd Seifert,** [d]**Norbert Hauptmann,** [d]**Christopher Kohler,** [d]**Manfred Klier** (hns); [b]**Gidon Kremer** (vn); [c]**Paul Tortelier** (vc); [a]**Daniel Barenboim** (pf); [a]**London Philharmonic Orchestra/Dietrich Fischer-Dieskau;** [b]**Philharmonia Orchestra/Riccardo Muti;** [c]**Royal Philharmonic Orchestra/Yan Pascal Tortelier;** [d]**Berlin Phiharmonic Orchestra/Klaus Tennstedt.** EMI Rouge et Noir CZS7 67521-2. Items marked [a] from HMV ASD3053 (3/75), [b]ASD143519-1 (10/83), [c]ASD3728 (10/79), [d]ASD3724 (12/79).
Piano Concerto in A minor, Op. 54[a]. Introduction and Allegro appassionato in D minor (Concertstück), Op. 92[a]. Violin Concerto in D minor, Op. posth[b]. Cello Concerto in A minor, Op. 129[c]. Konzertstücke in F major, Op. 86[d].

.•' ② 2h lm ADD 8/93

If ever a performance of Schumann's Piano Concerto stressed the principle of dialogue between soloist and conductor, then this is it. True, the Philharmonia's string ensemble isn't as water-tight under Fischer-Dieskau as it might have been under some other conductors; and poetry is invested at the premium of relatively low-level drama. Orchestral textures are absolutely right for Schumann — warm yet transparent, full-bodied yet never stodgy — and poetry is a major priority. Add Barenboim's compatible vision and keyboard finesse, and you indeed have a memorable reading. The more discursive *Introduction and Allegro appassionato* has plenty of interest, but remembering that this isn't exactly top-drawer Schumann, the performance could be more arresting. Conversely, the *Konzertstücke* has as much forthrightness as it could possibly take, certainly in terms of engineering: the four magnificent horns ring out with Olympian force, keenly supported by an animated BPO. The Cello Concerto is more smoothly recorded, but although Tortelier *père* had the measure of this fragile masterpiece's troubled spirit, his son was, at least at this stage in his career, less comprehensively perceptive. As for the Violin Concerto, one finds oneself frequently moved by Kremer's solo playing — his handling of the slow movement has a tonal richness — but less than happy with Muti's indulgent accompaniment. The repetitions in this work are frequently misunderstood as symptoms of creative decline rather than as the trenchant rhetorical devices that they in fact are, and Muti gives the impression of being unconvinced by them. Nevertheless, Kremer and Muti are, within the useful context of this competitively-priced set, certainly up to the task of communicating what is still a scandalously underrated work. They also have the benefit of good engineering.

Schumann. WORKS FOR CELLO. **Heinrich Schiff** (vc); [b]**Gerhard Oppitz** (pf); [a]**Berlin Philharmonic Orchestra/Bernard Haitink.** Philips 422 414-2PH. Item marked [a] recorded in 1988, [b] arranged Grützmacher, recorded in 1991.
Cello Concerto in A minor, Op. 129[a]. Adagio and Allegro in A flat major, Op. 70[b].
Fantasiestücke, Op. 73[b]. Funf Stücke im Volkston, Op. 102[b].

Ih DDD 6/93

Schumann's Cello Concerto is a fairly dark, troubled work, and sometimes cellists are tempted to adopt a somewhat overwrought approach when playing it. In fact, it responds best to a more balanced approach, as exemplified in this performance by Heinrich Schiff. His playing is very eloquent, and quite strong, but there is also a feeling of dignity and refinement in his response to the music. Everything is perfectly in scale, and the work's essential nobility is allowed to emerge in a most moving fashion. Schiff's technique is faultless, and his tonal quality is very beautiful. Haitink and the BPO seem totally in sympathy with the soloist, and the recording is warm and well-detailed. The three items with piano accompaniment comprise a series of short pieces which are for the most part sunnier in outlook than the Concerto, and they make an effective contrast to the larger-scale work. Again Schiff's playing is expressive, but his phrasing is full of subtlety and poetry, and Oppitz is a highly responsive partner.

Additional recommendations ...
Cello Concerto. Fantasiestücke. Fünf Stücke im Volkston, Op. 102. Adagio and Allegro. **Yo-Yo Ma** (vc); **Emanuel Ax** (pf); **Bavarian Radio Symphony Orchestra/Sir Colin Davis.** CBS Masterworks CD42663 — Ih llm DDD 10/88
Cello Concerto. Fantasiestücke. Fünf Stücke im Volkston. Adagio and Allegro. **Lluis Claret** (vc); **Rose-Marie Cabestany** (pf); **English Chamber Orchestra/Edmon Colomer.** Harmonia Mundi HMC90 1306 — Ih 3m DDD 5/90
Cello Concerto[a]. **Lalo.** *Cello Concerto in D minor*[a]. **Saint-Saëns.** *Cello Concerto in A minor, Op. 33*[b]. **János Starker** (vc); **London Symphony Orchestra/**[a]**Stanislaw Skrowaczewski,** [b]**Antál Dorati.** Mercury 432 010-2MM — Ih 5m ADD 4/92
Cello Concerto. **Schnittke.** *Cello Concerto No. 1.* **Natalia Gutman** (vc); **London Philharmonic Orchestra/Kurt Masur.** EMI CDC7 54443-2 *(see review under Schnittke; refer to the Index to Reviews)* — Ih 5m DDD 8/92
Cello Concerto[a]. *Piano Concerto in A minor, Op. 54*[b]. *Introduction and Allegro appassionato, Op. 92*[c]. [a]**Jacqueline du Pré** (vc); [a]**New Philharmonia Orchestra/Daniel Barenboim** ([b]pf); [bc]**London Philharmonic Orchestra/Dietrich Fischer-Dieskau.** EMI CDM7 64626-2 — Ih 14m ADD 3/93
Cello Concerto[a]. *Piano Trio No. 1 in D minor, Op. 63*[b]. *Funf Stücke im Volkston*[c]. [b]**Alexander Schneider** (vn); **Pablo Casals** (vc); [b]**Mieczyslaw Horszowski,** [c]**Leonard Mannes** (pfs); [a]**Prades Festival Orchestra/Eugene Ormandy.** Sony Classical Casals Edition SMK58993 — Ih 14m ADD 5/94

Schumann. Piano Concerto in A minor, Op. 54[b]. Piano Quintet in E flat major, Op. 44[a].
Alicia de Larrocha (pf); [a]**Tokyo Quartet** (Peter Oundjian, Kikuei Ikeda, vns; Kazuhide Isomura, va; Sadao Harada, vc); [b]**London Symphony Orchestra/Sir Colin Davis.** Victor Red Seal 09026 61279-2. Recorded in 1991.

lh 4m   DDD   5/93

One hopes it is not ungallant to note that Alicia de Larrocha was 70 when she made this recording of Schumann's best known chamber work and concerto, for it demonstrates the best qualities of age. Indeed, affection and experience are here allied to an untarnished technical command. The Piano Quintet, recorded in New York, moves along in a relaxed yet glowing way, with the pianist taking the overall lead but never in a dominating manner, while her colleagues of the Toyko Quartet clearly enjoy the first movement's friendly exchanges with her and each other. This is not to say that these artists miss the more dramatic aspects of the work, however, and thus the strangely march-like second movement has plenty of atmosphere, as has its resolution into more peaceful music towards the end. The *Scherzo* is rightly both forceful and dancelike, and the finale has melodiousness as well as momentum. Though this pianist must have played Schumann's Concerto hundreds of times, it has clearly not diminished her sympathy with this most loveable work, in which buoyancy of invention goes hand in hand with tenderness. Her playing here has been called both "mature" and "contented", and one can see what was meant: nothing is exaggerated, though no point is missed either, and instead the music is simply allowed to unfold in a spacious yet alert way, with a notably unhurried finale. "Ripeness is all", we feel: Shakespeare's words are an altogether suitable description for this performance, in which the London Symphony Orchestra under Sir Colin Davis are the most attentive of partners. This recording was made in EMI's Abbey Road Studios and the sound is rich yet natural.

Additional recommendations ...
Piano Concerto. **Grieg.** *Piano Concerto in A minor, Op. 16.* **Stephen Kovacevich** (pf); **BBC Symphony Orchestra/Sir Colin Davis.** Philips 412 923-2PH — lh lm ADD 10/86
Piano Concerto. **Grieg.** *Piano Concerto.* **Radu Lupu** (pf); **London Symphony Orchestra/ André Previn.** Decca Ovation 417 728-2DM — lh lm ADD 12/87
Piano Concerto[a]. *Davidsbündlertänze, Op. 6. Kinderszenen, Op. 15.* **Fanny Davies** (pf); [a]**Royal Philharmonic Society Orchestra/Ernest Ansermet.** Pearl mono GEMM CD9291 — lh 5m ADD 5/88 ▲
Piano Concerto. **Grieg.** *Piano Concerto.* **Murray Perahia** (pf); **Bavarian Radio Symphony Orchestra/Sir Colin Davis.** CBS CD44899 — lh DDD 5/89
Piano Concerto. **Schoenberg.** *Piano Concerto, Op. 42.* **Maurizio Pollini** (pf); **Berlin Philharmonic Orchestra/Claudio Abbado.** DG 427 771-2GH — 5lm DDD 7/90
Piano Concerto. **Grieg.** *Piano Concerto.* **Pascal Devoyon** (pf); **London Philharmonic Orchestra/Jerzy Maksymiuk.** Classics for Pleasure CD-CFP4574 — lh 3m DDD 2/91
Piano Concerto[a]. **MacDowell.** *Piano Concerto No. 2 in D minor, Op. 23*[b]. *Woodland Sketches, Op. 51 — No. 1, To a Wild Rose*[b]. **Van Cliburn** (pf); **Chicago Symphony Orchestra/**[a]**Fritz Reiner,** [b]**Walter Hendl.** RCA Victor Van Cliburn Collection GD60420 — lh ADD 10/91 ▲
Piano Concerto[a]. **Franck.** *Symphonic Variations, Op. 46*[b]. **Grieg.** *Piano Concerto in A minor, Op. 16*[c]. [a]**Friedrich Gulda,** [bc]**Clifford Curzon** (pfs); [a]**Vienna Philharmonic Orchestra/ Volkmar Andreae;** [b]**London Philharmonic Orchestra/Sir Adrian Boult;** [c]**London Symphony Orchestra/Øivin Fjeldstad.** Decca Headline Classics 433 628-2DSP (*see review under Franck; refer to the Index to Reviews*) — lh 16m ADD 1/92 ▲
Piano Concerto. **Grieg.** *Piano Concerto.* **Lars Vogt** (pf); **City of Birmingham Symphony Orchestra/Simon Rattle.** EMI CDC7 54746-2 — lh 2m DDD 1/93

New review
Schumann. Piano Concerto in A minor, Op. 54. Introduction and Allegro appassionato in D minor (Concertstück), Op. 92. Introduction and Allegro, Op. 134. **Michel Dalberto** (pf); **Vienna Symphony Orchestra/Eliahu Inbal.** Denon CO-75859. Recorded in 1993.

lh 2m   DDD   6/94

Whereas the current CD catalogue lists nearly 60 versions of Schumann's Piano Concerto, there are only four of the G major *Concertstück* that followed just four years later in 1849, and none at all of the D minor *Introduction and Allegro*, Op. 134, of 1853 — the year before Schumann's breakdown. So all praise to Dalberto and Denon for now giving us these three works on one and the same disc. Even if the G major *Concertstück* might be thought just a little protracted, its ideas are as graciously romantic and fresh as its scoring is delicate. The more demonstrative D minor work too, has its reminders of the romantic Schumann of old (the pathos of the piano's introductory rumination, for instance, and the cajoling lyricism of the *Allegro*'s second subject) to offset moments of laboured invention. Combining sensitivity with warmth, soloist and orchestra play both works with persuasive conviction. The concerto, with the keyboard much in the limelight, is a spirited performance that yet seems to lack an element of old-world mellowness and grace. Denon's tonal reproduction is acceptable.

Schumann. SYMPHONIES. **Staatskapelle Dresden/Wolfgang Sawallisch.** EMI Sawallisch Edition CMS7 64815-2. From HMV SLS867 (2/74). Recorded in 1972.
No. 1 in B flat major, Op. 38, "Spring"; No. 2 in C major, Op. 61; No. 3 in E flat major, Op. 97, "Rhenish"; No. 4 in D minor, Op. 120. Overture, Scherzo and Finale, Op. 52.

② 2h 28m ADD 11/93 Ⓑ

New review

Schumann. Bavarian Radio Symphony Orchestra/Rafael Kubelík. Sony Classical Essential Classics SBK48269/70. From CBS 79324 (10/79). Recorded 1978-9.
SBK48269 — No. 1 in B flat major, Op. 38, "Spring"; No. 2 in C major, Op. 61. *SBK48270* — No. 3 in E flat major, Op. 97, "Rhenish"; No. 4 in D minor, Op. 120. Manfred, Op. 115 — Overture.

② 1h 14m 1h 16m ADD 7/93 Ⓑ

Schumann's symphonies come in for a lot of criticism because of his supposed cloudy textures and unsubtle scoring, but in the hands of a conductor who is both skilful and sympathetic they are most engaging works. Sawallisch's recordings, brightly transferred, provide us with a much admired set. His style, fresh and unforced, is not as high powered as some other conductors but it is sensible, alert and very pleasing. He achieves great lightness in the First and Fourth Symphonies — there's always a sense of classical poise and control but never at the expense of the overall architecture of the pieces. The Second and Third Symphonies, larger and more far-reaching in their scope, again benefit from Sawallisch's approach. The playing of the Staatskapelle Dresden is superlative in every department, with a lovely veiled string sound and a real sense of ensemble. These are real bargains and with the *Overture, Scherzo and Finale* thrown in for good measure, definitely not to be missed.

It is difficult to understand why Kubelík's wonderful cycle failed to make an impact when it was first issued. His sensitivity to detail, his refusal to bully Schumann's vulnerable structures and his ability to penetrate occasional thickets of orchestration, make these especially memorable. Just listen to the cheeky bassoon backing clarinet, 1'44" into the *Spring* Symphony's fourth movement, the limpid phrasing of the *Rhenish* Symphony's *Nicht schnell* third movement, or the to-ing and fro-ing between first and second violins (usefully separated, as virtually always with Kubelík) in the last movement of the Second. Only the first movement of the Fourth seems a little heavy-handed, but then the poetry of the *Romanze* and the exuberance of the finale more than make amends. First movement repeats are observed and the playing throughout is rich in felicitous turns of phrase. The sound, though, is a minor stumbling block: violins are thin (one of the few disadvantages of having them separated is that their massed tone becomes mildly diluted), brass a little fuzzy and the whole production less focused than Sawallisch's set. But Kubelík's insights are too varied and meaningful to miss, and there is much pleasure to be derived from them. What with a stirring *Manfred* Overture added for good measure, they also constitute exceptional value for money.

Additional recommendations ...
Nos. 1-4. Cello Concerto in A minor, Op. 129[a]. *Piano Concerto in A minor, Op. 54*[b]. [a]**Justus Franz** (pf); [b]**Mischa Maisky** (vc); **Vienna Philharmonic Orchestra/Leonard Bernstein.** DG 423 099-2GH3 — ③ 3h 18m DDD 3/88 Ⓑ
Nos. 1-4. **Berlin Philharmonic Orchestra/Herbert von Karajan.** DG Symphony Edition 429 672-2GSE2 — ② 2h 12m ADD 7/90 Ⓑ
Nos. 1-4. **Suisse Romande Orchestra/Armin Jordan.** Erato 2292-45496-2 — ② 2h 11m DDD 12/90 Ⓑ
No 1. Manfred, Op. 115 — Overture. Overture, Scherzo and Finale, Op. 52. **Stuttgart Radio Symphony Orchestra/Sir Neville Marriner.** Capriccio CD10 063 — DDD 6/86 Ⓑ

Nos. 1 and 4. **Royal Concertgebouw Orchestra/Riccardo Chailly.** Decca 425 608-2DH
— •⁖ lh 3m DDD 12/90 ⁹ₛ Ⓑ

Nos. 2 and 3. **Staatskapelle, Dresden/Wolfgang Sawallisch.** EMI Studio CDM7 69472-2
— •⁖ lh llm ADD ll/88 Ⓑ

Nos. 2 and 3. **Berlin Philharmonic Orchestra/James Levine.** DG 423 625-2GH — •⁖
lh l2m DDD 2/89 ⁹ₚ Ⓑ

Nos. 2 and 3. **Baltimore Symphony Orchestra/David Zinman.** Telarc CD80182 — •⁖
lh l0m DDD 6/91 Ⓑ

Nos. 2 and 3. **London Philharmonic Orchestra/Kurt Masur.** Teldec 2292-46446-2 — •⁖
lh 6m DDD 12/91 Ⓑ

Schumann. Symphonies — No. 3 in E flat major, Op. 97, "Rhenish"; No. 4 in D minor, Op. 120. **London Classical Players/Roger Norrington.** EMI CDC7 54025-2.

•⁖ 57m DDD 3/91   Ⓑ 🖋

Spearheading the authentic brigade's excursion into romantic repertoire, it's surprising how euphonious Roger Norrington's ensemble sounds here. Gone is the braying brass obscuring fragile strings that was often a feature of period performance. Norrington controls his forces with an acute ear and intelligence for what is germane to the music, and the brass only 'open up' where structure demands it, or where the overall balance would be unaffected. The strength of purpose, separated violin desks and close balance are often reminiscent of the best of Klemperer's work for EMI in the sixties. There is too a similar lack of concern for mere beauty of sound. Textural revelations aside (they are too numerous to mention), the most striking feature of these accounts is their strict adherence to Schumann's explicit indications of tempo: the middle movements of both symphonies are much faster than usual. Some collectors may initially feel short changed on graceful singing lines and variety of moods but compensation lies in the revitalization of the music's rhythms, and its sense of direction. The Fourth Symphony, in particular, is experienced in one single sweep. It's a pity, here, in music that should be continuous, that the CD contains breaks between the first three movements.

Additional recommendations ...

No. 3. **Schubert.** *No. 8 in B minor, D759, "Unfinished".* **Concertgebouw Orchestra/Leonard Bernstein.** DG 431 042-2GBE — •⁖ DDD Ⓑ

No. 4. Manfred Overture. **Haydn.** *Symphony No. 88 in G major, "Letter V".* **Berlin Philharmonic Orchestra/Wilhelm Furtwängler.** DG mono 427 404-2GDO — •⁖ lh 6m AAD 6/86 Ⓑ ▲

No. 3. **Mendelssohn.** *Symphony No. 5 in D major, Op. 107, "Reformation".* **Berlin Philharmonic Orchestra/Herbert von Karajan.** DG Galleria 419 870-2GGA — •⁖ lh 9m ADD 4/88 Ⓑ

No. 3. **Schubert.** *No. 8[b].* [a]**Los Angeles Philharmonic Orchestra/Carlo Maria Giulini;** [b]**Philharmonia Orchestra/Giuseppe Sinopoli.** DG 3D Classics 427 818-2GDC — •⁖ lh 3m DDD 4/90 ⁹ₚ Ⓑ

No. 3. **Schubert.** *Symphony No. 3 in D major, D200.* **North German Radio Symphony Orchestra/Günter Wand.** RCA Victor Red Seal 09026 61876-2 — •⁖ 56m DDD 2/94 ⁹ₚ Ⓑ

Schumann. Piano Quartets — E flat major, Op. 47; C minor. **Young Uck Kim** (vn); **Heiichiro Ohyama** (va); **Gary Hoffman** (vc); **André Previn** (pf). RCA Victor Red Seal 09026 61384-2. Recorded in 1991.

•⁖ 47m DDD 5/93

Schumann lovers the world over owe a great debt of gratitude to André Previn and his colleagues for giving us the "world première recording" of Schumann's C minor Piano Quartet, written when he was still a law student of only 18. Though favourably impressing several Leipzig musical friends at an informal try-out in 1829, the work remained unpublished for 150 years until a performing edition was prepared by that dedicated Schumann scholar, Wolfgang Boetticher. The nimble *Minuetto* and tenderly spun *Andante* are its gems: Schumann himself subsequently described the trio of the *Minuetto* (containing a phrase destined to reappear in the fourth of his Op. 4 *Intermezzos* for solo piano) as the moment he knew he belonged to a new world of romance. Though the more classically inspired flanking movements need (and in this splendidly vivid performance receive) a few discreet cuts, both have irrepressible buoyancy of spirit. His familiar second and last Quartet in E flat followed towards the end of 1842, a year almost exclusively devoted to chamber music, by which time he had an eminently distinguished pianist wife to help promote it. With his clear texture and rhythmic crispness, Previn ensures that the important keyboard part never dominates. And even though just now and again (notably in the meltingly heartfelt *Andante cantabile*) the sensitive cellist lacks the warmest and richest tonal glow, the playing, no less than the recording, holds its own with all the catalogue's rivals.

Additional recommendations ...
Quartet, Op. 47[a]. Piano Quintet in E flat major, Op. 44[b]. **Beaux Arts Trio; [b]Dorf Bettelheim** (vn); [ab]**Samuel Rhodes** (va). Philips 420 791-2PH — .•* 58m ADD 2/88 ℗
As Philips. **Jiří Panocha** (vn); **Miroslav Sehnoutka** (va); **Jaroslav Kulhan** (vc); **Jan Panenka** (pf); **Smetana Quartet.** Supraphon 11 0367-2 — .•* 57m DDD 10/91
Quartet, Op. 47. Piano Quintet in E flat major, Op. 44. **Schubert Ensemble of London.** Hyperion CDA66657 — .•* 58m DDD 2/94

Schumann. Violin Sonatas — No. 1 in A minor, Op. 105; No. 2 in D minor, Op. 121. **Gidon Kremer** (vn); **Martha Argerich** (pf). DG 419 235-2GH.

.•* 49m DDD 1/87

The rapidity of composition of the two violin sonatas (four and six days respectively) is nowhere evident except perhaps in the vigour and enthusiasm of the music. Argerich and Kremer, both mercurial and emotionally charged performers, subtly balance the ardent Florestan and dreamily melancholic Eusebius elements of Schumann's creativity. This is even more striking in the Second Sonata, a greater work than its twin, thematically vigorous with a richness and scope that make it at once a striking as well as ideally structured work. Kremer and Argerich have established a close and exciting duo partnership and this fine recording shows what like minds can achieve in music so profoundly expressive as this.

New review
Schumann. PIANO WORKS. **Vladimir Horowitz.** CBS CD42409. Item marked [a] recorded live in Carnegie Hall, New York in 1968, [b] 1966.
Toccata in C major, Op. 7. Kinderszenen, Op. 15 (both from SBRG72117, 7/63). Kreisleriana, Op. 16 (72841, 12/70). Arabeske in C major, Op. 18[a] (72720, 1/69). Blumenstück in D flat major, Op. 19[b] (72794, 11/69).

.•* 1h 11m AAD 8/90 ℗

The programme was apparently selected by Horowitz himself from LPs of the 1960s. There is a characteristically impish delight in the *Toccata*'s passing quirks such as melodic syncopation, hidden inner voices and abrupt dynamic contrast. The *Arabeske* and *Blumenstück*, no mere drawing-room aquarelles in these ripely romantic readings, were both recorded live, allowing this otherwise studio-produced, excellently remastered disc to end in tumultous applause. However, the gem is *Kreisleriana*. This was a first choice in a BBC Radio 3 "Building a Library" programme way back in 1973. And despite the many fine versions that have come and gone since then, it would still be the one to take to a desert island — for its intensity and succulent melodic line in Eusebian introspection no less than for its Florestanian bursts of flame, and equally much for its relish of that vein of Hoffmannesque fantasy and caprice for which Schumann also finds a place in the work. Just this one performance alone would always keep Horowitz among the immortals.

Schumann. Piano Sonata No. 1 in F sharp minor, Op. 11. Fantasie in C major, Op. 17. **Maurizio Pollini** (pf). DG 423 134-2GH. From 2530 379 (5/74).

.•* 1h 3m ADD 5/88 ℗ Ⓑ

These works grew from Schumann's love and longing for his future wife Clara. Both perform-ances are superb, not least because they are so truthful to the letter of the score. By eschewing all unspecified rubato in the *Fantasie*, Pollini reminds us that the young Schumann never wrote a more finely proportioned large-scale work; this feeling for structure, coupled with exceptional emotional intensity, confirms it as one of the greatest love-poems ever written for the piano. His richly characterized account of the Sonata is refreshingly unmannered. Certainly the familiar charges of protracted patterning in the faster flanking movements are at once dispelled by his rhythmic *élan*, his crystalline texture and his ear for colour. The sound re-emerges with all its original clarity on CD.

Additional recommendation ...
Piano Sonata No. 1. Waldszenes, Op. 82. Kinderszenen, Op. 15. **Vladimir Ashkenazy** (pf). Decca
421 290-2DH — .•˙ 1h 14m DDD 2/89 ⁹ₚ Ⓑ
Fantasie. Fantasiestücke, Op. 12. **Brahms.** *Variations and Fugue on a Theme by Handel, Op. 24.*
Benno Moiseiwitsch (pf). Testament mono SBT1023 — .•˙ 1h 18m ADD 1/94 ⁹ₚ ▲ Ⓑ

Key to symbols

Price	Quantity/ availability	Timing	Recording mode	Review date
②	②	1h 23m	DDD	6/88

New review

Schumann. Allegro in B minor, Op. 8. Novelletten, Op. 21. Drei Fantasiestücke, Op. 111. Gesänge der Frühe, Op. 133. **Ronald Brautigam** (pf). Olympia OCD436. Recorded in 1993.

.•˙ 1h 19m DDD 6/94 ⁹ₚ

The note reminds us that even the eight *Novelletten* chosen as the centrepiece here are not often heard in sequence as a set. Brautigam prefaces them with the early (1931-2) B minor *Allegro* originally intended as the first movement of a sonata. They are followed by the last two suites Schumann ever wrote for the piano — the *Gesänge der Frühe* only a year before his final breakdown. Most enjoyable is Brautigam's vitality — vitality of imagination no less than of fingers. You are immediately gripped by his plunge into the Op. 8 *Allegro*, with its arresting octave 'motto'. His mercurial fancy and ear for hidden melodic strands in the ensuing stream certainly makes nonsense of hasty dismissal of this work as mere old-style virtuoso note-spinning. Moreover, such is his unflagging impulse in the eight *Novelletten* that never for a moment are you tempted to accuse Schumann of over-repetitively patterned figuration. Potently characterized and contrasted as are the three *Fantasiestücke*, Op. 111 of 1851, Brautigam leaves you in no doubt as to their unity as a set — as he does again, still more subtly and movingly, in the more elusive spiritual world of the five *Gesänge der Frühe*. The bright, clear tonal reproduc-tion is acceptable enough.

Schumann. Kinderszenen, Op. 15[a]. Faschingsschwank aus Wien, Op. 26[b]. Carnaval, Op. 9[b]. **Daniel Barenboim** (pf) DG Privilege 431 167-2GR. Item marked [a] from 2531 079 (6/79), [b] 2531 089 (7/79). Recorded in 1979.

.• 1h 13m ADD 8/91 ⁹ₚ Ⓑ

The extremely fine DG budget price recital of three of Schumann's finest works finds Daniel Barenboim at the peak of his pianistic power. Barenboim achieves both the virtuosity and interpretative prowess necessary to fully realize the brilliant miniatures within each work. Above all it is the strong sense of character which he imparts to Schumann's individual sound world that makes the disc as a whole so successful. The *Kinderszenen* ("Scenes from Childhood") contain some of Schumann's most eloquent and intimate piano writing and Barenboim brings a wonderful delicacy and wistfulness to this music. The more robust *Faschingsschwank aus Wien* ("Carnival Jest from Vienna") is given a performance of great vitality, more than sufficient to hide the work's occasional weaknesses. The crowning glory of the disc as a whole is a splendidly vibrant and intense performance of *Carnaval* which perfectly captures the extrovert intentions of Florestan, while equally successfully portraying the poetic side of Eusebius. The climax, with Schumann triumphing against the Philistines, is extraordinarily exhilarating. DG's sound is fully worthy of this magnificent example of romantic interpretation.

Additional recommendations ...
Kinderszenen. Kreisleriana, Op. 16. **Martha Argerich** (pf). DG 410 653-2GH — .•˙ 52m DDD
5/84 ⁹ₚ Ⓑ
Kreisleriana. Fantasia in C major, Op. 17. **Artur Rubinstein** (pf). RCA Gold Seal 09026 61264-2
— .•˙ 1h 6m ADD 2/93 ⁹ₚ Ⓑ

Schumann. Davidsbündlertänze, Op. 6. Waldszenen, Op. 82. Fantasiestücke, Op. 111.
Andreas Haefliger (pf). Sony Classical CD48036. Recorded in 1991.

⠶ **Ih 5m DDD I0/92**

Schumann. Davidsbündlertänze, Op. 6. Fantasiestücke, Op. 12. **Benjamin Frith** (pf). Naxos
8 550493. Recorded in 1991.

Ih 3m DDD 3/93

Although by 1851 Schumann had dropped overt references to that Laurel and Hardy of his
creative imagination, Florestan and Eusebius (referring, more or less, to the *yin,* and *yang* —
masculine and feminine, assertive and reflective — characters of individual pieces), frequent and
telling changes of mood remained an essential ingredient of his mature style. *Davidsbündlertänze,*
or "Dances of the League of David" exemplify this trend most vividly: two books, each containing
nine separate pieces, alternating fast with slow, humorous with serious and invariably maintaining
an element of surprise. There are two 'versions' of the *Davidsbündlertänze,* one from 1837, the
other from 1851 and Andreas Haefliger achieves a felicitous musical balance by combining
elements of both. His is an intelligent and thoughtful brand of pianism, sensitive to modulation
and wonderfully warm in tone; one was was often reminded of the similarly perceptive art of
our own much-loved (and much missed) master pianist, Solomon. What is most striking about
the *Davidsbündlertänze* is the way Schumann plots key changes from one miniature to the next,
effecting many magical contrasts, especially in the second book. Furthermore, the actual level of
invention is always high, and the closing sequence utilizes some of Schumann's most bewitching
invention: try, by way of example, the final pair — "Wie aus der Ferne" and "Nicht schnell"
(tracks 17 and 18). *Waldszenen* is less a sweeping inspiration than a series of lonely vignettes;
"The Prophet Bird" (track 25), a frequently performed 'encore' in its own right, is possibly the
most atmospheric evocation of tree-top bird song pre-Messiaen, an eerie, questioning *morceau* that
twists and turns with the unpredictability of its natural model. If *Waldszenen* takes us deep into
the woods, the late *Fantasiestücke* take us further still; here loneliness transforms to disorientation
(second movement), and youthful passion becomes defiant grandeur (third). Haefliger charts both
this and the disc's companion pieces with sure intuition, and he is most beautifully recorded. The
young prize-winning British pianist Benjamin Frith indulges the *Davidsbündlertänze*'s caprice,
highlighting the contrasts between fast and slower pieces, and summoning his excellent technique
for some exciting pianism. But then contrast lies at the very heart of Schumann's inspiration.
Frith is quite unlike Haefliger in that he favours impulse over refinement, and isn't afraid to
throw caution to the winds, if the mood dictates. His *Fantasiestücke,* too, are forthright and
outspoken, although "Des Abends", "Warum" and "Ende vom Lied" each contain plenty of poetry.
Naxos's recording is excellent. Certainly recom-mended, not only for the budget-conscious
collector, but for those who enjoy youthful pianistic exuberance.

Additional recommendation ...
Papillons, Op. 2. Davidsbündlertänze. Carnaval, Op. 9. Fantasie in C major, Op. 17. Etudes
Symphoniques, Op. 13. Kreisleriana, Op. 16. Kinderszenen, Op. 15. Piano Sonata No. 2 in G minor,
Op. 22. Arabeske, Op. 18. Bunte Blätter, Op. 99 — Novellette. Drei Romanzen, Op. 28. Humoreske,
Op. 20. Waldszene. Nachtstücke, Op. 23. **Wilhelm Kempff** (pf). DG 435 045-2GX4 — ⠶ **⦾**
4h 57m ADD 5/92 ꝗₚ

New review
Schumann. LIEDER. **Robert Holl** (bass); **András Schiff** (pf). Decca 436 123-2DH. Texts
and translations included. Recorded in 1990.
Liederkreis, Op. 39. Sieben Gedichte, Op. 90. Lieder, Op. 40 — No. 1, Märzveilchen; No. 2,
Muttertraum; No. 3, Der Soldat; No. 4, Der Spielmann. Lieder und Gesänge aus Wilhelm
Meister, Op. 98*a* — No. 4, Wer nie sein Brot mit Tränen ass; No. 6, Wer sich der Einsamkeit
ergibt; No. 8, An die Türen will ich schleichen. Nachtlied, Op. 96 No. 1.

⠶ **Ih 8m DDD 7/94**   ꝗₚ

The structure of this recital, and the way in which it works on the ear and the spirit from first
to last, is an inextricable part of the power of its performances: each one is typical of Robert
Holl's deeply absorbed imaginative examination of everything he sings, and of András Schiff's
minutely sentient accompanying. The Op. 39 *Liederkreis* is the central point of reference. Before
this come the seven little Lenau settings of Op. 90, approached by Holl very much as private

intimations and reflections, to be overheard by the listener. "Meine Rose" is a mere sigh in half-voice; a dark "Der schwere Abend" presages the state of mind of *Dichterliebe*'s "Ich hab' im Traum". As a group, these songs breathe out the very essence of the *Waldeinsamkeit* which appears overtly in the Op. 39 *Liederkreis*. For Holl, these are songs of far distant exile, the first poem whispering its intimations of mortality in a mere fraction of his mighty bass. He also adds the dark fairytale miniatures of the Hans Andersen Songs (Op. 40) and the tortured, forward-looking *Wilhelm Meister* Harper-Songs, ending, wonderfully, with one of Schumann's and Goethe's very greatest, "Über allen Gipfeln ist Ruh". An outstanding recital.

Schumann. LIEDER. **Peter Schreier** (ten); **Christoph Eschenbach** (pf). Teldec 2292-46154-2. Texts and translations included. Recorded in 1988.
Liederkreis, Op. 24. Liederkreis, Op. 39. Dichterliebe, Op. 48. Myrthen, Op. 25 — No. 1, Widmung; No. 2, Freisinn; No. 3, Der Nussbaum; No. 7, Die Lotosblume; No. 15, Aus den hebräischen Gesängen; No. 21, Was will die einsame Träne?; No. 24, Du bist wie eine Blume; No. 25, Aus den östlichen Rosen; No. 26, Zum Schluss, Lieder-Album für die Jugend, Op. 79 — No. 4, Frühlingsgruss; No. 7, Zigeunerliedchen; No. 13, Marienwürmchen; No. 26, Schneeglöckchen. Zwölf Gedichte, Op. 35 — No. 3, Wanderlied; No. 4, Erstes Grün; No. 8, Stille Liebe; No. 11, Wer machte dich so krank?; No. 12, Alte Laute. Liebesfrühling, Op. 37 — No. 1, Der Himmel hat eine Träne geweint; No. 5, Ich hab in mich gesogen; No. 9, Rose, Meer und Sonne. Fünf Lieder, Op. 40. Mein schöner Stern!, Op. 101 No. 4. Nur ein lächelnder Blick, Op. 27 No. 5. Geständnis, Op. 74 No. 7. Aufträge, Op. 77 No. 5. Meine Rose, Op. 90 No. 2. Kommen und Schneiden, Op. 90 No. 3. Lieder und Gesange, Op. 51 — No. 1, Sehnsucht; No. 3, Ich wandre nicht. An den Mond, Op. 95 No. 2. Dein Angesicht, Op. 127 No. 2. Lehn deine Wang, Op. 142 No. 2. Der arme Peter, Op. 53 No. 3.

③ 2h 45m DDD 6/91

This is a very fair conspectus of Schumann's genius as a Lieder composer and all the offerings are authoritatively performed. They include recommendable accounts of the three cycles appropriate for a male singer to tackle. Schreier with Eschenbach, who has made a special study of the composer, make the most of *Dichterliebe* and the two *Liederkreise*, identifying themselves with the various moods and characters depicted within. Schreier's idiomatic and pointed diction and accents allied to Eschenbach's exploratory and imaginative way with Schumann's highly individual writing for piano would be hard to better. The remainder of these three well-filled CDs is given over to single songs and to discerning choices from groups other than the cycles. Here are the most telling pieces from *Myrthen* and from the 12 Kerner settings, Op. 35. Late Schumann is acknowledged to be a more doubtful quantity, but he could still write great songs such as the poignant *Meine Rose* and the lovely Heine setting, *Dein Angesicht*. To these, as to the delightful *Zigeunerliedchen*, and much else, this pair of superb performers bring their unfailing artistry, always seeking and finding the heart of the matter. The well-balanced recording is an unobtrusive support.

Additional recommendations ...
Frauenliebe und Leben, Op. 42. Dichterliebe, Op. 48. **Lotte Lehmann** (sop); **Bruno Walter** (pf). CBS Masterworks Portrait CD44840 — 48m ADD 11/89
Myrthen, Op. 25 — No.1, Widmung; No. 3, Der Nussbaum; No. 7, Die Lotosblume; No. 9, Lied der Suleika; No. 11, Lied der Brait aus dem Liebesfrühling I; No. 12, Lied der Braut aus dem Liebesfrühling II; No. 15, Aus den hebräischen Gesängen; No. 21, Was will die einsame Träne?; No. 23, Im Westen. Sieben Gedichte, Op. 90. An den Sonnenschein, Op. 36 No. 4. Der Himmel hat ein Träne geweint, Op. 37 No. 1. Muttertraum, Op. 40 No. 2. Romanzen und Balladen, Op. 64 — No. 2, Das berlassne Mägdelein; No. 3, Tragödie. Melancholie, Op. 74 No. 6. Geisternähe, Op. 77 No. 3. Der Einsiedler, Op. 83 No. 3. **Mitsuko Shirai** (mez); **Hartmut Höll** (pf). Capriccio 10 445 — 1h 3m DDD 11/93

Schumann. LIEDER. **Eberhard Waechter** (bar); **Alfred Brendel** (pf). Decca 425 949-2DM. Texts and translations included. From SXL2310 (6/62). Recorded in 1961.
Dichterliebe, Op. 48. Liederkreis, Op. 24 — Schöne Wiege meiner Leiden; Mit Myrten und Rosen. Lehn deine Wang an meine Wang, Op. 142 No. 2. Mein Wagen rollet langsam, Op. 142 No. 4.

41m ADD 6/91

This recording of *Dichterliebe*, 31 years old and somewhat overlooked when first issued, is one of the most satisfying ever made of the cycle, by virtue of Waechter's total identification with the jilted man's sorrow expressed in warm, vibrant, wholehearted, never self-conscious singing. Here the romantic thoughts, melancholy, anger, torment, resignation, so memorably achieved in Schumann's setting of Heine, receives an answering identification on Waechter's part. Nowhere else in Schumann's output are the voice and piano so closely entwined as if in a single outpouring of inspiration. Here that achievement is fully realized through Brendel's discerning, probing execution. Always achieving rapport with his partner, Brendel is here caught before he became the famous pianist he is today. Anybody listening to his marvellously perceptive accounts of Schumann's ingenious postludes would hear what a masterly pianist he already was. The extra songs are given with just as much illumination on both sides.

Additional recommendations ...
Liederkreis, Op. 24. Frauenliebe und -leben, Op. 42. Tragödie, Op. 64 No. 3. Abends am Strand, Op. 45 No. 3. Lehn' deine Wang, Op. 142 No. 2. Mein Wagen rollet langsam, Op. 142 No. 2. **Brigitte Fassbaender** (mez); **Irwin Gage** (pf). DG 415 519-2GH — ⠕ 57m DDD 2/86 Ⓑ
Dichterliebe, Op. 48. Liederkreis, Op. 39. **Olaf Bär** (bar); **Geoffrey Parsons** (pf). EMI CDC7 47397-2 — ⠕ 54m DDD 9/86 ⁹ₚ Ⓑ
Dichterliebe. Liederkreis, Op. 39. **Josef Protschka** (ten); **Helmut Deutsch** (pf). Capriccio 10 215 — ⠕ 1h 2m DDD 12/88 ⁹ₚ Ⓑ
Dichterliebe. Der Nussbaum, Op. 25 No. 3. **Brahms:** *Deutsche Volkslieder — No. 1, Sagt mire, o schönste Schäf'rin; No. 4, Guten Abend, mein tausiger Schatz; No. 15, Schwesterlein, Schwesterlein; No. 34, Wie komm'ich denn zur Tür herein? Wiegenlied, Op. 49 No. 4.* **Prokofiev:** *Three Children's Songs, Op. 68. The Ugly Duckling, Op. 18 (all sung in German).* **Peter Schreier** (ten); **Wolfgang Sawallisch** (pf). Philips 426 237-2PH *(see review in the Collections section; refer to the Index to Reviews)* — ⠕ 1h 12m DDD 4/90 Ⓑ

Schumann (arr. Beecham). Manfred — Incidental Music, Op. 115. **Gertrud Holt** (sop); **Claire Duchesneau** (mez); **Glyndwr Davies, Ian Billington** (tens); **Niven Miller** (bar); **Laidman Browne, Jill Balcon, Raf de la Torre, David Enders** (spkrs); **BBC Chorus; Royal Philharmonic Orchestra/Sir Thomas Beecham.** Sir Thomas Beecham Trust mono BEECHAM4. From Fontana CFL1026/7 (2/59). Recorded 1954-56.

⠕ 1h 18m ADD 9/91   ⁹ₚ ▲

Schumann was haunted by Byron's autobiographically-inspired dramatic poem, *Manfred*, from a very early age. When eventually writing his incidental music for it (15 numbers and an overture) in 1848-9 he confessed to never having devoted himself to any composition before "with such lavish love and power". No one in this country has ever done more for it than Sir Thomas Beecham, who even staged it at the Theatre Royal, Drury Lane, London, way back in 1918, some 36 years before reviving it for the BBC and at the Festival Hall in performances leading to this now legendary recording. Score-followers will at once note Beecham's appropriation and scoring of two of the composer's roughly contemporaneous keyboard miniatures as additional background music for the guilt-wracked, soliloquizing Manfred. But their choice and placing is so apt that even Schumann himself might have been grateful. By present-day standards Laidman Browne might be thought a shade too overtly emotional in the title-role. But speakers (including a splendidly awesome Witch of the Alps and rustic chamois-hunter), like singers, orchestra and the magnetic Sir Thomas himself, are all at one in vividness of atmospheric evocation. Splendid remastering also plays its part in making this medium-priced disc a collector's piece.

New review
Schumann. GENOVEVA. **Julia Faulkner** (sop) Genoveva; **Keith Lewis** (ten) Golo; **Harald Stamm** (bass) Hidulfus, Caspar; **Alan Titus** (bar) Siegfried; **Renate Behle** (sop) Margaretha; **Carl Schultz** (bass) Drago; **Johann Tilli** (bass) Balthasar; **Hamburg State Opera Chorus; Hamburg Philharmonic Orchestra/Gerd Albrecht.** Orfeo C289932H. Notes, text and translation included. Recorded live in the Musikhalle, Hamburg in 1992.

⠕ ② 2h 58m DDD 1/94

Because of certain dramatic shortcomings, including a contrived, last-minute happy ending and an infusion of black magic once dismissed by George Bernard Shaw as "pure bosh", Schumann's one and only opera, *Genoveva*, never held the stage. After the unpardonably long omission of *Genoveva* from the British catalogue, we can now at last enjoy much lovely music in our armchairs through this Hamburg live recording under the directorship of that tireless champion of the unjustly neglected, Gerd Albrecht. Prime responsibility for the care of Genoveva, the luckless lady, wrongly accused of adultery while her husband is away at the war, rests with Golo, who is wracked by conscience about his secret passion for her until he is stung into vengeance by Genoveva's "Away, away, infamous bastard". The role is feelingly and lyrically sung by Keith Lewis. Genoveva herself, only fully portrayed in distress (Acts 2 and 4), is sung by the American, Julia Faulkner, with a pure-toned, girlish vulnerability. Albrecht sweeps the opera along with an effortlessly flowing, seam-concealing continuity that would have surely pleased the composer himself, who was anxious to emulate Wagner's ever-growing rejection of the self-contained operatic set-number. The sound quality offered by the Hamburg engineers is unfailingly mellifluous.

Further listening ...

Works for Piano Trio — Piano Trios: No. 1 in D minor, Op. 63; No. 2 in F major, Op. 80; No. 3 in G minor. Fantasiestücke, Op. 88. **Borodin Trio.** Chandos CHAN8832/3 (11/90).

Piano Sonata No. 2. Kreisleriana, Op. 16. Nověllette in F sharp minor, Op. 21 No. 8. **Vladimir Ashkenazy** (pf). Decca 425 940-2DH (4/92).

Four Fugues, Op. 72. Marches, Op. 76 — No. 2 in G minor. Toccata, Op. 7. Blumenstück, Op. 19. Vier Nachtstücke, Op. 23. **Sviatoslav Richter** (pf). Decca 436 456-2DH (3/93).

Das Paradies und die Peri, Op. 50. **Soloists; Lausanne Pro Arte Choir; Suisse Romande Chamber Choir and Orchestra/Armin Jordan.** Erato 2292-45456-2 (4/90).

Szenen aus Goethes Faust. **Soloists; Wandsworth School Choir; Aldeburgh Festival Singers; English Chamber Orchestra/Benjamin Britten.** Decca 425 705-2DM2 (7/90).

Heinrich Schütz

German 1585-1672

New review

Schütz. MOTETS. **Emmanuel Music Chorus/Craig Smith.** Koch International Classics 37174-2. Texts and translations included. Recorded in 1992.
Geistliche Chormusik, Op. 11 — O lieber Herre Gott, SWV381; Tröstet, tröstet mein Volk, SWV382; Ich bin eine rufende Stimme, SWV383; Ein Kind ist uns geboren, SWV384; Das Wort ward Fleisch, SWV385; Die Himmel erzählen, SWV386; Herzlich lieb hab isch dich, SWV387; Das ist je gewisslich, SWV388; Ich bin eine rechter Weinstock, SWV389; Unser Wandel ist im Himmel, SWV390; Selig sind die Toten, SWV391; Ich weiss, dass mein Erlöser lebt, SWV393. Ich weiss das mein Erlöser lebet, SWV457.

Ih 7m DDD 11/93

As the informative note observes, "Schütz is out to convince, to move, to exhort, literally to change your way of thinking". Nowhere in Schütz's music is this more apparent than in the motets from the 1648 collection. The glittering sound of the Emmanuel Music Chorus is just what is required for Schütz's six-part writing. The chorus's bright timbre lends itself extremely well to the varied textures of the motets recorded here, and Craig Smith obviously understands this music very well indeed. The chorus have an excellent command of the language, and a tremendous empathy with, and understanding of, the music. The magical unfolding of the opening phrase of *O lieber Herre Gott* and the handling of the subtle and unexpected harmonic writing of *Selig sind die Toten* are among the most memorable things on the disc, and blazing *forte* passages of splendour abound. Undoubtedly one of the best discs of Schütz available.

Schütz. MOTETS. **Tölz Boys' Choir/Gerhard Schmidt-Gaden** with **Roman Summereder** (org). Capriccio 10 388. Texts and translations included. Recorded 1989-90.
Ich hab mein Sach Gott heimgestellt, SWV305. Ich will dem Herren loben allezeit, SWV306. Was hast du verwirket, SWV307. O Jesu, nomen dulce, SWV308. O misericordissime Jesu,

SWV309. Ich leige und schlafe, SWV310. Habe deine Lust an dem Herren, SWV311. Herr, ich hoffe darauf, SWV312. Bone Jesu, verbum Patris, SWV313. Verbum caro factum est, SWV314. Hodie Christus natus est, SWV315. Wann unsre Augen schlafen ein, SWV316. Meister, wir haben die ganze Nacht gearbeitet, SWV317. Die Furcht des Herren, SWV318. Ich beuge meine Knie, SWV319. Ich bin jung gewesen, SWV320. Herr, wann ich nur dich habe, SWV321. Rorate coeli desuper, SWV322. Joseph, du Sohn David, SWV323. Ich bin die Auferstehung, SWV324.

1h 17m   DDD   4/93

Getting music published evidently encountered economic difficulties during the Thirty Years' War, for Heinrich Schütz had to issue his *Kleine Geistliche Konzerte* ("Little Sacred Concertos") — short motets for vocal soloists and continuo — in two parts in, respectively, 1636 and 1639. No. 24 from Part I and Nos. 1-19 from Part II comprise the programme for this second volume from soloists of the Tölz Boys' Choir and although, at first sight, this may seem too regimented an approach to produce satisfying listening for the whole disc, Schütz himself structured the items so that there is a progression throughout the set, not only in increased numbers of soloists but also in intensity and intellectual scope. The voices of the soloists here are typically very individual and characterful, and all are remarkably adroit and stylish, so the personal witness that is so pronounced in the text is particularly well portrayed. These are performers well used to the subtleties of baroque word setting and they highlight all the ingenuity that Schütz lavished on these seemingly simple texts. There is an evident delight in the way the composer deployed his limited resources, constantly ringing the changes on traditional formulas to produce a richness of ideas that it took a Bach or Handel to emulate. The rather close recording allows all these intricacies to emerge undiminished and although the resonance of the acoustic seems restrained, this is no bad thing for music that, despite its title, has the feel of chamber music.

Further listening ...

Freue dich des Weibes deiner Jugend, SWV453 (with Frieder Lang, ten). Ist nicht Ephraim mein teuer Sohn, SWV40. Saul, Saul, was verfolgst du mich, SWV415. Auf dem Gebirge, SWV396 (Ashley Stafford, Michael Chance, altos). Musicalische Exequien, SWV279-81 (Lang). **Monteverdi Choir; English Baroque Soloists; His Majesties Sagbutts and Cornetts/ John Eliot Gardiner.** Archiv Produktion 423 405-2AH (11/88).

Saul, Saul, was verfolgst du mich, SWV415. Ich danke dem Herrn, SWV34. Magnificat anima mia, SWV468. Stehe auf, meine Freundin, SWV499. *Coupled with* **G. Gabrieli.** Magnificat, Lieto godea. **M. Praetorius.** Meine Seele erhebt den Herren. **Monteverdi.** Gloria in excelsis Deo. **Schütz Academy/Howard Arman.** Capriccio 10 409 (5/93).

Arthur Schwartz
American 1900-1984

Suggested listening ...

A TREE GROWS IN BROOKLYN. **Original Broadway cast.** Sony Broadway CD48014.

Cyril Scott
British 1879-1970

Suggested listening ...

Aubade, Op. 77. Neapolitan Rhapsody. Three Dances, Op. 22. Suite Fantastique. Two Passacaglias on Irish Themes. **South African Broadcasting Corporation Orchestra/Peter Marchbank.** Marco Polo 8 223485 (7/94).

Two Pieces, Op. 47. Two Pierrot Pieces, Op. 35. Pierrette. Poems. Trois Danses tristes, Op. 74. Sonata, Op. 66. **Dennis Hennig** (pf). Etcetera KTC1132 (10/92).

James Scott
American 1885-1938

Suggested listening ...

Evergreen Rag. Modesty Rag. Peace and Plenty Rag. Troubadour Rag. *Coupled with* **Nazareth.** Apanhei-tecavaquinho. Cavaquinho. Vitorioso. Odeon. Nove de Julho. Labirinto. Guerreiro. Plangente. Cubanos. Fon-Fon! *Lamb.* Ragtime Nightingale. American Beauty Rag. Bohemia Rag. Topliner Rag. **Joshua Rifkin** (pf). Decca 425 225-2DH (4/92).

Alexander Scriabin
Russian 1872-1915

Scriabin. Piano Concerto in F sharp minor, Op. 20[a]. Prometheus, Op. 60[b]. Le poème de l'extase, Op. 54[c]. [ab]**Vladimir Ashkenazy** (pf); [b]**Ambrosian Singers;** [ab]**London Philharmonic Orchestra,** [c]**Cleveland Orchestra/Lorin Maazel.** Decca 417 252-2DH. Items marked [a] and [b] from SXL6527 (1/72), recorded in 1971, [c] SXL6905 (9/79), recorded in 1978.

Ih 6m ADD 4/89

This CD gives us the essential Scriabin. The Piano Concerto has great pianistic refinement and melodic grace as well as a restraint not encountered in his later music. With *Le poème de l'extase* and *Prometheus* we are in the world of *art nouveau* and Scriabin in the grip of the mysticism (and megalomania) that consumed his later years. They are both single-movement symphonies for a huge orchestra: *Prometheus* ("The Poem of Fire") calls for quadruple wind, eight horns, five trumpets, strings, organ and chorus as well as an important part for solo piano in which Ashkenazy shines. The sensuous, luminous textures are beautifully conveyed in these performances by the LPO and the Decca engineers produce a most natural perspective and transparency of detail, as well as an appropriately overheated sound in the sensuous world of *Le poème de l'extase.*

Additional recommendation ...
Piano Concerto[a]. *Le poème de l'extase.* [a]**Garrick Ohlsson** (pf); **Czech Philharmonic Orchestra/Libor Pešek.** Supraphon CO2047 — 53m DDD 11/89
Piano Concerto[a]. *Symphony No. 3.* [a]**Roland Pöntinen** (pf); **Stockholm Philharmonic Orchestra/Leif Segerstam.** BIS CD475 — Ih 17m DDD 1/91

Scriabin. ORCHESTRAL WORKS. **Philadelphia Orchestra/Riccardo Muti.** EMI CDS7 54251-2. Text and translation included.
Symphonies — No. 1 in E major, Op. 26 (with Stefania Toczyska, mez; Michael Myers, ten; Westminster Choir. From EL270270-1, 3/86); No. 2 in C minor, Op. 29 (CDC7 49859-2, 11/90); No. 3 in C minor, Op. 43, "Le divin poème" (CDC7 49115-2, 4/89). Le poème de l'extase, Op. 54 (Frank Kaderabek, tpt. CDC7 54061-2). Prometheus, Op. 60, "Le poème du feu" (Dmitri Alexeev, pf; Philadelphia Choral Arts Society, CDC7 54112-2).

③ 3h 8m DDD 7/91

Harken all hedonists! Herein are contained all Scriabin's symphonies — the *Poem of Ecstasy* and *Prometheus* couldn't possibly be referred to by anything as mundane as mere symphonic numbers — at last in performances that mingle dramatic fervour with an ability to float all those gorgeous *cantabiles*; and achieve climaxes that radiate enlightenment and, yea, cause the very earth to move. The first two Symphonies find the budding luminary still bound by the fetters of tradition (such stars in the firmament as Liszt, Tchaikovsky and Wagner exerting a strong gravitational pull). *The Divine Poem* (No. 3) shows Scriabin's universe magnificently broadening, using an enormous orchestra (to match the expanded mission), whilst the single movement *Poem of Ecstasy* and *Prometheus* represent the full flowering of his genius, and manage some startling musical innovations in the process. High Priest Riccardo Muti has at his command an orchestra whose opulent tones are here at their legendary best and a group of technical acolytes who see to it that the mystical waves of sound are aptly tidal.

Additional recommendations ...
No. 3. *Le poème de l'extase, Op. 54.* **New York Philharmonic Orchestra/Giuseppe Sinopoli.** DG 427 324-2GH — ⠶ 1h 10m DDD 6/89 ♀ₚ
No. 3. **Arensky.** *Silhouettes (Suite No. 2), Op. 23.* **Danish National Radio Symphony Orchestra/Neeme Järvi.** Chandos CHAN8898. — ⠶ 1h 6m DDD 10/91 ♀ₚ
No. 3. *Le poème de l'extase.* **Berlin Radio Symphony Orchestra/Vladimir Ashkenazy.** Decca 430 843-2DH — ⠶ 1h 10m DDD 11/91

New review
Scriabin. Mazurkas, Opp. 3, 25 and 40. **Artur Pizarro** (pf). Collins Classics 1394-2. Recorded in 1993.

⠶ 1h 17m DDD 6/94 ♀♭ₚ

Trespassing on Polish territory (the mazurka is, after all, the most indigenous of dances), Scriabin creates a dark opalescent magic and a narcotic languor that can affect one like some intense insinuating perfume. Very much mazurka-fantasies, these are essentially night pieces where dark imaginings bubble to the surface with frightening rapidity and immediacy. Leeds has not always been lucky in its first-prize winners, but 1990 was clearly a golden year. What freedom and rapture, what sultry declamation Pizarro finds in Op. 3 in particular, in music ranging from an obsessive wheeling round a single idea (No. 2, with its amusing prophecy of "Love is the sweetest thing") to the sudden welling up of dark, subterranean passions in No. 10. His rubato is lavish, his sense of Scriabin's continuous modulation colourful and dramatic, and repetitions always provide an opportunity for further experiment, for the most imaginative realignment of texture and voicing. Born in Portugal, but American-based, Pizarro could hardly sound more authentically Slavonic. The recordings are spacious and resonant.

Key to symbols

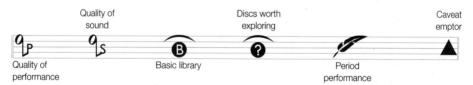

| Quality of sound | | Discs worth exploring | | Caveat emptor |

♀♭ₚ ♀ₛ Ⓑ ❓ ✒ ▲

| Quality of performance | | Basic library | | Period performance | |

Scriabin. PIANO WORKS. **Roger Woodward.** Etcetera KTC1126. Recorded in 1991. Piano Sonatas — No. 6, Op. 62; No. 10, Op. 70. Three Etudes, Op. 65. Two Dances, Op. 73. Five Preludes, Op. 74. Poèmes, Opp. 63, 67, 69 and 71. Poème-Nocturne, Op. 61. Vers la flamme, Op. 72

⠶ 1h 15m DDD 10/92 ♀♭ₚ

Although Roger Woodward is primarily known for his unflagging championship of contemporary avant-garde music, his repertoire in the concert-hall (though not necessarily apparent on disc) ranges from Beethoven through to the late-romantics. This recording of late Scriabin piano music is therefore a welcome addition to his discography. The shorter pieces on the disc are what William Blake would have described as "worlds in a grain of sand", and it is Woodward's ability to project this, together with the feeling that these are minor satellites inextricably linked by gravity to the larger bodies of the sonatas, that most impress. Good examples of this can be heard in the *Two Dances*, Op. 73, the two tiny Preludes, Op. 67 (the second of which comes over as a veritable cosmic-shimmer in the hands of Woodward) and the three spellbinding and demonically taxing *Etudes*, Op. 65. As for the Sixth and Tenth Sonatas, these are certainly amongst the most structurally convincing and logical accounts on disc at present. The Tenth exemplifies Woodward's linear approach to the music, with Scriabin's vaporescent material gradually opening out into wider and ever more expansive vistas, and in the spine-tingling Sixth Sonata we are privy to some exceptionally intense and concentrated playing. Woodward's tonal and dynamic range is extremely wide and this has been faithfully captured in the clear and atmospheric recording. Generous measure and a stunning addition to Scriabin's music on disc.

Additional recommendations ...

Fantaisie in B minor, Op. 28. Piano Sonatas — No. 1 in F minor, Op. 6; No. 2 in G sharp minor, Op. 19, "Sonata-fantasy"; No. 3 in F sharp minor, Op. 23; No. 4 in F sharp major, Op. 30; No. 5, Op. 53; No. 6, Op. 62; No. 7, Op. 64, "White Mass"; No. 8, Op. 66; No. 9, Op. 68, "Black Mass"; No. 10, Op. 70. Sonata in E flat minor. Sonate-fantaisie in G sharp minor. **Roberto Szidon.** DG 20th Century Classics 431 747-2GC3 — .•' ③ 3h ADD 4/92 ᑫₚ

Piano Sonatas Nos. 3 and 9. Three Pieces, Op. 2 — No. 1, Etude in C sharp minor; No. 2, Prelude in B major. Five Preludes, Op. 16. Four Preludes, Op. 22. Two Preludes, Op. 27. Four Preludes, Op. 31. Four Preludes, Op. 33. Five Preludes, Op. 74. **Graham Scott.** Gamut Classics CD520 — .•' 1h 7m DDD 10/91

Scriabin. COMPLETE ETUDES. **Piers Lane** (pf). Hyperion CDA66607. Recorded in 1992. Etude in C sharp minor, Op. 2 No. 1. 12 Etudes, Op. 8. Eight Etudes, Op. 42. Etude in E flat major, Op. 49 No. 1. Etude, Op. 56 No. 4. Three Etudes, Op. 65.

.•' **56m DDD 12/92**

Although Scriabin's *études* do not fall into two neatly packaged sets in the same way as Chopin's celebrated contributions, there is nevertheless a strong feeling of continuity and development running throughout the 26 examples produced between the years 1887 and 1912. This is admirably demonstrated in this excellent issue from Hyperion, which, far from being an indigestible anthology proves to be an intriguing and pleasurable hour's worth of listening charting Scriabin's progression from late-romantic adolescence, to harmonically advanced mystical poet. Indeed, although these studies can be counted as amongst the most digitally taxing and hazardous of their kind, Scriabin also saw them as important sketches and studies for his larger works, and as experiments in his gradually evolving harmonic language and mystical vision. Piers Lane attains the perfect balance between virtuoso display and poetic interpretation. Expressive detail and subtle nuance are finely brought out, and he is more than receptive to Scriabin's sometimes highly idiosyncratic sound-world; rarely, for instance, has the famous "Mosquito" *Etude* (Op. 42 No. 3) been captured with such delicate fragility as here, and in No. 1 of the three fiendishly difficult *Etudes,* Op. 65 (fifths, sevenths and ninths!) the tremulous, ghostly flutterings are tellingly delivered with a gossamer-light touch and an appropriate sense of eerie mystery. The clear, spacious recording is exemplary.

Additional recommendation ...

Piano Sonatas — No. 2 in G sharp minor, Op. 19, "Sonata-fantasy"; No. 9 in F major, Op. 68, "Black Mass". Etudes — Op. 8: No. 2 in F sharp minor; No. 4 in B major; No. 5 in E major. Op. 42: No. 3 in F sharp major; No. 4 in F sharp major; No. 7 in F sharp minor. Four Pieces, Op. 51. Vers la flamme, Op. 72. **Prokofiev.** *Visions fugitives, Op. 22.* **Nikolai Demidenko** (pf). Conifer CDCF204 — .•' 1h 13m DDD 8/91 ᑫₚ

Piano Sonata No. 3. Preludes — C major, Op. 11 No. 1; D major, Op. 39 No. 2; G major, Op. 39 No. 3; Op. 48 No. 2. Impromptu in B flat minor, Op. 12 No. 2. Etudes — B flat minor, Op. 8 No. 7; F sharp major, Op. 42 No. 4; D flat major, Op. 42 No. 6. **Rachmaninov.** *Preludes — C sharp minor, Op. 3 No. 2; D minor, Op. 23 No. 4; E flat major, Op. 23 No. 6. Etudes-tableaux, Op. 39 — No. 4 in B minor; No. 5 in E flat minor; No. 6 in A minor.* **Vladimir Sofronitzki** (pf). Multisonic Russian Treasure 310181-2 — .•' 58m ADD 5/94 ᑫₚ ▲

Peter Sculthorpe

Australian 1929-

Suggested listening ...

Four Little Pieces — Morning song; Sea chant; Little serenade; Left Bank waltz. Callabonna.
Night Pieces — Snow; Moon; Flowers; Night; Stars. Mountains. Djilile. Nocturnal. Sonatina.

Koto I. Koto II. Landscape. Sea chant (trans pf.) Left Bank waltz. *Coupled with* **W. Stanley** (ed. Sculthorpe). Rose Bay Quadrilles. **Max Cooke, Darryl Coote, Linda Kouvaras, Robert Chamberlain, Gudrun Beilharz, Alex Furman, Michael Hannan, Peter Sculthorpe** (pfs). Move MD3031 (3/92).

José Serebrier
Uruguain 1938-

Suggested listening ...

Poema elegíaco. Momento psicológico. *Coupled with* **Bloch.** Violin Concerto. Baal Shem. **Michael Gutman** (vn); **Royal Philharmonic Orchestra/José Serebrier.** ASV CDDCA785 (5/92).

Claudin de Sermisy
French c.1490-1562

Suggested listening ...

Chansons. *Coupled with* **Janequin.** Chansons. **Ensemble Clément Janequin.** Harmonia Mundi HMC90 1271.

Roger Sessions
American 1896-1985

New review
Sessions. Symphony No. 2.
Harbison. Oboe Concerto[a]. Symphony No. 2. [a]**William Bennett** (ob); **San Francisco Symphony Orchestra/Herbert Blomstedt.** Decca 443 376-2DH. Recorded in 1993.

1h 10m   DDD   7/94

The first movement of Sessions's Symphony (1946) typically alternates passages of frenetic activity and sumptuous lyricism, helped here by the really excellent orchestral sound. Response to its première performance wasn't encouraging — critics found the first movement and the *Adagio* too long at nine minutes each whereas the second, a mercurial *Allegretto*, lasts under two minutes: the boisterous finale is then welcome. These proportions may still seem perplexing but Sessions carries the day with his flair for orchestral colour. John Harbison, who was a pupil of Sessions at Princeton, now adds substantially to his rapidly growing representation on CD with the Symphony No. 2 (1987) and the Oboe Concerto (1991). These two orchestral works provide greater scope than some of his earlier works and, given more dramatic space, are more convincing without losing any of Harbison's personal type of unpredictability. The Oboe Concerto, marvellously played by the dedicatee William Bennett, is unusual in creating a jazz personality, including real bent notes, for the soloist — and big band effects in the finale. Harbison creates a series of decorative panels, almost Poulenc's technique, skilfully laid out and often with an energy comparable to Sessions.

Further listening ...

Piano Sonata No. 2. *Coupled with* **Griffes.** Piano Sonata in F sharp minor. **Ives.** Piano Sonata No. 1. **Peter Lawson** (pf). Virgin Classics VC7 59316-2 (2/94). *See review under Griffes; refer to the Index to Reviews.*

Rodion Shchedrin

Suggested listening ...

Stihira. *Coupled with* **Glazunov.** Violin Concerto in A minor, Op. 82[a]. ***Prokofiev.*** Violin Concerto No. 1 in D major, Op. 19[a]. [a]**Anne-Sophie Mutter** (vn); **Washington National Symphony Orchestra/Mstislav Rostropovich.** Erato 2292-45343-2 (3/89).

Bright Sheng

Suggested listening ...

H'un (Lacerations): In memoriam 1966-76[a]. The stream flows[b]. Three Chinese Love Songs[c]. My song[d]. [c]**Lisa Saffer** (sop); [b]**Lucia Lin** (vn); [c]**Paul Neubauer** (va); [c]**Bright Sheng,** [d]**Peter Serkin** (pfs); [a]**New York Chamber Symphony Orchestra/Gerard Schwarz.** New World 80407-2 (9/92).

John Sheppard

Suggested listening ...

Mass — "Be not afraide" (with plainsong Propers). *Sacred Choral Works* — Steven firste after Christ. Sancte Dei pretiose. Impetum fecerunt unanimes. Gaudete caelicole omnes. *Coupled with* **Sampson.** Psallite felices. **The Cardinall's Musick/Andrew Carwood.** Meridian CDE84220 (12/92).

Sacred Choral Works — In manus tuas Domine II. Gaude virgo Christiphera. Reges Tharsis et insulae. Libera nos, salva nos I. Libera nos, salva nos II. *Coupled with* ***Tye.*** Missa Euge Bone. Peccavimus Patribus nostris. **Clerkes of Oxenford/David Wulstan.** Proudsound PROUCD126 (5/90).

Church Music — Jesu salvator seculi, verbum. Deus tuorum militum II. Ave maris stella. Jesu salvator seculi, redemptis Missa "Cantate". Salvator mundi Domine. **The Sixteen/Harry Christophers.** Hyperion CDA66418 (12/92).

Church Music — Gaude gaude gaude Maria virgo. Dum transisset Sabbatum I. Spiritus Sanctus procedens II. In manus tuas II. Audivi vocem de caelo. Libera nos, salva nos II. Beata nobis gaudia. Impetum fecerunt unanimes. Sancte Dei pretiose. Sacris solemniis iuncta sint gaudia. **The Sixteen/Harry Christophers.** Hyperion CDA66570 (12/92).

Aeterne Rex altissime. Dum transisset Sabbatum II. Hostis Hérodes impie. In manus tuas III. Te Deum laudamus. Mass "The Western Wynde". The Second Service: Magnificat; Nunc Dimittis. **The Sixteen/Harry Christophers.** Hyperion CDA66603 (8/93).

Richard M. Sherman/Robert B. Sherman

Suggested listening ...

Mary Poppins — *original film soundtrack.* Pickwick/Disney DSMCD459.

Dmitry Shostakovich

Shostakovich. Cello Concertos — No. 1 in E flat major, Op. 107; No. 2, Op. 126.
Heinrich Schiff (vc); **Bavarian Radio Symphony Orchestra/Maxim Shostakovich.**
Philips 412 526-2PH. From 412 526-1PH (8/85).

 lh lm DDD 10/85

These two concertos make an obvious and useful 'coupling' for they are both vintage
Shostakovich. Indeed, the First occupies a commanding position in the post-war repertory and is
probably the most often-heard modern cello concerto. If the Second Concerto has not established
itself in the repertory to anywhere near the same extent, the reason may be that it offers fewer
overt opportunities for display. It is a work of grave beauty, inward in feeling and spare in its
textures. It is pensive, intimate and withdrawn and on first encounter its ideas seem fugitive and
shadowy, though the sonorities have a characteristic asperity. The recording's balance is generally
excellent: very natural yet very clear, and there is quite outstanding definition and realism.

Additional recommendations ...
No. 1[a]. *Piano Concertos No. 2 in F major, Op. 102. Piano Concerto in C minor for Piano, Trumpet and
Strings, Op. 35.* [a]**Mstislav Rostropovich** (vc); [a]**Philadelphia Orchestra/Eugene
Ormandy; New York Philharmonic Orchestra/Leonard Bernstein** (pf). CBS Maestro
CD44840 — lh 9m ADD 11/89
Nos. 1 and 2. **Natalia Gutman** (vc); **Royal Philharmonic Orchestra/Yuri Temirkanov.**
RCA Victor Red Seal RD87918 — lh 6m DDD 1/91
No. 1[a]. *Symphony No. 5 in D minor, Op. 47.* [a]**Miloš Sadló.** (vc); **Czech Philharmonic
Orchestra/Karel Ančerl.** Supraphon Crystal Collection 11 0676-2 — lh 12m ADD 8/93
Nos. 1 and 2. **Mstislav Rostropovich** (vc); **USSR Symphony Orchestra/Evgeni
Svetlanov.** Russian Disc RDCD11109 — 59m ADD 7/94
No. 1[a]. **Schumann.** *Cello Concerto in A minor, Op. 129* (arr. Shostakovich). **Mstislav
Rostropovich** (vc); [a]**USSR Symphony Orchestra;** [b]**Moscow Philharmonic
OrchestraPhilharmonic Orchestra/David Oistrakh.** Russian Disc RDCD11106 — 50m
ADD 7/94
Nos. 1 and 2. **Torleif Thedéen** (vc); **Malmö Symphony Orchestra/James DePreist.** BIS
CD626 — lh 5m DDD 7/94

Shostakovich. PIANO CONCERTOS AND PIANO WORKS. **Dmitri Shostakovich** (pf);
[a]**Ludovic Vaillant** (tpt); [b]**French Radio National Orchestra/André Cluytens.** EMI
Composers in Person mono CDC7 54606-2. Recorded 1958-59.
Piano Concertos — C minor for Piano, Trumpet and Strings, Op 35[ab]; No. 2 in F major, Op.
102[b]. Three Fantastic Dances, Op. 5 (all from French Columbia FCX769, 10/61). 24 Preludes
and Fugues, Op. 87 — No. 1 in C major; No. 4 in E minor; No. 5 in D major; No. 23 in F
major (FCX771); No. 24 in D minor (Parlophone PMC1056, 7/58).

lh 16m ADD 4/93 ▲

Before devoting himself entirely to composition Shostakovich pursued a successful parallel career as
a concert pianist, playing mostly romantic repertoire. These recordings were made at a time when
he still played his own works in public, and they show him to have been a highly skilled player. His
performances of both concertos are quite brilliant, and have a particularly vivacious, outgoing
quality. In the First Concerto Ludovic Vaillant plays the trumpet part with character and great
virtuosity, and the orchestral playing under Cluytens matches that of the composer in its joyous high
spirits. The three little *Fantastic Dances* are wittily brought to life. A different, far more serious and
academic world is evoked by Shostakovich in his Preludes and Fugues. Here the composer shapes
his own long contrapuntal lines with great skill, and these are very compelling, highly concentrated
performances. The mono recordings are all very acceptable, save that of the last Prelude and Fugue,
where a certain rustiness creeps into the sound. All these items have obvious historical importance,
but they also offer many rewards to the listener who is primarily interested in the music.

Shostakovich. Piano Concertos — C minor for Piano, Trumpet and Strings, Op. 35[a]. Piano
Concerto No. 2 in F major, Op. 102. The Unforgettable Year 1919, Op. 89 — The assault on

beautiful Gorky. **Dmitri Alexeev** (pf); [a]**Philip Jones** (tpt); **English Chamber Orchestra/ Jerzy Maksymiuk.** Classics for Pleasure CD-CFP4547. From CFP414416-1 (11/83).

48m DDD 1/89

Shostakovich's Piano Concertos were written under very different circumstances, yet together they contain some of the composer's most cheerful and enlivening music. The First, with its wealth of perky, memorable tunes, has the addition of a brilliantly-conceived solo trumpet part (delightfully done here by Philip Jones) that also contributes to the work's characteristic stamp. The Second Concerto was written not long after Shostakovich had released a number of the intense works he had concealed during the depths of the Stalin era. It came as a sharp contrast, reflecting as it did the optimism and sense of freedom that followed the death of the Russian dictator. The beauty of the slow movement is ideally balanced by the vigour of the first, and the madcap high spirits of the last. The poignant movement for piano and orchestra from the Suite from the 1951 film *The Unforgettable Year 1919*, "The assault on beautiful Gorky", provides an excellent addition to this disc of perceptive and zestful performances by Alexeev. He is most capably supported by the ECO under Maksymiuk, and the engineers have done them proud with a recording of great clarity and finesse. A joyous issue.

Additional recommendation ...
Concerto for Piano, Trumpet and Strings[a]. *Chamber Symphony in C minor, Op. 110a. Preludes, Op. 34*[b] — *Nos. 5, 6, 10, 13, 14, 17 and 24.* [ab]**Evgeni Kissin** (pf); [a]**Vassili Kan** (tpt); **Moscow Virtuosi/Vladimir Spivakov.** RCA Victor Red Seal RD87947 — 58m DDD 12/89
Concerto for Piano, Trumpet and Strings. **Lutoslawski.** *Paganini Variations.* **Rachmaninov.** *Rhapsody on a Theme of Paganini, Op. 43.* **Peter Jablonski** (pf); **Raymond Simmons** (tpt); **Royal Philharmonic Orchestra/Vladimir Ashkenazy.** Decca 436 239-2DH — 55m DDD 12/92

Shostakovich. Violin Concertos — No. 1 in A minor, Op. 99; No. 2 in C sharp minor, Op. 129. **Lydia Mordkovitch** (vn); **Scottish National Orchestra/Neeme Järvi.** Chandos CHAN8820. Recorded in 1989.

1h 9m DDD 4/90 🎵ₚ

These two heartfelt violin concertos are fine examples of Shostakovich's genius. It is the First, composed in 1948 for David Oistrakh, that is the better known and some people think it the finer work; but the Second was written for the same violinist two decades later and Lydia Mordkovitch, who studied with him in Moscow, reveals its sparer lines no less successfully than the big romantic gestures of No. 1. Her tone has a dark warmth that suits the soliloquizing lyrical music of these pieces admirably, but she is also not afraid to be uncompromisingly rough and tough (more so than Oistrakh himself) in the delivery of the scherzo and finale of the First Concerto as well as its great cadenza. Neeme Järvi is himself a committed performer of the Shostakovich symphonies who well understands the composer's style, and the Scottish National Orchestra sounds as Russian as anyone could wish, even to the tone of its brass section, which has the fine principal horn that both concertos require. The recording of the solo violin is closer than one would hear in the concert hall — Glasgow's City Hall in this case — and at times (for example, the cadenza of the First Concerto) positively tactile and percussive in effect, but with playing such as this few will complain. The orchestral sound is rich in the Chandos tradition and if it occasionally almost overwhelms the ear that is maybe what the composer intended. An exciting disc.

Additional recommendation ...
Nos. 1 and 2. **Dmitry Sitkovetsky** (vn); **BBC Symphony Orchestra/Andrew Davis.** Virgin Classics VC7 59601-2 — 1h 7m DDD 9/90 🎵ₚ

Shostakovich. The Golden Age — complete ballet. **Royal Stockholm Philharmonic Orchestra/Gennadi Rozhdestvensky.** Chandos CHAN9251/2. Recorded in 1993.

② **2h 14m DDD 5/94** ❓

The Golden Age (1930) is an industrial exhibition organized in a capitalist country, at which a group of Soviet sportsmen have been invited to compete. The general idea of Shostakovich's characterization is clearly to differentiate between goodies and baddies by assigning them respectively healthy-folk and decadent-bourgeois idioms. But then the trouble was, he couldn't stop himself enjoying being decadent. Not all of the 37 movements stand up independently of the stage-action. But the finales and the whole of Act 3 are top-notch stuff, at times surprisingly threatening in tone and symphonic in continuity; and there are several movements which could undoubtedly be promoted alongside the four in the familiar concert suite (the Tap Dance of Act 2 is especially appealing, for instance). Those who know their Shostakovich will be constantly intrigued by foretastes of *Lady Macbeth*, the Fourth Symphony and the *Hamlet* music, and by the appearance of Shostakovich's "Tea for Two" arrangement as an Interlude in Act 2. This first complete recording is a major coup for Chandos. Admittedly not even their flattering engineering can disguise a certain lack of confidence and idiomatic flair on the part of the Royal Stockholm Philharmonic Orchestra. But let that not deter anyone with the least interest in Shostakovich, or ballet music, or Soviet music, or indeed Soviet culture as a whole, from investigating this weird and intermittently wonderful score.

Shostakovich. Chamber Symphony, Op. 110*a*. Symphony for Strings in A flat major, Op. 118*a*. String Quartet No. 15 in E flat minor, Op. 144 (arr. Rachlevsky). **Kremlin Chamber Orchestra/Misha Rachlevsky.** Claves CD50-9115.

Ih 20m DDD 3/93

Shostakovich was not immune to flattery, and although he did not himself choose to arrange any of his 15 String Quartets for full string band he was happy to give such arrangements by others his blessing. A number of commentators have regretted that he did so — the gain in power in such versions tends to be offset by a loss of concentrated energy. But here is a recording which sweeps away any doubts. The Kremlin Chamber Orchestra was founded in September 1991. Not only does it sound as virtuosic as any of the specialist groups Russia has produced in recent years, but it also directs that virtuosity into subtler, less attention-seeking regions of characteriza-tion. Misha Rachlevsky encourages his players to achieve intensity as much through restraint as through abandon, and often with the barest minimum of vibrato. The sense of identity with the composer's message is almost tangible. Moreover, Rachlevsky has produced his own extremely convincing version of the funereal Fifteenth Quartet and contrived to fit all three performances on to a single, excellently recorded CD.

Additional recommendation ...
Chamber Symphony. Two Pieces, Op. 11 — Scherzo. **Bartók.** *Romanian Folkdances, Sz68. Divertimento, Sz113.* **Zagreb Soloists/Tonko Ninic.** Pickwick PCD1000 — .•* Ih Im DDD II/92

New review
Shostakovich. SYMPHONIES. [a]**London Philharmonic Orchestra;** [b]**Concertgebouw Orchestra/Bernard Haitink.** Decca Ovation 425 063/74-2DM. Texts and translations included.
425 063-2DM[a] (1h 5m) — No. 1 in F minor, Op. 10 (from SXDL7515, 5/81); No. 3 in E flat major, Op. 20, "The first of May" (with the London Philharmonic Choir. SXDL7535, 7/82). *425 064-2DM*[a] (1h 16m) — No. 2 in B major, Op. 14 (London Phil Ch. SXDL7535, 7/82); No. 10 in E minor, Op. 93 (SXL6838, 10/77). *425 065-2DM* (1h 8m) — No. 4 in C minor, Op. 43 (SXL6927, 11/79)[a]. *425 066-2DM* (1h 16m) — No. 5 in D minor, Op. 47 (SXDL7551, 12/82)[b]; No. 9 in E flat major, Op. 70 (SXDL7515, 5/81)[a]. *425 067-2DM*[b] (1h 14m) — No. 6 in B minor, Op. 54 (411 939-2DH2, 8/85); No. 12 in D minor, "The year 1917", Op. 112 (SXDL7577, 6/83). *425 068-2DM* (1h 19m) — No. 7 in C major, "Leningrad", Op. 60 (D213D2, 11/80)[a]. *425 069-2DM* (1h 13m) — No. 15 in A major, Op. 141 (SXL6906, 3/79)[a]; From Jewish Folk Poetry, Op. 79 (Elisabeth Söderström, sop; Ortrun Wenkel, contr; Ryszard Karczykowski, ten. 417 261-2DH, 3/87)[b]. *425 071-2DM* (1h 2m) — No. 8 in C minor, Op. 65 (SXDL7621, 11/83)[b]. *425 072-2DM* (1h 1m) — No. 11 in G minor, "The year 1905", Op. 103 (411 939-2DH2, 8/85)[b]. *425 073-2DM* (1h 4m) — No. 13 in B flat minor, Op. 113, "Babi Yar". (Marius Rintzler, bass; Concertgebouw Choir. 417 261-2DH, 3/87)[b]. *425 074-2DM*[b] (1h 12m) — No. 14, Op. 135 (Julia Varady, sop; Dietrich Fischer-Dieskau, bar. SXDL7532, 1/82). Six Marina Tsvetaeva Poems, Op. 143 (Ortrun Wenkel. 417 261-2DH, 3/87).

.•* ⓘⓘ ADD/DDD II/93

We used to see Shostakovich's output discussed in terms of public and private utterance. Rigorously 'public' symphonies — giving new life to a monumental form that, in the opinion of

Soviet ideologists, had become impossible to cultivate in the capitalist West — were ranged against ineluctably 'private' chamber works, intimate confessionals in which the composer was apt to reveal his secret heart. Paradoxically, despite today's much greater understanding of the symphonies' own allusive dimension, there have been few wholly successful recordings in recent years. As Western LPs of the 1960s and 1970s from conductors like Ormandy, Previn and Berglund have disappeared from the catalogue, so the more demonstrative Soviet tradition has splintered. The first complete Western cycle, that of Bernard Haitink, returns to the catalogue at mid-price, Decca having jettisoned a few minor works and decoupled several major ones. It is hard to argue with the new presentation when it includes modern annotations and full recording data. Concerned for tradition, and with the need to challenge it, the young Shostakovich could be classical and modern, polemical and prankish by turns.

Haitink, not entirely po-faced, turns in a thoroughly decent account of the First Symphony, missing just a little of the element of pastiche. The recoupling with the Third does strike sparks, the language of the later music variously foreshadowed in divergent contexts. In the Fourth Symphony, Haitink offers no stupendous revelations, content to bring out the dignity of the writing in a piece where we have come to expect something more sensational, less perfectly controlled. Even the hurtling *moto perpetuo* fugato passage for strings which triggers the main climax of the first movement seems just a little too studied. His outer movements are helpfully split, by additional cues — but his literalness and sobriety fall short of the ideal, as, marginally, does the playing. It is worth paying extra for Järvi's emotional candour (reviewed further on). Haitink's *Gramophone* Award-winning Fifth, deeply considered and almost indecently well-upholstered, is not easy to assess. Originally greeted with extreme reverence in these pages — its release followed hard on the heels of the publication of *Testimony* which surely influenced the critical response — it is an earnest attempt to make structural sense of the music's grand symphonic aspirations. It is only because the orchestral playing is generally so immaculate that one registers the curious glitch 2'13" into the *Largo*. That movement is generally less affecting than it can be, yet the preceding *Allegretto* is triumphantly brought off as a heavy-footed Mahlerian *Ländler*. Then again, the first movement's long-limbed second subject chugs along reluctantly, dourly unphrased, with none of the easeful balm to be found in other interpretations.

Haitink's Fifth is now generously paired with his solid, untrivial but scarcely earth-shattering Ninth. Readers should perhaps opt for Rozhdestvensky in the Ninth (reviewed further on); his coupling is yet another Fifth: differently well-intentioned, notably un-svelte and not at all like Haitink's. Haitink's Sixth and Twelfth is characterized by playing of predictable *gravitas* and tonal splendour. Indeed, this Twelfth could be seen as the 'best' modern version. The *Leningrad* is another matter. Rightly praised for its symphonic integrity and splendid sound, Haitink's *nobilmente* reappraisal is now a much cheaper option than Bernstein's two-disc epic on DG (reviewed further on), though some will respond more favourably to the raw authenticity of Rozhdestvensky. Haitink's stoical view of the Eighth is highly impressive, though not very varied in mood. Curiously, the finale is mis-cued. If you can accept far greater technical flaws, Mravinsky's live recording (reviewed further on) is in a different league, offering electrifying music-making of a kind seldom if ever heard from Western orchestras and, one fears, shortly to become a thing of the past in the new Russia. Speeds are generally much faster; the woodwind tear into their phrases like scalded cats, and the string sound is inimitably intense, big but never bland. Kurt Sanderling's reading (listed under Mravinsky) is also highly impressive. The Tenth has always seemed less dependent on a conductor steeped in the Russian tradition, and the only drawback of Haitink's well-played well-recorded account is his unsubtle, over-confident tone in the enigmatic third movement *Allegretto*. There is real demonic abandon in the scherzo. Karajan's Tenth is very desirable (reviewed further on) but he offers no makeweight. Haitink offers a carefully prepared account of No. 2, where the choral contribution has the odd awkward moment but the overall effect is very arresting. His Eleventh too has such weight and precision that his customary detachment is mostly less noticeable than his phenomenal control.

Haitink's Thirteenth boasts another of Decca's huge, reverberant recordings, here of such 'cinematic' brilliance and range that it threatens to dwarf the music-making. While chorus and orchestra are on terrific form, even this monolithic work ideally requires greater flexibility and plasticity than the conductor seems willing to provide. The soloist, Marius Rintzler, would seem to be at one with Haitink's brooding approach. Kondrashin's account, reviewed further on, makes a very recommendable alternative. As one of the first of Shostakovich's late scores to be taken seriously in the West, it is odd that the Fourteenth should have been so poorly represented in the CD catalogue. Haitink's polyglot reading (not quite that authorized by the composer, incidentally) does not really represent a viable solution — too much vital and specific tone colour is lost along with the original note-values. To make matters worse, Fischer-Dieskau is in hectoring mode and both soloists' proximity to the microphones makes for uncomfortable listening, though the orchestral contribution is excellent. Barshai (listed below) can lay claim to *absolute* authenticity. It is a fascinating document, as he and Vishnevskaya rage against the dying of the light in every song, slicing seconds (sometimes minutes) off the timings of the Western account. Reshetin is superb too, less inclined to histrionics. Generally speaking the sound is close and crude, by no means intolerable but sufficiently prone to distortion to inhibit a general recommendation. In its way, however, this disc is indispensable. Haitink's Fifteenth has always been highly regarded, despite some less than needle-sharp contributions from the percussion where it matters most. At medium price, and with a rather high-level transfer of its coupling (whose historical significance is ably outlined in the insert-note), this merits a place at or near the top of anyone's list. To sum up: Haitink's set, superbly engineered, is nothing if not reliable. For those who prize technical finesse over raw passion, Haitink remains a plausible first choice. These are endlessly fascinating, endlessly equivocal works.

Additional recommendations ...
No. 2[a]. October, Op. 131. Festive Overture in A major, Op. 96. The Song of the Forests, Op. 81[b]. [b]**Mikhail Kotliarov** (ten); [b]**Nikita Storojev** (bass); [b]**New London Children's Choir;** [ab]**Brighton Festival Chorus; Royal Philharmonic Orchestra/Vladimir Ashkenazy.** Decca 436 762-2DH — .·˙ 1h 12m DDD 7/94
No. 11. **Leningrad Philharmonic Orchestra/Evgeny Mravinsky.** Russian Disc RDCD11157 — .·˙ 56m ADD 1/94
Nos. 9[a] and 14[b]. [b]**Galina Vishnevskaya** (sop); [b]**Mark Reshetin** (bass); [b]**Moscow Chamber Orchestra/Rudolf Barshai;** [a]**USSR Symphony Orchestra/David Oistrakh.** Russian Disc RDCD11192 — .·˙ 1h 13m ADD 1/94

Shostakovich. Symphonies — No. 1 in F minor, Op. 10; No. 6 in B minor, Op. 54. **Scottish National Orchestra/Neeme Järvi.** Chandos CHAN8411. Recorded 1984-85.

.·˙ 1h 4m DDD 6/86   9ₚ 9s

The First Symphony, the 19-year-old composer's graduation piece from the then Leningrad Conservatory in 1925, may be indebted to Stravinsky, Prokofiev, Tchaikovsky and even Scriabin. But it rarely sounds like anything other than pure Shostakovich. The sophisticated mask of its first movement is drawn aside for a slow movement of Slav melancholy and foreboding, and the finale brilliantly stage-manages a way out. The Sixth (1939) takes the familiar Shostakovichian extremes of explosive activity and uneasy contemplation (that the composer reconciles in the finale of the First) and separates them into individual movements. Two swift movements (a mercurial but menacing *Scherzo*, and a real knees-up of a finale) follow on from an opening *Largo* whose slow lyrical declamations eventually all but freeze into immobility. Järvi has a will (and Chandos, the engineering) to explore the extremes of pace, mood and dynamics of both symphonies; his account of the First Symphony convinces precisely because those extremes intensify as the work progresses. Some may crave a fuller, firmer string sound, but the passionate intensity of the playing (in all departments) is never in doubt.

Additional recommendations ...
Nos. 1 and 6. **Royal Philharmonic Orchestra/Vladimir Ashkenazy.** Decca 425 609-2DH — .·˙ 1h 4m DDD 6/90
Nos. 6 and 12. **Royal Concertgebouw Orchestra/Bernard Haitink.** Decca Ovation 425 067-2DM — .·˙ 1h 14m DDD 11/93
Nos. 1[a], 5[b], and 7[c]. Prelude in E flat minor, Op. 34[d] (orch. Stokowski). [abd]**Philadelphia Orchestra,** [c]**NBC Symphony Orchestra/Leopold Stokowski.** Pearl mono GEMMCD9044 — .·˙ ② 2h 36m ADD 1/94 9ₚ ▲

Shostakovich. Symphony No. 4 in C minor, Op. 43. **Scottish National Orchestra/ Neeme Järvi.** Chandos CHAN8640.

.·˙ 1h 1m DDD 12/89   9s

Shostakovich withdrew the Fourth Symphony before its first performance and one can readily see why: Stalin would have loathed it. It is a work of extraordinary bitterness and anger, curdled with dissonance, raucous derision and eerie unease, the very model of what a Soviet symphony should not be, but at the same time the teeming cauldron from which much of the troubling ambiguity of Shostakovich's later style was cast. It needs a performance that takes risks, not least of setting the listener's teeth on edge and of terrifying him out of his wits. Järvi is prepared to allow his orchestra to yell at times to allow the occasional ugly, poisoned sound in a work that boils with discontent but also with sheer unreleased creative energy. No one who admires the Fifth Symphony should be without a recording of the Fourth that presents its towering frustration and disquiet at full strength. Järvi does so more successfully than any other conductor. Both his orchestra and the recording engineers hang on like grim death. The effect can only be described as magnificently appalling.

Additional recommendations ...
No. 4. Suite No. 1 for Jazz Band. **soloists ensemble; USSR Ministry of Culture State Symphony Orchestra/Gennadi Rozhdestvensky.** Olympia OCD156 — .·'' 1h 15m DDD/AAD 5/89
National Symphony Orchestra/Mstislav Rostropovich. Teldec 9031 76261-1 — .·'' 1h 5m DDD 11/92
No. 4. **Vienna Symphony Orchestra/Eliahu Inbal.** Denon CO-75330 — .·'' 1h 3m DDD 7/93 ꝗₚ

Shostakovich. Symphony No. 5 in D minor, Op. 47. Ballet Suite No. 5, Op. 27a. **Scottish National Orchestra/Neeme Järvi.** Chandos CHAN8650. Recorded in 1988.

.·'' **1h 16m DDD 4/90**   Ⓑ

There are more Shostakovich Fifths than you can shake a stick at in the CD catalogue at present, and several of them are very good. Järvi's makes perhaps the safest recommendation of them all: it has a generous coupling (which cannot be said of many of its rivals), it has no drawbacks (save, for some tastes, a slight touch of heart-on-sleeve in the slow movement) and a number of distinct advantages. A profound seriousness, for one thing, and an absolute sureness about the nature of the finale, which many conductors feel the need to exaggerate, either as brassy optimism or as bitter irony. Järvi takes it perfectly straight, denying neither option, and the progression from slow movement (the overtness of its emotion finely justified) to finale seems more natural, less of a jolt than usual. The SNO cannot rival the sheer massiveness of sound of some of the continental orchestras who have recorded this work, but while listening one hardly notices the lack, so urgent and polished is their playing. A very natural and wide-ranging recording, too, and the lengthy Suite (eight movements from Shostakovich's early ballet *The Bolt*, forming an exuberantly entertaining essay on the various modes that his sense of humour could take) makes much more than a mere fill-up.

Additional recommendations ...
No. 5. Five Fragments, Op. 42. **Royal Philharmonic Orchestra/Vladimir Ashkenazy.** Decca 421 120-2DH — .·'' 56m DDD 6/88 Ⓑ
No. 5[a]. Cello Concerto No. 1 in E flat major, Op. 107[b]. [a]**New York Philharmonic Orchestra/Leonard Bernstein;** [b]**Yo-Yo Ma** (vc); [b]**Philadelphia Orchestra/Eugene Ormandy.** CBS Maestro CD44903 — .·'' 1h 17m DDD 4/90 Ⓑ
Nos. 5 and 9. **Atlanta Symphony Orchestra/Yoel Levi.** Telarc CD80215 — .·'' 1h 18m DDD 6/90 Ⓑ
No. 5. Novorossisk Chimes. October — Symphonic Poem, Op. 131. Overture on Russian and Kirghiz Folk Themes, Op. 115. **Royal Philharmonic Orchestra/Enrique Bátiz.** ASV CDDCA707 — .·'' 1h 16m DDD 9/90 Ⓑ
No. 5. Festival Overture, Op. 96. **London Symphony Orchestra/Maxim Shostakovich.** Collins Classics 1108-2 — .·'' 59m DDD 9/90 Ⓑ
No. 5. **Hallé Orchestra/Stanislav Skrowaczewski.** Pickwick IMP Classics PCD940 — .·'' 48m DDD 8/91 Ⓑ
No. 5. **Leningrad Philharmonic Orchestra/Evgeny Mravinsky.** Erato 2292-45752-2 — .·'' 44m ADD 6/92 Ⓑ
No. 5. Cello Concerto No. 1 in E flat major, Op. 107[a]. [a]**Miloš** (vc); **Czech Philharmonic Orchestra/Karel Ančerl.** Supraphon Crystal Collection 11 0676-2 — .·'' 1h 12m ADD 8/93 Ⓑ
No. 5. **Berlin Symphony Orchestra/Kurt Sanderling.** Berlin Classics Eterna BC2063-2 — .·'' 51m ADD 7/94 Ⓑ

Shostakovich. Symphonies — No. 7 in C major, Op. 60, "Leningrad". No. 1 in F minor, Op. 10. **Chicago Symphony Orchestra/Leonard Bernstein.** DG 427 632-2GH2. Recorded live in 1988.

② 2h DDD 1/90

The *Leningrad* Symphony was composed in haste as the Nazis sieged and bombarded the city (in 1941). It caused an immediate sensation, but posterity has been less enthusiastic. What business has the first movement's unrelated long central 'invasion' episode doing in a symphonic movement? Is the material of the finale really distinctive enough for its protracted treatment? Michael Oliver, in his original *Gramophone* review wrote that in this performance "the Symphony sounds most convincingly like a symphony, and one needing no programme to justify it". Added to which, and no disrespect is intended by this observation, the work's epic and cinematic manner has surely never been more powerfully realized. These are live recordings, with occasional noise from the audience (and the conductor), but the Chicago Orchestra has rarely sounded more polished or committed under any conditions. The strings are superb in the First Symphony, full and weightily present, and Bernstein's manner in this Symphony is comparably bold and theatrical of gesture. A word of caution: set your volume control carefully for the *Leningrad* Symphony's start; it is scored for six of both trumpets and trombones, and in the above mentioned 'invasion' episode, no other recording has reproduced them so clearly, and to such devastating effect.

Additional recommendation ...
No. 7. **USSR Ministry of Culture State Symphony Orchestra/Gennadi Roszhdestvensky.** Olympia OCD118 — 1h 15m DDD 8/88

Shostakovich. Symphony No. 8 in C minor, Op. 65. **Leningrad Philharmonic Orchestra/Evgeni Mravinsky.** Philips 422 442-2PH. Recorded live in 1982.

1h ADD 6/89

Dedicated to Mravinsky, the Eighth Symphony, written in 1943, two years after the *Leningrad*, offers a wiser, more bitterly disillusioned Shostakovich. The heroic peroration of the Seventh's finale is here replaced by numbed whimsy and eventual uneasy calm. Whether the grim visions that the journey there depicts are wartime or peacetime ones, rarely can a performance have presented them with more lacerating force. The solo cor anglais, after the first movement's central climax, plays as if his very life depended on his lament being heard at the other side of the world. Speeds are generally faster than we are used to from western interpreters, and the standard of playing, given the risks taken, and that this is a one-off live performance, defies criticism. If you're cursed with perfect pitch you will notice that the whole Symphony is a semitone sharper than it should be; for the rest of us, only a restricted dynamic range mars an excellent piece of engineering. The Leningrad audience, clearly immobilized, maintain an awed silence.

Additional recommendations ...
No. 8. **Concertgebouw Orchestra/Bernard Haitink.** Decca Ovation 425 071-2DM — 1h 2m DDD
No. 8. **Washington National Symphony Orchestra/Mstislav Rostropovich.** Teldec 9031-74719-2 — 1h 1m DDD 10/92
No. 8. Funeral-Triumphal Prelude, Op. 130. Novorossiisk Chimes, "The Fire of Eternal Glory". **Royal Philharmonic Orchestra/Vladimir Ashkenazy.** Decca 436 763-2DH — 1h 7m DDD 4/94
No. 8. **Berlin Symphony Orchestra/Kurt Sanderling.** Berlin Classics Eterna BC2064-2 — 1h 7m ADD 7/94

Shostakovich. Symphonies — No. 9 in E flat major, Op. 70; No. 5 in D minor, Op. 47. **USSR Ministry of Culture State Symphony Orchestra/Gennadi Rozhdestvensky.** Olympia OCD113.

1h 13m DDD 5/89

Some of Rozhdestvensky's interpretations in his Shostakovich cycle on Olympia are quirky in the extreme. In the Fifth Symphony he is at his most restrained, and the result is one of the finest accounts on CD of this much-recorded work. Listening to it you wonder why so many conductors fail to achieve a natural flow, and why those who do achieve it often sound bland. Rozhdestvensky gives us just about the best of both worlds, as he does in the Ninth Symphony — a kind of not-the-Ninth-Symphony, written in 1945 in a spirit of deliberate non-celebration and full of black humour and evasiveness. Neither playing nor recording are in the highest class, but the communicative instincts are in the right place throughout and the coupling is a generous one.

Additional recommendations ...

No. 9. No. 15 in A major, Op. 141. **Royal Philharmonic Orchestra/Vladimir Ashkenazy.** Decca 430 227-2DH — ,·' 1h 5m DDD 10/92

Nos. 9[a] and 5[b]. [a]**London Philharmonic Orchestra;** [b]**Concertgebouw Orchestra/Bernard Haitink.** Decca 425 066-2DM — ,·' 1h 16m DDD 11/93

Nos. 9[a] and 14[b]. [b]**Galina Vishnevskaya** (sop); [b]**Mark Reshetin** (bass); [a]**USSR Symphony Orchestra/David Oistrakh;** [b]**Moscow Chamber Orchestra/Rudolf Barshai.** Russian Disc RDCD11192 — ,·' 1h 13m ADD 1/94

Shostakovich. Symphony No. 10 in E minor, Op. 93. **Berlin Philharmonic Orchestra/ Herbert von Karajan.** DG Galleria 429 716-2GGA. From SLPM139020 (1/69). Recorded in 1966.

,·' **51m ADD 8/90**   9 p   Ⓑ

Stalin died on 5 March 1953, the same day as Prokofiev. In the summer of that year Shostakovich produced a symphony which can be taken as his own return to life after the dark night of dictatorship — the last two movements included, for the first time in his output, his personal DSCH signature (the notes D, E flat, C, B natural, in the German spelling). In the West the Tenth Symphony is now widely regarded as the finest of the cycle of 15, not just for its sheer depth of personal feeling, but because it finds the purest and subtlest musical representation of that feeling. Perhaps this is why it is less dependent than some of Shostakovich's major works on a conductor steeped in the Russian idiom. Karajan's profound grasp of the overall drama unites with a superb instinct for atmosphere and mood to put the earlier of his two recordings into a class of its own. It is a performance of compelling integrity and sweep, with an almost palpable sense of what is at stake emotionally. The recording sounds a little bass-heavy in this digital remastering but is still far more realistic than Karajan's 1982 remake.

Additional recommendations ...

No. 10. Hamlet — Suite, Op. 32: excerpts[a]. **USSR Ministry of Culture State Symphony Orchestra/Gennadi Rozhdestvensky;** [a]**Leningrad Chamber Orchestra/Eduard Serov.** Olympia OCD131 — ,·' 1h 9m DDD/ADD 5/89 Ⓑ

No. 10. **Hallé Orchestra/Stanislaw Skrowaczewski.** Pickwick IMP Classics PCD955 — ,·' 52m DDD 10/91 Ⓑ

No. 10. **Lutoslawski.** *Funeral music.* **Cleveland Orchestra/Christoph von Dohnányi.** Decca 430 844-2DH — ,·' 1h 5m DDD 9/92 Ⓑ

New review

Shostakovich. Symphony No. 13 in B flat minor, Op. 113, "Babi Yar". **Vitaly Gromadsky** (bass); **USSR State Academic Choir; Yurlov Russian Choir; Moscow Philharmonic Orchestra/Kyrill Kondrashin.** Russian Disc RDCD11191. Text and translation included. Recorded live in Moscow in 1962.

,·' **57m AAD 3/94**   9 p

This will be a self-recommending issue for many readers, given the unavailability of all three previous Kondrashin performances. Rival Western accounts like Haitink's make a different sort of impact. More concerned with the symphonic than the dramatic, he brings a touch more subtlety to the ironic equivocations of "A Career" but is less successful in putting across the straightforward, 'dissident' anger of previous movements. Shostakovich confounds expectations not merely by selecting these vivid, dissenting verses (imagine Copland setting Bob Dylan c.1963) but by presenting them in an idiom of Mussorgskian simplicity, unimpeachably 'correct' from the official Soviet point of view. It is no accident that the composer follows the Twelfth's revolutionary *Dawn of Humanity* with a consecutive opus focusing on the enduring legacy of Stalinism. On Russian Disc's rediscovered (stereo) tape, the finer points are forgotten as every syllable of text is projected with maximum force. For anyone unconvinced by Haitink's reading — for all his technical assurance, he can seem to be missing the point — this new disc is the one to have, whatever its exact provenance. The choral singing is outstanding and, in place of Marius Rintzler's impassive manner (and occasional habit of sliding up to the note), we have Vitaly Gromadsky, risking more than critical disfavour by taking on this controversial new work, supremely committed (if not without moments of uncertain pitch), gloriously, unmistakably Russian. He does miss a vital cue in the desolate third movement, "In the store", here taken at an easy, flowing pace. As for the sound-quality, it is vivid enough and by no means impossibly crude. This is an indispensable piece of musical history.

Key to symbols

Price	Quantity/ availability	Timing	Recording mode	Review date
	② ②	1h 23m	DDD	6/88

Shostakovich. String Quartets — No. 1 in C major, Op. 49; No. 3 in F major, Op. 73; No. 4 in D major, Op. 83. **Brodsky Quartet** (Michael Thomas, Ian Belton, vns; Paul Cassidy, va; Jacqueline Thomas, vc). Teldec 2292-46009-2. Recorded in 1989.

1h 12m   DDD   6/90

The First, Third and Fourth Quartets make a particularly absorbing coupling, with hinted depths and plans for further exploration clearly audible beneath the acknowledgements to quartet tradition in the First (which also has a touch of very likeable open-eyed naïvety to it), an enormous step forward to the grandeur of the Third's impassioned slow movement and a path forward firmly indicated by the troubled ambiguities and poignancies of the Fourth. The Brodsky have the range for their projected complete cycle, there seems no doubt of that; already there is a fine balance between bigness of gesture and an expressive but strong lyricism. They are especially good at pacing and concentration over a long span, too, and they leap the technical hurdles with ease. A very clean and direct but rather close recording; but the sense of being amidst such responsive players, almost watching their intentness, has its own rewards.

Additional recommendation ...

No. 1. No. 2 in A major, Op. 68. Nos. 3 and 4. No. 5 in B flat major, Op. 92. No. 6 in G major, Op. 101. No. 7 in F sharp minor, Op. 108. No. 8 in C minor, Op. 110. No. 9 in E flat major, Op. 117. No. 10 in A flat major, Op. 118. No. 11 in F minor, Op. 122. No. 12 in D flat major, Op. 133. No. 13 in B flat minor, Op. 138. No. 14 in F sharp minor. No. 15 in E flat minor, Op. 144.
Fitzwilliam Quartet. Decca Enterprise 433 078-2DM6 — ⑥ 6h 17m ADD 6/92

Shostakovich. Piano Quintet in G minor, Op. 57[a]. String Quartets — No. 7 in F sharp minor, Op. 108; No. 8 in C minor, Op. 110. [a]**Sviatoslav Richter** (pf); **Borodin Quartet** (Mikhail Kopelman, Andrei Abramenkov, vns; Dmitri Shebalin, va; Valentin Berlinsky, vc). EMI CDC7 47507-2. From EL270338-1 (11/85).

1h 10m   ADD   10/87

The Seventh and Eighth Quartets are separated by only one opus number and both works inhabit a dark and sombre sound world. The Seventh is dedicated to the memory of his first wife, Nina, who died in 1954 and is one of his shortest and most concentrated quartets. The Eighth Quartet provides a perfect introduction to Shostakovich's music. It is very much an autobiographical work. The Piano Quintet is almost symphonic in its proportions, lasting some 35 minutes and has been popular with audiences ever since its first performance in 1940. Much of its popularity stems from Shostakovich's highly memorable material, particularly in the boisterous and genial Scherzo and finale movements. The Borodin Quartet play with great authority and conviction and in the Seventh Quartet there is a fine sense of poetry and intimacy. Richter's performance of the Piano Quintet matches the grandeur of the work, with playing that has tremendous power and strength. The recording, taken from a live performance, is rather dry with a slightly hard piano sound, but this does little to distract from so commanding a performance as this. The earlier studio recordings of the string quartets are well recorded. This disc would be an excellent introduction to the chamber music of Shostakovich.

New review

Shostakovich. Cello Sonata in D minor, Op. 40. Moderato for Cello and Piano.
Prokofiev. Cello Sonata in C major, Op. 119. **Lynn Harrell** (vc); **Vladimir Ashkenazy** (pf). Decca 421 774-2DH.

·•´ **5lm DDD 3/90**

This reading of the Shostakovich carries strong conviction. In the fine opening sonata-allegro — exactly the kind of movement which Shostakovich later claimed he was unable to write, Harrell and Ashkenazy bring out the shape beautifully, with the coda's *Largo* winding-down sounding not a bar too long, and the exposition repeat seeming appropriate. It is Yo-Yo Ma (listed below), however, who offers the strongest competition. His is a very compelling performance, and in the three later movements he finds more variety and still greater depths of feeling than Harrell and Ashkenazy. The latter pair's gritty, forceful *Scherzo* is impressive, and their *Largo* digs deeply. In the Prokofiev, Harrell and Ashkenazy are clear winners. Their opening *Andante grave* combines gravity and flowing eloquence in a way no other partnership can match and they communicate most strongly the sense of achievement Prokofiev wanted. Shostakovich's *Moderato* is a trifle. The performance is appealing but the interest is probably limited to Shostakovich connoisseurs. Cello and piano are well balanced.

Additional recommendation ...
Cello Sonata. Piano Trio No. 2 in E minor, Op. 67[a]. [a]**Isaac Stern** (vn); **Yo-Yo Ma** (vc); **Emanuel Ax** (pf). CBS CD44664 — ·•´ 59m DDD 6/89

Shostakovich. Violin Sonata, Op. 134. Viola Sonata, Op. 147. **Shlomo Mintz** (vn, va); **Victoria Postnikova** (pf). Erato 2292-45804-2. Recorded in 1991.

·•´ **1h 9m DDD 11/92** ⁹ₚ

These are two of the most unremittingly bleak works in the entire chamber repertoire — Shostakovich in his last decade was more or less free to choose whatever musical means would suit his message, and that message drains the cup of sorrow to its bitterest dregs. What strange force compels us then to listen? Perhaps it is simply our responsibility to commemorate even the darkest aspects of life in the twentieth century; perhaps it is also the sense that such experiences can be survived and transfigured through the creative will. Certainly performances as intense, yet subtle, as Mintz's and Postnikova's leave you awe-struck rather than simply despairing. Erato's recording could perhaps have been a little more immediate, and Mintz's viola sound is not as individual as some. But his grasp of the idiom is extraordinary, and Postnikova is an ideal partner. It is a joy to welcome playing which gets so consistently to the emotional core.

Shostakovich. 24 Preludes and Fugues, Op. 87. **Tatyana Nikolaieva** (pf). Hyperion CDA66441/3. Recorded in 1990.

·•´ **2h 46m DDD 3/91** ⁹ₚ ❓

Even if you didn't know that Shostakovich had written his 24 Preludes and Fugues specially for Tatyana Nikolaieva it would be difficult not to sense the unique authority. The playing isn't without the odd small blemish here and there (memory lapses?) and the reverberant acoustic adds a sustaining pedal effect of its own in one or two places, but for playing of such strength, character and insight one would willingly put up with far worse. Inevitably, particular pieces linger in the memory — the impassioned F sharp minor Fugue, the dancing A major Prelude or the haunted stillness of the B flat minor Fugue — but the most impressive aspect of Nikolaieva's interpretation is the way she communicates her belief that these 24 small pieces add up to a complete musical experience — after this it's very difficult to disagree: the monumental D minor Fugue really does feel like the final stage in a long and fascinatingly varied process. If you still think that Shostakovich's contribution to piano literature is relatively insignificant, try this.

Further listening ...

The gadfly — Suite, Op. 97a. **USSR Cinema Symphony Orchestra/Emin Khachaturian.** Classics for Pleasure CD-CFP4463 (4/89).

Symphony, Op. 73a (trans. Barshai). Chamber Symphony, Op. 83a (trans. Barshai). **Chamber Orchestra of Europe/Rudolf Barshai.** DG 435 386-2GH (8/92).

Cello Sonata in D minor, Op. 40. Moderato for Cello and Piano. *Coupled with* **Prokofiev.** Cello Sonata in C major, Op. 119. **Lynn Harrell** (vc); **Vladimir Ashkenazy** (pf). Decca 421 774-2DH (3/90).

24 Preludes, Op. 34. *Coupled with* **Alkan.** 25 Préludes dans les tons majeurs et mineur, Op. 31. **Olli Mustonen** (pf). Decca 433 055-2DH (10/91).

Hypothetically Murdered, Op. 31a (reconstructed McBurney). Five Fragments, Op. 42. Suite No. 1 for Jazz Band. Four Songs, Op. 46[a] (No. 4 orch. McBurney). [a]**Dmitri Kharitonov** (bass); **City of Birmingham Symphony Orchestra/Mark Elder.** United Recordings 88001-2 (1/94).

Suite on Verses of Michelangelo Buonarroti, Op. 145a[a]. Four Verses of Captain Lebyadkin, Op.146a. **Dietrich Fischer-Dieskau** (bar); **Radio-Symphonie-Orchester Berlin/ Vladimir Ashkenazy** ([a]pf). Decca 433 319-2DH.

LADY MACBETH OF THE MTSENSK DISTRICT. **Soloists; Ambrosian Opera Chorus; London Philharmonic Orchestra/Mstislav Rostropovich.** EMI CDS7 49955-2 (5/90).

Jean Sibelius

Finnish 1865-1957

New review

Sibelius. Violin Concerto in D minor, Op. 47[a]. Serenade in G minor, Op. 69 No. 2[a]. En saga, Op. 9. [a]**Julian Rachlin** (vn); **Pittsburgh Symphony Orchestra/Lorin Maazel.** Sony Classical SK53272. Recorded in 1992.

| ♪ 1h DDD 6/94 | q p q s |

Julian Rachlin was only 18 when he made this recording and here he is in one of the most challenging of concertos, whose difficulties he takes easily in his stride. He has consistent beauty of tonal colour, a pure silvery tone with intonation to match, and possesses the aristocratic quality this music calls for. He is technically flawless — stunning in fact — and his eloquence is unfailingly persuasive: for example, the beautifully articulate way in which he echoes the questioning phrase in the slow movement (track 2, 2'34"). The tiny mannerisms in which he indulges would not inhibit a placing alongside Cho-Liang Lin (reviewed under Nielsen; refer to the Index to Reviews), or such other classics as Oistrakh, Heifetz and Perlman. Certainly his artistry and sensitivity place him securely among the finest players of the day. The G minor *Serenade* is quintessential Sibelius. It has a poignant, wistful melancholy all its own, and there are few pieces which more keenly evoke the magic of the white nights of the Scandinavian summer. Rachlin, coming as he does from the Baltic, though he left Lithuania when he was six, would understand all that. Lorin Maazel's *En saga* is a straight, often very fast, but thoroughly atmospheric account of the score. The recording is splendidly balanced. Outstanding.

Additional recommendations ...
Violin Concerto[a]. **Glazunov.** *Violin Concerto in A minor, Op. 82*[b]. **Prokofiev.** *Violin Concerto No. 2 in G minor, Op. 63*[c]. **Jascha Heifetz** (vn); [a]**Chicago Symphony Orchestra/Walter Hendl;** [b]**RCA Victor Symphony Orchestra/Walter Hendl;** [c]**Boston Symphony Orchestra/ Charles Münch.** RCA Red Seal RD87019 (*see review under Glazunov; refer to the Index to Reviews*)
— ♪ 1h 9m ADD 10/86 q p Ⓑ ▲
Violin Concerto[a]. **Brahms.** *Violin Concerto in D major, Op. 77*[b]. **Ginette Neveu** (vn); **Philhar- monia Orchestra/**[a]**Walter Susskind,** [b]**Issay Dobrowen.** EMI Références mono CDH7
61011-2 — ♪ 1h 10m ADD 3/88 q p Ⓑ ▲

Violin Concerto. **Bruch.** *Violin Concerto in G minor, Op. 26.* **Shizuka Ishikawa** (vn); **Brno State Philharmonic Orchestra/Jiří Bělohlávek.** Supraphon Gems 2SUP 0002 — .·' 56m AAD 9/88 Ⓑ
*Violin Concerto*ᵃ. **Dvořák.** *Violin Concerto in A minor, B108*ᵇ. **Salvatore Accardo** (vn); ᵃ**Concertgebouw Orchestra,** ᵇ**London Symphony Orchestra/Sir Colin Davis.** Philips Silver Line 420 895-2PSL — .·' 1h 8m ADD 10/88 ꟼₚ Ⓑ
*Violin Concerto*ᵃ. *Overture in A minor. Menuetto. In Memoriam, Op. 59.* ᵃ**Silvia Marcovici** (vn); **Gothenburg Symphony Orchestra/Neeme Järvi.** BIS CD372 — .·' 54m DDD 1/89 Ⓑ
*Violin Concerto*ᵃ. **Prokofiev.** *Violin Concerto No. 2 in G minor, Op. 63*ᵃ. **R. Strauss.** *Violin Sonata in E flat major, Op. 18*ᶜ. **Jascha Heifetz** (vn); ᶜ**Arpád Sándor** (pf); ᵃ**London Philharmonic Orchestra/Sir Thomas Beecham;** ᵇ**Boston Symphony Orchestra/Serge Koussevitzky.** Biddulph mono LAB018 — .·' 1h 18m ADD 1/91 ꟼₚ Ⓑ ▲
Violin Concerto (original 1903-04 version and final 1905 version). **Leonidas Kavakos** (vn); **Lahti Symphony Orchestra/Osmo Vänskä.** BIS CD500 — .·' 1h 15m DDD 4/91 ꟼₚ ꟼₛ ⊚
Violin Concerto. Six Humoresques, Opp. 87 and 89a. Two Humoresques, Op. 69. Two Serenades, Op. 69. **Joseph Swensen** (vn); **Finnish Radio Symphony Orchestra/Jukka-Pekka Saraste.** RCA Victor Red Seal 09026 60444-2 — .·' 1h 6m DDD 1/93 Ⓑ
Violin Concerto. **Brahms.** *Violin Concerto.* **Tasmin Little** (vn); **Royal Liverpool Philharmonic Orchestra/Vernon Handley.** EMI Eminence CD-EMX2203 *(see review under Brahms; refer to the Index to Reviews)* — .·' 1h 12m DDD 2/93 ꟼₚ Ⓑ
Violin Concerto. **Beethoven.** *Violin Concerto in D major, Op. 61.* **David Oistrakh** (vn); **Stockholm Festival Orchestra/Sixten Ehrling.** Testament mono SBT1032 — .·' 1h 15m ADD 7/94 ꟼₚ Ⓑ ▲
Violin Concerto. **Tchaikovsky.** *Violin Concerto in D major, Op. 35.* **Nigel Kennedy** (vn); **City of Birmingham Symphony Orchestra/Simon Rattle.** EMI CDC7 54127-2 — .·' 1h 2m ADD ꟼₚ Ⓑ

New review

Sibelius. Kullervo, Op. 7. **Marianne Rørholm** (contr); **Jorma Hynninen** (bar); **Helsinki University Chorus; Los Angeles Philharmonic Orchestra/Esa-Pekka Salonen.** Sony Classical SK52563. Text and translation included. Recorded in 1992.

> .·' 1h 10m DDD 7/93   ꟼₚ

Sibelius's *Kullervo* was the symphonic poem-cum-symphony with which he made his breakthrough in Finland in 1892. Common to all recordings, including this newcomer, is the magisterial presence of Jorma Hynninen. Salonen keeps a firm grip on the proceedings and maintains a real sense of momentum throughout. Moreover, temptations to dwell on beauty of incident or to indulge in expressive emphasis are resisted, and this extraordinary piece is all the more telling as a result. The dramatic force of the central scena is vividly realized and both Marianne Rørholm and Jorma Hynninen are impressive — as indeed are the male voices of the Finnish chorus. An impressive performance, and the orchestral playing and recording are absolutely first class. This is arguably the best *Kullervo* we have yet had.

Additional recommendation ...
Eeva-Liisa Saarinen (mez); **Jorma Hynninen** (bar); **Estonian State Academic Male Choir; Helsinki University Male Choir; Helsinki Philharmonic Orchestra/Paavo Berglund.** EMI Matrix CDM5 650800 — .·' 1h 12m DDD 7/94

Sibelius. ORCHESTRAL WORKS. **Philharmonia Orchestra/Vladimir Ashkenazy.** Decca Ovation 417 762-2DM. From 417 378-1DM5. Recorded 1980-85. Finlandia, Op. 26. Karelia Suite, Op. 11. Tapiola, Op. 112. En Saga, Op. 9.

> .·' 1h 3m DDD 12/88   ꟼₚ ꟼₛ

More than 30 years separate *En Saga* and *Tapiola*, yet both works are quintessential Sibelius. The latter is often praised for the way Sibelius avoided 'exotic' instruments, preferring instead to draw new and inhuman sounds from the more standard ones; and the former is, in many ways, just as striking in the way Sibelius's orchestration evokes wind, strange lights, vast expanses and solitude. Both works suggest some dream-like journey: *En Saga* non-specific though derived from Nordic legend; *Tapiola* more of an airborne nightmare in, above and around the mighty giants of the Northern forests inhabited by the Green Man of the Kalevala, the forest god Tapio (the final amen of slow, bright major chords brings a blessed release!). Ashkenazy's judgement of long term pacing is very acute; the silences and shadows are as potent here as the wildest hurricane. And Decca's sound allows you to visualize both the wood and the trees: every detail of Sibelius's sound world is caught with uncanny presence, yet the overall orchestral image is coherent and natural. In addition, his *Finlandia* boasts some of the most vibrant and powerful brass sounds on disc.

Additional recommendations ...

Finlandia. Tapiola. Legends, Op. 22 — The swan of Tuonela. Kuolema, Op. 44 — Valse triste. **Berlin Philharmonic Orchestra/Herbert von Karajan.** DG 413 755-2GH — .·*' 44m DDD 1/85 ⁹ₚ

Tapiola. Pohjola's daughter, Op. 49. Rakastava, Op. 14. Andante lirico. **Gothenburg Symphony Orchestra/Neeme Järvi.** BIS CD312 — .·*' 56m DDD 6/87 ⁹ₚ ⁹ₛ

Finlandia. Karelia Suite. En Saga. The swan of Tuonela. Tapiola. Luonnatar, Op. 70ᵃ. ᵃ**Elisabeth Söderström** (sop); **Philharmonia Orchestra/Vladimir Ashkenazy.** Decca Ovation 430 757-2DM — .·*' 1h 13m DDD 7/93 ⁹ₚ ⁹ₛ

Finlandia (arr. H. Fricker). **Nielsen.** *Commotio, FS155.* **Alain.** *Litanies, Op. 79.* **Mulet.** *Carillon-sortie in D major.* **Sløgedal.** *Variations on a Norwegian Folk Tune.* **Lindberg.** *Organ Sonata in G minor, Op. 23 — Alla Sarabanda; Allegro con brio.* **Mozart.** *Orgelstück (Fantasia) für eine Uhr, K608.* **Lefébure-Wély.** *Marche.* **Elgar.** *Pomp and Circumstance March in G major, Op. 39 No. 4.* **Christopher Herrick** (org). Hyperion CDA66676 (*See review in the Collections section; refer to the Index to Reviews*) — .·*' 1h 15m DDD ⁹ₚ ⁹ₛ

New review

Sibelius. ORCHESTRAL WORKS. ᵃ**Dong-Suk Kang** (vn); **Gothenburg Symphony Orchestra/Neeme Järvi.** BIS CD472. Recorded in 1989.
Six Humoresques, Opp. 87 and 89ᵃ. Two Serenades, Op. 69ᵃ. Two Pieces, Op. 77ᵃ. Overture in E major. Ballet scene.

.·*' 1h 2m DDD 2/91 ⁹ₚ ⁹ₛ

The music for violin and orchestra here is marvellously rewarding and gloriously played. The six *Humoresques*, Opp. 87 and 89 come from the same period as the Fifth Symphony, at a time when Sibelius was toying with the idea of a second violin concerto, and some of the material of the *Humoresques* was possibly conceived with a concerto in mind. Sibelius wrote that these radiant pieces convey something of "the anguish of existence, fitfully lit up by the sun", and behind their outward elegance and charm, there is an all-pervasive sadness. This is even more intense in the *Serenades*, which are glorious pieces and quintessential Sibelius. Dong-Suk Kang is an outstanding player. His impeccable technique and natural musical instinct serve this repertoire well and he seems to have established an excellent rapport with Järvi and the Gothenburg orchestra. The two fill-ups are juvenilia and are only intermittently characteristc. The *Overture* is very much in his *Karelia* idiom, though they are of undoubted interest to all Sibelians. The recording is of the usual high quality one has come to expect from BIS.

New review

Sibelius. Pelleas and Melisande — Incidental Music, Op. 46. Swanwhite, Op. 54 — excerpts. King Christian II — Incidental Music, Op. 27ᵃ. ᵃ**Sauli Tiilikainen** (bar); **Iceland Symphony Orchestra/Petri Sakari.** Chandos CHAN9158. Text and translation included. Recorded 1992.
Swanwhite — The Harp; The Maiden with the Roses; The Prince Alone; Swanwhite and the Prince; Song of Praise.

.·*' 1h 19m DDD 7/93 ⁹ₚ ⁹ₛ

These performances are natural and unaffected and radiate immense care and pleasure in music-making. The *King Christian II* music includes "The Fool's Song", complete with soloist, and very good he is too, and a short "Minuet". Petri Sakari's performance is totally unaffected, plain and full of enthusiasm; the players sound as if they are enjoying this score and communicate their pleasure. Phrasing is attentive, musical through and through but never fussy. The *Pelleas and Melisande* has some pretty stiff competition to contend with, notably from Sir Thomas Beecham and the RPO in 1962 at mid-price (reviewed below). While it in no way displaces it, it is still a version many collectors would want to have. It is imaginative, totally musical, strong on atmosphere and observant of dynamic subtleties. There may be readers who might find some of the tempos on the slow side; they are unhurried, but in context they feel right. Unfortunately there is only room for five movements from the *Swanwhite* music. All are beautifully played; every detail is allowed to take its time and the phrasing, though attentive, is free of the slightest taint of narcissism. Let "Swanwhite and the Prince" serve as an example of how well thought out and natural in feeling the phrasing is! Added to this, the Chandos recording is beautifully transparent, warm and well-detailed. Recommended with enthusiasm.

Sibelius. ORCHESTRAL WORKS. **Royal Philharmonic Orchestra/Sir Thomas Beecham.** EMI Beecham Edition CDM7 63400-2. Recorded in 1955.
Pelleas and Melisande — Incidental Music, Op. 46. The Oceanides, Op. 73. Symphony No. 7 in C major, Op. 105 (all from HMV ASD468, 7/62). Tapiola, Op. 112 (ASD518, 4/63).

● 1h 16m ADD 7/90

Sibelius. ORCHESTRAL WORKS. [a]**Royal Philharmonic Orchestra;** [b]**BBC Symphony Orchestra,** [c]**London Philharmonic Orchestra/Sir Thomas Beecham.** EMI Beecham Edition mono CDM7 63397-2, recorded 1938-55.
The Tempest — Incidental Music, Op. 109 (from Philips ABR4045, 12/55)[a]. Scènes historiques: Op. 25 — No. 3, Festivo; Op. 66 (both from Columbia 33C1018, 11/53)[a]. Karelia Suite, Op. 11 — No. 1, Intermezzo; No. 3, Alla marcia (HMV DB6248. Recorded 1945)[b]. Finlandia, Op. 26 (Columbia LX704, 4/38)[c].

● 1h 13m ADD 7/90

Sibelius. ORCHESTRAL WORKS. [a]**London Philharmonic Orchestra,** [b]**Royal Philharmonic Orchestra/Sir Thomas Beecham.** EMI Beecham Edition mono CDM7 64027-2. Recorded 1937-47.
Symphonies — No. 4 in A minor, Op. 63[a] (from HMV DB3351/5, 3/38); No. 6 in D minor, Op. 104[b] (DB6640/42, 6/50). The Tempest — Incidental Music, Op. 109: Prelude[a] (DB3894, 12/39). Legends, Op. 22 — Lemminkäinen's Homeward Journey[a] (DB3355/6, 3/38). The bard, Op. 64[a] (DB3891, 12/39).

● 1h 19m ADD 3/92

One of the special things about Beecham's Sibelius was its sheer sonority: there was a fresh, vernal sheen on the strings quite different from the opulence of Koussevitzky or Karajan but with all their flexibility and plasticity of phrasing, and a magic that is easier to discern than define. Suffice it to say that his feeling for atmosphere in Sibelius was always matched by a strong grip on the architecture. The first CD collects together some of his greatest performances from the early days of stereo — *Pelleas*, *Tapiola* and *The Oceanides*, the latter recorded specifically at Sibelius's request. They are unsurpassed in atmosphere and poetic feeling. His 1956 recording of the two suites from *The Tempest* enjoys legendary status and is pure magic. The 1952 performances of four of the *Scènes historiques* have that similar ring of authenticity that transcend any sonic limitations. Beecham's stark account of the Fourth Symphony carries special authority since it was done after a long correspondence with the composer; and the 1947 RPO performance of the Sixth enjoyed Sibelius's imprimatur. The Prelude to *The Tempest* is as chillingly realistic as *Lemminkäinen's Homeward Journey* is exciting.

Additional recommendations ...
Legends. **Gothenburg Symphony Orchestra/Neeme Järvi.** BIS CD294 — ● 49m DDD 6/86
Legends. Luonnotar, Op. 70[a]. *The bard.* [a]**Phyllis Bryn-Julson** (sop); **Scottish National Orchestra/Sir Alexander Gibson.** Chandos Collect CHAN6586 — ● 1h 2m ADD 11/92
Pelleas and Melisande. Swanwhite — excerpts. *King Christian II* — Incidental Music, Op. 27[a]. [a]**Sauli Tiilikainen** (bar); **Iceland Symphony Orchestra/Petri Sakari.** Chandos CHAN9158 — ● 1h 19m DDD 7/93
Rakastava. Scènes historiques, Opp. 25 and 66. Valse lyrique. **Scottish National Orchestra/Sir Alexander Gibson.** Chandos CHAN6591 — ● 54m ADD 11/93

New review
Sibelius. Symphonies — No. 1 in E minor, Op. 39[a]; No. 7 in C major, Op. 105[b]. Karelia Overture, Op. 10[c]. **London Symphony Orchestra/Anthony Collins.** Beulah mono 1PD8.

Item marked [a] from Decca LXT2694 (8/52), [b] LXT2940 (12/54), [c] LW5209 (3/56). Recorded 1952-55.

♪♪ 1h 2m ADD 6/94

New review
Sibelius. Symphonies — No. 2 in D major, Op. 43[a]; No. 6 in D minor, Op. 104[b]. **London Symphony Orchestra/Anthony Collins.** Beulah mono 2PD8. Item marked [a] from Decca LXT2815 (10/53), [b] LXT5084 (11/55). Recorded 1953-55.

♪♪ 1h 9m ADD 6/94

New review
Sibelius. Symphony No. 3 in C major, Op. 52[a]. Pohjola's Daughter, Op. 49[b]. Pelleas and Melisande[c] — No. 2, Melisande; No. 6, Pastorale; No. 7, At the spinning wheel; No. 8, Intermezzo; No. 9, Death of Melisande. Nightride and Sunrise, Op. 55[d]. **London Symphony Orchestra/Anthony Collins.** Beulah mono 3PD8. Item marked [a] from Decca LXT2960 (12/54), [b] LXT2962 (12/54), [c] LXT5084 (11/55), [d] LXT5083 (10/55). Recorded 1954-55.

♪♪ 1h 8m ADD 6/94

The name Anthony Collins (1893-1963) probably doesn't mean a great deal to the majority of younger readers, but for quite a few serious Sibelius *aficionados* his 1950s Decca recordings hold cult status. In these transfers the original recordings are revealed for the fine achievements they were: beautifully balanced, clear and vivid, allowing us to hear these performances in intimate detail — which is how they deserve to be heard. Collins is a first-rate musical landscape-painter. He doesn't just give us the bold sweeping brush-strokes, important as they are; he shows how the landscapes team with minute life. Rustling string textures aren't blandly homogenized — tiny details catch the ear, and then vanish again. Woodwind bird calls or horn calls can be acutely expressive — some passages remind one of Sibelius's comments about quasi-human voices in the nature sounds around his forest-home. But exaggeration is alien to the Collins approach. Nothing is forced, almost everything is fresh and vital. But it isn't only in the symphonies that the Collins touch is refreshing. *Pohjola's Daughter* comes to life as effectively as the symphonies, and Vol. 3 contains a real rarity, an entirely satisfactory *Nightride and Sunrise*.

Sibelius. SYMPHONIES. **Philharmonia Orchestra/Vladimir Ashkenazy.** Decca 421 069-2DM4.
Symphonies — No. 1 in E minor, Op. 39 (from 414 534-1DH, 5/86); No. 2 in D major, Op. 43 (SXDL7513, 11/80); No. 3 in C major, Op. 52 (414 267-1DH, 8/85); No. 4 in A minor, Op. 63 (SXDL7517, 5/81); No. 5 in E flat major, Op. 82 (SXDL7541, 1/82); No. 6 in D minor, Op. 104 (414 267-1DH, 2/85); No. 7 in C major, Op. 105 (SXDL7580, 8/83).

♪♪ ④ 3h 52m ADD/DDD 12/87

Of all the cycles of Sibelius's symphonies recorded during recent years this is one of the most consistently successful. Ashkenazy so well understands the thought processes that lie behind Sibelius's symphonic composition just as he is aware, and makes us aware, of the development between the Second and Third Symphonies. His attention to tempo is particularly acute and invariably he strikes just the right balance between romantic languor and urgency. The Philharmonia play for all they are worth and possess a fine body of sound. The recordings are remarkably consistent in quality and well complement the composer's original sound-world.

Additional recommendations ...
Nos. 1-7. Finlandia. Tapiola. The swan of Tuonela. **Boston Symphony Orchestra/Sir Colin Davis.** Philips 416 600-2PH4 — ♪♪ ④ 4h 26m DDD 11/86
Nos. 1-7. The Oceanides. Kuolema — Scene with cranes. Night ride and sunrise, Op. 55. **City of Birmingham Symphony Orchestra; Philharmonia Orchestra/Simon Rattle.** EMI CMS7 64118-2 — ♪♪ ④ 4h 27m 2/92 DDD
Nos. 1-7. **Vienna Philharmonic Orchestra/Lorin Maazel.** Decca 430 778-2DC3 — ♪ ③ 3h 32m ADD 2/92
Nos. 1-7. Belshazzar's Feast — Incidental Music, Op. 51. Pohjola's daughter. Karelia Suite — Intermezzo; Alla marcia. Tapiola. **London Symphony Orchestra; Symphony Orchestra/ Robert Kajanus.** Finlandia mono FACD81234 — ♪♪ ③ 3h 7m ADD 2/92 ♪p ▲

Nos. 1 and 2[b]. Nos. 3 and 5[a]. *Belshazzar's Feast*[a]. *Pohjola's daughter*[a]. *Karelia Suite*[b] — *Intermezzo; Alla marcia. Tapiola*[a]. [a]**London Symphony Orchestra,** [b]**Symphony Orchestra/Robert Kajanus.** Finlandia mono FACD81234 — .•* ③ 3h 7m ADD 2/92 ♩ₚ ▲

Nos. 4 and 5. **Scottish National Orchestra/Sir Alexander Gibson.** Chandos CHAN8388 — .•* 1h 1m DDD 9/87

Nos. 4 and 5. **San Francisco Symphony Orchestra/Herbert Blomstedt.** Decca 425 858-2DH — .•* 1h 8m DDD 7/91 ♩ₚ ♩ₛ

Nos. 4 and 6. **City of Birmingham Symphony Orchestra/Simon Rattle.** EMI CDM7 64121-2 — .•* 1h 7m DDD 2/92 ♩ₚ

Nos. 4 and 6[a]. *The Tempest: Prelude. Legends* — *Lemminkäinen's return. The bard.* **London Philharmonic Orchestra,** [a]**Royal Philharmonic Orchestra/Sir Thomas Beecham.** EMI mono CDM7 64027-2 — .•* 1h 19m ADD 3/92 ♩ₚ ▲

Nos. 4 and 7. *Kuolema* — *Valse triste.* **Berlin Philharmonic Orchestra/Herbert von Karajan.** DG Galleria 439 527-2GGA — .•* 1h 6m ADD 5/94 ♩ₚ

Nos. 5 and 7. *Kuolema* — *Scene with cranes. Night ride and sunrise*[a]. **City of Birmingham Symphony Orchestra,** [a]**Philharmonia Orchestra/Simon Rattle.** EMI CDM7 69122-2 — .•* DDD 2/92 ♩ₚ ⑧

No. 5[a]. **Nielsen.** *Symphony No. 4, "The inextinguishable", FS76*[b]. *Pan and Syrinx, FS87*[b]. [a]**Philharmonia Orchestra;** [b]**City of Birmingham Symphony Orchestra/Simon Rattle.** EMI CDM7 64737-2 .•* 1h 18m DDD 11/93 ♩ₚ ⑧

Sibelius. Symphony No. 1 in E minor, Op. 39. Karelia Suite, Op. 11. Finlandia, Op. 26. **Oslo Philharmonic Orchestra/Mariss Jansons.** EMI CDC7 54273-2. Recorded in 1990.

.•* 1h 2m DDD 1/92 ♩ₚ ⑧

Jansons's account of the First Symphony was quite the most thrilling version to have appeared for some years. It has all the excitement and brilliance of the Vienna Philharmonic version under Bernstein without its exaggerations. Tempos throughout are just right, the phrasing breathes naturally and the sonority is excellently focused. Jansons never presses on too quickly but allows each phrase, each musical sentence to register so that the listener feels borne along on a natural currrent. Moreover, excitement is not whipped up but arises naturally from the music's forward momentum. The Oslo Philharmonic is a highly responsive orchestra of no mean virtuosity and they play with a splendid intensity and fire not only in the symphony but also the *Karelia Suite* and *Finlandia* which sound very fresh. All the artistic decisions in this reading seem to be right and the orchestral playing further enhances the high renown this ensemble now enjoys. Very good recording too.

Additional recommendations ...

Nos. 1 and 7. **Scottish National Orchestra/Sir Alexander Gibson.** Chandos CHAN8344 — .•* 58m DDD 1/85

No. 1. *Karelia Suite.* **Philharmonia Orchestra/Vladimir Ashkenazy.** Decca 414 534-2DH — .•* 57m DDD 5/86 ⑧

No. 1. *Karelia Suite.* **Berlin Philharmonic Orchestra/Herbert von Karajan.** EMI Studio CDM7 69028-2 — .•* 55m DDD 9/87 ⑧

Nos. 1 and 6. **Berlin Philharmonic Orchestra/Herbert von Karajan.** EMI CDD7 63896-2 — .•* 1h 9m DDD 7/91 ♩ₚ ⑧

No. 1. **Vienna Philharmonic Orchestra/Leonard Bernstein.** DG 435 351-2GH — .•* 41m DDD 4/92 ♩ₚ ⑧

Sibelius. Symphony No. 2 in D major, Op. 43. Romance in C major, Op. 42. **Gothenburg Symphony Orchestra/Neeme Järvi.** BIS CD252.

.•* 48m DDD 10/84

The Second Symphony possesses a combination of Italianate warmth and Nordic intensity that has ensured its wide popular appeal. None of Sibelius's other symphonies has enjoyed such immediate and enduring success. If it inhabits much the same world as the First, it views it through more subtle and refined lenses. As in the First Symphony, it is the opening movement that makes the most profound impression. Its very air of relaxation and effortlessness serves to mask its inner strength. Järvi's version has sinew and fire and the Gothenburg orchestra are splendidly responsive and well disciplined. There is an unerring sense of purpose and direction: the momentum never slackens and yet nothing seems over-driven. The performance is concentrated in feeling and has freshness and honesty. The short but charming *Romance* in C for strings, written at about the same time, is an excellent fill-up.

Additional recommendations ...

No. 2. **Scottish National Orchestra/Sir Alexander Gibson.** Chandos CHAN8303 — .•˙
4lm DDD 3/84 Ⓑ

No. 2. Finlandia. Kuolema — Valse triste. The Swan of Tuonela, No. 2. **Boston Symphony Orchestra/Sir Colin Davis.** Philips Silver Line 420 490-2PM — .•˙ 1h 9m ADD 6/87 Ⓑ

No. 2. **Royal Philharmonic Orchestra/Sir John Barbirolli.** Chesky CD-3 — .•˙ 44m ADD 6/91 Ⓑ ▲

Nos. 2, 5 and 7. Swanwhite — The Maidens with roses. Tapiola. Pohjola's daughter. **Boston Symphony Orchestra; BBC Symphony Orchestra/Serge Koussevitzky.** Pearl mono GEMMCDS9408 — .•˙ ② 2h 5m AAD 7/90 Ⓑ ▲

No. 2. **Dvořák.** *Symphony No. 8 in G major, Op. 88.* **BBC Symphony Orchestra, Royal Philharmonic Orchestra/Sir Thomas Beecham.** EMI Beecham Edition mono CDM7 63399-2 — .•˙ 1h 17m ADD 7/90 Ⓑ

No. 4. The Tempest — Suite No. 1. **Danish National Radio Symphony Orchestra/ Leif Segerstam.** Chandos CHAN8943 — .•˙ 1h 5m DDD 8/91 � ᑫₛ

No. 2. Finlandia. Karelia Suite. **Philharmonia Orchestra/Vladimir Ashkenazy.** Decca Headline 430 737-2DM — .•˙ 1h 12m DDD 8/92 Ⓑ

No. 2. Tapiola. Kuolema — Valse triste. **San Francesco Symphony Orchestra/Herbert Blomstedt.** Decca 433 810-2DH — .•˙ 1h 9m DDD 3/93 Ⓑ

No. 2. The swan of Tuonela. Kuolema — Valse triste. Andante festivo for Strings. **Oslo Philharmonic Orchestra/Mariss Jansons.** EMI CDC7 54804-2 — .•˙ 1h 1m DDD 7/93 Ⓑ

No. 2. Romance in C major, Op. 42. Kuolema — Valse triste. Finlandia. **Boston Symphony Orchestra/Vladimir Ashkenazy.** Decca 436 566-2DH — .•˙ 1h 5m DDD 10/93 Ⓑ

Sibelius. Symphonies — No. 3 in C major, Op. 52[a]; No. 2 in D major, Op. 43[b]. **City of Birmingham Symphony Orchestra/Simon Rattle.** EMI CDM7 64120-2. Item marked [a] from EL270496-1 (4/87), [b] EL270160-1 (1/85).

.•˙ **5lm DDD 2/92**

Sibelius's Third Symphony is a striking advance on his first two; whilst they speak the same language as the music of Tchaikovsky and Grieg, the Third strikes us because of its spareness of texture and concentration of ideas. The weight of string tone associated with Sibelius is here apparent and carries tremendous expressive power. The finale, in particular, is a remarkable movement possessing a power and inevitability that evolve from the Symphony's unusual structure. In the Second Symphony, Rattle's first movement is, perhaps, on the slow side. In general, though, both performance and recording are very fine.

Additional recommendations ...

Nos. 3 and 6. **Scottish National Orchestra/Sir Alexander Gibson.** Chandos CHAN8389 — .•˙ 54m DDD 9/87

Nos. 3 and 6. **Philharmonia Orchestra/Vladimir Ashkenazy.** Decca 436 478-2DM — .•˙ 58m DDD 2/94 ᑫₚ

New review

Sibelius. COMPLETE PIANO MUSIC, Volumes 1 and 2. **Annette Servadei.** Continuum CCD1058/9.
CCD1058 — Six Impromptus, Op. 5. 10 Pieces, Op. 24. 10 Bagatelles, Op. 34. CCD1059 — Kuolemo, Op. 44 No. 1 — Valse triste. Spagnuolo. Mandolinato. Morceau romantique sur un motif de M. Jacob de Julin. The cavalier. 10 Pensées lyriques, Op. 40. Six Finnish Folksongs. 10 Pieces, Op. 58. Longing.

.•˙ ② 1h 9m 1h 10m DDD 3/94

Generally speaking, Sibelius's piano music has had a bad press, the only and most distinguished exception being the monograph Erik Tawaststjerna published way back in 1957. It has never engaged the sympathy of concert pianists with the exception of Wilhelm Kempff, who never recorded any of it, and Glenn Gould, who did. Sibelius himself admitted his lack of sympathy for the instrument: "I do not care for the piano — it is an unsatisfying, ungrateful instrument which only one composer, Chopin has fully succeeded in mastering and two others, Debussy and Schumann have come on intimate terms". Be that as it may, one must recognize the justice of Gould's verdict that "Sibelius never wrote against the grain of the keyboard" (*The Glenn Gould Reader*: London: 1984). The time is ripe for a new cycle and the first two CDs in Servadei's survey augur well for the rest. And whether in the early Op. 5 *Impromptus* (which do sound like piano reductions, a charge to which much of Sibelius's early piano music is open), or in the Op. 58 set, which he thought "an improvement technically" on his earlier keyboard pieces, she proves a perceptive and sensitive advocate. It is only by the exalted standards Sibelius set elsewhere that his contribution to the keyboard repertoire seems so limited in breadth and inventive resource. There are many miniatures that are rewarding, particularly in the Op. 57 set, but few masterpieces. The recording quality is very truthful. It is fortunate that this artist plays with delicacy of colour and feeling, for the keyboard is at times just a shade too closely observed. Compare, say, the "Rêverie", which opens Op. 58, with the "Summer Song" and you will appreciate the difference. The former is excellent but the texture in the latter would have greater transparency in the middle register had the perspective been a shade more distant. A small point and one which does not diminish the artistic attractions of this pair of discs.

Sibelius. SONGS. **Anne Sofie von Otter** (mez); **Bengt Forsberg** (pf). BIS CD457. Texts and translations included.
Arioso, Op. 3. Seven Songs, Op. 17. Row, row duck. Six Songs, Op. 36. Five Songs, Op. 37. Pelleas and Melisande, Op. 46 — The three blind sisters. Six Songs, Op. 88. Narcissus.

57m DDD 6/90

In all, Sibelius composed about 100 songs, mostly to Swedish texts but his achievement in this field has, naturally enough, been overshadowed by the symphonies. Most music-lovers know only a handful like "Black roses", Op. 36 No. 1, and "The Tryst" and the most popular are not always the best. Sibelius's output for the voice has much greater range, diversity and depth than many people suppose. For collectors used to hearing them sung by a baritone, the idea of a soprano will seem strange but many of them were written for the soprano Ida Ekman. Anne Sofie von Otter not only makes a beautiful sound and has a feeling for line, but also brings many interpretative insights to this repertoire. The very first song from the Op. 17 set is a marvellous Runeberg setting, "Since then I have questioned no further" and it was this that Ida Ekman sang for Brahms. Von Otter captures its mood perfectly and has the measure of its companions too. Her account of "Black roses" is particularly thrilling and she is very persuasive in the weaker Op. 88 set. She sings throughout with great feeling for character and her account of "Astray", Op. 17 No. 6, has great lightness of touch and charm. The Opp. 36 and 37 sets are among the finest lyrical collections in the whole of Sibelius's song output, and they completely engage this artist's sensibilties. These are performances of elegance and finesse; Bengt Forsberg proves an expert and stylish partner and both artists are well recorded.

Sibelius. The Tempest — Complete Incidental Music, Op. 109. **Kirsi Tiihonen** (sop); **Lilli Paasikivi** (mez); **Anssi Hirvonen, Paavo Kerola** (tens); **Heikki Keinonen** (bar); **Lahti Opera Chorus and Symphony Orchestra/Osmo Vänskä.** BIS CD581. Text and translation included. Recorded in 1992.

1h 8m DDD 2/93

A first recording of the full score! Sibelius's music for *The Tempest,* his last and greatest work in its genre, was the result of a commission for a particularly lavish production at the Royal Theatre, Copenhagen in 1926. The score is far more extensive than the two suites and consists of 34 musical numbers for soloists, mixed choir, harmonium and large orchestra. Readers will be brought up with a start by the music for the "Berceuse", the second item, which uses a harmonium rather than the strings with which we are familiar from the two suites and although it is still more magical in the familiar orchestral suite, the original has an other-worldly quality all its own. The music is played in the order in which it was used in the 1927 production of the play and there are ample and excellent explanatory notes. The "Chorus of the Winds" is also different but no less magical in effect. Of course, taken out of the theatrical context, not everything comes off — but even if the invention is not consistent in quality, at its best it is quite wonderful. The singers and chorus all rise to the occasion and Osmo Vänskä succeeds in casting a powerful spell in the "Intermezzo", which opens Act 4. The recording is marvellously atmospheric though it needs to be played at a higher than usual level setting as it is a little recessed. For Sibelians this is a self-recommending issue.

Further listening ...

Scaramouche — Incidental Music, Op. 71. The Language of the Birds — Wedding March. **Gothenburg Symphony Orchestra/Neeme Järvi.** BIS CD502 (4/92).

Piano Quintet in G minor (1890)[a]. String Quartet in D minor, Op. 56, "Voces intimae". **Gabrieli Quartet** with [a]**Anthony Goldstone** (pf). Chandos CHAN8742 (2/90).

String Quartets — E flat major; A minor; B flat major, Op. 4; D minor, Op. 56, "Voces intimae". **Sibelius Academy Quartet.** Finlandia FACD209 (8/92).

THE MAIDEN IN THE TOWER. Karelia Suite, Op. 11. **Soloists; Gothenburg Concert Hall Chorus and Symphony Orchestra/Neeme Järvi.** BIS CD250 (3/85).

Robert Simpson
British 1921-

Suggested listening ...

Symphonies Nos. 2 and 4. **Bournemouth Symphony Orchestra/Vernon Handley.** Hyperion CDA66505 (12/92).

Symphony No. 3. Clarinet Quintet. **Bernard Walton** (cl); **Aeolian Quartet; London Symphony Orchestra/Jascha Horenstein.** Unicorn-Kanchana Souvenir UKCD2028 (6/90).

Symphonies Nos. 6 and 7. **Royal Liverpool Philharmonic Orchestra/Vernon Handley.** Hyperion CDA66280 (6/88)

Symphony No. 9. **Bournemouth Symphony Orchestra/Vernon Handley.** Hyperion CDA66299 (12/88).

Music for Brass Band: Energy — Symphonic Study. The Four Temperaments. Introduction and Allegro on a Bass by Max Reger. Volcano — Symphonic Study. Vortex. **Desford Colliery Caterpillar Band/James Watson.** Hyperion CDA66449 (1/91).

String Quartets Nos. 3 and 6. String Trio (Prelude, Adagio and Fugue). **Delmé Quartet.** Hyperion CDA66376 (7/90).

String Quartets Nos. 7 and 8. **Delmé Quartet.** Hyperion CDA66117 (2/90).

String Quartet No. 9. **Delmé Quartet.** Hyperion CDA66127 (2/90).

String Quartet No. 12. String Quintet[a]. **Coull Quartet;** [a]**Roger Bigley** (va). Hyperion CDA66503 (7/92).

Howard Skempton
British 1947-

Suggested listening ...

Lento. **BBC Symphony Orchestra/Mark Wigglesworth.** NMC NMCD005 (6/93).

Henry Smart

British 1813-1879

Suggested listening ...

Postlude in D major. Air and Variations and Finale Fugato. Three Andantes — G major; A major; E minor. Minuet in C major. Grand Solemn March in E flat major. **Anne Marsden-Thomas** (org). Priory PRCD368 (9/92).

Bedrich Smetana

Bohemian 1824-1884

Smetana. Má vlast. **Czech Philharmonic Orchestra/Rafael Kubelík.** Supraphon 11 1208-2. Recorded at a performance in the Smetana Hall, Prague in May 1990.

⠎ **Ih 18m DDD 9/91**   ⑨ℙ Ⓑ

Smetana's great cycle of six tone-poems, *Má vlast*, celebrates the countryside and legendary heroes and heroines of Bohemia. It is a work of immense national significance encapsulating many of the ideals and hopes of that country. What a triumphant occasion it was when Rafael Kubelík returned to his native Czechoslovakia and to his old orchestra after an absence of 42 years and conducted *Má vlast* at the 1990 Prague Spring Festival. Supraphon's disc captures that live performance — not perfectly, since the sound is efficient rather than opulent — but well enough to show off what is arguably the finest performance on record since Talich's early LP set. You would never imagine that Kubelík had emerged from five years of retirement and a recent serious illness, such is the power and eloquence of his conducting. Typically he takes a lyrical rather than a dramatic view of the cycle, and if there is strength enough in more heroic sections there is also a refreshing lack of bombast. Kubelík's intimate knowledge of the score (this is his fifth recording of it) shows time and time again in the most subtle touches. Even the weakest parts of the score are most artfully brought to life, and seem of much greater stature than is usually the case. "Vltava" flows beautifully, with the most imaginative flecks of detail, and in "From Bohemia's Woods and Fields" there are vivid visions of wide, open spaces. The orchestra, no doubt inspired by the occasion, reward their former director with superlative playing.

Additional recommendations ...
Royal Liverpool Philharmonic Orchestra/Libor Pešek. Virgin Classics VC7 59576-2 — ⠎ Ih 16m DDD 7/90 ⑨ℙ Ⓑ
Czech Philharmonic Orchestra/Václav Talich. Koch International Legacy mono 37032-2 — ⠎ Ih 19m ADD 2/91 ⑨ℙ Ⓑ ▲
Israel Philharmonic Orchestra/Walter Weller. Decca Headline Classics — ⠎ Ih 14m 1/92 Ⓑ
Czech Philharmonic Orchestra/Václav Talich. Supraphon mono 11 1896-2 — ⠎ Ih 14m ADD 1/94 Ⓑ ▲

Smetana. 14 Czech Dances, T112. Bagatelles and Impromptus, B40. **Radoslav Kvapil** (pf). Unicorn-Kanchana DKPCD9139. Recorded in 1992.

⠎ **Ih 13m DDD 10/93**

The *Czech Dances* fall into two groups; a set of four polkas (1877) and ten miscellaneous dances (1879). Kvapil's expert, sensitive performances touch delicately on the emotions lying beneath the music's surface. The polkas are elliptical, allusive pieces with some strange progressions and harmonic side-slips that are very far from the world of *The bartered bride*. The second set was in a sense a riposte to Dvořák, Smetana feeling that he could write dances which instead of being generally Slavonic could take their ideas from the detailed nature of specific Czech dances. They form an attractive and well-contrasted group. The earlier *Bagatelles and Impromptus* of 1844 are much simpler, and have a direct lyricism that was coloured by his love for his future wife Kateřina; they were an unusual form for a Czech composer in those years, and they presage much in his music as well as having plenty to offer the listener as pieces whose charm is by no means superficial.

Smetana. THE BARTERED BRIDE. **Gabriela Beňačková** (sop) Mařenka; **Peter Dvorský** (ten) Jeník; **Miroslav Kopp** (ten) Vašek; **Richard Novák** (bass) Kecal; **Jindřich Jindrák** (bar) Krušina; **Marie Mrázová** (contr) Háta; **Jaroslav Horáček** (bass) Mícha; **Marie Veselá** (sop) Ludmila; **Jana Jonášová** (sop) Esmeralda; **Alfréd Hampel** (ten) Circus master; **Karel Hanuš** (bass) Indian; **Czech Philharmonic Chorus and Orchestra/Zdeněk Košler.** Supraphon 10 3511-2. Notes, text and translation included. From 1116 3511 (7/82).

③ 2h 17m DDD 10/91

There is something special about a Czech performance of *The bartered bride* and this one is no exception. The hint of melancholy which runs through the work is wonderfully evoked, as well as its marvellous gaiety. Zdeněk Košler has the rhythm and lilt of the music in his bones, like any Czech conductor worth his salt. The Czech Philharmonic has long had one of the finest of all woodwind sections, and especially in this music they play with a sense of their instruments' folk background, with phrasing that springs from deep in Czech folk-music. This sets the musical scene for some moving performances. The warm, lyrical quality of Gabriela Benňačková's voice can lighten easily to encompass her character's tenderness in the first duet, "Věrné milováni", or "Faithful love", the considerable show of spirit she makes when Jeník appears to have gone off the rails. Her Act 1 lament is most beautifully song. Peter Dvorský as Jeník plays lightly with the score, as he should, or the character's maintaining of the deception can come to seem merely cruel. Even old Kecal comes to new life, not as the conventional village bumbler, but as a human character in his own right as Richard Novák portrays him — quite put out, the old boy is, to find his plans gone astray. In fact, all of the soloists are excellent. The chorus enjoy themselves hugely, never more so than in the Beer chorus. Altogether a delightful, touching and warming performance.

New review
Smetana. LIBUSE. **Gabriela Beňačková** (sop) Libuše; **Václav Zítek** (ten) Přemysl; **Antonín Svorc** (bass) Chrudoš; **Leo Marian Vodička** (ten) Stáhlav; **Karel Průša** (bass) Lubtor; **René Tuček** (bar) Radovan; **Eva Děpoltová** (sop) Krasava; **Věra Soukupová** (mez) Radmila; **Prague National Theatre Chorus and Orchestra/Zdeněk Košler.** Supraphon 11 1276-2. Notes, text and translation included. Recorded live in 1983.

③ 2h 46m DDD 4/94

Libuše is a patriotic pageant, static and celebratory, with such plot as there is concerning the mythical founder of Prague, Libuše, and her marriage to the peasant Přemysl, founder of the first Czech dynasty. Václav Zítek makes a fine, heroic Přemysl; but the triumphant performance comes, as it must, from Gabriela Beňačková. The opera concludes with a series of tableaux in which Libuše prophesies the future kings and heroes who will assure the stability and greatness of the nation. At the end of a long performance her voice is undimmed in its ringing splendour; and earlier, as near the very start, the beauty of her tone and line seeks out all the warmth, character and humanity which she proves to be latent in Smetana's spacious but seemingly plain vocal writing. *Libuše* is scarcely Smetana's greatest opera, as he liked to claim, but especially in so splendid a performance from Beňačková, and under the grave but impassioned direction of Zdeněk Košler, it makes compelling gramophone listening. The live recording includes some applause, but little other audience intervention.

Further listening ...

Symphonic Poems — Richard III, Op. 11; Wallensteins Camp, Op. 14; Hakon Jarl, Op. 16. Prague Carnival. *Coupled with* **Janáček.** Sinfonietta. **Bavarian Radio Symhony Orchestra/ Rafael Kubelík.** DG Galleria 437 254-2GGA (1/93).

THE TWO WIDOWS. **Soloists; Prague Radio Chorus and Symphony Orchestra/ Jaroslav Krombholc.** Praga PR250 022/3 (6/93).

THE BRANDENBURGERS IN BOHEMIA. **Soloists; Prague National Theatre Chorus and Orchestra/Jan Hus Tichý.** Supraphon 11 1804-2 (5/94).

Dame Ethel Smyth

Suggested listening ...

Violin Sonata in A minor, Op. 7[a]. String Quintet in E major, Op. 1[b]. Cello Sonata in A minor, Op. 5[c]. String Quartet in E minor[d]. [c]**Friedmann Kupsa** (vn); [bc]**Johanna Varner** (vc); [ac]**Céline Dutilly** (pf); [bd]**Fanny Mendelssohn Quartet.** Troubadisc TRO-CD03 (6/94).

Mass in D major[a]. THE BOATSWAIN'S MATE — Suppose you mean to do a given thing. March of the Women[b]. **Eiddwen Harrhy** (sop); [a]**Janis Hardy** (contr); [a]**Dan Dressen** (ten); [a]**James Bohn** (bass); **Plymouth Festival** [ab]**Chorus and Orchestra/Philip Brunelle.** Virgin Classics VC7 59022-2 (8/91).

Four Songs (1907)[a]. Three Songs (1913)[b]. Horn Trio in A major[c]. **Various soloists.** Troubadisc TRO-CD01405 (6/94).

Antonio Soler

New review

Soler. Quintets – No. 3 in G major; No. 4 in A minor; No. 5 in D major. **Concerto Rococo** (Nicolas Mazzoleni, Roberto Crisafulli, vns; Nadine Davin, va; Elena Andreyev, vc; Jean-Patrice Brosse, hpd). Pierre Verany PV792111. Recorded in 1992.

1h 11m DDD 4/94

Soler's delightful and melodious quintets were written in 1776 – that's to say at the same time as Mozart's *Haffner* Serenade – for private music-making in the villa near the Escorial (where Soler was a monk) of the music-loving Infante, Don Gabriel de Borbón. The Hispanicisms that fascinated Scarlatti, and appear in some of the keyboard sonatas of his disciple Soler, are rarely to be found here: the style is closer to that of Boccherini, and it is not without significance that the latter was in the Spanish royal service at the time. What is at once apparent is the vitality of Soler's writing: sparkling in the G major's first movement and boisterously bucolic in its third; full of agitation in the A minor's third movement and of fresh invention in its variation finale (in which viola and cello are suddenly allotted starring roles); fiercely energetic in the D major's second movement (in which there are echoes of the 'hunting' figures of Scarlatti's Kk159) and Haydnesque in its finale. The Concerto Rococo is an extremely good ensemble with the harpsichord a sweet-toned copy of a Cresci. The playing is notably neat and crisp throughout and the recording is excellent.

Soler. KEYBOARD SONATAS. **Maggie Cole** ([a]fp/[b]hpd). Virgin Classics Veritas VC7 59624-2. No. 18 in C minor[a]; No. 19 in C minor[a]; No. 41 in E flat major[a]; No. 72 in F minor[a]; No. 78 in F sharp minor[a]; No. 84 in D major[b]; No. 85 in F sharp minor[b]; No. 86 in D major[b]; No. 87 in G minor[a]; No. 88 in D flat major[b]; No. 90 in F sharp major[b]. Fandango.

1h 11m DDD 5/91

If Soler's name is not widely known, that is because he devoted much of his creative time to writing 120 keyboard sonatas which have been overshadowed by those of his predecessor Domenico Scarlatti — who was also his teacher. But they have a character of their own and are longer and more elaborate than Scarlatti's. Maggie Cole takes into account the fact that Soler knew both the fortepiano and harpsichord and sensibly divides the 12 here into two parts, playing the first six on the former and the second on the older instrument. The overriding character of the music is energy, and pieces such as Sonatas Nos. 84 and 88 (played on a three-manual Goble harpsichord after a Hamburg instrument of 1740) fairly burst out of the loudspeakers in a recording that will be too closely-miked for some tastes but is undeniably realistic. Still, there's enough variety in the invention for listening in sequence — though nothing is especially Spanish-sounding save for the *Fandango* on track 7. The fortepiano (by Derek Adlam and based on a Viennese instrument) is more expressive than many, as the gravely melancholy Sonata No. 18 demonstrates. This piece is one of the longest at nearly ten minutes, and is nicely complemented by the shorter and bouncier No. 19 that follows. Maggie Cole's playing is wonderfully crisp and clean, and by using discreet rhythmic flexibility (and tonal shading in the fortepiano pieces) she never allows busy passagework to become merely mechanical.

Additional recommendations ...

Sonatas — No. 1 in A major; No. 3 in B flat major; No. 24 in D minor; No. 25 in D minor; No. 28 in C major; No. 29 in C major; No. 30 in G major; No. 31 in G major; No. 96 in E flat major; No. 118 in A minor. Prelude No. 1 in D minor. **Bon van Asperen** (hpd). Astrée Auvidis E8768 — .·' lh llm DDD 7/92 ✍

Sonatas — No. 7 in C major; No. 8 in C major; No. 9 in C major; No. 20 in C sharp minor; No. 21 in C sharp minor; No. 34 in E major; No. 95 in A major. Prelude No. 3 in C major. **Bon van Asperen** (hpd). Astrée Auvidis E8769 — .·' lh 8m DDD 7/92 ✍

Sonatas — No. 10 in B minor; No. 11 in B major; No. 12 in G major, "de la Cordorniz"; No. 13 in G major; No. 14 in G major; No. 52 in E minor; No. 73 in D major; No. 74 in D major; No. 92 in D major, "Sonata de clarines"; No. 106 in E minor. Prelude No. 6 in G major. **Bon van Asperen** (hpd). Astrée Auvidis E8780 — .·' lh 9m DDD 7/92 ✍

Sonatas — No. 37 in D major; No. 46 in C major; No. 56 in F major; No. 98 in B flat major; No. 100 in C minor; No. 103 in C minor; No. 108 in C major, "del Gallo"; No. 109 in F major; No. 112 in C major. Fandango. Prelude No. 5 in D major. **Bon van Asperen** (hpd). Astrée Auvidis E8771 — .·' lh 17m DDD 7/92 ✍

Sonatas — No. 15 in D minor; No. 22 in D flat major; No. 23 in D flat major; No. 54 in D minor; No. 61 in C major; No. 75 in F major; No. 76 in F major; No. 80 in G minor; No. 81 in G minor; No. 84 in D major; No. 86 in D major. **Bon van Asperen** (hpd). Astrée Auvidis E8772 — .·' lh 10m DDD 7/92

Sonatas — No. 18 in C minor; No. 19 in C minor; No. 26 in E minor; No. 27 in E minor; No. 36 in C minor; No. 85 in F sharp minor; No. 90 in F sharp minor; No. 91 in C major. No. 94 in G major. **Bon van Asperen** (hpd). Astrée Auvidis E8773 — .·' lh 15m DDD 7/92 ✍

Sonatas — No. 36 in C minor; No. 72; No. 88; No. 119 in B flat major; Fandango. **D. Scarlatti.** A minor, Kk7. C minor, Kk84. F minor, Kk185. F minor, Kk187. E flat major, Kk193. A major, Kk208. D major, Kk491. D major, Kk492. **Virginia Black** (hpd). United Recordings 88005-2 (*see review under D. Scarlatti; refer to the Index to Reviews*) — .·' 58m DDD 8/94 ♀ₚ ✍

Stephen Sondheim
American 1930-

Suggested listening ...

FOLLIES. **Original Broadway cast.** EMI Angel ZDM7 64666-2

INTO THE WOODS. **Original London cast.** RCA Victor RD60752 (9/91).

SUNDAY IN THE PARK WITH GEORGE. **Original Broadway cast.** RCA Victor RD85042 (7/90).

PACIFIC OVERTURES. **English National Opera.** That's Entertainment CDTER21152 (8/88).

Fernando Sor
Spanish 1778-1839

Sor. GUITAR WORKS **Eduardo Fernández.** Decca 425 821-2DH. Recorded in 1989. Grand solo, Op. 14. Fantasia élégiaque, Op. 59. Sonatas — C major, Op. 15 No. 2; C minor, Op. 25. Etudes — Op. 6 Nos. 4, 6 and 8; Op. 29 No. 25; Op. 35 Nos. 16 and 17; Op. 21. "Les adieux".

.·' lh 9m DDD ll/91

Although best known for his guitar music Sor wrote much for other mediums; it was through his ballet music that he visited Russia. Stylistically, his music sits between that of Mozart and Beethoven, and little of it shows any trace of his Hispanic origins. Of his several sonata-form works, Op. 25 is the most developed of its time for the guitar, and the *Grand solo* is in effect one sonata-form movement. The *Fantasia élégiaque* is a lament on the death of his friend Charlotte Beslay — above the final bars is written "Charlotte! Adieu" and it is arguably the most moving piece written for the guitar before this century. Sor also wrote numerous pieces for didactic purposes (which they serve without sacrifice of musical appeal), including 97 studies under five opus numbers, of which there is a selection in this recording. Fernández's clean performances complement Eisenhardt's (listed below) and both provide an excellent introduction to Sor's music as it is perceived by today's guitarists.

Additional recommendation ...
Sonata in C minor, Op. 25. Variations on the Scottish Air, "Ye banks and braes", Op. 40. Six Airs from Mozart's "Die Zauberflöte", Op. 19. Le calme — caprice, Op. 50. **Lex Eisenhardt.** Etcetera KTC1025 — .•' 49m DDD I/89

Further listening ...

Introduction and Variations on a Theme by Mozart, Op. 9. Fantasia élégiaque in C minor, Op. 59. Etudes — Op. 6 No. 11; Op. 31 No. 12; Op. 35 No. 22. *Coupled with* **Coste.** Pièces originales, Op. 53 — No. 1, Rêverie. Morceaux episodiques, Op. 23 — No. 7, Les soirées d'Auteuil. Grande sérénade, Op. 30. **Raphaëlla Smits** (gtr). Accent ACC29182D (8/93). *See review under Coste; refer to the Index to Reviews.*

Kaikhosru Shapurji Sorabji

British 1892-1988

New review
Sorabji. Fantaisie espagnole. **Donna Amato** (pf). Altarus AIR-CD-9022.

.•' 18m DDD 7/93

New review
Sorabji. Le jardin parfumé. **Yonty Solomon** (pf). Altarus AIR-CD-9037.

.•' 26m DDD 7/93

Composed in 1923, *Le jardin parfumé* counts as one of Sorabji's better-known works and there is no better introduction to his style. Cast in his most characteristic 'tropical-nocturne' vein it is saturated in sensuality, yet at the same time somnambulistically sure-footed (nothing like a Sorabji piece for bringing out the alliterative poly-syllables). Quite why the composer should have denied the Scriabin connection is a mystery — the piece exudes late-Scriabin-sonata textures from virtually every pore. The *Fantaisie espagnole*, by contrast, takes off from the Granados of *Goyescas* and follows its own weird and wonderful path past the Hispanic impressionism of Debussy and Ravel, ending up not so very far from Gershwin. Both performances and recorded sound are very fine.

Further listening ...

Piano Sonata No. 1. **Marc-André Hamelin.** Altarus AIR-CD-9050 (5/91).

Opus clavicembalisticum. **John Ogdon** (pf). Altarus AIR-CD-9075 (9/89).

John Sousa

American 1854-1932

Suggested listening ...

GREAT AMERICAN MARCHES, Volume 1 — King Cotton. Hands across the sea. Solid Men to the Front. Gladiator. The Royal Welch Fusiliers. Marquette University March. Semper

Fidelis. The Legionnaires. The Northern Pines. The Belle of Chicago. The Daughters of Texas. The Gallant Seventh. Nobles of the Mystic Shrine. The Invincible Eagle. Golden Jubilee. New York Hippodrome. **Royal Marines Band/Lt-Col. G.A.C. Hoskins.** EMI Great American Series CDM7 64671-2.

GREAT AMERICAN MARCHES, Volume 2 — El Capitan. Hail to the Spirit of Liberty. The Charlatan. The Washington Post. From Maine to Oregon. The Lambs' March. The Beau Ideal. The Crusader. The Diplomat. The National Game. The Black Horse Troop. Powhatan's Daughter. On the Campus. The Kansas Wildcats. La Flor de Sevilla. The Fairest of the Fair. Sound Off. Jack Tar. The High School Cadets. The Thunderer. The Glory of the Yankee Navy. The Stars and Stripes Forever. **Royal Marines Band/Lt-Col. G.A.C. Hoskins.** EMI Great American Series CDM7 64672-2.

FENNELL CONDUCTS SOUSA. Sound Off. Nobles of the Mystic Shrine. Sabre and Spurs. The Picadore. Our Flirtation. The High School Cadets. The Invincible Eagle. Bullets and Bayonets. The Liberty Bell. Riders for the Flag. Solid Men to the Front. The Gallant Seventh. The Rifle Regiment. The Pride of the Wolverines. Golden Jubilee. The Gridiron Club. New Mexico. Sesqui-Centennial Exposition. The Black Horse Troop. The Kansas Wildcats. Manhattan beach. Ancient and Honorable Artillery Company (of Boston). The National Game. The Glory of the Yankee Navy. **Eastman Wind Ensemble/Frederick Fennell.** Mercury Living Presence 434 300-2MM.

Key to symbols

Price	Quantity/ availability	Timing	Recording mode	Review date
	② ②	1h 23m	DDD	6/88

Louis Spohr

German 1784-1859

Suggested listening ...

Symphonies — No. 1 in E flat major, Op. 20; No. 5 in C minor, Op. 102. **Košice State Philharmonic Orchestra/Alfred Walter.** Marco Polo 8 223363.

Clarinet Concerto No. 1 in C minor, Op. 26[a]. *Coupled with **Mozart.*** Clarinet Concerto in A major, K622[a]. ***Weber.*** Clarinet Concerto No. 2 in E flat major, J118. **Ernst Ottensamer** (cl, [a]basset cl); **Vienna Philharmonic Orchestra/Sir Colin Davis.** Philips 438 868-2PH (6/94). *See review under Mozart; refer to the Index to Reviews.*

Double Quartet in D minor, Op. 65. String Sextet, Op. 140. String Quintet in G major, Op. 33 No. 2. **L'Archibudelli** and **Smithsonian Chamber Players.** Sony Classical Vivarte SK53370 (4/94).

JESSONDA. **Soloists; Hamburg State Opera Chorus; Hamburg Philharmonic Orchestra/Gerd Albrecht.** Orfeo C240912H (11/91).

Sir John Stainer

British 1840-1901

Suggested listening ...

The Crucifixion — *Oratorio.* Come, Thou long-expected Jesus — *Hymn.* I saw the Lord — *Anthem.* **Richard Lewis** (ten); **Owen Brannigan** (bass); **St John's College Choir, Cambridge/George Guest.** Decca Headline 436 146-2DSP.

Carl Philipp Stamitz

Suggested listening ...

Clarinet Concertos — No. 3 in B flat major; No. 10 in B flat major; No. 11 in E flat major. *Coupled with* **J. Stamitz.** Clarinet Concerto in B flat major. **Sabine Meyer** (cl); **Academy of St Martin in the Fields/Iona Brown.** EMI CDC7 54842-2 (11/93).

Flute Concerto in C major. *Coupled with* **Mercadante.** Flute Concerto in E minor. **Mozart.** Flute Concerto No. 2 in D major, K314/285d. **Irena Grafenauer** (fl); **Academy of St Martin in the Fields/Sir Neville Marriner.** Philips 426 318-2PH (11/91).

Jan Stamitz

Suggested listening ...

Trumpet Concerto in D major (realized Boustead). *Coupled with* **Hummel.** Trumpet Concerto in E flat major. **Hertel.** Trumpet Concerto in D major. **Haydn.** Trumpet Concerto in E flat major, HobVIIe/1. **Håkan Hardenberger** (tpt); **Academy of St Martin in the Fields/Sir Neville Marriner.** Philips 420 203-2PH (12/87). *See review in the Collections section; refer to the Index to Reviews.*

Charles Villiers Stanford

New review

Stanford. Morning and Evening Services — B flat major, Op. 10; C major, Op. 115. Benedictus and Agnus Dei in F major. **Durham Cathedral Choir/James Lancelot** with **Keith Wright** (org). Priory PRCD437. Recorded in 1992.

Ih 20m DDD 4/94

The mastery of composition is there for all to see. Moreover, it is seen with all the greater clarity when the opus is performed complete, as here. Excellent notes tell in outline of the evidence which could be amassed in a much longer study of the unity of these works, the thematic material and detailed cross-reference which bind the individual numbers into a work of art; and that is the special function of the record. The Choir of Durham Cathedral is fresh-toned and homogeneous in sound, stylish in phrasing and nuance, precise in attack and articulation. Exemplary too is the work of the organist, especially in Op. 115 where Stanford appears to be thinking so much more in terms of orchestration. The balance between organ and choir is fine.

Further listening ...

Symphony No. 1 in B flat major. Irish Rhapsody No. 2 in F minor, Op. 84, "Lament for the son of Ossian". **Ulster Orchestra/Vernon Handley.** Chandos CHAN9049 (10/92).

Symphony No. 2 in D minor, "Elegiac". Clarinet Concerto in A minor, Op. 80[a]. [a]**Janet Hilton** (cl); **Ulster Orchestra/Vernon Handley.** Chandos CHAN8991 (1/92).

Symphony No. 3 in F minor, Op. 28, "Irish". Irish Rhapsody No. 5 in G minor, Op. 147. **Ulster Orchestra/Vernon Handley.** Chandos CHAN8545 (1/88).

Symphony No. 4 in F major, Op. 31. Irish Rhapsody No. 6, Op. 191[a]. Oedipus tyrannus, Op. 29 — Prelude. [a]**Lydia Mordkovitch** (vn); **Ulster Orchestra/Vernon Handley.**
Chandos CHAN8884 (3/91).

Morning Services — A major, Op. 12; C major, Op. 115. Evening Service in B flat major. *Coupled with* **Bairstow.** The Lamentation. **F. Jackson.** Benedicite in G major. **Noble.** Magnificat in A minor. **Ely Cathedral Choir/Paul Trepte** with **Jeremy Filsell** (org). Gamut Classics GAMCD527 (2/92). *See review in the Collections Section; refer to the Index to Reviews.*

Three Motets, Op. 38 — Justorum animae; Coelos ascendit hodie; Beati quorum via. *Coupled with* **Martin.** Mass for Double Chorus. **Duruflé.** Four Motets sur des thèmes grégoriens, Op. 10 — Ubi caritas; Tota pulchra es; Tu es Petrus; Tantum ergo. **Górecki.** Totus tuus, Op. 60. **Byron.** Verba. [a]**Rebecca Outram** (sop); **Schola Cantorum, Oxford/Jeremy Summerly.** Proudsound PROUCD129 (4/92). *See review in the Collections Section; refer to the Index to Reviews.*

Fantasia and Toccata in D minor, Op. 57. *Coupled with* **Reger.** Five Easy Preludes and Fugues, Op. 56 — No. 1 in E major. **Shostakovich.** Lady Macbeth of the Mtsensk district — Passacaglia. **Schmidt.** Chaconne in C sharp minor. **Ravanello.** Theme and Variations in B minor. **Keith John** (org). Priory PRCD370 (11/92). *See review in the Collections Section; refer to the Index to Reviews.*

John Stanley
British 1712-1786

Suggested listening ...

Organ Concertos, Op. 10 — No. 1 in E major; No. 2 in D major; No. 3 in B flat major; No. 4 in C minor; No. 5 in A major; No. 6 in C major. **Northern Sinfonia/Gerald Gifford** (org). CRD CRD3365 (10/92).

Voluntaries — A minor, Op. 6 No. 2; D minor, Op. 7 No. 4; G major, Op. 7 No. 9. *Coupled with* **Boyce.** Voluntary in D major. **Handel.** Fugue in G major. Voluntary in C major. **Heron.** Voluntary in G major. **Hook.** Voluntary in C minor. **Russell.** Voluntary in F major. **Stubley.** Voluntary in C major. **S. Wesley.** Voluntaries — E flat major, Op. 6 No. 7; B flat major. **Jennifer Bate** (org). Unicorn-Kanchana DKPCD9106 (11/91). *See review in the Collections section; refer to the Index to Reviews.*

Max Steiner
Austrian/American 1888-1971

Suggested listening ...

Film Scores: Now, Voyager — excerpts. King Kong — Suite. Saratoga Trunk — As long as I live. The Charge of the Light Brigade — Forward the Light Brigade. Four Wives — Symphonie moderne[a]. The Big Sleep — Suite. Johnny Belinda — Suite. Since You Went Away — Main Title. The Informer — excerpts[b]. The Fountainhead — Suite. [a]**Earl Wild** (pf); [b]**Ambrosian Singers; National Philharmonic Orchestra/Charles Gerhardt.** RCA Victor GD80136 (10/90).

Wilhelm Stenhammar
Swedish 1871-1927

Stenhammar. Piano Concerto No. 1 in B flat minor, Op. 1[a]. Symphony No. 3 — fragment. [a]**Mats Widlund** (pf); **Stockholm Philharmonic Orchestra/Gennadi Rozhdestvensky.** Chandos CHAN9074. Recorded in 1992.

```
♪ · 5lm  DDD  10/92
```

New review

Stenhammar. Piano Concerto No. 2 in D minor, Op. 23[a]. Serenade in F major, Op. 31[b]. Florez och Blanzeflor, Op. 3[c]. [c]**Ingvár Wixell** (bar); [a]**Janos Solyom** (pf); [a]**Munich**

Philharmonic Orchestra; [bc]Swedish Radio Symphony Orchestra/Stig Westerberg.
EMI Matrix CDM5 65081-2. Text and translation included. Items marked [a] from Swedish HMV
4E 063 34284 (8/81), [bc] Swedish HMV 4E 061 35148 (8/80). Recorded 1970-74.

.•˙ 1h 13m ADD 5/94

The First Piano Concerto comes from 1893, when Stenhammar was 22, and such was its success
during the 1890s that he was invited to play it with the Berlin Philharmonic under Richard Strauss.
In time, however, he grew tired of it and became careless as to its fate. Both the autograph and the
orchestral parts were destroyed when Breslau was bombed during the Second World War. But
recently a copy probably made for the American première came to light in the Library of Congress.
Chandos also offer a short fragment from the Symphony No. 3 in C, on which Stenhammar
embarked in 1918-9. At not much under 50 minutes it is perhaps overlong, but still has much
charm, and Widlund and Rozhdestvensky make a most persuasive case for it. The recording has
great depth and warmth and the strings of the Stockholm Orchestra have great richness of sonority
The Serenade is arguably Stenhammar's masterpiece. In its Overture the writing is vibrant and
luminous, full of subtly changing textures and colours, and like the finale is of symphonic
proportions. Apparently Stenhammar toyed at one stage with the idea of adding the word
selvaggio or "wild" to the title of the *Scherzo*, the mercurial centrepiece of the whole work, which
is played with captivating spirit here. Stig Westerberg's 20-year-old recording comes up very
fresh indeed though the upper strings don't have quite the same bloom as the Gothenburg under
Neeme Järvi (listed below). The latter offer the charming *Reverenza* movement that Stenhammar
eventually rejected but nothing else by way of fill-up. The playing throughout is ardent, sensitive
and vital. This issue offers two additional pieces, most notably János Solyom's brilliant account
of the Second Piano Concerto with the Munich Philharmonic, sounding as if it were recorded
yesterday. It is strongly indebted to Saint-Saëns, and the *Scherzo* has a Mendelssohnian effervescence and delicacy. The early and endearing if Wagnerian *Florez och Blanzeflor*, finely sung by
Ingvar Wixell, is the admirable makeweight.

Additional recommendation ...
Piano Concerto No. 1[a]. Two Sentimental Romances, Op. 28[b]. Florez och Blanzeflor, Op. 3[c]. [a]**Love
Derwinger** (pf); [b]**Ulf Wallin** (vn); [c]**Peter Mattei** (bar); **Malmö Symphony Orchestra/
Paavo Järvi.** BIS CD550 — .•˙ 1h 8m DDD 10/92

Sir William Sterndale Bennett

Suggested listening ...

Piano Concertos — No. 1 in D minor, Op. 1; No. 3 in C minor, Op. 9. Caprice in E major,
Op. 22. **Malcolm Binns** (pf); **London Philharmonic Orchestra/Nicholas Braithwaite.**
Lyrita SRCD204 (11/90).

Piano Concertos — No. 2 in E flat major, Op. 4; No. 5 in F minor. Adagio. **Malcolm Binns**
(pf); **Philharmonia Orchestra/Nicholas Braithwaite.** Lyrita SRCD205 (11/90).

William Grant Still

New review
W.G. Still. Symphony No. 2 in G minor, "Song of a New Race".
Dawson. Negro Folk Symphony.
Ellington (orch. Henderson). Harlem. **Detroit Symphony Orchestra/Neeme Järvi.**
Chandos CHAN9226.

.•˙ 1h 14m DDD 3/94

It would be foolhardy to hail William Grant Still's First Symphony as a major find, but it is an
affectingly lyrical, unpretentious offering. Not surprisingly, given Still's reputation as an expert

arranger, the scoring is assured and effective; indeed, the richly textured string writing in particular seems tailor-made for the legendary skills of the work's première performers, namely Leopold Stokowski and the Philadelphia Orchestra. The latter also first performed William Levi Dawson's *Negro Folk Symphony*. That was in 1934, but the composer later revised the piece after a visit to Africa in 1952. Again, it is thoroughly diverting stuff, stylishly orchestrated. It was John Mauceri who most recently drew our attention to the provocative charms of Duke Ellington's steamy 1950 portrait-in-sound, *Harlem*, yet the relaxed virtuosity displayed by Järvi's Detroit players makes for an experience just as swaggeringly enjoyable. Given such consistently idiomatic, polished advocacy and agreeably velvety Chandos sound, this release must be deemed a great success.

Further listening ...

Afro-American Symphony. *Coupled with* **Ellington.** The River — Suite. **Detroit Symphony Orchestra/Neeme Järvi.** Chandos CHAN9154 (4/93).

Karlheinz Stockhausen

German 1928-

Suggested listening ...

Michaels Reise um die Erde. **Markus Stockhausen** (tpt); **Suzanne Stephens** (basset-hn); **Kathinka Pasveer** (alto fl); **Ian Stuart** (cl); **Lesley Schatzberger** (cl/basset-hn); **Michael Svoboda** (tbn/bar hn); **Andreas Boettger, Isao Nakamura** (perc); **Michael Obst, Simon Stockhausen** (synths); **Karlheinz Stockhausen** (sound projection). ECM New Series 437 188-2 (3/93).

Mantra. **Yvar Mikashoff, Rosalind Bevan** (pfs); **Ole Orsted** (electronics). New Albion NA025CD (1/91).

Klavierstück XII-XIV. **Bernhard Wambach** (pf). Koch Schwann 310015 (5/90).

Aus den sieben Tagen — Setz die Segel sur Sonne verbindung. **Ensemble Musique Vivante/Diego Masson** with **Karlheinz Stockhausen** (filters/potentionmeters). Harmonia Mundi HMA190 795 (9/89).

Stimmung. **Singcircle/Gregory Rose.** Hyperion CDA66115 (2/87).

Alessandro Stradella

Italian 1644-1682

Suggested listening ...

San Giovanni Battista. **Catherine Bott, Christine Batty** (sops); **Gérard Lesne** (alto); **Richard Edgar-Wilson** (ten); **Philippe Huttenlocher** (bar); **Les Musiciens du Louvre/Marc Minkowski.** Erato 2292-45739-2 (10/92).

Key to symbols

Quality of sound	Discs worth exploring	Caveat emptor
Quality of performance	Basic library	Period performance

Eduard Strauss

Austrian 1835-1916

Johann Strauss I

Austrian 1804-1849

Johann Strauss III

Austrian 1866-1939

Josef Strauss

Austrian 1827-1870

Johann Strauss II

Austrian 1825-1899

New review

EIN STRAUSSFEST II. ªCincinnati Pops Chorale; Cincinnati Pops Orchestra/Erich
Kunzel. Telarc CD80314. Recorded 1991-92.
E. Strauss: Ohne Aufenthalt, Op. 112. **Josef Strauss:** Plappermäulchen, Op. 245.
Sphärenklänge, Op. 235. Jockey, Op. 278. **J. Strauss I:** Chinese Galop, Op. 20.
J. Strauss II: Egyptischer Marsch, Op. 335ª. Künstler–Quadrille, Op. 71. Kaiser–Walzer,
Op. 437. Freikugeln, Op. 326. Jubelfest–Marsch, Op. 396. Tritsch-Tratsch–Polka, Op. 214.
Geisselhiebe, Op. 60ª. Klipp Klapp, Op. 466. Wein, Weib und Gesang, Op. 333. Perpetuum
mobile, Op. 257.

Ih 8m   DDD   7/93

This collection deliberately sets out to adorn popular Strauss pieces with sound effects to
outdo anything one hears at a Vienna New Year Concert. It starts with a performance of
Eduard Strauss's *Ohne Aufenthalt* that is accompanied throughout by steam railway effects,
has bullets flying mercilessly in the *Freikugeln* Polka, and includes neighing nags and
swishing whips in the *Jockey* Polka. The fun is increased by the inclusion of the
Künstler–Quadrille, a sort of 1850s "Hooked on Classics" number that begins with
Mendelssohn's "Wedding March" and continues through the likes of Mozart's Symphony
No. 40 and Chopin's 'Funeral March' Sonata to Beethoven's *Ruins of Athens* and *Kreutzer*
Sonata. If the Viennese lilt is just a shade lacking in the waltzes, the playing is nevertheless
excellent and lively throughout. The Strausses themselves would have approved.

NEW YEAR'S DAY CONCERT, 1992. Vienna Philharmonic Orchestra/Carlos Kleiber.
Sony Classical SK48376. Recorded live in 1992.
J. Strauss I: Radetzky March, Op. 228. **J. Strauss II:** Stadt und Land, Op. 332.
Vergnügungszug, Op. 281. DER ZIGEUNERBARON — Overture. Eine Tausend und eine
Nacht, Op. 346. Neue Pizzicato Polka. Persischer Marsch, Op. 289. Tritsch–Tratsch Polka,
Op. 214. Unter Donner und Blitz–Polka, Op. 324. An die schönen blauen Donau–Waltz,
Op. 314. **Josef Strauss:** Dorfschwalben aus Oesterreich, Op. 164. Sphärenklänge, Op. 235.
Nicolai: DIE LUSTIGEN WEIBER VON WINDSOR — Overture.

Ih 17m   DDD   4/92

In every respect, this is superb, a 'must'. Carlos Kleiber's second New Year's Day
Concert, celebrating the arrival of 1992, was a delightful occasion in every way. Here is
proof positive of its musical enchantments. Kleiber combined in a single baton his father
Erich's discipline, Clemens Krauss's innate sense of rhythm, Karajan's elegance and Krips's
insinuating charm. It's a formidable brew. Anyone who saw and heard the concert on
television will know just how delightfully Kleiber, with his unorthodox, seemingly
effortless methods, achieves his aims and how willingly his compliant orchestra responds to
his peculiar gifts. Among the outright winners here is the champagne effervescence of *Eine
Tausend und eine Nacht*, the ethereal beauty of *Sphärenklänge,* the irresistible verve of the
Pizzicato Polka and the panache of *Unter Donner und Blitz*. To crown one's pleasure, the
recording is faultless: it has presence, warmth, depth, and captures ideally a sense of the
occasion. It is not merely a wonderful souvenir of a special event but a thing of joy
forever.

NEW YEAR'S DAY CONCERT, 1994. Vienna Philharmonic Orchestra/Lorin Maazel.
Sony Classical SK46694. Recorded live in 1994.
J. Strauss I: Radetzky March, Op. 228. **J. Strauss II:** Enfantillage, Op. 202. Ein Herz, ein
Sinn, Op. 323. Die Fledermaus — Csárdás. G'schichten aus dem Wienerwald, Op. 325.
Lucifer, Op. 266. An der schönen, blauen Donau, Op. 314. Caroussel–Marsch, Op. 133.
Accelerationen, Op. 234. Lieder–Quadrille, nach beliebten Motiven, Op. 275. **Josef Strauss:**
Ohne Sorgen, Op. 271. Aus der Ferne, Op. 270. Feuerfest!, Op. 269. **E. Strauss:** Mit Chic,
Op. 221. **Lanner:** Die Schönbrunner, Op. 200.

Ih 18m DDD 7/94

Lorin Maazel, not a conductor who by nature radiates fun, turned the 1994 concert into a party
of extraordinary effervescence, in which (alongside the Strausses) he was the life and soul. He
relaxed in a jovial way that one would hardly have expected, even remembering his earlier
appearances at New Year concerts, and the players seemed to warm to him as never before. His
triumph was crowned, when in *Tales from the Vienna Woods* he took up the violin, and with
Werner Hink from the orchestra played the saucy duet sections at the beginning and end, to the
Viennese manner born. This generous selection from the concert builds up to that coup, but
then curiously fails to mention Maazel's other supernumerary contribution. In the quick polka by
Josef Strauss, *Ohne Sorgen* ("Without a Care"), Maazel, using an instrument at his elbow, as the
television relay showed us, provided decorations on the glockenspiel. Though the booklet makes
no mention of that, happily the recording compensates, aptly highlighting the glockenspiel notes.
That polka is one of the sparkling rarities, ten of them out of a total of 15 items, which help to
give this 1994 offering its distinctive flavour. Only one is identified as a first-ever recording, the
Schönbrunner waltz of Joseph Lanner, light and charming if not specially characterful, but other
rare delights include the French polka, *Feuerfest!* by Josef Strauss with its clanging hammers and
anvils, the *Lucifer* polka with bangs on the drum and the gallumphing *Caroussel* march, both by
Johann Strauss, as well as *Mit Chic*, the one contribution from the long-lived Eduard Strauss. The
Sony sound is warm and atmospheric but some may find the disc has too much applause.

VIENNESE DANCE MUSIC. [a]**Wolfgang Schulz** (fl); [b]**Ernst Ottensamer** (cl); [c]**Alois
Posch** (db); [d]**Heinz Medjimoreč** (pf); [e]**Alfred Mitterhofer** (harm); **Alban Berg Quartet**
(Günter Pichler, Gerhard Schulz, vns; Thomas Kakuska, va; Valentin Erben, vc). EMI CDC7
54881-2. Recorded in 1992.
J. Strauss I (arr. Weinmann): Wiener Gemüths, Op. 116[c]. Beliebte Annen, Op. 137[c]. Eisele
und Beisele Sprünge, Op. 202[c]. **J. Strauss II:** Schatz, Op. 418 (arr. Webern)[de]. Wein, Weib
und Gesang, Op. 333 (arr. Berg)[de]. Kaiser–Walzer, Op. 437 (arr. Schoenberg)[abd]. **Lanner**
(arr. Weinmann): Marien–Walzer, Op. 143[c]. Steyrische–Tänze, Op. 165[c]. Die Werber, Op. 103[c].

Ih 2m DDD 6/94

In the Alexander Weinmann arrangements of Lanner and the elder Johann Strauss, one is able to
appreciate to the full the clear lyrical lines of works whose full orchestration is very much built
upon the foundation of the string quartet. Likewise, in the large-scale waltzes of the younger
Strauss one cannot but admire the skill and affection with which Webern, Berg and Schoenberg
used the limited resources available to their Society for Private Musical Performances. Indeed, if
string quartet, piano, flute and clarinet inevitably struggle to capture the full splendour of the
march introduction to the *Kaiser–Walzer*, the imaginative way in which Schoenberg finds a chamber
ensemble substitute for Strauss's full orchestral sound is perhaps the most impressive aspect of the
various arrangements here. On its own terms, the collection is extremely impressive. The Alban
Berg Quartet have made a fine selection of some of the most melodic works from over half a
century of prodigious invention, and they play them with affection and relish. From Lanner's
tender *Marien–Walzer*, through to Strauss junior's most magisterial waltz, the clarity and
refinement of the playing is tempered with a sense of lightheartedness and fun. If you fancy a
Viennese dance collection with a different slant, don't hesitate to go for this admirable release.

J. Strauss II. COMPLETE EDITION, Volumes 34, 35 and 36. [a]**Bratislava Radio
Symphony Orchestra/Michael Dittrich; Košice State Philharmonic Orchestra/**

[b]**Johannes Wildner,** [c]**Alfred Walter.** Marco Polo 8 223234/6. Volumes marked [ab] recorded 1991, [c] 1989-91.

8 223234[a] — Russischer Marsch, Op. 426. Slaven–Potpourri, Op. 39. Fünf Paragraphe, Op. 105. La favorite, Op. 217. Nikolai–Quadrille, Op. 65. Abschied von St Petersburg, Op. 210. Der Kobold, Op. 226. Im russischen Dorfe, Op. 355 (orch. Schönherr). Dolci pianti (with Jozef Sikora, vc). Niko–Polka, Op. 228. *8 223235*[b] — Zivio!, Op. 456 (orch. Fischer). Architecten-Ball–Tänze, Op. 36. Jäger, Op. 229. Accelerationen, Op. 234. Der Liebesbrunnen, Op. 10 (orch. Kulling). Die Zeitlose, Op. 302. Königslieder, Op. 334. Im Sturmschritt, Op. 348. Der Blitz, Op. 59 (orch. Babinski). Heut' ist heut', Op. 471 (orch. Babinski). Die Wahrsagerin, Op. 420. *8 223236*[c] — Matador–Marsch, Op. 406 (orch. Fischer). Kreuzfidel, Op. 301. D'Woaldbuama (Die Waldbuben), Op. 66 (orch. Babinski). Process, Op. 294. Elfen–Quadrille, Op. 16 (orch. Kulling). Mephistos Höllenrufe, Op. 101. Bitte schön!, Op. 372. Die Extravaganten, Op. 205. Fledermaus–Quadrille, Op. 363. Der Klügere gibt nach, Op. 401. Neu–Wien, Op. 342. Diplomaten–Polka, Op. 448.

③ 1h 9m 1h 14m 1h 8m DDD 7/94

Volume 34 offers a distinct Russian flavour. The most obviously familiar item is the opening *Russischer Marsch* while the waltz *Abschied von St Petersburg* will also be familiar to some. It's a fine swinging waltz, with an attractive cello solo in the introduction. *Dolci pianti*, one of three romances surviving from Strauss's Russian visits, provides further material for a cello soloist, while the piquant *Niko–Polka* offers as good an example as any of the delights to be found among the unfamiliar works of the Waltz King. Not the least attraction of Vol. 34 is the conductor Michael Dittrich and his alert, *echt-Wienerisch* performances here. On Vol. 35 Johannes Wildner's conducting shows up to much better effect than has often been the case. Marches have always been his strong point, and the collection thus gets off to a good start with *Zivio!* from the operetta *Jabuka*. There are other attractive pieces on offer, too, from the perpetual favourite *Accelerationen,* through the delicate polka–mazurka *Die Zeitlose* to the magisterial *Königslieder* (a waltz from Strauss's most successful period) and the polka–mazurka *Die Wahrsagerin* on melodies from *The Gipsy Baron*. Volume 36 offers perhaps the most attractive music of the three volumes. Again the performance of the haunting waltz *Mephistos Höllenrufe* may not erase memories of some previous versions, but such pieces as the *Neu-Wien* waltz and the excellently played *Fledermaus–Quadrille* are among the composer's most agreeable creations. Perhaps the most pleasant surprise of all comes from the waltz *Die Extravaganten* which, with its endearing themes and richly inventive harmonic and orchestral touches, shows above all the merits of Marco Polo's voyage of Straussian rediscovery.

J. Strauss I. Radetzky March, Op. 228.
J. Strauss II. WALTZES AND POLKAS. **Vienna Philharmonic Orchestra/Willi Boskovsky** (vn). Decca Ovation 417 747-2DM. Recorded 1958-73.
J. Strauss II. DIE FLEDERMAUS — Overture. Perpetuum mobile, Op. 257. Accelerationen–Waltz, Op. 234. Unter Donner und Blitz–Polka, Op. 324. Morgenblätter–Waltz, Op. 279. Persischer Marsch, Op. 289. Explosionen–Polka, Op. 43. Wiener Blut–Waltz, Op. 354. Egyptischer Marsch, Op. 335. Künstlerleben–Waltz, Op. 316. Tritsch-Tratsch–Polka, Op. 214. **J. Strauss II/Josef Strauss:** Pizzicato Polka.

1h 5m ADD Ⓑ

There have been no finer recordings of Johann Strauss than those by Boskovsky and the Vienna Philharmonic. The velvety sheen and elegance of the orchestra's sound, combined with the unique lilt that comes so naturally to Viennese players, produced magical results. For this compilation Decca have sensibly mixed seven of the most famous waltzes and polkas from those sessions with other popular Strauss compositions in various rhythms, from the celebrated *Die Fledermaus* Overture, through popular polkas and novelty pieces (for *Perpetuum mobile* Boskovsky himself can be heard explaining that it has no ending) to the ever-popular *Radetzky March*. The recorded sound is not up to the most modern digital standards, but reprocessing has produced a remarkably homogeneous sound for recordings originating over a 15-year period.

Additional recommendations ...
Künstlerleben. Rosen aus dem Süden–Waltz, Op. 388. DER ZIGEUNERBARON — Overture. G'schichten aus dem Wienerwald–Waltz, Op. 325. Kaiser–Walzer, Op. 437. DIE FLEDERMAUS — Overture. An die

schönen blauen Donau. **London Philharmonic Orchestra/Franz Welser-Möst.** EMI CDC7
54089-2 — .•* lh 6m DDD 12/91 Ⓑ
Frühlingsstimmen, Op. 410. Annen, Op. 117. Wo die Zitronen blü'n, Op. 364. Perpetuum mobile,
Op. 257. Persischer Marsch, Op. 289. Künsterleben, Op. 316. Vergnügungszug, Op. 281. Wein, Weib
und Gesang, Op. 333. Tritsch-Tratsch, Op. 214. G'schichten aus dem Wienerwald, Op. 325. **Joseph**
Strauss. *Dorfschwalben aus Osterreich, Op. 164.* **Vienna Opera Orchestra/Carl Michalski.**
Rose Collection 3209 — . lh l0m DDD 7/93 Ⓑ

J. Strauss II. COMPLETE EDITION, Volume 17. **Bratislava Radio Symphony
Orchestra/Alfred Eschwé.** Marco Polo 8 223217. Recorded in 1989.
Freiheits–Leider, Op. 52. Armenball, Op. 176. Melodien–Quadrille (on themes by Verdi),
Op. 112. Windsor–Klänge, Op. 104. 's gibt nur a Kaiserstadt!, 's gibt nur a Wien, Op. 291.
Bürgersinn, Op. 295. Liebchen, schwing dich, Op. 394. Feenmärchen, Op. 312. Fest–Polonaise,
Op. 352. Adelen–Walzer, Op. 424. Violetta, Op. 404. Kaiser Franz Joseph Marsch, Op. 67.

.•* lh 14m DDD 10/92 Ⓠp

J. Strauss II. COMPLETE EDITION, Volume 27. **Austrian Radio Symphony
Orchestra, Vienna/Peter Guth.** Marco Polo 8 223227. Recorded in 1991.
Künstler–Quadrille, Op. 71. Drollerie–Polka, Op. 231. Aeolstöne–Walzer, Op. 68.
Express–Polka schnell, Op. 311. Gruss an Wien–Polka française, Op. 225. Souvenir de
Nizza–Walzer, Op. 200. Spanischer Marsch, Op. 433. Annina–Polka Mazurka, Op. 415. Wein,
Weib und Gesang–Walzer, Op. 333. Sans-Souci–Quadrille, Op. 63. Durchs Telephon–Polka,
Op. 439. Frühlingsstimmen–Walzer, Op. 410·

.•* lh 9m DDD 8/92 Ⓠp Ⓠs Ⓑ

Balancing the familiar and unfamiliar, individual volumes of Marco Polo's complete Johann
Strauss Edition have inevitably varied in their appeal. However, the freshness of impact that
comes from unfamiliarity often outweighs any lesser invention. What is far more striking about
the series has been the variation in approach and grasp of idiom of the conductors. The two
here, both Viennese-trained but with slightly different approaches, come out very much at the
top of the range. Alfred Eschwé's style is essentially a relaxed one, though he understands the
crucial importance of differentiating one dance tempo from another. Having done so, he
encourages the music to speak for itself, allowing the waltzes to breathe and flow with a lilt too
often missing from conductors who seek to impose themselves on the music. For all their
unfamiliar titles, the contents too are a delight. The *Windsor-Klänge* waltzes, composed for a ball
at the British Embassy in Vienna, are splendid, and the quick polka *'s gibt nur a Kaiserstadt!* can
seldom have been so excitingly played. Perhaps even better, though, is the collection by the
Austrian Radio Symphony Orchestra under its leader Peter Guth. In quality of contents,
sensitivity of conducting, sprightliness of playing and clarity of recorded sound alike this is
outstanding. One marvels anew at how Vienna orchestras seem to have this music in their
blood. Under Guth they manage not merely extra lilt, but extra lift. Even in the more familiar
items such as *Frühlingsstimmen* and, above all, *Wein, Weib und Gesang* Guth has little to fear from
comparisons. In the latter waltz he brings out details that are usually unheard and he makes
more of its long introduction than perhaps any previous recording. Among the less familiar
items, the waltzes *Aeolstöne* and *Souvenir de Nizza* and the polkas *Gruss an Wien* and *Express*
(familiar for its use in the ballet *Graduation Ball*) are outstandingly enjoyable.

J. Strauss II. DIE FLEDERMAUS. **Dame Elisabeth Schwarzkopf** (sop) Rosalinde; **Rita
Streich** (sop) Adele; **Nicolai Gedda** (ten) Eisenstein; **Helmut Krebs** (ten) Alfred; **Erich
Kunz** (bar) Doctor Falke; **Rudolf Christ** (ten) Orlovsky; **Karl Dönch** (bar) Frank; **Erich
Majkut** (ten) Blind; **Luise Martini** (sop) Ida; **Franz Böheim** (bar) Frosch; **Philharmonia
Chorus and Orchestra/Herbert von Karajan.** EMI CHS7 69531-2. From Columbia
33CX1309-10 (11/55). Recorded in 1955.

.•* ② lh 50m ADD 11/88 Ⓠp Ⓑ ▲

Anyone less concerned with modernity of sound than with enjoying a well-proven, classic
interpretation of Strauss's operetta masterpiece can readily be recommended to EMI's 1955
recording. Herbert von Karajan, whose preference for slow tempos and beauty of sound above all
else was then still in the future, here directs with affection and *élan*. Amongst the principals

Elisabeth Schwarzkopf leads the cast majestically and ravishingly. Notably in the *Csárdás*, her firm lower notes swell gloriously into a marvellously rich and individual register. As her maid, Adele, Rita Streich is an agile-voiced, utterly charming foil, launching her "Laughing Song" with deliciously credible indignation. Nicolai Gedda also enters into the fun with supreme effect. Throughout he sings with youthful ardour and freshness, but he also has a high old time impersonating the stammering Blind in the Act 3 trio. Erich Kunz's rich, characterful baritone is also heard here to good effect as Doctor Falke, the character who arranges the 'bat's revenge' which forms the story of *Die Fledermaus*. Unconventionally, the young Prince is played by a tenor rather than the mezzo-soprano for whom the role was written. Purists may object, but the result is dramatically convincing, and musically could hardly be bettered when the singer is the sweet-toned Rudolf Christ. Altogether this set can still rival any later one in theatrical effectiveness and EMI have done a good job in refurbishing it, with the disc-break sensibly placed between Acts 1 and 2.

Additional recommendations ...

Die Fledermaus. **Soloists; Bavarian State Opera Chorus and Orchestra/Carlos Kleiber.** DG 415 646-2GH2 — .⁚ ② 1h 47m ADD 12/86 ⁹ₚ Ⓑ

Die Fledermaus (with Gala Sequence). **Soloists; Vienna State Opera Chorus and Orchestra/ Herbert von Karajan.** Decca 421 046-2DH2 — .⁚ 2h 23m ADD 12/87 ⁹ₚ Ⓑ ▲

Die Fledermaus. **Soloists; Philharmonia Chorus and Orchestra/Otto Ackermann.** Classics for Pleasure CD-CFPD4702 — .. ② 1h 53m ADD 2/89 Ⓑ

Die Fledermaus. **Vienna State Opera Chorus; Vienna Philharmonic Orchestra/André Previn.** Philips 432 157-2PH2 — .⁚ ② 1h 52m DDD 9/91 ⁹ₚ ⁹ₛ Ⓑ

Die Fledermaus[a]. New Year's Day Concert in Vienna, 1951[b] — *G'schichten aus dem Wienerwald–Waltz, Op. 325. Im Krapfenwald'l–Polka française, Op. 336. Eljen a Magyar!–Polka, Op. 332. Egyptischer Marsch, Op. 335. Vergnügungszug–Polka Galop, Op. 281.* **J. Strauss II/Josef Strauss:** Pizzicato Polka. **Josef Strauss:** *Mein Lebenslauf ist Lieb und Lust–Waltz, Op. 263. Die Libelle–Polka mazur, Op. 204. Jockey–Polka schnell, Op. 278.* **Soloists; Vienna State Opera Chorus; Vienna Philharmonic Orchestra/Clemens Krauss.** Decca Historic Series mono 425 990-2DM2 — .⁚ ② 2h 17m ADD 10/92 ⁹ₚ Ⓑ ▲

Die Fledermaus. **Soloists; Netherlands Opera Chorus; Concertgebouw/Harnoncourt.** Teldec 4509-91974-2 — .⁚ 1h 12m DDD 7/93 Ⓑ

Further listening ...

New Year's Day Concert in Vienna, 1987: DIE FLEDERMAUS — Overture. Annen–Polka, Op. 117. Vergnügungszug–Polka, Op. 281. Unter Donner und Blitz–Polka, Op. 324. Frühlingsstimmen–Waltz, Op. 410ᵃ. An die schönen blauen Donau–Waltz, Op. 314. *Coupled with* **J. Strauss I.** Beliebte Annen–Polka, Op. 137. Radetzky March, Op. 228. **J. Strauss II/Josef Strauss.** Pizzicato Polka. **Josef Strauss.** Sphärenklänge–Waltz, Op. 235. Delirien–Waltz, Op. 212. Ohne Sorgen–Polka, Op. 271. **Kathleen Battle** (sop); **Vienna Philharmonic Orchestra/Herbert von Karajan.** DG 419 616-2GH (11/87).

New Year's Day Concert in Vienna, 1989: Accelerationen–Waltz, Op. 234. Bauern–Polka, Op. 276. DIE FLEDERMAUS — Overture. Künstlerleben–Waltz, Op. 316. Eljen a Magyar!–Polka, Op. 322. Im Krapfenwald'l–Polka française, Op. 336. Frühlingsstimmen–Waltz, Op. 410. RITTER PASMAN — Csárdás. An die schönen blauen Donau–Waltz, Op. 314. *Coupled with* **J. Strauss I.** Radetzky March, Op. 228. **J. Strauss II/Josef Strauss.** Pizzicato Polka. **Josef Strauss.** Die Libelle–Polka Mazur, Op. 204. Moulinet–Polka française, Op. 57. Plappermäulchen–Polka schnell, Op. 245. Jockey–Polka schnell, Op. 278. **Vienna Philharmonic Orchestra/Carlos Kleiber.** Sony Classical SK45938 (2/91).

Richard Strauss
German 1864-1949

R. Strauss. ORCHESTRAL WORKS, Volume 1. ᵃᵇ**Peter Damm** (hn); ᶜ**Manfred Clement** (ob); ᵈ**Manfred Weise** (cl); ᵈ**Wolfgang Liebscher** (bn); ᵉ**Malcolm Frager** (pf); ᶠᵍ**Peter Rösel** (pf); **Staatskapelle Dresden/Rudolf Kempe.** EMI CMS7 64342-2. Items marked abcdefg from HMV SLS5067 (10/76), ʰ SLS894 (3/75), ⁱSLS861 (10/73), ʲSLS880 (6/74).

Horn Concertos — No. 1 in E flat major, Op. 11[a]; No. 2 in E flat major, AV132[b]. Oboe Concerto, AV144[c]. Duet Concertino, AV147[d]. Burleske in D minor, AV85[e]. Parergon, Op. 73[f]. Panathenäenzug Symphonic Study in the form of a Passacaglia, Op. 74[g]. Till Eulenspiegels lustige Streiche, Op. 28[h]. Don Juan, Op. 20[i]. Ein Heldenleben, Op. 40[j].

 3h 44m ADD 12/92

R. Strauss. ORCHESTRAL WORKS, Volume 2. [a]**Ulf Hoelscher** (vn); **Staatskapelle Dresden/Rudolf Kempe.** EMI CMS7 64346-2. Items marked [a] from HMV SLS5067 (10/76), [bfi]SLS894 (3/75), [cgh]SLS861 (10/73), [de]SLS880 (6/74).
Violin Concerto in D minor, Op. 8[a]. Sinfonia domestica, Op. 53[b]. Also sprach Zarathustra, Op. 30[c]. Tod und Verklärung, Op. 24[d]. Der Rosenkavalier — Waltzes[e]. Salome — Dance of the Seven Veils[f]. Le bourgeois gentilhomme — Suite, Op. 60[g]. Schlagobers — Waltz[h]. Josephslegende — Suite[i].

 3h 42m ADD 12/92

R. Strauss. ORCHESTRAL WORKS, Volume 3. [c]**Paul Tortelier** (vc); [e]**Max Rostal** (va); **Staatskapelle Dresden/Rudolf Kempe.** EMI CMS7 64350-2. Items marked [abd] from HMV SLS861 (10/73), [c] SLS894 (3/75), [ef] SLS880 (6/74).
Metamorphosen for 23 Solo Strings, AV142[a]. Eine Alpensinfonie, Op. 64[b]. Aus Italien, Op. 16[c]. Macbeth, Op. 23[d]. Don Quixote, Op. 35[e]. Dance Suite on Keyboard Pieces by François Couperin, AV107[f].

 3h 28m ADD 12/92

"From the store of glorious memories of my artistic career, the tones of this master orchestra ever evoke feelings of deepest gratitude and admiration" (thus spoke Richard Strauss when greeting the Dresden Orchestra in 1948 on its 400th Anniversary). You get the feeling that this orchestra is justifiably proud of its tones, and its Straussian associations; it takes only a few minutes of the wind concertos disc (the first CD in Volume 1), with the principals as soloists, to be aware of those tones, and to detect a special radiance that probably derives from that pride. Kempe, it seems, was the man to draw it out, and give it purpose; after his *Till Eulenspiegel*, for example, virtually all others either affect character, or are characterless. Some may find Kempe an occasionally circumspect Straussian, one who preferred decorum to decibels in the protracted cacophony that concludes the *Sinfonia domestica*, and who ensures that the famous "2001" opening to *Also sprach Zarathustra* isn't so awesome that the rest of the piece is an anti-climax. Neither did he have at his disposal the saturated sonorities of the Berlin Philharmonic that supported Karajan's breadth and power. It is difficult, though, to think of many other Straussians with the imagination and understanding to bring these scores to life from within. To catalogue Kempe's Straussian credentials would take up more space than is available; suffice it to say that, like Fritz Reiner, clarity of texture and a natural flexibility of pacing were prerequisites for the characterful animation and interaction of orchestral soloists or instrumental groups, but never at the expense of the long-term direction of the music. His technique, too, ensured the kind of feats of ensemble and precision that you might have expected from the Chicago Symphony Orchestra under Reiner, but Kempe's orchestra, of course, retains its warmer and cherishably Old World tones.

There are many self-evidently great Strauss performances here. A lithe, demon-driven *Don Juan*; perhaps the most vital and communicative *Don Quixote* ever recorded (greatly ennobled by Tortelier's presence); and *Ein Heldenleben* whose hero is drawn with humanity, even vulnerability and self-doubt (the reaction to the critics is unbearably sad; the scene with the hero's wife, properly reactive) and the ideal choice for those who find the work's egotism unpalatable. EMI have mixed the familiar with the unfamiliar in each box, and dedicated Straussians will find the by-ways explored with comparable commitment and skill. The recordings, made between 1970 and 1975 (the year before Kempe's premature death), vary in perspective from an ideally distanced, natural layout (*Till* and *Aus Italien*), to the closer and slightly 'contained' (*Eine Alpensinfonie* and *Ein Heldenleben*), and the vividly present (*Le bourgeois gentilhomme* and *Metamorphosen*). Clear, light-toned timpani with very little bass resonance further enhance Kempe's precise rhythmic control (even though they sound like tom-toms at the start of *Also sprach Zarathustra*), and soloists are invariably up-front, but rarely at the expense of orchestral detail. The whole invaluable enterprise benefits from the warm acoustics of the Lukaskirche in Dresden.

Additional recommendations ...

Horn Concertos. Weber. *Concertino for Horn and Orchestra in E minor, J188.* **Hermann Bauman** (hn); **Leipzig Gewandhaus Orchestra/Kurt Masur.** Philips 412 237-2PH — .ꞏ' DDD 6/85 ꝙₚ

Horn Concertos[a]. Hindemith. *Horn Concerto[b].* **Dennis Brain** (hn); **Philharmonia Orchestra/[a]Wolfgang Sawallisch;** [b]**Paul Hindemith.** EMI CDC7 47834-2 — .ꞏ' 49m ADD 10/87 ꝙₚ ▲

Metamorphosen for 23 Solo Strings. Tod und Verklärung. **Berlin Philharmonic Orchestra/ Herbert von Karajan.** DG 410 892-2GH — .ꞏ' 52m DDD 2/84

Don Juan. Tod und Verklärung. Also sprach Zarathustra. **Vienna Philharmonic Orchestra/ Herbert von Karajan.** Decca Ovation 417 720-2DM — .ꞏ' 1h 15m ADD 12/87 ꝙₚ ⒷⒾ ▲

Don Juan. Tod und Verklärung. Till Eulenspiegel. **London Philharmonic Orchestra/Karl Rickenbacher.** Classics for Pleasure CD-CFP4592 — .ꞏ 55m DDD ꝙₚ Ⓑ

Metamorphosen for 23 Solo Strings. Tod und Verklärung, Op. 24. Drei Hymnen, Op. 71[a]. [a]**Felicity Lott** (sop); **Scottish National Orchestra/Neeme Järvi.** Chandos CHAN8734 — .ꞏ' 1h 12m DDD 3/90

Aus Italien. Don Juan. **Berlin Philharmonic Orchestra/Riccardo Muti.** Philips 422 399-2PH — .ꞏ' 1h 1m DDD 9/90 Ⓑ

Don Juan. Don Quixote[a]. [a]**Franz Bartolomey** (vc); [a]**Heinrich Koll** (va); **Vienna Philharmonic Orchestra/André Previn.** Telarc CD80262 — .ꞏ' 1h DDD 10/91 ꝙₛ Ⓑ

Metamorphosen for 23 Solo Strings. **Schoenberg.** *Verklärte Nacht.* **Wagner.** *Siegfried Idyll.* **Sinfonia Varsovia/Emmanuel Krivine.** Denon CO-79442 — .ꞏ' 1h 4m DDD 12/92 Ⓑ

Don Quixote. Salome — Dance of the Seven Veils. **Miklos Perényi** (vc); **László Bársony** (va); **Hungarian State Orchestra/János Ferencsik.** Hungaroton White Label HRC081 — . 49m ADD Ⓑ

Also sprach Zarathustra. Ein Heldenleben, Op. 40. **Chicago Symphony Orchestra/Fritz Reiner.** RCA 09026 61494-2 — .ꞏ' 1h 16m ADD 4/93 ꝙₚ Ⓑ ▲

Metamorphosen for 23 Solo Strings. **Schoenberg.** *Verklärte Nacht.* **Wagner.** *Siegfried Idyll.* **Berlin Philharmonic Orchestra/James Levine.** DG 435 883-2GH — .ꞏ' 1h 19m DDD 8/93 Ⓑ

Oboe Concerto[a]. Violin Concerto[b]. Duett-Concertino[c]. [a]**Gordon Hunt** (ob); [b]**Boris Belkin** (vn); [c]**Dmitri Ashkenazy** (cl); [c]**Kim Walker** (bn); **Berlin Radio Symphony Orchestra/ Vladimir Ashkenazy.** Decca 436 415-2DH — .ꞏ' 1h 16m DDD 3/94

Metamorphosen for 23 Solo Strings. **Honegger.** *Symphony No. 2.* **Webern.** *Langsamer Satz (trans. Schwarz).* **Seattle Symphony Orchestra/Gerard Schwarz.** Delos DE3121 — .ꞏ' 1h 11m DDD 4/94 Ⓑ

New review

R. Strauss. COMPLETE MUSIC FOR WIND. [c]**Heinz Holliger** (ob); [ab]**Netherlands Wind Ensemble;** [c]**New Philharmonia Orchestra/Edo de Waart.** Philips 438 733-2PM2. Items marked [a] from 6500 097 (12/71), [b]6500 297 (10/72), [c]6500 174 (1/72). Recorded 1970-71. *Serenade, Op. 7[a]. Suite in B flat major, Op. 4[b]. Sonatina No. 1 in F major, "Aus der Werkstatt eines Invaliden", AV135[b]. Sonatina No. 2 in E flat major, "Fröhlicher Werkstatt", AV143[a]. Oboe Concerto, AV144[c].*

.ꞏ' ② 2h 12m ADD 7/94 ꝙₚ

Given the very positive projection of London Winds' Hyperion set, these classic performances of a previous generation should find a special niche in the catalogue. Advances in technology have made them sound more contained than one remembered, but there is much to be said for an intimate balance in these works. The Op. 7 *Serenade* is typical of the Ensemble at their best. Textures are blended with evident care, nothing is overbearing or ill-tuned, and there are appropriate premonitions of the later, 'autumnal' Strauss. The Op. 4 Suite comes off slightly less well; the sound-stage seems a little overcrowded and the music-making a little 'straight'. Edo de Waart's direction of the *Sonatina No. 1, Aus der Werkstatt eines Invaliden*, is outstandingly success-ful, more than just precise. Like Michael Collins and the London Winds, the Dutch group excels in the *Sonatina No. 2, Fröhlicher Werkstatt*; its outer movements are comparatively relaxed in mood, with the *Andantino* and minuet unobtrusively nuanced. As an added inducement, Philips have appended Heinz Holliger's 1970 recording of the Oboe Concerto to the complete music for winds. It is as expert as you might expect, though not exactly overflowing with charm. The transfers are excellent and there are full notes. Warmly recommended at mid price.

Additional recommendations ...
Suite in B flat major. Sonatina No. 1. **Norwegian Wind Ensemble/Gerard Oskamp.** Victoria
VCD19045 — ⸰⸱·' 1h 2m DDD 8/92
Suite in B flat major. Sonatinas Nos. 1 and 2. Serenade. **London Winds/Michael Collins.**
Hyperion CDA66731/2 — ⸰⸱·' ② 1h 45m DDD 8/93

R. Strauss. Divertimento, Op. 86. Le bourgeois gentilhomme — Suite, Op. 60. **Orpheus Chamber Orchestra.** DG 435 871-2GH. Recorded in 1991.

⸰⸱·' **1h 8m DDD 3/93**

This coupling should give much pleasure to those prepared to take a little New World zest and stringency with their Strauss; despite the absence of a conductor, there is nothing remotely bland or mechanical about the playing. The little-known *Divertimento* is often confused with the similar-sounding *Dance Suite* of 1923, also based on Couperin originals. The *Divertimento* came together as late as 1943 and has never established a firm place in the repertoire. Until now: the Orpheus Chamber Orchestra is mightily impressive here, eclipsing previous exponents by restoring something of the freshness of Couperin's *Pièces de clavecin* to Strauss's outrageous realizations. Behind the inauthentic, chocolate-box sonorities lurks an affecting undercurrent of nostalgia and there are obvious links with *Capriccio*'s pastiche of Passepied, Gigue and Gavotte. *Le bourgeois gentilhomme* is of course the stronger score and this stylish account of the suite is absolutely complete, unlike some famous versions of the past. Again, the players are on world-beating form, lacking perhaps the very last ounce of charm and flexibility but compensating with a dazzling display of technique. Sensitive microphone placement minimizes the problems of an over-resonant venue. This is modern music-making at its best.

R. Strauss. Eine Alpensinfonie, Op. 64. Don Juan, Op. 20. **San Francisco Symphony Orchestra/Herbert Blomstedt.** Decca 421 815-2DH. Recorded in 1988.

⸰⸱·' **1h 10m DDD 6/90**

The *Alpine* Symphony is the last of Richard Strauss's great tone-poems and is in many ways the most spectacular. The score is an evocation of the changing moods of an alpine landscape and the huge orchestral apparatus of over 150 players encompasses quadruple wind, 20 horns, organ, wind machine, cowbells, thunder machine, two harps and enhanced string forces. Its pictorialism may be all too graphic but what virtuosity and inspiration Strauss commands. Herbert Blomstedt's reading penetrates beyond the pictorialism into the work's deeper elements. It emerges as a gigantic hymn to nature on a Mahlerian scale. Tempos are slower, but these are justified by the noble expansiveness of the final pages, towards which the whole performance moves with impressive inevitability. The San Francisco Symphony's playing is magnificent, with subtle use of vibrato by the strings and superb performances, individual and corporate, by the wind sections. The recording is on a spacious scale to match the performance, the big climaxes really thrilling and the whole well balanced. The *Don Juan* performance is fine too.

Additional recommendations ...
Eine Alpensinfonie. **Concertgebouw Orchestra/Bernard Haitink.** Philips 416 156-2PH —
⸰⸱·' 50m DDD 7/86 ♀ₚ ♀ₛ Ⓑ
Eine Alpensinfonie[a]. *Songs*[b] — *Freundliche Vision, Op. 48 No. 1; Meinem Kinde, Op. 37 No. 3; Das Bächlein, Op. 88 No. 1; Morgen!, Op. 27 No. 4.* [a]**Felicity Lott** (sop); [b]**Edwin Paling** (pf); **Scottish National Orchestra/Neeme Järvi.** Chandos CHAN8557 — ⸰⸱·' 1h 1m DDD 12/87 ♀ₚ Ⓑ
Eine Alpensinfonie. Der Rosenkavalier — Suite[a]. [a]**Augmented Tivoli Orchestra, Bavarian State Orchestra/Richard Strauss.** Koch Legacy mono 37132-2 — ⸰⸱·' 1h 12m ADD 1/93 ♀ₚ Ⓑ ▲

R. Strauss. Ein Heldenleben, Op. 40. **Berlin Philharmonic Orchestra/Herbert von Karajan.** DG 415 508-2GH.

⸰⸱·' **47m DDD 4/86**

Karajan brings a particular wealth of experience to Strauss's exuberant account of a hero's life. The hero is of course Strauss himself and the heroine, his wife, but this is no Nietzschean superman; in Karajan's third stereo recording the characterization of the carping critics is as sharp as ever and the legendary Pauline provokes as well as consoles (with close-miked soloist Leon Spierer playing it deliberately straight). Perhaps the hero's exploits on the battlefield lack the last ounce of vigour and athleticism, but then this is an older man's view and there is surely ample compensation in the Berliners' rich yet detailed sonorities. Even here, after a slow start, the excitement builds in masterly fashion and there is a tremendous climax. Throughout the piece, Karajan's control of line never falters; phrases are long and immaculately tailored. There is never any danger of this life collapsing into a series of minutely characterized but disparate incidents. DG's recording brings an inconsistent, rather close focus at times and playing time is less than generous. Nevertheless, the magnificent overall sweep and glorious orchestral response make this a very special issue for admirers of an opulent brand of music-making which it has become fashionable to deprecate as heartless or insincere. Although no true Straussian will be without other versions, Karajan is still the major claimant for supremacy.

Additional recommendations ...

Ein Heldenleben. Don Juan. **Berlin Philharmonic Orchestra/Herbert von Karajan.** DG Galleria 429 717-2GGA — .·' ADD ⁹ₚ Ⓑ ▲

Ein Heldenleben. **Staatskapelle Dresden/Herbert Blomstedt.** Denon C37-7561 — .·' 46m DDD 12/84 ⁹ₚ ⁹ₛ Ⓑ

Ein Heldenleben. Macbeth, Op. 23. **Staatskapelle Dresden/Rudolf Kempe.** EMI Studio CDM7 69171-2 — .·' 1h 4m ADD 5/88 ⁹ₚ Ⓑ

Ein Heldenleben. Don Juan. **Vienna Philharmonic Orchestra/Clemens Krauss.** Decca Historic mono 425 993-2DM — .·' 59m ADD 9/92 ⁹ₚ Ⓑ ▲

Also sprach Zarathustra. Ein Heldenleben. **Chicago Symphony Orchestra/Fritz Reiner.** RCA Living Stereo 09026 61494-2 — .·' 1h 16m ADD 4/93 ⁹ₚ Ⓑ

Ein Heldenleben. Till Eulenspiegels lustige Streiche. **Cleveland Orchestra/Christoph von Dohnányi.** Decca 436 444-2DH — .·' 1h 1m DDD 10/93 Ⓑ

R. Strauss. Till Eulenspiegels lustige Streiche, Op. 28. Ein Heldenleben, Op. 40. **Chicago Symphony Orchestra/Daniel Barenboim.** Erato 2292-45621-2.

.·' 1h 3m DDD 8/91 ⁹ₚ ⁹ₛ Ⓑ

This disc kicks off with Barenboim's suave reading of *Till Eulenspiegel*. The performance is brilliant, combining tenderness (as in the introduction) with exuberance. His pacing and judging of the tricky corners is exemplary and his approach shows an awareness that this above all is a young man's music. For sheer splendour and opulence it is quite staggering. Barenboim's hero in *Ein Heldenleben* is impetuous and romantic and he gives the Chicago Symphony Orchestra a free rein to bring their customary flair and virtuosity to the work. The battle sequence is properly exciting while Samuel Magad's violin solo is sweet and seductive. This reading is a major claimant for supremacy. Erato have given Barenboim a big full sound, eminently suited to the music. The entire recording is very fine, with plenty of inner detail and for sheer opulence and splendour it surpasses other versions.

Additional recommendations ...

Till Eulenspiegels lustige Streiche. Ein Heldenleben. **London Symphony Orchestra/Michael Tilson Thomas.** CBS CD44817 — .·' 1h 3m DDD 5/89 ⁹ₚ ⁹ₛ Ⓑ

Ein Heldenleben[a]. Don Juan, Op. 20[b]. Till Eulenspiegels lustige Streiche[c]. [a]**Philadelphia Orchestra/Eugene Ormandy;** [bc]**Cleveland Orchestra/George Szell.** Sony Classical Essential Classics MK48272 — .· 1h 15m ADD 5/93 ⁹ₚ Ⓑ

New review

R. Strauss. Deutsche Motette, Op. 62[a]. Zwei Gesänge, Op. 34. An den Baum Daphne (epilogue to "Daphne"), AV137[b]. Die Göttin im Putzzimmer, AV120. [a]**Tina Kiberg,** [b]**Marianne Lund** (sops); [b]**Christian Lisdorf** (treb); [a]**Randi Stene** (contr); [a]**Gert Henning-Jensen** (ten); [a]**Ulrik Cold** (bass); [b]**Copenhagen Boys' Choir; Danish National Radio Choir/Stefan Parkman.** Chandos CHAN9223. Texts and translations included. Recorded in 1993.

.·' 57m DDD 5/94

Under Stefan Parkman the Danish National Radio Choir have established a reputation second to none. Parkman handles his singers as if they were a fully fledged symphony orchestra; which is not at all inappropriate in this programme by the supreme master of orchestral colour. From the heart of the 16 chorus parts of the *Deutsche Motette* a further seven are projected by solo voices emerging imperceptibly from the midst of a dense, luxuriant texture. The depth of colour and range of emotions are every bit as extensive in these works as in the great orchestral tone-poems; indeed few orchestral tone-poems evoke dusk and sunset so vividly as "Der Abend", the first of the 1897 *Zwei Gesänge*. There is a wonderfully luminous soundscape here; a combination of superb compositional skill, sensitive musical direction, superlative choral singing and a warm, full-bodied recording.

New review

R. Strauss. Four Last Songs, AV150. Zueignung, Op. 10 No. 1. Morgen, Op. 27 No. 4. **Wagner.** Wesendonk Lieder. **Elisabeth Meyer-Topsøe** (sop); **Copenhagen Philharmonic Orchestra/Hans Norbert Bihlmaier.** Kontrapunkt 32156. Notes, texts and translations included. Recorded in 1993.

50m DDD l/94

New review

R. Strauss. Four Last Songs, AV150
Wagner. Wesendonk Lieder. Tristan und Isolde — Prelude and Liebestod. **Cheryl Studer** (sop); **Staatskapelle Dresden/Giuseppe Sinopoli.** DG 439 865-2GH. Texts and translations included.

lh lm DDD 7/94

Here is a discovery, perhaps the most promising *Jugendlich-Dramatische* soprano to burst on the scene since Cheryl Studer. With a full, glowing tone that soars easily above the stave without let or hindrance, an even line, and an innate feeling for a long phrase, Elisabeth Meyer-Topsøe has chosen repertory that shows off her gifts ideally. She sings the *Wesendonk Lieder* with a truly Wagnerian amplitude of phrase and a fair feeling for the text. You only have to hear the generosity of "Stehe still!", with vibrato used to enhance the expression (a lovely "Wesen in wesen", a refulgent close), or the passage starting "Wohl ich weiss es" in "Im Treibhaus" to hear these matters made manifest. Others have, of course, found deeper shades in the songs, but these will surely come to this young artist in time. Similarly the sense of valediction in the *Four Last Songs* can be more easily encompassed by maturer singing, but few have managed the long, tricky phrases of "Beim Schlafengehen" with such a long breath or such daring, exciting fullness. The Wagner is faithfully recorded. In the Strauss items, the voice sometimes seems to go out of focus and the orchestra is lacking real definition. The conducting and playing are always adequate but not quite of the calibre this aspiring artist deserves.

In the Strauss Cheryl Studer need hardly fear comparison with the best of her predecessors (below), largely because her voice, lyrical yet with dramatic overtones, seems near-ideal for Strauss and for this work in particular, quite apart from the sheer beauty and technical accomplishment of her singing. In the first two songs there is the necessary ecstasy and longing in her singing as Strauss reviews, elegiacally, his musical credo. As an exemplar of the rest one could cite the loving treatment in "September" of the phrases beginning "Langsam tut er", the singer's tone poised, the shading of the line perfectly natural. It is the seamless legato and lovely voice that again make "Beim Schlafengehen" so rewarding while, in the final song, Studer is suitably hushed and reflective. Sinopoli and the Staatskapelle Dresden provide ideal support for their singer with the playing in all these works as lyrically expressive as the singing above it, all tempos ideally judged. Similar praise can be given to the reading of the *Wesendonk Lieder*. Here, once again, one notes Studer's amazing combination of vocal mastery and interpretative insight. Every dynamic and expressive mark is scrupulously followed (listen to the *piano* at "Luft" and "Duft" in the second song) in the pursuit of seamless phrasing and a due attention to the text. Her Liebestod makes one eager for her to sing the role on stage, or at least on CD. The richness of her singing, the thorough mastery of German diction and phraseology, make this another special performance. Sinopoli's reading of the Prelude to *Tristan* is flowing, intense and spontaneous and the playing is predictably superb, all adding to the disc's worth. The recordings are for the most part happily spacious and well focused.

R. Strauss. LIEDER. OPERA EXCERPTS. **Lisa della Casa** (sop); **Vienna Philharmonic Orchestra/[a]Karl Böhm; [b]Rudolf Moralt, [c]Heinrich Hollreiser.** Decca Historic mono 425 959-2DM. Texts and translations included. Recorded 1953-54.

Four Last Songs, AV150 (from LW5056, 12/53)[a]. ARABELLA — Er ist der Richtige nicht (with Hilde Gueden, sop. LW5029, 10/53)[b]; Der Richtige so hab ich stets zu mir gesagt (Paul Schoeffler, bass-bar. LXT5017, 4/55)[c]; Das war sehr gut, Mandryka (Alfred Poell, bar. LW5029)[b]. ARIADNE AUF NAXOS — Es gibt ein Reich[c]. CAPRICCIO — Closing scene (Franz Bierbach, bass. Both LXT5017)[c].

⠶ 1h 7m ADD 4/90 ⓆP Ⓑ ▲

Strauss's *Four Last Songs* are a perfect summation of the composer's lifelong love-affair with the soprano voice deriving from the fact that he married a soprano, Pauline Ahna. They are also an appropriate and deeply moving farewell to his career as a composer and to the whole romantic tradition and they have inspired many glorious performances. In recent times there has been a tendency to linger unnecessarily over what are already eloquent enough pieces. Lisa Della Casa, in her naturally and lovingly sung performance under Karl Böhm (the first-ever studio recording of the pieces back in 1953) makes no such mistake. In this new incarnation this is a wonderful offering at medium price backed by other invaluable Strauss interpretations from the Swiss diva. Her particular gift is to sing the pieces in a natural, unforced manner with gloriously unfettered tone. Her and Böhm's tempos tend to be faster than those employed by most of her successors.

Additional recommendations ...
Four Last Songs. Cäcilie, Op. 27 No. 2. Morgen, Op. 27 No. 4. Wiegenlied, Op. 41 No. 1. Ruhe meine Seele, Op. 27 No. 1. Meinem Kinde, Op. 37 No. 3. Zueignung, Op. 10 No. 1 (orch. Heger). **Jessye Norman** (sop); **Leipzig Gewandhaus Orchestra/Kurt Masur.** Philips 411 052-2 — ⠶ DDD 2/84 ⓆP Ⓑ

Four Last Songs[a]. CAPRICCIO — Morgen mittag um Elf[a]. ARABELLA[b] — Ich danke, Fräulein ... Aber der Richtige; Mein Elemer; Sie wollen mich heiraten; Das war sehr gut (all with Anny Felbermayer, sop; Josef Metternich, bar). **Dame Elisabeth Schwarzkopf** (sop); **Philharmonia Orchestra/ [a]Otto Ackermann, [b]Lovro von Matačic.** EMI Références mono CDH7 61001-2 — ⠶ 1h 8m ADD 4/88 ⓆP Ⓑ ▲

Four Last Songs[a]. Metamorphosen for 23 Solo Strings. Oboe Concerto[b]. [a]Gundula Janowitz (sop); *[b]Lothar Koch* (ob); **Berlin Philharmonic Orchestra/Herbert von Karajan.** DG Galleria 423 888-2GGA — ⠶ 1h 15m ADD 12/88 ⓆP Ⓑ

Four Last Songs. Bach. Cantata No. 199, "Mein Herze schwimmt im Blut" (**Dame Elisabeth Schwarzkopf** (sop); **Philharmonia Orchestra/Thurston Dart**). *Mass in B minor, BWV232 — Christe eleison; Laudamus te; Et in unum Dominum* (**Dame Elisabeth Schwarzkopf; Kathleen Ferrier,** contr; **Vienna Philharmonic Orchestra/Herbert von Karajan**). *Mozart. Nehmt meinen Dank, K383* (**Dame Elisabeth Schwarzkopf; Philharmonia Orchestra/Alceo Galliera**). *Gieseking. Kinderlieder* (**Dame Elisabeth Schwarzkopf; Walter Gieseking,** pf). EMI CDM7 63655-2 — ⠶ 1h 19m ADD 12/90 ⓆP Ⓑ

Four Last Songs[a]. All' mein Gedanken, Op. 21 No. 1[b]. Allerseelen, Op. 10 No. 8[b]. Begegnung, AV72[b]. Cäcilie, Op. 27 No. 2[b]. Hat gesagt, Op. 36 No. 3[b]. Madrigal, Op. 15 No. 1[b]. Malven, Op. posth[b]. Morgen, Op. 27 No. 4[b]. Muttertändelei, Op. 43 No. 2[b]. Die Nacht, Op. 10 No. 3[b]. Schlechtes Wetter, Op. 69 No. 5[b]. Ständchen, Op. 17 No. 2[b]. Zueignung, Op. 10 No. 1[b]. **Dame Kiri Te Kanawa** (sop); **[a]Vienna Philharmonic Orchestra/Sir Georg Solti** ([b]pf). Decca 430 511-2DH — ⠶ 50m DDD 9/91 ⓆP Ⓠs Ⓑ

Four Last Songs[a]. Tod und Verklärung, Op. 24[b]. Wagner. GOTTERDAMMERUNG[c] — Dawn and Siegfried's Rhine Journey; Siegfried's Death and Funeral Music. **[a]Lucia Popp** (sop); **[ab]London Philharmonic Orchestra; [c]Berlin Philharmonic Orchestra/Klaus Tennstedt.** EMI Digital CDD7 64290-2 — ⠶ 1h 10m DDD 8/92 ⓆP Ⓑ

Four Last Songs. Cäcilie, Op. 27 No. 2. Morgen, Op. 27 No. 4. Wiegenlied, Op. 41 No. 1. Ruhe meine Seele, Op. 27 No. 1. Meinem Kinde, Op. 37 No. 3. Zueignung, Op. 10 No. 1 (orch. Heger). **Jessye Norman** (sop); **Leipzig Gewandhaus Orchestra/Kurt Masur.** Philips 411 052-2 — ⠶ 2/84 ⓆP Ⓑ

R. Strauss. LIEDER[a]. Metamorphosen for 23 Solo Strings. **[a]Gundula Janowitz** (sop); **Academy of London/Richard Stamp.** Virgin Classics VC7 59538-2. Texts and translations included.
Lieder — Ruhe, meine Seele, Op. 27 No. 1; Waldseligkeit, Op. 49 No. 1; Freundliche Vision, Op. 48 No. 1; Morgen!, Op. 27 No. 4; Befreit, Op. 39 No. 4; Meinem Kinde, Op. 37 No. 3;

Winterweihe, Op. 48 No. 4; Wiegenlied, Op. 41 No. 1; Die heiligen drei Könige aus Morgenland, Op. 56 No. 6.

Ih DDD 2/91

Gundula Janowitz has given some of the most beautiful performances of the music of Richard Strauss in the last three decades. Why no one asked her to record more songs during her heyday is a great mystery, but here is a quite lovely collection that shows her musicality and fine feeling for the Strauss idiom at its best. Obviously, given the passing of the years, she is happiest in the gentler, more legato numbers where her quite exquisite breath control and beauty of tone reap rich rewards — the floated line in *Wiegenlied* is absolutely ravishing and her feeling for words has, if anything, deepened over the years. She instils appropriate drama into the ecstatic *Die heiligen drei Könige aus Morgenland*, a lovely song. Throughout the disc the Academy of London play with great feeling and a good regard for the sound-world that Richard Strauss's music demands. As a very substantial fill-up, Richard Stamp and his orchestra offer a sensitive reading of Strauss's heartrending *Metamorphosen*, that threnody for the great opera-houses of Germany destroyed by Allied bombing during the Second World War. The complex lines are interwoven with care and sensitivity, and the work's true character emerges powerfully in this passionate performance. The recording is rich and clear. A delightful disc.

Additional recommendation ...
Lieder — Meinem Kinde; Morgen; Du meines Herzens Krönelein, Op. 21 No. 2; Ich schwebe wie auf Engelsschwingen, Op. 48 No. 2; Die Nacht, Op. 10 No. 3; Allerseelen, Op. 10 No. 8; Mein Auge, Op. 37 No. 4; Schön sind, doch kalt die Himmelssterne, Op. 19 No. 3; Ich wollt' ein Sträusslein binden, Op. 68 No. 2; Ständchen, Op. 17 No. 2. Coupled with **Wolf.** *Mörike Lieder — Der Knabe und das Immlein; Er ist's; Das verlassene Mägdlein; Begegnung; Nimmersatte Liebe; Verborgenheit. Eichendorff Lieder — Verschwiegene Liebe. Italienisches Liederbuch — Auch kleine Dinge. Spanisches Liederbuch — In dem Schatten meiner Locken. Bescheidene Liebe.* **Barbara Bonney** (sop); **Geoffrey Parsons** (pf). DG 429 406-2GH — ⸫ 55m DDD 8/90

R. Strauss. SALOME. **Cheryl Studer** (sop) Salome; **Bryn Terfel** (bar) Jokanaan; **Horst Hiestermann** (ten) Herod; **Leonie Rysanek** (sop) Herodias; **Clemens Bieber** (ten) Narraboth; **Marianne Rørholm** (contr) Page; **Friedrich Molsberger** (bass) First Nazarene; **Ralf Lukas** (bass) Second Nazarene; **William Murray** (bass) First Soldier; **Bengt Rundgren** (bass) Second Soldier; **Klaus Lang** (bar) Cappadocian; **Orchestra of the Deutsche Oper, Berlin/Giuseppe Sinopoli.** DG 431 810-2GH2. Notes, text and translation included. Recorded in 1990.

② Ih 42m DDD 9/91

Strauss's setting of a German translation of Oscar Wilde's play is original and erotically explicit. It caused a sensation in its day and even now stimulates controversy. This recording is a magnificent achievement, mainly because of Cheryl Studer's representation of the spoilt Princess who demands and eventually gets the head of Jokanaan (John the Baptist) on a platter as a reward for her striptease ("Dance of the Seven Veils"). Studer, her voice fresh, vibrant and sensuous, conveys exactly Salome's growing fascination, infatuation and eventual obsession with Jokanaan, ending in the arresting necrophilia of the final scene. She expresses Salome's wheedling, spoilt nature, strong will and ecstasy in tones apt for every aspect of the strenuous role. She is supported to the hilt by Sinopoli's incandescent conducting and by Bryn Terfel's convincing Jokanaan, unflaggingly delivered, by Hiestermann's neurotic Herod, who makes a suitably fevered, unhinged sound as the near-crazed Herod, and Rysanek's wilful Herodias. The playing is excellent and the recording has breadth and warmth. This is eminently recommendable. For a newcomer to the work, Studer's superb portrayal just tips the balance in favour of Sir Georg Solti's famous version in which Birgit Nilsson offers a gloriously sung Salome and the playing of the Vienna Philharmonia is ravishingly beautiful..

Additional recommendation ...
Soloists; Vienna Philharmonic Orchestra/Sir Georg Solti. Decca 414 414-2DH2 — ⸫ ② Ih 39m ADD 7/85

R. Strauss. ELEKTRA. **Birgit Nilsson** (sop) Elektra; **Regina Resnik** (mez) Klytemnestra; **Marie Collier** (sop) Chrysothemis; **Tom Krause** (bar) Orestes; **Gerhard Stolze** (ten)

Aegisthus; **Pauline Tinsley** (sop) Overseer; **Helen Watts** (contr), **Maureen Lehane,**
Yvonne Minton (mezs), **Jane Cook, Felicia Weathers** (sops) First, Second, Third, Fourth
and Fifth Maids; **Tugomir Franc** (Tutor); **Vienna Philharmonic Orchestra/Sir Georg**
Solti. Decca 417 345-2DH2. Notes, text and translation included. From SET354/5 (11/67).

② 1h 48m 12/86

Elektra is the most consistently inspired of all Strauss's operas and derives from Greek mythology,
with the ghost of Agamamenon, so unerringly delineated in the opening bars, hovering over the
whole work. The invention and the intensity of mood are sustained throughout the opera's one-
act length, and the characterization is both subtle and pointed. It is a work peculiarly well-suited
to Solti's gifts and he has done nothing better in his long career in the studios. He successfully
maintains the nervous tension throughout the unbroken drama and conveys all the power and
tension in Strauss's enormously complex score which is, for once, given complete. The recording captures the excellent singers and the Vienna Philharmonic in a warm, spacious acoustic
marred only by some questionable electronic effects.

Additional recommendations ...
Soloists; Bavarian Radio Chorus and Symphony Orchestra/Wolfgang Sawallisch.
EMI CDS7 54067-2 — ② 1h 42m DDD 12/90
Excerpts[a] — *Allein! Weh, ganz allein; Was willst du, fremder Mensch?; Elektra; Schwester! SALOME —*
Dance of the seven veils[b]; Ach, du wolltest mich nicht deinen Mund küssen lassen[c]. [ac]**Inge Borkh** (sop)
Elektra, Salome; [a]**Paul Schoeffler** (bass-bar) Orestes; [a]**Frances Yeend** (sop) Chrysothemis;
[a]**Chicago Lyric Opera Chorus; Chicago Symphony Orchestra/Fritz Reiner.** RCA Gold
Seal GD60874 — 1h 7m ADD 5/93 ▲
Soloists; Hamburg State Opera Chorus and Philharmonic Orchestra/Eugene
Jochum. Acanta mono 44 2128 — ② 1h 47m ADD 7/93

R. Strauss. DER ROSENKAVALIER. **Dame Elisabeth Schwarzkopf** (sop) Die
Feldmarschallin; **Christa Ludwig** (mez) Octavian; **Otto Edelmann** (bass) Baron Ochs;
Teresa Stich-Randall (sop) Sophie; **Eberhard Waechter** (bar) Faninal; **Nicolai Gedda**
(ten) Italian Tenor; **Kerstin Meyer** (contr) Annina; **Paul Kuen** (ten) Valzacchi; **Ljuba**
Welitsch (sop) Duenna; **Anny Felbermayer** (sop) Milliner; **Harald Pröghlöf** (bar)
Notary; **Franz Bierbach** (bass) Police Commissioner; **Erich Majkut** (ten) Marschallin's
Majordomo; **Gerhard Unger** (ten) Faninal's Majordomo, Animal Seller; **Karl Friedrich**
(ten) Landlord; **Loughton high School for Girls and Bancroft's School Choirs;**
Philharmonia Chorus and Orchestra/Herbert von Karajan. EMI CDS7 49354-2.
Notes, text and translation included. From Columbia SAX2269/72 (11/59). Recorded in 1956.

③ 3h 11m ADD 1/88 Ⓑ ▲

Der Rosenkavalier concerns the transferring of love of the young headstrong aristocrat Octavian
from the older Marschallin (with whom he is having an affair) to the young Sophie, a girl of
nouveau riche origins who is of his generation. The portrayal of the different levels of passion is
masterly and the Marschallin's resigned surrender of her ardent young lover gives opera one of
its most cherishable scenes. The comic side of the plot concerns the vulgar machinations of the
rustic Baron Ochs and his attempts to seduce the disguised Octavian (girl playing boy playing
girl!). The musical richness of the score is almost indescribable with stream after stream of
endless melody, and the final trio which brings the three soprano roles together is the crowning
glory of a masterpiece of our century. This magnificent 1956 recording, conducted with genius
by Karajan and with a cast such as dreams are made of, has a status unparalleled and is unlikely
to be challenged for many a year. The Philharmonia play like angels and Elisabeth Schwarzkopf
as the Marschallin gives one of her greatest performances. The recording, lovingly remastered,
is outstanding.

Additional recommendations ...
Soloists; Vienna State Opera Chorus; Vienna Philharmonic Orchestra/Sir Georg
Solti. Decca 417 493-2DH3 — ③ 3h 20m ADD 3/87 Ⓑ
Soloists; Dresden Kreuzchor; Dresden State Opera Chorus; Staatskapelle Dresden/
Bernard Haitink. EMI CDS7 54259-2 — ③ 3h 43m DDD 9/91 Ⓑ
(Abridged). **Soloists; Vienna State Opera Chorus; Vienna Philharmonic Orchestra/**
Robert Heger. DIE AEGPTISCHE HELENA — *Helen's awakening; Funeral march; Bei jener Nacht;*

Zweite Brautnacht, Zaubernacht!; **Rose Pauly** (sop); **Berlin State Opera Orchestra/Fritz Busch.** *Breit über mein Haupt, Op. 19 No. 2. Morgen, Op. 27 No. 4.* **Robert Hutt** (ten); **Richard Strauss** (pf). Pearl mono GEMMCDS9365 — ⊙ ② Ih 55m ADD 3/90 ⁹ₚ Ⓑ ▲

R. *Strauss.* ARIADNE AUF NAXOS. **Gundula Janowitz** (sop) Ariadne; **Teresa Zylis-Gara** (sop) Composer; **Sylvia Geszty** (sop) Zerbinetta; **James King** (ten) Bacchus; **Theo Adam** (bass-bar) Music Master; **Hermann Prey** (bar) Harlequin; **Siegfried Vogel** (bass) Truffaldino; **Hans Joachim Rotzsch** (ten) Brighella; **Peter Schreier** (ten) Scaramuchio, Dancing Master; **Erika Wustmann** (sop) Naiad; **Annelies Burmeister** (mez) Dryad; **Adele Stolte** (sop) Echo; **Erich-Alexander Winds** (spkr) Major-Domo; **Staatskapelle Dresden/ Rudolf Kempe.** EMI Opera CMS7 64159-2. Notes, text and translation included. From HMV SAN215/7 (11/68).

⊙ ② Ih 58m ADD II/92

At mid-price this classic set cannot be recommended too highly. Nobody knew more about how to pace Strauss's operas than Kempe and he was at his best when working with the Dresden Staatskapelle, a group of players who have Strauss in their veins. This reading brings out all the sentiment and high spirits of this delightful work, and the results are beautifully recorded. Janowitz's golden tones were ideal for the title role, which she sings with poise and inner feeling, though she makes little of the text. Zylis-Gara is a suitably impetuous Composer in the engaging Prologue where 'he' meets and has a gently erotic encounter with the charming but flighty Zerbinetta, a role here taken with brilliant accomplishment by Sylvia Geszty, who made it her own in the 1960s. James King is a forthright though none too flexible Bacchus. The smaller parts are also well taken. The piece has fared well on disc, and some may prefer the elegant Karajan version in mono on EMI with Elisabeth Schwarzkopf's highly detailed, silver-voiced Ariadne, Rita Streich's appealing Zerbinetta, Irmgard Seefried as the most impulsive of all Composers and Rudolf Schock as an ardent Bacchus, but Karajan's reading lacks the heart of Kempe's. The more recent Masur version, with the admirable Leipzig Gewandhaus, has Jessye Norman as a stately Ariadne, Julia Varady as a fiery Composer, Edita Gruberová as a bright-eyed, dexterous Zerbinetta, Paul Frey as an anonymous Bacchus. Masur, like Kempe, is steeped in the work's performing tradition and is the best of modern sets.

Additional recommendations ...
Soloists; Philharmonia Orchestra/Herbert von Karajan. EMI mono CMS7 69296-2 — ⊙ ② 2h 8m ADD 4/88 ▲
Soloists; Leipzig Gewandhaus Orchestra/Kurt Masur. Philips 422 084-2PH2 — ⊙ ② Ih 58m DDD II/88
Soloists; London Philharmonic Orchestra/Sir Georg Solti. Decca Grand Opera 430 384-2DM2 — ⊙ ② 2h Im ADD 5/92

R. *Strauss.* DIE FRAU OHNE SCHATTEN. **Julia Varady** (sop) Empress; **Plácido Domingo** (ten) Emperor; **Hildegard Behrens** (sop) Dyer's Wife; **José van Dam** (bar) Barak the Dyer; **Reinhild Runkel** (contr) Nurse; **Albert Dohmen** (bar) Spirit-Messenger; **Sumi Jo** (sop) Voice of the Falcon; **Robert Gambill** (ten) Apparition of a Young Man; **Elzbieta Ardam** (mez) Voice from above; **Eva Lind** (sop) Guardian of the Threshold; **Gottfried Hornik** (bar) One-eyed Brother; **Hans Franzen** (bass) One-armed Brother; **Wilfried Gahmlich** (ten) Hunchback Brother; **Vienna Boys' Choir; Vienna State Opera Chorus; Vienna Philharmonic Orchestra/Sir Georg Solti.** Decca 436 243-2DH3. Notes, text and translation included. Recorded 1989-91.

⊙ ③ 3h I5m DDD 5/92 ⁹ₚ ⁹ₛ

This was the most ambitious project on which Strauss and his librettist Hugo von Hofmannthal collaborated. It is both fairy tale and allegory with a score that is Wagnerian in its scale and breadth. The Solti version presents the score absolutely complete in an opulent recording that encompasses every detail of the work's multi-faceted orchestration. Nothing escapes his keen eye and ear or that of the Decca engineers. The cast boasts splendid exponents of the two soprano roles. Behrens's vocal acting suggests complete identification with the unsatisfied plight of the Dyer's Wife and her singing has a depth of character to compensate for some tonal wear. Varady gives an intense, poignant account of the Empress's taxing music. The others, though never less than adequate, leave something to be desired. Domingo sings the Emperor with customary vigour and strength but evinces little sense of the music's idiom. José van Dam is likewise a vocally impeccable Barak but never penetrates the Dyer's soul. Runkel is a mean, malign Nurse as she should be though she could be a little more interesting in this part. It benefits from glorious, dedicated playing by the Vienna Philharmonic Orchestra.

Additional recommendations ...
Soloists; Tölz Boys' Choir; Bavarian Radio Chorus and Symphony Orchestra/ Wolfgang Sawallisch. EMI CDS7 49074-2 — .·˙ ③ 3h 11m DDD 9/88 ⁹ₚ
Soloists; Vienna State Opera Chorus; Vienna Philharmonic Orchestra/Karl Böhm. Decca Historic 425 981-2DM3 — .·˙ ③ 3h 16m ADD 10/91 ⁹ₚ ▲

New review
R. Strauss. ARABELLA. **Julia Varady** (sop) Arabella; **Helen Donath** (sop) Zdenka; **Dietrich Fischer-Dieskau** (bar) Mandryka; **Walter Berry** (bass) Waldner; **Helga Schmidt** (mez) Adelaide; **Elfriede Höbarth** (sop) Fiakermilli; **Adolf Dallapozza** (ten) Matteo; **Hermann Winkler** (ten) Elemer; **Klaus-Jürgen Küper** (bar) Dominik; **Hermann Becht** (bar) Lamoral; **Doris Soffel** (mez) Fortune Teller; **Arno Lemberg** (spkr) Welko; **Bavarian State Opera Chorus; Bavarian State Orchestra/Wolfgang Sawallisch.** Orfeo C169882H. Notes, text and translation included. From EMI SLS5224 (10/81).

.·˙ ② 2h 22m DDD 1/89

Complete except for a brief cut in Matteo's part in Act 3, Sawallisch's 1981 EMI recording of *Arabella* has been easily fitted by Orfeo on two CDs. Sawallisch is the most experienced conductor of Strauss's operas alive today and at his best in this one, his tempos just right, his appreciation of its flavour (sometimes sentimental, at others gently ironic and detached) unequalled. Helen Donath's delightful Zdenka is a perfect foil for Varady's Arabella. Varady's singing of the title-role is characterful and intelligent. One should be left with ambivalent feelings about this heroine; is she lovable or a chilling opportunist? Or both? And while Fischer-Dieskau's singing of Mandryka has not the total security of his earlier DG recording of the role with Keilberth (listed below), he remains the best Mandryka heard since the war.

Additional recommendations ...
Soloists; London Philharmonic Orchestra/Sir Georg Solti. Decca Grand Opera 430 384-2DM — .·˙ ② 2h 1m ADD 5/92 ▲
Soloists; Bavarian State Opera Chorus and Orchestra/Joseph Keilberth. DG 437 700-2GX3 — .·˙ ③ 2h 39m ADD 8/93

Further listening ...

Intermezzo — Four Symphonic interludes. Capriccio — Sextet. Die Schweigsame Frau — Potpourri. Guntram — Prelude. Die Frau ohne Schatten — Symphonic fantasy.**Rotterdam Philharmonic Orchestra/Jeffrey Tate.** EMI CDC7 54581-2 (4/93).

CAPRICCIO. **Soloists; Philharmonia Orchestra/Wolfgang Sawallisch.** EMI mono CDS7 49014-8 (9/87).

Igor Stravinsky
Russian/French/American 1882-1971

New review
Stravinsky. Concerto for Piano and Wind Instruments[a]. Ebony Concerto[b]. Capriccio[a]. Movements[a]. [a]**Olli Mustonen** (pf); [b]**Dmitri Ashkenazy** (cl); **Deutsches Symphony Orchestra, Berlin/Vladimir Ashkenazy.** Decca 440 229-2DH.

.·˙ 55m DDD 1/94

Mustonen's hotfoot, balletic pianism pays high dividends in the colourful *Capriccio*, where both the solo writing and its execution are nimbly virtuosic. In the Concerto, Mustonen and Ashkenazy realize the music's innate neo-classicism and the piano is nicely incorporated among the winds, thus allowing us immediate aural access both to unfamiliar detail and to the full force of the Deutsches Symphony Orchestra's sonorous brass section. The *Capriccio* is a quixotic, brightly coloured score and finds Mustonen in an even more extrovert frame of mind. His is a lean but brilliant reading, where the first movement's fanciful solo flourishes are despatched with a winning combination of elegance and panache and where Ashkenazy fully matches his enthusiasm. Ashkenazy's *Ebony Concerto* must yield to the incomparable and spectacularly well recorded Benny Goodman/Stravinsky version. Salonen offers a taut rigorously disciplined *Symphonies of Wind Instruments*, and in so doing provides a useful, musically revealing (and relevant) companion to the Concerto. In other respects, though, Mustonen, Ashkenazy and their engineers have come up with an agreeable programme, one that presents Stravinsky as less dry — and perhaps less imposing — than he often sounds.

Additional recommendations ...
Concerto for Piano and Wind Instruments. Capriccio. Movements for Piano and Orchestra. Symphonies of wind instruments. **Paul Crossley** (pf); **London Sinfonietta/Esa-Pekka Salonen.** Sony Classical SK45797 — ,•' 54m DDD 10/90

Stravinsky. The Rite of Spring. Apollo. **City of Birmingham Symphony Orchestra/ Simon Rattle.** EMI CDC7 49636-2.

,•' Ih 5m DDD II/89   q|p Ⓑ

Recordings of *The Rite of Spring* are legion, but it is rare to find Stravinsky's most explosive ballet score coupled with *Apollo*, his most serene. The result is a lesson in creative versatility, confirming that Stravinsky could be equally convincing as expressionist and neoclassicist. Yet talk of lessons might suggest that sheer enjoyment is of lesser importance, and it is perfectly possible to relish this disc simply for that personal blend of the authoritative and the enlivening that Simon Rattle's CBSO recordings for EMI so consistently achieve. Rattle never rushes things, and the apparent deliberation of *The Rite*'s concluding "Sacrificial Dance" may initially surprise, but in this context it proves an entirely appropriate, absolutely convincing conclusion. Rattle sees the work as a whole, without striving for a spurious symphonic integration, and there is never for a moment any hint of a routine reading of what is by now a classic of the modern orchestral repertoire. The account of *Apollo* has comparable depth, with elegance transformed into eloquence and the CBSO strings confirming that they have nothing to fear from comparison with the best in Europe or America. The recordings are faithful to the intensity and expressiveness of Rattle's Stravinsky, interpretations fit to set beside those of the composer himself.

Additional recommendations ...
The Rite of Spring. **Mussorgsky.** Pictures at an Exhibition. **Concertgebouw Orchestra/ Riccardo Chailly.** Decca Ovation 430 709-2DM — ,•' Ih 6m DDD 8/91 q|p Ⓑ
The Rite of Spring. Fireworks, Op. 4. Circus Polka. Greeting Prelude, "Happy birthday to you". **London Philharmonic Orchestra/Sir Charles Mackerras.** EMI Eminence CD-EMX2188 — ,•' 42m DDD 8/92 Ⓑ
The Rite of Spring. Symphony in E flat major. Symphony in Three Movements. Symphony in C. Symphony of Psalms[a]. [a]**Festival Singers, Toronto; Columbia Symphony Orchestra;** [a]**CBC Symphony Orchestra/Igor Stravinsky.** Sony Classical CD46294 — ,•' ② 2h 22m ADD 8/92 q|p Ⓑ
The Rite of Spring. Petrushka. **London Philharmonic Orchestra/Bernard Haitink.** Philips Insignia 434 147-2PM — ,•' Ih 9m ADD 8/92 q|p q|s Ⓑ
The Rite of Spring. Four Etudes. Scherzo à la russe. **Philharmonia Orchestra/Eliahu Inbal.** Teldec Digital Experience 4509-91449-2 — ,•' 50m DDD 7/93 q|p Ⓑ
The Rite of Spring. Petrushka. **Oslo Philharmonic Orchestra/Mariss Jansons.** EMI CDC7 54899-2 — ,•' Ih 7m DDD 1/94 Ⓑ

Stravinsky. The Rite of Spring. Perséphone[a]. [a]**Anthony Rolfe Johnson** (ten); [a]**Anne Fournet** (narr); [a]**Tiffin Boys' Choir; London Philharmonic** [a]**Choir and Orchestra/Kent Nagano.** Virgin Classics Duo VCK7 59077. Notes, text and translation included.

,•' ② Ih 23m DDD 6/92   Ⓑ

The American composer Elliott Carter described *Perséphone* as "a humanist *Rite of Spring*", so this makes a logical and thought-provoking coupling (timings are not generous on the two CDs but they do come at mid-price). Although 20 years separate both works they could not be more different. The primal energy of the earlier *Rite of Spring*'s very naturalistic setting of scenes from pagan Russia is almost wholly absent from the cool, hieratic beauty of *Perséphone*'s ritual, and predominantly lyrical mode of address. The latter fuses elements of melodrama (literally, speech with music), oratorio and ballet, is set in classical Greece and has a text that is spoken and sung in French. Nagano's recording is the first to have appeared since Stravinsky's own 1966 account (part of the Stravinsky Edition but not one of the items to be made available separately) and is, in many ways, finer. A modern dynamic range predictably benefits the thrilling theatre of the choral invocation for Perséphone's return from the underworld in the third part of the work (culminating in a triple *forte* cry of "Printemps" as powerful as anything in the *Rite*); and both Anne Fournet in the spoken role of Perséphone, and Anthony Rolfe Johnson as the priest of the Eleusinian mysteries are preferable to their predecessors. Nagano's tempos are swifter than Stravinsky's which, in music that is predominantly slow moving, will be welcomed by many. Nagano's *Rite* is balletic and sharply emphatic; closely miked in a way often reminiscent of Stravinsky's own, with strongly projected woodwind and a crisp, forceful, though never heavy presence for the percussion. Other versions may remind us more powerfully of the work's extremism, but Nagano is often strikingly individual — one thinks of the almost reptilian coiling of clarinets at the end of the "Ritual of the Ancestors" — with more expressive phrasing and pacing than usual in the work's mysterious moments.

Stravinsky. Le baiser de la fée — Ballet.
Tchaikovsky (arr. Stravinsky). The Sleeping Beauty — Bluebird pas de deux. **Scottish National Orchestra/Neeme Järvi.** Chandos CHAN8360. Recorded in 1984.

♪ 5lm DDD 7/85

Le baiser de la fée ("The Fairy's Kiss") was Stravinsky's 1928 "compatriotic homage" to Tchaikovsky, using the latter's songs and piano music, and imitating parts of *The Sleeping Beauty*. The scenario is based on Andersen's tale *The Ice Maiden*, as according to Stravinsky "it suggested an allegory of Tchaikovsky himself. The fairy's kiss on the heel of the child is also the music marking Tchaikovsky at his birth, though the muse did not claim Tchaikovsky at his wedding, as she did the young man in the ballet, but at the height of his powers." What this hauntingly beautiful performance proves is that the work has never really had the recognition it deserves because, until this one, no recording has done it full justice. Stravinsky's own 1965 account is, by comparison, dutiful and has a very restricted dynamic range. There are fine accounts available of the *Divertimento*: a suite that Stravinsky later extracted from the ballet, but the complete work is a must, not least for the penultimate scene where the Fairy lures the young man from his wedding: after a passionate but strangely troubled *crescendo*, the Fairy throws off her veil of disguise to a *subito piano* dissonance (track three at 19'32") that chills you to the marrow. The coupling is apt, and great fun.

Stravinsky. The Firebird — Ballet. Scherzo à la russe (versions for jazz ensemble and orchestra). Quatre études (1952 version). **City of Birmingham Symphony Orchestra/ Simon Rattle.** EMI CDC7 49178-2.

♪ lh 5m DDD 4/89

Diaghilev chose *The Firebird* as the subject of the first ballet which he himself created for his own company. Lyadov's tardiness in delivering the musical score caused the great impresario to take a risk in transferring his commission to a young and inexperienced composer, but Stravinsky seized his first important opportunity to great effect, and the result was an early masterpiece. Simon Rattle emphasizes the work's romantic influences rather than those elements which suggest a composer who would soon take a radically new path. We are reminded that Rimsky-Korsakov was Stravinsky's teacher, and that he was influenced at the time by Scriabin and Glinka. On its own terms it is a very fine, illuminating performance, brilliantly colourful and superbly played by the Birmingham orchestra. The four *Etudes*, completed in 1929, are neoclassical in style and Rattle delivers these pithy, pungent little pieces with wit and clarity. It's interesting to hear both the original orchestral version of *Scherzo à la russe*, written in 1944, and the composer's own arrangement of this poker-faced piece for Paul Whiteman's band, made later the same year. Both seem equally effective in their different ways. The recording is very good indeed to match

a high-quality, highly sympathetic performance.

Additional recommendations ...
The Firebird. Le chant de rossignol — Symphonic Poem. Fireworks, Op. 4. Scherzo à la russe. Tango.
London Symphony Orchestra/Antál Dorati. Mercury 432 012-2MM — ,·' Ih 14m ADD 11/91 ९ₚ Ⓑ

The Firebird (1910 version). Scherzo fantastique. Fireworks. **Montreal Symphony Orchestra/ Charles Dutoit.** Decca 414 409-2DH — ,·' Ih 3m DDD 12/86 ९ₚ ९ₛ Ⓑ

The Firebird. Scherzo à la russe. **Berlin Philharmonic Orchestra/Bernard Haitink.** Philips 426 317-2PH — ,·' 51m DDD 12/91 ९ₚ Ⓑ

The Firebird. Apollon musagète. **Detroit Symphony Orchestra/Antál Dorati.** Decca Headline 430 740-2DM — ,·' Ih 14m DDD 8/92 Ⓑ

The Firebird. Le chant de rossignol. **Danish National Radio Symphony Orchestra/Dmitri Kitaienko.** Chandos CHAN8967 — ,·' Ih 17m DDD 9/92 Ⓑ

The Firebird. Fireworks, Op. 4. Four Etudes. **Chicago Symphony Orchestra/Pierre Boulez.** DG 437 850-2GH — ,·' Ih DDD 11/93 ९ₚ Ⓑ

The Firebird. Symphonies of Wind Instruments. **London Philharmonic Orchestra/Franz Welser-Möst.** EMI CDC5 55030 — ,·' 56m DDD 6/94 Ⓑ

New review
Stravinsky. Symphony in C major[a]. Symphonies of Wind Instruments[b]. Scherzo fantastique, Op. 3[c]. Symphony in Three Movements[a]. [a]**Suisse Romande Orchestra,** [bc]**Montreal Symphony Orchestra/Charles Dutoit.** Decca Ovation 436 474-2DM. Items marked [a] from SXDL7543 (6/82), [b] 414 202-2DH (4/85), [c] 414 409-1DH (10/86). Recorded 1981-84.

,·' Ih IIm DDD 5/94 ९ₚ

In Geneva, Dutoit was conducting an orchestra with plenty of experience of these scores behind it; was recording with a company whose long-standing proven ability to reproduce this orchestra with needle-sharp definition reached a new high with these recordings (Ansermet's timps rarely sounded as good as this; Stravinsky's never); and in a hall (Victoria Hall) whose acoustics breathed just enough fresh, natural air into and around the proceedings. The inclusion of Dutoit's Montreal recordings of the *Scherzo fantastique* (like the composer's, daringly fast but more securely articulated) and the *Symphonies of Wind Instruments* (Montreal winds on peak form) generously extends what was in the 1980s *Gramophone*'s prime recommendation for the orchestral symphonies. It remains so now for the 1990s.

Stravinsky. Petrushka (1947 version)[a]. Symphony in Three Movements. [a]**Peter Donohoe** (pf); **City of Birmingham Symphony Orchestra/Simon Rattle.** EMI CDC7 49053-2.

,·' 57m DDD 5/88

Stravinsky's second great ballet score has been well served on disc from the earliest days of LP. He recorded it himself (rather indifferently) but there is in any event a good case for preferring the brilliance and clarity of digital sound in this of all works. Should this be your priority, Bernard Haitink's stunning (if synthetically recorded) Berlin Philharmonic version (listed below) makes a plausible choice. Simon Rattle's performance is most notable for its fresh look at details of scoring and balance, with pianist Peter Donohoe making a strong impression. The results are robust and persuasive, though one sometimes has the impression that the characters are being left to fend for themselves. The atmospheric sound with its generous middle and bass is certainly more natural than Philips's for Haitink. The symphony too is eminently recommen-dable, sounding more grateful and high spirited than it sometimes has, with Rattle particularly relishing the jazzy bits.

Additional recommendations ...
Petrushka (1911 version)[a]. Scènes de ballet. [a]**Philip Moll** (pf); **Berlin Philharmonic Orchestra/ Bernard Haitink.** Philips 422 415-2PH — ,·' 52m DDD 10/91 ९ₛ

Petrushka. Firebird —Suite. Pastorale (arr. Stokowski). **Shostakovich** (arr. Stokowski). Prelude in E minor, Op. 34 No. 14. **Philadelphia Orchestra/Leopold Stokowski.** Dutton Laboratories mono CDAX8002 — ,·' Ih ADD 5/93 ९ₚ ▲

Petrushka. **Borodin.** Symphony No. 2 in B minor. **Concertgebouw Orchestra/Kyrill Kondrashin.** Philips Collector Series 438 280-2PH — ,·' Ih 5m ADD 9/93 ९ₚ

Orpheus. Petrushka. **Philharmonia Orchestra/Esa-Pekka Salonen.** Sony Classical SK53274 — ,·' Ih 4m DDD 2/94 ९ₚ

Symphony in C. Symphony in Three Movements. Symphony of Psalms[a]. **London Symphony** [a]**Chorus and Orchestra/Michael Tilson Thomas.** Sony Classical SK53275 — .·´ 1h 11m DDD 7/94

Stravinsky. WORKS FOR TWO PIANOS. **Vladimir Ashkenazy, Andrei Gavrilov** (pfs). Decca 433 829-2DH. Recorded 1990-91.
Scherzo à la russe. Sonata for Two Pianos. Concerto for Two Solo Pianos. The Rite of Spring.

.·´ **1h 8m DDD 2/93**

Scant attention has been paid to Stravinsky's two-piano output on disc to date, so this disc is particularly valuable in that it brings together his two original works for the medium, together with the rarely heard 'piano-duet' version (arranged by the composer) of the *Rite of Spring* and the two piano version of the *Scherzo à la russe*. The latter, more often heard in either its orchestral or jazz ensemble versions, is an invigorating breath of Russian fresh air, which, although written in 1944 looks back to the folk inspired sound-world of *Petrushka*. The Sonata and Concerto, dating from 1931 and 1943 respectively, are much more astringent and classical in tone, but their spiky, contrapuntal textures and acute contrasts are splendidly projected here by Ashkenazy and Gavrilov, who lift what can often sound like two of Stravinsky's more academic essays into much more attractive and approachable works. Stravinsky once said, "All my life I have tried out my music as I have composed it, orchestral as well as any other kind, four hands at one piano". *The Rite of Spring* was no exception, and the initial piano-duet version of the work (heard on this disc in an arrangement for two pianos) was actually published in 1913, the year of *The Rite's* tumultuous orchestral première. Ashkenazy and Gavrilov's account is one of the most exciting and galvanizing renditions of this version on disc; no pale imitation, but a rhythmically incisive reading with every minute gear change, and every nuance of this complex and thrilling score finely judged and delivered. Excellent recording — a must!

New review
Stravinsky. PIANO WORKS. **Victor Sangiorgio** (pf). Collins Classics 1374-2. Recorded in 1991.
Piano-Rag Music. Circus Polka. Sonata. Serenade in A major. Tango. Four Studies, Op. 7. Scherzo. Sonata in F sharp minor.

.·´ **1h 11m DDD 9/93**

Victor Sangiorgio launches his Stravinsky programme with a superbly colourful account of the *Piano-Rag Music*. He commands an excellent variety of attack and resonance, and this combines with his natural rhythmic élan and his fine ear for textural voicing to make the *Circus Polka* and the *Tango* especially effective. The *Studies* go well too, especially the Chaplinified Scriabin of No. 4. The short 1902 *Scherzo* is the only seriously flawed performance, marred as it is by a tendency towards spasmodic over-punctuation. But at least Sangiorgio pays this slight piece, and the anything-but-slight F sharp minor Sonata, the compliment of meticulous preparation. Third-hand Tchaikovsky the Sonata may be, but there is still something irresistible about the Russian gung-ho of its finale as relished here by Sangiorgio. The recording is very immediate in its impact, with warmth and clarity.

Stravinsky. SONGS. [a]**Phyllis Bryn-Julson** (sop); [b]**Ann Murray** (mez); [c]**Robert Tear** (ten); [d]**John Shirley-Quirk** (bar); **Ensemble Intercontemporain/Pierre Boulez.** DG 20th Century Classics 431 751-2GC. Texts and translations included. From 2531 377 (7/82). Recorded in 1980.
Pastorale[a]. Deux poèmes de Paul Verlaine[d]. Two poems of Konstantin Bal'mont[a]. Three Japanese lyrics[a]. Three little songs, "Recollections of my childhood"[a]. Pribaoutki[d]. Cat's Cradle Songs[b]. Four Songs[a]. MAVRA — Chanson de Paracha[a]. Three Songs from William Shakespeare[b]. In memoriam Dylan Thomas[c]. Elegy for J.F.K.[d]. Two Sacred Songs (after Wolf)[c].

.·´ **58m ADD 2/92**

It may be true that this disc lacks the focus of a single major work, but it is also much more than a random compilation of unrelated miniatures. Principally, it offers an aurally fascinating contrast between two groups of pieces: Stravinsky's relatively early Russian settings, as he worked through his own brand of nationalism, reaching from the salon style of *Pastorale* to the folk-like vigour of a work like *Pribaoutki*; then the late serial compositions, written in America, which prove that the rhythmic vitality and melodic distinctiveness of the early works survived undimmed into his final years. Stravinsky may have regarded texts as collections of sounds whose natural rhythms had no role to play in their musical setting, but the essential meaning still comes through unerringly, whether it is that of the plaintive Paracha's song from the opera *Mavra* or the sombre *Elegy for J.F.K.* (to an Auden text). The disc is rounded off by the very late Wolf arrangements, and whilst one might quibble here and there about Boulez's choice of tempo, or the balance of voice and instruments, the disc as a whole is immensely satisfying as a comprehensive survey of an important repertory.

Key to symbols

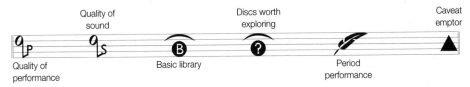

Quality of sound	Discs worth exploring	Caveat emptor
Quality of performance	Basic library	Period performance

The reviews which follow comprise part of "The Complete Edition" (Sony Classical S22K46290, medium price, 22 CDs, ADD, 7/91). The items reviewed here were subsequently issued as separate sets.

Stravinsky. THE COMPLETE EDITION. **Various artists/Igor Stravinsky.** Sony Classical SM3K46291 (Volume 1). Recorded 1959-62.
The Firebird (Columbia Symphony Orchestra. From CBS 72046, 9/62). Scherzo à la russe (Columbia Symphony Orchestra). Scherzo fantastique (CBC Symphony Orchestra). Fireworks (Columbia Symphony Orchestra. All from CBS GM31, 2/82). Petrushka (Columbia Symphony Orchestra. Philips SABL175, 4/61). The Rite of Spring (Columbia Symphony Orchestra. SABL174, 4/61). Les noces (Mildred Allen, sop; Regina Sarfaty, mez; Loren Driscoll, ten; Richard Oliver, bass; Samuel Barber, Aaron Copland, Lukas Foss, Roger Sessions, pfs; American Concert Choir; Columbia Percussion Ensemble). Renard (George Shirley, Loren Driscoll, tens; William Murphy, bar; Donald Gramm, bass; Toni Koves, cimbalom; Columbia Chamber Ensemble. Both from CBS SBRG72071, 12/62). L'histoire du soldat — Suite (Columbia Chamber Ensemble. SBRG72007, 6/62).

③ 3h 14m ADD 8/92

Inspiration for this collection of mainly stage music came from Stravinsky's native folk-song, folk-dance, folk-tale and folk ritual; and the set contains virtually all the music from Stravinsky's 'Russian' period, including the three great ballets. It is fascinating to chart his development from the 1908 *Scherzo fantastique* with its orchestral colours scintillating in the best Rimsky-Korsakovian manner, to the wholly original language of *Les noces* with its almost exclusively metrical patterns and monochrome scoring (soloists, chorus, pianos and percussion) begun only six years later. The links are there: witness the Rimskian bumble-bee that flies through the *Scherzo* to find its winged counterpart two years on in *The Firebird*; and the primitive rhythmic force of Kastchei's "Infernal dance" in *The Firebird* finding its fullest expression, another three years later, in *The Rite of Spring*; and so on. Each work is a logical, if time-lapse progression from the previous one. The set concludes with the 15-minute long animal rites of the farmyard opera-cum-burlesque *Renard* (1916); and *L'histoire du soldat* (1918), a morality play designed for a small touring theatre company (the Suite included here omits the speaking roles); both, like *Les noces*, leaving behind the lavish orchestra of *The Rite* for small and unusual instrumental and vocal combinations.

To have the composer at the helm, and a consistent approach to the way the music is recorded, ensures that those links are clearly established. And the orchestra that takes the lion's share of the task, the Columbia Symphony, was assembled by CBS to include many of the finest players in America. It is possible to criticize the recordings (made between 1959 and 1963) for close balances and spotlighting, but many modern contenders, more distantly recorded, will more often than not deprive you of adequate articulation of the music's linear and rhythmic ingenuity. The dynamic range and contours of *The Rite of Spring* do seem momentarily reduced and disturbed by the techniques, otherwise all these recordings reproduce with good tone, range, openness and presence. As to Stravinsky the conductor, only *Les noces* finds him at less than his usual rhythmically incisive self. This *Petrushka* is more representative: it pulsates with inner life and vitality — incidentally, Stravinsky uses his leaner, clearer 1947 revision, not the original 1911 score as the booklet claims.

Additional recommendation ...
Les noces[a]. Mass[b]. **Soloists; English Bach Festival Chorus;** [b]**Trinity Boys' Choir;** [a]**Martha Argerich,** [a]**Krystian Zimerman,** [a]**Cyprien Katsaris,** [a]**Homero Francesch** (pfs); [a]**English Bach Festival Percussion Ensemble;** [b]members of the **English Bach Festival Orchestra/ Leonard Bernstein.** DG 20th Century Classics 423 251-2GC — ⨪ 44m ADD 6/88 ◖P

Stravinsky. THE COMPLETE EDITION. **Various artists/Igor Stravinsky.** Sony Classical SM3K46292 (Volume 2).
Apollo (Columbia Symphony Orchestra). From SBRG72355, (11/65). Agon (Los Angeles Festival Symphony Orchestra. SBRG72438, 8/66). Jeu de cartes (Cleveland Orchestra). Scènes de ballet (CBC Symphony Orchestra). Bluebird — Pas de deux (Columbia Symphony Orchestra. All from SBRG72270, 5/65). Le baiser de la fée (Columbia Symphony Orchestra. SBRG72407, 5/66). Pulcinella (Irene Jordan, sop; George Shirley, ten; Donald Gramm, bass; Columbia Symphony Orchestra. SBRG72452, 7/66). Orpheus (Chicago Symphony Orchestra. SBRG72355).
⨪ ③ 3h 30m 8/92 ◖P

Volume 2 of Sony's Stravinsky Edition comprises ballets written between 1919 and 1957. *Pulcinella* was based on music originally thought to have been written by Pergolesi, but now known to be the work of various eighteenth-century composers. In 1919 Stravinsky had not long embraced neo-classical style, but here was a brilliant example of old wine in new bottles, with the melodies sounding as if they come from the pen of Stravinsky himself. The composer conducts a lively, sharply-accented account of the score. 1928 saw the production of two Stravinsky ballets. *Appolo*, a mainly quiet, contemplative score, written for string orchestra, has many passages of great beauty. Stravinsky the conductor does not linger over these, but allows the work's cool classical elegance to speak for itself. In *Le baiser de la fée* Stravinsky used themes by Tchaikovsky as the basis for his score. Once again, the music seems quite transformed, and the result is a most captivating work. Stravinsky's watchful, affectionate performance is perfectly proportioned. His arrangement of the "Pas de deux" from Tchaikovsky's *Sleeping Beauty* is no more than a reduction for small pit orchestra, however, and a mere curiosity.
In *Jeu de cartes*, which dates from 1936, Stravinsky used music by Rossini and others, but here the references are only fleeting, and merely enhance the humour of this robust, outgoing score. His performance brings out all the work's vigour and personality very effectively, but here and there rhythms become slightly unstuck, and a slightly hectic quality manifests itself. *Scènes de ballet* was written in 1944, and possesses a slightly terse quality in the main, though there are some more lyrical passages. Stravinsky does nothing to soften the work's edges in his performance, and it emerges as a strong, highly impressive piece. *Orpheus* was completed in 1947, and shows Stravinsky's neoclassical style at its most highly developed. Much of the music is quiet, after the manner of *Apollo*, but then the orchestra suddenly erupts into a passage of quite savage violence. Stravinsky conducts this passage with amazing energy for a man in his eighties, and elsewhere his performance has characteristic clarity and a very direct means of expression typical of a composer performance. Finally *Agon*, written in 1957, attracts the listener with its colourful opening fanfares, and then pursues an increasingly complex serial path in such a brilliant and highly rhythmical fashion that one is hardly aware that the technique is being used. This work, brilliantly conducted by Stravinsky, is an ideal introduction to his late style, and to the serial technique itself. Remastering has been carried out with the greatest skill, and all the recordings in this set sound very well indeed for their age.

Additional recommendations ...
Pulcinella[a]. Le chant du rossignol[d]. [a]**Ann Murray** (mez); [a]**Anthony Rolfe Johnson** (ten); [a]**Simon Estes** (bass); [a]**Ensemble Intercontemporain;** [b]**French National Orchestra/ Pierre Boulez.** Erato 2292-45382-2 — ⨪ ADD 5/86
Pulcinella[a]. Jeu de cartes. [a]**Teresa Berganza** (mez); [a]**Ryland Davies** (ten); [a]**John Shirley-Quirk** (bar); **London Symphony Orchestra/Claudio Abbado.** DG Galleria 423 889-2GGA — ⨪ 1h 2m ADD 1/89 ◖P
Pulcinella[a] (with original inspirations). Concerto in E flat major, "Dumbarton Oaks". [a]**Bernadette Manca di Nissa** (mez); [a]**David Gordon** (ten); [a]**John Ostendorf** (bass); **St Paul Chamber Orchestra/Christopher Hogwood.** Decca 425 614-2DH — ⨪ 1h 6m DDD 6/90

Orpheus. Jeu de cartes. **Royal Concertgebouw Orchestra/Neeme Järvi.** Chandos CHAN9014
— .• 53m DDD 3/92

Pulcinella. Danses Concertantes. **Soloists; City of London Sinfonia/Richard Hickox.** Virgin
Classics Virgo VJ5 61107-2 — . 59m DDD 1/94

Stravinsky. THE COMPLETE EDITION. **Various artists/Igor Stravinsky.** Sony Classical
SM2K46294 (Volume 4).
Symphonies — No. 1 in E flat major (Columbia Symphony Orchestra SBRG72569, 11/67).
Stravinsky in rehearsal. Stravinsky in his own words (GM31). Symphony in Three Movements
(Columbia Symphony Orchestra. SBRG72038, 9/62). Symphony in C (CBC Symphony Orchestra).
Symphony of Psalms (Toronto Festival Singers, CBC Symphony Orchestra. SBRG72181, 8/64).

.• ② 2h 23m 8/92

The word 'symphony' appears in the title of each work on these two discs, but this term covers
some very diverse material. Stravinsky was in his mid-twenties when he wrote his Symphony in
E flat, and the score is very much in the style of his teacher Rimsky-Korsakov. It has genuine
colour and flair, however, and the octogenarian conductor brings paternalistic affection and a
good deal of vigour to his performance. The *Symphony in C* dates from 1940, when Stravinsky
was in his neoclassical phase. The work has many beautiful pages, as well as much pungent wit.
In this performance Stravinsky drives the music much harder than he did in his 1952 mono
recording with the Cleveland Orchestra, and although there are some exciting moments the
music does tend to lose its elements of grace and charm. The performance of the *Symphony in
Three Movements* is also characterized by the use of fastish tempos. But this violent work, written
in 1945, and inspired by events in the Second World War, responds more readily to a strongly
driven interpretation. Stravinsky wrote his *Symphony of Psalms* in 1930, and this composition
reflects his deep religious convictions in varied settings from the Book of Psalms. His use of a
chorus is interestingly combined with an orchestra which lacks upper strings. Stravinsky conducts
a fervent, serious, beautifully balanced performance. All the 1960s recordings in this set sound
very well in their new CD transfers. In some quarters the elderly Stravinsky has been wrongly
portrayed as a frail, inadequate figure who only took over performances when works had been
thoroughly rehearsed for him. Nothing could prove more clearly that this was not true than the
rehearsal excerpts in this set, which show a vigorous, alert octogenarian very much in control of
proceedings, and rehearsing passages in some detail.

Additional recommendation ...
Symphony of Psalms^c. Pater noster. Credo. Ave Maria. Mass^c. Canticum sacrum. [a]**John Mark Ainsley**
(ten); [b]**Stephen Roberts** (bar); **Westminster Cathedral Choir;** [c]**City of London
Sinfonia/James O'Donnell.** Hyperion CDA66437 — .• 1h 8m DDD 9/91

Stravinsky. OEDIPUS REX[a]. Symphony of Psalms[b]. **Ivo Zídek** (ten); Oedipus; **Věra
Soukupová** (mez) Jocasta; **Karel Berman** (bass) Créon; **Eduard Haken** (bass); Tiresias;
Antonin Zlesák (ten) Shepherd; **Zdeněk Kroupa** (bar) Messenger; **Jean Desailly** (narr);
Czech Philharmonic Chorus and Orchestra/Karel Ančerl. Supraphon Historical 11
1947-2. Item marked [a] from SUAST50678 (1/68), [b] SUAST50778 (8/68). Recorded 1964-66.

.• 1h 13m AAD 3/93

Oedipus Rex is one of Stravinsky's most compelling theatre pieces, a powerful drama that re-
enacts the full force of a glorious highspot in ancient culture. The text is by Jean Cocteau, who
once said, pertaining to his work on *Oedipus,* that "any serious work, be it of poetry or music, of
theatre or of film, demands a ceremonial, lengthy calculation, an architecture in which the
slightest mistake would unbalance the pyramid" (quoted from *Diary of an Unknown*, pub. Paragon
House). The fusion of words and music in *Oedipus,* indeed its very 'architecture' is masterly and
arrests the attention consistently, from the animated severity of the opening narration, through
the cunningly calculated tension of its musical argument, to the tragic restraint of its closing
pages. Stravinsky has nearly always been well served by Czech musicians, and the late Karel
Ančerl was one of his most committed exponents. This particular recording of *Oedipus Rex* was
taped in the Dvořák Hall of the House of Artists, Prague, and earned itself at least three major
gramophone awards. Ančerl traces and intensifies salient points in the tragedy yet maintains a
precise, sensitive touch; his vocal collaborators include the noble Karel Berman (Créon) who,

like Ančerl himself, suffered considerably during the Nazi occupation of Czechoslovakia; then there's a fine Jocasta in Věra Soukupová and the convincing but occasionally unsteady Ivo Zídek singing the part of Oedipus. Both here and in the *Symphony of Psalms* — one of the most serenely perceptive performances of the work ever recorded — the Czech Philharmonic Chorus excels, while Supraphon's 1960s engineering (not, alas, the DDD suggested on the box) has an appealing brightness .

Additional recommendation ...
Soloists; Shin-yu Kai Choir; Saito Kinen Orchestra/Seiji Ozawa. Philips 438 865-2PH
— ,∙∙' 53m DDD 3/94

Further listening ...

Violin Concerto in D major. *Coupled with* **Mozart.** Violin Concerto in B flat major, K207. **David Oistrakh** (vn); **Orchestre des Concerts Lamoureux/Bernard Haitink.** Philips Collector 434 167-2PM (1/93).

Works for String Orchestra — Concerto in D major for String Orchestra. Double Canon, "Raoul Dufy in memoriam". Three Pieces. Apollon musagète. **Guildhall String Ensemble/Robert Salter.** RCA RD60156 (10/90).

Works for Chamber Orchestra — Divertimento (arr. from "La baiser de la fée"). Suites Nos. 1 and 2. Octet. Suite from "L'histoire du soldat". **London Sinfonietta/Riccardo Chailly.** Decca Enterprise 433 079-2DM (5/92).

MISCELLANEOUS WORKS. **Various artists.** EMI Composers in Person mono CDS7 54607-2 (5/93). Recorded 1928-34.
Les noces (sung in English. Kate Winter, sop; Linda Seymour, contr; Parry Jones, ten; Roy Henderson, bar; Berkeley Mason, Leslie Heward, Ernest Lush, Edwin Benbow, pfs; BBC Chorus; percussion ensemble/Igor Stravinsky). *Octet* (Marcel Moyse, fl; Emile Godeau, cl; Gustave Dhérin, Marius Piard, bns; Eugène Foveau, Pierre Vignal, tpts; André Lafosse, Raphaël Delbos, tbns/Stravinsky). *Capriccio* (Stravinsky, pf; Walther Straram Concerts Orchestra/Ernest Ansermet). *Symphony of Psalms* (Alexis Vlassov Choir; Straram Orchestra/Stravinsky). *Pastorale* (Louis Gromer, ob; Georges Durand, cor ang; André Vacellier, cl; Gabriel Grandmaison, bn; Samuel Dushkin, vn/Stravinsky). *Petrushka* — *Danse russe*. *The Firebird* — *Scherzo; Berceuse*. *Le chant du rossignol* — *Airs du rossignol; Marche chinoise* (all with Dushkin, vn; Stravinsky, pf). *Ragtime* (Lucien Lavaillotte, fl; Godeau, cl; Jean Devemy, hn; Foveau, tpt; Roger Tudesq, tbn; Roland Charmy, Henri Volant, vns; Etienne Ginot, va; Louis Juste, db; Aladar Racz, cimbalom; Jean Morel, perc/Stravinsky). *Piano-rag-music* (Stravinsky). *Suite italienne* — *Serenata; Scherzino*. *Duo concertant* (Dushkin; Stravinsky). *Serenade in A major* (Stravinsky). *Concerto for Two Pianos* (Soulima and Stravinsky, pfs).

THE RAKE'S PROGRESS. **Soloists; Sadler's Wells Opera Chorus; Royal Philharmonic Orchestra/Igor Stravinsky.** Sony Classical SM2K46299 (8/92).

Key to symbols

,∙∙'	② ②	lh 23m	DDD	6/88
Price	Quantity/ availability	Timing	Recording mode	Review date

Barbara Strozzi
Italian 1619-1664 or later

Suggested listening ...

Gite, o giorni dolenti. Questa è la nuova. Non mi dite. Soccorrete, luci avare. Amor, non dormir più. Voglio morire. Perle care. Amore è trandito. Rissolvetevi pensieri. *Coupled with*

Granata. Toccata. *Piccinini.* Toccata. **Glenda Simpson** (mez); **Camerata of London.**
Hyperion CDA66303 (10/89).

Jule Styne
American 1905-

Suggested listening ...

FUNNY GIRL. **Original Broadway cast.** EMI Angel ZDM7 64661-2.

GYPSY. **Original 1990 Broadway revival cast.** Elektra Nonesuch7559 79239-2.

Josef Suk
Bohemian 1874-1935

New review
Suk. Asrael, Op. 27. **Bavarian Radio Symphony Orchestra/Rafael Kubelík.** Panton 81
1101-2. Recorded in 1981.

·· lh 4m ADD I/94

To use large scale symphonic form for the purging of deep personal grief carries the danger that
the result will seriously lack discipline. In 1904-5 Suk's world was shattered by two visits from
Asrael (the Angel of Death in Muslim mythology): he lost his father-in-law (and revered teacher)
Dvořák, and his beloved wife, Otylka. Forgivably, Suk does perhaps linger a little too long in
the fourth movement's gentle, mainly lyrical portrait of Otylka, but elsewhere the progress is as
satisfying psychologically as it is symphonically. Much of the music has a concentrated dream-like
quality; at the extremes, spectral nightmare visions merge with compensatory surges of lyrical
ardour. It seems that *Asrael*'s time has well and truly come; there are now seven versions
currently available. Set Kubelík's reading alongside any of the modern versions and one is
immediately aware of a wholly compelling imaginative intensity and interpretative flair that
betoken a true poet of the rostrum. Kubelík's control throughout is awesome and he conjures
up playing of enormous expressive subtlety from his fine Munich orchestra. No other recorded
performance — not even Václav Talich's legendary 1952 Supraphon account — succeeds in
conveying the intensely personal nature of this music with such devastating emotional candour.
Technically, too, one need have no qualms about this Panton product — the Bavarian Radio
engineers secure most truthful results.

Additional recommendations ...
Asrael. **Royal Liverpool Philharmonic Orchestra/Libor Pešek.** Virgin Classics VC7
59638-2 — ·· lh 2m DDD 9/91
Asrael. **Dvořák.** *Stabat mater, B171.* **Soloists; Czech Philharmonic Chorus and Orchestra/**
Václav Talich. Supraphon Historical mono 11 1902-2 — ·· ② 2h 27m ADD 12/93 ⁹ₚ ▲
Asrael. **Russian State Symphony Orchestra/Evgeni Svetlanov.** Russian Disc RDCD11011
— ·· lh 4m DDD I/94

New review
Suk. Ripening, Op. 34ᵃ. Praga, Op. 26. **Royal Liverpool Philharmonic ᵃChoir and**
Orchestra/Libor Pešek. Virgin Classics VC7 59318-2. Recorded in 1992.

·· lh 7m DDD I/94

Completed in 1917, *Ripening* shows Suk at the height of his powers. This vast yet tightly
organized tone-poem shares many of the autobiographical concerns of both its large-scale
orchestral predecessors (namely *Asrael* and *A Summer Tale*). Throughout, Suk handles his
outsize forces with a truly Straussian confidence and virtuosity, nowhere more strikingly

than in the extended Fugue which attains a climax of truly devastating proportions; the profound serenity of the ensuing coda (where a wordless female chorus is used to magical effect) could not have been harder won. The coupling, *Praga*, is an affectionate, enjoyably grandiloquent portrait-in-sound of that fair city dating from 1904. Pesek's direction is imaginative, the RLPO's playing accomplished and communicative. The engineering, too, is first-class.

New review

Suk. CHAMBER WORKS, Volumes 1-3. [l]**Jiří Válek** (fl); [eghijlno]**Josef Suk**, [g]**Jitka Nováková**, [o]**Ludmila Vybíralová**, [o]**Miroslav Kosina**, [o]**Jaroslav Krištůfek**, [o]**Zdeněk Mann** (vns); [e]**Jan Talich** (va); [e]**Michaela Fukačová**, [k]**Marek Jerie**, [n]**František Host**, [o]**Ivo Laniar** (vcs); [o]**Tomáš Josífko** (db); [n]**Renata Kodadová** (hp); **Josef Hála** ([hl]pf/[n]harm); [eij]**Jan Panenka**, [f]**Pavel Stěpán**, [k]**Iván Klánský** (pfs); [o]**Josef Fousek**, [o]**Libor Kubánek** (perc); [cd]**Suk Trio** (Josef Suk, vn; Josef Chuchro, vc; [c]Josef Hála, [d]Jan Panenka, pfs); [abfmn]**Suk Quartet** ([afm]Antonín Novák, [bn]Ivan Straus, Vojtěch Jouza, vns; Karel Rehák, va; Jan Stros, vc). Supraphon 11 1874-2 (also available separately, as indicated below). Recorded 1966-92. *11 1531-2*: String Quartets — No. 1 in B flat major, Op. 11[a] (from 1111 2974, 10/82); No. 2, Op. 31[b]. Tempo di menuetto[b]. Meditation on an old Czech hymn, Op. 35a[b] (all from 1111 3370, recorded 1984). Quartet movement in B flat major[a] (recorded 1978, new to UK). *11 1532-2*: Piano Trio in C minor, Op. 2[c]. Elégie, Op. 23[d] (SUAST50863, 12/69). Piano Quartet in A minor, Op. 1[e]. Piano Quintet in G minor, Op. 8[f] (recorded 1978, new to UK). *11 1533-2*: Mélodie[g]. Minuet[h]. Balada in D minor[i] (SUAST5077, 8/68). Four Pieces, Op. 17[j] (SUAST5077). Ballade in D minor, Op. 3 No. 1[k]. Serenade in A major, Op. 3 No. 2[k] (both recorded 1983, new to UK). Bagatelle, "Carrying a bouquet"[l]. Barcarolle in B flat major[m]. Balada in D minor[m] (both recorded 1978, new to UK). Elégie, Op. 23[n]. Sousedská[o].

♪ ③ 1h 11m 1h 14m 1h 3m ADD/DDD 2/94

A treasure-trove of heartfelt music performed with refinement and flair. Volume 1 concentrates on Suk's string quartet output (Suk himself was the second violinist in the great Czech Quartet for 40 years). If the First Quartet (1896) doesn't quite show the same freshness or entrancing melodic vein of the String Serenade of four years earlier, it remains a delightfully unassuming creation with the genial presence of Suk's teacher Dvořák looming large over the proceedings. It is followed by a rare hearing for the alternative finale Suk composed some 19 years later in 1915. By this time, of course, the composer had already found his own strongly personal voice. Both the resourceful Second Quartet of 1911 (an ambitious one-movement essay of nearly 28 minutes' duration and considerable emotional variety) and the deeply-felt *Meditation on an old Czech Hymn* (1914) are works of some substance well worth exploring, and these passionate accounts enjoy excellent sound. The remaining two volumes perhaps contain more to interest Suk *aficionados* than newcomers, though the adorable *Four Pieces* for violin and piano, Op. 17, have always remained great favourites. Volume 2 features youthful offerings: the Piano Trio, the Piano Quartet, the likeable, if rather garrulous, Piano Quintet of 1893 and the touching *Elégie* for piano, violin and cello from 1902, written to celebrate the anniversary of the death of the poet and dramatist, Julius Zeyer. Apart from the *Four Pieces* already mentioned, the third and final volume also contains, amongst much else, the *Elégie* in its original guise for violin, cello, string quartet, harmonium and harp, no fewer than three different *Ballades* in D minor conceived for various instrumental combinations during Suk's days at the Conservatory, the "Barcarolle" slow movement of a very early String Quartet from 1888, as well as the composer's last completed piece from 1935, the engaging *Sousedská* for five violins, double bass, cymbals and triangle. Recording dates range from 1966 to 1992 (most of the material is designated as AAD), but the quality is consistently praiseworthy and the volumes are available either separately or gathered together within an attractive slipcase.

Further listening ...

Serenade in E flat major, Op. 6. *Coupled with* **Grieg.** Holberg Suite, Op. 40[a]. **Tchaikovsky.** Serenade in C major for Strings, Op. 48. [a]**Swiss Chamber Orchestra, Polish Radio Chamber Orchestra/Agnieszka Duczmal.** ASV CDQS6094 (3/94).

Arthur Sullivan

Sullivan. Cello Concerto in D major (reconstr. Mackerras and Mackie)[a]. Symphony in
E major, "Irish"[b]. Overture di ballo[b].
Elgar. Romance, Op. 62 (arr. vc)[a]. [a]**Julian Lloyd Webber** (vc); [a]**London Symphony
Orchestra/Sir Charles Mackerras;** [b]**Royal Liverpool Philharmonic Orchestra/Sir
Charles Groves.** EMI British Composers CDM7 64726-2. Items marked [a] from CDC7 47622-2
(2/87), recorded in 1986; [b] HMV ASD2435 (2/69), recorded in 1968.

> **Ih Ilm ADD/DDD 4/94**

Sir Charles Groves's sturdy yet affectionate reading of Sullivan's wholly charming *Irish* Symphony
was always one of the best of his EMI offerings with the RLPO and the 1968 recording remains
vivid. In the sparkling *Overture di ballo*, again, Groves conducts with plenty of character. There
are also first-rate performances of Sullivan's undemanding Cello Concerto from 1866 (in a fine
reconstruction by Sir Charles Mackerras — the manuscript was destroyed in Chappell's fire of
1964) as well as Elgar's wistful little *Romance* (originally for bassoon). This is a thoroughly
attractive mid-price reissue.

Sullivan. THE PIRATES OF PENZANCE. **Eric Roberts** (bar) Major-General Stanley;
Malcolm Rivers (bar) Pirate King; **Gareth Jones** (bar) Samuel; **Philip Creasy** (ten)
Frederic; **Simon Masterton-Smith** (bass) Sargeant of Police; **Marilyn Hill Smith** (sop)
Mabel; **Patricia Cameron** (sop) Edith; **Pauline Birchall** (mez) Kate; **Susan Gorton** (contr)
Ruth; **D'Oyly Carte Opera Chorus and Orchestra/John Pryce-Jones.** TER CDTER2
1177. Recorded in 1990.

> ② **Ih 25m DDD 9/90**

The revival of the D'Oyly Carte Opera Company produced the first digital recordings of
complete Gilbert and Sullivan scores, and this TER set is a very happy example. Philip Creasy is
an engaging and vocally secure Frederic, and Marilyn Hill Smith trips through "Poor wandering
one" with a delectable display of vocal ability and agility. The couple's interplay with the chorus
in "How beautifully blue the sky" is quite enchanting, and their exchanges in "Stay, Frederic,
stay" splendidly convincing. Eric Roberts makes the Major-General a thoroughly engaging
personality, and the dotty exchanges between Simon Masterson-Smith's Sargeant of Police and
his police force are sheer joy. Even such details as the girls' screams at the appearance of the
pirates in Act 1 have a rare effectiveness. John Pryce-Jones keeps the score dancing along. Those
who want the dialogue as well as the music must look elsewhere, but this version is certainly to
be recommended for its musical and acting values as well as its fine modern sound.

Additional recommendation ...
Soloists; Welsh National Opera Chorus and Orchestra/Sir Charles Mackerras. Telarc
CD80353 — *..* Ih 19m DDD 11/93 9p

Sullivan. THE MIKADO[a]. **John Holmes** (bass) The Mikado; **John Wakefield** (ten) Nanki-
Poo; **Clive Revill** (bar) Ko-Ko; **Denis Dowling** (bar) Pooh-Bah; **John Heddle Nash** (bar)
Pish-Tush; **Marion Studholme** (sop) Yum-Yum; **Patricia Kern** (mez) Pitti-Sing; **Dorothy
Nash** (sop) Peep-Bo; **Jean Allister** (mez) Katisha.
IOLANTHE[b] — excerpts. **Elizabeth Harwood, Elizabeth Robson, Cynthia Morey** (sops);
Heather Begg, Patricia Kern (mezs); **Stanley Bevan** (ten); **Eric Shilling, Denis Dowling,
Julian Moyle** (bars); **Leon Greene** (bass); **Sadler's Wells Opera Chorus and Orchestra/
Alexander Faris.** Classics for Pleasure CD-CFPD4730. Item marked [a] from HMV CSD1458/9
(10/62), [b] CSD1434 (7/62). Recorded in 1962.

> ② **2h 15m ADD 4/94**

At the core of these performances are some of the finest British singers of 30 years ago, all of whom
were chosen not just for their singing but for their sense of the theatricality and humour of Gilbert
and Sullivan. Just listen, for instance, to how John Heddle Nash gives full expression to every word

of Pish-Tush's "Our great Mikado". Here, too, is Marion Studholme's delicious Yum-Yum and Elizabeth Harwood's joyous Phyllis. If one singles out Clive Revill for special mention, it is because his Ko-Ko is uniquely well-judged and imaginative, combining superb comic timing, verbal clarity and vocal dexterity. His "little list" is hilarious, and one can almost feel one's hand gripped at the words "shake hands with you *like that*". At the helm in both works is Alexander Faris who knew supremely well how to capture the lightness and sparkle of operetta. The new Overture put together for *The Mikado* by Stephen Dodgson may come as a surprise, but it is apt and cleverly done. The sound is inevitably dated when compared to more recent recordings, but it scarcely mars the enjoyment.

Additional recommendations …
Soloists; D'Oyly Carte Chorus; Royal Philharmonic Orchestra/Royston Nash. Decca 425 190-2LM2 — .·ʹ ② 1h 30m ADD 1/90
Soloists; Welsh National Opera Chorus and Orchestra/Sir Charles Mackerras. Telarc CD80284 — .·ʹ 1h 19m DDD 5/92 ♀ₚ

Sullivan. THE YEOMEN OF THE GUARD. **Donald Maxwell** (bass) Sir Richard Cholmondeley; **David Fieldsend** (ten) Colonel Fairfax; **Terence Sharpe** (bar) Sergeant Meryll; **Julian Jenson** (ten) Leonard Meryll; **Fenton Grey** (bar) Jack Point; **Gary Montaine** (bass) Shadbolt; **Lesley Echo Ross** (sop) Elsie; **Janine Roebuck** (mez) Phoebe; **Jill Pert** (contr) Dame Carruthers; **Carol Lesley-Green** (sop) Kate; **D'Oyly Carte Opera Chorus and Orchestra/John Owen Edwards.** TER CDTER2 1195. Recorded in 1992.
.·ʹ ② 1h 55m DDD 5/93 ♀ₚ

This recording has a tremendous freshness and naturalness, theatricality and musicality about it. It is splendidly paced by the conductor, John Owen Edwards, who produces impressive solemnity in the more serious moments (including a really haunting Funeral March) but deliciously imparts life into lighthearted numbers such as "Here's a man of jollity" and "Rapture, Rapture". Among the cast, there is real pleasure in the singing of Lesley Echo Ross, who was Phyllis in TER's *Iolanthe* and is here a refreshingly clear, youthful Elsie Maynard, her voice soaring beautifully in the ensembles. Likewise Jill Pert, as Dame Carruthers, repeats the favourable impression she created in *The Gondoliers* and *Iolanthe*. Fenton Grey is a first-rate light baritone Jack Point, too, enunciating his words with considerable clarity. But why, in "O, a private buffoon", does he suddenly display a cockney accent that is totally missing elsewhere in his singing? Perhaps Janine Roebuck's imposing mezzo-soprano creates a somewhat mature-sounding Phoebe, but she and the other principals all contribute to a strong cast. The theatricality of the venture is nowhere better demonstrated than in the inclusion of the dialogue over the music that precedes "I have a song to sing, O!". This uniquely complete version also includes some extra, usually omitted verses and, in an appendix, an alternative version of "Is life a boon?" and two other discarded numbers.

Additional recommendations …
THE YEOMEN OF THE GUARD[a]. *TRIAL BY JURY*[b]. **Soloists; D'Oyly Carte Opera Chorus,** [a]**Royal Philharmonic Orchestra/Sir Malcolm Sargent;** [b]**Orchestra of the Royal Opera House, Covent Garden/Isidore Godfrey.** Decca 417 358-2LM2 — .·ʹ ② 2h 5m ADD 1/90 ♀ₚ
THE YEOMEN OF THE GUARD. **Soloists; Academy and Chorus of St Martin in the Fields/Sir Neville Marriner.** Philips 438 138-2PH2 — .·ʹ ② 1h 55m DDD 11/93 ♀ₚ

Sullivan. THE GONDOLIERS. Overture di Ballo (1870 version). **Richard Suart** (bar) Duke of Plaza-Toro; **Philip Creasey** (ten) Luiz; **John Rath** (bass) Don Alhambra; **David Fieldsend** (ten) Marco; **Alan Oke** (bar) Giuseppe; **Tim Morgan** (bar) Antonio; **David Cavendish** (ten) Francesco; **Toby Barrett** (bass) Giorgio; **Jill Pert** (contr) Duchess of Plaza-Toro; **Elizabeth Woollett** (sop) Casilda; **Lesley Echo Ross** (sop) Gianetta; **Regina Hanley** (mez) Tessa; **Yvonne Patrick** (sop) Fiametta; **Pamela Baxter** (mez) Vittoria; **Elizabeth Elliott** (sop) Giulia; **Claire Kelly** (contr) Inez; **D'Oyly Carte Opera Chorus and Orchestra/John Pryce-Jones.** TER CDTER2 1187. Recorded in 1991.
.·ʹ ② 1h 49m DDD 5/92

This is one of a series of recordings by the new D'Oyly Carte Opera Company that offers a vastly better quality of sound than any of its ageing competitors. Orchestral detail is the most immediate beneficiary, and the overture serves to demonstrate John Pryce-Jones's lively tempos and lightness of touch. Outstanding among the singers are perhaps John Rath, who gives Don Alhambra's "I stole the prince" and "There lived a king" real presence, and Jill Pert, a formidable Duchess of Plaza-Toro. Richard Suart not only provides the leading comedy roles with exceptionally clear articulation and musicality, but also adds considerable character to his portrayals; his "I am a courtier grave and serious" is a sure winner. David Fieldsend and Alan Oke provide attractive portrayals of the two gondoliers, and Lesley Echo Ross and Regina Hanley are also most agreeable. Seasoned listeners may note numerous changes of detail as a result of the purging of the performance material of changes made to the parts around the time of the 1920s Savoy Theatre revivals. There is no dialogue, but added value is provided by Sullivan's sunniest comic opera score being accompanied by the sparkling *Overture di Ballo*, played in its original version with some traditional cuts opened up.

Further listening ...

Songs — Let me dream again. Mary Morison. The Marquis de Mincepie. The moon in silent brightness. Five Shakespeare Songs — O mistress mine; Orpheus with his Lute; The Willow Song. The lost chord. Sweethearts. St Agnes's Eve. The Dove Song. Gone! Winter. What does little birdie say? The Absent-minded Beggar. **Jeanne Ommerle** (sop); **Sanford Sylvan** (bar); **Gary Wedow** (pf). Conifer CDCFC156 (9/87).

Overtures — HMS PINAFORE. THE PIRATES OF PENZANCE. PATIENCE. IOLANTHE. PRINCESS IDA. THE MIKADO. THE GONDOLIERS. THE YEOMEN OF THE GUARD. DI BALLO. RUDDIGORE. **New Sadler's Wells Opera Orchestra; D'Oyly Carte Opera Orchestra/John Pryce-Jones, Simon Phipps, John Owen Edwards.** TER CDVIR8316 (5/93).

HMS PINAFORE — *comic opera.* **Soloists; D'Oyly Carte Opera Chorus; New Symphony Orchestra/Isidore Godfrey.** Decca 414 283-2LM2 (1/90).

IOLANTHE — *comic operetta.* **Glyndebourne Festival Chorus/Pro Arte Orchestra/Sir Malcolm Sargent.** EMI CMS7 64400-2.

RUDDIGORE — *operetta.* THE PIRATES OF PENZANCE — *operetta.* **Soloists; Glynde-bourne Festival Chorus/Pro Arte Orchestra/Sir Malcolm Sargent.** EMI CMS7 64412-2.

Franz von Suppé

Austrian 1819-1895

Suggested listening ...

Overtures — Leichte Kavallerie. Tantalusqualen. Die Irrfahrt um's Glück. Die Frau Meisterin. Ein Morgen, ein Mittag, ein Abend in Wien. Pique-Dame. Wiener Jubel. Dichter und Bauer. **Academy of St Martin in the Fields/Sir Neville Marriner.** EMI CDC7 54056-2 (10/90).

Requiem. **Soloists; Franco-German Choir, Lyon; Bonn Youth Symphony Orchestra/ Wolfgang Badun.** BNL BNL112774 (1/92).

Tylman Susato

Flanders ?c. 1500-1561/4

New review
Susato. Dansereye — excerpts. **New London Consort/Philip Pickett.** L'Oiseau-Lyre 436 131-2OH. Recorded in 1991.

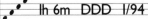 1h 6m DDD 1/94

Listening to this disc is, to the ear, what participating in a delectable wine-tasting is to the palate. These 34 dances are performed in different settings with an almost endless variety of groupings of an astonishingly high number of authentic sixteenth-century instruments. Among the impressive array of between 20 and 30 different kinds of musical instruments, we find, besides the more courtly lutes and viols, a number of less usual ones, such as the Flemish 'rumble-pot', jingle-bells, and the rackett. Some are clearly rustic, or folk instruments. But Pickett tells us his aim has been to present his listeners with a programme designed "along the lines of a very special evening's dancing and entertainment at one of the richest Flemish courts". Indeed, the chief fascination of this recording, quite apart from the quality of the performances, lies in the skilful musical planning of the whole diverse sequence of items, holding the listener's interest right through to the end.

Johann Svendsen
Norwegian 1840-1911

Suggested listening ...

Symphonies — No. 1 in D major, Op. 4; No. 2 in B flat major, Op. 15. Two Swedish folk-melodies, Op. 27. **Gothenburg Symphony Orchestra/Neeme Järvi.** BIS CD347 (11/87).

Jan Pieterszoon Sweelinck
Dutch 1562-1621

Suggested listening ...

Or soit loué l'Etérnal. Mon Dieu, j'ay en toy esperance. Qui au conseil des malins. Vous tous qui la terr' habitez. Revenge moy, pren la querelle. Mon am'en Dieu taut seulement. Les cieux en chacun lieu. Du Seigneur les bontez. Ne sois fasché. Or sus serviteurs de Seigneur. Jamais ne cesseray. Vouloir m'est pris. Le Toutpuissant à mon Seigneur. D'ou vient, Seigneur. Vous tous les habitans. **Trinity College Choir, Cambridge/Richard Marlow.** Conifer CDFC205 (8/92).

Karol Szymanowski
Polish 1882-1937

New review
Szymanowski. Violin Concertos—No. 1, Op. 35; No. 2, Op. 61.
Stravinsky. Violin Concerto in D major. **Chantal Juillet** (vn); **Montreal Symphony Orchestra/Charles Dutoit.** Decca 436 837-2DH. Recorded in 1992.

Ih I0m DDD I0/93

Although there are several of the Stravinsky to choose from, neither of the Szymanowski concertos are anywhere as near well served. The latter are among the most glorious and intoxicating works in the repertory. Their sound world is totally distinctive: an exotic luxuriance, a sense of ectasy and longing, a heightened awareness of colour and glowing, almost luminous textures that are quite magical. No scores cry out more strongly for the advantages of modern recording, and in this respect they are well served here. Dutoit is attentive to every detail as is his soloist who is scrupulous in matters of dynamics and refreshingly selfless in putting the score before all else. As in the Stravinsky the Decca recording is truthful in matters of balance: indeed some may feel the soloist needs just a little more help. Chantal Juillet produces a refined rather small tone and Decca have opted not to glamorize or beautify it. She also has the wiry vitality that the Stravinsky concerto needs and Dutoit's credentials as a Stravinskian are impeccable. This recording will give much pleasure.

Additional recommendations ...
Stravinsky. Violin Concerto[c]. *Lutoslawski.* Partita for Violin, Orchestra and Obbligato Solo Piano[a]. Chain 2 for Violin and Orchestra[b]. **Anne-Sophie Mutter** (vn); [a]**Phillip Moll** (pf); [ab]**BBC Symphony Orchestra/Witold Lutoslawki;** [c]**Philharmonia Orchestra/Paul Sacher.**
DG 423 696-2GH *(reviewed under Lutoslawski; refer to the Index to Reviews)* — **56m DDD 2/89** ⁹ₚ

Szymanowski. *Nos. 1 and 2. Violin Sonata in D minor, Op. 9ᵃ. King Rogerᵃ — Roxana's Song.*
Wanda Wilkomirska, ᵃ**Tadeusz Chmielewski** (vns); **Warsaw National Philharmonic**
Orchestra/Witold Rowicki. Polskie Nagrania PNCD064 —.•˙ 1h 12m ADD 7/90

Stravinsky. *Violin Concerto.* **Prokofiev.** *Violin Concertosᵃ — No. 1 in D major, Op. 19; No. 2 in*
G minor, Op. 63. **Kyung-Wha Chung** (vn); **London Symphony Orchestra/André Previn.**
Decca Ovation 425 003-2DM *(reviewed under Prokofiev; refer to the Index to Reviews)* — .•˙ 1h 12m
ADD 7/90 ⁹ₚ Ⓑ

Szymanowski. *String Quartets — No. 1 in C major, Op. 37; No. 2, Op. 56.*
Webern. *Slow Movement (1905).* **Carmina Quartet** (Matthias Enderle, Susanne Frank, vns;
Wendy Champney, va; Stephan Goerner, vc). Denon CO-79462-2.

.•˙ 45m DDD 3/92   ⁹ₛ 👁 ❓

Szymanowski's sound world is totally distinctive: there is an exotic luxuriance, a sense of ecstasy
and longing, a heightened awareness of colour and glowing, almost luminous textures. The two
quartets are separated by a decade: the First, whose sense of ecstasy and longing permeates its
opening, is a subtle and deeply-felt performance and much the same can be said of No. 2. Again
heady perfumes and exotic landscapes are in evidence, though with his increasing interest in folk-
music, the finale has slight overtones of Bartók. The Swiss-based Carmina Quartet play both
Szymanowski works with great understanding and emotional involvement, and technically they
are quite brilliant. If we associate Webern with brief, highly compressed atonal and serial works,
the Slow Movement for String Quartet shows the composer in his early twenties still writing in
a late-romantic style, appropriately enough for a piece which reflects for Webern the pleasures
of a walk through Austrian woods with his future wife. The Movement sprawls a little, but is
very pleasingly written. The Carmina Quartet give a sympathetic, warm-hearted performance of
this piece, and the sound obtained by Denon's largely Japanese team throughout the disc is very
detailed, but also has a very attractive bloom.

Additional recommendation ...
String Quartets. **Lutoslawski.** *String Quartet.* **Penderecki.** *String Quartet No. 2.* **Varsovia**
Quartet. Olympia OCD328 — .•˙ 1h 8m AAD 6/89 ❓

New review
Szymanowski. Stabat mater, Op. 53ᵃ. Litany to the Virgin Mary, Op. 59ᵇ. Symphony No. 3,
"The song of the night", Op. 27ᶜ. ᵃᵇ**Elzbieta Szmytka** (sop); ᵃ**Florence Quivar** (contr); ᶜ**Jon**
Garrison (ten); ᵃ**John Connell** (bass); **City of Birmingham Symphony Orchestra and**
Chorus/Sir Simon Rattle. EMI CDC5 55121-2. Texts and translations included.

.•˙ 56m DDD 8/94   ⁹ₚ ⁹ₛ

The first impression here is that Rattle is relatively new to Szymanowski. There's a huge
enthusiasm here, a missionary quality that bespeaks the recent convert. On the other hand the
care over matters of balance, the knowledge of just those points where Szymanowski's complexity needs very careful handling if it's not simply to blur into opacity, suggest a conductor who
has been there before and knows the dangers. You get the feeling that a conscious decision was
made to delay recording this music until the circumstances were right. The CBSO Chorus sound
not only thoroughly at home in the music but in the language too.The clincher on the decision
to go ahead with this recording might well have been Rattle's realization that in Elzbieta
Szmytka he had a soprano who might have been born to sing Szymanowski's pure, floated and
very high-lying soprano lines (in the *Stabat mater* and the *Litany*; in the symphony he uses a
tenor, which was Szymanowski's own first choice). The result is very fine indeed: one of the
most beautiful Szymanowski recordings ever made. And yet 'beautiful Szymanowski' isn't all that
hard if the orchestra's good enough and the conductor capable. Rattle's insistence that all of the
music be heard, its bones and sinews as well as its flesh, its urgency and passion as well as its
deliquescent loveliness, makes for uncommonly gripping Szymanowski as well. He reminds one
of how much more there is to the Third Symphony than voluptuous yearning: solemnity, for one
thing, and a fierce ardour that can indeed knock you sideways. The choice of soloists for the
Stabat mater is interesting: alongside Szmytka's radiant purity are Quivar's throaty vibrancy and
Connell's weighty darkness. Not a matching trio, but the contrast is appealing; it adds to the
rich differentiation of sonority that Rattle draws from his chorus and orchestra. Garrison in the

symphony is a touch hard and strenuous, less enraptured than one or two of the Polish tenors (and sopranos) who've recorded it, but he's a musicianly and likeable singer. The recording is outstanding: lucid, rich and spacious, with tremendous and perfectly focused climaxes.

Additional recommendation ...
Stabat Mater[a]. *Symphony No. 3*[b]. *Three Fragments from poems by Jan Kasprowicz, Op. 5*[c]. [ab]**Stefania Woytowicz** (sop); [ac]**Krystyna Szostek-Radkowa** (mez); [a]**Andrzej Hiolski** (bar); **Polish Radio and Television** [ab]**Choir and** [b]**Symphony Orchestra, Cracow;** [ac]**Polish Radio and Television Great Symphony Orchestra, Katowice/**[a]**Stanislaw Wislocki,** [b]**Tadeusz Strugala;** [c]**Jerzy Maksymiuk.** Koch Schwann 312652 — ⏱ 1h 10m ADD 4/94 ⁹ₚ

Further listening ...

Symphonies — No. 2 in B flat major, Op. 19[b]; No. 3, "The song of the night", Op. 27[a]. Concert Overture in E major, Op. 12[b]. [a]**Wieslaw Ochman** (ten); [a]**Cracow Polish Radio Chorus; Polish National Radio Symphony Orchestra/**[a]**Jerzy Semkow,** [b]**Jacek Kaspszyk.** EMI Matrix CDM5 65082-2 (7/94).

Four Etudes, Op. 4. Metopes, Op. 29. Fantasy, Op. 14. Masques, Op. 34. **Dennis Lee** (pf). Hyperion CDA66409 (7/91).

Songs with Orchestra — Love-songs of Hafiz, Op. 26; Songs of the infatuated muezzin, Op. 42; Songs of a fairytale princess, Op. 31. KING ROGER — Roxana's Song. Three Fragments from Poems by Jan Kasprowicz, Op. 5. **Soloists; Polish State Philharmonic Orchestra, Katowice/Karol Stryja.** Marco Polo 8 223294 (4/92).

KING ROGER[a]. Harnasie — Suite, Op. 55[b]. **Soloists; Warsaw National Opera Chorus and Orchestra/Mieczyslaw Mierzejewski,** [b]**Bohdan Wodiczko.** Olympia OCD303 (5/89).

Germaine Tailleferre

French 1892-1983

Suggested listening ...

Sonata for Violin and Piano No. 1[bd]. *Coupled with* **C. Schumann.** Piano Trio in G minor, Op. 17[a]. **Beach.** Piano Trio in A minor, Op. 150[a]. **Carreño.** String Quartet in B minor[bc]. **Mendelssohn-Hensel.** Piano Trio in G minor, Op. 11[a]. **Boulanger.** Pièces — Nocturne; Cortège[bd]. **Chaminade.** Piano Trio No. 1 in G minor, Op. 11[a]. [a]**Macalester Trio;** [b]**Joseph Roche,** [c]**Robert Zelnick** (vns); [c]**Tamas Strasser** (va); [c]**Camilla Heller** (vc); [d]**Paul Freed** (pf). Vox Box 115845-2. *See review in the Collections section; refer to the Index to Reviews.*

Toru Takemitsu

Japanese 1930-

Takemitsu. ORCHESTRAL, CHAMBER AND INSTRUMENTAL WORKS. **John Williams** (gtr); [a]**Sebastian Bell** (alto fl); [b]**Gareth Hulse** (ob d'amore); [c]**London Sinfonietta/Esa-Pekka Salonen.** Sony Classical SK46720.
To the Edge of Dream[c]. Folios — I, II and III. Toward the Sea[a]. Here, There and Everywhere. What a Friend. Amours Perdues. Summertime. Vers, l'Arc-en-ciel, Palma[bc].

⏱ 1h DDD 1/92

Toru Takemitsu is an original, refined composer and something of a latter-day impressionist, as titles like *To the Edge of Dream* suggest. It may therefore come as a surprise to find him arranging songs by Lennon and McCartney, Gershwin and others, for solo guitar. Yet these

prove to have attractive touches of the subtlety found in Takemitsu's own compositions, and they also provide useful contrast to the more substantial works on this beguiling disc. *Folios*, the earliest composi-tion included, already reveal Takemitsu's musical catholicity in its reference to a Bach chorale. *Toward the Sea* and *Vers, l'Arc-en-ciel, Palma* are both more expansive mood pieces, the former (for guitar and alto flute) almost too reticent and hesitant beside the richer textures of the latter, which is enhanced by the additional solo role given to the oboe d'amore as well as its beautifully laid out orchestral accompaniment. *To the Edge of Dream* is in effect a guitar concerto, with a wider range of mood and an even more developed role for the orchestra than *Vers, l'Arc-en-ciel, Palma*. It provides a particularly satisfying focus for a sensitively performed and well recorded disc. Even if we hear rather more of the guitar relative to the orchestra than we would in the concert-hall, there is nothing unreasonably artificial about the result.

Additional recommendation ...
To the Edge of Dream. **Arnold.** *Guitar Concerto, Op. 67.* **Rodrigo.** *Concierto de Aranjuez.* **Julian Bream** (gtr); **City of Birmingham Symphony Orchestra/Simon Rattle.** EMI CDC7 54661-2 *(see review under Arnold; refer to the Index to Reviews)* — .·˙ 58m DDD 7/93 ⁹ₚ

Further listening ...

November Steps[a]. Eclipse[b]. Viola Concerto, "A String around Autumn"[c]. [ab]**Katsuya Yokoyama** (shakuhachi); [ab]**Kinshi Tsuruta** (biwa); [c]**Nobuko Imai** (va); [ac]**Saito Kinen Orchestra/Seiji Ozawa.** Philips 432 176-2PH (8/92).

Rain Coming. Rain Spell. riverrun [a]. Tree Line. Water-ways. [a]**Paul Crossley** (pf); **London Sinfonietta/Oliver Knussen.** Virgin Classics VC7 59020-2 (9/91).

A Way A Lone. *Coupled with* **Barber.** String Quartet, Op. 11. **Britten.** String Quartet No. 2 in C major, Op. 36. **Tokyo Quartet.** RCA Victor Red Seal 09026 61387-2 (2/94). *See review under Barber; refer to the Index to Reviews.*

Corona. The Crossing. Far Away. Les yeux clos. Litany. Pause uninterrupted. Piano Distance. Rain Tree Sketch. **Roger Woodward** (pf). Etcetera KTC1103 (6/91).

Thomas Tallis

British c.1505-1585

Tallis. Lamentations of Jeremiah. MOTETS. **The Tallis Scholars/Peter Phillips.** Gimell CDGIM025. Texts and translations included.
Motets — Absterge Domine. Derelinquat impius. Mihi autem nimis. O sacrum convivium. In jejunio et fletu. O salutaris hostia. In manus tuas. O nata lux de lumine. Salve intemerata virgo.

.·˙ lh 8m DDD 5/92

This, the third volume of the survey by The Tallis Scholars of the music of the Tudor composer, Thomas Tallis, contains the well-known *Lamentations*, eight motets, and the extended motet *Salve intemerata virgo*. The *Lamentations* and motets are typical of the style of late Renaissance English composers. The overall mood is one of considerable austerity and their simplicity is indicative of the probability of their having been written for the private use of loyal Catholics rather than for formal ritual. *Salve intemerata virgo,* on the other hand, looks back to the glories of the late fifteenth century. In particular Tallis's use of the phrygian mode gives the work as a whole a strong sense of the medieval. Despite this disparity of styles the Tallis Scholars acquit themselves, as always, with great distinction. In the *Lamentations* and motets they achieve an appropriate sense of intimacy, while in *Salve intermerata virgo* they rise fully to the challenges of one of the more extended and demanding examples of Tudor choral composition. In addition the formidable challenges which this latter work sets for the conductor, such as the sense of pace, variation of dynamics, and overall architecture of the work, are all extremely well handled by Peter Phillips. Like much music of this era, the compositions of Thomas Tallis repay repeated listenings, and in these distinguished readings, aided by Gimell's fine recording, Tallis's genius is fully revealed.

Additional recommendation ...
Lamentations of Jeremiah. Salvator mundi II a 5. O sacrum convivium. Mass a 4. Absterge Domine. **The Hilliard Ensemble/Paul Hiller.** ECM New Series 833 308-2 — ‥ DDD 4/88

Tallis. SACRED CHORAL WORKS. [a]**Taverner Consort;** [b]**Taverner Choir/Andrew Parrott.** EMI Reflexe CDC7 49555-2. Texts and translations included.
Videte miraculum[b]. Homo quidam[b]. Audivi vocem[a]. Candidi facti sunt Nazarei[b]. Dum transisset Sabbatum[b]. Honor, virtus et potestas[b]. Hodie nobis[a]. Loquebantur variis linguis[b]. In pace, in idipsum[a]. Spem in alium (with Wim Becu, bass sackbut; Paul Nicholson, Alan Wilson, orgs)[ab].

‥ (2) 1h 2m 1h 8m DDD 5/89

Tallis, one of the greatest composers of sacred music, has been sympathetically and generously acknowledged by Andrew Parrott and the Taverner Choir with this disc of Latin church music. It includes the masterly 40-part responsary *Spem in alium* written, it would seem, in reply to a similarly ambitious one by Tallis's Italian contemporary, Alessandro Striggio. The performances are characterized by translucent textures, a wonderful feeling for structure and a fluent under-standing of the composer's contrapuntal ingenuity. Certainly there are occasional hints of vocal strain in the uppermost reaches of the part writing but they do little to spoil an affectionate, technically assured account of thrilling music. Parrott illuminates the music with his own deep understanding of it, but above all with the skilful deployment of vocal talent that he has at his command.

Additional recommendations ...
Spem in alium. Salvator mundi (I, II). Sancte Deus, sancte fortis. Gaude gloriosa Dei mater. Miserere nostri. Loquebantur variis linguis. **The Tallis Scholars/Peter Phillips.** Gimell CDGIM006 — ‥ 43m DDD 3/86 ⁹ₚ

O salutaris hostia. In jejunio et fletu. Salvator mundi I. Salvator mundi II. In manuas tuas, Domine. Lamentations of Jeremiah. O sacrum convivium. O nata lux de lumine. Te lucis ante terminum. Spem in alium (with Winchester College Quiristers; Vocal Arts; Timothy Byram-Wifield, org). **Winchester Cathedral Choir/David Hill.** Hyperion CDA66400 — ‥ 59m DDD 5/90

Further listening ...

Missa Salve intemerata virgo. Coupled with **Taverner.** *Mass a 4, "Western Wynde". Song, "Western Wynde".* **St John's College Choir, Cambridge/George Guest.** EMI· Eminence CD-EMX2155 (2/90).

Sergey Ivanovich Taneyev
Russian 1856-1915

Suggested listening ...

Symphony No. 4 in C minor, Op. 12. THE ORESTEIA — Overture. **Philharmonia Orchestra/Neeme Järvi.** Chandos CHAN8953 (4/92).

Alexandre Tansman
Polish/French 1897-1986

Suggested listening ...

Le Jardin du Paradis — Danse de la sorcière[abcde]. *Coupled with* **Saint-Saëns.** Caprice sur des airs danois et russes, Op. 79[abc]. ***d'Indy.*** Sarabande et menuet, Op. 72[abcde]. **Roussel.** Divertissement, Op. 6[abcde]. ***Françaix.*** L'heure du berger[abce]. **Poulenc.** Elégie[e]. ***Milhaud.*** Sonata for Flute, Oboe, Clarinet and Piano, Op. 47[abc]. [a]**Catherine Cantin** (fl); [b]**Maurice Bourgue** (ob); [c]**Michel Portal** (cl); [d]**Amaury Wallez** (bn); [e]**André Cazalet** (hn); **Pascal**

Rogé (pf). Decca 425 861-2DH (5/91). *See review in the Collections Section; refer to the Index to Reviews.*

String Quartets Nos. 2-8. Triptyque. **Silesian Quartet.** Etcetera KTC2017 (8/92).

Francisco Tárrega

Spanish 1852-1909

Suggested listening ...

Mazurka in G major. Study in A major. Marietta. Capricho árabe. Prelude in A minor. Recuerdos de la Alhambra. *Coupled with **Malats*** (arr. Tárrega). Serenata española. **Pujol.** Tango espagnol. Guajira. **Llobet.** Popular Catalan folksongs. **Julian Bream** (gtr). RCA Victor Red Seal RD60429 (7/92). *See review in the Collections Section; refer to the Index to Reviews.*

Giuseppe Tartini

Italian 1692-1770

Tartini. VIOLIN SONATAS. **Locatelli Trio** (Elizabeth Wallfisch, vn; Richard Tunnicliffe, vc; Paul Nicholson, hpd). Hyperion CDA66430. Recorded in 1990.
Sonate e una pastorale — No. 2 in F major; No. 8 in C minor; No. 10 in G minor, "Didone abbandonata"; No. 12 in F major. Pastorale in A major. Sonata in G minor, "Le trille du diable".

Ih 13m DDD 4/92

The members of the Locatelli Trio have an impressive pedigree as performers of baroque music. Here they bring their wealth of experience most fruitfully to bear upon six of about 42 authenticated violin sonatas by Giuseppe Tartini, the violin virtuoso and pedagogue who established such an influential school of playing in Padua in the second quarter of the eighteenth century. These sonatas are well selected to illustrate the range of Tartini's style and to produce a balanced, developing programme. Two important and better known works — nicknamed *Didone abbandonata* and *Le trille du diable* — frame others that are equally rich in graceful melody, dazzling passagework and innovative scoring but which perhaps lack a distinctive selling point. The three-movement *Pastorale* in A major is a particularly effective work, worthy of much wider dissemination in recital programmes. The multi-sectioned final movement is a triumph of novel ideas and balanced structure. This performance is especially affecting, with the lightness of approach nevertheless conveying a depth of feeling not always to the fore elsewhere on this disc. In general, warmth and invention abound in this playing, yet the galant style is never transgressed, the emotions never pushed to romantic proportions. Elizabeth Wallfisch's baroque violin has a full, rounded tone and she plays with admirable security of technique, even in the most demanding sections. The resonance of the ensemble is delightfully reflected in the spacious acoustic of the recording, further helping the cause of such fine music that has for too long been neglected.

Tartini. VIOLIN SONATA. **Locatelli Trio** (Elizabeth Wallfisch, vn; Richard Tunnicliffe, vc; Paul Nicholson, hpd). Hyperion CDA66485. Recorded in 1991.
D major, BD19; B flat major, BB1; A major, BA4, "sopra lo stile che suona il Prette dalla Chitarra Portoghese"; B flat major, BB5 (Op. 5 No. 6).

Ih 7m DDD II/92

The four works here are unfailingly inventive, ranging in style from the militaristic first *Allegro* of the D major Sonata to the delicate *Largo* of the B flat work. Each sonata here receives performances of the highest calibre from the Locatelli Trio, richly detailed and compelling in tone. Listen to the extraordinary Sonata, BA4 "In the style of the priest who plays the Portuguese guitar". The second movement *Andante* sets biting double-stopped dissonances of the violin against limpid pizzicato cello in such a manner as to sound almost improvised. Tempos are unfailingly apt — in the B flat Sonata, Op. 5 No. 6, the opening *Affetuoso* is given ample space before launching into the breezy *Allegro*, with Elizabeth Wallfisch throwing off the intricate figurations with effortless grace and impeccable tuning, even in the top-most registers, of which Tartini was inordinately fond. Unless the very thought of original instruments brings you out in a rash, there is much to delight here, both in the pieces and the performances. The immediate recording brings the players right into the room with the listener and the scholarly yet readable notes from Peter Holman set the works in their proper context.

Further listening ...

Violin Concertos — E minor, D56; A major, D96; A minor, D113. **Uto Ughi** (vn); **I Solisti Veneti/Claudio Scimone.** Erato Emerald 2292-45380-2 (11/91).

Phyllis Tate
British 1911-1987

Suggested listening ...

String Quartet in F major. *Coupled with* **Rubbra.** String Quartet No. 2 in E flat major. **P. Wishart.** String Quartet No. 3 in A major. **English Quartet**. Tremula TREM102-2 (12/93). *See review under Rubbra; refer to the Index to Reviews.*

John Tavener
British 1944-

Tavener. The Protecting Veil[a]. Thrinos.
Britten. Solo Cello Suite No. 3, Op. 87. **Steven Isserlis** (vc); [a]**London Symphony Orchestra/Gennadi Rozhdestvensky.** Virgin Classics VC7 59052-2.

Ih 14m DDD 3/92

The Protecting Veil is one of the feasts of the Mother of God, according to the ritual of the Orthodox Church. John Tavener's ability to transfer such a concept into a concert work of wide appeal and proven impact is indeed remarkable, even if its success has more to do with the simple, direct emotionalism of the music than with its specific religious connotations. Direct emotionalism, certainly — but the music's predominantly slow pace and sustained lyricism, offset by occasional, striking dramatic gestures of sorrow and lamentation, make huge demands on the stamina and technique of the performers. Both Steven Isserlis and Gennadi Rozhdestvensky, not normally one of the more self-effacing of conductors, deserve high praise for the way they sink themselves into the music's contemplative but far from monotonous ethos, and refugees from the battering of more complex contemporary music need look no further for solace and consolation. The brief lament of the unaccompanied cello piece Thrinos is no less affecting, while the Britten suite provides valuable contrast through music from which the intense and unshakeable religious faith of Tavener's work is conspicuous by its absence. Even by modern standards, the recording quality is outstandingly good.

New review
Tavener. String Quartets — The Last Sleep of the Virgin; The Hidden Treasure.
Pärt. String Quartets — Summa; Fratres. **Chilingirian Quartet** (Levon Chilingirian, Mark Butler, vns; Louise Williams, va; Philip De Groote, vc). Virgin Classics VC5 45023-2. Recorded in 1993.

Ih 14m DDD 5/94

Tintinnabulation (a tinkling ringing of bells), a word that Arvo Pärt uses for describing his style, might equally apply to John Tavener's meditative The Last Sleep of the Virgin (1992). "Still, quiet and intensely fragile" writes Tavener at the head of his score. Music such as this aims at suggestion rather than argument, and with production and performance standards that are uniformly high, it's best to take this work on its own terms and leave it at that. *The Hidden*

Treasure (1989) is another continuous piece, one that centres on the idea of longing for Paradise. Contrast is the key word here — forceful and static passages alternate, but words mean nothing, you *must* hear it for yourself! In fact, virtually the whole of Tavener's recent output is single-mindedly intent on defining and exploring areas beyond the busy prisons of language, a trend that Arvo Pärt has been exploring since the mid-1970s. *Fratres* and *Summa* are wordless prayers that take specific liturgy as their starting point and ultimately convey a universal message. Approach them as you might a lonely walk among hills or mountains at dusk, where (to paraphrase Pärt) the many-faceted is abandoned and "everything that is unimportant falls away". Anything more or less, and the point is lost entirely.

New review

Tavener. Hymn for the Dormition of the Mother of God. Hymn to the Mother of God. Little Lamb, who made thee? (The Lamb)[b]. The Tiger. Ikon of Light[a]. Today the Virgin. Eonia. **The Sixteen;** [a]**Duke Quartet** (Louisa Fuller, Rick Koster, vns; John Metcalfe, va; Ivan McCready, vc)**/Harry Christophers.** Collins Classics 1405-2. Item marked [b] from 1270-2 (12/90), recorded in 1990; remainder new to UK, recorded in 1993.

Ih 7m DDD 6/94

Lavish soundscapes, like *The Protecting Veil*, may have caught the public imagination, but perhaps Tavener's real genius is encapsulated in his two Blake settings. Just as the true believer can find more profound beauty in a tiny icon than a church full of frescos, so in these short works Tavener's spiritual and musical vision seems more intense than in his more expansive works. What's more, he reaches into the very soul of Blake's famous but none the less obscure poetry. It is not just the Blake settings that show Tavener focusing his writing without losing that intangible sense of depth and mystery which so informs the larger scores, and whether it is the gloriously full-bodied crescendo in the *Hymn to the Mother of God*, or the deliberate absence of colour and expression in *Eonia*, The Sixteen seem to have an instinctive feel for the inner spirit of the music, creating compelling performances of all six of these miniature *a cappella* masterpieces. With the *Ikon of Light*, though, maybe the more prayerful and distant style adopted by The Tallis Scholars is preferable. The Sixteen bring a satisfying warmth and richness, but is this entirely appropriate in a work of such mystery and spiritual intensity? It can be powerful — not least with the initial five gradually expanding choral statements of the word "Fos" ("light") set against the sparse back-drop of a string trio which here have all the blinding awesomeness of nuclear explosions.

Additional recommendation ...
Ikon of Light[a]. Funeral Ikos[b]. Carol — The Lamb[c]. Members of the **Chilingirian Quartet; The Tallis Scholars/**[ab]**Peter Phillips,** [c]**John Tavener.** Gimell CDGIM005 — 55m DDD 6/91

New review

Tavener. We shall see Him as He is. **Patricia Rozario** (sop); **John Mark Ainsley, Andrew Murgatroyd** (tens); **Britten Singers; Chester Festival Chorus; BBC Welsh Symphony Chorus and Orchestra/Richard Hickox.** Chandos CHAN9128. Text included. Recorded at a performance in the Royal Albert Hall, London in 1992.

Ih Im DDD I/93

We shall see Him as He is was given its first performance in the Chester Summer Music Festival in 1992. This recording is a remarkable achievement in every respect — balance and sound are superb and the spellbound audience are as quiet as mice. The text depicts, in simple but powerful words, various events in the life of Christ — His baptism, the miracle at Cana, the cleansing of the temple, His healing of the cripple, the Last Supper and the Crucifixion, to name a few. These are presented as a series of 12 musical episodes (ikons) headed by an introduction entitled "The Unfolding of the Great Mystery"; perhaps the best way for the listener to think of the work is as one large iconostasis comprising of 12 smaller ikons which gradually unfold as the work progresses. Although the piece could scarcely be described as modest in its scoring, Tavener's handling of the forces could hardly be more economical. Most of the musical focus is in the sumptuous and melismatic vocal writing, with the instrumental material providing iconographical colour and, at key points in the narrative, declamatory and monumental "blazes of light", as for example in the turning of water into wine and the healing of the cripple. Performances are astonishingly persuasive and committed in this compelling and intensely moving work. Those who have come to Tavener's music via *The Protecting Veil* will not be disappointed.

John Taverner
British c.1490-1545

New review

Taverner. CHORAL WORKS. **The Sixteen;** [a]**Fretwork** (Wendy Gillespie, Richard Campbell, treble viols; Susanna Pell, Julia Hodgson, Richard Boothby, bass viols; William Hunt, great bass viol)/**Harry Christophers.** Hyperion CDA66639. Texts and translations included. Recorded in 1992.
Hodie nobis caelorum Rex. Mater Christi sanctissima. Magnificat sexti toni. Nesciens mater. Quemadmodum a 6[a]. Missa Mater Christi sanctissima. In nomine a 4[a].

1h 5m DDD 3/94

The Sixteen offer an impressive account of the composer's five-part *Missa Mater Christi sanctissima*, based on his votive anthem of the same name. It is a lively and vigorous work, beautifully crafted, and this performance amply matches that craftsmanship. Harry Christophers attempts no liturgical reconstruction, concentrating instead upon sheer musical quality. Three female sopranos replace the boy trebles. The music is all pitched up a tone, which has the effect of adding brilliance to every climax. He demonstrates the surprisingly good acoustic of St Jude-on-the-Hill in Hampstead — an acoustic of space and definition, ideal for the interweaving of the strands of early Tudor polyphony; indeed, clarity and a sense of space are hallmarks of the recording. The supporting programme of the Christmas responsory, *Hodie*, the votive anthem *Mater Christi* and a four-part *Magnificat* is completed — unexpectedly, but most delightfully — by two pieces for viols.

Taverner. Missa Sancti Wilhelmi. MOTETS. **The Sixteen/Harry Christophers.** Hyperion CDA66427. Texts and translations included.
Motets — O Wilhelme, pastor bone. Dum transisset Sabbatum. Ex eius tumba.

52m DDD 4/92

The *Missa Sancti Wilhelmi* is not one of Taverner's best known works, but there is no reason why this should be the case. Though it does not have the sometimes rather wild melodic beauty of the six-voice Masses, it is nevertheless an impressive work in a more modern imitative style, in keeping with its model *O Wilhelme, pastor bone.* The Sixteen perform with their customary clarity and precision, and convey enthusiasm even in the somewhat syllabic *Gloria* and *Credo* movements of the Mass, something which is not always easy to do. While both the 'Wilhelm' works and *Dum transisset Sabbatum* are among Taverner's later works, there is no doubt at all that *Ex eius tumba* is one of the earliest. It is firmly late medieval in style, and the intricate tracery of its construction, so well captured here by The Sixteen, makes a thought-provoking contrast to the pieces in a more 'continental' imitative style. At 15 minutes this is a substantial composition, and one can only be surprised that it is so little-known: perhaps the large amount of chant which forms an integral part of the work has discouraged performers. *Dum transisset Sabbatum* is, however, the high point of the disc, and if The Sixteen do not quite attain the ecstatic heights achieved in the recording by The Tallis Scholars (reviewed above), neither do they fail to rise to Taverner's inspiration.

Additional recommendation ...
Dum transisset Sabbatum. Missa Gloria tibi Trinitatis. Kyrie a 4, "Leroy". **The Tallis Scholars/Peter Phillips.** Gimell CDGIM004 — 47m DDD 7/86

Further listening ...

Missa Corona spinea. *Motets* — Gaude plurimum; In pace in idipsum. **The Sixteen/Harry Christophers.** Hyperion CDA66360 (1/90).

Mass a 4, "Western Wynde". Mater Christi. *Coupled with **Tallis.*** *Motets* — Sancte Deus. Audivi vocem de caelo. Honor, virtus et potestas. O sacrum convivium. Salvator mundi I a 5. **New College Choir, Oxford/Edward Higginbottom.** CRD CRD3372 (4/89).

Missa Mater Christi. O Wilhelme, pastor bone. Mater Christi sanctissima. **Christ Church Cathedral Choir, Oxford/Stephen Darlington.** Nimbus NI5218 (4/90).

André Tchaikovsky

Polish/British 1935-1982

Suggested listening ...

String Quartet No. 2 in C major, Op. 5. *Coupled with **Wirén.*** String Quartet No. 3 in D minor, Op. 18. ***Hugh Wood.*** String Quartet No. 3, Op. 20. ***Barber.*** String Quartet, Op. 11. **Lindsay Quartet.** ASV CDDCA825 (1/93). *See review in the Collections section; refer to the Index to Reviews.*

Pyotr Ill'yich Tchaikovsky

Russian 1840-1893

New review
Tchaikovsky. Piano Concertos — No. 1 in B flat minor, Op. 23[a]; No. 2 in G major, Op. 44 (orig. version)[b]; No. 3 in E flat major, Op. 75[a]. Concert Fantasia, Op. 56[c]. **Peter Donohoe** (pf); **Bournemouth Symphony Orchestra/Rudolf Barshai** with **Nigel Kennedy** (vn); **Steven Isserlis** (vc). EMI CMS7 63658-2. Item marked [a] from EL749667-2 (4/89), [b] EL270603-1 (8/87), [c] new to UK.

② 2h 7m DDD 2/91 ⁹ₚ Ⓑ

Peter Donohoe's recording of Tchaikovsky's Second Piano Concerto deservedly won the *Gramophone* Concerto Award in 1988. The work had been most often heard in a truncated version but Donohoe and Barshai between them transformed the reputation of the much longer original version, with its *concertante* sections in the *Andante* — helped by fine contributions from Nigel Kennedy and Steven Isserlis. Barshai, also, by setting a sparkling pace for the first movement, counteracted the earlier view that this movement was inflated. The recording is worthy of the playing, with a firm, bold piano image realistically balanced against an orchestral sound that satisfyingly combines brilliance with body and warmth. The performance of the First Concerto is spacious and strong, yet does not match the Second in natural spontaneity. The *Andantino* is charmingly done and the finale has all the feeling of a Russian dance. In the coda there are stormy octaves from the soloist, and a broad, strongly moulded prepresentation of the main lyrical tune to match the breadth of the opening movement. The Third Concerto is in a single movement, lasting just over a quarter of an hour. There is no lack of spontaneity here, and soloist and conductor successfully hold together a work that needs cohesion, with a nicely judged balance between lyricism and drama. Again the sound is very good. The *Concert Fantasia* is laid out in two substantial movements, together lasting very nearly half an hour. It has a big, rumbustious cadenza at the centre of the first movement, which begins chirpily in the orchestra, sounding very like ballet music. Donohoe plays the cadenza very much in the grand manner. There is a degree of muddiness to the climax, and the pedalling contributes to this, so that one feels he is going over the top a bit. But the effect is powerfully commanding. The performers take the composer's markings very literally, and the fast music is raced through with exhilarating zest.

Additional recommendations ...
No 2. ***Grieg.*** *Piano Concerto in A minor, Op. 16*[a]. **Artur Rubinstein** (pf); **Boston Symphony Orchestra/Erich Leinsdorf;** [a]**Orchestra/Alfred Wallenstein.** RCA Gold Seal 09026-61262-2 — ⁣.•⁣ 1h 3m ADD ⁹ₚ Ⓑ
No 2. ***Rachmaninov.*** *Piano Concerto No. 2 in C minor, Op. 18.* **Alexei Sultanov** (pf); **London Symphony Orchestra/Maxim Shostakovich.** Teldec Digital Experience 9031-77601-2 —
.•⁣ 1h 10m DDD ⁹ₚ Ⓑ

No 2[a]. **Prokofiev.** *Piano Concerto No. 3 in C major, Op. 26*[b]. **Martha Argerich** (pf); [a]**Royal Philharmonic Orchestra/Charles Dutoit;** [b]**Berlin Philharmonic Orchestra/Claudio Abbado.** DG 415 062-2GH — .•' 1h 3m ADD 5/85 ⁹ₚ Ⓑ

No 2. **Dohnányi.** *Variations on a Nursery Song.* **András Schiff** (pf); **Chicago Symphony Orchestra/Sir Georg Solti.** Decca 417 294-2DH — .•' 59m DDD 12/86 ⁹ₚ Ⓑ

No 2[a]. **Chopin.** *Piano Concerto No. 2 in F minor, Op. 21*[b]. **Vladimir Ashkenazy** (pf); **London Symphony Orchestra/**[a]**Lorin Maazel;** [b]**David Zinman.** Decca Ovation 417 750-2DM — .•' 1h 6m ADD 1/89 Ⓑ

No 2[a]. *Violin Concerto in D major, Op. 35*[b]. [a]**Emil Gilels** (pf); [a]**New York Philharmonic Orchestra/Zubin Mehta;** [b]**Pinchas Zukerman** (vn); [b]**Israel Philharmonic Orchestra/ Zubin Mehta.** CBS Masterworks CD44643 — .•' 1h 9m DDD 9/89 ⁹ₚ Ⓑ

Nos. 1 and 3. **Emil Gilels** (pf); **New Philharmonia Orchestra/Lorin Maazel.** EMI Eminence CD-EMX2001 — .•' 52m ADD 8/90 Ⓑ

No 2. Concert Fantasia, Op. 56. **Mikhail Pletnev** (pf); **Philharmonia Orchestra/Vladimir Fedoseyev.** Virgin Classics VC7 59612-2 — .•' 1h 4m DDD 4/91 ⁹ₚ Ⓑ

No. 2. **Mozart.** *Piano Concerto No. 21 in C major, K467.* **Emil Gilels** (pf); **USSR Symphony Orchestra/Kyrill Kondrashin.** Mezhdunarodnaya Kniga MK417106 — .•' 1h 3m AAD 5/93 ⁹ₚ Ⓑ

Nos. 2 and 3. **Victoria Postnikova** (pf); **Vienna Symphony Orchestra/Gennadi Rozhdestvensky.** Decca Ovation 436 485-2DM — .•' 1h 8m DDD 6/94 Ⓑ

Tchaikovsky. Piano Concerto No. 1 in B flat major, Op. 23[b].
Prokofiev. Piano Concerto No. 3 in C major, Op. 26[a]. **Martha Argerich** (pf); [a]**Berlin Philharmonic Orchestra/Claudio Abbado;** [b]**Royal Philharmonic Orchestra/Charles Dutoit.** DG 415 062-2GH. Item marked [a] from 138349 (2/68), [b] 2530 112 (10/71).

.•' **1h 3m ADD 5/85** ⁹ₚ Ⓑ

By general consensus Martha Argerich's 1971 recording of Tchaikovsky's B flat minor Piano Concerto is still among the best of the currently available recordings. The opening of the first movement sets the mood of spaciousness and weight, with the lovely secondary material bringing poetic contrast. The *Andantino* has an appealing delicacy, with the centrepiece dazzling in its light-fingered virtuosity to match the exhilaration of the last movement. The admirably balanced recording has plenty of spectacle, the strings are full and firm and the piano image is strikingly real and tangible. The unexpected but inspirational coupling was one of Argerich's début recordings, and for those less familiar with Tchaikovsky's twentieth-century compatriot, the music itself will come as a refreshing surprise. The apparent initial spikiness soon dissolves with familiarity and Prokofiev's concerto reveals itself as very much in the romantic tradition. Its harmonies are more pungent than those of Tchaikovsky, but the melodic appeal is striking and the sheer vitality of the outer movements is irresistible as projected by Martha Argerich's nimble fingers.

New review
Tchaikovsky. Violin Concerto in D major, Op. 35[a].
Brahms (arr. Joachim). Hungarian Dances[b] — No. 1 in G minor; No. 2 in D minor; No. 4 in B minor; No. 7 in A major. **Sarah Chang** (vn); [b]**Jonathan Feldman** (pf); [a]**London Symphony Orchestra/Sir Colin Davis.** EMI CDC7 54753-2. Recorded 1992-93.

.•' **49m DDD 12/93** ⁹ₚ

The range of dynamic truthfulness conveyed in Sarah Chang's performance, helped by a clear, full, naturally-balanced recording, brings not just momentary delight in individual phrases but cumulative gain, in this reading which so strongly hangs together. Not only does Chang play with exceptionally pure tone, avoiding heavy coloration, her individual artistry does not demand the wayward pulling-about often found in this work. In that she is enormously helped by the fresh, bright and dramatic accompaniment provided by the LSO under Sir Colin Davis. In the outer movements Chang conveys wit along with the power and poetry, and the intonation is immaculate. Brahms *Hungarian Dances* are delectable, marked by the sort of naughty pointing of phrase and rhythm that tickles one's musical funny-bone just as the playing of Kreisler always did. Here is a young artist who really does live up to the claims of the publicists.

Additional recommendations ...
Violin Concerto. **Mendelssohn.** *Violin Concerto in E minor, Op. 64.* **Jascha Heifetz** (vn);
Chicago Symphony Orchestra/Fritz Reiner. RCA RD85933 —
Violin Concerto. Sérénade mélancolique in B minor, Op. 26. Souvenir d'un lieu cher, Op. 42 — No. 3,
Mélodie (orch. Glazunov). Valse-scherzo in C major, Op. 34. **Xue-Wei** (vn); **Philharmonia**
Orchestra/Salvatore Accardo. ASV CDDCA713 — •‿•' 54m DDD 9/90 Ⓑ
Violin Concerto[a]. **Bazzini.** *La ronde des lutins, Op. 25*[b]. **Bloch.** *Baal shem — Nigun*[b]. **Kreisler.**
Liebesleid[b]. **Prokofiev** *(arr. Heifetz). The Love for Three Oranges — March*[b]. **Tartini.** *Violin Sonata*
in G minor, "The devil's trill"[b]. **Tchaikovsky** *(arr. Kreisler). String Quartet No. 1 in D major, Op. 11*
— Andante[b]. **Wieniawski** *(arr. Kreisler). Caprice in A minor*[b]. **Itzhak Perlman** (vn); [b]**Janet**
Goodman Guggenheim (pf); [a]**Israel Philharmonic Orchestra/Zubin Mehta.** EMI CDC7
54108-2 — •‿•' 1h 12m DDD 2/91 Ⓑ
Violin Concerto. **Prokofiev.** *Violin Concerto No. 2 in G minor, Op. 63.* **Kyoko Takezawa** (vn);
Moscow Radio Symphony Orchestra / Vladimir Fedoseyev. RCA Victor Red Seal
09026 60759-2 — •‿•' 1h 3m DDD 12/93 Ⓑ
Violin Concerto. **Brahms.** *Violin Concerto in D major, Op. 77.* **Jascha Heifetz** (vn); **Chicago**
Symphony Orchestra/Fritz Reiner. RCA Living Stereo 09026 61495-2 — •‿•' 1h 4m ADD 4/93
Ⓑ ▲
Violin Concerto. Sérénade mélancolique in B minor, Op. 26. Valse-scherzo in C major, Op. 34. **Pierre**
Amoyal (vn); **Philharmonia Orchestra/Charles Dutoit.** Erato Libretto 2292-45971-2 —
•‿•' 51m ADD 5/93 ⁹ₚ Ⓑ
Violin Concerto. **Sibelius.** *Violin Concerto in D minor, Op. 47.* **Gil Shaham** (vn); **Philharmonia**
Orchestra/Giuseppe Sinopoli. DG 437 540-2GH — •‿•' 1h 7m DDD 9/93 Ⓑ

Tchaikovsky. 1812 — Overture, Op. 49. Capriccio italien, Op. 45. MAZEPPA — Cossack
Dance. **Cincinnati Symphony Orchestra/Erich Kunzel.** Telarc CD80041. From DG10041
(4/80).

•‿•' 35m DDD 12/83   ⁹ₛ Ⓑ

Kunzel's recording of the *1812* is an unashamed hi-fi spectacular, so much so that purchasers are
warned that the cannon at the end can damage loudspeakers with their extreme volume. At the
time of the recording it is claimed that windows nearby were shattered. In the *Capriccio italien*
too, another colourful popular favourite, this version uses the full range of high-fidelity digital
sound with the bass drum very prominent and astonishingly vivid in its exploitation of the lowest
register. The forwardness of such effects may detract from the purely musical qualities of the
performances, which are strong and energetic without being so perceptive or so exciting as
some, though very well played. Particularly enjoyable is the third item, the vigorous and
colourful "Cossack Dance".

Additional recommendation ...
Overture. Romeo and Juliet. Hamlet, Op. 67a. **London Philharmonic Orchestra/Sir**
Alexander Gibson. Collins Classics Quest 3048-2 — •‿•' 51m DDD Ⓑ

Tchaikovsky. Serenade in C major, Op. 48. Souvenir de Florence, Op. 70. **Vienna**
Chamber Orchestra/Philippe Entremont. Naxos 8 550404. Recorded in 1990.

• 1h 5m DDD 10/91   ⁹ₚ ⁹ₛ Ⓑ

This is one of the many CDs now on the market that dispel the myth once and for all that only
full-price recordings contain really outstanding performances. The Naxos label is just about as
'bargain' as you will get, and here they have given us superlative performances of two of
Tchaikovsky's most endearing works. The Serenade in C contains a wealth of memorable and
haunting music, beautifully and inventively scored and guaranteed to bring immense pleasure and
delight to those dipping their toes in to the world of classical music for the first time. Philippe
Entremont and the Vienna Chamber Orchestra give a marvellously polished and finely poised
performance full of warmth, affection and high spirits, and the famous second movement Waltz
in particular is played with much elegance and grace. The *Souvenir de Florence*, originally written
for string sextet, makes a welcome appearance here in Tchaikovsky's own arrangement for string
orchestra. This is a delightfully sunny performance, full of suavity, exuberance and romantic
dash, but always alert to the many subtleties of Tchaikovsky's skilful and intricate part-writing.

The *Adagio cantabile* is particularly notable for some extremely fine and poetic solo playing from the violin and cello principals of the VPO. The beautifully spacious recording does ample justice to the performances. A magnificent bargain.

Additional recommendations ...
Serenade. Suite No. 4 in G major, Op. 61, "Mozartiana". Elegy in G major in honour of Ivan Samarin. String Quartet No. 1 in D major, Op. 11 — Andante cantabile (orch. Serebrier). The Sleeping Beauty (orch. Stravinsky) — Variations de la Fée de lilas; Entr'acte. **Scottish Chamber Orchestra/José Serebrier.** ASV CDDCA719 — .•' Ih 17m DDD 3/91 ⁹ₚ Ⓑ
Serenade. **Grieg.** *Holberg Suite, Op. 40. Two Norwegian Melodies, Op. 63.* **Moscow Soloists/Yuri Bashmet.** RCA Victor Red Seal RD60368 — .•' Ih Im DDD 3/91 Ⓑ
Serenade. Souvenir de Florence. **Auvergne Orchestra/Jean-Jacques Kantorow.** Denon CO-75026 — .•' Ih 2m DDD 3/93 Ⓑ

Tchaikovsky. Romeo and Juliet — Fantasy Overture. The Nutcracker — Ballet Suite, Op. 71a. **Berlin Philharmonic Orchestra/Herbert von Karajan.** DG 410 873-2GH. From 410 873-1GH (2/84).

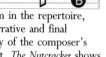

.•' **44m DDD 4/84** ⁹ₚ Ⓑ

It might be argued that *Romeo and Juliet* is the most successful symphonic poem in the repertoire, economically structured, wonderfully inspired in its melodies and with the narrative and final tragedy depicted with imaginative vividness. Karajan brings out all the intensity of the composer's inspiration and the playing of the Berlin Philharmonic creates much excitement. *The Nutcracker* shows the other side of the composer's personality, the most wonderfully crafted light music, and the suite is utter perfection. Each of the *danses caractéristiques* is a miracle of melody and orchestration and their charm never cloys, especially when they are played so winningly and with such polish. The recording is admirably clear and well balanced and though a little more warmth would have made the upper strings sweeter in the ballet music, this remains a very recommendable disc.

Additional recommendations ...
Romeo and Juliet (1869 version). Hamlet — Incidental Music, Op. 67a[a]. Festival Overture on the Danish national hymn, Op. 15. Serenade for Nikolai Rubinstein's name day. MAZEPPA — Battle of Poltava; Cossack Dance. [a]**Janis Kelly** (sop); [a]**Derek Hammond-Stroud** (bar); **London Symphony Orchestra/Geoffrey Simon.** Chandos CHAN8310/11 — .•' ② Ih 34m DDD 7/84 Ⓑ
Romeo and Juliet. Capriccio italien, Op. 45. Francesca da Rimini, Op. 32. Elegy in honour of Ivan Samarin. **Royal Philharmonic Orchestra/Vladimir Ashkenazy.** Decca 421 715-2DH — .•' Ih 6m DDD 8/89 Ⓑ
The Nutcracker — Ballet Suite. The Sleeping Beauty — excerpts. Swan Lake — excerpts. **Berlin Philharmonic Orchestra/Mstislav Rostropovich.** DG Galleria 429 097-2GGA — .•' Ih 9m ADD 4/90 ⁹ₚ Ⓑ
The Nutcracker — Ballet Suite[a]. The Sleeping Beauty — excerpts. Swan Lake — excerpts. [a]**Ambrosian Singers; London Symphony Orchestra/André Previn.** EMI CZS7 62816-2 — .•' ② 2h 28m ADD 3/92 Ⓑ
Romeo and Juliet. 1812 —Overture. Capriccio Italien, Op. 45. None but the lonely heart, Op. 6 No. 6 (arr. Riley). EUGENE ONEGIN — Faint echo of my youth. [b]**Ofra Harnoy** (vc); **Philharmonia Orchestra/**[ab]**Plácido Domingo** ([d]ten); **Randall Behr.** EMI CDC5 55018-2 — .•' Ih 8m DDD 4/94 Ⓑ

Tchaikovsky. ORCHESTRAL WORKS. **Royal Liverpool Philharmonic Orchestra/Sian Edwards.** EMI Eminence CD-EMX2152.
1812 — Overture, Op. 49. Romeo and Juliet — Fantasy Overture. Marche slave, Op. 31. Francesca da Rimini, Op. 32.

.•' **Ih 6m DDD 12/89** ⁹ₚ ⁹ₛ Ⓑ

It is an extraordinary achievement that the young British conductor, Sian Edwards, should have made her recording début with a Tchaikovsky programme of such distinction. She immediately achieves a splendid artistic partnership with the Royal Liverpool Philharmonic Orchestra, whose playing is so full of vitality, and whether in *1812* with its vigour and flair, its cluster of lyrical folk melodies, and a spectacular finale with thundering canon, or in *Marche slave*, resplendently patriotic, in a uniquely Russian way, together they bring the music tingling to life in every bar. *Romeo and Juliet*, on the other hand, needs a finely judged balance between the ardour and moonlight of the love music, the vibrant conflict of the battle, and the tragedy of the final denouement, which is uncannily well managed. Most intractable interpretatively is *Francesca da Rimini*, with its spectacularly horrifying picture of Dante's inferno which the composer uses to frame the central sequence depicting the lovers, Francesca and Paolo, and the doom-laden atmosphere which surrounds their intense mutual passion. Edwards's grip on this powerfully evocative sequence of events is unerringly sure, and she takes the orchestra through the narrative as only an instinctive Tchaikovskian could. The work opens with an unforgettable sense of nemesis and ends with a truly thrilling picture of the whirlwinds of Hell, into which the lovers are cast, still in their final passionate embrace. All in all this is one of the best Tchaikovsky discs in the mid-price catalogue and the fine EMI Eminence recording combines weight and sonority with brilliance, and brings a most attractive ambient effect.

Additional recommendations ...
Francesca da Rimini. Hamlet — Fantasy Overture, Op. 67. **New York Stadium Orchestra/ Leopold Stokowski.** dell'Arte CDDA9006 — .·' ADD 4/88 ♩ₚ Ⓑ
Romeo and Juliet. Capriccio italien, Op. 45. Francesca da Rimini. Elegy in honour of Ivan Samarin. **Royal Philharmonic Orchestra/Vladimir Ashkenazy.** Decca 421 715-2DH — .·' 1h 6m DDD 8/89 ♩ₚ Ⓑ
Romeo and Juliet. Francesca da Rimini. Mazeppa — Cossack Dance. Festival Coronation March in D major. **Leipzig Gewandhaus Orchestra/Kurt Masur.** Teldec 9031-76456-2 — .·' 53m DDD 5/93 ♩ₚ Ⓑ

Key to symbols

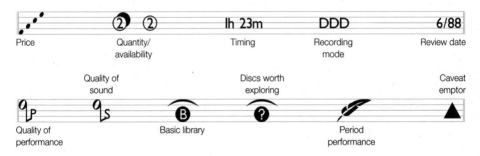

Price	Quantity/ availability	Timing	Recording mode	Review date

1h 23m ... DDD ... 6/88

Quality of sound ... Discs worth exploring ... Caveat emptor

Quality of performance ... Basic library ... Period performance

Tchaikovsky. Swan Lake, Op. 20 — Ballet. **Montreal Symphony Orchestra/Charles Dutoit.** Decca 436 212-2DH2. Recorded in 1991.

.·' ② 2h 34m DDD 2/93 ... ♩ₚ Ⓑ

No one wrote more beautiful and danceable ballet music than Tchaikovsky, and this account of *Swan Lake* is a delight throughout. This is not only because of the quality of the music, which is here played absolutely complete including additions the composer made after the première, but also thanks to the richly idiomatic playing of Charles Dutoit and his Montreal orchestra in the superb and celebrated location of St Eustache's Church in that city. Maybe some conductors have made the music even more earthily Russian, but it is worth remembering that the Russian ballet tradition in Tchaikovsky's time was chiefly French and that the most influential early production of this ballet, in 1895, was choreographed by the Frenchman Marius Petipa. Indeed, the symbiosis of French and Russian elements in this music (and story) is one of its great strengths, the refinement of the one being superbly allied to the vigour of the other, notably in such music as the "Russian Dance" with its expressive violin solo. This is a profoundly romantic reading of the score, and the great set pieces such as the Waltz in Act 1 and the marvellous scene of the swans on a moonlit lake that opens Act 2 are wonderfully evocative; yet they do not for that reason overshadow the other music, which supports and strengthens them as gentler hills and valleys might surround and enhance magnificent, awe-inspiring peaks, the one being indispensable to the other. You do not have to be a ballet aficionado to fall under the spell of this wonderful music, which here receives a performance that combines romantic passion with an aristocratic refinement and is glowingly recorded.

Additional recommendations ...

Swan Lake. **Royal Opera House Orchestra, Covent Garden/Mark Ermler.** Royal Opera House Records ROH301/03 — .·· ③ 2h 33m DDD 12/89 ⁹ₚ Ⓑ

Swan Lake. **Philharmonia Orchestra/John Lanchbery.** Classics for Pleasure CD-CFPD 4727 — .· ② 2h 34m DDD 9/89 Ⓑ

Swan Lake — excerpts. The Nutcracker — Ballet Suite. Romeo and Juliet. **Chicago Symphony Orchestra/Sir Georg Solti.** Decca Ovation 430 707-2DM — .·· 1h 10m DDD 8/91 Ⓑ

Swan Lake. **Slovak Radio Symphony Orchestra, Bratislava/Ondrej Lenárd.** Naxos 8 550246/7 — . ② 2h 20m DDD 12/91 Ⓑ

Swan Lake. **London Symphony Orchestra/Michael Tilson Thomas.** Sony Classical SK46592 — .·· ② 2h 29m DDD 4/92 ⁹ₚ Ⓑ

New review

Tchaikovsky. The Sleeping Beauty, Op. 66 — ballet. **Kirov Theatre Orchestra/Valery Gergiev.** Philips 434 922-2PH3. Recorded in 1992.

.·· ③ 2h 44m DDD 7/93   ⁹ₚ ⁹ₛ Ⓑ

Many authorities regard this as Tchaikovsky's finest ballet score and, indeed, one of the greatest ballet scores of all time. It has many wonderful things: the Waltz from Act One includes some wonderfully arching phrasing that soars with tremendous passion, while the "Panorama" of Act 2 is one of the composer's finest melodic ideas. The "Pas de six" of Act 1 and the contrasted Fairy dances of Act 3 bring the same almost Mozartian grace (combined with Tchaikovsky's own very special feeling for orchestral colour) that he displays in the *Nutcracker* characteristic dances, which turn simple ballet vignettes into great art. Valery Gergiev, the conductor of the Kirov Theatre Orchestra of St Petersburg is at home in this score. He secures splendidly alive and sympathetic playing from his orchestra and the Philips recording is full and sumptuous, with a rich theatrical atmosphere. Tchaikovsky's big climaxes expand properly, the strings are full and natural and the woodwind colours glow.

Additional recommendations ...

Sleeping Beauty (incomplete). **Philharmonia Orchestra/George Weldon.** Classics for Pleasure CD-CFPD4458 — .· ② 1h 57m ADD 1/89 Ⓑ ▲

Sleeping Beauty. **Philharmonia Orchestra/John Lanchbery.** EMI CDS7 49216-2 — .·· ② 2h 39m DDD 3/89 Ⓑ

Sleeping Beauty. **Royal Opera House Orchestra, Covent Garden/Mark Ermler.** Royal Opera House Records ROHCD306/8 — .·· ③ 2h 53m DDD 5/90 Ⓑ

Sleeping Beauty — excerpts. **Royal Opera House Orchestra, Covent Garden/Mark Ermler.** Royal Opera House Records ROHCD003 — .·· 1h 12m DDD 5/90 Ⓑ

Sleeping Beauty. **Czecho-Slovak State Philharmonic Orchestra/Andrew Mogrelia.** Naxos 8 550490-2 — . ③ 2h 53m DDD 4/93 Ⓑ

New review

Tchaikovsky. The Nutcracker. The Sleeping Beauty – Aurora's Wedding. **Montreal Symphony Orchestra/Charles Dutoit.** Decca 440 477-2DH2. Recorded in 1992.

.·· ② 2h 15m DDD 3/94   ⁹ₚ Ⓑ

Many of the favourite characteristic dances seem freshly minted, notably the "Dance of the Sugar-plum Fairy", with its deliciously liquid celesta, and the perky "Chinese Dance". The "Waltz of the Snowflakes" (Act 1) with the children's chorus also has great charm. The transparency of the recorded sound, which helps to make all this possible, is immediately noticeable in the delightful gossamer string textures of the "Miniature Overture". But the big Act 2 *Adagio*, too, is exceptionally satisfying, its histrionics conveyed with passionate flair, yet without hysterical rhetoric at the excitingly grand climax. The recording is extremely vivid: bright but without glare, and the balance between detail, weight and hall resonance seems exactly right. "Aurora's Wedding" is the very much truncated version of *The Sleeping Beauty* which Diaghilev adopted in repertory after his extravagant London production of the complete ballet in 1921 nearly bankrupted him. The music, after introducing both Carabosse and the Lilac Fairy, passes on to the christening, includes the hunting scene in Act 2, where the Prince has a vision of his sleeping princess, then moves on to the happy ending and the dances which form the highlight of the last act. Top choice for *The Nutcracker* can safely rest between Dutoit and Ashkenazy. Previn's mid-price 1972 LSO version also emerges very favourably against the competition.

Additional recommendations ...
Nutcracker. **Ambrosian Singers; Philharmonia Orchestra/Michael Tilson Thomas.** CBS CD42173 — .·ʼ ② DDD 3/87 ⁹ₚ Ⓑ
Nutcracker[a]. *QUEEN OF SPADES — Duet of Daphnis and Chloë*[b]. [b]**Cathryn Pope** (sop); [b]**Sarah Walker** (mez); [a]**Tiffin Boys' School Choir; London Symphony Orchestra/Sir Charles Mackerras.** Telarc CD80137 — .·ʼ ② 1h 28m DDD 5/87 ⁹ₚ ⁹ₛ Ⓑ
Nutcracker[a]. *Glazunov. The Seasons, Op. 67.* [a]**Finchley Children's Music Group; Royal Philharmonic Orchestra/Vladimir Ashkenazy.** Decca 433 000-2DH2 (*see review under Glazunov; refer to the Index to Reviews*) — .·ʼ ② 2h 11m DDD 4/92 Ⓑ
Nutcracker. Serenade in C major, Op. 48[a]. **London Symphony Orchestra,** [a]**Philharmonia Hungarica/Antál Dorati.** Mercury 432 750-2MM2 — .·ʼ ② 1h 9m ADD 9/92 ⁹ₚ Ⓑ ▲
Nutcracker. **Ambrosian Singers; London Symphony Orchestra/André Previn.** Classics for Pleasure CD-CFPD4706 — .·ʼ ② 1h 26m ADD 3/93 Ⓑ

Tchaikovsky. SYMPHONIES. **London Symphony Orchestra/Igor Markevitch.** Philips 426 848-2PB4. Recorded 1962-66.
No. 1 in G minor, Op. 13, "Winter Daydreams"[a]; No. 2 in C minor, Op. 17, "Little Russian"[b]; No. 3 in D major, Op. 29, "Polish"[c]; No. 4 in F minor, Op. 36[d]; No. 5 in E minor, Op. 64[e]; No. 6 in B minor, Op. 74, "Pathétique"[f]. Item marked [a] from SAL3578 (10/66), [b] SAL3601 (3/67), [c] SAL3549 (2/66), [d] SAL3481 (2/65), [e] SAL3579 (12/66), [f] 835126AY (10/62).

.·ʼ ④ 4h 16m ADD 3/91 ⁹ₚ Ⓑ

If you want to avoid routine in standard repertoire, then entrust its interpretation to a composer-performer. It's a formula that doesn't always work, but when it does the results are usually illuminating beyond belief. Igor Markevitch started life as a composer; in fact, before the Second World War he was considered one of Nadia Boulanger's most promising protégées, and his compositions were held in high esteem. Markevitch's approach to Tchaikovsky is refreshing, spontaneous and insightful; no wonder Stravinsky (another Markevitch speciality) felt such a deep love for this music, with its piquant scoring, acute sense of harmonic development and dramatic impact. Markevitch avoids a blanket approach to the six symphonies. He doesn't merely select and indulge those aspects of the music that appeal to him; rather, he treats each separate work as a unique phase in an ongoing symphonic journey. His are more recreations than interpretations; and although attentive to structure, he's quite willing to underline small details, varying the pulse to expressive ends — as he does in the first movements of the Fourth and Sixth Symphonies — and guiding us through musical events that we might otherwise have missed. But where a lesser conductor might turn selective observation into tiresome point-making, Markevitch always retains a sense of structural proportion. His handling of the Third Symphony's introduction is masterly, with the transition into the main *Allegro* as effective as it is cunning. He brings both expressive weight and balletic sensibility to the early symphonies, and although Bernard Haitink's versions (now reissued on a six-disc, bargain-price set) are not displaced, Markevitch's are especially supple, with the LSO strings and woodwinds excelling themselves in keenness of attack and clarity of articulation. The Fifth, too, is supremely alive and eager to yield its secrets, with a first movement that forges forwards and resists the temptation to linger over the big tunes. Musical punctuation can be a problem in Tchaikovsky, but Markevitch understands how to make this music breathe; and with clean, open recordings (just a little short on lustre), his work is borne to us much as it sounded on the day.

Additional recommendations ...
Nos. 1-6. Capriccio italien, Op. 45. Manfred Symphony, Op. 58. **Oslo Philharmonic Orchestra/ Mariss Jansons.** Chandos CHAN8672/8 — .·ʼ ⑦ 5h 19m DDD 1/89 ⁹ₚ Ⓑ
Nos. 4-6. Manfred Symphony[a]. **Philharmonia Orchestra,** [a]**New Philharmonia Orchestra/ Vladimir Ashkenazy.** Decca 425 586-2DM3 — .·ʼ ③ 3h 12m ADD 3/90 ⁹ₚ Ⓑ
No. 1[a]; *Nos. 2-6*[b]. *Romeo and Juliet — Fantasy Overture*[b]. [a]**New Philharmonia Orchestra,** [b]**Philharmonia Orchestra/Riccardo Muti.** EMI CZS7 67314-2 — .·ʼ ④ 4h 32m ADD 9/91 ⁹ₚ Ⓑ
Nos. 1-6. Romeo and Juliet. **Vienna Philharmonic Orchestra/Lorin Maazel.** Decca 430 787-2DC4 — .·ʼ ④ 4h 27m ADD 4/92 ⁹ₚ Ⓑ

Nos. 1-6. *Francesca da Rimini*, Op. 32. *Marche slave*, Op. 31. *Fate*, Op. 77. *Romeo and Juliet* —
Fantasy Overture. *Capriccio Italien*, Op. 45. *Swan Lake* — *Suite*. **Royal Philharmonic Orchestra/
Yuri Temirkanov.** RCA Victor Red Seal 09026 61821-2 — .·* ⑥ 6h 3lm DDD 5/94 Ⓑ
Nos. 1-6. *Romeo and Juliet*. *Manfred Symphony*. *Capriccio italien*. *1812* — *Overture*, Op. 49. *Marche
slave*, Op. 31. *Francesca da Rimini*. *The storm*, Op. 76. **Concertgebouw Orchestra,
Amsterdam/Bernard Haitink.** Philips Bernard Haitink Symphony Edition 442 061-2PB6 —
.·* ⑥ 7h 3m ADD 9/94 Ⓑ

Tchaikovsky. Symphony No. 1 in G minor, Op. 13, "Winter daydreams". **Oslo
Philharmonic Orchestra/Mariss Jansons.** Chandos CHAN8402.

.·* **44m DDD 2/86**

Tchaikovsky. Symphony No. 2 in C minor, Op. 17, "Little Russian". Capriccio italien,
Op. 45. **Oslo Philharmonic Orchestra/Mariss Jansons.** Chandos CHAN8460.

.·* **48m DDD II/87**

The composer himself gave the work the title *Winter daydreams*, and also gave descriptive titles to
the first two movements. The opening *Allegro tranquillo* he subtitled "Dreams of a winter journey",
while the *Adagio* bears the inscription "Land of desolation, Land of mists". A *Scherzo* and finale
round off a conventional four-movement symphonic structure. In the slow movement Jansons
inspires a performance of expressive warmth and tenderness, while the *Scherzo* is managed with
great delicacy and sensitivity. Both the opening movement and the finale are invested with vigour
and passion, and everywhere the orchestral playing is marvellously confident and disciplined. The
recording has not only impact and immediacy but also warmth and refinement. Jansons also has
the full measure of Tchaikovsky's Second Symphony. It is a direct performance — the first
movement allegro is relatively steady, but never sounds too slow, because of crisp rhythmic
pointing — and the second movement goes for charm and felicity of colour. The finale is properly
exuberant, with the secondary theme full of character, and there is a fine surge of adrenalin at the
end. The *Capriccio italien*, a holiday piece in which the composer set out to be entertaining, is also
played with great flair and the hint of vulgarity in the Neapolitan tune is not shirked. Again the
closing pages produce a sudden spurt of excitement which is particularly satisfying. The recording
here is just short of Chandos's finest — the massed violins could be sweeter on top, but the hall
resonance is right for this music and there is a proper feeling of spectacle.

Additional recommendations ...
No. 2 (*original version*). **London Symphony Orchestra/Geoffrey Simon.** Chandos
CHAN8304 — .·* 39m DDD 1/84
No. 1. *Variations on a Rococo Theme in A major*, Op. 33[a]. [a]**Mstislav Rostropovich** (vc); **Berlin
Philharmonic Orchestra/Herbert von Karajan.** DG Galleria 431 606-2GCE — .·* lh 4m
ADD 8/91 ⁹ₚ Ⓑ

Tchaikovsky. Symphony No. 3 in D major, Op. 29, "Polish". Capriccio italien, Op. 45. **St
Louis Symphony Orchestra/Leonard Slatkin.** RCA Victor Red Seal RD60433. Recorded
1988-89.

.·* **lh 3m DDD 8/92**

Leonard Slatkin and the St Louis Symphony Orchestra rise memorably to each successive challenge
in this most intractable of symphonies. Although the Third has its undoubted structural flaws, it
responds well to assertive yet unsentimental conducting, and Slatkin's ably considered reading keeps
its more obvious ambiguities firmly in check. Each of the five movements has its own particular
obstacles; Slatkin's handling of the difficult transition into the main section of the opening movement
is totally convincing, whilst no finer reading of the over-inflated development section exists on disc.
Slatkin's unusually fast tempos for the *Alla Tedesca* and of course the penultimate *Scherzo* hold no
terrors for the St Louis players, whose corporate virtuosity and refinement astound and delight the
ear in equal measure. There is warmth and ardent, dark-hued tenderness from every section in the
Andante, so often delegated to the role of inconsequential musical backwater in this symphony. The
finale, a glittering orchestral *Polonaise* (from which the work takes its subtitle Polish), offers playing
of enthralling brilliance. Slatkin draws resplendent, virile playing from his orchestra, and yet
manages to avoid any suggestion of brazen swagger during the anthem-like peroration which brings

the symphony to a thrilling conclusion. The disc also includes a refreshingly audacious performance of that perennial holiday journal, the *Capriccio italien*. Definitely the disc to have then, if you've previously harboured doubts about the Third, and easily the best version recorded to date.

Additional recommendations ...
No. 3. **Oslo Philharmonic Orchestra/Mariss Jansons.** Chandos CHAN8463 — ... 45m
DDD 7/86 ℗
No. 3. **Berlin Philharmonic Orchestra/Herbert von Karajan.** DG 419 178-2GH — ...
lh 4m 12/86 ℗
No. 3. Serenade in C major, Op. 48. **Berlin Philharmonic Orchestra/Herbert Von Karajan.**
DG Galleria 431 605-2GCE — ... lh l6m ADD/DDD 8/91 ℗ Ⓑ

Tchaikovsky. Symphony No. 4 in F minor, Op. 36. **Oslo Philharmonic Orchestra/ Mariss Jansons.** Chandos CHAN8361. From ABRD1124 (7/85).

... **42m DDD 9/86** ℗ Ⓑ

A high emotional charge runs through Jansons's performance of the Fourth, yet this rarely seems to be an end in itself. There is always a balancing concern for the superb craftsmanship of Tchaikovsky's writing: the shapeliness of the phrasing; the superb orchestration, scintillating and subtle by turns; and most of all Tchaikovsky's marvellous sense of dramatic pace. Rarely has the first movement possessed such a strong sense of tragic inevitability, or the return of the 'fate' theme in the finale sounded so logical, so necessary. The playing of the Oslo Philharmonic Orchestra is first rate: there are some gorgeous woodwind solos and the brass manage to achieve a truly Tchaikovskian intensity. Recordings are excellent: at once spacious and clearly focused, with a wide though by no means implausible dynamic range.

Additional recommendations ...
No. 4. No. 5 in E minor, Op. 64; No. 6 in B minor, Op. 74, "Pathétique". **Leningrad Philharmonic Orchestra/Evgeny Mravinsky.** DG 419 745-2GH2 — ... ② 2h 9m ADD 8/87 ℗ Ⓑ
No. 4. Marche slave, Op. 31. **London Symphony Orchestra/Gennadi Rozhdestvensky.**
Pickwick IMP Classics PCD867 — ... 53m DDD 12/87 ℗ Ⓑ
No. 4[a]. **Beethoven.** Egmont, Op. 84 — Incidental Music[b]. [b]**Pilar Lorengar** (sop); [a]**London Symphony Orchestra,** [b]**Vienna Philharmonic Orchestra/George Szell.** Decca Historic
425 972-2DM — ... lh 4m ADD 4/91 ℗ Ⓑ
Nos. 2 and 4. **New Philharmonia Orchestra/Claudio Abbado.** DG Galleria 431 604-2GCE
(this is also available on DG Privilege at bargain price: 429 527-2GR) — ... lh l5m ADD 8/91 ℗ Ⓑ
Nos. 2 and 4. **Polish National Radio Symphony Orchestra/Adrian Leaper.** Naxos 8
550488 — . lh l9m DDD 5/93 Ⓑ
Nos. 4-6. **London Symphony Orchestra/Igor Markevitch.** Philips Duo 438 335-2PM2
(same recordings as those reviewed above) — ... ② 2h l2m ADD 2/94 ℗ Ⓑ

Tchaikovsky. Symphony No. 5 in E minor, Op. 64. **Oslo Philharmonic Orchestra/ Mariss Jansons.** Chandos CHAN8351.

... **43m DDD 3/85** ℗ Ⓑ

Many of the remarks made about Mariss Jansons's performance of the Fourth Symphony also apply here, though it should be stressed that there isn't the vaguest hint of sameness about his interpretations. One's impressions in the Fifth are very different: the rich dark tones of the clarinets in the first movement's introduction, the beautiful tone and elegant phrasing of the horn in the *Andante cantabile*, the ardent, sweeping intensity of the strings at climaxes and, above all, Jansons's extraordinarily coherent vision of the Symphony as a complete utterance. This is a most recommendable version of the Fifth, despite the lack of a fill-up.

Additional recommendations ...
No. 5. Sérénade mélancolique[a]. [a]**Shizuka Ishikawa** (vn); **Czech Philharmonic Orchestra/ Lovro von Matačic,** [a]**Zdenek Kosler.** Supraphon Crystal Collection 11 0656-2 — ... 52m
ADD ℗ Ⓑ
No. 5. EUGENE ONEGIN — Tatiana's letter scene[a]. [a]**Eilene Hannan** (sop); **London Philharmonic Orchestra/Sian Edwards.** EMI Eminence CD-EMX2187 — ... 59m DDD 1/92 Ⓑ

No. 5. **Rimsky-Korsakov.** *Russian Easter Festival Overture, Op. 36.* **Philharmonia Orchestra/ Guiseppe Sinopoli.** DG 437 542-2GH — .•· lh lm DDD 3/94 Ⓑ
No. 5. *The Storm, Op. 76.* **Polish National Radio Symphony Orchestra/Antoni Wit.** Naxos 8 550716 — . lh lm DDD 7/94 Ⓑ

Tchaikovsky. Symphony No. 6 in B minor, Op. 74, "Pathétique". Marche slave, Op. 31. **Russian National Orchestra/Mikhail Pletnev.** Virgin Classics VC7 59661-2.

.•· 53m DDD 1/92   ♩♭ ♩ₛ Ⓑ

There's no denying that Russian orchestras bring a special intensity to Tchaikovsky, and this Symphony in particular. But, in the past, we have had to contend with lethal, virbato-laden brass, and variable Soviet engineering. Not any more. Pianist Mikhail Pletnev formed this orchestra in 1990 from the front ranks of the major Soviet orchestras, and the result here has all the makings of a classic. The brass still retain their penetrating power, and an extraordinary richness and solemnity before the Symphony's coda; the woodwind (soft, veiled flute tone, dark-hued bassoons) make a very melancholy choir; and the strings possess not only the agility to cope with Pletnev's aptly death-defying speed for the third movement march, but beauty of tone for Tchaikovsky's yearning cantabiles, and their lower voices add thunderous black density to the first movement's development's shattering intrusion. Pletnev exerts the same control over his players as he does over his fingers, to superb effect. The dynamic range is huge and is comfortably reproduced here with clarity, natural perspectives, a sense of instruments playing in a believable acoustic space, and a necessarily higher volume setting than usual. *Marche slave*'s final blaze of triumph, under the circumstances, seems apt.

Additional recommendations ...
No. 6. **Oslo Philharmonic Orchestra/Mariss Jansons.** Chandos CHAN8446 — .•· 44m DDD 5/87 ♩♭ Ⓑ
No. 6. **Leningrad Philharmonic Orchestra/Evgeny Mravinsky.** Erato 2292-45756-2 — .•· 45m DDD 6/92 ♩♭ Ⓑ
No. 6. *Romeo and Juliet — Fantasy Overture*[b]. **National Symphony Orchestra/Albert Coates.** Beulah mono 1PD6 — .•· lh 6m ADD 7/94 Ⓑ ▲

<ins>New review</ins>
Tchaikovsky. Manfred Symphony, Op. 58. **Philharmonia Orchesta/Riccardo Muti.** EMI Studio Plus CDM7 64872-2. Recorded in 1981.

.•· 59m DDD 3/94   ♩♭

This symphony "In four scenes" was inspired by a reading of Byron's dramatic poem. Tchaikovsky originally felt it to be "the best of my symphonic compositions" though he later refused Manfred admittance to his canon of numbered symphonies. Muti's is an aptly epic reading and thrilling sonically (especially at the climaxes of the outer movements). It has an onward sweep and vigour which do not prevent the memorable lyrical tunes at the centre of the *Scherzo* and in the *Andante*, blossoming fully. The Philharmonia play superbly.

Additional recommendations ...
Oslo Philharmonic Orchestra/Mariss Jansons. Chandos CHAN8535 — .•· 53m DDD 5/88 ♩♭
Manfred Symphony. Romeo and Juliet — Fantasy Overture. **NBC Symphony Orchestra/Arturo Toscanini.** RCA Gold Seal mono GD60298 — .•· lh 7m ADD 6/92 ♩♭
Bournemouth Symphony Orchestra/Andrew Litton. Virgin Classics VC7 59230-2 — .•· 57m DDD 3/93 ♩♭
Manfred Symphony. Hamlet — Fantasy Overture after Shakespeare, Op. 67. **Vienna Philharmonic Orchestra/Lorin Maazel.** Decca 425 051-2DM — .•· lh l3m ADD 11/93 ♩♭
Manfred Symphony. Hamlet — Fantasy Overture, Op. 67. **Vienna Philharmonic Orchestra/ Lorin Maazel.** Decca 425 051-2DM — .•· lh l3m ADD 11/93

<ins>New review</ins>
Tchaikovsky. String Quartets — No. 1 in D major, Op. 11; No. 2 in F major, Op. 22; No. 3 in E flat minor, Op. 30. Quartet Movement in B flat major. Souvenir de Florence — String Sextet, Op. 70[a]. [a]**Yuri Yurov** (va); [a]**Mikhail Milman** (vc); **Borodin Quartet** (Mikhail

Kopelman, Andrei Abramenkov, vns; Dmitri Shebalin, va; Valentin Berlinsky, vc). Teldec 4509-90422-2. Recorded in 1993.

② 2h 31m DDD 1/94

Who could fail to recognize the highly characteristic urgency and thematic strength of the F major Quartet's first movement development section, or miss premonitions of later masterpieces in the Third Quartet's *Andante funèbre*. None of these works is 'late' (the last of them predates the Fourth Symphony by a couple of years), yet their rigorous arguments and sweeping melodies anticipate the orchestral masterpieces of Tchaikovsky's full maturity. So why the neglect — that is, of all but the First Quartet? The most likely reason is our habitual expectation of orchestral colour in Tchaikovsky, a situation that doesn't really affect our appreciation of the early, almost Schubertian D major Quartet (the one with the *Andante cantabile* that moved Tolstoy to tears). The Second and Third Quartets are noticeably more symphonic and particularly rich in the kinds of harmonic clashes and sequences that Tchaikovsky normally dressed for the orchestral arena. Even minor details, like the quick-fire exchanges near the beginning of No. 3's *Allegretto*, instantly suggest 'woodwinds' (you can almost hear oboes, flutes and clarinets jostle in play), while both finales could quite easily have been transposed among the pages of the early symphonies. But if these and other parallels are to register with any conviction, then performers need to locate them, and that's a challenge the Borodins meet with the ease of seasoned Tchaikovskians. Generally speaking, the earlier performances (listed below) have the more incisive attack (especially in the First Quartet); but the newer ones are marginally more 'natural' and spontaneous, most noticeably in the first movement of the exuberant *Souvenir de Florence* sextet, and in that wonderful passage from the Second Quartet's first movement where the lead violin calms from agitated virtuosity to a magical recapitulation of the principal theme — an unforgettable moment, superbly paced in the Teldec reading. We also get a bonus in the shape of a 15-minute B flat Quartet movement — an appealing torso imbued with the spirit of Russian folk-song — which is accommodated partially at the expense of the First Quartet's last movement repeat (included in the 1979 recording).

Additional recommendation ...

Nos. 1-3. Souvenir de Florence[a]. **Borodin Quartet** with [a]**Yuri Bashmet** (va); [a]**Natalia Gutman** (vc). EMI CDS7 49775-2 — ② 2h 20m ADD 8/88

New review

Tchaikovsky. COMPLETE PIANO WORKS. **Victoria Postnikova.** Erato 2292-45969-2. Items marked [a] from 2292-45512-2 (6/92). Recorded 1990-92.
Two Pieces, Op. 1. Three Souvenirs de Hapsal, Op. 2. Valse caprice in D major, Op. 4. Romance in F minor, Op. 5. Valse-scherzo in A major, Op. 7. Capriccio in G flat major, Op. 8. Three Morceaux, Op. 9. Two Morceaux, Op. 10. Six Morceaux, Op. 19. Six Morceaux composés sur un seul theme, Op. 21. Impromptu in A flat major. Valse-scherzo in A major. Impromptu-caprice in G major. Aveu passione in E minor. Military March in B flat major. Piano Sonata in G major, Op. 37. Album for the young, Op. 39. Dumka, Op. 59. The Seasons, Op. 37*b*[a]. Piano Sonata in C sharp minor, Op. 80[a]. 50 Russian Folk Songs (with Gennadi Rozhdestvensky, pf, four hands). Potpourri on Themes from the opera "Voyevoda". Three Romances. Theme and Variations in A minor. 12 Morceaux, Op. 40. Six Morceaux, Op. 51. 18 Morceaux, Op. 72. Momento lirico in A flat major.

⑦ 8h 53m DDD 7/93

Why, given the indestructible popularity of the B flat Piano Concerto, should Tchaikovsky's solo piano music be so little heard? The solo works are no less gratefully written than the concertos — if anything they tend to suit the instrument rather better — and it is only at times in the later pieces, when Tchaikovsky looks self-consciously towards Lisztian layouts, that embarrass-ment ensues. Nor can the blame be laid at the door of Robert Schumann, the model for an overwhelming proportion of the writing. In fact the problem seems to be more that, without the colouristic resources of contrasting instruments to fall back on, as soon as Tchaikovsky wants to extend a miniature time-span into something dramatic he has a tendency to rant. Of course, not all these works had elevated artistic intentions. Some, like the *Potpourri*, were obviously pot-boilers. It would be absurd to expect consistency of inspiration here. And yet there are surprisingly few instances of zero musical interest, and in every cycle of shorter pieces there are items to be treasured. Postnikova brings to every single piece a virtually ideal blend of affection, respect and intelligence, not to speak of virtuoso command. Not only does this give the textures the best possible chance to 'come off the page', she also has the instinct for inflexions which get us to the heart of Tchaikovsky's individual moods. The piano tone is generally fine, though occasionally dry. A highly desirable library acquisition for all Tchaikovskians and serious lovers of the piano repertoire.

New review

Tchaikovsky. PIANO WORKS. **Sviatoslav Richter**. Olympia OCD334. Recorded in 1983. Morceaux — Op. 10 (Nos. 1 and 2 from Eurodisc 205 455, 9/84; remainder new to UK, recorded 1983); Op. 19 — No. 1, Rêverie du soir, No. 5, Capriccioso; Op. 40 — No. 2, Chanson triste, No. 8, Valse; Op. 51 — No. 1, Valse de salon, No. 3, Menuetto scherzoso, No. 5, Romance; Op. 72 — No. 5, Méditation, No. 12, L'espiègle, No. 15, Un poco di Chopin. Romance in F minor, Op. 5. Valse-scherzo in A major, Op. 7 (all from 205 455). The Seasons, Op. 37*b* — No. 1, January; No. 5, May; No. 6, June; No. 11, November (Eurodisc 610 075, 10/84).

·ᵖ Ih 20m DDD/ADD I/94

Richter elevates Tchaikovsky's miniatures far beyond the salon. No interpretative frills, just trenchant fingerwork and perfectly sculpted sound, so that slight unbendings become immensely touching. The effect is to convey not so much the surface melancholy of these pieces as their underlying strength of character. A curious sense of permanence comes through, as though the music is being contemplated rather than felt. Not for imitation, perhaps (and who could imitate such perfect harmonic and structural weighting?), but this is breathtaking, inspiring artistry, and it sets its own terms. Sound-quality is on the dry side. But Richter's is the sort of playing which positively benefits from close analytical scrutiny, and serious collectors of piano recordings should need no further encouragement.

New review

Tchaikovsky. SONGS. **Olga Borodina** (mez); **Larissa Gergieva** (pf). Philips 442 013-2PH. Translations included. Also includes a limited edition sampler of opera excerpts. Recorded 1993. My genius, my angel, my friend. Take my heart away. Songs, Op. 6 — No. 1, Do not believe, my friend; No. 2, Not a word, O my friend; No. 5, Why?; No. 6, None but the lonely heart. Cradle song, Op. 16 No. 1. Reconciliation, Op. 25 No. 1. The fearful minute, Op. 28 No. 6. It was in the early spring, Op. 38 No. 2. Songs, Op. 60 — No. 6, Frenzied nights; No. 7, Gipsy's song; No. 12, The mild stars shone for us. Songs, Op. 63 — No. 4, The first meeting; No. 5, The fires in the rooms were already out. Serenade, Op. 65 No. 1. Songs, Op. 73 — No. 2, Night; No. 4, The sun has set; No. 6, Again, as before, alone.

·ᵖ ② Ih DDD 6/94

Olga Borodina is among the most considered of Tchaikovsky interpreters on disc. In the "Cradle song", one of Tchaikovsky's most haunting pieces, Joan Rodgers (reviewed below) sounds carefree as she rocks her baby to sleep, where Borodina is heavier, sensing dark threats all around. Larissa Gergieva (Valery Gergiev's sister) adds to the unsettling atmosphere of that song by stressing the chromatic tensions in the accompaniment. In general, it might have been better to have had a pianist less amenable to slow speeds than Gergieva, but Borodina has such a range of colour and expression in her voice that she can fill the time profitably. One marvels at the beauty of the singing and admires its sustained intensity. In "Night" a darkness descends over the voice from the opening lines, but in "Again, as before, alone" she tries something even more daring, draining all the life and vibrancy from her tone in a way that is quite unforgettable. One would hardly dare play the final track often (Hvorostovsky is matter-of-fact by comparison). The booklet does not include Russian texts either in Cyrillic or transliteration, but there is a free CD, "Presenting Olga Borodina" in three excerpts from existing Philips opera sets. In fact, there is no need to persuade us that the young Russian mezzo is a star: Borodina is one of the major singers of her generation and this recital demands that she be accepted on her own terms.

Tchaikovsky. SONGS. **Joan Rodgers** (sop); **Roger Vignoles** (pf). Hyperion CDA66617. Texts and translations included. Recorded in 1992.
Op. 6 — No. 1, Do not believe, my friend; No. 2, Not a word, o my friend; No. 5, Why?; No. 6, None but the lonely heart. Cradle song, Op. 16 No. 1. The canary, Op. 25 No. 4.

Op. 28 — No. 3, Why did I dream of you?; No. 6, The fearful minute. Op. 38 — No. 2, It was in the early spring; No. 3, At the ball. Op. 47 — No. 1, If only I had known; No. 6, Does the day reign?; No. 7, Was I not a little blade of grass?. Op. 54 — No. 8, The cuckoo; No. 9, Spring song; No. 10, Lullaby in a storm. Op. 60 — No. 1, Last night; No. 4, The nightingale; No. 10, Behind the window in the shadow. Op. 63 — Serenade: O child beneath thy window. To forget so soon.

․․•⁕ lh 5m DDD 2/93

The features which make Tchaikovsky's great orchestral showpieces so universally popular — the profoundly human emotions, the unforgettable melodies — are also much in evidence in these songs. Indeed, condensed into this miniature form and shorn of opulent orchestral colour Tchaikovsky's outpourings have an even more direct appeal. *None but the lonely heart* is justly famous for its aching sense of loneliness, but others speak with equal intensity. *The nightingale*'s sorrowful mood is given greater poignancy by the echoes of its solitary song in the piano while *Was I not a little blade of grass?* tugs at the very heart-strings as the singer recounts the misery of an arranged marriage. But if this seems to suggest a CD full of unrelieved gloom, that's certainly not the case. Melancholia may be the dominant mood but this cleverly balanced programme includes songs of simple joy (*Cradle song* — written in celebration of the Rimsky-Korsakovs's first child) and at least one genuinely funny moment as an eponymous cuckoo reiterates her familiar call *ad nauseam*. Joan Rodgers does not give big, dramatic performances but her subtle, understated characterizations suit these songs admirably — the Russian texts may be incomprehensible to most readers (English translations are included), but no one can fail to understand their spirit from these appealing performances. As her partner (and the piano is no mere accompaniment to the voice) Roger Vignoles is ever sensitive, displaying by turn discretion and flair and adding real authority to these distinguished and delightful songs.

Additional recommendations ...
Six Songs, Op. 6 — No. 4, A tear trembles; No. 6, None but the lonely heart. Six Songs, Op. 25 — No. 1, Reconciliation. Six Songs, Op. 28 — No. 6, The fearful minute. Six Songs, Op. 38 — No. 1, Don Juan's Serenade. 12 Songs, Op. 60 — No. 4, The nightingale; No. 11, Exploit. Six Songs, Op. 63 — No. 2, I opened the window. Six Songs, Op. 73 — No. 6, Again, as before, alone. **Rachmaninov.** Six Songs, Op. 4 — No. 1, Oh no, I beg you, forsake me not; No. 3, In the silence of the secret night; No. 4, Sing not to me, beautiful maiden. Six Songs, Op. 8 — No. 5, The dream. 12 Songs, Op. 14 — No. 9, She is as lovely as the noon. 12 Songs, Op. 21 —No. 6, Fragment from Musset. 15 Songs, Op. 26 — No. 2, He took all from me; No. 6, Christ is risen; No. 13, When yesterday we met. **Dmitri Hvorostovsky** (bar); **Oleg Boshniakovich** (pf). Philips 432 119-2PH — ․․•⁕ 52m DDD 10/91

New review
Tchaikovsky. EUGENE ONEGIN. **Dmitri Hvorostovsky** (bar) Eugene Onegin; **Nuccia Focile** (sop) Tatyana; **Neil Shicoff** (ten) Lensky; **Olga Borodina** (mez) Olga; **Alexander Anisimov** (bass) Prince Gremin; **Sarah Walker** (mez) Larina; **Irina Arkhipova** (mez) Filipievna; **Francis Egerton** (ten) Triquet; **Hervé Hennequin** (bass-bar) Captain; **Sergei Zadvorny** (bass) Zaretsky; **St Petersburg Chamber Choir; Orchestre de Paris/Semyon Bychkov.** Philips 438 235-2PH2. Notes, text and translation included. Recorded in 1992.

․•⁕ ② 2h 21m DDD 12/93   **♀ₚ**

Entirely at the service of Tchaikovsky's marvellous invention, Semyon Bychkov illuminates every detail of the composer's wondrous scoring with pointed delicacy and draws playing of the utmost acuity and beauty from his own Paris orchestra — enhanced by the clear, open recording — and the St Petersburg Choir is superbly disciplined and alert with their words. Focile offers keen-edged yet warm tone and total immersion in Tatyana's character. Aware throughout of the part's dynamic demands, she phrases with complete confidence, eagerly catching the girl's dreamy vulnerability and heightened imagination in the Letter scene, which has that sense of awakened love so essential to it. Hvorostovsky is in his element. His singing has at once the warmth, elegance and refinement Tchaikovsky demands from his anti-hero. Together he, Focile and Bychkov make the finale the tragic climax it should be; indeed the reading of this passage is almost unbearably moving. Shicoff has refined and expanded his Lensky since he recorded it for

Levine and Anisimov is a model Gremin, singing his aria with generous tone and phrasing while not making a meal of it. Olga Borodina is a perfect Olga, spirited, a touch sensual, wholly idiomatic with the text — as, of course, is the revered veteran Russian mezzo Arkhipova as Filipievna, an inspired piece of casting. An outright recommendation for a magnificent achivement.

Additional recommendations ...
Soloists; John Alldis Choir; Orchestra of the Royal Opera House, Covent Garden/ Sir Georg Solti. Decca 417 413-2DH2 — ⦂⦂ ② 2h 23m ADD 8/87
Soloists; Sofia National Opera Chorus; Sofia Festival Orchestra/Emil Tchakarov. Sony Classical S2K45539 — ⦂⦂ ② 2h 23m DDD 3/91
Soloists; Bolshoi Theatre Chorus and Orchestra/Vassili Nebolsin. Dante Lys mono LYS10/11 — ⦂⦂ ② 2h 14m ADD 1/94 ▲

New review
Tchaikovsky. THE QUEEN OF SPADES. **Gegam Grigorian** (ten) Herman; **Maria Gulegina** (sop) Lisa; **Irina Arkhipova** (mez) Countess; **Nikolai Putilin** (bar) Count Tomsky; **Vladimir Chernov** (bar) Prince Yeletsky; **Olga Borodina** (mez) Pauline; **Vladimir Solodovnikov** (ten) Chekalinsky; **Sergei Alexashkin** (bass) Surin; **Evgeni Boitsov** (ten) Chaplitsky; **Nikolai Gassiev** (ten) Major-domo; **Gennadi Bezzubenkov** (bass) Narumov; **Ludmila Filatova** (mez) Governess; **Tatiana Filimonova** (sop) Masha; **Kirov Theatre Chorus and Orchestra/Valery Gergiev.** Philips 438 141-2PH3. Notes, text and translation included. Recorded in 1992.

⦂⦂ ③ 1h 46m DDD 10/93

There are major problems with all the current sets of *The Queen of Spades*, but Valery Gergiev, one of the outstanding Tchaikovskians of the day, here persuades a thoroughly Western-sounding Kirov Theatre Orchestra to what is surely the most refined account of the score yet recorded, and one that is never lacking energy or full-blooded attack. His is not so much a compromise approach as one which stresses fatalism and underlying sadness. The recording was made in the Kirov Theatre itself, and there is admittedly some constriction to the orchestral sound-picture; but for many the atmosphere of a real stage-venue will be a plus, and the all-important balance between voices and orchestra is just right. If the spine still fails to tingle as often as it should, that is mainly a reflection of the respectable but unexciting singing, though it would be folly to expect greater thrills from any of the three rival sets, and in many ways Gergiev's conducting elevates this new one above them all.

Additional recommendations ...
Soloists; Gouslarche Boys' Choir; Svetoslav Obretenov National Chorus; Sofia Festival Orchestra/Emil Tchakarov. Sony Classical S3K45720 — ⦂⦂ ③ 2h 39m DDD 12/90 ᵠₚ
Soloists; American Boychoir; Tanglewood Festival Chorus; Boston Symphony Orchestra/Seiji Ozawa. RCA Victor Red Seal 09026-60992-2 — ⦂⦂ ③ 2h 36m DDD 11/92 ᵠₚ

Further listening ...

Orchestral Suites[a] — No. 2 in C major, Op. 53; No. 4 in G major, Op. 61, "Mozartiana". Sérénade mélancolique in B minor, Op. 26[b]. Mélodie in E flat major, Op. 42 No. 3[b].
[a]**Carl Pini**, [b]**Pinchas Zukerman** (vns); [a]**Philharmonia Orchestra/Michael Tilson Thomas**; [b]**Israel Philharmonic Orchestra/Zubin Mehta.** CBS Digital Masters CD46503 (8/91).

Variations on a Rococo Theme in A minor, Op. 33. Nocturne in C sharp minor, Op. 19 No. 4. *Coupled with Miaskovsky.* Cello Concerto in C minor, Op. 66. *Shostakovich.* The Limpid Stream, Op. 39 — Adagio. **Julian Lloyd Webber** (vc); **London Symphony Orchestra/ Maxim Shostakovich.** Philips 434 106-2PH (5/92).

Symphony No. 7 in E flat major (cpted Bogatryryev). Piano Concerto No. 3 in E flat major, Op. 73[a]. [a]**Geoffrey Tozer** (pf); **London Philharmonic Orchestra/Neeme Järvi.** Chandos CHAN9130 (4/93).

Suite No. 3 in G major, Op. 55 — Theme and Variations. **Hungarian National Philharmonic Orchestra/Tibor Ferenc.** Pickwick IMP Classics PCD1016 (6/93).

Piano Trio in A minor, Op. 50. **Pierra Amoyal** (vn); **Pascal Rogé** (pf); **Frédéric Lodéon** (vc). Erato Libretto 2292-45972-2 (5/93).

Souvenir d'un lieu cher, Op. 42 — No. 1, Méditation in D minor. Valse-scherzo, Op. 34. *Coupled with* **Bartók.** Sonata for Solo Violin, Sz117. **Brahms.** Hungarian Dance No. 1 in G minor. **Chaminade** (arr. Kreisler). Sérénade espagnole. **Falla** (trans. Kochanski). Suite populaire espagnole. **Kyoko Takezawa** (vn); **Philip Moll** (pf). RCA Victor Red Seal 09026 60704-2 (2/93).

Alexander Tcherepnin   *Russian/French/American 1899-1977*

Suggested listening ...

Symphony No. 4, Op. 91. Suite, Op. 87. Russian Dances. Romantic Overture, Op. 67. **Košice State Philharmonic Orchestra/Win-Sie Yip.** Marco Polo 8 223380 (10/92).

Georg Philipp Telemann   *German 1681-1767*

New review
Telemann. OVERTURE-SUITES AND CONCERTOS. [b]**Franz Verster** (fl); [c]**Paul Doctor** (va); [a]**South-West German Chamber Orchestra/Friedrich Tilegant;** [bd]**Amsterdam Chamber Orchestra/André Rieu;** [c]**Concerto Amsterdam/Frans Brüggen** ([ab]rec). Teldec Das Alte Werk 9031-77620-2. Items marked [abd] recorded in 1967, [c] 1968. Overture Suite in A minor[a]. Concerto in E minor for Recorder and Flute[b]. Viola Concerto No. 1 in G major[c]. Overture des Nations: anciens et modernes for Strings and Continuo, TWV55[d].

· lh 9m ADD 7/93   **P**

Four performances of the highest calibre, marvellously recorded in the 1960s and now sounding as fresh as the day they were made. Two of them feature the great recorder player Frans Brüggen (who is now more often heard on disc as a conductor). He is at his inimitable finest, and this is very fine indeed, in the masterly Suite in A minor for recorder and strings (every bit as fine a work as the Bach B minor Suite for the same instrumentation) and the E minor Concerto for recorder, transverse flute and strings with its attractive interplay of solo texture. Here he is joined by Franz Verster. Brüggen then moves to the conductor's podium to direct the Concerto Amsterdam, joined by a superb viola player, Paul Doctor, in the justly famous G major Viola Concerto. The *Ouverture des Nations anciens et modernes* is another suite (comprising nine movements), full of the composer's most felicitious invention. The music is played with great verve and character and the CD transfer is exemplary. This is possibly one of the finest Telemann collections ever issued on CD.

Telemann. CONCERTOS, Volumes 1 and 2. **Collegium Musicum 90/Simon Standage** (vn). Chandos CHAN0519 and CHAN0512. Recorded 1990-91.
CHAN0519: Concertos — A minor for Violin; E minor for Flute and Violin (Rachel Brown, fl); G major for Four Unaccompanied Violins; A major for Four Violins (Micaela Comberti, Miles Golding, Andrew Manze, vns); E major for Violin. Orchestral Suite in G minor, "La Changeante". *CHAN0512*: Concertos — G major for Violin; D major for Two Flutes, Violin and Cello (Brown, Siu Peasgood, fls; Jane Coe, vc); F sharp minor for Violin; G major for Two Violins (Comberti). Orchestral Suite in B flat major, "Ouverture burlesque".

· ② lh 3m lh 4m DDD 4/92

It is difficult to mention Telemann without referring to the prolific and eclectic nature of his output, both of which are reflected in his very numerous concertos, and in these recordings the two works that are *not* concertos — *La Changeante* and *Ouverture burlesque*, both of which evoke the spirit of the *commedia dell'arte*. What changes in *La Changeante* is not only the moods of the movements but also their keys; only the first and last of the eight are in the home key of G minor, the others are in a variety of different ones, a most unusual feature at that time. The ouverture-suites are predominantly French in style but the concertos represent Telemann's highly individual variant of Venetian models. Whilst Vivaldi's concertos are predominantly in three movements (quick-slow-quick), Telemann's are usually in four or five, with no set pattern of pace, and they take both *da chiesa* and *da camera* forms. Telemann's muse seems rarely to have slept, likewise his acute sense of instrumental colour. When Playford wrote of "Sprightly and cheerful musick" he was referring to that of the cittern; had he lived a little longer he might have felt the same about that of Telemann, not least if he had heard it played so expertly by Collegium Musicum 90, who are brought into your home by most faithful recorded sound.

Additional recommendation ...
Concerto for Recorder, Viola da gamba and Strings in A minor.[ab]. *Overture Suites — D major, TWV55: D6*[b]*; A minor, TWV55: A2*[a]*. Sinfonia in F major, TWV50: 3*[ab]. [a]**Marion Verbruggen** (rec); [b]**Sarah Cunningham** (va da gamba); **Orchestra of the Age of Enlightenment/Monica Huggett.** Harmonia Mundi HMC90 7093 — .·' 1h 14m DDD 1/94 ✎

New review
Telemann. Overture Suites — C major, TWV55: C6; D major, TWV55: D19; B flat major, TWV55: B10. **The English Concert/Trevor Pinnock.** Archiv Produktion 437 558-2AH. Recorded in 1992.

.·' 1h 17m DDD 6/93

The three orchestral suites on this disc afford splendid examples of Telemann's seemingly inexhaustible invention in this sphere. The best-known of the suites is that in C major for three oboes, bassoon and strings. It's one of countless pieces that demonstrate Telemann's sympathy for and knowledge of the oboe. The movements are effectively contrasted with the composer juxtaposing for example a vigorous Bourrée *en trompette* with a drowsy "Sommeille" whose somnolent quavers have almost hypnotic powers. Pinnock revels in scene-painting of this kind, just as he invariably hits upon effective tempos for the dances. The Suite in D is much less often performed and has existed in only one other commercially recorded version; lastly, Pinnock has chosen a Suite in B flat, hitherto unrecorded on disc but unquestionably in Telemann's best manner. Fine music, fine playing and a sympathetic recorded sound. What more could one want?

Telemann. RECORDER WORKS. **Peter Holtslag** (rec); **The Parley of Instruments/ Peter Holman,** [a]**Roy Goodman.** Hyperion CDA66413. Recorded in 1989.
Overture Suite in A minor[a]. Concertos — F major; C major. Sinfonia in F major[a].

.·' 1h 6m DDD 10/91

Telemann professed a working knowledge of most of the standard instruments of his day and consequently wrote rewardingly for them. This is especially true in his treatment of woodwind instruments for which he has left a generous legacy. This disc, as well as containing two concertos, includes a suite and a sinfonia. The Suite in A minor is Telemann's best-known work for treble recorder; indeed, it is to recorder players what Bach's B minor Orchestral Suite is to flautists. The soloist, Peter Holtslag, is an accomplished player whose sensibilities exert a favourable influence over matters of texture, articulation and phrasing. He is a good judge of tempos and, almost alone among his competitors on disc, hits on an effective pace for the beautifully constructed French overture with which the Suite begins. The concertos are attractive pieces, too, that in F major concluding with an engaging pair of menuets. The Sinfonia, unusually scored for recorder, viola da gamba, cornett, three trombones, strings and continuo with organ introduces a distinctive splash of colour. The recording is most sympathetic.

Additional recommendations ...
Concertos — F major; B flat major; A minor. Suite in C major. **Cologne Musica Antiqua/ Reinhard Goebel.** Archiv Produktion 413 788-2AH — .·' 49m DDD 3/85 ✎

Overture Suite. Concerto in C major. Concerto for Recorder, Viola da gamba and Strings in A minor[a]. [a]**Mark Levy** (va da gamba); **New London Consort/Philip Pickett** (rec). L'Oiseau-Lyre 433 043-2OH — ⠶⠶ 1h 8m DDD 11/92 ✐

New review
Telemann. Sonates Corellisantes — No. 1 in F major, TWV42: F2. Paris Quartets, "Nouveaux quatuors en Six Suites" — No. 6 in E minor, TWV43: e4. Essercizii Musici — Trio No. 8 in B flat major, TWV42: B4. Quartets — A minor, TWV43: a3; G minor, TWV43: g4. **Florilegium Ensemble.** Channel Classics CCS5093. Recorded in 1992.

⠶⠶ 53m DDD 10/93 ⑨ℙ

A well chosen programme. The rarity is the *Sonata Corellisante* for two violins and continuo in which Telemann pays tribute to Corelli. The remaining works are the sixth and perhaps finest of the 1738 *Nouveaux Quatuors* or *Paris Quartets* as they have become known, a little *Quartet* (or *Quadro*) in G minor, a B flat Trio from the *Essercizii Musici* collection (*c.*1739) and a fine Concerto da camera (Quartet) in A minor, very much along the lines of Vivaldi's pieces of the same kind in which each instrument other than the continuo has an obbligato role. The finest work here is the *Paris Quartet* which consists of a Prelude, a sequence of dance-orientated movements and an elegiac Chaconne that lingers long in the memory. The performance is full of vitality and probes beneath the music's superficialities. There is, throughout the programme, an intensity and a youthful spontaneity about this playing which has considerable appeal; and the continuo line, furthermore, is handled with boldness and imagination.

New review
Telemann. ESSERCIZII MUSICI. [d]**Conrad Steinmann** (rec); [b]**Oskar Peter** (fl); [f]**Miguel Piguet** (ob); [a]**Paolo Pandolfo** (va da gamba); [abdf]**Imke David** (vc); [abdf]**Andreas Staier**, [ce]**Jesper Bøje Christensen** (hpds). Deutsche Harmonia Mundi 05472 77169-2. Recorded in 1990.
Trio No. 2 in G major, TWV42: G6[a]; Trio No. 4 in A major, TWV42: A6[b]; Solo No. 6 in C major, TWV41: 3 (arr. Christensen)[c]; Trio No. 8 in B flat major, TWV42: B 4[d]; Solo No. 12 in F major, TWV32: 4 (arr. Christensen)[e]; Trio No. 12 in E flat major, TWV42: Es 3[f].

⠶⠶ 1h 14m DDD 8/93

Telemann's *Essercizii Musici* (1739) is a collection of alternating "Solos" and "Trios" a summary of the composer's best work in these forms; but while the Trios have been frequently performed both in concert and on disc some of the Solos remain less well-known. This delightful programme devised and performed by members of the Schola Cantorum Basiliensis offers all the pieces in *Essercizii Musici* calling for obbligato harpsichord. The four Trios with obbligato harpsichord each has a different instrument to partner it and are captivating works, skilfully and appealingly written. They are among the most impressive testaments to his ability in writing in a form for which he was greatly admired by his own colleagues both at home and abroad. The performances are full of insight and sparkle with lively humour.

Telemann. VOCAL WORKS. René Jacobs (alto); **Berlin Academy for Ancient Music.** Capriccio 10 338. Texts and translations included. Recorded in 1989.
Cantatas — Tirsis am Scheidewege; Nach Finsternis und Todesschatten; Meines Bleibens ist nicht hier. Das Frauenzimmer verstimmt sich immer. Vergiss dich selbst, mein schönster Engel. An der Schlaf. Die Einsamkeit. Concerto grosso in E minor — Adagio.

⠶⠶ 1h DDD 11/92 ✐

Telemann lovers will find some rarities among the items chosen by the counter-tenor, René Jacobs, for his solo recital. By far the most extensive and consistently interesting of them is the cantata *In einem Tal, umringt von hohen Eichen* or *Tirsis am Scheidewege* as it is called in its modern performing edition. It comes from a collection of "Moral Cantatas" published in Hamburg in 1731. But do not be put off by such a collective title for the music is unfailingly entertaining and is engagingly sung by Jacobs with a small group of period instruments played by the Berlin Academy for Ancient Music. The remainder of the programme consists of two airs which Telemann included in his pioneering musical journal "Der getreue Music-Meister", a sacred cantata from his collection of "Harmonischer Gottes-Dienst", two songs and a further sacred cantata *Meines Bleibens ist nicht hier*. There is much here to please the listener and Jacobs's sensibility both to text and music brings the programme to life with style and charm. One purely instrumental item, an *Adagio* for strings from a *Concerto grosso*, acts as an overture to the programme. Full texts with translations are included.

Telemann. Ino[a]. Overture-Suite in D major. [a]**Barbara Schlick** (sop); **Cologne Musica Antiqua/Reinhard Goebel.** Archiv Produktion 429 772-2AH. Text and translation included. Recorded in 1989.

54m DDD 4/91

Telemann's dramatic cantata, *Ino,* is the product of an Indian summer which the composer enjoyed during the decade 1755-1765. He was, in fact, 84 when he composed *Ino* but we could easily be forgiven for believing it to be the work of a composer half his age. The Enlightenment poet Ramler's text is based on one of Ovid's *Metamorphoses* and concerns Ino, daughter of Cadmus and Hermione. She married Athamos who went mad, murdered one of their sons and attempted murder on the other. Ino, with husband in hot pursuit hurls herself into the sea clutching her child. Neptune comes to her aid, transforms her into the goddess Leukothea and her son into the god Palaemon. Telemann, with music wonderfully fresh in spirit, brings the tale to life in a manner hardly equalled and never surpassed by any of his earlier dramatic works. Barbara Schlick sounds cool in the face of such adversity as Ovid and Ramler place in her path, but there is an underlying passion in her interpretation and the result is musically satisfying. That is also true of Cologne Musica Antiqua under the informed and enthusiastic direction of Reinhard Goebel. This stylish ensemble comes into its own in a performance of another product of Telemann's Indian summer, the Overture-Suite in D major. A feast for lovers of this composer's music and one which offers delights that no baroque music enthusiast should overlook. Outstanding.

New review

Telemann. Der Tag des Gerichts[a]. Ino[b]. [a]**Gertraud Landwehr-Herrmann**, [b]**Roberta Alexander** (sops); [a]**Cora Canne-Meijer** (contr); [a]**Kurt Equiluz** (ten); [a]**Max van Egmond** (bass); [a]**Vienna Boys' Choir**; [a]**Hamburg Monteverdi Choir; Vienna Concentus Musicus/Nikolaus Harnoncourt.** Teldec Das Alte Werk 9031-77621-2. Texts and translations included. Item marked [a]2292-42722-2 (12/89, recorded in 1966), [b] 2292-44633-2 (4/91, recorded in 1988).

 ② 2h 1m ADD/DDD 7/93

Der Tag des Gerichts ("The Day of Judgement") is another one of Telemann's greatest achieve-ments from that miraculous decade of his creative rejuvenation. The work was first performed in Hamburg in 1762 when Telemann was 81 years old. From start to finish this beautiful score has all the freshness of invention and vitality that we might have expected from a man half his age. The text is by Wilhelm Alers who described it as a "Poem for Singing in Four Contem-plations". It must have appealed to the octogenarian composer who brings it to life with a wealth of instrumental colour, affective word-painting and striking contrasts. The disc further includes Telemann's masterly dramatic cantata, *Ino*, belonging to the same period. The performances are equal to almost everything in these vital and rapturous scores. Twenty-two years separate the recordings of the two works, revealing the remarkable consistency with which Harnoncourt's limpid sense of enactment has been pursued.

New review

Telemann. DON QUICHOTTE AUF DER HOCHZEIT DES COMACHO. **Raimund Nolte** (bass) Don Quichotte; **Michael Schopper** (bass) Sancho Pansa; **Silke Stapf** (sop) Pedrillo; **Mechthild Bach** (sop) Grisostomo; **Heike Hallaschka** (sop) Quiteria; **Annette Kohler** (mez) Comacho; **Karl-Heinz Brandt** (ten) Basilio; **Bremen Vocal Ensemble for Ancient Music; La Stagione/Michael Schneider.** CPO CPO999 210-2. Notes, text and translation included. Recorded live in 1993.

59m DDD

Telemann's delightful comic-opera/serenata, *Don Quichotte auf der Hochzeit des Comacho* ("Don

Quixote at Camacho's Wedding"), dates from 1761; he selected for a libretto a text by a young Hamburg poet, Daniel Schiebeler. Schiebeler took an episode from Part 2 of Cervantes's celebrated burlesque novel, in which the Knight of the Lions and his squire Sancho Panza encounter some rather strange wedding celebrations as they roam the world in search of adventure. The bride, Quiteria is to marry Camacho, a rich sheep farmer. But *she* loves Basilio who is, however, poor and therefore disqualified from marrying his childhood sweetheart. Just as the marriage is about to take place Basilio is led in with a dagger in his breast. He implores Quiteria to grant him one last wish — to give a dying man her hand in marriage, since that would strengthen his heart and give him breath for confession. Quiteria agrees to this, gives Basilio her hand and the priest blesses them, whereupon Basilio leaps to his feet pulling the dagger deftly from his breast. It was all a trick, he exclaims, jubilantly. Camacho is furious and demands instant justice but Don Quixote intervenes: "Quiteria was Basilio's, and Basilio Quiteria's, by Heaven's just and favourable decree". Drinking, dancing and merrymaking follow as Quixote and a reluctant Sancho leave the feast for the open road once more. Most sharply and wittily characterized is the role of Sancho, a character in whom Telemann, like us, clearly delighted. Athletic leaps accompany his recollection of an earlier unpleasant escapade when playful rogues tossed him in a blanket. Michael Schopper revels in the part, giving a larger-than-life picture of this lovable squire. Quixote is another bass role, here sung by Raimund Nolte. His, too, is a splendidly robust performance, as we can hear, for instance, in his vigorous chiding of the timorous tendencies in Sancho's nature (tracks 5 and 6). The remaining roles are smaller, but uniformly well sung and the choruses, often adorned with rhythmic and instrumental ideas which evoke splashes of local colour, are first-rate. In summary, here is a work which should have a wide appeal for its musical diversity, skilful characterization and captivating melodies. The sound is excellent.

Further listening ...

Musique de table — Productions I-III. **Vienna Concentus Musicus/Nikolaus Harnoncourt.** Teldec Das Alte Werk 2292-44688-2 (10/89).

Overture Suites — C major, TWV55: C6; D major, TWV55: D19; B flat major, TTWV55: B10. **The English Concert/Trevor Pinnock.** Archv Produktion 437 558-2AH (6/93).

Paris Quartets — Concerto No. 1 in G major; Sonata No. 1 in A major. Nouveaux Quatuors — No. 2 in A minor; No. 6 in E minor. **Wilbert Hazelzet** (fl); **Trio Sonnerie.** Virgin Classics Veritas VC7 59049-2 (3/92).

12 Fantaisies. **Patrick Gallois** (fl). DG 437 543-2GH (6/93).

Schwanengesang, TWV4: 6 Herr, strafe mich nicht in Deinem Trinitatis, TWV1: 771. **Soloists; La Stagione/Michael Schneider.** CPO CPO999 212-2 (7/94).

Missa brevis. Deus judicium tuum. Alles redet jetzt und singet. **Soloists; Rheinische Kantorei; Das kleine Konzert/Hermann Max.** Capriccio 10 315 (11/91).

PIMPINONE. **John Ostendorf** (bass) Pimpinone; **Julianne Baird** (sop) Vespetta; **St Luke's Baroque Orchestra/Rudolph Palmer.** Newport Classic NCD60117 (1/92).

Key to symbols

Gramophone Awards winners

Gramophone Editor's choice

Sigismond Thalberg

German/Austrian 1812-1871

Suggested listening ...

Fantasies on operas by Donizetti. **Francesco Nicolosi** (pf); Marco Polo 8 223365 (7/94).

Charles Thomas

French 1811-1896

New review

Thomas. HAMLET. **Thomas Hampson** (bass) Hamlet; **June Anderson** (sop) Ophélie; **Gregory Kunde** (ten) Laërte; **Denyce Graves** (mez) Gertrude; **Samuel Ramey** (bass) Claudius; **Jean-Philippe Courtis** (bass) Ghost; **Gérard Garino** (ten) Marcellus; **Michel Trempont** (ten) Polonius; **François Le Roux** (bar) Horatio; **Thierry Félix** (bar) First Gravedigger; **Jean-Pierre Furlan** (ten) Second Gravedigger; **Ambrosian Opera Chorus; London Philharmonic Orchestra/Antonio de Almeida.** EMI CDS7 54820-2. Notes, text and translation included. Recorded in 1993.

③ 3h 18m DDD 1/94

Variously described as a "powerful, dark-hued masterpiece" and as, dramatically, a travesty with some musical high spots amid a sea of commonplace sentimentalities, Thomas's *Hamlet* seems to demand being looked at afresh. Forget Shakespeare if you can, and though the contrived happy ending, with Hamlet being proclaimed king, takes some swallowing, responsibility for this lies not with Thomas but with the French audiences of the 1860s. For the Covent Garden produc-tion of *Hamlet* a year after the Paris première, the ending was changed as a sop to British sensibilities, and Hamlet kills himself. The present recording goes back to Thomas's original but also includes the Covent Garden ending in an appendix, to which is also banished the ballet (dramatically irrelevant) on which Parisian audiences insisted. Also as an appendix is the inclusion of a duet between Claudius and Gertrude only recently discovered. So, what impression does it make? There are indeed undistinguished sections, where Thomas lapses into the conventional, and lead-ins to arias are too often like ballet-dancers' "take up position" (though the introduction to "To be or not to be" is almost Verdian) — but against this must be set the tense scene of the ghost's appearance, Hamlet's highly dramatic confrontation of Gertrude, such arias as Claudius's prayer for forgiveness and Hamlet's "Comme une pâle fleur", and Thomas's orchestration — colourful and full of felicities. Almeida secures the utmost commitment from the LPO — the initial coronation march has tremendous impact and the Ambrosian Singers are splendidly firm-voiced and tonally sensitive. The casting is admirable: Anderson, with her seductive voice and sparkling technique, presents a touching and vulnerable Ophelia, and manages even to make the protracted mad scene that occupies all of Act 3 something more than the mere display-piece for prima donnas and canary-fanciers. Hampson's Hamlet is full of subtle shadings of tone and colour, and the recitatives (his as well as the others') are invested with life and character. Ramey brings weight to his portrayal of Claudius, Denyce Graves has a secure facility as Gertrude, and all the minor parts are well taken. In sum, listeners should give Thomas another chance.

Further listening ...

RAYMOND — Overture. *Coupled with* **Chabrier.** Joyeuse marche. España. **Dukas.** L'apprenti sorcier. **Satie** (orch. Debussy). Gymnopédies — Nos. 1 and 3. **Saint-Saëns.** SAMSON ET DALILA — Bacchanale. **Bizet.** Jeux d'enfants. **Ibert.** Divertissement. **Montreal Symphony Orchestra/Charles Dutoit.** Decca 421 527-2DH (6/89). *See review in the Collections section; refer to the Index to Reviews.*

Virgil Thomson

Suggested listening ...

Symphony on a Hymn Tune[b]. Symphony No. 2[b]. LORD BYRON[ac] — Alas! the love of woman!; A wanderer from the British world of fashion; Sweet Lady; I'd sooner burn in hell; Fare thee well thus disunited. Shipwreck and Love Scene from Byron's Don Juan[ac]. A Solemn Music[c]. A Joyful Fugue[c]. [a]**Martyn Hill** (ten); [b]**Monadnock Festival Orchestra;** [c]**Budapest Symphony Orchestra/James Bolle.** Albany TROY017-2 (4/90).

Dimitri Tiomkin

Suggested listening ...

Film Scores: Lost Horizon — Suite[a]. The Guns of Navarone — Prelude. The Big Sky — Suite. The Fourposter — Overture. Friendly Persuasion — Love scene in the barn. Search for Paradise — finale[a]. [a]**John Alldis Choir; National Philharmonic Orchestra/Charles Gerhardt.** RCA Victor GD81669 (5/91).

Michael Tippett

Tippett. ORCHESTRAL WORKS. [c]**Heather Harper** (sop); [abc]**London Symphony Orchestra/Sir Colin Davis;** [d]**Chicago Symphony Orchestra/Sir Georg Solti.** Decca London 425 646-2LM3. Item marked [a] recorded in 1975, [b] 1967, [c] 1973, [d] 1979-81. Symphonies — No. 1[a] (from Philips 9500 107, 10/76); No. 2[b] (Argo ZRG535, 1/68); No. 3[c] (Philips 6500 662, 1/75); No. 4[d], Suite in D major for the Birthday of Prince Charles[d] (both from Decca SXDL7546, 8/81).

③ 2h 5lm ADD/DDD 7/90

These four symphonies comprise one of the most considerable contributions to the genre by a British composer this century. Numbers 1 and 2 are examples of Tippett's earlier, still relatively traditional language, while Nos. 3 and 4 are more radical. Bounding energy is the predominant quality of Nos. 1 and 2, an energy whose individual attributes are by no means diminished by association with Stravinsky. But Tippett's more personal, magical lyricism is also prominent, especially in the marvellous slow movement of No. 2, and this lyricism forms a clear link to the more reflective passages of No. 3. This glorious, 55-minute work evolves from purely instrumental arguments about active and reflective states of mind into a series of songs (for soprano) that confront some of the most urgent social issues of our time. Though arguing the need to counter violence and repression with tolerance and love, the music offers its own irreconcilable confrontation between allusions to Beethoven's Ninth and Bessie Smith-style blues, swept up into a stark coda as uncompromising in its modernism as anything in Tippett's output. After this the Fourth Symphony is less hectic, though no less diverse in its materials, a half-hour single movement of dazzling colours and vivid emotions. Although the performances occasionally remind us of the difficulties Tippett presents to his interpreters, and the recordings are not, on the whole, of the latest digital vintage, this is — thanks mainly to the commitment and persuasiveness of Sir Colin Davis — a set of considerable distinction.

Additional recommendations ...
No. 4[a]. *Byzantium*[b]. [b]**Faye Robinson** (sop); **Chicago Symphony Orchestra/Sir Georg Solti.** Decca 433 668-2DH — 58m DDD 4/93
No. 4. *Fantasia on a Theme of Handel*[a]. *Fantasia Concertante on a Theme of Corelli.* [a]**Howard Shelley** (pf); **Bournemouth Symphony Orchestra/Richard Hickox.** Chandos CHAN9233 — 1h 6m DDD 11/93

Tippett. Praeludium. Symphony No. 3[a]. [a]**Faye Robinson** (sop); **Bournemouth Symphony Orchestra/Richard Hickox.** Chandos CHAN9276. Text included. Recorded in 1993.

Ih 4m DDD 6/94

The Third Symphony, first heard in 1972, is one of Tippett's most complex and highly charged attempts to create a convincing structure from the collision between strongly contrasted musical characteristics. The work evolves from a purely orchestral drama — fast first movement, slow second movement, both large-scale, followed by a shorter scherzo — to a less extended but also tripartite sequence of blues settings, the whole capped by a huge, climactic coda in which the soprano voice finally yields the last word to the orchestra. The first two movements (Part 1, as Tippett calls it) remain a considerable technical challenge, especially to the strings, but this performance manages to sustain an appropriate level of tension without sounding merely effortful, and without skimping on the opportunities for eloquence of phrasing. It could well be that Tippett has over-indulged the percussion in the slow movement, but this vivid and well-balanced Chandos recording lets us hear ample detail without exaggerating the bright colours and hyper-resonant textures. The later stages have the advantage of a superbly characterful singer in Faye Robinson. She has the power, the edge, and also the radiance, to make Tippett's progression from idiosyncratic blues to Beethoven-quoting peroration utterly convincing. The work ends, famously, on a question-mark, dismissing the unrestrained affirmation of Beethoven's *Choral* finale in favour of the unresolved opposition of loud brass and soft strings. Will that "new compassionate power/To heal, to love" which the text "senses" actually be achieved? Twenty years on, the jury is still out on Tippett's great humanist challenge. Meanwhile, there can be no questioning the achievement of this performance and recording, coupled strikingly with the highly characteristic *Praeludium* for brass, bells and percussion of 1962. Sir Colin Davis's account of the symphony (see above), will always be admired as a magnificent pioneering effort, but Chandos have given us the version for our time.

Tippett. String Quartet No. 5. **Lindsay Quartet** (Peter Cropper, Ronald Birks, vns; Robin Ireland, va; Bernard Gregor-Smith, vc). ASV CDDCA879.
Brown: Fanfare to welcome Sir Michael Tippett. **Purcell:** Fantasies — F major, Z737; E minor, Z741; G major, Z742. **Morris:** Canzoni Ricertati — No. 1, Risoluto; No. 6, Lento sostenuto. **C. Wood:** String Quartet in A minor.

Ih 16m DDD 1/94

This curious mixture of a programme is a precise re-creation of the concert at which Tippett's Fifth String Quartet had its first performance. Music by two of his teachers and one of his great inspirers is preceded by a greeting prelude that quotes both Purcell and Tippett himself. Tippett's Quartet is quite typical of him, both in its exquisitely singing lyricism and in the fact that it is by no means a mere looking back towards his earlier lyrical phases. Here intensification of expression is often achieved by distillation, towards such a simplicity of utterance that at crucial moments the music thins sometimes to one, often to no more than two, of the quartet's voices. R.O. Morris's *Canzoni Ricertati* subject faintly folk-like melodies to ingenious fugal and canonic treatment. In Charles Wood's quartet, the ingenious interplay of short motives in his scherzo is something that might have caught the young Tippett's ear, and his finale dresses up the Irish folk-song *The lark in the clear air* in its best Sunday clothes. The Purcell *Fantasies* point up Tippett's Purcell-ancestry rather touchingly as does Christopher Brown's miniature *Fanfare*. The Lindsay's beautiful performances are cleanly but not clinically recorded.

Tippett. A Child of Our Time. **Jessye Norman** (sop); **Dame Janet Baker** (mez); **Richard Cassilly** (ten); **John Shirley-Quirk** (bar); **BBC Singers; BBC Choral Society; BBC Symphony Orchestra/Sir Colin Davis.** Philips 420 075-2PH. Text included. From 6500 985 (11/75). Recorded in 1975.

Ih 4m ADD 11/87

A Child of Our Time takes as its narrative kernel the shooting in 1938 of a minor German diplomat by a 17-year-old Jew, Herschel Grynspan, and so causing one of the most savage anti-

Jewish pogroms seen in Nazi Germany. But the universality of the dilemma of an individual caught up in something he cannot control gives it a much broader relevance. Just as Bach used the Lutheran hymns for the chorale sections within his Passions, so Tippett uses the negro spiritual to tap a similarly universal vein. The soloists provide the narrative thread against the more reflective role of the chorus but they come together forcefully in the spirituals. Sir Colin Davis directs a powerful and atmospheric performance and his soloists are very fine. The 1975 recording sounds well.

Additional recommendations ...
Soloists; City of Birmingham Symphony Chorus and Orchestra/Sir Michael Tippett.
Collins Classics 1339-2 — .·⁚ lh 9m DDD 9/92 Ⓑ
Soloists; London Symphony Chorus and Orchestra/Richard Hickox. Chandos
CHAN9123 — .·⁚ lh l3m DDD 2/93 Ⓑ

Further listening ...

Concerto for Double String Orchestra. Fantasia Concertante on a Theme of Corelli. Little Music for Strings. **Academy of St Martin in the Fields/Sir Neville Marriner.** Decca London 421 389-2LM (8/89).

Choral Works — Dance, Clarion Air. The Weeping Babe. Plebs angelica. Bonny at Morn. Crown of the Year. Music. A Child of Our Time — Five Negro Spirituals. **Soloists; Christ Church Cathedral Choir/Stephen Darlington.** Nimbus NI5266 (1/91).

The Mask of Time. **Soloists; BBC Singers; BBC Symphony Chorus and Orchestra/ Andrew Davis.** EMI British Composers CMS7 64711-2 (10/93).

KING PRIAM. **Soloists; London Sinfonietta Chorus; London Sinfonietta/David Atherton.** Decca London 414 241-2LH2 (1/90).

THE ICE BREAK. **Soloists; London Sinfonietta Chorus; London Sinfonietta/David Atherton.** Virgin Classics VC7 59048-2 (2/92).

Loris Tjeknavorian
Iranian 1937-

Suggested listening ...

Danses fantastiques. *Coupled with* **Khachaturian.** The Widow of Valencia — Suite. Gayaneh — Suite No. 2. **Armenian Philharmonic Orchestra/Loris Tjeknavorian.** ASV CDDCA884 (3/94). *See review under Khachaturian; refer to the Index to Reviews.*

Henri Tomasi
French 1901-1971

Suggested listening ...

Trumpet Concerto. *Coupled with* **Jolivet.** Concertino for Trumpet, Piano and Strings[a]. **Hummel.** Trumpet Concerto in E flat major. **Haydn.** Trumpet Concerto in E flat major, HobVIIe/1. **Sergei Nakariakov** (tpt); [a]**Alexander Markovich** (pf); **Lausanne Chamber Orchestra/Jésus López-Cobos.** Teldec 4509-90846-2 (10/93). *See review in the Collections section; refer to the Index to Reviews.*

Thomas Tomkins

British 1572-1656

Suggested listening ...

Third Service — Magnificat and Nunc dimittis. *Cathedral Music* — O sing unto the Lord a new song. Then David mourned. My beloved spake unto me. Above the stars my saviour dwells. Glory be to God on high. Almighty God, the fountain of all wisdom. When David heard. My shepherd is the living Lord. Sing unto God. Behold, the hour cometh. O God, the proud are risen against me. **St George's Chapel Choir, Windsor/Christopher Robinson** with **Roger Judd** (org). Hyperion CDA66345 (3/90).

Third or Great Service. *Anthems* — Almighty God, the fountain of all wisdom; Be strong and of good courage; O God, the proud are risen against me; O sing unto the Lord; Then David mourned; When David heard; Woe is me. **The Tallis Scholars/Peter Phillips.** Gimell CDGIM024 (3/92).

Ernest Tomlinson

British 1927-

Suggested listening ...

Little Serenade. An English Overture. The Story of Cinderella — Fairy Coach; Cinderella Waltz. Kielder Water. Silverthorne Suite. Second Suite of English Folk-Dances. Lyrical Suite — Nocturne. Pastoral Dances — Hornpipe. Gaelic Sketches — Gaelic Lullaby. Nautical Interlude. Sweet and Dainty. **Bratislava Radio Symphony Orchestra/Ernest Tomlinson.** Marco Polo 8 223413 (12/92).

Giuseppe Torelli

Italian 1658-1709

New review

Torelli. 12 Concerti grossi, Op. 8 — No. 2 in A minor; No. 3 in E major; No. 6 in G minor; No. 8 in C minor; No. 9 in E minor; No. 12 in D major. **Mariana Sirbu, Antonio Perez** (vns); **I Musici.** Philips 432 118-2PH. Recorded in 1992.

53m DDD 1/94

Considering Torelli's importance in the development of the *concerto grosso*, his own have been given scant attention. His posthumously published 12 *Concerti grossi*, Op. 8 are mature works of which Nos. 1-6 are for two violins and strings and Nos. 7-12 are solo-violin concertos, signposts to the road taken by Vivaldi. Pre-Vivaldi and pre-Bach these concertos may be, but there is much to remind one that Torelli was himself a violin virtuoso; Sirbu and Perez follow splendidly in his footsteps: accurate, expressive but economical with vibrato. These sturdy works, without dance movements, have some interesting features: solo and tutti material differ, several pairs of movements are played virtually continuously, and near the end of Concerto No. 3/III the two soloists converse in quasi-cadenza fashion over a dominant pedal. These are invigorating performances of works that deserve attention and, as such, are warmly recommended.

Further listening ...

Concerto in E minor for Four Violins and Strings. *Coupled with* **Locatelli.** Introduttioni Teatrali and Concerti, Op. 4 — No. 12 in F major. **Leo.** Concerto in D major for Four Violins and Strings. **Mossi.** Concertos, Op. 4 — No. 12 in G minor. **Valentini.** Concerti grossi, Op. 7 — No. 11 in A minor. **Cologne Musica Antiqua/Reinhard Goebel.** Archiv Produktion 435 393-2AH (9/92). *See review in the Collections section; refer to the Index to Reviews.*

Michael Torke

American 1961-

Suggested listening ...

Colour Music — Green;. Purple; Ecstatic Orange; Ash; Bright Blue Music. **Baltimore Symphony Orchestra/David Zinman.** Argo 433 071-2ZH (2/92).

The Yellow Pages[e]. Slate[abcd]. Adjustable Wrench[d]. Vanada[d]. Rust[e]. **Michael Torke** (pf); [a]**Edmund Niemann, Nurit Tilles** (pf, four hands); [b]**James Pugliese** (xylophone); [c]**Gary Schall** (marimba); **London Sinfonietta/**[d]**Kent Nagano,** [e]**David Miller.** Argo 430 209-2ZH (12/90).

Veljo Tormis

Estonian 1930-

Suggested listening ...

Livonian Heritage. Votic Wedding Songs. Izhorian Epic. Ingrian Evenings. Vespian Paths. Karelian Destiny. **Estonian Philharmonic Chamber Choir/Tonu Kaljuste.** ECM New Series 434 275-2 (10/92).

Charles Tournemire

French 1870-1939

Tournemire. Suite Evocatrice, Op. 74.
Vierne. Symphony No. 3, Op. 28.
Widor. Symphonie Gothique, Op. 70. **Jeremy Filsell** (org). Herald HAVPCD145. Played on the Harrison and Harrison organ of Ely Cathedral. Recorded in 1991.

Ih IIm DDD 3/92

Compared with, say, the symphonies of Tchaikovsky or Sibelius the organ symphonies of Widor and his pupil Vierne are not particularly long. But in terms of organ music they are among the longest single works in the repertory. Within their five-movement form the composers set out to exploit the full expressive range of the organ and it was no coincidence that the organ symphony developed in turn of the century France. The great French organ builder Aristide Cavaillé-Coll was then producing instruments capable of hitherto undreamt-of colour and expression. Both Widor (at St Sulpice) and Vierne (at Notre Dame) had at their disposal the finest instruments in Paris and they indulged themselves fully in their symphonies. The subtitle of Widor's Ninth (*Gothic*) says it all. The structure is vast, intricately detailed, and almost forbidding in its grandness. Vierne's Third also presents an awesome spectacle, full of complex music and technically demanding writing, while Tournemire's neo-classical Suite provides a moment almost of light relief in such heavyweight company. Jeremy Filsell is an outstanding virtuoso player with a gift for musical communication and, in the Ely Cathedral organ, an instrument which produces the range of the great French instruments, but within an altogether clearer acoustic. These are performances of exceptional quality captured in a recording of rare excellence from the small independent company, Herald.

Eduard Tubin

Estonian-Swedish 1905-1982

Suggested listening ...

Symphonies Nos. 3 and 8. **Swedish Radio Symphony Orchestra/Neeme Järvi.** BIS CD342 (9/88).

Symphonies — No. 4, "Sinfonia lirica"[a]; No. 9[b]. Toccata[b]. [a]**Bergen Symphony Orchestra,** [b]**Gothenburg Symphony Orchestra/Neeme Järvi.** BIS CD227 (10/86).

String Quartet. Piano Quartet in C sharp minor[a]. Elegy. *Coupled with* **Pärt.** Fratres. **Tüür.** String Quartet. **Tallinn Quartet;** [a]**Love Derwinger** (pf). BIS CD574 (1/94). *See review under Pärt; refer to the Index to Reviews.*

Six Preludes. Piano Sonatas Nos. 1 and 2. Lullaby. Album Leaf. Three Pieces for Children. A little March, for Rana. Three Estonian Folk-dances. Prelude No. 1. Variations on an Estonian Folk Tune. Ballad on a Theme by Mart Saar. Four Folk-songs from my country. Sonatina in D minor. Seven Preludes. Suite on Estonian Shepherd Melodies. **Vardo Rumessen** (pf). BIS CD414/16 (three-disc set, 3/89).

Joaquín Turina
Spanish 1882-1949

Turina. ORCHESTRAL WORKS. **Bamberg Symphony Orchestra/Antonio de Almeida.** RCA Victor Red Seal RD60895.
Danzas fantásticas, Op. 22. La procesión del Rocío, Op. 9. Sinfonía sevillana, Op. 23. Ritmos, Op. 43.

Ih 3m DDD 7/92

An hour's worth of musical sunshine, with the occasional cloud drifting by just for tonal contrast. Turina was a magnificent orchestrator and although he was — as Antonio de Almeida points out in his useful booklet annotations — a "quintessential Sevillian", he was also acutely aware of musical trends beyond his own locality. His style approximates the youthful opulence of early Debussy (whose sensuous *Printemps* frequently comes to mind), yet the piquant instrumentation that graces, say, "Exaltación" from the *Danzas fantásticas*, or the whole of *La procesión del Rocío* is refreshingly individual — beautifully aired and crafted, with the sum of its gleaming parts amounting to an appealing tonal blend. Were it not for the give-away nature of specifically Spanish melodies, Dvořák (of the *Slavonic Dances*) would as likely come to mind as Falla — particularly in the *Danzas*. La procesión (1912) predates the other pieces on the disc, while *Ritmos* was composed as late as 1928. It was premièred by Casals, but here more than anywhere else on the disc, one is reminded of Almeida's great mentor, Sir Thomas Beecham. Just listen to the way he points *Ritmos*'s atmospheric "Danza lenta", or sample the excitement he generates in the "Danza exótica" from the same work; then turn back to "Fiesta en San Juan de Aznalfarache" from *Sinfonía sevillana* — awash with colour from the first bar to the last — and witness how the Bamberg players exploit Turína's varied tonal palette. As for the recording (a co-production between BMG Classics and Bavarian Radio), it's truly demonstration-worthy; a fair sampling point is the "Valse trágico" from *Ritmos*, which features a spectacular mushrooming tam-tam. But then Turina is the answer to a recording engineer's dream: his use of winds, brass and percussion, in particular, is as judicious as it is impressive, and he never overcrowds his orchestral climaxes. Quite simply, this disc is unalloyed delight from start to finish — *Fantásticas* in name *and* nature!

Further listening ...

Piano Trios — No. 1, Op. 35; No. 2, Op. 76. Círculo, Op. 91. **Munich Piano Trio.** Calig CAL50 902.

La oración del torero. *Coupled with* **Wagner.** Siegfried Idyll. **Wolf.** Italian Serenade. **Puccini.** Crisantemi. **Berlioz.** Rêverie et caprice, Op. 8[a]. **Sibelius.** Kuolema, Op. 44 — Valse triste. **Dvořák.** Nocturne in B major, B47. [a]**Guillermo Figueroa** (vn); **Orpheus Chamber Orchestra.** DG 431 680-2GH (10/91). *See review in the Collections Section; refer to the Index to Reviews.*

Rapsodia sinfónica, Op. 66. *Coupled with* **Albéniz** (orch. Halffter). Rapsodia española, Op. 70. **Falla.** Noches en los jardines de España. **Alicia de Larrocha** (pf); **London Philharmonic Orchestra/Rafael Frühbeck de Burgos.** Decca 410 289-2DH (10/84).

Poeme en forma de canciones. *Coupled with* **Padilla.** Valencia. **Grever.** Jurame. **F. Alonso.**
Maitechu mia. **Lara.** Granada. **Vives.** Doña Francisquita — Por el humo. **Soutullo.** Ultimo
romantico — Noche de amor. **Serrano.** Alma da Dios — Canción húngara. **Falla.** Canciones
populares españolas. **Mompou.** Combat del somni. **Obradors.** Canciones clásicas españolas —
Del cabello más sutil. Corazón porqué pasais. **José Carreras** (ten); **Martin Katz** (pf); **English
Chamber Orchestra/Robin Stapleton, Roberto Benzi, Antoni Ros Marbá.** Philips 432
825-2PM (7/92). *See review in the Collections Section; refer to the Index to Reviews.*

Mark-Anthony Turnage
British 1960-

Suggested listening ...

Three Screaming Popes. **City of Birmingham Symphony Orchestra/Simon Rattle.** EMI
TSP204681-2 (9/92).

Erkki-Sven Tüür
Estonia 1959-

Suggested listening ...

String Quartet. *Coupled with* **Pärt.** Fratres. **Tubin.** String Quartet. Piano Quartet in C sharp
minor[a]. Elegy. **Tallinn Quartet;** [a]**Love Derwinger** (pf). BIS CD574 (1/94). *See review under
Pärt; refer to the Index to Reviews.*

Christopher Tye
British c.1505-1572

Suggested listening ...

Consort Music — Complete Instrumental Works. **Hespèrion XX/Jordi Savall.** Astrée Auvidis
E8708 (11/89).

Sacred Choral Works — Kyrie, "Orbis factor". Mass, "Euge bone". Quaesumus omnipotens.
Miserere mei, Deus. Omnes gentes, plaudite. Peccavimus cum patribus. **Winchester
Cathedral Choir/David Hill.** Hyperion CDA66424 (1/91).

Marco Uccellini
Italian c.1603-1680

New review
Uccellini. SONATAS. **Arcadian Academy** (Elizabeth Blumenstock, Katherine Kyme, vns;
David Bowles, vc; David Tayler, lte, gtr)/**Nicholas McGegan** (hpd, org). Harmonia Mundi
HMU90 7066. Recorded in 1992.
Op. 2 — Sonata ottava a due violini. Op. 3 — Sonata quarta detta "La Trasformata"; Aria
quinta sopra "La Bergamasca"; Aria sesta sopra un balletto; Sonata nona a doi violini detta "La
Reggiana". Op. 4 — Sonata seconda detta "La Luciminia contenta"; Sonata quarta a violino solo
detta "La Hortensa virtuosa"; Aria undecima a doi violini sopra "Il Caporal Simon"; Aria decima
quarta a doi violini "La mia Pedrina"; Aria decima quinta sopra "La Scatola dagli agghi"; Sonata

decima ottava a doi violini; Sonata vigesima a doi violini; Sonata vigesima prima a doi violini; Sonata vigesima quinta; Sonata vigesima sesta sopra "La Prosperina"; Sonata vigesima settima. Op. 7 — Sonata nona.

1h 12m   DDD   7/94

The Arcadian Academy have here produced a superb recording by a relatively unknown composer. Marco Uccellini deserves to be better known — not merely because he was the first to publish music specifically for the violin, nor because he was a prolific composer who left nine published collections of sonatas, but because the music is so good. This recording includes sonatas for one or two violins and continuo from Uccellini's Second (1639), Third (1642), Fourth (1645) and Seventh (1668) Books. Their selection is expertly paced, framed by lively dialogue 'arias' with guitar accompaniment (in *L'Emenfrodito* from Op. 3 the violinists take delight in the roles of hen and cuckoo) and sonatas (*La Luciminia contenta* and *La Hortensa virtuosa*) in which Elizabeth Blumenstock, playing a 1687 Strad, and Katherine Kyme, on a 1769 Gaffino, eloquently express themselves in turn. The vitality and rhetoric with which they infuse these performances is emphatically illuminating. Though seemingly very idiomatically conceived for violins, these sonatas owe more to madrigals than to dance music. At times, as in the *Sonata decima ottava* from the Fourth Book, one can almost hear the text, so akin to speech are the lines. The players of the Arcadian Academy deftly mix different bass combinations of cello, harpsichord, organ, archlute and guitar. The result — never more delightful than in the single selection taken from the Seventh Book (track 13) — is a real cracker!

Viktor Ullmann

Austrian/Hungarian 1898-1944

New review

Ullmann. Piano Concerto, Op. 25[a]. Five Variations and Double Fugue on a Piano Piece of Arnold Schoenberg. Symphony No. 2 in D. [a]**Konrad Richter** (pf); **Brno State Philharmonic Orchestra/Israel Yinon.** Bayer BR100228. Recorded in 1992.

53m   DDD

This is the first in a series devoted to "the forgotten, lost and prohibited music of European composers in the 20th century" — an offshoot of the 1989 Baden-Württembergische Musikhochschultage which targeted the composer victims of two world wars. The highlight of the festival was the world première of Viktor Ullmann's 'Symphony No. 2' extrapolated from the copiously annotated manuscript of his Piano Sonata No. 7 by Bernhard Wulff, a professor at the Freiburg Musikhochschule. Even in its 'original' form, this is music which poses a raft of unavoidable (and unanswerable) aesthetic questions. Listening to Wulff's superbly effective realization is at once more harrowing and considerably more rewarding than the piano original. Given that the composer was transported to Auschwitz within weeks of its composition, normal critical evaluation might be thought almost impertinent. And yet this would be to do the composer a disservice. We do not need to approach these scores gingerly like tourists visiting a concentration camp. Ours is the generation for whom Mahler's 'Tenth' has become standard repertoire. Against far greater odds, the same fate could await Ullmann's 'Second'. Ullmann's Piano Concerto, on the other hand, seems likelier to remain a historical curio; it is not helped here by a hard piano sound and an uncertain first trumpet. His disturbing eclecticism is much less evident in the overtly Schoenbergian *Variations*, not the equal of the superb, Second Viennese-style Third String Quartet he completed in Theresienstadt (see below), but 'all of a piece' in a way not entirely characteristic of him. The 'Symphony' deploys his usual quota of stylistic reminiscences and yet Ullmann ensures that these no longer work against each other. There can be no doubt that the quixotic orchestration helps, adding acid wit to the first movement's vain attempt at innocence, edge to the grotesque *Alla marcia* and overwhelming emotional force to the slow movement which emerges as impassioned as well as compositionally rigorous. One cannot but be moved by the Hebrew melody which concludes the work, singing in the face of the murder of so many thousands. Schoenberg attempts something similar in his *Survivor from Warsaw*, but the sheer strength required to compose in Ullmann's circumstances threatens to make such comparisons as irrelevant as pointing out that the penultimate page of Bayer's booklet is printed upside down and the wrong way round. Otherwise, the documen-tation is admirably full. On the evidence of this first instalment, Bayer's Atlantis Series could prove essential listening indeed.

Further listening ...

String Quartet No. 3, Op. 43. *Coupled with* **Klein.** String Trio. Fantasie a Fuga. Piano Sonata[a]. String Quartet, Op. 2. **Hawthorne Quartet;** [a]**Virginia Eskin** (pf). Channel Classics CCS1691 (12/91). *See review under Klein; refer to the Index to Reviews.*

Fartein Valen

Suggested listening ...

Pastorale, Op. 11. Le cimitière Marin, Op. 20. Sonetto di Michelangelo, Op. 17 No. 1. Cantico di ringraziamento, Op. 17 No. 2. Nenia, Op. 18 No. 1. La isla de las calmas, Op. 21. Ode to Solitude, Op. 35. Ave Maria, Op. 4[a]. Zwei Chinesische Gedichte, Op. 8[a]. Darest Thou now, O soul, Op. 9[a]. Die dunkle Nacht der Seele, Op. 32[a]. [a]**Dorothy Dorow** (sop); **Oslo Philharmonic Orchestra/Miltiades Caridis.** Simax PSC3115 (6/93).

Symphonies — No. 1, Op. 30; No. 2, Op. 40; No. 3, Op. 41; No. 4, Op. 43. **Bergen Philharmonic Orchestra/Aldo Ceccato.** Simax PSC3101 (8/93).

Francisco Valls

Suggested listening ...

Missa Scala Aretina. *Coupled with* **Biber.** Requiem in F minor. **Soloists; Netherlands Bach Society Choir and Baroque Orchestra/Gustav Leonhardt.** Deutsche Harmonia Mundi 05472 77277-2 (8/93). *See review under Biber; refer to the Index to Reviews.*

Edgard Varèse

Varèse. VARIOUS WORKS. [a]**Rachel Yakar** (sop); [b]**Lawrence Beauregard** (fl); [c]**New York Philharmonic Orchestra;** [d]**Ensemble Intercontemporain/**[e]**Pierre Boulez.** Sony Classical MK45844. Texts and translations included.
Ionisation[ce]. Amériques[ce]. Arcana (All from CBS 76520, 6/78)[ce]. Density 21.5[b]. Offrandes[ade]. Octandre[de]. Intégrales (All from IM39053, 3/85)[de].

lh 17m ADD/DDD 10/90

These classic recordings make a welcome return to the catalogue, especially since the music of Varèse has been so poorly represented on disc and in the concert hall in recent years. Quite why so important a figure in twentieth-century music should be neglected like this is hard to say, and even more difficult to comprehend when one samples the quality of the music presented here. Varèse was a pioneer, a quester and above all a liberator. Music for him was a form of twentieth-century alchemy — the transmutation of the ordinary into the extraordinary, an alchemical wedding of intellectual thought with intuitive imagination. Indeed, it was the writings of the fourteenth century cosmologist and alchemist Paracelsus that formed the inspiration behind his orchestral work *Arcana*, a vast canvas of sound built entirely out of one melodic motive. Discernible are echoes of Stravinsky and others, but the totality of *Arcana* is pure Varèse. The same is true of *Amériques*, a title that Varèse emphasized was not to be taken as "purely geographical but as symbolic of discoveries — new worlds on earth, in the sky or in the minds of men". Here romanticism and modernism seem to coexist side by side, where allusions from works such as *La mer* and *The Firebird* seem like racial memories carried into his brave new world. The remaining items consist of smaller chamber works which display Varèse's most radical, though equally rewarding, styles. Boulez and his players give committed, virtuosic performances of these challenging and intriguing works. Well worth exploring.

Ralph Vaughan Williams

British 1872-1958

Vaughan Williams. Symphony No. 1, "A Sea Symphony". **Felicity Lott** (sop); **Jonathan Summers** (bar); **Cantilena; London Philharmonic Choir and Orchestra/Bernard Haitink.** EMI CDC7 49911-2. Text included. Recorded in 1989.

> • Ih IIm DDD 1/90   ⁹⌐ₚ

A firm hand on the tiller is needed to steer a safe course through this, Vaughan Williams's first and most formally diffuse symphony, completed in 1909. Haitink is clearly an ideal choice of helmsman and he is helped by a remarkably lucid recording that resolves details that would rarely be revealed in live performance. What might be more unexpected here is the obvious affinity he shows for this music: whilst never transgressing the bounds of Vaughan Williams's characteristically English idiom, he manages to place the work in the European mainstream, revealing a whole range of resonances, from Bruckner and Mahler to the Impressionists. Not all the glory should go to the conductor, of course. Both soloists are particularly fine, the vulnerability behind the spine-tingling power of Felicity Lott's voice providing excellent contrast to the staunch solidity of Jonathan Summers. The LPO Chorus, aided by Cantilena, are on top form and the whole enterprise is underpinned by the London Philharmonic's total commitment and expertise. Here is the recording of this glorious work for which the catalogue was waiting.

Additional recommendations ...
Margaret Marshall (sop); **Stephen Roberts** (bar); **London Symphony Chorus; Philharmonia Orchestra/Richard Hickox.** Virgin Classics VJ7 Virgo 59687-2 — • Ih 4m DDD ⁹ₚ
Joan Rodgers (sop); **William Shimell** (bar); **Royal Liverpool Philharmonic Choir and Orchestra/Vernon Handley.** EMI Eminence CD-EMX2142 — • Ih 10m DDD 2/89
Yvonne Kenny (sop); **Brian Rayner Cook** (bar); **London Symphony Chorus; London Symphony Orchestra/Bryden Thomson.** Chandos CHAN8764 — • Ih 6m DDD 2/90
Dame Isobei Baillie (sop); **John Cameron** (bar); **London Philharmonic Choir and Orchestra/Sir Adrian Boult.** Belart mono 450·144-2 — , Ih 8m ADD 7/94 ▲

New review
Vaughan Williams. Symphonies — No. 2, "A London Symphony"; No. 8 in D minor. **Royal Liverpool Philharmonic Orchestra/Vernon Handley.** EMI Eminence CD-EMX2209. Recorded in 1992.

> • Ih 12m DDD 8/93   ⁹⌐ₚ

There are greater depths to *A London Symphony* than mere pictorialism, not least an incredible symphonic structure and a universal message of social change, or to quote from H. G. Wells's novel *Tono-Bungay* with which the symphony has been linked: "a note of crumbling and confusion, of change and seemingly endless swelling, of a bubbling up and a medley of futile loves and sorrows". The ideal interpreter of this work is the conductor who can make the piece sound pertinent to London, who can bring out the universality at the heart of the work, as well as making the whole experience a 'symphonic' one. Vernon Handley achieves all these. It's all here: structural cohesion, symphonic breadth, the implications of a broader, universal message and a marvellous sense of atmosphere and place. In the slow movement the sense of evocation is strong — one can almost feel the chilly London mist envelope you, and the distant jingles really do loom from several streets away. Transition from the lively, nocturnal *Scherzo* (here incisively articulated and brilliantly coloured) to the tragic finale is exceptionally well captured, with a tremendous feeling of inevitability as the opening *fortissimo* outburst, like a collapsing star, leads us inevitably toward the symphony's sombre conclusion. Handley's account of the Eighth Symphony is every bit as splendid and commendable as his account of the *London*. Of the most striking features, it is the rhythmic incisiveness and glorious phrasing that most impress, but there are also some extremely fine solo contributions from the orchestra too; lovely solo flute playing at the beginning of the work, and a gorgeous violin solo in the slow movement. His approach is straightforward; no depth plumbing here, just down to earth, warm hearted music-making. The recordings are ideally balanced and spacious, and put the seal on a top contender for available versions of these symphonies.

Additional recommendations ...

No. 2. Partita for Double String Orchestra. **London Philharmonic Orchestra/Sir Adrian Boult.** Decca 430 366-2LM — .•* lh 6m ADD ⁹ₚ Ⓑ

No. 2. Fantasia on a Theme by Thomas Tallis. **London Philharmonic Orchestra/Bernard Haitink.** EMI CDC7 49394-2 — .•* lh 6m DDD 7/88 ⁹ₚ Ⓑ

No. 2. Concerto Grosso. **London Symphony Orchestra/Bryden Thomson.** Chandos CHAN8629 — .•* lh 5m DDD 10/89 ⁹ₚ Ⓑ

No. 2. Concerto Accademico[a]. *The Wasps — Overture.* [a]**James Oliver Buswell IV** (vn); **London Symphony Orchestra/André Previn.** RCA Gold Seal GD90501 — .•* lh llm ADD 3/91 ⁹ₚ Ⓑ

No. 2. Fantasia on a Theme by Thomas Tallis. **London Philharmonic Orchestra/Sir Adrian Boult.** EMI CDM7 64017-2 — .•* lh ADD 5/92 ⁹ₚ Ⓑ

Nos. 2 and 8. **Hallé Orchestra/Sir John Barbirolli.** EMI CDM7 64197-2 — .•* lh 14m ADD 6/92 ⁹ₚ Ⓑ ▲

Key to symbols

Quality of sound		Discs worth exploring		Caveat emptor
⁹ₚ ⁹ₛ	Ⓑ	❓	✒	▲
Quality of performance	Basic library		Period performance	

Vaughan Williams. Symphonies — No. 3, "A Pastoral Symphony"[a]; No. 4 in F minor. [a]**Alison Barlow** (sop); **Royal Liverpool Philharmonic Orchestra/Vernon Handley.** EMI Eminence CD-EMX2192. Recorded in 1991.

.•* lh 7m DDD 11/92   ⁹ₚ

Vaughan Williams composed his Third Symphony, *A Pastoral,* between 1916 and 1921, and since its first performance in 1922 its title has frequently led to misconceptions concerning the underlying inspiration behind the music. The music itself almost seems to encourage the idea of an idyllic English landscape complete with gently rolling hills and frolicking lambs, but as Vaughan Williams once explained to a friend: "It's really war-time music", and went on to describe how a great deal of it originated during his time as an ambulance driver in the battle fields of Ecoivres in the First World War. When heard with this in mind one can hear the uneasy tension that constantly permeates the score, and the predominantly quiet and contemplative music begins to reveal itself as the poignant elegy that it truly is — a requiem for the young men who sacrificed lives in this pastoral landscape. Ironically the Fourth Symphony has suffered the opposite fate to its predecessor in that images of war, and in particular the growing rise of Fascism at the time of its composition (1931-34), have frequently been aligned to the score's somewhat angry, dissonant mood. Vaughan Williams, however, vigorously denied any such programmatic undercurrent, and was adamant that the work was no more than just a description of a typical modern symphony. Today the symphony is viewed as such — a superb essay in symphonic argument and musical invention. Vernon Handley's accounts of both works are of the highest calibre; the Third glows with an aura of mystery, and features a very fine account of the wordless soprano lament by Alison Barlow, and the Fourth is given a reading that is every bit as compelling and electrifying as the composer's own recording. At mid-price this is a bargain not to be missed.

Additional recommendations ...

No. 3. Oboe Concerto in A minor[a]. **Yvonne Kenny** (sop); [a]**David Theodore** (ob); **London Symphony Orchestra/Bryden Thomson.** Chandos CHAN8594 — .•* 56m DDD 8/88

No. 4. Violin Concerto in D minor, "Concerto accademico"[a]. [a]**Kenneth Sillito** (vn); **London Symphony Orchestra/Bryden Thomson.** Chandos CHAN8633 — .•* 50m DDD 1/89 ⁹ₚ

Nos. 3 and 4. **Heather Harper** (sop); **London Symphony Orchestra/André Previn.** RCA Gold Seal GD90503 — .•* lh 13m ADD 3/91

No. 4[a]. **Holst.** *The Planets, H125*[b]. [a]**BBC Symphony Orchestra/Ralph Vaughan Williams;** [b]**London Symphony Orchestra/Gustav Holst.** Koch International Classics mono 37018-2 — .•* lh 9m ADD 4/91 ⁹ₚ ▲

Nos. 4 and 6. **New Philharmonia Orchestra/Sir Adrian Boult.** EMI CDM7 64019-2 — *..*
1h 9m ADD 5/92
Nos. 3[a] and 4. Fantasia on "Greensleeves". [a]**Linda Hohenfeld** (sop); **Philharmonia Orchestra/ Leonard Slatkin.** RCA Victor Red Seal 09026 61194-2 — *..* 1h 13m DDD 11/93 ♩ₚ ♩ₛ

New review
Vaughan Williams. Double Piano Concerto. Symphony No. 5 in D major. **Ralph Markham, Kenneth Broadway** (pfs); **Royal Philharmonic Orchestra/Sir Yehudi Menuhin.** Virgin Classics Virgo VJ5 61105-2. Recorded in 1987.

. 1h 9m DDD 1/94

The fine duo, Ralph Markham and Kenneth Broadway join Sir Yehudi Menuhin and the RPO for this performance of the Double Piano Concerto. This was arranged by the composer in 1946 from the (solo) Piano Concerto, the ending being altered to advantage. It remains a somewhat uneven work, but when presented so vigorously and persuasively, well worth exploring. Here is a case where a bargain price should tempt any Vaughan Williams *aficionado* to explore less well-known territory. More particularly so since Menuhin's strongly paced, yet passionately lyrical account of the glorious Fifth Symphony is quite different from the Vernon Handley version (reviewed below and still a front-runner in this work) and would grace any collection. The recording of both pieces is first-class.

Vaughan Williams. Symphony No. 5 in D major. Flos campi — Suite[a]. [a]**Christopher Balmer** (va); [a]**Liverpool Philharmonic Choir; Royal Liverpool Philharmonic Orchestra/Vernon Handley.** EMI Eminence CD-EMX9512. From EMX2112 (8/87). Recorded in 1986.

.. 1h 2m DDD 3/88

This disc is a bargain, both artistically and economically. The recording is full-toned and carefully balanced, preserving the luminous qualities of two of Vaughan Williams's most visionary and subtly devised scores; and the RLPO's playing under Vernon Handley is totally in sympathy with the music. The performance of *Flos campi* is outstandingly good. This work is deeply influenced by Ravel and has marvellous use of a wordless choir to intensify the erotic and sensuous longing of the music inspired by the *Song of Solomon*. The viola's impassioned and lyrical outpouring is beautifully played by Christopher Balmer, with excellent woodwind soloists in support, and the Liverpool Philharmonic Choir sings with secure intonation and flexible dynamic range. Handley's interpretation of the Fifth Symphony emphasizes the strength and passion in this music. His control of the architectural splendour of the first movement is masterly and he allows the ecstasy of the slow movement to unfold most naturally.

Vaughan Williams. Symphony No. 6 in E minor. Fantasia on a Theme by Thomas Tallis. The Lark Ascending[a]. [a]**Tasmin Little** (vn); **BBC Symphony Orchestra/Andrew Davis.** Teldec British Line 9031-73127-2. Recorded in 1990.

.. 1h 2m DDD 8/91

Andrew Davis has clearly thought long and hard before committing this enigmatic and tragic symphony to disc, and the result is one of the most spontaneous and electrifying accounts of the Sixth Symphony available. The urgency and vigour of the first and third movements is astonishing, leaving one with the impression that the work might have been recorded in one take. His treatment of the second subject's reprise in the closing pages of the first movement is more underplayed and remote than the beautifully sheened approach of some recordings, but is arguably more nostalgic for being so. The feverish, nightmare world of the *Scherzo* is a real *tour de force* in the hands of an inspired BBC Symphony Orchestra, and the desolate wasteland of the eerie final movement has rarely achieved such quiescence and nadir as here. Davis's searchingly intense *Tallis Fantasia* is finely poised with a beautifully spacious acoustic. The disc concludes on a quietly elevated note with Tasmin Little's serene and gently introspective reading of *The Lark Ascending*. The recording is excellent.

Additional recommendations ...
Fantasia on a Theme by Thomas Tallis[a]. *Fantasia on Greensleeves*[a]. **Elgar.** *Introduction and Allegro for*
String Quartet and Strings[a]. *Serenade in E minor*[a]. *Elegy for Strings*[b]. *Sospiri*[b]. [a]**Sinfonia of London;**

[b]**New Philharmonia Orchestra/Sir John Barbirolli.** EMI CDC7 47537-2 — ⠂•⠄ 58m ADD 2/87 ⁹ₚ ▲

Fantasia on a Theme by Thomas Tallis. Partita for Double String Orchestra. Oboe Concerto[a]. *English Folk-Song Suite (orch. Jacob). Fantasia on "Greensleeves" (arr. Greaves).* [a]**Jonathan Small** (ob); **Royal Liverpool Philharmonic Orchestra/Vernon Handley.** EMI Eminence CD-EMX2179 — ⠂•⠄ 1h 8m DDD 12/91

Vaughan Williams. Symphony No. 7, "Sinfonia antartica". **Sheila Armstrong** (sop); **London Philharmonic Choir and Orchestra/Bernard Haitink.** EMI CDC7 47516-2. From EL270318-1 (10/85). Recorded in 1984.

⠂•⠄ 42m DDD 1/87   ⁹ₚ ⁹ₛ

Scored for wordless soprano solo and chorus plus a large orchestra, this Seventh Symphony was based on the composer's music for the film *Scott of the Antarctic*. It comprises five movements; the Prelude, which conveys mankind's struggle in overcoming hostile natural forces; a *Scherzo*, which depicts the whales and penguins in their natural habitat; "Landscape", which portrays vast frozen wastes; Intermezzo, a reflection of the actions and thoughts of two members of the party; and "Epilogue", describing the final tragic assault on the South Pole. Bernard Haitink's conducting is highly imaginative, very concentrated and very committed and the LPO respond to him with some wonderfully atmospheric playing, full of personality and colour. Sheila Armstrong's eerie disembodied soprano voice and the remote chorus heighten the atmosphere, so that the score emerges as a powerful, coherent essay in symphonic form. Every detail has been captured by a magnificently sonorous and spacious recording.

Additional recommendations ...
No. 7[a]. *Toward the Unknown Region.* [a]**Catherine Bott** (sop); **London Symphony Chorus and Orchestra/Bryden Thomson.** Chandos CHAN8796 — ⠂•⠄ 55m DDD 4/90
No. 7[a]. *Serenade to Music.* [a]**Alison Hargan** (sop); **Royal Liverpool Choir and Orchestra/ Vernon Handley.** EMI Eminence CD-EMX2173 — ⠂•⠄ 57m DDD 9/91

Vaughan Williams. Symphony No. 9 in E minor. Piano Concerto in C major[a]. [a]**Howard Shelley** (pf); **London Symphony Orchestra/Bryden Thomson.** Chandos CHAN8941. Recorded in 1990.

⠂•⠄ 57m DDD 7/91

Alongside the scorching account of the apocalyptic Fourth Symphony, this clear-headed, perceptive traversal of the enigmatic Ninth has fair claims to be regarded as the best thing in Bryden Thomson's underrated VW cycle for Chandos. Thomson's urgent conception of the opening *Moderato maestoso* in particular has a sweep and momentum one might not have previously associated with this movement, yet the gain in terms of sheer concentration and symphonic stature is irrefutable. Granted, some may find the outer sections of the succeeding *Andante sostenuto* just a little too lacking in evocative magic, but there's no gainsaying the effectiveness of gallumphing woodwind in the oafish scherzo; certainly, the LSO's saxophone trio seem to be enjoying their day out hugely. In the finale, too, Thomson's approach is more boldly assertive than usual — not the way one would always want to hear this music, perhaps, but a thoroughly valid and convincing performance all the same. The coupling, Howard Shelley's distinguished remake of the same composer's craggily elusive Piano Concerto, is both imaginative and desirable. All in all, a highly recommendable disc: the LSO are in fine fettle throughout, whilst Chandos's glowing sonics come close to the ideal.

Additional recommendation ...
No. 8 in D minor. No. 9. *Flourish for Glorious John (Barbirolli).* **Philharmonia Orchestra/ Leonard Slatkin.** RCA Victor Red Seal 09026 61196-2 — ⠂•⠄ 1h 3m DDD 8/93

`New review`
Vaughan Williams. Dona nobis pacem[a]. Sancta civitas[b]. [a]**Yvonne Kenny** (sop); [b]**Philip Langridge** (ten); **Bryn Terfel** (bass-bar); [b]**St Paul's Cathedral Choir; London Symphony**

Chorus and Orchestra/Richard Hickox. EMI British Composers CDC7 54788-2. Texts included. Recorded in 1992.

lh 3m DDD 12/93

This is a generous and inspiring coupling of two of Vaughan Williams's most important choral utterances. Hickox coaxes magnificent sounds from the LSO throughout: in *Dona nobis pacem*, for example, the sense of orchestral spectacle during "Beat! Beat! drums!" is riveting in its physical impact. As ever, the contribution of the London Symphony Chorus combines full-throated discipline and sensitivity to nuance, and Hickox's trio of soloists are all excellent, with Bryn Terfel outstandingly eloquent. *Sancta civitas* is a work whose multi-layered scoring places great demands on both conductor and production team alike: suffice it to report, it is difficult to see Hickox's inspirational account of this still-underrated score (with its striking pre-echoes of *Job* and the Fourth Symphony) being surpassed for years to come. EMI's clean, wide-ranging sound sets the seal on a memorable pair of performances.

Additional recommendation ...
Dona nobis pacem[a]. *Five Mystical Songs.* [a]**Edith Wiens** (sop); **Brian Rayner Cook** (bar); **London Philharmonic Choir and Orchestra/Bryden Thomson**. Chandos CHAN8590 — 57m DDD 3/89

Vaughan Williams. VOCAL WORKS. [a]**Elizabeth Connell, [a]Linda Kitchen, [a]Anne Dawson, [a]Amanda Roocroft** (sops); [a]**Sarah Walker, [a]Jean Rigby, [a]Diana Montague** (mezs); [a]**Catherine Wyn-Rogers** (contr); [a]**John Mark Ainsley, [a]Martyn Hill, [a]Arthur Davies, [a]Maldwyn Davies** (tens); [acd]**Thomas Allen, [a]Alan Opie** (bars); [a]**Gwynne Howell, [a]John Connell** (basses); [b]**Nobuko Imai** (va); [bcd]**Corydon Singers; English Chamber Orchestra/Matthew Best.** Hyperion CDA66420. Texts included. Recorded 1990. Serenade to Music[a]. Flos campi[b]. Five mystical songs[c]. Fantasia on Christmas carols[d].

lh 8m DDD 8/90

In 1938 Sir Henry Wood celebrated his 50 years as a professional conductor with a concert. Vaughan Williams composed a work for the occasion, the *Serenade to Music*, in which he set words by Shakespeare from Act 5 of *The Merchant of Venice*. Sixteen star vocalists of the age were gathered together for the performance and Vaughan Williams customized the vocal parts to show off the best qualities of the singers. The work turned out to be one of the composer's most sybaritic creations, turning each of its subsequent performances into a special event. Hyperion have gathered stars of our own age for this outstanding issue and Matthew Best has perceptively managed to give each their head whilst melding them into a cohesive ensemble. A mellow, spacious recording has allowed the work to emerge on disc with a veracity never achieved before. The coupled vocal pieces are given to equal effect and the disc is substantially completed by Nobuko Imai's tautly poignant account of *Flos campi*, in which the disturbing tension between viola solo and wordless chorus heighten the work's crypticism. Altogether, an imaginative issue that is a must for any collection.

Additional recommendation ...
Flos Campi[a]. *Viola Suite*[b]. *Two Hymn-Tune Preludes*[c]. *The Poisoned Kiss — Overture*[c]. *The Running Set*[c]. [ab]**Frederick Riddle** (va); [a]**Bournemouth Sinfonietta Chorus; Bournemouth Sinfonietta/** [ab]**Norman Del Mar,** [c]**George Hurst.** Chandos Collect CHAN6545 — lh 6m ADD 11/92

New review
Vaughan Williams. On Wenlock Edge[a]. Songs of Travel[b].
Butterworth. Love blows as the wind blows[c].
Elgar. Pleading, Op. 48 No. 1[c]. Song Cycle, Op. 59[c]. Two Songs, Op. 60[c]. [ac]**Robert Tear** (ten); [b]**Thomas Allen** (bar); **City of Birmingham Symphony Orchestra/**[ab]**Simon Rattle,** [c]**Vernon Handley.** EMI British Composers CDM7 64731-2. Items marked [ab] from EL270059-2 (9/84), [c] HMV ASD3896 (9/80). Texts included. Recorded 1979-83.

lh 9m DDD/ADD 3/94

Neither of Vaughan Williams's song cycles was originally written with orchestral accompaniment. *On Wenlock Edge* was scored for accompaniment of piano and string quartet, while the

Songs of Travel were written with piano. Both lose a little when sung with orchestra but the gain seems to considerably outweigh any loss, especially when three such superb artists are involved. Tear's singing is notable for some wonderfully long phrases (as also is Allen's in the other cycle) together with the other Tear qualities, of clarity of words and such matters. The CBSO play especially well for Rattle, as they always do. All in all, superb performances that do real justice to Vaughan Williams's imagination, his care for words and his orchestration. The Tear/Handley Elgar and Butterworth items are rarities and were all première recordings. Throughout, Tear sings with his customary sensitivity and intelligent word-pointing. Equally, the CBSO under Handley tender irreproachably alert and imaginative support. EMI's warm-toned engineering is vivid and beautifully balanced. This is a most desirable reissue. Not to be missed.

Vaughan Williams. VOCAL WORKS. [a]**Sir John Gielgud** (narr); [a]**Lynne Dawson,** [d]**Linda Kitchen** (sops); [c]**Catherine Wyn-Rogers** (contr); [d]**John Mark Ainsley,** [b]**John Bowen,** [d]**Adrian Thompson** (tens); [d]**Alan Opie** (bar); [d]**Bryn Terfel** (bass-bar); [d]**Jonathan Best** (bass); [a]**John Scott,** [bce]**Roger Judd** (orgs); [a]**London Oratory Junior Choir; Corydon Singers; City of London Sinfonia/Matthew Best.** Hyperion CDA66569. Texts included. Recorded 1990-91.
A Song of Thanksgiving[a]. Three Choral Hymns[b]. Magnificat[c]. The Shepherds of the Delectable Mountains[d]. The Old Hundredth Psalm Tune[e].

⏺ **1h 13m DDD 8/92**

Welcome for many reasons, this is in the first place a timely filler-in of gaps. The *Magnificat* of 1930, for instance, is rarely heard, and so, more surprisingly perhaps, is *The Shepherds of the Delectable Mountains*. Both are works of great beauty, the *Magnificat* being set in a particularly imaginative way with solo flute and women's voices for the Angels of the Annunciation, while the three choral hymns from *Pilgrim's Progress,* relatively spare in texture and restrained in expression, reminds us of the composer's lifelong affection for Bunyan's allegory. There are various shorter pieces, including VW's splendid arrangement of the *Old Hundredth* psalm-tune as used in the 1953 Coronation. Then the other major work, *A Song of Thanksgiving* (or *Thanksgiving for Victory* as it was originally called in 1945), is a richly-scored work, rejoicing from a full heart and without taint of vainglory, national or otherwise. Sir John Gielgud as speaker confers further dignity and restraint, his voice no longer the sonorous instrument of earlier years but still beautiful in quality and usage. Distinguished among the other solo contributions are those of Bryn Terfel in *The Shepherds* and the flautist Duke Dobing in the *Magnificat*. The impressively massed forces of choir and orchestra are finely directed by Matthew Best, and the recorded sound has both clarity and spaciousness.

Additional recommendation ...
The Old Hundreth Psalm. Toward the Unknown Region. O taste and see. O clap your hands. Let us now praise famous men. Benedicite. **Walton.** *Orb and Sceptre. Set me as a seal upon thine heart. Jubilate Deo. A Litany. Coronation Te Deum.* **Soloists; Waynfelte Singers; Winchester Cathedral Choir; Bournemouth Symphony Orchestra/David Hill.** Argo 436 120-2ZH — ⏺ 1h 10m DDD 5/93 9ₚ 9ₛ

New review
Vaughan Williams. RIDERS TO THE SEA[a]. Merciless Beauty[b]. Epithalamion[c]. **Norma Burrowes** (sop) Nora; **Dame Margaret Price** (sop) Cathleen; **Helen Watts** (contr) Maurya; **Benjamin Luxon** (bar) Bartley; **Pauline Stevens** (mez) Woman; **Ambrosian Singers; Orchestra Nova of London/Meredith Davies.** [b]**Philip Langridge** (ten); [c]**Stephen Roberts** (bar); [c]**Jonathan Snowden** (fl); [c]**Howard Shelley** (pf); [b]members of the **Endellion Quartet** (Andrew Watkinson, James Clark, vns; David Waterman, vc); [c]**Bach Choir;** [c]**London Philharmonic Orchestra/Sir David Willcocks.** EMI British Composers CDM7 64730-2. Item marked [a] from HMV ASD2699 (9/71), recorded in 1970; [bc] CDC7 47769-2 (3/88), recorded in 1986. Texts included.

⏺ **1h 15m ADD/DDD 4/94**

Vaughan Williams completed his masterly setting of J.M.Synge's one-act drama, *Riders to the Sea*, in 1932. Although it has enjoyed the occasional revival, it remains one of the least-known and most under-appreciated of Vaughan Williams's major works. Indeed, with scoring that is both economical and intensely evocative, it can be a gripping experience, especially when presented as sympathetically as here. The cast is a uniformly strong one, and Meredith Davies inspires everyone to give of their very best. The 1970 sound has come up superbly, creating a rather more vivid impression, in fact, than its two digitally recorded partners here from 1986. These are also both considerable rarities. *Epithalamion* is a large-scale cantata from 1957 based on Edmund Spenser's love-poem of the same name: musically, it draws extensively on material used in Vaughan Williams's 1938 masque, *The Bridal Day*, and its emotional centrepiece, "The Lover's Song", boasts a viola solo of exquisite beauty. Finally, there is *Merciless Beauty*, three pithy Chaucer settings for tenor and string trio dating from 1921. Performances are once again all one could wish.

Further listening ...

Job — A masque for dancing. **David Nolan** (vn); **London Philharmonic Orchestra/ Vernon Handley.** Classics for Pleasure CD-CFP4603 (3/93).

Orazio Vecchi
Italian 1813-1901

New review
Vecchi. L'Amfiparnaso. Il convito musicale — o giardiniero; Lunghi danni; Bando del asino. **Clément Janequin Ensemble** (Jean-Louis Comoretto, alto; Bruno Boterf, Paul de los Cobos, tens; François Fauché, bar; Marc Busnel, bass; Eric Bellocq, lte; Matthieu Lusson, bass viol; Andrea Perugi, hpd/org)/**Dominique Visse** (alto). Harmonia Mundi HMC90 1461. Texts and translations included. Recorded in 1993.

59m DDD 12/93

Despite a career spent largely in the service of the church, Orazio Vecchi's main interest as a composer was in the lighter styles of madrigal writing. Designed as a sequence of narrative pieces loosely grouped around some familiar aspect of social life, his so-called madrigal comedies are interesting not as one of the forerunners of opera, but for their brilliance of characterization and variety of emotional expression achieved within a limited and compact style. As Lelio puts it in the Prologue to *L'Amfiparnaso*, this is a "spectacle that is understood by the mind into which it enters by the ears and not by the eyes", a piece of theatre which is played out in the imagination rather than on the stage. Dominique Visse and the Clément Janequin Ensemble have seized the essential spirit of this conception with enthusiasm and discrimination and, with deftness of touch and understanding of Vecchi's richly descriptive style, bring off these wryly amusing miniatures with bravura. Full of the sounds and colours of Italy, this is perfect entertainment for an English winter evening.

Giuseppe Verdi
Italian 1550-1605

Verdi. OVERTURES AND PRELUDES. **Berlin Philharmonic Orchestra/Herbert von Karajan.** DG 419 622-2GH. From 413 544-1GX2 (2/86). Recorded in 1975. NABUCCO. ERNANI. I MASNADIERI. MACBETH. IL CORSARO. LA BATTAGLIA DI LEGNANO. LUISA MILLER. RIGOLETTO. LA TRAVIATA. I VESPRI SICILIANI. UN BALLO IN MASCHERA. LA FORZA DEL DESTINO. AIDA.

1h 13m ADD 10/87

Karajan was one of the most adaptable and sensitive of dramatic conductors. His repertoire in the theatre is extraordinarily wide being at home equally in Verdi, Wagner, Richard Strauss and Puccini. In this selection from his celebrated 1976 collection of all of Verdi's overtures, he gives us some fine insights into the composer's skill as an orchestrator, dramatist and poet. Though Karajan had only recorded *Aida* complete his dramatic instincts bring some fine performances of the lesser known preludes. The earliest, *Nabucco* from 1842 (the collection is arranged chronologically), already shows a mastercraftsman at work, with a slow introduction promising much. *La Traviata* shows a quite different skill — the delcate creation of a sensitive poet working in filigree. The final four preludes are great works fully worthy of this individual presentation. Even the lesser known Preludes are enhanced by Karajan's dramatic instincts. Good recordings, though less than outstanding.

Verdi. Messa da Requiem[a]. OPERA CHORUSES. [a]**Susan Dunn** (sop); [a]**Diane Curry** (mez); [a]**Jerry Hadley** (ten); [a]**Paul Plishka** (bass); **Atlanta Symphony Chorus and Orchestra/ Robert Shaw.** Telarc CD80152. Texts and translations included.
DON CARLOS — Spuntato ecco il dì. MACBETH — Patria oppressa. OTELLO — Fuoco di gioia. NABUCCO — Va, pensiero, sull'ali dorate. AIDA — Gloria all'Egitto.

② 1h 53m DDD 3/88 — Ⓑ

Of all nineteenth-century choral works, Verdi's setting of the Requiem Mass is one of the most approachable. The choral writing is of the utmost splendour and conviction, and is a very personal statement of belief although written by an unbeliever. In many sections soloists and chorus are intermingled in a masterly fashion, and the writing for the orchestra is always appropriate to the text. Robert Shaw directs a performance that avoids histrionics and display and impresses by sheer musicianship. Tempos are well judged and rarely depart from the composer's markings. The team of soloists are well blended. The chorus are well drilled and full bodied and contribute lustily to the operatic choruses included as a bonus. The recording is very fine, spacious yet clear.

Additional recommendations ...
Messa da Requiem. Quattro pezzi sacri[a]. **Soloists; [a]Berlin RIAS Chamber Choir; St Hedwig's Cathedral Choir, Berlin; Berlin Radio Symphony Orchestra/Ferenc Fricsay.** DG Dokumente mono 429 076-2GDO2 — ② 2h 12m ADD 11/89 Ⓑ ▲
Messa da Requiem. Quattro pezzi sacri. **Soloists; Philharmonia Chorus and Orchestra/Carlo Maria Giulini.** EMI CDS7 47257-2 — ② 2h 9m ADD 4/87 Ⓑ
Messa da Requiem. Quattro pezzi sacri. **Soloists; Vienna State Opera Concert Chorus; Vienna Philharmonic Orchestra/Claudio Abbado.** DG 435 884-2GH — ② 2h 7m DDD 9/93 Ⓑ ⁹s
Messa da Requiem. **Soloists; Chicago Symphony Chorus and Orchestra/Sir Georg Solti.** RCA Victor Gold Seal 09026-61403-2 — ② 1h 22m ADD 9/93 ⁹p Ⓑ

New review
Verdi. OPERA CHORUSES. **Santa Cecilia Academy Chorus and Orchestra, Rome/ Carlo Rizzi.** Teldec 4509-90267-2. Texts and translations included.
NABUCCO — Gli arredi festivi; Va, pensiero, sull'ali dorata. MACBETH — Tre volte miagola; Patria oppressa! LA BATTAGLIA DI LEGNANO — Giuriam d'Italia. I LOMBARDI — Gerusalem!; O Signore, del tetto natio. IL TROVATORE — Vedi! le fosche. DON CARLO — Spuntato ecco il dì d'esultanza. OTELLO — Fuoco di gioia! AIDA — Gloria all' Egitto.

1h 1m DDD 8/93 — ⁹p Ⓑ

This is something special. The Choir of the Saint Cecilia Academy excels itself. The first test comes in "Va, pensiero" as the sopranos rise, invoking the "golden harp of prophetic bards" in thirds. Every voice is steady, every tone pure. Going with this is an unusual attention to detail, a well disciplined care for the rise and fall of the music. Then we have the chorus of virgins and Levites, firm and sensitive both. In *Macbeth* the *streghe* gain effect not by doing their celebrated impersonations of the Witch in *Snow White* but by pointing the words and sharpening the rhythm. Nor do they forego their Italian heritage: the voices are still rich, those of the basses especially so. Their chorus-master, Norbert Balatsch, has evidently done good work with them. Carlo Rizzi conducts with lively attentiveness and feeling for the swell of emotions in these marvellous pieces. And such a collection of excerpts does rekindle appreciation: for instance, of the desolate 'landscaping' of the refugees' scene in *Macbeth*, and the growth of inspiration among the pilgrims to Jerusalem in *I lombardi*. In short, a disc with a lot of pleasure in it.

Verdi. OPERA CHORUSES. **Chicago Symphony Chorus and Orchestra/Sir Georg Solti.** Decca 430 226-2DH. Texts and translations included. Recorded in 1989.
NABUCCO — Gli arredi festivi giù cadano infranti; Va, pensiero, sull'ali dorate. I LOMBARDI — Gerusalem!; O Signore, dal tetto natio. MACBETH — Tre volte miagola;

Patria oppressa. I MASNADIERI — Le rube, gli stupri. RIGOLETTO — Zitti zitti. IL TROVATORE — Vedi! le fosche notturne spoglie; Squilli, echeggi la tromba guerriera. LA TRAVIATA — Noi siamo zingarelle ... Di Madride nio siam mattadori (with Marsha Waxman, mez; David Huneryager, Richard Cohn, basses). UN BALLO IN MASCHERA — Posa in pace. DON CARLOS — Spuntato ecco il dí. AIDA — Gloria all'Egitto. OTELLO — Fuoco di gioia. REQUIEM — Sanctus.

lh 10m DDD 4/91

Verdi's choruses occupy a special place in his operas. They are invariably red-blooded and usually make a simple dramatic statement with great impact. The arresting "Chorus of the Hebrew Slaves" ("Va, pensiero") from *Nabucco* is probably the best-known and most popular chorus in the entire operatic repertoire, immediately tugging at the heart-strings with its gentle opening cantilena, soon swelling out to a great climax. Solti shows just how to shape the noble melodic line which soars with firm control, yet retaining the urgency and electricity in every bar. He is equally good in "Gli arredi festivi", from the same opera, not only in the bold opening statement, shared between singers and the resplendent sonority of the Chicago brass, but also later when the mood lightens, and women's voices are heard floating over seductive harp roulades. The dramatic contrasts at the opening of "Gerusalem!" from *I Lombardi* are equally powerfully projected, and the brass again makes a riveting effect in "Patria oppressa" from *Macbeth*. But, of course, not all Verdi choruses offer blood and thunder: the volatile "Fire chorus" from *Otello* flickers with an almost visual fantasy, while the wicked robbers in *I Masnadieri* celebrate their excesses (plunder, rape, arson and murder) gleefully, and with such rhythmic jauntiness that one cannot quite take them seriously. The "Gypsies chorus" from *La Traviata* has a nice touch of elegance, and the scherzo-like "Sanctus", from the *Requiem*, which ends the concert, is full of joy. But it is the impact of the dramatic moments which is most memorable, not least the big triumphal scene from *Aida*, complete with the ballet music, to provide a diverse interlude in the middle. The recording is in the demonstration class.

Additional recommendation ...
NABUCCO — *Gli arredi festivi già cadano infranti; Va, pensiero, sull'ali dorate.* MACBETH — *Patria oppressa.* IL TROVATORE — *Vedi! le fosche notturne spoglie; Ora co'dadi, ma fra poco.* LA TRAVIATA — *Noi siamo zingarelle; Si ridesta in ciel* (with Alena Cokova, mez; Stanislav Vrabel, bass). DON CARLOS — *Spuntato ecco il dì d'esultanza.* AIDA — *Gloria all'Egitto.* OTELLO — *Fuoco di gioia.* LA BATTAGLIA DI LEGNANO — *Deus meus, pone illos ut rotam* (Eva Jenisova, sop; Cokova); *Giuramento* (L'udovit Ludha, ten). ERNANI — *Si ridesti il Leon di Castiglia.* LA FORZA DEL DESTINO — *Rataplan! rataplan!* (Ida Kirilová, mez). **Slovak Philharmonic Choir; Slovak Radio Symphony Orchestra/Oliver Dohnányi.** Naxos 8 550241 — . 56m DDD 4/91

Verdi. STIFFELIO. **José Carreras** (ten) Stiffelio; **Sylvia Sass** (sop) Lina; **Matteo Manuguerra** (bar) Stankar; **Wladimiro Ganzarolli** (bass) Jorg; **Ezio di Cesare** (ten) Raffaele; **Maria Venuti** (mez) Dorotea; **Thomas Moser** (ten) Federico; **Austrian Radio Chorus and Symphony Orchestra/Lamberto Gardelli.** Philips 422 432-2PM2. Notes, text and translation included. From 6769 039 (10/80). Recorded in 1979.

② lh 49m ADD 3/90

This work is gradually gaining the reputation it deserves as companies and audiences realize its quality (it gains its first performance at Covent Garden in the 1992-3 season). It tells of Stiffelio, a Protestant clergyman, in a Catholic country, whose wife Linda has committed adultery and finds it in his heart, after her father has killed her lover, to forgive her. The work has elements that pre-echo *Otello* and is yet another example of Verdi finding the specific music for a specific predicament. This performance, firmly conducted by Gardelli, has an involved, involving assumption of the title-role by Carreras. This role is a gift for an accomplished tenor and he catches the moral fervour and uncertainties of the part with his open-hearted, spontaneous performance. Sylvia Sass also offers a rewarding, strongly emotional performance as Lina.

Verdi. MACBETH. **Piero Cappuccilli** (bar) Macbeth; **Shirley Verrett** (mez) Lady Macbeth;
| **Nicolai Ghiaurov** (bass) Banquo; **Plácido Domingo** (ten) Macduff; **Antonio Savastano**

(ten) Malcolm; **Carlo Zardo** (bass) Doctor; **Giovanni Foiani** (bass) Servant; **Sergio Fontana** (bass) Herald; **Alfredo Mariotti** (bass) Assassin; **Stefania Malagú** (mez) Lady-in-waiting; **Chorus and Orchestra of La Scala, Milan/Claudio Abbado.** DG 415 688-2GH3. Notes, text and translation included. From 2709 062 (10/76). Recorded in 1976.

③ 2h 34m ADD 9/86

Verdi's lifelong admiration for Shakespeare resulted in only two operas based on his plays. *Macbeth*, the first, originally written in 1847, was extensively revised in 1865. Without losing the direct force of the original, Verdi added greater depth to his first ideas. Once derided as being un-Shakespearian, it is now recognized as a masterpiece for its psychological penetration as much as for its subtle melodic inspiration. Abbado captures perfectly the atmosphere of dark deeds and personal ambition leading to tragedy, projected by Verdi, and his reading holds the opera's disparate elements in the score under firm control, catching its interior tensions. He is well supported by his Scala forces. Shirley Verrett may not be ideally incisive or Italianate in accent as Lady Macbeth, but she peers into the character's soul most convincingly. As ever, truly inspired by Abbado, Cappuccilli is a suitably haunted and introverted Macbeth who sings a secure and unwavering legato. Domingo's upright Macduff and Ghiaurov's doom-laden Banquo are both admirable in their respective roles.

Additional recommendations ...
Soloists; Berlin Deutsche Opera Chorus and Orchestra/Giuseppe Sinopoli. Philips 412 133-2PH3 — ③ 2h 15m DDD 2/85
Soloists; Metropolitan Opera Chorus and Orchestra/Erich Leinsdorf. RCA Victor GD84516 — ② 2h 10m ADD 9/88
Soloists; Chorus and Orchestra of the Santa Cecilia Academy, Rome/Thomas Schippers. Decca Grand Opera 433 039-2DM2 — ② 2h 1m ADD 5/92
Soloists; Ambrosian Opera Chorus; New Philharmonia Orchestra/Riccardo Muti. EMI CMS7 64339-2 — ② ADD 2/93

Verdi. LUISA MILLER. **Montserrat Caballé** (sop) Luisa; **Luciano Pavarotti** (ten) Rodolfo; **Sherrill Milnes** (bar) Miller; **Bonaldo Gaiotti** (bass) Count Walter; **Anna Reynolds** (mez) Federica; **Richard Van Allan** (bass) Wurm; **Annette Céline** (mez) Laura; **Fernando Pavarotti** (ten) Peasant; **London Opera Chorus; National Philharmonic Orchestra/ Peter Maag.** Decca 417 420-2DH2. Notes, text and translation included. From SET606/08 (5/76).

② 2h 24m ADD 10/88

This transitional work shows Verdi enhancing his skills and refining his musical style. The plot, based on a Schiller drama, involves the tragedy and death of Luisa and her beloved Rodolfo brought about by the evil Wurm, apt predecessor of Verdi's Iago. The title-role could not find a more appealing interpreter than Caballé, who spins a fine line and is highly responsive to Luisa's sad situation. She is partnered by Pavarotti at the height of his powers as Rodolfo. He excels in "Quando le sere al polacido", the work's most famous aria. As Luisa's equivocal father, Miller, Milnes gives one of his best performances on disc and Van Allan is a properly snarling Wurm. Maag, an underrated conductor, directs a strong, well-proportioned performance. He gives the impression of being in love with this opera and he goes right to the heart of the score, finding its seriousness as well as its fire. The last act is specially fine, containing what are regarded as among the gramophone classics, the two duets of Luisa, first with her father, then with Rodolfo. The production is unobtrusively effective in creation of atmosphere and is spaciously recorded.

Additional recommendation ...
Soloists; Chorus and Orchestra of the Royal Opera House, Covent Garden/Lorin Maazel. DG 423 144-2GH2 — ② 2h 13m ADD 5/88

Verdi. RIGOLETTO. **Tito Gobbi** (bar) Rigoletto; **Giuseppe di Stefano** (ten) Duke; **Maria Callas** (sop) Gilda; **Nicola Zaccaria** (bass) Sparafucile; **Adriana Lazzarini** (mez) Maddalena; **Giuse Gerbino** (mez) Giovanna; **Plinio Clabassi** (bass) Monterone; **William Dickie** (bar) Marullo; **Renato Ercolani** (ten) Borsa; **Carlo Forti** (bar) Count Ceprano; **Elvira Galassi**

(sop) Countess Ceprano; **Chorus and Orchestra of La Scala, Milan/Tullio Serafin.** EMI mono CDS7 47469-8. Notes, text and translation included. From Columbia 33CXS1324, 33CX1325/6 (2/56). Recorded in 1955.

② 1h 58m ADD 2/87

The story of the hunchbacked jester Rigoletto at the court of a licentious Duke who seduces the Fool's daughter Gilda by masquerading as a poor student, and the consequent attempts at revenge on the part of Rigoletto, produced from Verdi one of the most telling of his mid-period triumphs. His identification with each of the characters and the sheer energy and sensuous ardour of the score is quite remarkable. Nowhere else on record have these characterizations been delineated with such intelligence and commitment as by Gobbi, Callas and di Stefano on this 40-year-old set. Serafin presides over everything with an unerring grasp of Verdian timing.

Additional recommendations ...

Soloists; Chorus and Orchestra of La Scala, Milan/Rafael Kubelík. DG 435 050-2GH2 — ② 2h 3m ADD ⁹ₚ Ⓑ

Soloists; Vienna State Opera Chorus; Vienna Philharmonic Orchestra/Carlo Maria Giulini. DG 415 288-2GH2 — ② DDD 11/85 Ⓑ

Soloists; RCA Italiana Opera Chorus and Orchestra/Sir Georg Solti. RCA Victor GD86506 — ② 1h 53m ADD 9/88 Ⓑ

Soloists; Chorus and Orchestra of La Scala, Milan/Riccardo Muti. EMI CDS7 49605-2 — ② 1h 56m DDD 11/89 Ⓑ

Soloists; Chorus and Orchestra of the Teatro Communale, Bologna/Riccardo Chailly. Decca 425 864-1DH2 — ② 1h 47m DDD 1/90 ⁹ₚ Ⓑ

Soloists; Slovak Philharmonic Chorus; Czecho-Slovak Radio Symphony Orchestra/ Alexander Rahbari. Naxos 8 660013/4 — ② 1h 55m DDD 3/92 Ⓑ

New review

Verdi. LA TRAVIATA. **Tiziana Fabriccini** (sop) Violetta; **Roberto Alagna** (ten) Alfredo; **Paolo Coni** (bar) Germont; **Nicoletta Curiel** (mez) Flora; **Antonella Trevisan** (mez) Annina; **Enrico Cossutta** (ten) Gastone; **Orazio Mori** (bass) Baron; **Enzo Capuano** (bass) Marquis; **Francesco Musinu** (bass) Doctor; **Ernesto Gavazzi** (ten) Giuseppe; **Ernesto Panariello** (bass) Servant; **Silvestro Sammaritano** (bass) Messenger; **Chorus and Orchestra of La Scala, Milan/Riccardo Muti.** Sony Classical S2K52486. Notes, text and translation included. Recorded live in 1992.

② 2h 16m DDD 10/93 ⁹ₚ

An exciting and eloquent reading on all sides, this version must now be rated with the established frontrunners – but, as with some of those, most notably any of Callas's versions, it is not for the fainthearted, or for those who like their Violettas to have full, equally, produced voices. Fabriccini is evidently not an Act 1 Violetta. But even without assured coloratura and with problems at the *passagio*, she is one who is going to hold our attention and move us. In the Second Act so much bespeaks not only complete identification with Violetta's predicament but also vocal acumen of an exceptional kind, often based on the seemingly lost art of portamento. Because this is a live performance we are conscious that the singer's acting is part of the secret of the reading's success, that and the obvious youth of a soprano who is not yet a preening prima donna. The final tragedy is still better, very much modelled on Callas. The voice, more settled now than anywhere in the performance manages her role with long-breathed phrasing and pathetic accents, the result of a true understanding of Verdian style yet never self-conscious in its effect – this is undoubtedly great singing *and* interpretation. The death is deeply moving. Alagna, in the role that brought him to attention, is just the Alfredo for this Violetta; youthfully ardent, with keen-edged tone, finely attuned to the legato essential in Verdi. The recording is taken from four performances, given at La Scala, and is a theatrical view full of electricity, vitally executed by the forces of La Scala, as vital as any in the recorded history of the work. Don't miss it.

Additional recommendations ...

Soloists; Rome Opera Chorus and Orchestra/Fernando Previtali. RCA Gold Seal GD84144 — ② 1h 53m ADD ⁹ₚ Ⓑ

Soloists; **Bavarian State Opera Chorus and Orchestra/Carlos Kleiber.** DG 415 132-2GH2 — .·' ② 3/86 ℗ Ⓑ

Soloists; **Ambrosian Opera Chorus; Band of HM Royal Marines; Philharmonia Orchestra/Riccardo Muti.** EMI CDS7 47538-8 — .·' ② 2h 9m DDD 11/87 ℗ Ⓑ

Soloists; **Chorus and Orchestra of the Teatro Nacional de San Carlos, Lisbon/Franco Ghione.** EMI mono CDS7 49187-8 — .·' ② 2h 3m ADD 11/87 ℗ Ⓑ ▲

Soloists; **Chorus and Orchestra of La Scala, Milan/Carlo Maria Giulini.** EMI mono CMS7 63628-2 — .·' 2h 4m ADD 2/91 Ⓑ ▲

Soloists; **Metropolitan Opera Chorus and Orchestra/James Levine.** DG 435 797-2GH2 — .·' ② 2h 2m DDD 11/92 Ⓑ

New review

Verdi. IL TROVATORE. **Plácido Domingo** (ten) Manrico; **Aprile Millo** (sop) Leonora; **Vladimir Chernov** (bar) Conte di Luna; **Dolora Zajick** (mez) Azucena; **James Morris** (bass) Ferrando; **Sondra Kelly** (contr) Ines; **Anthony Laciura** (ten) Ruiz; **Glenn Bater** (bass) Old Gipsy; **Tim Willson** (ten) Messenger; **New York Metropolitan Opera Chorus and Orchestra/James Levine.** Sony Classical S2K48070. Notes, text and translation included. Recorded in 1991.

.·' ② 2h 9m DDD 6/94 ℗ Ⓑ

This is the most recommendable among modern versions of *Trovatore*, with a reading all-round that finely balances the lyrical and melodramatic elements in the score. Once Leonora appears, the reading takes on true Verdian style. Millo floats "Come d'aurato" effortlessly on a fine line and throughout her part is replete with the right kind of Verdian *spinto* sound, the correct phraseology. This is a reading to please the ear and move the heart. Immediately this Leonora is confronted with Conte di Luna, we hear the firm, vibrant, implacable tones of Chernov. His voice is surely now in its absolute prime and he sings everything with the confident panache that suggests as much. Our upright hero is Domingo, aged a little since his earlier recordings of Manrico for Mehta and Giulini (listed below). The artistry and management of the voice are as rewarding as of old and Domingo reserves his best for the last and greatest scene when both his sovereign phrasing — "Riposa, o madre" sung in a single breath — and his involvement take on the aura of active participation. Manrico's feelings of love for his mother, momentary contempt for Leonora and eventual tragic pathos are firmly targeted: we hear once more the noble tenor we know and can listen to in sappier voice for Giulini. As Azucena, Zajick gives an effective and strong-willed performance, wanting only the last ounce of character: she is also at her best in the final act. The Met chorus is no more than adequate on this occasion, but as ever the house's orchestra play with the virtuosity it reserves for its Musical Director. Levine's reading is well timed, properly earthy yet refined in the many delicate touches Verdi evinces in arias and duets. His is a more dramatically vital reading than Giulini's which is at times unconscionably slow (his version runs to three discs), and rivals Karajan's in projecting incisively the drama's essence.

Additional recommendations …
Soloists; **Saint Cecilia Academy Chorus and Orchestra/Carlo Maria Giulini.** DG 423 858-2GH2 — ② 2h 20m 2/85 ℗ Ⓑ

Soloists; **Chorus and Orchestra of La Scala, Milan/Herbert von Karajan.** EMI mono CDS7 49347-2 — .·' ② 2h 9m ADD 12/87 ℗ Ⓑ ▲

Soloists; **Ambrosian Opera Chorus; New Philharmonia Orchestra/Zubin Mehta.** RCA Red Seal RD86194 — .·' ② 2h 17m ADD 8/88 ℗ Ⓑ

Soloists; **Robert Shaw Chorale; RCA Victor Orchestra/Renato Cellini.** RCA Victor mono GD86643 — .·' ② 1h 57m ADD 8/88 ℗ Ⓑ ▲

IL TROVATORE[a]. LA FORZA DEL DESTINO[b] — *excerpts.* [ab]**Soloists;** [a]**Chorus of the Royal Opera House, Covent Garden;** [a]**London Philharmonic Orchestra/Vittorio Gui.** [b]**Chorus and Orchestra of RAI, Rome/Oliviero de Fabritiis.** Legato Classics mono LCD-173 — .·' ② 2h 38m ADD 2/94 ℗ Ⓑ ▲

Verdi. UN BALLO IN MASCHERA. **Giuseppi di Stefano** (ten) Riccardo; **Tito Gobbi** (bar) Renato; **Maria Callas** (sop) Amelia; **Fedora Barbieri** (mez) Ulrica; **Eugenia Ratti** (sop) Oscar; **Ezio Giordano** (bass) Silvano; **Silvio Maionica** (bass) Samuel; **Nicola Zaccaria** (bass) Tom; **Renato Ercolani** (bar) Judge; **Chorus and Orchestra of La Scala, Milan/**

Antonino Votto. EMI mono CDS7 47498-8. Notes, text and translation included. From Columbia 33CX1472/4 (10/57).

♪ ② 2h 10m ADD 9/87 ♪P ▲

Ballo manages to encompass a vein of lighthearted frivolity (represented by the page, Oscar) within the confines of a serious drama of love, infidelity, noble and ignoble sentiments. None of the more recent recordings has quite caught the opera's true spirit so truly as this one under Votto's unerring direction. Callas has not been surpassed in delineating Amelia's conflict of feelings and loyalties, nor has di Stefano been equalled in the sheer ardour of his singing as Riccardo. Add to that no less a singer than Tito Gobbi as Renato, at first eloquent in his friendship to his ruler, then implacable in his revenge when he thinks Riccardo has stolen his wife. Fedora Barbieri is full of character as the soothsayer Ulrica, Eugenia Ratti a sparky Oscar. It is an unbeatable line-up.

Additional recommendations ...
Soloists; Chorus and Orchestra of La Scala, Milan/Claudio Abbado. DG 415 685-2GH2 — ♪ ② DDD 9/86
Soloists; Haberdashers' Aske's School Girls' Choir; Medici Quartet; Royal Opera House Chorus, Covent Garden; New Philharmonia Orchestra/Riccardo Muti. EMI CMS7 69576-2 — ♪ ② 2h 7m ADD 11/88
Soloists; RCA Italiana Opera Chorus and Orchestra/Erich Leinsdorf. RCA Gold Seal GD86645 — ♪ ② 2h 8m ADD 11/88 ♪P
Soloists; Robert Shaw Chorale; NBC Symphony Orchestra/Arturo Toscanini. RCA Victor Gold Seal mono GD60301 — ♪ ② 2h 2m ADD 7/91 ▲
Soloists; Metropolitan Opera Chorus and Orchestra/Ettore Panizza. Myto mono 2MCD90317 — ♪ ② 2h 27m ADD 2/94 ▲

Verdi. LA FORZA DEL DESTINO. **Martina Arroyo** (sop) Leonora; **Carlo Bergonzi** (ten) Don Alvaro; **Piero Cappuccilli** (bar) Don Carlos; **Ruggero Raimondo** (bass) Padre Guardiano; **Biancamaria Casoni** (mez) Preziosilla; **Sir Geraint Evans** (bar) Melitone; **Antonio Zerbini** (bass) Marchese; **Florindo Andreolli** (ten) Trabuco; **Mila Cova** (mez) Curra; **Virgilio Carbonari** (ten) Mayor; **Derek Hammond-Stroud** (bar) Surgeon; **Ambrosian Opera Chorus; Royal Philharmonic Orchestra/Lamberto Gardelli.** EMI Opera CMS7 64646-2. Notes, text and translation included. From HMV SLS948 (3/70). Recorded in 1969.

♪ ③ 2h 48m ADD 6/93 ♪P

This wonderfully multifarious opera demands an array of principal singers who need to be skilled in an unusually wide range of vocal and dramatic skills. It is a 'chase' opera in which Carlos pursues Alvaro and Leonora through two countries, through cloister and convent, through scenes popular and martial, all treated on the most expansive scale. It is dominated by its series of magnificent duets that are composed so that the music marches with the development of situation and character. This reissue is an excellent and completely satisfying mid-price buy. It features Bergonzi, that prince among Verdi tenors, as an exemplary and appealing Alvaro, the best in any complete set, and Piero Cappuccilli — like Bergonzi at the peak of his powers when this set was made — as a full-blooded and Italianate Carlos. In the three all-important duets, their voices blend ideally. Leonora was the most successful of Arroyo's recorded roles, and she sings here with a feeling and urgency appropriate to Leonora's desperate situation. Casoni's vital Preziosilla, Raimondi's grave but over-lugubrious Padre Guardiano and Sir Geraint's keenly characterized Melitone complete a well-chosen cast. Over all presides Gardelli, a Verdi conductor with an instinctive feeling for the ebb and flow of his music, always attending to the needs of the music, never calling attention to himself. All of the versions listed here have much to commend them. The Levine is more opulently but not so stylishily sung and perhaps a little too hectically conducted. The *Gramophone* Award-winning Sinopoli is the stuff of which great music drama is made, especially in the opera's closing pages. It is wonderfully enacted by Paata Burchuladze (Padre Guardiano), Rosalind Plowright (Leonora) and José Carreras (Alvaro), with subtle changes of pace and perspective from Sinopoli and glorious string playing. The Serafin boasts the irreplaceable Callas and conducting on the Gardelli level but has some indifferent singing, significant excisions and a mono recording.

Additional recommendations ...
Soloists; Ambrosian Opera Chorus; Philharmonia Orchestra/Giuseppe Sinopoli. DG
419 203-2GH3 — .·˙ ③ 2h 58m DDD 5/87 ۹ₚ
Soloists; Chorus and Orchestra of La Scala, Milan/Riccardo Muti. EMI CDS7 47485-8
— .·˙ ③ 2h 44m 5/87 ۹ₚ
Soloists; Chorus and Orchestra of La Scala, Milan/Tullio Serafin. EMI mono CDS7
47581-8 — .·˙ ③ 2h 44m ADD 10/87 ۹ₚ ▲
Soloists; John Alldis Choir; London Symphony Orchestra/James Levine. RCA
RD81864 — .·˙ ③ 2h 5lm ADD 10/87

Verdi. DON CARLO. **Plácido Domingo** (ten) Don Carlos; **Montserrat Caballé** (sop)
Elisabetta; **Shirley Verrett** (mez) Princess Eboli; **Sherrill Milnes** (bar) Rodrigo; **Ruggero
Raimondi** (bass) Philip II; **Giovanni Foiani** (bass) Grand Inquisitor; **Delia Wallis** (mez)
Thibault; **Ryland Davies** (ten) Count of Lerma; **Simon Estes** (bass) A Monk; **John Noble**
(bar) Herald; **Ambrosian Opera Chorus; Royal Opera House Orchestra, Covent
Garden/Carlo Maria Giulini.** EMI CDS7 47701-8. Notes, text and translation included.
From SLS956 (7/71).

.·˙ ③ 3h 28m ADD 7/87

In no other Verdi opera, except perhaps *Aida*, are public and private matters so closely
intermingled, so searchingly described as in this large-scale, panoramic work, in which the
political intrigues and troubles of Philip II's Spain are counterpointed with his personal agony
and the lives and loves of those at his court. This vast canvas inspired Verdi to one of his most
varied and glorious scores. Giulini, more than any other conductor, searches out the inner soul
of the piece and his cast is admirable. The young Plácido Domingo makes a vivid and exciting
Carlos, whilst Montserrat Caballé spins glorious tone and phrases in encompassing Elisabeth's
difficult music. Shirley Verrett is a vital, suitably tense Eboli, Sherrill Milnes an upright, warm
Rodrigo and Ruggero Raimondi a sombre Philip. Throughout, the Covent Garden forces sing
and play with fervour and understanding for their distinguished conductor.

Additional recommendation ...
(Includes appendix). **Soloists; Chorus and Orchestra of La Scala, Milan/Claudio Abbado.**
DG 415 316-2GH4 — .·˙ ④ DDD 12/85

Verdi. AIDA. **Maria Callas** (sop) Aida; **Richard Tucker** (ten) Radames; **Fedora Barbieri**
(mez) Amneris; **Tito Gobbi** (bar) Amonasro; **Giuseppe Modesti** (bass) Ramfis; **Nicola
Zaccaria** (bass) King of Egypt; **Elvira Galassi** (sop) Priestess; **Franco Ricciardi** (ten)
Messenger; **Chorus and Orchestra of La Scala, Milan/Tullio Serafin.** EMI mono CDS7
49030-8. Notes, text and translation included. From Columbia 33CX1318/20 (1/56). Recorded
in 1955.

.·˙ ③ 2h 24m AAD ll/87 ۹ₚ Ⓑ ▲

Aida, the daughter of the Ethiopian king, is a prisoner at the Egyptian court where she falls in
love with Radames, an Egyptian captain of the guard; Amneris, the Egyptian princess, also loves
him. The tensions between these characters are rivetingly portrayed and explored and the
gradual build-up to Aida's and Radames's union in death is paced with the sureness of a master
composer. Callas's Aida is an assumption of total understanding and conviction; the growth from
a slave-girl torn between love for her homeland and Radames, to a woman whose feelings
transcend life itself represents one of the greatest operatic undertakings ever committed to disc.
Alongside her is Fedora Barbieri, an Amneris palpable in her agonized mixture of love and
jealousy — proud yet human. Tucker's Radames is powerful and Gobbi's Amonasro quite
superb — a portrayal of comparable understanding to stand alongside Callas's Aida. Tullio
Serafin is quite simply ideal and though the recording may not be perfect by current standards,
nowhere can it dim the brilliance of the creations conjured up by this classic cast.

Additional recommendations ...
**Soloists; Chorus of the Royal Opera House, Covent Garden; Trumpeters of the
Royal Military School of Music, Kneller Hall; New Philharmonia Orchestra/
Riccardo Muti.** EMI CDS7 47271-8 — .·˙ ③ 2h 28m 1/87 Ⓑ

Soloists; Rome Opera House Chorus and Orchestra/Sir Georg Solti. Decca 417 416-
2DH3 — ⋰ ③ 2h 32m ADD 9/87 Ⓑ
Soloists; Rome Opera House Chorus and Orchestra/Jonel Perlea. RCA Victor mono
GD86652 — ⋰ ③ 2h 29m ADD 8/88 �ᵠₚ Ⓑ ▲

Verdi. OTELLO. **Jon Vickers** (ten) Otello; **Leonie Rysanek** (sop) Desdemona; **Tito
Gobbi** (bar) Iago; **Florindo Andreolli** (ten) Cassio; **Mario Carlin** (ten) Roderigo; **Miriam
Pirazzini** (mez) Emilia; **Ferrucio Mazzoli** (bass) Lodovico; **Franco Calabrese** (bass)
Montano; **Robert Kerns** (bar) Herald; **Rome Opera Chorus and Orchestra/Tullio
Serafin.** RCA Victor GD81969. Text and translation included. From LDS6155 (1/61).
Recorded in 1960.

⋰ ② 2h 24m ADD 11/88 Ⓑ ▲

The role of Otello is notoriously demanding and there are few voices that one would say were
'made for it'. Jon Vickers's is certainly one of them. Simply as singing his is a magnificent
performance: the voice is at its most beautiful and the breadth of his tone in the upper notes is
astonishing. Stylistically, too, he is quite remarkably scrupulous, allowing himself no effect that is
not authorized in the score, and always exact in his observations of *piano* markings. Giving this
recording a unique distinction is Tito Gobbi as Iago, justly the most famous singer of the role in
post-war years and the Desdemona too is clearly a great artist. Serafin conducts in a way that
allows everything to be clearly heard, forfeiting some excitement but never cheapening by
exaggeration or sentimentality. He secures clean, spirited playing from the Rome orchestra and
keeps a control that is firm without being inflexible. This is a well-produced set that has scarcely
aged over the years.

Additional recommendations ...
Soloists; Chorus and Orchestra of La Scala, Milan/Lorin Maazel. EMI CDS7 47450-8
— ⋰ ② 2h 22m DDD 1/86 ᵠₚ Ⓑ
Soloists; Metropolitan Opera Chorus and Orchestra/Ettore Panizza. Music and Arts
mono CD645 — ⋰ ② 2h 19m AAD 9/91 ᵠₚ Ⓑ ▲
**Soloists; Metropolitan Opera Children's Chorus; Chicago Symphony Chorus and
Orchestra/Sir Georg Solti.** Decca 433 669-2DH2 — ⋰ ② 2h 9m DDD 11/91 ᵠₚ Ⓑ
Soloists; NBC Chorus and Symphony Orchestra/Arturo Toscanini. RCA Victor Gold
Seal mono GD60302 — ⋰ ② 2h 5m ADD 3/92 ᵠₚ Ⓑ ▲

Verdi. FALSTAFF. **Tito Gobbi** (bar) Falstaff; **Rolando Panerai** (bar) Ford; **Luigi Alva**
(ten) Fenton; **Elisabeth Schwarzkopf** (sop) Alice; **Anna Moffo** (sop) Nannetta; **Fedora
Barbieri** (mez) Quickly; **Renato Ercolani** (ten) Bardolfo; **Nicola Zaccaria** (bass) Pistola;
Tomaso Spatoro (ten) Dr Caius; **Nan Merriman** (mez) Meg Page; **Philharmonia Chorus
and Orchestra/Herbert von Karajan.** EMI CDS7 49668-2. Notes, text and translation
included. From SAX2254/6 (7/61). Recorded in 1956.

⋰ ② 2h ADD 9/88  ᵠₚ Ⓑ ▲

Verdi's *Falstaff* is one of those works that sum up a career with perfection, yet though it was his
last opera it was also his first comic opera. This classic EMI recording enshrines one of the finest
Falstaffs to have graced the stage in post-war years, Tito Gobbi. His assumption of the role is
magnificent, and the completeness with which he embraces the part tends to overshadow his
many successors. Assembled around this larger-than-life character is a near ideal cast, sprightly of
gait, sparklingly comic and above all, beautifully sung. Karajan's conducting is always deeply
cherishable as he leads the Philharmonia Orchestra surefootedly through the score and the
recording has come up sounding as fresh as the day it was set down.

Additional recommendations ...
**Soloists; Los Angeles Master Chorale and Philharmonic Orchestra/Carlo Maria
Giulini.** DG 410 503-2GH2 — ⋰ ② 2h 3m ADD 12/83 Ⓑ
*FALSTAFF. AIDA. Quattro pezzi sacri — Te Deum. Requiem. NABUCCO — Va, pensiero. LUISA
MILLER — Quando le sere al placido. Inno delle Nazioni.* **Soloists; Robert Shaw Chorale; NBC
Symphony Orchestra/Arturo Toscanini.** RCA Gold Seal mono GD60326 — ⋰ ⑦ 6h 13m

Further listening ...

I DUE FOSCARI. **Soloists; Austrian Radio Chorus and Symphony Orchestra/ Lamberto Gardelli.** Philips 422 426-2PM2 (12/89).

ATTILA. **Soloists; Chorus and Orchestra of La Scala, Milan/Riccardo Muti.** EMI CDS7 49952-2 (5/90).

I VESPRI SICILIANI. **Soloists; Chorus and Orchestra of La Scala, Milan/Riccardo Muti.** EMI CDS7 54043-2 (1/91).

SIMON BOCCANEGRA. **Soloists; RCA Chorus and Orchestra/Gianandrea Gavazzeni.** RCA Red Seal RD70729 (9/87).

Key to symbols

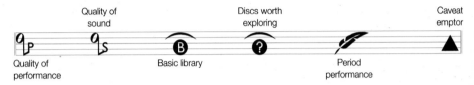

| Quality of sound | Discs worth exploring | Caveat emptor |

Quality of performance   Basic library   Period performance

Tomas Luis de Victoria

Spanish 1548-1611

Victoria (ed. Turner). Responsories for Tenebrae. **Westminster Cathedral Choir/David Hill.** Hyperion CDA66304. Texts and translations included.

lh l5m DDD 7/89

Westminster Cathedral is probably one of the few places where compositions of such noble inspiration may still be heard during the last three days of Holy Week. Such a living link with tradition goes to explain the inner understanding, the tremendous pathos of a superbly tragic and musically satisfying performance. The carefully chosen texts tell of the betrayal and arrest of Jesus, his passion and burial. The music expresses with anguish the suffering and sorrow of those days. Certain passages in the recording are particularly memorable: a gentle treble lead at the opening of "Una hora", the dramatic juxtaposition of the evil vigil of Judas and the naïvety of the disciples' sleep. Variations of tempo, especially that for the plotting of Jeremiah's enemies and the exact dovetailing, as in "Seniores", combine to heighten the dramatic effect. These pieces, of tragic magnificence, are performed with intensity and integrity, so that a great recording will now ensure that an incomparable treasure of Christian music will be safely preserved for future generations.

Additional recommendation ...
Responsories for Tenebrae. **The Sixteen/Harry Christophers.** Virgin Classics Veritas VC7 59042-2 — **lh l0m DDD 7/92**

Further listening ...

Missa O magnum mysterium. Missa Ascendens Christus in altum. *Motets* — O magnum mysterium. Ascendens Christus. **Westminster Cathedral Choir/David Hill.** Hyperion CDA66190 (9/87).

Officium defunctorum. **Westminster Cathedral Choir/David Hill.** Hyperion CDA66250 (9/87).

Missa O quam gloriosum. Motet — O quam gloriosum. Missa Ave maris stella. **Westminster Cathedral Choir/David Hill.** Hyperion CDA66114 (6/86).

Officium defunctorum. *Coupled with* **Lôbo.** Versa est in luctum. **The Tallis Scholars/Peter Phillips.** Gimell CDGIM012 (9/87).

Louis Vierne
French 1870-1937

New review
Vierne. Symphonies — No. 1 in D minor, Op. 14; No. 3 in F sharp minor, Op. 28.
Michael Murray (org). Telarc CD80329. Played on the Cavaillé-Coll organ of Saint Ouen Abbey Church, Rouen. Recorded in 1992.

lh l5m DDD 5/94	**9**s

Vierne's organ symphonies, the Third in particular, have fared well on CD. If you already have Jeremy Filsell's disc (see review under Tournemire; refer to the Index to Reviews) then rest assured Murray does not eclipse it. That said, this coupling, setting the dark, forbidding Third against the exuberant, optimistic First, is attractive and Murray has remarkable technical command, executing the detail of these demanding scores with total security, and playing this dense acoustic to full effect — hence a dangerously slow but spine-tinglingly exciting Final to the Third. However, this is essentially a New World approach to French culture, sharing an intense enthusiasm with those who will likely find in this music something of the exotic. What for some might be the only drawback with this recording will be for others its most attractive quality. The combination of a sizzling instrument, a steamy acoustic and Telarc's opulent recording has the effect of a kind of aural Turkish Bath.

Further listening ...

Triptyque, Op. 58. Pièces en style libre, Op. 31. **Colin Walsh** (org). Priory PRCD319 (3/92).

Henry Vieuxtemps
Belgian 1820-1881

Suggested listening ...

Violin Concerto No. 5 in A minor, Op. 37. *Coupled with* **Paganini.** Violin Concerto No. 1 in D major, Op. 6. **Viktoria Mullova** (vn); **Academy of St Martin in the Fields/Sir Neville Marriner.** Philips 422 332-2PH (10/89).

Heitor Villa-Lobos
Brazilian 1887-1959

New review
Villa-Lobos. The Discovery of Brazil — Suites Nos. 1-4. **Slovak Philharmonic Chorus; Slovak Radio Symphony Orchestra/Roberto Duarte.** Marco Polo 8 223551.

lh l9m DDD 8/94	**9**p

It has taken a very long time for *The Discovery of Brazil*, one of Villa-Lobos's most significant works, to reach the record catalogue. The original score —which incorporated orchestrations of three earlier pieces — was intended for a 1937 nationalist film, which however used only a fraction of it: the composer then expanded his version into the present four suites (totalling ten items), of which he conducted the first performance in Paris in 1952. Predictably picturesque and colourful in nature, the work depicts the journey of the caravels, with the varied feelings of the aristocrats and seamen on board, the arrival in the strange new continent, and the celebration, amid friendly Indian spectators, of the first Mass in Brazil on May 1st, 1500. For this, Villa-Lobos had recourse to a very large orchestra and a great diversity of styles — Indian chants, popular Portuguese dances and *saudades*, Andalusian rhythms and Moorish melodic contours (since Spaniards and Moors may have been among the crew), plainchant, the *Ave verum* and *Tantum ergo*. Taken as a whole it achieves a certain epic quality, as the composer intended: what it lacks in homogeneity is counterbalanced by the sheer exuberance of invention. The Fourth Suite, in which the orchestra is joined by the chorus, is the most substantial, and the finale the most musically impressive, with some remarkable counterpoint; but the elaborate intertwining of Indian elements and the liturgical would have been more effective with more secure intonation from the chorus, especially the sopranos. Except for occasional anxieties in the very highest register of the violins, the orchestra rises splendidly to the whole score.

Villa-Lobos. ORCHESTRAL WORKS. **Czecho-Slovak Radio Symphony Orchestra, Bratislava/Roberto Duarte.** Marco Polo 8 223357. Recorded in 1990.
Gênesis — Ballet. Erosño (Origem do rio Amazonas). Amazonas — Symphonic Poem. Dawn in a tropical forest.

lh 2m DDD 3/92

Do not be deterred by the thought of an Eastern European orchestra playing unfamiliar Villa-Lobos. The Czecho-Slovak Radio Orchestra is clearly a very skilled and flexible body, and the conductor Roberto Duarte, a Brazilian authority on Villa-Lobos, has instilled South American colour and rhythmic vitality into his players quite brilliantly. The best of the four works is probably the earliest, *Amazonas*, which was written in 1917. Here, at the age of 30, Villa-Lobos's imagination was extraordinarily fertile, and this early evocation of Brazilian folklore, with its use of unusual instruments and strange orchestral timbres, is remarkably advanced for its date. The short tone poem *Dawn in a tropical forest* is a late work dating from 1953, and this has a more lyrical, more classical style. The remaining two works also come from the last phase in Villa-Lobos's career, and have similar themes. *Gênesis*, written in 1954, is a large-scale symphonic poem and ballet which depicts its enormous subject with all the extravagant colour and use of complex rhythms which were the composer's trademark. *Erosño*, or *The origin of the Amazon*, composed in 1950, is another ambitiously complex work. All four items are captured in faithful, wide-ranging sound.

Villa-Lobos. CHAMBER WORKS. **William Bennett** (fl); [ae]**Neil Black** (ob); [a]**Janice Knight** (cor ang); [aef]**Thea King** (cl); [acf]**Robin O'Neill** (bn); [d]**Charles Tunnell** (vc); [b]**Simon Weinberg** (gtr). Hyperion CDA66295.
Quinteto em forma de chôros[a]. Modinha[b]. Bachianas brasileiras No. 6[c]. Distribuçiño de flôres[b]. Assobio a jato[d]. Chôros No. 2[e]. Cançño do amor[b]. Trio for oboe, clarinet and bassoon[f].

lh lm DDD 9/89   **Q P**

If there is one consistent feature in Villa-Lobos's enormous and diverse output, it is his unpredictability. His restless, supercharged mind never tired of experimenting with new sonorities, and he never felt inhibited, in the course of a work, from following unrelated new impulses. This has the effect of making his music at the same time attractive and disconcerting. The multi-sectional Quintet, the most significant item here, is highly complex but extremely entertaining in its quirky way; and it is played with marvellous neatness, finely judged tonal nuances and high spirits. The rarely heard Trio, the earliest work here, is a particularly spiky atonal piece, typical of its period (1921), depending almost entirely on exuberantly thrusting and counter-thrusting rhythm: it calls for virtuosity, and gets it. The sixth of the *Bachianas brasileiras* (easily the best available recorded performance) is most sensitively shaped, and the second *Chôros*, which makes great demands on the two players both individually and in mutual responsiveness, is outstandingly polished. A disc of outstanding artistry.

New review
Villa-Lobos. SACRED CHORAL WORKS. **Corydon Singers and** [a]**Orchestra/Matthew Best.** Hyperion CDA66638. Texts and translations included.
Missa São Sebastião. Bendita sabedoria. Praesepe (with Ansy Boothroyd, mez). Cor dulce, cor amabile. Panis angelicus. Sub tuum praesidium. Ave Maria (a 5). Ave Maria (a 6). Pater noster. Magnificat-alleluia (Elizabeth McCormack, mez)[a].

lh l7m DDD 8/93   **Q P**

Any listener not informed in advance and asked to identify the composer of all these religious works except the Mass (the earliest here) would be most unlikely to think of Villa-Lobos. That larger-than-life exotic, that extravagantly experimental and boisterous figure, the composer of such chastely restrained music, the sweetly gentle *Cor dulce*, the mellifluous imitative counter-point of the first of the *Bendita sabedoria* (six brief choral pieces on biblical texts), the controlled fervour of the *Pater noster*? Even the impressive and grandiose *Magnificat-alleluia* (written in 1958 at the request of Pope Pius XII to celebrate Lourdes Year) gives no hint of its country of origin. The one clue here might be that, of the two *Ave Marias*, the (earlier) five-part setting is in Portuguese. It is only the Mass that reveals all. Amid its austere style and purely diatonic, contrapuntal idiom the *Sanctus* suddenly seems to come from a different background: then one remembers that Sebastian is the patron saint of Rio de Janeiro; and looking into the score one finds that the liturgical heading of each movement is followed by a local one, the final *Agnus Dei* bearing the sub-title "Sebastian, protector of Brazil". In an exceptionally informative note, Simon Wright, besides sketching in the politico-social background to Villa-Lobos's religious music, also points out that vestiges of old magical beliefs brought by African slaves still tinge Catholicism in Brazil. This programme, all of unaccompanied music except for the *Magnificat-alleluia*, should not be listened to as a continuity if some feeling of sameness is to be avoided: the Corydon Singers are most efficient in all they do, even if their tone is not the most seductive, but the outstanding performance is that of the Mass.

Further listening ...

Guitar Concerto. Five Preludes. 12 Etudes. **Julian Bream** (gtr); **London Symphony Orchestra/André Previn.** RCA Red Seal RD89813 (2/87).

Piano Concertos Nos. 1-5. **Cristina Ortiz** (pf); **Royal Philharmonic Orchestra/Miguel Gómez-Martínez.** Decca 430 628-2DH2 (5/92).

String Quartets. **Danubius Quartet.** Marco Polo 8 223389/90 (11/92): *8 223389* — No. 1; No. 8; No. 13. *8 223390* — No. 11; No. 16; No. 17. *8 223391* — No. 4; No. 6; No. 14.

Piano Works — Bachianas brasileiras No. 4 (pf version). Guia prático. Poema singélo. Caixinha de música quebrada. Saudades das selvas brasileiras No. 2. As tres Marias. Valsa da dor. Cirandas — No. 4, O cravo brigou com a rosa; No. 14, A canôa virou. Ciclo brasileiro. **Cristina Ortiz.** Decca 417 650-2DH (12/87).

Philippe de Vitry

French 1291-1361

Suggested listening ...

De Vitry and the Ars Nova. **The Orlando Consort.** Amon Ra CD-SAR49 (10/91).

Antonio Vivaldi

Italian 1678-1741

New review

Vivaldi. CELLO CONCERTOS. **Ofra Harnoy** (vc); [a]**Igor Oistrakh** (vn); **Toronto Chamber Orchestra/Paul Robinson.** RCA Victor Red Seal 09026 61578-2. Recorded 1992. D major, RV404; D minor, RV407; F major, RV411; G minor, RV417; A minor, RV420. Concerto for Violin, Cello and Strings in F major, "Il Proteo o sia il mondo al rovescio", RV544[a].

59m DDD 1/94

With Vivaldi's music, Ofra Harnoy has the happiest empathy. She eloquently reveals the slow movements' tenderness and dignified pathos with no trace of sentimentality; the *Adagio* of RV420 and *Largo* of RV407 in particular are alone worth the price of the whole disc. In the outer movements her bow skips and dances, digging as deep as is appropriate, but never more, while those of the Toronto Chamber Orchestra do likewise, transparent but not thin in sound.

The 'world première' is the Concerto in D major, with solo-episodic figurations similar to those in Vivaldi's concertos for that other 'dual-register' instrument, the bassoon, and a brief but lovely *Adagio affetuoso*. In the curiously titled double concerto, RV544, Oistrakh proves a splendid match for her in style, weight and breadth of sound, and welcomely so in a work in which the soloists respond to one another, rather than play together. A clean and well-balanced recording completes the picture.

Vivaldi. CELLO CONCERTOS AND SONATAS. **Christophe Coin** (vc); **Academy of Ancient Music/Christopher Hogwood** (hpd). L'Oiseau-Lyre 433 052-2OH. Recorded in 1990.
Concertos — D minor, RV406; C minor, RV402; G major, RV414. *Sonatas* — A minor, RV44; E flat major, RV39; G minor, RV42.

1h 7m DDD 1/92

With this disc Christophe Coin completes his recording of Vivaldi's nine cello sonatas as well as including three of the composer's cello concertos. Vivaldi wrote rewardingly for the cello as the music on this issue demonstrates. Coin's feeling for dance rhythms, his clear articulation and musical phrasing and his sharp ear for detail bring the pieces alive in an infectious way. He is both firmly and imaginatively supported in the sonatas by a fine continuo group, and in the concertos by the strings of the Academy of Ancient Music. In the sonatas Christopher Hogwood varies the colour of the accompaniments by moving between harpsichord and organ while cello and baroque guitar add further variety and support. In the concertos, fast movements are characterized by vigorous, idiomatic passagework for the solo instrument punctuated by pulsating Vivaldian rhythms in the tuttis. In the slow movements, richly endowed with lyricism, the expressive intensity of the music is, on occasion, almost startling, revealing Vivaldi as a composer capable of far greater affective gestures than he is often given credit for. This music was intended to move the spirit, to appeal to the senses, and it seldom, if ever, fails to do so.

Additional recommendations ...
Cello Concertos — B minor, RV424; G minor, RV416; A minor, RV418; F major, RV412; C minor, RV401; G major, RV413. **Christophe Coin** (vc); **Academy of Ancient Music/Christopher Hogwood.** L'Oiseau-Lyre 421 732-2OH — 58m DDD 8/89
Cello Concertos — C minor, RV402; D major, RV403; D minor, RV406; F major, RV412; G major, RV414; A minor, RV422; B minor, RV424. **Ofra Harnoy** (vc); **Toronto Chamber Orchestra/Paul Robinson.** RCA Victor Red Sea RD60155 — 1h 13m DDD 4/90
Cello Sonatas — E flat major, RV39; E minor, RV40; F major, RV41; G minor, RV42; A minor, RV43; A minor, RV44; B flat major, RV45-RV47. **Anthony Pleeth, Suki Towb** (vcs); **Robert Woolley** (hpd/org). ASV Gaudeamus CDGAD201 — ② 2h 3m DDD 11/91

New review
Vivaldi. SIX FLUTE CONCERTOS, Op. 10. **Patrick Gallois** (fl); **Orpheus Chamber Orchestra.** DG 437 839-2GH. Recorded in 1992.

49m DDD 5/94

Patrick Gallois is a player of agility and sensitivity, an intelligent artist who can make his metal flute speak with all the subtlety of varied articulation and tone colour that some of us had come to assume was only possible on the wooden baroque instrument. These are deliciously light performances, in the best sense of the word; plenty of air allowed in, sparing and thoughtful use of vibrato, and above all an infectious bounce to the music-making in general. Gallois's sunny approach is matched by the excellent string players of the Orpheus Chamber Orchestra, whose stunning unanimity of ensemble, crispness of attack and sheer concentration-level once again make it hard to believe that they operate without a conductor. And both soloist and orchestra are equally responsive, too, to the uniquely tranquil beauties of the Vivaldian slow movement.

New review
Vivaldi. OBOE CONCERTOS. [a]**Stephen Hammer,** [b]**Frank de Bruine** (obs); [c]**Eric Hoeprich,** [c]**Antony Pay** (cls); **Academy of Ancient Music/Christopher Hogwood.** L'Oiseau-Lyre 433 674-2OH. Recorded in 1991.

Oboe Concertos — C major, RV447[b]; F major, RV457[a]; A minor, RV461[a]; A minor, RV463[b]; D minor, RV535[ab]. Concerto for Two Clarinets, Two Oboes and Strings in C major, RV559[abc].

♩• 1h DDD 7/93   **q ♩ p ✒**

This delightful miscellany of concertos by Vivaldi for one and two oboes — in a single instance, here, they are joined by a pair of clarinets — confirms Stephen Hammer as one of the very finest baroque oboe players around. He and Christopher Hogwood have achieved a happy partnership which realizes on the one hand the exuberant vitality of Vivaldi's rhythms, and on the other the rich seam of fantasy running through so much of his music. Few if any of Vivaldi's 18 or so surviving solo concertos for the instrument are disappointing. Stephen Hammer and Frank de Bruine have picked four of the best constructed and most alluring of them, taking two concertos each. They join forces in the D minor Concerto for two oboes, and are further joined by Eric Hoeprich and Antony Pay for one of Vivaldi's two concertos for two oboes and two clarinets. The latter piece is effectively written with the focus on the contrasting sonorities of the single and double reed families. Hammer negotiates the solo writing with consummate skill, athletic, precise in tuning and articulation and tasteful in his ornamentation and the remainder comes over with comparable panache. Both oboists unfailingly bring out the poetry in the music with sensibility and restraint. Fine recorded sound.

·*Vivaldi.* OBOE CONCERTOS. **Douglas Boyd** (ob); [a]**Marieke Blankestijn** (vn); **Chamber Orchestra of Europe.** DG 435 873-2GH. Recorded in 1991.
Oboe Concertos — C major, RV447; C major, RV450; D major, RV453; A minor, RV461; A minor, RV463. Concerto for Violin and Oboe in B flat major, RV548.

♩• 59m DDD 5/93

As well as being an inspired composer for his own instrument — the violin — Vivaldi could equally turn his hand to concertos for a great many other instruments. One of the principal beneficiaries of his skill was the oboe, for which he wrote 17 solo concertos, three for two oboes and another for oboe and violin. In this virtuoso programme the oboist, Douglas Boyd, has chosen five of the solo oboe concertos together with the more modestly conceived but no less captivating Concerto in B flat for oboe and violin. The oboe concertos have been selected discerningly, not only for their musical interest but also, it would seem, with an eye to their rarity value on the concert platform. Boyd, playing a modern oboe, gives fluent, sensitively shaped performances and is supported in a lively manner by the strings of the Chamber Orchestra of Europe. Boyd is expressive in slow movements — they almost invariably possess considerable lyrical appeal — and athletic in faster ones; and he needs to be, for Vivaldi seldom showed mercy on his soloists. From among the many beautiful movements here the *Larghetto* of the Concerto in A minor (RV461) stands out and may be ranked among Vivaldi's happiest creations for the oboe. Fine recorded sound.

Vivaldi. CONCERTOS. [a]**Stephen Marvin**, [b]**Chantal Rémillard**, [c]**Cynthia Roberts** (vns); [d]**Anner Bylsma**, [e]**Christina Mahler** (vcs); **Tafelmusik/Jeanne Lamon** ([f]vn). Sony Classical Vivarte SK48044. Recorded in 1990.
Concertos for Cello and Strings[d] — G major, RV413; A minor, RV418. Concerto for Violin, Cello and Strings in B flat major, RV547[df]. Concerto for Two Violins, Two Cellos and Strings in G major, RV575[adef]. Concerto for Four Violins and Strings in D minor, RV549[abcf]. Concertos for Strings — C major, RV117; E minor, RV134; F minor, RV143; A major, RV159.

♩• 1h 6m DDD 9/92   **q ♩ p ✒**

The Canadian period-instrument group Tafelmusik has been building up an impressive discography of music ranging from Corelli to Mozart. Here the players address themselves to Vivaldi in a first-rate recording of concertos for various combinations of strings. Though Vivaldi himself was a violinist he wrote for almost every other instrument of his day with informed skill. One of those to benefit was the cello which features as a solo instrument to a greater or lesser extent in five of the concertos in this programme. The soloist is the Dutch virtuoso Anner Bylsma whose animated playing generates a feeling of excitement and spontaneity by no means easily captured on disc. If he has a fault then it is that he is too often attracted by breakneck tempos and it is that which detracts from the opening movement of the G major Concerto (RV413). Apart from that one minor criticism the disc is one to be treasured not only for the excellence of the playing but also for the judicious choice of repertory. The Concerto in G major for two violins, two cellos and strings (RV575) is a beautifully crafted work with notably expressive writing for the solo instruments. The four concertos for ripieno strings, in which Vivaldi foreshadows the early classical symphonists, provide a rewarding contrast with the remaining programme and are played here with accomplishment and affection.

New review

Vivaldi. CHAMBER CONCERTOS. **Il Giardino Armonico.** Teldec 4509-91852-2. Recorded 1990-92.
D major, RV93. D major, RV94. F major, RV98, "La tempesta di mare". G minor, RV104, "La notte". G minor, RV107, A minor, RV108. F major, RV442. Trio Sonata in D minor, RV63.

Ih 7m DDD 7/94

There are baroque bands that are frankly dull and there are others on whom stylistic felicity sits naturally and gracefully. Il Giardino Armonico, an 11-strong group of young Italians, is one of the best. Italy, the birthplace of the baroque, has been curiously slow in coming forward with a specialized unit such as this, but the wait has been worthwhile; Il Giardino Armonico are as Italian as the music itself — brightly coloured, individualistic, confident, stylish, arrestingly decorated, bubbling with enthusiasm and ... add your own adjectives. The only un-Italian thing about them is their collective unanimity! Set these performances against any others in the catalogue and, with no detriment to the others, the differences are likely to deal you a blow to the solar plexus. Any sneaking fear that such unbridled *élan* leads to a uniformly vigorous approach is unfounded; equally 'Italian' is their wide dynamic range, dramatically exploited in RV104 and RV63, and all calls for serenity are answered. The recording is as bright and clear as the music.

Additional recommendation ...
RV98; RV104; RV90; RV101. Flute Concertos, Op. 10 — G major, RV435; F major, RV442. **Orchestra of the Eighteenth Century/Frans Brüggen** (fl/rec). RCA Red Seal Seon RD70951 —
53m DDD 2/87

New review

Vivaldi. CHAMBER CONCERTOS. **Philidor Ensemble.** Philips 434 995-2PH. Recorded in 1985.
A minor, RV86; C major, RV88; F major, RV99; G minor, RV103; G minor, RV105; G minor, RV107. Sonata for Recorder, Bassoon and Continuo in A minor, RV86.

53m DDD 9/93

In Vivaldi's chamber concertos, broadly speaking, each part other than the continuo has an obbligato role. The Philidor Ensemble has selected five from the 20 or so concertos of this type which have been handed down; and in addition, it plays the fine Sonata in A minor for treble recorder, bassoon and continuo. This is a rewardingly written piece with virtuoso passages for both soloists and a very beautiful third movement *Largo cantabile*. The remaining works include parts for violin, treble recorder, oboe and bassoon in various groupings. Technically speaking, the playing is of a high standard but, much more than that, the interpretations are enlivened by the artists' informed sense of baroque style. Rhythms are taut yet treated with an effective elasticity allowing phrases to breathe unhurriedly. Tempos are never rushed and the resonances of the instruments are carefully handled in the recording so that the character of each is able to assert itself clearly. A delightful programme, affectionately played and entirely free from any self-conscious, exaggerated mannerisms. The sound is excellent.

Vivaldi. 12 Violin Concertos, Op. 4, "La stravaganza". **Monica Huggett** (vn); **Academy of Ancient Music/Christopher Hogwood.** L'Oiseau-Lyre Florilegium 417 502-2OH2.

② Ih 4Im DDD 3/87

In *La stravaganza* Vivaldi makes a further decisive step towards the virtuoso solo violin concerto and though the quality of the music is a little uneven, the set nevertheless contains several movements of outstanding beauty. From among them we might single out the *Grave* of the Concerto No. 4 in A minor whose suspensions, chromaticisms and lyrical solo violin part cast a spell of almost fairy-tale enchantment, and the *Largo* of the Concerto No. 12 in G major with its ostinato bass above which a simple but haunting melody is treated to a series of variations. Monica Huggett gives a lively, inspired account of the music. Her warm tone, well-nigh impeccable intonation, sensitive dynamic shading and sheer virtuosity lead us to the heart of these pieces in a seemingly effortless fashion. There is a rich vein of fantasy coursing through *La stravaganza* and this is vividly realized in her communicative playing. The small string forces provide sympathetic support and Christopher Hogwood generates an enthusiastic atmosphere with well-judged tempos and tautly sustained rhythms.

Additional recommendations ...
Felix Ayo (vn); **I Musici.** Philips 426 935-2PM2 — .•' ADD 7/91 ✒
Academy of St Martin in the Fields/Sir Neville Marriner. Decca Serenata 430 566-2DM2 — .•' ② lh 50m ADD 2/92

New review
Vivaldi. Violin Concertos, Op. 8 — Nos. 1-4, "The Four Seasons"; No. 5 in E flat major, "La tempesta di mare"; No. 6 in C major, "Il piacere". **European Community Chamber Orchestra/Marieke Blankestijn** (vn); **Richard Lester** (vc); **Harold Lester** (hpd). Teldec 4509-91683-2. Recorded in 1993.

.•' 59m DDD 6/94 　　　　　　　　　　　　　　　　　　　　　ᖚP ⒷB

This is the first choice among available middle-of-the-road versions of *The Four Seasons*. Marieke Blankestijn is a most accomplished and accurate violinist, whose bowing ranges with rare sensitivity from the joyously vigorous to the merest whisper, and her flexibly moulded lines, drawn with just the right weight and with the 'right' notes 'squeezed', are never overladen with vibrato. She reacts refreshingly to the music and to those mysterious 'chicken or egg?' verses — Vivaldi's? — but without lapsing into theatricality, and the slow movements receive a little tasteful decoration where appropriate. Indeed, she has a fine grasp of style, shared by the ECCO, who play as though they were just discovering the music — and happy to be doing so. Neither she nor they are baroque specialists; these are modern-instrument performances at present-day pitch, but they cannot fail to enchant anyone whose 'purism' falls short of obsession. If all European Community affairs were as harmonious as this we would have little to worry about! The same admirable features are present in the other two concertos, equally crisply recorded.

Additional recommendations ...
Op. 8 Nos. 1-12. Flute Concerto in D major, RV429. Cello Concerto in B minor, RV424. **Stephen Preston** (fl); **Simon Standage** (vn); **Anthony Pleeth** (vc); **The English Concert/Trevor Pinnock.** CRD CRD3348/9 — .•' ② 2h 34m ADD 8/88 Ⓑ ✒
Op. 8 Nos. 1-12. **Felix Ayo** (vn); **I Musici.** Philips 426 943-2PM2 — .•' ② ADD 7/91 Ⓑ ✒
The Four Seasons. Violin Concerto in C major, RV171. Concerto in B flat major for Strings, RV163, "Conca". **L'Europa Galante/Fabio Biondi** (vn). Opus 111 OPS56-9120 — .•' 54m DDD 4/92 Ⓑ ✒
Op. 8 — Nos. 2 and 10. Violin Concertos, Op. 11 — No. 2 in C minor; RV199, "Il sospetto"; E major, RV271, "L'amoroso"; A major, RV335, "Il curcù". **Jaap van Zweden** (vn); **Combattimento Consort Amsterdam/Jan Willem de Vriend.** Sony Classical SK53265 — .•' 58m DDD 8/93 Ⓑ ✒

Vivaldi. 12 Violin Concertos, Op. 9, "La cetra". **Simon Standage** (vn); **Academy of Ancient Music/Christopher Hogwood** (hpd). L'Oiseau-Lyre 421 366-2OH2. Recorded in 1987.

.•' ② lh 50m DDD 4/89 　　　　　　　　　　　　　　　　　　　　　　

La cetra ("The lyre"), published in 1727, was Vivaldi's last great set of printed concertos. All but one of the 12 concertos are for solo violin, the odd one out being the ninth in the set which is scored for two violins; in this work Simon Standage, the soloist in each of the remaining concertos of the set, is partnered by Catherine Mackintosh. Two others, in A major (RV348) and B minor (RV391) require 'scordatura' or retuning of the solo violin. These are satisfying concertos, less obviously innovative than some of those in Vivaldi's earlier sets, but none the less containing a rich diversity of ideas and collectively representative of the composer's mature style. Christopher Hogwood has a refreshingly robust approach to the music, evident not only in his choice of lively tempos, but in the crisp, brightly articulated sound of the Academy of Ancient Music and in the imaginatively realized continuo, this last a feature of almost all Hogwood's recordings. Standage's tone quality matches that of the ripieno strings and his playing has something of that demonic virtuosity which we might imagine Vivaldi himself to have possessed. There is an infectious vitality in this playing which is very exciting. Intonation is not always impeccable nor is the playing invariably as refined as one would like. But the virtues easily outweigh the shortcomings and few will be other than captivated by the sort of performance qualities present in the finale of the Sixth Concerto (RV348), for instance. There is, in short, nothing of the routine or the world-weary in this recording.

Additional recommendations ...
Felix Ayo (vn); **I Musici.** Philips 426 946-2PM2 — ·· ② ADD 7/91 🎖
I Solisti Italiani. Denon CO-79475/6 — ·· ② 1h 56m DDD 9/92

New review
Vivaldi. Six Violin Concertos, Op. 11. **Stanley Ritchie** (vn); **Frank de Bruine** (ob); **Academy of Ancient Music/Christopher Hogwood.** L'Oiseau-Lyre 436 172-2OH. Recorded in 1991.

·· 1h 7m DDD 4/94

The solo violinist, Stanley Ritchie, has long been an agile and sympathetic exponent of Vivaldi's concertos. He is able to lightly articulate the passagework and to bring out the pleasing contours of Vivaldi's melodic writing. There is plenty of expressive variety in this music, ranging from the somewhat wistful violin melody of the slow movement of the First Concerto, with its limpid upper string pizzicato accompaniment, to the vigorous gestures which characterize many of the outer movements. Contrast is a feature, too, in the single Oboe Concerto (No. 6). Here the soloist is Frank de Bruine, who gives a fluent account of the outer movements and a lyrical one of the ostinato-based *Largo cantabile*. Christopher Hogwood and the Academy of Ancient Music provide lively and sympathetic support, Hogwood effectively ringing the changes between harpsichord and chamber organ continuo, and also sensibly engaging the services of a theorbo player, Tom Finucane. In short, an enjoyable disc with a notably expressive performance of *Il favorito*, whose slow movement is endowed with lyricism and expressive fantasy, neither of which is lost on Ritchie. Good recorded sound.

New review
Vivaldi. CONCERTOS. **L'Europa Galante/Fabio Biondi** (vn). Opus 111 OPS30-86. Recorded in 1993.
Violin and Strings in E minor, RV281; Strings in E minor, RV133; Cello and Strings in D minor, RV407; Violin and Strings in F major, "per la Solennità di S Lorenzo", RV286; Violin, Organ and Strings in D minor, RV541; Two Violins and Strings in D major, RV511; Two Cellos and Strings in G minor, RV531.

·· 1h 13m DDD 6/94

Of the seven concertos included on this disc only RV281 is new to the catalogue. All the others have appeared, at one time or another, though only RV531, for two cellos, at all frequently. In fact RV281, a Violin Concerto in E minor, is among the most interesting pieces here, full of commanding gestures in the tuttis and expressive fantasy in the virtuoso solo violin part. These are qualities in Vivaldi's music L'Europa Galante seek to highlight in their sprightly, mercurial performances, full of energy and spontaneity. The remainder of the programme has been carefully planned to provide the listener with contrast in texture if not always of tonality. The soloists are all drawn from the ensemble and very accomplished they are too. The cellist, Maurizio Naddeo, has a pleasingly warm tone and a good ear for detail and the Cello Concerto in D minor, a seldom heard piece, comes over persuasively. The two solo concertos, for two violins and two cellos respectively, are played with panache and an awareness of the bold and striking nature of Vivaldi's invention.

Vivaldi. L'estro Armonico, Op. 3. **Academy of Ancient Music/Christopher Hogwood.**
L'Oiseau-Lyre Florilegium 414 554-2OH2. From D245D2 (12/81).

② 1h 36m DDD 1/86 ⁹ₚ ⁹ₛ Ⓑ

This set of Concertos is arranged as a display of variety, and ordered in a kaleidoscopic way
that would maintain interest were it to be played in its entirety. These works are often
played with an inflated body of *ripieno* (orchestral) strings, but in this recording they are
played as Vivaldi intended them; only four violins are used. The contrast does not come
from antiphony or weight of numbers but is provided through the *tutti* versus episodic
passages. One could not assemble a more distinguished 'cast' than that of the AAM in this
recording, showing clearly just why this music is best played on period instruments, by
specialists in baroque style, who are not afraid to add a little embellishment here and there.
Neither the enchanting performances nor the quality of their recording could be better; this
is required listening.

Additional recommendations ...
Solisti Italiani. Denon CO-72719/20 — ② 1h 49m DDD 8/89 Ⓑ
Roberto Michelucci (vn); **I Musici.** Philips 426 932-2PM2 — ② ADD 7/91 Ⓑ
Academy of St Martin in the Fields/Sir Neville Marriner. Decca Serenata 430 557-
2DM2 — ② 1h 42m ADD 2/92 Ⓑ

New review
Vivaldi. CONCERTOS FOR STRINGS. **I Musici.** Philips 438 876-2PH. Recorded in 1992.
B flat major, RV163, "Conca". F major, RV136. C minor, RV118. D major, RV123. A major,
RV160. D minor, RV128. A major, RV159. G major, RV146. F minor, RV143. C major, RV117.

55m DDD 5/94

Here is a generous and varied selection from among the concertos which Vivaldi wrote for
strings without soloist. He composed over 40 such pieces of which ten are included here.
Anyone who still thinks that one Vivaldi concerto sounds much the same as another should
address himself to these vital, often forward-looking pieces. They are full of striking contrasts
and ideas which point strongly in the direction of the early symphony and the tautly constructed
fugues at the conclusion of the Concerto in D major (RV123) and the beginning of the Concerto
in F minor (RV143) are but two reminders of how effective a contrapuntist Vivaldi could be if
he so wished. I Musici give a lively view of these engaging concertos with tidy ensemble and
good intonation and should disappoint only those who no longer find enjoyment in listening to
baroque repertory played on modern instruments. Good recorded sound.

Vivaldi. DOUBLE CONCERTOS. **Collegium Musicum 90/Simon Standage** (vn).
Chandos Chaconne CHAN0528. Recorded in 1991.
Concertos for Two Violins and Strings — C major, RV505; D major, RV511; A minor, RV523
(Micaela Comberti, vn). Concerto for Two Cellos and Strings in G minor, RV531 (Jane Coe,
David Watkin, vcs). Concerto for Two Oboes and Strings in D minor, RV535 (Anthony Robson,
Catherine Latham, obs). Concerto for Two Violins, Oboe and Strings in C major, RV554.

1h 5m DDD 3/93

It was natural, with so many talented young ladies available at the Pietà, that Vivaldi should have
written a large number of concertos with two or more soloists. More than two dozen are for
two violins and most remain unrecorded; RV505 and 511 are both mature works, the former
leaning toward *galant* style and the latter 'unified' by elements that are common to its outer
movements. RV554, originally a triple concerto for violin, oboe and organ, was rewritten by
Vivaldi for oboe and two violins, in which latter form it is given in this recording. The Concerto
for two oboes, RV535, is 'Corellian' in its four-movement *da chiesa* form and in its
'conversations' between the soloists and the *ripieno* strings — a Vivaldian rarity. If Vivaldi wrote
a more eloquently pathetic melody than that of the *Largo* of the Double Cello Concerto, RV531,
it is hard to bring it to mind; it is an early work — why did he never return to that most
rewarding of media? Collegium Musicum 90 field a modest string band, which adds leanness of
sound to their other virtues of stylishness and crispness of ensemble. Excellent oboe soloists
contribute to the allure of this recording.

Vivaldi. CONCERTOS — ALLA RUSTICA. **The English Concert/Trevor Pinnock.**
Archiv Produktion 415 674-2AH.
G major, RV151, "Alla rustica"; B flat major for Violin and Oboe, RV548; G major for Two
Violins, RV516; A minor for Oboe, RV461; G major for Two Mandolins, RV532; C major, RV558.

— 53m DDD 9/86

The *Concerto con molti stromenti*, RV558, calls for a plethora of exotic instruments and Vivaldi's
inventiveness, everywhere apparent, seems to know no bounds. The vigorous melodies have
splendid verve whilst the slow movements are no less exciting. The concertos, which employ
plucked instruments, are particularly entrancing to the ear — here is virtuosity indeed, with
Pinnock sensibly opting for an organ continuo to emphasize the difference between the plucked
strings and the bowed. The Double Mandolin Concerto, RV532, is beautifully played with a real
build-up of tension in the tuttis. The playing of The English Concert is affectionate and
rhythmically precise and the recording is good with the gentler sounding instruments well
brought out of the fuller textures.

Vivaldi. STRING CONCERTOS. [a]**Adrian Chamorro** (vn); [b]**Maurizio Naddeo** (vc);
L'Europa Galante/Fabio Biondi (vn). Opus 111 OPS309004. Recorded in 1990.
C minor, RV761; D minor, RV129, "Concerto madrigalesco"; G minor, RV517[a]; B flat major,
RV547[b]; C minor, RV202; E flat major, RV130, "Sonata al santo sepolcro". Sinfonia in B minor,
RV169, "Sinfonia al santo sepolcro".

— 52m DDD 9/91

This invigorating programme contains well-known and less well-known concertos by Vivaldi.
The performances sparkle with life and possess an irresistible spontaneity. The Concertos for one
and two violins (RV761 and RV202) are comparative rarities and are played with agility and
insight by the soloist director Fabio Biondi and his alert and responsive ensemble. Biondi himself
is capable of light and articulate bowing and has a natural feeling for graceful turns of phrase.
Vivaldi's virtuoso writing occasionally finds chinks in his armour but with enlightened music-
making of this order it matters little. Everywhere Vivaldi's infectious rhythms are tautly
controlled and the music interpreted with character and conviction. Perhaps the highlight of the
disc is the Concerto in B flat for violin and cello. Outer movements are crisply articulated and
played with almost startling energy while the poignant lyricism of the *Andante* is touchingly
captured. A refreshing and illuminating disc whose imaginative and passionate interpretations
have few rivals in the catalogue. The recorded sound is clear and ideally resonant.

New review
Vivaldi. 12 VIOLIN SONATAS. **La Romanesca** (Andrew Manze, vn; Nigel North,
lte/theorbo/gtr; John Toll, hpd). Harmonia Mundi HMU90 7089/90. Recorded in 1992.
No. 1 in C major, RV3. No. 2 in D minor, RV12. No. 3 in G minor, RV757. No. 4 in
D major, RV755. No. 5 in B flat major, RV759. No. 6 in A major, RV758. No. 7 in C minor,
RV6. No. 8 in G major, RV22. No. 9 in E minor, RV17*a*. No. 10 in B minor, RV760. No. 11
in E flat major, RV756. No. 12 in C major, RV754.

② 2h 25m DDD 1/94

Vivaldi is so well-known for his concertos that we are apt to overlook his admittedly much
smaller output of sonatas. This set of 12 for violin and continuo was discovered in
Manchester's Central Music Library during the 1970s though five of them exist in versions
which have been known for much longer. It is probable that all of them date from the early-
to mid-1720s when Vivaldi assembled them to present to Cardinal Ottoboni on the occasion
of his visit to Venice, the city of his birth, in 1726. The violinist Andrew Manze has an
appealing rapport with this music and is expressive in his shaping of phrases. He reveals
sensibility towards Vivaldi's pleasing melodic contours. Indeed, this is a quality in which these
sonatas abound, not only in the varied Preludes with which each Sonata begins but also in the
brisker, sometimes very brisk allemandes and correntes. He ornaments the music with an
effective blend of fantasy and good taste and he dispenses with bowed continuo instruments,
preferring the lighter textures provided by harpsichord, archlute, theorbo or guitar. This is
music of great beauty and vitality which will delight most if not all lovers of the late baroque;
and it is sympathetically interpreted and warmly and intimately recorded.

Vivaldi. CONCERTOS AND CANTATAS. [a]**Catherine Bott** (sop); **Tom Finucane** ([b]mand/[c]lte); **New London Consort/Philip Pickett** ([d]rec). L'Oiseau-Lyre 433 198-2OH. Texts and translations included. Recorded 1989-90.

All'ombra di sospetto, RV678[a]. Lungi dal vago volto, RV680[a]. Vengo a voi, luci adorate, RV682[a]. Concerto for Two Mandolins and Strings in G major, RV532[b]. Chamber Concerto for Lute, Two Violins and Continuo in D major, RV93[c]. Chamber Concerto for Recorder, Two Violins and Continuo in A minor, RV108[d]. Concertos, Op. 10 — No. 3 in G minor, RV439, "La notte".

1h 13m DDD 1/93

This disc is a welcome incursion to one of the least explored areas of Vivaldi's music — the chamber cantata. As well as three cantatas the programme includes four well contrasted concertos by Vivaldi who was, of course, one of the greatest masters of the form. Catherine Bott gives sparkling performances. Her clear, well-focused voice and secure technique are a constant pleasure as is the intelligence with which she draws together text and music. This is indeed singing to enchant the ear and beguile the senses and all the more so when it is supported by sympathetic and stylish accompaniments. Continuo lines are imaginatively realized and there are attractive obbligatos for both recorder and violin. The concertos with which the cantatas are interspersed are among Vivaldi's more modestly conceived. Two of them feature plucked string instruments, a lute (RV93) and two mandolins (RV532). Thanks to the wonders of modern recording Tom Finucane takes both mandolin parts, playing with sprightly zeal and an ear for detail; and he gives an affecting performance of the wistfully alluring *Largo* of the Lute Concerto. Philip Pickett is the solo recorder player in the remaining concertos, giving performances which are fluent and full of vitality.

Vivaldi. Domine ad adiuvandum me festiana, RV593. Beatus vir, RV597. Stabat mater, RV621. Magnificat, RV610. **Ex Cathedra Chamber Choir and Baroque Orchestra/Jeffrey Skidmore.** ASV Gaudeamus CDGAU137. Texts and translations included. Recorded in 1991.

1h 10m DDD 12/92

This is an interesting and mainly successful attempt to place a handful of Vivaldi's sacred pieces in a liturgical context. The well-known work here is the *Stabat mater* for alto voice and strings, but the others deserve to be heard more often than they are. Ex Cathedra Chamber Choir is a well-disciplined, youthful sounding ensemble whose contribution to the recording is first-rate. And it is from the choir that solo voices emerge as required, giving the performances an homogeneity of sound and intent. The instrumentalists, too, make a strong contribution and together with the voices project interpretations which are full of vitality. There are, of course, rival versions on disc of all the music sung here but, on the strength of the thoughtful way it has been presented by the director of Ex Cathedra, Geoffrey Skidmore, this is perhaps the most affecting of them. Few will be disappointed, for example, by the gently inflected, poignant account of the *Stabat mater* by the male alto Nigel Short. Hardly a detail has been overlooked, even to the extent of allowing the listener to hear a distant bell during the opening Versicle. In short, only the painfully and unnecessarily small typeface of the accompanying texts fails to please.

Additional recommendations ...

Magnificat. In turbato mare irato, RV627. Concertos — D minor, RV129, "Concerto madrigalesco"; G minor, RV157; G major, RV151, "Concerto alla rustica". Lungi dal vago volto, RV680. **Soloists; Tafelmusik Chamber Choir and Baroque Orchestra/Jean Lamon** (vn). Hyperion CDA66247 — 57m DDD 12/87

Vestro Principi divino, RV633. Stabat mater. Filiae mestae, RV638. Nisi Dominus, RV608. **Gérard Lesne** (alto); **Il Seminario Musicale Ensemble.** Harmonic H/CD8720 — 58m DDD 3/91

Laudate pueri Dominum, RV600[a]. Stabat mater[b]. Deus tuorum militum, RV612[c]. Sanctorum meritis, RV620[d]. [ad]**Margaret Marshall** (sop); [bc]**Jochen Kowalski** (alto); [ad]**Jacques Ogg** (org); **Concertgebouw Chamber Orchestra/Vittorio Negri.** Philips 432 091-2PH — 49m DDD 2/92

New review
Vivaldi. SALVE REGINA. [a]**Gérard Lesne** (alto); [b]**Fabio Biondi** (vn); **Il Seminario Musicale.** Virgin Classics Veritas VC7 59232-2. Texts and translations included. Recorded in 1991.

Salve regina in C minor, RV616[a]. Introduzione al Miserere, RV641[a]. Introduzione al Gloria, RV637[a]. Salve regina in G minor, RV618[a]. Concerto for Violin and Strings in C major, RV581[b] ("per la Santissima Assenzione di Maria Vergine").

♪ **1h 17m DDD 6/93** ♀**P**

The principal works here are two settings of the Marian antiphon *Salve regina*, but the French counter-tenor Gérard Lesne follows this with an extended *Introduzione* to a *Miserere*, one of two by Vivaldi, and an *Introduzione* to a *Gloria*; and by way of making up a programme, he divides the four vocal pieces into two groups inserting a Violin Concerto between them. The main bias of this music is contemplative, often deeply so, as is the case with the darkly expressive, sorrowful introduction to the *Miserere non in pratis*. Lesne approaches the music with style. Indeed, a stronger advocate for these affecting compositions is hard to imagine since he is technically almost faultless. Then there is the Concerto in C major (*in due cori*), a splendid example of Vivaldi's skill in this medium, admirably played by the violinist Fabio Biondi with Lesne's own group Il Seminario Musicale. Vivaldi enthusiasts will require no further proof of this disc's merit, but readers in general should also find much to enjoy here, both in the singing and playing. The recorded sound is pleasantly resonant, serving the best interests of Lesne's voice and of the instruments too. A fine release.

Vivaldi. Juditha Triumphans, RV645. **Elly Ameling** (sop); **Birgit Finnilä, Annelies Burmeister, Ingeborg Springer** (mezs); **Júlia Hamari** (contr); **Berlin Radio Ensemble; Berlin Chamber Orchestra/Vittorio Negri.** Philips 426 955-2PM2. Text and translations included. From 6747 173 (10/75). Recorded in 1974.

♪ ② **2h 33m ADD 4/92**

This recording of Vivaldi's only surviving oratorio, *Juditha Triumphans*, was made in 1974 and though various new recordings have come and gone since then none have surpassed it. Vittorio Negri fields an orchestra of modern instruments, and a very good one it is too. The obbligato playing is first-rate although an over-ornate harpsichord continuo gives the performance a dated aspect. The soloists are excellent for the most part with Birgit Finnilä in the title role. Her "Quanto magis generosa" with viola d'amore, and the memorable "Veni, veni, me sequere fide" with an obbligato chalumeau are particularly affecting. Júlia Hamari brings a lively sense of theatre to her portrayal of the warrior, Holofernes, and his servant Vagaus is agilely sung by the soprano, Elly Ameling. Judith's servant, Abra, is portrayed with clarity and conviction by Ingeborg Springer. No male voice soloists here, since Vivaldi wrote the oratorio for the musically gifted girls of the Pietà orphanage in Venice where he worked on and off for most of his life. Negri brings as much drama to the piece as music and text will allow and the results are by-and-large rewarding. Full texts are included and the recorded sound is excellent.

Kevin Volans
South African 1949-

New review
Volans. String Quartets — No. 2, "Hunting: Gathering"; No. 3, "The Songlines". **Balanescu Quartet** (Alexander Balanescu, Clare Connors, vns; Bill Hawkins, va; Nick Cooper, vc). Argo 440 687-2ZH. Recorded in 1993.

♪ **57m DDD**

Both works here call on ideas from native African peoples, including the Hamar of Ethiopia and the Zulus, but Volans's style is also reminiscent of Western models, Stravinsky, Bartók and Messiaen most especially. In fact, the mesmeric, 19-minute second movement of *The Songlines* features one passage (roughly 12'00" to 15'00") that suggests the joint influence of Messiaenic bird song and Bartókian nocturnal atmosphere. Volans favours speech-like phrase constructions and punctuation, although his work appears not to have mirrored specific words. *Hunting: Gathering* is certainly the place to start: its language is less discursive than *The Songlines*, its melodic material easier to assimilate. There's even what sounds like a passing reference to the theme for the TV 'cop' show "Cagney and Lacey" (near the beginning of the second movement)! *The Songlines* was intended as "an extension in another medium" on Bruce Chatwin's novel of the same name and is altogether darker, more austere and more obviously outspoken than its predecessor. However, both works are beautifully realized, and the recordings have a clarity and refinement that reflects similar priorities on the part of the performers. Recommended.

Further listening ...

White man sleeps (1982[d] and 1986[a] versions). Mbira[b]. She who sleeps with a small blanket[c]. [bd]**Kevin Volans,** [b]**Deborah James,** [d]**Robert Hill** (hpds); [d]**Margriet Tindemans** (va da gamba); [bcd]**Robyn Schulkowsky** (perc); [a]**Smith Quartet.** United Recordings 88034 (10/91).

Key to symbols

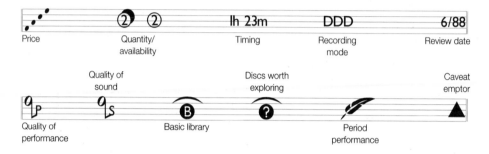

Price	Quantity/ availability	Timing	Recording mode	Review date

Quality of sound	Discs worth exploring	Caveat emptor

Quality of performance	Basic library	Period performance	

Jan Vořišek

Bohemian 1791-1825

Suggested listening ...

Six Impromptus, Op. 7. Fantaisie in C major, Op. 12. Variations in B flat major, Op. 19. Piano Sonata in B flat major, Op. 20. **Radoslav Kvapil** (pf). Unicorn-Kanchana DKPCD9145 (6/94).

Ladislav Vycpálek

Czechoslovakian 1882-1969

New review

Vycpálek. Cantata of the Last Things of Man, Op. 16[a]. Czech Requiem, Op. 24[b]. [a]**Drahomíra Tikalová,** [b]**Mariana Reháková** (sops); [b]**Marie Mrázová** (contr); [a]**Ladislav Mráz,** [b]**Theodor Srubař** (bars); **Czech Philharmonic Chorus and Orchestra/Karel Ančerl.** Supraphon Historical 11 1933-2. Texts and translations included. Item marked [a] from SUA10026 (4/61), recorded in 1957, [b] recorded at a performance in Prague in 1968 and new to UK.

② 2h 20m AAD 7/93

The *Cantata of the Last Things of Man* (1922) is a remarkable work, based on folk texts and setting out a threefold move from materialism through death to faith; and though it is grounded in a simple, direct idiom that takes much of its nature from Czech folk-music, it is also sophisticated in its contrapuntal usage and ancient in its references. There is more than a suggestion of Janáček in the splendour of the writing for brass and drums. If Vycpálek lacks Janáček's radiant idiosyncrasies, his idiom is original, elevating, and affirmatory. And this 1961 recording, despite a few gusty sounds, survives as a convincing account of a fervent and original work. The *Czech Requiem* dates from 1940, dark times for Czechoslovakia. It is cast in similar idiom, and draws on three sacred texts in a manner that is bound to recall Brahms's *German Requiem*. There resemblance ends: not only is the idiom utterly different, but Brahms's humanist pessimism is entirely absent from this strongly Christian work. The conviction of the perform-ance speaks much for what it means to Czechs, and is very moving. Karel Ančerl, its conductor, survived Auschwitz to return home; in 1968 he gave this performance before the Russian tanks rolled in. When they did he left, to die abroad. It is, then, a historic performance.

Richard Wagner

German 1813-1883

Wagner. ORCHESTRAL WORKS. **Philharmonia Orchestra/Yuri Simonov.** Collins Classics 1207-2.
GOTTERDAMMERUNG — Siegfried's Rhine Journey; Siegfried's Funeral March. PARSIFAL — Prelude, Act 1. SIEGFRIED — Forest Murmurs. TRISTAN UND ISOLDE — Prelude and Liebestod. DIE WALKURE — Ride of the Valkyries.

Ih 8m DDD 10/91

"The old poisoner" Debussy called him. Be it the dragon's blood, a love potion or sacrament from the Holy Grail, for those who prefer it administered in short, concentrated doses, this disc is an obvious choice. If there exists a more forceful paean of brass and timpani as Siegfried and Brünnhilde emerge to greet daybreak before the Rhine journey, it has yet to be heard. Yet this is no mere sonic spectacular: every phrase is lovingly turned and shaded, and the expression in each extract is finely attuned to its dramatic context. The brass intone the "Faith" motive from *Parsifal* with dignity and restraint, and while the playing at the climax of Isolde's Liebestod lacks nothing in passion, Simonov shows respect for Wagner's single *forte* marking. This is also one of the most coherent Wagner sounds on disc, offering separation of textures, a telling projection of the lower orchestral voices, and a real sense of space. You hear the pedal notes that evoke the stillness of the forest, you feel its depths, you rejoice with Siegfried at its natural wonders, and you understand why Debussy (despite his protestations) could never entirely cleanse himself of Wagner's influence.

New review
Wagner. OPERATIC HIGHLIGHTS. [b]**Tiana Lemnitz** (sop); [b]**Torsten Ralf** (ten); [g]**Herbert Janssen** (bar); [g]**Ludwig Weber** (bass); [bg]**Royal Opera House Chorus, Covent Garden; London Philharmonic Orchestra/Sir Thomas Beecham.** Dutton Laboratories mono CDLX7007. Item marked [a] from Columbia LX557 (12/36), [b] LX645/6 (10/37, recorded live in the Royal Opera House, Covent Garden in 1936), [c] LX732/3 (9/38), [d] LX768/9 (2/39), [e] LX733 (9/38), [f] LX482 (5/36), [g] LX636/7 (9/37. Royal Opera House, 1936).
DIE MEISTERSINGER VON NURNBERG — Prelude, Act 1[a]; Da zu dir der Heiland kam[b]; Wach auf![b]; Morgenlich leuchtend[b]. DER FLIEGENDE HOLLANDER — Overture[c].
TANNHAUSER —Overture[d]; Entry of the Guests[e]. LOHENGRIN — Prelude, Act 3[f].
GOTTERDAMMERUNG[g] — Hier sitz' ich zur Wacht; Hoiho! Ihr Gibichsmannen.

Ih 9m ADD 6/94

Beecham was a lifelong Wagnerian and these superlative performances make one regret all the more that he never recorded a Wagner opera complete in the studio. The greatest 'might have been' would be a complete Covent Garden *Die Meistersinger* of 1936, when a superb cast had been assembled: given that the recording facilities were there to make the sides included here, one wonders why the rest of the opera wasn't also committed to disc. A month after those excerpts were taken live Beecham went into the studio to record his masterly account of the Prelude to Act 1. Here the whole panoply of the score is set expectantly before us. The Royal Opera House Chorus sing well, though not exceptionally so. Ralf, a compact, musical tenor sings a pleasing, poetic Prize song, for which he duly receives the crown from Lemnitz's nonpareil of an Eva, perfect trill and all. Nine days after the *Meistersinger* extracts were made, EMI were back at Covent Garden for *Götterdämmerung*. All that officially resulted were two solos, in which we hear Weber as an implacable then fiendishly celebratory Hagen. The rest of the items demonstrate Beecham's ability to inject zestful conviction into pre-*Ring* Wagner without ever overblowing the sound, as so often happens today. These readings also confirm the virtuoso calibre of his pre-war LPO, who play with a precision and character that leap from the loudspeakers with amazing freshness and vitality in these faultless transfers, not a 78rpm surface to be heard, a tribute to Dutton Laboratories' skills in using the Cedar system to best advantage.

Wagner. TANNHAUSER — Overture. Siegfried Idyll. TRISTAN UND ISOLDE — Prelude and Liebestod[a]. [a]**Jessye Norman** (sop); **Vienna Philharmonic Orchestra/Herbert von Karajan.** DG 423 613-2GH. Text and translation included. Recorded live in 1987.

54m DDD 8/88

For the Wagner specialist who has a complete *Tannhäuser* and *Tristan* on the shelves, this disc involves some duplication. Even so, it is not hard to make room for such performances as are heard here. For the non-specialist, the programme provides a good opportunity for a meeting halfway, the common ground between Master and general music-lover being the *Siegfried Idyll*. This offers 20 minutes of delight in the play of musical ideas, structured and yet impulsive, within a sustained mood of gentle affection. The orchestration is something of a miracle, and it can rarely have been heard to better advantage than in this recording, where the ever-changing textures are so clearly displayed and where from every section of the orchestra the sound is of such great loveliness. It comes as a welcome contrast to the *Tannhäuser* Overture, with its big tunes and *fortissimos*, the whole orchestra surging in a frank simulation of physical passion. A further contrast is to follow in the *Tristan* Prelude, where again Karajan and his players are at their best in their feeling for texture and their control of pulse. Jessye Norman, singing the *Liebestod* with tenderness and vibrant opulence of tone, brings the recital to an end. There is scarcely a single reminder that it was recorded live.

Additional recommendations ...

Siegfried Idyll. **Bruckner.** *Symphony No. 8 in C minor.* **Royal Concertgebouw Orchestra/ Bernard Haitink.** Philips 412 465-2PH2 — *..·* ② 1h 44m DDD 7/86 Ⓑ
Siegfried Idyll. LOHENGRIN — *Preludes* — *Acts 1 and 3.* DIE MEISTERSINGER VON NURNBERG — *Prelude, Act 1.* DIE WALKURE — *Ride of the Valkyries; Wotan's Farewell and Magic Fire Music*[a]. [a]**John Tomlinson** (bass); **Philharmonia Orchestra/Francesco d'Avalos.** ASV CDDCA666 — *..·* 1h 4m DDD 3/90 Ⓟ Ⓑ
Siegfried Idyll. **Dvořák.** *Serenade for Strings in E major, B52. Romance in F minor, B39*[a]. **Scottish Chamber Orchestra/Jaime Laredo** ([a]vn). Pickwick IMP Classics PCD928 — *..·* 1h 4m DDD 4/90 Ⓑ
Opera Choruses — DER FLIEGENDE HOLLANDER. TANNHAUSER. LOHENGRIN. DIE MEISTER-SINGER VON NÜRNBERG. GOTTERDAMMERUNG. PARSIFAL. **Bayreuth Festival Chorus and Orchestra/Wilhelm Pitz.** DG Privilege 429 169-2GR — *..·* 53m ADD 4/90 ▲
DER FLIEGENDE HOLLANDER — *Overture.* LOHENGRIN — *Prelude, Act 1.* DIE MEISTERSINGER VON NURNBERG — *Prelude, Act 1.* TANNHAUSER — *Overture and Venusberg Music.* TRISTAN UND ISOLDE — *Prelude und Liebestod.* **Berlin Philharmonic Orchestra/Seiji Ozawa.** Philips 426 271-2PH — *..·* 1h 6m DDD 4/91 Ⓢ Ⓑ
RIENZI — *Overture.* TANNHAUSER — *Overture; Venusberg Music.* DIE MEISTERSINGER VON NURNBERG —*Prelude, Act 1.* LOHENGRIN — *Prelude Act 3.* DER FLIEGENDE HOLLANDER — *Overture.* **Orchestra of the Metropolitan Opera, New York/James Levine.** DG 435 874-2GH — *..·* 1h DDD 10/93 Ⓑ
TANNHAUSER — *Overture*[a]. LOHENGRIN — *Prelude, Act 1.* DIE WALKURE — *Ride of the Valkyries*[a]. GOTTERDAMMERUNG — *Prelude and Siegfried's Rhine Journey*[a]; *Siegfried's Funeral March; Starke Scheite*[b]. DER FLIEGENDE HOLLANDER — *Overture*[a]. TRISTAN UND ISOLDE — *Prelude and Liebestod*[c]. DIE MEISTERSINGER VON NURNBERG[a] — *Preludes* — *Acts 1 and 3; Dance of the Apprentices.* PARSIFAL — *Prelude and Good Friday Music*[c]. [b]**Kirsten Flagstad** (sop); [a]**Vienna Philharmonic Orchestra,** [b]**Philharmonia Orchestra,** [c]**Berlin Philharmonic Orchestra/ Wilhelm Furtwängler.** EMI Références mono CHS7 64935-2 — *..·* ② 2h 24m ADD 4/94 Ⓑ ▲

Wagner. RIENZI. **René Kollo** (ten) Cola Rienzi; **Siv Wennberg** (sop) Irene; **Janis Martin** (sop) Adriano; **Theo Adam** (bass) Paolo Orsini; **Nikolaus Hillebrand** (bass) Steffano Colonna; **Siegfried Vogel** (bass) Raimondo; **Peter Schreier** (ten) Baroncelli; **Günther Leib** (bass) Cecco del Vecchio; **Ingeborg Springer** (sop) Messenger of Peace; **Leipzig Radio Chorus; Dresden State Opera Chorus; Staatskapelle Dresden/Heinrich Hollreiser.** EMI CMS7 63980-2. Notes, text and translation included. From SLS990 (11/76). Recorded 1974-76.

..· ③ 3h 45m ADD 2/92

Rienzi is grand opera with a vengeance. Political imperatives count for more than mere human feelings, and politics means ceremony as well as warfare: marches, ballet music and extended choruses are much in evidence, while even the solo arias often have the rhetorical punch of political harangues. It could all be an enormous bore. Yet the young Wagner, basing his work on Bulwer Lytton's story of the tragic Roman tribune, did manage to move beyond mere tub-thumping into a degree of intensity that — for those with ears to hear — prefigures the mature genius to come. In the end, Rienzi himself is more than just a political animal, and the existential anguish of Tannhäuser, Tristan and even Amfortas glimmers in the distance. It would be idle to pretend that this performance is ideal in every respect, either musically, or as a recording. But its virtues outweigh its weaknesses by a considerable margin. Siv Wennberg was not in best voice at the time, but the other principals, notably René Kollo and Janis Martin, bring commendable stamina and conviction to their demanding roles. Above all the conductor Heinrich Hollreiser prevents the more routine material from sounding merely mechanical, and ensures that the whole work has a truly Wagnerian sweep and fervour. Moreover, it is the only complete recording in the current edition of *The Classical Catalogue*.

Wagner. DER FLIEGENDE HOLLÄNDER. **Robert Hale** (bass-bar) Holländer; **Hildegard Behrens** (sop) Senta; **Kurt Rydl** (bass) Daland; **Josef Protschka** (ten) Erik; **Iris Vermillion** (mez) Mary; **Uwe Heilmann** (ten) Steuermann; **Vienna State Opera Concert Choir; Vienna Philharmonic Orchestra/Christoph von Dohnányi.** Decca 436 418-2DHO2. Notes, text and translation included. Recorded in 1991.

② 2h 25m DDD 4/94

Singers, conductor, chorus, orchestra and engineers combine to make this the most successful recording of the work to date. In consequence its revolutionary character is fully realized. With the Vienna Philharmonic responding to Dohnányi's precise and energizing beat from start to finish the sea does really seem to course through the score as Wagner intended. Dohnányi emphasizes the raw, even untutored sound of much of the orchestration, giving the wind and brass the prominence they deserve. Taut, springy rhythms abound from the Overture onwards. He opts for the three-act version and the full ending. Hale is an exemplary Dutchman and sings with great depth and understanding. This is evident throughout a masterly traversal of his long monologue, where the required torment in the tone is revealed to the full. Behrens captures Senta's single-minded passion and infatuation, singing the quieter passages with refined sensitivity, the forceful ones with fearless attack; and satisfaction extends to the lesser roles. The chorus are superb as sailors, ghost crew and townspeople, singing with firm tone and exact attack. Nothing here is left unconsidered yet, amazingly, for the most part a real sense of the theatre is achieved throughout. For that we have to thank the Decca team. Balance, depth, perspectives all seem blessedly natural; undoctored and inevitable, so that one is able to take the sound-picture for granted.

Additional recommendations …
Soloists; Bayreuth Festival Chorus and Orchestra/Woldemar Nelsson. Philips 434 599-2PH2 — ② 2h 14m DDD 10/92
Soloists; Bayreuth Festival Chorus and Orchestra/Karl Böhm. DG 437 710-2GX2 — ② 2h 14m ADD 8/93
Soloists; Austrian Radio Chorus and Symphony Orchestra/Pinchas Steinberg. Naxos 8 660025/6 — ② 2h 19m DDD 9/93

Wagner. TANNHAUSER (Paris version). **Plácido Domingo** (ten) Tannhäuser; **Cheryl Studer** (sop) Elisabeth; **Andreas Schmidt** (bar) Wolfram; **Agnes Baltsa** (mez) Venus; **Matti Salminen** (bass) Hermann; **William Pell** (ten) Walther; **Kurt Rydl** (bass) Biterolf; **Clemens Biber** (ten) Heinrich; **Oskar Hillebrandt** (bass) Reinmar; **Barbara Bonney** (sop) Shepherd Boy; **Chorus of the Royal Opera House, Covent Garden; Philharmonia Orchestra/ Giuseppe Sinopoli.** DG 427 625-2GH3. Notes, text and translation included.

③ 2h 56m DDD 9/89

Plácido Domingo's Tannhäuser is a success in almost every respect. He evokes the erotic passion of the Venusberg scene and brings to it just the right touch of nervous energy. This is boldly contrasted with the desperation and bitterness of the Rome Narration after the hero's fruitless visit to the Pope seeking forgiveness: Domingo's description of how Tannhäuser avoided every earthly delight on his pilgrimage is delivered with total conviction. In between he berates the slightly prissy attitude of his fellow knights on the Wartburg with the dangerous conceit of someone who knows a secret delight that they will never enjoy in their measured complacency. His tenor must be the steadiest and most resplendent ever to have tackled the part, although his German is far from idiomatic with several vowel sounds distorted. Baltsa also has some problems with her German, but she has the range and attack, particularly in the upper register, for an awkwardly lying part. Here comparisons have to be made with Christa Ludwig for Solti (listed below), in one of her most successful assumptions. She is not only more familiar with the role but also has the more voluptuous voice and is superbly seconded by Solti; which brings us to Sinopoli. It is obviously his concern throughout to bring out every last ounce of the drama in the piece, both in terms of orchestral detail, which receives very special attention from the Overture, given a big, full-blooded reading, onwards, but also in his awareness in this opera of the longer line, often sustained by the upper strings. The Philharmonia's violins respond with their most eloquent playing. The kind of frisson Sinopoli offers is evident in the anticipatory excitement at the start of Act 2 and the iron control he maintains in the big ensemble later in the same act. Cheryl Studer's secure, beautiful voice has no difficulty coping with Sinopoli's deliberate tempos. She takes her part with total conviction, both vocal and interpretative, phrasing with constant intelligence. Andreas Schmidt is a mellifluous, concerned Wolfram, Salminen a rugged, characterful Landgrave and Barbara Bonney an ideally fresh Shepherd Boy. As knights, ladies and pilgrims the Covent Garden Chorus sing with consistent beauty of sound, and have been sensibly balanced with the orchestra. As Sinopoli has chosen to conduct the Paris version, the Solti set is its main rival. It has always been one of Solti's most recommendable opera recordings, and in its CD format it remains a formidable achievement. Domingo and Studer, however, incline one towards this version, as does the wide range of the finely engineered recording, which makes the excellent Decca seem just a shade dated.

Additional recommendation ...
Soloists; Vienna Boys' Choir; Vienna State Opera Chorus; Vienna Philharmonic Orchestra/Sir Georg Solti. Decca 414 581-2DH3 — .·' ③ 2/86 ॰ᵖ

New review
Wagner. LOHENGRIN. **Paul Frey** (ten) Lohengrin; **Cheryl Studer** (sop) Elsa of Brabant; **Gabriele Schnaut** (sop) Ortrud; **Ekkehard Wlaschiha** (bar) Telramund; **Manfred Schenk** (bass) King Henry; **Eike Wilm Schulte** (bar) Herald; **Bayreuth Festival Chorus and Orchestra/Peter Schneider.** Philips 434 602-2PH4. Recorded in 1990.

.·' ④ 3h 32m DDD 10/92

This is a splendidly absorbing performance of *Lohengrin*. The underrated Schneider conducts a straightforward, no-nonsense reading in the best Kapellmeister tradition, avoiding the extremes of tempo interpretation of some more highly-powered conductors. He obtains playing and singing of the highest calibre from the Bayreuth orchestra and chorus, sustains the long and sometimes tedious-seeming paragraphs of Acts 1 and 2 without ever allowing boredom to intervene, and brings extraordinary tension to such forward-looking scenes as Lohengrin's arrival, the Ortrud-Telramund dialogue and the psychologically intense duet for Elsa and Lohengrin in Act 3. Elsa was one of the roles with which Studer made her name on the international scene; she sings it here once more with refulgent tone, understanding of the text and comprehension of Elsa's dreamy then troubled personality. Particularly affecting is her desperate appeal to Lohengrin at the end of Act 2. Paul Frey is a sensitive, chivalrous Lohengrin, even if his voice hasn't quite the Heldentenor strength of some of his predecessors. Evil is reasonably well represented. Wlaschiha is a vital and nasty Telramund, keenly projecting the character's chip-on-the-shoulder malevolence of the words. Schnaut has an imposing, powerful soprano although more could have been made of the words than she achieves. Schenk is a well-routined King, Schulte a superb Herald. Incidentally, Schneider observes the traditional (Wagner's) cut just before Lohengrin's Farewell, although the passage is printed in full in the booklet. This set is well worth considering in a sparse recommendable field of available versions.

Wagner. TRISTAN UND ISOLDE. **Wolfgang Windgassen** (ten) Tristan; **Birgit Nilsson** (sop) Isolde; **Christa Ludwig** (mez) Brangäne; **Eberhard Waechter** (bar) Kurwenal; **Martti Talvela** (bass) King Marke; **Claude Heater** (ten) Melot; **Peter Schreier** (ten) Sailor; **Erwin**

Wohlfahrt (ten) Shepherd; **Gerd Nienstedt** (bass) Helmsman; **Bayreuth Festival Chorus and Orchestra/Karl Böhm.** Philips 434 425-2PH3. From DG 419 889-2GH3 (7/88). Notes, text and translation included. Recorded live in 1966.

③ 3h 39m ADD 10/91

Böhm's recording is a live Bayreuth performance of distinction, for on stage are the most admired Tristan and Isolde of their time, and in the pit the 72-year-old conductor directs a performance which is unflagging in its passion and energy. Böhm has a striking way in the Prelude and *Liebestod* of making the swell of passion seem like the movement of a great sea, sometimes with gentle motion, sometimes with the breaking of the mightiest of waves. Nilsson characterizes strongly and her voice with its marvellous cleaving-power can also soften quite beautifully. Windgassen's heroic performance in the Third Act is in some ways the crown of his achievements on record, even though the voice has dried and aged a little. Christa Ludwig is the ideal Brangäene, Waechter a suitably-forthright Kurwenal, and Talvela an expressive, noble-voiced Marke. Orchestra and chorus are at their finest.

Additional recommendations ...
Soloists; Bavarian Radio Chorus and Symphony Orchestra/Leonard Bernstein. Philips 438 241-2PH4 — ④ 4h 26m DDD
Soloists; Chorus of the Royal Opera House, Covent Garden; Philharmonia Orchestra/Wilhelm Furtwängler. EMI mono CDS7 47322-8 — ④ 3h 56m ADD 5/86 ▲
Soloists; Chorus of the Royal Opera House, Covent Garden; London Philharmonic Orchestra/Fritz Reiner, Sir Thomas Beecham. EMI Références mono CHS7 64037-2 — ③ 3h 32m ADD 1/92 ▲

New review
Wagner. DIE MEISTERSINGER VON NURNBERG. **Bernd Weikl** (bar) Hans Sachs; **Ben Heppner** (ten) Walther; **Cheryl Studer** (sop) Eva; **Kurt Moll** (bass) Pogner; **Siegfried Lorenz** (bar) Beckmesser; **Deon van der Walt** (ten) David; **Cornelia Kallisch** (contr) Magdalene; **Hans-Joachim Ketelsen** (bar) Kothner; **Michael Schade** (ten) Vogelgesang; **Hans Wilbrink** (bar) Nachtigall; **Ulrich Ress** (ten) Zorn; **Hermann Sapell** (bar) Eisslinger; **Roland Wagenführer** (ten) Moser; **Rainer Büse** (bass) Ortel; **Guido Götzen** (bass) Schwarz; **Friedmann Kunder** (bass) Foltz; **René Pape** (bass) Nightwatchman; **Bavarian State Opera Chorus; Bavarian State Orchestra/Wolfgang Sawallisch.** EMI CDS5 55142-2. Notes, text and translation included.

④ 4h 17m DDD 8/94

It is, surprisingly, 19 years since we had a new recording of Wagner's great comedy, although in the meantime several old and/or historic sets have been reissued or have appeared for the first time. We needed a new, carefully prepared performance employing modern technology, and here we have it. It is very much a version for today — profoundly musical, as it was bound to be under Sawallisch, sung with a consistent beauty of sound perhaps encountered in no other version, and recorded truly and spaciously. Anybody coming to the work for the first time, and wanting a version backed by modern sound, will find it a sensible choice, a performance for the most part measuring up to the score's many demands on its interpreters. Working with what were then his own Bavarian State Opera forces, Sawallisch obtains singing and playing on the highest level of achievement, observant of detail, rich in texture, sure in pacing and — very important in this score — anxious to move forward where there is any danger of the music seeming over-extended, as in the recital of the tones and the Act 2 episode of Beckmesser's courting. Sawallisch's reading also catches the warmth that pervades the whole opera, yet is also successful in deftly projecting its comedy. It must be said, however, that with Sawallisch the earth doesn't move, the spirit is seldom lifted as it should be — and can be, witness Karajan (until this edition, the *Guide*'s top recommendation, now sadly deleted) and Abendroth. On the other hand, nobody is better than Sawallisch at characterizing the disputes between the Masters in Act 1, or the pointed humour of the Act 2 Sachs/Beckmesser scene, and much else of that nature is unobtrusively right. Where the recording itself is concerned, great care has been taken over the placing of the singers in relation to one another and the correct distancing of the voices where called for. The balance in relation to the orchestra seems just about ideal. In the modern manner the chorus is placed a little too far back. Karajan's Dresden account would present a strong challenge to the newcomer were it available, and the inspiriting, marvellously sincere Hermann Abendroth (what feeling in every bar here!). None of these is so note perfect, so exact or well considered as the Sawallisch, but thay all suggest that frisson of a live performance occasionally missing in the new set. Even so, Sawallisch takes an honoured place in this company and context. His reading is full of thoughtful *apercus* and natural flow, and displays a sensible overview of the score. Vocally it will satisfy all but those with the most demanding tastes in, and/or, long experience in Wagnerian interpretation.

Additional recommendation ...
Soloists; Bayreuth Festival Chorus and Orchestra/Hermann Abendroth. Preiser mono 90174 — .·' ④ 4h 22m ADD 2/94 ⁹ₚ ▲

New review
Wagner. DAS RHEINGOLD. **John Tomlinson** (bass) Wotan; **Linda Finnie** (mez) Fricka; **Graham Clark** (ten) Loge; **Helmut Pampuch** (ten) Mime; **Günter von Kannen** (bar) Alberich; **Eva Johansson** (sop) Freia; **Kurt Schreibmayer** (ten) Froh; **Bodo Brinkmann** (bar) Donner; **Birgitta Svendén** (mez) Erda; **Matthias Hölle** (bass) Fasolt; **Philip Kang** (bass) Fafner; **Hilde Leidland** (sop) Woglinde; **Annette Küttenbaum** (mez) Wellgunde; **Jane Turner** (mez) Flosshilde; **Bayreuth Festival Orchestra/Daniel Barenboim.** Teldec 4509-91185-2. Notes, text and translation included. Recorded live in 1991.

.·' ② 2h 29m DDD 10/93 ⁹ₚ Ⓑ

New review
Wagner. DIE WALKURE. **Poul Elming** (ten) Siegmund; **Nadine Secunde** (sop) Sieglinde; **Anne Evans** (sop) Brünnhilde; **John Tomlinson** (bass) Wotan; **Linda Finnie** (mez) Fricka, Siegrune; **Matthias Hölle** (bass) Hunding; **Eva Johansson** (sop) Gerhilde; **Eva-Maria Bundschuh** (sop) Helmwige; **Ruth Floeren** (sop) Ortlinde; **Shirley Close** (mez) Waltraute; **Hebe Dijkstra** (mez) Rossweisse; **Birgitta Svendén** (mez) Grimgerde; **Hitomi Katagiri** (mez) Schwertleite; **Bayreuth Festival Orchestra/Daniel Barenboim.** Teldec 4509 91186-2. Recorded live in 1992.

.·' ④ 3h 53m DDD 10/93 ⁹ₚ Ⓑ

These are enthralling performances. Tomlinson's volatile Wotan is the most potent reading here. He manages to sing every word with insistent meaning and forceful declamation while maintaining a firm legato. His German is so idiomatic that he might have been speaking the language his whole life and he brings breadth and distinction of phrase to his solos at the close of both operas. Anne Evans has a single, important advantage over other recent Brunnhildes in that her voice is wholly free from wobble and she never makes an ugly sound. Hers is a light, girlish, honest portrayal, sung with unfailing musicality if not with the ultimate insights. Linda Finnie is an articulate, sharp-edged Fricka, and Graham Clark a sparky, incisive Loge. Nadine Secunde's impassioned Sieglinde is matched by the vital, exciting Siegmund of Poul Elming and Matthias Hölle as both Hunding and Fasolt is another of those black basses of which Germany seems to have an inexhaustible supply. The whole of *Das Rheingold* is magnificently conducted by Barenboim, a more expansive Wagnerian than Böhm. By 1991 he had the full measure of its many facets, brought immense authority and power to building its huge climaxes, yet finds all the lightness of touch for the mercurial and/or diaphanous aspects of this amazing score. He has the inestimable advantage of a Bayreuth orchestra at the peak of their form, surpassing — and this says much — even the Metropolitan orchestra for Levine, and Barenboim's reading is more convincing as a whole than Levine's. Similar qualities inform his interpretation of *Die Walküre*. Barenboim has now learnt how to match the epic stature of Wagner's mature works, how to pace them with an overview of the whole and there is an incandescent, metaphysical feeling of a Furwänglerian kind in his treatment of such passages as Wotan's anger and the Valkyrie ride. Again, the orchestra are superb. They are backed by a recording of startling presence and depth, amply capturing the Bayreuth acoustic.

Additional recommendations ...
Das Rheingold. **Soloists; Bavarian Radio Symphony Orchestra/Bernard Haitink.** EMI CDS7 49853-2 — .·' ② 2h 29m DDD 12/89 ⁹ₚ Ⓑ
Das Rheingold. **Soloists; Metropolitan Opera Orchestra/James Levine.** DG 427 607-2GH3 — .·' ③ 2h 37m DDD 7/90 Ⓑ
Die Walküre. **Soloists; Bayreuth Festival Orchestra/Clemens Krauss.** Foyer mono 4-CF2008 — .·' ④ 3h 32m ADD 6/88 ⁹ₚ Ⓑ ▲

| *See also Karl Böhm's versions reviewed below.*

Wagner. DER RING DES NIBELUNGEN.
DAS RHEINGOLD. **Theo Adam** (bass-bar) Wotan; **Annelies Burmeister** (mez) Fricka;
Wolfgang Windgassen (ten) Loge; **Erwin Wohlfahrt** (ten) Mime; **Gustav Neidlinger**
(bass) Alberich; **Anja Silja** (sop) Freia; **Hermin Esser** (ten) Froh; **Gerd Nienstedt** (bass)
Donner; **Vera Soukupova** (mez) Erda; **Martti Talvela** (bass) Fasolt; **Kurt Boehme** (bass)
Fafner; **Dorothea Siebert** (sop) Woglinde; **Helga Dernesch** (sop) Wellgunde; **Ruth Hesse**
(mez) Flosshilde; **Bayreuth Festival Chorus and Orchestra/Karl Böhm.** Philips 412 475-
2PH2. Notes, text and translation included. Recorded at a performance in the Festpielhaus,
Bayreuth in 1967. From 6747 037 (9/73). Recorded in 1967.

 ② 2h 17m ADD 7/85

DIE WALKÜRE. **James King** (ten) Siegmund; **Leonie Rysanek** (sop) Sieglinde; **Birgit
Nilsson** (sop) Brünnhilde; **Theo Adam** (bass) Wotan; **Annelies Burmeister** (mez) Fricka,
Siegrune; **Gerd Nienstedt** (bass) Hunding; **Danica Mastilovic** (sop) Gerhilde; **Liane Synek**
(sop) Helmwige; **Helga Dernesch** (sop) Ortlinde; **Gertraud Hopf** (mez) Waltraute; **Sona
Cervená** (mez) Rossweisse; **Elisabeth Schärtel** (contr) Grimgerde; **Sieglinde Wagner**
(contr) Schwertleite; **Bayreuth Festival Chorus and Orchestra/Karl Böhm.** Philips 412
478-2PH4. Notes, text and translation included. Recorded live in 1967. From 6747 037 (9/73).

④ 3h 30m ADD 2/85

SIEGFRIED. **Wolfgang Windgassen** (ten) Siegfried; **Theo Adam** (bass) Wanderer; **Birgit
Nilsson** (sop) Brünnhilde; **Erwin Wohlfahrt** (ten) Mime; **Gustav Neidlinger** (bass)
Alberich; **Vera Soukupova** (mez) Erda; **Kurt Boehme** (bass) Fafner; **Erika Köth** (sop)
Woodbird; **Bayreuth Festival Orchestra/Karl Böhm.** Philips 412 483-2PH4. Notes, text
and translation included. Recorded live in 1967. From 6747 037 (9/73).

④ 3h 43m ADD 8/85

GOTTERDAMMERUNG. **Birgit Nilsson** (sop) Brünnhilde; **Wolfgang Windgassen** (ten)
Siegfried; **Josef Greindl** (bass) Hagen; **Gustav Neidlinger** (bass-bar) Alberich; **Thomas
Stewart** (bar) Gunther; **Ludmila Dvořáková** (sop) Gutrune; **Martha Mödl** (mez)
Waltraute; **Dorothea Siebert** (sop) Woglinde; **Helga Dernesch** (sop) Wellgunde; **Sieglinde
Wagner** (contr) Flosshilde; **Marga Höffgen** (contr) First Norn; **Annelies Burmeister** (mez)
Second Norn; **Anja Silja** (sop) Third Norn; **Bayreuth Festival Chorus and Orchestra/
Karl Böhm.** Philips 412 488-2PH4. Notes, text and translation included. Recorded live in
1967. From 6747 037 (9/73).

④ 4h 9m ADD 5/85

Wagner's *Der Ring des Nibelungen* is the greatest music-drama ever penned. It deals with the
eternal questions of power, love, personal responsibility and moral behaviour, and has always
been open to numerous interpretations, both dramatic and musical. For every generation, it
presents a new challenge, yet certain musical performances have undoubtedly stood the test of
time. One would recommend the recording made at Bayreuth in 1967 because, above all others,
it represents a true and living account of a huge work as it was performed in the opera house
for which it was largely conceived. Every artist who appears at Bayreuth seems to find an extra
dedication in their comportment there, and on this occasion many of the singers and the
conductor surpassed what they achieved elsewhere. Böhm's reading is notable for its dramatic
drive and inner tension. For the most part he also encompasses the metaphysical aspects of the
score as well, and he procures playing of warmth and depth from the Bayreuth orchestra. Birgit
Nilsson heads the cast as an unsurpassed Brünnhilde, wonderfully vivid in her characterization
and enunciation, tireless and gleaming in voice. Wolfgang Windgassen is equally committed and
alert as her Siegfried and Theo Adam is an experienced, worldly-wise Wotan. No *Ring* recording
is perfect or could possibly tell the whole story but this faithfully recorded, straightforward
version conveys the strength and force of the epic's meaning.

Additional recommendations ...
DER RING DES NIBELUNGEN. **Vienna State Opera Chorus; Vienna Philharmonic
Orchestra/Sir Georg Solti.** Decca 414 100-2DM15 — ①⑤ 14h 37m ADD 3/89 ▲
DER RING DES NIBELUNGEN. **Soloists; Chorus and Orchestra of RAI, Rome/Wilhelm
Furtwängler.** EMI mono CZS7 67123-2 — ①③ 15h 2m ADD 2/91 ▲
DAS RHEINGOLD. **Soloists; Bayreuth Festival Orchestra/Clemens Krauss.** Foyer mono
3-CF2007 — ③ 2h 25m ADD 6/88 ▲

DIE WALKURE. **Soloists; Bayreuth Festival Orchestra/Clemens Krauss.** Foyer mono
4-CF2008 — .·' ④ 3h 32m ADD 6/88 ⁹ₚ Ⓑ ▲
SIEGFRIED. **Soloists; Bayreuth Festival Orchestra/Clemens Krauss.** Foyer mono
4-CF2009 — .·' ④ 3h 57m ADD 6/88 ⁹ₚ Ⓑ ▲
SIEGFRIED (sung in English). **Soloists; Sadler's Wells Opera Orchestra/Sir Reginald
Goodall.** EMI CMS7 63595-2 — .·' ④ 4h 38m ADD 3/91 ⁹ₚ Ⓑ
GOTTERDAMMERUNG. **Soloists; Bayreuth Festival Orchestra/Clemens Krauss.** Foyer
mono 4-CF2010 — .·' ④ 4h 20m ADD 6/88 ⁹ₚ Ⓑ ▲
GOTTERDAMMERUNG. **Soloists; Metropolitan Opera Chorus and Orchestra/James
Levine.** DG 429 385-2GH4 — .·' ④ 4h 30m DDD 8/91 ⁹ₚ Ⓑ
GOTTERDAMMERUNG (sung in English). **Soloists; English National Opera Chorus and
Orchestra/Sir Reginald Goodall.** EMI CMS7 64244-2 — .·' ⑤ ADD 11/92 ⁹ₚ Ⓑ
GOTTERDAMMERUNG — excerpts. **Soloists; English National Opera Chorus and
Orchestra/Sir Reginald Goodall.** EMI CMS7 64244-2 — .·' 1h 6m ADD 11/93 Ⓑ

Wagner. PARSIFAL. **Jess Thomas** (ten) Parsifal; **George London** (bass-bar) Amfortas;
Hans Hotter (bass) Gurnemanz; **Irene Dalis** (mez) Kundry; **Gustav Neidlinger** (bass)
Klingsor; **Martti Talvela** (bass) Titurel; **Niels Möller** (ten) First Knight; **Gerd Neinstedt**
(bass) Second Knight; **Sona Cervená** (mez), **Ursula Boese** (contr), **Gerhard Stolze, Georg
Paskuda** (tens) Squires; **Gundula Janowitz, Anja Silja, Else-Margrete Gardelli,
Dorothea Siebert, Rita Bartos** (sops), **Sona Cervená** (mez) Flower Maidens; **Bayreuth
Festival Chorus and Orchestra/Hans Knappertsbusch.** Philips 416 390-2PH4. Notes,
text and translation included. Recorded live in 1962. From SAL3475 (11/64).

.·' ④ 4h 10m ADD 6/86 ⁹ₚ

There have been many fine recordings of this great Eastertide opera, but none have so
magnificently captured the power, the spiritual grandeur, the human frailty and the almost
unbearable beauty of the work as Hans Knappertsbusch. This live recording has a cast that has
few equals. Hotter is superb, fleshing out Gurnemanz with a depth of insight that has never been
surpassed. London's Amfortas captures the frightening sense of impotence and anguish with
painful directness whilst Thomas's Parsifal grows as the performance progresses and is no mean
achievement. Dalis may lack that final degree of sensuousness but gives a fine interpretation.
Throughout Knappertsbusch exercises a quite unequalled control over the proceedings; it is a
fine testament to a great conductor. The Bayreuth acoustic is well reproduced and all in all it is
a profound and moving experience.

Additional recommendations ...
**Soloists; Berlin State Opera Chorus; Berlin Philharmonic Orchestra/Daniel
Barenboim.** Teldec 9031-74448-2 — .·' ④ 4h 16m DDD 10/91 ⁹ₚ ⁹ₛ
Soloists; Bayreuth Festival Chorus and Orchestra/Hans Knappertsbusch. Teldec
Historic Series mono 9031-76047-2 — .·' ④ 4h 32m ADD 8/93 ⁹ₚ ▲

Charles Waldteufel
French 1837-1915

Suggested listening ...

Waltzes — España. Les patineurs. Estudiantina. Acclamations. *Coupled with* **Offenbach.** Gaîteé
parisienne[a]. **Monte-Carlo Philharmonic Orchestra/[a]Manuel Rosenthal, Willy
Boskovsky.** EMI Studio CDM7 63136-2 (12/89).

Johann Gottfried Walther
German 1684-1748

Suggested listening ...

Concertos — del Signor Torelli; del Signor Taglietti; del Signor Telemann in G major and
C minor; del Signor Meck. *Chorale Preludes* — Herr Jesu Christ, ich weiss gar wohl; Es ist das

Heil uns kommen her; Hilf mir Gott, dass mir's gelinge; Herr Gott, nun schleuss der Himmel auf; Schmücke dich, o liebe Seele. *Partita — Jesu meine Freude.* **Stephen Farr.** Meridian CDE84213 (8/92).

William Walton

British 1902-1983

Walton. Violin Concerto. Viola Concerto. **Nigel Kennedy** (vn, va); **Royal Philharmonic Orchestra/André Previn.** EMI CDC7 49628-2. From EL749628-1 (1/88).

57m DDD 4/88

These Concertos are among the most beautiful written this century. Walton was in his late twenties when he composed the viola work and in it he achieved a depth of emotion, a range of ideas and a technical assurance beyond anything he had so far written. Lacking in the brilliance of the violin, the viola has an inherently contemplative tonal quality and Walton matches this to perfection in his score, complementing it rather than trying to compensate as other composers have done. There is a larger element of virtuosity in the Violin Concerto, but it is never allowed to dominate the musical argument. Nigel Kennedy gives wonderfully warm and characterful performances which are likely to stand unchallenged as a coupling for a long time. He produces a beautiful tone quality on both of his instruments, which penetrates to the heart of the aching melancholy of Walton's slow music, and he combines it with an innate, highly developed and spontaneous-sounding sense of rhythmic drive and bounce which propels the quick movements forward with great panache. Previn has long been a persuasive Waltonian and the RPO respond marvellously, with crisp and alert playing throughout. The recordings are very clear and naturally balanced with the solo instrument set in a believable perspective.

Additional recommendation ...
Violin Concerto. Violin Sonata. Two Pieces. **Lydia Mordkovitch** (vn); **London Philharmonic Orchestra/Jan Latham-Koenig.** Chandos CHAN9073 — 1h 9m DDD 10/92

New review
Walton. Façade — Suites Nos. 1-3[a]. Siesta[b]. Sinfonia Concertante[ca]. Portsmouth Point[a].
Arnold. Popular Birthday[a]. [c]**Eric Parkin** (pf); **London Philharmonic Orchestra/**[a]**Jan Latham-König,** [b]**Bryden Thomson.** Chandos CHAN9148. Recorded 1990-92.

59m DDD 1/94

The *Sinfonia Concertante* (1926-7) with its sharply memorable ideas in each movement and characteristically high voltage, has never had the attention it deserves, and that is all the more regrettable when there is such a dearth of attractive British piano concertos. The soloist, Eric Parkin, is perfectly attuned to the idiom, warmly melodic as well as jazzily syncopated. He points rhythms infectiously and shapes melodies persuasively, though the recording sets the piano a little backwardly, no doubt to reflect the idea that this is not a full concerto. Jan Latham-König proves most understanding of the composer's 1920s idiom, giving the witty *Façade* movements just the degree of jazzy freedom they need. The Third Suite, devised and arranged by Christopher Palmer, draws on three apt movements from the *Façade* entertainment, ending riotously with the rag-music of "Something lies beyond the scene". That is a first recording, and so is Constant Lambert's arrangement of the Overture, *Portsmouth Point. Siesta* is given an aptly cool performance under Thomson, and the *Popular Birthday* is Malcolm Arnold's fragmentary linking of *Happy Birthday to You* with the "Popular Song" from *Façade,* originally written for Walton's seventieth birthday. The impact of some of the pieces, notably in *Façade,* would have been even sharper, had the warmly atmospheric Chandos recording placed the orchestra a fraction closer.

Walton. ORCHESTRAL WORKS. **London Philharmonic Orchestra/Bryden Thomson.** Chandos CHAN8968.

Overtures — Johannesburg Festival; Portsmouth Point; Scapino. Capriccio burlesco. The First Shoot (orch. Palmer). Granada Prelude. Prologo e Fantasia. Music for Children. Galop final (orch. Palmer).

Ih 10m DDD 11/91

While enthusiasts for Walton's music may justifiably complain that there is not enough of it, they usually concede that what there is is readily available in good recorded performances. However, thanks to the dedicated and skilful work of Christopher Palmer, still more of it is now coming to light. How many people, one wonders, have ever heard *The First Shoot*, a miniature ballet written for a C.B. Cochran show in 1935, the *Granada Prelude* devised for that television company in the 1960s, or the *Prologo e Fantasia* which was the composer's last work, written for Rostropovich and his National Symphony Orchestra of Washington. Such fresh and welcome goodies as these appear along with familiar material such as the splendidly open-air, nautical overture *Portsmouth Point* that Walton wrote nearly 40 years earlier at the very start of his career. The Cochran piece, as orchestrated by Palmer, has five little sections that are delightfully jazzy in a way that recalls *Façade* and one's only regret is that there's not more of it. All this music is in the excellent hands of Bryden Thomson and the LPO, and Palmer's booklet essay is a model of stylish, informative writing. The recording is richly toned in the successful Chandos style, which takes some edge off the composer's characteristically sharp scoring but is still most enjoyable.

Walton. Symphony No. 1 in B flat minor. Cello Concerto[a]. [a]**Lynn Harrell** (vc); **City of Birmingham Symphony Orchestra/Simon Rattle.** EMI British Composers CDC7 54572-2. Recorded 1990-91.

Ih 14m DDD 12/92

Simon Rattle's version of Walton's First Symphony is as intelligent and dynamic a traversal as one would expect from this talented figure. Texturally speaking, the inner workings of Walton's score are laid bare as never before, aided by what sounds like a meticulously prepared CBSO. Some may find a touch of contrivance about Rattle's control of dynamics in the scorching first movement, but there's absolutely no gainsaying the underlying tension or cumulative power of the whole. Under Rattle the *Scherzo* darts menacingly (the most convincing account of this music since the classic 1966 Previn account), whilst the slow movement is an unusually nervy, anxious affair. Certainly, the finale is superbly athletic and lithe, though by now one is beginning to register that EMI's sonics are, for all their transparency and natural perspective, perhaps a little lightweight for such enormously red-blooded inspiration. Overall, though, Rattle's is a very strong account – indisputably one of the finest we've had in recent years – and his disc's claims are enhanced by the coupling, a wholly admirable performance of the same composer's luxuriant Cello Concerto. Here Rattle and Lynn Harrell form an inspired partnership, totally dedicated and achieving utter concentration throughout — no mean feat in this of all works, whose predominantly slow-moving progress demands so much from both performers and listeners.

Additional recommendations ...
Nos. *1*[a] . *2*[b]. [a]**London Philharmonic Orchestra,** [b]**London Symphony Orchestra/ Sir Charles Mackerras.** EMI Eminence CD-EMX2206 — Ih 14m DDD 12/89
No. 1. **Vaughan Williams.** *The Wasps — Overture.* **London Symphony Orchestra/André Previn.** RCA Victor Gold Seal GD87830 — 52m ADD 2/89
No. 1[a]. *Viola Concerto*[b]. *Façade — excerpts*[c]. [b]**Frederick Riddle** (va); [c]**Dora Stevens** (sop); [c]**Hubert Foss** (pf); **London Symphony Orchestra/**[a]**Hamilton Harty,** [b]**Sir William Walton.** Dutton Laboratories mono CDAX8003 — Ih 12m ADD 12/93 ▲

Walton. Symphonies — No. 1 in B flat minor; No. 2. **Royal Philharmonic Orchestra/ Vladimir Ashkenazy.** Decca 433 703-2DH. Recorded in 1991.

Ih 12m DDD 4/93

Even in the face of intense competition from the similarly coupled EMI Eminence issue with Sir Charles Mackerras, Ashkenazy's pairing has a lot going for it. Although not quite as glowingly rich as some of this company's previous efforts from Walthamstow Assembly Hall, Decca's production is a splendidly analytical affair, and the ear revels in the thrilling amount of detail captured by the engineers in these superbly orchestrated scores. The RPO, too, respond with no little dash or commitment; certainly, the *Scherzo* of the First Symphony is delivered with impressive poise and rhythmic (indeed almost balletic) flair, and if one might crave a rather larger, more refulgent body of string tone on occasion (as in the gorgeous Mediterranean seascape which comprises the Second Symphony's slow movement), the brass playing has exemplary thrust and flashing brilliance throughout. Ashkenazy's conception of the First is laudably clear-sighted and undisruptive. What's missing, however, is simply that last ounce of crackling tension one finds on rival readings from the likes of Rattle, Mackerras and, above all, Previn (see above). Indeed, the last-mentioned's blistering 1966 LSO account remains pre-eminent, and in the Second, too, many will understandably prefer the greater emotional pungency of Mackerras and sheer orchestral spectacle of George Szell's famous Cleveland recording from 1961 (listed below). Still, the present coupling is a generous one, and no-one will be disappointed with either Ashkenazy's achievement here nor the impact of the Decca engineering.

Additional recommendation …
No. 2. Partita. Variations on a Theme by Hindemith. **Cleveland Orchestra/George Szell.** CBS Masterworks CD46732 — .•' Ih 5m ADD 12/91 ꝙp

Walton. Belshazzar's Feast[a]. Coronation Te Deum. Gloria[b]. [b]**Ameral Gunson** (contr); [b]**Neil Mackie** (ten); [a]**Gwynne Howell**, [b]**Stephen Roberts** (bars); **Bach Choir; Philharmonia Orchestra/Sir David Willcocks.** Chandos CHAN8760. Texts included. Recorded in 1989.

.•' Ih 2m DDD I/90

With Sir David Willcocks in charge of the choir which he has directed since 1960, one need have no fears that the composer's many near-impossible demands of the chorus in all three of these masterpieces will be met with elegance and poise. There is as well, in *Belshazzar*, a predictably fine balance of the forces to ensure that as much detail as possible is heard from both chorus and orchestra, even when Walton is bombarding us from all corners of the universe with extra brass bands and all manner of clamorous percussion in praise of pagan gods. Such supremely musical concerns bring their own rewards in a work that can often seem vulgar. The revelation here is the sustained degree of dramatic thrust, exhilaration and what Herbert Howells called "animal joy" in the proceedings. How marvellous, too, to hear the work paced and scaled to avoid the impression of reduced voltage after the big moments. Gwynne Howell is the magnificently steady, firm and dark toned baritone. The *Gloria* and *Coronation Te Deum* are informed with the same concerns: accuracy and professional polish are rarely allowed to hinder these vital contributions to the British choral tradition. The recording's cathedral-like acoustic is as ideal for the *Te Deum*'s ethereal antiphonal effects, as it is for *Belshazzar*'s glorious spectacle; and Chandos match Willcocks's care for balance, bar by bar.

Walton. Façade[a]. Overtures — Portsmouth Point; Scapino[b]. Siesta[b].
Arnold. English Dances, Op. 33[c]. [a]**Dame Edith Sitwell**; [a]**Sir Peter Pears** (spkrs); [a]**English Opera Group Ensemble/Anthony Collins**; [bc]**London Philharmonic Orchestra/Sir Adrian Boult.** Decca London mono 425 661-2LM. Items marked [a] from LXT2977 (11/54), [b] LXT5028 (6/55), [c] LW5166 (6/55).

.•' Ih 14m DDD ꝙp ▲

This is the classic and authoritative reading of the fully approved selection of *Façade* settings. Dame Edith herself reads two-thirds of the numbers, Sir Peter the remaining third. The poetess herself reads them with such *joie de vivre*, such a natural feeling for her own verses and inflections that nobody could be expected to rival her. Her timing is perfect, her delivery deliciously idiosyncratic, the intonations obviously what she and presumably Walton wanted. Sir Peter isn't far behind her in ability to relish the writing and the instrumental ensemble plays with refinement allied to virtuosity. The 1950s mono recording stands the test of time remarkably well.

Additional recommendations …
Façade[a]. **Sitwell.** Poems: Two Kitchen Songs. Five Songs — Daphne; The Peach Tree; The Strawberry; The Greengage Tree; The Nectarine Tree. On the Vanity of Human Aspirations. Two Poems from "Façade"

— The Drum; Clowns' Houses. The Wind's Bastinado. The Dark Song. Colonel Fantock. Most Lovely Shade. Heart and Mind. **Prunella Scales, Timothy West** (spkrs); [a]members of **London Mozart Players/Jane Glover.** ASV CDDCA679 — .·' lh 4m DDD/ADD 4/90

Façade — Suites Nos. 1 and 2. **Bliss.** Checkmate — Suite. **Lambert.** Horoscope — Suite. **English Northern Philharmonia/David Lloyd-Jones.** Hyperion CDA66436 — .·' lh l4m DDD 3/91

New review

Walton. THE BEAR. **Della Jones** (mez) Madame Popova; **Alan Opie** (bar) Smirnov; **John Shirley-Quirk** (bar) Luka; **Northern Sinfonia/Richard Hickox.** Chandos CHAN9245. Text included. Recorded in 1993.

.·' 53m DDD 1/94 — — — — — — — — — — — — — — —

New review

Walton. TROILUS AND CRESSIDA — excerpts. **Dame Elisabeth Schwarzkopf,** [a]**Marie Collier** (sops); **Monica Sinclair** (contr); **Richard Lewis,** [a]**Sir Peter Pears, Lewis Thomas** (tens); **John Hauxvell** (bar); **Geoffrey Walls** (bass-bar); **Philharmonia Orchestra,** [a]**Orchestra of the Royal Opera House, Covent Garden/Sir William Walton.** EMI British Composers mono CDM7 64199-2. Text included. From Columbia 33CX1313 (11/55), except item marked [a] from Decca SET392/3 (12/68). Recorded in 1955
Is Cressida a slave?; Slowly it all comes back; How can I sleep?; Is anyone there?[a]; If one last doubt; Now close your arms; Interlude; From isle to isle chill waters; All's well; Diomede! ... Father!

.·' 55m ADD 1/94 — — — — — — — — — — — — — — ▲

If Walton's sense of humour was firmly established from the start in *Façade*, his one-acter, *The Bear*, among his later works brings out very clearly how strong that quality remained throughout his life. In this Chekhov tale, Walton times the melodramatic moments marvellously — notably the climactic duel between the mourning widow and her husband's creditor (the bear of the title) and Hickox brings that out most effectively. Walton also deftly heightens the farcical element by introducing dozens of parodies and tongue-in-cheek musical references, starting cheekily with echoes of Britten's *Midsummer Night's Dream*. Hickox brings out the richness of the piece as well as its wit, helped by the opulent Chandos recording which still allows words to be heard clearly. The casting of the three characters is as near ideal as could be. Della Jones is commanding as the affronted widow, consistently relishing the melodrama like a young Edith Evans. Alan Opie as Smirnov, 'the bear' is clean-cut and incisive, powerfully bringing out the irate creditor's changing emotions, while John Shirley-Quirk, still rich and resonant, is very well cast as the old retainer, Luka. With the duel scene leading delectably to an amorous *coup de foudre* — *The Bear* in many ways comes off even better on disc than on stage. Similarly the power and passion of *Troilus and Cressida*, the grandly tragic opera which Walton wrote for Covent Garden, has never come over more tellingly than in the fine collection of excerpts recorded in 1955 only five months after the première in the previous December. Sadly Walter Legge advised his wife, Elisabeth Schwarzkopf, not to sing the work on stage, and her heartfelt performance on this recording makes one regret that all the more. Richard Lewis as Troilus was at his peak too, strong and clear. With the excerpts rightly concentrating on high-points in the lovers' music, one marvels how rich Walton's invention is, with Cressida in particular inspiring melodies of Puccinian memorability. This CD reissue adds to the original EMI selection a tiny fragment originally recorded by Decca that allows one to sample the incomparable characteriza-tion which Peter Pears brought to the comically camp role of Pandarus. The transfer of the EMI mono sound is first-rate, with the voices given fine presence, so that the contrast with the Decca stereo is not obtrusive.

Further listening ...

The Quest — Ballet (ed. Palmer). The Wise Virgins — Ballet Suite. **London Philharmonic Orchestra/Bryden Thomson.** Chandos CHAN8871 (4/91).

String Quartets — No. 1[a]; A minor[b]. **Gabrieli Quartet.** Chandos CHAN8944 (10/91).

Piano Quartet[a]. Violin Sonata. **Kenneth Sillito** (vn); [a]**Robert Smissen** (va); [a]**Stephen Orton** (vc); **Hamish Milne** (pf). Chandos CHAN8999 (3/92).

Henry V — a Shakespeare scenario (arr. Palmer). **Christopher Plummer** (narr); **Westminster Abbey Choristers; Chorus and Academy of St Martin in the Fields/Sir Neville Marriner.** Chandos CHAN8892 (4/91).

Film Music, Volume 2 — Spitfire Prelude and Fugue. A Wartime Sketchbook (arr. Palmer). Escape Me Never — Suite (arr. Palmer). The Three Sisters (ed. Palmer). The Battle of Britain — Suite. **Academy of St Martin in the Fields/Sir Neville Marriner.** Chandos CHAN8870 (12/90).

Magnificat and Nunc dimittis. Cantico del sole. Antiphon. Set me as a seal upon thine heart. Missa brevis. Where does the uttered music go?. Jubilate Deo. A Litany. The Twelve. *Carols* — All this time; What cheer?; King Herod and the Cock. Make we joy now in this fest. **Trinity College Choir, Cambridge/Richard Marlow.** Conifer CDCF164 (5/89).

Key to symbols

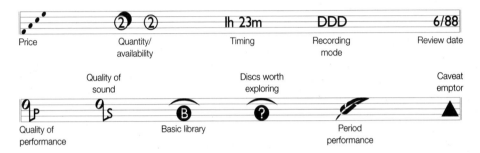

Price	Quantity/ availability	Timing	Recording mode	Review date
Quality of sound		Discs worth exploring		Caveat emptor
Quality of performance	Basic library		Period performance	

Peter Warlock

British 1894-1930

Suggested listening ...

A Cornish Carol. I saw a fair maiden. Benedicamus Domino. The full heart. The rich cavalcade. Corpus Christi. All the flowers of the Spring. As dew in Aprylle. Bethlehem Down. A Cornish Christmas Carol. *Coupled with* **Moeran.** Songs of Springtime. Phyllida and Corydon. **Finzi Singers/Paul Spicer.** Chandos CHAN9182 (10/93). *See the review under Moeran; refer to the Index to Reviews.*

Unico Wilhelm, Graf van Wassenaer

The Netherlands 1692-1766

New review

Wassenaer. CONCERTI ARMONICI. **The Brandenburg Consort/Roy Goodman.** Hyperion CDA66670. Recorded in 1993.
No. 1 in G major. No. 2 in B flat major. No. 3 in A major. No. 4 in G major. No. 5 in F minor. No. 6 in E flat major.

Wassenaer was a Dutch nobleman, diplomat and amateur musician. When his *Concerti Armonici* was published by Carlo Ricciotti, an Italian violinist, in 1740, he dedicated it to another Dutch nobleman who was wrongly named as the composer when Walsh republished the works in 1755. A nineteenth-century manuscript copy by a Polish composer, Francois Lessel, attributed them to Pergolesi and this led to their inclusion in Pergolesi's *Opera Omnia* — from which Stravinsky imported several themes 'by Pergolesi' for his ballet *Pulcinella*. Though this attribution has long been doubted it was only in 1979 that a manuscript was discovered, in an unknown hand but with an introduction in Wassenaer's own, which places his authorship of the *Concerti Armonici*

beyond doubt. Such is their marvellous quality, not least their harmonic richness, that it is impossible to believe that they could have been his only works, and it makes one wonder what happened to the rest — maybe lurking amongst the spurious or doubtful ones by others. All are in four-movement *da chiesa* form and reflect Wassenaer's wide knowledge of the music of his time, with his taste for Italian composers well to the fore — and even with the occasional hint of Bach! The Brandenburg Consort use Walsh's edition and adhere to the original complement of strings with an enhancing variety of continuo instruments. Their finely shaped and affectionate performances, beautifully recorded, are a major addition to the recorded repertory of the period.

Franz Waxman

German/American 1906-1967

Suggested listening ...

Film Scores: Prince Valiant — Suite. A Place in the Sun — Suite. The Bride of Frankenstein — Creation of the female monster. Sunset Boulevard — Suite. Rebecca — Suite. The Philadelphia Story. Old Acquaintance — Elegy for Strings. Taras Bulba — Ride to Dubno. **National Philharmonic Orchestra/Charles Gerhardt.** RCA Victor GD80708 (11/91).

Rebecca — *film score.* **Bratislava Radio Symphony Orchestra/Adriano.** Marco Polo 8 223399 (10/92).

The Bride of Frankenstein — *film score.* **Westminster Philharmonic Orchestra/Kenneth Alwyn.** Silva Screen FILMCD135 (3/94).

Carl Maria von Weber

German 1786-1826

Weber. Clarinet Concertos — No. 1 in F minor, J114; No. 2 in E flat major, J118. Clarinet Concertino in E flat major, J109. **Orchestra of the Age of Enlightenment/Antony Pay** (cl). Virgin Classics VC7 59002-2.

| 52m DDD 10/88 | |

Among the major composers, it was Weber who most of all enriched the solo repertory of the clarinet. He was inspired by his acquaintance with a fine player, in this case Heinrich Bärmann, and for this recording Antony Pay has used a modern copy of a seven-keyed instrument of around 1800, to which two extra keys have been added to come nearer to the ten-keyed instrument that Bärmann played. The orchestra also uses period instruments and in several passages, such as the hymnlike one with horns in the slow movement of the F minor Concerto, one hears this in their subtly different tone. The music itself is consistently fluent and elegant, witty and attractive and is stylishly played, with lovely clarinet tone in all registers.

Additional recommendation ...
As above. **Paul Meyer** (cl); **Royal Philharmonic Orchestra/Günther Herbig.** Denon CO-79551 — 50m DDD 10/92

Weber. Piano Sonatas — No. 1 in C major, J138; No. 2 in A flat major, J199. Rondo brillante in E flat major, J252, "La gaîté". Invitation to the dance, J260. **Hamish Milne** (pf). CRD CRD3485. Recorded in 1991.

| 1h 16m DDD 9/92 |

Weber's piano music, once played by most pianists, has since suffered neglect and even the famous *Invitation to the dance* is now more often heard in its orchestral form. Since he was a renowned pianist as well as a major composer, the neglect seems odd, particularly when other pianist composers such as Chopin and Liszt are at the centre of the concert repertory; but part of the trouble may lie in the difficulty of the music, reflecting his own huge hands and his tendency to write what the booklet essay calls "chords unplayable by others". Hamish Milnes makes out a real case for this music, and his playing of the two sonatas is idiomatic and resourceful, even if one cannot banish the feeling that Weber all too readily used the melodic and harmonic formulae of eighteenth-century *galanterie* and simply dressed them up in nineteenth-century salon virtuosity. From this point of view, a comparison with Chopin's mature sonatas or Liszt's magnificent single essay in the form reveals Weber as a lightweight. A hearing of the first movement in the First Sonata will quickly tell you if this is how you may react, while in its *Presto* finale you may praise a Mendelssohnian lightness but also note a pomposity foreign to that composer. Leaving aside the musical quality of these sonatas, this is stylish playing which should win them friends. The *Rondo brillante* and *Invitation to the dance* make no claim to be other than scintillating salon music, and are captivating in Milne's shapely and skilful performances. The recording is truthful and satisfying.

Additional recommendations ...
No. 2. **Brahms.** *Four Ballades, Op. 10.* **Alfred Brendel** (pf). Philips 426 439-2PH — .•• 53m DDD 6/91

Nos. 1 and 2. **Martin Jones** (pf). Pianissimo PP20792 — .•• 58m DDD 9/92

New review
Weber. LIEDER. **Dietrich Fischer-Dieskau** (bar); **Hartmut Höll** (pf). Claves CD50-9118. Texts and translations included. Recorded in 1991.
Meine Lieder, meine Sänge, J73. Klage, J63. Der Kleine Fritz an seine jungen Freunde, J74. Was zieht zu deinem Zauberkreise, J86. Ich sah ein Röschen am Wege stehn, J67. Er an Sie, J57. Meine Farben, J62. Liebe-Glühen, J140. Uber die Berge mit ungestüm, Op. 25 No. 2. Es stürmt auf der Flur, J161. Minnelied, J160. Reigen, J159. Sind es Schmerzen, J156. Mein Verlangen, J196. Wenn ich ein Vöglein war', J233. Mein Schatzerl is hübsch, J234. Liebesgruss aus der Ferne, J257. Herzchen, mein Schätzchen, J258. Das Veilchen im Thale, J217. Ich denke dein, J48. Horch'!, Leise horch', Geliebte, J56. Elle était simple et gentilette, J292.

.•• **52m DDD 11/93** 𝄞 P

"In my opinion the first and most sacred duty of a song-writer is to observe the maximum of fidelity to the prosody of the text that he is setting." Weber was writing in defence of a number he composed for an obscure play, but his words can stand as an apologia for his 90-odd songs. His contribution to German song has been underrated, for his ideas were different from those of his contemporaries. Fischer-Dieskau used to resist suggestions that he might take up Weber's songs, and it is good that he has done so, even late in his career. Always sensitive to words, he now responds with the subtlety of understanding that comes from many years of closeness to German poetry. Only very occasionally is there the powerful emphasis on the single expressive word that sometimes used mar his interpretations, keeping them too near the surface of the poetry. He can still use individual colour marvellously: the tonal painting of 'blue', 'white' and 'brown' in *Meine Farben* is exquisitely done. But more remarkable, here and in other songs, is the manner in which he follows the novel melodic lines which Weber has contrived out of the poetry. *Ein steter Kampf* is a masterly example; so is *Was zieht zu deinem Zauberkreise*, one of the few songs in which Weber enters Schubertian territory; so are *Es stürmt auf der Flur* and *Liebesgruss aus der Ferne*. Not even Fischer-Dieskau can quite bring off the coy *Der Kleine Fritz* by slightly sending it up (the only hope), and there is something a bit hefty about *Reigen*, a very funny wedding song full of "Heissa, lustig!" and "Dudel, didel!", though Hartmut Höll does wonders with the clanking accompaniment. Höll varies his tone so much here from the warmth and depth of his touch elsewhere that one wonders if the engineers did not take a small hand: why not? These are charming, touching, witty, colourful verses, often by minor figures of Weber's circle, and they drew from him music that heightens their point. Fischer-Dieskau's intelligent artistry could not more eloquently support the praise for Weber from Wilhelm Müller, poet of *Die schöne Müllerin* and *Winterreise*, as "master of German song".

Weber. DER FREISCHUTZ. **Peter Schreier** (ten) Max (Hans Jörn Weber); **Gundula Janowitz** (sop) Agathe (Regina Jeske); **Edith Mathis** (sop) Aennchen (Ingrid Hille); **Theo Adam** (bass) Caspar (Gerhard Paul); **Bernd Weikl** (bar) Ottokar (Otto Mellies); **Siegfried**

Vogel (bass) Cuno (Gerd Biewer); **Franz Crass** (bass) Hermit; **Gerhard Paul** (spkr) Samiel; **Günther Leib** (bar) Kilian (Peter Hölzel); **Leipzig Radio Chorus; Staatskapelle Dresden/Carlos Kleiber.** DG 415 432-2GH2. Notes, text and translation included. From 2720 071 (11/73).

> ② 2h 10m ADD 11/86

This opera tells of a forester Max and his pact with the forces of darkness to give him the ability to shoot without missing. Carlos Kleiber's recordings are always fascinating and for this one he went back to the manuscript seeking out details rarely heard in the standard opera house text. His direction is imaginative and where controversial (his tempos do tend to extremes) one feels he presents a strong case. His cast is very fine too: Schreier's Max is more thoughtful than some, though always ready to spring back after his hellish encounters. Janowitz is a lovely Agathe and Mathis a perky Aennchen, whilst Adam's Caspar is suitably diabolic. The use of actors to speak the dialogue does take a little getting used to, but the recording is good and the Dresden orchestra play magnificently.

Additional recommendation ...
Soloists; Chorus of the Deutsche Oper, Berlin; Berlin Philharmonic Orchestra/ Joseph Keilberth. EMI CMS7 69342-2 — ② 2h 14m ADD 9/89

Further listening ...

Invitation to the Dance. *Overtures* — Der Beherrscher der Geister; Euryanthe; Oberon; Abu Hassan; Der Freischütz; Peter Schmoll. **Berlin Philharmonic Orchestra/Herbert von Karajan.** DG Galleria 419 070-2GGA (6/88).

Grand Duo Concertant, J204. *Coupled with* **Brahms.** Clarinet Sonatas, Op. 120 — No. 1 in F minor; No. 2 in E flat major. **Paul Meyer** (cl); **François-René Duchable** (pf). Erato 2292-45480-2 (9/90).

PETER SCHMOLL UND SEINE NACHBURN. **Soloists; Hagen Philharmonic Orchestra/ Gerhard Markson.** Marco Polo 8 223592/3 (4/94).

OBERON. **Soloists; Bavarian Radio Chorus and Symphony Orchestra/Rafael Kubelík.** DG 419 038-2GX2 (12/91).

Anton Webern

Austrian 1883-1945

Webern. Passacaglia, Op. 1. Six Pieces, Op. 6. Five Pieces, Op. 10. Variations, Op. 30. **Bach** (arr. Webern). Musikalisches Opfer, BWV1079 — Ricercar a 6. **Schoenberg.** A Survivor from Warsaw, Op. 46[a]. [a]**Gottfried Hornik** (narr); [a]**Vienna State Opera Chorus; Vienna Philharmonic Orchestra/Claudio Abbado.** DG 431 774-2GH. Text and translation included. Recorded 1989-92.

> 50m DDD 5/93

Claudio Abbado has recorded rather more in the way of progressive twentieth-century music over the years than many other star conductors. It would be good to have much more. Meanwhile, we must be grateful for these recordings of Webern, including a fine reading of the rarely-heard and forcefully dramatic Variations, Op. 30. Abbado and the VPO are predictably responsive to the romantic intensity of the early Passacaglia, with nothing routine in their performance, and the sets of expressionist miniatures are even more convincing in their blend of delicacy and power. The fourth piece from Op. 6, the closest Webern ever came to concentrating the essence of a Mahlerian funeral march, and ending with an ear-splitting percussion crescendo, is all the more effective for Abbado's refusal to set a self-indulgently slow tempo. Technically, these recordings outshine the competition, though both Boulez and Karajan remain memorable as interpreters — Boulez especially in Op. 30, Karajan most notably in Op. 6. Given the evident rapport between Webern and Abbado it seems odd that the disc doesn't include more of Webern's music — for example, the Symphony, Op. 21. The Bach arrangement is nevertheless an ear-opening exercise in passing baroque counterpoint through a kaleidoscope of expressionist tone-colours, and Schoenberg's *A Survivor from Warsaw* retains its special power to move and disturb.

Passacaglia. Five Movements, Op. 5. Six Piece. Symphony, Op. 21. **Berlin Philharmonic Orchestra/Herbert von Karajan.** DG 20th Century Classics 423 254-2GC — .•' 46m ADD 7/88 ⁹ₚ
Passacaglia. Six Pieces. Five Pieces. Symphony. Variations. **Mozart.** *Symphonies — No. 35 in D major, "Haffner", K385; No. 36 in C major, "Linz", K425; No. 38 in D major, "Prague", K504; No. 39 in E flat major, K543; No. 40 in G minor, K550; No. 41 in C major, "Jupiter", K551.* **Cleveland Orchestra/Christoph von Dohnányi.** Decca 436 421-2DH3 — .•' ③ 3h 18m DDD 10/93

Webern. COMPLETE WORKS, Opp. 1-31. **Various artists.** Sony Classical M3K45845. Notes, texts and translations included. From 79204 (12/78). Recorded 1967-72.
Passacaglia, Op. 1 (London Symphony Orchestra/Pierre Boulez). Entflieht auf leichten Kähnen, Op. 2 (John Alldis Choir/Boulez). Five Songs from "Der siebente Ring", Op. 3. Five Songs, Op. 4 (Heather Harper, sop; Charles Rosen, pf). Five Movements, Op. 5 (Juilliard Quartet). Six Pieces, Op. 6 (LSO/Boulez). Four Pieces, Op. 7 (Isaac Stern, vn; Rosen, pf). Two Songs, Op. 8 (Harper, sop; chamber ensemble/Boulez). Six Bagatelles, Op. 9 (Juilliard Qt). Five Pieces, Op. 10 (LSO/Boulez). Three Little Pieces, Op. 11 (Gregor Piatigorsky, vc; Rosen, pf). Four Songs, Op. 12 (Harper, sop; Rosen, pf). Four Songs, Op. 13. Six Songs, Op. 14 (Harper, sop; chbr ens/Boulez). Five Sacred Songs, Op. 15. Five Canons on Latin Texts, Op. 16 (Halina Lukomska, sop; chbr ens/Boulez). Three Songs, Op. 18 (Lukomska, sop; John Williams, gtr; Colin Bradbury, cl/Boulez). Two Songs, Op. 19 (John Alldis Ch, mbrs LSO/Boulez). String Trio, Op. 20 (mbrs Juilliard Qt). Symphony, Op. 21 (LSO/Boulez). Quartet, Op. 22 (Robert Marcellus, cl; Abraham Weinstein, sax; Daniel Majeske, vn; Rosen, pf/Boulez). Three Songs from "Viae inviae", Op. 23 (Lukomska, sop; Rosen, pf). Concerto, Op. 24 (mbrs LSO/Boulez). Three Songs, Op. 25 (Lukomska, sop; Rosen, pf). Das Augenlicht, Op. 26 (John Alldis Ch, LSO/Boulez). Piano Variations, Op. 27 (Rosen, pf). String Quartet, Op. 28 (Juilliard Qt). Cantata No. 1, Op. 29 (Lukomska, sop; John Alldis Ch; LSO/Boulez). Variations, Op. 30 (LSO/Boulez). Cantata No. 2, Op. 31 (Lukomska, sop; Barry McDaniel, bar; John Alldis Ch; LSO/Boulez). Five Movements, Op. 5 — orchestral version (LSO/Boulez). **Bach** (orch. Webern): Musikalischen Opfer, BWV1079 — Fuga (Ricercata) No. 2 (LSO/Boulez). **Schubert** (orch. Webern): Deutsche Tänze, D820 (Frankfurt Radio Orchestra/Anton Webern. Recorded live in 1932).

.•' ③ 3h 43m ADD 6/91

Webern is as 'classic' to Pierre Boulez as Mozart or Brahms are to most other conductors, and when he is able to persuade performers to share his view the results can be remarkable — lucid in texture, responsive in expression. Despite his well-nigh exclusive concern with miniature forms, there are many sides to Webern, and although this set is not equally successful in realizing all of them, it leaves the listener in no doubt about the music's sheer variety, as well as its emotional power, whether the piece in question is an ingenious canon-by-inversion or a simple, folk-like *Lied*. From a long list of performers one could single out Heather Harper and the Juilliard Quartet for special commendation; and the smooth confidence of the John Alldis Choir is also notable. The recordings were made over a five-year period and have the typical CBS dryness of that time. Even so, in the finest performances which Boulez himself directs — as indicated in the review above, the *Orchestral Variations*, Op. 30 is perhaps the high point — that remarkable radiance of spirit so special to Webern is vividly conveyed. It is a fascinating bonus to hear Webern himself conducting his Schubert arrangements — music from another world, yet with an economy and emotional poise that Webern in his own way sought to emulate.

Movement. String Quartet (1905). Five Movements. Six Bagatelles. String Quartet, Op. 28. **Quartetto Italiano.** Philips 420 796-2PH — .•' 53m ADD 4/88
Five Movements. Six Bagatelle. String Quartet, Op. 28. Trio. Movement (1925). String Quartet (1905). Slow Movement (1905). Rondo (c. 1906). **Arditti Quartet.** Disques Montaigne 789008 — .•'
lh 6m DDD 12/91

Matthias Weckmann

German c.1616-1674

Suggested listening ...

Cantatas — Weine nicht, es hat über wunde. Zion sprecht, der Herr hat mich verlassen. Herr, wenn ich nur dich habe. Wie liegt die Stadt so wüste. Dialogo von Tobias und Raguel. Kommet her zu mir alle. Wenn der Herr die Gefangen zu Zion erlösen wird. Angelicus coeli chorus. Gegrüsset seist du, Holdselige. Rex virtutum. Der Tod ist verschlungen. Es erhub sich ein Streit[a]. **Greta de Reyghere, [a]Jill Feldman** (sops); **James Bowman** (alto); **Ian Honeyman, [a]Guy de Mey** (tens); **Max van Egmond** (bass); **[a]Capella Sancti Michaelis/Erik van Nevel; Ricercar Consort.** Ricercar RIC109097/8 (4/93).

Thomas Weelkes

British 1576-1623

Suggested listening ...

Cathedral Music — Alleluia, I heard a voice. All laud and praise. Laboravi in gemitu meo. Give the king thy judgements. O Lord, arise. If King Manasses. When David heard. O how amiable are they dwellings. Gloria in excelsis Deo (Sing my soul to God). O Jonathan, woe is me. Hosanna to the Son of David. Pavane[a]. Evening Service for Trebles — Magnificat; Nunc dimittis.Voluntaries I and II[a]. **Winchester Cathedral Choir/David Hill** with **[a]Timothy Byram-Wigfield** (org). Hyperion CDA66477 (10/92).

Cathedral Music — Alleluia, I heard a voice. Give ear, O Lord. Hosanna to the Son of David. When David heard. O Lord, grant the King a long life. Give the King thy judgements. Gloria in excelsis Deo (Sing my soul to God). Evening Service a 5. Ninth Service. **Christ Church Cathedral Choir, Oxford/Stephen Darlington.** Nimbus NI5125 (3/89).

Kurt Weill

German/American 1900-1950

New review

Weill. Concerto for Violin and Wind Orchestra, Op. 12[a]. Kleine Dreigroschenmusik. **[a]Naoko Tanaka** (vn); **St Luke's Orchestra/Julius Rudel.** Music Masters 67007-2.

48m DDD 2/94

Weill's Violin Concerto, although composed four years before *Die Dreigroschenoper*, is a definite precursor of the sound we associate with the more obviously popular music he wrote for his theatre pieces with Brecht. The parallel is especially striking in the scoring for wind orchestra and the flirtatious second movement, which Naoko Tanaka plays with a seemingly relaxed manner, in fine contrast to the 'duel' of the first, more skeletal movement. The Concerto has a handful of recordings, but Rudel's sympathetic conducting makes this the natural contender for first choice. The suite from *Dreigroschenoper*, first performed by an ensemble from the Berlin Opera under Klemperer, is one of Weill's most frequently performed works. Rudel's direction of the suite is beautifully light and elegant, with a splendid feel for the wit and balletic subtlety of Weill's orchestration.

Additional recommendations ...
Concerto[a]. *Kiddush*[b]. *Kleine Dreigroschenmusik.* **[a]Yuval Waldman** (vn); **[b]Grayson Hirst** (ten); **[b]Ray Pellerin** (org); **[b]Amor Artis Chamber Choir and Orchestra/Johannes Somary.** Newport Classics NCD60098 — 55m DDD 12/91

Concerto. **Berg.** *Chamber Concerto for Violin, Piano and 13 Wind Instruments*[a]. **Eivind Aadland** (vn); **[a]Einar Henning Smebye** (pf); **Norwegian Wind Ensemble, Ole Kristian Ruud.** Simax PSC1090 — 1h 3m DDD 8/93

Kleine Dreigroschenmusik. Symphonies — No. 1; No. 2. **Lisbon Gulbenkian Foundation Orchestra/Michel Swierczewski.** Nimbus NI5283 — 1h 14m DDD

Weill. SONGS. **Ute Lemper** (sop); **Berlin Radio Ensemble/John Mauceri.** Decca New Line 425 204-2DNL. Texts and translations included.

Der Silbersee — Ich bin eine arme Verwandte (Fennimores-Lied); Rom war eine Stadt (Cäsars Tod); Lied des Lotterieagenten. Die Dreigroschenoper — Die Moritat von Mackie Messer; Salomon-Song; Die Ballade von der sexuellen Hörigkeit. Das Berliner Requiem — Zu Potsdam unter den Eichen (arr. Hazell). Nannas-Lied. Aufstieg und Fall der Stadt Mahagonny — Alabama Song; Wie man sich bettet. Je ne t'aime pas. One Touch of Venus — I'm a stranger here myself; Westwind; Speak low.

· ·′   **50m DDD 3/89**   ♀♪

The songs in this collection are mostly from the major works Weill composed between 1928 and 1933, but also included are one from his years in France and three items from the 1943 Broadway musical *One Touch of Venus*. The collection introduces a most exciting talent in the person of Ute Lemper. By comparison with the husky, growling delivery often accorded Weill's songs in the manner of his widow Lotte Lenya, we here have a voice of appealing clarity and warmth. What distinguishes her singing, though, is the way in which these attributes of vocal purity are allied to a quite irresistible dramatic intensity. Her "Song of the Lottery Agent" is an absolute *tour de force*, apt to leave the listener emotionally drained, and her *Je ne t'aime pas* is almost equally overwhelming. Not least in the three numbers from *One Touch of Venus*, sung in perfect English, she displays a commanding musical theatre presence. With John Mauceri on hand to provide authentic musical accompaniments, this is, one feels, how Weill's songs were meant to be heard.

Weill. Die Dreigroschenoper. **Lotte Lenya,** Jenny; **Erich Schellow,** Macheath; **Willy Trenk-Trebitsch,** Mr Peachum; **Trude Hesterburg,** Mrs Peachum; **Johanna von Kóczián,** Polly Peachum; **Wolfgang Grunert,** Tiger Brown; **Inge Wolffberg,** Lucy; **Wolfgang Neuss,** Streetsinger; **Günther-Arndt Choir;** members of the Dance Orchestra of **Radio Free Berlin/Wilhelm Brückner-Rüggeberg.** CBS Masterworks CD42637. Notes, text and translation included. From 77268 (12/72). Recorded in 1958.

· ·′   **1h 18m ADD 3/89**   ♀♪ ▲

In *Die Dreigroschenoper* ("The Threepenny Opera") Kurt Weill sought to match the satire of Bertolt Brecht's updating of John Gay's *The Beggar's Opera* with numbers in the dance rhythms and jazz-tinged orchestrations of the time. The number that later became famous as "Mack the Knife" is merely the best known of the many catchy numbers in a score that none the less bears the hallmark of a cultivated musician. This 1958 reading has eclipsed all others. It has the distinction of featuring the composer's widow, Lotte Lenya, in the role of Jenny that she had created back in 1928. The recording carries about it an undeniable feeling of authenticity in the pungency of its satire and the catchiness of its score. Johanna von Kóczian is a charming Polly, Erich Schellow a winning Macheath, and Trude Hesterberg a formidable Frau Peachum, while Wilhelm Brückner-Rüggeberg has just the right feel for Weill's dance rhythms. This is an absolutely complete recording of the score, including the once expurgated "Ballad of Sexual Dependency" and the usually omitted "Jealousy Song". Despite its age, the recorded sound remains good, and the whole is a compelling experience.

Additional recommendation ...
Soloists; Berlin RIAS Chamber Choir and Sinfonietta/John Mauceri. Decca 430 075-2DH — · ·′ 1h 14m DDD 3/90 ♀♪

New review
Weill. Die Sieben Todsünden[a]. Songs[b] — Complainte de la Seine; Youkali; Nannas Lied, "Meine Herren, mit Siebzehn Jahren"; Wie lange noch?; Es regnet; Berlin im Licht. **Brigitte Fassbaender** (mez); [a]**Karl-Heinz Brandt,** [a]**Hans Sojer** (tens); [a]**Hidenori Komatsu** (bar); [a]**Ivan Urbas** (bass); [a]**Hanover Radio Philharmonic Orchestra/Cord Garben** ([b]pf). Harmonia Mundi HMC90 1420. Texts and translations included. Recorded 1992-93.

· ·′   **55m DDD 12/93**   ♀♪

Weill and Brecht's *Seven Deadly Sins*, written in haste just after their flight from Hitler's Germany, was their last major collaboration. The question of its interpretation will always be bound up with the memory of Lotte Lenya, who created the role of Anna I. Brigitte Fassbaender is the first great Lieder singer to record it, the others have all been singing actresses or opera stars; her performance is stupendous — one of the best things she has ever done on disc. Of course she sounds rather aristocratic compared with the knowing street-singer style adapted by Lemper on Decca, but just compare her in "Lust", the very heart of the work, and marvel at the detail she extracts from both text and music. The rest of Fassbaender's disc is a judiciously chosen selection of Weill songs, all of which have some bearing on *The Seven Deadly Sins*. Cord Garben's conducting and the soloists in the male quartet are fine but compared with Rattle's interpretation, the pacing sounds a bit pedestrian. One cannot, however, imagine a dancer being able to keep up with Rattle's frantic speed in the Schneller Walzer section of "Pride". Elise Ross's performance (for Rattle) has been generally underrated, her singing is full of interesting detail, but inevitably she sounds pale compared with Fassbaender.

Additional recommendations ...
Die Sieben Todsünden. Kleine Dreigroschenmusik. **Soloists; London Symphony Orchestra/ Michael Tilson Thomas.** CBS Masterworks CD44529 — .•' 55m DDD 3/89
Die Sieben Todsünden. Mahagonny-Gesänge[a]. **Ute Lemper** (sop); [a]**Susanne Tremper** (sngr); **Helmut Wildhaber, Peter Haage** (tens); **Thomas Mohr** (bar); **Manfred Jungwirth** (bass); **Berlin RIAS Sinfonietta/John Mauceri.** Decca 430 168-2DH — .•' 1h 6m DDD 4/91
Die Sieben Todsünden[a]. **Stravinsky.** *Pulcinella*[b]. **Soloists;** [b]**Northern Sinfonia,** [a]**City of Birmingham Symphony Orchestra/Simon Rattle.** EMI CDM7 64739-2 — .•' 1h 13m DDD/ADD 12/93

Weill. STREET SCENE. **Kristine Ciesinski** (sop) Anna Maurrant; **Richard Van Allan** (bass) Frank Maurrant; **Janis Kelly** (sop) Rose Maurrant; **Bonaventura Bottone** (ten) Sam Kaplan; **Terry Jenkins** (ten) Abraham Kaplan; **Meriel Dickinson** (mez) Emma Jones; **Angela Hickey** (mez) Olga Olsen; **Claire Daniels** (sop) Jennie Hildebrand; **Fiametta Doria** (sop) First Nursemaid; **Judith Douglas** (mez) Second Nursemaid; **English National Opera Chorus and Orchestra/Carl Davis.** TER Classics CDTER21185. Recorded in 1989.

.•' ② 2h 26m DDD 11/91

Street Scene is the most ambitious product of Weill's American years. It's something of a *Porgy and Bess* transferred from Catfish Row to the slum tenements of New York. Where *Porgy and Bess* is through-composed with recitatives, though, *Street Scene* offers a mixture of set musical numbers, straight dialogue, and dialogue over musical underscoring. The musical numbers themselves range from operatic arias and ensembles to rousing 1940s dance numbers. This complete recording is one of two resulting from a joint Scottish Opera/English National Opera production of 1989. This one offers the cast and conductor of the ENO production, with just a couple of relatively minor substitutions. Of the two recordings this is probably the more consistently well sung, particularly where style is concerned. Weill described the work as a "Broadway opera", and it demands a vernacular rather than a classical operatic singing style. This it duly gets from Kristine Ciesinski as Anna Maurrant, while Janis Kelly's beautifully clear but natural enunciation and her sense of emotional involvement make daughter Rose's "What good would the moon be?" a performance of real beauty. Praiseworthy too is Richard Van Allan as the murderous husband, his "Let things be like they always was" creating a suitably sinister effect. Among the subsidiary attractions is the appearance of Catherine Zeta Jones, of ITV's *The Darling Buds of May*, performing the swinging dance number "Moon-faced, starry-eyed".

Additional recommendation ...
Soloists; Scottish Opera Chorus and Orchestra/John Mauceri. Decca 433 371-2DH2 — .•' ② 2h 28m DDD

New review
Weill. Lost in the Stars. **Gregory Hopkins** (ten) Leader; **Arthur Woodley** (bass-bar) Stephen Kumolo; **Reginald Pindell** (bar) Absalom, John, Man, Villager; **Cynthia Clarey** (sop) Irina; **Carol Woods** (sngr) Linda; **Jamal Howard** (treb) Alex; **Richard Vogt** (spkr)

Stationmaster, Judge; **New York Concert Chorale; St Luke's Orchestra/Julius Rudel.**
Music Masters 67100-2. Recorded in 1992.

Lost in the Stars is subtitled "A Musical Tragedy" and was adapted by Maxwell Anderson from
Alan Paton's novel *Cry the Beloved Country*. Weill and Anderson's use of a chorus to comment on
the action and advance the story makes the play difficult to stage, and Anderson's sentimentaliza-
tion of the Paton original has made it one of the most dated of Weill's works. Julius Rudel
conducted a production of *Lost in the Stars* for the New York City Opera in 1959, and observes
in the booklet that he found these recording sessions "somewhat akin to a religious experience".
This certainly communicates itself, especially in the choral sequence "Cry the beloved country"
which frames the death-cell confrontation between father and son. Without much recorded
dialogue, the condescending sugariness of the Anderson contribution is reduced and Weill's
experimentation with the choruses as well as his usual high quota of great melodies make this
one of the finest modern recordings of his work. In the main role of the black preacher,
Kumolo, Arthur Woodley sings with fervour and fine diction and the Orchestra of St Luke's
manages an accurate 1940s sound; a real achievement. This is a major addition to the catalogue
and essential to any collection of Weill's work — or of twentieth-century opera.

Further listening ...

Der Silbersee. **Soloists; Cologne Pro Musica; Cologne Radio Symphony Orchestra/
Jan Latham-König.** Capriccio 60 011-2 (8/90).

Leó Weiner
Hungarian 1885-1960

Suggested listening ...

Suite on Hungarian Folk-tunes, Op. 18. *Coupled with* **Bartók.** The miraculous mandarin, Sz73
— ballet[a]. [a]**London Voices; Philharmonia Orchestra/Neeme Järvi.** Chandos CHAN9029
(3/92). *See review under Bartók; refer to the Index to Reviews.*

Three Hungarian Rural Dances. *Coupled with* **Kodály.** Seven Pieces, Op. 11. **Liszt.** Csárdás
macabre, S224. **Dohnányi.** Gavotte and Musette. **Bartók** (trans. cpsr.). Dance Suite, Sz77.
Kurtág. Plays and Games for Piano, Book 3 — excerpts. **Szöllösy.** Paesaggio con morti. **Peter
Frankl** (pf). ASV CDDCA860 (6/93). *See review in the Collections section; refer to the Index to Reviews.*

Judith Weir
Scottish 1954-

Suggested listening ...

The Consolations of Scholarship — Chinese Yuan drama[a]. King Harald's Saga[b]. [a]**Linda Hirst** (sop);
[b]**Jane Manning** (sop); [a]**Lontano/Odaline de la Martinez.** United Recordings 88040 (3/90).

Silvius Weiss
German 1686-1750

Suggested listening ...

L'Amant malheureux in A minor. Capriccio in D major. Plainte in B flat major. Prelude in
D major. Prelude in E flat major. Suite I — B flat major; D minor; F major. Suite II in
G minor. Suite in A major "L'esprit italien". **Lutz Kirchhof** (lte). Sony Classical S2K48391

Sonata in A minor, "L'infidèle". Prelude, Fantasia and Fugue in C major. Tombeau sur la mort de M. Comte de Logy. *Coupled with* **Vivaldi** (trans. North, after Bach): Concerto in D major, RV230. **Bach** (trans. North): Partita in D minor, BWV1004 — Chaconne. **Nigel North** (lte). Linn Records CKD006 (12/92). *See review in the Collections section; refer to the Index to Reviews.*

Richard Wernick

American 1934-

Suggested listening ...

String Quartet No. 4. *Coupled with* **Harbison.** String Quartet No. 2. **Schuller.** String Quartet No. 3. **Emerson Quartet.** DG 437 537-2GH (11/93). *See review under Harbison; refer to the Index to Reviews.*

Samuel Wesley

British 1766-1837

Suggested listening ...

Symphonies — No. 3 in A major; No. 4 in D major; No. 5 in E flat major; No. 6 in B flat major. **Milton Keynes Chamber Orchestra/Hilary Davan Wetton.** Unicorn-Kanchana DKPCD9098 (10/91).

Samuel Sebastian Wesley

British 1810-1876

Suggested listening ...

Anthems — Ascribe unto the Lord. Blessed be the God and Father. Cast me not away. Thou wilt keep him in perfect peace. Wash me throughly. The wilderness and the solitary place. *Organ works* — Andante in E minor. Choral Song and Fugue. Larghetto in F minor. **New College Choir, Oxford/Edward Higginbottom** (org). CRD CRD3463 (10/91).

Percy Whitlock

British 1903-1946

Suggested listening ...

Hymn Preludes — Darwall's 148th; Song 13. *Coupled with* **C.S. Lang.** Tuba tune. **Howells.** Three Psalm-Preludes (Set 1), Op. 32. **Elgar.** Organ Sonata No. 1 in G major, Op. 28. **Vaughan Williams.** Three Preludes on Welsh Hymn Tunes — Rhosymedre. **Cocker.** Tuba tune. **Gareth Green** (org). Naxos 8 550582 (3/93). *See review in the Collections section; refer to the Index to Reviews.*

Charles Marie Widor

French 1844-1937

Widor. ORGAN WORKS. **Thomas Trotter.** Argo 433 152-2ZH. Played on the Cavaillé-Coll organ of Saint François-de-Sales, Lyon, France. Recorded in 1990.

Symphonies, Op. 42: No. 5 in F minor — Adagio; Toccata. No. 6 in C minor — Allegro. No. 7 — Moderato cantabile; Allegro. Symphonie gothique in C minor, Op. 70. Trois Nouvelles Pièces, Op. 87.

Ih I4m DDD I0/92

Two pieces of organ music stand head and shoulders above anything else in sheer popularity. After Bach's Toccata and Fugue in D minor, Widor's Toccata has justifiably attracted admiration from generations of music-lovers. Any church organist will tell you that it's requested as frequently for weddings as any music, and in performance it displays not only the player's virtuosity but also the power and glory of the instrument itself. But to assess Widor's qualities as a composer on the strength of this one piece is to do him a major disservice. Let's say straight away that Thomas Trotter's sturdy performance is the equal of any, and this full-throated French organ makes a simply wondrous noise. The Toccata comes from one of ten full-scale symphonies Widor wrote for the organ, attempting to recreate in scope and range on one instrument what other symphonists achieve through the medium of a large orchestra. These organ symphonies exploit a vast array of colours and effects and in addition to a complete symphony (the aptly named *Gothic*) Trotter has selected a number of individual movements — the majestic opening of the Sixth, the lyrical *moderato cantabile* from the Eighth and not only the Toccata but the reflective *adagio* which precedes it in the Fifth (and without which no performance of the Toccata should be considered complete). Argo have captured these splendid performances in a most atmospheric recording which will hopefully inspire the inquisitive listener to delve beyond the flamboyant Toccata.

Further listening ...

Sinfonia sacra, Op. 81[a]. Symphony No. 3, Op. 69[b]. **Paul Wisskirchen** (org); [a]**Cologne Gurzenich Orchestra,** [b]**Philharmonia Hungarica/Volker Hempfling.** Motette CD40071.

Key to symbols

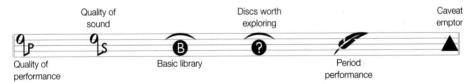

Quality of sound	Discs worth exploring	Caveat emptor

Quality of performance — Basic library — Period performance

Adolf Wiklund

Swedish 1879-1950

Suggested listening ...

Piano Concertos — No. 1 in E minor, Op. 10[a]. No. 2 in B minor, Op. 17[b]. Summer night and sunrise — Symphonic Poem, Op. 18. [a]**Ingemar Edgren,** [b]**Greta Erikson** (pfs); **Swedish Radio Symphony Orchestra/Stig Westerberg; Gothenburg Symphony Orchestra/ Jorma Panula.** Caprice CAP21363.

Henryk Wieniawski

Polish 1835-1880

Suggested listening ...

Violin Concerto No. 2 in D minor, Op. 22. *Coupled with* **Saint-Saëns.** Violin Concerto No. 3 in B minor, Op. 61. **Julian Rachlin** (vn); **Israel Philharmonic Orchestra/Zubin Mehta.** Sony Classical SK48373 (12/92). *See review under Saint-Saëns; refer to the Index to Reviews.*

Philip van Wilder

New review

Wilder. Concerto for Oboe, String Orchestra and Percussion.
Barlow. The Winter's Past. Piece for Oboe and Improvisatory Percussion[a].
Bloom. Requiem. Narrative.
Corigliano. Aria. **Humbert Lucarelli** (ob); [a]**Mark Wood** (perc); **Brooklyn Philharmonic Orchestra/Michael Barrett.** Koch International Classics 37187-2. Recorded in 1993.

∴ 5lm DDD 7/94

Although John Corigliano receives top billing for his intensely moving *Aria* (an effective arrangement for strings and oboe from the slow movement of his Concerto for oboe and orchestra), it is Alec Wilder's catchy, easygoing Concerto for Oboe, String Orchestra and Percussion which occupies the lion's share of this CD (roughly half its playing time, in fact). Wilder's work ranges in tone from 'classical' music to popular ballads; Sinatra is one of his great fans (he made a famous record of Wilder's beautiful song, *I'll be Around*) and many other prestigious artists have espoused his cause. Yet mindless categorizing has sometimes inhibited a fuller appreciation of his skills as a 'serious' composer. The concerto's gentle demeanour and subtle echoes of various contemporary masters (Lucarelli himself suggests Gershwin, Poulenc and Villa-Lobos) make for an utterly bewitching 25 minutes. Then there's Wayne Barlow's vernal *The Winter's Past*. His style reflects lazy, sun-soaked afternoons, rather in the manner of Copland or Vaughan Williams. Here, as elsewhere in this warming miscellany, Lucarelli weaves a warm, sinewy tone and receives responsive support from the Brooklyn Philharmonic under Michael Barrett. Robert Bloom's nicely crafted, neo-romantic Requiem (with its Hebraic undertones) and his rather more 'personal' *Narrative* are both prime contenders for any oboist's repertoire. Lucarelli ends his programme with Wilder's wistful, upbeat *Piece for Oboe and Improvisatory Percussion* — a pleasant encore to an altogether charming, well-recorded disc.

Charles Williams

Suggested listening ...

The Dream Of Olwen — Piano and Orchestra (from the film "While I live"). *Coupled with* **Addinsell.** Warsaw Concerto (from the film "Dangerous Moonlight"). **Rózsa.** Spellbound Concerto (from the film "Spellbound"). **Bath.** Cornish Rhapsody (from the film "Love Story"). **Gershwin.** Rhapsody in Blue. **Daniel Adni** (pf); **Bournemouth Symphony Orchestra/Kenneth Alwyn.** Classics for Pleasure CD-CFP9020.

John Williams

Suggested listening ...

Flute Concerto[a]. Violin Concerto[b]. [a]**Peter Lloyd** (fl); [b]**Mark Peskanov** (vn); **London Symphony Orchestra/Leonard Slatkin.** Varèse Sarabande VSD5345.

Dracula — *original film soundtrack.* Varèse Sarabande VSD5250.

E.T.: The Extra-Terrestrial — *original film soundtrack.* MCA DMCL1878.

Hook — *original film soundtrack.* Epic 469 349-2.

Jurassic Park — *original film soundtrack.* MCA MCD10859.

| Schindler's List — *original film soundtrack.* MCA MCD10969.

Star Wars Trilogy — *original film soundtracks.* Fox 07822 11012-2.

Film scores — Close Encounters of the Third Kind; Star Wars. **National Philharmonic Orchestra/Charles Gerhardt.** RCA Victor GD82698.

Meiron Williams

Suggested listening ...

Aros Mae'r Mynyddau Mawr (The mountains remain). Gwynfyd (Paradise). Awelon y Mynydd (Mountian breezes). O Fab y Dyn (O! son of man). Y lyn (The lake). Cloch y Llan (The Church bell). Rhosyun yr Haf (Summer rose). Ora Pro Nobis (Pray for us). Ffarwel iti, Cymru (Farewell, fair Wales). Pan Ddaw'r Nos (When night comes). Adlewych (Reflection). **Bryn Terfel** (bass-bar); **Annette Bryn Parri** (pf). Sain SCDC2013 (8/93).

Meredith Willson

Suggested listening ...

THE MUSIC MAN. **Original Broadway cast.** EMI Angel ZDM7 64663-2.

Sandy Wilson

Suggested listening ...

THE BOY FRIEND. **Original 1984 London revival cast.** That's Entertainment CDTER1095 (3/87).

Dag Wirén

Suggested listening ...

Wirén. String Quartet No. 3 in D minor, Op. 18. *Coupled with* **A. Tchaikovsky.** String Quartet No. 2 in C major, Op. 5. **Hugh Wood.** String Quartet No. 3, Op. 20. **Barber.** String Quartet, Op. 11. **Lindsay Quartet.** ASV CDDCA825 (1/93). *See review in the Collections section; refer to the Index to Reviews.*

Peter Wishart

Suggested listening ...

String Quartet No. 3 in A major. *Coupled with* **Rubbra.** String Quartet No. 2 in E flat major. **Tate.** String Quartet in F major. **English Quartet**. Tremula TREM102-2 (12/93). *See review under Rubbra; refer to the Index to Reviews.*

Hugo Wolf

Wolf. Intermezzo. Italian Serenade. String Quartet in D minor. **Artis Quartet** (Peter Schumayer, Johannes Meissl, vns; Herbert Kefer, va; Othmar Muller, vc). Accord 22080-2. Recorded in 1987.

57m DDD 6/90

Wolf's astonishing String Quartet suggests that his early death and the discouragingly contemptuous treatment his larger works received during his lifetime, robbed us of a great composer of chamber music. The Quartet is without the slightest shadow of doubt a masterpiece. For a composer not yet 20 to have had such a mastery of large-scale structure, such skilled command of complex thematic working and such confidence in handling big and dramatic ideas is nothing short of breathtaking. But these profoundly serious qualities are combined with a youthful prodigality of invention and an exuberance of spirit that are winning as well as awesome. Only the work's huge difficulty in performance can have kept it on the furthest fringes of the repertory for so long. How fortunate that for its first recording in many years it should have been taken up by such an urgently communicative as well as such a virtuoso group as the Artis Quartet. The popular *Italian* Serenade, charmingly done, is a welcome supplement; the *Intermezzo*, still more neglected than the String Quartet, shares its qualities and adds to them a measure of enchanting humour. Excellent recorded sound, too: unreservedly recommended.

New review
Wolf. Italienisches Liederbuch. **Barbara Bonney** (sop); **Håkan Hagegård** (bar); **Geoffrey Parsons** (pf). Teldec 9031-72301-2. Texts and translations included. Recorded in 1992.

1h 16m DDD 7/94

We have here a reading of *Italienisches Liederbuch* from these three vital and well-equipped interpreters that can be spoken of in the same breath as the superb generation of Wolf interpreters (listed below). Bonney and Hagegård are both highly versed in Lieder interpretation, both possess attractive and individual voices allied to sound techniques, so we can take the vocal and verbal accomplishments as such for granted. Both enter fully into the spirit of these charmed miniatures; both have the art of immediately setting the mood of each song and shaping it swiftly into a convincing whole, keenly supported by Parsons. Bonney catches the petulant anger of "Wer rief dich denn?", then she relaxes into the wheedling urgency, two songs later, of "Nun lass uns Frieden schliessen". In "Ihr jungen Leute" she is to the life the worried girlfriend taking leave of her soldier. The dramatic power and range of emotional colour she can release in her voice come into play in "Lass sie nur gehen" and the succeeding song "Wie soll ich fröhlich sein" and she ends the CD with an exuberant "Ich hab' in Penna". Hagegård can also encompass every mood in his far-ranging interpretations. The ninth song, "Dass doch gemalt" can stand as an exemplar for the rest — a hushed and wondrous start, then a fine line and shaping to a heroic climax. He manages the ecstatic love songs that lie at the Book's centre with a beauty and strength that would be hard to beat. "Und willst du deinen Liebsten" and "Wir haben beide lange Zeit" have the touch of greatness on them; so, later on, does "Benedeit die sel'ge Mutter". Parsons is a model of discernment and unexaggerated musicianship throughout, never missing an interpretative point yet never underlining any to excess. He is ideally balanced with the voices and the recording is truthful.

Additional recommendations ...
Elisabeth Schwarzkopf (sop); **Dietrich Fischer-Dieskau** (bar); **Gerald Moore** (pf). EMI CDM7 63732-2 — 1h 19m ADD 12/90
Irmgard Seefried (sop); **Dietrich Fischer-Dieskau** (bar); **Erik Werba, Jörg Demus** (pfs). DG Dokumente 435 752-2GDO — 1h 15m ADD 11/92

New review
Wolf. GOETHE LIEDER. **Wolfgang Holzmair** (bar); **Thomas Palm** (pf). Collins Classics 1402-2. Texts and translations included. Recorded live in 1988.
Harfenspieler I-III; Der Rattenfänger; Coptisches Lied I; Frech und froh I and II: Epiphanias; Genialisch Treiben; Der Schäfer; Blumengruss; Frühling übers Jahr; Anakreons Grab; Phänomen;

Ob der Koran von Ewigkeit sei?; Trunken müssen wir alle sein!; So lang man nüchtern ist; Sie haben wegen der Trunkenheit; Hätt' ich irgend wohl Bedenken; Komm, Liebchen, komm!; Wie sollt ich heiter bleiben; Wenn ich dein gedenke; Ganymed.

♪ **55m DDD 9/93** ♀P

Holzmair is a refreshing and challenging singer. He follows no known school and quite avoids the influence of Fischer-Dieskau. His voice is individual and tangy; his interpretations here, as elsewhere, are apparently spontaneous (the live recording helps) and unmarked by convention. His tone doesn't please everyone; it has a quick vibrato of a kind more frequently encountered in the earlier decades of the century than in the later, and it can harden under pressure. That's part of the price of taking risks: like Wolf he isn't always well behaved — and he's all the more stimulating for his immediacy of manner. Nowhere is that more apparent than in *Ganymed* where the wonder of the poem and its setting is wholly conveyed in this soaring interpretation. At the other end of the emotional scale in the inexhaustible variety of the Goethe settings is the desolation of the *Harfenspieler* ones, in the first of which the line "Dann bin ich micht allein" carries all the inner torment of the mysterious old man. Nor at the end of the next verse is Holzmair averse to bursting out in operatic-like pain at "Mich Einsamen die Pein". The all-important piano parts are in the safe hands of Thomas Palm, a most sensitive player. He is placed a shade too far backward in relation to the voice but this probably reflects what you would have heard in the concert-hall. Too much applause is included and the length is short by today's standards on CD. But, as they say, the quality is what matters and here it is high.

New review

Wolf. LIEDER. **Dame Elisabeth Schwarzkopf** (sop); **Gerald Moore** (pf). EMI Festspiel-dokumente mono CDH7 64905-2. Texts included. Recorded live in 1958.
Mörike Lieder — Im Frühling; Auf eine Christblume I; Lied vom Winde. Goethe Lieder — Philine; Mignon; Der Schäfer; Blumengruss; Frühling übers Jahr; Anakreons Grab; Phänomen; Ganymed. Spanisches Liederbuch — Mühvoll komm' ich und beladen; In dem Schatten meiner Locken; Bedeckt mich mit Blumen; Wer tat deinem Füsslein weh; Wehe der, die mir verstrickte. Italieniches Liederbuch — Nun lass uns Frieden schliessen. Sechs Lieder für eine Frauenstimme — Mausfallen-Sprüchlein. Sechs alte Weisen.

♪ **lh llm ADD 10/93** ♀P ▲

New review

Wolf. MORIKE LIEDER. **Brigitte Fassbaender** (mez); **Jean-Yves Thibaudet** (pf). Decca 440 208-2DH. Texts and translations included. Recorded in 1992.
Der Knabe und das Immlein; Jägerlied; Das verlassene Mägdlein; Begegnung; Nimmersatte Liebe; Fussreise; Verborgenheit; Im Frühling; Auf eine Wanderung; Der Gärtner; Auf ein altes Bild; In der Frühe; Schlafendes Jesuskind; Zum neuen Jahr Kirchengesang; Gebet; An den Schlaf; Peregrina I; Peregrina II; Lebe wohl; Denk' es, o Seele!; Der Feuerreiter; Gesang Weylas; Storchenbotschaft; Bei einer Trauung; Selbstgeständis.

♪ **lh 7m DDD 8/93** ♀P

"A blissful experience of the purest lied art" reported the *Salzburger Nachrichten* on Schwarzkopf's recital. The recording derives from the Austrian Broadcasting Corporation's archive. It gives a marvellous sense of presence, recalling most vividly what it was that made the memory of Schwarzkopf's song recitals precious. First, the quality of voice, caught here at its purest and most radiant; then the full concentration of a total sensibility, emotion and intellect fused, upon the songs: every one of them lived a special life on each separate occasion. The riches of this recital are beyond the scope of a short review. Every song here deserves a paragraph to itself, and the appreciation of Gerald Moore's work would have a large share in each. The disc, for one who cares for Wolf's songs and the art of their performance, is beyond price.

The 1992 Fassbaender recording is exemplary in balance and sense of atmosphere and is, of course, in stereo. The peculiar intensity that is Fassbaender's special gift and Thibaudet's probing, big-scale playing fulfil virtually every need of these often complex and occasionally puzzling songs. Nobody could do more to convince doubters of their greatness than these two artists who have obviously struck up an ideal rapport, the strengths of one feeding off those of the other. Once again Fassbaender unerringly finds the apt emphasis for a word or a phrase. The line "Sohn der Jungfrau, Himmelskind!" in *Schlafendes Jesuskind*, besides showing the innate beauty of the mezzo's tone, is the very essence of wondering repose here predicated by Wolf.

Thibaudet's wide-ranging technique allied to his intellectual control are of a calibre to match the spontaneous, piercing insights of his singer. Note the airy, delicate playing, just right, in *Der Knabe und das Immlein*, suggestive of summer calm. He reaches a zenith of excellence in the fearsomely difficult *Feuerreiter*; few pianist-accompanists could manage it like this. Of course, the complete *Mörike* is available in Fischer-Dieskau's classic recording (listed below). But any Wolfian, indeed any Lieder-lover, should also want to acquire these absorbing issues.

Additional recommendation ...
Mörike Lieder[a]. *Michelangelo Lieder*[b]. **Dietrich Fischer-Dieskau** (bar); **Gerald Moore** (pf). EMI [a]mono/[b]stereo CMS7 63563-2 — .ᐟ ② 2h 8m ADD 9/90 ⁹ₚ

Further listening ...

Penthesilea[a]. DER CORREGIDOR — Prelude; Intermezzo. Italian Serenade[a]. Scherzo and Finale. **Orchestre de Paris/Daniel Barenboim.** Erato 2292-45416-2 (4/90).

Ermanno Wolf-Ferrari
Italian 1876-1948

Suggested listening ...

IL SEGRETO DI SUSANNA — Overture; Intermezzo. I QUATTRO RUSTEGHI — Overture; Intermezzo. LA DAMA BOBA — Overture. IL CAMPIELLO — Intermezzo; Ritornello. L'AMORE MEDICO — Overture; Intermezzo. I GIOIELLI DELLA MADONNA — Festa popolare; Intermezzo; Serenata; Danza napoletana. **Academy of St Martin in the Fields/Sir Neville Marriner.** EMI CDC7 54585-2 (3/93).

Stefan Wolpe
German/American 1902-1972

New review
Wolpe. Quartet for Oboe, Cello, Percussion and Piano[a]. Sonata for Violin and Piano[b]. Trio in Two Parts[c]. [c]**Harvey Sollberger** (fl); [a]**Stephen Taylor** (ob); [b]**Jorja Fleezanis** (vn); [ac]**Fred Sherry** (vc); [a]**Daniel Kennedy** (perc); [a]**Aleck Karis**, [b]**Garrick Ohlsson**, [c]**Charles Wuorinen** (pfs). Koch International Classics 37112-2. Recorded in 1991.

.ᐟ **1h 8m DDD 2/94**

Stefan Wolpe was a committed abstract expressionist — he admired the painters of this school too — and a determined post-Webern composer. He was much admired by Elliott Carter and younger composers on the New York scene such as Charles Wuorinen and Harvey Sollberger, who formed The Group for Contemporary Music in 1962. This group supported Wolpe in the 1960s and 1970s and now adds some magnificently dedicated performances to those already available. First comes the première recording of the resourceful Quartet for Oboe, Cello, Percussion and Piano (1955). This is splendidly done, with Stephen Taylor's athletic and mellifluous oboe playing under Sollberger's direction. The Sonata for Violin and Piano (1949), at nearly half an hour, is a major work of its period although somewhat over-extended even in this virtuoso performance. The *Trio in Two Parts* from the mid-1960s is closest to post-Webern manners. Fragments of material ricochet from one instrument to the other in a tireless demonstration of energy. Like Dallapiccola and Gerhard, both affected by Schoenberg's discoveries, Wolpe shows an unswerving integrity which in his case is expressed in rather remote abstract terms. These well-recorded performances make the best possible case for the music.

Further listening ...

In Two Parts[c]. Three Lieder[ac]. Quartet[c]. Hamlet[c]. Piece for Two Instrumental Units[c]. To the Dancemaster[ac]. Solo Piece for Trumpet[b]. Piece for Trumpet and Seven Instruments[bc]. [a]**Joyce**

Castle (mez); [b]**Raymond Mase** (tpt); [c]**Parnassus/Anthony Korf.** Koch International Classics 37141-2 (12/92).

Charles Wood

Irish 1866-1926

Suggested listening ...

St Mark Passion[a]. *Coupled with* **Holloway.** Since I believe in God the Father Almighty. [a]**William Kendall** (ten); [a]**Paul Robinson**, [a]**Kwame Ryan** (bars); [a]**Peter Harvey** (bass); **Gonville and Caius College Choir, Cambridge/Geoffrey Webber** with **Richard Hill** (org). ASV CDDCA854 (5/93).

Haydn Wood

British 1882-1959

Suggested listening ...

Sketch of a Dandy. Serenade to Youth. Mannin Veen. Three London Cameos — Suite. Mylecharane. Moods Suite No. 6, "Joyousness". A Brown Bird Singing. Apollo. The Seafarer. **Bratislava Radio Symphony Orchestra/Adrian Leaper.** Marco Polo 8 223402 (8/92).

Hugh Wood

British 1932-

Suggested listening ...

String Quartet No. 3, Op. 20. *Coupled with* **Wirén.** String Quartet No. 3 in D minor, Op. 18. **A. Tchaikovsky.** String Quartet No. 2 in C major, Op. 5. **Barber.** String Quartet, Op. 11. **Lindsay Quartet.** ASV CDDCA825 (1/93). *See review in the Collections section; refer to the Index to Reviews.*

Piano Concerto, Op. 31. **Joanna MacGregor** (pf); **BBC Symphony Orchestra/Andrew Davis.** Collins 20th Century Plus 2007-2 (6/93).

William Wordsworth

British 1908-1988

Suggested listening ...

Symphonies — No. 2 in D major, Op. 34; No. 3 in D major, Op. 48. **London Philharmonic Orchestra/Nicholas Braithwaite.** Lyrita SRCD207 (11/90).

Robert Wright

American 1914-

Suggested listening ...

KISMET (Wright/Forrest, after Borodin). Cast includes **Valerie Masterson, Donald Maxwell, David Rendall, Richard Van Allan, Judy Kaye; Ambrosian Chorus; Philharmonia Orchestra/John Owen Edwards.** TER Classics CDTER2 1170 (7/90).

Iannis Xenakis

Romanian/French 1922-

Suggested listening ...

Palimpsest. Dikhthas[a]. Epeï. Akanthos[b]. [a]**Irvine Arditti** (vn); [a]**Claude Helffer** (pf); [b]**Penelope Walmsley-Clark** (sop); **Spectrum/Guy Protheroe.** Wergo WER6178-2.

Jalons[a]. Phlegra[b]. Thalleïn[b]. Keren[c]. Nomos Alpha[d]. [c]**Benny Sluchin** (trombone); [d]**Pierre Strauch** (vc); **Ensemble Intercontemporain/**[a]**Pierre Boulez,** [b]**Michel Tabachnik.** Erato 2292-45770-2.

Naama[b]. A l'Ile de Gorée[bc]. Khoai[b]. Komboï[ab]. [a]**Sylvio Gualda** (perc); [b]**Elisabeth Chojnacka** (hpd); [c]**Xenakis Ensemble/Huub Kerstens.** Erato MusiFrance 2292-45030-2 (10/90).

Metastasis. Pithoprakta. Eonta[a]. **French Radio National Orchestra/François Le Roux;** [a]**Paris Contemporary Music Instrumental Ensemble/Konstantin Simonovic.** Le Chant du Monde LCD278 368.

ORESTIA. **Strasbourg University Music Department; Colmar Women's Voices; Anjou Vocal Ensemble; Basse-Normandie Ensemble/Dominique Debart.** Salabert Actuels SCD8906 (9/90).

Key to symbols

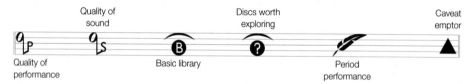

Quality of sound — Discs worth exploring — Caveat emptor

Quality of performance — Basic library — Period performance

Eugène Ysaÿe

Belgian 1858-1931

Suggested listening ...

Caprice d'après l'etude en forme de valse de Saint-Saëns. *Coupled with* **Saint-Saëns.** Introduction and Rondo capriccioso, Op. 28. **Massenet.** THAIS — Méditation. **Sarasate.** Zigeunerweisen, Op. 20. **Chausson.** Poème, Op. 25. **Ravel.** Tzigane. **Joshua Bell** (vn); **Royal Philharmonic Orchestra/Andrew Litton.** Decca 433 519-2DH (1/92). *See review in the Collections section; refer to the Index to Reviews.*

Solo Violin Sonatas, Op. 27 — No. 1 in G minor; No. 2 in A minor; No. 3 in D minor, "Ballade"; No. 4 in E minor; No. 5 in G major; No. 6 in E major. **Lydia Mordkovitch** (vn). Chandos CHAN8599 (5/88).

Riccardo Zandonai

Italian 1883-1944

Suggested listening ...

FRANCESCA DA RIMINI[a] — Act 2: E ancora sgombro il campo del comune? ... Date il segno, Paolo, date ... Un'erba io m'avea, per sanare ... Onta et orrore sopra. Act 3: No, Smadragedi, no! ... Paolo, datemi pace! ... Ah la parola chi i miei occhi incontrano. Act 4: Ora andate ... E così, vada s'è pur mio destino. *Coupled with* **Giordano.** FEDORA[b]. **Soloists;** [a]**Monte-Carlo**

Opera Orchestra/Nicola Rescigno; ^bMonte-Carlo Opera Chorus and Orchestra/
Lamberto Gardelli. Decca Grand Opera 433 033-2DM2 (3/92). *See review under Giordano; refer
to the Index to Reviews.*

Jan Dismas Zelenka

Bohemian 1679-1745

Zelenka. The Lamentations of Jeremiah. **Michael Chance** (alto); **John Mark Ainsley**
(ten); **Michael George** (bass); **Chandos Baroque Players.** Hyperion CDA66426. Texts and
translations included. Recorded in 1990.

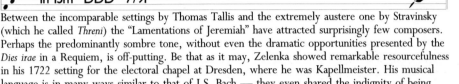

Ih I3m DDD 7/9l

Between the incomparable settings by Thomas Tallis and the extremely austere one by Stravinsky
(which he called *Threni*) the "Lamentations of Jeremiah" have attracted surprisingly few composers.
Perhaps the predominantly sombre tone, without even the dramatic opportunities presented by the
Dies irae in a Requiem, is off-putting. Be that as it may, Zelenka showed remarkable resourcefulness
in his 1722 setting for the electoral chapel at Dresden, where he was Kapellmeister. His musical
language is in many ways similar to that of J.S. Bach — they even shared the indignity of being
thought old-fashioned for the apparent severity and complexity of their styles — but there are also
daring turns of phrase which are entirely personal. The six *Lamentations* feature each singer twice;
this performance is intimate, even mystical, slightly spacious in tempo and with a resonant acoustic.

New review
Zelenka. Trio Sonatas — Nos. 2, 5 and 6. **Ensemble Zefiro** (Paolo Grazzi, Alfredo
Bernardini, obs; Alberto Grazzi, bn; Roberto Sensi, db; Rolf Lislevand, theorbo; Rinaldo
Alessandrini, hpd/org). Astrée Auvidis E8511. Recorded in 1993.

52m DDD 6/94

For sheer *élan* and spirit the baroque instrumental players on this disc take some beating.
Zelenka's six sonatas for two oboes, bassoon and continuo are among the most rewarding and at
times most difficult pieces of baroque chamber music in the oboe repertory. Indeed, pieces
demanding such virtuosity from these instruments were probably without precedent at the time
(1715). We can only speculate as to the circumstances which led to their composition but the
writing is often such as to make us wonder if they were destined for friends or enemies of the
composer. Here, then, is splendidly invigorating playing of music which offers a great deal beyond
face value. The sounds of the solo instruments themselves, together with an effective continuo
group of double-bass, harpsichord/organ and theorbo are admirably captured in the recording.

Further listening ...

Capriccios — No. 1 in D major; No. 2 in G major; No. 3 in F major; No. 4 in A major;
No. 5 in G major. Concerto a 8 in G major. Sinfonia a 8 in A minor. Hipocondrie a 7 in
A major. Overture a 7 in F major. **Berne Camerata/Alexander van Wijnkoop.** Archiv
Produktion 423 703-2AX3 (1/89).

Alexander Zemlinsky

Austrian 1871-1942

Zemlinsky. Lyrische Symphonie, Op. 18. **Julia Varady** (sop); **Dietrich Fischer-Dieskau**
(bar); **Berlin Philharmonic Orchestra/Lorin Maazel.** DG 419 261-2GH. Texts and
translations included. From 2532 021 (3/82).

44m DDD 6/87

Zemlinsky's powerful symphonic song cycle for soprano and baritone employs the vast forces of
the late-romantic orchestra at its most opulent. The poems by the composer gradually build up,

if not to a narrative, then to a series of symbolist portrayals of the spirit of love. The male singer contributes a more abstract, more idealized yearning after the "dweller in my endless dreams", the soprano a more down-to-earth evocation of emotional longing. Dietrich Fischer-Dieskau and his wife Julia Varady cope well with the tormented legato phrasing and tortured harmonies as the vision of an idealized love shimmers before their eyes just beyond their reach. The Berlin Philharmonic play this unfamiliar score with great virtuosity, strongly conducted by Lorin Maazel and have been recorded in a wonderfully mellow acoustic.

Further listening ...

String Quartets — No. 1 in A major, Op. 4; No. 2, Op. 15; No. 3, Op. 19; No. 4, Op. 25. *Coupled with* **Apostel.** String Quartet No. 1, Op. 7. **LaSalle Quartet.** DG 427 421-2GC2 (8/89).

Die Seejungfrau. Psalm 13, Op. 24[a]. [a]**Ernst Senff Chamber Chorus; Berlin Radio Symphony Orchestra/Riccardo Chailly.** Decca 417 450-2DH (6/87).

Gesänge nach Maeterlinck, Op. 13[a]. *Coupled with* **Reger.** Variations and Fugue on a Theme of J.A. Hiller. [a]**Hedwig Fassbender** (mez); **Czech Philharmonic Orchestra/Václav Neumann.** Supraphon 11 1811-2 (7/93).

EINE FLORENTINISCHE TRAGODIE, Op. 16. **Doris Soffel** (mez) Bianca; **Kenneth Riegel** (ten) Guido Bardi; **Guilermo Sarabia** (bass) Simone. **Berlin Radio Symphony Orchestra/ Gerd Albrecht.** Koch Schwann CD11625 (12/85).

DER KREIDERKREIS. **Soloists; Berlin Radio Symphony Orchestra/Stefan Soltesz.** Capriccio 60016-2 (1/92).

Bernd Zimmermann

German 1918-1970

New review

Zimmermann. Concertos — Oboe and Small Orchestra[a]; Trumpet and Orchestra, "Nobody knows the trouble I see"[b]; Canto di speranza[c]; Cello and Orchestra, "en forme de pas de trois"[c]. [a]**Heinz Holliger** (ob); [b]**Håkan Hardenberger** (tpt); [c]**Heinrich Schiff** (vc); **South-West German Radio Symphony Orchestra/Michael Gielen.** Philips 434 114-2PH. Recorded 1989-92.

Ih Ilm   DDD   11/93

The Oboe Concerto (1952) vigorously confronts the central postwar challenge: if you want to embrace the new (serialism) alongside the old (neo-classicism), how do you keep your balance? The answer, for Zimmermann, was 'precariously'. In the Trumpet Concerto (1954) the absorption of a negro spiritual and elements of jazz serve to intensify the trauma of a search for stylistic equilibrium. Yet again the result is an impressive work of art strongly built and progressing inexorably to a bleak conclusion. *Canto di speranza* (1953-7) brings us still closer to the apocalyptic modernism of the opera *Die Soldaten* (begun in 1958) as models — notably Webern — become objects of mockery. The Cello Concerto *en forme de pas de trois*, written after the opera in 1965-6, completes the process of recreative rejection. It is a haunting fantasy, at once ballet score and concert work, a parody of nineteenth-century terpsichorean conventions which is as bitter in tone as it is beguiling in sound. Philips have assembled three star soloists for this well-recorded disc, and with sterling orchestral support they do the music proud.

New review

Zimmermann. Enchiridion[b]. Cello Sonata[a]. Four Short Studies[a]. Intercommunicazione[ab]. [a]**Michael Bach** (vc); [b]**Bernhard Wambach** (pf). CPO CPO999 198-2. Recorded in 1992.

Ih 2m   DDD

In common with his other compositions for cello, hope is in short supply and although the path Zimmermann negotiates through his modern wasteland is not unrelievedly bleak, it is unsparingly intense. The major work here is the relatively late *Intercommunicazione* for cello and piano (1967), in which a form progressing to what Zimmermann terms the "combination of incompatible instruments" is powerfully built: the more powerfully, in fact, for not involving a traditional kind of progress at all. The music's increasing density leads to a brief recollection of the kind of neo-expressionist explosions that occupy centre stage in the earlier Sonata for solo cello of 1960. The sonata has dated, but it retains a core of vitality and lyric eloquence, and benefits greatly, as does *Intercommunicazione*, from the finely graded playing of Michael Bach. Zimmermann's concern to humanize his instinctive reclusiveness is movingly recalled in the brief solo studies composed in 1970, the year he took his own life. The disc underlines the distance Zimmermann travelled from the early *Enchiridion* for piano (1949-52). These 13 short pieces chart an initial escape from neo-classicism into avant-garde expressionism and end — in a way Bernhard Wambach's playing makes explicit — with the question that haunted Zimmermann from then on: "where can we go from here?". This is a well-recorded disc, and leaves one grateful that Zimmermann was able to make so much enduring music out of his acute sense of the ephemeral.

Collections

Orchestral

AMERICAN MUSIC. Boston Symphony Orchestra/Serge Koussevitzky. Pearl mono GEMMCD9492.
Foote: Suite in E minor, Op. 63 (from RCA Victor 11-8571/2. Recorded in 1940). *McDonald:* San Juan Capistrano (RCA Victor 17729. 1939). **Copland:** El salón México (HMV DB3812/13, 10/40). **Harris:** Symphonies — No. 1 (American Columbia 68183/6. 1934); No. 3 (DB6137/8, 12/42).

·♪ Ih I9m AAD I2/9I ▲

Music lovers with a romantic hankering for the American desert and the Great Outdoors may well know Roy Harris's high, wide and handsome Third Symphony already, but the chances of having heard Serge Koussevitzky's 1939 recording of it are somewhat more remote. If you can accept and enjoy the sound-tracks of classic westerns, then you'll have no trouble with this CD: the playing of the Boston Symphony burns through a veil of surface hiss with the ease and accuracy of a blow-torch, and Koussevitzky's conducting tends to confirm the judgement of many, that this is indeed the greatest American symphony. It's a tremendous experience, and although the work is barely 17 minutes long, it none the less constitutes an epic journey. Koussevitzky was a great musical pioneer, and his recordings of Copland's saucy *El salón México* and Arthur Foote's delightful Suite (easily as appealing as, say, Grieg's *Holberg* Suite) are rightly regarded as classics. Add Harris's First Symphony — a poorer recording, but a fascinating prophecy of greater work to come — and Harl McDonald's colourful essays, and you have the basis of an absorbing concert, one that you're likely to replay many times.

BAROQUE CLASSICS. Taverner Players/Andrew Parrott. EMI Reflexe CDM7 69853-2.
Handel: Solomon — Arrival of the Queen of Sheba. Harp Concerto in B flat major, Op. 4 No. 6 (with Andrew Lawrence-King, hp). **Purcell:** Three Parts upon a Ground. A Suite of Theatre Music: The Indian Queen — Trumpet Overture, Symphony, Dance. Abdelazer — Rondeau; The Gordion Knot Unty'd — Chaconne. **Pachelbel:** Canon and Gigue. **Bach:** "Wir danken dir, Gott, wir danken dir", BWV29 — Sinfonia. "Ich steh mit einem Fuss im Grabe", BWV156 — Sinfonia. "Der Himmel lacht! die Erde jubiliert", BWV31 — Sonata. "Ich liebe den Höchsten von ganzem Gemüte", BWV174 — Sinfonia. Christmas Oratorio, BWV248 — Sinfonia. "Gottes Zeit ist die allerbeste Zeit", BWV106 — Sonatina. "Herz und Mund und Tat und Leben", BWV147 — Chorale, "Jesus bleibet meine Freude" ("Jesu, joy of man's desiring") (with Taverner Consort).

·♪ Ih DDD I2/88 ✍

If you have ever felt the desire to hear 'baroque classics' as the composer might have heard them, but have been deterred by the unfriendly sounds and deadpan renditions offered by some early-instrument groups, you may do the former without suffering the latter by adding this disc to your collection. Though the performances have every benefit of stylistic scholarship and early-instrumental mastery they are in no way 'dry', nor are there any chalk-on-blackboard sounds to set the teeth on edge; on the contrary, the late David Reichenberg's oboe playing is likely to be a delightful revelation. Like other baroque composers, Bach was wont to rework some of his music for other media: thus you may recognize the Sinfonias from Cantatas 29, 156 and 31 as being related to the *Preludium* of the Third Violin Partita (BWV1006), the *Largo* of the F minor Harpsichord Concerto (BWV1056) and the first movement of the Third Brandenburg Concerto (BWV1048). This represents a doorway to the appreciation of baroque music in authentic performance, through which you may enter with as much enthusiasm as do the Taverner Players.

CONCERTANTE CELLO WORKS. Steven Isserlis (vc); **Chamber Orchestra of Europe/John Eliot Gardiner.** Virgin Classics VC7 59595-2.

Tchaikovsky: Variations on a Rococo Theme, Op. 33. Pezzo capriccioso, Op. 62. Nocturne, Op. 19 No. 4. Andante cantabile, Op. 11. *Glazunov:* Two Pieces, Op. 20. Chant du menestrel, Op. 71. *Rimsky-Korsakov:* Serenade, Op. 37. *Cui:* Deux morceaux, Op. 36 — Scherzando; Cantabile.

1h 4m   DDD   10/90

This delicious collection of Russian concertante works for cello offers the immediate advantage of a version of Tchaikovsky's *Rococo* Variations that aligns closely with the composer's original intentions for the work — many other recordings use heavily edited and reordered versions. Its second advantage is the considered, clean-toned playing of Steven Isserlis, one of a mighty handful of first-rate cello soloists that the UK can now boast. His style is not as demonstrative as that of some, though he is quite capable of opening the emotional floodgates when it is appropriate, and his delicacy and stylish phrasing bring out the best in this programme. Whether the music is lyrical, introspective, or playful, his restraint lends it another level of meaning that illuminates its inner life. Praise must also go to John Eliot Gardiner and the Chamber Orchestra of Europe. Accompanying of this sort is never easy, as expert control is demanded for long periods with few attendant moments in the spotlight. Gardiner and the engineers have attained an ideal balance between soloist and orchestra and the players demonstrate an intuitive feel for the late nineteenth-century idiom of the music.

CONCERTOS FOR FOUR VIOLINS. Cologne Musica Antiqua/Reinhard Goebel.
Archiv Produktion 435 393-2AH.
Torelli: Concerto in E minor for Four Violins and Strings. *Mossi:* Concertos, Op. 4 — No. 12 in G minor. *Valentini:* Concerti grossi, Op. 7 — No. 11 in A minor. *Locatelli:* Introduttioni Teatrali and Concerti, Op. 4 — No. 12 in F major. *Leo:* Concerto in D major for Four Violins and Strings.

1h 6m   DDD   9/92

Even the most assiduous collectors and discerning connoisseurs of baroque concertos are likely to find novelties in this 'off the beaten track' programme from Cologne Musica Antiqua. Mossi, Valentini and Locatelli belong to the Roman school, though the latter shows marked Venetian leanings, while the remaining two composers are products of Bologna (Torelli) and Naples (Leo). Whatever doubts there may be concerning the intrinsic merit of these works they nevertheless provide a fascinating and valuable glimpse of what composers other than Corelli (Rome) on the one hand or Vivaldi (Venice) on the other were up to. Reinhard Goebel who, alas, was unable to lead his group from the violin in his usual manner, following an injury to his arm, directs effectively. The textures in these concertos are rich and contrasting and the players draw subtle resonances from them. The opening *Largo* and ensuing fugue of the Valentini work affords striking examples of Musica Antiqua's skill in pointing up the variety of string sound inherent in this repertory. This is a fascinating programme performed with Musica Antiqua's customary *élan* and precision.

CONTEMPORARY WORKS FOR ORCHESTRA. [a]Istvan Matuz (fl); Ensemble Intercontemporain/[b]Pierre Boulez; [c]Peter Eötvös. Erato 2292-45409-2.
Dufourt. Antiphysis for Flute and Chamber Orchestra[ab]. *Ferneyhough.* Funérailles — versions I and II for Strings and Harp[b]. *Harvey.* Mortuos Plango, Vivos Voco — Concrete Sounds processed by Computer[c]. *Höller.* Arcus for 17 Instruments and Tape[c].

1h 12m   AAD

Not easy listening granted, but for those interested in exploring what the outer limits of contemporary music have to offer then the rewards are great indeed. Jonathan Harvey's *Mortuos Plango, Vivos Voco* is arguably one of the most successful pieces of tape montage to have emerged in recent years. The title and text are taken from the inscription on the great tenor bell at Winchester Cathedral: "I count the hours which fly past, I weep for the dead and I call the living to prayer". From this, and the electronic manipulation of a boy's voice and the great tenor bell itself, Harvey constructs a colourful and chilling atmosphere in which he says: "One must imagine the walls of the concert-hall enclosing the [listener] like the side of the bell around which the soul of the young boy flies freely". The hyper-complexities of Ferneyhough's

| *Funérailles* I and II for harp and strings are less easily assimilated but no less fascinating, and

subsequent hearings yield up more of its inner secrets and labyrinthine workings. Ferneyhough calls them: "Rite[s] taking place behind a curtain, or in the far distance". Dufourt's *Antiphysis* for flute and chamber orchestra, and Höller's *Arcus* for 17 instruments and tape, both date from 1978, and in their own utterly different ways, reflect the extraordinary virtuosity and artistry of the Ensemble Intercontemporain, for whom they were written, and who play with such stunning conviction on this disc. Exceedingly well recorded.

FETE A LA FRANCAISE. Montreal Symphony Orchestra/Charles Dutoit. Decca 421 527-2DH.
Chabrier: Joyeuse marche. España. *Dukas:* L'apprenti sorcier. *Satie* (orch. Debussy): Gymnopédies — Nos. 1 and 3. *Saint-Saëns:* SAMSON ET DALILA — Bacchanale. *Bizet:* Jeux d'enfants. *Thomas:* RAYMOND — Overture. *Ibert:* Divertissement.

1h 10m DDD 6/89

With great style and huge amounts of panache Charles Dutoit presides over a highly enjoyable collection of French 'lollipops'. Moving forward from Chabrier's *Joyeuse marche*, this *fête* includes such favourites as *The sorcerer's apprentice*, deliciously pointed and coloured, Chabrier's tribute to Spain, *España*, and Saint-Saëns's steamy Bacchanale from *Samson et Dalila*. A cool, limpid interlude is provided by two Satie *Gymnopédies*, here in orchestrations by Debussy. The whole programme is rounded off with tremendous fun by Ibert's outrageous *Divertissement* in a truly winning performance. The Montreal Symphony Orchestra are, without doubt, a first-rate orchestra and their grasp of French repertoire is certainly not equalled by any native band. Add to that a recording of quite breathtaking brilliance and you have a disc to treasure and delight.

New review
FRENCH BAROQUE HARPSICHORD WORKS. Sophie Yates. Chandos Chaconne CHAN0545. Recorded in 1993.
D'Anglebert: Pièces de Clavecin — Suite in G minor; Tombeau de M. de Chambonnières. *F. Couperin:* L'Art de toucher le clavecin — Prélude in D minor. Livre de clavecin, Deuxième ordre — Seconde Courante; Sarabande, "La Prude"; Les Idées heureuses; La Voluptueuse. *Forqueray:* La Rameau; La Boisson; La Sylva; Jupiter. *Rameau:* L'enharmonique. L'Egyptienne. La Dauphine.

1h 11m DDD 11/93

Sophie Yates has a real understanding of the French style — so difficult to capture, with its special conventions and elaborate ornamentation. Her phrasing is subtle as well as musical; and she proves herself capable of the flexibility proper to this music without risk to the underlying pulse or to continuity. Her reading of *La Dauphine*, Rameau's last harpsichord piece, is justifiably free and improvisatory, since it is thought to be a transcription of Rameau's extemporization at the wedding of the Dauphin in 1747. She savours Rameau's bold enharmonics, too, shows drive and energy in his *L'Egyptienne*, impressive dignity in Forqueray's tribute to his great contemporary and in a d'Anglebert sarabande, expressiveness in Forqueray's *La Sylva* and a sense of enjoyment in the trenchant drama of the flashing thunderbolts of his *Jupiter*. Yates also has the advantage of admirable recording of a particularly beautiful and rich-sounding instrument (a copy of a Goujon).

FRENCH ORCHESTRAL WORKS. [a]French Radio National Orchestra; [b]Royal Philharmonic Orchestra/Sir Thomas Beecham. EMI Beecham Edition CDM7 63379-2.
Bizet: Carmen — Suite No. 1 (from HMV HQS1108, 12/67)[a]. *Fauré:* Pavane, Op. 50 (HMV ASD518, 4/63)[a]. Dolly Suite, Op. 56 (orch. Rabaud. HQS1136, 5/68)[a]. *Debussy:* Prélude à l'après-midi d'un faune (ASD259, 6/59)[b]. *Saint-Saëns:* Le rouet d'Omphale, Op. 31 (ASD259)[b]. *Delibes:* Le Roi s'amuse — Ballet Music (HQS1136)[b].

1h 8m ADD 7/90

Even to those who never heard him in the flesh there is no mistaking Beecham's relish in, and flair for, the French repertoire. His combination of mischievous high spirits, almost dandyish elegance, cool outer classicism masking passionate emotion, swagger, refined nuance and delicate charm was perhaps unique — not matched even by such committed Francophiles as Constant

Lambert. *Elan* is at once in evidence here in the *Carmen* prelude, and subtle dynamic gradations in the entr'actes to Acts 2 and 4; there is lightness, vivacity and tenderness in Fauré's *Dolly* suite and a true Gallic reserve in his *Pavane*; and he enters with prim finesse into Delibes's pastiche dances. Debussy's erotic study, on repeated hearings of this performance, becomes the more Grecian and effective for its conscious understatement; and only the Saint-Saëns symphonic poem, for all the RPO's delicacy, seems to hang fire. But four or five bull's-eyes out of six is a pretty good score, and at medium price not to be missed.

New review

HARMONICA CONCERTOS AND VIRTUOSO WORKS. Tommy Reilly (harmonica); [a]Basle Radio Symphony Orchestra/Cedric Dumont; [b]orchestra/Robert Farnon; [c]Munich Radio Orchestra/Charles Gerhardt; [d]South West German Radio Orchestra/ Emmerich Smola. Chandos CHAN9248. Recorded 1968-81.
Arnold: Harmonica Concerto, Op. 46[a]. *Farnon:* Prelude and Dance[b]. *Moody:* Toledo, A Spanish fantasy[c]. *Spivakovsky:* Harmonica Concerto[c]. *Villa-Lobos:* Harmonica Concerto in A minor[d].

• • 1h ADD 5/94 ·· ℗

The Spivakovsky has a catchy tune in the first movement (much like a Leroy Anderson encore), another semi-pop romantic melody for its centre-piece and an infectious *moto perpetuo* finale. Tommy Reilly plays it superbly. The Malcolm Arnold work is exuberantly melodic in the manner of the *English Dances,* the orchestra most effectively scored without woodwind to give the soloist a strong, reedy profile. Its centre-piece is unexpectedly dirge-like, with dark brass sonorities and percussion providing a sombre accompaniment. The Villa-Lobos, scored for a small orchestra, has a neo-classical opening movement which is pastoral in feeling, then produces a quite beautiful melody for the *Andante*. The finale has a few piquant hints of the composer's usual Brazilian geography and here Reilly substitutes his own cadenza. Farnon's nostalgic *Prelude and Dance* (a light-hearted yet bittersweet waltz) calls for virtuosity and dash, plus a ready response to quicksilver changes of mood. These Reilly takes in his stride and the harmonica has seldom, if ever, been so well caught on disc.

ITALIAN FLUTE CONCERTOS. Jean-Pierre Rampal (fl); I Solisti Veneti/Claudio Scimone. Sony Classical SK47228.
Romano: Concerto in G major. *Cecere:* Concerto in A major. *Alberti:* Concerto in F major, "Con sordini". *Sammartini:* Concerto in G major.

• • 52m DDD 2/92 ··

Italy was slower than most other countries to favour the transverse flute over its fipple relative, as Vivaldi's well known concertos testify, but there were composers who responded to the flute's siren song, possibly persuaded by approaches from Margrave Carl Friedrich, a player and enthusiast thereof, in whose large collection of music (housed in Karlsruhe) there are numerous flute works. Some of these composers were Italian and four of their flute concertos, unpublished and otherwise unrecorded, form the programme of this recording; indeed, only the name of Sammartini was to be found in *The Classical Catalogue* prior to this recording, and of Romano and Cecere it may be said that "little is known of their lives". Alberti's Concerto is high baroque and, time and taste having marched on, Sammartini's is both 'high-transitional' and virtuosic; the others inhabit the middle ground. What they all have in common is clean-cut, melody-rich charm, persuasively displayed by Rampal, the most seductive of flautists, with the spruce support of I Solisti Veneti in a pristine recording. It isn't for instrumental purists but it is certainly for anyone who enjoys happy, uncomplicated and unfamiliar music, played with a smile.

New review

MARCHES AND OVERTURES A LA FRANCAISE. Detroit Symphony Orchestra/Paul Paray. Mercury Living Presence 434 332-2MM. Items marked [a] from AMS16077 (3/61), [b]AMS16121 (11/62), [c]sex15050 (3/62), [d]sex15024. Recorded in 1959.
Meyerbeer: Coronation March[a]. *Gounod:* Marche funèbre d'une marionnette[a]. *Saint-Saëns:* Suite algérienne in C major, Op. 60 — March militaire française[a]. Marche héroïque in E flat major, Op. 34[a]. *Rouget de Lisle:* La marseillaise[a]. *Adam:* Si j'étais roi — Overture[b].

Boieldieu: La dame blanche — Overture[b]. *Offenbach:* La belle Hélène — Overture[c]. Orphée aux enfers — Overture[c]. Les contes d'Hoffmann — Prelude[c]. *Rossini:* Guillaume Tell — Overture[d].

⠕ 1h 6m ADD 11/93 ▲

They don't make collections like this any more! Or so it seems. Yet can musical tastes really have changed so radically from the days when people would patiently turn over a 78rpm record for the second half of Boieldieu's *La dame blanche* Overture? Unlikely, and there must surely be a welcome for such a collection of charmingly melodious, unpretentious and yet well-crafted pieces as on this CD. Paul Paray (1886–1979) was a genuine son of Normandy who in his seventies could still bring out the Gallic warmth, excitement and sparkle of these pieces. The recording sounds just a shade raw with the violins at the top of their range, but generally the warmth and richness of sound make it quite unbelievable that these recordings are now 35-odd years old.

New review
DAVID OISTRAKH. The Historical Recordings. **David Oistrakh** (vn); [a]**Moscow State Symphony Orchestra/Kyrill Kondrashin; USSR State Orchestra/**[b]**Kondrashin,** [d]**Dmitry Kabalevsky;** [c]**USSR Radio Symphony Orchestra/Gabril Yudin.** Monitor Collectors Series mono MCD72073. Items marked [a] from MK DO3041, [b]Supraphon LPM7 (6/54), [c]DO2611/2, [d]DO14029 (1/66). Recorded between 1940s and 1950s; dates unknown. *Chausson:* Poème, Op. 25[a]. *Ravel:* Tzigane[a]. *Glazunov:* Violin Concerto[b]. Mazurka-Oberek[c]. *Kabalevsky:* Violin Concerto[d].

⠕ 1h 12m AAD 𝄽**p** ▲

David Oistrakh delivers the most confidential of Chausson *Poèmes*, an intimate, warm-textured reading, generous of tone and phrased with consummate good taste, although the mono Russian recording relegates Kondrashin's orchestra to an unhelpful distance. *Tzigane* suggests cultivated urbanity rather than gipsy camp-fires, although there is no lack of violinistic fireworks, especially in the opening cadenza. The Glazunov Concerto is given a performance in a million — broad, romantic and with that unique sense of timing that only the greatest artists command. Alas, the sound is dim and synthetic but the musicianship is of a calibre that easily transcends sonic limitations. Kabalevsky's blandly tuneful Concerto was composed in 1948 and provides Oistrakh with a palatable but lightweight vehicle for his skills: the *Andantino cantabile* has a song-like simplicity, and the closing *Vivace giocoso* is full of sparkling figurations. Which leaves Glazunov's lilting *Mazurka-Oberek*, the kind of piece that Oistrakh could play in his sleep, albeit with a degree of style and panache that most other violinists could barely achieve, even in their dreams! Monitor's transfers are based on Russian originals that date from the 1940s and 1950s; no recording dates are given, but the sound is generally clean and the CD is issued with useful musical annotation. A marvellous disc and required listening for all lovers of great violin playing.

ORCHESTRAL WORKS. [a]**Guillermo Figueroa** (vn); **Orpheus Chamber Orchestra.** DG 431 680-2GH.
Wagner: Siegfried Idyll. *Turina:* La oración del torero. *Wolf:* Italian Serenade. *Puccini:* Crisantemi. *Berlioz:* Rêverie et caprice, Op. 8[a]. *Sibelius:* Valse triste, Op. 44. *Dvořák:* Nocturne in B major, B47.

⠕ 1h 2m DDD 10/91

The Orpheus Chamber Orchestra, of some 25 instrumentalists who play without a conductor, are an American group founded in the 1980s who have achieved success with every one of their discs — and this collection of seven pieces from seven European countries (if we count Wolf's sprightly, single movement *Italian Serenade* as Italian) is another winner. Wagner wrote his *Siegfried Idyll* as a birthday present for his wife, and it was first played in their home to waken her on that day in 1870 (which happened also to be Christmas Day); it is unusually tender music and one of his most immediately attractive works which here receives a loving performance. At 19 minutes this is the longest piece in the programme; the others last under nine, but each of them still comes across strongly. Another example of instrumental music from an opera composer is Puccini's *Crisantemi* ("Chrysanthemums"), an elegiac piece, originally for string quartet, that he wrote in memory of Duke Amadeo of Savoy but which later provided material for his opera *Manon Lescaut*. Like the Puccini, Wolf's *Serenade* was originally for just four players but sounds well when played by larger forces. Guillermo Figueroa is a persuasive soloist in Berlioz's *Rêverie et caprice*, which is suavely passionate and very Gallic. Indeed, everything in this well chosen programme — a European musical tour — is worth hearing and even the familiar *Valse triste* (Sibelius in waltz time, but mysteriously so) comes up freshly and strongly. The recording is richly atmospheric.

ORCHESTRAL WORKS. Cristina Ortiz (pf); **Royal Philharmonic Orchestra/Moshe Atzmon.** Decca 414 348-2DH. From 414 348-1DH (5/86).
Rachmaninov: Piano Concerto No. 2 in C minor, Op. 18. *Addinsell:* Warsaw Concerto.
Litolff: Concerto Symphonique No. 4 in D minor, Op. 102 — Scherzo. *Gottschalk* (orch. Hazell): Grande fantaisie triomphale sur l'hymne national brésilien, RO108.

58m DDD 9/86   9 P Ⓑ

The C minor Concerto of Rachmaninov symbolizes romanticism at its ripest. Its combination of poetry and sensuous warmth with languorously memorable melodic lines balanced by exhilarating pianistic brilliance happily avoids any suggestion of sentimentality. The simple chordal introduction from the soloist ushers in one of the composer's most luscious tunes, yet the slow movement develops even greater ardour in its melodic contour, and the composer holds back a further haunting expressive idea to bring lyrical contrast to the scintillating finale. The couplings here are most apt. The genuinely inspired pastiche *Warsaw Concerto* by Richard Addinsell has a principal theme worthy to stand alongside those of Rachmaninov and its layout shows satisfying craftsmanship. Ortiz plays this main theme with great affection and she is equally beguiling in the delicious Litolff *Scherzo*. The effect here is of elegance rather than extrovert brilliance: this is reserved for the Gottschalk *Grande fantaisie triomphale*, which is played with a splendid panache that almost covers its inherent vulgarity and certainly emphasizes its ingenuous charm. Throughout the recording balance is realistic and the reverberation adds the most attractive bloom.

SAXOPHONE CONCERTOS. John Harle (sax); **Academy of St Martin in the Fields/ Sir Neville Marriner.** EMI CDC7 54301-2.
Debussy (ed. Harle): Rapsodie. *Glazunov:* Saxophone Concerto in E flat major, Op. 109. Out of the Cool. *Ibert:* Concertino da camera. *R.R. Bennett:* Saxophone Concerto. *Villa-Lobos:* Fantasia.

1h 11m DDD 1/92   9 P

As the issue of a mixed marriage the saxophone has had problems in gaining general acceptance in 'respectable' (musical) society. Sigurd Rascher did wonders for it in the pre-war years, but overall its image has remained what it has been throughout this century, that of an instrument which rose to fame in houses of ill repute and smoky dens in which jazz developed — and from which came the players with the most fluent techniques. At the same time the saxophone's potential as a solo instrument was recognized by a number of notable composers, among them Glazunov and Ibert in the 1930s, Villa-Lobos in 1958 and, some decades later, by Bennett and Heath — the last a composer with a jazz pedigree. Debussy preceded all these but, writing for a lady of his acquaintance who had breathing problems, didn't really have his heart in it; his *Rapsodie* is here presented with worthier orchestration by John Harle. Harle is the virtuoso for whom the saxophone may have long been waiting; the selected works show his splendid musicianship and spectacular technical command to good advantage. If you have any prejudice against the saxophone that is less than incurable, this outstanding disc could easily change your mind — as well as introducing you to some unfamiliar and attactive music.

SCANDINAVIAN SUITES. Guildhall String Ensemble/Robert Salter. RCA Victor Red Seal RD60439.
Nielsen: Little Suite in A minor, FS6. *Grieg:* Holberg Suite, Op. 40. Two Elegiac Melodies, Op. 34. Two Melodies, Op. 53. *Sibelius:* Romance in C major, Op. 42. *Wirén:* Serenade for Strings, Op. 11.

1h 10m DDD 3/92   9 S

All of these, with the possible exception of the Sibelius *Romance*, are popular repertoire pieces, and are eminently well served by the excellent Guildhall String Ensemble and Robert Salter. *The*

Classical Catalogue lists few alternatives of the Nielsen and the Wirén that are finer; and although the Grieg pieces are far more generously represented on disc the Guildhall Strings can more than hold their own. Indeed these performances are touched with distinction. Tempos are sensibly judged and their phrasing and blend are admirable. Yet while they are attentive to every detail of dynamic nuance and tonal finesse, there is no trace of self-consciousness. The second of the Grieg *Melodies*, Op. 53, is particularly affecting in their hands. The recording, made at Forde Abbey, Chard in Somerset, is spectacularly good, having altogether excellent range, body and presence.

New review

STRINGS! THE DEFINITIVE COLLECTION. Guildhall String Ensemble/Robert Salter. RCA Victor Red Seal 09026 61275-2. Item marked [a] from RD87907 (2/90), remainder new to UK. Recorded in 1992.
Pachelbel: Canon and Gigue in D major. **Bach:** Orchestral Suite No. 3 in D major, BWV1068 — Air. *Vivaldi:* Concerto for Strings in G major, "Alla rustica", RV151. *Hoffstetter:* String Quartet in F major, Op. 3 No. 5 — Serenade. *Elgar:* Salut d'amour, Op. 12. *Purcell* (arr. Britten): Chaconne in G minor for strings, Z730. *Marais:* La Gamme — Sonnerie de Sainte-Geneviève du Mont. *Barber:* Adagio for Strings, Op. 11. *Handel:* Serse — Ombra mai fu. Concerto grosso in B flat major, Op. 6 No. 7[a]. *Boccherini:* String Quintet in E major, G275 — Minuet. *Albinoni:* Adagio in G minor.

Ih 10m DDD 2/94

In what terms might this collection be described as 'definitive'? It's a silly title but it isn't a silly record. The programme, comprising a selection of baroque 'pops' and a sprinkling of other later-period ones, is aimed at those who like the sound of a string orchestra (and who have progressed beyond Mantovani), and are not unduly jolted by excursions from one period to another — and back. The Bach Air comes 'as is', uncomplicated by embellishment, and the movements by Haydn, Marais (How did he get in here? His piece became a TV theme!) and Boccherini are beefed up by larger string contingents than their composers specified. The augmentation of forces is done in the best possible taste, with no pandering to lovers of the big, lush, throbbing sound of massed strings, just pleasing performances of variously attractive music. The seasoned collector may already have much of this repertory in selected versions, but for others it may open doors and provide much enjoyment — and in that role it is most welcome.

New review

TANGAZO. MUSIC OF LATIN AMERICA. New World Symphony/Michael Tilson Thomas. Argo 436 737-2ZH. Recorded in 1992.
Chávez: Sinfonía India. *Copland:* Danzón cubano. *Roldán:* Suite from "La Rebambaramba". Rítmica V. *Revueltas:* Sensemayá. *García Caturla:* Tres danzas cubanas. *Piazzolla:* Tangazo. *Ginastera:* Suite from "Estancia".

Ih 14m DDD 6/93

There are some surprising inter-relationships here: for instance, Chávez's Second Symphony (based on repetitive Indian melodies and rhythms and employing platoons of native percussion) has a second section that bears a curious resemblance to Copland's usual folky style. The latter is represented here by the entertaining pastiche that has been called "An American in Cuba"; but it is from two other composers that the authentic Cuban voice is heard. Amadeo Roldán's most famous work, the ballet *La Rebambaramba* (1926/7) about Havana low life in 1830, relies on very heavily accented Afro-Cuban rhythms; his *Rítmica V* is for percussion only. From exactly the same time and background come the three *Cuban dances* by García Caturla (a pupil of Nadia Boulanger who, as a magistrate, was assassinated by a criminal he was about to try), but these reveal a far greater subtlety of harmony and instrumentation, particularly in the second movement. Sophistication of nationalist material is to be found in the dances from Ginastera's ballet *Estancia*, depicting a day on an Argentinian ranch: the virtuosic final *malambo* is frenetically exciting, but the peaceful "Dance of the wheat" is hauntingly lovely. Far more 'civilized' and elegant than nearly all these works, however, is the ingenious, sensitively written and attractive symphonic study of the Argentine tango by Piazzolla, another Boulanger pupil: it would be a knock-out at the Proms. Altogether a highly recommendable disc, brilliantly recorded with demonstration quality.

THE TOSCANINI COLLECTION. New York Philharmonic Orchestra/Arturo Toscanini. RCA Gold Seal mono GD60318.
Gluck: Orfeo ed Euridice — Ballet in D minor (from HMV D1784, 7/30). *Rossini:* Il barbiere di Siviglia — Overture (D1835, 10/30). L'italiana in Algeri — Overture (HMV DB2943, 10/36). Semiramide — Overture (DB3079/80, 3/37). *Verdi:* La traviata — Preludes, Acts 1 and 3 (D1672, 6/30). *Wagner:* Götterdämmerung — Dawn and Siegfried's Rhine Journey (DB2860/61, 7/36). Lohengrin — Preludes: Act 1 (DB2904, 9/36); Act 3 (DB2861).

ADD 1h 4m 11/92 (9)P ▲

RCA's Toscanini Collection contains many very desirable reissues, but this disc has a particular quality in that it shows very clearly several outstanding but differing aspects of the great conductor's genius. The recordings, made in 1929 and 1936, have been made to yield a quality of sound which most listeners will find perfectly acceptable, and they date from a period when, as chief conductor of the New York Philharmonic Orchestra, Toscanini was in his artistic prime. Those who still imagine him always to be a hard, relentless interpreter should hear the exquisitely poised Gluck ballet music, or the tender, extraordinarily eloquent *Traviata* preludes. The Rossini Overtures are certainly propelled with a good deal of energy, but there's plenty of air in the rhythms, and some elegant phrasing amid the virtuoso playing of the magnificent New York Philharmonic. Wagner was particularly near to Toscanini's heart: the *Lohengrin* Act 1 Prelude has a wonderfully luminous quality, and "Siegfried's Rhine Journey" is played with tremendous strength and majesty.

TRUMPET CONCERTOS. Håkan Hardenberger (tpt); **Academy of St Martin in the Fields/Sir Neville Marriner.** Philips 420 203-2PH.
Hummel: Trumpet Concerto in E flat major. *Hertel:* Trumpet Concerto in D major. *J. Stamitz* (realized Boustead): Trumpet Concerto in D major. *Haydn:* Trumpet Concerto in E flat major, HobVIIe/1.

59m 12/87 (9)P

This recording made such a remarkable impression when it first appeared in 1987 that it created overnight a new star in the firmament of trumpeters. The two finest concertos for the trumpet are undoubtedly those of Haydn and Hummel and Hardenberger plays them here with a combination of sparkling bravura and stylish elegance that are altogether irresistible. Marriner and his Academy accompany with characteristic finesse and warmth, with the lilting dotted rhythms of the first movement of the Hummel, seductively jaunty. The lovely *Andante* of the Haydn is no less beguiling and both finales display a high spirited exuberance and an easy bravura which make the listener smile with pleasure. He is no less distinctive in the lesser concerto of Johann Hertel and the other D major work attributed to Johann Stamitz but probably written by someone with the unlikely name of J.B. Holzbogen. This takes the soloist up into the stratosphere of his range and provides him also with some awkward leaps. The Hertel work also taxes the soloist's technique to the extremities but Hardenberger essays all these difficulties with an enviably easy aplomb and remains fluently entertaining throughout. The recording gives him the most vivid realism and presence but it is a pity that the orchestral backcloth is so reverberant; otherwise the sound is very natural.

New review
TRUMPET CONCERTOS. Sergei Nakariakov (tpt); [a]**Alexander Markovich** (pf); **Lausanne Chamber Orchestra/Jésus López-Cobos.** Teldec 4509-90846-2. Recorded 1993.
Jolivet: Concertino for Trumpet, Piano and Strings[a]. *Hummel:* Trumpet Concerto in E flat major. *Tomasi:* Trumpet Concerto. *Haydn:* Trumpet Concerto in E flat major, HobVIIe/1.

56m DDD 10/93 (9)P

The young Russian, Sergei Nakariakov is in his element in the opening Jolivet Double Concerto, standing well out in front of his partner, Alexander Markovich. The balance is less than ideal, with the piano set rather backwardly and the orchestra in a dryish acoustic. The piano emerges more strongly in the very florid finale, the bubbling animation of the playing reaching a frenzy of activity towards the end. The Tomasi (1901-71) is an even better piece and could hardly be better played. In the Haydn and Hummel, the Nakariakov/López-Cobos performances do not quite match the famous version by Håkan Hardenberger, who has the inestimable advantage of wonderfully smiling accompaniments from Marriner and the ASMF. However, the lovely *Andante* of the Haydn is so gracefully phrased by Nakariakov, that the ear is ravished and the finale sparkles delectably, as does, for that matter, the finale of the Hummel. As a whole this new CD is a distinctive compilation, and confirms Nakariakov's position as one of the world's leading trumpeters. The Teldec recording is truthful.

TWENTIETH-CENTURY FLUTE CONCERTOS. Jennifer Stinton (fl); [a]**Geoffrey Browne** (cor ang); **Scottish Chamber Orchestra/Steuart Bedford.** Collins Classics 1210-2. *Honegger:* Concerto da camera[a]. *Ibert:* Flute Concerto (1934). *Nielsen:* Flute Concerto, FS119. *Poulenc* (orch. L. Berkeley): Flute Sonata.

 Ih 6m DDD 8/91

This is basically a vehicle for the artistry of the flautist Jennifer Stinton who presents two flute concertos (by Nielsen and Ibert) plus a transcription of the Poulenc Flute Sonata and a duo concertante by Honegger for flute, cor anglais and strings dating from the period of the Fourth Symphony. The Honegger in which Jennifer Stinton is joined by Geoffrey Browne will come as a surprise to those music-lovers who have not encountered it before; it is pastoral in character and has enormous charm and these artists play with great sympathy for the idiom. Gallic charm is a feature of the Ibert Concerto which also comes off very well. Stinton gives thoroughly expert performances both of this lollipop and Sir Lennox Berkeley's arrangement of the no-less delightful Poulenc. The note reminds us that Honegger was present at the first performance of the Nielsen Concerto (which took place in Paris in 1926), which as the only Scandinavian piece is the 'odd-man-out' here. Though it is less brilliant than the Gallois performance, it is well played and the recording is very good in respect to balance, naturalness and presence.

TWENTIETH CENTURY PLUS. [f]**Andrew Marriner** (cl); [ace]**BBC Sympony Orchestra/** [a]**Peter Eötvös,** [c]**Matthias Bamert,** [e]**Lothar Zagrosek;** [b]**BBC Philphmonic Orchestra/ Sir Peter Maxwell Davies;** [f]**London Symphony Orchestra/Michael Tilson Thomas;** [d]**English Chamber Orchestra/Steuart Bedford.** Collins Classics 2001/5-2. Items marked [a] recorded at a performance in the Royal Albert Hall, London on August 30th, 1990, [b] Cheltenham Town Hall, July 12th, 1990, [c], [d] and [e] recorded in association with the Arts Council.
2001-2: *Birtwistle:* Earth Dances[a]. 2002-2: *Maxwell Davies:* Caroline Mathilde — Concert Suite from Act One[b]. 2003-2: *Saxton:* In the beginning[c]. Music to celebrate the resurrection of Christ[d]. 2004-2: *Mason:* Lighthouses of England and Wales[e]. 2005-2: *Tavener:* The Repentant Thief[f].

(5) 37m 25m 30m 16m 20m DDD 3/92

No, not a five-CD set, but five separately available CD singles, each featuring the music of a contemporary British composer. At first sight the overall title "Twentieth Century Plus" may seem a contradiction in terms (the longest CD has a duration of only 37 minute) but when one considers that the price of each CD is considerably less than that of a full-price issue and that both performances and recordings are of exceptionally high quality then these are bargains indeed. The most important (and long awaited) issue here is perhaps Birtwistle's large and impressive orchestral work — *Earth Dances*. Though massively complex in its construction and organization of material, *Earth Dances* can be a richly rewarding experience for the listener. Its title relates both to the 'geological' strata-like layers of the music, and often violent surface energy that almost makes the earth dance. Tavener's *The Repentant Thief* for clarinet and orchestra is built around a rondo-like structure made up of 10 segments — five "Refrains", three "Dances" and two "Laments", and its title refers to the thief who was crucified with Jesus on Golgotha. It was composed shortly after Tavener had finished work on two large scale works (*Resurrection* and the opera *Mary of Egypt*) and is described by the composer as "a shorter, simple and rather primitive piece". Its simplicity, clear-cut formal scheme and tunefulness make it an immediately accessible and absorbing experience, and this is all the more enhanced by a magical performance of the solo clarinet part by Andrew Marriner. Like the *Eight Songs for a Mad King* before it, the Concert Suite from Act 1 of the ballet *Caroline Mathilde* by Maxwell Davies explores the subject of madness — Caroline Mathilde was the wife of the unbalanced King

Christian VII of Denmark. The ballet traces the King's gradual mental deterioration, and his wife's subsequent love affair with the King's physician (Dr Struensee) through a series of short tableaux that mix Maxwell Davies's musical parody style with his more acerbic and intricate methods of composing. The remaining discs feature music by the younger composers Benedict Mason and Robert Saxton. The highly original, if somewhat unusual *Lighthouses of England and Wales* reveals Mason to be a composer of a striking individuality, not to mention an extremely gifted orchestrator, and Saxton's richly colourful pieces — *In the beginning* and *Music to celebrate the resurrection of Christ* — continue the composer's interest in the religious theme of darkness into light.

WIEN MODERN. [a]**Vienna Jeunesse Choir; Vienna Philharmonic Orchestra/Claudio Abbado.** DG 429 260-2GH. Texts and translations included. Recorded at performances in the Musikverein, Vienna in October 1988.
Boulez: Notations I-IV (1945/78). *Ligeti:* Atmosphères (1961). Lontano (1967). *Nono:* Liebeslied (1954)[a]. *Rihm:* Départ (1988)[a].

46m DDD 4/90

Live recordings of contemporary music concerts are, understandably, rare. Too much can go wrong: in particular, the playing, however well-rehearsed, can develop the rough edges of anxiety and even hostility which make for dispiriting listening, especially when repeated. All the more reason, then, to celebrate the fact that *Wien Modern* is something of a triumph. Even without the crowning glory heard at the actual event, Berg's great set of *Three Orchestral Pieces*, Op. 6, the programme has the strong central focus of two of Ligeti's hypnotic orchestral soundscapes, played with brilliant precision under Abbado's strong yet never overbearing control. The Boulez miniatures — reworkings of early piano pieces — are no less riveting. The rarity, Nono's early exercise in 12-note lyricism, and the novelty, Wolfgang Rihm's specially-composed Rimbaud setting, are not on the same high level of inspiration, but in these secure, confident performances, with an electric, live concert atmosphere conveyed in a first-class recording, they contribute substantially to what was, unmistakably, a very special musical occasion.

WORKS FOR HORN AND ORCHESTRA. Hermann Baumann (hn); **Leipzig Gewandhaus Orchestra/Kurt Masur.** Philips 416 380-2PH. Recorded in 1985.
Glière: Horn Concerto in B flat major, Op. 91. *Saint-Saëns:* Morceau de concert in F minor, Op. 94. *Chabrier:* Larghetto. *Dukas.* Villanelle (orch. Bujanowski).

47m DDD 5/93

The combination of the virtuoso horn player Hermann Baumann, the conductor Kurt Masur and the great Leipzig Gewandhaus Orchestra in an unbeatable recording presents current German music-making at its finest. And the extraordinary bonus about this recording, quite apart from the superlative performances, is the imaginative and interesting repertoire. The music of the Russian composer Reinhold Glière has existed in a kind of twilight, overshadowed by the more familiar names of Tchaikovsky, Rachmaninov, and Prokofiev. Yet his works are shot through with a lush late romanticism which exerts a strong fascination. The Horn Concerto is a highly typical work: wide arching lyric themes; brilliantly orchestrated, and unsparing in its demands upon the soloist. With many backward glances to Tchaikovsky, this is a most welcome addition to the romantic concerto repertoire for the horn. The three shorter pieces which complete this CD are all by French composers of the late nineteenth century. None of these works is of the calibre of the Glière concerto, but each one is both an effective display piece for the horn and a composition of some musical imagination. Hermann Baumann's playing is beyond reproach and he sails through all the trials of each work effortlessly and with burnished tone. Masur's direction of the Gewandhaus is impassioned as well as disciplined, and the recorded sound is suitably rich and excellently balanced.

WORKS FOR OBOE AND ORCHESTRA. John de Lancie (ob); [a]**London Symphony Orchestra/André Previn;** [b]**chamber orchestra/Max Wilcox.** RCA Victor Gold Seal GD87989. Items marked [a] from SB6721, 11/67, [b] Recorded in 1987 and new to UK.

Français. L'horloge de flore[a]. *Ibert.* Symphonie Concertante[a]. *Satie* (orch. Debussy). Gymnopédie No. 1[a]. *R. Strauss.* Oboe Concerto[b].

1h 12m ADD/DDD 12/91

This delightful collection focuses on the career and talent of the American oboist John de Lancie. De Lancie was the American soldier who in 1945 asked Strauss to write him a few bars of music for the oboe — the result, no less, was the delightfully sunny Oboe Concerto. De Lancie's return to the United States prevented him from attending the première, but a few years later Strauss granted him permission to give the work its American première. Bureaucracy and protocol intervened however, and in the event the solo part was entrusted to Mitchell Miller. This 1987 recording (and a very fine one it is too) therefore closes the circle that began over 45 years ago in the Bavarian Alps. It was de Lancie too, who commissioned Françaix's gorgeous suite for oboe and orchestra, *L'horloge de flore* ("The flower clock"). Each of its seven movements represent a flower (and the time of day that the bloom opens), in the Flower Clock developed by the Swedish botanist Carl von Linne. Quite why this charming and melodious work should not be more well known and indeed performed is a complete mystery — it would certainly be a winner with any audience. Inexplicable, too, is the apparent neglect in the catalogue at present of Ibert's *Symphonie Concertante* for oboe and strings. This substantial work is a fine example of Ibert's natural gift for seamless melodic invention and exquisite string writing; if you know and love the Flute Concerto then this work should be next on your list of acquisitions. The Françaix and Ibert items were recorded in 1966 but are remarkably fresh and clear, with Previn and the LSO providing most sympathetic accompaniments.

WORKS FOR VIOLIN AND ORCHESTRA. Joshua Bell (vn); **Royal Philharmonic Orchestra/Andrew Litton.** Decca 433 519-2DH.
Saint-Saëns: Introduction and Rondo capriccioso, Op. 28. *Massenet:* THAIS — Méditation. *Sarasate:* Zigeunerweisen, Op. 20. *Chausson:* Poème, Op. 25. *Ysaÿe:* Caprice d'après l'etude en forme de valse de Saint-Saëns. *Ravel:* Tzigane.

1h DDD 1/92

The Spaniard, Pablo de Sarasate, and the great Belgian virtuoso, Eugene Ysaÿe, both travelled to study in Paris during the second half of the last century, and although both were celebrated as distinguished exponents of violin technique, their collective influence upon the composers active in France at much the same time proved to be far more significant, as this brilliant selection of virtuoso showpieces will readily confirm. The young American violinist, Joshua Bell, himself a grand-pupil of Ysaÿe via his teacher, Joseph Gingold, is heard to superb advantage here in commanding performances of music which will captivate as much as it will astonish. Bell captures the heady bravura of Saint-Saëns *Introduction and Rondo capriccioso* with breathtaking ease, and his spiccato playing in the coda is little short of phenomenal. Sarasate's perennial favourite *Zigeunerweisen* will also astound, with Bell's mastery of the whole panoply of technical effects, including multiple-stopping and left hand pizzicato, contributing to an authentic gypsy-style performance. No recording of this kind would be complete without the celebrated "Méditation" from Massenet's *Thaïs*, made especially compelling here, in Bell's affectionately rich-toned account. The same tonal refinement and sensitivity characterize his elegiac reading of the *Poème* by Chausson, ably supported by the Royal Philharmonic Orchestra under Andrew Litton. Ysaÿe's *Caprice d'après l'etude* is another, although rather less familiar *tour de force*, affording every possibility for virtuosic display, although it does not challenge Ravel's devilish *Tzigane* in terms of pure technical difficulty. This truly hair-raising rendition of the *Tzigane* would bring any concert audience to its feet, and Bell is wholly at ease with its Bartókian gypsy style. This thrilling playing crowns a hugely enjoyable collection from this dazzling young virtuoso. The clear and incisive Decca sound ensures that the forces are balanced effectively, and the natural ambience of Watford Town Hall lends a realistic dramatic weight to full orchestral climaxes, without undue spotlighting of the soloist. An admirable and meticulous release, then, whose appeal will gain Joshua Bell many new admirers.

Chamber

AMERICAN PIANO TRIOS. Hartley Piano Trio (Jacqueline Hartley, vn; Lionel Handy, vc; Carolin Clemmow, pf). Gamut Classics GAMCD536.
Beach: Piano Trio in A minor, Op. 150. **Ives:** Trio. **Bloch:** Three Nocturnes. **Copland:** Vitebsk (Study on a Jewish theme). **Cowell:** Trio.

Ih 13m   DDD   6/94

The Hartley Piano Trio are an excellent ensemble, well balanced, invariably musical and utterly satisfying to listen to in all the styles represented here. Well recorded too. Amy Beach wrote her romantic Trio in A minor as late as 1938, sticking to her guns as if the nineteenth century had never ended. Her slow movement could have come from Elgar or Rachmaninov and there is only an occasional syncopation in the finale to ruffle her Boston decorum. This elegant perform-ance brings out the same quality in Beach's music. Quite different is the Trio by Ives, a rarely heard substantial piece, and Ives set great store by substance. It has to be reckoned with alongside his two string quartets. The joke *Scherzo* is a crazy *mélange* of superimposed quotations and the extended finale ends memorably, saturated with hymn-tune references of a kind that could only have come from Ives. The performance is just as sympathetic and idiomatic as the Beach — two parallel routes to genuine musical discovery. The more familiar Copland is a further contrast, with his characteristic hard-edged sound of the late 1920s and less familiar quarter-tones. The sound is clean and harsh with some very nifty passagework from all three players in the *Allegro*. Bloch's *Three Nocturnes* are mellifluous rarities, in recognizably his own emotional territory, and the Cowell Trio, with a different combination of instruments for each movement, finally brings all three players together with a movement of real serenity.

AMERICAN WORKS FOR WIND QUINTET. Reykjavik Wind Quintet (Bernhardur Wilkinson, fl; Dadi Kolbeinsson, ob; Einar Jóhannesson, cl; Joseph Ognibene, hn; Hafsteinn Gudmundsson, bn). Chandos CHAN9174. Recorded 1991-92.
Barber: Summer Music, Op. 31. **Beach:** Pastorale. **Fine:** Partita. **Harbison:** Quintet for Wind. **Villa-Lobos:** Quinteto em forma de chôros. **Schuller:** Suite.

Ih 6m   DDD   II/93

American music, Icelandic instrumentalists, British venue. Barber's *Summer Music* is delightfully relaxed and playful here, helped by the familiar glow of The Maltings' acoustic. Schuller's little Suite, his first published work, is a teenage *jeu d'esprit* which already shows him experimenting with aspects of jazz in the central Blues movement. Harbison's Wind Quintet is certainly serious in intent, its musical language not always as approachable as we expect from this composer though the outer movements are immediately striking. While eminently lean, lucid and fluent, Beach's brief *Pastorale* risks sounding old hat after this — its idiom would have been considered antiquated in 1942 — and the programme ends on a slightly disconnected note with one of Villa-Lobos's less shapely utterances. Even so, this is a thoroughly recommendable package.

BALANESCU QUARTET. Balanescu Quartet (Alexander Balanescu, Clare Connors, vns; Bill Hawkes, va; Caroline Dale, vc). Argo 436 565-2ZH.
Byrne: High Life. **Moran:** Music from the Towers of the Moon. **Lurie:** Stranger than Paradise. **Torke:** Chalk.

52m   DDD   3/93

All four of the American composers represented here write in easily approachable styles. Each work is excellently served by highly dedicated, expert performances from the Balanescu Quartet, and by a faithful, well-defined recording. David Byrne's *High Life* is the shortest piece on the disc, and consists of syncopated, repeated patterns over which apparently random, free-floating ideas come into being and then dissolve away. Robert Moran's contribution uses material from his opera *From the Towers of the Moon* and is in four short sections. His style is readily enjoyable, with fresh and energetic ideas, and attractive melodic invention. John Lurie's *Stranger than Paradise* is based on music written for a film of the same name: six descriptive episodes form a pleasantly evocative work which is influenced by blues and minimalist styles. *Chalk* is Michael Torke's word for the resinous residue formed by the action of a bow drawn strongly across a stringed instrument. The basic pulse of his piece is constant, in the style of the minimalists, and indeed there is plenty of vigorous, even hectic writing for the four instruments. Torke's insert-notes indicate that he much admires the Balanescu players, and they certainly play their hearts out for him.

BOREALIS. [a]**Siri Torjesen** (sop); **Borealis Ensemble/Christian Eggen.** Aurora ACD4973.
Janson: Tarantella. *Nordensten:* Ricochet, Op. 75. *Söderlind:* A Poem of Longing, Op. 35[a]. *Bibalo:* The Savage.

1h 10m DDD 9/93

This disc makes a fine showcase for the Norwegian ensemble Borealis. Alfred Janson's *Tarantella* (1990) is a wild, striking affair, really sounding (for once) like the dance of someone poisoned by a spider. *Ricochet* (1990) by Frank Tveor Nordensten is something of a mishmash stylistically, although entertaining in the way its diverse elements bounce around (hence, one presumes, the title). Ragnar Söderlind is the foremost Norwegian composer of his generation and the best work on this disc is his chamber aria *A Poem of Longing* (1982) which also exists in versions with piano or orchestra. For reference the chamber scoring here is: flute/piccolo, soprano saxophone, horn, percussion, piano, violin, viola and double bass. The most complex work is the longest: Antonio Bibalo's suite *The Savage* (1983). What is fascinating is the extraordinary resourcefulness with which Bibalo handles his curiously-comprised ensemble (which includes a synthesizer). A crackingly well-performed and recorded recital.

BY ARRANGEMENT. Tetra ([a]Stephen Goss, [a]Peter Howe, [a]Paul Thomas, [b]Graham Roberts, Richard Storry, gtrs). Conifer CDCF903. Recorded 1989-91.
Bernstein (arr. Storry): West Side Story — Medley[a]. *Weill* (arr. Goss): Der Dreigröschen-oper — Songs[a]. *Prokofiev* (arr. Goss): Lieutenant Kijé, Op. 60 — Romance, Kijé's Wedding; Troika[a]. *Bock* (arr. Storry): Fiddler on the Roof — Medley[a]. *Walton* (arr. Goss): Façade — excerpts[b].

1h 6m DDD 11/93

Beethoven once described the guitar as a "miniature orchestra" — and would surely have said no less if he had heard a quartet such as this one. Tetra works wonders with four 'standard' instruments. The oneness of their attack (the guitar is a percussive instrument) and variation of nuance speaks of countless hours of rehearsal — by players of first-rate technical control and sensitive musicianship. All this would be futile in a programme of 'borrowed' music if the arrangements were not of comparable quality — which they *are*. Put the original forms of this music out of your mind; eschew comparisons and enjoy it in its new dress. Arrangements are neither good nor bad by definition; these are good because they *sound* well. The quality of the recording is superb. If you aren't actually allergic to guitars, buy and enjoy this fine issue.

CAPRICCIO DI FLAUTI. Amsterdam Loeki Stardust Quartet (Daniel Brüggen, Bertho Driever, Paul Leenhouts, Karel van Steenhoven, recs). L'Oiseau-Lyre 440 207-2OM. Items marked [a] from 414 277-2OH (8/86), [b]421 130-2OH (4/88), [c]436 155-2OH, [d]430 246-2OH (2/92).
Merula: La Lusignuola[a]. *R. Johnson II:* The Temporiser a 4[a]. *Byrd:* Sermone blando a 3, BE17/23[a]. *Anonymous:* Istampita, "Tre fontane"[a.] Prince Edward's Paven[c]. The Queine of Ingland's Paven[c]. *Bach:* The Art of Fugue, BWV1080 — Contrapunctus I[b]. Fugue in G major, BWV550[b]. Brandenburg Concerto No. 3 in G major, BWV1048 — Allegro. *Sweelinck:* Mein junges Leben hat ein End'[b]. *Frescobaldi:* Capriccio V sopra la Bassa fiammenga[d]. Canzon prima[a]. *Conforti:* Ricercar del quarto tono[d]. *Palestrina:* Lamentationum Hieremiae

prophetae[d]. **Trabaci:** Canzon francesa terza[d]. **Aston:** Hugh Ashton's Maske[c]. **Taverner:** In nomine a 4[c]. **Shott:** Aan de Amsterdamse Grachten (new to UK).

♪ 1h 4m DDD

The annotator begins by quoting Cherubini: "What could be more tedious than a recorder?". Certainly the tone of recorders, minimally enhanced by partials, is somewhat neutral, but when they play in consort the ear is thus drawn to the lines and structure of the music itself, unseduced by specific beauties of individual sounds. Interest resides in the quality of the music and its performance, and in neither respect is this recording to be found lacking. In their precision and stability of pitch, unanimity of attack and technical agility, the Amsterdam Loeki Stardust Quartet are unsurpassed — had he heard them Cherubini might have thought differently about the instrument. Tedious they are not. Sharper-edged tongues have never 'spoken' than in Johnson's *The Temporiser* (the most 'capricious' item on offer), the interplay of the lines in the second *Allegro* of the Third *Brandenburg Concerto* has never been more clearly heard, and *Aan de Amsterdamse Grachten*, their parting Shott, is a well-known barrel-organ tune of the 1950s, a reminder that caprice is still alive and kicking — and that the ALSQ are refreshingly ready to revel in the twentieth century. Here is a programme in which caprice in its playful sense is sharply contrasted with un-capricious solemnity and seriousness of purpose, the music skilfully arranged for the medium and played in immaculate style. Recorder lovers will not need the strong recommendation I make to others.

New review

CELLO SONG. Julian Lloyd Webber (vc); **John Lenehan** (pf). Philips 434 917-2PH. Recorded in 1992.
Villa-Lobos: O Canto do capadócio. **Bach:** Cantata No. 156, Ich steh mit einem Fuss im Grabe, BWV156 — Sinfonia. **Castelnuovo-Tedesco:** Sea murmurs, Op. 24a. **Schumann:** Five Stücke im Volkston, Op. 102 — No. 2, Langsam. **Scriabin:** Etudes, Op. 8 — B flat minor. **Rachmaninov:** Romance in F minor. **Grieg:** Lyric Pieces, Book 3, Op. 43 — To the Spring. **Delius:** Hassan — Serenade. **Elgar:** Romance, Op. 62. **Chopin:** Cello Sonata in G minor, Op. 65 — Largo. **Brahms:** Five Lieder, Op. 105 — Wie Melodien zieht es mir. **Dvořák:** Seven Gypsy Melodies, B104 (Op. 55) — Songs my mother taught me. **Debussy:** Beau soir. **Messiaen:** Quatuor pour la fin du temps — Louange à l'Eternité de Jésus. **Traditional:** The Star of the County Down.

♪ 53m DDD 10/93

As the title of this disc implies, all the pieces are rather in the same slowish-paced, lyrical vein, but their sequence has been cleverly chosen so that there is still plenty of variety to keep the listener's attention. Some of the items are original cello and piano pieces, others are skilful arrangements, and there is a good mixture of well-known and unusual offerings. Elgar's bassoon *Romance* translates particularly well to the cello, as do the Brahms, Debussy and Dvořák songs. The Messiaen excerpt is the longest and the most profound item, and it exists quite happily as an entity away from the rest of the *Quatuor*. Throughout the programme Julian Lloyd Webber plays with exceptional sensitivity, sympathy and tonal beauty — in fact it would be difficult to find better performances of this kind of repertoire anywhere on records of today or yesterday. John Lenehan gives good support, and Philips have provided a mellow, roomy quality of recording.

New review

CHAMBER WORKS BY WOMEN COMPOSERS. [a]**Macalester Trio;** [b]**Joseph Roche,** [c]**Robert Zelnick** (vns); [c]**Tamas Strasser** (va); [c]**Camilla Heller** (vc); [d]**Paul Freed** (pf). Vox Box 115845-2.
C. Schumann: Piano Trio in G minor, Op. 17[a]. **Beach:** Piano Trio in A minor, Op. 150[a]. **Tailleferre:** Violin Sonata No. 1[bd]. **Boulanger:** Pièces — Nocturne; Cortège[bd]. **Mendelssohn-Hensel:** Piano Trio in G minor, Op. 11[a]. **Carreño:** String Quartet in B minor[bc]. **Chaminade:** Piano Trio No. 1 in G minor, Op. 11[a].

♪ ② 2h 21m ADD

Four of the seven works here are première recordings. For such chivalrous acts of rescue gratitude is primarily due to Joseph Roche, leader of the Macalester Trio. Hearing Fanny

Mendelssohn-Hensel's Piano Trio alongside the by now familiar G minor Piano Trio by Fanny's renowned pianist acquaintance, Clara Schumann, it reveals Clara as the neater craftswoman but Fanny as the more urgent communicator — especially its surging first movement. Too bad that as wife of the Prussian court painter, Wilhelm Hensel, the professional concert platform for her was decidedly out of bounds. Not so for this disc's sole American representative, Amy Marcy Cheney, who after marriage at 18, in 1885, pursued an active career as a pianist and composer under the name of Mrs H.H.A. Beach for her remaining 59 years. Dating from 1938, her Op. 150 Piano Trio testifies to a generously romantic heart, albeit occasionally too openly worn on the sleeve in so far as melody is concerned. In the last of the four piano trios we meet the young Cécile Chaminade, already anticipating later conquests with the ear-catching charm of this work's fancifully scored *Scherzo*. The solitary string quartet (like the last two works new to the catalogue) comes from that legendary Venezuelan firebrand, Teresa Carreño, here in surprisingly assuaging, quasi classical trim — even to the inclusion of a fugal episode (as if in emulation of Clara Schumann) in the finale. Each work included merits its place, but none, surely, more than those for just violin and piano. Lili Boulanger's "Nocturne" and "Cortège" is sensitive and subtle. As for Tailleferre's finely crafted, emotionally sophisticated First Sonata in C sharp minor, its previous omission from the catalogue is inexplicable. Apart from a bland account of Clara Schumann's Trio, the playing throughout is as acceptable as the recording.

New review

CLARINET VIRTUOSI OF THE PAST: SIMON HERMSTEDT. [acde]**Elizabeth Ritchie** (sop); **Victoria Soames** (cl); [b]**Anna Coleman** (vn); [b]**Matthew Souter** (va); [b]**Alastair Blayden** (vc); [acdef]**Jennifer Purvis** (pf). Clarinet Classics CC0006. Notes, texts and translations included. Recorded in 1992.
Mozart: La clemenza di Tito — Parto, parto (arr. Bergmann)[a]. *Müller:* Quartet No. 2 in F sharp minor[b]. *Paer:* Sargino, ossia l'allievo dell'amore — Una voca al cor mi parla (arr. Weston and Voxman)[c]. *Spohr:* Sechs Lieder, Op. 103[d]. Faust — Ich bin allein[e]. Variations in B flat major on a Theme from "Alruna"[f].

1h 13m   DDD   3/94

Considering the fact that the clarinet has been around for nearly three centuries and inspired Mozart and Brahms to write masterpieces, it is a pity that its solo repertory remains small and that much of it is music of the second rank. That description undoubtedly fits the *Sechs Lieder* that Spohr wrote for Simon Hermstedt in 1837. However, they have charm; indeed, in a letter to the composer, Mendelssohn praised No. 2 for "its perfectly natural sweetness". Elizabeth Ritchie, Victoria Soames and Jennifer Purvis bring freshness and skill to this music, while the clarinettist's performance has the tonal flexibility to remind us that Hermstedt modelled himself on the best violinists of his day. The rest of the programme is also enjoyable and demonstrates the skill and interpretative range of the singer as well as that of the clarinettist and her instrumental colleagues. The recording, made in the ample acoustic of St George's, Brandon Hill, Bristol, is well balanced.

New review

CLASSICAL WORKS FOR HORN AND STRINGS. Hermann Baumann, [a]**Vladimir Dshambasov** (hns); **Gewandhaus Quartet** (Karl and Conrad Suske, vns; Dieter Hallmann, va; Jürnjakob Timm, vc); [b]**Olaf Hallmann** (va); [c]**Christian Ockert** (db). Philips 426 440-2PH. Recorded in 1992.
Mozart: Horn Quintet in E flat major, K407/K386c[b]. *Haydn:* Divertimento a tre in E flat major, HobIV/5. *M. Haydn:* Romanze in A flat major. *Beethoven:* Sextet in E flat major, Op. 81b[a]. *Reicha:* Horn Quintet, Op. 106[c].

1h 13m   DDD   9/93

In the insert-notes, horn-player Hermann Baumann describes the pieces on this disc as "the essential chamber works for horn and strings of the Classical and Romantic periods". The core work of the recording is Mozart's Horn Quintet and, according to Baumann, the horn part is the most difficult that Mozart wrote for the instrument. Michael Haydn's *Romanze*, an arrangement of the slow movement from Mozart's Third Horn Concerto, K447, is affectionately played with satisfying warmth of tone and unity of ensemble, and Joseph Haydn's E flat Divertimento provides an entertaining contrast. Antoine Reicha (1770-1836) is best known as a theorist. However, his E major Quintet, Op. 106, recorded here for the first time, blends virtuosity and lyricism in music of rhythmic and contrapuntal ingenuity, and deserves to be better known. These are excellent performances, superbly recorded.

New review

COMPOSERS IN PERSON. [a]**Maria Barrientos,** [b]**Ninon Vallin** (sops); [c]**Enrique Granados,** [d]**Federico Mompou,** [b]**Joaquin Nin** (pfs); **Manuel de Falla** ([a]pf/[e]hpd); [e]**instrumental ensemble.** EMI Composers in Person mono CDC7 54836-2 Texts and translations included.

Granados: Danzas españolas, Op. 37[c] — No. 7, Valenciana; No. 10, Danza triste (both from Odeon 68649/50). Goyescas — No. 7, El pelele[c] (68651. All recorded c.1912). *Falla:* Siete canciones populares españolas[a] (French Columbia D11701 and PFX1/2. 1928-30). El amor brujo[a] — Canción del fuego fátuo. Soneto a Córdoba (PFX2. 1930). Harpsichord Concerto[e] (French Columbia LFX92/3. 1930). *Mompou*[d]: Scènes d'enfants — No. 5, Jeunes filles au jardin. Suburbis — No. 1, El carrer, el guitarrista i el vell cavall. Cançons i dansas — No. 5 (all from French Columbia FCX184); No. 6 (previously unpublished); No. 8. Paisajes — No. 1, La fuente y la campana (FCX184. All 1950). *Nin*[b]: Cantos populares españolas — No. 3, Tonada de la niña perdida; No. 4, Montañesa; No. 6, Malagueña; No. 7, Granadina; No. 19, Canto Andaluz; No. 20, Polo (Odeon 188693/5. 1929).

Ih 18m   ADD   II/93   ▲

With few exceptions all Spain's leading composers in the early part of this century were excellent pianists. Granados is represented by some 1912 discs. Despite their surface noise (very heavy in an improvised ramble on "El pelele"), his qualities are evident, particularly in a light, airy and crisply rhythmic "Valenciana". The major part of the present disc is given over, reasonably enough, to Falla, an indisputably greater composer than the others and a conspicuously first-class keyboard player. His playing of the Harpsichord Concerto is masterly, especially of the *Lento* which, exemplifying his plea that it should be taken as slowly as humanly possible, is enormously atmospheric and evocative of great bells during the Corpus Christi procession. Falla is equally outstanding in the seven folk-songs accompanying Maria Barrientos. Ninon Vallin's bright, clear voice is artlessly attractive in the folk-song settings of Nin, a virtuoso pianist who is evidently enjoying himself in the "Malagueña". In a totally different style, far more introspective and subtle, is the playing of Mompou. He takes the dance of the fifth *Can o i dansa* slower than usual, gives a fine lift to the sixth (dedicated to Rubinstein), and is utterly seductive in the sentimental tune of "Jeunes filles au jardin", played very slowly and freely.

DEBUT. Sarah Chang (vn); **Sandra Rivers** (pf). EMI CDC7 54352-2.
Sarasate: Concert Fantasy on "Carmen", Op. 25. *Elgar:* Salut d'amour, Op. 12. La Capricieuse, Op. 17. *Khachaturian:* Gayaneh — Sabre Dance. *Kreisler:* Tempo di Menuetto in the style of Pugnani. *Paganini:* Caprices, Op. 1 — No. 1 in E major; No. 15 in E minor. *Chopin* (arr. Milstein): Nocturne in C sharp minor, Op. posth. *Shostakovich* (arr. Zyganow): Preludes, Op. 34 — No. 10 in C sharp minor; No. 15 in D major. *Gershwin* (trans. Heifetz): Porgy and Bess — It ain't necessarily so. *Liszt* (arr. Milstein): Consolations, S172 — Lento placido. *Tchaikovsky:* Souvenir d'un lieu cher, Op. 42 — Mélodie in E flat major. *Prokofiev* (arr. Heifetz): The Love for Three Oranges — March.

51m   DDD   I/93

This astonishing disc heralds the recording début of another much-vaunted violinistic phenomenon, the 11-year-old Sarah Chang. A student of the acclaimed pedagogue Dorothy DeLay, Chang actually made this recording at the age of nine, playing a quarter-sized violin. With an impressive catalogue of major orchestral engagements to her credit, she is now continuing her studies at the Juilliard School in New York. Her taxing programme opens with an impeccable account of Sarasate's *Carmen* Fantasy, in an edition prepared by Zino Francescatti; dazzling playing, even if that last *frisson* of excitement is held in check. The two Elgar favourites are charming, even if slightly mannered, but Chang's bristling performances of Khachaturian's "Sabre Dance" and the famous Heifetz transcription of the March from Prokofiev's *The Love for Three Oranges* are both sensational. Her Paganini, too, is electrifying — she despatches the First and Fifteenth *Caprices* with the confident *élan* of a seasoned virtuoso. The same technical assurance is evident in two Preludes by Shostakovich, but undemonstrative offerings are marginally less convincing perhaps, at this very early stage, with some inflexibility in the Tchaikovsky and Kreisler works. She is a shade unyielding in her approach to Nathan Milstein's winning Chopin and Liszt arrangements, but her natural spontaneity works to greater advantage in "It ain't necessarily so", from *Porgy and Bess*, in the famous Heifetz version. "Sarah Chang is the most ideal violinist I have ever heard" was Sir Yehudi Menuhin's verdict on this monumentally gifted young virtuoso. Her recording début will enthral and captivate in equal measure — hear it as a matter of priority!

JACQUELINE DU PRE — HER EARLY BBC RECORDINGS. Jacqueline du Pré, [f]William Pleeth (vcs); [deg]Ernest Lush, [c]Stephen Kovacevich (pfs). EMI Studio mono CDM7 63165/6-2. Recorded at broadcast performances on [a]January 7th, 1962, [b]January 26th, 1962, [c]February 25th, 1965, [dg]March 22nd, 1961, [e]September 3rd, 1962, [f]March 17th, 1963. *CDM7 63165-2* — *Bach:* Solo Cello Suites — No. 1 in G major, BWV1007[a]; No. 2 in D minor, BWV1008[b]. *Britten:* Cello Sonata in C major, Op. 65 — Scherzo and March[c]. *Falla* (arr. Maréchal): Suite populaire espagnole[d]. *CDM7 63166-2* — *Brahms:* Cello Sonata No. 2 in F major, Op. 99[e]. *F. Couperin:* Nouveaux Concerts — Treizième Concert[f]. *Handel* (arr. Slatter): Oboe Concerto in G minor, HWV287[g].

② 1h 52m ADD 9/89 ▲

We owe the BBC and EMI a debt of gratitude for making these valuable recordings available on disc. The performances date from her mid- to late- teens, and reveal a maturity and passion that is rare in so young a performer. This, together with her wonderful gift of communication, make these performances very special indeed. The two Bach Cello Suites have a magical, intimate poetry that transfixes the attention from the very first note and her beautifully phrased and lyrical readings more than compensate for any slight imperfections of articulation. Sadly we have only the Scherzo and March movements from the Britten Cello Sonata, and judging by the quality of these, a complete performance would surely have been a recording to treasure. These are sparkling performances, full of wit and good humour, reflecting the obvious rapport between the two young artists. The recording of Falla's *Suite populaire espagnole* dates from 1961 when du Pré was only 16 but is no less assured or technically accomplished. The performance is full of life and rhythmic vitality, with some very tender and expressive playing, as in the cantabile melodies of the "Nana" and "Cancion" movements. The mono recordings are not of the highest quality (the Bach Suites are taken from transcription discs, so there are traces of surface noise and clicks) but this is of little relevance when we are presented with playing as beautiful and captivating as this.

New review

FRENCH BAROQUE FLUTE MUSIC. Rachel Brown (fl); Mark Caudle (viol); James Johnstone (hpd). Chandos Chaconne CHAN0544. *Leclair:* Trio Sonatas — No. 1 in E minor, Op. 2; No. 7 in G major, Op. 9. *Blavet:* Trio Sonata No. 2 in D minor, "La Vibray", Op. 2. *Rameau:* Pièces de clavecin en concerts — Cinquième concert. *M. La Barre:* Sonate l'inconnuë in G major, Book 2 No. 9. *Hotteterre:* Airs et Brunettes.

1h 11m DDD 2/94

Rachel Brown's all-French programme gains most of its substance from two Leclair sonatas placed at the beginning and the end, and from the fifth *concert* from Rameau's *Pièces de clavecin en concerts* in the middle. Not only are these the best music, they also get the best performances, with Brown combining taste, passion and a sort of languid, expansive freedom that seems the very essence of good baroque manners. In between come an athletic though comparatively straightforward sonata by Blavet, a suite by La Barre whose main interest lies in a vigorous Chaconne, and a collection of Hotteterre arrangements of vocal originals. From beginning to end this is still a disc of high-quality flute-playing — expressive, controlled, easy on the ear, and crisply accompanied too.

FRENCH CHAMBER MUSIC. [a]Catherine Cantin (fl); [b]Maurice Bourgue (ob); [c]Michel Portal (cl); [d]Amaury Wallez (bn); [e]André Cazalet (hn); Pascal Rogé (pf). Decca 425 861-2DH.

Saint-Saëns: Caprice sur des airs danois et russes, Op. 79[abc]. **d'Indy:** Sarabande et menuet, Op. 72[abcde]. **Roussel:** Divertissement, Op. 6[abcde]. **Tansman:** Le Jardin du Paradis — Danse de la sorcière[abcde]. **Françaix:** L'heure du berger[abce]. **Poulenc:** Elégie[c]. **Milhaud:** Sonata for Flute, Oboe, Clarinet and Piano, Op. 47[abc].

·ɔ̣· 1h 7m DDD 5/91

French composers are noted for their special fondness for writing for wind instruments, but their wide diversity of styles is illustrated by this attractive disc, which is notable for superbly clean and sensitive playing by musicians in complete accord with each other and in instinctive sympathy with the music. Of the three works here for wind quintet and piano, the Roussel *Divertissement* is a particular delight, in turn sprightly and seductive; the d'Indy movements (transcribed from an earlier suite for the curious combination of trumpet, two flutes and string quartet) are an expressively contrapuntal sarabande and an oddly chirpy minuet; and the pungent Tansman dance is from an unfinished ballet. Jean Françaix's habitual spirit of *gaminerie* reigns in his three portraits for wind quartet and piano, written with his usual consummate craftsmanship. The works for wind trio and piano could scarcely be more unlike: Saint-Saëns's suave confection on (reputedly bogus) Danish and Russian airs, with a brilliant piano part, and Milhaud's often abrasive sonata (despite a pastoral opening), which ends with a dirge for victims of a Spanish influenza epidemic. And there's Poulenc's elegy for Dennis Brain, its broad lament tinged with just a touch of the humour that Dennis himself would have enjoyed.

THE LINDSAYS: 25 YEARS. Lindsay Quartet (Peter Cropper, Ronald Birks, vns; [a]Robin Ireland, [b]Roger Bigley, vas; Bernard Gregor-Smith, vc). ASV CDDCA825. Taken from BBC broadcast performances.
Wirén: String Quartet No. 3 in D minor, Op. 18 (recorded in 1987)[a]. **A. Tchaikovsky:** String Quartet No. 2 in C major, Op. 5 (1978)[b]. **Hugh Wood:** String Quartet No. 3, Op. 20 (1980)[b]. **Barber:** String Quartet, Op. 11 (1988)[a].

·ɔ̣· 1h 17m ADD 1/93

As its name suggests, this issue celebrates the Lindsay String Quartet's twenty-fifth anniversary, with all but the present violist Robin Ireland chalking up over 20 years membership. The quartet has played works ranging from the classics to the less familiar modern ones by André Tchaikovsky and Hugh Wood that feature here. Indeed, what we have here is in no way central twentieth-century repertory: no 'great' composer at all, some will say, and regret it. Furthermore, these are recordings of BBC concert performances from 1978-88, and inevitably there are a few rustles that would otherwise have been edited out and applause after each work except the Tchaikovsky. However, such is the vitality of the playing that one can overlook these matters, and the overall quality of the sound is good. Dag Wirén is a Swedish composer known mainly for just one work, a Serenade for Strings, but his Third Quartet has plenty of personality although in a conservative idiom. André Tchaikovsky was Polish-born but spent much of his life in England before dying by his own hand at the age of 46; a fine pianist as well as a composer, he had a prickly personality that is strongly reflected in his Second Quartet, written for the Lindsays and first played by them in this BBC performance of January 1978. Hugh Wood's Third Quartet, which the Lindsays premièred, is also a tough piece, and relies heavily on Second Viennese School gesturings that now sound very dated, but the Lindsays play it with commitment. Finally, Samuel Barber's Quartet is maybe the best music here. Its celebrated central *Adagio* sounds strikingly fresh played in context on four instruments instead of alone in the usual version for string orchestra. It is a pleasure to salute the Lindsays and to welcome this excellent tribute disc.

New review
MADE IN AMERICA. Yo-Yo Ma (vc); [c]**Ronan Lefkowitz**, [d]**Lynn Chang** (vns); [ab]**Jeffrey Kahane**, [c]**Gilbert Kalish** (pfs). Sony Classical SK53126. Recorded 1991-92.
Bernstein (trans. Ma): Clarinet Sonata[a]. **Gershwin** (arr. Heifetz, trans. Ma)[b]: Three Preludes. **Ives:** Trio for Violin, Clarinet and Piano[c]. **Kirchner:** Triptych[d].

·ɔ̣· 1h 5m DDD 4/94

In Ives's Trio you have the feeling that Ives's only way of coping with his love for the 'old tunes' was to send them up; yet he did so with such aplomb, daring and imagination that one can't help but respond gratefully. Ives's Trio is the final work in Yo-Yo Ma's absorbing programme. The first, Bernstein's wartime Clarinet Sonata, was arranged with the composer's authorization and is pure delight from start to finish: mild, melodious and ultimately high-spirited. Which leaves Gershwin and Kirchner, the former represented by a sensuous re-working of Heifetz's famous *Prelude* transcriptions, the latter by an astonishingly outspoken *Triptych*. Scored, respectively, for "Cello Solo" and "Violin and Cello Obbligato" (the movement subtitles), *Triptych* ends with a vigorous *Presto*. The entire programme is superbly performed, the Ives being particularly adroit, the Gershwin smoochy and playful. This is the sort of recital that will have you reaching for *The Classical Catalogue* in search of more of the same.

MUSIC FOR WIND ENSEMBLE. Aulos Quintet ([a]Peter Rijkx, fl; [a]Diethelm Jonas, ob; [a]Karl-Theo Adler, cl; [a]Ralph Sabow, bn; Dietmar Ullrich, hn). Koch Schwann Musica Mundi 310087.
Briccialdi: Wind Quintet, Op. 124. *Lefébure:* Suite, Op. 57. **Rossini:** Wind Quartet No. 6[a]. *Taffanel:* Wind Quintet.

59m DDD 10/91

The image of wind music for some people is of something faintly comic, even perhaps of piping, burping and blasting, according to whether the instruments are high or low and playing softly or loudly — certainly not music offering the expressive sophistication that we associate with piano or strings. Nevertheless, in the hands of first-class players these instruments are as refined and subtle as any others. It's a pity that some of the great composers — Mozart is a notable exception — gave us little music for wind alone, though they often wrote splendidly for these instruments in orchestral music. Still, Rossini is a great figure, and even if the others represented in this nineteenth-century programme are not, they make up for lack of depth by writing superbly for the players. The members of the Aulos Wind Quintet are totally equal to this music and the performances are a delight — but then, so is the music itself, mainly on the lighter side and presented here with tremendous panache as well as affection. Each work here has its own kind of charm, and each player brings both skill and refinement to a satisfyingly well-blended whole; the second movement of Rossini's Quartet is particularly good at showing them off individually in a series of variations. The recording is clear, atmospheric and well balanced. This is a disc to give much delight.

ROMANTIC MUSIC FOR VIOLIN AND PIANO. Vera Vaidman (vn); **Emanuel Krasovsky** (pf). CDI/Pickwick PWK1137.
Tchaikovsky: Méditation, Op. 42 No. 1. Valse-Scherzo, Op. 34. Mélodie, Op. 42 No. 3. *Dvořák:* Violin Sonatina in G major, B183. **Schubert:** Violin Sonata in A minor, D385. *Kreisler:* Schön Rosmarin. Liebesleid. Liebesfreud.

1h 11m DDD 6/90

Here is a splendid collection of inspired music for violin and piano, marvellously played and given a digital recording of great realism and immediacy. The Dvořák *Sonatina* was written in New York at around the same time that the great Czech composer created his most popular work, the *New World* Symphony, and it deserves to be equally well known. All four movements are brimming over with the same kind of memorable melody that makes the symphony such a favourite with the public. The first movement makes an impression of great vigour and impulse, the *Larghetto* sings beguilingly, the *Scherzo* dances vivaciously and the finale sparkles and introduces another quite lovely lyrical folksy melody which is instantly memorable and stays in the mind long after the work has concluded. Vera Vaidman's performance has great sympathy and spontaneity and her partner, Emanuel Krasovsky gives all the support she could ask for, though it is she who dominates — for that is the way the music is written. The programme opens with an engaging Tchaikovsky triptych, each miniature strikingly characterful and the third, *Mélodie*, having that bittersweet Russian melancholy for which the composer is famous. The Schubert *Sonata* which follows the Dvořák has a disarming, simple lyricism. Like the Dvořák it is in four movements: the *andante* is gently eloquent, and the finale flows with captivating innocence. The programme ends with three Kreisler lollipops, dashingly played, to end the recital exuberantly. This disc is in the bargain price range and the recording is in the demonstration class: on a minor label, with an Israeli source, it could be so easily passed by, but it should be sought out, for its rewards are very considerable.

JOSEPH SZIGETI. The Recordings with Béla Bartók and Andor Foldes. **Joseph Szigeti** (vn); [a]**Andor Foldes,** [b]**Béla Bartók** (pfs). Biddulph mono LAB070/71. From American Columbia and New Music Quarterly originals; recorded 1940-41.

Bartók: Rhapsody No. 1, Sz86[b]. Contrasts, Sz111[b] (with Benny Goodman, cl). *Bloch:* Baal Shem[a]. *Debussy:* Violin Sonata in G minor[a]. *Ives:* Violin Sonata No. 4, "Children's Day at the Camp Meeting"[a]. *Schubert:* Violin Sonatina in D major, D384[a]. Also includes works by *Bach, Brahms, Corelli, Debussy, Dvořák, Falla, Hubay, Kodály, Lalo, Milhaud, Mussorgsky* and *Schubert.*

(2) 2h 9m ADD   P ▲

Ever the thinker among conjurors, Joseph Szigeti didn't so much transcend pyrotechnics as harness them to expressive ends. Szigeti's technique was in good working order on this set and fully up to realizing the sensuality implicit in works like Debussy's Sonata and "Clair de lune" from the *Suite bergamasque* (heard here in Rölens's effective arrangement). *Baal Shem* is gripping in its confessional ardour, enshrining profoundly insightful interpretations. It was also fascinating to encounter the rare Ives Fourth Sonata. It is difficult to imagine the tender, central *Largo cantabile* sounding with greater melancholy than it does here. It is a strangely alluring piece, full of stylistic contradictions and ending with an engagingly off-beam *Allegro*. The Milhaud and Falla items (the booklet prints them in reverse order) are delightfully adroit, but Szigeti's own transcription of the *Háry János* Intermezzo is rather discursive and heavy-handed. The Bartók *Rhapsody* is given with appropriate rustic gaiety, while *Contrasts* — heard here in its best CD transfer yet — has just the right feeling of improvised burlesque. The Bach, Corelli and Schubert items convey the very essence of Szigeti's violinistic personality, his warmth, elegance and superior intelligence. The Corelli *La folia* will stop you in your tracks, especially the closing cadenza with its felicitous chord-work, a remarkable piece of playing by any standards. The Schubert D major *Sonatina*'s opening *Allegro molto* displays acute sensitivity to line, while in the carefree *Rondo* (taken from the big D major Piano Sonata, D850) Szigeti's quick-wristed, capricious phrasing is reminiscent of Heifetz's. The Bach *Bourrée* is typically crisp, deliberate and rhythmically supple. Quite honestly, everything here is so rich in incident that no amount of listening will dull its appeal. Joseph Szigeti's art is truly inexhaustible!

TWENTIETH-CENTURY CHAMBER WORKS. Jascha Heifetz (vn); [a]**Gregor Piatigorsky** (vc); [b]**Emanuel Bay,** [c]**Artur Rubinstein** (pfs). RCA Victor Gold Seal GD87871.

Debussy[b]: Violin Sonata in G minor. Préludes — Book 1, No. 8, La fille aux cheveux de lin (arr. Hartmann. Both mono and new to UK). *Respighi:* Violin Sonata in B minor[b] (new to UK). *Ravel* (arr. Roques): Sonatine in F sharp minor — Menuet[b] (from RB16243, 6/61). Piano Trio in A minor[ac] (HMV mono DB9620/22, 6/51). *Martinů:* Duo[a] (SB6661, 7/66).

1h 13m ADD 9/90   P S ▲

Though the twentieth century has produced many fine violinists, the name of Jascha Heifetz still inspires a special awe, not least among fellow musicians, for his playing had exceptional eloquence and personality alongside a technical command that he displayed not only in dexterity but more often than not by imparting a subtle, inimitable colour to his tone when shaping a phrase. The works here are of the violinist's own time, for he had already made his début aged five a decade before Debussy wrote his Violin Sonata towards the end of the First World War. He recorded that Sonata with Emanuel Bay in 1950, but we would not know it when hearing the sound as successfully remastered here, and this is playing of real distinction, even if the elusive middle movement is arguably over-forceful. Heifetz and his celebrated colleagues are also impressive in the Ravel Trio recorded in the same year, also a wartime work but of a different kind, having great power and feeling, though the gentle little Minuet from the piano Sonatine is taken too briskly. The Respighi and Martinů pieces are perhaps less striking at first, but here too we are fully held by the authority of the playing. As already suggested, little apology need be made for the sound in the major works despite the age of the recordings, though there is 78-type needle hiss in *La fille aux cheveux de lin* and one misses really quiet tone in the Ravel Trio. This disc is for everyone, not just for connoisseurs of fine violin playing.

VIOLIN RECITAL. Kyoko Takezawa (vn); **Philip Moll** (pf). RCA Victor Red Seal 09026 60704-2.

Bartók: Violin Sonata, Sz117. **Brahms:** Hungarian Dance No. 1 in G minor. **Chaminade** (arr. Kreisler): Sérénade espagnole. **Falla** (trans. Kochanski): Suite populaire espagnole. **Tchaikovsky:** Souvenir d'un lieu cher, Op. 42 — No. 1, Méditation in D minor. Valse-scherzo, Op. 34.

1h 5m   DDD   2/93

Brave indeed is the violinist who elects to open a début recital disc with the Bartók solo sonata! Kyoko Takezawa's fearless performance is outstandingly good; her playing has idiomatic refinement and formidable virtuosity, sufficient to guarantee success in this most taxing of works for unaccompanied violin. For the remainder of her programme, this 1986 Gold Medal winner at the 1986 Indianapolis Violin Competition, and former student of Dorothy DeLay at the Juilliard School is joined at the piano by Philip Moll. Their Tchaikovsky performances are particularly memorable; affecting and nostalgic in the "Méditation" in D minor, and appropriately zestful in the case of the "Valse-scherzo". Takezawa's dazzling account of de Falla's *Suite populaire espagnole* (Paul Kochanski's arrangement) has an intuitive flair and individuality, also much in evidence in the other Spanish-flavoured offering here, Chaminade's *Sérénade espagnole*, once a regular Kreisler encore piece, but seldom heard these days. Takezawa shows her true mettle in a spirited rendition of the *Hungarian Dance* No. 1 by Brahms, which concludes the programme. This is an outstanding release, a brilliantly played and perceptively chosen programme crowned by a stunning version of the Bartók Sonata. A must for all lovers of the violin.

New review
VIRTUOSO WORKS FOR VIOLIN AND PIANO. Maxim Vengerov (vn); **Itamar Golan** (pf). Teldec 9031-77351-2. Recorded in 1993.
Wieniawski: Polonaise No. 1 in D major, Op. 4. Légende, Op. 17. **Paganini:** I palpiti, Op. 13. **Kreisler:** Schön Rosmarin. Tambourin chinois. Caprice viennois. **Bloch:** Baal shem — Nigun. **Tchaikovsky:** Souvenir d'un lieu cher, Op. 42 — No. 2, Scherzo in C minor; No. 3, Mélodie in E flat major. **Messiaen:** Theme et Variations. **Sarasate:** Caprice basque, Op. 24. **Bazzini:** La Ronde des lutins, Op. 25.

1h 7m   DDD   4/94

Maxim Vengerov may not be the most creative fiddler around, but he is such a masterful musician that everything he touches turns to gold. Firstly, his intonation is impeccable. The purity and steadiness of Paganini's *I palpiti* is such that one never has the impression of his being under any strain. The double-stopping episodes in Wieniawski's *Légende* appear to come as naturally to him as single notes. He captures the mawkish Slavonic melancholy with real intensity. In the Kreisler selection Vengerov is gentle and generous-spirited, charmingly pure in *Schön Rosmarin* and idiomatic for the tongue-in-cheek *Tambourin chinois*. The Bazzini has terrific attack too though it might have been more impish. The music is undeniably inconsequential, but one is left gawping at the phenomenal accuracy and confidence of the left-hand pizzicato section at the end. In conclusion it must be said that rarely if ever does one hear the Tchaikovsky *Mélodie* played with more eloquence and refined tone colour.

WORKS FOR CELLO AND PIANO. Maria Kliegel (vc); **Raimund Havenith** (pf). Marco Polo 8 223403.
Cassadó: Dance of the Green Devil. **Popper:** Fantasy on Little Russian songs, Op. 43. Serenade, Op. 54 No. 2. **Bach** (trans. Rose): Suite in D major, BWV1068 — Air. **Schubert:** Schwanengesang, D957 — Ständchen. **F. Schubert II:** Bagatelle, Op. 13 No. 9. Die Biene. **Granados:** Goyescas — Intermezzo. **Shostakovich:** The gadfly, Op. 97 —Tarantella. **Ravel:** Sites auriculaires — Habanera. **Debussy:** Préludes, Book 1 — La fille aux cheveux de lin. **Senaillé:** Violin Sonata No. 5 in D minor — Allègro spirituoso. **Vieuxtemps:** 36 Etudes, Op. 48 — No. 24, Cantilena. **Barchet:** Images de Menton — Boulevard de 'Garavan. **Offenbach:** Danse bohémienne, Op. 28. **Rachmaninov:** Vocalise, Op. 34 No. 14. **Gershwin:** Short Story.

1h 15m   DDD   9/92

With just over 75 minutes of superb playing, and a programme of rewarding variety and scope, this recital disc from German-born Maria Kliegel and Raimund Havenith ranks with the finest now available. A casual glance at the repertoire reveals quite a few surprises; the selections are fascinating, striking an ideal balance between the adventurous and the reassuringly familiar, all heard in performances of spectacular quality. Gaspar Cassadó's *Dance of the Green Devil* (Falla's influence is obvious!) is incisively played, and Kliegel is especially fine in two works by the "Paganini of the cello", David Popper. The Bach Air and "Ständchen" from Schubert's *Schwanengesang* will be familiar, as will "La fille aux cheveux de lin", transcribed from Book 1 of Debussy's *Préludes*. As transcriptions, all are remarkably effective, but Kliegel's virtuosity comes very much to the fore in the Intermezzo from *Goyescas* and the Ravel "Habanera", whilst her account of Shostakovich's witty "Tarantella", from orchestrations for the 1955 film *The Gadfly*, has flair and brilliance. An introspective reading of the familiar Rachmaninov *Vocalise* could have benefited from a degree of extra flexibility perhaps, but Kliegel gives a fascinating performance of Barchet's pizzicato study of vaguely flamenco idioms, "Boulevard de Garavan". Gershwin's *Short Story* offers a total contrast to the remaining items by Vieuxtemps and Offenbach, completing an unusually distinguished recital, vividly played and glowingly recorded. Definitely worth investigating.

WORKS FOR CLARINET AND PIANO. Michael Collins (cl); **Kathryn Stott** (pf). EMI Virtuosi CDC7 54419-2.
Schumann: Fantasiestücke, Op. 73. **Debussy:** Première rapsodie. **Poulenc:** Clarinet Sonata. **Lovreglio:** Fantasia on Verdi's "La traviata", Op. 45. **Weber:** Grand Duo Concertant, J204. **Messager:** Solo de concours.

> 1h 7m DDD 9/92

WORKS FOR CLARINET AND PIANO. Victoria Soames (cl); **Julius Drake** (pf). Clarinet Classics CC0001.
Copland: Clarinet Sonata. **Tailleferre:** Arabesque. Sonata for Solo Clarinet. **Honegger:** Sonatine. **Poulenc:** Clarinet Sonata. **Milhaud:** Sonatine, Op. 100. Duo Concertant, Op. 351.

> 1h 8m DDD 9/92

One wishes that more music existed for the clarinet as a solo instrument, and it seems unfair that an instrument loved by Mozart, Weber and Brahms (to name but three composers) has such a small solo repertory. But there it is, and besides music by the men just mentioned there are other works of importance such as Schumann's *Fantasy Pieces,* Debussy's *Rapsodie* and the Poulenc Sonata which appears on both these British discs. Michael Collins is one of the finest clarinettists playing today, and certainly earns the title of virtuoso with the performances on the EMI disc. Messager's "competition solo" demands and receives great agility and panache, and Debussy's later piece is no less well served by this artist's refinement and subtlety. Weber's *Grand duo concertant* is a sonata in all but name, with fine melodies in its central *Andante* and a theatrical finale, and here Kathryn Stott matches Collins in her handling of the challenging piano part. The recording is excellent.

On the Clarinet Classics disc, Copland's Clarinet Sonata nominally dates from the very end of his life but proves to be an expert reworking of the Violin Sonata which he composed four decades earlier in 1943. This was a vintage period for him and he described the work as mainly lyrical, with little virtuosity. In fact there is an American purity of flavour here that is uniquely his and which we also find in other works of this time such as the ballet, *Appalachian Spring.* Victoria Soames and Julius Drake give this Sonata guts as well as quiet poetry, and they are no less good in Poulenc's, which has the same blend of energy and tenderness, although Collins and Stott bring even more brilliance to its finale. The music by four members of Les Six is not all of the same stature, and although Milhaud's two pieces (separated by some three decades) are good value in their quirky way, the Honegger is not so interesting until its vivid finale. But it is good to have all these works together and the performances by Soames and Drake are unfailingly stylish, while the recording is well balanced and faithful.

WORKS FOR FLUTE AND PIANO. Peter Lloyd (fl); [a]**Rebecca Holt** (pf). Pickwick IMP Classics PCD991.
Gaubert: Flute Sonata No. 1[a]. **Caplet:** Rêverie et petite valse[a]. **Fauré:** Fantaisie, Op. 79[a]. **Saint-Saëns:** Romance in D flat major, Op. 37[a]. **Busser:** Prélude et Scherzo[a]. **Poulenc:** Flute Sonata[a]. **Roussel:** Andante and Scherzo, Op. 51[a]. **Ferroud:** Trois Pièces.

> 1h 6m DDD 9/92

Poulenc's Flute Sonata forms the focal point of this superb recital from Peter Lloyd,
accompanied at the piano by Rebecca Holt. The recording was made in Henry Wood Hall,

London, whose warm acoustic ambience imparts a sensuous glow to the flute sound, and gives the piano a degree of natural transparency and weight without too much technical intervention. Lloyd's Poulenc is particularly satisfying; effortlessly played, and yet perceptive enough to reveal the sinister undercurrents concealed behind the obvious melodic appeal of the music. Gaubert's First Flute Sonata is possibly less stimulating; its language is certainly less demonstrative, but it is hardly less enjoyable for all that. Lloyd's account is effective and the sensitivity of his playing more than compensates for any passing deficiencies in the music itself. Henri Busser's *Prélude et Scherzo* and the *Rêverie et petite valse* by Caplet are undemanding, yet undeniably charming, and like the *Trois pièces* by Ferroud, they typify their genre with a certain romantic innocence. Much the same could be said of the Fauré and Saint-Saëns items too, but the performances are consistently excellent and raise the musical worth of these slender offerings to an altogether higher level. The duo also include Albert Roussel's *Andante and scherzo*, in an ideally balanced performance which makes the most of the languorous and outwardly virtuosic possibilities of this unfamiliar work. An enjoyable disc then, offering first rate recorded sound and performances of great distinction.

Instrumental

AMERICAN PIANO SONATAS, Volume 1. **Peter Lawson.** Virgin Classics VC7 59008-2. *Copland:* Piano Sonata in E flat major, Op. 26. *Ives* (ed. Cowell): Three-page Sonata. *Carter:* Piano Sonata. *Barber:* Piano Sonata, Op. 26.

Ih 16m   DDD   5/91

This disc offers four relatively unfamiliar but highly characterful American piano works in authoritative performances by a British-born pianist who clearly has their idiom at his fingertips — as well as their pretty challenging notes. As played here, the Copland Piano Sonata of 1941 has softness as well as strength, and for all its powerful utterance there is a strangely compelling lyricism at work too; one can see why the young Leonard Bernstein adored the work and played it. The recording matches the music, being on the close side but extremely lifelike as piano sound. Ives's *Three-page Sonata*, which at over seven minutes is longer than the miniature that its title suggests, is a gnomic utterance, but as always with this composer we feel that he has something to say that could be said in no other way. Carter's Piano Sonata is an early work of 1946, which the composer revised much later in 1982; its debt to Copland is evident, but there is also a personal voice and the scope and sweep of the music is deeply impressive. Barber's Sonata (1949), which was written for Horowitz, is less radical in idiom than the other works played and thus more immediately approachable if by no means conventional, being a work of considerable power and eloquence, very well written for the piano.

New review

AVANT-GARDE GUITAR. Eduardo Fernández (gtr). Decca 433 076-2DH. Recorded 1990.
Berio: Sequenza XI. *Britten:* Nocturnal after John Dowland, Op. 70. *Brouwer:* La Espiral Eterna. *Takemitsu:* All in Twilight. *Torres:* Mil y una caras. *Yocoh:* Sakura.

Ih 14m   DDD   7/93

Rarely can one wholeheartedly commend a guitar record to the attention of lovers of twentieth-century music, without reference to the instrument, but this is one of those occasions. Britten's *Nocturnal* lasts a little longer than usual but, in both its component movements and its overall conception, it is finely judged and dramatically telling. Yocoh's koto-haunted variations and Takemitsu's delicate miniatures are very different oriental faces of contemplation and are here given their appropriate time and space. The works by Brouwer and Torres are differently concerned with evolution — Brouwer's from the growth of a small cell, Torres's by the gradual transition of one pitch-group to another; this being in itself a gradual process, they too unfold in unhurried ways and both employ a strange array of effects. Berio is, on the contrary, concerned with the synthesis of disparate elements in his explosive *Sequenza XI*. Fernández is in supreme command of his demanding programme, both in the vividly recorded performance of it and in his understanding of it.

SIMON BARERE. THE COMPLETE HMV RECORDINGS, 1934-6. **Simon Barere** (pf). APR mono CDAPR7001.
Liszt: Etudes de Concert, S144 — La leggierezza (from HMV DB2166, 7/34). Années de pèlerinage, Deuxième année, S161, "Italie" — Sonetto 104 del Petrarca. Etudes de Concert, S145 — Gnomenreigen (both from DB2167, 9/34). Réminiscences de Don Juan, S418 (two versions. DB2749/50. Recorded 1934 and 1936). Valse oubliée, S215 No. 1. Rhapsodie espagnole, S254 (DB2375/6, 6/35). **Chopin:** Scherzo No. 3 in C sharp minor, Op. 39 (APR7001, 12/85. 1935). Mazurka in F sharp minor, Op. 59 No. 3 (two versions — DB2674, 1/37; second previously unpublished. 1935-6). Waltz in A flat major, Op. 42 (DB2166).
Balakirev: Islamey — Oriental Fantasy (two versions. DB2675, 4/36). **Blumenfeld:** Etude for the Left Hand. **Glazunov:** Etude in C major, Op. 31 No. 1 (DB2645, 12/35). **Scriabin:** Etudes — C sharp minor, Op. 2 No. 1 (1934); D sharp minor, Op. 8 No. 12 (two versions. 1934-5). **Lully** (arr. Godowsky): Gigue in E major. **Rameau** (arr. Godowsky): Tambourin in E minor (both 1934. All from APR7001). **Schumann:** Toccata in C major, Op. 7 (three versions — two on DB2674, 1/37; third previously unpublished. 1935-6).

② 2h 6m ADD 5/91

For many years following his death in 1951 Simon Barere was simply a legendary name to conjure with, whose phenomenal pianism appeared to have been lost to future generations of music lovers. Then in the late 1980s a small specialist company, Appian Recordings, began to reissue his recordings — all extremely rare — in a series of three volumes. This, the first, contains all of the recordings (including rejected takes) which Barere made for HMV between 1934 and 1936, following his emigration from Russia and then Germany to the USA where his reputation was firmly, if briefly, established. Barere was part of the generation of super-pianists, including Horowitz, who succeeded the first wave of Russian virtuosos such as Rachmaninov and Lhévinne. For musicians such as these the normal peaks of the piano literature became mere starting points for complete and thorough investigations of the musical and technical capabilities of the instrument itself. The HMV sessions included such monumental tests of virtuosity as Balakirev's fantasy *Islamey*, Liszt's *Réminiscences de Don Juan*, and "Gnomenreigen", together with a whole range of shorter but equally testing pieces by Schumann, Chopin, Scriabin, Godowsky and Barere's final teacher, Blumenfield. To all of this music Barere brought a technique which knew no difficulties and a sense of musical taste which kept vulgar display firmly at bay. The results are frankly benchmarks of performance by which all aspiring virtuosos must be tested and which few will ever equal. Simon Barere's playing is simply breathtaking in its unrestrained vigour and superb technical control, both laid at the feet of a unique and powerful musical insight. This two-CD set is an essential memorial to one of the greatest, if unsung, heroes of the piano this century. The production by Bryan Crimp is faultless, with full and highly faithful transfers from the original 78s, and completely comprehensive accompanying documentation. No lover of truly great piano playing can afford to be without this issue.

New review

BAROQUE GUITAR TRANSCRIPTIONS. Sergio and **Odair Assad** (gtrs). Elektra Nonesuch 7559-79292-2. Transcriptions by S. Assad unless otherwise stated. Recorded in 1991.
D. Scarlatti: Keyboard Sonatas — D minor, Kk9 (trans. Pujol); A minor, Kk54; D major, Kk96; D major, Kk140; D minor, Kk141; C major, Kk251 (all trans. S. Abreu); E major, Kk162 (trans. T. Bitterman); G major, Kk432 (trans. O. Caceres); F minor, Kk466; Kk531.
Rameau: Pièces de clavecin — Allemande; Gigues I and II; Le rappel des oiseaux; Rigaudon; Musette en rondeau; Les tendres plaintes; La follette; Les cyclopes; Le lardon. **F. Couperin:** Le Bavolet-Flotant. Le Carillon de Clithére. **Bach:** Das wohltemperirte Klavier — Prelude and Fugue No. 3 in C sharp major, BWV848.

Ih 14m DDD 10/93

The Assad brothers were born in Brazil and have now been settled in France for some years. In a world in which there are now many guitarists with virtuosic techniques the Assads are unique in their total, seemingly effortless command of their instruments; all things seem possible to them and, in every nuance and bending of tempo, they are in as tight accord as the two hands of any keyboard player. Every item in this programme is from the harpsichord repertory and one is reminded of Falla's description of the guitar as "a harpsichord, but expressive". Though their use of dynamic shading exceeds anything of which the harpsichord is capable it is utterly musical and enchanting, as is their exploitation of the guitar's greater facility in making changes of tone-colour. The fast items (and there are many) bubble and sparkle joyously, there is contrasting tenderness in, for example, Kk466, and Rameau's birds have never called more beguilingly than they do here.

BAROQUE ORGAN MUSIC. Peter Hurford (org). Argo 414 496-2ZH. Played on the Blank organ of the Bethlehemkerk, Papendrecht, The Netherlands.
G. Böhm: Prelude and Fugue in C major. Vater unser im Himmelreich. Auf meinen lieben Gott. Von Himmel hoch da komm'ich her. **L. Couperin:** Branle de basque. Fantaisie in G minor. **J.K. Kerll:** Capriccio sopra il cucu. **Buxtehude:** Mensch, willt du leben seliglich. Wir danken dir, Herr Jesu Christ. Vater, unser im Himmelreich. **Walond:** Voluntary No. 5 in G major. **G.B. Pescetti:** Sonata in C minor. **Pachelbel:** Ciaccona in D minor. **Sweelinck:** Unter der Linden grüne. **Stanley:** Voluntary in C major, Op. 5 No. 1.

Ih Ilm DDD 10/87

At first glance we may be a little dismayed to find an anthology called "Baroque Organ Music" which omits a single note of Bach. More careful scrutiny of the contents, however, may well persuade us that it is for our own good since Peter Hurford has chosen a programme of all too seldom-heard music by composers who were also noted organists of their day. The outstanding figures here are Jan Pieterszoon Sweelinck, Georg Böhm, Dietrich Buxtehude, Johann Pachelbel and Louis Couperin and although these works form the main body of the recital, listeners are unlikely to be disappointed by the several smaller, lighter-textured pieces with which Hurford makes discerning contrast, as well as showing off the appealing character of the organ.

BLACK ANGELS. Kronos Quartet (David Harrington, John Sherba, vns; Hank Dutt, va; Joan Jeanrenaud, vc). Elektra Nonesuch 7559-79242-2.
Crumb: Black Angels. **Tallis** (arr. Kronos Qt): Spem in alium. **Marta:** Doom. A sigh. **Ives** (arr. Kronos Qt/Geist): They are there! **Shostakovich:** String Quartet No. 8 in C minor, Op. 110.

Ih 2m DDD 4/91

This is very much the sort of imaginative programming we've come to expect from this talented young American quartet. With an overall theme of war and persecution the disc opens with George Crumb's *Black Angels*, for electric string quartet. This work was inspired by the Vietnam War and bears two inscriptions to that effect — *in tempore belli* (in time of war) and "Finished on Friday the Thirteenth of March, 1970", and it's described by Crumb as "a kind of parable on our troubled contemporary world". The work is divided into three sections which represent the three stages of the voyage of the soul — fall from grace, spiritual annihilation and redemption. As with most of his works he calls on his instrumentalists to perform on a variety of instruments other than their own — here that ranges from gongs, maracas and crystal glasses to vocal sounds such as whistling, chanting and whispering. *Doom. A sigh* is the young Hungarian composer István Marta's disturbing portrait of a Roumanian village as they desperately fight to retain their sense of identity in the face of dictatorship and persecution. Marta's atmospheric blend of electronic sound, string quartet and recorded folk-songs leave one with a powerful and moving impression. At first sight Tallis's *Spem in alium* may seem oddly out of place considering the overall theme of this disc, but as the sleeve-notes point out the text was probably taken from the story of Judith, in which King Nebuchadnezzar's general Holofernes besieged the Jewish fortress of Bethulia. Kronos's own arrangement of this 40-part motet (involving some multi-tracking) certainly makes a fascinating alternative to the original. A particularly fine account of Shostakovich's Eighth String Quartet (dedicated to the victims of fascism and war) brings this thought-provoking and imaginative recital to a close. Performances throughout are outstanding, and the recording first class.

New review

CARNEGIE HALL HIGHLIGHTS. Artur Rubinstein (pf). RCA Victor Gold Seal 09026 61445-2. Items marked [a] from SB6504 (9/62), [b]RL13850 (7/81). Recorded live in Carnegie Hall, New York in 1961.

Debussy: Préludes — La cathédrale engloutie; Ondine[a]. Images — Hommage à Rameau; Poissons d'or[a]. **Szymanowskxsi:** 20 Mazurkas, Op. 50 — Nos. 1-4[a]. **Prokofiev:** Vision fugitives, Op. 22 — Nos. 1, 2, 3, 6, 7, 9, 10, 11, 12, 13, 14, 16[a]. **Villa-Lobos:** Próle do bébé, Book I[a]. **Schumann:** Arabeske in C major, Op. 18[b]. **Albéniz:** Navarra[a].

·.· 1h 4m   ADD   10/93

Artur Rubinstein had a unique flair for live musical communication and these concert performances have great spontaneity. In fact, the whole disc might have been billed as The Essential Rubinstein, thus providing one of the few occasions where the 'essential' epithet would have been fully justified. And it's certainly all here — the wistful reverie (*Arabeske*), the mastery of rhythm and exotic colours (Szymanowski *Mazurkas*, *Navarra*, *Próle do bébé*), acute sensitivity to miniature forms (*Visions fugitives*), unforced virtuosity employed to musical ends (*Próle*) and a natural inclination towards musical impressionism (Debussy). RCA are more active with their back catalogue than most of their rivals so we can only hope that more Rubinstein is waiting in the wings.

EIGHTIETH BIRTHDAY RECITAL, Volume 2. **Shura Cherkassky** (pf). Decca 433 654-2DH. Recorded at a performance in Carnegie Hall, New York in December 1991.
Bach (arr. Busoni): Partita in D minor, BWV1004 — Chaconne. **Schumann:** Etudes Symphoniques, Op. 13. **Chopin:** Nocturne in F minor, Op. 55 No. 1. Tarantelle in A flat major, Op. 43. **Ives:** Three-page Sonata, Op. 14. **Hofmann:** Kaleidoskop, Op. 40. **Pabst:** Concert Paraphrase from Tchaikovsky's "Eugene Onegin", Op. 81. **M. Gould:** Boogie Woogie Etude.

·.· 1h 18m   DDD   1/93

Shura Cherkassky has long enjoyed the slightly dubious reputation of being a pianist's pianist. Capable of transforming familiar masterpieces into delectable kaleidoscopes of nuance and voicing he can be enchanting or infuriating according to taste. But when he is really on form it is difficult for even the hardest-hearted listener to resist. Big occasions tend to bring the best out of him, and they don't come much bigger than an eightieth-birthday concert at Carnegie Hall. That recital is here complete save for three items scheduled to appear on a future disc; a patching session took place the following day but was apparently not used for the CD. Spontaneous enjoyment is here in abundance. The extraordinary freedom in the repeated sections of the Schumann is one obvious proof of that; and the relishing of the last three lightweight pieces is another. But more deeply rewarding virtues are to be found too — in the dramatic pacing of the Bach/Busoni *Chaconne*, in the breathtaking poetry of the Chopin pieces, and not least in the full-blooded assault on Ives's craggy *Three-Page Sonata* which Cherkassky learned especially for the occasion. Here, and after each of the encores, the Carnegie Hall audience goes into justifiable raptures. Decca's recording has been done with exemplary care for balance and perspective.

New review

SHURA CHERKASSKY LIVE, PIANO RECITALS, Volumes 3 and 4. **Shura Cherkassky** (pf). Decca 433 650/1-2DH. Recorded between 1973 and 1991.
433 650-2DH: **Chopin:** Piano Sonatas — No. 2 in B flat minor, Op. 35; No. 3 in B minor, Op. 58. Fantasie in F minor, Op. 49. *433 651-2DH:* **Paderewski:** Humoresque de concert, Op. 14 — Menuet célèbre. **Tchaikovsky** (arr. Nagel): None but the lonely heart, Op. 6 No. 6. **Chopin:** Waltz in E minor, Op. posth. **Rachmaninov:** Polka de W. R. Morceaux de fantaisie, Op. 3 — Elégie in E flat minor. **Shostakovich:** Polka from "The Golden Age". **Scriabin:** Etude in C sharp minor, Op. 2 No. 1. **Balakirev:** Islamey. **Cherkassky:** Prélude pathétique. **Sinding:** Rustle of Spring, Op. 32 No. 3. **Albéniz** (arr. Godowsky): España, Op. 165—Tango. **Mozart:** Piano Sonata in A major, K331/K300i — Rondo alla turca. **Debussy:** Arabesque No. 1. **Rebikov:** The Christmas tree. **Moszkowski:** Liebeswalzer in A flat major, Op. 57 No. 5. **Sibelius:** Romance in D flat major, Op. 24 No. 9.

·.· ②   1h 3m   1h 3m   ADD/DDD   6/93

There are few pianists around who have the innate intelligence and resourcefulness to explore the possibilities of a score as does Cherkassky. His mastery of tone-colour is unique in today's world, where there are so many musicians who fail to produce an individual piano sound. Always more at home in the recital hall, where he can be in complete control of the proceed-ings, the octogenarian Russian commands the attention not as a musician too frequently capable of distorting a score, but as a man wholly dedicated to communicating the beauty and drama of the music he plays. Of course, one accepts and embraces some of the weird and wonderful inner lines that surface in familiar pieces by Chopin, but these highlights serve to add to the polyphonic richness of the score, rather than detract from the overall effect. Cherkassky is *the* pianist for encores, and the selection presented here is a delight. The Russian items are the most deep-felt. Rachmaninov's early "Elégie", influenced by Tchaikovsky, is incomparable. The phrasing is pliable, yet not pulled about. Another high point must be the *Polka de W. R.*, also by Rachmaninov, which could scarcely have been better played, not even by Horowitz. Here one encounters Cherkassky in a real celebratory mood. All taken from live recitals, the sound-quality varies but is nearly always true to Cherkassky's tone. Altogether, not be missed by anyone who loves really fine piano-playing.

ENGLISH ORGAN MUSIC. Gareth Green. Naxos 8 550582. Played on the organ of Chesterfield Parish Church.
C.S. Lang: Tuba tune. *Howells:* Three Psalm-Preludes (Set 1), Op. 32. *Elgar:* Organ Sonata No. 1 in G major, Op. 28. *Vaughan Williams:* Three Preludes on Welsh Hymn Tunes — Rhosymedre. *Whitlock:* Hymn Preludes — Darwall's 148th; Song 13. *Cocker:* Tuba tune.

·lh 4m DDD 3/93

Most large English church and cathedral organs boast at least one tuba stop — making a huge, fat, trumpet-like noise so powerful it can overwhelm every other stop on the organ. The *Tuba tune*, of which there are two classic examples on this CD, is a uniquely English creation in which the tuba stop is pitted against the rest of the instruments in a light-hearted, tuneful battle. C.S. Lang's jovial romp with its instantly-singable tune is certainly the most famous tuba tunes of all while Norman Cocker's slightly more demanding one runs it a close second. The Chesterfield organ possesses a fine tuba which brings these two pieces thrillingly to life in this thoroughly enjoyable CD. The remainder of the programme represents the very best of early twentieth-century English organ music with a handful of characteristic pieces; memorable for their fine melodies and stirring qualities. Gareth Green has an instinctive feel for this music and plays it all with great aplomb and this organ suits it to a tee — although Naxos's recording might have been a little clearer.

THE ESSENTIAL HARPSICHORD. Virginia Black. Collins Classics 5024-2.
Arne: Keyboard Sonata No. 3 in G major. *D. Scarlatti:* Keyboard Sonatas — C major, Kk159; G major, Kk337; E major, Kk380. *J.S. Bach:* Italian Concerto, BWV971. *Balbastre:* Pièces de clavecin I — La Suzanne. *Daquin:* Pièces de clavecin I — Le coucou. *Duphly:* Pièces de clavecin III — Le Forqueray. *F. Couperin:* Livre de clavecin II — Les baricades mistérieuses; Le dodo; Le tic-toc-choc. *Handel:* Keyboard Suites — No. 5 in E major, "Harmonious Blacksmith"; No. 7 in G minor — Passacaille. *Mozart:* Piano Sonata in A major, K331/300*i* — Rondo alla turca. *Paradies:* Toccata in A major. *Rameau:* Les cyclopes. *W.F. Bach:* Polonaise in E minor.

·lh 14m DDD 5/91

Virginia Black has assembled a delightful programme of music which should conquer all ears not yet won over by the sound of a harpsichord. She is a communicative player, spontaneous in transferring her thoughts to the keyboard and with a lively sense of poetry. These qualities and others too may be sensed in her interpretation of Bach's *Italian Concerto*. This is the most substantial piece in her recital and it comes over well with clearly articulated phrases, rhythmic elasticity and well-chosen tempos. There are occasions when Miss Black pushes the music along just a little harder than is good for it — listeners may sense that in the concluding Variations of Handel's famous so-called *Harmonious Blacksmith* theme — but her liveliness of temperament ensures her performances against any accusations of stuffy convention or dullness. Only the W.F. Bach Polonaise seems perhaps not to speak from the heart. A recital, in short, which deserves to win friends. Few are likely to be disappointed either by her choice of music or her colourfully imaginative treatment of it.

FRENCH ORGAN WORKS. Simon Lindley. Naxos 8 550581. Played on the organ of Leeds Parish Church, UK.

Guilmant: Grand Choeur in D major, "alla Handel". Cantilene pastorale, Op. 19. **Vierne:** 24 Pièces en stile libre, Op. 31 — Epitaphe; Berceuse. Stele pour un enfant défunte. **M-A. Charpentier:** Te Deum, H146 — Prelude. **Langlais:** Trois méditations (1962). **Bonnet:** Romance sans paroles. **de Maleingreau:** Suite mariale. **Boëllmann:** Suite gothique, Op. 25. **Widor:** Symphony No. 5 in F minor, Op. 42 No. 1 — Toccata.

Ih I4m DDD 3/93

Two of the most popular organ showpieces are here — Widor's Toccata and the Toccata which comes as the last movement of Boëllmann's *Suite gothique*. In addition there is the majestic *Te Deum* Prelude by Charpentier (familiar to a wide audience as the Eurovision signature tune) and the gentle *Berceuse* which Vierne wrote for his baby daughter. Alongside these evergreens, mainstays of any organ-lover's CD collection, are some more unusual but no less enjoyable pieces: Guilmant's glorious *Grand Choeur "alla Handel"*, Bonnet's delightful *Romance sans paroles* and Paul de Maleingreau's *Suite mariale*. In short, a real feast of some of the best French organ music. Simon Lindley, organist at the musically-renowned Leeds Parish Church, gives fine, no-nonsense performances which should appeal especially to those exploring this music for the first time. The organ makes a super noise, and the Naxos recording is highly commendable. It may not be an instrument which the *cognoscenti* of French organ music would immediately approve of, but there is enough sensitivity and interpretative insight in Lindley's performances to make this a worthwhile buy for casual listener and specialist alike.

FROM STANLEY TO WESLEY, Volume 6. **Jennifer Bate** (org). Unicorn-Kanchana DKPCD9106. Played on the organs of Adlington Hall, Cheshire; The Dolmetsch Collection, Haslemere, Surrey; The Chapel of St Michael's Mount, Cornwall; The Iveagh Bequeast, Kenwood, London; Killerton House, Broadclyst, Exeter, Devon and The Chapel of Our Lady and St Everilda, Everingham, Yorkshire.

Boyce: Voluntary in D major. **Handel:** Fugue in G major. Voluntary in C major. **Heron:** Voluntary in G major. **Hook:** Voluntary in C minor. **Russell:** Voluntary in F major. **Stanley:** Voluntaries — A minor, Op. 6 No. 2; D minor, Op. 7 No. 4; G major, Op. 7 No. 9. **Stubley:** Voluntary in C major. **S. Wesley:** Voluntaries — E flat major, Op. 6 No. 7; B flat major.

Ih 5m DDD II/91

Whilst most people would regard Bach and his North German contemporaries as synonymous with all that is best in eighteenth-century organ music there was also a significant school of organist-composers thriving in England. Chief amongst these was John Stanley whose music was greatly admired at the time, in particular by a recent immigrant from Germany, one George Frederic Handel (two fine examples of his own organ music are to be found on this CD). But while the German composers were writing for their great, majestic organs, their English counterparts were faced with something far humbler in scope and more delicate and intimate in character. To hear this music played on such an instrument is to have its true beauty revealed: here it is played not just on one authentic contemporaneous instrument, but the Unicorn-Kanchana team have scoured the length and breadth of England, from Cornwall to Yorkshire, to unearth six classic, and virtually unaltered examples. Jennifer Bate's immense musical and technical powers and her innate, native sense of style, imbues this disc with compelling musical authority which, added to the captivating sound of these six delightful organs, makes it an intriguing historical document — real 'living history', if you like. This CD is the sixth in a series and while each is a valuable addition to the recorded legacy of English music, this one in particular gives the less specialist collector a representative and varied selection of this wonderful, yet woefully overlooked area of our musical heritage.

GREAT EUROPEAN ORGANS, Volume 26. **Keith John** (org). Priory PRCD370. Played on the organ of Gloucester Cathedral, UK.

Stanford: Fantasia and Toccata in D minor, Op. 57. **Reger:** Five Easy Preludes and Fugues, Op. 56 — No. 1 in E major. **Shostakovich:** Lady Macbeth of the Mtsensk district —

Passacaglia. **Schmidt:** Chaconne in C sharp minor. **Ravanello:** Theme and Variations in
B minor.

> **Ih I3m DDD II/92**   ♪ₚ ♪ₛ

On the face of it this CD might look as if its appeal is purely for those with a specialist taste in
large-scale post-romantic organ music. Certainly Schmidt's gargantuan *Chaconne* represents a
daunting prospect both to player and listener, while Shostakovich's only organ solo begins with
the kind of chilling dissonance which would certainly scare off those of a delicate disposition.
Similarly neither Stanford nor Reger usually attract a crowd when their organ music played —
and who has ever heard of Ravanello? But if ever a recording was made to shatter
preconceptions, this is it. For a start the Gloucester organ makes a wondrous sound and Priory's
recording is in a class of its own; in terms of sound alone this surely ranks as one of the best
ever organ CDs. Then Keith John quite literally pulls out all the stops to produce an
unparalleled display of virtuosity and musicianship. His technical prowess turns the Schmidt into
a thrilling *tour de force* while few could question, after hearing his performances, that the
Stanford is one of the best organ works ever written by a British composer or that Ravanello's
music doesn't deserve the neglect it currently suffers. An essential disc in anyone's CD
collection — what more is there to say?

LA GUITARRA ROMANTICA. Julian Bream (gtr). RCA Victor Red Seal RD60429.
Tárrega: Mazurka in G major. Study in A major. Marietta. Capricho árabe. Prelude in
A minor. Recuerdos de la Alhambra. **Malats** (arr. Tárrega): Serenata española. **Pujol:** Tango
espagnol. Guajira. **Llobet:** Popular Catalan folk-songs.

> **48m DDD 7/92**

It was in Spain that the guitar's revival began after the instrument's mid-nineteenth century
eclipse. The prime mover was Francisco Tárrega, a concert virtuoso, teacher and composer, who
also laid the foundations on which modern playing technique has been built. Tárrega's
compositions were for the most part charming miniatures, some of which paid tribute to Spain's
Moorish past; the *Capricho árabe* and *Recuerdos de la Alhambra* (his most famous and evocative
piece) are two of these. It was also Tárrega who developed the art of arranging 'other' music
for the guitar, a means by which its repertory has been greatly enlarged since then; it is
principally through his arrangements that Malats's *Serenata* and Alard's Study in A major are now
remembered. His Catalonian pupils, Miguel Llobet and Emilio Pujol were concert performers
and also attractive composers in a similar romantic vein; Llobet died at the age of 50, whilst
Pujol eventually found his true calling to be that of a teacher and musicologist. Llobet is
represented by his delightful settings of folk-songs from his native land, Pujol by two
transatlantic glances (to Argentina and Cuba). This music could not have a more eloquent
advocate than Julian Bream in a very vivid recording.

VLADIMIR HOROWITZ. PIANO WORKS. RCA Gold Seal mono/ᵃstereo GD60377.
Prokofiev: Piano Sonata No. 7 in B flat major, Op. 83 (from RB6555, 12/63. Recorded
1945). Toccata, Op. 11. **Poulenc:** Presto in B flat major (both from HMV DB6971, 1947).
Barber: Piano Sonata in E flat major, Op. 26 (RB6555. 1950). **Kabalevsky:** Piano Sonata
No. 3, Op. 46 (new to UK. 1947). **Fauré:** Nocturne No. 13 in B minor, Op. 119ᵃ (RL12548,
2/78. 1977).

> **Ih 5m ADD 6/92**   ♪ₚ ▲

Even today, when there is a six-deep queue of virtuosos that, laid end to end, would stretch
halfway round the world, Vladimir Horowitz's playing is something to make the listener gasp
and sit up. He has been called, with justification, "the greatest pianist alive or dead". Horowitz
was associated with all three of these sonatas from their very beginnings. Prokofiev wrote his
Seventh Sonata in 1942, and Horowitz gave the first American performance less than two years
later. He sent a copy of this 1945 recording to the composer, and Prokofiev sent him an
autographed copy of the score in return, inscribed "to the miraculous pianist from the
composer". The performance is indeed superlative, with playing of extraordinary virtuosity, and
Horowitz responds with equal flair to the sonata's 'barbaric' and lyrical elements. Kabalevsky's
Third Sonata dates from 1946, and Horowitz gave the American première in February 1948,
two months after he made this recording. The work is of lesser stature than the Prokofiev, but

its three well-contrasted movements make up an effective enough sonata. Again, Horowitz plays brilliantly and very sympathetically throughout the work. The world première of Barber's Piano Sonata was given by Horowitz in 1949. This piece is brilliantly written and technically very difficult to play — a perfect vehicle, in fact, for Horowitz the virtuoso. The great pianist brings great flair to the shorter Poulenc and Prokofiev items: the Fauré was recorded at a later stage of his career, and is played in a more deliberate, though perfectly idiomatic fashion. Four of the items have been transferred from 78s in good sound. The Barber and Fauré come from tape sources and sound well — the latter is even in stereo. This is a disc all pianists and piano enthusiasts should have — and it's mid-price too!

VLADIMIR HOROWITZ. THE LAST RECORDING. **Vladimir Horowitz** (pf). Sony Classical SK45818.
Haydn: Keyboard Sonata in E flat major, HobXVI/49. *Chopin:* Mazurka in C minor, Op. 56 No. 3. Nocturnes — E flat, Op. 55 No. 2; B major, Op. 62 No. 1. Fantaisie-impromptu in C sharp minor, Op. 66. Etudes — A flat major, Op. 25 No. 1; E minor, Op. 25 No. 5. *Liszt:* "Weinen, Klagen, Sorgen, Zagen", Präludium, S179. *Wagner/Liszt:* Paraphrase on Isolden's Liebestod from "Tristan und Isolde", S447.

58m DDD 8/90

More than any other pianist of his generation, Vladimir Horowitz was a legend in his lifetime, not only for his staggering technique but also for the personality and authority of his playing. Other pianists such as Rubinstein and Arrau may have been finer all-rounders (there were gaps in his repertory even in the classical and romantic field), but none has left so many performances distinguished by a special individuality that is covered, though hardly explained, by the word magic. As Murray Perahia has written, from the point of view of a pianist over 40 years his junior, "he was a man who gave himself completely through his music and who confided his deepest emotions through his playing". The performances in this last of his recordings, made in New York in 1989 and with superlative piano sound, are wonderfully crystalline and beautifully articulated, yet there is warmth too in the Haydn sonata that begins his programme and nothing whatever to suggest that octogenarian fingers were feeling their age or that his fine ear had lost its judgement. The rest of the disc is devoted to Chopin and Liszt, two great romantic composers with whom he was always associated, the last piece being Liszt's mighty transcription of Wagner's *Liebestod*, in which the piano becomes a whole operatic orchestra topped by a soprano voice singing out her love for the last time. Apparently this was the last music Horowitz ever played, and no more suitable ending can be imagined for a great pianistic career informed by a consuming love of music that was expressed in playing of genius. A uniquely valuable record.

New review
THE HUNGARIAN ANTHOLOGY. Peter Frankl (pf). ASV CDDCA860.
Liszt: Csárdás macabre, S224. *Dohnányi:* Gavotte and Musette. *Kodály:* Seven Pieces, Op. 11. *Bartók* (trans. cpsr.): Dance Suite, Sz77. *Weiner:* Three Hungarian Rural Dances. *Kurtág:* Plays and Games for Piano, Book 3 — excerpts. *Szöllösy:* Paesaggio con morti.

1h 18m DDD 6/93

An important reminder, this, of how and where Hungarian piano music is progressing. The last piece of Peter Frankl's programme dates from 1988; the *Paesaggio con morti* by András Szöllösy, an impressive, 11-minute study in musical shades and textures. Working back from there, and tracing the general direction of Szöllösy's route, is a relatively simple task. Oddly, Kodály more than Bartók seems — in this case, at least — the overriding influence: his *Seven Pieces*, Op. 11 have never sounded more engaging than here, and the largest of them, "Epitaphe", is surely among the composer's most dramatic inspirations. With György Kurtág's *Plays and Games for Piano*, credits revert back to Bartók. Leo Weiner's spicy *Hungarian Rural Dances* include a "Ronde de Marosszek"; but here again, it's more Bartók than Kodály who springs to mind. Bartók's own *Dance Suite* is, of course, a pivotal creation in its use of Eastern European and Arabic modes, and the way they are so expertly welded on to the work's overall structure. And then to Dohnányi and Liszt, although the former's pleasant *Gavotte and Musette* seems more a side-long glance at Smetana than an extension of the bold, bald and audacious world of Liszt's menacing *Czárdás macabre*. Here we can locate the seeds of Bartók's mature style, sown not merely among the realms of local folklore (although this disturbing *Czárdás* is profoundly Hungarian in spirit), but deep within the furthest recesses of our collective musical unconscious. Performances and recording are sympathetic.

New review

EILEEN JOYCE. Works by *d'Albert, Bach, Brahms, Chopin, Debussy, Grieg, Liszt, Mozart, Rachmaninov, Schumann, C. Scott, Shostakovich* and *R. Strauss*. Eileen **Joyce** (pf). Pearl mono GEMMCD9022 From Parlophone and Columbia originals; recorded 1933-41.

Ih IIm AAD 2/94

Tasmanian-born Eileen Joyce (1912-91) was a pianist of unique charisma whose radiance and volatility held her vast audiences transfixed until her dangerously high-pitched career became submerged in a welter of publicity and a pace too fast for her — or anyone else — to bear. Within a short time she became a tragic victim of her own success, virtually retiring from public life at the age of 42. Joyce specialized in romantic show-stoppers, and although d'Albert's *Scherzo* is sadly cut here, it is reeled off with a witty and scintillating disregard for difficulty that will enthral all lovers of pianistic wizardry. Her tone, too, whether magisterial in Bach/Liszt or delicate in Mozart, is a marvel of variety, clarity and refinement. Her Debussy "Toccata" (*Pour le piano*) suggests, in its mischievously twinkling and inflected detail, how her playing evolved with a truly glorious disregard for received wisdom, French or otherwise; few pianists have communicated such unalloyed joy in music-making. Small wonder that her admirers included Glenn Gould, Ivan Davis and Earl Wild, to name but three. Pearl's transfers of recordings dating from Joyce's great years are impressive.

New review

PIET KEE AT THE CONCERTEGBOUW. Piet Kee (org). Chandos CHAN9188.
Franck: Fantaisie in A major. *Mendelssohn:* Organ Sonata in C major/minor. *Schumann:* Fugue on B-A-C-H, Op. 60 No. 3. *Andriessen:* Sonata da chiesa. *Saint-Saëns:* Fantaisie in C major, Op. 157. *Alain:* Deuxième fantaisie. Le jardin suspendu. *Messiaen:* Les corps glorieux — Joie et clarté des corps glorieux.

Ih I2m DDD I0/93

Kee has made an ingenious choice of pieces which all treat the organ orchestrally, while at the same time finding some of these composers' finest, yet less familiar, creations. Alain's *Deuxième fantaisie* ranks considerably higher in musical worth than almost anything else he wrote — and if you doubt this, listen to the stimulating performance here. It is good, too, to see the name of Hendrik Andriessen appear on record again. A couple of decades or so ago he seemed to be all the rage; now representation of his music in the catalogues is minimal, to say the least, and to have his *Sonata da chiesa* back again alone makes this an invaluable release. For the most part these are outstanding performances. Kee is a master in the art of organ colour and, coupled with his meticulous and scholarly approach, one can't seriously question either the authority or sincerity of anything here — from a disarmingly delicate *Jardin suspendu* to a magisterial reading of the Mendelssohn sonata.

EVGENI KISSIN IN TOKYO. Evgeni Kissin (pf). Sony Classical SK45931. Recorded live in 1987.
Rachmaninov: Lilacs, Op. 21 No. 5. Etudes tableaux, Op. 39 — No. 1 in C minor; No. 5 in E flat minor. *Prokofiev:* Piano Sonata No. 6 in A major, Op. 82. *Liszt:* Concert Studies, S144 — La leggierezza; Waldestauschen. *Chopin:* Nocturne in A flat major, Op. 32 No. 2. Polonaise in F sharp minor, Op. 44. *Scriabin:* Mazurka in E minor, Op. 25 No. 3. Etude in C sharp minor, Op. 42 No. 5. *Anonymous* (arr. Saegusa): Natu — Wa Kinu. Todai — Mori. Usagi.

Ih I3m DDD II/90

One reason for buying this CD is that it contains dazzling piano playing by a 15-year-old Russian set fair for a career of the highest distinction. A better reason is that the recital contains as full a revelation of the genius of Prokofiev as any recording ever made in any medium. The Sixth

Sonata is the first of a trilogy which sums up the appalling sufferings of Russia under Stalin in a way only otherwise found in Shostakovich's 'middle' symphonies. Kissin plays it with all the colour and force of a full orchestra and all the drama and structural integrity of a symphony, plus a kind of daredevilry that even he may find difficult to recapture. As for the rest of the recital only the Rachmaninov pieces are as memorable as the Prokofiev, though everything else is immensely impressive (the Japanese encore-pieces are trivial in the extreme, however). Microphone placing is very close, presumably in order to minimize audience noise; but the playing can take it, indeed it may even be said to benefit from it.

New review
THE LAST ROSE OF SUMMER. Ann Murray (mez); **Graham Johnson** (pf). Hyperion CDA66627. Recorded in 1992.
Traditional: The last rose of summer. Believe me if all those endearing young charms. The Meeting of the Waters (all arr. J. A. Stevenson). The Leprechaun. The Next Market Day. The Bard of Armagh. I have a bonnet trimmed with blue. A young maid stood in her father's garden. Monday, Tuesday. The Stuttering Lovers. I will walk with my love. The Cork Leg (all arr. H. Hughes). She moved thro' the fair. Danny Boy. The Coulin. *Stanford:* The falling star. The Beautiful City of Sligo. The stolen heart. *P. Tate:* The lark in the clear air. *H. and P. French:* Ach, I dunno. Phil the Fluter's Ball. Gortnamona. *Colahan:* Galway Bay. *E. Ball:* Mother Machree. *Britten:* Folk Song Arrangements — How sweet the answer; Oft in the stilly night; The last rose of summer; O the sight entrancing.

lh l3m   DDD   8/93   **P**

Though it's not short of a toot of the flute and the twiddle on the fiddle-o, nor yet deprived utterly of a drop of the mountain dew, a prattle o' the praties and spiel of the spalpeens, yet the songs and the record as a whole have an appeal that goes well beyond that of the souvenir shop and the travel poster. No doubt the art of singer and pianist should in themselves be potent enough to assure of that much in advance, and indeed not in the profoundest Schubert, the most exquisite Fauré, has either of them performed with more delicacy and refinement, more tenderness, humour, and, on the rare occasions that evoke it, passion, than they do here. Ann Murray sings within happily appropriate limits and makes us realize more clearly than ever just how wide the boundaries of her art are set. Graham Johnson turns everything beautiful-side-out: some of these accompaniments could sound stodgy or hamfisted in other, less imaginatively guided, hands. Here everything has grace and wins favour, *Phil the Fluter's Ball*, *Mother Machree* and all. One other feature is the variety and skill of four arrangers. A sure winner.

LATE ROMANTIC MASTERWORKS. **Andrew Fletcher** (org). Mirabilis MRCD903. Played on the organ of St Mary's Collegiate Church, Warwick.
Andriessen: Thema met variaties. *Bridge:* Three Organ Pieces, H63 — Adagio in E major. *Dupré:* Cortège et litanie, Op. 19 No. 2. *Howells:* Siciliano for a High Ceremony. *Pach:* Introduction and Fugue. *Peeters:* Aria, Op. 51. Variations on an Original Theme, Op. 58. *Reger:* Benedictus, Op. 59 No. 9. *Schmidt:* Prelude and Fugue in D major, "Hallelujah". *Willan:* Introduction, Passacaglia and Fugue.

lh 2lm   DDD   ll/91   **S   ❓**

St Mary's Church, Warwick, boasts an extraordinary organ. In fact it is two quite separate organs housed at opposite ends of the church but playable from just one console. Listening to this disc using an UHJ Ambisonic decoder the spatial effect is most vividly recreated: Mirabilis's 'surround-sound' recording places the West End organ through the front pair of speakers while the Transept organ speaks from the rear speakers. The effect is aurally astonishing, but it could be a recipe for musical disaster. As it is, Andrew Fletcher knows better than almost anyone what its strengths and weaknesses are — what works and what doesn't; he was responsible for its present design and in this thoroughly enjoyable recital guides us expertly through its manifest glories. Fletcher not only shows the organ off to best effect, he also plays this entire programme with impressive fluency. Most of these pieces are old favourites to church organists but neither the music nor, in many cases, the names of the composers will be familiar to those outside the intimate world of organ aficionados. But don't be put off, everything here from Flor Peeter's appealing *Aria* to Healey Willan's dramatic *Introduction, Passacaglia and Fugue* is well worth exploring, and you can rest assured that Fletcher's stirring playing, the organ's wonderful wealth of sounds and Mirabilis's top-notch recording provides an exceptionally generous programme of real delights.

THE LAST RECITAL FOR ISRAEL. Artur Rubinstein (pf). RCA Victor Red Seal 09026 61160-2. Recorded in 1975.
Beethoven: Piano Sonata No. 23 in F minor, Op. 57, "Appassionata". *Schumann:* Fantasiestücke, Op. 12. *Debussy:* La plus que lente. Pour le Piano — Prélude. *Chopin:* Etudes — C sharp minor, Op. 10 No. 4; E minor, Op. 25 No. 5. Nocturne in F sharp major, Op. 15 No. 2. Polonaise in A flat major, Op. 53.

.•˙   1h 15m   ADD   3/93   9⌐P

Ever a supporter of youth in music, Artur Rubinstein gave a special concert in January 1975 at Ambassador College (California) for the benefit of the International Cultural Centre for Youth in Jerusalem; it was merely days before his eighty-eighth birthday. The event was sponsored entirely by contributions, and Rubinstein played to a packed house, which of course was no great surprise. However, what does truly amaze is the vitality and concentration of the performances. It might seem something of a cliché to say that Rubinstein plays the *Appassionata* like a man half his age, but it also happens to be the truth: the sheer energy and panache of the first movement so far exceeds expectations that one finds oneself checking the recording date to make sure that this isn't a reissue of an earlier Rubinstein recording. And in truth, the recording — taken from a video sound-track — tends, unlike the playing, to sound older than it is. In addition to barnstorming Beethoven and endearingly warm-hearted Schumann, Rubinstein plays two Chopin *Etudes* that, believe it or not, he never recorded commercially: Op. 25 No. 5 and Op. 10 No. 4. Both are remarkable, as is a battle-scarred but riveting A Flat Polonaise (a Rubinstein speciality). But best of all is the famous E flat Nocturne, Op. 15 No. 2 — an intimate, beautifully phrased performance, so typical of the man and the best possible way to remember him. A simultaneously-released RCA video contains the entire programme, but the best items are on this CD. A life-affirming experience.

LUTE WORKS. Nigel North. Linn Records CKD006.
Weiss: Sonata in A minor, "L'infidèle". Prelude, Fantasia and Fugue in C major. Tombeau sur la mort de M. Comte de Logy. *Vivaldi* (trans. North, after Bach): Concerto in D major, RV230. *Bach* (trans. North): Partita in D minor, BWV1004 — Chaconne.

.•˙   1h 1m   DDD   12/92

Bach was a friend, admirer and almost exact contemporary of Sylvius Leopold Weiss, the greatest lutenist of his time and famed for his skill as an improviser. The tale of the unsuccessful attempt by a jealous violinist to bite off Weiss's thumb has often been told. Most of his 600-plus works for the baroque lute are preserved in manuscripts held in London and Dresden, the rest are spread around various (often surprising) places. The title of the Sonata *L'infidèle* reflects the current interest in Turkish music as fashionable exotica, the *Tombeau sur la mort de M. Comte de Logy,* marking the death of another famous lutenist, is a poignant elegy that can hold its own in any company; the other three pieces fit well together, though not so coupled by Weiss. In adapting the famous *Chaconne* of Bach to a plucked-string instrument, North is not the first in the field, but he is among the most successful. Vivaldi's RV230, a violin concerto, was arranged for solo harpsichord by Bach. North has rearranged Bach's version for the lute — and why not, when it is so well done ? North, one of today's best lutenists, adds comely embellishments where fitting, preserving some of Weiss's improvisatory spirit, in one of the finest and best-recorded discs of lute music on the market.

New review
NOCTURNAL. Julian Bream (gtr). EMI CDC7 54901-2. Recorded in 1992.
Martin: Quatre Pièces Brèves. *Britten:* Nocturnal after John Dowland, Op. 70. *Brouwer:* Guitar Sonata. *Takemitsu:* All in Twilight. *Lutoslawski:* (trans. Lutoslawski): 12 Folk Melodies.

.•˙   1h 13m   DDD   4/94   9⌐P   9⌐S

No one can truly reach into the depths of Britten's *Nocturnal* until Life has taught them some hard lessons, nor, perhaps, can they perceive the *Innigkeit* of Martin's work; Bream, now in his sixties and with his technical armoury totally at the service of his emotions, demonstrates the truth of this in performances of moving intensity. Age has not dimmed his enthusiasm for pastures new: Brouwer's strong, and in places wryly humorous, Sonata with its teasing references to the composers to whom its three movements pay tribute, and Takemitsu's introspective *All in Twilight*, were written at his behest and are communicated with wonderful clarity. What Gareth Walters, the annotator, aptly describes as the "simple charm" of Bream's arrangements of Polish folk-melody settings by Lutoslawski brings the recital to a lighter conclusion. The old wine has matured beautifully and the new is of vintage status. The temptation to say that Bream has rarely played (or been recorded) better than here is too strong to resist!

ORGAN FIREWORKS, Volume 3. Christopher Herrick. Hyperion CDA66457. Played on the organ of St Eustache, Paris.
Batiste: Offertoire in D minor. *Bossi:* Pièce héroïque in D minor, Op. 128. Scherzo in D minor, Op. 49 No. 2. *Dubois:* Grand Choeur in B flat major. *Dupré:* Cortège et Litanie, Op. 19 No. 2. *Jolivet:* Hymne à l'Univers. *Lefébure-Wély:* Marche in F major, Op. 122 No. 4. *Lemare:* Concert Fantasy on "Hanover", Op. 4. Marche héroïque in D major, Op. 74. *Saint-Saëns:* Allegro giocoso in A minor, Op. 150 No. 7.

Ih IIm   DDD   9/91

Here is something truly spectacular. The brand new organ in St Eustache's Church, Paris was designed by the organist Jean Guillou who made sure it was an instrument fit for the finest of players and the greatest of music. In addition to a large array of stops, manuals and pipes it also boasts such extravagances as two consoles and a playback facility which enables the organ to play unattended. For this disc Christopher Herrick took advantage of this latter facility so that performances made during the day could be recorded in the small hours when extraneous noise was at a minimum. But the organ itself makes such a tremendously powerful, not to say, awesome noise, that one would have thought such a precaution unnecessary. Hyperion's vivid recording of this magnificent instrument stands out as one of the best recordings of an organ currently available on CD. Herrick's programme shows both the instrument and his own amazing virtuosity off to brilliant effect. There is great fun to be had from these pieces, none of which can really be said to be well-known. This is a disc of pure, unadulterated pleasure.

New review
ORGAN FIREWORKS, Volume 5. Christopher Herrick (org). Hyperion CDA66676. Played on the Virtanen organ in Turku Cathedral, Finland.
Alain: Litanies, Op. 79. *Sibelius* (arr. H. Fricker): Finlandia, Op. 26. *Sløgedal:* Variations on a Norwegian Folk Tune. *Mulet:* Carillon-sortie in D major. *Lindberg:* Organ Sonata in G minor, Op. 23 — Alla Sarabanda; Allegro con brio. *Mozart:* Orgelstück (Fantasia) für eine Uhr, K608. *Lefébure-Wély:* Marche. *Nielsen:* Commotio, FS155. *Elgar:* Pomp and Circumstance March in G major, Op. 39 No. 4.

Ih I5m   DDD

This disc mines a rich seam of repertoire ranging from the sublime (Mozart's *Fantasia*) to the ridiculous (Lefébure-Wély's *Marche*), from the obscure (Sløgedal's *Variations*) to the familiar (Elgar's *Pomp and Circumstance*). All have in common a virtuosity, be it simple showiness or something of greater musical substance, which, articulated by such an able player as Christopher Herrick and on an organ the mere sound of which can send shivers down the spine, means that we are treated to a thoroughly satisfying, carefully balanced display of aural pyrotechnics. Breathtaking clarity and an almost electrically charged brilliance of tone are the hallmarks of this magnificent Finnish organ. Never has *Finlandia* sounded quite so thrilling as it does with these flashing trumpets; never has Mulet's evergreen *Carillon-sortie* crackled as it does in this cold, clear Northern atmosphere. It gives a wonderful radiance to those less overtly flashy pieces and, combined with Herrick's intuitive musicianship, we have here performances of the Mozart *Orgelstück*, and Nielsen's mammoth *Commotio*, of great stature. This is a splendid disc as thrilling and truly spectacular as anything Hyperion have so far produced.

ORGAN TRANSCRIPTIONS. Thomas Trotter (org). Decca 436 656-2DH. Recorded 1992. *Elgar:* Pomp and Circumstance March in D major, Op. 39 No. 1 (trans. Lemare). Chanson de matin, Op. 15 No. 2 (trans. Brewer). *Gounod* (trans. Best): Marche funèbre d'une marionette. *Mendelssohn* (trans. Warren): A Midsummer Night's Dream — Overture. *Rossini* (trans. Lemare): Guillaume Tell — Overture. *Suppé* (trans. Evans): Dichter und Bauer — Overture. *Tchaikovsky* (trans. Goss-Custard): The Nutcracker, Op. 71a — Miniature Overture; Dance of the reeds; Waltz of the flowers. *Wagner* (trans. Lemare): Tannhäuser — Pilgrims' Chorus. Die Walküre — Ride of the Valkyries.

• Ih 14m DDD 4/94

That Thomas Trotter still frequently plays these transcriptions at his regular Birmingham recitals and clearly believes them worthy of committing to record is a testament not only to the magnificence of the instrument itself but also to his intelligent handling of the contradictory demands made by the music. His remarkable virtuosity ensures that everything sounds gloriously facile (belying the fact that here is some of the most technically demanding of all organ writing), his flamboyant streak cheerfully surmounts even the most outrageously non-organistic pieces (notably Best's grotesque *Marche funèbre d'une marionette*) and above all he has genuine musical integrity; how could anyone who didn't know exactly how Tchaikovsky's harp cadenza in the *Nutcracker*'s "Dance of the reeds" sounds bring off so convincingly Goss-Custard's decidedly glib re-working of this passage? A disc of immense fun and surprisingly good taste.

PIANO RECITAL. Claudio Arrau. Philips Insignia 438 305-2PM. *Liszt:* Liebesträume. S541 — No. 3, O lieb, so lang du lieben kannst (S298). Etudes d'exécution transcendante, S139 — Harmonies du soir. *Chopin:* Nocturnes — B major, Op. 62/1; E major, Op. 62/2. *Brahms:* Scherzo in E flat minor, Op. 4. *Beethoven:* Rondos, Op. 51 — No. 2 in G major. *Schubert:* Impromptus, D899 — No. 3 in D flat major. *Schumann:* Waldszenen, Op. 82 — No. 7, Vogel als Prophet. Three Romanzen, Op. 28 — No. 2 in F sharp major. Arabeske in C major, Op. 18. *Debussy:* Estampes — Soirées dans Grenade. Images, Book 2 — Poisson d'or.

• Ih 19m ADD 10/93

The late lamented Claudio Arrau took recording very seriously, although at times that robbed his playing in the studio of the last degree of spontaneity. Thus, in Liszt's *Liebesträume* No. 3, which opens his recital, and the two Chopin *Nocturnes* which follows, Arrau's gentle, poetic nudgings of the melodic line sound a little self-conscious. However, then he gives us his fine Brahms *Scherzo* in E flat minor and the wonderful Schubert *Impromptu* in D flat from D899, which he plays magically. His Schumann is pretty impressive, too — "Vogels als Prophet" (from *Waldszenen*), the *Romance* in F sharp, Op. 28 No. 2 and the *Arabeske* in C, Op. 18. These pieces are followed by another composer pianist he understood so well: Debussy — "Soirée dans Grenade" from *Estampes* and a superb "Poisson d'or'" (*Images*, Book 2). The recital ends with a dazzling "Harmonies du soir" (from Liszt's *Etudes d'exécution transcendante*). All reveal extremely distinguished playing, backed by a recorded sound that is very real. One would certainly have had to pay far more for a good seat at an Arrau recital, and that is just what one has here with this disc.

PIANO RECITAL. Maurizio Pollini. DG 419 202-2GH. Items marked [a] from 2530 225 (6/72), [b] 2530 893 (7/78). *Stravinsky:* Three Movements from "Petrushka"[a]. *Prokofiev:* Piano Sonata No. 7 in B flat major, Op. 83[a]. *Webern:* Variations for Piano, Op. 27[b]. *Boulez:* Piano Sonata No. 2 (1948)[b].

• Ih 9m ADD II/86

The capacity to stupefy is not the only measure of greatness in a performer; but it is an important factor, and in very few piano recordings is it embodied to the extent of this one. It is there from the very first bar of the first *Petrushka* movement — few pianists have ever attempted the tempo Pollini takes. Similarly, the Boulez Second Sonata has never been recorded with anything approaching this accuracy, glinting articulation and incandescent vigour. The bitterness at the heart of Prokofiev's slow movement with its remorseless tolling of bells is starkly revealed, and Pollini responds no less acutely to the distilled poetry behind the apparently arid surface of Webern's *Variations*. Clearly the Russian works are the more likely to grab the first-time listener; the Webern and Boulez may leave you utterly cold, or else touch regions of your psyche you did not know you had. With Pollini as exponent and with exemplary DG recording, the second possibility should not be ruled out. Intellectually, dramatically, lyrically, virtuosically, whichever way you look at it, this is a superlative disc.

New review

PIANO RECITAL. Rosalyn Tureck. VAI Audio VAIA1024-2. Recorded live in 1992.
Bach: Adagio in G major, BWV968. Chromatic Fantasia and Fugue in D minor, BWV903. Partita for Solo Violin in D minor, BWV1004 — Chaconne (arr. Busoni). Partita in B flat major, BWV825 — Gigue. Goldberg Variations, BWV988 — Variation 29. Musette in D major, BWVAnh126. *Mendelssohn:* Song without Words in E major, Op. 19 No. 1. *Schubert:* Moments musicaux, D780 — No. 2 in A flat major; No. 3 in F minor. *Brahms:* Variations and Fugue on a Theme by Handel, Op. 24.

② lh 24m DDD 8/93   ⑨ₚ

Rosalyn Tureck playing Mendelssohn, Schubert, Brahms and Bach? Surely there must be some mistake. Touchingly and often gloriously the answer is no. This live recital is a highly individual occasion, undisguised by the limited recording. The Mendelssohn and Schubert have a winning gentleness and the Brahms is exceptionally majesterial. Her Bach-Busoni, too, is only occasionally marred by pedantry or over-emphasis and it is her 'straight' Bach, particularly the *Chromatic Fantasia and Fugue* that will provoke raised eyebrows as well as happiness. Yet none of Tureck's decisions have been lightly arrived at and her seeming idiosyncrasy is based on years of devoted scholarship and experience. Unlike Glenn Gould, who so despised the *Chromatic Fantasia and Fugue*, she views it as a vital cornerstone of the repertoire and her reading, which features a gentle and meditative propulsion of the fugue, is deeply refreshing. The Bach encores, too, show this pianist at her greatest and are offered up with an undimmed zest and resilience, a sheer joy in living.

New review

TCHAIKOVSKY AND HIS FRIENDS. Margaret Fingerhut (pf). Chandos CHAN9218. Recorded in 1992.
Arensky: Intermezzo in F minor, Op. 36 No. 12. Le ruisseau dans la forêt. Romance, Op. 53 No. 5. *Glazunov:* Etudes, Op. 31 — No. 2 in C minor; No. 3 in E minor. Prelude in D major, Op. 25 No. 1. *Liadov:* Two Bagatelles, Op. 17. Prelude in B minor, Op. 11 No. 1. Prelude in F sharp minor, Op. 39 No. 4. *Rachmaninov:* Canon in E minor. Morceaux de fantaisie, Op. 3 — No. 1, Elégie in E flat minor; No. 3, Mélodie in E; No. 4, Polichinelle in F sharp minor. *Taneyev:* Scherzo in E flat minor. Andante semplice. *Tchaikovsky:* Humoresque in E minor, Op. 10 No. 2. Nocturne in C sharp minor, Op. 19 No. 4. Chant sans paroles in A minor, Op. 40 No. 7. Dumka, Op. 59.

lh 18m DDD 4/94

The Russian salon piano piece, owing a good deal to song and therefore to French example, was an immensely popular genre in Moscow and St Petersburg circles, and Tchaikovsky set examples both good and risky. The lively pieces, such as his wonderfully catchy *Humoresque*, not only put Russian folk idioms into currency, but could seize the sharpest of twentieth-century Russian ears, Stravinsky's, and go into *The Fairy's Kiss* with his own rhythmic bounce. The tender ones could veer in the direction of sentimentality, and sometimes lurch over the margins of good taste. A good variety is represented here. Margaret Fingerhut has chosen intelligently. She has a real understanding of the genre, and can knock off the rapid fancy (Taneyev's *Scherzo*) and the sudden, almost manic burst of energy (Liadov's F sharp minor Prelude), as well as the dreamy meditation (Liadov's first Op. 17 Bagatelle, "La douleur" or Tchaikovsky's own Nocturne or Rachmaninov's *Mélodie*) and a genre piece such as Arensky's pretty little picture of a brook running through a forest. Her greatest talent is for a flexibility of phrasing that always sings. These are in the best sense sympathetic performances, and should give pleasure.

Early Music
Medieval — Renaissance
12th–15th centuries

New review

THE SWEET LOOK AND THE LOVING MANNER. Sinfonye/Stevie Wishart. Hyperion
CDA66625. Texts and translations included. Recorded in 1992.
Carenza/Alais/Iselde: Na Carenza. *Anonymous:* Soufrés, maris. Toute seule, passerai.
Por coi me bait mes maris?. Bona domna, un conseil vos deman. C'est la gieus en mi les prez.
C'est desoz l'olive en mi les prez. La jus desouz l'olive. Et une chambre cointe et grant. Main
s'est levee Aëlis. Tout leis en mi les prez. Bele Doette as fenestres se siet. Avant hier en un vert
pre. Li debonnaires Dieus. *Iseut de Capio/Almuc de Castelnau:* Domna N'Almucs, si-us
plages. **Beatriz de Romans:** Na Maria. *Beatriz de Dia:* Estat ai en greu cossirier. A
chanter m'er de so qu'eu no volria (arr. Wishart). *Bernart de Ventadorn:* Non es meravilla
s'eu chan. *Dregnau de Lille:* Mout m'abelist quant le voi. *Audefroi le Bastart:* Bele
Emmelos.

♪♪ **1h 10m DDD 8/93**

The musicians of Sinfonye go from strength to strength. This is their third record for Hyperion,
and brings increasing admiration for the wonderfully tactful and resourceful drumming of Jim
Denley, the range of colours and textures Stevie Wishart can draw from her fiddle, the
inventive playing of Paula Chateauneuf on the oud and particularly the superbly sensitive way in
which Vivien Ellis projects the troubadour songs. Using for the most part what is effectively a
slow isosyllabic style, she presents the songs primarily as poems that happen to have a melodic
line attached to them. But perhaps the most important feature of the recording is that the
instrumental interludes are so well designed. The arrangements here are without exception
musically compelling, normally derived by speeding up the original melody. The performances
show a new and compelling approach to the ever-fraught problems of presenting early
monophonic song.

MUSIC FOR THE LION-HEARTED KING. Gothic Voices/Christopher Page. Hyperion
CDA66336. Texts and translations included.
Anonymous Twelfth Century: Mundus vergens. Novus miles sequitur. Sol sub nube latuit.
Hac in anni ianua. Anglia, planctus itera. Etras auri reditur. Vetus abit littera. In occasu sideris.
Purgator criminum. Pange melos lacrimosum. Ver pacis apperit. Latex silice. *Gace Brulé:* A la
doucour de la bele seson. *Blondel de Nesle:* L'amours dont sui espris. Ma joie me semont.
Gui IV, "Li chastelain de Couci": Li nouviauz tanz.

♪♪ **1h DDD 10/89**   ♩♭ ❓ ✒

Christopher Page has a remarkable gift for creating enthralling programmes of early music bound
together by a brilliantly-chosen central theme, or appellation. This new collection is no less
distinguished and every bit as fascinating, musically and historically. Whether or not Richard
himself ever actually listened to any of these pieces is beside the question: they are all
representative of the period of his lifetime and are gathered together here in his name for the
800th anniversary of his coronation (1189). Two types of twelfth-century vocal music are
represented: the *conductus* — which can be written for one, two, three or even four voices and
the *chanson*, or noble, courtly love song. The singers cannot be applauded too highly for
performances marked by an extraordinary insight into how this music should be tackled, that is,
with a fair degree of restraint as well as know-how, given the sort of audience it might have had
in Richard's day: the royal court or the household of some high-ranking ecclesiastic.

THE COURTS OF LOVE. MUSIC FROM THE TIME OF ELEANOR OF AQUITAINE.
Sinfonye (Mara Kiek, voc; Andrew Lawrence-King, medieval hp; Jim Denley, perc)/**Stevie
Wishart.** Hyperion CDA66367. Texts and translations included.
Gui d'Ussel: Si be'm partetz, mala domna, de vos. *Raimbaut de Vaqeiras:* Calenda
maya (vocal and instrumental versions). *Anonymous 12th Century:* L'on qui dit q'amors est
dolce chose. *Bernart de Ventadorn:* Ara'm conseillatz seignor. Conartz, ara sai au be. Quan

vei la lauzeta mover. **Cadenet:** S'anc fuy belha ni prezada (vocal and instrumental versions). **Giraut de Bornelh:** S'ie'us queir conseil, bel' amig' Alamanda. **Gace Brulé:** Quant je voi la noif remise. Quant voi le tens bel et cler. Quant flours et glais et verdues s'esloigne. Quant li tens reverdoie.

1h 4m DDD 8/90

This recital consists of songs and instrumental pieces dating from the end of the twelfth century and derived from the "courts of love" of Aquitaine, Champagne, Flanders and elsewhere. The courts of love, created around aristocratic figures such as Marie of Champagne and Eleanor of Aquitaine, were essentially a charade of the medieval law courts, to which lovers could bring their complaints. Thus the texts of the songs are concerned with the dilemmas of infidelity, betrayal and unrequited love. All that survives of this music is melodies for singing: these have been sensitively arranged by Stevie Wishart for a small selection of medieval instruments, including the symphony, a sort of hurdy-gurdy, medieval fiddles, lutes and percussion. All the players of Sinfonye are both expert and relaxed, projecting the music with great character. Six of the pieces are sung by Mara Kiek with considerable feeling: her unusual voice production and tone help to give a sense of 'distance' to the performances, and throughout strike a suitably plaintive note. Hyperion's recording catches all the vocal and instrumental inflexions with great fidelity and a most natural sense of balance. All in all, a fascinating glimpse of music and manners from a remote if influential corner of medieval civilization.

BELLA DOMNA. THE MEDIEVAL WOMAN: LOVER, POET, PATRONESS AND SAINT. **Sinfonye** (Mara Kiek, voc; Andrew Lawrence-King, medieval hp; Jim Denley, perc)/**Stevie Wishart** (medieval fiddle, symphony). Hyperion CDA66283. Texts and translations included. **Martin Codax:** Cantigas de Amigo. **Anonymous Thirteenth Century:** Domna, pos vos ay chausida. Estampies Royals — No. 3; No. 4; No. 6. Danse Royale. **de Fournival:** Onques n'amai tant que jou fui amee. **La Comtesse de Die:** A chantar m'er de so qu'ieu non volria. **Anonymous Fourteenth Century:** Lasse, pour quoi refusai.

1h DDD 6/88

This intriguing CD collection of medieval songs joined together by the themes of woman as lover, poet, patroness and saint was originally released in 1988 and represented the début of Stevie Wishart's group Sinfonye. The performances of this elusive music have all the freshness and excitement of first encounter. The musical centre stage is held predominantly by the extraordinary vocalist Mara Kiek, whose plaintive as well as idiosyncratic tone ideally matches the distance of the music between its composition and the present day: this is genuinely music from another time and place, with hardly any relationship to the present day at all. Stevie Wishart's playing of the medieval fiddle, used predominantly as a drone instrument and the symphony, a kind of hurdy-gurdy, well matches in its freedom and espressivity Kiek's singing, as does the supportive percussion playing of Jim Denley on two types of medieval drum. The fourth and final member of the group is the harpist Andrew Lawrence-King, whose playing adds tremendous colour to these intriguing recreations of the medieval woman's expression of emotions such as betrayal and violation. The harshness as well as vigour of the medieval era is powerfully recreated in these performances. Hyperion's recording is appropriately neutral, catching at times some of the claustrophobia of the emotions expressed in the music. An extremely interesting recital of music unlikely to be encountered elsewhere.

THE PILGRIMAGE TO SANTIAGO. New London Consort/Philip Pickett. L'Oiseau-Lyre 433 148-2OH2. Texts and translations included.
Including Cantigas de Santa María (collected/composed by Alfonso el Sabio), the seven Cantigas de Amigo by Martin Codax and other medieval vocal and instrumental works from the Codices Las Huelgas and Calixtinus.

② 2h 6m DDD 7/92

In recent years a far higher standard of performance together with more rigorous scholarship has come to be expected from those who choose to perform this kind of repertoire. Philip Pickett has been in the forefront of this impressive rise in confidence (as much about what is not known as is definitely known) as this two-disc set amply demonstrates. What may perhaps be surprising to some is the quality of the music itself. The Cantigas remain some of the most enticing melodies ever written, and the New London Consort do them full justice with an array of instrumentalists and singers who are, however, used with discretion. Similarly the moving *Cantigas de Amigo* of Martin Codax are beautifully sung with a restraint that pays expressive dividends, though they do not have quite the transcendent quality of Maria Kiek's recording with Sinfonye (Bella Domna; refer to the Index to Reviews). The polyphonic music from the Las Huelgas and Calixtinus manuscripts completes, with a flourish, the survey tied together by the "Santiago" label. If there is early polyphony that sounds fresher than the four-part *Belial vocatur*, for example, it has yet to be recorded. In addition to polyphonic works of various genres, Pickett has also chosen to record the four *planctus* settings from the Las Huelgas Codex: moving music in themselves, they are valuable also for their historical associations, as is explained in the comprehensive notes to the set.

VOX IBERICA I. SONS OF THUNDER. **Sequentia/Benjamin Bagby, Barbara Thornton.** Deutsche Harmonia Mundi RD77199. Texts and translations included.
Codex Calixtinus — Ad superni regis decus. Alleluia: Vocavit Ihesus Iacobum. Annua gaudia, Iacobe debita. Benedicamus Domino. Congaudeant catholici. Cum vidissent autem. Cunctipotens genitor deus. Dum pater familias. Dum esset. Exultet celi curia. Gratulantes celebremus festum. Huic Iacobo. Iacobe sancte tuum repettio. Iacobi virginei. In hac die laudes cum gaudio. Jocundetur et letetur. Misit Herodes. Nostra phalans. O adiutor. Regi perhennis glorie. Rex immense, pater pie. Vox nostra resonet.

Ih 14m   DDD   12/92

VOX IBERICA II. CODEX LAS HUELGAS. **Sequentia/Benjamin Bagby, Barbara Thornton.** Deutsche Harmonia Mundi 05472-77238-2. Texts and translations included.
Codex Las Huelgas — Audi, pontus. Ave Maria, gracia plena. Benedicamus Domino cum cantico. Benedicamus: Hic est enim precursor. Benedicamus virgini matri. Casta catholica. Catholicorum concio. Ex illustri. Fa fa mi fa/ut re mi ut. In hoc festo gratissimo. Maria, virgo virginum. Mater patris et filia. Mundi dolens de iactura. O gloriosa Dei genitrix. O, plangant nostri prelati. O plena gracia. Psallat chorus in novo carmina. Qui nos fecit ex nichilo. Resurgentis Domini. Salve regina glorie. Stabat iuxta Christi crucem. Verbum patris hodie. Virgo sidus aureum. Four Planctus — Plange Castella misera; Quis dabit meo aquam; Rex obiit et labitur Castelle gloria; O monialis concio Burgensis.

Ih 15m   DDD   12/92

VOX IBERICA III. CANTIGAS DE SANTA MARIA. **Sequentia/Benjamin Bagby, Barbara Thornton.** Deutsche Harmonia Mundi 05472-77173-2. Texts and translations included.
Alfonso el Sabio: Por nos, Virgen Madre. Como o nome da Virgen. Sobelos fondos do mar. Nenbre-sse-e, Madre de. Dized', ai trobadores. Maldito seja quen non loara. Quantos me creveren loaran. Quen bõa dona querrá. Pero que seja a gente. Santa Maria, strela do dia. Pois que Deus quis da Virgen. Macar poucos cantares acabei e con son. En todo logar á poder.
Riquier: Humils, forfaitz, repres e penedens. ***Anonymous Thirteenth Century:*** *Kharajas* — Que faray, mamma?; Meu sidi Ibrahim; Gar si yes devina; Gardi vos ay yermanellas.

Ih 18m   DDD   12/92

These three generously-filled discs provide a fascinating insight into Spain between the twelfth and fourteenth centuries. The country's history and culture as encompassed in the texts and music of the three repertories recorded is brought to life by Sequentia with all the immediacy of an illuminated miniature in a mediaeval manuscript. The music comes from three famous Spanish mediaeval manuscripts — the Las Huelgas manuscript, the Codex Calixtinus, and the collection of Cantigas de Santa María compiled at the court of King Alfonso "El Sabio" of Castille. What strikes one immediately is the freshness and imagination of virtually every piece here recorded. Sequentia's performances are commensurate with these qualities — listen, for example, to the magical textures of the women's choir singing *Sobelos fondos do mar* from the Cantigas collection, or the robust, steely harmony projected by the men in the organa from the Calixtinus manuscript. Surely one of the most remarkable pieces of the Middle Ages is the enormous *Virgo sidus aureum*, a prosa *"de Sancta Maria"* lasting over 14 minutes, whose text is a radiant mystical contemplation of the Mother of God. Liturgico-poetic parallels for it may well be sought in the East rather than the West — the Greek *Akathist* hymn from several centuries earlier, for example — but if Hildegard of Bingen, the "feather on the breath of God" is brought to mind, that would also be no surprise. It must be said that the poetic quality of all three of these collections is so high that the music could hardly fail to be of the same level of inspiration. This astonishing piece is given a splendid, coherent rendition (no easy task with a monophonic work of this length) by two soloists, female choir and symphonia, and one only has to listen to it after one of the rather shorter three-part conductus, such as *Mundi dolens de iactura*, or one of the powerful *organa* for St James, the "Son of thunder", from the Calixtinus collection, to gain some idea of the impact and the extent of the variety to be found on these discs. The Cantigas collection convincingly conveys the accomplishments of the court of the king who "while he was pondering the heavens and looking at the stars...lost the earth and his kingdom", and places the Cantiga repertory in the context not only of the troubadours (in particular Guirault Riquier) but also the Mozarabic *kharjas* (or *jarchas*), whose music has been reconstructed, with some success, by Benjamin Bagby. This testament to the richness of musical life in mediaeval Spain should not be missed: it has lost none of its power over the centuries.

New review

WORCESTER FRAGMENTS. English Sacred Music of the Late Middle Ages. **Orlando Consort** (Robert Harre-Jones, alto; Charles Daniels, Angus Smith, tens; Donald Grieg, bar). Amon Ra CD-SAR59. Texts and translations included.

58m DDD 8/93

In this recording the Orlando Consort provide the listener with the chance to gain an overall impression of how music developed in England during the thirteenth and early fourteenth centuries — a development distinguished by its intriguing variety, creativity and undoubted beauty, its peculiar sweetness being marked by the constant harmonic use of the interval of a third. The Orlando Consort manage to achieve a balance between the type of buzzing vocal timbre, believed to have been that of the Middle Ages with its roughness of approach, and their own good solid modern standards of professional musicianship. The Consort also attempts to reproduce what scholars now believe to have been the way in which Ecclesiastical Latin was pronounced in medieval England.

THE MARRIAGE OF HEAVEN AND HELL. THIRTEENTH-CENTURY FRENCH MOTETS AND SONGS. **Gothic Voices/Christopher Page.** Hyperion CDA66423. Texts and translations included.
Anonymous: Je ne chant pas. Talens m'est pris. Trois sereurs/Trois sereurs/Trois sereurs. Plus bele que flors/Quant revient/L'autrier jouer. Par un martinet/Hé, sire!/Hé, bergier! De la virge Katerine/Quant froidure/Agmina milicie. Ave parens/Ad gratie. Super te Jerusalem/Sed fulsit virginitas. A vous douce debonnaire. Mout souvent/Mout ai esté en doulour. Quant voi l'aloete/Dieux! je ne m'en partiré ja. En non Dieu/Quant voi la rose. Je m'en vois/Tels a mout. Festa januaria. **Blondel de Nesle:** En tous tans que vente bise. **Colin Muset:** Trop volontiers chanteroie. **Bernart de Ventadorn:** Can vei la lauzeta mover. **Gautier de Dargies:** Autre que je ne seuill fas.

46m DDD 12/90

The reasons for the dazzling success of Gothic Voices both in the recording studio and in the concert-hall are once again evident in this collection. It is both an entertaining and well-planned recital and, if one chooses to take it that way, reading Christopher Page's insert-notes while listening, a detailed lecture-recital. The music, all French and dating from the thirteenth century, is that seemingly impenetrable repertoire of polytextual motets, unexpectedly compared and contrasted with monophonic trouvère songs. The comparison is illuminating, and the performances of both genres of music are up to Gothic Voices' usual standards: intonation is perfect, textures are finely balanced, the performances are always conceived just as much melodically as harmonically, and the greatest respect is always paid to the words (even when there are three texts at the same time, as is often the case here!). The clever juxtaposition of the trouvère Bernart de Ventadorn's *Can vei la lauzeta mover* with the triple-texted motet *Quant voi l'aloete/Dieux! je ne m'en partiré ja/NEUMA* encapsulates the thinking behind this recording: a compelling musical experience and a provocative intellectual one.

New review

THE STUDY OF LOVE. FRENCH SONGS AND MOTETS OF THE FOURTEENTH CENTURY. **Gothic Voices/Christopher Page.** Hyperion CDA66619. Texts and translations included.
Machaut: Dame, je suis cilz/Fins cuer. Trop plus/Biauté paree/Je ne suis. Tres bonne et belle. Se mesdisans. Dame, je vueil endurer. *Pycard:* Gloria. *Solage:* Le basile.
Anonymous: Pour vous servir. Puis que l'aloe ne fine. Jour a jour la vie. Combien que j'aye (two versions). Marticius qui fu. Renouveler me feïst. Fist on dame. Il me convient guerpir. Le ior. En la maison Dedalus. La grant biaute. En esperent. Ay las! quant je pans.

♪ lh DDD 6/93   ♪ₚ ♪s

The title of the disc speaks of the ways in which the discourses of love (and 'love') in the late Middle Ages are partly, perhaps largely, derived from books — the Bible, classical poetry and myths, the earlier medieval literary tradition — rather than some expression of unmediated personal feeling. But music was a powerful means for the late medieval artist to attempt to transcend the bookish intertextualities of the literary texts. Rarely has Gothic Voices, both as individuals and together, sounded more alive and present: it is even almost possible to listen to the whole disc at one sitting without surfeit. The accord of vowel colour between the singers in some of the fully texted pieces is marvellous, a feature pointed up the more by juxtaposition with those works in which Page continues his experiments with lower-voice vocalization. Where some slight untidiness creeps in, the impression often (though not invariably) given is the positive one of risk being happily taken in the recording sessions, the very absence of which has so often been the downfall of lesser groups (and not just in medieval music). A wonderful addition to the catalogue, and the recorded sound is superlative.

IL SOLAZZO. The Newberry Consort/Mary Springfels. Harmonia Mundi HMU90 7038. Texts and translation included.
Anonymous Fourteenth Century Italian: La Badessa. Bel fiore danza. Nova stella. Cominciamento di gioia. Trotto. Principe di virtu. *Jacopo da Bologna:* Non al suo amante. *Landini:* La bionda treccia. Dolcie signorie. Donna, s'i, t'o fallito. El gran disio. *Ciconia:* O rosa bella. Ligiadra donna. *Zacharo de Teramo:* Rosetta. Un fior gentil. *Bartolino da Padova:* Alba columba.

♪ lh 2m DDD 7/93

If medieval Italian music pales somewhat in comparison to the glories of opera from the nineteenth century onwards, there are still riches to be discovered in this collection of *trecento* vocal and instrumental works. The Chicago-based ensemble, The Newberry Consort, use a mere five performers to provide over an hour of entertainment. This was the era of writers such as Dante, Petrarch, Boccaccio, but also of Simone Prodenzani — the author of a cycle of sonnets entitled *Il Solazzo*, many of which were later set to music. Whilst some of the *Solazzo* texts are presented here in musical form (the scurrilous *La Badessa* is one), Italian ballata from leading composers of the time are also represented — Ciconia's *O rosa bella* and Landini's *La bionda treccia*, for example. The vocal numbers are all taken by mezzo Judith Malafronte and counter-tenor Drew Minter who clear the hurdles of tricky pronunciation and flamboyantly complex vocal lines to give a thoroughly communicative performance of this wonderful music. Mary Springfels provides elegant and musical direction as well as that essential ingredient to a disc such as this — the informative booklet. If the prospect of an hour of early Italian song sounds daunting, fear not, for the instrumental dances on the disc (especially the anonymous *Cominciamento di gioia*) are played with a vitality that will make you want to jump up and join in! Explorers of the riches from Italian times long gone by need have no qualms when sampling from this lively, superbly performed disc.

THE MEDIEVAL ROMANTICS. FRENCH SONGS AND MOTETS, 1340-1440. **Gothic Voices/Christopher Page.** Hyperion CDA66463. Texts and translations included.
Solage: Joieux de cuer en seumellant estoye. *De Porta:* Alma polis religio/Axe poli cum artica. *Machaut:* C'est force, faire le weil. Tant doucement me sens emprisones. Comment qu'a moy lonteinne. *Tenorista:* Sofrir m'estuet et plus non puis durer. *De Senleches:* En ce gracieus tamps joli. *Dufay:* Je requier a tous amoureux. Las, que feray? Ne que je devenray?

G. Velut: Je voel servir plus c'onques mais. *De Lymburgia:* Tota pulcra es, amica mea. *Anonymous:* Various works.

○● 56m DDD 3/92

A revelatory disc, this. As with Gothic Voices' previous recordings, a large and almost completely unknown selection of medieval repertoire is presented with cordon bleu elegance and panache. Christopher Page's excellent insert-notes provide the rationale behind this particular anthology, and if the ravishing sound of the ensemble does not convince you that this music is of the highest quality, then nothing will. The connections between pieces by composers such as Solage and Senleches with later music by Dufay are brought into sharp relief in this well-planned collection. Page's enlightening dissection of Solage's extraordinary *Joieux de cuer en seumellant estoye* in the commentary is the focal point of a wider discussion of the way in which composers of the fifteenth century reacted to the accomplishments of the fourteenth; and the concrete result of these speculations is the delightful programme here recorded. Listen to the Johannes de Lymburgia's smoothly consonant *Tota pulchra es* immediately after the eccentric harmonies of the Solage song and ask yourself whether music history was ever so absorbing.

LANCASTER AND VALOIS. Gothic Voices (Margaret Philpot, contr. Rogers Covey-Crump, Andrew Tusa, Charles Daniels, Leigh Nixon, tens; Stephen Charlesworth, Donald Grieg, bars; Andrew Lawrence-King, hp)/**Christopher Page** (lte). Hyperion CDA66588. Texts and translations included.
Machaut: Donnez, signeurs. Quand je ne voy ma dame. Riches d'amour et mendians. Pas de tor en thies pais. *Solage:* Tres gentil cuer. *Cesaris:* Se vous scaviez, ma tres douce maistresse. Mon seul voloir/Certes m'amour. *Cordier:* Ce jur de l'an. *Pycard:* Credo. *Sturgeon:* Salve mater domini/Salve templum domini. *Fonteyns:* Regali ex progenie. *Anonymous:* Puis qu'autrement ne puis avoir. Soit tart, tempre, main ou soir. Le ior. Avrai je ja de ma dame confort? Sanctus. Je vueil vivre au plaisir d'amours.

○● 59m DDD 9/92

This is the tenth recording to come from Christopher Page's Gothic Voices and, the considerable success of their previous recordings notwithstanding, this is perhaps their best yet. In the space of 11 years, Page and his group have reinvented performance practice in medieval and fifteenth century music, as powerful and popularizing an influence as David Munrow and his Early Music Consort of London in the 1970s. "Lancaster and Valois" takes its name from the chosen repertoire: French secular songs of the late fourteenth and early fifteenth centuries juxtaposed with sacred English pieces from around 1400. Much thought has been given to the ordering of the pieces and the grouping of the voices, resulting in the greatest possible diversity. In *Tres gentil cuer* by Solage, Page sets an ideally lilting tempo, with the text finely enunciated by Margaret Philpot, the tenors (in this instance Charles Daniels and Leigh Nixon) adding definition but never threatening to engulf. This is followed by a *Credo* by the English composer Pycard, the longest and most stately piece on the disc, exploiting the richer timbres of tenors and baritones. With excellent sound and entertaining and scholarly notes by Christopher Page, this is an irresistible disc.

New review
THE VOICE IN THE GARDEN. SPANISH SONGS AND MOTETS, 1480-1550. **Gothic Voices/Christopher Page** with **Christopher Wilson** (vihuela) and **Andrew Lawrence-King** (hp). Hyperion CDA66653. Texts and translations included. Recorded in 1993.
Encina: Mi libertad en sosiego. Los sospiros no sosiegan. *Peñalosa:* Por las sierras de Madrid. Ne reminiscaris, Domine. Precor te, Domine. Sancta Maria. *Mena:* Yo creo que n'os dió Dios. La bella malmaridada. *Enrique:* Mi querer tanto vos quiere. *Anonymous:* Pase el agoa, ma Julieta. Harto de tanta porfia. Dindirín, dindirín. Ave, Virgo, gratia plena. Dentro en el vergel. Entra Mayo y sale Abril. *Instrumental works* — *Narváez:* Fantasía II tono; Fantasía III tono. Paseávase el rey moro. *Fernández Palero:* Paseávase el rey moro. *Milán:* Fantasías 10, 12 and 18. *Segni:* Tiento. *Anonymous:* A la villa voy.

○● 52m DDD 2/94

As usual with Gothic Voices, there is a mixture of all-vocal and solo-instrument performances, never the twain meeting and a mixture of what used to be called sacred and secular: motets by

Peñalosa sit cheek by jowl with love songs and instrumental fantasies, giving an unusual and intriguing picture of the repertory. In general the record has all the qualities that make anything by Gothic Voices a required purchase for collections that aim at serious coverage of early centuries; and the resourceful selection of music makes it an important contribution to the understanding of Spanish culture. A note of special praise for Christopher Wilson's performances of the vihuela solos which have a control and eloquence that are truly impressive. Andrew Lawrence-King characteristically throws new light on some of this repertory with his immaculate range of colours and textures on the harp.

THE BRIGHTEST HEAVEN OF INVENTION. New London Chamber Choir/James Wood. Amon Ra CD-SAR56. Texts and translations included.
Regis: O admirabile commercium. *Obrecht:* Factor orbis. Salve crux. *Josquin Desprez:* Praeter rerum seriem. *Brumel:* Nato canunt omnia. *Busnois:* In hydraulis. Anthoni usque limina. *Dufay:* Ave regina celorum.

Ih DDD 3/93

The motets on this disc are linked by much more than their Flemish origin and the period of their composition (about 1450-1525). First, there is their sheer originality: even from the outset, with *O admirabile commercium* by Johannes Regis, we are in the world of unconventionality and innovation. Secondly, riddles and cryptic references enliven the task of realizing these scores — even to the extent, in Busnois's *Anthoni usque limina*, that we are still unsure as to how the cryptograph for the tenor part is to be interpreted! Thirdly, many of these composers obviously knew and respected each other: Antoine Brumel's *Nato canunt omnia* is a parody work based on the Regis motet. Above all, these motets are connected by a general attitude of approach, based on the development from a secure tradition for a discerning audience that would be able to follow the new paths to be trod. The New London Chamber Choir performs on a semi-professional basis and offers urgently committed performances that do not always display subtleness of balance or dynamic shading, and have their moments of rawness, but which ultimately convince by the strength of their imagination. A lucid recording, set in a lively-enough ambience, complements the whole.

THE ROSE AND THE OSTRICH FEATHER. Music from the Eton Choirbook, Volume 1.
The Sixteen/Harry Christophers. Collins Classics 1314-2. Notes and texts included.
Fayrfax: Magnificat ("Regale"). *Hygons:* Salve regina. *Turges:* From stormy wyndis. Stabat iuxta Christi crucem. *Anonymous:* This day day dawes. *Cornysh:* Salve regina.

Ih 3m DDD 4/92

The sacred music of early Tudor England (the end of the fifteenth century) has been unjustly neglected on CD and the welcome extended to this Collins release is further enhanced by the fact that Harry Christophers and his ensemble have since added two further volumes to this series dedicated to music from the Eton Choirbook. The destruction of great swathes of manuscript in the sixteenth century has left us with only isolated jewels such as this to remind us in sound what the eye can behold in the Perpendicular style of the architecture of the cathedrals of Canterbury, Worcester, Winchester and the Minster at York. Both architecture and music present soaring vaulted vistas and an attention to florid and ornate tracery. The Rose and the Ostrich Feather? These were both potent symbolic emblems of members of the royal house of Tudor and the words are incorporated into the two secular songs with English texts. The white rose was also an image closely associated with the Virgin Mary and most of the scores in the Choirbook are dedicated to her. Sadly, the disc is without translations of the Latin works but there is a fascinating essay by John Milsom. This music finds The Sixteen at their best, especially attentive to the severe tuning demands placed on the singers, for whom there is no instrumental accompaniment. Particularly notable is the control that Christophers exerts over the sound of his singers in this very taxing music (four of the performances on the disc last for over ten minutes). The recorded sound expertly captures and balances the expressive singing. Whether used as an aural accompaniment to a great architectural style or enjoyed purely for its sharply-defined reflection of one of the greatest periods of English music (existing within the choral traditions which continues to this day), this disc is altogether outstanding and should not be missed.

New review

THE PILLARS OF ETERNITY. Music from the Eton Choirbook, Volume 3. **The Sixteen/ Harry Christophers.** Collins Classics 1342-2. Texts and translations included.
Cornysh: Ave Maria, mater Dei. **Davy:** O Domine caeli terraeque. A myn hart remembir the well. A blessid Jhesu. **Lambe:** Stella caeli. **Wilkinson:** Credo in Deum/Jesus autem. Salve regina.

Ih Im DDD 7/93

This disc opens with Richard Davy's *O Domine caeli*, a vast and complex work lasting just over a quarter of an hour in performance, but apparently composed within a single day at Magdalen College, Oxford. It goes on and on in the most exalted, but perhaps inconsequential manner until its final resounding "Amen". What should a choir do with it except sing it as well as possible in terms of ensemble and intonation, as The Sixteen certainly do, and let the glorious sounds wash over the dumbfounded listener? Still more perplexing is Robert Wilkinson's *Credo in Deum/Jesus autem*, a 13-voice canon in which the individual voice parts represent Jesus and the 12 disciples. The net effect has been aptly described as "harmonious chaos", which it surely is, although, in common with all multi-voiced works of this period, it is harmonically static in a way that should delight minimalist fans. Symbolism is also the key to the structure of Wilkinson's setting of the *Salve regina* — the nine voice parts each representing a designated rank in the nine-fold hierarchy of angels. This is vintage Eton Choirbook, the composer pitting the full and sonorous directness of the tutti acclamations against the flights of fantasy in the solo sections. Another must for any self-respecting collection of renaissance polyphony.

New review

THE FLOWER OF ALL VIRGINITY. MUSIC FROM THE ETON CHOIRBOOK, Volume 4. **The Sixteen/Harry Christophers.** Collins Classics 1395-2. Texts and translations included. Recorded om 1993.
Kellyk: Gaude flore virginali. **Nesbet:** Magnificat. **Fayrfax:** Most clere of colour. **Browne:** O Maria Salvatoris mater. Salve regina. **Anonymous:** Ah, my dear son. Afraid, alas.

Ih 3m DDD 2/94

We know a good deal about the context for which the Marian music in the Eton Choirbook was composed: each evening members of the College choir were to gather before an image of the Virgin and sing an antiphon in her honour (the College was itself dedicated to Mary). During Lent they were to perform the *Salve regina*, and throughout the rest of the year 'an antiphon of the Blessed Virgin' is all that is stipulated in the College statutes. This is the repertory represented on this disc, together with a Magnificat and three songs with texts that can be loosely described as Marian. It is magnificent music: the sheer scale of the two Marian motets and the monumental approach of their composers Kellyk and Browne, is quite staggering. It is not difficult to imagine these works being sung on a major Marian feast with the chapel singers before the lectern in a supreme act of Marian piety. The Sixteen, of course, are now well sung in this repertory and they perform it wonderfully, with an instinctive feel for the contrasts of sonority that so often define its structure.

Late Renaissance   16th–17th centuries

TUDOR CHURCH MUSIC. Worcester Cathedral Choir/Donald Hunt with **Raymond Johnston** (org). Abbey Alpha CDCA943. Texts included.
Weelkes. Hosanna to the Son of David. Gloria in exelsis Deo. When David heard. **Byrd.** Teach me, O Lord. Cantate Domino. Ave verum corpus. Sing joyfully unto God our strength. **Tomkins.** When David heard. Almighty God, the fountain of all wisdom. **Tallis.** Salvator mundi, salva nos I. If ye love me. Hear the voice and prayer. **Gibbons.** O Lord, in thy wrath rebuke me not. This is the record of John. Hosanna to the Son of David.

5Im DDD 5/93

Its church music was one of the glories of Tudor England, and the standard as represented by relatively minor composers was as high as the output was generous. But here we have the masters, "the big five", all heard in some of their finest and most famous works, so that the recital presents a small but useful anthology, ideal for adding to collections which otherwise have nothing of this sort in them. The Choir of Worcester Cathedral have many recordings to their credit but probably none better than this. They are a fine example of the Cathedral tradition in England; and one does not have to have just finished reading Joanna Trollope's *The Choir* to feel strongly convinced of the need for its preservation. The first sound of Weelkes's *Hosanna to the Son of David* itself tells of a rich culture, especially when the luxury of a choice in settings arrives later with the version by Orlando Gibbons. There are also two settings of the lament *When David heard*, both of them superbly 'built' by the singers as well as the two composers, Weelkes and Tomkins. Some of the anthems have organ accompaniment and soloist; most are sung *a cappella*, in recorded sound that does not (as is frequently the case) place the choir in too distant a perspective.

AWAKE, SWEET LOVE. [a]**James Bowman** (alto); [b]**David Miller** (lte); [c]**King's Consort of Viols** ([d]Wendy Gillespie, Richard Boothby, William Hunt, [e]Mark Caudle). Hyperion CDA66447. Notes and texts included.
Dowland: Can she excuse my wrongs[abc]. Flow my teares[abe]. A fancy, P5[b]. Sorrow stay[abe]. Queene Elizabeth, her Galliard[b]. Goe nightly cares[abde]. Now, O now I needs must part[ab]. Preludium[b]. A Fantasie, P1[b]. Say love if ever thou didst finde[ab]. Frogg Galliard[b]. Awake sweet love, thou art returned[ab]. Tell me, true Love[abc]. *Campion:* Author of light[abe]. Oft have I sigh'd[abe]. *Ford:* Since first I saw your face[ab]. *Johnson:* Eliza is the fairest queen[ac]. *Ferrabosco:* Pavin[b]. *Danyel:* Eyes, look no more[abe]. Thou pretty bird how do I see[abe]. I doe whenas I do not see[ab]. *Hunnis:* In terrors trapp'd[ac]. *Anonymous:* Come, tread the paths[ac].

﹒﹒﹒ 1h 12m DDD 10/91	♩ P ❓ 🖋

Domestic music-making flourished in the times of Good Queen Bess, when many households boasted the odd lute, maybe a chest of viols, and citizens whose singing voices could be heard (not only at bathtime); many were those who rewarded the publishers of music for their use and delight. This situation is mirrored in the programme of songs (with lute or consort) and lute solos, by James Bowman and the King's Consort. The music of Dowland lies naturally at the heart of the matter and here it frames that of some of his distinguished contemporaries. The inclusion of the viol part specified in some of the lute songs restores a dimension of beauty that is often sacrificed in present-day performances. In keeping with the album title, many of the songs deal with aspects of love — even the lute-solo *Frogg Galliard* pokes fun at the unrequited love of Mounsier le Duc d'Alençon for the Queen herself. James Bowman brings more than two decades of experience and devotion to bear in these memorable performances, and he is most sympathetically supported by the King's Consort, amongst whom David Miller should be singled out for special mention for his clear and intelligent playing of the lute solos. Happy the family that spent its leisure hours with this music, and happy the owner of this disc.

New review
A PLAY OF PASSION SONGS AND DANCES FOR THE ELIZABETHAN STAGE. [a]**Jeremy Budd** (treb); [b]**Michael Chance** (alto); **Fretwork** (Wendy Gillespie, Richard Campbell, Julia Hodgson, Sarah Groser, William Hunt, Richard Boothby, viols). Virgin Classics Veritas VC5 45007-2. Texts included. Recorded in 1990.
Anonymous: In Paradise[b]. The dark is my delight[a]. What meat eats the Spaniard?[ab]. Come, tread the paths[b]. Ah, silly poor Joas[b]. Allemande and Galliard. *A. Holborne:* Infernum and Galliard. Three Pavans and Galliards. *Albarti:* Pavan and Galliard. *Farrant:* Ah, alas, you salt-sea gods[a]. *A. Ferrabosco II:* Almayne a 5. Pavan and Alman a 5. *E. Johnson:* Eliza is the fayrest quene[a]. Come again[ab]. *Cobbold:* Ye mortal wights[a]. *Byrd:* Fair Britain Isle[b]. *Gibbons:* The silver swan[a]. Pavan and Galliard a 6. What is our life?[ab].

﹒﹒﹒ 1h 12m DDD 7/94	

The introverted side of the Elizabethan psyche prevails in this recording but melancholy is attractively offset by an assorted selection of instrumental numbers and lighter-veined songs. No less than a quarter of the works are by anonymous composers, the most alluring example *In Paradise* (closely followed by *Ah, silly poor Joas*) in which Michael Chance intones the sensuous text with extraordinary nobility above Fretwork's resonant support. Chance's co-partner is Jeremy Budd who is strong and unperturbable. His contributions are always notable for the sense he brings to the texts and some intuitive colouring of vowels. Fretwork perform with their usual delicacy of nuance, evenness of tone and textural transparency. Indeed, no one can doubt their pre-eminence as one of Britain's leading chamber ensembles. The final Holborne Pavan, and the exquisite Ferrabosco too, are eloquently shaped. The closing item, *What is our life?*, leaves us reflecting on one of the most delectable fruits of the consort song repertory.

New review

THREE PARTS UPON A GROUND. John Holloway, Stanley Ritchie, Andrew Manze (vns); **Nigel North** (theorbo); **Mary Springfels** (va da gamba); **John Toll** (hpd/org). Harmonia Mundi HMU90 7091. Recorded in 1993.
Purcell: Fantasia upon a Ground, Z731. **Buonamente:** Sonata a tre violini. **G. Gabrieli:** Canzone et Sonate — Sonata per tre violini. **Marini:** Sonata in Ecco con tre violini. Sonatae, Op. 22 — Sonata terza a tre. **Uccellini:** Sinfonici, Op. 9 — Sinfonia nona a tre violini. **Fontana:** Sonate a 1, 2, 3 — Sonata seidici. **Constantin:** Pavan. **Schmelzer:** Sonata a tre. **Hacquart:** Harmonia parnassia — Sonata decima. **Rosier:** Suite for Three Violins. **Pachelbel:** Canon and Gigue in D major.

Ih 5m   DDD   1/94

While everyone will know the Purcell and Pachelbel grounds that frame the programme, the rest will be revelatory. The early Italian sonatas for three violins are, like their vocal counterparts, rhetorical and virtuosic. There are solo passages, imitative passages, dialogues between one violin and the others (especially in the Gabrieli sonata), thrusting scales and delicate asides (in the Uccellini sinfonia), and harmonically directed passages of resonant homophony. The rapport between the violinists is particularly evident in Marini's *Sonata in Ecco*, where not only is the spatial effect of the echoes brought off extremely effectively, but the slowing cascading echoes over an organ pedal enchant by their novelty. The performances are polished and interactive with Holloway, Ritchie and Manze approaching the music with a mixture of enthusiasm, stylishness and control. In sum: extremely entertaining.

New review

A GIFT OF NATURE. SEVENTEENTH-CENTURY ENGLISH CHAMBER MUSIC. Trio Sonnerie (Monica Huggett, vn; Sarah Cunningham, va da gamba; Gary Cooper, virg/org); **Stephen Stubbs** ([a]theorbo/[b]gtr); **Andrew Lawrence-King** ([c]hp/[d]org). Teldec Das Alte Werk 4509-90841-2.
Baltzar: A Prelude for the Violin by Senior Balshar, a Germaine. Divisions on "John Come Kiss me Now"[ac]. **Schop:** Lachrime pavaen[b]. **N. Matteis:** Ayres for the Violin, Book 4[bc] — Ground after the Scotch Humour; Passagio a solo; Allegro Prestissimo; Ground; Aria Amorosa; Ground in D, la sol re. **Brade:** Coral. **W. Lawes:** Fantasia-Suite No. 8 in D major. **C. Simpson:** Prelude. Divisions on a Ground. **Jenkins:** Fantasia in D minor. **Byrd:** John Come Kiss me Now, BK81. **Farinel:** Faronell's Ground[b]. **Anonymous:** A Division for a trible viol to play with a virginall[ad]. Paul's Steeple[ac].

Ih 10m   DDD   5/94

New review

HENRY PURCELL AND HIS TIME. Scaramouche (Andrew Manze, Caroline Balding, vns; Jaap ter Linden, bass viol; Ulrike Wild, hpd/org); [a]**Foskien Kooistra** (vn); [b]**Konrad Junghänel** (theorbo). Channel Classics CCS4792.
Locke: The Broken Consort — Suites Nos. 3[b] and 4. **W. Lawes:** Fantasia-Suite No. 7 in D minor. **Jenkins:** Fantasia in three parts. **C. Simpson:** Prelude. Divisions on a Ground[b]. **Baltzar:** Divisions on "John Come Kiss me Now"[b]. **Purcell:** Pavans — B flat major, Z750; G minor, Z752[a]. Fantasia upon a Ground, Z731[ab].

Ih DDD   5/94

The contents of these two discs of English seventeenth-century chamber music may look alike, but no one finding themselves in possession of both should consider their money wasted. It's not just that, a little surprisingly, no piece appears twice; rather, it's that the respective approaches to programming and interpretation are happily complementary, so you can take your pick as your mood carries you. In the Teldec release the emphasis is on fleeting 'divisions' or variation sets by relatively minor figures, mostly on catchy popular tunes and mostly for violin. They are despatched with effortless ease by Monica Huggett and happily enhanced by the gentle and spacious acoustic of The Maltings, Snape. There's a solo spot for each of Trio Sonnerie's other members, however, and a constantly changing array of guest continuo instruments (including, unusually for this repertoire, a harp). For Channel Classics, Scaramouche offer a more homogeneous selection of music and instrumental combinations. (The disc advertises itself, by the way, as offering the music of "Henry Purcell and His Time", a claim whose level of accuracy — Lawes, for one, died over a decade before Purcell was born — is eloquently symbolized by a portrait of an unmistakably Elizabethan lady on the front of the box!) Here the innocent charm of the Trio Sonnerie selection is largely replaced by the weightier, more sober pronouncements of Lawes, Locke and Purcell, but also by a bold interpretative vigour which makes it just as lively a listen in its own way. Jaap ter Linden's rendition of his Simpson piece is a little more poetic than Sarah Cunningham's is of hers, while Andrew Manze's version of *John Come Kiss me Now* has a Turkey-in-the-Straw ending that will make you chuckle.

New review

MUSIC FROM RENAISSANCE PORTUGAL. Cambridge Taverner Choir/Owen Rees.
Herald HAVPCD155. Texts and translations included. Recorded in 1992.
P. de Cristo: Magnificat. Ave Maria. Sanctissimi quinque mar tires. De profundis. Lachrimans sitivit anima mea. Ave Regina caelorum. **D. Lôbo:** Missa pro defunctis. **Anonymous:** Si pie Domine. **A. Fernandez:** Libera me Domine. Alma redemptoris mater. **Carreira:** Stabat mater.

lh 9m   DDD   1/94

This is one of those rare examples of scholarship and musicianship combining to result in performances that are both impressive and immediately attractive to the listener in excellent music, totally neglected till now. There is a wonderful glow about this recording that reflects the skilful engineering on the part of Herald as well as the imagination of the sonority on Rees's part. The striking feature of his approach is the emphasis on the meaning of the words. This choir sings of the Day of Judgement or the rejoicing due to the Virgin as if they really mean it: Rees is not afraid to shape phrases, to use dynamics, to vary the intensity of the sound in the service of the words which, though even more familiar to the monks and chapel singers who originally performed these pieces at the monastery of Santa Cruz in Colmbra, would have had an immediacy and a reality for them that it is hard to recapture today. How graphic those texts, in fact, are, and how well this choir brings them to life.

ITALIAN RECORDER MUSIC. Amsterdam Loeki Stardust Quartet (Daniel Brüggen, Bertho Driever, Paul Leenhouts, Karel van Steenhoven, recs). L'Oiseau-Lyre 430 246-2OH.
Battiferri: Ricercare secundo. **Cima:** Canzon la Capriccio. **Conforti:** Ricercar del quarto tono. **Frescobaldi:** Capriccio sopra la Spagnoletta. Canzon decima detta la Paulini. Ricercare terzo. Capriccio V sopra la Bassa Fiamenga. **Guami:** Canzons — La Bastina; La Brillantina; La Gentile. **Merula:** Canzons — La Ghirardella; La Merula. Dum Illuscescente Beati. Iste est Joannes. O Glorioso Domina. **Palestrina:** Lamentationes Hieremiae. **Trabaci:** Canto fermo primo del primo Tono. Canzona franzesa quinta sopra dunque credete ch'io. Canzona franzesa terza.

lh 2m   DDD   2/92

None of the music in this programme was written for recorders but this is not important: it dates from a time when the boundaries between instrumental and vocal music were far less clear than they later became, and in which the music was very often more important than the identity of the instruments on which it was played. What mattered most was that the interwoven lines should be heard clearly and in proper balance. Italy was the Alma Mater of such music and it was also the country in which the recorder resisted the onslaught of the transverse flute for the longest. Few sounds are more depressing than that of an ensemble of mediocre recorder players, but few are more suited to presenting music of the above kind with the clarity and (thanks to the recording engineers) precise balance, and without a variety of tone-colours to seduce the ear in the direction of one line or another, than a recorder consort of the impeccable quality of the Amsterdam Loeki Stardust Quartet. For those who delight in hearing contrapuntal lines, mellifluously and ingeniously spun, this disc is custom-made.

THE LUTE IN DANCE AND DREAM. Lutz Kirchhoff (lte). Sony Classical Vivarte SK48068.
Anonymous: Italiana. Galliarda. Passamezzo moderno. Sarabande. La Cardinalle. *Milano:* Fantasia di M. Francesco Milanese. *Mudarra:* Fantasia que contrahaze la harpa en la manera de Ludovico. *R. Godard:* Ce mois de May. *Reis:* Courante. *Hassler:* Canzon. *Mertel:* So wünsch ich ihr eine gute Nacht. *Dowland:* A dream, P75. The shoemaker's wife, A toy, P58. *Ballard:* Branles de village. *Mouton:* Menuet. Prelude. *Dubut:* Chaconne. *D. Gaultier:* Gigue. *Durante:* Carillon. *E. Gaultier:* Chaconne. *Falkenhagen:* Variations on "Wer nur den lieben Gott lässt walten". *Weiss:* Tombeau sur la mort de M. Comte de Logy. *Kapsperger:* Libro I d'intavolatura di lauto — Gagliarda 1a. Libro I d'intavolatura di chitarrone — Aria di Fiorenze; Corrente 2a.

Ih DDD II/92

This disc should be of particular interest to those who may excusably have formed the impression that the world of lute music is overly concerned with solemnity and academicism — and no less to those who have not. Kirchhoff, a strong and stylish player, has assembled a programme of European music for both the renaissance and baroque lutes — Mudarra's *Fantasia* was written for the vihuela, not the lute, but it suits the latter just as well and its uniqueness entitles it to an honorary 'boarding pass'. Dances were a staple of early instrumental music and there are plenty in this programme, albeit mostly of renaissance genres; Weiss's *Tombeau sur la mort de M. Comte de Logy* is in the form of an allemande. The programme lives up to the promise of its name: songs appear as intabulations or as the subject for variations. The 'dream' element is that of the composer's fancy, the 'abstract' fantasias and the like, and Dowland's miniature that lends its name to the album as a whole. The lute repertory represents a microcosmic overview of the music of its times, and this well chosen selection of it, played with sensitivity and vitality (and pristinely recorded), does it full justice.

VIHUELA MUSIC OF THE SPANISH RENAISSANCE. Christopher Wilson. Virgin Classics Veritas VC7 91136-2.
Milán: Libro de musica de vihuela de mano, "El Maestro", Book 1 — Fantasias I, VIII, XI and XII; Pavanas IV and VI. *Narváez:* Los seys libros del Delfin — Guardame las vacas (two versions); Milles regres; Fantasia; Baxa de contrapunto. *Mudarra:* Tres libros de música en cifra para vihuela — Romanesca: O guardame las vacas; Pavana de Alexandre; Gallarda; conde claros; Fantasia que contrahaze la harpa en la manera de Ludovico. *Valderrábano:* Silva de Sirenas — Fantasia; Soneto lombardo a manera de dança; Soneto. *Fuenllana:* Orphenica Lyra — Duo de Fuenllana; Tant que vivray; Fantasia de redobles; De Antequera sale el moro. *López:* Fantasia. *Pisador:* Libro de Musica de Vihuela — Dezilde al cavallero que; Madona mala vostra; Pavana muy llana para tañer. *Mendoza:* Diferencias de folías. *Daza:* El Parnasso — Quien te hizo Juan pastor; Fantasia. *Anonymous Sixteenth Century:* La morda.

59m DDD 4/91

This generously filled disc reflects virtually the entire vihuela repertory from Luis Milán (1536) to the much less familiar Esteban Daza (1572). The vihuela is a member of the viol family but whose strings, typically arranged in six or seven courses, each paired in unison, are plucked rather than bowed. Christopher Wilson, better known to us as a lutenist, has chosen his programme well though the quality of the music is, almost inevitably, uneven. The most impressive pieces belong to the earliest of the composers represented here — Milán, Mudarra and Narváez. Between them they produced music rich in fantasy and varied both in colour and form. Wilson brings their compositions to life imaginatively, rhythmically and with a fluent technique that should win many friends. The recording itself is admirable, capturing the wide range of colours of which both instrument and performer are capable.

A VENETIAN CORONATION, 1595. Gabrieli [a]Consort and Players/Paul McCreesh. Virgin Classics Veritas VC7 59006-2. Texts and translations included.
G. Gabrieli: Intonazioni — ottavo tono; terzo e quarto toni; quinto tono alla quarta bassa (James O'Donnell, org solo). Canzonas — XIII a 12; XVI a 15; IX a 10. Sonata VI a 8 pian e forte. Deus qui beatum Marcum a 10[a]. Omnes gentes a 16[a]. *A. Gabrieli:* Intonazioni — primo tono (O'Donnell); settimo tono (Timothy Roberts, org). Mass Movements[a] — Kyrie a 5-12; Gloria a 16; Sanctus a 12; Benedictus a 12. O sacrum convivium a 5[a]. Benedictus

Dominus Deus sabbaoth (arr. Roberts. O'Donnell, Roberts). **Bendinelli:** Sonata CCC-XXXIII. Sarasinetta. **M. Thomsen:** Toccata I.

`..•'  lh llm  DDD  5/90                                    9 p  ✎`

The coronation of a new Doge of Venice was always a special occasion, and never more than when Marino Grimani (1532-1605) was elected to that office. We do not know what music was played then, but the whole ceremony is notionally and credibly reconstructed in this recording by Paul McCreesh and his cohorts. The recording was made in Brinkburn Priory, a church whose acoustic (aided by some deft manipulation of the recording controls) is spacious enough to evoke that of the Basilica of St Mark, the site of the original event. Space *per se* is vital to the music of the Gabrielis, who excelled in using it by placing instrumental and vocal groups in different parts of the building — which thereby became an integral part of the music. A fine selection of music that *could* have been played then is enhanced by the opening tolling of a bell, a crescendo marking the leisurely approach of the ducal procession, and the impression of architectural space created by changing stereo focus. It would be difficult to speak too highly of the performances, supplemented by first-class annotation, in this memorable recording. A trip to Venice would cost a lot more than this disc but, though you could visit the real St Mark's, it would not buy you this superb musical experience.

New review

SACRED MUSIC FROM VENICE AND ROME. The Sixteen/Harry Christophers with [a]**Laurence Cummings** (org). Collins Classics 1360-2. Texts and translations included. Recorded in 1992.
Caldara: Crucifixus. **A. Gabrieli:** De profundis clamavi. **Frescobaldi:** Fiori musicali, Op. 12 — Toccata cromatica per l'Elevatione; Toccata per l'Elevationea. **Cavalli:** Salve Regina. **Monteverdi:** Domine, ne in furore. **G. Gabrieli:** Hodie completi sunt. **Lassus:** Tui sunt coeli. Missa Bell'Amfitrit altera.

`..•'  57m  DDD  l0/93                                      9 p`

Clearly the starting-point was the colour and richness of the Venetian tradition from the Gabrieli to Caldara, and it is certainly good to have available works such as Andrea's *De profundis* and Giovanni's *Hodie completi sunt*, comparatively little-known motets that are not otherwise currently available in the catalogue. But the Lassus Mass, which takes up more than a third of the record, fits rather awkwardly into this scheme despite its eight-voice texture and characteristic manipula-tion of sonority and texture. However, it is the performances themselves that matter, and here The Sixteen produce a sequence of finely-turned and thoughtful interpretations. Their approach is uniformly sturdy and muscular, with plenty of controlled power in the lower voices and an attractively clear brightness in the upper ones. Harry Christophers, guided by an unerring sense of mobility and contrast, encourages his singers in readings which never fail to extract every last nuance of the text. The dialogue exchanges in Cavalli's well-known *Salve Regina* are beautifully executed, and the vivid sense of drama in that performance is carried through to particularly good effect in the Monteverdi which follows it. This is one of the best records of these repertories to appear for some time.

VENETIAN VESPERS. Gabrieli Consort and Players/Paul McCreesh with [a]**Timothy Roberts** (org). Archiv Produktion 437 552-2AH2. Texts and translations included.
Sacristy bell. **Gabrieli** (ed. Roberts): Intonazione[a]. *Versicle and response:* Deus in adiutorium; Domine ad adiuvandum. **Rigatti:** Dixit Dominus. **Grandi:** O intemerata. *Antiphon:*Beata es Maria. **Monteverdi:** Laudate pueri. **Banchieri:** Sùonata prima[a]. *Antiphon:* Beatam me dicent. **Monteverdi:** Laetatus sum. **Finetti:** O Maria, quae rapis corda hominum. *Antiphon:* Haec est quae nescavit. **Rigatti:** Nisi Dominus. **Banchieri:** Dialogo secondo[a]. *Antiphon:* Ante thronum. **Cavalli:** Lauda Jerusalem. **Grandi:** O quam tu pulchra es. **Anonymous:** Praeambulum[a]. *Chapter:* Ecce virgo. **Monteverdi:** Deus qui mundum crimine iacentem. *Versicle and response.* Ave maria; Dominus tecum. *Antiphon.* Spiritus Sanctus. **Rigatti:** Magnificat. **Marini:** Sonata con tre violini in eco. *Collect:* Dominus vobiscum — Deus, qui de beatae Mariae. *Dismissal:* Dominus vobiscum — Benedicamus Domino. **Monteverdi:** Laudate Dominum. **Fasolo** (ed. Roberts): Intonazione — excerpts[a]. **Rigatti:** Salve regina.

`..•'  ②  lh 36m  DDD  4/93                                 9 p  ✎`

Paul McCreesh's sense of adventure made quite an impact with his reconstruction of Doge Grimani's Coronation in 1595. This follow-up takes as its starting point a Vespers service "as it might have been celebrated in St Mark's, Venice 1643", and it is no less striking a speculation. McCreesh is wisely not attempting to re-create a historical event but to provide a rejuvenating context for some more wonderful Venetian church music. There can be little doubt that listening to psalm settings within a liturgical framework illuminates the theatricality and significance of the works in a unique way, barely possible in an ordinary format where one work simply follows another. Yet the quality of the music is what really counts and this is where McCreesh deserves the greatest praise. He has skilfully blended a range of diverse concerted works with equally innovative and expressive solo motets, each one offset by ornate organ interludes and home-spun plainchant. Monteverdi is well represented, as one would expect, but by introducing resident composers (who were regularly employed by the great basilica) a strong Venetian sensibility prevails in all these works despite the many contrasting styles of the new baroque age. The little-known Rigatti is arguably the sensation of this release with his highly dramatic and richly extravagant sonorities. The settings of *Dixit Dominus* and *Magnificat* are almost operatic at times though they maintain the spatial elements inspired by St Mark's. The Gabrieli Consort and Players are a group with an extraordinary homogeneity of sound and focused energy: Monteverdi's *Laetatus sum* is one of the many examples where they reach new heights in early seventeenth-century performance. The solo performances are deliciously executed too, particularly those involving the falsettists. The purity and control in Finetti's *O Maria, quae rapis* knows no bounds. This CD is an achievement of the very highest possible order.

LAMENTO D'ARIANNA. VARIOUS SETTINGS. **The Consort of Musicke/Anthony Rooley.** Deutsche Harmonia Mundi Editio Classica GD77115. Texts and translations included. From 1C 165 169504-3 (2/85).
Monteverdi: Lamento d'Arianna a voce sola. Lamento d'Arianna a 5. Pianto della Madonna voce sola. *Bonini:* Lamento d'Arianna in stile recitavo. *Pari:* Il lamento d'Arianna. *Costa:* Pianto d'Arianna a voce sola. *Il Verso:* Lasciatemi morire a 5. *Roscarini:* Reciproco amore a 3.

② 1h 48m ADD 12/90

This is an historic recording and it recalls a moment of particular significance in the history of music. Monteverdi's *Arianna* first saw the light of day in Mantua in 1608. None of it survives except for Arianna's great dramatic lament after she has been abandoned by Teseo. The lament, which had apparently moved the Mantuan audience to tears, was central to the whole opera and it became extremely popular in its own right. Other composers imitated it and a new style of dramatic composition for solo voice was born as a result. In 1984 Anthony Rooley had the splendid idea of searching out some of these other seventeenth-century compositions and bringing them all together in a single programme. The two resulting LPs are now reissued as CDs and we can enjoy, first and foremost, Monteverdi's own original version, ably sung with profound understanding by Emma Kirkby, with accompaniment for chitarrone; and also the composer's well-known five-part madrigal using the same material (1614), as well as his much later (1640) reworking of this music, transformed into a somewhat sentimental meditation, for solo voice and organ, a religious lament placed in the mouth of the Madonna at the foot of the Cross. The five lesser-known compositions have each something new to offer: Bonini's dramatic setting may well come closest to the action of the original opera; Pari's contribution is a series of 12 madrigals analysing the successive emotions of the heroine. Costa's solo lament (Emma Kirkby again) is totally restrained and dignified. Antonio il Verso's madrigalian version, for all its extravagance, is clearly derived from Monteverdi's model. Roscarini, the latest of the six (1695), pushes extravagance to its limits. All of this is delightfully performed. This is a recording that throws much fascinating light on the way music changed course during the seventeenth century, but it is no less enjoyable for fulfilling such a useful purpose.

Choral and Song

ARIE ANTICHE. Cecilia Bartoli (mez); **György Fischer** (pf). Decca 436 267-2DH. Texts and translations included.
A. Scarlatti: Già il sole dal Gange. Son tutta duolo. Se Florindo è fedele. O cessate di piagarmi. Spesso vibra per suo gioco. *Giordani:* Caro mio ben. *Lotti:* Pur dicesti, o bocca

bella. **Cesti:** Intorno all'idol mio. **Paisiello:** Nel cor più non mi sento. Il mio ben quando
verrà. Chi vuol la zingarella. **Anonymous:** O leggiadri occhi belli. **Marcello:** Quella fiamma
che m'accende. **Caldara:** Selve amiche. Sebben, crudele. **Caccini:** Tu ch'hai le penne, amore.
Amarilli. **Parisotti:** Se tu m'ami. **Cavalli:** Delizie contente. **Vivaldi:** Sposa son disprezzata.
Carissimi: Vittoria, vittoria!

1h 6m DDD 12/92

With Scarlatti and Vivaldi among the composers, these *arie antiche* are not necessarily very old.
Italian singers have long been accustomed to lumping together all songs earlier than Mozart (or
perhaps Haydn) under this heading, piously including them at the start of a recital so as to
establish a classical tone and give them time to try out their voices before entering on the more
strenuous and popular part of their programme. Bartoli here devotes a whole disc to them, as
things delightful in themselves, varied in mood and style, and calling in turn on almost all the
essential arts of a good singer. No one can come away with a feeling of having been short-
changed at the end of this. Her voice is ideal, both silken and chaste, finely controlled, cleanly
produced. With a simple, direct song such as the famous *Caro mio ben* she will never fuss or
show off; with Vivaldi's *Sposa son disprezzata* she exploits the most deliciously languishing tone
and sometimes one more frankly passionate and 'operatic'. Most of the items are gems, and to
all of them György Fischer brings the touch of the expert jeweller, knowing exactly how best to
set off the beauties of voice and melody.

New review
THE ART OF ARLEEN AUGER. Arleen Auger (sop); [a]members of the **Saint Paul
Chamber Orchestra** and the **Minnesota Orchestra/Joel Revzen** ([bc]pf). Koch International
Classics 37248-2. Items marked [a] recorded 1986-91. Texts and translations included.
Larsen: Six Sonnets from the Portuguese[a]. **Purcell** (ed. Britten): If music be the food of
love, Z379 No. 3. The Libertine — Nymphs and shepherds[b]. Pausanias — Sweeter than roses.
Schumann: Myrthen, Op. 25 — No. 1, Widmung; No. 3, Der Nussbaum; No. 11, Lied der
Braut I; No. 12, Lied der Braut II. Romanzen und Balladen, Op. 64 — No. 1, Die
Soldatenbraut. **Mozart:** Das Veilchen, K476. Dans un bois solitaire, K308/K295b. Das Lied
der Trennung, K519. Als Luise die Briefe, K520[c]. Abendempfindung, K523.

55m DDD 4/94

Here is a record to cherish, and with it, of course, a memory. The late Arleen Auger was loved
for her voice, her art and herself. All items here are taken from live performances, and the
recorded balance favours the accompaniment, but a great and very special beauty remains. Libby
Larsens's settings of six of Elizabeth Barrett-Browning's sonnets were written for the singer, and
they suit her to perfection. The idiom is lyrical, the writing for voice full of understanding about
what should and should not be asked of a singer. Auger sings unerringly, with great beauty of
tone and feeling for words. This, the Purcell songs, and the Mozart (Schumann on the whole
suits her less well) are a lovely memorial: the fine legato (in Mozart), the even runs (in Purcell)
and the gentle beauty of tone throughout. At the end of the programme comes Mozart's
Abendempfindung with its quiet presentiment of death and its modest wish for remembrance, a
wish that the record aptly helps to fulfil.

CABARET CLASSICS. Jill Gomez (sop); **John Constable** (pf). Unicorn-Kanchana
DKPCD9055. Texts and translations included.
Weill: Marie Galante — Les filles de Bordeaux; Le grand Lustucru; Le Roi d'Aquitaine;
J'attends un navire. Lady in the Dark — My ship. Street Scene — Lonely house. Knicker-
bocker Holiday — It never was you. **Zemlinsky:** Songs, Op. 27 — Harlem Tänzerin; Elend;
Afrikanischer Tanz. **Schoenberg:** Arie aus dem Spiegel von Arcadien. Gigerlette. Der
genügsame Liebhaber. Mahnung. **Satie:** La diva de l'Empire. Allons-y, Chochotte. Je te veux.

57m DDD 6/88

Schoenberg writing cabaret songs with a popular touch? Yes, and quite catchy ones too, as can
be heard particularly in *Gigerlette* — prompting the intriguing speculation of what might have
been had he not concentrated on *Gurrelieder*. On the other hand, his *Der genügsame Liebhaber* and
Zemlinsky's three songs would have been most unlikely to go down with cabaret audiences,
however intellectual. At the other end of the spectrum are Satie's café-concert songs (the

sentimental waltz *Je te veux* is languidly attractive) and the Weill items, which were not written for cabaret but are drawn from a 1934 Paris play and post-war Broadway musicals. That all these songs do not require a gin-sodden voice or raucous delivery is demonstrated with the utmost artistry by Jill Gomez, in turn seductive, pathetic, sly, sweet, swaggering, passionate, salacious — or simply singing beautifully. Her performance of Weill's *Lonely house* (one of his best) remains hauntingly in the mind.

CANTICLES FROM ELY. Ely Cathedral Choir/Paul Trepte with **Jeremy Filsell** (org). Gamut Classics GAMCD527.
Bairstow: The Lamentation. **F. Jackson:** Benedicite in G major. **Noble:** Magnificat in A minor. **Stanford:** Morning Services — A major, Op. 12; C major, Op. 115. Evening Service in B flat major.

52m DDD 2/92

For Matins the *Te Deum*, with *Benedicite* or *Jubilate* for a somewhat rare change, for Evensong *Magnificat* and *Nunc Dimittis*: these were the canticles sung or recited at Church of England services throughout the centuries, and in most cathedrals they are so still. Setting them to music has also been a preoccupation of British composers through the ages. In late Victorian times and the early part of the twentieth century it was almost a national industry, with Sir Charles Villiers Stanford as its High Master. He wrote ten services altogether, the one in B flat being the most popular, that in C probably the most admired among musicians. A notable feature in their time was the independence of the organ parts, but to modern listeners it is the richness of sound, the unfailing tunefulness and the sure professionalism of craftsmanship that are likely to be most striking. The Morning Service in A, written in 1880, is also remarkable for boldness of invention with some fine modulations and a particularly inspired breadth at the end of the *Jubilate*. In between the three Stanford services heard here come others by three organists of York Minster: Tertius Noble (represented by a less well-known and on the whole less successful setting than his B minor service), Sir Edward Bairstow, and Francis Jackson (a colourful, and in this company distinctly modern, setting of the *Benedicite*). The *Lamentations* of Jeremiah are designed for alternative use in Lent but, while Bairstow's music is resourceful, it is probably not sufficiently so to justify the length of the piece on musical grounds alone. The Choir of Ely Cathedral sing with fine tone and precision, the organ accompaniments are distinguished by imaginative registration and a strong rhythmic sense, and the disc is well produced.

THE CHRISTMAS ALBUM. FESTIVE MUSIC FROM EUROPE AND AMERICA. **Taverner Consort, Choir and Players/Andrew Parrott.** EMI Reflexe CD46672. Texts and translations included.
Billings: Methinks I see an heaven'ly host. A virgin unspotted. **J. Foster:** While shepherds watched their flocks. **Cererols:** Serafin, que con dulce harmonia. **Vidales:** Los que fueren de buen gusto. **M. Praetorius:** Magnificat super "Angeles ad pastores". **Charpentier:** In nativitatem Domini Nostri Jesu Christi canticum, H414. **Pascha:** Christmas Mass — Gloria. Arr. **Greatorex:** Adestes, fideles.

1h 3m DDD 12/92

Here is a Christmas record for all the year round. It also takes a good round trip to countries far and near, beginning and ending in New England, where William Billings, a one-legged, one-eyed tanner and "arguably the first American composer with a truly individual voice", provides carols of spirited simplicity and uninhibited gusto. Also from the New World comes a religious pop-song, a *jàcara*, from 1702 performed originally by the nuns of the convent at Pueblo, a charming poem set to a catchy tune with syncopations and knocks on the guitar. Europe, after that, seems a little tame. Lower Saxony offers a *Magnificat* on the carol *Angelus ad pastores* by Praetorius, based on a motet by Lassus, France a courtly musical shepherds-play by Charpentier, and Slovakia a kind of miniature Christmas oratorio, with shepherd-pipes and alphorn. The English contribution comprises early versions of *While shepherds watched their flocks* in Haydnesque scoring by John Foster of Sheffield, and *Adeste, fideles* as it was heard in London in the spring of 1797. Most delightful, perhaps, is the piece from Catalonia, gracefully sung by Emily Van Ethera and Timothy Wilson. Andrew Parrott's singers and players give pleasure throughout, and the disc owes much to the work of Clifford Bartlett as musical editor and writer of the informative notes.

ENGLISH CHURCH MUSIC, Volume 1. **Queen's College Choir, Oxford/Matthew Owens** with [a]**David Went** (org). ASV CDDCA851. Texts included.
Howells: Chichester Service[a]. A Hymn for St Cecilia[a]. Salve regina. O salutaris hostia. My eyes for beauty pine[a]. Like as the hart[a]. *Leighton.* Second Service, Op. 62[a]. Give me wings of faith[a]. O sacrum convivium. Solus ad victimam[a]. Crucifixus pro nobis, Op. 38[a].

Ih 14m DDD 5/93

Herbert Howells was at Queen's College, Oxford, in 1916, and Kenneth Leighton read Classics there in 1947, so it is appropriate that they should be brought together by their college choir. A quality they had in common was their sure instinct for choral sound, and at the take-over point in this recital (the opening of Leighton's *Second Evening Service*) the succession is felt to be a very close and natural one. Both are well represented. A lot of Howells's choral work has been recorded recently, but the selection here overlaps very little with other desirable records: *Like as the hart* is the principal exception, and as this is a particularly lovely performance the duplication is easily justified. The Chichester Service has its first recording: a fine work, rising in characteristic ecstasy. Leighton's Service is also impressive, the *Magnificat*'s "Gloria" swaying slowly, while that of the *Nunc Dimittis* ends in subdued fashion, beautiful in its quietness. The other major work, the *Crucifixus pro nobis*, is probably better served by a tenor soloist, but this is a fine, urgent performance with excellent work by the choir, as indeed there is throughout the recital.

FAREWELL TO SALZBURG. Christa Ludwig (mez); **Charles Spencer** (pf). RCA Victor Red Seal 09026 61547-2. Texts and translations included. Recorded in 1993.
Brahms: Lieder, Op. 19 — No. 4, Der Schmied; No. 5, An eine Aolsharfe. Dein blaues Auge, Op. 59 No. 8. Vergebliches Ständchen, Op. 84 No. 4. Mädchenlied, Op. 95 No. 6. Immer leiser wird mein, Schlummer, Op. 105 No. 2. Ständchen, Op. 106 No. 1. *Mahler:* Lieder aus "Des Knaben Wunderhorn" — Das irdische Leben; Rheinlegendchen. Rückert-Lieder — Ich bin der Welt abhanden gekommen; Um Mitternacht. *Schumann:* Stille Tränen, Op. 35 No. 10. Myrthen, Op. 25 — No. 3, Der Nussbaum; No. 15, Aus dem hebräischen Gesängen. Marzveilchen, Op. 40 No. 1. Der Himmel hat ein Träne geweint, Op. 37 No. 1. Liederkreis, Op. 39 — No. 4, Die Stille; No. 5, Mondnacht. *R. Strauss:* Gefunden, Op. 56 No. 1. Begegnung, Av72. Du meines Herzens Krönelein, Op. 21 No. 2. Die Nacht, Op. 10 No. 3. Lieder, Op. 27 — No. 1, Ruhe, meine Seele; No. 4, Morgen.

Ih 9m DDD 10/93

The inevitable loss of some of the voice's characteristic bloom and mobility, and the passing moments of instability at the bottom of the register do nothing to compromise the projection of character and spirit in everything Christa Ludwig sings here. Two songs from Mahler's *Des Knaben Wunderhorn* settings reveal that fusion of winsome, folk-art simplicity with the sense of a darker vision beyond which she, like Mahler, excels at conveying. Ludwig's voice warms to the tender containment of Richard Strauss's writing in songs like the little Goethe setting *Gefunden*, and finds a particular solemnity of concentration for *Ruhe, meine Seele* and a daringly slow *Morgen*. Schumann and Brahms celebrate the intimate confidence of Ludwig as Lieder singer, *Der Nussbaum* and *Die Stille* seem dream-like extensions of speech, even thought. By contrast, Byron's Hebrew melody and Brahms's Blacksmith light a bright flare, still burning effortlessly at the top of the voice. Most telling, though, are the more harmonically and methodically elusive songs: the secrets of sleep and of the Aeolian harp are now what Ludwig understands best and re-creates most affectingly.

THE FIRST PLACIDO DOMINGO INTERNATIONAL VOICE COMPETITION. [a]**Ainhoa Arteta,** [b]**Inva Mula-Tchako,** [c]**Nina Stemme** (sops); [d]**Plácido Domingo** (ten); [e]**Kwangh-chul Youn** (bass); **Paris Opéra-Bastille Orchestra/Eugene Kohn.** Sony Classical SK46691. Recorded live in 1993.
Bellini: I PURITANI — Qui la voce[b]. *Catalani:* LA WALLY — Ebben? Me andrò lontana[c]. *Donizetti:* L'ELISIR D'AMORE — Caro elisir! ... Chi e mai ... Esulti pur la barbara ... Tran, tran, tran, tran[bd]. *Gounod:* FAUST — Mais ce Dieu ... A moi les plaisirs; O merveille![de]. *Massenet:* MANON — Je marche sur tous les chemins[a]. *Meyerbeer:* L'AFRICAINE — Pays merveilleux ... O paradis[d]. *Mozart:* DON GIOVANNI — Là ci darem la mano[be]. LE NOZZE DI FIGARO — Sull'aria ... Ricevete o padroncina[ac]. *Penella:* EL GATO MONTES — Me

llamabas, Rafaeliyo?[ad]. **Puccini:** LA BOHEME — O soave fanciulla[ad]. **Sorozabal:** LA TABERNERA DEL PUERTO — No puede ser[ad]. **Verdi:** LA FORZA DEL DESTINO — Io muoio! Confessione! ... Non imprecare, umiliata[cde]. OTELLO — Già nella notte densa ... Venga la morte! [cd]. LA TRAVIATA — Libiamo, ne'lieti calci[abcde].

∴ **1h 10m DDD 6/94**   **⑨**ₚ

The great tenor acts as a kind of a father-figure to the four winners of the first competition held in his name, inviting them to sing alone and in duet with him while he throws in a couple of solos. In the presence of the young he himself is, Faust-like, rejuvenated, singing with an amazing freedom in a kind of conspectus of his own repertory, opening the night with a wonderfully open-throated reading of "O paradis" and later giving an ebullient, golden account of Leandro's Romance from *La Tabernera del puerto*, the first of four encores that he graciously announces in charmingly fractured French. All the singers are worthy winners. The three sopranos are, in differing ways, highly promising. The Swedish Nina Stemme, who ought to have won the Cardiff Singer of the World contest, is the most affecting among them with a warm, appealing voice of sensuous overtones, ideal for La Wally's eloquent solo to which she brings appropriate vibrancy. Then she proves a thoroughly worthy Desdemona, phrasing with Verdian breadth, for Domingo's sovereign Otello, here caught on even more heroic form than on his complete sets. The Albanian soprano Inva Mula-Tchako sounds like the young Freni, floating line and tone tenderly in "Qui la voce", then joining Domingo in an engaging, astutely characterized account of the duet from *Elisir*. Ainhoa Arteta is a more French-like soprano, with a lighter, shallower tone, a slightly acid Manon, more at home in the duets from *El gato montés* and *Bohème* with Domingo, where her Spanish temperament is very much to the fore. The Korean Kwanghchul Youn comes into his own as a suave Giovanni to Mula-Tchako's Zerlina. The well-filled disc is faithfully recorded: once again in a live performance a natural rather than a manufactured acoustic is caught with the Bastille orchestra present but not too prominent.

New review

GLYNDEBOURNE RECORDED. Glyndebourne Festival [a]Chorus and [b]Orchestra, [c]Royal Philharmonic Orchestra, [d]London Philharmonic Orchestra, [e]orchestra/[f]Fritz Busch, [e]Michael Mudie, [g]Vittorio Gui, [h]Sir John Pritchard, [i]Bernard Haitink, [j]Simon Rattle. EMI mono/stereo CDH5 65072-2.
Mozart: LE NOZZE DI FIGARO — Cinque, dieci[di] (Gianna Rolandi, sop; Claudio Desderi, bar. From CDS7 49753-2, 7/88); Riconosci in quest'amplesso[bg] (Graziella Sciutti, sop; Monica Sinclair, contr; Daniel McCoshan, ten; Sesto Bruscantini, bar; Franco Calabrese, Ian Wallace, basses. HMV ALP1312/5, 1/56); Sull'aria; Ricevete o padroncina[abf] (Audrey Mildmay, Aulikki Rautawaara, sops. Both from HMV DB2591, 1/36). COSI FAN TUTTE — Una bella serenata[bf] (Heddle Nash, ten; Willi Domgraf-Fassbaender, John Brownlee, bars. DB2654, 5/36); Soave sia il vento[di] (Carol Vaness, sop; Delores Ziegler, mez; Desderi. CDS7 47727-8, 7/87); Il core vi dono[bf] (Blanche Thebom, mez; Erich Kunz, bar. DB21119, 12/50). DON GIOVANNI — Là ci darem la mano[di] (Elizabeth Gale, sop; Thomas Allen, bar. HMV SLS143655-3, 7/84); Ah, dove il perfido?[bf] (Ina Souez, Luise Helletsgruber, Mildmay, sops; Koloman von Pataky, ten; Roy Henderson, bar; Salvatore Baccaloni, bass. DB2983, 7/37). IDOMENEO — Vedrommi intorno[bf] (Richard Lewis, ten. World Records SH294, 11/79. Recorded 1951); Spiegarti non poss'io[bh] (Sena Jurinac, sop; Léopold Simoneau, ten. ALP1515/7, 10/57). DIE ENTFUHRUNG AUS DEM SERAIL — Ach, ich liebte[dh] (Dame Margaret Price, sop. CfP CFP40032, 12/72).
Gay: THE BEGGAR'S OPERA[e] — O Polly, you might have toy'd and kissed; My heart was so free; When I laid on Greenland's coast (Mildmay; Constance Willis, mez; Michael Redgrave, Henderson, bars. HMV C3159/60, 6/40). **Rossini:** LA CENERENTOLA — Signor, una parola[bg] (Marina de Gabarain, mez; Bruscantini; Wallace. ALP1147/9, 7/54). LE COMTE ORY — O bon ermite[abg] (Sari Barabas, sop; Cora Canne-Meijer, mez; Juan Oncina, ten. ALP1473/4, 7/57). IL BARBIERE DI SIVIGLIA — Ah! qual colpo[cg] (Victoria de los Angeles, sop; Luigi Alva, ten; Bruscantini. HMV SAN114/6, 10/63). **Monteverdi:** L'INCORONAZIONE DI POPPEA — Pur ti miro[ch] (Magda László, sop; Lewis. SAN126/7, 6/64). **Gershwin:** PORGY AND BESS — Bess, you is my woman now[dj] (Cynthia Haymon, sop; Willard White, bass. CDS7 49568-2, 6/89).

∴ **1h 16m ADD/DDD 6/94**   **⑨**ₚ ▲

We begin at the beginning with reminders of the delicate beauty of Mildmay and Rautawaara in
the *Ur-Figaro* of 1934 (the first-ever 'complete' recording of a Mozart opera in any form)

followed by the elegance and dash of Nash, Domgraf-Fassbaender and Brownlee in the classic 1935 *Così fan tutte*, both coming up in pristine transfers. The Epilogue to *Giovanni* shows off the best of the 1936 cast, most notably Souez, von Pataky and Helletsgruber, perhaps unsurpassed as Anna, Ottavio and Elvira heard in the house. "Il core vi dono" is a glowing performance from the 1950 *Così* extracts, in which Kunz's warm Guglielmo is memorable. All these examples demonstrate Busch's distinction as a supreme Mozartian, just as four of the next five extracts reveal Gui's strengths in Rossini and Mozart, too, recalling the house's second golden age with Gui in charge. Whatever may be thought of Leppard's over-lush Monteverdi, it's hard to resist László's Poppea and Lewis's Nero celebrating illicit love at the close of Monteverdi's opera. Price's "Ach, ich liebte" from highlights of *Entführung* in 1972 is a souvenir of her pure, technically irreproachable Mozart singing and of a happy revival. The examples from Haitink's Da Ponte sets remind us of how he continued that essential tradition of Glyndebourne, faultless ensemble in Mozart, during the 1980s. The disc ends fittingly with an extract from the mould-breaking *Porgy and Bess*. As a whole the disc is a worthy representation of what has been achieved in capturing the unique experience of Glyndebourne.

New review

GOETHE LIEDER. Irmgard Seefried (sop); **Erik Werba** (pf). Orfeo D'Or mono C297921B. Recorded live in 1957.
Mozart: Das Veilchen, K476. Das Kinderspiel, K598. **Beethoven:** Egmont — Incidental Music, Op. 84: Die Trommel gerühret!; Freudvoll und leidvoll. Wonne der Wehmut, Op. 83 No. 1. **Schubert:** Suleika I, D720. Suleika II, D717. Heidenröslein, D257 (includes a false start). Der König in Thule, D367. Ganymed, D544. Gretchen am Spinnrade, D118. Im Frühling, D882. Ave Maria, D839. **Schumann:** Myrthen, Op. 25 — No. 9, Lied der Suleika. **Wolf:** Mignon I; Mignon II; Mignon III; Mignon ("Kennst du das Land?"); Blumengruss; Die Bekehrte; Frühling übers Jahr; Anakreons Grab.

Ih IIm ADD 9/93

Unlike her other Lieder recitals (reviewed elsewhere in this section), all these performances are taken live from a single recital (devoted entirely to Goethe settings), a singer caught at the peak of her powers at a Salzburg recital of 1957. Listen to just four examples of her art and you will know all; the repeat of "Trocknet nicht" in Beethoven's Wonne der Wehmut, the first line of Schumann's ineffably beautiful and touching Lied der Suleika or the erotic close to Schubert's "Was bedeutet die Bewegung" (Suleika I) or the start of Wolf's "So lass mich scheinen" (Mignon III). Here caught on the wing is the kind of sincere, innig singing that can't be learnt: it is instinctive. But, of course, that is not the end of it. Seefried knew as well as anyone that essential in Lieder performance: how to shape a song from start to finish in speeds that never ever drag, evident throughout this arresting recital, but most particularly in Wolf's Mignon, "Kennst du das Land?" (the intensity evinced here not equalled even by Schwarzkopf herself — how searing are the repeated cries of "Kennst du es wohl?") and Gretchen am Spinnrade, which — probably because this is a real event and not a studio invention — has a cumulative, riveting effect seldom if ever heard matched; eternal longing expressed in simple yet overwhelmingly poignant diction and expression — slight signs of strain at the top here wholly appropriate. We are given the recital unedited except for the excision of some applause. Thus endearingly we hear a Heidenröslein where the singer 'dries', makes an amusing apology and starts again. Erik Werba was the perfect pianist for this singer. An unforgettable recital, worth every penny even at full price. Don't miss it.

New review

GREAT CATHEDRAL ANTHEMS, Volumes 3-5. [a]**Southwark Cathedral Choir/Peter Wright;** [b]**Lincoln Cathedral Choir/Colin Walsh;** [c]**Truro Cathedral Choir/David Briggs** with [a]**Stephen Layton,** [b]**James Vivian,** [c]**Simon Morley** (orgs). Priory PRCD435/454/429. Texts included.
PRCD435[a] — *Elgar:* The Apostles, Op. 49 — The Spirit of the Lord. **S. S. Wesley:** Blessed be the God and Father. **W. H. Harris:** Faire is the Heaven. **Mendelssohn:** Symphony No. 2 in B flat major, "Hymn of Praise", Op. 52 — I waited for the Lord. **Gibbons:** Drop, drop slow tears. **Bairstow:** Lord, I call upon Thee. **Boyle:** Thou, O God, art praised in Sion. **Purcell:** Thy word is a lantern unto my feet, Z61. **Howells:** O pray for the peace of Jerusalem. **Vaughan Williams:** Wither's Rocking Hymn. **Hadley:** My beloved spake.

Wood: Hail, gladdening light. *Britten:* Jubilate Deo. PRCD454[b] — *A. Gabrieli:* O sacrum convivium. *Byrd:* Teach me, O Lord. *Gibbons:* Great Lord of Lords. *Greene:* Lord, let me know mine end. *Bruckner:* Os justi. Ave Maria. Tota pulchra es. Locus iste. *Elgar:* Ave verum corpus, Op. 2 No. 1. The Light of Life, Op. 29 — Seek Him that maketh the seven stars. *Ley:* Evening Hymn of Charles I. *Bairstow:* Though I speak with the tongues of men. Lord, Thou hast been our refuge. *Talbot:* O praise God in His Holiness. *Howells:* A Hymn for St Cecilia. Holy spirit, ever dwelling. Like as the hart. PRCD429[c] — *Weelkes:* Hosanna to the Son of David. *Eccard:* When to the temple Mary went. *Tallis:* O nata lux de lumine. *Taverner:* Dum transisset Sabbatum I. *Howells:* Take him, earth, for cherishing. *Bairstow:* Blessed City, heavenly Salem. *Gray:* What are these that glow from afar?. *Mozart:* Ave verum corpus, K618. *Wood:* Expectans expectavi. *Weir:* Illuminare, Jerusalem. *Vaughan Williams:* Mystical Songs — Let all the world in every corner sing.

③ 3h 23m DDD 7/94

These issues follow no particular theme or period in their choice of programme, and, while giving due weight to the term 'cathedral' in the series-title, they have included also some shorter anthems, more readily within the scope of the parish church choir. The items are not restricted to British composers, though in the cathedral tradition they naturally preponderate. The choirs themselves are not among those that are generally recognized as the 'star' recording choirs, but what each of them has shown is the high standard achieved countrywide and also an individual character in each in terms of choral tone, style and repertoire. For the value of that repertoire the series provides an excellent advertisement. Volume 3 has some of the acknowledged masterpieces: Purcell's *Thy word is a lantern*, Wesley's *Blessed be the God and Father*, Britten's *Jubilate in C*, for example. In Vol. 4, Greene's *Lord, let me know mine end* is a particularly fine work, and Howells's *Like as the hart* has much of the essence of its composer concentrated within its short span. Weelkes's *Hosanna to the Son of David*, Tallis's *O nata lux* and another of Howells's most inspired anthems, *Take him, earth, for cherishing*, written in memory of President Kennedy, are all highlights in the fifth volume. But then there are the surprises: the expert transcription of the Prologue to *The Apostles* in the Southwark recital, the Bruckner group by Lincoln, and Judith Weir's *Illuminare, Jerusalem* on the Truro disc. Each, too, will bring its discovery, or its happy reminder of something long forgotten. The Volume by the Choir of Lincoln Cathedral is the one to have prime recommendation. The trebles are surely as fine as any in the country, and there is that something individual about the roundness and strength of their voices so welcome in a choir. Their record gives great pleasure, and the sound of these splendid trebles soaring to their high notes in the Bruckner motets or re-entering with "Like as the hart" in the Howells anthem remains a very special memory. Truro also have a distinctive quality, but here it is more a matter of the blend and texture of sound, enriched by some genuine basses. They also exhibit remarkable accomplishment in their confident mastery of difficult unaccompanied modern music. Southwark bring an affectionate touch, but the programme would benefit from more that might encourage crispness and energy. This issue also suffers, compared with the other two, in not being supplied with printed texts. In all three, the organ is well recorded, and the standard of playing is high.

HAIL, GLADDENING LIGHT. Cambridge Singers/John Rutter. Collegium COLCD113. Texts and translations included.
Anonymous: Rejoice in the Lord. *Purcell:* Remember not, Lord, our offences, Z50. *J. Amner:* Come, let's rejoice. *Tomkins:* When David heard. *Bairstow:* I sat down under his shadow. *J. Goss:* These are they that follow the lamb. *Taverner:* Christe Jesu, pastor bone. *Philips:* O beatum et sacrosanctum diem. *Howells:* Nunc dimittis. *Vaughan Williams:* O vos omnes. *Dering:* Factum est silentium. *Stanford:* Justorum animae, Op. 38 No. 1. *C. Wood:* Hail, gladdening light. *Tavener:* A hymn to the mother of God. Hymn for the dormition of the mother of God. *Elgar:* They are at rest. *Walton:* A litany. *Morley:* Nolo mortem peccatoris. *Tallis* O nata lux. *Rutter:* Loving shepherd of Thy sheep. *R. Stone:* The Lord's Prayer. *J. Sheppard:* In manus tuas. *W.H. Harris:* Bring us, O Lord God.

  1h 12m DDD 4/92

This has the subtitle "Music of the English Church" and it is arranged under four main headings: anthems and introits (these count as one), Latin motets, settings of hymns and other poetry, and prayer-settings. Each of them is well represented in a programme that varies delightfully in period and style, and in performances which are remarkably consistent in quality. Some of the items will come as discoveries to most listeners: for example, the anthem *Come, let's rejoice*, a splendid, madrigal-like piece written by John Amner, organist from 1610 to 1641 at Ely Cathedral where these recordings were made. Others are equally impressive in their present performance: a deep quietness attends the opening of Richard Dering's *Factum est silentium*, which ends with rhythmic Alleluias set dancing with subdued excitement. Among the hymn-settings is one by a 16-year-old called William Walton. Included in the prayers is the choirmaster's own setting, characteristically made for pleasure, of *Loving shepherd of Thy sheep*. All are unaccompanied, and thus very exactingly test the choir's blend of voices, its precision, articulation and feeling for rhythm. In all respects they do exceptionally well; the tone is fresh, the attack unanimous, the expression clear and sensitive, the rhythm on its toes. These are young and gifted singers, formed with disciplined enthusiasm into a choir with a distinctive style — and, incidentally, recorded with admirable results by a family firm which operates from a studio built at the bottom of the garden.

HEAR MY PRAYER. [a]**Jeremy Budd** (treb); **St Paul's Cathedral Choir/John Scott** with [b]**Andrew Lucas** (org). Hyperion CDA66439. Texts and translations included.
Allegri: Miserere (with Nicholas Thompson, treb; Wilfred Swansborough, alto; Timothy Jones, bass)[a]. *B. Rose:* Feast Song for St Cecilia (Simon Hill, alto; Alan Green, ten)[a]. *Brahms:* Ein deutsches Requiem — Ich hab nun Traurigkeit (sung in English)[ab]. *Britten:* Festival Te Deum, Op. 32[ab]. *Harvey:* Come, Holy Ghost (Andrew Burden, ten; Nigel Beaven, bass)[a]. *Mendelssohn:* Hear my prayer[ab]. *Stanford:* Evening Canticles in G major (Jones)[ab]. *Tavener:* I will lift up mine eyes. *Wise:* The ways of Zion do mourn (Charles Gibbs, bass)[ab].

♪ 1h 16m   DDD   10/91

The special distinction of this disc is the work of the treble soloist, Jeremy Budd. He sings in a programme which is very much the choirboy's equivalent of an operatic soprano's "Casta diva" and more of that sort (come to think of it, Master Budd could probably have sung a splendid "Casta diva" into the bargain). As it is, he crowns the Allegri *Miserere* with its five top Cs, spot-on, each of them (rather like Melba singing "Amor" at the end of Act 1 in *La bohème* five times over). He commands the breath, the long line and the purity of tone needful for the solo in Brahms's Requiem and copes with the difficult modern idiom of Jonathan Harvey's *Come, Holy Ghost* with an apparent ease that to an older generation may well seem uncanny. Other modern works are included. John Tavener's *I will lift up mine eyes*, written for St Paul's in 1990, has its characteristic compound of richness and austerity; and in this, the words penetrate the mist of echoes more successfully than do those of the *Feast Song for St Cecilia*, written by Gregory Rose and set to some very beautiful music by his father Bernard. It is good, as ever, to hear Stanford's Evening Service in G, with its almost Fauré-like accompaniment finely played by the excellent Andrew Lucas; and for a morning canticle there is Britten's *Te Deum* with its effective build-up to "Lord God of Sabaoth" and its faint pre-echo of *The Turn of the Screw* at "O Lord, save Thy people". There is also a melancholy anthem by Michael Wise, whose fate it was to be knocked on the head and killed by the watchman to whom he was cheeky one night in 1687.

INTERMEDIOS DEL BARROCO HISPANICO. [a]**Montserrat Figueras** (sop); **Hespèrion XX/Jordi Savall** (va da gamba). Astrée Auvidis E8729.
M. Romero: Caiase de un espino[a]. *Aguilera de Héredia:* Tiento de Batalla. Ensalada. *Lope de Vega/Anonymous:* De pechos sobre una torre[a]. Como retumban los remos[a]. *F. Guerrero:* Si tus penas[a]. *J. Cabanilles:* Pasacalles V. Tiento Ileno. Corrente italiana. *J.K. Kerll:* Batalla Imperial. *M. Machado:* Afuera, afuera que sale[a]. *Correa de Arauxo:* Batalla des Morales. *J. Blas de Castro:* Desde las torres del alma[a]. Entre dos Alamos verdes[a]. *J. Marin:* Ojos, que me desdenais[a]. *Anonymous:* No hay que decirle el primor[a].

♪ 1h 11m   DDD   2/92

A heady Hispanic baroque cocktail. All the vocal numbers here are settings of texts by the colourful and astonishingly prolific Spanish poet and dramatist Lope de Vega (1562-1635), described by Cervantes as "a monster of nature". They range from blithe, folkish pieces through the powerful *De pechos sobre una torre*, in whch a woman laments her lover who has sailed for England with the Armada, to Guerrero's haunting prayer to Jesus, declaimed over a bare string bass and culminating in an extraordinary spoken climax. The instrumental items interspersed with the vocal settings include several rousing battle pieces — a popular seventeenth-century genre — and, for contrast, three beautiful polyphonic numbers by one of the greatest figures of the Spanish Baroque, Joan Cabanilles. If Jordi Savall has touched up the scoring of some of the pieces, no matter: the performances are exciting, sensual, dramatic, with kaleidoscopically varied instrumental colouring, from the entertaining percussion effects of Machado's *Afuera, afuera que sale* to the grave viol consort of Cabanilles's *Pasacalles V* (strong Purcellian associations here). And Savall's wife, Montserrat Figueras, with her distinctive, plangent tone, makes a subtle, stylish, richly imaginative soloist. An irresistible disc, and an ideal introduction to the largely unexplored treasures of the Spanish Baroque.

New review
ITALIAN SONGS. Cecilia Bartoli (mez); **András Schiff** (pf). Decca 440 297-2DH. Texts and translations included. Recorded in 1992.
Beethoven: La Partenza, WoO124. Four Ariettas, Op. 82. In questa tomba oscura, WoO133.
Mozart: Ridente la calma, K152/K210a. **Schubert:** Didone abbandonata, D510. Im Haine, D738. An die Leier, D737. La Pastorella al Prato, D528. Vier Canzonen, D688. Pensa, che questo istante, D76. Willkommen und Abschied, D767. **Haydn:** Arianna a Naxos, HobXXVI*b*/2.

· 68m DDD 11/93

It is good to be reminded of these composers' responses to the Italian muse in this particularly well-cast recital. Central Europe, in the person of András Schiff, meets Italy, in Cecilia Bartoli, to delightful, often revelatory effect. The simple form and undemanding vocal line of Beethoven's little *La Partenza* makes for a truthfulness of expression which Bartoli's clear, light-filled enunciation recreates to the full. With her warm breath gently supporting the voice's lively, supple inflexion, she reveals Beethoven's own skill in word-setting both here and in two fascinatingly contrasted settings of "L'amante impaziente" in the *Ariettas*, Op. 82. Schubert's ten *Canzone* selected here show a wide range of treatment, from the compressed lyric drama of Dido's lament "Vedi quanto adoro", in which Bartoli's lives intensely from second to second, to the honied Goldoni *pastorella* and the thrumming, pulsating serenade of "Guarda, che bianca luna", D688 No. 2. A gently, fragrantly shaped Mozart *Ridente la calma*, and a Haydn *Arianna a Naxos* of movingly immediate and youthful response complete this unexpectedly and unusually satisfying recital.

LIEDER RECITAL. Dame Janet Baker (mez); **Martin Isepp** (pf). Saga Classics SCD9001. Texts and translation included. From STXID5277 (4/66).
Schumann: Frauenliebe und -leben, Op. 42. **Brahms:** Die Mainacht, Op. 43 No. 2. Das Mädchen spricht, Op. 107 No. 3. Nachtigall, Op. 97 No. 1. Von ewiger Liebe, Op. 43 No. 1.
Schubert: Heimliches Lieben, D922. Minnelied, D429. Die abgeblühte Linde, D514. Der Musensohn, D764.

· 47m AAD 3/92

AN ANTHOLOGY OF ENGLISH SONG. Dame Janet Baker (mez) **Martin Isepp** (pf). Saga Classics SCD9012. From STXID5213 (8/66).
Vaughan Williams: Five mystical songs — The call. Songs of travel — Youth and love.
Ireland: A Thanksgiving. Her song. **Head:** A piper. **Armstrong-Gibbs:** This is a sacred city. Love is a sickness. **Dunhill:** The cloths of heaven. To the Queen of heaven. **Warlock:** Balulalow. Youth. **Howells:** King David. Come, sing and dance. **Gurney:** Sleep. I will go with my father a-ploughing. **Finzi:** Let us garlands bring, Op. 18 — Come away, death; It was a lover and his lass.

· 45m AAD 3/92

These recordings were rapturously reviewed in *Gramophone* when they first appeared, and there was no doubt that a singer of great achievement and still greater promise had arrived in our midst. Over the next many years, the name of Janet Baker (Dame-to-be) graced the monthly lists of new recordings and unfailingly brought distinction with it. Her interpretative powers were to mature, and she was certainly to be better recorded, but it is quite likely that nothing brought greater pleasure in the sheer sound of the voice than these early recitals, one of English

| song, one of Lieder. Her *Frauenliebe und -leben* here has the mark of a great interpreter upon it

particularly in the song of happy motherhood, "An meinem Herzen"; but earlier, the conviction of her singing irradiates the performance, and in the last song the fine dark tone and change of expression on the 'face' of the voice are both eloquent and moving. In the Schubert group, her *Musensohn* has a joyous unselfconsciousness, and in the Brahms her *Von ewiger Liebe* still ranks among the finest of all. The selection of English songs is a joy in itself, with Howells's *King David* and *Come, sing and dance* as perhaps the most memorable of all. And nothing could be lovelier than Finzi's setting of *Come away, death* or this performance of it. Some listeners may be deterred by the level of tape-hiss; regrettable too are the short playing times of both discs and the failure of the presenters to give the dates of the original recordings. These are small matters, however, and there is nothing small about such singing.

New review

LIEDER. Karl Erb (ten); **Bruno Seidler-Winkler** (pf). Preiser Lebendige Vergangenheit mono 89208. From HMV and Electrola originals; recorded 1934-9.
Lieder by *Adam, Bach, Beethoven, Brahms, Liszt, Loewe, Schoeck, Schubert, Schumann, Wolf* and *Zilcher.*

(2) · 2h 29m · AAD · 6/94 · P · ▲

Erb's career, voice and style closely resemble those of Peter Schreier today; their voices are uncannily similar in timbre, for they possess a tone of strange, plangent beauty that can on the other hand sound a shade piercing and uncomfortable. Almost all of the first CD is devoted to Erb's Schubert, covering a wide range of the better-known songs. Few, except perhaps for Schreier himself, have come closer to conveying the inner desolation and/or loneliness of such pieces as *Wanderers Nachtlied II, Dass sie hier gewesen,* "Der Wegweiser" and "Das Wirtshaus". The piercing, sad quality of tone, the acute accentuation of words are here wholly appropriate. Yet Erb can lighten his voice and manner for such charmers as *An Sylvia* and *Liebesbotschaft.* The second disc in the main comprises Erb's Beethoven, Schumann, Brahms and Wolf. Some of his Schumann is beyond praise. His intimate, spontaneous readings of such favourites as *Meine Rose, Mondnacht* and *Der Nussbaum* sound newly minted. The same can be said of Brahms's glorious *O wüsst' ich doch den Weg zurück.* Again, his reading of Wolf's religious (Mörike and Ocana) settings are held on a thread of perfectly sustained legato. The transfers are excellent.

LIEDER AND SONG RECITAL. Peter Schreier (ten); **Wolfgang Sawallisch** (pf). Philips 426 237-2PH. Texts and translations included. Recorded in 1984.
Brahms: Deutsche Volkslieder — No. 1, Sagt mire, o schönste Schäf'rin; No. 4, Guten Abend, mein tausiger Schatz; No. 15, Schwesterlein, Schwesterlein; No. 34, Wie komm'ich denn zur Tür herein? Wiegenlied, Op. 49 No. 4. **Prokofiev:** Three Children's Songs, Op. 68. The Ugly Duckling, Op. 18 (all sung in German). **Schumann:** Dichterliebe, Op. 48. Der Nussbaum, Op. 25 No. 3.

· 1h 12m · DDD · 4/90

This live recital caught Schreier and his pianist, Sawallisch, at the top of their form as a partnership. Their account of *Dichterliebe* encompasses every facet of the cycle, holding the attention from start to finish through the intensity of its utterance and flights of imagination. The grief, so poetically and movingly expressed by Heine and Schumann, is here delineated with raw immediacy yet no sense of exaggeration. The troubled, abandoned lover sings, in Schreier's plangent tones, with a poignant, tearful feeling that goes to the heart of things and Sawallisch's playing is fully supportive of the tenor's reading. As compared with Bär (refer to the Index to Reviews), Schreier sings in the original keys throughout: his is a more overtly emotional reading, but both deserve recommendation. In the Brahms, Schreier and Sawallisch rightly adopt a lighter, yet equally pointed style. The Prokofiev group shows Schreier equally adept in a very different idiom. Here, instead of attempting phonetic Russian, he very sensibly uses his own German translations and thus makes the most of the text. The audience noises, applause apart, are minimal and the recording conveys the sense of a real occasion.

New review

LIEDER. Irmgard Seefried (sop); **Erik Werba** (pf). DG Dokumente mono/stereo 437 348-2GDO2. Recorded 1953-62.

Works by *Bartók, Brahms, Mozart, Mussorgsky, Schubert, Schumann, R. Strauss* and *Wolf.*

② 2h 15m ADD 7/93

"A thing of beauty is a joy forever." Of no singer could that be more truly spoken than of Seefried. In her singing on these two discs we hear someone whose every utterance bespeaks natural sincerity and truthful feeling. That made her the perfect advocate of Mozart's songs. As Karl Schumann writes in his perceptive note, rightly headed "The Art that conceals Art", she gave to them a new stature, one that realized the depth of emotion beneath the apparently simple surface. *Das Lied der Trennung* is a template of all that she had to offer in this repertory: the creamy tone, easy, unruffled legato, the unforced treatment of the text, and a realization that it isn't necessary to lay on the artistry with a trowel or engage in slow tempos to make your points. The same comments apply to her Schubert and Brahms. On the same disc she also offers three examples of her skills in Wolf, three Mörike settings — catching the other-worldly thoughts of *An eine Aeolsharfe*, the intimate sorrow of *Das verlassene Mägdlein*, the tone sounding full of an appropriate lassitude and sadness, and the erotic charge of *Begegnung*. A sole Strauss item, the familiar *Ständchen*, is wonderfully light and eager. The second CD features, among other pleasurable items, Seefried's much-admired account of Schumann's *Frauenliebe und -leben*, where she unerringly encompasses the joy, excitement and final sorrow of the cycle, subtly varying her tone for the various states of emotion, catching to perfection the *Innigkeit* of "Süsser Freund". Finally, more Schubert and Strauss, among them an intense version of Schubert's *Die junge Nonne* and a dreamy one of Strauss's *Traum durch die Dämmerung*. This cornucopia of delights is faultlessly transferred to CD at medium price with all texts and translations included. What more can those who love this singer want.

New review

LIEDER. Lieder by *Brahms, Flies, Mozart, Schubert* and *Wolf.* Irmgard Seefried (sop) with various artists. Testament mono SBT1026. From Columbia originals; recorded 1946-53.

1h 14m ADD 9/93

Another 'must' for anyone who loves Seefried. In these wonderfully immediate and faithful transfers of performances made between 1946 and 1953 in Vienna and London, Seefried is heard at the peak of her powers, when her voice was at its freshest and easiest. In the Mozart whether the mood is happy, reflective or tragic, Seefried goes unerringly to the core of the matter. Here we have the archness of *Die kleine Spinnerin*, the naughty exuberance of *Warnung*, the deep emotion of *Abendempfindung* and *Unglückliche Liebe*. We are offered five Schubert songs, including an unsurpassed *Auf dem Wasser zu singen*, so airy and natural; a pure, elevated *Du bist die Ruh* and a poised, ravishing *Nacht und Träume*. The lullabies of Flies, Schubert and Brahms are all vintage Seefried. The Wolf items are a real treasure trove: a sorrowful, plangent account of *Das verlassene Mägdlein* (perhaps the most compelling interpretation of all here; unutterably moving), an enchanting, spontaneous *Elfenlied* (with Gerald Moore marvellously delicate in this). For the most part, Moore is in attendance to complete one's pleasure in an irresistible and generously filled disc.

New review

MISERERE AND OTHER CHORAL WORKS. Trinity College Choir, Cambridge/Richard Marlow. Conifer CDCF219. Recorded in 1993.
Parry: I was glad. Jerusalem. **Schubert:** Deutsche Messe, D872 — Sanctus. Ave Maria, D839. *Barber:* Agnus Dei, Op. 11. *Burgon:* Nunc dimittis. *Bach:* Cantata No. 129, "Gelobet sei der Herr, mein Gott" — Dem wir das Heilig itzt (sung in English). *Allegri:* Miserere. *Mendelssohn:* Hear my prayer. *Gardiner:* Evening Hymn. *Walford Davies:* God be in my head. *Berlioz:* L'Enfance du Christ — Shepherds' Farewell. *Franck:* Panis angelicus. *Purcell:* Hear my prayer, O Lord, Z15. *C. Wood:* Hail, gladdening light. *Mozart:* Ave verum corpus in D, K618. *Gounod:* Ave Maria. *Vaughan Williams:* The Old Hundredth Psalm Tunes. O taste and see.

1h 19m DDD 2/94

The choir is at its absolute best here in Barber's arrangement of his famous *Adagio* for strings as an *Agnus Dei* for unaccompanied voices. In texture and balance, as in the precision of attack and chording, they are really superb. *Jerusalem* is phrased with breadth and care for sense. Breadth, too, distinguishes the performance of *I was glad*, the choir's fine sustaining power serving them well. They are expert in making the most of their resources, so that the quiet "O pray for the peace of Jerusalem", like the solo choir in the Allegri *Miserere*, makes doubly effective the rich sonority to come. All the solo work is good, with a remarkably authentic treble tone supplied by Andrea Cockerton in Mendelssohn's *Hear my prayer*. Purcell's *Hear my prayer* is probably the gem of the whole programme, which is broadly popular in character, a generous mix of periods and styles, with the choir's own style helping to impose a unity and always guaranteeing performances that will be careful in preparation and scrupulous in beauty of tone.

ON WINGS OF SONG. SONGS AND DUETS. [a]**Felicity Lott** (sop); [b]**Ann Murray** (mez); **Graham Johnson** (pf). EMI CDC7 54411-2. Texts and translations included.
Purcell (arr. Britten): Come ye sons of art, away, Z323 — Sound the trumpet[ab]. The Indian Queen — I attempt from love's sickness[b]. Lost is my quiet for ever, Z502[ab]. King Arthur — Fairest Isle[a]. What can we poor females do, Z518[ab]. *Mendelssohn:* Wasserfahrt[ab]. Duets, Op. 63[ab] — No. 5, Volkslied; No. 6, Maiglöckchen und die Blümelein. Auf Flügeln des Gesanges, Op. 34 No. 2[b]. Neue Liebe, Op. 19a No. 4[ab]. Abendlied[ab]. *Rossini:* Soirées musicales — No. 1, La promessa[a]; No. 10, La pesca[ab]. Péchés de vieillesse, Book 1 — Anzoletta co passa la regata[b]. Duetto buffo di due gatti[ab]. *Gounod:* La siesta[ab]. *Delibes:* Les trois oiseaux[ab]. *Massenet:* Rêvons, c'est l'heure[ab]. Joie![b]. *Paladilhe:* Au bord de l'eau[b]. *Aubert:* Cache-cache[ab]. *Balfe:* Trust her not[ab]. *Sullivan:* Coming home[ab]. *Quilter:* It was a lover and his lass, Op. 23 No. 3[ab]. *Britten:* Mother comfort[ab]. Underneath the abject willow[ab].

lh l6m DDD 7/92

These expert duettists (fellow contributors to the Songmakers's Almanac, Marschallin and Octavian in many a *Rosenkavalier*, and recently back from a European tour at the time of publication) have already one highly successfully disc ("Sweet Power of Song" — reviewed further on) to their joint credit, and now achieve what often proves the more difficult task of providing an equally good sequel. But of course this is not really a double-act but a trio, and Graham Johnson is, as ever, more than accompanist. When he arranges a programme, delight follows as sure as night follows day. Here the delight lies partly in discovery (for instance, there is a charmer of Gounod's, in Spanish style, the voices in dreamy thirds, the ending softly delicate). Then there is the range of mood, from Purcell's assured, outward-going "Sound the trumpet" at the start to the desolation that burrows within Britten's haunting *Mother comfort* near the end. Solos are deftly chosen to bring out the best in each singer, as in the clean style and unostentatious manner of Felicity Lott's "Fairest Isle" and Ann Murray's finely phrased, evenly sustained *Auf Flügeln des Gesanges*. Then there are the charming oddities: Sullivan's "Coming home" turns out to be a duet from *Cox and Box* (but with different words), and 'Rossini's' cat-duet is now attributed to that singularly unpredictable minor genius, Robert Pearsall. The recording is exemplary.

New review
PASTORAL. [b]**Judith Howarth** (sop); **Emma Johnson** (cl); [a]**Malcolm Martineau** (pf). ASV CDDCA891.
Ireland: Fantasy-Sonata in E flat major[a]. *Vaughan Williams:* Six Studies in English folk song[a]. Three Vocalises for Soprano Voice and Clarinet[b]. *Bax:* Sonata for Clarinet and Piano[a]. *Bliss:* Pastoral (posth.)[a]. Two Nursery Rhymes[b]. *Stanford:* Sonata for Clarinet and Piano, Op. 129Af.

lh l4m DDD 7/94

A lovely programme, radiantly performed and most judiciously chosen. Things get under way in fine style with John Ireland's marvellous *Fantasy-Sonata*: beautifully written, passionately argued and encompassing (for Ireland) a wide range of moods; it's certainly a work that shows this underrated figure at the height of his powers. The Clarinet Sonata by Ireland's teacher, Stanford, is one of that composer's most successful works: formally elegant and most idiomatically laid out, it boasts a central *Adagio* (entitled "Caoine" — an Irish lament) of considerable eloquence. Johnson is a gloriously mellifluous exponent in both Vaughan Williams's Six *Studies* and the Bax Sonata, and in the first movement of the latter she manages to convey a slumbering mystery that is somehow almost orchestral in its imaginative scope. Judith Howarth joins Johnson for the haunting *Three Vocalises* (one of Vaughan Williams's very last utterances from his final year) and makes an equally agile showing in Bliss's delightful *Two Nursery Rhymes* and touching *Pastoral*. A real pleasure, then, from start to finish and Malcolm Martineau proffers superb accompaniments.

A PROGRAM OF SONG. Leontyne Price (sop); **David Garvey** (pf). RCA Living Stereo 09026 61499-2. Texts and translations included. Recorded in 1959. New to UK.
Fauré: Clair de lune, Op. 46 No. 2. Notre amour, Op. 23 No. 2. Au cimetière, Op. 51 No. 2. Au bord de l'eau, Op. 8 No. 1. Mandoline, Op. 58 No. 1. *Poulenc:* Main dominée par le coeur. Miroirs brûlants. Ce doux petit visage. *R. Strauss:* Allerseelen, Op. 10 No. 8. Schlagende Herzen, Op. 29 No. 2. Freundliche Vision, Op. 48 No. 1. Wie sollten wir geheim, Op. 19 No. 4. *Wolf:* Mörike Lieder — Der Gärtner; Lebe wohl. Lieder für eine Frauenstimme — Morgentau. Spanisches Liederbuch — Geh' Geliebter, geh' jetz.

40m ADD 5/93

There can be few recordings which so vividly resemble the sound of singer and pianist performing live in one's own home. This forward, warts-and-all 1959 RCA recording has a disconcerting immediacy, but it's not just the recorded sound which creates this sense of close intimacy. Leontyne Price sings with a captivating directness which belongs more to the domestic room than the concert-hall — or even the opera house, for it was here that her reputation was made, becoming revered as one of the foremost Verdi sopranos. Her recorded legacy encompasses major roles from Mozart through Berlioz and Puccini to Gershwin and Samuel Barber, but this CD is special. This was her recording début made in the Town Hall, New York City, and shows her in repertoire with which she has not generally been associated. Yet she sings it with an intuition and sensitivity which would be the envy of singers whose lifetimes' work has been in *Lieder* and *chanson*. The French and German accents have an unmistakable American twang, but it's not the words which matter so much as the sense of involvement she brings to each and every one of these beautiful and memorable songs. A CD of great historic and artistic value.

New review

A SALUTE TO AMERICAN MUSIC. [a]**Leontyne Price,** [b]**Maureen O'Flynn,** [ei]**Renée Fleming,** [f]**Karen Holvik,** [l]**Denise Woods,** [o]**Carol Vaness** (sops); [b]**Phyllis Pancella,** [j]**Tatiana Troyanos,** [n]**Frederica von Stade,** [q]**Marilyn Horne** (mezs); [bhi]**Jerry Hadley,** [b]**Paul Groves** (tens); [b]**Daniel Smith,** [b]**Jeff Mattsey,** [dm]**Sherrill Milnes,** [c]**Robert Merrill** (bars); [p]**Samuel Ramey** (bass); [gikl]**Collegiate Chorale; Metropolitan Opera Orchestra/ James Conlon.** RCA Victor Red Seal 09026 61509-2. Recorded live in 1991.
S. Ward: America the Beautiful[a]. *Menotti:* Amelia al ballo — Overture. *Weill:* Street Scene — Ice-Cream Sextet[b]. Knicker-bocker Holiday — September Song[c]. *V. Thomson:* Five Songs from William Blake — Tiger! Tiger! burning bright[d]. *Griffes:* Fiona Macleod Poems, Op. 11 — The Lament of Ian the Proud[e]. *Foster:* Ah! May the red rose live alway[f]. *Bernstein:* Chichester Psalm No. 1[g]. West Side Story — Maria[h]. Candide—Make our garden grow[i]. *Copland:* Old American Songs, Set 2 — At the river[j]. *Bolcom:* The Tyger[k]. *Gershwin:* Porgy and Bess — Leavin' for the Promised Land[l]. *M.D. Levy:* Mourning becomes Electra — Too weak to kill the man I hate[m]. *Barber:* Vanessa — Must the Winter come so soon?[n]. Antony and Cleopatra — Give me my robe[o]. *Floyd:* Susannah — Hear me, O Lord[p]. *Berlin:* God bless America[q].

1h 12m DDD 6/93

This 'look at an era just gone by' starts with a great lift-off: *America the Beautiful* sung by Leontyne Price. At the age of 63 she can still summon enough patriotic fervour to make non-Americans want to apply for citizenship papers on the spot! And she isn't the oldest performer by any means. Robert Merrill is ten years her senior and delivers Weill's "September Song" touchingly. One of the most moving performances is Karen Holvik in Stephen Foster's immaculate *Ah! May the red rose live alway*, with piano (Steven Blier). More calculating, but equally polished nostalgia comes from Barber, especially "Must the winter come so soon" from *Vanessa*, hauntingly sung by Frederica von Stade. Tatiana Troyanos sings Copland's setting of Robert Lowry's "At the river" with impressive, quiet dignity. Bernstein is the only composer who gets in three times — the Collegiate Chorale is on form for the first of the *Chichester*

Psalms; Jerry Hadley sings "Maria"; and there's an ensemble from *Candide*. Finally, in case you didn't sign on for US citizenship, Marilyn Horne gives a truly commanding performance of Berlin's classic *God bless America*. This is not just an anthology which works — it's a wow!

New review
SINGERS OF IMPERIAL RUSSIA, Volumes 1-4. 35 singers with various accompaniments.
Pearl mono GEMMCDS9997/9, GEMMCDS9001/03, GEMMCDS9004/06 and GEMMCDS9007/09 (four three-disc sets, only available separately).
GEMMCDS9997/9 — recorded 1900-11 (3h 27m): *Soprano* — Medea Mei-Figner. *Tenors* — Ivan Ershov, Nikolai Figner and Leonid Sobinov. *Baritone* — Ioakim Tartakov. *Basses* — Adamo Didur and Vasili Sharonov. *GEMMCDS9001/03* — 1901-11 (3h 29m): *Sopranos* — Natalia Ermolenko-Juzhina and Maria Michailova. *Mezzo-soprano* — Antonina Panina. *Tenors* — David Juzhin, Andrei Labinsky and Gavril Morskoi. *Baritones* — Oskar Kamionsky and Polikarp Orlov. *Basses* — Dmitri Bukhtoyarov, Vladimir Kastorsky, Vasili Sharonov and Lev Sibiriakov. *GEMMCDS9004/06* — 1901-24 (3h 42m): *Sopranos* — Irena Bohuss, Anna El-Tour, Janina Korolewicz-Wayda, Maria Kuznetsova, Lydia Lipkowska and Nadezhda Zabela-Vrubel. *Contralto* — Evgenia Zbrueva. *Tenors* — Dmitri Smirnov and Eugene Witting. *Bass* — K. E. Kaidanov. *GEMMCDS9007/09* — 1901-14 (3h 41m): *Sopranos* — Maria Michailova and Antonia Nezhdanova. *Mezzo-soprano* — Galina Nikitina. *Contralto* — Evgenia Zbrueva. *Tenors* — Alexandr Alexandrovich, Alexandr Bogdanovich, Alexandr Davidov, Andrei Labinsky and Eugene Witting. *Baritone* — Nikolai Shevelev. *Basses* — Vladimir Kastorsky and Lev Sibiriakov.

··⁴ 4 ③ AAD 6/93

This is the equivalent, in terms of gramophone history, of one of those exhibitions for which queues form long and deep and daily outside the Tate Gallery or the Royal Academy: in fact, if a similar exhibition of paintings, furniture and porcelain from the Tsar's palaces were mounted in London it would surely be a sell-out. Quite simply, there has never been a published collection to match this, both in the quality of the items and in its extensiveness. Of the singers of Imperial Russia, the world came to know Chaliapin, who eclipsed the rest. He is not among the artists presented here, but we have, among the basses, two who at least for vocal splendour are his equal: Adamo Didur, the Pole who was New York's first Boris Godunov (preceding Chaliapin there), and Lev Sibiriakov, another giant of a man with a magnificently produced voice to match. The tenors include Smirnov and Sobinov, a kind of collector's Tweedledum and Tweedledee, though in fact very unalike indeed. New to most listeners will be Ivan Ershov, heard in Siegfried's Forging Song from St Petersburg, 1903, with piano and anvil accompaniment: an astonishing voice and most accomplished in technique. Evgenia Zbrueva the contralto, sopranos Nezhdanova, Ermolenko-Jushina, Mei-Figner and the superbly recorded Korolewicz-Wayda are also plentifully represented. Most amazing of all, perhaps, is the vividness of sound. These are some of the world's rarest recordings and, almost without exception, they are in pristine condition.

SONGS BY FINZI AND HIS FRIENDS. [a]Ian Partridge (ten); [b]Stephen Roberts (bar);
Clifford Benson (pf). Hyperion CDA66015. Texts included.
Finzi: To a Poet, Op. 13a[b]. Oh fair to see, Op. 13b[a]. *Milford*[a]: If it's ever spring again. The colour. So sweet love seemed. *Farrar:* O mistress mine![a]. *Gurney*[b]: Sleep. Down by the salley gardens. Hawk and Buckle. *Gill:* In Memoriam[b].

··⁴ 5lm ADD 9/91

This is a record that drew from its original reviewer, Trevor Harvey, high and unstinting praise when it appeared in 1981 as part of the commemoration of Finzi 25 years after his death. Finzi was never an avant-garde composer and during his lifetime received quiet and grateful acknowledgement from kindred spirits rather than anything more spectacular. In the last 20 years or so, appreciation has deepened and become more widespread. His songs, particularly, have a depth of feeling that is not always apparent at first hearing, and their idiom is that of a writer to whom overstatement or any other kind of cheapening would have been abhorrent. In this selection most of the chosen poems are affectionate and gentle, but F.L. Lucas's *June on Castle Hill* contains "whispers of wars to come", and George Barker's "Ode on the Rejection of St Cecilia" is a strong and sombre utterance that evokes an uncommonly hard-hitting style in the composer. His friend, Robin Milford, sets Hardy and Bridges with comparable sensitivity, and

Ernest Farrar (killed in 1918) is remembered by his charmingly nonchalant "O mistress mine!". Stephen Roberts is an admirable singer of the songs by Ivor Gurney, and Ian Partridge gives a lovely account of Finzi's Op. 13*b* songs. Clifford Benson is the excellent accompanist throughout and recording and presentation are first-rate.

New review

SONGS AND DANCES OF DEATH. Dmitri Hvorostovsky (bar); **Kirov Theatre Orchestra/Valery Gergiev.** Philips 438 872-2PH. Texts and translations included. Recorded in 1993.
Rimsky-Korsakov: SADKO — The paragon of cities; Beautiful city! KASHCHEY THE IMMORTAL — In this, night's darkest hour. SNOW MAIDEN (second version) — Under the warm blue sea. THE TSAR'S BRIDE — Still the beauty haunts my mind. *Borodin:* PRINCE IGOR — No sleep, no rest. *Rubinstein:* THE DEMON — Do not weep, my child; On the airy ocean; I am he whom you called. NERO — Vindex's Epithalamium: I sing to you, Hymen divine! *Rachmaninov:* ALEKO — Aleko's cavatina. *Mussorgsky:* Songs and Dances of Death.

• Ih 2m DDD 5/94

In the scenes from Rubinstein's *The Demon* Hvorostovsky, superbly supported by Valery Gergiev and his Kirov orchestra recorded in their own theatre, has done nothing better than his impersonation of the devil; in the scenes from the third he projects the gloating demon to the life. This is splendid stuff. So is Vindex's rollicking Epithalamium from the same composer's *Nero*, sung with wonderful breadth and confidence. Then he changes character again to bring before us the emotional torment of Rachmaninov's Aleko as he recalls the love Zemfira once had for him. The best of the Rimsky items as regards music and interpretation are Nizgir's aria from the *Snow Maiden* and Gryaznoy's musing on past triumphs in the field of love from *The Tsar's Bride*. Here Hvorostovsky varies his tone more successfully than in the other Rimsky items. Mussorgsky's *Songs and Dances of Death* really need an imposing bass rather than a lyric baritone to make their true mark, yet these are more than acceptable performances on what is undoubtedly Hvorostovsky's most enjoyable recital to date, immeasurably helped by the support and the excellent recording. This is a fascinating disc.

THE SPLENDOUR OF SPAIN. José Carreras (ten); **Martin Katz** (pf); **English Chamber Orchestra/Robin Stapleton, Roberto Benzi, Antoni Ros Marbá.** Philips 432 825-2PM. Recorded 1978-85.
Padilla: Valencia. *Grever:* Jurame. *F. Alonso:* Maitechu mia. *Lara:* Granada. *Vives:* Doña Francisquita — Por el humo. *Soutullo:* Ultimo romantico — Noche de amor. *Serrano:* Alma da Dios — Canción húngara. *Falla:* Canciones populares españolas. *Mompou:* Combat del somni. *Obradors:* Canciones clásicas españolas — Del cabello más sutil. Corazón porqué pasais. *Turína:* Poeme en forma de canciones.

• Ih 4m ADD/DDD 7/92

To celebrate "The Splendour of Spain" Philips have plundered their archives to come up with a series of discs each reflecting a different facet of Spanish music. This CD, devoted to song, has that greatest of all Spanish voices, José Carreras, beginning in classic Carreras fashion with big, crowd-pulling displays of vocal power and emotional extravagance. Never can Augustin Lara's classic *Granada* have packed quite such a punch, with opulent orchestral accompaniment (including that archetypically Spanish instrument, the guitar) and Carreras giving it his all, while the semi-operatic *Alma da Dios* positively oozes Eastern magic casting a spell few could resist. But the real highlights of this CD are a group of more intimate and subtle art songs by Falla, Mompou, Obradors and Turína. Here the true measure of Carreras's artistry is to be found. He sings with warmth, sensitivity and remarkable control. Martin Katz's piano accompaniments, especially in Mompou's three songs *Combat del somni* are in a class of their own. Only a singer of the calibre of Carreras could bring off such a diverse programme with such utter conviction and he has been served well by consistently high quality recordings.

SWEET POWER OF SONG. Felicity Lott (sop); **Ann Murray** (mez); **Graham Johnson** (pf) with [a]**Galina Solodchin** (vn) and [a]**Jonathan Williams** (va). EMI CDC7 49930-2. Texts and translations included.

Beethoven[a]: 25 Irish Songs, WoO152 — Sweet power of song; English Bulls. 12 Irish Songs, WoO154 — The Elfin Fairies; Oh! would I were but that sweet linnet. **Berlioz:** Pleure, pauvre Colette. Le trébuchet, Op. 13 No. 3. **Brahms:** Vier Duette, Op. 61. **Chausson:** Two duos, Op. 11. **Fauré:** Pleurs d'or, Op. 72. Tarantelle, Op. 10 No. 2. **Gounod:** D'un coeur qui t'aime. L'Arithmétique. **Saint-Saëns:** Pastorale. El desdichado. **Schumann:** Liederalbum für die Jugend, Op. 79 — No. 15, Das Glück; No. 19, Frühlings Ankunft; No. 23, Er ist's; No. 26, Schneeglöckchen.

Ih 2m DDD II/90

This is a delightful presentation of an entertaining programme. The singers' careers have run concurrently with growing success on the international scene yet faithful to Graham Johnson as founding members of the Songmakers' Almanac. Here they recall many evenings of happy duetting at that group's recitals. They sing together with an instinctive rapport that is most gratifying. Johnson has devised a programme for them that provides an ingenious variety of mood and style. Beethoven's Irish Songs may not be great music but they are given vivid advocacy here. So are the more attractive and deeper duets by Schumann and Brahms. The Berlioz pieces, nicely contrasted, are well done; so are the Gounod, Fauré and Chausson items, even if a shade more accenting of words would have been welcome here. The real winner among the French items — surely a collector's item of the future — is Gounod's *L'Arithmétique*, an amusing lesson in Victorian thrift delivered in both French and English. Johnson supplies appropriate accompaniments and interesting notes. The recording naturally balances voices and piano.

New review
TWENTIETH-CENTURY ENGLISH SONGS. Anthony Rolfe Johnson (ten); **David Willison** (pf). Pickwick IMP Classics PCD1065. Items marked [a] from Polydor 2460 236 (2/75), [b]2460 258 (1/76). Recorded 1974-75.
Vaughan Williams: Songs of Travel[a]. **Butterworth:** A Shropshire Lad[b]. **Ireland:** The Land of Lost Content[b]. **Gurney:** Down by the Salley Gardens[b]. An Epitaph[b]. Desire in Spring[b]. Black Stitchel[b]. **Warlock:** My Own Country[b]. Passing by[b]. Pretty Ring Time[b].

Ih 8m ADD 4/94

These songs rank with the best in any language. John Ireland's writing may have an elusive strength but for the rest (including the lovely things by Gurney and Warlock) they belong (to adapt Housman) to "the land of *found* content". A very special contribution is David Willison's. The accompaniments to the *Songs of Travel* and Butterworth's *A Shropshire Lad* do not appear to be difficult, and the composers have placed them well within the scope of an amateur. But what a richness of texture they have when played with such intelligent and sensitive professionalism. Everywhere he brings a touch which clarifies and endears. Rolfe Johnson's singing too is masterly in so many respects. He phrases with easy breadth, and brings off perfectly points of unsuspected difficulty such as the ending of "The Roadside fire" from *Songs of Travel*. In "Whither must I wander" he catches the emotion but does not overplay it, while in Butterworth's "Is my team ploughing?" he differentiates the voices of dead and living without exaggeration. The recordings are fine.

VOCAL RECITAL. Régine Crespin (sop); [b]**John Wustman** (pf); [a]**Suisse Romande Orchestra/Ernest Ansermet.** Decca 417 813-2DH. Texts and translations included. Items marked [a] from SXL6081 (3/64), [b]SXL6333 (6/68).
Berlioz: Les nuits d'été. **Ravel:** Shéhérazade[a]. **Debussy:** Trois chansons de Bilitis[b].
Poulenc: Banalités[b] — Chansons d'Orkenise; Hôtel. La courte paille[b] — Le carafon; La reine de coeur. Chansons villageoises[b] — Les gars qui vont à la fête. Deux poèmes de Louis Aragon[b].

Ih 8m ADD II/88

Some recordings withstand the test of time and become acknowledged classics. This is one of them. Crespin's voluptuous tone, her naturally accented French and her feeling for the inner meaning of the songs in both these cycles are everywhere evident. Better than most single interpreters of the Berlioz, she manages to fulfil the demands of the very different songs, always alive to verbal nuances. In the Ravel, she is gorgeously sensuous, not to say sensual, with the right timbre for Ravel's enigmatic writing. The other songs on this CD enhance its worth.

Crespin offers a highly evocative, perfumed account of the Debussy pieces and is ideally suited to her choice of Poulenc, of which her interpretation of "Hôtel" is a classic. Ansermet and his orchestra, though not quite note perfect, are — like the singer — right in timbre and colour for both these rewarding cycles. The sound is reasonable given the age of the recording. This is a most desirable acquisition.

WHERE THE MUSIC COMES FROM. AMERICAN SONGS. **Cynthia Haymon** (sop); **Warren Jones** (pf). Argo 436 117-2ZH. Texts included.
Hoiby: Where the music comes from. Always it's Spring. **Rorem:** See how they love me. Early in the morning. O you whom I often and silently come. **Burleigh:** Among the fuchsias. Till I wake. Worth while. The prayer. **Barber:** O boundless, boundless evening. Sleep now. **Nordoff:** Embroidery for a faithless friend. **Farwell:** Wild nights! Wild nights! **Beck:** Songs of devotion. **Logan:** Marrow of my bone. **Hundley:** Strings in the earth and air. Come ready and see me. **Dougherty:** Love in the dictionary. **Griffes:** In a myrtle shade. **Lekberg:** The spring and the fall.

· · · 54m DDD 12/92

Seeing a CD devoted to American songs most people would probably think of Gershwin, Bernstein and the big numbers from smash-hit Broadway musicals. In presenting her own very personal selection portraying the 'many shades of love', Cynthia Haymon is displaying an altogether different side of twentieth-century American music. All 20 of these songs show a simplicity and gentleness which seems worlds away from the brashness of the Broadway stage, yet there is still something uniquely American in their openness and unashamed romanticism. Haymon, whose reputation largely rests on her operatic and stage roles (most recently as Bess in *Porgy and Bess* and Coretta King in the recording of the musical *King*) seems here to be baring her true self. She sings with a directness and unpretentiousness which seems like a mere extension of a sensitive yet exuberant personality and which suits this gentle programme perfectly. Accompanied by the ever-astute Warren Jones, she passes easily from the turn-of-the-century salon style of Burleigh's *Among the fuchsias* to Ned Rorem's somewhat austere *See how they love me*, always singing with absolute conviction and sincerity. An all-too brief CD of intimate moments to soothe the heart and refresh the soul.

Operatic highlights and recitals

THE ART OF THE PRIMA DONNA. Dame Joan Sutherland (sop); **Chorus and Orchestra of the Royal Opera House, Covent Garden/Francesco Molinari-Pradelli.** Decca 425 493-2DM2. Texts and translations included. From SXL2556/7 (12/60).
Arne: ARTAXERXES — The soldier tir'd. **Bellini:** LA SONNAMBULA — Care compagne ... Come per me sereno ... Sopra il sen. NORMA — Sediziose voci ... Casta diva ... Ah! bello a me ritorna. I PURITANI — Son vergin vezzosa; O rendetemi la speme ... Qui la voce ... Vien, diletto. **Delibes:** LAKME — Ah! Où va la jeune Indoue. **Gounod:** FAUST — O Dieu! que de bijoux ... Ah! je ris. ROMEO ET JULIETTE — Je veux vivre. **Handel:** SAMSON — Let the bright Seraphim. **Meyerbeer:** LES HUGUENOTS — O beau pays de la Touraine! **Mozart:** DIE ENTFUHRUNG AUS DEM SERAIL — Martern aller Arten. **Rossini:** SEMIRAMIDE — Bel raggio lusinghier. **Thomas:** HAMLET — A vos jeux, mes amis. **Verdi:** OTELLO — Mia madre aveva una povera ancella ... Piangea cantando. LA TRAVIATA — E strano ... Ah fors' è lui ... Sempre libera. RIGOLETTO — Gualtier Maldè ... Caro nome.

· · ② 1h 49m ADD 1/90

Those who have not heard Dame Joan until recent times can only speculate on the full beauty of her voice in its prime. This album, from 1960, preserves the real Sutherland quality as well as any of her records have done and it is a delight from start to finish. Sutherland and her husband, Richard Bonynge, have long been interested in the history of opera and particularly of its singers, so *The Art of the Prima Donna* was arranged to relate each of the solos to a famous soprano of the past. Arne's *Artaxerxes* recalls Mrs Billington, and the final items are associated with more recent artists such as Tetrazzini and Galli-Curci. It presents a brilliant conspectus, with Sutherland mastering the most fearsome of technical demands and showing a wonderfully complete command of the required skills. She was then fresh from the triumph at Covent Garden in *Lucia di Lammermoor* which brought her international fame in 1959. Her voice was at its purest, and her style had not developed the characteristics which later partly limited the pleasure of her singing. What the record may not quite convey is the sheer house-filling volume of her voice. Even so, nobody who hears these recordings can be in any doubt about her mastery or about the aptness of the title, bestowed on her by the Italians, of "la stupenda".

MARIA CALLAS. RARITIES. **Maria Callas** (sop); [a]**Paris Conservatoire Orchestra/ Nicola Rescigno;** [b]**Maggio Musicale Fiorentino Orchestra/Tullio Serafin;** [c]**Rome RAI Orchestra/Alfredo Simonetto;** [d]**Philharmonia Orchestra/Antonio Tonini;** [e]**Paris Opera Orchestra/Georges Prêtre.** EMI CDC7 54437-2. Texts and translations included. Items marked [c] recorded at a concert in San Remo, Italy in 1954.
Beethoven: Ah! perfido, Op. 65[a] (from Columbia SAX2540, 8/64). *Mozart:* Don Giovanni — Non mi dir[b] (CMS7 63750-2, 11/91. Recorded in 1953). Die Entführung aus dem Serail — Martern aller Arten[c] (sung in Italian. New to UK). *Weber:* Oberon — Ozean du Ungeheuer![d] (English. Previously unpublished. 1962). *Rossini:* Armida — D'amore al dolce impero[c] (EX769741-1, 4/89). *Donizetti:* Lucrezia Borgia — Tranquillo ei posa ... Com'è bello![d] (1961). *Verdi:* Don Carlos — O don fatale[d] (1961). I vespri siciliani — Arrigo! ah, parli[d] (1960). Il trovatore — Vanne ... lasciami ... D'amor sull'ali rosee[a]. I lombardi — Te, Vergin santa[a] (all previously unpublished). Both recorded in 1964/5. Aida — Pur' ti riveggo ... Fuggiam gli ardor[e] (with Franco Corelli, ten. New to UK. 1964).

♪ 1h 18m ADD 2/93 ▲

'Rarity' is one of those tricky words which, being really only quantitative, seems to imply something about quality as well. So the reader may well look doubtfully at the title: the "Callas Rarities" may indeed be rarities for the best of reasons, that of inferiority to versions and recordings that are less rare. In this instance, though, they are genuinely well worth having. For example, here is the Nile Duet from *Aida* with Franco Corelli, sole survivor of a projected album of duets to be recorded in 1964. Corelli provides the vocal thrills, sometimes even responding in kind to the dramatic intensity which characterizes Callas's performance from the start. Her voice is sometimes raw, and the soft B flat on "fuggiam" only just arrives and stays put. But always there is something distinctive: here it is the nostalgia, "Là tra foreste" being sung as a wistful, private vision of the homeland. Then there are the two incredibly brilliant solos from a concert at San Remo in 1954 ("Martern aller Arten" and "D'amore al dolce impero"); also previously unpublished versions, not alternative 'takes' but different performances, products of a different session. Usually one can see why they were not issued at the time, but here it is easier to see why they deserve to see the light of this later day.

COVENT GARDEN ON RECORD, Volumes 1-4. 143 singers with various accompaniments. Pearl mono GEMMCDS9923/6 (four 3-disc sets: only available separately).

♪ 3h 33m 3h 25m 3h 47m 3h 42m AAD 7/92 ꝗP ▲

An Aladdin's cave, where whatever the torch lights upon is treasure. At the entrance: Adelina Patti, well past her prime to be sure, but in that *Ah, non credea mirarti* what heartfelt pathos when she comes to the lines "Mi ravivar l'amore il pianto mio non puèo", what delicacy in the soft tones and the trill, and, after all, what a miracle that we should be able to hear as clearly as this, from the 63-year-old woman in retirement at her Welsh castle in 1906, the beauty remaining to the most world-renowned voice of her century. Further in among the treasures, the first Otello, the first Falstaff; near to them, a baritone, one Mario Ancona of 1904, almost forgotten today but truly superb in his Donizetti as, by his side, is the bass Marcel Journet, sonorous and with a funny old chorus to support him in a passage from that epitome of nineteenth-century grand opera, *Les Huguenots*. Into the next chamber, and a voice arises celebrating the fickleness of womankind — the voice of the god of tenors, Enrico Caruso. His Irish friend McCormack, his business-partner Melba, his Neapolitan *amico* Scotti: all are there. Deeper in, and we have come through the First World War, to where British singers — Walter Widdop, Heddle Nash and Joan Cross among them — mingle freely and quite rightly with tip-top company such as Lotte Lehmann, Elisabeth Rethberg and Friedrich Schorr. At the end of the journey we reach the ominous date 1939: for the chambers of this Aladdin's cave of records have also been the years of the Covent Garden Opera House, with singers heard there, in the present theatre, as early as 1871, up to the end of the international seasons and the outbreak of World War Two. The singers are heard in the roles they sang, and are sometimes recorded 'live' from the stage, as with Chaliapin in 1928 and Gigli in 1939. Many of the recordings are of extreme rarity, and thanks to the expertise of Keith Hardwick, who compiled the programme and effected the transfers, a sizeable proportion of them are heard to greater advantage than ever before on CD or LP. Not everything is perfect, either in the singers themselves (they don't always do what we want them to), or the selections (nothing of some famous Covent Garden roles such as Caruso's Canio and Turner's Turandot) or even the transfers (a certain harshness in some of the later recordings). But the four albums, three CDs to a volume and each volume available separately, comprise one of the best of anthologies. They also document a fascinating period in the history of a great opera house: an extraordinary concentration of enterprise, historical time, musical talent and in some instances genius, all within the compass of these 12 small discs.

FAVOURITE SOPRANO ARIAS. Luba Orgonasova (sop); **Bratislava Radio Symphony Orchestra/Will Humburg.** Naxos 8 550605.
Bellini: I PURITANI — Qui la voce. I CAPULEI ED I MONTECCHI — Oh! quante volte. LA SONNAMBULA — Come per me sereno. *Donizetti:* LINDA DI CHAMOUNIX — O luce di quest'anima. Lucia di Lammermoor — Il dolce suono; Ardon gl'incensi; Alfin son tua; Spargi d'amaro pianot. *Puccini:* TURANDOT — Signore, ascolta!; Tu, che di gel sei cinta. GIANNI SCHICCHI — O mio babbino caro. LA RONDINE — Chi il bel sogno di Doretta. *Verdi:* RIGOLETTO — Tutte le feste.

58m DDD 2/93

Here is a young and excellent singer in the fresh prime of her voice and with her artistry developed quite far enough to make her an effective communicator. She comes (like Edita Gruberová before her) from Bratislava and has enjoyed considerable success at Salzburg. Her voice is deliciously clear, and though in the category of light soprano she nevertheless has a certain depth and richness of tone which impart a warmer humanity to her singing than is often found among singers in this repertory. Limitations are felt from time to time: a musical one, for instance, when she gives a push to the final B flat in Liù's "Signore, ascolta!", and a dramatic one when she seems not to feel the pathos of Gilda's narrative in "Tutte le feste". Yet the solos from *Lucia di Lammermoor* and the Bellini operas are touching in their emotional warmth as well as being sung with a charming sweetness and remarkable technical skill. She is sympathetically accompanied and well recorded: in sum, one of the most enjoyable recitals by a relative newcomer, and especially good value at its super-bargain price.

New review
CLAUDIA MUZIO. OPERA ARIAS AND SONGS. **Claudia Muzio** (sop) with various artists. Romophone mono 81005-2. From HMV and Edison originals; recorded 1911-25.
Adriana Lecouvreur, L'africaine, L'amico Fritz, Andrea Chénier, Bianca e Fernando, La bohème, Carmen, Les contes d'Hoffmann, Eugene Onegin, La forza del destino, Hérodiade, I lombardi, Loreley, Madame Sans-Gêne, Mefistofele, Pagliacci, Paride e Elena, Rinaldo, Salvator Rosa, La traviata, Il trovatore, I vespri siciliani, La Wally and Zazà; songs by Bachelet, Buzzi-Peccia, Chopin, Guagni-Benvenuti, Herbert, Mascheroni, Monahan, Pergolesi, Rossini and Sodero.

② 2h 33m ADD 1/94

The crackles and surface noise that usually afflict Edison reproduction have all but been eliminated, so that we can hear Muzio's voice in its absolute prime without, as it were, the effort of listening through a sea of interference. The sheer beauty of the soprano's voice and her wonderful intensity of expression can now be experienced with astonishing immediacy. All the Muzio gifts, including that of refined, exquisite phrasing combined with that peculiarly heart-rending intensity that was hers alone, are heard in that enchanting song by Bachelet, *Chère nuit* (the first disc, track 8). If your dealer will let you hear that, even if you are sceptical about singers of the past, you are sure to make off home with this set, eager to hear the rest. A feast of captivating interpretations from one of the century's three or four greatest singing-actresses.

OPERA ARIAS AND DUETS. Giovanni Martinelli (ten); [a]**Metropolitan Opera Chorus and Orchestra/Giulio Setti;** [b]**Josef Pasternack,** [c]**Rosario Bourdon.** Preiser Lebendige Vergangenheit mono 89062. Recorded 1926-7
Verdi: RIGOLETTO — La donna è mobile. Il trovatore — Quale d'armi fragor ... Di quella pira[a] (with Grace Anthony, sop). LA FORZA DEL DESTINO — Oh, tu che in seno; Invano Alvaro ... Le minacciei fieri accenti (with Giuseppe de Luca, bar). AIDA — Se quel guerrier io fossi ... Celeste Aida[b]; Nume, custode e vindici (with Ezio Pinza, bass). *Giordano:* ANDREA CHENIER — Un dì all'azzurro spazio[b]; Come un bel dì di maggio[c]. FEDORA[b] — Amor ti vieta; Mia madre, la mia vecchia madre. *Mascagni:* CAVALLERIA RUSTICANA[c] — O Lola; Mamma, quel vino è generoso. *Leoncavallo:* PAGLIACCI — Recitar! ... Vesti la giubba[c]; Per la morte! smettiamo ... No, Pagliaccio non son[a] (with Grace Anthony). ZAZA — E un riso gentil[c]. *Puccini:* LA BOHEME — Che gelida manina[b]. TOSCA — E lucevan le stelle[b].

 1h 8m AAD 3/93 ▲

Here is one of the most fascinating of singers. He can also be one of the most thrilling, his voice having at its best a beauty unlike any other, his art noble in breadth of phrase and concentration of tone. It also has to be said that his records hardly make easy or restful listening, but what at first may even repel soon becomes compulsive, the intensity of expression and individuality of timbre impressing themselves upon the memory with extraordinary vividness. Martinelli's career was centred on the Metropolitan, New York, where he sang first at the height of the Caruso era, inheriting Caruso's more dramatic roles in 1921. This selection makes an unrepresentative start with "La donna è mobile", but the excerpts from *Il trovatore* and *La forza del destino* have the very essence of the man, masterly in his shaping and shading of recitative, or in the long curves of his melodic line and the tension of his utterance. There are also superb performances of solos from *Andrea Chénier* and *Pagliacci*, the involvement of his "No, Pagliaccio non son" unequalled before or since. These are recordings from 1926 and 1927, the period in which his vocal and artistic qualities were probably best matched. The transfers are fine apart from the song from Leoncavallo's *Zazà* which plays below pitch.

New review
OPERA ARIAS AND DUETS. Elisabeth Rethberg (sop) with various artists. Preiser Lebendige Vergangenheit mono 89051. From Odeon and Brunswick originals; recorded 1920-25.
L'africaine, Andrea Chénier, The bartered bride, La bohème, Carmen, Madama Butterfly, Le nozze di Figaro, Tosca, Die Zauberflöte and Der Zigeunerbaron; songs by Bizet, Mozart, Pataky and R. Strauss.

1h 11m AAD 7/94 ▲

Elisabeth Rethberg died in 1976, when little notice was taken of the passing of a singer once voted the world's most perfect. The year 1994 is the centenary of her birth, so this fine selection of her early recordings is well timed. The earliest catch her at the charming age of 26 (the voice settled, but still that of a young woman), and the last of them, made in 1925, find her just into her thirties, mature in timbre, feeling and artistry. It is doubtful whether a judicious listener would at any point cry "Ah, it's an Aida voice!", but Aida became the part for which she was most famous. In Countess Almaviva's first aria, her legato is the next thing to perfection; in Pamina's "Ach, ich fühl's" the head tones are beautifully in place, the portamentos finely judged, emotion always implicit in the singing. The duets with Richard Tauber include the music of Micaëla and Don José sung with unrivalled grace and intimacy, Rethberg shading off the end of her solo most elegantly, Tauber softening in his so as to welcome and not overwhelm the soprano's entry, and both singers phrasing like the consummate artists they were. The songs are equally delightful.

New review
OPERA ARIAS AND SONGS. Lucien Fugère (bar) with various artists. Symposium mono 1125. From French Columbia originals; recorded 1928-30.
La basoche, Le jongleur de Notre-Dame, L'ombre, Die Zauberflöte, Don Giovanni, Le roi malgré lui, Dinorah, Le val d'Andorre, Louise, Les saisons, Le medecin malgré lui, La rencontre imprévue, Le maître de chapelle; songs by Chaminade, Couperin, Henrion, Levadé and Widor.

1h 18m AAD 6/93 ▲

Dates to keep in mind: 1848, 1928, 1930, 1933 and 1935. On the first, Lucien Fugère was born, on the second he made the first of the records heard here, on the third he made the last;

in 1933 he gave his last operatic performance, and two years later he died. A little mental arithmetic establishes that he was 80 when he recorded (for example) the solos from Massenet's *Le jongleur de Notre-Dame*; having listened to them, one has to do the sum again, this time counting up on one's fingers to make sure, for otherwise his age would be scarcely credible. Actually, the recordings made at 80 are not the best; 81 was better, 82 best of all. The year 1930 brought the 'Grand Air' from Paër's *Le maître de chapelle*, which is Fugère's masterpiece. This enacts in brief a miniature opera on the subject of Cleopatra, and vocally it uses every trick in the book: an exercise of brilliant resource, performed with wit, elegance, technical skill and the infinite variety of Cleopatra herself. And the voice does sound even younger, even more assured here than in the first sessions, the acoustic being less boxy and allowing more room for expansion. The transfers are clear and natural.

New review

OPERA ARIAS AND SONGS. Amelita Galli-Curci (sop) with various artists. Conifer Happy Days mono CDHD201. From Victor originals; recorded 1917-29.
Arias from Don Pasquale, The Golden Cockerel, Lucia di Lammermoor, Rigoletto, Semiramide, La sonnambula, La traviata and Il trovatore; songs by Bishop, A. Scarlatti and Yradier.

Ih 10m ADD 3/94 ▲

New review

OPERA ARIAS AND SONGS. Amelita Galli-Curci (sop) with various artists. Romophone mono 81003-2. From Victor originals; recorded 1916-20.
Arias from Il barbiere di Siviglia, Dinorah, Don Pasquale, Lakmé, Lucia di Lammermoor, Manon Lescaut (Auber), Martha, Le nozze di Figaro, I puritani, Rigoletto, Roméo et Juliette, La sonnambula and La traviata; songs by Alvarez, Benedict, Bishop, Buzzi-Peccia, David, Delibes, Giordani, Grieg, Massenet, Proch, Samuels and Seppilli.

② **2h 39m ADD 3/94** ▲

These two issues complement each other very happily, the Romophone going up to 1920, the Conifer concentrating on later recordings, with an overlap of only three items. In *Gramophone* in 1923 the Editor wrote: "One of the most solid grounds I have for facing the coming of old age with equanimity is the reasonable hope that I shall spend it listening to as many records of *la diva* Galli-Curci's voice as there are of Caruso's". The purity of her voice was certainly a delight; it was at that time firm and even throughout its wide compass; and her fluency in scalework, precision in staccato, and ability to swell and diminish on a long-held high note were exceptional. She was an artist who could phrase and nuance exquisitely and who, within the boundaries of a more or less pretty joy and sadness, could be quite poignantly expressive. In the years of her greatest fame and success, roughly the decade from 1916 to 1926, her operatic repertoire was the standard one for the 'coloratura' soprano, and it is well represented by her records. What they also have, making them treasurable beyond anything that such a summary might suggest, is a personal flavour, a caress, a way of making words sound like water purling gently on a summer's afternoon, a dreaminess that can awaken to fun and affection though she could also flatten rather sadly in pitch. For completeness and also for the fine quality of the transfers many will want the Romophone. The Conifer selection is certainly a good one, including rarities such as the Scarlatti cantata (*Solitudini amene, apriche collinetti*), "Bel raggio" and "Ah, non giunge". On the whole, the early records have been transferred on this CD more enjoyably than the electricals.

OPERA ARIAS AND SONGS. Beniamino Gigli (ten) with various artists. Memoir Classics mono CDMOIR417. From HMV originals. Recorded 1921-39.
Arias from — L'AFRICAINE; ANDREA CHENIER; LA BOHEME; CAVALLERIA RUSTICANA; L'ELISIR D'AMORE; LA FORZA DEL DESTINO; MARTHA; MEFISTOFELE; LES PECHEURS DE PERLES; RIGOLETTO. *Songs by* **Bixio, Cottrau, De Curtis, Denza, Di Chiara and Toselli.**

Ih 5m AAD 6/93 ⁰p ▲

Of all the famous Italian tenors, Gigli was the one whose voice seemed most to embody the sweets of nature — the sunshine, the fruit filled "with ripeness to the core" and so forth. He sang as though for the love of it, though of course collecting a substantial fee too (and in fact rather than submit to the indignity of a reduction in salary he quit the Metropolitan in their financial crisis of 1932). The records included here come from the years either side of that date and show him in his magnificent prime, the leading lyric-dramatic tenor of the world. The programme begins with his "Che gelida manina" of 1931, one of the top best-sellers in the HMV catalogues for many a year. His appeal lies not only in the sweetness, the easy power and ring of his well-rounded voice, but also in a personality that is almost winsomely human: a chubby chuckle, a boyish pleading, lightens up the 'face' of his singing. There is fervour in his *Andrea Chénier*, good humour in his "La donna è mobile", and appropriate bad temper in his *Cavalleria rusticana* duet with the formidable Dusolina Giannini. Then, in a selection of shamelessly tuneful Italian songs, he woos beguilingly, sometimes in the honeyed half-voice, ultimately with the thrilling vibrancy of his *fortissimo*. Two of the items (from *Mefistofele* and *La forza del destino*) are reproduced a semitone too high, but in general the quality of transfers is fine and the selection excellent. A superb performance.

OPERA ARIAS AND SONGS. Maria Ivogün (sop); [a]**Michael Raucheisen** (pf); [b]**orchestra;** [c]**Berlin State Opera Orchestra/Leo Blech.** Nimbus Prima Voce NI7832. *Bishop:* Lo, here the gentle lark[b] (from Brunswick 10174, 11/25). *Handel:* L'allegro, il penseroso ed il moderato, HWV55 — Sweet bird[b] (Polydor 85313, recorded 1925). *Donizetti:* DON PASQUALE — Ah! un foco insolito[b] (85302, recorded 1924). LUCIA DI LAMMERMOOR — Ardon gl'incensi[b] (Odeon 76977, recorded 1917). *Rossini:* Il BARBIERE DI SIVIGLIA — Una voce poco fa[b] (85309, recorded 1925). *Verdi:* LA TRAVIATA — E strano ... Ah, fors'è lui ... Sempre libera[b] (sung in German. 76982/3, recorded 1916). *Chopin:* Nocturne in E flat major, Op. 9 No. 2[b] (arr. sop/orch. 76975). *Meyerbeer:* LES HUGUENOTS — Une dame noble et sage[b] (German. 76997). *Nicolai:* DIE LUSTIGEN WEIBER VON WINDSOR — Nun eilt herbei[b] (76811. All recorded 1917). *Schubert:* Ständchen (Horch! Horch! die Lerch), D899[b]. Winterreise, D911 — Die Post[b] (both from Brunswick 15075, 9/24). *J. Strauss II:* Frühlingsstimmen, Op. 410[b] (85313, recorded 1924). G'schichten aus dem Wienerwald, Op. 325[b] (10174). An die schönen, blauen Donau, Op. 314[c]. DIE FLEDERMAUS — Klänge der Heimat[c] (HMV DB4412, 6/34). *Kreisler:* Liebesfreud[b] (Brunswick 50050, 12/24). *Anonymous:* O du liebs Angeli[a]. Z'Lauterbach han i'mein Strumpf verlor'n[a]. Gsätzli. Maria auf dem Berge[a] (all from HMV DA4402, 6/33).

⠶ Ih 18m ADD 8/92 ⓠ |P ▲

Somewhere or other, after much searching of the memory, ransacking of the catalogues and phoning around among connoisseurs, it might be possible to discover a more delightful example of the coloratura's art than that of Maria Ivogün as displayed in her recording of Kreisler's *Liebesfreud*, made in 1924: if so, one such does not spring to mind now. With the most pure and delicate of tones, nothing shrill or piercing about them, she sings way above a normal mortal's reach, ease and accuracy in the purely technical feats going along with a lilt and feeling for the idiomatic give-and-take of waltz rhythm that are a joy musically. Turn to Handel, with the solo from *Il penseroso*, and the same art is put to lovely use in a different idiom. Her *Traviata* aria has warmth and spontaneity; her Frau Fluth in *Die lustigen Weiber von Windsor* is a woman of charm and energy; and the 1934 recording of the Czardas in *Die Fledermaus* shines as bright in spirit as in clarity of timbre. From the same period comes the set of four songs, Swiss and German, that show most touchingly her command of the art to be simple. This is an admirable introduction to a most lovely singer, and it represents the Prima Voce series at its best.

OPERA ARIAS AND SONGS. Adelina Patti (sop); various artists. Nimbus Prima Voce mono NI7840/1. Recorded 1902-28.
Mario Ancona, Mattia Battistini, Emma Calvé, Fernando De Lucia, Edouard de Reszke, Emma Eames, Lucien Fugère, Wilhelm Hesch, Lilli Lehmann, Félia Litvinne, Francesco Marconi, Victor Maurel, Dame Nellie Melba, Lillian Nordica, Adelina Patti, Pol Plançon, Maurice Renaud, Sir Charlles Santley, Marcella Sembrich, Francesco Tamagno and Francesco Viñas.

⠶ ② 2h ADD 7/93 ▲

This is a 'historical' issue for straightforward enjoyment. Although the originals were made in the very earliest years of recording, they are reproduced here with a vividness that calls for very little in the way of 'creative listening', making allowances and so forth. It starts in party mood with the first Falstaff of all, Victor Maurel, singing to a bunch of cronies in the studio of 1907 the "Quand'ero paggio" which he sang at La Scala in the première of 1893. They cheer and call for an encore, which he gives them, then again (and best of all) this time in French. The record has been transferred many times to LP and CD, but never has it been so easy for the listener to 'see' it and feel part of it. The magnificent bass Pol Plançon follows with King Philip's solo from *Don Carlos*, beautifully even in production and deeply absorbed in the character and his emotions. The hauntingly pure, well-rounded soprano of Emma Eames in Tosti's *Dopo* (a real passion there despite its restraint), and then the miraculously spry and elegant 80-year-old Lucien Fugère lead to the first of the Patti records: the one her husband thought unladylike and asked to be withdrawn from the catalogue, *La calesera*, and the most joyous she ever made. Tamagno, Melba, Nordica, Renaud: they are all here, and on thrillingly good form. The copies of these rarities have been selected with great care, and, while other transfers have, technically, got more "off" the record, none has captured the beauty of the voices more convincingly.

OPERA CHORUSES. Chorus and Orchestra of the Royal Opera House, Covent Garden/Bernard Haitink. EMI CDC7 49849-2. Texts and translations included.
Beethoven: FIDELIO — O welche Lust (with John Mark Ainsley, ten; Alistair Miles, bar).
Berlioz: LES TROYENS — Royal Hunt and Storm. **Bizet:** CARMEN — Les voici! voici la quadrille! (Haberdashers' Aske's School Boys' Choir). **Donizetti:** LUCIA DI LAMMERMOOR — Per te d'immenso giubilo; D'immenso giubilo. **Giordano:** ANDREA CHENIER — O pastorelle, addio. **Mascagni:** CAVALLERIA RUSTICANA — Easter Hymn (Helen Field, sop). **Verdi:** AIDA — Gloria all'Egitto. NABUCCO — Va, pensiero. OTELLO — Fuoco di gioia. IL TROVATORE — Vedi! le fosche notturne spoglie. **Wagner:** LOHENGRIN — Treulich geführt. **Weber:** DER FREISCHUTZ — Was gleicht wohl auf Erden dem Jägervergnügen.

Ih Im DDD 12/89   P Ⓑ

After an evening at the opera it is usually the arias and soloists that come in for remark and discussion, but quite often what actually brings the greatest enjoyment and remains in the memory as most vivid and colourful is a chorus or a passage of ensemble. Composers tend to reserve their broadest tunes for the chorus, and in this selection we have the Easter Hymn, Anvil Chorus, Wedding March and Chorus of Hebrews, all among the world's best. Less obvious, and a delight in context (both here and in the opera), is the Pastoral from *Andrea Chenier*. Altogether deeper in feeling, and most moving of all, is the Prisoners' Chorus from *Fidelio*. In each of the excerpts, the Covent Garden Chorus (so often overlooked in reviews) show themselves fully worthy of the attention bestowed on them. Haitink, never insensitive, sometimes misses the full effect of a climax, but the Orchestra are in fine form and give a particularly good account of the "Royal Hunt and Storm" from *The Trojans*. For the general listener it is a disc that will give pleasure in itself and in stirring up a determination to go and see the operas again; for the Covent Garden *habitué* it will bring back memories, almost as if one were turning the pages of a picture-book, as the scenes and evenings return vividly to mind.

OPERA RECITAL. Ezio Pinza (bass) with various artists. Pearl mono GEMMCD9306.
Verdi: AIDA — Mortal diletto ai Numi (Metropolitan Opera Orchestra, New York/Giulio Setti); Nume custode vindici (Giovanni Martinelli, ten; Metropolitan Opera Chorus and Orchestra. Both from Victor 8111). ERNANI — Che mai vegg'io ... Infelice! (orchestra/Rosario Bourdon. HMV DB1750). DON CARLOS — Dormiro sol nel manto mio regal (orchestra/Bourdon. DB1087, 3/28). I VESPRI SICILIANI — O patria ... O tu Palermo (orchestra/Bourdon. DB1087). Messa da Requiem — Confutatis maledictis (orchestra/Bourdon. HMV AGSB103). SIMON BOCCANEGRA — A te l'estremo addio ... Il lacerato spirito (chorus and orchestra/Carlo Sabajno. DB699, 6/24). IL TROVATORE — Di due figli ... Abbietta zingara (chorus and orchestra/Sabajno. DB828). **Mozart:** DON GIOVANNI — Finch'han dal vino; Deh vieni alla finestra (orchestra/Bourdon. HMV DA1134, 10/31). DIE ZAUBERFLOTE — O Isis und Osiris (sung in Italian. Orchestra/Bourdon. DB1088, 3/28). **Meyerbeer:** ROBERT LE DIABLE — Nonnes, qui reposez (sung in Italian. Orchestra/Bourdon. DB1088). **Thomas:** LE CAID — Enfant chéri ... Le tambour-major (orchestra/Bourdon. DB1086, 3/28). **Gounod:** FAUST — Le veau d'or (Metropolitan Opera Chorus and Orchestra/Setti. DA1108, 9/38). **Bellini:** NORMA — Ah del tebro (Chorus and orchestra/Sabajno. DA566, 5/25). I PURITANI — Cinta di fiori (Orchestra/Sabajno. HMV VB70, 6/52). **Donizetti:** LA FAVORITA — Splendon più belle (orchestra. DA708). LUCIA DI LAMMERMOOR — Dalle stanze (chorus and orchestra/Sabajno. VB70). **Boito:** MEFISTOFELE — Ave Signor (orchestra.

DB829); Son lo spirito (orchestra/Sabajno. DA567). *Halévy:* LA JUIVE — Si la rigeur (sung in Italian. Orchestra/Sabajno. DB698, 11/24); Vous qui du Dieu vivant (sung in Italian. Orchestra. DB829).

Ih 16m AAD 2/89 ⓠ P ▲

The first half of the century brought forth three fine Italian basses: Nazzareno de Angelis, Tancredi Pasero and Ezio Pinza. Of these it was Pinza who gained the greatest international fame, partly through the beauty of his voice and partly through the strength and vividness of his personality. Eventually it was the musical *South Pacific* that made him a household name, but his success here owed much in turn to the fact that he came to the Broadway show from the Metropolitan Opera House where he was leading bass from his house début in 1926 until 1948. Before coming to America he had sung at La Scala under Toscanini, his repertoire then ranging from the role of Pimen in *Boris Godunov* (he was later to sing Boris himself) to King Mark in *Tristan und Isolde*. At the Metropolitan he sang mostly in the Italian and French operas, with an increasing interest in Mozart, whose Don Giovanni became his most famous role, which he sung also at Salzburg and Covent Garden. This is represented in the present selection (called "The Golden Years") by two short solos, which may well be found to be the least satisfying of the performances. Sarastro's "O Isis und Osiris", on the other hand, sung in Italian as "Possenti numi" is magnificent in the sonority of tone and dignity of style. There is also some superb Verdi, above all the aria from *Ernani*, sung with deep feeling and subtlety of shading, and the "Confutatis" from the *Requiem*, ideally smooth, resonant and authoritative. In these and the earlier pre-electrical recordings Pinza shows clearly why he is so widely regarded as having been the supreme *basso cantate* of the century.

New review

OPERETTA ARIAS. Barbara Hendricks (sop); [a]**Claire Henry** (sop); [a]**Shirley Minty**, [a]**Linda Richardson** (mezs); [b]**Gino Quilico** (bar); [c]**Ambrosian Singers**; **Philharmonia Orchestra/Lawrence Foster.** EMI CDC7 54626-2. Texts and French translations included. *Lehár:* Giuditta — Meine Lippen, sie küssen so heiss. Die lustige Witwe — Es lebt eine Vilja, ein Waldmägdelein. Friederike — Warum hast du mich wachgeküsst? *Stolz:* Der Favorit — Du sollst der Kaiser meiner Seele sein. *Zeller:* Der Vogelhändler — Schenkt man sich Rosen in Tirol. *J. Strauss II:* Die Fledermaus — Klänge der Heimat. *Messager:* Madame Chrysan-thème — Le jour sous le soleil béni. L'amour masqué — J'ai deux amants. *Offenbach:* La vie parisienne — Autrefois plus d'un amant. Le voyage dans la lune — Monde charmant. *Sullivan:* The Pirates of Penzance — Poor wandering one[c]. The Mikado — The sun, whose rays are all ablaze. *Romberg:* The New Moon — One kiss[c]; Lover, come back to me[b]. *F. Loewe:* My Fair Lady — I could have danced all night[a]. *Herbert:* Naughty Marietta — Ah! sweet mystery of life; Italian Street Song[c].

Ih IIm DDD 8/93 ⓠ P

This is the first time a singer has sought to encompass such a wide cross-section of the international operetta repertoire in original languages on a single disc. And what a delight it proves to be! To be sure, Hendricks is hardly right for the tempestuous Giuditta, and her *Fledermaus* Csárdás ends with a less than perfect final note. But in the more lyrical, more tender numbers, and also in the cuter ones, she is a joy. The generally slow tempos adopted help give a number such as Stolz's "Du sollst der Kaiser meiner Seele sein" a delightfully dreamy quality. Then, when one imagines that nothing could top the charm and elegance of Lehár's "Warum hast du mich wachgeküsst?", along comes Hendricks's effortlessly characterful singing of the glovemaker's song from *La vie parisienne*. Perhaps even better is Messager's "J'ai deux amants", with the pouting lips almost audible, and an irresistible laugh at the end. This is the first recording of Offenbach's *Voyage dans la lune* waltz song, and the *Fledermaus* Csárdás includes the 16 bars usually omitted. In addition, "I could have danced all night" has the servants' interjections, and "Lover come back to me" offers the introductory incidental music as well as the baritone's entrance. In nearly 40 years of listening your writer has found no recital more captivating.

New review

RCA/MET 100 SINGERS, 100 YEARS. RCA Victor 09026 61580-2. Recorded 1903-80. From RL85177.

Singers include **Licia Albanese, Carlo Bergonzi, Jussi Björling, Grace Bumbry, Montserrat Caballé, Enrico Caruso, Giuseppe di Stefano, Plácido Domingo, Kirsten Flagstad, Mirella Freni, Amelita Galli-Curci, Beniamino Gigli, Marilyn Horne, Alfredo Kraus, John McCormack, Dame Nellie Melba, Lauritz Melchior, Sherrill Milnes, Birgit Nilsson, Ezio Pinza, Lily Pons, Rosa Ponselle, Leontyne Price, Renata Scotto, Dame Kiri Te Kanawa, Luisa Tetrazzini, Richard Tucker, Shirley Verrett** and **Leonard Warren.**

⑥ 6h 30m ADD 4/94 ⑨ₚ ▲

"100 years of operatic brilliance ... World's greatest voices ... Deluxe commemorative book ... Colourful wall chart." These are the headings on the back of the big oblong box (very handsome but making havoc of the storage system). As to the performances: with voice, virtuosity and vividness of character, there is a nice symmetry in Schumann-Heink's *Le Prophète*, magnificently clear despite its age near the start, and Marilyn Horne's *L'italiana in Algeri* near the end. Among the early singers Plançon is superb, the gay smile of his serenading Mephistopheles (Berlioz's) cheekily accompanying the impeccably aristocratic manners of his singing. Johanna Gadski's Senta, Alma Gluck's Nedda, McCormack's Alfredo, these are distinct successes. Less expected is the duet from *Boris Godunov* by Paul Althouse, the Met's first Dmitri, and the too rarely remembered Margarethe Arndt-Ober. Other duets lovely to hear again are Sachs and Eva's (Act 3) by Schorr and Rethberg, and later Bumbry and Domingo opulent in Act 4 of *Aida*. The first voice to give that sudden thrill which one always hopes for in these collections is Lauri-Volpi's in *Norma*; in modern times Bergonzi's in *Macbeth*. There are fine examples of Tibbett (*The King's Henchman*), Warren (*Faust*), Di Stefano (*Bohème*) and Björling (*Manon Lescaut*). Less happily represented are Corelli (*Carmen*), Kraus ("La donna è mobile"), Pinza (Don Giovanni's Serenade) and Caruso (*La Juive*). This is a valuable anthology: pick one track before lunch and another after dinner, and the day's pleasure will be enhanced.

New review

RUSSIAN OPERA CHORUSES. Bolshoi Theatre Chorus and Symphony Orchestra/ Alexander Lazarev. Erato 4509-91723-2.
Rimsky-Korsakov: Snow Maiden — Carnival procession; Chorus of blind psalterists; Song of the Grain. Mlada — Procession of the Nobles. The Tsar's Bride — Hop-Pickers' Chorus. Christmas Eve — Koliadka. Invisible city of Kitezh — The disaster is approaching. *Glinka:* A Life for the Tsar — Introduction, Polonaise and final chorus. *Mussorgsky:* Boris Godunov — Kromy Forest scene. *Borodin:* Prince Igor — Be firm, Countess; Villagers' Chorus; Polovtsian Dances.

lh 5m DDD 5/94

Secretly, let's face it — or is this one of those heresies with which the guilty soul has to live companionless? — the moments in performances of Russian opera when the heart leaps up and gives a naïve little cry of "Oh, I *am* enjoying this!" tend to occur during the choruses. For one thing, they are often the most Russian part of it, having a basis of folk-song and bringing out of the voices something of the national character. More elemental and elementary, perhaps, is their colourfulness. All the choruses on this record are rich in colouring. Some (*Mlada* and the finale of *A Life for the Tsar*, for instance) are choruses of rejoicing; others (the psalterists in *Snow Maiden*, the *Christmas Eve* "Koliadka" carol) are religious; and it is good to have, for stiffening, the communal panic of the *Invisible city of Kitezh* and the Revolutionary scene in *Boris Godunov*. As for performance, chorus and orchestra are fine individually, and it is only this wretched habit in modern times of depriving choirs of any real immediacy of presence that limits enjoyment. The "Polovtsian Dances" bring the disc to a splendid conclusion.

HAROLD WAYNE COLLECTION, Volume 8. **Suzanne Adams, Emma Calvé** (sops)); **Antonio Scotti, Maurice Renaud** (bars); **Anton van Rooy** (bass-bar); **Pol Plançon** (bass); **Sir Landon Ronald** (pf). Symposium mono 1100. From G&T originals. Recorded in 1902 with piano accompaniment.
Suzanne Adams — excerpts from Faust and Roméo et Juliette; songs by Stern, Vidal and Bishop. **Emma Calvé** — Carmen and Cavalleria rusticana. **Scotti** — Méssaline, Don Giovanni, Faust, Carmen and Falstaff; songs by Rotoli and Tosti. **Maurice Renaud** — Tannhäuser; song by Holmès. **Anton Van Rooy** — Die Walküre, Die Meistersinger von Nürnberg, Tannhäuser

and Das Rheingold. **Pol Plançon** — Philémon et Baucis, Roméo et Juliette, Le caïd and Les huguenots; songs by J-B. Faure and Godard.

♪♪ 1h 19m AAD 3/93 ▲

Though this is the eighth volume of a remarkable series, it is probably the first that can be recommended with assurance to a wider public than those listeners who have a specialized interest in the singers recorded during the early years of the gramophone. Those on the present disc were all made in London in 1902: they were the 'London Reds', beloved of collectors and now worth a small fortune. The first likely surprise for a newcomer is how vividly the voices come through. The great French bass Pol Plançon is heard in the opening tracks, and the immediacy and naturalness of reproduction are often astonishing. So too is the singing, with sonority and refinement, superb fluency of scales and triplets, a brilliantly articulated trill, the well-bound evenness of cello tone, and a lively sense of fun. Not all are as satisfyingly caught as Plançon: the famous Carmen of the time, Emma Calvé, proves more elusive, though her little asides and exclamations are entertaining. Harold Wayne is the owner of one of the world's finest private collections, and his generosity has allowed these rarities to become public property. It is an opportunity to gain a privileged glimpse of another age and of singers who are far too special, both as voices and artists, to be merely forgotten.

Films and Show Music

Suggested listening ...

BIG WAR THEMES. **Jarre:** Lawrence of Arabia. Is Paris Burning?. **Tiomkin:** The Guns of Navarone. **Goodwin:** Battle of Britain. Where Eagles Dare. 633 Squadron. **Coates:** The Dam Busters — march. Eighth Army march. **Anka:** The Longest Day. **E. Bernstein:** The Great Escape. **Rózsa:** The Green Berets. **Myers:** The Deer Hunter — Cavatina. **Cobert:** The Winds of War. **Farnon:** Colditz. **Parker:** Sink the Bismark. **Rodgers:** Victory at Sea — excerpts. **King:** We'll Meet Again. **Addison:** Reach for the Sky. **Geoff Love and His Orchestra.** Compacts for Pleasure CC211.

CAPTAIN BLOOD: CLASSIC FILM SCORES FOR ERROL FLYNN. **Steiner:** The Adventures of Don Juan — Suite. They Died With Their Boots On — Suite. Dodge City — Suite. **Korngold:** The Sea Hawk — Suite[a]. Captain Blood — Ship in the night. The Adventures of Robin Hood — Suite. **Waxman:** Objective, Burma! — Parachute drop. **Friedhofer:** The Sun Also Rises — Prologue; The lights of Paris. [a]**Ambrosian Singers; National Philharmonic Orchestra/Charles Gerhardt.** RCA Victor GD80912 (11/91).

CASABLANCA: CLASSIC FILM SCORES FOR HUMPHREY BOGART. **Steiner:** Casablanca — Suite. Passage to Marseille — Rescue at sea. The Treasure of the Sierra Madre — Suite. The Big Sleep — Love Themes. The Caine Mutiny — March. Virginia City — Stagecoach; Love scene. Key Largo — Suite. **Waxman:** To Have and Have Not — Main Title. The Two Mrs Carrolls — Suite. **Hollander:** Sabrina — Main Title. **Young:** The Left Hand of God — Love Theme. **Rózsa:** Sahara — Main Title. **National Philharmonic Orchestra/Charles Gerhardt.** RCA Victor GD80422 (10/90).

CLASSIC BRITISH FILM MUSIC. **Vaughan Williams:** Coastal Command — Suite. **Easdale:** The Red Shoes — Ballet. **Schurmann:** Attack and celebration. **Bliss:** Conquest of the Air — Suite. **Philharmonia Orchestra/Kenneth Alwyn.** Silva Screen FILMCD713.

CLASSIC FILM SCORES FOR BETTE DAVIS. **Steiner:** Now, Voyager — It can't be wrong. Dark Victory — excerpts. A Stolen Life — Main Title. In This Our Life — Suite. Jezebel — waltz. Beyond the Forest — Suite. The Letter — Main Title. All This and Heaven Too — Suite. **Korngold:** The Private Lives of Elizabeth and Essex — Elizabeth. Juarez — Carlotta. **Waxman.** Mr Skeffington — Forsaken. **Newman:** All About Eve — Main Title. **National Philharmonic Orchestra/Charles Gerhardt.** RCA Victor GD80183 (3/90).

GREAT WESTERN THEMES. *Moross:* The Big Country. Wagon Train. *Morricone:* A Fistful of Dollars. For a Few Dollars More. The Good, the Bad and the Ugly. Once Upon a Time in the West. *Young:* Shane — The call of the faraway hills. *Newman:* How the West Was Won. *Tiomkin:* The Alamo — The green leaves of summer. Gunfight at the OK Corral. High Noon. Rawhide. *E. Bernstein:* The Magnificent Seven. True Grit. *Fielding:* The Wild Bunch. *Livingston:* Cat Ballou. *Faith:* The Virginian. *Buttolph:* Maverick. *Darby/Gertz:* The Legend of Jesse James. *Bacharach:* The Man who Shot Liberty Valance. *Rose:* Hombre. *Duning:* The Big Valley. *Mockridge:* Laramie. *Spencer:* Gunsmoke. **Geoff Love and His Orchestra.** Compacts for Pleasure CC204.

A HISTORY OF HITCHCOCK: DIAL M FOR MURDER. *Gounod:* Funeral March of the Marionette. *Waxman:* Rebecca — Suite; Suspicion — excerpts. *Rózsa:* Spellbound — Concerto for Orchestra. *Addinsell:* Under Capricorn — Suite. *Tiomkin:* Dial M for Murder — Suite. *Herrmann:* Vertigo; North by Northwest; Psycho; Marnie — excerpts. *Jarre:* Topaz — March. *Goodwin:* Frenzy — London Theme. **City of Prague Philharmonic Orchestra/Paul Bateman.** Silva Screen FILMCD137 (3/94).

HOLLYWOOD DREAMS. *Schoenberg:* Fanfare for the Hollywood Bowl. *Rodgers:* Carousel — Waltz. *Steiner:* Gone with the Wind — Main Title. *Stravinsky:* The Firebird — Lullaby; Finale. *Newman:* 20th Century-Fox fanfare. Street scene. *Waxman:* A Place in the Sun — suite. *Bernstein:* On the Waterfront — Love Theme. *Arlen/Stothart:* The Wizard of Oz — Suite. *Prokofiev:* Semyon Kotko — Southern night. *Korngold:* The Adventures of Robin Hood — excerpts. *Gore:* Defending Your Life — finale. *Barry:* Dances with Wolves — Theme. *Williams:* ET — Flying. **Hollywood Bowl Orchestra/John Mauceri.** Philips 432 109-2PH.

Marc Minkowski

Sir Charles Mackerras

Anne-Sophie Mutter

Riccardo Muti

Information

Gramophone Blue riband dealers

The *Gramophone Blue riband* dealer scheme is designed to identify record dealers throughout the UK who can be relied upon to provide a certain level of classical record availability and service to customers.

The dealers listed below are all *Gramophone Blue riband* dealers and are identified as follows:

*S*R *Gramophone Blue riband* specialist dealers will be those recognized as having extensive product and specialist musical knowledge. They will offer a superior service and a true depth and comprehensiveness of stock. Many such dealers will be identified by record companies and distributors and endorsed by *Gramophone* readers as being qualified for this category.

*C*R *Gramophone Blue riband* classical dealers will carrry a worthwhile stock of classical recordings together with additional items such as publications, videos, accessories, etc. Staff expertise should be considerable, complementing an overall specific commitment to classical recordings.

*B*R *Gramophone Blue riband* dealers. A fundamental requirement is that the dealer carries a stock of classical recordings and provides a good standard of service. Although the level of commitment to classical recordings may be modest, a desire and ability to order recordings not stocked is obligatory.

*M*R *Gramophone Blue riband* mail order dealers (appearing as a group at the end of this list) will be able to offer customers an extensive and efficient service by post. A number of dealers will fall into the above categories but will also offer a mail order service. Once again, the skill and standing of this type of dealer will be recognized by the classical record industry as a whole.

London

Les Aldrich Music Shop *C*R
98 Fortis Green Road, Muswell Hill, London N10 3BH.
081-883 5631

Arcade Music *S*R
13-14 Grand Arcade, Tally-Ho Corner, Finchley, London N12 0EH. 081-445 6369

Bush Books & Records *B*R
113 Shepherds Bush Centre, Shepherds Bush, London W14 9HP. 081-740 5342

Caruso & Co *S*R
10 Charlotte Place, London W1P 1AP. 071-636 6622

The CD Shop *B*R
206 Field End Road, Eastcote, Pinner, Middlesex HA5 1RD. 081-866 0017

Classic CDs *S*R
72 Heath Street, London NW3 1DN. 071-431 5161

Classical Discs *S*R
38 Great Queen Street, London WC2R JAA. 071-430 0240

Covent Garden Records *S*R
84 Charing Cross Road, London WC2H 0JA. 071-379 7427

Dillons The Bookstore *S*R
82 Gower Street, London WC1E 6EQ. 071-636 1577

Earfriend *B*R
8 Broad Street, Teddington, Middlesex TW11 8RF. 081-977 0348

Farringdons Records *S*R
64-72 Leadenhall Market, London EC3V 1LT. 071-623 9605

Farringdons Records *S*R
Royal Festival Hall, South Bank Centre, London SE1 8XX. 071-620 0198

Grahams Hi-Fi *B*R
Canonbury Yard, 190a New North Road, London N1 7BS. 071-226 5500

Harrods Sound and Vision *S*R
Harrods, Brompton Road, Knightsbridge, London SW1X 7XL. 071-730 1234 ext. 2185

Thomas Heinitz Ltd, Music in the Home *S*R
35 Moscow Road, Bayswater, London W2 4AH. 071-229 2077

Herga Music *B*R
2a High Street, Wealdstone, Harrow, Middlesex HA3 7AA. 081-861 1590

HMV *C*R
2 Waterglade Centre, Ealing Broadway, London W5 2ND. 081-566 2590

HMV *S*R
150 Oxford Street, London W1N 0DJ. 071-631 3423

HMV *S*R
363 Oxford Street, London W1R 2BJ. 071-629 1240

HMV *C*R
70 George Street, Richmond, Surrey TW9 1HE. 081-940 9880

HMV *B*R
Trocadero, 18 Coventry Street, London WC1. 071-439 0447

Harold Moores Records *S*R
2 Great Marlborough Street, London W1V 1DE. 071-437 1576 / 439 9206

Music and Video Club *C*R
132 Uxbridge Road, Ealing, London W13 8QT. 081-566 3560

Music and Video Club *C*R
344-348 Station Road, Harrow, Middlesex HA1 2DR. 081-861 5344

Music and Video Club *C*R
119-121 Brent Street, Hendon, London NW4 2HH. 081-203 9888

Music Discount Centre *S*R
1 Creed Lane, St Pauls, London EC4V 5BR. 071-489 8077
Mail order 071-236 0060

Music Discount Centre *S*R
29 Rathbone Place, London W1P 1AD. 071-637 4700

Music Discount Warehouse *S*R
33-34 Rathbone Place, London W1P 1AD. 071-636 5850

Music Discount Centre *S*R
46 Thurloe Street, South Kensington, London SW7 2LT. 071-584 3338

Music Discount Centre *S*R
437 The Strand, London WC2R 0RN. 071-240 2157

Music Discount Centre at ENO *S*R
31 St Martin's Lane, London WC2N 4ER. 071-240 0270

Royal Opera House Shop *S*R
Royal Opera House Box Office, Floral Street, Covent Garden, London WC2E 9DD. 071-240 1200 ext. 343

Simply Classics *C*R
23 Old Brompton Road, Kensington, London SW7 3HZ. 071-225 2111

WH Smith Ltd *C*R
Brent Cross Shopping Centre, Brent Cross, London NW4 3FB. 081-202 4226

Templar Records *S*R
Leicester Square Bookstore Ltd, 9A Irving Street, London WC2H 7AT. 071-930 3579

Tower Records *S*R
62-64 Kensington High Street, Kensington, London W8 4PL. 071-938 3511

Tower Records *S*R
1 Piccadilly Circus, London W1R 8TR. 071-439 2500

Tower Records *C*R
Unit 001B Whiteleys of Bayswater, Queensway, London W2 4YR. 071-229 4550

Trumps Records and Tapes Ltd B℞
28 Station Lane, Hornchurch, Essex RM12 6NJ. *0708 446810*
Turntable B℞
40 Station Road, North Chingford, London E4 7BE.
081-524 3917
Virgin Retail C℞
527 Oxford Street, London W1R 1DD. *071-491 8582*
Virgin Megastore S℞
14-16 Oxford Street, London W1R 7DD.
071-580 5822/071-631 1234
Wanda's Classics C℞
82a High Street, Wimbledon Village, London SW19 5EG.
081-946 3556

South East
Abbey Music Store B℞
7 Church Street, Romsey, Hampshire SO51 8BT.
0794 513149
Andys Records B℞
53-54 High Street, Chelmsford, Essex CM1 1DH.
0245 344800
Andys Records B℞
4 Longwyre Street, Colchester, Essex CO1 1LH. *0206 44334*
Bastow's Classics C℞
50a North Street, Chichester, West Sussex PO19 1MQ.
0243 533264
Blumlein's S℞
9a Dragon Street, Petersfield, Hampshire GU31 4JN.
0730 266605
Brentwood Hi Fidelity Ltd S℞
2 Ingrave Road, Brentwood, Essex CM15 8AT. *0277 221210*
Broadway Classical C℞
148 The Broadway, Leigh-on-Sea, Essex SS9 1AA.
0702 711249
Camden Classics S℞
5 Grosvenor Road, Tunbridge Wells, Kent TN1 2AH.
0892 515705
Camulo's Classics S℞
49 Crouch Street, Colchester, Essex CO3 3EN. *0206 369310*
Caruso's C℞
3 Upper Brook Street, Winchester, Hampshire. *0962 842383*
Chew & Osborne C℞
70 South Street, Bishop's Stortford, Hertfordshire CM23 3AZ.
0279 656401
Chew & Osborne C℞
148 High Street, Epping, Essex CM16 4AG. *0992 574242*
Chew & Osborne C℞
26 King Street, Saffron Walden, Essex CB10 1ES.
0799 523728
Classical Longplayer S℞
31 Duke Street, Brighton, East Sussex BN1 1AG.
0273 329534
Classical Longplayer S℞
6 St Peter's Street, Canterbury, Kent CT1 2AT. *0227 768888*
H & R Cloake Ltd S℞
29 High Street, Croydon, Surrey CR0 1QB. *081-681 3965
(Classical) / 081-686 1336 (Pop/Jazz)*
The Compact Discount Centre S℞
5 Headgate Buildings, Sir Isaacs Walk, Colchester, Essex
CO1 1JJ. *0206 762422*
James Dace & Son Ltd C℞
33 Moulsham Street, Chelmsford, Essex CM2 0HX.
0245 352133
Dillons The Bookstore S℞
Unit 59, The Bentall Centre, Kingston-upon-Thames, Surrey
KT1 1TR. *081-974 6811*
Dillons The Bookstore C℞
Units 23-24, Marlands Shopping Centre, Civic Centre Road,
Southampton, Hampshire SO1 0SJ. *0703 222255*
Discus Music B℞
14 Bridge Street, Bishops Stortford, Hertfordshire CM23 2JU.
0279 755861
Disques B℞
64 High Street, Heathfield, East Sussex TN21 8JB.
0435 866920

Fine Records C℞
32 George Street, Hove, East Sussex BN3 3YB. *0273 723345*
Fives B℞
22 Broadway, Leigh-on-Sea, Essex SS9 1NN. *0702 711629*
Grammar School Records B℞
The Old Grammar School, High Street, Rye, East Sussex
TM31 7JF. *0797 222752*
HMV C℞
61-62 Western Road, Brighton, East Sussex BN1 2HA.
0273 747221
HMV C℞
90-92 High Street, Bromley, Kent BR1 1EY. *081-313 0727*
HMV C℞
137 North End, Croydon, Surrey CR0 1TN. *081-686 5557*
HMV C℞
Units 11/12, 1st Floor, Bentalls Centre, Kingston-upon-
Thames, Surrey KT1 1TR. *081-974 8037*
Hollycourt Records C℞
10 Holly Court, Billericay, Essex CM12 9AP. *0277 633809*
Just Classics S℞
Unit 8, Royal Star Arcade, Maidstone, Kent. *0622 693670*
Langley's Records B℞
466 Walton Road, West Moseley, Surrey KT8 2JG.
081-979 3648
Michael's Classical Record Shop S℞
183 Montague Street, Worthing, East Sussex BN11 3DA.
0903 207478
Music and Video Club C℞
31-32 South Street, Chichester, West Sussex PO19 1EL.
0243 539137
Music and Video Club C℞
42-46 Crouch Street, Colchester, Essex CO3 3HN.
0206 577407
Music and Video Club C℞
Unit 2, 4 Worthing Road, Horsham, West Sussex RH13 7BP.
0403 275080
Music and Video Club C℞
309 High Street, Orpington, Kent BR6 0NN. *0689 891720*
The Music Centre C℞
Grove Hill Road, Tunbridge Wells, Kent TN1 1RZ.
0892 526659
Nicholls Bros Ltd C℞
82 High Street, Braintree, Essex CM7 7JP. *0376 326694*
Octave Recorded Music Specialist B℞
18 High Street, Lewes, East Sussex BN7 2LN. *0273 473611*
Orpheus S℞
27 Marmion Road, Southsea, Hampshire PO5 2AT.
0705 812397
Record Corner C℞
Pound Lane, Godalming, Surrey GU7 1BX. *0483 422006*
Record House C℞
84 Sycamore Road, Amersham, Buckinghamshire HP6 5DR.
0494 433311
Seaford Music S℞
24 Pevensey Road, Eastbourne, East Sussex BN21 3HP.
0323 732553
Second Spin B℞
14 Sackville Road, Bexhill-on-Sea, East Sussex TN34 3JL.
0424 210894
Showells B℞
94 High Street, West Wickham, Kent BR4 0NF. *081-777 5255*
WH Smith Ltd C℞
The Bentalls Centre, Kingston-upon-Thames, Surrey KT1 1TR.
081-549 7631
WH Smith Ltd C℞
54 The Harlequin, Watford, Hertfordshire WD1 2TF.
0923 211388
Sound Barrier S℞
24 Tunsgate, Guildford, Surrey GU1 3QS. *0483 300947*
C W A Ticehurst Ltd B℞
39 High Street, Heathfield, East Sussex TN21 8HU.
0435 862222
Tower Records S℞
17 Fife Road, Kingston-upon-Thames, Surrey KT1 1SB.
081-541 2500

Trax B℞
82 Station Road, Birchington-on-Sea, Kent CT7 9RA.
0843 848494

Trumps B℞
257 High Road, Loughton, Essex IG10 1AD. *081-508 4565*

The Turntable B℞
1 Corner House Parade, Ewell, Surrey KT17 1NX.
081-393 1881

Virgin Retail C℞
157-161 Western Road, Brighton, East Sussex BN1 2BB.
0273 323216

Virgin Retail C℞
Unit 18-22 Drummond Centre, Croydon, Surrey CR0 1TQ.
081-686 8386

Virgin Megastore S℞
93-105 Clarence Street, Kingston-upon-Thames, Surrey KT1
2QN. *081-549 9977*

Whitwams Ltd C℞
70 High Street, Winchester, Hampshire SO23 9DE.
0962 865253

Wisemans B℞
13 The Broadway, Portswood Road, Southampton, Hampshire
SO2 1WE. *0703 557705*

The Woods C℞
12 The Arcade, Bognor Regis, West Sussex PO21 1LH.
0243 827712

South West

Amadeus Classical Records S℞
7 Frankfort Gate, Plymouth, Devon PL1 1QA. *0752 671992*

Audiosonic (Gloucester) Ltd S℞
6 College Street, Gloucester, Gloucestershire GL1 2NE.
0452 302280

Bath Compact Discs S℞
11 Broad Street, Bath, Avon BA1 5LJ. *0225 464766*

Bristol Classical Discs S℞
59 Broad Street, Bristol, Avon BS1 2EJ. *0272 276536*

Cantabile C℞
4 Dove Lane, Sidmouth, Devon EX10 8AN. *0395 578517*

Cantata C℞
1 Truro Lanes, Kenwyn Street, Truro, Cornwall TR1 3DJ.
0872 222832

Classics C℞
Devon Square Gallery, 81 Queen Street, Newton Abbot,
Devon TQ12 2AU. *0626 55099*

The Collectors Room S℞
Suttons Music Centre, 3 Endless Street, Salisbury, Wiltshire
SP1 1DL. *0722 326153*

Compact Classics S℞
7-8 Criterion Arcade, Old Christchurch Road, Bournemouth,
Dorset BH1 1BU. *0202 558407*

Compact Disc Centre B℞
5 The Old Pannier Mall, High Street, Honiton, Devon
EX14 8LS. *0404 45693*

Compact Records & Tapes B℞
31 High Street, Falmouth, Cornwall TR11 2AD. *0326 311936*

The Cry of the Gulls B℞
4 Fore Street, Fowey, Cornwall PL23 1AQ. *0726 833838*

Dorchester Music B℞
15 High West Street, Dorchester, Dorset DT1 1JP.
0305 264977

The Dorset Music House C℞
The Green, Sherborne, Dorset DT9 3HX. *0935 812914*

Duck, Son & Pinker S℞
59 Bridge Street, Swindon, Wiltshire SN1 1BT. *0793 522220*

Duck, Son & Pinker C℞
51 Oxford Street, Weston-Super-Mare, Avon BS23 1TL.
0934 621174

Gillian Greig Music C℞
44 Kingston Road, Taunton, Somerset TA2 7SG.
0823 333317

Hancock & Monks Music Emporium S℞
65 Westbury Hill, Westbury-on-Trym, Bristol, Avon BS9
3AD. *0272 623251*

Hickies C℞
153 Friar Street, Reading, Berkshire RG1 1HG. *0734 575771*

HMV C℞
13-15 Stall Street, Bath, Avon BA1 1QE. *0225 466681*

HMV S℞
138-141 Friar Street, Reading, Berkshire RG1 1EY.
0734 560086

HMV B℞
16-17 Regents Street, Swindon, Wiltshire SN1 1JQ.
0793 420963

C Milsom and Son S℞
12 Northgate, Bath, Avon BA1 5AS. *0225 465975 ext 136*

Music and Video Club C℞
1 Sevendials, 43 Monmouth Street, Bath, Avon BA1 1EW.
0225 311206

Music and Video Club C℞
31-32 Westover Road, Bournemouth, Dorset BH1 2BL.
0202 311044

Music Masters C℞
28 Fore Street, Lostwithiel, Cornwall PL22 0BL.
0208 873525

John Oliver B℞
33 Fore Street, Redruth, Cornwall TR15 2AE. *0209 216494*

Opus S℞
The Gallery, Guildhall Centre, Exeter, Devon EX4 3HW.
0392 214044

Opus Music . C℞
21 Pydar Street, Truro, Cornwall TR1 2AY. *0872 223327*

Ottakar's C℞
15 Eastgate Street, Gloucester, Gloucestershire GL1 1NS.
0452 422464

Rayners Compact Disc C℞
84 Park Street, Bristol, Avon BS1 5LA. *0272 273936*

The Record Shop B℞
99 High Street, Crediton, Devon EX17 3LF. *0363 774299*

Record Select B℞
Polmorla Road, Wadebridge, Cornwall PL27 7NB.
0208 812625

Solo Music Ltd C℞
22a Market Arcade, Guildhall Shopping Centre, Exeter, Devon
EX4 3HW. *0392 496564*

Sounds Good S℞
26 Clarence Street, Cheltenham, Gloucestershire GL50 3NU.
0242 234604

Square Records B℞
14 High Street, Wimborne, Dorset BH21 1HU. *0202 883203*

Trax Music C℞
59 High Street, Christchurch, Dorset BH23 1AS.
0202 499629

Virgin Retail S℞
The Galleries, Union Gallery, Broadmead, Bristol, Avon BS1
3XD. *0272 297798*

Virgin Retail S℞
140 Armada Way, Plymouth, Devon PL1 1JB. *0752 254400*

Virgin Retail C℞
1-5 Oxford Road, Reading, Berkshire RG1 7QG.
0734 575222

Channel Islands

Seedee Jons C℞
4 Colomberie, St Helier, Jersey, Channel Islands JE2 4QA.
0534 67858

Sound Engineering Ltd C℞
6 Columberie, St Helier, Jersey, Channel Islands JE2 4QA.
0534 21735

Soundtrack B℞
Church Square, St Peter Port, Guernsey, Channel Islands.
0481 722178

Teleskill Ltd B℞
3-4 Market Street, St Peter Port, Guernsey, Channel Islands.
0481 722323

East Anglia

Amberstone Bookshop C℞
49 Upper Orwell Street, Ipswich, Suffolk IP4 1HP.
0473 250675

Andys Records B℞
90 St Johns Street, Bury St Edmonds, Suffolk IP33 1TZ.
0284 767502

Andys Records *B*℞
31-33 Fitzroy Street, Cambridge, Cambridgeshire B1 1ER.
0223 61038

Andys Records *B*℞
8 Buttermarket Centre, St Stephen's Lane, Ipswich, Suffolk
IP1 1DT. *0473 258933*

Andys Records *B*℞
14-16 Lower Goat Lane, Norwich, Norfolk NR2 1EL.
0603 617047

CMS Records *S*℞
1A All Saints' Passage, Cambridge, Cambridgeshire CB2 3LT.
0223 460818

Compact Music *C*℞
17 North Street, Sudbury, Suffolk CO10 6RB. *0787 881160*

Galleon Music *C*℞
High Street, Aldeburgh, Suffolk IP15 5AX. *0728 453298*

Garon Records *C*℞
70 King Street, Cambridge, Cambridgeshire CB1 1LN.
0223 62086

Heffers Sound *S*℞
19 Trinity Street, Cambridge, Cambridgeshire CB2 3NG.
0223 358351 ext.336

HMV *B*℞
23 Market Street, Cambridge, Cambridgeshire CB2 3NZ.
0223 322521

Millers Music Centre *S*℞
12 Sussex Street, Cambridge, Cambridgeshire CB1 1PW.
0223 354452

Prelude Records *S*℞
25b St Giles Street, Norwich, Norfolk NR2 1JN.
0603 628319

Virgin Retail *C*℞
Castle Mall, Castle Meadow, Norwich, Norfolk NR1 8DD.
0603 767376

Wells *B*℞
14 Queen Street, Southwold, Suffolk IP18 6EQ.
0502 723906

Words and Music *B*℞
3a Cumberland Street, Woodbridge, Suffolk IP12 4AH.
0394 383098

Midlands

Russell Acott *C*℞
124 High Street, Oxford, Oxfordshire OX1 4DE.
0865 241195

Andys Records *B*℞
37 Bridge Street, Peterborough, Cambridgeshire PE1 1HA.
0733 345252

Andys Records Ltd *B*℞
Unit 38, Waterside Centre, High Street, Lincoln, Lincolnshire
LN2 1AP. *0522 568476*

James Beattie plc *C*℞
71-80 Victoria Street, Wolverhampton, West Midlands
WV1 3PQ. *0902 22311*

Berry's Music *C*℞
23 Bridge Place, Worksop, Nottinghamshire S80 1DT.
0909 473532

Blackwells Music Shop *S*℞
38 Holywell Street, Oxford, Oxfordshire OX1 3SW.
0865 792792

The Book Castle *B*℞
12 Church Street, Dunstable, Bedfordshire LU5 4RU.
0582 605670

Chappell of Bond Street *B*℞
21 Silbury Arcade, Central Milton Keynes, Buckinghamshire
MK9 3AG. *0908 663366*

Classic Music *C*℞
7 Lime Street, Bedford, Bedfordshire MK40 1LD.
0234 357221

Classic Tracks *S*℞
21 East Bond Street, Leicester, Leicestershire LE1 4SX.
0533 537700

Classical CD *S*℞
27 Heathcote Street, Nottingham, Nottinghamshire NG1 3AG.
0602 483832

Collectors Record Centre *C*℞

6 Duckworth Square, Derby, Derbyshire DE1 1JZ.
0332 45957

Complete Discery *C*℞
Wallace House, Oat Street, Evesham, Worcestershire
WR11 4PJ. *0386 442899*

I M E Counterpoint *C*℞
1a Clarburgh House, 32 Church Street, Malvern,
Worcestershire. *0684 561860*

David's Music *B*℞
12 Eastcheap, Letchworth, Hertfordshire SG6 3DE.
0462 483459

Dillons The Bookstore *S*℞
128 New Street, Birmingham, West Midlands B2 4DB.
021-631 4333

Durrant Records *C*℞
84 Wyle Cop, Shrewsbury, Shropshire SY1 1UT.
0743 351008

Easy Listening Ltd *B*℞
1135 Warwick Road, Acocks Green, Birmingham B27 6RA.
021-707 1620

Forsyth Bros Ltd *C*℞
6 The Midway, Newcastle-Under-Lyme, Staffordshire
ST5 1QG. *0782 616177*

HMV *S*℞
38 High Street, Birmingham, West Midlands B4 7SL.
021-643 0177

HMV *B*℞
212 The Potteries Shopping Centre, Market Square, Hanley,
Staffordshire ST1 1PS. *0782 283232*

HMV *S*℞
44-46 Cornmarket Street, Oxford, Oxfordshire OX1 3HA.
0865 728190

HMV *B*℞
9-17 High Street, Leicester, Leicestershire LE1 4FP.
0533 539638

Music and Video Club *C*℞
6 Mardol, Shrewsbury, Shropshire SY1 1PY. *0743 343247*

Music Box *B*℞
5 Kings Walk, Guildhall Street, Grantham, Lincolnshire
NG31 6NL. *0476 72151*

Music Room *C*℞
Paddock Lane, Ablewell Street, Walsall, West Midlands WS1
2EG. *021-556 2434*

Not Just Books *B*℞
7a Market Place, Uppingham, Rutland LE15 9QH.
0572 821306

Oakstone Classics *S*℞
23 Reindeer Court, Worcester, Worcestershire WR1 2DS.
0905 619629

Ottakar's *C*℞
16 High Street, Banbury, Oxfordshire OX16 8EE.
0295 270498

The Outback *C*℞
19a Church Street, Hereford, Herefordshire HR1 2LR.
0432 275063

Presto Music *S*℞
23 Portland Street, Leamington Spa, Warwickshire CV32 5EZ.
0926 334834

Record House *C*℞
36 High Street, Aylesbury, Buckinghamshire HP20 1SF.
0296 20770

WH Smith Ltd *C*℞
29 Union Street, Birmingham, West Midlands B2 4LR.
021-631 3303

WH Smith Ltd *C*℞
14-16 Listergate, Nottingham, Nottinghamshire NG1 7DD.
0602 582919

Sounds Expensive *S*℞
12 Regent Street, Rugby, Warwickshire, CV21 2QF.
0788 540772

Spinadisc Records *B*℞
83-87 Lower Precinct Coventry, West Midlands CV1 1DS.
0203 632004/5

Spinadisc Records *B*℞
75a Abington Street, Northampton, Northamptonshire
NN1 2BH. *0604 31144*

Stamford Music Shop   *C*R
11 St Mary's Hill, Stamford, Lincolnshire PE9 2DP.
0780 51275
St Martins Records   *S*R
23 Hotel Street, Leicester, Leicestershire LE1 5AW.
0533 539292
Brian Sunderland (Music)   *B*R
62 Earlsdon Street, Coventry, West Midlands CV5 6EJ.
0203 714272
Tower Sounds   *C*R
9 Market Place, Cirencester, Gloucestershire Gl7 2NX.
0285 654283
Virgin Retail   *S*R
98 Corporation Street, Birmingham, West Midlands B4 6SX.
021-236 2523
Virgin Retail   *C*R
40-44 The Precinct, Coventry, West Midlands CV5 6EJ.
0203 634346
Virgin Retail   *S*R
6-8 Wheelergate, Nottingham, Nottinghamshire NG1 2NB.
0602 476126

North East

Adagio Classical Records   *C*R
Westminster Arcade, Harrogate, North Yorkshire HG1 2RN.
0423 506507
Banks & Son (Music) Ltd   *S*R
18 Lendal, York, North Yorkshire YO1 2AU. *0904 658836*
Blake Head Record Shop   *C*R
89 Micklegate, York, North Yorkshire YO1 1NA.
0904 625482
Calm & Classical   *S*R
144 West Street, Sheffield, South Yorkshire S1 4ES.
0742 755795
The Classical Record Shop   *S*R
2 Merrion Centre, Leeds, West Yorkshire LS2 8NG.
0532 452059
Bernard Dean   *C*R
10-12 St Thomas Street, Scarborough, North Yorkshire
YO11 1DR. *0723 372573*
The Den   *B*R
38 Cavendish Street, Keighley, West Yorkshire BD21 3RG.
0535 606086
Forsyth Bros Ltd   *C*R
St George House, 40 Great George Street, Leeds, West
Yorkshire LS1 3DL. *0532 444494*
HMV   *B*R
1-13 Schofields Centre, Leeds, West Yorkshire LS1 6JB.
0532 442992
HMV   *C*R
46-48 Northumberland Street, Newcastle-upon-Tyne, Tyne &
Wear NE1 7TT. *091-232 7470*
HMV   *C*R
121-123 Pinstone Street, Sheffield, South Yorkshire S1 2HL.
0742 751445
HMV   *C*R
10a Coney Street, York, North Yorkshire YO1 1NA.
0904 640218
Metro Music   *C*R
12 Victoria Road, Scarborough, North Yorkshire YO11 1SD.
0723 379471
Musidisc   *B*R
39 Ladygate, Beverley, North Humberside HU17 8BH.
0482 868033
Playback   *C*R
122-124 Linthorpe Road, Middlesbrough, Cleveland TS1 2JR.
0642 219133 (Classical CDs), 250060
Record Collector   *C*R
233-235 Fulwood Road, Broomhill, Sheffield, South Yorkshire
S10 3BA. *0742 668493*
Teesdale Music   *C*R
9 Galgate, Barnard Castle, County Durham DL12 8EQ.
0833 31201
Time & Tune   *C*R
Grove Bookshop, 10 The Grove, Ilkley, West Yorkshire
LS29 9EG. *0943 817301*

Virgin Retail   *B*R
94-96 The Briggate, Leeds, West Yorkshire LS1 6BR.
0532 443681
Virgin Retail   *C*R
Monument Mall, 15-21 Northumberland Street, Newcastle-
upon-Tyne, Tyne & Wear NE1 7AE. *091-230 5959*
Virgin Retail   *S*R
Orchard Square, Fargate, Sheffield, South Yorkshire S1 2HD.
0742 731175
Westside Music   *C*R
959 Ecclesall Road, Sheffield, South Yorkshire S11 8TN.
0742 670718
J G Windows Ltd   *S*R
1-7 Central Arcade, Newcastle-upon-Tyne, Tyne & Wear
NE1 5BP. *091-232 1356*
J Wood & Sons Ltd   *C*R
38 Manningham Lane, Bradford, West Yorkshire BD1 3AE.
0274 307636
J Wood & Sons Ltd   *C*R
11-15 Market Street, Huddersfield, West Yorkshire HD1 2BH.
0484 427455

North West and Isle of Man

Action Replay   *B*R
24 Lake Road, Bowness-on-Windermere, Cumbria LA23 3AP.
05394 45089
Andys Records   *B*R
27-29 Victoria Square, Bolton, Lancashire BL1 1RJ.
0204 373388
Andys Records   *B*R
2 Marble Place, Southport, Merseyside PR8 1DF.
0704 549222
Aston Audio   *B*R
4 West Street, Alderley Edge, Cheshire SK9 7EG.
0625 582704
Blackwell's Academic Bookshop   *B*R
149-153 Oxford Road, Manchester, Greater Manchester
M13 9RU. *061-274 3331*
Bluebell Bookshop & Music   *B*R
Angel Square, Penrith, Cumbria CA11 7BP. *0768 66660*
Bookcase   *C*R
17 Castle Street, Carlisle, Cumbria CA3 8TP. *0228 44560*
Chester Compact Disc Centre   *C*R
18 Paddock Row, Grosvenor Precinct, Chester, Cheshire
CH1 1ED. *0244 311991*
Circle Records   *S*R
33 Victoria Street, Liverpool, Merseyside L1 6BG.
051-236 1000
Concert Corner   *S*R
94b-96b Lord Street, Southport, Merseyside PR8 1JR.
0704 533883
Dillons the Bookstore   *B*R
14-16 Bold Street, Liverpool, Merseyside L1 4DS.
051-708 6861
Forsyth Brothers Limited   *S*R
126 Deansgate, Manchester, Greater Manchester M3 2GR.
061-834 3281
Kenneth Gardner Ltd   *C*R
28 New Street, Lancaster, Lancashire LA1 1EG.
0524 841398
Gibbs Bookshop Ltd   *S*R
10 Charlotte Street, Manchester, Greater Manchester M1 4FL.
061-236 7179
HMV   *C*R
48-50 Foregate Street, Chester, Cheshire CH1 1HA.
0244 310307
HMV   *S*R
22-36 Church Street, Liverpool, Merseyside L1 3AW.
051-709 1088
HMV   *S*R
90-100 Market Street, Manchester, Greater Manchester
M1 1PD. *061-834 8550*
HMV   *B*R
51-53 Merseyway, Stockport, Cheshire SK1 1PW.
061-460 0548
Kovary's Opus III   *C*R
44 Market Place, Cockermouth, Cumbria CA13 9NG.
0900 822314

Lancaster Classical Music	C℞

Lancaster Classical Music C℞
26 Sun Street, Lancaster, Lancashire LA1 1EW.
0524 842434

Margin Music B℞
3 Market Place, Macclesfield, Cheshire SK10 1EB.
0625 619013

New Kelly's Music Shop C℞
101 Church Street, Barrow-in-Furness, Cumbria LA14 2HW.
0229 822973

Ken Palk Ltd B℞
Shopping Centre, Bramhall, Stockport, Cheshire SK7 1AW.
061 439 8479

Rare Records S℞
13 Bank Square, Wilmslow, Cheshire SK9 1AN. *0625 522017*

Reidy's Home of Music C℞
9-13 Penny Street, Blackburn, Lancashire BB1 6HJ.
0254 265303

Rushworths Music Limited C℞
31a Bridge Street, Chester, Cheshire CH1 1NG. *0244 325252*

Rushworths Music House Ltd C℞
42-46 Whitechapel, Liverpool, Merseyside L1 6EF.
051-709 9071

WH Smith Ltd C℞
5-7 Foregate Street, Chester, Cheshire CH1 1HH.
0244 321106

WH Smith Ltd C℞
10-16 Church Street, Liverpool, Merseyside L1 3EG.
051-709 1435

Smiths of Wigan B℞
41 Mesnes Street, Wigan, Lancashire WN1 1QY.
0942 42810/46270

Smyth's Records B℞
123-125 Highgate, Kendal, Cumbria LA9 4EN. *0539 729595*

Virgin Retail S℞
32-36 Foregate Street, Chester, Cheshire CH1 1HA.
0244 322212

Virgin Retail S℞
52-56 Market Street, Manchester, Greater Manchester
M1 1QA. *061-833 1111/2*

Isle of Man

Island Compact Disc Centre C℞
80 Parliament Street, Ramsey, Isle of Man. *0624 815521*

Scotland

Bauermeister Booksellers S℞
15-16 George IV Bridge, Edinburgh EH1 1EH. *031-226 5561*

Bruce Millers C℞
363 Union Street, Aberdeen AB9 1EN. *0224 592211*

Casa Cassettes Ltd B℞
325 Sauchiehall Street, Glasgow G2 3HW. *041-332 1127*

Concorde B℞
15 Scott Street, Perth PH1 5EJ. *0738 21818*

John M Hay (Stirling) Ltd B℞
Friars Gait, 29-31 Friars Street, Stirling FK8 1HE.
0786 473573

HMV B℞
247-251 Union Street, Aberdeen AB1 2BQ. *0224 575323*

HMV C℞
129 Princes Street, Edinburgh, EH2 4AH. *031-226 3466*

HMV C℞
Unit 6, Lewis's Centre, Argyle Street, Glasgow G2 8AD.
041-204 4787

HMV C℞
154-160 Sauchiehall Street, Glasgow G2 3DH. *041-332 6631*

McAlister Matheson Music Ltd S℞
1 Grindlay Street, Edinburgh EH3 9AT. *031-228 3827*

Melody Centre B℞
86 High Street, North Berwick, East Lothian EH39 4HD.
0620 892616

The Musicmongers C℞
151 South Street, St Andrews, Fife KY16 9UN. *0334 78625*

James Thin Ltd C℞
53-59 Southbridge, Edinburgh EH10 4QR. *031-556 6743*

Top Note C℞
123 Crown Street, Aberdeen AB1 2HN. *0224 210259*

Tower Records S℞
217-221 Argyle Street, Glasgow G2 8DL. *041-204 2500*

Virgin Retail S℞
133 Union Street, Aberdeen AB1 2BH. *0224 213050*

Virgin Retail C℞
Unit G Level 1, The Wellgate Centre, Dundee, Tayside DD1
2DB. *0382 200755*

Virgin Retail S℞
131 Princes Street, Edinburgh EH2 4AH. *031-225 4583*

Virgin Retail C℞
28-32 Union Street, Glasgow G1 3QX. *041-221 0103*

Virgin Retail C℞
Unit 4, Lewis' Building, Argyle Street, Glasgow G1 2AQ.
041-221 2606

Wales

Abergavenny Music S℞
23 Cross Street, Abergavenny, Gwent NP7 5EW.
0873 853394

Cerdd Ystwyth Music C℞
7 Upper Portland Street, Aberystwyth, Dyfed SY23 2DT.
0970 623382/617626

City Radio S℞
27a Morgan Arcade, Cardiff, South Glamorgan CF1 2AF.
0222 228169

Clwyd Books B℞
Harmony House, St George's Place, Llandudno, Gwynedd.
0492 877510

HMV B℞
51 Queen Street, Cardiff, South Glamorgan CF1 4AS.
0222 227147

Marjan Music B℞
190 High Street, Prestatyn, Clwyd LL19 8SR. *0745 853160*

The Muse C℞
43 Holyhead Road, Bangor, Gwynedd LL57 2UE.
0248 362072

Naughty Cat Records C℞
at J P Williams-Jones Booksellers, Eldon Square, Dolgellau,
Gwynedd LL40 1PS. *0341 422173*

Swales Music Centre Ltd C℞
2-6 High Street, Haverfordwest, Pembrokeshire, SA61 2DJ.
0437 762059/763261

Virgin Retail S℞
Units 7-9, Capitol Arcade, The Capitol, Queen Street, Cardiff,
South Glamorgan CF1 4HQ. *0222 388273*

Northern Ireland

Classical Tracks S℞
14 Donegal Arcade, Belfast BT1 1PT. *0232 333868*

Koinonia S℞
6 Pottinger's Entry, High Street, Belfast BT1 2JZ.
0232 247873

Virgin Retail C℞
Unit 1C, Castlecourt, Royal Avenue, Belfast BT1 1DD.
0232 236623

Mail order

CDX Classical M℞
The Olde Coach House, Windsor Crescent, Radyr, South
Glamorgan CF4 8AE. *0222 844443/843890*

City Radio M℞
24 Charles Street, Newport, Gwent NP9 1JT. *0633 840728*

Club 50/50 Music & Video M℞
PO Box 1277, Chippenham, Wiltshire SN15 3YZ.
0249 445400

Compact Classics Ltd M℞
87 Portland Road, London W11 4LN. *071-221 1735*

Crotchet & Company M℞
Church Stretton, Shropshire SY6 6DR. *0694 722982*

Eden Compact Discs M℞
41 Hever Road, Edenbridge, Kent TN8 5DH. *0732 863392*

Europadisc M℞
89-91 North Street, Sudbury, Suffolk CO10 0AR.
0787 375743

Hale CDs M℞
405 Hale Road, Hale Bans, Altrincham, Cheshire WA15 8XX.
061-980 7093

MDT Classics Ltd *M'R*
6 Old Blacksmiths Yard, Sadler Gate, Derby, Derbyshire
DE1 3PD. *0332 368251*

Music Established Ltd *M'R*
2 Dukes Court, Princess Way, Prudhoe, Northumberland
NE42 6DA. *0670 511744*

The Music Group *M'R*
West Haddon, Northamptonshire NN6 7AA. *0788 510693*

Opus 1 Music *M'R*
19 Brunswick Road, Bangor, County Down BT20 3DY.
0247 457775

Records-by-Post *M'R*
P.O Box 32, Southport, Merseyside PR8 2HR.

C G Robson Imports *M'R*
39 Winchcombe Road, Eastbourne, East Sussex BN22 8DE.
0323 725376

Silver Service CD *M'R*
24 Touch Wards, Dunfermline, Fife KY12 7TG. *0383 738159*

Squires Gate Music Centre *M'R*
Squires Gate Station Approach, St Anne's, Lancashire FY8 2SP.
0253 44360

Tandy's Records Limited *M'R*
24 Islington Row, Birmingham, West Midlands B15 1LJ.
021-455 8866

Wings Mail Order *M'R*
Paddock Lodge, Dummer, Basingstoke, Hampshire RG25 2AF.
0256 397099

Second hand specialists

Bargain Classical Records
9 The Arcade, High Street, Eltham, London SE9 1BE.
081-859 5836

Ben's Collectors Records
101 West Street, Farnham, Surrey GU9 7NS. *0252 734409*

Ben's Collectors Records
5 Tunsgate, Guildford, Surrey GU1 3QT. *0483 301165*

Cheapo Cheapo Records
53 Rupert Street, London W1V 7HN. *071-437 8272*

Garon Records
65-66 The Covered Market, Oxford, Oxfordshire OX1 3DX.
0865 246887

Simply Classical
93 Mansfield Road, Nottingham, NG1 3FN. *0602 799250*

West Midlands Classical Records
204 Smethwick Enterprise Centre, Rolfe Street, Smethwick,
Warley, West Midlands B66 2AR. *0721 555 5549*

Yarborough House Bookshop
The Square, Bishops Castle, Shropshire SY9 5BN. *0588 638318*

The 78 Record Exchange
9 Lower Hillgate, Stockport, Cheshire SK1 1JQ.

Import specialists

Michael G Thomas
5a Norfolk Place, London W2 1QN. *071-723 4935*

Manufacturers and Distributors

Entries are listed as follows: **Manufacturer** or **Label**—UK Distributor *(Series)*

Acanta Pilz UK
Accent Gamut
Accord (Musidisc) Harmonia Mundi
Adda Gamut
Adès Harmonia Mundi
Albany Albany
Altarus Albany
Amon Ra (Saydisc) Gamut/Harmonia Mundi
APR Harmonia Mundi
Arabesque Seaford Music
Archiv Produktion PolyGram Record
  Operations *(Archiv Produktion, Archiv Produktion
  Galleria)*
Argo PolyGram Record Operations
Arion Discovery Records
ASV Koch International *(ASV, Gaudeamus,
  Quicksilva, White Line)*
Athene Albany
Auvidis Koch International *(Astrée, Valois)*
Aurora Gamut
Bay Cities Albany
Bayer Priory
Beecham Trust Sir Thomas Beecham Trust
Belart PolyGram Record Operations/Gamut
Berlin Classics Koch International
Beulah Priory
Biddulph Scott Butler
BIS Conifer
Bluebell Scott Butler
BNL Priory
Bridge Complete Record Co.
British Music Society British Music Society
Cala Complete Record Co.
Calliope Harmonia Mundi
Campion RRD (Distribution)
Capriccio Target
Caprice Complete Record Co.
Cascavelle Scott Butler
Catalyst BMG UK
CBC Records Kingdom
CBS Sony Music Entertainment *(Masterworks,
  Masterworks Portrait, Maestro, Digital Masters)*
CdM Russian Season Harmonia Mundi
Centaur Complete Record Co.
Chandos Chandos *(Chandos, Chaconne, Premium,
  Collect)*
Channel Classics Select
Chanticleer RRD (Distribution)
Chesky New Note
Christophorus Select
Claremont Complete Record Co.
Classics For Pleasure Music for Pleasure
Claves Complete Record Co.
Cloud Nine Silva Screen

Collegium Gamut/Koch International
Collins Classics Conifer *(Collins Classics, Quest,
  20th Century)*
Conifer Conifer
Continuum Select
CPO Koch International
CRD Select
Dabringhaus und Grimm Priory
Dacapo (Marco Polo) Select
Dante Scott Butler *(Lys, Historic Piano Collection)*
Decca PolyGram Record Operations *(Decca, New
  Line, London, Ovation, Entartete Musik, Enterprise,
  Grand Opera, Headline, Historic, Serenata,
  Weekend)*
Dell'Arte Harmonia Mundi
Delos Conifer
Denon Conifer *(Denon, Aliare)*
Deutsche Harmonia Mundi BMG UK
  (Deutsche Harmonia Mundi, Editio Classica)
DG PolyGram Record Operations *(DG, DG
  Galleria, 3-D Classics, 20th Century Classics,
  Mozart Masterpieces, Resonance, Grieg Edition,
  Classikon, Compact Classics, Dokumente, Karajan
  Symphony Edition, Privilege)*
Disques Montaigne Koch International
Dutton Laboratories Complete Record Co.
Dynamic RRD (Distribution)
Earthsounds Scott Butler
EBS Kingdom
ECM New Series New Note
Elektra Nonesuch Warner Classics
EMI Eminence Music for Pleasure
EMI EMI *(Angel, EMI, Reflexe, Studio, Beecham
  Edition, British Composers, Composers in Person,
  Digital Classics, Digital Twins, Elgar Edition,
  L'Esprit Français, Great American, Great Recordings
  of the Century, Legendary Interpretations, Matrix,
  Phoenixa, Références, Rouge et Noir, Studio Plus)*
EMI Laser Music for Pleasure
Epic Sony Music Entertainment
Erato Warner Classics *(Erato, MusiFrance, Libretto,
  Emerald)*
Etcetera Scott Butler
Eurodisc BMG UK
Europa Music Koch International
Finlandia Warner Classics
First Night Records Pinnacle
FNAC Music Nimbus
Fonè UK Distribution
Forlane Scott Butler
Four Hands Music Gamut
Fox BMG UK
Foyer RRD (Distribution)
Gamut Classics Gamut

Gimell Conifer
Hänssler Classic Select
Harmonia Mundi Harmonia Mundi *(Harmonia Mundi, Musique d'abord)*
Harmonic Records Complete Record Co.
Hat Hut Harmonia Mundi
Helicon Helicon
Herald Gamut
Hungaroton Conifer *(Hungaroton, White Label)*
Hyperion Select *(Hyperion, Helios)*
Intercord Scott Butler *(Gielen Edition, Classical Creations)*
Intrada Koch International/Silva Screen
Isis Records Priory
Jade Complete Record Co.
Jecklin Disco Scott Butler
Keyboard Records Scott Butler
Kingdom Records Kingdom
Koch International Classics Koch International
Koch Schwann Koch International
Kontrapunkt Impetus
Largo Complete Record Co.
LaserLight *(Capriccio)* Target
Le Chant du Monde Harmonia Mundi
Legato Classics Complete Record Co.
Léman Classics Scott Butler
Linn Records PolyGram Records Operations
Lyrita Conifer
L'Oiseau-Lyre PolyGram Record Operations
Marco Polo Select *(Marco Polo, British Light Music)*
MCA BMG UK
Medici-Whitehall Gamut
Memoir Classics Target
Mercury PolyGram Record Operations
Meridian Gamut
Metier Albany
Mezhdunarodnaya Kniga Complete Record Co.
Mirabilis Mirabilis
Mode Impetus
Motette Priory
Multisonic Koch International
Music and Arts Harmonia Mundi
Musica Oscura Complete Record Co.
Musica Sveciae Gamut
Musical Observations Albany
Musidisc Harmonia Mundi *(Musidisc, Gâité-Lyrique)*
MusicMasters Nimbus
Naxos Select
New Albion Harmonia Mundi
New World Harmonia Mundi
Newport Classic RRD (Distribution) *(Newport Classics, Premier)*
Nimbus Nimbus
NKF Gamut
NM Classics Impetus
NMC Complete Record Co.
Novalis Gamut

Nuova Era Complete Record Co.
Ode Discovery Records
Olympia Complete Record Co. *(Olympia, Explorer)*
Ondine Koch International
Onyx Scott Butler
Opera Rara Scott Butler
Opus III Harmonia Mundi
Opus 3 May Audio Marketing
Orfeo Koch International
Ottavo Priory
Panton RRD (Distribution)
Pavane Kingdom
Pearl (Pavilion) Harmonia Mundi
Philips PolyGram Record Operations *(Philips, Silver Line, Duo, Insignia, Baroque Classics, . Collector, Legendary Classics, Mozart Edition, Musica da Camara, Concert Classics)*
Pianissimo Albany
Pickwick Pickwick/Gamut *(IMP Masters, IMP Classics, IMP Red Label, Golden Legacy of Recorded Sound)*
Pierre Verany Kingdom
Point Music PolyGram Record Operations
Point Records Gamut
Polskie Nagrania Complete Record Co.
Polydor PolyGram Record Operations
Praga Harmonia Mundi
Preiser Harmonia Mundi
Priory Priory
Proudsound Gamut
Pyramid Records Priory
RCA BMG UK *(RCA Victor, Red Seal, Gold Seal, Julian Bream Edition, Living Stereo, Van Cliburn Edition, Papillon, Seon, Victrola)*
Redcliffe Recordings Complete Record Co.
Reference Recordings Quantum Audio
Regent Records Dervorguilla
Relief Albany
REM Editions Priory
Ricercar Gamut *(Ricercar, Secondo)*
Rose Collection Gamut
Royal Opera House Records Conifer
Russian Disc Koch International
Saga Classics Complete Record Co.
Sain Scott Butler
Salabert Actuels Harmonia Mundi
Silva Screen Conifer
Simax Gamut
Sine Qua Non Sine Qua Non
Sony Classical Sony Music Entertainment *(Sony Classical, Vivarte, Essential Classics, Broadway, Casals Edition, Glenn Gould Edition, Bernstein Royal Edition)*
Soundboard Records Soundboard Records
Stradivari Michèle International
Stradivarius Priory
Supraphon Koch International
Telarc Conifer
Teldec Warner Classics *(Teldec Classics, British Line, Das Alte Werk, Digital Experience, Das Alte Werk Reference)*

TER Classics Koch International

Testament Gamut

Tremula Scott Butler

Tring International Tring International/Priory

Troubadisc Complete Record Co.

Unicorn-Kanchana Harmonia Mundi *(Unicorn-Kanchana, Souvenir)*

United Recording Complete Record Co.

Vanguard Classics Complete Record Co. *(Vanguard Classics, Bach Guild)*

Varèse Sarabande Pinnacle

Victoria Gamut

Virgin Classics EMI *(Virgin Classics, Veritas, Virgo, Duo)*

Voiceprint Voiceprint

Vox Complete Record Co. *(Vox Legends, Vox Box)*

Wergo Harmonia Mundi

For additional information on Manufacturers and Distributors, refer to *The Gramophone Classical Catalogue* (published by General Gramophone Publications).

Record Company Names and Addresses

Unless otherwise indicated all the companies listed below are based in the UK; addresses for record companies from outside the UK are given, where available (telephone numbers should be prefixed with the appropriate international dialing code).

Accent Records Eikstraat 31, 1673 Beert, *BELGIUM* (32 2 356 1878)

Accord 3-5 Rue Albert de Vatimesnil, 92305 Levallois, *FRANCE* (33 4758 1290)

Adès 54, Rue Saint Lazare, 75009 Paris, *FRANCE* (33 1 4874 8530)

Albany Records UK *UK* PO Box 12, Carnforth, Lancashire LA5 9PD (0524 735873) *US* PO Box 5011, Albany, NY12205 *USA* (1 518 453 2203)

Altarus Records Easton Dene, Bailbrook Lane, Bath BA1 7AA (0225 852323)

Appian Publications and Recordings (APR) PO Box 1, Wark, Hexham, Northumberland NE48 3EW (0434 220627)

Arabesque Recordings 10 West 37th Street, 5th floor, New York, NY10018 *USA* (1 212 279 1414)

Archiv Produktion 1 Sussex Place, Hammersmith, London W6 9XS (081-846 8515)

Argo 1 Sussex Place, Hammersmith, London W6 9XS (081-846 8515)

Arion 36, Avenue Hoche, 75008 Paris, *FRANCE* (331 4563 7670)

ASV 1 Beaumont Avenue, London W14 9LP (071-381 8747)

Athene D&J Recording, 7 Felden Street, London SW6 5AE (071-736 9485)

Aurora c/o The Norwegian Society of Composers, Galleri Oslo, Tøyenbekken 21, PO Box 9171, Grønland, 0134 Oslo, *NORWAY* (47 22 170190)

Auvidis 47 Avenue Paul Vaillant Couturier, 94251 Gentilly Cedex, *FRANCE* (33 1 4615 8800)

Bayer AG Ku-Mipine-Makrolon (Dept), 51368 Leverkusen, *GERMANY* (49 214 30 8507)

Sir Thomas Beecham Trust Denton House, Denton, Harleston, Norfolk IP20 0AA (098686 780)

Belart PO Box 1425, Chancellors House, 72 Chancellors Road, Hammersmith, London W6 9QB (081-910 5000)

Grammofon AB BIS Bragevägen 2, 18264 Djursholm, *SWEDEN* (46 8 755 4100)

Biddulph Recordings 35 St George Street, London W1R 9FA (071-491 8621)

BMG Classics Bedford House, 69-79 Fulham High Street, London SW6 3JW (071-973 0011)

BMG UK Lyng Lane, West Bromwich, West Midlands B70 7ST (021-525 5545)

BNL Productions 28 Rue Louis Nouveau, 06400 Cannes, *FRANCE* (33 9292 2584)

Bridge Records GPO Box 1864, New York, NY10116, *USA* (1 516 487 1662)

British Music Society 7 Tudor Gardens, Upminster, Essex RM14 3DE (071-454 6480)

Scott Butler Disc and Tape Factors Unit 2, Lansdowne Mews, Charlton Lane, London SE7 8AZ (081-858 9190)

Cala Records 17 Shakespeare Gardens, London N2 9LJ (081-883 7306)

Calliope 14 Rue de la Justice, Boîte Postale 166, 60204 Compiègne Cedex, *FRANCE* (33 4423 2765)

Campion 13 Bank Square, Wilmslow, Cheshire SK9 1AN (0625 527844)

Capriccio Zur Mühle 2, 50226 Frechen, *GERMANY* (49 2234 60060)

Caprice Records Box 1225, 111 82 Stockholm, *SWEDEN* (46 8 791 4600)

Cascavelle 23 Ch Bellefontaine, 1223 Cologny, Genève, *SWITZERLAND* (41 22 735 7862)

Catalyst Bedford House, 79 Fulham High Street, London SW6 3JW (071-973 0011)

CBC Records PO Box 500, Station A, Toronto, Ontario M5W 1E6, *CANADA* (1 416 205 3501)

CBS Records *see* SONY MUSIC ENTERTAINMENT

Centaur Records 8867 Highland Road, Suite 206, Baton Rouge, LA70808, *USA* (1 504 336 4877)

Chandos Records Chandos House, Commerce Way, Colchester, Essex CO2 8HQ (0206 794000)

Channel Classics Records Jacob van Lennepkade 334 e, 1053 NJ Amsterdam *THE NETHERLANDS* (31 20 6161775)

Chesky Records 311 West 43rd Street, Suite 702, New York, NY10036, *USA* (1 212 586 7799)

Classics for Pleasure 1-3 Uxbridge Road, Hayes, Middlesex UB4 0SY (081-561 8722)

Claves Records Trüelweg 14, 3600 Thun, *SWITZERLAND* (41 3323 1649)

Cloud Nine 8 Oakington Road, London NW9 2DH (071-286 0705)

Collegium Records PO Box 172, Whittlesford, Cambridge CB2 4QZ (0223 832474)

Collins Classics Electron House, Cray Avenue, St Mary Cray, Orpington, Kent BR5 3PN (06898 33076)

The Complete Record Co. 12 Pepys Court, 84 The Chase, London SW4 0NF (071-498 9666)

Conifer Records Horton Road, West Drayton, Middlesex UB7 8JL (0895 447707)

CPO Lübeckerstraße 9, 49124 Georgsmarienhütte, *GERMANY* (49 5401 851 261)

CRD PO Box 26, Stanmore, Middlesex HA7 4XB (081-958 7695)

Dabringhaus und Grimm Bachstraße 35, 32756 Detmold, *GERMANY* (49 5231 24001)

Dacapo (Marco Polo) Nikolaj Plads, 1,2. tv, 1067 Copenhagen, *DENMARK* (45 3393 2930)

Dante 2 Rue d'Issy, 92170 Vanves, *FRANCE* (33 1 4638 3022)

Decca Classics 1 Sussex Place, Hammersmith, London W6 9XS (081-846 8515)

Dell'Arte Records PO Box 26, Hampton, Middlesex TW12 2NL (081-979 2479)

Delos International Hollywood and Vine Plaza, 1645 North Vine Street, Suite 340, Hollywood, California CA90028, *USA* (1 213 962 2626)

Denon/Nippon Columbia 14-14, Akasaka 4-Chome, Minatu-Ku, Tokyo 107-11, *JAPAN* (81 3 3584 8271)

Dervorguilla PO Box 363, Oxford OX1 4HB (0865 725301)

Deutsche Grammophon 1 Sussex Place, Hammersmith, London W6 9XS (081-846 8515)

Discovery Records The Old Church Mission Room, King's Corner, Pewsey, Wilts SN9 5BS (0672 63931)

Dutton Laboratories PO Box 576, Harrow, Middlesex HA3 6YW (081-421 1117)

Dynamic Edizione Discografiche e Musicale, Via Mura Delle Chiappe 39, 16136 Genova, *ITALY* (39 10 27 2284)

Earthsounds PO Box 1, Richmond, North Yorkshire DL10 5GB (0748 825959)

EBS Records Postfach 1230, 72121 Pliezhausen, *GERMANY* (49 7127 88633)

ECM Postfach 600331, 81203 München, *GERMANY* (49 89 851048)

Elektra Nonesuch: *US* 75 Rockefeller Plaza, New York NY10019, *USA* (1 212 484 7200); *UK* 46 Kensington Court, London W8 5DP (071-938 5542)

EMI Records Customer Services Dept, 20 Manchester Square, London W1A 1ES (071-487 4442)

EMI Sales & Distribution Centre, Hermes Close, Tachbrook Park, Leamington Spa, Warwickshire CV34 6RP (0926 888888)

Erato: FRANCE 50 Rue des Tournelles, 75003 Paris, *FRANCE* (33 1 4027 7000); *UK* 46 Kensington Court, London W8 5DP (071-938 5542)

Etcetera Keizersgracht 518, 107 EK Amsterdam, *THE NETHERLANDS* (31 20 23 48 05)

First Night Records 2/3 Fitzroy Mews, London W1P 5DQ (071-387 7767)

FNAC Music 99 Rue du Cherche Midi, 75006 Paris, *FRANCE* (33 1 4439 5100)

Fonè 50-54 Via Goldoni, 57125 Livorno *ITALY* (39 586 884069)

Forlane 15 Rue de l'Ancienne Mairie, 92100 Boulogne Billancourt, *FRANCE* (33 1 4825 0217)

Four Hands Music 15 Birchmead Close, St Albans, Herts AL3 6BS (0727 58485)

Gamut Distribution Gamut House, Lancaster Way, Ely, Cambridgeshire CB6 3NP (0353 662366)

Gimell Records 4 Newtec Place, Magdalen Road, Oxford OX4 1RE (0865 244557)

Hänssler Classic Postfach 12 20, 73762 Neuhausen, *GERMANY* (49 7158 1770)

Harmonia Mundi: *UK* 19-21 Nile Street, London N1 7LR (071-253 0863); *FRANCE* Mas de Vert, 13200 Arles, (33 9049 9049); *USA* 2037 Granville Avenue, Los Angeles, CA90025, *USA* (1 310 478 1311)

Harmonic Records Parc de Montigny, Maxilly-sur-Léman, 74500 Evian-les-Bains, *FRANCE* (33 5075 6900)

Hat Hut Box 461, 4106 Therwil, *SWITZERLAND* (41 61 721 6655)

Helicon PO Box 9, Hastings, East Sussex TN34 3JA (0424 422061)

Herald Audiovisual Publications The Studio, 29 Alfred Road, Farnham, Surrey GU9 8ND (0252 725349)

Hungaroton Vörösmarty tér 1, 1051 Budapest, *HUNGARY* (36 1 1187 193)

Hyperion Records PO Box 25, Eltham, London SE9 1AX (081-294 1166)

Impetus Distribution PO Box 1324, London W5 2ZU (081-998 6411)

Isis Records 52 Argyle Street, Oxford, OX4 1SS (0865 726553)

Jade 1 Square Puccini, 78150 Le Chesnay, *FRANCE* (33 1 4242 1717)

Jecklin & Co Rämistraße 42, 8024 Zürich, *SWITZERLAND* (41 1 261 7733)

Keyboard Records 418 Brockley Road, London, SE4 2DH (081-699 2549)

Kingdom Records 61 Collier Street, London N1 9BE (071-713 7788)

Koch International: *UK* 24 Concord Road, London W3 0TH (081-992 7177); *USA* 177, Cantiague Rock Road, Westbury, NY11590, *USA* (1 516 938 8080)

Koch Schwann PO Box 7640, AM Wehrahn 1000, 4000 Düsseldorf 1, *GERMANY*

Kontrapunkt PO Box 35, Slottsalleen 16, 2930 Klampenborg, *DENMARK* (45 31 644 244)

Largo Records Hohenstaufenring 43-45, 50674 Köln *GERMANY* (49 221 2402234)

Le Chant du Monde 108 Rue Vieille-du-Temple, 75003 Paris, *FRANCE* (33 1 4276 0997)

Legato Classics Lyric Distribution, 18 Madison Avenue, Hicksville, NY11801, *USA* (1 516 932 5503)

L'Oiseau-Lyre 1 Sussex Place, Hammersmith, London W6 9XS (081-846 8515)

Lyrita 99 Green Lane, Burnham, Slough, Bucks SL1 8EG (0628 604208)

May Audio Marketing 83 Main Street, Burley-in-Wharfdale, West Yorkshire LS29 7BU (0943 864930)

Marco Polo 58 Pak Tai Street, 8th Floor, Kai It Bldg, Tokwawan, Kowloon, *HONG KONG* (852 760 7818)

Memoir Classics PO Box 66, Pinner, Middlesex HA5 2SA

Mercury 1 Sussex Place, Hammersmith, London W6 9XS (081-846 8515)

Meridian Records PO Box 317, Eltham, London SE9 4SF (081-857 3213)

Metier Fleet House, 173 Haydons Road, London SW19 8TB (0772 866178)

Michèle International Michèle House, The Acord Centre, Roebuck Road, Hainult, Essex IG6 3TU (081-500 1819)

Mirabilis Records Springwood Works, Water Street, Huddersfield, West Yorkshire HD1 4BB (0532 685123)

Mode PO Box 375, Kew Gardens, New York, NY11415, *USA* (1 212 595 6089)

Motette-Ursina Neusser Weg 63a, 40474 Düsseldorf, *GERMANY* (49 211 434864)

Music and Arts Programs of America PO Box 771, Berkeley, Claifornia CA94701, *USA* (1 510 525 4583)

Music for Pleasure 1-3 Uxbridge Road, Hayes, Middlesex UB4 0SY (081-561 8722)

MusicMasters 1710 Highway 35, Ocean, NJ 07712-2910, *USA* (1 908 531 3375)

Musica Sveciae Knugl, Musikalaiska Akadamien, Blasieholmstorg 8, 111 Stockholm, *SWEDEN* (46 8 611 1870)

Musidisc 3-5 Rue Albert de Vatimesnil, 92305 Levallois Cedex, *FRANCE* (33 1 4758 1290)

Naxos 58 Pak Tai Street, 8th Floor, Kai It Bldg, Tokwawan, Kowloon, *HONG KONG* (852 760 7818)

Naxos/Marco Polo (UK) PO Box 576, Sheffield, Yorkshire S10 1AY (0742 678958)

New Albion Records 584 Castro Street, Suite 515, San Francisco, CA94114, *USA* (1 415 621 5757)

New Note Unit 2, Orpington Trading Estate, Sevenoaks Way, St Mary Cray, Orpington, Kent BR5 3SR (06898 77884)

New World Records 701 Seventh Avenue, 7th Floor, New York, NY10036, *USA* (1 212 302 0460)

Newport Classic 106, Putnam Street, Providence, Rhode Island RI02909, *USA* (1 401 421 8143)

Nimbus Records Wyastone Leys, Monmouth, Gwent NP5 3SR (0600 890682)

NKF c/o The Norwegian Society of Composers, Galleri Oslo, Tøyenbekken 21, PO Box 9171, Grønland, 0134 Oslo, *NORWAY* (47 22 170190)

NMC Francis House, Francis Street, London SW1P 1DE (071-828 3432)

Nuova Era Records Corso Marconi, 39, Torino 10125, *ITALY* (39 11 669 8903)

Ode Record Co 2 York Street, Parnell, Box 37-331, Auckland, *NEW ZEALAND* (64 9 358 5491)

Olympia Compact Discs 31 Warple Way, London W3 0RX (081-743 6767)

Ondine Fredrikinkatu 77 A 2, 00100 Helsinki, *FINLAND* (35 8 492 348)

Opera Rara 25 Compton Terrace, London N1 2UN (071-359 1777)

Opus 111 37 Rue Blomet, 75015 Paris, *FRANCE* (33 1 4567 3344)

Orfeo International Music Augustenstraße 79, 8000 München 2 *GERMANY* (49 89 522031)

Ottavo Recordings Westeinde 10, 2512HD Den Haag, *THE NETHERLANDS* (31 70 346 9494)

Panton Radlická 99, 150 00 Praha 5, *CZECH REPUBLIC* (42 202 5341 378)

Pavane Records 17 Rue Ravenstein, 1000 Bruxelles, *BELGIUM* (32 2 513 0965)

Pavilion Records Sparrows Green, Wadhurst, East Sussex TN5 6SJ (0892 783591)

Philips Classics 1 Sussex Place, Hammersmith, London W6 9XS (081-846 8515)

Pianissimo Ridgeway Road, Pyrford, Woking, Surrey GU22 8PR (0932 345371)

Pickwick Group The Waterfront, Elstree Road, Elstree, Hertfordshire WD6 3BE (081-207 6207)

Pierre Verany 15 Rue Guyton-de-Morveau, 75013 Paris, *FRANCE* (33 1 4581 1414)

Pinnacle Electron House, Cray Avenue, St Mary Cray, Orpington, Kent BR5 3RJ (06898 70622)

Pilz UK The Broadway, Didcot, Oxon OX11 8ES (0235 811796)

PolyGram Classics and Jazz 1 Sussex Place, Hammersmith, London W6 9XS (081-846 8515)

PolyGram Record Operations PO Box 36, Clyde Works, Grove Road, Romford, Essex RM6 4QR (081-590 6044)

Polskie Nagrania 6, Goleszowska Street, 01249 Warsaw, *POLAND* (48 2 373794)

Priory Records Unit 9b, Upper Wingbury Courtyard, Wingrave, Nr. Aylesbury, Bucks HP22 4LW (0296 682255)

Proudsound 61 Iffley Road, Oxford OX4 1EB (0865 723764)

Quantum Audio PO Box 26, Kilmarnock, Ayrshire KA1 1BA (0563 71122)

RCA Bedford House, 69-79 Fulham High Street, London SW6 3JW (071-973 0011)

Redcliffe Recordings 68 Barrowgate Road, London W4 4QU (081-995 1223)

Reference Recordings Box 7725X, San Francisco, California CA94107, *USA* (1 415 355 1892)

Regent Records PO Box 524, London SE25 6AN (081-771 6645)

REM Editions 4 Rue Sainte Marie des Terreaux, 69001 Lyon, *FRANCE* (33 7830 0571)

Ricercar Burnaumont 73, G912 Anloy, Liban, *BELGIUM*

Royal Opera House Records *see* Conifer Records

RRD (Distribution) 13 Bank Square, Wilmslow, Cheshire SK9 1AN (0625 549862)

Russian Disc 577 Brown Brook Road, Southbury, CT06488, *USA* (1 203 264 4073)

Sain Llandwrog, Caernarfon, Gwynedd LL54 5TG (0286 831111)

Saydisc Chipping Manor, The Chipping, Wotton-under-Edge, Glos GL12 7AD (0453 845036)

Seaford Music 24 Pevensey Road, Eastbourne, East Sussex BN21 3HP (0323 732553)

Select Music and Video Distributors 34a Holmethorpe Avenue, Holmethorpe Estate, Redhill, Surrey (0737 760020)

Silva Screen 261 Royal College Street, London NW1 9LU (071-284 0525)

Simax Sandakerveien 76, PO Box 4379, Torshov, 0402 Oslo 4, *NORWAY* (47 2271 0140)

Sine Qua Non Sine Qua Non Society, The Old Forge, 2 Bridge Street, Hadleigh, Suffolk IP7 6BT (0473 828494)

Sony Music Entertainment 10 Great Marlborough Street, London W1V 2LP (071-911 8200)

Sony Music Operations Rabans Lane, Aylesbury, Buckinghamshire HP19 3RT (0296 395151)

Soundboard Records PO Box 5, Stanley, Co. Durham DH9 7HR

Stradivarius Via Andrea Costa 7, 20131 Milano, *ITALY* (39 2 261 43119)

Supraphon Palackého 1, 11299 Praha 1, *CZECH REPUBLIC* (42 2 24 225831)

Target Records 23 Gardner Industrial Estate, Kent House Lane, Beckenham, Kent BR3 1QZ (081-778 4040)

Telarc International 23307 Commerce Park Road, Cleveland, Ohio OH44122, *USA* (1 216 464 2313)

Teldec Classics 46 Kensington Court, London W8 5DP (071-938 5542)

TER Classics 107 Kentish Town Road, London NW1 8PB (071-485 9593)

Testament 14 Tootswood Road, Bromley, Kent BR2 0PD (081-464 5947)

Tremula PO Box 1491, Windsor, Berkshire SL4 2PE (0753 860522)

Tring International Triangle Business Park, Wendover Road, Aylesbury, Bucks HP22 5BL (0296 615800)

UK Distribution 23 Richings Way, Iver, Bucks SL0 9DA (0753 652669)

Unicorn-Kanchana Records PO Box 339, London W8 7TJ (071-727 3881)

United Recording Threeways House, 40-44 Clipstone Street, London W1P 7EA (071-436 5054)

Vanguard Classics 27, West 72nd Street, New York, NY10023, *USA* (1 212 769 0360)

Varèse Sarabande 13006 Saticoy St, North Hollywood, CA91605, *USA* (1 818 764 1172)

Victoria Sandakerveien 76, PO Box 4379, Torshov, 0402 Oslo 4, *NORWAY* (47 2271 0140)

Virgin Classics *see* EMI Records

Voiceprint PO Box 5, Stanley, Co. Durham, DH9 7HR

Warner Classics (UK) 46 Kensington Court, London W8 5DP (071-938 5542)

Wergo Postfach 3640, 55026 Mainz, *GERMANY* (49 06131 246891)

Birgit Nilsson

Indexes

Erich Leinsdorf

Dame Kiri Te Kanawa

Sergei Rachmaninov

Index to Artists

Index to Reviews

Collections

Films and Show Music